7th Edition

The fun, fast, and easy way to get productive online

New Riders' Official

Internet and World Wide Web YELLOW PAGES

New Riders Publishing
A Division of Macmillan Computer Publishing
201 West 103rd Street Indianapolis, IN 46290 USA

This directory is publised by:

New Riders Publishing
201 West 103rd Street
Indianapolis, IN 46290 USA

Printed in the United States of America 1 2 3 4 5 6 7 8 9 0

CIP data available upon request

Warning and Disclaimer

This book is designed to provide information about the World Wide Web. Every effort has been made to make this book as complete and as accurate as possible, but no warranty or fitness is implied.

The information is provided on an "as is" basis. The author(s) and New Riders Publishing shall have neither liability nor responsibility to any person or entity with respect to any loss or damages arising from the information contained in this book or from the use of the disks or programs that may accompany it.

Publisher *John Pierce*

Executive Editors *Karen Reinisch*
Lorna Gentry

Managing Editor *Thomas F. Hayes*

Trademark Acknowledgments

All terms mentioned in this book that are known to be trademarks or service marks have been appropriately capitalized. New Riders Publishing cannot attest to the accuracy of this information. Use of a term in this book should not be regarded as affecting the validity of any trademark or service mark.

Acknowledgments

Thank you to all who worked at a frantic pace to produce a quality product. Special thanks go to Jill Bond, Robin Drake, Lori Lyons, Katy Stallings, and Faithe Wempen. New Riders' would also like to thank the following contributing editors who worked so feverishly to help author this book:

Mark Bibler
Fraun Blauw
Jill Bond
Kelli Brooks
Cheri Clark
Erik Dafforn
Sandy Doell
Robin Drake
Kezia Endsley
Mitzi Foster
Mary Inderstrodt
Stephanie Kirchner
Amy Lepore
Rita Lewis
Lisa Lord
Annie Owen
Cliff Shubs
Katy Stallings
Faithe Wempen

Acquisitions, Development, and Editor
Jill D. Bond

Production Editor
Lori A. Lyons

Editorial Assistant
Jennifer L. Chisholm

Cover Designer
Sandra Schroeder

Cover Production
Casey Price

Book Designer
Glenn Larsen

Graphics Image Specialists
Sadie Crawford
Wil Cruz
Oliver Jackson

Production Team Supervisor
Victor Peterson

Production Team
Angela Perry
Daniela Raderstorf
Megan Wade

Indexers
Kevin Fulcher
Sandra Henselmeir

TABLE OF CONTENTS

About the Authors

Mark Bibler is a long-time role-playing fanatic and information geek, which certainly qualifies him to survey and write about most Internet and World Wide Web sites. He holds a Bachelor of Arts in History and English from Ball State University in Muncie, Indiana, and is an avid reader, owning a library of several thousand books.

Fran Blauw, although financially independent, enjoys working as a freelance editor strictly for kicks. She spends most of her time alphabetizing her list of countless suitors. Strangely, though, she has managed to memorize every Nick At Nite episode. When not being whisked off to Paris or Rome, Fran enjoys consulting her Magic 8-Ball for answers to the mysteries of the universe.

Jill Bond is a freelance writer and editor for Macmillan Computer Publishing. She has been in the computer book publishing industry since 1989 and has since worked on a bagillion books, including programming, software application, and Internet topics. She lives in Columbus, Indiana with her husband and two daughters. In her spare time, she enjoys boating, music, and drinking Coors Light with friends while hanging out at home.

Kelli Brooks provides freelance editing, desktop publishing, and writing services to various businesses and organizations. She worked in editorial for Macmillan Computer Publishing's Que for two years before leaving to be a full-time wife, mother, and freelancer. Prior to working at Que, she worked as Marketing Manager for a rehabilitation facility in Indianapolis where she ghostwrote medical articles for staff physicians. In addition to this book, she was recently a contributing author for a career resource book, *What Can I Do Now?* (published by J.G. Ferguson Publishing of Chicago), geared toward the high school student exploring different career opportunities. Kelli graduated from Anderson University in 1990 with a B.A. in mass communication. She lives in the Indianapolis area with her husband, Brett, and daughter, Paige, and is expecting another child in the Spring of '98. She loves music, traveling South, movies, and spending time with her family and friends.

Cheri Clark has been editing professionally for 11 years—first at *The Saturday Evening Post* magazine, then in-house at Macmillan Computer Publishing, and for the past 5 years at home in Crawfordsville, Indiana. She enjoys being a "work at home" mom, raising her two boys, Nathan and Matthew, with the help of her husband, Jeff.

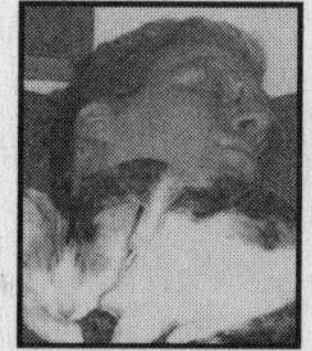

Erik Dafforn is an Indianapolis-based editor and writer whose passion for witty social commentary is eclipsed only by his addiction to dairy products. He feels that in addition to the archived wisdom of `alt.tv.simpsons`, the Internet has many lessons to teach us—most importantly, that your computer can now be much more than a $2,000 typewriter. It can also be a $2,000 radio, phone book, CD player, and telephone. Now that's progress.

Robin Drake has been editing and writing computer-related text since 1985. Always willing to experiment, her motto is, "I'll click anything. I'll double-click anything." She holds an M.A. in English and Philosophy from Ball State University in Muncie, Indiana.

Sandy Doell is a freelance editor who lives in Indianapolis, Indiana with her husband Dave. In her spare time, she enjoys camping, reading, wildlife watching, and writing. She has four sons, whose hobbies include hunting, archery, skiing, trucks, and song writing, so finding sites about those topics was a family venture. Sandy's main passion is hunting morel mushrooms in the spring, but there was no morel category in this edition. Maybe next year....

Kezia Endsley is an Indianapolis-based editor, writer, and student with interests ranging from contemporary literature to long-distance running to environmental science. She is known for her peculiar habit of attracting abandoned cats, most of whom she has offered refuge. The Internet, she notes, is useful in at least two or three ways, but mostly to get cheat codes for Crash Bandicoot.

Mitzi Foster has over seven years of writing and editing experience from a wide variety of fields, including the newspaper, public relations, legal, and publishing industries. While earning her B.S. in Journalism at Ball State University, she interviewed, researched, and wrote feature articles for the university's Public Information Office. Since 1993, she has edited over 45 books for Macmillan Computer Publishing including *Entertainment on the Net, The Brain Makers, Internet Graphics Gallery, The 10-Minute Guide to Teams and Teamwork,* and *100 Best Freelance Careers.* She currently is Senior Editorial Account Manager for Trinity Productions, which she founded in 1995 to provide writing, proofreading, and editorial services to corporate clients.

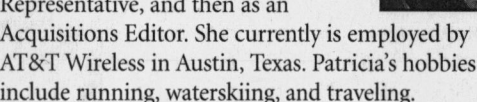

Patricia Guyer is a graduate of Indiana University - Bloomington with a Bachelor of Science degree in Business, Marketing. She worked for Macmillan Computer Publishing for three years: first as a Sales Representative, and then as an Acquisitions Editor. She currently is employed by AT&T Wireless in Austin, Texas. Patricia's hobbies include running, waterskiing, and traveling.

Mary Inderstrodt is a graduate of Purdue University, with degrees in English and Anthropology. Before going freelance, she worked in-house as an editor for Macmillan. Her hobbies are writing, reading, driving across the country, and trying to grow citrus trees.

Stephanie Kirchner is a student at Marian College in Indianapolis, Indiana, majoring in Education. She will be continuing her education by attending graduate school to attain her degree in Social Work. She enjoys reading, music, and helping others.

Amy Lepore is a freelance editor and project manager who lives in Westfield, New Jersey. She is a '94 graduate of Butler University in Indianapolis and has worked in computer publishing ever since. Aside from computers, Amy's interests include traveling, Broadway shows, and watching the Chicago Bulls.

Rita Lewis has applied her MA in anthropology to the study of computers, and especially Macintosh computers. After fifteen years as a proposal manager using Macs to sell mainframes and UNIX, Rita set out on her own. In the seven years she has been freelancing, she has written 11 books on various topics including networking, Macintosh operating systems, and various applications. Her most recent and best-received titles include *PageMill 2 Handbook* (Hayden Books 1996) and *Maclopedia* (Hayden Books 1995).

Lisa Lord edits computer books for fun and profit and to maintain her jet-set lifestyle. Her hobbies include perfecting the double-click, singing the entire score of *The King and I*, adding to her collection of bad puns, and embarrassing her son by laughing at the dancing-candy commercial in movie theaters.

Annie Owen is a freelance editor and writer who lives in Indianapolis with her husband, David Bartley, and their two labradors, Emerson and Mazzy Star. She enjoys reading/writing fiction, travel, gardening, and restoring their historic 1912 craftsman home.

Cliff Shubs graduated from the University of Vermont. After graduation, he worked as a reporter and columnist for the *Western Star* newsweekly in Warren County, Ohio. In 1994, he became an editor for New Riders Publishing in Indianapolis. Cliff worked on the very first *Yellow Pages* in the Fall of 1994 and has helped on subsequent editions. Cliff left New Riders in 1997 to pursue a career as a freelance editor and writer. His interests include NPR, PBS, bicycling, aerobics, good food, movies, and music, for which he has an affinity for "hippie" music.

Faithe Wempen left the corporate world to become a freelance writer and editor, and has been happy ever since. She has an M.A. in English from Purdue University, and got interested in computers through a temp job working on an IBM mainframe back in the 80s. Now a self-described computer geek, her favorite activities are surfing the Internet and convincing strangers at parties that they need to buy home computers. She lives in Indianapolis with Margaret (an engineer and ex-rugby player) and their two shetland sheepdogs, Sheldon and Ashley.

Introduction

The Internet is a collection of interconnected computer networks from around the world that provides a wealth of information on nearly any topic you can imagine. The World Wide Web, often simply called the Web, is a subsystem of the Internet. The Web has become the definitive "hot spot" for Internet users primarily because it allows for anyone to graphically and visually "advertise" themselves or a specific cause, and have this representation 24 hours a day. Many individuals do not have the need to create their own Web page, as this type of representation is called, but they do want to have access to and be able to view the Web sites of others. Whatever your situation, you will be utterly amazed by the tremendous variety and amount of information available on the World Wide Web and captured in this book.

Features and Uses of the World Wide Web

The Web can link together information from anywhere in the world and make it available to anyone. A grade-school student can jump from Dun & Bradstreet's financial information to a pictorial tour of the Croatia's capital, Zagreb, to the state of the Internet in southern Africa, without ever leaving his or her desk.

There's far more to the Web than just information. You can learn static facts from any encyclopedia. The information stored in the Web is constantly updated. With the Web, you'll always have the freshest information at your fingertips.

The Web also dynamically links information into a seamless whole. You may start your information hunt next door and finally track down your quarry somewhere in Singapore. From where you sit, however, the distance between the two online data sources makes no difference. The Web enables you to move around the world as easily as to the local library—with a click of a mouse.

Although the Web has existed for a relatively short time, it is already being used in numerous areas by both public and private institutions. Businesses have discovered the benefits of advertising and performing transactions on the Web. Educational institutions also are making more information available on the Web, and students are discovering that they can get increasingly more research done by searching Web pages rather than library books. You can make travel plans, buy houses, read about your favorite hobby, and make new friends via the Web.

Business

Individual companies have set up advertisements on the Web. Before long, it will be almost unprofitable for any major company—especially one that deals in new technologies—to exist without its own site to show advertisements and product information. Moreover, buyers are rapidly finding out that it is far easier to take a look at a new product by going to a business's Web page than by physically going to the store to look for a product or searching advertisements in the newspaper. In addition to finding advertisements on the Web, consumers can do their shopping on the Web as well.

Do you want to actually purchase an item that you've been viewing? Step into a shopping mall. These malls allow users to place orders for items that can then be shipped to their homes or businesses. Holiday shopping couldn't be easier! No longer will you have to stand in lines at stores or wait on hold for the attendant at the mail-order company to take your order. Instead, you can find the item you want and enter your credit information to have it shipped right away.

Users can order almost anything from the Web: chocolate, books, games, clothing, music, or anything else they might desire. This directory contains listings for numerous stores and shopping centers.

Education

Many educational resources already are available through the Web. Libraries are adding their catalogs and universities are posting information about degree programs. You can find research documents containing information about almost any subject. Before long, traveling to a library to find this information will become a nearly obsolete venture. Instead, students will be able to find information they need without leaving their desks.

The possibilities for education on the Web are amazing. Many college and university classes presently create Web pages for semester class projects. Research papers on many different topics are also available. Even elementary school students are using the Web to access information and pass along news to other students. Exchange students can communicate with their classmates-to-be long before they actually arrive at their new school. It won't be long before students will be able to take language classes that are actually taught in the country where the language is spoken.

Many elementary and secondary schools have created and are maintaining Web pages. Students and teachers work together to decide what information should be included on the site and prepare it for publication. By doing this, not only do they make more information available to the community, but students gain useful knowledge of new technologies and their use.

Travel

Planning a vacation? There are many sites on the Web that can help you solidify your travel plans, or give you ideas of places you might want to visit. These sites offer information about tours and hotel accommodations, as well as car rentals, airfare, and other forms of transportation. Cruise lines have Web pages that outline various types of cruise packages and describe destinations. Many cities sponsor Web pages as well, where you can learn about restaurants, sightseeing, shopping opportunities, and local points of interest.

About this Directory

This directory lists more than 10,000 selected World Wide Web sites. Each listing presents the site's title and URL, as well as a brief description of the site.

The sites have been placed in categories, such as Career & Employment, Health & Fitness, Kids Only, Music, Religion & Philosophy, and Travel, and are then presented alphabetically in subcategories. Because New Riders Publishing wanted to present as many sites as possible in this directory, maximum effort has been made to avoid site duplication from category to category, even if the site's contents qualifies it for more than one category (for example, a site about church music could conceivably fall under either the Music or Religion category).

Further Reading

There are many books and articles about the World Wide Web; moreover, any relatively recent book about the Internet will contain some material on the subject of the Web. Some possible sources for further information include:

Inside the World Wide Web, Second Edition, New Riders Publishing.

Designing Web Graphics .2, Lynda Weinman, New Riders Publishing.

Web Concept and Design, Crystal Waters, New Riders Publishing.

New Riders Publishing

The staff of New Riders is committed to bringing you the very best in computer reference material. Each New Riders book is the result of months of work by authors and staff who research and refine the information contained within its covers.

As part of this commitment to you, the reader, New Riders invites your input. Please let us know if you enjoy this book, if you have trouble with the information and examples presented, or if you have a suggestion for the next edition.

Please note, however: New Riders staff cannot serve as a technical resource for the World Wide Web or for related questions about software- or hardware-related problems. Moreover, the World Wide Web is a dynamic environment that changes daily. Because changes will inevitably have taken place between the time of this book's compilation and its publication date, New Riders welcomes and solicits your feedback regarding inaccuracies or possible improvements and additions for subsequent editions.

If you have a question or comment about any New Riders book, there are several ways to contact us. We will respond to as many readers as we can. Your name, address, or phone number will never become part of a mailing list or be used for any purpose other than to help us continue to bring you the best books possible. You can write us at the following address:

New Riders
Attn: Publisher
201 W. 103rd Street
Indianapolis, IN 46290

If you need assistance with the information in this book, contact Macmillan Technical Support by phone at **317/581-3833** or via e-mail at **support@mcp.com**.

Also be sure to visit Macmillan's Web resource center for all the latest information, enhancements, errata, downloads, and more. It's located at **http://www.mcp.com/**.

NRP is an imprint of Macmillan Computer Publishing. To obtain a catalog or information, or to purchase any Macmillan Computer Publishing book, please contact our Customer Service Department at **800/858-7674** or fax us at **800/835-3202** (International Fax: 317/228-4400). Or visit our online bookstore at **http://www.mcp.com/**.

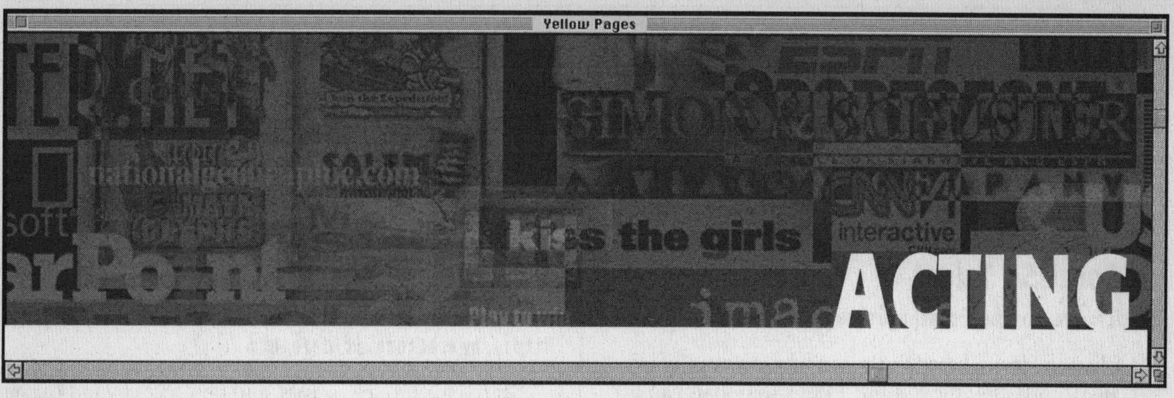

A fter all, what am I? Just the greatest actor in the world.

Basil Underwood in It's Love I'm After *(1937)*

Academy Kids Management

http://www.academykids.com/

A Hollywood talent agency for actors ages 18 years and under. They offer workshop and coaching for young actors and their parents.

The Academy of Television Arts & Sciences

http://www.emmys.org/

Provides information, background, and a hall of fame for The Academy of Television Arts and Sciences. Includes information about the Emmy awards, education programs, and current academy news.

Academy of Theatrical Combat

http://www.catalog.com/academy/

The home page for a company that specializes in teaching actors how to stage realistic fight scenes. Part of the nonprofit Association of Kinetic Artists.

Acting Workshop Online

http://www.execpc.com/~blankda/acting2.html

Provides information for the aspiring actor. Includes a great amount of basic practical advice for someone wanting to become an actor. Includes an acting FAQ, information on how to deal with stage fright, royalties, and much more. This is an interesting site even for the non-thespian.

NRP TOP PICKS

The Academy of Television Arts & Sciences
http://www.emmys.org/

Actor's WorldLink
http://members.aol.com/aworldlink/index.htm

The Academy of Motion Picture Arts and Sciences (AMPAS)
http://www.lightside.com/ampas/

DIDASKALIA: Ancient Theatre Today
http://www.warwick.ac.uk/didaskalia/didaskalia.html

Hollywood Actors Network
http://www.hollywoodnetwork.com/hn/acting/index.html

Playbill On-Line
http://www1.playbill.com/playbill/

TalentWorks: The Online Casting Service
http://www.talentworks.com/

The Actors Group

http://www.actorsgroup.com/

This organization holds seminars and workshops for its members and helps actors and actresses market themselves. Members can also post their own Web pages at this site with their photos and resumes.

Actors Online

http://www.actorsonline.com/

Provides an online actor and actress directory that includes pictures and resumes. Includes entertainment and theater industry news and links to other related sites. Also includes an actor/actress of the week feature.

Related Sites

http://webhome.idirect.com/~aaction/aaction-1.html

http://www.actingstudio.com/

A B C D E F G H I J K L M N O P Q R S T U V W X Y Z

Actor's WorldLink

http://members.aol.com/aworldlink/index.htm

Provides online display of actors and actress pictures and resumes. Includes current acting news and links to many different casting agencies.

AdComUSA Talent

http://www.bostonadcom/pages/talent.html

A listing service based in Boston where actors, voice talent, and other theatre and TV professionals can list their credentials.

Aisle Say: Home Page

http://www.escape.com/~theanet/AisleSay.html

Provides an online magazine dedicated to theater reviews, opinion, and much more. Includes an index of articles, stories, and links to related theater and acting sites.

The Academy of Motion Picture Arts and Sciences (AMPAS)

http://www.lightside.com/ampas/

Site includes information about AMPAS, the Academy Awards, press releases, and current news.

Auditions On-Line

http://www.auditions.com/

Provides an online audition and casting service for the California theatre and film industry. Includes a great amount of information about casting calls in the Los Angeles, San Francisco, and Northern California areas.

Calgary Professional Arts Alliance

http://www.culture.net.ucalgury.ca/cpaa/index.html

Information about participating in and joining this organization, which supports arts and culture in the Calgary area. Includes contact information for the Calgary Actors Equity Association.

Casting Connection

http://members.aol.com/rlshelly/rlshelly.htm

Provides casting information for actors, actresses, models, and other talent. Includes casting call, audition, and talent search information.

Casting Guild

http://www.castingguild.com/

Provides links and information about casting calls, auditions, and talent showcases for union, non-union, and university productions. Includes links to many related sites.

Casting on the Web

http://www.actors.it/defe.htm

Search for models, actors, and new faces by indicating the type of person you need. This service for casting directors and show organizers includes a detailed form for narrowing your search. Includes complete information on models and talent.

CastingOnline

http://hookomo.aloha.net/~wrap/

A one-stop cybercasting site for the performing arts industry. Click the continent of your choice or read about the latest casting projects nationwide. Includes casting info for actors, musicians, voice-overs, and multimedia projects.

Celebrity Archives

http://geocities.com/Hollywood/set/1150/index.html

A well-organized network of links to fan pages for many actors and other celebrities.

Children's Theatre

http://pubweb.acns.nwu.edu/~vjs291/children.html

Provides information and resources covering children's theatre. Includes many different links and a state-by-state entry of children's theatre companies.

Dan Vera's Impersonation Showcase Tribute

http://www.impersonationshowcase.com/

Learn how to book this interesting all-impersonator show, featuring "tributes" to Elvis, Patsy Cline, Janis Joplin, The Blues Brothers, and lots of other great old acts.

Related Sites
http://www.fas.harvard.edu/~art/institute.html
http://www.jmbloom.com//index.htm
http://home.ica.net/~coco/index.htm

Creative Outlet Theatre Company

http://members.aol.com/CreatvOutl/creative.htm

A nonprofit organization that produces live theatre, providing a forum for young actresses and actors. Young people high school age and above can arrange theatrical internships through this group.

DIDASKALIA: Ancient Theatre Today

http://www.warwick.ac.uk/didaskalia/didaskalia.html

Provides an online publication about acting and theatre of Greek and Roman drama as they are performed today. Includes many different articles, essays, and features covering many different related subjects.

East 15 Acting School

http://web.ukonline.co.uk/east15.acting

Provides online information about the East 15 Acting School based in London and York England. Includes a prospectus, school tour, course summary, and grant information.

Ed Hooks Theatrical Workshops

http://www.best.com/~edhooks/

Ed Hooks, author of several acting books including *The Audition Book*, presents a series of workshops for actors of all levels, preparing them for film, TV, and commercial work.

English Actors at the Turn of the 20th Century

http://www.siue.edu/COSTUMES/actors/pics.html

Provides information and pictures of many different actors and actresses of American theatre at the turn of the 20th century. Spotlights actors and actresses such as Sarah Bernhardt, Walter Passmoor, and many more.

Hollywood Actors Network

http://www.hollywoodnetwork.com/hn/acting/index.html

Lists advertisers who can help you break into Hollywood and articles on people in the business. This site includes a number of directories you can join or examine detailing information on acting, broadcasting, and screen writing. Provides links to everything imaginable regarding Hollywood and the entertainment industry.

Impronet

http://www.mono.org/impronet/

Provides information about the Impronet group of improvisational actors who perform comedy based on and inspired by the Internet. Includes detailed explanation of how the troupe works and where it will be performing.

Improv Across America

http://http.tamu.edu:8000/~fslip/ImprovAmerica/

Provides news and contact information for improvisational acting troupes across the United States. Includes links to many other related improv and acting sites.

Improv Page

http://sunee.uwaterloo.ca/~broehl/improv/index.html

Provides information about improvisational theatre and troupes. Includes an index of improv groups, history of improvisational theatre, book listings, glossary of terms, and much more.

MUSE NET

http://www.cybercom.net/~alonigro/

Provides information about the Priscilla Beach Theatre. Includes current show information for adults, children, and the Priscilla touring company. Also includes a casting directory and current news.

The Musicals Home Page

http://musicals.mit.edu/musicals/

Provides a comprehensive list of sites dedicated to musicals and other related information. Includes news, reviews, and articles about musical theatre.

Related Sites

http://www.filmbiz.com/essentials/Acting.html

http://www.valentinestudio.com/

http://www.mrshowbiz.com/

http://www.e-zines.com/TheComedyCoach/

http://www.uwindsor.ca/faculty/arts/dramatic/voice/v+s.html

A B C D E F G H I J K L M N O P Q R S T U V W X Y Z

Playbill On-Line

http://www1.playbill.com/playbill/

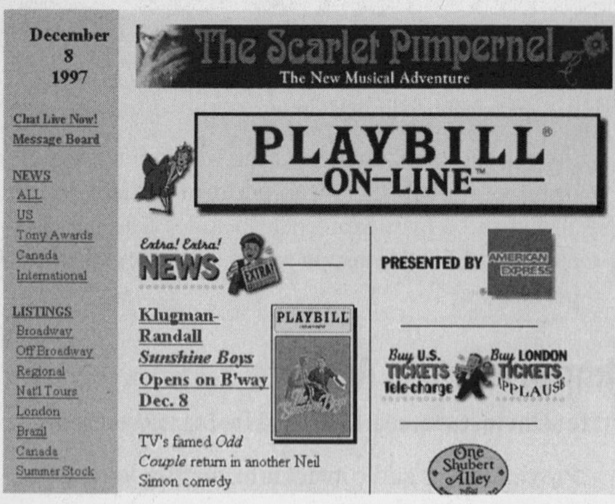

Provides show dates for theatres in the United States, Canada, England, and more. Includes previews, reviews, and articles about theatre productions.

Raymond Interactive Theatre, Ltd.

http://www.rit.com/

Based on the same technologies as computer games, this interactive theater enables you to interact online with the production. Includes information about becoming a RIT ticketholder. If computer game shoot-'em-ups have become stale, then this may be the entertainment option you have been waiting for.

Steppenwolf Theatre Company

http://www.steppenwolf.org/

Information about this popular Chicago theatre, including current and future productions, actor profiles, and directions/parking information for patrons.

The Studio Theatre

http://www.studiotheatre.org/

Provides information about the Washington, D.C. based The Studio Theatre. Includes theatre group background, current productions, and upcoming productions information.

Take One Film Casting

http://www.kdcol.com/~rvon/take1.html

This site belongs to Utah's largest full-service casting agency. Among other shows, this agency casts the TV show *Touched By an Angel.* Find out how to be an extra in a production filmed in Utah.

TalentWorks: The Online Casting Service

http://www.talentworks.com/

An online community of actors and other entertainment professionals, this site lists casting calls, offers actors the opportunity to network, and provides space for members to post their own home pages.

Theatre InSight

http://www.utexas.edu/students/ti/

Provides an online journal covering performance and theatre studies. Includes papers, essays, and discussion on many topics in theatre.

Theatre-Express Home Page

http://www.theater-express.com/

Provides an online magazine dedicated to acting and the theatre. Includes reviews, casting calls, audition information, and articles about theatre productions.

The Tony Awards Online

http://www.tonys.org/

Provides information about the American Theatre Wing, the League of American Theatres, and Producers' Tony Awards, given for achievement in live theatre. Includes theatre news, reviews, a Tony database, and much more.

TVI Actors Studio Home Page

http://www.tvistudios.com/

Provides online site for TVI Actors Studio, a Los Angeles and New York based acting school. Includes alumni list, courses offered, and school history.

VCV Stunts—Stuntmen on the Net

http://www.procom.com/~daves/vcvstunt.html

Offers professional stunt actors for live action, motion pictures, and video.

The Virtual Headbook

http://www.xmission.com/~wintrnx/virtual.html

Provides a collection of actors' resumes and head shots that casting directors, agents, and directors can search for free. Actors can join online, get tax help, or sign with a California agent. Sound and video clips of actors at work are also available.

> Perhaps the greatest social service that can be rendered by anybody to the country and to mankind is to bring up a family.
>
> *George Bernard Shaw*

Adoption Benefits: Employers as Partners in Family Building
http://www.adopting.org/employer.html

AdoptioNetwork
http://www.adoption.org

Faces of Adoption—America's Waiting Children
http://www.adopt.org/adopt/

Treasure Maps
http://www.firstct.com/fv/tmapmenu.html

GROWING FAMILIES

Adoption Advocates: Adoption Policy Resource Center

http://www.fpsol.com/adoption/advocates.html

Provides federal and state legislative news and analysis (including statutes and court decisions), adoption assistance (subsidy) information resources, legal resources, and advocacy resources.

Adoption Benefits: Employers as Partners in Family Building

http://www.adopting.org/employer.html

Provides information about company-sponsored adoption benefit plans, including who is eligible for benefits, how company-sponsored benefit plans actually work, covered expenses and when they are paid, the types of adoption the benefit plans cover, adoption leave of absence from the workplace, a list of companies that offer adoption benefits, as well as other adoption assistance programs. If you are considering adopting a child, this is a great place to go for information regarding company-sponsored benefits.

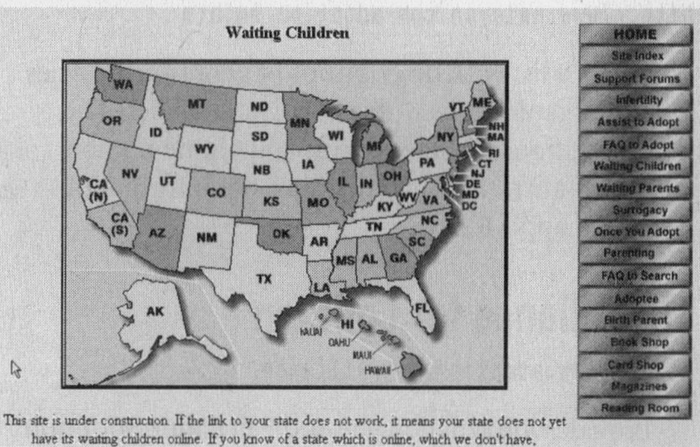

Adoption Newsletters in the United States

http://www.helping.com/family/ad/adnlu.html

A sizable directory of newsletters and magazines on adoption. The site lists subscription rates and also includes selected periodicals on the search for birth parents or for children given up for adoption.

Adoption—Where Do I Start?

http://www.infi.net/adopt/iii1st.html

Offers information about the process of adoption, including the type of children available for adoption, who is eligible, steps for agency adoption and independent adoption, guide books, and a list of national adoption organizations.

A
B
C
D
E
F
G
H
I
J
K
L
M
N
O
P
Q
R
S
T
U
V
W
X
Y
Z

AdoptioNetwork

http://www.adoption.org

Provides information that encompasses the broad scope of adoption, including lists of agencies and photo-listings, legal resources, information about international adoptions, FAQs for children about adoption, a walk-through of the adoption home study process, and much more.

The Adoptions Connections Project: Women's Journeys

http://www.sover.net/~adopt/index.html

Site geared toward women that offers stories of adoptees, birthmothers, and adoptive mothers. Provides conference and workshop information and a free monthly online publication called "The Adoption Connections Newsletter." Great support site for women touched by adoption.

AIS Exchange List 1996—Community Resources

http://www.halcyon.com/adoption/04.htm

Offers a list with descriptions of adoption agencies and organizations within the United States. The descriptions include address and phone number information, fees, and membership information (when applicable).

The Alliance for Children

http://www.adoption.com/alliance/

Provides information about the Ecuador Adoption Program, the Romania Adoption Program, and the China Adoption Program provided by this agency. Also includes a list of criteria for which adoptive parents must qualify.

Christian World Adoption

http://www.cwa.org/cwa.html

Site of a nonprofit international child placement agency. In conjunction with local service agencies, places children from other countries, such as Russia, Paraguay, Brazil, and Mexico, in families throughout the United States.

Domestic Infant Adoption Advice

http://www.openadoption.org/bbetzen/

Written by Bill Betzen, this site concentrates on providing information about "open adoptions," including information to anyone considering the placement of an infant (including a checklist to use when searching for an agency), recommendations for anyone considering the adoption of an infant, and infant adoption cost questions and issues.

Faces of Adoption—America's Waiting Children

http://www.adopt.org/adopt/

Comprehensive site that provides 143 pages of photo-listings of children available for adoption, categorized by age and sex. Also includes information on legislation, the adoption process, lists of adoption agencies and organizations, conferences and seminars, and other material pertinent to all aspects of adoption. This is a must visit!

Help the Children

http://www.adopting.org/htc.html

Site of a private, not-for-profit, adoptive-parent-led corporation, specializing in the preparation and support of families and single persons wishing to adopt from the United States and several countries around the world. Includes licensing information, fee structure, and general information about international adoption and policies. This site also has a comprehensive photo-listing of children available for adoption that includes health and development information, circumstances under which children came into custody, and recommendations for placement.

Holt International Children's Services

http://www.holtintl.org/

Provides services to reunite children with birth families, or places them with adoptive families in the country of their birth or another country.

Independent Adoption Center Home Page

http://www.webcom.com/~nfediac/welcome.html

Provides information and support for birthparents and adoptive parents, information and resources for professionals in the adoption field, and links to other Web sites that provide information about adoption.

National Adoption Organizations

http://www.infi.net/adopt/nao.html

Lists branches of the federal government concerned with adoption, national organizations concerned with adoption, and other groups with specialized interest in adoption, such as advocacy, education, and financial support. Also includes links for international, national, and regional adoption exchanges, and photo-listings.

Resources for Adoptive Parents—Adoption Information on the Internet

http://www.precious.org/

Provides photo-listings of children from the former Soviet Union and China. The site of Association of American Nonprofit Adoption Agencies, Inc. is an Arkansas corporation that does not place children for adoption, but rather contracts with licensed agencies to coordinate adoptions from the former Soviet Union and in some cases China. Although the individual listings do not provide as much health and development information as other sites, you can request video tapes and further information from AANAA, Inc. This site also provides a list of adoption agencies associated with AANAA, Inc. You can find other information related to adoption, such as a list of books, country-specific adoption and general adoption information, and resources for special-needs children.

Roots and Wings Adoption Magazine

http://www.adopting.org/rw.html

Quarterly magazine that contains articles that cover the broad scope of adoption. Included are personal stories, specialized columns, and advice for adoptees, adoptive parents, and birth parents.

Voices of Adoption

http://www.ibar.com/voices/

Adoptee and birthparent stories, adoption issues, and search stories are a few of the offerings of this site. Also includes reader responses and links to other adoption sites.

SEARCHING FOR BIRTHFAMILY

Adoptee & Genealogy Page from Carrie's Crazy Quilt!

http://www.mtjeff.com/~bodenst/page3.html

Offers a wealth of information regarding searching for a birthparent or relinquished child, from information you will need to get started on your search (and how that info will help) to links to other adoption/search sites. If you are searching, you will appreciate the numerous links provided.

Adoption on the Usenet

http://www.webcom.com/kmc/adoption/faqs.html

This comprehensive site contains tons of important information for those searching for birthparents, children, or siblings. You can find booklists (with reviews), legislative information, newsgroups (alt.adoption), FAQs regarding the alt.adoption newsgroup, and a list of support groups, broken down by country and state. This site also contains links to must-read information if you are considering the use of a searcher in your quest. A+!

Jeff Hartung's Adoptees Resources Home Page

http://psy.ucsd.edu/~jhartung/adoptees.html

Provides up-to-date information about adoption-related events and legislation, lists of books related to searching for children and birthparents, other links, newsletters, and newsgroups. This is a must-visit for anyone searching.

Treasure Maps

http://www.firstct.com/fv/tmapmenu.html

Great site with many tools for searching and tracking your family history. Useful in searching for birthfamily. This site contains helpful tools, such as suggestions for "getting past the stone wall," a tutorial on the U.S. Federal Census, research outlines, and collections of compiled and original family records.

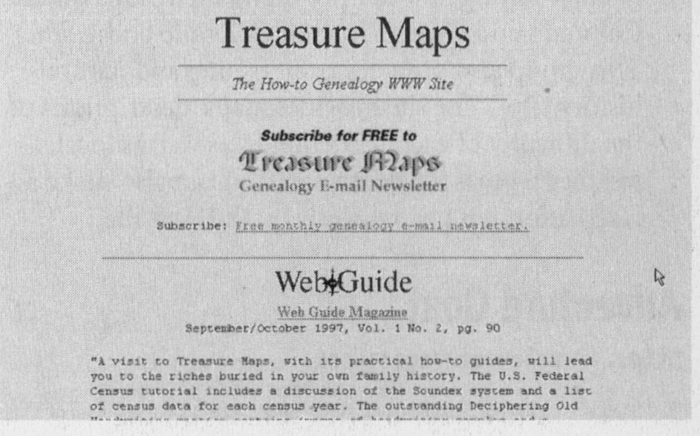

Treasure Maps
The How-to Genealogy WWW Site
Subscribe for FREE to
Treasure Maps
Genealogy E-mail Newsletter
Subscribe: Free monthly genealogy e-mail newsletter.
WebGuide
Web Guide Magazine
September/October 1997, Vol. 1 No. 2, pg. 90
"A visit to Treasure Maps, with its practical how-to guides, will lead you to the riches buried in your own family history. The U.S. Federal Census tutorial includes a discussion of the Soundex system and a list of census data for each census year. The outstanding Deciphering Old

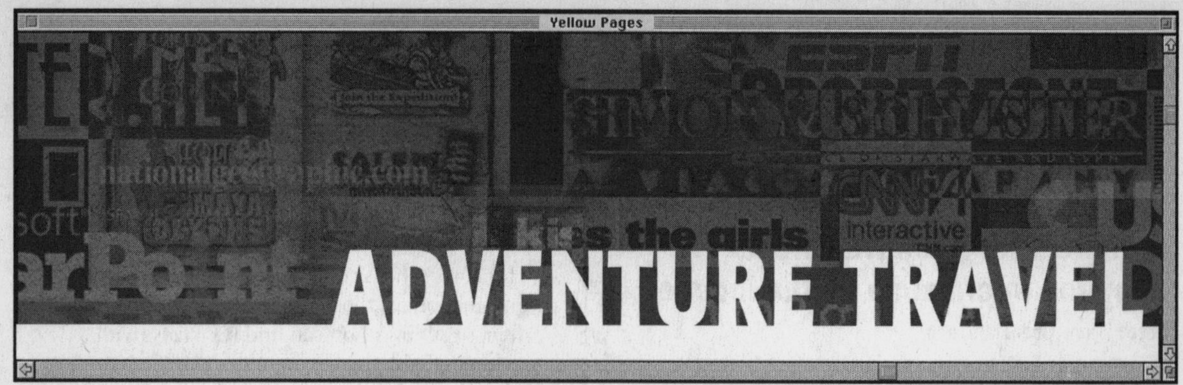

> Life is either a daring adventure or nothing at all.
>
> *Helen Keller*

Above All Travel

http://www.aboveall.com/AAT.html

A full-scale travel agency specializing in exotic and unusual travel destinations. Links include destinations to Tahiti, Antarctica, French waterways, European skiing, and tropical scuba diving adventures. The site has many large graphics making it slow to navigate, and several "front doors" to pass through before getting to the meat of the site.

Adventure Bound River Expeditions

http://www.raft-colorado.com/

A water rafting outfitter providing excursions on the Colorado and Green Rivers of Colorado and Utah. This group also provides trout fishing and natural history trips. The site provides maps, descriptions of the difficulty of each trip's rapids, as well as local weather reports for the region. You can also make a reservation for a trip directly on the Web site.

Adventure Goat

http://www.adventuregoat.com/

Take a virtual outdoors trek without leaving your armchair. Adventure Goat provides reviews of outdoor gear, links to adventure outfitters for booking trips, and detailed descriptions of a large array of adventures. You can link to travel descriptions by subject and geographic location. An Alta Vista-based search engine is also included so that you can go to other adventure sites on the World Wide Web.

Adventure Travel Society
http://www.sni.net/ats/

Adventure Out

http://www.gorge.net/business/adout/

This site describes Adventure Out, a Mount Hood guide company providing rock climbing, Lead Climbing, Natural History Hikes, van tours, and winter trips. Adventure Out also sponsors winter skiing excursions on Mount Hood's North Face. Adventure Out specializes in team-building programs.

Adventure Quest

http://www.adventurequest.com/adven/

Adventure Quest provides a one-stop shopping site for over 1,000 adventure travel outfitters worldwide. You can search the site by company name, geographical location, and type of adventure.

Adventure Tour Directory

http://www.sni.net/trips/

A complete compendium of Web sites offering adventure travel tours and outfitting support in one handy place. The site is sponsored by On The Mark Adventures. On The Mark Adventures invites tour companies and groups to join their consortium via an online sign up form. A voluminous list of catalog links is also included for your enjoyment.

Adventure Travel Society

http://www.sni.net/ats/

Links are provided for travel agency sites, the Seventh Annual World Congress on Adventure Travel and Ecotourism and Expo in Quebec, adventure travel business issues, descriptions of various adventure travel destinations, and a link to a publications site.

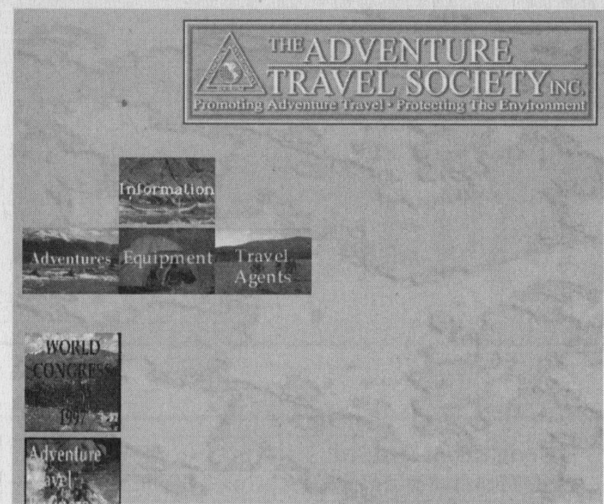

Adventures Abroad Home Page

`http://www.adventures-abroad.com`

They provide tours to 84 countries. Their specialties are Adventure Travel, International Tours, Small Group Tours, and Worldwide Tours. They also provide services as Travel Agents and Tour Operators.

African Safari Scene

`http://www.accesstravel.com/africa/africa.html`

This site is provided by Access Travel and lists various African safari travel packages to Kenya and East Africa. You can book your trip via a link to Access Travel.

Arctic Adventours, Inc.

`http://www.oslonett.no/html/adv/AA/AA.html`

Advertises Arctic Adventours, a Norwegian company that specializes in creating exciting expeditions and explorations in the Arctic area, including Northern Norway, Jan Mayen, Spitzbergen, Franz Josef's Land, and Northern Russia/Siberia.

EarthWise Journeys

`http://www.teleport.com/~earthwyz/`

Provides information about adventure travel packages with an ecological and socially responsible philosophy. Provides information about socially responsible travel, packages available, and a lengthy company background.

Mt. McKinley, Alaska

`http://www.inch.com/%7Edipper/ak.html`

Denali, as the locals call it, is Alaska's beacon to the world. This is adventure travel at its best, not to mention at its most dangerous. But armchair travel is fun too. If you have VRML (virtual reality software) installed, click on the 360-degree views of Denali offered as links from this site. Click on personal links to Mt. McKinley sites.

New Brunswick, Canada Outdoor Adventures

`http://www.csi.nb.ca/tourism/`

Advertises Outdoor Adventures vacation packages, which include whale watching, scuba-diving, sailing, kayaking, canoeing, hiking, bird-watching, and cycling in various national parks and other locations.

The Official Home Page of the Acadia National Park

`http://www.nps.gov/acad/w95026aa.html`

The National Park Service sponsors this Web site to present information about Acadia National Park. Links are provided to pages providing information about planning your visit, concessions, off-season visits, as well as books and literature. Links also are provided to other natural history sites, cultural history sites, and photographs of Acadia.

Resort Sports Network

`http://www.rsn.com/`

Provides information on packages, rates, and opportunities for the avid athlete and vacationer. Neat Web cam provides realtime photographs of various sport locations. Includes wind, surf, and snow conditions for the extremist on vacation.

Sumatra Adventure

`http://www-wfcb.ucdavis.edu/www/pub/tim.html`

A travelogue by Tim Lee called "A Quest for Riches in Sumatra." The article is filled with wildlife photography and first-person accounts of various trips through Sumatra.

Wildwest Travel, Inc.

`http://www.webcom.com/~wildwest/`

Provides information about western adventure travel packages, such as snowmobile tours, cowboy vacations, Alaskan cruises, and wilderness travels. Provides package background, pricing, and includes contact information.

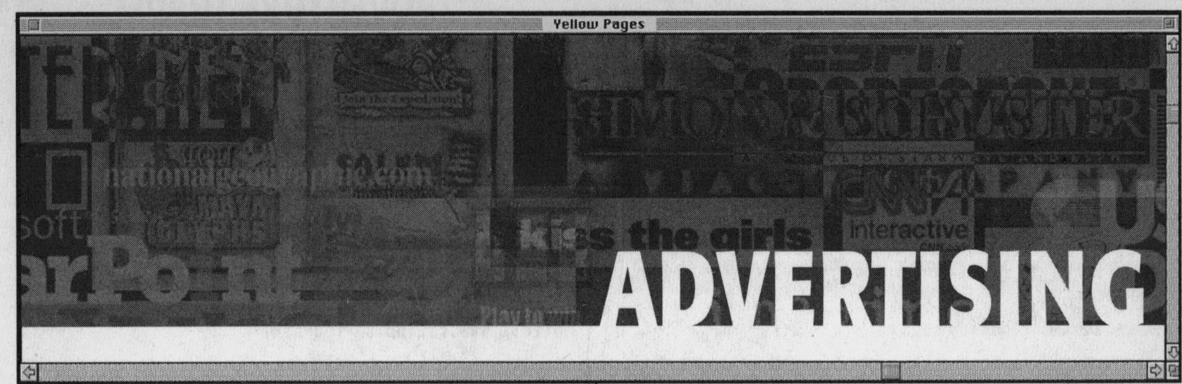

A B C D E F G H I J K L M N O P Q R S T U V W X Y Z

> Advertising is selling Twinkies to adults.
>
> *Donald R. Vance*

Accipiter AdManager

`http://www.accipiter.com/Products/index.html#TOP`

A product enabling Web site managers to perform targeted advertising as well as keep track of visitors to their sites. Includes an overview of the product and a live demo. There are also sample reports (publishers, visitors, and demographics).

Ad Council

`http://www.adcouncil.org/`

Home page of the Advertising Council, a private non-profit corporation conducting public service advertising campaigns. Contains a list of public service advertising campaigns as well as a calendar of events.

Ad FX

`http://www.ad-fx.com/`

Helps you to generate more business from your Yellow Pages ad by giving it a makeover. Includes eye-catching samples of some of their work.

Ad Juggler

`http://www.adjuggler.com/`

Displays randomly rotating banner ads hyperlinked to advertiser's Web sites. Sites are searchable. Sites that use Ad Juggler are listed. Also contains statistics, technical information, and ordering information.

Advertisement Pictures
`ftp://ftp.sunet.se/pub/pictures/advertisments/`

Advertising and Marketing Helper Directory
`http://www.geocities.com/WallStreet/3584/`

Federal Trade Commission
`http://www.ftc.gov/`

NRP TOP PICKS

Advertisement Pictures

`ftp://ftp.sunet.se/pub/pictures/advertisments/`

A site containing pictures from some of the most well-known ad campaigns. For example, a picture from the Absolut Vodka campaign featuring the Brooklyn bridge can be found here.

Advertising and Marketing Helper Directory

`http://www.geocities.com/WallStreet/3584/`

An extensive index of resources for advertisers. Includes associations, awards and festivals, conferences, books, advertising for children, ad critique, Web hot sites, and more. If you're bored, you can find links to brands, media, marketing, magazines and publications, and so on.

Advertising Educational Foundation

`http://www.aded.org/`

Addresses fundamental questions people have about advertising: Is advertising misleading; does it make people buy things they don't need; does anyone in the advertising industry have ethics? Includes information on the visiting professor and ambassador programs as well as educational materials.

Advertising Law

http://www.webcom.com/~lewrose/home.html

Read the text of three important documents related to advertising law. Includes relevant articles, FTC literature, testimony and speeches, other sites, and more. Also links to a discussion forum.

Advertising Media Internet Center

http://www.arfsite.org/

Links to media software, market segments, news service, a research monitor, rates, dates and data, media guru, ad talk, ad jobs, and more. Many of these sites require membership, which is free.

Advertising, Boelter & Lincoln

http://www.advbl.com/

Provides Web site advertising and marketing along with traditional advertising. Site provides complete company history, capabilities (technical and otherwise), data of the firm's effectiveness, and a list of Web sites Boelter & Lincoln created. Also provided is a group of affiliations and customers.

AfterHours Communications Corp.

http://www.ahours.com

Provides complete advertising services, including online marketing and advertising. Includes Web site design and construction. Also provides a list of customers and their sites, "Top 10 Ways to Tell if You have a Sucky Home Page," and "Top 10 Tips to Better Web Sites."

Allen & Associates, Ltd.

http://www.radix.net/~eallen/

Provides company background, portfolio, and gallery for marketing communications graphic arts studio. Includes Web site nexus of sites created by Allen & Associates.

AmericaMall Classifieds

http://1second.com/1america.htm

Enables you to submit your ad to this site for free. Ads cover advertising, arts and antiques, auctions, automotive, business opportunities, real estate, travel, employment, work at home, and more.

American Association of Advertising Agencies

http://www.commercepark.com/AAAA/index.html

The trade association representing the American advertising business. Encompasses management, media, print and broadcast production, secondary research on advertising and marketing, international advertising, and more. Includes an update of the Washington scene. Many AAAA members are small sized companies.

Another Color, Inc.

http://www.csgi.com/AC/

Contains information and background of services offered by this graphic designs firm based in Washington, D.C. Provides extensive list of clients with portfolios of work in marketing promotion, package design, corporate identity, Web site creation, and other related work.

Austin Knight's KnightNet

http://www.ak.com/

Provides U.S. home site for worldwide advertising agency. Includes company history, profile, listings of service, international location sites, portfolio of work done, and awards received.

Automated Resource Data Entry Network (ARDEN)

http://www.arden-inc.com/

Contains listings, current resumes, and home page links of advertising professionals. For freelancers, photographers, illustrators, art studio personnel, graphic designers, account services, media, research, financial, human resources, and others. Includes an application for new members, an edit mode, and a way to search for individuals, ad agencies, and advertisers. A secure server site.

B.A.A.S. Boating Advertising, Advice, and Service

http://www.dataplace.nl/baas

Specializes in advertising for the marine market, represents yachting magazines, b-to-b and consumer magazines, and Webvertising.

BackChannel

`http://www.commercepark.com/AAAA/bc/`

The quarterly newsletter of the American Association of Advertising Agencies (AAAA). Online issues date from current to April, 1995. Pointers and chat room news constantly updated. Links to AAAA home page.

Bernard Hodes

`http://www.hodes.com/`

Specializes in recruitment advertising and human resource connections. Services include direct mail, broadcast campaigns, collateral design, referral programs, and even a presence on the Internet. Several interactive features, including an "HR Plaza" and the "Career Mosaic."

Better Business Bureau

`http://www.bbb.org/advertising/index.html`

Arm of the Better Business Bureau that promotes honest advertising. Contains information pertaining to local advertising review programs and national advertising review programs, including the National Advertising Division (NAD), and the Children's Advertising Review Unit (CARU).

Blacklist of Internet Advertisers

`http://math-www.uni-paderborn.de/~axel/BL/blacklist.html`

A list of those who have misused the Internet (junk email and user groups) for advertising. Describes who gets on the list and for how long, the philosophy behind the list, spamming, ways of dealing with commercial junk, and so on. Updated regularly.

Blain/Olsen/White/Gurr

`http://www.bowg.com/main.html`

An advertising agency that caters to a high-tech clientele. You can view a portfolio of their works, a list of clients, and so on.

Carter Waxman

`http://www.carwax.com`

Provides home site for the Carter Waxman advertising agency based in the Silicon Valley. Includes company background and portfolio of work. The most interesting part of the site is a weird, lurid, and yes, fictional soap opera called "The Valley of the Chips." This self-described "continuing saga of lust and intrigue in an era of technology" is rather funny, if not just strange. You will see nothing comparable in any other business site.

Casie Guiding Principles of Interactive Media Audience Measurement

`http://www.commercepark.com/AAAA/bc/casie/guide.html`

This paper is the result of a joint venture of the Association of National Advertisers, Inc. and the American Association of Advertising Agencies. Provides guidelines on the control of interactive media with regard to cyberspace and television. Includes a bibliography.

Chase Online Marketing Strategies

`http://advert.com/`

This is the home page of the "Online Ad Agency." Information on consulting includes various articles written by Larry Chase. Subscribe to the e-journal, Web Digest for Marketers.

Chase Online Marketing Strategies

`http://www.chaseonline.com/`

Offers links to other marketing-related sites. Also offers advertising- and catalog-related information.

Chiat/Day, Inc.

`http://www.chiatday.com/factory/`

This site is under construction. Provides home site for Chiat/Day Inc. and TBWA advertising firms that have recently merged. Includes merger reasoning and preview of services to come to this site.

Children's Advertising Review Unit (CARU)

`http://www.bbb.org/advertising/childrensMonitor.html`

The arm of the Better Business Bureau that handles inappropriate and misleading advertising, and advertising to children ages 12 and under. Contains lists of supporters, academic advisors, and business advisors. Also includes self-regulatory guidelines and a parent's guide.

Classified Advertising Network (C.A.N.)

`http://www.texoma.com/donrey/classified/newspaper/advertising/`

Feel that newspaper advertising is still the best way of securing clients? From this site you can place ads in

55 papers. Can also place ads to sell personal items and homes. Includes rates, markets, circulation by city, map of markets, and so on.

Cohn & Wells

http://www.cohn-wells.com/

Provides marketing, advertising, and communications services across many types of media. Provides company profile, philosophy, services, and capabilities. Includes links to clients' Internet pages.

Communications Week Interactive

http://techweb.cmp.com/ia/iad_web_/

An online magazine designed to enhance commerce over the Web. Particularly for the Information Technology (IT) specialist. Many important links and articles. Contains searchable archives.

The Conaghan Report

http://www.naa.org/news/webcount.html

This site tracks audience and advertising on the Web. Includes reports on meetings such as the Internet Advertising Bureau and links to articles such as "Do Web sites that sell advertising really need third-party audits?" Also includes numerous resources on counting, auditing, tracking, analyzing, and other business transactions.

Cortex Marketing Resources

http://www.cortex.net/

Provides high-end consulting and Internet software. Compiles marketing resources. Concentrates on listing agencies, suppliers, publications, and so on, that are not presently on the Internet.

curious pictures

http://found.cs.nyu.edu/curious/

Provides full-service graphics production for TV commercials, computer graphics, and interactive media. Based in New York City, curious pictures has worked on many recognizable on-air spots and commercials. Site includes company profile along with full services-offered listings. Also includes internship information, career opportunities, and an online guided tour of the offices.

CyberAtlas

http://cyberatlas.com/

Measurement tool describes the Web in terms of: market (demographics, usage patterns, and so on); segments (e-commerce, Intranets, and so on); tools (servers, software, and so on); and other resources (FAQs, glossary, links, and so on).

Design Productions

http://www.designproductions.com/

This Canadian-based agency specializes in advertising, marketing, printing, Web page design, photography, multimedia, digital imaging, and 3D rendering. Can download free software. Will offer you a free presentation of the work they'd do for you.

Dissect an Ad

http://www.pbs.org/pov/totk/dissect.html

Developed by the Center for Media Literacy to teach you the points of critiquing presidential election ads. Tells you who the target audience is, what the ad is trying to sell, how the ad sells, what facts it uses, and so on. Also contains "P.O.V. (Point Of View)" interactive.

DoubleClick

http://www.doubleclick.com/

An Internet advertising network that provides Web advertising tools and products. Also tells you how to secure a place on some of the most highly visible sites.

Farago Advertising

http://www.farago.com

Provides home site for Farago Advertising, which provides full-service advertising for traditional media and new media alike. Includes services offered, client listings, and an "ask the 8-ball" section to answer questions. Also includes contact information.

Federal Trade Commission

http://www.ftc.gov/

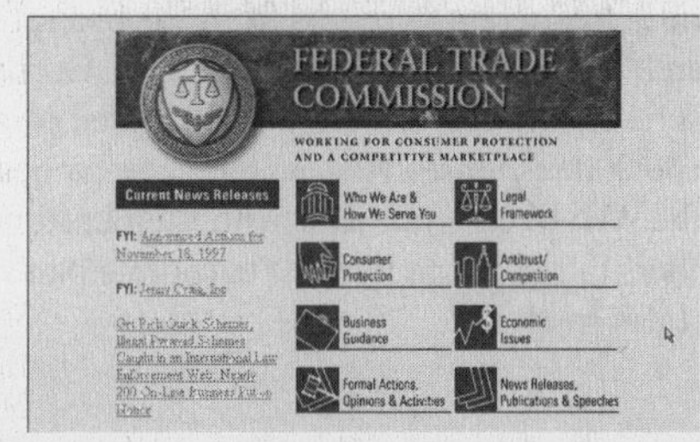

A B C D E F G H I J K L M N O P Q R S T U V W X Y Z

Enforces a number of federal anti-trust and consumer protection laws. Contains several new articles (including scholarship scams), news releases, commission actions, speeches, conferences, hearings, and workshops. Also links to FTC consumer line and business line.

Forest Green Media

http://fgreen.com/fgm/

Company that provides interactive marketing for the Web and multimedia. Specializes in unique, high-tech graphics. Provides links to current projects, clients, demos, as well as net stocks, what's new, and Internet search engines.

Free Link Sites

http://www.goodnet.com/~ej77486/linkmeu.htm

This site gives you access to over 300 sites that will in turn provide access to yours. Includes reciprocal text links, reciprocal banner links, and free Web pages.

GBH Handsfree Communication

http://nia.com/headsets/

GBH provides hands-free communications equipment, such as headsets, teleconferencing, telecommuting, and videoconferencing products for the ergonomically correct office. Links are provided to their products with descriptions and pictures. Links to ordering info also are provided.

Goswick Advertising

http://www.goswick.com/

An advertising firm capable of creating broadcast and print advertising, multimedia services on the Internet, and commercial online service marketing. Includes links to past and current projects, the agency, and the advertising team.

HERMES, Consumer and Corporate Surveys

http://www.umich.edu/~sgupta/hermes/

Provides free access to results from the project's research on commercial uses of the Web. Currently offers results from four user surveys, based on more than 30,000 responses. Also enables companies who use the Web to communicate with their customers or suppliers to register to become corporate panel members (also free).

Ingalls, Quinn, & Johnson

http://www.iqj.com/

Advertising, PR, and multimedia solutions for your business, especially clients in TV, radio, and print. Provides links to numerous arms of their agency, as well as employment opportunities.

Institute for the Study of Business Markets

http://www.smeal.psu.edu/isbm/

Contains current information related to ISBM activities, including seminars, research projects, publications, and membership in the organization.

Internet Advertising Guide

http://www.voyager.net/adv/internet-advertising-guide.html

This is a resource for those wanting to use the Internet as an advertising medium. "Advertising Primer" contains several e-zines as well as an online advertising discussion list. Other sections include unique Internet advertising formats, Web measurement, Internet advertising networking, and a discussion of search engines.

Kern Media Associates

http://www.maine.com/kern/

Radio, TV, and cable ad agency located in Gloucester, Maine. Links to free newsletters and services, clients, creative services, and more.

Liggett Stashower

http://www.liggett.com/

A marketing communications company based in Cleveland, Ohio. Their clients range from local charities to international organizations. Includes links to services, marketing, consulting, creative services, and more.

Marcus Advertising

http://www.marcusad.com/marcus/

A long-time, full-service advertising agency specializing in creative services, print and broadcast production, PR, multimedia, Web publishing, and much more. Provides access to their clients and their current projects.

Market Place Media

http://www.marketmedia.com/

A marketing company to help you target your product with the right media to the right audience—students, seniors, military, or minorities. Expert in direct marketing, posters, radio, specialized newspapers and magazines, promotions, and more.

Marketing Ally

http://www.westerndirect.com

Provides support for telemarketing, Internet services, and other direct marketing campaigns.

McMonigle and Associates

http://www.primenet.com/~mands/index.html

An advertising, design, and marketing firm specializing in a variety of services, including corporate development, design, media planning, TV and radio production, audio/video, and promotion.

McSpotlight

http://www.envirolink.org/mcspotlight/home.html

A critical response to McDonald's $1.8 billion in annual advertising. Includes information on various lawsuits, issues related to their business practices, their censorship strategy and other insights on their company, campaigns against McDonald's and other multi-nationals, and much more. Includes a debate room as well.

Michael J. Motto Advertising

http://www.gti.net/motto/

If you have advertising or marketing needs on or off the Internet, Michael J. Motto Advertising will handle your questions by phone or you can stop in for a visit (the first visit's on them). They can help your company maximize your profit potential using the Internet.

Mousetracks—NSNS Marketing Resources

http://nsns.com/MouseTracks/

Offers links to and commentary on marketing activities and resources available on the Net for educational and professional use.

National Association for Promotional and Advertising Allowances (NAPAA)

http://www.napaa.org/

A national nonprofit trade association that focuses on trade allowance programs. Site contains a new, live chat line, services for members, a directory of resources, and a glossary of terms.

O'KEEFE WORLD

http://www.okeefe.com

The home of O'Keefe Marketing, a full-service ad agency integrating Web site development with traditional marketing.

Poppe Tyson

http://www.poppe.com/

This full-service advertising agency provides public relations, database marketing, database management, and direct mail. Specializes in "branding applications," Internet-based applications that help companies increase their brand equity. Has won many awards for its work.

Project 2000

http://www2000.ogsm.vanderbilt.edu/

A project at Vanderbilt University devoted to studying the marketing implications of the World Wide Web and other computer media environments. Contains debate, papers, newsworthy items, courses, and site stats. Includes several interactive sessions.

Saatchi and Saatchi Business Communications

http://www.saatchibuscomm.com/

Focuses on integrating worldwide business communications. Other services include print, broadcast, collateral, Yellow Pages, and direct. Much of their work for clients can be viewed here.

Sales Plus

http://www.salesplus.com/

Contains information related to sales and marketing. Contains prospecting, video and audio tapes, books and software, trade shows, and consulting information related to sales and marketing.

A B C D E F G H I J K L M N O P Q R S T U V W X Y Z

SCI Design and Communications

ftp://users.aol.com/scides/home/index.html

The home page for a firm specializing in advertising and design.

Sharrow Advertising and Marketing Information Resource Center

http://www.dnai.com/~sharrow/register.html

Hosts marketing topics, including a mail-order catalog, advertising opportunities, and lists of advertising and marketing resources on the Web.

Sidea

http://www.sidea.com/

Provides home site for SIDEA (Service, Information, Demonstrations, Evaluations, Assistance), a retail marketing company. SIDEA produces demonstration booths and set-ups so customers can experience products in the store. Includes services, products, and contact information.

TAL Marketing Services, Inc.

http://moose.erie.net/~talerie

Offers extensive experience in print, media, multimedia, audio/video, interactive, broadcast, direct mail, and outdoor marketing.

TEAMS Marketing and Sales Assessment Software

http://mtg-teams.com

Offers TEAMS (Total Evaluation and Analysis of Marketing and Sales), a sales and marketing assessment software program designed to evaluate and improve your company's marketing and sales activities. Includes samples of the TEAMS questionnaire and report and an electronic order form.

University of Texas Advertising World

http://www.utexas.edu/coc/adv/world/

A directory of marketing communications for students, teachers, and professionals. The extensive index goes from A to W and includes account planning, direct advertising, event planning, social marketing, student interest, and much more.

Wahlstrom & Company

http://www.wahlstrom.com/

Provides yellow page advertising consulting and services. Publishes the Wahlstrom Reports newsletter about directory advertising and new electronic media. Includes clients' listings and contact information.

Wall Street Journal

http://www.adnet.wsj.com/

Online guide for advertising on the Net, Web sites, and general Internet directory. Lets you search the directory by category and alphabetically. Also includes lists of companies advertising in the Wall Street Journal related to catalog shopping, travel planning, mutual funds, education, corporate annual reports, and an annual subscription guide.

Web Advertising Brokers

http://www.acme.com/ad_brokers/

Evaluates Web brokers—middlemen between advertisers and page providers. Among those reviewed are Burst! Media, Commonwealth, DoubleClick, eAds, Narrowcast Media, Internet Banner Network, WebConnect, and Webvertising.

White Palm's Effective Banner Design

http://www.photolabels.com/betterbanners.shtml

Provides numerous articles on banner design and banner advertising. Plenty of banner samples. Also contains list of link swapping sites.

Winkler McManus

http://www.winklermcmanus.com/

Provides home site for Winkler McManus Advertising. Includes portfolio, company philosophy, profile, news, and contact information.

Young & Roehr, Inc.

http://www.teleport.com/~davidwh/

Provides full advertising services from direct mail to new media. Provides handling of Web site creation, public relations, and strategic planning. Includes services offered, client listings, artwork samples, and links to sites created.

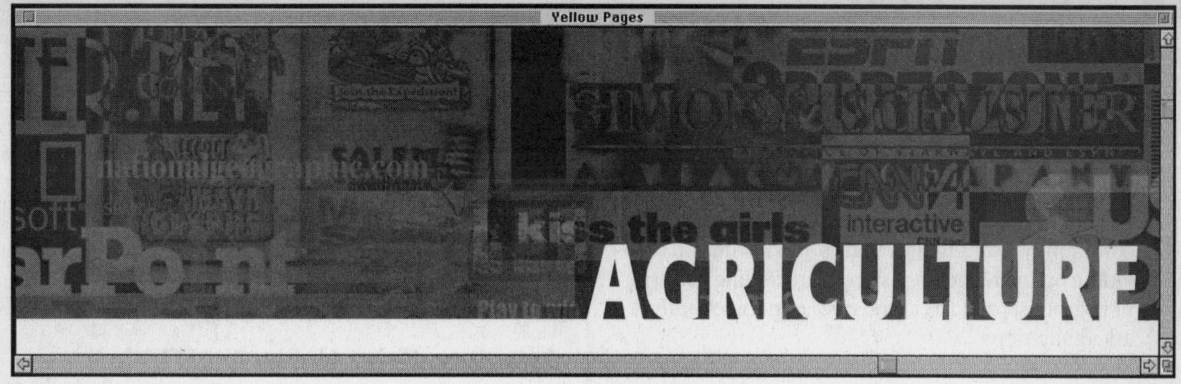

A B C D E F G H I J K L M N O P Q R S T U V W X Y Z

> When tillage begins, other arts follow. The farmers therefore are the founders of human civilization.
>
> *Daniel Webster*

NRP TOP PICKS

Agrinet
`http://www.spectramedia.com/agrinet/`

Beef Today
`http://www.beeftoday.com/index.dbm`

Chicago Board of Trade (CBOT)
`http://www.cbot.com/menu.htm`

Farm Journal Today
`http://www.farmjournal.com/`

National Corn Growers Association (NCGA)
`http://www.ncga.com/`

Purdue Weather Processor (WXP)
`http://wxp.atms.purdue.edu/`

Voice of Agriculture
`http://www.fb.com/home.shtml`

A*L*O*T Angus Association

`http://www.erinet.com/carl/alot.html`

Detailed information on cattle sales, breeding, and advantages of Black Angus by the Arkansas * Louisiana * Oklahoma * Texas (A*L*O*T) Angus Association. Links to other members, calendar of events, related Black Angus, ranching, and agricultural sites. Up-to-date information on Mad Cow Disease.

Ag Answers

`http://www.aes.purdue.edu/AgAnswrs/AgAnswers.html`

Problem-solving information for Ohio and Indiana farmers. Searchable database of questions and answers, event calendar, research information, and agricultural news. Connects to Purdue University and Ohio State University home pages.

Ag Electronics Association

`http://www.agriculture.com/aea.html`

Devoted to the use of electronics in agriculture. Includes membership information, links to past issues of agINNOVATOR, and council meeting minutes and schedules.

Ageless Iron

`http://www.agriculture.com/contents/sf/ageless/agiindex.html`

Special site for antique farm machinery hobbyists, traders, and clubs. Articles on news in the field, maintaining and repairing valuable equipment, and restoration.

Ag-Links

`http://www.gennis.com/aglinks.html`

Features news, weather, professional and nonprofessional associations, research, and newsletters related to the agriculture industry. Also contains links to other agricultural sites.

Agri-Alternatives

`http://www.agrialt.com/`

Online magazine specializing in farm technology and management, published by a family of farmers. Selected articles from back issues available. Subscribe, sign the guest book, purchase T-shirts, and use the links to jump to selected sites.

Agricultural Network Information Center (AgNIC)

http://www.agnic.org/

Lists of resources and activities for the agricultural community. Links to universities and institutions providing online reference assistance, including listservs, newsgroups, products and services, and frequently asked questions.

Agriculture Online

http://www.agriculture.com/

Contains current news of interest to the agricultural community. Also offers links to sites on the Internet related to agriculture issues, agriculture-related discussions, and articles.

AgriGator Commercial Agriculture Sites

http://www.ifas.ufl.edu/WWW/AGATOR/HTM/AGCOMMERCIAL.HTM

Contains extensive links to businesses on the Internet related to agriculture, including subjects on gardening, farming, fishing, birds, insects, forestry, food research, and other topics.

Agrinet

http://www.spectramedia.com/agrinet/

General agricultural resource site offering links to farm, ranch, family, and commercial sites. Includes classified ads—farm equipment, computers, employment, opportunities, and more. Listings are free for 30 days. Site provides great starting place for agricultural sites.

AgriOne-Internet Ag Marketing

http://www.agrione.com/

Agricultural buying and selling service on the Net, specializing in hogs and pork products, classified ads. Extensive links to other agriculture-related businesses.

American Dairy Science Association (ADSA)

http://www.adsa.uiuc.edu/

Association meetings and information. Articles from the *Journal of Dairy Science*, including an index searchable by author or content and instructions on submitting manuscript for publication. Also includes links to other dairy- and agriculture-related sites.

American Farmland Trust

http://www.farmland.org/

Concerned with preserving farmland and wildlife habitats. Includes statistics on the loss of farmland to urban sprawl and details on what the user can do, as well as links to related resources and other organizations.

American Paint Horse Association (APHA)

http://www.apha.com/

Association membership info and products, merchandise exchange, programs, and clubs. News and press releases, history of the breed, and breeding information. Links to other equine sites.

American Soybean Association (ASA)

http://www.oilseeds.org/asa/

ASA background and history, news about the soybean industry. Membership information and activities, chart depicting soybean utilization, and sponsorship information for the Web site.

Association of Agricultural Computing Companies

http://www.agriculture.com/aacc.html

Concerned with using computer technology in agriculture. Links to manufacturers, public and private institutions, agricultural suppliers, and so on. Includes membership information, employment referral service, and AACC Newsletter.

Beef Today

http://www.beeftoday.com/index.dbm

Magazine for beef producers. Online articles, surveys, discussion groups, new product info, and market research. Links to veterinary and extension sites, as well as government sites.

Cattlemen on the Web

http://www.ncanet.org/

Home page of the National Cattlemen's Beef Association. Current articles about hot topics in the industry, membership information, and links to other sites. CowTown America section features cattle-related information for non-industry readers, including a number of articles on water usage, manure, the importance of grass, and other interesting topics.

Census of Agriculture

`http://govinfo.kerr.orst.edu/ag-stateis.html`

Census Bureau data from 1982, 1987, and 1992. Search data by state, zip code, or county. Detailed information on cropland acreage, farm production, cattle sales, and much more. Dozens of specific tables available for download.

Center for Soybean Tissue Culture and Genetic Engineering

`http://mars.cropsoil.uga.edu/homesoybean/index.htm`

Describes efforts to develop and refine a complete soybean genetic engineering system. Contains a number of links to other pages discussing soybeans or biotechnology.

Ceres Online

`http://www.ceresgroup.com/col/`

Specializes in providing information for agriculture. Search functions connect to other professionals in the agriculture industry. Calendar database lists hundreds of upcoming events; weather maps include world, national, and hot spot info. NetTools section connects to download locations for browsers, graphics software, and more.

Chicago Board of Trade (CBOT)

`http://www.cbot.com/menu.htm`

News, announcements, and commentary, grain futures quotes (delayed 10 minutes), and other info for those interested in trading commodities. Frequent MarketPlex updates on current market information, charts and analysis, and details for media reps.

Chicago Mercantile Exchange (CME)

`http://www.cme.com:80/index.html`

News and views on futures and options, including educational resources, membership lists, government regulations, and links to related financial institutions and other exchanges and agencies. CME price quotes are delayed 10 minutes.

Communicating for Agriculture

`http://ca.cainc.org/`

Site for farmers, ranchers, and rural businesses. News on legislation, lobbying efforts, and business; back issues of CA Highlights articles; opinion polls; research database on high-risk insurance pools.

Conservation Technology Information Center (CTIC)

`http://www.ctic.purdue.edu/ctic.html`

Sections on farming programs, farm and urban land management practices, survey data on crop residues. Links to members' home pages, and upcoming events.

Cooperative State Research Education & Extension Service (CSREES)

`http://www.reeusda.gov/new/csrees.htm`

Searchable index of CSREES-sponsored programs. Lists of grants and funding opportunities. Newsletter, calendar of events, job bank.

Earth Online

`http://farm.fic.niu.edu/earth/home.html`

Web site of Foundation EARTH (Environment, Agriculture, Research & Technology in Harmony), an environmental organization. Harmony Farms link provides "virtual tours" of Harmony Farms Program demonstration sites. Pledge to Earth section displays pledges made by farmers to change their practices to be more environmentally sound.

EarthWatch Communications, Inc.

`http://www.earthwatch.com/`

Weather on Demand service shows storms in progress, radar conditions, and forecasts. State, local, national, and international weather; interesting links to weather-related merchandise.

Economic Research Service (USDA)

`http://www.econ.ag.gov/`

Provides economic and social science information and analysis for public and private decisions on agriculture, food, natural resources, and rural America. Features reports, catalogs, publications, USDA data statistics, and employment opportunities. Also offers other agriculture-related links.

Family Farm Alliance

`http://www.whiteknight.com/Alliance/`

Home page for this nonprofit organization dedicated to the preservation of irrigated agriculture in the western U.S. Site includes details about the organization, membership, meetings and conferences, government regulations, and more.

A
B
C
D
E
F
G
H
I
J
K
L
M
N
O
P
Q
R
S
T
U
V
W
X
Y
Z

Farm Journal Today

http://www.farmjournal.com/

Articles on farming industry topics, headline news (updated twice daily), lists of upcoming industry events, and a variety of farm-related links, including a handy link that lets you specify your state and county to see a running weather forecast.

Farm Safety 4 Just Kids

http://www.fs4jk.org/

Site advocates farm safety and prevention of farm-related injuries. Information on membership and becoming a sponsor, chapter listings, Dr. Danger's safety tips, and catalog of items to help teach kids about farm safety. Kids section is graphical and fun.

Farmland Information Library

http://farm.fic.niu.edu/fic/home.html

Site devoted to individuals interested in agriculture. Contains information about upcoming events, legislation, literature, Internet resources, farm statistics (U.S., by state), and an agricultural library.

GrainGenes

http://wheat.pw.usda.gov/graingenes.html

Database sponsored by the USDA that provides molecular and phenotypic information on wheat, barley, rye, oats, and sugarcane.

HorseNet

http://www.horsenet.com/

Equestrian books and videos, library of online magazines and periodicals, links to racing and equestrian sites—magazines, breeders, associations, racing fans, farriers, and others.

Implement & Tractor Online

http://www.ag-implement.com/

Site dedicated to sharing information for farmers, manufacturers, and dealers of farm equipment. News articles, equipment locator service, classified advertising, weather, business/finance contacts, links to other agricultural sites.

Information Services for Agriculture (ISA)

http://www.aginfo.com

Market and futures information from various mercantile exchanges and universities, a searchable index of thousands of agriculture-related documents, links to other agriculture sites, and contact information for getting your agriculture-related business onto the Web.

Iowa State University Agronomy Department

http://www.ag.iastate.edu/departments/agronomy/

Details on department services, research projects, and programs. Faculty, staff, and student info. The extension service offers publications, weather information, software services, census data, and even an online quiz.

John Deere–Agricultural Equipment

http://www.deere.com/ag/index.htm

Offers product information on entire farm machinery line, as well as other Deere products. Includes lists of dealers in the U.S. and Canada.

Kansas City Board of Trade (Kansas City, Missouri)

http://www.kcbt.com/

Detailed articles about wheat and natural gas futures, historical and trading information, membership information and connections, links to other exchange centers.

Livestockplus Online

http://206.107.180.50:80/livestockplus/

Nationwide news and highlights on livestock-related topics. Details on fairs and cattle shows. Links to other stock-related topics.

Mainstreet-USA

http://www.mainstreet-usa.com/

Sponsored by Farm Credit Services, this site uses a graphical "town" to connect the agricultural community. Clicking one of the "buildings" in the town graphic displays related information. Farmers will be particularly interested in the Feed Store and Farm Supply Store. Use the Grapevine Message Board to post messages and read other postings.

National 4-H Council

http://www.fourhcouncil.edu/

Information on getting kids involved in agricultural education. Historical and membership information, current programs, news and events, and other 4-H sites to visit.

National Agricultural Library (NAL)

http://www.nalusda.gov/

Part of the USDA, this site is a resource for ag research, education, and applied agriculture. Huge collection of downloadable agricultural images. Government documents, access to assistance from special research sites, links to other Internet agriculture sites. AGRICOLA database provides millions of agriculture-related citations from publications.

National Christmas Tree Association

http://www.christree.org/

Site dedicated to growers of Christmas trees and related industries. Includes a special section for tree purchasers on how to maintain a tree at home, along with facts on buying real Christmas trees versus artificial trees. Membership services section includes access to American Christmas Tree Journal online, insurance, and more.

National Corn Growers Association (NCGA)

http://www.ncga.com/

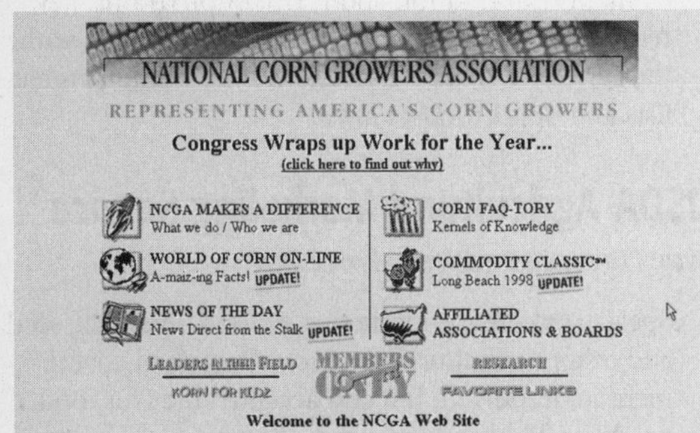

Interesting statistics on corn crops. News and headlines for corn growers, including NCGA radio report (requires RealAudio player). Searchable archive of past news articles. Announcements of upcoming industry trade shows.

National Pork Producers Council

http://www.nppc.org/

Section of consumer info includes recipes and ideas for using pork in your diet. Information for producers includes current news, articles of interest, market summaries, and information on such topics as government regulation and swine care. There's even a section for kids.

National Water Resources Association (NWRA)

http://www.nwra.org/

Home page for this national nonprofit organization concerned with management and conservation of water and water resources and with state and federal water policies. Analysis of legislation related to water management. Links to congressional and legislative sites.

NewCrop (New Crop Resource Online Program)

http://www.hort.purdue.edu/newcrop/

Part of Purdue University's Indiana Center for New Crops & Plant Products. Provides detailed descriptions about many kinds of crops, as well as access to reference material. Also contains links to experts on specific crops, upcoming events, import-export restrictions and permits, and more.

Not Just Cows

http://www.snymor.edu/~drewwe/njc/njcmain.htm

Subtitled "A Guide to Internet Resources in Agriculture and Related Sciences," this site directs the user to a myriad of agriculture-related sites on the Internet and Bitnet, including newsgroups, electronic magazines, discussion groups, newsletters, and libraries with agriculture collections.

Pest Management & Crop Production Newsletter

http://www.entm.purdue.edu/entomology/Pest&Crop/index.html

Site offers the latest information on pests and their impact on crops. Several back issues of the periodical are accessible from this site (Adobe Acrobat Reader required). A publication of Purdue University.

Purdue University School of Agriculture

http://www.agad.purdue.edu/

Lists of international programs, agricultural alumni, connections to other Purdue agriculture-related departments: agronomy, biochemistry, botany, entomology, agricultural economics, and more. Each connected department has its own lists of sites, details about programs, and research info.

Purdue Weather Processor (WXP)

http://wxp.atms.purdue.edu/

Maps and data on current and archived weather patterns and forecasts including high-resolution plots of data from weather balloons, radar, and so on. For meteorologists and others who need detailed weather information on an immediate basis. Hundreds of GIF images, loaded by click rather than automatically to save download time.

Renewable Fuels Association

http://www.ethanolrfa.org/

Dedicated to promoting the use of ethanol in the transportation and agriculture industries. Newsletters, press releases, calendar of events, association news, and membership information. Links to related bioenergy sites.

Shiloh Creek Farm

http://www.leanbeef.com/

Cost and price information on various kinds of cattle. Graphics of Shiloh prize cattle and lists and descriptions of awards they've won. Descriptions of Shiloh breeding programs and links to related sites.

Small Farm Resource

http://www.farminfo.org/

Site filled with general information for owners of small farms or rural property. The site warns that much of the info may be hearsay and therefore unreliable. Includes links to sites on barns, bees, bats, dozens of kinds of crops and livestock, pests, equipment, and property management.

Small Grains

http://www.rrtrade.org/smallgrains/

News and information for the small grain grower. Production library includes answers to typical problems in growing and storage; Wheat Facts section allows searching for data on world wheat production; back issues of *Prairie Grains* magazine online.

Spectrum Commodities

http://www.mcn.net/~spectrum/

Commercial site providing brokerage service to agribusiness for trading in futures. Market research, grain and business quotes, CropCast weather maps, precipitation estimates, and free publications.

Today's Market Prices

http://www.todaymarket.com/

Listing of worldwide wholesale market prices on fruits and vegetables. Product prices reported by product and location of origin; extensive searchable index. Links to university and government agriculture, horticulture, agronomy, biology, and many other related departments.

USA Today Weather

http://www.usatoday.com/weather/wfront.htm

Nationwide regional forecasts, data designed specifically for teachers, pilots, and others. Graphical design with world weather, wind chill, storm forecast, and other topics available at a click.

USDA (United States Department of Agriculture)

http://www.usda.gov

Contains information about USDA programs, news releases, current events, and legislation dealing with the agricultural industry. Also contains employment lists and opportunities links.

USDA Agricultural Marketing Service

http://www.ams.usda.gov/index.htm

Specialized site for marketing of food, livestock, seed, and other agricultural products. Published government invitations to bid and accepted bids for food products. Publications, news releases on shipping rates, transportation workshops, and other related topics.

USDA Economics and Statistics System

http://usda.mannlib.cornell.edu/usda/usda.html

Reports and info on agriculture-related topics from the economics agencies of the USDA. Search by title, subject, or keyword and download the desired report(s) or data set(s). Reports are generally in ASCII format and data sets in Lotus 1-2-3 format for use in spreadsheets.

Voice of Agriculture

http://www.fb.com/home.shtml

Provides links to agricultural, ranching, and farm-related sites as well as state and county farm bureaus. Also offers links to national and rural news and educational materials and bulletin boards where members of the agricultural community share information and ideas.

WeatherNet

http://cirrus.sprl.umich.edu/wxnet/

Sponsored by the University of Michigan, WeatherNet is a one-stop source for current weather information for travelers, skiers, and anyone with a need to know the current forecast and radar conditions. Includes color weather maps and an archive of weather software, most of it shareware.

LISTSERVS

AGENG-L—Agricultural Engineering

You can join this group by sending the message "sub AGENG-L your name" to

listserv@gwdg.de

AG-EXP-L—Ag Expert Systems Mailing List

You can join this group by sending the message "sub AG-EXP-L your name" to

listserv@vm1.nodak.edu

AGRIC-L—Agriculture Discussion Mailing List

You can join this group by sending the message "sub AGRIC-L your name" to

listserv@uga.cc.uga.edu

AGWOMEN-L—Women in Agriculture List

You can join this group by sending the message "sub AGWOMEN-L your name" to

majordomo@peg.apc.org

AQUA-L—Aquaculture Discussion List

You can join this group by sending the message "sub AQUA-L your name" to

listproc@upei.ca

BEEF-L—Beef Specialists Discussion List

You can join this group by sending the message "sub BEEF-L your name" to

listproc@listproc.wsu.edu

BEE-L—Bee Biology Discussion List

You can join this group by sending the message "sub BEE-L your name" to

listserv@uacsc2.albany.edu

BIOSPH-L—Biosphere and Ecology Discussion List

You can join this group by sending the message "sub BIOSPH-L your name" to

listserv@ubvm.cc.buffalo.edu

BIOTECH—Biotechnology Discussion List

You can join this group by sending the message "sub BIOTECH your name" to

listserv@umdd.umd.edu

CSANR-L—Center for Sustainable Agriculture and Natural Resources

You can join this group by sending the message "sub CSANR-L your name" to

listproc@listproc.wsu.edu

DAIRY-L—Dairy Discussion List

You can join this group by sending the message "sub DAIRY-L your name" to

listserv@umdd.umd.edu

D-MGT—Dairy Management

You can join this group by sending the message "sub D-MGT your name" to

listproc@listproc.wsu.edu

EQREPRO-L—Equine Reproduction Mailing List

You can join this group by sending the message "sub EQREPRO-L your name" to

listproc@cornell.edu

EXT-MEAT—Meat Specialists Extension Group Discussion

You can join this group by sending the message "sub EXT-MEAT your name" to

listserv@vm1.spcs.umn.edu

FAOLIST—Food and Agriculture Organization Open Discussion List

You can join this group by sending the message "sub FAOLIST your name" to

listserv@irmfao01.bitnet

FARMCHAT—Hastings Federation of Agriculture Mailing List

You can join this group by sending the message "sub FARMCHAT your name" to

Majordomo@main.telos.ca

FARM-MGT—Farm Management Discussion List

You can join this group by sending the message "sub FARM-MGT your name" to

istserv@vm1.nodak.edu

GOATS—Discussion List for Goat Managers and Lovers

You can join this group by sending the message "sub GOATS your name" to

`listproc@listproc.wsu.edu`

GRAZE-L—Grazing Discussion List

You can join this group by sending the message "sub GRAZE-L your name" to

`istserv@taranaki.ac.nz`

HERB—Medicinal and Aromatic Plants Discussion List

You can join this group by sending the message "sub HERB your name" to

`istserv@vm.egu.edu.tr`

IRRIGATION-L—Irrigation Theory and Practice Discussion List

You can join this group by sending the message "sub IRRIGATION-L your name" to

`listserv@vm.gmd.de`

MULCH-L—Mulch-Based Agriculture Discussion Group

You can join this group by sending the message "sub MULCH-L your name" to

`listproc@cornell.edu`

NEWCROPS—New Crops Discussion List

You can join this group by sending the message "sub NEWCROPS your name" to

`listserv@vm.cc.purdue.edu`

NIPMN-L—National Integrated Pest Management Network

You can join this group by sending the message "sub NIPMN-L your name" to

`listproc@cornell.edu`

PIGFARM—Pig Farming Discussion Group

You can join this group by sending the message "sub PIGFARM your name" to

`listserv@ist01.ferris.edu`

PLTRYNWS—Poultry Health, Production and Management News

You can join this group by sending the message "sub PLTRYNWS your name" to

`listserv@sdsuvm.sdstate.edu`

SHEEP-L—Sheep Discussion Group

You can join this group by sending the message "sub SHEEP-L your name" to

`listserv@listserv.uu.se`

SOILS-L—Soil Science Discussion Group

You can join this group by sending the message "sub SOILS-L your name" to

`listserv@unl.edu`

SUSTAG-L—Discussions about Sustainable Agriculture

You can join this group by sending the message "sub SUSTAG-L your name" to

`listproc@listproc.wsu.edu`

SWINE-L—Swine Practitioners Discussion Group

You can join this group by sending the message "sub SWINE-L your name" to

`listserv@vm1.spcs.umn.edu`

TRICKLE-L—Trickle or Drip Irrigation Mailing List

You can join this group by sending the message "sub TRICKLE-L your name" to

`listserv@unl.edu`

VETMED-L—Veterinary Medicine Discussion List

You can join this group by sending the message "sub VETMED-L your name" to

`listserv@uga.cc.uga.edu`

NEWSGROUPS

`ab.gov.agriculture.barley`

`alt.agriculture.fruit`

`alt.agriculture.misc`

`alt.agriculture.misc`

`alt.business.import-export.food`

`alt.sustainable.agriculture`

`bionet.drosophila`

`bionet.immunology`

`bionet.photosynthesis`

`bionet.plants`

`clari.biz.market.commodities`

`misc.rural`

`rec.equestrian`

`rec.gardens`

`sci.agriculture.beekeeping`

`sci.agriculture.poultry`

`sci.agriculture.poultry`

`sci.agriculture.ratites`

`sci.bio.botany`

`sci.bio.conservation`

`sci.bio.ecology`

`sci.bio.entolomology`

`soc.culture.scientists`

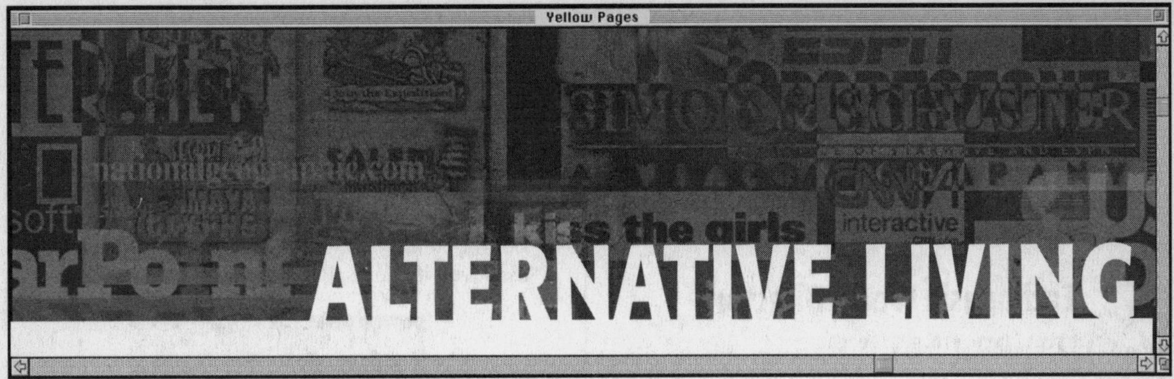

Those of us who refuse to risk and grow get swallowed up by life.

Patty Hansen

American Civil Liberties Union

http://www.aclu.org/

Provides information on every front at which the ACLU is battling, including Net censorship, separation of church and state, abortion rights, the death penalty, and immigrant rights. Closely follows the ACLU v Reno anti-CDA trial and argues against anti-terrorism legislation resulting from the Oklahoma bombing.

American Civil Rights Review

http://webusers.anet-stl.com/~civil/index.html

Civil rights and the constitution explored and presented at this extremely active site. Articles for and against current thinking on diversity and multiculturalism, subsidized housing, immigration, bussing, slavery, and much more.

Amnesty International Online

http://www.amnesty.org/

Human rights defenders go online to provide information about rights violations and what you can do to help. Topics include China and women.

American Civil Liberties Union
http://www.aclu.org/

Amnesty International Online
http://www.amnesty.org/

Euthanasia World Directory
http://www.efn.org/~ergo/

Global Vision: Media for the Millenium
http://www.igc.apc.org/globalvision/

Center for Democracy and Technology

http://www.cdt.org/

Links to a host of issues concerning civil liberties. Includes updated headlines of articles regarding the Internet, with further links to the events that caused issues to come to the forefront of the public's attention.

Cohousing Network

http://www.cohousing.org/

This group developed in response to the impersonal living experienced in many suburbs in America. It provides links to a state-by-state list of communities throughout the country that have adopted this manner of living, and it explains the benefits of the lifestyle.

Cornucopia of Disability Information Gopher Server

gopher://val-dor.cc.buffalo.edu/1

With links to sites pertaining to disability issues from a local to an international level, this site is not just for the disabled, but also for people who provide them with services.

Eco-Village Information Service

`http://www.gaia.org/`

Eco-villages are primarily concerned with integrating comfortable living spaces with their surroundings. This site provides background and links to successful communities.

Euthanasia World Directory

`http://www.efn.org/~ergo/`

This very delicate subject is handled well and extensively by the Euthanasia Research & Guidance Organization's page. It contains comprehensive lists of links to right-to-die organizations, as well as information on their stands and legislation they would like to see passed.

Fair Housing Institute, Inc..

`http://www.mindspring.com/~fairhous/index.html`

Consulting company offering services and information about U.S. housing laws. A good place for anyone concerned with fair housing. Property owners and managers, landlords, tenants, and others can read newsletter articles and pick up helpful advice.

Fear—Forfeiture Endangers American Rights

`http://www.fear.org/`

Dedicated to reforming the country's recent, unconstitutional forfeiture laws that impose double jeopardy on undeserving defendants by taking property without a hearing, while convicting the person to jail and heavy fines.

Fellowship for Intentional Community

`http://www.well.com/user/cmty/fic/`

Promoting the ideals of cooperative living, this page is a springboard to help you find communities throughout the country, as well as links to places that will assist you if you're already living in a cooperative.

Global Vision: Media for the Millenium

`http://www.igc.apc.org/globalvision/`

Links to areas throughout the world keep you updated on current events in human rights. Lists shows pertaining to the issues covered in the page and where they can be viewed, as well as the transcripts from previous shows.

Human Rights Web

`http://www.hrweb.org/`

A globally comprehensive list of links for information about human rights, who's trying to violate them, and what you can do to protect those rights.

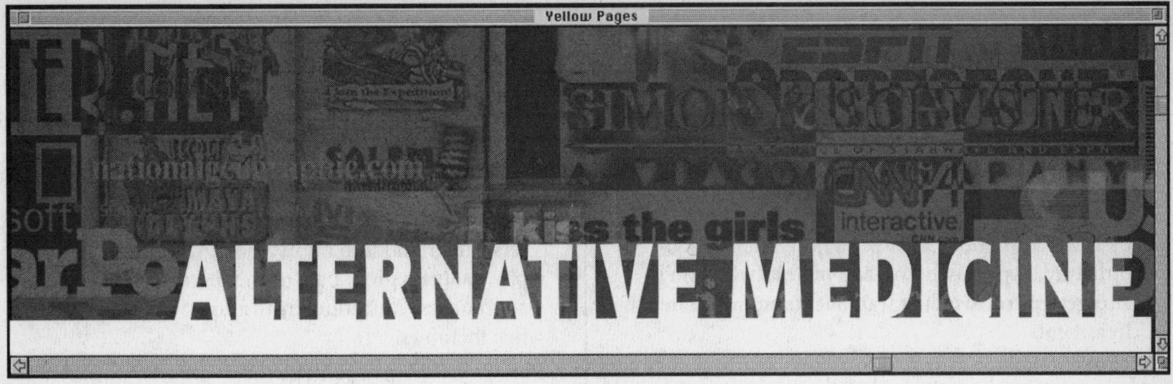

ALTERNATIVE MEDICINE

> America does not seem to remember that it derived its wealth, its values, its food, much of its medicine, and a large part of its "dream" from Native America.
>
> *Paula Gunn Allen*

Acupuncture Home Page

http://www.demon.co.uk/acupuncture/index.html

Find info about acupuncture, including conditions treated, training, research, practitioners, and other resources.

Alexandra Health Center

http://www.homeop.com

At this site, you'll learn about natural medicine and homeopathy. You also get concise descriptions of the medicine for sale.

Alternative Medicine Connection

http://www.arxc.com/arxchome.htm

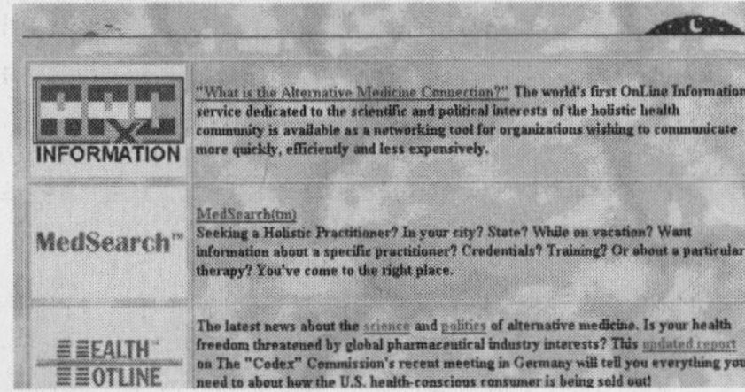

Health Care Information Resources—Alternative Medicine
http://www-hsl.mcmaster.ca/tomflem/altmed.html

New Age Journal Online
http://www.newage.com/Journal/

Offers the latest news about the science and politics of alternative medicine. Gives you access to MedSearch, which helps you find a holistic practitioner, view his or her credentials, and get info on a specific therapy. Also offers a patient information exchange, where people describe how they have benefited from holistic therapies.

Alternative Medicine Digest

http://www.alternativemedicine.com/alternativemedicine/

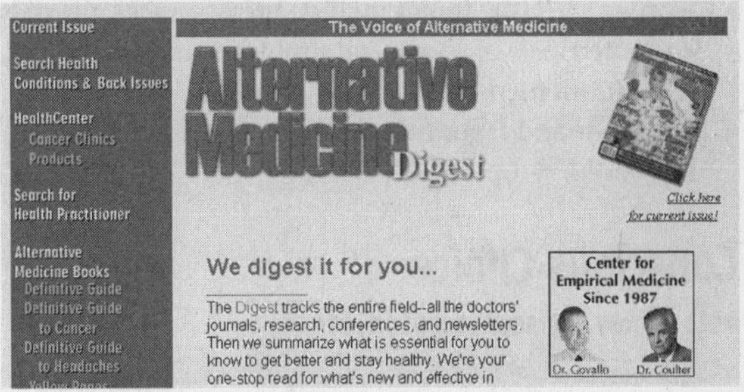

This site tracks the alternative medicine field—doctors, journals, research, conferences, and newsletters—and summarizes it.

The Alternative Medicine Home Page from Falk Library of the Health Sciences, University of Pittsburgh

http://www.pitt.edu/~cbw/altm.html

Serves as a jumpstation for sources of info on unconventional, unorthodox, unproven, alternative, complementary, innovative, and integrative therapies.

A B C D E F G H I J K L M N O P Q R S T U V W X Y Z

Alternative Medicine/Unconventional Therapy

http://www.mel.lib.mi.us/health/health-alternative.html

Gives you tips on choosing whether alternative therapy is right for you. You'll see subjects such as acupuncture, hypnosis, herbs, and biofeedback. You'll also get tips on avoiding fraudulent, unproven health treatments.

The Black Health Net

http://www.blackhealthnet.com/departments/alternative.asp

Offers timely info on alternative medicine for those of African descent. Check out topics such as acupuncture, naturopathy, herbology, chiropractic, ayurveda, therapeutic touch, aromatherapy, guided imagery, and nutrition. You'll also learn about alternative or complementary therapies for some of the illnesses common to African Americans. Includes a Q&A section.

The Center for Complementary & Alternative Medicine Research in Women's Health

http://cpmcnet.columbia.edu/dept/rosenthal/Women.html

This site gives you a database of published research worldwide in all areas of alternative medicine for women's health. Topics include breast cancer, fibroids, endometriosis, menopausal problems, menstrual regulation, menstrual-related disorders, pregnancy, pre-labor and labor management, and vaginal infections/symptoms.

Conscious Choice

http://www.consciouschoice.com/

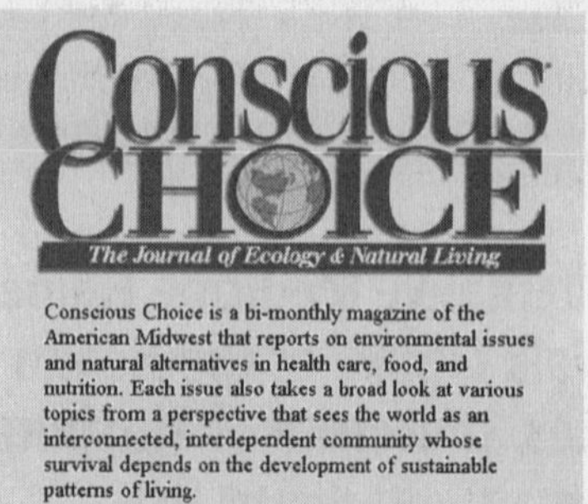

Conscious CHOICE
The Journal of Ecology & Natural Living
Conscious Choice is a bi-monthly magazine of the American Midwest that reports on environmental issues and natural alternatives in health care, food, and nutrition. Each issue also takes a broad look at various topics from a perspective that sees the world as an interconnected, interdependent community whose survival depends on the development of sustainable patterns of living.

This online, bimonthly, Midwestern magazine reports on environmental issues and natural alternatives in health care, food, and nutrition.

General Complementary Medicine References

http://www.forthrt.com/~chronicl/archiv.htm

Provides links to Web pages, networks, discussion groups, mailing lists, e-zines, journals, and newsletters. You'll find info on psychology, religion, philosophy, wellness programs, music therapy, metaphysical approaches, education, institutions, and other alternative therapies.

Get Well

http://www.moreinfo.com.au/getwell/

Topics include herbal medicine, healthy recipes, and info on topics such as folic acid, beta-carotene, and the prevention of gastric irritation. Get advice from accredited naturopaths and book recommendations. View a listing of health food distributors around the world. Get access to free publications on topics such as acne, Altzheimer's disease, digestive disorders, migraines, and hypertension.

HANS—The Health Action Network Society

http://www.hans.org/

This site covers current issues such as acupuncture, chiropractic topics, diseases, fluoride, food, government, pesticides, vitamins, and water. You'll find offers on films, books, and videos for sale.

Healing Arts Magazine

http://www.healing-arts.com/

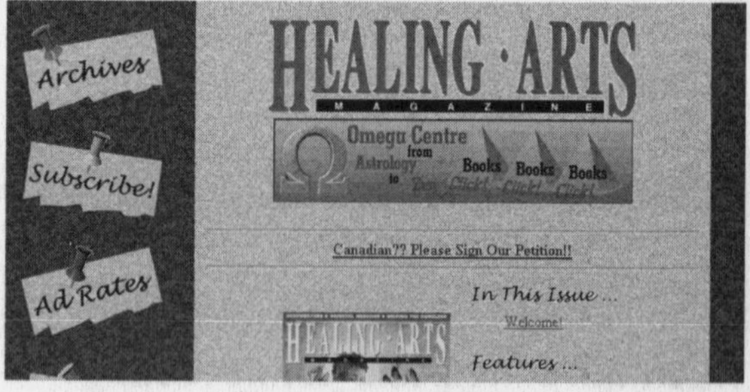

Features articles such as "Breaking Free of Stress," "Breast Cancer: Tipping the Scales in Your Favour," "Healthwatch: Osteoporosis," and "Hands that Heal: The Art of Therapeutic Touch." This site provides a huge amount of links to just about every alternative medicine resource you could imagine. It's easy to find any specific topic and a wealth of information on it through the links.

Health Care Information Resources—Alternative Medicine

http://www-hsl.mcmaster.ca/tomflem/altmed.html

Explores various alternative therapies. Gives you links to info on holistic healthcare. Also provides info on events, seminars, workshops, practitioners, and books.

HealthWWWeb Integrative Medicine, Natural Health, and Alternative Therapies

http://www.amrta.org/

Gives you info on topics such as acupuncture, herbs, homeopathic remedies, immunology, holism, and phytotherapy. Also provides a two-year global calendar of events for healthcare professionals and others. Check out links to other sites on topics such as AIDS/HIV resources, alchemy, spirituality, shaminism, ayurveda, yoga, hypnotherapy/imagery in healing, longevity, and osteopathic medicine. Includes a global listing of universities and institutes with alternative medicine-related info. Includes a list of recommended publications.

Holistic Internet Community Learning Center

http://www.holistic.com/essays/index.html

Read essays on holistic living, healing, and growth. Articles include "A Physician in Transition to a More Holistic Practice," "17 Ways to Prevent Heart Attacks," and "How Music Heals: Trends in the Use of Music and Sound for Healing."

National Institute of Health, Office of Alternative Medicine

http://altmed.od.nih.gov/

Get info on the NIH OAM, which identifies and evaluates unconventional healthcare practices. You'll find the latest info on research, training, education, and development for complementary and alternative medicine. Investigate areas such as alternative therapies, bioelectromagnetics applications, diet/nutrition/lifestyle changes, herbal medicine, manual healing methods, mind/body interventions, and pharmacological/biological treatments. Also includes a FAQ.

Natural Health and Longevity Resource Center

http://www.all-natural.com/index.html

Provides alternative and holistic approaches to healing and the exposure of health hazards in modern society. You'll get info on articles, health news updates, nutrition, recommended books, and links to other health sites. Includes an herbal reference library.

Nature's Medicine

http://www.halcyon.com/jerryga/welcome.html

Provides natural alternatives to Western medicine. Specializes in targeted nutritionals for better health. Offers more than 200 products.

New Age Journal Online

http://www.newage.com/Journal/

Get tips on finding an alternative healthcare practitioner. Use the Holistic Health Directory—a state-by-state listing of more than 6,000 practitioners in nearly 140 treatment categories. Includes articles on fitness and exercise, mind and spirit, "green" living, whole foods, and holistic health. Also includes a classified ad section.

People's Place

http://peopleplace.com

Get info and resource listings for health, personal growth, alternative medicines and therapies, healthy eating, fitness, yoga and meditation, books, vegetarianism, macrobiotics, and ayurveda. You'll also find lists of resorts, retreats, and related workshops and events.

Qi: The Journal of Traditional Eastern Health & Fitness

http://www.qi-journal.com/

Browse through articles on acupuncture, meditation, Qigong, Tai Chi, Yoga, TCM, herbs, and health exercises.

WHOLELIVING.COM

http://www.wholeliving.com

Provides a database of alternative and holistic health info and resources. Lists events and expos going on in the Maryland area.

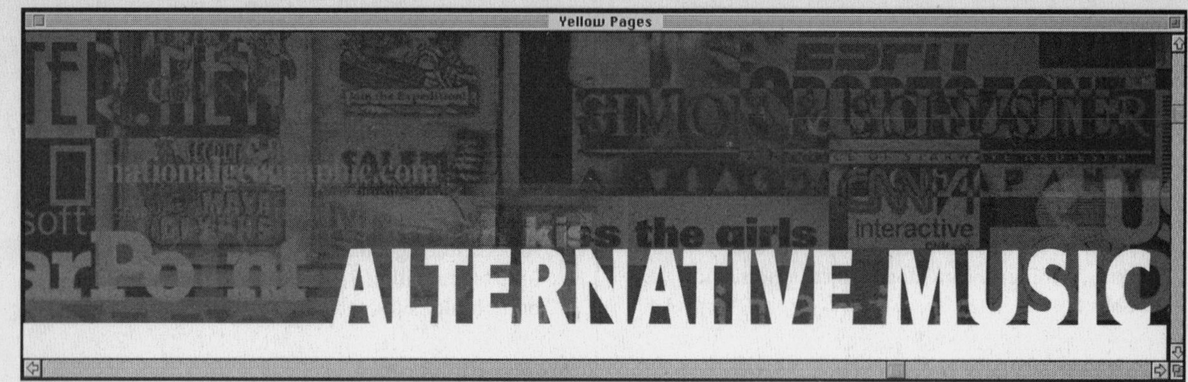

A B C D E F G H I J K L M N O P Q R S T U V W X Y Z

Furthermore, you are to stick to playing normal modes of music, not weird stuff. Those who we'd find acceptable here would include Lawrence Welk, Jim Nabors, Mantovani ...

Lt. Steven Hauk in Good Morning, Vietnam *(1987)*

Action Park: The Big Black/Rapeman/Shellac Pages

`http://tezcat.com/~andy/actionpark/`

This site is about the punk rock bands Big Black, Rapeman, and Shellac; all are fronted by guitarist/recording engineer Steve Albini. Includes articles, lyrics, discographies, and links to other related sites. Warning: Some language not for the faint of heart, but I did find this comment from the page author pretty funny: "Email all comments to andy@tezcat.com, but don't even THINK of askin' me anything that's on the list of Questions I Get Asked Every Damn Week."

A Gentle Introduction to the Wonderful and Frightening World of The Fall

`http://www.dcs.ed.ac.uk/home/cxl/fall/index.html`

Here you'll find articles, interviews, a history, and a discography of the U.K. rock group The Fall. Includes lyric transcriptions, mailing list information, and much more. This site is very detailed and highly recommended to fans of The Fall or anyone curious about their music.

NRP TOP PICKS

ALL.RADIO.COM- Radio for the 21st Century
`http://www.allradio.com/`

Brave Combo
`http://brave.com/bo/`

The Cave Inn: Nick Cave and the Bad Seeds
`http://www.zephyr.net/users/cave/`

D'CuCKOO
`http://www.well.com/user/tcircus/Dcuckoo/index.html`

High Lonesome
`http://www.highlonesome.com/`

The Indie Index
`http://www.indieindex.com/`

Indie Label List
`http://www.cs.ucl.ac.uk/external/T.Wicks/ill/index.html`

The R.E.M. Home Page
`http://www.svs.com/rem/`

Squirrel Nut Zippers
`http://www.mammoth.com/mammoth/bands/snz/`

Sub Pop Records Onlines
`http://www.subpop.com/`

ALL.RADIO.COM - Radio for the 21st Century

`http://www.allradio.com/`

It's like having a big jukebox in your computer! Choose from almost any genre imaginable, including Alternative Alley, World Beat, The Dance Mix, Gothic Den, and Hip Hop Stop. Different artists are spotlighted, with accompanying trivia contests. There are free CD offers, links to other cool stuff—it's fun, so check it out. Just make sure you read the info on the first page about what your computer needs to listen to the music.

Austin Axis

http://www.awpi.com/AustinAxis/index.html

Primarily a site about Austin, Texas, but there's an *excellent* music section. After all, as the site says, Austin is the live music capital of the Southwest! Lots of info on local and visiting performers and groups, upcoming bands, festivals and concerts, but make sure you check out *Arena Magazine* about the local music scene. Good stuff, Maynard.

BONG & Depeche Mode Home Page

http://www.commline.com

This page on the eclectic alternative band Depeche Mode includes lyrics, song parodies, FAQs, dozens of pictures, and several links to other Depeche Mode resources. You can also get information on how to subscribe to the BONG mailing list. Listen to some MIDI files while you're browsing the site.

Brave Combo

http://brave.com/bo/

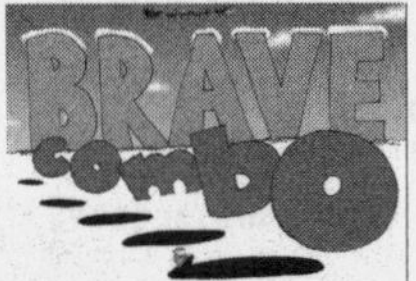

"Nuclear polka" is probably the best way to describe this Texas-based group, one of my favorite discoveries of the past year. This great-looking site with content to match is an excellent reflection of the group's talent. You'll find a discography, band profiles, a calendar of upcoming appearances, and more. If you've never heard their oddly addicting music, check out the "Hava Nagila Twist" in the Sound Samples section.

CAKE Online

http://www.grunge.com/

Here's the online home of *CAKE* magazine, an excellent place to find the latest info on bands and record labels, as well as all kinds of other entertaining articles. Check out the link to their back issue on the 1997 Music & Arts Guide for tons of info about new and alternative bands and upcoming concerts and festivals.

Can

http://www.io.com/~jwc/rock/can.html

Here's the unofficial home for the German progressive rock band known as Can. Includes band member backgrounds, discography, and a history of the group, as well as links to other related sites. Note that this page does tend to focus on the group's music during the 1970s. Cool graphics.

The Cave Inn: Nick Cave and the Bad Seeds

http://www.zephyr.net/users/cave/

This unofficial site dedicated to the gothic blues rock music of Nick Cave and The Bad Seeds includes current news, articles, interviews, and links to other related sites in a well-organized format. Nice, clean-looking graphics. You can also find a complete discography and pictures of Nick Cave.

The Cure: Stiff as Toys and Tall as Men

http://miso.wwa.com/~anaconda/cure2.html

A very cool site map takes you to sections on fan club information and 'zines, lyrics, images, a discography, books, interviews, and more. Also includes some sound clips and links to other sites. Check out "Speak My Language" in the Sounds section for a collection of humorous quotes from The Cure.

D'CuCKOO

http://www.well.com/user/tcircus/Dcuckoo/index.html

The techno-tribal band is made up of six women from Oakland who build and play their own percussion instruments, including 6-foot bamboo "trigger sticks." Features the band's interactive "showtoys"

MidiBall, as seen on the Discovery Channel, and RiGBy, an animated, 3D, computer-generated puppet—honest! Their music mixes sophisticated pop vocals and lyrics with techno, dance, and world music influences.

EnoWeb '97

`http://www.hyperreal.com/music/artists/brian_eno/`

As it says on the welcome page, this site has been "serving your Eno needs with impunity since 1993." Great site for the Eno fan who documents his music and artwork. Includes articles, interviews, a chronology, contact addresses, a discography, and more.

High Lonesome

`http://www.highlonesome.com/`

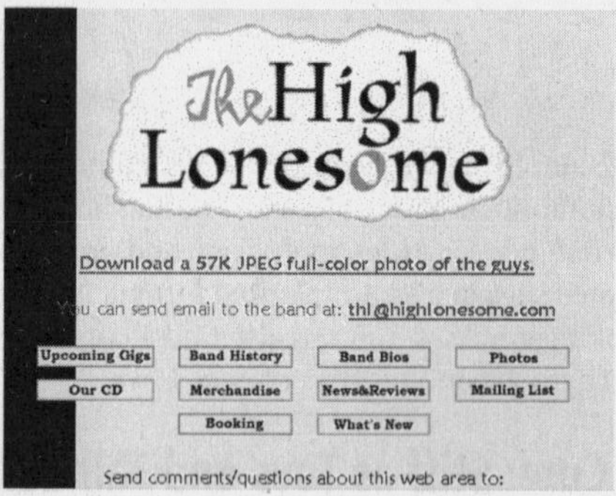

This well-crafted site on the band The High Lonesome features bios, history, lyrics, photos, ordering information, upcoming gigs, and more. Listen to 30-second samples of the band's eclectic music in WAV or AIFF format, then e-mail the band to tell 'em what you think. No flashy graphics or bells-and-whistles here—just a good solid site, with easy navigation and engaging writing that give you an excellent introduction to the band and its music.

Home Page Replica

`http://www.shiningsilence.com/hpr/`

This nicely organized site is a home for the music of Captain Beefheart and his Magic Band. Includes band bios, articles, album artwork, and links to related sites.

Hyperreal

`http://hyperreal.com/`

Hyperreal bills itself as a site for alternative culture, music, and expression. It has a huge archive of artists, and sections for anyone interested in raves or dance music. You'll find tons of links to music info, other cool sites, and a helpful library of audio and video tools.

The Indie Index

`http://www.indieindex.com/`

Great site—organized layout and very cool graphics, with a lot of black-and-white photos. You'll find everything you need to know about indie music; there are sections on artists, bands, and labels, along with tons and tons of links to other indie sites and even a search feature. A different artist or group is featured each week. You can also jump on the Indiering here, a Webring of independent music sites.

Indie Label List

`http://www.cs.ucl.ac.uk/external/T.Wicks/ill/index.html`

If you like independent-label music, then this organized site has a boatload of information for you. Search for general info, music lists, and label info, or follow the links to the featured label of the day. Well-written commentaries on each entry; for example, the info in the Label list gives you phone numbers, e-mail and mailing addresses, featured artists, and a link to that label's home page, if one's available. Great resource!

Indie Web

`http://www.indieweb.com/`

A wealth of information on independent labels in an easy-to-access format. You can also find info on starting up an indie label and manufacturing and distribution. Check out Elsewhere on the Web for indie info in Australia, Canada, and Sweden, as well as an alphabetized-by-state listing of independent music resources in the United States.

IUMA

`http://www.iuma.com/`

This site offers lots of information, sounds, and links to independent musicians worldwide. Includes links to many different labels, bands, online magazines, and other related sites. Also includes a weekly online band-of-the-week contest and contact information.

Lou Reed and the Velvet Underground

`http://www.rocknroll.net/loureed/`

You'll find info about Lou Reed, the Velvet Underground, and more here. Includes, among other things, a bootleg gallery, a discography, an image gallery, and comments on the latest tour.

Lunar-cy: The Official Moonshake Web Site

http://www.students.uiuc.edu/~j-javen/moonshake.html

Click the photo of the rock group Moonshake to start this site up. Be prepared, though; this graphics-intensive page takes a while to load completely. Once there, you'll find sound clips, a discography, song lyrics, a discussion forum, photos of the group, and band news and touring information. The group disbanded in May, 1997, however, so that last item probably won't be of much help. Still, for fans or those wanting to know more, this site has plenty to offer.

The Metaverse: Vibe Main Menu

http://alterworld.com/vibe/index.html

Check out The Delivery Room to listen to unsigned bands.

Nettwerk Productions

http://www.nettwerk.com/

Home of Nettwerk Records. Sarah McLachlan is probably its biggest name, but check out the Unforscene Music section for information on other alternative artists and groups signed with this label. There's currently a section on the Lilith Fair, too.

No-Fi Records

http://www.no-fi.com/

Home of No-Fi Records, featuring such groups as Last Days of May, Colorsound, and The Roswell Incident. You'll find discographies, band backgrounds, pictures, and more. No-Fi will even email you updates on new releases.

The Offspring.Net

http://www.theoffspring.net

Tons of information about the rock band The Offspring. Includes guitar tabs, lyrics, discography, articles, images, sound clips (in WAV and RealAudio) and interviews, with links to other related Offspring sites.

Orbital - Stopped Clock

http://www.york.ac.uk/~wjb101/orbital.htm

This unofficial home for the electronic music group Orbital offers background information, a discography, and news and articles about the group. Check out the new Live section for a collection of info about the group's appearances. You'll also find links to other electronic music sites.

Pet Shop Boys - Virtually

http://www.petshopboys.com

Here's the site for those of you who can't get enough of the Pet Shop Boys. Check out the huge picture library, fan club information, monthly updates, and audio and video clips. Also includes a FAQs list, news hotlines, biographies, articles, reviews, a pricing guide, and links to other sites.

PJ Harvey

http://www.polygram.com/polygram/island/artists/harvey_pj/PJBio.html

Polygram Record's official site for PJ Harvey has a biography, a discography, images of her CD cover art, info on tours and concerts, and a separate section for her latest release, "To Bring You My Love." Check out the link to PJ Harvey poster art, too.

The Punk Page

http://www.webtrax.com/punk/

The title of the site says it all! Look no further for all your punk music needs and news. You'll find articles, record reviews, and links—for both the old school and new school of punk—to sites about many different punk rock bands and labels worldwide. Cool graphics and lettering, and there are even links to skateboarding sites.

The R.E.M. Home Page

http://www.svs.com/rem/

Not an "official" R.E.M. site, but you R.E.M.-heads, like me, will find plenty at this organized site to satisfy you. Includes news and reviews, FAQs, info on joining the official fan club, links to other R.E.M. sites, bootlegs and collectibles, and a chat room. You'll also find a discography, guitar chord sheets, sound and video clips, lyrics (how *did* they do that? I'm still figuring out "The End of the World As We Know It"), and a huge photo archive. Check out the transcript of Michael Stipe's interview on AOL.

Sonic Truth Homepage

http://www.xs4all.nl/~bigron/sonic/index.html

Click one of the playing cards to find lyrics, articles, interviews, and a biography of the New York City–based band Sonic Youth. Includes photos, tour information, and links to many different related sites.

Squirrel Nut Zippers

http://www.mammoth.com/mammoth/bands/snz/

This page of the Mammoth Records site is devoted to the Squirrel Nut Zippers (read the welcoming blurb to find out where they got their name), a "Hot Music" group from the Chapel Hill, NC area. Click an illustration of one of their CDs to get a discography; some include RealAudio sound clips. The page also has links to sites hosted by fans of the Squirrel Nut Zippers.

Sub Pop Records Online

http://www.subpop.com/

This site, the online home for Sub Pop Records, covers the underground Seattle music scene. Get reviews and hear samples of upcoming hot bands and artists, find out about tours and appearances, and check out the links to fun stuff. Entertaining writing, clean payout, and cool graphics, especially the animation of the exploding head on the welcome page.

Talking Heads

http://129.237.17.3/Heads/Talking_Heads.html

Get your Talking Heads information here. This site spares nothing—it offers digitized songs, images, links to all kinds of Talking Heads Web resources, and more. Sign up for the Talking Heads mailing list and check out the "The Members: Life After Heads" section.

They Might Be Giants: Home-Away-From-Homepage

http://www-personal.engin.umich.edu/~athaler/TMBG/TMBG.html

This unofficial site for They Might Be Giants has an excellent introduction describing the group's music. Currently, there's a section on TMBG's latest tour. You'll also find lyrics, graphics, FAQs, and a recommendation for another TMBG site.

Third Eye Blind

http://www.slip.net/~3eb/

Information about the band, albums, articles, tour dates, sound and video clips, and e-mail. Interesting graphics, by the way.

The Tragically Hip - Tales from the Hip

http://www.thehip.com/

Check out this official home for the Canadian band The Tragically Hip. You'll find lots of pictures from past tours, find out how to join their mailing list, get on the Tragically Hip Webring, read bios and reviews, and more. Check out the section on their latest release, "Live Between Us."

Turmoil's Seattle Music Web

http://seattlemusicweb.com/

This site on underground music in Seattle offers many WAV clips and whole songs. Also has a Seattle music calendar, related art and photos, and more. Check out the section "So, You Want To Be a SeattleMusicWeb Band?" and the links to other Seattle music sites.

Ubu Web: Pere Ubu's Avant Garage Online

http://www.dnai.com/~obo/ubu/

Here's a detailed, well-crafted history, discography, and graphics of the Cleveland-based "Avant-Garage" rock group Pere Ubu. Includes album artwork, articles, FAQs, interviews, links to related sites, and ordering and contact information. Cool graphics, especially the garage!

You can be thirty years old or seventy years young. Decide in your favor.

Unknown

Anheuser-Busch Theme Parks
http://www.4adventure.com/

Paramount's Great America
http://www.pgathrills.com/

Universal Studios Florida Universal Studios Hollywood
http://www.mca.com/unicity/http://www.usf.com/

Adventure City

http://www.imenu.com/adventurecity/

This affordable California theme park is built especially for younger kids. Site contains info about the available rides, petting farm, shows, and so on.

Adventure World

http://www.adventure-world.net/

Water and theme park featuring over 100 rides, shows, and attractions. The latest addition is Skull Island, which contains the new Typhoon Seacoaster. The Adventure World SpokesHero is Cal Ripkin Jr., so it must be pretty cool.

Anheuser-Busch Theme Parks

http://www.4adventure.com/

Contains links to all Anheuser-Busch parks across America, including Sea World, Busch Gardens, Water Country USA, Adventure Island, and Sesame Place. They're all over, so one surely is located near you.

Cedar Point

http://www.cedarpoint.com/

This 364-acre amusement park/resort is located in Ohio, but that shouldn't stop you from going. This park claims to host the largest collection of rides (59) and roller coasters (12) in the world. You gotta see it to believe it.

Coaster Zombies

http://members.aol.com/SteelForce/index.html

Site dedicated to roller coaster enthusiasts everywhere. This club is for anyone who loves theme parks and wants to share their favorites with others. You can even buy a Coaster Zombies T-shirt or mouse pad.

Coney Island

http://www.brooklynonline.com/coneyisland/

Brooklyn's famous national treasure, where the concept of the roller coaster originated. Site says nothing will "scare the willy's out of you" like the Cyclone, the famous 80-years-old coaster. My personal favorite is the Disco Bumper Cars.

Disney.com–The Web Site for Families

http://www.disney.com/

Contains links to all things Disney, which by now is more than just a cute little mouse. Includes information about its theme parks as well as movies, the TV channel, videos, books, its cruise line, and much more.

Frontier Movie Town

http://www.onpages.com/frontier_movie_town/

Create and film your own Western! Where else do people offer to "dress you then shoot you"? Also contains Western Heritage Museum & Little Hollywood Museum. Yee-haw!

Funtricity Family Entertainment Park

http://www.funtricity.com/

Site contains general park info for this family entertainment park. Rides and attractions include the Vicksburg 500, Kidtricity Kastle, Home Run batting cages, Bayou Bumpers, and the Space Shuttle America.

Gold Rush City

http://www.goldrushcity.com/

This resort consists of three theme parks (Gold Rush City, Wildlife Park and High Tech Park), a water park, and more. Also contains commercial, residential, and retail properties.

Great Escape and Splashwater Kingdom

http://www.thegreatescape.com/

This New York-area theme park contains over 125 rides, shows, and attractions. For roller coaster enthusiasts, the site boasts that The Comet was rated the Best Wooden Coaster by readers of Inside Track magazine.

Libertyland

http://www.libertyland.com/

One of the cheeriest-looking Web sites you'll ever see. Libertyland is home to one of the oldest all-horse carousels as well as the Zippin Pippin, Elvis' favorite ride.

Medieval Times

http://medievaltimes.com/

Knights, jousting, a feast you eat with your hands… You'll think you're back in the times of King Arthur. This unique experience gives new meaning to the phrase dinner "theater." I've actually been and I loved it!

Paramount's Great America

http://www.pgathrills.com/

This official site provides a virtual tour of the park and its attractions. Also contains employment and season ticket information, as well as section about what's new for 1998.

Paramount's Kings Island

http://www.pki.com/

Visit the amusement park choice of the Brady Bunch! (Remember the infamous tube mix-up?) Take an online tour of the park and discover the latest live stage shows.

Ponderosa Ranch

http://www.ponderosaranch.com/

Originally the home to the TV Western, "Bonanza," today it's a Western theme park at Lake Tahoe. You can take guided tours of the set and view authentic stagecoaches and historic pieces from that era.

Six Flags Theme Parks

http://www.sixflags.com/

The largest regional theme park company in the country, with 12 parks throughout the U.S. According to the site, "85% of all Americans live within just a day's drive from a Six Flags Theme Park."

Spooky World

http://www.spookyworld.net/

This seasonal horror theme park is open from October 1 to November 1 every year. Offers plenty of frights for all ages, with a special play area called Booville for kids under 10.

Theme Park Review

http://www.themeparkreview.com/

Contains a photo gallery and trip reports from some of the world's best theme parks and roller coasters. Check the puke factor before riding the ride!

Universal Studios Florida
Universal Studios Hollywood

http://www.mca.com/unicity/
http://www.usf.com/

Where to go to experience the movies firsthand. Features many high-tech attractions with movie tie-ins, including Jurassic Park and Back to the Future. No experience can truly compare.

Related Sites

http://world.std.com/~fun/clp.html

http://www.800hershey.com/park/

http://www.adventurelanding.com/

LISTSERVS

PARKEMAIL—Park e-mail
You can join this group by sending the message "sub PARKEMAIL your name" to

listserv@euronet.be

SPRENET—Society of Park & Recreation Educators
You can join this group by sending the message "sub SPRENET your name" to

listserv@uga.cc.uga.edu

FTP SITES

ftp://ftp.cdrom.com/.12/internet/rtfm/rec/parks/theme

ftp://ftp.cs.columbia.edu/archives/faq/rec/parks/theme

ftp://ftp.cs.virginia.edu/pub/uigroup/alice/park/amusementPark/

ftp://ftp.csie.nctu.edu.tw/Documents/FAQ/rec/arts/disney/parks/

ftp://ftp.csie.nctu.edu.tw/Documents/FAQ/rec/parks/theme

ftp://ftp.eunet.fr/FAQ/disney-faq/parks

ftp://ftp.gwu.edu/pub/rtfm/rec/parks/theme

ftp://ftp.rediris.es/docs/faq/rec/parks

ftp://ftp.tol.it/software/FAQ/rec/parks

ftp://ftp.ulpgc.es/docs/faq/rec/arts/disney/parks

ftp://ftp.ulpgc.es/docs/faq/rec/parks/theme

ftp://ftp.uni-trier.de/pub/info/faq/rec/parks/theme

NEWSGROUPS

alt.disney.disneyland

rec.arts.disney.parks

rec.parks.theme

rec.roller-coaster

Related Sites

http://www.casinopier-waterworks.com/

http://www.freerun.com/napavalley/outdoor/marinewo/marinewo.html

http://www.holidayworld.com/

http://www.knotts.com/

http://www.pkd4fun.com/

http://www.santasvillage.com/

http://www.wild-adventure.com/

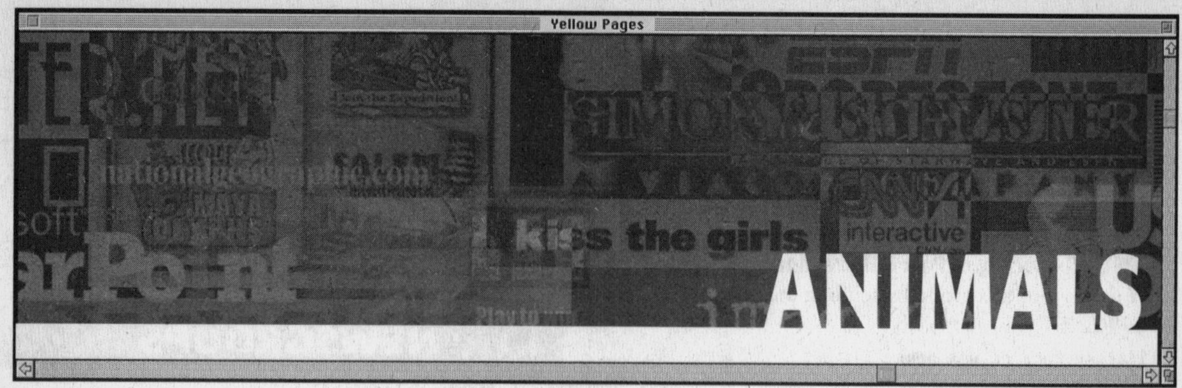

> In wilderness I sense the miracle of life, and behind it our scientific accomplishments fade to trivia.
>
> *Charles A. Lindbergh*

Birmingham Zoo-Animal Omnibus
http://www.bhm.tis.net/zoo/ao

The House Rabbit Society Home Page
http://www.rabbit.org/

Pet Grief Support
http://www.petloss.com

Animal Rights Resource Site

http://envirolink.org/arrs/index.html

The Animal Rights Resource Site, sponsored by the Envirolink Network, provides information for those involved in the support of animal rights. An icon-based menu takes you to FAQs, journals, the latest news, and extra resources. Includes information about the annual International Animal Rights Symposium in Washington, DC. Information on vegetarianism and veganism is also available.

Birmingham Zoo-Animal Omnibus

http://www.bhm.tis.net/zoo/ao

Designed primarily for children, this site is enjoyable and informative for all ages. It contains a massive index of animal photos and information pertaining to each species. The index is searchable by the common name for an animal and by geographic location. Teachers will find the resources pages, maps, and links to other sites useful.

The Pet Place

http://www.ddc.com/petplace

Dogs, cats, birds, and amphibians are featured on this site, along with pet rescue operations and tips on how individuals can aid these efforts. Also find stories, training tips, and product information for your pets. You can even submit your pet's photo and biographical sketch for possible publication on the page.

Donald Firsching's Chicken Page

http://ccwf.cc.utexas.edu/~ifza664/index.html

Did you know that the average American eats 20 chickens a year? That's according to Firsching Enterprises, the sponsor of this site. This page includes other "cool chicken facts" and "great chicken connections" (links to other sites/info). Contains links to information on the history of chickens, the poultry industry, and how to raise and care for chickens. Also offers hen and rooster .WAV sound files.

Endangered Species

http://www.nceet.snre.umich.edu/EndSpp/Endangered.html

Provides information on endangered species. Contains a large list of extinct species and clickable image maps that identify at-risk species by region.

Getting a Pet

http://www.tezcat.com/~ermiller/getapet.html

This sight will come in handy for those who are thinking of getting a dog or cat and need advice on where/how to get started. The site offers information on choosing a breed, descriptions of different types of animal shelters, advice on why you should avoid pet stores, and the truth about puppy mills. Includes links to related sites.

The House Rabbit Society Home Page

http://www.rabbit.org/

The House Rabbit Society is a nonprofit organization that works to rescue abandoned rabbits and find permanent homes for them. The Society also educates the public and assists humane societies. This Web site offers information about rabbits that are available for adoption, plus pictures and bios. It also offers links to Web sites of HRS local chapters, and provides general information about rabbits as house pets.

Inter-species Telepathic Communication

http://www.CyberArk.com/animal/telepath.htm

Do you believe humans can communicate telepathically with pets? If so, you're not alone. This site describes one dog owner's experiences in communicating telepathically with her dog, and includes submissions by other pet owners who detail similar communications with their animals. This page also refers you to reading material on the subject, videos, and workshops around the country on inter-species communication.

Nature Collections

http://secondnature.com/nature.htm

This photo- and graphics-laden site features photographic artwork of animals in their natural habitat. It also includes screen savers of nature shots that users can download—for a small fee. Includes photos of other nature venues and links to other sites about nature and travel.

Man is the most intelligent of the animals—and the most silly.

Diogenes

Pet Grief Support

http://www.petloss.com

For pet owners who are grieving over the death of a pet or an ill pet, this site offers support and encouragement. One highlight is the Monday Evening Candle Ceremony, a weekly event in which people across the country (who have lost a pet) light candles in memory of their departed companions. The site also includes the Rainbow Bridge story, which provides an answer to the question: "Where do our pets go when they die?" (You might want to keep a tissue handy for this one.)

PetBunny Home Page

http://www.mit.edu:8001/people/klund/bunny/bunny.html

PetBunny, which includes a mailing list for rabbit owners, is an open forum for people who are interested in discussing rabbits. The discussion includes such topics as diet, behavior, and medical problems. The site includes a few links to specific rabbit home pages.

The Remembrance Page

http://www.primenet.com/~meggie/bridge.htm

This site, which offers an outlet for grieving pet owners, includes poems, tributes, and photos from owners who want to share memories of animals. Visitors can also access links to pages that contain tributes to specific dogs, cats, and birds.

LISTSERVS

To subscribe, send an email message to listserv@listserv.net with SUBSCRIBE (LIST NAME) in the body. Do not use brackets. Leave subject line blank. Do not use signature.

List names

1. PETS-L
2. RAPTOR-C
3. VETINFO

ANMGT-L—Animal Management Discussion Forum
University of Nebraska Computing Services Network, Lincoln, NE

You can join this group by sending the message "sub ANMGT-L your name" to

`listserv@unlvm.unl.edu`

ANSCI-L—Animal Science Students
You can join this group by sending the message "sub ANSCI-L your name" to

`listserv@listserv.okstate.edu`

AQUARIUM—Fish & Aquaria
You can join this group by sending the message "sub AQUARIUM your name" to

`listserv%emuvm1.bitnet@listserv.net`

AZARCOL—Aquariums Research Coordinators
Kansas State University; Manhattan, KS

You can join this group by sending the message "sub AZARC-L your name" to

`listserv@ksuvm.ksu.edu`

CANINE-L—Discussion Forum for Dog Fanciers
Pennsylvania State University

You can join this group by sending the message "sub CANINE-L your name" to

`listserv@psuvm.psu.edu`

CAT-CHAT
You can join this group by sending the message "sub CAT-CHAT your name" to

`istserv@lsv.uky.edu`

CONSGIS—Biological Conservation and GIS
You can join this group by sending the message "sub CONSGIS your name" to

`listserv%uriacc.bitnet@listserv.net`

DAIRY-L—Dairy Discussion List
University of Maryland CSC, College Park, MD 20742-2411

You can join this group by sending the message "sub DAIRY-L your name" to

`listserv%umdd.bitnet@listserv.net`

EMBRIO—Basic Embryology for Medical Students
Temple University, Philadelphia, PA 19122

You can join this group by sending the message "sub EMBRIO your name" to

`listserv@vm.temple.edu`

EQUINE-L—Discussion Forum for Horse Fanciers
Pennsylvania State University

You can join this group by sending the message "sub EQUINE-L your name" to

`listserv@psuvm.psu.edu`

FELINE-L—Discussion Forum for Cat Fanciers
Pennsylvania State University

You can join this group by sending the message "sub FELINE-L your name" to

`listserv@psuvm.psu.edu`

FERRET—The Domestic Ferret Electronic Mailing List (FML)
City University of New York/University Computing Center

You can join this group by sending the message "sub FERRET your name" to

`listserv@cunyvm.cuny.edu`

GERBILS—Gerbil Discussion List
Rice University Information Systems, Houston, Texas

You can join this group by sending the message "sub GERBILS your name" to

`listserv@ricevm1.rice.edu`

GISAB-L—Gibbs Sampling in Animal Breeding
University of Nebraska Computing Services Network, Lincoln, NE

You can join this group by sending the message "sub GISAB-L your name" to

`listserv@unlvm.unl.edu`

GROOMERS-L—Pet Groomers Helping Each Other
You can join this group by sending the message "sub GROOMERS-L your name" to

`listserv@home.ease.lsoft.com`

KSUPET-L—KSU Pet Health News
Kansas State University; Manhattan, KS

You can join this group by sending the message "sub KSUPET-L your name" to

`listserv@ksuvm.ksu.edu`

MAMMAL-L—Mammalian Biology
Smithsonian Institution, Washington, DC 20560

You can join this group by sending the message "sub MAMMAL-L your name" to

`listserv@sivm.si.edu`

MARMAM—Marine Mammals Research & Conservatoin Discussion
University of Victoria, Victoria, BC

You can join this group by sending the message "sub MARMAM your name" to

`listserv@uvvm.uvic.ca`

MATBI-L—Marine All Taxa Biological Inventories
Smithsonian Institution, Washington, DC

You can join this group by sending the message "sub MATBI-L your name" to

`listserv@sivm.si.edu`

PETBUNNY—Forum for Folks with Companion Rabbits
You can join this group by sending the message "sub PETBUNNY your name" to

`listserv@lsv.uky.edu`

POODLE—All Poodle Discussion Group
eWorld, Apple Online Services, Cupertino, CA, USA

You can join this group by sending the message "sub POODLE-L your name" to

`listserv@mail.eworld.com`

PROTECTION-DOGS-L—Protection Dogs Discussion List
eWorld, Apple Online Services, Cupertino, CA, USA

You can join this group by sending the message "sub PROTECTION-DOGS-L your name" to

`listserv@mail.eworld.com`

URBWLF-L—Urban Wildlife Working Group: Ecology, Education, Planning
You can join this group by sending the message "sub URBWLF-L your name" to

`listserv%uriacc.bitnet@listserv.net`

WDAMAGE—Wildlife Damage Management
You can join this group by sending the message "sub WDAMAGE your name" to

`listserv@listserv.nodak.edu`

WLREHAB—Wildlife Rehab List
You can join this group by sending the message "sub WLREHAB your name" to

`listserv@listserv.nodak.edu`

ZOOGNUSNews from the National Zoological Park, Washington, DC
Smithsonian Institution, Washington, DC 20560

You can join this group by sending the message "sub ZOOGNUS your name" to

`listserv@sivm.si.edu`

ZOOGRAD—Department of Zoology Grad Students
Arizona State University, Tempe, AZ

You can join this group by sending the message "sub ZOOGRAD your name" to

`listserv@asuvm.inre.asu.edu`

NEWSGROUPS

`alt.animals`

`alt.animals.badgers`

`alt.animals.bears`

`alt.animals.dolphins`

`alt.animals.felines`

`alt.animals.foxes`

`alt.animals.raccoons`

`alt.aquaria`

`alt.chinchilla`

`alt.fan.lemurs`

`alt.pets.ferrets`

`alt.pets.hamsters`

`alt.pets.rabbits`

`alt.skunks`

`alt.support.grief.pet-loss`

`alt.wolves`

`rec.animals.wildlife`

`rec.aquaria`

`rec.aquaria.tech`

`rec.equestrian`

`rec.hunting.dogs`

`rec.pets`

`rec.pets.birds`

`rec.pets.cats`

`rec.pets.dogs`

`rec.pets.dogs.rescue`

`rec.pets.herp`

A B C D E F G H I J K L M N O P Q R S T U V W X Y Z

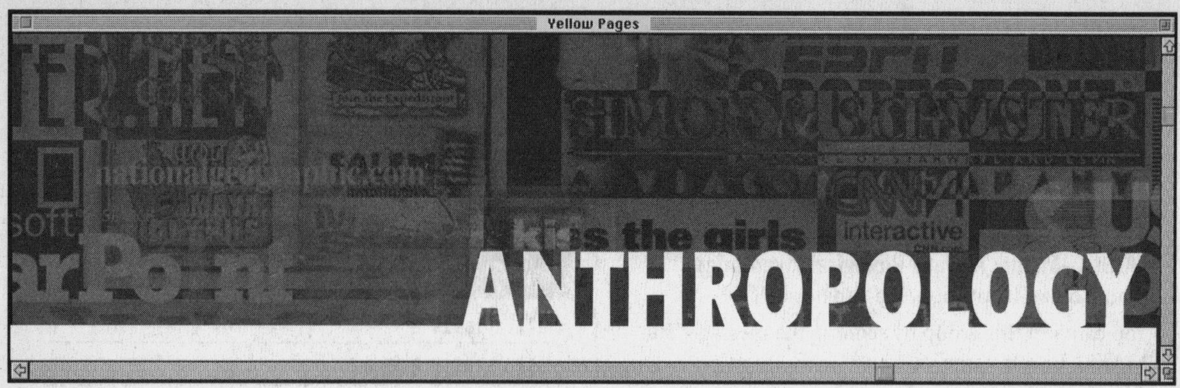

ANTHROPOLOGY

> Man is an animal suspended in webs of significance he himself has spun...
>
> *Max Weber from* Cliffard Geertz

American Indian Mother Earth Prayers

http://www.indians.org/welker/earth.htm

This is another personal site dedicated to preserving Native American earth mother prayers. Links are provided to various people's prayers accompanied by natual history photographs that invoke the spirit of the poems.

The ANTHAP Home Page

http://www.acs.oakland.edu/~dow/anthap.html

The Society for Applied Anthropology maintains this Web site to provide information about its activities. Links include various research papers, meetings, courses of study, and employment. An extremely comprehensive collection of materials on the topic.

AnthroLink

http://www.buckley.pvt.k12.ca.us/AnthroLink/

A beautifully designed site dedicated to sharing information pertaining to the teaching of Anthropology at secondary schools and community colleges. Teaching materials, course outlines, and a a huge collection of related links are provided via clever hominid skull graphics.

Related Site

http://www.ameranthassn.org/

Rabbit In The Moon

http://www.halfmoon.org/index.html

Anthropology Resources at the University of Kent

http://lucy.ukc.ac.uk/

This is the oldest site containing Anthropological resources on the Web. The site is supported by the Center for Social Anthropology and Computing and contains information on research projects, information resources, calendar of events of interest to anthropologists, and transcripts of talks on various topics of interest. You can perform keyword-based searches of CSAC's archives, bibliographies, and theses.

Dazhdbog's Grandchildren

http://sunsite.unc.edu/sergei/Grandsons.html

This is a personal site designed with the assistance of Sergei Naumov and the University of North Carolina at Chapel Hill. The site provides cultural information on the "Rus" people including their music, humor, folktales, and more. Note that most of the materials on the server are in Russian. Software is provided as well as instructions on how to display Cyrillic type in your browser.

The Encyclopedia Mythica

http://www.pantheon.org/mythica/

This is an ongoing exercise to build a comprehensive pictoral and textual encyclopedia of all of the world's mythology. Entries are provided by both subject and alphabetical order. Accomodation is provided for those browsers that cannot handle frames.

Related Site

http://www.archaeology.la.asu.edu/vm/mesaum/teo/

Ethnographic.com

http://www.ethnographic.com/

A professionally developed site providing information for both the dilitente and professional ethnographer on both the material and cultural aspects of indigenous peoples. Emphasis is placed on reviewing ethnographic sites based on their usefulness and accuracy. Links are organized by ethnographic subject, such as fashions, music, books, museums, art dealers, and so forth.

Field Work: The Anthroplogy of the Field

http://www.truman.edu/academics/ss/faculty/tamakoshil/index.html

A gorgeously graphic site providing insite into ongoing research by Dr. Laura Zimmer-Tamakoshil in Papua New Guinea. The frame-based site provides information on planning, resources, writing research proposals, logistics, and actual field notes during her experience.

Indigenious People's Literature

http://38.15.30.162/glenwelk/natlit.htm

Glen Welker is collecting indigenous people's folklore in a comprehensive archive organized by indigenous people. Stories can be viewed using Adobe Acrobat. English and Spanish versions of the site are provided.

Internet Resources for Anthropology

http://nsccux.sccd.ctc.edu/~tlc/anthro.html

A very spare site that contains a collection of links to other Anthropology-related sites. Very dull.

Lords of the Earth

http://www.realtime.net/maya/

A beautiful site providing links to mesoamerican anthropology pages. The page does have a decided political bent in support of the many indigenous revolutions occuring in Central America.

Materials for the Study of Women and Gender in the Ancient World—Nereids

http://www.uky.edu/ArtsSciences/Classics/Nereids/Index.html

This site presents an academic compendium of information concerning Nereids (water nymphs) as they were used in Roman mosaics. The site is written in French with very few links to anywhere else.

Mayan Epigraphic Database Project Home Page

http://jefferson.village.virginia.edu/med/home.html

This is the front-end to an extensive database of Mayan glyphs and their linguistic meanings. The site lets you enter verbal values and see the corresponding Mayan glyph. An excellent tool for translating epigraphic materials.

Myths and Legends

http://pubpages.unh.edu/~cbsiren/myth.html

This is a bare-bones site dedicated to collecting links to Web sites, published articles, and analytical sites dealing with myths and legends. The site is updated often as the collection grows.

Rabbit In The Moon

http://www.halfmoon.org/index.html

This is one of the most beautiful sites on the Internet. Rabbit In the Moon is dedicated to sharing up-to-date information about the Classic Maya. Links are provided to pages explaining Mayan glyphs and writing, architecture, languages, academic meetings, and other Mayan sites. The Rabbit In the Moon site provides interactive games to teach about Mayan writing and calendrics, projects to teach about architecture, as well as a search engine.

Science World of Discovery—Ancient Life: Early Man

http://members.aol.com/mlhuestis/sciworld/earlyman.htm

This is an extremely comprehensive collection of information about evolution, paleontology, and ancient life throughout the world. Links included on the Page include Journals and Publications, various search engines for other Paleontology sites, FAQs, career information, and dictionaries.

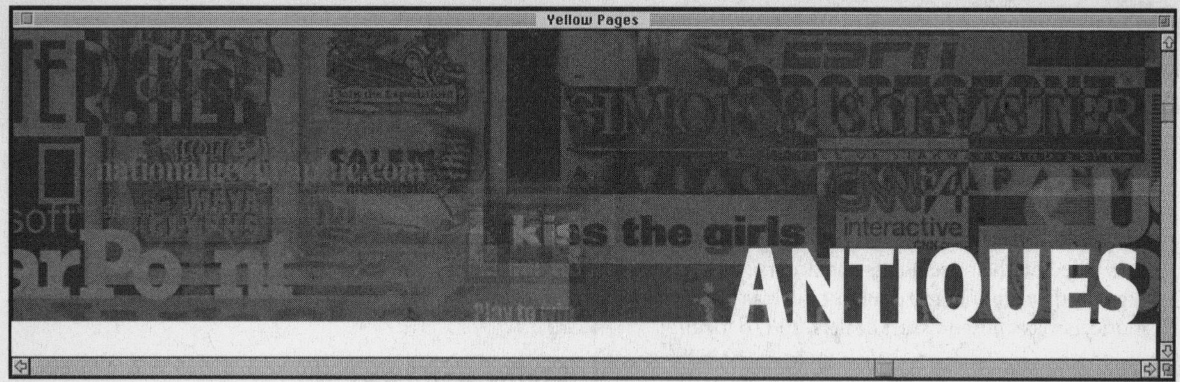

> O, good old man, how well in thee appears.
> The constant service of the antique world.
>
> *William Shakespeare*

100s of Antiques and Collectibles

http://www.tias.com/stores/100s/

If you are looking for a specific item, this site enables you to run a search, and the results tell you which online dealers or galleries have it in stock. Searches may take three forms: Quick, Complete, and Auction.

Antique Alley

http://bmark.com/aa/

Antique Alley's page allows you to search for a specific item or shop; peruse a giant list of shops around the country; or guides you to others antiques pages, in case a search comes up empty.

Antique Networking

http://www.antiqnet.com/

The main focus of this site is to help collectors find sellers by providing an exhaustive search engine that changes daily. They also help collectors find suitable interior designers, antique insurance agents, and others.

Related Sites

http://web2.airmail.net/~pezmgl/#TABLETOP

http://www.antiquephono.com/

http://www.sfautomobilia.com/automobilia.htm

http://WWW.ANTIQUE-QUILTS.COM/

Antiques Road Show
http://www.pbs.org/wgbh/pages/roadshow/

Antique Radio Restoration & Repair

http://www.neca.com/~radiodoc/

Whether you want to buy an antique radio or have an old television restored, this Connecticut-based specialty business thrives on old technology. You may learn more about vintage radios, TV, and other personal electronics here and on several pages linked to it.

Antiques Road Show

http://www.pbs.org/wgbh/pages/roadshow/

Even if you're an inexperienced antiquer, PBS's *Antiques Road Show* is a great show and Web site to visit to get into it. The show visits antique conventions all around the country where they have experts appraise items that regular people bring in and are clueless about. They also appraise fakes, to help the viewer gain knowledge about how to avoid them. Check out the appraisal contest.

Auction! Auction!

http://auctionauction.com/

If you like to attend auctions to buy your antiques, give the Auction! Auction! page a try. Select by state, region, or even country or continent. You will see a list of available items at auctions being held in your region.

Augie's 45 RPM Vinyl Record Sale

http://home.earthlink.net/~augustl/45_RPM_Sale.html

Augie has been collecting records since the 1950s, so it is not surprising that you have your choice from 6,000 titles. An alphabetic index will list all of the titles he has available.

The Doll House

http://www.csmonline.com/barbie/

For every doll collector, there is the Doll House Web site, which specializes in Barbie. Join discussion groups, search classified ads, and download images of Barbies you didn't even know existed. The site also links to articles by renowned Barbie expert, Jane Sarasohn-Kahn.

Early American History Auctions, Inc.

http://www.earlyamerican.com/

The online site for the EAHA specializes in antique Americana, such as maps, civil war memorabilia, newspapers, coins, and so on. Check out the price list of current items and submit a bid, either by email, fax, or snail mail.

Famous Furniture

http://famous-furniture.com/

We all have a little antiquer within us, yearning to grasp the old and rare. Famous Furniture imports antiques from all over the world and presents them well in this information-rich site.

Know Knew Books Online

http://www.knowknew.com/

Have you been looking for that special first edition Ayn Rand forever? Know Knew Books has collectible books for many categories: art & photography, fiction, history, Westerns, music, humor, children's, science fiction, and more.

The Life Archive

http://snowdens.bc.ca/LIFE/lindex.html

This is a Web site devoted to collectors of *Life* magazine, which are divided into the following year categories: 1940 and Older, every individual year 1941 through 1951, and then 1952 and Newer. The site is run by a bookstore in British Columbia.

Net Stamps

http://www.netstamps.com/index2.htm

Stamp collectors all over the world can come to Net Stamps' site to view articles about the stamp-collecting world's governing body, read and place classified ads, and learn about new stamp releases from the United States Post Office.

Political Memorabilia Marketplace

http://207.36.66.177/index.html

Whether you collect Presidential campaign pins, flags, plates, or what not, this site covers it. You can perform searches, follow links to related sites, or check out the latest items from recent campaigns, such as Perot '96 or Inauguration '97.

Sign It

http://www.signit.com/

Sign It deals in autographs of movie and TV stars, musicians, athletes, and others. Glance over their price lists. A secure server enables you to make online transactions safely.

Star Show

http://www.starshow.com/

Star Show is your one-stop Web shop for Star Wars, Star Trek, and other sci-fi collectibles. This site will remind you why never to sell any toys after they are outgrown.

Topps

http://www.topps.com/

Famous for its baseball cards, Topps originally started as a bubble gum manufacturer. Use their site to learn more about the company and its history, as well as their collectibles, which include baseball, basketball, and entertainment cards, candy and gum, comics, and more.

Related Sites
http://www.classicengland.co.uk/historic.html
http://www.bear-paw.com/
http://www.centralcarpet.com/
http://slip.net/~hpytrail/
http://www.bradex.com/
http://www.sonic.net/~rod/epb.html

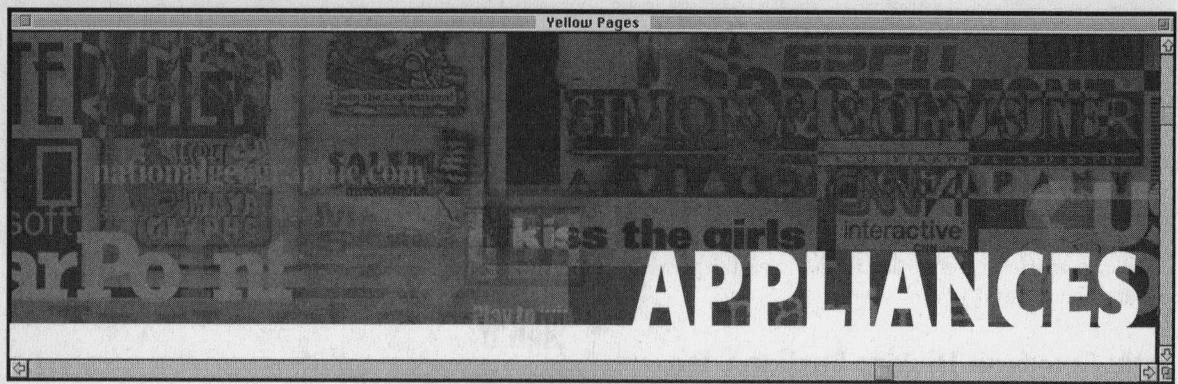

> My husband and I have figured out a really good system about the housework: neither one of us does it.
>
> *Dottie Archibald*

As Seen on TV

http://www.asontv.com/

If you have ever regretted not calling that "800" number to buy some appliance you saw for sale on TV, this site will thrill you. You can buy all those gadgets and appliances right here online, and for less money than they were originally advertised for in many cases.

Association of Home Appliance Manufacturers

http://www.aham.org/

This site is home for the professional organization for people and companies that make appliances. It's mostly specialized industry stuff, but their "Just for Consumers" section offers a useful guide for selecting an appliance.

Binatone Products

http://www.binatone.com/

Most people have never heard of Binatone Products, a Swiss appliance company, but their online catalog is classy and professional. A good example of a well-designed product sales site.

Hamilton Beach/Proctor Silex
http://www.hambeach.com/

Braun Home Page

http://www.braun.de/home.htm

Information about Braun goods, those classy coffee makers and other small appliances sold in upscale department stores. In keeping with that image, this site is dark, sleek, and understated.

Cuisinart

http://www.cuisinart.com/

Home page of "the food processor people," this clean-looking site enables you to order replacement parts and accessories and find out more about other appliances you may want to buy at your local retailer. You can also download free recipes that you can make using (surprise!) your Cuisinart food processor.

Disabled Persons Furniture and Appliances

http://www.tradepages.co.uk/sector/disabled.html

A comprehensive list of appliance suppliers that provide specially made appliances that are easier for people with disabilities to use than regular models.

Frigidaire

http://www.frigidaire.com/

The usual product information offerings and technical specs, plus customer service, a dealer locator, and some innovative kitchen and laundry room design ideas.

Related Sites

http://www.appliances.com/

http://www.dakgourmetproducts.com/

GE Appliances

http://www.ge.com/index.htm

Not a lot of hype, but plenty of good information. A searchable database of GE products helps you compare various models before making a purchase, and you can schedule a service call online. You'll also find technical information, from which vacuum bags to buy to the height of a particular refrigerator.

Hamilton Beach/Proctor Silex

http://www.hambeach.com/

Plenty of information about Hamilton Beach and Proctor Silex kitchen appliances, plus a great recipes section and extensive Q&A about using and maintaining individual product lines and models.

Hotpoint Ltd.

http://www.hotpoint.co.uk/
http://www.ge.com/appliances/usa/hotpoint/index.htm

Hotpoint is a division of General Electric, and its U.S. site is merely a section of the larger GE site (http://www.ge.com). However, the United Kingdom site is very different, with clever animated icons and an entirely different feel, and worth visiting just for entertainment value even if you are a U.S. user.

The Kitchen Collection

http://www.kitcol.com/

A sort of factory outlet mall online, specializing in kitchen appliances and gadgets. Includes famous brands like WearEver and Hamilton Beach, at prices that approximate those of factory outlet stores.

Maytag Home of Dependability

http://www.maytag.com/index.cgi

A friendly, easy-to-use online showroom of Maytag appliances. You can get detailed product specifications and warranty information, find out about special promotions and rebates, order parts and service, and even locate a dealer in your area. A great one-stop shopping site that may make you want a Maytag even if you had already decided on another brand.

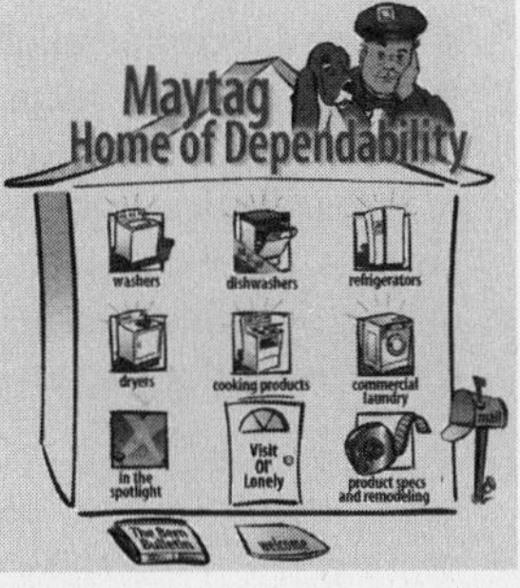

Philips Domestic Appliances and Personal Care

http://www.dap.philips.com/

Philips is a multi-division company that makes everything from televisions to CD-ROM drives. This site is devoted to the "DAP" division (Domestic Appliances and Personal Care) and showcases an amazing array of products from deep fryers to electric toothbrushes.

Sears, Roebuck and Company

http://www.sears.com/

One of the biggest department stores, Sears puts on a good Web site that looks and feels a lot like their catalog (before they stopped producing it, that is). You can order from their online catalog, which includes a full line of their famous Kennmore appliance line, locate a store in your area, or send a message to Customer Service.

Whirlpool Home Appliances

http://www.whirlpool.com/index.shtml

A nicely designed site where you can find out more about Whirlpool's large family of appliances, from washing machines to air conditioners. Includes a Dealer Locator and an online problem troubleshooting process.

Related Sites
http://www.dartmouth.edu/~boyo/engs4/appliances.html
http://www.in-sink-erator.com/
http://www.jennair.com/
http://kitchenaid.com/index.shtml
http://www.carico.com/
http://www.adg-bosch.com/saltlake/
http://www.aastore.com/aashopdirectory/
http://www.vita-mix.com/

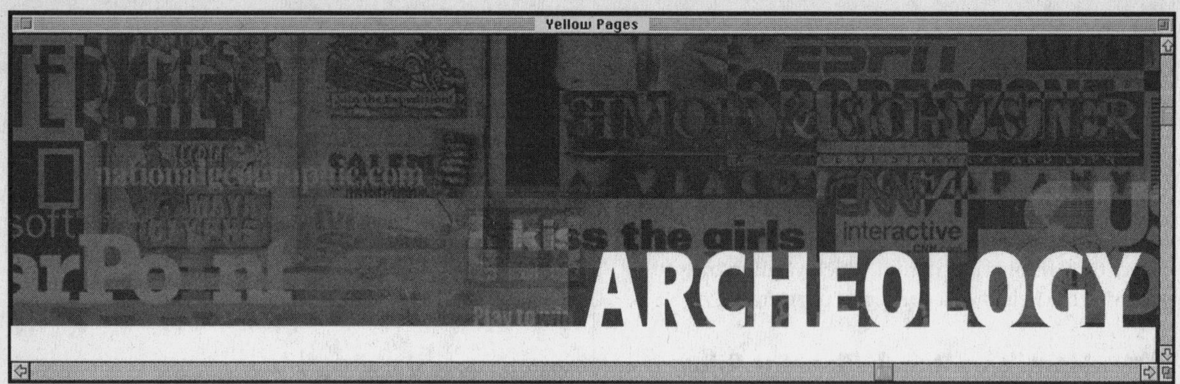

> What a fitting end to your life's pursuits. You're about to become a permanent addition to this archaeological find. Who knows? In a thousand years, even you may be worth something.
>
> *Belloq in* Raiders of the Lost Ark *(1981)*

The Ancient Sites Directory

http://www.henge.demon.co.uk/

A photographic compendium of the major archeological sites of the United Kingdom. This is a Frames-based site that also provides glossary terms, maps, and short descriptions for each excavation.

The Archeological Adventure

http://tqd.advanced.org/3011/indexge.htm

A student-built Web site providing extensive information on how archeologists perform their work, exciting finds, and an interactive forum for discussions about archeology and its practioners. Links are provided to other sites of interest to archeology students.

The Institute of Egyptian Art and Archaeology
http://www.memst.edu/egypt/main.html

Archeology World

http://artalpha.anu.edu.au/web/arc/arcworld.htm

An overview of archeological activities on the Pacific rim, including Australia, Polynesia, and Micronesia. A series of pages on "Unconventional Archeology" invites responses from traditional scientists to non-academic archeological research including New Age and Neopaganistic work.

ArchNet: Main Menu

http://www.lib.uconn.edu/ArchNet

Provides links to and information regarding archaeology on the Internet. Includes the following subject areas: archeometry, ceramics, educational materials, ethnohistory, ethnoarchaeology, geo-archaeology, and a fabulous list of links to museum Web pages.

Classics and Mediterranean Archaeology Home Page

http://rome.classics.lsa.umich.edu/welcome.html

A rather dry compendium of Archeological source materials primarily focused on Mediterranean and classical archaeology. Also provides access to all sorts of archaeological links, including articles, journals, projects, exhibits, images, related academics, museums, geographic information, other Internet resources, and more. An excellent resource.

GIS and Remote Sensing for Archaeology: Burgundy, France

http://deathstar.rutgers.edu/projects/france/france.html

A description of a specific remote sensing project undertaken by Rutgers University in Burgundy, France. Sums up most of the major modern technological techniques for excavating and sensing underground. Very slow to download since the GIS images are very large.

Gopher and WWW Servers

http://www.cr.nps.gov/ncptt/irg/irg-servers.html

This is an index of Usenet newsgroups and WWW servers sponsored by the Internet Resources for Heritage Conservation, Historic Preservation, and Archeology. Describes what you can find on Web servers dedicated to archaeology. Offers links to historical societies, archaeology sites, museums, architectural preservation sites, gophers, FAQs, and servers.

The Institute of Egyptian Art and Archaeology

http://www.memst.edu/egypt/main.html

Presents exhibits from the University of Memphis, TN Institute of Egyptian Art and Archeology online that include mummies and other artifacts. Offers the chance to see the relics of old or take a Web tour of Egypt.

Maya Research Group

http://www.qvision.com/MRP/

The Maya Research Group (MRP) is dedicated to the preservation of Mayan archeological sites. This Web site provides discussion areas, research papers, and digging opportunities related to Mayan archeology. The Web site also provides a bookstore with secure commercial server where you can purchase books on related subjects.

National Archeological Database

gopher://riceinfo.rice.edu/11/Subject/Anth

A gopher site listing an extensive array of Usenet newsgroups on a multitude of topics concerning Archeology. Numerous university archives are listed as well as many of the Web sites described in this section.

Newstead Project

http://www.brad.ac.uk/acad/archsci/field_proj/newstead/newstead.html

Focuses on the archeological exploration of settlements surrounding a Roman fort, called Trimontium, in southern Scotland.

Oriental Institute Archaeology

http://www-oi.uchicago.edu/OI/PROJ/OI_Archaeology.html

Covers many ongoing excavations and other archaeological projects by the Oriental Institute at the University of Chicago. Offers links to many different projects.

OWAN

http://www.wesleyan.edu/classics/OWAN.html

The *Old World Archaeology Newsletter (OWAN)* covers the conferences, research, and publications concerning archaeology. Includes editorials and announcements.

The Ohio State University Excavations at Isthmia

http://www.acs.ohio-state.edu/history/isthmia/isthmia.html

Covers the excavations at The Sanctuary of Poseidon at Isthmia (Greece). Examines the work and describes several points of interest in the area.

The Sacred Landscape

http://www.sonic.net/yronwode/sacredland.html

This is a definitely off-beat Web site dedicated to the description of archeological sites in terms of their sacred geometry. Free Mason theology and pseudo-science articles on the astro-calendric meanings of classic sites are presented along with photographs.

Stone Pages

http://joshua.micronet.it/utenti/dmeozzi/HomEng.html

A gorgeous Web site providing descriptions of megalithic sites throughout England, Ireland, and Scotland. Provides recent updates including information about newly discovered sites. Quicktime VR movies of various megaliths are presented as well as statistical and research data about the sites. Pages provided in both Italian and English.

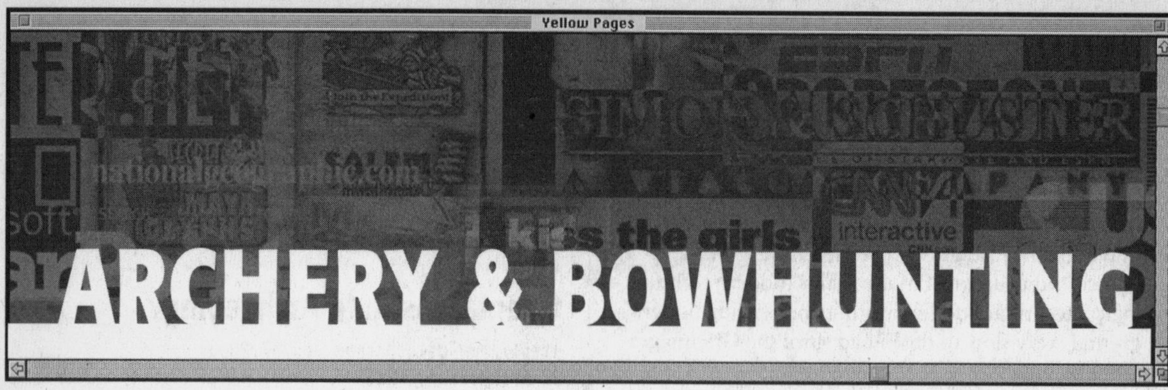

> He stakes his quiver,
> bow, and arrows,
> His mother's doves, and
> team of sparrows.
>
> *John Lyly*

Angus Duggan's Archery Page

http://www.dcs.ed.ac.uk/home/ajcd/archery

This simple (no graphics) page is packed with dozens of links to FAQs, Usenet newsgroups, and other archery links. Angus also provides photographs, lists of tournaments and awards, rankings, and some personal observations on the sport.

Archery Dynamics, Inc.

http://www.bowhunting.net/archerydynamics/default.htm#top

Archery Dynamics is a manufacturer of archery products. This site provides a list of their products with ordering information. You'll also find links to other manufacturers of archery equipment, links to other archery sites, and some great photos of hunters with their prey.

Blue Mountain Home Page

http://www.telmarcorp.com/bluemt/

This commercial site contains information about Blue Mountain Archery equipment. It also provides searchable regulations for all 50 states and some awesome wildlife photography.

Related Site

http://207.17.189.22/login

Lenny's Archery Page for Cheshire County Bowmen
http://www.pthwaite.demon.co.uk/

Bowhunter Magazine

http://www.bowhunting.net/bowhunter/default.htm#top

The Internet site of *Bowhunter Magazine*, complete with articles, editorials, photos, and advertising. You'll find deer and elk forecasts for the current season plus advice and tips from experts. The site contains links to national and state alerts.

Bowhunting.Net's Main Navigation Page

http://www.bowhunting.net/index.html#listing

Here's a well-maintained, updated site packed with informative articles, the latest news in the archery industry, and links to many other sites. From here you can access a live chat room complete with classified ads, news of upcoming events, and more. There are directories of pro shops and dealers, and the site sponsors a regular sweepstakes.

Browning Home Page

http://www.browning.com/brwnfram.htm

Browning, the rifle/shotgun manufacturer, also makes state-of-the-art bows. You'll find everything you need for the hunt right here—a large selection of bows and all the accessories. There's a complete list of dealers, and contact information for requesting free catalogs. Check out this site and hear the sounds of the wild via the audio clip that accompanies the home page.

Related Sites

http://info.htcomp.net/bhn/clubs.nsf/d18055b9f3523b3d862563dc0062dcbd?OpenView

http://info.htcomp.net/bhn/dealers.nsf

FITA Home Page

http://www.worldsport.com/sports/archery/home.html

FITA, the International Archery Federation, with headquarters in Lausanne, Switzerland, is the recognized world governing body for the sport of target and field archery. Here you'll find official reports of plans for the 2000 Olympics in Sydney, newsletters from participating countries, and lots of official news about the sport of archery. Find out about upcoming archery events, or register as a member of FITA. You can view the page in either English or French, and order videos of archery competition at the 1996 Atlanta Olympics.

Idaho Archery

http://members.aol.com/idarchery/index.html

The best feature of this site is its archive of stories from bowhunters. If you're wondering what the allure is that causes someone to drive sometimes hundreds of miles into the wilderness and then walk more miles, all before the break of day, check out these stories from hunters in the field. You'll find the usual pictures of hunters with their prey with the addition of the events that led up to the kill and information about the exact equipment used. There's much more at this site, including deer and elk forecasts, upcoming competitions, and links to other pages, but the real-life stories are the best.

Lenny's Archery Page for Cheshire County Bowmen

http://www.pthwaite.demon.co.uk/

Here you can learn about the sport of field archery in England. There's news of upcoming shoots, information about official organizations, and links to other archery pages. Be sure to visit the "Fun and Entertainment" section; this is actually a primer in archery, complete with illustrations, where you can learn what to expect at a shoot, what you should wear, bring to eat, and more. There are definitions of field, target, and clout archery, along with illustrations of longbows, recurve, and more.

Links Archers

http://www.sol.co.uk/l/linksarchers/

Learn about archery in Scotland here. There's a section about news and scores from Scotland, articles by and about individual archers, some with photos, and lots of tips and hints for improving your form.

Sagittarius Twente, University Archery Club

http://snt.student.utwente.nl/~sagi/

This site, from the Netherlands, has a unique site map in the form of an archery target. It's well-constructed with pages of articles by and for archers. Don't miss the Excuses page.

The US Archer

http://www.bowhunting.net/usarcher/default.htm#top

At this Web site you'll find the entire contents of the *US Archer* magazine, a bimonthly publication. The current and archived issues are here in their entirety, but there's also the offer of free books with a subscription. There are articles, editorials, photographs—everything you'd find in the real magazine. You'll also find links to all the official archery organizations and other sites of interest to archers. This magazine covers all aspects of archery, from field and target archery to 3D shoots to bowhunting.

NEWSGROUPS

rec.sport.archery

alt.archery

FAQs are at:

http://www.dcs.ed.ac.uk/home/ajcd/archery/faq/index.html

Related Sites

http://info.htcomp.net/bhn/manufac.nsf/58f6144a65441958862563dc0062e101?OpenView

http://www.archerydynamics.com/

http://www.yahoo.com/Recreation/Sports/Archery/

http://www.usarchery.org/

http://www.gnas.u-net.com/

http://www.usarchery.org/results/97od/97od.htm

http://www.thebowman.com/

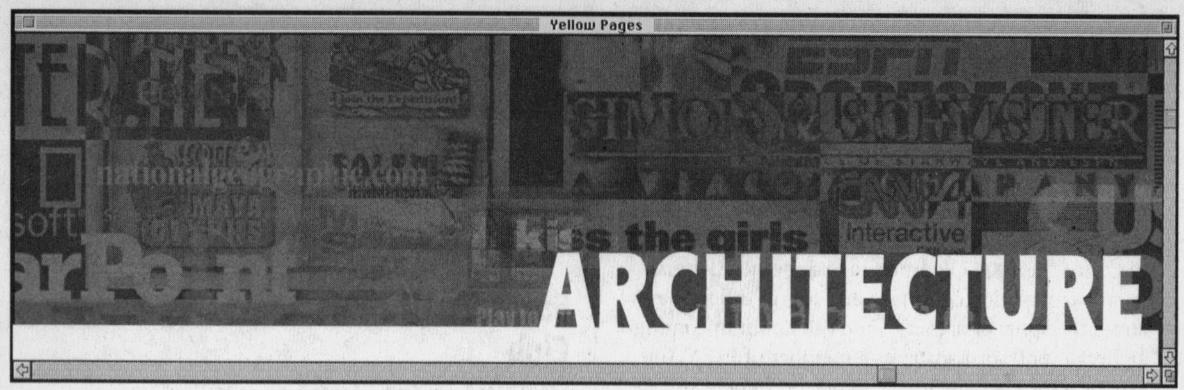

A doctor can bury his mistakes, but an architect can only advise his clients to plant vines.

Frank Lloyd Wright

The American Institute of Architects and the American Architectural Foundation

http://www.aia.org/

The collective voice of America's architects, this organization has advanced the profession since 1857. The Web site serves 58,000 members and provides information on their mission statement, history, events, chapter offices, and member services. The educational resources of the Foundation are also highlighted.

The American Institute of Architects and the American Architectural Foundation
http://www.aia.org/

Design Basics Home Online Planbook
http://www.designbasics.com/feat06.htm

The Pritzker Architecture Prize
http://www.pritzkerprize.com/

Architects Checklist for Custom Homes

http://www.arteriors.com/site/index.htm

A step-by-step checklist for selecting a site for your new home. Categories of questions include location, amenities, physical characteristics, available utilities and services, and building codes and other restrictions.

Art for Architecture

http://www.artarch.com/

A service company for architects and designers. AFA works closely with clients on projects that require artwork in various mediums.

Design Basics Home Online Planbook

http://www.designbasics.com/feat06.htm

Design Basics, Inc. provides single family home plans with available technical support and custom design options. Build your dream home with plans that are also marketed through catalogs, newsstand magazines, and home building industry trade publications.

HBA Architecture and Interior Design

`http://www.hbaonline.com/index.htm`

Describes HBA Architecture and Interior Design's current projects, lists key personnel and shows examples of their work.

MBT Architecture

`http://www.mbarch.com`

Advertises the firm that offers services in project management. Provides an online gallery and brochure. Learn about the latest projects they have been involved with, visit the Galleries of Architecture, Interiors, Laboratories, and Renderings. Employment opportunities are also available.

Open Building Architecture For Residential Construction

`http://www.access.digex.net/~david/OB.html`

Open Building (OB) is a set of principles for making an architecture of variety and coherence. It is a new approach to housing construction and marketing. These principles are useful for constructing and renovating buildings when decisions are organized on several levels among a number of parties who prefer to act independently while expecting a coherent architecture to result.

Plan Net

`http://www.plannet.com/`

An informational site about architecture, which includes The Daily Plan Net, The Studio, The Library, The Showcase, and a Net Index. Vital product information, CAD demos, and architectural forums are all included.

The Pritzker Architecture Prize

`http://www.pritzkerprize.com/`

The Pritzker Architecture Prize is sponsored by the Hyatt Foundation, and is the world's most prestigious architecture award. Learn about its Laureates and about their international traveling exhibition, "The Art of Architecture."

V.C.net

`http://www.webfac.com/VCnet/`

V.C.net is an educational tool for architecture students and a place to visit to learn more about architecture.

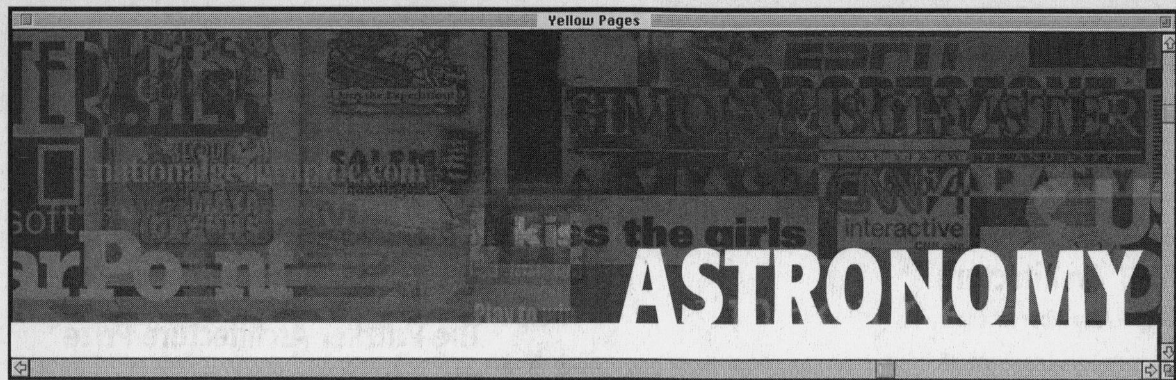

> No one ever injured his eyesight by looking on the bright side of things.
>
> *David Kaplan*

American Astronomical Society

`http://www.aas.org/`

Provides general astronomy information of interest to professionals and amateur enthusiasts. Maintains links to other astronomy resources on the Net.

Art of Renaissance Science: Galileo and Perspective

`http://bang.lanl.gov/video/stv/arshtml/lanlarstitle.html`

Features the life of Galileo, including many images from the period; based on a videotape entitled "The Art of Renaissance Science: Galileo and Perspective."

Astro!Info

`http://www.astroinfo.ch/index_e.html`

Provides general information about a variety of astronomical events. Available in German, English, or French. (The listed link is for the English version.)

Astro!Info
`http://www.astroinfo.ch/index_e.html`

Astronomy-Related Web Sites
`http://www.skypub.com/links/astroweb.html`

CCD Images of Galaxies
`http://zebu.uoregon.edu/galaxy.html`

Mount Wilson Observatory
`http://www.mtwilson.edu/`

NASA World Wide Web Information Services
`http://www.gsfc.nasa.gov/NASA_homepage.html`

Solar System Live
`http://www.fourmilab.ch/solar/solar.html`

WebStars: Astronomy Resources on the World Wide Web
`http://www.stars.com/WebStars/`

Astronomical Data Center

`http://nssdc.gsfc.nasa.gov/adc/adc.html`

Element of the National Space Science Data Center (NSSDC) / A World Data Center for Rockets and Satellites (WDC-A-R&S). Part of an international federation of astronomical data centers. Acquires, verifies, formats, documents, and distributes files that contain astronomical data in computer-readable form. Also develops and maintains software tools to access these data.

Astronomical Museum in Bologna

`http://boas3.bo.astro.it/dip/Museum/MuseumHome.html`

Provides background on the history of astronomy and the instruments at this museum. (Mostly in Italian.)

Astronomy HyperText Book

http://zebu.uoregon.edu/text.html

A hypertextual astronomy textbook written at the college level. Contains interactive information about astronomy. Also offers links to sites that offer astronomy assistance.

Astronomy-Related Web Sites

http://www.skypub.com/links/astroweb.html

Offers an extensive listing of astronomy-related Web sites and includes brief descriptions.

AstroWeb Astronomy/Astrophysics on the Internet

http://msowww.anu.edu.au/~anton/astroweb/

Provides a searchable index of information about astronomy and astrophysics that you can find on the Internet. Contains a keyword or string search option.

Caltech Space Society

http://www.seds.org/seds/chapters/css/CSS.html

Provides information about space-related projects, such as conferences and educational programs, that are open to the public.

CCD Images of Galaxies

http://zebu.uoregon.edu/galaxy.html

Presents a collection of images that specializes in photographs of galaxies. Also offers educational resources.

Center for Advanced Space Studies (CASS) Home Page

http://cass.jsc.nasa.gov/CASS_home.html

Provides information about this national research center, as well as general information about space science.

Compton Observatory Science Support Center

http://cossc.gsfc.nasa.gov/cossc/cossc.html

Contains links to various instrument home pages, bulletin board access, announcements, and public data archives.

CyberSky

http://www.cybersky.com

CyberSky is an educational shareware program that allows you to turn your computer into an animated traditional planetarium.

HEASARC Video Archive

http://heasarc.gsfc.nasa.gov/docs/heasarc/videos/videos.html

Contains a directory of video clips that highlight high-energy astrophysics missions (in various formats).

High Energy Astrophysics Science Archive Research Center

http://heasarc.gsfc.nasa.gov/docs/HEASARC_HOME_PAGE.html

Contains general information on supernovae, x-ray binaries, and black holes.

Institute for Space Astrophysics C.N.R

http://titan.ias.fra.cnr.it/ias-home/ias-home.html

Offers some links in Italian but the majority in English. Includes the "Electronic Atlas of Dynamical Evolutions of Short-Period Comets."

International Astronomical Union

http://www.lsw.uni-heidelberg.de/iau.html

Contains access to current and past bulletins, as well as reports posted by association members.

International Occultation Timing Association (I.O.T.A.) Home Page

http://www.sky.net/~robinson/iota.htm

Specializes in organizing reliable ways to view occultations and eclipses. Provides information on how nonmembers can become involved. Offers a list of members' addresses to help you locate a member near you who would be willing to help you properly view occultations and eclipses.

The Long Duration Exposure Facility

http://setas-www.larc.nasa.gov/setas/ldef.html

Describes the LDEF satellite, which contained 57 experiments and spent 69 months in space. Provides the baseline on space environments and their effects.

Mount Wilson Observatory

http://www.mtwilson.edu/

Overviews several ongoing astronomy projects using innovative techniques and modern detectors. Provides information for professionals, amateurs, tourists, and educators.

NASA World Wide Web Information Services

http://www.gsfc.nasa.gov/NASA_homepage.html

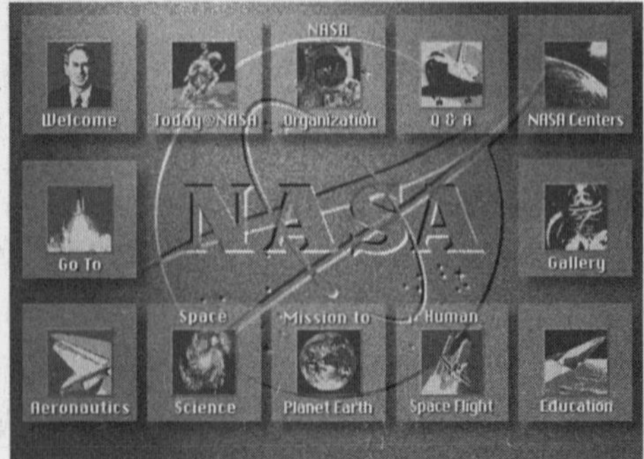

Contains news and resources of value to a variety of people. Provides scientific information for professionals as well as educational information for teachers and students.

Purdue SEDS (Students for the Exploration and Development of Space)

http://roger.ecn.purdue.edu/~seds/

Provides information about the Purdue SEDS group and serves as a place to discuss space exploration and development.

SEDS Internet Space Warehouse

http://seds.lpl.arizona.edu/

Contains many links to space resources on the Internet, a few multimedia documents, and information about the organization.

Sensors and Instrument Technology Planetary Tour Guide

http://ranier.oact.hq.nasa.gov/Sensors_page/Planets.html

Contains links to Web sites that have tours of the planets.

Sky Online Home Page

http://www.skypub.com/

Contains astronomy-related information and a large number of resources. Also contains a regularly updated listing of astronomical events.

Solar System Live

http://www.fourmilab.ch/solar/solar.html

Allows you to view a model of the solar system. Offers adjustable settings so you can see how the solar system would be at any given time or on any given date.

Southern Cross Astronomical Society

http://www.scas.org/

Enables you to check out the Southern Cross Astronomical Society.

Space Explorer's Guide

http://nyquist.ee.ualberta.ca/~wanigar/spacelink/space_explorer.html

Contains links to space resources all over the globe by country. Provides information on space news and jobs.

Space Settlement

http://www.nas.nasa.gov/NAS/SpaceSettlement/

Provides information on developing orbital space settlements, including who, what, where, when, and how much.

StarBits—Acronyms, Abbreviations, and More

http://cdsweb.u-strasbg.fr/~heck/sfbits.htm

Furnishes a searchable dictionary/glossary of astronomy acronyms, abbreviations, and terms.

StarWorlds—Astronomy and Related Organizations

http://cdsweb.u-strasbg.fr/~heck/sfworlds.htm

Furnishes a searchable listing of the addresses of organizations, institutions, associations, companies, and other groups involved in astronomy and related space sciences.

STELAR Project Demos

http://ssdoo.gsfc.nasa.gov/stelar/stelar_demos.html

Study of Electronic Literature for Astronomical Research. Explores the use of electronic means for improving access to scientific literature, and using astronomical publications to evaluate distribution, search, and retrieval techniques for full text and graphics display. Contains a listing of hypertext journal articles on astronomy.

Usenet FAQs Space

http://www.cis.ohio-state.edu/hypertext/faq/usenet/space/top.html

Presents FAQ list of general questions about planetary probes or information about solar system bodies.

Views of the Solar System

http://www.hawastsoc.org/solar/homepage.htm

Offers an educational view of the solar system. Contains images and information about the sun, planets, moons, asteroids, comets, and meteoroids.

Web Nebulae

http://seds.lpl.arizona.edu/billa/twn/top.html

Contains a collection of images of various objects in our galaxy. Includes images and explains how to classify nebulae.

WebStars: Astronomy Resources on the World Wide Web

http://www.stars.com/WebStars/

Provides information about astronomy. Contains online journals as well as searchable indexes and listings of other sites.

Welcome to Loch Ness Productions

http://www.lochness.com/

Specializes in producing planetarium program materials. Includes access to samples of planetarium music and art, as well as a listing of planetariums around the world.

Welcome to Project CLEA

http://www.gettysburg.edu/project/physics/clea/CLEAhome.html

Contemporary Laboratory Experiences in Astronomy. Contains educational resources that can be used to incorporate astronomy into science curriculum.

Welcome to the Planets

http://pds.jpl.nasa.gov/planets/

Presents collection of photos from NASA, organized by planet, and the space craft that took the picture. Also includes textual explanations of the photos.

World Wide Web Home Page of the Canadian Astronomy Data Centre (CADC)

http://cadcwww.dao.nrc.ca/CADC-homepage.html

Contains general information on astronomy. Enables users to access programs and full-text copies of articles from several CD-ROMs.

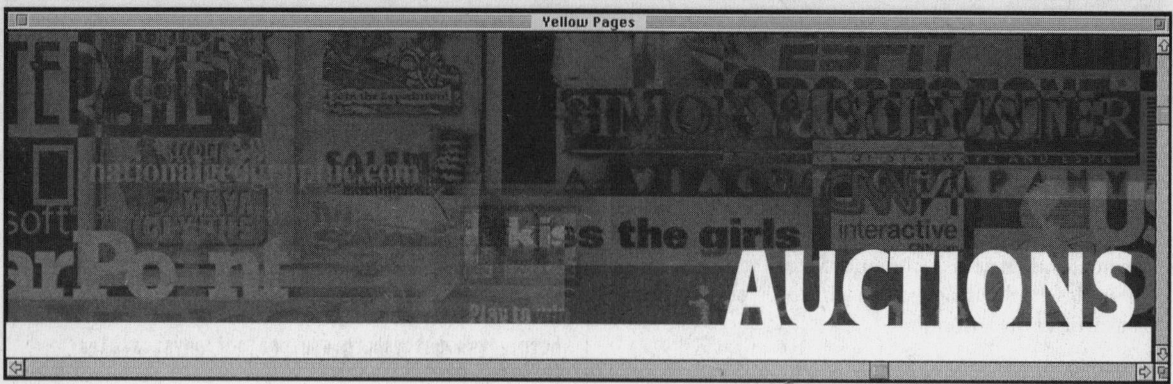

A
B
C
D
E
F
G
H
I
J
K
L
M
N
O
P
Q
R
S
T
U
V
W
X
Y
Z

But we're late for the charity auction.

Morticia in The Addams Family *(1991)*

Airline Auctions

http://www.flightauctions.com/

Planning a trip? Save on the air fare by checking out flight auctions. Just register and bid. Choose your destination and see what's available. There's also a QuickSaver option, where the prices are fixed, but low, for round-trip airfares.

Artists Online

http://www.onlineart.com/home1.html

Look at the art. Read the artists' biographies. See their portfolios. Search by color, mood, subject matter, and more for just the right painting, sculpture, tapestry, photograph, or drawing. Then bid on the one you must have. Each work can be enlarged; you'll save hours of searching through galleries looking for just the right contemporary art. Thousands of artworks by hundreds of artists. Don't miss this one.

Auction Master

http://www.cam.org/~bbrochu/auction.html

Auctioneers and auction managers should check out this site. Download a free demo copy of Auction Master, an auction management program that tracks buyers, consignors, and sale of lots, and prints invoices and reports.

Related Sites

http://www.antiquephoto.com/

http://www.idevelop.com/atc/

Sotheby's
http://www.sothebys.com/index.html

Auctionpage Auctions

http://auctionpage.com/

From this page you can search 250 auction sites to find just the item you want. Main topics are Collectibles, Antiques, Computers, Software, and Merchandise. You can also post news of your own auctions and services here.

Emerald Asset Management

http://www.eamllc.com/

This site specializes in auctions of computer equipment. Click "Click Here" to register and receive information about upcoming auctions in your area and to enter their sweepstakes and win prizes.

Excite Shopping Channel: Auctions and Bargains

http://www.excite.com/channel/shopping/bargains/

This is a good place to begin your search for just the right auction for you. There are links to several auctions, along with some just plain good bargains and free stuff.

Hoss' Auction Town

http://www.auctionhosstown.com/

Here you can browse for what's on sale this week, submit a bid, or sell something of your own. If you've never attended an auction, check out Karen's Tips for advice on how they work. Hoss also posts a joke of the week, and your favorite joke could be the next one posted. Just go to the joke of the week and click "Click here to enter your joke."

Internet Auction List

http://www.internetauctionlist.com/

Click a category (art, militaria, horses and livestock, and many more) and choose from dozens of online auctions. Go to the calendar and see which auctions are being held on a particular date. Check for links to other auction sites or subscribe to the free newsletter. This is the most complete list of auctions available on the Web.

Miles of History: Online Auction

http://www.collectorsnet.com/miles/auction/index.html

Here's an auction site that specializes in Civil War memorabilia. Browse through the items, read the auction rules, and submit your bid. Lots of links to other good auction and Civil War sites.

The National Auctioneers Association

http://www.auctionweb.com/naa/

This is the official page of the National Auctioneers Association with links to members' home pages, excerpts from "The Auctioneer," the official publication of the association, and much more. Learn about the auctioneers' code of ethics; learn how auctions work; read the mission statement of the association; and learn how to join.

NETIS—Auctions on the Web

http://www.auctionweb.com/

Find a list of upcoming auctions in your area. Search by date, geographical area, or category. Locate a member auctioneer in your state. This site is an affiliate member of the National Auctioneers Association. Whatever you're looking for—real estate, collectibles, antiques—there's an auction listed here that specializes in it.

Sotheby's

http://www.sothebys.com/index.html

This, as you might expect, is a classy Web page. Read about upcoming auctions, order catalogs, learn how to begin a collection, but best of all, check out the interactive "Auction Adventures." Follow a young couple as they purchase furnishing for their new house, try to guess which watch a young Londoner will choose, and follow a wine connoisseur as he checks out the merchandise in a wine auction.

Super Auction: Live Internet Auction House

http://superauction.com/

This site specializes in computers and components. Brand new printers start at $25; modems at $10. Click an item and see the bid history and the current "winner" and winning bid. There are some real bargains to be had here, and it's all name brand components and systems.

Related Sites

http://www.uauction.com/atc/
http://www.azww.com/cc/auction.shtml
http://www.iaoauction.com/
http://cayman.ebay2.com/aw/
http://www.christies.com/
http://www.tcwc.com/chicago/
http://www.rm-smythe.com/
http://www.easyauction.com/

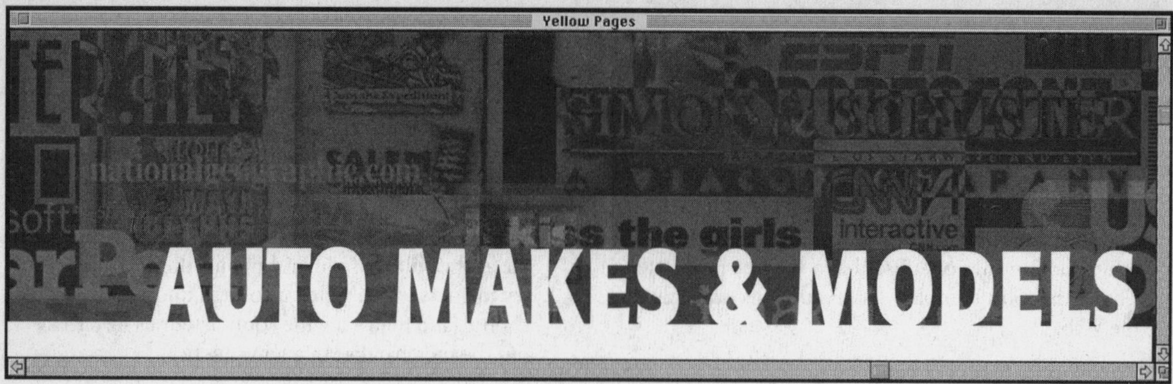

> If the automobile had followed the same development cycle as the computer, a Rolls-Royce would today cost $100, get a million miles per gallon, and explode once a year, killing everyone inside.
>
> *Robert X. Cringely,* InfoWorld

AC Cobra Page

http://www.xs4all.nl/~luukb/

The AC Cobra isn't just a car, it's a way of life; this Web page is dedicated to it. Here you will find listings of Cobra owners on the Web, the history of Carrol Shelby, pictures, stories, and much more. Of interest to anyone who's ever dreamed of owning one of these roadsters.

Acura

http://www.acura.com/

The classy Acura has become an urban status symbol, and you can find out why on this page. It provides information about the new RL Navigation System offered on the 1998 Acura, plus service and benefit information for current owners.

Related Sites

http://www.craftsmenlimousine.com/

http://www.ingway.co.jp/~daihatsu/

Isuzuville
http://www.isuzu.com/

Alfa Romeo GTA

http://www.xmission.com/~gtaj/

A page dedicated to this light racing car that the Italian auto maker put out in the 1960s. Includes information about all the various flavors of the car, and an image gallery of every GTA the author has ever seen.

BMW of North America

http://www.bmwusa.com/index2.html

Whether you're a current BMW owner or a wannabe, you'll find plenty of information at this site. Learn about the new 1998 models at the Showroom, or visit the Pre-Owned area to find out how you can acquire a gently-used BMW. You can even check out BMW motorcycles.

Buick

See General Motors

Cadillac

See General Motors

Chevrolet

See General Motors

Chevy Trucks

See General Motors

Chrysler Corporation

http://www.chrysler.com

Your one-stop shopping spot for all the models made by Chrysler Corporation, including Dodge, Chrysler,

Plymouth, Jeep, and Eagle. Visit the Motor Mall to see the latest models, or visit the Service Center for up-to-date service and maintenance information.

Dodge

See Chrysler Corporation

Eagle

See Chrysler Corporation

Ferrari North America

`http://www.ferrari.com/Menu/index.asp`

Everything for the Ferrari lover, from a history of the company to a list of authorized dealers. Includes a showcase of current and past models, plus an interesting Java applet called Paint Your Own Ferrari that lets you see how certain models look in different colors. (Quite cool.)

Ford Motor Company

`http://www.ford.com/`

The master page from which you can access all the model-specific pages for vehicles made by the Ford Motor Company. These include Ford, Lincoln, Mercury, Ford Heavy Truck, SVT, and Jaguar.

General Motors

`http://www.gm.com/index.cgi`

This page is the jumping-off point for individual Web sites for the various models made by General Motors, including Chevrolet, Geo, GMC, Buick, Pontiac, Saturn, Chevy Trucks, Cadillac, and Oldsmobile.

Geo

See General Motors

GMC

See General Motors

Honda 98

`http://www.honda.com/index.html`

Check out all the latest Honda models here, locate nearby dealers, and visit the Honda corporate headquarters, all in one trip. One very cool feature called myHONDA.com lets you customize the Web page for the specific models you are interested in.

Hyundai Motor Company

`http://www.hmc.co.kr/`

This easy-to-navigate site offers profiles on the new Hyundai models, a company profile, and current company news. The content is a bit thinner than at many American car sites, but you can get a general idea of the company's offerings.

Infiniti

`http://www.infinitimotors.com/`

"Own one and you'll understand" is this company's motto, and their site focuses on the superior safety and comfort features of their product. You'll find comprehensive safety data, model pictures and specs, and the opportunity to order a free hard-copy brochure.

Jaguar

See Ford Motor Company

Javelin AMX Home Page

`http://www.javelinamx.com/`

A page dedicated to the Javelin, a sports car produced by American Motors in the early 1970s. Here you will find a bevy of information and links including images, original artwork, humor, cars owned by the site's visitors, and much more.

Isuzuville

`http://www.isuzu.com/`

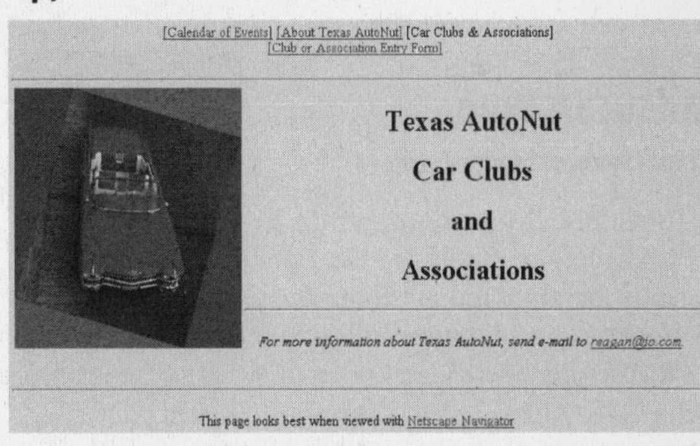

The Isuzu site is proof that you don't have to have the fanciest graphics and animation to produce an effective site. This charming site is set up with a "small town" metaphor, in which you visit the Bank for financing, Floyd's Gas for maintenance and fuel economy tips, and so on. Very inventive and different!

Jeep

See Chrysler Corporation

A B C D E F G H I J K L M N O P Q R S T U V W X Y Z

A B C D E F G H I J K L M N O P Q R S T U V W X Y Z

Lexus Home Page

`http://www.lexus.com/`

This classy site has a European feel to it. The theme is "The Lexus Centre of Performance Art," and the usual sections (model specs, dealer lists, and more) are folded into categories like Events Centre and Patrons Circle. The only trouble with it is that sometimes it's hard to stretch the metaphors enough to figure out what you're going to see in each area.

Lincoln

See Ford Motor Company

MAZDA

`http://www.mazda.com/`

Learn all about the latest Mazda models in this online Mazda showroom. All the standard sales information is here, plus a cool interactive timeline showing the history of the company.

Mercedes-Benz

`http://www.mercedes-benz.com/e/mbe1.htm`

Not just your average snooty expensive car site! This site has innovative content, including information about the very strange looking but aerodynamically superior A-Class vehicles. You can also find out about Mercedes-Benz racing teams here.

Mercury

See Ford Motor Company

Mitsucars.com

`http://www.mitsucars.com/`

Mitsubishi Motors presents dealer listings, financing information, model specifications, and motorsports information. Find out about the very hot 3000GT sports car or the sport-utility Montero from this easy-to-use site.

Nissan: Enjoy the Ride

`http://www.nissan-usa.com/`

Not only does Nissan have great TV commercials, but they also have a great Web site. Check out the funky graphics, obviously picked out by the same creative folks who do the TV commercials. Then browse the latest models and take a "joyride" through Nissan history and future plans.

Oldsmobile

See General Motors

Plymouth

See Chrysler Corporation

Pontiac

See General Motors

Saturn

See General Motors

SVT

See Ford Motor Company

> **Interested in Selling?**
>
> If you are interested in selling rather than buying a vehicle, you could try listing your vehicle in your local newspaper online (`http://www.newspapers.com/npcom1.htm`). Other sites include 2BuySell (`http://www.2buysell.com/`), Yahoo Automotive Classifieds (`http://classifieds.yahoo.com/auto.html`), or the Buy and Sell Marketplace (`http://emporium.turnpike.net/N/nexus/buysell/re_comha.htm`).

Toyota

`http://www.toyota.com/`

Toyota's "Everyday" theme from their TV commericials is carried over into their Web site, with pics and quotes from ordinary people enjoying their Toyota vehicles. Configure a new Toyota, locate a used one, or just browse the news and corporate info.

Waletail's Porsche and 959 Home Page

`http://www.olemiss.edu/~waletail/ben.htm`

True Porsche lovers live by the motto "Porsche: There is no Substitute." At this site you can find information and photos from every major Porsche produced, from a humble 11 horsepower Porsche tractor to the sleek new 986 convertible.

Welcome to VW

`http://www.vw.com/`

This Volkswagon site is fun and active, geared to the young and hip Web audience. The specs are not terribly detailed, but there's enough to point you toward your local dealer for more information. It includes a "favorite roads" section for taking scenic, winding drives, which is a nice break.

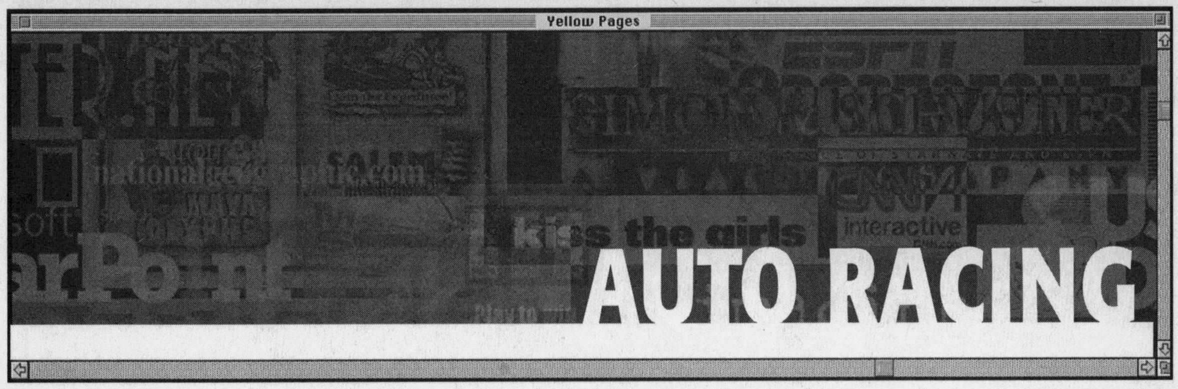

> By sensation, and not by calendars, and each moment is a day, and the race a life.
>
> *Benjamin Disraeli*

candelaMotorsport

http://www.candela.com.au/motorsport

Provides all the latest news, press releases, pictures, and generally anything involving motorsports in Australia and the rest of the world.

GALE FORCE F1

http://www.monaco.mc/f1/

Provides Formula One motor racing results and track information. Also offers a subscription to a mailing list that provides up-to-date race results via email.

Indy Car Racing Magazine

http://www.icr.com/

Exclusive coverage of the PPG CART World Series and the Indy Racing League, including the latest racing reports in RealAudio format.

Matt's Solar Car Page

http://www-lips.ece.utexas.edu/~delayman/solar.html

Provides race information, team listings (United States and Canada), and official results of previous races. Also offers images of solar cars, as well as a race route map across Australia.

The Racer Archive
http://student-www.eng.hawaii.edu/carina/ra.home.page.html

Motorsports Media Service International Home Page

http://www.west.net/~webpages

Provides information about auto racing—drivers, teams, sponsors, art and photography, merchandise, and more.

The Racer Archive

http://student-www.eng.hawaii.edu/carina/ra.home.page.html

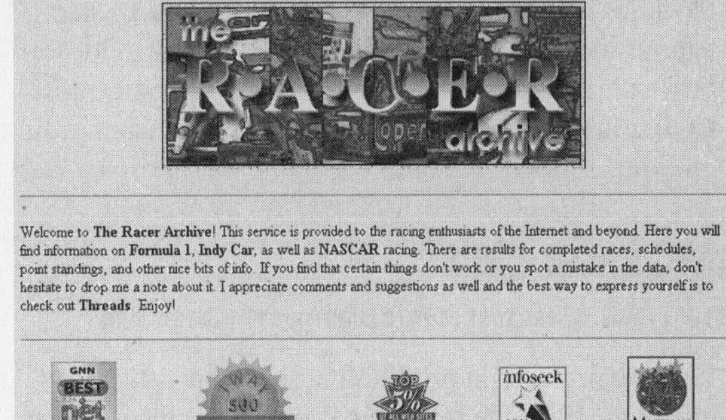

Provides information about Formula One, IndyCar, and NASCAR racing. Also includes race results, point standings, schedules, history, links to other sites, anecdotes, and more.

A B C D E F G H I J K L M N O P Q R S T U V W X Y Z

AUTOMOTIVE CLUBS & ORGANIZATIONS

> You never can tell by how much noise the horn makes, how much gas is in the tank.
>
> *Unknown*

AAA Online

http://www.aaa.com/

Go directly to your state's "Triple A" office by entering your zip code. You already know about their famous Triptiks and the 24/365 road service that offers car lockout help, jump starts, and fixed flats. But what about their travel reservations and discounts, domestic and international tours, and $1,000 arrest bonds? These are among the 67 reasons that AAA wants you to join.

AMC Pacer Club

http://www.classicar.com/clubs/pacer/pacer.htm

Although it was in production only from 1975 through 1980, the futuristic Pacer's pop culture acceptance didn't take hold until years later (perhaps due to *Wayne's World*?). Pacer owners are encouraged to register their cars and keep all documentation. Members receive the newsletter, but you don't have to own one of the famous bubble cars to join! The site also features Warholesque Pacer art.

The National Motorists Association
http://www.motorists.com/

American Truck Historical Society

http://www.the-matrix.com/aths/truck.html

An organization dedicated to the assimilation of information regarding the history of the American trucking industry. The society publishes *Wheels of Time*, a magazine distributed to members worldwide. They maintain a reference library and archives, and hold a truck show every year.

The Antique Automobile Club of America

http://www.aaca.org/

The AACA is not just for people who like old cars. Actually, they want to preserve and celebrate all modes of "self-propelled vehicle," by which they mean any vehicle meant to carry people that runs on gasoline, diesel, steam, and electricity. Founded in 1935, the AACA has over 400 chapters all over the world, and their Web site is exhaustive in its coverage of history, legislation, film and video, museums, links, and much more.

Bill Lavender's Driving Online

http://www.driving.co.uk/

A Britain-based site about every aspect of safety and driving you could conceive: skid control, accident investigation, motorcycles and "lorries," "tarmac terrorism," and much more. Includes stories from the road, such as the one about the man who survived a crash with a utility pole, but who died when he touched the downed 11,000-volt wire.

CHVA

http://www.classicar.com/clubs/chva/chva.htm

The Contemporary Historical Vehicle Association is a club dedicated to the preservation of vehicles from the Action Era, which is defined as any car 25 years old or older, back to 1928. Members receive free classified ads, access to an extensive club library, and CHVAID, a volunteer-based roadside assistance program.

The Electric Auto Association

http://www.eaaev.org/

The EAA is a nonprofit organization dedicated to the advancement and adoption of the electricity-powered car. The EAA is based in the fact that electric vehicles (EVs) are more efficient and better for the planet than those that run on standard fossil-fuel. A long list of links to other EV-related sites is provided.

EVOOA: Emergency Vehicle Owners and Operators Association

http://www.intrlink.net/evooa/index.htm

If you thought the Blues Brothers were the only civilians to own their own police car, consider the 200 members of the international EVOOA. If you have any interest in or want to buy any type of public-safety vehicles, from classic police cruisers to tow trucks, this site for the Spokane, Washington, club is the first stop for you.

Great Drives

http://users.why.net/ajax/gdrives.htm

Great Drives is a list compiled from contributors far and wide who've gone down the road feeling casual. Featured drives include detailed road descriptions and sights to see from Astoria to Portland, San Francisco to Oakland, and all points Yellowstone National Park. So fill the tank and pack a lunch because it's time to cruise.

Hudson-Essex-Terraplane Club, Inc.

http://www.classicar.com/clubs/hudson/Hethome.htm

A worldwide organization founded in 1959 that is dedicated to the preservation of the automobiles produced by the Hudson corporation, and later by American Motors. Members enjoy parts locators, annual meetings, and "The White Triangle," a 60-page bimonthly magazine. Includes chat room now in beta testing for members to help each other.

Los Angeles Hearse Society

http://pages.prodigy.com/CA/LA/hearse/

If you stop for every funeral procession to admire the shiny black paint and sober motion of the hearse, this site is for you. Actually, hearses are as diverse as their owners, who have leanings toward all things "weird and wonderful." Activities include grand tours of grand cemeteries.

Mid-America Old Time Auto Association

http://www.classicar.com/clubs/motaa/motaa.htm

MOTAA was devised in 1958 to be a collection of small antique car clubs, since most of the larger clubs were too far away to be of any use. The organization publishes a bimonthly newsletter, "The Antique Car Times." Membership in member auto clubs is not required for MOTAA membership, but it is recommended.

The National Motorists Association

http://www.motorists.com/

The NMA exists to protect your rights as a driving citizen. Among their many services, the NMA lobbies for sensible road traffic laws and engineering, argues for your right to drive whatever you want, helps you fight tickets, and opposes camera-based enforcement, as well as speed traps designed to generate revenue.

The National Woodie Club

http://www.classicar.com/clubs/woodie/woodhome.htm

Though the subject of many a joke, the wood-paneled station wagon has its own hardcore fans, who recognize that their "woodies" have crossed over from tongue-in-cheek kitch to art in motion. Woodies were the vehicle of choice for the country's original surfers, but does this mean that Web surfers will take to wood-paneled computers?

Partnership for a New Generation of Vehicles (PNGV)

http://www.ta.doc.gov/pngv/

In 1993, the government combined forces with Ford, Chrysler, and GM with the goal to build a "supercar," which would be an environmentally friendly car with three times the fuel efficiency, without sacrificing performance, affordability, or safety.

RADAR: Radio Association Defending Airwave Rights, Inc.

http://www.radar.org/

RADAR is concerned with the driver's right to use radar and laser detectors, but it also provides info about defending yourself from unjust speeding tickets. Did you know that regular radar guns make mistakes 10 to 30 percent of the time! The site provides links to related sites, important information regarding relevant legislation, and much more.

Rolls-Royce Owners' Club

http://www.virtualforum.com/rroc/

For those lucky enough to own a Rolls-Royce or Bentley automobile, this club provides a variety of services. There is a parts exchange service and national events. The Web site also includes a FAQ and maintenance tips.

The Sports Car Club of America

http://www.scca.com/

If you've ever driven down the street and made car racing noises to yourself, then the SCCA is the club for you. You are encouraged not only to love sports cars and racing, but to enter racing school and go racing yourself. This site provides a huge list of pro and amateur races and other events. Do you have a teenager with a heavy foot? How about entering them in the Speed Freakz program?

Texas AutoNut Car Clubs and Associations

http://www.io.com/~reagan/autonut/carclubs.html

The Lone Star State hosts many clubs for many different kinds of cars, and the Texas AutoNut site is the place to start. Clubs exist for models including Avanti, Studebaker, Chrysler muscle cars, and even Nissans. Web surfers may fill out forms to inform others of clubs, associations, and events.

Women On Wheels

http://www.vancouver-bc.com/WomenOnWheels/index.html

Angry about poor prices, service, and treatment of single women looking for cars, the Women on Wheels Webmaster started her site to help members protect themselves. WOW's mission is to provide a trustworthy referral service for repairs and sales, empower and educate female drivers about what to look for, and offer other benefits to members. All women are encouraged to recommend businesses that have done them right.

Women's Auto Help Center

http://www.womenautohelp.com/

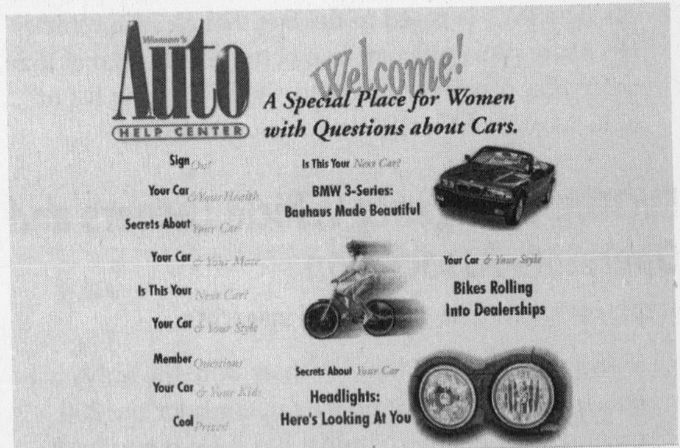

Membership is free at the Women's Auto Help Center, and you will find more articles and help than you can shake a stick shift at. The Center's Advisory Board is comprised of women from all aspects of the automotive industry, all dedicated to help women make the best automotive decisions they can through dealers who will treat them fairly. Related topics include cars and how they relate to men, children, and style.

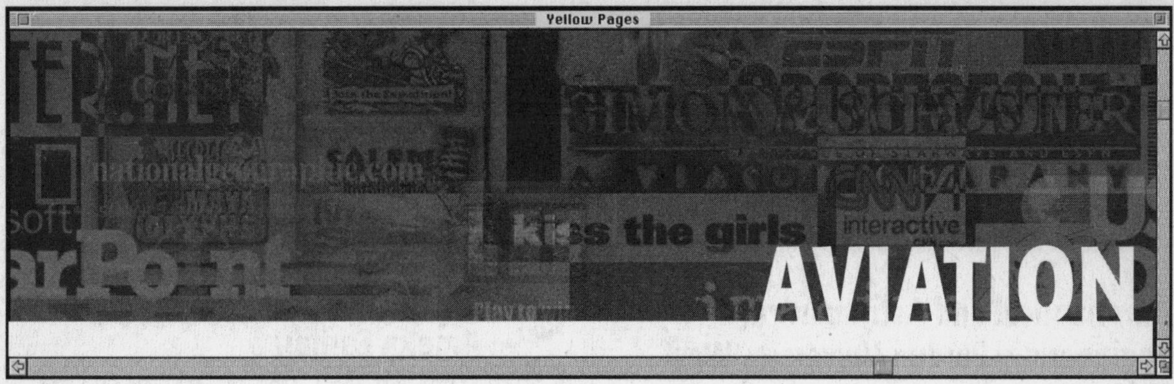

> Flying a plane is no different from riding a bicycle. It's just a lot harder to put baseball cards in the spokes.
>
> *Captain Rex Kramer, in the movie* Airplane

For all aviation and aircraft buffs, this category offers sites about air and space, air combat, aircraft archives, and aeronautical engineering, to name a few. The sky's the limit!

01: Bermuda Shorts

http://www.parascope.com/en/bermuda1.htm

Afraid to fly over the Bermuda Triangle? This site should help dispel some of the myths associated with the area.

1 GOLDEN: Aviation Yellow Pages

http://www.aviationdirectory.com/golden.htm

This site is an aviation yellow pages. You can look here for listings of businesses and their Web pages (if available) that relate to aviation.

AIR&SPACE Smithsonian Magazine

http://www.airspacemag.com/ASM_Magazine.html

Learn about this magazine, which was created by the Smithsonian Institution's National Air and Space Museum. You can see what is featured in the latest issue or subscribe online.

AIR&SPACE Smithsonian Magazine
http://www.airspacemag.com/ASM_Mag

ACES HIGH: The Finest in Aviation Photography
http://www.aviation.ca/aces/aceshigh.html

Amelia Earhart
http://www.ionet.net/~jellenc/eae_intr.html

Basics of Space Flight Learners' Workbook
http://www.jpl.nasa.gov/basics/

Landings: Weather
http://www.landings.com/_landings/pages/weather.html#direct

NATIONAL AIR & SPACE MUSEUM HOMEPAGE
http://www.nasm.edu/NASMpage.html

Stalag 13 Aviation Links
http://users.aol.com/dheitm8612/page2.htm

ACES HIGH: The Finest in Aviation Photography

http://www.aviation.ca/aces/aceshigh.html

Whether for personal enjoyment or to spice up a presentation, look at this site for downloading aviation photography. This site also offers tips for taking your own photographs.

AERIUS, INTERNATIONAL ASSOCIATION FOR STUDENTS OF AVIATION

http://student.fee.uva.nl/aerius/index.htm

The main goal of this association is to obtain internships for students. Check out this site to learn more about the association and how to join.

Aeronautical and Astronautical Engineering, Purdue University, West Lafayette, Indiana

http://aae.www.ecn.purdue.edu/AAE/

Provides information about undergraduate and graduate Aeronautical and Astronautical Engineering programs at the university. Enables you to investigate the provided facilities and research opportunities as well as become familiar with the teaching staff. Provides a link to the university home page.

Air Affair

http://www.airaffair.com/

Focuses on different types of flying machines. Includes a calendar of flying shows, a listing of aviation fuel prices, and an aviation library.

Air charters, fishing trips and seaplane tours with Sound Flight

http://www.soundflight.com/

This company can fly you on a scenic sightseeing tour, take you on a fishing trip, and fly you to a lakeside picnic. Other flying possibilities are available. They will even fly supplies to you on your yachting excursions! Check out this site for more details.

Air Combat USA

http://www.aircombatusa.com/

Find out how you can fly actual air-to-air combat in a real, state-of-the-art military aircraft! You won't even need a pilot's license.

Aircraft Images Archive

http://www.cs.ruu.nl/pub/AIRCRAFT-IMAGES/

Collection of pictures of mainly military aircraft. All photos are in JPEG format.

Airship The Home Page for Lighter-Than-Air Craft

http://spot.colorado.edu/~dziadeck/airship.html

Offers links for finding information about lighter-than-air craft. Includes information on these craft in fiction, models, and pictures; a bibliography; and links to Internet resources and discussion groups.

Amelia Earhart

http://www.ionet.net/~jellenc/eae_intr.html

Interested in Amelia Earhart? This site provides a nice biography detailing her life from her youth until her last flight. It also has some nice pictures.

Aviation Directories

http://www.sportflyer.com/directry.htm

As the name suggests, the site is simply a directory with links to other aviation sites. This could be a good starting place when looking for something.

Aviation Directory

http://www.arts-online.com/aviation.htm

The Aviation Internet Directory is a biannual publication listing Internet sites for several aviation-related topics. See this site if you want to order this directory or if you want to have a Web site posted in it.

AeroWeb: The Aviation Enthusiast Corner

http://omni.brooklyn.cuny.edu/rec/air/air.html

Provides many resources, including picture libraries, air show information, and aircraft locators.

Aviation Jobs Online - Home Page

http://www.aviationjobsonline.com/index.html

Looking for a job in the aviation field? Here is a great place to start. It isn't just for pilots, either. This site supports jobs for all areas of aviation.

AviationWeb Homepage

http://www.aviationweb.com/

This site contains a database for finding a U.S. flight school near you. Pilot schools can also come here to create a profile for themselves to be entered into the database.

Aviators Welcome

http://www.canovair.com/

This page offers aviation publications intended to help train professional pilots. Simulator profiles, system schematics, and other topics are covered.

The Avion Online Newspaper

http://avion.db.erau.edu/

This is an online aviation newspaper directed at students. You can check out the current issue, look at archived issues, or subscribe online to the hard copy version. Information about topics like trade shows and air shows can be found. Contains many good pictures.

Balloon Federation of America Home Page

http://www.bfa.ycg.org/

Find out what is going on in the Balloon Federation of America. You can fill out an application to join or just check out the latest news. Offers links to other sites.

Basics of Space Flight Learners' Workbook

http://www.jpl.nasa.gov/basics/

Provides orientation to space flight and related topics, including the solar system, gravity and mechanics, interplanetary trajectories, orbits, electromagnetic phenomena, space craft types, telecommunications, onboard subsystems, navigation, and phases of flight.

The Boeing Home Page

http://www.boeing.com/

Home page for the world's largest producer of commercial jetliners. Provides information on employment opportunities and company news as well as background information and facts about the company's families of airplanes. Contains interesting, downloadable pictures of their airplanes.

Canard's Aviator's Page

http://www.canard.com/

Provides information for the aviation enthusiast. Offers links to Canard aircraft that provide information on each aircraft and other related information.

Delta SkyLinks Home Page

http://www.delta-air.com/index.html

Loads of useful information for those interested in flying with Delta. You can check flight schedules, reserve tickets, or just read news about the company.

Embry-Riddle Aeronautical University

http://www.db.erau.edu/

Learn about the world's largest aeronautical university. This site contains admission information, research opportunities, and a virtual tour of campus.

Helicopter Adventures, Inc.

http://www.heli.com/

Learn about this helicopter flight-training school and how you can learn to fly helicopters. This site also contains several links to other helicopter-related sites.

Helicopter Association International

http://www.rotor.com/

This association is dedicated to advancing the civil helicopter industry. Check out this site to learn more about them and how to join.

Jeremy Harkin's Military Aircraft Archive

http://www.rpi.edu/~harkij/airpics.html

Very comprehensive archive boasting 223 featured aircraft. Aircraft are neatly divided into categories such as World War I, World War II, Post War/Modern. Contains loads of pictures and technical data.

Landings

http://www.landings.com/aviation.html

Excellent and informative site that provides a wide variety of aviation information for all levels, including recent news items and editorials.

Landings: Weather

http://www.landings.com/_landings/pages/weather.html#direct

One of the best weather sites available. Find weather information from around the globe. Also contains endless links to other aviation-specific topics.

Launch.net—Hot Air Ballooning!

http://www.launch.net/

Interested in hot air balloons? Check here to learn how they work, how to get a ride in one, and how to become a pilot. Several good links, too.

Learjet, Inc.

http://www.learjet.com/

Offers information about the jet aircraft manufacturer. This includes company history, employment opportunities, and specifications and photos of their product.

NAA - National Aeronautic Association

http://www.naa.ycg.org/

Their home page states that "by promoting safety, rights of access, and better public understanding of aviation and air sports, the NAA is not only for the experienced pilot, but for aviation enthusiasts of all kinds." See their home page to learn about the association and how to become a member.

NASA Dryden Flight Research Center

http://www.dfrf.nasa.gov/dryden.html

Provides information about the activities of this research center. Includes a photo archive of research aircraft, research documents, and program information.

NASA Home Page

http://www.nasa.gov/

Acts as the starting point for all of NASA's Web-based information. Offers links to resources, including space shuttle information, home pages for the NASA centers around the country, space images, and educational resources.

NASA Space Shuttle Web Archives

http://shuttle.nasa.gov/

Provides data about the current space shuttle mission. Includes images, schedules, mission information, video clips, and technical information. Contains statistics and goals of every mission ever flown by a shuttle.

NASA Television on CU-SeeMe

http://btree.lerc.nasa.gov/NASA_TV/NASA_TV.html

Helps visitors learn how to access live images and audio from NASA using CU-SeeMe software. Provides a link for obtaining the CU-SeeMe software.

NATIONAL AIR & SPACE MUSEUM HOMEPAGE

http://www.nasm.edu/NASMpage.html

This site describes the museum very well. It includes a very thorough description of the museum's exhibits, complete with many photos.

Parks College of Saint Louis University

http://www.slu.edu/colleges/parks/parks_home.html

This site offers information about another aviation college. Read about the history of the school as well as about its available courses and programs.

Pilot Supplies from AI Pilot Shop

http://www.aipilotshop.com/

Offers a wide range of pilot supplies from several manufacturers. Pictures and descriptions of goods are available as well as an online order form.

Planes of Fame Home Page

http://www.winternet.com/%7Epof/

Take a virtual tour of this museum boasting more than 20 World War II aircraft. This site comes with pictures and documentation for each plane. Fighters, bombers, and training aircraft are featured.

R/C Links!

http://www1.primenet.com/~bhenley/rclinks.html

This is a page of links to sites concerning radio-controlled devices. Radio-controlled airplanes make up the majority of the links.

Sky Warriors, Inc.

http://www.skywarriors.com/

Sky Warriors is a company that allows pilots and non-pilots the opportunity to fly real fighter planes and dogfight with an opponent. They also provide training for pilots to become accustomed to unusual flying conditions, and they provide formation training.

Stalag 13 Aviation Links

`http://users.aol.com/dheitm8612/page2.htm`

This is THE granddaddy of all aviation pages. This site contains hundreds of alphabetized, aviation-related links. If there is an aviation page in existence, there is a good chance you will find it here.

To Fly is Everything

`http://hawaii.cogsci.uiuc.edu/invent/airplanes.html`

This site bills itself as "a virtual museum of the invention of the airplane." It contains a good written history of the first airplanes. It also has several movies (in QuickTime format) and photographs of early pilots. Definitely a good source of information about the Wright brothers.

The Ultralight Home Page

`http://www.cs.fredonia.edu/~stei0302/www/ultra/ultralight.html`

This site is intended to make it easy for people to learn more about flying ultralights. It does a fine job of this and even contains links to other ultralight pages.

United Airlines

`http://www.ual.com/`

Check flight schedules or reserve tickets. You can also learn some background information about the company. Check out the company's Mileage Plus program to see how you can earn free miles.

The UNOFFICIAL Seattle Museum of Flight Home Page

`http://www.airfax.com/mof/`

Read about museum tour times and prices as well as museum history. Several photos of airplanes displayed in the museum are available.

Up Ship!

`http://www2.giant.net/people/mbrown/`

About 30 pictures of zeppelins including, of course, the Hindenburg. Offers some links to other sites.

Vintage Aircraft Supply

`http://www.aerobrake.com/vas/`

This site offers hard-to-find airplane parts. Control wheels, gun sights, data plates, and stick grips are some examples of what you can find. Check out this page if you're interested in selling authentic relics, too.

Welcome to Banyan Air Service

`http://www.banyanair.com/`

This is a good place to look if your airplane needs servicing. They can do several kinds of repairs as well as sell parts.

The World Wide Web Virtual Library: Aviation

`http://macwww.db.erau.edu/www_virtual_lib/aviation.html`

This site covers practically every imaginable aspect of aviation. It is a library containing links to dozens of other related sites. This would be an excellent place to begin a search into the area of aviation.

Wright Brothers Medal

`http://www.sae.org/ABOUT/AWARDS/wright.htm`

Learn about the Wright Brothers Medal presented annually by the Society of Automotive Engineers. It recognizes the author of the best paper covering the "development, design, construction, or operation" of an aircraft or spacecraft.

NEWSGROUPS

- rec.aviation.aerobatics
- rec.aviation.hang-gliding
- rec.aviation.homebuilt
- rec.aviation.marketplace
- rec.aviation.military
- rec.aviation.piloting
- rec.aviation.products
- rec.aviation.questions
- rec.aviation.rotorcraft
- rec.aviation.simulators
- rec.aviation.soaring
- rec.aviation.stories
- rec.aviation.student
- rec.aviation.ultralight
- rec.models.rocket
- sci.aeronautics

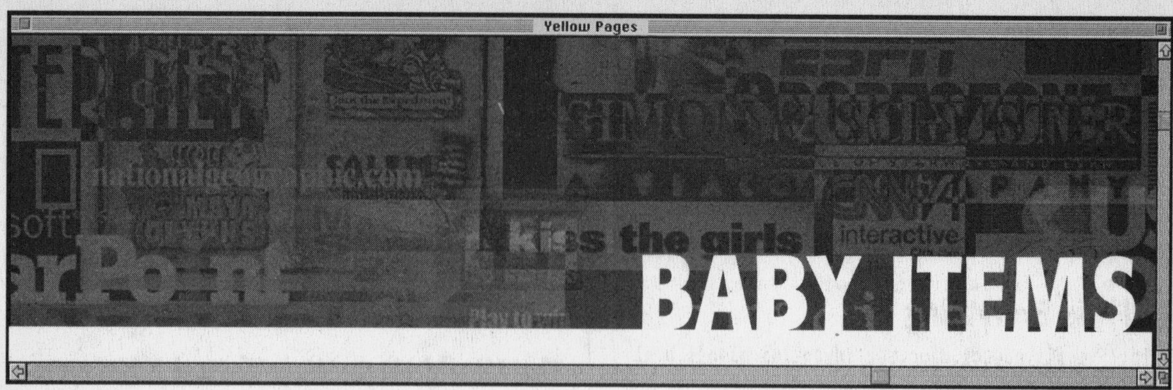

> It is far easier to explain to a three-year-old how babies are made than to explain the processes whereby bread or sugar appear on the table.
>
> *Dervla Murphy*

All About Teaching Babies, Infants, and Toddlers

http://www.infantlearning.com/

Can babies really learn to read? This site tackles that question and offers a video and information to help stimulate learning and teach your baby to read, using a multisensory approach. Also offers Q&A, news, parenting resources, and educational links.

American Academy of Pediatrics

http://www.aap.org/

Offers the full gamut of information relating to the mental, physical, and social health of infants through young adults. A searchable, easy-to-navigate site filled with valuable information for parents.

THE BABY AND CHILD PLACE

http://www.babyplace.com/

Go here for information on caring for your babies and children. Articles by staff members as well as stories and photos submitted by readers (you can submit yours too). Includes product recall information, product reviews, listing of healthcare organizations, home-safety information, links to other sites, and more.

NRP TOP PICKS

American Academy of Pediatrics
http://www.aap.org/

Babycare Corner
http://www.familyinternet.com/babycare/babycare.htm

Babyworld Home Page
http://www.babyworld.com/nindex2.htm

TheBabyNet
http://thebabynet.com/

Baby Bumpers

http://www.babybumpers.com/

The Baby Bumpers company sells HEARTHGUARD bumper products to help safeguard babies and toddlers against the dangers of a fireplace hearth. Products can be special ordered—free quotes available.

Baby Freebies

http://members.tripod.com/~jkeri/babyfreebies.htm

This site has an alphabetical listing of free products, offers, services, coupons, and contests of interest to parents. Also links to other baby/new parent Web sites, as well as other (nonbaby) freebie sites.

Baby Games

http://www.cyserv.com/dstoll/BGinfo.html

Sells Baby Games, computer software designed to introduce young children ages 18 months through 4 years to the computer. Software teaches the alphabet, numbers, shapes, colors, and animals.

The Baby Soother for Parents

http://www.parentsplace.com/shopping/soother/index.html

Offers an audiocassette that helps soothe colicky babies by playing "pink noise." Also offers a tape for preschoolers and expectant moms of all-instrumental music that calms the listener and evokes positive feelings.

Baby Stuff

http://www.baby-stuff.com/catalog.html

Twenty full-screen photos show beautiful baby bedding sets available for order. Also links to other baby resources. A narrowly focused but visually pleasing site.

Baby Web

http://www.netaxs.com/~iris/infoweb/baby.html

Offers baby and parenting information, including pregnancy and birth FAQs, parenting FAQs, and baby care. Also gives links to baby-related newsgroups, sites offering services to new and expectant parents, and the Baby Web Store. A good jumping-off point for additional baby info.

Babycare Corner

http://www.familyinternet.com/babycare/babycare.htm

Offers health, safety, and medical information for infancy through adolescence. Includes searchable references for dental health, common injuries, medication, illness symptoms, nutrition, immunizations, genetics, and much more.

Babyhood Home Page

http://www.babyhood.com/

Focuses on babies birth to 24 months. Baby home pages, childcare, health and safety, parenting, products and services, read-aloud, recreation, and miscellaneous categories are all available at this site. Also has some cute baby pictures.

Baby's Art Gallery InfoHaus Page

http://www.infohaus.com/access/by-seller/Babys_Art_Gallery

A storefront offering Baby's Art Gallery—a set of high-contrast images designed to stimulate newborns. You can download and print these '90s versions of the traditional black-and-white images (in JPG format) or view them onscreen with your baby. Includes a list of baby links.

Babyworld Home Page

http://www.babyworld.com/nindex2.htm

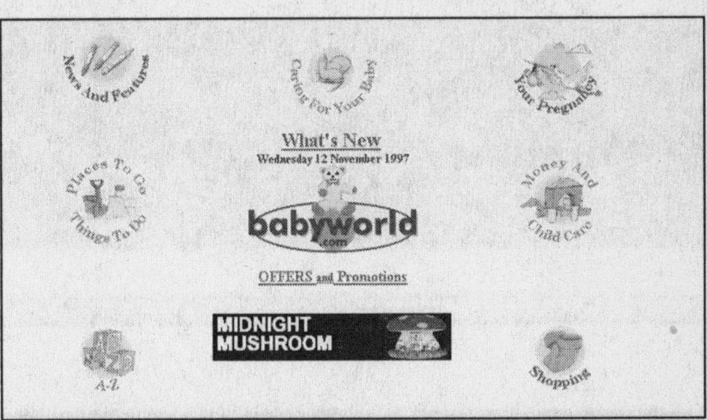

An excellent searchable site with a wealth of information on childcare, pregnancy, birth, and baby products. You could easily spend all afternoon exploring the related pages and links.

December Fifth Creations

http://www.dfcreations.com/Welcome.html

Offers baby-naming software for sale. Also gives hints on baby naming, provides baby shower games and gift-giving ideas, and lists other interesting baby-related Web sites.

Heaven Railroad

http://www.heavenrr.com/

This site offers an online catalog of cribsets, bedding, and accessories with a Christian (railroad) theme. Also offers tips on arranging and lighting your baby's room for safety and security. A "Hot List" leads you to an extensive list of sites related to babies, children, and parenting. A wholesome, helpful site.

Jellinek's Baby Name Chooser

http://www.namechooser.com/baby/index.shtml

Be sure to visit this site if you are having difficulty choosing a baby name. Selects boys' or girls' names at random. Also includes listings of most popular names and latest names and allows you to add names to the list. Offers links, a name forum, Java chat, and baby cards you can send via email free.

Super Baby Food Book

http://www.superbabyfood.com/mainmenu.htm

Visit this site to order the *Super Baby Food Book*, a 460-page reference book on feeding your baby. Site offers various example chapters so that you can sample before you buy. Includes links to other sites of interest.

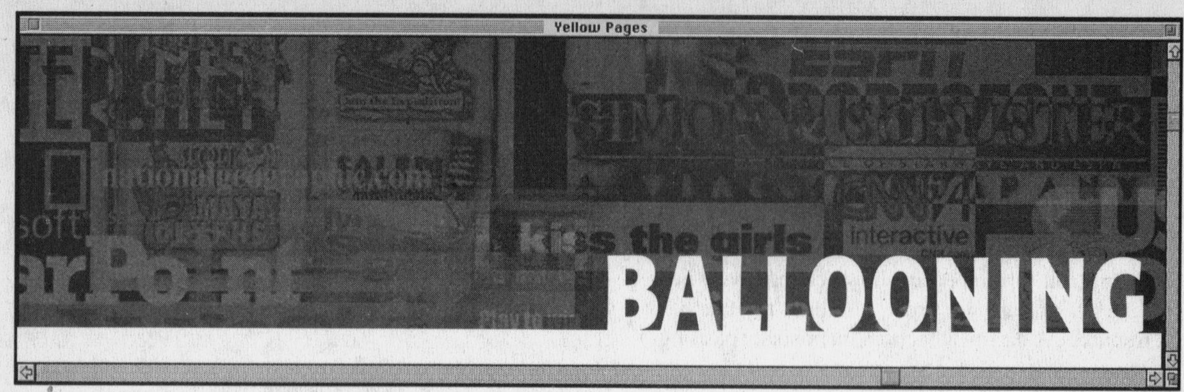

> There 's something in a flying horse,
> There 's something in a huge balloon.
>
> *William Wordsworth*

1998 U.S. Hot Air Balloon Championships

http://www.balloonchamps.com/

A complete program, schedule, and entry forms for this prestigious ballooning competition. Buy your advance souvenirs, find out about attractions and accommodations, and more.

Airship and Blimp Resources

http://www.hotairship.com/index.html

A volunteer-run site with resource information catering to a wide variety of interest and experience levels. This site focuses on the history and current status of airships and blimps rather than balloons, but a lot of the general information is applicable to ballooning as well.

AUNTY MONKEY – The Balloon Fanzine

http://www.users.fl.net.au/~monkey/menu.html

Aunty Monkey is a nonprofit, nonpolitical ballooning fanzine, focusing on the lighter, fun side of ballooning. It's a very cool, graphical site with a decidedly Generation-X feel to it and lots of good solid ballooning information. You can also subscribe to the hard-copy version.

AUNTY MONKEY – The Balloon Fanzine
http://www.users.fl.net.au/~monkey/menu.html

Balloon Pages on the World Wide Web
http://www.euronet.nl/users/jdewilde/index.html

Hot Air Balloons USA
http://www.hot-airballoons.com/

Balloon Central

http://www.gkco.co.uk/balloon-central.html

All the details about around-the-world balloon racing teams attempting a world flight in 1997-1998. Includes all the press releases pertaining to each team, and links to related sites.

Ballooning Resource Guide

http://www.campus.ne.jp/~sugawara/

A very nice global ballooning site, with links to ballooning information all over the world, broken down by location and site purpose (clubs, organizations, balloon rides, commercial sites, and so on).

Balloon Life Magazine

http://www.balloonlife.com/bl.htm

This site doesn't provide much in the way of free samples; you must subscribe to the magazine to access most of the content. However, subscribers will find a wealth of information about ballooning, including articles on insurance, photography, special events, and contests.

Balloon Pages on the World Wide Web

http://www.euronet.nl/users/jdewilde/index.html

Wow! What a comprehensive list of Web addresses for all things related to ballooning. From here you can jump to sites for various "Around the World" attempts, as well as pages and pages of ballooning history, advice, and photography.

Hot Air Balloons USA

http://www.hot-airballoons.com/

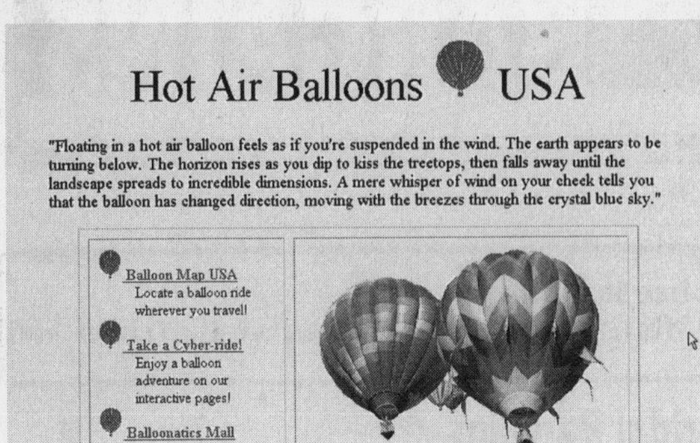

A colorful, complete, and thoroughly enjoyable site. Features an interactive "Take a Cyber-Ride" balloon ride expedition, a mall area for shopping for balloon-related items, and a map showing balloon ride vendors all over the U.S.

Incredible Journeys

http://www.sa-homepage.com/balloon/

A site offering adventures in Hot Air Ballooning, including rides, instruction, and equipment sales. Available for parties, weddings, and sightseeing flights around historic San Antonio and the surrounding hill country.

Innovation Ballooning

http://innovation-ballooning.co.uk

A company that provides hot air balloon flights for the able and disabled. The baskets of Innovation's balloons are specially adapted to allow easy access and perfect views from a wheelchair. Very cool, if you happen to be in the U.K.

National Scientific Balloon Facility

http://master.nsbf.nasa.gov

The NSBF is a NASA facility managed by the Physical Science Lab of New Mexico State University. They launch, track, and recover scientific balloon experiments all over the world, and this page shows some of their PR materials and photographs. Interesting in a science-geek sort of way.

The Balloon Federation of America

http://www.bfa.ycg.org/

The site of the major American ballooning organization. Includes membership information, events, competition standings, and products for sale, all geared to the experienced ballooner.

World Balloon Corporation

http://www.worldballoon.com/

A must-bookmark site for the serious balloon enthusiast, this New Mexico-based company sells and repairs balloon equipment, prints banners for the balloons, and even manages balloon events.

NEWSGROUPS

rec.aviation.balloon

rec.aviation.homebuilt

rec.aviation.ultralight

rec.aviation.piloting

MAILING LISTS

LTA-builder

This list discusses all aspects of building lighter-than-air vehicles including hot air and gas balloons and airships (thermal or gas, rigids and blimps).To subscribe send mail to ltabuilder@launch.net, "subscribe" (w/o the quotes) must be the subject.

LTA-forsale

This list is intended for trading, buying and selling of balloon related items. To subscribe send mail to lta-forsale@launch.net, "subscribe" (w/o the quotes) must be the subject.

Airship-List

This list covers more general airship topics such as the history, future, and philosophy of airships. To subscribe send mail to listproc@lists.colorado.edu. The message (no subject) should contain the following: Subscribe airship-list "your name".

Balloon@lboro.ac.uk

The group is here to discuss any topics in relation to LTA aircraft (Lighter Than Air). This includes Hot Air Balloons, Gas Balloons, Airships, and Hot Air Airships. To subscribe, send email to majordomo@lboro.ac.uk and in the body of the message, put "subscribe balloon."

A B C D E F G H I J K L M N O P Q R S T U V W X Y Z

> **If** the best things in life are free, why am I in the red?
>
> *Bernadette McCarver Snyder*

#1 Travel Bargains

http://www.real-travelbargains.com/

Save over 40 percent on your favorite airline tickets. Get information on international travel, car rental, and travel clubs.

Air tickets Direct

http://www.airtickets.co.uk/

Gives a phone number and info on planning your trip, tickets, car rentals, insurance, news, and specials on traveling products.

Baby Bargains

http://www.bhome.com/baby.htm

This site has links to Beanie Babies Store, Furniture Stores, and backpacks. Also allows you to email with baby item requests.

Bonus Bargains

http://www.elitemall.com/brbg.html

Sign up to receive exciting, bargain offers via email that usually sell out with a few hours.

Related Sites

- http://cycling.org/
- http://wesell.com/
- http://iypn.com/bill/

Free Stuff Bonanza
http://www.bargains-mall.com/free-stuff/index.html

Bridal Bargains

http://www.windsorpeak.com/bridalbargains/default.html

Order the Bridal Bargains book or just browse through the overview, tips, or articles at this site. A mailbag with letters from other customers gives an insight on the book also.

CD Bargains.com

http://www.cdbargains.com/

Used or new CD catalog online. Order online or through fax, phone, or email. Choose from thousands of CDs under $9.00 and two thousand under $5.99!

The Dynamic Wizard Home Page

http://www.dynamicwizard.com/

Shop in the wizard mall, CD blowout link, and save 50 percent on your groceries link. Receive a newsletter through email that contains many bargains.

Free Stuff Bonanza

http://www.bargains-mall.com/free-stuff/index.html

This fun site gives links to many other sites that offer free stuff. Some of the free stuff links are free food samples, introductory magazine free, beauty item samples, and other free links.

Related Sites

- http://www.aone.com/~scotlitl/barg1.html
- http://www.aone.com/~scotlitl/barg3.html
- http://www.chinatowns.net/

Note Before you buy, be sure to check out the retailer's privacy policy. Make sure the site offers a secure server, especially if you are paying for your purchases with a credit card. The better stores will have a privacy policy and should be able to tell you what they are going to do with the data they receive from you.

Hot Buyz

http://www.hotbuyz.com/

Immediately buy bargains that include software, furniture, and cellular phones. Offers secrets of furniture discounts and answers to frequently asked furniture questions.

Mall Bargains

http:http://yellowpage.net/main.htm

Provides lists of retail sites from which you can order merchandise. Products available range from computers, traders and wholesalers, and cameras to voice mail systems.

MediaMart Winter Video Bargains

http://www.netvideo.com/mediamart/video/v.bargains.html

Order videos online that relate to New Year's resolutions, winter sports, and winter dreams.

Net-Bargains

http://www.net-bargains.com/

Northern Virginia's site for online coupons 24 hours a day. Click different categories that you can save on: beauty supplies, automobiles, dry cleaning, and photo processing.

United States Auctions

http://www.usauctions.com/index5.htm

A live 24-hour auction site! Bid on computers, hardware, software, printers, and other electronics.

Wacky Stacky's Weekly Bargains

http://www.wackystackys.com/

This exciting site offers weekly bargains on things from electronics, sports, toys, and miscellaneous. Includes picture and information on the product for sale.

Related Sites

http://www.talking-pages.com/do06000.htm

http://www.wipd.com/~go/mgenw4.htm

http://www.airbargainstravel.com/

http://www.aone.com/~scotlitl/barg2.html Mall Bargains

http://yellowpage.net/main.htm

A B C D E F G H I J K L M N O P Q R S T U V W X Y Z

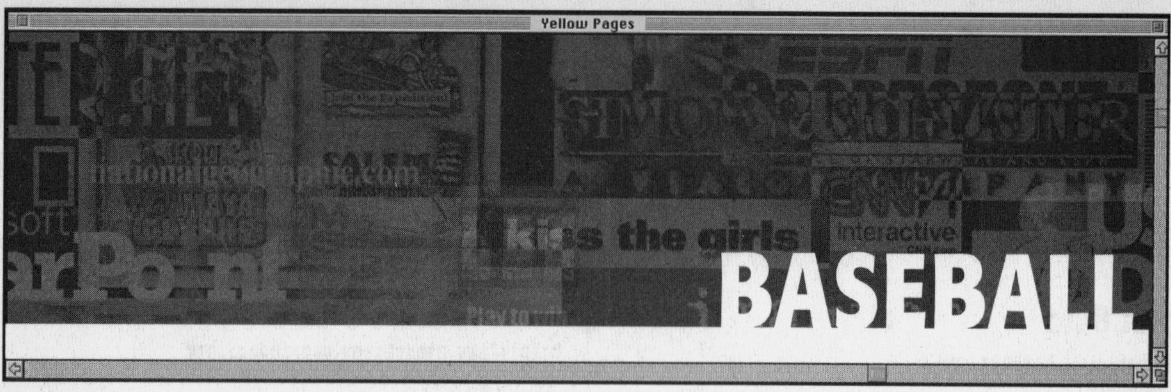

BASEBALL

Where have you gone, Joe DiMaggio?

Paul Simon

The following are Web sites for Major League Baseball teams:

Team	URL
Atlanta Braves	http://www.atlantabraves.com/
Chicago Cubs	http://www.students.uiuc.edu/~k-jerbi/Cubs/home.html
Cleveland Indians	http://www.indians.com/
Houston Astros	http://www.astros.com/
Minnesota Twins	http://www.wcco.com/sports/twins/
New York Yankees	http://www.yankees.com/
Oakland A's	http://www.oaklandathletics.com/
Pittsburgh Pirate	http://www.pirateball.com/
San Francisco Giants	http://www.sfgiants.com/
Seattle Mariners	http://www.mariners.org/
St. Louis Cardinals	http://www.stlcardinals.com/
Toronto Blue Jays	http://www.bluejays.ca/bluejays/

Baseball Hall of Fame

http://www.baseballhalloffame.org/index.html

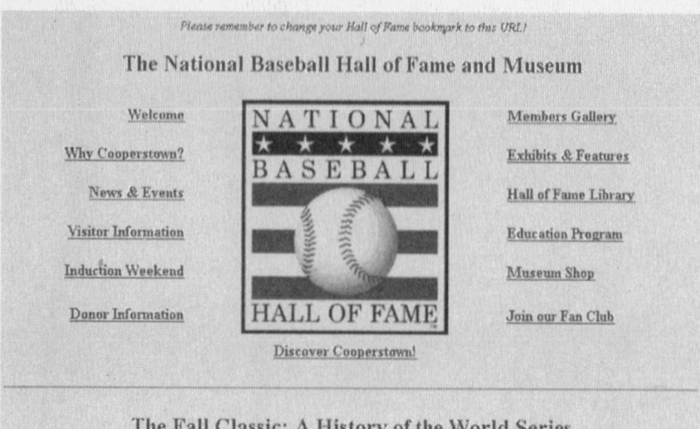

Baseball Hall of Fame
http://www.baseballhalloffame.org/index.html

ESPNet SportsZone: Major League Baseball
http://espnet.sportszone.com/mlb/

Little League Baseball
http://www.littleleague.org/

Major League Baseball
http://www.majorleaguebaseball.com/

The Hall of Fame site provides admission prices and hours of operation. You can link to directions on how to get to Cooperstown, access the Hall of Fame newsletter "Around the Horn," and view online special exhibits like the current one on the history of the World Series.

ESPNet SportsZone: Major League Baseball

http://espnet.sportszone.com/mlb/

A site with everything you've come to expect from ESPN, just concentrated on baseball. Here you'll find links to the top stories of the day, but you'll also find 1997 attendance figures, team payroll lists, and the latest injury reports. Subscription information available; ideal for both the casual observer and baseball enthusiast.

Fastball

http://www.fastball.com/

With scores and stats updated every three minutes, this is a great resource for followers of the game. There is hometown coverage of the Braves, Rockies, Reds, Astros, Marlins, and Rangers just a click away. Dugout Chatter is a unique link to chat rooms and baseball topics.

Instant Baseball

http://www.InstantSports.com/baseball.html

Truly instant in the sense that game updates are done about every two minutes so you can follow the game without your television or radio. They are currently running beta tests that will bring animated games live to the Web. Now available are up-to-the minute standings, statistics, and schedules for all MBL teams.

Japanese Professional Baseball

http://www.inter.co.jp/Baseball/

Provides final statistics in this league from 1936 to the present. Team rosters, schedules, and statistics are provided as well.

Little League Baseball

http://www.littleleague.org/

Provides lists of past state champions and a thorough FAQ page. The World Series link details the happenings of that event. Information on summer camps is provided along with gift and equipment supply purchasing information.

Major League Baseball

http://www.majorleaguebaseball.com/

Official site of Major League Baseball contains an up-to-date scoreboard, photo of the day, and a section for kids. Also included are links to each team that provide individual team member stats and career highlights, as well as links to each team's home page. The MLB Library and Digest are useful for learning facts about the game.

Nando Baseball Server

http://www.nando.net/SportServer/baseball/

The baseball link of the Nando SportServer breaks down the MBL by leagues and divisions. Each league section has a listing of that day's starting pitchers. Also included are current statistics, team transactions, and a preview of that day's games.

New York Yankees Home Plate

http://www.yankees.com/

Yankee fans can order season tickets, subscribe to *Yankee Magazine*, and order merchandise from this site. Team rosters and statistics for both the Yankees and their minor league affiliates are also available.

World Youth Baseball

http://www.brandonu.ca/~ennsnr/WYB/

Unofficial server of World Youth Baseball. Provides links to league standings and schedules. Teams from all over the world play in this league. The site provides words to the official song of the WYB and a link to find out about former WYB players now in the major leagues.

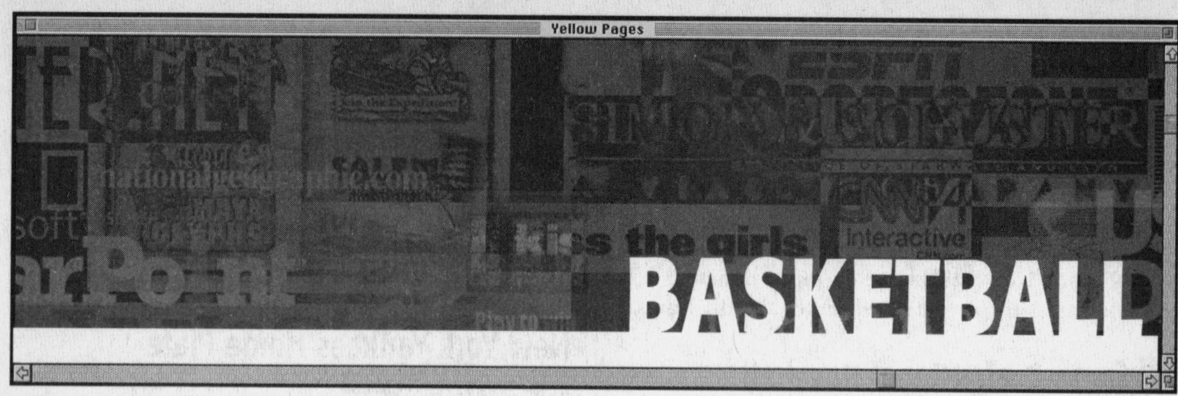

> In sports, you simply aren't considered a real champion until you have defended your title successfully. Winning it once can be a fluke; winning it twice proves you are the best.
>
> *Althea Gibson*

The following are the home pages for teams of the National Basketball Association:

Team	URL
Atlanta Hawks	http://www.nba.com/hawks/
Charlotte Hornets	http://www.nba.com/hornets/
Chicago Bulls	http://www.nba.com/bulls/
Cleveland Caveliers	http://www.nba.com/cavs/
Dallas Mavericks	http://www.nba.com/mavericks/
Denver Nuggets	http://www.nba.com/nuggets/
Detroit Pistons	http://www.nba.com/pistons/
Houston Rockets	http://www.nba.com/rockets/
Indiana Pacers	http://www.nba.com/pacers/
Los Angeles Lakers	http://www.nba.com/lakers/
Milwaukee Bucks	http://www.nba.com/bucks/
New York Knicks	http://www.nba.com/knicks/
Orlando Magic	http://www.nba.com/magic/
Philadelphia 76ers	http://www.nba.com/sixers/
Sacramento Kings	http://www.nba.com/kings/
Utah Jazz	http://www.nba.com/jazz/
Washington Wizards	http://www.nba.com/bullets/

Harlem Globetrotters Online
http://www.harlemglobetrotters.com/

Journal of Basketball Studies
http://www.tsoft.com/-deano/index.html

Basketball Explorations

http://library.advanced.org/12006/

This Web site seeks to teach kids about math, physics, art, and other disciplines through the game of basketball, which helps to pique and hold the interest of children whose minds might otherwise wander.

Basketball Hall of Fame

http://www.hoophall.com/

More hoop trivia than you can dribble a ball at. The site has every conceivable bit of information about inductees, this day in basketball history, articles, the Hall of Fame building and location, and more.

The Basketball Highway

http://www.bbhighway.com/

This is the site of the Coaches Information Resource Network, which exists to help coaches improve their game. They may search the site for specific topics, jump to other basketball pages, and learn more about the CIRN database.

Boxscore Basketball

http://www.arrowweb.com/BSBB/toc.html

Boxscore Basketball is a video game of sorts in which players use statistics to plays games with existing, but virtual, players. The site offers an evaluation version and the rules manual, and you're invited to purchase the full version, of course.

College Basketball Page

http://www.onlysports.com/bball/

Has all the usual: schedules, rosters, conference breakdowns, and team nicknames. But, this site also includes All-American lists, recruiting information, academic standards, and rule changes for the next season. Includes information for both men and women, Division IA and below.

Full Court Press

http://www.fullcourt.com/

Full Court Press covers women's b-ball at the high school, college, professional, and international levels. The site is full of articles about players, teams, conferences, and coaches. An article in a recent issue asks the question, "Will female atheletes handle their power better than men?"

Harlem Globetrotters Online

http://www.harlemglobetrotters.com/

The Globetrotters have been entertaining us and beating the Washington Generals for decades, and now you can find them on the Web. The site is offered in many languages, and covers the history, the 1997 schedule, the players, and all things Globetrotter.

HoopsChat

http://www.4-lane.com/sportschat/newsc/hp_index.html

HoopsChat is simply a chat group that anyone can join. Just enter the name you want to use and off you go to discuss basketball in every possible light.

Hoops for Hope

http://www.hoopsforhope.org/

Hoops for Hope is a tournament that travels the country and raises funds to help charities of the Matthew 25 Foundation. The Web site provides a full mission statement, schedule of events, and lists of benefactors and sponsors.

Indiana Basketball Hall of Fame

http://web.hoopshall.com/hall/mainmenu.html

Perhaps no other state in the country claims basketball for itself than does the Hoosier State, which has seen the likes of Larry Bird, Oscar Robertson, and countless others leave rubber streak marks on wooden floors. Though the Hall is located in New Castle, IN, their Web site offers info to the prospective visitor, articles about upcoming events, and more.

Journal of Basketball Studies

http://www.tsoft.com/~deano/index.html

The Journal is perhaps the most detailed scientific following of the professional sport on the Web. On the one hand, it's a wonderful tool for students to learn the use of statistics in a practical, fun environment; on the other, the articles are interesting, regardless of their purpose.

Nando Basketball Server

http://www.nando.net/SportServer/basketball/

The basketball link of the Nando SportServer. Provides links to national and collegiate level teams, scores and statistics. Also includes links to important sports stories like tournament results and happenings such as Jordan's return to basketball.

National Wheelchair Basketball Association

http://www.nwba.org/

The NWBA consists of 22 conferences with 181 teams, which figures out to a lot of wheels! They have teams for men, women, students, and children of all ages. The Web site has a team directory, the official rules, the history of wheelchair basketball, and more.

NBA.Com Players

http://www.nba.com/playerindex.html

Part of the official NBA Web site, the Players page provides statistics and backgrounds for every NBA athlete, as well as career highlights, career transactions, and personal info. The site also provides team links, a Global Game, and more.

On Hoops

http://www.onhoops.com/

A forum for those who love to discuss and critique basketball, its players, coaches, and referees as much as they love to watch the games. You won't find just a list of stats and team rosters here. You will find links to the Police Blotter which chronicles the latest NBA player brushes with the law, as well as a place to vote for your favorite chump player. A nice change of pace for basketball enthusiasts.

The Refeream Site

http://ww1.comteck.com/~jighm/index.html

Ever want to explode after witnessing a game go down the tubes because of poor officiating? This site offers a place to blow off steam. What exactly is it to be "refereamed"?

Scottie Pippen's Home Court

http://www.33online.com/

The complete guide to Pippen's career including links to both his college and professional stats. There are over 20 photos to download and video files highlighting memorable plays and games from the past season.

SlamOnline

http://www.slamonline.com/

The abridged version of their regular magazine. Slam contains the best articles from the latest edition.

Ultimate Basketball Home Page

http://www.odyssey.com.au/sports/bball.html

This site is very graphics-oriented. You can download logos from NBA teams as well as photos of several current NBA players. This site also provides links to popular sports pages by ESPN and featuring Michael Jordan.

USA Basketball.Com

http://www.usabasketball.com/

USA Basketball is the governing body of men's and women's b-ball and is recognized by the International Basketball Federation and the United States Olympic Committee. The organization selects and trains USA teams for national and international play. Their Web site offers a FAQ, news releases, photos, links, and athlete bios.

WNBA

http://www.wnba.com/

The official site of the Women's National Basketball Association offers articles on individual players and teams, sound and video bites via QuickTime and RealAudio, the schedule of games, a gift shop, and more.

Related Sites

http://www.woods.demon.co.uk/britball.html

http://www.geocities.com/Colosseum/5290/

http://www.njbl.org/

http://www.basketball.demon.co.uk/

http://revolution.3-cities.com/~eclipse/

http://www.cris.com/~Hopep/ball.html

http://www.geocities.com/WestHollywood/4606/

http://outreach.mac.cc.cmu.edu/WBPeople/EECM/Ray/hoops

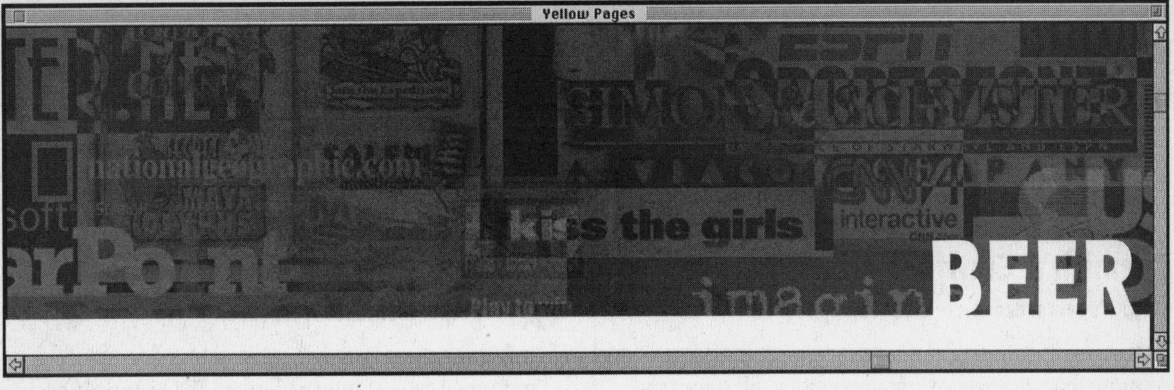

> Let schoolmasters puzzle their brain,
> With grammar, and nonsense, and learning,
> Good liquor, I stoutly maintain,
> Gives genius a better discerning.
>
> *Oliver Goldsmith*

1-800-MICROBREW

http://www.800-microbrew.com/

This microbrew-of-the-month club promises each member will receive 12 bottles of fine microbrew each month, six from two different breweries. Site also contains recipes for such delicacies as cheesy beer bread and beef braised in igloo ale.

Acats Internet Bar Pages

http://www.epact.se/acats/

Consider this site your online bartender. Contains an exhaustive index of mixed drink recipes available in a searchable database by drink name or type of liquor. Learn the tools of the trade and check out postings for employment opportunities. Visit Jim's Saloon for some humorous barkeep stories.

Related Sites

http://www.beerclub.de/

http://www.beerparadise.ltd.uk/

NRP TOP PICKS

Bud On-Line
http://www.budweiser.com/

Cat's Meow 3: Internet Beer Recipe Database
http://realbeer.com/brewery/cm3/recs/index.html

Guinness
http://www.guinness.ie/

Union Liquors Microbeer and Craft Beer Catalog
http://www.union-liquors.com/

Association of Brewers

http://beertown.org/index.html

This site features Beertown, a place dedicated to "the pursuit of quality beer." Contains links to the American Homebrewers Association, the Institute for Brewing Studies, Brewers Publications, and the Great American Beer Festival.

B.A. Brewmeister

http://www.beerbeer.com/

Come and brew your own beer at this Virginia Beach store. If that's not in your neighborhood, you can order a five-gallon beer kit to brew in the comfort of your own home. And, as beermaking tip #5 says, don't forget to "aerate your wort." That's fine advice for us all.

Barley, Malt & Hops

http://www.bmh-club.com/jul_beers.html

Site that provides members monthly sampler packs of all-natural craft-brewed beers.

Related Sites

http://www.brewnews.com/

http://www.hogshead.com/

http://www.juneau.com/akbrew/

A B C D E F G H I J K L M N O P Q R S T U V W X Y Z

Bass Ale

http://www.bassale.com/

This tongue-in-cheek site pokes fun at silly promotions, art, advice columns, and more. Also contains some amusing classified ads that are mostly unrelated to beer.

Beamish & Crawford Brewery

http://www.aardvark.ie/beamish/

Brewing Beamish Genuine Irish Stout in Cork for more than 200 years. Contains a movie file about the brewery.

Beer Across America

http://www.beeramerica.com

Offers online ordering, beer specials, recipes, newsletters, beer chat, and more.

Beer at Home

http://beerathome.com/~beer

Equipment, supplies, information, and recipes for the making of beer, wine, mead, and cider. Their motto is "Beer, we like making it, drinking it and talking about it."

Beer Drinkers of America

http://www.beerdrinkers.com/

This consumer organization works hard not only to protect beer drinkers' rights but to fight against proposed beer tax increases. Find out more about what this organization stands for, and check out 10 helpful tips to enjoy a beerfest.

Beer Master's Tasting Society

http://BeerMasters.com/BeerMasters/

No matter what kind of beer you like, this site wants to hear your thoughts and feelings about it. Use the Beer Glossary to brush up on the latest terminology so you can impress your local bartender. Subscribe to the The Tap Times News or check out the latest in glassware.

Beers of the World

http://www.BeersoftheWorld.com/

This New York store carries over 1500 different beers from all over the world. Unfortunately, this huge selection cannot be shipped out of state. Search alphabetically for your favorite lager, microbrew, or regular old Bud.

BreWorld

http://www.breworld.com

Europe's largest beer and brewing site. Beer, brewing, organizations, breweries, publications, and much more.

Bud On-Line

http://www.budweiser.com/

A colorful, innovative site from Budweiser, the King of Beers. Features information on the history of beer and how Budweiser is improving the quality of beer. Order Budweiser paraphernalia, check out the latest Budweiser sponsored/endorsed events, and download the Budweiser screensaver.

BYOB (Be Your Own Brewmaster, Inc.)

http://www.634brew.com/

Learn how to brew your own beer and make custom labels. You also can purchase malts, grains, hops, and other ingredients. Specials are also available.

Cat's Meow 3: Internet Beer Recipe Database

http://realbeer.com/brewery/cm3/recs/index.html

The quintessential site for home brewers and microbreweries alike. Hundreds of recipes ranging from traditional lagers to herb and spiced beers. Recipes dating from the 1500s to the present day are classified and well-organized in an exhaustive index. The site also contains detailed information for the first-time brewer, as well as links for beer recipe formulating software for most operating systems and platforms. If you consider yourself a beer aficionado, be sure to bookmark this site—you'll be returning frequently.

Foster's Beer

http://www.fostersbeer.com/

More than just great beer. You can learn how to speak Australian, how to purchase authentic outback apparel, and the history of Foster's beer. What more could you ask for in a "mate?"

Guinness

http://www.guinness.ie/

This detailed site invites you to visit St. James' Gate, the home of Guinness beer. Learn about the beer, the can, and much (and I mean MUCH) more. You can even download a Guinness screensaver. You also can choose between the Shockwave or regular versions of this site.

Heineken

http://www.Heineken.nl/

Provides history of the Heineken brewery and offers a virtual tour. Send customized email postcards and participate in Heineken's online game to win prizes. As a service, Heineken provides a running clock displayed in all time zones—worth a bookmark just for this fact.

Hempen Ale Home

http://www.hempenale.com/

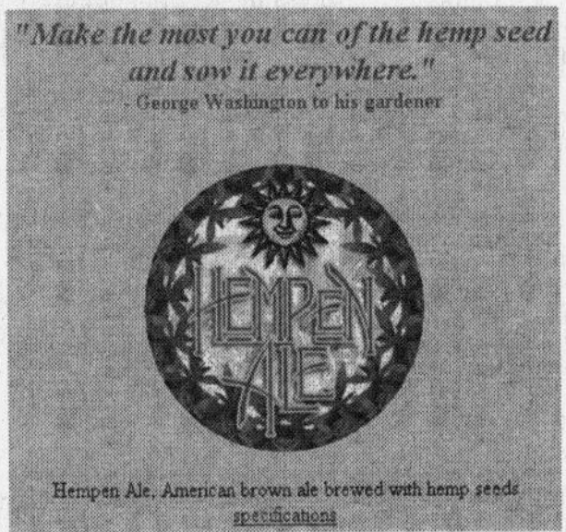

Site contains extensive press coverage about this beer brewed from hemp seeds. Also provides a history of industrial hemp, one of today's hip causes in Hollywood.

King and Barnes Ltd—Brewers of Fine Sussex Ales

http://www.kingandbarnes.co.uk/

The site provides descriptions of the history of the brewery and its beers, a listing of all the pubs in the UK that serve King & Barnes beers, a listing of the latest brands and any seasonal beers currently being offered, a listing of the bars and pubs in the USA that serve the beers, an email page for contacting King & Barnes directly, and an order form for ordering beer-related memorabilia.

Leinenkugel's Leinie Lodge

http://www.leinie.com/

Learn all about this Wisconsin brew and other specialties in the Leinenkugel family of beers. Any company with a beer called Big Butt is a company you gotta love.

Michael Jackson's Beer Hunter Online

http://www.beerhunter.com/

An online magazine to complement Michael Jackson's Beer Hunter and World Beer Hunter CD-ROMs, featuring Mr. Jackson, the world's foremost beer journalist. New articles every Thursday, including news, events, in-depth features, homebrewing (with recipes!), and more, from the best beer writers around the globe.

MGD Taproom

http://www.mgdtaproom.com/index.html

Not just a beerfest, this site also contains information about Miller-sponsored events, such as sports and concerts. And Brewmaster can answer any questions about beer that you could possibly have. All this plus the chance to critique Miller beer, the site, their commercials, and more.

Northwest Brew News

http://www.wolfenet.com/~nwbrew

The essential newsletter for the beer enthusiast. Reviews of breweries, beers, pubs, and alehouses throughout the northwest region. Pocket beer guide, jokes, trivia, and more.

The Oxford Brewing Company

http://shell.idt.net/~ericm9/oxford/

Mid-Atlantic company that combines the British brewing heritage and American microbrewing process to produce new, flavorful brews. Links to ordering brewing information and clothing.

Pabst Brewing Company

http://www.pabst.com/

Provides a history of beer in general as well as of this brewing company, one of the oldest in America. Also under the Pabst umbrella are Olympia, Hamm's, Pearl, and other labels.

Pete's Brewing Company

http://www.peteswicked.com/

This site contains lots of financial info about this company, including a business overview, earnings statements, investor resources, and more. Very different from most beer-related sites.

A B C D E F G H I J K L M N O P Q R S T U V W X Y Z

The Pub Brewing Company

http://www.pubbrewing.com/

Thinking about opening your own brew pub? This is the company to show you the ropes. They provide layouts, equipment, installation, training, inspections, and more. Your comprehensive guides to getting into the brew business.

Redhook Brewery

http://www.redhook.com/

Provides information on the Washington state-based microbrewery that has begun to make its existence known nationwide for its diversity and excellence. Take a virtual tour of the brewery. Evaluate the stock value of this up-and-coming brewery.

Siebel Institute of Technology

http://www.siebel-institute.com/welcome/

The classes many college students dream about are offered at this brewing training establishment. Take courses such as Advanced Brewing Technology, Beverage Packing, or Flavour Evaluation. Lab services also are offered and you can consult the institute's newsletter.

S.P.S. Beer Stuff

http://www.beerstuff.com/index.htm

A visually impressive site presenting an online catalog of homebrewing equipment and supplies. The catalog includes over 100 varieties of malt extracts from around the world. Also includes some brewing recipes from visitors. *The* site for homebrewers.

Union Liquors Microbeer and Craft Beer Catalog

http://www.union-liquors.com/

This online catalog features over 600 varieties of beer, available for shipping to most U.S. locations. Browse the site by name, style, flavor, brewery, state, or country. If the local LiquorLand doesn't have it, chances are Union Liquors does!

Virtual Pub

http://lager.geo.brown.edu:8080/virtual-pub/

An award-winning web site where beer aficionados exchange information on their favorite brews. Also contains an eclectic collection of information on beer with a healthy representation of links to other beer-related sites.

The World's Top Ten Beers Of The Month

http://www.geocities.com/southbeach/4769

Come to the top ten page that lets you be the judge. Submit your vote on The Top Ten Beers Of The Month. No preselected lists, just you and your vote.

USENET NEWSGROUPS

alt.beer

alt.beer.like-molson-eh

fido7.at.beer

fido7.kharkov.beer

fido7.mo.beer

fido7.ru.beer

muc.lists.beer.homebrew

rec.beer

sci.homebrew

uiuc.org.homebrewers

LISTSERVS

ADD-L—Forum for discussion of concerns of drinking and driving

You can join this group by sending the message "sub ADD-L your name" to

listserv@admin.humberc.on.ca

CD—Cybercenter for controlled drinking/drug use discussion

You can join this group by sending the message "sub CD your name" to

listserv@maelstrom.stjohns.edu

Related Sites

http://www.microbility.com/

http://www.philadelphia.around-town.com/home/of/independence.html

http://www.shenandoahbrewing.com/

http://www.sierra-nevada.com/

http://www.srv.net/shop/lostarts/welcome.html

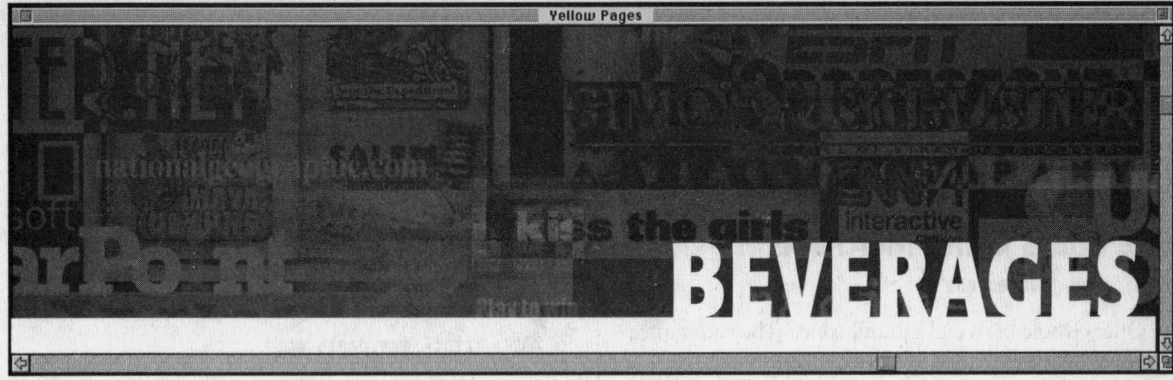

> If this is coffee, please bring me some tea; but if this is tea, please bring me some coffee.
>
> *Abraham Lincoln*

COFFEES AND TEAS

All Hawaii Coffee

http://www.mauigateway.com/~coffee

Offers types of gourmet coffee from Hawaii's volcanic soil. Order via the Web.

Baronet Coffee

http://www.cyberusa.net/baronet/

Shop online or receive their mail order catalog. Gift baskets, rare coffees, coffee clubs, coffee supplies, and much more.

Cafe Gourmet Coffees

http://www.usit.net/hp/cafegour/homepage.html

This site offers consumer and wholesale prices. Emphasizes the social aspect of coffee and calls for a return to the old world elegance of coffee drinking.

Cafe MAM

http://mmink.cts.com/mmink/dossiers/cafemam.html

An environmentally conscious and socially responsible Mayan cooperative with a wide variety of fine coffee roasts and blends and other Cafe MAM paraphernalia available for online ordering.

NRP TOP PICKS

Peet's Coffee and Tea
http://www.peets.com/

Jolt Cola
http://www.joltcola.com/

Capulin Coffee

http://emall.com/ashcreek/

Offers a traditionally dried 100% natural jungle coffee grown on Mexico's Pacific coast. Proceeds from the sale of Capulin benefit a conservation project, which grows and harvests these beans.

China Mist Tea Company

http://www.chinamist.com

Retail store over the Internet that offers many types of teas.

Coffee Tea & Spice

http://www.best.com/~blholmes/coffeeandtea/

A Haight Ashbury-based coffee shop since 1973, this site offers a wide variety of coffees and teas. All orders are roasted expressly for shipment.

Cool Brew Coffee from New Orleans Coffee Company

http://www.coolbrew.com/

Features concentrated, cold-filtered, gourmet coffee extract.

Fortunes International Teas

http://www3.pgh.net/~fortunes

The ultimate tea site. Offers 100 percent Pure Ceylon Teas, information on tea growing, cultivating, and Sri Lanka. Everything you wanted to know, but were afraid to ask.

A B C D E F G H I J K L M N O P Q R S T U V W X Y Z

Hipberry Tea Room

http://hipberry.com

Hipberry Tea carries more than 100 specialty teas and exotic herbal blends from around the world.

Java DocUs Coffee Merchants

http://www.javadoc.com

Offers whole bean and ground coffee. They guarantee you'll love their coffee and prices! Visit to win free coffee and gifts.

Java Hut

http://www.javahut.com/

Delivers whole bean coffee right to your door. Offers more than 15 distinctive roasts, straights, and blends. Gift boxes are available.

Mother City Espresso

http://www.halcyon.com/zipgun/mothercity/mothercity.html

Provides a guide to the culture of Seattle coffee houses with reviews of the best and worst bean roasters and coffee house environments. Contains addresses and telephone numbers to order from with a 20 percent discount.

Moxie Collector's Page

http://www.xensei.com/users/iraseski/

Learn all there is to know about the first soft drink, which was endorsed by Ted Williams and remains a staple in most New England refrigerators. The only commercial product to become synonymous with a personal attribute, Moxie even played a role in history. Download rare movie footage of an alien drinking Moxie.

Notes from Latte Land

http://www.foodetc.com/latte.html

Recommended by the founders of *food etc.*, this site contains tips from Caffe Ladro on how to make great espresso at home. Suggestions on the proper equipment as well.

Orleans Coffee Exchange

http://www.orleanscoffee.com

Gourmet coffee from the heart of the French Quarter. They offer a free pound of java with your first order.

Over the Coffee

http://www.cappuccino.com/

Lets you express your personal opinions about a good cup of joe. Read the opinions of your fellow coffee lovers, or access other coffee-related sites on the Internet. You know, coffee talk! No big whoop.

Peet's Coffee and Tea

http://www.peets.com/

Order online for home delivery. Visitors to this site can browse through the owner's journal from his travels as he searches for fine coffee. Also includes a page on coffee news and wisdom for tips on how to brew the best cup of java possible.

Praiswater Coffee Roasters

http://www.webbranch.com/coffee/index.html

Provides information about their story of growing coffee in Kona, Hawaii, an overview of the coffee process, an up-to-date product listing (including their famous Kona coffee), and an online order form for direct purchasing. Wholesale inquiries welcome.

Sally's Place

http://www.bpe.com/drinks/coffee/index.html

Insights into coffee shops and cafes around the world. Suggestions on brewing the best coffee. Even includes a definition of coffee buzzwords for confused novices.

Tea Traders: Teas From Around The World

http://www.teatraders.com

Teas from around the world. The best place to get a wide variety of teas and tea accessories. They have just about everything that deals with tea!

The Gourmet Coffee Club

http://www.gourmetcoffeeclub.com/members/6162.html

Free club. Have gourmet coffee, tea, and cocoa delivered right to your door.

Top 10 Signs You Are Drinking Too Much Coffee

http://www.geocities.com/SunsetStrip/2324/011.html

A humorous top 10 list. A must for coffee drinkers!

SOFT DRINKS

Almdudler

http://www.almdudler-us.com/frames.htm

A natural herbal soft drink that, according to the site, can be successfully mixed with red or white wine, beer, or any kind of liquor. The manufacturer says there is no comparable product in the U.S. What does this stuff taste like? Order it to find out.

Almost Official Coca-Cola Page

http://www.geocities.com/capecanaveral/1743/coke.htm

Information on the world's leading soft drink manufacturer. Cool pics and great info.

Antarctica Soft Drinks

http://www.antarctica.com.br/english/softd.htm

Full of the names, major ingredients, and descriptions of soft drinks produced in Antarctica. You've most likely never heard of these drinks, but with the help of this site you could be the first on your block to set a new trend.

Coca-Cola

http://www.coca-cola.com

Provides information about the most renowned soft drink company. Buy, sell, and trade Coca-Cola paraphernalia online. Check out Coca-Cola–sponsored sporting events. See how Coca-Cola is doing in the business world before you decide to buy some stock in soft drinks.

Jolt Cola

http://www.joltcola.com/

Arguably one of the best sites on the Web now. With the advantage of having a computer-oriented core audience, Jolt presents a Java-powered site featuring information on the beverage of choice of hackers and college students. Test your vital signs on the Jolt-o-meter. See the impact Jolt has had on the entertainment industry. Get a glimpse of Jolt culture. A good site for pure entertainment value.

Pepsi Russia

http://www.pepsi.ru/

The first Pepsi site in Russia with links to other Pepsi sites and the history of Pepsi in Russia. You can even see your name appear in Russian atop the Kremlin wall.

Perrier

http://www.perrier.com/

Nature's original beverage refresher in bottled form. Perrier's site provides information about the company and offers a restaurant guide to New York, Los Angeles, Chicago, Washington, D.C., and New Orleans. View Perrier's past, present, and future advertising artwork. Enter the bottle art contest or order some Perrier apparel and paraphernalia.

Snapple

http://www.snapple.com/

Made from the best stuff on earth, Snapple's site offers information on its current and future flavored beverages—vote for your favorite! Enter the Snapple-a-day sweepstakes and win free Snapple products.

The Royal Crown Cola Story

http://www.cyborganic.com/people/fuzzy/rcstory.htm

A history of Royal Crown Cola, some photos, and various promotional information. This site appears to belong to a reeeaaallly devoted fan of the soft drink.

Yoo-Hoo on the Net

http://http.tamu.edu/~bar8201/yoohoo/

A humorous look at an old favorite—Yoo-Hoo. Site includes frequently un-asked questions, mix ups, and a Yoo-Hoo gallery.

Related Sites
http://www.beans-brews.com/bbtips.htm
http://i-sis.com/cafe.html
http://www.essetti.com/tips.htm
http://www.cw-usa.com/gifts.html
http://www.roadsideamerica.com/set/drink.html
http://www.hoovers.com/sample_his.html
http://www.javaventures.com/costrica.html
http://www.mendocinosoda.com/
http://www.nbcfiz.com/products/
http://www.er.uqam.ca/merlin/hj891806/twedel2.html

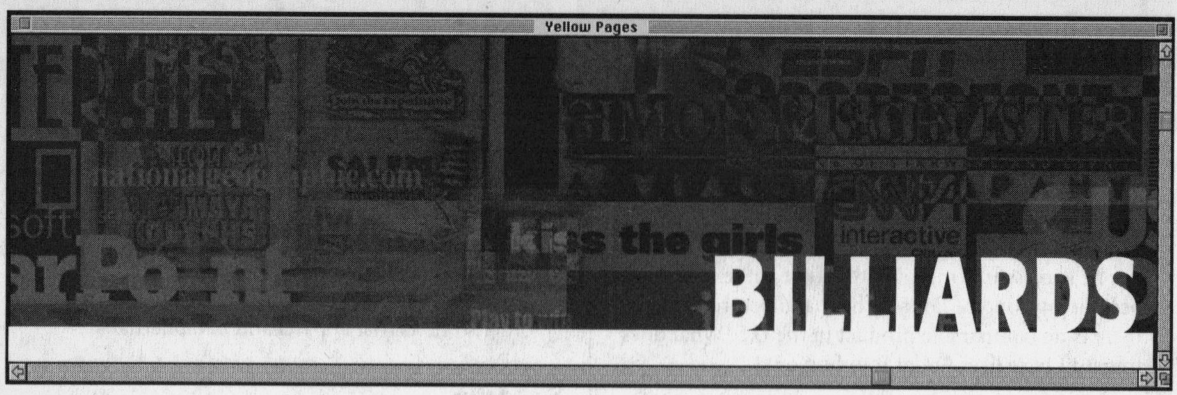

> It is impossible to imagine Goethe or Beethoven being good at billiards or golf.
>
> *H. L. Mencken*

American Poolplayers Association

http://www.poolplayers.com/

Geared primarily toward the competition-minded player, this site offers complete rules for the games of 8-ball and 9-ball, plus an opportunity to join the APA or start up an APA tournament franchise. Also includes a link to American Poolplayer Magazine articles.

Billiard Congress of America

http://www.bca-pool.com/

The Billiard Congress of America is the governing body for the sport of pocket billiards in North America. Their site is primarily educational, providing official rules and guidelines for equipment, but you can also join the organization from here and read about their publications. Surprisingly deep and detailed content in a wide range of areas, ranging from the history of the sport to the latest tournaments.

Billiard Pro Shop, Inc.

http://www.billiardpro.com/

An online store where you can purchase the very finest cues, cases, and table fabrics. This is pricey equipment ($500 and up for a cue), but if billiards is your life, it's no doubt worth the expense.

Billiard Congress of America
http://www.bca-pool.com/

Billiard World Web Magazine
http://www.billiardworld.com/

Mark Avlon's List of Interesting Pool, Billiard, and Snooker Links
http://www.accessone.com/~mavlon/

Billiards Digest Interactive

http://www.billiardsdigest.com/

The online complement to the most comprehensive magazine in billiards. Rather than replacing the magazine, the site offers features that supplement the paper copy, such as coverage of upcoming tournaments, chat rooms, and opinion polls.

Billiard World Web Magazine

http://www.billiardworld.com/

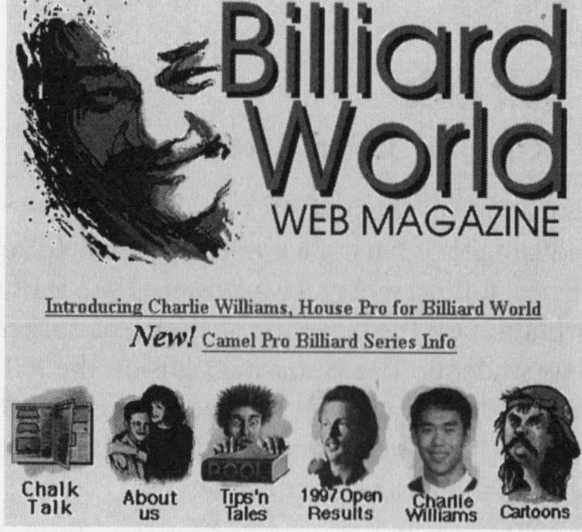

Nicely done online magazine, including all the features you would expect from a paper mag. There's an advice column, feature articles, letters to the editor, cartoons—you get the idea. Definitely worth the stop!

Cyber-Pool

http://www.cybercanarias.com/pool/

A site where you can play a computer pool game online with other players from around the world. Just the thing for anybody who can't get enough pool in his or her real life.

Frequently Asked Questions About Pool

http://www.gla.ac.uk/Clubs/WebSoc/~9407795b/intro.htm

Loads of helpful information for the pool novice, in question-and-answer format. (Note that this is not the official FAQ from the rec.sport.billiard newsgroup.)

Mark Avlon's List of Interesting Pool, Billiard, and Snooker Links

http://www.accessone.com/~mavlon/

A huge list of other sites on the Web pertaining to billiards and related sports. Not fancy, but quite thorough.

Oran Green's Very Extensive Billiards, Cues, Pool, and Snooker Links

http://www.cland.net/~faxsell/cue4b.htm

Another huge list of cue-sports links, including commercial vendors, clubs and organizations, and personal pages created by fans of the sport.

Pool Jargon List

http://www.accessone.com/~mavlon/jargon.html

A text-only glossary of pool-related terms. Very helpful for a beginner trying to understand the lingo at a tournament!

Professional Cuesports Association

http://www.cuesports.com/

A view from the pro billiards circuit, including player spotlights, tournament photos, schedules, and (of course) genuine PCA merchandise for sale.

Saffron Billiards on the Internet

http://www.saffrons.com/

A nicely constructed online sales catalog for pool tables, cues, and billiard room accessories with many pictures. A great resource for comparison-shopping many brands and models. They also sell foosball and air hockey tables.

The Billiard Zone

http://www.sound.net/~jimbarr/pplofkc/

Thoroughly researched and easy-to-navigate information about cue sports brought to you by the Players Pool League of Kansas City. Many good articles, including one on how to spot and avoid hustlers.

The Mining Company

http://billiardspool.miningco.com/

Frequently updated, professional-quality site with articles about billiard playing, on both the amateur and professional level. There is also a chat area and a list of events.

Women's Professional Billiard Association

http://www.wpba.com/

Part organizational info, part fanzine, this site provides profiles and the latest stats for the top WPBA players and offers posters and other souvenirs for sale. You can also find out how to join the organization in any of several capacities. (They have a Patron class of membership for those who want to support the sport but don't play competitively themselves.)

NEWSGROUPS

rec.sport.billiard

Rec.sport.pool

Related Sites

http://www.fhi-berlin.mpg.de/~unger/cue_links.html

http://gabn.org/

http://zenon.inria.fr:8003/koala/jma/hobbies/Snooker/Snooker-Referees.html

http://www.caves.org/~roger/

http://www.bca-pool.com/nwba/

http://24.112.6.1/~newscues/

http://www.playcraft.com/

http://www.freespace.net/~elmark/pool1.htm

http://www.nakisa.ca/software/billiard.html

http://www.netins.net/showcase/bcahome/wpa/wpa_epbf.htm

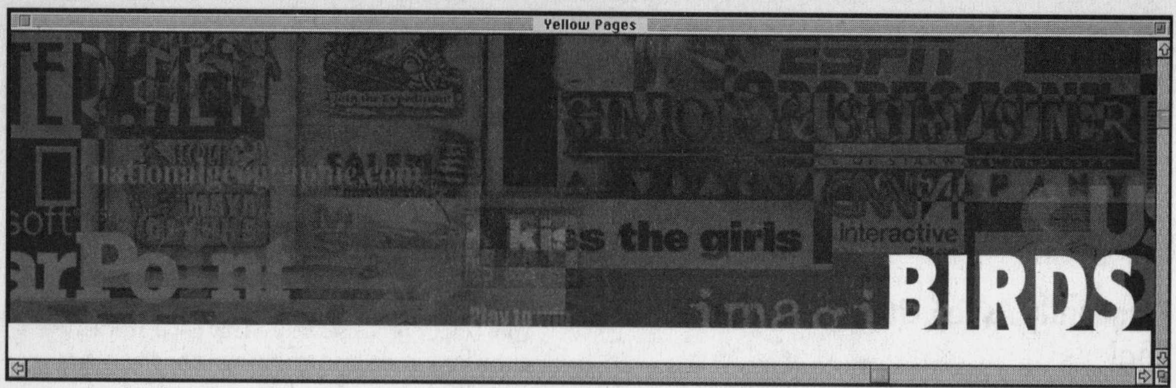

A B C D E F G H I J K L M N O P Q R S T U V W X Y Z

Oh the little birds sang east, and the little birds sang west.

Elizabeth Barrett Browning

The Baltimore Bird Club

http://www.bcpl.lib.md.us/~tross/baltbird.html

This site is not just for Maryland residents. There are rare bird alerts posted for the entire east coast region, links to bird societies, and an extensive list of additional sites on the adventures of birding in America.

Birding on the Web, the Next Generation

http://www-stat.wharton.upenn.edu/~siler/birding.html

An extensive collection of related sites, Hot Lists of bird sightings, and FAQs about all aspects of birding. Also find recommended reference works, computer software, books, and travel tips for the best birding opportunities. The information is sorted geographically and by specific bird types.

Caring for Your New Bird

http://www.ddc.com/~kjohnson/birdcare.htm

This 23-page book includes information such as listings at local pet stores, mail-order supply catalogs, veterinarians, and bird clubs. Includes info on choosing breeders and choosing a bird, the first few days, handling your new bird, household safety, nutrition, diseases and injuries, and more. This page was chosen as a Hot Site by Starting Point, a WWW database searching tool.

Birding on the Web, the Next Generation
http://www-stat.wharton.upenn.edu/~siler/birding.html

National Audubon Society
http://www.audubon.org

PETBird
http://www2.upatsix.com/

God gives every bird its food, but he does not throw it into the nest.

J.G. Holland

The Eagle Page from Rocky Mountain High

http://www.sky.net/~emily/eagle.html

Pays homage to birds of prey and provides a resource list of other related sites. A diverse site that provides info (or points you in the right direction) about the U.S. Bald Eagle Protection Act, information on adopting an eagle, and poems and song lyrics about eagles.

The Fabulous Kakapo (Strigops Habroptilus)

http://www.resort.com/~ruhue/kakapo.html

Focuses on the Kakapo bird, a rare nocturnal, flightless parrot that's native to New Zealand. Once prevalent throughout the area, the Kakapo population is slowly diminishing. There are only about 56 Kakapo left. This site details how New Zealanders are working to help the population recover. This site is now mirrored in Japan.

National Audubon Society

http://www.audubon.org

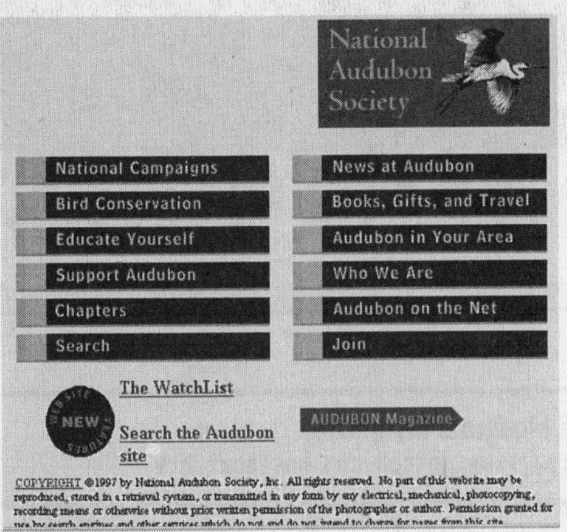

This site, the home page of the National Audubon Society, provides information on the conservation issues and programs the Society is currently working on. Those campaigns currently target the marine ecosystems of the world and bird sanctuaries that protect wildlife habitats. Learn about the Audubon's action agenda for the 104th Congress. You can also get travel, education, and membership information.

The Pet Bird Page

http://aloha.net/~granty/

With facts about everything from the Maroon Bellied Conure to the African Gray Parrot, this site serves as a guide to pet birding. Includes FAQs and newsgroup connections in addition to specific information on most of the major breeds of commonly domesticated birds.

PETBird

http://www2.upatsix.com/

Introduces aviary practices, FAQs, and links to numerous breeders, vendors, and avian associations. Also features a lost or stolen page where you can report missing pets. Provides software on aviculture and birding.

United States Fish and Wildlife Service Home Page

http://www.fws.gov/

Offers information on numerous species (both endangered and non-endangered), including migratory habits and habitats. There is also a searchable database of publications of the Fish and Wildlife Service.

Virtual Birding in Tokyo

http:ux01.so-net.or.jp/~koike

Provides exquisite pictures of wild and domestic birds in Tokyo, Japan.

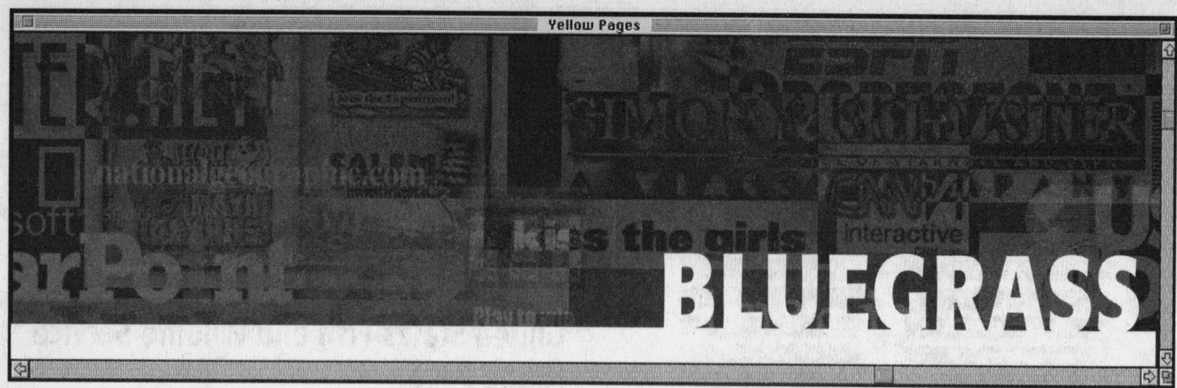

BLUEGRASS

> Bluegrass gives you the best of everything—dance, rhythm, fellowship, in a festival setting.
>
> *Roger Banister*

Beppe Gambetta

http://www.pangea.it/music/gambetta/

An accomplished Italian acoustic guitarist who performs his traditional American guitar playing all over the world. Schedule him for your next acoustic music festival, workshop, or concert by contacting his national managing agent. Note his list of credentials, discography, and published works.

the bluegrass connection

http://www.gotech.com/homepgxt.htm

Online resource where you can locate festivals and bluegrass music products and information. Also find out about record companies, manufacturers of bluegrass equipment, and instrument supply companies.

the bluegrass connection
http://www.gotech.com/homepgxt.htm

BlueGrassRoots MASTER CATALOG SEARCH

http://BGR.ee/MUSIC/

Enormous database of bluegrass musicians and record labels. Search the database for your favorite musician, band, or album. You can also search by the label or the year. A master catalog is available for download.

Central Texas Bluegrass Association

www.zilker.net/~ctbg/

Offers information about the Central Texas Bluegrass Association, a nonprofit corporation. Includes a calendar of events, as well as workshop and membership information.

CYBERGRASS

http://www.banjo.com/BG/

Online music magazine dedicated to bluegrass music. Everything bluegrass can be found here: news, album reviews, festivals and events, artist profiles, associations, books, and publications—even bluegrass definitions. If you don't see what you're looking for in the table of contents, search the database.

Doc Watson

http://sunsite.unc.edu/doug/DocWat/DocWat.html

Contains a brief biography, a discography, a concert schedule, and a performance by Doc Watson accompanied by his son Merle. Includes links to pages on other bluegrass greats, such as Bill Monroe.

Full Moon Rising

http://shell.rmi.net/~brain/music/fmr.html

Bluegrass band out of Colorado Springs, Colorado. Meet the band, plan around their upcoming performances, and find out the latest news from festivals and events they've attended.

Harmonic Arts

http://www.harmonicarts.com/

Full service music store located in Lawrence, Kansas. Check their full range of guitars, banjos, violins, fiddles, amps, and percussion instruments. They also post specials online. To order, call the toll-free number. They also have a selection of used instruments and equipment for sale and house a repair shop.

Heart of America BlueGrass and Old-Time Music

http://www.microlink.net/~habot/

Music club out of Kansas City, Missouri. Meets once a month and provides a concert (free to the public) of three or four bluegrass and old-time music bands. You can even listen to a radio segment from the Bluegrass Radio Network.

Huck Finn Jubilee!

http://www.Huckfinn.com/

This country and bluegrass festival in Southern California lasts three days and also includes horseback riding, clogging, catfishing, boating, and crafts. Make a reservation, check the maps on how to get there, and check out the activities available.

Intermountain Acoustic Music Association

http://www.xmission.com:80/~iama/

Nonprofit organization devoted to promoting and preserving acoustic music, including bluegrass, folk, and old-time music. The IAMA sponsors various seminars, workshops, and concerts; check out the Event Calendar. There's also a monthly newsletter for members; become one by filling out the online form and sending in your membership fee.

International Bluegrass Music Association

http://www.ibma.org/IBMA/

The IBMA is an international trade organization dedicated to the promotion of bluegrass music. Get membership information, find out who your regional representatives are, look at current industry press releases, or visit the International Bluegrass Music Museum.

Old Time Music Bulletin Board

http://140.190.128.190/oldtime/oldtime.html

Enables readers to exchange and sell instruments and discuss banjo playing, fiddling, songs and lyrics, reviews, and anything else regarding American old-time music. Lets you post messages to the Anything Else? page.

The Pacific Bluegrass Network

http://www.healey.com.au/~mkear/pbn.htm

Formed by the International Bluegrass Music Association to encourage the development of bluegrass music in the Pacific Rim countries. Meet the representatives from Australia, New Zealand, China, Indonesia, Japan, and Hawaii; and read their objectives, which includes encouraging local radio play of bluegrass music.

The Rosine Association

http://www.gotech.com/rosine/homepg.htm

Memorial Web site to Bill Monroe, Father of Bluegrass Music. The Rosine Association is raising funds to build a monument in his honor at his birthplace, Rosine, Kentucky. View a graphic of the monument and find out how you can show your support by donating money and affixing your personal message and name to the monument for posterity.

Welcome to Planet Bluegrass!

http://www.csn.net:80/planet/

Blue Planet Music, organizers of the legendary Telluride Bluegrass Festival, is now online. Contains festival schedule and information, as well as information about Blue Planet recordings and their mail-order operation.

A B C D E F G H I J K L M N O P Q R S T U V W X Y Z

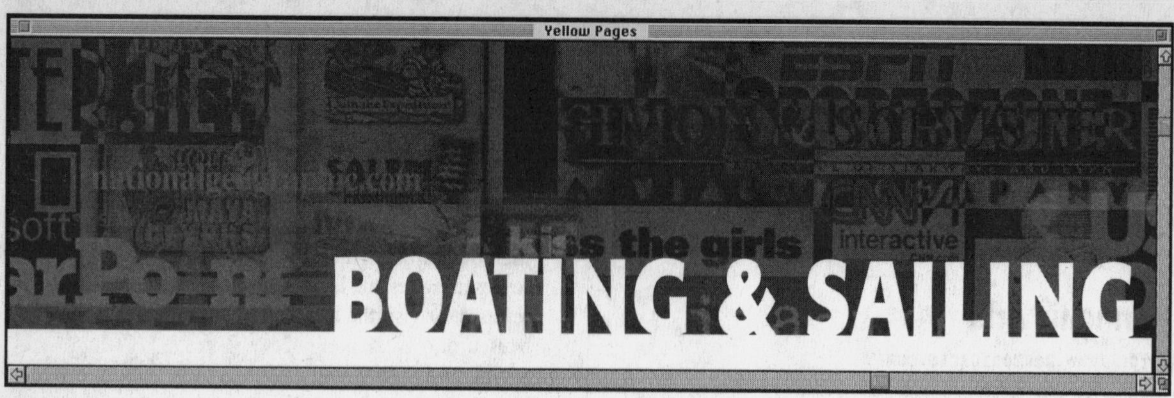

BOATING & SAILING

> It's not the towering sail but the unseen wind that moves the ship.
>
> *Unknown*

American Sail Training Association

http://tallships.sailtraining.org/

The ASTA does more than teach people how to sail. It has access to many different kinds of ships and offers programs for diverse peoples who come to learn sailing and perform academic experiments, have a corporate retreat, adventure vacations, and more. For whatever reason they come, they all take home newfound pride, humility, bravery, strength, and other positive personal characteristics.

American Sailing Association

http://www.american-sailing.com/

Aspiring sailors will likely find a school near them—no matter where they live—that is staffed by instructors who have earned ASA certification through rigorous training and studies.

Boatnet

http://www.boatnet.com/boatnet/

Initially focused on the Northwest, Boatnet is expanding to include information for the entire country. You can find out about new and used boats for sale, chartered trips, as well as links to online publications.

Related Sites

http://www.usboat.com/gardner/

http://www.goals.com/sailscin/sailscin.htm

Mark Rosenstein's Sailing Page
http://www.apparent-wind.com/sailing-page.html

Cutty Sark Tall Ships' Races

http://www.cutty-sark.com/tall-ships/

This site contains pictures and artwork, a history of the race, and information regarding the youth program whereby young people from all over the world get a chance to learn about sailing, the sea, teamwork, self-discipline, and the competitive spirit. This race began in 1956.

Dave Culp SpeedSailing

http://www.dcss.org/speedsl/

For anyone into or interested in boats that run fast on wind. Read up on speed sailing rules, see the latest edition of SpeedWeek '97, peruse the photo gallery, and learn about the cool boats that are pulled by kites!

David Dellenbaugh's Speed and Smarts

http://www.paw.com/sail/speedsmarts/

This page, by an ex-America's Cup sailor, has all the tips and techniques you need to learn to sail faster, based on Dellenbaugh's monthly newsletter of the same name.

Institute of Maritime History

http://www.maritimehistory.org/

Join chat groups, read articles, and otherwise learn about the good work of the IMH and the projects they've undertaken, such as the excavation of a sunken shipwreck.

Mariner's Net

http://www.aztec.com/pub/aztec/mariner/

Another thorough links page to get you to sites about sailing schools, sailing vacations, weather, and sailing magazines, as well as links to sailing chats, discussions, bulleting boards, and the like.

Mark Rosenstein's Sailing Page

http://www.apparent-wind.com/sailing-page.html

An extensive sailing resource where you can get the latest sailing news, information about maritime museums and magazines, individual stories from around the world, and much more.

Philadelphia Wooden Boat Factory

http://www.libertynet.org/~pwbf/

The PWBF is a nonprofit organization that provides youth programs centered on boat building and sailing. The skills learned help the participants to empower themselves to take on new challenges throughout life and work.

Sailing

http://www.sailnet.com/sailing/

The online version of the magazine. Read back issues, as well as the current one. Leave messages on the Message Center, and surf through the many sailing links.

Sailing Alternatives

http://www.sailingalternatives.org/

Sailing Alternatives is an organization dedicated to helping disabled (and "abled") persons sail together on ships appropriately modified or otherwise fitted. Physical therapy and rehab are integrated with the sailing as needed.

Sailing the Dream

http://www.coconutinfo.com/sailingthedream/cover.html

The full story of Dr. John F. McGrady, who sailed around the world in his 30-foot boat. Check out the prologue, study the glossary, and then delve into the text of this adventurer's tale.

United States Power Squadrons Web Page

http://www.usps.org/

Presents USPS, a private boating organization. Focuses on USPS's Basic Boating Course and the purpose of the club. Provides a FAQ and link, and tells how to locate a squadron near you.

U.S. Naval Institute

http://www.usni.org/

Although the Institute was established in 1873, their very modern Web page offers the cybersailor access to their store, contests, *Proceedings* magazine, publishing house, and more, including seminars on a wide range of topics.

U.S. Sailing

http://www.ussailing.org/

The home page of the official governing body of the sport of sailing in America, the United States Sailing Association, offers surfers info on sailing publications, racing events and schedules, educational courses, Olympic sailing, and more.

The Waterfront

http://www2.interpath.net/jef/Waterfront/index.html

This site handles all of your seagoing affairs: boating, diving, fishing, and so on. Learn about upcoming events, find different marinas in your area, examine classified ads for boats and stuff, and remember to turn on the lighthouse.

WWW Sailing Index

http://www.ualberta.ca/~sjones/urls.html

A list of links to other sailing/yachting pages as well as to online publications, clubs, and sailing series results.

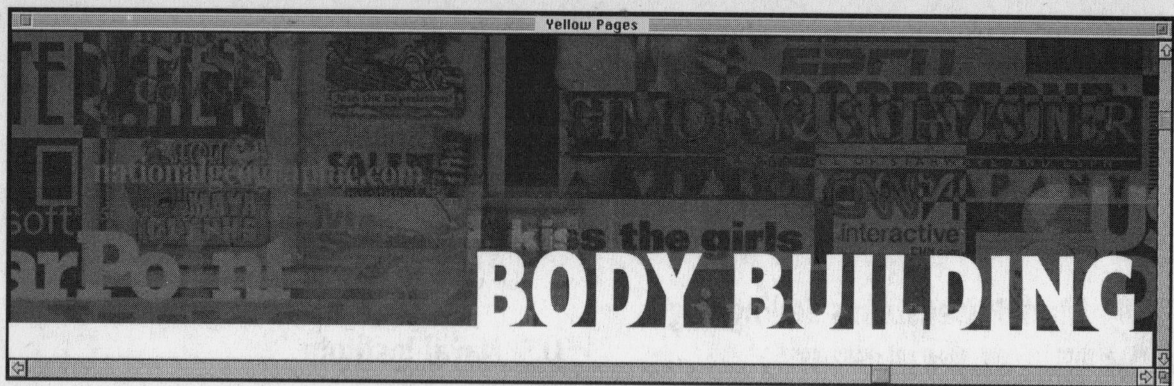

BODY BUILDING

> It is men, not women, who have promoted the cult of brutal masculinity; and because men admire muscle and physical force, they assume that we do too.
>
> *Elizabeth Gould Davis*

Amateur Female Bodybuilding Gallery

`http://www.frsa.com/fgallry.html`

Pictures, pictures, pictures! This site contains nothing but competition and publicity shots of the top female bodybuilders. If that's what you're looking for, you won't be disappointed; the selection here is truly impressive.

American Bodybuilding

`http://www.getbig.com/abb1.htm`

This site has a great section containing rules, judging criteria, and schedules for many bodybuilding and fitness federations and contests. It also includes info on fitness magazines, fitness centers, and links to other sites.

Betterbodz

`http://www.betterbodz.com/`

This site promises to replace the "science fiction" of nutrition and training with scientific facts. The highlight of the site is the library of articles, through which you can get information about everything from antioxidants to weight loss. A great browsing resource for the non-hardcore amateur bodybuilder.

Hardgainer's Home Gym Home Page
`http://www.monmouth.com/~rclodfelter/`

Musclenet: The Virtual Gym
`http://www.musclenet.com/`

Cyberpump!

`http://www.geocities.com/Colosseum/4000/`

A great site for hardcore HIT (high-intensity training) bodybuilding enthusiasts, including articles, a search engine, training guidance, a Q&A section, and a reader feedback system. A whole online community waits for you here!

Faith Sloan's Bodybuilding Site

`http://www.frsa.com/bbpage.shtml`

Partly a fan page for Faith Sloan, a leading female bodybuilder, and partly an educational site. Lots of articles about training and nutrition and its own bulletin board where users can communicate with one another.

Hardgainer's Home Gym Home Page

`http://www.monmouth.com/~rclodfelter/`

This personal site has some great resources for the person who works out in his or her home. There are several calculators for figuring up your reps, many articles about setting up your own home gym, sections with tips for particular exercises, a nutrition analysis tool, and a Body Mass Ratio (BMR) calculator.

Muscle & Fitness Online

`http://www.muscle-fitness.com/`

The online edition of the popular print magazine Muscle & Fitness, this site contains some great information for the amateur bodybuilder, including training, nutrition, and sports medicine articles. There are even articles on S-E-X (nothing dirty, but rather topics such as "Vascectomy Health Risks"). Definitely worth checking out!

Muscle Media: The Art & Science of Body Building

`http://www.musclemedia.com/`

An online version of the popular newsstand magazine, this site offers much more than the usual "teasers" that print magazines often provide online. There are many meaty articles, including an advice column, and audio clips from your favorite bodybuilding experts.

Muscle Memory

`http://musclememory.com/`

This site is dedicated to preserving the history of competitive bodybuilding. Its central feature is a search engine with which you can search for a bodybuilder's name and find out what competitions he or she has won. You can also see alphabetical lists of people or chronological lists of contests.

Musclenet: The Virtual Gym

`http://www.musclenet.com/`

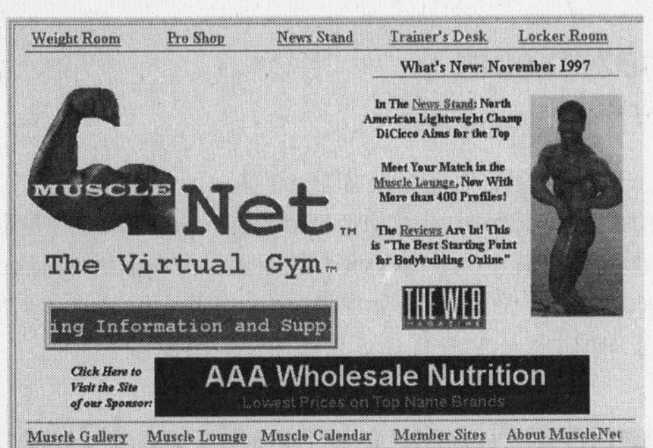

Something for everyone! You can search a database of gyms for a place to work out, buy equipment and workout apparel, link to over a dozen bodybuilding magazines online, post messages in a member forum, and tons more. There is so much content here, you'll find it hard to tear yourself away to go work out!

National Bodybuilding and Fitness Magazine

`http://nbaf.com/nbaf/home.html`

Geared toward the beginning bodybuilding enthusiast, this site has loads of helpful articles from the current and previous issues of the print magazine of the same name. You can also access message boards and a moderated bodybuilding forum.

National Physique Committee

`http://www.getbig.com/info/npc.htm`

NPC is the official amateur organization of bodybuilding and fitness for the IFBB (International Federation of Body Builders). Like the minor leagues in baseball, the NPC serves as a training ground for amateurs who are on their way to the pros. Learn all about the upcoming matches at this site, and order NPC-logo clothing.

Natural Physique Systems

`http://www.indiana.net/~thekid/phys.htm`

A great place for the beginner interested in natural (drug-free) bodybuilding. You can learn how to pose for the judges, read about upcoming contests, get training tips, and more.

POWERLIFTING.com

`http://nbaf.com/fit/direct/start.html`

A gateway to powerlifting information on the Web, this site provides loads of links in categories such as events, rules, publications, training routines, commercial sites, clubs, and image libraries. A great place to start your search for powerlifting info.

The Female Bodybuilder Ring

`http://www.bomis.com/rings/femalebodybuilder/`

Over 30 links (at last count) to Web sites featuring news and information on female bodybuilding. There are links for fan pages for individuals as well as general links that provide basic information about the sport.

NEWSGROUPS

`alt.sport.weightlifting`

`misc.fitness.weights`

Related Sites

`http://www.musculardevelopment.com/`

`http://www.geocities.com/Colosseum/Track/6812/`

`http://www.geocities.com/HotSprings/1205/`

`http://www.cyberiron.com/`

`http://userwww.service.emory.edu/~librpj/bbind.html`

`http://www.wesnet.com/rickc/`

`http://www.aristotle.net/~bphillips/building.html`

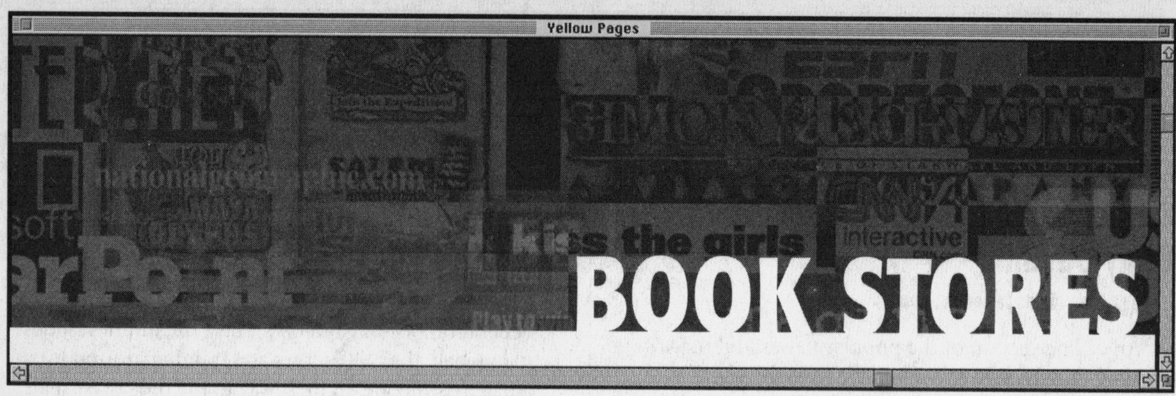

A B C D E F G H I J K L M N O P Q R S T U V W X Y Z

For books are not absolutely dead things, but do contain a potency of life in them; they do preserve as in a vial the purest efficacy and extraction of that living intellect that bred them.

John Milton

12 GO Web Directory-Publishers

http://www.12go.com/publis.htm

A Web directory by specific subject with absolute links to publishers' sites. Also, free links and free marketing contest.

2001

http://tucson.com/2001/

2001 includes links to access resources for book publishers and for book lovers.

AAA Books on the Net

http://www.inter-mall.com/books

Find publishers, publicists, authors and more. Books for sale. A unique bookstore promoting up-and-coming authors in all categories of fiction and nonfiction.

The Elliott Bay Book Company
http://www.elliottbaybook.com/ebbco/

All Outdoors Bookstore

http://www.alloutdoors.com/bookstore/

This site is the outdoor person's dream. Here you'll find books on fishing, hunting, and outdoor adventure. Visit the Coffee Shop and chat with fellow anglers and outdoor people. Make a stop at the Adventure Travel section to find that perfect Canadian lodge and outfitter. Pull on your waders, don your hunting gear, and sit back, and select the book and adventure that's right for your outdoor needs.

Amazon.com

http://www.amazon.com/

Touted as the "Earth's Biggest Bookstore," Amazon.com maintains and sells over one million titles. With a well-developed search engine, you can search by just about anything you know about a book or author—even if it is just one word.

American Studies Journals and Zines

http://xroads.virginia.edu/~journal/index.html

Links to journals and e-zines in American Studies and related fields; includes synoptic versions of some journals.

Antiquarian Booksellers' Association of America

http://www.abaa-booknet.com

Specializes in rare and antiquarian books, maps, and prints. Provides a search service by specialty and location, catalogs and links to other services for over 140 booksellers, current information on book fairs nationwide, links to online public access catalogs at libraries worldwide, and articles of interest to book sellers and book collectors from the ABAA Newsletter.

Association of American University Presses (AAUP) Online Catalog/Bookstore

http://aaup.pupress.princeton.edu/

Online bookstore that is a made up of member university presses. Open for business but still under construction, the AAUP introduction states that it expects to have more than 100,000 titles from almost 100 imprints. Provides links to individual university presses. Includes the ability to search for an entire association or by individual university imprint.

Astrology et al Bookstore

http://www.astrologyetal.com/

Features online catalog of astrology, occult, pagan, UFO, metaphysical, and other related titles. Includes a listing of out-of-print and hard to find books that they have in stock.

Audiobook Source

http://www.webcom.com/absource/

Audiobooks online. Enables you to search the catalog and place orders for more then 7,000 titles. Holds monthly specials and has sale items.

Banned Books On-line

http://www.cs.cmu.edu/Web/People/spok/banned-books.html

Banned Books On-line celebrates the freedom to read. There are links to e-texts on the Web featuring authors who have at one time been banned in America and elsewhere. Also present is some censorship history of the books featured on the page.

Bantam Doubleday Dell Online

http://www.bdd.com

Catalogs, forums, puzzles, and interviews with the authors of new books. Check out their author of the week. Science fiction fans should check out the Spectra SF Forum.

Body Mind & Soul

http://www.powersource.com/bmsbooks

Body Mind & Soul is a metaphysical bookstore specializing in the healing and rejuvenation of your entire being. Here you can order books and learn ways to improve your life mentally, physically, and spiritually.

Bonder Bookstore Inc.

http://www.bonder.com

Provides online sales site for the Montreal, Quebec based bookstore. Includes order form for purchasing any book in print over the Web.

Book Banning, Burning, and Censorship

http://www.banned.books.com/

A multimedia experience concerning banned books, censorship, and their impact on the world. There are quotes, pictures, audio files, and the use of client-side pull to present its case. Make sure you are using a Netscape-compatible browser to experience this site to its fullest.

Book Express OnLine

http://www.bookexpress.com

A discount bookstore offering great savings of 30 to 90 percent. Here you find books on tape, computer books, children's books, novels, health books, reference books, books on religion, business books, and out-of-print books.

Book Hunter

http://www.i1.net/~bhunter/

Provides a book finding service specializing in, but not limited to, technical books. Includes price quote service, search, and order forms. Also includes company profile and account establishment information.

Bookbinding, a tutorial

http://www.cs.uiowa.edu/~jones/book/

An instruction guide to repairing books that might be falling apart, this site has been carefully researched and represents the work of a true bibliophile.

A B C D E F G H I J K L M N O P Q R S T U V W X Y Z

Booklegger's

http://www.bookleggers.com/

A used bookstore in Chicago dealing in rare and used books. You can also find audio cassettes, books on tape, videos, and compact discs.

BookLink

http://www.intac.com/~booklink

Specializes in distributing ESL (English as a Second Language) and multicultural books. Also sells children's books and any British book in print.

Bookmasters Electronic Marketplace

http://www.bookmasters.com

Bookmasters not only sells books online, it also typesets, prints, binds, and distributes books for the publishing industry. Visit the Reading Room to sample some books or stop by the Coffee House Chat to see what readers think about certain books.

Books Stacks Unlimited, Inc.

http://www.books.com/

A huge online bookstore with more than 350,000 titles in stock, generous discounts, great service, discussion groups, author pages, and more. Updated daily.

BookSite

http://www.booksite.com/

An online bookstore that provides search tools for a two-million-book database, new release information, and ordering information. Includes testimonials from satisfied customers.

Bookstore at Houghton Mifflin

http://www.hmco.com/trade/

Provides online sales for one of the largest printing houses in the world. The store is broken down into six sections with book listings, book excerpts, news, and discussion groups. Also included are links and resources for related information and research.

BookWorld

http://www.bookworld.com/

A very useful reference site for anyone who buys books or wants to publish books of their own. This site has samples of hundreds of titles under myriad subjects. It also provides information about publishing and marketing a book over the Internet, and it includes links to many publishers and related services.

Borders Books and Music

http://www.borders.com/

Enables you to search for books and then order them from Borders' large selection of books and magazines. Also provides a list of store locations and enables you to browse their titles.

Bruce E. Southworth Reviews

http://www.Words-n-Deeds.com

Drawing on many years of print and television experience, Words-n-Deeds provides reviews of both fiction and non-fiction books, interviews with authors, and links to publishers, bookstores, and other related organizations.

Canadian Publishers' Council

http://www.pubcouncil.ca

Association representing book publishers in Canada since 1910. Site includes links to publishing related sites, FAQs, industry studies, and statistics and information on copyright.

Christian Book Connection

http://seercom.com/cbc/

Online Christian bookstore. Features a catalog of nearly 30,000 items including books, Bibles, Bible software, CDs, and cassettes. Also presents the monthly Christian best-sellers lists of books and music.

Conservation OnLine

http://palimpsest.stanford.edu/

A guide to preserving books, articles, pictures, and other media for professionals and amateurs alike. This site is dedicated to the preservation of information of many media.

Curious George Goes to WordsWorth

http://curiousgeorge.wordsworth.com

Offers a wide selection of books for children of all ages. You can also find toys, CD-ROMs, books on tape, artwork (prints and posters), T-shirts, and gifts. Anything Curious George-related is here.

David Morrison Books

`http://www.teleport.com/~morrison/`

Provides catalog and online sales for David Morrison Books, which specializes in titles on art, architecture, decorative arts, and photography. Includes book descriptions and information.

Deep Politics Bookstore

`http://www.copi.com/deepbook.htm`

Provides home site and sales for political texts and books. Includes book and author background, as well as ordering information.

The Elliott Bay Book Company

`http://www.elliottbaybook.com/ebbco/`

At this Seattle, Washington, independent bookstore's site, you find book reviews from the staff (including reviews of children's books), a list of in-store publications, including a newsletter, and book ordering information. This site includes a list of visiting authors (an average of ten a week) to the bookstore, and you can even order signed modern first editions and signed numbered limited editions. If you get the chance, visit the store in person. The service, selection, and atmosphere are exceptional!

Fast Books

`http://www.moreinfo.com.au/fastbooks/`

Provides online book sales specializing in self-publishers. Includes company catalog, self-publishing information, previews, and ordering information.

Future Books Online Discount Bookstore

`http://www.futurebooks.com/`

At this online bookstore, just pick up your shopping cart, put it in gear, and away you go! You can find any book you're looking for. It is especially helpful to writers, painters, and graphic designers. It offers a newsletter, and you can get their self-publishing kit to help you get your own work published.

Gareth Stevens Publishing

`http://market.net/literary/gsinc/index.html`

Provides online catalog of Gareth Stevens series books, descriptions of titles, prices, and ordering information. Books are indexed by category (nature, science, social studies, biography, picture books, reference, and bibliotherapy).

Henry Miller Library

`http://www.henrymiller.org`

Peruse rare Miller books, literature, an online bookstore, gallery, interactive forums, and more at the online home of the Henry Miller Library, located in Big Sur, CA.

Houghton Mifflin Company

`http://www.hmco.com/`

Houghton Mifflin Company online. Publishes educational books and materials for elementary through college levels. Includes links to subsidiaries.

House of Science Fiction

`http://www.xenoscience.com/sf/`

Online bookstore specializing in science fiction novels and periodicals, and science fiction, horror, and fantasy anthologies.

A Hundred Highlights from the Koninklijke Bibliotheek

`http://www.konbib.nl/100hoogte/hh-en.html`

This large, Dutch library has a searchable index of resources. There are also many pictures present that were either created specifically for the library or are archived at the library. This library mainly houses older books, so this presentation is to bring them to the public in a way that makes them less vulnerable to battery and the caustic effects of being in the open.

Hungry Mind Review Discussion

`http://www.bookwire.com/webx?14@@.ee6b2b2`

A place to discuss titles, subjects, genres, or just about anything concerning reading. There are archives of discussions from the past. Feel free to join any of the many discussions.

Index

http://www.bookwire.com/links/other_booksellers/other_booksellers.html

If you're looking for a particular type of book, click the links, and the list of booksellers will appear. Provides links to computer, gay and lesbian, science fiction, children's, travel booksellers, and many, many more. Also gives a link to other bookseller sites.

internet-books.com

http://www.internet-books.com

A Web site for book lovers. A source of information about books, publishers, authors, and libraries. Essentially a site providing links to other sites, but providing information as content is made available.

It's a Mystery

http://www.mysterybooks.com/

If you're looking for collectibles or just browsing for a new hard-cover mystery book, this is the site for you. Also join the book club and check out the fun and mysterious links.

JourneyWare Media

http://www.journeyware.com/

Software products and books for lifelong learning, family relationships, and responsible living. Browse the online catalog or place an order.

L'Art Medical Antiquarian Books

http://www.xs4all.nl/~artmed/

The history of medicine, antique books, and a place to register in a "wish-list" for certain titles. There are links to a mailing list and the Netherlands Antiquarian Bookseller's Network.

Law Stuff USA

http://www.lawstuffusa.com

This is an online legal bookstore with the law student in mind. You find casebooks and supplements, legal references, and study guides.

The Library

http://personalwebs.myriad.net/hewett/library.htm

The Library contains links to book publishers, online bookstores, libraries, and other sites that serious book collectors will find useful.

Loganberry Books

http://www.logan.com/loganberry/

Offering book-of-the-month clubs specializing in women's, children's, arts, and out-of-print books. Choose the club that is right for you.

Login Brothers Book Company

http://www.lb.com/

A book company specializing in books and videos for the health professional. Search for medical, nursing, or health-related profession titles. Also carries a limited selection of legal texts including Blonds Legal Notes and the Blackletter series.

Macmillan Publishing USA (The Information SuperLibrary)

http://www.mcp.com/

The Information SuperLibrary is full of interesting and useful information about computer-related titles, including a link to the online version of this book, *New Riders' Official Internet and World Wide Web Yellow Pages.*

Mage Publishing

http://gpg.com/mage/

Persian literature and culture, English language publisher. Order from their catalog or even from books out of print.

Mare's Nest Publishing

http://www.poptel.org.uk/password/marenest.html

Publisher of Nordic poetry and fiction in the United Kingdom, some new, some in translation dating back over one thousand years. Links to their catalog, stock list, and the Password home page.

McGraw-Hill Bookstore

http://www.bookstore.mcgraw-hill.com/

This bookstore offers a huge selection of science and technical, reference, professional, business, and computer books from all publishers—not just McGraw-Hill titles.

Midnight Special Bookstore

http://msbooks.com/msbooks/

A social and cultural, independent bookstore featuring political, social science, history, and related books, weekly events, video and Web connections. Provides access to other independent bookstores and asks you to bypass the chains and support the independent booksellers.

Moe's Books

http://moesbooks.com/

Contains more than 500,000 titles in stock at a discount. Includes rare children's books, hard-to-find import titles, new books, remainder books, and used books. Also offers free searches if you can't find the book you want.

Navrang Inc.

http://catalog.com/navrang/

Comics, books, or magazines published in or about India or by Indian authors. Links to ordering information as well as other interesting links on or about India.

New World Books

http://branch.com/books/books.html

You can order any book in print by mail and save up to 30 percent, as long as you know the author/title. Provides links to book news, university presses, book summaries, and more.

New Zealand Books On-Line

http://www.nzbooks.co.nz

New Zealand Books On-Line is the Web home of the NZ publishing and book selling industry. Includes a searchable catalogue of NZ books, indexes of books sorted by title, author and subject, directories of New Zealand publishers and book shops, as well as sections devoted to new releases, best sellers, book reviews, and more.

Next Wave Consulting

http://www.access.digex.net/~dwiley/nextwave.html

Next Wave helps publishers create and market electronic publications, including designing online catalogs, creating CD-ROMs, and developing comprehensive strategic plans for electronic product development.

Notable Children's Books

http://www.ala.org/alaorg/alsc/notbooks.html

This site, sponsored by the Association for Library Service to Children, is filled with suggested reading for children and is organized to separate younger, middle, and older children's books. There are also suggested readings for children of all ages.

The Old Bookroom

http://www.ozemail.com.au/~oldbook/

A secondhand and antiquarian bookshop specializing in books, prints, and maps on Asia, Africa, and the Middle East.

Oneida Indexing Services

http://www.mnsinc.com/juniee

Experienced indexer putting together high-quality indexes at reasonable prices and fast turnaround time. Geographical distances are not a problem!

Pantera Publishing

http://www.iquest.net/~kingman/book.html

Provides information and online sales for the book *Tall Weeds and Big Dogs* by John Kingman. This book is a career and job-survival handbook. Includes testimonials and reviews of the work.

Pas de chance

http://www.interlog.com/~ian/

Produces and provides small print-run, obscure writings and poetry. Includes company catalog, artwork, and ordering information. Pas de chance is definitely not your usual publishing house.

The Penguin Bookery Online Bookstore

http://www.kiva.net/~penguin

The Penguin Bookery is a small-town bookstore that also offers mail-order service to U.S. addresses. They perform free searches for any title.

Polonia Bookstore

http://www.polonia.com/

Provides sales of books for Polish-Americans. Includes catalog of books in English with Polish themes and books, magazines, and newspapers in Polish. Also includes book previews, links to Polish sites, and ordering information.

The Preservation Educators' Exchange

http://www.well.com/user/bronxbob/presed-x/presed-x.html

A site to exchange information that might be valuable to anyone who wishes to learn more about archiving or preserving books and library science. There are announcements of upcoming events, items of interest, and even syllabi of library science classes at different universities.

Publishers Marketing Association (PMA) Online

http://www.pma-online.org/

PMA is the largest nonprofit trade association representing independent publishers of books, audio, video, and CDs. Site includes member directories, information, discussion forums, and more.

PUBNET®

http://www.pubnet.org

PUBNET is an electronic data interchange (EDI) service sponsored by book publishers and trade associations in the book industry. It offers a low-cost method for sending orders to publishers via a central network, and provides faster and more accurate ordering than most traditional and some electronic methods. PUBNET connects booksellers, with one link, to over 80 major publishers with 400+ imprints and is available 24 hours a day, 7 days a week. PUBNET is linked with over 25 inventory control systems used by stores and publishers and provides software free of charge that runs on IBM-compatible PCs for member stores. Currently there are over 3,800 sites using PUBNET.

ReadersNdex

http://www.readersndex.com/

This is a great site if you love books. Provides links to authors, publishers, book stores, discussion panels, and a reading room of articles and book samples. Includes personalized subscription services that provides information based on interests.

The Romance Pages

http://www.ivdev.com/booksource/romance/index.html

Maintained by Integrated Visions, this site lists many contemporary romance authors and their newest works (including some excerpts and scans of book covers).

Science Express, Inc.

http://www.sci-exp.com/

Provides online sales of a large catalog of computer books. The catalog covers nearly all topics from a range of publishers. Includes searchable index, book descriptions, and reviews. Also includes online ordering information.

Secret Staircase Bookshop

http://www.secretstaircasebooks.com/

Provides online sales for the Secret Staircase Bookshop. Specializes in children's books and adult mysteries. Includes a listing of autographed books in stock, reviews, catalogs, a store calendar, and ordering information. Also provides links to reading and other related sites.

Shen's Books and Supplies

http://www.shens.com/

Provides online catalog sales of children's books from Asia, South America, Europe, and Australia. Offers titles in English and other languages. Includes indexed catalog and company recommendations. Also includes company history, new release information, and monthly themes.

A Sherlockian Holmepage

http://watserv1.uwaterloo.ca/~credmond/sh.html

Contains many links to electronic Holmes and Conan Doyle resources.

Small Business Bookstore & Information Center

http://www.inklingpubs.com

If you own a small business or are thinking of starting your own business, this site has what you need. Besides the books listed here, you can get their print catalog, listing other books of interest to the small-business owner.

Speedy Research Service

http://www.geocities.com/athens/6282

Information collection, journal photocopying, and research. A one-person company that provides fast and inexpensive access to journals and scholarly information. Comprehensive results in all fields, and specializes in medicine and biochemistry.

Stone Bridge Press

http://www.stonebridge.com/~sbp/

Provides online catalog and sales for Stone Bridge Press books, software, and videos. Specializes in books and products about Japan. Includes complete catalog, excerpts, cover artwork, reviews, and author profiles.

Svoboda's Books Online: State College, PA

http://www.epicom.com/svobodas

Specializes in academic and technical titles, but offers access to anything in American Books-in-Print. Lets you place book orders from your computer.

Time-Life Explorer

http://www.timelife.com

Enables you to explore the many products Time-Life offers in books, music, and videos.

Ultimate Romance Novel Website

http://www.icgnet.com/romancebooks/

Enables you to offer your opinions on romance novels you've read. Take a look at their gallery of cover art and read up on publishers, writers, illustrators, and cover models.

Ulysses

http://www.antiquarian.com/ulysses

This bookstore's specialty is modern first editions, modern illustrators, and poetry. They conduct searches for that hard-to-find book. For easy shopping, get on their mailing list and receive five to six catalogs a year to order your favorite books.

Vintage Books Reading Group Guides

http://www.randomhouse.com/knopf/read/

A novel idea about the reading group (and perhaps a very good way to promote books, too), the Vintage Books Reading Group Guides are like the discussion questions you might find at the end of a story in a high school anthology (only for adults). There is more here, though: there is author biography, pictures of the books and authors, and a selected further reading list. If you are in charge of a reading group and can't think of a good place to start discussion, try this site first.

Willy Wonka Lyrics

http://condor.stcloud.msus.edu/~triskm01/hazel/wonka/lyrics.htm

The lyrics to each song from the movie, including the songs of the Oompa Loompas.

A Woman's Spirit

http://www.womanspirit.com/

This site is a woman's virtual bookstore where you can order books, buy gifts, and utilize a women's business directory—and even list your woman-owned business. You can use the Book Search to find that special or out-of-print book. Learn more about your favorite author and even "meet" her in a virtual chat session.

Words of the Web

http://www.telepath.com/sewedel/wordweb.html

Words of the Web is a site for anyone interested in literature: writers, agents, publishers, or readers. Links to author, agent, and publisher sites, as well as links to other places of interest to readers and writers.

WordsWorth Books

http://www.wordsworth.com/

Besides offering a wonderful selection of books at a discounted price, WordsWorth Books is a book lover's dream, with its book selection of the day; interviews with authors; great selection of children's books; contests for adults and children; autographed copies of books; the independent bestseller list; and all literary awards winners, for fiction, nonfiction, and children's literature. Plan to stay at this site for a while; it's very refreshing.

Zanadu Comics

http://www.aa.net/~zanadu

Specializes in alternative and mainstream comics, graphic novels, and more. Features reviews by staff and customers, promotions, a trivia contest, and a virtual catalog.

NEWSGROUPS

news://alt.books.reviews

news://alt.books.technical

news://rec.arts.books

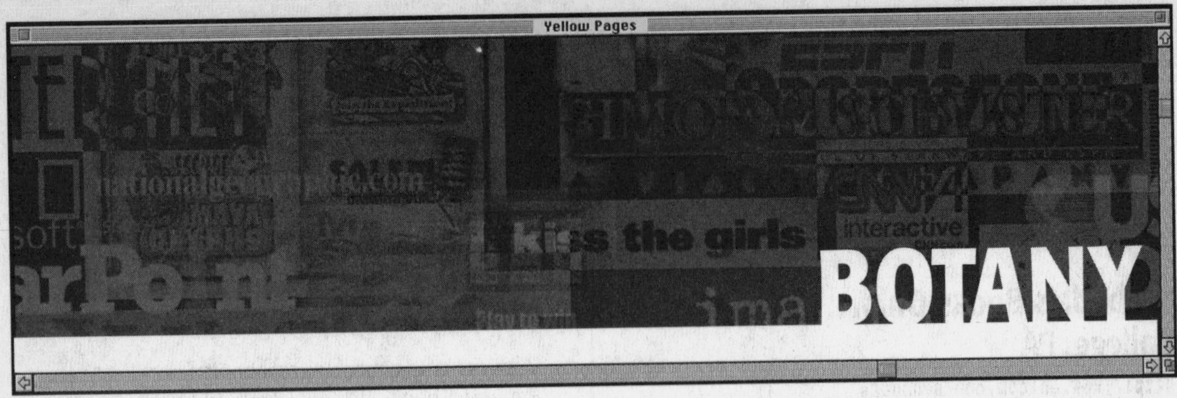

A B C D E F G H I J K L M N O P Q R S T U V W X Y Z

> And all their botany is Latin names.
>
> *Ralph Waldo Emerson*

Balogh Scientific Books

http://www.balogh.com/~balogh/

Publisher and bookseller specializing in botany. Features information on books, an online ordering desk, new book releases, and news about botany. Also offers a mailing list and book trading list.

Connecticut Botanical Society

http://www.vfr.com/cbs/

Site describes the activities of the botanical society: field trips, programs, ecology, and conservation. Also gives information about membership.

Internet Directory for Botany

http://www.helsinki.fi/kmus/botmenu.html

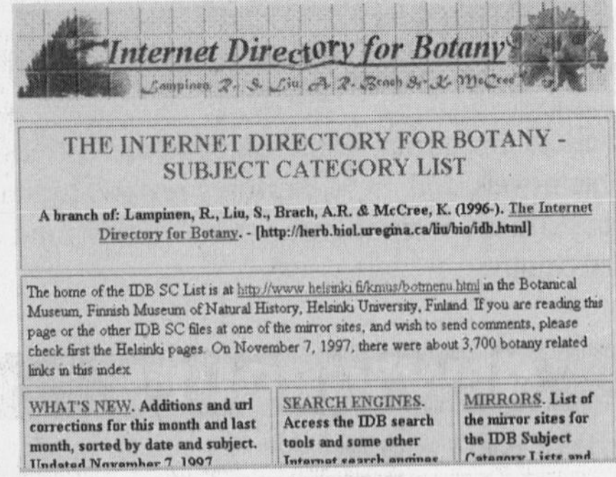
Internet Directory for Botany

Lampinen R. S. Liu A. R. Brach & K. McCree

THE INTERNET DIRECTORY FOR BOTANY - SUBJECT CATEGORY LIST

A branch of: Lampinen, R., Liu, S., Brach, A.R. & McCree, K. (1996-). The Internet Directory for Botany. - [http://herb.biol.uregina.ca/liu/bio/idb.html]

The home of the IDB SC List is at http://www.helsinki.fi/kmus/botmenu.html in the Botanical Museum, Finnish Museum of Natural History, Helsinki University, Finland. If you are reading this page or the other IDB SC files at one of the mirror sites, and wish to send comments, please check first the Helsinki pages. On November 7, 1997, there were about 3,700 botany related links in this index.

WHAT'S NEW. Additions and url corrections for this month and last month, sorted by date and subject. Updated November 7, 1997

SEARCH ENGINES. Access the IDB search tools and some other Internet search engines

MIRRORS. List of the mirror sites for the IDB Subject Category Lists and

Site provides many botanical sites in science, economy, universities, and applicable software. Also provides mirror sites in nine countries.

Internet Directory for Botany
http://www.helsinki.fi/kmus/botmenu.html

National Institute of Agricultural Botany

http://www.open.gov.uk/niab/niabhome.htm

Includes comprehensive index to the science and study of botany. Features articles on training, lab tests, and chemical and plant diseases.

Nature Described: Learning to Look at the World

http://www.ncsa.uiuc.edu/SDG/Experimental/vatican.exhibit/exhibit/g-nature/Nature.html

Provides historical data about nature and botany.

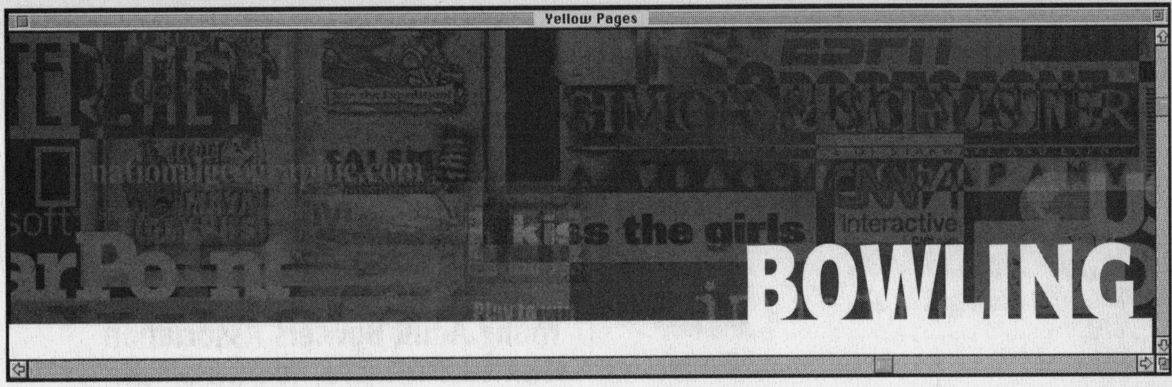

Normally, someone would have to go to a bowling alley to meet someone of your stature.

Hobson in Arthur *(1981)*

Brunswick Online
http://208.206.43.10/

Complete Bowling Index
http://www.bowlingindex.com/

The History of Bowling
http://www.icubed.com/users/allereb/faq2.html

ABC/WIBC Bowling Page

http://www.foxnet.net/users/bowling/abc.html

The newsletter of the American Bowling Congress, this page includes rules, articles (for example, there's one called "The Economic Impact of Bowling"), bowling news, and advisories of interest to bowlers and their supporters.

AMF Bowling Centers

http://www.kokodir.com/amfbowling/

At this site, you can locate the nearest AMF Bowling Center in your area, and print out a coupon good for a free game once you get there.

Bowling Home Page

http://www.icubed.com/users/allereb/bowling.html

An eclectic mix of bowling sites, including bowling organizations and tournaments, a ball survey, bowling instruction, bowling clip art, and more.

Bowling Mart

http://www.bowlingmart.com/

An online store where you can buy bowling equipment (balls, bags, shoes, and so on) for discount prices.

Bowling World

http://www.bowlingworld.com/

An online magazine that spotlights professional bowling, including articles, columns, a scoreboard, and classified ads.

Brunswick Online

http://208.206.43.10/

Whether you're interested in building a bowling alley or just building your average, this site points the way. Find out about the Brunswick products that can help. There is also a Blockbuster Bowling online game you can play (if your browser supports Shockwave).

CDE Software

http://www.cdesoftware.com/welcome.html

This company produces software for league management and tournament management, as well as bowling clip art and T-shirt designs. Find out more about CDE products here, or download a free rulebook and/or screen saver.

Central Canada's Main Bowling Index

http://www.foxnet.net/users/bowling/index.html

Lots of links for bowling in Canada, including tournament standings, bowling associations, and rulebooks.

Complete Bowling Index

http://www.bowlingindex.com/

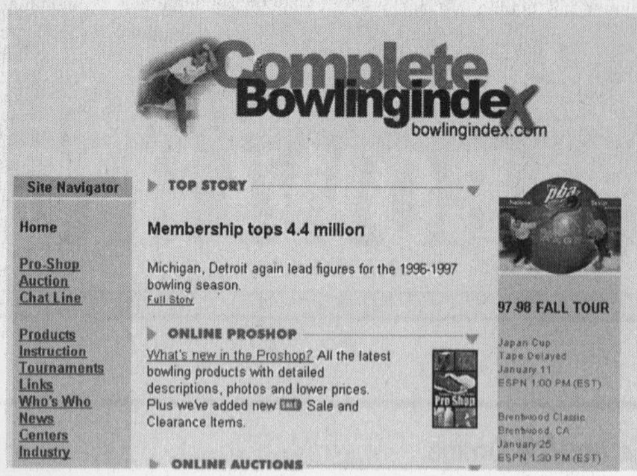

A great site with lots of resources, including a Pro Shop, an online bowling equipment auction, a chat area, lots of links—the works.

Dick Ritger Bowling Camps

http://www.ritgerbowlingcamp.com/

Information about a training camp that bowlers can attend to help improve their game. Summer and winter sessions are offered, plus instructor certification.

The History of Bowling

http://www.icubed.com/users/allereb/faq2.html

An interesting article chronicling the history of the sport from ancient Egypt to the present.

PBA Tour

http://www.pbatour.com/pbatour/home.asp

The official site of the Professional Bowlers Association tour, this site profiles the key competitors, provides updated scores and standings, and lets you know when various bowling tournaments will be broadcast on television.

Young Adult Bowlers Association

http://www.interlog.com/~jimt/bowling/yaba/

Online newsletters (and back issues) for this organization for bowling enthusiasts between 19 and 35.

NEWSGROUP

alt.sport.bowling

Related Sites

http://ourworld.compuserve.com/homepages/polymedia/

http://www.icubed.com/users/allereb/faq3.html

http://members.aol.com/bucjewell/greatlakesnabi.htm

http://www.igbo.org/

http://www.intac.com/~jserico/bowlnews.html

http://www.iinet.net.au/~roderic/Bowling/List1.html

http://www.twsu.edu/~cacwww/camptop.htm

http://www.shef.ac.uk/~sutbc/

http://www.worldwidebowlingsupply.com/

http://www.yahoo.com/Recreation/Sports/Bowling/

BOXING

> A thousand pardons. Assault and battery not permitted without license from boxing commission.
>
> *Charlie Chan in* The Black Camel *(1931)*

Boxing Buzz

http://www.uhu.com/boxing/buzz/buzz.htm

An online monthly pugilistic potpourri of inside news, gossip, results, fight predictions, ratings, opinions and miscellany. Each issue is text-only, but full of information.

Boxing: CBS SportsLine

http://www.sportsline.com/u/boxing/index.html

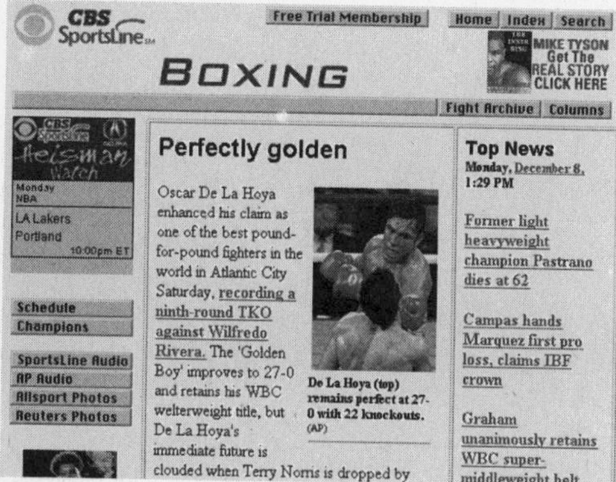

A nicely designed online newspaper that focuses on professional boxing. Includes articles and current scores, as well as photos from major competitions.

NRP TOP PICKS

Boxing: CBS SportsLine
http://www.sportsline.com/u/boxing/index.html

Boxing Online
http://www.boxingonline.com/

ESPN SportZone: Boxing
http://espn.sportszone.com/box/

Boxing Monthly

http://www.boxing-monthly.co.uk/

Sample articles from the current print issue of this popular boxing magazine, plus information about subscribing.

Boxing Online

http://www.boxingonline.com/

A very nicely done site devoted to professional boxing. Includes schedules, reviews, fight reports, photos, profiles, rankings, and a boxer directory.

Boxing on the Web

http://www.ipcress.com/writer/boxing.html

Schedules and rankings for professional boxers, plus division and rule information, and even a table listing boxers' birthdays.

Boxing Times

http://www.squaredcircle.com/boxingtimes/dec97/

In-depth boxing analysis, including extensive preview coverage to help you pick the winners, whether you wager for fun or for money. Also includes post-fight analyses and world rankings.

Related Sites

http://axiscom.com/15th_round/

http://www4.nando.net/newsroom/sports/oth/1995/oth/box/feat/box.html

ESPN SportZone: Boxing

http://espn.sportszone.com/box/

The latest boxing news stories from ESPN. Updated daily, this is your best source for up-to-the-minute coverage.

International Boxing Hall of Fame

http://www.ibhof.com/

An attractive tribute to the great fighters in boxing history, this site spotlights many boxing legends and provides information about the newest inductees.

LadyBoxer Online

http://www.femboxer.com/ladybxer/index.htm

The first magazine devoted to women's boxing, this online edition contains much of the content of the newsstand copy, including articles, standings, and photos.

Muhammad Ali: THE GREATEST Web Site

http://www.theslot.com/ali/

A tribute site for Muhammad Ali, boxing legend. Includes many photos.

Oscar De La Hoya

http://www.oscardelahoya.com/

The official online channel for this World Champion boxer. The site includes fan club information, news, an upcoming fights calendar, photos, and much more.

Shadowboxing

http://www.dev-null.com/shadowbox.html

Here you can learn about getting started with shadowboxing, a very good fitness workout.

Yahoo! Sports: Professional Boxing

http://sports.yahoo.com/box/

Easy-to-follow links to the latest scores and news reports from professional boxing.

Women's Boxing on the Web

http://femboxer.com/

A comprehensive and serious look at women's professional boxing, including news, fight reports, and video clips.

World Boxing News

http://www.world-boxingnews.com/

This site is sponsored by Panix Promotions. It is home to the Lennox Lewis fan club and also provides current articles and recent boxing rankings.

NEWSGROUP

rec.sport.boxing

Related Sites

http://www3.sympatico.ca/biz.of.boxing/

http://www.cyberbouts.com/index.ihtml

http://cyberboxingzone.com/boxing/cyber.htm

http://www.fightresults.com/

http://www.hbo.com/boxing/

http://ifba.com/

http://netboxing.com/

http://www.worldboxing.com/

BROWSERS & INTERFACES

But honey, I wouldn't be up so late on a faster machine.

Unknown

A-Web

http://www.amitrix.com/aweb.html

This is a browser for the Amiga computer system (an oldie but a goodie). It supports Netscape plug-ins, frames, and tables.

About Web/Genera

http://gdbdoc.gdb.org/letovsky/genera/genera.html

Offers Web/Genera, a software package that uses Mosaic 2.4 to integrate Sybase databases into the Web. Offers downloadable alpha-mode (pretest) software.

Adobe Acrobat

http://www.adobe.com/prodindex/acrobat/main.html

You can download Adobe Acrobat Reader here, a program that lets you read PDF files that you find on some Web sites. (What you want here is the free reader, not the full version of Adobe Acrobat, which costs money.)

Arachne

http://www.naf.cz/arachne/

This program enables DOS users (without Windows) to browse the Web graphically. This site can be busy, so you may want to try the mirror site link at the top of the page.

NRP TOP PICKS

Adobe Acrobat
http://www.adobe.com/prodindex/acrobat/main.html

Internet Explorer Component Download
http://www.microsoft.com/ie/ie40/download/rtw/x86/en/download/addon95.htm

Netscape Communications
http://www.netscape.com

Jargon

Browser: An interface that enables you to manage information on the Web. The browser speaks to the servers to which you are connecting, grabs the Web pages you want, and displays the files within the browser interface.

WWW servers: Computers that store and "serve," or provide access to, Web documents.

BrowserWatch Home Page

http://browserwatch.internet.com/

Frequently updated information about Web browsers in general—which programs have what capabilities, and so on. You can also download plug-ins for the most popular browsers here.

CineWeb

http://www.digigami.com/cineweb/

This site is home to a great tool that enables you to play a variety of multimedia files, including QuickTime, Video for Windows, MPEG, and Autodesk Animator.

Cyberspace Connection

http://www.main.com/~kirton/index.html

Offers a variety of resources, from search engines to personal and commercial Web links. Provides "your jumppoint to Cyberspace."

Hill Holliday Advertising

http://www.hhcc.com/

A site that provides links to download Shockwave, Java, and Netscape. Other than that, all links return the user to this page.

Internet Explorer

http://www.microsoft.com/ie/

The home of Microsoft Internet Explorer, one of the most popular Web browsers available. You can download whatever version is appropriate for your computer from this site.

Jargon

Home page: This is the first page of a Web site. It usually includes a summary or links to the information provided in the whole Web site.

Link: A link works as a pointer to another location or document. It also is called a hypertext link.

Dead link: This is a hypertext link that is outdated and leads you to an error message.

Surf: People move through Web documents by surfing. Sit back, relax, and ride the Web waves. See? You're surfing!

URL: An acronym for Uniform Resource Locator, an URL basically is a Web document address.

Internet Explorer Component Download

NRP TOP PICKS

http://www.microsoft.com/ie/ie40/download/rtw/x86/en/download/addon95.htm

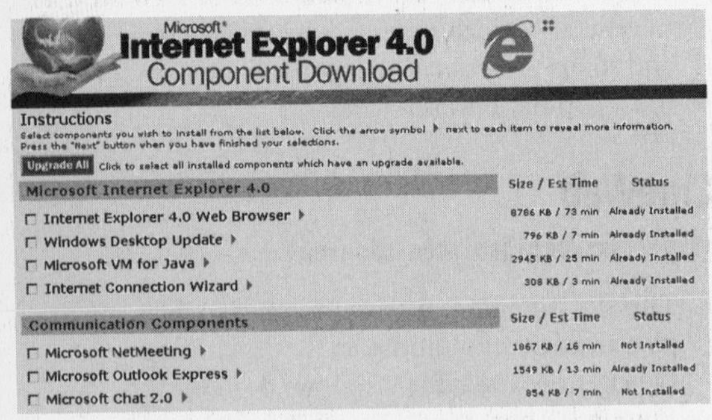

Enhance Internet Explorer 4.0 with accessories and plug-ins direct from Microsoft. You can download and automatically install them from this page. It also checks your current setup and determines which components need adding or upgrading. Very cool!

IBM Web Explorer

http://www.networking.ibm.com/WebExplorer/

Need an OS/2 Warp Web browser? Check out this page, where you can download one or get support for your existing copy.

Internet Group/Internet Business Center

http://home.tig.com/cgi-bin/genobject/index

A Web and Internet resource and home page provider. Offers Manage! IT, a browsing tool.

Lynx Information

http://lynx.browser.org/

Lynx is a text-only Web browser, one of the few still being updated these days. The Web without graphics may be dull, but if you are using a system that cannot display graphics, it may be your only choice!

Types of Browsers

Browsers come in several different flavors. Graphical interface browsers display the images, links, and test in full color. The most popular graphical browsers include Netscape Navigator, Microsoft Internet Explorer, and NCSAS Mosaic. Internet service providers, such as America Online and CompuServe, give their own graphical browsers to their subscribers. Many online services, however, offer their users a choice between the ISP browser and a commercial browser, such as Microsoft Internet Explorer or Netscape Navigator.

MacZilla

http://maczilla.com/

Macintosh users can download a program here that enables them to play a variety of multimedia files that are commonly found on Web pages, including movies (QuickTime/AVI/MPEG) and music clips (au/wav/midi/aiff/mp2) from inside Netscape Communicator for Macintosh.

Microsoft Desktop Gallery for Internet Explorer 4.0

http://www.microsoft.com/ie/ie40/gallery/?/ie/ie40/gallery/gal_main.htm

One of the Active Desktop features of IE4 is the ability to set up active objects on your Windows 95 desktop (for example, a stock ticker that continually updates and displays prices for your favorite stocks). You can download these active components from this section of the Microsoft Web site.

Netscape Communications

http://www.netscape.com

Find out about Netscape Communicator, the most popular Web browser and suite of Internet tools. You can download a copy for whatever computer system you are using, or explore the hefty but well-organized links section.

Netscape Plug-Ins

http://www.tiac.net/users/mdw/imap/xplugingif.html

A very handy page from which you can download a wide variety of plug-ins (add-in programs) for Netscape Navigator.

RealAudio RealPlayer

http://www.real.com/products/player/index.html

You will need this program to play RealAudio clips you find on some Web pages. Download a free copy of the player from this site.

VDONet Corp

http://www.vdo.net/

The home of VDOLive plug-in, which enables you to play VDO clips you find on some Web pages. Get your free copy of the player here, or buy the commercial version with more capabilities.

Related Sites

http://www.browserwars.com/

http://www.cyberdog.apple.com/

http://java.sun.com/products/hotjava/index.html

http://www.talentcom.com/icomm/index.html

http://www.netphonic.com/home.htm

http://www.threetoad.com/main/Browser.html

http://www.vapor.com/voyager/

http://www-dsed.llnl.gov/documents/WWWtest.html

http://www.delorie.com/web/wpbcv.html

http://www.nanospace.com/~lee/xspace/

A B C D E F G H I J K L M N O P Q R S T U V W X Y Z

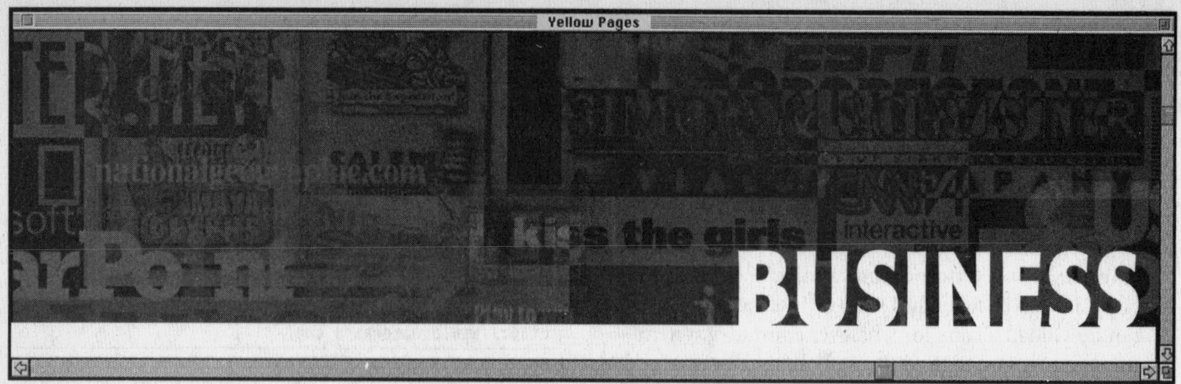

> By working faithfully eight hours a day you may eventually get to be boss and work twelve hours a day.
>
> *Robert Frost*

Not just for the "business-minded," this category also contains sites that pertain to consumer issues, patent information, and taxes!

The Benchmarking Exchange

http://www.benchnet.com

Information and communication system dedicated to benchmarking, reengineering, process improvement, and quality improvement.

NCI Navatar Canada Inc.

http://www.navatar.ca/

Offers up-to-date information on BPR and change management. Offers links to other sites covering business process reengineering, business process redesign, IT, public service reengineering projects, treasury board IQE, and related subjects. Also lists upcoming BPR seminars and courses.

The Business Incorporating Guide
http://www.corporate.com/

EXPOguide Home Page
http://www.expoguide.com/

FedEx Home Page
http://www.fedex.com/

LEXIS-NEXIS Communication Center
http://www.lexis-nexis.com/

MTAC Home Page
http://oracle.mtac.pitt.edu/WWW/MTAC.html

Nijenrode Business Webserver
http://www.nijenrode.nl/nbr/index.html

SCREENWRITERS ON LINE
http://screenwriter.com

CORPORATE HOME PAGES

3M Innovation Network

http://www.mmm.com

Provides information about 60,000 innovative 3M products for the home, business, and industry. Also offers information on market centers, worldwide operations, and company news.

AT&T Home Page

http://www.att.com/

Includes information about AT&T products and services, activities, news, employment opportunities, and investment information.

FedEx Home Page

http://www.fedex.com/

Features free package tracking with the identification number. Also contains information related to available services, free downloadable software, and delivery options.

GE Home Page

http://www.ge.com/index.htm

Includes information about GE products and services, company news and events, current stock quotes, and research, development, investment, and employment opportunities.

Goodyear Tire and Rubber Company

http://www.goodyear.com/

Provides information about specifications and preferences regarding tires. Gives advice on the purchase and care of tires. Includes a catalog of Goodyear tires. Also gives contact information to the nearest Goodyear store, including hours and services offered.

JCPenney Home Page

http://www.jcpenney.com/

Provides information on investor relations, gift registry, and online shopping. Includes a store locator and a customer survey.

McDonnell Douglas Aerospace

http://pat.mdc.com/MDA_Houston.html

Includes some corporate information, as well as information on robotics and 3D animated human mannequins. Uses the 3D human modeling system to analyze human body fit and function within a geometric structure.

MCI Home Page

http://www.mci.com

Takes you on a virtual tour of MCI. Offers links to Internet MCI, Gramercy Press, MCI Developers Lab, and the Small Business Center. Describes available products and services, and offers online customer service.

Shell Oil Company

http://www.shellus.com

Provides information about Shell's activities, products, and research.

SONY Online

http://www.music.sony.com/

Contains information about Sony products and services. Includes categories of music, movies, games, electronics, television, theaters, radio, and merchandise.

Tandy Corporation

http://www.tandy.com/

Encompasses Radio Shack, Computer City, and Incredible Universe. Provides history of Tandy and information on future activities, press releases, and investments.

UPS Home Page

http://www.ups.com/

Contains service information, software, UPS news, and contact information. Also contains a section on package tracking.

Walgreen Co

http://www.walgreens.com

Includes Walgreen's corporate information, career opportunities, company history, store locations, and links to other pharmacy-related sites.

MISCELLANEOUS BUSINESS SITES

Acer America Career Opportunities

http://www.acer.com/aac/jobs/index.htm

Provides online career opportunities in numerous fields within the corporation, including customer service, engineering, manufacturing, marketing, sales, and Web teams. Also includes capability to apply over the Web for all fields.

AdMorInk

http://www.focusoc.com/admorink/

A small publisher of booklets on various subjects. Site provides information, catalogs, and samples of many of their assorted titles. Subject matter varies from do-it-yourself booklets to travel and art titles.

A B C D E F G H I J K L M N O P Q R S T U V W X Y Z

Aquatic Network

`http://www.brainiac.com/aquanet`

Serves as an information server for the aquatic world. Includes information on aquaculture, conservation, fisheries, marine science and oceanography, maritime heritage, ocean engineering, and seafood.

American Computer Resources, Inc.

`http://www.the-acr.com/`

Provides wholesale sale of IBM, Compaq, Packard Bell, and other computer companies' products. Includes product listings, technical support, company history, and import/export library. Also provides services such as a study web and an international calling code directory.

Automation Specialists

`http://www.cyberport.com/mall/autospec/`

Provides sales of application design engineering and automation solution products. Also provides sales of transducers, generators, solar panels, and batteries. Includes a description of the technical features of products that are offered.

The Business Incorporating Guide

`http://www.corporate.com/`

Contains details on how to form your own corporation in any state. Also provides information on the advantages of incorporating, types of corporations, Internet resources, and incorporating software.

Broadway Video, Inc.

`http://www.broadwayvideo.com/`

Provides home site for Broadway Video, Broadway Comics, and the Broadway Interactive Group. Includes BV forum and chat rooms. Also includes previews of upcoming titles and listings of comic retailers nationwide.

Bubble Technology Industries Inc.

`http://intranet.on.ca/~bubble/`

Produces radiation protection products and services. Includes company and product profiles with photographs. Text background is currently under construction.

Chastain Research Group, Inc.

`http://www.best.com/~chastain`

Serves as a consulting firm dedicated to meeting the requirements of biotechnology/pharmaceutical companies and professionals.

Duoforce Enterprises, Inc.

`http://www.netwave.net/duoforce/`

Provides consulting, skills training, and seminar services on networking, office communications, and public relations. Includes listing of services and products offered. Also includes contact information and a communications skills test.

EXPOguide Home Page

`http://www.expoguide.com/`

Offers details about trade shows, conferences, exhibitions, and links to related associations and resources.

Farg's Cost Accounting Home Page

`http://darkwing.uoregon.edu:80/~nfargher/`

Home page for cost accounting at the University of Oregon. Includes class notes and references to related articles and accounting resources.

Global Business Network

`http://www.gbn.org/`

A membership organization specializing in scenario thinking and collaborative learning about the future. Brings together members from business, science, the arts, and academia to explore uncertainties and to reframe executives' mental models and increase the organization's perceptive powers.

Global Trade Center

`http://www.tradezone.com/welcome.html`

Provides resources and information for people interested in world trade and mail order. Provides links to trade resources and sites around the world, trade news, business opportunities, and much more.

Habia Cable AB

`http://www.habia.se/english/welcome.html`

A German company with offices in Europe offering cable to meet any industrial or business requirement. Provides links and descriptions of products and ordering information.

HADCO Corporation

`http://www.hadco.com:8080/`

For those in the electronics industry, offers printed circuit board technological excellence. Links to services, volume manufacturing, and tech centers.

Harris Digital Telephone Systems

`http://www.dts.harris.com/`

Provides telecommunications platforms and software, switching systems, wireless communications products, and so on, for public telephone networks and private switching environments. Provides links to product info, training and employment opportunities, what's new, contact information, and more.

Inland Answering Service

`http://www.citivu.com/usa/ias/index.html`

A personal, professional, nationwide telephone answering service. Will take orders, send messages to your voice mail or pager, schedule appointments, or broadcast faxes. Check out their long list of services for your business.

International Typeface Corporation

`http://www.esselte.com/itc/`

This corporation has designed and licensed typeface designs for numerous companies. Links to license, sales, and marketing info, press releases, stuff to download, and more.

Internet Bankruptcy Library

`http://bankrupt.com`

Provides worldwide troubled-company resources for the bankruptcy and insolvency professional, including discussion groups, a worldwide directory of professionals, and notices of conferences.

ISO Easy

`http://www.exit109.com/~leebee/`

Provides assistance in understanding and implementing the ISO 9000 model for quality assurance. Contains a FAQ list and links to other sites on quality assurance standards and other ISO 9000 resources.

Jones, Hall, Hill, and White

`http://www.jhhw.com`

A professional law corporation practicing exclusively in the area of municipal finance as bond counsel, underwriter's counsel, special tax counsel, and rebate compliance counsel. Includes links to other public finance resources as well.

LEXIS-NEXIS Communication Center

`http://www.lexis-nexis.com/`

An online legal, news, and business information retrieval, storage, and management service. Describes the services and products available worldwide.

McDonnell Information Systems

`http://www.mdis.com/`

Provides software, hardware, management, training, consulting, maintenance services, computer solutions, and development tools for your company. Links to a variety of sales groups.

MTAC Home Page

`http://oracle.mtac.pitt.edu/WWW/MTAC.html`

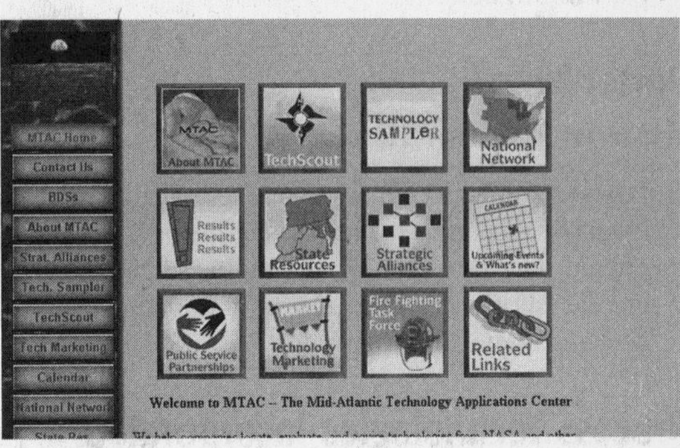

Mid-Atlantic Technology Applications Center. One of six regional technology transfer centers funded by NASA. Promotes use of NASA technologies in the private sector to help U.S. firms improve their competitiveness.

Nijenrode Business Webserver

`http://www.nijenrode.nl/nbr/index.html`

Webserver at the Netherlands Business School. Provides resources relevant to students, faculty, and researchers at business schools. Offers links to information about careers, business news, other business schools, and other business-related directories.

ODIN Oil Network

http://www.oil.net

Presents an Internet network designed for companies and individuals involved in the international oil industry. Enables people involved with exploration and drilling, production, seismic, and personnel to get in touch with one another and with the service and supply companies they need to access.

Paracel, Inc.

http://www.paracel.com

Develops leading-edge information filtering and categorizing technologies for the Internet, enterprise, bioinformatic, and government industries.

Peters-de Laet, Inc.

http://www.pdel.com/

Distributes electronic, electrical, and fastener products including connectors, sockets, fasteners, and much more. Includes catalog, new product, and company information.

Porter Novelli

http://www.porternovelli.com/

Provides public relations services specializing in new media applications. Includes client listings, services offered, and the CyberLifestyle online services demographic information. Includes links to many related sites and contact information.

Process Technologies Incorporated

http://www.execpc.com/~pti

Manufactures glass photo-tooling on a small scale. Produces chromium and iron-oxide photo tools for the microelectronics industries.

Research Dynamics

http://www.resdyn.com/

Provides home site for Research Dynamics. Includes corporate structure, job listings, and contact information.

The Resource Group

http://www.in.net/resource/index.html

Assists organizations and individuals in working toward personal and professional growth and development through using the tools of the information age. The group has three divisions: Technical Resources, The Resource Group Bookstore, and The Resource Group Consulting.

Rodex Technologies for the Manufacturing Industry

http://www.magi.com/~rodex/

Supplies manufacturing technologies such as equipment, software systems, and engineering expertise from Canada to manufacturers worldwide.

Rogers Communications Inc.

http://www.rogers.com/

Provides home site for Rogers Communications Inc., a large Canadian telecommunications, media, and cable television corporation. Includes corporate profile and detailed information about Rogers' services and products. Also includes facilities tour, job openings, cable channel line-ups, and contact information for all divisions.

Scope Systems—Worldwide Industrial Electronics Repair and Services

http://www.charm.net/~scope

Specializes in the repair and remanufacture of industrial electronic circuit boards and assemblies. Includes analog, digital, power supplies, A/C and D/C drives, video monitors, and process control systems.

SCREENWRITERS ON LINE

http://screenwriter.com

Offers trade secrets, advice, and insider information from professional screenwriters. Publishes "The Screenwriter's Insider Report," a subscription-based industry newsletter that features insider interviews with screenwriters, studio heads, and agents.

Seven Technologies

http://www.sevent.dk

A Danish software company working toward professional solutions for professional computer users. Provides process visualization, automation tools, graphical user interfaces, supervision systems, transaction systems, security management systems, and information about how to get in touch with the company.

Shape Memory Applications, Inc.

http://www.sma-inc.com/

Supplies and uses NiTi shape memory and superelastic alloys. Provides information on products and services offered, as well as technical and industry news.

STAT-USA

http://www.stat-usa.gov/

Provides daily economic news, statistical releases, export and trade databases and information, and domestic economic databases and information.

Submarine Cables of the World

http://www.ptcable.com/~ptc/iscw/iscw.shtml

Provides information about underwater cable protection. Includes committee background, resources guide, and very detailed information about underwater cables.

The TechExpo on WWW

http://www.techexpo.com/

Provides information about high technology companies in the areas of engineering and life sciences. Includes information on their products and services, societies, universities, magazines, and newsletters.

Tele-Communications, Inc. (TCI)

http://www.tcinc.com/

Provides home site for TCI telecommunications. Includes links to many sites and contact information.

TeleService Resources, Inc.

http://www.amrtsr.com/tsr_home.htm

Provides online reservation services for the travel and hotel industry. Includes listing of services offered, company partners, company profile, and contact information.

WingsNet

http://www.vphi.com/cgi-bin/choose.pl

Produces and provides sales of The Signature Line of training videos. Includes lengthy company catalog, program information, company profile, philosophy, and ordering information.

Waters Corporation

http://www.waters.com/

Analytic instrument and chromatography chemistries manufacturer, specializing in High Performance Liquid Chromatography (HPLC) technology. Provides information about the company, its products, and related technologies.

World of Commercial Ballooning

http://www.aero.com/ballooning/commercial/main.htm

Provides information and details about commercial ballooning and its advertising uses. Provides ample information about the technical, media, and marketing angles for using a hot air balloon.

LISTSERVS

ALSBNEWS—Academy of Legal Studies in Business (ALSB) News

Miami University, Oxford, OH

You can join this group by sending the message "sub ALSBNEWS your name" to

listserv@miamiu.muohio.edu

AOL-EZONE—"Your Business Newsletter" - America Online's Weekly Small Bus

America Online, Inc. (1-800-827-6364 in USA/Canada)

You can join this group by sending the message "sub AOL-EZONE your name" to

listserv@listserv.aol.com

BETS-L—Business Ethics Teaching Society

University of Illinois at Chicago, Chicago, IL

You can join this group by sending the message "sub BETS-L your name" to

listserv@uicvm.uic.edu

BIZNEWS—News Service Business News Releases

Purdue University, West Lafayette, IN

You can join this group by sending the message "sub BIZNEWS your name" to

listserv@vm.cc.purdue.edu

BSN-D—Business Sources on the Net - Distribution List

You can join this group by sending the message "sub BSN-D your name" to

listserv@listserv.kent.edu

BTECH94—Business Technology

University of Missouri-St. Louis

You can join this group by sending the message "sub BTECH94 your name" to

listserv@umslvma.umsl.edu

BUSHEA—Health-Related Information for Business and Industry

Southern Illinois University at Carbondale, Carbondale, IL

You can join this group by sending the message "sub BUSHEA your name" to

`listserv%siucvmb.bitnet@listserv.net`

BUSLAW-L—Business Law List

Humber College, Toronto, ON

You can join this group by sending the message "sub BUSLAW-L your name" to

`listserv@admin.humberc.on.ca`

BUSLIB-L—Business Libraries Discussion List

Boise State University, Boise, ID

You can join this group by sending the message "sub BUSLIB-L your name" to

`listserv@idbsu.idbsu.edu`

BUSREC—Business Recovery

Wayne State University, Detroit, MI

You can join this group by sending the message "sub BUSREC your name" to

`listserv@cms.cc.wayne.edu`

CORP-L—Corporate Accountability List

The American University, Washington, DC

You can join this group by sending the message "sub CORP-L your name" to

`listserv@american.edu`

EHCOLUMN—Economic History Columns

Miami University, Oxford, OH

You can join this group by sending the message "sub EHCOLUMN your name" to

`listserv@miamiu.muohio.edu`

INBUSINESS—Internet in Business Discussion List

America Online, Inc. (1-800-827-6364 in USA/Canada)

You can join this group by sending the message "sub INBUSINESS your name" to

`listserv@listserv.aol.com`

KSINDX-L—KS Index of Leading Econ. Indicators

Kansas State University, Manhattan, KS

You can join this group by sending the message "sub KSINDX-L your name" to

`listserv@ksuvm.ksu.edu`

LABOR-L—Forum on Labor in the Global Economy

You can join this group by sending the message "sub LABOR-L your name" to

`listserv@yorku.ca`

MBA-L—BA Discussion List

University of Missouri-St. Louis

You can join this group by sending the message "sub MBA-L your name" to

`listserv@umslvma.umsl.edu`

NASIRN-L—North American Service Industries Research Network List

America Online, Inc. (1-800-827-6364 in USA/Canada)

You can join this group by sending the message "sub NASIRN-L your name" to

`listserv@listserv.aol.com`

NDSRB-L—Students for Responsible Business

University of Notre Dame, Notre Dame, IN

You can join this group by sending the message "sub NDSRB-L your name" to

`listserv@vma.cc.nd.edu`

PCBR-L—Pacific Business Researchers Forum (PCBR-L)

You can join this group by sending the message "sub PCBR-L your name" to

`listserv%uhccvm.bitnet@listserv.net`

ROUNDTABLE—International Business Roundtable

You can join this group by sending the message "sub ROUNDTABLE your name" to

`listserv@home.ease.lsoft.com`

TOES97—The Other Economic Summit USA 1997

Syracuse University

You can join this group by sending the message "sub TOES97 your name" to

`listserv@listserv.syr.edu`

NEWSGROUPS

`alt.business`

`alt.business.home.pc`

`alt.business.hospitality`

`alt.business.import-export`

`alt.business.insurance`

`alt.business.internal-audit`

`alt.business.misc`

`alt.business.multi-level`

`alt.business.seminars`

`alt.internet.commerce`

`alt.society.labor-unions`

`biz.books.technical`

biz.clarinet
biz.clarinet.sample
biz.comp.accounting
biz.comp.mcs
biz.comp.telebit
biz.config
biz.control
biz.digex.announce
biz.digital.announce
biz.digital.articles
biz.general
biz.jobs.offered
biz.marketplace.computers.discussion
biz.marketplace.computers.mac
biz.marketplace.computers.other
biz.marketplace.computers.pc-clone
biz.marketplace.computers.workstation
biz.marketplace.discussion
biz.marketplace.international
biz.marketplace.international.discussion
biz.marketplace.non-computer
biz.marketplace.services.computers
biz.marketplace.services.discussion
biz.marketplace.services.non-computer
biz.next.newprod
biz.oreilly.announce
biz.pagesat
biz.pagesat.weather
biz.stolen
biz.tadpole.sparcbook
biz.test
biz.univel.misc
biz.zeos.announce
biz.zeos.general
clari.biz.briefs
misc.consumers.frugal-living
misc.entrepreneurs
misc.invest.real-estate
misc.invest.stocks
misc.invest.technical

A B C D E F G H I J K L M N O P Q R S T U V W X Y Z

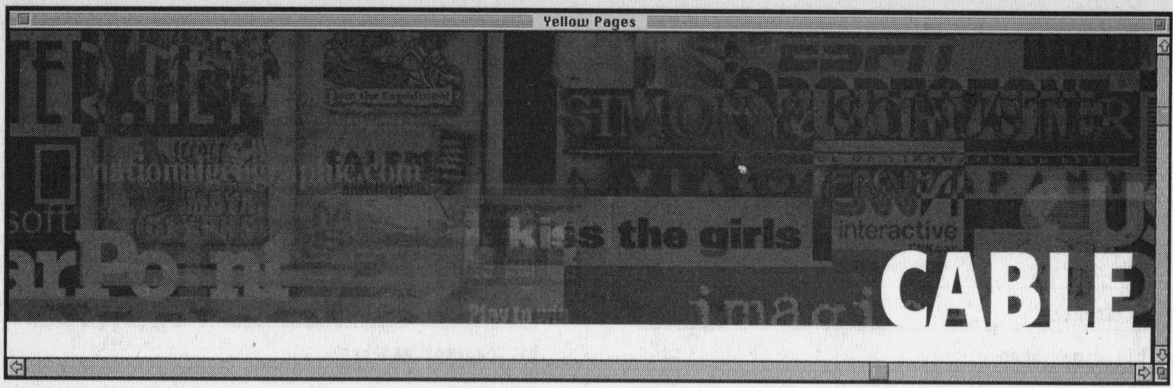

> Yes, I still live with my parents, which I admit is both bogus and sad. But I have this awesome cable access show, and I still know how to party.
>
> *Wayne in* Wayne's World *(1992)*

A&E

http://www.aetv.com/index2.html

Sneak peaks of shows coming up on the A&E cable network, plus daily listings and a trivia quiz. Lots to see and do here!

American Movie Classics

http://www.amctv.com/

Information about your favorite classic movies and movie stars, as well as upcoming movies on the AMC cable channel.

Ben's Cable Box

http://www.geocities.com/SiliconValley/Park/3254/cabletv.htm

Equipment reviews and instructions for normal people who don't understand technical jargon but want to run their cable boxes. Great stuff!

Related Sites
http://members.aol.com/bryce115/index.html
http://www.cable-link.com/
http://www.cablenet.org/

NRP TOP PICKS

Cable Connect
http://www.cableconnect.com/

Cable Online
http://www.cable-online.com/

Cinemax
http://www.cinemax.com/

BRAVO TV

http://www.bravotv.com/

Program listings for the BRAVO cable network, plus film reviews, contests, and information about the Bravo in the Classroom program.

Cable Connect

http://www.cableconnect.com/

Lots of great information and links dealing with the cable television industry. Get the latest news about individual cable companies, find out what's behind popular cable channels, and more.

Cable World Magazine

http://www.mediacentral.com/CableWorld

An online magazine aimed primarily at cable operators and stockholders in cable companies.

Cable Online

http://www.cable-online.com/

An "insider site" for the cable TV industry, with job listings, associations, events, and programmer/operator information.

Cinemax

http://www.cinemax.com/

An innovative site featuring more than just the usual program listings. You can use the interactive Movie Matchmaker to get recommendations of movies you might like, or check out the Max for Me page that lets you create a personalized printout of the schedule for the movies you want to see.

CNN Interactive

http://www.cnn.com/

The Web version of the popular cable network, this site includes late-breaking news stories in many categories, including sports, travel, international, weather, and style.

C-SPAN

http://www.c-span.org/

Program listings, as well as RealAudio clips from the Senate and House of Representatives that deal with the key issues of today. There is also a searchable archive.

Free Speech TV

http://www.freespeech.org/

Free Speech TV is a Web-based video broadcast hub, housing over 300 on-demand RealMedia files, with new programs posted daily. This may well be the future of television, folks! Remember, you saw it here first.

Nick at Nite & TV Land

http://nick-at-nite.com/

TV nostalgia buffs will find a lot to love here, including video clips of old commercials, schedules, contests, and other fun goodies.

Sam's Interactive Cable Guide

http://www.teleport.com/~samc/cable1.html

Wow! Tons and tons and TONS of links to pages representing every aspect of the cable industry. Each page (and there are several) has literally hundreds of links on it. A great place to start browsing.

Sundance Channel

http://www.sundancechannel.com/

Everything you wanted to know about the Sundance Film Festival plus the Sundance Channel on cable TV. Includes archives and a Sundance Store.

The Weather Channel

http://www.weather.com/twc/homepage.twc

Check the latest weather in your area or around the world at this site, which operates in conjunction with the cable channel of the same name.

NEWSGROUPS

rec.video.cable-tv

alt.cable-tv

alt.cable-tv.re-regulate

Related Sites

http://www.comcast.com/

http://www.discovery.com/

http://www.cablemaven.com

http://www.lifetimetv.com/

http://www.multichannel.com/

http://www.buttle.com/tv/schedule.htm

http://www.ultimatetv.com/UTVL/utvl.html

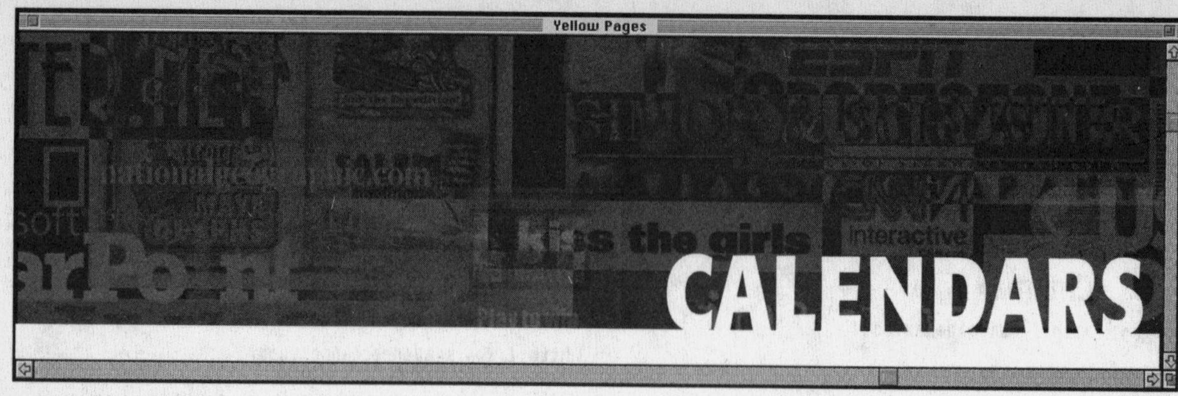

It's just another Wednesday. The calendar's full of 'em.

Jeff in Rear Window *(1954)*

Ancient Calendars

http://physics.nist.gov/GenInt/Time/ancient.html

A fascinating tour of ancientpast methods of marking time, from clocks to calendars.

Asian Astrology Calendar Converters

http://w3.baobei.com/astro/astroindex.html

Billed as the Internet's first and foremost resource for the study of Asian astrology. Includes calendar coverters for Chinese, Tibetian, and Vietnamese calendars. Very interesting!

The Calendar FAQ

http://www.pip.dknet.dk/~pip10160/calendar.html

An overview of the Christian, Hebrew, and Islamic calendars in common use. It will provide a historical background for the Christian calendar, plus an overview of the French Revolutionary calendar and the Mayan calendar.

CalendarLand

http://www.juneau.com/home/janice/calendarland/

Offering a list of links to other calendar pages, CalendarLand is a comprehensive resource of general, event, celestial, interactive, and cultural and religious calendars. The site also offers links to calendar indexes and directories, calendar information and resources, and calendar software.

CalendarLand
http://www.juneau.com/home/janice/calendarland/

Ecclesiastical Calendar
http://cssa.stanford.edu/~marcos/ec-cal.html

Literary Hyper Calendar
http://sparc1.yasuda-u.ac.jp/LitCalendar.html

Virtual Jerusalem Calendar
http://www.virtual.co.il/city_services/calendar/

Calendars and Their History

http://astro.nmsu.edu/~lhuber/leaphist.html

This site reprints an essay by L. E. Doggett about the history of various calendars, including the Gregorian, the Julian, the Hebrew, the Islamic, the Indian, and the Chinese. Additionally, the essay explains the astronomical bases of calendars, calendar reform movements, and historical eras and chronologies. This site is an important first step for anyone trying to understand where calendars originate and how they are created.

CALENDR-L: The Calendar Mailing List

http://ecuvax.cis.ecu.edu/~pymccart/calndr-l.html

A Web page that provides information about the email mailing list devoted to discussion of the social, historical and philosophical dimensions of Calendars and Time Reckoning.

The Catholic Calendar Page

http://www.easterbrooks.com/personal/calendar/index.html

Look up the liturgical year, find out when the next holy day of obligation is coming up, or just check out the suggested Bible readings for the day at this informative Catholic-run site.

Chinese Astrology Calendar

http://found.cs.nyu.edu/liaos/calendar.html

By using this simple interface, you can click any year in the Twentieth Century and be given a chart that tells you, for example, that 1996 was the Year of the Rat and that 1997 was the Year of the Ox. The backgrounds at this site are beautiful, but might be slow to download.

Doug Zonker's Today's Date

http://www.cs.washington.edu/homes/dougz/date.html

Lists today's date in a variety of calendar formats, including French, Mayan, Islamic, Hebrew, Astronomical, Julian, and ISO.

Ecclesiastical Calendar

http://cssa.stanford.edu/~marcos/ec-cal.html

The Ecclesiastical Calendar site offers Christian calendars for any year you specify. The calendar calculates when Easter and its attendant Christian holidays (Ash Wednesday, Good Friday, and others) will fall in a particular year and also when other feast days in the Roman Catholic tradition will occur. The Web author explains the various algorithms used to calculate Easter's date, discusses when certain cultures adopted the Western method for determining the Easter date, and even posits that current formulas for determining the Easter date might not be valid in the far future.

The ESO Sky Calendar

http://archive.eso.org/obs-prep/skycalc/

The European Southern Observatory's adaptation of John Thorstensens (of Dartmouth College) skycalc program. It produces a nighttime calendar of phenomena for a single site including sun rise and set times, astronomical twilights, both in civil time and LST, and moon rise and set times and phase for each night in the month.

Gregorian-Hijri Dates Converter

http://bert.cs.pitt.edu/~tawfig/convert/

Converts Gregorian dates into the Islamic calendar.

Heavenly Details

http://www.almanac.com/cgi-bin/heaven.pl?mooninput=current

The Old Farmer's Almanac offers herewith the dates and locations of solar and lunar eclipses for the year, as well as the days of the full moon for seven years.

The Hebrew Date for Today

http://www.doe.carleton.ca/doebin/dfs_dispatch?hebdate

This site translates today's Gregorian date into the Hebrew calendar (for example, 20 April 1996 is 1 Ayar 5756) and offers a list of upcoming holidays.

Home Page for Calendar Reform

http://ecuvax.cis.ecu.edu/~pymccart/calendar-reform.html

This site details several attempts that have been made to reform the Gregorian calendar. Included here are the World Calendar, the 13-month calendar, and the Positivist Calendar, in addition to a history of calendar reform.

Indonesian National Holidays

http://hastu.com/holidays.html

This site shows all the Indonesian national holidays up through the year 2000, including religious festivals of Moslem, Christian, Hindu Dharma, and Buddhist faiths.

The Islamic Calendar for North America

http://www.erols.com/shaukat/calendar.html

Calculate the Crescent Moon's visibility from this site, and check out the 1998 and 1999 calendars with Islamic dates.

Literary Hyper Calendar

http://sparc1.yasuda-u.ac.jp/LitCalendar.html

Offering a "this day in literary history" service, the Literary Hyper Calendar has an interface consisting of the calendar for the current month. The calendar is a clickable imagemap and you simply click the date in which you are interested. In addition, you can choose from a list of other months and days.

Millennium Resources on the Internet

http://www.panix.com/~wlinden/calendar.shtml

A very comprehensive set of links to resources from the Millennium Institute.

The Moon's Phase

http://imagiware.com/astro/moon.cgi

The page generates a calendar for the given range of months which contains, for each day, the Julian Date, sun rise and set times, and moon rise and set times.

One-World Global Calendar

http://www.zapcom.net/phoenix.arabeth/1world.html

Offering festivals, celebrations, and holidays from ancient and modern cultures around the world, this is an excellent multicultural resource. The calendar is updated weekly.

Ron Smith Oldies Calendar

http://www.oldiesmusic.com/cal.htm

This calendar offers a this-week-in-rock-and-roll-history service, which details the anniversaries of births, deaths, and famous events occurring in that week.

Space Calendar (JPL)

http://newproducts.jpl.nasa.gov/calendar/

Space-related activities and anniversaries for the coming year, compliments of NASA's Jet Propulsion Laboratory.

Virtual Jerusalem Calendar

http://www.virtual.co.il/city_services/calandar/

Calendar

Kislev

Su	M	Tu	W	Th	F	Sh
1	2	3	4	5	6	7
8	9	10	11	12	13	14
15	16	17	18	19	20	21
22	23	24	25	26	27	28
29	30	1				

Rosh Chodesh (1st Kislev)

- *Ya'aleh ve-yavo* is included in the Amidah
- Half-Hallel is recited after Shacharit
- Torah reading: BeMidbar 28: 1-15
- Mussaf for Rosh Chodesh

Shabbat, Parshat Vayeitzei (7th Kislev)
Haftarah: Hoshei'a 12:13 - 14:10

Shabbat, Parshat Vayishlach (14th Kislev)
Haftarah: Ovadyah 1:1 - 21

Shabbat, Parshat Vayeshev (21st Kislev)
Haftarah: Amos 2:6 - 3:8

Chanukah, First Day - Wednesday (25th Kislev)
Begins *Tuesday* Evening

Index/Map | News | Calendar | Lists | Join! | About

Includes all Jewish holidays and events. Click a calendar date to see that day's significance, along with suggested Torah readings and activities.

The World Wide Holiday and Festival Page

http://www.smiley.cy.net/bdecie/

Explains and calculates movable holidays (that is, those that don't happen on the exact same date every year) for almost every culture, country, and religion.

Related Sites

http://host.ld.centuryinter.net/McDaniel/cc.htm

http://www.payvand.com/calendar/intro.html

http://tehran.stanford.edu/Calendar/calendar.html

http://www.public.iastate.edu/~rjsalvad/scmfaq/calendar.html

http://members.tripod.com/~PHILKON/index.html

http://www.bcca.org/~glittle/today.html

http://www.panix.com/~wlinden/calendar.shtml

http://www.boutell.com/birthday.cgi

http://www.intellinet.com/CoolTools/CalendarMaker/

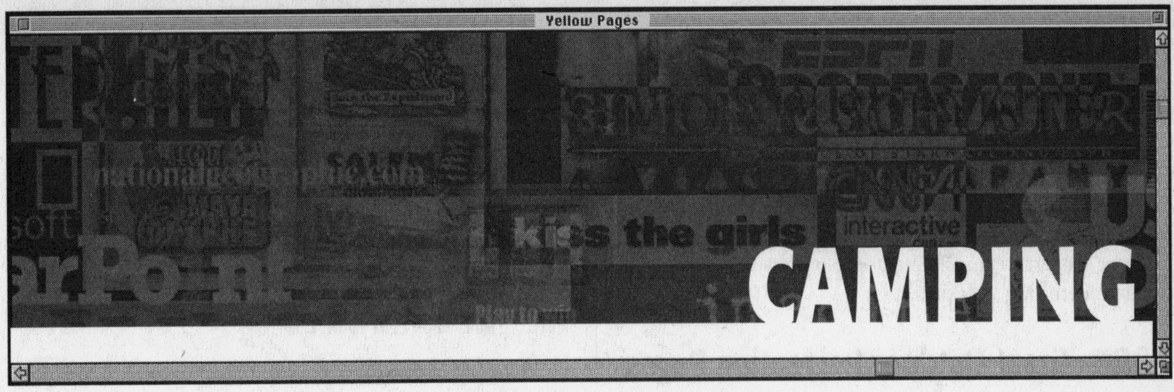

> Why is my survival kit held together with paper clips?
>
> *Bernadette McCarver Snyder*

American Park Network—Camping

http://www.americanparknetwork.com/activity/camping.html

Planning a camping trip to a national park? Check here first for site availability, activities you'll find in the park, fees, and much more. Camping in some national parks requires reservations, and you'll find contact information here; some park campgrounds are available on a first-come, first-served basis, and this site provides information on how to make sure you get a site.

Backcountry Home Page

http://io.datasys.swri.edu/Overview.html

For the more adventurous camper. You'll find lightweight recipes for backpackers, tips from experienced hikers, pages and pages of backpacking and hiking information. Includes links to pages the backpacker will find of interest, such as manufacturers of equipment, government pages, and more. There's a lot to see here.

Related Sites
http://www.gorefabrics.com/backpacking/backpack.htm?
http://www.barefooters.org/hikers/
http://www.outdoorlink.com/
http://members.aol.com/CMorHiker/backpack/index.html
http://www.cotswold-outdoor.co.uk/1camp.html
http://www.goodsamclub.com/

Basecamp
http://www.intx.net/basecamp/

The Back-Country Kitchen—Northern Trails Press

http://www.gorp.com/northtrails/

Camp food does not have to be limited to hot dogs and trail mix. Learn some of the finer points of cooking on a camp stove, which vegetables travel well in a backpack, and cold-weather outdoor cooking. Pick up some tips, try some highlighted recipes, and order a camping cookbook. There are lots of links to other outdoor cooking sites, too.

Backpacker Magazine's Basecamp

Http://www.bpbasecamp.com/

Here's a magazine for the backpacker with features, articles, and forums. There's a special page for and about women and a searchable encyclopedia of camping terms. There are links here to other sites of interest to campers and backpackers, too.

Basecamp

http://www.intx.net/basecamp/

The people at Basecamp manage to communicate the joy of camping. This is a lively site with lots to do and see. The staff actually takes you with them on a hike through several different places. Be sure to follow Mom and Darby as they motorhome through Canada to Alaska. There are recipes, art, poetry, links to other sites; this is a happening site.

A B C D E F G H I J K L M N O P Q R S T U V W X Y Z

Camping World Online

http://www.campingworld.com/index.shtml

Camping World is a leading supplier of products for RVs in particular and camping in general. Order a free catalog. Check out some of their products. Get special online bargains. Find the Camping World store closest to you. There are also links to some other great camping web sites.

GORP—Great Outdoor Recreation Pages

http://www.gorp.com/default.htm

So what do people actually *do* when they camp? Learn about all the great outdoor activities here—fishing, hiking, canoeing, bicycling, and more. Learn about little-known and uncrowded camping places in National Parks and Forests and some State Parks and Forests. Ever wonder how those campground hosts got their jobs? Click on "Jobs in the Outdoors" for links to dream jobs.

KOA Homepage

http://www.koakampgrounds.com/

If you like plenty of luxury while you're camping—hot showers, recreation rooms, convenience stores—KOA is the way to go. Check here for a list of the KOA campgrounds across North America, an explanation of the different ways to camp at a KOA, services available, and, if you're looking for an enjoyable and profitable way to earn your living, how to open a KOA of your very own.

L.L. Bean Welcome Page

http://www.llbean.com/

Keeping warm is a primary concern when you're camping, and L.L. Bean is the place to go for warm clothes, snowshoes, and more. Order a free catalog; check out the online product guide; definitely use their park search page. With hundreds of national and state parks, forests, and wildlife refuges, it's a handy tool.

Minnesota State Parks

http://www.dnr.state.mn.us/outdoor/parks/parks.htm

If we had to pick only one state to highlight in the camping section, Minnesota would be the one. Whether on the prairie, in a hardwood forest, or near the Great Lakes, Minnesota State Parks offer every possible camping experience from canning and portaging the Boundary Waters to just sitting outside your RV listening to the wolves howl. Find the park you'd like to visit and make your reservations—all at this site.

Ocean City, MD's Frontier Town Campground

http://www.frontiertown.com/

Here's a unique family camping experience. This campground features more than 500 sites, a pizza parlor, and access to many area attractions, including golf courses and harness racing.

RV Lifestyle—Fulltiming America

http://fulltiming-america.com/index.html

A site by and for full-time RVers—those people who carry their homes with them as they move from majestic mountains to peaceful seashores. Read the evaluations of campgrounds across America. Watch this site as it grows. Contribute to its growth with your own evaluations. There's also a list of contacts in each state for tourism and travel information.

Visit Your National Parks

http://www.nps.gov/parks.html

This is an official National Park Service page. Learn about the National Parks. Pick one that is right for your camping needs. Find out what the fees are. Make reservations. There's a featured park of the month and a guide to lesser-known parks, along with lots of useful and up-to-date information.

NEWSGROUPS

rec.outdoors.camping

rec.outdoors.rv-travel

rec.backcountry

Related Sites

http://www.outdoorlink.com

http://www.gorp.com/gorp/resource/US_National_Forest/main.htm

http://www.gorp.com/gorp/resource/us_ns/fl/camp_gul.htm

http://www.lnt.org/

http://virtualroadtrip.com/visitor.shtml

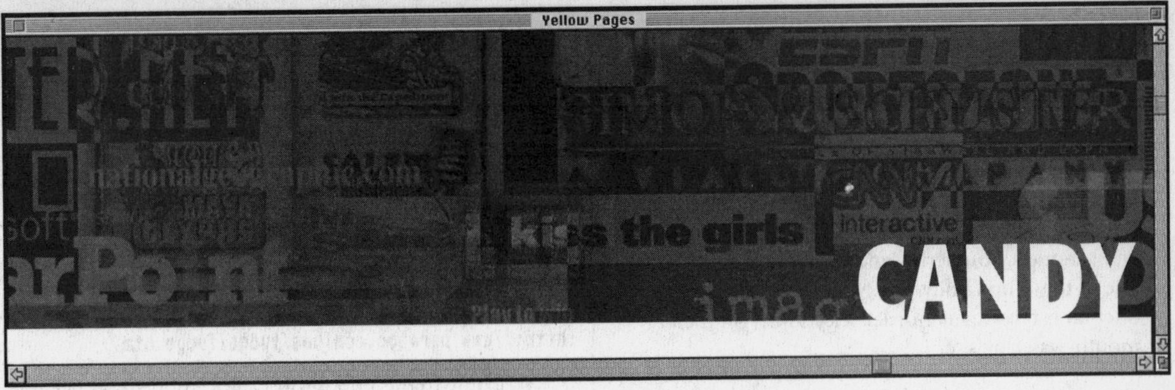

> Actually, I have been trying this new fat free diet I invented. All I've had to eat for the past six days are gummy bears, jelly beans, and candy corns.
>
> *Romy in* Romy and Michele's High School Reunion *(1997)*

C & C Candies

http://www.pottsville.com/CCcandies

Unique hand-painted molded chocolate novelties. Choose from more than 300 seasonal and all-occasion molds.

Candy Bouquet International

http://www.franchise1.com/comp/cndybok1.html

Candy Bouquet shops offer floral-like gifts made from different candies and chocolates.

Chilham Village British Candies

http://qb.island.net/~candies

Chilham Village British Candies is a retailer of candies and sweets. You can order online and they will send an order within 24 hours of your request.

Godiva Chocolatier
http://www2.godiva.com/

Esther Price Candies

http://www.estherprice.com

Esther Price Candies and Chocolates claims that all it takes is one taste to realize that this is the finest candy you'll find anywhere. Online ordering and delivery throughout the U.S. and Canada.

GAYETY'S Chocolates

http://www.mcs.net/~candy/home.html

For more than 75 years GAYETY'S has been hand-dipping its own chocolate-covered candies, using 100-percent natural ingredients and no preservatives.

Godiva Chocolatier

http://www2.godiva.com/

Offering some of the best chocolate in the world, this site enables you to order online or locate the nearest Godiva retailer near you. Even the graphics make your mouth water. Definitely a stop for chocoholics.

Hershey Chocolate North America

http://www.hersheys.com/hcna/

Includes info on Hershey's chocolate, as well as pasta, Hershey's grocery, and an online cookbook.

Southern Candy Makers

http://www.fqmall.com/southern

Southern Candy Makers is a world-renowned family-owned and operated confectionary in New Orleans, LA. Their candy recipes are derived from classic New Orleans formulas, particularly their various pralines and caramels. Southern Candy Makers was just voted one of the "Top Candy Makers In The World." They offer an extensive mail-order selection. Visit their mouth-watering site.

Sweet Charlotte's of New Orleans

http://www.neworleans.com/candy/

A quaint Victorian candy shop located in the historic area of Rivertown in Kenner, LA, 10 minutes from downtown New Orleans. They specialize in New Orleans-style original pralines, handmade chocolates such as pecan hash, truffles, turtles, and a special handmade-in-Louisiana basket made of peppermint candy and filled with chocolates. The basket is completely edible. They also have a very extensive selection of the finest sugar-free chocolates made. They ship nationwide and have reasonable prices.

Wisconsin Dells Candy Stores

http://www.baraboo.com/bus/fudge/fudge.htm

Welcome to the Wisconsin Dells Candy Stores, where you can order fudge, chocolates, and gourmet candies online, or by using their 800 number.

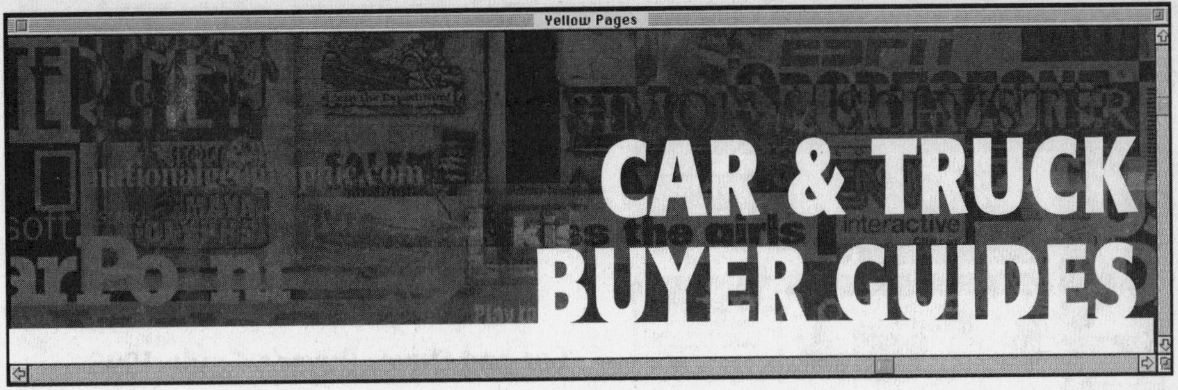

CAR & TRUCK BUYER GUIDES

> If speedometers are so important, why do something like 85 percent of all drivers ignore them and drive according to road conditions and their best judgment?
>
> *Brock Yates,* Car and Driver

Action Auto Buyer's Guide

`http://www.autobuyersguide.com/`

A great resource for finding the automobile of your dreams, or selling the one of yesterday's dreams. Scan current ads or place an ad (for free!) to sell your car, truck, van, or vehicle-related items. There are alphabetical and geographical listings of and links to auto dealers on the Net. Or link to the Kelley Blue Book, a car loan calculator, or a site where you can look up various insurance rates.

America's Automall

`http://www.aautomall.com/`

Automall is a searchengine designed specifically to find vehicles (new and used) over the Internet. Find the dealerships located nearest you by searching the database of more than 600 dealership Web sites. The AutoForm feature uses a price quote email form which you send to multiple dealerships; they then send you their best price. The Pre-owned Vehicle database lets you search for used cars. You also have access to pricing guides, insurance quotes, and recall information.

autoweb.com
`http://www.autoweb.com/`

Automotive Database

`http://www.vaxxine.com/adbase/`

A database of automobiles for sale and automobiles wanted. You can search by make and region. It's also a database of auto parts to find or sell. Automotive discussions are the talk in this site's chat room.

AutoPlus

`http://www.autoplus.com/`

A car buyer's guide aimed mainly at the Boston area, but applicable elsewhere as well. You'll find a listing of used cars for sale and can add yours if you like. There also is information about new cars, including a searchable database of over 16 years of car reviews done by the Boston Globe.

AutoSite

`http://www.autosite.com/`

Billing themselves as "the ultimate automotive buyer's guide," AutoSite covers everything from dealer invoices on new cars to used car book values to automobile recalls to manufacturers' toll-free phone numbers. There's also a handy troubleshooting and question and answer section on car repairs.

Related Sites

`http://www.autorebate.com/`
`http://www.carprice.com/`
`http://www.aiada.org/`
`http://www.auto.com/`
`http://www.myclassiccar.com/`
`http://www.caranddriver.com/`
`http://www.kitcar.com/cgscbook.html`
`http://www.autoexchange.com/`

A B C D E F G H I J K L M N O P Q R S T U V W X Y Z

autoweb.com

http://www.autoweb.com/

autoweb.com partners with USAToday to bring you an online "auto superstore." This is the first and only automotive Web site to be awarded PC Magazine's Top 100 Website Award. Not only can you browse their Virtual Lot, search their database of dealers for your ideal car, and advertise your car for $19.95 per month, you can even arrange to have a car delivered to your home for a test drive.

Auto Stop

http://www.theautostop.com/

Auto Stop is an auto-buying service that guarantees low, competitive prices on both new and previously owned vehicles. Within 48 hours after choosing the vehicle you want, Auto Stop's nearest subscribing dealership calls you with a quote, guaranteed to be fleet price, not retail price. You also have access to a large database of classifieds for used vehicles.

Buying a Car Online

When you consider purchasing a vehicle online, the first thing you thing you should think about is whether you want to buy a new or used auto. You can easily cut down on your search time by deciding this question early on in the process. To help you make this decision, you could look up prices for vehicles in the Kelley Blue Book (listed in this section). All you have to do here is enter the make and model you are interested in buying and the site will give you a pricing report.

To receive a quote from a dealer near you, try AutoWeb Interactive (`http://www.autoweb.com`). this site enables you to type in a make and model and a dealer near you will return a price quote.

Auto World

http://www.autoworld.com/

Unlike the Kelley Blue Book (a competitor of Auto World), Auto World updates its Vehicle Information and Pricing Service on a daily basis and takes into account variations in regional pricing. In addition to dynamic pricing reports, you can get a quote on a car or read tips on buying a car.

Car and Driver Buyer's Guide 1996

http://www.caranddriver.com/hfm/cgi-unprot/bg

The official buyer's guide of the famous automotive magazine. Pick a manufacturer, price range, and vehicle type, and browse the results complete with photos. Or take the shortcuts and browse by all of any one category. Vehicle specifications are also provided.

Car Buying Pain Relief

http://www.autobytel.com/

If you know the model of car you want, Autobytel can put you in contact with dealers in your area. Find both new or used cars. The site also includes new and used car pricing information and a weekly auto market report for the latest on the car world. A French language site is also available.

Car Tips

http://www.tex-net.net/tex-net/cartips.html

When buying a car from a dealership, do you feel like you're walking into a spider's web? These tips are provided to make you feel less like a victim and more in control of your automobile purchase. Tips include what time of the month you can get the best price, what to do before going to the dealership, and what cars really cost the dealer.

Car Trackers

http://www.cartrackers.com/

Perform a new or used car search, read the buyer's guide, or participate in online community events like auto-related games and chat room discussion. This site also provides a host of reviews of various automobiles. Or, advertise your used vehicle, be it a car, truck, watercraft, snowmobile, bus, RV, or ATV.

CARveat Emptor

http://www.well.com/user/kr2/

An enlightening set of tips for dealing with dealers when buying a car. The site shows you common tricks of the trade to look out for and methods you can use to get a better deal. Read all of this lengthy advice, and you'll be more than ready for your next purchase.

DealerNet

http://www.dealernet.com/

A very comprehensive guide to buying a car via the Internet. Enter your specific search criteria on the make, model, year, price range, and dealership location of your desired vehicle, and *voilà*! DealerNet gives you a list of options. You can also check out New Car Test Reviews. Or go to a chat room and discuss automotive topics with other auto lovers.

Edmund's Automobiles Buying Guides

http://www.edmunds.com/

The place to go when thinking of buying a new or used car. A multitude of information is available, including price guides, dealer cost information, buyer advice and recommendations, recall information, and much, much more. Best of all, it's absolutely free.

Internet Car Guide

http://www.carguide.com/

Select a car by looking through makers, models, and classes. When you narrow your search down to a single vehicle, you are presented with a photo and the option of viewing all of its specifications. A glossary is also provided, which is very useful for giving meaning to sometimes cryptic automobile terms.

Kelley Blue Book

http://www.kbb.com./

Get free pricing reports on new and used vehicles from this renowned company. Or, if you prefer to physically thumb through the Blue Book pages, order the book online. After you settle on a price you are willing to pay, buy a car online by linking to dealerships and auto buying services.

Microsoft Carpoint

http://carpoint.msn.com/

Microsoft's Carpoint has been chosen the official Web site of the 1998 North American International Auto Show (NAIAS). In addition to extensive coverage of the Detroit convention, Carpoint offers new and used car information, interactive classifieds, 360 degree views of cars and trucks, Kelley Blue Book pricing reports, side-by-side comparisons, and news and advice on car-related issues.

Stoneage

http://www.stoneage.com/

Stoneage specializes in putting consumers in touch with new and used car dealers and sellers over the Internet. Find a specific dealer in your area and schedule an appointment or ask for a quick quote. Before buying that used car, purchase a vehicle history report for $19.95. Learn the benefits of extending that manufacturer's warranty. For one fee, get the three major credit reports in one easy-to-read report.

Tallweb—Cars

http://www.bluplanet.com/tallweb/cars.html

Without giving any consideration whatsoever to the performance of the vehicles, a bunch of tall people sat in a bunch of cars and decided which were the best (and worst) based solely on interior room and comfort. Trucks, sport-utilities, mini-vans, and even subcompacts are compared.

Used Car Buying Guide

http://lyre.mit.edu/~powell/sherman/files/used_car.html

A very lengthy set of questions designed to completely evaluate the condition of a used car before purchasing it. Included are questions you should ask of the seller and of yourself, and checklists for inside, outside, and under the car. A plain text version of this document is available and would be very handy to print out and take when looking at a car.

Vehicle Information and Pricing Buyers Guide

http://www.carpricing.com/

Check dealer invoice pricing, search for the wholesale value of your used vehicle, or get an actual price quote from one of more than 4,000 dealers. Pricing information is provided by National Automobile Bankers Associates. Other features include a loan calculator and an auto news section with press releases from the manufacturers.

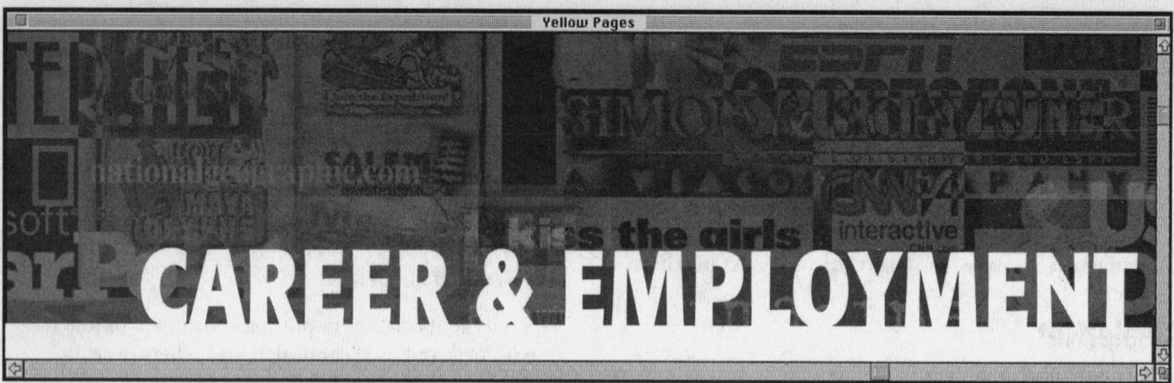

A B C D E F G H I J K L M N O P Q R S T U V W X Y Z

Going to work for a large company is like getting on a train. Are you going sixty miles an hour or is the train going sixty miles an hour and you're just sitting still?

J. Paul Getty

NRP TOP PICKS

America's Employers
http://www.americasemployers.com/

Career Magazine
http://www.careermag.com/

Career Mosaic
http://www.careermosaic.com/

Career Resource Center
http://www.careers.org/

Colossal List of Career Links
http://www.emory.edu/CAREER/Links.html

Cool Works
http://www.coolworks.com/showme/

DICE (Data processing Independent Consultants Exchange)
http://www.dice.com/

E-Span
http://www.espan.com/

Hoover's Online
http://www.hoovers.com/

JobHunt
http://www.job-hunt.org/

The McKinley Group, Inc.
http://www.itgonline.com/McKinley

The Monster Board
http://www.monster.com/

Resume'Net
http://www.resumenet.com/

The Salary Calculator
http://www.homefair.com/homefair/cmr/salcalc.html

100 Careers in Cyberspace

http://www.globalvillager.com/villager/CSC.html

This site is devoted to helping individuals find Internet-related jobs. "Job opening" ads can be posted or searched, as can "job wanted" ads. Search function allows user to specify job title, job location, and educational requirements (or you can see the entire listing at once).

1st Steps in the Hunt

http://www.interbiznet.com/hunt/

1st Steps in the Hunt is a Web guide for job searchers. Formatted like a magazine and updated almost daily, this site provides short profiles of a variety of career-related Internet sites (with links), and discusses issues relevant to job seekers. The site also maintains a nice collection of links to a variety of useful resources. A very good site with an excellent design.

Access Careers & Jobs Resources

http://www.hawk.igs.net/jobresources/

A site prepared for career-minded individuals who want to access useful links to a variety of different utilities that may help them find a job. Examples include links to a personality profile, a research mechanism, and a résumé bulletin board are at this site.

Achievement Corporation

http://www.acorp.co.uk/

Bringing a range of Human Resources and Internet communications services to you from the Web. Check out links to different services that might help you find a job.

ACME Training, Inc.

http://www.gus.com/acme/

A supplier of custom training for corporate clients, Acme training also specializes in Adobe Acrobat (PDF) documents for many uses. Their home page will direct you through several pages, including a company philosophy, a list of projects, and examples of their work.

Advanced Training Professionals

http://www.trainingpros.com/

Providing training services at below-industry standard prices, Advanced Training Professionals is dedicated to delivering world-class training to all forms of industries. Whether you are in business, education, or just want to learn, ATP promises they can help.

Advertising & Media Jobs Page

http://www.nationjob.com/media

Search for jobs in advertising and media by location, position type, salary, and key-word. The "P.J. Scout" can locate jobs of interest and mail them to you each week. For both employers and job seekers.

The Airbase

http://www.airforce.com/

Filled with information about joining the U.S. Air Force. This is where you need to go if you want even more information about becoming an Airman or Airwoman.

The Airline Employment Assistance Corps

http://www2.csn.net/AEAC/

Often visited, the AEAC helps people find jobs in the airline field.

America's Employers

http://www.americasemployers.com/

There are résumé banks, company databases, job search FAQs, and other links that might help you find a job available at this site.

American Management Association

http://www.tregistry.com/ama.htm

The AMA provides the business community with a complete management resource. This page gives you information about membership and what it takes to get in contact with this group.

America's Job Bank

http://www.ajb.dni.us/

Your tax dollars being put to work for you! America's Job Bank is a free service provided by the U.S. Department of Labor and state public Employment Service Agencies. For the job seeker, this site contains over 250,000 job listings (most of which are in the private sector). Employers may post job openings at no cost.

Amerisoft

http://www.apk.net/amerisoft/

If you are from the U.S. and want to be an executive abroad, or if you are an executive in another country who wants to work in the U.S., check out this site. Mostly specializing in data processing and automation consulting, this firm has much information for bright and eager candidates at its Web site.

The Analysis Group

http://www.nichecom.com/~analysis/

Founded in 1988, the Analysis Group offers candidate development services, including full search and recruitment and training in all aspects of recruiting and sourcing.

The Ankarlo Training Group Home Page

http://www.ankarlo.com/

This home page is filled with information about how to advance in today's competitive business environment. It stresses creativity and leadership to attain those goals and gives advice on how to seek them.

A B C D E F G H I J K L M N O P Q R S T U V W X Y Z

Asian Career Web Home Page

http://www.rici.com/acw/

This site is designed to match job seekers who are bilingual in English and an Asian language with international employers. A site for individuals who speak English and the local language of China, Hong Kong, India, Indonesia, Japan, Korea, Malaysia, Philippines, Singapore, Taiwan, Thailand, or Vietnam, and employers looking for such individuals.

Asia-Net, Inc.

http://www.asia-net.com/

Designed for bilingual professionals who are proficient in Japanese, Chinese, or Korean, as well as English. Job seekers can subscribe to a free mailing list that will email job openings to members. Employers looking for bilingual professionals can post job openings.

Atlantic Management Resources

http://users.aol.com/amrecruit/amr.htm

A list of current positions, special openings, interviewing tips, and other information is available at this site.

Benefit Associates

http://www.benefitassociates.com/

Benefit Associates is a recruiting company that specializes in the placement of human resources and employee benefit personnel. There are links to different specializations, as well as jobs and candidates available.

The Best Jobs in the USA Today

http://www.bestjobsusa.com/index.html

For both potential employees and employers, this site hosts many links to aid in employment. There is a Best Jobs Database, a Recruiter's Boardroom, and other important links to assist in your search.

Bolack Total Travel Academy

http://www.bolack.com/school.htm

This site has information for people who are already in travel or who are considering a career in travel. Includes links to seminars, class schedules, and other important aspects of discovering success in the travel business.

Boldface Jobs

http://www.boldfacejobs.com/

At the Boldface Jobs' Web site, job seekers can add their résumés to the online database or search for job openings by specialization and location. Employment agencies and recruiters can add company profiles to the database or post jobs and candidates that they have available.

Broadcast Employment Services–TV Jobs

http://www.tvjobs.com/index_a.htm

A site devoted to the broadcasting profession. Broadcasting professionals can post résumés and search an online Job Bank that lists job openings from around the country. Freelancers can post "situations wanted" ads. Employers can locate individuals with suitable skills. This site also contains a nice set of links to useful resources.

The Business Job Finder

http://www.cob.ohio-state.edu/dept/fin/osujobs.htm

Maintained by the Fisher College of Business at the Ohio State University, the Business Job Finder is a very highly regarded and informative Web site. This site contains information on a variety of business career areas, listings of current jobs, and a variety of other reference material. The information and links the Business Job Finder provides can help you to make wise career decisions.

Butterfass, Pepe & MacCallan, Inc.

http://www.bpmi.com/

With links to the executive search process, principals, specialization, and other areas of functional expertise, this site promises to give information for managers, consultants, and executives.

CaBiT Development

http://rampages.onramp.net/~cabit/

CaBiT Development stands for Computer Based Training Development & Delivery Tools. It consists of a suite of several Windows-based programs that run on PCs used in client/server network environments. This site is where you can find information about obtaining this service.

Caldwell Partners On-line Directory

`http://www.caldwellpartners.com/`

An executive search formed in 1970, this firm's clients are businesses and public organizations who want to fill positions within their respective assemblages. Check this site for professional resources, contacts, and a directory.

Career Center

`http://www.netline.com//Career/career.html`

This site contains a good collection of links to career and employment-oriented Web sites. Short descriptions accompany the links so that you can get an idea of what to expect from the linked sites. Also contains a listing of relevant Internet newsgroups.

Career Center

`http://www.vmedia.com/books/business/sec5/index.htm`

Maintained by Internet Business 500, this site contains a collection of links to employment resources on the World Wide Web. Categories of linked sites include career malls and job fairs, placement resources, want ads, career advisors, headhunters, and Fortune 500 companies.

Career Crafting

`http://www.careercraft.com/`

This site is home to a type of reconsideration therapy. Find out here how to quit the job you always hated, get the job you always wanted, and how not to fear bills and other obstacles.

Career Expo

`http://www.eos.net/careerex/`

If you are looking to become involved in a job fair, this company is the place to check out. They have been organizing fairs for about fifteen years, bringing together engineering, information systems, computer science, and many other professionals with leading U.S. and Canadian companies.

Career Magazine

`http://www.careermag.com/`

An online magazine that provides much more than just feature articles about careers and job hunting. This Web site also includes lists of job openings, employer profiles, a résumé bank, a career forum, directories of recruiters and consultants, a list of job fairs, links to colleges, relocation resources, and other career information. A great resource!

Career Management International

`http://www.cmi-lmi.com/`

Specializing in human resources, there are many links here useful for business-oriented career professionals.

Career Mosaic

`http://www.careermosaic.com/`

Developed by the Bernard Hodes advertising agency, this is an interactive job search tool. You can post your own résumés, look at others, participate in online job fairs, examine a career resource center, and read about entry-level opportunities for college students.

Career Planning Process

`http://www.cba.bgsu.edu/class/webclass/nagye/career/process.html`

Not sure which career to pursue or which career you are suited for? The Career Planning Process site can help. By offering pointers from career counselors and a series of exercises, this site takes a visitor through a number of steps that will help the user define goals and competencies, explore career options, and prepare for a job search or graduate school.

Career Resource Center

http://www.careers.org/

A comprehensive online directory of career resources, this site contains a large collection of links to job listings, employers, career Web sites and publications, educational institutions, and more. All resources are cross-indexed by geographical location (which encompasses North America, Western Europe, Japan and New Zealand).

Career Resource Home Page

http://www.rpi.edu/dept/cdc/homepage.html

This site is filled mainly with links. You can look at career services at universities, an Internet Job Surfer, professional societies, and more.

Career Résumés

http://branch.com/cr/cr.html

With the idea that a résumé should be a marketing tool instead of a simple history, Career Résumés has opportunities for both job seekers and corporations.

career.com

http://www.career.com/

HEART Advertising Network maintains career.com as a service to match job hunters with employers. Job seekers can search the online jobs database by company, location, or discipline. This service is free. Employers can post job openings on the database for a fee. This site also maintains a real-time virtual job fair.

CareerBuilder

http://careerbuilder.com/

CareerBuilder offers personalized job searching services. Individuals can tailor their job search by company, job type, location, and salary, and can electronically submit their résumé if they find an opening that they are interested in. CareerBuilder also offers Personal Search Agents that scan job postings daily and emails summaries of openings that match the member's specifications.

CareerCity

http://www.adamsonline.com/

CareerCity's Web site has three main searchable databases: Job Listings, Job Newsgroups, and Corporate Recruiting Links. Searches in all the databases can be customized so that you can find just what you are looking for.

CareerCity

http://www.careercity.com/

CareerCity's Web site contains a large online database of job openings that can be searched. Employers may post job openings for free. Job searchers can post their résumés to the database if they want. This site also contains a nice collection of resources about job hunting, writing cover letters and résumés, and interviewing.

CareerLab

http://www.careerlab.com/

This site is very user-friendly. There are links to an online bookstore, a quick tour, a testing and assessment area, and information about the company.

CareerMart

http://www.careermart.com/

An extensive career search based on the familiar job fair that you might find at the local university or armory. Search by region, state, or just about in any other fashion.

CareerMosaic

http://www.careermosaic.com/

CareerMosaic is a large Web site with plenty of useful resources for job hunters. This site includes a job and résumé databank, employer profiles, job fair listings, a special section for students and recent graduates, an international gateway, and a career resource center with tips on job-hunting, résumé writing, and links to professional organizations. A great place to start your job search.

CareerPath.com

http://www.careerpath.com/

CareerPath.com posts tens of thousands of job ads each month. Ads are updated by newspapers around the country. Job seekers can specify which newspaper's ads to search, and can specify the job type to search for.

Careers Accounting

http://www.accounting.com/

A site for professionals in accounting and finance. This site allows visitors to add their résumés to the database and search job listings. Also provides links to accounting placement agencies. Businesses can add company profiles to the database as well.

CareerWEB

http://www.cweb.com/

CareerWEB is an extensive search tool useful for just about anyone seeking information about a professional career. There are listings, a résumé pool, and all other sorts of information.

Chancellor and Chancellor, Inc.

http://www.chancellor.com

A brokerage firm offering comprehensive placement services for computer technology professionals. Specializes in services for contractors, contract employees, and full-time software professionals. Contains resources for contractors and links to related sites.

The Chronicle of Higher Education–Academe This Week–Job Openings

http://chronicle.merit.edu/.ads/.links.html

This site is an online listing of academic and administrative job openings in higher education. Visitors can browse job openings by academic field or keyword. Searches can be limited to specific regions, the entire United States, or openings outside of the United States.

ClearWord Communications and Training

http://www.clearword.com/

Clear Modern English for international business and industry is stressed here. Obviously, language is important on both sides—native speakers need to avoid colloquialisms and other turns of phrase that are allusive to non-natives.

College Grad Job Hunter

http://www.collegegrad.com/

You've earned your college degree and now face the prospect of looking for a job. Now what? This site can help sharpen your job-searching skills. From preparations for the job search, to writing cover letters and résumés, to interviewing and negotiating a contract, College Grad Job Hunter contains an array of resources that can help you land that job. Also contains a list of job postings that you can search and a link to the Job Hunter E-zine.

Colossal List of Career Links

http://www.emory.edu/CAREER/Links.html

Maintained by Emory University, this is a fantastic site for the job hunter who is looking for useful sites on the Internet. Not only does the Colossal List contain a great collection of links, but all of the linked sites are thoroughly described and rated. A great help in finding Web sites that will fulfill your needs. Also contains links to resources about graduate and professional schools.

Conceptual Systems, Inc.

http://www.concepsys.com/

Creative solutions to complex problems can be found by seeking the help of CSI. Their Web page has links to people, products, CSI news, and clients.

Cool Works

http://www.coolworks.com/showme/

Slackers and college students rejoice! This site can help you to find a seasonal job in a great place. Search for jobs in resorts, cruise ships, summer camps, National Parks, or ski resorts. As the Cool Works site says, "check out what it takes to live and work in the kinds of places that most people only get to visit."

Cromwell Partners Interactive

http://www.cromwell-partners.com/

Cromwell Partners Interactive is a company that wants to help place people into executive positions. If you are qualified, please check out this well-developed site for more information.

CyberFair

http://www.career.com/cyberfair.html

A new twist on the conventional job fair, this site features a place for employers and job seekers to send for information about potential employment.

Cybermania!

http://www.vni.net/~murtaza/chem395/

CyberMania! is designed to provide chemists and biochemists links to employment opportunities. Whether you are a chemist, a biotechnician, or in medicine, you can find all the links you need at this site.

Cyberspace Jobs

http://www.best.com/~lianne/index.html

Just what kind of job opportunities are there in the world of cyberspace? If you are unsure, you can visit this site to find out. The Cyberspace Jobs page contains profiles of many different types of Internet-related jobs. Also provides links to relevant Web sites and newsgroups for further information.

Damar Group

http://www.dgl.com/cspromo.html

This site presents two different packages and a new approach to training. Both courses are designed to give you training on the Internet.

DICE (Data processing Independent Consultants Exchange)

http://www.dice.com/

This site provides a job search database for computer consultants and high-tech professionals. Offering free services for job seekers, DICE is a "national job advertising service utilized by recruiting firms seeking high tech data processing professionals." Contains current job listings, along with contact information for each.

The Direct Marketing World

http://www.dmworld.com

Contains links to the DM World Job Center; mailing lists and databases; professional listings; a library that includes news, articles, and glossaries; and a DM calendar of events. There are also connections to current news headlines.

DXI Corporation

http://isotropic.com/dxicorp/dxihome.html

Provides contract services to the information processing industry. Lists positions available for contractors. Also includes a newsletter and a list of reasons for hiring contractors.

E-Span

http://www.espan.com/

The first place to look if you are considering using the Web as an employment search tool is E-Span. The site provides a ResumePro Database that you can submit your résumé to for employers to peruse, or you can try either the CareerPro MasterFile Database or the CareerPro Database to search for new job listings.

Edwards and Associates

http://www.worldleader.com/eaa/

Need a part-time manager for your small business? Then this site might have what you are looking for. Browse around corporate magazines, FAQs, or get in contact with this firm.

The Employment Channel Online

http://www.employ.com/

A companion to the Employment Channel, this online site provides information about the TV show, an interactive jobs database, an employment CyberFair, and an employment center which provides information to those looking for work.

Employment Resources for People with Disabilities

http://www.disserv.stu.umn.edu/TC/Grants/COL/listing/disemp/

This site provides a good collection of links to a wide variety of resources available for disabled individuals. The linked sites are briefly described. While most linked sites seem to be in the United States, several are located in Canada and the UK.

Employment Search Productions

http://www.employvideo.com/

If you want to find another job, are unemployed, or simply feel that you are underpaid, you should look at this site. There are links to video self-teaching programs, tips, and other useful links located at this site.

Employnet, Inc.

http://employnet-inc.ksi.com/

Recruiters can register with Employnet online to search a database filled with résumés of potential employees. Job seekers and employers alike should peruse this Web site for help in the job search.

EngineeringJobs.com

http://www.engineeringjobs.com/

This site is devoted primarily to listing jobs in the engineering field and allowing engineers to post their résumés online. EngineeringJobs.com also includes links to engineering references, engineering societies, and other job and résumé Web sites.

Equal Opportunity Publications

`http://www.eop.com/homepage.html`

Home page for the publisher of several magazines devoted to women, minorities, and people with disabilities in the workplace. This site provides information about their magazines, links to businesses seeking employees, listings of job fairs, and a resource page continuing selected articles from their magazines.

executives.ch

`http://executives.ch/`

The executives.ch Web site is an international employment exchange focused on Germany, Austria, and Switzerland. Job listings can be searched by field or geographical region. The site also provides "positions sought" ads and company profiles. A French language version of this site is available at `http://emploi.ch/`. Italian language version of the site is available at `http://imphieghi.ch/`. German language versions of the site is available at `http://stellen.ch` and `http://stellen.com`.

Federal Jobs Digest

`http://www.jobsfed.com/`

This site is the online companion to the *Federal Jobs Digest* periodical. The site contains federal government job listings in a variety of fields—engineering, science & math, computers, medicine, social science & law, law enforcement, accounting & auditing, administration & management, secretarial, clerical, and trade & postal.

Fortune Personnel Consultants

`http://www.conterra.com/fortune/`

This page is geared toward finding qualified candidates for staffing the needs of your company. At this site, you'll find positions in manufacturing and legal positions, as well as information about how to contact this leading placement firm.

Forty Plus of Northern California

`http://www.sirius.com/~40plus/`

Forty Plus is a nonprofit, cooperative organization designed to assist individuals over the age of 40 with career transitions. This site provides information about membership in Forty Plus, provides links to other Forty Plus chapters (located in several states and Toronto, Canada), and provides a listing of member résumés.

FranInfo

`http://www.franinfo.com/`

Looking to own your own business? Or perhaps to franchise the business you already own? If so, this site may help. FranInfo provides a variety of information about buying franchises and franchising your business. The site also contains a list of franchise opportunities.

FSG Online Jobs in Biotechnology, Pharmaceuticals and Medicine

`http://www.medmarket.com/tenants/fsg/`

This site provides a variety of resources for employers and job seekers in the field of science. Job hunters can search for positions and post résumés. Employers can advertise jobs and search the online résumé database. The site also includes some articles on careers in the sciences and job hunting.

GET A JOB

`http://www.getajob.com/`

GET A JOB's Web site allows job seekers to search an online listing of job openings and post résumés to the site's database. Employers can search the résumé database to find suitable candidates. The site also contains some articles on careers and a large, linked list of employment newsgroups.

Get TOP $$$ in a JOB You Love

`http://isdn.net/nis/`

FAQs, résumés, and other answers for the career-minded professional. You can even email career questions to this site's professional staff.

Getting Past Go

`http://www.mongen.com/getgo/`

Getting Past Go is a resource for new and recent college graduates. There is plenty of documentation here that will help you find exactly what you are looking for.

Good Works

`http://www.tripod.com/work/goodworks/`

Is what you do more important to you than how much you make? Do you want to work at a job that is socially responsible? If so, you may want to visit Good Works. Good Works is a national directory of social change organizations. You can search the Good Works job database by organization, position, or location.

Groupweb

`http://groupweb.com/opening/jobs.htm`

A Web site dedicated to employers and job seekers. Employers can post job openings, while seekers can submit résumés.

A Guide to Job Resources by US Region

`http://www.wm.edu/csrv/career/stualum/jregion.html`

Provided by the College of William and Mary, this is an excellent collection of links to career resources on the Web. Visitors can link to sites that contain job listings for particular regions of the United States, comprehensive job listing pages, or pages devoted to particular career fields. A very good place to start your search.

High Technology Careers

`http://www.hightechcareers.com/`

Career management and development, technology trends, and future outlooks are what you'll find available at this site. You can submit your résumé to this site, and they'll post it for you.

Hispanstar

`http://hispanstar.com/`

This Web site is the official home site of *Hispanic Business* magazine. At this site, you can browse through information from Hispanic Business, HispanTelligence research services, and HispanData professional services. The site also contains job listings and offers you the opportunity to submit a résumé to HispanData.

Hoover's Online

`http://www.hoovers.com/`

Hoover's Online bills itself as the ultimate source for company information. This site provides links to company Web sites, company profiles, as well as business and investment information. Job hunters can search the online database, which can be focused upon specific companies, locations, or industries.

Hot Jobs

`http://www.career.com/PUB/hotjob.html`

A simple listing of jobs that are available from mostly electronics companies.

How to Find a Creative Job in the Real World

`http://www.ici.net/cust_pages/dawnl/dawnl.html`

This site is essentially a "CyberEd" course in looking for artistic jobs. You can read stories and check resources here as well.

Human Resource News and Issues

`http://www.newspage.com/browse/46587/46590/`

This page is simply filled with links about today's human resource issues.

The Human Resource Professional's Gateway to the Internet

`http://www.teleport.com/~erwilson/`

Eric Wilson's home page serves as a gateway to Internet sites of interest to Human Resource professionals. Categories of links to be found at this site include HR Web pages, HR and related Listservs, job search sites, HR related companies, and WWW search tools. Most links are annotated to give you a sense of what they contain.

The Image Maker

`http://www.intranet.on.ca/~jwaisvisz/`

A training company based in the U.S. and Canada, the Image Maker has skills seminars offered in English and French. This page has many links that describe the information here.

InfoDesign Group

`http://www.infodsn.com/`

This company offers complete documentation, technical support, and training design and development services. This site has such links as Helping Business into the Future and What InfoDesign Can Do for Your Company. Note that this site currently is undergoing construction.

The Information Professional's Career Page

`http://www.brint.com/jobs.htm`

This Web site contains a wealth of resources relevant to careers in Information Systems. Some of the information contained in this site includes discussions of the changing roles of information executives, issues of professional development, résumé and interview skills, professional associations and societies, career links, and much more. A great resource for information systems professionals.

InPursuit's Employment Network

http://www.inpursuit.com/e-network/

Built from the success of Shawn's Internet Résumé Center, InPursuit has built an entire employment network. Consisting of many career-related services and products, this network allows "the job seeker and the employer to come together."

The Insurance Career Center

http://connectyou.com/talent/

Insurance professionals can search for jobs at this Web site and post their résumés online. Employers can post job openings and search the résumé bank. The site also includes corporate profiles and a directory of national recruiters.

International Homeworker's Association

http://www.homeworkers.com/

The International Homeworker's Association provides services to help those working in their homes to prosper. Their Web site has a members forum, a listing of job postings, and an online résumé bank. The site also describes publications available through the IHA.

The Internet Fashion Exchange

http://www.fashionexch.com/

The Internet Fashion Exchange Web site is a centralized employment marketplace for the fashion and retail industry. The site contains a Candidate Profile area, which can be posted to or searched, as well as a Positions Offered area, which can be searched or added to. The site also includes links to career resources and human resource services.

ISG Computing Careers Online

http://www.isgjobs.com/

Located in the Greater Toronto area, ISG is a firm specializing in the placement of individuals in the information technology field. This Web site allows you to search ISG's Job Bank for contract and permanent positions. The site also maintains a Career Resource Centre, which contains a variety of information and links.

The Jacks Institute

http://www.jackstax.com/

A trainer of tax industry professionals, the Jacks Institute's Web site has links to tax courses and books, tax tips, and a guest book.

Job Fair Home Page

http://www.iupui.edu/it/jobfair/

Select from two different fairs—the Indiana Collegiate Job Fair or the Multicultural Job Fair. Check out employer lists, or contact the coordinator of the fair.

Job Resources by US Region

http://www.wm.edu/csrv/career/stualum/jregion.html

Provided by the College of William and Mary, this is an excellent collection of links to career resources on the Web. Visitors can link to sites that contain job listings for particular regions of the United States, comprehensive job listing pages, or pages devoted to particular career fields. A very good place to start your search.

Job Search and Employment Opportunities: Best Bets from the Net

http://asa.ugl.lib.umich.edu/chdocs/employment/

This guide from the University of Michigan describes and provides links to some of the best career and employment resources on the Internet. The resources are grouped by general fields: Education and Academics, Humanities and Social Sciences, Science and Technology, Business and Government, and Career Development Resources. A good starting point for your searches.

JobCenter

http://www.jobcenter.com/

JobCenter's Web site allows individuals to search job ads and place their résumé online for a fee. JobCenter also offers members the service of having an intelligent agent automatically search job ads and email results. Employers can post job ads at JobCenter for a fee.

JobClips by Internet

http://www.jobclips.com/

JobClips specializes in helping individuals find jobs in the engineering, computer and information science fields. JobClips will search for job openings that meet your specifications and will email results to you weekly.

The JobExchange

http://www.jobexchange.com/

Featuring membership opportunities for job search and recruiting, this site also boasts a candidate database to help search for qualified individuals to fill positions.

JobHunt

http://www.job-hunt.org/

This Web site rightly bills itself as "A Meta-list of Online Job-Search Resources and Services." JobHunt contains a great collection of links to job listings, companies, newsgroups, recruiting agencies, résumé banks, university career resource centers, and more. Well worth a visit.

Jobs & Careers Online

http://www.servonet.com/jobs

This site contains an online listing of classified ads. The classifieds are broken down into categories, which include administration, finance, sales, education, medical and dental, technical, and more.

JobServe

http://www.jobserve.com/

The JobServe Web site is a good source for individuals in the Information Technology field who are looking for employment in the United Kingdom. This site allows the visitor to search the online Job Server, and offers the opportunity to subscribe to a mailing list that sends email messages daily listing the latest job vacancies.

JobSmart

http://jobsmart.org/index.htm

Maintained by Bay Area public libraries, this site is a good source of information for job seekers in Northern California. JobSmart provides access to career guides, information about résumés and salaries, job ads, job hotlines, and job fairs.

JOBTRAK

http://www.jobtrak.com/

JOBTRAK works in partnership with colleges, universities, and career centers across the U.S. to provide a centralized source of job listings and information for recent or prospective graduates. This Web site includes online job and résumé databanks, links to recruiters and graduate school programs, and job searching tips.

JobWeb

http://www.jobweb.org/

JobWeb is a huge collection of links to resources on the Internet. If you need information about jobs, the job search, human resources, or career planning, chances are that you will find what you are looking for here. A service provided by the National Association of Colleges and Employers.

Library Job Hunting

http://tigger.cc.uic.edu/~aerobin/libjob.html

If you are looking to find hands-on experience and are in Library Science, this is the place to look. This page was written by a person who collected information in a search for a job for himself.

Marketing Classifieds

http://www.marketingjobs.com/

This site focuses on marketing jobs and is for both employers and job seekers. For the former, you can post a job and search a résumé database. For the latter, search the marketing classifieds, email the marketing classifieds your résumé, and examine company profiles.

The McKinley Group, Inc.

http://www.itgonline.com/McKinley

This home page for the McKinley Group provides information about their developmental workshops made to meet a company's specific needs. It also includes links related to this company's service.

Michael Latas & Associates, Inc.

http://www.latas.com/

A full-service executive search and professional recruiting firm, Michael Latas & Associates has an ideology of divide and conquer; they have divisions that work exclusively in different areas of expertise. Check out this site to request information or read more about this firm's ideology and impressive record.

Michigan Association of Personnel Services

http://www.michjobs.com/

The Michigan Association of Personnel Services was founded in 1945 with the objective of providing personnel services to clients within Michigan and the United States. This site has links to Officers and Directors, member firms, and geographical location of employment opportunities.

MMWIRE Classifieds

http://www.mmwire.com/classifieds.html

MMWIRE Classifieds contains job opportunities in multimedia, video games, interactive entertainment, and online services. Job seekers can search for employment opportunities by specific company or by position.

The Monster Board

http://www.monster.com/

This site is called the Monster Board for a reason. It is filled with plenty of links associated with jobs, careers, and companies.

NACCB Online Job Board & Resume Bank

http://computerwork.com/

This free service is provided by the National Association of Computer Consultant Businesses. Devoted to helping individuals find technical jobs and contract opportunities, the site allows you to post your résumé to their databank and search their online job board. Also allows for searches of local NACCB member companies.

National Business Employment Weekly

http://www.nbew.com/

The online companion to the print version of the *National Business Employment Weekly*. This Web site provides a table of contents of the current issue, as well as selected full text articles from current and past issues. The site also provides information about print subscriptions and books that can be purchased.

National Center for Tooling & Precision Components (NCTPC)

http://www.utoledo.edu/www/nctpc/

This Web site for the nonprofit organization formed to provide programs in training, education, technical and business assistance, and research and development to "improve the competitive positions of U.S. tooling and manufacturing companies."

National Directory of Emergency Services

http://www.policejobs.com/

Sponsored by Eagle Visions, this Web site contains current job listings for fire and police departments. Membership in Eagle Visions is required to view the database, and is available at this site.

National Diversity Journalism Job Bank

http://www.newsjobs.com/

Sponsored by the Florida Times-Union, this site is designed to help journalists find jobs. The National Diversity Journalism Job Bank allows you to search for jobs on the online database or post your résumé. It also provides links to other job banks and a nice collection of journalism resources.

NationJob Online Jobs Database

http://www.nationjob.com/

The NationJob is a nationwide jobs database with a Midwest focus. Search the online database or sign up for the free P.J. Scout service, which will search the listings for you and e-mail you the results. You can also search for jobs at particular companies or look at company profiles at this Web site.

NetConnections

http://www.christworks.net/

A career networking organization, NetConnection groups different resources by region. You can also peruse the NASS Membership Directory, the PARW Membership Directory, or other links at this site.

Online Career Center

http://www.occ.com/index.html

The Online Career Center allows you to search a job listing database, a résumé database, and a database of company information and profiles. Job seekers can sign up for automated "agents" which will search job listings for them and allow them to see the results the next time they log in.

Online Sports Career Center

http://www.onlinesports.com./pages/CareerCenter.html

The Online Sports Career Center's Web site contains a job bank that lists sports-related career opportunities. The site also includes a résumé bank which can be searched or posted to, as well as a set of links to other career resources.

Pemberton and Associates

http://www.biddeford.com/pemberton/

A "comprehensive human resource solution," this site is filled with information about this company's services. Whether you need compensation and benefit administration, recruitment services, or training and development programs, this company can help.

Peritas Online

http://www.peritas.com/

A well-formatted page, there is an online training promotion available at this site. You can also check out the KnowledgePool consortium—the World's largest commercial training education group.

Physicians Employment

http://www.physemp.com/

This Web site lists employment opportunities for physicians, nurses, and allied health care professionals. Also included in the site is a listing of fellowship and residency programs. Hospitals and Clinics, as well as health care recruiting firms, can post a limited number of job openings on the site for free.

Practical Management, Inc.

http://www.practmgt.com/

Management and instructor development are what you'll find at Practical Management's home page. There is much information here, as well as links to some courses.

ProMatch '97

http://www.promatch.org/

A page filled with links, it can help with program outlines, a résumé profile, and an industry council. You can join this organization, so check out the link called Membership Requirements if this group meets your career needs.

Radio/Recording Career Connection

http://www.sna.com/musicbiz/

On-the-job training for qualified individuals of audio recording can be found from the company who owns this site. You'll find information about how to contact this firm, as well as other information about what they do.

Recruiters OnLine Network

http://www.ipa.com/

Recruiters OnLine Network is an online association and resource for the employment industry. Their Web site contains a jobs database that can be searched by job seekers or posted to by member firms and recruitment services. Those searching for employment can also post a résumé or CV to the online database for free.

Recruiters OnLine Network

http://www.ipa.com/

As a worldwide online association and resource to help discover meaningful employment, this site has many links to help you find a job. RON is a large association of individuals and firms linked together in the online community as a virtual association of employment professionals. Check out the different links that give listings, résumés, and associates for the latest information in your job search.

Resume Innovations

http://www.résumé-innovations.com/

Resume Innovations can help you develop a professional and effective résumé. Services that they provide include assisting you in preparing your résumé, printing your résumé and cover letters, and posting an online version of your résumé. This site also allows employers to search the online résumé bank.

Resume'Net

http://www.resumenet.com/

Resume'Net wants to help you put your résumé on the World Wide Web. In addition to offering résumé development and printing services, Resume'Net will also allow you to create a Web page that contains your résumé. Their Web site also contains a nice set of links to other career services available on the Internet.

Riccione & Associates, Inc.

http://www.riccione.com/

Riccione & Associates specializes in executive search and placement services for individuals in the computer hardware and software industries. They handle both permanent placement and contract work, and have job listings for both areas in their Web site.

The Riley Guide–Employment Opportunities and Job Resources on the Internet

http://www.jobtrak.com

Compiled by Margaret Riley, this guide provides a great deal of information about how to use the Internet to aid in your job search. The site contains lots of links to various resources of interest, and is a good starting place for anyone who is looking for work and wants to tap into the wealth of information contained on the Internet.

Ronaldi's MBA Job Finder

http://www.wvu.edu/~colbe/person/students/résumés/marcus.htm

This page is provided by West Virginia University in order to provide a clearinghouse of career-related information for MBA students. Whether you are seeking a job with a worldwide employer, in a particular city, or by a particular type of company, you'll find what you need at this address.

RootLearning, Inc.

http://rootlearning.com/

They call themselves pioneers in the emerging technology of Learnegy. Filled with Macromedia documents, this page claims that everyone "from the CEO to the shop floor operator" must "understand and respond to the vital economic, competitive, productivity, and customer (quality and value) issues that will shape the organization's future." Note that this site currently is being redesigned.

The Salary Calculator

http://www.homefair.com/homefair/cmr/salcalc.html

You are thinking of relocating to another city, but are unsure whether you can afford to do so. The relocation calculator allows you to determine the salary you would need to make in a new city, based on cost-of-living differences. The site also automatically provides links to relocation services and Realtors that serve the city you are considering moving to.

Saludos Web

http://www.saludos.com/

Saludos Web, a service provided by *Saludos Hispanos* magazine, is devoted exclusively to promoting Hispanic careers and education. This site allows you to view articles from the magazine, explore information about education and careers, and search a national listing of jobs. Saludos Web also provides links to Hispanic-related Internet resources, as well as other employment resources on the Internet.

Science Professional Network

http://recruit.sciencemag.org/

A service provided by Science Online, the Science Professional Network contains a searchable database of Science classified advertisements, a resource center, lists of meetings and career fairs, and links to academic science departments.

SENET Career Expo Home Page

http://www.senetcareer.com/

A source employment network, SENET Career Expo wants to provide job placement through career expos, diversity and minority job fairs, effective résumé writing skills, and other career programs. There are many links at this site to peruse.

SHRM Online

http://www.shrm.org/

This is the Web site for the Society for Human Resource Management. SHRM Online contains a great deal of information for human resource professionals, including links to HR News and HR Magazine, seminar and conference listings, white papers, job openings, and more. A good resource for those in the HR field.

Silicon Valley Employment Opportunities

http://www.netview.com/jobs/

The Silicon Valley Employment Opportunities page contains a collection of links to specific businesses and recruitment firms located in Silicon Valley, Web sites specializing in employment in California, as well as national employment Web sites.

SkillSearch

http://www.internet-is.com/skillsearch/faq.html

SkillSearch bills itself as a service for individuals who aren't actively looking for a job. They provide links between experienced professionals and companies that could use their skills. Members of this service have a personal database record, which SkillSearch compares with employer requests. If they find a potential match, they will send the member's résumé directly to the employer.

Source Services Home Page

http://www.experienceondemand.com/

Source Services is located in more than 50 cities across the United States and Canada, and has 8 divisions that handle a number of different industries and job types. Their Web site explains the various services that they offer, provides advice to job seekers, and offers you the opportunity to search their job listings.

Stressmaster

http://www.stressmaster.com/

The self-proclaimed "Leader in Stressmastery Training and Products," this site is very businesslike in approach—simple, dignified. Read lists of different types of programs or follow links to programs offered by the company.

StudentCenter.com

http://www.StudentCenter.com/

StudentCenter helps college, graduate students, and recent graduates identify their personal strengths, define their career goals, and learn about those companies that best match their interests. They provide advice and information about all phases of a job search. They also provide information about major cities in the United States and abroad, which can be helpful to those considering relocating.

Success Express Journal

http://www.success.ie/

Success Express Journal online is host to a weekly magazine. Check out the Tips from the Top, Book Reviews, and more at this site.

Summer Jobs

http://www.summerjobs.com/

Summer Jobs is a database of seasonal and part-time job opportunities. Although focusing primarily upon the U.S., the database contains opportunities in other countries as well. The jobs database can be searched by job location or type. Employers can post job openings to the database.

TechCareers

http://www.techweb.com/careers/careers.html

TechCareers is a useful Web site for employers and professionals in the high technology field. Employers can post job openings to the online database. Job seekers can search the database for free. The site also contains weekly news columns about high tech careers, salary surveys, and a collection of links to other Internet resources.

Technology Registry

http://techreg.com/

Technology Registry is an interactive, online employment database. Professionals in the technology field can submit profiles to be added to the database, whether they are actively looking for employment or would like to keep abreast of interesting opportunities. Employers can find suitable job candidates by searching the database.

TLC Seminars

http://www.tlcsem.com/

A training seminar based in choice. There are links to several different types of training sessions, including Presentation Skill Training, Instructor Training, and Custom Training Development.

TOPjobs USA

http://www.topjobsusa.com/

The TOPjobs USA Web site has won honors in several Internet employment ratings. This site contains a searchable job database, employer database, and consultant database, as well as providing career advice and links to other Internet career resources.

Total Human Resources

http://www.totalhr.com/thr/

If you are looking for fair policies for your company that are current and uphold today's federal and state laws, this site is for you. Total Human Resources is a consulting firm with comprehensive help.

Training Express

`http://www.trainx.com/`

Not only nice looking, the Training Express Web site is filled with information about their systems, how to order them, and an online catalog of training materials. There is also a page filled with links concerning training.

unisoft.net

`http://www.unisoft.net/`

Bandwidth-heavy, but very nice-looking; unisoft.net offers a program called CVexe. In an attempt to help make your résumé more attractive to potential employers, CVexe wants to help present your résumé in a unique and accessible way.

The Virtual Job Fair

`http://www.vjf.com/`

The Virtual Job Fair is exactly what it says it is. Includes a library, links to searches and expos, a résumé center, and high tech careers. Formatted for both graphical browsers and text-only browsers, you can look at a table of contents or use an image map of the fair to navigate the site.

Vital Learning Corporation

`http://www.vital-learning.com/`

The Vital Learning Corporation is an online training academy that offers state-of-the-art tools developed for computer-based training. At this site, you can request more information, read about products, and join a mailing list.

Welcome to Advance: The Home Page of High-Tech Careers

`http://philanet.com/news/advance/table.html`

This site is a companion to Advance: The Magazine of High-Tech Careers. The Advance Web site contains subscription and advertising information about the magazine, as well as a listing of high-tech job opportunities.

Westech Career Expo

`http://www.vjf.com/pub/westech/`

At this site, you can put your résumé in a database or check out job fairs that are close to your hometown—they even include maps. You can also peruse other resources, such as careers magazines and other resources.

What Color is Your Parachute: The Net Guide

`http://washingtonpost.com/parachute`

The Washington Post and Dick Bolles, author of the well-known book *What Color is Your Parachute*, present this site as an online resource to help job seekers. Full of advice on how to utilize the Internet in a job hunt, as well as recommendations on the best Internet sites to visit. Bolles regularly appears online to answer questions posed by visitors to the site.

whatNOW?

`http://www.halcyon.com/whatnow/`

Techniques to land the job that you want are located at this site. There are links to tips, topics, career resource centers, and experts that you can look at, or if you'd rather, you can purchase the video that promises to "turn interviews into job offers."

Which Job Fair is Right for You?

`http://www.psijobfair.com/a-fair.html`

This site consists of a list of different types of job fairs. Each description is relatively short, and has links to locations, times, and dates.

WITI Campus—Women in Technology International

`http://www.witi.com/`

Women in Technology International's WITI Campus Web site is a great source of information for women working in the high technology field. This is a well-designed and comprehensive Web site that covers a number of different areas, including career resources for women in the technology field. Job hunters will want to visit the job opportunities section of the site.

The World Wide Web Employment Office

`http://www.harbornet.com/biz/office/annex.html`

The World Wide Web Employment Office provides job listings and résumé banks that can be searched by visitors. Job seekers are offered the opportunity to have their résumés posted to the online database. Jobs and résumés can be searched by field of interest. The site provides job and résumé information for the United States and abroad.

world.hire

`http://world.hire.com/`

The world.hire site is an online employment recruiting service. At this site, employers can recruit suitable candidates over the Internet, and job seekers can post their résumés to gain maximum exposure.

Xplore Business

`http://www.xplore.com/xplore500/medium/business.html`

The Xplore Business Web site contains a collection of links to various business-related resources on the Internet. Whether you are looking for business-related career pages, governmental agencies, or online magazines, Xplore Business may have the link that you need.

LISTSERVS

ALIENS-L—Taxation/Witholding/Reporting Requirements for Payments to Aliens

You can join this group by sending the message "sub ALIENS-L your name" to

`listserv@utkvm1.utk.edu`

BLIND-JOBS-L—Employment Issues Concerning Blind People

You can join this group by sending the message "sub BLIND-JOBS-L your name" to

`listserv@sjuvm.stjohns.edu`

CAREER-L—SUNY-wide Career Development Organization List

You can join this group by sending the message "sub CAREER-L your name" to

`listserv@bingvmb.cc.binghamton.edu`

ECOLOG-L—Ecological Society of America: Grants, Jobs, News

University of Maryland CSC, College Park, MD

You can join this group by sending the message "sub ECOLOG-L your name" to

`listserv%umdd.bitnet@listserv.net`

FEDJOBS—Federal Job Bulletin Board

Dartmouth College, Hanover, NH

You can join this group by sending the message "sub FEDJOBS your name" to

`listserv@listserv.dartmouth.edu`

ICEN-L—ICEN-L International Career and Employment Network (NAFSA)

University Computing Services, Indiana University

You can join this group by sending the message "sub ICEN-L your name" to

`listserv@iubvm.ucs.indiana.edu`

JOB-LIST—Job Offers from EARN Institute members

You can join this group by sending the message "sub JOB-LIST your name" to

`listserv@gumncc.terena.nl`

JOB-TECH—Technology and Employment Conference

University of Illinois at Chicago, Chicago, IL

You can join this group by sending the message "sub JOB-TECH your name" to

`listserv@uicvm.uic.edu`

JOBANALYSIS—Jobanalysis Discussion List

Virginia Tech

You can join this group by sending the message "sub JOBANALYSIS your name" to

`listserv@listserv.vt.edu`

JOBPLACE—JobPlace (Self Directed Job Search Techniques and Job Placement)

National Association of Colleges and Employers, Bethlehem, PA

You can join this group by sending the message "sub JOBPLACE your name" to

`listserv@news.jobweb.org`

JOBVAC-L—OSU Job Vacancy Listings

You can join this group by sending the message "sub JOBVAC-L your name" to

`listserv@listserv.okstate.edu`

LABNEWS—News of Labor Unions & Workplace Organizing

You can join this group by sending the message "sub LABNEWS your name" to

`listserv@ucbcmsa.bitnet`

LIBJOBS—Library and Information Science Jobs mailing List

National Library of Canada, Ottawa, Ontario, Canada

You can join this group by sending the message "sub LIBJOBS your name" to

`listserv@infoserv.nlc-bnc.ca`

MBACAREER-L—Career Counsellors for MBA Students

You can join this group by sending the message "sub MBACAREER-L your name" to

`listserv@pdomain.uwindsor.ca`

MOONLIGHT-L

You can join this group by sending the message "sub moonlight-l your name" to

`listserv@netcom.com`

SLAJOB—Special Libraries Association Employment Opportunities

University Computing Services, Indiana University

You can join this group by sending the message "sub SLAJOB your name" to

`listserv@iubvm.ucs.indiana.edu`

STC—School to Careers: The Purpose of Public Education

You can join this group by sending the message "sub STC your name" to

`listserv@listserv.syr.edu`

STUDEMP—Issues Related to Student Employment

University of Arizona, Tucson, AZ

You can join this group by sending the message "sub STUDEMP your name" to

`listserv@listserv.arizona.edu`

SUMMJOBS—Summer Job Information List from Career Services

You can join this group by sending the message "sub SUMMJOBS your name" to

`listserv@ricevm1.rice.edu`

SWJOBS—AD&A Software Jobs Weekly

L-Soft International, Inc.

You can join this group by sending the message "sub SWJOBS your name" to

`listserv@peach.ease.lsoft.com`

TESLJB-L—Jobs and Employment Issues (TESL-L sublist)

You can join this group by sending the message "sub TESLJB-L your name" to

`listserv@cunyvm.cuny.edu`

NEWSGROUPS

`ab.jobs`

`atl.jobs`

`atl.resumes`

`aus.ads.jobs`

`austin.jobs`

`az.jobs`

`ba.jobs.agency`

`ba.jobs.contract`

`ba.jobs.misc`

`ba.jobs.offered`

`ba.jobs.resumes`

`balt.jobs`

`bc.jobs`

`be.jobs`

`bermuda.jobs.offered`

`bionet.jobs`

`bionet.jobs.offered`

`bionet.jobs.wanted`

`biz.jobs`

`biz.jobs.offered`

`can.jobs`

`chi.jobs`

`cmh.jobs`

`dc.jobs`

`dfw.jobs`

`dod.jobs`

`fl.jobs`

`hepnet.jobs`

`houston.jobs`

`houston.jobs.offered`

`houston.jobs.wanted`

`hsv.jobs`

`ie.jobs`

`iijnet.jobs`

`il.jobs.misc`

`il.jobs.offered`

`in.jobs`

`ithaca.jobs`

`kc.jobs`

`kw.jobs`

`la.jobs`

`li.jobs`

`lou.lft.jobs`

`memphis.employment`

`mi.jobs`

`milw.jobs`

`misc.jobs.contract`

`misc.jobs.fields.chemistry`

`misc.jobs.offered`

`misc.jobs.offered.entry`

`misc.jobs.resumes`

`mn.jobs`

nb.jobs
ne.jobs
ne.jobs.contract
nebr.jobs
nj.jobs
nm.jobs
nv.jobs
nyc.jobs.contract
nyc.jobs.misc
nyc.jobs.offered
nyc.jobs.wanted
oh.jobs
ont.jobs
osu.jobs
ott.jobs
pa.jobs.offered
pa.jobs.wanted
pdaxs.jobs
pdaxs.jobs.clerical
pdaxs.jobs.computers
pdaxs.jobs.construction
pdaxs.jobs.delivery
pdaxs.jobs.domestic
pdaxs.jobs.engineering
pdaxs.jobs.management
pdaxs.jobs.misc
pdaxs.jobs.resumes
pdaxs.jobs.retail
pdaxs.jobs.sales
pdaxs.jobs.secretary
pdaxs.jobs.temporary
pdaxs.jobs.wanted
pgh.jobs.offered
pgh.jobs.wanted
phl.jobs.offered
phl.jobs.wanted
qc.jobs
sac.jobs
sat.jobs
sdnet.jobs.offered
sdnet.jobs.services
sdnet.jobs.wanted
seattle.jobs.offered
seattle.jobs.wanted
slac.jobs
slo.jobs
stl.jobs
swnet.jobs
tnn.jobs
tor.jobs
triangle.jobs
tx.jobs
uark.jobs
ucb.jobs
ucd.jobs
us.jobs.contract
us.jobs.offered
us.jobs.resumes
ut.jobs
utcs.jobs
va.jobs
vegas.jobs
wyo.jobs
za.ads.jobs

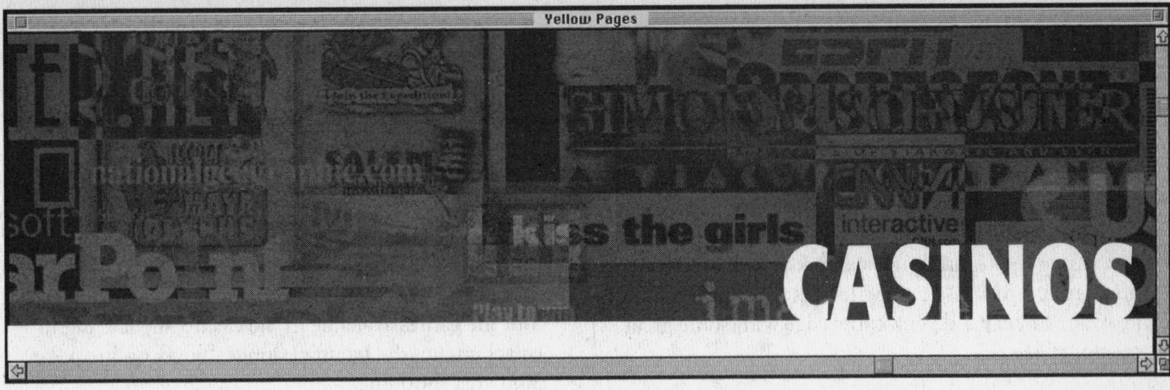

A B C D E F G H I J K L M N O P Q R S T U V W X Y Z

The gambling known as business looks with austere disfavor upon the business known as gambling.

Ambrose Bierce

American Indian Casinos Directory

http://www.bhw.com/lonestar/

Gaming on Indian reservations is big business these days. Twenty-six states now have Indian gaming, all in rural, less traveled areas. Find out where they are by ordering the Directory of American Indian Casinos and Bingo Halls. Fill out your request and receive your information in moments.

British Casino Association

http://www.british-casinos.co.uk/

The BCA is the casino industry's trade association in Great Britain where there are 115 licensed casinos located in the cities and provincial towns of Great Britain, including Scotland and Wales. Read up on the gaming regulations of the industry in this country, which are considered to be the most strictly regulated in the world. This site lists addresses and phone numbers of all 115 by location.

Casino Boat News & Gaming Report

http://members.aol.com/CasinoBoat/cbn.html

Monthly newsletter of America's shipboard and riverboat gambling tracks the operations of day cruise ships and riverboat casinos across the U.S. Check out the current headlines or search the archives for past news. You can also link to state gaming sites that offer specific news about the gaming industry in that area.

Casino Center
http://www.casinocenter.com/

Casino Center

http://www.casinocenter.com/

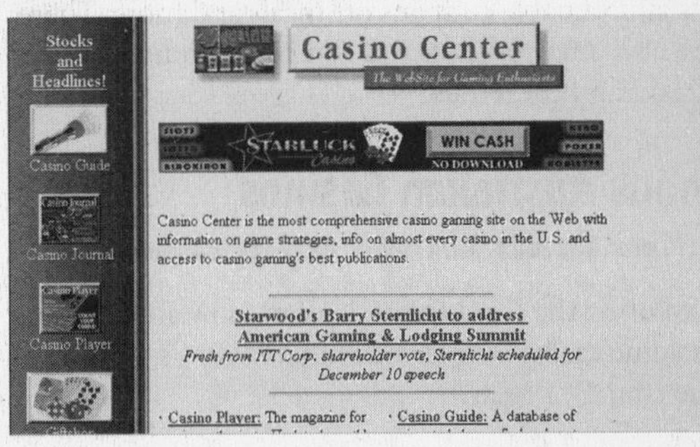

The gaming enthusiast needs to bookmark this comprehensive site. Brush up on your gaming tips and strategies with the online gaming magazine, find out information on hundreds of casinos across the country from an extensive database, and learn the rules of all the casino games from Keno to blackjack. Also, you can check out current stock prices and company news from the industry's publicly owned companies.

Casino City

http://www.casinocity.com/

This glitzy site makes you feel like you're on the Strip in Vegas. Browse the Bookstore and order online. Search the casino database. Try your hand at the Virtual Casino. Or go to Wall Street and take a gamble on gaming stocks. And for the diehard enthusiast, there's a Who's Who of casino executives.

Related Sites

http://www.casinomagic.com/

http://www.cliffcastle.com/

http://www.casino-network.com/lodg.html

Cyn's Casinos and Gaming Web Guide

http://pages.prodigy.com/CasinoGaming/index.htm

A great guide to the many casino and gaming sites on the Web. If you're looking for a casino in Argentina, you can find a link to it on the Casinos page. If you want to chat about the latest in craps playing, the Discussing the Games page will link you to a host of newsgroups, forums, mailing lists, and bulletin boards. Plus, expand your knowledge with some great casino trivia.

Discounts at Las Vegas Hotels & Casinos

http://www.vacationweb.com/userx/LVHotCas/LVHotCas/discounted-hotels-casinos.html

Are you a bargain hunter? Check out the vacation discounts available through this site. Not only can you get great rates, but you can score some free show tickets and valuable coupons off meals and more. There are also links to where you can get discount airline tickets and car rentals.

Famous Australian Casinos

http://www.wps.com.au/travel/clients/casiohm.htm

Exploring the Land Down Under? How about taking in some casinos while you're there? Here's a listing of the country's best.

Hilton Hotels Corporation

http://www.ballys.com/

Bally's Hotels and Casinos of Las Vegas, Atlantic City, New Orleans, and Mississippi can all be accessed here. You can find room rates, casino information, entertainment schedules, and more for each of these Bally resorts.

Mississippi Casinos

http://www.mississippicasinos.com/

Thirteen casinos populate the Mississippi Gulf Coast. Discount gaming vacation packages and free stuff are for the taking, and this is the place to cash in. Also, check out the area weather, maps, entertainment, and golf opportunities. There are also links to Mississippi's Memphis area casinos.

Player's Edge

http://www.playersedge.com/

Player's Edge is an e-zine devoted to gaming and casino issues. Features cover various industry topics, specific casinos, and even book reviews. Visit the Ask the Pro column for answers to your gambling questions. You can also download freeware and check the odds on different sporting events.

Royal Cabana Casino

http://www.royalcabana.com/

Navigate through Aruba's largest casino resort. Check out the games available in the casino, the late night snack menu, the Iguana Lounge, bingo, online poker, and area shopping.

Sands Hotel & Casino

http://www.acsands.com/

One of Atlantic City's best casinos comes to your desktop. This resort offers the latest games, world-class performers, and high-quality dining. Reservations are just a mouse click away. If you're feeling lucky, enter the online sweepstakes to win a BMW. Or check out the company's financial report and job opportunities.

Spirit Mountain Casino

http://www.spirit-mountain.com/

This casino, offering the best in casino games and entertainment, is operated by the Confederated Tribes of the Grand Ronde Community of Oregon and is located well away from the bustle of the city. Check out the complimentary shuttle bus service from Portland and Salem. There's also an interesting page covering where and how casino revenues are being invested in the community.

The Casino Net

http://www.the-casino-net.com/

A comprehensive directory of casinos and casino-related news. Search the casino database by location, name, or type of game. Visit casinos located around the world or in your backyard and even make reservations online. Also, read up on the latest in gaming news. Fill out the guestbook and enter yourself in a weekly prize drawing.

Trump Casino

http://www.trumpindiana.com/

Visit Trump Casino, a mega-yacht just outside Chicago, in Northwest Indiana. In addition to travel packages and casino information, find out about the Trump Club, a way to redeem instant cash, complimentary meals, Trump products, and more.

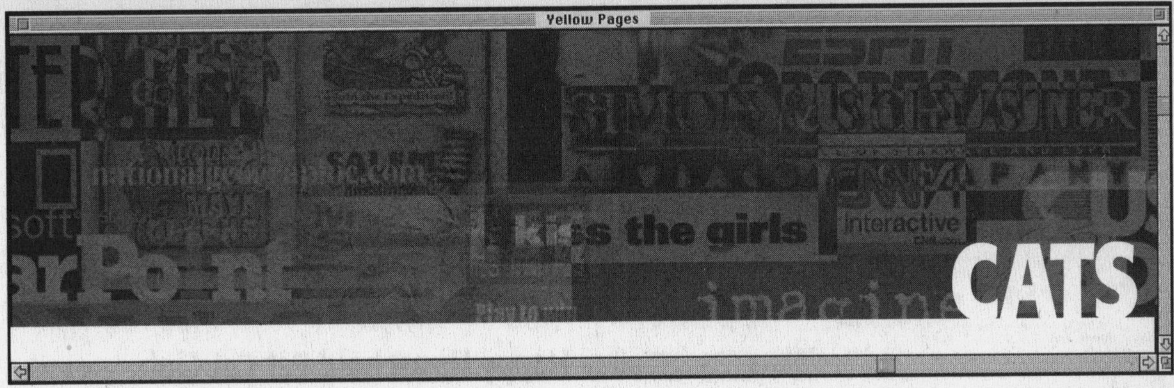

> Dogs come when they're called, cats take a message and get back to you.
>
> *Mary Bly*

Bad Kitty!

http://geog.utoronto.ca/reynolds/pethumor/badkitty.html

A very long list of promises that a family cat makes to its owners, including which annoying habits will stop, how bathroom etiquette is to be observed, how bodily functions will no longer interfere with their lives, and much more. The site also included lists for dogs, rabbits, iguanas, and horses.

Beware of Cat!

http://www.geocities.com/Heartland/Meadows/6485/

Surfing all of these cat sites may give you a taste for them. If you decide to add cat pages to your own site, come here to find a wide array of feline graphics, animation, backgrounds, and icons.

Big Cats On Line

http://dialspace.dial.pipex.com/agarman/

This offers information regarding all aspects of nondomestic cats, including their conservation. Many links to other sites are provided.

Related Sites

http://dccorner.bayside.net/Other/youcanhelp.html

http://www.indy.net/~catshavn/

http://ourworld.compuserve.com/homepages/PAL/

http://www.xmission.com/~emailbox/catring.html

Why Cats Paint
http://www.netlink.co.nz/~monpa/index.html

Catsbuzz Bookstore

http://members.aol.com/catsbuzz/SCREEN.htm

Books, books, and more books about cats—books about specific breeds, books with general information, books for kids, and books for Christmas. Link over to Catsbuzz Central and check out cats in the news, great cat links, and cat poetry.

Cat Fanciers' Home Page

http://www.fanciers.com/

Provides cat-related information. Offers numerous FAQs on different cat breeds, feline health, and care issues. Offers links to show schedules, cat organizations, FTP and gopher sites, as well as links to commercial sites, picture sites, and cat owners' home pages.

Cat House (EFBC/FCC) Home Page

http://www.cathouse-fcc.org/

Contains pictures and some audio clips straight from the cat's mouth. The Cat House (a.k.a. the Feline Conservation Center) is a desert zoo that contains a variety of wild cat species. More than 50 cats, representing 13 species, live at the compound. Includes photos of recent births.

Cats

http://www.reallyuseful.com/Cats/index.html

Based on a series of T.S. Eliot poems, the musical *Cats* has become one of the most popular musicals ever. You can use this site to buy Cats merchandise and tickets, learn about Cats-related news, and join a forum dedicated to discussing the show.

The Cheetah's Workshop

http://bigcats.com/index.html

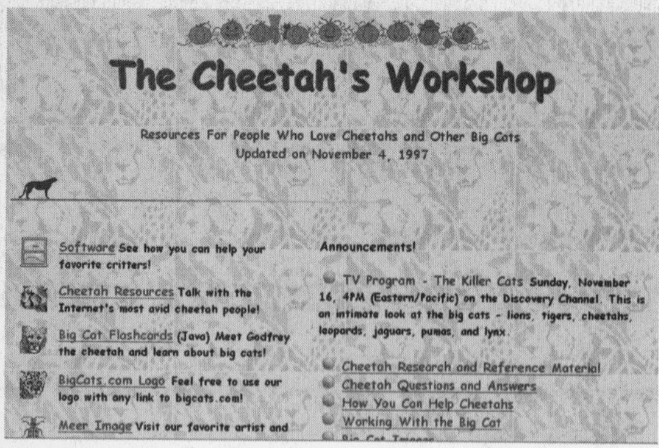

This site indexes societies, parks, government agencies, and volunteer organizations devoted to preservation of animals in the wild and their habitats. The Workshop offers their own software creations to visitors with the request that donations be sent to further their efforts. Be sure to visit the photo galleries and the BIG CATS page.

Cindy's Cat Pages

http://www.afn.org/~afn47757/

Contains resources for feline information, but also has extensive reviews of other cat sites. Check out the cat poetry, the Black Panther Awards, cat "tales," book reviews, and more. Forms are provided for application to membership into CLAW, the most exclusive club for cats.

Dr. PepperSauce–Counselor

http://www.getnet.com/~slick/drpep.html

Sponsored by an honest-to-goodness animal psychologist, Dr. PepperSauce a cat counselor—a cat who is a counselor, that is—who "paws" questions from around the globe concerning cat behavior, health, and nutrition.

Feline Information

http://www.animalclinic.com/catpage.htm

This page offers extensive info and advice concerning major diseases that cats suffer, from leukemia to diabetes. The style is in a familiar question & answer format, so even non-veterinarians can understand.

Feline Information Page

http://www.best.com/~sirlou/cat.shtml

How do you say "cat" in Hawaiian? Find that out and more at this fun site filled with stories, photos, and factual information on the care and feeding of cats. In addition, you can study the history and evolution of cats as a species. (By the way, "cat" in Hawaiian is Popoki!)

Happy Household Pet Cat Club

http://www.best.com/~slewis/HHPCC/

The Happy Household Pet Cat Club (HHPCC), a 28-year-old international organization, is geared toward cat owners who want to exhibit their feline companions in cat shows. HHPCC's Web site offers access to a bi-monthly newsletter, membership information, and info on how you can get the most out of showing your household cat in shows.

How to Toilet Train Your Cat

http://www.rainfrog.com/mishacat/toilet.shtml

If you're tired of buying cat litter and emptying it, it may be time to consider toilet training. No, really, you can toilet trian your cat! This site offers its own advice and techniques and mentions those given by a host of books on the subject.

Index of /multimed/pics/feline

http://sunsite.sut.ac.jp/multimed/pics/feline/

Lets visitors view and/or download images of lions, tigers, cougars, cheetahs, and other large cats.

LAL Cat Archive

http://www.imall.com/archives/cat.html

Offers pictures of cats—many cat pictures in GIF format, many of them quite large. Also contains links to more cat pictures as well as other cat-related sites. Enables you to send your cat's picture for display.

Mystic Molly of the Web

http://web.ukonline.co.uk/Members/keith.dumble/

Molly is a furry fortune teller and horoscope reader. Lottery players will appreciate her methods for picking this week's numbers. Occasionally, Molly makes live Web appearances, and be sure to get your Mystic Molly T-shirt.

PetCat

http://www.petcat.com/petcat/

This site provides more information than you can shake a tail at. Enter your cat's name and which kinds of information you are most interested in to personalize the site to your needs. You also can ask questions ranging from cat ailments to nutrition. There's also a distinct focus on cat psychology.

Savage Studios Homepage

http://www.awod.com/gallery/wgd/savage/

Features information on cats of all shapes and sizes. Offers links to big cat organizations and the Zoe Foundation, which is dedicated to helping endangered, large cats survive.

The Tame Beast

http://www.tamebeast.com/7c.htm

In addition to the traditional information about cats, this site offers extensive links to clubs, services, and products. A long list of shelters and vets will help you to find a place to keep your cat while away or a place to find more cats when you are ready to adopt another.

The Traditional Cat Association Home Page

http://www.covesoft.com/tca/

The Traditional Cat Association (TCA) is a non-profit organization dedicated to preserving the health, longevity, and physical characteristics of cats. The group's objectives include establishing a registry for Traditional cat breeds, and to bring back and maintain the "old style" look of each breed. This site includes links to cat breeders, a newsletter, photos, membership information, and more.

Virtual Kitty

http://www.virtualkitty.com/

Very much like the popular Tamagotchi pets, Virtual Kitty lets you adopt your own online cat (or dog). Keep your kitty alive by visiting it every day and giving it food and attention. Treating it poorly or ignoring it will cause it to die.

The Virtual Pet Cemetery

http://www.lavamind.com/pet.html

All pet owners must eventually deal with the loss of a pet. The Virtual Pet Cemetery offers a place to give your pet a virtual burial and to say your goodbyes. This site has numerous, touching accounts of people and the pets they lost. The site has won many awards.

Why Cats Paint

http://www.netlink.co.nz/~monpa/index.html

Did you know that the Egyptians knew of some cats' ability to "paint" 3,000 years ago? Or that some cats' work is sold at auction? One "famous" painter sold paintings for up to $7,000. This site explores the creative aspects of the feline, recently re-inspired by the international best-seller, *Why Cats Paint.*

The Zoe Foundation

http://www.awod.com/gallery/probono/zoe/index.html

The Zoe Foundation is dedicated to helping endangered large cats avoid extinction. Funds are raised through product sales, licensing, and donations. The special focus of the foundation is on the Indochinese tiger, panthera tigris corbetti. View photos of some big cats, get info about foundation products, and learn how you can join the preservation effort.

Related Sites

http://www.acmepet.com/feline/library/febreed.html

http://www.sonic.net/~pals/

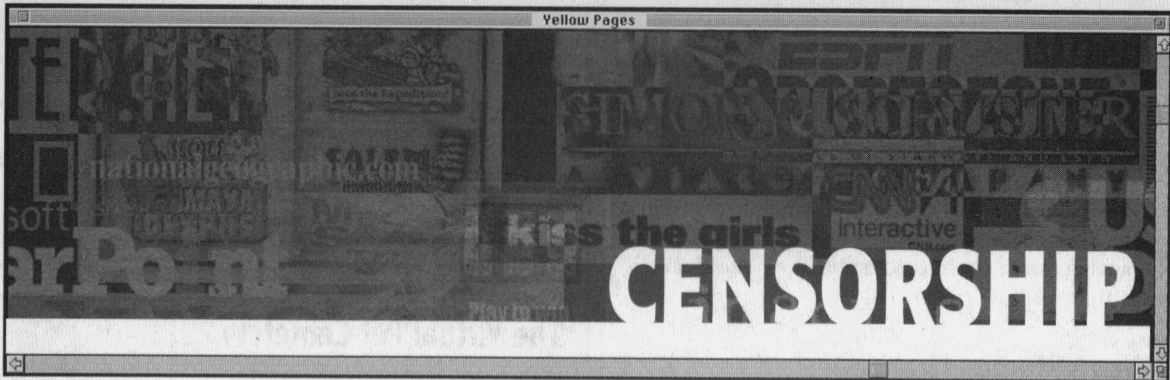
Yellow Pages
CENSORSHIP

> Thanks to television, for the first time the young are seeing history made before it is censored by their elders.
>
> *Margaret Mead*

Banned Books and Censorship

http://www.bookstore.com/censorship/banned.htm

Lists sites dealing with books in the U.S. and around the world that have been challenged. Not all these books end up getting banned.

NRP
TOP PICKS

Blue Ribbon Campaign for Online Free Speech

http://www.eff.org/blueribbon.html

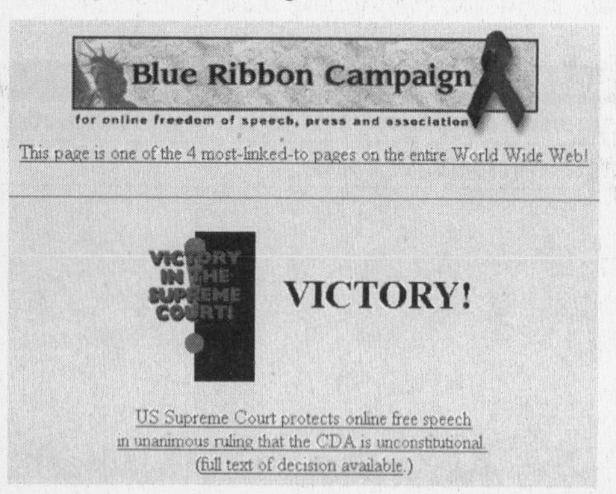
Blue Ribbon Campaign
for online freedom of speech, press and association
This page is one of the 4 most-linked-to pages on the entire World Wide Web!
VICTORY!
US Supreme Court protects online free speech
in unanimous ruling that the CDA is unconstitutional
(full text of decision available.)

Blue Ribbon Campaign for Online Free Speech
http://www.eff.org/blueribbon.html

The Indecency Page
http://cctr.umkc.edu/userx/bhugh/indecent.html

Know Your Enemies
http://www.eff.org/pub/Groups/BCFE/bcfenatl.html

One of the premier sites dealing with electronically relayed free speech and press. Extensive material and global links covering this issue. The origin of the Blue Ribbon icon of support for the cause. Ranks number six on the Webcrawler "Top 25 Most Linked to Sites." Contains the full text of the Communications Decency Amendment of the 1996 Telecommunication Act.

Bonfire of Liberties: Censorship of the Humanities

http://www.humanities-interactive.org/bonfireindex.html

If the opportunity does not present itself to see this traveling showcase on the history and roots of censorship, this site is the next best thing.

Citizens Internet Empowerment Coalition

http://www.ciec.org/

Rulings and reactions from officials involved, as well as concerned observers, regarding the Communications Decency Act. Regularly updated with new developments in the case, as well as links to the background of the case and those involved in it.

The Indecency Page

http://cctr.umkc.edu/userx/bhugh/indecent.html

Dedicated to making as much fun of the Communications Decency Act as possible, though this page could in no way be called indecent. Links to many related sites.

Index on Censorship

http://www.oneworld.org/index_oc/index.html

The most recent and back issues of this magazine are available in their entirety online. Look here for well-written articles on the repercussions of freedom of speech in our everyday lives.

Know Your Enemies

http://www.eff.org/pub/Groups/BCFE/bcfenatl.html

Where to go to find brief summaries on many of the more notorious enemies of free speech. Within each description are links to other articles dealing with their histories and cohorts.

National Coalition Against Censorship–Censorship News

http://www.ncac.org/onhome.html

Lists articles from the NCAC's newsletter, Censorship News, which is published quarterly. Includes articles about freedom of expression, school censorship, free flow of information, obscenity laws, and more. Also includes information about the NCAC and its purpose.

Project Censored

http://censored.sonoma.edu/censored/

Devoted to listing online news stories that impact all of us, but that weren't well publicized. Not the place to go if you want to remain in a good mood. This site might cause the hairs on your neck to rise and fists to form.

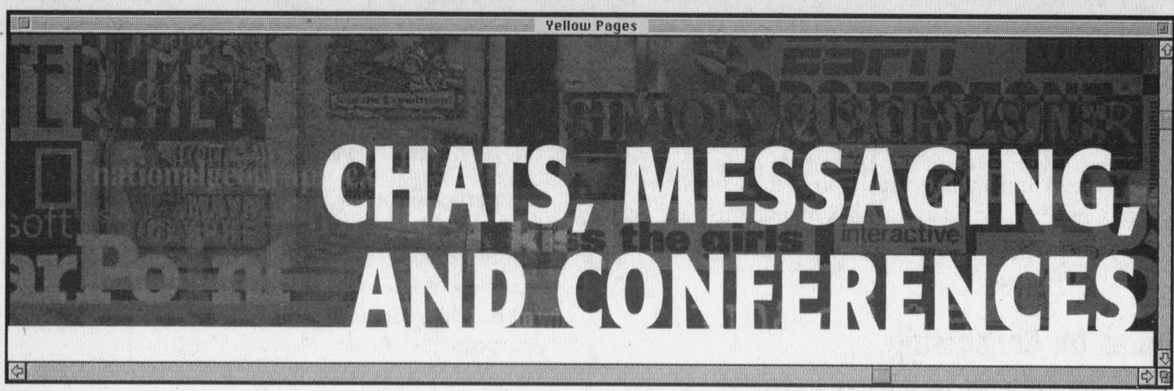

> I do wish we could chat longer, but I'm having an old friend for dinner.
>
> *Dr. Hannibal Lecter in* The Silence of the Lambs *(1991)*

Action Chat

http://www.ten-percent.com/chat/

Access free Java chat rooms for your Netscape site. There's also a how to chat page where novice users learn step-by-step how to find and join a chat room.

AudioVision

http://www.smithmicro.com/products/Prodavis.htm

Video telephone software for your PC. Hook it up to the Internet or an intranet, or strictly use it on your personal telephone line. VideoLink Mail is a video email feature; the player and a demo are available for download.

CHAT—The Ultimate Chat Links

http://www.abeamoflight.com/hot/chat-a.htm

From AA Chat to ZTV Chat and links to every kind of chat room in between. Alphabetical listing of chat room links and books that offer chat room instruction.

Chat with Beeson.Com's WWW Chat

http://www.beseen.com/

WWW Chat operates several thousand unmoderated chat rooms. Download the latest version of the Vinyl Edition Upgrade for the new features such as banning, word filter, sex symbols, and graphic titles.

IRdg
http://www.irdg.com/

DaveCentral Conferencing Software, Freeware, Demos and Betas

http://www.davecentral.com/conf.html

Software archive of various computer conferencing products. Lists the latest additions and updates and offers search capabilities for looking for a specific product of interest.

Electronic Messaging Association

http://www.ema.org/

EMA promotes the use and usefulness of the electronic messaging industry. Find out about breakthroughs in new electronic messaging technology and upcoming events within EMA and view articles and publications related to the electronic messaging industry.

ICQ—World's Largest Internet Online Communication Network

http://www.icq.com/

Download ICQ's time-limited beta for chatting, sending messages and files, and setting up other real-time communication. Developed by Mirabilis LTD, this is a very comprehensive site, offering lots of valuable information on this ICQ suite of Internet tools.

International Messaging Associates

http://www.ima.nextel.es/

Software development company that supports global corporate email communication. Products include Internet Exchange for cc:Mail v2.11 and Internet Exchange for Lotus Notes. The latest version of Internet Exchange for cc:Mail is Year 2000-compliant.

Internet Relay Chat Games

http://calypso.cs.uregina.ca/Games/

Offers information and history on the most popular games played on the IRC network. Offers information on Risky Business, Chaos, Boggle, and Acrophobia.

IRdg

http://www.irdg.com/

Company that specializes in developing advanced communication and messaging systems. iPost Universal Courier is a monthly service system that allows you to check your voice, fax, or page messages through your existing email account.

Messaging Central

http://www.messagingcentral.com/

Collection of cross-platform messaging product and service information. Get the latest on messaging issues, news, technical papers and specifications, product demos, and training and consulting services.

mIRC

http://www.mirc.co.uk/

This program enables you to connect to the Internet Relay Chat (IRC) network. Learn more about mIRC and IRC and download the latest version for free.

Protecting Groupware Messaging Systems: Virus Protection and Backup

http://www.cheyenne.com/Product-Info/WhitePapers/31010.html

White paper by Cheyenne Software on the importance of protecting groupware or messaging systems. Call the company or visit them online (at http://www.cheyenne.com) for information on their software suite.

Quarterdeck Global Chat

http://www.qdeck.com/chat/

Formerly owned by Prospero. Focuses on adding live interaction to the Web. Allows you to download the software for free, and also offers discussion areas.

RealCall Internet Telephony

http://www.callme.co.uk/unification.htm

RealCall is a Web-to-telephone service, similar to a toll-free 1-800 number. Clicking a RealCall button tells a Web site host to call you back. Try out the online demo and find out how to get this unique service.

Screen Porch

http://screenporch.com/welcome.htm

Offers the Caucus 3.1 software, which adds interactive, conferencing capabilities to Web sites. Demo online, download a free 30-day trial version, or order an upgrade or full version of the application.

TeamWARE AB

http://www.pro.icl.se

A Swedish company that provides the Internet e-mail and Web product EMBLA.

Tribal Voice–The PowWow Page

http://www.tribal.com/PowWow/

PowWow is a Windows application that you use to communicate over the Internet with up to nine people; ideal for chatting, transferring files, and surfing the Web with friends or family. There's also a Kids PowWow version for children designed to offer them the same services but with added protection against predators. Download or learn about the program here.

World Wide Web Consortium

http://www.w3.org/pub/WWW

Offers information about the upcoming WWW International Conference. Also contains a wealth of information on various Web issues, such as security, HTTP, and graphics standards.

Worlds Chat

http://www.worlds.net/wc/

Provides a 3D multiuser chatting system. Allows you to use images and sound while you chat with others, interacting *through* your computer instead of with it.

Related Sites
http://www.ema.org/html/ssummit.htm
http://www.banyan.com/messaging/im.html
http://www.zdnet.com/pcmag/issues/1517/pcmg0023.htm
http://www-lmmb.ncifcrf.gov/lemkin/XconfMan.html
http://www.honeysw.com/honeycom.htm
http://www.donnyworld.com/local/what1.htm
http://www.cixt.cuhk.edu.hk/gtalk/

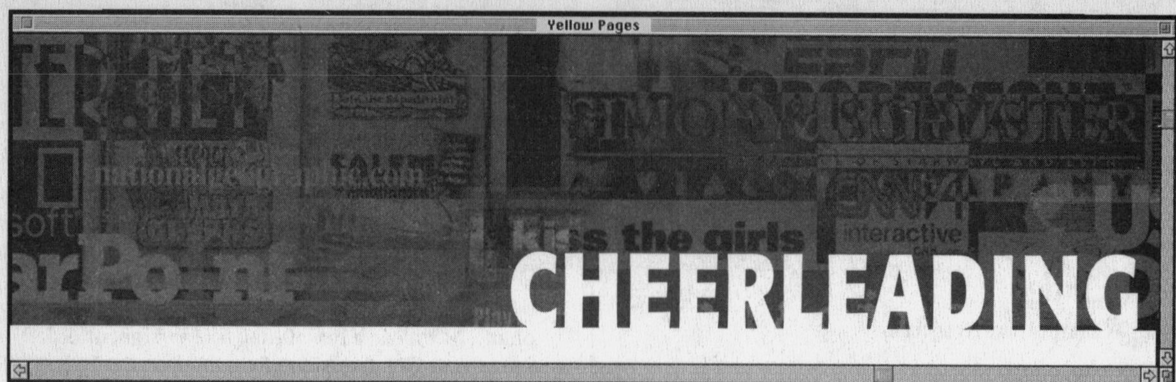

> The loudest boos always come from those in the free seats.
>
> *Unknown*

AmeriCheer

http://www.m8.com/americheer/cheerleading.html

AmeriCheer, an Ohio-based organization, promotes the growth of cheerleading. Access their newsletter and find information on summer camps, cheerleading classes, and squad and individual instruction. You can also read the results of the national championship and check out the latest cheerleading apparel from Victory Wear.

Cheer LTD Today—A Spirited Tradition

http://www.oldmp.com:80/cheerltd/

Cheer LTD provides coaches and cheerleaders with the tools needed to perfect their skills and their squads. This site is designed to inform the public of Cheer LTD's programs. Find out about the latest cheerleading and dance championships, who won Cheerleader of the Year, what's available at the Cheerleader Shoppe, and upcoming camps, clinics, conferences, and choreography.

Cheerleader Central

http://www.cheerleader.com/Cheer/index.nt.html

This site specializes in selling cheerleader merchandise and licensed NFL cheerleader apparel for women and girls. You can also join the Cheerleader Central mailing list where you can find out when and where professional cheerleading squads will be making appearances.

Universal Cheerleaders Association Online
http://www.danceuda.com/uca/index.html

Collegiate Cheerleading Company

http://members.aol.com/cccsprt/index.html

CCC offers training for coaches and cheerleaders and even provides custom squad analysis. Find out about the many camps and clinics offered to various levels—college, varsity, junior varsity, junior high, and midgets.

EssesCo Athletic and Cheerleading Supply

http://www.essesco.com/

An online catalog for cheerleading and sports supplies. View full-color pictures illustrating their line of merchandise of uniforms, shoes, poms, warmups, jackets, and more.

Mid American Pompon Inc.

http://www2.pompon.com/pompon/

Mid American Pompon creates, instructs, and judges pompon and dance routines. In addition to information on training camps and workshops and an online catalog, Mid American's site conducts surveys on various issues relating to cheerleading. There's also an Expert's Corner page where you can present your difficult coaching situation and receive expert advice.

San Francisco 49ers Gold Rush Cheerleaders

http://www.geocities.com/Colosseum/5338/gr.html

Meet members of this NFL cheerleader squad, tour a photo gallery of them in action, order merchandise such as trading cards, CD-ROMs, calendars, and videos, join the fan club, and link to the football team's NFL site.

Spiritwear

http://www.ramgraphics.com/

Spiritwear offers a wide range of cheerleading apparel that you can order online. Choose from their cheerleading line of products including special Camp Packs and Cheer Accessories, or have something custom made for your squad. Inventory reduction items are available through the Closeouts page.

Team Cheer Online

http://www.teamcheer.com/

Whether you want poms, jackets, team bags, or cheer shoes, Team Cheer Online offers competitive pricing based on volume (the more you buy, the better price you get). Browse the online catalog and call (toll free), fax, or mail your order in.

Texas Cheerleading Association

http://www.cheertca.com/

TCA holds competitions for cheerleaders across the state of Texas. Check out championship winners, competition results, and camp and clinic schedules and fees. This site also has a page devoted to fundraising ideas.

The Varsity Mall

http://www.varsity.com/html/mall/index.html

Imagine a mall of just cheerleader stuff and you've imagined this site. Complete the online order form or phone in your order to receive a wide array of cheerleading paraphernalia including campwear, competition music, videos, mats, signs, and uniforms.

United States Competitive Cheerleaders Association

http://www.uscca.com/

This association hosts cheer and dance competitions across the United States. Check out the competition schedule and results, summer camps offered, and join the mailing list to stay on top of upcoming events. Your school can offer to host a competition through the Competition Host page. Or, if you are looking for a career in this area, check out the Employment page.

Universal Cheerleaders Association Online

http://www.danceuda.com/uca/index.html

Welcome to Universal Cheerleaders Association Online!

- Cheerleading Resource Center! (new!)
- The Online Scholarship Guide
- The Varsity Mall
- Find Your Local Rep
- Mascot Central
- Competition Information - Regionals Results and ESPN airdates!
- Our Sponsors!
- Link to UCA!

UCA

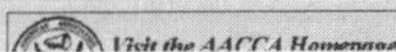

A great resource for cheerleaders. There's a Resource Center where you can look up new chants and cheers, get advice on preparing for a tryout, and get ideas for fund-raisers. You can search for schools that offer scholarships in cheerleading and dance. Or, UCA has representatives all over the country; search for the one nearest you. There's also a special mascot page.

Virginia Tech Cheerleaders

http://sports.vt.edu/Cheer/

Home page of the Virginia Tech cheerleading squad. Financial aid contact information on the college and cheerleading and mascot program information for those interested in trying out for the squad.

WorldWide Cheerleader Homepage

http://www.telepath.com/jennifer/cheer/

Improve your cheerleading skills by learning the basics of jumping, new chants and cheers, and tryout tips. Other WorldWide Cheerleader resources for the spirit-filled cheerleader include listings of cheerleader associations, camps, and supply companies.

Related Sites
http://www.lehigh.edu/~incheer/cheer.html
http://www.danceuda.com/danceuda/index.html
http://www.ttsd.k12.or.us/schools/tuhs/Cheer/tuhscheer.shtml
http://www.americancheerleader.com/
http://www.aacdscholarship.com/
http://www.delanet.com/~usaigc/
http://www.expresspages.com/c/cheerleadingunlimited/
http://www.sisite.com/cheerleading/
http://www.sportsteam.com/cheer2.html
http://www.dvbiznet.com/BRYNMAWR/

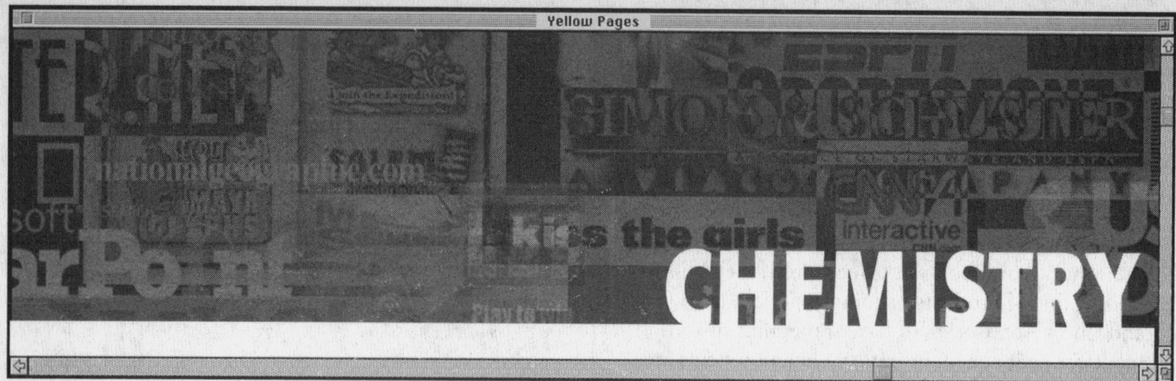

> Organic chemistry is the chemistry of carbon compounds. Biochemistry is the study of carbon compounds that crawl.
>
> *Mike Adams*

The American Chemical Society

http://www.acs.org/

Site provides access to the American Chemical Society products and news, all ACS journals, as well as limited access to Chemical Literature Abstracts. Also provides access to U.S. chemical patents from 1971 to the present. Excellent site for anyone in an academic or professional chemical field.

ChemCAI: Instructional Software for Chemistry

http://www.sfu.ca:80/chemed/

Contains links to software sources, demonstration materials, and other information for chemists.

Chemistry Hypermedia Project

http://www.chem.vt.edu/chem-ed/vt-chem-ed.html

Provides a library of hypermedia tutorials related to chemistry.

Chemistry Teacher Resources
http://rampages.onramp.net/~jaldr/chemtchr.html

George Goble (GHG) Extended Home Page
http://ghg.ecn.purdue.edu/

Los Alamos National Laboratory of Energetic Materials
http://sonhp.lanl.gov/DX2/dx2home.html

Chemistry Teacher Resources

http://rampages.onramp.net/~jaldr/chemtchr.html

Provides resources for teachers and high school students of chemistry and original documents created by a science teacher.

Composite Materials Research Group—University of Mississippi

http://cypress.mcsr.olemiss.edu/~melackey

Features research conducted by the Composite Materials Research Group at the University of Mississippi. Focuses on the optimization of the pultrusion process for the manufacture of composite materials and mechanical and physical property characterization of composite materials. Features faculty research, facilities and equipment, and graduate school opportunities.

CTI Centre for Chemistry Software Catalogue

http://www.liv.ac.uk/ctichem/catmain.html

Lists software you can use in many areas of science, including general science, crystallography, and all areas of chemistry. Covers a wide variety of software types and platforms.

Dalton Chemical Laboratories, Inc.

http://www.dalton.com/

Specializes in the synthesis of phosporamidites, oligonucleotides, custom synthesis, and research contracts.

George Goble (GHG) Extended Home Page

http://ghg.ecn.purdue.edu/

Among the many quirky treasures here, you can view JPEG images of an outdoor barbecue with liquid oxygen. Also contains audio tracks and an MPEG movie of the grill lighting and subsequent disintegration of the grill.

Introduction to Alchemy

http://www.levity.com/alchemy/index.html

Site describes the past of chemistry in alchemy (as well as the future), current applications, and uses of alchemy. Site gives links to mysticism, metaphysical, and allegorical journeys in alchemy. Also provides links to alchemical literature and alchemical societies.

Jane's Brain Page

http://maui.net/~jms/brainuse.html

Presents study of how brain chemicals affect emotion, personality, and sexuality. Also offers links to related sites.

Los Alamos National Laboratory of Energetic Materials

http://sonhp.lanl.gov/DX2/dx2home.html

Site features fantastic images of exploding objects, as well as information on new explosives, unique applications of explosives, explosives safety, and remediation. Site also stresses the availability of internships and employment at the National Laboratories.

SoftShell Online

http://www.softshell.com/

Offers discussions and information on chemistry topics, including electronic publishing, the free ChemWeb GIF structure editor, and other chemistry software (such as ChemWindow and ChemIntosh). Focuses on worldwide access to chemical information. Presents a magazine in which anything can be published. Serves as a resource, a classroom, a library, a bulletin board, and a hangout.

Software Reviews from the CTI Centre for Chemistry

http://www.liv.ac.uk/ctichem/swrev.html

Reprints software reviews from the Centre's journal *Software Reviews.* Helps educators and researchers locate appropriate chemistry-related software.

STM Image Gallery

http://www.almaden.ibm.com/vis/stm/gallery.html

Site features a virtual tour of Scanning Tunneling Microscopy Image gallery. Also features many nanoscale images of quantum interference, as well as images of the famous Quantum Corrals.

Understanding Our Planet Through Chemistry

http://helios.cr.usgs.gov/gips/aii-home.htm

Explains the history of the earth and the chemistry concepts involved in its formation.

A B C D E F G H I J K L M N O P Q R S T U V W X Y Z

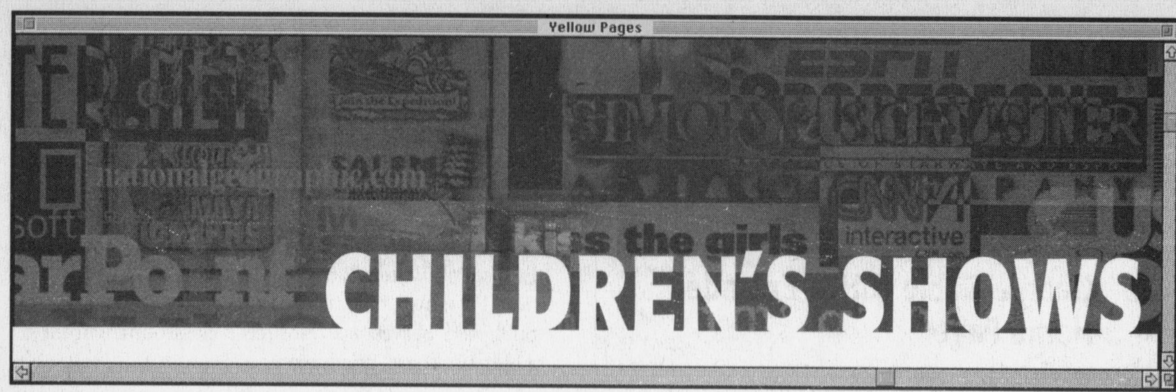

CHILDREN'S SHOWS

> Oh, there's nothing wrong with the children. Only the governesses.
>
> *Captain Von Trapp in* The Sound of Music *(1965)*

NRP Top Picks

Arthur
http://www.pbs.org/wgbh/pages/arthur/

The School House Rock Page
http://genxtvland.simplenet.com/SchoolHouseRock/

Scooby-Doo
http://TBSsuperstation.com/disaster/scooby.htm

2 Stupid Dogs

http://www.sn.no/~tbk/2stupid.html

Produced by Hanna Barbera, *2 Stupid Dogs* is about, well, two dogs that aren't that smart. There are plenty of pictures, sounds, and links available at this site. (And, if you can get here, then you are probably smarter than our heroes.)

The Adventures of Pete and Pete

http://www.cs.indiana.edu/entertainment/pete-and-pete/

Nickelodeon's television program *The Adventures of Pete and Pete* chronicles the adventures of two brothers who experience very strange happenings. There is always someone interesting on the show, ranging from Iggy Pop to Hunter S. Thompson to Adam West.

The alt.tv.tiny-toon FAQ

http://kumo.swcp.com/synth/tta-faq.html

A comprehensive site for fans of Fox's *Tiny Toons.* Includes every conceivable question possible about this cartoon.

Related Sites

http://www.con.wesleyan.edu/~clemens/bullwinkle/bullwinkle.html

http://www.garfield.com/

http://www.foxkids.com/goose.htm

Animaniacs

http://www.wbanimation.com/bin/wb.cgi?MIval=an_100.htm

Yakko, Wacko, and Dot (the cute one) have their home page here on the Warner Brothers studio lot. Check out the information, downloads, credits, and a bunch of other stuff that you can't get anywhere else on the Web.

Arthur

http://www.pbs.org/wgbh/pages/arthur/

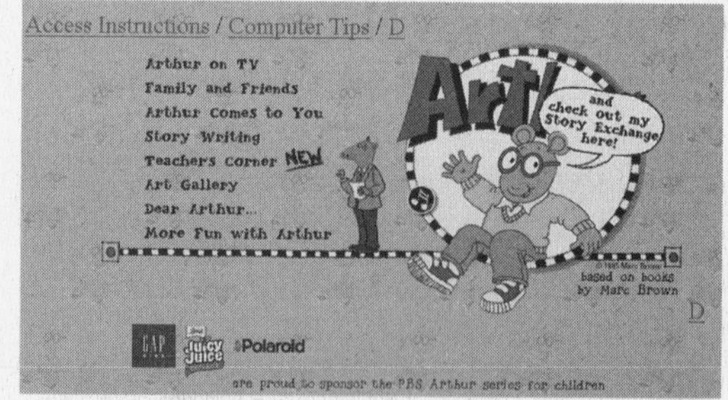

Click on any date in Arthur's calendars (three month's worth) to see a description of the episode on that day. Look up the important facts and history of Arthur's family and friends: Binky Barnes, The Brain, D.W., Baby Kate, Buster, Francine, Muffy, Nadine, Pal, Mr. Ratburn, and Mr. and Mrs. Read. Join the story-writing exchange, where classrooms across the country send Arthur their best stories about Arthur and his friends; Arthur might decide to post your story at his site. Each week, Arthur chooses four Arthur-related drawings by kids and displays them in his online gallery. If you're a teacher, investigate Teacher's Corner for ideas on hands-on activities for second-grade students. Also, check out the dates and descriptions of special Arthur events around the country.

Barney

`http://www.barneyonline.com/Barney/Nav/home.html`

Personally, I could live without this cuddly purple dinosaur, but this site is very interactive for the kids who love him. Barney has a photo gallery where he displays pictures kids have drawn. He also gives kids interactive games to play with adults; the adults ask the kids whether they can find certain items, and they click them. Kids can also participate in a sing-along game, painting activities, and a coloring book. Or, play the memory match game and get info on Barney's fan club and magazine. If you're in the mood to shop, enter the Barney store to browse for videos and books.

Battle of the Planets and G Force

`http://www.vacuform.com/Gatchaman/`

Provides information about the English version of the Japanese cartoons *Battle of the Planets* and *G Force.* Popularized in the 1980s, these cartoons continue to have fans today. Includes an episode guide, pictures, and much more.

Beakman's World Home Page

`http://www.spe.sony.com/Pictures/tv/beakman/beakman.html`

The MTV generation's version of Mr. Wizard, *Beakman's World* started as a syndicated info-comic strip and has become a Saturday morning show. There's much to learn about science, so look here for a head start.

Big Bad Beetleborgs

`http://www.pazsaz.com/bborgs.html`

They're big, bad, and they're Beetleborgs. This site provides an episode guide, pictures, and much more about the Fox children's show *Big Bad Beetleborgs.* Includes links to other related sites.

Camp Cariboo

`http://camp.cariboo.com/`

Provides an online site for the children's show *Camp Cariboo,* hosted by Tom and Mark. Includes pictures, an episode guide, and a parents' resource.

Captain Caveman

`http://www.hype.com/nostalgia/tv/capcav/capcavin.htm`

"What can't he pull out of his fur?" is the question of the hour with this superhero. Look here for some Captain Caveman quotations, pictures, and other info about this popular kids' cartoon.

Captain Planet

`http://www.turner.com/planet/`

Shown on the Turner Broadcasting System, *The Adventures of Captain Planet* provides a superhero for the '90s. Smart. Ecological. Blue. This is his official Web page, and it has lots of stuff to look at and download.

Cartoon World

`http://www.cet.com/~rascal/`

Cartoons through the ages reside at this site. There are pictures and information here that you thought you'd never see again. A cartoon lover's paradise!

Children's Television Workshop

`http://www.ctw.org/`

From the people who bring you *Sesame Street,* this page gives parenting information and stuff for kids to do. It includes some nice pictures of *The Muppets* (and the like) and coloring pages for printing out.

Chip & Dale's Rescue Rangers

`http://www.cybercomm.net/~paltiel/CDRR/EverythingRR/listing.html`

You'll find just about everything here you'll need to know about this popular Disney cartoon series. Includes pictures, an episode guide, fan art, toy information, and more.

Clarissa Explains It All

`http://www.ee.surrey.ac.uk/Contrib/Entertainment/Clarissa/`

Check out the episode guides, interviews, and other information about Nickelodeon's young adult comedy *Clarissa Explains It All.*

Count Duckula Page

`http://www.ghgcorp.com/vision/Lupine/Duckula/index.html`

Count Duckula was one of the original wacky ducks presented for kids' amusement (after Daffy but before Darkwing). This page is his unofficial site.

A B C D E F G H I J K L M N O P Q R S T U V W X Y Z

A B C D E F G H I J K L M N O P Q R S T U V W X Y Z

Danger Mouse

http://www.charm.net/~altera/dm/

Download images and sounds of this popular Nickelodeon cartoon. Includes info on the show's characters, a lengthy video list, and links to fan pages.

Darkwing Duck

http://www.geocities.com/Hollywood/4526/

Provides a wealth of information about the popular Disney animated series *Darkwing Duck.* Includes an episode guide, pictures, character profiles, and much more.

Earthworm Jim

http://www.wbanimation.com/bin/wb.cgi?MIval=ej_500.htm

Based on a popular game for the Nintendo Entertainment System, Earthworm Jim lives in a very strange world where goldfish are evil and, well, an earthworm is a superhero. You can download sounds, movies, and other stuff from this official Web site.

The Flintstones Unofficial Home Page

http://www.powerup.com.au/~ves/

This is a great page with a desktop theme for Windows 95, pictures, a broadcast schedule, and updated sites for kids. These pages have also been translated into Ukrainian and Russian (just in case you were wondering).

Fraggle Rock

http://www.clark.net/pub/cvaughn/html/frindex.htm

This page is dedicated to the Muppet-like Fraggles. It offers a complete Fraggle Rock guide and other information of interest.

Freakazoid!

http://www.wbanimation.com/bin/wb.cgi?MIval=f_600.htm

Presented by Steven Spielberg, *Freakazoid!* is a popular Warner Brothers cartoon with a teenage superhero. Actually, Freakazoid was once mild-mannered Dexter Douglas but was transformed by a "crash on the information superhighway." See where the Internet will get you?

Go-Go Gadget (An Inspector Gadget Homepage!)

http://members.tripod.com/~inspector1/

Come to this site for facts on all your favorite characters: Inspector Gadget, Penny, Brain, Capeman, Chief Quimby, Dr. Claw, MAD Cat, and various MAD agents. Browse the gallery of pictures from the show. Listen to the theme song and well-known quotations from Inspector Gadget. Or, check out the list of Gadget's gadgets.

Gumby on the Web

http://www.emsphone.com/gumby/

Complete with the Gumby theme song, pictures, and other wonderful Gumby memorabilia, Gumby on the Web can satisfy any person's appetite for green clay. There's even a link to an essay on Gumby's Eastern mystic philosophy.

The Home Page of One Wile E. Coyote, Super Genius

http://www.accessone.com/~curtiss/wile_e/

Includes Wile's resume, including his work history. Browse through the galleries of photos and sounds. Check out the videos for sale. Includes Chuck Jones' 10 rules that must always be obeyed in the Coyote-Road Runner series. Also offers links to other pages.

H.R. Pufnstuf

http://www.west.net/~popomatic/pufnstuf.html

Check out this site for info on the Saturday morning live-action puppet TV show in the '70s by Sid & Marty Krofft. Sing along with the theme song and check out the lyrics, just in case you can't remember them. Refresh your memory with a list of the cast, as well as descriptions of all 17 30-minute episodes. You also might be interested in the H.R. Pufnstuf collector's shopping list (games, comic books, lunch boxes, and more).

The Jetsons

http://TBSsuperstation.com/disaster/jetsons.htm

The Jetsons was one of Hanna Barbera's family cartoons aimed at both kids and adults. Not as successful as *The Flintstones, The Jetsons* eventually won over many fans and now has its home on TBS. This site has pictures and trivia from the futuristic family.

Jonny Quest

`http://www.illuminatus.com/quest`

Provides a detailed episode guide, pictures, and much more about the popular cartoon *Jonny Quest.* Try out the video clips, sound bytes, FAQs, and a fan-voting booth for your favorite episodes.

Keeper's Cartoon Files

`http://www2.cruzio.com/~keeper/toons.html`

This isn't a pretty site, but it does include a ton of information on Warner Brothers' cartoons, such as *Animaniacs* and *Pinky and The Brain.* Download a complete episode list of Warner cartoons, lyrics, and screenplays of particular shows, and learn more about the Warner Internet Fan Association.

Kids Incorporated

`http://www.interlog.com/~m9/`

Provides an episode guide, cast background, and parents' recommendations of the children's show Kids Incorporated. Includes links to other Kids, Inc. sites.

The Life with Louie Homepage

`http://www.geocities.com/TelevisionCity/2210`

Life with Louie is a 30-minute animated comedy on FOX. It's about a not-so-typical family in the '70s and is based on the life of comedian Louie Anderson. This site includes sounds and videos from the show, as well as descriptions of Pvt. Anderson, Mrs. Anderson, and Louie. Also includes a show FAQ.

Mighty Morphin Power Documents

`http://members.nova.org/~wynstorm/mmpr.html`

Start morphin, folks! This site has everything for the fan of the *Mighty Morphin Power Rangers.* Includes a season-by-season episode guide, a lengthy FAQ, and links to other Ranger sites.

Mister Rogers' Neighborhood

`http://www.pbs.org/rogers/`

Of course Mister Rogers has a home page. One of the nicest parts of his page, though, is his use of Real Audio with his information. Fred's site includes lyrics to songs and a book list for suggested reading.

Muppets Home Page

`http://www.ncsa.uiuc.edu/VR/BS/Muppets/muppets.html`

Although this site is thin on sounds and images, valuable info for Muppets fans abounds. Must-sees are the episode guides for all of Jim Henson's productions, including *The Muppet Show, Fraggle Rock,* and *Dinosaurs.* Travel to official and fan-related Muppets sites on the Web and read online articles on The Muppets. Die-hard Muppets fans should check out the Muppo-graphy, a list of everything known with Muppets in it.

New Zoo Revue

`http://www.newzoorevue.com/`

Provides information about the '70s children's show *The New Zoo Revue.* Includes an episode guide, many pictures, and music from the show. Also includes links to other children's Web sites.

Nickelodeon

`http://www.nick.com/`

This site gives you general info on kid's shows, Nick facts, and descriptions of today's episodes and the next episodes. Learn about shows such as Ahhh!!! Real Monsters, The Angry Beavers, Doug, Hey Arnold!, KABLAM!, Looney Tunes, Muppet Babies, The Ren & Stimpy Show, Rocko's Modern Life, Rugrats, Rupert, Snick, Space Cases, What Would You Do?, and Wild & Crazy Kids.

Pee Wee's Playhouse

`http://www.peewee.com/index.html`

This is the official Web site for the popular children's show *Pee Wee's Playhouse,* staring Paul "Pee Wee Herman" Reubens. Includes ordering information and much more.

Phil's Faboo Animaniacs Web Page

`http://www.novia.net/~wakko/warner.html`

This fan page for the *Animaniacs* cartoon includes images, funny sound clips, and links to other fan pages. You can also join the Animaniacs' Life fan club if you love the show and also have time for a real life—difficult!

A B C D E F G H I J K L M N O P Q R S T U V W X Y Z

Pinky and The Brain

http://www.wbanimation.com/bin/wb.cgi?MIval=pb_300.htm

Pinky and The Brain are the Odd Couple of lab rats. Apparently, they've moved their scheme to take over the world to the World Wide Web.

The ReBoot Home Page

http://uts.cc.utexas.edu/~ifex534/main.html

Come here for information on the characters of the Saturday morning cartoon show *ReBoot*. You can also read the episode guide and general info. Check out the episode guide and the Did You Notice section for funny info on the show's more subtle additions.

The School House Rock Page

http://genxtvland.simplenet.com/SchoolHouseRock/

Conjunction Junction, what's your function? Any Generation Xer will remember these songs. Check out Grammar Rock, America Rock, Science Rock, and Multiplication Rock. Sing along with the songs and read the lyrics. Which song is your favorite—Interjections?

Scooby-Doo

http://TBSsuperstation.com/disaster/scooby.htm

"Scooby Doo " can be seen Monday- Friday on TBS at 6:35 AM and 4:05 PM (E). On the Weekends, check "Scooby Doo" out at 8:35AM on Saturday and at 8:05AM and 5:05PM on Sunday
DiSAsTeR AREA DiSAsTeR AREA

Find out everything you ever wanted to know about "those pesky kids": Daphne, Fred, Scooby Doo, Shaggy, and Velma. Check out the typical sayings and responses, such as "Jeepers!" and "Jinkies!" Take the Scooby quiz of little-known facts. Did you know that Shaggy was the first vegetarian in cartoons? See a list of celebrity guests and a history of how the show has changed. Includes a coloring book with images you can print out and then color. Also presents a schedule of times you can catch Scooby-Doo on TV.

The Superfriends Archive

http://fantasia.ncsa.uiuc.edu/Doug/superhtml/

With the Flash, Batman and Robin, Superman, Aquaman, and Wonder Woman, the Superfriends are here! Of course, you can download pictures, sounds, and other stuff from the site. You can also check out the complete listing of Superfriends, just in case you've forgotten some of their names.

Superhero Cartoon Database

http://www.pazsaz.com/scotpage.html

This is the place for info on more than 80 superhero cartoons. Each superhero page comes with facts about episodes and the cast, and most pages have pictures. Check out your favorite cartoon. Is it *Batman: The Animated Series, The Arabian Knights, Flash Gordon, Gargoyles, Men in Black, Mortal Kombat, Return to the Planet of the Apes, Shazam!, Space Ghost, Spider-Man, Thundercats*, or *X-Men: The Animated Series*?

The Sylvester and Tweety Mysteries

http://www.wbanimation.com/bin/wb.cgi?MIval=st_400.htm

Based on the characters from the series that produced television legend Bugs Bunny, the Sylvester and Tweety Mysteries Web site has bios, credits, sounds, and movies to download. You can also consult a schedule of times the show airs.

That's Warner Bros.!

http://www.wbanimation.com/bin/wb.cgi?MIval=wb_200.htm

Bugs Bunny, Sylvester, Yosemite Sam, and Pepe LePew (you remember these guys, right?) call this their official Web page. It is based at the Warner Brothers server and has plenty of stuff to look at, download, and read about.

Thunderbirds

http://www.ludd.luth.se/~kavli/Tbirds.html

The *Gerry Anderson TV* series produced in the '60s has been popular for years. Presented in claymation, the famous cold-war jet-plane show now has information on the Web. This site includes pictures, info, and a Gerry Anderson FAQ.

Underdog Home Page

http://web.cps.msu.edu:80/~bennet96/Underdog.html

If you always root for the Underdog, you might want to check out this site for character and episode information, Underdog pictures and sounds, and theme song lyrics. Also offers links to other sites and info on Underdog videos.

The Unofficial Beany and Cecil Page

http://www.megalink.net/~cooke/beany-cecil/index.html

Browse through this info on the original series (1962) and the revised series (1988), as well as links to other Beany & Cecil sites. Check out the pictures and sounds featuring Beany, Captain, Cecil, Lil' Ace, Dishonest John, Pop Gunn, Go Man Van Gogh, and more.

The Unofficial Pink Panther Page

http://www.high-tech.com/panther/

This site plays the Pink Panther theme song (but just once, so you don't go crazy) and then lets you choose to listen to any (or all!) of the six versions of the song. Review the history of the Pink Panther and check out the image archive of animation cells. View pictures from Julie Tapia's Pink Panther Museum, located in Santa Rosa, CA. You can also download files, such as a Pink Panther animated cursor, a screen saver, and an icon. Also includes Pink links.

The Unofficial Rugrats Home Page

http://www.gti.net/azog/rugrats/

Find out all the facts and read up on the history of your favorite characters, such as the Pickles, Finster, and DeVille families. Or, learn about the minor characters, such as Cynthia, Reptar, and the Dummi Bears. Look over the brief descriptions of all the episodes. Or, investigate the section of unanswered or "did you notice" questions submitted by viewers.

The Unofficial Sid and Marty Krofft Home Page

http://www.west.net/~popomatic/Krofft.html

This page is dedicated to the brothers Krofft, creators of shows such as *H.R. Pufnstuf* and *Bugaloos.* This is a beautifully designed page and has many links, including theme songs, "Krofftware," and a family photo album.

An Unofficial Where on Earth is Carmen Sandiego? Page

http://www.geocities.com/Hollywood/4118/sandiego.html

Check out this site's collection of fan fiction, art, essays, and parodies. See how well you do on the Carmen trivia quiz. Read over information from a Q&A session with Broderbund Software. View character biographies, articles about the show, an episodes guide, the photo gallery, and the merchandise page. Includes sounds, common sayings from the characters, and theme-song lyrics (both versions). Also presents links to more Carmen sites.

Worldwide Wishbone

http://www.wwwishbone.com/WWWishbone/MyBooks/saltydog.html

Preview shows for the next season by reading the descriptions. Order Wishbone books and CD-ROMs from the Lyrick Studios Store. Play Wishbone games online. Pick out an image from the coloring book. Listen to sound bites and save them on your computer. Or, view the Wishbone photo collection and Quicktime video clips. Help Wishbone finish his stories or join in the discussion area. Get updates on contests and events, and learn how to join the fan club. Includes a Q&A section.

NEWSGROUPS

alt.fan.pooh
alt.fan.power-rangers
alt.tv.animaniacs
alt.tv.beakmans-world
alt.tv.muppets
alt.tv.nickelodeon
alt.tv.sesame-street

Related Sites

http://www.emunix.emich.edu/~vlong/muppets.html
http://www.nucleus.com/~stevep/toon.htm
http://www.pbs.org/readingrainbow/
http://www.aap.org/family/smarttv.htm
http://www.eecis.udel.edu/~markowsk/anime/speed/startup/
http://www.cs.rose-hulman.edu/~stinerkt/Tick.html
http://www.geocities.com/Hollywood/6859/tj.html

A B C D E F G H I J K L M N O P Q R S T U V W X Y Z

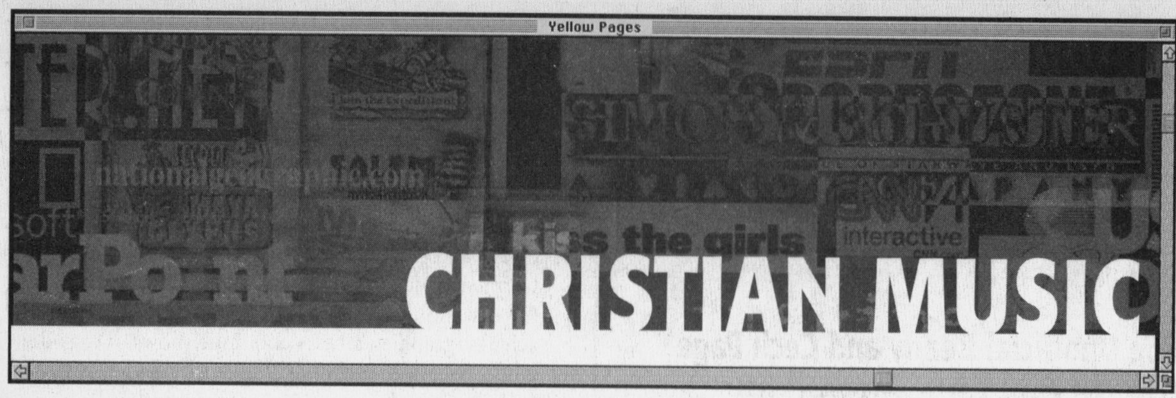

CHRISTIAN MUSIC

> In the faces of men and women I see God.
>
> *Walt Whitman*

Susan Ashton

`http://www.rendall.com/ashton`

Serves as a resource page for contemporary Christian singer Susan Ashton. Includes the expected Net resources, as well as many metalinks that point to other Christian music resources.

Christian Music Online

`http://www.cmo.com/cmo/index.html`

Provides information about different types of Christian music, including contemporary, alternative, praise/worship, and rap. Includes concert dates, artists' biographies, and sound files.

Jamsline: The Christian music information source

`http://www.jamsline.com/`

Cool looking site that offers hundreds of titles for purchase, including Amy Grant, Jars of Clay, Anointed, and more. CDs are reasonably priced at $12.99 and tapes for $8.99.

Jars of Clay

`http://www.jarsofclay.com/`

Official site of the Christian rock group Jars of Clay. Here you'll find band and tour info, merchandise, sound bites, and more. Great looking page!

Michael W. Smith

`http://www.cs.rose-hulman.edu/~schaefsm/mws/`

Focuses on contemporary Christian/pop artist Michael W. Smith. Includes information on contacting the fan club and the Michael's Best Friend newsletter.

The Official Michael Card Web Site

`http://michaelcard.com/`

Official site for the Christian composer and musician. Offers lyrics, music, bio information, new release info, song titles, and more. Great site and well organized.

TLem CHRISTIAN MUSIC RESOURCES

`http://tlem.netcentral.net/cmr/`

Huge database that provides artist contact information, links to other Christian Music sites, and a Christian Music Comparison Chart. This site has won many awards. It's a must see!

YMC – Christian Music

`http://ebc.iso.net/smrc/chmusic.html`

Another huge database that contains all kinds of Christian Music info, including tour dates, artist bios and booking info, radio charts, and more.

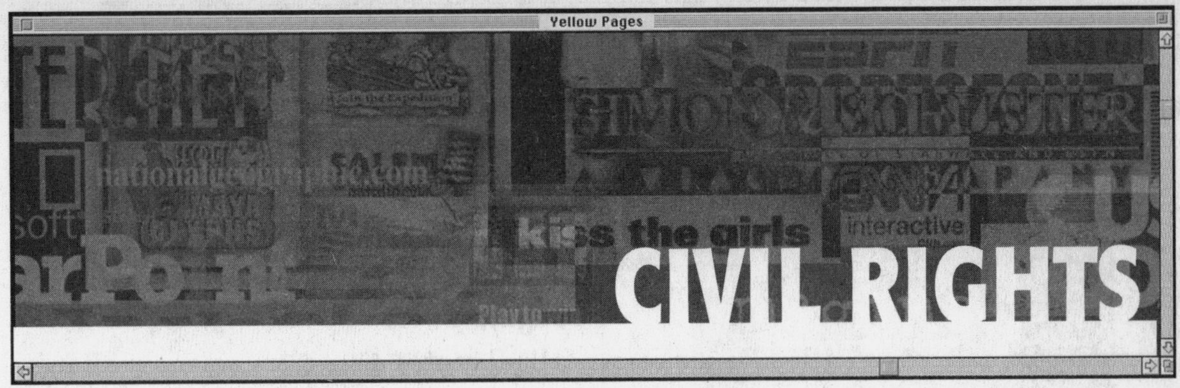

> Give no bounties:
> Make equal Laws:
> secure life and prosperity
> and you need not give alms.
>
> *Ralph Waldo Emerson*

The American Civil Liberties Union

http://www.aclu.org/

Lots of info about this powerful organization, which fights for the rights of minorities of all types to be fairly represented. Learn about the latest legal cases in areas ranging from racial preferences to the separation of church and state.

Constitutional Rights Foundation

http://www.crf-usa.org/index2.html

Constitutional Rights Foundation (CRF) is a non-profit, non-partisan, community-based organization dedicated to educating America's young people about the importance of civic participation in a democratic society. Their Web site explains their publications, events, and programs.

Freedom of Expression Links

http://insight.mcmaster.ca/org/efc/pages/chronicle/censor.html

A big list of interesting sites that deal with freedom of ideas and expression, including organizations, documents, legal cases, and newsgroups.

Leadership Conference on Civil Rights
http://www.civilrights.org/

The ROBIN Report
http://www.hamline.edu/robin/

Greensboro Justice Fund

http://www.gjf.org/

Named after the 1979 Greensboro Massacre, the Greensboro Justice Fund provides grants to individuals and groups fighting bigotry in the South today. You can find out how to apply for a grant here, or view a list of current and past grant recipients.

Historic Audio Archives

http://www.webcorp.com/civilrights/index.htm

Subtitled "Voices of the Civil Rights Movement," this site provides RealAudio clips of famous civil rights speeches, including those by Martin Luther King and Malcolm X.

Law Research: The United States Department of Justice

http://www.lawresearch.com/v2/cusdoj.htm

A huge collection of links to every imaginable division of the Department of Justice.

Related Sites

http://www.amnesty.org/

http://www.cccr.org/

http://www.freedomhouse.org/

http://www.lchr.org/

http://www.envirolink.org/orgs/magnuscentre/

http://socsci.colorado.edu/~jonesem/montgomery.html

http://www.seattletimes.com/mlk/movement/PT/phototour.html

Leadership Conference on Civil Rights

http://www.civilrights.org/

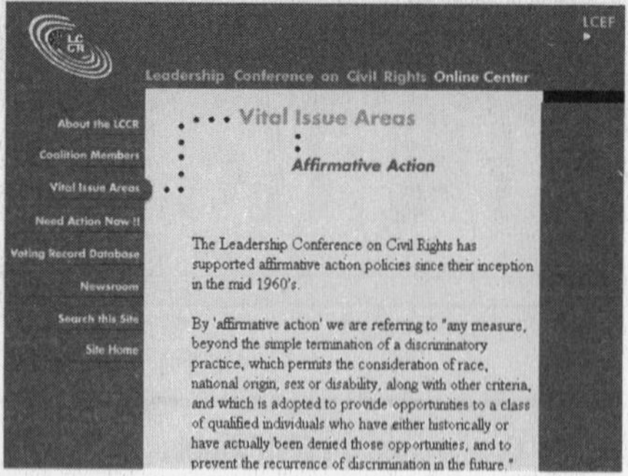

Home to both the Leadership Conference on Civil Rights and the Leadership Conference Educational Fund, this site explains both organizations and provides a wealth of information and links.

Minority Rights Group International

http://www.minorityrights.org/

An international non-governmental organization that promotes the rights of ethnic, linguistic and religious minorities.

National Civil Rights Museum

http://www.mecca.org/~crights/

A collection of Civil Rights artifacts, including Dr. Martin Luther King's speeches and replicas of civil rights monuments.

Religious Freedom International

http://www.article18.org/

A human rights group that acts in behalf of religious minorities worldwide. Read their newsletters here and find out more about what they do and how you can help if you wish to.

The ROBIN Report

http://www.hamline.edu/robin/

The Religion or Belief Information Network (ROBIN) is a non-governmental information network, reporting on issues relating to freedom of religion or belief and public policy. They are committed to furthering support for the 1981 United Nations Declaration on the Elimination of All Forms of Intolerance and of Discrimination Based on Religion or Belief.

Second Amendment Law Library

http://www.2ndlawlib.org/

A rather serious and scholarly site with information about past and current legal cases involving second amendment rights (the right to bear firearms).

United States Commission on Civil Rights

http://www.usccr.gov/

The United States Commission on Civil Rights (USCCR) is an independent, bipartisan, fact-finding agency of the Executive Branch. Check out their publications, regional office locations, and information about filing a complaint.

Votelink...the Voice of the Net

http://www.votelink.com/

A highly interactive site that encourages you to voice your opinion about pertinent civil rights issues of the day. You can vote or just read about the pro and con sides to an issue, as well as participate in a forum discussion on the topic.

NEWSGROUPS

alt.activism.youth-rights
alt.censorship
alt.civil-liberty
alt.privacy
alt.privacy.anon-Server
alt.society.civil-disob
alt.society.civil-liberties
alt.society.civil-liberty
clari.news.censorship
clari.news.civil rights
fj.soc.human-rights
info.firearms.politics
soc.rights.human
talk.politics.guns

Related Sites

http://www.powerup.com.au/~dmcclure/progr.htm
http://www.calyx.com/~refuse/altindex.html
http://www.ed.gov/offices/OCR/

> The soul of music slumbers in the shell till waked and kindled by the master's spell; And feeling hearts, touch them but rightly, pour a thousand melodies unheard before!
>
> *Samuel Rogers*

Allegro, Baroque, and Beyond

http://www.netroplex.net/~allegro/

The home page of a performing group dedicated to understanding historical perspectives and using past traditions with period instruments to recreate the musical heritage of the 17th, 18th, and 19th centuries.

Beethoven the Immortal

http://magic.hofstra.edu:7003/immortal/index.html

This site is devoted to the life and works of Ludwig von Beethoven. Contains pictures, audio/MIDI files, as well as a detailed history of his life and a complete listing of his works. Includes famed letters to his immortal beloved.

BMG: Classics World

http://www.classicalmus.com/

A large online store where you can order almost any classical recording currently in print.

The Classical Guitar Aficionados' Page
http://fly.hiwaay.net/~marklong/class/

The Classical Guitar Aficionados' Page

http://fly.hiwaay.net/~marklong/class/

This well-written, interesting site includes playing guides, a FAQ about classical guitars, myriad classical guitar links, and sheet music. Tricks and techniques for guitar playing are provided by the author, whose love and devotion to classical guitar comes through in his prose.

Classical Insites

http://www.classicalinsites.com/

A comely and functional site that provides the browser with a bounty of classical music information. A gallery of featured artists, histories of the masters, discussion of the historical periods of music, and information on various instruments are just a few of the features offered at this site. Links to other resources abound. If you are moved by classical music, don't miss this site!

A B C D E F G H I J K L M N O P Q R S T U V W X Y Z

The Classical MIDI Connection

http://midiworld.com/cmc/

Contains a load of classical MIDI sequences at your perusal. You can browse the site and listen to or save any of the sequences available. This site is well organized and you can search via composers as well as via style of music.

Classical Music Education Foundation

http://www.clef.org/

Clef states its purpose as singular: to bring music to the ears of anyone who will listen. An elegant-looking site that includes a well-organized list of related links. A music database is under construction.

Classical Net

http://www.classical.net/

A point-of-entry into a wide array of informational files about classical music, as well as links to other interesting Web sites. Includes a CD buying guide, composer data, reviews, and more.

Classical Piano Solo Home Page

http://www.geocities.com/Vienna/2027/

Provides MIDI files of classical piano solos and orchestral arrangements created by the author of the site. Boasts that all MIDI files on the site are original. Composer index is alphabetical, and includes interpretations of Beethoven, Chopin, Haydn, Liszt, and more. Includes file size and play time with each file.

Franz Schubert Page

http://home1.swipnet.se/~w-18046/schub.html

Love Schubert? So does the author of this site! Listen to a continuous Schubert loop as you browse this page that includes information on Schubert's life, works, and the historical times surrounding this young composer's life. You won't want to leave, for the music alone.

The George Gershwin Page

http://www.redestb.es/personal/racsoft/George1.htm

This page features a biography, discography, lyrics, and MIDI files of this Jazz-age composer. Get a feel for the genius of Gershwin at this site; provided in both Spanish and English. Music plays while you browse.

Great Women Composers

http://www.geocities.com/EnchantedForest/3744/

This site offers a biographical account of the many forgotten women Opera librettists, singers, and harpsichordists. Includes pictures, music, writings, and biographies of these women. Graphics are beautiful, although text color is hard to read at times.

KlassikNet

http://www.culturekiosque.com/klassik/index.htm

An online magazine for classical music fans, including articles, performer and composer interviews and biographies, reviews, and schedules. Some articles in both French and English.

Medieval & Renaissance Music

http://home.hkstar.com/~mulcheng/home.html

States that it is a site for beginners rather than scholars and provides history and timeline for both medieval and renaissance music. Includes lists of literature and manuscript resources for more information about this music.

National Association of Composers, USA

http://www.thebook.com/nacusa/

NACUSA, founded in 1933, is devoted to the promotion and performance of music by Americans. The site includes members links, recent and upcoming concert schedules, chapter information, and a plethora of links to other music-related sites. Check this one out for the links alone!

New York Philharmonic Gateway

http://www.nyphilharmon.org/

Information for fans and friends of the New York Philharmonic, including educational guides, historical information, ticket information, and news releases.

OPERA America

http://www.operaam.org/

OPERA America is an organization that serves the field of opera by providing informational, technical, and administrative resources to the public in regards to opera. Its mission is to promote opera as exciting and accessible to individuals from all walks of life. The site includes information about advocacy and awareness programs, professional development, an artists database of OPERA America members, and a season and schedule database.

Orchestra Net

http://www.orchestranet.co.uk/

An excellent point of entry for classical music searches, this sites says it's an unbroken chain of hundreds of classical music Web sites ranging greatly in content and style. Includes lists of orchestras, concerts, CDs, books, and music-related news.

Piano on the Net

http://www.artdsm.com/music.html

Always wanted to learn how to play the Piano, but never had the time to learn? This site provides Piano lessons online. Each lesson takes about 35 minutes to complete and you must have QuickTime installed.

The Piano Page

http://www.ptg.org/

A site solely devoted to the piano, including news, events, conventions, music, teachers, manufacturers information, images, advice on buying a piano, and more! Louis Moreau Gottschalk's Souvenir d'Andalousie plays in the background as you browse the site. Piano lovers shouldn't miss this one; the links alone are worth the time.

Symphony Orchestra Information

http://www.hoptechno.com/symphony.htm

Find information on the major symphony orchestras in the world. Organized by geographical area, it includes historical background, Web sites, email addresses, and concert schedules of many major symphony orchestras.

CLASSICAL MUSIC NEWSGROUPS

rec.music.classical

rec.music.classical.guitar

rec.music.classical.performing

rec.music.classical.recordings

rec.music.compose

rec.music.opera

Related Sites

http://pages.nyu.edu./~whitwrth/

http://www.atlantisopera.org/

http://www.chopin.org/

http://www.edepot.com/beethoven.html

http://www.e-universe.com/lmfhome/

http://www.music.vt.edu/faculty/aq/audubon.html

http://www.orbis.net/cmp/

http://www.sai-national.org/phil/composers/composer.html

http://www.xs4all.nl/~etaoin/Glass/

http://www4.interaccess.com/baroque/

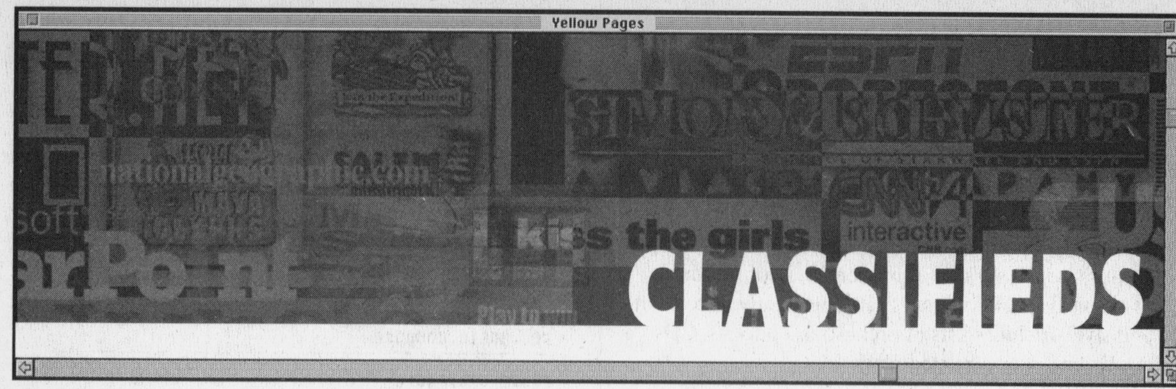

> They send messages through the personal ads, that's how they hook up. Last year she was in Mexico City, then Los Angeles, now New York. Desperate. I love that word.
>
> *Roberta in* Desperately Seeking Susan *(1985)*

A-Z Free Classifieds

http://www.freeclassifieds.com/

You can view the ads via an index, view ads via area codes, place an ad (free of charge), or review the statistics area, which tells you number of hits per category per month. Categories range from business services to child care to dance instruction.

Ads Be Us

http://www.adsbeus.com/

You can advertise with AdsBeUs for $5.00 per month (with a three month minimum). Ads runs for three months, or until you terminate the ad, whichever comes first. You simply send the ad via email, listing the category you want the ad placed in. Includes corporate and banner ads.

Related Sites

- http://classifieds.yahoo.com/personals.html
- http://webcom.com/~abc/abchome.html
- http://www.canadacoupons.com/
- http://www.he.net/~dro/tme.html

Arts and Crafts Internet Mall
http://www.artcraftmall.com/

Adult Personal Ads

http://www.adultpersonals.com/

Features uncensored classified ads posted by adults along with pictures and links to homepages. Includes private "Members Only" live chat and private email box issued with every membership.

Alana's Online Ads

http://ajordan.com/class.html

You'll find ad after ad listed here, from psychics to Chile recipes to Christmas letters from Santa. Everything you could think of is for sale here. Submitting ads is free and requires only submission of a form.

AllAbout Center

http://www.icemall.com/allabout/inmark.html

The free classifieds section of this site includes links to various other free classifieds sections, regional and national, as well as ads of its own. A good point of entry if you are looking for a ton of classified sites.

Amused Amigos

http://www.amused.com/penpal.html

A pen pals site that specifically prohibits inappropriate chatting, includes an impressive amount of registered pen pals from around the globe. Also includes links to other pen pal sites. Ages typically range from 13 to 40.

Related Sites

- http://www.sgn.com/4sale.html
- http://www.texoma.com/donrey/classified/newspaper/advertising/

Arts and Crafts Internet Mall

http://www.artcraftmall.com/

Provides purchasing information about dolls, wood crafts, wreaths, Barbie clothes, herbal bath soaps, Santas, gourds, doll clothing, gifts, and more. Read about the craft of the week or browse the other arts and crafts resources listed at this site. You can submit free classified ads, which run for two months.

Buy and Sell.Net

http://www.buyandsell.net/

You can post and search this large collection of ads as well as update your ad at any time. Ad categories range from travel to antiques to video games to crafts. Automatically picks Usenet newsgroups appropriate to your ad.

CyberPages Business Classifieds

http://www.cyberpages.com/business

Organized by advertising category and within category, by city, this service includes free section for personal items. Business items, irrespective of value, must be entered in the free section. Also includes services such as missing persons, dating services, interesting polls, stocks, and commodities.

Net Classifieds

http://www.netclassifieds.com.au/

When browsing the Net Classifieds, you'll find product categories such as art, baby needs, boats, electronics, and others. Each category has a related links section as well. Search by category or by index.

One-Stop Web Classifieds

http://www.netbizusa.com/

Here you can browse the ads, submit your own ad, go to the chat room, or review the ad rates. Categories vary from antiques to real estate to child care to personal ads. A good way to get in touch with other buyers or sellers.

Porsche Classifieds Digest

http://www.haphazard.com/pcd/

A compilation of 2000 or more Porsche-related classified ads from all over the Internet; updated daily. Browse via Porsche model, look for Porsche-related employment, or perform a custom search. You're bound to find the Porsche or Porsche-related product you are looking for here.

Surfing Classifieds: Dahuna Online

http://www.dahuna.com/

The one-stop shop for all your surfing needs, whether it be world links, the surf shop, surf and tide reports, or an extensive classified section. Search the classifieds for surfboards of all types, wetsuits, books, and various surfing paraphernalia.

Telephone Directories on the Web

http://www.contractjobs.com/tel/

Reports itself to be the most detailed listing of online white pages, yellow pages, and fax directories on the Web. Rated top 1,000 World Sites by Web Statistics. Includes areas from Argentina to Israel to Taiwan and more. Email address directories are also available.

WorldPhoto

http://www.worldphoto.com/

Resources for photographers worldwide. You can share a photographic tip or trick, or post a photo-related problem in the help forum. Comprehensive free classified ad section for photo equipment and related services.

NEWSGROUPS

alt.ads

alt.business

alt.business.misc

alt.personals.ads

alt.marketplace.fun

misc.forsale

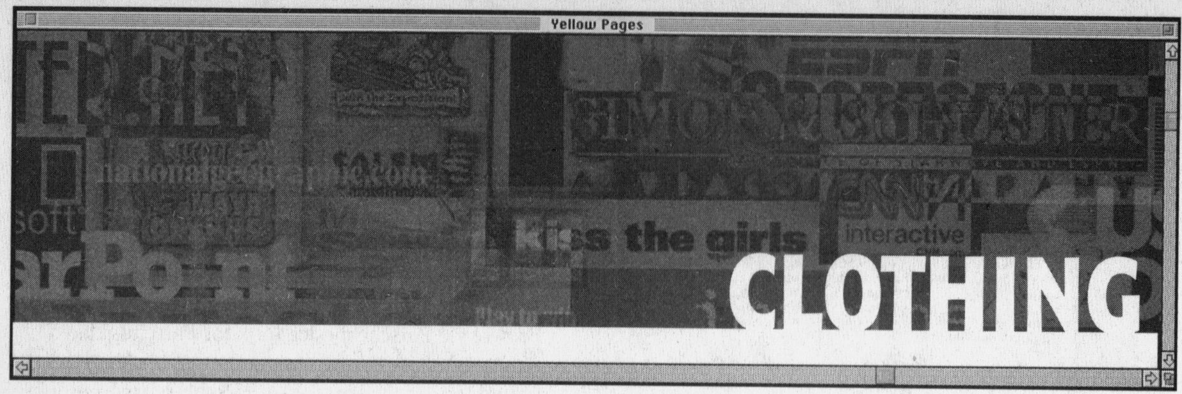

> I love to go shopping. I love to freak out salespeople. They ask me if they can help me, and I say, "Have you got anything I'd like?" Then they ask me what size I need, and I say, "Extra medium."
>
> *Steven Wright*

2(x)ist Underwear

`http://www.2xist.com/`

Provides a virtual catalog of men's underwear. Includes a closer view of boxers, briefs, tanks, and tees, as well as a size chart and guarantee.

Abercrombie & Fitch: A Cool Yule

`http://www.abercrombie.com/`

Proving that it's more than just a men's and women's clothing store, this site offers links to the hottest Internet games, Abercrombie & Fitch-approved music, and other cool sites. Order their quarterly catalog ($10) and receive even more news, cultural information, and, of course, check out the latest styles.

America's Tall Catalog

`http://www.cottonshirt.com/`

Offers 100-percent cotton and button-down pinpoint oxfords for the big and tall. Web-direct, same day shipping. Prices and sizes available are listed.

Welcome to BackCountry, Inc.
`http://www.backcountryinc.com/`

Apparel Catalogs

`http://www.apparelcatalogs.com/`

Database of clothing catalogs for men, women, and children and how to order them. Lists description of the type of apparel sold, customer service phone numbers, addresses, and costs of the catalog.

Baby Armadillo Clothing

`http://www.albany.net/%7Esmiles/`

Your infants and toddlers will be adorable dressed in this line of clothing, all made of 100-percent combed cotton knits. View their current designs and prices and find out how to order.

Bonté Casuals

`http://www.catalog.com/corner/bonte`

Offers children's casual wear made with environmentally friendly fabrics. For every garment sold, the company purchases 25 square feet of rainforest or wetlands acreage or helps sponsor a whale. If you send in your hangtag, they give you the deed to the property.

Camalgori A Representative Collection of Fashion Made in Italy

`http://www.nettuno.it/btw/cmlgr`

Offers the Camalgori collection of women's clothing.

Capitol Clothing Corporation

`http://www.netpatrol.com/members/capitolc.html`

Boys clothing manufacturer based in Miami, Florida. Choose from two lines of clothing: Little Baron, sizes infant to 7, a Capitol Boys, sizes 8 to 14. For more information, contact them by phone, mail, or email.

Eddie Bauer Online Store Home Page

`http://www.eddiebauer.com/eb/index.asp`

Casual and dress casual clothing for men and women, including footwear, outerwear, underwear, and skiwear. Also sells luggage, home decor items, and other accessories. After checking their weekly specials, you can order online. Join EB Exclusive for a special online shopping experience. You can even fill out a wish list online for friends and family to view.

Express Online

`http://express.style.com/`

Provides news about fashions, trends, and upcoming merchandise. Ask the Express fashion director for fashion tips and tricks. Members are eligible for exclusive offers from Express.

Frederick's of Hollywood Home Page

`http://www.fredericks.com/`

Retail clothing company specializing in women's lingerie, swimwear, hosiery, sportswear, and dresses, but also offers some menswear. Print out their free coupon for 15 percent off any item in one of their retail stores. There's also a Museum of the Frederick's clothing worn by celebrities in various film and television roles.

Genius T-Shirts

`http://www.a1.com/shirt/t-shirt.html`

Carries a collection of 50 artistic, scholarly T-shirts and sweatshirts, including Einstein, Socrates, Mozart, Geronimo, Dickinson, and more. Will ship internationally.

Grand Illusions Clothing Company

`http://grand-illusion.com/`

Features authentic reproductions of clothing and uniforms worn through America's history. The clothing has appeared in various films including Gettysburg, Dances with Wolves, and Glory. A vast online selection of men's and women's mid-nineteenth century garments and accessories. Online ordering available or visit their retail store in Newark, Delaware.

Finding & Buying Just About Anything Online

Shops and malls are as diverse in the products they carry as their offline counterparts, and they number almost as many. While online shopping is relatively new (only a few years old), some of the online stores rival their offline siblings in the sheer number of products they carry. Because there are so many shopping sites online, new database sites are springing up to help consumers choose between and find some of the many sites out there. One example of this is the Computer ESP Cyberstore (`http://www.uvision.com/`). This site enables you to search for a word or phrase to find that product in their database, or you can look at the over 46,000 products listed by category and choose a product. The database will pull up all the different companies selling the products you are interested in, and then it will show the actual product and its price.

Graphiti

`http://libertynet.org/~graphiti`

Lets you design your own T-shirts, sweatshirts, jackets, caps, and more. Lets you order as many or as few items as you want.

Hot Couture Clothing Company

`http://www.hotcouture.com`

Designs and manufactures clothing for women. Designs and sews every garment individually to produce distinctive garments that represent the wearer's individual sense of style.

J.J. Skivvee Clothing Company

`http://www.jjskivvee.com/`

A small, but impressive, line of basic, casual clothing for men and women. Choose from boxers, Sherpa top, tunic, or cardigan, Saturday pants, Mission shirt, Mid-Nite shirt or Stuff-it blanket. Online ordering available.

Latter-Day Specialties

`http://www.valor.net/mormon/clothing.htm`

Clothing designed for the Mormon community. View the catalog, fill your shopping cart, and place your order all online.

A B C D E F G H I J K L M N O P Q R S T U V W X Y Z

Lebow Bros. Clothing for Men and Boys

http://www.tiac.net/users/lebow/

Offers fine clothing for men and boys, including sizes for the hard-to-fit individual. (In English and Chinese.)

Menswear Unlimited

http://www.mens-wear.com/

Presents a catalog of men's tailored clothing.

Ms. Jill's Vintage Clothing and Retro Clothing

http://www.msjills.com/

Sells men's and women's clothing from the 40s, 50s, and 60s, as well as jewelry and other accessories. Note Ms. Jill's Fashion Tip of the Week. Humorous quips and descriptions from Ms. Jill make this site quite entertaining.

Planet Greek

http://www.nemonet.com/planet/plntgrek.htm

Offers a selection of custom screen-printed and embroidered Greek apparel, including event T-shirts and elaborately embroidered fraternity or sorority crests.

Rainbow Rags

http://www.promotion.com/rainbow/

Offers high-quality, durable children's clothing featuring embroidered and appliquéd trim for a unique look.

Rick Vela's Clothing Store

http://www.rickvelaclothing.com/

Men's traditional and contemporary corporate clothing store based in Waco, Texas. View photos, prices, and descriptions. You don't have to travel to Waco to order, just send them an email or call.

Specially For You—Clothing for the Physically Challenged

http://www.icontrol.net/speciallyforyou/

Clothing tailored to fit men and women with special needs. Check out the different types of clothes available. Or, if you need something you don't see, contact them and they will do their best to meet your specific need.

The UV and Sun Protection Shop

http://www.ilos.net/%7Ewcic/sunprotection.htm

Clothing designed to protect you from harmful UV rays of the sun, which are proven to cause skin cancer. Solarweave clothing blocks 95 to 99 percent of UV radiation. Buy men's, women's, and children's clothing or, if you want to make something yourself, you can order the fabric.

Welcome to BackCountry, Inc.

http://www.backcountryinc.com/

BackCountry sells hunting gear, including camouflage clothing made with Omnitherm, a machine washable wool fabric. Online ordering available.

Welcome to L.L. Bean

http://www.llbean.com/

Sporting gear and apparel for men, women, and children. Order from more than 1,000 L.L. Bean products shown in the online store or place your catalog order while online and find out availability instantly.

Related Sites
http://www.ski-north.com/clothing.html
http://www.quikpage.com/N/naturalfib/
http://www.gymboree.com/
http://www.pbm.com/%7Elindahl/rialto/idxclothing.html
http://www.quikpage.com/L/laniado/
http://kleids.com/index.html
http://www.purefilth.com.au/surfgear.htm
http://www.lakeland.com/
http://commerce.best.com/~inetmall/achldrnsclthng.html
http://www.cdpnet.com/bellyband/

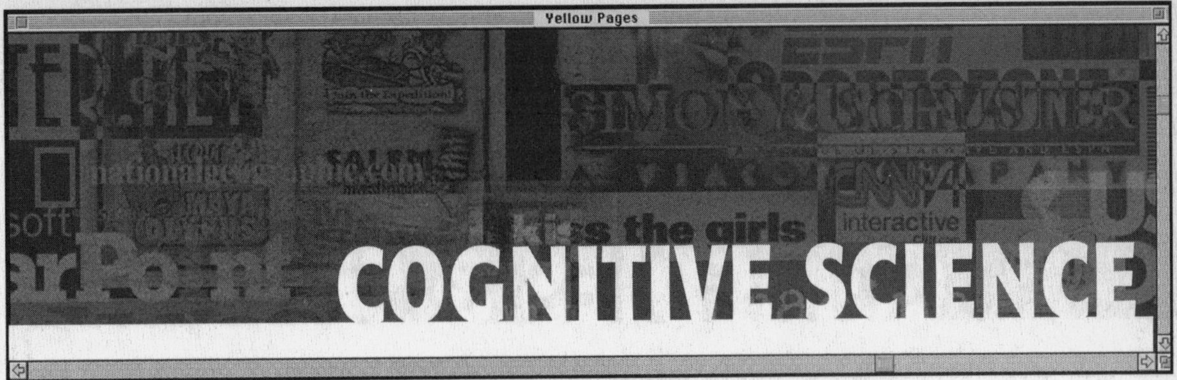

> The brain is a wonderful organ. It starts working when you get up in the morning and doesn't stop until you get to the office.
>
> *Robert Frost*

Esoteric Psychology

http://users.aol.com/psychosoph/intropsych.html

Provides an alternative look at psychology and relationships based on spiritual ideas and values. Also contains links to interesting charts on soul evolution, auras, and energies.

Internet Resources for Cognitive Science

http://gort.ucsd.edu/ds/sophia/cogsci.html

Site provides links to major cognitive science academic departments. Also contains links to the library of the University of California at San Diego.

Interpsych

http://www.shef.ac.uk/%7Epsysc/InterPsych/inter.html

Site provides an Internet forum discussion of mental health issues and contains links to electronic conferences on topics such as addiction, group-psychotherapy, hypnosis, neuropsych, and many more.

MIT Artificial Intelligence Laboratory
http://www.ai.mit.edu/

MIT Artificial Intelligence Laboratory

http://www.ai.mit.edu/

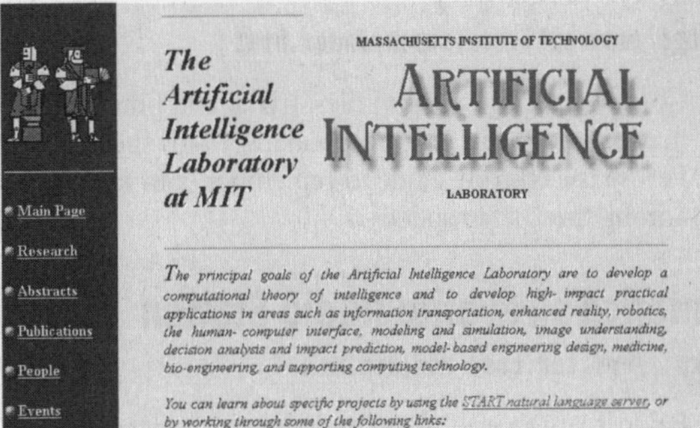

Provides information and publications about MIT's latest work on artificial intelligence, including information on computer vision, humanoid robotics, and artificial muscles.

Neurosciences on the Internet

http://www.lm.com/~nab

Lists sites suggested as starting points for exploring neuroscience. Also lists some essential biological and medical resource sites and some World Wide Web sites invaluable for any type of information retrieval.

Psych Central–Dr. John Grohol's Mental Health Page

http://www.grohol.com/web.htm

Site provides comprehensive links to psychological and mental health topics. Links are broken into two categories—general and professional resources. Site provides a good place to begin searching for information about psychological disorders.

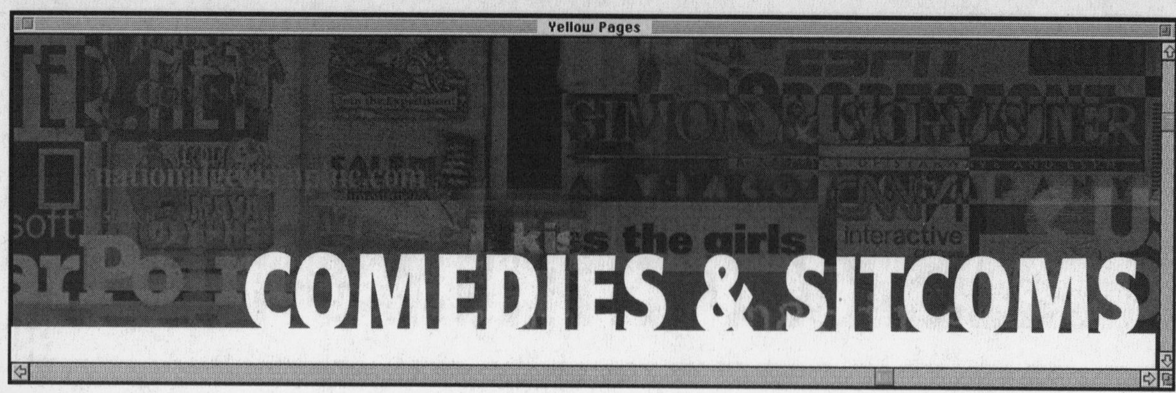

A
B
C
D
E
F
G
H
I
J
K
L
M
N
O
P
Q
R
S
T
U
V
W
X
Y
Z

These pretzels are making me thirsty.

Cosmo Kramer from Seinfeld

All in the Family

http://www.aitf.com/index/index.html

Contains pictures, sound files, trivia, and other information about this ground-breaking 1970s show. Peruse the episode guide to remember your favorites among the 202 episodes.

America's Favorite Radio Station

http://www.tir.com/~rtw/krp.htm

Baby, if you've ever wondered, this site concentrates on *WKRP in Cincinnati.* It calls itself a fan guide and has articles, photos, stories, and other remembrances from the late '70s–early '80s sitcom.

Beavis and Butthead: The Episode Guide

http://www.mcs.net/~batcave/public_html/bnbguide.html

Site takes a while to load, but for die-hard fans, it's worth it. Lists episodes by season and includes the original air date, a synopsis, and a list of the videos shown. Someone just has too much time on their hands…

The Benny Hill Information Page

http://pages.prodigy.com/PA/mrbrittas/Benny.html

Provides information about the popular British sketch comedy program *The Benny Hill Show.* Includes cast profiles, songs, and much more.

Beavis and Butthead: The Episode Guide
http://www.mcs.net/~batcave/public_html/bnbguide.html

Cheers Home Page
http://s9000.furman.edu/~treu/cheers.html

The Unofficial Addams Family Website
http://www.addamsfamily.com/

Better Dead Than SMEG

http://www.dwarflander.com/reddwarf.htm

The Red Dwarf unofficial Web page is bandwidth-heavy and extremely Netscape formatted, but deserves a look if you are a fan of the almost-famous British comedy.

Bewitched Home Page

http://www.persephone.com/bewitched/

Elizabeth Montgomery and her TV show have many fans, but none seem as Web-savvy as the creator of this site. It has the look and feel of the television program and much information about people related to the show.

The Bob Newhart Unofficial Homepage

http://www.bob-newhart.com/

This page is dedicated to all of Bob Newhart's shows from 1972–present, but concentrates mainly on *The Bob Newhart Show,* which lasted from 1972–1978. There are links to episode guides, broadcast listings, trivia, and other pieces of Newhart interest.

Bosom Buddies Home Page

http://www.ozemail.com.au/~peterv/bb/index.html

Remember Kip and Henry? They lived in an all-women's apartment complex and worked in an advertising agency. Well, anyway, this is their Web site, and it's very complete—there's an episode guide, reviews, sounds, and loads of other information about this show that helped start Tom Hanks's career. (No offense to Peter Scolari, of course.)

The Brady Bunch Gallery

http://weber.u.washington.edu/~schell/brady.html

Provides many different pictures and articles about the wildly popular 1970s television show *The Brady Bunch.* Includes links to other Brady sites.

Brady World

http://members.aol.com/BradyBFan/brady.htm

Contains nearly everything you ever wanted to know about the popular 1970s sitcom *The Brady Bunch.* Includes many different pictures, an episode guide, and information about the new movies.

The British Comedy Library

http://homepages.enterprise.net/achwong/Comedy/index.html

Fans of British comedy will enjoy this collection of information and links. Provides lots of information about the '80s hit, *The Young Ones,* and its cast.

Cafe Nervosa

http://www-personal.umich.edu/~geena/frasier.html

This site is dedicated to the NBC comedy *Frasier,* starring Kelsey Grammer and Moose the dog (as Eddie). With the theme song, photos, and much more to come, this page is well worth seeing. It has some nice animated GIFs and other stuff that are, well, Frasier-riffic!

The Carol Burnett Show Episode Guide

http://www-personal.umich.edu/~mcgee/cbsguide.txt

Just what it says it is: a no-nonsense text file filled with information about The *Carol Burnett Show,* which aired from 1968–1979.

Caroline in the City

http://www.nbc.com/tvcentral/shows/carolineinthecity/index.html

Describes the whole convoluted history of the relationship between Caroline and Richard. Also provides cast bios and links to transcripts of their online chat sessions.

Cheers Home Page

http://s9000.furman.edu/~treu/cheers.html

Online fan site of the TV show *Cheers.* Includes an archive of pictures, audio of famous *Cheers* quotes, information about every cast member, and the lyrics to Woody's classic "Kelly's Song."

C'mon, Get Happy!

http://www.geocities.com/Hollywood/5255/

This is the unofficial home page of the Partridge family. It has pictures, links, and other stuff relating to the show *The Partridge Family* and its original cast.

The Comedy Store Fan Club Home Page

http://www.macom.co.il/Channel2/ComedyStore/index.html

Next time you are in Israel, check out this popular Hebrew program. But if you can't make it there and are curious what happens on Israeli TV, you can access it from this fan club home page.

Dharma & Greg

http://www.abc.com/primetime/dharma_greg/

This site doesn't just describe the popular new show and its stars, it helps you determine how compatible you are with your mate. Also provides synopses for upcoming episodes.

The Dick Van Dyke Show

http://hampshire.edu/~tdzF94/DVD.html

Provides a good amount of information about the popular 1960s television show *The Dick Van Dyke Show.* Includes cast profiles, character backgrounds, an episode guide, trivia, sound bytes, and much more. Includes links to other related sites.

The Dick Van Dyke Show

http://www.geocities.com/TelevisionCity/1190/

Provides trivia questions, pictures, and an episode guide of the popular sitcom *The Dick Van Dyke Show.* Includes sound bytes, cast profile, and a "what are they doing now" segment.

Related Sites

http://members.aol.com/iluvmattl/blove.html

http://pages.prodigy.com/PA/mrbrittas/Benny.html

http://www.foxworld.com/koth/index.htm

Dinosaurs

http://www.sci.kun.nl/thalia/funpage/dinosaurs/dinos_en.html

You can read this page in both English and Dutch, but what you'll get is basically the same content. It has pictures, cast member bios, a sound library, and more dino-oriented stuff.

Dr. Katz

http://home.dwave.net/~jscott/katz.html

Almost as neurotic as his patients, Dr. Katz sees a couple of stand-up comedians an episode. Oh yeah, he's a therapist. And a cartoon.

Dream On

http://www.mca.com/tv/dreamon/

The popular HBO adult sitcom has come to Comedy Central on cable TV. There are bios, credits, a forum, and more available for your perusal at this site.

Duckman!

http://bluejay.creighton.edu/~jduche/duckman.html

Tons of information about this crazy animated show. Check out random Duckman! quotes, synopses of each season, and graphics from the show. Great wallpaper!

Eerie, Indiana

http://www.imc.sfu.ca/eerie/

This strange, short-lived program has many fans, and this Web site was written by one of the most fanatic. It is very complete with links, credits, pictures, sounds, an episode guide, and a mailing list.

Ellen

http://www.tvplex.com/Touchstone/Ellen/

Provides pictures, video clips, sound bytes, and cast profiles about the popular television comedy *Ellen*. Includes episode backgrounds and links to other related sites.

Encyclopedia Brady

http://www.primenet.com/~dbrady/

The encyclopedia Brady is comprehensive in nature, filled with a FAQ, an episode guide, links to other Brady sites, and a glossary. If you are addicted to Mike and Carol and Sam and Alice, you'll love this site.

Everybody Loves Raymond

http://www.cbs.com/prime/raymond/index.htm

Contains your basic information, including a description of the show, a summary of the next episode, cast bios, and contact information. This show has jumped in the ratings since it switched nights, much to the delight of the critics that loved it (but doesn't everybody?).

The Facts of Life Unofficial Home Page

http://fly.hiwaay.net/~djberry/ns3-fol.htm

You take the good, you take the bad, you take some Netscape extensions. Anyway, this page is very complete with everything you probably forgot about this *Diff'rent Strokes* spin-off. Be warned, though, this page is graphics-heavy and formatted to the nines.

Fawlty Towers Episode Guide

http://www.cm.cf.ac.uk/Fun/FawltyTowers.html

Perfect for those PBS British comedy extravaganzas, the *Fawlty Towers* episode guide will give you a description of each episode, including what the sign outside says.

Friends

http://www.nbc.com/entertainment/shows/friends/index.html

The official *Friends* home page. Click your favorite character to see a bio of the actor.

The Get Smart Home Page

http://www.bcpl.lib.md.us/~cbirkmey/getsmart.html

This site is devoted to Maxwell Smart and all his buddies at Control. This site disseminates all sorts of information, including cast lists, episode guides, and other Smart-related info.

Gilligan's Island

http://www.lookup.com/homepages/58181/homea.html

This site has daily quizzes, a free *Gilligan's Island* information package, and a three-hour tour. There is also information about every character present on the show. Did you know that Mrs. Howell's name was actually Eunice?

Related Sites

http://www.geocities.com/Hollywood/Lot/9904/greenmain.html

http://www.geocities.com/TelevisionCity/3657/

The Golden Girls

http://www.innotts.co.uk/~kburton/gg/

The show with Bea Arthur, Rue McClanahan, Betty White, and Estelle Getty finds its home at this site. There are character bios, the title song, and a book of scripts located here.

Home of Home Improvement Cyberfans

http://www.morepower.com/homeimpr.html

More information than you probably ever wanted about Tim Allen, *Tool Time*, or that hunky Jonathan Taylor Thomas. This page has won all kinds of awards and is worth seeing even if just out of respect for the sheer amount of time taken to create it.

The Honeymooners Picture Depot

http://www.intercall.com/~python/honymoon/honymoon.htm

This page has information about Jackie Gleason, Art Carney, and Joyce Randolph, as well as the popular '50s TV show, *The Honeymooners.*

Hope & Gloria

http://www.lifetimetv.com/thetube/hope/index.html

Provides information about the Lifetime television comedy program *Hope & Gloria.* Includes an episode guide, character profile, and chat information.

Larry Sanders Cast

http://www.hbo.com/larry/

Demonstrates why this show is so popular and appealing. Provides detailed episode highlights, including parts of the actual scripts with pictures. All the background information you need to enjoy this show to its fullest is available here.

The Leave It To Beaver Home Page

http://www.geocities.com/Hollywood/Hills/2993/

Provides information about the very popular 1950s television comedy *Leave It To Beaver.* Includes character background, cast profiles, pictures, and news about the Leave It To Beaver movie.

Related Sites

http://www.idreamofjeannie.com/

http://www.lifetimetv.com/tv/DESIGNING/INDEX.HTM

http://www.nbc.com/tvcentral/shows/justshootme/

Love & Marriage

http://www.spe.sony.com/tv/shows/married/index.html

Provides the official home page for the comedy show *Married...With Children.* Includes show background, cast profiles, and much more.

Mad About You

http://www.spe.sony.com/tv/shows/mad/index.html

Check out Paul and Jamie's family tree to see how they became who they are today. The episode guide provides the definitive history of this favorite couple from the very beginning. Also links to the show's soundtrack and a game called "Murray's Mad Dash."

Mama's Family

http://www.labs.net/mfreier45/mamaeg.htm

The official unofficial *Mama's Family* site, complete with an episode guide, quotes, cast information, and other links.

Maniac Mansion

http://alcor.concordia.ca/~vipond/maniac.htm

From the show starring Joe Flaherty as Fred Edison, this home page is dedicated to what many believe to be the "funniest television program in history." Of course, those people are probably Canadian.

The Many Loves of Dobie Gillis

http://www.worldsite.net/~furthur/

Includes about anything one needs to know about the popular comedy *The Many Loves of Dobie Gillis* that starred Dwayne Hickman as Dobie and Bob Denver as Maynard G.Krebbs (later Gilligan on *Gilligan's Island*). Provides many pictures, cast profiles, and information where Dobie Gillis is on television these days.

Married...With Children Home Page

http://bundy.simplenet.com/mwc/

If you were looking for information or links for *Married...With Children,* this is the place to go. It has episode guides, pictures, and the coveted Bundybase.

Related Sites

http://www.persephone.com/bewitched/

http://www.wdfn.com/brackets/sitcom.html

A B C D E F G H I J K L M N O P Q R S T U V W X Y Z

Monty Python's Flying Circus

http://www.dcscomp.com.au/sdp/tvseries/index.htm

Ever wondered what the heck is a Monty Python? This site can answer your every question. The series guide links to the over 400 sketches performed, and you can listen to almost 100 sound bytes from the show. You also can watch a video of the opening animation.

Moon Over Parma

http://www.geocities.com/Hollywood/6663/parma.htm

A tribute to *The Drew Carey Show*, Moon Over Parma is very complete. It has an episode guide, pictures, bios, and links to other Drew Carey-oriented Net sites.

Moonlighting, on the Web

http://www.ici.net/cust_pages/ddemelo/moonlighting.html

The show that launched Bruce Willis's career and revived Cybill Shepherd's finds a great fan page here. There are links to background information, an episode guide, related pages, and even an IRC chat channel.

The Nanny Unofficial Home Page

http://www.thenanny.com/

This site has FAQs, an episode guide, links, pictures, and cast references about the popular CBS show *The Nanny*. It also has sound bytes, but who would want Fran Drescher's voice on their SoundBlaster card?

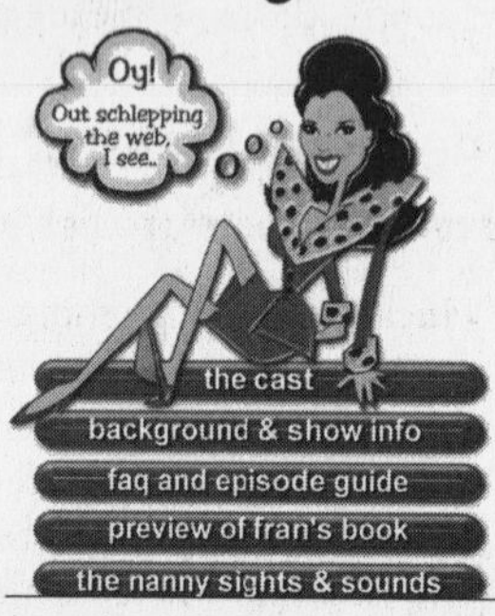

The New Web Site of Love Mystery Science Theatre 3000

http://tazer.engrs.infi.net/mst3k/

Find out the latest on MST3K's move from Comedy Central and their film. This site also includes episode guides, FAQs, and ratings of each show.

Parker Lewis Can't Lose

http://www.geo.mtu.edu/flamingo/

Digests; archives; and the whos, whats, whens, and wheres of the short-lived cult-followed Fox television program.

The R.M.P.S.S.

http://ugWeb.cs.ualberta.ca/~stuart/monty.cgi/

Every time you access this site, a different Monty Python sketch appears. You can also choose to see any of dozens of Monty Python TV and movie skits.

Saturday Night Archives

http://www.best.com:80/~dijon/tv/snl/

A number of FAQs on characters, parodies, song lyrics, *Wayne's World*, band information, and more are provided at this site. This site also includes a monthly schedule of SNL, links to Web sites of former cast members, and of course the Deep Thought of the Day.

Seinfeld

http://www.nbc.com/entertainment/shows/seinfeld/index.html

Provides the official NBC Web site for the wildly popular show *Seinfeld*. Includes upcoming episode previews, chat transcripts, cast profiles, and character background.

Seinfeld Index Page

http://seinfeld.sogaard.com/

If you are a fan of the NBC comedy *Seinfeld*, then this site is for you. This site provides an index site for nearly all of the *Seinfeld* pages on the Internet, along with having quite a bit of information on the popular comedy. Provides an episode guide, character guide, and much more.

Sergeant Bilko

http://www.bilko.u-net.com/index.htm

This site provides an episode guide and other information about the classic comedy program *Sergeant Bilko*, also known as *The Phil Silvers Show*. Includes cast profiles and links to related sites.

The Simpsons Archive

http://www.snpp.com/

Find out how many different chalkboard and couch gags have been used in the opening credits. Peruse all references to *The Simpsons*—whether in newspapers, magazines, political cartoons, or other sources—in the complete bibliography. All Simpsons fanatics can find much of interest here.

Since 1975, Saturday Night Live

http://members.itw.com/~bradleys/snl.html

Find out about late-breaking SNL news, read transcripts of past Weekend Updates, and see what others thought of recent shows. This in-depth site also lists all the different casts since the beginning of the show. The FAQ alone has 67 questions and answers.

Sitcom!

http://www.geocities.com/TelevisionCity/1233/index.html

This site-in-progress is putting together a central location to find links to your favorite sitcoms. *Friends* alone has over 75 links here. Definitely a site to keep your eye on.

Sitcom Architects Registry

http://www.funhaus.com/tvthesis/arcreg.html

Answers the question everyone has been desperately seeking the answer to: How many architects have there been in TV sitcoms? This list identifies the character, the actor, the series, and the dates. What a big weight off—now we don't have to hunt them down on our own.

Sledge Hammer! Arsenal

http://www.phrank.com/sh/

Remember David Rasche? Remember when comedy was wacky? Alright, maybe that's a bit too cheesy, but if you remember this show, you'll be glad to know that there is now a place to get sounds, pictures, and information about this short-lived ABC sitcom.

Spin City

http://www.abc.com/primetime/spin_city/index.html

This is the official site of the hip new comedy set in and around the New York City mayor's office. Includes show synopsis, cast bios, and a guide to past and future episodes.

South Park

http://www.comcentral.com/southpark/

This cartoon is definitely *not* for kids, but the raunchy little group of boys from South Park has gained a huge following. Visit the South Park Playland to play games such as Sliders, Stack Up, and a hilarious Word Jumble.

The State's Virtual Whatever

http://www.thstate.com/

The State comedy troupe has now set up a Web site with email links to each of the members and information about what they are all now doing. Originally brought to TV by MTV, the State has a new show on Comedy Central.

Sup's Blackadder Page

http://www.geocities.com/televisioncity/8889/bladder.htm

The British comedy starring Rowan Atkinson as Blackadder has a very well-done fan page here. This site hosts many sounds; an interview; and other links related to Rowan Atkinson, Blackadder, and British comedy.

The Unofficial Addams Family Website

http://www.addamsfamily.com/

This complete Addams family site contains not only downloadable clips, photos, and trivia about the TV series, but about the cartoons and movies as well. Lists all guest stars of the series and provides a full history of the works of Charles Addams, the creator.

Welcome to the Official Mr. Bean Website

http://www.mrbean.co.uk/

If you like Mr. Bean, you'll love this goofy site. Much of it is written in first person as the character himself, so it contains lots of nonsensical information. Also provides clips from his self-titled movie.

What's Happening

http://www.geocities.com/Colosseum/6667/heyheyhey.html

Provides information about the sitcom *What's Happening* and the later show *What's Happening Now*. Includes a cast profile, character background, pictures, sound files, and much more.

Whose Line Is It Anyway?

http://www.geocities.com/WestHollywood/1770/wliia.html

Read about this improvisational game show, which has aired since 1988 in England. You can find the show on Comedy Central and read more about the rules and stars. Be sure to read about the Drinking Game!

A B C D E F G H I J K L M N O P Q R S T U V W X Y Z

The Wonder Years

http://www.sfc.keio.ac.jp/~t93272at/wonder.html

A site for the complete *Wonder Years* fan. This page contains loads of information about Kevin Arnold and his entourage. Join the mailing list, read the articles, but most of all, enjoy the site.

LISTSERVS

FRIENDSZ—Friend Zone—The NBC comedy Friends fans

You can join this group by sending the message "sub FRIENDSZ your name" to

listserv@listserv.dartmouth.edu

SITCOM—Sitcom Writing Discussion List

You can join this group by sending the message "sub SITCOM your name" to

listserv@maelstrom.stjohns.edu

NEWSGROUPS

alt.comedy

alt.comedy.air-farce

alt.comedy.british

alt.comedy.british.blackadder

alt.comedy.firesgn.thtre

alt.comedy.improvisation

alt.comedy.jerrylewis

alt.comedy.laural-hardy

alt.comedy.marx-bros

alt.comedy.paul-reubens

alt.comedy.slapstick

alt.comedy.slapstick.3stooges

alt.comedy.standup

alt.comedy.vaudeville

alt.comedy-central

alt.fan.adams.family

alt.fan.beavis-n-butthead

alt.fan.monty-python

alt.tv.ab-fab

alt.tv.absolutely-fabulous

alt.tv.beavis-n-butthead

alt.tv.boston-common

alt.tv.brady-bunch

alt.tv.caroline-city

alt.tv.dr-katz

alt.tv.frasier

alt.tv.friends

alt.tv.hermans-head

alt.tv.home-imprvment

alt.tv.kids-in-hall

alt.tv.mad-about-you

alt.tv.mash

alt.tv.mr-belvedere

alt.tv.mwc

alt.tv.newsradio

alt.tv.ren-n-stimpy

alt.tv.roseanne

alt.tv.seinfeld

alt.tv.simpsons

alt.tv.simpsons.itchy-scratchy

alt.tv.sitcom

alt.tv.southpark

alt.tv.spin-city

alt.tv.the-nanny

alt.tv.wings

alt.tv.wonder-years

rec.arts.tv.uk.comedy

FTP SITES

ftp://ftp.cdrom.com/.12/internet/rtfm/rec/arts/tv/uk/comedy

ftp://ftp.csie.nctu.edu.tw/Documents/FAQ/rec/arts/tv/uk/comedy

ftp://ftp.doc.ic.ac.uk/media/tv/collections/tardis/uk/comedy/SitcomList

ftp://ftp.io.com/pub/usr/pablo/Favorites/entertainment/Television/Duckman.url

ftp://ftp.isc.org/pub/usenet/control/alt/alt.tv.sitcom.Z

ftp://ftp.ntua.gr/pub/audio/sounds/series/seinfeld

ftp://ftp.rat.org/pub/miles/midi/THEMES/TV/Seinfeld.mid

ftp://ftp.stgenesis.org/pub/tv/comedy

ftp://ftp.surreycmc.gov.uk/Favorites/Entertainment/Television/TheSimpsons.url

ftp://ftp.umr.edu/.pub/faqs/text/tv/frasier

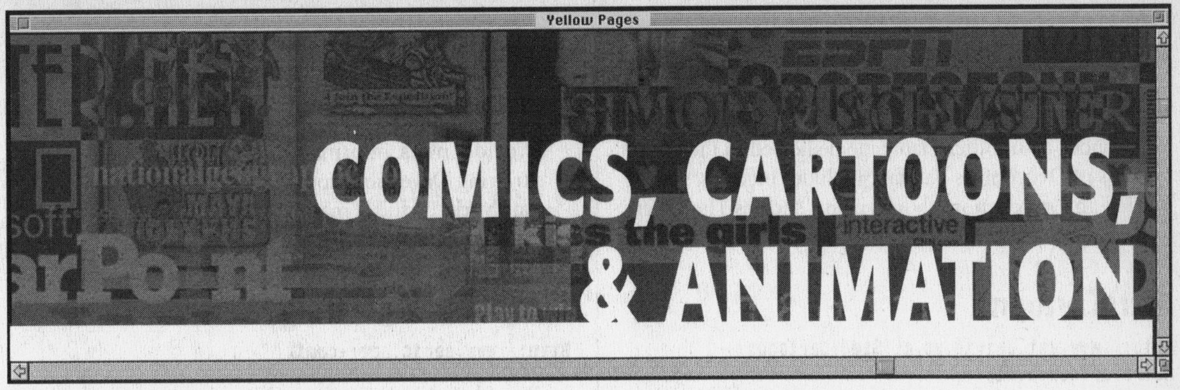

Boy, you don't know nothing. Mighty Mouse is a cartoon. Superman's a real guy. There's no way a cartoon could beat up a real guy.

Teddy in Stand by Me *(1986)*

The 3-D Zone

http://www.leonardo.net/3dzone/

Publishes comic books in 3D, including work by Steve Ditko, Bill Ward, and others. Read about the latest publications, or pull out your 3D glasses and click 3-D Fun.

The 86th Floor

http://members.aol.com/the86floor/index.html

Provides an online site for fans of the pulp fiction and comic book hero Doc Savage. Includes Doc Savage news, information, a virtual comic, and much more.

Amazing Spider-Man Page

http://pilot.msu.edu/user/haleysco/spiderman/

Provides an unofficial fan page dedicated to Marvel Comic's Spider-Man. Includes artwork, news, and an interview with Marvel Comic guru Stan Lee.

Kids' Cool Animation
http://www.kaleidoscapes.com/kc_intro.html

Animation Links

http://pearl.cs.pusan.ac.kr/~sskim/page/animate.html

This site gives you close to 50 links to different animation sites, including MTV online animation, Animation resources on the net, plus many more.

Animation World Network

http://www.awn.com/

Anyone interested in animation should check this site out! It includes links to Animation World Magazine, a Career Connection, and an animation village, gallery, and vault.

The Anime Web

http://www.itsnet.com/~bug/animeweb/

Provides information, news, and pictures from many different Japanese animation films. Includes club entries from all over the world with links to other related sites.

Animecca

http://animecca.com/

This is the site for anyone interested in animation, especially Japanese Animae. Includes reviews, articles, artwork, and links to many related animation sites. Also includes a discussion forum, news, and upcoming release information.

ARKHAM ASYLUM

http://copper.ucs.indiana.edu/~jeffsmil/

Provides an unofficial fan page dedicated to the villains of DC comic's Batman. Includes pictures, stories, and much more about villains such as The Joker, Catwoman, and more.

AstroCartoons

http://www.ast.univie.ac.at/Stud/Cartoons/AstroCartoon.html

This hilarious site links you to different cartoons/comics that have an astronomical theme to them.

Beyond Comics!

http://www.cdsnet.net/Business/Beyond/beyond1.htm

This site has a lot of the great classic comics, including Superman and Marvel and Dark Horse. This site also includes card and role-playing games.

Bigfire Anime!

http://www.bigfire.com/

Provides news, reviews, articles, sound bytes, and much more covering animation, especially Japanese Animae. Includes links to many other related sites.

Calvin and Hobbes on the World

http://eos.kub.nl:2080/calvin_hobbes/

If you like the comic strip, you'll be in heaven when you click Gallery and scroll down to an exhaustive list of Calvin information. Peruse the book list, and then examine the latest Calvin and Hobbes picture books. This site also includes icons and desktop patterns, a popularity poll, a random picture generator, links to newsgroups, and interviews with the creator, Bill Watterson. Although this site is unofficial, it is incredibly thorough.

The Cartoon Factory

http://www.cartoon-factory.com/

Search for your favorite cartoon at this fun site. This resource guides you through the net directly to the characters and cartoons you want to view.

Related Sites

http://www.e-help.com/cartoons_comics_humor_animation1.htm

http://www.cs.uidaho.edu/~fricke/misc/cartoons.html

Cerebus the Page

http://www.redweb.com/Cerebus/index.html

Provides news, information, artwork, and much more covering Dave Sim's comic book Cerebus the Aardvark. Includes many different articles and interviews with Sim and links to related sites.

Comic Book Clearing House

http://www.sonic.net/~comix/

Provides a home site for independent and small comic book publishers on the Internet. Includes cover artwork, samples, reviews, previews, and much more.

Comic Collector Home Page

http://www.xnet.com/~rich/cc.html

Provides news, information, and discussion for comic collectors. Includes links to many related comic book sites.

Comics 'n Stuff

http://www.phlab.missouri.edu/~c617145/comix.html

This award-winning site contains hundreds of Web sites that include actual comics you can read. You can also access a Web chat room, perform a comics query search, or download FAQs about comics and the Web.

Computer Animation

http://www.bergen.org/AAST/ComputerAnimation/

Anything you need to know about computer animation and graphics. Discusses evolution, tools, applications, and other sites associated with animation and computers.

Cyber Namida!

http://www.namida.com/

Provides news and information about Japanese Animae and Manga (comics). Includes pictures, reviews, articles, and links to many related sites.

Dark Horse Comics Home Page

http://www.dhorse.com/

Provides news, information, artwork, and upcoming release information for Dark Horse Comics, publisher of the Star Wars, Aliens, and many more titles. Includes many different articles about Dark Horse titles and artists.

Darkhugh's Den's Guide to Spider-Man

http://members.aol.com/Darkhugh/spmcomic.htm

Provides information, news, and pictures of Marvel Comic's Spider-Man. Includes a listing of every appearance of the super-hero, and links to other related comic book sites.

DC Comics Title Chronology

http://www.cris.com/~scotth/dc.html

Provides a chronology and publishing history of all of the titles released by DC Comics, publishers of Superman and Batman, among many. The chronology is very lengthy and should be interesting to any fans of DC comics.

DC Heroes

http://copper.ucs.indiana.edu/~rmaple/table.html

Provides information, pictures, stories, and articles about DC Comic book heroes such as Adam Strange, Superman, Batman, and Wonder Woman. Includes links to other related comic book sites.

Diamond Comic Distributor, Inc.

http://www.diamondcomics.com/

This comic distributor's online page has comic news, previews, and a catalog. Find out many interesting facts at this fun page!

Disney Comics

http://www.update.uu.se/~starback/disney-comics/

Provides an unofficial fan page about Disney Comics. Includes articles, artwork, and discussion about artists such as Carl Barks and much more.

Disney.com

http://www.disney.com/

A great Web site for families to explore together! Has links to some of Disney's best known cartoons, along with activities for kids and families. Also has a Disney shop online!

The Dreaming

http://www.holycow.com/dreaming/

Provides a fan page dedicated to the comic writing of Dave Gaiman and fantasy titles such as *The Sandman*. Includes graphics, articles, interviews, and much more.

Event Comics

http://www.eventcomics.com/

Download titles, covers, and illustrations from your favorite event artist. Also has a chat feature that allows you to talk with other collectors!

EX: The On-line World of Anime & Manga

http://www.spja.com/ex/

Provides an online magazine dedicated to Japanese Anime and Manga. Includes back issue and subscription information. EX features many different articles, pictures, and much more dealing with Anime.

Fortress of Solitude

http://www-scf.usc.edu/~dsilvers/supes1.html

Provides news, information, and pictures dealing with DC Comic's Superman and related titles. Includes a rogues gallery, explanation of Superman's powers, and much more.

The Home Page of One Wile E. Coyote, Super Genius

http://www.accessone.com/~curtiss/wile_e/

Wile E. Coyote fans here!! This site is devoted to the genius of Wile E. Includes gallery photos, sound clips, a résumé, and video sales of this fun loving coyote.

Iguana's Comic Book Cafe!

http://www.iguanas-cbc.com/index.html

This café is a gaming and comic book mail ordering service. Also specializes in toys, Beanie Babies, and Manga videos.

Jonah Weiland's Comic Book Resources

http://envisionww.com/jonahw/comics/comiclinks.html

Nice site that includes special sections with hundreds of links regarding Marvel, DC, Dark Horse, miscellaneous, independent, and self-published comics. One of the few Web pages that can be considered a decent proxy for Marvel's absence on the Web.

Kids' Cool Animation

http://www.kaleidoscapes.com/kc_intro.html

Create your own animations through tutorials and other links at this fun site. View animations of other visitors.

Kryptonian Cybernet Home Page

http://www.ms.uky.edu/~sykes/kc/index.html

Provides an online monthly magazine dedicated to DC comic's Superman. Includes articles, pictures, reviews, and upcoming release information about *Superman* and other related titles. Also includes information about the Lois and Clark television series and links to other related sites.

Lighten Up with United Media

http://www.unitedmedia.com/home.html

Read the daily comics at this fun site! Click which comic you want to view and find today's comic along with an archive of past comics. Contains Snoopy, Dilbert, For Better or For Worse, and Editorial Comics.

Logan Fan Club Home Page

http://gopher.uwsuper.edu/~kforslun/logan/

Provides a fan club site for Marvel Comics superhero Logan (a.k.a. Wolverine). Includes many different pictures, fan stories, current Wolverine news, and upcoming release information.

Lori's X-Men Page

http://web2.spydernet.com/lori/x-men.htm

Provides an unofficial home page tribute to Marvel Comics' X-Men titles. Site includes fan fiction, artwork, and links to many other comic-related sites.

Mantle of the Bat

http://www.cire.com/batman/

Provides an Internet magazine dedicated to DC Comic's character Batman. Includes many different articles, artwork, fan fiction, and links to other related sites.

The Nonstop Looney Tunes Page

http://home.worldonline.nl/~4704922/looneytunes/

This site has moving pictures and sounds of the Looney Tune characters. You can also view a photo gallery, listen to the Looney Tune theme, or download a screen saver.

Related Sites

http://www.rapidramp.com/MainTopics/HumorComics.html

http://www.universe.digex.net/~pfeifer/toons.html

http://www.cybercomm.net/~dano/comics.html

Notes from the President Archive

http://www.teleport.com/~ennead/ampersand/sim/

Provides an archive of essays and articles written by Cerebus Creator and comic industry critic Dave Sim. Includes an index of topics covered and links to other related sites.

Planet Millennium

http://www.planet-millennium.com/

A graphically rich page focusing on ways to build up your self-esteem. Click anywhere on the large planet to begin your journey toward resolving a conflict. This site also provides information on Planet Millennium comic books devoted to self-esteem.

Reviews from the Forbidden Planet Archive

http://www.maths.tcd.ie/mmm/ReviewsFromTheForbiddenPlanet.html

Provides reviews, news, and upcoming release information about comics and science fiction novels. Includes an index of reviews by publisher and title.

RM's Cartoon Guide

http://www.blisreel.com.au/rm/cartoon.htm

This site links you to many different cartoon and comic sites. Click the title of a cartoon to find out more about it.

Sirius Entertainment

http://www.insv.com/sirius

This comic book publisher enables you to examine its titles, which include Dawn, Animal Mystic, Poison Elves, Akiko, and more. Be sure to visit the Sirius Gallery for hot .JPEG files of its art.

Small Press Comics Chat

http://www.sentex.net/~sardine/small.press.html

Provides information, articles, reviews, and a discussion room about small press and independent comics. Includes links to artist and other related small press comic sites. Also includes information about how to publish your own comics.

Related Sites

http://www.microweb.com/wolfy/html2/Cartoons.html

http://www.ara-animation.com/misc.htm

http://www.cms.livjm.ac.uk/www/homepage/cmsdgoo1/comics.htm

Small Press Zone

http://www.cloudnet.com/~hamlinck/spz.htm

Includes an archive of information dealing with independent and small press comic books and their artists. Provides links to many related sites. Also includes artwork, articles, reviews, and much more.

Super Marketing: Ads from the Comic Books

http://www.steveconley.com/supermarketing.htm

This site is dedicated to the classic ads and advertising pages that appeared in Golden and Silver age comics. Some ads for such things as the Hypno-coin, six tapes for $1.49, and much more are quite humorous.

Virtual Comics

http://www.virtualcomics.com/

Provides home site for Virtual Comics, publishers of CD-ROM interactive comic titles such as The Skull and others. Includes artwork, previews, and information about Virtual Comic's titles.

Warner Brother's DC Comics

http://www.dccomics.com/

Provides the official home page for DC Comics, publisher of Superman, Batman, Wonder Woman, and many more. Includes articles, previews, an online radio show, and much, much more.

Wolverine's REALM

http://www.smartlink.net/~falcon/comics/wolverine.html

Provides an unofficial fan page for Marvel Comics' character Wolverine. Includes facts, origin information, artwork, fan pictures, and much more.

X PAGE

http://www.mallorn.com/~m-blase/xpage/

Provides a plethora of information, stories, and artwork about Marvel Comics' The X-Men. Includes links to other fan pages and related comic book sites.

Related Sites
http://www.cartoonsforum.com/default.html
http://www.rpi.edu/~bulloj/comicsbib/comicsbib.html

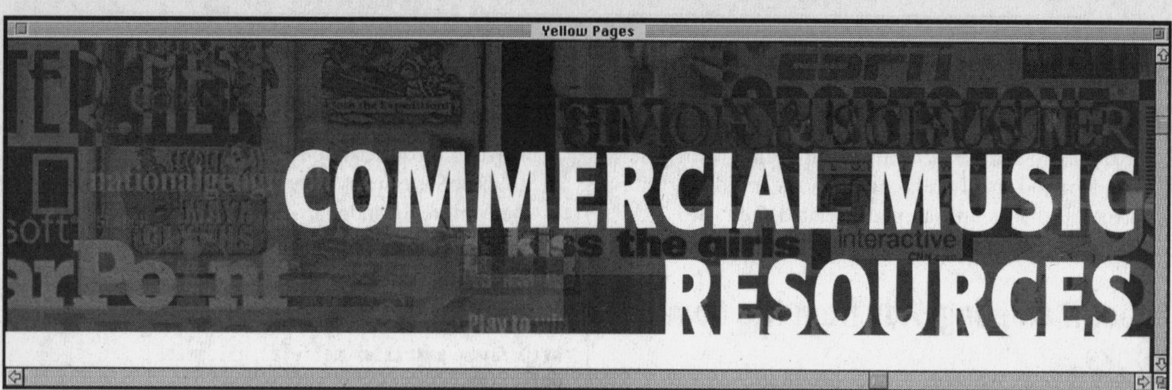

> I don't know anything about music. In my line you don't have to.
>
> *Elvis Presley*

Ace Ticket Service—Concert Tickets

http://www.mindspring.com/~acetix/concerts.html

Buys and sells tickets to concerts and other events. Search for concert information by artist, city, or venue. Also features an artist of the week, tour gossip, and information on new and top ten tours.

Akers Mic

http://www.oslonett.no/akersmic/musikk/ztv.html

Online CD store. Presents a catalog and other offerings within multimedia, surround-sound, and high-end HIFI. Contains more than 62,000 titles.

Alafia Publishing and Music Sales

http://www.alafia.com/

Alafia is a Tampa Bay mail order music house. They take orders by phone, fax, or mail. Order from the list of music for all parts of the orchestra, chamber music, or even music software.

Alfred Publishing Co., Inc.

http://www.alfredpub.com/

The publisher of Alfred's Basic Guitar Method, this company promises over 12,000 titles in its catalog, with over 500 new additions each year. The site contains tips for musicians of all stripes, from piano to drums. Also has links to Alfred dealers, guitar sites, and music software information.

Pitter Patter Music
http://www.asis.com/pitter/

Argus Music Searcher

http://www.fuzzlogic.com/argus/

With this search tool, you can look for music via the artist's name (individual or group), and/or album title. Searches Web and Usenet groups.

BMG Music Service

http://www.bmgmusicservice.com/

This is one of the companies famous for offering tons of CDs for a small amount of money in the Sunday paper. Well, the offer still stands online, and you're free to sign up for membership, browse the list of artists and albums, and fill up your cart with goodies. Contains full membership details, including your responsibilities after getting your large, cheap batch of music. You can now decline the selection of the month by email, thus saving that precious stamp.

Boom Theory

http://www.boomtheory.com/

Boom Theory specializes in Spacemuffins, which are electronic and electro-acoustic drums. Spacemuffins are upgradable, so they'll never be obsolete. Read the interesting and lengthy saga behind the creation of Spacemuffins and check out the entire product line and price structure.

CDnow

http://cdnow.com/

Claiming to be the world's largest music store, CDnow promises a huge selection, low prices, secure credit card transactions, and fast delivery. The site says delivery usually takes place within three to six working days for US orders, or less than three weeks for foreign orders. Read reviews, listen to RealAudio clips of your favorite tunes, and more.

Columbia House Online

`http://www.columbiahouse.com/`

Another of the "get a lot for a little" music vendors. The music catalog is large and the site is well organized, and it's connected to Columbia House's clubs for videos and CD-ROMs. Music is categorized nicely and is easy to find.

Dale Music Company Inc.

`http://www.dalemusic.com/`

Dale specializes in choral and organ music, boasting over 100,000 titles in their musical warehouse. They've taken the time to chart their products nicely in tables, including a description of the piece. They also sell sheet music by most major publishers and contain links to many of those publishers.

Fender World

`http://www.fender.com/`

The official site of Fender Guitars, this site says that the history of this 50-year-old company is nothing compared to its future. Find Fender dealers around the world, check out the guitar and bass setup guide (written with Fender products in mind), and see the full product line (unfortunately, without suggested retail prices).

GEMM Homepage

`http://www.gemm.com/`

The Global Electronic Music Marketplace claims over a million new and used CDs, LPs, and other memorabilia. The site is competitive, so if you're selling or buying, gauge your price accordingly. Search for that missing piece of your musical collection or sell that hard-to-find classic you found in your parents' attic.

Harknett Musical Services

`http://www.harknettmusic.com/`

This Canadian family has set up a site with lots of information and a sense of humor thrown in for good measure. Browse the large selection of sheet music (make sure to check the latest releases), new and used instruments, and the rent-to-own plans for instruments.

IRVINGTON MUSIC

`http://www.irvmusic.com/`

Irvington Music buys and sells hard-to-find classical and opera LPs and reel-to-reel recordings. Search their large database by composer, instrument, or recording medium. Also send them the information about a recording you're looking for, and they can help you track it down.

Jazz Music Stores Around the World

`http://www.acns.nwu.edu/jazz/lists/stores.html`

Serves as a guide to jazz record stores worldwide, arranged alphabetically by location. Includes useful information on shops' strengths in terms of formats and new/used, bargains, and more.

Marshall Worldwide

`http://www.marshallamps.com/`

The company famous for its amps, Marshall has set up a cool site loaded with Shockwave effects. Check out the new and classic product lines, and find amp tips such as the lifespan of valves and tricks to properly set your impedance settings.

Peavey Drums Interactive

`http://www.peavey.com/division/mi/drums/index.html`

Peavey has many irons in the fire, and drums is one of the big ones. See the product line and hear RealAudio recordings of the pros banging on Peavey drums. Take a virtual tour of the factory and see how the drums are made.

Pitter Patter Music

`http://www.asis.com/pitter/`

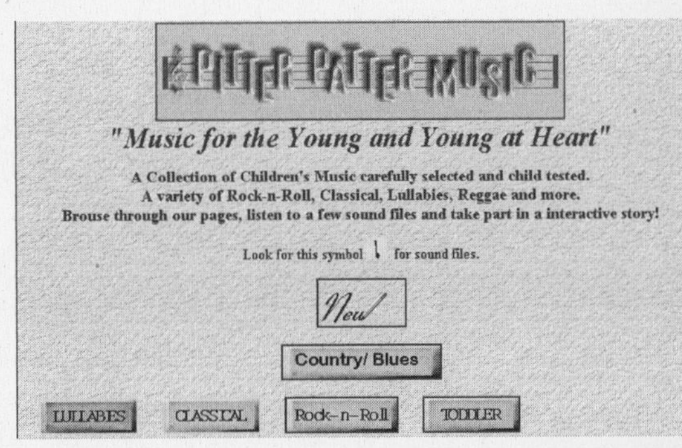

PITTER PATTER MUSIC
"Music for the Young and Young at Heart"
A Collection of Children's Music carefully selected and child tested.
A variety of Rock-n-Roll, Classical, Lullabies, Reggae and more.
Brouse through our pages, listen to a few sound files and take part in a interactive story!
Look for this symbol for sound files.
New
Country/ Blues
LULLABIES
CLASSICAL
Rock-n-Roll
TODDLER

Pitter Patter specializes in musical recordings for children. Categories include country/blues, classical, rock-n-roll, and lullabies and also include a special section for toddlers. See album covers and listen to sound clips from songs. Pitter Patter is also a secure site, and thus is one of the few stores that accepts online orders.

Ticketmaster Online!

http://www.ticketmaster.com/

Like it or not, Ticketmaster is one of the largest ticket brokers in the world, selling over 60 million tickets per year. Visit the site to see where your nonrefundable convenience surcharge is going. Search the national listing of events, and check out the seating plan of your venue to find out exactly where your seats are.

Transatlantic Management

http://euphoria.org/home/transmgt/index.html

Provides management and marketing services to unsigned musicians and bands. Includes company background, artist roster, and contact information.

Virtual Radio

http://www.microserve.net/vradio/

Do you want to hear new music? Here is an online service that does not offer sound byte clips—it offers entire songs. Virtual Radio provides a listener programmable station. Includes index by band with musician biographies and songs. This is a cool site.

Yahoo! Billboard Music Charts

http://la.yahoo.com/external/bpi/music_chart/

Links to chart current chart toppers in all categories—singles, albums, mainstream rock, modern rock, country, adult contemporary, R&B, rap, Latin tracks, and more.

Yahoo! Music and Recording News

http://newspage.yahoo.com/newspage/yahoo2/003idx.html

Contains press releases on the latest news in the recording industry.

NEWSGROUPS

rec.music.classical

rec.music.classical.recordings

rec.music.collecting.cd

rec.music.collecting.misc

rec.music.collecting.vinyl

Related Sites

http://music123.com/

http://pages.prodigy.com/bargains_galore/firstpag.htm

http://www.all-music.com/

http://www.anet-dfw.com/~gflat/brookmays.html

http://www.a-zuc.com/music/

http://www.businessquest.com/campbell/campbellmusic.html

http://www.mt.net/~piccolom/

http://www.songbirdmusic.com/

http://www.tapmusic.com/

http://www.westwindmusic.com/

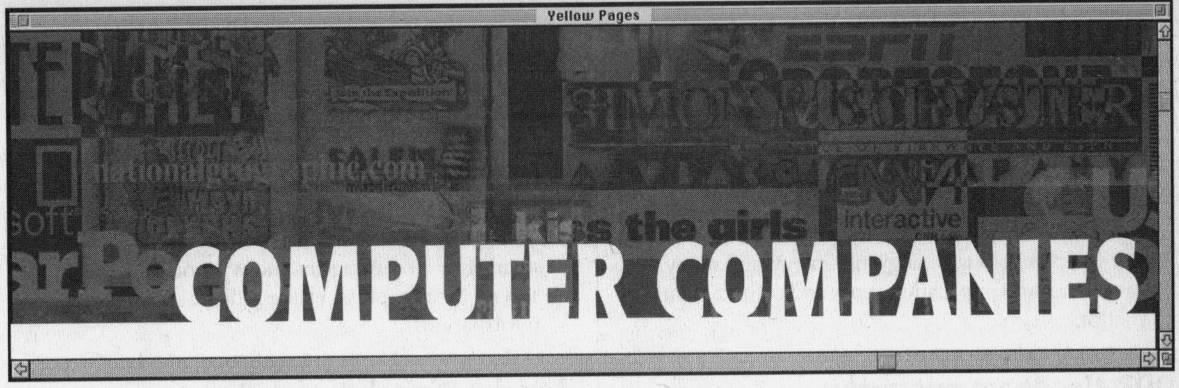

COMPUTER COMPANIES

> I am not a computer nerd. I prefer to be called a hacker!
>
> *Lex in* Jurassic Park *(1993)*

COMPUTER SERVICES

American Digital Network

http://www.adnc.com/

Provides USR 56K28.8 v.34 digital modems, full digital ISDN, Web services, and Web site design. Includes full product information, technical support, service listings, software, and sales contacts.

CGI Systems, Inc.

http://www.cgisystems.com/home.nsf
http://www.cgisystems.com/

CGI is an IBM company that designs and delivers custom-produced hardware, software, and applications packages created to serve client needs and structures. Specializes in Lotus Notes sales automation and the creation of networks, groupware, and work applications. Provides lengthy company background with detailed listings of services and products offered.

Client Systems, Inc.

http://www.clientsys.com/

Distributes and provides support for Hewlett-Packard and Oracle hardware, software, services, and other miscellaneous products. Includes lengthy company profile, Oracle news, HP updates, and hardware and software products listings. Also provides contact numbers and email addresses for all of North America.

> **Apple Computer Home Page**
> **http://www.apple.com/**

Cunningham & Cunningham, Inc.

http://www.c2.com/

Specializes in computer training and custom programming. Includes company profile, contact information, and philosophies utilized in services. Includes links to Web pages created by Cunningham & Cunningham.

Data Exchange Corporation

http://www.dex.com/

Provides a wide range of technical repair services for everything from hard drives to printers. Also provides technical support services, spare parts, and a wide array of other services. Includes services offered, contact information, job opportunities, and data exchange.

Database Excelleration Systems

http://www.desdbx.com/

Produces DES Database Excellerator products that improve speed and performance through their solid state design. These products are compatible with Sybase, Oracle, or RBDMS networking systems. Includes services offered, product background, and specifications. Also includes contact information.

Dataserv Middle East & Africa Ltd

http://www.wp.com/dataserv/home.html

Supplier of second hand IBM mini- and main-frame equipment to countries in the Middle East and Africa.

A B C D E F G H I J K L M N O P Q R S T U V W X Y Z

DataWave Technologies

`http://www.dwavetech.com/`

Researches, develops, and produces custom-designed software and hardware for the scientific and medical fields. Includes technologies packages for data acquisition and data analysis for disciplines such as neuroscience, psychology, biology, neurology, and many more. Includes application types and contact information.

DDB Needham Interactive Communications

`http://www.ddbniac.com/`

Develops and produces applications for data management, telecommunications, interactive media, and multimedia. Includes Internet design, communications, video conferencing, digital library, and many other products. Includes work samples, art gallery, and contact information.

IBM Corporation

`http://www.ibm.com`

This is a cool site that looks like a television commercial. You can reach all of IBM's myriad divisions from the home page. You can also read about IBM systems solutions via articles. Take online training courses, attend real-time seminars, or chat with people with similar interests. An extensive search engine is also provided for navigating this very large corporate site.

HARDWARE COMPANIES

Acer America on the Web

`http://www.acer.com/aac/index.htm`

Home page for Acer North America. Acer manufactures personal computer clones. The Acer America Site provides online shopping, FAQs, and information about the Acer Group, including employment opportunities. There are 16 Acer-related sites on the Web.

Acorn Group, Plc.

`Http://www.acorn.com/acorn/`

Acorn Computer is a British company that manufactures RISC-based personal computers, network computers, and peripherals. Acorn's Home page has links to descriptions of their products, technology, services, and Acorn in the news. The site also provides links to private Internet areas for use by Acorn employees.

Amdahl Corporation Home Page

`http://www.amdahl.com/`

Amdahl Corporation was recently bought by its major stockholder, Fujitsu Corporation. Amdahl manufactures and markets IBM-compatible large-scale computers and open system architecture equipment. The Home page includes product information, service listings, press release index, and technical information.

Apache Digital Corporation

`http://www.apache.com/`

Provides information on ALPHA-based, NeXTSTEP, Linux/BSD UNIX, Windows NT, SPARC-based, and other custom design systems that they sell. Also provides online custom design form, company background, policies, and detailed additional product information.

Apple Computer Home Page

`http://www.apple.com/`

Apple introduces a new marketing strategy "Think Different" and their Web site prominently displays this theme. Apple now provides an online storefront where you can purchase customized hardware configurations of your favorite Macintosh models. Provides information on Apple's latest products and also supplies software updates. Although the rumor mills are flying about this company's fate, Apple's Web site obviously is full of information on new products and software enhancements. Check out this site for the latest on Apple technology.

Compaq Access

`http://www.compaq.com/`

Access Compaq's Web services for corporate information, worldwide service center directories, technical support, and press releases on Compaq's newest Web servers and pricing.

Related Sites
`http://www.borland.com/`
`http://www.sgi.com/ss.home.page.html`
`http://www.tandem.com/cgi-bin/webdriver.exe?MIval=iHomePage`
`http://www.parc.xerox.com/parc-go.html`
`http://www:think.com/`

DayStar Digital

http://www.daystar.com/

This manufacturer of high-performance multiprocessor upgrades for Macs provides a simple, graphical Web site for registering products, downloading updates and related Mac software, or learning more about Daystar's product line. Also learn about their new Genesis system of Mac-compatible systems.

Dell.com

http://www.dell.com/

This Site provides secure online shopping for Dell personal computer products. You can custom-configure a system and buy it online. The site also lets you search for information by types of users as well as provides the standard corporate information.

Digital PC

http://www.pc.digital.com/

Aside from Digital's typical Web services, such as technical support, current product information, and International center addresses, is their own search engine—Alta Vista. Add this to your list of favorites in case your current search engines disappoint.

Fujitsu Systems Business of America Home Page

http://fsba.com/

Provides online Help, CAD, and desktop conferencing products. This site also explains the corporate structure of Fujitsu Japan, a $30 billion per year company.

Gateway International 2000 USA

http://www.gateway.com/

This is a cool, interactive site providing two ways to access information about Gateway personal computers. You can select a link from a list of types of users, or go directly to information about a specific system. The site also provides access to technical support and corporate information.

Hewlett-Packard

http://www.hp.com/

The leader in desktop hardware and network servers provides a multi-lingual Web site that is much more international than most other computer manufacturers. Jump from this site to learn about HP's Latin American division, their newest systems in other countries, and technical information on HP printers.

Intel

http://www.intel.com/

This site provides all the information you ever wanted to know about Intel's integrated circuits, and especially the Pentium II chip. The site showcases software running on Intel-based hardware, hardware implementations, and offers business opportunities as well as the standard technical support and news briefs.

Motorola

http://www.mot.com/

Manufacturer of PowerPC chips and other integrated circuits as well as computers and peripherals. The Motorola Homepage provides information about the corporation, its products, divisions, and activities, including the Motorola Western Open tournament.

PERIPHERALS COMPANIES

Alps Electric USA

http://www.alpsusa.com/cgibin/var/alpsusa/index.html
http://www.alpsusa.com/

Alps Electric manufactures high-end color printers and other peripherals. This site provides product information, technical support, and drivers for manufacturers of computer peripherals equipment. Includes full product line and background along with purchasing information. Also provides contact to Alps components division. A rebate form for the new Alps MD-1000 color printer is included along with an online catalog where you can order your Alps products via the Web.

Altera Home Page

http://www.altera.com/

Provides company background, training information, product listings, employment opportunities, sales information, and distributors list for this manufacturer of programmable logic devices and computer-aided logic development tools. Sight also includes an electronic access contact sight for technical support and general product information.

Bell Microproducts, Inc.

http://www.bellmicro.com/bellmicro/default.asp
http://www.bellmicro.com/

Distributers of many various computer products including superconductors, storage subsystems, digital optical equipment, and various software packages. Provides technical support, product information, company profile, and services listings.

Comdisco Inc.

http://www.comdisco.com/

Designs, produces, and provides disaster recovery software, systems integration services, and risk consultations. Products include CLASS and ComPAS disaster recovery products. Includes complete listing of services offered that range from disaster recovery consulting to computer leasing.

Data-Doc Electronics, Inc.

http://www.datadoc.com/

Supplies sales for connection products such as interface cables, adapters, and printer share equipment. Includes detailed product catalog with technical specifications and contact information.

SOFTWARE COMPANIES

Adobe Systems, Inc.

Http://www.adobe.com

Adobe Systems manufactures an array of software for publishing and graphic image production and management. This site is comprehensive in scope, offering case studies, white papers, business opportunities, demos, and a full type foundry where you can download type fonts after purchasing them.

Ariel's Story Studio

http://www.disney.com/DisneyInteractive/mermaid/index.html

When you click the Disney Interactive URL you are taken under the sea to a very musical, active site advertising Disney Interactive's newest CD-ROM. You are given a chance to try out its features online, order a copy online, or link to other Disney Interactive CD-ROM sites.

Claris Corporation Main Page

http://www.claris.com/index.html

Claris Corporation is a wholly owned subsidiary of Apple Computer. Claris provides an extensive array of Macintosh and Windows productivity software. This site provides information about new products, opportunities to demo products before purchasing, and information about Claris Corporation (such as employment and business opportunities).

Corel Corporation Homepage

http://www.corel.ca/

Corel Corporation provides a suite of business software including WordPerfect, CorelDraw, Quatro Pro, and Paradox. The Corel site offers a one-stop shopping area for researching, testing, and purchasing Corel products. Training information and corporate information are also provided at the site.

Deneba Software Homepage

http://www.deneba.com/

Deneba makes Canvas, a Macintosh-originated vector drawing program. The Deneba Site provides the opportunity to demo Canvas, learn about its features, technical support, and obtain updates. Deneba also offers job opportunities online.

Farallon Home Page

http://www.farallon.com/

Farallon provides innovative networking solutions for PCs and Macintoshes. Ethernet, LAN, and communications software are Farallon's specialty. This site provides access to software reviews, online shopping, technical support, and white papers pertaining to networking hardware and software.

IMSI Homepage

http://www.imsisoft.com/index.html

IMSI provides utilities, clip art, CAD, and other productivity software products. This site provides technical support, online purchasing, updates, and news about IMSI products. It also offers corporate information and job opportunities.

Micrografx

http://www.micrografx.com/

This is a cool Web site with Java enhancements offering information about Micrografx' array of graphics tools. The design of the site says a lot about the innovative nature of Micrografx' products. Corporate information, product information, and technical support is provided.

Microsoft Corporation Homepage

`http://www.microsoft.com/microsoft.htm`

This is the official corporate home page of Microsoft Computer. The site provides links to a personal home page site and product-based sites. The corporate site provides technical support, event and seminar lists, news briefs, reviews, white papers, and demos of Microsoft products, as well as corporate information.

Netscape Homepage

`http://www.netscape.com/`

Netscape's home page is a multifaceted Web site providing access to both Netscape's products (browsers, servers, and Web suites), but also Java-enhanced windows to Netcenter (Netscape's consumer personal home page), ABC news feeds, and special offers. Netscape plug-ins, updates, and software are available for demos and purchasing. A SmartUpdate system automates installing new software components from Netscape on to your computer.

Novell Worldwide

`http://www.novell.com/`

Novell manufactures network server software for Intranets and LANs. This is a glitzy site featuring Java-based news feeds and articles about Novell products. Corporate information and how to purchase Novell products is also provided through various links.

Oracle Corporation Homepage

`http://www.oracle.com/`

Oracle manufactures large-scale relational database software and associated network products. This Web site presents news briefs about Oracle, Larry Ellison (Oracle's president), and Oracle-related events. The Site also provides all of the standard corporate support information such as technical support, white papers, business opportunities, and job opportunities.

Quark, Inc. Homepage

`http://www.quark.com/`

This busy pulsing Site provides access to QuarkXpress and other Quark desktop publishing products, including demos, technical support, online shopping, and news. An extensive array of xTensions for Quark products are also offered, as are training tips.

Sun Microsystems

`http://www.sun.com/`

The home page from the creators of the new Java Web language is a must-see for Web fanatics. Click their Search icon to access Java information quickly, or to find info on specific topics. The monthly e-zine SunWorld Online provides a wealth of information about Web servers, diagnostic software, and recent Net information.

Sybex Inc.

`http://www.sybex.com/`

Produces a large catalog of tutorial, reference, handbook, and network products. Includes software, books, and manuals. Provides online catalog, contact, and ordering information.

Related Sites
`http://www.adaptec.com/`
`http://www.be.com/`
`http://www.dayna.com/`
`http://www.supermac.com/`
`http://www.cisco.com/`

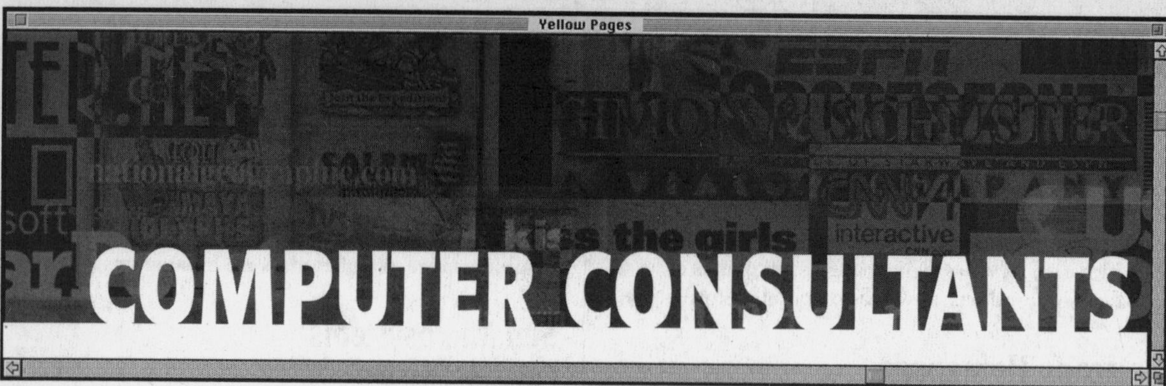

COMPUTER CONSULTANTS

> Never trust a computer bigger than you can lift.
>
> *Micro Credo*

ActionCall Help Desk Service

`http://www.actioncall.com`

Provides a calling card that you can use 24 hours a day, 7 days a week and call for computer help. Page provides different packages, including the Action Call Gold Card.

AHK & Associates

`http://www.value.net/ahk/html/`

Provides a complete list of services, products and support to be used with ISDN products. Site includes a full equipment catalog, consulting services, Internet accessing with ISDN, and Web site of interest to ISDN subscribers.

Amadeus Consulting

`http://www.wolfgang.com/`

Develops 32-bit, object-oriented applications. Amadeus also designs Internets and firewalls. Provides listings of software, Web services, company background, their clients, development information, and listings of public Internet introductions.

Related Sites

`http://www.ccs-corp.com/`

`http://www.nitebird.com/`

`http://www.wooden-nickel.net/redletter/`

`http://www.compu-consult.com/`

Hesperus Computer Consulting
`http://www.hesperus.com/`

Bennett Products—Computer Sales/Networking/Consulting/Internet

`http://www.bennettpro.com`

Provides computer sales, consulting, networking, and Internet access and support. Their ftp site provides a small collection of the best shareware and freeware available.

Bozeman Legg, Inc.—Environmental Computer Consulting

`http://www.bozemanlegg.com/`

Environmental industry solutions for data management needs using advanced network and database technologies. Also offers help for the Year 2000 problem, including a freeware program that helps to analyze your system software and pick out potential problems. Environmental applications include EDMS, EDF, EDCC, and COELT.

Cambridge Technology Partners

`http://www.ctp.com/`

Installs, implements, and integrates business computing systems. Specializes in working on fast and tight time frames. Includes company profile, lengthy service listings, and representative work with clients. Also provides consulting and investment information.

Commonwealth Data Systems, Inc.

`http://www.mnsinc.com/bradshaw/`

Provides consultation specializing in customized software development in various system languages including DELPHI, C++, Pascal, and many more.

Services include development and integration for Windows, LAN, and TurnKey systems. Includes example work done for OSHA.

Communicopia Environmental Research and Communications

http://communicopia.bc.ca/

Provides Internet and media-consulting services to environmental- and natural resource-based companies and government agencies. Services include Web page, communications, system, and database design and development.

CompAdept Corporation

http://www.compadept.com/

Personal computer and network consulting company.

Comport Consulting Corporation

http://www.comport.com/

Provides consulting, technical support and sales for Digital Equipment products. Also provides software applications in warehousing distribution. Includes company profile and product specifications with current news on each.

Compusult Limited

http://www.compusult.nf.ca/

Provides computer consulting services and custom computer products for the scientific and technical areas for businesses and government agencies. Includes listing of services offered and specialized software systems. Also includes information about Applications for Rural Communities (ARC) and Compusult Integrated Data Access Systems (CIDAS) specialized software.

The Computer Consulting Service Home Page

http://www.ccs.com/

Specializes in computer consulting for medical practices in the Mid-Atlantic region of the United States. Uses The Medical Manager software as its healthcare management system and bundles it with the proper hardware and peripherals needed for a successful, growing practice.

Related Sites

http://login.dknet.dk/~mortenf/mfd/index.html

http://gray.maine.com/people/tcolkitt/Cstone.html

Computer Consulting Toolkit

http://www.entrepreneurmag.com/resource/toolkit/compcon.hts

Looking to start your own computer consulting business? This site by *Entrepreneur* magazine offers an in-depth look into what the market looks like, what you'll need, how much it will cost, and what your chances are of succeeding. You can also order their Start-Up Guide, which takes you through the steps and covers all the details of starting this new business.

Computer Power Group

http://www.cpsg.com.au/cpg/welcome.html

Provides computer systems consulting and training for Australia and the Asian Basin. Includes full service listings, group profile, press releases, and contact information. Also includes stock reports and investment information.

Computerized Data Management

http://www1.minn.net/~cdm

Offers training and support for the home user and small business owner in the St. Paul and Minneapolis areas.

ConsultLink Inc.

http://www.consultlink.com/consultlink/

Directory of more than 19,000 computer consultants and contractors. The database includes the following computer specialists: Technology Strategy, Programming, System Administration, Networking, Technical Writing, Support, Graphics, Hardware, Marketing, and Business Strategy. Simply search to find the perfect candidate and then pay a $15 for the contact information.

CooperSoft

http://www.getnet.com/~joeco/

Specializes in custom software applications, Web site design, and network creation. Includes links to pages CooperSoft created and search engines. Provides contact information.

CoreLAN Communications, Inc.

http://www.corelan.com/

Provides consultation services and products specializing in network communications, database systems, and Internet access integration. Includes client and technological partners links. Also includes full service listings and corporate profile.

A B C D E F G H I J K L M N O P Q R S T U V W X Y Z

CSI.NET, Inc.

http://www.csi.net/

Provides and produces network and Internet consulting along with custom designed applications and software. Includes consultation information on firewalls, ISDN services, Internet access, connectivity issues, and specialized applications creation. Also includes company profile and contact information.

Dokken Software Inc.

http://imt.net/~dokken/

Provides consulting software development, relational database creation, and Internet relations. Specializes in object-oriented software, graphical user interfaces, and databases. Includes listing of services offered, technologies utilized, and clients. Also includes company profile and contact information.

Dowdell Business Services

http://www.dowdell.com

Consultant for Windows NT/Novell real-time database interfaces. Check out the link to the atomic clock in Boulder, Colorado.

Durango Computer Classroom

http://animas.frontier.net/~mkatz/

Provides computer consulting and training services. Specializes in software design and groups applications training. Includes courses listings, company news, and hiring opportunities.

Eccosys, Ltd.

http://www.eccosys.com/ECCOSYS/es.html

Provides and produces Internet consulting, custom Internet software development, and systems integration services. Includes service listings, current projects, and contact information. Also includes career opportunities.

ESDX

http://www.esdx.org/esdhome.html

Provides a home site for ESDX, a nonprofit management information technology association for companies specializing in health, environmental, and safety. Includes association news, abstracts, members, and cases featured. Also includes links to member companies and a search index.

The Expert Marketplace

http://expert-market.com/index.html

More than 200,000 consulting firms are listed in this directory. Many free services offered to members, and membership is free, too. Also a resource for consultants looking for exposure.

EZTech

http://rand.nidlink.com/%7Ephelpsj/

An Idaho-based consulting company. Provides consulting on Web page construction worldwide. Check out the HTML client portfolio and link to sites written by EZTech. Local services include tutoring, computer setup and configuration, virus protection and recovery, and hardware and software installation for IBMs and IBM clones.

The FIEN Group

http://www.fiengroup.com/

Provides consulting on a wide range of computer system needs. Consulting services include client/server application development, WWW publishing, Folio Views Infobase Technology uses, and much more. Provides technical partner listings, links to sites created, and contact information.

Fly-By-Day Consulting

http://www.mindspring.com/~cavu

Provides software consulting services in C and UNIX, specializing in communications and porting. Also offers many aviation links, including current weather observations and forecasts.

Folio Corporation

http://www.folio.com/

Provides for the professional user links to download Folio's award winning Web retriever, access to their computer products buyer's guide, educational services, intranet seminars, and an application for their beta test program.

For-to-Win

http://www.sigma-research.com/for2win/for2win2.htm

Company to rewrite and convert your DOS/Fortran programs to make them compatible with Win 3.1/ Win95. Provides link to download a financial engineering demo written in Fortran 90 and converted to Win 3.1 or Win95. Consultants possess over 20 years of experience.

Full Spectrum Communications

http://www.fsc.com/fsc/

Provides professional consulting and educational services in networking. Can fine-tune an existing network or design from the ground up. Provides links to complete profiles of consulting and educational services and well as information on their more popular classes: internetworking on the Internet and design optimization of networks.

Galaxy Systems Inc.

http://www.interport.net/galaxy/

An employment site for computer consultants. Provides links and descriptions to consulting positions, some permanent, as well as the Galaxy Office and staff. Send your resume.

Garbee and Garbee

http://www.gag.com/

This is the personal home page of Bdale and Karen Garbee, who do pro bono consulting particularly for Amateur Radio and Amateur Satellite Services. Provides links to their current undertakings.

Genoa Technology

http://www.gentech.com

Genoa Technology will design and develop test solutions for manufacturers of computer printers and facsimile devices to ensure interoperability. Links are provided to testing services, products, training classes, publications, and so forth.

GulfNet Technologies

http://199.44.46.2/

A small business in Perry, Florida offering several computer-related services to businesses and individuals such as Accounting Systems, Internet Access, Desktop Computer Systems, and Networks.

Guru Technologies, Inc.

http://www.gurutech.com/

Develop hardware and software solutions for semiconductor, networking, and graphics systems companies. Provide tech support and productivity enhancement. Provides links to clients, courses, professional associations, and company information.

Hartford Computer Group

http://www.awa.com/hartford/

Sells, services, and leases a full line of computers, peripherals, and equipment from manufacturers such as Apple, IBM, Compaq, NEC, AST, and Texas Instruments. Offers free technical support, fast delivery, warranties, and more.

HD Industries

http://www.Infoservice.com/HDIndustries/

Consulting firm based in Sacramento, California for the Macintosh user, database solutions written in 4th Dimension or Panorama. Current consulting projects include sports teams off the coast of Africa and recreation districts in California.

Hesperus Computer Consulting

http://www.hesperus.com/

Located in Great Falls, Montana, this consultant provides services in Web design and hosting, custom programming of software applications, computer upgrading, and general computer consulting. They boast competitive rates; you can check them out on their Web pages.

Hieroglyphics

http://www.webcom.com/~hiero/welcome.html

Web Consultants offering Internet/Intranet, Graphic Design, Multi-media, Catalog and Newsletter design, and much more for your business. Provides links to clients' pages, services, pricing, Java, plug-ins, animation, and other groovy sites.

hot-n-GUI

http://www.hotngui.com/

A large application cross-platform developer. Links to their consulting services, add ons (commercial and freeware), and other useful pages.

Ian Freed Consulting, Inc.

http://www.ifc.com/

Telecommunications and computer consulting for your business or organization. Provides links to company profile, projects, clients, lab, and employment opportunities.

A B C D E F G H I J K L M N O P Q R S T U V W X Y Z

IC Group, Inc.

http://pobox.com/icg/fromyahoo.html

Basic and extended WWW services, email, and technical and future-oriented consulting for your business or organization. Provides links to clients, projects, and other information.

Inacom Corp.

http://www.inacom.com/

Helping your business utilize the full capacity of information technology. Inacom offers your company desktop management, LAN design, training, consulting, and much more. Provides access to company profile, tech links, and what Inacom can do for you.

Index

http://www.telematrix.com/

The International Telecom Center is for anyone, business or individual, who would like to advertise their goods and services on the Internet. Browse the store or check out their advertising and consulting services.

Information Builders Inc.

http://www.ibi.com

Home page for this large, multinational computer consulting firm and software developer for client/server environments. Uses FOCUS EDA/SQL, and LEVEL5 in their work.

Integrated Systems Solutions Corporation

http://www.issc.ibm.com/

An IBM subsidiary that helps its business customers manage their information technology more efficiently or develop new services. Links to services, publications, and career and contact information.

InterComp Internet, UNIX, and World Wide Web services

http://www.panix.com/~tab/intercomp/

A custom programming, training, and consulting firm for your business. Links to services, company background, and experience.

Related Sites

http://www.cbi-net.com/

http://www.surpass.com/

Internet Communications & Marketing

http://www.icommark.com/

Offers consulting, application conversions, and training services. This site includes Windows NT Server Setup and training in Seattle, Washington and Windows 95 Setup and Training in San Jose, California and Seattle. Site also provides numerous links to many search engines on the Net.

Jackson-Reed, Inc.

http://www.halcyon.com/prreed/jackreed.html

Educational and consulting services to support the computing environment. Onsite courses offered. Some client/server products offered are Microsoft/SQL server, Oracle, Java, UNIX, and more.

Janet Ruhl's Computer Consultant's Resource Page

http://www.javanet.com/~technion/

Janet Ruhl, the author of several books, is a consultant's consultant, offering advice on how to manage your computer consulting business. There's a computer consultant's message board where you can talk and share tips with other consultants. A big portion of the site is devoted to the Real Rate Survey where you can see how your consulting rates measure up.

Jewell, Chris

http://www.wco.com/~jewellcj/

The personal home page of Chris Jewell with a link to Jewell Consulting, which provides software solutions for businesses. Uses object-oriented technology and familiar with AS/400 systems.

J.F.T.R.

http://www.jftr.com/

Just For The Record, a multimedia development company, specializes in Web site development and Internet marketing. Find out who they are, look up their services and rates, and meet their staff. And, after you contact them, you can check out their other clients' sites.

JimWare Inc.

http://www.prairienet.org/~jdpierce/homepage.html

Tool and utilities for OS/400 and VM used by system professionals. Links to JimWare, product catalog and ordering, other interesting links, and search engines.

JM Consulting and Cheap Advice

http://pages.prodigy.com/IL/jomoor/

A brief home page with a link to the consulting page and information about "what JM Consulting knows." Will answer your PC questions or questions about Chicago restaurants!

Keystone Technology

http://www.keytech.com/

Oklahoma City company providing Internet access, Web services, and any computer-related solutions your business requires. Mac, Intel, LAN, WAN, networking, telephony, and many more solutions.

Kinchlea Computer Consulting on Denman Island

http://kinch.ark.com/kcc/

Based in British Columbia, Dave Kinchlea offers a wide range of consulting services over the Internet. Email him your tough questions and he will reply with an answer. He also handles online administration of networks and custom programming.

Kitchen Wisdom Publishing

http://www.wiskit.com/

Kitchen Wisdom, a one-time publisher of cookbooks, now offers software development and consulting based on their own problems with desktop publishing. Provides consulting for UNIX, Internet connections, and will run a free custom network diagnosis on your system.

Lavallée & Associates

http://www.lcl.ca

Company specializing in Web and Internet applications, business re-engineering, systems analysis, project management, and more. Contact them for your consulting needs.

MacMedic

http://www.pacificrim.net/~macmedic/

Networking solutions, hardware and software troubleshooting, hardware repair, telecommunications, training, and phone support for the Mac user.

MBS Industries, Inc.

http://www.mbsii.com/mbs/

For your Internet presence needs, training, consulting, software and Web page development.

MC^2

http://www.mc2-csr.com/

A virtual marketing and consulting firm for all your company's Internet needs. Links to their services, customers, upcoming events, other links of interest, and more.

MediaGlobe

http://www.mediaglobe.com/

Company providing businesses the assistance needed to connect to and exploit the Internet. Check out their FTP Archive, product info and catalog, and services.

MetaCase Consulting

http://www.jsp.fi/metacase/

A software company specializing in system integration and modeling and object-oriented graphics. Their software features MedaEdit Personal, MetaEdit+, and MetaEdit+ Method Workbench. Access to product descriptions, press releases, ordering info, and more.

Micwil Computer Consulting

http://www.micwil.sk.ca/micwil/index.html

Canadian company that provides help on buying a computer system (including hardware and software) and training on how to use it. Use the Brand Rating's Guide to evaluate which manufacturer's components are best for you. There's also Quote Builder page where you can build your own system and find out how much it costs.

Mike Salitter Consultant Services

http://knet.flemingc.on.ca/~msalitte/mscs.html

Network consulting and troubleshooting for many environments including Windows, Novell NetWare, Windows for Workgroups, UNIX, and others, plus many platforms and languages.

A B C D E F G H I J K L M N O P Q R S T U V W X Y Z

A B C D E F G H I J K L M N O P Q R S T U V W X Y Z

Minerva Technology

http://www.minerva.ca/

Client/server consulting firm with links to services, jobs, awards and news, company, and contact information.

Multitech Consulting

http://www.mypersonalconsultant.com/sgnframe.htm

Personal computer consulting company. Fill out the online form telling Multitech who you are, what kind of computer you own, what your family uses it for, and what level of computer experience you have, and you're assigned your own consultant. Ask hardware-related or configuration-related questions and receive an email reply within 48 hours.

MVS Training, Inc.

http://www.pittsburgh.net/MVS/

A training provider for individuals who work with mainframe computers, midrange, and PC computers. Will also deliver basic writing and speaking skill training. Check out their long list of training offerings and client testimonials.

Mystech Enterprises

http://www.primenet.com/~valenti/index.html

A company providing client/server solutions as well as custom photography (because of the owner's hobby). Links to current consulting projects and software solutions—and recent photographs from Yosemite Park.

NACCB Online

http://computerwork.com/

The National Association of Computer Consultant Businesses provides career resources to computer contractors. If you're looking for work, submit your resume or take a look at the job board. Search for the NACCB member nearest you. Find out about upcoming job fairs and special events.

Netplan ApS. Consultants in Telecommunications

http://www.netplan.dk/netplan/enetp1.htm

Danish telecommunications and computing consulting firm with an English language Web page. This site provides a few links that describe Netplan's services. Descriptions are nicely done although a few translation mistakes occur. Can you find them?

Pangea Visions

http://www.fortnet.org/~pangea/index.html

Provides Web site consulting, advertising, home site design, and database creation. Includes services offered, company profile, resources utilized, and links to Web sites created. Also includes WWW use statistics and facts.

Phoenix Systems Internet Publishing

http://www.biddeford.com/phoenix/

Provides a wide array of Internet services including consulting, publishing, Web site creation, Internet research, and systems installation. Includes client listings, technical archive, and services offered.

PLATINUM Solutions

http://www.platsol.com/

A company dedicated to creating "Customer Based Solutions" via education, consulting, task insourcing services, and integration. Their core services include information and systems management, applications solutions, and education services.

PRC Inc. Home Page

http://www.prc.com/

Unusually plain home page for a huge government contractor that provides computer system integration, software development, facilities management, and energy-related engineering services. Find out about PRC's corporate culture and strategy, and learn more about recent work.

Relational Information Systems, Inc.

http://wl.iglou.com/ris/

Provides consulting and custom software development services. Specializes in UNIX-based, database management systems. Includes information about CA-INGRES and CA-UNICENTER products. Also includes contact information.

SAIC Los Altos Home Page

http://www.saic.com/

Employee-owned research and development company based in San Diego that specializes in energy, environment, information technology, health care, telecommunications, and transportation. Click an industry of interest (telecommunications, for example) to read about SAIC services or to learn more about recent client work.

Sistemas

http://www.sistemas.com/

Bilingual (English and Spanish) company providing computer consulting, computer training, and systems support. Sistemas is a Trenton, New Jersey office where you can go for computer education, training, upgrading and repairing, and technical support services. You can order computer books online. Check out their impressive client list.

Software Dynamics Consulting

http://www.sdcnet.com/

Provides Oracle and Microsoft consultation services. Specializes in software, project management, and methods development. Includes links to Midwest Oracle Users Group Papers and contact information.

Spire Technologies

http://www.spiretech.com/

Provides a wide range of consulting and other services. Includes Web site design, AutoCAD design, Internet provisions, and connectivity solutions. Includes products and services offered listings along with links to clients' sites.

Sterling Information Group

http://www.sterinfo.com

Software and management consultants, and custom software developers based in Austin, Texas. This simple site discusses Sterling services.

STS

http://www.alaska.net/~lafferty/sts.html

Provides home site for STS (Scientific Technical Services) which provides system consultation and custom programming services. Includes company profile and contact information.

TechLund International Co.

http://www.techlund.com/

Consulting firm specializing in Web site design and hosting. Other services include setting up communications infrastructure. Check out their Qualifications page for credentials. There's also a search engine where you can search the site for information on your specific need.

Technology Futures, Inc.

http://www.tfi.com/

Provides corporate computer consulting and reporting services. Includes listing of clients, reports made, seminars offered, and publications created. Provides contact information.

TeKnowlogy Education Centers

http://www.teknowlogy.com/

Provides training, education, and testing services on many different computer systems, languages, and applications. Includes course dates, classes offered, and services provided. Also includes business partners, company profile, and contact information.

Telecommunications Technology Corp.

http://www.teltechinc.com/

Provides computer system consulting services and products to the banking, transportation, and manufacturing industries. Includes information about systems development, database management, and custom software applications design. Provides listing of clients served and contact information.

Word Master, Inc.

http://www.interaccess.com/wmi/wm/

Provides consulting and custom systems design services. Specializes in OMNIS consulting and custom applications development. Also includes Web page design services.

Xephon

http://www.xephon.co.uk/

Provides consultation, information, and products about IBM-compatible enterprise systems. Includes listings of Xephon publications, services, and information about IBEX mainframes. Also includes contact information and links to other enterprise system sites.

Zip Consulting & Design

http://www.sonic.net/~richw/zip.html

Provides consulting services and products for companies utilizing MS-DOS and especially Paradox based systems. Includes information about custom database set-up and advantages. Also includes technical specifications and background of work done.

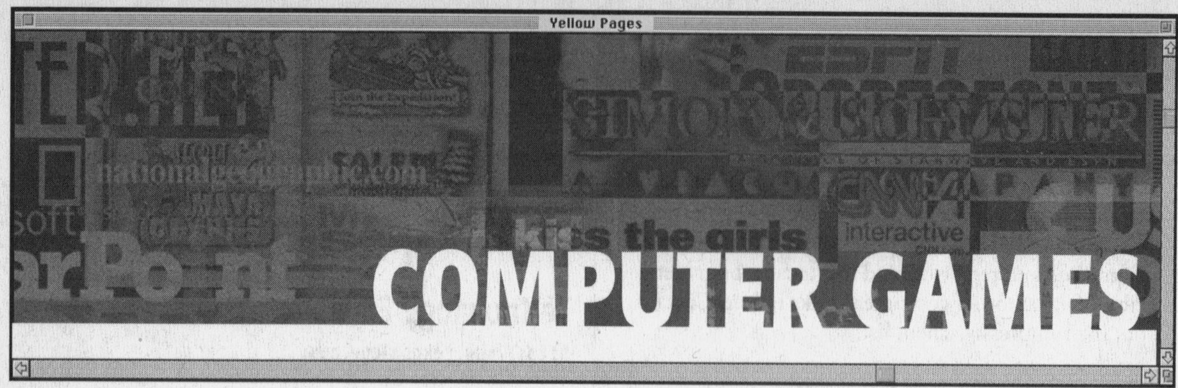

> Whatever games are played with us, we must play no games with ourselves.
>
> *Ralph Waldo Emerson*

For those of you who are game lovers, this category offers many places to start in game playing. You can find sites on 3D action and strategy games, adventures, simulators, MUDs, and sports-related games. Have fun!

3D ACTION GAMES

The 3D Gaming Scene

http://www.pol.umu.se/html/ac/mainpage.htm

Describes in detail every 3D action game available, beginning with the original—Wolfenstein 3D. Download working demos and shareware versions from this page, or just read a helpful description of each game. Includes a screen shot from each game, the type of 3D engine used in the game, and provides cheat FAQs and walk-throughs.

The All-Time Best Doom Levels

http://doomgate.cs.buffalo.edu/~williams/

The best DOOM and DOOM II add-on levels are now available in one place. You no longer have to hunt far and wide for add-on DOOM levels, only to find that they stink. This page provides dozens of the best levels available. Most of these levels include new monsters; new textures, lighting, and sound; and even new weapons. Get ready to die!

Frag dot Com

http://www.frag.com/

Quake fans will want to check out this one-stop online resource every chance they get to stay on top of what's new and evolving with the mother of all 3D action games. This page offers news, letters, reviews, land links to all things Quake with new issues being published online every week. If you miss a week just check out this site's extensive news archive, cataloged by week.

GameNet

http://www.gamenet.com/

A Mac gamer subscriber service. Provides 24-hour access to BBS and server (for play) devoted to Mac games such as Marathon, Power Poker, and Chuck Yeager's Air Combat. Subscribers can order games at discount prices.

id software

http://www.idsoftware.com/

Home page of the creators of Doom, Doom II, and the long-awaited Quake. The success of id software's games is so great that accessing this site is almost impossible. Check out similar sites first to see if the software updates, levels, or patches you need are available.

Mech Warrior 2 and Clan of the Ghost Bear Page

http://www.lookup.com/homepages/69636/mw/mech2.html

Complete resource for the 3D battle simulator MechWarrior II, from Activision. This site includes detailed information on the best way to fight different

'Mechs and all the cheat codes for Mech-warrior II and the expansion pack. In addition, an invaluable list of utilities includes 'Mech editing software, patches for version 1.1 and Windows 95, information on running the game from the hard drive, and custom .AVIs.

3D STRATEGY GAMES

Justin's Command and Conquer Web Page

http://www.cam.org/~jlee06/cc.html

A detailed site dedicated to Command & Conquer, voted by many as the best PC game of 1995. This site is filled with tips for beating your opponents, getting out of messes, and multiplayer tactics. Invaluable is the files section, which includes the latest patches and a new level editor, CCEDIT. Includes links to other interesting sites dedicated to Command & Conquer.

Player's Lists

http://www.zorda.com/playlst/

Join a players list for Hexen, DOOM I/II, CivNET, Command & Conquer, and Warcraft II. Simply choose the game, click Add Yourself to the <game> List, then fill out the form. A great resource for 3D game strategists.

ADVENTURE GAMES

The Myst Hint Guide

http://www.astro.washington.edu/ingram/myst/index.html

Clues to solving those vexing puzzle problems in Myst are now available. This site, one of the top 5% visited on the Web, provides hints organized by world. There is no walkthrough at this URL, but the hints should help you solve traps when you're completely stumped. If you ever wondered why such a mentally torturous game was ever created, FAQs near the end of the page will answer your questions.

Review of Phantasmagoria

http://www.ozemail.com.au/~larme/phantas.html

Detailed Web site for Sierra On-Line's mysterious, beautiful, and controversial adventure game Phantasmagoria. This site includes all the hints, cheats, and walkthrough information you'll need if you get really stumped. More interesting, however, is a detailed account on why this game has been banned in Australia! If you haven't played the game yet, this site will certainly pique your interest.

Riven: The Official Site

http://www1.riven.com/

Operated by the folks at Cyan, you can rest assured that this site contains a wealth of information about this magnificent sequel to Myst. In addition to extensive lore about the game, including the story of Riven and a complete recap of Myst, you'll also learn about some of fascinating behind-the-scenes stories regarding the making of the game. Analyze this game's uniqueness to its predecessor or just come to appreciate the detail in its design with a visit to breathtaking the Riven image gallery. If you're not totally impressed with Riven before you check out this site, you will be before you leave.

CHEAT CODES

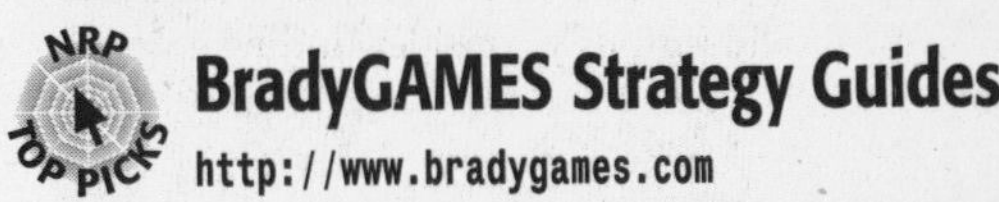

BradyGAMES Strategy Guides

http://www.bradygames.com

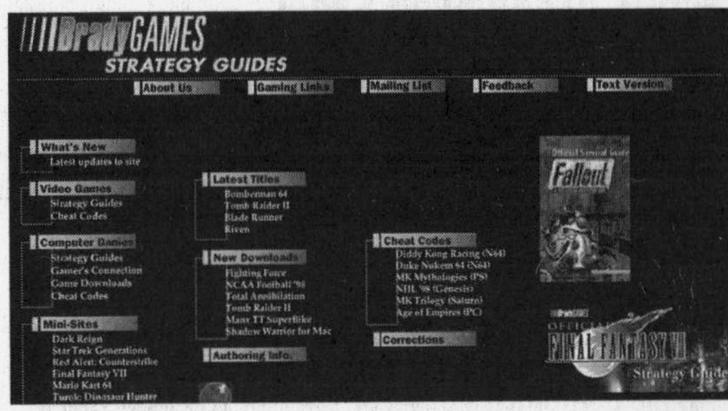

This is the place to go to find out what BradyGAMES, publisher of strategy guides for all the latest video and PC game titles, has put on the shelves lately. However, if you'd rather get your game secrets for free, this site also features an extensive list of cheat codes (both video and PC) for all the hot games. These cheats are updated often, so it's a good idea to check the Web site out frequently (even if you've already purchased a strategy guide) for late-breaking codes.

Cheater's Guild

http://www.cheatersguild.com/

Looking for the invincibility code for the newest shooter? Or maybe you'd like to know how get an unfair advantage with that old, obscure adventure game that nobody plays anymore? Chances are, the game you seek to cheat is included in this site's Cheat

Vault, which features a list of over 1,100 games—and still growing! The Vault presents you with 27 options (A-Z, plus #) to begin your search. Simply select the first character of the game you're looking for to access the list of games beginning with that character. Some games listed feature walkthrough strategy rather than cheats.

The Cheater's Guild

http://www.thecheatersguild.com/

Sure, it's almost the same name and Web site address as the previous listing, but this is a different site, with a comparable list of cheats and some unique features. The Cheater's Guild motto is, "I came, I tried, I lost, I tried again, I cheated, I won." If you can sympathize with this philosophy, you've come to the right place. This site is organized similarly to its counterpart, "Cheater's Guild," but in a slightly more intuitive fashion—it's a bit easier to navigate through the cheat archives and various other fun options "The" Cheater's Guild offers. Basically, if it's an old game and you can't find it here or the other site with the "The," you should seriously consider finding a new hobby.

Secrets of the Sega Sages

http://www.segasages.com/

With a name like this, you might expect to find only codes for Sega games, but this site actually features an admirable list of PC cheats, as well as codes for all of the console systems. It bills itself as "The Cure for the Common Code." That may or may not be true, but it does deliver is a plethora of codes submitted by visitors to the site. You can surf through the submissions in the traditional alphabetic style, or you can "speed-dial" the game you're searching for via Sega Sage's cheat code search engine. Although you may find this site to be quicker, caveat emptor—these codes were sent in by error-prone humans like you and me, and may not always be totally accurate.

COMPANIES

3D Realms

http://www.3drealms.com/

Essential for fans of the alien-obliterating hero Duke Nukem. Stop by this site to keep your finger on the pulse of what's in store for the game that just keeps evolving. It's also a great place to check out the other impressive games developed by this division of Apogee Software—including *Prey*, *Shadow Warrior*, and *Terminal Velocity*. This site features support, downloadable demos, as well as screenshots of games still in development.

7th Level

http://www.7thlevel.com/

These guys have been busy, and it shows. Read about the latest gaming project, check out their Free Demos section, visit the Company Store, or try out their Chat feature, where you can communicate with other gaming fiends.

Aristoplay, Ltd.

http://intergalactic.com/aris.htm

Provides company information and a catalog for this maker of educational computer games. Also provides Aristokids, a free newsletter that offers games and fun facts.

Epic Megagames

http://www.epicgames.com/

See some examples of why Epic's motto is "Only for Pentium. Only for Windows 95." This site provides information on Epic's latest releases and tantalizing upcoming products. Download demos of their latest 2D and 3D shoot 'em ups, contact Epic employees, or read the latest news on their collaboration with other game companies.

Interplay Productions

http://www.interplay.com

The "By Gamers, For Gamers" people who brought you *Star Trek: Starfleet Academy*, *Fallout*, *Redneck Rampage*, and many others have put together an impressive, albeit long-to-load, site. Visit here to get support on your latest gaming addiction, check out what's coming soon, download some demos, or even pick out something new from their online store—there's always lots to choose from!

LucasArts Entertainment Company Presents

http://www.lucasarts.com/menu.html

If you've got a few minutes, enter this page's URL, then go grab a cold one. Although the graphics are a little ambitious for a 28.8 connection, the page provides unique, useful links not found at other sites. Check out LucasArts' Entertainer magazine, shop the company store, or download demos from their library of games. The Recruitment Center is for all those who dreamed of working in the gaming business.

Microprose Software

http://www.microprose.com/mpshp.html

Creators of the award-winning Civilization and X-Com strategy games. This humorous site includes info on future projects, Cool Stuff—Microprose products—and technical help.

Pop Rocket, Inc.

http://www.poprocket.com/

Provides home site for Pop Rocket games, producers of Total Distortion. Includes game background, links to the Shockwave Game Arena, Rocket Shop, press releases, and interviews with the game designers. Also includes online contests, merchandise, and ordering information.

Shadow Island Games

http://www.pbm.com/

Play by electronic mail (PBEM) Olympia and Arena at this site. Provides game background, dice server services, and information about PBEM games.

Sierra On-Line

http://www.sierra.com/

This opening page and the Guest page for Sierra On-Line is small compared to the Welcome page you can access if you join their "club." Click Join to sign up for Sierra's club; click on Members if you are already a member. If you can find their Demos link, you will have hit pay dirt. This site is updated daily.

Virgin Zesty Bytes

http://www.virgin.com/

Virgin Interactive's home page provides a number of snack treats for the gaming addict. Dip into the Tasty Samples to read about Virgin's current product line and to download several working demos. The publisher of the immensely popular 11th Hour sequel to 7th Guest, provides links and information for this salty brain stumper.

Virtual Entertainment

http://www.cts.com/~vrman/

Provides information about VR Slingshot interactive virtual sport games. Includes detailed descriptions, pictures, and ordering information. Provides online test version of VR Slingshot.

FLIGHT SIMULATORS

Air Havoc Controller for Windows

http://com.primenet.com/rainbow/

Instead simulating flying the plane, this time you simulate being an air traffic controller. Air Havoc utilizes 3D graphics at 640×480 resolution along with 28 different aircraft. Site provides sample images and video clips of the game.

Battlecruiser 3000AD Unofficial FAQ and Home Page

http://www.geocities.com/SiliconValley/9579/battle.html

Find out the status of Take 2's Battlecruiser 3000AD. Read the gossip on its delays and beta pirates, download the demo, check out screen shots and the latest FAQ, and read email from the game's principal developer.

Embry-Riddle Flight Simulation Links

http://macwww.db.erau.edu/www_virtual_lib/aviation/flightsim.html

Can you think of a better place to access flight simulator links than from the largest flying school in the country? This page includes dozens of links to the best Web sites on flying games and flight simulators.

First Eurofighter Air Wing

http://www.ef2000.com/

For pilots of the flight simulator Eurofighter 2000, published by Ocean Software. Visit with other pilots in the Officer's Club, find that cheat code you've heard about in the Pilot Forum, download the latest patch and FAQ file, or ask for technical help in the Maintenance Hanger. A thorough site for Eurofighter fans.

A B C D E F G H I J K L M N O P Q R S T U V W X Y Z

Flight Unlimited

http://www.lglass.com/flight.html

Considered by many to be the most realistic flight simulator to date, the home page for this amazing program provides screen shots and descriptions of different planes and courses in the game. Really only an introduction to Flight Unlimited.

Military Simulations Inc.

http://www.military-sim.com/

Professional-type flight simulators for your personal computer. Check out their newest title, "Back to Baghdad—The Ultimate Desert Storm Simulation." Other products and ordering information also provided.

Military Simulations Back to Baghdad

http://www.military-sim.com/

Can Falcon Gold be eclipsed? Find out if Back to Baghdad's F-16 is more accurate. This page describes the game's development, provides a contest for registered users, and includes links to companies that helped develop the game, including SPOT satellite imagery, Thrustmaster, CH, and Digital Workshop.

TekMate Home of the Skunks

http://rampages.onramp.net/~tekmate/

The makers of Virtual Skunks, plane add-on software to Microsoft Flight Simulator and Flight Sim's Aircraft Factory includes free downloadable airplanes, a gallery of aircraft, and a "plane locator." If you're interested in flying your favorite WW II bomber, Thompson Trophy classic, 90's jet airliner, or anything else, chances are good you'll find it in one of TekMate's 23 plane collections.

Thrustmaster Home Page

http://www.thrustmaster.com/

The manufacturer of the most advanced flight controls available provides help setting up controllers in Windows 95, patches and updates, technical support, FAQs about Thrustmaster products, developer support, and the latest news.

Related Sites
http://www.io.com/~vga2000/
http://www.frontiernet.net/~mmadigan/
http://www.auricvision.com/frameh.htm
http://www.trailerpark.com/tango/mgp

U.S. Navy Fighters The Unofficial Home Page

http://wwwedu.cs.utwente.nl/~kamps/usnf.html

This highly detailed fan page for Electronic Arts' U.S. Navy Fighters provides secret key codes and cheats for the game, lengthy help and information on the Ukraine 1997 Campaign and Marine Fighters add-ons, information on EA's ATF flight simulator, and files that let you fly any plane. This page also contains a number of custom missions.

The USENET Guide to Falcon 3

http://cactus.org/~knutson/UGF3/UGF3.book.html

Incredibly detailed listing of USENET threads about Spectrum Holobyte's famous Falcon 3.0 flight simulator. This well-organized site has ten sections, including Trivia, Setup, Tips and Strategy, and Quirks and Bugs. These categories are broken down into hundreds of subcategories. If you can't find it here, you dreamt it!

Warbirds Internet Multi-Player Flight Simulation

http://www.icigames.com/

Download the Warbirds software, then sign up to fly against other Internet gaming fanatics. This site provides a FAQ to answer all your questions (a must read), the demo for downloading, and rates for playing on the Warbirds Internet network. Exciting!

GAME DEVELOPER SITES

3D Engine List

http://www.cs.tu-berlin.de/%7Eki/engines.html

Check out the Special Categories sidebar on this page; it includes dozens of demos, shareware engines, and even a full working engine for developing your own 3D action game. This nicely organized site includes tons of 3D gaming information.

Digital Dialect

http://www.primenet.com/~mcase/

Develops 3D game engines and 3D games for Sega, Sony Playstation, and the PC. Read about Digital Dialect's latest 3D game engine, CANCUN, which boasts sloping walls, correct perspective at all angles (even looking up and down), 6 degrees of camera movement, dynamic lighting, and 3D monsters.

G.A.C. Computer Services

`http://rampages.onramp.net/~campbel/`

Develops games for BBSs, PCs, and Web servers. Provides catalogs and demos of products, which you can download and pay for via credit card. Game modules include Lucky Star Casino Ship, InterLORD, and the Realm of Vanadia.

BBS

Acronym for Bulletin Board Service.

IBM OS/2 Games Home Page

`http://www.austin.ibm.com/os2games`

IBM home page for OS/2 game developers and game enthusiasts. Includes product announcements, demos, press releases, a developer's corner, and gaming tips.

Jeff Lander's Home Page

`http://www.lainet.com/~jeffl/`

Showcases the Dagger 3D engine, which is being used to develop a new game called Varuna's Forces for Sega, Sony Playstation, PC, and other platforms. Examine the technical specs on this engine and several utilities included with it, such as the Havoc renderer and Height Mapping Terrain System.

Pie in the Sky Software

`http://www.catalog.com/psky/`

Provides sales of Pie's 3D GCS (Games Creation System) software. Includes detailed product background, links to games created with GCS, downloadable demos, and ordering information.

HARDWARE

CH Products

`http://www.chproducts.com/`

If you're a die-hard flight simulator fanatic, check out the F-16 Series link on the Gaming Gear page. CH's F-16 Fighterstick, Pro Peddles, and Pro Throttle will turn heads (watch your six!). This page also lets you leave messages for the company, download CH drivers and other free software, and get technical specs on all CH "sticks."

Creative Zone

`http://www.creaf.com/zonemenu.html`

Creative Technologies' Web site provides three publications: Music Pub, Entertainment Arcade, and Business Center. Check out these publications to see the latest in gaming and sound technology. The Creative Zone also includes links to a directory of every Web page they have, information on anything you'd ever want to know about their Sound-, Modem-, and VideoBlaster products, and an online newsstand. This is a huge Web site.

Diamond Multimedia

`http://www.diamondmm.com/`

Click Entertainment and Visual Systems to read about Diamond's newest 3D graphics accelerators and video cards. Read about their next trade show, employment opportunities, and product specs.

Forte Vfx1

`http://www.fortevr.com`

VR headsets are hot these days, and Forte's Web site shows why the Vfx1 is one of the hottest. Download the newest drivers for their headset, play with beta drivers for Windows 95, see how you can use this headset with VRML, and find out which games are compatible with this device.

Mag zine

`http://www.maginnovision.com/`

Tired of your 14-inch monitor you bought with that AT back in 1990? Check out Mag's DX17T monitor or choose the perfect monitor using their Select-A-Screen decision maker. This site also enables you contact tech support, learn more about monitors using their Glossary of Monitor Terms, and email Mag employees.

Virtual I/O

`http://www.vio.com/`

See what free stuff is available for the Virtual I/O glasses, locate retailers, see which games are compatible, talk to developers, and read company info. Currently these glasses are the leader in VR headset sales.

HORROR GAMES

Computer Games Rating Guide

http://www.ozemail.com.au/~larme/phguide.html

Read what it takes to get an RC, MA, M, or G rating on a computer game. This measuring system is similar to the National Motion Picture Rating Association's movie ratings. This page also discusses the possible reasons why Phantasmagoria was banned in several countries.

Fade to Black

http://www.atw.fullfeed.com/~jkrutke/f2b.htm

A violent, nerve-wracking 3D game with villains and monsters that resembles the older, less sophisticated Alone in the Dark. This page provides hints, lets you download the demo, displays screen shots taken from the game, and provides technical information.

Gabriel Knight Help and Hints Home page

http://www.westga.edu/~jgibson/gk2/

Reviews the original Gabriel Knight game and the sequel: The Beast Within. Download patches for the original Sins of the Fathers, sign the Guestbook, and download the complete walk through. This site also provides email help. If you get stuck, send off an email to the Webmaster of this page. Very helpful!

Into the Void

http://www.playmatestoys.com/pages/pie/itv.htm

Will you survive against alien races bent on your destruction? Read about this space simulation that takes place largely in the nebulous void of empty space. This page provides a detailed synopsis of the game and screen shots.

Psychic Detective

http://www.ea.com/eastudios/psychic/psychic.html

What's so frightening about this Electronic Arts game? Check out the screen shots on this page to see the types of characters you'll be dealing with to solve this murder mystery. This site also provides a downloadable film of the intro (it's 10MB!).

Related Sites

http://www.basementmag.com/games/

http://www.stuck-hints.com/

http://www.doggysoft.co.uk/gaming/

Shivers

http://www.iinet.net.au/~quandary/issue5/shiv.html

Provides a lengthy review of Sierra's spooky horror game for teenagers.

HUMOROUS GAMES

Cannon Fodder II

http://happypuppy.com/games/link/canfod2.htm

Download a working demo of one of the silliest "strategy" games made. The only instructions that come with this game are "Kill all enemies." Black humor at its finest in the gaming world.

Earthworm Jim II

http://www.playmatestoys.com/pages/pie/ewjpc.htm

Download the demo to this hilarious weirdfest with Earthworm Jim and his sidekick Snott. This page includes .WAVs of Jim's infamous expressions, screen shots from the game, and the story line. Fun!

Information about Lemmings 3D the Demo

http://www.cs.umu.se/~mnlchm/l3demo.html

This fan page provides links for downloading Pygnosis' latest Lemmings adventure—Lemmings 3D. You can also download the cheat codes and the walk-through, or contact other Lemmings nuts at the Lemming newsgroup.

You Don't Know Jack

http://www.berksys.com/www/products/ydkj.html

The hottest game on the party circuit has a Web page with info on question packs, a free demo, system requirements, and press releases. If you think one of the answers is in error, you can email the Webmaster. If you do, be funny!

LIFE SIMULATORS

The Civilization Page

http://www.lilback.com/civilization/

A detailed Netscape 2 Web page for the Microprose simulation Civilization. This Web site discusses in detail the purpose of the computer game and Avalon Hill's original board game. You can also download

FAQs, files from sections for the Mac, Amiga, and PC, and get information on CivNet and Civilization II, the sequel to this popular game.

Jerry Moore's Sim Stuff Web Page

`http://www.vcnet.com/jmoore/simstuff.htm`

Download cheat programs written in Visual Basic for SimCity 2000, Simlife, SimAnt, and other Maxis simulators. A description for each program is provided. This page also includes different winning cities created by Jerry Moore and other SimCity addicts.

Maxis, Inc. Home Page

`http://www.maxis.com/index.html`

If this page doesn't look right and you become a little concerned, you probably need to be playing more games. This detailed Web site for the largest computer "simulation" gaming company includes a company store, tips and hints, the latest Maxis news, and game demo downloads.

MAGAZINES

Computer Gaming World

`http://www.zdnet.com/gaming/`

This popular gaming magazine provides tons of reviews of the latest games, an online archive of back issues, a library of patches and demo files, and the latest Features stories and cover articles. The What's New link also provides daily industry news. The only way to get to this page was through the Ziff-Davis Home Page.

Game Informer

`http://www.gameinformer.com/`

You can subscribe to the real "paper lovers" edition of this video gaming mag (the kind you get by snail mail), or just peruse the links on this page. Check out the Back Issues link for select articles found in the magazine. The Secret Access: Codes of the Week choice is a must-see if you think you've done everything possible on that Playstation game you wore out.

NEXT Generation Magazine

`http://www.next-generation.com/`

A busy site filled with live chat, the latest reviews of games for every PC, Mac, and video gaming platform, and a number of downloadable videos of gaming in progress. Their well-organized archives let you search by platform: hundreds of reviews and news flashes are available. This site is updated daily.

Nuke InterNETWORK

`http://www.nuke.com/`

Check out the great interface of this online magazine and magazine publisher that strives to use the hottest technology available. Sendai, the parent company of such popular gaming magazines as Electronic Gaming Monthly, Computer Games Magazine, and Cinescape, provides a number of unique features at this Web site. Their Chat forums on gaming let you communicate in real-time with anyone else. Register for their monthly contest.

PC Gamer Online

`http://www.pcgamer.com/`

Check the contents of the latest issue of PC Gamer, contact PC Gamer staff, or read about their new CD that comes with the magazine. The Demos area lists a number of game demos you can download that aren't on the monthly CD-ROM.

SHAREWARE/FREEWARE GAME DIRECTORIES

Games Domain

`http://www.gamesdomain.co.uk/`

The oldest gaming resource on the Web now has sites in the U.K., U.S., and Russia. You can search for a particular game using the search engine at the top of the page. This page also provides the latest news on additions to the Domain and information on GD Magazine.

Happy Puppy's PC Hit 100 Game Downloads

`http://happypuppy.com/games/link/index.html`

Your one-stop HQ for demos/crippleware/ shareware of the 100 hottest games on the market. Scroll through the candy aisle and click your game of interest. Stop by the Boneyard for downloads of slide shows and demos of older games. This well-designed site should be bookmarked if you're addicted to gaming.

shareware.com

http://www.cnet.com/Resources/Software/

Part of the excellent c/net electronic magazine, this well-designed site provides over 100,000 programs for downloading. To see the latest and greatest shareware, demos, and freeware for PCs and Macs, try to find the c/net selections choice. This Web site is considered by many to be the shareware and freeware resource.

Welcome to the New Guru Online

http://www.anime.net/~go/

Site devoted to rating video games, game machines, and magazines. After you register, you can vote on a number of different topics. Although this is purely for video games and has no downloads to speak of, the Vote and Sponsored Pages links may give you ideas about your next game purchase.

ONLINE GAMING

2AM Games

http://www.2am.com/

The creators of this site are strong believers in the philosophy that games were meant to be played with others (not alone, person vs. computer). The site seeks to attract not only those interested in the games that are offered, but also those who are interested in the joy of meeting other people with a mutual interest in challenging game competition. You have a choice of several games ranging from Chess to combat simulators. Pay a modest fee to play all the games you like for a few months or purchase individual games and enjoy unlimited multiplayer access.

Battle.net

http://206.79.254.170/index.htm

Tired of playing Diablo or Starcraft by yourself? This site provides a forum for fans of these Blizzard games to go head to head against one another in multiplayer format—for free! To do battle over the Internet with other players worldwide, all you need to do is select the Battle.net option from within the game of your choice.

MPLAYER

http://www.mplayer.com/

Another great site to compete in multiplayer games with people from all over, MPLAYER has an unbelievable selection of games to choose from including Quake, Command & Conquer, MechWarrior 2, Terminal Velocity, and Warcraft. In the mood for something a little more pensive? This site also offers classic board game adaptations like Scrabble, Risk, and Battleship. Very polished and easy to navigate, MPLAYER features many special features like "Player of the Week," as well as informative news articles on upcoming releases.

SPORTS-RELATED GAMES

The Unofficial Need for Speed Page

http://www.atw.fullfeed.com/~bix/nfs.htm

This fan page for the road racing simulator by Electronic Arts includes secret cheat codes and hints, technical information on the cars, reviews and email, and the downloadable demo. You can submit your best lap times, download a Track Editor, and contact other fans on the Need For Speed mailing list.

VR Soccer

http://www.vrsports.com/website/products/soccer.html

A 360-degree field of vision and 20-player network capability make this one of the hottest sports titles available. Download the demo or check out screen shots from the game.

Welcome to My NBA Live 96 Page

http://www.msilink.com/~solso/nbalive96.html#Hardware

An excellent site if you're researching EA's latest NBA PC game. This site includes personal email and reviews from dozens of NBA Live fanatics. Sounds from the game, troubleshooting, patches, player editors, and more make this site more valuable than EA's own NBA Live 96 site.

WAR SIMULATIONS

Enemy Lock On!

http://www.elo.com/elomag/

Online gaming magazine devoted to combat simulators. Download previous issues of Enemy Lock On!, read the latest rumors, download artwork, or check out their detailed Links page.

Related Sites

http://w3.one.net/~tlewis/hawk.html

http://www.compulink.co.uk/~mirage/

http://gw2.s-gimb.lj.edus.si/~moses/pcgames.html

The Goat Locker

http://www.mbnet.mb.ca/~moreau/harpoon.html

Web site for the Harpoon and Harpoon II submarine simulation. Information on Harpoon USENET groups, mailing lists, and Department of Defense Web sites are included. You can also download a number of Harpoon (I and II) scenarios created by fans of the game.

HPS Simulations

http://www.cris.com/~sturmer/

Index page for games offered, such as Tigers on the Prowl, Point of Attack, Panthers in the Shadows. Anything for the military game enthusiast, such as the military history calendar.

Multiplayer Games and Simulations

http://www.teleport.com/~caustic/

Provides information on every multiplayer game available. Find out about Internet gaming, online games, commercial and BBS game servers, gaming groups, and network game help. Click a game of interest in the Games and Resources section to access Web pages and FAQs. Consider adding this to your bookmarks.

The Tanker's Homepage

http://www.rapidramp.com/tanker/

An excellent resource for the war strategy gaming fanatic. This incredibly detailed site provides information on computer games and board games. Topics are organized as Gaming, Military History, Movie Reviews, Online Discussions, Free Software, and What's New. The Gaming section is divided in Ground Warfare, Aerial Warfare, and Naval Warfare. The reviews of these games are thorough and helpful.

The War Page

http://aylic.com/War/war.html

This thorough site lists every known computer war game in the Computer Wargames section. This site also has information on military history, political theory, weapons, and military science. A valuable site if you're looking for a particular war game.

LISTSERVS

A3R—A Discussion List for the Games ADVANCED THIRD REICH and RISING SUN

You can join this group by sending the message "sub A3R your name" to

listserv@sjuvm.stjohns.edu

ADND-L—Advanced Dungeons and Dragons Discussion List

You can join this group by sending the message "sub ADND-L your name" to

listserv@utarlvm1.uta.edu

ALTEREGO-L—Alter Ego Games Discussion List

Wizards of the Coast, Inc.

You can join this group by sending the message "sub ALTEREGO-L your name" to

listserv@oracle.wizards.com

ARIA-L—Last Unicorn's Aria Game List

Brown University, Providence, RI

You can join this group by sending the message "sub ARIA-L your name" to

listserv@brownvm.brown.edu

CHESS-L—The Chess Discussion List

You can join this group by sending the message "sub CHESS-L your name" to

listserv@nic.surfnet.nl

CONSIM-L—Conflict Simulation Games

You can join this group by sending the message "sub CONSIM-L your name" to

listserv@listserv.uni-c.dk

GAMEHENDGE—Gamehendge MUSH Users Mailing List

NetSpace Project, Brown University, Providence, RI

You can join this group by sending the message "sub GAMEHENDGE your name" to

listserv@netspace.org

GAMES-L—Computer Games List

Brown University, Providence, RI

You can join this group by sending the message "sub GAMES-L your name" to

listserv@brownvm.brown.edu

GMAST-L—Gamemasters Interest Group

University of Tennessee at Chattanooga

You can join this group by sending the message "sub GMAST-L your name" to

listserv@utcvm.utc.edu

A B C D E F G H I J K L M N O P Q R S T U V W X Y Z

GSPE-NL—Discussion List in the Field of Gaming, Simulation

University Center of Information

You can join this group by sending the message "sub GSPE-NL your name" to

`listserv@nic.surfnet.nl`

ISAGA-L—Int'l Simulation and Gaming Association Forum

You can join this group by sending the message "sub ISAGA-L your name" to

`listserv%uhccvm.bitnet@listserv.net`

MIDGARD-L—Midgard PBM Game ;Discussion List

You can join this group by sending the message "sub MIDGARD-L your name" to

`listserv@home.ease.lsoft.com`

MUD-L—Multi-User Dungeons and Other Simulated Real-Time Environments

You can join this group by sending the message "sub MUD-L your name" to

`listserv@vm3090.ege.edu.tr`

MYTHUS-L—Mythus Fantasy Roleplaying Game List

Brown University, Providence, RI

You can join this group by sending the message "sub MYTHUS-L your name" to

`listserv@brownvm.brown.edu`

PC-GAMES-NEW—Shareware.com PC-Games-New List

You can join this group by sending the message "sub PC-GAMES-NEW your name" to

`listserv@dispatch.cnet.com`

PC-GAMES-TOP—Shareware.com PC-Games-Top List

You can join this group by sending the message "sub PC-GAMES-TOP your name" to

`listserv@dispatch.cnet.com`

QMS-L—QM Studio Games List

You can join this group by sending the message "sub QMS-L your name" to

`listserv@brownvm.brown.edu`

UD-L—Ultimate Dungeon List

You can join this group by sending the message "sub UD-L your name" to

`listserv%uriacc.bitnet@listserv.net`

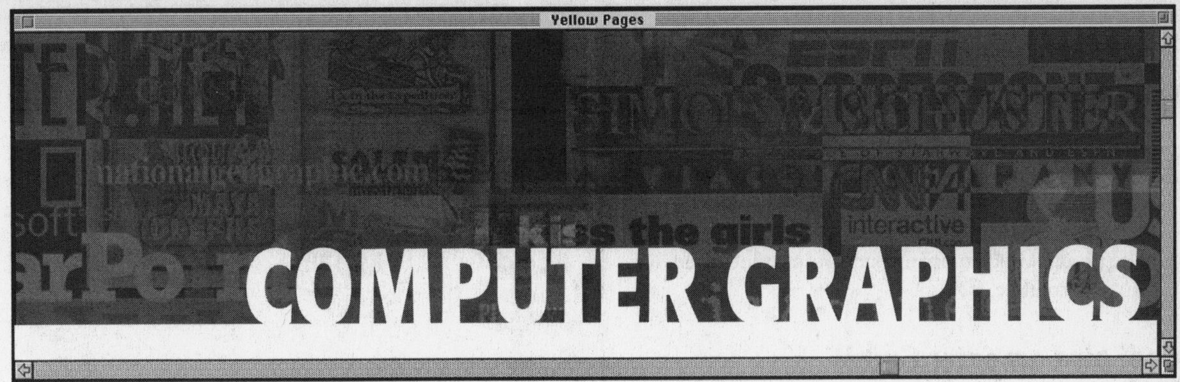

COMPUTER GRAPHICS

> Why look at the computer when you can look at the real thing?
>
> *Vulcanologist in* Dante's Peak *(1997)*

Agfa Digital Imaging and Electronic Prepress Systems

http://www.agfahome.com/

Agfa is the premiere producer of prepress products including scanners, type fonts, prepress software, and services. The Agfa site offers links to information about their products, the ability to download updates, and purchase software and hardware online. The site also provides access to corporate information.

Animated GIF Artists Guild

http://www.agag.com/

An organization dedicated to furthering the expertise and mutual interests of animated GIF designers. The site contains links to portfolios, tips and trips, discussion groups, and information about AGAG. Please do not copy any animations from this site without giving due credit or permission.

AnimaTek, Inc.

http://www.animatek.com/

Developers of 3D technologies, virtual environments, and artificial inhabitants. Provides information about 3DS BonesPro IPAS, AnimaTek's World Builder landscape editor, and other products. Also provides lists of development services and technologies for sale.

Click 3x
http://www.click3x.com

Anton's Freehand Page

http://www.euro.net/ecompany/afpindex.html

One of the best stops for everything Freehand. Besides the standard links to Usenet groups and mailing lists, this page includes links to Freehand demos and updates, bugs and problems FAQs, information on enhancing Freehand, and FAQs for fixing printing problems.

Artifice, Inc.

http://artifice.com/foyer.html

Creates tools, software and media for environment designers. Provides company background, extensive product information, great buildings showcase, technical support and press release library. Includes great detail about DesignWorkshop technical background and features.

Astrobyte

http://www.astrobyte.com/

Producers of BeyondPress software that enables conversions from Xpress to HTML. Provides product overviews, reviews, links to sites using Astrobyte software, downloadable evaluation tools, and information on Japanese versions of their software. Includes links to reference and learning of HTML.

Blue Sky Research

http://www.bluesky.com/

Produces Textures, LaTeX, TeX, and font software. Also produces technical manuals that go with their products. Provides technical support, company news, upgrade information, and relevant links such as CTAN, the "Comprehensive TeX Archive Network."

Baystate Technologies Web.

http://www.cadkey.com/

Produces CAD products including systems, hardware, and software. Includes lengthy product descriptions, company history, technical support, press releases, features in trade magazines, and online order forms. The product and company backgrounds are extensive and informative.

CadSoft Computer GmbH

http://www.CadSoft.DE/

Provides information about CadSoft's EAGLE software, which allows you to design printed circuit boards. Provides the usual technical support and online product descriptions, but also includes an exhaustive world-wide list of distributors, and a link for downloading updates, new drivers, and a free, fully functional demo version of EAGLE.

Caema Ltd.

http://www.sci.fi/~tsuomine/caema.htm

Produces MecDesign software applications for MicroDesign, MicroStation, and PowerDraft systems for use in the mechanical design and engineering fields. Provides online demonstrations, product descriptions, technical support, developmental business partners, and tutorials.

Canto Software

http://www.canto-software.com/

Canto Software produces Cumulus 4.0 to manage electronic media via Windows NT servers. The Web site provides examples of Cumulus' usefulness, technical support, online updates, and information about purchasing the software.

Cimio CADCAM Conversion software

http://www.cimio.co.uk/

Cimio's ConvertX CADCAM data exchange software enables you to freely exchange CADCAM data among AutoCAD (DWG and DXF rev 10-13), CADDS3, CADDS4X, CADDS5, CATIA V3, I/EMS, IDEAS drafting, Medusa (rev 5, 6, 7, 12), and Microstation environments.

Click 3x

http://www.click3x.com

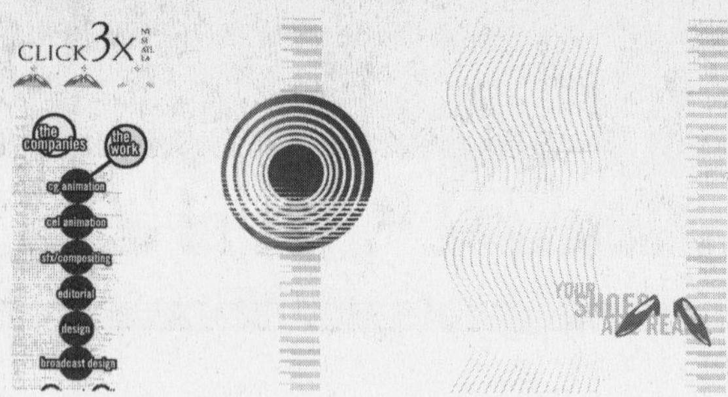

Produces and provides full-service computer graphics services including animation, and interactive production. Includes studio equipment and staff listings. Also provides computer graphics created for many commercials and companies.

ComCom Systems, Inc.

http://www.comcomsystems.com/image.html

Produces ELA Office and ELA Office Batch, Windows based OCR, and image database software. Office Batch eliminates the need to type and file forms; you simply scan in the forms and Office Batch reads them. ELA View and ELA Network are advanced document imaging systems that can handle tens of thousands of documents per day.

Computer Graphics Systems Development Corporation (CGSD)

http://www.cgsd.com

Produces simulation and virtual reality products. Also produces a computer graphics industry newsletter *Real Time.* Provides consulting and specialized software design. Includes information about systems integrations research, visual stimulation real-time systems, and other software products.

CyberTec Commercial Art Inc.

http://www.wln.com/~grafx/index.html

Provides full-service computer and traditional graphics services. Includes Web site creation, brochures, T-shirts, and layout and design. Also includes company logo creation, four-color process separations, and camera-ready artwork. Site provides full-service listings, samples of work done, and contact information.

Cytopia Software Incorporated

http://www.cytopia.com/

Designs and produces graphics software and applications. Includes information about SocketSet, PhotoLab, and Image Xpress ScanPrepPro products. Includes technical specifications, downloadable samples, technical support, and an art portfolio. Also includes press releases and contact information.

DNA Graphics Created with PovChem

http://ludwig.scs.uiuc.edu/~paul/DNA.html

This guy produces models of DNA double helices in many different styles, such as Celtic. Animations of DNA are displayed as well as a portfolio of the artist's work is presented.

Data Image Systems

http://bigweb.com/mall/don/index.html

Provides sales on graphics equipment and software. Includes product specifications and contact information. Also includes links to other graphics-related sites.

DesignSphere Online

http://www.dsphere.net/

Provides industry news and information on a number of topics that tie with computer graphics, multimedia design, lithography, and other visual forms. Includes links to online zines, career opportunities, graphics businesses, portfolios, and numerous tips.

Digio Media

http://www.digio.com/

Provides home site for Digio Media, a full-service graphics firm based in Seattle, Washington. Includes links to clients and staff credentials. Also includes a performance lab with examples of work done.

Edifika

http://ournet.clever.net/edifika/hp.html

Produces graphics software, applications, and products that are used in architecture, Web design, and computer animation. Specializes in the use of OTVR virtual reality technologies from Apple. Includes services offered, work examples, and contact information.

Electronic Design Automation Companies

http://www.edac.org/

Provides home site and information for the Electronic Design Automation industry. Includes publications directory, services, and listings with links to all member companies. Also includes resources information, job listings, and contacts.

Evans & Sutherland Computer Corporation

http://www.es.com/

Designs and produces real-time 3D graphics systems for simulation and virtual reality needs. Includes company product catalog, technical specifications, and examples of real-time movies along with other graphics. Provides contact information and links to related sites.

Fractal Design Corporation

http://www.fractal.com/

Download working demos of the award-winning Fractal Design Painter or Dabbler—an easy-to-use Paint program—or learn more about new Fractal products, such as Poser. A must-see is the Art Gallery, a collection of amazing artwork created with Fractal products.

The Graphics Gallery

http://www.infi.net/~gallery/

Experienced designers, artists, and technicians will take your business file or document and convert it to another format, create slides, develop advertising media—anything that can be done! Provides links to services, prices, new media, technical info, and so on.

Hamrick Software

http://www.primenet.com/~hamrick/

Check out VuePrint image viewer for Windows to print or download Internet images. Links to more product info, tech support, and "fun things to do."

ICE

http://www.iced.com/

High performance graphics—the Desktop RealTime Engine series— for GFLOPS throughput used by movie directors to engineers. Access to links about product information, application and development, and technical information.

A B C D E F G H I J K L M N O P Q R S T U V W X Y Z

Intergraph Corp

http://www.ingr.com/usa/index.html

Find out about Intergraph, a Huntsville, Alabama company, that makes high-end 3D drafting and design workstations and software. Learn more about their new TDZ multiple-Pentium Pro systems, which use Windows NT and the OpenGL standard for 3D graphics. To see what Intergraph systems are capable of, search for Golden Mouse in their search engine. Amazing!

KATMEKAT

http://www.mindspring.com/~katmekat/

This is a beautifully designed site that invites you to use their services in graphic design and Web site creation. Continually updated, this site provides links to examples of their work in 3D imagery, interactive software, Web graphics, and games. Specialization in Japanese is also displayed.

Lightscape Technologies, Inc.

http://www.lightscape.com/

The Lightscape Visualization System is the "most powerful visualization application on the market today." View images, models, and see the possibilities for your graphics needs.

Live Picture, Inc.

http://www.livepicture.com/

For the high-end professional market, imaging software and technologies for designers, production specialists, photo labs, and photographers. Check out their new software, live picture network, other cool links, and more.

MacroMedia Freehand Page

http://www.macromedia.com/Tools/Freehand/index.html

Home page for the main competitor to Adobe Illustrator. Check out the Macromedia's Gallery to see what Freehand designers have created with this powerful program.

Management Graphics, Inc. USA

http://www.mgi.com/

If you're in the digital color graphics industry, this site will provide quality printing and imaging solutions for you. Offers a complete line of film recorders and support as well as news, announcements, and links to other sites.

Marine Graphics, Inc.

http://nwlink.com/graphics/

"Virtual Relettering" for your boat. They will take the picture you send, scan it, and create a full size vinyl graphic that you can preview on the Internet in only a few days to see what it will look like on your boat. If you're in the Seattle area, they'll install it too. If you're not, they provide complete installation instructions.

MaxVision Online

http://www.maxvision.com/

CAD experts specializing in modeling, visualization, and CAD graphics on MaxVision Symbion Workstations. MaxVision will provide the support you need for your workstation, or do the work for you.

Mentor Graphics Corporation

http://www.mentorg.com/

Integrated system design products and services, including hardware and software design, education, and training. Check out their many benefits for your business.

Nova Development

http://www.novadevcorp.com/

Nova Development publishes terrific collections of Web clipart called Web Explosion and Web Animation Explosion as well as an extensive array of terrific EPS color clipart and games. The Nova Development site features descriptions of their products, a free clipart download area, technical support, the capability to order their products online, and information about the company.

Number Nine Visual Technologies

http://www.nine.com/

Graphic display solutions for personal computers, for the novice to the experienced user. Links to customer support, product information, and specifications.

Optix The Internet Document Management System

http://www.blueridge.com

Web site for Blueridge Technologies' Optix document management system. This page describes Optix features, such as COLD (Computer Output to Laser Disk) and OCR (Optical Character Recognition); permits you to access technical support, and includes links to imaging-related sites.

Parallel Performance Group

http://www.ppgsoft.com/ppgsoft/loox.html

Produces the LOOXS interactive graphics development system and applications. Includes product features, advantages, and system requirements.

Parametric Technology Corporation

http://www.ptc.com/

Produces support software for the Pro/ENGINEER mechanical design system. Includes company profile, product specifications, consulting services offered, and investment background. Also includes resellers listings and contact information.

Pathtrace Systems

http://mfginfo.com/cadcam/edgecam/pathtrace.htm

Produces CAD/CAM-based manufacturing design software, applications, and products. Includes information about EdgeCam, EdgeMilling, and other related products. Provides technical specifications and contact information.

Pattern Corporation

http://www.patterndom.com/

Provides a wide range of multimedia design services. Includes examples of works done, resources utilized, and contact information. Also includes links to many related sites.

Paul Mace Software

http://www.pmace.com/

Designs and produces Expo (GRASP) animation graphics systems along with other related products. Includes technical support, pricing, downloadable demos, online Expo demonstration, and contact information.

Performing Graphics Company

http://www.pgc.com/

Provides home site for Performing Graphics which specializes in real-time meetings pages and performance graphics. Meetings pages are sites set up for teleconferencing with graphics exchanged for companies. Includes articles about the utilization of graphics and icons. Also includes service listings including Web site design, and telefacilitation training.

PhotoModeler

http://www.photomodeler.com/

Find out about this bizarre software, which converts objects in photograph into 3D objects on the computer. Visit their VRML pages (you need a VRML viewer to do this), read FAQs about the capabilities of this software, download demos, and link to other related pages. A fascinating site for photographers and artists.

Photoshop Folder FTP Site

ftp://ftp.asi.com/pub/photoshop

A small but valuable site for Photoshop and Kai's users who want to try out freeware and shareware filters and other Photoshop add-ons.

The Pixel Foundry

http://the-tech.mit.edu/KPT/KPT.html

The best jumping off point for Kai's Power Tool users. This site includes links to online galleries, tips and tricks for Kai's users, and newsletters full of Photoshop tips. The Background Gallery is a must-see for Web page designers.

Play Incorporated

http://www.play.com/

Designs and produces the Snappy Video Snapshot digital image producer. The Snappy can take any image from a camcorder, VCR, or a TV and make a digital still for a PC. Includes detailed technical specifications and features. Provides downloadable demo software. Also includes company profile and upcoming product information.

Precision Graphics of Texas

http://mfginfo.com/service/precision/precision.htm

Provides graphics design and production in new and old media. Includes services and products offered by Precision Graphics. Also includes a search engine of professional graphic resources.

Quadrat Communications

http://www.interlog.com/~quadrat/

Provides graphic design and other publication services. Includes service listings, artwork portfolio, and contact information for this small Toronto, Ontario firm.

Renaissance Technologies

http://www.rentech.com/

Provides graphics services and products. Services include Web site creation, custom graphics production, and access service. Also includes sales of Sitescapes graphic templates for WWW publishing and Rainbow color selection applications.

Render-Cam Images

http://www.crl.com/~rci/rci.htm

Supplies graphics and 3D production services, including computer animation, morphing, modeling, and 3D layout. Includes company portfolio and links to WWW sites created. Provides services offered listing and contact information.

Scientific Visualization Sites

http://www.nas.nasa.gov/RNR/Visualization/annotatedURLs.html

Collection of links to every known scientific visualization site on the Web. Each Web page from related universities that have such projects is described and compared to other Web sites. Very helpful for scientists interested in modeling their experiments.

Silicon Surf

http://www.sgi.com/

Besides the usual complement of product specs, customer support, and reseller directories, this Web site includes Silicon's unique Extreme Tech, Serious Fun, and Surf Zone links. Check out the Serious Fun link to download freeware, join SGI's Surf Zone club (a 3D Web navigator), and SGI's Image gallery.

Software Publishing Corporation Home Page

http://www.spco.com

Developers of Harvard Graphics and the new ASAP WordPower program, which lets you create presentation quality graphics from text files. Check out the ASAP Webshow Gallery for downloads of presentations created with SPC products.

Stephens Design

http://www.opendoor.com/StephensDesign/

Provides graphic design and production services for advertising, Web publishing, and more. Includes example graphics created, portfolio of artwork, and company profile.

Subia

http://www.subia.com/subia/

Provides a wide array of graphics and related design services. Includes detail color scanning, Web site creation, graphic design production, and digital proof services. Includes services background and contact information.

team smartyPANTS!

http://www.eden.com/~smarty/

Provides a wide range of graphics and Web publishing services. Includes 3D artwork creation, Web site design, writing HTML, and much more. Offers links to sites created, example artwork, and contact information.

Triffet Design Group

http://www.primenet.com/~martman/TDG.html

Creates fashion and packaging design graphic design services. Includes client list and contact information.

Ultimate PhotoShop Compendium

http://www.sas.upenn.edu/~pitharat/photoshop/main.html

This is a fabulous collection of tips, tricks, filters, and plug-ins for Adobe PhotoShop. The site design is inviting and provides simple access to the many tools for PhotoShop users. An extremely useful site.

Virtus Corporation

http://www.virtus.com/

Produces desktop 3D graphics and virtual reality software. Includes information about the 3D Web site Builder, WalkThroughPro, and other graphics tools. Provides company history, product background, and contact information.

WebFlow Communications Group

http://fox.nstn.ca/~webflow/

Provides graphic design, Web site creation, digital imaging, and other services. Includes clients listing, example work, and company contacts.

Zycad Corporation

http://www.zycad.com/

Produces computer design software and tools for engineering, prototyping, and simulations applications. Includes information about the Paradym XP Simulation Accelerator and other products. Provides company profile, press releases, financial information, office locations, and contacts.

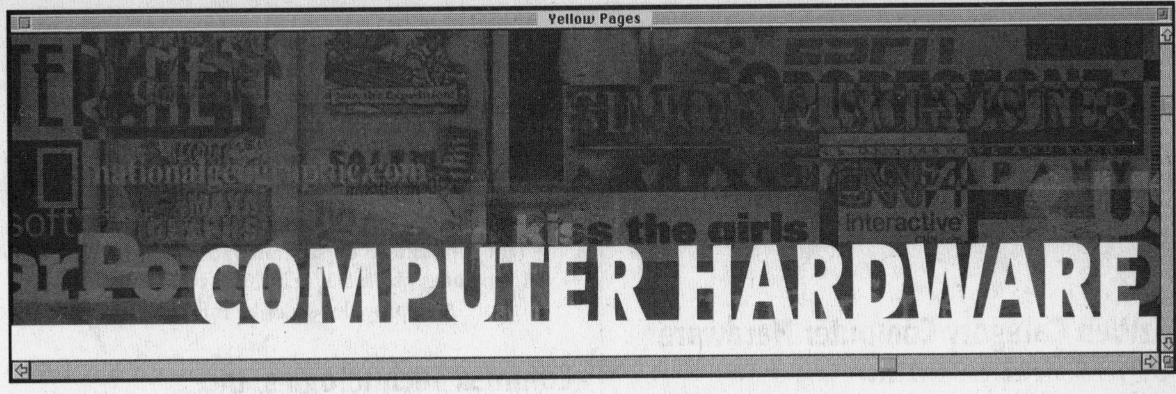

> To err is human, but to really foul things up requires a computer.
>
> Farmers' Almanac, *1978*

1st Solutions, Inc.

http://www.firstsol.com/

Provides sales for 50 Series Hardware in the United States and Canada. Also provides licensed hardware and software, consulting for Prime users, and the offering of a self-developed multi-host RAID7 that can run simultaneously on Prime or other CPU platforms.

ACCESS Computer Hardware

http://www.electriciti.com/~access/

Provides sales, set-up, service, support, and consulting for small to medium sized technology companies that are moving into international markets or looking to expand export business. Also provides information on the use of Sparc Clone Workstations, hard drives, and other products.

Advanced Computer Design

http://www.adcomp.com/

Online catalog of various computer hardware products. Browse the catalog or use the search engine to find what you're looking for. A VeriSign Authentic site, it offers secure online ordering.

Worldwide Technologies Desktop & Mobile Computing Solutions
http://www.worldwidetechnologies.com/index.html

Altair Electronics Ltd.

http://altair.on.ca/

Designs and manufactures custom-made computers. Sells PC and Mac systems and peripherals. Email the company for more information and prices.

American Power Conversion

http://www.apcc.com/

Click one of APC's uninterruptible power supply products to read about its features and capabilities. You can also view a picture of each product, download demo software, and leave questions for their marketing department.

Apason Distributors

http://blackboard.com/apason/

Sells motherboards, hard drives, video cards, multimedia kits, cases, memory, CPUs, and modems. Warranty information, pricing, and shipping rates (AirBorne Express) are available online.

ATI Technologies Online

http://www.atitech.ca/

The colorful home page for this successful manufacturer of video accelerator boards and multimedia products provides links to Public Relations, and provides information for investors and developers. The Products section discusses in-depth ATI video products. Click Current Drivers to download the latest ATI drivers.

A B C D E F G H I J K L M N O P Q R S T U V W X Y Z

Autotime Corp.

http://www.teleport.com/~autotime/

Producers of memory converters, HYPERcable printer cables, and LASERBuddy printer forms. This site is currently under construction, but will eventually feature technical support. Includes product features and pricing.

BizWeb Category Computer Hardware

http://www.bizweb.com/keylists/computer.hardware.html

This long list of computer hardware-related Web sites has hundreds of links to such companies as DEC, Cray, Creative Labs, Epson, and GammaLink. If you can't find the company you're looking for here, it doesn't exist! A thorough site.

Black Box Corporation

http://www.blackbox.com/

Provides online catalog for Black Box, who produces and sells data communications and digital connectivity products. Includes a searchable catalog, technical support services, online reference guide, and product background information. Also provides capability to receive hard copy version of catalog through the mail.

BVM

http://www.bvmltd.co.uk/

Develops and manufactures VMEbus boards, controllers, disc modules and other related hardware along with software supports. Provides detailed product background, press releases, and news clippings about BVM and their products.

Central Data

http://www.cd.com/

Produces SCSI and ethernet connectivity and host interface products such as serial port controllers, modem, and terminal servers. Includes product benefits and pricing information along with listings of support services. The site also provides technical support and a customer feedback column.

Related Sites
http://computermax-inc.com/
http://icemall.com/mall/computers.html
http://www.sellhorn.com/hard01.htm
http://www.webpost.net/spelts/bookstore/hardware.html

Colorgraphic Communications Corporation

http://www.colorgfx.com/

Produces multi-screen video adapters for Windows and Microstation products. Enables user to run different applications on separate monitors from one PC. Includes product specifications and technical support. Also provides ordering information.

Commax Technologies, Inc.

http://www.commax.com/

Produces computer hardware specializing in Pentium Processor CD-ROM notebooks. Includes company news, technical support, and contact information. Provides links to mobile technology sites on the Web.

Computer Companies and Vendor WWW home pages

http://www.acd.ucar.edu/computing/www.pages.html

Nicely organized site lists computer hardware manufacturers on the Web. Other categories and links on this page include Computer Software, Vendors, and Supplies. Worth a visit!

Computer Hardware Page

http://infotique.lm.com/cgi-bin/phpl.cgi?comphard.html

MegaMall site for new and used computer hardware. Many different brands and types offered. Provides an A-to-Z search index and ordering information.

Computer Hardware Resources, Inc.

http://www.chrhq.com/

Located in Houston, Texas, CHR sells new and refurbished terminals, printers, PCs, and Stratus equipment. Leasing of certain brands is available. Services products from Stratus, DEC, IBM, Link, Okidata, Televideo, Wyse, and Falco. CHR also buys used equipment.

The Computer Hardware Technical Support Page

http://sunflower.singnet.com.sg/%7Esehsuan/comsup.html

Personal home page devoted to giving free advice about hardware issues such as computer parts and problems. Contains a link to TipWorld where you can learn all kinds of tricks of the computer trade.

The Computer House of Rochester, Inc. Online

http://www.thecomputerhouse.com/MainPage.htm

Full service computer sales, service, and consulting company out of Rochester, New York. Hardware products can be accessed from the Virtual Sales Department page.

DTK Computers, Inc.

http://www.gan.net/dtk/

Produces Novell authorized microcomputer products and services. Includes product reviews, service, ordering, and contact information. Provides background for the GAN family of workstations.

GEW's Computer Hardware Shop

http://www.gardian.com/hardware/

Choose from CPUs, motherboards, memory, hard drives, video cards, modems, CD-ROMs, sound cards, and backup systems. Simply download the order form, fill it out while browsing the merchandise, and mail it in. Be sure to check out the weekly specials.

Global Bandwidth Exchange

http://www.bbi.com/

Provides exchange for buying and selling of digital circuits. Includes listing of products on hand and services information. Also provides CyberBell Online Trading database.

Hauppauge Computer

http://www.hauppauge.com/hcw/index.htm

Provides digital video boards for PCs. Provides links to product listings, products specs, image files, software, service and support info, and special offer and ordering info.

Hewlett-Packard Products

http://hpcc997.external.hp.com:80/ahp/home.html

One of the most successful computer hardware manufacturers in the U.S. provides a number of links on their Products page. Find out more about HP's computer equipment, including laptops, palmtops, printers, desktop and tower computers, servers, monitors, and more. This site also provides links to HP's medical, chemical, and test measurement equipment.

HI-TECH MARKETING

http://www.hitechmktg.com/

Extensive selection of computer hardware for sale, including motherboards, CPUs, modems, hard drives, scanners, printers, Ethernet cards, video and sound cards, monitors, mice, joysticks, trackballs, keyboards, and cables. For some good deals, check out the Specials page. Order by phone, fax, or secure order form.

ICS

http://www.relay.net/~gcw/memory.html

Simm memory/CPU distributor for home or office. Motherboard and multi-media upgrades, Web consulting. Provides links to product info, prices, upgrade kits.

The Image

http://www.lainet.com/image/

An Internet monitor repair center for monitors used for CAD workstations, graphics design, and medical imaging. Provides pricing and order information. Also offers monitors for sale.

Image Manipulation Systems

http://www.imageman.com/

Offers video output (I/O, JPEG CODEC) cards and teleconferencing cards for company needs. Provides information on software support, sites of interest, and product inquiries.

Information Data Products Corp.

http://www.planet.net/idpc/

Wide area networking products including new and refurbished hardware. Links to products, specials, hardware and other resources of interest.

Intel Information for Developers

http://www.intel.com/design/

The king of computer hardware provides an easy-to-use "quick navigator" for developers interested in a specific Intel CPU or technology. This page also provides important news, links to Intel's online magazine, and specific language information for programmers.

Intergraph Corporation

http://www.ingr.com/

Hardware and software for the technical desktop. Software for engineering, publishing, mapping/geographical systems. Links to products and services, user groups, news, and related search engines.

Maintech Hardware Services

http://www.maintech.com/HW1.htm

Offers hardware support service for Sun product line, UNIX systems, most third-party peripherals, IBM/RS6000, Silicon Graphics equipment, DEC computer hardware, and Axil products. Services Box Hill disk drives and high volume data storage equipment. Also authorized to sell and service Compaq computers, AST equipment, and Digital hardware. Staff authorized A+, MSCE, CNE, and Sun® technicians.

Maxtor Current Product Information

http://www.maxtor.com/products.html

Read about Maxtor's 2.5-inch and larger hard disk drives, which range in size from 837MB to 2GB. This page provides links for their notebook and desktop products, FAQs, and retail sales outlets.

Memory USA

http://www.mu.com/

If you're looking to upgrade your memory on your home or business computers, Memory USA will buy, sell, or trade memory for competitive prices.

Micro House International

http://www.microhouse.com/

Service and support for the PC hardware including hard drive and modem tech support guides. Find out more about their products and services as well as browse links to "hot deals" and other sites of interest.

MIPS

http://www.mips.com/

Provides information on MIPS' RISC-based UNIX computers. Read about MIPS' powerful computers that use the MIPS RISC chip. Extensive detail on available products and services, including training and documentation.

P.C. Kleen Plus, Inc.

http://www.pckleenplus.com/

Custom configures PCs systems and offers technical support. Check out the Build It Yourself special where they send the computer parts and you put it together yourself.

Power Computing Corporation

http://www.powercc.com/

Produces the 225MHz PowerTower Pro desktop system, the fastest desktop currently being made. Includes PowerTower technical specifics, magazine reviews, technical support, reference materials, and ordering information. Also includes company profile.

Praegitzer Industries Web Server

http://www.pii.com/

Designs and manufactures printed circuit boards. Includes company profile, services offered, technologies utilized, and corporate philosophy. Provides investor information, trade show appearance dates, job openings, and future technology previews.

ProComp Inc.

http://www.procomp-bmt.com/frames.htm

Computer, parts, network, and service company serving the Beaumont, Texas area. Stocks computers and computer parts from various manufacturers, including Fujitsu, Quantum, Practical Peripherals, Seagate, and Matrox.

Rockwell Collins Printed Circuits

http://www.rockwell.com/rockwell/bus_units/cca/cpc/

Produces multi-layer circuit boards for the telecommunications, military, microwave, and other industrial technology needs. Includes company profile, services offered, price quote form, and contact information.

Samsung Group

http://www.samsung.co.kr/news/news.html

How is Samsung involved in electronics? The question should be, "What aren't they involved in?" Find out about Samsung's 1 GB RAM chips, their latest semiconductor plants, camera operations, and computer CD-ROM drives. The company also makes chemicals, the world's largest ships, and even office buildings!

SCEPTRE

http://www.gus.com/emp/sceptre/sceptre.html

Produces 486 notebook computers, and 17- and 15-inch color monitors. Includes technical specifications, features, and contact information.

Silicon Reality

http://www.sireal.com/

Manufactures high-performance 3D graphics accelerators and multimedia products. Their product, The TAZ Core, is used in 3D graphics animation, multimedia, and virtual reality applications.

Sound & Vision

http://www.eclipse.net/%7Esoundvis/index.html

Sells computer systems, parts, and accessories. Price lists and specials are listed on the site. Order online or by phone and pay by check, moneyorder, or Visa/Mastercard. There's also an extensive list of links to manufacturers' sites.

Storage Computer in Japan

http://www.storage.com/

Produces enterprise-wide storage systems. Includes product technical information, customers listings, and contact information.

Tadpole Technology

http://www.tadpole.com/

Produces the SPARCbook family of portable notebook computers and the Alphabook 1 software development notebook. Includes product specifications, technical support, resellers listings, and contact information.

Thinking Machines Corporation

http://www.think.com/

The company that introduced parallel computing to the world now is also a software developer. Find out more about their CM-5x parallel computer products, including the massive CM-500, which can have up to 4,096 separate super-SPARC processors!

TouchWindow

http://www.touchwindow.com/

Provides information and features on the TouchWindow monitors. TouchWindow monitors are screen interaction enabled. Includes detailed product background and ordering information.

TTi Technologies, Inc.

http://www.hypermart.com/tti/default.htm

Provides online sales and service of a large catalog of computer hardware. Includes distribution of BIOS upgrades and sales of motherboards, hard drives, and computer systems. Includes detailed catalog and ordering information.

The Ultimate Industry Connection

http://www.hardware.com/complist.html

All the hardware companies from Acer Computers to Zida Technologies Limited. Lists hundreds of links to manufacturers of computer hardware in alphabetical order.

ViewSonic Corporation

http://www.viewsonic.com/

Produces a large line of color monitors. Includes product features, company profile, reviews, technical support, and resellers listings.

Worldwide Technologies Desktop & Mobile Computing Solutions

http://www.worldwidetechnologies.com/index.html

Large dealer of computers, hardware, and peripherals at discount prices. Also includes links to sites offering technical support for computer hardware problems. Good source of links to hardware-related newsgroups.

Related Sites

http://www.cruzio.com/bus/computers/hardware/index.html

http://www.okcmasters.com/

http://www.avsweb.com/richarnold/index.htm

http://www.innovatorsnet.com/hardware/gridhrd.html

http://www.pricewatch.com/

http://www.globalvillage.com/

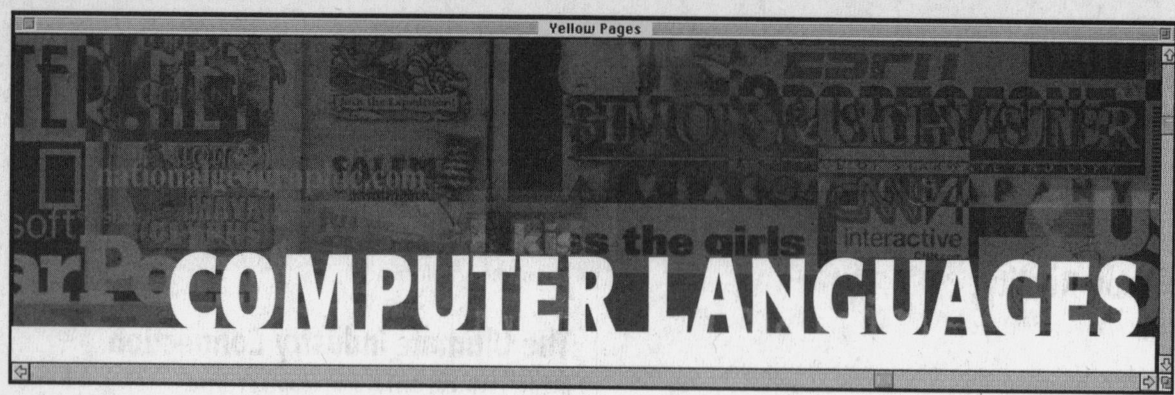

A B C D E F G H I J K L M N O P Q R S T U V W X Y Z

> I do not fear computers. I fear the lack of them.
>
> *Isaac Asimov*

Amzi! Prolog + Logic Server

`http://www.amzi.com/`

Produces Amzi! Prolog + Logic Server, a software add-on you embed in C++ and other programming languages to create logic-based intelligent agents and intelligent components, which are used in software that relies on artificial intelligence. Amzi!'s products assist programmers who need to create software that configures, schedules, diagnoses, advises, recognizes, lays out, plans, understands, or teaches. Downloadable demos and tutorials are provided to show how this Prolog-based programming language works.

The C Programmer's Pages

`http://pitel-lnx.ibk.fnt.hvu.nl/~rbergen/cmain.html`

Personal Web page for the beginning programmer in C. Gives history and background of the language, teaches basic skills, and offers pointers, tips, and tricks. Includes some C source code.

C Programming v.2.6

`http://www.cit.ac.nz/smac/cprogram/default.htm`

Download FAQs and online books about C programming. This site also provides many C utilities and compilers.

Programmers Heaven
`http://www.programmersheaven.com/`

The C++ Virtual Library

`http://info.desy.de/user/projects/C++.html`

A great resource for C++ beginners and intermediate users. This site includes information on upcoming conferences, free C++ software and reviews of commercial packages, and a number of tutorials for the beginner.

Computational Syntax and Semantics at New York University

`http://www.nyu.edu/pages/linguistics/`

Web site of the New York University Linguistics Department showing how to use a computer to process human language data. Covers the research opportunities and coursework available in computational syntax and semantics.

CONSULTIX, the UNIX Training Experts

`http://www.halcyon.com/yumpy/`

Provides UNIX training and other advanced language training for Fortune 500 companies and the Federal Government. This site lists upcoming classes, their structure, and how they fit into certification programs. CONSULTIX teaches the following languages: C, AWK, Bourne shell, and Korn shell languages, UNIX System administration, UNIX security, and Linux (the UNIX look-alike system).

FAQ: BETA Programming Language

http://www.daimi.aau.dk/~beta/FAQ/

Links to where you can get the BETA programming language FAQ, a question and answer list of basics about the language. You can get it via FTP, email, or it's listed on this Web site. Also check out version changes.

Free Compilers and Interpreters

http://cuiwww.unige.ch/cgi-bin/freecomp

Enter the name of the free (public-domain) compiler, compiler generator, interpreter, or assembler you need and the search engine will find it. You can also search by category.

GLU Parallel Programming Toolkit

http://www.csl.sri.com/GLU.html

Create platform-independent, adaptive, scaleable, parallel applications with the GLU (Granular Lucid) toolkit. Explains the features of GLU and provides links to downloadable files, demonstrations, applications, publications, and more.

Did you know

We've heard of people getting "hooked on Java," but that doesn't just mean they're addicted to caffeine. Java, created by Sun Microsystems, is a programming language that has taken the World Wide Web by storm. If you see graphics moving like Mexican jumping beans at a Web site, it's usually a Java applet at the helm of the mini-animation. These Java programs make the Web more interactive, but they also require some higher-end hardware. You can turn off Java in your Web browser, but if you want to see the Web in full action, consider getting a fast CPU processor. It's hard to go wrong with a Pentium processor that is at least 133 MHz.

The Haskell Home Page

http://haskell.org/

General purpose, purely functional language. The Haskell 1.4 Report and The Haskell 1.4 Library Report define the language and can be accessed on the Web site or downloaded. There's also a tutorial available.

hav.Software

http://www.hav.com/default1.html

Provides two C++ Neural Net libraries for C++ developers in PC-DOS, Windows, NT, and UNIX—IBM, HP, SUN, SGI. Also provides contract and custom software development and project management services to business, scientific, and research interests.

Hyperparallel Technologies

http://www.ppgsoft.com/ppgsoft/hc_main.html

HyperC is a programming language used to program parallel computers from Hyperparallel Technologies. Provides links to features and characteristics, technical information, and programming examples.

Index of /1/perlinfo/scripts

http://www.metronet.com/1/perlinfo/scripts/

An amazingly spartan page with a number of downloadable scripts written in Perl. There's no home page button or anything else except PERL scripts. This site is only for the serious PERL tinkerer.

J15

http://www4.interaccess.com/infopro/x3j15/

The National Committee for Information Technology Standards (NCITS) Technical Committee J15 has developed an ANSI standard for PL/B, a programming language for business. PL/B is used by more than 250,000 workstations in over 40 countries. Nine independent compiler companies offer a range of hardware and operating systems using PL/B. Learn who developed the standard, why they did it, and how they did it.

LEARN C/C++ TODAY

http://www.cis.ohio-state.edu/hypertext/faq/usenet/C-faq/learn-c-cpp-today/faq.html

A detailed page for C++ beginners. Includes reviews of dozens of C++ books, TXT, and FAQ files; recommends C++ packages for a number of platforms, and discusses the best way to start learning this important language. Although the site is rarely updated, the information is still relevant and valuable.

A B C D E F G H I J K L M N O P Q R S T U V W X Y Z

NESL: A Parallel Programming Language

http://www.cs.cmu.edu/~scandal/nesl.html

Developed by a group at Carnegie Mellon University, NESL is a parallel language that is loosely based on the ML programming language. This site gives the basics of NESL and provides a tutorial, library of algorithms, research papers, quick reference guide, and tells where to download it.

OC Systems AdaMania Page

http://ocsystems.com/

Develops the Powerada compiler for the Power PC.

PC AI—The Dylan Programming Language

http://www.pcai.com/pcai/New_Home_Page/ai_info/pcai_dylan.html

Dylan is an object-oriented programming language currently being developed by Apple. Links to sites offering information about Dylan, Dylan vendors, Dylan FAQs, and Dylan newsgroups.

Pennington/XTRAN

http://www.pennington.com/xtran.htm

Pennington Systems Incorporated developed XTRAN, an expert system which provides translation, analysis, reengineering, standardization, and code generation. XTRAN's rules language is like C in syntax but is similar to Lisp in semantics.

PolyJ—Java with Paramaterized Types

http://www.pmg.lcs.mit.edu/polyj/

MIT Laboratory for Computer Science's Programming Methodology group developed this portable compiler. It accepts an extended version of Java. Link to the paper defining this language.

Related Sites
http://www.duke.edu/eng169s2/group1/lex4/prot4.htm
http://union.ncsa.uiuc.edu/HyperNews/get/computers/languages.html
http://www.cs.mun.ca/~donald/bsc/node6.html
http://www.acm.org/sigplan/
http://www.math.uio.no/doc/gnu/emacs/program_modes.html
http://www.demon.co.uk/ar/Prolog/

Programmers Heaven

http://www.programmersheaven.com/

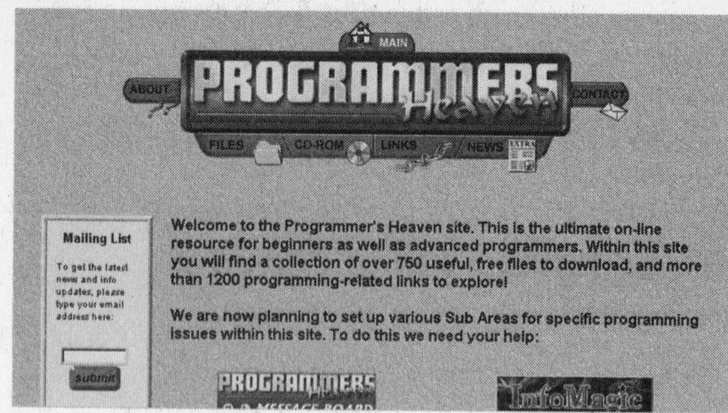

Online resource for beginner to expert programmers. Download source code and files for various programming languages or order them on CD-ROM. There are also more than 1200 links to programming-related sites. Subscribe to their mailing list to receive email updates.

Quadralay's C++ Archive

http://www.austinlinks.com/CPlusPlus/

Quadralay is a developer of software products that produce and distribute documents in standard electronic formats. Archive lists links to C++ programming information, career resources, where you can learn C++, and other related sites.

Rigal Language Home Page

http://www.ida.liu.se/labs/pelab/members/vaden/rigal/

Learn about the Rigal language, which uses atoms, lists, and labeled trees for data structures. Download published papers, see code examples, and read FAQs from the University of Latvia's ftp site.

Software Translation Tools

http://www.netusa.net/~mpsinc

Develops software translators, converters, and provides translation services in a number of languages. This company also makes fertility forecasting software for hospitals. Download demonstration programs of these conversion and migration tools.

Related Sites
http://feenix.metronet.com/1h/perlinfo/perlinfo.html
http://www-swiss.ai.mit.edu/scheme-home.html
http://www.cs.arizona.edu/sr/www/index.html
http://cuiwww.unige.ch/eao/www/Visual/comp.lang.visual.FAQ

Task Parallelism and Fortran

http://www.mcs.anl.gov/fortran-m/FM.html

Argonne National Laboratory looks at High Performance Fortran (HPF) and Fortran M (FM), a small set of extensions to Fortran. There are four papers available on HPF and many links to FM-related documentation and contacts.

Theta

http://clef.lcs.mit.edu/Theta.html

An object-oriented programming language to be used by Thor, a distributed object-oriented database. Currently being developed by the Programming Methodology Group of the MIT Laboratory for Computer Science. Lists features and gives links to Theta Reference Manual.

Tutorials–Need help with C/C++ and other languages?

http://www.andrews.edu/~maier/tutor.html

An online library that provides a number of FAQs and entire books online that you can download to teach yourself C++, ANSI C, UNIX, HTML, vi, and email. All the documents at this site are public domain or freeware. An excellent site for novice programmers in any of these languages.

The Unprotectability of Computer Languages Under Copyright

http://gopher.ieee.org/usab/DOCUMENTS/FORUM/LIBRARY/POSITIONS/complang.html

A Position Statement by the Institute of Electrical and Electronics Engineers. In the United States, IEEE members number more than 220,000 electrical, electronics, and computer engineers.

Unofficial FutureBASIC Web Page

http://www.ids.net/~paumic/FutureBasic/

FutureBASIC is a powerful BASIC programming language for the Macintosh. This site includes source code, utilities and demos, chat groups, and articles on this easy-to-use language.

Welcome to the WWW Home of COBOL

http://www.cobol.org/

An organization of hardware manufacturers and COBOL software developers that provides information about COBOL developments. Read about the Great COBOL Debate that took place at DB Expo in December 1995 to see into the future of COBOL.

A B C D E F G H I J K L M N O P Q R S T U V W X Y Z

> Computer Science is no more about computers than astronomy is about telescopes.
>
> *E. W. Dijkstra*

Argonne National Laboratory: Mathematics and Computer Science Division

http://www.mcs.anl.gov/

Scaleable parallel computing, high-performance I-WAY networks, and High-Performance Computing and Music research are currently under way at this federally funded institute. Another fascinating research project is the CAVE, a ten-foot cube that provides a stereo optical, real time, virtual environment. Check out how this works!

Brussels Free University (ULB) Computer Science Department: Bookmarks

http://www.ulb.ac.be/di/bookmarks/book.html

Collects bookmarks about computer science, mathematics, computer firms, technical reports in these fields, bibliographies, and more.

Graphics, Visualization, and Usability Center
http://www.cc.gatech.edu/gvu/

Chicago Journal of Theoretical Computer Science

http://cs-www.uchicago.edu/publications/cjtcs/

Hosted by the University of Chicago's Computer Science department, this site has several years' worth of back issues of the journal. Subscribe to the journal from the site, or go right to the articles. The site has a special area for discussing the articles online.

Computer Oriented Abbreviations and Acronyms

http://www.access.digex.net/~ikind/babel95b.html

A lengthy glossary of computer-oriented abbreviations and acronyms, updated three times a year (January, May, and September). This page takes a while to load because of its length, but its thoroughness is worth a bookmark or a printout.

Computer Science Undergraduate Tutor Service

http://ww2.netnitco.net/users/suchoza/tutor.htm

Computer programmer Richard Suchoza put up this site to help students with undergrad-level CS questions. Submit your contact information, deadline, and a brief summary of your problem and Richard promises that someone will reply with loose guidelines for solving your problem in the time allotted.

Computer Vision and Image Processing Group

http://poseidon.csd.auth.gr:80/

Covers digital image processing and related areas. Includes the areas of multichannel and color image processing, parallel image processing, medical signal processing, ultrasonic image processing and storage, fast algorithms and architectures for digital filtering and image processing, morphological image analysis.

Computing Center, Academy of Sciences, Russia

http://sunny.ccas.ru/

Provides computing services to the institutes of the Academy and other users.

The Collection of Computer Science Bibliographies

http://liinwww.ira.uka.de/bibliography/index.html

Getting information from a variety of sources, this site claims over 750,000 references to computer science articles from publications all over the world. A few of the categories include compiler technology, parallel processing, and logic programming. This site boasts over 2.2 million hits in the last three years.

Cornell Theory Center

http://www.tc.cornell.edu

One of four supercomputing centers funded by the National Science Foundation. This center experiments with powerful parallel processing structures in a number of disciplines, including aerospace engineering, economics, epidemology, physics, and visualization.

Cray Research

http://www.cray.com/

If you think your desktop Pentium is powerful, check out Cray's latest desktop systems, some of which are wireless.

CS-100 The History of Computing

http://calypso.cs.uregina.ca/Lecture/

A detailed discussion of the history of computing presented in a slide show format. Find out about Charles Babbage's infamous "Difference Engine," Blaise Pascal's revolutionary "Pascaline," ENIAC, and the Altair computer. A thorough and well-designed trip through computing history.

Dartmouth Experimental Compression Systems

http://www.cs.dartmouth.edu/~jmd/decs/DECSpage.html

Join the Dartmouth gang as they try to develop systems that improve the performance of applications that have limited bandwidth capacity. Find information on specific projects, the people involved, recent publications, and how it could affect you.

The Data Mine

http://www.cs.bham.ac.uk/~anp/TheDataMine.html

Hosted by the Computer Science department of the UK's University of Birmingham, this site is devoted to furthering the study of data mining—the potentially useful extraction of previously unknown information from data. Read papers, check bibliographic sites, and contribute your own research findings to the site.

Electronic Desktop Project Home Page

http://vflylab.calstatela.edu/Welcome.html

Focuses on improving the way science is taught and learned by bringing the power of advanced workstation technology to introductory science students in both major and general education classes. Details some of EDP's projects and offers links to interactive demonstrations.

Electronic Visualization Lab

http://www.evl.uic.edu/EVL/index.html

Merges art, computers, and science in electronic visualization. Contains visualization projects, as well as student home pages that display visualizations.

European Software Institute (ESI)

http://www.esi.es/

Provides information about Europe's movement toward improving the competitiveness of the European software industry. Includes training information, a list of upcoming events, and new improvements to their server.

Graphics, Visualization, and Usability Center

http://www.cc.gatech.edu/gvu/

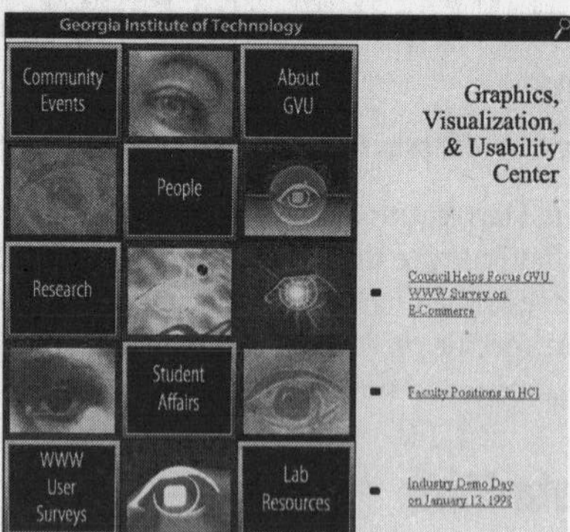

Part of the Georgia Institute of Technology site, the GVU strives to make the union of people and computers more harmonious. Specific disciplines include animation, virtual reality, cognition, Internet tools, and many more. The site also discusses the new graduate program in Human Computer Interaction.

Historic Computer Images

http://ftp.arl.mil/ftp/historic-computers/

Download large GIF photos of famous, early computers, such as the ENIAC, EDVAC, ORDVAC—a fascinating Web site.

Human Genome Project Information

http://www.ornl.gov/TechResources/Human_Genome/home.html

Sponsored by the US Department of Energy, the Human Genome Project is a 15-year study begun in 1990 with the goal of discovering and documenting all 60,000–80,000 human genes. Scientists and students from 18 coutries are contributing to the research. This site contains all sorts of information on the topic, from a status timeline to funding information.

Human-Computer Interaction Institute

http://www.cs.cmu.edu/afs/cs.cmu.edu/user/hcii/www/hcii-home.html

Part of Carnegie Mellon's School of Computer Science, this institute has the goals of creating technology that people can successfully interact with and teach that skill to others. Find out about current research projects as well as information on undergraduate and masters degrees.

IBM Technical Journals

http://www.almaden.ibm.com/journal/

Part of IBM's site, this is the online home of the IBM *Journal of Research and Development* and the IBM *Systems Journal*. Read dozens of back issues on topics such as proximal probe microscopies, optical lithography, and scalable parallel computing.

IEEE Communications Society Technical Committee on Gigabit Networking

http://www.ccrc.wustl.edu/pub/ieee-tcgn/tcgn.html

Lists upcoming Gigabit Workshops and IEEE white papers and reports on gigabit computing. Includes links to other gigabit networking projects, researchers, and sites.

The Innovation Network

http://innovate.si.edu/

Founders of the Computerworld Smithsonian Awards, which have honored individuals who creatively used information technology (also known as IT) to improve humanity. Check out the Applications of Technology Information link and the Interviews link to find out how recent winners of this award used IT in their projects.

Intelligent Systems Integration Program

http://www.augusta.co.uk/isip

Joint initiative by the Department of Trade and Industry (DTI) and the Engineering and Physical Sciences Research Council (EPSRC) to encourage the use of intelligent systems in UK business. This site describes the technology transfer clubs, special interest groups, demonstration projects, and latest news of the ISIP program, which strives to incorporate these pattern-recognition agents in standard software development toolkits.

Los Alamos Group XTM Home Page

http://www-xdiv.lanl.gov/XTM/

Supports X-Division's mission by developing state-of-the-art computational tools to investigate and solve complex problems in radiation hydrodynamics and transport. Applies these tools to problems that are important to the nation's security and well-being.

MetaCenter Computational Science Highlights

http://www.tc.cornell.edu/Research/MetaScience/

Provides information in the form of text, images, sound, and animations on more than 10,000 National Science Foundation research projects. All the sites listed on this Web page have used NSF facilities to conduct research. Download computer animations of Comet Shoemaker-Levy impacting Jupiter, theoretical 3D models of action inside the sun, and many more fascinating images.

The Mind Switch

http://www.phys.uts.edu.au/~asearle/m_switch.html

This Australian site is hosted by the University of Technology, Sydney. The Mind Switch project is based on the research of two UTS faculty, and revolves around the fact that a particular brain signal increases when a person's eyes shut for more than a second. What are the practical applications for this knowledge? Find out here.

MIT Artificial Intelligence Laboratory

http://www.ai.mit.edu/index.html

The MIT AI lab's research ranges from learning and vision and robotics to development of new computers. Check out the Our Research link to read about projects in Machine Vision, Robotic Touch, Virtual and Enhanced Reality, and SodaBot software agents.

MIT Press Science and Technology Journals

http://mitpress.mit.edu/journals-in-category.tcl?category=Science%20and%20Technology

Just one of MIT Press's journal categories, the science and technology section contains such journals as *Computational Linguistics*, the *International Journal of Robotics Research*, and *Videre: A Journal of Computer Vision Research*. Find links to each journal's Web site, find out about submitting papers, and get subscription information about the paper versions.

NASA High Performance Computing and Communications

http://cesdis.gsfc.nasa.gov/hpccm/factsheets.html

This program works with American businesses and universities to accelerate the development of high-performance computing technologies for use in future NASA Earth and space missions. Find out what a teraflop is (a trillion floating point operations per second), and the size of a petabyte, which is equivalent to 2,300 years of digitized video!

Neural Networks at your Fingertips

http://www.geocities.com/CapeCanaveral/1624/

This site contains software simulators for eight neural network architectures. The simulators are in ANSI C and are available in such categories as pattern recognition and time-series forecasting.

North Carolina Supercomputing Center Home Page

http://www.ncsc.org/

Find out how NCSC promotes the use of supercomputing at North Carolina schools. Read about their new Cray "flyer" computer, and find out more about research being conducted with their equipment.

PARC Xerox Palo Alto Research Center

http://www.parc.xerox.com/

Find out more about the 25th anniversary of the computing center that invented laser printers, graphical user interfaces, ethernet technology, and Object Oriented Programming languages. Check out personal pages of PARC researchers and employees and find out about current projects, such as nano-technology and machine vision. A prerequisite for any true technophile is to download the map to PARC's campus.

Pattern Matching Pointers

http://www.cs.purdue.edu/homes/stelo/pattern.html

If you study pattern matching, you need to visit this site. It contains an alphabetical reference of the top students and scientists engaged in the field right now (most are linked to their home pages), as well as a bibliography of books and journals, software resources, newsgroups, and mailing lists.

Projects in Scientific Computing

http://www.sdsc.edu/MetaScience/welcome.html

National Science Foundation Research Center. Online version of the Pittsburgh Supercomputing Center (PSC)'s annual publication. Features current research in various fields, written at a nonspecialist level.

A B C D E F G H I J K L M N O P Q R S T U V W X Y Z

San Diego Supercomputer Center

http://www.sdsc.edu

National laboratory for computational science and engineering established in 1985. Advances research and promotes United States economic competitiveness with state-of-the-art computational tools. Features a variety of collaborative research and educational programs, high-performance computational and visualization tools, and a nationally recognized staff.

Smithsonian Computer History

http://www.si.edu/resource/tours/comphist/computer.htm

Take an online tour of this recent Smithsonian exhibit, which includes the original ENIAC computer, WWII German ENIGMA encryption devices, and high definition TV. Download a slide show of the exhibit, and read what famous scientists, such as Robert Ballard and Seymour Cray, have to say about the age of information.

Software Tools for Logistics Problem Solving

http://primal.iems.nwu.edu/~levi/tools.html

Group of researchers and students who develop software for supply chain/logistics/vehicle routing applications using geographic information systems (GIS). If you like puzzles or demo software and you're running Netscape 2.0 in Windows 95 or UNIX, click the Software Demonstration button for an example of their software. Cool maps!

Solving Rubik's Cube Using the "Bestfast" Search Algorithm and "Profile" Tables

http://www.sunyit.edu/~millerd1/RUBIK.HTM

SUNY Computer Science grad student David Miller has developed a complex solution to a complex problem—'80s brainteaser Rubik's Cube. Find out how he did it without using conventional algorithms. The strangest thing is, Miller still claims he can't solve the cube, but his *program* can.

Spectral Research Technologies

http://www.tenn.com/srt/srt.html

Provides research and produces SPECTRA6 quantitative analysis systems. SPECTRA6 is utilized in data analysis of radiation from stellar sources and related thermodynamic properties.

Sun Technology and Research

http://www.sun.com/tech/

Get a futuristic perspective from the folks that brought you Java. See what Sun is up to regarding collaborative research with universities, speech recognition, and more.

UCSD Optoelectronic Computing Group

http://soliton.ucsd.edu/

Researches and develops massively parallel optoelectronic computer systems using the optimal utilization of microelectronic and photonic technologies. Pursues a plan of research that spans the areas of optoelectronic materials and devices, diffractive and micro-optics, nonlinear optics, optical storage technologies, parallel computing algorithms and architectures, including database and neural systems, computer modeling, and optoelectronic packaging.

Welcome to The Computer Museum

http://www.net.org/

The largest computer museum in the U.S., based in Boston, Massachusetts, continually updates and expands this Web address with information on new exhibits, museum clubs for adults and kids, upcoming events, and behind the scenes of their most popular exhibits.

NEWSGROUPS

bionet.neuroscience

comp.soft-sys.math.scilab

soc.culture.scientists

Related Sites

http://www.cs.umn.edu/scg98/

http://www.cs.umr.edu/ijcs/

http://www-east.elsevier.com/ida/Menu.html

http://www.mcs.net/~jorn/html/ai.html

http://www.interlog.com/~r937/doomsday.html

http://www.mines.edu/students/d/drferrin/Cool_Beans/GeneMachiene.html

http://robotics.stanford.edu/~suresh/theory/theory-home.html

http://www.cenparmi.concordia.ca/

http://kona.ee.pitt.edu/todaes/

http://eve.physics.ox.ac.uk/QCresearch/cryptoanalysis/qc.html

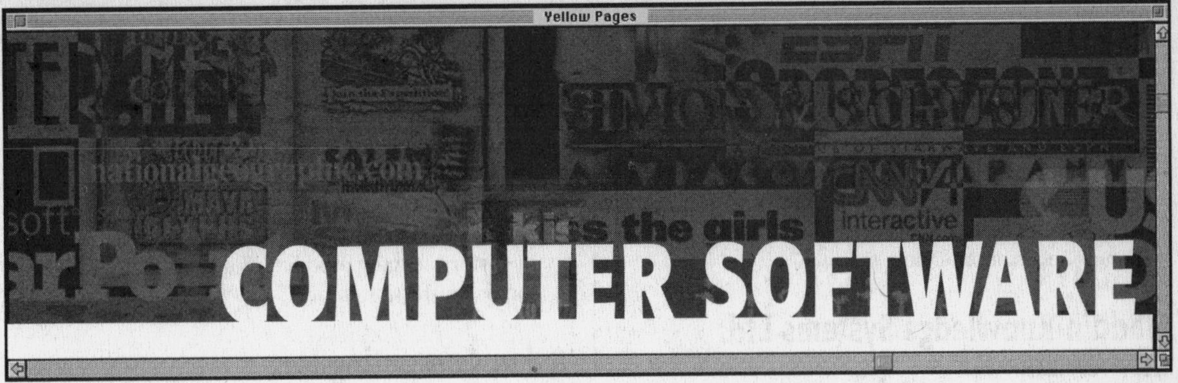

> If it's in the computer, they believe anything.
>
> *Jessica in* Sleepless in Seattle *(1993)*

20/20 Software

http://www.twenty.com/~twenty/

Develops and markets PC-Install, an installation program for developers and consumers. Also produces PC-Loan, a graphical analysis tool for analyzing mortgages, car loans, and other types of money borrowing.

4GL Computing Ltd

http://www.demon.co.uk/4gl/

Provides Silicon Grafics Workstations, software sales, support and services for the United Kingdom. Site also provides a full product guide.

Ablaze Business Systems, Inc.

http://www.ablaze-inc.com

Provides information, sales, and support in association management software. Also provides Internet services ranging from page creation to Internet training to Java development.

Absoft Corporation

http://www.absoft.com/

Provides information, sales, technical support for FORTRAN 77, Fortran 90, and C/C+ software. Also provides download product information, Absoft Fortran Newsletter, and "Fred's Link O' The Week".

WinZip Home Page
http://www.winzip.com/

Abstract Technologies

http://www.abstract.co.nz/

Manufactures peripherals for IBM RISC System/8000 workstations. Site provides information about products, support and technologies used. This includes downloadable software, product guides, and links to IBM technical tips and techniques.

Accsys Corporation

http://www.accsys-corp.com/

Provides information about custom designed software, little language design, and Newton Products. Includes information about AMIGO, a software application English/Spanish dictionary and reference translation system for Newton Software.

Advanced Paradigms, Inc.

http://www.paradigms.com/

Provides software development, training, systems consulting, and engineering for federal agencies and other companies. A.P.I. is a certified Microsoft trainer, and has a highly certified staff of engineers and developers. Also provides a list of contracts, partners and affiliates.

Advanced Quick Circuits, L.P.

http://www.iu.net/aqc/

Provides products and services specializing in quick-turn, high layer count, multi-layer, dense packaging, advanced technology. Site also provides a general price quote service online, PCB problems survey, technical updates, and employment opportunities at Advanced Quick Circuits.

Agorics, Inc.

http://www.agorics.com/~agorics/

Provides design and production of custom software packages. Includes a full history of the company, technology background, customer listings, technical library, and a list of hot links to related technical papers and economic sites.

Aladdin Knowledge Systems Ltd.

http://www.hasp.com/

Provides information and history on Aladdin Knowledge Systems and their products. Includes corporate and investors forum, Next Generation smartcard development information, FAST team merger background. Also provides links to HASP protections systems and HOPE programming environments.

Aliah, Inc.

http://www.aliah.com/

Provides background, software demos, methodologies, training, and support information for AliahTHINK. Includes features such as computer-based training, AliahSTRATEGY evaluations, and free software.

Alpha Microsystems Services Operation

http://www.alphamicro.com/

Provides company background, product information, services listings, technical support, AlphaCONNECT news, and AlphaSEARCH for more specific questions. Also provides Alpha stock information and employment opportunities.

Applix, Inc.

http://www.applix.com/

Developers of Anyware software that utilizes Java technology. Provides company background, product information, technical support, alliances, demos, and overview of Anyware's capabilities. The graphic design and artwork of this site is very well done.

Archive Comparison Test (A.C.T)

http://www.mi.net/act/act.html

A monthly report that compares 45 different compression programs (archivers) for speed and compression sizes. If you work with graphics and often have to archive or transfer them, click the bitmap graphic test to see where your archiver stands. WinZIP, for example, is one of the slowest and most average compression utilities.

Ashlar Inc.

http://www.ashlar.com

Produces computer-aided design software for drafting and design companies. Features background and technical information about Vellum 3D CAD software packages. Includes technical support, service, company history, lengthy product information, and customer satisfaction notices.

Aslan Computing Inc.

http://www.aslaninc.com/

Produces problem solving and custom designed developmental support software for Microsoft systems. Also produces database building and Web site creation packages. Site provides company background, problem-solving listings, product information, clients list with links, and technical development partners list with links.

Provides information, technical support, company background, and distributors list for this manufacturer of support products for Fast Ethernet and Ethernet networks. Includes listing of trade shows Asante will be attendance.

ATI Technologies

http://www.atitech.ca/

Produces multimedia applications software, graphics accelerators, and other related products. Provides feature and specifications for all ATI products. Also provides driver information, press releases, and developer relations information.

Austin Software Foundry

http://www.foundry.com/

Software development company that creates applications for client/server architectures using an object-oriented development approach. Uses Powerbuilder, Lotus Notes, and proprietary software to develop corporate solutions.

Automata Design, Inc. (ADI)

http://www.adiva.com/

Produces Pro Circuit Builder software for the printed circuit fabrication industry. Provides sales, support, and product information.

Axis Communications AB

`http://www.axis.se/`

Develops and produces CD-ROM servers and print servers. Provides product information, distribution network, company profile, and technical support services. Includes Axis T-shirt online contest.

Bentley Systems

`http://www.bentley.com/`

Produces MicroStation and other engineering-use software. Includes Mechanical Engineering, Geo-Engineering, and Building/Plant Engineering lines of products. Provides extensive product information, technical support, listing of services, and the Bentley Gallery of images created with their software. Also provides links to Bentley Europe, Mid-World and Africa online.

Bernstein & Associates, Inc.

`http://www.b-and-a.com/`

Provides software, training, and consulting. Includes work with VAX, ALPHA, UNIX, and Windows NT. Also includes lists and links of Berstein & Associates' clients.

BGS Systems

`http://www.bgs.com/`

Develops BEST/1 Performance software and systems. Provides product information, sample graphics, technical support, and company news. Also provides contact addresses for BGS Systems world wide, including email links.

Bismarck Group

`http://www.bismarck.com/`

Produces customized software and integration packages. Provides downloadable software samples, and links to clients sites. Also includes hiring information.

Bluestone, Inc.

`http://www.bluestone.com/`

Produces developmental software packages and tools for use with Java, Motif, and Windows. Bluestone provides training, technical services, and consulting. Site includes corporate profile, services background, and product information.

Blyth Software

`http://www.blyth.com/index.html`

Produces OMNIS products for developmental client and server applications. Site provides downloadable software, product information, technical support, consulting, and training services.

BMC Software, Inc.

`http://www.bmc.com/`

A worldwide developer and vendor of software for the automation of applications and data on different types of computers in host-based and open systems environments. This site includes the latest news on applications and application suites BMC uses with clients, a calendar of free seminars in specific cities, and includes forums for questions and answers with BMC Software's research and development staff.

Brickell Research, Inc.

`http://www.shadow.net/~roland/soap.html`

Designs and produces custom software, tools and systems that are used in the medical field for information storage and billing. Also produces document imaging technology systems. Provides product and service information along with hot links to other medical sites.

Brightware Corporation

`http://www.brightware.com/`

Supplies technology products and software application consulting. Produces ART*Enterprise client/server retrieval software tools for systems building. Provides product background, service listings, and work done for clients.

CACI Products Company

`http://www.caciasl.com/`

Creates modeling and simulation software for the use in system and network design. Produces COMNET III, SIMPROCESS, MODSIM III, and SIMSCRIPT II.5 simulation tools and language. Provides information and background on these and other products. Includes company profile and listings of trade shows that CACI will be in attendance.

Caldera Inc.

http://www.caldera.com/

Creates and markets network support software and workstations based upon Linux operating systems. Provides company profile, product specifications, technical support, online network documentation, development resources, and a link to Linux online reference. Also provides dealer and reseller information for the world.

Cambridge Computer Corp.

http://www.cam.com/

Produces connectivity products for Windows and communications software for Macintosh. Includes vxConnect and vxServer for Microsoft Windows computers and mxConnect and mxServer for Apple Macintosh computers. Provides product specifications and contact email addresses.

Camellia Software Corporation

http://www.halcyon.com/camellia/

Produces Batch Job Server, a batch job management program for Windows NT. Download a free working version of the program, access technical support, or order the full version of the program.

Candle Corporation

http://www.candle.com/

Develops and produces software applications including the Candle Command Center for Distributed Systems. This system can be configured to be used with UNIX, Oracle and Sybase, Windows NT, NetView for AIX, and Netware. This nicely organized site provides ample product information, company history, and customer support. Also includes job listings with Candle Corporation.

Caravelle Networks Corporation

http://www.caravelle.com/

Develops and produces monitoring software that works with hardware systems and applications of networks, intranets, and the Internet. Caravelle's WATCHER family of products and services are toolkits that monitor and report systems online availability, speed, and performance. Provides company background, product specifics, and technical support. Includes downloadable demonstration software.

CastCAE

http://www.castech.fi/

Produces CastCAE software for use in engineering applications such as tool and die, moldings, and other casting creation. Includes details about CastCAE 2.0's new features. Provides information about CastCHECK structural analysis design software for the metals industry.

Catron Custom Software

http://www.tiac.net/users/cgb/catron/

Specializes in custom designed software for business or home use. Also provides data conversions. Includes email and telephone contacts.

CE Software

http://www.cesoft.com/

Producers of QuicKeys, WebArranger, and other software for use with Macintosh and Microsoft computers. CE Software centers around use with email and Web service applications. Includes company background, product information, press releases, and technical support services. Includes links to different areas within the company from sales to employment opportunities.

CEO Software

http://www.the-wire.com/usr/ceo/

Develops financial planning corporate software. Also offers financial software consulting. Site provides information about products such as CEO*Plan, CEO*PlanPlus, CEO*Risk, and CEO*Demographics software. Also provides company history and product reviews.

Chicago-Soft, Ltd

http://www.quickref.com

Developers of mainframe software, such as MVS/Quick-Ref and MVS/Quick-Ref for Windows, which enable you to access online message descriptions and programming information on VMS systems.

Classic Variety AIPS

http://info.cv.nrao.edu/aips/aips-home.html

Develops and produces AIPS (Astronomical Image Processing System) software packages for tasks use in the gathering and processing of astronomical data.

Specializes in software for radio astronomy. Includes software specifications, samples of image processing, and links to other astronomy sites. Provides ordering information.

Clayton Wallis

http://www.claytonwallis.com/index.html

Produces software, applications, and other tools like CompExec for use in finance, human resource, and consultant offices and firms. Includes editions for the desktop and office. Provides product background, company profile, downloadable software, and a guide to human resource-related Web sites.

clySmic Software

http://www.albany.net/~rsmith/

Produces shareware for DOS, Windows, Windows NT, and Windows 95. Includes catalog listing of products, free downloadable software, product specifications, and technical support. Includes hot links to many different sites like the Louvre, Sherlockian Holmes page, and many more.

Coconut Info

http://www.dublclick.com/coconutinfo

Develops and offers software, training, and technical support for business and education under many systems, especially Macintosh. Includes company profile, product catalog, and listing of services offered. Also includes a hot link listing of sites ranging from Hawaiian weather forecast to pictures on Mars.

Cogent Computing Software

http://www.rt66.com/sjburke/

Provides software designed for public and educational institutions. Budget Director manages grants & contracts; C-Quest creates exams, quizzes, and questionnaires; and CC-Track manages tasks.

Collabra Software, Inc.

http://www.collabra.com/

Designs and produces "groupware" packages for companies for use in desktops and networks. Includes articles and press releases about Collabra and groupware systems. Provides product information, pricing, downloadable demos and evaluation software. Collabra Software, Inc. has been acquired by Netscape. Web site is in transition.

Columbia Data Products, Inc.

http://www.cdpi.com/

Produces SnapBack network software for disaster recovery and live backup. Includes background and technical specifications on the SnapBack family of products. Provides company profile and contact information world wide.

Computers and Learning A/S

http://www.oslonett.no/html/adv/Candle/candle.html

Develops and produces CANDLE software development platform products. Includes listing of products and services available. Provides extensive background and technical specifications for the Candle Authoring System and its related software products. Includes downloadable shareware and software demos.

Computervision Corp.

http://www.cv.com/

Produces and offers desktop and network product development including PDM products for data management and CAD/CAM software for automated design companies. Includes detailed product information and services offered listings. Provides Computervision stock and investor information.

Compuware Corporation

http://www.compuware.com/

Produces UNIFACE applications development software along with products for custom designed products. Includes company profile and in-depth overview of products and services provided. Also includes Compuware news and upcoming trade shows.

Confluent, Inc.

http://www.confluent.com

Offers Visual Thought, a multipurpose UNIX diagramming and flowcharting tool. Provides product information and lets you place orders.

Connectivity Custom Controls

http://www.toupin.com/~etoupin/ccc.html

Provides information about Plug-n-Play connectivity software products. Includes brief synopsis of Connectivity Custom Control Pack for network communications capabilities. Also provides contact information.

A B C D E F G H I J K L M N O P Q R S T U V W X Y Z

Core Systems

http://www.win.net/~core/

Produces Internet-Connect networking software packages for accessibility to the Internet. Includes product specifications, downloadable demonstration software, and contact information.

Cornelius Concepts

http://www.teleport.com/~concepts/

Develops and produces software applications using Delphi Rapid Application Development (RAD) environment for Windows. Includes company profile, clients listings, and personal background of Cornelius Concepts key officers.

Cort Directions, Inc.

http://www.empnet.com/cort/

Specializes in payroll and human resources software for client/server (Windows) and the HP3000.

CPI Electronic Publishing

http://www.citation.com/

Produces environmental, health, and safety compliance software. Includes information about the Regulatory Compliance CD-ROM that includes registration with the Federal Environmental and Safety Authority (FESA). Provides links to other related sites.

CPsoft Consulting

http://www.azstarnet.com/~cpsoft/index.html

Produces Easy Time Payroll software for automated payroll systems. Includes product information, download sample software, and ordering information. Also provides links to Game Cheats, IU Music Resources, and Grendel's Archive sites.

Crescent Division

http://www.progress.com/crescent/

Designs and produces the PROGRESS line of software, applications, and products for professional IS organizations that are system databased in Oracle, Sybase, SQL Server, ODBC, and DB2/400. Includes product and service background technical information. Provides technical support, press releases, and ordering information.

CrossWind Technologies, Inc.

http://www.crosswind.com/

Produces the SYNCHRONIZE cross-platform task scheduling management software family of products. Includes lengthy product background and technical information. Also includes downloadable sample software, company news, and ordering information.

Custom Innovative Solutions (CIS)

http://www.cisc.com/

Develops and produces custom designed software and applications packages. Provides a large company profile and product information background. Includes downloadable software and company philosophies. This includes the "Loser User Awards", a strange yet enlightening group of quotes and email, dealing with copyright infringement and company ethics.

CVS Bubbles

http://www.loria.fr/~molli/cvs-index.html

Produces CVS simultaneous file configuration software family. Includes tutorials, product specifications, trade publication articles, and contact information. Also includes links to FTP and WWW sites for related CVS products.

CyberMedia

http://www.cybermedia.com/

Produces AutoFix family software and other products for computer self maintenance and reference. Includes information about Oil Change for Windows 95 and First Aid 95 software. Provides technical specifications, product information, and ordering contacts.

Cyclic Software

http://www.cyclic.com/

Specializes in software support applications for CVS, including porting new platforms and custom enhancements. Includes product specifications, free software, and company profile.

Cygnus Support Information Gallery

http://www.cygnus.com/

Provides commercial support and maintenance for free software. Includes working with G++, GDB, PRMS, and GAS. Site includes many different types of downloadable Groupware, technical support, and manuals. Also includes company profile and contact information.

Databyte

http://www.databyte.com/home.html

Developer of Flexx, accounting software for client\server environments. Check out the JavaMania choice to download pre-built Java applets from Databyte.

DataViz

http://199.186.148.129/

Develops and produces file translation, conversion, and connectivity software applications for interaction between Macintosh and PCs. Includes information about MacLinkPlus, MacOpener, Conversions Plus, and other translation products. Provides technical specifications, resellers information, distributors contacts, company profile, and news.

Delphic Medical Systems

http://www.delphic.co.nz/

Designs and produces medical laboratory computer applications and products. Provides company profile, technical specifications, and support. Includes links to other New Zealand companies and sites.

DGA

http://www.dga.co.uk/

Designs and produces connectivity software, applications, and products. Specializes in gateways that link Lotus Notes and cc:Mail to IBM SNADS and NJE mail systems. Produces the Gateway family of products. Includes company profile, technical specifications, and links to other related sites.

Diskovery Educational Systems

http://www.diskovery.com/Diskovery/

Furnishes an electronic pricing guide for computer software, hardware, CD-ROMs, books, videos, and laser discs. Also offers a printed catalog. Categorizes products by title, category, and publisher.

Dragon's Eye Software

http://dragonseye.vservers.com/

Produces K-Free software that monitors free memory, disk space, and system resources. Includes product background and ordering information.

Dubl-Click Software

http://www.dublclick.com

Makes products for the Macintosh, Windows, and Newton computer. Download demos of their Calculator Construction Kit, Calx for Newton advanced calculator.

Electric Gypsy Software & Consulting

http://www.tyrell.net/~elecgpsy/

Provides consulting and development of custom software for UNIX, Windows, or DOS. Includes service listings and contact information.

emotion, Inc.

http://www.emotion.com/emotion/

Produces the Creative Partner family of software for Macintosh and Microsoft computers that enable distribution of data for collaborative work across networks and beyond. Includes product specifications, company profile, technical support, and contact information.

Engineering Graphical Solutions

http://www.egsx.com/

Designs and produces Graphical User Interfaces (GUI) and development software for UNIX-based computers utilizing the X Window System. Includes lengthy company profile and product technical specifications. Provides related links and contact information.

EnviroAccount Software

http://wheel.dcn.davis.ca.us/go/earthaware/

Produces environmental awareness and education software. EarthAware is an environmental literacy educational tool for use in schools and the home. Includes product background and ordering information.

Environmental Systems Research Institute

http://www.esri.com/

Produces GIS geographic information system technologies and desktop mapping software. Includes full product information along with reviews and press releases. Includes technical support, career opportunities, technical partners, and ordering information.

A B C D E F G H I J K L M N O P Q R S T U V W X Y Z

Eòlas Technologies Incorporated

http://www.eolas.com/

Produces FastApp Internet software and other application tools for intranet development, management, security, and tracking. Includes company profile and product technical specifications. Provides downloadable demonstration software, Web search index, and contact information.

ERDAS

http://www.erdas.com/

Produces ImagingGIS software and products. Includes product specifications, customer testimonials, company profile, ordering information, and upcoming trade show appearances. Provides technical support, upgrade information, and new product news.

ExperTelligence

http://www.expertelligence.com/

Designs and produces an extensive line of development tools, systems, and software applications. Includes information about Action! interface development tools and specialized applications for needs as diverse as air tanker refueling and aircraft seat layout. Includes product specifications, company profile, and contact information.

FCR Software

http://www.fcr.com/homepage.html

Develops portable network LAN and WAN software for OEM systems products. Includes product catalog, technical support, dealers listings, and company profile. Also includes job opportunities information.

Fineware Systems

http://www.fineware.com

Makers of the distinguished shareware products, Peeper, 1st Alert, Space Hound, and File Ferret. Read about these products, download them, and see if they'll help your work.

Fundamental Software

http://www.funsoft.com/funsoft.html

Company describes itself as "the only System/370 Plug Compatible Mainframe manufacturer able to put the mainframe in a laptop." Provides links to various OPEN/370 models and configurations.

Futuristic Software & Computing Group

http://www.entrepreneurs.net/futuregroup/

Computer software company offering Visual Basic and C programming, multimedia services, Web page design, as well as links to free software sites, shopping and points of interest on the Web, and much more.

Gamma Productions, Inc.

http://www.gammapro.com/

Supplier of Unicode-based Internet-enabled ActiveX technology for windows and UNIX users. Links to ordering info, press releases, and other interesting sites.

Gemini Systems Software, Inc.

http://www.geminisystems.com/

Gemini Systems provides software for POS/Inventory Control/Accounting for the building materials industry. Provides links to the software, ordering info, testimonials, company info, and press releases of their most recent products.

GeneCraft

http://www.genecraft.com/vectdir/

GeneCraft manufactures the Vector Detector, gene cloning software for Macintosh users. Provides links to information explaining intelligent cloning software, advanced features, ordering/downloading info, pricing info (academic discounts), and company info.

Generator

http://www.iea.com/~stevem/brochure.html

Generator is designed to be used with Microsoft Excel on IBM compatibles. It is a computer program designed to solve any mathematical problem you can define on an Excel spreadsheet. Provides definitive links to genetic algorithms, what generator can do, demos to download, and performance and application information.

GIS/Solutions, Inc.

http://www.giskey.com/

Offers industry-standard software to environmental professionals who manage chemistry, geology, and hydrology information on PC compatibles. Provides 3D visualization capability. Links to sales representative.

GrafTek Inc.

`http://web.idirect.com/~graftek/index.html`

GrafTek developed LabelView for Windows/DOS. It is a bar-code label design package for businesses and is easy to use. Provides links to a demo copy as well as to their other releases, most recently one that includes drivers for thermal transfer pictures.

Gryphon Software Corporation

`http://www.gryphonsw.com/`

This five star site provides software for two distinct groups: video professionals and graphic designers, and software for children. They are most known for their MORPH software. Provides links to other software products, pricing and ordering info, demos, beta info, and other Web sites of interest.

Harlequin

`http://www.harlequin.com`

Provides symbolic processing, electronic publishing, and custom applications. Programs in C, C++, Dylan–, Lisp, ML, PostScript–, and Prolog.

Hearne Scientific Software

`http://www.hearne.com.au/`

Mathematical, statistical, and graphing and forecasting software distributor in Australia and New Zealand. Provides links to products, catalogs, product samples, and ordering and pricing info.

Helios Software

`http://www.helios.de/`

A software company based in Germany, provides client/server solutions for Macintosh, PCs, and UNIX/Risk-based systems. Also provides color management solutions. Complete software descriptions and information provided.

HK Systems - San Diego (formerly VantageWare)

`http://www.industry.net/hk.systems`

Produces MasterMove warehousing and distributions software. Includes product features, technical support, and ordering information.

HMS Software

`http://www.wst.com/hms`

Project management software and services, training and consulting, for your project management needs.

Honeysuckle Computing

`http://pages.prodigy.com/GA/honeysoft/honeysoft.html`

Multimedia and windows software development for the home or business. Provides links to shareware products for your home business such as Santa, Valentine, and Easter letters software, and software to start and organize your home day care business.

Hummingbird Software

`http://www.primenet.com/~awong/legaudit.html`

Provides software to streamline the legal auditing process. Fee $aver will save your firm time and money. If you have a big job, Hummingbird will process it for you. Links to software, ordering and pricing information.

iambic Software

`http://www.iambic.com/iambic/`

Company that designs, manufacturers, markets software applications for the personal digital assistant market. Provides links to the company, products, ordering, employment, support, other links, and news.

I-Kinetics, Inc.

`http://www.i-kinetics.com/`

CORBA component software for Enterprise Information Systems for businesses and organizations. Several new links to company info, products and services, press releases, seminars and training, and more.

ImageFX

`http://www.imagefx.com`

Multimedia and imaging components for any sort of Web publishing. Provides demos, product and announcement links. FXTools version 4.0 for special effects publishing on CD-ROMs, presentations, ads, demos is available. Product and technical information provided for other software as well.

A B C D E F G H I J K L M N O P Q R S T U V W X Y Z

Imageware

http://www.iware.com/

Business software for point processing, reverse engineering, and rapid prototyping used by hundreds of companies. Provides links to product info, support info, current customers.

Imagix

http://www.teleport.com/~imagix

Offers program understanding tools for software developers working with legacy or complex software. Download a trial copy of Imagix 4D, get pricing info, customer support, other products and Web sites of interest.

Imaja Home Page

http://www.imaja.com/imaja/

Offers animation, multimedia, educational, and music software for the Mac user. Provides access to software demos and samples, artwork, calendars, other info of interest.

IMB Managing for Profit

http://www.imb.com

Home page for the developer of PEOPLE-PLANNER, labor management software, which projects business and labor requirements and creates optimum employee schedules. The Resource Center button helps you determine the best type of labor management software to use; Customers Say describes in detail how existing customers take advantage of People Planner software.

InContext Systems

http://www.incontext.ca/

SGML and Web software for your business. Provides links to customer support, demos to download, business info, new products, tech info, and much more.

INERTIA

http://www.ppgsoft.com/ppgsoft/inertia.html

Desktop software for design engineers, cutting your design and production time incredibly. Software will interface with your system's hardware, for complete integration and multi-tasking.

Inference

http://www.inference.com/

A cool site for information management software for your business or organization. Watch their upcoming events scroll across the bottom of your screen. Access to products, services, support, customers, and more.

INFORIUM, The Information Atrium Inc.

http://www.e-commerce.com/inforium.htm

Information management software that uses SGML and SQL relational database technology, solving your open information exchange needs. LivePAGE will manage graphics, text, and multimedia in a relational database. Links to company info, products, services, contacts.

Information Builders, Inc.

http://www.ibi.com/

Independent software solution vendor for any level of business that needs products and services for business analysis, reporting, data warehousing, and more. Provides links to products, tech support, user group, bookstore, consulting and training, press releases and announcements, and demo software to download.

Insight Designs, Inc.

http://www.phoenix.net/~insight/

Provides software in order for your company to make the transition to filing your financial documents electronically, using the electronic data gathering and analysis system of the US Securities and Exchange Commission. Links to software and database information, and other useful sites of interest.

Insignia Solutions

http://www.insignia.com/

Software allowing your business to use Windows applications on many different platforms. Information links for Mac and PC users. Links to products, catalog, tech support, press releases, and more.

Interactive Software Engineering

http://www.eiffel.com/

Provider of Eiffel, the method and language to revolutionize software by reusing software components. Links to many Eiffel related topics, training sessions, subscription info, downloading info, and much more.

International Knowledge Systems

http://iks.com/

Internet software development and consulting company experienced in JAVA applications.

International Software Systems Inc.

http://www.issi.com/issi/issi-home_page.html

If your organization or business is looking for an integrated, graphical adaptable software package with services for process improvement, check out the ProSLCSE™ products. Links to products and services, employee home pages, and other interesting links.

Interpretive Software

http://www.execpc.com/~isi/

Business education software for computer-based simulations. Links to simulations, products descriptions and ordering, newsletter, and more.

ISPW

http://www.ispw.com/

ISPW—Integrated Software Processing Workframe—will help increase the productivity of your application development and maintenance staff. Access to a technical overview, base system and options, benefits, FAQs, and more.

J-MAC System Inc.

http://www.j-mac.co.jp/

Based in Sapporo, Japan, a software company for the medical industry. Software to file, analyze, and transfer images. Links to company, software, staff pages, and more.

JOBSCOPE Manufacturing Management System

http://web.sunbelt.net/~jobscope

Manufacturing management software for your contract-driven company. Special services if you are an aircraft repair and overhaul facility. Links to product information, services, employment opportunities, and more.

KE Software Pty Ltd

http://www.ke.com.au/

Company in Australia that develops database software, specializing in structured and textual data high speed retrieval. Links to products, clients, demos, courses, and more.

KeyStone Learning Systems Corporation

http://www.keylearnsys.com

Provides video training for Windows applications. Describes their video training library and provides order forms.

LandWare

http://www.landware.com/

Software solutions for the Mac, PDA, or Windows users who are existing Landware customers. Browse through their list of new products and press releases.

Law Enforcement/Police Software

http://www.augusta.net/alert1.htm

Windows-based records management system for law enforcement agencies. Links to demos, features, tech support, and employment opportunities for law enforcement officers.

Layer Eight Systems, Inc.

http://www.eight.com/

Provides financial engineering and software systems for the financial derivatives market. Describes their interest rate derivatives real-time pricing software system.

Legal Computer Solutions

http://www.lcsweb.com/

Software, management, and training applications for law offices. Links to research sites, the news room, and more.

Lex Systems

http://www.link.ca/~lex/

LEXIFILE is library automation software for PCs and can run on a LAN. Download a sample program or get more information and links.

Lexitech, Inc.

http://www.lexitech.com/

Software to bridge standard kiosk operation and the Internet. Download a sample, read customer testimonials, get up-to-date news, and more.

LifeGuide

http://www.compuoffice.com/lg.html

Canadian-based life insurance software system for comparisons, surveys, quotes, and information necessary to agents, brokers, and financial planners. Download the demo or order the software.

Lighten, Inc.

http://www.lighten.com/

Provides Advance 1.0 for Windows, a tool used for business modeling and analysis. Offers an evaluation guide and an animated demo.

Lighthouse Software, Inc.

http://www.lighth.com/~lighth/

Business productivity tools and software development on many operating systems and in many computer languages. Links to their products and support services.

Lilly Software Associates, Inc.

http://mfginfo.com/cadcam/visual/visual.htm

VISUAL Manufacturing is integrated manufacturing software developed by Dick Lilly for one to one thousand users. Explore the specifications and benefits this software can offer you or your company.

LMSoft

http://www.lmsoft.ca/

HyperPage multimedia software integrates animation, video, sound, images, and hypertexts easily for use on the Web. Order a free demo CD or download other cool stuff.

Look Software Systems Inc.

http://look.com/

Anti-virus software for your home or office. Links to products, support, and performance information.

Lumina Decision Systems, Inc.

http://www.lumina.com/

A computer software and services company that develops and markets software for modeling and decision support. Contains a product description and links to information about decision risk analysis.

Mabry Software

http://www.halcyon.com/mabry/

A computer software company based in Seattle, Washington. Products include MIDI Pack (to create and manipulate data from Visual Basic), an Internet Pack with new controls, IniCon OCX, and Wave OCX. Check out their site and download sample software.

MacNeal-Schwendler Corporation

http://www.macsch.com/

For those in the field of computer-aided engineering, software designed for finite element analysis and modeling. Links to products and support, technology, their featured "model of the month," and more.

Macola Software from Osiris

http://www.osiris.com/osiris/products/macola/index.html

Develops accounting software for DOS, UNIX, and Windows. Download a PowerPoint presentation of their latest Windows Macola package.

Magna Computer Corp.

http://magna.magna.net/

Computer software for the resort industry, timeshare resort hardware and software, consulting, support, and opportunities. Provides a long list of resort clients.

Maui Software

http://www.mauisoftware.com/

Creator of TimeTracker software for the Macintosh. All programs are shareware and are free to download. TimeTracker, an easy-to-use application for recording time tasks on the Macintosh, is also supported at this site. Check out the latest updates to TimeTracker and find out about TimeSlice, a more powerful time-tracking product.

Mayflower Software

http://www.maysoft.com/

Basic computer solutions software, disaster recovery, and specialty products for Lotus ™ Notes.

MECC

http://www.mecc.com/

Contains information about its innovative and fun software programs for kids of all ages. Offers technical support and links to various other Internet sites of interest to kids, parents, and teachers. Includes titles such as The Oregon Trail, MathKeys, Storybook Weaver, MayaQuest, and Science Sleuths.

Medlin Accounting Shareware

http://community.net/~medlinsw/

Accounting shareware for Windows or DOS, including payroll, accounts payable/receivable, and general ledger. Click the links to download.

MentorPlus Software, Inc.

http://www.webcom.com/~criteria/mentorp/

MentorPlus specializes in navigational software for pilots. Links to their products, news, and job information.

Merlin Software

http://www.deltanet.com/merlin/

Merlin Software features Proposal Wizard, a proposal generation software for systems integrators. Check out their Pro and Lyte versions, Mac and Windows updates, Beta testing, tech support, computers for sale, and other links.

MetaWare Incorporated

http://www.metaware.com/

If you are a professional programmer, check out MetaWare's software development kits with components such as assembler, compiler, debugger, and others. Links to technology descriptions, customers, tech support, and more.

MicroExcel Software

http://www.microexcel.com/mxsoft/mxweb.htm

Perfect Recall software allows you to store anything you find on the Internet and then load it into any other software package you prefer to use. Or load the images into another browser off-line.

Micro-Frame Technologies, Inc.

http://www.microframe.com

The largest manufacturer of software for managing government contract costs and schedule reports in the U.S. Find out about training seminars, new updates to Micro Frame Program Manager and other products, access technical support, and new developments at this successful software company.

Microstar Software Ltd.

http://www.microstar.com/

Computer Aided Document Engineering along with document design and authoring make Microstar the provider of end-to-end document management solutions for your corporation. Check our what they can do for your company, as well as download their free software.

Microsystems Software, Inc.

http://www.microsys.com

Developers of security and accessibility software, such as CyberPatrol, which protects kids from adult material on the Net, and CyberSentry, a program that monitors employees' use of the Internet. Download time-restricted working demos, read company publications and press releases, or read about their support of free speech. Their Route 6-16 link connects you to a list of Web sites that are safe for kids and suitable for family interests.

Milestone Technologies, Inc. (MTI)

http://spadion.com/mti/

Data broadcasting applications software and consulting, including SATX ™ file transfer software. Can be used to transfer data over any broadcasting network including cable television, Direct Broadcast Satellites, FM subcarriers, and others.

MKS Source Integrity Product

http://www.mks.com/useful/

Software configuration management for client/server and Web development for your organization. Their Integrity Products help to manage teams across remote locations. Check out their demo software, sales, training opportunities, and more.

MLL Software and Computers

`http://www.ppgsoft.com/ppgsoft/wz_main.html`

Check out their breakthrough WIZDOM-Pro that will change object-oriented technology to an effective development environment. Links to concepts, features, development facilities, product info, site licenses, and more.

Modular Software Corporation

`http://www.primenet.com/~modsoft/`

This company offers a variety of software packages including PicLan Networking software and FULL-VIEW for windowing. Check out their full line of products and support.

NeoLogic Systems

`http://www.neologic.com/~neologic/`

Object-oriented applications for software developers. Download NeoLogic software or find out more about their products, support, success stories, information, and jobs.

NeuroSolutions—The Neural Network Simulation Environment

`http://www.nd.com/`

Provides information on NeuroSolutions, a neural network design and simulation software product for UNIX and Windows. Includes a demo and ordering information.

new stuff inc.

`http://www.newstuff.com/`

Manufacturer of fashion software including B. Famous on Stage for the fashion or costume designer. Check out their product demonstration or order your own copy.

ObjectSpace Inc.

`http://www.objectspace.com`

Offers object-oriented software products, consulting, and training. Provides information on training classes and schedules, product descriptions, and support information.

Ovation Software Testing, Inc.

`http://world.std.com/~ovation/ovation.html`

Specializes in software test automation technology. Provides technical information and information on training programs and implementation guidelines and modules.

Pacific Numerix Corporation

`http://www.crl.com/~pacnum/pnc.html`

Develops electronic design validation tools and related software applications. Includes technical specifications, demonstration slide show, and contact information.

Peninsula Advisors, Inc.

`http://www.best.com/~iris/`

Creates IRIS (Integrated Real Estate Information Systems) management software for portfolio tracking, contract, and client services. Includes product specifications and services offered by Peninsula. Provides company profile, contact information, and links to real estate-related sites.

Personal Library Software, Inc.

`http://www.pls.com/`

Produces information retrieval software that has graphical interfaces as well as textual. Includes detailed technical background and features on PL Web, PL Sync, and other Personal Library Software products. Provides downloadable demos, technical partners information, career opportunities, and clients using PL Web.

Pierian Spring Educational Software

`http://www.pierian.com/`

Creates educational software for schools and individuals. Includes product profile, company background, and links to many educational sites. Provides a media gallery and online ordering information.

Pinnacle Software

`http://members.aol.com/psoftinfo/index.html`

Produces custom designed software and consulting services along with a series of Pinnacle developed applications. Includes services and products offered with detailed specifications. Provides free demos, shareware, and links to many other sites.

Praxis International

http://www.praxisint.com/

Provides software and consulting for database, data replication, and data warehouse applications. Page includes information on their data replication, training classes, and professional services.

Prime Time Freeware

http://www.cfcl.com/ptf/

Publishes mixed-media CD-ROMs, books, and provides collections of free software. Includes company catalog, ordering, and contact information.

Process Analysts, Inc.

http://www.pai-colo.com/pai/

Produces custom designed automation and management software and applications. Specializes in process integration, environmental monitoring, and data acquisition systems. Includes technical support, job opportunities, and contact information.

Prode

http://www.prode.milano.it/prode.html

Produces software for the chemical industry and scientific chemistry research. Includes information about the Prode Calculator graphical interface database tool. Provides company background, products catalog, and contact information. Also provides links to related sites.

ProSoft International, Inc.

http://www.webcom.com/~prosoft/

Provides information and demos of FileView developers utility software and applications. Includes technical specification, technical support, pricing, and ordering information.

Quadrillion Data Analysis Software for Semiconductor Manufacturers

http://www.quadrillion.com/

Developer of Q-Yield, analysis software for semiconductor engineers, provides technical product information, information on obtaining free working demos, training information, and links to other semiconductor sites.

Quality America Incorporated

http://www.qa-inc.com/

Produces analysis, planning, and training software specializing customization for client needs. Includes product and service background with articles about Quality America's business and development philosophies. Provides information about training services, foreign distribution, and contacts worldwide.

Quality Software Management

http://www.tiac.net/users/lehotsky/

Provides custom software design, process improvement, and language creation consulting, services and products. Includes in depth company philosophy, services, and background.

Quality Software Management

http://www.utopia.com/companies/qsm/home.html

Provides custom software design, process improvement, and language creation consulting, services and products. Includes in depth company philosophy, services, and background.

Quest Software Inc.

http://quests.com/

Produces the Netbase Suite, VistaPlus, and many other families of output and database management software tools. Includes product technical specifications and features along with performance reviews. Provides company profile, technical support, services offered, and contact information.

RABA Technologies, Inc.

http://www.raba.com/

Develops and produces UNIX-based custom software, applications and systems. Also provides systems integration and consulting services. Includes technical references, product specifications, and services offered listings.

Robert McNeel & Associates

http://www.mcneel.com/

Provides home site for Robert McNeel & Associates, developers of Rhino modeling software and other development and rendering products. Includes technical specifications and features, technical support, and training information.

A B C D E F G H I J K L M N O P Q R S T U V W X Y Z

Sage Solutions, Inc.

http://www.sagesoln.com/

Develops custom-designed software applications and products. Includes clients list, company philosophy, and contact information. Provides detailed accounting of company resources and allocations.

Sanctuary Woods Multimedia

http://www.sanctuary.com/

Designs and produces interactive educational software for schools and individuals. Includes information about Major League Math software. Provides company background, link to education sites, and contact information.

Scandinavian Softline Technology

http://www.softline.fi/

Produces the SST Server, Open Edicom, and GMS SMS families of communications software. Includes technical specifications, company background, and online product updates.

Seagate Software, Inc.

http://www.arcada.com/

Develops tools and applications in data management for storage, management, and information access. Provides extensive product information. Also provides company background, trade show appearance dates, and information for doing business with Arcada.

Second Nature Software, Inc.

http://www.secondnature.com/

Develops and produces custom screen saver packages. Includes downloadable samples, licensing information, and available packages. Provides many artwork examples and dealers information.

Sequent Computer Systems, Inc.

http://www.sequent.com/public/index.html

Creates client/server platforms, software, and systems for a wide range of companies. Includes information about Sequent SMP systems, company philosophies, resources, and clients. Includes detailed company and product background.

Shana Corporation

http://www.shana.com/

Provides home site for Shana Corporation and the Informed line of form creation and processing software and products. Includes company profile and product background. Also includes job opportunities and links to technical partners sites.

Simucad

http://www.simucad.com/

Produces SILOS III Simulation Environment logic EDA software. Includes company profile, product background, demo software, press releases, and contact information.

Skylonda Group

http://www.skylonda.com/skyhome.html

Produces environmental, health, and safety software and products for companies. Includes consulting information, custom systems development, and product background. Provides clients listings, technical partners, and contact information.

Smithmicro

http://www.smithmicro.com/

Produces communications and connectivity products. Includes information about AudioVision video phone software, HotFax for Windows, and HotDisk products. Includes technical specifications, online ordering, and contact information.

SoftSell Business Systems Inc.

http://www.softsell.com/

Designs and produces the VersaTest and Relate testing, simulation, and support software and products. Includes technical specifications, client listings, and contact information.

Software Consulting Services

http://nscs.fast.net/

Provides consulting and software products for newspapers and other periodicals. Includes information about Layout-8000 products. Also includes company profile, customer, and contact information.

Software Tailors

http://www.traveller.com/~rew/tailors.html

Provides custom software development, Web site creation, and Internet training. Includes listings of services offered, products utilized, company philosophies, and contact information.

Solid Oak Software, Inc.

http://www.solidoak.com/

Produces Internet software systems like CyberSitter adult material filters, Re:PLY email applications, Re:PUBLIC client Internet software, and other products. Includes technical specifications, company news, technical support, and online ordering.

SouthWare Innovations, Inc.

http://www.excelco.com/swinfo.html

Produces the Excellence Series of business software and other office products. Includes information about inventory and management software products. Provides technical specifications, features, and ordering information.

SPARTA, Inc.

http://www.huntsville.sparta.com/

Provides software development, corporate management, systems engineering, and other technology services. Includes listing of services offered, technologies utilized, SPARTA resources, clients, and contact information.

Specialized Business Solutions

http://www.some.com/sbs/

Produces Keystroke point-of-sale software and products. Includes product specifications and features along with downloadable demonstration software. Provides dealers and contact information.

SpeedSim, Inc.

http://www.speedsim.com/speedsim/

Provides a home site and information about Cycle-Based Simulation software that validates logic designs. Includes information about the SpeedSim line of simulation software. Also includes information about support products for Windows NT and Linux operating systems. Provides detailed company profile and contact information.

SST Inc.

http://www.webcom.com/~sstinc/

Provides information about SST Inc. (Systems, Software, and Technology). Produces Winsock debugging tools and the TraceStock family of products. Includes technical specs, ordering and contact information.

Stonehand Inc.

http://www.stonehand.com/

Develops and licenses software text-formatting tools and products. Includes information about the Stonehand Composition Toolbox formatting library. Provides technical reference and contact information.

StrandWare Home Page

http://www.ecnet.com/strandware/www/index.html

Provides bar code design and printing software for the personal computer. Includes a corporate profile, product fact sheet, and industry newsletter, Automatic I.D. News. If you're lost, click the Where is Eau Claire, Wisconsin link to see a nice map and learn about this exciting little city.

Strawberry Tree, Inc.

http://www.strawberrytree.com/

Provides data acquisition and analysis software applications solutions and products. Includes company history and facts about WorkBench products. Includes ordering information and distributors for the United States and international customers.

Subtle Software

http://world.std.com/~subtle/index.html

Produces the Subtleware product line for use with Windows systems. Products are used for creation of database applications and database creation. Includes product specifics and contact information.

Sunbelt Software

http://www.ntsoftdist.com/ntsoftdist

Provides Windows NT utilities, such as event log, fault tolerance, virus protection, and batch job programs. Order online or link to other Windows NT sites.

A B C D E F G H I J K L M N O P Q R S T U V W X Y Z

Sunquest Information Systems, Inc.

`http://www.sunquest.com/`

Provides laboratory information systems and computer solutions to hospitals in the U.S., Canada, and Europe.

Sunvalley Software

`http://www.kwanza.com/~embleton/service.html`

Produces QuickTime VR interactive media software and Custom Kiosks applications. Includes technical specifications and discussions on virtual reality. Provides ordering information.

Superlative Software Solutions

`http://www.cat.syr.edu/3Si/`

Provides custom software development and training services. Specializes in Java client/server applications and C++ operation services. Includes training service listings, company profile, and contact information.

SurfWatch Software

`http://www.surfwatch.com/`

Provides information about Spyglass Inc.'s SurfWatch adult material filter software. SurfWatch helps to filter out adult-oriented and explicit Web sites for families and organizations. Includes product specifics and contact information.

SW International Systems Pte Ltd

`http://www.swi.com.sg/`

Develops client/server, research, and development software for the health industry. Includes company profile, products offered, and contact information.

SymCon Software

`http://www.interlog.com/~symcon/`

Produces software for accounting needs, desktop publishing, and Web design. Also provides custom software development and programming. Includes services offered and contact information.

Synapse Communications, Inc.

`http://www.synapse.com`

Develops Windows software for connecting to IBM AS/400 computer system. Find out about their software products, access tech support, read the latest news, and read about new products.

Syntax

`http://www.syntax.com/`

Produces the TotalNET line of network operating and systems integration software. Includes TotalNET features and technical specifications, Internet access services, training schedule, and contact information.

Systemcorp

`http://www.systemcorp.com/index.html`

Produces ready-made data and document management software on CD-ROMs. Includes information about the TrackFlow 9000 task management software. Provides product specifications and contact information.

Systems Alliance, Inc.

`http://www.access.digex.net/~golshan/alliance.html`

Provides custom software development and consultation services. Includes technical partners information, company resources, and contact services.

TEC Solutions

`http://www.tecs.com/tecs`

Produces the TECS WebServer line of software and products. Includes company profile, product technical specifics, and contact information.

TECHCO

`http://www.primenet.com/~techco/`

Provides network engineering, systems integration, custom software design, and database development services. Includes list of services and consultation available.

Technetix UNIX/Internet Tools

`http://teknetix.com/UNIX.html`

Produces email interoffice message software. Includes product specifics and ordering information.

The Attachmate Internet Products Group

`http://www.twg.com/`

Produces the EMISSARY line of desktop Internet software and products. Includes company profile, product technical specifics, and contact information.

The Information Systems Manager, Inc.

http://www.infosysman.com/

Creates multi-platform application tools for software and system development. Includes information about PowerFlex architecture and services offered by ISM. Provides corporate profile, product features, and contact information.

The Message Board System

http://www.netins.net/showcase/message/tmb.html

Provides information about The Message Board System of programs and applications that provide conference attendance message and registration capabilities. Includes product features, customers served, and contact information.

The Molloy Group, Inc.

http://www.planet.net/molloy

Developers of Cognitive Processor software for technical support departments. Find out what cognitive processing is and how it is used in this software.

The Numerical Algorithms Group Ltd

http://www.nag.co.uk/

Develops and produces scientific and technical software for mathematical problem solutions. Includes online catalog and a detailed background of the NAG group. Also provides white pages, reviews, and contact information.

The Plant Software, Inc.

http://www.theplant.com/

Produces E-Glue annotation utility for Windows-based systems. Includes product features and contact information.

Thermal Solutions

http://www.sauna.com/tsi/

Produces Sauna thermal design and electronic equipment modeling software. Includes product features, online technical support, pricing, and demo information.

Thinque Systems Corporation

http://www.thinque.com/isis/

Develops and produces software for the mobile communications and retail sales industries. Includes information about the ThinqNet Mail Gateway, Instant Wireless, Sales Traq, and other software products. Provides technical specifications, press releases, and contact information.

Thomson Software Products

http://www.thomsoft.com

Developer of application development and information management software. Read about their Nomad, Ada, and TeleUse language products, contact technical support, or examine their Site Index to find exactly the information you need.

Thunderstone Software

http://www.thunderstone.com/

Produces business software and applications for data management solutions. Includes information about the Metamorph and Texas families of software. Provides company profile, product background, job openings, and contact information.

TimeLess Technologies Schedule Wizard Software

http://www.timelesstech.com/

Makers of Schedule Wizard Sports Scheduling Software, easy-to-use software for creating round-robin schedules for any type of sport. Download a demo of this product, a trial version, or check out links to other sports-related Web pages.

Tosoft Children's Educational and Quit Smoking Page

http://www.teleport.com/~tosoft/

Download free demo copies of their Dinosaur database for kids, Memory game, and Quit Smoking scheduler.

Tower Concepts, Inc.

http://www.tower.com/

Produces Razor integrated problem tracking and management software system. Includes online technical manual and contact information.

Trax Softworks, Inc.

http://www.webcom.com/~traxsoft/

Produces TeamTalk group information sharing applications and Cypress authoring tools. Includes product specifications, company profile, and contact information.

A B C D E F G H I J K L M N O P Q R S T U V W X Y Z

Tumbleweed Software Corp

http://www.twcorp.com/

Developers of Novell Envoy, a document viewer, Tumbleweed Publishing Essentials, and other electronic document viewing products. Download the Envoy plug-in for Netscape or other Tumbleweed products, talk to the Web master, or read the latest news on Tumbleweed products.

Ubi Soft

http://www.ubisoft.com/

Provides the worldwide home site for Ubi Soft, developer of educational and entertainment software and applications products. Includes product background, technical support, trade show appearance dates, and contact information.

UNIBOL

http://www.unibol.com/

Produces the Unibol 36 and Unibol 400 native environments for open systems families of products. Includes technical specifications, product support, and contact information.

Uniplex

http://www.uniplex.co.uk/

Produces business applications and software for use with the Open Enterprise Workgroup environment. Includes information about onGo workgroup software products and the Uniplex line. Provides technical specifications, worldwide resellers listings, and contact information.

Uptime Computer Solutions, Inc.

http://www.uptime1.com/

Produces Lotus Notes workgroup software and other database applications. Includes product specifics, company philosophy, Web publishing services, and client listings.

Van Dyke Technologies

http://www.vandyke.com/vandyke/

Produces the CRT windsock terminal that supports Telnet and roglin protocol. Includes technical specifications, online product registration, and contact information.

Veritas Software

http://www.veritas.com/

Produces storage maintenance and management products. Also produces FirstWatch high availability management software. Includes company profile, technical white papers, and contact information.

VersaFax

http://www.cosi.com/

Provides product features, technical support, and contact information about VersaFax software. VersaFax is a fax command line interface broadcasting and transmission tool.

Viewpoint Software Solutions

http://www3.servtech.com/viewpoint/

Produces LabVIEW and VisualBasic systems integrations software and tools. Provides custom software development services. Includes product features, service listings, links to related sites, and contact information.

Virtual AdVentures

http://www.virtualadventures.com

Produces multimedia travel and adventure experiences, including "Fly Fishing: Great Rivers of the West," and "Virtual AdVentures, Grand Canyon." Includes reviews and ordering information.

Visigenic

http://odbc.visigenic.com/

Produces database and distributed object connectivity software. Includes information about the VisiODBC sereics and the Visibroker for Java and C++. Includes company profile, product features, technical partners listings, and ordering information.

Vision XXI

http://www.vxxi.com/

Specializes in the creation of software and applications for use in credit union automated loan systems. Includes information about the Inhouse system and LoanLink automated system. Provides detailed product background and contact information.

VYSOR Integration Inc.

http://www.synapse.net/~vysor/welcome.htm

Develops Windows software developer and image systems integrator. Includes information about the V-Image Remote System and PiXCL Tools interpreted language products. Includes online FAQ files, technical support, and ordering information.

Wall Street Software

http://www.fastlane.net/homepages/wallst/wallst.html

Produces PC investment monitoring, ordering, and management software. Includes information about Stock Watch 2000 and other investment applications and products. Provides ordering and contact information.

Welcome to Computer Associates

http://www.cai.com/

CA's Web site lets you leave messages for CA consumer relations, examine CA products, read press releases, and even check on the company's financial situation. Their Search This Site function simplifies searches for a specific topic or product.

Welcome to HPI on the World Wide Web

http://www.instalit.com/

Develops installer programs for several computer platforms. Visual Release for Windows lets you develop a sophisticated installation (setup) program. Download a working demo, read about HPI's installers for other platforms, or send email for technical help.

Welcome to Microsoft

http://www.microsoft.com/

Select a specific software package using Microsoft's Select a Product field, or select one of 16 countries to see a Web page in your language. The home page for the king of software includes daily news releases, free downloads of their Explorer Web browser, directories of Microsoft partners and resellers, and lists of upcoming events.

Wind River Systems

http://www.wrs.com/

Produces embedded development software and tools. Includes detailed information about the Tornado line of products. Site provides white papers, product reviews, company profile, and ordering information.

Wingra Technologies

http://www.wingra.com/

Produces Missive messaging software systems and Jnet connectivity products. Includes product technical specifications, company news, and links to related sites.

WinZip Home Page

http://www.winzip.com/

Way cool software that enables you to zip (compress) your files. Great for archiving, reducing large files to send over the Internet, and making more room on your hard drive.

Wireless Data Systems, Inc. (WDS)

http://www.gate.net/~pdwhitt/

Develops, produces and installs portable data terminals and software products. Specializes in real-time warehouse and inventory management software. Includes client list of installations and contact information.

Zinc Software Inc.

http://www.zinc.com/

Produces C++ libraries and utilities for applications creation. Includes company background, technical partners, product technical specifications, and contact information.

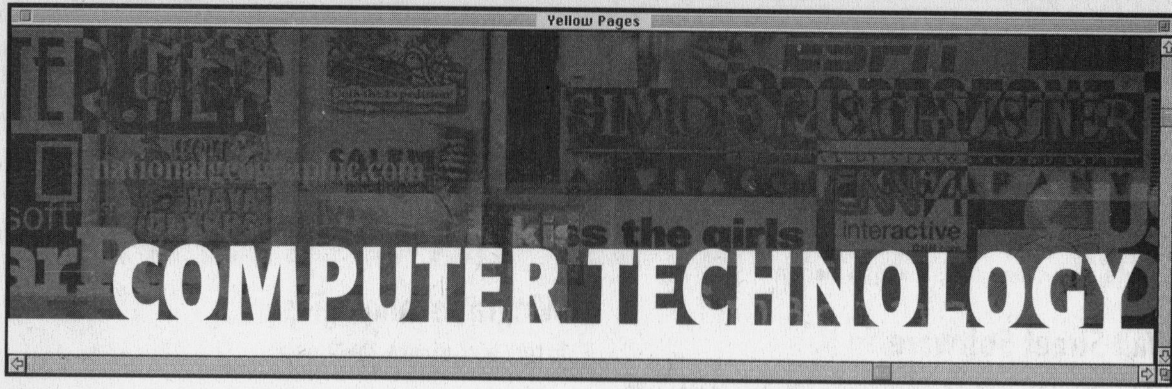

A B C D E F G H I J K L M N O P Q R S T U V W X Y Z

> The personal computer market is about the same size as the total potato chip market. Next year it will be about half the size of the pet food market and is fast approaching the total worldwide sales of pantyhose.
>
> *James Finke*

ASYNCHRONOUS TRANSFER MODE (ATM)

ATM Forum

http://www.atmforum.com

If you are interested in reading about the Asynchronous Transfer Mode (ATM) technology, head over to the ATM Forum. Here you can read white papers about ATM, access the ATM Forum Newsletter, and find out more about the ATM Fax-On Demand service being promoted. ATM is still not a ubiquitous service, but it does have a great deal of support by many people. You can find out why here.

Related Sites

ftp://ftp.sdsc.edu/pub/vrml/software/browsers/

http://www.afterdark.com/

http://www.borland.com/

Frank Condron's World O'Windows
http://www.conitech.com/windows/index.asp

Cell Relay Retreat

http://cell-relay.indiana.edu/cell-relay

Before the triple-jump was introduced to the modern day Olympics, there was the cell relay. For conditioning concerns, the participants were required to attend the cell-relay retreat, which consisted of learning terms such as AVSSCS (Audio-Visual Service Specific Convergence Sublayer), MTP3 (Message Transfer Protocol 3), and Traffic Contract. Those who weren't ready sat for hours until the next cell-relay retreat.

net2net

http://www.net2net.com/

Established in 1993, net2net focuses solely on ATM technology and its applications in business. The site has press releases and recent articles, troubleshooting guides for its products, and an online demonstration of CellBlaster, its online ATM analyzer.

SECANT Network Technologies

http://www.secantnet.com/

SECANT focuses on network system architecture and the hardware and software to go along with it. The site includes information on SECANT's product line—encryption accelerators, ATM network encryptors, and ATM network analyzers. Also included are links to ATM forums and research sites.

Related Sites

http://www.incommon.com/

http://www.surfwatch.com/

http://www.webcom.com/~optimax/delphi.html

http://www.woll2woll.com/

C++ PROGRAMMING LANGUAGE

Ask The MFC Pro

http://www.inquiry.com/techtips/mfc_pro

Troubled with something in your C++ program? Come to the Ask The MFC Pro to read questions and answers about classes, communication concerns, controls, dialogs, and MDI. While here, you should check out the Discussion Forums page for discussions on development news, gossip, and rumors.

Borland C++

http://www.borland.com/borlandcpp/

Borland C++ 5.0 is one of the top selling C++ programs on the market. This Web site includes press releases about Borland C++, the latest patch for version 5.01, technical support information, and bug information. There's also a link to other sites devoted to Borland C++.

Microsoft Visual C++

http://www.microsoft.com/VISUALC

"Welcome to object-oriented nirvana," this Microsoft site proudly proclaims. Now that you found it, what do you do? You can download patches, read FAQ on Visual C++, and find out about upcoming events and promotions. The site is categorized by user type to help you find the content right for you. This includes sections for new Visual C++ users, students, technical managers, business partners, and advanced developers.

Mumit's STL Newbie Guide

http://www.xraylith.wisc.edu/~khan/software/stl/STL.newbie.html

You can find a beginner's guide to the Standard Template Library (STL) language. This is not a highly graphical site, but then again it doesn't need to be. It shows how to write container objects, how to store derived objects in an STL container, and more.

Pacific Galaxy C++ Development Club

http://www.pgdc.com/

Worried about what to do this weekend? Join the Pacific Galaxy C++ Development Club and leave your worries behind. With a free membership to this club, you can get assistance on getting up to speed with C++. Regardless of whether you're a novice programmer, or someone conversant in another programming environment, this site can help you understand more about C++.

Quadraley's C++ Archives

http://www.austinlinks.com/CPlusPlus/

This site includes a number of links that point to C++ programming information. You can find links to guides for understanding Microsoft Foundation Classes (MFCs), get a list of C++ library archives, and career resource links. The Learn C++ section includes a number of links to books, tutorials, and classes that will help you understand C++ better.

Shareware Files for OWL Programmers

http://www.pfdpf.state.oh.us/msawczyn/owl/files/owlfiles.htm

OWL stands for Object Windows Library for Borland C++. This site includes over 100 shareware OWL files that you can download. The site is set up in two frames: the left frame lets you search for specific tools; the right frame displays the search results, with hyperlinks to the files. There are also buttons that display OWL resources, OWL-related chats, and mailing lists devoted to OWL.

ELECTRONIC MAIL SOFTWARE AND TECHNOLOGY

Claris Em@iler

http://www.claris.com/products/claris/emailer/emailer.html

Find out what's up with the latest version of one of the hottest e-mail programs for the Mac. Em@iler 2.0 supports multiple accounts and signatures and automatically sorts incoming messages with criteria that you establish.

Common Ground

http://www.commonground.com

Although Common Ground does not develop or distribute email software, you can obtain information about their document distribution products. These products, such as Common Ground Desktop Edition, enable you to convert Windows and Macintosh files to a common DigitalPaper format. You then can distribute that file over email (or via a Web page, floppy disk, or network) to others and they can read and print your document, without worrying about which document or operating system the document was created on.

E-Mail AutoResponder

http://www.phoenix.net/~enn/$autoenn.html

If you run a marketing company or department and want to automatically respond to email messages sent to you, you should invest in auto responder software for your Internet email server. You can find out about the E-Mail AutoResponder product at this site.

Eudora E-Mail Software

http://www.eudora.com

One of the best, if not the best email software programs available can be found at this site. You can download trial versions of Eudora Lite and get a beta copy of the latest Eudora Pro for Windows 3.01. If you already have an email application you use and love, give Eudora a try. You might end up dumping your old one and sticking with Eudora.

Infinite Technologies

http://www.ihub.com/index.html

Infinite Technologies is a company that sells communications products and services for local area networks. Some of their products include WebMail, ExpressIT, and MHS Toolkit for Netware.

InfoScan

http://www.machinasapiens.com/english/products/infoscan/infoscanang.html

InfoScan is a product that filters incoming messages of all types—email, newsgroup, databases, local networks, and so on. Incoming messages are scanned for keywords that you choose. The results are graphically presented in a radar-like screen. Those messages closest to the bulls-eye are the ones that are most worthy of your attention. Download a free trial version.

Inter-Network Mail Guide

http://www.nova.edu/Inter-Links/cgi-bin/inmgq.pl

Forget how to send e-mail from America Online to CompuServe? Use the handy form on this page to enter a computer network you want to send mail from (such as AOL) and the target network (such as CompuServe) to see how to address the email.

Johnson Consulting: The cc:Mail Experts

http://www.jconsult.com/

Face it. Sometim es you need to call in an expert to help you with a problem. The Johnson Consulting Web page details how they (Johnson Consulting) can help you with your Lotus cc:Mail problems. They offer cc:Mail migration courses, as well as third-party product support and services. You also can click a link called Dale's auto-racing pictures to see two images of racing cars you can download for wallpaper images.

Lotus cc:Mail

http://www.ccmail.com

Lotus cc:Mail is the most popular email application used on local area networks (LANs). From this site, you can read the cc:Mail upgrade planning guide, read about the recently release cc:Mail Release 6 product, and download pre-release evaluation software. You can also find out about available jobs at Lotus, if you happen to be looking for one.

L-Soft Products

http://www.lsoft.com/products.html

LISTSERVE software is software designed to manage mailing lists on the Internet. This site is devoted to LISTSERV, one of the top selling LISTSERVE applications on the market. You also can read about LSMTP for sites that are not fortunate enough to have high-end hardware, and EASE, a list hosting service that users can use to create their own mailing lists.

Mailbot Autoresponder Service

http://www.mailback.com

DataBack Systems distributes and supports email autoresponder software. You can read about DataBack's new Slow Poke autoresponder, find out about how some of DataBack's customers are using their software, and find out about DataBack's product line, including their custom email packages.

Microsoft Exchange Server

http://www.microsoft.com

Find out the latest news about the Microsoft Exchange Server at this site. Exchange Server is a high-end messaging and email service that runs on Windows NT. With the soon-to-be-released version 5, Exchange Server finally gets built-in Internet and

World Wide Web services. If you are evaluating Exchange Server, you can find out how it compares to Lotus Notes, Netscape Suitespot, and Novell Groupwise by clicking the Compare Exchange button.

Millennium Cybernetics

http://www.icybernetics.com/

Millennium Cybernetics is the maker of EchoMail, an intelligent mailing platform. The product is built for companies that need to automatically route and respond to massive amounts of electronic mail every day. EchoMail won the 1997 IBM/Lotus Beacon Award for the Best Messaging Solution.

Pegasus Mail

http://www.pegasus.use.com

Another very fine email application is Pegasus Mail. One of the best things about Pegasus Mail is that it is free. You can download a copy of it from this Web site, as well as learn about how to use it and order manuals for it. This is another email application that once you try it, it's hard to go back to another program.

Privacy Petition to Protect Our Personal Information

http://cyberhost.com/ragis/petition.html.

Did you know that "our names and addresses are sold for over $5 billion every year" to direct marketing firms to send us junk mail? Did you know that your Social Security number is sold "to lawyers who want to track [you] without a warrant"? If not, think about how telemarketers and junk mail operators get your name and address. If you want to stop this invasion of your privacy, hit this site and fill out the petition to protect your private information.

TSW's eFilter

http://catalog.com/tsw/efilter

If you want to delete some of the junk mail reaching your inbox, try the eFilter shareware software. This software searches your messages while they're still on the server and deletes those messages that contain specific keywords that you select to delete. You can download a free 10-time trial version of the software to see if you like it.

FTP SITES

Computer Science Techreports

ftp://fas.sfu.ca/pub/cs/techreports/

Large archive of technical computer science reports, arranged by institution.

Wiretap Technical Information Archive

ftp://ftp.spies.com/Library/Techdoc/

All sorts of technical information dealing with computers. Topics available range from hardware info, networking, CPUs.

INTRANET

Building a Corporate Intranet

http://webcom.com/wordmark/sem_1.html

Did your boss just leave your office telling you to get an intranet set up in your company? Did you say, "Right away sir," without any knowledge of how to get it done? If so, visit this site developed by Wordmark to get an overview of what intranets are and how to implement an intranet, and get some advice on accessing the Internet from an intranet. You also can get information on purchasing courseware and seeing live presentations of this material.

Creating Private Intranets: Challenges and Prospects for IS

http://www.strom.com/pubwork/intranetp.html

In this white paper, author David Strom discusses key features of corporate intranets and how to make a transition from SNA networks to intranets. Strom is the founder of CMP's *Network Computing* magazine.

Forrester Defines The Full Service Intranet

http://www.forrester.com/hp_mar96nsr.htm

This site includes a report by Forrester's, "Network Strategy Service," that discusses the next-generation intranet. In it, there are five standard services that are predicted to do away with network operating systems (such as Novell NetWare) as we know them today. These services include file, directory, print, email, and network management. You'll need to register with Forrester before you can read the report. (The registration is free.)

Intranet Design Magazine

http://www.inergy.com

Intranet Design Magazine is one of the premier online magazines (comes out biweekly) devoted to designing and implementing intranets. Some of the resources you can find here include articles, intranet FAQs, back issues, and comments. If you do anything with intranets, you need to visit and bookmark this site.

The Intranet Exchange

http://www.innergy.com/ix/index.html

The Intranet Exchange is part of the Intranet Design Magazine Web site. It provides an active and lively discussion area for those interested in discussing intranet topics. The page is set up so that threads are organized together, enabling you to see how long threads are and who participates in them.

Intranet Information Page

http://webcompare.iworld.com/intranet.html

The Intranet Information Page is located on the Internet World magazine Web site. It includes articles about intranets, links to white papers that discuss intranets (such as *Netscape's Intranet Vision Paper*), and links to other intranet-related sites.

Intranet Journal

http://www.intranetjournal.com

Another fantastic resource for intranet news, information, expert advice, and intranet-related software is the Intranet Journal. One nice area of this site is the Expert's Corner, which provides articles by intranet guest experts on selected topics, such as NT vs. UNIX, document management concerns, and Web site administration.

Intranet Resource Center

http://www.cio.com/WebMaster/wm_irc.html

If you read *Web Master* magazine and work with intranets, you might want to check out this site. You can find case studies, reports, information on seminars, events, and links to other sources here.

Intranet—A Guide to "Intraprise-Wide" Computing

http:///www.htscorp.com/intrawp.htm

Don't let the title fool you. This document is a nice introduction to what an intranet is, how an organization can use one, what tools are needed, and what tools are available. You'll want to supplement this document with a tutorial on putting all this together, but this is a good place to start.

Novell's Business Guide to Intranets and the Internet

http://www.novell.com/icd/nip/nbg2ii.html

You can read the second edition of the *Novell's Business Guide to Intranets and the Internet* at this site. Some of the chapters include "Tap Into the Power of Intranets and the Internet," "What is an Intranet," and "Bringing Intranets and the Internet to Your Network." Even if you are not a Novell NetWare administrator, you can still appreciate this book and find some useful intranet-related information you can apply in your company.

Red Traktor Demo Intranet

http://www.redtraktor.com/

If you want to see how an intranet works, this site won't disappoint you. After you hit this site and check out the old Farmall tractor background image, click the Enter button. Input the username and password shown on the left side of the screen and click OK. You now are in an interactive intranet demonstration.

JAVA

A Brief History Of Java

http://smoke.thepipe.com/java.html

As the site name implies, this is a concise guide to the Java programming language. Although you can come away with a nice little applet (the ubiquitous "Hello World" program), you should use this as a launch pad to other sources of documentation on Java.

Gamelan

http://www.gamelan.com

Almost as soon as Java became a household word for programmers and Web gurus, Gamelan became THE site to view and download Java applets. It still is the premier site devoted to Java applets, and includes a number of directory categories for applets, including arts and entertainment, educational, publications, special effects, and more. If you want to view a Java applet, visit this site first. It probably has what you're looking for.

Java Centre, The

http://www.java.co.uk/

This UK-based Web site provides the latest news about Java applets and features an applet-of-the-month. A directory of Java developers will help you find a developer in the UK. The site also issues the "famed" Golden Duke Award for the best Java applet.

Java Games

http://weber.u.washington.edu/~jgurney/games/

If you fancy computer games, try out some of the Java games at this site. This site is divided into two sections—games of strategy and games of skill. Treasure Hunt, Othello (great game), BlackJack, Rubik's Cube, Solitaire, and Pong, just to name a few.

JavaSoft Home Page

http://java.sun.com

The JavaSoft Home Page is where your understanding of Java should begin. This site is developed by Sun Microsystems and is devoted to developers who want to use Java to create dynamic applications for the Web or other system. You can download the JDK 1.1 SDK here, read about HotJava News, and download Java applets.

JavaWorld

http://www.javaworld.com

JavaWorld is one of the premier publications about Java and the Java community. Resources, news, tutorials, tips, and tricks about Java are located on the JavaWorld Web site. A number of third-party products are featured as well, including Visual Café Pro from Symantec, SuperCede, and Visual Basic 5.0. A list of Java events is helpful for those looking to attend seminars on Java.

Making Sense of Java

http://reality.sgi.com/employees/shiffman_engr/Java-QA.html

Is Java easy to use? Will Java replace C++? Will Java save planet Earth from alien invasion? Except for the last question, you can get the real lowdown on Java from a Silicon Graphics developer evangelist at this site. This is not a tutorial site, but it does counter some of the claims presented in the press and misunderstandings about Java.

TechTools Hands-On: Java

http://www.techweb.com/tools/java/java.html

Presented by CMP's TechWeb publication, this Java section contains helpful information on JavaScript, building your own Java applets, finding Java resources, and more. The Java Applet Tutorial link is a good tutorial for learning how to program in Java. You also can link to a tutorial on JavaScript.

Unofficial Java Workshop Troubleshooting Guide, The

http://rampages.onramp.net/~ranger/java_workshop.html

Do you have a Java problem? If so, hit this site for a no-nonsense approach to finding your answer. This site has several small tables that include two parts: Problem and Solution. Read the problem, which is stated in clear and concise language. Then read the solution, which is also stated in clear and concise language (if you know anything about Java, that is).

JAVASCRIPT

JavaScript 411

http://www.freqgrafx.com/411/

The JavaScript 411 site includes tutorials, FAQs, and a library of JavaScipt information. The Snippet Library contains code snippets you can plug into your applications to help speed up your development time. You also submit your code to the library for others to re-use.

JavaScript Authoring Guide

http://home.netscape.com/eng/mozilla/Gold/handbook/javascript/index.html

The JavaScript language is developed by Netscape Communications. This site is documentation for writing JavaScript applets. You'll need a browser that supports frames for this site.

JavaScript Mailing List

http://www.netural.com/javascript/

Visit this site to subscribe to a mailing list devoted to JavaScript programming. You also can jump to a couple of different JavaScript-related sites. The site also includes a few JavaScript example applets. To see the code for these applets, just view the source code of the HTML page in your browser.

A
B
D
E
F
G
H
I
J
K
L
M
N
O
P
Q
R
S
T
U
V
W
X
Y
Z

JavaScript Resources

http://home.netscape.com/comprod/products/navigator/version_2.0/script/script_info/index.html

This Netscape site provides several links to JavaScipt information and tutorials. You also can link to examples of JavaScript applets, including a JavaScript applet for calculating your income tax.

Martin's HTML and JavaScript Guide

http://web.ukonline.co.uk/members/claire.weekes/mjm/guide.htm

This page is set up in two categories: HTML Stuff and JavaScript Stuff. Click on the link that interests you most. If you click on the JavaScript-Stuff link, you are advised that you'll need a JavaScript-enabled browser to see the JavaScript applets work. Once inside, you can review the code for several JavaScript applets, including still messages, moving messages, flashing messages, reverse text, and more.

MOBILE COMPUTING TECHNOLOGY

Andrew Seybold's Outlook

http://www.outlook.com/

This site is devoted to wireless technology and features the *Outlook on Communications and Computing* publication. It covers information on a number of wireless topics, including hardware, middleware and software, services, mobile implementations, and the Internet. You can request to receive a free copy of this publication by filling out a form.

MobiDick Group

http://www.ct.monash.edu.au/~mobidick

Interested in mobile computing research? The MobiDick Group, which stands for MOBIle Databases, Interoperability, Computing, Knowledge, is dedicated to that mission. You can submit articles about mobile computing, as well as read MOBIDICK papers. There is also a nice list of mobile computing links provided.

Mobilis

http://www.volksware.com/mobilis/

Mobilis is the mobile computing lifestyle magazine. You can find featured articles here, table of contents of issues, and a what's new section. The "Ask Ms. PDA" section lets you asks questions about mobile computing, such as which PDA (Personal Digital Assistant) is best for you. Back issues of the magazine can be viewed as well.

Psion PLC

http://www.psion.com/

Learn about the Psion line of mobile computing and communications products. This site includes technical support pages, product information, references for developers, and a what's new page. You also can read about how Psion and Nokia Mobile Phones have an agreement to make modems and phones more compatible.

Ubiquitous Computing

http://www.ubiq.com/hypertext/weiser/UbiHome.html

There is a joke that everything available for the personal computer was created at Xerox PARC (the Xerox research and development institute in Palo Alto, CA) in the 1960s. For the most part this is probably true, including the term ubiquitous computing. This site explains what ubiquitous computing is, why it is just the opposite of virtual reality, and what types of applications are being designed to make ubiquitous computing a reality. You also can find some neat cartoons about ubiquitous computing.

Windows CE

http://www.microsoft.com/windowsce/default.asp

Microsoft Windows CE is a new operating system designed for hand-held computers, such as those manufactured by Casio, Compaq, NEC, and Hewlett Packard. This site contains a wealth of information about Windows CE, how to develop applications for it, links to other mobile computing sites, and general marketing information about Windows CE.

Wireless Initiative

http://www.ini.cmu.edu/wireless/Wireless.html

Carnegie Mellon University runs this site, which describes the Information Networking Institute (INI). Divided into three dimensions—research, infrastructure, and applications—INI is devoted to making wireless networks useful and cost-effective. Some of the research information you can find here includes protocols for adaptive mobile and wireless networking, wearable computers, and human factors analysis of mobile computing.

NETWORKING TECHNOLOGIES

ADSL Forum

http://198.93.24.23/home.html

The byline for this page is "Making the future happen sooner." The ADSL Forum promotes the ADSL (Asymmetric Digital Subscriber Line) technology to whoever wants to increase the bandwidth of the Internet and make things happen much more quickly while online. You can link to information about the technical side of ADSL, as well as marketing information about ADSL.

Black Box Reference Center

http://www.blackbox.com/bb/refer.html/tigf012

The goal of Black Box is to provide links and resources covering all aspects of networking and connectivity. Browse the glossary of communication terms, then dive into the docs about LAN/WAN technology, remote data transmission, wireless communication, cables and connectors, and much more.

ISDN Primer

http://www.interforce.com/technology/isdnprimer.html

ISDN (Integrated Services Digital Network) is another networking technology that provides high-speed phone and data communications. The ISDN Primer site provides an introduction to ISDN, as well as information on where to find additional references on ISDN.

ISDN Tutorial

http://www.ziplink.net/~ralphb/ISDN/

For an introduction to ISDN, including pictures, visit this site. The information is organized in ten pages, including topics on history of ISDN, its advantages, layer protocols, and sources and references. It also includes an ISDN "book store" link to a page that lists some of the third-party reference books available on ISDN.

Microsoft BackOffice

http://www.microsoft.com/backoffice

Microsoft BackOffice is a family of products designed to work together, with Windows NT Server as its main component. The family includes Microsoft Exchange Server, Merchant Server, Proxy Server, SNA Server, SQL Server, Systems Management Server, Transaction Server, Index Server, and Internet Information Server. This Web site includes information on all these products, as well as how to implement BackOffice in your enterprise.

MONET Home Page

http://fury.nosc.mil

MONET is a Department of Defense network that stands for High Data Rate MObile interNET. This site, which contains no classified information, defines MONET, how it will someday interoperate with the public-carrier networks in the future, and how it will achieve high data rate transfers using mobile RF communication links.

Network Computing's ISDN Online

http://techweb.cmp.com/nc/isdn/

Network Computing magazine's Web site devoted to ISDN. You can find information about ISDN product and services, the latest news about ISDN, issues and concerns surrounding ISDN, and articles relating to ISDN. The Interaction page includes newsgroups and mailing list information about ISDN.

Novell NetWare

http://www.novell.com

Novell NetWare is the most widely used networking operating system in the world. You can find product information, press releases, and links to support files here. The training and certification page includes updated information about obtaining your CNE, CAN, Master CNE, and other certifications.

SNMP and CMIP

http://www.inforamp.net/~kjvallil/t/snmp.html

SNMP is the Simple Network Management Protocol. CMIP is the Common Management Information Protocol. Both of these protocols are very important to the management of networks. If you are new to these protocols or just interested in them, visit this site for "newbie guides" to SNMP and CMIP.

User's Guide To CMU SNMP for Linux

http://www.cris.ufl.edu/~dadavis/cmu-snmp.html

Carnegie Mellon University (CMU) provides free SNMP software for Linux, a freely distributed UNIX version. You can find out about how the CMU SNMP works on Linux, as well as get updated information on SNMP version 2. Some of this information is dated, but this site does provide helpful discussions on using CMU SNMP for Linux.

Windows 95 Starting Page

`http://www.dylan95.com`

This is a site devoted to Windows 95, including tips, reviews, links to other resources, interactive discussions, and help. The site operator, Dylan Greene, has designed three different views of this site: frames and JavaScript; frames and Java; and tables. You can select which type of view you want to use.

The Windows 95 TCP/IP Setup How-To FAQ

`http:///www.aa.net/~pcd/slp95faq.html`

Windows 95 is one of the easiest operating systems to use. But when you have to configure Windows 95 to communicate over a TCP/IP network, you might as well set aside a few hours of time for the task. If you need to do this (and you happen to have Web access), visit this site to get a detailed description of how to set up TCP/IP on Windows 95.

OPERATING SYSTEMS

Frank Condron's World O'Windows

`http://www.conitech.com/windows/index.asp`

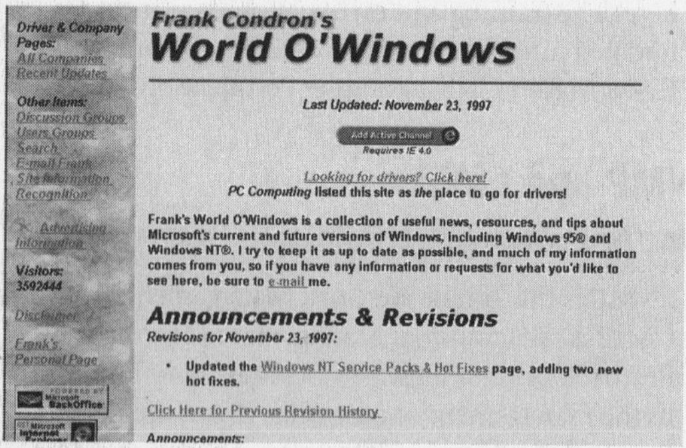

Frank just keeps cranking out the news we want. His Windows 95 site was one of the Net's most popular—if his numbers tell the truth, he's logged almost 4 million hits—and now that Windows 98 is on the horizon, he hasn't slowed down a bit. Get the latest industry information on tentative release dates, bugs, fixes, current versions of NT, Office, and more.

FreeBSD

`http://www.freebsd.org`

FreeBSD is an advanced UNIX operating system for PCs. FreeBSD is usually used as an Internet server or network operating system for a local area network. One of the strong features of FreeBSD is that it is free and you get the source code for it, which is like getting free ice cream to all those computer programmers out there.

IBM OS/2 Warp 4

`http://www.software.ibm.com/os/warp/html3/index.html`

OS/2 was originally developed by IBM and Microsoft. Now it is owned exclusively by IBM. OS/2 Warp 4 is the latest version of this advanced PC operating system and you can get information about its features, how it incorporates voice recognition technology and Java, and how its graphical user interface is improved. There are also links to recent press releases and news items about OS/2.

Linux International

`http://www.li.org`

Linux is a monkey that solves crimes on television. No, that was Linus, I think. Linux is a free "re-implementation" of UNIX. UNIX is an operating system that is popular on workstations and in colleges. At the Linux International Web site, you can get documentation about Linux, read press clippings, link to Linux mailing lists, and get descriptions of newsgroups devoted to Linux. There are also links to sites where you can obtain Linux.

Mac OS Web

`http://www.macos.apple.com`

The Apple Macintosh was the first operating system that was easy to use (except for one developed back in the 1960s at Xerox PARC, of course). This Web site features information about the latest Macintosh version, press releases about Apple's purchase of NeXT, and a history of the Macintosh.

MacOS8.com

`http://www.macos8.com/`

The gang at MacOS8.com spends its time keeping you informed about all aspects of the latest Mac OS, from potential future interaction with Microsoft down to getting the right price when you're ready to buy. Read editorials, articles, and trade show reports, and get quick answers from the help desk.

MicrosoftWindows98.com

http://www.microsoftwindows98.com/

At first glance, some might think this is a genuine Microsoft site, and others might think it's a spoofing parody site. It's neither. A service of Cornerstone Communications, the site looks like an actual Windows desktop, but it contains quite a bit of information on Windows 98. Check out upgrades and patches, find a large tips and tricks section (complete with screenshots), and check in frequently to the online discussion.

MyDesktop Network

http://www.win98.net/

This site (actually, a group of sites) claims over 10,000 pages of Windows-related information. Covers Windows 98, NT 5.0, and IE 4.0. For current news, industry gossip, beta reports, and interviews, check the site often.

Oak Repository—CP/M Archive

http://oak.oakland.edu/oak/cpm/index-cpm-pre.html

CP/M is dead; long live CP/M. Before the Apple, before DOS, before Windows, CP/M ruled the desktop. Now you can't buy it. You can, however, find a number of applications written for CP/M that you can download.

Simtel.Net MS-DOS Page

http://oak.oakland.edu/simtel.net/msdos.html

This site includes a collection of software and resources for the MS-DOS operating system. Although many users have migrated to Windows 95 and left MS-DOS behind, many users (including those who still use older versions of Windows) still have DOS on their computers. If you're one of them and need to find an application, hit this site. It has, for instance, about 100 different text editors you can download.

Sun Microsystem's Solaris

http://www.sun.com/solaris/index.html

Recently, Sun revolutionized computing with its Java programming environment. For a long time, however, Sun has been known for its Solaris operating environment, which is a version of UNIX that resides on workstations. Many Internet and Web servers use Solaris as their operating system because of its advanced capabilities. This Web site includes information about Solaris, Internet solutions with Solaris, networking features of Solaris, and more. You also can download a copy of Joe, which combines Java and Solaris NEW to create Web applications.

Windows 95

http://www.microsoft.com/windows95/

Probably the best part of the Microsoft's Windows 95 Web site is that it includes links to free software you can download. This software includes updates, patches, software included only on the CD-ROM version of Windows 95, and shareware. You also can link to the Windows 95 Resource Kit, which is a *must* have if you do any systems support for Windows 95.

Windows Information Network Home Page

http://www.mbnet.mb.ca/win/winhome.html

The Windows Information Network is devoted to providing information and resources about the Microsoft Windows line of operating systems, including Windows 3.1, 3.11, 95, and NT. A collection of Win News newsletters dating back to February 1994 is included at this site.

Windows NT Server 4.0

http://www.microsoft.com/ntserver/default.asp

The premier networking operating system for small to medium sized businesses is probably Windows NT Server 4.0. Find out how to plan and deploy NT Server 4.0 in your company, how to evaluate it against its competitors (Novell NetWare, NT Server 3.51, and Netscape Enterprise Server), and get service packs. You also can download a copy of Microsoft's Internet Information Server (IIS) 3.0.

Windows NT Workstation 4.0

http://www.microsoft.com/ntworkstation/default.asp

For organizations that need a powerful, 32-bit operating system that doesn't require you to reboot it three times a day, Windows NT Workstation 4.0 is ideal. You can learn about NT Workstation 4.0 at this Web site, as well as download updated software, shareware, and the Microsoft Personal Fax for Windows software.

A B C D E F G H I J K L M N O P Q R S T U V W X Y Z

REFERENCE INFORMATION

Guide To Network Resource Tools, The

http://www.earn.net/gnrt/notice.html

The Internet has come a long way in the past two or three years. However, the Internet is more than just the World Wide Web. You can read about searching engines, email, FTP, and other services available on the Internet at this location.

High Bandwidth Web Page

http://plainfield.bypass.com/~gzaret/hiband.html

Remember in the old days when your television received only three stations, but you wished you had more? Now that you have more, do you wish you had even more? If so, come to the High Bandwidth Web Page and read about how higher bandwidth on the Internet is analogous to more television channels. Just think, in a short time you could be watching the *Brady Bunch* on the Internet.

High Performance Networks and Distributed Systems Archive

http://hill.lut.ac.uk/DS-Archive

Read about current news in the high performance networks and distributed systems business. You'll be on the edge of your seat reading about gigabit test-beds, advanced telecommunications programs at LLNL, and the Asynchronous Transfer Mode (ATM) technology. A comical sidebar link about the divisions between current ATM supporters is provided as well, called HotWired's "Netheads vs. Bellheads."

Main Street Earth

http://www.mainstreetearth.com/

This gigantic site features archive after archive, including reviews of top Web sites by topic, white and yellow pages, dictionaries, people-finders, search engines, and libraries of libraries. Software archive links point you to vast collections of shareware, fonts, applets, Web graphics, and much more.

SunSITE Communications Archive

http://www.sunsite.unc.edu/dbarberi/papers

Interested in reading about virtual communities, chats, IRC (Internet Relay Chat), MUDs, and MOOs? Hit this site and read through the papers collected here. You can also link to the white paper discussion called "TinySex is Safe Sex," by Claire Benedikt.

TELECOMMUNICATIONS

Association for Local Telecommunications Services (ALTS)

http://www.alts.org/

The ALTS Web page provides up-to-date information about ALTS, which is a national association that promotes local telecommunications competition. It was founded in 1987. You can find current news about local telecommunications, as well as regulatory information about the industry here.

Investors Edge

http://www.investorsedge.com/

Although this site is not devoted to helping you learn about Visual Basic Script, you can learn how to implement VBScript on your Web site. The Investors Edge Web site uses extensive VBScripting, as well as JavaScript to bring alive their side. Scrolling stock quotes, flashing advertisements, and updated corporate reports are included here.

Phreaker Abatement

http://www.visual-traffic.com/hacker.html

Phreakers are computer hackers that break into telecommunication systems illegally. This site is devoted to helping companies prevent phreaker intrusion. A list of "Immediate Actions" is provided, such as change all passwords, know where every serial port is in your company, which phone codes to deny (such as 700, 809, and 900 prefixes), and more. If you are a systems manager or information services person, visit this site to learn about how to prevent phreaking in your company. It will be worth your time.

Telecom Digest Home Page

http://hyperarchive.lcs.mit.edu/telecom-archives/

The Telecom Digest Home Page provides archives of past comp.dcom.telecom newsgroup digests. You also can chat with other people about the telecommunications industry and link to the newsgroup. Click on the Main Gate link to see an index of the archived digests.

United States Telephone Association (USTA) World Wide Web Site

http://www.usta.org/

This site provides information about USTA. Click on the Regulatory Initiatives to read about how USTA promotes the interests of its members. You can join USTA by clicking on the USTA Membership link. You also can read about the latest legislative acts (such as the Telecommunications Act of 1996) by clicking on the Legislative Initiatives link.

VISUAL BASIC AND VBSCRIPT

Alan's VBScript Examples

http://www.coolnerds.com/vbscript/vbindex.htm

Well-known computer author Alan Simpson posts some of his best scripts for your perusal. If you like the controls, just view the HTML source to get the code. Includes scripts tackling currency, date, and color problems.

Ask the VB Pro

http://www.inquiry.com/thevbpro

Ask the VB Pro is a well-designed site that provides information about the Visual Basic programming environment. You can find a comprehensive list of questions and answers categorized by topics (such as callbacks, MDI forms, Windows Help, and so on). Version icons to the right of the Q&A sections let you know which Visual Basic version (3 or 4) the topic is discussing.

Microsoft VBScript Start Page

http://www.microsoft.com/vbscript/

Who knows more about VBScript than the people who invented it? Microsoft gives you tons of information on this site, from facts about scripting upgrades and additional links to a full VBScript Language Reference and tutorial. Also includes all sorts of free downloadable goodies. If you're looking for A–Z coverage about VBScript, this is the place.

Microsoft Visual Basic

http://www.microsoft.com/vbasic/

Microsoft's Visual Basic Web site should be your first stop when looking for Visual Basic help on the Web. It is a well-designed site, with information about how to use Visual Basic, where to download software related to Visual Basic development, and information on VBA.

Scribe

http://www.km-cd.com/scribe/

Scribe is a resource for VBScript writers of all skill levels. The site serves as a catalogued listing of other sites that employ VBScript or other cool technologies, such as ActiveX or other interesting multimedia effects. Find a site you like, then find out how the author created the effects.

VBScripts.com

http://www.vbscripts.com/

This non-Microsoft site is run by Paul Lomax, a veteran VB programmer and author. Check out the working code examples, ask or answer a question in the message forums, or browse through the listing of VB books designed to help beginning and experienced VB programmers.

Visual Basic Online

http://www.codd.com/vb-mag/

This site features an online magazine devoted to Visual Basic. Links to articles, the VBO Joke Center, reviews of VB controls, and more are offered at this site. If you feel the need to volunteer to keep the VB Online site the "greatest Visual Basic Online Magazine around," click on the Get Involved with VB Online to see how you can help.

NEWSGROUPS

alt.computer

alt.technology

comp.lang.basic.visual.database

comp.lang.c++

comp.lang.javascript

comp.os.ms-windows.networking.win95

comp.windows.news

Related Sites

http://www.caligari.com/

http://www.cuj.com/

http://www.digitalfocus.com/

A B C D E F G H I J K L M N O P Q R S T U V W X Y Z

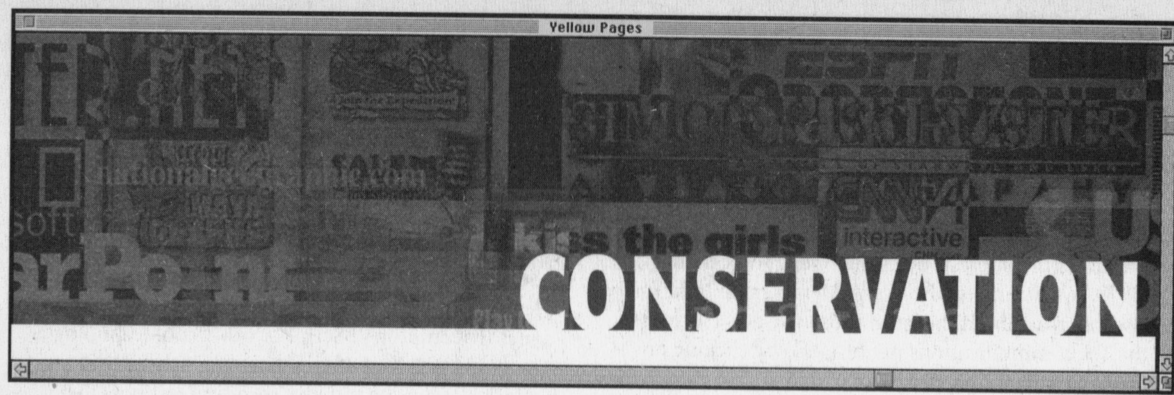

CONSERVATION

> Like the resource it seeks to protect, wildlife conservation must be dynamic, changing as conditions change, seeking always to become more effective.
>
> *Rachel Carson*

Arbor Day
http://arborday.vservers.com/home.htm

Conservation Breeding Specialist Group
http://www.cbsg.org/

Northeast Document Conservation Center
http://www.nedcc.org

Wildlife Conservation Society/ Bronx Zoo
http://www.wcs.org

Arbor Day

http://arborday.vservers.com/home.htm

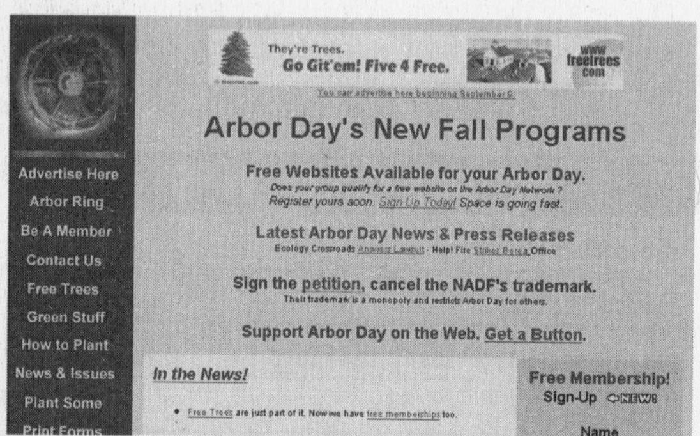

Learn how you can help the environment by planting a tree in your community. Learn about the many Arbor Day programs for supplying trees to communities and educating the population about the importance of trees.

Atlantic Salmon Federation

http://www.flyfishing.com/asf/

As if the salmon of North America didn't have enough trouble having to swim upstream, now they have to contend with the possibility of extinction. The ASF's goal is to find solutions to all issues that could possibly affect the salmon's survival.

Butterfly Website: Conservation and Ecology, The

http://mgfx.com/butterfly/ecology/index.htm

Provides articles calling for the conservation of butterflies. Also has articles describing the Montes Azules Biosphere Preserve, which includes butterfly ranching among its many projects.

Conservation Breeding Specialist Group

http://www.cbsg.org/

A conservation group whose mission is "to assist conservation of threatened animal and plant species through scientific management of small populations in wild habitats, with linkage to captive populations where needed." Check out their site to learn more about their programs and publications, read the current issue of their newsletter, or find out how you can assist.

Conservation International

http://www.conservation.org/

Learn all about the company that works in rain forests, coastal and coral reef systems, dry forests, deserts, and wastelands in over 22 countries. Also, find out what you can do to assist actor Harrison Ford, Intel Chairman/CEO Gordon Moore, and the rest of CI in their ongoing fight to conserve our environment.

The Coral Reef Alliance

http://www.coral.org/

This site is the diving-in point for an alliance made up of snorkelers, divers, and others who realize the value of our coral reefs and are working to preserve them. The alliance sponsors a number of conservation projects which you can sign up for online.

Endangered Plants: Images

http://www.nceet.snre.umich.edu/EndSpp/ESimages/ESplants.html

When one thinks of endangered species, one typically thinks solely of animals. Several species of plants, however, are threatened and endangered as well. They are shown here along with information regarding their status and location.

Endangered Species

http://www.nceet.snre.umich.edu/EndSpp/Endangered.html

View recent additions to the endangered species list, as well as the entire list sorted by group or region. View a list of extinct animals. This site also contains many images of creatures on the list.

GreenLife Society—North America

http://nceet.snre.umich.edu/greenlife/index.html

The goal of the GLSNA is to contribute to the protection and conservation of endangered flora and fauna. They feel that every species has a right to exist regardless of whatever resource value they hold for man. The organization was founded in 1983 and is staffed primarily by volunteers.

International Palm Society

http://www.palms.org/

The IPS is a group consisting of almost 3,000 members in over 80 countries dedicated to study, culture, and preservation of palm trees around the world. Their Web site gives general information about the society, membership information, and offers access to several palm oriented publications.

International Wildlife Education & Conservation (IWEC)

http://www.iwec.org

A great resource for people who want to learn about wildlife conservation and how to get involved in hands-on projects. IWEC's unique projects include: wildlife adoption, animal-assisted therapy, enrichment for captive wildlife, endangered species reproduction, wildlife rehabilitation, ecotravel, wildlife kits, and many others. This is a new no-nonsense, grassroots organization that believes in the reinforcement of the human-animal bond and the respect and well-being of all living creatures.

John Muir Exhibit

http://www.sierraclub.org/john_muir_exhibit/

Learn about the great naturalist, conservationist, and founder of the Sierra Club. The site includes pictures, a time line of Muir's life, his writings, and more. Learn how to celebrate John Muir Day.

League of Conservation Voters

http://www.lcv.org/

The League believes that the best way to achieve environmental results is through successful environmental legislation. Their goal is to elect members to congress who truly care about the environment. They provide a scorecard, which lets the public know how the House and Senate rate in environmental voting, in addition to providing a means to contact representatives to let them know that you care and are watching them.

Maine Solar House

http://solstice.crest.org/renewables/wlord/index.html

A great way to conserve energy (thereby reducing strain on the environment) is by using sustainable forms of energy. This site is an example of the practical use of solar energy in a home. It includes house plans and information about solar heat and energy.

Marine Fish Conservation Network, The

http://www.netspace.org/MFCN/

Due to decades of overfishing, our nation's marine life is severely depleted, and fisheries are going bankrupt. Learn how you can be part of the solution to this marine crisis.

Mr. Solar Home Page

http://www.netins.net/showcase/solarcatalog/

"Mr. Solar" is a man in Utah who along with his wife has been living on solar energy for over eighteen years. His goal is to help everyone become as self sufficient as he and his wife have been. His site includes the "Ask Mr. Solar" column, over 100 articles on alternative energy, and how-tos on setting up your own solar electric system.

National Association of Service and Conservation Corps

http://www.nascc.org

The National Association of Service and Conservation Corps (NASCC) is the membership organization for youth corps programs. NASCC serves as an advocate, central reference point and source of assistance for the growing number of state and local youth corps around the country.

National Audubon Society

http://www.audubon.org/

Get background information on the Society, its namesake John James Audubon, and his natural art. Find your local chapter and get membership information. You can even join online.

National Recreation and Park Association (NRPA) Home Page

http://www.nrpa.org/

Home page of the National Recreation & Park Association (NRPA). NRPA is committed to advancing parks, recreation, and environmental conservation efforts that enhance the quality of life for all people.

Northeast Document Conservation Center

http://www.nedcc.org

The Northeast Document Conservation Center specializes in the conservation of paper-based materials including books, documents, art on paper, and photographs. NEDCC also offers microfilming and photographic duplication services, disaster assistance, preservation consulting, and educational outreach.

Redwood Region Audubon Society

http://www.rras.org/rras

The Redwood Region Audubon Society is a local chapter of the National Audubon Society. Its parent organization is among the oldest and largest private conservation organizations in the world. The society works on behalf of natural heritage through environmental education and conservation action. It protects wildlife in more than seventy sanctuaries from coast to coast.

Sempervirens Fund

http://reality.sgi.com/employees/ctb/sempervirens/

A nonprofit land conservancy (the oldest in California), the fund works to protect redwood forests from threats such as population growth and logging. Learn how you can help keep these magnificent trees available for public enjoyment.

Surfrider Foundation USA

http://www.surfrider.org

This grassroots eco-surf organization is dedicated to the preservation of biological diversity on our coasts. They emphasize low-impact "surfaris" and environmental education among surfers and others to maintain a synergy between man and beach.

USDA—Natural Resources Conservation Service

http://www.ncg.nrcs.usda.gov/Welcome.html

The NRCS helps private landowners to develop conservation systems suited to their land. They also work with rural and urban communities alike to reduce erosion, conserve water, and solve other resource problems.

Wildlife Conservation Society/Bronx Zoo

http://www.wcs.org

The Wildlife Conservation Society, headquartered at the Bronx Zoo, is dedicated to the conservation of wildlife around the world.

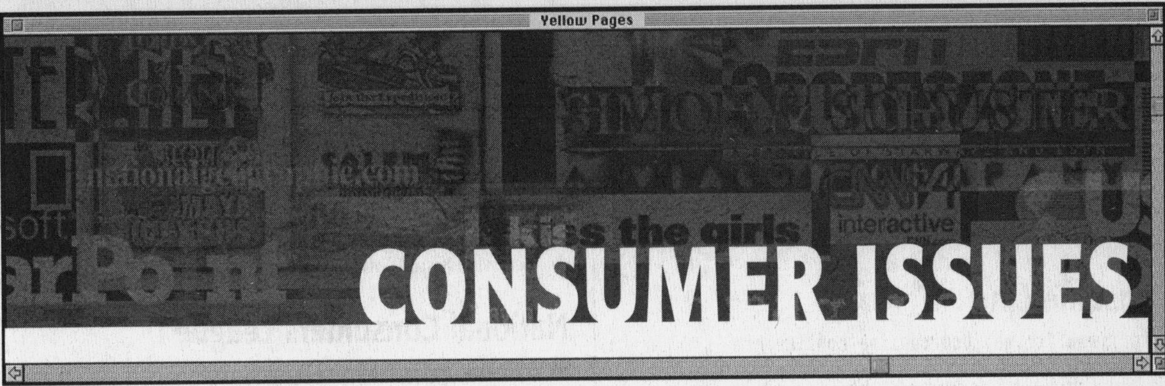

> The most important word in the vocabulary of advertising is *TEST*. If you pretest your product with consumers and pretest your advertising, you will do well in the marketplace.
>
> *David Ogilvy*

Angryconsumer.com

http://www.angryconsumer.com/index5.htm

A place to share your consumer experiences (good and bad) online. Email your experiences of serious problems, annoyances, and good stuff and they are placed on the site. The Reporting Consumer Fraud page gives direction in what to do in if you have had a fraudulent experience.

Bicycle Helmet Safety Institute Home Page

http://www.bhsi.org/

The helmet advocacy program for the Washington Area Bicyclist Association. There's a consumer pamphlet, a toolkit for organizing bicycle helmet programs, plus the latest issue of *The Helmet Update*, a newsletter devoted to discussing helmet news.

Related Sites

http://ag.arizona.edu/AREC/WEMC/consumerissue.html

http://www.directnet.com/~rbrennan/

http://www.consumer.org.nz/

The Dental Consumer Advisor
http://www.toothinfo.com/

Consumer Fraud Alert Network

http://www.world-wide.com/homebiz/fraud.htm

Provides information about the latest scams that professional con men and scam artists are using to rob you of your money. Offers advice about how you can protect yourself from being ripped off and who you can contact for help.

Consumer Information Center

http://www.pueblo.gsa.gov/

Access 200 federal publications regarding consumer issues. Their catalog offers information on a wide range of areas, such as cars, healthcare, food, travel, and children. You can also order the entire catalog.

The Consumer Law Page

http://seamless.com/alexanderlaw/txt/intro.html

Provides information related to consumer law. Offers articles on topics such as insurance fraud and product liability, brochures on topics, such as automobiles, funerals, and banking, and useful links to other resources related to consumer law.

The Consumer Project

http://www.consumerwatchdog.org/

Company dedicated to protecting the rights of the consumer, taxpayer, and medical patient. Find out the latest in consumer news and events, or search for your area of interest. You can even donate funds or volunteer to help out the cause.

Related Sites

http://www.igc.apc.org/pirg/aapc/index.htm

http://www.epic.org/

Consumer World

http://www.consumerworld.org/

Consumer resource guide to more than 1500 Internet consumer resources from reporting fraud to looking for the best airfare. Search the database for your specific consumer issue. Read the latest consumer news.

ConsumerLine

http://www.ftc.gov/bcp/conline/conline.htm

The Office of Consumer and Business Education of the Bureau of Consumer Protection operates this online service. Find published articles on various consumer issues (in English or Spanish), read about current consumer problems, report a consumer complaint, or check out educational campaigns.

CORPORATE WATCH

http://www.corpwatch.org/

Web site designed for investigating corporate activity. Get the hottest consumer news, learn about the organization's latest campaigns, and learn the research techniques needed to "dig up dirt on your favorite company."

The Dental Consumer Advisor

http://www.toothinfo.com/

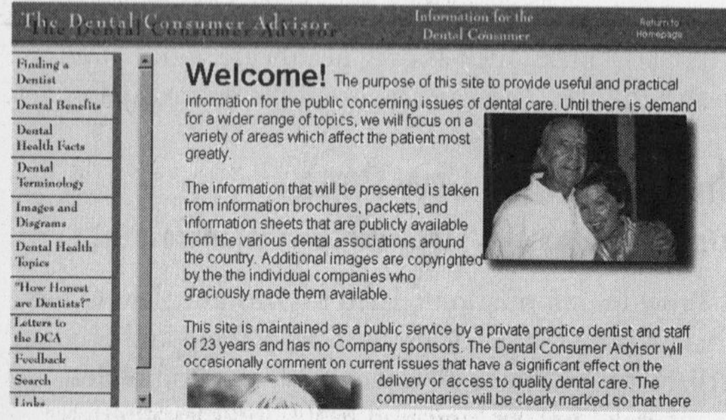

Useful and practical information on dental issues. Areas covered include dental terminology, insurance, and finding a dentist. Write in about your own dental experiences or ask the Advisor questions. Extensive list of links related to dentistry.

FDA Consumer Magazine

http://www.fda.gov/fdac/fdaconsumer.html

Publication of the U.S. Food and Drug Administration and includes reports of unsafe or worthless FDA products. Electronic copies are available through the Web site, or you can subscribe to the magazine by sending in the online form.

Internet ScamBusters

http://www.scambusters.com/

Free online newsletter dedicated to exposing Internet fraud and protecting consumers from misinformation and hype. Subscribe to the newsletter, share your own Internet scam experience, or enter their Internet ScamBusting Contest.

National Consumers League

http://www.natlconsumersleague.org/

Founded in 1899, this advocacy group represents consumers on workplace and marketplace issues. Find out the latest on consumer scams. Learn how to become an NCL member and when and where their next event is scheduled.

The National Fraud Information Center

http://www.fraud.org/

Originally formed in 1992 to battle telemarketing fraud, the NFIC now has a toll-free hotline for reporting telemarketing fraud, asking for advice about telemarketing calls, and investigating Internet fraud. The Web site also offers a section on fraud targeting the elderly.

The PIRGs—Fighting For Consumers

http://www.pirg.org/consumer/index.htm

The Public Interest Research Groups battle against consumer abuses. Some of their campaigns are against rising bank fees, credit company errors and abuses, dangerous products, and the tobacco industry's marketing to children.

U.S. Consumer Product Safety Commission

http://www.cpsc.gov/

Protects Americans against possible injury and death caused by consumer products. If you have experience with an unsafe product, report it on the Talk to Us page. Check out the latest recalled products. There's a special 4 Kids page that addresses issues such as the risks of inline skates, the importance of wearing bike helmets, and how to play baseball safely.

Related Sites

http://www.sec.gov/consumer/cyberfr.htm

http://www.pueblo.gsa.gov/1997crh/res_pg71.txt

http://www.nhtsa.dot.gov/cars/problems/

http://solar.rtd.utk.edu/~ccsi/csusa/business/consumer.html

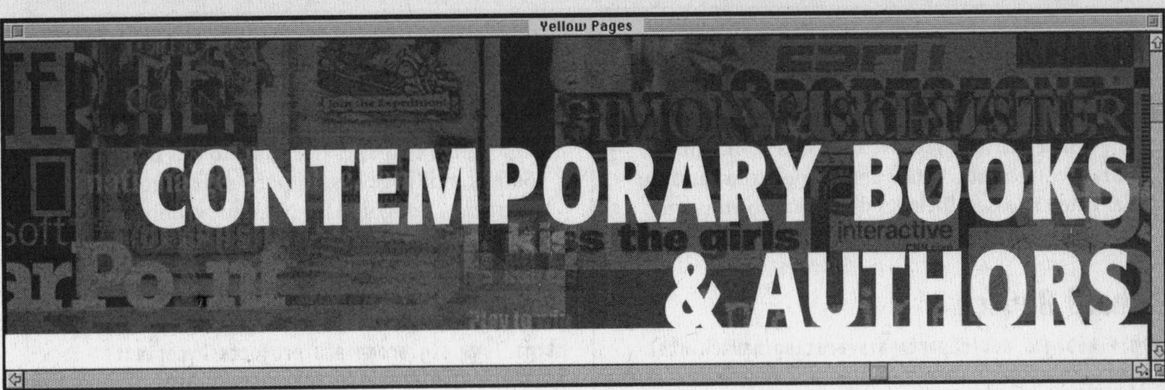

CONTEMPORARY BOOKS & AUTHORS

Learn to love good books. There are treasures in books that all the money in the world cannot buy, but the poorest laborer can have for nothing.

Robert G. Ingersoll

AUTHORS

Douglas Adams

http://www.umd.umich.edu/~nhughes/dna/

Several links to FAQs, lists of works by Adams that are available online, and membership information for the semi-official fan club, ZZ9 Plural Z Alpha. There's even a search engine, in case you want to find out exactly where in Adams' works the Babel fish is first mentioned. The site is maintained by the maintainer of the `alt.fan.douglas-adams` FAQ.

Louisa May Alcott

http://www.coppersky.com/louisa/

Explains why the author of *Little Women* was named after a moon crater and what her life was like in a commune. This site provides links to photos and other Alcott sites.

V.C. Andrews

http://www.csh.rit.edu/~cwalker/vcandrews/

Another book list, with descriptions of most of the books. Also has a family tree of the Foxworth family from the *Flowers in the Attic* series.

NRP TOP PICKS

Charles Dickens
http://lang.nagoya-u.ac.jp/~matsuoka/Dickens.html

Fyodor Dostoevsky
http://members.aol.com/KatharenaE/private/Philo/Dostoy/dostoy.html

Jack Kerouac
http://www.charm.net/~brooklyn/People/JackKerouac.html

Oscar Wilde
http://www.jonno.com/oscariana/1.html

Isaac Asimov

http://www.clark.net/pub/edseiler/WWW/asimov_home_page.html

A wonderful site for Asimov fans! Comprehensive booklists, stores and publishers that sell them, transcripts of reviews and interviews, and even sound files of Asimov himself.

Margaret Atwood

http://www.cariboo.bc.ca/ae/engml/friedman/atwoodbiblio.htm

An easy-to-follow table of contents lets you link to Atwood's poetry, novels, children's stories, dramatic works, and anthologies. You can also find sound files and film works. Follow more links at the bottom of the page to other Atwood sites.

Nicholson Baker

http://www.cts.com/browse/jwalk/nbaker/

The Nicholson Baker Fan Page is a page filled with facts about the books and the life of Nicholson Baker. There are links to reviews and comments, and perhaps most enjoyably, the first sentence of each novel is present in its description.

Clive Barker

http://www.wols.demon.co.uk/

The official Clive Barker Web site lists books, films, games, comics, and details about book tours and special video releases. Includes discussion forums and transcripts of IRC interviews with Barker.

Richard Bausch

http://web.gmu.edu/departments/writing/bausch.html

An instructor at George Mason University, writer Richard Bausch is widely published and acclaimed. His works have been featured in such periodicals as *The Atlantic, Harper's, The New Yorker,* and *Esquire.*

Greg Bear

http://www.kaiaghok.com/gregbear/gregbear.htm

Biography, bibliography, and some original work by Bear himself, exclusive to the Web ("for the time being"). Also contains bitmaps of some of Bear's paintings.

Samuel Beckett

http://www-personal.umich.edu/~kadaca/beckett.html

Provides an online source of information on twentieth century playwright and author Samuel Beckett. Presents many different articles and essays about Beckett's works such as *Endgame* and *Waiting for Godot.* Site includes a bibliography, biography, pictures, and links to other related sites.

Aphra Behn Page

http://ourworld.compuserve.com/homepages/r_nestvold/

This site is dedicated to the first professional woman writer in the English language. A prolific playwright (second only to John Dryden in the Restoration), Aphra Behn is known largely for her prose. This site has links to information about Aphra Behn and other women writers.

Jorge Luis Borges

http://www.rpg.net/quail/libyrinth/borges.html

Provides a history, bibliography, fictional bookshelf, biography, and works of Borges. You can also find images (made for postcards) and links to other Borges sites.

Richard Brautigan

http://www.riza.com/richard/

One of the only sites dedicated to this British Black Satirist, this page has a library and a "Trader's Corner." Configured for Netscape-compatible browsers.

Charlotte Brontë

http://www.stg.brown.edu/projects/hypertext/landow/victorian/cbronte/bronteov3.html

Dedicated to the Victorian author of *Jane Eyre,* this site also boasts links to literary and artistic relations, as well as a cultural context section.

Rita Brown

http://mchip00.med.nyu.edu/lit-med/lit-med-db/webdocs/webauthors/brown283-au-.html

This page concerns Rita Mae Brown, lesbianism, and medicine in the humanities. This page has links to these and other issues.

Charles Bukowski

http://realbeer.com/buk/

Strange that a drunk, self-described "dirty old man" would have such a nice home on the Web. There is a biography, a newsletter, an art section, and letters to the author.

Edgar Rice Burroughs

http://www.tarzan.com/

Probably as close as a person can come to an "official" Edgar Rice Burroughs page, this site has an autobiographical sketch, essays, and other information about the writer of the Tarzan series (and other fantasies).

William S. Burroughs

http://www.hyperreal.com/wsb/

Whenever a person begins to study William S. Burroughs, there are usually words of warning or at least a *caveat lector.* This site keeps with that tradition but gives great insight into the life of the writer of books such as *Naked Lunch* and *Junky.* This site offers a Web memorial to Burroughs.

Albert Camus

http://www.sccs.swarthmore.edu/~pwillen1/lit/indexa.htm

Although this page is probably too heavily formatted, the information presented is at least interesting. There are several essays about Camus, a biography, and photographs of the Algerian/French Absurdist.

Truman Capote

http://www.sgi.net/marbles/zeno/capote.html

Mainly dedicated to the new-journalistic novel *In Cold Blood*, this site also has biographical information and other points of interest about Truman Capote.

Jim Carroll

http://home.forbin.com/~laverne/carroll/carroll.html

Jim Carroll's home on the Web seems to want to dispel anything known by the public about the author of *The Basketball Diaries*. Indeed, Carroll is a multi-practiced artist in music, letters, and spoken-word performance; however, this site claims him the messiah of the nouveau Renaissance.

Lewis Carroll: An Overview

http://www.stg.brown.edu/projects/hypertext/landow/victorian/carroll/carrollov.html

Lewis Carroll (née Charles Dodgson) was not only the writer of the famous Alice in Wonderland stories, he also was a mathematician and scientist. This site houses information about Carroll as a whole person—his literary tactics, religion and philosophy, and his work in a political and social context.

Raymond Carver

http://world.std.com/~ptc/

This site has biographical information and essays about Raymond Carver. His stories have become very popular in the recent past, perhaps because of Robert Altman's film *Short Cuts*; however, Carver died of cancer in 1988. This page is the only one of its kind.

Neal Cassady

http://www.geocities.com/SoHo/5160/

Cassady's only book, *The First Third*, was an autobiography that went unpublished until he died. Cassady is a cultural icon, the infamous Dean Moriarty character in Kerouac's *On the Road*. This site leads to information about Cassady's life, friends, and influences. Also, find links to other beat writings and poetry. And, read *The Great Sex Letter*, which Cassady wrote to Kerouac, and which shows, if not defines, some of the quick jazz-flow writing of the beat generation.

Willa Cather

http://icg.harvard.edu/~cather/

A well-formatted site available from the Harvard Web server, this page has information about Cather, her work, and scholarly conferences in her honor. Her very astute picture of America in the early twentieth century should be impetus enough for a reader to look at the information included at this site.

Miguel de Cervantes

http://csdl.tamu.edu/cervantes/

A project of the Cervantes International Bibliography Online and the Anuario Bibliográfico Cervantino, this site is dedicated to solve the "problem of currency, thoroughness, and accessibility which now hampers research on Cervantes." There is a record of the books, articles, dissertations, reviews, and other points of interest included here to this end.

Agatha Christie

http://www.nd.edu/~rwoodbur/christie/christie.htm

Provides a chronological listing of most of Christie's works, grouped optionally by featured detective. This site also offers a collection of plays and short stories. The maintainer of the page promises that all the books and plays listed will eventually have complete descriptions (including whodunnit, for the impatient!).

Arthur C. Clarke Chapter of "The Silicon Jungle"

http://www.clark.net/pub/rothman/jungle.htm

Relates one person's experiences communicating with Clarke via telecommunications satellite in 1985, before the Internet was known outside of military and research institutions.

Joseph Conrad

http://www.americanliterature.com/HD/HDINDX.HTML

Here is the online version of *Heart of Darkness*, the story upon which the movie *Apocalypse Now* was based. The book is broken into chapters, and the site's suggestion is to read one chapter a day. Conrad's sultry writing will make you think you are in the jungle, not sitting in front of your computer.

Stephen Crane

http://www.en.utexas.edu/~mmaynard/Crane/crane.html

This page was written by several students at the University of Texas at Austin for a project in their English class; however, this doesn't diminish its relevance to the study of Stephen Crane. It is quite complete and has biography, bibliography, and excerpts from Crane's work—both audio and text.

Michael Crichton

http://www.globalnets.com/crichton/crichton.html

The writer of such novels as *Jurassic Park, The Eaters of the Dead*, and *Congo*, and all-around American media entrepreneur Michael Crichton finds a welcome home at this page. There are many good links to information about his life, books, and other entertainment efforts.

Cyber-Seuss

http://www.afn.org/~afn15301/drseuss.html

A good Dr. Seuss page, with all kinds of links, including information on the "Great Grinch Debate."

Charles Dickens

http://lang.nagoya-u.ac.jp/~matsuoka/Dickens.html

The home page includes a painting of Charles Dickens, by William Powell Frith (1859). This site is absolutely exhaustive in resources about Dickens, author of such fabulous books as *The Pickwick Papers* and *Great Expectations.* The site's dynamic quality is that it is constantly being updated to include new information about Dickens. You can link to archives back to April of 1997—and all the historical information is very up-to-date and useful.

Related Sites

http://www.vanderbilt.edu/AnS/english/flackcj/LitIndex.html

http://www.myunicorn.com/index1.html

http://www.bibliomania.com/

http://www.go-campus.com/

http://www.dingir.org/WebOS/omf/dingir/authors/

http://www.lib.vt.edu/Subjects/English_L&L.html

http://www.apocalypse.org/pub/u/batalion/english.shtml

Fyodor Dostoevsky

http://members.aol.com/KatharenaE/private/Philo/Dostoy/dostoy.html

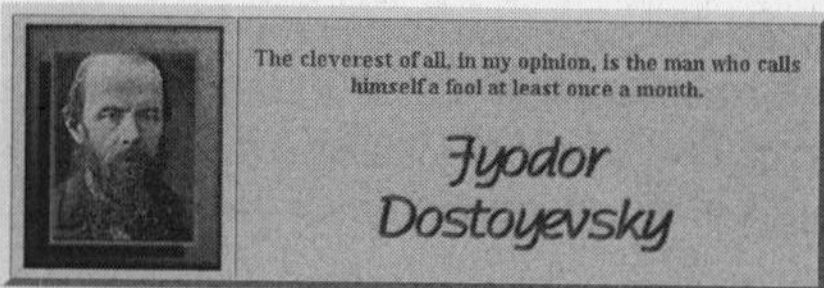

Great site about the stellar Russian author of books such as *Crime and Punishment* and *The Brothers Karamazov.* The site begins by telling you a little about Dostoevsky's life and about famous people who were influenced by his writing. There are also links to study guides of all his major works as well as links to other Dostoevsky sites.

Umberto Eco

http://www4.ncsu.edu/eos/users/m/mcmesser/www/eco.html

A computer-friendly semiotician, Umberto Eco's work has been hailed by philosophers, scholars, and readers all over the world. This site provides a good overview of the work of this important Italian writer.

T.S. Eliot

http://virtual.park.uga.edu/~232/eliot.taken.html

This site provides information on American poet T.S. Eliot. Includes a biography, bibliography, and poetry by Eliot. Also includes links to other related sites.

William Faulkner

http://www.mcsr.olemiss.edu/~egjbp/faulkner/faulkner.html

The site to visit for any sort of information about William Faulkner. John B. Padgett, currently a Ph.D. student at the University of Mississippi (located at Oxford, whence Faulkner hailed), maintains this completists' page with more information on it than anyone could want.

F. Scott Fitzgerald

http://www.csd.scarolina.edu/fitzgerald/index.html

Based at the University of South Carolina, this site dedicated to F. Scott Fitzgerald is in celebration of the centennial of his birth. The mission statement of the page states that "this site celebrates his writings, his life, and his relationships with other writers of the 20th century." True to this, you'll find biography, writings, and beautiful photos of the famous author from the Roaring '20s.

Ian Fleming

http://www.mcs.net/~klast/www/fleming.html

You might think, the Ian Fleming Web page might as well be called "oh, yeah, and for the guy who actually created James Bond;" however, this page is filled with history, biography, and news clips relating to the British author. Of course, you'll find plenty of 007, too.

Thomas Hardy

http://pages.ripco.com:8080/~mws/hardy.html

A large site about the author, it includes what you might expect—biography, e-texts, pictures—as well as some very entertaining sound bites of excerpts of works by Hardy, and Monty Python's take on him.

Nathaniel Hawthorne

http://www.tiac.net/users/eldred/nh/hawthorne.html

"Dedicated to enhancing our understanding and appreciation of Hawthorne's writings and life," this site has complete e-texts of his novels and stories. There are readings, pictures, and information about this American author of the 19th century.

Ernest Hemingway (The Papa Page)

http://www.ee.mcgill.ca/~nverever/hem/cover.html

Probably the definitive Hemingway site, the Papa Page brings pictures, bibliographies, and biography of Ernest Hemingway to the World Wide Web. There are good references here to print resources that can be obtained at any bookstore or library.

L. Ron Hubbard

http://www.lronhubbard.org/

A wonderful site to visit for its accessibility, layout, and information on L. Ron Hubbard. It offers a profile of Hubbard, his poetry, songs and music, philosophy, and (of course) his books. There's also a link to the Church of Scientology. Includes audio clips of some of his lectures and writings.

Zora Neale Hurston

http://pages.prodigy.com/zora/

A site dedicated to the writer of the famous novel *Their Eyes Were Watching God.* There are links, many photographs, and links to other Hurston and literature sites.

Robert Jordan

http://www.cc.gatech.edu/ftp/people/viren/www/jordan/jordan.html

A whimsical FAQ to Robert Jordan's work, with humor, language guides, and more.

James Joyce (Work in Progress)

http://www.2street.com/joyce/

There are many joys to this site—pictures of the author, his family, and those people mentioned in his work; important songs and readings by Joyce himself; links to articles and Internet groups who study Joyce; and maps of the places mentioned in his work. Give yourself some time, though, this site is worth it.

Franz Kafka—Constructing

http://info.pitt.edu/~kafka/intro.html

Provides bibliography (both of Kafka and critical works), biography, pictures, and more about the author of works such as *The Castle, The Trial,* and *Amerika* (among more). Includes a listing of Kafka's library and links to other related sites.

Franz Kafka Photo Album

http://www.cs.technion.ac.il/~eckel/Kafka/kafka.html

This site provides a well put together visual guide to the life of Franz Kafka. Includes many pictures of the Austrian writer and links to other Kafka sites.

Jack Kerouac

http://www.charm.net/~brooklyn/People/JackKerouac.html

A Literary Kicks page that provides a biography, bibliography, excerpts, and pictures of Beat author Jack Kerouac. Kerouac is known as the person who coined the term "beatnick," and his prose and style is still popular among the Bohemian-type culture today. This site includes a guide to character names, publications, and much more.

Stephen King

http://wwwcsif.cs.ucdavis.edu/~pace/king.html

Full of many interesting links that one might not imagine Stephen King would relate himself with. In other words, you will find photos, FAQs, and biographies about King here, but you will also find a guess at his mailing address and a copy of some liner notes King wrote for Michael McDermott's album.

Barbara Kingsolver

http://www.csc.eku.edu/honors/kingsolver/

Pictures of her book covers, essays by students, and a biography compose this site dedicated to the writer of *Pigs in Heaven.*

Dean Koontz

http://www.dkoontz.com/

This site is written and maintained by a Koontz fan club, so you know they are really charged with the excitement of his writing. This is not just a static Web experience (although there are some great links to other Koontz sites and online information). From this site you can chat with Koontz fans, join a club, send a Koontz postcard, join a discussion group, or play a trivia contest.

Milan Kundera

http://www.georgetown.edu/irvinemj/english016/kundera/kundera.html

Provides a bibliography, biography, and essays about writer Milan Kundera, the author of *The Unbearable Lightness of Being* and many others. Includes links to site about Prague, Kundera, and other literary pages.

Katherine Kurtz

http://arrogant.itc.icl.ie/KatherineKurtz.html

Contains listings of Katherine Kurtz's works and a short biography, as well as a Deryni FAQ.

Louis L'Amour

http://louis-lamour-fan.com/

A self-proclaimed "celebration of American History and the Wild West," this site gives more than just information about L'Amour and his prolific amount of novels—it approaches all things from the American West. The author of this site has written it in such a way that is very inviting, and he has included reviews, pictures, and (kindly) a list of updates made on the page.

Related Sites

http://www.just-so.com/ecard/scripts/select.cgi

http://www.stg.brown.edu/projects/hypertext/landow/SSPCluster/theorists.html

http://www.geocities.com/Athens/Forum/1504/index.htm

Ursula K. Le Guin

http://www.uic.edu/~lauramd/sf/leguin/

A biography, contact and agent information, lists of awards won by Le Guin, and a complete bibliography, arranged both chronologically and by type of work (poetry, novel, and so on).

C.S. Lewis (Into the Wardrobe)

http://cslewis.cache.net/

Into the Wardrobe has many tidbits and large chunks of useful information for the scholar, reader, and fan of C.S. Lewis. One of the best parts of this site is its completist attitude toward studying Lewis and his work—it even includes a Useful Contacts page.

H. P. Lovecraft

http://www.primenet.com/~dloucks/hpl/

Biography, chronological list of tales, a Lovecraft FAQ, information regarding the "Necronomicon," and a photo-tour of New England locations related to Lovecraft's work.

Anne McCaffrey

http://arrogant.itc.icl.ie/AnneMcCaffrey.html

Contains links to bibliographies, a list of awards, and sample chapters from Anne McCaffrey's latest books. There's also a link to DragonWeb, and a list of fan clubs.

Cormac McCarthy

http://www.cormacmccarthy.com/

The Cormac McCarthy Home Page is a good place to start for someone interested both in the writing of Cormac McCarthy and the literature of the American Southwest. Often compared to William Faulkner, McCarthy has recently become very popular among certain literary circles. Perhaps with the proliferation of novels such as *All The Pretty Horses*, reading will again become an American pastime.

Herman Melville

http://www.melville.org/

Alright, so maybe you didn't like reading *Moby Dick* in high school; that doesn't mean that it wasn't worthwhile, though, right? Melville is actually a pretty approachable author, not to mention his importance to the American tradition. Try him again here—you'll find a comprehensive amount of information about the author of arguably "the great American novel."

James Michener

http://www.cwrl.utexas.edu/~mmaynard/Michener/

Most readers will remember Michener as a writer who could go all the way back to the beginning of *time*, practically, in order to add to his books all the historical, philosophical, and political reference they could possibly have. This site captures his life and work by providing links to Michener's chronology, reviews about his books, and literary works.

N. Scott Momaday

http://users.mwci.net/~lapoz/Momaday.html

A very ambitious Web page, this page promises to provide links to information "about every article and book written by or about N. Scott Momaday." Already present (as of this writing) are biographical and bibliographical information and reviews of Momaday's work.

Toni Morrison

http://www.en.utexas.edu/~mmaynard/Morrison/home.html

Provides a biography, bibliography, and pictures of 1993 Nobel Prize winning author Toni Morrison. Includes articles about Morrison's books such as *Tar Baby*, *Sula*, *Beloved*, and many more.

Haruki Murakami

http://www.geocities.com/Paris/3954/haruki1.htm

Provides information about Japanese author Haruki Murakami, best known for his books *Hear the Wind Sings* and *The Trilogy of the Rat.* Includes a biography, bibliography, pictures, and an interview with Murakami.

Vladmir Nabokov (Zembla)

http://www.libraries.psu.edu/iasweb/nabokov/nsintro.htm

A formidable presence on the World Wide Web in terms of layout, content, and conciseness, Zembla offers a great amount and breadth of information concerning Vladmir Nabokov, the author of novels such as *Lolita* and *Bend Sinister.*

Anaïs Nin

http://www.informatik.uni-leipzig.de/privat2/beckmann/public_html/nin.html

This home page includes links to resources concerning Anaïs Nin's work, a bibliography, and a biography. Includes links to other Nin-related sites.

Joyce Carol Oates (Celestial Timepiece)

http://storm.usfca.edu/~southerr/jco.html

Celestial Timepiece gives a full view of author Joyce Carol Oates. Provides a great amount of information on Oates, the author of many novels, including *You Must Remember This* and *The Triumph of the Spider.* This site features a well-laid out table of contents that covers her life and gives access to resources for research on Oates and her writing.

George Orwell

http://www.levity.com/corduroy/orwell.htm

Had Orwell known that someday "big brother" might be watching him, in the form his picture and life story being on the Web for the world to see... well, he might have been pleased. This site provides a biography of Orwell's life and has a few links to related sites.

Edgar Allen Poe

http://www.cs.umu.se/~dpcnn/eapoe/ea_poe.html

Author of "The Raven," Edgar Allen Poe is also famous for his short stories that were meant to "expand the human soul." This Web site is very popular, and deservedly so—it features biography, links to e-text, and a chat room.

Thomas Pynchon: HyperArts Pynchon Pages

http://www.hyperarts.com/

Provides indexes and Web guides to the writings of the mysterious American author Thomas Pynchon. Includes detailed background and articles on Pynchon novels such as *Gravity's Rainbow*, *Vineland*, and *V.*

A B C D E F G H I J K L M N O P Q R S T U V W X Y Z

Ayn Rand

http://www.aynrand.org/

Dedicated to Rand's novels and philosophy, there are many links to biographies, bibliographies, mission statements, and objectivism. The philosophy of reason and egoism lives here.

Anne Rice

http://www.personal.psu.edu/users/l/m/lms5/aboutar.html

A very large site in honor of the horror writer from New Orleans. Anne Rice's books have become very popular in the last few years, and this site is testimony to that. There are pictures, biographies, bibliographies, sounds, and even information about Rice's house in New Orleans.

Tom Robbins (The AFTRLife)

http://www.rain.org/~da5e/tom_robbins.html

A self-described Tom Robbins playground, the AFTRLife is a fun place to look around and learn about Tom Robbins' work. It is Java enhanced, and is well formatted. A good place to spend a few minutes if you are looking for the author of *Still Life With Woodpecker.*

Philip Roth

http://omni.cc.purdue.edu/~royald/roth.htm

A straightforward page concerning Philip Roth's work as a novelist and critic. There are biographies, bibliographies, interviews, and articles present here.

Antoine de Saint-Exupery

http://www.westegg.com/exupery/

Perhaps known mostly for his book *The Little Prince,* Antoine de Saint-Exupery was also an adult novelist and pilot. At this site, there are links to quotes, a bibliography, and e-texts available in several languages.

J.D. Salinger (The Bananafish Home Page)

http://slf.gweep.net/~sfoskett/jds/index.html

Provides information about J.D. Salinger, the author of the *Catcher in the Rye.* The site includes articles, essays, and more about Salinger's writing.

Mary Shelley

http://www.netaxs.com/~kwbridge/maryshel.html

This site houses information about Mary Shelley, Percy Shelly, the Romantics, and, of course, her popular novel *Frankenstein.* Newly updated, there is a gothic air to this site, including a musical background.

Gertrude Stein

http://www.magibox.net/~stein/

The most "official" Gertrude Stein page, this site features a reproduction of the wallpaper Stein and Alice B. Toklas bought for their Paris apartment. Of course, too, there are some pictures and quotes from the author. Includes a bibliography, articles, and much more.

John Steinbeck

http://www.sjsu.edu/depts/steinbec/srchome.html

San Jose State University is home to the Steinbeck Research Center, and this is its home on the Web. There are chronologies, biographical information, bibliographies, and an interesting link called Steinbeck Country with pictures and other tidbits. Includes links to other Steinbeck-related sites.

Harriet Beecher Stowe

http://www.cs.cmu.edu/People/mmbt/women/StoweHB.html

A Celebration of Women Writers presents a bibliography of Stowe, including a link to the complete text version of *Uncle Tom's Cabin.* The text was scanned, and is introduced by plenty of legal notices. Also, this site offers several related links.

Amy Tan

http://www.luminarium.org/contemporary/amytan/

Amy Tan On The Web gives excerpts, sound bites, interviews, links, and pictures of this influential contemporary American author. Her work has been widely translated and deserves the recognition that it has attained.

Ananta Toer

http://www.access.digex.net/~bardsley/prampage.html

Provides a biography, bibliography, and more on Indonesian writer Pramoedya Ananta Toer. Includes an extensive list of essays, articles, reviews, abstracts, letters, and interviews.

Lev Nikolayevich Tolstoy

ftp://users.aol.com/Tolstoy28/tolstoy.htm

This site does not look like much from the get-go, but it contains some very useful information, as well as offers online books (yep, you can read them online) of the author of *Anna Karenina* and *War and Peace.* The site also links to biographies and literary criticisms of Tolstoy.

Mark Twain (Ever the Twain Shall Meet)

http://www.lm.com/~joseph/mtwain.html

This site seems to know its stuff. It has links to e-text versions of several of Twain's novels—both downloadable and in HTML—and other very interesting links to Twain around the Web.

John Updike: The Centurian

http://www.users.fast.net/~joyerkes/

Provides information and a discussion area for the works of American author John Updike, best known for the *Witches of Eastwick, A Month of Sundays,* and *Rabbit Run* (among many others). Includes a bibliography (both of critical and Updike works), a biography, essays, articles, and pictures.

Jules Verne

http://avery.med.virginia.edu/~mtp0f/flips/jules.html

A well-maintained, chatty site dedicated to the author of *20,000 Leagues Under the Sea* and *Around the World in 80 Days* (among others), this page is easily navigated and has good links to biography, reviews, pictures, and the like.

Kurt Vonnegut

http://www.cas.usf.edu/english/boon/vonnegut/kv.html

Provides information about the writings of American author Kurt Vonnegut. Includes pictures, essays, articles, and links to other sites for the author of *Slaughterhouse Five* and many more. Also includes a list of books about Vonnegut.

Alice Walker

http://www.luminarium.org/contemporary/alicew/

Essays, articles, criticism, poetry, short stories, excerpts—you name it, you'll find it here. Includes a wealth of information about Alice Walker, the author of *The Color Purple* and many other titles.

Oscar Wilde

http://www.jonno.com/oscariana/1.html

Don't come to this site unless you are prepared to relax for awhile as you go through a textual and visual tour of Oscar Wilde's biography. During this tour, you will read about his life, see photographs, view letters and telegrams to and from Wilde, and get a sense of who the author was. When you get to the end, select "About this project" to see other Wilde links on the Web. This is a truly gratifying experience.

Thomas Clayton Wolfe

http://www.cms.uncwil.edu/~connelly/wolfe.html

Provides a biography, chronology, pictures, and quotes of American author Thomas Wolfe, best known for his novel *Look Homeward, Angel.* Includes a list of critical studies, examples of humor used in his writing, and information about a commemorative stamp campaign.

Virginia Woolf

http://www.aianet.or.jp/~orlando/VWW/

The Virginia Woolf Web has quotes, e-texts, and information about Bloomsbury group with which Woolf is associated. This page is consistently updated, and contains information about Woolf that is found nowhere else on the Web. Includes a vast amount of links to other literature related sites.

LITERATURE

The Libyrinth

http://www.microserve.net/~thequail/libyrinth/index.html

A very large and intricate Web unto itself, the Libyrinth features information and links about twentieth century authors and their influence on (and by) Magical Realism or Post Modernism. Several authors are included here, and several more are in the midst of being added. Those featured at the time of this writing are listed (along with their Web address within the Libyrinth) in the following listing:

Author	URL
Jorge Luis Borges	http://www.microserve.net/~thequail/libyrinth/borges.html
Umberto Eco	http://www.microserve.net/~thequail/libyrinth/eco.html
Gabriel García Márquez	http://www.microserve.net/~thequail/libyrinth/garcia.marquez.frame.html
James Joyce	http://www.microserve.net/~thequail/libyrinth/joyce.html

Literary and Critical Theory

http://www.stg.brown.edu/projects/hypertext/landow/SSPCluster/theorists.html

Provides a wide array of information on literary theory and theorists. Includes many different essays and links to other literary criticism sites.

Literary Kicks

http://www.charm.net/~brooklyn/

This extensive site provides an introduction and background information on Beat era writers such as Lawrence Ferlinghetti, Greg Corso, Allen Ginsberg, William S. Burroghs, and more. Includes biographies, bibliographies, pictures, and links to other beat related sites.

Literary Resources

http://www.geocities.com/SoHo/9214/

Provides assistance for those who want to use the Web to find literary links. Search by first letter of the last name to find an author, browse through movement (Modernism, Victorian, Romanticism, and so on) for types of writing, and check out the online books page.

Modernism Timeline 1890–1940

http://weber.u.washington.edu/~eckman/timeline.html

Provides a timeline of literary works and their historical context in the modernism era (1890–1940). Includes a search index and many links to other literary based sites.

NEWSGROUPS

alt.arts.storytelling

alt.books.anne-rice

alt.books.arthur-clarke

alt.books.beatgeneration

alt.books.brian-lumley

alt.books.bukowski

alt.books.chesterton

alt.books.clive-barker

alt.books.crichton

alt.books.cs-lewis

alt.books.dean-koontz

alt.books.deryni

alt.books.h-g-wells

alt.books.iain-banks

alt.books.isaac-asimov

alt.books.julian-may

alt.books.kurt-vonnegut

alt.books.larry-niven

alt.books.m-lackey

alt.books.moorcock

alt.books.phil-k-dick

alt.books.pratchett

alt.books.raymond-feist

alt.books.reviews

alt.books.robert-rankin

alt.books.sf.melanie-rawn

alt.books.stephen-king

alt.books.technical

alt.books.terry-brooks

alt.books.toffler

alt.books.tom-clancy

alt.comp.shareware.authors

alt.fan.authors.stephen-king

alt.fan.douglas-adams

alt.fan.eddings

alt.fan.harlan-ellison

alt.fan.heinlein

alt.fan.pern

alt.fan.piers-anthony

alt.fan.pooh

alt.fan.pratchett

alt.fan.tolkien

alt.fan.tom-clancy

alt.fan.tom-robbins

alt.fantasy.conan

alt.jokes.limericks

alt.legend.king-arthur

alt.sex.stories

alt.sex.stories.d

alt.startrek.creative.erotica

asu.books.exchange

aus.org.acs.books

biz.books.technical

humanities.lit.authors.shakespeare

misc.books.technical

misc.writing.screenplays

rec.arts.books

rec.arts.books.childrens

rec.arts.books.hist-fiction

rec.arts.books.marketplace

rec.arts.books.reviews

rec.arts.books.tolkien

rec.arts.erotica

rec.arts.mystery

rec.arts.sf.written

rec.arts.sf.written.robert-jordan

rec.arts.startrek.current

rec.arts.startrek.reviews

relcom.fido.su.books

sdnet.books

slac.rec.books

soc.libraries.talk

tnn.books

tnn.books.magazine

tnn.books.new

ucb.market.books

ucd.swap.books

uiuc.misc.bookcoop

uk.media.books.sf

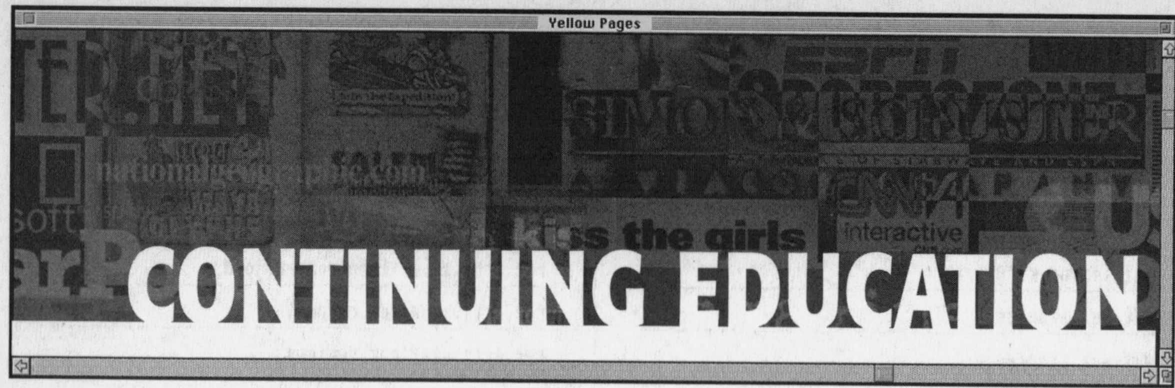

> The things taught in schools and colleges are not an education, but the means of education.
>
> *Ralph Waldo Emerson*

APHA: Continuing Education

http://www.apha.org/science/ce/index.html

Site maintained by the American Public Health Association. The APHA annual meeting holds specific conferences for various disciplines in the public health field. Continuing Education Units are available for each.

Automotive Management Institute AMIONLINE

http://www.amionline.org/

Members of the automotive service industry can find out about AMI's continuing education programs at AMIONLINE. Check the calendar of upcoming AMI events or the catalog for specific coursework offered.

Biomedical Communications

http://www.lvm.com/biomed/

Offers Continuing Medical Education (CME) programs and training materials for the following areas of medicine: Colposcopy, Cervical Intraepithelial Neoplasia, Gynecology, Laser Surgery, Electrosurgery, LEEP and Abnormal Pap Smears. Shop the mall for books, videos, and CD-ROMs related to your area.

SPIE Education Programs
http://www.spie.org/web/education_home.html

Colorado School of Mines Special Programs and Continuing Education

http://gn.mines.colorado.edu/Outreach/Cont_Ed/

Conferences and programs offered to chosen off-campus groups. Topics include mine safety and health, environmental issues, and industrial minerals processing. Some of the courses include post-conference online discussion.

Continuing Education at the University of Missouri-Rolla

http://www.umr.edu/~conted

Offers continuing Education courses and conferences sponsored by the University of Missouri-Rolla in all disciplines. Continuing Education courses in Civil and Electrical Engineering. Conferences in Mining, Asphalt, Concrete, Geotechnical Engineering, Explosives, Earthquakes, Machine Foundation, and numerous others.

Continuing Education for Professional Social Workers

http://www.brynmawr.edu/Adm/pubs/conted/fall97/registration.html

License renewal, tuition, transportation information—all you need to know about continuing education options for social workers at Bryn Mawr College in Bryn Mawr, Pennsylvania. Gives a detailed list of registration information needed and where to send that information.

Continuing Education on the Web

http://www.ce4psych.com

Continuing education courses for psychologists on the Web and Internet. Get CE credit directly on your computer.

Continuing Education—www.DentalGlobe.com

http://dentalglobe.com/ce.html

Extensive list of links to continuing education programs and courses in dentistry. Some of the programs are even available online.

Dalhousie University Maritime School of Social Work Continuing Education Program

http://is.dal.ca/socialwork/coned/

Serves the need for Social Work continuing education in the maritime provinces and concentrates on the Nova Scotia area. Also welcomes United States and Canadian students. Check out the workshops and certificate programs available.

Division of Continuing Education—University of Nevada, Reno

http://www.dce.unr.edu

Serving all of your continuing education needs, the DCE at UNR offers courses in Gaming Management, Professional Development, Correspondence Study, and the list goes on.

Division of Extended & Continuing Education at the University of Connecticut

http://www.ucc.uconn.edu/~wwwece

The Division provides educational opportunities for professionals, adult learners, and traditional students. They provide certificate, degree, credit, and non-credit courses.

Foundations In Continuing Education

http://www.concentric.net/~fice

Foundations In Continuing Education provides quality Self Study (Home-Study) Continuing Education for Dental Professionals. ADA CERP Recognized Provider. AGD National Sponsor. Courses approved by DANB.

Law Journal Seminar-Press Home Page

http://www.legalseminars.com/

Offers continuing legal education programs. Approved continuing professional education (CPE) sponsor; gain CPE credits by attending their seminars. Check out the calendar of events or request to be notified via email of seminars specializing in your area of practice.

Midwest Center for Occupational Health and Safety Continuing Education

http://www.healthpartners.com/mcohs/mc_continuing_education.html

The Midwest Center is an effort between the University of Minnesota School of Public Health and St. Paul Ramsey Medical Center. It provides a full range of professional continuing education courses in the areas of occupational medicine, industrial hygiene, safety and occupational health nursing, and the management of hazardous substances such as asbestos and lead. Check out their current programs and upcoming ones.

NYU's School of Continuing Education

http://www.nyu.edu/sce/

NYU's School of Continuing Education offers more than 2,000 credit and noncredit courses in over 100 fields for adults to advance their careers, enhance their lives, and keep ahead of a constantly changing world.

Physical Therapy Continuing Education Conferences and Workshops

http://www.tpta.org/conf_wks.htm

Web page of the Texas Physical Therapy Association. Lists upcoming courses and seminars in and around the Texas area.

RNonline: Online Continuing Education in Nursing

http://www.learnwell.org/~edu/rnonline.shtml

Short courses for nursing professionals and other medical professionals. The entire process in done online: select a course, study the material and participate in interactive cases, print the online test form, fill it in, mail it in with your $15 fee, and await your results. Two weeks later, given a passing score, you receive your Continuing Education Certificate in the mail.

San Jose State University Continuing Education

http://conted.sjsu.edu/

Find out about SJSU's many current continuing education programs. Improve your current career or pursue a new one with the Professional Development Programs; learn English as a Second Language; browse the summer session schedule; or, if you live far away, check into the Video-Assisted Learning opportunities.

SPIE Education Programs

http://www.spie.org/web/education_home.html

Courses and continuing education programs in optical engineering by the International Society for Optical Engineering (SPIE). The Annual Continuing Education Catalog is available online. Check out upcoming courses, including some video courses that can be viewed at home. There are also courses broadcast over the National Technological University satellite network.

Texas Tech University Division of Continuing Education

http://www.dce.ttu.edu/

Catalog of the Division of Continuing Education at Texas Tech University, containing courses for high school, college, and adult students, as well as Credit by Examinations (CBEs) for elementary, middle school, and high school students. TEA-accredited high school diploma program and Texas Tech University-approved college curriculum.

University of Berkley: 'College without Classes' Degree Programs

http://www.berkley-u.edu

Alternative education, adult distance learning (correspondence school). No residency. Earn college degrees without classroom work. Low tuition, credit for life experience.

University of North Alabama Continuing Education

http://www.una.edu/conted/index.html

The Continuing Education department of UNA offers a wide variety of courses for adults, youth, and various professions, including accounting and auditing, nursing, human resources and personnel, industrial hygiene/occupational health and safety, and quality improvement. Check out the many courses designed for the person who simply wants to learn a new skill like gardening or learn how to use a computer.

University of San Diego, Continuing Education

http://www.electriciti.com/~cont_ed

The University of San Diego, Division of Continuing Education offers career advancement opportunities for educators by providing credential and certificate programs, workshop, lecture series, and professional development courses. All of these offerings meet the requirements set forth by the state for the professional development of teachers.

WebEd University

http://ceus.com

WebEd is a virtual University for professionals to obtain Continuing Education Credits on the Internet. They have several colleges for a variety of professions.

Western CPE: Continuing Education for Accountants CPA

http://www.umt.edu/ccesp/wcpe/

Sponsored by the University of Montana, this organization teaches courses to accountants seeking continuing professional education. Courses are either conducted in a resort setting or are self-study programs.

Related Sites
http://www.gse.rutgers.edu/adult/
http://www.concentric.net/~Fice/oc.htm
http://www.baylor.edu/~cont_ed/Welcome.html
http://www.csmc.edu/pediatrics/new.html
http://www.fvcc.cc.mt.us/depts/ce/
http://med-www.stanford.edu/center/events/cme/
http://www.cam.ac.uk/CambUniv/ContEd/
http://www.state.nv.us/boards/nsbn/contedu/cereg.htm
http://www.una.edu/conted/professions.html
http://www.cma-canada.org/english/cma19.html
http://chppm-www.apgea.army.mil/trng/describe.crs/d6401.htm

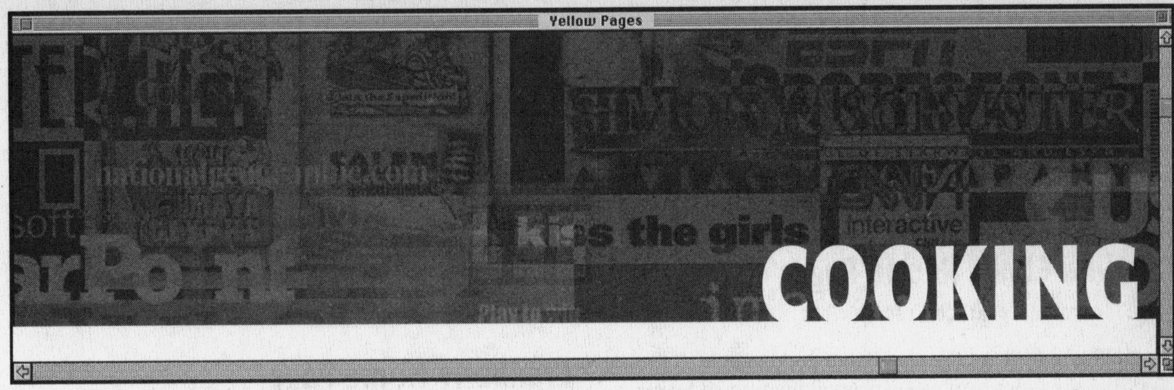

> Cooking is like love. It should be entered into with abandon or not at all.
>
> *Harriet Van Horne*

B's Cucumber Page

http://www.lpl.arizona.edu/~bcohen/cucumbers/info.html

For those interested in cucumbers and their various uses, this page provides recipes and information about commercial and greenhouse growing of cucumbers. Also included are 20 reasons why cucumbers are at least as good as men.

Bagel Page

http://jaka.ece.uiuc.edu/~scott/bagels/

Recipes and other information about bagels. Also contains links to other bagel-related sites

Black Rose's Recipes & Links

http://www.cchat.com/recipes.htm

Black Rose's Recipes & Links includes 800+ links to other recipes sites, and 300+ recipes and growing! New recipes added weekly.

Bread

http://www.cs.cmu.edu/~mjw/recipes/bread/bread.html

Provides an index of bread recipes.

Official French Fries Page
http://www.select-ware.com/fries/

SOAR–Searchable Online Archive of Recipes
http://soar.berkeley.edu/recipes/

Breakfast Cereal Hall of Fame

http://198.3.117.222/

A good deal of information about breakfast cereal. There is a featured "cerealebrity" about which you can view more information. There are also articles on the price of cereal, cereal art, and more.

Broccoli Central

http://ucsu.colorado.edu/~banasn/Home.html

Everything you could possibly want to know about the green vegetable and quite a few things that you didn't. That is, of course, unless you were looking for information on how to cook and eat it, which is nowhere to be found on this page.

Buffalo Chicken Wing Home Page

http://www.moran.com/htmld/bcw/

A page that takes Buffalo wings very seriously. Learn why Buffalo claims them, where they originated, and who makes the best wings. Vote for your favorite wing restaurant, and collect or submit Buffalo wing recipes.

Burrito Page

http://www.infobahn.com/pages/rito.html

A humorous look at a staple Mexican food item. Practices burritology—learn about yourself through the burrito toppings you choose. Contains links to other sites about burritos that enable you to learn about, order, and deconstruct the mystery of the burrito.

A B C D E F G H I J K L M N O P Q R S T U V W X Y Z

Callahan's Cookbook

http://www.ruhr-uni-bochum.de/callahans/cookbook.html

An eclectic collection of recipes contributed by readers of the alt.callahans newsgroup

Carolina Chat's Recipe Page

http://carolina-chat.com/recipes.htm

A place to find good recipes from good people. A lot of links, recipes, and you can email them to add your recipes and sites too!

Cheeseburger in Paradise

http://www.fdu.com/fdu/cburger.htm

A listing of the best places to find a cheeseburger of world-class caliber. No matter if you're in Chicago or Cairo, there's always a good cheeseburger somewhere.

CheeseNet 95

http://www.wgx.com/cheesenet/

The graphics-rich cheese bible of the Web—how to make it, its history, the different variations, a picture gallery, cheese literature, and cheese language. Features a cheese-making demonstration.

Chil E-Heads

http://neptune.netimages.com/~chile/

Chile pepper culture: recipes, restaurants, botany, festivals, and trivia.

Cookbooks On/Line Recipe Database

http://www.cookbooks.com/reg.htm

Cookbooks On/line recipe database is the largest recipe database on the Web. If you are looking for any recipes, this is the place to start!

The Cooking Couple Clubhouse

http://www.cookingcouple.com

Jump out of the frying pan and into the fire with the best-selling Cooking Couple on a Web site dedicated to food, romance, love, and lust.

Cooking Recipes of the Institute of Nuclear Chemistry

http://quasar.physik.unibas.ch/~tommy/nanni/recipes.html

Contains easy-to-make and inexpensive recipes collected by German chemists and physicists. Recipes are available in both English and German. Includes a metric conversion chart.

Cranberry Home Page

http://www.scs.carleton.ca/~palepu/cranberry.html

Contains much information about cranberries: cranberry products, cranberries and the urinary tract, cranberry beer, and even some recipes for making things with cranberries.

Creole and Cajun Recipe Page

http://www.webcom.com/~gumbo/recipe-page.html

"New Orleans food is as delicious as the less criminal forms of sin." (Mark Twain, 1884). A comprehensive guide with recipes that distinguishes the fine art of New Orleans Cajun and Creole cuisine. Also contains links to several online cookbooks and food-related sites.

Culinary World Tour

http://www.webcom.com:80/~gumbo/world-food.html

Provides a nice representation of international recipes ranging from African Bobotie, a curried bread custard with lamb, to Kloi Buad Chi, a dessert from Thailand.

Dan's Doner Kebab Registry

http://student.uq.edu.au/~cs315886/Dan/kebab.html

Doner Kebabs, also known as gyros, are considered by some to be the food of the gods. Dan certainly is taken with them and offers reviews of kebab shops from around the world, kebab recipes, and links to other kebab pages.

Dawn's Collection of 'Net Recipes

http://www.hcc.cc.fl.us/services/staff/dawn/recipes.htm

Like new recipes? Then you will enjoy this Web page that includes recipes available via the Net and a recipe of the month.

Dinner Co-Op

http://dinnercoop.cs.cmu.edu/dinnercoop/home-page.html

This site offers more than your run-of-the mill food-related site. Over 1,500 links to sites concentrating on recipes, culinary education, restaurant reviews, and online food stores. Well-organized and useful—definitely worth a bookmark!

FATFREE Vegetarian Mailing List Archive

http://www.fatfree.com/

Contains 2,391 fat-free and lowfat vegetarian recipes that can be accessed from a searchable archive. Also contains links to other lowfat/vegetarian-oriented Internet resources.

Filipino Cuisine

http://pubweb.acns.nwu.edu/~flip/food.html

Provides information on Filipino restaurants, cookbooks, recipes, and substitutions for hard-to-find ingredients. Also contains links to other Filipino cooking-related sites.

Food Resource

http://www.orst.edu/food-resource/food.html

A comprehensive index of food-related sites. Choose from a plethora of links to recipe sites, restaurant databases, colorful images of food, sites on culinary education, and anything else even remotely connected with food.

FoodPlex

http://www.gigaplex.com/wow/food/index.htm

Possibly the most entertaining food-related site on the Web, the FoodPlex contains humorous information about food, as well as other trivia such as the distribution of animals in a box of animal crackers. There are also sections on taste-testing dog biscuits, where to find the best ice cream in America, and a guide to enjoying TV dinners. Don't pass this site by!

Friends and Partners Kitchen

http://solar.rtd.utk.edu/friends/life/cookbooks/master.html

Offers American, Russian, and International cuisine recipes. Also supports an international chef chat room for culinary tips and treasures. Contains links to other online cookbooks.

FYNet's Collection of Malaysian Recipes

http://ucsee.eecs.berkeley.edu/~soh/recipe.html

Looking to try something a little different? Try this site which contains links to four Internet recipe sources of Malaysian cuisine.

Garlic Page

http://www.broadcast.com/garlic/

Provides information on how to grow garlic, how to prepare garlic, garlic recipes, the different varieties of garlic, and what makes the variations of garlic special. Also explains how you can use garlic to improve your health.

Good Cooking

http://www.goodcooking.com

Good Cooking features food, wine and cooking with professional recipes, submitted recipes, recipe links, good cooking information, nutritional links, consumer information, fish/shellfish recipes, culinary schools links, food facts, wine links, wine information, free recipe submission, travel information, food definitions, culinary information, fun facts, and brain food. Advertise food, wine, cooking, and travel products.

Hawaiian Electric Kitchen

http://www.hei.com/heco/ekitchen/ekitchen.html

A Web site based on the TV show by the same name. Features Hawaiian dishes ranging from Pineapple-Macadamia Nut Bread to Jellyfish salad. Also contains a link to their Gopher site that contains recipe archives from 1994 and 1995.

Hawaii's Favorite Recipes

http://hisurf.aloha.com/Recipes.html

Aunty Leilani posts new recipes each week for those who like the flavor of the islands.

Hot Roast Beef Sandwiches

http://members.aol.com/donwdowney/HotRoastBeefSandwiches.html

Searches America for the perfect roadside hot roast beef sandwich. Restaurants are critiqued by their roast beef's forkiness, as well as by their choice of bread and side items.

A B C D E F G H I J K L M N O P Q R S T U V W X Y Z

Idaho Potato Expo

http://www.sisna.com/Idaho_Potato_Expo/

Take a virtual tour of the Expo, which is located in the "Potato Capital of the World," Blackfoot, Idaho. Also check out potato recipes and gift items from Idaho.

International Recipes OnLine

http://eden-backend.rutgers.edu/~davidg

Here over 18,000 people worldwide share recipes of their heritage. Visit this page to get just about any recipe you could possibly want and also receive information on being included in the group!

The Italian Food Market

http://www.italianfood.com/

It's enough to make you want to lick your screen. Everything from ciabatta to tagliatelli to soppresata. Get out the credit card because it's going to be hard not to place an order.

Ketchum Kitchen

http://www.recipe.com/

Considering themselves pioneers in cooking, the people of Ketchum Public Relations Worldwide in San Francisco prove themselves worthy with two online cookbooks (time consuming and time cutting), seasonal cooking tips, featured celebrity chefs, and a Dear Sandy column devoted to culinary topics.

Kosher Express

http://www.marketnet.com/mktnet/kosher/recipes.html

A generous collection of Kosher recipes for Passover. Also contains links to Usenet Kosher recipe archives.

La Comeda Mexicana

http://mexico.udg.mx/Cocina/menu.html

Read about the history of Mexican food, and try out recipes for both traditional and interesting dishes from south of the border. This site is available in both English and Spanish.

La Pagina dela Salsa Mole

http://www.slip.net/~bobnemo/mole.html

Mole is a spicy chili-chocolate sauce used in traditional Mexican cooking. This site contains a fairly complete listing of recipes, a geographical listing of where to locate hard-to-find ingredients, and interesting facts on the history of Mole, as well as a list of links to other food-related sites.

Mama's Cookbook

http://www.eat.com/cookbook/index.html

A graphics-rich collection of Italian-style recipes using Ragu products. Contains a pasta and cooking glossary for those just starting out.

Medieval/Renaissance Food Home Page

http://www.pbm.com/~lindahl/food.html

Offers references and recipes for anyone who wants to make a medieval feast or sample medieval cooking just for themselves. Includes references for European and Islamic dishes.

My Favorite Recipes

http://www.ece.ucdavis.edu/~darsie/recipes.html

A personal collection of vegetarian recipes presented in simulated easy-to-follow, bulleted recipe cards.

National Pork Producer's Council

http://www.nppc.org/

Find out all there is to know about "the other white meat," including industry facts, health statistics, pig facts, and the quintessential pork recipe of the day.

New England Lobster

http://www.nelobster.com/

Offers fresh lobster, guaranteed overnight delivery. Provides online ordering through a secure server. Be sure to check out the extensive indexed collection of seafood recipes.

New Mexico Secrets

http://www.nmsecrets.com/recipes.html

Their Recipes of the Week page allows New Mexico Secrets to share with the rest of the world their wonderful New Mexico recipes. Be sure to bookmark this page so you won't miss any of their culinary delights.

Official French Fries Page

http://www.select-ware.com/fries/

Fun-filled information about the world's most popular side dish. Besides the normal uses for french fries (eating), find out the legal specifications of french fries, how to make them, learn about their history, and find out about alternative condiments and applications of the world's greatest snack food.

Pasta Home Page

http://www.ilovepasta.org/

Answers to frequently asked questions about pasta, information about the National Pasta Association and their brands, pasta nutritional information, information about various pasta shapes and which sauces to use them with, and several pasta recipes.

Pedro's Kitchen

http://superior.carleton.ca/~pwigfull/pedro.html

A collection of authentic Brazilian recipes from a self-proclaimed Renaissance man.

Pickle Preservation Society

http://www.ithaca.edu/orgs/pickle/pickle1/pickleweb.html

The place for pickle lovers of all sorts to come together and discuss their gherkins. Find out all sorts of pickle tidbits, including recipes. Also find out about starting your own chapter of the society.

Potato Miscellany

http://www.infi.net/~cksmith/famine/Miscellany.html

Links to a variety of pages that all deal with the potato. Read about new potatoes in Ireland, a better potato, potatoes as dust containment and paint removers, and more.

Prapapun's Hobby Kitchen

http://www.gezi.com:80/gzworld/recipe.html

Traditional Thai recipes with a little cooking humor mixed in. Try your hand as a chef in the guest kitchen where you submit recipes via e-mail.

Ranch Worship Page

http://www.math.grin.edu/~boley/ranch/

Dedicated to enlightening the world about the many values of ranch dressing (sometimes also known as "House"). There is a list of ranch's top 10 uses, and a form for submitting your favorite to be added to the list.

The Raspberry Web Page

http://www.xnet.com/~mego/raspberry/index.html

Intended to be the most comprehensive site on raspberries, this page provides raspberry recipes, general raspberry info, raspberry art & photos, and a variety of raspberry links.

Recipe Archive Index

http://www.cs.cmu.edu/~mjw/recipes/

A master recipe archive collected by Amy Gale ranging from crockpot recipes to ethnic dishes.

Recipes for Traditional Food in Slovenia

http://www.ijs.si/slo/country/food/recipes/

An award-winning site providing recipes for traditional Slovenian dishes as well as some information concerning wine making and a guide to "virtual" Slovenia.

Recipes, Recipes...

http://www.intex.net/~dlester/pam/recipe/recipes.html

This site contains the recipe of the week, recipe links, kid's cooking page, kid's recipe links, and more.

RECIPES—10 Authentic German Recipes

http://www.4-1-1.com/info/minka.htm

Ten Authentic German Recipes by Karin Krumes, translated into English. These are either old family recipes that have been handed down from generation to generation, or are her own creations. Minka Enterprises, Inc.

Restaurant Le Cordon Bleu

http://sunsite.unc.edu/expo/restaurant/restaurant.html

A graphics-rich site from the renowned French cooking school. Offers recipes for seven full menus—one for each day of the week.

Rhubarb Compendium

http://www.clark.net/pub/dan/rhubarb/rhubarb.html

The history and description of rhubarb, how to grow, harvest, store, and use rhubarb, tons of rhubarb recipes, and a rhubarb photo gallery.

Ridiculously Easy Recipes

http://www.sar.usf.edu/~zazuetaa/recipe.html

A collection of easy-to-make recipes put together by college students for college students or anyone looking for the easy way out of preparing a meal.

Rolling Your Own Sushi

http://www.rain.org/~hutch/sushi.html

Learn the Japanese fine art of preparing raw fish as an edible delicacy. Acquire the basic skills with terminology, equipment, and food supplies, or extend your own knowledge with the several different styles presented with graphics and text.

Snax.Com

http://www.snax.com/

A site catering to those who like crunchy snack foods. Sample the audio files and see if you can guess the snack associated with the crunch. Try your hand at some new chip dips, no matter what your eating habits are. Enter the Snax.Com contest and win a T-shirt. If you have time to be a couch potato, you have time to visit this site.

SOAR–Searchable Online Archive of Recipes

http://soar.berkeley.edu/recipes/

Planning an exotic meal? Forgot a recipe to an old family favorite? SOAR can help. The archive has more than 10,000 recipes from around the world. They have recipes for all occasions, religions, cultures, and diets. Come explore this site to plan your next meal.

Spam Page

http://www.rsi.com/spam/

More than you ever wanted to know about Spam, the amazing meat product from Hormel. Includes the Spam story, Spam recipes, brewing with Spam, and Spam haiku.

Strawberry Facts Page

http://www.jamm.com/strawberry/facts.html

An award-winning site containing recipes and everything you ever wanted to know about "the perfect berry."

Stuart's Chinese Recipes

http://www.dcs.gla.ac.uk/~blairsa/Chinese_Recipes.html

An impressive collection of Chinese food recipes gathered from submissions by visitors of the site. Visitors are encouraged to add their Chinese culinary wisdom to the present collection.

TexMex

gopher://spinaltap.micro.umn.edu/11/fun/Recipes/TexMex

Provides a small collection of traditional TexMex foods. A good foundation of dishes sure to please the palate suited for spicy food.

Thai Fruits

http://www.su.ac.th/thailand/fruits/fruits.html

An overview of the many fruits indigenous to Thailand. Learn about mangoes, jackfruit, rambutan, and perhaps the most coveted fruit of all, the durian.

Turkish Cuisine

http://www.metu.edu.tr:80/~melih/recipes.html

Authentic recipes from Turkey. Cooking difficulties range from amateur to expert.

USENET Cookbook

http://www.astro.cf.ac.uk/misc/recipe/

Online archive of recipes collected from various newsgroups. Recipes can be found from a searchable index or scanning the alphabetical listing. Measurements available in metric and non-metric formats.

VNO: Food–Cooking and Recipes

http://yatcom.com/neworl/food/recipes/bytype.html

Offers New Orleans-style cooking including the traditional gumbo, jambalaya, and red beans and rice recipes.

Wild Mushrooms

http://www.ijs.si/slo/country/food/gobe/

Provides information on how to pick, prepare, cook, and eat your own wild mushrooms without making a fatal error. Contains a list of good, and bad and ugly (poisonous) mushrooms, as well as a glossary, and several recipes.

YACB: Yet Another CookBook

http://www.csrd.uiuc.edu/koufaty/yacb/

A large collection of traditional Venezuelan recipes available in English and Spanish. Some non-Venezuelan recipes are thrown in at the end for good measure.

VEGETARIAN & NATURAL FOODS

Algy's Herb Page

http://www.algy.com/herb/index.html

A Netscape-enhanced site devoted to herbs. Provides information about obtaining seeds, how to use herbs ornamentally, enhance your cooking with herbs, and find online herb catalogs.

Dechenne Raw Vegetarian Catalogue

http://www.direct.ca/promotionalguides/drvc

This company offers Raw Vegetarian or Living Food products and services. It includes books, resources and other information to maintain and improve your health.

Don't Panic, Eat Organic

http://www.rain.org/~sals/my.html

A site devoted to the science of organic farming and living. The cherimoya, fruit of the Incas, and reputed to be one of the finest fruits on God's green earth is spotlighted. Provides links to other sites centered on the organic movement.

Earthrise Spirulina Home Page

http://www2.earthrise.com/spirulina/

Offers a natural food product catalog of spirulina blue green algae, green superfoods, and nutriceuticals. Also offers a spirulina scientific reference library. Explains how spirulina is ecologically grown at Earthrise Farms in California.

Garden Feasts (A Totally Vegetarian Cookbook)

http://www.sirius.com/~ice

The Garden Feasts vegetarian cookbook features gourmet menus & recipes, poems of love & friendship, an Albert Bigelow Paine story from 1898, and J.M. Conde's classic illustrations.

Gardenburger

http://www.gardenburger.com/

An environmentally conscious company that offers a healthier, meatless alternative to the traditional hamburger. The site provides recipes, product information, and a searchable database to help you find Garden-burgers, Gardendogs, and Gardensausage in your local restaurants and food stores.

Herbs & Spices

http://www.teleport.com/~ronl/herbs/herbs.html

For the naturalist in all of us, this site provides a graphics-rich index of herbs and spices with recipes and information about growing, storing, and cooking with your own bit of mother nature.

Index to Gluten-Free and Wheat-free Diets pages

http://www.wwwebguides.com/nutrition/diets/glutenfree/

A vital guide for those requiring gluten-free or wheat-free diets. Also contains information and links to sites dealing with the Celiac condition.

Mycelium

http://www.hcds.net/mushroom/welco.html

Everything you ever wanted to know about mushrooms but were afraid to ask. Provides recipes, mushroom anatomy, tips on mushroom gathering, and links to other sites about this deliciously edible fungus.

Native American Foods

http://www.jrthorns.com/FosterFoods/

Order a variety of traditional Native American food products, including naturally grown wild rice, nuts, syrups, berries, and more.

Oils of Aloha

http://www.oils-of-aloha.com/

The Hawaiian source for Kukui and Macadamia nut oils.

Tamilian Cuisine

http://www.cba.uh.edu/~bala/tamilnadu/food.html

Collection of Tamil recipes and links to Tamil/vegetarian newsgroups.

Vancouver Island Vegetarian Association Home Page

http://www.islandnet.com/~viva/homepage.htm

The Vancouver Island Vegetarian Association home page contains their latest newsletters, schedule of events, and links to many other vegetarian and environmentally oriented sites on the World Wide Web.

Vegetarian Celebrations

http://ourworld.compuserve.com/homepages/nanetteb

Vegetarian Celebrations provides gourmet recipes and entertaining tips plus great vegetarian resources from *Tis the Season: A Vegetarian Christmas Cookbook* by Nanette Blanchard.

Vegetarian Country

http://www.vegcountry.com

Vegetarian Country is an entertaining and educational enterprise dedicated to the communication and promotion of the benefits of a vegetarian lifestyle.

Vegetarian Pages

http://www.veg.org/veg/

An award-winning site that is the definitive guide to Internet resources for vegetarians and vegans. If you're curious to see what's online and devoted to vegetarianism, you'll most likely find it here.

Vegetarian Society of the District of Columbia

http://envirolink.org/arrs/vsdc/index.html

Founded in 1927, the Vegetarian Society of the District of Columbia, Inc. (VSDC) is the nation's oldest vegetarian society. It is a non-profit educational organization that seeks to promote the benefits of a vegetarian diet and to unite vegetarians and those interested in vegetarianism in the Washington, D.C. metropolitan area.

Veggies Unite!

http://www.vegweb.com/

A well-designed site for committed and noncommited vegetarians, replete with a searchable recipes archive, nutritional information, a guide to vegetarian-minded events, and links to other vegetarian sites.

Very Vegetarian

http://www.cyber-kitchen.com/pgvegtar.htm

Very Vegetarian is a comprehensive page of Web resources dedicated to those interested in a healthy lifestyle. It includes links to recipes, organizations and even travel sites around the world.

GOPHER & FTP SITES

Alt.gourmand Archives

ftp://gatekeeper.dec.com/pub/recipes

Recipe archive of recipes posts to the alt.gourmand Usenet news group.

Usenet cookbook

gopher://spinaltap.micro.umn.edu/11/fun/Recipes

The Usenet cookbook, available via gopher. The recipes are searchable, so you can find the recipe you need quickly.

More Internet Recipes

gopher://ftp.std.com/11/obi/book/HM.recipes/TheRecipes

A site containing even more recipes gathered from online sources. Most recipes offered on this site are of dishes that can be prepared for general, everyday consumption.

World Guide To Vegetarianism

ftp://catless.ncl.ac.uk/veg/Guide/

An international targeted site providing lists and links of vegetarian organizations, publications, cooking schools, and travel agencies devoted to vegetarians. The most useful aspect of the site is a searchable database, by city, of restaurants that cater to vegans and vegetarians.

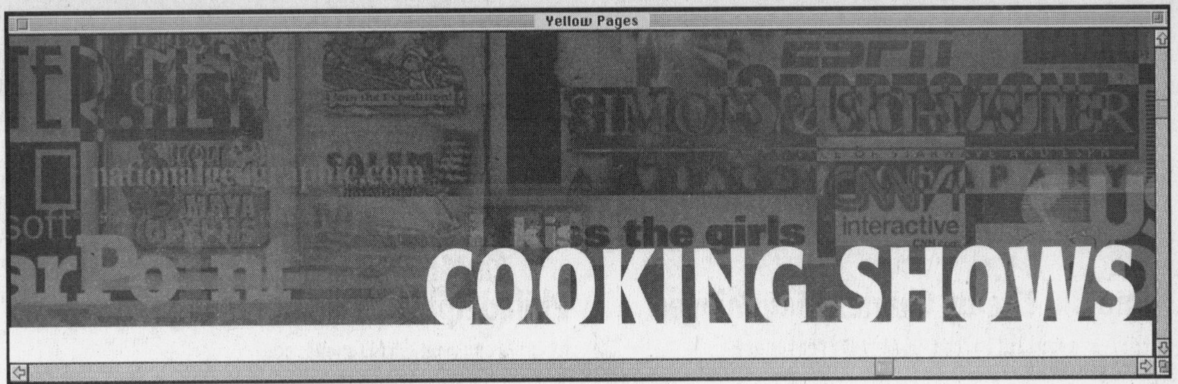

> Cookery is become an art, a noble science; cooks are gentlemen.
>
> *Robert Burton*

5:30 with Jude

http://tvone.co.nz/programmes/jude/index.html

New Zealand home show featuring tips from Jude on cooking, gardening, and crafts. The site lists current recipes (Christmas Mincemeat Doughnuts) and gives links to archives of recipes from past shows (Breakfast Bruschetta with Tomatoes and Bacon).

Border Grill

http://bordergrill.com/

Santa Monica, California restaurant featuring Mexican and Central American cuisine. Restaurant chefs, Mary Sue Milliken and Susan Feniger, host the Too Hot Tamales television show (on the Television Food Network) and the Good Food radio show (KCRW in Southern California). Download a recipe featured on the radio show or in one of the latest cookbooks.

Related Sites

- http://www.gpb.org/gptv/pastprev/oct96/octcook.htm
- http://baking.miningco.com/library/weekly/aa070797.htm
- http://www.channela.com/food/yancancook/yccgroup.html
- http://www.nueva.pvt.k12.ca.us/~akosut/st/l/list/tccs
- http://www.mpt.org/mpt/programming/home.html
- http://www.croninco.com/videochef.html
- http://www.hei.com/heco/ekitchen/history.html
- http://www.ktv-i.com/ktv_release003.html

Border Grill
http://bordergrill.com/

Cooking with Caprial!

http://www.pacificharbor.com/caprial/

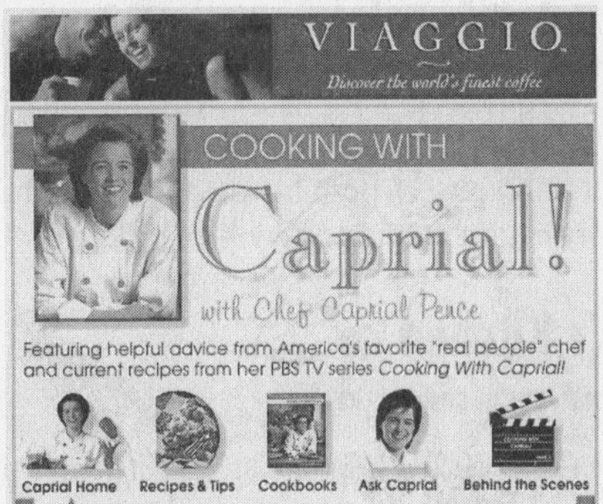

Hostess of a public television cooking show, Caprial Pence shares her best recipes and tips. Find out about her latest cookbook and order it online. Email your important or trivial cooking questions. You can even put her Portland, Oregon restaurant that she runs with her husband (where she also teaches cooking classes) on your travel itinerary.

CyberKitchen Programs

http://www.foodtv.com/programs.htm

Brought to you by the Food Network, this site is a complete resource for those who love to cook. Includes a listing of the network's 19 food-related television programs. Get information on food-related news, dining, and health. Shop the CyberMarket for specialty food and cooking items or ask the CyberChef your most pressing culinary question.

Related Sites

- http://www.asahi.co.jp/aguri/riskyE.html
- http://www.news-observer.com/daily/1997/10/08/food00_side2.html

Great Chefs Online—TV Schedule

http://www.greatchefs.com/tv/

Lists the great chefs and the dishes they prepared on television. You can search for the chef, the restaurant, or the key ingredient to find the information you need to get the recipe.

Honolulu Lite by Charles Memminger

http://starbulletin.com/96/04/17/features/memminger.html

Humorous article written by Memminger, a columnist for the Honolulu Star-Bulletin, about his appearance on *Sam Choy's Kitchen*. This cooking show is taped in Honolulu at Sam Choy's restaurant.

Jacques Pepin's Public Television Series

http://www.kqed.org/fromKQED/TV/jp/

KQED produces *Today's Gourmet with Jacques Pepin* and several other series featuring the culinary expertise of Jacques Pepin. Pepin served as personal chef to several French heads of state, including Charles De Gaulle. Find recipes from his latest shows and a link to information on his new cooking products.

Karen's Kitchen

http://www.turq.com/go-karen/

Karen Claffey is the host of Karen's Kitchen, a popular radio cooking show in Montreal. The show plans to hit the television networks soon. Plan your next meal with the help of her cookbook, *Fast and Fun Food*, or her recipe of the month.

The Malt Show

http://members.macconnect.com/~maltshow/

Access Houston, a cable access television station for Houston, Texas, airs this program featuring micro-brewed beer and single malt scotch whisky. Tour breweries and distilleries, get the lowdown on various brewing methods, learn about home brewing, and visit Houston pubs and beerfests. Check the schedule for showtimes. If you aren't in the Houston area, email your order for four episodes of the show for $15.

Michael's on 40

http://www.mfw.com/moe/on40.html

Broadcasting to Florida's Gulf Coast, this weekly television cooking show features the culinary techniques of Michael Klauber. Not only can you access his recipes, but you can download a Quicktime movie of the show.

New Cooking Shows

http://www.wceu.org/cooking.htm

Highlights the newest cooking shows in the Daytona Beach, Florida area, broadcast by WCEU 15. Gives detailed descriptions of the shows, who the hosts are, and when they air.

Philadelphia Online Cooking Show

http://cooking.phillynews.com/

Online cooking program. View the recipe or download the video to see how it's done. Each recipe gives presentation pointers and nutritional information. Search the recipe database for new dishes using key ingredients as keywords.

Pisto's Kitchen On-Line

http://www.montereybay.com/Pisto/!pisto.html

Chef John Pisto is the restaurateur and television host of *Monterey's Cookin' Pisto Style*. Check out his greatest recipes, his award-winning restaurants (there are four), and his line of kitchen/cooking products.

Television with Nathalie Dupree

http://www.nathalie.com/tv.html

Nathalie Dupree Cooks is a half-hour television cooking show on public television. Her radio presence can be heard on "The Home Cooking Minute with Nathalie Dupree," which is sponsored by Pepcid AC. Check this site for local radio locations. Look up her many published books and find out how to order. Of course, recipes and tips are also provided online.

Vegetarian Country

http://www.vegcountry.com/

The vegetarian lifestyle is promoted on this entertaining cooking show and Web site. Airs on public access television stations across the country; check this site for a station near you. Also included are recipes, a vegan quiz, and FAQs about vegetarians.

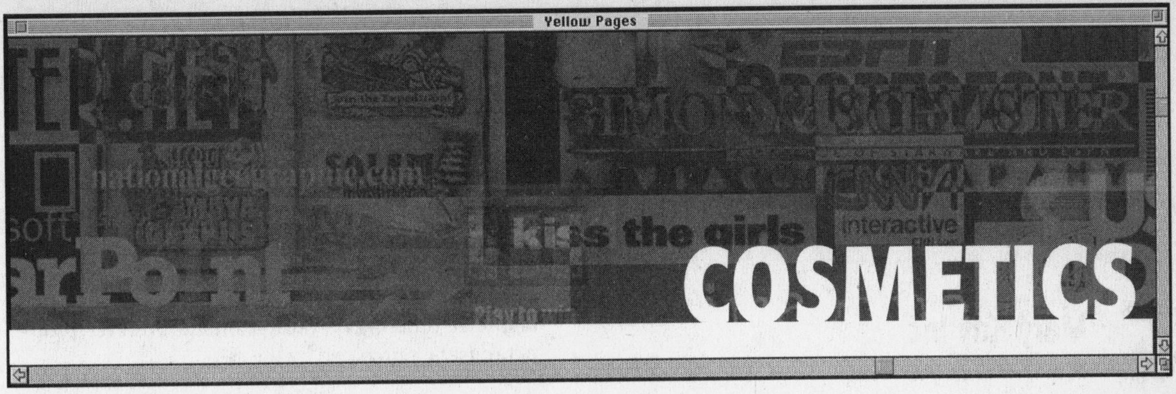

> I was going to have cosmetic surgery until I noticed that the doctor's office was full of portraits by Picasso.
>
> *Rita Rudner*

Arval Laboratories—Swiss Cosmetics

`http://www.arval.ch/`

Switzerland-based biological lab specializing in skin care products. Brands include Arval, Nadja Avalle (made with natural plant extracts), Monitor (offers sun protection), and Arolla.

Avon

`http://www.avon.com/`

Global company selling cosmetics and beauty-related products for men and women. Order from a select number of products online or request a catalog listing all Avon's products. Join the A-List to find out via email of new products and specials.

Bonne Bell

`http://www.bonnebell.com/`

Hip, fun, and innovative line of beauty products. Don't know where to find Bonne Bell products? Check the Where to Shop! page. Some of Bonne Bell's old favorites aren't available everywhere anymore, but you can order them online.

Mary Kay Inc.
`http://www.marykay.com/`

Clinique

`http://www.clinique.com/main.html`

Line of cosmetics sold in finer department stores. Thanks to Macy's Department Store, you can even order select Clinique products online. Get a personal consultation or ask an expert your toughest skin care problems. There's also a bridal guide for brides-to-be.

The Cosmetics Connoisseur

`http://www.makeuplesson.com/`

Book by Twila Shakespeare, beauty advisor. Learn some beauty tips and find out how to order the book.

Cosmetics Links

`http://www.users.wineasy.se/bjornt/clinks1.html`

Links to various cosmetic Web sites from Aveda to Zhen Cosmetics. Includes well-known and not-so-well-known cosmetics companies.

Crabtree & Evelyn

`http://www.crabtree-evelyn-usa.com/`

Fragrances and toiletries manufactured in Europe, England, and the United States. They also sell potpourri, candles, and food items. Buy it all by printing the order form and mailing it in. Or locate stores closest to you; they can be found in 37 countries across the world.

Related Sites

`http://www.lorealcosmetics.com/`

`http://www.shiseido.co.jp/e/index5.htm`

A B C D E F G H I J K L M N O P Q R S T U V W X Y Z

A B C D E F G H I J K L M N O P Q R S T U V W X Y Z

The IMAN Collection

http://www.sheen.com/sheen/iman/iman.htm

Supermodel Iman brings you her own line of cosmetics and skin care. Her Second to None Cream Foundation comes in 16 shades and sells at J.C. Penney and other department stores for about $17.50.

Mary Kay Inc.

http://www.marykay.com/

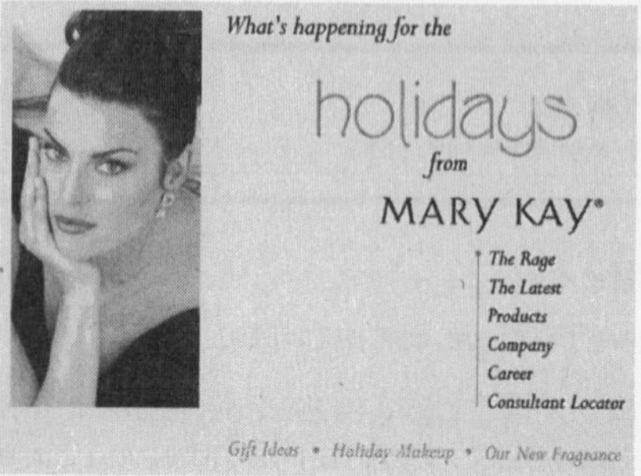

What's happening for the
holidays
from
MARY KAY
The Rage
The Latest
Products
Company
Career
Consultant Locator
Gift Ideas • Holiday Makeup • Our New Fragrance

Offers wide range of skin care and body care products and makeup to men and women. Listed as one of the Most Admired Corporations in America by *Forbes* magazine in 1995, Mary Kay also offers many career opportunities. To order Mary Kay products, use the Consultant Locator to find the consultant nearest you.

Mind Over Makeup—Roxanna Floyd's Guide for Women of Color

http://www.womenslink.com/beauty/makeup.html

Part of the Women's Link Web site, Mind Over Makeup is a regular feature. Makeup artist Roxanna Floyd, who has brought out the best in celebrities such as Angela Bassett and Whitney Houston, shares her best tips and techniques specific to an African-American woman's needs.

The National Accrediting Commission of Cosmetology Arts & Sciences

http://naccas.org/

Independent accrediting commission and national agency for the institutional accreditation of cosmetology schools and programs. Approximately 1,000 schools offer more than 20 programs in cosmetology arts and sciences. There's a listing of accredited schools as well as a job bank for those looking for employment in the field.

NEEM Cosmetics

http://www.neem1.com/index.html

Manufactured by Anthony Pharmaceuticals and Cosmetics, NEEM products help prevent skin against aging, acne, dryness, psoriasis, and eczema. They contain a quality NEEM oil known for its effective fight against psoriasis and other skin disorders. It also has sunscreen and insect repellent properties. Wholesale and retail ordering is available online; however, product must be purchased by the case.

Sandy O's Faces

http://www.SandyO.com/

Site of Sandy Oringer, owner of a personal face design studio in Cold Spring Harbor, New York. Get her beauty advice and receive an online makeover. Send her a close-up, color photo and a detailed description of your skin, coloring, and lifestyle. In return, you get an enlargement of your photo with an overlay of colors you should be wearing. Also receive simple instructions on application and suggestions on hair, eyebrows, frame shape for eyeglasses and more.

Welcome to Lite-Cosmetics, USA

http://www.seniorcosmetics.com/

Anti-aging skin care products. Created for aged skin but found to be effective for sensitive, allergic, and damaged skin of all ages. Browse through their various products, prices, and descriptions. There's also a skin problem question and answer page.

World Wide Web by LANCÔME

http://www.lancome.com/france/cgi-bin/get

This site is as aesthetically pleasing as the beauty it promotes. Lancôme, based in France, manufactures beauty products ranging from fragrances to makeup to skin care. Site offers information on various products and which ones are best for your look and personality.

Related Sites

http://www.skincaremall.com/

http://www.chanel.fr/

http://www.covergirl.com/

http://www.vmakeup.com/

http://www.xmission.com:80/~jafravh/

http://www.vitaminb3.com/beauty.htm

http://www.vitagen.com/beauty.htm

http://www.montero.com/

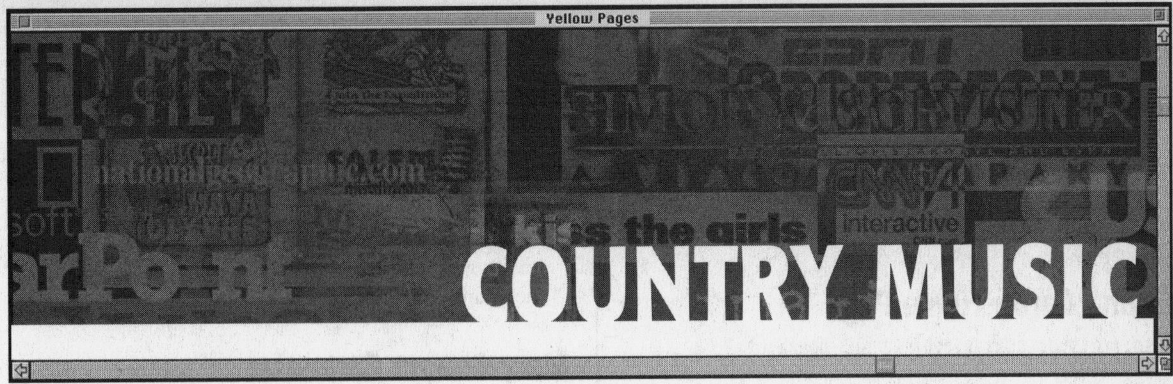

A
B
C
D
E
F
G
H
I
J
K
L
M
N
O
P
Q
R
S
T
U
V
W
X
Y
Z

Oh, we got both kinds. We got country *and* western.

Claire in The Blues Brothers *(1980)*

The ACME Dolly Parton Page

http://www.bestware.net/spreng/dolly/index.html

Chosen by CelebSite as the best Dolly Parton site on the Web. Contains the latest news about the singer as well as many photos, lists of albums and singles, and information about TV and film appearances. Also offers an excerpt from her 1994 autobiography and a link to buy it.

Alan Jackson

http://ajackson.com/

Official site for fans of this popular entertainer. Offers tour and fan club information, and introduces you to his band. Did you know his favorite TV show is *The Andy Griffith Show*?

Basket Full of Country

http://www.hcc.cc.fl.us/services/staff/dawn/basketc.htm

Offers a personal collection of country-related sites for country western music fans and cowboys. Also provides fan club information and a pen pal list.

Related Sites

http://www.countrystars.com/artists/mccready.html

http://www.diamondrio.com/

http://www.geocities.com/Nashville/4244/

NRP TOP PICKS

The ACME Dolly Parton Page
http://www.bestware.net/spreng/dolly/index.html

George Strait Online
http://www.georgestraitfans.com/

Oak Ridge Boys
http://www.oakridgeboys.com/

Randy Travis
http://www.randy-travis.com/

Reba McEntire
http://www.reba.c

Vince Gill
http://www.vincegill.com

Blackhawk

http://www.alasoft.com/chris/blackhawk/

Find out how this band got its name at this site. Listen to music clips and read through song lyrics, or find out where to catch them on tour. You can purchase their CDs online, including their wonderful self-titled debut album.

Brooks & Dunn Online

http://www.brooks-dunn.com/

Provides tour information, the opportunity to order merchandise and albums. Also provides an email address.

Charlie Daniels Band

http://charliedaniels.com/

Everybody knows "The Devil Went Down to Georgia," but there's more to Charlie Daniels than that. Check out his latest album and peruse the timeline of his life. See what he looked like before the beard.

The Clint Black Website

http://www.clintblackfans.com/main.html

See what this dimpled crooner has been up to lately and when he'll be appearing near you. Listen to sound clips, brush up on your lyrics, watch videos, or read recent articles about him.

Deana Carter Home Page

http://uts.cc.utexas.edu/~wonsup/deana.html

This "official unofficial" site provides information about one of the most popular newer country artists Deana (pronounced Dean-a, not De-an-a) Carter. Vote for your favorite Deana song and check out concert reviews.

George Strait Online

http://www.georgestraitfans.com/

Visit the George Strait General Store to pick up items such as pillowcases, ornaments, clocks, and notepads—all bearing the likeness of your favorite hat act! Or you can visit the Swap Shop, read the latest fan newsletter, and chat with other fans. A very complete site.

History of Country Music

http://www.roughstock.com/history

Focuses on influential country artists as far back as the beginning of country music itself. Features history on artists such as Roy Acuff, Hank Williams, Gene Autry, Patsy Cline, Charley Pride, and more. Includes country styles such as western swing, urban cowboy, honky tonk, the Nashville sound, and others.

Kenny Rogers Road

http://members.aol.com/Mixer5000/index.html

He's not just a gambler, he's also a photographer. Read about his flourishing side career, as well as checking out his complete discography, tour dates, and most recent wedding.

LeAnnR.com–The LeAnn Rimes Page

http://www.leannr.com/

This famous teenager made a huge splash with her debut album, "Blue," and her glorious "I-can't-believe-she's-only-13" voice. This unofficial site contains photos, lyrics, a bio (she's now a mature 15), tour dates, and much more, and was created by someone who obviously adores her.

Martina McBride Home Page

http://www.martina-mcbride.com/

Contains many sections of information and clips from this popular singer. The From the Vaults section contains an "internet-only radio production" brought to you exclusively by this official site. You can join the mailing list and fan club here, as well as catch up on news and TV appearances.

Mary-Chapin Carpenter

http://www.servtech.com/public/mrs7764/MCC/index.html

Provides a fan page for country/folk singer Mary-Chapin Carpenter. Site includes a biography, discography, pictures, and links to other related pages.

Oak Ridge Boys

http://www.oakridgeboys.com/

This award-winning group has had members come and go in its 50-year history, but most people know the current members whose hits include "Elvira" and "Y'All Come Back Saloon." Site contains tons of photos, clips, group history, and everything a fan could want.

The Official Johnny Cash Page

http://www.johnnycash.com/

Contains a long, long list of career highlights and a summary of his recently published biography (October 97). Check out the selection of classic audio clips from this legendary country performer.

Patty Loveless

http://www.music.sony.com/Music/Nashville/PattyLoveless/index2.html

Listen to some of Patty's songs, read through her detailed bio, and join the fan club. This CMA Female Vocalist of the Year winner has earned her following by producing hit after hit record. Check out this site to see why.

planet garth

http://www.planetgarth.com/

Provides the latest on country sensation Garth Brooks. Includes tour information, reviews, chart positions, pictures, and downloadable songs in RealAudio format.

Randy Travis

http://www.randy-travis.com/

Brush up on your Travis trivia at this site, which includes both his musical accomplishments and his recent foray into acting. (Did you see him tackle Jon Voight in "The Rainmaker?") Also contains clips from his Greatest Hits Volumes I & II.

Reba McEntire

http://www.reba.com/

The official site for devotees of the country music singer. Links include the album, chat, the book, and off the record.

The Shania Twain Mailing List

http://www.shania.com/

Provides links to vote for Shania's latest singles on various video and record charts. Join the mailing list to receive updates and newsletters about this love-her-or-hate-her artist.

Tim McGraw

http://www.funzone4mcgraw.com/

Become a mcgrawfunaddict (in other words, join the fan club) at this site. Contains all the latest info about this hunky singer and his wife, country singer Faith Hill.

Trace Adkins Official Website

http://www.Nashville.Net/~sarepta/

Listen to a message from Trace or the songs from his latest album. Also contains the usual bio, tour dates, gift shop, and fan club information.

A Tribute to Patsy Cline

http://www.nola.ovik.se/pj/patsy/

Viewers can share stories and memories about this artist who died prematurely in a 1963 plane crash. Read quotes about Patsy from people who knew her, and view the events calendar commemorating the achievements of her life and career.

Related Sites

http://www.bogguss.com/

http://www.cbvcp.com/c2/john.html

http://www.claywalker.com/

http://www.conwaytwitty.com/

http://www.leeroy.com/

The Trisha Yearwood Fan Page

http://members.aol.com/lovntrisha/kedogn1.html

Track the singer's hits as they travel the record charts. Post to the fan page message board and take a fan survey. Also includes current news, a biography, photos and audio clips, and more—all dedicated to fans of this powerfully voiced country star.

Vince Gill

http://www.vincegill.com

Contains information on upcoming concerts and special appearances. You can listen to his latest hit single and read bios about Vince and his band and staff. Also offers the words to many of his hits. Read Vince Gill's thoughts on his latest album.

Willie Nelson's Page

http://www.justicerecords.com/~nancy/arp16.html

This is the official site from Justice Records, Willie's current label. Read about his more than 100 albums and the twists and turns of his long career.

NEWSGROUPS

alt.music.country.classic

alt.music.garth-brooks

rec.music.artists.emmylou-harris

rec.music.country.old-time

rec.music.country.western

LISTSERVS

ALLMUSIC—Discussions on all forms of Music

You can join this group by sending the message "sub ALLMUSIC your name" to
listserv@american.edu

CCML—The Country Music Mailing List

You can join this group by sending the message "sub CCML your name" to
listserv@maelstrom.stjohns.edu

COUNTRY-L—A discussion list for country music

You can join this group by sending the message "sub COUNTRY-L your name" to
listserv@listserv.indiana.edu

Related Sites

http://www.mca-nashville.com/mav/mavalbum.htm

http://www.wbr.com/nashville/dwightyoakam/

A B C D E F G H I J K L M N O P Q R S T U V W X Y Z

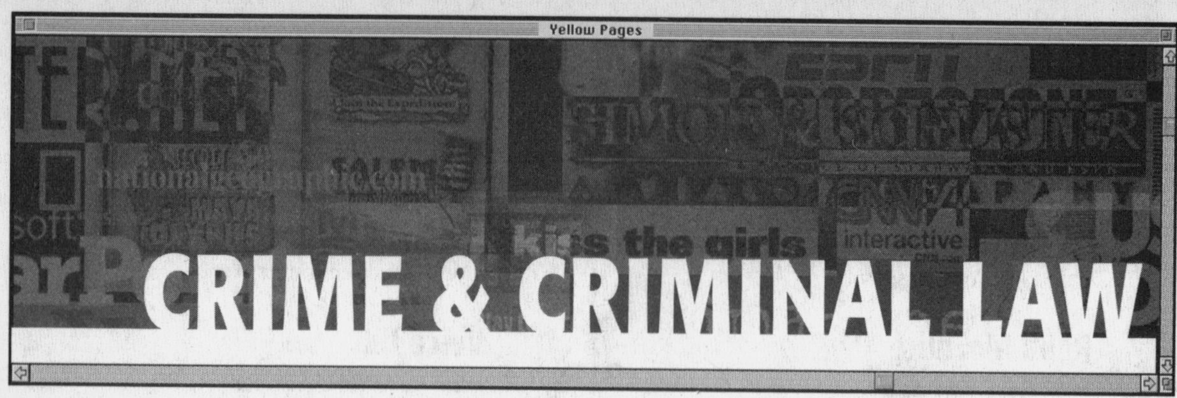

> The real crime is not failure but low aim.
>
> *Robert H. Schuller*

Are You Being Stalked?

`http://www.privacyrights.org/fs/fs14-stk.html`

Learn about state and federal laws against stalking. Includes stalking-prevention tips and security recommendations for stalking victims—including office, home, and vehicle stalking. Includes links to other resources.

Bureau of Justice Statistics Home Page

`http://www.ojp.usdoj.gov/bjs/`

BJS collects, analyzes, and publishes info on crime, criminals, victims, and the operation of justice systems at all levels of government. Read statistics, reports, and surveys on topics such as drugs, law enforcement, prosecution, courts and sentencing, corrections, and expenditure and employment. Check out key facts on trends in crime, Federal investigations and prosecutions, and felony convictions in state courts. Search through the BJS publications alphabetically or by topic. This scholarly-looking site might seem a bit hard to wade through at first, but it provides a huge amount of info.

Related Sites

- `http://www.thomson.com/rcenters/cj/cole/index.html`
- `http://amdahl.com/ext/iacp/pslc1.toc.html`
- `http://www.fbi.gov/ucr/hatecm.htm`
- `http://www.synapse.net/~arrakis/jpp/jpp.html`
- `http://www.icpsr.umich.edu/NACJD/home.html`
- `http://www.missingkids.org/`

NRP TOP PICKS

The Federal Bureau of Investigation
`http://www.fbi.gov/homepage.htm`

Justice Information Center
`http://www.ncjrs.org/`

Computers, Freedom & Privacy Video Library

`http://www.forests.com/cfpvideo/`

This site contains an extensive library of videos that address issues surrounding electronic communications. You'll see videos on topics related to the Internet, constitutional law, privacy, censorship, computer crime, hackers, info-wars, access to government info, surveillance, workplace issues, and medical discrimination. The title of each video and run time are given, along with order instructions.

Cop Talk

`http://www.geocities.com/CapitolHill/3945/`

Read true stories about police work by real cops from around the world. Includes an Ask a Cop section and covers current events in the LAPD. Related articles are taken from the *Los Angeles Times*. Includes links to related sites.

The Counter-Terrorism Page

`http://www.terrorism.net/`

Enter chat rooms to discuss general terrorism, security and personal protection, international law enforcement, intelligence, and counter-terrorism policy. Read articles on workplace violence, recent trends in terrorism, product tampering, kidnapping, assassinations, citizen militias, the Unabomber, Middle-Eastern terrorism, and more. Travel advisories let you get up-to-date info by selecting the country you want to visit—including info on health conditions and requirements for entering various countries. Use the search engine to enter a query and get related info. Includes links to terrorism, intelligence, and crime-related sites.

The Crime Files

http://www.emeraldcity.com/crimefiles/crimes2.html-ssi

Visit this site for detailed descriptions of unsolved crimes from law enforcement agencies around the world. Look at composites of suspects, crime-scene photos, and videos of actual crimes. See police reports and reports of crimes from individuals. You can also report a crime you have seen or know about; rewards are offered.

Crime-Free America

http://announce.com/cfa/cfa.htm

Crime-Free America is a grassroots, not-for-profit group dedicated to putting an end to America's crime epidemic. Crime Forum discusses the impact of crime and explores effective ways of preventing and deterring it. Crime Data offers crime statistics and links to the FBI and Bureau of Justice Web sites. Crime Watch profiles recent news stories of crimes, criminals, and the criminal justice system.

Crime Prevention Initiatives

http://www.crime-prevention.org.uk/

Find online guides to teach you how to better protect yourself, your home, and your belongings. Not intended to replace the need for police officers, but to help them help you.

Crime Stoppers International, Inc.

http://c-s-i.org/world.htm

Find the name and phone number of a Crime Stoppers program in your area. In most cases, you'll also find a TIPS phone number so that you can call with info about a crime.

Criminal Justice Resources on the Web

http://www.fsu.edu/~crimdo/cj.html

This is an exhaustive resource for links and info on criminal justice; you can find national and international links and sources in a variety of areas. You'll find info and links to federal agencies, police agencies, the FBI, the U.S. Secret Service, White House policies, the Justice Technology Information Network, the CIA, the IRS, and the Immigration and Naturalization Service.

Domestic Violence

http://www.s-t.com/projects/DomVio/

Explore domestic violence, its causes, its victims, and some solutions. Includes a special help site with resources for victims of domestic violence. Also includes links to related guides and articles on the Internet.

Ethics Updates

http://ethics.acusd.edu/death_penalty.html

Enter one of the discussion forums. Topics include punishment and the death penalty. Recent suggestions for discussion questions include "Time Off for Informing?", "The Rights and Privileges of Prisoners," "Justice and Money," "Justice and Race," "The Death Penalty, IQ, and Age," "Wrongful Murder Convictions and the Death Penalty," "Executions and Suffering," "Punishment and Chronic Sex Offenders," and "Justice in Sentencing?"

The Federal Bureau of Investigation

http://www.fbi.gov/homepage.htm

Go here for an inside look at how the FBI works. See the photographs and names of the Ten Most Wanted, and get the latest crime statistics. Read all about the investigations that made headlines and much more. This is a very comprehensive and complete guide; it's a great place to visit and stay for awhile.

Fugitive Watch Web Site

http://www.fugitive.com/

This site gives you names, pictures, and info about fugitives from the law and gives you a place to submit tipster information. You'll also read about cases that have been solved. Visit It's the Law for info on topics such as "Living Trust vs. Will: Which is For Me?" and "Drug Testing in the Work Place." Be sure to check out "Busting Up: Tall Tales in the World of Crime" for strange or humorous crime stories. This site also includes a section on missing persons, which offers a database of missing children. Check out the tips on keeping your children safe, and find listings of community and law enforcement services.

Instant Technologies, Ltd.–Missing Persons Page

http://www.instantech.com/missing_person/index.html

View open missing persons reports, or submit a missing persons report. This is a free service supported by private donations and corporate sponsors. View success stories as well. Includes a FAQ and links to other sites.

International Association of Chiefs of Police (IACP)

http://www.amdahl.com/ext/iacp/

IACP is the world's senior law enforcement executive association; it was founded more than 100 years ago. It includes more than 14,000 members from 80 nations and addresses contemporary issues facing law enforcement. You'll find the IACP Private Sector Liaison Committee publications index here. You'll also find a wide variety of literature, such as "Combating Workplace Violence," "Product Tampering," and "Drugs in the Workplace."

International Associations of Crime Analysts (IACA)

http://web2.airmail.net/iaca/execs.htm

Offers communication among police chiefs, police officers, crime analysts, detectives, security personnel, and other people interested in tracking and analyzing crime data in a scholarly manner. The IACA promotes professional standards in crime analysis, provides practical educational opportunities, and creates an international network for the standardization of analysis techniques. Learn about the organization and how to register. Includes an application and bylaws.

International Law Enforcement–www.copnet.org

http://police.sas.ab.ca/

Learn about international jobs in law enforcement. Or, take a look at the soon-to-be published *COPNET CHRONICLES*—a free, online newsletter published by a policeman and featuring articles on law enforcement subjects. This site includes extensive links to police agencies and public services. You'll also find info on corrections institutions, electronic crime, firearms, forensics, cults, Satanism, terrorism, missing persons, the FBI's most wanted, family support, traffic, and more.

Justice Information Center

http://www.ncjrs.org/

This service of the National Criminal Justice Reference Service (NCJRS) is one of the most comprehensive online clearinghouses of criminal justice information. Use the NCJRS Abstracts Database to view summaries of criminal justice literature—government reports, journal articles, books, and more. Get information on crime statistics, gang suppression and intervention, violence, and victimization. Also learn about stalking, sexual assault, preying on the elderly, fraud, victim's rights, drunk driving, and workplace violence. You can download hundreds of reports and studies from government agencies from this site.

Justice Net

http://www.igc.org/justice/

This site is for groups and individuals addressing prisons, the criminal prosecution system, and related justice issues. It's a library for grassroots activists, educators, and people fighting for human rights and social justice. Use this site as a networking tool and a library of info; it distributes regular news, updates, alerts, and analyses about prisons, police, and other justice issues. Also offers on-site training and equipment for grassroots organizations.

Juvenile Justice Home Page

http://www.abanet.org/crimjust/juvjus/home.html

Promotes reform and positive change in the juvenile justice system and gives you valuable resources. Works with ABA entities, bar associations, and local and state advocacy groups to monitor and influence juvenile justice policies and practices. Gives you updates of federal developments, behind-the-scenes insight, and analyses of legislation that will affect kids. You'll find up-to-date info on the latest state legislation, policies, and correctional activities. You'll also have access to in-depth articles on state-level developments and juvenile justice news from around the country. You'll find information on the Due Process Project, which examines causes of inadequate representation, offers recommendations to improve kids' legal services, and provides technical assistance and training. Includes juvenile justice articles from *Criminal Justice Magazine*.

Knowledge is Power (K.I.P.)—Crime Victim Rights

http://ourworld.compuserve.com/homepages/victim/

This home page for a community group in Clarksville, Tennessee offers emotional support and assistance to crime victims. Victims are invited to contact the group, and times are posted for the weekly meetings. Includes interesting links, as well as KIP's telephone number, fax number, and e-mail address.

MADD ON-LINE

http://www.madd.org/

This Mothers Against Drunk Driving site includes drunk-driving statistics and information on traffic fatalities (including statistics organized by holiday and state). You'll find information on arrests and convictions, blood-alcohol levels, and sobriety checkpoints. Read about the research on youth driving under the influence of liquor or drugs, as well as the risks to other drivers and pedestrians. The Hot Issues section includes MADD's reactions and suggestions to the latest items in the news. You'll also be able to read MADD's position statements and goals, and find out how you can get involved with legislation and grassroots campaigns.

The National Fraud Information Center

http://www.fraud.org/

Includes information and warnings against telemarketing fraud, Internet fraud, and fraud against the elderly. Take a look at the latest fraud-related stories in the news. Includes a FAQ and info on how to report a fraud.

National Victim Center

http://www.nvc.org/

Stop here if you have been a victim of crime. This site offers information about what you and supporters can do to fight for victims' rights. Read about legislation and public policy, as well as litigation and legal issues. You'll also find crime-related statistics and links to other victims' sites.

National Victims' Constitutional Amendment Network

http://www.nvc.org/nvcan/

Check here to find up-to-date information on what is being done to preserve the rights of crime victims under the U.S. legal system. Read about the proposed amendment to the U.S. Constitution to protect the rights of crime victims, and use the database to take a look at each state's laws on victims' rights. Read stories from survivors of the Oklahoma City bombing. Includes links to C-SPAN Online, MSNBC, Court TV, and CNN Interactive.

National Youth Gang Center (NYGC)

http://199.44.41.30:80/nygc/

This site from the Office of Juvenile Justice and Delinquency Prevention (OJJDP) includes info on the NYGC and its findings. NYGC expands and maintains the body of critical knowledge about youth gangs and effective responses to them. It assists state and local jurisdictions in the collection, analysis, and exchange of information on gang-related demographics, legislation, literature, research, and program strategies. It also coordinates the activities of the OJJDP Youth Gang Consortium—a group of federal agencies, gang program representatives, and service providers.

NOVA's Homepage

http://www.access.digex.net/~nova/

The National Organization for Victim Assistance works on behalf of victims of crime and disaster. NOVA provides direct services to victims and serves as an educational resource and support to victim-assistance professionals. You'll get information on National Crime Victim Rights Week 1998 (April 19–25) and the campaign for the constitutional amendment for victims' rights. You can also read the draft amendments to the U.S. Constitution for both the Senate and the House of Representatives. Includes an extensive list of phone numbers and web links for crisis resources, and offers training manuals, books, audio cassettes, and info packets for sale.

Parents of Murdered Children

http://www.metroguide.com/pomc/

This organization provides emotional support and information about surviving the loss of a loved one to murder. Members help one another by sharing experiences, feelings, and insights. Includes info on related programs and special services.

Previous Criminal Justice Myths of the Month

http://www.ncianet.org/ncia/myth96.html

Presents a list of myths along with the pertinent info to support the reality. Each month, a new myth is discussed. You can check out all the myths; they are arranged by year and month. You'll find links to statistics and reports to support the reality versus the myth. Previous myths include "Random Murder Increasing" and "More Police Lead to Less Crime."

Prison Legal News

http://www.prisonlegalnews.org/

The *Prison Legal News* is an online monthly newsletter published and edited by two Washington State prisoners. It's geared toward other prisoners, their friends, and loved ones. The articles pertain to prisoners' rights and analysis in America and throughout the world. Includes reports on court decisions that affect prisoners and contains information to help prisoners exercise their rights in the judicial system. Back issues available.

Rate Your Risk

http://www.Nashville.Net/~police/risk/

Take three quizzes to rate your risks. Quiz 1: Are you going to be raped, robbed, stabbed, shot, or beaten? Quiz 2: Are you going to be murdered? Quiz 3: Is someone going to break in and burglarize your home? Answer simple questions to these tests, which use known risk factors taken from executive security courses, police detectives, and security consultants. This site also offers a virtual police academy so that you can see what it's like to be an officer. You'll also see info on self-defense techniques, as well as info and warning signs of domestic violence.

Security on Campus, Inc.

http://www.soconline.org/

SOC, Inc. is a national organization for the prevention of campus violence and crimes. It helps campus victims enforce their legal rights, builds awareness, and increases safety at colleges and universities. Students, parents, and the community will get info on topics such as the date-rape drug and U.S. crime statistics at schools. You'll also learn about the enactment of various state laws and major legislation regarding campus crime. Site visitors may recognize recent laws addressing this issue as changes that have been brought about by SOC activities. Includes many articles and reference materials, as well as links to related sites.

Sexual Assault Information Page

http://www.cs.utk.edu/~bartley/saInfoPage.html

This site provides info on acquaintance rape, child sexual abuse, date rape, domestic violence, incest, sexual assault, sexual harassment, post-traumatic stress disorder, and more. Includes links to related literature and newsletters, men's resources (as victims and secondary victims), and crisis centers. You'll also get info on offenders, self-defense tips, and a FAQ.

United States Department of Justice

http://www.usdoj.gov/

The Department of Justice is here to serve you, so find out what they're doing and what's on their minds. You can link to other justice servers and government sites or explore the different branches of the Justice Department. Use the search engine to explore the Justice Department WWW Server, all DOJ WWW servers, and all federal government servers. Includes a DOJ Web page for kids, which includes sections for Kindergarten to 5th grade, youth (6th to 12th grade), parents, and teachers. Kids get info on topics such as "hateful acts" against different races, religions, and cultures.

U.S. Most Wanted Criminals

http://cpcug.org/user/jlacombe/wanted.html

Includes information on people from the FBI's Most Wanted List; the FBI's Other Most Wanted List; the U.S. Marshals Service Most Wanted List; Drug Enforcement Agency Fugitives; Bureau of Alcohol, Tobacco, and Firearms; and the U.S. Customs Service. You'll also see info on the Bureau of Diplomatic Security Counter-Terrorism Rewards program. Also, the U.S. Postal Inspection Service provides info on people from its most-wanted posters. You can also view wanted criminals listed by state and region or county.

Welcome to OJJDP

http://www.ncjrs.org/ojjhome.htm

Learn how the Office of Juvenile Justice and Delinquency Prevention fights against juvenile violence and victimization and promotes practical solutions to juveniles' problems. Its goal is to prevent youth from becoming delinquent by focusing on prevention programs for at-risk youths and improving the juvenile justice system response to delinquent offenders. You'll get juvenile justice info and resources from around the country. You'll also see contact lists for state agencies and organizations, highlights and contact info for agency grantees, news highlights, and legislation. Includes highlights from and links to juvenile justice-related publications.

LISTSERVS

listserv@vm.temple.edu

listserver@chicagokent.kentlaw.edu

majordomo@law.usyd.edu.au

lists@list.cdc.gov

listproc@essential.org

listserv@weber.ucsd.edu

CJUST-L@cunyvm.cuny.edu

CSPPLIST@weber.ucsd.edu

firearms-politics-request@tut.cis.ohio-state.edu

listserv@indycms.iupui.edu

listserv@indycms.bitnet

listserv@umdd.umd.edu

listserv@umdd.bitnet

listproc@ncjrs.aspensys.com

Listproc@nra.org

prison@hypoxia.hsc.colorado.edu

listserv@unmvma.unm.edu

listserv@unmvma.bitnet

almanac@esusda.gov

listproc@ncjrs.org

bikecops-request@dps.sdsu.edu

LISTSERV@american.edu

copjobs-l-request@ListService.net

listserv@cunyvm.cuny.edu

greg@firearmstraining.com

listserv@cunyvm.cuny.edu

majordomo@tcomeng.com

majordomo@law.usyd.edu.au

listproc@essential.org

listserv@cunyvm.cuny.edu

listserv@vm.temple.edu

listserv@albany.edu

listproc@ncjrs.aspensys.com

listserv@indycms.iupui.edu

listserv@unmvma.unm.edu

majordomo@reeusda.gov

LISTSERV@URIACC.URI.EDU

FTP SITES

ftp://ftp.cdc.gov

ftp://ucs.ubc.ca

ftp://ncjrs.org/pub/ncjrs/

ftp://128.204.33.18/uncjin/wsavail/

ftp://ftp.census.gov

ftp://ncjrs.org/pub/ncjrs/

ftp://128.204.33.18/uncjin/wsavail/

ftp://ucs.ubc.ca

GOPHER SITES

gopher://wiretap.spies.com:70/11/Library/Untech

gopher://gopher.nyc.pipeline.com:70/11/society/aclu

gopher://uacsc2.albany.edu:70/11/newman

gopher://gopher.uchicago.edu:70/11/ustudent/sexab/AcquaintanceRape

Related Sites

http://www.cyber-quest.com/home/ron/home.htm

http://unsolved.com/wanted.html

http://www.ojp.usdoj.gov/ovc/justice/statues.htm

http://www.feminist.org/gateway/vs_exec2.html

A B C D E F G H I J K L M N O P Q R S T U V W X Y Z

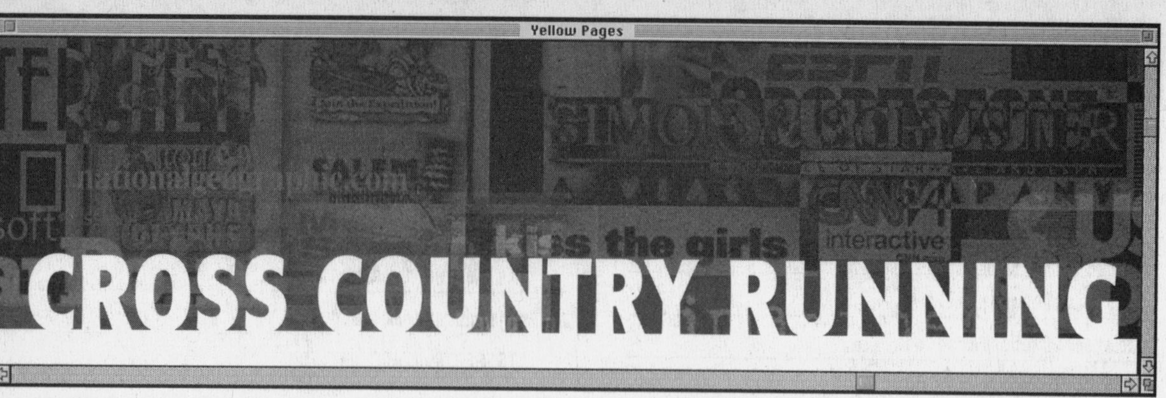

CROSS COUNTRY RUNNING

> He who does not tire, tires adversity.
>
> *Martin Tupper*

Cool Running

http://www.coolrunning.com/

Comprehensive site showing the latest running news, calendar of running events, and race results. There's a Runner's Voice page where a successful runner is interviewed each month (you can listen with RealAudio). Also find out about racing locations and events around the world.

Cross Country '97 at Haney's Shoe Express

http://www.ncweb.com/biz/haney/cross_country/

Features cross country footwear by Nike, Asics, and Saucony. You can view pictures of the shoes and other accessories. If you don't see your favorite shoe, email them and they'll respond. You can also request to be notified by email of any new gear. Online ordering is available.

Cross Country Girl

http://www.geocities.com/Yosemite/4229/

Personal Web page of Chinelo, a college-aged girl from Minnesota, and a cross country running enthusiast. There are links to her favorite cross country running teams, publications like Runner's World, and a list of running rules. Or chat with her in her own private chat room.

USATF on the Web
http://www.usatf.org/

Dr. Pribut's Running Injuries Page

http://www.clark.net/pub/pribut/spsport.html

Dr. Stephen Pribut, D.P.M. (podiatrist) from Washington DC, offers his expertise on various running injuries, how to avoid them and how to treat them. He also shares tips on what to look for in a good running shoe and a good sports physician.

EASYWARE—Software for Swimming and Track

http://bud.dot-net.net/dabineri/

Easy Meet Manager is a software product designed for your track and field, cross country, and road race meet management needs. Send email for more information or call to order.

High School Track and Cross Country Recruiter

http://www.shentel.net/track/

Listing of high school athletes who are interested in running in college. Includes athletes' performances and stats. More than 150 colleges and universities were informed of this site, which gives coaches the ability to view all kinds of information on potential recruits. You can sign up to include your name and information in the database for $14.95. Updates are allowed three times a year.

Related Sites

http://www.coolrunning.com.au/

http://www.cc.geneseo.edu/%7Excountry/xc_coach.htm

http://members.aol.com/mossman4/sihs/xc.html

Road Race Management

`http://www.rrm.com/`

Information, products, and services for race directors and race enthusiasts. Read about what others are doing in the Race Directors' Survey or register for the next Race Directors' Meeting and Trade Exhibit. Check out the Race Director Tip of the Week.

Road Runners Club of America

`http://www.rrca.org/`

The RRCA is a national association of not-for-profit running clubs, the largest grassroots running organization in America. Find out how your club can join. Clubs and events are listed by state. Check out the many programs they sponsor and publications they produce.

RUN THE PLANET

`http://www.dada.it/rtp/`

Operated by *Podismo*, an Italian running magazine, this site lists running events in 530 cities all over the world. There's also a Run the Planet Traveller's Survival Kit where you can find dictionaries of running terms in Danish, German, Italian, Portuguese, Spanish, and Swedish. You can even print your own customized Runners' Travel Pocketbook.

RunMichigan.com!

`http://www.runmichigan.com/`

Resource for Michigan runners. View results for regional, state, and local meets of all levels. Check out marathon results and photos. Look at the race calendar of upcoming events. Search the site for your specific interest.

Running Amuck!

`http://userzweb.lightspeed.net/%7Edoogie1/links.html`

Hundreds of Web site links related to running, including triathlons and races, coaching associations, clubs and organizations, online stores and catalogs, and much more. Also, if you're looking for information on the FinishLynx Timing System for your school, email the Webmaster.

The Running Page

`http://sunsite.unc.edu/drears/running/running.html`

Source of running information found on the Web—running clubs, scheduled running events, chat rooms, information on running injuries, and products such as software, heart rate monitors, and shoes. There's even information on a study that you can join on the relationship between exercise and the risk of breast cancer.

Southern Comfort Hash House Harriers

`http://www.randomc.com/~german/schhh.html`

A club originating in Malaysia in 1938, hashing is a combination of running trails and partying with 20 to 40 other men and women. Clubs exist all over the world and this site's club is out of Atlanta, Georgia. Find out when and where the next trail begins.

Steve Prefontaine

`http://weber.u.washington.edu/~cbeahm/PRE_PAGE/PRE.html`

All about Steve Prefontaine, one of America's greatest distance runners who died a premature death from injuries obtained in a car accident. Check out his stats, his bio, and the movie about his life and accomplishments.

USATF on the Web

`http://www.usatf.org/`

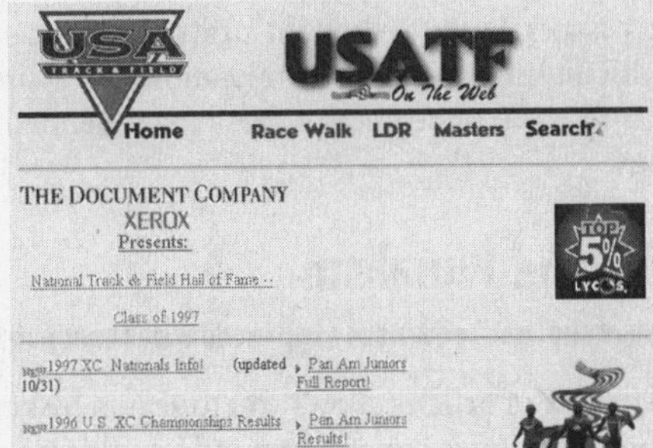

Chosen for Lycos' Top 5 percent of the Web sites awards, this site is home of USA Track & Field, the national governing body for track and field, long distance running, race walking, and cross country. USATF's more than 2,500 members are from clubs, colleges and universities, schools, and other organizations across the country. You can search the site for just about anything related to running: championship results, annual meetings, membership information, bios on today's stars, coaching schools, youth programs, records and stats, and much more.

Related Sites

`http://wso.williams.edu/orgs/track/`

`http://www.csbsju.edu/public.affairs/sju.sports/cross.html`

`http://www.purdue.edu/DFA/athletes/mtr.htm`

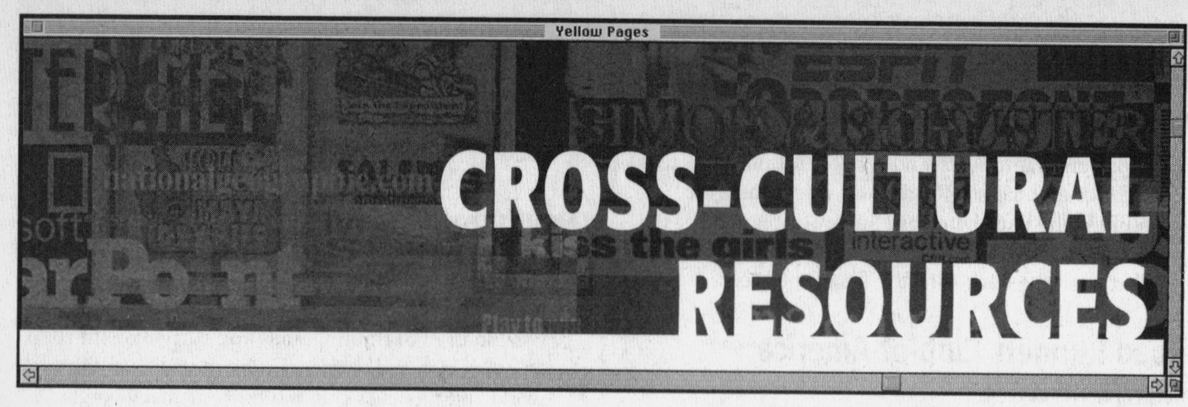

CROSS-CULTURAL RESOURCES

> Don't judge a man until you have walked a mile in his moccasins.
>
> *C. Geronimo*

Center for Equal Opportunity

http://www.ceousa.org/

Think tank seeking to influence public policy to become colorblind. Organization addresses several primary issues. Links to thought-provoking articles on multicultural education, immigration and assimilation, and racial preferences. Gives recommended readings.

Diversity and Pluralism

http://www.msue.msu.edu/msue/imp/moddp/masterdp.html

This database of articles allows you to search by keyword or letter, and is cross-referenced by subject and author. The links are varied and the directions clear, making it a good starting point for information.

The ERaM Programme

http://www.brad.ac.uk/bradinfo/research/eram/eram.html

To find out about current trends in the area of ethnicity and racism studies, take a look at this page. If you'd like to read more, link to The ERaM WWW pages to look at the sources that went into the research you've just read about.

NRP TOP PICKS

In Motion
http://www.cts.com/browse/publish/index3.html

Library-in-the-Sky
http://www.nwrel.org/sky/

The Web of Culture
http://www.worldculture.com/

In Motion

http://www.cts.com/browse/publish/index3.html

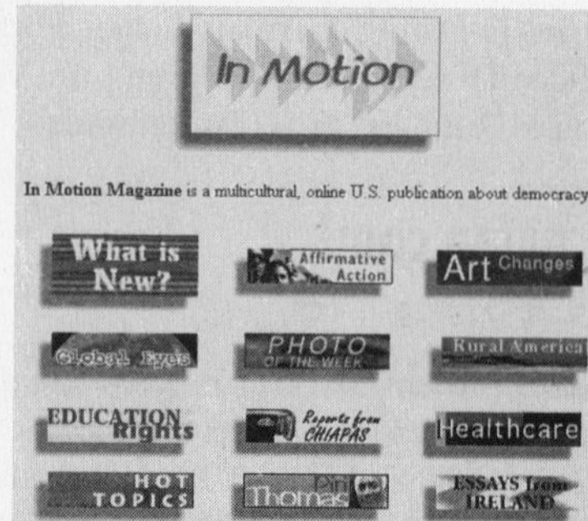

Online magazine promoting social change. Covers the diverse national and international cultures that make up our world. A rich mix of links to places around the world. Lots of photos.

Interracial Voice

http://www.webcom.com/intvoice/

Published every other month to serve the mixed-race/interracial community. Advocates universal recognition of mixed-race individuals as constituting a separate "racial" entity and supports the initiative to establish a multiracial category on the 2000 Census.

Library-in-the-Sky

http://www.nwrel.org/sky/

As with any good library, the contents of this site are organized by the subjects of interest to specific user groups: Categories of Subjects, Emerging Areas and Support, Fun Stuff and Resources. Five access windows reveal holdings for Teachers, Students, Parents, Librarians, and Community. A fun site organized for easy exploration. See also link to Schoolhouse.

Multicultural Media

http://www.multiculturalmedia.com/

Interesting site for finding the music and books of the world on video, audio, or CD-ROM. Each of the thousands of entries are described in a brief paragraph. Indexed by country name from A to Z. Click the searchable world map.

Multicultural Pavilion

http://curry.edschool.Virginia.EDU/go/multicultural

The University of Virginia provides this resource for educators and students with a shared interest in cross-cultural learning and information sharing. Areas include Hypernews Discussion, a Listserv, and the details about working on an international Web publishing project. Online material and links to good stuff for K–12 teachers on the Teachers Corner page.

Museum of Tolerance

http://www.wiesenthal.com/mot/

A high-tech, hands-on experiential museum that focuses on two themes through unique interactive exhibits: the dynamics of racism and prejudice in America, and the history of the Holocaust. Includes info about visiting the museum's 3D site in LA.

National Civil Rights Museum

http://www.mecca.org/~crights/

Take a tour of this Memphis-based museum, which starts from the beginning—Brown v Board of Education—and provides links to related sites.

The National Multicultural Institute

http://www.nmci.org/

Provides a forum for the discussion of the critical issues of multiculturalism through conferences in February, June, and November, and through training and consulting programs.

Ward Hill Press

http://bookzone.com/wardhill/

Book lovers everywhere will appreciate this site for its cross-cultural book selection. Boasts of having won acclaim and serious attention. Links lead to book reviews and author biographical information. Also has a link to books available online.

The Web of Culture

http://www.worldculture.com/

Designed to educate and entertain on the topic of cross-cultural communications. Offers useful info to the student and the educator on global language (and a body language page is under construction), religion, embassies, business and currency, and more.

Weber State University Clearinghouse for Multicultural/Bilingual Education

http://www.weber.edu/MBE/htmls/MBE.HTML

Public-private clearinghouse for educators. Sponsored by the university and participating companies and organizations out of Ogden, Utah and parts of the West.

Yellow Pages

CYBER LAW & CYBERSPACE ISSUES

> My favorite thing about the Internet is that you get to go into the private world of real creeps without having to smell them.
>
> *Penn Jillett*

The Internet Movie Database
http://www.imdb.com/

Computers and Law Web Site

http://wings.buffalo.edu/law/Complaw/

Brought to you by the University at Buffalo School of Law, this lists student law papers that cover computer legal issues. There are also links to other helpful law-related sites.

Cyber Law Centre, Internet Law, Intellectual Property

http://www.cyberlawcentre.org.uk/

Directory of Intellectual Property resources on the Internet. Cyber Law Centre's Recommended Legal Links page is an extensive, alphabetical listing of online legal resources.

Cyberlaw Encyclopedia

http://gahtan.com/techlaw/

Listing of sources related to Internet law and other online issues. Source topics range from Censorship to Spamming to Online Banking.

Cyberspace Legal Issues

http://www.gcwf.com/cyberleg.htm

Various articles and publications concerning computers and the law. Also find links to the full text of U.S. Copyright Law, U.S. Trademark Law, and U.S. Patent Law.

Related Sites

http://www.aclu.org/issues/cyber/censor/censor.html

http://www.cyberpass.net/%7Ex/home.html

http://www.ctr.columbia.edu/citi/cybcompap/citirs.htm

Blacklist of Internet Advertisers

http://math-www.uni-paderborn.de/~axel/BL/blacklist.html

One of several blacklists targeting Internet advertisers who violate "netiquette" when hawking their wares. Provides more information on the issue and advice on what to do to avoid getting blacklisted when you advertise on the Internet.

c|net: the computer network

http://www.cnet.com/

c|net: the computer network, creators of c|net online and the television series c|net central, is an on-air and online interactive showcase for computers, multimedia, and digital technologies.

Censorship and the Internet

http://dis.strath.ac.uk/people/paul/Control.html

Offers a growing collection of links about censorship and associated issues on the Internet. Provides resources on the legal and ethical issues of running a Web service.

EFFweb–The Electronic Frontier Foundation

http://www.eff.org/

A nonprofit civil liberties organization working in the public interest to protect privacy, free expression, and access to online resources and information. Includes many online resources and references. Contains its publication *EFFector Online.*

Executive Guide to Marketing on the New Internet

http://www.industry.net/guide.html

An online paper that focuses on the effects of the Internet on business. Talks about the changing role between the Internet and the marketing executive and speculates on the future on the Internet.

Hermes Project

http://www.umich.edu/~sgupta/hermes

Presents an ongoing research project that is trying to determine the commercial uses of the Web. Offers an online consumer survey for people on the Web.

Information Economy

http://www.sims.berkeley.edu/resources/infoecon/

Formerly called Economics and the Internet, this site provides a collection of documents related to information goods, intellectual property, and related issues. Includes high-resolution slides.

Internet Society

http://www.isoc.org/

The closest thing to a governing organization to be found on the Net. Offers information services, ISOC chapter data, conferences and papers, and Internet standards.

Mapping the Internet

http://www.uvc.com/gbell/promo.html

Presents Gordon Bell, one of the pioneers of the Internet, discussing his views on the direction in which the Internet should now proceed. Discusses his proposal for ending the problems with limited bandwidth and the increased traffic on the Internet. Includes a slide show and sound bites with the presentation.

NCSA Main Menu

http://www.ncsa.com/

The National Computer Security Association is an organization devoted to improving and promoting computer security through NCSA certifications and research. Other on-site topics include finding out if your firewall and anti-virus software are certified by the NCSA; and learning 50 ways to keep your computer safe.

NetWatchers Legal Cyberzine

http://www.ionet.net/~mdyer/netwatch.shtml

A monthly e-zine that reports on legal developments in cyberspace and the online world.

SurfWatch Home Page

http://www.surfwatch.com/

Presents SurfWatch, a program for reducing the risk of children uncovering sexually explicit material on the Internet.

What's New in Japan

http://www.ntt.co.jp/WHATSNEW/index.html

Provides information on recent happenings or recent changes on the Web in Japan. Offers a Japanese language version of the site.

WWW.LAW-CYBER.COM

http://www.law-cyber.com/

Web site of Stephen Sabludowsky, Louisiana-based attorney specializing in Internet and Technology Law. Access recent news, links, articles, and publications on Internet privacy, security, Internet commerce, and Web site development.

EDUCATIONAL & TUTORIAL LISTINGS

Center for the Application of Information Technology

http://www.cait.wustl.edu/cait/

A consortium whose mission is "to be a center of learning in the field of information management and to provide our member companies with world-class educational and leadership programs."

A B C D E F G H I J K L M N O P Q R S T U V W X Y Z

Demystifying the Internet

http://www.udel.edu/alex/demyst/

The University of Delaware maintains this site for users new to the Internet. Coverage includes the history of the Internet, all the Internet tools and what they do, and tutorials that teach you how to use the various Internet tools.

FutureNet

http://www.futurenet.co.uk/netmag/Issue1/Easy/index.html

Europe's leading electronic magazine. Serves as a complete in-depth Internet beginner's guide. Provides information on how to hook up your machine, how to use information to your advantage, and more. Also provides a history of the Internet.

Gestalt Systems, Inc.

http://www.gestalt-sys.com/

Provides links to computer training classes, courseware, educational support, and information for downloading its training software.

Global Institute for Interactive Multimedia

http://www.thegiim.org/

Provides information and guides for teaching people how to create a home page. Divides the information according to the audience; for example, provides a different tutorial for teachers than for business owners.

Glossary of Internet Terms

http://www.matisse.net/files/glossary.html

Lists and defines Internet and computer-related terms and acronyms.

How To Search a WAIS Database

http://town.hall.org/util/wais_help.html

Provides information on how to begin and structure a Wide Area Internet Server search. Describes how to use Boolean operators, wild cards, relevance ranking, and so on. Offers a tutorial on using a WAIS search engine.

INFO Online

http://www.pona.com

Focuses on "Information Networking For Oncologists," and specifically provides information for physicians dealing with networks, integration, and pharmaceutical companies. Also offers information for people involved with oncology, including patients.

INFOMINE

http://lib-www.ucr.edu/

An online library at the University of California-Riverside. Aims to make resources available to UCR students and staff, but is open to the public. Offers many online card catalogs and articles.

Information Management Group

http://www.imginfo.com/

A Windows development and Internet educational and consulting firm offering university courses, consulting, and tips and tricks for developers. Provides links to services and classes offered.

Inter-Links

http://www.nova.edu/Inter-Links/start.html

A site for browsing the Internet and locating specific resources. Features Internet resources, guides and tutorials, news and weather, library resources, fun and games, a reference shelf, and a miscellaneous section. Includes several original search engines as well. Millions of visitors can't be wrong.

Internet Learning Center

http://oeonline.com/~emoryd

Offers tutorial columns and "where to go" columns. Also includes links to the UNIX Reference Center, the Hypertext Guide, Rinaldi's Netiquette, Odd de Presno's Online World book, and other Internet resources. Past columns are archived.

Internet Web Text

http://www.december.com/web/text/index.html

A hypertext guide to the Internet, written by Net guru John December. Begins with Internet orientation and clicks through all the major Internet tools. Highly recommended.

Introduction to the Internet II

http://uu-gna.mit.edu:8001/uu-gna/text/internet/index.html

One of several prototype classes and texts sponsored through the Globewide Network Academy. Introduces the user to various resources available via the Internet, with particular emphasis on allowing a neophyte to access GNA services as quickly as possible.

Kids on Campus (Cornell Theory Center)

http://www.tc.cornell.edu/cgi-bin/Kids.on.Campus/top.pl

The Cornell Theory Center sponsors Kids On Campus as part of its celebration of National Science and Technology Week. The purpose of this event is to increase computer awareness and scientific interest among Ithaca, New York-area third, fourth, and fifth grade students. Hands-on computer activities, innovative videos, and exciting demonstrations help the children develop interest and excitement in computers and science.

Learning Edge Corp.

http://www.io.org/~tle/

Offers products and services to the private and public sectors, including courseware and training, animation, videos, interfaces, and more. Contains links to clients, services, portfolio, and more.

Library Solutions Institute and Press

http://www.internet-is.com/library/

Internet training information and seminars for both students and trainers. Self-paced tutorials including HTML tutorial, K–12 resources, publications, and more.

Magnett Internet Gateway

http://www.magnet.ca/

Links to various Internet browsers and gateways such as software archives, helper applications, Netscape questions and answers, and customer service for subscribers of Magnett Internet Gateway.

Management Concepts Inc.

http://www.MgmtConcepts.com/

A corporation providing training in personal property management, property leasing, grants management, and computer and financial applications.

Provides access to new courses and special events, publications, and links to other sites of related interest.

MicroMedium, Inc.

http://www.micromedium.com/

Check out MicroMedium's Digital Trainer Professional® multimedia computer-based training software for your organization. Already in use by AT&T, MCI, Long John Silver's, and others. Includes links to product reviews, demos, tech support, the MicroMedium training library, and ordering information.

Multimedia Help Page

http://www.sdcs.k12.ca.us/people/schumsky/greg.html

Provides quick access to sources of multimedia tools and tips on the Web. Also provides links and tips for video production, search engines, and production tools for the Apple Newton.

Net Guru Technologies, Inc.

http://www.ngt.com/

On-site training and consulting by certified Webmasters. Some courses include these topics: Webmaster specialists, security and firewalls, UNIX, networking, TCP/IP, and more. If you register online, you will receive a rebate!

Net: User Guidelines and Netiquette, by Arlene Rinaldi

http://www.fau.edu/rinaldi/net/index.html

Offers a collection of Internet user guidelines and netiquette. Discusses legal and ethical issues involved.

Netscape Tutorial

http://w3.ag.uiuc.edu/AIM/Discovery/Net/www/netscape/index.html

Gives a step-by-step tutorial on using Netscape—it can be very in-depth. Allows for different levels of expertise.

Online World Resources Handbook

http://login.eunet.no/~presno/

Provides practical advice on using the Internet to get information or programs. Breaks topics down into various topics, such as how to get free expert assistance, how to read your electronic daily news, and more.

A B C D E F G H I J K L M N O P Q R S T U V W X Y Z

Patrick Crispen's Internet Roadmap

`http://www.brandonu.ca/~ennsnr/Resources/Roadmap/Welcome.html`

This is the Internet Roadmap online training course, available in HTML. This is a well-written tutorial and is very user-friendly. A must for any Internet coordinator's bookmark list!

SquareOne Technology Free Online WWW/Internet Tutorials

`http://www.squareonetech.com/`

Everything you wanted to know about the Internet but were afraid to ask—that's what you find in this beginner's guide to the Net. Ask the Answer Guy any question without fear of embarrassment. Get the basics on using the Internet and find out the meaning behind some of the most common technical terms. There's even a Recommended Software section for help in sifting through the many software options out there.

UK Index Beginner's Guide: the Net

`http://www.ukindex.co.uk/begin0.html`

Serves as a beginners guide to using the Internet, and includes pointers to more resources.

U-Wanna-What Internet Education

`http://www.uwannawhat.com/NetCourse/index.html`

Free, online educational courses that teach Internet and HTML basics to the novice computer user. Learn about the WWW, email, newsgroups, and Net communication. Also learn how to create simple Web pages with HTML.

Winsock Connections

`http://omni.cc.purdue.edu/~xniu/winsock.htm`

Explains both the hardware and software issues concerning setting up your Windows PC to access the Internet. Explains where to get the software you need and how to configure it. Also provides information on creating HTML documents.

Writing the Information Superhighway

`http://www.umich.edu/~wbutler/UC153Syl.html`

Offers information regarding how to write literature for the Internet (originally an online class at University of Michigan). Lets you direct questions to the professors who originally taught the class. Also includes a linked bibliography of other sites.

Youth Quake

`http://emall.com/yq/home.html`

Serves as a destination for computer-literate youth. Plans to cater to education all around the world.

Zen and the Art of the Internet

`http://www.cs.indiana.edu/docproject/zen/zen-1.0_toc.html`

A beginner's guide to the Internet. Offers information on the search engines available and even a section on how to create a newsgroup.

GUIDES, TOURS, & COOL SITE RESOURCES

Cool Site of the Day

`http://www.infi.net/cool.html`

Connects you to the cool site of the day on the Internet, determined by the moderator. This works better than a random-site connector because the sites are more likely to be pretty cool.

George Coates Performance Works

`http://www.georgecoates.org/`

Just a diversional site where you fill out a questionnaire (it's short) and are then matched with a character who most fits your personality type. Your character is described, and you can change characters often. You are encouraged to visit your multiple personalities often!

Glass Wings

`http://www.aus.xanadu.com/GlassWings/`

A site whose stated purpose is "to have fun, help improve the state of the world, inform, provide an interesting and useful commercial site, and have fun (yes, I intentionally mentioned fun twice)." Provides a collection of links and a search site only for fun and nonbusiness-oriented stuff. Includes an online mall where you can buy things, links to humorous sites, and more.

GO! Online Communications

`http://www.jumppoint.com`

An exclusive Internet club of advertisers. Includes links to businesses, professionals, employment opportunities, Kids Corner, and more.

Greene Communications Design, Inc.

`http://www.greene.com/`

A graphics design firm expanded to Web publishing. Greene will design anything for the business, educational, advertising or marketing executive (including letterheads, logos, promotional or educational materials, press releases, and so on). Provides links to projects, clients, and the Internet development group.

Hajjar/Kaufman New Media Lab

`http://www.hkweb.com/`

A small marketing and development company that gives you all the benefits and expertise of a large company. Hajjar/Kaufman will develop your business Web site. Provides links to clients and to contact information.

Handy Guide

`http://www.ahandyguide.com/`

Serves as a complete guide to thousands of sites on the Internet and Web. Lets you search by category or company name, and teaches American Sign Language (ASL) as you go.

High-Tech Investor

`http://www.want2know.com/invest/invest.htm`

Written by an investment and markets reporter at the *Toronto Globe and Mail*, this site discusses investment-related resources on the Web and offers a collection of links to some of those resources.

Hit The Beach!

`http://www.hitthebeach.com/`

If you like the beach, you'll love this site. Provides links to a chat café, the swimsuit shot of the week, a virtual trip to the beach, a beach shop, and food. Register to win a trip to Cancun or to Jamaica, mohn. Also a beach-related search engine.

Hybrid Communications

`http://gs1.com/homepages/dir.HTML`

A virtual metropolis of culture, government, art and antiques, restaurants, public service, business, retail, travel, and entertainment sites. Click whatever interests you.

The Internet Movie Database

`http://www.imdb.com/`

Huge database of movies and movie information. Search by movie title, character name, or cast or crew member. Or the more advanced search lets you search by location, two or more people working together, year, or production company. For the fastest service, choose to search from one of three servers nearest you: UK, US, or Italy. In addition to the database service, read up on the latest daily movie news, browse through current movies in production, and get current movie reviews.

Internet ProLink SA/AG

`http://www.iprolink.ch/`

Provides links to businesses on the Web, Web tools and services, and the "culture café." Also available in other languages.

Internet Resources

`http://www.brandonu.ca/~ennsnr/Resources/`

Contains pointers to more than 100 guides, lists, and indices of documents that help you learn how to use the Internet. Includes pointers to The December and Yanoff Lists, Patrick Crispen's Internet Roadmap (in HTML), The Awesome List, and many others.

Kids World 2000: Cool Sites Just For Kids

`http://www.now2000.com/bigkidnetwork/otherkidssites.html`

Links to all kinds of sites of interest to children. Includes links to Planet Zoom, CyberAngels Internet Safety Patrol, and The Headbone Zone.

Meta-list of What's New Pages

`http://homepage.seas.upenn.edu/~mengwong/whatsnew.list.html`

Offers a collection of links to all the different Internet What's New sites for the Web. By the author's own admission, "the Web is growing so fast that this document can be considered, at best, a historical artifact."

Net Trek Cafe

`http://www.nettrek.com.au/`

The first Internet café in Australia, offering a variety of links and services, including Internet training, a business directory, links to Internet search engines and catalogs, Australian links, outer space and *Star Trek* links, links for kids and music lovers, sports, news media, and much much more.

nicejob Media

`http://www.earthlink.net/~mrnicejob/`

An odd assortment of home pages, including Two Moms Named Alma, An Illusion Dog, Unexplained Art, and more. If you're looking for an interesting site, look no further.

NickNet

`http://www.pinc.com/nburger/home.html`

More than 3,200 links to dazzle and amaze you! If Web surfing were any more fun, they would have to ban it! Everything you could ever want is here and categorized so it is all easy to find. Web addicts beware!

Overall Knowledge Company, Inc.

`http://www.okc.com`

Overall Knowledge Company, Inc. is a general Web presence provider with an emphasis on the film and television trades as well and the arts and entertainment industries. Also publishes several industry-specific directories on the World Wide Web.

Platinum 100—The Top 100 Sites of 1997

`http://www.catalog.com/krs/plat.html`

Collects nominations of the best sites on the Web and then posts their favorite 100. This year's group of 100 was chosen from more than 800,000 nominations sent in from January to November 1997.

Point Survey and Escort

`http://www.pointcom.com/`

Provides a large collection of reviews of Web sites. Rates sites for content, presentation, and experience. Includes more than 1,000 reviews across many categories. Helps you get started on the Web with answers to common questions and guided tours of browsing software and sites.

Sapphire Swan Web Guide

`http://www.sapphireswan.com/webguide/`

Directory of resources on the Web. Choose from the alphabetical listing of topics ranging from Airlines to Yellow Pages.

Thousand Points of Sites

`http://inls.ucsd.edu/y/OhBoy/randomjump1.html`

Sends you to a Web site randomly selected from its listings.

ThreadTreader's WWW Contests Guide

`http://www.4cyte.com/ThreadTreader/`

Presents ThreadTreader's WWW Contests Guide, a complete, current compilation of contests on the Web. Provides easy ways to browse through an extensive index of online contests, drawings, raffles, sweepstakes, and other prize-oriented promotions. Even lets you add your own contest to the ThreadTreader's Guide.

Today Page

`http://www.vossnet.co.uk/local/today/index.html`

Offers a collection of links to sites that change daily; for example, includes links to news, your horoscope, and weather photos.

Unusual or Deep Site of the Day

`http://adsint.bc.ca/deepsite/`

Offers links to sites that provide some sort of intellectually stimulating purpose.

Virtual Tourist Pre-Home Page

`http://www.vtourist.com/`

Geographical guide and directory to World Wide Web servers around the world. For example, if you are interested in Kenyan Web sites and servers, click Africa and then Kenya on the world and country maps.

WebCounter Top Sites

`http://www.digits.com/top/`

Listing of top sites ranked by the number of hits per day they receive. There's a Top 10 list and a Top 100 list. There's also an alphabetical listing and a listing of adult theme sites.

Related Sites
`http://www.bway.net/%7Ehbograd/cyb-acc.html`
`http://www.tigerden.com/junkmail/moreinfo.html`
`http://www.fenwick.com/pub/cyber.html`
`http://www.aber.ac.uk/%7Edgc/munich.html`
`http://www.fcj.com/int-ref.html`

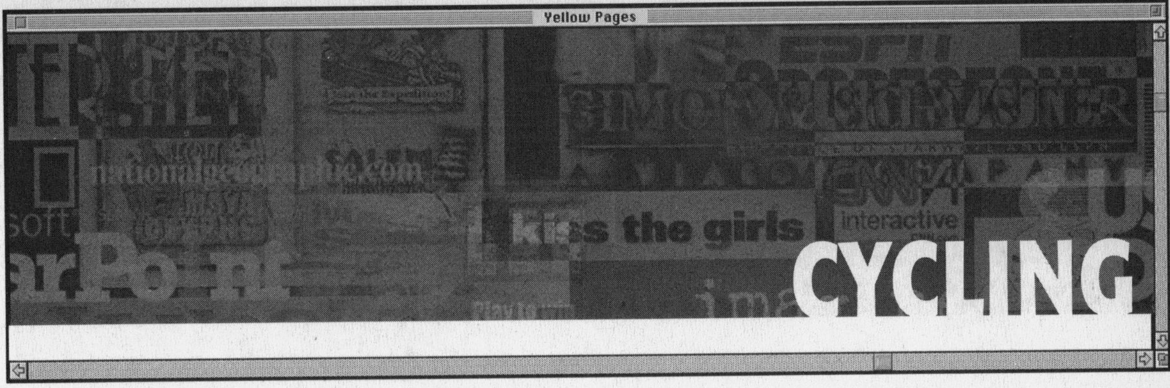

> A woman without a man is like a fish without a bicycle.
>
> *Gloria Steinem*

Cyber Cyclery

http://cyclery.com/index.html

Provides links to cycling manufacturers, publications, tour organizations, and associations for both bicycle racing and mountain biking. Shown in both graphic and quick link formats.

Emory Bicycle Manufacturing Company

http://www.tdg.com/emory/emory.html

Factory direct bicycles. Forty years in the bicycle business. Offers products ranging from beach cruisers to collectibles to mountain bikes.

MuDsLuTs

http://www.mudsluts.com/pigseye/index2.html

Home page of Northwest Mountain Biking. Provides links to maps of the top trails in the Northwest United States as well as updates on product recalls, and direct links to biking suppliers and manufacturers all over the country.

VeloNet
http://www.cycling.org/

The WWW Bicycle Lane
http://www.cs.purdue.edu/homes/dole/bikelane.html

VeloNet

http://www.cycling.org/

Information center for the Global Cycling Network. Provides links to mailing lists of cycling clubs throughout the U.S. and the world. This is a sister site to Cyber Cyclery, listed previously, but includes links for things like BMX racing and Tandem riding as well as links to relevant publications.

The Velonews

http://www.velonews.com

A journal of competitive cycling. Offers news, Tour De France info, and links to other pages. Can also browse the classified section, which lists bikes for sale, clinics, and a calendar of events.

The WWW Bicycle Lane

http://www.cs.purdue.edu/homes/dole/bikelane.html

Similar to other cycling sites in content by providing links to manufacturers and publications. The section on Bicycle Commuting and Advocacy is worth checking out; Bikelane offers links to other popular cycling sites as well.

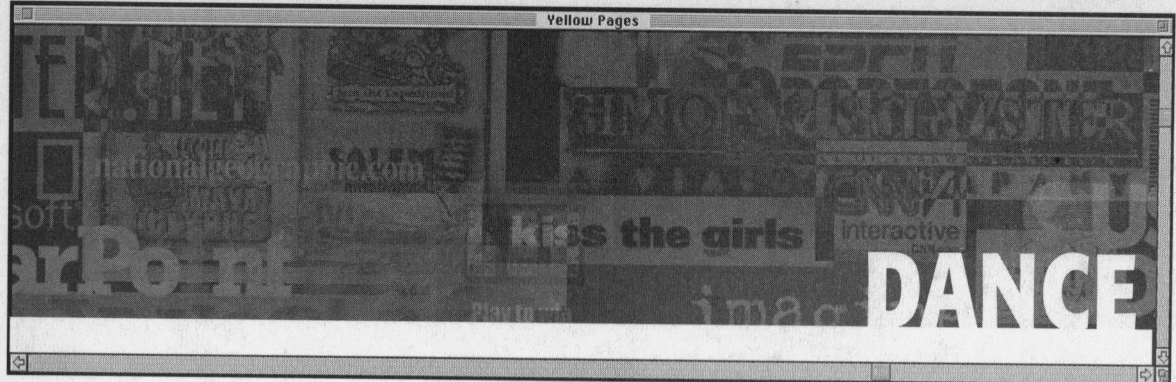

I have no desire to prove anything by dancing. I have never used it as an outlet or a means of expressing myself. I just dance. I just put my feet in the air and move them around.

Fred Astaire

American Ballet Theatre

http://www.abt.org/

An information site for this touring classical dance company. Includes performance schedules, photos, and information about the ballets performed and the dancers in the company.

Ballet Terms

http://www.recruitex.com/dancex/

A glossary of ballet and dance terms.

Ballet Web

http://www.novia.net/~jlw/index.html

A personal Web site devoted to classical ballet. A lot of good stuff here, including an "Electric Ballerina" with short QuickTime clips illustrating ballet steps and movements.

Dance Jump
http://artworks.qtime.com/dance/

The Ballroom Dancing Pages

http://ourworld.compuserve.com/homepages/skeffington/quasar.htm

Includes information about the Blackpool dance festival, variations of ballroom dancing (modern versus Latin American), and links to other ballroom dancing sites. You can order videos and CDs on this site as well.

The Clogging Page

http://www.access.digex.net/~jmangin/clogging.htm

Although not a particularly beautiful site, it contains a lot of pertinent information about clogging. Find terms and definitions, performing groups and instructors, reviews of clogging books, videos, and audio recordings, as well as related home pages and newsgroups. A good place to start for all your clogging needs.

CyberDance: Ballet on the Web

http://www.thepoint.net/~raw/dance.htm

A collection of over 2000 links to dance-related Web sites (classical ballet and modern dance).

Related Sites

http://members.tripod.com/~PHRESHPHUNC/Breakers.html

http://www.angelfire.com/ca/kurrupt209/index.html

http://rowlf.cc.wwu.edu:8080/~n9344199/bd/music.html

http://www.sirius.com/~jstbbs/

http://pages.prodigy.com/bellydance

Dance Jump

http://artworks.qtime.com/dance/

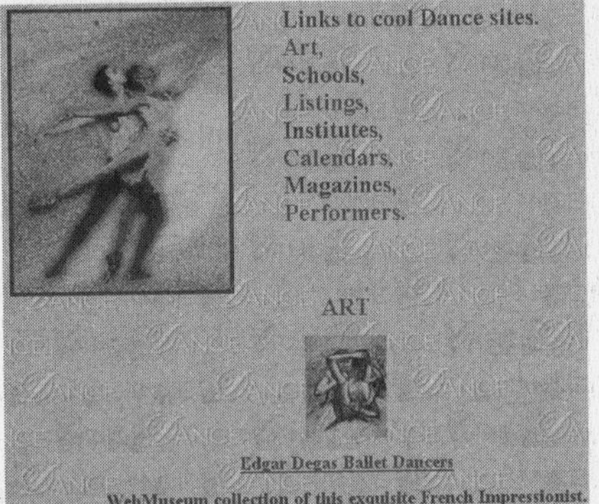

A point of entry that links performers, magazines, institutions, art, and schools related to various forms of dance. An elegant-looking site with a great many links to every kind of performance dancing you can imagine.

Dance Magazine

http://www.dancemagazine.com/

Highlights of the current print issue of *Dance Magazine*, plus links, reviews, and editorials.

Dance Pages

http://www.ens-lyon.fr/~esouche/danse/dance.html

A French site listing many dance companies' home pages, including European pages that it may be difficult to find information about in the United States.

Dance Teacher Now Magazine

http://www.dance-teacher.com/

Samples from the current issue, plus a library of back issues to peruse and writers' guidelines for article submissions. A great resource for any dance instructor.

Dance USA

http://www.danceusa.com/

Calls itself the Web site for the dance industry and includes advice and resources on costumes, choreography, fundraising, competitions, make-up, and more. Slanted more for dance and drill teams and instructors.

Related Sites
http://www.syspac.com/~parker
http://www.doveman.com/showcase/index.html
http://www.well.com/user/cwj/bacds/

Dancer's Delight

http://pilot.msu.edu/user/okumurak/

All about hip-hop and house dancing. Contains descriptions, history, and pictures of different styles of dancing such as B-boying, locking, popping, house, hip-hop, and capoeira. Discusses famous dancers and the international dancing scene as well.

DanceX Dancers Exchange

http://www.recruitex.com/dancex/

An interactive newsletter for dancers, including articles by professionals from all corners of the world and information about upcoming auditions.

Dancing Deep in the Heart of Texas

http://members.aol.com/CactusStar/home.htm

Covers many issues related to square dancing and country/western dancing in Texas and is hosted by two instructor/dancers. Definitions of square dancing, related sites, good nightclubs in Texas, and top ten line dances of the week are just a few of the features at this site.

Dandy's Dance Videos

http://www.infoarea.com/video/dance.htm

Email or 1-800 order these instructional videos and learn how to dance just about any dance you can imagine, including tap, line dancing, west coast swing, ballroom, ballet, jazz, point by point, square, shape-up, Texas two step, and belly. Videos range from $9.99 to $39.99.

Irish Set Dancing in North America

http://www.execpc.com/~jimvint/setdance/

Set dancing is a traditional social dance popular in Ireland in which four couples dance in a square. It usually consists of three to six figures with a short pause between each. This site provides background and history, as well as special events, instructors, and dance studios in North America that teach set dancing.

Latin Music Online

http://www.lamusica.com/welcome.html

All you ever wanted to know about Latin dancing and music, including club, concert, and tour guides for U.S. and Europe. Includes resources to dance classes, books, radio, and TV shows. Covers Latin music and dancing in the news.

A B C D E F G H I J K L M N O P Q R S T U V W X Y Z

List of Ballets

http://www.ens-lyon.fr/~esouche/danse/ballets.html

An alphabetical list of ballets, including composers and brief descriptions.

Native American Dancing

http://www.scsn.net/users/pgowder/dancing.htm

Native American dancing of this style is called Pow Wow dancing. This site covers various forms of men's and women's Pow Wow dancing, including grass, fancy shawl, jingle, traditional, and buckskin dancing. Learn about the etiquette, the instruments (drums), and the songs used in Pow Wow dancing as well. Includes calendar of events.

SalsaWeb Magazine

http://www.salsaweb.com/

Salsa-related information which includes city guides, features and reviews, artist pages, news and events, a chat board, and links to related sites. Boasts to be the largest compilation of Salsa resources on the Net.

Shagger Online

http://www.shagger.com/

Covers Carolina shag dancing, music, festivals, and events. Find out all about shag dancing, shag instructors, DJs, entertainers, and bands here. Contains past issues of Shagger magazine as well as stories and photos of shaggers and shagging.

Shapiro and Smith Dance Company

http://members.aol.com/dancedoggy/index.html

Learn all about this New York City-based dance company that specializes in athletic-oriented artistic dance. Site includes newsletter, reviews, gallery, and schedule of performances. Company is composed of seven members.

Square Dancing

http://www.square-dancing.com/

All you would ever need to know about square dancing. Contains a square and round dancing Webring, which includes resources and links to regional and national clubs, individuals, suppliers, and commercial sites all related to square dancing.

What Is Contra Dance?

http://www.rain.org/~gshapiro/contradance.html

Informational page all about Contra dancing, including various descriptions of what it is, a history and origin of the name, as well as links to other contra dancing sites. Provides advice on newcomers on how to best learn to contra dance.

NEWSGROUPS

alt.arts.ballet

alt.dance.newsba.dance

rec.arts.dance

rec.folk.dancing

rec.music.country.western

Related Sites

http://www.tiac.net/users/latte/lcfd/campfrm.html

http://www.ncl.ac.uk/~nsdwww/

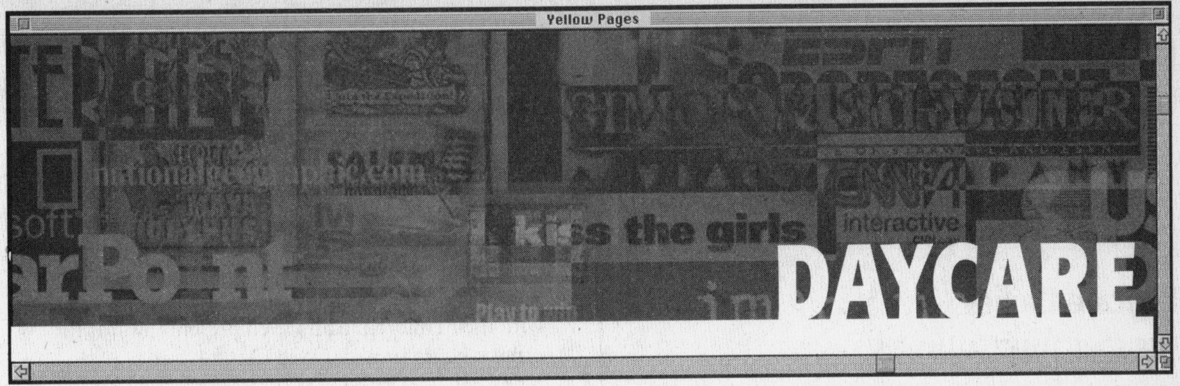

> A three year old child is a being who gets almost as much fun out of a fifty-six dollar set of swings as it does out of finding a small green worm.
>
> *Bill Vaughan*

AFDS, Inc.

Http://www.afds.com/

The American Federation of Daycare Services, Inc. Provides insurance for in-home daycare providers. You can research insurance plans and get an online price quote on this site.

American Childcare Solutions

http://www.parentsplace.com/readroom/ACS/daycare.html

This is an exhaustive listing of resources for daycare providers and parents. The site provides examples of forms providers can develop, how to get accredited, links to toy providers, and other daycare provider sites. The site is sponsored by the ParentsPlace.

Bizzy Bee Daycare

http://www.cyberplus.ca/~bkcooper/webpage.htm

A home-based daycare center's personal page offering many links to educational resources for daycare providers, resources for working parents, and information about the Bizzy Bee center in Ottawa, Canada.

Childcare Directory.com

http://www.childcare-directory.com/

This is a comprehensive site dedicated to providing information on childcare services. The site is oriented around providing resources for childcare providers, au pares, nannies, and home schoolers. A link is provided for software for managing home-based daycare centers. The site also provides a discussion forum on daycare issues as well as chat rooms related to daycare.

Childfun Mailing List Page

http://Prairie.Lakes.com/~mrsrickw/

This is the home page of the Childcare Webring. Webrings are a series of personal pages and mailing lists that bring people with similar interests together. This Webring is used by childcare providers to share information about childcare issues, cooking hints, recipes, humor, marriage counceling, and other child-related issues.

Daycare is for Parents, not Infants and Toddlers

http://www.bconnex.net/~cspcc/daycare/

Sponsored by the Canadian Society for the Prevention of Cruelty to Children, this site explores societal values and other issues surrounding contemporary child care and other family concerns.

A B C D E F G H I J K L M N O P Q R S T U V W X Y Z

Daycare Lister

http://www.daycarelister.com/

Looking for daycare in northern California? This site, geared toward residents (and especially those new to the area), offers a map which locates those centers nearest your work or home.

Daycare Dailies

http://www.daycaredailies.com/

This is a fantastic resource for working parents in the southern California area. Daycare Dailies is updated daily providing a list of daycare providers. The site also provides helpful hints on finding and retaining good daycare as well as a way for daycare providers to advertise their services.

Daycare Providers Home Page

http://www.icomm.ca/daycare/

A superb site for anyone interested in daycare. Established by one provider to share techniques, ideas, problems and solutions, this site offers a wealth of information and resources, including an IRC channel, a variety of craft and activity ideas, and links to a host of daycare-related sites—sites for pre-school development, pre-school activities, daycare businesses and daycare software, and many, many more!

Idea Box

http://www.worldvillage.com/ideabox/index.html

The Idea Box is a site presented to offer early childhood education and activity resources. The site contains an extensive set of educational tools, activities, recipes, and other early childhood learning resources. A parenting message board and teacher-to-teacher discussion group area is also provided.

Kiddie Campus U

http://www.kiddiecampus.com

Kiddie Campus U owns and operates daycare centers in the New York area. In addition to the KCU program and consulting options, the site serves as a primer for daycare considerations and includes a number of "kiddie links."

Laura's Home Daycare

http://www.erols.com/ouremail/index.htm

This personal Web site provides information about Laura's daycare business. It is cute and easy to navigate, providing links to the author's philosophy and skills. The Web site also provides links to fun and games pages, recipes, a seasonal page, and many activities that other daycare providers and parents can do with their children. Laura even presents awards for other daycare provider Web sites.

Monday Morning Moms

http://www.MondayAm.com/MondayMorning.html

This is a company that provides paperwork and management support for childcare providers and their employers. Monday Morning Moms helps working parents find quality care, performs the tax paperwork in support of the care provider, and monitors his or her activities to ensure quality. This site explains Monday Morning Moms services in detail.

Nanny's Room

http://www.erols.com/ouremail/Nanny's_Room.htm

This is a personal Web site of a daycare provider. The Nanny's Room provides helpful links for other home-based daycare providers. The site has a whimsical approach to presenting its lists of daycare provider's home pages.

Related Sites

http://www.childcare-ppin.com/

http://www.geocities.com/Heartland/Plains/1231/

http://www.geocities.com/Heartland/7402/

http://www.fortunecity.com//millenium/falmouth/8/mac340.html

http://www.geocities.com/Heartland/Meadows/2612/

http://www.open.org/kelly/ccpic/index.html

http://www.childrensdefense.org/

http://serendip.brynmawr.edu/

http://ericps.ed.uiuc.edu/nccic/nccichome.html

http://www.indiana.edu/~eric_rec/fl/pcto/menu.html

DEATH & DYING

> Things to remember: 1) The worth of character; 2) The improvement of talent; 3) The influence of example; 4) The joy of origination; 5) The dignity of simplicity; 6) The success of perseverance; 7) The value of time; 8) The pleasure of working; 9) The obligation of duty; 10) The power of kindness; 11) The wisdom of economy; 12) The virtue of patience.
>
> *Marshall Field*

The Bereavement Education Center

`http://bereavement.org/`

Includes the Men's Grief Resource and information on support, resources, conferences and workshops, and email courses.

DeathNET

`http://www.rights.org/~deathnet/`

Offers pages related to the legal, moral, medical, historical, and cultural aspects of human mortality.

DeathNET
`http://www.rights.org/~deathnet/`

International Association for Near-Death Studies
`http://www.iands.org/iands/`

Euthanasia World Directory

`http://www.efn.org/~ergo/`

Includes pages on the Euthanasia Research and Guidance Organization, the World Federation of Right to Die Societies, and acts, laws, and news about euthanasia.

International Association for Near-Death Studies

`http://www.iands.org/iands/`

IANDS The International Association for Near – Death Studies

"Do you remember how electrical currents and 'unseen waves' were laughed at? The knowledge about man is still in its infancy." - Albert Einstein

Welcome!

Welcome to the Home Page for the International Association for Near-Death Studies, Inc. (IANDS).

This page is provided as a service for those who have an interest in near-death experiences; those who have had a near-death experience (or related phenomena) and their loved ones; those who research these phenomena; those health-care professionals who care for the critically ill; those who are seriously ill; and those who have an interest in understanding the nature of human consciousness. Enjoy your visit!

- The Near-Death Experience (NDE)
- If You Have Had a Similar Experience
- If Someone You Know Has Had an NDE

For those with an interest in near-death experiences, those who have had near-death experiences, and those who research the phenomena.

Internet Cremation Society

`http://www.cremation.org/`

Contains links to cremation providers and societies, scattering options, and U.S. and Canadian society participants.

Natural Death Centre

http://newciv.org/worldtrans/naturaldeath.html

A nonprofit project established to support dying people both at their home life and their careers, and to help them arrange funerals. Includes lists of publications and articles.

Sociology of Death and Dying

http://www.trinity.edu/~mkearl/death.html

Contains pages dealing with how people die, death across cultures and time, death and religion, moral debates, and personal impacts of death.

Summum Mummification

http://www.summum.org/mum.htm

Offers ideas on modern mummification, philosophical examination of mummification, and pet memorials.

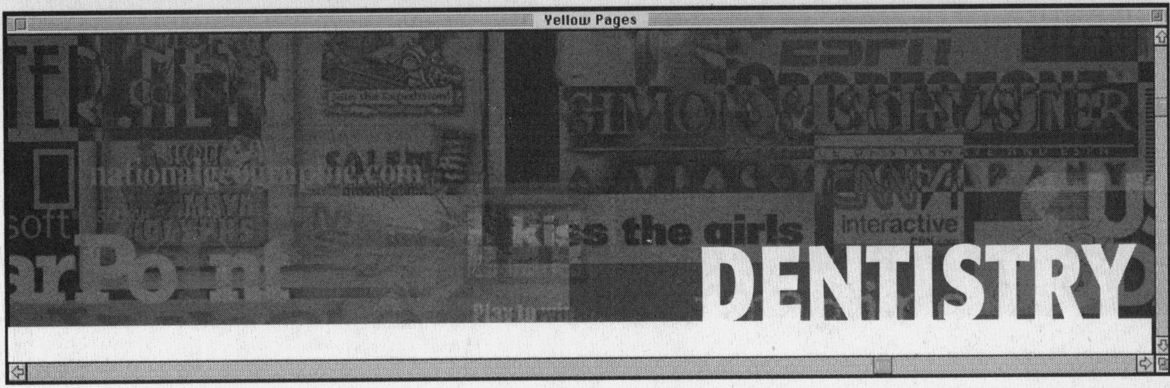

DENTISTRY

> Sans teeth, sans eyes, sans taste, sans everything.
>
> *William Shakespeare*

Dental Ethics

http://ourworld.compuserve.com/homepages/SEYMOUR_YALE/

Seeks to "address the future of American dentistry" through a discussion of modern dental ethics.

Dental Implant Home Page

http://www.dental-implants.com/

Provides information on placing and restoring dental implants. Includes seminars, articles, study groups, and patient treatment overviews.

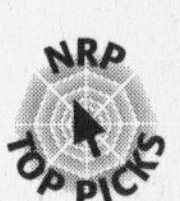

Dental Related Internet Resources

http://www.nyu.edu/Dental/intres.html

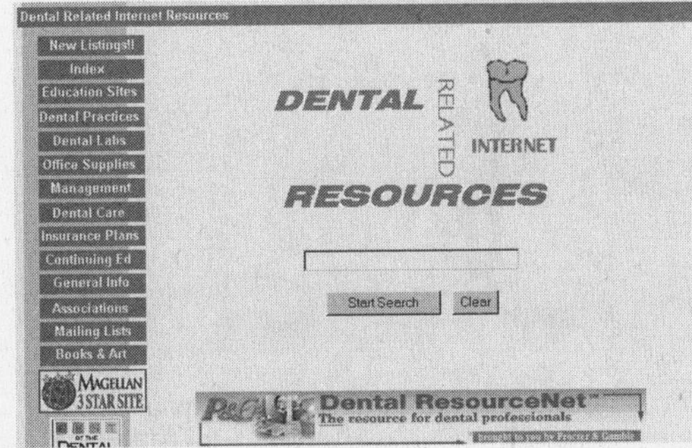

New York University College of Dentistry provides connections to other dental education sites, office supplies, government-related information, and insurance.

Dental Related Internet Resources
http://www.nyu.edu/Dental/intres.html

Frequently Asked Questions
http://www.dentistinfo.com/topics/faq.htm

So, You Want to be a Dentist?
http://www.vvm.com/~bond/home.html

DENTal TRAUMA Server

http://www.unige.ch/smd/orthotr.html

Dedicated to the dissemination of basic and therapeutic knowledge of dentofacial trauma.

Frequently Asked Questions

http://www.dentistinfo.com/topics/faq.htm

A FAQ sheet with in-depth information on such subjects as root canal therapy, crowns, and gum disease.

Mercury Page

http://vest.gu.se/~bosse/MercuryPage.html

At this site you find text, links, and abstracts related to mercury and amalgam as environmental and health issues, and the facts, prejudices, thoughts, and ideas that may be contained in them.

Oral Health Country Profiles

http://www.whocollab.odont.lu.se./index.html

Presents information on dental diseases and oral health services for countries around the world.

So, You Want to be a Dentist?

http://www.vvm.com/~bond/home.html

For those considering dentistry as a career. Covers different types of dentists, how to care for teeth, and how to become a dentist.

DEPARTMENT STORES & MALLS

> I may be a beginner at some things, but I've got a black belt in shopping!
>
> *Phyllis in* Troop Beverly Hills *(1989)*

1Cat

http://www.shopathome.com/

A site devoted to providing you with a one-stop source for free catalogs. Boasts more than 650 free catalogs of products ranging from western apparel to Range Rovers; you are bound to find the catalog or product you want here. Includes spotlight and newest catalog entries.

800 Shopping

http://www.800shopping.com/

The idea is simple: You browse the array of books, music, software, flowers, contact lenses, and such and then order through a 1-800 number. Prevents you from having to give credit card numbers over the Web. Selections are limited.

Amazon Bookstore

http://www.amazon.com/

As close to the real bookstore experience as a virtual one will ever be, you might even get a faint whiff of freshly brewed coffee when you enter it. Books are reported as up to 40 percent off retail prices. If you can't find the book you want, this is the place to go. Searching features include searching by subject, author, by bestsellers, by award winners, or by recommendation of the staff. Includes online reviews. You get the feeling these people love books—if you do too, don't miss this site.

The Gap
http://www.gap.com/

America Shopping Mall

http://www.asmall.com/

Includes areas to advertise, classified ads, and an impressive selection of shopping categories ranging from religion to computers to astrology. Helps narrow your search.

Bloomingdale's

http://www.bloomingdales.com/

Includes online shopping, shopping by catalog, and shopping by personal shopper. The events page tells about upcoming sales and seasonal happenings in its various stores. Get design and style tips from the home design experts page.

The Gap

http://www.gap.com/

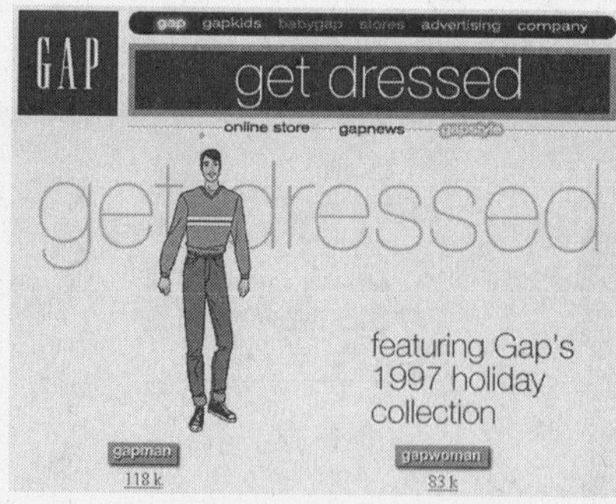

Check out the interactive dolls that let you mix and match clothes from current clothing lines! Includes a store locator, online shopping, gift shop for gift ideas, and company information. As you might have guessed, this site is simple yet cool.

Lycos Shopping Network

http://www.lycos.com/commerce/shopnet/

A good point of entry, this site includes an impressive list of shopping categories as well as special features such as Aardvark, the online shopping experience with gifts for pets and the people who love them, and Andy's garage, gift ideas for men. Find the department store you are looking for from here.

Mall of America

http://www.americamall.com

With a detailed and easy-to-use directory, this mall is inviting to browsers. The site uses graphics sparingly, a plus if you have a slow modem. Shopping areas include collectibles, insurance, seminars, florists, food and beverages, and number over 20.

One Virtual Place

http://www.1virtualplace.com/

A funky site with products relating to computers and electronics. Also has a card shop, a gifts and gadgets shop, and personal care products. The Black Tie flowers section allows you to send flowers to a loved one, online, complete with your personal message.

Registering DOES Have Its Benefits

Having a mall membership sometimes enables you to be eligible for a discount in the stores, so look at the home page before starting to shop. Also look at the hope page to see what types of deals the site can offer you. For example, the World Shop (http://www.worldshop.com), which includes stores from all over the world, not only offers its members a discount on the stores in the mall, but also provides a link to a free stuff page. Changing all the time, this page shows mall stores that offer free catalogs, samples, and provides a link to their sites. Free products, contests and awards, discounts and good deals make online malls great additions for shopping pleasures.

One World Center

http://www.1worldcenter.com/

This is a stylish site that provides a local business locator and a product-oriented search engine. The shopping directory provides links to such categories as famous brand names, art, automotive, health and fitness, and books, to name a few. Somewhat graphics intensive.

One World Plaza

http://www2.clever.net/1world/plaza/shop.htm

Looking for apparel, books, collectibles, gifts for kids, or health and beauty items? Try this site as a jumping off place. A good way to find the unusual or obscure.

Outlets Online

http://www.outletsonline.com/

Provides nationwide information on outlet and factory store shopping. Includes Virtual Outlets, which allow you to order merchandise or request catalogs from online outlet stores. An online magazine and Q&A from other readers let you get in touch with fellow shoppers.

Pier 1 Imports

http://www.pier1.com/

Checking a bridal registry online, applying for jobs, and finding gift ideas are just some of the things you can do at this site. Includes special section for sale items and store locator. All items include prices and descriptions.

ShopFind

http://www.shopfind.com/

A search engine devoted to making your online shopping experience more satisfying. You simply enter items you wish to purchase and ShopFind returns a detailed list of places to start. Site is simple and easy to use.

Target Stores

http://www.targetstores.com/

This friendly site features a store locator, great list of available video games, bridal and baby gift registry, and featured sales. You also can sample new musical releases in the Movies, Music, and Books section or learn about Target's donations to charities.

NEWSGROUPS

alt.business

alt.business.home

alt.business.misc

alt.fashion

biz.marketplace

alt.marketplace.funky-stuff.forsale

biz.marketplace.services

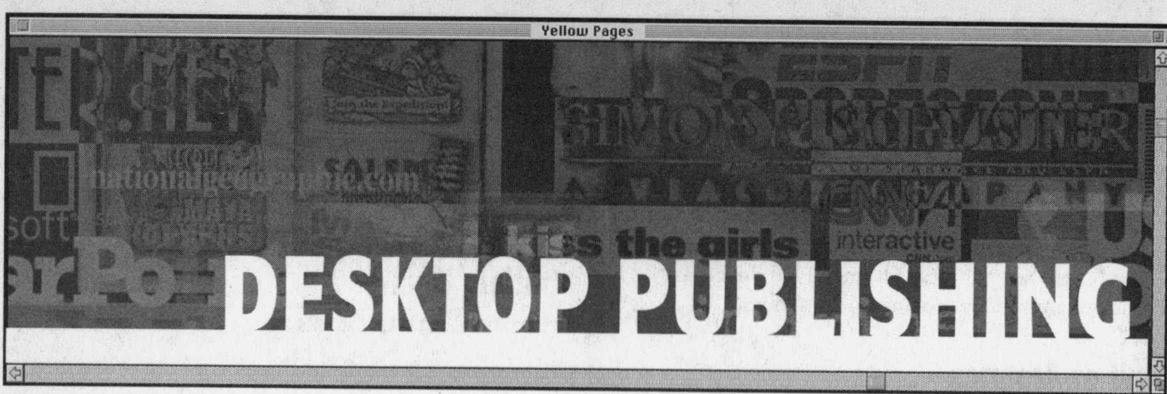

DESKTOP PUBLISHING

> The stroke of a brush does not guarantee art from the bristles.
>
> *Kosh Naranek in* Babylon 5 *(1993)*

Advanced Web Offset (AWO) Homepage

`http://207.67.226.117/awo/content.html`

AWO provides 4-color offset printing services. Their cleverly designed site offers information about the equipment they use, and their cost structure and bidding process, as well as software downloads.

Attention Earthling Type Foundry

`http://www.attention-earthling.com/`

This cool site provides a frame-based way to view fonts that you can order online using their secure purchasing system. Each font family is about $39 for both TrueType and Type 1 fonts. A FAQ is included to explain how Attention Earthling Type Foundry works.

Attention Earthling Type Foundry
`http://www.attention-earthling.com/`

A First Guide to PostScript

`http://www.cs.indiana.edu/docproject/programming/postscript/postscript.html`

An excellent site for desktop publishers and programmers who want to learn more about the PostScript language. If you have been using PostScript for years and still aren't sure how it works, or if you want to learn more about the language, check out this site. Includes topics on graphics, transformations in PostScript, and more. Check out the Funky Stuff link for info on modifying the printout of a document.

Adobe Systems Incorporated

`http://www.adobe.com/`

Download a free copy of Adobe Acrobat or check to see if a patch or update is available for Photoshop or any other Adobe product. The Customer Spotlights page includes articles detailing how Adobe products are used by various companies—a great way to get ideas for your next project.

Avista Products

`http://www.allamericanmusic.com/avista/Avista.html`

This is a fabulous multimedia extravaganza that accurately advertises the work of Avista—desktop and Webtop design. Avista specializes in Microsoft PowerPoint presentations, broadcast and Web-based animations, and musical compositions. The site presents the products offered in a very accessible manner. In addition, there is a large list of favorite links to other design and music-oriented sites.

Boxtop Interactive, Inc.

http://www.boxtop.com/home.html

Boxtop Software produces online brand awareness for its clients through innovative software such as iVisit Web conferencing, Web and print design, and animations. The site is a beautiful reflection of what Boxtop is selling and worth visiting just to see its animations and uses of graphic images.

Fonts Online

http://www.fontsonline.com/html/enter.html

This site is featured in David Siegel's "Killer Web Sites" book and site. The interactive features invite you to try out various fonts and then place your order online. Search for Alphabets, Inc.'s fonts by category, alphabetical name, or purpose. You can also order a CD-ROM full of fonts that you can unlock as needed.

Freedom System Integrators, Inc.

http://southwind.net/fsi/

Provides products, brochures, and tools for desktop publishers and newspaper publishing. Provides links to other desktop publishing pages and college newspapers. Also provides a key word search engine.

i am Iomega

http://www.iomega.com/

Fun site from the manufacturer of the ZipDisk, a removable diskette that is popular with graphic designers and page layout staff. Although your only choices are Cool Products, Tech Stuff, and New Stuff, you can still find out about Iomega's products, access tech support, and read all the news that's fit to print.

Macromedia Software

http://www.macromedia.com/Tools/Fontographer/

Macromedia is the foremost publisher of graphic tools including Freehand, Xres, Fontographer, Director, Shockwave, and now a new HTML WYSYWYG editor called Dreamweaver. This very large site provides contests, white papers, demos, corporate information, updates, and reviews of all of Macromedia's products. The site uses Macromedia Shockwave to enhance your experience browsing.

New World Graphics and Publishing

http://www.nwgraphics.com/

Sit back and pop a cold one while this image-heavy page crawls across the Web. Puts small businesses on the WWW in Spanish and English. Find out how much this service costs, and what other clients have signed up.

Quark, Inc.

http://www.quark.com/

Creates desktop publishing, graphics, and multimedia software applications tools. Includes information about the QuarkImmedia graphics viewer, QuarkXpress publishing software, and other applications. Includes technical specifications, links to related sites, product reviews, and contact information.

Serif, Inc.

http://www.serif.com/

Produces desktop publishing and graphics software and products. Includes a company profile and information about PagesPlus, ArtPacks, and DesignerPage software. Provides product features, reviews, and technical specifications.

The WRITE Desktop

http://www.writedesktop.com/

A commerical desktop publishing and Web design company whose work has appeared in many computer-related journals and magazines. The site contains many examples of the group's work and resumes. Very slick presentation.

Web Developer's Journal

http://nctweb.com/webdev

A fabulous e-zine dedicated to desktop publishing and Web publishing issues. Contains book reviews, tips and tricks, software reviews, links to shopping areas, articles on related topics, and beautiful layout and design.

Related Sites
http://www.desktoppublishing.com/open.html
http://www.ledet.com/prepress/
http://www.vitalnet.com/grav/
http://imalchemy.com/
http://www.sheffieldgroup.com/
http://www.baxsie.com/
http://www.imageclub.com/
http://www.metacreations.com/
http://www.hillustration.com/page1.html

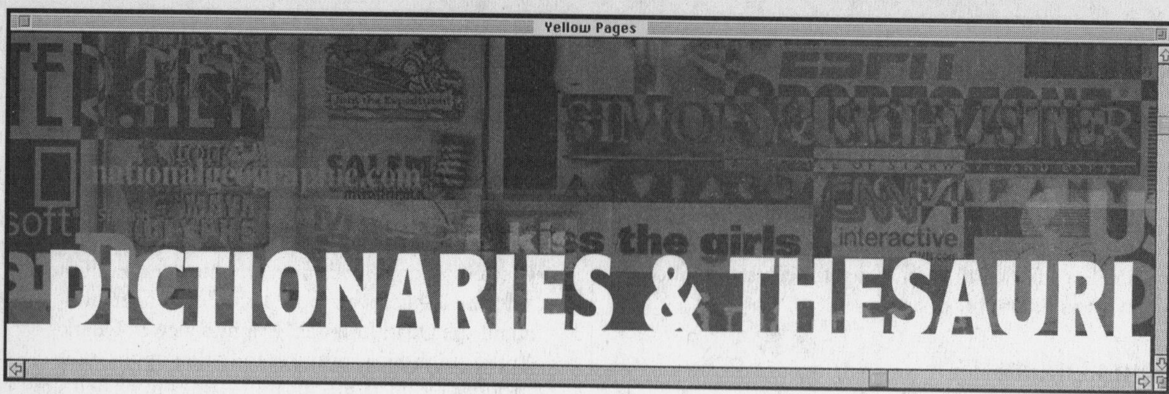

DICTIONARIES & THESAURI

> What's another word for thesaurus?
>
> *Steven Wright*

Acronym lookup site

http://www.ucc.ie/cgi-bin/acronym

Are you bombarded with acronyms and abbreviations every day? Can't remember whether you should call AA or AAA when your car won't start? This easy-to-use site can help you out of your dilemma. Just type in the letters you're trying to decipher and the Acronym lookup site gives you an immediate definition.

ARTFL Project: ROGET'S Thesaurus Search Form

http://humanities.uchicago.edu/forms_unrest/ROGET.html

The ARTFL (American and French Research on the Treasury of the French Language) Project, located at the University of Chicago, has provided this online version of Roget's Thesaurus. The interface is simple—type in the word you want, and the form will return synonyms and antonyms. This site is among *PC Magazine*'s Top 100 Web Sites.

The Astronomy Thesaurus

http://msowww.anu.edu.au/library/thesaurus/

This is an extensive thesaurus of words related to astronomy. Just click a word and the list of synonyms appears onscreen. The thesaurus is available in English, French, German, Spanish, and Italian.

Dictionary of Custom License Plate Terms
http://www.wenet.net/~olivier/plates/index.html

A.Word.A.Day Home Page

http://www.wordsmith.org/awad/index.html

Become a subscriber to the mailing list and receive a word, with its definition, every day. Increase your vocabulary this fun, easy way. The site also contains an anagram solver. Just submit a word you'd like to have an anagram for, and await the results.

The Climbing Dictionary

http://www.fm.bs.dlr.de/misc/climbing/climbing_dict.html

Browse the only dictionary of rock/mountain climbing terms in English, along with translations in German, French, Dutch, Italian, Spanish, Swedish, and Polish.

Dictionary of Cell Biology

http://www.mblab.gla.ac.uk/~julian/Dict.html

Searchable cell biology index. Is the online counterpart to *The Dictionary of Cell Biology*, 2nd ed., plus some additions.

Related Sites

- http://clever.net/cam/encyclopedia.html
- http://www.oclc.org:5046/oclc/research/panorama/contrib/liamquin/baileys/headwords.html
- http://www.june29.com/HLP/
- http://www.notredame.ac.jp/cgi-bin/ej
- http://www.notredame.ac.jp/cgi-bin/spell
- http://www.c3.lanl.gov:8064/
- http://www.geocities.com/SoHo/Studios/9783/phond1.html
- http://math-www.uni-paderborn.de/HTML/Dictionaries.html

Dictionary of Custom License Plate Terms

http://www.wenet.net/~olivier/plates/index.html

Additions 11/5/97: 22, 2LN, 404, 411, 50, 911, L, SQP (a number-heavy night!)

0 = zero, nothin'
000 = nothin' (as seen in IOU 000)
1 = one, want
10C = Tennesse
10S = tennis
10SE = Tennesse
1CE = once
1DR = wonder
1DRFL = wonderful
1E6 = a million (calculator humor)
1E9 = a billion
2 = to, too, two (also start of any "to" sounding word, like 2DAY)
2 = Q (cursive Q) = cue, queue
22 = Tues. (Tuesday)
2DAY = today
2ISHN = tuition
2LN = toolin'
2LY = truly
2M8O = tomato
2N = tune
2Q = took you
2TH = tooth
4 = for, fore, four
4 = replacement for letters 'fo' in many words (e.g., 4ORD)
404 = not found (yes it's gone from esoteric web error code to slang-land)
411 = information
44UM = foresome

An entertaining list of the terms used on those custom license plates you see every day: *EIEIO* on a farmer's car, *GDAYM8* (an Australian greeting). This whimsical site has a dictionary of common terms used on vanity plates and a list of plates spotted (you're invited to submit new ones).

Dictionary Society of North America Homepage

http://www.csuohio.edu/dsna/index.html

This society is dedicated to dictionaries, their history and use. There's a suggested reading list, application for membership, newsletters, and information about the purpose of the Society.

The Free On-Line Dictionary of Computing

http://wombat.doc.ic.ac.uk/

Searchable dictionary of computer terms. Along with the definition of the term, the site also provides hypertext links to the terms in the dictionary alphabetically immediately before and immediately after the requested term. Also includes a list of links to other reference sites—some general Internet reference sites, some specifically computer reference sites.

Related Sites

http://www2.echo.lu/edic/

http://www.cs.washington.edu/homes/kgolden/wordbot.html

Hypertext Webster Interface

http://c.gp.cs.cmu.edu:5103/prog/webster/

A simple way to look up word definitions on the Web. Type in the word you want, click Look up definition, and, within seconds, the Interface returns the definition of the word. For example, a search on "frontier" brought back the word, broke the word down into its components (fron-tier), and provided the definition.

Merriam-Webster Online

http://www.m-w.com/home.htm

In addition to a dictionary and a thesaurus, you'll find a word of the day, a game to play, and other interesting word-related items. Check out Words from the Lighter Side if you enjoy knowing the latest slang terms and their meanings.

OneLook Dictionaries

http://www.onelook.com/

This site works like all the searchable dictionaries, with one slight difference: It searches 188 dictionaries. There are links to all the dictionaries and some related sites.

The Oxford English Dictionary Online

http://www.oed.com/demo.html

This address will take you to the demonstration pages. The OED Online is an ongoing project and is restricted to registered users. There is much to see and do on the demonstration pages, though, and you can register to be on the mailing list.

Roget's Internet Thesaurus

http://www.thesaurus.com/

This is the complete Thesaurus. You can browse alphabetically, choose one of the six classes of words, or type in a word to search for. Then click the word, and receive a list of synonyms.

A semantic rhyming dictionary

http://www.link.cs.cmu.edu/dougb/rhyme-doc.html

Trying to write a poem? Stymied for a word that rhymes with hungry? Check out this page. Simply type the word you want to find a rhyme for, and click the Submit button.

STING software engineering glossary

http://dxsting.cern.ch/sting/glossary-intro.html

Searchable by keyword. In addition to definitions of terms, also provides links to sites with more information about selected term.

The Word Wizard

http://wordwizard.com/

Not a dictionary in the strictest sense, but a site where words are celebrated. You must register to participate, but there are contests with prizes and just plain fun stuff to do with words. You can also Ask the Word Wizard for help with definitions, usage, or word origins.

WordNet 1.5 Vocabulary Helper

http://www.notredame.ac.jp/cgi-bin/wn

This is a simple but powerful site. Just type in a word, any word, and you'll be rewarded with every possible meaning of the word: synonyms, antonyms, hyponyms, coordinate terms…the list goes on.

The WorldWideWeb Acronym and Abbreviation Server

http://www.ucc.ie/info/net/acronyms/acro.html

As simple as it sounds, this site offers a dictionary of acronyms and abbreviations. You can even offer new acronyms to add to their list or request an acronym definition via email if you cannot access the Web!

NEWSGROUPS & GOPHER

alt.usage.english newsgroup

alt.fan.word-detective

mail.wordsmith

gopher://gopher.niaid.nihgov/77/deskref/Dictionary/enquire

A B C D E F G H I J K L M N O P Q R S T U V W X Y Z

A B C D E F G H I J K L M N O P Q R S T U V W X Y Z

How can I find a weigh out before the weigh in?

Bernadette McCarver Snyder

The Calorie Control Council
http://www.caloriecontrol.org/

CyberDiet
http://www.cyberdiet.com/

Weight Watchers
http://www.weight-watchers.com/

Ask the Dietician

http://www.dietitian.com/

Get nutritional advice from Dr. Joanne Larsen MS RD LD. Search the provided categories of questions and answers before sending a new question. Categories include different vitamins, eating disorders, diseases, and much more.

The Calorie Control Council

http://www.caloriecontrol.org/

Contains sections that discuss everything from low calorie sweeteners to trends and statistics. Use the calorie counter calculator to determine the fat grams and calories in what you eat.

Conquer Your Cravings

http://www.nocravings.com/

Site promotes the book *Conquer Your Cravings* by Suzanne Geisemann. If you aren't affected by the dessert names scrolling across the top of this page, you probably don't need this book.

CyberDiet

http://www.cyberdiet.com/

Contains pages on food facts, menus and meal plans, recipes, and exercise. Search the database of foods, use the daily food planner, or assess your nutritional profile.

Diettalk.com

http://www.diettalk.com/

Site was created to provide daily support to struggling dieters. When a moment of weakness strikes, you can always find someone here to talk it over with. You also can gain motivation from others' success stories that are posted here.

FITE—Fat is the Enemy

http://www.bright.net/~fite/

A support and advocacy group being formed for overweight Americans. Excess dietary fat is one of America's leading killers, and this group feels that something needs to be done to stop it.

Gail's Weight Loss Page

http://www.spessart.com/users/ggraham/weight.htm

The sole purpose of this site is sharing. There are no sales pitches, no products to buy, just support. Gail keeps her journal online for others to read, as well as her favorite recipes and a list of diets.

Health Vision

http://www1.mhv.net/~donn/diet.html

Offers links to FAQs on different exercises, diet and food myths, and a "powerful but spooky technique" to help start the diet journey.

Healthy Kitchen

http://members.aol.com/hgourmet/index.html

Provides quick and easy dinner recipes that fit the busy lifestyle of today's families. Have your eating habits and recipes analyzed, or send in your healthy cooking questions.

Healthy Weight Loss

http://www.ComSource.net/~bwelch/healthy.html

Determine out your percentage of body fat and your Basal Metabolic Rate (BMR). Site also discusses vitamins and minerals as well as the benefits of a healthier lifestyle.

Helping Your Child Lose Weight the Healthy Way

http://members.aol.com/diet4child/healthyway/index.html

Site supports the above-titled book, which helps parents deal with their children's weight and health issues. Provides fat-lowering strategies aimed at kids and suggests snack alternatives.

International No Diet Day

http://www.fatso.com/fatgirl/largesse/indd/

An informational page about the holiday. Designed to warn people about the dangers of obsessive and compulsive dieting. INDD aims to make people feel good about themselves no matter what size they are.

Largesse: The Network for Size Esteem

http://www.fatso.com/fatgirl/largesse

A feminist resource center and clearinghouse for non-diet and size rights communities worldwide.

Light Cooking

http://www.lightcooking.com/

A great place to swap recipes with others. Site posts a Recipe of the Week and a Tip of the Day. Also provides an indexed archive of past recipes and tips. There also is a kids' cooking corner and a place to convert your recipes.

Low-Fat Living

http://www.xe.net/lowfat/

Join the mailing list to receive free low-fat recipes by email. Site contains book reviews, tips for dining out, articles, recipes, and more.

Magic of Believing

http://www.geocities.com/Athens/1953/

Provides information on joining Magic of Believing, a support group that discusses diets, obesity, medical advances, fitness, and nutrition.

The Magic of Believing

http://www.swlink.net/~colonel/morris2.html

A nonprofit group of individuals dedicated to supporting those who are overweight. Membership is free and includes a forum for sharing strategies and methodologies for weight loss, as well as giving and getting emotional support.

Medical Sciences Bulletin

http://pharminfo.com/pubs/msb/seroton.html

Reprint of an article on serotonin and eating disorders.

Modern Methods—Fat Burning Specialists

http://fatloss.com/dd.htm

Provides background information on metabolism and how your body burns fat. After you are given the background information, you are granted the opportunity to purchase the diet plan claimed to be the "most effective fat burning diet ever."

Michael D. Myers MD Inc./Myers Information Services

http://www.weight.com/

Written by a physician, this page contains overviews of eating disorders, treatments and current topics related to obesity, and obesity-related medical conditions.

MSO Weight Management Information Page

http://www.drrossfox.com/

This site, sponsored by the Medical Services Organization, L.L.C, describes its surgical weight loss program and procedures for obese people. Qualifying criteria and other issues are discussed, and success stories are displayed.

Nourish Net

http://www.nourishnet.com/index.html

Join the Nourish Net Club for personal weight tracking or just peruse the site for new ideas. This group recommends keeping daily logs and provides several samples. Also provides weight charts to see where you stand.

Nutri/System Online

http://www.nutrisystem.com/

At Nutri/System's Web site, you can read about the features and benefits of joining, read testimonies from clients who have had success with Nutri/System, find out where the centers are located, and sign up for free stuff.

Physicians Weight Loss Centers

http://www.pwlc.com/

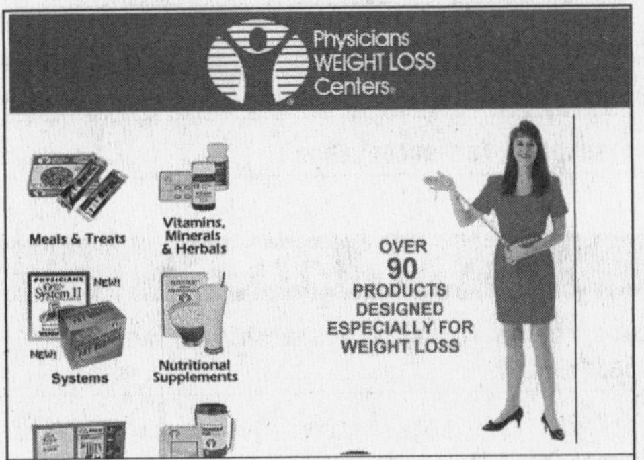

Describes the systems available through these centers as well as the meals and treats. Also discusses vitamins and minerals and other nutritional supplements. Motivational books and tapes are also provided.

The Science of Weight Management

http://www.DrOliver.com/

This site provides a daily column written by David Oliver, Ph.D. Previous columns are archived for review and readers can submit topic suggestions.

Stop the Insanity Home Page

http://www.susanpowter.com/

Discusses Susan's latest book and vitamin program as well as her radio show. Also provides access to a Susan Powter chat room for new ideas, recipes, and information.

Tell-Me-Y, Inc.

http://www.cnct.com/~tellmey/

Provides the phone number for The Solution Hotline, a charge-per-minute connection to discussions of topics including hypnotherapy and food addiction.

TOPS—Take Off Pounds Sensibly

http://www3.ns.sympatico.ca/stoner/tops.html

An unofficial TOPS page created by one of its members. Included is information on how and why to join TOPS, nifty ideas for TOPS programs, information on TOPS retreats, and more.

Weight Loss Control Center Home Page

http://www.arbon.com/weight/home.htm

Features a tip of the day and a newsletter to which you can subscribe. Past tips are archived for reference. Also provides a link to another diet page.

Weight Management Centers

http://www.weightmanagement.com/

Site offers a history of the company and biographies of staff professionals. Also includes information about bariatric medicine and the health risks of obesity.

Weight Watchers

http://www.weight-watchers.com/

The online page of the popular weight loss program. Gives information about Weight Watchers and its many plans. Also includes an interactive portion where users can read and post success stories, challenges & solutions, exercise, and recipes.

The Yo-Yo Diet Syndrome

http://www.hayhouse.com/books/yoyo.htm

Site provides the outline of this book by Doreen Virtue, Ph.D. Also includes part the introduction and a description of the book's intended audience.

The Zone Files

http://www.enterthezone.com/

From best-selling author Dr. Barry Sears, this site continues what his controversial books started. It defines and discusses the Zone and how to stay in it. Testimonials are provided and research news is posted.

A B C D E F G H I J K L M N O P Q R S T U V W X Y Z

LISTSERVS

ATKINS-NEW—New Diet Revolution List
You can join this group by sending the message "sub ATKINS-NEW your name" to
listserv@maelstrom.stjohns.edu

CADIS—CADIS Carbohydrate Addicts Diet Information & Support
You can join this group by sending the message "sub CADIS your name" to
listserv@maelstrom.stjohns.edu

EAT-DIS—EAT-DIS Eating Disorders List
You can join this group by sending the message "sub EAT-DIS your name" to
listserv@maelstrom.stjohns.edu

FIT-L—Exercise/Diet/Wellness List
You can join this group by sending the message "sub FIT-L your name" to
listserv@etsuadmn.bitnet

FOODTALK—Read it... Do it: Food, Nutrition, Food Safety
You can join this group by sending the message "sub FOODTALK your name" to
listserv@unlvm.unl.edu

NLC—NLC The Net Loss Club, weight-loss support group
You can join this group by sending the message "sub NLC your name" to
listserv@maelstrom.stjohns.edu

NUTCOM-L—AABP Nutrition Committee
You can join this group by sending the message "sub NUTCOM-L your name" to
listserv@uga.cc.uga.edu

PALEOFOOD—Paleolithic Eating Support List
You can join this group by sending the message "sub PALEOFOOD your name" to
listserv@maelstrom.stjohns.edu

RAW-FOOD—Raw Food Diet Support List
You can join this group by sending the message "sub RAW-FOOD your name" to
listserv@maelstrom.stjohns.edu

SCD—Specific Carbohydrate Diet List
You can join this group by sending the message "sub SCD your name" to
listserv@maelstrom.stjohns.edu

Related Sites

http://dmi-www.mc.duke.edu/dfc/home.html

http://KingsFans.com/clinic.htm

WELLNESS—Lifetime wellness program planning and discussion
You can join this group by sending the message "sub WELLNESS your name" to
listserv@list.uvm.edu

WELLNESS—Support Group for Wellness
You can join this group by sending the message "sub WELLNESS your name" to
listserv@msu.edu

NEWSGROUPS

alt.food.fat-free

alt.food.low-fat

alt.personals.fat

alt.sex.weight-gain

alt.support.big-folks

alt.support.diet

alt.support.obesity

sci.med.nutrition

soc.support.fat-acceptance

FTP SITES

ftp://ftp.cs.columbia.edu/archives/faq/alt/support/diet

ftp://ftp.csie.nctu.edu.tw /Documents/FAQ/alt/support/diet

ftp://ftp.gwu.edu/pub/rtfm/alt/support/diet

ftp://ftp.rediris.es/docs/faq/alt/support/diet

ftp://ftp.sinica.edu.tw/doc/USENET-FAQ/alt/support/diet

ftp://ftp.uni-paderborn.de/ftp/disk1/doc/faq/sci/med/nutrition

ftp://ftp.vhdl.org/eda/diet

ftp://ftp.webcom.com/pub4/ns/www/weightloss.html

GOPHER

American Heart Association
gopher://gopher.amhrt.org/

Related Sites

http://www.bearware.net/clinique-nutrition/

http://www.carbohydrateaddicts.com/

http://www.fatfree.com/

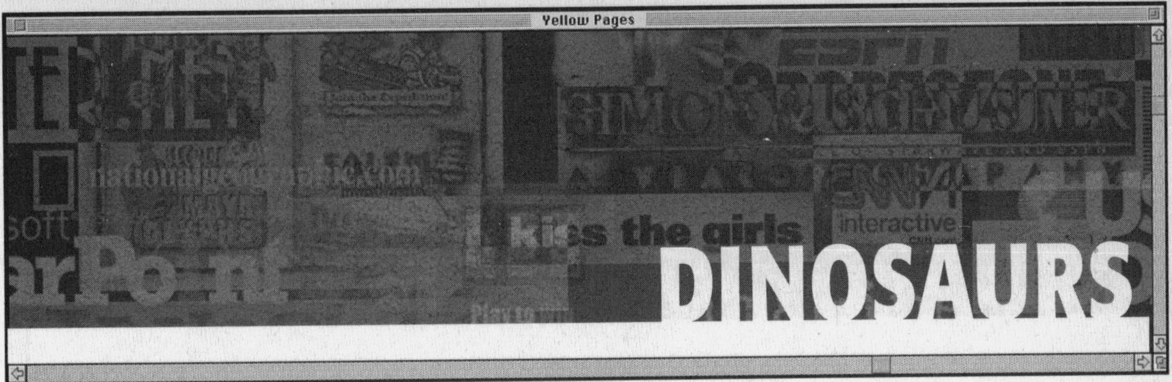

The Dodo never had a chance. He seems to have been invented for the sole purpose of becoming extinct and that was all he was good for.

Will Cuppy

Dinosaur Fact Sheet

http://www.slsc.org/docs/mod3/mod3_2/mod3_22/ep2538g.htm

The St. Louis Science Center maintains this site filled with great graphics and easy-to-understand information on the amazing dinosaurs. Great fun.

Dinofest '98: The World's Fair of Dinosaurs

http://www.dinofest.org/

Features exhibits by scientists, educators, and paleontologists; artwork, and live and fossil plants. The exhibit is the third of its kind in the U.S. and is sponsored by the Academy of Natural Science in Philadelphia.

IPL Dr. Internet Dinosaurs

http://ipl.sils.umich.edu/youth/DrInternet/Dinosaurs.html

Tour the dinosaurs in the Hawaii exhibit and see a baby Hypselosaurus hatch. Then skip over to the Field Museum of Natural History in Chicago and view the ancient birds and dinosaurs featured in the Life Over Time exhibit.

Dinofest '98: The World's Fair of Dinosaurs
http://www.dinofest.org/

The Lost World of Dinosaurs
http://www.id.iit.edu/~doe/alphadmo_07a/dinosaur.html

The Lost World of Dinosaurs

http://www.id.iit.edu/~doe/alphadmo_07a/dinosaur.html

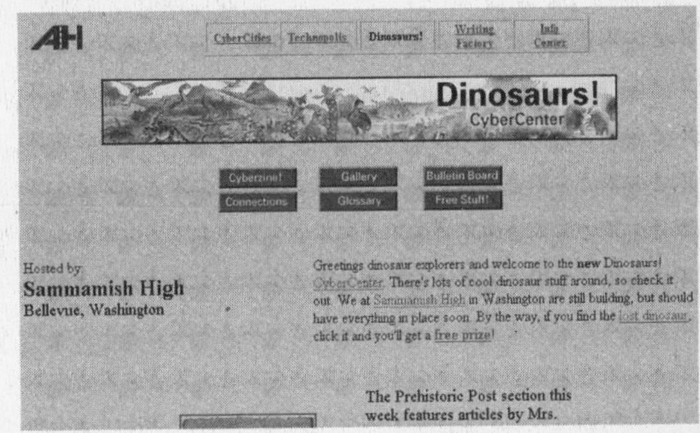

High school students in Bellevue, Washington maintain this bulletin board for elementary students to post messages, ask questions, or make comments on any topic dealing with dinosaurs. Students are also asked to make submissions to the newsletter *Prehistoric Post.* There is an online dictionary of terms used on the Web site and links to other sites.

Yahoo!-Science and Oddities: Dinosaurs

http://www.yahooligans.com/Science_and_Oddities/Dinosaurs

An audio Dinosaur Dictionary has pronunciations of the names of all the dinosaurs. You can also view QuickTime video clips from *Jurassic Park* and *The Lost World.* Link to dinosaur exhibits at several museums and an online magazine for children.

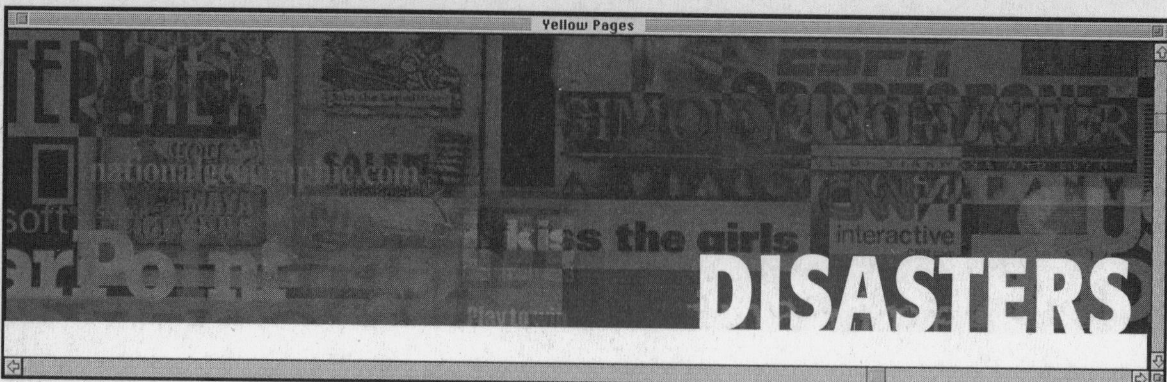

> The greatest test of courage on earth is to bear defeat without losing heart.
>
> *Robert Green Ingersoll*

American Red Cross

http://www.redcross.org/

One of the best-looking sites in this category, with nice clean graphics, an easy-on-the-eyes layout, and helpful navigation. Besides that, it offers lots of good information on safety tips, organized by type of disaster; a link to making online donations to disaster victims; background on Red Cross services, organized in an outline format; recent news stories; a monthly calendar of events nationwide; and a multimedia library. One cool feature is the American Red Cross Virtual Museum; choose a time period (I picked 1900–1919) and find photos, documents, and historical highlights, or go on the automated tour.

Chelyabinsk: The Most Contaminated Spot on the Planet

http://ww1.logtv.com/webpages/grunberg/chelya/chel.html

Dedicated to the victims of radiation in Chelyabinsk, Russia, this site has information about the calamities that have befallen the area. Learn why the area was closed to foreigners for over 45 years. This site also has a description of the documentary by Slawomir Grunberg.

American Red Cross
http://www.redcross.org/

Disaster Finder
http://ltpwww.gsfc.nasa.gov/ndrd/disaster/

Disaster Forum '98
http://freenet.edmonton.ab.ca/disaster/index.html

DisasterRelief.org - Worldwide Disaster Aid and Information Via the Internet
http://www.disasterrelief.org

EPICENTER - Emergency Preparedness Information Center
http://theepicenter.com

FEMA - Federal Emergency Management Agency
http://www.fema.gov/

Natural Hazards Center - Information on Human Adaptation to Disaster
http://www.Colorado.EDU/hazards

Disasters and Catastrophes

http://members.tripod.com/~dogw/index.htm

If you think disasters are fascinating—as I do—then visit this site created by someone who shares your interest. Site sections include Featured Disasters (from the *Titanic* to Chelyabinsk), Personal Accounts (such as the author's account of a fire at his junior high school—honestly!), and Disasters in the News (links to news services and online newspapers). Offers a bibliography with reviews and tons of links to other sites. There's also a link to the Odd & Unusual (which the author admits is "usually disgusting").

Related Sites

http://www.weatherstore.com/1001natd.htm

http://www.unr.net/~lbevan/adpac/

Disaster Finder

http://ltpwww.gsfc.nasa.gov/ndrd/disaster/

No, it's not a meeting place for Typhoid Marys, Klutz Supremes, and other accidents-waiting-to-happen. This site uses the Excite search engine to index 585—yes, you heard me, 585—disaster-related sites. You can use keywords or choose category buttons to get a list of sites and a helpful preview of what's offered at each one, so you can decide whether you want to visit.

Disaster Forum '98

http://freenet.edmonton.ab.ca/disaster/index.html

Home page for the International Conference in Edmonton, Alberta on June 26–July 1, 1998. The conference will focus on coming up with solutions to handling disasters for those employed or interested in emergency preparedness and response. As of now, there's a preliminary conference schedule that features a disaster response simulation; the site will be updated periodically. Also offers links to other sites on related seminars and meetings.

The Disaster Preparedness and Emergency Response Association, International

http://www.disasters.org/deralink.html

This site has warnings, alerts, listings of conferences and workshops, and links to news services and is the host site for "Emergency Management Gold." It's also a good resource for training emergency and disaster preparedness professionals.

Related Sites
http://www.lifelink.com/
http://www2.xoom.com/Hazards/
http://www.disasters-hazardmit.org/

DisasterRelief.org - Worldwide Disaster Aid and Information Via the Internet

http://www.disasterrelief.org

Great, information-packed site that's also well-organized and easy to navigate. It reports on worldwide disasters and relief efforts and includes referrals for providing or getting aid for specific disasters. World at a Glance covers the top disaster stories of the day, and Today in Disaster History takes a look back at disasters that happened on the current date. There's an extensive library with sections on Preparedness, U.S. Disasters, World Disasters, and more; the coolest feature in the library is a test to find out your Disaster I.Q. With the help of my 8-year-old son, I got 17 out of 20 answers correct, so I was invited to join the Red Cross Disaster Action Team! Plenty of links to other related sites, too.

Disaster Report Archive

http://www.eqe.com/publications/disaster.html

Sponsored by EQE International, a consulting firm on earthquake and structural engineering, this page links to reports on earthquakes, wildfires, hurricanes, and other natural disasters. Each report has a table of contents and references for more information. I found the Earth Science section of the table of contents particularly interesting; for example, the report on the earthquake in Kobe, Japan had a map of the tectonic plates in the area, along with a ground-motion map and photos. Not an exhaustive list of disasters, but each report is thorough.

Earth Shakes

http://www.earthshakes.com

Although the site has informative disaster preparedness tips that are updated monthly, the focus seems to be selling emergency survival packs for earthquakes and other natural disasters. Good place to get ideas for what you might need to survive an emergency, like solar-powered radios, dust masks, and waterproof matches. My favorite was the Double Delight; for only $59.50, you get enough supplies to see a couple comfortably through three days—and hey, you get playing cards and a whistle thrown in, too!

EPICENTER - Emergency Preparedness Information Center

http://theepicenter.com

Practical information on how to come up with a family disaster plan; you even get a checklist you can print out. Although the site does offer products you can buy for your emergency preparedness kit, it also gives you tips on assembling your own from resources you can find close to home. Check the Emergency Preparedness Tip o' da Week to find out just how disorganized and unprepared you are (in my case, very!). EPICENTER is even thoughtful enough to have tips for including your pets in your disaster planning. And I swear I'm not making this up—there are even recipes to make dried food and emergency rations taste delectable.

Extension Disaster Education Network

http://www.aces.uiuc.edu/~eden/prepare.html

EDEN is a cooperative effort among Extension Services across the country to pool resources and information for improving disaster planning. By coordinating state research and education programs, it hopes to increase awareness of disaster preparedness and recovery measures. The site has a database you can search for articles and reports on preparing for disasters, and lists of upcoming seminars, conferences, and workshops.

FEMA - Federal Emergency Management Agency

http://www.fema.gov/

Whew! More than 4,000 pages of information—everything you wanted to know about disaster preparedness, but quaked to ask. Plenty of informative sections, such as Project Impact: Building a Disaster Resistant Community and Help After a Disaster, but the coolest, in my opinion, is the FEMA for Kids section. Click the cartoon tornado character to find pages with online games, stories, tips on becoming a Disaster Action Kid, and lots of clear information on what causes disasters and how to prepare for them. There's even a resource section for teachers. FEMA also has a comprehensive, well-organized virtual library.

Fire Station Earth/Globalwatch

http://www1.shore.net/~globalw/

Home page for Globalwatch, whose aim is to improve awareness of global environmental problems and natural disasters. The organization offers the Global 100, which awards best practices in disaster preparedness. One recent award, which you can link to from this site, went to the United Nations Global Programme for the Integration of Public Administration and the Science of Disasters. You can find links to articles, reports, and recent conferences.

Global Disasters Report

http://hypnos.m.ehime-u.ac.jp/GHDNet/WADEM/GDR96.htm

Text-heavy site packed with information on all kinds of disasters; the site is divided into "human-caused" disasters, such as civil strife and industrial accidents, and natural disasters, like hurricanes, earthquakes, and floods. The brief entries emphasize statistics; for example, a typical entry lists the type of disaster, its current stage, number of people affected, current recovery/relief activity, and a short description of the event. Not a bad starting place, if you need, say, a listing of earthquakes in the past year.

History of Atlantic Disasters

http://www.gov.nb.ca/pss/hoad.htm

Lists in chronological order all kinds of disasters, including shipwrecks and fires; indexed by Canadian province. Interesting historical perspective.

ICES Disaster Resources

http://www.ag.uiuc.edu/~disaster/disaster.html

ICES, the Illinois Cooperative Extension Services, offers this list of resources for information on preparing for and recovering from natural disasters. Published by the University of Illinois at Urbana-Champaign, it has lots of links to other related sites, including the Extension Disaster Education Network (covered earlier in this section).

Major Airline Disasters

http://www.d-n-a.net/users/dnetGOjg/Disasters.htm

Chronological database of more than 600 major commercial airline disasters from 1920–1997. Offers details, in table format, of dates, locations, plane type, airline, and likely reasons for the crash. Includes an index to search by year or plane type, and a link to Skynet Server for further research and an information-exchange forum.

Natural Disaster Safety Tips

http://www.usatoday.com/weather/wsafe0.htm

A list of Web pages and online resources for disaster safety tips and information. Includes links to NOAA Weather Radio to get up-to-date weather information, watches, and warnings and FEMA (Federal Emergency Management Agency). This site also has an index of recent news stories on weather and safety tips.

Natural Hazards Center - Information on Human Adaptation to Disaster

`http://www.Colorado.EDU/hazards`

You won't find a lot of fancy graphics, but this site of full of excellent information. The Natural Hazards Center at the University of Colorado in Boulder acts as an international clearinghouse of information on natural disasters and how people respond and adjust to them. They offer an annual workshop and the HazLit database, which you can search by subject. There's an electronic newsletter; a publications catalog, including disaster-related books and periodicals; lists of upcoming conferences, universities that offer emergency management courses, and institutions that study hazards; and a great list of Web sites that's organized into categories.

Oil Spill Public Information Center

`http://www.alaska.net/~ospic/`

In March 1989, the Exxon Valdez spilled 11 million gallons of oil into Prince William Sound. This site has a wealth of data about this major ecological disaster, including maps, photos, and information about the effects of the spill on wildlife. You can even download an audio file of Captain Hazelwood reporting the ship's grounding.

NEWSGROUPS

`alt.disasters.aviation`

`alt.disasters.earthquake`

`alt.disasters.misc`

`alt.disasters.planning`

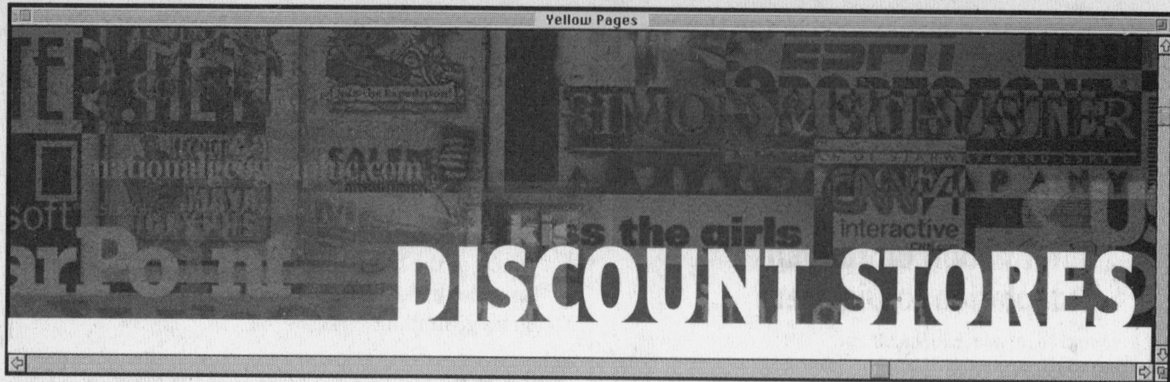

> Now, you might ask, "How do I get one of those complete home tool sets for under $4?" An excellent question. Go to one of those really cheap discount stores...
>
> *Dave Barry*

NRP TOP PICKS

Target
http://www.target.com

Wal-Mart Online
http://www.wal-mart.com

1-800-314-BAGS and Luggage

http://www.1800314bags.com/

A discount site for online ordering of sporting goods, luggage, business and computer cases, and travel accessories. Lowest, direct-to-consumer prices on major brands. Money-back guarantee.

All Discount Home Page

http://www.alldiscount.com/

This site was designed to become a virtual storefront for Internet shoppers. Set up your own virtual storefront to sell to netizens. Pages still under construction.

America's Computers Hardware and Software Discount Warehouse

http://www.consumer-online.com/computer.html

An online computer discount warehouse selling new computer systems, laptop computers, hardware, and software.

Book Express on Line

http://www.sunshine.on.ca/books/

A large discount bookstore serving Internet, retail, and wholesale customers. Savings of 60–90% off books in a wide range of categories (audio, children, health, out-of-print, religion, and more). You can order or check your order status online.

Consolidated Stores

http://www.cnstore.com/

Leads you to information on Odd Lots/Big Lots and KB Toys, subsidiaries of Consolidated Stores Corp. Find Odd Lots/Big Lots store locations and view the weekly flyer at the Storefront, or click the KB Toys shortcut to learn about toys.

The Discount Store

http://www.syncnet.com/store/index.htm

The Discount Store is like a wholesale store. A limited number of items can be ordered via phone, fax, mail, or email. Product categories include infomercial products, Sporting Goods, Ladies Only, Kids Stuff, Handy Man, Household Items, Seasonal Gifts, and Specials.

Discount Store Merchandise Fashion Jewelry Wholesale

http://www.norwich.net/~jewelry/discount.htm

Wholesalers of fashion jewelry and hair accessories. Selling primarily to discount stores; $100 minimum purchase.

Discount Store News Online!

http://www.discountstorenews.com/

"The online authority in power retailing." This online publication gives the daily news on what's happening with various retailers and provides an archive of back issues. Targeted audience includes CEOs, presidents, general merchandise managers, buyers, and managers of retail establishments internationally.

Dollar Discount Stores of America

http://www.dollardiscount.com/

At this site you can learn how to set up a Dollar Discount Store of your own (where all merchandise is $1). Entrepreneurs, take note.

DOLLAR GENERAL

http://www.dollargeneral.com

Up-to-date stuff on Dollar General. Get Company Culture information and Investor information. Of limited interest to customers; mostly for investors.

Goodwill Industries International

http://www.goodwill.org

Searchable site gives you the scoop on Goodwill Industries. Learn more about who they are and what they do, read press releases, find your local Goodwill store, learn how you can get involved, and dig into some FAQs and facts.

> **Finding Deals Online**
>
> Just like any other store, online stores have sales. After you find a few stores you like, go to the store sites periodically to check and see what is on sale. Sometimes you will see a hyper-ad talking about a big sale when you go under a search engine page. These sales are sometimes only on one brand, such as IBM computers, but sometimes they include an entire store's inventory. Don't forget to comparison shop—you can find lower prices on some products just by shopping around.

Kmart!

http://www.kmart.com

Gives you an in-depth look at Kmart, with the latest Kmart news, as well as info about the Kmart celebrities, Community Outreach programs, Baby of Mine Club, Kmart Cash Card, and Kmart Credit Card. You can also take a virtual tour through Kmart, view the current sales circular, enter a sweepstakes, and locate a store near you. Searchable site.

Meijer

http://www.meijer.com

Provides information about Meijer, store locations, contests, employment opportunities, lists of current top-selling books, and fun family events.

New York Golf Center

http://www.newyorkgolf.com/

New York Golf Center superstores have gone online to offer their line of golf clubs and accessories at discount prices.

Retail Stores

http://www.geocities.com/WallStreet/7049/retail.html

An international listing of retail stores that have a presence on the Web.

SAM'S Club

http://www.samsclub.com/

Learn all about SAM'S Club. Locate a SAM'S Club near you, learn about member benefits, purchase a membership, and shop securely with SAM'S Club Online. Also find out what's new at the club and join the Product Forum.

Target

http://www.target.com

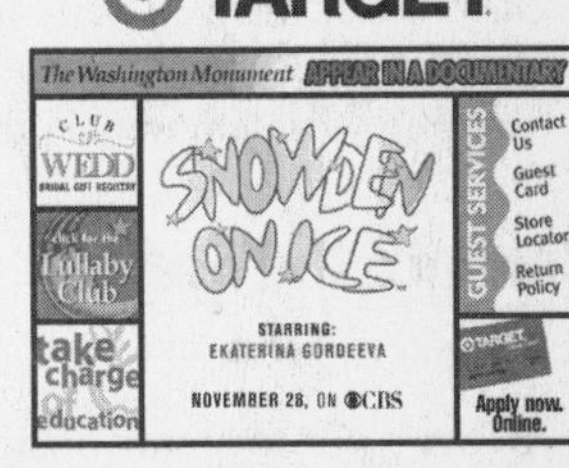

A sharp site detailing all of Target's programs and offerings, such as the Lullaby Club, Club Wedd, Take Charge of Education, School Fundraising Made Simple, 5% Back to the Community, TREAT-SEATS, the Target Guest Card, and various guest services. You can even access sound clips of new music available at Target.

Wal-Mart Online

http://www.wal-mart.com

Find Wal-Mart product and price information at this site, and order your goodies online. Search the store for what you want; you'll be rewarded with photos and details on each item. You'll have a great time filling up your virtual shopping cart. Also, locate the Wal-Mart nearest you.

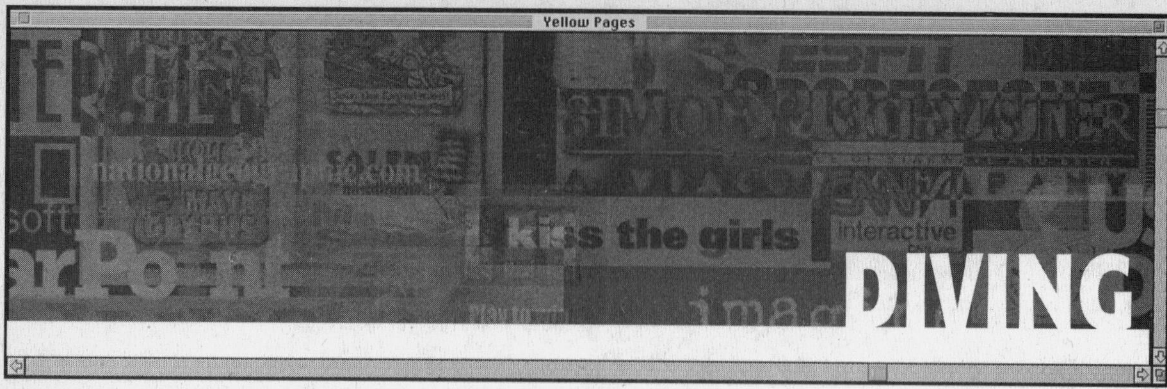

> Fame is a pearl many dive for and only a few bring up.
>
> *Louisa May Alcott*

Aloha Dive (Scuba)

http://alohadive.com/

Want to scuba dive on the outer edge of the big island of Hawaii? The Aloha Dive Company offers a unique experience in that you learn the historical and geological significance of each site as you visit it. Whether you want to see humpbacks, photograph creatures underwater, or just take lessons, you can find what you want at this family-run business.

Beneath the Sea

http://www.cyberus.ca/~bts/

BTS is a not-for-profit organization that works toward increasing awareness of the earth's oceans and sport of scuba diving. BTS helps promote the protection of marine wildlife via grants to other nonprofit groups. Includes links to seminars, workshops, mailing lists, and other diving-related sites.

Catalina Deep Sea Divers

http://www.diver.org/

This organization specializes in unique and adventurous scuba diving, salvage, and treasure hunting all over the world. Read about adventure diving, lost treasures, and ocean exploration as well.

Aloha Dive (Scuba)
http://alohadive.com/

Cayman Diving Lodge (Scuba)

http://site210083.primehost.com/index.html

This family-owned lodge is a full-service all-inclusive dedicated dive resort. Reportedly located on the secluded east end of Grand Cayman Island, the resort has only 10 rooms and guarantees full-service on-site dive operation and dive shop as well as private sand beach and boat dock.

Deep Sea Divers Den

http://www.ozemail.com.au/~diveden/

Based in Far North Queensland, Australia, and includes scuba diving to the Great Barrier Reef. Offers scuba diving courses in Cairns, Australia at all levels and live-aboard and one day trips to the Great Barrier Reef for snorkellers and divers. PADI certification available.

Dive Team Hawaii (Scuba)

http://www.scubahawaii.com/

Includes diving off Hawaii, Maui, and Kauai. A good point of entry page for all their sites on these various islands. Offer experience and know-how in order to make your diving experience as worry-free and satisfying as possible.

Luis Cabanas Scuba Diving and Instruction (Mexico)

http://www.cozumel.net/diving/luis/

Luis, a PADI Master Scuba Diver Trainer, has logged in over 250 dives to Punta Sur. Web site includes quotes from satisfied customers, photographs of dives in progress, and descriptions of basic dives for beginners. Also offers fishing trips, jungle adventure tours, underwater camera rentals, fast boat dive trips, and cave diving. Group discounts available.

Maui Diving Scuba Center/Snorkel Shop

http://members.aol.com/div4me/frames.html

Promises cheaper rates than the hotels, and caters the dive to your experience level. Claims to have the best safety record on all of Maui. Offers NAUI and PADI certification. For ages 12 and up.

North Caribbean Research (Wreck Diving)

http://www.oldship.com/

A joint collaboration of North Caribbean Research and the Dominican Government, this is a program for qualified divers. You join the Search and Salvage Team of N.C.R. at its facilities on Monte Cristi Bay. Adventure involves hands-on experience with search and salvage equipment. You will use differential global positioning systems and laser track plotters as you look for the lost ships of the 1563 fleet. Receive P.A.D.I. or B.S.A.C. certification as well.

Ocean Divers Home Page (Florida)

http://www.oceandivers.com//index.htm

Based in Key Largo, Florida, this outfit offers reef diving, wreck diving, charters, classes and instruction, and dive/hotel packages. Web site describes reef and wreck diving sites in detail, including depths and points of interest.

San Diego Dive Boat Page (Scuba)

http://www.thenerve2.com/sandiego/boatpage.html

A comprehensive index to all the boats in San Diego with Web pages. A great point of entry if you plan to be diving or snorkeling in the San Diego area. Includes diving gear rentals and purchases as well as words of wisdom when diving.

Scuba Central

http://scubacentral.com/

A great point of entry for all scuba divers, this site includes top 20 scuba links, Web chat about scuba diving, bulletin board area, online magazine "About Diving," photo gallery, industry guide, and shopping area. If you have a VRML-capable browser, you can even swim around in their virtual oceans.

ScubaPro

http://www.jwa.com/

A breathtakingly beautiful site that really captures the beauty of scuba diving and water-related sports. Offers diving, fishing, and camping sites around the world.

Twin Otter Diving (California)

http://www.whps.com/twin_otter/

Based in Monterey, California, Twin Otter offers diving off the Silver Prince, a charter boat for up to 20 people. Diving is to the off-shore reefs of Monterey Bay, Carmel Bay, Carmel Highlands, and Yankee Point south to Granite Canyon. For experienced divers; divers must bring their own equipment. Web site includes monthly dive schedules.

Yachts Are Us (Virgin Islands)

http://www.yachts-are-us.com/

Features yachting, snorkeling, and diving in the Virgin Islands. You charter your own yacht. Site includes map of the Virgin Islands, hotel information, featured yachts, and details about the vacation package such as FAQs, charter agreements, and more.

NEWSGROUPS

hawaii.sports

rec.scuba

rec.scuba.locations

rec.boats

rec.travel.caribbean

Related Sites

http://divenet.com/

http://ourworld.compuserve.com/homepages/roger_mathison/

http://touchthesea.com/

http://www.ambergriscaye.com/amigosdive/

http://www.batnet.com/seeandsea/

http://www.greatabaco.com/

http://www.neuro.fsu.edu/dave/docent.htm

http://www.oceanfest.com/

http://www.okeanos.com/

http://www.scubanetwork.com/

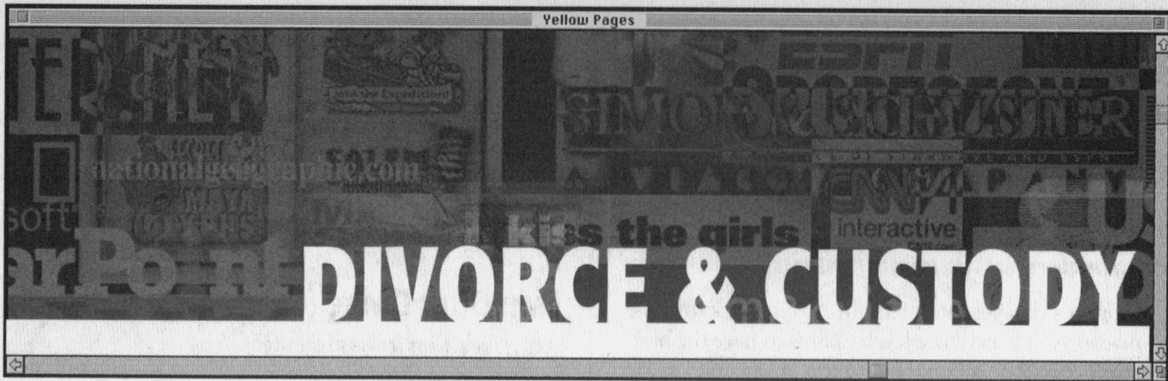

> Being divorced is like being hit by a Mack truck—if you survive you start looking very carefully to the right and left.
>
> *Jean Kerr*

CCADE Web
http://forensic.nova.edu/

Divorce Online
http://www.divorce-online.com/

Family Law Advisor Home Page
http://www.divorcenet.com/welcome.html

10 Questions About Child Custody

http://kpix.com/xtra/keane/QA-01Feb-162305-L.html

Informative page by KPIX Legal Analyst, Peter Keane. The 10 questions are those frequently asked by parents when trying to determine custody issues. The 10 questions cover topics such as the definition of custody, mediation and arbitration, the best interest of the child, and modification of current custody agreements.

C.H.I.L.D: Children Hurt in Legal Decisions

http://www.cei.net/~canichol/child.html

Site of a nonprofit organization dedicated to monitoring courts and decisions so that the best interest of the child is the primary concern of decision makers. Offers case scenarios, email, objectives, and general information regarding "the best interest of the child."

CCADE Web

http://forensic.nova.edu/

Site where professionals interested in child custody and dependency evaluation can meet and discuss topics of mutual interest. Provides online and other custody and dependency resources (legal, psychological, general, and professional), mailing lists for those involved in custody evaluations, conference announcements, and the capability to search this site for specific information.

Child Custody in the USA

http://www.islandnet.com/~wwlia/us-cus.htm

Incredible site with a wealth of information about the issue of child custody in the United States. Some topics included are types of custody arrangements and how those decisions are made, influences on decision-making, the child's wishes, mediation, and modifiability of custody and access orders.

Child Support Home Page

http://www.acf.dhhs.gov/ACFPrograms/CSE/index.html

Provides helpful information about the child support system, including basic child support program facts, newsletters and announcements, recent policy documents, and opportunity to offer feedback. Be sure to visit the External Information link for information about child support guidelines specific to your state.

Children's Rights Counsel Home Page

http://www.vix.com/crc/aboutcrc.htm

Site of Children's Rights Council (CRC), a national, non-profit, tax exempt, IRS 501(c)(3) children's rights organization based in Washington, D.C. Provides information about children's rights, legislation regarding children's rights, and data on the state and national levels.

Divorce

http://www.maricopa.gov/supcrt/ssc/sscinfo/divorce/divorce.html

Ongoing site that provides court information to the public. The information available is general but in easy-to-understand language and covers legal terminology used in divorce, child custody and child support issues, court papers, and property and debt.

Divorce Care Home Page

http://www.divorcecare.com/

Site of the Divorce Care support group. Provides a list of Divorce Care support groups in your area, resources for self help, information on children and divorce, financial survival, and more.

Divorce Helpline Webworks

http://206.214.38.18/SC/C11Real.html

Part of Divorce Helpline, this site provides a clear but gentle explanation about the differences between "legal" and the emotional, spiritual, and practical divorce.

Divorce Online

http://www.divorce-online.com/

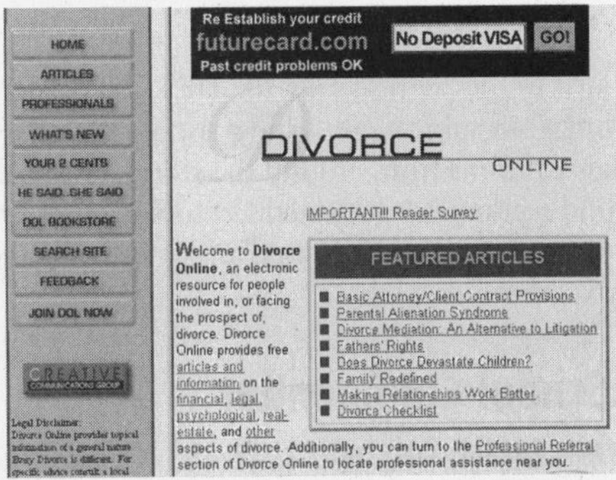

An electronic resource for people involved in, or facing the prospect of, divorce. Offers free articles and information on divorce-related topics and contains a Professional Referral section to locate help locate professional assistance near you. Also contains a FAQs section that applies to divorce.

Divorce Roadmap: Help Around the Legal System

http://www.divorcehelp.com/../SC/C12Map.html

Walks you through the complicated route of the law and divorce. Includes definitions for those great legalese terms, diagrams of the divorce process, and tips on how to get what you want from divorce. This is a great place for straightforward information. Be sure to click the "beat the system" link for more valuable info.

Family Law Advisor Home Page

http://www.divorcenet.com/welcome.html

Contains FAQs to the most common questions pertaining to divorce and family law, an online newsletter and index, a state-by-state resource center, an interactive bulletin board, international and national laws pertaining to child abduction along with a link to the U.S. State Department, and more. Also contains helpful information regarding child custody and child support.

Family Law Advisor Message Board

http://www.divorcenet.com/messages/msgs.html

Bulletin Board on which you can post questions and answers pertaining to family law. Updated daily. Good place for support and sharing experiences as well as sharing knowledge.

Family Law Links

http://www.value.net/~markwelch/famlaw.htm

Comprehensive list of links to other sites that cover family law, divorce, child custody and support issues, self-help for those experiencing separation or divorce, long-distance parenting, and more. Great site to visit when you're not sure what to search for in the family law arena.

Kids' Turn

http://members.aol.com/kidsturn/

Good site for kids and parents going through separation or divorce. Geared toward the "child's" best interest, this site offers suggestions for guiding kids through the "divorce zone," workshop information, list of suggested readings, and links to other organizations.

A B C D E F G H I J K L M N O P Q R S T U V W X Y Z

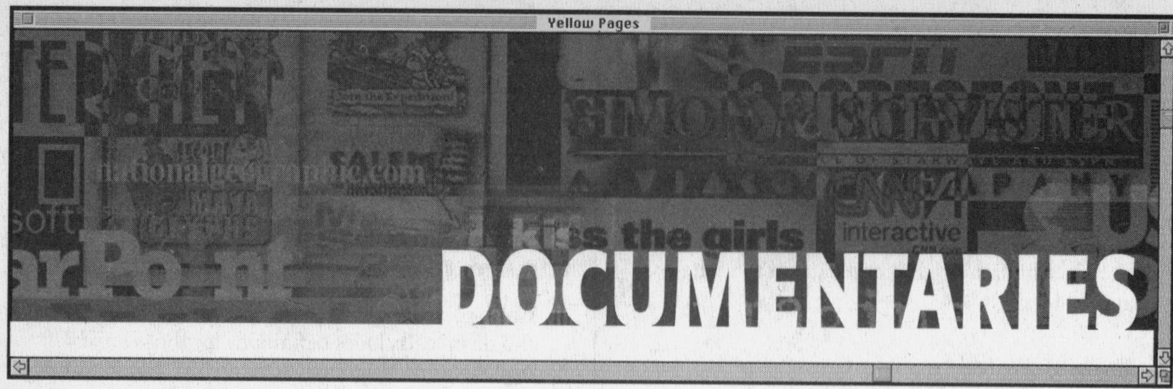

> It is difficult to produce a television documentary that is both incisive and probing when every twelve minutes one is interrupted by twelve dancing rabbits singing about toilet paper.
>
> *Rod Serling*

A&E

http://www.aetv.com/index2.html

Known for its popular "Biography" series, A&E is a cable television network that strives to make history accessible to the channel-surfing masses. Check current listings and go behind the scenes at the network's latest projects.

Anne Frank Remembered

http://www.spe.sony.com/Pictures/SonyClassics/annefrank/index.html

This is the official site of the film that won an Oscar for Best Documentary. Of special interest are an interview with Jon Blair, who wrote, produced, and directed the film, and the production notes, which discuss the facts surrounding the film's creation.

Related Sites

http://www.city.yamagata.yamagata.jp/yidff/en/home.html

http://www.jhfestival.org/

http://www.estacao.ignet.com.br/kinoforum/itsalltrue/

Liberty! The American Revolution
http://www.pbs.org/ktca/liberty/

The Center for Documentary Studies

http://aaswebsv.aas.duke.edu/docstudies/cds/index.html

Located at Duke University, the Center's mission is to examine dosumentaries in a new light, one that shows the documentary's effects on education and community structure. Find links to film resources, photodocumentary sites, and several literary sites.

CRUMB

http://www.spe.sony.com/Pictures/SonyClassics/crumb/crumb.html

Get the behind-the-scenes story on R. Crumb, the strange cartoonist of *Keep on Truckin'* fame that also happens to be part of the world's most dysfunctional family. Read extensive production notes and get a deeper glimpse into the neurotic world of the film's main character.

Documentary Filmsite

http://www.dds.nl/~damocles/

Located in the Netherlands, the DFS isn't drenched in American subjectivity. Find a list of critically acclaimed films from around the world. Find background reading on documentary topics, enter the chatroom, find out about upcoming festivals, and maybe even find a job.

Film School Confidential

http://www.lather.com/fsc/

This site is the home page of the book *Film School Confidential: The Insider's Guide to Film Schools,* written by Tom Edgar and Karin Kelly. Contains parts of the book, a list of MFA film schools, and guides about what you should expect from a film school and what it will expect from you.

Hoop Dreams

http://www.flf.com/hoop/index.htm

Although the film itself has long been gone from the "New Releases" category, this site is worthy of investigation based on the interesting biographies of its filmmakers and the lengthy production notes section. Also included is a transcript from an AOL conference with Producer and Director of Photography Peter Gilbert.

Internet Movie Database

http://www.imdb.com/

Search the massive database by film title, director, narrator, or more. Write a review or give a film your own star rating. An extensive linking system lets you find all films of a given topic, by a certain director, featuring the same actors, and so on.

Lewis and Clark

http://www.pbs.org/lewisandclark/

One of the latest joint ventures between master documentarian Ken Burns and PBS. This site features a timeline of the journey into the new American territory, commentary by historians, journals written by the explorers, and even a Lewis and Clark screensaver.

Liberty! The American Revolution

http://www.pbs.org/ktca/liberty/

Part of the PBS Web site, this area focuses on *Liberty!*, a production of Twin Cities Television and Middlemarch Films. Get historical background on the series' content, play a revolutionary game, read interviews with the filmmakers, and find out about the scholars that give PBS films that intellectual edge.

PBS Online

http://www.pbs.org/

At the official site of Public Broadcasting Services, you'll find information on current programming and fully stocked sites about PBS's current and recent documentaries, such as *Lewis and Clark, Hoop Dreams, Rock and Roll*, and more. The most interesting parts are the behind-the-scenes interviews with cast and crew members and reading the goals of the filmmakers.

Sundance Film Festival

http://cybermart.com/sundance/institute/festival.html

Documentary films are given special attention at the Sundance Film Festival, the organization that featured the debuts of *Hoop Dreams* and *Crumb*. The site features highlights of the festival since 1990 and a call for entries for next year's competition.

When We Were Kings

http://www.reellife.com/wwwkings/home-wwwkings.html

This is the official site of the award-winning documentary that covers the "Rumble in the Jungle"—the 1974 heavyweight championship fight between Mohammed Ali and George Foreman. Read the reviews, find out what went into making the film, and learn about the politics that set the stage for the fight.

NEWSGROUPS

alt.movies.cinematography

alt.movies.independent

rec.arts.movies.current-films

rec.arts.movies.lists+surveys

rec.arts.movies.people

rec.arts.movies.production

rec.arts.movies.reviews

rec.arts.movies.tech

Related Sites

http://www.localnet.com/~billj/document.html

http://www.mpimedia.com/wpa/index.html

http://www.users.interport.net/~kermit/livproof.html

http://www.ibmpcug.co.uk/lff.html

http://www.itvs.org/programs/BIBA/index.html

http://www-leland.stanford.edu/dept/communication/

http://www.graduate/film&video/index.html

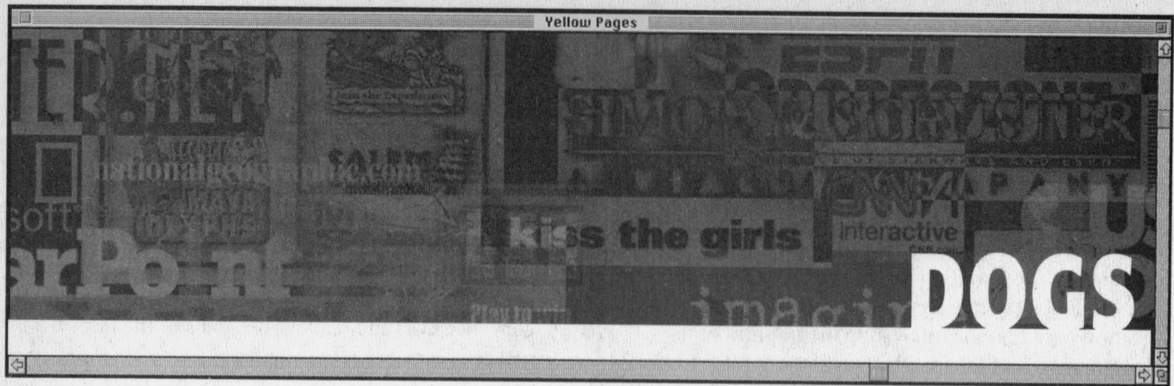

DOGS

> A dog teaches a boy fidelity, perseverance, and to turn around three times before lying down.
>
> *Robert Benchley*

The Actual Dog Show

http://www.neca.com/~szeder/dogshoh.html

Written by a veterinarian, this site dedicates itself to dog fanciers who show their dogs. Learn what happens at dog shows, why you should want to go, and why "bitch" is not a dirty word. You'll finally find out what these things are: the grooming area, the obedience ring, and the breed ring.

Adopt a Greyhound

http://www.adopt-a-greyhound.org/

Greyhounds may have been famous for their speed and grace on the track, but recently, people have begun to adopt them upon retirement, saving them from euthanasia or worse. This site provides a huge amount of information, as well as links to other sites. Check out the many adoption agencies specializing in greyhounds.

Adopt a Greyhound
http://www.adopt-a-greyhound.org/

Akbash Dog Home Page

http://www.upei.ca/akbash/akbash.htm

The Akbash Dog is a livestock-protection dog found in rural Turkey. This site enables you to view pictures of Akbash dogs, read their history and breed description, and learn about Ashkash Dogs International and its rescue program.

Bernese Mountain Dog Home Page

http://www.prairienet.org/~mkleiman/berner.html

Focuses on the Bernese Mountain dog. Includes photos, links to mailing lists, FAQs, information about getting a Bernese puppy, and links to owner sites.

Border Collies

http://mendel.berkeley.edu/dogs/bcs.html

Picture-filled site that provides special information on border collie email lists and an FTP site dedicated to border collie information. Includes information for those individuals thinking about getting a border collie, as well as an online training manual.

Borzoi Info Online

http://www.clark.net/pub/bdalzell/borzoiinfo.html

Provides information on the Borzoi breed. The Borzoi is a large hunting dog of Russia. Includes pictures and a link to the Borzoi Genealogy Database. Also offers articles and links to additional general dog-related information.

Canine Activity Calendar

http://www.acmepet.com/canine/civic/k9_act.html

Provides a one-stop-shopping list of canine shows scheduled throughout North America.

Canine Companions for Independence

http://www.caninecompanions.org/

We're all familiar with seeing eye dogs for the blind, but CCI trains dogs to help people with other disabilities. Learn about their puppy training program, learn what kinds of dogs are eligible, jump to related sites, and be sure to pick something up from the gift shop.

Canine Vaccination Schedule

http://www.acmepet.com/canine/k9vacsch.html

If you're a pet owner, you know how difficult it can be to keep up with your pet's inoculation schedule. However, there is an easier way: visit this site, which contains a schedule for canine vaccinations from age 6 weeks up to 18 months. The site also provides descriptions on how each vaccine is administered and describes the illness the vaccine treats.

Caucasian Ovcharka Info

http://pasture.ecn.purdue.edu/~laird/Dogs/Ovcharka/

Focuses on the Caucasian Mountain dog, a flock guardian that has served as a livestock guard, a home guardian, and a fighting dog. Includes special information on the national club for this breed, and contact information for the Caucasian Mountain Dog Club of America, Inc.

Choosing a Dog Breed

http://www.acpub.duke.edu/~hendrix/choosing.html

Offers guidance and suggestions to those who are thinking about getting a dog. Includes answers to a list of frequently asked questions. Includes a list of reading resources, including books and links to other sites.

The Deaf Dog Web Page

http://www.kwic.net/~cairo/deaf.html

This site is an offshoot of a mailing list for people with deaf dogs. You will learn about the BAER test for deafness, special collars, and more. Should you get another dog to provide companionship? Is there such thing as a "hearing ear" dog for other dogs?

Dog & Cat Computer Corner

http://dccorner.bayside.net/home.htm

The place for pet lovers to find dog and cat screen savers, themes, and wallpaper, and help to install them. You can also find trivia, games, funnies, and more. Take the dog and cat trivia quiz to see how much you actually know.

Dog Breeding

http://www.clark.net/pub/bdalzell/21stcent.html

Covers how to properly care for and raise a dog. Includes tips. Discusses aspects of several different breeds. Includes the electronic version of the Merck Veterinary Manual and information about CompuPed, a pedigree management program.

Dog-O-Gram

http://www.dogs-of-soho.com/

Some wonderful photography of dogs in Soho. Train your dog with helpful advice, send "postcards" of your dog over the internet, and view lots of city dogs in black-and-white photography. Also, the humorous "Dog Psych Clinic" is available to help you analyze puppies' idiosyncrasies.

Dog Play

http://www.dog-play.com/

Gives pet owners something different to think about—animal-assisted therapy. The author of this site details the experience of using dogs to help reach out to the elderly and confined individuals. The site includes links to organizations involved in animal-assisted therapy, books and publications on therapy dogs, and links to other dog-related sites.

Dog Term Glossary

http://pasture.ecn.purdue.edu/~laird/Dogs/glossary.html

Presents terminology both common and uncommon to the canine field. Provides many links to additional sites, as well as pointers to other parts of the glossary. Also contains contact information for Humane Societies and the American Kennel Club.

Foggy Mountain Dog Coats

http://www.impactsitedesign.com/dogcoat/

Have you ever wondered where old Mrs. Smith down the street got that itty bitty coat for her corgi? Maybe she ordered it from Foggy Mountain. They feature many different styles for dogs of all sizes. They even have rain wear, so your dog won't have to shake himself dry in your dining room.

GORP: Great Outdoor Recreation Pages

http://www.gorp.com/gorp/eclectic/pets.htm

Tired of walking the dog just around the block or the local park? These pages detail countless destinations that will cater to you and your canine. Provided are complete lists by activity, region, interest, and lodging.

Greyhound Starting Gate

http://pasture.ecn.purdue.edu/~laird/Dogs/Greyhound/

Did you know you can play a greyhound's ribs like an air guitar? Well, not really, but at this site, you *can* learn the other "Top 10" reasons you should adopt a greyhound. This site focuses on finding homes for retired racing greyhounds. It provides background information on the greyhound and its history in the United States.

Index of Famous Dogs

http://www.evl.uic.edu/caylor/dogindex.html

A surprising number of dogs and other animals have important roles in TV and movies or are owned by famous people. This site is dedicated to listing them all, even the obscure ones. For example, what is the name of the dog who pulls down the bikini of the little girl in the old Coppertone ads? What was the name of Santa's Little Helper's "wife?" How about all their puppies?

Jackson Hole Iditarod Sled Dog Tours

http://jackson-hole.com/activities/dogsled/jhdogsled/

While your friends burn themselves on some crowded beach somewhere, take your next vacation over scenic trails in a warm dog sled lead by dogs trained by an experienced Iditarod racer.

NaturalDogFood.com

http://www.naturaldogfood.com/

Ever wonder whether the canned food you feed your dog is actually good for it? This site's Webmaster is sure that her dog's diet of "people" food helped it live a healthy life, and she cites experts. The site provides some recipes, a FAQ, suggested reading, and more.

Police Dog Homepage

http://www.best.com/~policek9/rollcall.htm

This site is dedicated to the dogs who are placed in the line of fire everyday. Information is provided for K9 academies, associations, availability, and more. Most touching are poetry and stories of K9s and handlers who were killed in the line of duty.

Pomeranian Dog Home Page

http://www.u-net.com/~galley/

Provides information on the Pomeranian. Includes links to pictures, history, and breed standards, as well as information on other links related to the Pomeranian.

Portuguese Water Dog Index

http://pasture.ecn.purdue.edu/~laird/Dogs/PWD/index.html

Offers information on the Portuguese Water Dog, also referred to as the Fisherman's Dog. Offers links to other related sites, including the Pacific NW Portuguese Water Dog Club site, which incorporates HTML 3.0 background imaging techniques.

The Pug Dog Home Page

http://www.camme.ac.be/~cammess/www-pug/home.html

This thorough site presents the Pug dog, a member of the Toy group. Find out why this dog is a great choice for potential pet owners who live in a dwelling with no outdoor yard or dog run. The site also provides a guest book to record comments for passers-by.

Rhodesian Ridgebacks

http://warthog.cns.udel.edu/richard/RhoRidge/rrfaq.html

Offers information on email lists of owners of the Ridgeback dog (sometimes called the African Lion Hound), a native of South Africa. Presents a list of frequently asked questions, for potential owners of Ridgebacks.

SaraQueen: Queen of all dogs in the Universe

http://members.aol.com/saraqueen/index.html

A humorous account of existence through the eyes of SaraQueen. She has a chat room, a doggy Prozac alternative, Devotee of the Month, a Dogs Against Gates campaign (yes, both kinds of "Gates"), and more.

Schipperke Page

http://www.eskimo.com/~baubo/schip.html

Includes information and pictures on the Schipperke breed of dog (pronounced "schipperkey"). Features a list of additional sites that offer information on canines, including medical projects and veterinary studies.

Shy Dogs Links Page

http://www.geocities.com/Heartland/9820/

Not all dogs are as brave as Rin Tin Tin or as outgoing as Lassie. Among other dog-related links are pages dedicated to the quiet, soft-spoken dogs—the ones the neighbors don't even know they have. Perhaps a visit from a few more Web surfers will help these dogs break out of their furry shell.

Three Dog Bakery

http://www.threedog.com/

After stocking up on your own sticky buns and cake, remember to stop by this Web site to order some treats for Spot. Their doggie treats were a knee-jerk reaction to commercial biscuits that had up to 50 ingredients, and pups all over the world love them, including Oprah's!

Tibetan Mastiff Home Page

http://www.idyllmtn.com/tm/

Focuses on the Tibetan Mastiff breed of dog. Includes Tibetan Mastiff-related links to clubs, pictures, purchasing, and information on relevant health matters.

The Visual Rhodesian Ridgeback

http://wintermute.sr.unh.edu/ridgeback/ridgeback.html

Focuses on the Rhodesian breed. Contains some links to adorable pictures of the young Ridgeback and the owners that love them. Also provides additional links to other canine sites.

Related Sites
http://www.imt.net/~sleddogadventure/
http://www.herb-doc.com/petcare.htm
http://www.netpet.com/articles/choc.tox.html

A B C D E F G H I J K L M N O P Q R S T U V W X Y Z

A
B
C
D
E
F
G
H
I
J
K
L
M
N
O
P
Q
R
S
T
U
V
W
X
Y
Z

DOMESTIC VIOLENCE, CHILD ABUSE, & MISSING CHILDREN

The point of nonviolence is to build a floor, a strong new floor, beneath which we can no longer sink.

Joan Baez

Blain Nelson's Abuse Pages

http://marie.az.com/%7Eblainn/dv/index.html

Great site that provides personal experience with abuse (the giving and receiving end), questions to help you determine whether you are an abuser or have been abused, information about the "cycle of abuse," and links to other sites that pertain to this subject.

C.A.P.A. - The Child Abuse Prevention Association

http://www.childabuseprevention.org/

Child abuse prevention tips and responsibilities, calendar of events, programs, and ways to get involved in prevention methods are all highlighted at this informative site.

Child Abuse Awareness Association

http://sdcc3.ucsd.edu/~caaa/

University of California at San Diego newly formed group devoted to preventing child abuse through education, volunteering, and articles all featured at this site.

Family Violence Prevention Fund
http://www.igc.apc.org/fund/index.html

The Polly Klaas Foundation
http://www.pollyklaas.org/index2.htm

Child Abuse Prevention

http://www.medaccess.com/abuse/abuse_toc.htm

A picture of an innocent child portrays the importance of this site. It has answers to FAQ, as well as a definition of child abuse and a fact sheet.

Child Abuse Prevention Network

http://child.cornell.edu/

This site is dedicated to enhancing Internet resources for the prevention of child abuse and neglect. Offers list of state-level programs on the prevention of child abuse, electronic newsletter that keeps you up-to-date on the developments of this site, and links to other helpful sites.

Child CyberSEARCH: English Home Page

http://www.childcybersearch.org/ccscengl.htm

Canadian site that provides a database of missing children, a list of Canada's missing children agencies, a library that contains helpful tips, pamphlets, special interest articles about missing children, child-care, and parenting. Mostly geared toward Canadians, but some information is universal.

Child Quest International

http://www.childquest.org/

Site dedicated to the recovery of missing, abused, and exploited children. Offers safety tips to keep your kids safe, lists of other resources that can answer questions you may have, and links to other important sites dedicated to the safety of children.

Child Search: National Missing Children's Center

http://www.childsearch.org/

Provides support services for those whose children are missing, such as crisis counseling, search assistance, photo distribution assistance. Also provides photo-listings of missing children, child ID kits, and safety tips for parents.

Child Sexual Abuse

http://www.cs.utk.edu/~bartley/sacc/childAbuse.html

Not a lot of bells and whistles at this sight, but really good, must-know information about child sexual abuse. Offers sections on symptoms, feelings the child (and the parent) may have, protecting kids, and listening to children.

Childhelp USA

http://www.childhelpusa.org/

In-depth access to child abuse information and facts, names of celebrity ambassadors, Childhelp USA advisory board, and lists of Childhelp facilities. Also gives immediate help to those who are being abused.

Children's House Home Page

http://childhouse.uio.no/

Site that is an interactive resource center—a meeting place for the exchange of information that serves the well-being of children. Offers workshops and training, information resources on the well-being of children, information about early childhood, and a spot about children's rights.

Children's Safety Network Home Page

http://www.edc.org/HHD/csn/

Contains publications and resources produced by CSN and other EDC injury prevention projects that include full-text in HTML format that can be viewed, downloaded, and printed directly from this site.

CyberPages International Inc: Missing Children

http://www.cyberpages.com/MISSING.HTM

Provides a list of missing children. This page is free of charge and enables you to add to the list. Also provides a list of other sites on the Internet that provide a similar service.

Domestic Violence Page

http://www.iquest.net/~gtemp/famvi.htm

Site devoted to fighting all forms of family violence. Great info here, such as facts about domestic violence, readers stories, suggestions for where to get help, suggested reading list, and links to other sites that pertain to domestic violence.

Domestic Violence Quiz

http://www.igc.apc.org/fund/quiz/

Take this domestic violence quiz to test your knowledge on domestic violence related issues. After submitting each answer, an explanation is given about the correct answer.

Family Violence Awareness Page

http://www.famvi.com/

Statistical informatiopersonal essays, hotlines, questions, T-shirt sales, and links devoted to preventing occurrences of domestic violence.

Family Violence Prevention Fund

http://www.igc.apc.org/fund/index.html

This informative site gives facts, news, personal stories, celebrity input, and more on domestic violence. It discusses the impact on children, adults, and the workplace.

International Center for the Search and Recovery of Missing Children

http://www.icsrmc.org/

This site allows you to choose Spanish or English as the spoken language and then continues by showing pictures of missing children and also has an intake package which allows for immediate reporting of a missing child.

The KEYEYE Making Kids Safe Page

http://www.keyeye.com/

Site dedicated to teaching personal safety to children. Offers videotapes that help teach your child how to recognize ploys of abductors, safety tips for parents and children, and links to other safety pages.

Related Sites

http://www.nccn.net/~dvcoaltn/

http://www.nvc.org/gdir/safety.htm

http://www.quinlan.com/

Kathy's Resources on Parenting, Domestic Violence, Abuse, Trauma, and Disassociation

`http://www.mcs.net/~kathyw/home.html`

Offers tons of information about the different aspects of violence, including information for parents; data and info on trauma and disassociation, abuse, rape, and domestic violence; and a Net ratings guide.

Mental Health Net: Responding to Sexual Child Abuse

`http://www.cmhcsys.com/factsfam/rspdabus.htm`

Site that contains suggestions for adults who suspect child abuse or are approached by a child indicating that he or she has been abused. Suggestions are specific to your reaction to the child and what you should do after the discussion with the child.

Minnesota Higher Education Center Against Violence & Abuse

`http://www.umn.edu/mincava/newstuff.htm`

Site of an electronic clearinghouse via the World Wide Web for issues that pertain to domestic violence. Offers information about domestic violence in the forms of research papers and book suggestions, support for professionals, school safety info, list of treatment guidelines, gallery of children's art, poetry and prose by survivors, and links to help resources and other sites.

Missing Children at Lost Kids

`http://www.lostkids.org/`

This site has thumbnail pictures of missing kids and by clicking the pictures, find out more information of the missing children. The site has a phone number if you have any information on any of the children.

National Center for Missing and Exploited Children

`http://www.missingkids.org/`

Site of a private, non-profit organization working in cooperation with the U.S. Department of Justice dedicated to the search for missing children and pursuit of child protection. Offers training for those involved in child protection and recovery, search assistance to those looking for missing children, and provides publications and resources pertinent to the safety of children. Also provides access to a missing children database.

PeaceDove

`http://www.wam.umd.edu/~dove/pd2.html`

Provides links to missing children sites. The other sites aren't necessarily huge, but the info contained at those sites are equally as important.

The Polly Klaas Foundation

`http://www.pollyklaas.org/index2.htm`

Named after an abducted child, this site has pictures and information of missing children. It also has relevant information on how to keep your children safe and how to educate the public.

Stop Child Abuse Now

`http://www.efn.org/~scan/`

Exploration of child abuse topics through personal stories and pleas to prevent the vicious cycle of child abuse from continuing.

Suggested Readings on Domestic Violence

`http://www.cybergrrl.com/planet/dv//bib.html`

This site lists titles and reviews on suggested books that deal with domestic violence. Also has links to SafetyNet Home page and Cybergrrl Webstation.

Survivor Organizations and Agencies

`http://www.csbsju.edu/isti/03txt.html`

Provides list of organizations and agencies in the United States for victims and survivors of child abuse and includes addresses, phone numbers, and fax numbers.

Want to Contact Your Runaway Child?

`http://www.wwwsite.com/runaway/index.shtml`

Contact your runaway child via the World Wide Web! This site is made in the off chance that your runaway child has access to the Internet. Post a message and read responses.

Related Sites
`http://www.nccn.net/~dvcoaltn/`
`http://www.nvc.org/gdir/safety.htm`

Yellow Pages

DRAMAS

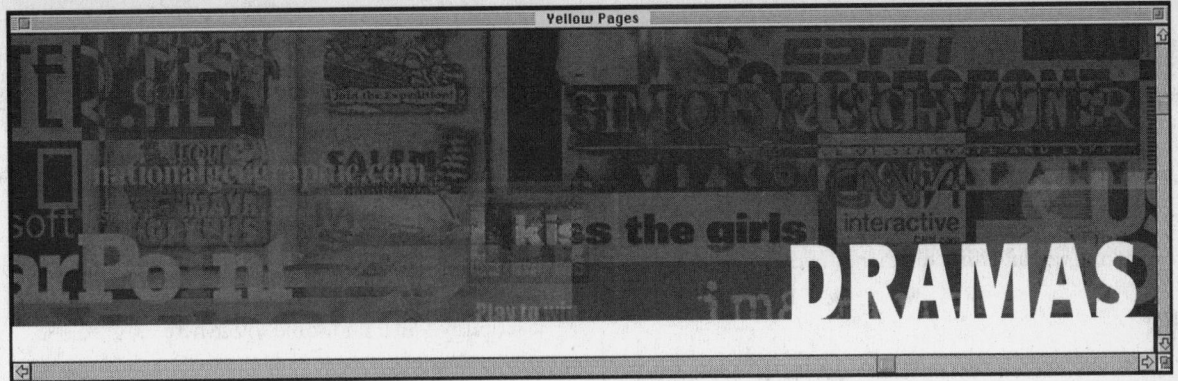

> Seeing a murder on television...can help work off one's antagonisms. And if you haven't any antagonisms, the commercials will give you some.
>
> *Alfred Hitchcock*

413 Hope Street

http://www.foxworld.com/413indx.htm

413 Hope Street is the drama created by Damon Wayans about a teen crisis center in New York City. Shockwave movies about the show, biographies of stars, and background/pilot information included.

The A-Team

http://www.xs4all.nl/~jmm/a-team/

An unofficial *A-Team* site which includes archives of the electronic newsletter about the A-Team called "On the Jazz," information about an upcoming A-Team movie, FAQ about the series, the standard episode guide, and sounds from the series. Get in touch with fellow A-Teamers here.

Angelic Heaven

http://www.charliesangels.com/

If you are a fan of *Charlie's Angels*, check out this site. Includes newsletter, merchandise, bios, and current work of actors, as well as links to other angel sites. Newsletter is full of nostalgic recollections of the show.

Profiler
http://www.nbc.com/thrillogy/profiler/

The Avengers

http://nyquist.ee.ualberta.ca/~dawe/avengers.html

Provides an unofficial home page for the 1960s British adventure drama show *The Avengers*. Includes an episode guide, pictures, sound files, and much more.

Bay Watch

http://www.baywatchtv.com/

Includes many pictures and videos of the stars clad in their bathing suits, this is the official Bay Watch site. Episode updates, fun facts, cast information, and email forums are just some of the things you'll find here.

Brooklyn South

http://home.imsweb.net/~kamala/bk-south.htm

An unofficial Web site, this includes cast information, links to other sites, episode updates and summaries, picture galleries, a chat room, and more. A good site to get in touch with other fans.

Chicago Hope Home Page

http://www-cs-students.stanford.edu/~clee/chicagohope.html

The Chicago Hope Home Page is based on the CBS drama that centers around a hospital and its doctors. This site is filled with pictures, FAQs, and episode guides, as well as other information about this popular show.

The Complete X-Files Episode Guide

http://www.geocities.com/CollegePark/Quad/4303/xftable.html

A comprehensive guide, organized by director and writer, to Chris Carter's show about the supernatural. Includes information on upcoming episodes, reviews and ratings, and links to other *X-Files* databases.

ER

http://www.nbc.com/entertainment/shows/er/index.html

This show is wildly popular on Thursday nights. It stars Anthony Edwards, George Clooney, Julianna Margulies, Maria Bello, and Eriq La Salle as doctors and nurses at County General Memorial Hospital. Written by Michael Crichton, this show takes place in Chicago. And, of course, you can read all about it at this site on the Web.

Hawaii Five-O Guide

http://world.std.com/~olorin/h5o.html

Provides an episode guide, cast profiles, interviews, and pictures from the police drama *Hawaii Five-O.* Includes links to other fan club and convention pages.

Homicide: Life on the Street

http://www.nbc.com/homicide/

Provides the official NBC site for the show *Homicide.* Includes cast profiles, episode information, and sound files. Also includes links to other related sites.

Kung Fu: The List Continues

http://thunder.ocis.temple.edu/~cbaconsm/kflist.html

Provides information about the television show *Kung Fu*, including details about the new series. Includes many pictures, an episode guide, a FAQ, and much more.

Law and Order

http://www.mca.com/tv/laworder/

Last year's Emmy Winner for outstanding drama series. This site includes a NetForum, awards and nominations, and lengthy bios of the stars. The theme song plays as you visit the site.

Little House on the Prairie

http://www.angelfire.com/tx/LittleHouse/

All you ever wanted to know about *Little House on the Prairie*, including episode guide, actor bios, pictures, interviews, and audio clips. You can listen to the theme song or join the mailing list.

Lost in Space

http://web2.airmail.net/pokeys/lis.htm

Calls itself the irreverent guide to this campy show, and includes episode guides, games, puzzles, and a drinking game. If you enjoy this show, but don't take it seriously, you'll find some solace here.

Melrose Place

http://www.geocities.com/Hollywood/5639/melrose.html

Provides a fan site for the Fox drama *Melrose Place.* Includes a current story line synopsis, character backgrounds, cast profiles, pictures, and links to many other Melrose Place sites.

Millennium

http://www.foxworld.com/millnium/index.htm

Provides the official Fox home site for the drama *Millennium.* Includes an episode guide, character profiles, behind the scenes articles, and many different pictures.

The Moose's Guide to Northern Exposure

http://www.netspace.org/~moose/moose.html

Online guide to Northern Exposure. Includes graphics, sound bytes, FAQs, episode guides, rerun schedules, and a lengthy bibliography.

My So-Called Life

http://www.tc.umn.edu/nlhome/g564/lask0008/mscl.html

Information, multimedia, feedback, images, scripts, and links are present at this page. This show that had a strange air-life can sometimes be caught now on MTV, but there is no real rhyme or reason to when they show it. Just like being a teenager.

Nothing Sacred

http://www.abc.com/primetime/nothing_sacred/index.html

New drama from ABC about a Catholic priest in the inner city trying to make sense of his calling and of the things going on around him. Somewhat controversial, this show invokes strong reactions on both fronts. Chosen as best new drama from Viewers for Quality Television.

NYPD Blue Home Page

http://src.doc.ic.ac.uk/public/media/tv/collections/tardis/us/drama/NYPDBlue/index.html

Includes detailed info for each episode and text files on the cast, characters, the NYPD drinking game, and several FAQs.

Party of Five

http://www.csua.berkeley.edu/~byron/PartyOf5/

Fan page for the Fox TV show, *Party of Five*, including an episode guide, a FAQ list about the show, recent publicity, and links to other fan sites.

The Perry Mason Pages

http://www.ozemail.com.au/~jsimko/

This unofficial Perry Mason home page features links and suggested readings to all things Perry Mason. Don't forget to check out the episode guides to find out which case Perry lost.

The Pretender

http://www.nbc.com/thrillogy/pretender/

Part of NBC's "thrillogy," this series is about "Jarod"—a genius, kidnapped and studied by the government as a child, who can master virtually any profession. Fights for justice as he runs from the government agency that wants to capture him and use his mind.

Profiler

http://www.nbc.com/thrillogy/profiler/

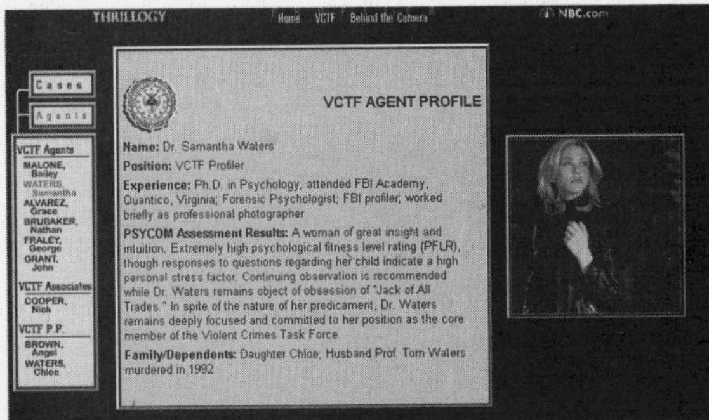

Part of the NBC's "thrillogy," this series is about a forensic psychologist who can see into the criminal mind and thus finds herself chasing down serial killers. This unique site includes agent profiles and case descriptions written from the point of view of an FBI database. The show, and the site, have graphic content.

The Quincy Examiner

http://www1.mhv.net/~mbatira/quincy/

Called the online home to fans of *Quincy, M.E.*, includes a FAQ, trivia, and character profiles. Includes the standard pictures and multimedia, along with search engine and AOL chat transcripts from Jack Klugman.

Ranger Territory: Walker Texas Ranger

http://members.aol.com/companyb97/wtr.htm

Stars Chuck Norris as a lone star ranger. This site devoted to the show includes an e-zine, fan art, news, rumors, and gossip about the show. Myriad links to other ranger sites.

The Real World

http://www.grrl.com/real.html

The Real World's unofficial Web site is for "all the folks out there who enjoy watching a group of young people whine, cry, bitch, laugh, talk, and share their constant confessions." There is a FAQ list, episode guide, and other stuff for *The Real World* fanatic.

The Rockford Files Home Page

http://busboy.sped.ukans.edu/~asumner/rockford/

Helps you find out where on television you can see reruns of this drama about the ex-con private eye played by James Garner. Includes an exhaustive list of episode guides from all six seasons, including the pilot. Directly linked to the newsgroup, `alt.tv.rockford-files`, as well. Contains pictures, multimedia, the works.

The Starsky and Hutch Page

http://www-personal.umich.edu/~llarkins/green.html

Provides an unofficial home site dedicated to the 1970s police drama *Starsky and Hutch*. Includes many pictures, an episode guide, and cast profiles. Also includes information about Starsky and Hutch books and links to other related sites.

The thirtysomething Episode Guide

http://duplox.wz-berlin.de/people/oswald/30/guide.ascii

This is the printable episode guide for the *thirtysomething* fan. Perhaps you forgot what exactly happened in an episode, or you were wanting a reference by which to write a drinking game. Here, you've found it.

The Unofficial Picket Fences Home Page

http://www.lewis.edu/fences/fences.html

At this site you'll find information about the show starring Tom Skerritt as the sheriff of a small town. There is a FAQ list, cast photos and info, links, and sounds from this popular CBS drama.

NEWSGROUPS

alt.tv.dallas

alt.tv.due-south

alt.tv.chicago-hope

alt.tv.homicide

alt.tv.nypd-blue

sg.rec.tv

rec.arts.tv

Related Sites

http://sqx.simplenet.com/tv/ally/index.html

http://web.ukonline.co.uk/tvqueen.t/dynasty1.htm

http://www.netspace.org/~moose/moose.html

http://www.scifi.com/bionics/bionicw.html

http://www.gdn.net/~marcm/Insanity/Sheila.html

http://home.ican.net/~duchess/drquinn/story1.htm

http://www.iup.edu/~vbyprdb/emergency.html

http://home.earthlink.net/~vegemite/index.html

http://www.uoguelph.ca/~mrathwel/Hulk/Hulk.html

http://www.nashbridges.com/

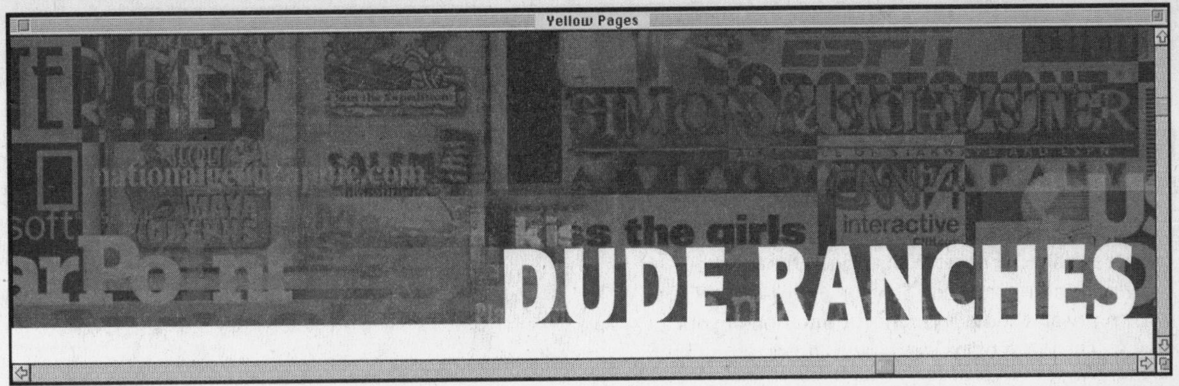

O Mary, go and call the cattle home,
And call the cattle home,
And call the cattle home,
Across the sands o' Dee!

Charles Kingsley

Bar BK Muleshoe Ranch

`http://www.muleshoe-ranch.com/`

Claiming to be the oldest working cattle ranch in the area, Arizona's Bar BK spans more than 43 square miles. Take an overnight horse ride, take a long swim, or pan for gold. If you're good, you can help the ranch hands mend fences or plow the fields.

Bucks and Spurs Guest Ranch

`http://www.bucksandspurs.com/`

Bucks and Spurs is located in the Missouri Ozarks and offers many different types of activities, from riding in a horse-drawn wagon to canoeing in the nearby waters. When you've been out on the range all day, come back home to a cowboy-style steak dinner with all the trimmings.

The Dude Ranchers' Association

`http://www.duderanch.org/`

Formed in 1926, this organization helps you create your dream vacation at a dude ranch. Use their guide to determine what type of ranch is best for you. The group claims strict admission criteria to be able to join their association and that if you stay at a DRA ranch, you've made the right choice.

Ranchweb–Worldwide Ranch Headquarters
`http://www.ranchweb.com/`

The Dude Ranches Home Page

`http://www.duderanches.com/`

The folks at duderanches.com have assembled a directory of ranches in 33 states and Canada. Search the map to find the ranches in a particular state, or comb through the list of "favorites" compiled by the staff. If you're looking for a job on a ranch, submit your personal information, which will then be forwarded on to prospective employers.

Granite Creek Guest Ranch

`http://www.srv.net/~granite/`

Located in the mountains of Idaho, Granite Creek offers cattle drives of varying lengths, calf roping, and scenic views of the Tetons. Have you wrangled one of Idaho's famous Cutthroat Trout? And don't just hop on a pre-saddled horse. This gang teaches you how to saddle and care for them yourself.

Hartley Guest Ranch

`http://www.duderanch.org/hartley/index.htm`

Located about 200 miles from Albuquerque, the Hartley Guest Ranch invites you to partake in New Mexico's breathtaking beauty. Have an experienced guide show you dinosaur bones, ancient Indian sites, and unique rock formations. Come at the right time of the season and help out with the cattle branding.

Homeplace Ranch

`http://www.cadvision.com/homeplaceranch/`

The Homeplace Ranch lies at the base of the Canadian Rockies in Alberta's "high cattle country." The ranch hands will match you with a horse that suits your riding experience. Enjoy the Calgary nightlife or the quiet Homeplace sunsets.

Hunewill Guest Ranch

http://www.guestranches.com/hunewill.htm

Located in Bridgeport, California, Hunewill claims over 1,200 head of cattle, and the staff needs your help rounding them up. Stay for a week and get your own private saddle horse for the duration of your stay. The ranch offers classes and clinics throughout the season.

Medicine Bow Lodge and Guest Ranch

http://www.medbowlodge.com/

During the summer, fish the lakes and streams or take a horseback ride through the mountains. During the winter, try your luck at cross-country skiing or snowmobiling, Try to be there over the weekend—Saturday nights, they promise, are prime rib nights.

Nine Quarter Circle Ranch

http://www.duderanch.org/9quarter/index.htm

This site features a handy "what to bring" guide so that you won't get caught with your chaps down. Also peruse the history section, which traces the history of the area from the 18th century to the present day. All guests stay in secluded cabins complete with wood-burning stove.

Pinegrove Dude Ranch

http://www.pagelinx.com/pinegrove/

The Pinegrove Dude Ranch is nestled on 600 acres in New York's Catskill Mountains. Join the cattle drive, take a long horseback ride, or relax and spend some time pitching horseshoes. Keep the kids busy in the day camp specially designed for them.

Ranchweb–Worldwide Ranch Headquarters

http://www.ranchweb.com/

Gene Kilgore and his staff have assembled a comprehensive site featuring travel information, maps, and additional information about dude ranch locations in the U.S. and Canada. Also included is information on fly fishing, hunting, cattle driving, whitewater rafting, and skiing. Don't forget to take a look at the real estate listings, where a few million dollars will buy you a ranch of your very own.

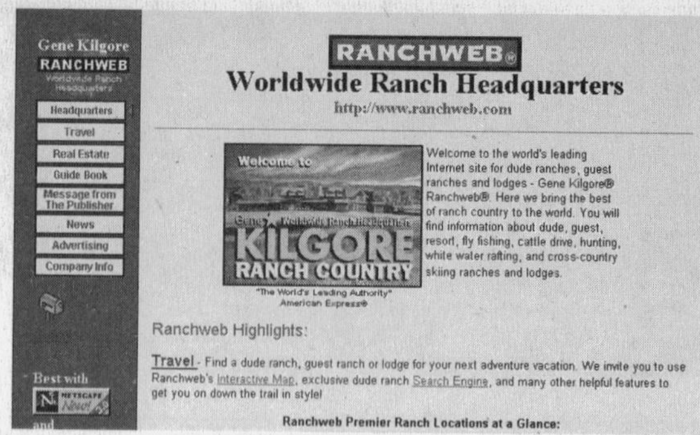

Rock Springs Guest Ranch

http://www.rocksprings.com/

More than a ranch, Rock Springs is also a fully functional conference center. Plenty of fun for kids and adults, this resort promises the services of a tennis pro (at designated times), local golf and fishing, and plenty of family activities.

Scott Valley Resort and Guest Ranch

http://www.scottvalley.com/

Take an Ozark canoe trip down the White River while the kids have fun at the petting zoo. The resort is also minutes away from fishing and water sports such as jet skiing, sailing, and scuba diving.

Wagon Wheel Ranch

http://www.wagonwheel.com/

West Texas is home to the Wagon Wheel, where the sky is big and the horses are tame and ready to be ridden. This site features a RealAudio greeting from the ranch's owner and promises three squares a day to all visitors. Bring your valid Texas hunting license and spend the day hunting quail.

Related Sites

http://www.duderanch.com/

http://www.duderanch.org/bald-eagle/index.htm

http://www.duderanches.com/RockingHorse/RockingHorse.html

http://www.dudesville.com/

http://www.paradiseranch.com/

http://www.texasusa.com/ranches/silvspur.html

http://www.trianglex.com/

http://www.vcn.com/server/business/dccgs/dude.html

http://www.virtualcities.com/ons/wy/h/wyhc501.htm

http://www.wyoming.com/~dte/guest-ranch/absaroka/

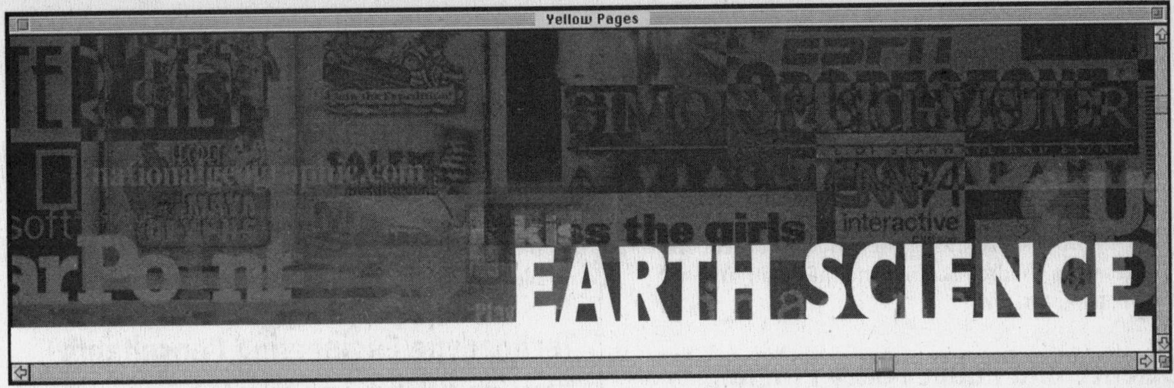

> The most beautiful thing we can experience is the mysterious. It is the source of all true art and science.
>
> *Albert Einstein*

EOS Buchantiquariat Benz

http://www.iprolink.ch/eos/

Catalog of antiquarian books concerning botany, earth science, geology, natural history, paleontology, and zoology. Also contains a search tool, some illustrations, terms and ordering information, and links to other earth science related sites.

Hanford Site

http://www.hanford.gov/

Department of Energy Web site supporting programs in waste management, environmental science restoration, and energy. Contains information on news and events, projects and activities, business opportunities, and the history of Hanford. Also features searchable database and links to other related Web sites.

Rain Forest Action Network Home Page
http://www.ran.org/ran/

VolcanoWorld
http://volcano.und.nodak.edu/

Lockheed Martin Idaho Technologies Corporation

http://www.inel.gov/

Site dedicated to the research in basic and applied sciences to solve problems related to the environment, energy production and use, economic competitiveness, and national security. Features educational resources, news releases, calendar events, environmental articles, and links to other environmental related sites.

National Center for Atmospheric Research

http://www.ucar.edu/oceanmodel.html

Presents a high-resolution simulation of the North Atlantic Ocean that represents circulation, designed to show the utility of some current scientific visualization tools to interpret highly complex data, making this data both meaningful and instructive to the viewer.

Online Earth Science Journals

http://www.epcc.ed.ac.uk/geo/petroleum/journals_FAQ.html

Lists online resources for earth science.

Rain Forest Action Network Home Page

http://www.ran.org/ran/

Discusses environmental issues of the rain forest. Includes numerous reports, statistics, information on other groups, and lists of companies to boycott. Also presents a children's corner and information about what you can do.

Science and Public Policy Program

http://www.uoknor.edu/spp/

Contains general information about the program, new trends, activities, and publications concerning policy research on environmental, energy, and sustainable development.

Science and Technology Corporation (STC)

http://www.stcnet.com/

Specializes in the atmospheric and environmental sciences.

Science Applications International Corp. (SAIC)

http://www.saic.com/

Firm devoted to high-tech products and services in the fields of national security, environment, health, energy, transportation, and systems integration. Features separate categories on energy, environment, government, information technology, health care technology, the Internet, telecommunication, transportation, a search tool, and career opportunities.

Supplements to Atmospheric & Oceanic Publications

http://www-cmpo.mit.edu/met_links/index.html

Provides data sets, source codes, and other supplements to published papers on the Web. Includes the means for visitors to the listing to add their own supplemental material if appropriate.

Technadyne Engineering Consultants

http://www.highfiber.com/~technady/

Consulting firm specializing in energy applications, earth sciences, environmental, and defense-related issues. Site features information about the firm and their clients and reports on some of their projects.

VolcanoWorld

http://volcano.und.nodak.edu/

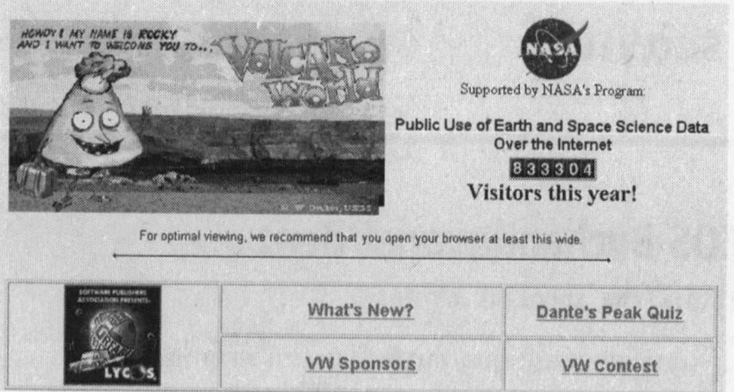

Provides information on volcanoes. Includes current news, images and articles about eruptions, background information, and an online expert who answers questions.

A B C D E F G H I J K L M N O P Q R S T U V W X Y Z

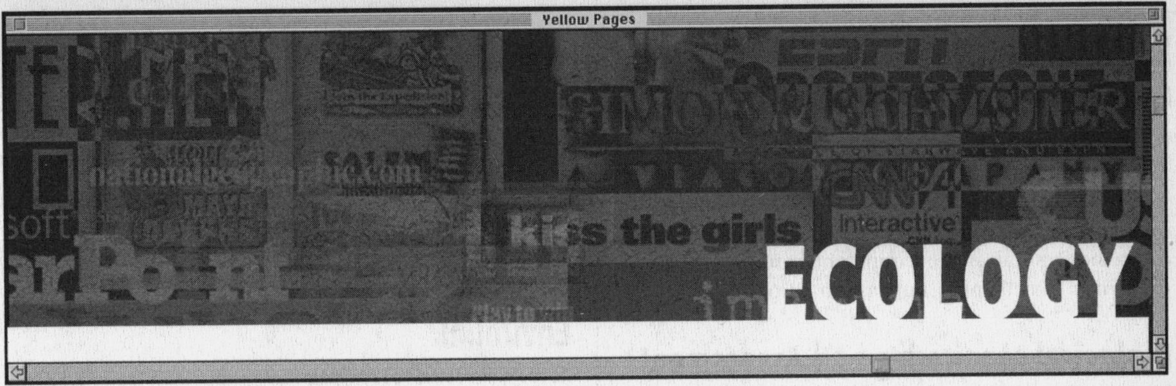

> People who decide they came to Earth to work, who make work their personal philosophy, are kept very busy.
>
> *Constantine Karamanlis*

NRP TOP PICKS

Abbey's Web
`http://www.abalon.se/beach/aw/abbey.html`

Earth Watch
`http://www.earthwatch.org/`

EcoLink
`http://www.envirolink.org/EcoLink/`

Greenpeace
`http://www.greenpeace.org/`

Sierra Club
`http://www.sierraclub.org/`

Abbey's Web

`http://www.abalon.se/beach/aw/abbey.html`

Site honors the militant environmentalist Edward Abbey and provides information about his writings and current ecological causes he promoted. Site also contains interesting links to outdoor photos.

The Access Fund

`http://www.sportsite.com/accessfund/`

Seeks to preserve America's diverse rock climbing areas through education, instruction in conservation, and promoting environmentally sound climbing practices. Site also contains board of directors information, as well as information regarding participation and protection of areas.

Cliff Ecology Research Group

`http://www.uoguelph.ca/botany/cerg/cerg.htm`

A group of ecologists dedicated to the study of cliffs. Learn about ancient cedars on cliffs, effects of human trampling, and cryptoendolithic organisms.

Coastal America National Website

`http://www.csc.noaa.gov/coastalamerica/`

The Coastal America program is a collaborative effort between organizations to protect the ecological systems and wildlife of America's coastal regions. Provides general information on the program itself and placeholders for more specific information yet to come.

Earth Watch

`http://www.earthwatch.org/`

A nonprofit membership organization that sponsors scientific field research projects. Their mission is "to improve human understanding of the planet, the diversity of its inhabitants, and the processes that affect the quality of life on Earth."

EcoLink

`http://www.envirolink.org/EcoLink/`

Online eco-Web journal. Delves into one ecological topic each week, including real-life stories, photos, and scientific information. Offers links to related Net resources.

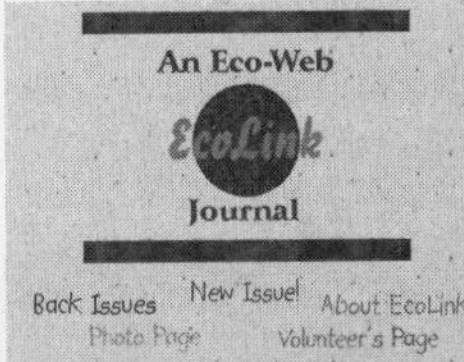

Ecologia

http://ecologia.nier.org/ecologia/

ECOlogists Linked for Organizing Grassroots Initiatives and Action is a group that "replaces cold war competition with environmental cooperation." Headquartered in the U.S., this group's mission is to provide assistance to environmental groups in the Former Soviet Union and Eastern Europe.

Ecological Monitoring and Assessment Network

http://www.cciw.ca/eman-temp/intro.html

EMAN is a network where ecologists from around the globe can share research, experiments, and ideas. Here ecologists can discuss emerging issues and trends and also develop options for future ecological policies.

Ecology Action Centre

http://www.cfn.cs.dal.ca/Environment/EAC/EAC-Home.html

The EAC have been protecting the environment since 1972. Their site contains several environmental FAQs, including definitions for the ever-growing list of environmental acronyms. The Information Centre also contains access to their library, policy papers, and their quarterly magazine "Between the Issues."

Ecology and Human Rights Information

http://paul.spu.edu/~koberst/green/green.html

Site contains various links to general ecological resources on the WWW, domestic and foreign. Site contains lists of major environmental and human rights special interest groups.

Ecology And the Conservation of Natural Resources

http://www.utm.edu/departments/ed/cece/ecology.shtml

Culminating experience whose mission is aided by knowledge of biology, chemistry, and geology. Includes content topics, corresponding performance objectives, correlation with National Science Education Standards.

Ecovote Online

http://www.ecovote.org/ecovote/

Site features the platform of the California League of Conservation Voters. Contains links to environmental issues, press releases, an environmental scorecard, 1996 bill tracking, and links to other WWW environmental resources.

Envirolink

http://www.envirolink.org

Envirolink provides a comprehensive amount of up-to-date environmental resources. Fellow environmentalists can communicate here via live video conferencing and chat rooms as well as access an environmental library and real-time environmental data.

Greenpeace

http://www.greenpeace.org/

Promoter of biodiversity and enemy of ecological and environmental pollution, Greenpeace and its links are accessible through this site. Links include the biodiversity campaign, the North Sea oil rig tour, a hotpage, and more.

International Center for Tropical Ecology

http://ecology.umsl.edu/

Combining the expertise of ecologists and systematists from both the University of Missouri-St. Louis and the Missouri Botanical Garden, the ICTE promotes research and education in biodiversity, conservation, and the sustainable use of tropical ecosystems.

Missouri Botanical Garden

http://www.mobot.org/

The MBG's Web site contains beautiful photographs of some of the many rare plants grown at their greenhouse. Information is also available from the research division in the field of biodiversity. A collection of online books is also accessible.

Natural Disaster Reference Database

http://ltpwww.gsfc.nasa.gov/ndrd/

The Natural Disaster Reference Database is a bibliographic database on research, programs, and results that relate to the use of satellite remote sensing for disaster mitigation. The database was created because there is at present no single source from which the scientific or disaster management communities can obtain information on the accomplishments and capabilities of remote sensing for disaster reduction. The database is a compilation of abstracted-from articles published since 1981.

PlanetKeepers

http://www.realtime.net/~waynep/plankeep.htm

An environmental site that features readings, inspirational quotes, a list of upcoming events, and a list of things that you can do today to help keep our Earth beautiful and healthy.

Sierra Club

http://www.sierraclub.org/

Home page for the non-profit public interest conservation organization. Site focuses on activist news, current critical "ecoregions," Sierra Club National Outings Program, as well as an internal Sierra Club search engine.

U.S.D.A. Natural Resources Conservation Service

http://www.ncg.nrcs.usda.gov/

Site describes the goals and services of the Natural Resources Conservation Service (NRCS). Formerly the Soil Conservation Service, the NRCS provides assistance to preserve the natural resources. Site also contains workforce organizations and state directories.

U.S. Fish and Wildlife Service–National Wetlands Inventory

http://www.nwi.fws.gov/

Site provides a list of the national wetlands and news related to them. Nineteen files are available for downloading, including a list of plant species that are found in wetlands. Also contains links to product information, ecology, and educator information.

World Forum for Acoustic Ecology

http://interact.uoregon.edu/MediaLit/WFAEHomePage

Seeks to investigate natural and human-made soundscapes. Offers links to sound resources and links to the online discussion forum.

NEWSGROUPS

news:sci.environment

news:talk.environment

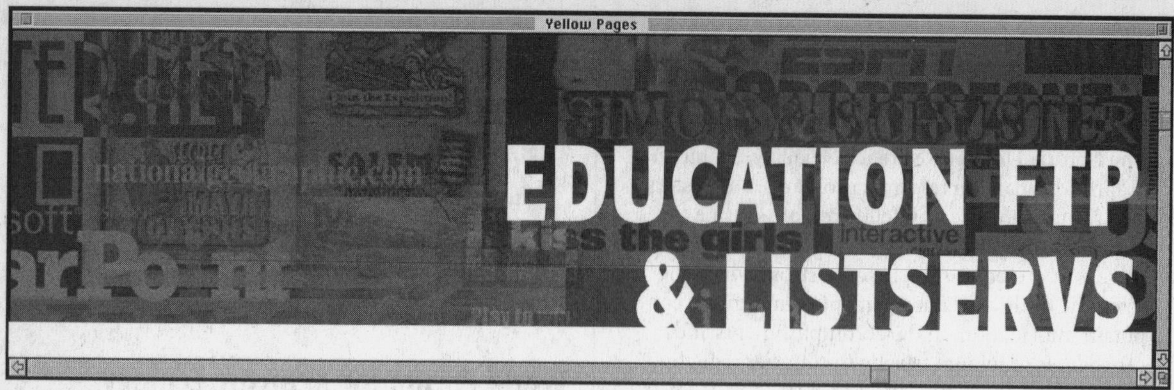

Let us think of education as the means of developing our greatest abilities, because in each of us there is a private hope and dream which, fulfilled, can be translated into benefit for everyone and greater strength for our nation.

John F. Kennedy

TELNET & FTP SITES

Health Sciences Libraries Consortium

`telnet://shrsys.hslc.org`

Login:cbl

The health sciences libraries consortium (HSLC) computer-based learning software database contains listings of PC-compatible and Macintosh programs used in health sciences and education.

Higher Education Resources and Opportunities (HERO)

`telnet://fedix.fie.com`

Login: New

A 24-hour, online database service that provides access to valuable information from colleges and universities on scholarships, grants, fellowships, conferences, faculty and student development, and research opportunities for minorities and women.

MicroMUSE

`telnet://michael.ai.mit.edu`

Login: guest

An educational multi-user simulated environment.

National Reference Center Master File

`telnet://locis.loc.gov`

Login: organizations

This site provides thousands of descriptions of organizations qualified and willing to answer questions and provide information on many topics in science, technology, and the social sciences. The file is updated weekly, and each entry in the file lists the name of the organization, mailing address, and other information.

LISTSERVS

AACSB–Business School Accredidation

University of Missouri-St. Louis

You can join this group by sending the message "sub AACSB your name" to

`listserv@umslvma.umsl.edu`

AEPDCC—Adult Basic and Literacy Education Professional Development Discussion

Texas A&M University Computing Services Center

You can join this group by sending the message "sub AEPDCC your name" to

`listserv@tamvm1.tamu.edu`

AERA—American Educational Research Association List (AERA)

Arizona State University, Tempe, AZ

You can join this group by sending the message "sub AERA your name" to

`listserv@asuvm.inre.asu.edu`

AJCUFAID—AJCU Financial Aid Directors

You can join this group by sending the message "sub AJCUFAID your name" to

`listserv@listserv.georgetown.edu`

CALIBK12—California K-12 Librarians

San Jose State University, San Jose, CA

You can join this group by sending the message "sub CALIBK12 your name" to

`listserv@sjsuvm1.sjsu.edu`

CCE—Council of Counselor Educators

University of Central Florida

You can join this group by sending the message "sub CCE your name" to

`listserv@ucf1vm.cc.ucf.edu`

CELVR001—CEL's Virtual Classroom 001

Central Michigan University, Mt. Pleasant, MI

You can join this group by sending the message "sub CELVR001 your name" to

`listserv@cmuvm.csv.cmich.edu`

COENEWS—College of Education Employee Discussion

University of South Florida, Tampa, FL

You can join this group by sending the message "sub COENEWS your name" to

`listserv@cfrvm.cfr.usf.edu`

CRITTHINKT-L—Teaching Critical Thinking

University of Illinois, Urbana, IL

You can join this group by sending the message "sub CRITTHINKT-L your name" to

`listserv@postoffice.cso.uiuc.edu`

CSTEP—Academic and Scholarship Information for Students

Syracuse University

You can join this group by sending the message "sub CSTEP your name" to

`listserv@listserv.syr.edu`

DEOS-L—The Distance Education Online Symposium

Pennsylvania State University

You can join this group by sending the message "sub DEOS-L your name" to

`listserv@psuvm.psu.edu`

DEOSNEWS—The Distance Education Online Symposium

Pennsylvania State University

You can join this group by sending the message "sub DEOSNEWS your name" to

`listserv@psuvm.psu.edu`

DR-ED—Medical Education Research and Development

Michigan State University, East Lansing, MI

You can join this group by sending the message "sub DR-ED your name" to

`listserv@msu.edu`

DSSHE-L—Disabled Student Services in Higher Education

State University of New York at Buffalo

You can join this group by sending the message "sub DSSHE-L your name" to

`listserv@ubvm.cc.buffalo.edu`

A B C D E F G H I J K L M N O P Q R S T U V W X Y Z

EAIE-L—A Discussion List for International Educators in Europe and be+

University Center of Information services (UCI), Nijmegen, The Netherlands

You can join this group by sending the message "sub EAIE-L your name" to

`listserv@nic.surfnet.nl`

ECENET-L—Early Childhood Education/Young Children (0-8)

University of Illinois, Urbana, IL

You can join this group by sending the message "sub ECENET-L your name" to

`listserv@postoffice.cso.uiuc.edu`

ECEOL-L—Early Childhood Education On-Line mailing list

University of Maine System, Orono, ME

You can join this group by sending the message "sub ECEOL-L your name" to

`listserv@maine.maine.edu`

ED220—Issues in Distance Education

The George Washington University Computer Center, Washington, DC

You can join this group by sending the message "sub ED220 your name" to

`listserv@gwuvm.gwu.edu`

EDINTL-L—Education School International Committee

Purdue University, West Lafayette, IN

You can join this group by sending the message "sub EDINTL-L your name" to

`listserv@vm.cc.purdue.edu`

EDLIB-L—Academic Education Librarians

Wayne State University, Detroit, MI

You can join this group by sending the message "sub EDLIB-L your name" to

`listserv@cms.cc.wayne.edu`

EE246—EE246-TCHG MATH ELEMENTARY SCHOOL

University of Missouri-St. Louis

You can join this group by sending the message "sub EE246 your name" to

`listserv@umslvma.umsl.edu`

FAMSTECH—Financial Aid Systems - Technical Discussion List

Arizona State University, Tempe, AZ

You can join this group by sending the message "sub FAMSTECH your name" to

`listserv@asuvm.inre.asu.edu`

FINAID-L—ADMINISTRATION of USA Financial Aid Offices

Pennsylvania State University

You can join this group by sending the message "sub FINAID-L your name" to

`listserv@psuvm.psu.edu`

FLTEACH—Foreign Language Teaching Forum

State University of New York at Buffalo

You can join this group by sending the message "sub FLTEACH your name" to

`listserv@ubvm.cc.buffalo.edu`

GC-L—Global Classroom: International Students E-mail Debate

You can join this group by sending the message "sub GC-L your name" to

`listserv%uriacc.bitnet@listserv.net`

GLB-HLT—Global Forum on Medical Education and Practice

University of Illinois at Chicago, Chicago, IL

You can join this group by sending the message "sub GLB-HLT your name" to

`listserv@listserv.uic.edu`

GRAPH-TI—Discussion of TI Graphing Calculators in Education

L-Soft International, Inc.

You can join this group by sending the message "sub GRAPH-TI your name" to

`listserv@peach.ease.lsoft.com`

HEALTH-L—International Discussion on Health Research

University College Dublin, Ireland

You can join this group by sending the message "sub HEALTH-L your name" to

`listserv@irlearn.ucd.ie`

HMEDRSCH—Home Education Research Discussion List

East Texas State University, Commerce, TX

You can join this group by sending the message "sub HMEDRSCH your name" to

`listserv@etsuadmn.etsu.edu`

IMSE-L—Institute for Math and Science Education

University of Illinois at Chicago, Chicago, IL

You can join this group by sending the message "sub IMSE-L your name" to

`listserv@listserv.uic.edu`

IRSU-L—International Relations Student Union List

Yale University Computer Center, New Haven, CT

You can join this group by sending the message "sub IRSU-L your name" to

`listserv@yalevm.cis.yale.edu`

ISSSAB-L—International Student and Scholar Services Advisory Board List

State University of New York at Buffalo

You can join this group by sending the message "sub ISSSAB-L your name" to

`listserv@ubvm.cc.buffalo.edu`

I_STUD—Members of the Student Chapter of the Institute for Op. Research

University of Missouri-St. Louis

You can join this group by sending the message "sub I_STUD your name" to

`listserv@umslvma.umsl.edu`

K-12GEOGED—ND K-12 Geography Educators

You can join this group by sending the message "sub K-12GEOGED your name" to

`listserv@listserv.nodak.edu`

K12ADMINK-12 Educators Interested in Educational Administration

Syracuse University

You can join this group by sending the message "sub K12ADMIN your name" to

`listserv@listserv.syr.edu`

K12SMALL—A Forum for Education in Small or Rural Schools

University of Arkansas Main Campus - Fayetteville

You can join this group by sending the message "sub K12SMALL your name" to

`listserv@uafsysb.uark.edu`

KINDED—Discussion Group for Course Education in Kindergarten

You can join this group by sending the message "sub KINDEDU your name" to

`listserv@listserv.kent.edu`

LRN-ED—Provide Support and Information to K12 Teachers

Syracuse University

You can join this group by sending the message "sub LRN-ED your name" to

`listserv@listserv.syr.edu`

A B C D E F G H I J K L M N O P Q R S T U V W X Y Z

MAC_ED-L—AOL Mac Education & Technology Forum Newsletter

America Online, Inc. (1-800-827-6364 in USA/Canada)

You can join this group by sending the message "sub MAC_ED-L your name" to

`listserv@listserv.aol.com`

MIDDLE-L—Middle level education/early adolescence (10-14)

University of Illinois, Urbana, IL

You can join this group by sending the message "sub MIDDLE-L your name" to

`listserv@postoffice.cso.uiuc.edu`

MIFINAID—Federal Education Loan Program

Michigan State University, East Lansing, MI

You can join this group by sending the message "sub MIFINAID your name" to

`listserv@msu.edu`

MSIRE-L—RI Math & Science Resource Discussion List

You can join this group by sending the message "sub MSIRE-L your name" to

`listserv%uriacc.bitnet@listserv.net`

MULTC-ED—Multicultural Education Discussion

University of Maryland CSC, College Park, MD

You can join this group by sending the message "sub MULTC-ED your name" to

`listserv%umdd.bitnet@listserv.net`

MUSIC-ED—MUSIC-ED Music Education

University of Minnesota, St. Paul Computing Services, St. Paul, MN

You can join this group by sending the message "sub MUSIC-ED your name" to

`listserv@vm1.spcs.umn.edu`

MWERA-H—Midwest Education Research Assn - H

The University of Akron, Akron, OH

You can join this group by sending the message "sub MWERA-H your name" to

`listserv@vm1.cc.uakron.edu`

NAFSA8-L—NAFSA: AIEE (Association of International Educators)

Temple University, Philadelphia, PA

You can join this group by sending the message "sub NAFSA8-L your name" to

`listserv@vm.temple.edu`

NETINTRO—Workshops For Grades K-12: Applications of the Internet

University Computing Services, Indiana University

You can join this group by sending the message "sub NETINTRO your name" to

`listserv@iubvm.ucs.indiana.edu`

NETSRCH—Workshops For Grades K-12: Internet Searching for Educators

University Computing Services, Indiana University

You can join this group by sending the message "sub NETSRCH your name" to

`listserv@iubvm.ucs.indiana.edu`

NEXUS-L—Nexus-L Research and Studies

FUNET (CSC / Finnish University and research NETwork), Espoo, Finland

You can join this group by sending the message "sub NEXUS-L your name" to

`listserv@fiport.funet.fi`

NYSFA-L—NYS Student Financial Aid List

State University of New York - Central Administration, Albany, New York

You can join this group by sending the message "sub NYSFA-L your name" to

`listserv%snycenvm.bitnet@listserv.net`

OISNEWS—News for IU International Students and Scholars

University Computing Services, Indiana University

You can join this group by sending the message "sub OISNEWS your name" to

`listserv@iubvm.ucs.indiana.edu`

ONLINEED—Faculties of Education Online Education Forum

Queen's University Computing Services

You can join this group by sending the message "sub ONLINEED your name" to

`listserv@qucdn.queensu.ca`

QUALRSED—Qualitative Research in Education

University of New Mexico, Albuquerque, NM

You can join this group by sending the message "sub QUALRSED your name" to

`listserv@unmvma.unm.edu`

RPE-L—Restructuring Public Education Discussion List

You can join this group by sending the message "sub RPE-L your name" to

`listserv%uhccvm.bitnet@listserv.net`

SA—Student Association Information and Discussion

Rice University Information Systems, Houston, TX

You can join this group by sending the message "sub SA your name" to

`listserv@ricevm1.rice.edu`

SERVICE—Student Service Leaders

University of Notre Dame, Notre Dame, IN

You can join this group by sending the message "sub SERVICE your name" to

`listserv@vma.cc.nd.edu`

SNURSE-L—An International Nursing Student List

State University of New York at Buffalo

You can join this group by sending the message "sub SNURSE-L your name" to

`listserv@ubvm.cc.buffalo.edu`

SSMP-L—Student Success Mentoring Program

Rensselaer Polytechnic Institute, Troy, NY

You can join this group by sending the message "sub SSMP-L your name" to

`listserv@vm.its.rpi.edu`

STCOAL—Student Coalition of Disabled Students

You can join this group by sending the message "sub STCOAL your name" to

`listserv@listserv.iupui.edu`

SUNYTRC—SUNY Teaching Resource Centers List

State University of New York at Buffalo

You can join this group by sending the message "sub SUNYTRC your name" to

`listserv@ubvm.cc.buffalo.edu`

SUPERK12—High Performance Internet & Computer Apps in K-12 Schools

Syracuse University

You can join this group by sending the message "sub SUPERK12 your name" to

`listserv@listserv.syr.edu`

T321-L—Teaching Science in Elementary Schools

University of Missouri-Columbia, Columbia, MO

You can join this group by sending the message "sub T321-L your name" to

`listserv@mizzou1.missouri.edu`

A B C D E F G H I J K L M N O P Q R S T U V W X Y Z

TAG-L—Talented and Gifted Education

You can join this group by sending the message "sub TAG-L your name" to

`listserv@listserv.nodak.edu`

TAMHA—Teaching American History

Wayne State University, Detroit, MI

You can join this group by sending the message "sub TAMHA your name" to

`listserv@cms.cc.wayne.edu`

TARPS—Teachers as Research Partners

Texas A&M University Computing Services Center

You can join this group by sending the message "sub TARPS your name" to

`listserv@tamvm1.tamu.edu`

TEACH-L

Purdue University, West Lafayette, IN

You can join this group by sending the message "sub TEACH-L your name" to

`listserv@vm.cc.purdue.edu`

TEACH-RI—News and Information for K-12 Teachers in Rhode Island

You can join this group by sending the message "sub TEACH-RI your name" to

`listserv%uriacc.bitnet@listserv.net`

TEACHART—NMAA Art Curriculum Teacher Conference

Smithsonian Institution, Washington, DC

You can join this group by sending the message "sub TEACHART your name" to

`listserv@sivm.si.edu`

TERSG-L—NRC: Teacher Education Research Study Group

State University of New York at Buffalo

You can join this group by sending the message "sub TERSG-L your name" to

`listserv@ubvm.cc.buffalo.edu`

TOW—The Online World Book Info

You can join this group by sending the message "sub TOW your name" to

`listserv@listserv.nodak.edu`

UBITA-L—International Teaching Assistants

State University of New York at Buffalo

You can join this group by sending the message "sub UBITA-L your name" to

`listserv@ubvm.cc.buffalo.edu`

VIRTCOL1—Virtual College Course 1

St. John's University, Jamaica, NY

You can join this group by sending the message "sub VIRTCOL1 your name" to

`listserv@sjuvm.stjohns.edu`

VIRTED—SJU Virtual Education List

St. John's University, Jamaica, NY

You can join this group by sending the message "sub VIRTED your name" to

`listserv@sjuvm.stjohns.edu`

VT-HSNET—VT K-12 School Network

Virginia Tech

You can join this group by sending the message "sub VT-HSNET your name" to

`listserv@vtvm1.cc.vt.edu`

WIOLE-L—Writing Intensive Online Learning Environments

University of Missouri-Columbia, Columbia, MO

You can join this group by sending the message "sub WIOLE-L your name" to

`listserv@mizzou1.missouri.edu`

WOMYNWIT—Women Professors of Adult Education

Texas A&M University Computing Services Center

You can join this group by sending the message "sub WOMYNWIT your name" to

`listserv@tamvm1.tamu.edu`

NEWSGROUPS

alt.education.alternative

alt.education.bangkok

alt.education.bangkok.cmc

alt.education.bangkok.databases

alt.education.bangkok.planning

alt.education.bangkok.research

alt.education.bangkok.student

alt.education.bangkok.theory

alt.education.disabled

alt.education.distance

alt.education.email-project

alt.education.higher.stu-affairs

alt.education.home-school.christian

alt.education.ib

alt.education.ib.tok

alt.education.research

alt.education.student.government

alt.education.university.vision2020

aus.education.bio-newtech

bit.listserv.slart-l

comp.edu

comp.edu.composition

comp.edu.languages.natural

comp.lang.logo

k12.chat.elementary

k12.chat.junior

k12.chat.senior

k12.chat.teacher

k12.ed.art

k12.ed.business

k12.ed.comp.literacy

k12.ed.health-pe

k12.library

k12.ed.comp.literacy

k12.ed.life-skills

k12.ed.math

k12.ed.music

k12.ed.science

k12.ed.soc-studies

k12.ed.special

k12.ed.tag

k12.ed.tech

k12.lang.art

k12.lang.deutsch-eng

k12.lang.esp-eng

k12.lang.francais

k12.lang.russian

k12.sys.projects

misc.education

misc.education.adult

misc.education.home-school.christian

misc.education.home.school.misc

misc.education.language.english

misc.education.medical

misc.education.multimedia

misc.education.science

rec.arts.books.childrens

sci.edu

sci.cognitive

sci.med.pharmacy

sci.op-research

sci.stat.edu

soc.college.teaching-a sst

uk.education.misc

uk.education.teachers

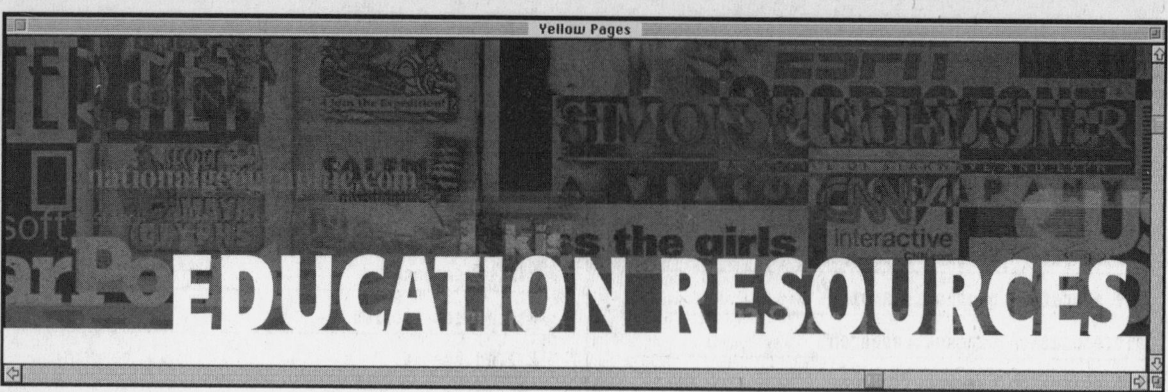

A B C D E F G H I J K L M N O P Q R S T U V W X Y Z

I have never let my schooling interfere with my education.

Mark Twain

Adult Education

http://galaxy.einet.net/galaxy/Social-Sciences/Education/Adult-Education.html

Offers links to several resources on adult education. Enables the combination of distance education, adult education, and the Internet to deliver instruction. Invites contributions to the collection of resources.

The Amistad Research Center

http://www.arc.tulane.edu/

Archives African-American history and culture. Also contains information about many other minority groups. Offers links to the center's manuscript collection, several art collections, traveling history exhibits, and library.

The AskERIC Virtual Library

http://ericir.syr.edu

Contains select resources for both education and general use. Includes lesson plans, ERIC digests, information guides and publications, reference tools, government information, and educational Listserv archives.

NRP TOP PICKS

The AskERIC Virtual Library
http://ericir.syr.edu

Education Virtual Library
http://www.csu.edu.au/education/library.html

ISN KidNews
http://www.vsa.cape.com/~powens/Kidnews.html

The Math Forum
http://forum.swarthmore.edu/

The New York Open Center
http://www.panix.com/~openctr

The World Lecture Hall
http://www.utexas.edu/world/lecture/

Biology (Science)

http://galaxy.einet.net/galaxy/Science/Biology.html

Offers links to all things scientific that might be of use to teach K–12 or university teachers and students. Categorizes sections by subset of biology, most recent additions, software, and collections, to name a few.

CALI: The Center for Computer-Assisted Legal Instruction

http://cali.org/

Nonprofit consortium of more than 155 United States law schools. Supports the production, distribution, and use of computer-based instructional materials.

CIC, Center for Library Initiatives

http://www.cic.net/cic/cli.html

Provides information for librarians, educators, and institutions, particularly those within the CIC (Big Ten universities, plus the University of Chicago).

The Comer School Development Program

http://info.med.yale.edu/comer

Provides information about the School Development Program, a national school reform project directed by James P. Comer, M.D., the renowned child psychiatrist at the Yale Child Study Center.

Cornell Theory Center Math and Science Gateway

http://www.tc.cornell.edu:80/Edu/MathSciGateway/

Provides links to resources in mathematics and science for educators and students in grades 9–12. Divides the resources into standard subject areas and includes links to online field trips and museums. Also offers journal and research articles.

The Cyber Classroom

http://www.cyg.net/~ddoctor

A collection of educational resources for students, parents, and educators, as well as some fun and games.

Department of Clothing, Design, and Technology, MMU

http://www.doc.mmu.ac.uk/hol/cdt.html

Details courses, staff, students, and the work done in this department. Contains examples of designs produced by students and staff and also details some of the conferences and shows scheduled.

The Digital Frog

http://www.sentex.net/~dfi

Focuses on producing high-quality educational software. Features The Digital Frog CD-ROM. Describes DFI and contains a full-featured Web version of The Digital Frog.

Education Resource Center

http://www.hec.ohio-state.edu/famlife/edu3.htm

This is a sub-site dedicated to providing educational resources about parenting, adolescents, divorce, families in the city, and more!

Education Virtual Library

NRP TOP PICKS

http://www.csu.edu.au/education/library.html

Alphabetically catalogs several interesting curriculum resources from around the world. Helps you research trends in education and creates multicultural or foreign language units. Also highlights links to a Web site created in Russian using the Cyrillic alphabet.

EDUCOM–Homepage

http://educom.edu:80/

Offers searchable archives of EDUCOM Review, archives of the Listserv EDUPAGE, and other online documents. Supports EDUCOM's focus on educational technology in higher education. Also offers links to several other telecom/educational technology-related site and programs.

Eriksdale School Educational Sites Page

http://www.escape.ca/~eriksdale/edusites.html

Comprehensive list of educational sites by discipline (including math, science, English, and social studies and also a general educational links category) and level (Elementary, Se condary).

Hillside Elementary School

http://hillside.coled.umn.edu/

Contains activities and projects. Lets students make their own home pages and have email addresses, and use the Internet for research.

Houghton Mifflin School Direct

http://www.schooldirect.com

School Direct, online K–8 educational resource store, offers quality educational materials for the student, teacher, and parent. Offers selected reading/language arts, mathematics, social studies, and technology materials—all from Houghton Mifflin Company, a publisher of textbooks, instructional technology, multimedia entertainment products, assessments, and other educational materials for the elementary and secondary school and college markets.

IPL Building Directory

http://ipl.sils.umich.edu:80/bldg.dir/

Consists of four main divisions—reference, youth services, services for librarians and information professionals, and the education division. Contains resources, interactive exhibits, and discussion areas.

ISN KidNews

http://www.vsa.cape.com/~powens/Kidnews.html

News service for students and teachers around the world. Allows you to use stories from the services as long as you credit the author, and enables you to submit stories. Encourages comments about news gathering, teaching, and computer-related issues in the discussion sections for students and teachers.

KidStore on the Net

http://www.kidstore.com/index.html

Specializes in fun and educational toys for children. Offers a list of resources for educators, parents, and kids on the Net.

Magic Learning Systems

http://www.xmission.com/~stageone/mls.html

Develops and markets educational and self-improvement software and shareware, combining the latest technologies with time-tested educational methods for the individual, the classroom, and the home.

Math and Science Gateway (Cornell Theory Center)

http://www.tc.cornell.edu/Edu/MathSciGateway/

Provides a wide range of educational services to the national community. Provides links to resources in mathematics and science for educators and students in grades 9–12.

The Math Forum

http://forum.swarthmore.edu/

Focuses on math education. Offers links to resources such as the Coalition of Essential Schools, a Web-based lesson on vectors, a geometry Listserv, and more. Also offers a section on projects for students, such as "Ask Dr. Math."

MATHMOL—K-12 Mathematics and Molecules

http://www.nyu.edu/pages/mathmol/

Provides students, teachers, and the general public information about the rapidly growing field of molecular modeling. Also provides K–12 students with basic concepts in mathematics and their connection to molecular modeling. Contains supporting materials for this project, such as a hypermedia textbook, a library of 3D molecular models, and online challenges for students.

The Media Literacy On-line Project Homepage

http://interact.uoregon.edu/MediaLit/HomePage

Provides information and resources to educators, producers, students, parents, and others interested in the influence of electronic media on children, youth, and adults. Contains a database on media literacy, as well as links to Internet resources related to the topic.

Medical/Clinical/Occupational Toxicology Resource Homepage

http://www.pitt.edu/~martint/welcome.htm

Provides information for practitioners, educators, and researchers in medical, clinical, and occupational toxicology. Also provides poison information.

Mount St. Helens

http://volcano.und.nodak.edu/vwdocs/msh/msh.html

Provides image maps of more than 1,490 still images of the mountain before, during, and after the eruption. Provides information about the people, Mount St. Helens and other volcanoes, other Mount St. Helens resources, plants and animals, and curriculum.

MU CoE Links to Education Resources

http://tiger.coe.missouri.edu/Resource.html

Offers many links on education and resources. Includes an entire section devoted to mathematics, science, and technology.

NASA Education Sites

http://quest.arc.nasa.gov/OER/

Offers a collection of servers specifically geared for teachers, students, and administrators. Offers a selection of math and science education resources, connectivity to numerous education servers, journals, and grant and project participation information.

Network Nuggets

http://www.etc.bc.ca/~tcoop/index.html

Shares information about educationally relevant Internet resources. Provides list members with a message each day during the school year to help them find resources on the Internet. Offers an organized main index, and the Listserv is one way to keep up with the Internet one day at a time.

The New York Open Center

http://www.panix.com/~openctr

Nonprofit center for holistic learning and culture in New York City. Offers nearly 1,000 courses annually on topics of alternative health and bodywork disciplines, depth psychologies, sociocultural issues, spiritual and meditative teachings, and multicultural arts. Includes program information and a preview of the center's journal.

The OSPI Math, Science, and Technology Server

http://www.ospi.wednet.edu/

Contains a collection of online math and science resources, as well as information on WEdNet. Also offers links to public and private online schools and Washington state colleges and universities.

Persimmon Software for Children

http://www.dnai.com/persimmon

Chooses a different monthly aspect of the arts and humanities to create an interactive, multimedia presentation that engages children and promotes creative learning.

Peterson's Education Center

http://www.petersons.com:8080/

Seeks to catalog all United States K–12 schools, colleges, and universities, both public and private, as well as community and technical colleges. Also plans to offer transcript services and scholarship information.

Placer County Office of Education

http://placercoe.k12.ca.us

Lists California K–12 and community colleges, as well as several links for teachers, students, and administrators.

Private School Resource

http://www.brigadoon.com/psrnet/

Presents a collection of many resources for private, independent, and religiously affiliated schools. Includes separate sections for organizations, school home pages, private school resources guides, and vendor information.

Project Libellus

http://osman.classics.washington.edu/libellus/libellus.html

Contains free classic Greek and Latin electronic texts. Offers pointers to other classic e-texts found at other archives, organized by institution or archive.

Scholary Electronic Forums Web Page

http://www.oise.on.ca/~arojo/forums.html

Offers contextualized information on scholarly electronic discussion groups. Provides information for potential and present users and listowners. Serves as a resource for electronic communication scholars, practitioners, and students.

SciEd: Science and Mathematics Education Resources

http://www-hpcc.astro.washington.edu/scied/science.html

Offers an organized math and science virtual bookshelf. Offers pointers to online scientific and mathematical reference works and charts, as well as links to the usual science and math subject areas. Also includes information on ethics in science and software and equipment suppliers.

Second Nature

http://www.2nature.org

Nonprofit environmental organization that helps institutions of learning, such as colleges and universities, produce graduates who will become environmental leaders. Provides information about Second Nature's unique educational philosophy.

SERESC

http://reg.seresc.k12.nh.us/

Contains links to a short list of very useful educational Internet resources. Also offers information on grants, government agencies, and museums.

Small is Beautiful

http://www.nas.nasa.gov/NAS/Education/nanotech/nanotech.html

Lists resources on nanotechnology. Includes DNA nanotechnology, molecular manufacturing, and computational nanotechnolgy.

Special Education Resources

http://www.intac.com/~washngtn/sped1.htm

Special Education resource for parents, teachers and administrators. Contains essential information and hotlinks to other sites.

Street Cents Online

http://www.screen.com/streetcents.html

Tied to the Canadian television show "Street Cents," which teaches young people how to be informed consumers. Covers all of the highlights of the week's program, and also offers a kids club and discussion list.

The Tecla Homepage from Birkbeck College London

http://www.bbk.ac.uk/Departments/Spanish/TeclaHome.html

Text magazine written for learners and teachers of Spanish, produced weekly during the school year. Provides text in Spanish, with vocabulary listed below the text.

Tele-School Online

http://www.teleschool.cableol.co.uk

Tele-School Online is an educational resource site. They have bookmarks, listed by subject and school home pages, listed by country.

TESL-EJ Master Page

http://violet.berkeley.edu/~cwp/TESL-EJ/index.html

Online journal. Covers teaching English as a second language from many perspectives.

Theodore Tugboat

http://www.cochran.com/

Based on a Canadian TV show, "Theodore Tugboat," and designed for young children. Enables kids to send a postcard to a friend, download a coloring book page, and help write an interactive story. Also offers a parent/teacher area.

UEWeb

http://eric-web.tc.columbia.edu/

Provides information on and for urban students, their families, and the educators who serve them. Includes manuals, brief articles, annotated bibliographies, reviews publications, and conference announcements in urban education, among other features.

The United States Education Department/OERI

http://gopher.ed.gov

Offers an information server that acts as a reference desk for all things educational. Includes educational software, Goals 2000 information, as well as primary, secondary, and vocational information.

Videodiscovery

http://www.videodiscovery.com/vdyweb

Provides information about interactive CD-ROM and laserdisc multimedia for science and math education, plus cool science facts, a guide to Internet education resources, educational technology primers, and more.

Virtual School Library Media Center

http://falcon.jmu.edu/~ramseyil

Library of educational resources for language arts, English, social studies, mathematics, networking, Internet, Shakespeare, Holocaust, children's literature, young adult literature, intellectual freedom, library science, science.

VOTEC Homepage

http://hre.ed.uiuc.edu/

Provides information about vocational/technical education. Includes information on workplace literacy, tech prep, thinking skills, and training.

The Washington Center for Internships & Academic Seminars

http://www.twc.edu/

Proposes the idea that the key to student success is active involvement in the educational process. Provides internships and academic seminar programs to college students that challenge them personally and professionally. Students apply academic theory through practical experience, discover their professional strengths and weaknesses, question chosen career paths, interact with students from across the country, and develop a broad sense of civic and professional responsibility.

Web 66

http://web66.coled.umn.edu

Seeks to be a catalyst that integrates the Internet into K–12 school curricula. Facilitates the introduction of Internet technology into K–12 schools by helping them set up servers, design home pages, and find other online schools.

Web66: K–12 Schools Registry

http://web66.coled.umn.edu/schools.html

Consists of a clickable map of the United States, Canada, and Mexico, and each click takes you to a different region's online schools. Provides the same information in a text format. Also offers school listings by country. Helps find keypals or partners for an online project.

Welcome to MegaMath

http://www.c3.lanl.gov/mega-math/welcome.html

Aims to bring unusual and important mathematical ideas to elementary school classrooms so that young people and their teachers can think about them together. Provides an online workbook with activities for teachers and students, as well as lesson plans and curriculum guides.

Whales: A Thematic Web Unit

http://curry.edschool.Virginia.EDU/~kpj5e/Whales/Contents.HTML

Focuses on K–5 kids. Contains images, activities and project ideas.

Window-To-Russia Homepage

http://www.kiae.su/www/wtr/

Offers resources in both Russian and English, as well as links that tell you how to install a Netscape-readable Cyrillic font. Offers online art exhibits, an interactive Russian-English dictionary, basic country information, and more.

WisDPI—The Wisconsin Department of Public Instruction

http://www.state.wi.us/agencies/dpi/

Includes resources about education and libraries. Contains a variety of K–12 projects, lesson plans, and educational links.

Women in Higher Education

http://www.itis.com/wihe

Presents Women in Higher Education, a monthly newsletter for women university administrators, faculty, and staff. Includes news and articles and current job listings.

The World Lecture Hall

http://www.utexas.edu/world/lecture/

Offers links to faculty world-wide who use the Web to deliver class materials. Includes syllabi, assignments, lecture notes, exams, multimedia textbooks, and resource materials on almost any subject.

The World of Benjamin Franklin

http://sln.fi.edu/franklin/rotten.html

Provides multimedia information about Ben Franklin using pictures, documents, and movies. Covers his family, inventions, diplomacy, philosophy, and leadership. Provides a bibliography for further study of Franklin, his accomplishments, and the time period.

A B C D E F G H I J K L M N O P Q R S T U V W X Y Z

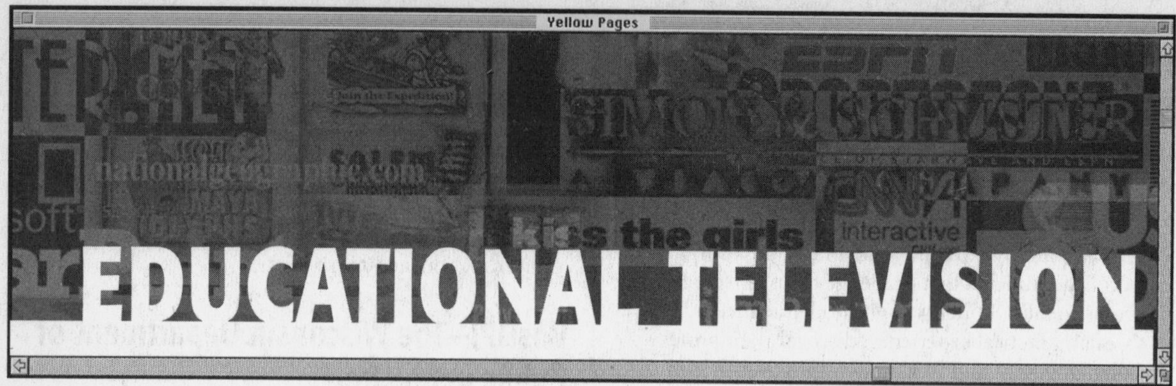

EDUCATIONAL TELEVISION

> Thanks to television, for the first time the young are seeing history made before it is censored by their elders.
>
> *Margaret Mead*

Barney Online

http://barneyonline.com/Barney/Nav/home.html

Welcome to Barney's home! If you enjoy what this purple dinosaur has to say, visit his homey site. Includes a play page with songs and games, a Barney store, and a Barney fan club.

Bill Nye the Science Guy's Nye Labs Online

http://nyelabs.kcts.org/

One of the hippest geeks on television, Bill Nye is from Seattle and sometimes has the guests to prove it. Entertaining as well as educational, Bill Nye the Science Guy's Web site has listings, a search mechanism, and other goodies.

Biography

http://www.biography.com/

A Web site based on the A&E program of the same name, Biography has a 15,000 person search engine, quizzes and games, and chapters from written biographies of important people. You can also get VDO clips and a calendar of upcoming programs.

Children's Television Workshop
http://www.ctw.org/

Children's Television Workshop

http://www.ctw.org/

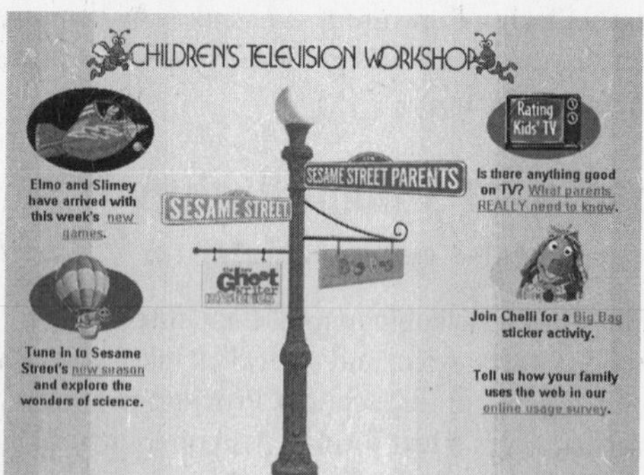

Offers many features for kids and parents alike, including a lineup of Sesame Street's new season, ratings of various children's television shows for parents, information about the Ghost Writer series among others, and online games galore for children. The parents section includes discussions of child development, education, product reviews, behavior and discipline, and others! Parents of young children should not miss this site.

Collecting Across America

http://www.collectin.com/

A program airing on Public Television, *Collecting Across America* spotlights what you'd think it would—collectors and the things they hoard. If you'd like to be on the show or have a suggestion, there is a reply form where you can voice your opinions.

Related Sites

http://www.igc.apc.org/greentv/

http://www.illusionstv.com/

http://www.voyager.com/~julian/Chem_TV/chemtv.html

The Creatures Connection

http://members.aol.com/cgzoo/

The Creatures Connection is a cable access television show that tries to provide viewers with a basic understanding of the animals in the world around them. Includes advice on how to properly care for pets and a detailed list of animal-related links.

The Discovery Channel

http://www.discovery.com

Cable channel covering history, technology, nature, exploration, and science-related issues. The site has special feature sections and "did you know" facts (such as why the *Titanic* sunk) that make it a unique experience from watching the channel. Includes the standard programming schedules as well as sections on kids-related programming.

The Doctor Is In

http://www.dartmouth.edu/~drisin/

Shown on PBS, *The Doctor Is In* has links to letters, awards, reviews, and dossiers of the production team. Also, every episode from the program is featured with a link to a quick description and videotape purchase information.

Engineering Television

http://www-etv.uta.edu/

The College of Engineering Center for Distance Learning, part of the University of Texas at Arlington, provides distance learning opportunities for graduate students in several areas of Engineering. Programs offered include Aerospace Engineering, Computer Science, Electrical Engineering, and Mechanical Engineering. Courses are via live interactive television throughout the North Texas area. Selected courses are also offered via videotape.

Great Canadian Parks

http://www.interlog.com/~parks/

Great Canadian Parks is shown Tuesdays on the Discovery Channel. It "explores the diverse natural and human histories within one of the most comprehensive parks systems in the world." A different park is showcased every week.

The Joy of Painting with Bob Ross

http://bobross.com/

Bob Ross's legacy of painting for the common person lives on at this, the official, *Joy of Painting* Web site. If you like happy trees, you'll love this site!

The Learning Channel

http://www.discovery.com/diginets/learning/learning.html

Cable channel devoted to programming about history, science, and world culture, as well as commercial-free programs for pre-schoolers. Site includes programming schedules and information about upcoming shows.

Newton's Apple

http://ericir.syr.edu/Projects/Newton/

Newton's Apple is a program shown on PBS affiliates around the nation. Each show has a particular theme and has guests who explain certain scientific concepts.

No Dogs or Philosophers Allowed

http://www.access.digex.net/~kknisely/philosophy.tv.html

Although it has a tricky title, this program is a philosophy program and is available only in a limited area. Check the site out even if you haven't seen it, though—you might like it enough to beg your cable company to get it.

PBS Online

http://www.pbs.org/whatson/

Check out what's on PBS television. A full listing, including picks and previews. Search functions allow you to search any subject or keyword according to month or start time. The guide to public television you have been looking for!

Reading Rainbow

http://www.pbs.org/readingrainbow/

This PBS-sponsored educational series is designed to encourage and motivate children to read and to visit their local libraries. Hosted by LeVar Burton. Site includes program descriptions and broadcast schedules, as well as activity suggestions to get your kids interested in reading. Sponsors a yearly Young Writers and Illustrators contest.

A B C D E F G H I J K L M N O P Q R S T U V W X Y Z

School House Rock

http://genxtvland.simplenet.com/SchoolHouseRock/

Remember these campy '70s edu-cartoons? Whether you are looking for a bit of nostalgia or want to teach your children all about conjunctions and the ethnic diversity of America, you'll find an exhaustive list of these tunes here. There are high and low graphics versions from which you can choose. Includes the lyrics and graphics of the standards: Grammar Rock, America Rock, Multiplication Rock, and Science Rock.

Science Gladiators

http://www.angelfire.com/ar/sg2000/

Public access television show for kids who enjoy science. Game-show format with kids as hosts and contestants. This site was written mostly by the grade-school age hosts and has allure for children.

The Science and Engineering Television Network, Inc.

http://www.setn.org/

SETN consists of scientific societies, corporations, government agencies, and universities dedicated to supporting scientific publishing in television. A good point of entry if you are looking for organizations in the science television markets.

Stephen Hawking's Universe

http://www.pbs.org/wnet/hawking/html/home.html

The show, on PBS, addresses the big bang theories, why the universe is the way it is, where we come from, and other cosmic questions in an entertaining way accessible to all adult audiences. The site includes standard schedule of programs, teacher's guide, and a strange stuff explained section, which discusses black holes and antimatter, among other topics.

Termite Television Collective

http://www.termite.org/index.shtml

The Termite TV Collective is a Philadelphia-based concern that produces a show called *This Is Only A Test*, a cable access series that confronts social issues through a low-budget, documentary approach. Includes episode guide.

This Old House

http://www.pathfinder.com/TOH/

The site about this public-access show includes FAQs as well as previews and updates about the current house being restored. See photos and read about restoration processes. You can also search by topic for information covered are various episodes.

Viewers for Quality Television

http://www.vqt.com/

Viewers for Quality Television (VQT) is a viewer organization that wants to influence the commercial networks to retain their critically-acclaimed quality series, despite insufficient Nielsen numbers. The site includes new season roundups, show endorsements, and short descriptions of best loved shows.

Where in the World Is Carmen Sandiego?

http://www.pbs.org/wgbh/pages/carmen/index.html

The popular geography computer game has gone from the computer to the television screen and back to the computer via the World Wide Web. Based at Boston's public television station, WGBH, this site has many links for students, teachers, and others who enjoy the game and the program.

NEWSGROUPS

alt.cable-tv

alt.tv

alt.tv.networks

misc.education

misc.kids

news:alt.tv.public-access

Related Sites

http://www.jou.ufl.edu/ITVAFOUND/

http://www.internetland.net/~kellbros/

http://www.foundation.reuters.com/

http://www.unctv.org/ncllink/adult/adult00.htm

http://www.uvsg.com/uvtvhome.htm

http://www.mpbc.org/

http://www.ciconline.com/

http://www.pbs.org/learn/scienceline/

http://www.jec.edu/

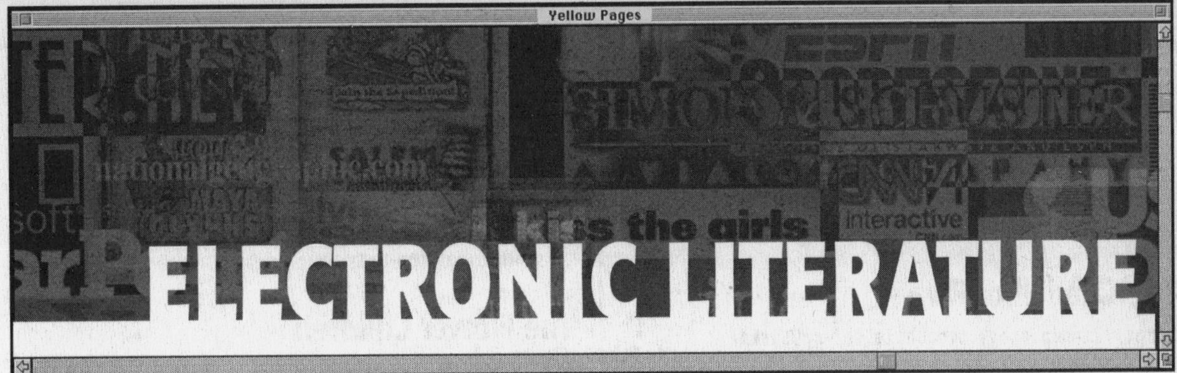

> You know who critics are? The men who have failed in literature and art.
>
> *Samuel Taylor Coleridge*

The Adventures of Tom Sawyer

http://www.cs.cmu.edu/Web/People/rgs/sawyr-table.html

The complete text, from the Project Gutenberg edition, linkable by chapter.

Alice's Adventures in Wonderland

http://www.cstone.net/library/alice/alice-w.html

The complete text, linkable by chapter, with colorized versions of the John Tenniel illustrations.

The Ancient Wisdom Home Page

http://www.primenet.com/~subru/Ancient_wisdom.html

An eclectic compilation of writings taken from ancient and contemporary authors on various facets of the Universal Wisdom Teaching—both Eastern and Western traditions.

American Literary Classics

http://www.mindport.net/~arezis/

A great site to visit if you want to catch up on reading you know you should be doing, but don't have much time to dedicate to it. This site gives a chapter a day of a classic American novel. (For instance, *The Red Badge of Courage* was featured at the time of this writing.) In addition to the chapter, the rest of the novel is present if you'd like to read it in its entirety, and links to the author of the featured book and some other interesting links are also available.

Candlelight Stories
http://www.candlelightstories.com/testnav.htm

Baker Street Connection

http://www.citsoft.com/holmes.html

Contains the texts of the Sherlock Holmes novels and short stories. Also includes scans of illustrations from Holmes books, and a canon word search feature.

Banned Books Online

http://www.cs.cmu.edu/People/spok/banned-books.html

Includes electronic versions of dozens of books that have been the objects of censorship and banning attempts. The books range from *Candide* to *Huckleberry Finn* and include commentary on banning and censorship attempts currently underway.

BerryWorks

http://www.speakeasy.org/berry/

Short pieces of fiction, poetry, and other writings by contemporary author Don Berry.

Candlelight Stories

NRP TOP PICKS

http://www.candlelightstories.com/testnav.htm

This award-winning site is a repository for children's online literature. From *Rumpelstiltskin* to *Thumbelina*, you can read your children these online classics. Includes a bookstore, international gallery, and spelling machine game. Story and illustrations submissions are welcome.

#cb Online Reading Club

http://www.mozzie.com/bookclub.htm

An online reading group that you can easily join by sending email. Club reads one book per month. Site includes top ten picks, monthly selections, and reviews.

The Citadell of Riva

http://linnea.asogy.stockholm.se/~mp95askm/David_Eddings/

Provides a biography of writer David Eddings, scans of artwork, and links to other pages. Also contains some excerpts from some of Eddings' works.

Classic Short Stories

http://www.bnl.com/shorts/

Site devoted to lovers of short stories and short prose, it includes an impressive selection of short stories from Edgar Allan Poe to Virginia Woolf. You can search by story name as well as by author.

The Commonplace Book

http://sunsite.unc.edu/ibic/Commonplace-Book.html

Traditionally, a "commonplace book" is a place to put notable passages people find in their reading to memorialize those ideas. This page is an electronic version of one of those books made by a variety of readers.

The Electronic Labyrinth

http://www.ualberta.ca/~ckeep/elab.html

Home to hypertext in literature, there are links to articles, e-texts, and other resources concerning hypertext in the area of writing. Essays by important authors are also present and link to other related articles.

The Electronic Library

http://www.books.com/scripts/lib.exe

This virtual library is available for the free dissemination of e-texts by thousands of different authors. There is a nice search engine that is available to find anything present in the "stacks."

Related Sites

http://www.casafuturatech.com/Personal/Stories/2Fiction/MLC/chapter1.html

http://www.teleport.com/~bcmetter/

http://www.internetv.com/austin/index.htm

The Fiction Network

http://www.fictionnetwork.net/

Provides a collection of short stories and works of serial fiction written by fellow Web browsers. Submissions are welcome. Includes stories of humor, fantasy, science fiction, mystery, children's, and other traditional fiction types.

The Flower Children

http://www.flowerchildren.com/

Here you'll find online children's stories from Germany, with beautiful illustrations. Legendary German fairy tales about mythological flower-children will delight children and adults. In German and English.

Great Books of Western Civilization

http://www.ilinks.net/~lnoles/grtbks.html

A self-study sort of course that should give the reader a well-rounded liberal education. The interesting twist on this, however, is that the books in the course are online (for the most part—some would infringe on copyrights).

Gutter Press

http://www.io.org/~gutter/

Provides radical literature and fiction to the reader of new or dangerous fiction. Provides links to other small presses, quarterly publications, and new and existing titles and authors.

HyperLiterature/HyperTheory

http://ebbs.english.vt.edu/hthl/HyperLit_Home.html

HyperLiterature/HyperTheory has an annotated bibliography, some readings, and some works by students who are studying this exciting new field.

Literary Works: Mark Twain

http://www.literature.org/Works/Mark-Twain/

Contains the complete text of *Huck Finn* and *Connecticut Yankee*, with more to come.

Little Women-DataText

http://www.datatext.co.uk/library/alcott/littlew/chapters.htm

The complete text of the book, linkable by chapter.

The Lost World (Randomhouse)

`http://www.randomhouse.com/site/lostworld`

A page maintained by the publisher, devoted to the *Jurassic Park* sequel. Contains ordering info, excerpts. Also contains links to other sites' articles on such subjects as dinosaurs, electric/hybrid vehicles, and chaos theory.

Mark Twain: Huckleberry Finn

`http://etext.lib.virginia.edu/twain/huckfinn.html`

Browse the complete text, chapter by chapter if you like, and look at the first edition illustrations. Includes early reviews and "the obscene sales prospectus illustration."

The Martian Chronicles Study Guide

`http://www.wsu.edu:8080/~brians/science_fiction/martian_chronicles.html`

Maintained by Washington State University, this is a useful page for those wishing to study and critique Bradbury's writing style.

Michigan Electronic Library

`http://mel.lib.mi.us/`

A project sponsored in part by Michigan's libraries, includes collections of online excerpts, stories, and reports in categories such as education, humanities and the arts, and science and the environment. Includes a reference desk, as well as a periodicals section.

The Mystery Corner

`http://www.cruzio.com/~mystcor/`

The Mystery Corner supplies short stories and samples of novels on a weekly basis and provides general discussions of interactive fiction. You are the detective and decide which clues to follow as you read along and discover the motive and plot of the story.

Narrative of the Life of Frederick Douglass

`http://downwithopp.com/lit/douglass/`

Read this heart-wrenching autobiographical account of Frederick Douglass' life. Born a slave around 1817, he learned to read and write from his master's wife and by teaching himself. He spent his life fighting for abolishment of slavery and the rights of free men.

Online Books FAQ

`http://www.cs.indiana.edu/metastuff/bookfaq.html`

A Frequently Asked Question list concerning the availability of online works, with links to archives and other directories, and information about public domain laws.

The Online Books Page

`http://www.cs.cmu.edu/books.html`

An excellent collection of online books, including categories such as prize winners and women writers. Provides search capabilities via author, title, subject, and what's new.

Project Gutenburg

`http://www.promo.net/pg/`

This award-winning site contains a collection of electronically stored books, mostly classics, that can be downloaded free of charge and viewed offline. Gopher searches for your favorite author reveal various options for downloading.

Ryer Reading Room

`http://members.aol.com/mryer/`

Electronic literature, some previously published, now for free. Poetry by Milly Ryer, short stories by Molly Ryer, humor by Rufus Jarman, a new mystery in serial by Marion Ryer, novels by Anne Silleck. Updated on the first of the month.

TeleRead

`http://www.clark.net/pub/rothman/telhome.html`

A project to bring books and reading to everyone. It includes articles, links, and papers written by scholars in support of electronic publishing.

The Ten Commandments

`http://rogue.northwest.com/~crt/hist/lewten0c.htm`

Includes complete and detailed reproduction of the Ten Commandments, as well as commentary on differences in the books of Exodus and Deuteronomy, comparison of Hebrew, Catholic, and Protestant versions, and more. Printed by Joseph Lewis.

Texts and Contexts

http://paul.spu.edu/~hawk/t&c.html

Site devoted to the expansion of knowledge regarding influential texts and authors in history. Submissions and additions are welcome. You an search via author and subject matter.

Tree Fiction on the World Wide Web

http://www.cl.cam.ac.uk/users/gdr11/tree-fiction.html

Gareth Rees's paper concerning hypertext and the World Wide Web presents differing ideas about the use of hypertext in today's literature. He even offers that certain games are a form of hypertext; in fact, he maintains that these are the most interactive type.

Washington Post Book Group

http://www.washingtonpost.com/wp-srv/style/longterm/books/bookgrp/bookgprules.htm

Read along with the *Washington Post* book club, an online forum that reads scheduled books and participates in discussion about the book. Books read here include *All the Pretty Horses*, by Cormac McCarthy and *The Wedding* by Dorothy West. Includes tips on creating your own book group.

Willy's Web of Bedtime Tales

http://www.willysweb.com/

Includes stories for children updated twice weekly. Read about Willy the Spider, who spins his Web of stories, as well as other characters. Good way to introduce the Web and reading to a young child.

The Wonderful Wizard of Oz

http://www.literature.org/Works/L-Frank-Baum/wizard/

The complete text of the book, linkable by chapter.

NEWSGROUPS

alt.books

alt.books.reviews

humanities.classics

rec.arts.books

Related Sites

http://www.geocities.com/Athens/Acropolis/9093/

http://eldarco.com/istory/mira/

http://www.deere.com/jdkids/johnny/index.htm

http://www.buylink.com/m7/syl/syl.html

http://pages.prodigy.com/lemus/lemus.htm

http://newt.blackboard.com/winter/guide/

http://www.wp.com/fictionreview/

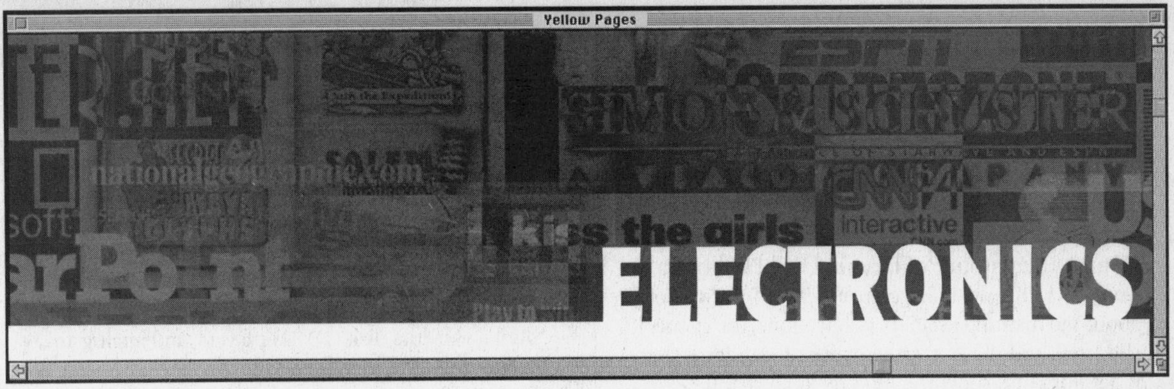

The primary cause of failure in electrical appliances is an expired warranty. Often, you can get an appliance running again simply by changing the warranty expiration date with a 15/64-inch felt-tipped marker.

Dave Barry

Alpine of America

http://www.alpine1.com/

Known for its high-end car stereos and speakers, Alpine also has a full product line of CD changers, head units (components that combine CD and cassette players, receivers, equalizers, and more), and auto security systems. Get full product features and links to Alpine sites in other coutries.

America's Discount Electronic Xpress

http://www.go-amdex.com/

AMDEX boasts over 10,000 products ready to ship. Find an extensive catalog of consumer electronics, from palmtop computers to karaoke machines to camcorders. Order before 4 p.m., and your shipment will be sent out the same day.

Tek Discount Warehouse
http://tekgallery.com/

Bose Corporation

http://www.bose.com

One of the leaders in high-end consumer audio, Bose prides itself on using non-conventional thinking and products to solve conventional problems. The company offers company history, current news and contests, and a secure site where you can purchase popular Bose models.

The Consumer Electronics Directory

http://electronics.net/

This site is a directory for dealers and manufacturers of home electronics. Add your electronics site to the list, and also add your name to the mailing list, which informs you of new product information, liquidation sales, and more.

ECS Refining

http://www.ecsrefining.com/

What happens to all those old circuit boards and circuits left over from obsolete machines? If companies are smart, they take them to a place like ECS, where the valuable and reusable components such as precious metals are extracted and recycled. Check out their techniques, policies, and their "no-landfill" philosophy.

Gernsback Publications, Inc.

http://www.gernsback.com/

This site is the host of *Popular Electronics* and *Electronics Now* magazines. Campy and fun, the site is equally suited for the professional electronic technician and enthusiastic hobbyist. Search current and recent issues, browse the FTP site, and leave a message on the boards.

IEEE Home Page

http://www.ieee.org

Home of the Institute of Electrical and Electronics Engineers, this site holds a great deal of information about the institute itself, its publications, the events it sponsors, and the ever-growing list of standards that it develops and supports. Find regional chapters and learn about training and career development programs through the organization.

Jerry Raskin's Needle Doctor

http://www.needledoctor.com/

Just because digital is the latest thing, don't think that analog is dead. The Needle Doctor specializes in keeping the vinyl sound alive with catalogs of new turntables, needles, cartidges, and belts. You're not the only one out there still listening to records. Come home to someone else who still cares. Order via phone or fax, or take the risk and order online from the not-yet-secure site.

MEGA HERTZ

http://www.megahz.com/

This online shop specializes in the broadcasting and receiving end of the electronics spectrum. Products include amps, antennas, demodulators, satellite receivers, and TVs and monitors.

Radar City

http://electronics.net/RadarCity/

Radar City features a small but standard set of the usual home electronics—TVs, camcorders, and stereo equipment. In addition, however, the store carries a large selection of radar detectors and scanners, which many of the large online stores don't bother with. Orders are accepted online, or via phone or fax.

Radio Shack

http://www.radioshack.com/

Radio Shack is still one of the leaders in consumer electronics. Find out about its many products, including mini-satellite TV, toys, cellular services, and home security. Also get the details on the international franchise program and employment opportunities.

Raytheon Electronics Semiconductor Division

http://www.raytheonsemi.com/sd/

Raytheon might not be as recognizable a name as Intel and some of the other electronics giants, but they're well-known within the electronics industry. Products include voltage regulators for Pentium and next-generation Intel chips, digital video encoders for digital versatile disk (DVD) players, and analog-to-digital converters. Find out how to take advantage of Raytheon's state-or-the-art facilities for your integrated circuit needs.

Satellite Broadcasting & Communications Association

http://www.sbca.com

If you're interested in a digital satellite for your home but don't know where to begin, start here. The SBCA represents all parts of the home satellite industry. Check out the section about finding a good satellite dealer in your area, and browse through the extensive glossary of DTH (direct-to-home) terms.

Tek Discount Warehouse

http://tekgallery.com/

Tek offers an enormous supply of appliances and electronics and promises a substantial savings from the manufacturer's suggested retail price. Products include stereo (home, car, and personal), microwaves, electric razors, camcorders, fax machines, telephones, copiers, digital cameras, vacuum cleaners, and much more. Order online or use the toll-free telephone number. The company promises quick ship times and a variety of payment methods.

Related Sites

http://www.4deals.com/

http://www.bgoods.com/

http://www.circuitservices.com/

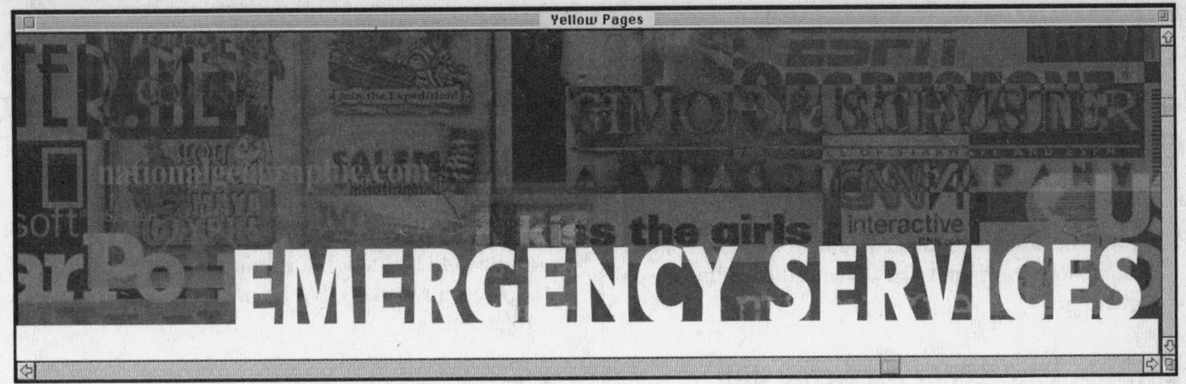

> In time of crisis, we summon up our strength. Then, if we are lucky, we are able to call every resource, every forgotten image that can leap to our quickening, every memory that can make us know our power.
>
> *Muriel Rukeyser*

1-800-MED-ALERT

http://www.800medalert.com/

This site is home to the Med Alert system, a way to make emergency contact with operators who can send the proper personnel to assist you. Pressing the button quickly establishes hands-free two-way communication. The unit is free with a monitoring subscription.

Abbey Group Consulting

http://www.abbeygroup.com/

The Abbey Group provides full consulting services in the public safety areas of fire services and law enforcement. Services include hazardous materials management systems, EMS reporting systems, wireless, on-the-job computing solutions.

Public Training Safety Consultants
http://www.pstc911.com/

AFTERDISASTER

http://www.afterdisaster.com/

If your home or business has been damaged by fire, flood, or other natural disaster, this group promises to get you back on your feet as soon as possible while minimizing your loss and downtime. Specializing in responding to fire and water damage, the company has skills in document drying, deodorization, mold/mildew treatment, getting clean water to your site, and much more.

American College of Emergency Physicians

http://www.acep.org/

This site holds a warehouse of information about the ACEP, its policies and guidelines, and current news. Features a large "members-only" section, but much of it is focused on non-members too. Find out about ACEP's views on managed care and other current concerns, as well as membership and dues information for doctors, residents, and med school students.

American Red Cross

http://www.redcross.org/

The jewel in the emergency services crown, the Red Cross exists to aid disaster victims and help people prevent and prepare for emergencies. Find out about the organization's current interests, locations in which it is currently helping disaster victims, and how to volunteer.

A B C D E F G H I J K L M N O P Q R S T U V W X Y Z

Canine Search and Rescue Gear by Lewis and Clark

http://www.dhinet.com/lewisclark/

This site features everything you need to outfit your rescue squad. Featuring doggy floatation devices, avalanche beacons, portable folding water bowls, and much more, Lewis and Clark offers quick online ordering.

EMBBS: Emergency Medicine and Primary Care Home Page

http://www.embbs.com

Provides educational resources and job opportunities for emergency and primary care physicians and health care providers.

Emergency

http://www.catt.citri.edu.au/emergency/

Hopes to provide an insight into emergency services around the world through action photos, a virtual emergency, a training room, and a notice board.

Emergency Preparedness Information eXchange

http://hoshi.cic.sfu.ca/epix/

Promotes the exchange of ideas about the prevention of, preparation for, and recovery from natural and sociotechnological disasters.

EmergencyNet

http://www.emergency.com/

The news service of the Emergency Response and Research Institute, EmergencyNet carries up-to-the-minute worldwide news regarding all sorts of catastrophes, from terrorist attacks to natural disasters. Also contains current articles and links for law enforcement, EMS operators, military operations, infectious diseases, and much more.

Event Medical Services, Inc.

http://www.eventmedical.com/

EMS sets up shop at conventions, sporting events, private parties, and wherever else you need them (as long at you're in California). Fully insured, EMS promises to take the worry away from hosting major events. They also carry a full line of emergency equipment and products.

FireFighting.Com

http://www.firefighting.com/

This jam-packed, energized site is like a giant rec room for emergency-services workers of all flavors. Featuring news, articles, links, a chat area, and even poetry and other writing, FireFighting.Com caters mostly to firefighters, but it will also interest law enforcement workers, EMTs, and other public safety professionals.

LifeGard

http://www.getsafe.com/lifegard/pers.html

LifeGard is a personal emergency alert system that lets authorities know when you need help. Comes with a tabletop model and a portable unit that you carry with you. Additional features include home carbon monoxide detectors and fire alarms.

Medic Aid Response Systems

http://www.medicaid-canada.com/

Based in Halifax, Nova Scotia, Medic Aid is a Canadian distributor of medical alarms. Search the products catalog, which includes a special "Alzheimer's-friendly" phone, and find an office near you with the store locator.

Mountain Rescue Association

http://www.mra.org/

A volunteer organization that provides mountain safety education and volunteers for search and rescue operations.

National Collegiate EMS Foundation Home Page

http://www.ncemsf.org/

Clearinghouse of information for campus Emergency Medical System groups. Also maintains two email discussion lists and information on conferences.

Paramedicine.com

http://www.paramedicine.com/

This site's goal is to be a resource to paramedics and those interested in paramedicine. Includes a chat/forum area, essays, and sections that detail EMS protocols and procedures in various states.

Public Training Safety Consultants

http://www.pstc911.com/

Based in California, this company hosts seminars for 911 dispatchers, first responders, and hotline call takers. Class topics include specific stress management for dispatchers, post-trauma stress courses, dispatching responses to workplace violence, and many more. Check the site often for specific locations and dates.

Rock-N-Rescue

http://www.rocknrescue.com/

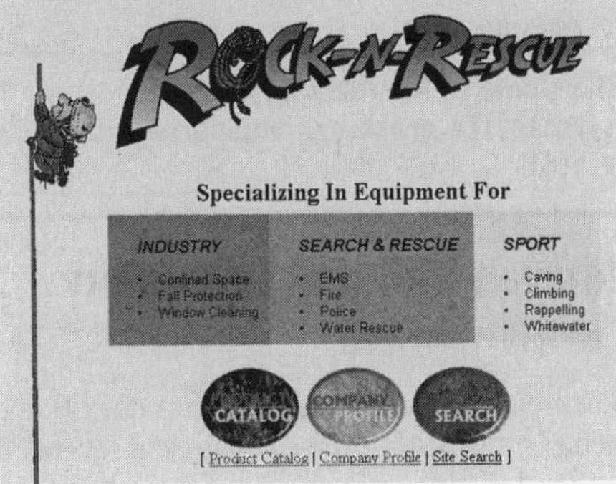

This company specializes in equipment for the narrow field of rock climbing and rope rescue. Browse their large catalog of ascending and rappelling devices, ropes and pulleys, and media resources. Whether your need is industrial, sport-based, or for a rescue squad, this site has what you need.

Skyblazer Signal Products

http://www.skyblazer.com/

Skyblazer makes flares and other emergency signaling products. Browse their line of flares and complete the survey to find out information on the Coast Guard's requirement for flares, the difference between marine and wilderness flares, and more.

Team Dispatch

http://www.sitegroup.com/teamdisp/

Program designed to bring more awareness to EMS, Fire and Rescue, and police and sheriff department dispatchers.

UBC (University of British Columbia) MultiCentre Research Network

http://www.interchg.ubc.ca/emerg_vh/ubc_multicentre.html

Emergency medicine research consortium made up of the emergency medicine research divisions of three teaching hospitals, Royal Columbian Hospital, St. Paul's Hospital, and Vancouver Hospital. Outlines information about the network's current and recent research activities. Also outlines recent publications, abstracts, presentations, and text book chapters. Functions as a bulletin board-type service, whereby members can post intra-network messages using a password-controlled link. Also offers links to a faculty-wide email directory.

NEWSGROUPS

alt.med.ems

misc.emerg-services

Related Sites

http://emer.paonline.com/

http://www.911.com

http://www.aaa.com/

http://www.geocities.com/Heartland/Plains/7841/

http://www.hurstjaws.com/

http://www.land-shark.com/

http://www.prepareandsurvive.com/

http://www.rescuebreather.com/

http://www.sos-rations.com/

http://www.viking-life.com/

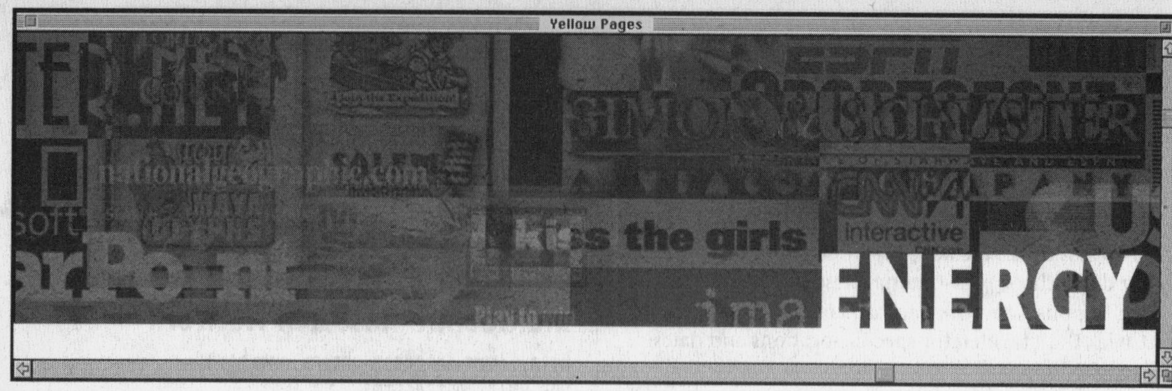

> Discontent and disorder were signs of energy and hope, not despair.
>
> *Cicely Veronica Wedgwood*

The American Nuclear Society

http://www.ans.org/

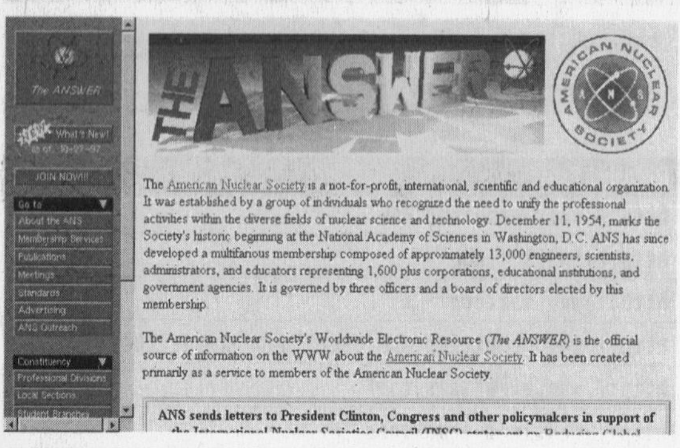

Provides information on membership, upcoming conferences, links to student chapters, and links to other WWW resources.

Bioenergy

http://calvin.biotech.wisc.edu/jeffries/

Resource page for bioenergy, bioconversion, and bioprocess technology. Contains an archive of related papers, information on liquid fuels from feedstocks and enzymatic methods. Personnel offer to assist in bioprocess development.

The American Nuclear Society
http://www.ans.org/

CREST'S Guide to Alternative Energy
http://solstice.crest.org/online/aeguide/index.html

Brookhaven National Laboratory

http://www.pubaf.bnl.gov/

Department of Energy research laboratory is dedicated to basic and applied investigation in several scientific disciplines. Contains an educational section geared for all ages, calendar of events, bulletin board, weekly newspaper, and departmental information.

Clustron Science Corporation

http://www.gslink.com/~ncmcn/Clustron/

Features information about the Nucleon Clustron Model of the atomic nucleus. Also contains company information and an atomic and nuclear periodic table of elements and isotopes.

CREST'S Guide to Alternative Energy

http://solstice.crest.org/online/aeguide/index.html

Contains features and articles related to alternative energy. Also includes links to other related sites and a searchable database.

Ed's News Page

http://www.hubcom.com/edsnews/index.html

Daily newspaper devoted to the oil and gas industry. Contains images, news summaries, and links to other news sources.

Energy Science and Technology Software Center

http://www.doe.gov/html/osti/estsc/estsc.html

Features software for sale funded by the Department of Energy or The Nuclear Regulatory Commission. Contains a searchable database, title information, ordering specifications, and other general information about the center.

Home Power Magazine

http://www.homepower.com/hp/

Magazine designed to assist home or business owners in lowering electric costs through solar, hydroelectric or wind energy. Contains articles and stories, subscription information, and links to other alternative energy-related sites.

Investigating Wind Energy

http://sln.fi.edu/tfi/units/energy/windguide.html

Set up in an educational format by The Franklin Institute Science Museum, this site contains discussions and articles relating to wind energy, information on building windmills, and different ideas and exhibits.

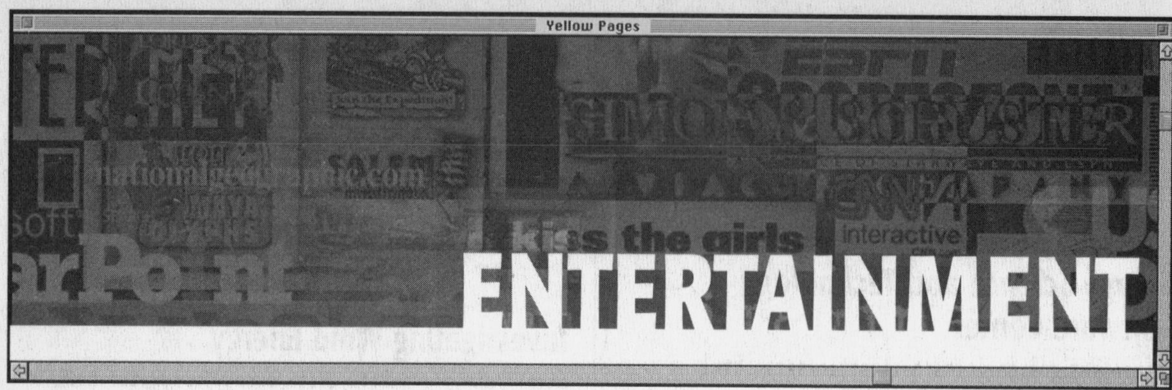

ENTERTAINMENT

> If it weren't for Philo T. Farnsworth, inventor of the television, we'd still be eating frozen radio dinners.
>
> *Johnny Carson*

101 Hollywood Blvd.

http://www.101hollywood.com/index.htm

A creative site featuring the faces of many famous people intertwined into a gripping plot lightly speckled with beer. Don't miss Hugh Grant's mug shot.

Campfire Tales

http://www.netlink.co.uk/users/avid-eye/jackanory/

Read one of four frightening fables of intrigue from this site. Also contains a very nice cowboy image on the home page.

Enter Magazine

http://www.entermag.com/

Provides an online magazine concentrating on issues in the transition between college and the workplace. Includes articles on practical subjects such as work, money, play, and has many online features. This site is highly recommended to anyone.

Marvin the Martian
http://www.frii.com/~engserv/marvin.htm

Hell's Buddha's

http://www.hellsbuddhas.com/

This site serves as the contact point for an ongoing five month motorcycle road trip through the country of India. In charge is Asokananda, the lead singer of a German punk rock band. Follow them through their journey to spiritual destinations.

The Magic 8 Bra

http://www.cyborganic.com/people/carla/Rumpus/Toychest/8bra/

Believe in a higher cup size and your fortune will flow. Just follow the directions and receive this questionable wisdom. Site also provides some strange links worth trying.

Marvin the Martian

http://www.frii.com/~engserv/marvin.htm

Marvin the Martian
Marvin Information
Marvin the Martian was created in 1948 by Chuck Jones. Marvin's voice was that of Mel Blanc. Marvin's first co-starring role was with Bugs Bunny in "Haredevil Hare" - 1948. He went on to co-star in at least four more roles with Bugs, "The Hasty Hare" - 1952, "Hare-Way to the Stars" - 1958, "Mad as a Mars Hare" - 1963 & "Bugs Bunnys' Lunar Tunes" - 1991. Along the way he also co-starred with Daffy Duck in "Duck Dodgers in the 24 1/2 Century" - 1953. In more recent years Marvin has be seen on such shows as "Tiny Toons", "Animaniacs" & "Tazmania ". Marvin has finally made his break-through to the big screen. He stars in the movie "Space Jam" with Micheal Jordan, Bugs Bunny & the rest of the Looney Tune cast.

The country's favorite little green man is back from the pages of Looney Tunes. Look here for some nicely done GIF images of Marvin, his dog, Bugs Bunny, and Duck Dodgers.

Net Frog

http://teach.virginia.edu/go/frog

This interactive frog dissection was designed for high school students, but it is fun for all—that is, assuming you were not emotionally scarred enough the first time you did this.

The Sneeze Page

http://www.claritin.com/Sneeze/Sneeze.html

Whether it is entertainment or not, who knows? Check out these ten downloadable sneezes. Ranging from a nasal sneeze to an allergy sneeze.

Southern California Real Time Traffic Report

http://www.scubed.com/caltrans/transnet.html

Look here if you are really in need for some random entertainment or if you are traveling in southern California. Site features online traffic reports, including accidents.

Planetary: The Artificial Intelligence Playground

http://www.planetary.net/

Lots of miscellaneous fun listings created by an artificial intelligence generator, such as fictitious grunge band names and tabloid headlines.

Virtual Flowers

http://www.virtualflowers.com/

Send a free online bouquet of flowers from this site to your sweetheart or significant other. Browse around the site for other floral shop items.

The Virtual Keyboard

http://www.xmission.com/~mgm/misc/keyboard.html

The name says it all. Yes, a virtual keyboard that is so slow, it takes five minutes to play *Mary Had a Little Lamb.* The page author also adds some useful suggestions to possible applications for the WWW virtual keyboard.

Welcome to the Adventures of Spacedog

http://www.spacedog.org/

The contact site for all your Spacedog needs, including fan club information, fun links, and movies. Site also contains links to other fun links checked out by "webmom."

LISTSERVS

ANIME-L—rec.arts.anime Newsgroup

Virginia Tech

You can join this group by sending the message "sub ANIME-L your name" to

listserv@vtvm1.cc.vt.edu

ASUENTER—ASU Entertainment Press Release Distribution List

You can join this group by sending the message "sub ASUENTER your name" to

listserv@asuvm.inre.asu.edu

DQMW-L—Dr. Quinn Medicine Woman TV Show

You can join this group by sending the message "sub DQMW-L your name" to

listserv%emuvm1.bitnet@listserv.net

ENTERTAINMENT-NEWS—Entertainment Channel Newsletter

You can join this group by sending the message "sub ENTERTAINMENT-NEWS your name" to

listserv@listserv.aol.com

ER-L—ER-L Discussions on ER (Crichton's TV Series)

Pennsylvania State University

You can join this group by sending the message "sub ER-L your name" to

listserv@psuvm.psu.edu

FILMUS-L—Film Music Discussion List

University Computing Services, Indiana University

You can join this group by sending the message "sub FILMUS-L your name" to

`listserv@iubvm.ucs.indiana.edu`

FKFIC-L—Forever Knight TV Show Stories

Pennsylvania State University

You can join this group by sending the message "sub FKFIC-L your name" to

`listserv@psuvm.psu.edu`

FKSPOILR—Forever Knight TV Show - Spoiler Topic List

Pennsylvania State University

You can join this group by sending the message "sub FKSPOILR your name" to

`listserv@psuvm.psu.edu`

FORKNI-L—Forever Knight TV Show

Pennsylvania State University

You can join this group by sending the message "sub FORKNI-L your name" to

`listserv@psuvm.psu.edu`

FRIENDS—The NBC Comedy Friends

Dartmouth College, Hanover, NH

You can join this group by sending the message "sub FRIENDS your name" to

`listserv@listserv.dartmouth.edu`

GIGGLES—House of Laughter, Jokes, Stories, and Anecdotes

You can join this group by sending the message "sub GIGGLES your name" to

`listserv@listserv.vt.edu`

GOODIES-L—Discussion List for the Goodies

America Online, Inc. (1-800-827-6364 in USA/Canada)

You can join this group by sending the message "sub GOODIES-L your name" to

`listserv@listserv.aol.com`

GS-L—Game Shows Discussion List

Ege University Bornova, Izmir, Turkey

You can join this group by sending the message "sub GS-L your name" to

`listserv@vm3090.ege.edu.tr`

HIGHLA-L—Highlander Movies and TV Series

Pennsylvania State University

You can join this group by sending the message "sub HIGHLA-L your name" to

`listserv@psuvm.psu.edu`

HLFIC-L—Highlander TV Show Stories

Pennsylvania State University

You can join this group by sending the message "sub HLFIC-L your name" to

`listserv@psuvm.psu.edu`

HORROR—Horror in Film and Literature

University Computing Services, Indiana University

You can join this group by sending the message "sub HORROR your name" to

`listserv@iubvm.ucs.indiana.edu`

HUMOR—Good Clean Funny Stuff

You can join this group by sending the message "sub HUMOR your name" to

`listserv@listserv.dartmouth.edu`

HUMORUG—A Humor List

You can join this group by sending the message "sub HUMOR your name" to

`listserv@uga.cc.uga.edu`

HUMORSCOPE—A Humorous Horoscope by Ron Lunde

You can join this group by sending the message "sub HUMORSCOPE your name" to

`listserv@listserv.aol.com`

LAZARUS-L—The Lazarus Man Discussion List

In the body of the message, type SUBSCRIBE LAZARUS-L. You can join this group by sending email to

`maiser@mirkwood.ucc.uconn.edu`

LAW-AND-ORDER—Discussion of the TV Series

America Online, Inc. (1-800-827-6364 in USA/Canada)

You can join this group by sending the message "sub LAW-AND-ORDER your name" to

`listserv@listserv.aol.com`

LOISCLA—The Lois & Clark: The New Adventures of Superman Discussion List

You can join this group by sending the message "sub LOISCLA your name" to

`listserv@vm3090.ege.edu.tr`

MERELEWIS—Life & Works of C.S. Lewis

You can join this group by sending the message "sub MERELEWIS your name" to

`listserv@listserv.aol.com`

MISC-HUMOR-L—Miscellaneous Humor Mailing List

You can join this group by sending the message "sub MISC-HUMOR-L your name" to

`listserv@listserv.aol.com`

MOPO-L—Movie Poster Discussion

The American University, Washington, DC

You can join this group by sending the message "sub MOPO-L your name" to

`listserv@american.edu`

PARTNERS—Discussion of the FOX sit-com Partners

You can join this group by sending the message "sub PARTNERS your name" to

`listserv@listserv.dartmouth.edu`

RRA-L—Romance Readers Anonymous

You can join this group by sending the message "sub RRA-L your name" to

`listserv@listserv.kent.edu`

SCREEN-L—Film and TV Studies Discussion List

You can join this group by sending the message "sub SCREEN-L your name" to

`listserv@ua1vm.ua.edu`

STCMD-L—Internet Star Trek Command Council

University of Arkansas Main Campus - Fayetteville

You can join this group by sending the message "sub STCMD-L your name" to

`listserv@uafsysb.uark.edu`

STHL-L—The Star Trek Humour League

University Center of Information services (UCI), Nijmegen, The Netherlands

You can join this group by sending the message "sub STHL-L your name" to

`listserv@nic.surfnet.nl`

THEATRE-SOUND—Discussion List for People Working in Sound for Live Theatre

You can join this group by sending the message "sub THEATRE-SOUND your name" to

`listserv@listserv.aol.com`

TWAIN-L—Mark Twain Forum

You can join this group by sending the message "sub TWAIN-L your name" to

`listserv@yorku.ca`

NEWSGROUPS

`alt.acting`

`alt.animation.spumco`

`alt.animation.warner-bros`

`alt.ascii-art.animation`

`alt.binaries.multimedia.d`

alt.binaries.pictures.anime
alt.cartoon.reboot
alt.comedy.firesgn-thtre
alt.comedy.improvisation
alt.comedy.standup
alt.comics.alternative
alt.comics.batman
alt.comics.classic
alt.comics.dilbert
alt.comics.image
alt.comics.lnh
alt.comics.peanuts
alt.comics.superman
alt.fan.actors
alt.fan.actors.dead
alt.fan.british-actors
alt.fan.dave_barry
alt.fan.don-imus
alt.fan.don-n-mike
alt.fan.howard-stern
alt.fan.kroq
alt.fan.mark-brian
alt.games
alt.geek
alt.home-theater.misc
alt.humor.best-of-usenet
alt.humor.bluesman
alt.humor.puns
alt.internet.talk-radio
alt.misc.forteana
alt.neo-tech
alt.radio.college
alt.radio.digital
alt.radio.networks.cbc
alt.radio.networks.npr
alt.radio.online-tonight
alt.radio.paul-harvey
alt.radio.pirate
alt.radio.scanner
alt.radio.scanner.uk
alt.radio.talk
alt.radio.uk
alt.radio.uk.talk-radio
alt.revenge
alt.rush-limbaugh
alt.sports.radio
alt.stagecraft
alt.tasteless.jokes
alt.toys.gi-joe
ba.broadcast
bit.listserv.radio-l
chi.media
chile.comics
dc.media
fido7.humor.filtered
fj.jokes
fj.rec.animation
fj.rec.comics
han.rec.humor
kw.theatre
misc.news.east-europe.rferl
nebr.humor
no.alt.radio-tv.irma-1000
no.radio-tv
pdaxs.arts.radio
phl.media
phl.theatre
rec.antiques.radio+phono
rec.arts.animation
rec.arts.anime.misc
rec.arts.anime.music
rec.arts.comics.alternative
rec.arts.comics.creative
rec.arts.comics.dc.lsh
rec.arts.comics.dc.universe
rec.arts.comics.dc.vertigo
rec.arts.comics.elfquest
rec.arts.comics.info

A B C D E F G H I J K L M N O P Q R S T U V W X Y Z

rec.arts.comics.marvel.universe
rec.arts.comics.marvel.xbooks
rec.arts.comics.misc
rec.arts.comics.strips
rec.arts.disney.animation
rec.arts.theatre
rec.arts.theatre.musicals
rec.arts.theatre.plays
rec.gambling
rec.gambling.misc
rec.gambling.other-games
rec.games.backgammon
rec.games.board
rec.games.bridge
rec.games.chess
rec.games.chess.computer
rec.games.chess.misc
rec.games.chess.play-by-email
rec.games.chess.politics
rec.games.chinese-chess
rec.games.design
rec.games.go
rec.games.misc
rec.games.pinball
rec.games.trading-cards.jyhad
rec.games.trading-cards.startrek
rec.games.video.arcade
rec.games.video.marketplace
rec.games.video.misc
rec.humor
rec.humor.funny
rec.models.rc.air
rec.models.rc.land
rec.models.rc.misc
rec.models.rc.water
rec.puzzles
rec.puzzles.crosswords
rec.radio.amateur.antenna
rec.radio.amateur.digital.misc
rec.radio.amateur.equipment
rec.radio.amateur.homebrew
rec.radio.amateur.misc
rec.radio.amateur.space
rec.radio.broadcasting
rec.radio.cb
rec.radio.info
rec.radio.noncomm
rec.radio.scanner
rec.radio.shortwave
rec.sport.paintball
relcom.comp.animation
relcom.humor
relcom.humor.lus
relcom.radio
relcom.radio.diagrams
relcom.radio.ham
sanet.radio.packet
sbay.hams
sci.med.radiology
slac.rec.ham_radio
talk.bizarre
tamu.kanm.radio
tnn.internet.itr
tnn.radio.amateur
tnn.radio.life
triangle.radio
tw.bbs.rec.radio
tw.bbs.talk.joke
uiuc.org.anime
uiuc.org.synton
uk.media.radio.archers
uk.radio.amateur
uwarwick.societies.amateur-radio
z-netz.freizeit.video

A
B
C
D
E
F
G
H
I
J
K
L
M
N
O
P
Q
R
S
T
U
V
W
X
Y
Z

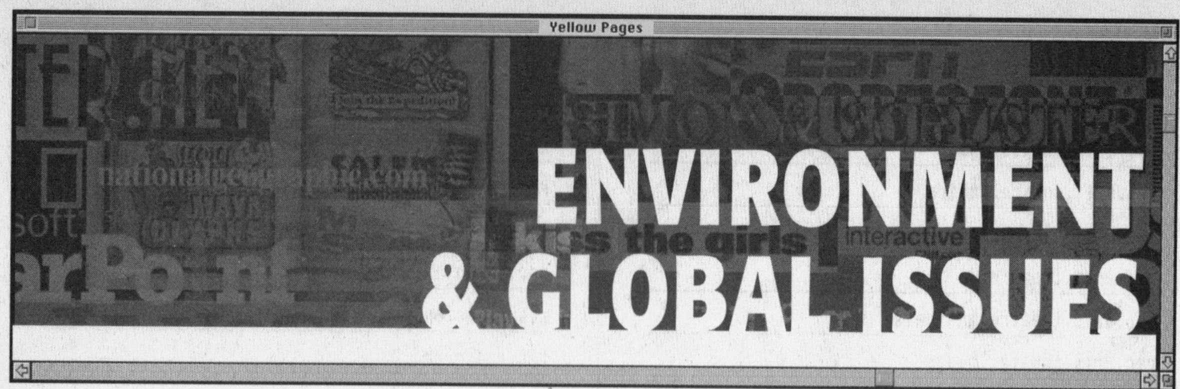

> It isn't pollution that's harming the environment. It's the impurities in our air and water that are doing it.
>
> *Vice President Dan Quayle*

EDUCATION

Academy for Conservation and Ecology

http://www.shore.net/~sace/

The Academy for Conservation and Ecology (ACE) is a nonprofit institution providing a unique opportunity for high school students to study conservation and ecology in the field.

Arizona EarthVision

http://earthvision.asu.edu/

Utilizing communications methods such as CU-SeeMe video conferencing and audio transmissions, this site provides high school students with an infusion of environmental education. An email discussion list is also available. Many guest speakers have their speeches broadcast from here.

Arizona EarthVision
http://earthvision.asu.edu/

National Environmental Trust
http://www.eic.org/

FICUS
http://www.arch.usf.edu/ficus/default.htm

Keep America Beautiful, Inc.
http://www.kab.org/index.html

CNN—Environment News Main Page
http://www.cnn.com/EARTH/index.html

GREEN PAGES—The Global Directory for Environmental Technology
http://eco-web.com

Ask An Earth Scientist

http://www.soest.hawaii.edu/GG/ASK/askanerd.html

The Department of Geology and Geophysics at the University of Hawaii generously provides this question answering service. If you have a question about geochemistry, the environment, pollution, or other earth-related subjects, the faculty will do their best to provide you with an answer.

Association of University Environmental Health Sciences Centers

http://www.envmed.rochester.edu/wwwrlp/niehsc/

The AUEHSC is a consortium of research centers, funded by an NIEHS program dedicated to the study of environmental health problems. The site is an outreach intended to 1) educate the public of the purpose of the program, and 2) inform members and the public of contacts/events/available resources to help solve environmental health problems.

Connecting With Nature

http://www.pacificrim.net/~nature/

The University of Global Education presents Project Natureconnect, a project which has as its goal the reconnection of humans with nature. Take advantage of PNC's books, email courses, workshops, and mailing list to help gain back personal and global sanity.

Destination Conservation: Environmental Education

http://www.ccinet.ab.ca/dc/

The Destination Conservation site graphically presents the success this educational program has had helping hundreds of schools reduce energy use, water consumption and waste production.

The Earth System Science Community Home Page

http://www.circles.org/

When learning Earth Science, students need resources that are not always readily available in the classroom. Enter the ESSC. Their goal is to provide students and teachers with advanced scientific resources via the WWW which will enable them to quickly and easily begin learning about the Earth system.

EE Link

http://nceet.snre.umich.edu/

Focuses on spreading information and ideas that help educators and students explore the environment together. Contains classroom resources and activities, educational contacts, reference material, and more.

EnviroNet

http://earth.simmons.edu/

EnviroNet is a network of teachers, scientists, environmental educators, and others who utilize telecommunication to enhance environmental science education. EnviroNet began in 1992 as a Teacher Enhancement Project at Simmons College in Boston which is funded by the National Science Foundation. The purpose of the project is to enhance environmental science education in the K–12 community throughout New England and the nation with the use of telecommunication technology.

Environmental Education Services, Inc.

http://homepage.interaccess.com/~eesinc/

Environmental workbook/magazine publisher for elementary school level. Also offers tailor-made environmental curriculum.

Environmental Education Workshops

http://rmcclos.idbsu.edu/env/ee.htm

List of hands-on, field and activities-based science and EE workshops designed for everyone including teachers and resource agency personnel. List includes available scholarships.

National Environmental Trust

http://www.eic.org/

The NET serves as a "war room" for public environmental education in the areas of protecting America's endangered species and ecosystems, protecting drinking water supplies, and reacting to global climate change. The site contains articles, links, and a RealAudio program.

Environmental Management Science Program

http://www.em.doe.gov/science

The Environmental Management Science Program is sponsoring targeted, long-term basic research so that "transformational" or breakthrough approaches will lead to significantly reduced environmental cleanup costs and risks, and is serving as a stimulus for focusing the nation's science infrastructure on environmental management problems.

FICUS

http://www.arch.usf.edu/ficus/default.htm

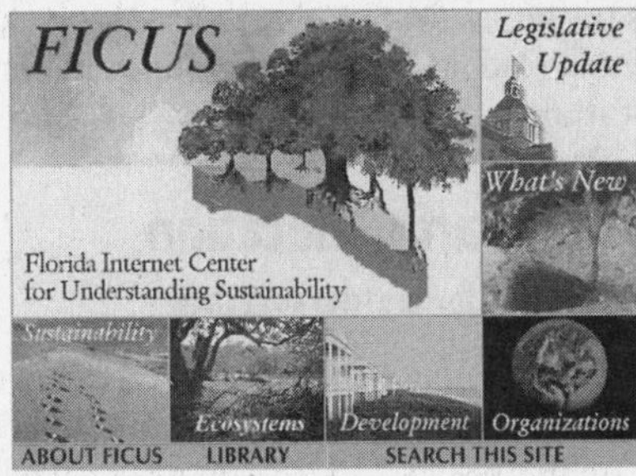

The Florida Internet Center for Understanding Sustainability seeks to provide a forum for the exchange of information about Florida's ecosystem, biodiversity, water, and exotic species.

The Global Environment Information Centre

http://www.geic.or.jp

The Global Environment Information Centre is a joint initiative of the United Nations University and the Environment Agency of Japan. It is founded on UN's Agenda 21 and is a center for global projects, networking and information on environmental issues. It will foster mechanisms to link NGOs with international policy-making processes.

The GLOBE Program

http://www.globe.gov/

Global Learning and Observations to Benefit the Environment is a group of students, teachers, and scientists who work together to learn more about our Earth. GLOBE students, with the help of their teachers, gather scientific data at their schools and pass it along to other students via the Internet. Scientists analyze the data and share their findings. The result is a better understanding of the Earth system.

GREENGUIDE—How to Trim Your Office Waste

http://www.pnl.gov/esp/greenguide/appa.html

This page contains practical guidelines for making your office a more efficient, waste-free organization. You'll learn how electronic publishing, use of recycled materials, and efficient purchasing can reduce waste. (And you might even save some money to boot!)

Handbook for a Better Future

http://www.mit.edu:8001/people/howes/environ.html

Developed as a guide to show what individuals can do to make the future better. Divided into two parts, "Situation" and "Solutions", the handbook contains articles by top scientists and authors. Also included is a suggested reading list for background environmental education.

Institute for Earth Education

http://slnet.com/cip/iee/default.htm

Dedicated to creating educational experiences that instill good feelings for the natural world, lessen our impact on our planet, and develop personal relationships with the earth and its systems. Many educational products are available, including books, pamphlets, and more.

Keep America Beautiful, Inc.

http://www.kab.org/index.html

Provides information on litter prevention and solid waste management (i.e., recycling, composting, waste-to-energy, sanitary landfilling). Offers lesson plans for teachers, awards programs, and links to community affiliates. All of their free publications are now available on-line.

Okefenokee Joe's Natural Education Center

http://www.gravity783.com/joe1.html

Visit Joe's "Critter Center" and learn about the residents of the Okefenokee swamp, a 700 square mile area that is one of the last remaining places where natural balance exists. Also visit the "Natural Garden" to learn more about Okefenokee's plant life.

Olympic Natural Resources Center

http://www.onrc.washington.edu/

Research and Education Facility of University of Washington, College of Forest Resources and Ocean and Fisheries Sciences. Finding pragmatic solutions to forest and marine sustainable resource management.

Plastic Bag Information Clearinghouse

http://www.plasticbag.com/

This site provides information that will prepare you for the next time you hear "Paper or plastic?". In addition, an environmental IQ test, free lesson plans available for teachers, and a section just for kids is available.

State Education and Environment Roundtable

http://www.seer.org/

Provides research reports about education, education reform, and education about the environment. Also offers links to education and environment web sites.

Texas Environmental Center

http://www.tec.org/

Access to environmental resources concerning water quality resources, documentaries, the Texas Environmental Almanac, GreenBeat!, and other environmental Internet resources.

World Transformation

http://newciv.org/worldtrans/

Is a page dedicated to helping people change their lifestyle in an attempt to become more harmonious with the earth. Includes sections such as Positive Vibrations, New Civilization, Spiritual Evolution, and more.

PRODUCTS & SERVICES

Black-Gold Oil Conditioning Systems

http://www.ozarksonline.com/blackgold/

Black-Gold Enterprises offers companies a means to reclaim their wasted oil, thus cutting down on waste. Oil reclamation saves the company money and saves our environment from unnecessary pollution.

Buy Green

http://www.buygreen.com/

This site is an excellent resource for learning to buy more "green" items. It maintains a list of companies that have developed guidelines and standards for green products, and a list of green products.

Earth Folk Catalog

http://www.gravity783.com/index.html

Here you can purchase products from naturalist artists such as Doug Elliot, James Billie, and Okefenokee Joe. Products include videos, cassettes, T-shirts, and more.

Earth Shirts

http://www.mind.net/darnell/

Earth Shirts is a cottage company from the woods of Southern Oregon that offers ecosafe T-shirts, biodegradable cleanup cloths, coffee mugs, and an incredible meat-free burger mix.

Eco-Heads

http://www.eco-heads.com/

Lovers of baseball caps and the environment rejoice! Eco-heads provides a complete line of caps produced entirely from organic cotton and wool. Caps are also available with environmental logos from organizations such as Greenpeace and The Wilderness Society.

Eco-Motion

http://www.halcyon.com/slough/ecomotion

A company that specializes in electric automobiles. The site explains the advantages of owning and operating an electric car, the costs involved, and it's practicality. This site also provides many links to "anyone who has anything to do with electric cars."

Electronic Lobbyist for Renewable Energy, The

http://www.pic.net/~stevie2/pages/cemail.html

At this site you can find out who your congressperson is, check their voting record on renewable energy, and lobby them by sending e-mail in support of wind, biomass, solar, and hydroelectric energy.

Environmental Site Assessment

http://www.flash.net/~softshel

Environmental Site Assessment is Windows software for the preparation of Phase 1 environmental liability reports. Environmental software written by an environment professional.

Environmental Software Resources

http://www.envirosw.com/software.html

The Environmental Software Resource Guide is a maintained database containing information for over 2,200 environmental software products from over 600 software vendors. Information is provided concerning the programs' major functions and what environmental media they deal with.

Frank Mikesh Natural History Books

http://www.netvista.net/~natscibooks

Specializing in out-of-print natural history books in over 30 searchable categories in current on-line catalogs.

Geotechnical & Geo-Environmental Software Directory

http://www.ibmpcug.co.uk/~bedrock/gsd/

Provided as a free resource for all geotechnical and geo-environmental engineers, this directory catalogues over 600 pieces of software dealing mainly with Soil Mechanics, Rock Mechanics, and Geotechnical Engineering. Listings are free for all software suppliers.

A B C D E F G H I J K L M N O P Q R S T U V W X Y Z

Green Bean

http://yourinfo.com/green/bean.html

A source for environment friendly products such as biodegradable toothbrushes, "save the earth" lunch bags, homemade soaps and shampoos, flannel diapers, and more.

GreenDesign

http://www.envirolink.org/greenmarket/greendesign/

A Web page design company that specializes in pages for socially and environmentally responsible organizations. Services include Web site design, photo scanning, Web site promotion, Web hosting, and CGI scripting.

Greenway

http://pages.prodigy.com/CA/palm/behpage1.html

Take the "How Green are You?" test, and then increase your score by using Greenway's environmentally sound products. Greenway offers products for home and personal care, as well as tips to help you get your home clean without the use of toxic chemicals.

Jade Mountain

http://www.indra.com/jade-mtn/contents.html

Jade Mountain is an environment friendly company that dates back to 1972. Their 112 page catalog contains over 4,000 products including energy efficient lighting, air purification devices, plans for electric transportation, cotton shower curtains and much, much more.

Mother Nature's General Store

http://www.mothernature.com/

A supplier of environmentally sound products, the General Store has items for sale in the areas of appliances, diet products, bath and dental supplies, groceries, herbs, pet supplies, vitamins, books, and more.

Real Goods

http://www.realgoods.com

Real Goods provides tools to promote a sustainable living environment, emphasizing independent living and energy self-sufficiency. Those interested in solar-powered housing, electric automobiles, and renewable energy will find this site particularly appealing.

Smokeless Cooking Products

http://www.ecomall.com/class/bbq.htm

Those aware of the harmful by-products of charcoal and wood burning will cherish being able to cook using only the power of the sun. With these smokeless grills, not only will you be sparing our environment, you'll also never burn your hot dogs again.

The Sun's Joules Multimedia CD-ROM on Renewable Energy

http://solstice.crest.org/

The Sun's Joules CD-ROM is an interactive multimedia encyclopedia on renewable energy and the environment. It includes sections on solar, wind, geothermal, hydropower, biomass, transportation, economics, and the environment with 60 video clips, 10 interactive exercises, and more.

The Video Project

http://www.videoproject.org/videoproject/

An abundance of videos about the environment. Videos are available concerning all aspects of the environment, from endangered species to sustainable development, water, and wildlife.

ZAP Power Systems

http://www.sonic.net/zap/

Zero Air Pollution (ZAP) Power Systems promotes the use of electric vehicles as a cleaner means of transportation. Their line is a collection of electric-powered bicycles for use by young and old alike. They also sell a patented power system that can be installed on an existing bicycle.

PUBLICATIONS

AHC Corporate Environmental Strategy: The Journal of Environmental Leaders

http://www.rpi.edu/dept/mgmt/SOM.pages/EMP/ces.html

AHC Corporate Environmental Strategy: The Journal of Environmental Leadership (CES) is a quarterly publication devoted to describing the connection between strategic environmental management and sound business strategy. The journal welcomes submissions with the corporate executive practitioner or public policy maker in mind.

Atlantic Monthly Election Connection: Environment, The

http://www.theatlantic.com/atlantic/election/connection/environ/environ.htm

This environmental page of *The Atlantic Monthly*, a publication "Devoted to Politics, Society, the Arts, and Culture since 1857" contains many well-written articles about our environment.

CNN—Environment News Main Page

http://www.cnn.com/EARTH/index.html

In addition to being a news superchannel on cable television, CNN also maintains a large WWW presence. Tune in to their environment page to keep abreast of the latest breaking environmental news as it happens.

Conscious Choice

http://www.consciouschoice.com/

The Journal of Ecology & Natural Living. This bimonthly publication of the American Midwest focuses on environmental issues and natural alternatives in health care, food, and nutrition. Regular departments include News of the Earth, Legislative Action, The Holistic M.D., Eco Surf, and Veggie Links, as well as book and movie reviews.

Duke Environment Magazine

http://www.env.duke.edu/Duke-Env/magazine.html

Published twice yearly by Duke University, this magazine contains articles devoted to valuing nature, ecology, wetlands, recycling, and more.

The Dying Sea

http://www.sacbee.com

The Sea of Cortez, one of the great natural wonders of the world, is being destroyed. This is a touching series that gives pertinent information about the destruction with photos.

E Online

http://www.emagazine.com/

E/The Environmental Magazine also has an online version which provides valuable environmental insights. Those who are interested in leading a "green" life will enjoy the articles that *E* provides. Also available is Ask E, where one can submit environmental questions to be answered by the knowledgeable staff of *E*.

Earth First! Journal

http://www.envirolink.org/orgs/ef/

Are you a radical ecologist? Do you believe in "monkeywrenching" and "ecotage"? If so, you'll likely enjoy this collection of journals that are intentionally provocative, controversial, and fun. Incidentally, the Earth First! Journal is published eight times a year, once on each Pagan holiday.

The Earth Times Home Page

http://earthtimes.org

Earth Times is an environmental newspaper published twice a month. Bill Clinton, Al Gore, Jimmy Carter, George Bush, and many other world leaders have been known to grace the opinion pages here. You can find out how to subscribe to the print edition, or browse recent issues online.

EcoLink

http://www.envirolink.org/EcoLink/new.html

The current issue of this journal hosted by the Envirolink Network is dedicated to articles about nonindiginous species. Previous issues of the journal devote their pages to Tropical Rainforests and Landscape Ecology. Also available is a photo page which contains all of the photos from all articles of the current issue collected on one page.

Ecology Law Quarterly

http://www.law.berkeley.edu/~elq/

One of the most respected and widely-read journals on environmental law and policy, Ecology Law Quarterly provides fresh insights and analysis from leading authors on critical environmental affairs. Synthesizing legal and technical matters, ELQ's articles are cited frequently in court opinions, by legal institutions, and by attorneys.

Electronic Green Journal

http://drseuss.lib.uidaho.edu:70/docs/egj.html

The Journal is an electronic publication with new issues being made available on an irregular basis by the University of Idaho Library. Currently five issues are available, each with a wealth of articles and reviews on the subjects of: assessment, conservation, development, disposal, education, hazards, pollution, resources, technology, and treatment.

A B C D E F G H I J K L M N O P Q R S T U V W X Y Z

Environmental Ethics Journal

http://www.cep.unt.edu/enethics.html

This site plays home to a vast collection of articles that concentrate on the philosophical side of environmental issues. Through this site you can access The Whole Earth Review, Green Earth Observer, and The Bear Essential.

Environmental News Network

http://www.enn.com/

The ENN see themselves as "your one stop on the Internet for timely news and information on the environment." This may well be true. Featured here are listings of companies who offer environmental products and services, a calendar of upcoming events and workshops, an environmental newsletter and much, much more.

Environmental Protection Magazine Online

http://www.eponline.com

Visit Environmental Protection Online! Read articles from past issues, email editors, find related sites, and discuss environmental issues in the EP Forum.

GREEN PAGES—The Global Directory for Environmental Technology

http://eco-web.com

A single reference source for government departments, utility companies, engineering consultants, development agencies, importers and traders, educational institutes, non-governmental organizations and individuals engaged in environmental activities.

GreenBeat!

http://www.tec.org/greenbeat/index.html

An Internet magazine published monthly by the Texas Environmental Center. Issues are available back to November 1995 and are devoted to Drought, Air Quality, Earth Day, Pathways to Involvement, Wastewater, Bioregionalism, Green Building, and Water Quality, respectively.

GREENLines

http://www.defenders.org/gline-h.html

GREENlines is a one page environmental news sheet published each and every day. This site is perfect for those who want a quick update on relevant environmental happenings but don't have a lot of time to read in-depth articles.

The Online Better World Magazine

http://www.betterworld.com/index.htm

An electronic magazine that offers feature articles on living a "greener" life. The magazine also features editorials, opinions, book reviews, and interactive discussions.

Our Environment—Online

http://maui.net/~jstark/ournvmag.html

This issue, number four, deals primarily with energy facts, technology, and conservation. The first three issues are also available, entitled "The Alarming Language of Pollution", "How Hot Is It?", and "Where Have All the Flowers Gone?".

People and the Planet

http://www.oneworld.org/patp/index.html

Provides a means to subscribe to the print version of the magazine or just browse the articles online. Articles have various environmental content. Videos are also available.

Rachel's Environment & Health Weekly

gopher://ftp.std.com:70/11/FTP/world/periodicals/rachel

An extensive collection of articles on the subjects of pesticides, sustainable development, global warming, waste management, and much more.

Ranger Rick

http://www.nwf.org/nwf/lib/rr/index.html

Remember *Ranger Rick*? This children's magazine now has several of its articles published on the Net, not to mention an index of topics that goes all the way back to 1968!

Science & The Environment

http://www.cais.net/publish/voyage.htm

This bimonthly magazine contains chapters on Biodiversity & Wildlife, Health, Population & Agriculture, Marine Ecology, Clean Water, Alternative Energy & Fuels, Climate Change & Atmospheric Studies, Waste Management & Recycling, and Clean Air.

SCOPE Newsletter

http://www.asi.fr/scope/

The Newsletter, published by the Scientific Committee on Phosphates in Europe is devoted to information concerning phosphates, detergents, sewage treatment, and the environment. The Newsletter contains objective articles containing scientific information on the effects of detergents, phosphate and non-phosphate, on the environment.

Viva La Tortuga!

http://www.earthisland.org/ei/strp/strpindx.html

Viva La Tortuga! is the newsletter of the Sea Turtle Restoration Project of Earth Island Institute. Inside you can find information on sea turtle activism, including where to buy turtle-safe shrimp.

The WWW Virtual Library—Environment

http://ecosys.drdr.virginia.edu/Environment.html

A directory of many environmental articles based on the subjects of Biodiversity & Ecology, Earth Sciences, Energy, Environmental Law, Forestry, Landscape Architecture, Oceanography, and Sustainable Development.

LISTSERVS

ACTIV-L—Activists Mailing List

University of Missouri-Columbia, Columbia, MO

You can join this group by sending the message "sub ACTIV-L your name" to

listserv@mizzou1.missouri.edu

AERE-L—Association of Environmental and Resource Economists

You can join this group by sending the message "sub AERE-L your name" to

listserv@lsv.uky.edu

AQUIFER—Pollution and Groundwater Recharge

Tecnopolis CSATA Novus Ortus - Valenzano (BA), Italy

You can join this group by sending the message "sub AQUIFER your name" to

listserv%ibacsata.bitnet@listserv.net

CERES-L—Collaborative Environments for Conserving Earth Resources

West Virginia Network for Educational Telecomputing

You can join this group by sending the message "sub CERES-L your name" to

listserv@wvnvm.wvnet.edu

CONSLINK—CONSLINK - The Conservation Network

Smithsonian Institution, Washington, DC

You can join this group by sending the message "sub CONSLINK your name" to

listserv@sivm.si.edu

CUSEN-L—Canadian Unified Student Environmental Network

Queen's University Computing Services

You can join this group by sending the message "sub CUSEN-L your name" to

listserv@qucdn.queensu.ca

ECDM—Environmentally Conscious Design & Mfg List

University of Windsor

You can join this group by sending the message "sub ECDM your name" to

listserv@pdomain.uwindsor.ca

ECOLOGIC—EcoLogic Mailing List

Rensselaer Polytechnic Institute, Troy, NY

You can join this group by sending the message "sub ECOLOGIC your name" to

listserv@vm.its.rpi.edu

ENTREE-L—Environmental Training in Engineering Education

University Center of Information services (UCI), Nijmegen, The Netherlands

You can join this group by sending the message "sub ENTREE-L your name" to

listserv@nic.surfnet.nl

ENVINF-L—List for Environmental Information

University Center of Information services (UCI), Nijmegen, The Netherlands

You can join this group by sending the message "sub ENVINF-L your name" to

listserv@nic.surfnet.nl

ENVIRON—Miami University Environmental Information
Miami University, Oxford, OH

You can join this group by sending the message "sub ENVIRON your name" to

`listserv@miamiu.muohio.edu`

ENVST-L—Environmental Studies Discussion List
Brown University, Providence, RI

You can join this group by sending the message "sub ENVST-L your name" to

`listserv@brownvm.brown.edu`

GREENGRP—Inst. for the Environment
The George Washington University Computer Center, Washington DC

You can join this group by sending the message "sub GREENGRP your name" to

`listserv@gwuvm.gwu.edu`

COASTNET—Coastal Management Conference
You can get info on this group by sending the message "info coastnet your name" to

`listserv@uriacc.uri.edu`

CUSN-L—Canadian Unified Student Environmental Network
You can get info on this group by sending the message "info Cusn-l your name" to

`listserv@qucdn.queensu.ca`

GROUNDWATER—GROUNDWATER
Type the command "subscribe GROUNDWATER in the body" and send to

`majordomo@ias.champlain.edu`

H-ASEH—American Society for Environmental History
You can join this group by sending the message "sub H-ASEH your name" to

`listserv@h-net.msu.edu`

ISEA-L—International Students for Environmental Action
University Center of Information services (UCI), Nijmegen, The Netherlands

You can join this group by sending the message "sub ISEA-L your name" to

`listserv@nic.surfnet.nl`

ONE-L—Organization and the Natural Environment
Clarkson University Schuler Resouces Center

You can join this group by sending the message "sub ONE-L your name" to

`listserv@clvm.clarkson.edu`

PS085—PS085-GLOBAL ECOLOGY
University of Missouri-St. Louis

You can join this group by sending the message "sub PS085 your name" to

`listserv@umslvma.umsl.edu`

QEN-L—Queen's Environmental Network
Queen's University Computing Services

You can join this group by sending the message "sub QEN-L your name" to

`listserv@qucdn.queensu.ca`

SEAUGA—Students for Environmental Awareness
The University of Georgia, Athens, GA

You can join this group by sending the message "sub SEAUGA your name" to

`listserv@uga.cc.uga.edu`

NEWSGROUPS

`alt.earth.system.science`

`alt.org.earth-first`

`alt.politics.greens`

`alt.politics.scorched-earth`

`alt.save.the.earth`

`ca.environment`

`earth.general`

`sci.bio.conservation`

`sci.environment`

`talk.environment`

`uk.environment`

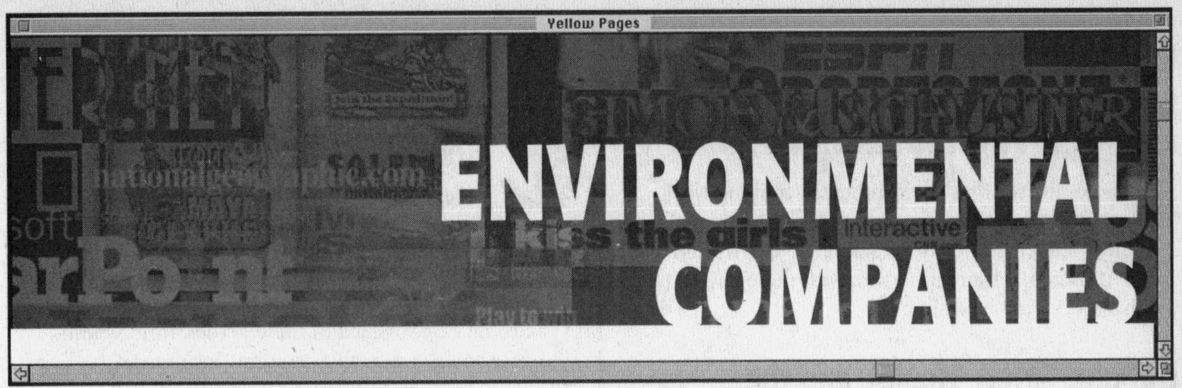

ENVIRONMENTAL COMPANIES

> We won't have a society if we destroy the environment.
>
> *Margaret Mead*

Amway

http://www.amway.com/amway/partners/environ/

Documents Amway's environmental efforts including the on-complex recycling center, participation in cleanup programs, Amway's environmental sponsorships, and their environmental awards.

BASF Ecology

http://www.basf.com/eco/

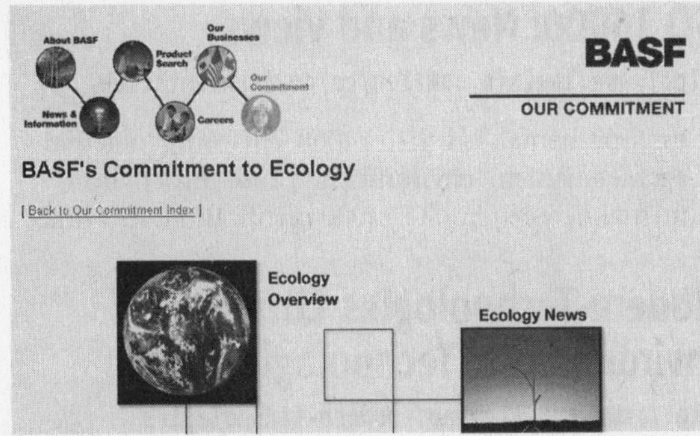

BASF is a very large international company well known for its manufacture of chemicals, plastics, nylon fibers, magnetic media, and more. They are committed to pollution prevention, ecology, and environmental care. This page contains much information about BASF's dedication to environmental preservation.

NRP TOP PICKS

BASF Ecology
http://www.basf.com/eco/

Envirobiz Environmental Professional Services
http://www.envirobiz.com/buttons/services.htm

Goldman Prize Winners
http://www.goldmanprize.org/goldman/

Benchmark Environmental Consulting: Business & Sustainable Development

http://www.mindspring.com/~benchmark

Benchmark undertakes research and policy projects seeking innovative responses to the interface between international business, economic development, and environmental protection. Current research areas include environmental management systems; trade-investment-and-environment; public participation; and agricultural biodiversity. Services are available through a publication program, through contracted consultant services, and through an active conference speaking and training schedule.

Chrysler Corporation—Recycling & Conservation

http://www.chryslercorp.com/community/index.html

Chrysler's environmental page which documents their push to minimize waste. Recycling projects and conservation procedures are documented. Also available are full size images of Chrysler's print ads on environmental goals, conservation, and recycling.

Department of the Navy Environmental Programs

http://enviro.navy.mil/

This site documents the U.S. Navy's environmental programs, including conservation, compliance, cleanup, pollution prevention, technology, and environmental planning.

A B C D E F G H I J K L M N O P Q R S T U V W X Y Z

Disaster's Edge Environmental Education Center

http://www2.third-wave.com/cccd/disaster.html

This company offers environmental training workshops targeted at specific groups. Children, high school students, and adults alike can benefit from an environmental training session with these guys. They also do custom workshops.

DuPont: Safety, Health, and the Environment

http://www.dupont.com/corp/gbl-company/she/index.html

DuPont's dedication to the environment is clearly demonstrated at their Web site. You can read their commitment, view their Environmental Audit, and review their official report to the EPA at this site.

ECS Underwriting, Inc.

http://www.ecsuw.com

Environmental insurance protection for industry worldwide. Environmental risk management case studies, lists of exposures, insurance coverage offered. Articles by environmental insurance experts. Find out how to manage environmental liability risk.

Envirobiz Environmental Professional Services

http://www.envirobiz.com/buttons/services.htm

Envirobiz Environmental Professional Services includes a searchable directory of world-wide environmental consulting firms, transporters and facilities; links; and a directory of environmental trade associations.

Environmental Search Home Page

http://www.sound.net/~esi/

Environmental Search, Inc. searches environmental records specializing in high quality geocoded mapping and reporting of environmental sites for ASTM standard site assessments and transaction screenings.

Ford Environmental Report

http://www.ford.com/corporate-info/environment/ERintro.html

This site is the environmental report from Ford Motor Company. Alternatives to gas-powered vehicles, automotive recycling, and "How to Drive Green" are among the topics explored.

Goldman Prize Winners

http://www.goldmanprize.org/goldman/

In 1996, the Goldman Environmental Foundation of San Francisco awarded a total of $450,000 to six environmental heroes from around the world. This page tells the story of each of these heroes, from whom every environmentalist can draw inspiration.

GreenWare Environmental Systems, Inc.

http://www.greenware.ca

GreenWare Environmental Systems Inc. integrates environmental law, business management and environmental accounting and auditing expertise with its strength in information technology. Visit the site for more information on environmental management and auditing software, environmental publications and an annotated list of online environmental resources.

Industry Canada—Canadian Environmental Solutions

http://strategis.ic.gc.ca/CES

CES is a multimedia tool designed to provide an instant response to environmental problems. In seconds, specific solutions to problems can be found, along with profiles of the companies that provide these solutions.

ISO 14000: News and Views

http://www.lawinfo.com/law/ca/environmentallaw/

Environmental, law, ISO 14000, environmental management system, environmental auditing, environmental newsletter, ISO 14000 certification, ISO links.

Modern Technologies Corp—Environmental Technologies Div

http://www.industry.net/modern-technologies

Describes MTC's environmental, health, and safety services and software, including the LINDEN Environmental Management System, InforM Safety Data System, Compliance Assistant. Also describes ISO 14000 services, MSDS Management services, Chemical Management Outsourcing, Environmental Reporting, and more. Includes press releases and demo program downloads.

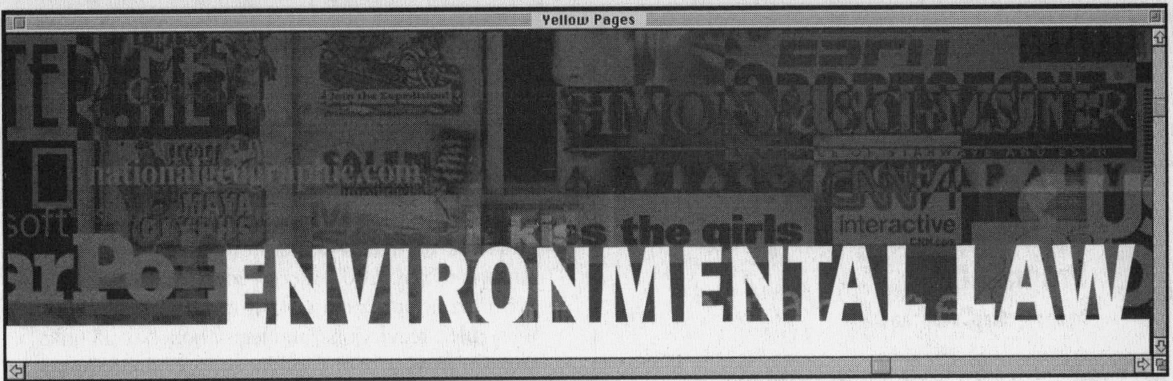

> The environment that people live in is the environment that they learn to live in, respond to, and perpetuate. If the environment is good, so be it. But if it is poor, so is the quality of life within it.
>
> *Ellen Swallow Richards*

Environmental Law Alliance Worldwide

`http://open.igc.org/elaw/`

Site is virtual home to the E-LAW. Contains the newsletter issued by the U.S. office. Each issue is a hot link: Click and read. You can also access the Telnet session, and join a electronic discussion conference. If you would rather, you can just browse the index of topic discussed in this electronic conference. See who participated in the E-LAW annual meeting, or meet some of its members. Site's basic purpose is to promote understanding of E-LAW.

Environmental Law World Wide Web Site
`http://www.webcom.com/~staber/welcome.html`

United Nations Environment Programme
`http://unep.unep.no/`

U.S. Environmental Protection Agency
`http://www.epa.gov/`

Environmental Law Around the World

`http://www.igc.org/igc/issues/el/`

Click the area of the world whose environmental law interests you, and you are whisked away to a page containing links to treaties, papers, and organizations for individual countries in that part of the world. Areas include Middle East, Europe, Asia, Americas, and Africa. Site also has connection to treaties and other links involving environment and the law.

Environmental Law Resources

`http://www.brunel.ac.uk/research/cer/resource/law.htm`

Site contains articles—sources of environmental law and regulations from the Internet—along with some discussion from the environmental newsgroups. Links include Standards, Law, Environmental Conventions, and Ecotaxes. Covers international environmental laws and regulations.

Environmental Law World Wide Web Site

`http://www.webcom.com/~staber/welcome.html`

Site is a plethora of information about environment and the law. Divided into sections: What's new, United States Environmental Law at a Glance, Recent Information Regarding Environmental Law, Articles,

A B C D E F G H I J K L M N O P Q R S T U V W X Y Z

Speeches, Press Releases and Announcements Concerning Environmental Law, and Environmental Forum. Each section contains links to various types of information including laws, statutes, articles, and press releases.

United Nations Environment Programme

`http://unep.unep.no/`

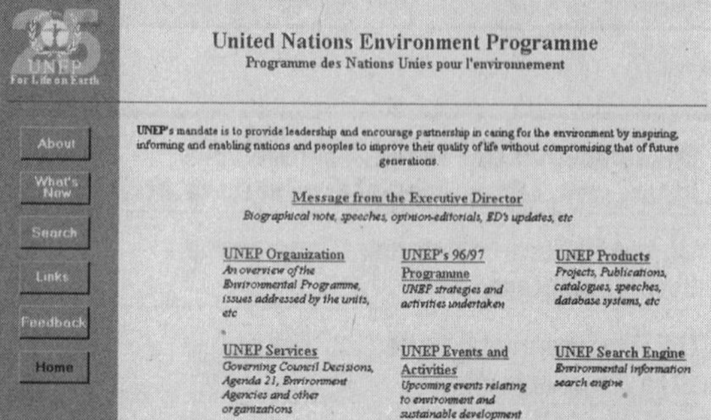

Find out what the UN is doing to promote the environment. Link to a discussion of what the UNEP is, access the UNEP Internet Information Exchange, read about Environmental Current Events, or search documents at UNEP. Page also can link you to other UN organizations, and the UNEP staff.

U.S. Environmental Protection Agency

`http://www.epa.gov/`

The home page of the U.S. Environmental Protection Agency boasts access to mountains of information. Links include standards about the EPA, what's new, and what's hot. Also, offices, programs, EPA news and events, contracts, grants, environmental financing, jobs, rules, regulations, and legislation. Not all links that are provided are listed here. Page has access to other Internet resources, and has a searchable database and index.

The WWW Virtual Library: Law: International & Environmental Law

`http://www.law.indiana.edu/law/intenvlaw.html`

Part of the WWW Virtual Library, this site has links and links and links to conferences, papers, collections, services, laws, and on and on about international and environmental law. Materials are organized alphabetically by source.

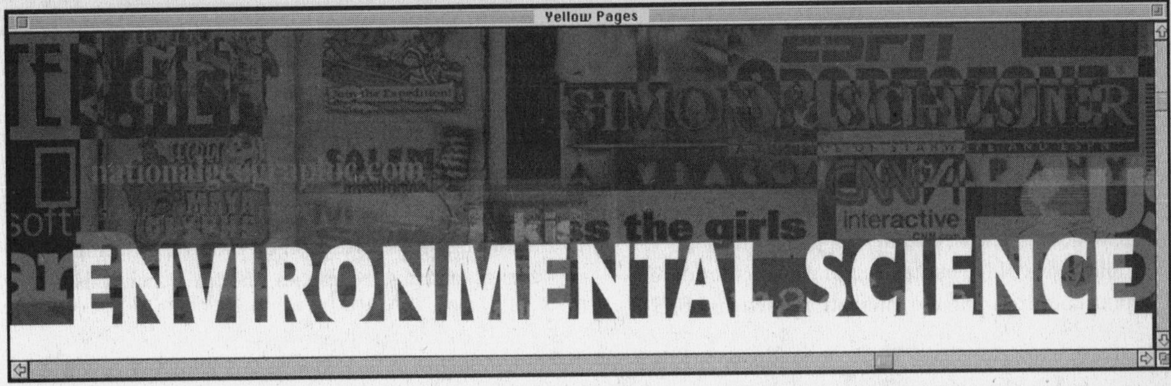

> To focus internally is made almost impossible for young people. The environmental impact is overwhelming.
>
> *Laura Huxley*

BCRI On-Line

http://www.bcr.bc.ca

Centre for Alternative Transportation Fuels. Focuses on forest biotechnology, environment, advanced transportation systems, ocean engineering, and ergonomics.

Earth and Environmental Science

http://info.er.usgs.gov/network/science/earth/earth.html

Site is a registry of Earth and environmental science Internet resources, maintained by the U.S. Geological Survey. Mainly provides links to university departments of Earth and environmental science.

EMF-Link

http://infoventures.com

Serves as a resource on biological effects of electric and magnetic fields for the general public and professionals. Contains key documents, resources, and literature for those interested in possible health effects from power lines, computer monitors, magnetic resonance imaging equipment, radio communications, cellular telephones, radar, microwave transmissions, and other sources.

Giovanni Guglielmo's Research Page on Salt Tectonics
http://www.utexas.edu/research/beg/giovanni/

Infrastructure Technology Institute (ITI)
http://iti.acns.nwu.edu/

Florida Center for Environmental Studies' Home Page

http://www.ces.fau.edu/

Provides environmental resources concerning the management of Florida ecosystems and other tropical and subtropical water dominated freshwater and estuarine ecosystems worldwide.

Giovanni Guglielmo's Research Page on Salt Tectonics

http://www.utexas.edu/research/beg/giovanni/

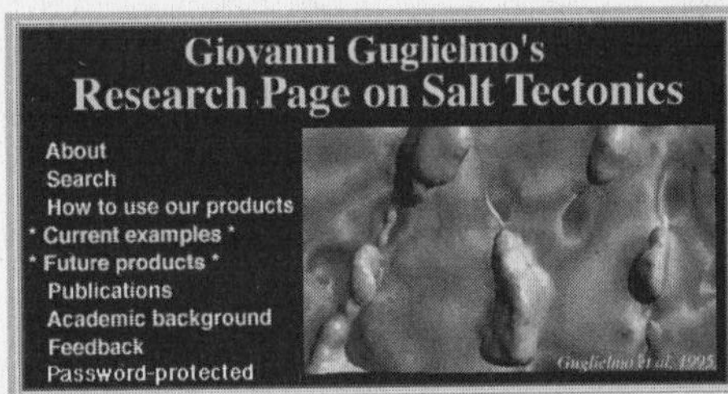

Contains free computer animations, 3D visualization, and interpretations of physical and finite element models of salt tectonics.

Greenspan Technology

http://peg.pegasus.oz.au/~greenspan/

Specializes in leading-edge water quality monitoring technology for the water resources, environmental, and pollution markets. Offers services ranging from the deployment of single water quality sensors, installation of sophisticated multiparameter monitors, to project management of major hydrological studies worldwide.

A B C D E F G H I J K L M N O P Q R S T U V W X Y Z

IFIAS

http://www.ifias.ca/index1.html

A global network of scientific research institutions that collaborate on projects relating to science, technology and innovation policy, ecosystem management, gender science and development, the implications of the human genome project for developing countries, and the international system of science.

Infrastructure Technology Institute (ITI)

http://iti.acns.nwu.edu/

Provides information about current research, technology transfer, and education regarding America's infrastructure.

United Nations Environment Programme (UNEP), Geneva

http://www.unep.ch/

Contains many treaties and programs on preserving the environment. Includes information on topics including the "Convention on Biodiversity," climate change, endangered species, and toxic chemicals.

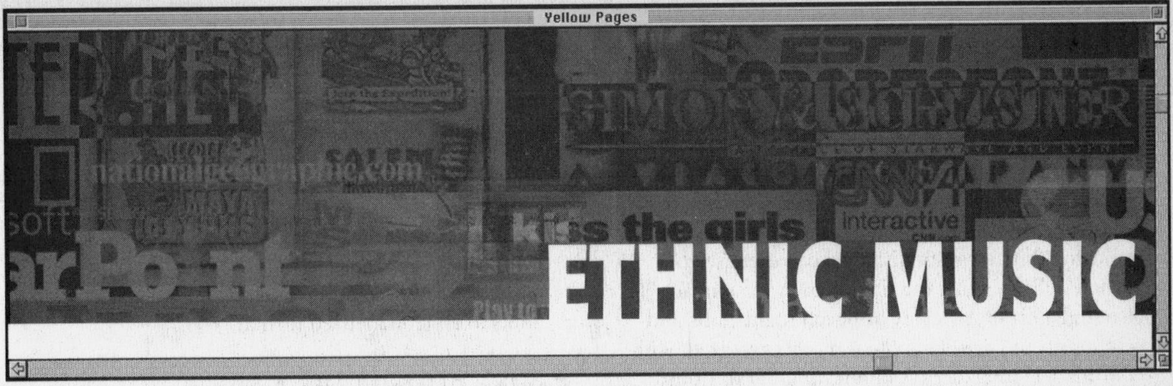

A B C D E F G H I J K L M N O P Q R S T U V W X Y Z

In the future skateboarders will hum Indonesian ditties to an African beat mixed by a DJ in London...wearing clothes designed by a former grunge guitarist bought over a website based in Mexico.

from the Luaka Bop page at http://www.wbr.com/luakabop/cmp/home.html

Abayudaya Jews in Uganda: Music

http://www.intac.com/PubService/uganda/music.html

Documents the songs of the Abayudaya people of Uganda, who converted to Judaism in the 1920s. You can download several audio files of songs, most of which are versions of American-Jewish songs. Also offers photos and information on the history and culture of the Abayudaya people.

African Music Encyclopedia
http://matisse.net/~jplanet/afmx/ahome.htm

Afro-Caribbean Music
http://www.ina.fr/Music/index.en.html

Ari Davidow's Klezmer Shack
http://www.well.com/user/ari/klez/

Irish and Celtic Music on the Internet
http://www.celticmusic.com/

Japanese Kabuki Music
http://www.fix.co.jp/kabuki/sound.html

Mbira Home Page
http://www.tiac.net/users/smurungu/home.html

Russian Music
http://mars.uthscsa.edu/Russia/Music/

The Sydney Folk Music Web Site
http://www.chepd.mq.edu.au/boomerang/SFP/folkhome.htm

Welcome to Bali & Beyond
http://www.pacificnet.net/gamelan/

African Music Encyclopedia

http://matisse.net/~jplanet/afmx/ahome.htm

There's lots of information here on African and African-influenced music and musicians from all over the world, including South America and the Caribbean, in an organized format. It includes articles, artist profiles, and sound samples and offers links to home pages of the different countries. You can start by clicking the letter representing the country of your choice, or page down and browse through the contents. You'll also find an alphabetized artist list, related African links, and African music sources. Along the way, look at some of the great photographs.

Afro-Caribbean Music

http://www.ina.fr/Music/index.en.html

Yes, there's reggae music here, but there's also everything from Afro Funk to Ziglibithy to suit your musical tastes. Explore Africa and the Caribbean by artist, geographical location, and style. If you get tired exploring this site in English, you can exercise your French skills by using the site's French version. You'll also find a list of African/Caribbean night clubs and restaurants in Paris. This site is nicely organized, with colorful 3-D musical notes indicating the sections, and the graphics and layout are very clean and crisp. You'll find an excellent page of links to other related Web resources, too.

Ain't Whistlin' Dixie

http://mothra.nts.uci.edu/~dhwalker/dixie/

This site gets "Best Title" in this category. It offers a collection of Irish, Scottish, and English traditional tunes played on the pennywhistle and ocarina. Each tune is presented in AU and AIFF formats. Note: AIFF takes two to three times longer to download.

Amorn Chomchoey's Web Page of Thailand

http://www.amorn.baremetal.com/thai.htm

A huge page of links for the many aspect's of Thailand's culture and history. Check out the links for traditional and contemporary Thai music in the "Music and Cinema" and "Thai Sound Files" sections.

Angus Og's Hot Links to the Celts

http://celt.net/og/ethmusic.htm

Wow! Pages and pages of links to Celtic music sites, alphabetized by site title. If you're interested in where to find Celtic music on the Web, this site should be your first stop.

Ari Davidow's Klezmer Shack

http://www.well.com/user/ari/klez/

Focuses on the klezmer musical blend of traditional Jewish folk music, blues, and jazz. You'll find articles, artist profiles, CD reviews, concert and festival information, a guide to radio programs, and contact information for klezmer musicians. There are also links to sites where you can buy klezmer CDs and a great annotated section on other klezmer-related resources on the Web.

Australian Music World Wide Web Site

http://www.amws.com.au/

This goal of this site is to supply information about as many Australian musicians and musical organizations as possible. Currently, the site lists over 1,410 Australian musicians of all kinds, and 564 of them have links to Web pages. The Other Links section offers a wealth of music- and other media-related links in an alphabetized format.

Ceolas Celtic Music Archive

http://celtic.stanford.edu/ceolas.html

This site claims to have the largest collection of Celtic music information that's available online. Irish and Scottish music predominate, but the music of Wales and Brittany is also represented. You'll find a guide to Celtic music resources, artist profiles, discographies, reviews, sound samples, and concert and festival schedules. Also featured are tune indexes, music software, a guide to musical instruments, and links to countless other sites.

Chinese Music Page

http://vizlab.rutgers.edu/~jaray/sounds/chinese_music/chinese_music.html

Here's an archive of Chinese and Taiwanese music from the pre- and post-liberation eras. The site has many audio samples of traditional instrumental and vocal forms, music from the folk, ceremonial, and military music genres, and a few related links to other Chinese music sites.

Classical Music Home Page: N.S.Sundar

http://www.cis.ohio-state.edu/~sundar/

This site offers information on North and South Indian classical music, Indian classical dance forms, FAQs for rec.music.indian.classical, and an eclectic gallery of photos ranging from musicians to Hindu deities to Mahatma Gandhi. Also includes databases of song lyrics and great personalities of Carnatic (South Indian) music.

Cultures of the Andes

http://www.andes.org/

Music, pictures, and literature from the Andes mountains of South America; offerings in English, Spanish, and the Quechua Indian language. You can also see movie clips of dances. There are English translations of the lyrics, and most sound clips are available in both AU and WAV format.

Delta Blues - The Digital Tradition Folk Song Database

http://www.deltablues.com/folksearch.html

You can search for folk music from around the world with a *very* cool search engine. I typed in "australian folk" and got a list of songs; on a whim, I picked "We'll Rant and We'll Roar" and got the lyrics, a brief but interesting history of the song, and a MIDI clip of the song. Now, here's a coincidence for you: The song just happened to be a version of the tune Quint sang in the movie *Jaws*, which was one of my favorite scenes. You can also get info here about *The Mudcat Cafe*, an online magazine about blues and folk music.

Dirty Linen

http://www.dirtynelson.com/linen/73toc.html

Dirty Linen is an online magazine for folk and world music. At its home page, you can find a table of contents, a list of back issues, a "gig guide," and more. Well worth checking out.

Flamenco Home Page

http://solea.quim.ucm.es/flamenco.html

This site covers on the flamenco scene in Madrid. Tourists and flamenco aficionados can find useful information about where to see live flamenco performances. There are links to other flamenco sites on the Web, too. Some information is in Spanish.

The Flamenco Guitar Home Page

http://www.guitarist.com/fg/fg.htm

More information on flamenco, with an introduction for beginners. There are discographies for both dancers and guitarists and MIDI sound files available. You'll also find dozens and dozens of links to related sites.

Hawaiian Jamz

http://www.mauigateway.com/~jamz/

Great site on Hawaiian music and culture! You need RealAudio to hear the clips and shows, however. Clean, clear graphics and organization; I liked the little pineapples scattered over the background. Each show is about an hour long and revolves around a particular theme, such as "Traditional Hawaiian Falsetto." There's a list of related sites, too.

Hindi Movie Songs

http://www.cs.wisc.edu/~navin/india/songs/index.html

This site focuses on Indian movie songs in the Hindi language, with song information and full lyrics. Includes categorized indexes of singers, music directors, lyricists, films, actors/actresses, as well as a searchable song title index.

Indonesian Music

http://www.umanitoba.ca/indonesian/music.html

Features information on different types of Balinese, Javanese, and Sundanese music and instruments, including the *gamelan* (Indonesian percussion orchestra) and *angklung* (a bamboo instrument). Also offers Indonesian song lyrics and links to North American gamelan orchestra pages.

Irish and Celtic Music on the Internet

http://www.celticmusic.com/

CelticMusic.Com, an online magazine, focuses on Celtic music; check out the site's magazine index for a helpful listing of back issues and links to the home pages of featured artists. The site also includes sheet music for traditional tunes, reviews of recent CDs, audio excerpts (for the titles with dancing musical notes next to them), and more in the Virtual Tunebook section. Lovely graphics, particularly the band of Celtic knots running along the left margin, and the site is easy to navigate around.

Japanese Kabuki Music

http://www.fix.co.jp/kabuki/sound.html

Fascinating information on kabuki and the instruments commonly used in kabuki, such as the taiko drum and the three-stringed shamisen. You can also hear samples of some of the instruments and examples of kabuki fans shouting out support for their favorite actors; these shouts are called *kakegoe*.

KiwiFolk: Folk and Acoustic Music in New Zealand

http://www.earthlight.co.nz/users/mikem/

This site organizes a wealth of information about New Zealand folk and acoustic music. You'll find upcoming events, festival news, bios of "kiwi" artists, and links to other related pages.

A B C D E F G H I J K L M N O P Q R S T U V W X Y Z

Larry Aronson Home Page

http://www.interport.net/~laronson/WorldBeat.html

You'll find a variety of information on Afro-pop music, particularly Soukous, a variety of pan-African dance music that originated in Zaire and the Congo. Features recommendations on bands, CDs, and other useful information, including related links with helpful annotations.

Mbira Home Page

http://www.tiac.net/users/smurungu/home.html

This page is an excellent introduction to *mbira*, the traditional music of Zimbabwe. It also covers Shona traditions, customs, and literature as they relate to mbira. For a site that the author warns is still under construction, there's a lot of good information here. You can listen to a sampler of mbira music, and check out the calendar of events.

MIZIK

http://www.unik.no/~robert/mizik/mizik.html

Here's an eclectic collection of world music information and extensive links to other ethnomusicology-related sites. Includes discographies (with images from the CD covers), sound samples, reviews, and more. You'll hear music from Asia, the French Antilles, and Africa, to name a few. (Note: Cool illustration of Calvin and Hobbes getting down on the welcome page!)

Norwegian Music Information Centre

http://www.notam.uio.no/nmi/index.html

You'll find all kinds of information on Nowegian music here—biographies on many, many composers; articles covering Norwegian music history, early and church music, and more recent pop, rock, and jazz; info on festivals and other events; and links to many other related sites.

Panther's Hawaiian Music Page

http://www.nahenahe.net/panther/hawaii2.html

This is an excellent place to start if you're looking for Web resources on Hawaiian music. You'll find lots of links to Hawaiian music sites and Web pages here.

Related Sites
http://www.bluepearl.com/latinlnks/#mus
http://www.wbr.com/luakabop/cmp/home.html
http://www.hnh.com/rahome/rampc.htm

Puro Mariachi

http://www.geocities.com/TheTropics/2703/

You'll find just about everything you wanted to know about mariachi music here, including a history of mariachi, recommended books and CDs, the lyrics to probably every Mexican song ever written (I'm not kidding!) alphabetized by first line of the song, and dozens and dozens of links to Mexican music and cultural sites. Cool background on the welcome page—it looks like a music notebook, with the spiral running along the lefthand side.

Richard Robinson's Tunebook

http://www.leeds.ac.uk/music/Info/RRTuneBk/tunebook.html

Offers a collection of sheet music of traditional tunes, primarily from the Celtic lands, Scandinavia, France, and the Balkans. You can access them by title, country, or type (jig, reel, waltz, and so on). This site offers lots of links, too, and I liked the author's conversational writing style. He offers lots of tips on how to download and view the files.

Russian Music

http://mars.uthscsa.edu/Russia/Music/

An informative, well-organized site with an archive of Russian singers and their songs, including photos, discographies, song lyrics, and audio and video clips. Also offers recommended recordings and where to buy them, as well as links to other sites. Includes pop music, but check out the sections on Russian folk and romantic music, too.

Sami's Urdu/Hindi Film Music Page

http://www.lehigh.edu/sm0e/public/www-data/sami.html

Here's a site for fans of Urdu and Hindi film music. Offers articles on singers, musical directors, and lyricists and gives you lists of songs indexed by singer, music director, and so forth. You can also find the notes and chords of songs and see many photos.

Santa Fe Guitar Quartet

http://nwselp.epcc.edu/stf/stf.html

Their repertoire encompasses music from the Renaissance, traditional tango, and the modern tango of Astor Piazzolla. The members of the quartet are all students taught at the Carlevaro Guitar School based in Montevideo, Uruguay. Using Abel Carlevaro's techniques, the four guitars create a miniature orchestra. Check out the 30-second sound clips available at this site.

Shimamura: English Index

http://www.shimamura.co.jp/english/eindex.html

At first, this site just looks like an advertisement for the music store and its new locations. However, if you go down to the links on traditional music and instruments, you'll find some excellent information. I chose the shamisen section and found not only an AU file, but an informative description of the instrument, an illustration, the type of music it's used for, and more. Fascinating stuff, but I'll warn you; the background graphics on some of the pages makes the text a little hard to read.

Some Peruvian Music

http://www.rcp.net.pe/snd/snd_ingles.html

This page from the World Wide Web Server of Peru—Red Cientifica Peruana—has sound files of Andean flute music as well as links to related Peruvian music topics.

Songs of Indonesia

http://www.geocities.com/SoHo/1823/index.html

This is an archive of Indonesian songs, divided into pop, traditional, and national songs, some in MIDI format. You'll find links to related sites, too.

The Sydney Folk Music Web Site

http://www.chepd.mq.edu.au/boomerang/SFP/folkhome.htm

This site covers Australian folk music and even offers a search feature. You'll also find interviews, news of local folk clubs in the Sydney area, and links to folk music sites in Australia, Ireland, the UK, and the USA. You'll find short bios of Australian folk musicians, news of upcoming festivals and events, and "folksie" organizations, all in a clear, nicely organized format.

Tara Publications: The World of Jewish Music

http://www.jewishmusic.com/

Offers a wide variety of Jewish music selections. You'll find an online catalog and links to other Jewish music sites. There are a few articles, too, and an artists section with links to their home pages. Check out the RealAudio library.

Temple Records

http://www.rootsworld.com/temple/

Provides home site and online ordering for Temple Records, which specializes in Scottish traditional music. Includes an online catalog, artist descriptions, and ordering information.

Turkish Music Home Page

http://vizlab.rutgers.edu/~jaray/sounds/turkish/turkish.html

Hosgeldiniz! This site has a Turkish music archive and an index to other Turkish music sites. Includes articles on Turkish music genres; audio files; discographies; and links to classical, folk, religious, and other music styles from Turkey and Cyprus.

The Unofficial Clannad Website

http://www.empire.net/~whatmoug/clanhome.htm

Excellent site, organized into sections with a discography, lyrics, images, interviews, sound bytes, and information about the Irish band Clannad. You'll also find links to other Clannad sites.

Welcome to Bali & Beyond

http://www.pacificnet.net/gamelan/

Bali & Beyond is a Los Angeles–based performing arts company inspired by the culture of Indonesia. The ensemble tours nationwide, featuring a variety of music, theater, and educational presentations. This colorful site is is their home page, with lots of information about upcoming concert schedules and events. However, check out the Kechat section for background on the Indonesian culture and music and Maria's corner for all kinds of interesting gift items. There's even a Fun and Gamelan section with yes, gamelan trivia questions! You can see audio and video clips of the performances; there are helpful tips on the plug-ins you need to view them.

NEWSGROUPS

alt.music.hawaiian

alt.music.mexican

alt.music.world

rec.music.indian.classical

rec.music.indian.misc

A B C D E F G H I J K L M N O P Q R S T U V W X Y Z

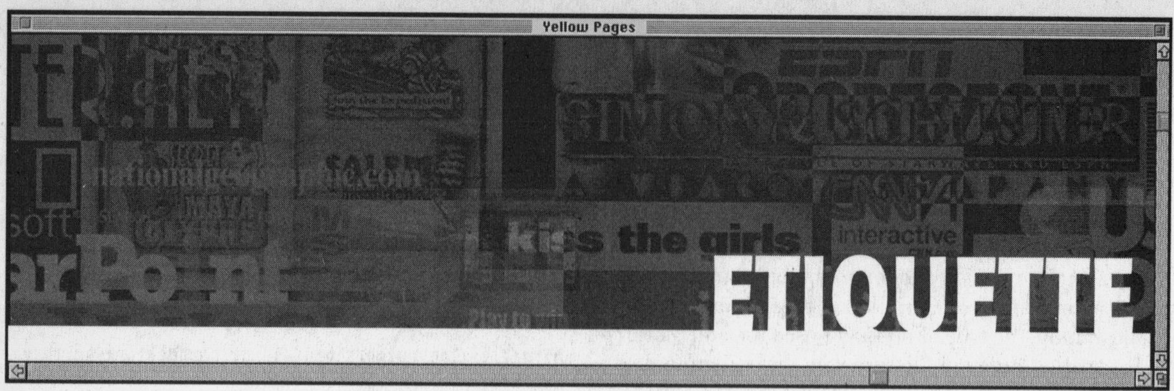

It is far more impressive when others discover your good qualities without your help.

Miss Manners (Judith Martin)

Beth Bloom-Wright Etiquette-Protocol-Image

`http://bethbloomwright.com/`

According to Beth Wright, people's perception of you is formed in eight seconds. Join employees of American Express, Hallmark, and IBM in taking her company's one-day seminar, which specializes in improving workers' professionalism in corporate environments.

Dance Floor Etiquette

`http://www.apci.net/%7Edrdeyne/flooretq.htm`

Provides a diagram of a dance floor with the dance areas outlined (line dances, flow dances, swing dances, and more).

Etiquette International

`http://www.consultants-mall.com/hilka.htm`

Etiquette International provides information and workshops for companies and individuals to boost their knowledge of business etiquette, entertaining, and international protocol. Read testimonials from past seminar participants and get detailed descriptions of the available seminars.

Pachter & Associates
`http://www.pachter.com/`

Good Housekeeping Advice

`http://homearts.com/gh/toc/osadvice.htm`

This is the index site for several Good Housekeeping advice columns, including Peggy Post's "Etiquette for Today." Search the list by topic, or just scroll through all the questions. If you have a question of your own, send it to Peggy via email.

International Protocol and Business Etiquette Training for Executives

`http://www.lettgroup.com/`

The Lett Group runs seminars that teach that one way to beat the competition is to outclass them. Find out details on seminars that are up to five days long, which cover topics such as introductions, business meals, telephone skills, and many more.

The Lou Kennedy Company

`http://www.loukennedy.com/`

Lou Kennedy is a speaker and expert on business etiquette and professional development. Read about her book, find out about the many programs that her company runs, and take a business etiquette quiz.

Mosh Pit Etiquette

`http://www.southern.com/BeastieBoys/Info/MoshPit.html`

Presented by the rock group the Beastie Boys, this guide can help you make it out of the concert alive, if that's your goal. Find out the maximum weight for a "certified waif"—someone who is allowed to "float" above the pit—and find out what gets you thrown into the moshing penalty box.

Mr. Golf Etiquette

http://www.mrgolf.com/

Promising to "make an asset" of himself, Mr. Golf set up this site to help you do your part in keeping golf a game of ladies and gentlemen. Read current or archived "Ask Mr. Golf" columns, or play a game in which you're shown a picture and challenged to determine the golfing etiquette rule being violated.

National League of Junior Cotillions

http://www.nljc.com/

This North Carolina-based organization trains and licenses those who wish to offer cotillion programs in their local areas. The groups teach young people the basics of etiquette, ethics, and good behavior to give them a head start at building character and confidence. Check out the Q&A section or find out how to start a program in your area.

Netiquette Home Page

http://www.albion.com/netiquette/index.html

This site features excerpts from Virginia Shea's book *Netiquette.* Read the 10 core rules of the Internet, take a netiquette quiz, and even join a mailing list to stay current on the newest ways to be polite online.

The Original Tipping Page

http://www.cis.columbia.edu/homepages/gonzalu/tipping.html

How much *do* you tip a skycap at the airport? This site gives recommended tipping standards for 10 different service categories, covering dozens of different service workers and situations. Includes ushers at sports arenas, manicurist, cruise ship cabin boy, and much more.

Related Sites

http://homepage.interaccess.com/~gmb/manners.htm

http://www.algonet.se/~dfl-tea/hemp/smoking_etiquette.html

Pachter & Associates

http://www.pachter.com/

Pachter & Associates specializes in corporate training and keynote speakers dedicated to etiquette, communication, and assertiveness in business. The site also boasts a large selection of related books and audiotapes that you can order by mail or fax.

Pastoral Etiquette

http://www.cremationconsultants.com/crem8me/pastrleq.htm

This page gives instruction to clergy regarding funerals and memorial services. The list includes judging the right amount of assistance to give to the grieving family, proper and respectful timing, and what to do after the funeral or memorial.

Square Dance Etiquette

http://www.glyphic.com/iagsdc/etiquette.html

Do you know when to introduce yourself to dancers you don't know? F. William Chickering, a member of the Times Squares Square Dance Club, has compiled this list. You probably know the simple rules, such as not to come to a dance drunk, but others might surprise you.

U.S. Flag Code

http://suvcw.org/flag.htm

Part of the Sons of Union Veterans of the Civil War site, this page reprints Chapter 10 of Title 36 of the United States Code. Included in this document are occasions and time for display, how to properly raise and lower the flag, and proper disposal of old flags.

USENET Etiquette

http://unix1.sncc.lsu.edu/internet/usenet/usenet-etiquette.html

Provides information about politely posting messages to Usenet newsgroups.

Related Sites

http://www.calweb.com/~dmurry/etiq.html

http://www.clari.net/brad/emily.html

http://www.claris.com/products/claris/emailer/eguide/index.html

http://www.eskseries.com/

http://www.fau.edu/rinaldi/netiquette.html

http://www.infocom.net/~elogan/etiquett.html

http://www.jostens.com/college/Etiquette/

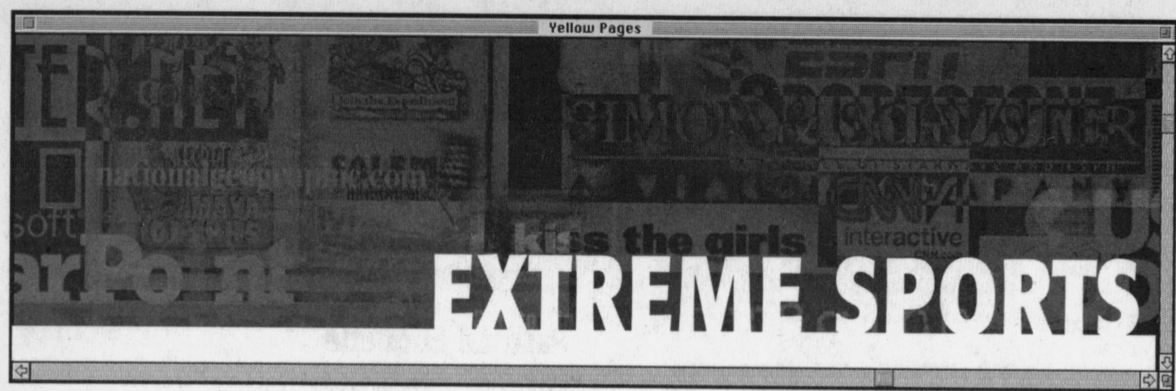

By sports like these are all their cares beguil'd;
The sports of children satisfy the child.

Oliver Goldsmith

ISF World Snowboarding Rankings

http://snowboardranking.com/

Presents International Snowboard Federation World & National Ranking lists, compiled from snowboarding competition results received from all over. Covers primarily Parallel Slalom, GS, Halfpipe, and Boarder Cross.

The Maui Windsurfing Report

http://maui.net/~mauiwind/MWR/mwr.html

The MWR is the center of windsurfing on the WWW. Offers action photos, news and views, contest to win a sail, and weather reports.

Parachute Industry Association

http://www.pia.com/

The objectives of the Parachute Industry Association are to advance and promote the growth, development, and safety of parachuting and to engage and serve participants in the parachute industry. The PIA consists of companies and individuals united by a common desire to improve business opportunities in this segment of aviation. Site contains PIA publications, parachuting "Yellow Pages", a product listing, meeting schedule, and more.

NRP TOP PICKS

Parachute Industry Association
http://www.pia.com/

Skydive Archive
http://www.afn.org/skydive/

Sailboard Vacations

http://www.sailboardvacations.com/

Offers detailed travel information on the finest windsurfing spots. Features the latest in quality windsurfing equipment from Mistral. Provides information on how to windsurf.

SkyDance SkyDiving

http://www.skydance.net/

Here you can find out where to learn to dive, but also find out how much any level of dive will cost. The site provides an online newsletter, a list of related skydiving sites, and memorable images to download.

Skydive Archive

http://www.afn.org/skydive/

A resource for those who want to learn to skydive, and learn about safety and training techniques. Link to the different disciplines of skydiving. Find out where to dive and what organizations you can join.

Windsight Windsurfing Wind Reports

http://www.windsight.com/

Provides text, graphic, and video coverage of windsurfing sites in the Columbia River Gorge, Oregon Coast, San Francisco Bay, Baja, and Maui. Also covers meteorological concepts as they apply to windsurfing. Explains how to use Windsight's 800 number voice phone service and the Windsight software.

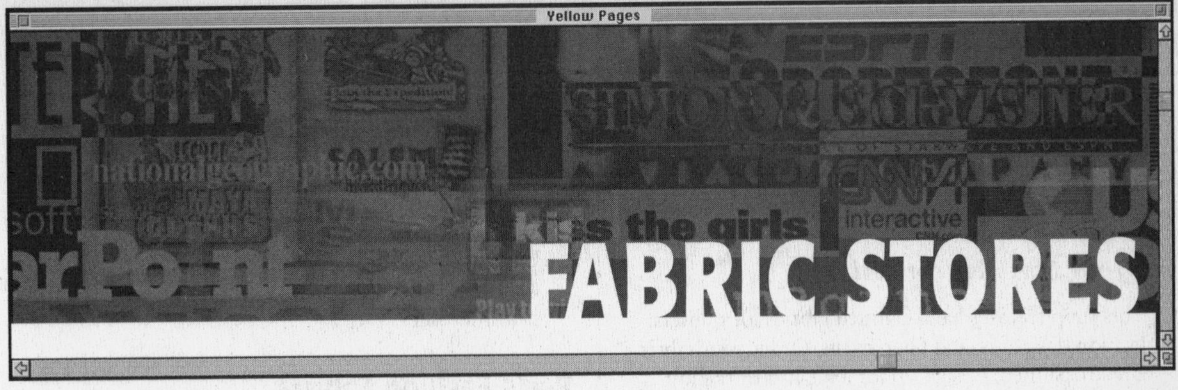

It is in his pleasure that a man really lives; it is from his leisure that he constructs the true fabric of self.

Agnes Repplier

American Textile Exchange

`http://www.ameritex.com/`

Need 100 yards of rayon in a hurry? American Textile Exchange stocks a million yards of closeout apparel fabric in its various warehouses across the country. The company deals primarily in fabric for women's and children's clothing and sells only in bulk. If you have excess fabric to sell, this could be the place.

Calico Corners

`http://www.calicocorners.com/`

With more than 90 stores in the US, Calico Corners specializes in fine fabrics, linens, and furniture upholstery. Glance through the online catalog and select a nice sofa and the pattern you want to cover it.

Carriage House Fabrics

`http://www.farmtek-fti.com/crghouse/index.html`

Browse the huge online catalog of fabric samples, featuring 10 different categories of cotton fabrics, as well as huge selections of rayons and flannels. The site features hundreds of full-color swatch samples and a slick order form. Operating only online, this site is more than just an electronic billboard.

Carriage House Fabrics
`http://www.farmtek-fti.com/crghouse/index.html`

Edinburgh Imports, Inc.

`http://www.edinburgh.com/`

Teddy Bear makers, look no further. Edinburgh imports and distributes original Schulte mohair, which is known worldwide for its superior bear-making qualities. Get the latest information about Teddy-making classes, featuring experts from around the world. In addition to mohair, Edinburgh also carries over 900 other specialty fabrics.

Fabric Land

`http://www.fabricland.com/main.html`

Not to be confused with Canada's largest fabric chain, Fabric Land is a New Jersey establishment specializing in window treatments and home fashions. If you think curtains and draperies are the same thing, swag on over for a free consultation.

Fabricland

`http://www.fabriclandwest.com/`

With over 170 stores nationwide, Fabricland is Canada's largest retail fabric store. Get the latest sale prices on thread, lace, felt, patterns, and of course, fabric. Even learn how to make projects with online patterns and instructions. You can also learn how to join the Fabricland Sewing Club, but the club is open only to those who live in Western Canada. Sorry.

Fabrics To Dye For

`http://www.fabricstodyefor.com/`

This shop features hand-painted fabrics for quilters, fashion designers, and fiber artists. Order your fabric already painted, or sign up for a kit and workshop and learn to paint it yourself.

Global Village Imports

`http://www.globalfabric.com/~gvi/`

Take a look at the ways that handwoven Guatemalan fabric is used. Available in a variety of weights, this cotton textile comes wildly and beautifully colored and is useful for clothing, home decorating, and quilting. Buy in bulk, or check out the deals on smaller quantities

Jeffrey Thomas Fabrics

`http://www.weblane.com/jtfabrics/`

This shop carries popular tapestries often used for handbags, luggage, and re-upholstery. Many of the fabrics in the Jeffrey Thomas showroom were designed by its staff, and thus won't be found anywhere else. You can also order imported tapestry pillows, or learn to make your own.

Kids Only Fabrics

`http://www.pe.net/~kidsonly/`

Find out what sort of corduroy today's smart toddler is wearing. Order yards of denim and make Sally her own overalls, by gosh. Place an order, join the fabric swatch service, or get the latest information on the hottest dobbies. *Dobbies?*

Linda's—Your UltraSuede Specialist

`http://www.oxford.net/~lindas/`

So you're too good for regular suede, eh? Lucky for you, Linda's will ship her inventory of UltraSuede, UltraSuede Light, and UltraLeather from Ontario to anywhere in the world. Find out why ultra-fabrics mean ultra-happiness for animals, as well as how Linda will make that wacky metric system work for you.

Mendels & Far Out Fabrics

`http://www.mendels.com/`

Sick of the tired cotton-poly blend? Mendels, broadcasting from the heart of San Francisco's Haight-Ashbury neighborhood, offers an alternative perspective to fabrics and their potential uses. Featuring special sections about tie dying and hemp, Mendels boasts a staff of artists who specialize in the stuff they sell.

Peg's Fashion Fabrics

`http://www.sewingstuff.com/Pegs/`

If you don't want to go to the store, let the store come to you. Check the schedule—Peg's moble fabric store sets up at local sewing expos, quilting shows, and convention centers all across the US. Many pieces are from New York design houses and would be quite difficult for the home sewer to find—even online.

Softworld's Sewing Resource Guide

`http://softworld.com/sewing/sewroom.htm`

This online directory gives links to dozens of worthwhile links. Search various categories for fabric dealers, quilting workshops, accessories, patterns, notions, textile history, and much more. This site is why the bookmark feature was made.

The Unique Spool

`http://www.uniquespool.com/`

Join the tour and see the latest in fabrics and styles from Africa, Australia, and Indonesia. If you long for the easy-going Victorian era, take a look at the reproduction prints based on 1880s U.S. fabrics. Better yet, check out the fabrics designed to look like fur, scales, wool, and skin.

NEWSGROUPS

`alt.sewing`

`rec.crafts.textiles`

Related Sites

`http://ares.redsword.com/dduperault/qsource.htm`

`http://www.a2zbiz.com/shop.shtml`

`http://www.burrows.com/lace.html`

`http://www.designwave.com/dwrc/library/silk.html`

`http://www.his.com/~queenb/feedsack.html`

`http://www.ilinks.net/~sewnuts/`

`http://www.libeco.be/`

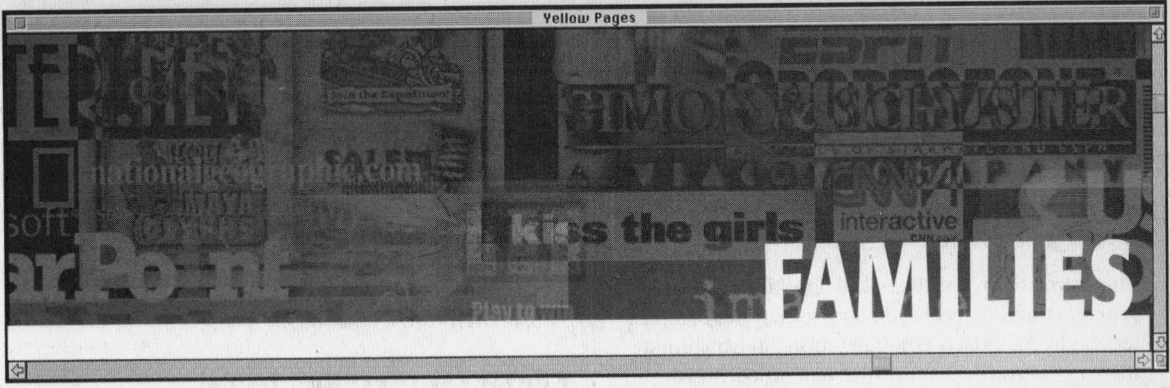

> The family is one of nature's masterpieces.
>
> *George Santayana*

FAMILY PLANNING, PREGNANCY AND CHILDBIRTH

Childbirth Resource Center

http://www.socalbirth.org/

Although the services cover only the Southern California area, the site provides a lot of information about holistic midwifery and home birthing as an option to childbirth, including holistic exercises, suggested reading, postnatal care suggestions, and links to many other sites.

Childbirth.org

http://www.childbirth.org/

This award-winning site provides a wealth of information on every aspect of childbirth, from the pros and cons of episiotomies to the history of Cesarean deliveries. Pages are both informational and personal, aiming to educate consumers on the many facets of childbirth while helping expectant mothers secure the best possible care.

Cutting Edge Press

http://www.childbirth.org/CEP.html

Cutting Edge Press offers books, video tapes, and birth bags for nurses, midwives, childbirth educators, and expectant parents. The books section is worth the trip alone.

ParentTime
http://www.pathfinder.com/ParentTime/

NARAL—Promoting Reproductive Choices

http://www.naral.org/home.html

The home page of the National Abortion and Reproductive Rights Action League (NARAL) offers an extensive and insightful exploration of reproductive health issues, including the many options currently available for family planning.

Noble Birth, Inc.

http://www.kcw.com

This site includes information, supplies, and support for childbirth, breast-feeding and infant care. Includes information on midwifery and home birth supplies; baby, maternity, and nursing apparel.

Online Birth Center

http://www.efn.org/~djz/birth/birthindex.html

This broad-based site encompasses all aspects of midwifery, pregnancy, birth, and breast-feeding. Some popular sub-sections include The Parent's Page, High-Risk Situations, and Alternative Health Resources. The site contains a myriad of articles and resources, and visitors to the site can search its extensive archives for information on a specific topic.

Planned Parenthood Federation of America

http://www.ppfa.org/ppfa/index.html

Includes sexual and reproductive health information in English and Spanish. Includes links and directories of Planned Parenthood affiliates and related organizations, as well as health information and resources regarding issues ranging from sex education to abortion to teen pregnancy.

Prenatal Testing

http://www.familyweb.com/faqs/prenattest_stories.shtml

This listing of Frequently Asked Questions (FAQ) provides useful information on a sometimes complex topic. The material is especially strong in explaining the types of tests available, such as amniocentesis, and screening for gestational diabetes or certain disabilities. A good starting point for learning about prenatal testing.

SANDS(vic)

http://www.vicnet.net.au./~sands/sands.htm

SANDS, an acronym for Stillbirth and Neonatal Death Support, is a wonderful site for those experiencing such grief. The site is an especially personal approach to the subject and offers articles, grief and bereavement resources and an assortment of related links.

Surrogate Mothers, Inc.

http://www.surrogatemothers.com/

This organization helps couples unable to conceive, single, and/or gay men and women find a surrogate mother. A full-service agency and one that openly works with gay and lesbian couples.

Unassisted Home Birth

http://www.kjv.com/family/homebirth.hts

A family-created site about a family of six (soon to be seven) who has birthed the last four children at home. No midwife or other health professional were present. It's just the husband, the wife, a few friends, and a birth tub. A personal take on this new fad.

HEALTH, DISABILITIES & SPECIAL NEEDS

ADA & Disability Information

http://www.public.iastate.edu/~sbilling/ada.html

This site offers an extraordinary assortment of links for ADA (Americans with Disabilities Act) resources and disability information. Categories of links include legal resources, newsletters and Listservs, products and services, and specific disabilities, among others.

Beach Center on Families and Disability

http://www.lsi.ukans.edu/beach/beachhp.htm

A useful site for those coping with a family member's disability. The Beach Center offers several newsletter, including Friendships, Parent-to-Parent Programs, and Dads and Disability, along with a series of fact sheets with helpful advice on advice on difficult issues, such as How to Encourage Friendships for Children with a Disability.

Center for Disability Policy

http://www.muskie2.usmacs.maine.edu/~cdispol/c-home.htm

The Center for Disability Policy at the University of Southern Maine works toward integrating those with disabilities into community life, and it conducts a wide range of applied research projects toward that end. The Center's home page explains its philosophy and areas of expertise.

Disabled Peoples International

http://www.dpi.org/

DPI promotes the human rights of people with disabilities. It focuses on development, human rights, communications, advocacy, and public education about and for disabled persons. Cross-disability and operates in over 100 countries.

Family Resource Network

http://www.paradisedirect.con/sea/frn.htm

"Bringing together families of children with special needs," this exceptional site offers a number of excellent services , including one-on-one emotional support (putting parents in touch with others in similar circumstances), a lending library of books and videos, and workshops and seminars. Especially valuable are the Network's Information Packets, which offer material on a myriad of topics, such as autism, developmental delays, epilepsy, spina bifida, and medically fragile infants. A very worthwhile site!

Family Village

http://www.familyvillage.wisc.edu/

The quintessential site for disability-related resources, the Family Village offers a wealth of information in a clear format with excellent graphics. Established as "a global community that integrates information, resources and communication opportunities," the site is designed to simulate a real village—click the Coffee Shop and find the family gathering place, with parent groups, sibling programs, and chat rooms. Drop in on the University and find links to disability research programs (including descriptions!) Move on to Sports and Recreation and tap into a bonanza of recreational resources for those with disabilities, from camps to Special Olympics. This is a super site!

Guide to Using the Internet for Parents of Children with Disabilities or Chronic Health Conditions

http://www.familyvillage.wisc.edu/search/guide.htm

Another extraordinary resource from the Family Village Project, this site serves as a primer for those venturing on to the Internet to learn of a medical condition. Sections include The Basics, Communicating Online, and Finding Information. This is the place to find common health acronyms, newsgroups, information on search engines, even online periodicals of interest to parents of children with special needs.

KidsHealth.org

http://kidshealth.org/

Provides info about the health of kids, ranging from child behavior and development, to nutrition, general health, surgery, and immunizations. Offers a section for children that contains health FAQs for kids, games, and more. Also contains many tips and fun facts to know and tell! A lot of good info at this site!

LD Online

http://www.ldonline.org/

An interactive guide designed as an information source for parents, teachers and children, the LD Online site includes an in-depth explanation of learning disabilities, an update on what's new in the field, bulletin boards, audio clips, and several other categories.

National Information Center for Children and Youth with Disabilities

http://www.nichcy.org/

A national information and referral center that provides information about disability-related issues for families as well as educators and health care professionals. Focus is on children and youth, up to age 22. Services include access to publications and databases as well as referrals to other organizations.

Our Kids

http://rdz.stjohns.edu/library/support/our-kids/

Web site dedicated to parents who raise kids with special needs. Provides a reading list for kids, nutrition information, as well as links to other parenting resources. Provides links and support for specific challenges, such as ADD, Chromosome X, and Down Syndrome; and access to national databases, such as GCRC Rare Disorder Network Database and NORD (National Organization for Rare Diseases).

PEDINFO: A Pediatrics WebServer

http://www.uab.edu/pedinfo/index.html

This broad-based site is not just for doctors, but for anyone interested in children's health. A sampling of categories includes publications, a directory of children's hospitals, information on congenital illness, disabilities and special health care needs, and parenting.

Special Needs Resources Online

http://www.scsn.net/~nhelman/famconn/other.html

This site provides an extensive index of special needs resources, including newsgroups, university programs, general information, and links to support pages such as the Asthma Page, the Easter Seals Home Page, and Parents Helping Parents.

PARENTING

365 TV-Free Activities

http://family.starwave.com/funstuff/activity/tvtoc.html

Great site that really does offer numerous suggestions of things to do with your kids that do NOT involve the television. Activities are listed by category, such as Arts and Crafts, Indoor/Outdoor Play, Tire 'em Out (one of my favorites!), and Older Kids Play, just to name a few. Excellent place to visit!

All About Kids Online

http://www2.aak.com/aak/

Way cool site that is about families and parenting. Features great articles about hot topics, such as choosing prenatal care, education in the United States, Attention Deficit Disorder, and so on. Also offers a "virtual community," calendar of family events, and a parent's forum.

D.O.S.A. Parent Page

`http://www.mbnet.mb.ca/~ahawkins/`

Site that provides all kinds of information for parents, such as tips for taming your child (great perspective!), and links to recommended sites for parents.

The Dads Den

`http://megamach.portage.net/~rborelli/children.html`

Geared toward new fathers, the goal of this site is an ambitious one—utilizing the "global village" concept to discuss problems and determine solutions for the future of children worldwide. In the short term, parents can share insights and wisdom of child rearing. Subject matter ranges from tips on combating colic to advice on marital relationships.

Early Childhood Educators and Family Web Corner

`http://www.nauticom.net/www/cokids/index.html`

Delightful and informative site conceived for educators but loaded with useful material for parents with young children. A sampling of topics includes health and nutrition, child safety concerns, social issues, family and holiday activities—even a section on using the Web. The Family Pages category features a plethora of site links with descriptions of each. A truly superb site!

Family Issues Page

`http://www.fix.net/~rprewett/fam.html`

The scope of this Christian-based site is reflected in the title. Along with separate Theology and Health Pages, it provides an extensive selection of articles, resources and links on pregnancy, education, and parenting trends and pitfalls.

Family Matters: Have Realistic Expectations of Small Children

`http://tera.oscs.montana.edu/wwwpb/home/real.html`

A simple but worthwhile site that explains preschoolers perceptions of the world at various developmental stages, and the importance of realistic expectations for them.

Family Planet Home Page

`http://family.starwave.com/`

Web magazine for families with kids 12 and under. Provides family news, expert advice for FAQs, Web site reviews, movie reviews, community opportunities with other parents, and the capability to send and receive responses to what's offered at this site. Good stuff here!

Family Web Home Page

`http://www.familyweb.com`

"An informative place for families to gather from around the world." An interesting site with a number of sections and an extraordinary collection of FAQs from the misc.kids newsgroups. The FAQs alone are well worth the visit and include pages on such things as nutrition, breast pumps, car seats, and SIDS—even a FAQ on raising street-smart kids.

family.com

`http://www.family.com/`

Super cool site that offers information on the following topics—activities, computing, education, travel, entertainment, and finance sections are just for starters. These sections are then broken down into sections of the United States. This site makes topics easy to find and provides great articles and information. This is a must-visit!

Fathering Magazine

`http://www.fathering.com`

A great online magazine for dads, with news, stories and games for the paternal set. The publication takes on serious issues as well—a recent issue featured an article on "The Sexual Abuse Industry."

Foster Parent Home Page

`http://www.rainbowkids.com/needs1296.html`

An excellent site covering the spectrum of foster care, including information on states and counties, children's issues and special needs. The site also offers a number of links to related subjects.

GrandsRuS

`http://www.eclypase.com/GrandsRuS/dir.htm`

Focusing on "grandparents and special others raising children," this is an attractive site with substance. The directory includes informational areas on rearing abused, adopted or special needs kids, grandparent chat sites and support groups, and a GrandsRuS newsletter. There are sections on Kids Pages, Home Management and Computer Tips. The producers of this site didn't miss much!

A B C D E F G H I J K L M N O P Q R S T U V W X Y Z

Home and Family Web Site

http://www.homeandfamily.com/

Web site about the *Home and Family Show* on The Family Channel (cable-access channel). Includes show diary and schedules, classifieds, a breast cancer forum, and information about parenting. If you like the show, be sure to check out the site.

Idea Central: Welfare and Families

http://epn.org/idea/welfare.html

Produced by the electronic policy forum, this site provides in-depth information on welfare issues, the true size of the welfare budget, and the cost of welfare reform, as well as its impact on families. It also includes an analysis of government policies on such issues.

Kid Safe Sites

http://www.cwa.co.nz/edu/kidsafe.html

A great resource for parents concerned about their children using the World Wide Web. This page offers a cornucopia of sites that have been screened and recommended as "kid-safe," as well as a capsule description of each.

The Mommy Times

http://www.mommytimes.com/

Site written and maintained by moms for moms (dedicated to preserving the sanity of all moms). Offers support network on the Web for moms, articles about motherhood, suggestions for all types of working mothers (those inside and outside of the home), and opportunities to share your experience with others. Great site for new moms, providing you can find the time!

Nashville Parent

http://www.nashvilleparent.com/

Great online, monthly magazine that has feature articles (April's issue included "Educating Your Children About HIV and AIDS" and "Preparing Kids for the Dentist", just to name a couple), a section that addresses parenting matters, and other links for parents and kids. Be patient, however; the graphics are great, but seem to take forever to load.

Related Sites

http://www.cherryvalleybooks.com/

http://childrensbooks.miningco.com/

National Child Care Information Center Home Page

http://ericps.ed.uiuc.edu/nccic/nccichome.html

Offers information about child care and federal programs for child care, tips for looking for and finding child care, a list of organizations serving child care and related professions, and links to other child care-related sites on the Net.

OUDPS: Kids Safety on the Internet

http://www.uoknor.edu/oupd/kidsafe/start.htm

Provides an array of topics on which you would want to educate your child, such as Internet safety, drugs and alcohol, home safety, stranger danger, and so on. This is a site that you can share with your children.

Parents-at-Home Page

http://iquest.com/~jsm/moms/

Way cool site that is geared toward parents that forgo outside employment and stay at home with kids, although not exclusive to stay-at-home parents. Offers an email pen pal page for kids, at-home moms and dads, and grandparents; parenting tips and resources that include Internet access and family health and safety; books and magazine lists; online medical help; links to other parenting sites; and more! This site has just about everything you could ask for in a parenting/family site—and what it doesn't have, you will find a link! Great site. Great site for new moms, providing you can find the time.

ParenthoodWeb

http://www.parenthoodweb.com/

This award-winning site offers a potpourri of resources on parenting issues—notices on product recalls, popular baby names, tips on handling holiday stress and an article on protecting your child from lead poisoning, to name a few. Parents can ask a pro questions on childrearing or solicit advice from the member discussion group. Bookmark this site—you'll return to it often.

Parenting New Mexico

http://www.net-publish.com/pnm/resource.html

Good site that offers articles and online resources. Also provides calendar of events, but unless you actually live in New Mexico, the calendar probably won't be of much use. The articles, however, address daily issues that parents face, such as home video reviews, info on Montessori, and children facing death and dying. Also has online resources to other sites.

ParentingMatters

http://lifematters.com/parentn.html

Great site that features a parent support interactive forum, articles on respectful parenting, four goals of misbehavior, handling kid's aggression, bridging the generation gap, and more. This site even contains a grandparenting column!

Parents and Children Together Online

http://www.indiana.edu/~eric_rec/fl/pcto/menu.html

An online magazine for parents and children whose focus is family literacy. Offers opportunities for you and your children to write and share family stories; features articles geared toward grades preschool through 3, 4 through 6, and older; and book reviews. Also offers interactive story telling—very cool! This is a great site for family interaction.

Parent's Place.Com

http://www.parentsplace.com/

Home-based site that offers info on midwifery, nutrition, education for your kids, adolescent and teen info, and single parenting. Also has daily and weekly features, such as violence in the family and sibling rivalry. Also offers online shopping where merchandise is geared towards the parenting market.

ParentTime

http://www.pathfinder.com/ParentTime/

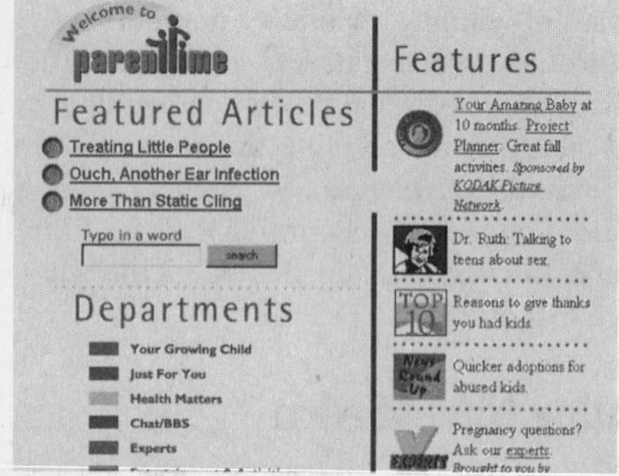

An attractive, fun site that personalizes your visit by having you enter the age(s) of your child(ren) as you enter. Includes information on pregnancy, a weekly newsletter, and an impressive assortment of articles and resources for every age group. Parents shouldn't miss this one.

Platypus Family Fun Pages

http://www.orst.edu/~dickt/playroom/playroom.html

Platypus Software produces educational software for children, and it extends that educational commitment to its online site. Its Family Fun Pages feature stories, songs, activities and games in both English and Spanish, so children can learn in both languages! A fun site to visit.

Positive Parenting Home Page

http://www.positiveparenting.com/

Features parenting tips, such as "9 things to do instead of spanking," "How to handle sibling rivalry," and "Saying, I love you." Also provides articles on parenting and online resources for parents and professionals.

ReadyWeb

http://ericps.ed.uiuc.edu/readyweb/readyweb.html

Geared toward parents and educators, ReadyWeb is sponsored by the ERIC Clearinghouse on Elementary and EarlyChildhood Education. The electronic collection of resources addresses the subject of "school readiness" from two perspectives: getting children ready for schools, and getting schools ready for children. The site also provides links to several publications.

Twins Magazine Home Page

http://www.twinsmagazine.com/

Site that offers information on twin pregnancy, childhood, and adulthood. Features monthly articles and back articles about issues that parents and twins face.

The Wonderwise Parent Home Page

http://www.ksu.edu/wwparent/wondhome.htm

Site interested in teaching parent/child interaction. Features articles on responsive discipline (how do I, as a parent, react?), an encyclopedia of parenting, and humor pages that offer anecdotes and quips.

SINGLE PARENTING

Jill's Single Parent Support Page

http://www.nucleus.com/~jlassali/

An interesting page with a personal approach, a professional presentation and great graphics, this site offers advice and comments on surviving single parenthood. There are sections on Kids and Divorce, Helpful Ideas, and links to related sites. A particularly nice feature on the opening page is the picture and statistics of a missing child. The image rotates every 10 minutes and features 12 of the most recently reported missing children. If you have information, a click on the child's photo will put you in contact with the Center for Missing and Exploited Children.

National Congress for Fathers and Children

http://com.primenet.com/ncfc/mission.html

With the stated goal of assisting "parents who desire to remain actively involved in the lives of their children," this group works to coordinate local efforts and encourage national initiatives that promote increased participation of fathers in their children's lives, especially non-resident parents. The site explains the goals and educational objectives of the organization.

Parents Without Partners, Inc.

http://www.parentsplace.com/readroom/pwp/

This is the online site for the international organization which focuses on issues and interests of single parents and their children. The site offers a listing of local chapters and events, resources and articles for single parents, and the opportunity to interact with other members through live chat sessions and bulletin boards.

Single Dad's Index

http://www.vix.com/pub/men/single-dad.html

A broad-based source of information from the World Wide Web Virtual Library, this is a great starting point for those seeking to learn more on the subject of single fatherhood. The index includes essays and studies on custody, economic and statistical material on child support, and commentary and legal information on visitation and access, paternity and child support, among others.

The Single Father's Lighthouse

http://www.av.gnet.com/~rlewis3/mail.html

Geared toward dads who are beginning the journey of single fatherhood, this site is both personable and informative, sharing the author's discoveries as he tracks down information, resources and links on single parenting. The conversational style and simple explanations ("Do you know about Listservs? I'm no expert...but these can really be great.") give a sense of camaraderie to the site.

Single Mothers by Choice

http://www.parentsplace.com/readroom/smc/index.html

An organization devoted to providing support and information to single mothers as well as those considering single motherhood. Includes advice from women who have done it, an online newsletter, membership forms, and contact information.

Single Parent Project–Kodiak College

http://www.alaska.net/~rwarner/spphtml.htm

Based in Kodiak, Alaska, the Single Parent Project has as its goal the self-sufficiency of low-income, single parent families through education. With that in mind, the site offers a variety of links on political information, government aid, and single parent support groups.

The Single Parent Resource

http://www.parentsplace.com/readroom/spn/index.html

This bi-monthly newsletter addresses issues important to single parents and children. The online version features more than 50 selected articles covering issues as diverse as custody arrangements, single parenting myths, household chores, legal matters, and utilizing family time.

Single Parent Resource Center

http://rampages.onramp.net/~bevhamil/singleparentresourcece_478.html

A useful site that includes information for single moms and dads about coping with divorce, understanding family law, handling financial issues, finding spirituality, as well as standard parenting and child-related issues. Includes publications, resources to other information, and links to single parents' Web pages.

Sole Mothers International

http://home.navisoft.com/solemom/

Sole Mothers International exists "for the benefit and encouragement of single parents." This expansive site covers a multitude of issues, such as money matters, the perils and pleasures of parenting, domestic violence, career issues, and a host of articles and resources. There's even a forum where members can present their thoughts on several key issues, such as daycare, welfare reform, and being a single dad. While the site is devoted to single parents, everyone can benefit from the information posted.

ADOPTION RESOURCES

Adopted Child

http://www.moscow.com/Resources/Adoption/

A newsletter, access to books, tapes, and additional links, as well as information for waiting or new adoptive parents are just a few of the things you'll find at this site. Includes informational articles relating to adoption.

Adoption.com

http://www.adoption.com/index.shtml

Graphics-intensive site that includes information for birthmothers with unplanned pregnancies, parents looking to adopt, as well as babies looking for adoptive parents.

Internet Adoption Resources

http://www.adopting.com/

A good point of entry, this site has myriad links to adopting agencies, facilitators and attorneys, information about support groups, information on adoptees' rights and perspectives, as well as waiting children photos.

LISTSERVS

ABLETECH-L—For parents, teachers, and others concerned with disabilities

You can join this group by sending the message "sub ABLETECH-L your name" to

listserv@listserv.okstate.edu

ABUSE-L—Professional Forum for Child Abuse Issues

State University of New York at Buffalo

You can join this group by sending the message "sub ABUSE-L your name" to

listserv@ubvm.cc.buffalo.edu

ABUSE-PARTNERS-L—Support for Partners of Abuse Survivors

You can join this group by sending the message "sub ABUSE-PARTNERS-L your name" to

listserv@sjuvm.stjohns.edu

ADOPTEES—List Adoptees/Adoptees Mailing List

St. John's University, Jamaica, NY

You can join this group by sending the message "sub ADOPTEES your name" to

listserv@sjuvm.stjohns.edu

BLINDFAM—SJU List for Families of the Blind

St. John's University, Jamaica, NY

You can join this group by sending the message "sub BLINDFAM your name" to

listserv@sjuvm.stjohns.edu

CARINGPARENTS—How Do Kids Cope with Illness?

You can join this group by sending the message "sub CARINGPARENTS your name" to

listserv@sjuvm.stjohns.edu

CEL-KIDS—Celiac/Coeliac Wheat/Gluten-Free Children List

St. John's University, Jamaica, NY

You can join this group by sending the message "sub CEL-KIDS your name" to

listserv@sjuvm.stjohns.edu

CO-OCCURRING-DISORDERS—Discuss Co-occurring Mental Health & Substance Abuse Disorders

You can join this group by sending the message "sub CO-OCCURRING-DISORDERS your name" to

listserv@listserv.aol.com

CPPARENT—Discussion for Parents of Children with Cerebral Palsy

St. John's University, Jamaica, NY

You can join this group by sending the message "sub CPPARENT your name" to

listserv@sjuvm.stjohns.edu

DADVOCAT—Dads of Children with Disabilities or Special Health+

You can join this group by sending the message "sub DADVOCAT your name" to

listserv@lsv.uky.edu

FAM-MATH—Family Math

You can join this group by sending the message "sub FAM-MATH your name" to

listserv@uicvm.uic.edu

FAMCOMM—Marital/Family & Relational Communication

Rensselaer Polytechnic Institute, Troy, NY

You can join this group by sending the message "sub FAMCOMM your name" to

listserv@vm.its.rpi.edu

FAMILY-L—Academic Family Medicine Discussion

You can join this group by sending the message "sub FAMILY-L your name" to

listserv@lsv.uky.edu

Related Sites

http://www.naturalchild.com/

http://www.earthnet-ltd.com/motherchild

FATHERS—US Department of HHS: Fatherhood and Social Service Programs

You can join this group by sending the message "sub FATHERS your name" to

`listserv@ulist.nih.gov`

FREE-L—Fathers' Rights and Equality Exchange

You can join this group by sending the message "sub FREE-L your name" to

`listserv@listserv.iupui.edu`

GERINET—Geriatric Health Care Discussion Group

You can join this group by sending the message "sub GERINET your name" to

`listserv@ubvm.cc.buffalo.edu`

HEALING—Healing: Survivors of Intimate Abuse

You can join this group by sending the message "sub HEALING your name" to

`listserv@sjuvm.stjohns.edu`

MFTC-L—MFTC-L Marriage and Family Therapy Counseling Discussion

You can join this group by sending the message "sub MFTC-L your name" to

`listserv@sjuvm.stjohns.edu`

MOMSONLINE—Moms Online Main Mailing List

You can join this group by sending the message "sub MOMSONLINE your name" to

`listserv@listserv.aol.com`

NFWNET-L—Nebraska Family Wellness Network

You can join this group by sending the message "sub NFWNET-L your name" to

`listserv@unlvm.unl.edu`

OPEN-ADOPTION—Open Adoption List (formerly BRTH-PRNT)

You can join this group by sending the message "sub OPEN-ADOPTION your name" to

`listserv@home.ease.lsoft.com`

PARENTING-L—Discussion of Parenting

University of Illinois, Urbana, IL

You can join this group by sending the message "sub PARENTING-L your name" to

`listserv@postoffice.cso.uiuc.edu`

PARENTS—Announcements, Information and Discussion Related to Parenting

You can join this group by sending the message "sub PARENTS your name" to

`listserv%uriacc.bitnet@listserv.net`

PSNEWS—Parent Soup Newsletter

You can join this group by sending the message "sub PSNEWS your name" to

`listserv@listserv.aol.com`

REGAYN—Drug Abuse Prevention

You can join this group by sending the message "sub REGAYN your name" to

`listserv@lsv.uky.edu`

S-YOUTH—Stolen Youth Mental Health, Abuse Problems of Youth

You can join this group by sending the message "sub S-YOUTH your name" to

`listserv@sjuvm.stjohns.edu`

SP-SUBSTANCE-ABUSE-LIST—Substance Abuse Information

You can join this group by sending the message "sub SP-SUBSTANCE-ABUSE-LIST your name" to

`listserv@listserv.acsu.buffalo.edu`

TCS—Taking Children Seriously: Non-coercive Parenting/Education

You can join this group by sending the message "sub TCS your name" to

`listserv@listserv.aol.com`

UIUCPARENT-L—U of I Parents Advocacy Group

University of Illinois, Urbana, IL

You can join this group by sending the message "sub UIUCPARENT-L your name" to

`listserv@postoffice.cso.uiuc.edu`

WS238-L—Women, Work, and Family in the 20th Century

State University of New York at Buffalo

You can join this group by sending the message "sub WS238-L your name" to

`listserv@ubvm.cc.buffalo.edu`

NEWSGROUPS

`alt.adoption`

`alt.child-support`

`alt.missing-kids`

`alt.parenting.solutions`

`alt.parenting.twins-triplets`

`alt.support.divorce`

`alt.support.single-parents`

`alt.support.step-parents`

`soc.culture.jewish.parenting`

`soc.support.depression.family`

Related Sites

`http://www.homearts.com/`

`http://www.parent-education.com/`

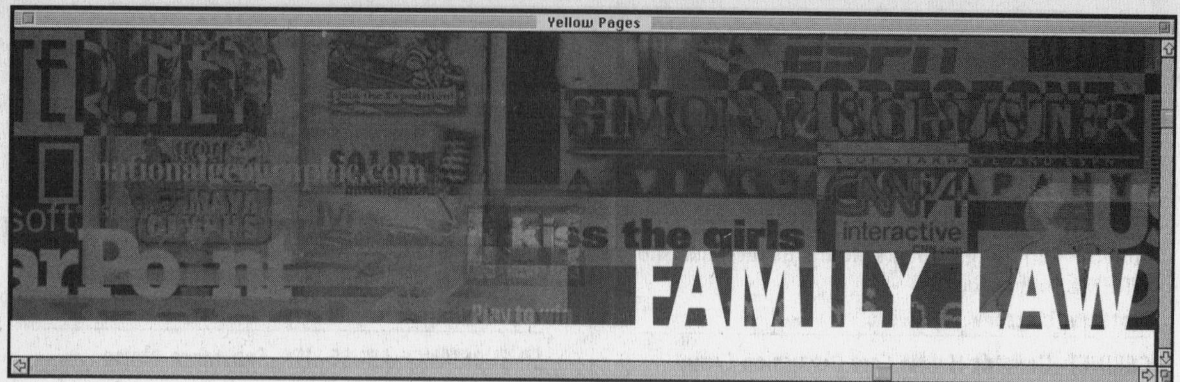

> There are vast untapped resources of faith and talent that can be discovered only in adversity.
>
> *Robert H. Schuller*

Divorce Helpline Home Page

http://www.divorcehelp.com/

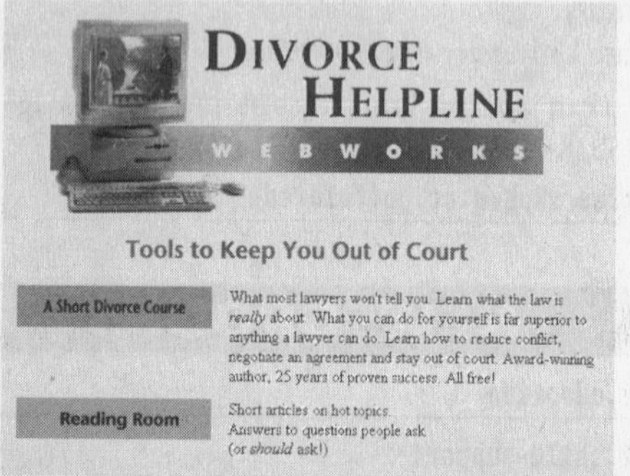

Keep the law out of your divorce! This site provides resources to the consumer who is looking to stay out of court for his or her divorce. Divided into sections: Helpline Center, Short Course, Directory, Book Shop, Work Room, and Reading Room. Also includes link to Divorce Helpline's California Center and a Directory of Self-help Services. Obligatory links to other sites included.

Divorce Helpline Home Page
http://www.divorcehelp.com/

Family Law Advisor Home Page
http://www.divorcenet.com/law/

The Equal Marriage Rights Home Page
http://www.ucc.gu.uwa.edu.au/~rod/gay/marriage.html

Family Law Advisor Home Page

http://www.divorcenet.com/law/

Site provides support and legal information for persons going through or having gone through a divorce. Divided into sections: Frequently Asked Questions, Online Newsletter and Index, State-by-State Resource Center, Interactive Bulletin Board, Paternity Establishment, Lawyer to Lawyer, and International Parental Abduction. Link to information through each of these sections. Page also includes a search engine that covers the entire site. Other legal and law links are available through this site, too.

Fathers' Rights and Equality Exchange

http://www.vix.com/free/index.html

Site contains much information about the legal rights of fathers. You can find out about the first annual F.R.E.E. conference, join F.R.E.E., discover the benefits of F.R.E.E., read the F.R.E.E. case file, and read a message from the founder of F.R.E.E. Other links include the F.R.E.E. file and testimonies from F.R.E.E. members.

Legal dot Net—Family Law, and Overview

http://www.legal.net/family.htm

An overview of family law and what is involved in the legalities of divorce. Covers the legal talk about negotiated settlements, discovery, disclosure statements, temporary orders, petitions, and responses. Site also links to other legal sites, and attorney and non-attorney topics.

The Equal Marriage Rights Home Page

http://www.ucc.gu.uwa.edu.au/~rod/gay/marriage.html

Site contains much legal information about same-sex marriages, including which states have banned them, which states have failed to ban them, and which states are currently trying to ban them. Also access same-sex lobby groups, the marriage mailing list, and articles on same-sex relationships and marriage. General information about how solid gay unions are is also included.

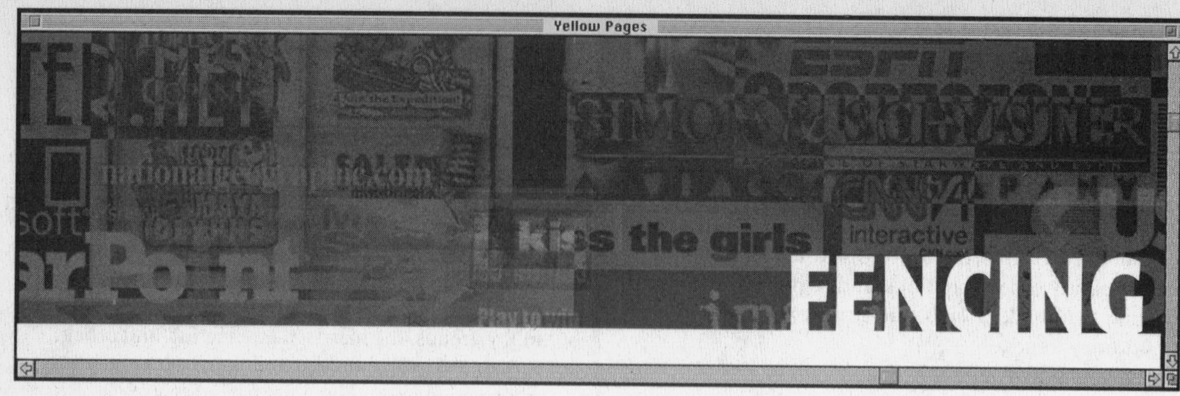

> The knight's bones are dust,
> And his good sword rust;
> His soul is with the saints,
> I trust.
>
> *Samuel Taylor Coleridge*

American Fencing Magazine HomePage

http://www.uncg.edu/student.groups/fencing/AmericanFencing/

The site of the official publication of the United States Fencing Association. Search the archives to find electronic versions of back issues dating back to 1987. Read the current issue, which contains columns and articles for competitors, coaches, and those interested in the administrative side of fencing.

British Fencing on the Internet

http://www.netlink.co.uk/users/afa/index.html

Formerly known as the Amateur Fencing Association, British Fencing constructed this site to serve as the electronic home of *The Sword*, the organization's quarterly print journal. Stay current with rule changes, membership news, and the organization's calendar of upcoming events.

Related Sites

http://www.calvacom.fr/fie/

http://www.cis.ohio-state.edu/hypertext/faq/usenet/sports/fencing-faq/top.html

http://www.ii.uib.no/~arild/fencing/faq/Top-view.html

British Fencing on the Internet
http://www.netlink.co.uk/users/afa/index.html

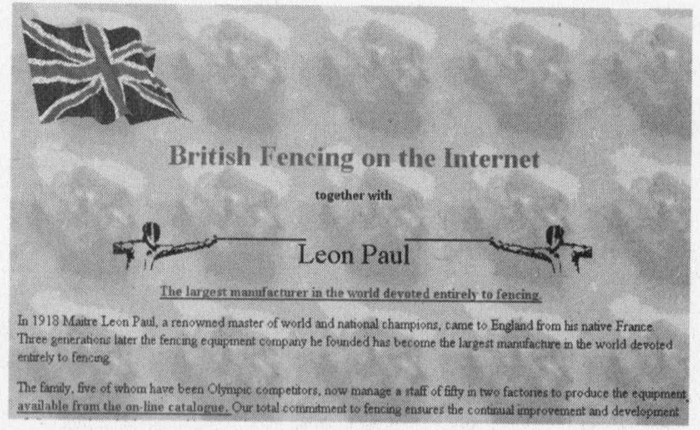

British Kendo Association News

http://ourworld.compuserve.com/homepages/S_Flowers/index.htm

Kendo, or "the way of the sword," is the Japanese martial art of fencing. The BKA site contains introductory information about the sport, a list of dojos in the UK, letters and editorials, and a list of upcoming events.

Canadian Fencing Federation

http://www.fencing.ca/

The governing body of fencing in Canada, the CFF built this site to keep you informed of current rankings and upcoming events. Order fencing-related items from the online boutique, and find biographies of the Canadian fencing squads.

The Fencing Post

http://www.thefencingpost.com/

Contains a full catalog of epees, foils, and sabres, with many pictures. Also included is a large selection of fencing shoes, tools, and accessories. The site promises a good discount for all online orders.

The Fencing Center of San Jose

http://www.fencing.com/

This nonprofit organization provides information to Bay-Area fencers. Read out about local workshops and peruse the schedule of group lessons.

Glossary of Terms

http://www.synec-doc.be/escrime/dico/engl.htm

Part of the *L'escrime en Belgique* (Belgian fencing) site, this terms list comes in both French and English. A must for the beginning fencer, and probably for the expert too. This glossary contains over 130 terms, from "absence of blade" to "yellow card." The site also links to many other French-language sites.

Leon Paul Fencing Equipment

http://www.netlink.co.uk/users/afa/leonpaul/lp1.htm

This British company was an official supplier to the Atlanta Olympic Games. The large online catalog accepts credit card orders, and the company will ship around the world. The site also contains current updates in fencing regulations.

LSU Fencing Club

http://sarah.rsip.lsu.edu/fencing/fencing.home.html

Up since 1994, this site is the oldest club site at LSU. Features great background information on the sport as well as rules, penalty guides, and links to other clubs around the world.

Martinez Classical Fencing and Historical Swordsmanship

http://pages.prodigy.com/kmoser/fencing.htm

Return to another era in Ramón Martínez' school of classical swordsmanship. In addition to classical fencing (foil, epee, and sabre), Maestro Martínez teaches the smallsword and rapier out of his Manhattan studio. He specializes in the historical and cultural events that shaped classical Spanish sword fighting.

NBC Sports—Olympic Fencing

http://olympic.nbc.com/sports/fencing/index.html

While the 1996 Atlanta Olympic Games are long gone, this site is still useful for finding out about the men's and women's teams, rules, and background on the sport. Also contains an interesting list of fencing facts and comparisons of the different competing countries. Watch this site as the 2000 Games in Sydney approach.

Professional Fencing League

http://www.profence.com/

The PFL site opened to serve the PFL membership and other interested parties. Find a list and bios of current members and check on the next tournament in your area. Also check the massive rule book so that you know what's going on in pro vs. amateur fencing.

Twin Cities Fencing Club

http://www1.stpaul.gov/stpaul/distcouncil/supc/tcfc/index.html

Located in Minnesota, the TCFC site lets you take a look at its practice facilities and stay up to date with the club schedule. Also features a comprehensive collection of local, national, and international tournament information.

United States Fencing Association

http://www.usfa.org/

The official site of the USFA. This extensive resource contains program descriptions, rules and regulations, current point standings by division, and more. Also find the rosters for the National Team and find the biographies of the 1996 Olympians.

Welcome to Wheelchair Fencing

http://www.ams.med.uni-goettingen.de/~ubartma/wheelchairfencing.html

This site contains a wealth of information for the wheelchair fencer. Includes rules, a listing of competitions, and highlights from recent Paralympics Games. Also provides links to other wheelchair fencing resources.

NEWSGROUP

rec.sport.fencing

Related Sites

http://www.ii.uib.no/~arild/fencing/patch2/www_pages.html

http://www.kismeta.com/digrasse.html

http://www.mit.edu:8001/activities/fencing/home.html

http://www.sport-hq.com/rex/combat/fenceorg.shtml

http://www.triumf.ca/people/morgan/faq_FENC.html

http://www.ugrad.cs.jhu.edu/~baker/usfca.html

http://zipmall.com/fencing_links.htm

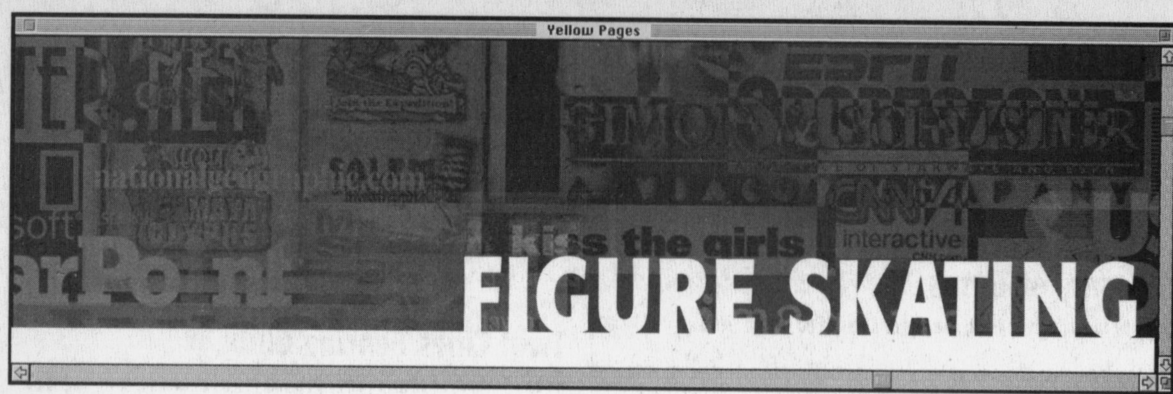

A B C D E F G H I J K L M N O P Q R S T U V W X Y Z

The connection between conscious and unconscious poses particular problems in the dancer because the body is the soul of action.

Marion Woodman

CBS SportsLine Olympic Figure Skating

`http://skating.iprolink.ch/lausanne97/`

Contains competition schedules and results, audio, and video of Olympic skaters.

Enchantment on Ice

`http://www.aiminc.com/iceskate/`

An online catalog featuring figure skating dresses, skates, videos, jewelry, and more.

EuroSkating

`http://skating.iprolink.ch/`

Dedicated to European figure skaters, this site contains info on competitions and skaters. Also has a search database visitors can use to find information on specific skaters.

Figure Skating

`http://www.figureskating.com/`

Visitors can specialize their searches according to dance, ladies, men, and pairs categories.

United States Figure Skating Association
`http://www.usfsa.org/`

Figure Skating Fan Page

`http://onramp.uscom.com/~alaynew/skate.htm`

Site contains photos, competitions, results, and TV and show schedule.

Figure Skating Page for Newcomers

`http://ourworld.compuserve.com/homepages/doug_coughtry/`

This site features explanations of the words, customs, procedures, and rules of figure skating in non-technical language.

Gymstytch

`http://www.gymstytch.com/`

This site belongs to a company that designs, manufactures, and sells skating wear. Shop, size, and order online.

International Figure Skaters Association

`http://w3.iprolink.ch/krupp/ifsa.htm`

This site is the official information source of the International Figure Skaters Association.

The Armenian National Figure Skating Team Web Site

`http://ourworld.compuserve.com/homepages/hagop/`

Contains pages listing team sponsors, team members, photo gallery, upcoming competitions, and past competition results. Also, fans can send their well wishes to the athletes via an email link.

The Insider's Guide with Debbi Wilkes

http://www.debbiwilkes.com/

This site is hosted by Debbi Wilkes, Olympic silver medalist and television commentator. Visitors can get the inside scoop about the skating community.

The Unofficial Russian Figure Skating Page

http://www.geocities.com/Colosseum/Track/4383/

Information on Russian figure skaters complete with photos and competition and show reports.

United States Figure Skating Association

http://www.usfsa.org/

An extensive site featuring results from a wide variety of competitions, standings, USFSA schedules and placements, lots of links, and more.

Related Sites

http://www.webcom.com/~dnkorte/sk8_0000.html

http://members.aol.com/revjoelle/index.html

http://members.aol.com/sk8judgs/index.htm

http://www.figureskating.com/ladies/amateur/kwan/kwan.htm

http://www.mts.net/~ghymers/

http://www.toe-picks.com/home.htm

A B C D E F G H I J K L M N O P Q R S T U V W X Y Z

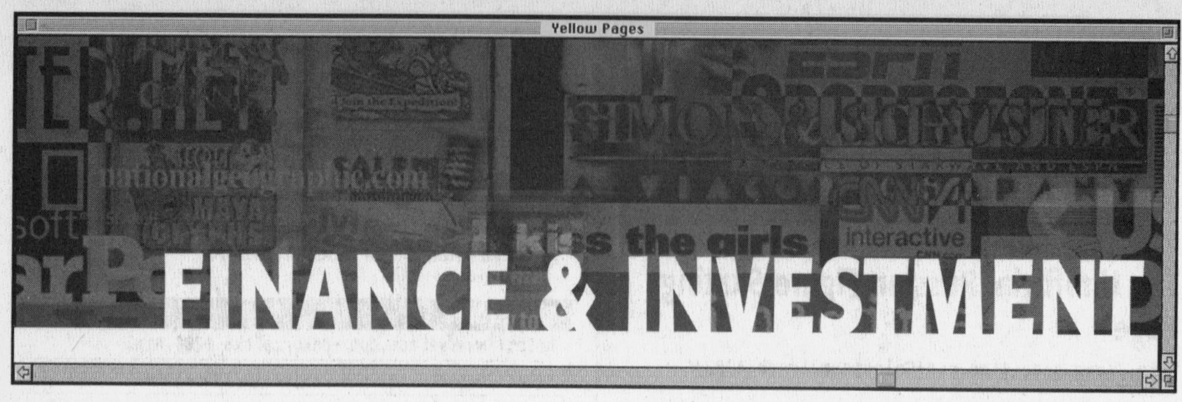

FINANCE & INVESTMENT

> Only a fool holds out for the top dollar.
>
> *Joseph P. Kennedy*

It doesn't matter whether you are a financial guru or just beginning to dabble in the investment market or finance, you'll find sites that have great information for all levels of experience. This category includes sites on banking, brokerage houses, exchanges, investment clubs and information, mutual funds, and more.

NRP TOP PICKS

- **The Credit Union Home Page** http://www.cu.org/
- **Trade History** http://www.tradehistory.com
- **DLJ Direct** http://www.dljdirect.com/
- **NASDAQ** http://www.nasdaq.com
- **GreenMoney On-Line Guide** http://www.greenmoney.com/
- **IPO Central** http://www.ipocentral.com/
- **Motley Fool** http://www.fool.com/

BANKS

The Credit Union Home Page

http://www.cu.org/

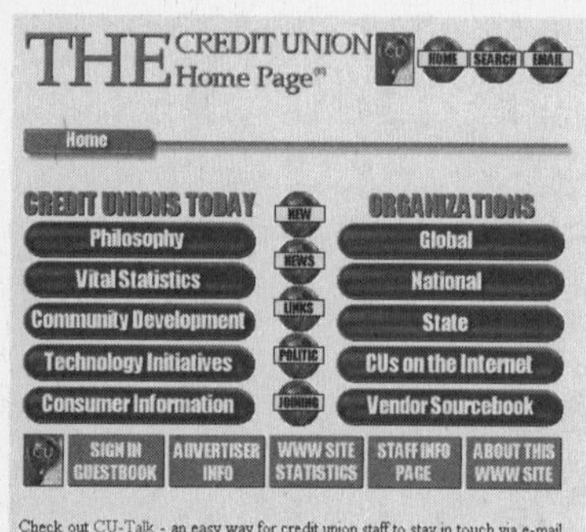

Serves as a gathering place for credit unions on the Internet, featuring information on credit unions ranging from joining a credit union to running one. Includes information on the philosophy of credit unions, consumer information, and services available.

Infogroup S.p.A.

http://www.infogroup.it/UK/home_uk.htm

Based in Florence, Italy, Infogroup offers software for the banking industry. Quality information systems are their main focus. Access to descriptions and services is offered.

The World Bank Home Page

http://www.worldbank.org/

This site provides information about the World Bank, including current events, press releases, bank news, publications, research studies, and country- and project-related information.

World Currency Converter

http://www.dna.lth.se/cgi-bin/kurt/rates

Enables you to choose a currency of the world, and then choose another currency to compare against it, which gives you the exchange rate. Rates are provided by the Federal Reserve Bank of New York and are updated daily.

BONDS

Bonds Online

http://www.bonds-online.com/

Extensive market information for tax-free municipal bonds, treasury/savings bonds, corporate, bond funds, and brokers. Bond investment information is available from the Bond Professor.

Trade History

http://www.tradehistory.com

Trade History covers bond market trade history. The site provides a database of actual trades in the bond market. As the database grows in size, its statistical value for investors will also grow. An OID calculator is now available, you can now calculate income and adjustments of Original Issue Discount Bonds as well as capital gains and losses.

BROKERAGES

DLJ Direct

http://www.dljdirect.com/

DLJ Direct (formerly PC Financial Network) is one of the best known and most popular financial sites on the Net. DLJ Direct offers online trading, real-time quotes and news, research, and portfolio tracking. Commissions for trades using DLJ Direct are lower than at most other services.

eBroker

http://www.ebroker.com/

eBroker provides quotes, account access, and online trading for independent investors. eBroker also provides discount brokering services. Their $12 per trade rate is one of the best available on the Internet.

e.Schwab Online Investing

http://www.eschwab.com/

The online trading service from Charles Schwab, e.Schwab offers discount brokering services to the individual investors. Trading online with e.Schwab offers convenience and control, at low stock commissions of $29.95.

E*Trade

http://www.etrade.com/

E*Trade is another online trading service geared toward the individual investor. With E*Trade you can buy and sell securities online for NYSE, AMEX, and NASDAQ. Stock performance information and company information is available.

Fidelity Investments

http://www.fid-inv.com/

A comprehensive site full of investment information. Fidelity provides services to the personal and institutional investor. Fidelity is a well known and trusted investment firm, and their site is worthwhile reading for anyone wanting to use their services.

Fin-Atlantic Securities, Inc.

http://www.gate.net/~stocks

Investment banking and securities brokerage firm. Offers stocks, bonds, options, mutual funds, new issues, and other securities. Offers Internet users one free no-commission trade.

Lombard Institutional Brokerage

http://www.lombard.com/

Lombard is dedicated to providing customers in the Internet community with a wide variety of investment options through the use of cutting edge technology. Lombard Brokerage offers real-time online trading. An online Research Information Center provides customers with the latest financial information.

Net Investor

http://paws.secapl.com/invest.html

Net Investor brings you online trading from PAWWS Financial Network. Among the services offered are: Free quotes & graphs, free online financial news, research and analysis, and free online access to PAWWS portfolio reporting. One of the most unusual services offered on this site is free checking and cash management. The Net Investor provides a convenient new way to manage investments that gives investors more control over their brokerage account than ever before. Net Investor provides 24-hour, online access to true low-cost trading and the tools needed to effectively manage a portfolio.

Pawws Financial Network

http://pawws.com

Provides information for investors. Allows quick access to the vast amounts of information necessary for successfully managing a securities portfolio. Seamlessly integrates services for portfolio accounting, securities and market research, and online trading.

Trading Room, Inc.

http://www.tradingroom.com/

TRI offers a FREE 800 Hotline & Fax service for investors. TRI is also a leader in electronic order placement. By utilizing technology TRI is able to offer clients blazing fills electronically from their computers. If you need access to electronic trading, this site is for you.

EXCHANGES

American Stock Exchange The Smarter Place to Be

http://www.amex.com/

Provides all kinds of financially related information, including market information, market news, listed companies, options and derivatives, and an information exchange section. Claims to be the first U.S. stock market on the Web.

Chicago Board of Trade

http://www.cbot.com

World's leading futures and commodities exchange. The CBOT home page provides market news and specialized information for traders. An educational area, named the Academic Hall, is geared to teachers and students who are interested in teaching about, or learning about the commodities markets.

Chicago Mercantile Exchange

http://www.cme.com/

Contains financial-related information. Provides information related to products and prices, educational resources, and CME member firms. Includes a CME news center, general information about CME, and links to other financial resources.

NASDAQ

http://www.nasdaq.com

The market known for its offering of high-tech stocks has a home on the Web. Market information is the staple of this site, offering information on the NASDAQ 100, the most active stocks, and so on. Stock quotes are also offered on this site.

The Philadelphia Stock Exchange

http://www.libertynet.org/~phlx/

The oldest stock exchange in the nation and the first on the Net (although they are not the only ones to claim this honor). Includes a history of the exchange, information on sectors index options, currency options, equity options, and links to other financial sites. Also includes a QuickTime VR scene of the Philadelphia Stock Exchange options floor.

FUTURES AND OPTIONS

Cyber-Futures

http://www.cyberfutures.com/

The Internet source for managed futures information. Cyberfutures was formed with the goal of providing a unified and complete Internet source for the futures industry. Not sure what managed futures are? The site provides a handy introduction to managed futures. There is also a vast index of Internet futures resources called the Internet Library.

Pacific Rim Futures and Options

http://www.teleport.com/~futures/

One of the most useful futures sites on the Web. Pacific Rim Futures and Options offers trading accounts and access to a database of closing prices. Online tutorials are available on the basics of futures and options trading. The tutorials offer good introductions to the commodities and option markets.

Lind-Waldock & Co.

http://www.lind-waldock.com

The World's Largest Discount Futures Brokerage Firm. Opening calls, market updates, and technical indicators are all available on the site. There is a section called "Ask an Expert" that attempts to answer your futures trading questions. An index of links to other futures/financial Web sites is offered.

A B C D E F G H I J K L M N O P Q R S T U V W X Y Z

Metal Prices

http://nickelalloy.com/

This site provides various metals prices updated daily from the London Metal Exchange. Although the site provides prices for many metals, it focuses mainly on nickel. Nickel investment charts, prices and a newsletter are featured on this site.

The Precious Metal & Gem Connection

http://www.pm-connect.com

The Precious Metal & Gem Connection provides investors with real time precious metal quotes, a dealer directory, bullion spreads, and exotic metals. A diamond price guide is available on the site. Online interactive conferencing is also provided to users.

World Link Futures, Inc.

http://www.worldlinkfutures.com

World Link Futures, Inc. is a New York Futures and Options Broker that goes out of its way to serve the beginning futures trader. The site provides lots of valuable information in trading for beginners all for free. A five lesson trading series is available online.

INVESTMENT CLUBS

EzTrade Club

http://www.eztrade.com

An online investors club featuring online charts and interactive analysis for stocks, options, and commodity futures. Extensive database including option volatilities updated daily. A Helpful options tutorial is available.

H$H Investment Forum

http://www.hh-club.com/

The H$H Investment Forum is an investment club that focuses on NASDAQ stocks priced at or below $1.25. Resources include investment strategies and company information. There are also online forums for discussion of investment-related topics. The club requires a subscription.

MoneyWorks!

http://www.mind-over-money.com/

The goal of MoneyWorks! is to make money for investors—small and large—by using the same sophisticated techniques of stock selection and portfolio management used on Wall Street. MoneyWorks! is open to people from all over the world.

Smart Money Club

http://www.bhw.com/smart/

A worldwide investors club providing investment opportunities, ideas, and financial reports. Online tax help is available. The site also includes discussion forums and electronic newsletters.

INVESTMENT INFORMATION

Accel Partners

http://www.accel.com

Invests in entrepreneurial companies of selected technology-driven markets. Provides links for company background, investment strategy, and resources for entrepreneurs.

Allegiance Financial Advisors

http://www.ibp.com/pit/allegiance/

Specializes in individualized asset management for individuals, businesses, retirement plans, and trusts.

The American Stock Report, Inc.

http://www.awod.com/gallery/business/asr/

Newsletter targeted at the busy individual who wants to build equity by purchasing stock in American companies. Provides a review of selected growth stocks rated favorably by established and widely read American financial publications.

A.S.K. Financial Digest

http://www.cloud9.net/~dkirchen/ask

Monthly newsletter that helps investors trade stocks, bonds, and mutual funds for intermediate financial cycles.

CyberFund

http://www.cyberfund.com

The CyberFund Investment Account program is a managed investment advisory service of Hammer Capital Management, Inc. It is designed to participate in the growth of the computer, telecommunications, and advancing technology industries. It invests only in publicly traded companies listed on the major U.S. and foreign stock exchanges.

Datastream International

http://www.datastream.com/

Datastream is a provider of global economic and financial data and software services for the investment community. Datastream's site provides information on the financial research services the company makes available to investors.

Ethical Investments

http://www.ethicalinvestments.co.uk

A site offering advice to individuals, small businesses and other organizations who want ethical considerations to have a bearing on their investment decisions. Provides information on companies with good environmental records.

GreenMoney On-Line Guide

http://www.greenmoney.com/

An information resource from the *GreenMoney Journal* for people interested in socially and environmentally responsible business, investing, and consumer resources. Information on companies' environmental track records is available, along with tips for socially responsible investing.

Hoover's Online

http://www.hoovers.com

A great research tool for investors. Hoover's provides company profiles plus free access to records on public and private companies. Here you can find out how well a company has done in the past.

How to Become a Real-Time Commodity Futures Trader—From Home

http://www.futures-trader.com/

Presents a trading guide recommended by *Futures Magazine.* Covers details from initial home setup to advanced strategies.

InterQuote

http://www.interquote.com

Provides a collection of affordable Internet-based financial information services, including real-time, delayed, and end-of-day information on stocks, options, indices, mutual funds, and futures from most United States and Canadian exchanges.

Investor's BusinessDaily

http://www.investors.com/

Investor's Business Daily is a magazine focusing on issues important to today's investor. On this site you can read today's *Investor's Business Daily.* IBD also offers access to a free online IBD investment education course.

IPO Central

http://www.ipocentral.com/

IPO Central offers access to the latest SEC filing information on companies that have filed to go public, including S-1s, company profiles, stock quotes, and more. Maybe you can find the next Netscape!

Kiplinger

http://kiplinger.com/

Kiplinger puts financial events in perspective on a daily basis. Stock quotes, mutual fund rankings, financial FAQs, and interactive resources are available.

Motley Fool

http://www.fool.com/

The Motley Fool is a well-known online financial forum originating on America Online. This is the Motley Fool's home on the WWW. The Fool provides individual investors with investment tips and advice. The Motley Fool Web site offers THE FOOL'S SCHOOL, an online investment guide that is subtitled "13 Steps To Investing Foolishly."

Olsen & Associates

http://www.olsen.ch/

Provides economic research in the field of financial markets. Specializes in the forecasting and historical analysis of foreign exchange rates. Also provides trading models and a currency ranking analysis.

Precision Investment Services, Inc.

http://powertrader.com

Presents PowerTrader, a fully integrated, real-time stock quotation, technical analysis, and portfolio management suite of software products. PowerTrader software reads the data you receive from your data service and displays the delayed or real-time quote information on your monitor. Enables you to collect data and analyze up to 32,000 instruments in any market: equities, options, futures, indices, bonds, money markets, and mutual funds.

PRESSline

http://www.pressline.com/

Company news and information are very important to investors, and PRESSline delivers. PRESSline contains a database of over 20,000 press releases, with keyword searching. Find out what companies around the world are doing.

Quote.Com

http://www.quote.com

Provides financial market data to the Internet community, including current quotes on stocks, options, commodity futures, mutual funds, and bonds. Also provides business news, market analysis and commentary, fundamental data, and company profiles.

SEC EDGAR Database

http://www.sec.gov/edgarhp.htm

EDGAR stands for Electronic Data Gathering, Analysis, and Retrieval. EDGAR is an online database of company financial information provided by the Securities and Exchange Commission. Provides access to company SEC filings, earning reports, and more.

Security APL Quote Server

http://www.secapl.com/cgi-bin/qs

Provides online trading, real-time quotes, information on portfolio accounting, financial calculators, news, and research.

SGA Goldstar Research

http://www.sgagoldstar.com/sga/

Presents a daily financial newsletter that offers the opinions and recommendations of successful stock market experts. Contains information on stocks, bonds, options, futures, securities, gold, the NYSE, and American and NASDAQ stock exchanges, as well as Dow Jones, over the counter, and Canadian stocks.

The Siegel Group, Inc.

http://www.fredsiegel.com

Specializes in providing financial news analysis and consulting to the broadcast media, primarily to local radio and television affiliates of the national networks. Includes links to several sites that provide commentary about activity in the financial markets.

Silicon Investor

http://www.techstocks.com/

Consists of five innovative areas for technology investors: Company Profiles, Groups, Chart Generator, StockTalk, and Spotlight. These areas enable you to participate in discussion forums, create individual charts and comparison charts, view company profiles, and get quotes and other financial information.

S-R-Invest

http://www.inusa.com/srinvest/

An informative, useful guide to information on responsible investing. The information available on this site is useful to anyone who is concerned about how their investments affect the environment and the world around them.

Streetnet

http://www.streetnet.com/

Streetnet provides Corporate Annual Reports, 10-Q's and 10-K's on the Web, and serves as a launching pad to all other financial services on the Net. Streetnet also provides investors with investment ideas and free stock quotes. There are individual listings for each American stock market.

Stockdeck Online

http://www.stockdeck.com/

Features corporate profiles on more than 600 publicly traded companies. Enables you to request additional information, such as financial reports or news releases online, as well as 15-minute delayed stock quotes.

StockMaster at MIT

http://www.stockmaster.com/

Provides recent stock market information, including current prices and the previous day's closing prices, one-year graphics of stock movements, and ticker symbols. Also contains links related to finance. Categories include daily stock charts, bimonthly mutual fund charts, and top stocks.

A B C D E F G H I J K L M N O P Q R S T U V W X Y Z

A Trader's Financial Resource Guide

http://www.libertynet.org/~beausang/

Serves as a financial resource guide to sites dealing with stocks, currencies, exchanges, banks, brokers, mortgages, futures, newspapers, sports pages, research, and search utilities.

Wall Street City

http://www.wallstreetcity.com/home.html

Telescan's Wall Street City is a next-generation financial Web site, where you can get the answers to your investment questions. Custom-design your own stock and mutual fund searches with the most powerful search engine in the world covering over 700 different criteria. You can access real-time and delayed quotes on over 300,000 domestic and international securities, and run full technical analysis on stock graphs from 1 day to 23 years.

Wall Street Net

http://www.netresource.com/wsn/home.html

Provides the latest news in the world of corporate debt and equity financing for issuers and investment bankers. Also contains archival data on transactions over the past twelve months.

Wall Street Online

http://www.wso.com/wso/

Presents a collection of daily investment advisory services, including Prostock, Instant Advisor, IPO Outlook, and The Pristine Day Trader.

Woodbridge and Associates

http://www.calypso.com/woodbridge/

Offers information on increasing the profitability of your investments through investing in emerging growth companies.

World Stock & Commodity Exchanges 1995

http://www.lpac.ac.uk/ifr/

Provides details of their handbook to more than 250 exchanges in 65 countries. Includes information for traders, brokers, dealers, bankers, treasurers, custodians, analysts, fund managers, and data vendors. Information listed for each exchange includes address and phone number, trading hours, holiday schedules, description of the trading system, and more.

MARKET SIMULATIONS

EduStock

http://tqd.advanced.org/3088/

A stock market simulation that is designed to teach what the stock market is, and how it can work for you. The site also offers tutorials on how to pick good stocks. The simulation available on this site happens in real-time.

Final Bell

http://www.sandbox.net/finalbell/pub-doc/home.html

The Final Bell is a stock market simulation game. Buy low, sell high, and trade simulated stocks daily through the site. Multiple prizes are awarded for the most successful traders.

Web Market Game

http://www.webmarketgame.com

An online simulation of the stock market using Web pages instead of company shares. Buy stocks in different web pages. The price of stock changes by how many hits a page has. This simulation is free and prizes will be awarded to the best traders.

MUTUAL FUNDS

American Century Investments

http://www.americancentury.com

A site for information on mutual funds managed by American Century Investments. Includes an online portfolio tracker that can be used to track your portfolio. Educational materials to help you determine and work toward your financial goals are available, along with fund profiles and historical performance information.

Dreyfus Corporation

http://www.dreyfus.com/funds/

The Dreyfus Online Information Center provides listings and descriptions of some of the mutual funds offered by Dreyfus, along with the Dreyfus services. The site provides information that can help investors get a clearer sense of the direction to take to meet their investment objectives. In addition to general information on investing, you will also find current economic commentaries on the financial markets updated weekly by Dreyfus portfolio managers.

Janus Funds

http://www.janusfunds.com

Janus Funds provides access to information on the funds they manage. You can check your funds' latest share price and account value 24 hours a day, 7 days a week. You can also find projected year-end dividends for each fund. All account information is accessed through security enhanced Web pages utilizing SSL.

The Mutual Fund Home Page

http://www.brill.com/features.html

Features articles on what's happening in the mutual fund industry, including topics such as "Investing for Retirement" and "The Best Choices in Variable Annuities."

Scudder, Stevens & Clark

http://www.scudder.com/

Provides information on all mutual funds managed by Scudder, Stevens & Clark. The site allows users to create a personalized page to access all of the information available on the site. Fund performance, daily prices, interactive worksheets, and fund prospectuses are offered. Includes an informative retirement planning section.

Strong Funds

http://www.strong-funds.com/

Information for anyone interested in the Strong family of mutual funds. Fund performance information and portfolio management tips are available. Strong also offers retirement investing help and general investment help with Strong's Learning Center.

Templeton Management

http://www.templeton.ca/

Templeton Management Limited currently manages in excess of $7 billion on behalf of more than 600,000 account holders in a diversified family of 12 mutual funds. This site makes available investment information on each fund offered by Templeton. The Templeton organization continues to follow today the investment tenets established by its founder, Sir John Templeton, over 50 years ago.

United Services Funds

http://www.usfunds.com/

Information on investment opportunities in United Services no-load mutual funds. Includes investment research reports daily fund prices, weekly investor alert, prospectuses, and shareholder reports.

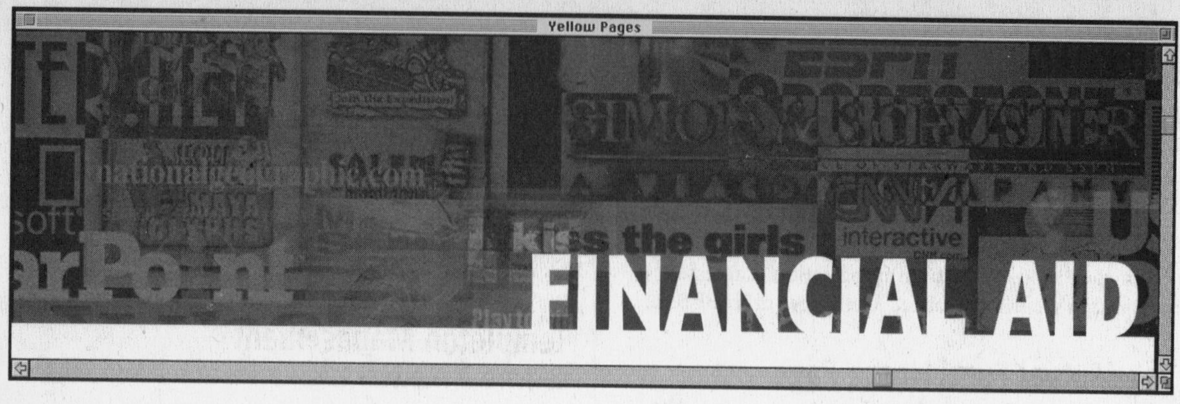

> A lot of people go to college for seven years.
>
> *Tommy in* Tommy Boy *(1995)*

The At-a-Glance Guide to Grants

`http://www.sai.com/adjunct/nafggrant.html`

You'll get links to agencies, databases, email lists, templates, and tutorials.

College Financial Aid Checklist

`http://www.rehab.uiuc.edu/pursuit/dis-resources/high-school/preparing/financial-aid.html`

Gives you suggestions and resources for paying for college. Includes a checklist of what to do during your junior and senior years of high school, as well as during your college years. Includes disability info resources. Also includes science, engineering, and mathematics resources.

fastWEB! (Financial Aid Search Through the Web)

`http://www.fastweb.com/`

Set up a personalized profile that will match your skills, abilities, and interests to fastWEB's database of more than 275,000 scholarships. Then check your fastWEB mailbox for updates and new awards. Come back regularly for info on hot new awards and updates on current scholarships. Look in the More About Local and Federal Aid section for detailed info on other loan, work-study, and grant programs. If your school is registered with fastWEB, you'll find info on local awards, too.

fastWEB! (Financial Aid Search Through the Web)
`http://www.fastweb.com/`

Great Lakes College Financial Aid Service

`http://www.glcfas.com`

This educational financial aid service lets you submit an online document to see how much financial aid you qualify for before you pay GLCFAS anything.

The Innovation Grants Competition

`http://www.ml.com/woml/forum/innovation/`

Over the next year, The Merrill Lynch Forum will award up to $150,000 in grants to recent Ph.D.s from universities worldwide through the Forum's Innovation Grants Competition. The competition challenges doctoral candidates in the sciences, liberal arts, and engineering fields to examine their dissertations in light of their commercial product or service potential.

MOLIS Scholarship Search

`http://www.fie.com/molis/scholar.htm`

This search service provides information about scholarship opportunities for qualified minority applicants.

Rhodes Scholarship Program

`http://www.colorado.edu/UCB/StudentAffairs/OIE/admin/rhodes2.html`

The Rhodes Scholarship Program was created by Cecil Rhodes to enable students from the colonies and the U.S. to spend two or three years at Oxford University. This would enable young people who would become leaders of their own countries to become familiar with the values and culture of England. The program is open to men and women of any race or religion. It is well-suited for students who plan to go on in such fields as law or business, as well as those who are seeking an academic career.

Scholarship Scams

http://www.ftc.gov/WWW/bcp/conline/edcams/scholarship/

Check this site for warnings about scholarship fraud from the Federal Trade Commission.

Student Services, Incorporated

http://web.studentservices.com/

Student Services has a database of more than 180,000 scholarships, grants, fellowships, and loans representing billions of dollars in private-sector funding for college students living in the U.S. Enter your major into the search engine to look up scholarships in that area.

Welcome to the Harry Truman Scholarship Foundation

http://www.truman.gov/

The Harry S. Truman Scholarship Foundation was established by Congress in 1975 as the official federal memorial to honor our thirty-third President. The Truman Scholarship is a highly competitive, merit-based award offered to U.S. citizens and U.S. nationals who want to go to graduate school in preparation for a career in public service. The scholarship offers recognition of outstanding potential as a leader in public service, membership in a community of persons devoted to helping others and to improving the environment, and a $30,000 grant ($27,000 of this is designated for graduate study in the U.S. or abroad in a variety of fields). Read the *Bulletin of Information* for guidelines and procedures.

Yahoo!—Education:Financial Aid:College Aid Offices

http://www.yahoo.com/Education/Financial_Aid/College_Aid_Offices/

Offers links to the College Aid Office for each university in the U.S. You'll get info on all the financial aid opportunities at each university.

NEWSGROUP

soc.college.financial-aid

GOPHER SITE

gopher://gopher.usia.gov/11s/education/fulbright/student

Related Sites

http://www.el-dorado.ca.us/~grants/seekers.shtml

http://www.collegeboard.org/fundfinder/bin/fundfind01.pl

http://www.finaid.org/

http://www.collegexpress.com/student-aid/index.html

http://www.nasfaa.org/DoIt-AffordIt/publicfront.html

http://users.plinet.net/~reisa/

http://www.nhsf.org/

http://www.nsf.gov/home/grants.htm

http://www.uic.edu/depts/ovcr/ors1.html

http://www.petersons.com/resources/finance.html

http://easi.ed.gov/

http://iwc.pair.com/scholarshipage/

http://www.devnet.net/usap/

http://www.iie.org/fulbright/

http://www.naas.org/

http://www.finaid.org/finaid/faqs/finaid.faq

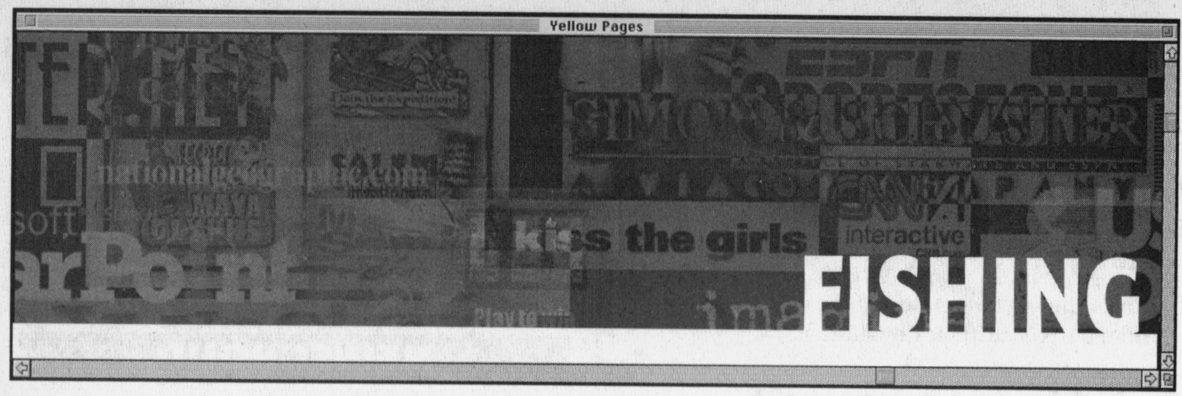

> The one who goes fishing gets something more than the fish he catches.
>
> *Mary Astor*

Anglers Outlet

http://www.anglers-outlet.com/

Order bait, tackle, and plenty of accessories from the online catalog. The site features specials found only on the Web, not in their regular catalog. There's also a separate area in which you can post information and results of fishing tournaments.

Bass Anglers Sportsman Society

http://www.outdoors.net/bass/

Home of *BASSMASTER Magazine*, the B.A.S.S. site gives you information on fishing technique seminars, membership information, and more. Find tournament information and get tips from fellow bass anglers.

Carping Online

http://www.page-builder.com/carp/

Carp fishing might not be as popular as bass fishing, but this site speculates that it will be. Here you'll find a ton of information about carp fishing, from the proper bait to a carp chat room. When you're finished with the day's catch, find the right recipes here too.

Related Sites

http://home.earthlink.net/~basstrainers/

http://host.fptoday.com/bassclub/

Ol' Paw's Fishin' Page
http://www.pagebiz.com/pawfish.html

Field & Stream Online

http://www.fieldandstream.com/

This popular magazine has set up a very extensive site that features a Q&A section, RealAudio fishing tips, and current articles. Search the large reference section for a vast selection of books, tips, and charts to prepare yourself for a successful fishing trip. What time will the sun rise in Jackson Hole on June 11? Find out here.

Fish & Game Finder Magazine

http://www.fishandgame.com/

Read the latest news about fishing and hunting. Plan your next fishing vacation with the help of vendors and site sponsors. Stay current with the latest articles, columns, and product reviews.

Fishing Secrets

http://www.fishingsecrets.com

Stressing that this site is completely non-commercial, a group of Florida fishermen compiled this collection of fishing reports, tips, and related links that cover aspects of many types of fishing. Post a message on the board about a particular fishing trip you've had, or feel free to ask for help from the site's regular visitors.

Flyfishers Online

http://www.flyfishers.com/

This site offers an extensive guide to flyfishing conditions in both North and South America. Find out from the up-to-date Event Calendar about the expos and conventions in your area. Also features an extensive equipment section that refers you to a list of appropriate online dealers.

Great Outdoor Recreation Pages

`http://www.gorp.com/gorp/activity/fishing.htm`

This site details the fishing hotspots across the U.S. and throughout the world. Prepare for your trip by visiting GORP's many links to tackle, apparel, and freeze-dried food vendors.

Grossenbacher Guides

`http://www.gomontana.com/Grossenbacher.html`

Let Brian and Jenny Grossenbacher plan your next flyfishing excursion in Southwest Montana. The site features information on women-only fishing trips, flyfishing conditions near Yellowstone Park, and a list of links to nearby lodges and other things to do while you're on vacation.

Gulf Coast Angler's Association

`http://www.gcaa.com/`

This group exists to help you plan the perfect fishing vacation. The site contains links and information about marinas, guides, bait and tackle, weather, and tides and currents in the Gulf states—Florida, Alabama, Mississippi, Louisiana, and Texas.

International Fishing Angling Information Page

`http://www.geocities.com/Yosemite/2215/iflinkg.html`

This site contains dozens of links to personal and commercial fishing pages. Check out the best Alaskan fishing locations, then click over to a page about flyfishing in Japan and Australia. Includes many links to fishing tips pages. Did you know that Indiana University has a bass fishing club? You do now.

King Crow

`http://www.fishandgame.com/kingcrow/index.html`

Are your ice-fishing trips too, well, cold? King Crow makes ice fishing houses that are so luxurious that you'll think you're pulling a bluegill from your living room floor. They're bigger than a college dorm room and if the pictures are accurate, quite a bit nicer.

Nautical Net

`http://www.nauticalnet.com`

A recreational water sports site that contains a tackle shop, marine electronics, boat brokers and manufacturers, clubs, fishing reports, and links to charter boats.

Nor'east Saltwater Magazine

`http://www.noreast.com`

A weekly sportfishing magazine for New York's saltwater anglers. Includes weekly fishing reports, sportfishing news, new product information, boats for charter, party boat schedules, weekly saltwater flyfishing column, editorials, reader feedback, classifieds, and more. Updated weekly from April to November, monthly from December to March.

Ol' Paw's Fishin' Page

`http://www.pagebiz.com/pawfish.html`

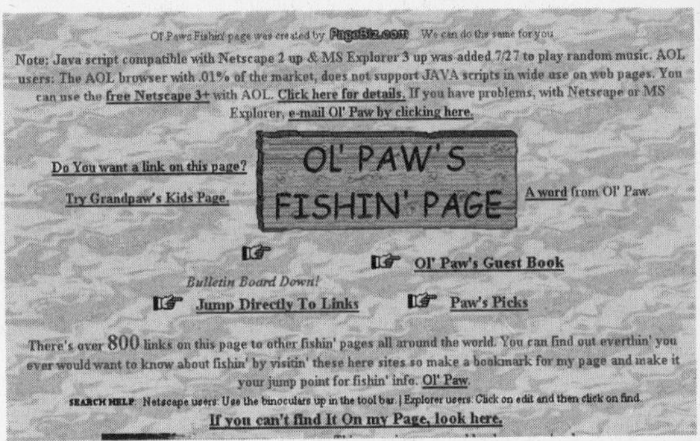

This site is an angler's dream database that claims to have over 800 links. Categories include Radio and TV shows; fishing magazines; links for the Americas, New Zealand, and all points in between; and plenty of information about bait, flies, and tackle. The site also contains links to dozens of newsgroups and bulletin boards.

United States Fish & Wildlife Service

`http://www.fws.gov/`

The FWS, a division of the Department of the Interior, created this site to tell you a little about itself. Find out what the group does to protect endangered species, and learn what the government—and you—can do to keep your old fishin' hole clean and healthy.

Virtual Flyshop

http://www.flyshop.com/

Comprehensive page that has reports of fishing conditions on Canadian rivers. Offers an online magazine, a forum that includes an interactive discussion, and an "Ask the Experts" section.

Walleye Central

http://walleyecentral.com/

A site that caters exclusively to walleye fishermen. Find out about walleye software, chat with other walleye lovers, and sign up for "Walleye In-Sider" Magazine. Get tips from the world's best Walleye fishermen.

World of Fishing

http://www.fishingworld.com

Offers all types of fishing information, services, products, tournament information, magazines, and servers as a place to visit other fishermen.

NEWSGROUPS

alt.fishing

alt.fishing.catfish

alt.tv.fishmasters

rec.outdoors.fishing

rec.outdoors.fishing.bass

rec.outdoors.fishing.fly

rec.outdoors.fishing.fly.tying

rec.outdoors.fishing.saltwater

Related Sites

http://maniac.deathstar.org/users/jvitor/html/af_ice.html

http://members.aol.com/macneil1/fishing.htm

http://tritonboats.com/

http://www.axionet.com/hansons/index.html

http://www.marketzone.com/cfhnb/cfhnb.html

http://www.scotangling.com/report.htm

http://www.scottyusa.com/

http://www.troutpond.com/

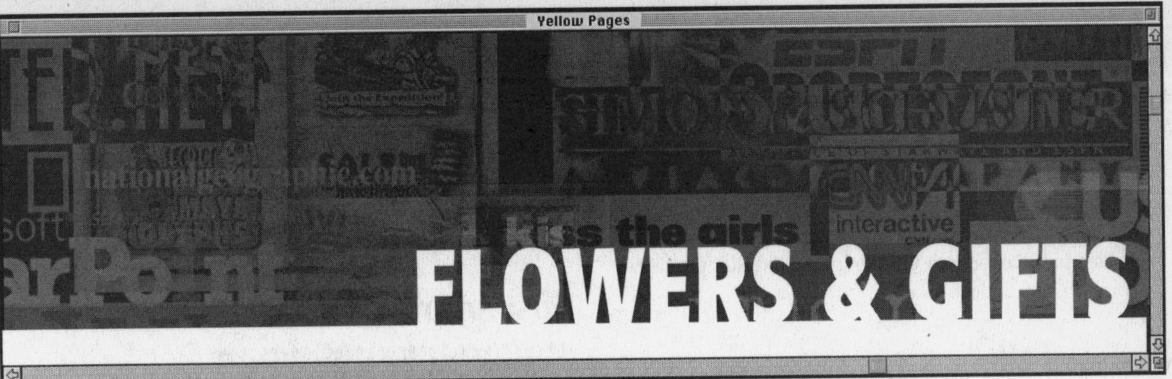

Yes, I'd like to order some flowers for my husband. Yeah, how much is the big "Please Forgive Me" bouquet? ...Okay, how 'bout the small "Please Get Over It" bouquet?

Lisa in Life's Work *(1996)*

1-800-FLOWERS

http://www.800flowers.com/

Advertises the services and products of 1-800-FLOWERS. Offers home decorating ideas, card message suggestions, and the latest in floral trends. Shop by occasion, product category, or price range. Special contests and promotions available.

1-800-Roses

http://www.1stresource.com/r/roses/default.htm

Specializes in long-stem roses. Other floral arrangements available. Open 24 hours. Free delivery. Order flowers over the Internet or by calling the toll free number.

1-800-USA-4-Flowers

http://usa4flowers.com/

You can click the state you want to send to, and a map selection guide helps you find florists in the closest area. State-by-state links are also available. Guarantees secure ordering and accepts all major credit cards. Same day delivery in the continental U.S.

Victoria's Garden
http://www.victoriasgarden.com/

à la Gift Basket Headquarters

http://www.gifthq.com/gifthq/

Offers 30 different food, wine, and all-occasion gift baskets. Secured credit card ordering nationwide. A detailed catalog provides prices and shipping and handling information for each basket.

Absolutely Fresh Flowers

http://www.cts.com/~flowers/

Specializes in nearly 150 different kinds of miniature carnations. Sells and ships flowers directly all over the U.S. via next day service. Offers satisfaction guarantee.

All Occasion Gifts and Baskets

http://www.alloccasiongifts.com/

Online store of this award-winning site includes basket categories such as the Christmas shop, men's gifts, wedding gifts, garden gift baskets, get well gift baskets, new arrival gift baskets, and more. You can order online or toll free. Also offers teapots and other collectibles.

Angela's Orchids

http://www.hawaii-shots.com/angelas/

Guarantees safe and timely delivery of dendrobium orchids from Hawaii via two-day Federal Express to anywhere in the continental U.S. Orchids are securely packed in a cardboard box. Also comes with an instruction sheet on care for the orchids.

A B C D E F G H I J K L M N O P Q R S T U V W X Y Z

Archie McPhee

http://www.mcphee.com/

Calls itself the outfitters of popular culture and includes gag gifts such as rubber chickens, punching nuns, lawn flamingos, and others. You can order online, request a catalog, browse through McPhee's classic picks, or search via the index. Excellent collection of sci-fi collectibles.

Circles of Life

http://circlesoflife.com/

Offers all natural, grapevine, and floral wreaths which are sent to any cemetery in the world for graveside placement. The bereaved (next of kin or friend) will receive an engraved card. Wreaths are 17-inch biodegradable circles which may be placed in any cemetery that doesn't allow artificial flowers.

Christmas Shop

http://www.ChristmasNet.com

Offers gifts for children year round. Specializes in Steinbach Nutcrackers, Department 56 villages, and ornaments of all types, sizes, and shapes. Lets you visit Santa in Long Grove, Illinois, where we all know he keeps a summer home.

Crafter's Showcase

http://www.northcoast.com/unlimited/product_directory/cs/cs.html

Provides color photographs and information about a wide array of items including dolls and plaques. Also provides pricing and ordering information.

Custom Made Wooden Jigsaw Puzzles

http://www.algorithms.com/users/markcapp/home.html

Provides personalized "one of a kind" wooden jigsaw puzzles hand crafted by Mark G. Cappitella. Uses your enlarged personal photos, favorite fine art prints, company logos, postcards, and so on. You also can choose from prints in the online art gallery.

Earthly Goods, Inc.

http://www.earthlygoods.com/

Earthly Goods is a supplier of wildflower seeds, wildflower seed mixtures, and grass seeds. Online product catalog, advice on growing from seeds and garden planning, and online ordering are a few of its features.

Erre Esse Gifts

http://www.erresse.com/erresse/index.html

Advertises fine silverware and sterling silver gifts. Includes tea and coffee sets, jewel cases, candelabras, and children's gifts. Contains prices and images of various pieces, as well as ordering information.

First American Flowers

http://www.1stamericanflowers.com/

Includes free same-day delivery all over the United States and Canada. Use a toll-free number to order the flowers of your choice, and they do the rest. Shop from the best values page, or choose your flowers by occasion. Gourmet baskets of fruit and flowers are available.

Forever Roses

http://www.foreverroses.com/

Company provides dried wreaths, hearts, swags, and topiaries. New England-based company uses only natural dried materials, and every arrangement contains their signature roses. Includes tool-free ordering number. Site includes pictures of many arrangements from which to choose.

FTD Internet

http://www.ftd.com/

Offers FTD's official flower catalog. Provides domestic and international delivery. Contains images of the products available and a free personal reminder service.

Gift Certificates Unlimited

http://www.imall.com/stores/gift_certificates/

Includes gift certificates from many well-known retailers from department stores, to restaurants, to book stores, and others. You place the order using the 1-800 number and Gift Certificates Unlimited sends the gift certificate, with card and package, directly to your recipient. Site includes exhaustive list of available retailers.

JC Penney Online Gift Registry

http://www.jcpgift.com/

Nationwide gift registry database of weddings and baby showers alike. You can search via the bride, groom, mother or father of the bride or groom, as well as via expecting mother or father. A convenient way to determine what gifts you want to buy before you get there.

Never Forget Again!

http://members.aol.com/timzebra/index.htm

A reminder service that sends you postcards one week prior to every date you want to be reminded of. Great for birthdays, anniversaries, corporate dates, car maintenance dates, and more. You can provide an unlimited amount of reminders and update them at any time.

Off the Deep End

http://www.offthedeepend.com/

Called shopping therapy for the culturally depraved, this site furnishes various campy gift items including over 100 kinds of salsa. Also offers flamingos galore, hats and disguises, and various Betty Boop paraphernalia.

Parkleigh World-Wide

http://www.parkleigh.com

Offers a selection of coffees, chocolates, writing instruments, stationery, and other fine gifts.

The Private Source

http://metroux.metrobbs.com/PrivateSource/index.htm

Advertises Private Source's collection of personal gifts through an online catalog.

PS I Love You

http://www.ps-iloveyou.com/

Provides personalized songs for every occasion. Song you pick comes complete with names, milestones, and other personal details that you provide. Each song comes on a cassette with a custom-printed lyric sheet. Site includes song catalog, separated into occasions.

StarLight Daylily Gardens

http://www.starlightdaylilies.com/

Includes an online daylily catalog with over 200 images of daylily varieties available from this Indiana-based garden. Browse the gardens, look through the collection packages for the best savings, or order a gift certificate. All you would ever want to know about daylilies.

Related Sites

http://www.star-gift-registry.com/star.htm

http://www.fly.net/~tom/weirdos_html/thingy.html

http://www.1q.com/copernicus

A Tisket, A Tasket

http://www.atisket-atasket.com/

You can create you own basket or choose from this New York-based company's creations. Toll free number and shipping all over U.S. makes this easy and convenient. Includes reminder service; you can also order online.

Total Flower Exports

http://www.iinet.net.au/~total/

Provides information about this exporter of fresh and dried flowers located in Australia. Enables you to view some unusual flowers and order a sampler of dried flowers.

Victoria's Garden

http://www.victoriasgarden.com/

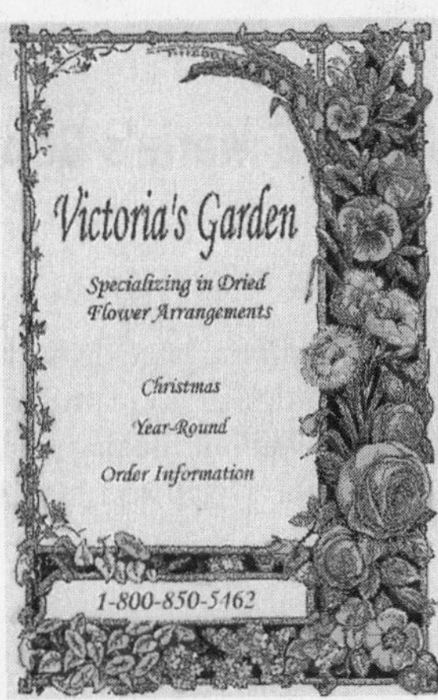

Florida-based, two-woman run company that specializes in dried flower arrangements, including centerpieces, sprays, and wreaths. Site includes pictures and prices on standard items. Order toll-free from a 1-800 number, online, or via regular mail.

NEWSGROUPS

alt.ads.forsale

alt.biz

alt.crafts.professional

alt.forsale.nutrition

alt.marketplace

alt.romance

rec.antiques.marketplace

rec.crafts.marketplace

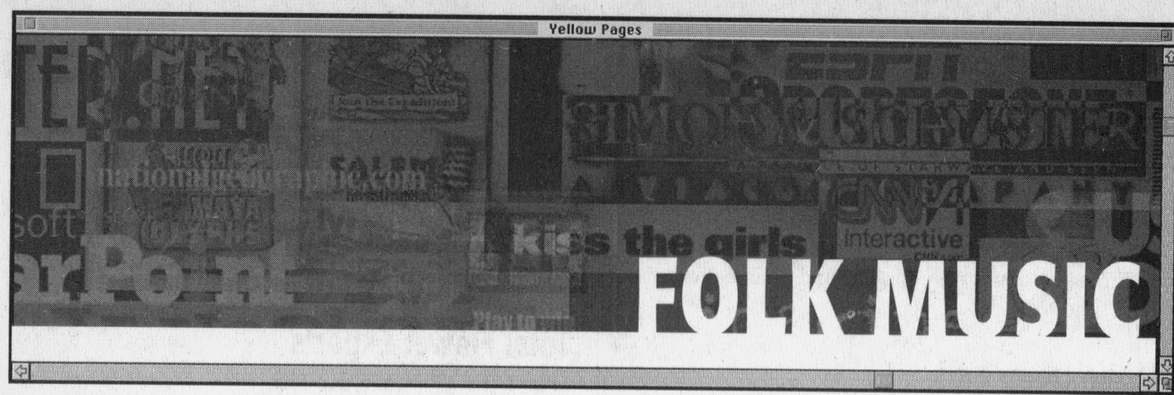

FOLK MUSIC

> Music washes away from the soul the dust of everyday life.
>
> *Berthold Auerbach*

Absolutely Cynthia Marie's Bob Dylan Page

http://www.geocities.com/SoHo/2615/

This is a very personal home page dedicated to Bob Dylan. Its multimedia design is creative and busy, but if you want to know all about the page's author and her feelings towards Bob Dylan and Joan Baez, visit here.

The Carlton Folk Club

http://www.btinternet.com/~geoff.white/carlton.htm

This folk music club based in Nottingham, England offers a very musical and animated site in conjunction with the activities of the physical club. You can learn who is playing when, learn about the performers, and hear clips of their music.

Christine Lavin Home Page

http://www.christinelavin.com/

Christine Lavin is a personality as well as a very talented songstress. She maintains this Web site to further her own career as well as to introduce fans to other folk musicians. The site is filled with contests, games, and musical exercises. You can also order Christine Lavin's albums and those of her protégés online. A link to amazon.com provides access to Christine's books.

Christine Lavin Home Page
http://www.christinelavin.com/

Christine Lavin

Big League Babe

Welcome to the Christine Lavin Home Page! This little bit of cyberspace is dedicated to a woman who is not only a great singer/songwriter, but also a generous promoter of other people's music, and an altogether wonderful and very funny person (not that we're biased!) We frequently update this site with new information directly from Christine, so keep an eye out for exciting new material. If you have any comments or suggestions, we'd love to hear from you. Have fun! Thanks for visiting!

Color Me Indigo

http://www.stwing.upenn.edu/~abstein/colormeindigo/

This site is dedicated to all things Indigo Girls. The site provides a place to talk about the group, learn where they are playing, their discography, chords and lyrics to their music, pictures of the group, and music clips.

Fasola Home Page

http://medinfo.labmed.umn.edu/Docs/.www/fasola_homepage.html

Provides information resources for Sacred Harp (a form of early American three- and four-part a cappella folk music that traces its roots back to Reformation and Renaissance England) and other American Shape Note traditions of singing.

Folk Alliance of America

http://www.hidwater.com/folkalliance/

The Folk Alliance was organized to preserve authentic folk music and dance. This site provides a way to donate to the alliance, become a member, and read scholarly articles about specific folk artists or genres.

Folk on the Radio

http://www.hidwater.com/folkdj/folkdj.html

Provides information on folk and bluegrass music on the radio, submitted by the programs' disk jockeys. Contains station lists, show profiles, and play lists.

Folkbook

http://www.cgrg.ohio-state.edu/folkbook/folkbook.html

An online compendium of information about accoustic music including artist biographics, guitar tablatures, tour dates and times, where you can purchase music by favorite artists, and an extensive list of Usenet newsgroups. This site is part of the Folk Music Web Ring.

FolkWeb

http://www.folkweb.com/

This is a neat site that lets you purchase accoustic and folk music online. The site lets you browse by artist's name, record label, and music category. You can also perform intense searches by artist, album, or song title. If you have RealAudio or Shockwave plug-ins installed, you can sample selected artists online. Each week another artist is featured. You can purchase CDs online via their secure purchasing system.

Fox Valley Folklore Society Home Page

http://www.mcs.net/~hammerd/fvfs/

This is a valuable site for folk music lovers in the Chicago area. The site lists folk music, storytelling, and dance events in the Chicago area throughout the year. The site provides links to other folklore organizations, newsletters, and to information about the Fox Valley Society.

John Stewart UK Fan Page

http://easyweb.easynet.co.uk/~slowcoach/jstewart/index.html

This is a very personal site dedicated to John Stewart. The Webmaster provides his own autobiography as well as information about John Stewart with emphasis on the United Kingdom. The site provides concert schedules, music clips, a guest book, and even a John Stewart chat room.

Related Sites

http://www.artsci.wustl.edu/~davida/woody.html

http://www.arlo.net/

The Kingston Trio Place

http://home.att.net/~SAVAIIKEN/kingston.htm

This is a Kingston Trio fan site set up as an e-zine about the Trio. There are trivia contests, music clips, information about new releases. The site provides a "Pick of the Month" as well as touring schedules, and a chat room.

Kiwi Folk and Accoustic Music

http://www.earthlight.co.nz/users/mikem/kiwifolk.html

This site brings visitors information about folk and accoustic music happenings in New Zealand. The site lists festivals, clubs, concert dates, and locations where readers can purchase instruments on New Zealand. A humor section and links to New Zealand artists are included.

Mother of Moth Home page

http://www.lycaeum.org/~pha2012/Index.htm

This is an eclectic site that is heavily philosophical in nature. The authors wish to promote alternative lifestyle choices based on the music of Mother of Moth. Reviews of the music, ideas for lifestyle changes based on the music, and sound clips are provided.

Music of the Sea

http://members.aol.com/Pintndale/index.htm

This site is dedicated to the admiration of the music of William Pint and Felicia Dale of Seattle, Washington. The site provides biographical information, tour schedules, a discography, and links to other folk music groups.

Peter, Paul, and Mary

http://www.downeast.net/ppm/

This site is dedicated to the music of Peter, Paul, and Mary. An extensive array of links is provided, including cartoons, lyrics, chords, song books, video releases, and concert dates. Links to solo sites are provided.

Southern Folklife Collection

http://ils.unc.edu/barba/sfc.html

Contains archives of Southeastern American tradition-derived music that includes numerous photographs, interviews, oral histories, video and film documentaries, books, and periodicals. Contains pages on music and musicians in the following categories: early country music, old-time string bands, gospel and spiritual song, and southeastern blues traditions, all illustrated with photos. This site was a student product and is no longer maintained.

Spirit Song

http://spiritsong.com/

A Web site hosting many different folk and accoutic music artists' Web pages centered in North Georgia, but encompassing the world. A beautifully designed site with much information about different types of muscians. The authors also design Web pages and host sites.

Stone Soup Arts Foundation

http://www.soup.org/users/stonsoup/

This is the accompanying Web site of a famous folk music club in New England that has introduced Patty Larkin, Tom Paxton, Cheryl Wheeler, and many other folk acts. The site presents information about current happenings at Stone Soup, as well as how to get tickets.

Tribute to the Limelighters

http://members.tripod.com/~sierran/limeliters.html

This a a simple site that presents information about the famous folk group the Limelighters. In fact, this site has everything you ever wanted to know about every permutation of the group from its earliest incarnation to today. Schedules of concerts, discography, historic concert information, and separate links to each member and former member of the group are provided.

Related Sites

http://www.maine.com/outergreen/

http://www.maine.com/outergreen/schoonerfare/sfdisc.html

http://www.bethwood.com/cynthiafta/tp.htm

http://celtic.stanford.edu/artists/Stivell.html

http://www.well.com/user/ari/klez/

http://pages.prodigy.com/keshlam/whatfilk.html

http://www.ozemail.aust.com/~mclean/loc.html

A B C D E F G H I J K L M N O P Q R S T U V W X Y Z

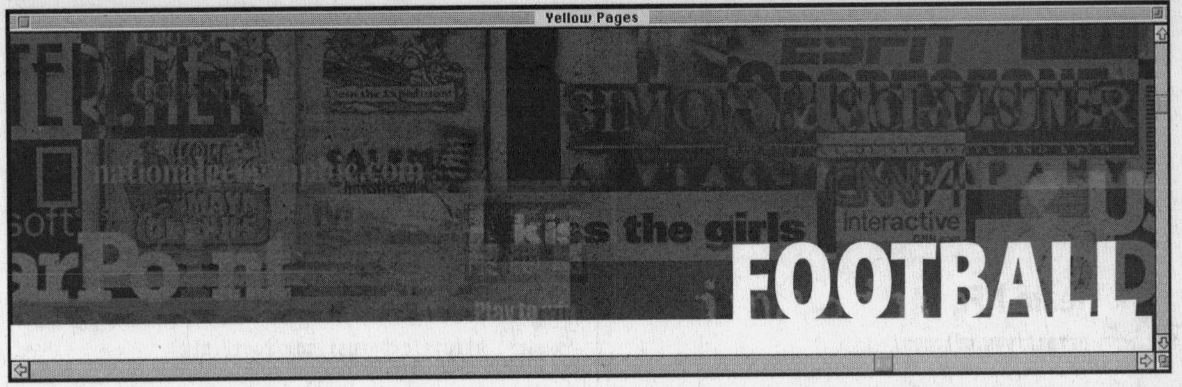

> It's not whether you get knocked down, it's whether you get up again.
>
> *Vince Lombardi*

Team NFL
http://www.nfl.com/

USA Football Center Online
http://cybergsi.com/foot2.htm

The following are home pages for National Football League teams:

Team	URL	Team	URL
Arizona Cardinals	http://nfl.com/cardinals/	Miami Dolphins	http://nfl.com/dolphins/
Atlanta Falcons	http://nfl.com/falcons/	Minnesota Vikings	http://nfl.com/vikings/
Buffalo Bills	http://nfl./bills/	New England Patriots	http://nfl.com/patriots/
Carolina Panthers	http://nflcom/panthers/	New Orleans Saints	http://nfl.com/saints/
Chicago Bears	http://nflcom/bears/	New York Giants	http://nfl.com/giants/
Cincinnati Bengals	http://nfl.com/bengals/	New York Jets	http://nfl.com/jets/
Cleveland Browns	http://nfl.com/browns/	Oakland Raiders	http://nfl.com/raiders/
Dallas Cowboys	http://nfl.com/cowboys/	Philadelphia Eagles	http://nfl.com/eagles/
Denver Broncos	http://nfl.com/broncos/	Pittsburgh Steelers	http://nfl.com/steelers/
Detroit Lions	http://nfl.com/lions/	San Diego Chargers	http://nfl.com/chargers/
Green Bay Packers	http://nfl.com/packers/	San Francisco 49ers	http://nfl.com/49ers/
Tennessee Oilers	http://nfl.com/oilers/	Seattle Seahawks	http://nfl.com/seahawks/
Indianapolis Colts	http://nfl.com/colts/	St. Louis Rams	http://nfl.com/rams/
Jacksonville Jaguars	http://nfl.com/jaguars/	Tampa Bay Buccaneers	http://nfl.com/buccaneers/
Kansas City Chiefs	http://nfl.com/chiefs/	Washington Redskins	http://nfl.com/redskins/

College Football WWW Site

http://www.engr.wisc.edu/~dwilson/rsfc/

Along with the usual schedules, preseason magazines and notes on each conference, this site links you to all the team logos, as well as information about stadiums, fight songs, and rules of the game.

College Sports Internet Channel

http://www.xcscx.com/colsport/

Provides access to Division 1A football teams by conference as well as by choosing from a map of the states. Links to other Sports Channel supported sites are also listed.

Nando Football Server

http://www.nando.net/SportServer/football/

The football arm of the Nando SportServer, this site gives access to professional and collegiate levels, a Cyber Road to the Superbowl, and a look back at seasons past.

Team NFL

http://www.nfl.com/

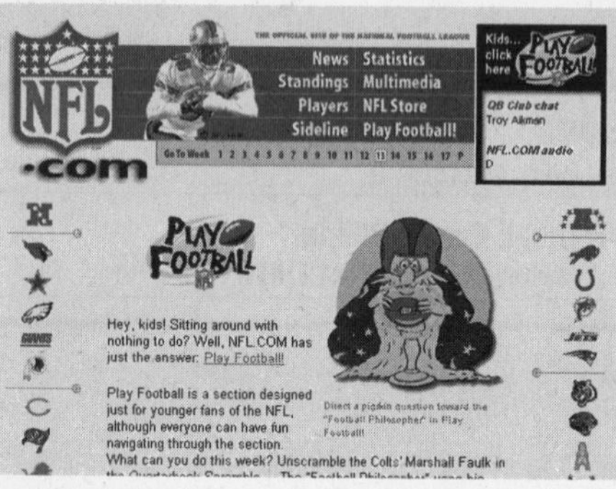

Provides top-notch reports of football happenings like the draft and playoffs. Links to NFL headlines, and Free Agent Q & A keep the football fan well-informed. There are also links for kids and places to find out more about your favorite NFL broadcaster.

Traveller Information Service

http://www.traveller.com/sports/ncaa_fb/

You can vote for the best Division 1A team, check out this week's picks, preview upcoming games, see who won last week, and access information for NCAA football teams.

USA Football Center Online

http://cybergsi.com/foot2.htm

Provides scores and updates to college and pro football games, standings, player stats, betting lines, and weekly stats. Also features a pregame show that talks about the games to be played that day, and provides the picks of the day.

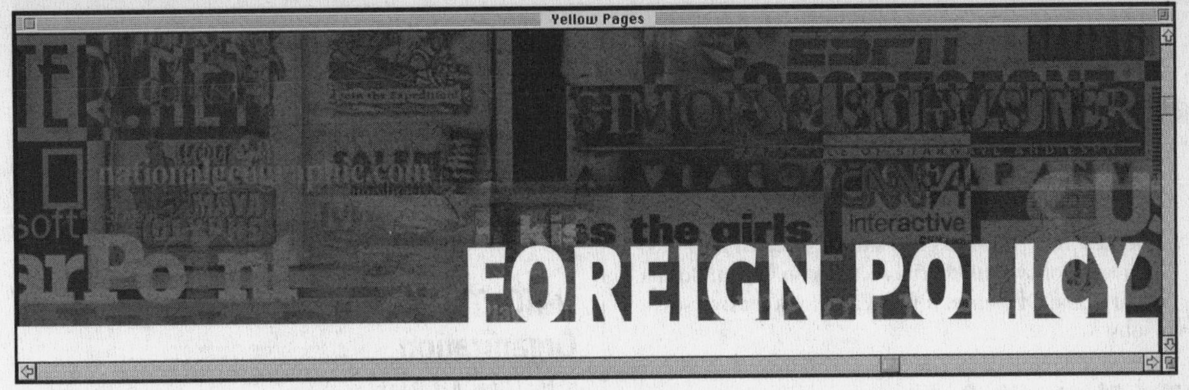

FOREIGN POLICY

> For my name and memory, I leave it to men's charitable speeches, to foreign nations, and to the next ages.
>
> *Francis Bacon*

American Diplomacy

American Diplomacy
`http://www.unc.edu/depts/diplomat/`

DOSFAN: Department of State Foreign Affairs Network
`http://dosfan.lib.uic.edu/index.html`

The Embassy Page
`http://www.embpage.org/`

The United Nations
`http://www.un.org/`

American Diplomacy

`http://www.unc.edu/depts/diplomat/`

An electronic journal of commentary, analysis, and research on American foreign policy and its practice. Published with the cooperation of the Triangle Institute for Security Studies.

American Foreign Service Association

`http://www.afsa.org/`

The Web site of AFSA, the professional association of U.S. Foreign Service, is an excellent resource for those interested in diplomacy and international affairs. The site includes educational programs, reference materials, publications, speakers, conferences, and more.

Canadian Foreign Policy

`http://www.carleton.ca/npsia/cfpj`

The Canadian Foreign Policy journal, published three times a year by Carleton University in Ottawa, Canada, provides a uniquely Canadian perspective on foreign policy issues.

Carnegie Council on Ethics and International Affairs

`http://www.cceia.org`

Carnegie Council is an independent, nonpartisan, nonprofit organization dedicated to increasing understanding of ethics and international affairs.

The Center for Security Policy

`http://www.security-policy.org`

The Center for Security Policy exists as a nonprofit, nonpartisan organization to stimulate and inform the national and international debate about all aspects of security policy, notably those policies bearing on the foreign, defense, economic, financial, and technology interests of the United States.

Department of Foreign Affairs, Dublin, Ireland

`http://www.irlgov.ie/iveagh`

Advises the government on all aspects of Ireland's external relations and acts as the channel of official communications with foreign governments and international organizations.

DOSFAN: Department of State Foreign Affairs Network

http://dosfan.lib.uic.edu/index.html

If you plan a trip overseas, you might want to check the travel advisories put out by the U.S. Department of State first. This is a great site for research into U.S. foreign policy, with special sections on China, Bosnia, and Cuba. Of course, you can also look for overseas jobs.

The Electronic Embassy

http://www.embassy.org/

Links to the staffs and resources of the Washington D.C. embassy community. Contacts in business and industry, education, the press, and government.

The Embassy Page

http://www.embpage.org/

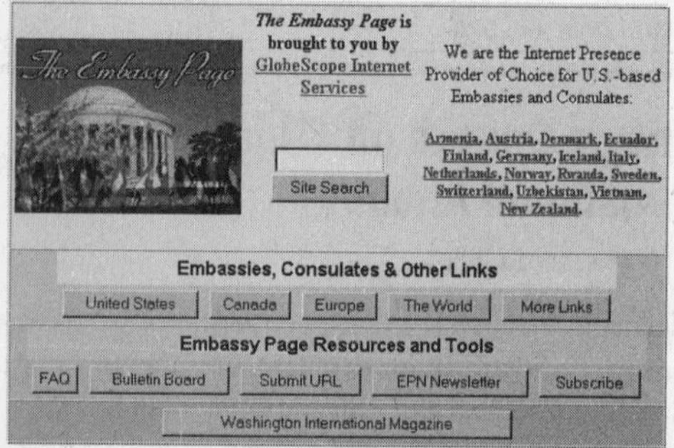

The Embassy Page is a connection to most of the U.S.-based embassies and consulates. Part of GlobeScope Internet Services.

International Analysis

http://www.cris.com/~intan

International Analysis is an analysis of pivotal economic and world events in a forecasting mode. The events are listed with provocative commentary on future probabilities.

NATO: The North Atlantic Treaty Organization

http://www.nato.int/

If you want to know what the international organization that beat communism in Europe has planned for an encore, plug this one in. It's a pretty informative site and one of the better-looking governmental sites.

The United Nations

http://www.un.org/

If you have the information resources of all the nations on earth, then you can put up a pretty good Web site. Hence, the U.N. Web site is a pretty good one. Students and teachers can use this site to its utmost. There's a lot of information here.

Women in International Security (WIIS)

http://www.puaf.umd.edu/wiis/

The official home page of Women In International Security (WIIS), dedicated to enhancing opportunities for women working in foreign and defense policy. An international, nonprofit, nonpartisan network and educational program, WIIS is open to both men and women at all stages of their careers.

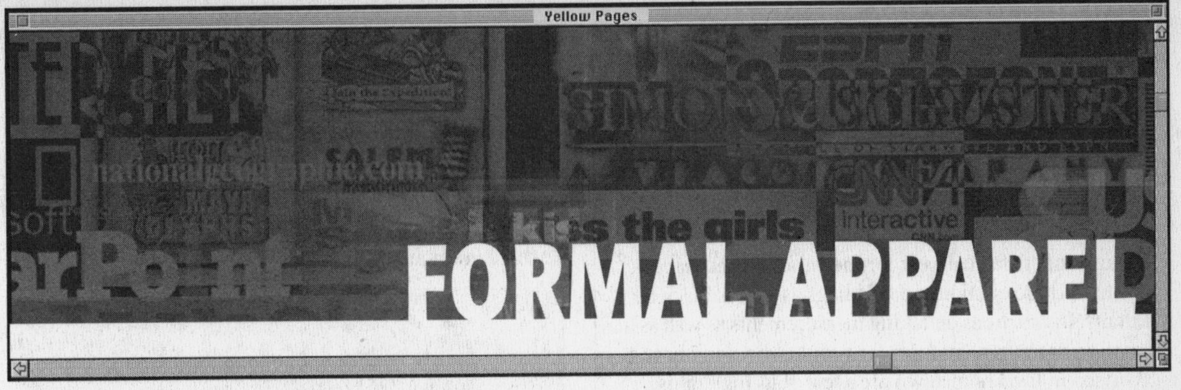

Remember the prom? You got so thin by then.

Michele in Romy and Michele's High School Reunion *(1997)*

A Great Deal

http://www.4-agreatdeal.com/

Includes business suits and formal and casual wear for women at reduced prices. All items are available in a range of sizes and colors and can be ordered online. Items include photographs and descriptions. Has a liberal return policy.

A Victorian Elegance

http://gator.net/~designs/

Specializes in vintage clothing, vintage wedding gowns, vintage men's apparel, and vintage accessories. Items range from 1800s through the 1900s. It boasts having over 1,000 items currently listed in its online showcases. Each item contains a full description and a photograph. Site includes sections on weekly specials, newest items, and information on collecting vintage items. Also offers layaway. A must-see sight for the eccentric wedding-goer.

Apparel Concepts for Men

http://www.apparelconcepts.com/

Includes a large variety of dress shirts, pants, dress suits, sport coats, and accessories for men. Various names and styles, all reported at below retail prices. Shipping is free on orders of $100 or more. Site is well organized and easy to maneuver.

The French Shop
http://www.frenchshop.com/

Budget Bridal Outlet Store

http://www.eskimo.com/~stopper/gown/gown.html

This bridal outlet service is a one-woman show that boasts up to 50% off retail prices for bridal dresses from makers such as Mirabella, Lamour, and Alexa. Includes sizing charts, warranties on dresses, and a FAQ about wedding dresses. Available sizes range from 4-48. All dresses are accompanied with pictures, which can be enlarged and printed. Orders can be faxed or emailed. Includes a section on men's tuxedos as well.

Change of A-Dress

http://www.coadress.proweb.co.uk/

Boasts to be the UK's Premier Designer Dress Agency and provides nearly new designer dresses for the fashion-conscious. Fashions include Mondi, Versace, Armani, YSL, Dior, and others.

Denise Byrd Designs

http://members.aol.com/TweetHeart/index.htm

Denise Byrd Designs boasts a wholesale supply of wedding gowns and bridesmaid dresses to bridal shops; complete cut, make, and trim services for bridal shops and designers; and creation of unique, one-off dresses as part of its myriad services. Online catalog and brochures available.

Dress Connection

http://www.dressconnection.com/

Dress Connection's goal is to provide high-quality dresses at competitive prices. Dresses are stated to be at least 30 percent off retail. A wide variety of styles and sizes (including misses, petite, and women's) is available. Each item has a detailed description, complete with material and cleaning needs.

Gingiss Formal Wear

http://www.gingiss.com/

Gingiss offers formal wear for men and women nationwide. Includes sections on weddings as well as black tie affairs. Instructions on taking measurements as well as a mail-in measurement form for people who don't have a Gingiss in their hometown are a few of its highlights. Sections on planning the wedding, as well as picking appropriate attire, make this site worth browsing.

Jim's Formal Wear

http://www.jimsfw.com/

The formal wear showcase section of this attractive site includes tuxedos and accessories from Demetrios, Chaps Ralph Lauren, Christian Dior, and Perry Ellis, to name a few. Photos of all tuxedos are provided. All tuxedos are guaranteed.

Naughty By Nature Fashions

http://www.nautybynature.com/

Although Naughty By Nature is not for the faint of heart and does include a lot more than evening gowns, the gowns section includes a cornucopia of alluring, figure-enhancing gowns in nylon, lycra, and spandex, among other synthetic fabrics. Each dress can easily be ordered online in various colors and sizes, including queen sizes. Orders can be taken by fax or toll-free phone calls. Site is relatively fast and easy to manipulate.

PZAZ NewYork

http://www.pzaz.com/prom97.htm

This site includes a large selection of formal wear dresses, including seasonal dresses, holiday attire, prom dresses, and more. Each dress is accompanied by a picture, description, color and size ranges, as well as prices. Ordering can be done online as well as through a 1-800 number. You can ask on on-site fashion expert questions about style, as well as read what other browsers have asked. Online fashion chat allows you to communicate or commiserate with fellow debutantes.

The French Shop

http://www.frenchshop.com/

The French Shop is a Web site of a family-owned dress shop established in 1936 and based in Bakersfield, California. The shop offers a complete line of formal wear for weddings, including bridal gowns (Watters & Watters, Jessica McClintock, and Ursula of Sweden) and clothing for members of the wedding party. Also includes bridal veils, gloves, honeymoon lingerie, and bridesmaid dresses. If the store is as quaint as the site, you might just make the trip there, no matter where you live!

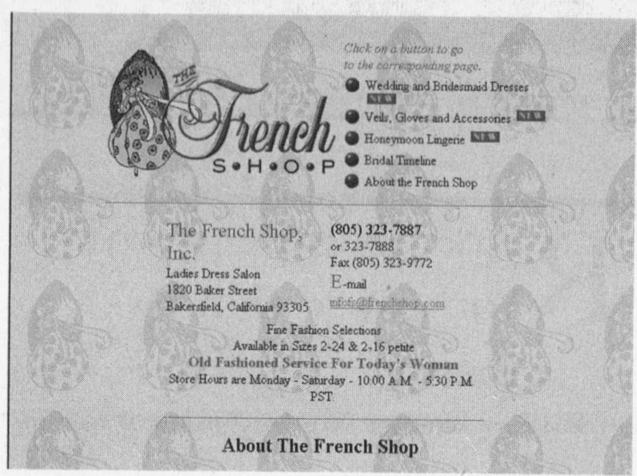

TuxOnTheNet

http://tuxonthenet.com/

TuxOnTheNet is a flashy site with attractive graphics of its tuxedos, career apparel, formal wear, and uniforms for men. Tuxedos can be rented and bought online. TuxOnTheNet also offers alterations and embroidery work. Includes tips on picking lapel sizes and cummerbunds, as well as information on the latest styles. This site is well-organized and easy to navigate after the graphics are loaded.

WedNet

http://www.wednet.com/

Although not exclusively about wedding attire, this site provides access to hundreds of wedding vendors. Gives advice about making your own wedding veil as well as how to establish a theme wedding. You can subscribe to the free monthly newsletter. If you are looking for various wedding services, this is a good place to start.

Related Sites
http://home1.gte.net/cmb2/index.htm
http://members.aol.com/allbridal/index.htm
http://www.3000.com/clubuno/
http://www.bigmen.com/
http://www.billyblue.com/
http://www.elegantforever.com/
http://www.starlighter.com/pursdrs/
http://www.suityourself.com/

A B C D E F G H I J K L M N O P Q R S T U V W X Y Z

> Now, I owe it to myself to tell you, Mr. Griswold, that if you are thinking of taking the tribe cross-country, this is the automobile you should be using. The Wagon Queen Family Truckster. You think you hate it now, but wait till you drive it.
>
> *Ed in* National Lampoon's Vacation *(1983)*

4WD: Four Wheel Drive and All Wheel Drive

http://www.sofcom.com.au/4WD/4WD.html

An Internet magazine devoted to off-roading. FAQs and pictures can be found about all sorts of vehicles including military, amphibious, and vehicles with as many as eight wheels. There is also an events page, with off-road events posted from all over the world, although the majority are Australian.

America's 4×4 4U Video Magazine

http://www.4x44u.com/pub/k2/am4x44u/4x4.html

Get the lowdown on trails, technical truck information, clubs and events, and 4×4 products. Then zoom on into the 4×4 chat room and talk shop with fellow off-roaders.

Four Wheeler Magazine
http://www.fourwheeler.com/

Dakar Official Site

http://www.dakar.com/

All the information on the famous Dakar road rally. Browse route information, information on the Dakar organization, photos from the race, and view the sponsors.

Fakawee!!

http://www.geocities.com/Baja/Dunes/3000/

This site was developed by a group out to dispel the myth that the Bay Area has no good off-roading locations. The site posts details of past and future California treks, but the real surprise is the extensive set of links to clubs, dealers, parts and accessories manufacturers, and more.

Flatlander's World Wide Web of 4-Wheeling

http://www.4x4now.com/

This large site features tons of adventure stories, trail guides and reviews, and listings of upcoming events. Contains a full selection of books and videos for 4×4 enthusiasts and a section about safety in off-road driving.

Related Sites

http://members.aol.com/offroadron/ieoa.htm
http://www.4x44u.com/pub/k2/orshops.htm
http://www.bekkoame.or.jp/~makoto-h/index.htm
http://www.bryancollins.demon.co.uk/
http://www.buffnet.net/~mudness/index1.htm
http://www.mesagroup.com/claw/
http://www.monstermania.com/

Four Wheeler Magazine

`http://www.fourwheeler.com/`

Read about adventures written by fourwheelers just like you. Find out where to go on vacation and what to do when you get there, and make sure to read about trail etiquette before you start your journey. Also make sure to check out the vehicle reviews and Best Buys section.

HUMMER.COM

`http://www.hummer.com/`

Of course HUMMER.COM is in all capital letters. This site is dedicated to the vehicle that proudly refuses labels and categories. Find out about both civilian and industrial versions of the Hummer, and see why it feels at home in conditions that would make other vehicles cry for Mommy.

Jeep Home Page

`http://www.jeepunpaved.com/alt_home.html`

Find out more information about this popular manufacturer of on/off-road vehicles. Trace the vehicle's history back through several wars and find out where the name "Jeep" might have come from. Read more information about how to do your off-road driving safely and ecologically.

Land Rover WWW

`http://www.landrover.com/`

Maker of the famous Range Rover, Land Rover offers this site to tell you about its various models and how to outfit your vehicle (and yourself) with the right gear. Request a free copy of the SUV comparison guide and make your own decisions.

Locator Online

`http://www.partslocator.com/`

This electronic version of *Locator Magazine* is a salvage yard that specializes in helping you find those elusive parts for your car or truck. The site can direct you to a dealer in your area, and it also can get you in touch with wholesale distributors and dismantlers.

My Jeep Adventures

`http://www.halcyon.com/csutton/myjeepadventures`

An ongoing story by Chris Sutton about his adventures with his 1952 flat-fender jeep. Details are provided about everything from buying the jeep and fixing it up with various parts, to coping with particular off-road situations.

Off-Road.com

`http://www.off-road.com/`

A well-put-together site of interest to off-road aficionados. Features include various articles on anything from a specific vehicle to land use. Also available are photo galleries, links to manufacturers' home pages, and a classified service where you can advertise your vehicle or parts.

Pirates of the Rubicon Extreme 4WD Club

`http://www.netsiteworld.com/rubicon/`

This multimedia-rich site features a chat room and a list of classified ads to buy and sell four-wheelers. Send in a picture of you and your rig to post to Viewers in Action.

ROCKCRAWLER.COM

`http://www.rockcrawler.com/`

This online magazine features trail reports, technical how-to articles, and adventure reports from readers. Also has serialized diaries from on-the-road contributors.

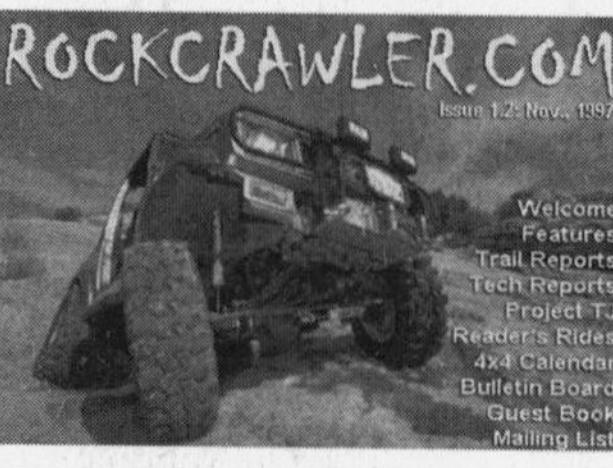

SUV Online

`http://www.suv.com`

A site devoted to the latest in motor trends, the sport utility vehicle. Get current industry news, statistics, and reviews. Features special sections for every major SUV model and an owner's forum, where you can post questions and comments in over 30 different categories about any aspect of the SUV scene.

The Ultimate Jeep Site

`http://www.ultimatejeep.com/`

Although not affiliated with Jeep or Chrysler, this site contains a wealth of information about one of the world's favorite vehicles. See product showcases and reviews, link to parts suppliers, and contact other Jeep owners in chat rooms and forums.

The Ultimate Poseur's Sport Utility Page

http://www.southern.edu/~jkarolyi/poseur/

True 4×4 fans will appreciate this humorous jab at those who buy SUVs for prestige only. Features the top ten reasons not to buy an SUV, facts and figures designed to "end the trend," and a list of alternative vehicles that meet the specifications of true 4×4 aficionados.

United Four Wheel Drive Associations

http://www.ufwda.org/

The UFWDA attempts to unite all 4×4 drivers, from weekend SUV driver to dedicated mud bogger. Find information on the awareness training program and get details on their yearly convention. Also provides current land use and legislative facts.

The World of Monster Trucks

http://www.truckzone.com/

Chat with drivers and other enthusiasts at designated times every week. Find out results of recent events, and browse through the huge picture gallery. Also contains a large list of links to other monster truck and motorsport sites.

The World's Largest Monster Truck Homepage

http://dcweb.designcraft.com/monster/trucks/

Hosted by motorsport photographer Eric Stern, this site claims over 475 photos of monster trucks in action. Also check out the latest industry news and events.

NEWSGROUPS

alt.auto.subaru

alt.autos.dodge.trucks

alt.autos.macho-trucks

rec.autos.4x4

rec.autos.driving

rec.autos.makers.jeep+willys

rec.autos.tech

Related Sites

http://www.off-road.com/4x4web/jeepster/

http://www.ok4wd.com/

http://www.wildhorses4x4.com/

A B C D E F G H I J K L M N O P Q R S T U V W X Y Z

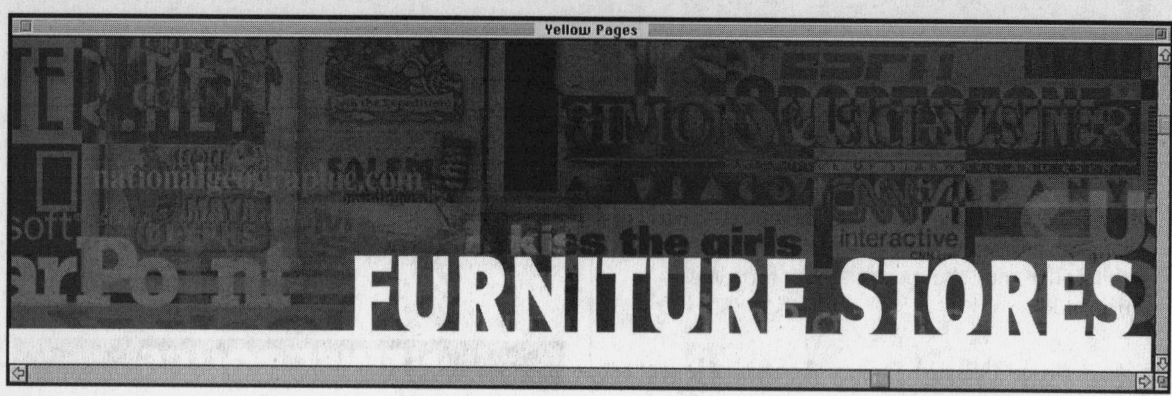

> Even when opportunity knocks, you still must get out of your chair to open the door.
>
> *Nuggets*

The Atrium Furniture Mall

http://theatrium.com/furniture/

Promising 40 to 50 percent discounts, the Atrium is a collection of 37 furniture stores that fit under one giant, North Carolina roof. Stroll through the galleries, then submit a form to get additional information about a specific type of furniture.

ANZANIA DESIGNS inc.

http://www.azania.com/

This Boston company specializes in custom wood furniture and doors. Pick from their designs, or submit your own specs and get a fast quote on one of the most detailed order forms you'll ever see.

Ecologic, Inc.

http://www.ecoloft.com/

Discover space-saving dormitory and bedroom furniture made entirely of recycled materials. Features lofts, desks, chairs, and more bunk beds. Also includes children's beds that look like covered wagons, castles, and more.

Related Sites

http://www.berne.com/

http://www.bluetomatoes.com/

http://www.butcherblockbarn.com/

Futon Express and Planet Ironworks
http://www.futonexpress.demon.co.uk/

Furniture City USA

http://www.furniturecity.com/

Although the entire world is welcome to visit the actual Wisconsin showroom, Furniture City ships only to Wisconsin, Northern Illinois, and Northern Michigan. Features furniture for the living room, dining room, and bedroom.

Futon Express and Planet Ironworks

http://www.futonexpress.demon.co.uk/

This British company specializes in cast iron furniture, futons, and related accessories. What says rigid flexibility like a cast-iron chaise lounge?

Hooker Furniture

http://www.hookerfurniture.com

Hooker is a company known for its high quality and traditional tastes. In addition to the usual array of dining room, living room, and bedroom sets, the company features a wide variety of home theater and entertainment center pieces.

La-Z-Boy

http://www.lazboy.com

Known for ages as an icon in the recliner field, La-Z-Boy sets out to prove that the company is anything but lazy. Features a furniture glossary, decorating tips, and its full showcase of sofas, loveseats, sectionals, and of course, recliners. The site also includes a program that lets you try different upholstery patterns on the same piece of furniture.

Majestic Woodworks

http://www.majwood.com/

The Majestic Woodworks site features hand-finished shaker reproductions in authentic shaker colors. Where else can you get a salt box in eight colors? Get full descriptions of their clocks, benches, and tables, and find out what happens if you decide to combine two colors!

Neto Furniture, Ltd.

http://www.globes.co.il/Neto/

Check out the contemporary designs featured at this Israeli site. Featuring both Hebrew and English text, the Neto site carries the latest in accessories for all rooms in the house and proves that cool Art Deco isn't dead, it's just chilling out on the Mediterranean.

Office Furniture USA

http://www.officefurniture-usa.com/

View the catalog of the company that promises everyday savings of 50 percent. Includes both new and used office furniture. Features include an online catalog and password-protected bulletin boards for dealers and manufacturers to share their secrets.

OFFICE@HOME

http://www.officehome.com/

Specializing in computer desks, file cabinets, and computer armoires, this site promises everything you need for your home office. The online showroom, however, carries only some of the things that the company sells.

Relax The Back Store

http://www.relaxtheback.com/

This site features ergonomic furniture and equipment, mostly for back pain. Discover things you never knew existed for sleep disorder, lumbar tension, and excessive vertebrae compression. Find a store location near you anywhere in North America with the store locator.

The Retail/Wholesale Futon Outlet Page

http://www.eskimo.com/~futon/index.html

If budget is a consideration, cruise by here to look for your futon. Order frames, mattresses, and slipcovers at discount prices.

The Spring Wood Smith

http://www.thewoodman.com/

Woody doesn't show his face, apparently because he's too busy handcrafting original cupboards and hutches and shaker-era accessories. Check out the hard-to-find specialties, such as handpainted fireplace covers and spoon racks.

Texwood Furniture Corporation

http://www.texwood.com/

Texwood manufactures several different lines of library and office furniture. The company offers assistance in designing your own media center, library, or computer room, or it will be happy to refer you to any of its dealers across the U.S. The site also features many facts about its shelves, computer desks, and so on, and it includes many tips about what to look for in library furniture.

NEWSGROUPS

alt.binaries.pictures.furniture

pdaxs.ads.furniture

rec.antiques

rec.woodworking

Related Sites

http://www.deco-echoes.com/

http://www.ergo-ws.com/

http://www.futon.org/

http://www.ggtc.com/

http://www.hofs.com/

http://www.romanart.com/

http://www.thetraveller.com/thetraveller/zivneys/zivneyshome.html

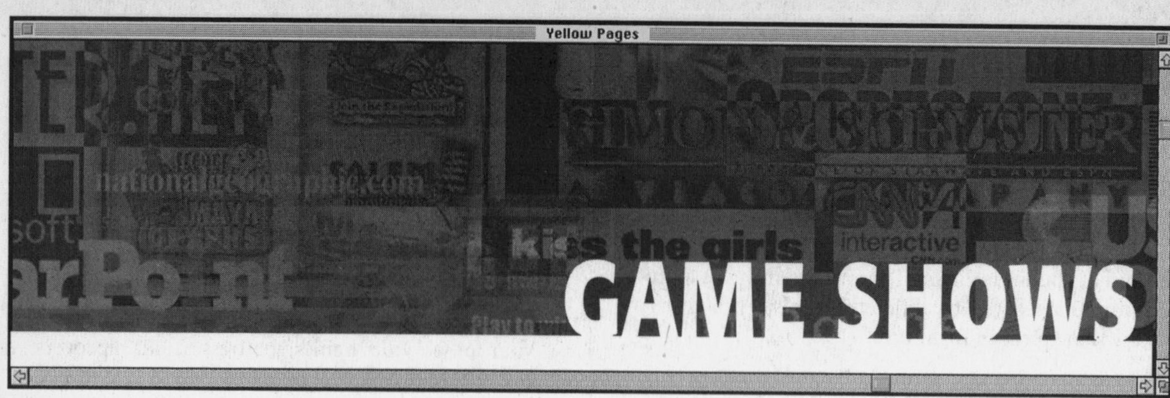

A
B
C
D
E
F
G
H
I
J
K
L
M
N
O
P
Q
R
S
T
U
V
W
X
Y
Z

Come on down!

The Price is Right

DEBT

http://www.lifetimetv.com/thetube/debt/index.html

Lifetime's new game show, DEBT with Wink Martindale, has a fun site full of the usual show history, host bio, and contestant information plus some cool tips on how to get out of your own credit card debt and a credit card survey. A chat room is also available.

DISCOMAN'S Price Is Right Home Page

http://home.ptd.net/~discoman/

Synthesized TPIR theme music plays in the background as you browse this site. It offers an enormous list of the show's games, their rules, and tips on how to win at them if you are lucky enough to make it to Contestants Row. Even better than the official TPIR home page.

Jeopardy

http://www.spe.sony.com/Pictures/tv/jeopardy/jeopardy.html

What is America's #1 game show? This official Jeopardy site contains facts about the show's host Alex Trebek, a schedule of upcoming special events and contestant searches, show highlights, historical big winners, and an online game. Be sure to give your answers in the form of a question!

DISCOMAN'S Price Is Right Home Page
http://home.ptd.net/~discoman/

Jeopardy
http://www.spe.sony.com/Pictures/tv/jeopardy/jeopardy.html

The Game Show Zone
http://www.geocities.com/TelevisionCity/3791/gsz.html

Match Game

http://php.indiana.edu/~wlambert/MG.html

A fan-created site with information on the host, Gene Rayburn, and those wacky regulars, Charles Nelson Reilly, Richard Dawson, and Brett Somers. Also includes rules and .wav files of bloopers and quotes.

The Game Show Network's WWW Site

http://www.spe.sony.com/Pictures/GSN/index.html

The Game Show Network offers the most popular game shows in television history from the '50s through the '90s, in addition to new, live interactive games shows.

The Game Show Zone

http://www.geocities.com/TelevisionCity/3791/gsz.html

A site with tons of trivia and news about any and all game shows—past and present. Also offers instructions on playing Internet versions of your favorite game shows and links to other sites.

The Games of Love

http://www.geocities.com/TelevisionCity/2765/

This site is dedicated to shows such as The Dating Game, Bzzz!, Personals, and more. Shows are amusingly summarized into categories such as the host; premise; the good, bad, and ugly about each show.

The Gong Show Fan Page

http://members.tripod.com/~wrcw/

This site pays homage to the goofiest of game shows. Several photos and facts that will take you back to the days of the gong.

The Newlywed Game

http://www.spe.sony.com/tv/shows/newlywed/index.html

The show that made the term "whoopee" famous gives you everything from weekly polls and live chat rooms to the show history at this site. You can even view the show set in 3D!

The Password Page

http://www.public.usit.net/sbeverly/password.htm

This fan-created site is full of facts about the show and its history. It also contains a great link to the Game Show Web Ring, which will take you to *Jeopardy*, *The Price Is Right*, *Wheel of Fortune*, and *Pictionary* sites.

The Price Is Right

http://www.cbs.com/daytime/price/

Home of the longest running game show in history, this site contains cast bios, ticket information, taping schedules, and a contact address. Sorry die-hard TPIR fans, but there aren't any online versions of the show available at this site.

The Unofficial Concentration Home Page

http://www.mindspring.com/~russellm/cncindx.htm

This unofficial site based on the NBC game show offers a puzzle that is revealed gradually through a series of four "snapshots" with the last snapshot revealing the entire puzzle. Also includes the rules, photos from the original show, and links to other game show sites.

Wheel of Fortune Home Page

http://www.spe.sony.com/tv/shows/wheel/

Home of America's #1 television game show in syndication, this site has a BBS discussion board, a ticket offer to view a taping of the show, and a contestant registration form—a must for any true fan! Of course, the site also gives visitors an opportunity to play the game online.

Win Ben Stein's CyberMoney

http://www.comedycentral.com/bstein/index.shtml

Based on Comedy Central's trivia game, this site has an online game you can play and explains the rules and differences from the actual TV game. It includes instructions on how to become a contestant on the TV game show. One player each day will be randomly chosen to win a Comedy Central T-shirt. Also, this site is full of links to other cool Comedy Central show home pages.

Related Sites

http://bookzone.com/topshelf/gameshow.html

http://www.gamesmania.com/english/news/business/gameshow.htm

http://www.fas.harvard.edu/~ilagan/guide10.html

http://www.fas.harvard.edu/~ilagan/trebek.htm

http://www.ox.compsoc.org.uk/~dickson/GS/atgs/

http://www.negia.net/~justind/badshow.html

http://www.fas.harvard.edu/~ilagan/gslibrary.htm

http://www.ox.compsoc.org.uk/~dickson/GS/gs.html

http://home.sprynet.com/sprynet/agallego/Top_15_Hosts.html

http://www.fas.harvard.edu/~ilagan/gslinks.htm

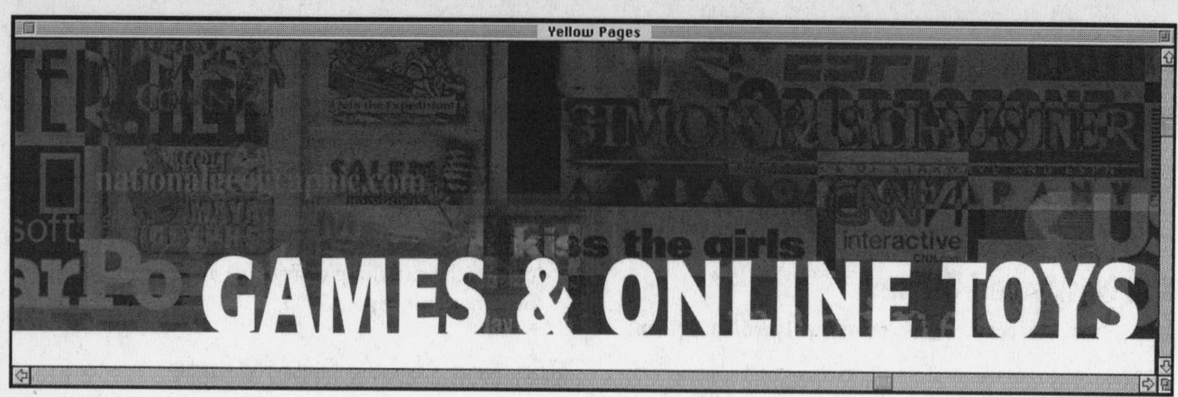

And I their toys to the great children leave.

James Thomson

Caissa's Web Home Page
http://caissa.com/

Crossword Puzzle Game
http://www.dareware.com/cross.htm

Heretical Rhyme Generator
http://zenith.berkeley.edu/seidel/Po/

Kooks Museum
http://www.teleport.com/~dkossy/

Apple Corps

http://jubal.westnet.com/apple_corps/apple_corps.html

The game you lost all the pieces to as a child is back. Mr. Potato Head is here, under an online, non-copyrighted form, except now he's an apple. You are able to place eyes, nose, teeth, mouth, whatever, onto the apple. A new twist is also available—change the vegetable if you like.

A Simple Rhyming Dictionary

http://bobo.link.cs.cmu.edu/cgi-bin/dougb/rhyme.cgi

This page offers a simple online rhyming dictionary that provides a list of words that rhyme with any entered word. Also provides homonyms, as long as the entered word is in the dictionary.

Ariel's Simpsons Trivia Quiz

http://www.geocities.com/Athens/1530/simptriv.html

Provides an online trivia quiz about the popular television show *The Simpsons.* Includes many different questions and links to other related sites.

Bluedog Can Count

http://kao.ini.cmu.edu:5550/bdf.html

A toy for your mathematical enjoyment. Blue dog will bark out the answer to any simple math problem you can input. But be careful about imaginary numbers.

Caissa's Web Home Page

http://caissa.com/

Provides a page where Caissa members can play chess live over the Internet. Includes membership rules and information.

Carlo's Coloring Book

http://www.ravenna.com/coloring/

Choose one of seven images to color from Carlo's page. Coloring book consists of templates pasted on a limited version of Paintbrush.

ChessLink

http://members.aol.com/alexgru/chesslink/index.htm

Provides a home page for ChessLink software that enables people to play chess across the Internet. Includes details about the software and links to other Chess-related sites.

Complaint Letter Generator

http://www-csag.cs.uiuc.edu/individual/pakin/complaint

Generate your own personalized complaint letter by entering a few details and facts. Just sit back and enjoy the complaint generated in as many paragraphs as you like.

Cool Lego Site of the Week

`http://www.fibblesnork.com/lego/cool/`

Check out this site to see the amazing things they are doing with Legos these days, not just the lunar lander you had as a kid. Also features links to other Lego pages.

Crejaculabryrinth

`http://www.xs4all.nl/~kessels/Puzzel04.html`

Learn how to make a straight angled line, if you dare. This site is another fun logic game that will have you bouncing off your bedroom walls.

Crossword Puzzle Game

`http://www.dareware.com/cross.htm`

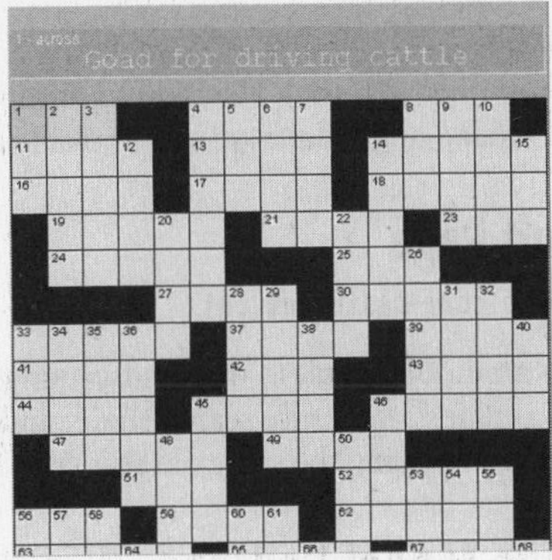

Provides many different crossword puzzle games. Includes links to other online game sites.

The Cyrano Server

`http://www.nando.net/toys/cyrano.html`

This site was created for the shy and unimaginative person in love. Cyrano will write your love letters for you and mail them electronically. Cyrano will also perform that nasty breakup, if necessary, so you won't have to go through the anguish.

The Daily 100

`http://www.80s.com/Entertainment/Movies/Daily100/`

A fantastic site featuring 80s movie trivia. They provide the clip, you provide the actor, movie, and year it debuted. Site keeps track of players; that is, it's a contest. Closed on weekends.

The Destruction Derby Games

`http://www.psygnosis.com/secure/derby/`

An online destruction derby is found at this site. Click an image of an older automobile. Then watch the destruction via blunt instruments.

Dogz

`http://www.dogz.com/`

Download a digital dog for free from the site. You can choose a Mac or PC dog or cat. He'll even fetch a bone on your screen.

Drinking Games

`http://www.rain.org/~uring/tvdrink/tv.htm`

A page for the entertainment of college students or other procrastinator types. Site features a large number of network shows turned into drinking games. Click the show, and a set of rules are shown.

Duck Hunt–Find the Fowl

`http://aurora.york.ac.uk/ducks.html`

The people from York University bring us an online duck hunt. In the spirit of the "Where's Waldo®" game, find the duck in these pictures. Also contains some fun links.

Ferret Frenzy

`http://www.delphi.co.uk/delphi/interactive/ferrets/intro.html`

With good reason, this is the only online Ferret racing game. Choose your ferret, place a bet, and watch the race.

The Fruit Game

`http://www.2020tech.com/fruit/index.html`

Offers the challenging "fruit game." Players remove fruit from the screen; the last player to remove fruit loses. Try this mathematical adventure.

Fun with Grapes

`http://www.sci.tamucc.edu/~pmichaud/grape/`

A theatrical and scientific study is performed here concerning the effect on grapes exposed to high levels of microwave radiation. Amusing results and discussions describe the experiment as well as the page in general.

A B C D E F G H I J K L M N O P Q R S T U V W X Y Z

Funny Bunny Trail

http://banzai.neosoft.com/citylink/easter/default.html

Hunt for Easter eggs on the WWW by surfing sites. Game is based on the USA Citylink Project. If you are really good, you could win some money. Check out this site for more information.

Guess the Dictator and/or Television Sitcom Character

http://sp1.berkeley.edu/dict.html

Those wacky Berkeley kids brought us another way to kill time. This game is based on the premise that you are your favorite dictator or television sitcom star. The site will ask you yes/no questions and tell you which dictator/star you are. It's amazing.

Handy Spanish Phrase

http://www.umr.edu/~tommy/span1.html

Need a handy Spanish phrase to interject into a conversation? Look no further. The handy Spanish phrase generator is here to supply you with phrases such as "Su prima es en fuego," which means "Your cousin is on fire."

Heretical Rhyme Generator

http://zenith.berkeley.edu/seidel/Po/

Generates a rhyme for every line entered by the browser. Don't be surprised if you are slightly appalled by the assault on the aesthetic.

Hit the Unabomber

http://ccwf.cc.utexas.edu/~jondough/jon2.htm

Do you have something against the Unabomber? This site provides some revenge. As the title says, the site allows a person to hit the Unabomber.

Home Appliance Shooting

http://www.csn.net/~dcbenton/has.html

Take out your aggressions here on those troublesome home appliances. Features the destruction of a gas grill and a television set.

Homers

http://student.uq.edu.au/~s335193/homers.html

This site is an online game that requires you to put Homer Simpson's head on straight. Includes rules and links to other online games.

How Bored Are You

http://www.kfu.com/~nsayer/bored/

Features a game called "How bored are you." Game involves following the rules and doing absolutely nothing while the page counts the seconds.

IBM—The Electric Origami Shop

http://www.ibm.com/Stretch/EOS/

The electric origami shop features kaleidoscope shots, fractals, high tech art, and some very tough puzzles for the mathematically inclined. Also features an interesting site traveler that one could explore for days.

ID Archives—Doom

http://www.idsoftware.com/archive.html

You can download a wealth of Doom levels and scenarios from this Web site. "Heretic and Shadow of the Serpent Riders" and Quake are also available here.

The Insult Page

http://www.io.com/~rasto/ins.cgi

Provides a random insult to the unsuspecting browser. Also contains a very nice search engine index if you are tired of doing the same old searches.

Interactive Model Railroad

http://rr-vs.informatik.uni-ulm.de/RR/RR.html

An online model railroad that you can operate from your Web browser, brought to you from the University of Ulm. Site also contains other railroad-related links.

Joe's Amazing Relationship Problem Solver

http://studsys.mscs.mu.edu/~carpent1/probsolv/rltprob0.html

This amazing page will solve all your relationship problems, maybe. You must answer several yes/no questions to have your problem solved for you. It is also recommended you read the disclaimer.

Kooks Museum

http://www.teleport.com/~dkossy/

The title describes it all. Take a course in crackpotology, kookology, and archaic. Also features the "Hall of Hate" and "Library of Questionable Scholarship."

Kurt Cobain's Talking Eight Ball

http://www.xworld.com/

In true bad taste, this page provides a bit of wisdom from the former grunge icon Kurt Cobain. Site requires the appropriate plug-in software.

Lemonade Stand

http://www.feist.com/~jmayans/lemonade/lemonade.cgi

Provides an online version of the popular computer game. You operate a lemonade stand in an attempt to make as much money as possible and retire to the Hall of Fame. It is not as easy as it sounds, either.

Lloyd's Coke Machine

http://www.ugcs.caltech.edu/~walterfb/coke/coke.html

Look here for an interactive Coke machine located at Caltech. You can send an LED message to a real Coke machine. Check out the schematics for a description of some amazing work. Cheers to the Caltech Coke machine guys.

Looney Tunes Karaoke

http://www.kids.warnerbros.com/karaoke/cmp/list.htm

Here are your favorite Looney tunes songs sung on your very own PC. Application requires Real Audio software plug-in. Choose from nine songs to sing along with your PC.

Manic Maze

http://www.worldvillage.com/maze.htm

Interactive online maze featuring prizes and other fun stuff. Check out some other fantastic links while you're at it.

Mark's Apology Note Generator

http://net.indra.com/~karma/formletter.html

Let Mark help you deal with life with his apology generator. Look here for a fill-in-the-blank ad-lib apology note that will be electronically mailed.

Mindgames

http://weber.u.washington.edu/~jlks/mindgame.html

Stump your friends with these amazing feats of psychological wizardry. Choose from five mind games and four puzzles. Site also features links to Behavior Online.

Mine Sweep

http://www.bu.edu/htbin/mines

Provides a Web version of the popular game Minesweeper. Includes instructions and a list of high scorers.

Oeno Phile's Mood Detector

http://www.chrysalis.org/oeno/testmood.htm

If you didn't get enough of these in the seventies, or if you weren't around in the seventies, this site is for you. This online mood ring site may tell you what you do not want to hear.

Optical Illusions—A Collection

http://lainet3.lainet.com/~ausbourn/

Very nicely done optical images can be viewed at this site. Explanations of the illusion and descriptions of what to expect are given as well. Very nice images.

PhoNETic

http://www.soc.qc.edu/phonetic/

If you lack creativity, this site will tell you what word your phone number will spell based on the corresponding letters on a telephone keypad. User can set parameters for 3 to 10 numbers or even go from words to numbers.

Piercing Mildred

http://streams.com/pierce/

Creativity is not lacking at this site. Choose from three characters and apply tattoos, piercing, and scars as your heart desires. Site requires quite of bit of instruction. You'll have to read it.

Pig Latin Converter

http://voyager.cns.ohiou.edu/~jrantane/menu/pig.html

Converts Web pages from English into Pig Latin by simply entering the URL address. A language rarely seen in print, Pig Latin is very difficult for the untrained eye to read, but try it if you have the spare time.

Play Chess on the Net

http://www.outland.com/OutlandChess.html

Play the ancient game in a real-time online form. Site features optional game clocks, chat boxes, and UCSF Player Ratings.

A B C D E F G H I J K L M N O P Q R S T U V W X Y Z

Punch John Tesh

http://www.well.com/user/vanya/tesh.html

Do you like the music and broadcasting of John Tesh? Well if you do not, here is a site for you. This site allows one to pummel (virtually) the face of John Tesh.

Riddle du Jour

http://www.dujour.com/

An online sphinx will ask the riddle. Can you solve it? Hone your wits, for there are prizes at stake. Site also contains a Labryinth and "Mondo Trivia."

Rock Mall's Trivia Challenge

http://www.rockmall.com/arcade.htm

Sharpen your wits, trivia junkies, for here is your site. Cruise through this site if you know everything about nothing important. Some questions here will stump all challengers.

Rock, Paper, Scissors

http://www.shadow.net/~proub/rps.html

The famous game that entertained you as a child and left you with bruised arms when you lost is back and online. Site also features a "cheat" option for those who can't take losing. Also contains a comments and doomsday philosophy page.

Salon Betty's Interactive Paper Doll

http://www.imusic.com/Paperdoll/

Provides an image of Betty, who can be dressed in one of four "grunge" outfits. Music is also available to download from this site.

Send an Electronic Postcard

http://linux.hartford.edu/~azmizar/postcard/

Choose from a variety of postcards from a selection of locations. Type in a message and send your friend a postcard.

Speedbump

http://www.sandbox.net/mines/pub-doc/speedbump.html

Provides rules, information, and more about the game Speedbump. The game Speedbump is similar to the popular game Minesweeper. There is no cost to play Speedbump, but with registration the player becomes eligible for prizes.

Star Trek: The Next Generation—The Daily Test

http://www.sci.kun.nl/thalia/funpage/startrek/

Features an online challenge for the *Star Trek* fan. You must match a picture from a specific episode with the episode title. Good luck. Engage.

The Tele-Garden

http://www.usc.edu/dept/garden/

Conceptual genius defines this site, a tele-robotic installation that enables WWW users to view and interact with a remote garden filled with real live plants. By using an industrial robot arm, you can watch the progress as the plants grow. You need a valid email address and a caring hand.

Test Borkifier

http://astro.queensu.ca/~dursi/borker.html

Enables you to take any English phrase and transform it into "Swedish chef" mumblings. An amazing feat to mystify your friends with your new form of speech.

Tetris

http://www.mit.edu:8001/people/nathanw/java/Tetris.html

This site allows one to play the popular game of Tetris online. Includes rules and a high scores list.

The Tick's Dart Games

http://www.islandnet.com/~cwalker/sites.html

Help the Tick destroy some forms of evil present in today's society. Like Garfield. You can choose one of several media icons or political figures to throw darts at.

Tic-Tac-Toe

http://http.bsd.uchicago.edu/~e-pikat/TicTacToe/ttt.html

If you didn't get enough of this game as a child, or if you have too much free time, try this site. We all know how the game will finish. But try it nonetheless.

The Ultimate Oracle—Pray Before the Head of Bob

http://www.resort.com/~banshee/Misc/8ball/index.html

The online version of the legendary Magic Eight Ball. Ask Bob any question and you are sure to get a response. You can even ask in four different languages.

The Vain Game

http://www.xs4all.nl/~kessels/Puzzel.html

Try this site if you need a good intellectual humbling. The game is challenging and entertaining and will, of course, suck your time from you.

Virtual Media

http://www.iaw.on.ca/~virtualm/

Home site for the video clip and sound byte of the week. Includes site background and information.

Web-a-Sketch

http://www.digitalstuff.com/web-a-sketch/

In the true spirit of the immortal Etch-a-Sketch comes Web-a-Sketch. The lines are a great deal harder to draw, but let's face it—you got the time. If your picture is good enough, it might make drawing of the week.

WebBattleship

http://info.gte.com/gtel/fun/battle/battle.html

The online version of the classic game, except you cannot choose where you want to place your battleships. Always entertaining, and the computer is pretty formidable.

Webcube

http://info.gte.com/cgi-bin/cube/cube?RESET

The "Rubic's Cube" game you hated as a child, but that caught on as a cultural phenomena. The only catch is that you can't take this one apart in order to win.

Welcome to Faces

http://www.corynet.com/faces/

This site enables you to create police sketches of famous celebrities by combining heads, eyes, and mouths of different individuals.

Welcome to Find-the-Spam

http://sp1.berkeley.edu/findthespam.html

One of the many Spam worshipping pages on the Web. The game here is Find the Spam. It is not as simple as one would think, either.

Welcome to the Web Wumpus

http://www.bu.edu/Games/wumpus.html

Look here for an online version of the game "Hunt the Wumpus." Your goal is to hunt the wumpus and shoot it before it gets you. Site includes game instructions.

Wizards of the Coast, Inc.

http://www.wizards.com/

Provides home site and information for Wizards of the Coast, producers of the popular "Magic: The Gathering" card came. Includes information about Magic and other games produced by the Wizards. Also includes company background and news.

WWW Anagram Generator

http://csugrad.cs.vt.edu/~eburke/anagrams.html

Take any of your favorite words or phrases and generate quite a few anagrams of it. Also contains news and upcoming features of the anagram generator.

The WWW Fortune Cookie Machine

http://www.mind.net/sage/fortune/

Receive a piece of distilled silicon wisdom from this page, without a bland cookie. You can also submit a fortune, if you think you have the karma it takes.

WWW Interactive Crossword

http://www.phillynews.com/crossword/

An online crossword puzzle brought to you by the Philadelphia newspapers. Choose from a slew of previous newspaper puzzles put online to play. You can even choose an "easy" mode.

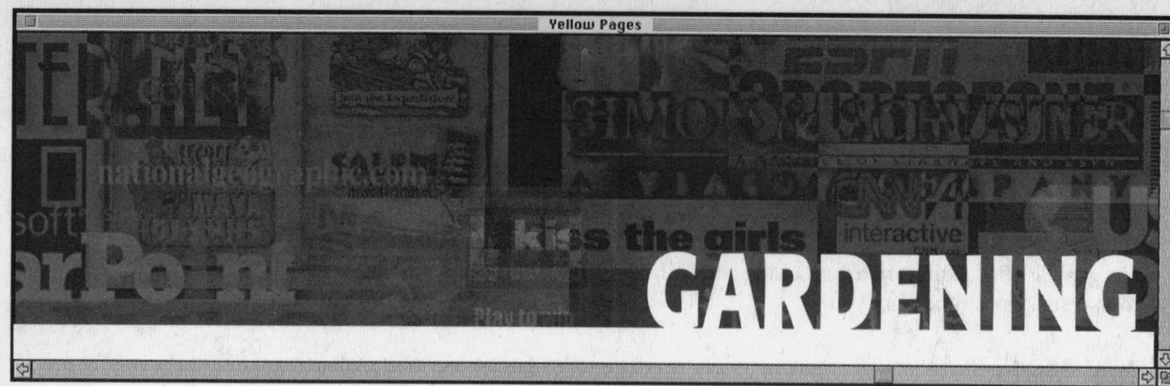

> The trouble with gardening is that it does not remain an avocation. It becomes an obsession.
>
> *Phyllis McGinley*

FLOWERS AND SHRUBS

American Horticultural Society

http://www.emall.com/ahs/

For the "horticulture connoisseur." Provides links to several articles from *The American Gardener*. Membership in the AHL and subscription to *The American Gardener* permit you to order several varieties of seeds for free in the month of January. The member is graced with many other privileges as well.

The Flower Link

http://www.flowerlink.com/

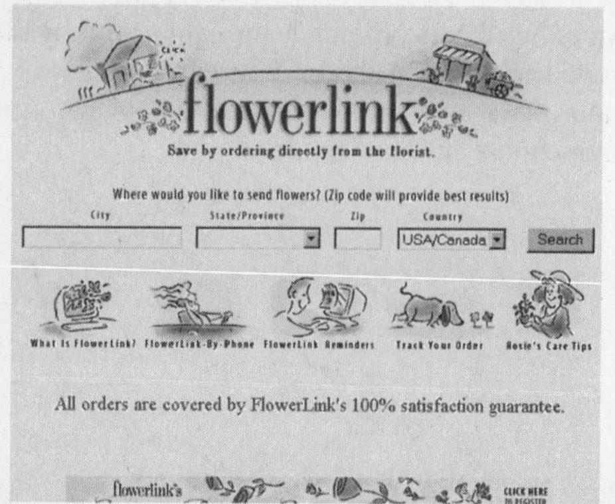

The Flower Link
http://www.flowerlink.com/

The Tree Doctor
http://www.1stresource.com/t/treedoc/

Enables you to order from budding flower shops across the U.S. and Canada. Many of these florists even provide same day delivery. What distinguishes this service is that that there are no accompanying service or transfer charges, saving you as much as 30 percent.

TREES

Arboriculture On-Line

http://spectre.ag.uiuc.edu/~isa/

A WWW resource designed by The International Society of Arboriculture (ISA) and the University of Illinois Cooperative States Research, Education, and Extension Service (ICSREES) to assist tree care professionals. Offers links to information at universities and other institutions throughout the world as well as "Arborist News," newsletter of the ISA.

The Tree Doctor

http://www.1stresource.com/t/treedoc/

This is the place to go to find answers to your urban tree questions. Find out about tree diseases and pests, tree topping, and organic bio-stimulants. There is also a directory of professional arborists. The Tree Care Doctor will gladly answer your questions.

Trees of the Pacific Northwest

http://www.orst.edu/instruct/for241/

From Oregon State University, challenges you to identify coniferous tree types of the Pacific Northwest by use of a "dichotomous key." If you don't have a conifer handy, you can try to identify a pictured "mystery tree." Also provides links to other tree-related sites.

Yellow Pages

GAY/LESBIAN/ BISEXUAL/TRANS

What concerns me is not the way things are, but rather the way people think things are.

Epictetus

COLLEGES AND UNIVERSITIES

cmuOUT

http://www.contrib.andrew.cmu.edu/org/out/

Local and regional information for gay and lesbian students at Carnegie Mellon University (Pittsburgh). A surprisingly content-rich site including info about bars, local businesses, travel, films, and more.

Harvard Gay & Lesbian Caucus

http://www.actwin.com/hglc/

Harvard Gay & Lesbian Caucus members include over 1,700 gay, lesbian, and bisexual Harvard and Radcliffe alumni/ae, faculty, and staff. This site, run primarily for Caucus members, details the organization's goals and activities.

Lesbian Gay Bisexual Alliance of Princeton University

http://webware.princeton.edu/stulife/womenctr/newwrg/wrslgb.htm

A colorful and attractive site with information for gay/lesbian students and alumni, an online edition of a gay newspaper, a list of campus meetings, and much more.

NRD TOP PICKS

Purdue's LesBiGay Home Page
http://expert.cc.purdue.edu/~triangle/

The Gay and Lesbian National Hotline
http://www.glnh.org/

PlanetOut
http://www.planetout.com/

Queer Resources Directory (QRD)
http://www.qrd.org/qrd/

Virtual AIDS Quilt
http://www.mcpsys.com/quilt/

Parents and Friends of Gays and Lesbians (PFLAG)
http://www.pflag.org/

Partners Task Force for Gay and Lesbian Couples
http://www.buddybuddy.com/toc.html

National Gay and Lesbian Task Force (NGLTF)
http://www.ngltf.org/

Whosoever
http://www.whosoever.org/

Ladyslipper Music
http://www.ladyslipper.org/

Wolfe Video
http://www.wolfevideo.com/

Penn State Pride Page

http://128.118.50.35:80/psupride/

This page provides information specific to the gay, lesbian, bisexual, and transgendered community at Penn State. There is a calendar of events, a resource list, and links to other sites. See also the Penn State Lesbian, Gay, and Bisexual Student Alliance page at http://www.smeal.psu.edu/pride/lgbsa/.

Purdue's LesBiGay Home Page

http://expert.cc.purdue.edu/~triangle/

Meeting schedules and upcoming campus events for Purdue University's gay, lesbian, and bisexual support organizations.

PlanetOut–Youth: Colleges

http://www.planetout.com/pno/netqueery/browse.html?subj/youth

There are many more college gay organizations than appear in these Yellow Pages. For a fairly comprehensive list of them, check out this site.

University of Texas at Austin Lesbian Bisexual Gay Student Association

http://www.utexas.edu/students/lbgsa/

Information about campus gay organizations, meeting times/places, and Austin, Texas area gay-friendly businesses and clubs.

University of California Lesbian Gay Bisexual Association

http://www.infoqueer.org/queer/orgs/uclgba/uclgba.html

UCLGBA is composed of representatives and organizations from each of the University of California's nine campuses. UCLGBA works on issues that affect l/g/b people throughout the UC system, such as domestic partnership benefits and system-wide recognition of l/g/b concerns. This site contains meeting information and minutes, information about each campus's organizations, and a WAIS information server of l/g/b information.

Related Sites

- http://www.amherst.edu/~lbga
- http://mariner.rutgers.edu/biglaru/
- http://www.duke.edu/lgb/
- http://www.columbia.edu/cu/gables/
- http://www.gwu.edu/~lgba/
- http://stuact.tamu.edu/stuorgs/glba/
- http://www.indiana.edu/~glbserv/
- http://bsuvc.bsu.edu/~d000lbgsa/index.html
- http://www.uic.edu/orgs/lgbt/
- http://www.nwu.edu/gluu/
- http://www.yahoo.com/Society_and_Culture/Cultures_and_Groups/Lesbians__Gays__and_Bisexuals/Education/Organizations/College_and_University/

CRISIS INTERVENTION AND COUNSELING

Community United Against Violence

http://www.xq.com/cuav/

Community United Against Violence (CUAV) is a nonprofit agency which addresses and prevents hate violence directed at lesbians, gay men, bisexuals, and transgender persons. CUAV also provides services to gay men who are battered by their partners. CUAV offers crisis intervention, short term counseling, advocacy with the criminal justice system, support groups, and a 24-hour crisis line.

The Gay and Lesbian National Hotline

http://www.glnh.org/

A non-profit, tax-exempt organization dedicated to meeting the needs of the gay and lesbian community by offering free and totally anonymous information, referrals, and peer-counseling. They offer a toll-free phone number that anyone can call for gay/lesbian support and information (1-888-THE-GLNH), and you can also submit email from their Web site and get a confidential reply.

WOMAN Inc. Lesbian Domestic Violence Project

http://www.best.com/~dvp/womaninc/

A San Francisco-based organization that combats violence against women, focusing on the lesbian community. They have a 24-hour hotline and offer legal assistance and counseling.

Youth Assistance Organization (aka Youth Action Online)

http://www.youth.org/

Youth Assistance Organization is a service run by volunteers, created to help self-identifying gay, lesbian, bisexual, and questioning youth. YAO exists to provide young people with a safe space online to be themselves. Their pages contain links to useful sites and a FAQ devoted to questions like "I think I may be gay; what do I do?"

Related Sites

- http://www.valinet.com/~lifecour/
- http://www.neosoft.com/~mcc/

GAYS AND LESBIANS OF COLOR

The Blacklist

http://www.udel.edu/nero/lists/blacklist.html

A resource site for the writings of gay, lesbian, bisexual, and transgendered people of African descent. It contains an excellent bibliography of writings, in many cases with Web links.

The Black Stripe

http://qrd.tcp.com/qrd/www/culture/black/blackstripe.html

Articles, booklists, and discussion for gays, lesbians, bisexuals, and transgendered people of African descent.

GLBPOC (Gay/Lesbian/Bisexual People of Color)

GLBPOC is a LISTSERV that discusses issues of interest to gay/lesbian/bisexual people of African descent. To subscribe to GLBPOC, send mail to: `majordomo@abacus.oxy.edu`. In the mail message, enter ONLY the words: `subscribe glbpoc`.

National Black Gay and Lesbian Leadership Forum

http://www.nblglf.org/

The current issue of this organization's newsletter is available online, as well as a few back issues. There is also information about their national conference.

Sistanet

http://persephone.hampshire.edu/~sistah/

A site for African-American lesbians, bi and transgendered women. There is also an associated LISTERV; to subscribe, send e-mail to `majordomo@igc.org` with the subject bio and the first line of the message body: `subscribe sistanet <your e-mail address>`. Then add a brief bio, which will be posted on the list.

Related Sites

http://www.blk.com/

http://www.blsg.com/astrolinks.htm

http://www.catchsplace.com/

http://www.brotha.com/

http://www.wam.umd.edu/~street/1BH.html

GENERAL INFORMATION AND LINKS

Answers to Your Questions About Sexual Orientation and Homosexuality

http://www.apa.org/pubinfo/orient.html

This site for the American Psychological Association provides just plain answers to the most common questions about sexual orientation. Text format, very readable, fact-based and backed up with hard clinical research—but not overly medical in tone.

The Bisexual Resources List

http://www.qrd.org/qrd/www/orgs/brc/brl-toc.html

A great list of links to other sites of interest to bisexuals.

CyberQueer Lounge

http://www.cyberzine.org/html/GLAIDS/glaidshomepage.html

An attractive frame-based site, nicely organized with an alphabetical list. Offers all the standard g/l/b information including classifieds, resource lists, and a very fun "Showcase" feature—just click the button to be whisked off to some randomly selected g/l/b site.

Gay and Lesbian Signs and Symbols

http://www.ncf.carleton.ca:12345/freeport/sigs/life/gay/symbols/menu

From the Lambda to the Rainbow Flag and pink triangle, everything you wanted to know about gay/lesbian culture symbolism. No fancy graphics, but a wealth of information.

Gay Links Navigation Page

http://www.io.com/~eighner/linkgay.html

A Texas-based personal page with a variety of links broken down into well-organized categories, including gay college and university sites and links to the gay leather community.

The Lesbian History Project

http://www-lib.usc.edu/~retter/main.html

Site dedicated to record, archive, and publicize works on lesbian history in any geographic area or time period, with an emphasis on lesbians of color in general and southern California in particular.

PlanetOut

http://www.planetout.com/

Definitely one of the cooler queer sites, especially for the 20-something set. The home page features exploits and the latest graphics of people that actually jump and dance around if your browser supports that sort of thing. The content is cool too; you can shop, read the latest news, check out other gay/lesbian links—the works.

Queer Resources Directory (QRD)

http://www.qrd.org/qrd/

Widely thought to be the biggest and best gay and lesbian information source on the Internet. The Queer Resources Directory breaks down all kinds of resource information into easy-to-understand categories; you can surf the categories, or jump directly to the Resource Tree (http://www.qrd.org/qrd/www/tree.html) for a more graphical, easy-to-browse look at the site.

QWorld

http://www.qworld.org/

All the standard fare you would expect from a site (news, politics, opinions, etc.), plus a few interesting extras, such as downloadable queer-themed sound files and icons and live chatrooms.

Rainbow Query

http://www.glweb.com/RainbowQuery/

The largest and most comprehensive gay-only index of the Web. Search in one of 12 categories or by using keywords. Very easy to use!

Related Sites
http://members.aol.com/detroit209/index.html
telnet://bbs.eyecon.com
http://www.geocities.com/~risqilly/

HIV/AIDS TREATMENT AND PREVENTION

alt.sex.safe

alt.sex.safe (Newsgroup)

A newsgroup devoted to discussions about promoting and practicing safe sex.

Emotional Support Guide

http://asa.ugl.lib.umich.edu/chdocs/support/emotion.html

Although this site has a general focus on all illnesses, not just HIV/AIDS, it provides a wealth of information for patients and caregivers facing chronic illness and death.

Gay Men's Health Crisis

http://www.gmhc.org/

Gay Men's Health Crisis (GMHC), founded by volunteers in 1981, is the nation's oldest and largest not-for-profit AIDS organization. GMHC offers hands-on support services to more than 9,500 men, women and children with AIDS and their families in New York City annually, as well as education and advocacy for hundreds of thousands nationwide.

The Safer Sex Page

http://www.safersex.org/

Safe sex information for everyone (gay/lesbian/bi/het), with an excellent selection of text articles on subjects ranging from condoms to counselor information. This site is one of the original plaintiffs in ACLU v. Reno, the challenge to the Communications Decency Act.

Virtual AIDS Quilt

http://www.mcpsys.com/quilt/

Like the original AIDS Quilt, but in cyber form. You can read panels posted by friends and relatives of AIDS victims, or design and post your own tribute to a lost friend or loved one.

Related Sites
http://204.179.124.69/network/index.html
http://theory.doc.ic.ac.uk/~kcl/bash.html
http://www.cdc.gov/nchstp/hiv_aids/dhap.htm
http://www-hsl.mcmaster.ca/tomflem/top.html
http://www.cybersurf.co.uk/takecare/

HOME AND FAMILY

Equal Marriage Rights Home Page

http://www.ucc.gu.uwa.edu.au/~rod/gay/marriage.html

Articles and other news about recent court cases that may be clearing the way for the eventual recognition of same-sex marriages, plus lots of links. Includes news items broken down by state.

Gay and Lesbian Support Groups

http://www.inet.net/adopt/supgrp1.html

A text page containing contact information for a variety of organizations that support gay and lesbian families and partnerships.

Lesbian Mothers Support Society

http://www.lesbian.org/lesbian-moms/index.html

Lesbian Mothers Support Society (LMSS) is a Canadian non-profit group that provides peer support for lesbian parents (biological and nonbiological) and their children, as well as those lesbians considering parenthood. Great links to reference articles of interest to lesbian parents.

Parents and Friends of Gays and Lesbians (PFLAG)

http://www.pflag.org/

PFLAG promotes the health and well-being of gay, lesbian and bisexual persons, their families and friends through support, education, and advocacy. They provide counseling to help straight family and friends accept and support their gay and lesbian loved ones, and organize grassroots efforts to end discriminatory practices toward gays and lesbians.

Partners Task Force for Gay and Lesbian Couples

http://www.buddybuddy.com/toc.html

Information and resources for gay and lesbian couples seeking ways to ensure their rights as a family. Includes discussion of marriage laws, surveys, legal information, and political news.

Related Sites

http://javanet.com/~famphoto/

http://www.studio8prod.com/familyq/

http://www.freedomtomarry.org/

MEDIA AND CULTURE

Dykes to Watch Out For

http://www.visi.com/~oprairie/bechdel/bechdel.html

This Open Prairie Syndicate page contains some sample cartoons from this very funny syndicated lesbian comic strip.

Dyke TV

http://www.dyketv.org/index.html

A weekly show produced by lesbians for lesbians, the show mixes news, commentary, and the arts. Lesbian film-makers all around the country are encouraged to help create the public access show's segments.

Famous Queers, Queens, and Dykes

http://www.efn.org/~mastrait/famousqueers.html

A fascinating and impressive list of famous people who were definitely or rumored to be gay or lesbian, along with links in many cases to more information about their lives.

The Gay and Lesbian Association of Choruses

http://www.galachoruses.org/

This umbrella organization unites and supports gay and lesbian choral groups all over the United States. They hold a yearly choral festival, which you can read about, as well as their other activities, on this page.

Gay and Lesbian Bands of America

http://agora.rdrop.com/~joe/lgba.html

Lesbian and Gay Bands Of America (L.G.B.A.) is the national musical organization comprised of concert and marching bands from cities across America. Find out here about the 22 member bands and their parade and concert appearances.

The Gaylaxians

http://gaylaxians.org/

The Gaylaxians Science Fiction Society is a non-profit organization for gay, lesbian, bisexual people and their friends interested in science fiction, fantasy, and horror. The Gaylaxians is the Boston, Massachusetts affiliate of The Gaylactic Network, There are chapters in various cities throughout North America. You can get a master list of all the regional clubs at this site, as well as a list of upcoming science fiction conventions.

Gay/Lesbian/Bisexual Television Characters

http://home.cc.umanitoba.ca/%7Ewyatt/tv-characters.html

This amazingly comprehensive list catalogs gay, lesbian, and bisexual television characters on 23 networks worldwide, from 1961 to the present.

Hothead Paisan

http://www.marystreet.com/hh/

The home page for an outrageous lesbian cartoon strip that plays out the notion: 'what if a radical lesbian feminist suddenly went crazy and said and did everything she wanted to?' A must-read for any lesbian fed-up with the patriarchy.

International Association of Gay Square Dance Clubs

http://www.glyphic.com/iagsdc/

The IAGSDC is the International Association of Gay Square Dance Clubs, a lesbian and gay organization that is the umbrella organization for gay square dance clubs in the United States, Canada, and Australia, formed by and for lesbians and gay men in their community and for their friends.

International Gay Rodeo Association

http://www.igra.com/

There is actually a gay rodeo association, and they hold their own rodeos all over the country, including not only gay meccas like Los Angeles and Washington D.C. but smaller cities like Billings, Montana, and Omaha, Nebraska. Get their full touring schedule here, and find out how to become a member.

The Isle of Lesbos

http://www.sappho.com/

Well-designed pages of poetry, art, and links to other lesbian-related sites. Coverage of Sapphic poetry is extensive.

The LGBQ Vegetarian Page

http://www.alumni.caltech.edu/~brett/qveg.html

Articles and links devoted to vegetarian issues, provided for a gay, lesbian, and bisexual readership. Includes lists of famous queer vegetarians, events, and media clippings.

Sisters on Stage

http://www.qworld.org/DykesWorld/sweetmusic.html

A lot of links and interesting information about self-identified lesbian or bisexual musicians and performers.

Women in the Arts

http://www.a1.com/wia/

WIA is the organization that produces the National Women's Music Festival, the oldest and largest all-indoor festival of women's music and culture (primarily lesbian), each June. Find out what they have in store for this year's festival, and learn more about this non-profit organization.

POLITICAL AND LEGAL

alt.politics.homosexuality

alt.politics.homosexuality

A newsgroup devoted to discussions of the current political issues affecting gay and lesbian people.

American Civil Liberties Union—Gay and lesbian Issues

http://www.aclu.org/issues/gay/hmgl.html

A whole branch of the ACLU is devoted to gay and lesbian rights, and their section of the ACLU Web site provides updates on recent court rulings and bills coming up in Congress. You'll also find information about joining the ACLU here.

Digital Queers

http://www.dq.org/

The Digital Queers (DQ) are gay and lesbian computer professionals and hobbyists who raise money for hardware and software for gay, lesbian, bisexual, and transgender community organizations. DQ is also a forum for a social and professional network for gays and lesbians in the computer industry.

Gay and Lesbian Alliance Against Defamation (GLAAD)

http://www.glaad.org/

GLAAD bills itself as "Your online resource for promoting fair, accurate, and inclusive representation as a means of challenging discrimination based on sexual orientation or identity." If you or a gay or lesbian person you know has been the victim of discrimination or abuse, this is the group to contact to find out what you can do.

The Gay & Lesbian National Hotline

http://www.glnh.org/

A nonprofit organization that provides a vital service to the gay community by providing nationwide toll-free peer counseling, information, and referrals. Offers links, a business referral database, and the opportunity to join the hotline.

Gay Workplace Issues

http://www.nyu.edu/pages/sls/gaywork/

Find out which corporations have gay-friendly policies, and learn how to fight on-the-job discrimination, at this informative site.

Grassroots Queers

http://critpath.org/~tracy/gq/queers.html

Dedicated to fighting hatred and bigotry and promoting equal rights for queers through networking, organizing, and direct action.

Human Rights Campaign

http://www.hrcusa.org

The Human Rights Campaign is the U.S.A.'s largest lesbian and gay political organization. They work to end discrimination, secure equal rights, and protect the health and safety of all Americans. This good-looking site contains a lot of political news for anyone interested in gay and lesbian issues.

National Gay and Lesbian Task Force (NGLTF)

http://www.ngltf.org/

NGLTF is a leading progressive civil rights organization that, since its inception in 1973, has been at the forefront of every major initiative for lesbian, gay, bisexual, and transgender rights. They're at work at national, state, and local levels, combating anti-gay violence, battling Radical Right anti-gay legislative and ballot measures, advocating an end to job discrimination, working to repeal sodomy laws, demanding an effective governmental response to HIV, reform of the health care system, and much more.

PUBLICATIONS

The Advocate

http://www.advocate.com/html/home/home.html

One of the oldest and most respected gay magazines. You can browse article summaries for the current issue (but you have to buy the print edition for the full text) and participate in the Advocate's latest poll.

Anything That Moves

http://www.anythingthatmoves.com/

A publication for bisexuals, including comics, fiction, poetry, articles, and more.

Girlfriends Magazine

http://www.gfriends.com/

The online edition of the very popular Girlfriends print magazine, featuring articles, horoscopes, and a monthly advice column by the ever-controversial Pat Califia.

Lavender Magazine Online

http://www.lavendermagazine.com/

A very cool and slick online magazine for the Twin Cities gay/lesbian/bisexual/trans community. Nice graphics and plenty of articles.

POZ Magazine

http://poz.com

This magazine is for HIV-positive people and seems targeted primarily toward gay men. It's a very slick, graphical site that contains the full contents of the current newsstand issue, including most graphics.

Sapphic Ink: A Lesbian Literary Journal

http://www.lesbian.org/sapphic-ink/

Fiction, poetry, and book reviews by, for, and about lesbians. Published quarterly.

Visibilities

http://www.qworld.org/Visi/visib_home.html

A totally online lesbian publication, Visibilities offers all the standard magazine fare: articles, columns, cartoons, book reviews, etc. It replaces the print version of the magazine, which was published from 1987 to 1991.

Whosoever

http://www.whosoever.org/

A great magazine for gay/les/bi/trans Christians, including theological articles, inspiration, and political action alerts. Recommended!

RELIGION

Affirmation: Gay and Lesbian Mormons

http://www.teleport.com/~affadmin/

With chapters around the world, Affirmation serves the needs of gays, lesbians, bisexual LDS and their supportive family and friends through social and educational activities. This site includes news, events, and support resources.

AXIOS: Eastern and Orthodox Gay and Lesbian Christians

http://qrd.tcp.com/qrd/www/orgs/axios/

A page with many links to information about AXIOS and the Orthodox church in general, including information about same-sex unions in history.

Dignity

http://www.dignityusa.org/

Dignity is an international organization for gay, lesbian, and bisexual Roman Catholics. There are chapters in most major cities. Visit their Web site or join their LISTSERV by sending email to `listserv@american.edu` with one line in the body of the email reading: `subscribe dignity (Full Name)`.

Ontario Consultants on Religious Tolerance

http://www.religioustolerance.org/ocrt_hp.htm

A very interesting site that compares and explains the varying levels of tolerance and acceptance for gays and lesbians in almost every religion you have ever heard of (and some that you probably haven't).

The Evangelical Anglican Church in America

http://www.dircon.co.uk/aglo/evangeli.htm

This branch of the Anglican Church is committed to inclusivity, including gay and lesbian believers. Their page includes information about the church's beliefs and links to other supportive groups.

Rainbow Wind: Lesbigay Pagans

http://users.aol.com/RainboWind/rbwintr.htm

Support information for gay and lesbian pagans of all denominations. Includes information about Rainbow Wind Magazine and links to other queer pagan sites.

Seventh Day Adventist Kinship International

http://www.sdakinship.org/

Seventh-day Adventist Kinship International, Inc. is a support group which ministers to the spiritual, emotional, social, and physical well-being of Seventh-day Adventist lesbians, gay men, bisexuals, and their families and friends. SDA Kinship facilitates and promotes the understanding and affirmation of homosexual and bisexual Adventists among themselves and within the Seventh-day Adventist community through education, advocacy, and reconciliation.

Unitarian Universalist Association

http://www.uua.org/

The Unitarian Universalist Church is a "big tent" group that welcomes a wide variety of believers, including gay and lesbian people of all beliefs. Find out more about their organization at this page.

United Church of Christ

http://www.ucc.org/

A lot of general information about the United Church of Christ here, including their organization, beliefs, and member churches.

Universal Fellowship of Metropolitan Community Churches

http://www.ufmcc.com/

MCC is a church fellowship designed specifically to minister to the spiritual needs of gay and lesbian people. This page directs you to their ministries all over the world.

Related Sites

http://www.nyu.edu/pages/sls/jewish/gjonline.html

http://www.geocities.com/WestHollywood/Heights/8977/

http://www.princeton.edu/~meneghin/oasis/oasis.html

http://student.uq.edu.au/~re116274/faeries.htm

A B C D E F G H I J K L M N O P Q R S T U V W X Y Z

SEXUALITY

BadPuppy Online Services

http://www.badpuppy.com/

A nicely run sexually-oriented service for gay men with some cute cartoon graphics. You have to download their software and buy a subscription to take advantage of some areas.

CMU Gender and Sexuality Links

http://eng.hss.cmu.edu/gender/

A page of links to articles and sites relating to gender and sexuality, especially gay and lesbian. Some links are to other sites; others to the text of scholarly articles. A good resource for research.

Gay Male S/M Activists

http://www.ability.net/gmsma/

GMSMA is the world's largest organization of men seriously interested in safe, sane, consensual S/M. Their site includes many articles, an event calendar, and more.

Glossary of Sexual Terms

http://eng.hss.cmu.edu/gender/sex-glossary.txt

This text-only page provides definitions of sexual terms and sexual slang. You may never speak a sentence with a straight face again after you've read all the sexual meanings of words you thought were perfectly ordinary!

Leather Links

http://www.io.com/~eighner/leather.html

A short but helpful list of leather groups on the Internet, mostly focused on the gay leather community.

Related Sites

http://www.gl.email.net/

http://www.gaymensmall.com/megalink.html

http://www.gaypersonals.com/

http://bestmatch.com/lesbianmatch/

http://www.maleness.com/

http://www.creative.net/~jetlag/sexguide/

http://www.shadesbeyondgray.com/

http://www.wpkn.org/wpkn/amazon/index.html

http://www.i2k.com/~verbeek/books/gaysuper.html

SHOPPING

A Different Light Bookstore

http://www.adlbooks.com/

Browse and order gay and lesbian books and videos from this large, friendly store. A Different Light also has retail outlets in San Francisco and West Hollywood.

A Gay Place in Cyberspace©

http://www.maui.net/~randm/gp.html

A lesbian and gay shopping mall, resource guide, and a lot of fun all packaged in one. You can enter shops, resorts and B&Bs, and hear a little gay gossip.

GayWeb

http://www.gayweb.com/menu.html

A guide to gay and lesbian businesses that operate on the Web. This colorful and attractive site points your way to dozens of businesses eager to sell you everything from cologne to real estate.

Ladyslipper Music

http://www.ladyslipper.org/

A record store (mail order and online) that sells only music by women artists, with a large selection of lesbian music. You can listen to cuts from many albums online, right from your browser!

The Rainbow Mall

http://www.rainbow-mall.com/index.html

A collection of links to gay-friendly and gay-owned businesses that will help you spend your money while keeping it "all in the family." Includes merchants, travel agents, realtors, long-distance companies, support agencies, wineries, and more.

Wolfe Video

http://www.wolfevideo.com/

This site sells gay and lesbian videotapes. Their annotated listing of films is impressive, and the monthly film reviews posted by users are entertaining.

Related Sites

http://www.beproud.com/

http://www.gaymall.com/index.html

http://www.gaymart.com/

TRANSGENDER

BoyChicks Home Page

http://www.e-zines.com/boychicks/

A good assortment of links to resources and sites for butch and transgendered women and FTM men.

The ClubKid Page

http://www.cris.com/~Kalina/Vamp/ClubKid.html

Transgendered page with host/hostess Kalina Isato. Plenty of links to interesting sites for cross-dressers, entertaining info on some of Kalina's own adventures, and, of course, great makeover and dressing advice from an expert.

FTM International

http://www.ftm-intl.org/index.html

A peer support group for female-to-male transvestites and transsexuals. They offer information and networking for women who are exploring their gender identity issues, or who need a safe place to explore their male personae, as well as for men who are in the process of transition, or who have completed the change. They also provide educational services to the general public on transgender issues.

The Gender Home Page

http://www.GenderWeb.org/

A personal page, but a very nice one, including scrolling graphics and a good list of transgender resources and a searchable database.

Intersex Society of North America (ISNA)

http://www.isna.org/

Support and advocacy group for intersexuals, defined here as "individuals born with anatomy or physiology which differs from cultural ideals of male and female." Very heavy on medical terminology; parents who are concerned about dealing with these issues should find this site enlightening but may need a medical dictionary handy.

The National TransGender Guide

http://www.tgguide.com/

Michelle's Mid Day Break is the main feature of this drag-oriented e-zine, put together by a cross-section of folks from around the country (okay, pun intentional). Chat rooms, plenty of shopping and other resources, personals, anonymous newsletters and mailing lists for subscribing, and, of course, the lovely Michelle, who enjoys "being a girl."

soc.support.transgendered

soc.support.transgendered

A newsgroup. According to their FAQ, "This is a place to discuss issues related to transsexuality, transvestitism, crossdressing, cultural and social problems, support groups and forums, conflicts with sexuality, and just generally coming to terms with one's self and knowing that one is not alone. Sexually explicit material is generally discouraged in this forum as well as transphobic statements. This forum is not a personals column." See also `alt.transgendered`.

TG FAQ

http://ezinfo.ucs.indiana.edu/~mberz/faqs.html

A Web page with links to basic transgender information. Includes the multi-part Transgender Frequently Asked Questions document of the soc.support.transgendered newsgroup, the FAQ for alt.transgendered, and a basic glossary.

Transexual Menace

http://www.apocalypse.org/pub/tsmenace

An international non-violent action group focusing on the issues facing the transgender community. (They also have some cool t-shirts for sale.)

TRAVEL

Damron Lesbian and Gay Travel Guides

http://www.damron.com/

Damron is a gay-owned/operated travel company offering exclusively gay vacation packages as well as "traditional" travel-related services (like airline tickets and hotel/car reservations). They bill themselves as "your one-stop travel consultant for Business and Vacation."

Gaytravel.com

http://www2.gaytravel.com/gaytravel/

A well-stocked directory of online travel resources for gays and lesbians. Includes travel agent and tour operator referrals.

Olivia Travel

http://www.oliviatravel.com/

Olivia Travel hosts cruises and all-inclusive vacations for women only. Get their latest cruise and vacation information here, request a brochure, and (at selected times) enter a sweepstakes to win a free cruise.

Pride Travel InfoNET

http://www.pridetravel.com/indexn.htm

A nice-looking site with lots of links to all kinds of travel experiences, including cruises and all-inclusive vacations, resorts, B&Bs, and more.

Rancho Mirage Travel

http://www.gay-travel.com/

A resource site for the gay and lesbian traveler. Information is available on cruises, foreign and domestic travel and tours, airfares, hotels, car rentals, and more.

Related Sites

http://www.abovebeyondtours.com/

http://www.alysonadventures.com/

http://www.tiac.net/vacation/gay_travel/

http://www.arrowweb.com/DestinQ/

http://www.gayholidays.com/

http://www.safari.net/~journeys/

http://www.q-net.com/qnet.htm

http://www.venture-out.com/home.html

http://www4.gaytraveling.com/gaytraveling/index.html

http://www.geocities.com/WestHollywood/6271/

http://home.cc.umanitoba.ca/~wyatt/tv-characters.html

http://mason.gmu.edu/~barmitag/dcavengers.htm

http://www.nyu.edu/pages/sls/gaywork/gaywkpl.html

http://abacus.oxy.edu/~ron/queerlaw.html

http://www.tyger.co.uk/sig/index.html

http://www.turnleft.com/out/

http://www.zzapp.org/awes/egcm/

http://www.genremagazine.com/

http://www.hglc.org/hglc/review.htm

http://www.hotspotsmagazine.com/

http://www.lesbiannews.com/

http://planetq.com/

http://www.pinkzone.com/

http://www.qmall.com/

http://www.wereeverywhere.com/

http://www.zebraz.com/

http://www.wavefront.com/~raphael/raq/raq.html

http://www.lumina.net/OLD/gfp/

http://www.3dcom.com/tg/gic/index.html

http://www.tgni.com/resource/resource.htm

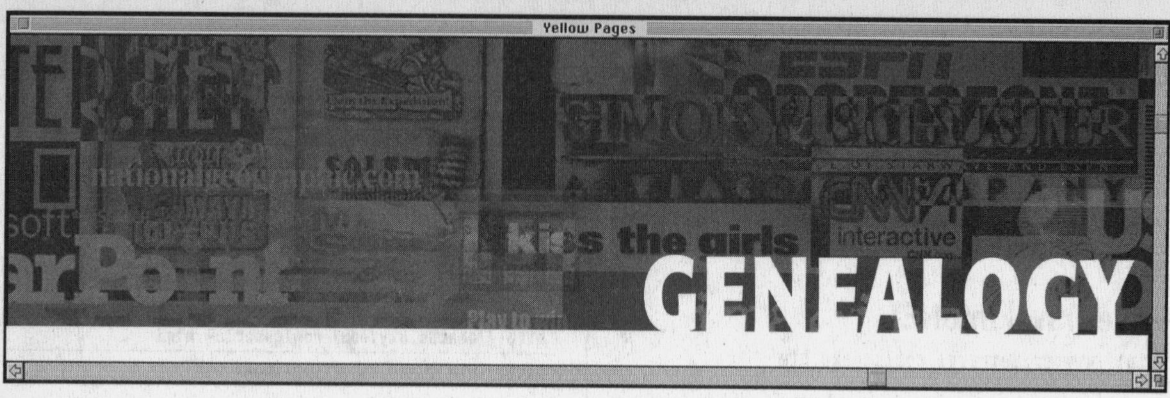

GENEALOGY

> What family doesn't have its ups and downs?
>
> *Queen Eleanor of Aquitaine in* The Lion in Winter *(1968)*

American Heritage Genealogy

http://www.a-h-i-inc.com/

This site offers census records on CD and genealogy software. Order the CDs online.

Celtic Family Roots

http://www.itw.ie/roots/

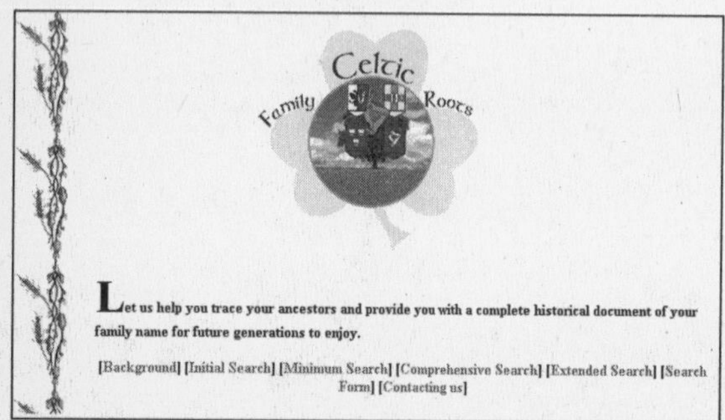

Celtic
Family Roots
Let us help you trace your ancestors and provide you with a complete historical document of your family name for future generations to enjoy.
[Background] [Initial Search] [Minimum Search] [Comprehensive Search] [Extended Search] [Search Form] [Contacting us]

This Irish genealogy site will trace your ancestry and family name, and compile a family tree for generations to come.

Cool Site of the Month for Genealogists

http://www.cogensoc.org/cgs/cgs-cool.htm

The Colorado Genealogy Society sponsors this site, which provides links to sites that meet the following criteria: They are not widely known to genealogists working on the Web, they provide an example of good genealogical work, or they contain valuable information for genealogists.

Celtic Family Roots
http://www.itw.ie/roots/

Find a Friend

http://www.findafriend.com/find_a_friend/index2.htm

Looking for that long lost family member? This site will help you find them. You can search by name, and if you have a birthdate, last known address, and specific location, that will narrow the search.

The Genealogy Home Page

http://www.genhomepage.com/

This extensive set of pages offers information about maps and geography, communication with other genealogists, a compendium of genealogy databases, a list of other genealogy home pages, and other genealogy resources, both in North America and around the world.

Genealogy Resources on the Internet

http://www-personal.umich.edu/~cgaunt/gen_int1.html

Chris Gaunt and John Fuller, creators of this site, offer a comprehensive list of genealogy information accessible through mailing lists, newsgroups, Telnet, email, FTP, Gopher, and World Wide Web sites.

Genealogy Resources on the Internet

http://pmgmac.micro.umn.edu/genealogy.html

Paula M. Goblirsch offers another comprehensive list of Internet resources devoted to genealogical research, plus a collection of German surnames that she is researching.

Roots Surname List Name Finder

http://searches.rootsweb.com/cgi-bin/Genea/rsl

This forms-based site contains over 92,000 surnames contributed by over 6,000 genealogists. It enables you to type in any surname and, if a match is found, it will display the surname along with a list of people researching that name.

Scotgen

http://www.scotgen.com/

Search for your Scottish ancestors at this site, which uses a Scottish-based researcher. Receive a full printed report and receive a family tree.

Genealogy Online!

Did you know that a growing sector of Internet users are aspiring genealogists? With connections to databases and family histories online, it is becoming easier and easier to do part of your genealogy searching online. If you are new to it, there are sites that explain the basics of getting started. Other sites provide specific data, including the U.S. Bureau of the Census (http://www.census.gov). If you want information on a certain surname, you can look at a directory, such as the International Telephone Directories on the Web (http://www.contractjobs.com/tel/). Whether you are just beginning your genealogy research or you want additional information, you are almost guaranteed to find something on the Web that can help you.

Treasure Maps: The "How-To" Genealogy Site

http://www.firstct.com/fv/tmaps.html

Offering a wealth of information about researching family history, this site offers tips for newcomers to genealogy and what to do if you "hit a wall" in your research.

Related Sites

http://www.rootscomputing.com/

http://www.ctssar.org/index.html

http://www.geo.ed.ac.uk/home/scotland/genealogy.html

http://www.ancestry.com/

http://www.open.gov.uk/gros/groshome.htm

http://www.spcc.com/ihsw/lhsresor.htm#GENEALOGY

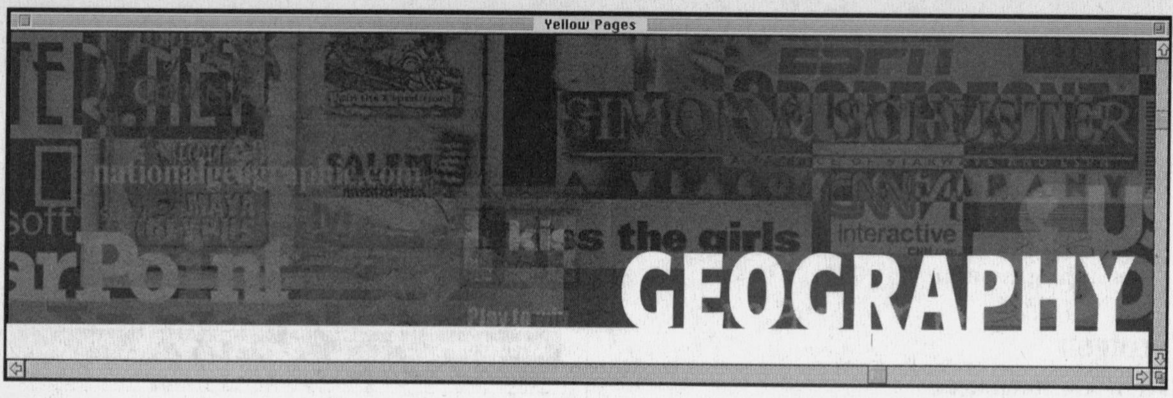

> What a long, strange trip it's been.
>
> *Grateful Dead*

NRP Top Picks

Color Landform Atlas of the United States
`http://fermi.jhuapl.edu/states/states.html`

Internet Resources for Geographers
`http://www.utexas.edu/depts/grg/virtdept/resources/contents.htm`

Chesapeake Bay Program

`http://www.epa.gov/r3chespk`

Page contains information on the health and history of the waterway. Features trends in pollution and restoration projects of Chesapeake Bay that are underway. Also contains links to scientific data and research about the bay and other bay resources.

Color Landform Atlas of the United States

`http://fermi.jhuapl.edu/states/states.html`

Color Landform Atlas of the United States

AK Alaska	MA Massachusetts	OR Oregon
AL Alabama	MD Maryland	PA Pennsylvania
AR Arkansas	ME Maine	RI Rhode Island
AZ Arizona	MI Michigan	SC South Carolina
CA California	MN Minnesota	SD South Dakota
CO Colorado	MO Missouri	TN Tennessee
CT Connecticut	MS Mississippi	TX Texas
DE Delaware	MT Montana	UT Utah
FL Florida	NC North Carolina	VA Virginia
GA Georgia	ND North Dakota	VT Vermont
HI Hawaii	NE Nebraska	WA Washington
IA Iowa	NH New Hampshire	WI Wisconsin
ID Idaho	NJ New Jersey	WV West Virginia
IL Illinois	NM New Mexico	WY Wyoming
IN Indiana	NV Nevada	
KS Kansas	NY New York	U.S. Links
KY Kentucky	OH Ohio	
LA Louisiana	OK Oklahoma	

Site provides beautiful colorform maps of the United States. Topographic maps and a "virtual tourist" of each state can be found, as well as an elevation key.

Geography—A Diverse Discipline

`http://www.umanitoba.ca/faculties/arts/geography/geoginfo.html`

Site is part of the geography department of the University of Manitoba. This page gives a broad overview of the disciplines of geography, as well as an explanation of the different disciplines. A good place to start for the novice interested in geography and its subfields.

Internet Resources for Geographers

`http://www.utexas.edu/depts/grg/virtdept/resources/contents.htm`

Provides WWW resources and information for geographers and laymen alike. Also contains great satellite imagery, mapping information, and other geographically relevant links.

TIGER Mapping Service

`http://tiger.census.gov/`

Allows you to generate a high-quality, detailed map of anywhere in the United States, using public geographic data.

United States Gazetteer

`http://tiger.census.gov/cgi-bin/gazetteer/`

Identifies places you can use the Tiger Map Server and the 1990 Census Lookup to view. Lets you search for a place by entering the name and state abbreviation.

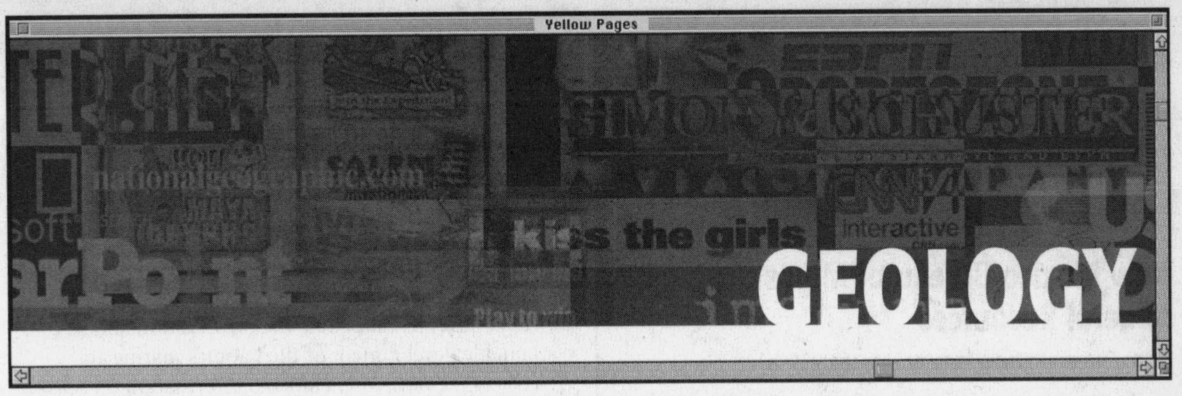

> God hid the fossils in the rocks in order to tempt geologists into infidelity.
>
> *Sir Edmund Gosse*

Centre for Earth and Ocean Research–University of Victoria

http://ceor.seos.uvic.ca/

Focuses on Earth and ocean research.

Civil Engineer's Calendar

http://audrey.fagg.uni-lj.si/ICARIS/dates.ce/

Provides information about upcoming events of interest to civil engineers, in a searchable index or obtainable by email.

IRI/LDEO Climate Data Library

http://rainbow.ldgo.columbia.edu/datacatalog.html

Presents a catalog of climate-related datasets, with an interface that enables you to make plots, tables, and files from any dataset, its subsets, or processed versions thereof.

IRI/LDEO Climate Data Library
http://rainbow.ldgo.columbia.edu/datacatalog.html

Geographic Nameserver
http://www.mit.edu:8001/geo

Smithsonian Gem and Mineral Collection
http://galaxy.einet.net/images/gems/gems-icons.html

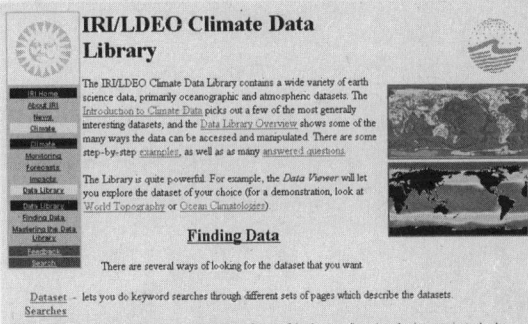

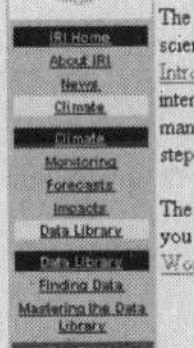
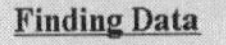

IRI/LDEO Climate Data Library
The IRI/LDEO Climate Data Library contains a wide variety of earth science data, primarily oceanographic and atmospheric datasets. The Introduction to Climate Data picks out a few of the most generally interesting datasets, and the Data Library Overview shows some of the many ways the data can be accessed and manipulated. There are some step-by-step examples, as well as as many answered questions.
The Library is quite powerful. For example, the Data Viewer will let you explore the dataset of your choice (for a demonstration, look at World Topography or Ocean Climatologies).
Finding Data
There are several ways of looking for the dataset that you want.
Dataset Searches - lets you do keyword searches through different sets of pages which describe the datasets.

Data Zoo

http://www-ccs.ucsd.edu/ccs/about_datazoo.html

Contains data collected by various California coastal data collection programs and studies.

Earthquake Info from the U.S.G.S.

http://quake.wr.usgs.gov/

Provides earthquake information. Includes plots, news, regional studies, maps, and references.

Geographic Nameserver

http://www.mit.edu:8001/geo

Provides geographic information about a specific location, including county, state, country, population, area code, latitude, longitude, and elevation.

A B C D E F G H I J K L M N O P Q R S T U V W X Y Z

Nevada Bureau of Mines and Geology

`http://www.nbmg.unr.edu`

Conducts research and publishes results of the studies for the general public, as well as geologic and minerals specialists.

New Mexico Bureau of Mines and Mineral Resources

`http://www.nmt.edu/~nmbmmr/homepage.html`

Provides a database of mineral images from New Mexico as well as a geologic map.

Smithsonian Gem and Mineral Collection

`http://galaxy.einet.net/images/gems/gems-icons.html`

Contains nearly 100 images and short descriptions of gems and minerals.

United States Department of the Interior/Geological Survey/Pacific Marine Geology

`http://walrus.wr.usgs.gov/`

Strives to address key marine and coastal issues, increase understanding of geological processes affecting these realms, and ultimately improve predictive capabilities to help guide the preservation and sustainable development of the nation's marine and coastal regions. Offers links to information on seismic activity, information on the Monterey bay area, and sea floor images. Also features a link to a more graphic-intensive version of the site. Contains many resources.

United States Geological Survey: Earth and Environmental Science

`http://info.er.usgs.gov/network/science/earth/earthquake.html`

Offers links to pages about earthquakes, federal emergency management, oceanography, Earth science, geology, and more.

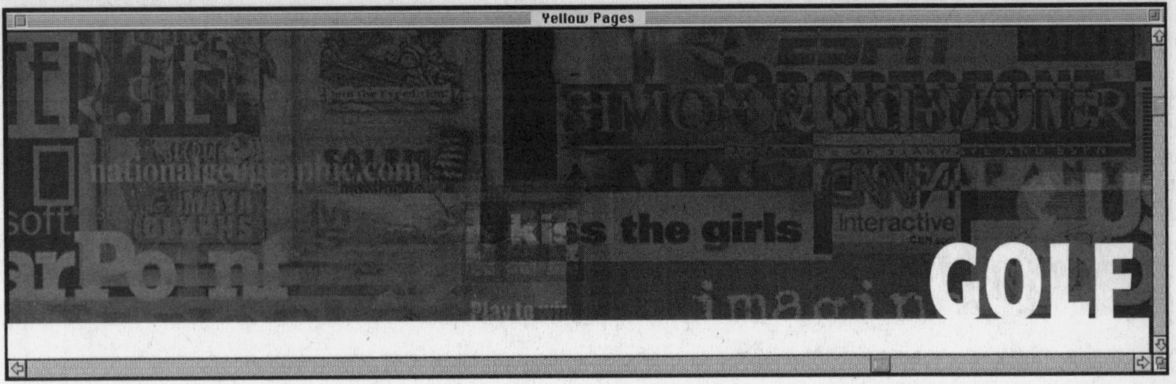

> The place of the father in the modern suburban family is a very small one, particularly if he plays golf.
>
> *Bertrand Russell*

The 19th Hole

http://www.sport.net

Serves as a place where fans and participants of the sport can gather, share a few stories, and settle a bet or two. Provides Daily Golf News, an Almanac, and an Art section. Also includes classified ads.

The Golf Circuit

http://www.sdgolf.com/

Thorough site that offers golf products for sale and provides the PGA schedule. Features many golf related topics and provides tips on everything from putting to the psychology of golf. Also contains an Internet golf directory that lists schools, golf product manufacturers and other related sites.

Golf Magazine

http://www.golfonline.com/

An online version of the current issue of Golf Magazine, you can also link to updates about past and future tournaments. A unique feature provided is a link to the current day in golf history. Information about Golf Magazine subscriptions is also available.

The Golf Circuit
http://www.sdgolf.com/

Golf Web
http://www.golfweb.com/

Golf Web

http://www.golfweb.com/

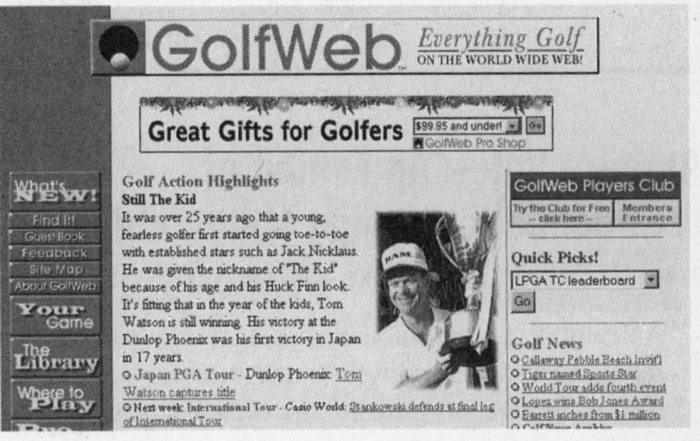

Here you can access the regular golf stuff: tournament results, online pro shops, an so on. But you can also link to the Lesson Tee for golfing tips, go to a link for Women in Golf as well as write a personal message to the winner of a current tournament.

Princeton Golf Archives

http://dunkin.princeton.edu/golf

Offers an education in designing a golf club and calculating slope and handicaps. Provides information about GolfData Online—a bulletin board that offers a database of 14,000 golf courses, tips from Jeff Maggert (PGA professional), discount coupons, and more (including GIF and BMP).

A B C D E F G H I J K L M N O P Q R S T U V W X Y Z

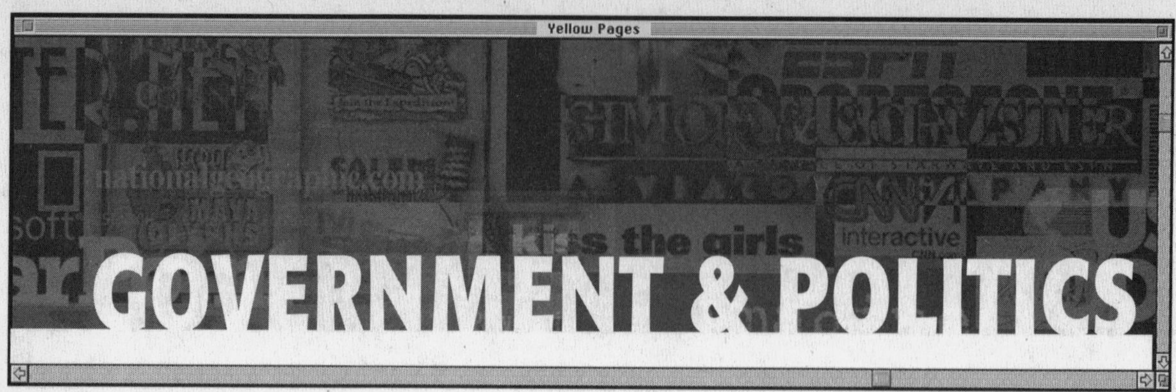

GOVERNMENT & POLITICS

> Politics I supposed to be the second-oldest profession. I have come to realize that it bears a very close resemblance to the first.
>
> *Ronald Reagan*

America Votes: An Exhibit of Presidential Campaign Memorabilia

http://scriptorium.lib.duke.edu/americavotes/

An exhibit of memorabilia from American presidential campaigns, including buttons, bumper stickers, leaflets, letters, sheet music, and even T-shirts.

American Political Items Collectors

http://www.collectors.org/apic/

APIC, non-profit and non-partisan, is the umbrella organization for political item collectors & scholars. Site provides support to those interested in U.S. political campaign memorabilia.

aristotle.org

http://www.aristotle.org

Aristotle is America's leading non-partisan supplier of software and voter list databases to political professionals. Campaign Manager software, a nationwide list of voters and fat cats on CD-ROM are used by candidates and parties seeking to win elections.

National Committee for an Effective Congress
http://www.ncec.org

NJ Capital Report
http://www.cpanj.com/

National Committee for an Effective Congress

http://www.ncec.org

The National Committee for an Effective Congress, a political committee which supports progressive House and Senate candidates with the full range of strategic campaign planning and tactics, now has a site on the World Wide Web. Currently, the site offers: articles from NCEC's Election Update newsletter; A searchable database of candidates, including campaign finance data; Information about NCEC-endorsed candidates.

NJ Capital Report

http://www.cpanj.com/

The Capital Report is a non-partisan monthly political magazine on New Jersey politics. It features sections on Governor Whitman, the Legislative Branch, political campaigns, and more.

Primary Colors

http://www.randomhouse.com/site/election96/primarycolors/

For as long as Random House keeps hyping this book, this site will be pretty cool. It gives background on all the characters and excerpts from the book. You can even find out who Anonymous is.

The Right Company

http://www.bnt.com/jester/rightco/

Did you ever wonder where you could find a Republican mouse pad? Just pull up the Right Company home page for all kinds of right-wing merchandise.

Taking on the Kennedys

http://www.pbs.org/pov/totk

Spinning off a revealing and sobering PBS show about the Congressional campaign run by Patrick Kennedy (Ted Kennedy's son) against a respected local opponent, this site is an innovative resource for the study of electoral campaigns with interactive features for evaluating and thinking critically about campaigns and their impact, a comprehensive set of links to voter resources and information, and a virtual "town hall" section for online discussion.

A B C D E F G H I J K L M N O P Q R S T U V W X Y Z

Yellow Pages

GOVERNMENT AGENCIES & OFFICES

> Sure there are dishonest men in local government. But there are dishonest men in national government too.
>
> *Richard Nixon*

NRP TOP PICKS

Census Bureau
http://www.census.gov/

CIAWEB: Central Intelligence Agency Web Site
http://www.odci.gov/cia

The Library of Congress Home Page
http://lcweb.loc.gov/

U.S. Postal Service
http://www.usps.gov

Board of Governors of the Federal Reserve

http://www.bog.frb.fed.us/

The Federal Reserve Board of Governors is the central government agency, that, along with the twelve regional Federal Reserve Banks, comprises the Federal Reserve System, the central bank of the United States.

BosniaLINK

http://www.dtic.dla.mil/bosnia/

This is the Department of Defense's link to information on the military's operations in the former Yugoslavia. You can access maps, charts, transcripts of operation briefings, and even NATO command email addresses.

Census Bureau

http://www.census.gov/

This has to be one of the most expansive sites in the Net. You can get data maps of every county and major city in the nation. There is so much data available through this site that you just have to go there. If you need population information, they've got it.

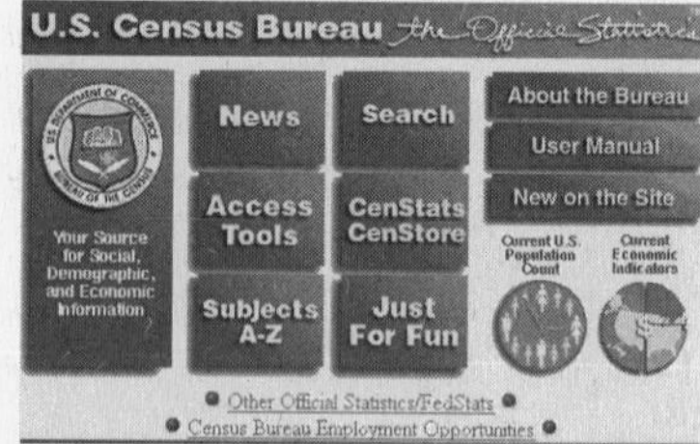

CIAWEB: Central Intelligence Agency Web Site

http://www.odci.gov/cia

For an organization that has an image of being secretive, this is a pretty large information site. You can take a virtual tour of CIA headquarters, order publications, and even send email to the director. But don't expect to find top secret documents.

DefenseLINK

http://www.dtic.mil/defenselink/

This is the Department of Defense's main link to the Office of the Secretary, the Joint Chiefs, the Army, Navy, Marine Corps, Air Force, Coast Guard, Reserves, and the worldwide defense theatres of command. A great starting place for U.S. defense research.

Division of Workforce Development—National Institutes of Health

http://www-urc.od.nih.gov/dwd/dwdhome.html

The Division of Workforce Development at the National Institutes of Health provides performance-based training and development courses and services to NIH and other government agencies.

Federal Election Commission

http://www.fec.gov/

Find out the laws and rules regulating compaign finance and contributions. You can also download the national mail-in voter registration form.

Federal Information Exchange

http://web.fie.com/

The FIE is the interface between the federal government and America's institutions of higher learning. An excellent research platform for linking up with various university computer systems. There's a good link here called MOLIS that links the nation's minority colleges.

The Federal Web Locator

http://www.law.vill.edu/Fed-Agency/fedwebloc.html#doj

Posted by the Villanova Center for Information Law and Policy, this site is a large list of links to federal agencies—especially the Department of Justice. No direct information here, but the links will take you just about anywhere you want to go in the federal government's Web.

FedWorld Information Network

http://www.fedworld.gov/

FedWorld links to every federal government Web site there is. It is pretty easy to get around in and has some of the most valuable links listed on the main page, including listings of all federal job openings and a way to download all tax forms.

The House of Representatives WWW Service

http://www.house.gov

Students needing information on the legislative process for school could not find a better source. All the committees, legislation, and, of course, the congressional members are accessible here. You can search alphabetically by name or by state. However, only postal or "snail-mail" addresses are provided. You can get to the House email gopher, but it looks like an antique.

The Kentucky Long-Term Policy Research Center

http://www.lrc.state.ky.us/ltprc/home.htm

The Kentucky Long-Term Policy Research Center is a unique government agency in the United States. Their mission is to change the way decisions are made in the Commonwealth of Kentucky by bringing a new perspective to policy making.

The Library of Congress Home Page

http://lcweb.loc.gov/

This site has links to all the Congressional sites and other government sites. The National Digital Library, Library Reading Rooms, and access to copyright laws and information make this a pretty useful site allowing researchers to access library services.

Metropolitan St. Louis Sewer District—MSD

http://www.msd.st-louis.mo.us

Regional Governmental Agency providing sewage and storm water service to both St. Louis city and St. Louis county, Missouri.

The National Endowment for the Arts

http://arts.endow.gov/

Listings of upcoming NEA events and the 56 state and jurisdictional arts agencies across the country.

Northern Sierra Air Quality Management District

http://www.nccn.net/~nsaqmd/

Three-county air quality special district government agency. Provides information regarding air quality, fire hazards, and more.

The Office of Management and Budget

http://www.whitehouse.gov/WH/EOP/omb

The OMB is the department of the executive branch that handles budgeting. You can get copies of the Federal Register and the budget reports. If you are looking for a federal job, there's a listing of all the OMB job openings and how to apply.

Pension Benefit Guaranty Corporation

http://www.pbgc.gov

The Pension Benefit Guaranty Corporation, a federal government agency, protects the pensions of nearly 42 million workers in about 55,000 private defined benefit pension plans.

Social Security On Line

http://www.ssa.gov/SSA_Home.html

All SSA questions can be answered here. There is a special feedback section for emailing complaints and problems regarding program benefits. There is a great deal of statistical data available here, and there are explanations of benefits and programs available in Spanish.

Thomas: The U.S. Congress

http://thomas.loc.gov/

Named after Thomas Jefferson, this site allows researchers to analyze legislation in the making and the voting records of those bills. It's a good use of the Library of Congress' resources. Easy to get around in, and you can download the Constitution.

U.S. Department of Justice

http://www.usdoj.gov/

Attorney General Janet Reno's Justice Department is accessible here. View press releases and link up with the Federal Bureau of Investigation, the Drug Enforcement Administration, or any of the other Justice divisions.

U.S. Agency for International Development

http://www.info.usaid.gov

The U.S. Agency for International Development is the independent U.S. government agency which administers foreign assistance and humanitarian aid programs on behalf of the people of the United States.

U.S. Department of Agriculture

http://www.usda.gov/

You might be surprised by some of the offices under the auspices of the USDA, including the Forestry Service and the Department of Natural Resources. The USDA even runs its own graduate school to which you can link.

U.S. Department of Commerce: Stat-USA

http://www.stat-usa.gov/

The D.O.C. calls it "the world's largest source of trade, business, and economic information." It's a great place for research with statistical data on the foreign and domestic economy and a daily economic report. You can also order Commerce publications.

U.S. Department of Education

http://www.ed.gov/

Find out about grants, contracts, and any of the Secretary's initiatives like Goals 2000; School-to-Work; Direct Loans; Safe, Disciplined, and Drug-free Schools; the Individuals with Disabilities Education Act (IDEA).

U.S. Department of Energy

http://www.doe.gov/

The most exciting part of the DOE site is the Electronic Exchange which has lots of software to download and computer hardware designs.

U.S. Department of Health and Human Services

http://www.os.dhhs.gov/

This site has access to information on all HHS programs including the National Institute of Health, the Food and Drug Administration, and the Administration on Aging. One important note: the Social Security Administration became a separate agency on March 31, 1995.

U.S. Department of Housing and Urban Development

http://www.hud.gov/

Community planning agencies can use this site to download information and access fair housing laws. The section called Doing Business with HUD is valuable to those business people seeking an avenue into government contracts.

U.S. Department of Labor

http://www.dol.gov/

The DOL has information here on labor laws and trends. There is information here on grants and government labor contracts and, if you are looking for a job, search America's Job Bank.

U.S. Department of Transportation

http://www.dot.gov/

Check out the latest from the Federal Aviation Administration, the Federal Highway Administration, the Federal Railroad Administration, the National Highway Traffic Safety Administration, and more.

U.S. Patent and Trademark Office

http://www.uspto.gov/

Here's where you can go to order the proper papers and materials to get legal protection for your intellectual property. It's also a good place to search for previously patented devices that may be of use to you or your business.

U.S. Postal Service

http://www.usps.gov

The Postal Service has built a site you can use. Here you can find your ZIP code by street or get tips on how to make business mailings more efficient and effective. Of course, you can also see and order the latest stamps.

The United States Senate WWW Server

http://www.senate.gov/

This is a lot like the House of Representative's server legislatively, but it offers more. The "gallery" link allows surfers to peruse the Senate art gallery and see photos of all the senators. Even more impressive is the virtual tour of the halls of congress.

The White House Home Page

http://www2.whitehouse.gov/WH/Welcome.html

This site takes a while to load if you have a slower modem, but it's worth it. Besides looking great, it's full of resources. It's an excellent historical site and provides access to all the most recent White House press briefings. You can even send email to the President, Vice President, and First Lady. Major go-getters can look into the White House fellowships.

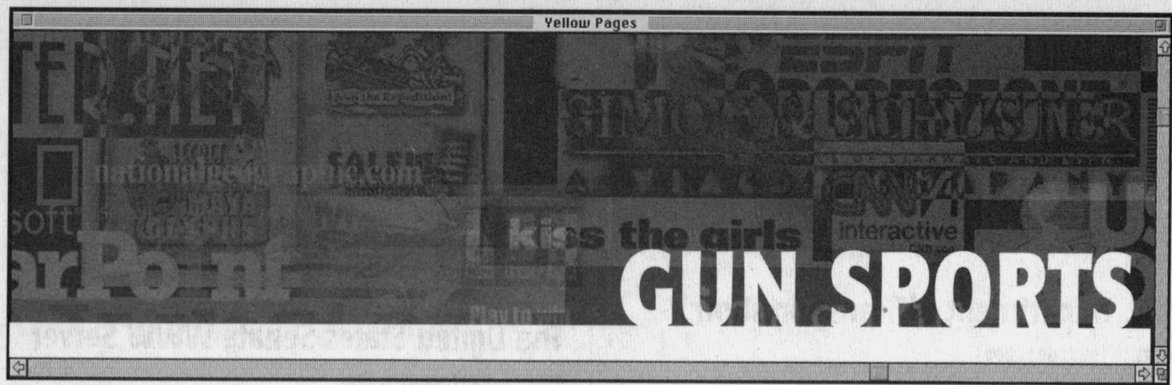

> A gun rack...a gun rack. I don't even own a gun, let alone many guns that would necessitate an entire rack. What am I gonna do...with a gun rack?
>
> *Wayne in* Wayne's World *(1992)*

AWARE: Arming Women Against Rape and Endangerment

`http://www.aware.org/index.html`

Society has never been a completely safe place, but as long as violent crime remains a threat people have the right to protect themselves. AWARE is a non-profit group that organizes courses that women can take to learn self defense, which includes everything from the use of mace to shotguns.

"The Burner" Jerry Barnhart

`http://ic.net/~burner/`

To say this guy is good would be a serious understatement. Mr. Barnhart is a champion shooter of too many competitions to list. You can ask him questions, view his equipment, and read tips about all aspects of target shooting perfection.

Clay Pigeon Shooting Association

`http://www.cpsa.co.uk/`

Become a member of the CPSA, check out scores, news, and links, and learn where the next competitions will be held.

NRP TOP PICKS

Clay Pigeon Shooting Association
`http://www.cpsa.co.uk/`

GunHoo
`http://www.gunsgunsguns.com/gunhoo/`

Doug's Shooting Sports Interest Page

`http://www.users.fast.net/~jasmine/`

Doug provides information about skeet, trap, pin, and more. He also provides links to the NRA, the USA shooting team, and firearm laws, and, to keep things light, there's a Joke of the Week.

Ducks Unlimited, Inc.

`http://www.ducks.org/`

Here is the site for the famous conservation group that works to nurture waterfowl and 900 other species all over North America. It includes info about their many science projects, a FAQ page, and a page to "Stump the Swamp Doctor," as well as links to related TV, radio, and printed page sites.

Fast Draw and the World Fast Draw Competition

`http://www.gunfighter.com/fastdraw/index.html`

What's the world record for drawing, cocking, aiming, and firing a gun *and* hitting a target? You won't believe it! Fast Draw has gained in popularity in recent years, and this site chronicles every aspect of it. It includes official rules and records, as well as lists of upcoming contests.

GunGames

`http://www.gungames.com/`

The current issue of the online version of the magazine includes an article about "shotgun golf," shooting tips, a rifle centerfold, and more. You can share stories and chat with other shooters, and be sure to notice the country singers who grace the cover.

GunHoo

http://www.gunsgunsguns.com/gunhoo/

GunHoo is an all-inclusive search engine for every conceivable topic on guns: accessories, ammunition, the Second Amendment, literature, safety, and more. Just like Yahoo, you can enter key words and conduct Web searches.

Home Appliance Shooting

http://www.csn.net/~dcbenton/has.html

Ever wonder what it would be like to take your old appliances and other household items out to pasture to blow them to pieces with 12-gauge shotguns? Well, this guy did it, again and again and again. He may have some deep, psychological fear of microwave ovens.

The Shooting Sports Website

http://www.shootingsports.com/home.html

This site provides links to every other Web site you can imagine regarding guns, shooting, and its sports. It also has its own articles, including a bunch of recipes for pheasant and partridge.

Shotgun Sports

http://www.shotgunsports.org/

Every aspect of the shooting life is covered here. It provides guides for clay and wing shooting, dog clubs, game bird breeders, gun rights groups and other organizations, shooting news, and more. Enter their talk groups with all your questions and comments.

United States Practical Shooting Association

http://www.uspsa.org/

This is the non-profit group that oversees the sport of "practical shooting," which is basically the shooting of targets that represent what guns of all makes and power will reasonably be expected to strike during their intended use. The site has a huge number of links for USPSA rules, information, classification and much more.

The Unofficial Tommy Gun Page

http://www.cybergate.net/~gjames/tsmghome.htm

Not only will you find links and pages related to collecting "Tommies," you'll also find a detailed history of the gun, which was so ahead of its time, that the Armed Forces didn't start adopting it until 1930, nine years after the first Model 1921 came off the line. The original could fire 1,200 rounds per minute.

Related Sites

http://www.recguns.com/gunPictures.html

http://members.aol.com/longSharps/index.html

http://www.prairienet.org/guns/

http://130.184.141.97/people/rcordell/SWZone.nclk

http://www.shooters.com/gunlinks/

A B C D E F G H I J K L M N O P Q R S T U V W X Y Z

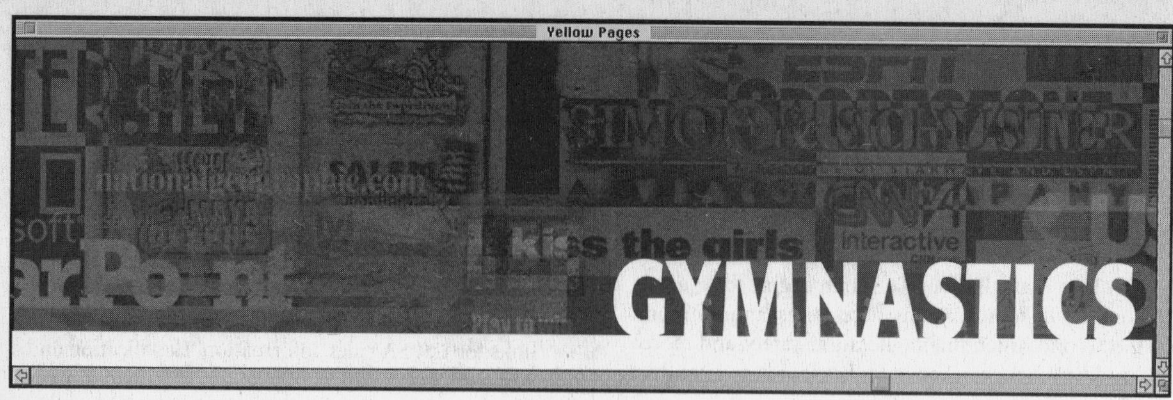

A
B
C
D
E
F
G
H
I
J
K
L
M
N
O
P
Q
R
S
T
U
V
W
X
Y
Z

You were going to be a gymnast.

Harry in When Harry Met Sally... *(1989)*

A Few Good Men

http://www.iloveusa.com/fewgoodmen/

Entertainment and educational information about men's gymnastics in the U.S. Also includes details, staff, dates, cost, and a sign up form for GYMJAM camp for boys and girls ages nine and up.

American Academy of Gymnastics

http://www.aaog.com/

Located in Bakersfield, California, AAG promotes gymnastics as a way to teach kids to have respect for themselves and others, to give them a sense of loyalty, responsibility, self-discipline, and commitment. A healthy approach in a sport that has often been criticized for pushing young people too far for success.

Artistic Gymnastics

http://easyweb.easynet.co.uk/~piggies/artgymru.htm

A photograph site featuring Russian, Romanian, and American gymnasts in various poses.

Body Expressions Dancewear, Inc.

http://www.paglinx.com/bdxdwr/

Owned by a mother and daughter team, this shop offers an online catalog of gymnastics and dance apparel and accessories by well-known makers such as Capezio, Danstar, Bloch, Leo's, and more. Offers coupons and a special savings link too.

American Academy of Gymnastics
http://www.aaog.com/
Rhythmic Sportive Gymnastics
http://www.rsg.net/rsg/

Gymnastics Videos

http://www.videos4you.com/gymnastics2.htm

An archive of instructional and educational gymnastic videos and CD-ROMs. Click the catalog icon, select the sports category, and then scroll through the alphabetical listing of videos and CD-ROMs to find what you want.

International Gymnastics

http://www.intlgymnast.com/

This site offers several options, but the most original is the "Ask Bart & Nadia" feature. Gymnasts can email questions to international champions Bart Conner and Nadia Comaneci, who then answer selected questions about every two weeks.

NCAA Gymnastics

http://www.usatoday.com/sports/other/socg.htm

USA Today's gymnastics site with current news stories related to the world of gymnastics. Also features links to NCAA men's and women's championship results.

Rhythmic Sportive Gymnastics

http://www.rsg.net/rsg/

This site features news, chat rooms, competitions, events, and photos related to the sport of rhythmic gymnastics. A link connects you to individual gymnasts' pages with stats, coach and contact info, bios, and photos.

Summer Gymnastics Camp Directory

http://www.ascx.com/gcd.htm

An alphabetical listing of camps in the U.S. Also has a supplies directory and a link to Magic Melodies Studios for gymnastics music.

The Gymnastics Home Page

http://tghp.simplenet.com/index.html

Features a survey for visitors to answer a question relating to recent gymnastics issues. This site's links to news, scores, profiles, events, and live chat rooms are probably the best.

USA Gymnastics Online

http://www.usa-gymnastics.org/

The official Web site of USA Gymnastics, a non-profit organization that sets the rules and policies of gymnastics in the U.S. Information here includes athlete profiles and news, tips, features, history of gymnastics, and scoring explanations.

Women's Gymnastics

http://www.welwyngymbook.com/

This site is based on the book *Women's Gymnastics A History* by Monot Simmons, II. It is first in a series of four books. Volume 1 covers gymnastics from 1966 to 1974.

Related Sites

http://members.tripod.com/~Domino213/

http://www.gymcan.org/pasthigh.html

http://www.olympic.nbc.com/

http://www.olympic.org/acog/newtop/d-newtop.html

http://www.leggs.com/olympics/gym/armchair.html

http://www.suite101.com/topics/page.cfm/410

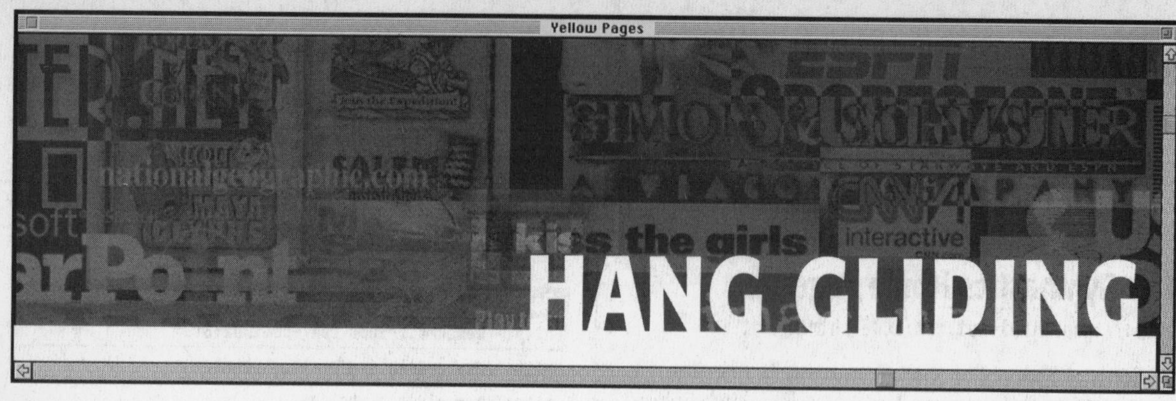

> # Oh Zephyr Winds which blow on high, lift me now so I can fly!
>
> *Isis in Isis (1975)*

Adventure Productions

`http://www.adventurep.com/`

Does your school or club need videos of hang gliding or paragliding to help raise revenues or membership? This may just be the place for you. Based in Reno, NV, Adventure Productions offers a variety of stock visuals as well as custom filming, production, and animation services.

AviationNet Aviation Web Directory

`http://aeps.com/aeps/awhang.html`

An extensive listing of links to sites all over the world related to anything in the air. The hang gliding/paragliding index provides dozens of listings for these specific air sports, but you can also check out listings for airshows and events, jets for sale, helicopters, and more at the main site at `http://aeps.com/aeps/avnetwd.html`.

FLISS (Paragliding and Hang-gliding)

`http://lappc-th4.in2p3.fr/fliss/`

Cross-country distance listings, plenty of background info and interesting articles, links to related sites. Check out the weather section for aviation forecasts and some terrific Webcams of flying regions!

Sky Adventures: Directory of Hang Gliding and Paragliding
`http://www.sky-adventures.com/hang/HGMPSHomePage.html`

NRP TOP PICK

Free Flight Glossary

`http://lapphp0.in2p3.fr/~orloff/FF/dic/`

Sky sports are about as international as possible, which can lead to interesting language problems—and the terminology of the sports is constantly changing. Check out this searchable site for a list of common terminology, searchable in English, German, Italian, French, or Spanish. The site creators are asking for contributions; can you help to expand the glossary?

Free Flying in Europe

`http://lapphp0.in2p3.fr/~orloff/FF/Welcome.html`

An eclectic collection of information for and by gliding enthusiasts. Some threads of online chat between pilots on various topics, a list of books about flying, links to meteorological sites, other sites related to hang gliding, and more. If you're a flying novice, read the FAQ for answers to a lot of the basic questions you'll undoubtedly have.

The Hang Glider/Paraglider Marketplace

`http://www.pacificnet.net/~kites/ads/hang.ads.html`

Sponsored by Ventura County Hang Gliding of Ventura county, CA, this site provides free listings for anyone wanting to sell or buy equipment. One very nice feature of this listing service is the equipment database, which lists manufacturer, model/size, USHGA rating, and comments that may be particularly useful for people unfamiliar with the various brands and models.

Hang Gliding Digest

http://itdcomm.com/hgdigest/

Hang gliding may be quiet in the air, but it's noisy on the net! This searchable digest of online conversations tracks discussions on issues of all kinds—even seemingly unrelated topics like spell checkers—some of it argumentative, but all of it interesting. Also includes links to hang gliding clubs and schools.

Hang Gliding WWW Server

http://www.web-search.com/hang.html

Plenty of browseable photos, movies (in QuickTime and MPEG format), and even a collection of hilarious hang-gliding-related comics. Links to pilot home pages, bulletin boards, and a new pilot chat page (requires Java), state-sorted list of schools and clubs. Many other useful links.

Hellenic Hang Gliding Federation

http://www.forthnet.gr/hhgf/

Interested in gliding from the mountains and isles of Greece? Events, calendar of game listings, and so on are in Greek, but weather information is in English with beautiful satellite images. Other site listings from around the world.

Landings: Hanggliding/Paragliding Links

http://www.landings.com/_landings/pages/hanggliding.html

Links to everything aviation. In the hang gliding/paragliding index, an alphabetical link list of schools, clubs, manufacturers, instructors, associations, repair shops, training camps, and more. For more general aviation topics and news updates, see `http://www1.drive.net/_landings/pages/landings.html`.

New Zealand Hang-Gliding and Paragliding Association

http://www.forthnet.gr/hhgf/

Except for lambing season (August to November), Down Under looks good for flying. Start with this site, which provides details on the rules of flying in the country, along with a nice map of sites on the islands that are appropriate for this sport. Pop in for details on upcoming hang gliding competitions, along with results of completed events.

Sky Adventures: Directory of Hang Gliding and Paragliding

http://www.sky-adventures.com/hang/HGMPSHomePage.html

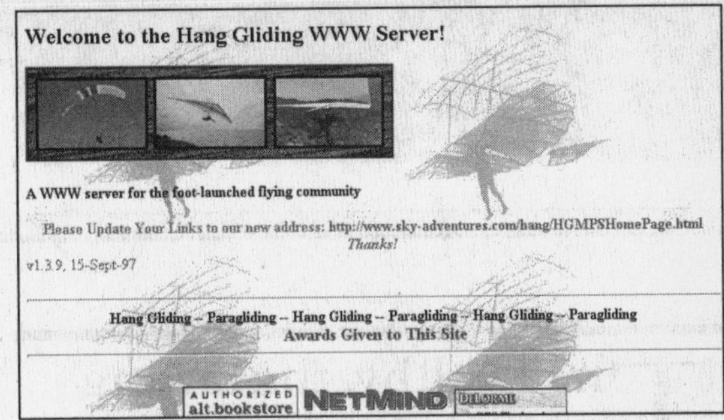

Whether you're an expert flyer, just getting started, or an enthusiast who just likes to observe this graceful sport, this Web site provides plenty of details. Hundreds of links to all sorts of sky-sport sites for hang gliding, paragliding, ultralights. Home page links are divided into U.S. listings and world listings for easy access to your favorite locations. Connect to instructor sites, employment listings, weather sites, tours, classifieds, legal issues, and much more.

Skywings on the Web

http://www.bhpa.co.uk/bhpa/

Skywings on the Web is the official Web site of the British Hang Gliding & Paragliding Association. It's a busy site, listing nearly 30,000 hits in the past year. Includes some online articles from recent editions of their publication, *Skywings*. Find BHPA clubs or schools in particular regions by clicking a regional map or searching alphabetically. Links to sites providing details on local weather are also provided.

United States Hang Gliding Association

http://www.ushga.org/

The Association's Web page provides plenty of useful information for the hang gliding professional, including the latest in regulations and details on pilot ratings (how to earn your rating, available endorsements, etc.), as well as info on membership benefits, local USHGA chapters, and upcoming competitions and other events.

Related Sites

- http://www.aerosoft.com.au/hanging.htm
- http://www.birdsinparadise.com/
- http://www.paraglide.co.uk/
- http://www.wpi.edu/~flying/hang.html

A B C D E F G **H** I J K L M N O P Q R S T U V W X Y Z

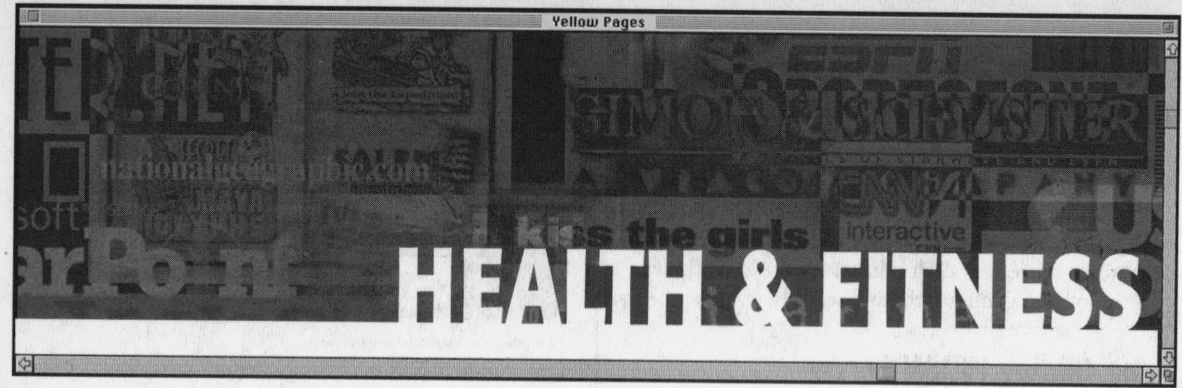

The healthy, the strong individual, is the one who asks for help when he needs it. Whether he has an abscess on his knee or in his soul.

Rona Barrett

COMPANIES

D&M Sales

http://www.srv.net/~dia/vitamins/opening.html

Provides company catalog and ordering information for Vitamin Power products. Includes ordering information and D&M Sales satisfaction guarantees.

Designs for Health

http://branch.com/vitamin/vitamin.html

Provides catalog information about DFH Discount Supplements. Includes a contact email address and phone numbers.

E-Zee Vision Prescription Eyeglasses

http://www.eyeglass.com

Offers prescription eyeglasses, factory-direct. Features high-resolution color images and sound.

NRP TOP PICKS

Disability Net
http://www.disabilitynet.co.uk/

American Heart Association National Center
http://www.amhrt.org/

CDC National AIDS Clearinghouse
http://www.cdcnac.org/

The Blonz Guide to Nutrition, Food Science, and Health
http://www.blonz.com/blonz/index.html

Mirkin Report
http://www.wdn.com/mirkin/

OSHA: Occupational Safety and Health Administration
http://www.osha.gov/

International Traveler's Clinic
http://www.intmed.mcw.edu/ITC/Health.html

Pharmavite Corporation

http://www.vitamin.com/

Offers information on vitamins and nutritional supplements.

DISABILITIES

Ability OnLine Support Network

http://www.ablelink.org/

An electronic bulletin that connects young people with disabilities or chronic illness to disabled and non-disabled peers and mentors.

Access Ability Travel

http://www.disabled-travel.com/

Specializes in vacations that meet the special needs of travelers with disabilities.

Archimedes Project

http://kanpai.stanford.edu/arch/arch.html

Seeks to promote equal access to information for individuals with disabilities by influencing the early design stages of tomorrow's computer-based technology.

Blind Childrens Center, Inc. Home Page

http://www.primenet.com/bcc/

Nonprofit organization. Provides resources and assistance to visually impaired children and their families. Offers information on an educational preschool program, family services, the current newsletter, and a calendar of upcoming events. Also lists links to other related sites.

Deaf World Web

http://deafworldweb.org/dww/

Lists some information in German and French, as well as English, and is fairly international in scope. Provides information on deaf studies, deaf culture, useful services, and more.

Disability Net

http://www.disabilitynet.co.uk/

A non-political service for people with disabilities run *by* people with disabilities.

Mankato State University Department of Communication Disorders

http://www.mankato.msus.edu/dept/comdis/kuster2/welcome.html

Covers topics including child language disorders, dysphagia, fluency disorders, stuttering, and hearing disabilities.

National Sports Center for the Disabled

http://www.nscd.org/nscd/

Discusses its role as the largest and most successful outdoor recreation program for those with disabilities. Includes both winter and summer activities.

DISEASES & CONDITIONS

AIDS Education and Research Trust

http://www.avert.org/

Provides timely information for all ages, including what AIDS is, what causes it, and how one might become infected.

Alzheimer Disease Web Site

http://med-www.bu.edu/Alzheimer/home.html

Serves as a reference site for clinicians, investigators, and caregivers interested in Alzheimer's disease and other related dementias.

American Diabetes Association

http://www.diabetes.org/

Take a simple test and determine your risk for diabetes. Then find the diabetes center that is closest to you. Learn about living with diabetes and what you can do to help out the association and those who suffer from diabetes.

American Heart Association National Center

http://www.amhrt.org/

The American association that fights heart disease and stroke. They maintain an extensive heart and stroke guide that contains over 300 articles from the association on various subjects such as aspirin, cigarette smoking, and exercise.

American Lyme Disease Foundation

http://www.w2.com/docs2/d5/lyme.html

Information about Lyme Disease, including how to spot early symptoms and general precautions for avoiding ticks, thus avoiding the disease altogether.

A B C D E F G H I J K L M N O P Q R S T U V W X Y Z

Arthritis—Doctor's Guide to the Internet

http://www.pslgroup.com/ARTHRITIS.HTM

Medical news and alerts about arthritis. Includes an overview of arthritis and a study of rheumatoid arthritis. Provides links to discussion groups and newsgroups and other sites that have arthritis-related information.

Bad Breath Research

http://www.tau.ac.il/~melros/Welcome.html

Interesting reading on the subject of halitosis. The questions and answers, articles, and online publications should be of interest to anyone who suffers from oral malodor or has a spouse that does.

Breast Cancer Information

http://nysernet.org/bcic/

Many things women should know about breast cancer, including how to detect breast cancer, toll-free numbers for information hotlines, questions and answers about cancer, and much more.

Cardiovascular Institute of the South

http://www.cardio.com/

Center for the advanced diagnosis and treatment of heart and circulatory disease. Offers a wide range of reports covering the full spectrum of prevention, diagnosis, and non-surgical and surgical treatment of circulatory problems.

Caring for People With Huntington's Disease

http://www.kumc.edu/hospital/huntingtons/

Although not intended to be an authoritative work, this page provides valuable information about Huntington's disease. The helpful tips at this page include communication strategies, help for eating and swallowing, and more. Also provides links to other HD sources.

CDC National AIDS Clearinghouse

http://www.cdcnac.org/

A searchable database of AIDS/HIV information, including information from the XI International Conference on AIDS and the Presidential Advisory Council on HIV/AIDS Progress Report. Also includes a gallery of AIDS-awareness posters.

Down Syndrome WWW Page

http://www.nas.com/downsyn/

Information on Down Syndrome, including articles, health care guidelines, a worldwide list of organizations, and education resources. The site also features a "brag book" containing photos of a number of children with the syndrome.

Endometriosis

http://www.ivf.com/endohtml.html

A variety of information on the puzzling disease. The site includes a lengthy FAQ, case studies, and a number of articles on the subject. A photo gallery is also included.

Eye Diseases and Conditions

http://www.eyenet.org/public/faqs/faqs.html

The American Academy of Ophthalmology has developed a collection of FAQs answering questions about a variety of eye diseases. Here you can find information about cataracts, glaucoma, amblyopia, and more.

Gastroenterology Consultants

http://www.gastro.com/

Drs. Peter Gardner and Stuart Waldstreicher provide an informational page about gastroenterology and liver disease, as well as their own practice treating such disorders. Links are provided to descriptions of symptoms, videos of intestinal surgery, facts and stats on digestive disease, and more patient information.

HYPHECAN Fingertip Cap

http://www.eskimo.com/~vanming/hpc_intro.html

A doctor-developed fingertip cap for fingertip injuries. Recommended by medical professionals. Links to usage information, free samples, and business opportunities for distributions.

Introduction to Skin Cancer

http://www.maui.net/~southsky/introto.html

Intended as a general introduction to skin cancer, this page provides basic information such as determining what causes skin cancer, what it is, what your personal risks are, and how to reduce those risks.

Jeffrey Modell Foundation

`http://www.mssm.edu/peds/modell/home-pag.html`

Dedicated to Primary Immune Deficiency, an inherited defect in the immune system.

Medicine OnLine

`http://meds.com`

Serves as a commercial online medical information service. Provides health care professionals and consumers a convenient place to obtain medical information. Serves as a gateway to access other health information services on the Internet. Currently focuses on cancer information.

The Merck Manual

`http://www.merck.com/!!rGBNN2da4rGBNN2da4/pubs/mmanual/html/sectoc.htm`

A definitive source of information about disease. Topics covered range from infectious diseases to nutritional and metabolic disorders to neurologic and psychiatric disorders. The manual has an extensive list of tables and figures and is very technical in nature.

Muscular Dystrophy Association

`http://www.mdausa.org/`

Learn all about the MDA and what it does to help combat neuromuscular diseases. Also learn about what you can do to help besides just watching the Jerry Lewis telethon.

National Osteoporosis Foundation

`http://www.nof.org/`

The NOF seeks to reduce the incidences of osteoporosis by making the public more informed about it. Its site provides background information on the disease, information about who's at risk, and prevention and treatment ideas.

NewsFile

`http://www.newsfile.com/1m.htm`

The world's only news weekly dedicated entirely to medical and health news. Headlines and glimpses of the stories are available for free, but to get the full articles, you must subscribe. Sample issues are available.

Parkinson's Web

`http://neuro-chief-e.mgh.harvard.edu/parkinsonsweb/Main/PDmain.html`

Serves as a resource directory, pointing you to sources of information on Parkinson's disease.

Pediatric Rheumatology Home Page

`http://www.wp.com/pedsrheum`

Provides information for children and young adults who have arthritis and other rheumatic diseases of childhood, their families, and the physicians who care for them.

Prostate Cancer InfoLink

`http://www.comed.com/Prostate/`

Includes pages on screening for prostate cancer, understanding diagnosis and treatments, and where to find support groups.

Rehabilitation Learning Center

`http://weber.u.washington.edu/~rlc/`

Seeks to create a computer-based multimedia rehabilitation environment designed to educate and train individuals with acute or chronic spinal cord injuries so they can successfully leave the in-patient rehabilitation environment and function in society. Provides information about their plans and progress.

Roxane Pain Institute

`http://www.Roxane.com`

Offers cancer and AIDS pain management services. Serves as a resource for pain sufferers and clinicians. Offers educational materials, including newsletters, clinical articles, presentation slides on cancer pain management, and a schedule of upcoming pain management seminars.

Scoliosis

`http://www.rad.washington.edu/Books/Approach/Scoliosis.html`

An article on the skeletal disease, written by Dr. Michael L. Richardson, MD. The article shows the various classifications of scoliosis and provides illustrations to further demonstrate the effects of the disease.

The Skin (Diseases) Page

http://www.pinch.com/skin/

The home to archives of various skin disease-related Usenet newsgroups. Also provides descriptions of the various skin diseases and links to other skin-related sites.

Sudden Infant Death Syndrome (SIDS) Information Home Page

http://q.continuum.net/~sidsnet/

Provides information about Sudden Infant Death Syndrome. "This page will grow and evolve as we progress up the learning curve together. Your patience, understanding, and contributions to this page will make it grow into a true network of people and information dedicated to stopping SIDS, the number one killer of infants between the ages of one month and one year." —Chuck Mihalko, President, SIDS Network.

World of Multiple Sclerosis

http://www.ifmss.org.uk/

FAQs, publications, research, products, services, forums, book reviews, a glossary of terms, and other information of interest to anyone involved in any way with multiple sclerosis.

FITNESS

Aerobics!

http://www.turnstep.com

Contains a FAQ sheet, a library of aerobics patterns, and a calendar of fitness events.

The Blonz Guide to Nutrition, Food Science, and Health

http://www.blonz.com/blonz/index.html

Authored by Ed Blonz, Ph.D., this site is designed to help you discern the valuable nutrition sites on the Web from those that are mere cyberjunk. The page provides many links to the sites that are considered the best and is also available in a version that contains frames and Java.

CyberNutrition Online

http://www.dole5aday.com/

An excellent source for kids and parents alike to find out the values of eating fruits and vegetables on a daily basis. Remember, "Five a day is the magic rule—more is OK, less is uncool!"

Dole 5 A Day

http://chd.syr.edu/chd/CyberNutrition2.html

Sponsored by the Syracuse College for Human Development, this page enables you to send in nutritional questions which are answered and then presented in archive form for the benefit of all. Ask about anything from riboflavin deficiencies to the healthful qualities of beer and pizza.

Balance: Fitness on the Net

http://hyperlink.com:80/balance

Online magazine covering sports nutrition and therapy and the International Register of Personal Trainers, as well as general fitness and exercise.

Food & Nutrition Information Center

http://www.nalusda.gov/fnic/

Provides information about healthy eating, dietary guidelines, food labeling, and other nutritional information. Contains links to many "nutritional" sites.

Food Pyramid

http://www.ganesa.com/food/index.html

Getting good nutrition is easy if you follow the food pyramid guide. This page is a graphical representation of the pyramid, with each food group depicted being a link to a short discussion about its nutritional qualities.

Hiking and Walking Home Page

http://www.teleport.com/~walking/hiking.html

Offers hiking and walking resources, organizations, philosophy, and updates on gear.

IFIC Foundation

http://ificinfo.health.org/

The home page of the International Food Information Council. Provides information for health professionals, educators, parents, and consumers. Includes FAQs and other publications.

Krispin Komments

http://www.krispin.com/

Contains two very informative articles, the Potassium Chronicles, and Protein Basics. Includes information on getting enough of each of these in your daily diet, complete with recipes.

Noah's Natural Foods

http://www.interlog.com/~noahs/

The best health supplements, herbs, green foods, high-end vitamins, and beauty-related products at the lowest prices. Browse the catalog, place an order, or link to other health-related sites.

NutriGenie

http://pages.prodigy.com/CA/nutrigenie/

A nutrition software publisher, including titles for weight loss, disease and nutrition, high blood pressure, heart disease, special diets, sports, allergies, and much more. Also includes other health-related sites and information for downloading.

Mirkin Report

http://www.wdn.com/mirkin/

Breakthroughs in health, fitness, nutrition, and sexuality. Includes discussions of scientific discoveries and information about Dr. Mirkin's radio programs and books.

The Nutrition Pages

http://deja-vu.oldiron.cornell.edu/~jabbo/

Contains a "Current Topics" section where articles can be read and submitted, and a "Just the FAQs" section that answers questions about nutrition. Check this page out and find out why a healthful diet is "funkier than chitlins with gravy and grits…".

MSU Athletic Training

http://vax1.mankato.msus.edu/~k061252/MSUATC.html

Provides information for people interested in the athletic training profession. Provides information about Mankato State University and a curriculum program and information concerning it. Also offers a number of other athletic training or related links, such as program information, alumni information, history, an athletic training Listserv discussion directory, and staff.

Professor Geoff Skurray's Food & Nutrition Information

http://www.hawkesbury.uws.edu.au/~geoffs/

A wealth of nutritional information, including information on reducing fat and improving athletic performance through proper nutrition; and dietary guidelines for adults, adolescents, and children.

Peak Performance

http://www.siteworks.co.uk/pperf/conts.htm

A scientific newsletter devoted to improving stamina, strength, and fitness.

GENERAL HEALTH

Good Health Web

http://www.social.com/health/index.html

Provides daily health news (and an archive), a library of health articles, discussions, and lists of FAQs, newsgroups, and mailing lists.

Health Resource

http://www.coolware.com/health/joel/health.html

Provides information about health, stress, sexuality, and many other health problems that people can encounter.

Healthtouch

http://www.healthtouch.com/

Provides updates on health, diseases, wellness and illness, a resource directory guide to organizations and government agencies, access to pharmacies in your community, and a drug search program that enables you to find information about prescription and over-the-counter drugs.

International Health News

http://www.perspective.com/health/index.html

Presents a monthly electronic newsletter and discussion group for people who want to gain a better understanding of news and research on the relationship between health, nutrition, and lifestyle.

Linda Sy Skin Care

http://www.fractals.com/sy/html/sy_intro.html

Skin-care products for sensitive skin, developed by dermatologists. Browse the products and place your order directly from your computer.

MEDMarket Virtual Industrial Park

http://www.frontier.net/MEDMarket/

The medical industry's Internet headquarters. Includes links to featured services, announcements, and MEDMarket tenants.

Minority Health Network

http://www.pitt.edu/~ejb4/min/

Lists minority health resources by minority group, by subject, and by disease. Also includes lists of upcoming events and publications.

World Health Network

http://www.worldhealth.net/

Dedicated to health, vitality, and longevity. Contains information on anti-aging, nutrition and exercise, and traditional and alternative health care.

HEALTH ADMINISTRATION

American College of Healthcare Executives

http://www.ache.org/

A professional membership society for health care executives. Offers publications, policy statements, and educational programs.

Aspen Publishers, Inc.

http://www.aspenpub.com/

Lists products and articles on administration, health care, and law and business.

BONES: The Biomedically Oriented Navigator of Electronic Services

http://bones.med.ohio-state.edu

Provides faculty, staff, and students in the health sciences with a starting point for Internet exploration.

Healthcare Financial Management Association

http://www.hfma.org/

A membership organization for financial management professionals. Provides a common ground for the exchange of ideas related to hospital finance.

Healthcare Information and Management Systems Society

http://www.himss.org/

A not-for-profit organization dedicated to promoting a better understanding of health care information and management systems.

Innervation Technology Corp.

http://www.innervation.com/inner/

Consulting and support services for those in the health care industry. Links to the company overview, products and services available on the Web, and other sites of interest to the medical community.

National Association of Health Authorities and Trusts

http://www.nahat.net/

Brings together NHS health authorities, Scottish health boards, and Northern Ireland health and social services boards to exchange information on support services, conferences, research, and publications.

Society for Medical Decision Making

http://www.nemc.org/SMDM

Focuses on promoting rational and systematic approaches to decisions about health policy and the clinical care of patients. Includes decision analysis, applications of quantitative methods in clinical settings and medical research, studies of human cognition and the psychology of clinical reasoning, medical ethics, medical informatics and decision making, artificial intelligence, evaluation of medical practices, and cost-effectiveness or cost-benefit assessments.

HEALTH CARE

Center for Rural Health and Social Service Developers

http://www.siu.edu/~crhssd/

Seeks to bring together university resources and health care agencies to address health concerns. The center conducts research and training, tests new models of health care delivery, and develops policy recommendations to improve the health of the rural populations.

Chiropractic Page

http://www.mbnet.mb.ca/~jwiens/chiro.html

Primarily serves as a pointer to health-related subjects, focusing on information for chiropractors, students, other health care practitioners, and interested laypersons. Offers many sites and links.

Colorado HealthNet

http://bcn.boulder.co.us/health/chn/index.html

Provides information on chronic illnesses, complementary therapies, health care plans, and information on state and federal agencies.

Internal Capsule

http://www.voicenet.com/1/voicenet/homepages/levinson/index.html

Provides resources and information on physical therapy, including music-related injuries and a PT student page.

Internet Medical Products Guide

http://www.medicom.com

Provides a database of medical product sales and technical information for health care providers.

Marijuana as a Medicine

http://www.calyx.com/~olsen/MEDICAL/medical.html

Continues the controversy of using marijuana to relieve medical ailments.

MDB Information Network

http://www.mdbinfonet.com

Provides objective information for health care decision-makers. Helps health care providers reduce risk, contain costs, and increase efficiencies by providing reliable data, strategic analysis, and counsel. Delivers services through three divisions: MDB Technology Services, MDB Information Services, and MDB Financial Network.

Patti Peeples' Guide to Health Economics, Medical, and Pharmacy Resources on the Net

http://www.exit109.com/~zaweb/pjp/

Lists national and international links to biotech firms, medical libraries, journals, employment opportunities, and health databases.

Physical Therapy WWW Page

http://www.mindspring.com/~wbrock/pt.html

Provides general information about physical therapy. Includes physical therapy today, research, treatment, typical work settings, specialization, and credentials.

SPA in Italy

http://www.travel.it/ter/

Promotes the belief that the hot springs in Italy can bring relief from every type of problem, from allergies to metabolism to stress.

HEALTH INSURANCE

AFLAC

http://www.aflac.com/

Provides guaranteed renewable supplemental health insurance.

Employers Health Insurance

http://www.employershealth.com/

Focuses on helping small businesses provide benefits.

FHP Health Care

http://www.fhp.com

Targets anyone who wants to assess his or her own health or learn more about HMOs.

Inscon: Insurance Consultants, Inc.

http://inscon.com/

Writes and administers insurance programs for colleges nationwide and K–12 institutions in a ten state region.

A B C D E F G H I J K L M N O P Q R S T U V W X Y Z

Insurance for Students, Inc.

http://www.ins-for-students.com/

Includes policies for colleges and universities, international programs, nursery and daycare, athletics, and camps.

Managed Health Care

http://ourworld.compuserve.com/homepages/MANDR/

Home page for a consulting firm that offers assistance in Medicaid consulting, HMO products and mergers, self-insured health plans, and insurance company consulting.

Worldwide Med

http://www.silo.com/services/wwmed/medsrc.htm

Independent insurance brokers offering temporary medical plans.

INSTITUTES

Arkansas Children's Hospital

http://www.ach.uams.edu/

Private, nonprofit institution. Offers children comprehensive medical care from birth to age 21, from every county in Arkansas and from many nearby states, regardless of a family's ability to pay.

Catholic Health Association of Wisconsin

http://www.execpc.com/~chaw

Nonprofit state association that serves more than 100 Catholic health care facilities in Wisconsin. Provides information about the association's purpose, educational programming, newsletters, and ethical information.

Dartmouth's Interactive Media Lab

http://iml.dartmouth.edu/

Part of the Dartmouth Medical School. Specializes in using computers, media, and communications technologies for medical simulations.

International Cancer Alliance

http://www2.ari.net/icare/

ICA is a nonprofit organization ensuring that high-quality, focused, patient-centered cancer information is available to patients and physicians. Includes information on programs and background and a sign-up site for more information.

Missouri Institute of Mental Health

http://www.missouri.edu/~mimhmj

Highlights the research, education, and multimedia efforts with which the Missouri Institute of Mental Health is currently involved.

New England Medical Center

http://www.nemc.org

Provides information about the tradition and history of the prestigious New England Medical Center. Offers comprehensive inpatient and outpatient care for adults and children.

Radiation Effects Research Foundation

http://www.rerf.or.jp/

Dedicated to studying the effects of the atomic bombings of Hiroshima and Nagasaki during World War II.

OSHA: Occupational Safety and Health Administration

http://www.osha.gov/

From the U.S. Department of Labor. Establishes and enforces protective standards and offers technical assistance to protect the American workplace.

MEDICAL HISTORY

Health History Research Center (HHRC)

http://www.med.umich.edu/HCHS/

Contains archival, manuscript, and museum materials; images of documents, photographs, graphic art and artifacts; exhibits and galleries on special topics; educational products; and online assistance.

Scientific and Medicinal Antiques

http://www.duke.edu/~tj/sci.ant.html

Includes information on electrical and magnetic items, calculating, surveying, surgical instruments, bloodletting, pharmaceuticals and medical chests, electrotherapy devices, and more.

TRAVEL RESOURCES

AEE Wilderness Safety and Emergency Care

http://www.princeton.edu/~rcurtis/wildsafe.html

Covers workshops and conferences and lists first-aid resources for planning a wilderness trip.

Executive Registry

http://www.med.cornell.edu/nyhexr/exr5.html

A network of medical centers designed to assist executive travelers. A consulting service and an emergency evacuation service.

Healthy Flying

http://www.maui.net/diana/

Tips for airplane travel. Covers jet lag, fear of flying, airline food, time zones, and blocked ears.

International Traveler's Clinic

http://www.intmed.mcw.edu/ITC/Health.html

Includes tips on traveling while pregnant and packing a travel medicine kit; lists environmental hazards, such as altitude and motion sickness and auto accidents; and gives an overview of different diseases and vaccinations.

Outdoor Action Guide to High Altitude Acclimatization and Illness

http://www.princeton.edu/~rcurtis/altitude.html

Discusses symptoms, what causes high altitude illnesses, and how to prevent them. Also covers the different types of illnesses.

World Wide Drugs

http://community.net/~neils/new.html

Lists medical and pharmaceutical hospitals and sites.

A
B
C
D
E
F
G
H
I
J
K
L
M
N
O
P
Q
R
S
T
U
V
W
X
Y
Z

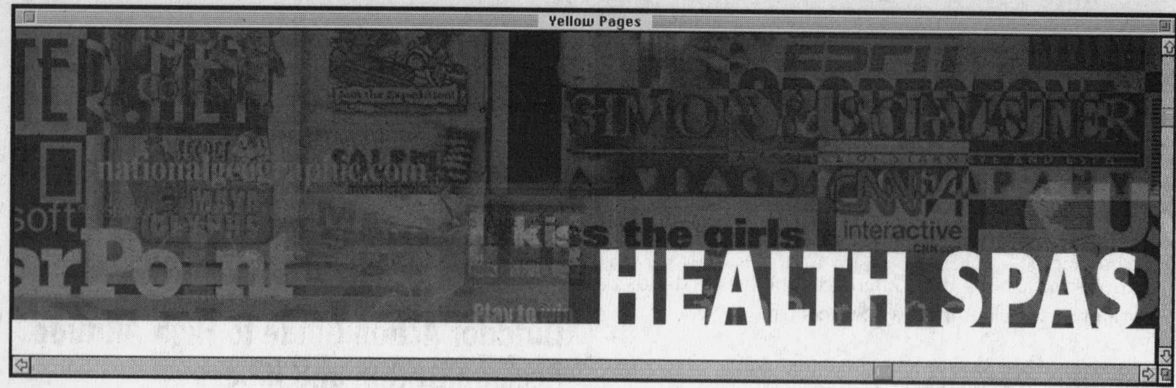

It's a whirlpool bath, Sir. I think you'll enjoy it.

Coleman in Trading Places *(1983)*

Alternative Inns, Resorts, Spas, and Camps Directory

http://www.medmarket.com/tenants/reiddds/herbplus/info/altinns.html

Listed by geographic area, this directory features alternative health inns, resorts, spas, and camps around the world.

Celebrities Health Secrets

http://www.celebhealthsecrets.com/

Find out how you can stay young, beautiful, and healthy the way the stars do. (No this isn't a plastic surgery site!)

Club Spa USA

http://www.clubspausa.com/

This site belongs to the Day Spa Association. Day spas have become increasingly popular in recent years as people look for an affordable way to pamper themselves and unwind.

Eco Travel Nature & Wilderness Retreats

http://naturalregistry.com/ecotravel/retreats.html

A listing of retreats, resorts, and spas specializing in alternative medicine, natural health, lifestyle, ecology trips, and holistic health.

Spa-finders Spa Source
http://www.spafinders.com/

Health Spa Napa Valley

http://www.napavalleyspa.com/

This day spa offers complete fitness and spa services. Make your reservations online.

Hippocrates Health Institute's Life Change Center

http://www.hippocratesinst.com/

Located in Florida, this resort promotes self-improvement and well-being through responsible and conscious living. Teaches clients to follow a natural lifestyle complete with enzyme-rich, living-foods vegetarian cuisine and supports the belief that positive thinking creates immunity to disease.

Jeffrey Joseph Spa of the Year Award

http://worldspas.com/award.htm

Spa Managemenet magazine highlights the spa of the year. Finalists in the seven catagories are also listed in alphabetical order and winners are at the top of each list.

The Natural Resource Directory

http://www.itlnet.com/natural/nrd/sect2c.html

A list of businesses focused on health, bodywork, and fitness. Directory is divided into categories according to specialization.

The Palms at Palm Springs

http://www.keho.com/palms/index.htm

Promoting a stress-free way to lose pounds and inches in the California sun. Voted one of the top 10 spas in the U.S. by *Conde Nast Traveler.* This site also features an online guided tour option.

The QuikPage National Business Website Directory

http://www.quikpage.com/

Click the Beauty, Health, & Fitness icon to search for spas in your area or an area you specify. A good resource to find a place to relax or get in shape.

SPA Natural Health and Beauty Products of Colorado

http://www.spa-products.com/

Natural, cruelty-free, evironmentally friendly beauty products. The site offers online shopping too.

Spa-finders Spa Source

http://www.spafinders.com/

Features a search engine to locate the right spa for you. You can also book your vacation online. Great gift ideas.

Related Sites

http://www.bodymassage.com/

http://www.icanect.net/fitlife/10.htm

http://www.gbdirect.co.uk/leisure/henlow/

http://www.st-martin-st-maarten.com/service/Peters/peterspa.html

http://www.portablespas.com/links.html

http://www.princeville.com/resort/63spa.html

http://www.salzburg.com/SalzburgerLand_e/texte/kur.htm

http://www.spahapuna.com/vitae.html

http://www.citysearch11.com/E/V/RDUNC/0003/04/78/6.html

http://www.2kweb.net/voyageur/AboutVoy.html

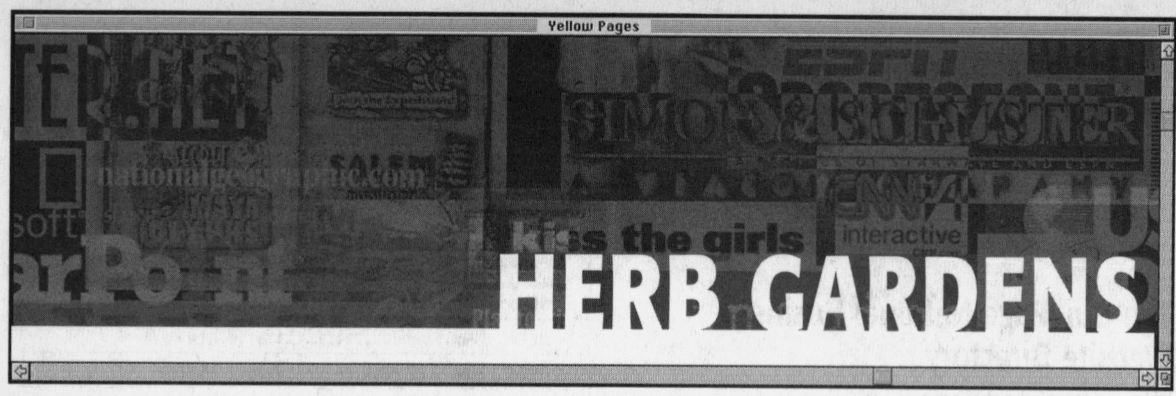

A B C D E F G H I J K L M N O P Q R S T U V W X Y Z

> **W**ho loves a garden loves a greenhouse too.
>
> *William Cowper*

Algy's Herb Page

http://www.algy.com/herb/menu.shtml

Featuring a recipe exchange, tips on growing your own herbs, medicinal herbs, an herb discussion group, and more. This site is an exhaustive source for the herb enthusiast.

Falcon Quest Alpaca & Herbs

http://www.falconquest.com/

This site specializes in ginseng, garlic, and goldenseal. (By the way, alpacas are similar to llamas.)

Golden Cabinet Herbs

http://www.acupuncture.com/GoldCab/GCIndex.htm

A great source for herbal formulas for weight loss, relaxation and stress relief, energy, rejuvenation, and cold prevention. Also lists return to youth and special women's formulas.

Green Leaf Gourmet Gift Baskets

http://www.greenleafgourmet.com/

Specializing in gourmet and herbal gift baskets, this site also has an herbal store. Great gifts for the herbalist in your life.

Algy's Herb Page
http://www.algy.com/herb/menu.shtml

Herbs 'N' More
http://www.cobweb.net/~wfaust/Herbs_N_More.html

Harvest Moon Natural Foods

http://www.harvest-moon.com/mailordr.html

This site features online shopping for vitamins, minerals, herbs, and specialty health items. A 10% discount is offered for orders of more than $100.

Herb Research Foundation: Herbs and Herbal Medicine for Health

http://sunsite.unc.edu/herbs/

This nonprofit foundation studies the use of herbs in health, environmental conservation, and international development. Provides frequently updated links to the latest herb-related news, features, information, and other related sites. You can also join and subscribe to their magazine.

Herbs First

http://www.herbsfirst.com/

This site strives to educate people on the proper use of herbs. Also offers high quality, affordable herbal health food products, books, videos, and tapes.

Related Sites

http://www.gourmetherbs.com/

http://www.ns.sympatico.ca/healthyway/LISTS/B1-C02_res1.html

http://www.herbnet.com/

http://www.sk.sympatico.ca/Contents/Health/HEALTHYWAY/feature_gar3.html

Herbs for Male and Female Systems

http://www.healthfree.com/schulze/herbs/malefema.htm

Herbal recipes for male and female reproductive health. Part of a health and natural healing program.

Herbs 'N' More

http://www.cobweb.net/~wfaust/Herbs_N_More.html

A complete resource on herbs and how they work on the body's systems. Lots of choices and an opportunity to get into specific problems or target areas.

Hilton Herbs

http://www.hiltonherbs.com/

Promotes the use of natural herbal health care for horses and dogs. Includes aromatherapy, homeopathy, and phytotherapy pages as well.

Moonrise Herbs

http://www.botanical.com/moonrise/index.html

This site promotes a complete lifestyle in balance with the cycles of nature. The goal is to use herbs and natural products to aid the healing process. Customer satisfaction is guaranteed.

Myrddin Herbs & Oils

http://www.biolab.co.nz/~alin/

This site encourages a natural approach to relieving stress, energizing the body, and creating a sense of well being by using herbs and essential oils. The aromatherapy rocks!

The Nickel & Thyme Shoppe

http://www.theherbshop.com/

Lots of great stuff here. The site has an online catalog, herb recipes, and an herbal reference guide.

Related Sites
http://www.campus.net/arts/ciao/cherbs.html
http://www.webshed.com/ns/default.htm
http://www.jps.net/keiran/plant.htm
http://www.mostunusual.com/shop/prodpages/herbs.html
http://www.wholeherb.com/

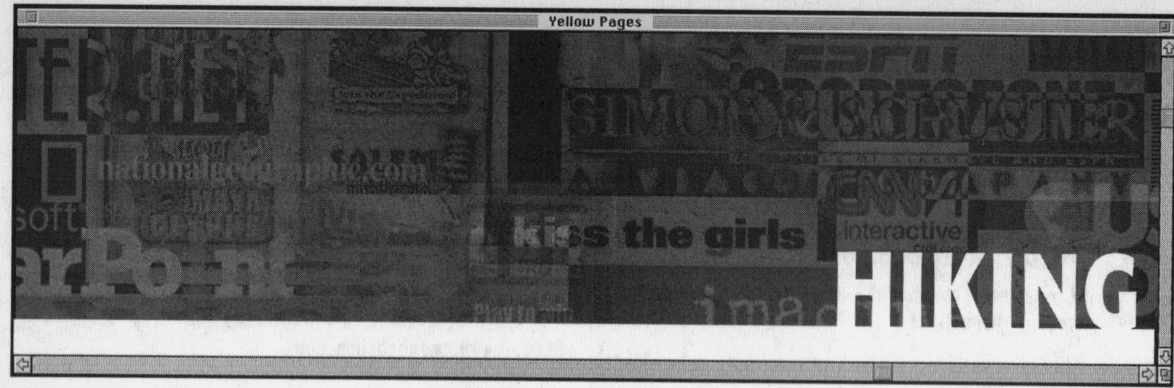

There is a pleasure in the pathless woods; There is a rapture on the lonely shore; There is society, where none intrudes, By the deep sea, and music in its roar: I love not man the less, but Nature more.

Lord Byron

About Hiking

http://www.abouthiking.com/

Online store and informational guide to backpacking and hiking. Read several feature stories, find books and software giving hiking tips and news, or take a virtual hike at this site. Easy to navigate, this site also branches off to other outdoor recreational sports information, such as snowboarding, skiing, and mountain biking.

American Discovery Trail

http://www1.discoverytrail.org/discoverytrail/

Site that offers information and the political history of a coast-to-coast hiking, biking, and equestrian trail that extends from Point Reyes National Seashore in California to Cape Henlopen State Park in Delaware. See state-by-state reports, photos, and current legislation regarding the American Discovery Trail.

Kings Canyon and Sequoia Wilderness Hikes
http://lennon.pub.csufresno.edu/~jwf16/

The Lightweight Backpacker
http://www.isomedia.com/homes/clindsey/

Views from the Top
http://www.lexicomm.com/whites/index.html

Appalachian National Scenic Trail

http://www.nps.gov/aptr/

The Appalachian Trail is 2,158 miles long and transverses 14 states. This is the National Park's Service Web site for the famous Appalachian Trail. The site offers basic information about hiking the trail and gives addresses to write to for more information. Link to information about Shenandoah and Great Smoky Mountains National Park hiking as well.

Chet Fromm's Backpacker Guide

http://www.geocities.com/Yosemite/1140/

Opens with some patriotic music. (You need a special plug-in to view the site in its totality; you can download the plug-in when you load the site.) Chet gives descriptions of his own experiences on the following trails: Appalachian, Florida, Pacific Crest, North Country, and Continental Divide. You get the feeling he knows what he's talking about when he gives the recipe for a brew to soak your feet in. This site links to several other interesting hiking sites.

Hiking and Walking Homepage

http://www.teleport.com/~walking/hiking.html

Site with an exhaustive amount of information about walking and hiking. (Click the Mining Company button to see more links about walking.) Find out what's new all over the world in regards to hiking. Link to everything from Usenet groups to suggested treks and tours. Get tips on where to buy gear and read tutorials on such things as Backpacking 101. This site also offers a chat service.

Hiking in the Carpathian Mountains

http://www.cs.umd.edu/~cpopescu/Carpathians/index.html

Offers beautiful photographs and reports about hiking in the Carpathian Mountain range (the Transylvanian Alps) in Europe and the Ukraine. Get trail tricks and helpful maps here. This site also links to other sites about the Carpathians.

Kings Canyon and Sequoia Wilderness Hikes

http://lennon.pub.csufresno.edu/~jwf16/

Gives reports, tips, and links to hiking in the Sierra Nevada mountains. The author of the site offers trip logs (mileage, number of days a trek takes to hike, and personal experiences on the trail) and photographs. You can also send an electronic postcard from this site; each postcard has a beautiful scenic view from a hiking spot in the mountains.

Newfoundland Backcountry

http://www.stemnet.nf.ca/~cpelley/homepage.htm

Opens with beautiful, full-color photos of the mountains in Newfoundland. You can select from a panel of trails and hiking places to get more information. The link to The Outdoor Experience brings you to an online store, where you can order backpacking gear.

The Lightweight Backpacker

http://www.isomedia.com/homes/clindsey/

Begins by giving you definitions of backpacking weights, and then leads you to the next page, which offers several links to good information about how to pack gear, what to buy, what not to buy, how to pack for a one-day hike as opposed to a three-day hike, and so on. This site links to numerous tips and other URLs; you are likely to find everything you need to know about packing and planning for a hiking trip here.

Sörmlandsleden

http://www.sormlandsleden.se/

Offers German and English translations about the Sörmlandsleden Trail in Sweden. This site gives information about the Stockholm area, the trail, weather, distances, accommodations, and area cottages. Also, view breathtaking photos of the trail.

Wilderness and Wildlands

http://www.nwrain.net/~outdoor/toppage.html

Gives a unique look at our world's wilderness areas. Get information about wilderness and hiking areas. The opening graphic is very clever, too. Link to other hikers' home pages. Also, if you are looking for a companion to hike with, see the Hiker's Companion link, which includes a fairly large list of personal ads.

Views from the Top

http://www.lexicomm.com/whites/index.html

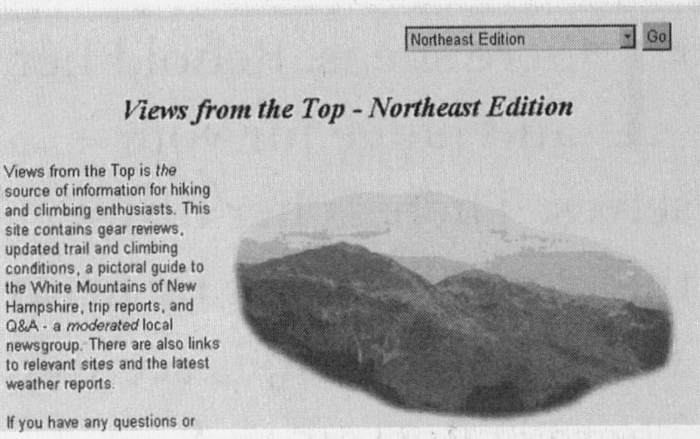

An excellent online guide to hiking. This site gives news and tips about the southeastern and northeastern U.S, and the southern and northern ranges of the Rocky mountains. Very easy to navigate, this site offers a lot of useful information about different geographical hiking places. You can get ice and weather reports, view photo galleries, join a moderated newsgroup, and read about rescue reports.

Yosemite Trails

http://www.geocities.com/Yosemite/Trails/

Select the Hiking or Backpacking menu option when you get to this site. Then, read about the several trails at Yosemite National Park in California. Each link offers information; some links have photos. Follow the link back to the main page to get more Yosemite information, such as photography, mountains, wildlife, and boy/girl scout recreation.

Related Sites
http://www.alaska.net/~paoletti/AGA/AlpineGuides.html
http://www.mortimer.com/brasiltr/
http://www.canyondreams.com/default.htm
http://www.discoveralberta.com/moonshadow/
http://www.members.aol.com/hikernet/index.html
http://www.pathfinderadventures.com/
http://www.bena.com/nepaltrek/profmg/profmg.html
http://www.worldwidequest.com/

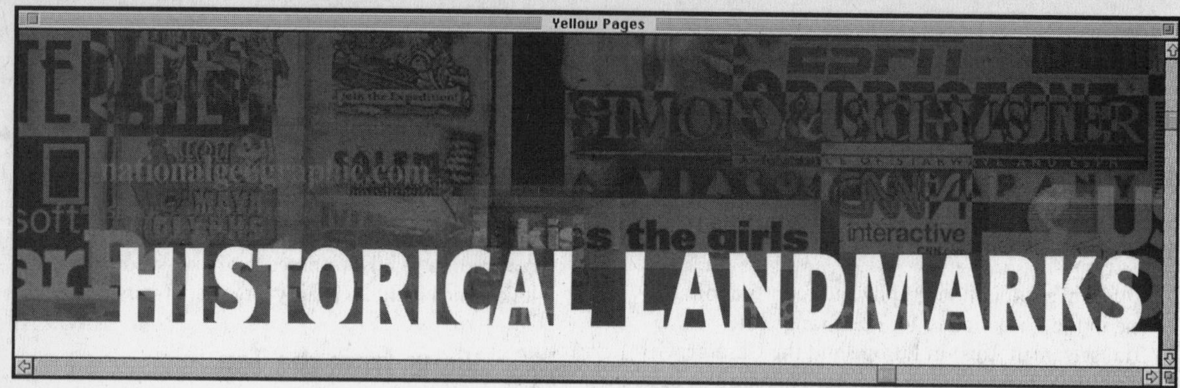

HISTORICAL LANDMARKS

> There she is. Behold her, and judge for yourselves. There is her history; the world knows it by heart. The past, at least, is secure. There is Boston and Concord and Lexington and Bunker Hill; and there they will remain forever.
>
> *Daniel Webster*

California State Historical Landmarks

http://www.donaldlaird.com/landmarks/

This site is named a Recommended Site by the History Channel. Visit over one thousand California historical landmarks. Use the site's search engine to see your favorite historical California landmark. The author has photographed many of them and has been to over 700 of the sites already.

European Walking Tours

http://www.gorp.com/ewt/

Take a walking tour and see historic landmarks in Italy, Austria, Finland, Lapland, Norway, Scotland, England, Switzerland, Canada, Yellowstone, and the Beartooths. Brochures are available upon request.

Guggenheim Museum
http://www.guggenheim.org/srgm.html

Frank Lloyd Wright Building Guide

http://www.geocities.com/CapitolHill/2317/flwbuild.html

This site lists over 120 buildings designed by the great architect Frank Lloyd Wright. The index lists the buildings by region and state. There are links for individual buildings and the most notable buildings.

Frank Lloyd Wright Home & Studio

http://www.oprf.com/flw/H&S.html

Take a tour of Frank Lloyd Wright's home and studio. He and his family lived here from 1898 to 1909. See where the Prairie School of architecture was born. Check out where Wright experimented with designs in his home and studio before he shared them with clients. If you're in the Oak Park, Illinois, area, you can visit the house in person; the site lists the tour hours.

Guggenheim Museum

http://www.guggenheim.org/srgm.html

Read about the museum's history and architecture; its numerous programs including tours; upcoming exhibitions; becoming a member and all the benefits of membership; and the museum store, where you can buy art books, gifts, jewelry, children's books and toys, and signature Guggenheim products.

Henry Ford Estate—Fair Lane

http://www.umd.umich.edu/fairlane/

Visit the estate of automotive pioneer Henry Ford. You can take a virtual tour of the estate and visit the beautiful rooms. If you're in the Dearborn, Michigan, area, you can visit the estate in person; check out the list of tour times. Christmas is a special time at Fair Lane, with things to do for the whole family, including Ginger Bread House making; breakfast with Santa; tea; a sumptuous, traditional Christmas dinner; and a candlelight tour.

Landmark Center

http://www.mtn.org/landmark/LMC2genl.html

Learn about St. Paul, Minnesota's beautiful Landmark Center. Read about its restoration and its wide array of activities for entertainment and culture.

The National Parks Service Links to the Past

http://www.cr.nps.gov/

Learn about the Civil War, visit historical sites, find out about historical lighthouses and preserved vessels, read about the Native American Graves Protection and Repatriation Act, and learn about the National Park Services Tribal Preservation Program. Find out about tax credits and grants related to historic preservation.

National Register Travel Itineraries

http://www.cr.nps.gov/nr/tourism.html

Want to take a historical vacation? The National Register offers about 50 sites you can visit around the country, while soaking up history. Itineraries are listed by region and city. You get maps, photos, descriptions, and addresses.

Oyster Bay Historical Society

http://www.servenet.com/OBHistory/

This Long Island-based site lists plenty of activities for everyone. Read about the museum's hands-on tour for children, where they can visit Oyster Bay in the 18th and 19th centuries and see how early residents lived. They're working on a railroad museum and rail excursions on restored Long Island Rail Road Locomotive #35. If you visit the museum in person, you may see the ghost of Teddy Roosevelt in the library.

Portland Whitehouse

http://www.travelbase.com/destinations/portland/portland-whitehouse/

Visit this beautiful Portland, Oregon, historic house and marvel at its elegance. Stay in any of its several beautifully decorated rooms.

Santa Cruz Beach Boardwalk

http://www.beachboardwalk.com/

Check out upcoming events at the historic beach boardwalk in Santa Cruz, California. They have concerts and a Christmas Craft and Gift Festival. You can read about more fun things to do at California's seaside amusement park.

Susan B. Anthony House Museum and National Landmark

http://www.frontiernet.net/~lhurst/sbahouse/sbahome.htm

Take an online tour of the Susan B. Anthony house. Learn about this great women's suffrage leader and anti-slavery activist. Be a part of history and donate to the capital campaign drive to help preserve and expand the house so that people may visit the site for years to come. Visit other historical links to learn more about famous women in history.

The United States Capitol

http://www.aoc.gov/

Learn the history of the Capitol building's construction, its architects, the architecture of this Washington, D.C., monument, and the artwork inside the Capitol. Visit the U.S. botanic gardens and learn about future Capitol projects. If you plan to visit the Capitol in person, check out the schedule of operation.

The USS Hornet CV-12, CVA-12, CVS-12 Home Page

http://tmx.com/hornet/

Read about the Aircraft Carrier Hornet Foundation's goal of acquiring and restoring the national historic landmark USS Hornet to be used as a U.S. Naval Air and Sea Museum and a technology education center. They also plan to use the USS Hornet as a ceremonial ship. Learn about the history of the Hornet and the aircraft carrier's role in World War II.

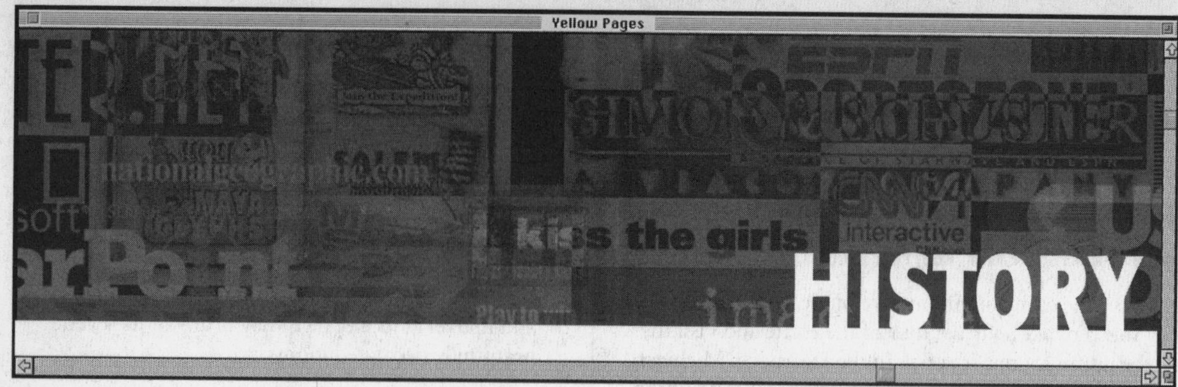

A B C D E F G H I J K L M N O P Q R S T U V W X Y Z

In the tumult of men and events, solitude was my temptation; now it is my friend. What other satisfaction can be sought once you have confronted History?

Charles DeGaulle

Rich in content, this category contains sites about history, including information about American history, ancient history, European history, and more. Learn more about the past that has brought us where we are today.

AMERICAN HISTORY

African American History

http://www.msstate.edu/Archives/History/USA/Afro-Amer/afro.html

A page devoted to the history of African Americans, with text and documents relating to Buffalo soldiers, the history of slavery in the United States, African American scientists, writers, musicians, and much more. Links to related sites.

American Civilization Internet Resources
http://www.georgetown.edu/departments/amer_studies/internet.html

Life Histories–American Memory Project
http://lcweb2.loc.gov/wpaintro/wpahome.html

Diotima: Women & Gender in the Ancient World
http://www.uky.edu/ArtsSciences/Classics/gender.html

The Victorian Web
http://www.stg.brown.edu/projects/hypertext/landow/victorian/victov.html

Ari's Today Page
http://www.uta.fi/~blarku/today.html

The National Inventors Hall of Fame
http://www.invent.org

American and British History Resources

http://info.rutgers.edu/rulib/artshum/amhist.html

Provides a large archive of links to material concerning American and British history. Offers maps, online books and essays by such people as Francis Bacon, Samuel Johnson, John Locke, William Penn, Thomas Paine, Benjamin Franklin, and Thomas Jefferson.

American Civil War Home Page

http://funnelweb.utcc.utk.edu/~hoemann/cwarhp.html

A gateway to numerous Civil War-related sites, including timelines, letters, graphic images, specific battles, and much more. A must for Civil War enthusiasts.

American Civilization Internet Resources

http://www.georgetown.edu/departments/amer_studies/internet.html

An immense compilation of links concerning American studies, from revolutionary war topics to current history.

American History

http://www.academic.marist.edu/history/hisamer.htm

A massive series of links to all major periods of American history, each with additional links. A wonderful starting point for related searches.

American Memory

http://lcweb2.loc.gov/amhome.html

Contains collections of American culture and history, mostly derived from Library of Congress special collections. Photographic panoramas, sound files, movies, photos, and documents can be found in abundance.

Anti-Imperialism in the United States, 1898–1935

http://web.syr.edu/~fjzwick/

Focuses on presenting information and literature about the Anti-Imperialist movement in the United States, including several documents penned by Mark Twain. Focuses on the period 1898–1935 and provides numerous links to texts by people and organizations active at that time in the movement. Provides backgrounds for different pieces.

Indiana Historical Society

http://www.ihs1830.org/ihs.html

Nonprofit membership organization. Collects, preserves, and promotes the history of Indiana. Features information on the Society's collections, exhibitions, publications, and numerous other activities.

Life Histories–American Memory Project

http://lcweb2.loc.gov/wpaintro/wpahome.html

Presents a collection of life histories sponsored by the Manuscript Division of the Library of Congress and written for the United States Works Progress Administration's Federal Writer's Project between 1936 and 1940. Includes 2,900 documents that represent the work of more than 300 writers from 24 states. Enables you to access these documents by various search means, including by region or state.

Oregon–World War II Farming

http://arcweb.sos.state.or.us/osuhomepage.html

Exhibits "Fighters on the Farm Front: Oregon's Emergency Farm Labor Service, 1943–1947," which includes more than 60 images and printed documents.

United States–History

gopher://wiretap.spies.com/11/Gov/US-History

Contains texts of historically significant United States documents, including the Declaration of Independence, Emancipation Proclamation, Monroe Doctrine, W.W.II surrenders of Germany and Japan, Tonkin Gulf Resolution, and more.

ANCIENT HISTORY

ABZU

http://www-oi.uchicago.edu/OI/DEPT/RA/ABZU/ABZU.HTML

Provides information concerning the ancient Near East including information and pictures about specific sites, museum exhibits, journals, and so forth. Provides a number of resources to ancient Egypt and Mesopotamia, including architectural information and texts.

Akkadian Language (Babylonian and Assyrian Cuneiform Texts)

http://www.sron.ruu.nl/~jheise/akkadian/index.html

Contains an introduction to the culture and history of ancient Mesopotamia, including documents in cuneiform and transliterations. Discusses grammar of Akkadian and Semitic languages and contains links to many related sites.

Alexandria, Egypt

http://pharos.bu.edu/Egypt/Alexandria

Provides information about the ancient Egyptian city of Alexandria. Includes history, maps, and visitor information.

Ancient City of Athens

http://www.indiana.edu/~kglowack/Athens/Athens.html

Includes many images of the historical sites of Athens, Greece, as well as insights into Greek history. Offers links to other sites concerning Greek history and architecture.

Archaeological Survey in the Eastern Desert of Egypt

http://rome.classics.lsa.umich.edu/projects/coptos/desert.html

A thorough archaeological study of the ancient site of Coptos, providing information about the trans-desert trade routes between the Nile Valley and the Red Sea which linked early Mediterranean civilizations with those of the Indian Ocean between 300 B.C. and A.D. 400.

Didaskalia: Home Page

http://www.warwick.ac.uk./didaskalia/

Provides information about ancient dance, drama, and music. Also provides access to Didaskalia itself (a journal on the Greek and Roman theater) and other related Internet sites.

Diotima: Women & Gender in the Ancient World

http://www.uky.edu/ArtsSciences/Classics/gender.html

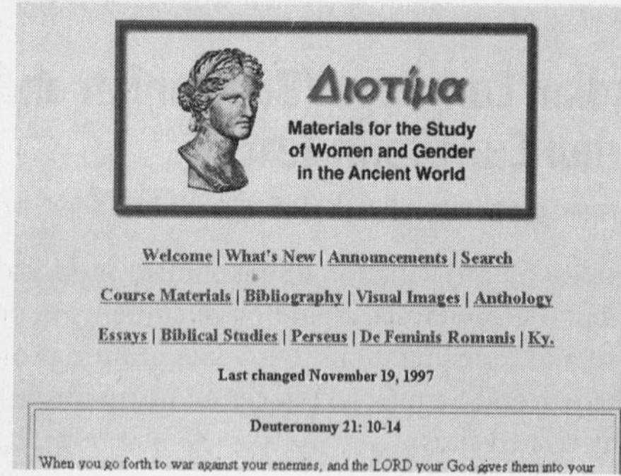

A resource specifically designed for historical information concerning women in the ancient Mediterranean. Features documents, discussions, images, and links.

Exploring Ancient World Cultures

http://cedar.evansville.edu/~wcweb/wc101

Not only does this site provide detailed information on eight ancient cultures, it also provides links to other fascinating (and highly specialized) historical Web sites, including the International Museum of the Horse.

Oriental Institute

http://www-oi.uchicago.edu

Provides information about the University of Chicago's Oriental Institute museum and philology projects. Includes information and visual images on ancient Near East regions, through ABZU, an immense database of links. Also includes a new bibliographic reference, "Women in the Ancient Near East."

Perseus Project Home Page

http://medusa.perseus.tufts.edu/

Presents an interactive multimedia database on ancient Greece. Includes ancient texts and information about sites and artifacts. Includes a searchable database for finding coins, vases, and more.

Pompeii

http://www.tulane.edu/pompeii/text/pompeii.html

Features interesting topics from Pompeii, including the famed mosaic of the Battle of Issus (between Alexander the Great and Darius) and pictures of the House of Faun, one of the largest and most elegant homes of Pompeii.

Pompeii Forum Project

http://jefferson.village.virginia.edu/pompeii/page-1.html

Includes maps and pictures of the unfortunate (but well-preserved) Roman city of Pompeii. Also serves as a forum for discussions about Pompeii and Roman architecture in general.

EUROPEAN HISTORY

Armenian Research Center Home Page

http://www.umd.umich.edu:80/dept/armenian/

Provides Armenian culture and history, as well as information on the Armenian genocide. Offers a link to the Society for Armenian Studies.

Berlin Wall Falls Project

http://192.253.114.31/Berlin/Introduction/Berlin.html

Presents the collaborative Web project, "Berlin Wall Falls: Perspectives from 5 Years Down the Road." Involves students and researchers around the globe.

Europe/Russia/Eastern Europe

http://execpc.com/~dboals/europe.html

An enormous series of links to sites connected to European history, from ancient days to modern times. A great starting place for more specific searches.

Germany—Database of German Nobility

http://www8.informatik.uni-erlangen.de/IMMD8/

Targets historians and geneologians. Focuses on the family tree of Charlemagne, but also features a database of biographies and portraits of German nobility.

The Historical Text Archive

http://www.msstate.edu/Archives/History

Award-winning site that contains links to East and West European history topics. Historical information, images, and documents relating to many countries, including Estonia, Iceland, France, the Netherlands, and more.

History Pages

http://ux1.cso.uiuc.edu/~kundert/josh/../history/history.html

Focuses on Celtic history. Plans to add pages on Saxon and Frankish history. Provides information on the Celts, including maps and links to other Celtic sites.

Hungarian Images and Historical Background

http://www.msstate.edu/Archives/History/hungary/hungary.html

Richly detailed summaries of the salient points of Hungarian history. Features images of coats of arms, crown jewels, maps, and more.

Irish Potato Famine

http://www1.cc.emory.edu/FAMINE

Images and contemporary reports and interviews about the Irish Potato famine (1845-1851) and related Web sites.

Irish History on the Web

http://wwwvms.utexas.edu/~jdana/

A vast number of links relating to Irish history. Features information on many historical and contemporary topics, including an "This Week in Irish History" page.

REESWeb: Russian and East European Studies

http://www.pitt.edu/~cjp/rees.html

A massive collection of links to historic and contemporary information about Russia and Eastern Europe. Anything from maps of the former Soviet Union to the home page of Bucharest can be found here.

Russian Information

http://www.valley.net/~transnat/russsubj.html

A good starting point for Russian history on the Web. Features a chronology of Russian history, an illustrated history of Russia and the USSR, links to Mikhail Gorbachev's home page, and more.

Soviet Archives: Entrance Room

http://sunsite.unc.edu/expo/soviet.exhibit/entrance.html

Provides the Library of Congress Soviet Exhibit, divided into two categories: The Internal Workings of the Soviet System and the Soviet Union and the United States.

The Victorian Web

http://www.stg.brown.edu/projects/hypertext/landow/victorian/victov.html

An expansive collection of information on 19th century British culture, with documents, links, and images.

HISTORICAL FIGURES

Abraham Lincoln Online

http://www.netins.net/showcase/creative/lincoln.html

Documents, images, speeches and links to other sites relating to Abraham Lincoln. A great source of information about the great emancipator.

Educational Sources for George Washington

http://www.mountvernon.org/image/george.html

Many documents on the first American President, George Washington. Discusses his life history, myths about George Washington, anecdotes, and excerpts from his journal.

Empires Beyond the Great Wall: The Heritage of Genghis Khan

http://vvv.com/khan

A virtual exhibit of the great Khan's artifacts, period clothing and armor, pottery, documents, and a biography of Genghis Khan.

Fair Play

http://rmii.com/~jkelin/fp.html

Online magazine. Focuses on giving Lee Harvey Oswald a fair shake. Presents articles concerning various views on the JFK assassination.

JFK Resources Online

http://users.southeast.net/~cheryl/jfk.html

A page devoted to JFK. Includes his inaugural address, memories of those who knew him, selected quotes, samples of his humor, photos, and sound bites. Also covers information about President Kennedy's assassination. Has many links to other pages, mostly devoted to the assassination controversy.

Leonardo da Vinci Museum

http://cellini.leonardo.net/museum/gallery.html

Sketches, paintings, drawings, and information about the life and times of this Renaissance genius. Offers additional links

MEDIEVAL STUDIES

Avalon: Arthurian Heaven

http://Reality.sgi.com/employees/chris_manchester/guide.html

The place to be if you're interest in both the historical and mythical King Arthur. Many links to other sites, including one that features the Monty Python *Holy Grail* script.

Byzantium: The Byzantine Studies Page

http://www.bway.net/~halsall/byzantium.html

A gateway to the numerous (and constantly growing) sites dedicated to the history, culture, and art of the Eastern Roman Empire. While western Europe struggled through the dark ages, civilization was alive and well in Byzantium.

Labyrinth WWW Home Page

http://www.georgetown.edu/labyrinth/labyrinth-home.html

Provides complete information about medieval studies on the Web. Also provides search capabilities.

Vikings Home Page

http://control.chalmers.se/vikings/viking.html

Provides topics on Viking cults, the Vikings of Russia, and Vikings of today. Also features a Swedish-Viking-English dictionary and offer links to other Viking-related Web servers.

WWW Medieval Resources

http://ebbs.english.vt.edu/medieval/medieval.ebbs.html

Offers links to different resources relating to medieval times.

MILITARY HISTORY

Cold War Hot Links

http://www.stmartin.edu/~dprice/cold.war.html

Films, images, documents, and links concerning the cold war, including formerly classified documents, information on McCarthy, period speeches, and much more.

Cybrary of the Holocaust

http://remember.org

Provides information on the Holocaust. Offers details on the rise of Nazism in Germany and its subsequent effects on the Jews. Includes pictures, eyewitness descriptions of concentration camps, and historical perspectives.

D-Day

http://192.253.114.31/D-Day/Table_of_contents.html

Provides Army and Navy news reels, past issues of the *Stars & Stripes* newspaper, famous speeches from the National Archives, and a collection of maps and battle plans from the Center for Military History.

Gulf War Photo Gallery

http://users.aol.com/andyhosk/gulf-war.html

Presents a Gulf War photo gallery, compiled by Ronald A. Hoskinson. Displays images taken primarily from the personal collection of Norman Jarvis. Offers a few links to other Gulf War sites.

Korean War Project

http://www.onramp.net/~hbarker/

Photos, maps, casualty lists, and historical documents, all related to the Korean War. Numerous links to related sites.

Military History

http://www.cfcsc.dnd.ca/links/milhist/

A good access of links through many of the world's most famous (infamous?) wars. Find links to the Hundred Years War, the French Revolution, or even the Persian Gulf War. If you're looking for military history, this is the place to start.

Operation Desert Storm Debriefing Book

http://www.leyden.com/gulfwar/

Provides information concerning military and political aspects of the Gulf War. Includes backgrounds on politicians, descriptions of military hardware, statistics, and links to other Gulf War sites.

Remembering Nagasaki

http://www.exploratorium.edu/nagasaki/

Observes the 50th anniversary of the dropping of atomic bombs on Hiroshima and Nagasaki. Includes photographs taken by Yosuki Yamahata of Nagasaki the day after, which create a backdrop for discussion and reflection on issues concerning the atomic age. Lets you share your views and read those of others.

Salzburg 1945–1955: Introduction

http://www.image.co.at/image/salzburg/

Presents Austrians and American G.I.'s sharing remembrances of the "Era of Occupation" of Salzburg, Austria, subsequent to the defeat of Nazi Germany in 1945. Includes links to images and text interviews.

Vietnam Veterans Home Page

http://www.vietvet.org/

Focuses on Vietnam veterans from both sides of the conflict. Provides a forum for exchange of information, stories, poems, songs, art, pictures, and experiences.

Worlds of Late Antiquity

http://ccat.sas.upenn.edu/jod/wola.html

A home page devoted to Late Roman and early Medieval information. No images, but many interesting documents.

World War I (1914-1918)

http://www.cfcsc.dnd.ca/links/milhist/wwi.html

A page dedicated to World War I, featuring links to many Great War subjects: propaganda, aerial combat, trench warfare, the Versailles treaty, lost poets, and more.

World War II on the Web

http://www.bunt.com/~mconrad/

A long list of links to sites concerning the second world war, including art, photos, documents, information for memorabilia collectors, access to films, and much else.

MISCELLANEOUS HISTORICAL SITES

ADFA History: History on the Internet

http://www.adfa.oz.au/HISTORY/links.html

A gargantuan series of links to historical sites, with photos, documents and multimedia resources on virtually any historical subject.

Ari's Today Page

http://www.uta.fi/~blarku/today.html

A great source of information for what happened today in history. Features birthdays of famous people, historical information, and important calendar days for the Jewish and Muslim faiths as well as important U.S.-oriented dates.

BUBL Information Service Web Server

http://www.bubl.bath.ac.uk/BUBL/History.html

Offers links to various history sites on the Net. Includes many topics other than history. Contains links to Russian, Vietnam War, United States, French and Indian War, Viking, Medieval, and Civil War historical sites.

Castles on the Web

http://fox.nstn.ca/~tmonk/castle/castle.html

Provides a collection of sites that offer information about and pictures of castles from around the world.

Gangsters!

http://www.well.com/user/mod79

If you want information on gangsters, start here. Offers history, images, biographies of criminals and crime fighters, a bibliography of organized crime in print and on film, and links to related sites.

The Heritage Post Interactive

http://heritage.excite.sfu.ca/hpost.html

Tidbits of Canadian history and information about current Canada. Features documents and images.

The Historical Text Archive

http://www.msstate.edu/Archives/History/index.html

Archives historical texts from various countries and periods. Includes a large collection from the United States. Offers many links to other historical resources.

History Computerization Project

http://www.directnet.com/history/

Provides a database for libraries, historians, museums, libraries and more, dedicated to the exchange of historical information. Includes access to many other directories of interest.

The History of Costume by Braun

http://www.siue.edu/COSTUMES/history.html

An online version of an old German book that features fashion through the ages, from Egypt to Russian folk dress of the late nineteenth century. Excellent graphics.

EXPO WWW Exhibit Organization

http://sunsite.unc.edu/expo

Provides an index to exhibits that include the Library of Congress's "Scrolls of the Dead Sea," "The 'Palace' of Diocletian at Split," and exhibits of paleontology, the Soviet Union, the Vatican, and more. Offers a list of terms relating to Middle Eastern and classical terms. Includes downloadable JPEG and GIF files.

Intentional Communities

http://www.well.com/user/cmty/index.html

Seeks to be an inclusive title for information on eco-villages, co-housing, residential land trusts, communes, student co-ops, urban housing cooperatives, and other related projects.

Mary Rose Virtual Maritime Museum

http://www.synergy.net/homeport.html

Offers a fascinating look at a recovered Tudor-period warship that sank in 1545. Provides links to other sites featuring ships of old.

Maya

http://www.realtime.net/maya/

Includes history, geography, geology, astronomy, archaeology, anthropology, and art forms related to the Americas before Christopher Columbus's discovery. Includes information on the Maya, Aztec, and American Indians.

The Maya Astronomy Page

http://www.astro.uva.nl/michielb/maya/astro.html

Focuses on Mayan civilization. Presents the Mayan creation story. Provides information about Mayan astronomy, mathematics, and their calendar. Offers links to other Mayan sites.

A B C D E F G H I J K L M N O P Q R S T U V W X Y Z

Media History, Studies, and Education

http://omnibus-eye.rtvf.nwu.edu/links/studies.html

A large number of links to history as recorded by film and other media. Many interesting sites, from the Documentary Educational Resources to the National Public Broadcasting Archives, scholarly works on Chinese Cinema, the D-Day News Reels Archive, and more.

Mithraism

http://www.lglobal.com/~hermes3/mithras.htm

Presents a look at Mithraism, a religion of the pre-Christian Roman Empire, for those interested in the roots of Western religion.

Musei

http://www.christusrex.org/www1/vaticano/0-Musei.html

Provides around 600 images of holdings of the Vatican museums. Also offers links to hundreds of images of the Sistine Chapel and the Raphael Stanze. Includes writings of John Paul II, access to News from the Holy SEE, and more.

The Museum Professional

http://www.sirius.com/~robinson/musprof

Serves as a starting point for accessing online resources in the museum field. Includes links to museum Web site lists, virtual museums, and specialization resources. Has a new forum for people in the museum field to share information.

The National Inventors Hall of Fame

http://www.invent.org

Biographies, images, and inventions of famous inventors. Additional information on virtual exhibits and information on B.F. Goodrich's Collegiate Inventor's Program. An interesting stop.

Native American Cultural Resources on the Internet

http://hanksville.phast.umass.edu/misc/NAculture.html

A massive series of links to Native American sites. A good source of related history, documents, and current information.

Papyrology Home Page

http://www-personal.umich.edu/~jmucci/papyrology

Provides access to papyrology collections world-wide, literature from and concerning the collections, and images of papyri including fragments from the *Book of the Dead.*

Paris Museums

http://www.paris.org/Musees/

Contains images and information for more than 20 museums in Paris, including the Louvre, Centre Pompidou, L'Orangerie, Auguste Rodin, and la Cite des Sciences et de l'Industrie.

Pirates

http://orion.it.luc.edu/~tgibson/pirates/pirates.html

The page for swashbucklers and rogues, featuring facts, myths, and legends about piracy, the history of piracy, famous people, places and images connected to pirates.

Romarch List Home Page

http://www.umich.edu/~pfoss/ROMARCH.html

Provides a "crossroads for Web resources on the art and archaeology of Italy and the Roman provinces, from ca. 1000 B.C. to A.D. 600." Offers many links to sites that contain images of Roman art and architecture.

Shikhin

http://www.colby.edu/rel/Shikhin.html

A site dedicated to helping find and identify the lost city of Shikhin in Israel. Presents the story of Shikhin, known for its pottery in its day, with text, pictures, and maps.

Shore Line Trolley Museum

http://www.panix.com/~christos/TrolleyPage.html

Exhibits the Shore Line Trolley museum of East Haven, CT. Provides information about museum operations, including hours and directions, as well as a tour of some streetcars in Shore Line's collection.

Voice of the Shuttle Home Page

http://humanitas.ucsb.edu/

A Web page devoted to the study of humanities, offering many links to humanities topics: archaeology, anthropology, architecture, art, general humanities, history, linguistics, literature, minority studies, philosophy, religious studies, women's studies, and more.

SCIENCE & TECHNOLOGY

The Art of Renaissance Science

http://www.setn.org/pubs/index.html

Photos, sound, animation, and documents tell the history of astronomy, anatomy, architecture, and art of the Renaissance, as narrated by Professor Joseph Dauben.

History of Astronomy

http://aibn55.astro.uni-bonn.de:8000/~pbrosche/astoria.html

Focuses on the history of astronomy and in general, on science. Contains links to biographies of important people, images from observatories around the world and other archives, museums, and astronomy exhibits on the Net.

History of Science, Technology, and Medicine

http://www.asap.unimelb.edu.au/hstm/hstm_ove.htm

Keeps track of information facilities in the field of the history of science, technology, and medicine. Also offers links to organizations, biographies, institutions, museums, and electronic journals.

History of Space Exploration

http://bang.lanl.gov/solarsys/

Provides information on the history of space exploration. Includes images of spacecraft and planets.

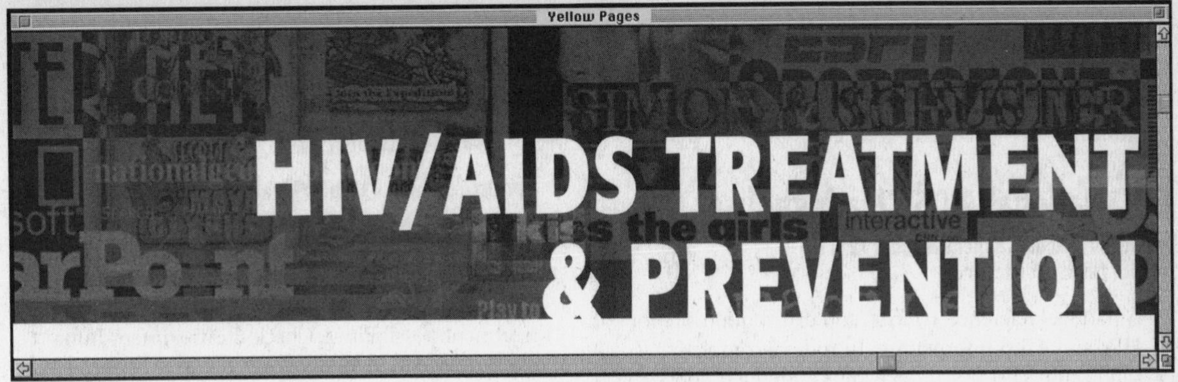

The challenge of having AIDS is not dying of AIDS, but *living* with AIDS.

Terry Boyd (ftp://hwbbs.gbgm-umc.org/library/stories/living.txt)

AIDS Clinical Trials Information Service

http://www.actis.org/

The search goes on for a cure. This site provides details on current clinical trials in progress, upcoming trials, and new FDA approvals, and includes two online databases (one on trial protocols, the other on drugs).

AIDS Clock

http://www.vers.com/aidsclock/

As of this writing, approximately 28 million people worldwide were infected with HIV. The AIDS Clock at the United Nations Population Fund Web site continues to add to this number at the discouraging rate of six people per minute. (Shockwave required to view the clock.) In addition to a variety of related links, this site includes connections to WHO, UNICEF, UNFPA, UNESCO, UNDP, and World Bank, the sponsors of UNAIDS, as well as the UNAIDS site.

Related Sites

- http://florey.biosci.uq.oz.au/hiv/HIV_EMIR.html
- http://text.nlm.nih.gov/ftrs/pick?ftrsK=0&collect=atis&t=880942927
- http://www.aidsauthority.org/news.html
- http://www.ainy.org/
- http://www.carfax.co.uk/aic-pers.htm

AIDS Outreach Center
http://www.aoc.org/resource.htm

AIDS Outreach Center

http://www.aoc.org/resource.htm

This organization, based in Fort Worth, TX, has one of the most complete resource listings available online for HIV/AIDS. Links are indexed by category and alphabetically for quick access. AOC also offers quite a variety of services; information on each is available from the Web site.

AIDS Virtual Library

http://planetq.com/aidsvl/index.html

Sponsored by Planet Q, this site deals with sociopolitical and medical topics related to HIV and AIDS prevention and treatment. An ample site list is provided for jumping off to other related sites.

alt.sex.safe

alt.sex.safe (Newsgroup)

A newsgroup devoted to discussions about promoting and practicing safe sex.

The Body: A Multimedia AIDS and HIV Information Resource

http://www.thebody.com/cgi-bin/body.cgi

In addition to selected coverage of AIDS, HIV, and related issues in the news, this site provides various forums with questions answered by a team of medical experts. Connections to government, commercial, and service sites. Also includes a section with many photos from the thought-provoking Loel A. Poor photographic essay, "AIDS: The Challenge to Educate."

CDC National AIDS Clearinghouse

gopher://cdcnac.aspensys.com:72/11/1
http://www.cdcnac.org/

A national reference, referral, and distribution site for HIV and AIDS information. Includes a complete publications list from which you can request documents.

Children With AIDS Project

http://www.aidskids.org/

Children With AIDS Project of America is a publicly supported 501C-3 nonprofit organization, providing support, care, and adoption programs for children infected with HIV/AIDS. Details on services and fees; register to become an adoptive parent, learn how to help the cause.

Condomania Online

http://www.condomania.com/

An interesting—and, okay, entertaining—site that also provides some good educational material on safe sex. Find your "magical condom" with the help of the Condom Wizard. Novelties, gifts, books, catalogs, and more available online or via mail.

Emotional Support Guide

http://asa.ugl.lib.umich.edu/chdocs/support/emotion.html

Although this site has a general focus on all illnesses, not just HIV/AIDS, it provides a wealth of information for patients and caregivers facing chronic illness and death.

Gay Men's Health Crisis

http://www.gmhc.org/

Gay Men's Health Crisis (GMHC), founded by volunteers in 1981, is the nation's oldest and largest not-for-profit AIDS organization. GMHC offers hands-on support services to more than 9,500 men, women and children with AIDS and their families in New York City annually, as well as education and advocacy for hundreds of thousands nationwide.

HIV/AIDS Treatment Information Service

http://www.hivatis.org/

Sponsored by six Public Health Service agencies, this site provides information about federally approved treatment guidelines for HIV and AIDS. Check the What's New page for updates on the latest news on antiretroviral agents, protease inhibitors, and other treatment possibilities. Check the Treatment Information page for history, glossary, current treatment information, more.

The International Council of AIDS Service Organizations (ICASO)

http://www.web.apc.org/~icaso/icaso.html

This organization's purpose is to unite and support community-based and non-governmental AIDS organizations around the world. Emphasis is on support and activity within the community, although international conferences, meetings, and events are listed.

JAMA HIV/AIDS Information Center

http://www.ama-assn.org/special/hiv/hivhome.htm

This Journal of the American Medical Association site is a resource for health care workers and physicians, with a broad range of coverage on treatment, testing, patient information, and other topics that will interest the public as well. Plenty of links to other sites, updated treatment and drug information, more.

Just Say Yes (Coalition for Positive Sexuality)

http://www.positive.org/cps/Home/index.html

Aimed at teenagers who are—or intend to be—sexually active, this site provides a positive spin on sex, but with a safe-sex outlook. Provides straight-up information and a place where people can exchange ideas, get questions answered, and share their feelings. Additional resource links are also provided.

Magic Johnson Foundation, Inc.

http://www.magicjohnson.org/

Co-sponsored by AT&T, this organization's thrust is raising money to support organizations that provide HIV/AIDS education, prevention, and care for young people. Information on educational resources, available grants, and how you can help.

Mediconsult.com

http://www.mediconsult.com/aids/

Site for patients with chronic illnesses. Medical news, information on clinical trials, connections to support groups, online ordering of medical products, and more. The MediXperts fee-based service provides access to medical experts on a variety of topics and promises complete privacy.

National Association of People with AIDS

http://www.thecure.org/

Based in the U.S., this organization serves as the voice for people infected with (or affected by) HIV and AIDS. Information on programs (education and outreach, health and treatment, and public policy), news updates, current events, and resources.

Safer Sex

http://www.safersex.org/

Safe sex information for everyone (gay/lesbian/bi/het), with an excellent selection of text articles on subjects ranging from condoms to counselor information. This site is one of the original plaintiffs in ACLU v. Reno, the challenge to the Communications Decency Act.

Stop AIDS Project

http://www.stopaids.org/

Based in San Francisco, CA, this organization's aim is to reduce the transmission of HIV and help the community of "self-identified gay and bisexual men." Educational materials and training manuals are free for downloading and adaptation (crediting the site, of course). Calendar of events and meetings, news updates, answers to common questions, an extensive list of resources, and more.

Virtual AIDS Quilt

http://www.mcpsys.com/quilt/

Like the original AIDS Quilt, but in cyber form. You can read panels posted by friends and relatives of AIDS victims, or design and post your own tribute to a lost friend or loved one.

NEWSGROUPS

clari.tw.health.aids

misc.health.aids

sci.med.aids

FTP & GOPHER SITES

ftp://atlas.lanl.gov/pub/aids-db/IMMUNO-DB

ftp://ftp.harbor.cove.com/virtual/tetraftp/pub/

gopher://gopher.hivnet.org/

gopher://gopher.niaid.nih.gov:70/11/aids/comm/teach

gopher://itsa.ucsf.edu/00/.i/.q/.d/quickies/glossary/27

gopher://odie.niaid.nih.gov/11/aids

gopher://psupena.psu.edu/1%24k%20AIDS

gopher://ucsbuxa.ucsb.edu:3001/11/.Journals/.A/.AIDS/

MAILING LISTS

4ACURE-L

aids

aidsact

AIDSBKRV

aids-d

aids-digest

aids-email

caregivers

cdcsumms

info-aids

These are just a few of the more than 50 mailing lists available on HIV and AIDS. For more listings, go to the Lizst site at http://www.liszt.com/ and search on **AIDS**.

Related Sites

http://www.csmc.edu/./hawc/aids.html

http://www.epibiostat.ucsf.edu/epidem/aids_surv.html

http://www.gnofn.org/~noaids/welcome.html

http://www.interserver.com/aidspage/

http://www.unaids.org/

A B C D E F G H I J K L M N O P Q R S T U V W X Y Z

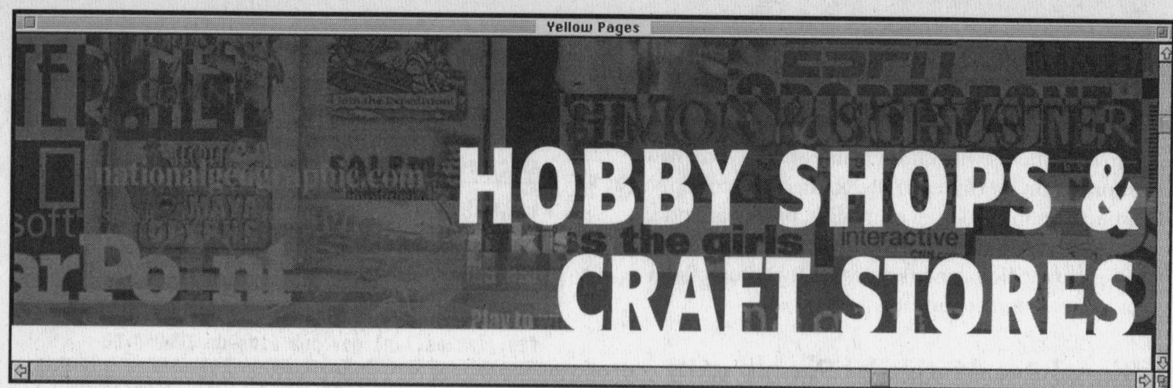

A
B
C
D
E
F
G
H
I
J
K
L
M
N
O
P
Q
R
S
T
U
V
W
X
Y
Z

I have a hobby. I have the world's largest collection of sea shells. I keep it scattered on beaches all over the world. Maybe you've seen some of it.

Stephen Wright

A.C. Moore Home Page
http://www.acmoore.com

Biggest Little Craft Mall
http://www.craftmall.com/

Fabri-Centers
http://www.joann.com/index.stm

Hobby Lobby Home Page
http://www.hobbylobby.com/

Michaels-THE Arts and Crafts Store
http://www.michaels.com

A.C. Moore Home Page

http://www.acmoore.com

Site of A.C. Moore, an arts, crafts, and floral shop. The site features a store locator, handy info about individual stores, projects to dig into, a Kids Club for fun, and a Teachers Club offering discounts to teachers.

Art Glass World

http://www.artglassworld.com/

A searchable site specializing in stained art and art glass. See visitors' glass artwork or display your own at the Visitors Gallery. Grab some free patterns, order stained-glass books, find a list of suppliers, join a live chat, locate retail stores, discover what's new in glass art, peruse glass art magazines, and dig into the Q&A section.

Arts N Crafts N Things

http://www.stitching.com/artsncrafts/

This site offers a text (no pictures) catalog of craft items you can mail-order. Email the store to ask about products or place an order. Specializing in needlework, knitting, crochet, ribbon embroidery, acid-free scrapbooking/photo albums, adult coloring books, and beads/glitter.

Basketpatterns.com

http://www.basketpatterns.com/index.html

Using an online shopping-cart system, you can purchase basket patterns, as well as basket-weaving tools, accessories, and books. You can also order finished baskets. The site also supplies some basketry-related links.

BFK - The Kite Store

http://www.kitestore.com/kite/index.htm

Bills itself as the world's largest online kite catalog. A searchable site offering kites, parts, and accessories. You can view the catalog online, ask for a printed catalog, or download the PDF version. You can also view the kite gallery's hundreds of photos. And visit BFK's new yo-yo store "for more fun on a string."

Biggest Little Craft Mall

http://www.craftmall.com/

A crafters' resource, with a mall analogy. Check out new vendors; search for crafts by keyword, category, or listing; sell your own crafts; read the classifieds; follow links to other places of interest to crafters; join a message forum; buy crafting books and magazines; and join the Crafters Club.

COMIX & CARDZ etc.

http://edgeworld.com/comix/

This site features a one-stop hobby shop that carries all comic books from Marvel, DC, and Image, as well as major brands of sports cards and game cards. You can currently request information online but should soon be able to order online.

Fabri-Centers

http://www.joann.com/index.stm

Site for Jo-Ann, ClothWorld, and New York Fabrics & Crafts stores, dealing in fabrics and crafts. Find your local store, enter a drawing, subscribe to the store newsletter, visit the investor relations page, find out about in-store specials, or post a message in Message Central to ask questions or share tips. Best of all, visit the Creative center for loads of crafts and sewing ideas and information.

Gemco International

http://www.madriver.com/gemco/index.html

A cyber store that supplies jewelers, gem collectors, and lapidary hobbyists with rough and cut gems from around the world at affordable prices. Some photos can be accessed for specials that are available only via the Web.

Hobby Lobby Home Page

http://www.hobbylobby.com/

Hobby Lobby's searchable Internet Catalog is a good way to get details on the products you're interested in. There are lots of other things to check out on the home page too—including weekly specials, television goings-on, craft projects, store locations and information, affiliated companies, and visitors' correspondence. You can even print off an Internet coupon and take it to the store on your next visit.

Hobby Shop Mall

http://www.hobbystores.com/

A listing of links to hobby shops that maintain a Web presence. Primarily covering plastic models, railroading, Lionel products, radio control, and Nascar collectibles.

HOBBYLINC

http://www.hobbylinc.com/

A full resource of hobby supplies—more than 10,000 items available. View an extensive graphical catalog, and take advantage of links, hints for hobbyists, biweekly specials, and educational information about various hobbies. Place or check the status of your order.

Michaels-THE Arts and Crafts Store

http://www.michaels.com

At this site you can get craft tips and new project ideas, find out about upcoming store activities, have fun on the Kids Club pages, join in the online activities and interactive crafts, or find the Michaels nearest you—even find investor information. A fun and noteworthy site.

Quilt Store

http://www.jandaweb.com/wtq/store.shtml

The online store of Whiffle Tree Quilts, a quilt shop in Silicon Valley. You can order supplies (kits, patterns, fabrics, and books) online or by phone.

Roll Models, Inc.: The Internet Model Shop

http://www.battlehobbies.com/

A hobby shop for plastic scale modelers. Offers pictures of completed models, a catalog, modeling hints and tips, a list of related organizations, links, and info about the company. Order online or via phone or fax.

Stamp Addicts Rubber Stamps & Supplies

http://stampaddicts.pair.com/

An online shopping resource for rubber stamp enthusiasts. Offers at least 30% off retail prices on stamps, papers, markers, and other accessories. Also order various stamping catalogs. Site includes links to other stamping resources.

The Wax House 1997 Online Catalog

http://www.execpc.com/~mfrend/

Offers an online catalog of all types of candlemaking supplies for beginners through experts. Sells starter kits for novices. You can also pose candle-making questions or discuss problems via email, or you can order copies of the Wax House Newsletter.

Yellow Medicine Trading Post

http://www.showmeweb.com/yellow/

Features a complete line of Indian craft supplies, including feathers, beads, hides, bone hairpipe, and miscellaneous items. Browse through the store and place your order.

NEWSGROUPS

rec.crafts.beads

rec.crafts.marketplace

rec.crafts.metalworking

rec.crafts.misc

rec.crafts.polymer-clay

rec.crafts.textiles.misc

rec.crafts.textiles.needlework

rec.crafts.textiles.quilting

rec.crafts.textiles.sewing

rec.crafts.textiles.yarn

rec.models.railroad

rec.models.rc.air

rec.models.rc.land

rec.models.rockets

rec.models.scale

rec.toys.cars

rec.woodworking

HOCKEY

> You don't have to think, Mike. It's hockey.
>
> *Commentator in* Sudden Death *(1995)*

Ice Age - The Official AHL Web Site
`http://www.canoe.ca/AHL/home.html`

Science of Hockey: Home
`http://www.exploratorium.edu/hockey/`

Temp\text
`http://www.theihl.com/`

Wayne Gretzky Home Page
`http://www.gretzky.com/`

Crease Monkey Hockey

`http://members.aol.com/todnielson/creasemonkey.html`

A sort of online hockey scrapbook for fans. You can watch the hockey scores scroll by at this site, which also offers player profiles, message boards, features, a photo gallery, and general hockey links. The site focuses on the AHL and NCAA Division I college hockey.

Doctor Hockey

`http://library.advanced.org/10187/`

The Doctor Hockey site, which targets athletes ages 15–19, was designed to teach students who are involved in the sport of hockey about the common injuries and how to prevent them. It can also give students an insight into the field of sports medicine.

First Base Sports' On-line Hockey Sports Terms

`http://www.firstbasesports.com/glossaries/hkyglos.htm`

A handy glossary of hockey terms. Jump to the desired description by clicking the first letter of the term and then scrolling down. If you're not sure what the crease lines are or exactly what part of the ice constitutes the neutral zone, this is one way to find out.

The Hockey News On-Line

`http://www.thn.com/`

The online version of *The Hockey News* magazine. Take a look at the latest issue, take part in this week's poll/drawing, and access all sorts of other timely and interesting online articles.

HockeyNewsLink: Main

`http://www.hockeynewslink.com/`

This is your source for all things hockey—your connection to resources and info. Jump to newspaper coverage of various teams, daily news, stats, periodicals, leagues, associations, people, and other hockey-related links.

Ice Age - The Official AHL Web Site

`http://www.canoe.ca/AHL/home.html`

Fans of the American Hockey League should visit this site. Gives you team and player info, broken down by conference and division. Also provides minute-by-minute game updates and scores, info on future games, player profiles, AHL record book data, hockey forums, and all the other good stuff related to the AHL.

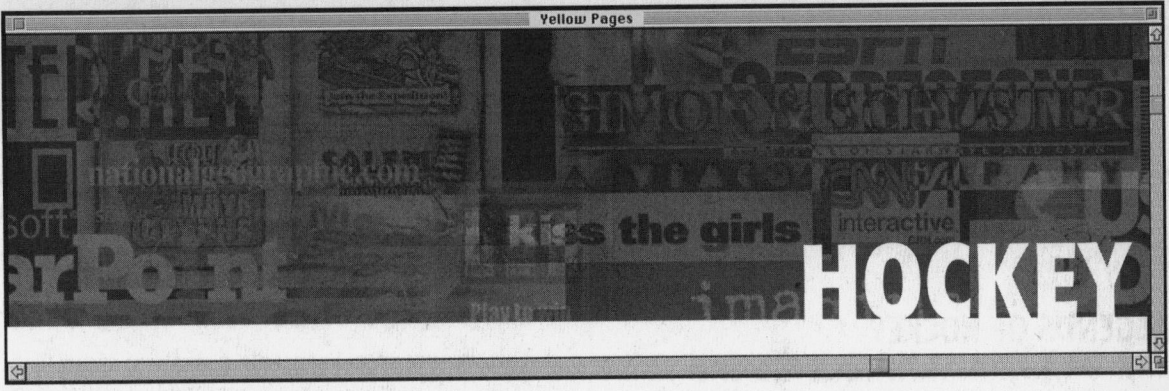

Iceman's Hockey Rules Page

http://www.afn.org/~afn56636/rules/rules.htm

Offers official NHL rule information, such as the full text of the NHL Rulebook and official signals; player and officials information, such as the all-time penalty leaders; and other hockey information, such as links to NHL sites.

LEGENDS OF HOCKEY

http://www.geocities.com/Colosseum/Field/2918/

Get the scoop on your favorite hockey legends—active legends, forwards, defensemen, goaltenders, international stars, and pioneers of hockey. Plus, play trivia games and participate in polls.

Science of Hockey: Home

http://www.exploratorium.edu/hockey/

The Science of Hockey takes you inside the game of hockey, utilizing RealAudio and Video to bring you science bits from leading physicists and chemists. It also gives you insight from NHL players and coaches from the San Jose Sharks. Want to know why ice is slippery or how to shoot a puck 100 miles per hour? Check it out.

SLAM! Women's Hockey Home Page

http://www.canoe.com/HockeyWomen/home.html

Gives you women's hockey news stories, plus such interactive offerings as the LIVE! Scoreboard, Photo Gallery, Hockey Talk (NHL), Puck Talk (Jr.), Fan Breakaway (AHL), and Cup Talk (playoffs). You can also get news, scores, and standings from the World Women's Championship.

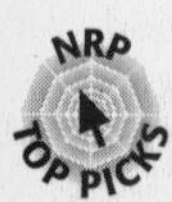

Temp\text

http://www.theihl.com/

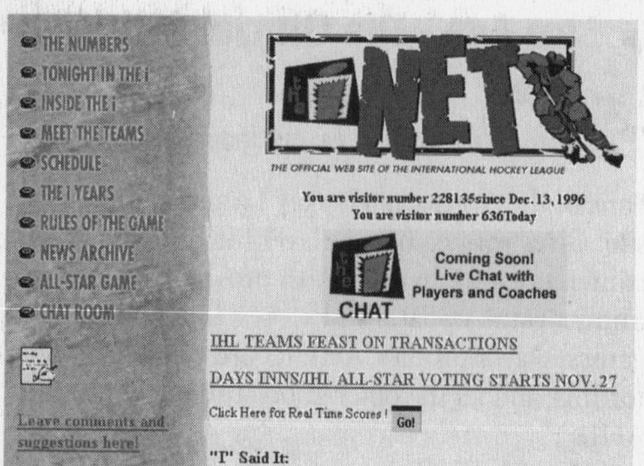

This is iNet, the official web site of the IHL. You'll find IHL news, info on the player and goaltender of the week, team notes, rules of the game, the league schedule, daily updates and recaps, and much more. You can also "meet" your favorite players from each division.

United States Hockey Hall of Fame

http://www.ushockeyhall.com/

This site showcases the people, places, and events that define the American hockey community. Dedicated to U.S. hockey, this site offers info on USHHF membership, an online gift shop, the Arena of Honor, hockey news and feature articles, a virtual tour of the site, and more.

USA Hockey

http://www.usahockey.com/

The official site of USA Hockey. The Main Menu asks you to pick from Players Only, Coaches & Officials, National Teams, USA Hockey InLine, News & Information, Rinks & Arenas, Fan Forum, Merchandise, and National Team Development Program. Come skate through it for yourself.

U.S. College Hockey Online

http://uscollegehockey.com/

Get college hockey scores, news stories, features, team and conference information, live broadcasts, and publications through this site. You can order college and pro licensed sportswear, and a USCHO bookstore is scheduled to open soon.

Wayne Gretzky Home Page

http://www.gretzky.com/

What would a lineup of hockey sites be without one dedicated to Wayne Gretzky? Learn about the life and career of "The Great One," including photos and even some video footage from his early years. And there's much more you can do at this site: access hockey news, get in on some chat, go inside the Shop or the Sports Store, play a game online, or take a virtual-reality tour of Gretzky's life. You won't want to miss this one.

A B C D E F G H I J K L M N O P Q R S T U V W X Y Z

Twas the night before
Christmas, when all
through the house;
Not a creature was stirring,
not even a mouse;
The stockings were hung by
the chimney with care,
In hopes that St. Nicholas
soon would be there.

Clement C. Moore

All About Christmas

`http://www.christmasdepot.com/`

An online Christmas store complete with trees, wreaths, ornaments, collectibles, letters to Santa, and gift ideas. A "View Shopping Cart" feature ensures that you don't overload!

Affordable Gifts Store

`http://www.1stkids.com/shop/`

This site features a large selection of unique and affordable gifts for family and friends. A great place to shop to avoid spending all of your money and losing your holiday spirit!

Happy Christmas
`http://www.happychristmas.com/`

April Fools on the Net

`http://www.2meta.com/april-fools/`

Listing of top 20 fools, which includes the headline "MicroSoft Bids to Acquire the Catholic Church" and more. Also lots of other foolish links. Come here to get a leg up on your friends this April 1st.

Cinco de Mayo

`http://latino.sscnet.ucla.edu/demo/cinco.html`

An important date (May 5th) in Mexican and Chicano communities, it marks the victory of the Mexican Army over the French at the Battle of Puebla, which came to symbolize Mexican unity and patriotism. Visit this site for the complete history and photos.

Christmas around the World

`http://www.christmas.com/christmas.html`

Asia, Europe, Latin America, the Middle East, and the Netherlands are among the regions with Christmas traditions explained on this site. Here you will also learn how to say "Merry Christmas" in over 30 languages and you will find a list of other holidays that fall around the Christmas season.

Easter in Cyberspace: A Christian Perspective

`http://members.aol.com/REMinistry/devotionals/easter.html`

This page reminds Easter celebrants of the "true meaning" of the holiday. You might not find jelly beans or bunnies, but you will find a collection of links about the death and resurrection of Jesus Christ.

A B C D E F G H I J K L M N O P Q R S T U V W X Y Z

The Easter Page

http://www.execpc.com/~tmuth/easter/sermon.htm

This site offers a collection of articles, sermons, essays, and devotions posted by Christians of all denominations. A handy reminder that there was an Easter long before the Easter bunny joined in.

The Fourth of July

http://wilstar.net/july4.htm

This patriotic site plays "Yankee Doodle Dandy" when you open the homepage. Filled with links to historic documents such as the Magna Carta, Declaration of Independence, Constitution, Emancipation Proclamation, and more. Also contains flag flying rules.

Hallmark Seasons and Reasons

http://www.hallmark.com/seasons_bin/seasons.asp

The site theme and features change with the seasons and holidays. Includes gift ideas and wrapping projects, address for online letters to Santa, and Kwanzaa and Hanukkah ideas. A really helpful site full of festive ideas.

Happy Birthday, America!

http://banzai.neosoft.com/citylink/usa/

Offering audio files of Vice President Al Gore and the Star Spangled Banner, this page celebrates the Fourth of July with multimedia, in addition to providing links to important governmental and historical sites.

Happy Christmas

http://www.happychristmas.com/

Keep the merry in your Christmas holiday by visiting this site for funny stories, gift ideas from silly to practical to useless, lists of holiday movies, and more. There's even a list of pizza places that are open on Christmas Day just in case!

Heather's Happy Holidaze Pages

http://www.shadeslanding.com/hms/

Most national holidays as seen through the eyes of a 7-year-old girl. This site has won several awards and it is easy to see why: The links are complete and relevant! An entertaining site to visit whether you have kids or not.

Jewish Holidays and Festivities on the Net

http://www.jewishpost.com/holidays/

A colorful site featuring the names and brief explanations of Jewish holidays. Categories include high holy days, Shavuot, Purim, and others.

Kitchen Link

http://www.kitchenlink.com/thanksgiving.html

Featuring Thanksgiving recipes, you can also find recipes for other holidays using the search engine provided here. Plenty of yummy turkey, stuffing, side dishes, dessert, and vegetarian recipes here to fill you up until next year.

Kwanzaa Information Center

http://www.melanet.com/kwanzaa/

Here you'll find reams of information about the background and purpose, symbols, and principles of Kwanzaa, as well as a schedule for Kwanzaa Celebration.

Martin Luther King Jr.

http://wwwstud.uni-giessen.de/%7Es410/king1.htm

This site is dedicated to the memory of slain civil rights leader Dr. Martin Luther King, Jr. and the national holiday that honors him. It features a biography and links to his famous "I Have a Dream" speech and more.

Passover in Israel

http://israeliculture.miningco.com/library/weekly/aa042497.htm

This site features the history of Passover, the differences in Passover in Israel compared to the rest of the world, recipe suggestions, and more. A newsletter, chat room, and BBS are also available here.

Passover on the Net

http://www.holidays.net/passover/

This beautifully illustrated page offers the story of Passover, information about the Seder meal (plus recipes), and a collection of downloadable Passover songs in MIDI format. Be aware though that the lavish backgrounds won't show up in all browsers and the graphics might be a memory drain.

Starnet Happy Holidays

http://www.azstarnet.com/public/holiday/holiday.html

Forget those snail mail cards! This site sends your electronic holiday greeting via the Internet.

Twelve Days of Christmas Holiday Guide

http://www.kinderguide.com/holiday.html

Twelve days of holiday crafts and spirited activities for the entire family. Try them this year to keep your holidays fun.

World Wide Holidays and Events

http://www.classnet.com/holidays/

This cool, searchable calendar lists the holidays and events celebrated on any given day. You can look up the holidays that fall on the day you access the calendar (April 13 is Songkran Day in Thailand, for example) or you can search the full calendar for a day of your choosing.

The Yom Tov Page

http://www.torah.org/learning/yomtov/index.html

On this page is a collection of links and information about the Jewish holidays.

Related Sites
http://www.njweb.com/stpats.html
http://www.night.net/thanksgiving/index.html-ssi
http://usacitylink.com//cupid/default.html
http://freezone.com/tmf/motherscard/
http://virtual-markets.net/vme/memorial/dvm_mem.html
http://perfect.presentpicker.com/fathersday/father.html
http://www.joi.org/edutain/rosh/
http://shamash.org/reform/uahc/congs/pa/pa001/fallhldy.html
http://members.aol.com/jewfaq/holiday4.htm
http://www.oct31.com/
http://www.vfw.com/amesm/origins.shtml

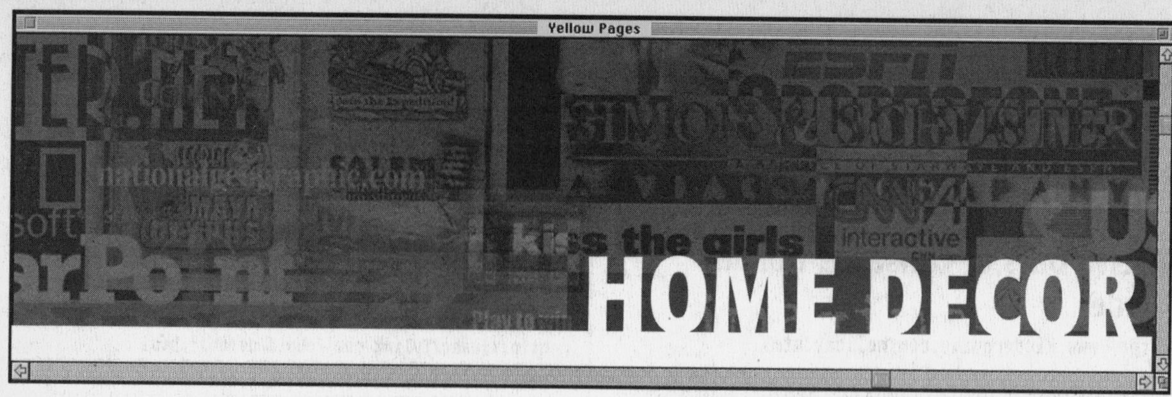

> A house is made of walls and beams; a home is built with love and dreams.
>
> *Anonymous*

Accents! for Your Home

http://www.accents.com/index.html

For your shopping pleasure, you can pick one of three music selections to play as you browse the site. This store offers a refined collection of home furnishings, designer accessories, fine art, and sculpture. Categories include the Art Gallery, Window Fashions, Home Accessories, and Garden.

Antique Alley Home Page

http://bmark.com/aa/

Bills itself as the Internet's Antiques Marketplace. Take a stroll down Antique Alley, stopping to enjoy the online catalogs of the shops that catch your fancy. Or use the powerful search engine to find what you want. You can also access a list of more than 35,000 antiques shops and dealers across the nation.

Country Gifts and Home Decor

http://www.garden.net/thegifthouse/

An online catalog of country gifts and decorations. Free discount coupon with your first purchase. Includes links to other sites.

NRP TOP PICKS

Accents! for Your Home
http://www.accents.com/index.html

Rustic Creations Homepage
http://www.ksmnet.com/rustic_creations/

The Country Mouse

http://www.ij.net/ps/countrymouse/index.html

A store of handcrafted gifts and distinctive home decor. The site features photos and ordering info for Country Candles (handcrafted candles and accessories), Hometown Treasures (a custom-created replica of your home in wood), and Country Style Cutting Boards (made of five hardwoods).

Country Sampler's Decorating Ideas

http://www.sampler.com/decideas/decideas.html

Online version of the popular decorating magazine. You'll find do-it-yourself project ideas, tips from Projects Editor Christy Crafton, a chance to peek at the latest issue, and an idea-exchange forum.

CUDDLEDOWN OF MAINE Online Outlet

http://www.cuddledown.com/

Offers fine home fashions and more—down comforters, bed linens and other sewn items, furniture, and accessories. Special discounts on discontinued and overstocked items.

Garbe's Lighting and Home Furnishings

http://www.garbes.com/

Store featuring distinctive lighting and home decor items. Departments include decorative hardware, door chimes/mailboxes, ceiling fans, everything for the bath, architectural products, and wall decor. Take a virtual tour and learn the FAQs of light.

Handpainted Art on Tiles

http://home1.gte.net/jaweb/artontile/match.html

Offers handpainted tiles to match your home's decor. Send the artist a piece of wallpaper or cloth—even a picture of your pet—and the artist will implement your idea on tiles, murals, countertops, and accessories. Or choose from the predesigned Classics Collection. View pictures of the artist's work at the site.

Home Decor Press—Do It Yourself

http://www.atl.mindspring.com/~homedec/home.html

Various articles and a Q&A section provide consumer advice and information for do-it-yourself decorators. Also read about money-saving books, and submit your own feedback via email.

Longaberger Baskets

http://www.longaberger.com/

Introduces you to the Longaberger company and all the Longaberger products, including baskets, pottery, fabrics, home decor, and home accessories. The site does not allow you to purchase products directly, but it does help you locate an independent sales consultant. Jump to the kitchen, dining room, library, and living room areas to see the goods available and get valuable information.

Rustic Creations Homepage

http://www.ksmnet.com/rustic_creations/

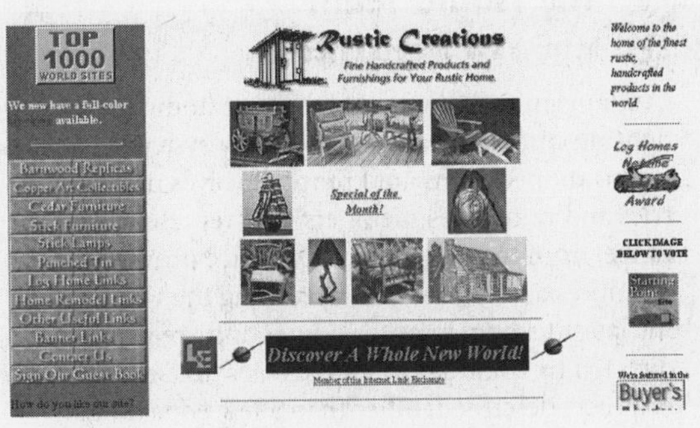

Fine rustic, handcrafted products for the home. You'll just have to see for yourself the things this master craftsman has made—such as an antique stagecoach replica, made of old barnwood, and one-of-a-kind rustic stick chairs. Site also has various links such as log home links and home remodeling links.

STANLEY HOME DECOR

http://www.stanleyworks.com/SHD1.htm

The popular toolmaker now has a line of affordable home decor items, and you can view them at this site. Also learn about other new Stanley products, and access some free project plans.

Stencil Ease Home Decor and Craft Stencils

http://stencilease.com/index.htm

Flip through the Stencil Ease catalog and order online. Stencils, paints, brushes, decorating stamps, and accessories are available. One page also gives detailed instructions on how to stencil. You can also order the Stencil Ease Decorator Catalog.

Vermont Natural Stoneworks Slate Products

http://www.sover.net/~stone/

Quality slate products to accent your home or yard. Slate quarried in the Vermont area is crafted by local artisans into products such as gas-stove mats, flooring, and walkway-to-go patios and walkways. Online order form.

Victoria's Garden

http://www.victoriasgarden.com/index.html

Beautiful dried flower arrangements for the home. Visit this site for photos of the arrangements, pricing information, and ordering instructions. Custom orders also available.

wiltjer pottery

http://www.maine.com/shops/wiltjer/welcome.htm

Unique ceramic clay designs. View the gallery of pottery vases and bowls, and see the handthrown sinks. Also, take advantage of the offered links.

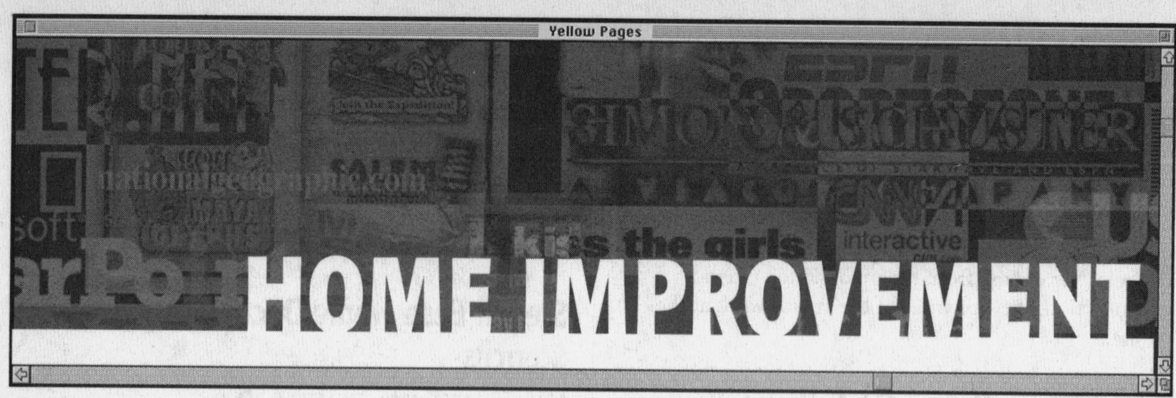

> You cannot push anyone up the ladder unless he is willing to climb himself.
>
> *Andrew Carnegie*

AUTOMATION

CBI Systems, Inc.

http://www.hyperf.com/cbi/

A Kentucky-based company that designs and installs control systems for homes and businesses. A listing is provided for several different packages for residential and business needs.

DHSL: Data Home Systems Limited

http://Fox.nstn.ca/~datahome/

A Hantsport, Nova Scotia company, employing the latest in electrical system technologies and offering an alternative to conventional wiring systems. The benefits that are explained are cost savings, security, entertainment, increased value, and ecology.

Home Automation Association

http://www.hometeam.com/haa/

You are invited to join others who manufacture, distribute, install, and service home automation products. Provides objectives of the association and the benefits of becoming a member.

The Home Team
http://www.hometeam.com/

The Construction Zone
http://www.construction-zone.com/

The Sound Home Resource Web Home Page
http://www.soundhome.com

The Woodworking Catalog
http://www.woodworking.com/

The National Wood Flooring Association
http://www.woodfloors.org/

Home Central
http://homecentral.com/

Lowe's Home Improvement Warehouse
http://www.lowes.com/

Orkin Home Page
http://www.orkin.com/

The Home Team

http://www.hometeam.com/

Contains information on intelligent home design, lighting controls, standards, security systems, communication systems, and more. Involves many industries and numerous members who represent a wide range, from manufacturing to service providers. Members are dedicated to spreading the word about the latest technologies for homes and are primarily directed by trade associations. Does not sell any of the products described, other than a few educational products. Provides information and remains neutral and unbiased to the industry.

JDS Technologies

http://www.hometeam.com/jds/

Manufacturer of telephone and computer control products for intelligent homes. Products are described in detail. A free home control software demo can be downloaded.

Media Dimensions

http://www.floridaguide.com/media/

Media Dimensions creates and installs custom home entertainment systems. Additional information is provided for worldwide services, home theater automation, and yacht and aircraft entertainment areas.

ProSpec

http://ilab.com/prosphme.htm

Interactive Labs' ProSpec Home Electronics Database is a free resource for consumers to view products from many manufacturers. Full color pictures and text for thousands of products covering the spectrum of home electronics. The site is geared toward the custom installation industry and has many useful features for consumers. The service is free to users. Manufacturers can submit their products for free.

The Spectacular Powerhouse Page

http://csbh.mhv.net/~powerhouse/mainmenu.html

A necessary page for electricians, engineers, and home owners. Provides information regarding the electrical industry by featuring subjects such as Q & A, help wanted page, and various links to other related Web sites for information on a particular topic of interest.

Vantage

http://www.transera.com/vantage/

Vantage provides advanced automation systems for lighting, HVAC, audio/visual, and home theater control systems. With a combination of superior technology and fabulous design, they produce a very sophisticated home automation system.

CONSTRUCTION & WOODWORKING

The Construction Zone

http://www.construction-zone.com/

Provides a resource for your home improvement needs. Their growing service offers listings of contractors and related businesses specializing in home repair, home improvement, remodeling and other related services covering the U.S. Visit their free handy hints forum or join their monthly online newsletter for ideas and tips. Contractors can also find out how to list their companies with this national registry.

Cyberwood Express

http://www.woodexpress.com/

Dedicated to the "small shop" woodworker. Provides information about hand-crafted products, wooden toys, and more. Welcomes suppliers of quality wood products.

The Dulux Paint Assistant

http://www.dulux.com

Describes the Dulux paint range of decorative paint products for buildings. The site has a paint selection program, a paint calculator, and painting tips to help solve your paint problems. A valuable resource for the home improvement enthusiast and the professional decorator.

Home Improvement Net

http://www.teleport.com/~plans/

A "how to" informational resource for home improvement activities. Advertisers welcome!

HomeSource

http://www.earthlink.net/~donvander/

Columnist and author Don Vandervort provides free home improvement information and ideas for remodelers and do-it-yourselfers.

Jonathan Press Woodworking and Home Improvement Books and Plans

http://members.aol.com/jonpress/index.html

A source for home improvement and woodworking books and plans, such as projects for gazebos, arbors, deck, outdoor furniture, and storage units. Includes a sign-up feature for a free six-month trial subscription to Home & Workshop Online quarterly magazine.

A B C D E F G H I J K L M N O P Q R S T U V W X Y Z

KraftMaid

http://www.kraftmaid.com/

Browse a virtual showroom of cabinets for kitchen, bathroom, laundry or other specialty uses. Find your nearest dealer, check the cabinet glossary, find out how to begin a remodeling project, or order a video and brochure.

New Home Builders

http://www.NewHomeBuilders.com/

The Ultimate national resource for new home construction. Use the database to select a state, city, neighborhood, or subdivision. Then set your price limit, the number of bedrooms and bathrooms you want, and you're well on your way to finding the home of your dreams. There are also lists of builders and industry-related articles.

New Home Interactive Cyber Home Building Site

http://www.emi.net/newhome

New Home Interactive allows you to create your own dream home. Visit the site to download a short demo program.

Pete's Dry Dock

http://www.pacificharbor.com/whpier/pdd/

Home maintenance and remodeling advice from handyman Pete Prlain. Help for do-it-yourselfers from deck repair and tool suggestions to drippy faucets and leaky roofs.

Professional Woodgraining Kits

http://members.aol.com/ffreeze

Details about products and services available to produce professional woodgraining results at home.

Quality Woodwork & Supply, Inc.

http://www.metrolink.net/quality/quote.htm

Carries a wide variety of woods, from the common to the exotic, as well as an array of other woodworking supplies. Offers an online price lookup system that enables you to enter the type and amount of wood you need and gives a price for the wood.

Remodeler Online

http://www.remodelers.com

A homeowners guide to finding home improvement remodelers across the country. Encourages listings from remodelers.

The Sound Home Resource Web Home Page

http://www.soundhome.com

A comprehensive site of home improvement and construction information for homeowners and prospective homeowners.

The Taunton Press

http://www.taunton.com/

Publishers of *Fine Woodworking, Fine Homebuilding,* and *Home Furniture* magazines for the builder and woodworking enthusiast. Continue your search for expert advice in the Book Shop and Video Room.

TrussPros

http://www.trusspro.com/index.shtml

Explore the world of wood building components, including building information, a glossary, and discussion areas.

W5: WoodWorking on the World Wide Web

http://www.iucf.indiana.edu/~brown/hyplan/wood.html

A collection of useful links to publications, shareware, CAD programs, and commercial sites for the woodworker, woodturner, and wood carver.

The Woodworking Catalog

http://www.woodworking.com/

Contains useful information on lumber, hardware, power tools, finishing supplies, books and plans, woodworking schools, workshops, stores, accessories, hand tools, wooden products, and machinery. Also contains a collection of links to otherwoodworking-related sites. Offers a downloadable DOS program called Woodpro (a lumber database and wood selection expert system).

EDUCATION

Books That Work

http://www.btw.com/

Books That Work publishes software to assist the consumer with home and garden projects. Subjects include kitchen and deck design, home improvement and Garden encyclopedias, and applets that estimate paint usage and calculate spans. Register for special promotions or order products online from this site.

DO IT YOURSELF HQ

http://pwp.usa.pipeline.com/~sivprob

Money-saving information and links for the home handyman and do-it-yourself practitioner.

Do It Yourself, Inc.

http://www.remarketing.com/diy/

One of the country's oldest and largest producers of educational videos, including award-winning titles on home improvement and woodworking. Most are accompanied by a fully diagrammed support booklet.

Home Improvement

http://www.learninglane.com/Learning/hmimprov.html

Visit any one of their classrooms with this site's Learning Lane. Provides instructional videos on the following subjects: home improvement and interior decorating, carpentry and woodworking, construction, home buying/selling, repair/remodeling, and home security.

Home Improvement On The Net

http://rampages.onramp.net/~homeline/il.htm

An easy-to-navigate chart of useful links to home improvement events, advice, and tips. Technical questions can be forwarded via email to "Mr. Fix-It."

Hometime

http://www.hometime.com/

Home page of the popular PBS television series. Offers text and still frame highlights from the show and step-by-step instruction on several home improvement projects.

Lamb Home Videos U-DO IT YOURSELF

http://www5.electriciti.com/homefix/

Award-winning do-it-yourself instructional videos. Learn to do-it-yourself from professional, certified instructors. Step-by-step instruction on the proper tools and techniques you'll need to get the job done. Subjects include tile setting for floors, walls or counters; installation of marble or Mexican tile; faux finishing (decorative painting techniques); installation of glass block; and basic plumbing.

Materials Engineering and Research Laboratory

http://donews.do.usbr.gov/merl/reprhome.html

Provides information on the research of new materials and methods for concrete maintenance, repair, and preservation. Also presents publications on the results of technical studies about conventional and new repair methods and materials.

Paint It Yourself

http://www.serv.net/faux/

Choose from a library of faux finishes or order a custom design, complete with instructions and suggested materials. Samples of wood, marble, antique, and specialty finishes are available.

Touch of Design's Interior Design Book Collection

http://www.electriciti.com/todesign/

This Southern California publisher lists books that are of interest to professionals and to consumers with an interest in products and services. Reports are included on finding your own style or staring your own interior design business.

FLOORING

Anderson Hardwood Floors

http://www.andersonfloors.com

Provides information on one of America's leading manufacturers of prefinished, laminated hardwood floors.

A B C D E F G H I J K L M N O P Q R S T U V W X Y Z

Carpet One

`http://www.carpet1.com/index.html`

Learn more about Carpet One and how to buy the right carpet for your home. Also visit the Bigelow Carpet Collection and learn the history of Bigelow carpet.

Central Carpet

`http://www.centralcarpet.com/prod01.htm`

Central Carpet is a direct importer and manufacturer of carpet, area rugs, and broadloom located in New York City. It is part of a 27-store chain. The site explains the product offerings, care and maintenance, and history of the company.

Country Oak Flooring

`http://www.hway.net/oakfloor/`

Quality T&G Oak Flooring at discount prices. Delivered factory direct anywhere in the USA.

Dalton Carpet Outlets

`http://www.hickory.nc.us:80/ncnetworks/carpets.html`

Provides a listing of carpet dealers in Dalton, GA, home of more than 100 carpet outlets and dealers.

Floor Coverings International

`http://kaos.deepcove.com/carpet/`

Advertises products offered by Floor Coverings International. Obtain information on carpet terminology, types of carpet styles and fibers, carpet cleaning, and answers to frequently asked questions (FAQs) related to carpets. Visit their showroom and check out the Hit Lists.

The National Wood Flooring Association

`http://www.woodfloors.org/`

A wealth of information on wood species, grades, installation, maintenance, and care.

Sculptured Carpet Selections

`http://scsi-inc.com/carpet/`

Specializes in affordable decorator rugs using inlay and sculpting techniques. Almost any design can be incorporated in these high quality carpet creations, including company logos. These rugs can be ordered in any size or color(s). Some design samples are shown at this site.

TrustMark

`http://www.shawinds.com/trustmark/`

Play the TrustMark Wheel of Fortune Sweepstakes for cash rebates and prizes while you learn about carpet construction, performance, and durability factors. Receive decorating tips and find your nearest TrustMark carpet retailer among more than 1,750 participants.

Vermont Natural Stoneworks Slate Products

`http://www.sover.net/~stone/`

Get back to nature with entryways, flooring, patio walkways, boot mats, plant mats, and pet feeding mats created from slate quarried in Vermont. Six subtle colorations are offered in these products that are shown in residential photographs. The slate products are suitable for installation by homeowners and builders.

Vintage Lumber

`http://www.VintageLumber.com/`

Source for antique flooring, rescued from buildings that are on the brink of destruction. Vintage pine, oak, chestnut, poplar, and beech are among the species available.

GENERAL HOME IMPROVEMENT

Cove's Home Improvement Page

`http://www.cove.com/homeimpv.html`

Site provides links to home improvement, plumbing, and handyman tips as well as access to the Thomas Register and chat rooms.

Fiberglass Insulation by Owens Corning

`http://owenscorning.com/`

Get in the pink with information about the fiberglass insulation products this company has developed for homes, as well as other products including roofing, vinyl siding, windows, and patio doors. Join the Owens Corning Homeowner Club at Panther Place, a centralized resource for home-related info, fun, and games.

Home Central

http://homecentral.com/

Your first stop home improvement resource, this search tool provides answers to specific how-to questions. Estimators, a tool dictionary, and reviews of products and services in fifteen categories are provided.

Home Ideas

http://www.homeideas.com

Offers articles to help you plan home projects, a guide to Internet sites, and a request section to get free catalogs and brochures sent to you by mail. A joint project between Home Mechanix magazine and Build.com.

Home Line Talk Radio

http://rampages.onramp.net/~homeline

Home improvement, house building, construction, and remodeling questions are answered on-the-air and on the Internet with Home Line Talk Radio, Houston, TX.

Home Repair Hotline

http://www.deltanet.com/allstar/homerepr.htm

Provides information about a 1-900 number that gives instructions related to the following topics: plumbing improvements, electricity, small and large appliances, heating and cooling units, and home improvement projects ($2.49 a minute).

Lowe's Home Improvement Warehouse

http://www.lowes.com/

Lowe's Companies, Inc. is one of America's top 30 retailers serving home improvement, home decor, home electronics, and home construction markets. Lowe's Web site offers step-by-step guides for home improvement projects, featured products, and tips from Lowe's Home Safety Council. There's also a store locator, recent corporate financial data, and a list of employment opportunities.

National Consumer Alert Hotline

http://www.deltanet.com/allstar/conalert.htm

Provides information on recalls and product warnings. Provides information on many types of appliances, as well as service providers, such as motels, dentists, and carpet cleaners.

On The House with The Carey Brothers

http://www.onthehouse.com/

On The House is a weekly syndicated radio talk show offering advice, hints, and solutions relating to all aspects of home maintenance, repair and improvement.

Pella Windows and Doors

http://www.pella.com/

Research the world of windows, and find the latest products this company has to offer. Terminology and energy efficiency are explained.

Southface Energy Institute

http://southface.org/

Southface Energy Institute is dedicated to research and education in environmentally sound energy technologies. Areas of energy efficient home building and affordable housing are explored.

This Old House

http://pathfinder.com/@@*CibrwcAB1zAhSf7/TOH/

An interactive doorway into This Old House, featuring articles and columns from the magazine, as well as topics related to building, renovation and restoration. Current news, information on personal appearances by the TV series crew, and project house updates are posted regularly.

INSPECTION

Accu-Spect Home Inspection Institute

http://javanet.com/~rgrant/

You can learn the tools of the home inspection business through Accu-Spect Home Inspector Institute. Certification available upon completion. These comprehensive videos are based on over a decade of residential home inspections. The videos also explain details and guide you through the home inspection business.

Advanced Home Inspection

http://www.hmw.com/advanced_home/

Answers frequently asked questions regarding the home inspection process. Provides information to buyers such as knowing what the contract should include, what are some causes for alarm, and how to deal with problems that arise. Sellers learn about issues such as how an inspection can help set a realistic price for the house and how the "Buyer Beware" catch phrase can become "Seller Beware."

American Society of Home Inspection

http://www1.mhv.net/~dfriedman/ashihome.htm

Provides information on the Association as a whole. Contains sections that give information on what new things homeowners, buyers, and inspectors should be aware of. Assists in finding a certified home inspector. Provides information on specific topics relating to electrical wiring, plumbing, the environment, structural foundations, heating systems, and chimneys and flues.

AmeriSpec Home Inspection Service

http://www.io.org/~amrspec/Overview.html

AmeriSpec is a franchised company that provides information on how to pursue a franchise opportunity. Frequently asked questions from buyers are answered.

Home Inspection Resources

http://pages.prodigy.com/LHKF55D/main.htm

Provides information in the following categories: home buyers assistance, market messages, home inspection forum, and Web site information.

HomeSpec 101

http://www3.islands.com/coral/authors.html

Describes a pamphlet that is purchased by first-time home buyers, retired people, or people interested in learning what to look for when purchasing a house. Site also features future pamphlets that will be available.

Orkin Home Page

http://www.orkin.com/

Orkin Exterminating Company provides information for homeowners battling household pests, or anyone curious about the insect world. Questions can be posed to the experts.

Professional Home Inspections, Inc.

http://www.discoverit.com/at/phi/

Provides sample home inspection reports that describe the exact services the company performs.

Many color radon graphs are available to learn more about radon.

Wedgwood Service Group, Inc.

http://www.wwsg.com/index.htm

Provides information and answers to the following topics: real estate inspection; seminars, audio tapes, marketing services, and a monthly industry newsletter for real estate inspectors; and a professional discussion forum.

INTERIOR DESIGN & DECORATING

American Society of Interior Designers

http://www.interiors.org/

An online referral service for the largest organization of professional interior designers in the world. Find information about the organization that has over 20,000 designers, educators and media members, over 7,000 student members and 3,500 industry foundation members. Learn how designers work, or find the right designer for your project.

Ask a Designer

http://www.askadesigner.com/

Pose your building, remodeling, or redecorating question to the pros at this site, and receive a reply with no required fee. The Dear Designer column is updated with answers to questions that have been submitted.

Cascade Blinds

http://www.youdo.com

Order factory direct blinds at wholesale prices.

Colton, Inc.

http://www.cc.utah.edu/~jc3908/colton.htm

Advertises the products of Colton Inc., a drapery manufacturing company in Salt Lake City, Utah.

Cuvs Factory Outlet Store

http://www.cuvs.com

Offers information about slipcovers for casual furniture cushions, picnic tables, accent pillows, window treatments, lamp shade covers, dust ruffles, and pillow shams.

Decorating Dimensions Inc.

http://www.decdim.com/homepage.htm

Carries decorating products for the home. Wall covering (wallpaper), window coverings, floor coverings (carpet, vinyl, wood flooring), and paint.

Decorating Online

http://www.netrix.net/saverud

Professionals at Saverud Paint Shop provide customers with decorating products and advice. Saverud's is a full-service decorating center that offers paint, wallpaper, window blinds, and related items.

Designer Stencils

http://www.designerstencils.com/

Presented by The Stencil Shoppe, Inc., this site offers products for beginners or those experienced with stencils. View and order stencils from the collections, or order a catalog of designs.

Home Decorating on a Shoestring

http://members.aol.com/decor8d/index.htm

A newsletter format from Pam Damour, with excerpts from the show "Home Matters" on the Discovery Channel. An Ask Pam feature and resources for decorating problems, including reviews of books and videos, are included.

Home Decorator

http://www.homefurnish.com/hmdeco_m.htm

Offer home decorating and interior design information, tips, and ideas. Subjects include furniture placement and room arrangement, accessorizing your home, color themes, combining patterns, and monthly design topics.

Home Fashion Information Network

http://www.thehome.com/

Find information on a variety of home furnishing topics under one roof, displayed in rooms for convenience. Topics include tips and tricks, how to select items, and assistance with your bridal registry.

The International Interior Design Association

http://www.iida.com/

There are more than 9,000 international members of this organization, which was formed through the unification of three influential interior design associations. Connect with the interior design community through this site, which has events listings and resources available.

J. R. Burrows & Company

http://www.burrows.com/

A source for English traditional home furnishings, including Arts & Crafts movement items, Victorian designs and Scottish lace curtains. History, online catalog, and ordering information is included.

Mainely Shades

http://www.maineguide.com/maineshade

Add to your home decoration with lampshades (cut and pierced, traditional, victorian) that you create. Complete kits available through mail order.

National Decorating Products Association

http://www.hygexpo.com/ndpa

Provides consumer information on decorating products and industry information for decorating product retailers and manufacturers.

Southwest Decor

http://swdecor.cpeq.com

Includes over forty pages (including pictures) of information. Specialize in Southwestern, western, and contemporary furnishings, decorating accessories, and gifts.

Steptoe & Wife Antiques, Ltd.

http://www.steptoewife.com/defaultf.htm

Architectural restoration products from iron staircases to drapery hardware are offered by this Canadian company whose motto is "100 years behind the times." Listings of products and distributors are provided.

Sudberry House

http://connix.com/~sudberry/

Displays fine wood accessories used for mounting needlework and crafts, as well as an online color catalog, a factory tour, and many needlework designs.

Suzanne Seely's "Make it Beautiful" Decorating Newsletter

http://www.aiminc.com/seely

Suzanne Seely brings her knowledge of styles, design, color, resources, and years of interior decorating experience to Internet subscribers in her newsletter.

Symbol-Talk

http://www.teleport.com:80/~symbol/index.html

Advertises meditation pillows made by Symbol Talk. Provides information on the various types and styles of pillows, cloth color, and how to order.

Wall Bear Wallpaper Stripping Tips

http://www.wallbear.com/PaperStripping.html

For anyone attempting to remove wallpaper, this site offers advice and a guide to tools and products to make the job easier. Step-by-step instructions work with Wall Bear proprietary stripper or any other brand.

PLUMBING

Best Mfg. Co.

http://pages.prodigy.com/best/

Offers wholesale plumbing supplies. Some of the products in their line include faucets, water heaters, fixtures, pipes, valves, and fittings.

CyberBath Catalogue

http://www.baths.com/index.htm

A comprehensive list of luxury bath and kitchen fixtures from major manufacturers. A new product is featured each month, as well as a current list of overstocked and closeout items.

Delta Faucet Company

http://www.deltafaucet.com/

Find out what is new at Delta Faucet, maker of lifetime warranted single handle faucets and a variety of kitchen and bathroom plumbing items. Locate the nearest dealer, or find replacement parts.

Faucet Outlet Online

http://www.faucet.com/

Contains selections of faucets. Provides information about installing, choosing, and selecting a faucet.

GROHE

http://www.grohe.com/

This company is known for its faucet brands used in custom homes and upscale remodeling projects. Lists the latest products, as well as how to contact GROHE. Also, look at a showroom and learn about their various promotional programs for dealers.

Pipe Trades Association

http://www.PipeTA.org/

The Pipe Trades Association's purpose is to bring together members of the Bay Area Local Unions. This site describes the Association and provides information regarding Local Unions 342, 343, and 467. Also lists topics such as craftsmanship, training and education, quality, contractors, labor management cooperation, hot links, and a discussion forum.

Splashnet

http://www.splashnet.com/

New England kitchen and bath showrooms featuring the latest products and designs. Look for new ideas or hot design tips.

theplumber.com

http://www.theplumber.com/

Hills Plumbing page provides answers to frequently asked questions. Offers a selection of plumbing links and newsgroups. Also learn about the history of plumbing.

Let us think of education as the means of developing our greatest abilities, because in each of us there is a private hope and dream which, fulfilled, can be translated into benefit for everyone and greater strength for our nation.

John F. Kennedy

Biblical Foundations for Christian Homeschooling

http://pages.prodigy.com/C/H/C/christianhmsc/home.htm

Directed toward Christian homeschooling families, this family-sponsored page traces its educational philosophy to God's instruction in Deuteronomy 6:5-7. The site includes homeschooling essays, national documents, news on homeschooling issues and links to other homeschooling family pages.

Benjamin Franklin Academy

http://www.benfrk.com

Home school assistance, home school links, home school curriculum, and distance learning provided by the Benjamin Franklin Academy.

Homeschool World
http://www.home-school.com/

Keystone National High School
http://www.keystonehighschool.com/

The Unschooling Homeschooler
http://www.islandnet.com/~bedford/home_lrn.html

Home School Learning Books

http://www.home-school.com/mall/esp/esp.html

Home School Learning Resources for Grades K–7. The entire year in one book. All subjects available.

The Home Schooling Advantage

http://www.concentric.net/~skiplac/

Information on home schooling, ADD/ADHD, learning challenged children, Web links to other educational sites, and general information on multimedia and its importance to education.

The Home School Legal Defense Association

http://www.learnathome.com/hslda.htm

Created to establish a low-cost method of obtaining quality legal defense for home schooling families. The online site provides information on current court battles and legal issues.

HomeFront Education

http://www.ebicom.net/~rileyafr

HomeFront Education provides helpful articles and helps for Home School parents including home school links.

Homeschool World

http://www.home-school.com/

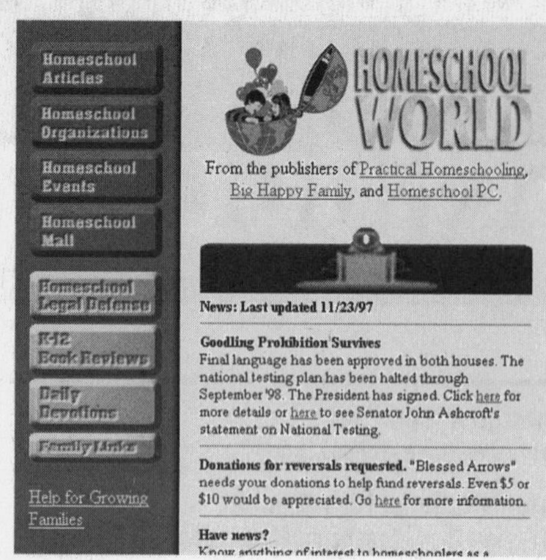

This award-winning site features a Home Life catalog, a listing of homeschool support groups, directories of courses and lesson plans, and a mammoth Homeschool Mall, where shoppers can find hundreds of items.

Keystone National High School

http://www.keystonehighschool.com/

Keystone High School offers a fully accredited distance education program for 9th through 12th grade students. Their online site details the homeschooling program offered. Features include a Parent Planning Guide, Course Descriptions, Policies and Guidelines, and other information.

Oregon Home Education Network

http://www/teleport.com/~ohen/index.html

A non-profit organization established to support Oregon's homeschooling families, the Oregon Home Education Network (OHEN) acts as a clearinghouse for homeschooling activities and resources at the local, state and national level. The online site includes FAQS about homeschooling, Oregon Administrative Rules, and a number of homeschool resources.

The Unschooling Homeschooler

http://www.islandnet.com/~bedford/home_lrn.html

As opposed to homeschooling, unschooling advocates disagree with the idea that children should be forced to learn in any structured environment. This unschooling site encourages students to "follow passions and explore interests", and it offers an index of resources to guide the process. An elaborate index includes links to animal, music, math and art sites, to name a few. There are also articles about homeschooling and a section on famous home learners. An intriguing site.

A B C D E F G H I J K L M N O P Q R S T U V W X Y Z

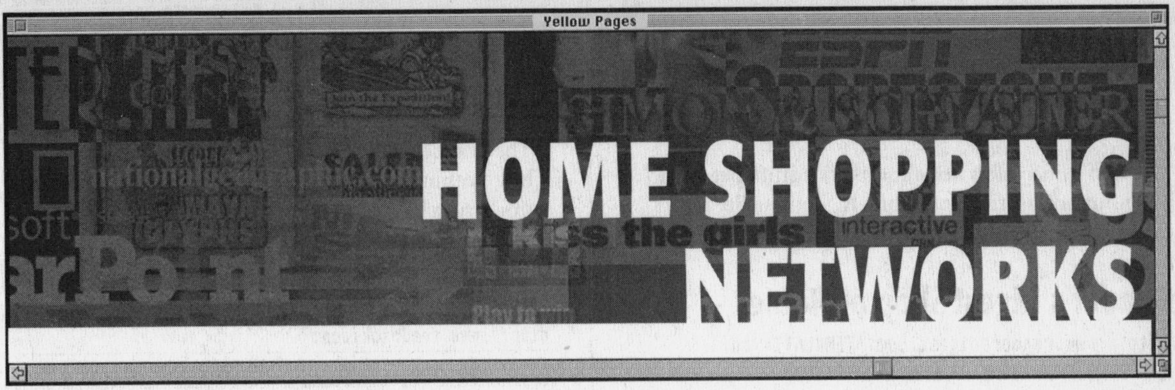

> We shop at home, we surf the Web, at the same time we're emptier.
>
> *Palmer Joss in* Contact *(1997)*

NRP TOP PICKS

CatalogLink
`http://cataloglink.com/cl/`

QVC Home Page
`http://www.qvc.com/`

African American Shopping Mall

`http://www.bnl.com/aasm/`

Created to provide a place to showcase African-American merchants' wares and offer products and services of interest to African-American consumers. Includes lots of choices and categories.

CatalogLink

`http://cataloglink.com/cl/`

Select the catalogs you want to receive from the categories at this site to help you with your home shopping. There are also several links to the companies' home pages for online shopping.

Eddie Bauer

`http://www.eddiebauer.com/eb/ShopEB/frame_line.asp`

Quality basics at good prices are available online at this site. Shoppers can log in their wish lists and shopping lists.

FAO Schwarz

`http://www.faoschwarz.com/`

This ulitmate online toy site is brought to you from the ultimate toy store. (One word of advice: Turn down your speakers for this site. The rocking horse sound will drive you insane.)

Gift Connection

`http://accessories.com/homepage.htm`

Several gift ideas in various price ranges. This site offers gift wrapping and overnight shipping.

Harry and David

`http://www.harryanddavid.com/`

This site belongs to the company that has the best pears found anywhere in the world. Anything you order here will be appreciated and devoured.

Innovations

`http://www.innovations.com.au/`

This site has lots of categories, including a handy "Gift Ideas Over $50" and an even handier "Gift Ideas Under $50" page. Also includes a find feature to help you quickly locate what you want.

JC Penney

`http://www.jcpenney.com/`

At this site you can use the electronic order form to order from the print catalog or shop the online store. You can also see what's happening in the stores or order the latest catalogs.

jcrew.com

`http://www.jcrew.com/`

The jcrew site offers on online catalog and an opportunity to order a copy of the paper catalog. Also has text and visual directories and gift ideas.

A B C D E F G H I J K L M N O P Q R S T U V W X Y Z

Land's End

http://www.landsend.com/spawn.cgi?ZEROPAGE&GRAPHIC&NULLPAGE&0

Land's End offers decorations, kids stuff, pet gifts, home accessories, and more. A good quality mail order merchandiser with a nicely designed Web site.

Reader's Digest Shop at Home

http://www.readersdigest.com/*TEMPLATE=/rd/commerce/htp/index.htp@session=fmj8r5

Offering books, music, videos, audio books, CD-ROMs, magazines, and more. A good wholesome site for family gifts.

Sam's Club

http://www.samsclub.com/forum/buylin10.shtml

This site has photos, descriptions, price information, and more for select toys. Not as many items as you would expect from this superwarehouse.

QVC Home Page

http://www.qvc.com/

The granddaddy of all home shopping pages! You can buy clothing, jewelry, electronics, home decor items, office supplies, and more at this site.

Related Sites

http://www.crutchfield.com

http://www.fredricks.com

http://www.fossil.com

http://www.gap.com

http://www.goodstuffcheap.com

http://www.llbean.com

http://www.spiegel.com

http://www.disney.com

http://www.sharperimage.com

http://www.studiostores.warnerbros.com

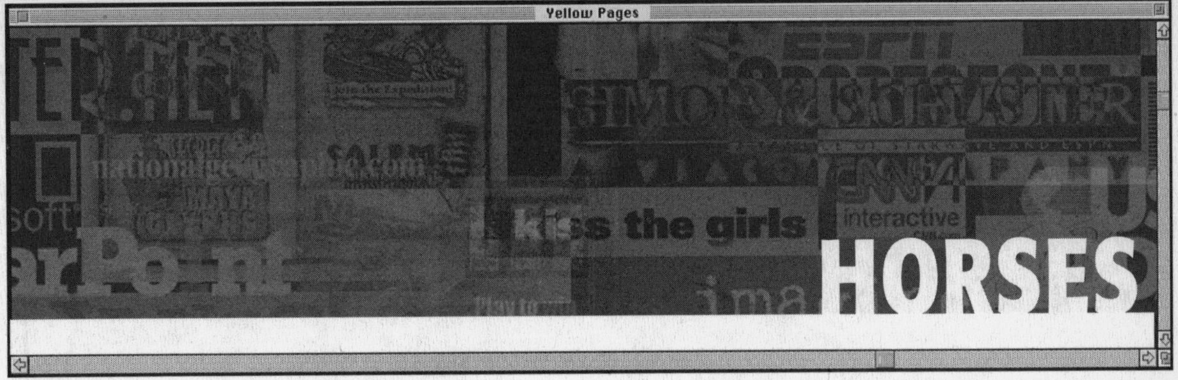

> Horse sense is the thing a horse has which keeps it from betting on people.
>
> *W.C. Fields*

The American Saddlebred Horse

http://www.american-saddlebred.com/

Anyone interested in horses, and show horses in particular, will enjoy viewing the video clips of the various gaits displayed during competitions. Detailed descriptions and diagrams of the horse's structure and history of the breed are also featured. The site includes a small photo gallery and links to saddlebred horse museums and national organizations.

EquiLinQ

http://www.wsmith.com/equilinq/

Provides sales information about horses and horse-related gear. Includes links to the red bluff bull and gelding sale and access to the online magazine *Ride!*.

The American Saddlebred Horse
http://www.american-saddlebred.com/

The Horseman's Advisor
http://www.spyder.net/horseadvice/

The Horse Zone

http://www.horsezone.com

If you're looking for a horse to buy, or need a saddle or other riding gear, the Horse Zone might be what you're looking for. This site contains that information and more. Home of the Equestrian Resource Center, this page contains a listing of classified ads, a discussion group, and a photo gallery of horses.

The Horseman's Advisor

http://www.spyder.net/horseadvice/

Serves as a clearinghouse for articles and products on horse-related topics. Includes a discussion forum, classifieds, and links to other sites.

Horsenet™

http://www.horsenet.com/

Horsenet offers information on equestrian vacations worldwide and videos of the 1996 Olympic equestrian events. A large classified section offers breeding, sale, and equipment information as well as dates and locations of upcoming shows like Equine Affaire-The Great American Horse Exposition.

WWW Library—Livestock Section

http://www.ansi.okstate.edu/library/equine.html

Provides a listing of horse resources, including information on breeds and selection, horse publications, publications on diseases, disorders, parasites of the horse, and general information such as behavior and training, buying a horse, care and horse shoeing, nutrition and feeding, and more.

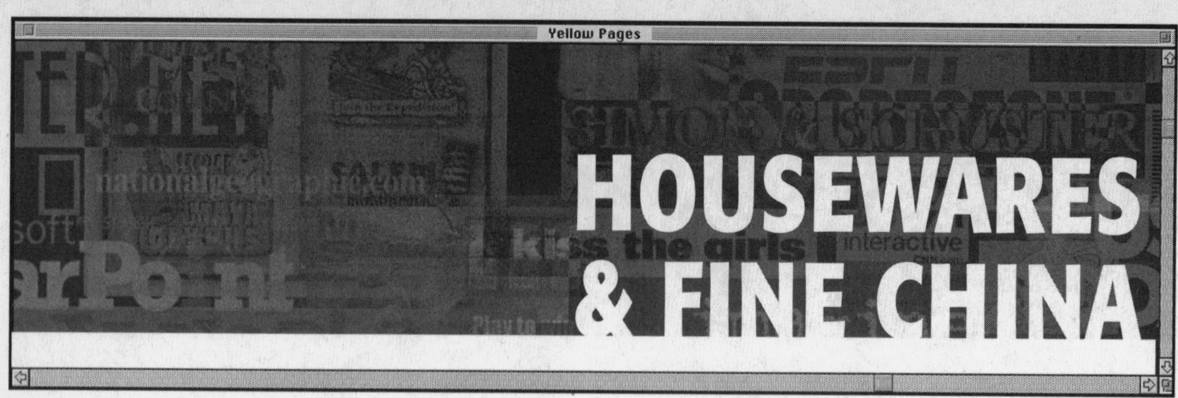

> Put it on a plate, son.
> You'll enjoy it more.
>
> *Mrs. Maddox in* Repo Man *(1984)*

NRP Top Picks

Chrisofle
`http://www.christofle.com/`

Fine China and Porcelain Repair
`http://infoweb.magi.com/~fcpr/fcprhome.html`

Gabriel's Trumpet
`http://www.gabrielstrumpet.com/`

Almost and Perfect Fine Discount China

`http://www.almostandperfectchina.com/china/default.html`

This site offers incredible prices on Baccarat, Royal Worcester, Wedgwood, Royal Copenhagen, Aynsley, Royal Doulton, and others. Help coordinating colors and patterns, selecting pieces, and bridal registry are also offered. Monograms, gift wrap, and gift certificates are available.

Apple Dream Fine China and Gifts

`http://www.appledream.com/`

Based in Atlanta, this site offers tableware, flatware, and giftware from well-known manufacturers such as Spode, Wedgwood, Royal Copenhagen, Haviland, Richard Ginori, and Bernardaud. Some discontinued patterns are offered too.

Atlantic Silver & China

`http://www.atlanticsilver.com/indexa.htm`

This site belongs to a company that buys and sells silver and china. It is also an authorized dealer of silver, crystal, and china for many major manufacturers. It offers a bridal registry at wholesale prices, gift services, pattern matching, and many more services. Definately worth a look if you are in the market to purchase or sell fine items.

Berkshire China Home Page

`http://www.profnet.co.uk/bkschina/`

Specializes in personalized fine bone china mugs for corporate promotions, gifts, incentive programs, businesses, schools, clubs, tourist venues, or whoever might order them.

China Traders Replacement Service

`http://www.chinatraders.com/`

The owner of this site locates additional pieces of discontinued china patterns, offers information on china appraisals and selling your china, and gives the definitions of various china terms. The site also contains helpful hints such as caring for your china and lead poisoning warnings.

Chrisofle

`http://www.christofle.com/`

Beginning with the homepage, this site gives visitors a sense of luxury that is associated with this legendary manufacturer of fine silverware, holloware, porcelain, and table linens. Christofle has recently launched its own line of crystal stemware and barware, which will undoubtedly become as coveted by collectors as its other product lines. In addition to the usual offerings, this site includes an etiquette page and a museum page complete with a photo and brief history of each piece.

Fine China and Porcelain Repair

http://infoweb.magi.com/~fcpr/fcprhome.html

A Canadian business that restores and repairs china and porcelain objects. The Archives link of this site contains photos and brief histories of objects that have been restored. It also has a FAQ that covers most of the questions visitors might have including the difference between restoring and repairing items.

Fulbreit China Locators

http://www.harlequinchina.com/

This company buys, sells, and locates china for people. It specializes in American, Bavarian, French Haviland, Fiesta, Harlequin, Russel Wright, Metlox, Eva Zeisal, and others. Site also requests information from visitors on specific pieces—visit that page for details. Whether you are looking for an entire set or a few pieces to complete the china set you inherited from your great-aunt, this is the place to look.

Gabriel's Trumpet

http://www.gabrielstrumpet.com/

Consignment antiques, china, silver, crystal, and decorative accessories for the home. Rated #1 consignment store by *The Chicago Tribune*, this store based in Wheaton, Illinois, has exceptionally fine quality merchandise. The site is full of clear photos of the items available for sale arranged by category. The only negative about this site is that no prices are provided. Visitors interested in purchasing an item or offering merchandise for consignment are instructed to contact the store via email.

Lenox Collections Home Page

http://www.lenoxcollections.com/

This elegant site offers Lenox classics and collections, as well as the company's history. It includes FAQs, information on favorite collectibles, the production process, and a free catalog offer. This is site is partially completed, but shows promise.

Old China Patterns Limited

http://www.chinapatterns.com/

This site offers a worldwide replacement matching service to help visitors locate or sell items. The company maintains an instock inventory of thousands of items plus more listed for sale by retailers, wholesalers, and individuals around the world. The service if free and your contact information is kept confidential.

Seaway China Company's Royal Doulton Site

http://www.seawaychina.com/

This company offers Royal Doulton figurines, characters, and new and discontinued collectibles. Includes Bunnykins and Beatrix Potter figurines.

Special Settings

http://www.shewey.com/wedding/ssetting/

This site offers Wedgwood, Lenox, Spode, Royal Worcester, Royal Crown Derby, Oneida, Gorham, and Reed & Barton priced according to the company's policy of "the more you buy, the less you pay." Special prices are available for customized packages of certain patterns—visit the site for details.

Stockwell China

http://www.stockwellchina.co.uk/

This site belongs to a 75-year-old Scottish company offering fine china, crystal, cutlery, and giftware. The site also has an online catalog and order service available.

The Story of Spode

http://www.spode.co.uk/

This Spode site contains an online tour of the oldest English pottery, which has been operating at the same site since 1770. Visitors are invited to join The Spode Society—a organization for collectors and Spode fans.

Related Sites

http://www.rubbermaid.com/home/h1main.htm

http://www.thetraveller.com/thetraveller/twoplatesfull/twoplatesfull.html

http://www.peddlers-cottage.com/

http://www.placemats.com/

http://www.Scenic-Idaho.com/PinehavenPottery/

http://www.web-images.com/clouds/

http://www.organized.com/

http://www.kitcol.com/

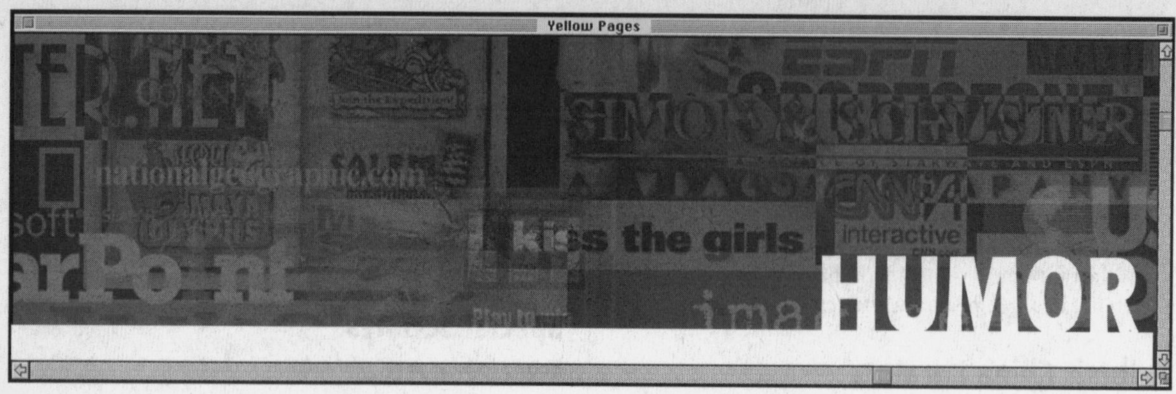

A gainst the assault of laughter nothing can stand.

Mark Twain

Air Guitar

http://www.digitalrag.com/mirror/air/air.html

Tired of watching your friends play air guitar at the Steve Miller concert and wishing you had that talent? Well, take an online lesson here. Also has 100 links to other entertaining sites.

The Amazing Pecking Chicken

http://www.vanderbilt.edu/~dotedu/staff/cluck/

Investigate this site of extreme silliness for images of a disco chicken, a pecking chicken, and the history of the pecking chicken home page. Read the top five "super-neato quotes from cluck worshipers" and find out how the power of the chicken has changed the lives of countless (OK, about 12) others.

The Anti-Telemarketer Source

http://www.izzy.net/~vnestico/t-market.html

Do you hate it when telemarketers bother you? This site is about the revenge of the customer. Offers techniques, stories, and more about dealing with telemarketers—finally, a site that's both funny *and* useful! Make sure you check out the "Hall o' Fame" section.

NRP PICKS

Bob's Fridge Door
http://www.bobsfridge.com/

Centre for the Easily Amused
http://www.amused.com/

CONK! Daily - Humor in the News
http://www.conk.com/

Conversational Terrorism
http://www.best.com/~vandruff/art_converse.html

Cruel Site of the Day
http://www.cruel.com/

Dave's Web of Lies
http://www.cs.man.ac.uk/~hancockd/lies.htm

Funny But No...
http://www.shoebox.com/funny/funny.asp

Goofiness Dot Com
http://www.goofiness.com/

The Herald Link - Dave Barry
http://www.herald.com/tropic/barry/

Lip Balm Anonymous
http://members.aol.com/LipBalmA/

The Lunacy Catapult
http://www.epix.net/~wayne26/

Quotes! of the Moment
http://www.hooked.net/users/davew/quotes.html

Spatula City
http://pixelscapes.com/spatulacity/

Twisted Tunes Home Page
http://www.twistedtunes.com/

Archive of Email Forwards

http://www.BL.net/forwards/

The author of this page suggests stopping off here to post your amusing story or joke, instead of the same email jokes and stories being forwarded over and over to countless people. Come on, think about it—how many times have you seen those variations on "Why did the chicken cross the road?" You can submit your own collection of bon mots, one-liners, light-bulb jokes, and so on, or browse through the archives of what the author says he was actually glad he got by email.

Baby Shark's Lawyer Joke Website

http://www.primenet.com/~russelb/Lawyer.html

Don't like lawyers? Then this site may be for you. Includes many different lawyer jokes and humorous stories, recommended reading, a link to Yahoo!'s index of lawyer jokes, and more.

The Bathrooms of Madison County

http://www.nutscape.com/~fluxus/

A well-done parody of the popular novel *The Bridges of Madison County* that includes pictures and a story told in seven parts about, literally, the bathrooms of Madison County in Iowa. The backgrounds used on some of the pages are a subtle touch; they look like bathroom tiles, outhouse siding, and so on.

Bob's Fridge Door

http://www.bobsfridge.com/

Created by Bob Hirschfield, this page offers satirical, humorous coverage of the news and other topics. Check out the sections Internet Insanity, Skewpoint, Annoying Computers, Funny Features, and, of course, Bob's Fridge Door. There's even a chat room. Cool graphics, especially the little animation of a fly being swatted.

The Bottom 95%

http://www.dartmouth.edu/~jaundice/bottom95/

Tired of all the "Top 5 percent of the Web" icons? Here's the pirate site that professes to list the remaining 95 percent; it offers a logo that pages can use to proudly proclaim they're in the "Bottom 95%." You'll also find a link to the page that lists the sites not listed by Point's survey.

Centre for the Easily Amused

http://www.amused.com/

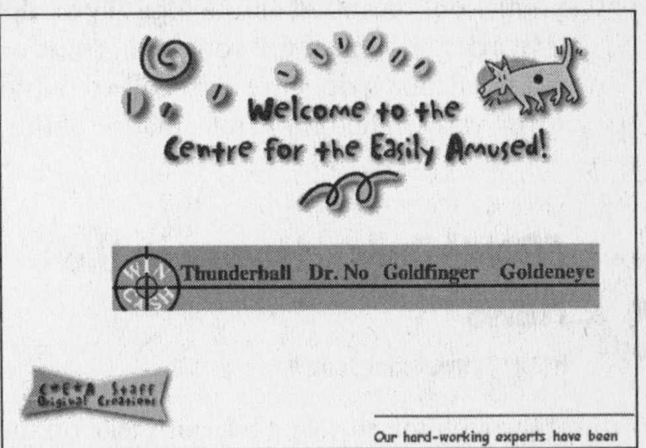

A phenomenal site where you can waste huge amounts of time browsing. The site's links are organized by category, like "Sites That Do Stuff" or "Random Silliness," to make up one the best lists of odd humor on the WWW. You'll also find trivia games, daily jokes, and chat rooms.

Clowns Are Evil Incarnate: The Anti-Clown Site

http://www.geocities.com/Colosseum/2430/clown.html

Who knows what tragic childhood event drove the author of this site to his current anti-clown beliefs? Nevertheless, he backs up his theory with news articles, dozens of stories from readers who have had horrifying clown experiences, and even a picture gallery of clowns doing very bad, un-clownlike things. Contribute your own story or picture, and help stamp out clowns (while wearing big floppy shoes, of course)!

College Dropout Alumni Association

http://www.geocities.com/CollegePark/7734/cdoaa.html

This humorous site lists famous alumni who dropped out of college; some of the names you'll see are almost unbelievable. Rosie O'Donnell? Bill Gates? William Faulkner? Includes stories, articles, and other offbeat items about dropping out of college and supplies membership information.

Compendium of Misunderstood Lyrics

http://www.flash.net/~trevas/

Surely I'm not the only one who thought Creedence Clearwater Revival was singing "There's a bathroom on the right"? If you're prone to misunderstanding lyrics, too, check out this site and feel less alone. Read past submissions organized chronologically or alphabetized by lyric line, or submit your own. Some of the best misunderstood lyrics have been collected into book form; you can find more information about it here.

CONK! Daily - Humor in the News

http://www.conk.com/

Browse through this site for a hilarious take on the daily news. You'll also find daily fun facts and quotes, games and puzzles, over 100 of your favorite comic strips, and more ways to goof off than you thought possible.

Conversational Terrorism

http://www.best.com/~vandruff/art_converse.html

I don't know about you, but I plan to print or email *several* copies of the guidelines suggested at this site to friends, loved ones, and not-so-loved ones. The author has grouped the most common conversational pitfalls into the categories of Ad Hominem Variants, Sleight of Mind Fallacies, Delay Tactics, Question as Opportunity, and General Irritants. Examples of each type of faux pas are given, too, but I'm sure *you're* not guilty of any of them—right?

Cruel Site of the Day

http://www.cruel.com/

Tired of a Pollyanna outlook? This site offers a cynical look at the Web by awarding sites that are the most perturbing and cruel, yet entertaining. "Our Cruel Heritage," an index to past award-winning sites, gives you a great starting point for what's warped, obscure, and peevish on the Web.

Cursing in Swedish

http://www.bart.nl/~sante/enginvek.html

Study sharp, succinct swearing in Swedish. According to the introduction, the Swedish language is remarkably limited when it comes to using four-letter words. If you're Swedish and short-tempered, or just interested in expanding your repertoire, let this page help you take out your aggressions. WAV files are supplied so you can learn to pronounce your curses properly.

The Daily Muse

http://www.cais.com/aschnedr/muse.htm

Tired of the daily news as reported by the well-groomed authoritative media? Look here for a cynical twist to the news, heavily seasoned with political humor. Choose from dozens of sections, such as Wordly Muse, Muse Briefs, and Bizmuse, or peruse the archives of back issues.

Dave's Web of Lies

http://www.cs.man.ac.uk/~hancockd/lies.htm

Dave's crack team of researchers haunt the Web looking for lies packaged as the truth (and if you believe *that*...). Choose the Lie of the Day, or go for A Week of Lies, or—better yet—search the Database of Lie by topic or by liar to find a lie useful for almost any situation. For special occasions, you might want to consult the Celebrity Liar.

David Hasselhoff is the AntiChrist

http://www.indirect.com/www/warren/baywatch.html

This Web site author proposes one of the scariest possible theories in show business. He's got lots of proof, including photos! Decide for yourself whether you subscribe to this eerie possibility about the favorite star of "Baywatch."

Funny But No...

http://www.shoebox.com/funny/funny.asp

Ever wondered what happens to the greeting card concepts that don't make it to the store shelves? Wonder no more—they've been collected here at Shoebox's site. Pick a week and see the greeting card rejects for that period, such as thanking a very fertile aunt for giving you lots of cousins. Prepare to be amused, horrified, or both.

The Gallery of Advertising Parody

http://www.dnai.com/~sharrow/parody.html

This site offers many different ad parodies (view the images in JPEG format) and other humorous features. Includes articles, pictures, and links to other humor/parody sites.

Georgetown Gonzo

http://sunsite.unc.edu/martin/gonzo.html

A Georgetown underground journalist put together this little gem in the true spirit of "gonzo journalism." Biting satire and a willingness to hold nothing sacred make this site enjoyable. Make sure you browse through the anthology of bad poetry!

Goofiness Dot Com

http://www.goofiness.com/

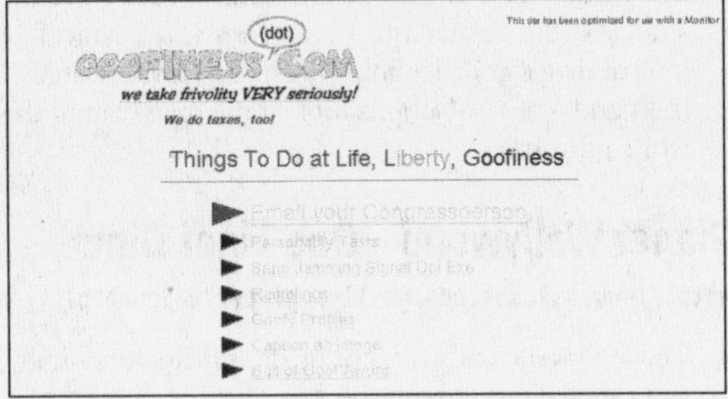

Who knew wasting time could be so much fun? At Goofiness Dot Com, you'll discover all kinds of new ways to fritter away your productive hours. Supply captions for pictures, take personality tests, read the Random Prediction and Random Quote of the day, and see the winners of the Ball of Goof Award.

Heather Has Two Mommies

http://www.swiss.ai.mit.edu/zoo/heather-has-two-mommies.html

A parody of the popular children's book *Heather Has Two Mommies*. The page author's cynical views of modern gender issues might be hilarious to some and dismaying to others, so use your judgment. The device of striking out certain words and phrases and replacing them with politically correct substitutes is amusing (and makes a point). At any rate, it's comforting to discover I'm not "lazy"; I'm "energetically-challenged."

The Herald Link - Dave Barry

http://www.herald.com/tropic/barry/

Here it is—the home of Dave Barry, humor columnist for *The Miami Herald*. You could spend quite a few hours browsing through Dave's Digest, a collection of past columns, and laughing yourself sick, or you could just check out his most recent gem. You can't email Dave from here, but you can contribute to his HeraldTalk bulletin board. There are some links to other Dave pages, such as those for his latest book or his band, the Rock Bottom Remainders.

The Infamous Big Green Button

http://www.geocities.com/Hollywood/5945/press01.html

Creative genius spawned this captivating site. It might be silly and useless, but you'll keep coming back to it. It features a—oh, how do I say this?—big green button to push. Check out the BGB comments page and for the bold, you can try out Big Green Button 2, the sequel.

Internet Squeegee Guy

http://www.website1.com/squeegee

Stop off at this page to get the inside of your monitor washed when you pull up to a stoplight on the information dirt road. You can choose to give the squeegee guy some change or to look the other way.

It's the French Fries

http://www.select-ware.com/fries/

They're hot, tasty, and a staple of the American diet, so look here for everything you never wanted to know about the skinny deep-fried potatoes. Learn about the history of the French fry, see some French-fry art, get recipes for making your own, and more.

Jim's All New, Fresher Smelling Home Page

http://www.cruzio.com/~jimg/index.html

This page, characterized by a dry, skewed sense of humor that the overeducated will enjoy thoroughly, is worthy of several minutes of uninterrupted surfing. Nicely done introductory pictures, too. Check out the section "My Idea of Humor" for links to all kinds of funny stories and humor tidbits.

Lip Balm Anonymous

http://members.aol.com/LipBalmA/

This site promotes the casting out of all lip balms based on their psychologically addictive tendencies. Read about the history of lip balm and "The Industry of Addiction," and please…share this site with someone you love.

The Lunacy Catapult

http://www.epix.net/~wayne26/

A site constructed for pure silliness and amusement. View the "Goofy Picture Show," browse through the archive of skits in the "Play a Day Center," check the progress of the presidential campaign of Fig Bar Man, and, if you're brave, try the Renegade Button of Doom.

The Mama Page

http://watt.seas.virginia.edu/~jwb7w/mom/home.html

Wade through a nearly endless list of "your Mama" jokes; to help you out, there's an index by joke subject. You can also submit your own "your Mama" jokes to the site.

Mefco's Random Joke Server

http://www.totalweb.com/ent/jokehome.html

Choose the type of joke you want from a large list of categories, including "Light Bulb Jokes," "Murphy's Law," "Jokes for Nerds," and so on. Read some funny stories, too, or submit your own joke, if you like.

The Miraculous Winking Jesus

http://www.fastlane.net/~sandman/jesus/

A mild spoof of the religious miracles observed around the world. The Winking Jesus page shows a detailed sketch of Jesus that periodically winks. You can also submit your own observations, depending on what you saw.

My Boss Sucks!

http://members.aol.com/btrumanz/gripe.htm

This site is being revamped, so not everything is ready at the time this book went to press. However, what's planned sounds good: Read the winning bad-boss story, submit your own to see whether it wins "Gripe of the Month," check out "Dumb Things My Boss Has Said," and investigate the links to other sites.

The NEW Mirsky.Com

http://mirsky.com/wow/

Home of what used to be Mirksy's Worst of the Web. Some funny stuff is still here, however, for you to check out. Read the first (and only) issue of *The Mirsky Monthly* newsletter, take the Mirsky Drunk Browsing Test™, and more.

The Oracle of Bacon at Virginia

http://www.cs.virginia.edu/~bct7m/bacon.html

Another site professing the power of Kevin Bacon. Find out your favorite actors' "bacon number," and play the linking game with *any* other actor. There are other games to play, and check out the new section "The Center of the Hollywood Universe."

PElvis

http://www.princeton.edu/~pelvis/

The King lives in the mind and jeans of the Princeton students who created this page. Gives you a cynical look at drugs and alcohol, with several Elvis-related links and a not-so-serious look at the man behind the white jumpsuit.

Planet Wallywood - One Liner Diner

http://www.halcyon.com/gwally/cgi-pvt/welcome.pl

Check this site daily for a pithy or amusing one-liner you can use throughout the day. The one-liners are randomly generated, so you might get the same one twice when you click "One more."

Public Domain

http://www.iminet.com/ccoats/

An online site for the newspaper column of the same name that includes a chat room, bulletin boards, stories, links, and more. An interactive feature lets you help solve problems submitted to this humorous advice column.

The Pun Starts Here

http://gdbdoc.gdb.org/~nazar/puns/punp1.html

You'll find puns of every type and for every occasion here. Some are organized by category, and some are very long stories ending in a pun that will make you groan or giggle, depending on your response to puns. Punsters will probably want to bookmark this page.

Punch Rush Limbaugh Page

http://www.indirect.com/www/beetle87/rush/index.html

That's right—punch everyone's favorite politically untrained conservative radio personality; he looks even better when you give him a black eye. Check out the Rush Limbaugh anagrams, too. Oh, and did I mention I bookmarked this page?

Quotes! of the Moment

`http://www.hooked.net/users/davew/quotes.html`

Get your fix of absurdist and off-the-wall humor here. This site offers a different quote or joke by Steven Wright or a different Deep Thought™ by Jack Handey each time you visit. Or you can sit there and keep clicking Reload to get one new quote after another—not that *I* personally tried that.

The Rock and Roll Hall of Shame

`http://pathfinder.com/@@q2StgAcAbwY4*3GW/people/hall/`

Is your music collection littered with bad drum solos and big-haired performers? If so, you'll love this site. Even the classic artists are assaulted here. Features a lengthy list of intolerable groups, downright embarrassing song lyrics, and bad film appearances by rock stars.

Rodney Dangerfield Home Page

`http://www.rodney.com/`

Rodney's home page features a joke of the day and the "no respect" contest. You can also download sound files and an answering-machine message in Rodney's voice.

The Scamizdat Memorial

`http://www.well.com/user/jerod23/clam.html`

The site gives you a scathing, yet humorous, look at the Church of Scientology from many different perspectives. Most of the articles at this site are taken from email messages, collected to leave a lasting impression of the religion. Check out some of the links to other related sites.

Solid Space

`http://redwood.northcoast.com/~shojo/Solid.html`

Here's a page of random bits of fun. Hear Fabio welcome you to his fan club, check out the online ViewMaster, investigate the "Dark Side of Pez" (it's scary, but true!), check out the Awful Music section, and more.

Spam Haiku Archive

`http://pemtropics.mit.edu/~jcho/spam/`

Learn how to create poetry in the rigorous haiku/Spam format. More than 4600 "Spamkus," most of which aren't so funny as they are curiously silly.

Spatula City

`http://pixelscapes.com/spatulacity/`

You'll find more than just pancake flippers at this cool virtual spatula store. The site offers a wealth of information, organized into groups of "The Silly Zone," "Fiction and Faction," "Black Light Special," and "Kitchenware n' Candybars." Go to the "Checkout Lane" to see a list of links to related sites.

Top Ten Ways to Tell if You Have a Sucky Home Page

`http://www.glover.com/sucky.html`

Does your home page just not make the cut? Look here for clues hinting at a bad home page, as well as links on how to get on track. Although the writing is humorous, the author makes some excellent points. You can even order the "Totally Un-Sucky Web Site Starter Kit" CD-ROM!.

Trailer Trash Tribune

`http://www.webserve.com/phrantic/tribune.htm`

Enjoy the working-class humor of this page written by white-collar people. The "landlords" of this site have, so they claim, been providing shelter for the homeless of the Internet since 1994. This online trailer park community might amuse you if you find the right link. Link to the "Phrantic's Public Housing Project," which is leading the fight for squatting rights in cyberspace.

Twisted Tunes Home Page

`http://www.twistedtunes.com/`

This site is a must for the loyal "Weird Al" Yankovic fan. Features parodies of rock-and-roll songs, updated weekly. Seasonal favorites are available, too. Requires RealAudio, which is available for download from this site.

WWWF Fights

`http://www.lightlink.com/grudge/`

Grudge matches against media personalities are featured here. Whether it's "Joe Camel fights Spud Mackenzie" or "The Sweat Hogs versus WKRP," the suspense is gripping.

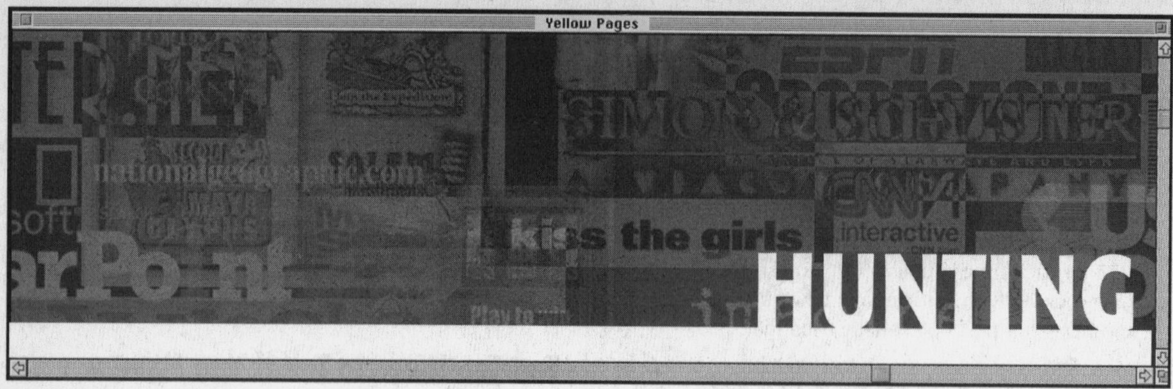

The horn of the hunter is heard on the hill.

Anne Crawford

Browning Home Page

http://www.browning.com/brwnfram.htm

Shotguns, rifles, archery equipment, huntingwear, gun cases, knives—Browning makes it all, and you can find ready access to ordering and price information on their home page. Order a catalog or check out job opportunities. There are also links to other hunting-related sites here.

Crock Pot Venison and Game Recipes

http://southernfood.miningco.com/library/crock/blgame.htm

After you've field dressed your deer or cleaned your birds, what do you do with all that meat? If you're getting tired of just plain old venison roasts or deer meat chili, the folks at Southern American Cuisine have gathered some wild game recipes here. This research was done during deer season, so the recipes are mostly for venison, but check it out during other seasons for quail, pheasant, and rabbit recipes.

Field & Stream Online

http://www.fieldandstream.com/

The outdoorsman's bible has a site on the Internet. The current issue is here with features, articles, and editorials. You can even pick an area of the country and find out what's in season and where to hunt.

The Virtual Wild Turkey Hunting Network
http://www.bowhunting.net/wildturkey.net/default.htm#top

Hunting Information Systems—An Online Guide

http://www.huntinfo.com/index.htm

Lots of products and outfitters listed here, and the site is updated often. Check out the recommended outfitters or suggest one of your own. You'll find the latest hunting news here, including alerts, state and regional information, news about swap hunts, and lots more.

Hunting New Zealand

http://www.fishnhunt.co.nz/hunting.htm

The Chat Room here is an interesting place to go, with Canadian hunters talking to New Zealand hunters talking to you. There's also all sorts of information about hunting in New Zealand and in general, along with jokes and tips. Be sure to check out the list of guides and safaris in New Zealand.

Maine Guides Online

http://www.maineguides.com/Welcome.html

Considering a hunting trip to Maine? Check out this site and then go to either Big Game Hunting, Small Game Hunting, or Bowhunting. You'll find everything you need right here: places to stay, places to hunt, guides, hunting equipment retailers, and things to do when you're not hunting. A very well maintained site.

North American Sportsman

http://www.outlaw.com/noramspo.html

An online magazine complete with articles, departments, advice, and recipes from the experts. There are links to other good sites here too.

NRA's Hunter Services Department

http://www.nra.org/hunter-svcs/hsd.html

The National Rifle Association's Hunter Services Department has information and links for youth hunter education, a code of ethics that all hunters should abide by, and information about who to contact in your state to participate in a local Hunters for the Hungry effort. Check all the links to other NRA pages.

The Longhunter

http://www.nmlra.org/longhunter.htm

This site, sponsored by the National Muzzleloading Rifle Association, is dedicated to hunting with muzzle loaders. Find out how to enroll in the organization and get tips on this challenging sport.

The Virtual Wild Turkey Hunting Network

http://www.bowhunting.net/wildturkey.net/default.htm#top

This site is filled with goodies. There are seminars on many aspects of turkey hunting, such as tips for beginners, information about turkey behavior, and taxidermy tips, along with links to other great sites. Bonus items: downloadable turkey calls, free wallpaper for your PC, and killer recipes—Cajun fried turkey sounds incredible.

The Wildlife Legislative Fund of America

http://www.wlfa.org/

This is the place to go if you want to get serious about wildlife management and the future of hunting, fishing, and trapping. This is the only organization whose sole mission is the conservation of natural resources. Learn about their mission and how to join.

Winter Outdoor Journal

http://outdoor-journal.com/currentmag/currentcover.html

This magazine is dedicated to outdoor sports with an emphasis on hunting and conservation. You'll find interviews with a game warden, deer hunting stories, reports from the field, and articles about guns, dogs, and planning a canoe trip. There are links to previous issues and political news that affects outdoorsmen.

NEWSGROUPS

rec.hunting

rec.hunting.dogs

Related Sites

http://www.huntersmall.com/

http://www.quality-pro.com/hunting/

http://www.bird-dog-news.com/GSP/GSP4sale.html

http://www.mercerwi.com/mikestevens/

http://www.outlaw.com/index2.html

http://www.bowsite.com/home7.html

http://www.galtpond.com/

http://www.huntinfo.com/wildlifeadven/bear.htm

http://www.nra.org/hunter-svcs/yhpages/yhphome.html

http://www.wildharvestvideos.com/

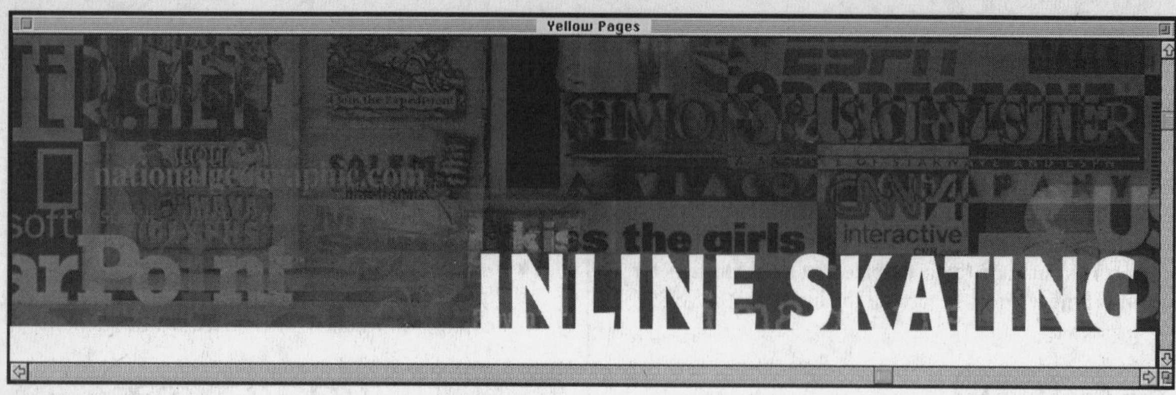

INLINE SKATING

> **I** never take my skates off.
>
> *Dirk Diggler in Boogie Nights (1997)*

Aggressive Skaters Association (ASA)

`http://www.aggroskate.com/index.html`

The ASA develops and oversees professional and amateur competitions in the aggressive skating field, and is working on developing a training-and-certification program for judges. Membership comes in three different flavors: General, Competition (includes insurance!), and Professional. Details on upcoming events, approved skate shops, more.

Aggressive Skating Online

`http://agskate.simplenet.com/aso/`

(Address will be changing to http://www.3RDimension.com/aso/ eventually.)

Lots of interesting/useful stuff. Info on waxing, ramp plans, schedule for skating on TV, tutorials on trick skating, more. Plenty of links and searches. Detailed reviews on new gear, including photos.

Charged

`http://www.charged.com/`

E-zine with updates on the latest news related to "action sports/extreme leisure." If you're into biking, skating, boarding, or anything else that's outdoors and high-speed, see this mag for plenty of interesting reading. Be sure to check out the Gear section for reviews of new equipment.

GenX - Aggressive Inline Skating

`http://www.irl.org.uk/genx/aggrosk8.html`

If you're just getting started at learning street tricks or vert tricks, this is a great place to start. The "non-macho guide" to frontside grinds is detailed enough to include specifics on what kind of equipment you need and how to adjust your skates. Some links to other sites as well.

Hardcore Inline Skating

`http://www.aggressive.com/inline/`

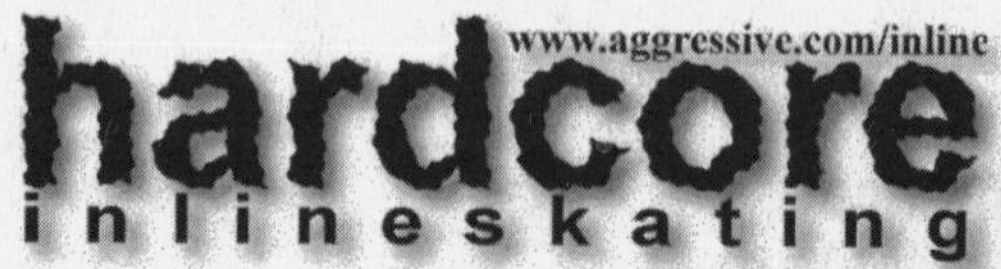

Inline skating is all about fun. It's not about who is the best, or who is sponsored, or who has the most respect. It IS about skating for yourself and helping those around you have a great time too. To that end I've made this web site that details most of what I know. If you feel that some skating bit is missing and should be here, please mail me!

contents

Chat
Check out the **Bulletin Board**, java chat and guestbook! Also sign up to the skating mailinglist.

Inline help area
Here's the tutorials on the technical, street, ramp and hockey moves.

Product Reviews
Check out the latest skates,

Introduction

Chat line, tutorials, product reviews, plenty of pictures and videos, all the latest gossip—even a helpful section on treating skating injuries. Believe it or not, this site includes a special section for/about girl skaters.

IISA National Skate Patrol

`http://www.iisa.org/nsp/`

Developed by the New York Road Skaters Association (NYRSA) and International Inline Skating Association (IISA), this organization's goal is to encourage the safety and enjoyment of inline skating. The patrol helps skaters learn the basics. They're also in touch with local police and park departments. Check out their site for details on how you can provide some help to new skaters.

InLine: The Skate Magazine

http://www.inlinemagazine.com/

Cool e-zine you can read online—when you're not out on wheels! The Movie Arcade shows you step-by-step exactly how to do some of your favorite tricks. Check out the lists of parks, rinks, clubs, skating events. Plenty of links to skate-related sites.

In-Line Skating Injuries: Epidemiology and Recommendations for Prevention

http://aepo-xdv-www.epo.cdc.gov/wonder/prevguid/p0000450/p0000450.htm

Nobody likes to talk about it, but the fact is that inline skating has some dangers associated with it. This site is a good one for adults to read before considering taking up this sport. Plenty of statistics are provided on the kinds of injuries that occur—but also some good advice on the kind of protective gear to use to prevent those injuries. Check it out.

Quest For The Holy Rail

http://fside.com/

You'll find references to this video on many of the aggressive skating sites. Although you can't order "Quest" or "Quest II" directly from this site, an 800 number is provided, and you can preview pics taken during the filming of both movies.

Rollerblade.com

http://www.rollerblade.com/

Obviously, these folks are up on what's new in skating gear, who's hot among skaters, and where the action is (click Skate Scenes or Events for details). Searchable index of skate parks, rinks, instructors, etc. And of course you can also find the details on their latest products at this site.

Scum Magazine

http://wwwvms.utexas.edu/~havoc/scum/index.html

Definitely aimed at the younger set, and the language may be objectionable to some viewers. Plenty of great pictures and video, though, along with fairly lengthy articles and interviews.

Skating the Infobahn

http://www.skatecity.com/index/

The skatecity.com site claims to be the most comprehensive inline skating index on the Web. With more than 1,400 sites listed, that just might be accurate! Links include new and hot categories, clubs and organizations, online magazines, skateparks and rinks, and more. Covers rollerhockey, speedskating, and traditional rollerskating.

Team Adventures

http://www.teamadventures.com/

Team Adventures is a group of 20 California skaters, aged 10–18, who travel the U.S. competing and performing at schools. They even do commercials! The site includes tryout information, upcoming events, bios and pics of the team members, the team magazine. A media gallery is also in the works.

Toxboe SkatePark

http://catch-up.com/toxboe/

Great trick guides—color-coded pictures for some of the instructions, so you can learn exactly where to place your feet for the best results. Detailed reviews on all kinds of skating gear, and guides on how to maintain your equipment. Good selection of links.

NEWSGROUPS

rec.skate

rec.sport.skating.inline

FTP SITE

ftp://ftp.sunet.se/pub/pictures/sports/skating/inline/

Related Sites

http://www.dul-x.com/sport/inline.htm

http://www.igs.net/~breakaway/

http://www.inline.co.nz/

http://www.landskaters.org/

http://www.nashville.net/~inline/maintain.html

http://www.outaline.com/

http://www.razors.ch/

http://www.rhinolaces.com/inline.htm

http://www.sk8net.com/icb/

http://www.ultrawheels.com/hockey/hocskate/hocskate.htm

A B C D E F G H I J K L M N O P Q R S T U V W X Y Z

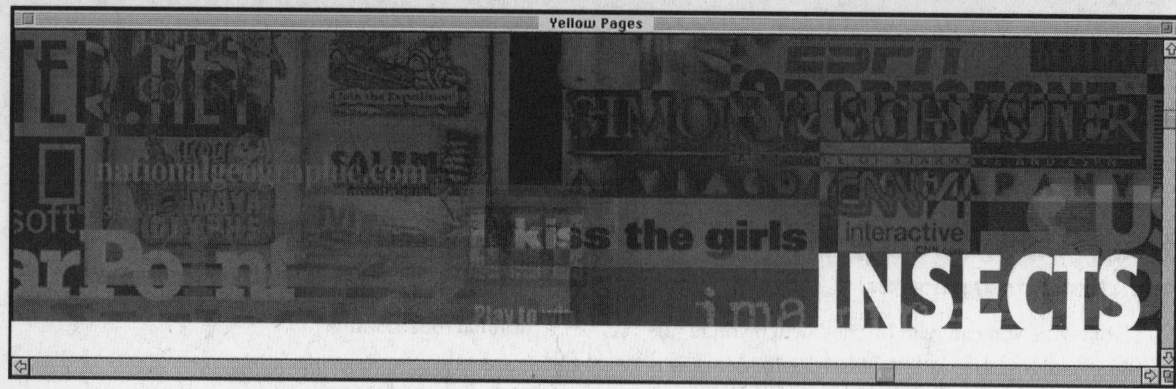

> Tush! tush! fear boys with bugs.
>
> *William Shakespeare*

Bug Baffler

http://www.bugbaffler.com/outofthegates/bb1.htm

Online retailer that specializes in mesh protective clothing. Not for the fashion conscious, to be sure!

The Butterfly Website

http://mgfx.com/butterfly/

Join a discussion group, learn how to raise butterflies, or become part of the efforts to preserve butterfly habitats. The impressive photo gallery will help you identify the various species of moths and butterflies and you can visit many butterfly gardens and zoos.

Cultural Entomology

http://www.insects.org

Insects in poetry, literature, and music? Discover how these creatures have played a part in the arts and humanities down through the ages. The issue of *Cultural Entomology*, available at this site, includes photographs, essays, and links to additional sites in Hawaii, California, and Brazil.

Forest Insects Lab–University of Missouri

http://forent.insecta.missouri.edu/ento/forent/index.htm

Offers information on research, publications, and abstracts. If you are serious about your bugs, you can get information here.

The Butterfly Website
http://mgfx.com/butterfly/

The Yuckiest Site on the Internet
http://www.nj.com/yucky/

Iowa State's Entomology Image Gallery

http://www.ent.iastate.edu/imagegallery.html

They may not win an Academy Award, but the Tick and Beetle movies that can be viewed at this Website are a fascinating look at the lives of these industrious creatures. The site also contains an entomology index and special features on mosquitoes, lice, and corn borers.

Pictures of Insects

http://surf.eng.iastate.edu/%7Ekarie/tutorials/insects.html

Ever wondered what the head of a beetle really looks like? Muse no more—while this site is still under construction, it currently offers images of insects, up close and personal.

The Yuckiest Site on the Internet

http://www.nj.com/yucky/

"Yuckiest" is not a distinction many Web sites would want, but Wendall the Worm and Rodney the Roach take great pride in introducing you to their world. Read all the exciting facts about the creepy crawlers then take the Cockroachworld Quiz. Let Rodney give you the lowdown on all his friends including the earthworm and the bearded worm. A lot of fun as well as informative.

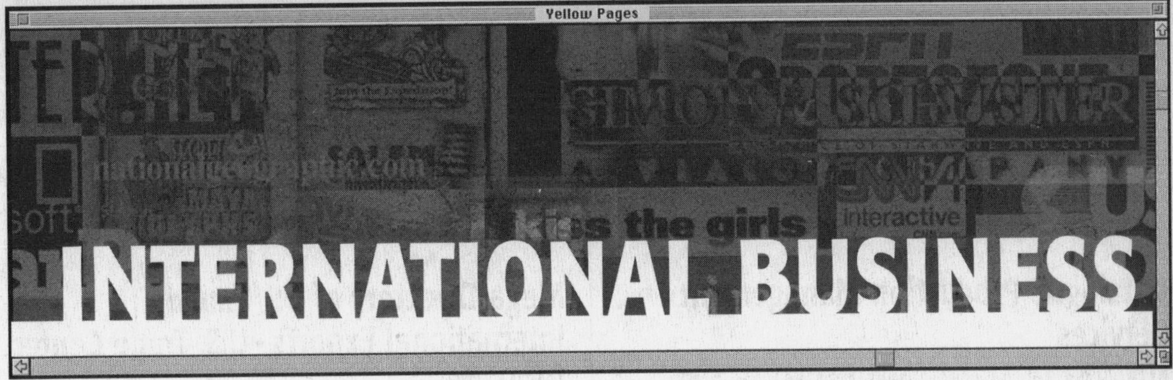

> Those that are above business... in the hands of any, till they are first proved and found fit for the business they are to be entrusted with.
>
> *Matthew Henry*

How to Do Business in Mexico
`http://daisy.uwaterloo.ca/~alopez-o/busfaq.html`

U.S. Council for International Business
`http://www.uscib.org/`

Valore International
`http://www.florin.com/valore/`

Welcome to Molson Canadian
`http://www.molson.com/canadian/`

Adnet

`http://www.adnet.ie/Adnet/`

Provides an interactive resources directory of Ireland. Site has links to various Irish businesses and chambers of commerce. A good place to start when inquiring about business in Ireland.

Agora Language Marketplace

`http://www.agoralang.com:2410`

Provides a place for vendors and consumers of language-related publications, materials, and services to congregate. Offers an online newsletter also available by subscription. Permits people to post their queries directly to the pages that relate to their request, including publications, study abroad, language services, and workshops. Also contains extensive resources for foreign language professionals.

Ask Us For

`http://www.webcom.com/~wrsl/askusfor.html`

Offers monthly newsletters by email about the international business sector in Bermuda. Also contains reports on other related issues.

Australian Pacific Advertising

`http://www.nt.com.au/apa/`

Provides Internet advertising and marketing for Australia and the Pacific rim. Site is still under construction, so many of the links are not yet established. Features information and links on real estate, services, and general features in Australia.

Australian Stock Market Web Page

`http://www.wp.com/paritech`

Includes information on Australian stock exchange data vendors, Australian companies and brokers on the Net, and Australian and overseas data for purchase.

Austrian Worldport Austrian Business Connection

`http://www.worldport.co.at/worldport/`

Serves as database of commerce. Contains about 3,000 business home pages from all over the world, including major business sites in Austria, international trade, technology, industry, manufacturing, services, tourism, culture, and entertainment. (In English and German.)

A B C D E F G H I J K L M N O P Q R S T U V W X Y Z

Batey Ads Singapore

http://bateyads.com.sg/

Provides advertising services throughout Asia and Australia. Includes extensive company history and policies along with listings of resources and clients. Also provides a creative showcase of work done.

Catalogue Production Management Services

http://www.webcom.com/~thames/cpms/welcome.html

Helps United States direct mail companies into Europe. Provides information about direct marketing in Europe, including sources for the most competitive print and paper prices.

How to Do Business in Mexico

http://daisy.uwaterloo.ca/~alopez-o/busfaq.html

Provides general information about Mexican business practices, including business hours, dress codes, negotiations, the wage structure, social practices, and sources of help and information.

INFOCENTRO

http://www.infotec.conacyt.mx/info_i.shtml

Provides information about Mexico, including commercial, culture, travel, education, science and technology, and state governments. Includes a search engine that lets you search Hispanic written documents on the Internet, as well as specialized directories. (Also in Spanish.)

Ingvar's Home Page

http://www.ingvar.is

Icelandic firm that provides information on engineering and consulting, import and export, and aqua- and mariculture. (Also in German and Icelandic.)

Internet World Publishing Systems

http://www.wps.com.au/

Provides and publishes World Wide Web services for Australia and the Asian Basin. Features an Australian travel page, business page, and real estate page. These pages cover many subsections and have links to many businesses and services throughout Australia. Also features listings of Australiasian World Publishing Systems multimedia services and prices. For the travel and business pages alone, this is a valuable resource to utilize. This site also is in Japanese and Korean.

The London Mall Magazine and HQ

http://www.londonmall.co.uk/

A combination magazine, shopping center, showcase, and information source. Offers articles and information on topics ranging from politics to weather to beer.

Mega-Directory of US/Canada International Exports—U.S. Trade Center Directory

http://www.grasmick.com/ustrade.htm

Contains directory of professionals who can assist Canadians exporting to and doing business with the United States. Offers categorized listing. Also includes information on Canadian companies sending employees to the U.S. and U.S. companies hiring Canadians.

Mobile Phones for UK Users

http://www.mobiles.co.uk/

Provides information on mobile phones, including specifications, special features, prices, and networks available in the United Kingdom.

Moscow Libertarium

http://feast.fe.msk.ru/libertarium/

Features information and articles on liberal movement, thinking, and studies. (In Russian and English.)

OCEANOR—Oceanographic Company of Norway

http://www.oceanor.no

Specializes in the marine environment. The company has developed marine environmental and performance monitoring and forecasting systems through a combination of expertise in meteorology, oceanography, biology, ocean engineering, and instrumentation. Markets these systems worldwide.

Octagon Technology Group, Inc

http://www.otginc.com

Provides worldwide business and financial services that allow companies to compete in the international marketplace. Provides multilingual and multi-jurisdictional sales, marketing, and distribution services.

Pristine Communications

http://www.pristine.com.tw/

Provides a wide range of communications services for companies looking to business in Asia. Offers translation, interpretation, media, and WWW services for Asia. Concentrates focus upon South Korea, China, and Japan. Includes services offered and contact information.

Selling Your Products Abroad

http://www.kcilink.com:80/brc/marketing/v2n10.html

Contains general information for product export, market opportunities, and market research. Also provides information on locating foreign markets and financing.

The South African Futures Exchange

http://www.safex.co.za/

Offers information about the financial and agricultural derivatives market in South Africa, as well as downloadable statistics and prices.

TN-1 NAFTA Home Page

http://www.grasmick.com/nafta.htm

The TN-1 permit is a U.S. immigration permit only for Canadians. The law office of Joseph C. Grasmick provides information relating to applying for immigration and work permits.

U.S. Council for International Business

http://www.uscib.org/

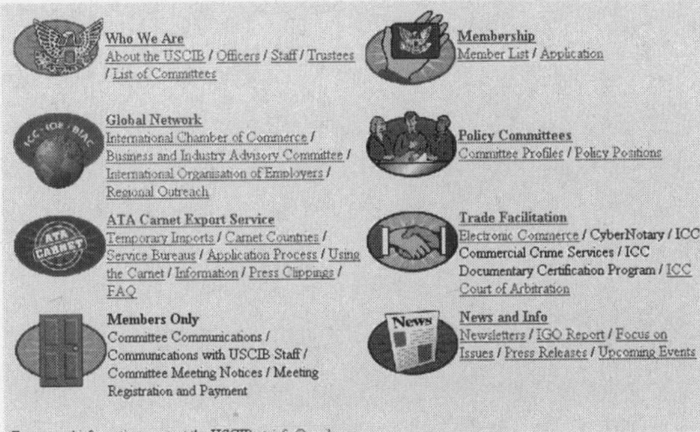

Describes the functions and purpose of the U.S. Council for International Business. Provides a section on ATA Carnet, the merchandising passport for doing business in foreign countries. Provides links to information concerning exporting.

Valore International

http://www.florin.com/valore/

An electronic journal covering issues in international trade and development. Provides articles and related links.

Virtual Business Plaza

http://zocalo.net/cz/

Presents the Czech and Slovak market, companies, classified ads, and other information. (In English and Czech.)

VR Cargo International Home Page

http://www.kolumbus.fi/cargo/

Provides information about Finnish railways as a transportation link between the West and East. Includes links to Russian and railroad Web sites, statistics about Finland, maps, and a traffic survey.

Welcome to Molson Canadian

http://www.molson.com/canadian/

Focuses on Canada: culture, events, travel in Canada, and hockey. Also offers email, bulletin boards, and a well-developed chat facility.

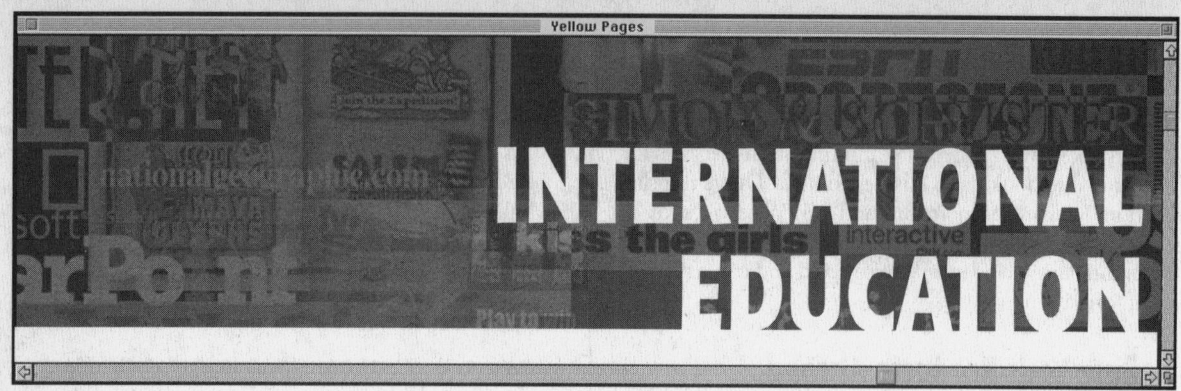

International Education

> Well, education has always been under-valued in the West, hasn't it?
>
> *Song Liling in* M. Butterfly *(1993)*

The Digital Education Network

http://www.edunet.com

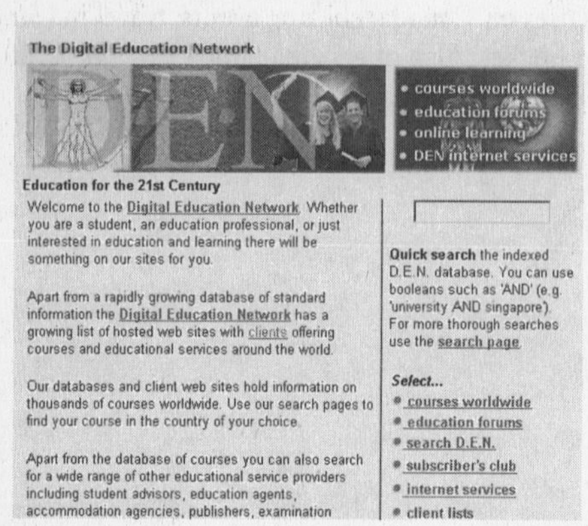

The site provides a wide range of resources for students and professionals interested in international education. Many schools offering courses to international students are featured on the site and information can be found on language schools, universities, business schools, colleges, and vocational schools. The site also hosts a number of award-winning learning resources such as the On-line English Grammar and the El-Online Centre.

The Digital Education Network
http://www.edunet.com

International Bulletin Board Reference

http://darkwing.uoregon.edu/~oieehome/

Good place to add your Web site, especially for its content on International Education with information such as International Education & Exchange Offices, International Student Organizations, Overseas Study Program, International Student Offices, etc. in various Universities, colleges, and schools. U.S. students and international students would definitely benefit from this site, especially for those people planning to study abroad.

The International Education Forum

http://www.csc.fi/forum

The International Education Forum provides specialized information on international educational exchange and mobility and intercultural area studies involving Europe, Finland and the United States.

It would be interesting to impress your memory engrams on a computer, doctor. The resulting flood of illogic would be most entertaining.

Spock in Star Trek *(1966)*

3Dimensions

http://www.3Dimensions.net/

Produces 3D computer graphics and animation for video, CD-ROMs, the Web, gaming, print, and film.

1997 International Digital Media Awards

http://www.multimediator.com/idma/

This site is dedicated to recognizing and rewarding excellence in the production of digital media. Includes lists of winners, finalists, judges, and sponsors. Also contains information on how to enter the 1998 competition.

After Hours Media Duplication Service

http://www.afterhours.com/

Provides CD mastering and duplication, floppy disk duplication, audio cassette and video cassette duplication, international video standards conversion, and film to video transfer.

Chips & Salsa
http://www.chipsnsalsa.com/

Allegro New Media

http://www.allegronm.com/

Publishes interactive multimedia CD-ROMs. Includes Allegro Home PC Library, the growing "Learn To Do" series, business references, cooking, travel in Europe, and educational titles.

Adaptive Media

http://www.adaptmedia.com/

Adaptive Media provides audio, video, and software solutions for corporations. This site allows visitors to preview products, read industry news, and investigate job opportunities with the company.

Animated Design

http://www.animateddesign.com/

Creates multimedia from interactive CDs to Web sites for corporate, commercial, and educational markets.

Atomic Vision, Inc.

http://www.atomicvision.com/

Produces and develops digital media products. Includes client listings, case studies, company processes, and purchasing information. The visuals of this site are very well done. Includes writings about the digital medium covering all pertinent subjects from the technical to the philosophical aspects of the new media. This is a business site that is not only selling the product, but raising questions about the technology and its direction.

Auricle Control Systems

http://www.webcom.com/~auricle/

Home site for the Oscar winning Auricle multimedia music composition tools. Professional composers and movie fans alike would find this site interesting. Provides product information, technical background, and pricing. Also provides information about how music for films is made, the art of film music, examples of where technology was used, and photo gallery of composers at work.

Avalanche Systems, Inc.

http://www.avsi.com/

Produces interactive media products. Includes list of services offered and links to clients sites on the Web.

AVM Summit

http://www.avmtechnology.com/

The "semi-official" source for information on AVM PC audio technical products. Includes product background, availability, support numbers, and troubleshooting tips.

AzTech Interactive

http://www.bigjam.com/aztech/index.html

Multimedia and WWW production studio based in Austin, TX. Produces CD-ROM, enhanced CD, and electronic brochures, and designs WWW sites for clients.

CA Natalie Associates

http://www.cana.com/cana/

Provides Web and Internet services ranging from site creation to database programming. Concentration of services are based in Web marketing, publishing, and WWW server work. Site includes company profile, work done with clients, service listings, and pricing. Also provides listings of job opportunities with CA Natalie Associates.

CD Learn: Personalized Training For Your Favorite Application Packages

http://www.refinery.com/cdlearn/

Offers CD-ROMs that provide interactive, CD-ROM lessons and reference guides for popular applications such as Microsoft Word, Word Perfect, Excel, and Windows 95.

CD Warehouse

http://www.ecn.com/cd_warehouse

Provides more than 3,000 CD-ROM titles at low warehouse prices. Check out the new weekly specials or download an online catalog.

CD Works

http://www.cdworks.com/

Produces and replicates CD-ROMS along with handling sales of CD recording hardware and software. Includes formats and guidelines for data and label artwork for submission. Provides company background, services provided, and links to other pertinent CD-ROM sites.

Chick Enterprises Ltd.

http://www.infomatch.com/~chick/chick.htm

Provides and produces a wide range of computer-based multimedia services and World Wide Web home page creation duties. Includes company background and full listings of services offered. On a humorous note, this site also provides links to various chicken sites.

Chips & Salsa

http://www.chipsnsalsa.com/

This site offers multimedia training programs that incorporate strong content with intuitive learning styles for corporations, non-profit organizations, and individuals. Fantastic site design.

Cinax Designs, Inc.

http://www.cinax.com/

Creates and Develops iFilm interactive film software products. Includes iFilmStudio digital editing software and iMotion seamless playback servers. These technologies are for use by filmmakers, game builders, and in the creation of interactive software. Includes iFilm samples, technology explanations, product background, client and portfolio listings. Provides "The Bench" an interactive movie. An interesting site for someone interested in multimedia technologies and their applications.

Constant Synthesis Project

http://www.sanctuary.com/haven/consynpro/

Provides site for a small network of San Francisco area artists who work in CD-ROM, Internet, and computer graphics technologies. Includes artist listings, gallery sampling of work, and collective projects. There is some nice artwork here done in the new media.

Crystal River Engineering

http://www.cre.com/cre

Creator of AudioReality, a 3D sound technology for entertainment, multimedia, virtual reality, and professional audio. Download free demos of Audio-Reality software and sample 3D spatial sounds, which can be played on any stereo system.

Darim Vision, Co.

http://www.darvision.com/

Designs and produces a wide array of multimedia hardware and software products for the individual and/or companies. Includes information about MPEGator, MARS, DVMPEG, and TeleGenesis products with full product specifications. Also includes technical support, downloadable software, and contact information.

DayStar Digital, Inc.

http://www.daystar.com/

Produces Genesis MP workstations, software, and applications that are used in media publishing such as 3D graphics and animation. Includes performance papers, technical specifications, full product catalog, and technical support. Provides company store, history, and resellers index.

Demo and Tutorial Builders from MIKSoft, Inc.

http://www.cnj.digex.net/~mik/

Produces StDemo and ShowBasic Development Kit, two script-based Windows Demo players. This site explains the program's advantages over Windows Recorder and lets you download a copy of StDemo Player—a demo builder. Also includes an opportunity to watch a unique demo presentation of ShowBasic—a demo/tutorial/CBT/presentation development kit for Windows. If this is what you need, order by email or on the phone.

Digital Creators

http://www.digitalcreators.com/

Specializes in multimedia, Web site page development, and computer graphics creation. Services offered include training, animation, CD-ROM, and home page creation. Includes links to sites created, graphics portfolio, CD-ROMs developed, and contact information.

Digital Movie News

http://spider.lloyd.com/~dmnews/

Interested in the latest issue of the E-zine Digital Movie News? This site's Table of Contents link includes exclusive articles on hundreds of topics, including software reviews, interviews with movie makers, and conference information. The home page includes a number of FAQs for those interested in starting their own digital movie-making enterprise.

EDGE Interactive Media, Inc.

http://www.edgegames.com/

Produces and provides interactive games, 3D multimedia systems, EDGE PCs, EDGE magazine, and various Web services. Includes job opportunities, product and service information.

Edit & Copy Communications

http://www.smartpages.com/editcopy/

Provides wide array of multimedia and graphics services for use in Web page design, graphics creation, and video tape and CD-ROM production. Includes Internet and production services offered. Also includes technology demonstrations, client listings, and information about electronic publishing. Provides contact information and company profile.

EMA Multimedia, Inc.

http://www.emamulti.com/

Provides a wide array of services including logo creation, packaging, interactive media, Web site design, and other multimedia productions. Includes examples of work, links to sites created, and contact information.

Entertainment Through Technology Consortium

http://www.ibmpcug.co.uk/~ettc/

Provides home site for ETTA, an association of entertainment and technology companies. The goal of the organization is to merge together new technologies and entertainment. Includes links to member organizations and a shared information database. Also includes membership and contact information.

A B C D E F G H I J K L M N O P Q R S T U V W X Y Z

HJF Digital Media

http://www.aloha.com/~redmond/

Provides digital media, graphics and sound production, to businesses and individuals. Provides links to animation, 3D, audio and video CD ROM production, desktop publishing, Web page services and promotional screen savers.

IBM 3D Interaction Accelerator

http://www.research.ibm.com/3dix

Workstation-based interactive 3D software that enables real-time visualization and inspection of large and complex mechanical and architectural CAD models. Web site outlines latest features of this accelerator and provides examples of how this product is being used by customers. A must-see is the Pictures and Animations link, which provides large images you can download of 3D environments. Be sure to check out the Frauen Kirche project by IBM of Germany.

IDM

http://www.jaring.my/at-asia/idm/id_hpage.html

Interactive Digital Media campaign for businesses and companies. Provides links to past projects, services, and contact information.

Incite

http://www.incite.com/

High bandwidth multimedia communications at peak performance. Check out Desktop Multimedia or Conversational Media™ for your performance needs. Links to support, marketing, contact info and much more.

Innovate Online

http://innovate.sgi.com/

Silicon Graphics' site is an information resource and interactive community for content creators. Features tips on how to use technology for multimedia development.

Interactive Video and Digital Solutions

http://www.ivs-web.com/

Offers products, services, and guidance in selecting training solutions based on interactive video multimedia technology. Provides products and services for business and educational organizations.

Internet Daily News

http://www.tvpress.com/idn/idnfp.htm

This site offers information on business and technology, careers, entertainment, and other multimedia topics.

Jack

http://www.cis.upenn.edu/~hms/jack.html

Jack is a human modeling and simulation system developed at the University of Pennsylvania. Provides a 3D interactive environment for a variety of applications. Links to news, information, demos, and more.

Loviel Computer Corporation

http://www.loviel.com/

Manufacturer of external SCSI storage devices, specializes in digital video, multimedia, and video conferencing, and offers services such as media integration, computer peripherals, value added services, set-up, tech support, training, and more.

MediaLive

http://www.xpand.com/

Produces and provides multimedia and virtual reality technology products and services. Includes information about the Xpand family of products and other multimedia creation tools. Also includes service listings such as Web creation, Internet consulting, and training. Site provides art portfolio, links to sites created, downloadable demos, company profile, pricing models and contact information.

Metatec Corporation

http://www.metatec.com/

A company offering network support, software development, and optical disc manufacturing and distribution for your publishing needs. Find out more about the company's bio, events, press releases, clients, and more.

MidiMan's Official Web Site

http://www.midiman.net/

If you're into musical production via computer, then check out this site. Lots of product and ordering information, troubleshooting ideas, and new ideas to try. Check out their newsgroup or FTP site, too.

Multimedia Archives

http://sunsite.nus.sg/ftpmultimedia.html

A treasure trove of sounds, images, and MPEG animations for adding to your multimedia presentations. The multimedia exhibit links are a must-see, although you can't use their images in your work.

Multimedia/Entertainment Industry Law and Business Information Center

http://www.dnai.com/~pzender/index.html

This site, which belongs to a multimedia attorney, is devoted to legal, business, and general information regarding multimedia, entertainment, and high tech industries.

Murray MultiMedia

http://www.murraymedia.com/

Creative interactive and print media including advertising, packaging, exhibits and displays, photographs, announcements, and more. Links to demos, media, info, and jobs.

Music Screeners

http://www.sony.com/Music/Screeners

Download a free trial of Sony Music Video's Screeners, which are editable music video screen savers.

Net-One System's Personalized CDs

http://www.primenet.com/~net-one

Small outfit that makes personalized CD-ROMs of music or data. This site is still under construction.

North Communications

http://www.infonorth.com/

Interactive multimedia technology developer among North American, European, and Australian offices. Powerful solutions to government, businesses, and individuals.

NuReality

http://www.nureality.com/

Incredible 3D products for your home theater, computer, or game system. Links to demos, stores, reviews, and other cool sites.

Pangea Creative Media

http://www.magi.com/~brett/pangaea.html

Provides multimedia services including Web site construction, The Cyberlink multimedia newsletter, Web publishing, and graphic design. Includes contact information and links to related sites.

Photodex Corporation

http://www.photodex.com/

Produces CompuPic (CPIC) graphics software and media library CD-ROMs. Includes product background and contact information. Provides links to online multimedia forums.

Pinnacle Post

http://www.halcyon.com/pinnacle/welcome.html

Provides home site for Pinnacle Post, a multimedia graphics production company. Includes services offered, pricing, company news, and contact information.

Punch & Brodie Productions

http://home.earthlink.net/~lbrodie/punch/

Provides live animation for video, film, and live productions. Specializes in corporate events, training videos, and commercials and entertainment.

QuickMedia

http://www.quickmedia.com

Produces Living Album multimedia software that enables photo prints, audio, and video storage on floppy disks and CDs. Includes product technical specifications, reviews, and ordering information.

Ramworks

http://www.ramworks.com/ramworks/

Provides home site for Ramworks, a multimedia graphics and publishing production studio. Includes information about Shockwave graphics software, clients listings, services offered, and contact information.

Scala Computer Television AS (Norway)

http://www.scala.com/Welcome.html

Develops multimedia technology products and software. Specializes in applications that enable multimedia presentations to work similar to television.

Produces the Human Touch graphical user interface and Scala Interactive Television (ITV) software. Includes product features, corporate profile, technical support, and contact information.

Sealworks, Inc.

http://www.sealworks.com/

Sealworks is a multimedia and Internet consulting and product company. Includes services, products, and resources utilized. Provides seminar dates, training services, and client listings.

Sound & Vision Media

http://www.svmedia.com/svmedia/

Provides a wide range of multimedia services and products. Includes Web site development, multimedia database design, and graphics creation. Site includes links to sites created, artwork examples, and information about The Presence Engine online catalog creation software.

Sprite Interactive

http://www.cityscape.co.uk/users/di50/

Offers multimedia production and related software development. Services includes Web site design, graphics creation, 3D modeling, and many more. Develops custom Photoshop, QuarkXPress, HTML, and others. Includes company background, portfolio, and contact information.

StarMan Group, Multimedia Productions

http://www.primenet.com/~star-man

Provides a wide range of multimedia services and products. Specializes in Java database development software and business site creation.

Station Graphics, Inc.

http://www.pic.net/~station/

Produces the VideoShow family of multimedia presentation products. Includes company profile and information about the VideoShow HQ Multimedia System. Provides technical specifications and contact information.

Related Sites

http://www.instanet.com/~iv/

http://www.kingproducts.com/

http://www.knowledgesystems.com/

Two Guys Named Hank

http://www.twohanks.com

Provides multimedia services including Web site design, computer animation, 3D modeling, and video production. Includes company background, and examples of work done.

Virtual Artists

http://www.va.com.au/va/

Provides a wide range of multimedia services including Web site creation, 3D graphics, computer animation, and other interactive media productions. Includes detailed company and personal background along with examples of work done.

Visionary Designs

http://www.visdesigns.com/

Provides a wide array of multimedia services and products. Includes computer animation, 3D graphics, CD-ROM creation, Web site design, and other multimedia services. Site includes company history, staff background, work examples, product listings, and contact information.

vivid studios

http://www.vivid.com/

Provides Web site construction, CD-ROM production, specialized interface creation, and other multimedia production services. Includes company profile, sites created, current projects, and links to many different sites.

Welcome to macromedia.com

http://www.macromedia.com/index.html

Headquarters for the producer of such hot multimedia authoring packages as Freehand, Director, Fontographer, and Authorware. Choose Low Bandwidth at this opening screen if you are using anything slower than a 28.8 modem.

X Communications Multimedia

http://www.webcom.com/~xcomm/

Provides multimedia services such as Web page design. Includes links pages to created by X Communications, the magic "8-ball", and linky links. From this site you can access quite a few music and entertainment pages.

My favorite thing about the Internet is that you get to go into the private world of real creeps without having to smell them.

Penn Jillett

EDUCATIONAL & TUTORIAL LISTINGS

Center for the Application of Information Technology

http://www.cait.wustl.edu/cait/

A consortium whose mission is "to be a center of learning in the field of information management and to provide our member companies with world-class educational and leadership programs."

FutureNet

http://www.futurenet.co.uk/netmag/Issue1/Easy/index.html

Europe's leading electronic magazine. Serves as a complete in-depth Internet beginner's guide. Provides information on how to hook up your machine, how to use information to your advantage, and more. Also provides a history of the Internet.

UK Index Beginner's Guide: the Net
http://www.ukindex.co.uk/begin0.html

Youth Quake
http://emall.com/yq/home.html

NickNet
http://www.pinc.com/nburger/home.html

Gestalt Systems, Inc.

http://www.gestalt-sys.com/

Provides links to computer training classes, courseware, educational support, and information for downloading its training software.

Global Institute for Interactive Multimedia

http://www.thegiim.org/

Provides information and guides for teaching people how to create a home page. Divides the information according to the audience; for example, provides a different tutorial for teachers than for business owners.

Glossary of Internet Terms

http://www.matisse.net/files/glossary.html

Lists and defines Internet and computer-related terms and acronyms.

How To Search a WAIS Database

http://town.hall.org/util/wais_help.html

Provides information on how to begin and structure a Wide Area Internet Server search. Describes how to use Boolean operators, wild cards, relevance ranking, and so on. Offers a tutorial on using a WAIS search engine.

INFO Online

http://www.pona.com

Focuses on "Information Networking For Oncologists," and specifically provides information for physicians dealing with networks, integration, and pharmaceutical companies. Also offers information for people involved with oncology, including patients.

INFOMINE

http://lib-www.ucr.edu/

An online library at the University of California-Riverside. Aims to make resources available to UCR students and staff, but is open to the public. Offers many online card catalogs and articles.

Information Management Group

http://www.imginfo.com/

A Windows development and Internet educational and consulting firm offering university courses, consulting, and tips and tricks for developers. Provides links to services and classes offered.

Inter-Links

http://www.nova.edu/Inter-Links/start.html

A site for browsing the Internet and locating specific resources. Features Internet resources, guides and tutorials, news and weather, library resources, fun and games, a reference shelf, and a miscellaneous section. Includes several original search engines as well. Millions of visitors can't be wrong.

Internet Learning Center

http://oeonline.com/~emoryd

Offers tutorial columns and "where to go" columns. Also includes links to the UNIX Reference Center, the Hyptertext Guide, Rinaldi's Netiquette, Odd de Presno's Online World book, and other Internet resources. Past columns are archived.

Internet Web Text

http://www.december.com/web/text/index.html

A hypertext guide to the Internet, written by Net guru John December. Begins with Internet orientation and clicks through all the major Internet tools. Highly recommended.

Introduction to the Internet II

http://uu-gna.mit.edu:8001/uu-gna/text/internet/index.html

One of several prototype classes and texts sponsored through the Globewide Network Academy. Introduces the user to various resources available via the Internet, with particular emphasis on allowing a neophyte to access GNA services as quickly as possible.

Kids on Campus (Cornell Theory Center)

http://www.tc.cornell.edu/cgi-bin/Kids.on.Campus/top.pl

The Cornell Theory Center sponsors Kids On Campus as part of its celebration of National Science and Technology Week. The purpose of this event is to increase computer awareness and scientific interest among Ithaca, New York-area third, fourth, and fifth grade students. Hands-on computer activities, innovative videos, and exciting demonstrations help the children develop interest and excitement in computers and science.

Learning Edge Corp.

http://www.io.org/~tle/

Offers products and services to the private and public sectors, including courseware and training, animation, videos, interfaces, and more. Contains links to clients, services, portfolio, and more.

Library Solutions Institute and Press

http://www.internet-is.com/library/

Internet training information and seminars for both students and trainers. Self-paced tutorials including HTML tutorial, K–12 resources, publications, and more.

Magnett Internet Gateway

http://www.magnet.ca/

Links to various Internet browsers and gateways such as software archives, helper applications, Netscape questions and answers, and customer service for subscribers of Magnett Internet Gateway.

Management Concepts Inc.

http://www.MgmtConcepts.com/

A corporation providing training in personal property management, property leasing, grants management, and computer and financial applications. Provides access to new courses and special events, publications, and links to other sites of related interest.

MicroMedium, Inc.

http://www.micromedium.com/

Check out MicroMedium's Digital Trainer Professional® multimedia computer-based training software for your organization. Already in use by AT&T, MCI, Long John Silver's, and others. Includes links to product reviews, demos, tech support, the MicroMedium training library, and ordering information.

Multimedia Help Page

http://www.sdcs.k12.ca.us/people/schumsky/greg.html

Provides quick access to sources of multimedia tools and tips on the Web. Also provides links and tips for video production, search engines, and production tools for the Apple Newton.

Net Guru Technologies, Inc.

http://www.ngt.com/

On-site training and consulting by certified Webmasters. Some courses include these topics: Webmaster specialists, security and firewalls, UNIX, networking, TCP/IP, and more. If you register online, you will receive a rebate.

Net: User Guidelines and Netiquette, by Arlene Rinaldi

http://www.fau.edu/rinaldi/net/index.html

Offers a collection of Internet user guidelines and netiquette. Discusses legal and ethical issues involved.

Netscape Tutorial

http://w3.ag.uiuc.edu/AIM/Discovery/Net/www/netscape/index.html

Gives a step-by-step tutorial on using Netscape—it can be very in-depth. Allows for different levels of expertise.

Online World Resources Handbook

http://login.eunet.no/~presno/

Provides practical advice on using the Internet to get information or programs. Breaks topics down into various topics, such as how to get free expert assistance, how to read your electronic daily news, and more.

Patrick Crispen's Internet Roadmap

http://www.brandonu.ca/~ennsnr/Resources/Roadmap/Welcome.html

This is the Internet Roadmap online training course, available in HTML. This is a well-written tutorial and is very user-friendly. A must for any Internet coordinator's bookmark list.

UK Index Beginner's Guide: the Net

http://www.ukindex.co.uk/begin0.html

Serves as a beginners guide to using the Internet, and includes pointers to more resources.

Winsock Connections

http://omni.cc.purdue.edu/~xniu/winsock.htm

Explains both the hardware and software issues concerning setting up your Windows PC to access the Internet. Explains where to get the software you need and how to configure it. Also provides information on creating HTML documents.

Writing the Information Superhighway

http://www.umich.edu/~wbutler/UC153Syl.html

Offers information regarding how to write literature for the Internet (originally an online class at University of Michigan). Lets you direct questions to the professors who originally taught the class. Also includes a linked bibliography of other sites.

Youth Quake

http://emall.com/yq/home.html

Serves as a destination for computer-literate youth. Plans to cater to education all around the world.

Zen and the Art of the Internet

http://www.cs.indiana.edu/docproject/zen/zen-1.0_toc.html

A beginner's guide to the Internet. Offers information on the search engines available and even a section on how to create a newsgroup.

GUIDES, TOURS, & COOL SITE RESOURCES

Cool Site of the Day

`http://www.infi.net/cool.html`

Connects you to the cool site of the day on the Internet, determined by the moderator. This works better than a random-site connector because the sites are more likely to be pretty cool.

George Coates Performance Works

`http://www.georgecoates.org/`

Just a diversional site where you fill out a questionnaire (it's short) and are then matched with a character who most fits your personality type. Your character is described, and you can change characters often. You are encouraged to visit your multiple personalities often.

Glass Wings

`http://www.aus.xanadu.com/GlassWings/`

A site whose stated purpose is "to have fun, help improve the state of the world, inform, provide an interesting and useful commercial site, and have fun (yes, I intentionally mentioned fun twice)." Provides a collection of links and a search site only for fun and nonbusiness-oriented stuff. Includes an online mall where you can buy things, links to humorous sites, and more.

GO! Online Communications

`http://www.jumppoint.com`

An exclusive Internet club of advertisers. Includes links to businesses, professionals, employment opportunities, Kids Corner, and more.

Greene Communications Design, Inc.

`http://www.greene.com/`

A graphics design firm expanded to Web publishing. Greene will design anything for the business, educational, advertising or marketing executive (including letterheads, logos, promotional or educational materials, press releases, and so on). Provides links to projects, clients, and the Internet development group.

Hajjar/Kaufman New Media Lab

`http://www.hkweb.com/`

A small marketing and development company that gives you all the benefits and expertise of a large company. Hajjar/Kaufman will develop your business Web site. Provides links to clients and to contact information.

Handy Guide

`http://www.ahandyguide.com/`

Serves as a complete guide to thousands of sites on the Internet and Web. Lets you search by category or company name, and teaches American Sign Language (ASL) as you go.

High-Tech Investor

`http://www.want2know.com/invest/invest.htm`

Written by an investment and markets reporter at the *Toronto Globe and Mail*, this site discusses investment-related resources on the Web and offers a collection of links to some of those resources.

Hit The Beach!

`http://www.hitthebeach.com/`

If you like the beach, you'll love this site. Provides links to a chat café, the swimsuit shot of the week, a virtual trip to the beach, a beach shop, and food. Register to win a trip to Cancun or to Jamaica, mohn. Also a beach-related search engine.

Hybrid Communications

`http://gs1.com/homepages/dir.HTML`

A virtual metropolis of culture, government, art and antiques, restaurants, public service, business, retail, travel, and entertainment sites. Click whatever interests you.

Internet ProLink SA/AG

`http://www.iprolink.ch/`

Provides links to businesses on the Web, Web tools and services, and the "culture café." Also available in other languages.

Internet Resources

http://www.brandonu.ca/~ennsnr/Resources/

Contains pointers to more than 100 guides, lists, and indices of documents that help you learn how to use the Internet. Includes pointers to The December and Yanoff Lists, Patrick Crispen's Internet Roadmap (in HTML), The Awesome List, and many others.

Meta-list of What's New Pages

http://homepage.seas.upenn.edu/~mengwong/whatsnew.list.html

Offers a collection of links to all the different Internet What's New sites for the Web. By the author's own admission, "the Web is growing so fast that this document can be considered, at best, a historical artifact."

Net Trek Cafe

http://www.nettrek.com.au/

The first Internet café in Australia, offering a variety of links and services, including Internet training, a business directory, links to Internet search engines and catalogs, Australian links, outer space and *Star Trek* links, links for kids and music lovers, sports, news media, and much much more.

nicejob Media

http://www.earthlink.net/~mrnicejob/

An odd assortment of home pages, including Two Moms Names Alma, An Illusion Dog, Unexplained Art, and more. If you're looking for an interesting site, look no further.

NickNet

http://www.pinc.com/nburger/home.html

More than 3,200 links to dazzle and amaze you. If Web surfing were any more fun, they would have to ban it. Everything you could ever want is here and categorized so it is all easy to find. Web addicts beware. This site is being revamped as this book goes to press.

Overall Knowledge Company, Inc.

http://www.okc.com

Overall Knowledge Company, Inc. is a general Web presence provider with an emphasis on the film and television trades as well and the arts and entertainment industries. Also publishes several industry-specific directories on the World Wide Web.

Point Survey and Escort

http://www.pointcom.com/

Provides a large collection of reviews of Web sites. Rates sites for content, presentation, and experience. Includes more than 1,000 reviews across many categories. Helps you get started on the Web with answers to common questions and guided tours of browsing software and sites.

Thousand Points of Sites

http://inls.ucsd.edu/y/OhBoy/randomjump1.html

Sends you to a Web site randomly selected from its listings.

ThreadTreader's WWW Contests Guide

http://www.4cyte.com/ThreadTreader/

Presents ThreadTreader's WWW Contests Guide, a complete, current compilation of contests on the Web. Provides easy ways to browse through an extensive index of online contests, drawings, raffles, sweepstakes, and other prize-oriented promotions. Even lets you add your own contest to the ThreadTreader's Guide.

Today Page

http://www.vossnet.co.uk/local/today/index.html

Offers a collection of links to sites that change daily; for example, includes links to news, your horoscope, and weather photos.

Unusual or Deep Site of the Day

http://adsint.bc.ca/deepsite/

Offers links to sites that provide some sort of intellectually stimulating purpose.

HTML & OTHER LANGUAGES

Bare Bones Guide to HTML

http://werbach.com/barebones/

Lists every HTML 2.0 tag and most of the 3.0 tags, with a special section on Netscape extensions.

Beginner's Guide to HTML

http://www.ncsa.uiuc.edu/General/Internet/WWW/HTMLPrimer.html

Talks about linking to other documents, troubleshooting, and creating forms. Focuses on Mosaic, but includes other browsers.

ColorEditor for Windows

http://www.bbsinc.com/colorEditor_FAQ.html

Provides standalone MS Windows shareware to assist the Web page author develop an HTML page color scheme using extensions to the HTML 3.0 specification. Also provides a Style Box that enables users to edit, save, and retrieve color schemes. Runs on Windows 3.1, Windows 3.1 for Workgroups, Windows 95, and Windows NT 3.5.

Introduction to HTML: Table of Contents

http://www.cwru.edu/help/introHTML/toc.html

Presents a guide to authoring Web pages. Divides sections by different images, lists, and anchors, and offers information on how to take advantage of Netscape functions.

Personal Home Page of Bob Hunter

http://www.awinc.com/users/bhunter/

Focuses on testing HTML coding examples and pushing the limits of HyperText Markup Language and all of its extensions.

Primer for Creating Web Resources

http://www-slis.lib.indiana.edu/Internet/programmer-page.html

Offers a list of links to HTML resources. Also offers links to Perl and CGI languages for creating top-of-the-line Web pages.

Web Letter, a Guide to HTML/Web Publishing

http://www.writething.com/

Serves as an HTML resource. Includes a newsletter, a video, and training books, as well as numerous links to help you build your own Web.

Web Resources

http://www.wwwa.com/resource.html

Serves as a complete Web resource site with HTML commands, software for publishing, searches, libraries, and high-speed Web host connections for your company or home page.

RESOURCES

All-Internet Shopping Directory

http://www.webcom.com/~tbrown/

Serves as an easy-to-use, fast-loading central hot link to products, services, malls, and stores on the Web. Selected as one of *PC Magazine's* top 100 Web sites (2/13/96).

Ansible's Web Page Design Services

http://www.cyberenet.net/center/

Helpful to anyone from newbies to expert Internauts, this site offers links to online Internet resources, software, search tools, and a list of favorite Internet sites.

Argus/Univeristy of Michigan Clearinghouse

http://www.clearinghouse.net/

"The Premier Internet Research Library," this site serves as a clearinghouse for subject-oriented Internet resources guides. Allows you to submit your own guides or obtain guides written on various Internet-related topics.

Aspen Systems Corp.

http://www.aspensys.com

Provides complete Internet services. Also discusses requirements and needs analysis, Internet publishing services, systems support, and customer support. Specializes in identifying, gathering, and analyzing online information.

Association of University Technology Managers

http://autm.rice.edu/autm/

Features resources for the technology transfer field, once called the "unknown profession." Offers links to other resources and includes information about AUTM (publications, membership, events), job postings, and a way to search lists of technologies you can license from more than 20 different university, government, and organizational sites in one query (via a harvest gatherer).

Autopilot

http://www.mit.edu:8001/people/mkgray/autopilot.html

Uses Netscape and connects you to a different Web site every 12 seconds. Helps you find totally random sites with little effort. Also allows you to change the amount of time between connections.

Canada Net Pages

http://www.visions.com/netpages

This page's stated goal is to "be recognized as the most comprehensive resource of Canadian business and finance data." Also provides links for various pages, such as Canada Net Financial Pages and Canada Net Business Directory.

Canadian Internet Handbook/ Advantage Home Page

http://www.csi.nb.ca/handbook/

Presents guides to Internet access in Canada. Lets you add your Canadian Internet address to the handbook, find out more about its publications, send the authors email, and more.

Cnet-Canada

http://cnet.unb.ca/cnet/

Provides information specific to Canada. Allows you to search the database by clicking the geographical regions on a map or by using standard keywords.

Common Internet File Formats

http://www.matisse.net/files/formats.html

Provides information on the different file types and formats on the Internet. Each blurb about a specific file type also gives links to obtaining readers for that type.

CRAYON–CReAte Your Own Newspaper

http://www.eg.bucknell.edu/~boulter/crayon/

Serves as an interactive news agent. Lets you choose from sections such as News, Sports, Entertainment, and others to find the best periodical information on the Internet. Enables you to organize it into your own personal newspaper—you may never read a print publication again.

Economics of Networks Internet Site

http://edgar.stern.nyu.edu/networks/

Provides information and links to the economics behind all networks. Includes downloadable papers on topics ranging from network compatibility to financial networks.

EINet Galaxy

http://www.einet.net

A search site provided free of charge by Trade-Wave Corp. Includes general topics and sublists under each of these. Also offers a list of job opportunities.

E-Minder Free Reminder-By-E-mail Service

http://www.netmind.com/e-minder/

Offers to send you automatically generated reminder messages for any event or occasion for which you register. Requires an email address, but otherwise is completely anonymous. Lets you specify the number of days in advance you want a reminder. It also provides a simple email interface that you can use to list or delete reminders.

FLFSoft, Inc. Home Page

http://www.flfsoft.com/

Develops Windows-based utilities and Internet software and services. Features Web Spinner, a Windows-based HTML editor.

FutureMedia Services

http://www.futuremedia.com/

Provides Internet access to small businesses interested in taking their services to the Internet. Provides Web site development and consulting services, FTP and Gopher service space, and links to current projects.

FutureTel, Inc.

http://www.ftelinc.com

Possesses leading technology in both compression and telecommunications, so it is uniquely positioned to serve the needs of the digital video publishing and distribution markets. Provides the most complete solution to the challenges of distributing and publishing digital video on CDs and wired and wireless networks. The company's digital video publishing product line includes PrimeView, a family of real-time PC-based MPEG encoders; and MPEG-WORKS, a comprehensive encoding control software package for human-assisted or pass-through compression.

G.T.A. Business Solutions

`http://www.elknet.com/gta/hpgta.html`

Provides businesses and organizations presence on the Internet with Web page design, training and classes. Includes access to price lists and sample client pages.

Glistening Trail Records

`http://membrane.com/`

For those in Pennsylvania (primarily the Philadelphia area), this site lists places for adventure, music, food, shopping, real estate opportunities, computer and business services, churches, credit card services, medical services, and more. Click individual listings for more descriptions and some pictures.

HFSI

`http://www.hfsi.com/`

Workflow and imaging technologies, providing products and services for the federal government and government contractors. Provides links to products, services, resource centers, and education and training opportunities. Offers workload management seminars to help your office run more efficiently and on less paper.

Home Run Pictures

`http://www.zdepth.com/homerun/`

This company creates online animation and special effects for ad agencies, corporations, TV stations, and interactive producers. Includes links to samples, contacts, and pricing information.

Information Age, Inc.

`http://www.informationage.com/`

A software- and data-intensive Web site development company with links to applications, articles, services, the Information Age team, and general information.

Innovative Computer Associates, Inc.

`http://www.icai.com/icai/`

A software engineering firm for database and Web page development, located near Denver, Colorado. Provides information about Internet classes offered and services such as online application development, multimedia marketing campaigns, corporate training, cross-platform application development, and much more.

Instruction Set, Inc.

`http://www.inset.com/`

Broad curriculum of courses for the software development technology of today. Links to courses and seminars, consulting, courseware development services, employment opportunities, and more.

InteliSys Technologica, Inc.

`http://www.intelinet.net/`

Networking and programming solutions for businesses around the world. Will also provide Web development services. Links to Web services. Watch up-to-date company info scroll across the bottom of your screen.

Interactive Data Systems, Inc.

`http://www.idsinc.com/`

A software engineering service provider, especially for object-oriented tools. Includes links to services, database and development environment info and software, freeware, and other interesting links.

Interactive Voice Applications

`http://www.tc.net/voice/`

Streaming audiofile technology to enable you to send voice messages around the world for a fraction of the regular cost. Expedite your business transactions while also reducing expenditures. Includes access to demos, contact info, and many other services.

Internet Resources Newsletter

`http://www.hw.ac.uk/libWWW/irn/irn.html`

A free monthly Web newsletter. Focuses on higher education and the Internet. Features lists of new Internet resources and other items of interest.

Internet Servers for the Mac OS

`http://www.freedonia.com/ism/`

Contains many links to Macintosh-specific software packages for running a Mac-based server. Topics include mail servers, mail gateways, ftp servers, Telnet servers, and more.

Internet Systems, Inc.

http://www.isi.net/

Business, educational, and government institution Internet services. Provides site architecture, access, service, and maintenance for your high volume site. Also provides access to clients' pages.

Internet World

http://pubs.iworld.com/iw-online/

An online version of this popular magazine devoted to the Internet. Allows you to search back issues by cover or by keyword.

INTRANET Technologies, Inc.

http://intranet.on.ca/

A full-service provider for everything from Web access to LANs to custom systems. Includes links to services, support, Web community and exposure info, and more.

Island Services Network

http://www.isn.net/

The Internet Company for Prince Edward Island. Provides access to search engines, user services, news and entertainment, local weather, and other Internet services.

iWORLD

http://www.iworld.com/

Touting itself as "all Net, all the time," this site offers Internet news, features, resources, and tools. Supported by Mecklermedia, publisher of *Internet World* magazine.

Knighted Computers

http://www.knighted.com/

An Internet service provider based in Fulton, New York, with links to local newspapers, games, software, hardware, services, and more.

Knossopolis

http://www.knosso.com/

A Web site design and architecture, training, teaching, and consulting firm with links to its resources and information, clients, projects, and more.

Life on the Internet

http://www.screen.com/understand/welcome.html

Provides a large collection of links to many resources on the Internet. Gives sources for browsers, software, page development, and more.

List of WWW Archie Services

http://pubweb.nexor.co.uk/public/archie/

Offers a list of hypertext links to Archie (archive) servers. Helps you find files anywhere on the Internet and lists Archie servers that use forms and others that don't.

Logical Operations

http://www.logicalops.com

Training products and services for professional trainers.

LookUp!

http://www.lookup.com/

Offers a directory service that provides easy-to-use names to email address mapping.

Lopez Communications

http://www.interport.net/peoplelink/

Lopez Communications offers a variety of on- and offline services, including integrated marketing to progressive organizations, online publishing, Web design, and other Web projects for socially responsible companies.

Marketing Masters

http://surveysaid.ostech.com:8080/

An Internet host with links to hosted sites, including Ham Radio Forums, Marketing Masters, and JF Computer Leasing.

Media Connection of New York–Links Page

http://www.mcny.com/linkspage/

Offers a collection of links to Web resources in or about New York City.

A B C D E F G H I J K L M N O P Q R S T U V W X Y Z

Miramar Productions

http://useattle.uspan.com/miramar/

Browse Miramar's catalog of latest releases, or go to its Top Five section for interactive previews, video and audio clips, computer animation, performance samplers, and much much more.

Newton Online

http://www.newtonline.com

Newton Online provides business consulting (and a quirky sense of humor) for companies who want to compliment marketing and communications strategies by using the Internet.

Norcov Research

http://www.norcov.com/

Offers scientific research, programming, Internet services, and UNIX administration. Check out the complete list of products and services as well as the Norcov customer pages.

Novia Internetworking

http://www.novia.net/

A personal and business connection to the Internet. Check out its partial list of hosted business pages, LAN integration capability, and its services and search engines.

Omega West

http://cascade.cs.ubc.ca:12000/omega/omega.html

A site with something for everyone. Well-organized into a hierarchical structure, it includes everything from business resources and financial tips to a broad spectrum of entertainment and Web developer resources. Omega West, an international distribution and services company, will soon have an "intelligent interface" that is capable of adapting to users' actions. This, of course, will mean that return visits and continued interaction will provide users with a personalized interface.

Premiere Technologies

http://www.tc.net/

Harnesses the power of audio on the Internet. Provides applications that enable you to instantly update your Web page or email applications by simply picking up your telephone and calling a fully automated system. Also qualifies as an authorized AT&T 900 service bureau, so you can set up and run any 900 or 800 voice or data application.

Presence—An Information Design Studio

http://www.presence.com/

Focuses on providing innovative and effective marketing solutions through the Internet. Also includes many interesting Internet-related links.

Q-D Software Development

http://www.q-d.com

Presents the creators of WebForms, the Web forms generator; and WinBrowse, the multiple-PC database utility. Also includes a variety of shareware programs available for download.

RealAudio Home Page

http://www.realaudio.com/

Provides RealAudio, software you can use to both record and play your own sound. Many Web sites on the Internet use RealAudio to provide sounds.

Sibylla: The WWW Software Development Kit

http://www.ariadne.it/sibylla/sibylla.en.html

Provides information on Sibylla, a development kit geared toward creating Web software, whose purpose is to provide access to information sources (such as company databases) through the Web. Also provides pricing information on the software.

Strategis

http://strategis.ic.gc.ca/engdoc/site.html

A business information site sponsored by the Canadian federal government's economic flagship department, dedicated "to the success of all Canadian businesses at home and abroad."

SWITCH—Swiss Academic and Research Network

http://www.switch.ch/

Presents SWITCH, an Internet service provider that interconnects all Swiss universities, many libraries, and research labs, as well as other Swiss and international organizations. Also presents the WWW Rent-A-Page service.

Timothy W. Amey Resource Links

`http://www.netins.net/showcase/amey/twa`

Offers a collection of resource links and information regarding OS/2 resources, OS/2 advocacy, Lotus resources, Intel alternatives, religion, Ford advocacy, and IT/IS resources.

Virtual Tourist

`http://www.vtourist.com/webmap/europe.htm`

Provides a graphical map interface that you can click to find and then jump to Web servers operating in many countries around the world.

Web Week

`http://pubs.iworld.com/ww-online/`

An electronic publication that serves as a repository of Web-related topics. Categories include News, Commercial, Intranet, Products, Under Construction, Industry, and Opinion.

Welcome to Netscape

`http://home.mcom.com/`

Offers information about the new security measures being built into HTML; also offers a downloadable version of Netscape for Windows 95 and technical support.

Windows95 InterNetworking Headquarters

`http://www.windows95.com`

Offers Windows 95 shareware, Internet setup information, networking across the Internet, and more.

WorldTel Global Marketing Network

`http://www.worldtel.com/home.html`

Lists businesses and individuals offering products, services, or opportunities to the world market.

SEARCHERS & DATABASES

Business Directions International

`http://www.business.com.au/`

An Internet search directory using numerous search engines to find business sites on the Internet.

Business Researcher's Interests

`http://www.brint.com/interest.html`

Provides more than 2,800 sites relevant to contemporary organizational issues concerning information processes, information systems, and information technology. Categories include electronic markets, organizational learning, emerging organizations, WWW design, and journals and magazines.

College and University Home Pages

`http://www.mit.edu:8001/people/cdemello/univ.html`

Provides links to the Web pages of more than 750 colleges and universities around the world. Allows you to search alphabetically or just browse.

COMMA Hotlist Database

`http://arachnid.cm.cf.ac.uk/htbin/AndrewW/Hotlist/hot_list_search.csh`

Provides a graphical, searchable Web database. Choose your search criteria from their list, and then it searches and gives you an output list. Also enables you to add your own hot list to the database.

Database Demos

`http://bristol.onramp.net/`

Shows you how to set up your Oracle-based database management system (DBMS) for access via the Web. Good for creating your own search engine or providing Web access to large bodies of information.

Four11 White Page Directory

`http://www.Four11.com/`

Enables you to search for people and their email addresses and Web pages. Contains more than 5.5 million listings. Allows you to register and put your name on the directory.

High Performance Cartridges

`http://www.netpoint.net/hpcart/hpcart.html`

A re-manufacturer of laser toner cartridges for large institutional settings. Also provides a search engine, a database of shareware on the Internet, and other cool links with software to download.

A B C D E F G H I J K L M N O P Q R S T U V W X Y Z

Index

http://www.library.vanderbilt.edu/law/acqs/pubr.html

If you're looking for a publisher or vender on the Internet, this is the database to search. Search by name, subject, email address, or geographic location.

Index of Australian Indexes

http://www.moreinfo.com.au/ausindex/

A meta-index of Australian Web site indexes. Over a dozen are described, with links to each.

InfoCafé

http://www.infocafe.com/

A complete bookstore on the Web. Members may order any book currently in print, or even books out of print, and InfoCafé will do the search. Books are indexed by department—for example, computers, business, fiction.

International Business Resources on the WWW

http://ciber.bus.msu.edu/busres.htm

Serves as an index of business, economics, trade, marketing, and government sites with an international focus.

Internet Pearls Index

http://www.execpc.com/~wmhogg

Features collections of the best of the Internet. Includes sections for beginners as well as comprehensive coverage of topics such as business, medicine, jobs, cinema, shareware, astronomy, futuristic technologies, fun, cartoons, comics, virtual reality, and more.

Internet Sleuth

http://www.isleuth.com/

Offers a collection of more than 500 searchable databases on a wide variety of subjects. includes links to a search form or a page that lists a number of related searchable databases. Also allows you search by keyword or browse alphabetically or by category.

InterNIC Directory of Directories

http://ds.internic.net/ds/dsdirofdirs.html

Contains an index of links to various resources, products, and services on the Net, including agriculture, the arts, business, dictionaries, education, health and medicine, religion, sports and hobbies, and weather. Allows you to add your site.

Lycos Home Page: Hunting WWW Information

http://lycos.cs.cmu.edu/

Provides a Web search engine. Contains more than 5.5 million Web pages in its database. Provides context for evaluating whether a document or page is relevant to your search.

Media Logic's Index of Economic and Financial Resources

http://www.mlinet.com/mle/

This index of resources is provided by Media Logic as a service for the Internet community. It provides a searchable index of data, news, and services that are of interest to investors, researchers, and other members of the financial community. Unlike many other Internet indexes, all entries here are subject to editorial review to ensure that they are useful, relevant, and current.

Micro Service & Training

http://www.ici.net/cust_pages/jsouza/jsouza.html

This is a resource database for computer hardware, software, and training. If you are searching for hardware or software, or if you need training or consulting for your business or organization, you can search for it here.

Mother-of-all BBS

http://wwwmbb.cs.colorado.edu/~mcbryan/bb/summary.html

Seeks to collect all Web addresses of all companies, universities, research centers, government agencies, research projects, and hardware and software announcements into one searchable database.

New User's Directory

http://hcs.harvard.edu/~calvarez/newuser.html

Presents a large collection of links to information. Offers tips for specific kinds of computers (MAC, IBM, UNIX, and so forth), links to search engines, and more. Also provides information on how to create Web pages and download software.

NlightN: Finding What You Want To Know Now

http://www.nlightn.com

Claims to be "the Web's largest library of meaningful information." With a single query, the NlightN Universal Index searches the Web, World News, Online Databases, and traditional reference sources.

shareware.com

http://www.shareware.com/

Formerly the Virtual Software Library, offers a tool for searching for shareware and freeware on the Internet.

Starting Point

http://www.stpt.com/

Offers "everything you need to work the Web every day." Provides a starting site for finding information on the Web. Offers many links.

Starting Points for Internet

http://www.ncsa.uiuc.edu/SDG/Software/Mosaic/StartingPoints/NetworkStartingPoints.html

NCSA's comprehensive links to Internet resources. Includes Gopher, Veronica, Finger, Usenet, WAIS, and many others. Also presents representative Web home pages. Highly recommended (nay, essential).

URL-Minder: Your Own Personal Web Robot

http://www.netmind.com/URL-minder/URL-minder.html

Presents the URL-minder, your own personal Web robot, which retrieves your registered URLs regularly and reports back to you by email when they change. The URL-minder also runs searches on Web databases regularly and lets you know when anything new that matches your search shows up. It also keeps track of the places you've been, so you can spend your time (and money) doing new things on the Web.

VSL Front Desk at the OAK Repository

http://www.acs.oakland.edu/cgi-bin/vsl-front

Enter a keyword, and the engine searches the major Internet shareware archives for the program you want.

WAIS Access Through the Web

http://www.ai.mit.edu/the-net/wais.html

Provides information about WAIS, a system that enables you to retrieve documents from databases via full-text searches. Allows you to search by name or by topic.

Yahoo!

http://www.yahoo.com

Possibly the most popular search site on the Web. Considered to be the place to go for anything, as long as it isn't too technically oriented. Offers links only to sources, which is different from something such as Lycos, which also searches directories and files themselves.

STATISTICS & HISTORY

Economic FAQs about the Internet

http://gopher.econ.lsa.umich.edu/FAQs/FAQs.html

Presents a collection of FAQs about the economics behind the Internet. Discusses the technology behind the Internet, the NSF backbone.

Rampages

http://rampages.onramp.net/new/index.html

A service provider that offers automated usage statistics, bookmarks, counters, and online tutorials. High-powered clients are also candidates for the Rampage of the Month. Web directories are organized by user name.

World Wide Web: Origins and Beyond

http://homepage.seas.upenn.edu/~lzeltser/WWW/

Gives the origins of the Web and also talks about some of the other uses of hypertext, such as the Xanadu project. Also discusses some disadvantages of the Web.

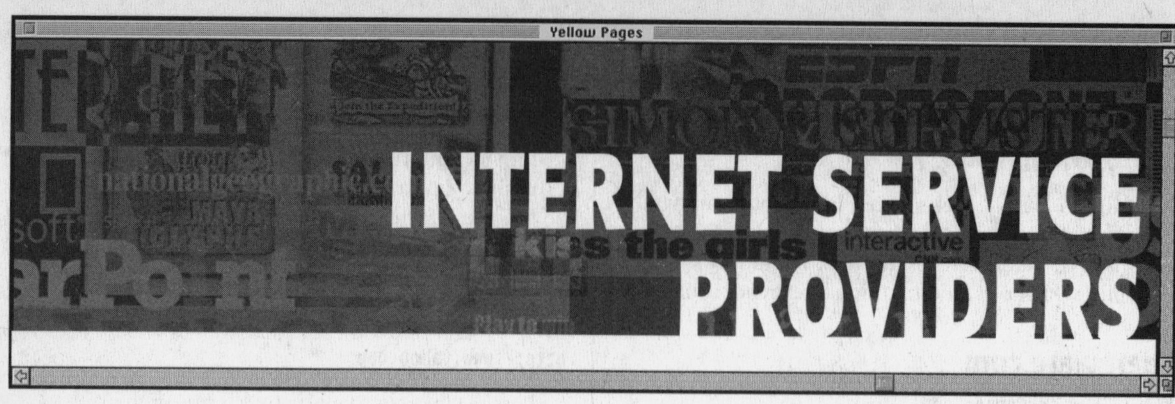

INTERNET SERVICE PROVIDERS

> Let's not start with the nerd jokes just because I enjoy the internet. You know, there's some pretty racy stuff on here.
>
> *Clark Edwards in* The Faculty *(1996)*

Charm Net Personal IP Page

`http://www.charm.net/pip.html`

Provides information on how to connect your computer directly to the Internet. It includes information for users of Macs, Windows, Windows NT, and OS/2.

CyberSight

`http://cybersight.com/cgi-bin/cs/s?main.gmml`

The information hotline for online hipsters. It also just happens to be a service provider and consultant to some of the largest corporations in the world, including Visa, Pepsi, and K2 Sports.

EFF's (Extended) Guide to the Internet

`http://www.eff.org/papers/bdgtti/eegtti.html`

Features a list of Internet providers, organized by state, and describes email, Usenet groups, FTP, Telnet, and BBSs.

NRP TOP PICKS

Fountainhead Internet Systems
`http://www.fountainhead.com/`

Imagine.com
`http://www.imagine.com/`

Internet Access Phoenix Arizona
`http://neta.com/`

Internet Interface Systems
`http://www.webnet.com.au/`

Enterprise Internet Services

`http://www.enterprise.net`

Acts as a major provider of Internet Services, based in the Isle of Man, British Isles. It also specializes in providing Web-based applications that utilize a secure Netscape Commerce Server. Offers a diverse and extensive Web server for all applications.

ExoCom

`http://www.exo.com`

Serves Los Angeles and Orange counties of southern California. Offers dial-up and dedicated access, and Web-hosting services. Has reasonable rates.

Fountainhead Internet Systems

`http://www.fountainhead.com/`

A full-service Internet provider based in Los Angeles. Provides Internet hookups, consulting, Web page design, and training. Also publishes the Los Angeles Superstation.

GeoCities

http://www.geocities.com/

Award-winning Internet provider based in Beverly Hills, California, with more than one million members. Contains hundreds of free home pages, organized into neighborhoods reflecting various sites, such as Wall Street or Hollywood. Presents a thriving community, including live video feeds from all over, as well as the freshest hot lists.

GHG Corp

http://www.ghgcorp.com/ghg/InternetServices/

A Houston company offering computer training and consulting services such as Web page development for businesses. Provides links to business home pages and newsgroups of interest.

Icanect

http://members.icanect.net/

Provides Internet consulting to get you connected with a service provider and up and running on the Internet. Provides downloads of Web and Internet software, along with contests, giveaways, and much more. This site has new Java and download sections.

ICNet: The Original Internet Provider for the Eastern Shore

http://www.intercom.net/

This provider for the eastern U.S. provides links to Internet and computer classes, computer resellers, search engines, local weather, news, and entertainment.

Imagine.com

http://www.imagine.com/

A service provider in Hartford, Connecticut, connecting individuals, businesses, government, and educational institutions to the Web. Offers Web site development, links to Imagine.com offerings (Web servers and firewalls), users' pages, and other creative services.

Industrial Peer-to-Peer

http://www.ippc.com/

Based in California, a network integration product and service provider for your organization. Includes links to products and services, management profiles, clients, and contact info.

Infonet

http://www.infonet.com/

A service provider that also presents information on navigation aids and search utilities, help files and FAQs, and other Internet services. Infonet also offers voice, fax, and data communications software.

InReach

http://www.inreach.com/

An Internet access provider for the Northern California area. Provides connection and service information as well as local job openings, news, and related sites.

Inspiration Software

http://www.rdrop.com/

Dial-up access for those in the Portland, Oregon area. Includes links to search engines, software to download, HTML info, movies, and other interesting Web sites.

Internet Access Phoenix Arizona

http://neta.com/

An access provider in Phoenix, Arizona, with links to information and renting Web space, business and personal home pages, Internet shopping, search engines, interesting sites, and more. Features new sites often.

Internet Application Services, Inc.

http://www.mindspring.com/

Internet Service provider for the Atlanta, Georgia, area. This site has a very well-done graphical layout.

Internet Channel

http://www.inch.com/

New York City–based Internet service provider. Links to services, accounts, clients, and the home page creator.

Internet Delaware

http://www.delnet.com/

Offers Internet access and Web publishing for individuals and businesses. A cool site with many, many links to search tools, software, Web sites, government info, products, and more.

What Type of Connection Do You Have?

Most online services offer Internet connectivity these days, and more and more people are taking advantage of the simplicity and extra help that an *online service* provides. Examples of these are America Online, CompuServe, and the Microsoft Network.

A *dial-up Internet Service Provider* (ISP) does not provide its own content. Because of this, these types of providers can undercut the online services on price and are a better deal for experienced users who want only to use the Internet. Examples of ISPs are SpryNet, Iquest, and GNN.

The third type of connection is a *direct connection through a LAN*. If you access the Internet from work, your company may have a full-time Internet connection through your LAN. That means you don't need a modem, and you'll be surfing ten times (or more) the speed of modem users. Lucky you!

Internet Express, Inc.

`http://www.inxpress.net/`

An access provider based in Madison, Wisconsin, with many links to services, subscriptions and rates, news access, global and local links, search engines, business and personal pages, and new user info.

Internet Front

`http://www.internetfront.com/`

An Internet service provider for businesses. Includes links to images, movies, software, other products, and more.

Internet Interface Systems

`http://www.webnet.com.au/`

An Internet access provider for businesses and individuals in Australia. A really cool interactive site with links to search engines, clients, games, newsgroups, and much more.

Internet Light and Power

`http://www.ilap.com/`

A Canadian-based Internet access provider for individuals and businesses in North America. Includes links to client services, search tools, cool sites, and more.

Internet MainStreet

`http://www.mainstreet.net/`

A full-service Internet provider for your business. Based in California, it provides links to other Web pages on its server.

Internet North

`http://www.internorth.com/`

An Internet service provider for Northern Canada. Includes links to Northern Canada's Net Index, local weather info, user's home pages, and more.

Internet On-Ramp, Inc.

`http://www.ior.com/`

A full-service Internet service provider based in Spokane, Washington. Includes links to support, Web info, businesses, members, AltaVista search engine, and more.

Internet Services Montana

`http://www.ism.net/index.html`

A full-service Internet provider based in Montana. Provides links to user pages, cool sites, businesses, Web searches, support, and more.

IntrepidNet

`http://www.intrepid.net/`

Internet access for individuals or businesses in eastern West Virginia and Washington County, Maryland. Provides access to businesses on the Internet, services, support, local sites, and more.

LavaNet, Inc.

`http://www.lava.net/`

Honolulu's Internet connection. Includes links to tech support, service and rates, clients' Web pages, the Hawaii home page, and more.

LI.Net

`http://www.li.net/`

The Internet service provider for the Long Island area. Includes links to resources, news, service, local living, and more.

Linkage Online

http://www.hk.linkage.net/

An Internet service provider for all your business needs, and the largest service provider in Asia. Find out about what it offers, businesses online, free classifieds, and more.

Magnetic Page

http://www.magpage.com/

An Internet service provider for Delaware, New Jersey, and Pennsylvania. Provides links to its corporate user pages, other user pages, subscriber services, Web searchers, and more cool stuff. Magpage now has an online newsletter, too.

Note A few online services let you use alternate email programs. CompuServe, for example, can be accessed through Microsoft Exchange, the Windows 95 email program, if you set it up correctly. See the Help system in Exchange to learn more about setting this up.

Medius Communications, Inc.

http://www.medius.com

Medius Communications, Inc., provides corporate Internet access and presence services, enabling organizations to plan, build, implement, and promote complete online information and application services.

Michigan Internet Cooperative Association

http://www.mica.net/

A full-service Internet service provider for businesses, offering high-bandwidth/low-cost connectivity. Check out its product announcements, its press releases, the Business Solutions Group, and more.

Minnesota MicroNet

http://www.mm.com/

An Internet service provider for the Minneapolis/St. Paul, Minnesota area. Includes links to business directories, community pages, customer support, and services.

Minnesota Regional Network (MRNet)

http://www.mr.net/MRNet.html

The most experienced Internet service provider located in Minnesota. Includes links to services, members, and resources.

MonadNet

http://www.monad.net/

An Internet service provider for individuals or organizations in the Monadnock area of New Hampshire. Includes links to how to get started, services and tech support, and FAQs.

Mountain Internet

http://www.mountain-inter.net/

An Internet service provider for areas in British Columbia, Canada. In addition to links to member services, it includes links to summer camps for kids, flight instruction classes, logger sports, auto racing, real estate, magazines, and other sites of local interest.

Nantucket.Net

http://www.nantucket.net/NN/

The Internet service provider for Nantucket Island. All the information you need to get started, including access info and pricing.

National Knowledge Networks, Inc.

http://www.nkn.edu/

The Internet service provider for North Texas, with links to Web info, services, news, and ideas. A new Web site is coming soon.

NetAxis

http://www.netaxis.qc.ca/

An Internet access provider based in Montreal, with links including local sites and businesses, search engines, local and community events and culture, and health sites, as well as links to sister sites.

NETCOM Online Communications Services, Inc.

http://www.netcom.com

Contains information about Netcom, one of the nation's largest Internet provider. Offers local access numbers online for subscribers on the go. Subscription information is also available online.

NetDepot

http://www.netdepot.com/

Internet access and services for individuals. Provides information about using and navigating the Internet, skills, and fun places to go.

NETHEAD

http://www.nethead.co.uk/

An Internet service provider for most of the United Kingdom. Offers Web publishing and consulting services to clients.

NetPoint Communications, Inc.

http://www.netpoint.net/

An international Internet service provider based in Miami, Florida, for individuals and corporations. Internet consulting provided in both English and Spanish. Provides access to a long list of interesting sites.

NetPress Communications

http://www.netpress.com/

NetPress Communications provides links to the following home pages: Collabra Software, Institute for Management Studies, Lithocraft, Inc., the Law Office of Kirsten Keith, and Bay Rep, Inc.

NetReach

http://www.reach.net/

An Internet service provider for the Quinte region located in Canada. Includes links to products and services, community and school information, Web sites, and resources.

Did you know...

Hardcore email users sometimes maintain two separate Internet accounts—one on an online service and one with an ISP. That way, they can have two different email addresses, and can keep their business and personal mail separated.

Netropolis

http://www.dash.com/

A local Internet service provider for the Denver, Colorado, area. Includes many links to art, business, education, government, entertainment, shopping, news, weather, and other sites.

Netside Network

http://www.netside.com/index.html

Internet access, computer sales, and networking for the southeastern U.S., with links to search engines, software sites, news and weather, user pages, advertising, and subscribing information.

Northwest Link

http://nwlink.com/

An Internet service provider for the Seattle, Washington area, with links to local news and weather, personal pages, new sites, rates, and service information.

Novagate

http://www.novagate.com

West Michigan's Internet service provider, with gateway information, services and pricing, yellow pages, local city information, and more.

Related Sites

http://web.cnam.fr/Network/Internet-access/how_to_select.html

http://www.instanet.com/

http://www.iquest.net/

http://ispfinder.com/

http://thelist.internet.com/

http://www.mojoski.com/nettools.html

http://www.barkers.org/online/index.html

http://www.taloncc.com/

http://www.thedirectory.org/

http://www.vli.ca

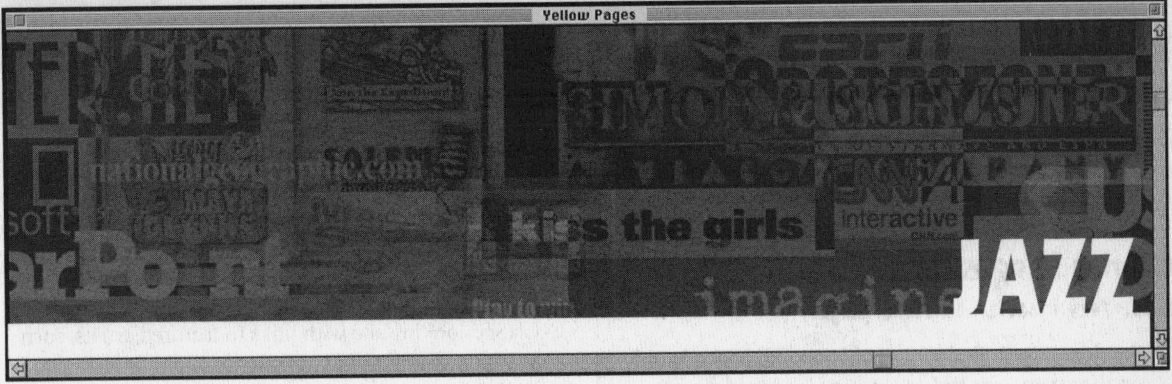

The memory of things gone is important to a jazz musician. Things like old folks singing in the moonlight in the back yard on a hot night or something said long ago.

Louis Armstrong

Jazz Central Station
http://jazzcentralstation.com/

Just Jazz
http://www.geocities.com/BourbonStreet/1114/

Milestones: A Miles Davis World Wide Web Site
http://charlotte.acns.nwu.edu/larryt/miles/milestones.html

Louis Armstrong Discography

http://www.foppejohnson.com/armstrong/

The home page contains several pics of the famous trumpeter in his different moods. The discography page includes information about sideman, hot 5 & 7, Stardom, the 30s, all-star, pure gold, and twilight discs. Also on this page are an interesting biography and related Armstrong links.

Alabama Jazz Hall of Fame

http://www.the-matrix.com/jazz/aljazz.html

Contains information about the organization whose stated mission is "to foster, encourage, educate, and cultivate a general appreciation of the medium of jazz music." Includes information on jazz events, their museum, instrument recycling, and the Jazz In Schools Program.

Albert Ayler: His Life And Music

http://ernie.bgsu.edu/%7Ejeffs/ayler.html

Presents a well-researched, well-written account of the free jazz music of Albert Ayler. Includes a very lengthy essay about Ayler's life and music. Also provides sound examples, album artwork, and a discography. This site has been put together by someone who loves Ayler's music and is well recommended.

Arizona Jazz, Rhythm and Blues Festival

http://www.infomagic.com/~azjazz/index.html

Offers complete schedules and ticket information for this fairly new jazz and blues event held in Flagstaff and brought to you by the organizers of the famous Telluride Jazz Festival. Also provides information on travel and accommodations.

Beeblebrox Homeworld

http://copper.ucs.indiana.edu/~mherzig/beeblebrox.html

Provides home site for the Bloomington, Indiana-based jazz quintet Beeblebrox. Site includes a band bio, tour dates, recording background, and links to other related sites.

Bill Frisell Home Page

http://www.geocities.com/Hollywood/2251/frisell.html

Includes a lengthy discography, articles, and a biography of jazz guitarist Bill Frisell. Provides links to other Frisell- and jazz-related sites.

Charles Mingus Home Page

http://www.siba.fi/~eonttone/mingus/

Provides a great deal of information and background on the jazz bassist and composer Charles Mingus. Includes a discography, articles, interviews, and other features. Includes links to other jazz and related sites.

Chet Baker: Lost and Found

http://home.ica.net/~blooms/bakerhome.html

Great site that contains tons of sound files (MPEG and AU formats) from Chet Baker's famous bop trumpeting. This site also includes a biography, album information, lyrics, and a four-part discography.

Contemporary List of Jazz Links

http://www.pk.edu.pl/~pmj/jazzlinks/

This site links to 1,326 other jazz-related sites. You'll find everything from festival information to jazz artists on the Web. Also, you can learn how to play jazz. Yep. Just follow the "Education" link.

Dave Brubeck

http://www.book.uci.edu/Jazz/CDLists/DaveBrubeck_CDL.html

This is a link off the University of California, Irvine, Bookstore site, but is about the best coverage on the Web for Dave Brubeck, the "cool jazz" pianist. The site gives a brief biography and offers plenty of images and an album list.

Electric Gallery

http://www.egallery.com/jazz.html

Dedicated to blues and jazz, this page offers beautiful, high-resolution images of artists such as B.B. King and Gary Patterson. Take the gallery tour (a walking tour or a shortcut) to see images or read about the artists featured at this site. Also, browse the online store to purchase jazz-related items.

Electric Gallery

http://www.egallery.com

Features paintings and sound samples of blues and jazz greats.

GRP: The Home of Contemporary Jazz

http://www.mca.com/grp/grp/index.html

Classic-looking site with links to featured artists, such as Chick Corea and Arturo Sandoval. It also has catalog listings of greats such as Dizzy Gillespie. Select GRP Talk to post to a discussion board or add yourself to the mailing list.

Hard Bop Cafe

http://www.mbnet.mb.ca/~mcgonig/hardbop.html

Serves as a complete guide to jazz in Canada. Includes concert and festival information, jazz on the radio, jazz publications, CD reviews, and more.

Harmolodic

http://www.harmolodic.com/begin.html

Provides home page for Ornette Coleman's Harmolodic productions. It includes background information about Ornette Coleman's music and philosophies of free jazz. Includes contact information, liner notes, and a Coleman discography. This site is a great source of information for jazz fans.

Jaco Pastorius

http://www.geocities.com/SunsetStrip/7831/

Provides a tribute home page to jazz bassist Jaco Pastorius. Includes a detailed discography that also outlines Pastorius' session work. Also includes articles, pictures, and links to other bass- and jazz-related sites.

Jazz Artists

http://www.erb.com/jazzartists/

Offers a great search engine to help you find the jazz artist you are looking for. Or, you can search for an artist by searching by musical instruments. Also, get listings of jazz clubs and festivals on the Internet.

Jazz Central Station

`http://jazzcentralstation.com/`

With a fabulous graphical stage, this site offers something for your visual and listening pleasure. Vintage images are what you select for going to different site areas, such as the Jazz Café, which is a chat link. This site features a biography and discography for at least one artist (currently, it's John Coltrane). You'll find numerous articles, links, and places to get information from this hot stop.

Jazz Central Station

`http://www.jazzcentralstation.com`

Features worldwide club, concert, and festival information, interactive reviews from JazzTimes magazine, recent and upcoming releases, artist reviews, the Jazz Cafe, and the Jazz Market. Also includes official site for the International Association of Jazz Educators.

Jazz Corner

`http://www.jazzcorner.com/`

An impressive and animated image map—and cool, hushed jazz music—introduces you to this site. Here, you can go to the Recording Studio to find more about jazz artists, shop at the Bop 'n Shop, get information on concerts and club dates at the Nitespot, and learn more about the business of jazz from the Office Suites link. Join the Speakeasy for an online discussion, too.

Jazz Fan Attic

`http://www2.magmacom.com/~rbour/index.html`

Wow, you name it, it's here. The home page offers you a list from which you can choose to link to anything from acid jazz to ragtime to blues. Based in Ottawa, this site also gives some information about local artists and clubs. The "Mainstream/Contemporary Jazz" selection has a cool portrait of Charlie Parker as well as 449 links to other jazz sites.

Jazz Improvisation

`http://gopher.adp.wisc.edu/jazz/`

Presents a series of articles for a course on jazz improvisation, taught at the University of Wisconsin. Serves as an introduction to the subject. Includes many images of musical notation and photos of jazz musicians.

Jazz in France

`http://www.jazzfrance.com/us/`

Surveys the entire French jazz scene, including festivals, magazines, musicians, jazz on radio and TV, and jazz awards. Provides texts in English and French.

Jazz Net

`http://www.dnai.com/~lmcohen/index.html`

Your guide to jazz on the Internet. Offers weekly updates and reviews of new jazz sites, as well as links to jazz-related sites.

Jazz: A Brief History

`http://www.rpa.net/jazz/`

Gives informative early history of jazz, from early African culture to Dixieland to swing. Also offers a page all set up for you to search for jazz in the major search engines of today.

John Coltrane: A Love Supreme

`http://sd.znet.com/~bydesign/coltrane.john/`

Presents the music and the man that is John Coltrane. Includes many different pictures, sound bytes, album artwork, and a very complete discography. Provides many different articles, interviews, and stories about Coltrane and his music. Also provides links to other Coltrane sites and links to other jazz sites. This site is highly recommended to any music fan.

John Coltrane: My Favorite Things

`http://www1.sanderso.org/sanderso/coltrane.html`

Includes many<$Coltrane, John> quotes from the jazz giant and a lengthy detailed thesis of Coltrane's music. Provides links to other jazz sites, a bibliography, and a gallery of photos. This is a well-crafted site.

A B C D E F G H I J K L M N O P Q R S T U V W X Y Z

John Zorn

http://mars.superlink.net/marko/jz.html

This is a well done unofficial site dedicated to the avant-jazz music of John Zorn. Includes articles, essays, and liner notes from Zorn releases. Also includes links to other related sites.

Just Jazz

http://www.geocities.com/BourbonStreet/1114/

The word "just" in the title page is an understatement! This is multimedia jazz heaven, with MIDI files, images of artists, slideshows, movie files, live radio, and so much more. You can read up on your favorite artist, listen to some jingling jazz in the background, browse through tons and tons of links, and find out what's hot in the jazz world.

Milestones: A Miles Davis World Wide Web Site

http://charlotte.acns.nwu.edu/larryt/miles/milestones.html

This is an example of what Web sites should be like. Easily navigable, graphically pleasing, and textually informative, this site offers so much about the great jazz trumpeter Miles Davis. Get news and a biography about Miles, order books and CDs online, listen to AU files or watch a QuickTime movie, and browse the endless links to related sites

Milestones: A Miles Davis WWW Site

http://miles.rtvf.nwu.edu/miles/milestones.html

Provides a thorough discography, articles, and photographs of jazz great Miles Davis. Includes interview sound bytes, album artwork, and links to other Davis and jazz sites. This site is a great introduction to the art of Miles Davis.

My Favorite Things

http://www.sanderso.org/coltrane.html

Very nice site with sultry images of John Coltrane blowing his sax. From the home page, link to thesis, bibliography, discography, and photo gallery sites. Also, you can find related Coltrane and jazz links.

Pacific Blues & Jazz

http://www.speakeasy.org/nwjazz/

Contains a potpourri of jazz information, pertaining to the northwestern United States (mostly Washington). Includes area artists and their recordings, concert and festival schedules, jazz publications, and visual art.

Pages of Fire

http://www.cs.ut.ee/~andres_d/mclaughlin/home.html

This site is dedicated to the music of jazz guitarist John McLaughlin and the Mahavishnu Orchestra. Includes discography, tour dates, album reviews, articles, and sound bytes. This site is lovingly put together and is recommended to fans and neophytes alike.

Pat Metheny Web Server

http://www.gilman.com/Metheny/home_page.html

This is the official home page of jazz guitarist and composer Pat Metheny. Includes upcoming tour dates and releases information. Also provides a complete discography, articles, and answers to frequently asked questions. This site is very well done.

Rude Interlude: A Duke Ellington Home Page

http://www.ilinks.net/~holmesr/duke.htm

Very resourceful site that offers you just about everything you'd want to find on the Web regarding the Duke. There are sound files, essays, information about the traveling Smithsonian Duke Ellington exhibition, and cover art for Duke's albums. Also find links and good descriptions to related sites.

Real Mingus Web

http://www.mingusmingusmingus.com/

Provides the official Charles Mingus Internet site. Includes a letter from Sue Mingus and detailed articles about the life and music of Charles Mingus. Also provides Mingus' writings and listings of authorized recordings. This is a great site for any jazz fan.

Thelonius Monk

http://www.achilles.net:80/~howardm/tsmonk.html

Provides a history, discography, and pictures of jazz pianist and composer Thelonius Monk. Includes current news, album reviews, and links to other jazz-related sites.

Traditional Jazz (Dixieland)

http://www.best.com/~kquick/dixie.html

Focuses on Dixieland music. Provides information on the bands, festivals, publications, societies, and places to hear Dixieland on the radio all over North America. Offers many links to newsgroups, mailing lists, and other jazz Web sites.

William Ransom Hogan Archive of New Orleans Jazz

http://www.tulane.edu/~lmiller/JazzHome.html

Contains oral history interviews, recorded music, photographic collections and film, sheet music and orchestrations, and numerous files containing manuscript materials, clippings, and bibliographic references. Contains information about the archive, photos, sound clips, and a complete index to the oral history interviews.

WNUR-FM JazzWeb

http://www.acns.nwu.edu/jazz/

Contains information on jazz. Includes essays on the different styles of jazz (accessible from a unique hypermap that reveals their interrelationships), artist bios, discographies, and reviews. Also offers information on festivals, venues, regional concerts, instruments, jazz in the media (radio, television, press), jazz art, and various jazz resources. Continually updated.

Yellow Jazz Pages

http://www.interjazz.com/yelowpag/yellpage.html

Great site for jazz professionals who want to get contacts and further their careers. You'll find booking agencies, venues, labels, clubs, and even live sound engineers—plus so much more. In the future, you'll be able to add your own listing to this site.

Related Sites

http://www.soros.org.mk/mk/skopje/jazz/en/count.htm

http://www.charm.net/~brooklyn/Topics/JanssenOnJazz.html

http://www.batnet.com/jazmin/

http://www.ohio.net/~osvaths/

http://www.acns.nwu.edu/jazz/artists/

http://miso.wwa.com/~blewis/

http://www.ragtimers.org/

http://members.aol.com/Jlackritz/jazz/index.html

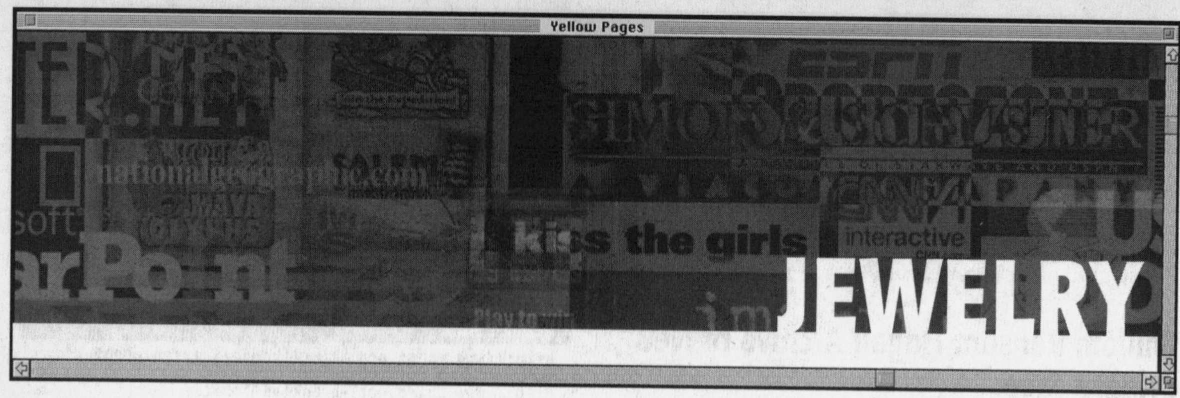

I take Him shopping with me. I say, 'OK, Jesus, help me find a bargain.'

Tammy Faye Bakker

Diamond Palace Superstore
http://www.diamondpalace.com/

Natalia Collection
http://www.nataliajewelry.com/

Under $99 Fine Jewelry
http://www.under99.com/

1-800-GEM-RING

http://gemring.simplenet.com/

Everything you could possibly want in the way of jewelry—rings, pendants, bracelets, earrings, and charms. Check out the price lists or request a catalog with photos.

The Amber Lady

http://goldray.com/amberlady/

Features genuine 40 million-year-old insects in polished honey-colored amber, as seen in *Jurassic Park* and featured in Smithsonian Magazine. Also offers more traditional amber jewelry.

AURAR/Victorian Reflections Jewelry

http://www.imageplaza.com/aurar/

Moderately priced period jewelry that is made in limited quantities. Amethysts, garnets, and pearls are used to make reproductions of jewelry from the Victorian Era.

The Bone Art Place

http://www.marketing.co.nz/bone/index.html

Site contains hand-crafted bone art and jewelry, and no two pieces are exactly alike. Send for a catalog that contains art in the shape of dolphins, whales, modern shapes, and more. The art is based on traditional New Zealand Maori carvings.

Celtic Motifs: Jewellery by John Frayne

http://www.thingzoz.com/celtic/index.htm

Offers silver and pewter Celtic jewelry by an Irish/Australian craftsman. Choose from a large selection, including bangles, earrings, bracelets, rings, and pendants. Order online or download a color catalog.

Ciel Azure Jewelry

http://www.ostrea.com/ciel/

Custom-designed jewelry for brides, bridesmaids, flower girls, and other special occasions. They try to accommodate your ideas or colors, and photos are posted of past clients with their creations.

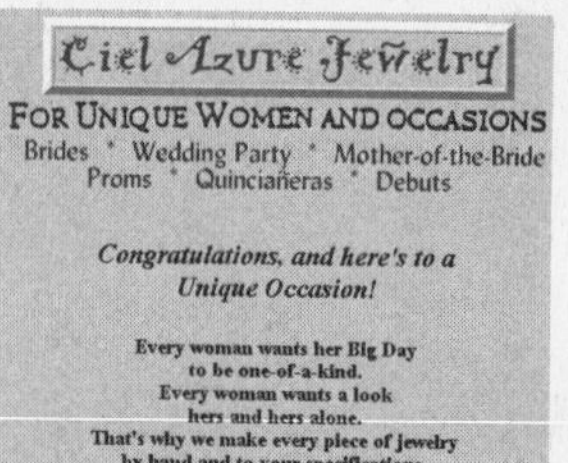

Cindy's Jewelry Store

http://www.webcom.com/toys/jewelry.html

This New York City store is a fine jewelry and pearl specialist. It offers custom design and stringing, and promises personal service and value pricing.

Colorburst Studios Online Catalog

http://www.teleport.com/~paulec/catalog.html

Order hand-crafted jewelry made from Niobium, a metallic chemical element that, when polished, resembles platinum. Designs are categorized and have names such as Man in the Moon, Global Forest, Umbrellas, Dolphins, and more. Check out the craft fair schedule to see if they'll be near you soon.

David Craig Jewelers

http://www.catol.com/dcj/

Specializes in diamonds, estate jewelry, and antique jewelry. Read David's monthly article and view his featured selections. Also lists other available services and links to other professional affiliations.

Diamond Palace Superstore

http://www.diamondpalace.com/

Contains many diamond-related links, from how diamonds were created to the magical properties of diamonds. Explains diamond color and clarity, carat weight, how diamonds are cut, and more. Also contains links to collectable coins.

Fast Fix Jewelry Repairs

http://www.fastfix.com/

Search the map at this site to find the location nearest you. If there's not one nearby, you can check out the franchise information available here. Also contains employment opportunities.

Gem Search International

http://www.pixi.com/gem_international/

Advertises the products of Gem Search International and contains diamond buying and selling information guides. Also offers diamond purchasing procedures.

Hollands Fine Western Jewelry

http://home1.gte.net/hollands/

Manufacturer of belt buckles and western jewelry for more than 60 years. Read through the history of the company or browse the online catalog. You also can request a color catalog with prices.

Ida's Gems and Designs

http://www.idasgems.com/

Home to both engagement and wedding rings as well as birth stones and loose gemstones. The site often features jewelry made using the current month's birthstone, and the store has many one-of-a-kind pieces.

J & M Coin, Stamp, and Jewelry Ltd.

http://www.jandm.com

J & M buys, sells, and trades coins, stamps, bullion, and jewelry. Offers a current list of products and a monthly commentary on coin collecting.

The Jewelers of Las Vegas

http://www.manifest.com/Jewelers

Manufacturers, wholesalers, importers, and distributors of fine jewelry. Offers an online catalog of products, as well as information about custom-made jewelry and advice on how to shop for jewelry.

Jewelers' Secret

http://tcguide.com/jewel/

As seen on TV! You can purchase this battery-powered polishing kit for jewelry from this site. Select either the deluxe or standard kit, both of which are hand-held. Restore the original shine and color to your jewelry.

Jewelry by Ponce

http://www.gayweb.com/113/ponce.html

This site offers rings, charms, pendants, and body jewelry. It also includes a special "Pride Collection" that features jewelry based on Aids awareness and gay pride. You can order online, or you can phone, fax, or mail in your order.

The London Cufflink Company

http://www.cufflinks.co.uk/

Designers and manufacturers specializing in cufflinks and wedding jewelry. The six-page online catalog contains designs in silver, but gold is also available. Company claims you can find a cufflink for all occasions at a great price.

Milne Jewelry Company

http://www.xmission.com/~turq

Presents an online catalog of Southwestern jewelry, including traditional Navajo, Zuni, and Hopi designs. Provides sections on "Guide to Southwest Indian Jewelry" and "Care of Silver and Turquoise Jewelry." (In English and Japanese.)

Natalia Collection

http://www.nataliajewelry.com/

Offers hand-painted wooden jewelry in the tradition of Russian and European art. Includes earrings, necklaces, brooches, bracelets, and jewelry boxes. The jewelry has three themes: floral, Nordic, and Russian nature and churches.

Pacific Craft House Creations

http://aloha-mall.com/pch/

Specializes in Hawaiian heirloom jewelry and other unique Hawaiian arts, crafts, and specialty gifts. Contains thumbnail photos you can click to see descriptions and ordering info. You also can find out your Hawaiian name at this site.

Puka Creations–Fine Handmade Jewelry

http://www.pukacreations.com/

Home of rice necklaces and other handmade jewelry. Site also contains letter necklaces and bracelets. Ordering and wholesale information also is available here.

Reflections of Ireland

http://users.aol.com/roireland/claddagh.html

Importers of traditional Irish jewelry, including claddagh and celtic rings. Find out how to wear the claddagh ring and what it means, as well as the legend behind it.

Rhinestone Jewelry Word Pins

http://www.rhinestone.com/rhinestone

Provides online sales of Austrian Crystal rhinestone jewelry. Includes catalog with pictures and ordering information.

Under $99 Fine Jewelry

http://www.under99.com/

Site contains a list of what's currently hot in jewelry, including anklets, baby jewelry, initials, sports, and much more. All these categories link to sample pieces of jewelry including prices and ordering info.

NEWSGROUPS

pdaxs.ads.jewelry

rec.crafts.jewelry

FTP & GOPHER SITES

ftp://ftp.hkstar.com/.1/netinfo/faq/news.answers/bodyart/piercing-faq/jewelry

ftp://ftp.fred.net/pub/users-www/iw/mall/class/jewelry

ftp://ftp.mhv.net/pub/users/j/jewelry

ftp://ftp.ultra.net/pub0/j/jewelry

ftp://ftp.webcom.com/pub4/myimage/www/jewelry

ftp://ftp.netins.net/showcase/mall/.web/jewelry

gopher://tucana.ualr.edu/11/Jewelry

Related Sites

http://www.abbeylane.com/

http://www.accessrex.com/Ambiance.htm

http://www.bel-cg.com/

http://www.connect.net/exgold/

http://www.idleidol.com/

http://www.illumina-gallery.com/

http://www.jewelry-direct.com/

http://www.martinandmartin.com/

http://www.photoscribe.com/

http://www.rust.net/~janken/index.html

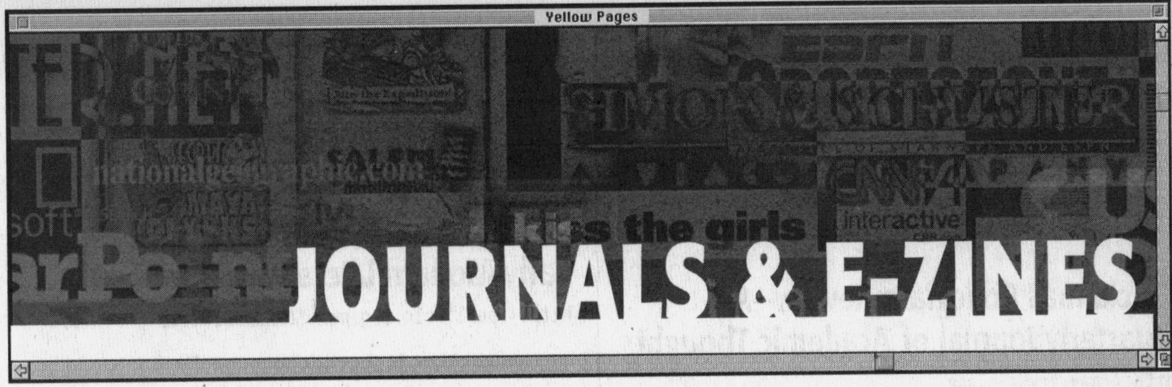

> Imagine if every Thursday your shoes exploded if you tied them the usual way. This happens to us all the time with computers, and nobody thinks of complaining.
>
> *Jeff Raskin*

NRP TOP PICKS

Blue Raincoat Journal	http://www.akula.com/~liap/home.html
CrossConnect	http://tech1.dccs.upenn.edu/~xconnect/
Mystery Readers Journal	http://www.slip.net/~whodunit/mystery
Sapphic Ink	http://www.lesbian.org/sapphic-ink/

@Ezine

http://www.vitter.com/ezine/@ezine.htm

Essays, commentary, short fiction, poetry, visual arts, and cultural interest grace the pages of this well-designed e-zine. There are also links to many of the artists' home pages and galleries.

American Drama

http://www.uc.edu/www/amdrama

American Drama is the journal of the American Drama Institute. The American Drama Website features complete tables of contents and a bibliography for all ten issues of the journal, a subscription page, playwright interviews (at present featuring interviews with Arthur Miller and August Wilson), and links to theater resources on the Internet. In the future, the Web edition will feature more playwright interviews, book reviews and abstracts for all articles featured in future issues of the journal.

American Planet Galactic News

http://www.americanplanet.com/

This quirky e-zine features poetry, links, current events, public affairs, and pictures that might be of interest to young adults.

Anagram

http://www.jhu.edu/~anagram/

This is a literary journal based at The Johns Hopkins University and dedicated to Asian-Americans. Although most of the contributors are students at Johns Hopkins, there are also writers from other venues presented.

Blue Raincoat Journal

http://www.akula.com/~liap/home.html

Quarterly literary journal with award-winning fiction, poetry, photography, and sequential art.

The Bull Street Journal

http://members.aol.com/BullStreet

The Bull Street Journal is a hysterical, unauthorized, full-length parody of the Wall Street Journal, not available in stores.

The Central California Poetry Journal

http://www.solopublications.com/journal.htm

The Central California Poetry Journal publishes poetry online by poets who write in or about Central California. Poems and articles are requested. The Journal is published by Solo Publications.

Clackamas Collegiate Review—A Quarterly Journal of Academic Thought

http://www.trybaja.com/ClackamasCollegiateReview.html

The Clackamas Collegiate Review is a student-run quarterly journal of academic thought.

The Cream City Review

http://www.uwm.edu/People/noj/tccr/about.htm

Based at the University of Wisconsin at Milwaukee, this is the literary journal of their English department. The name comes from the town's nickname, "The City of Cream-colored Bricks."

CrossConnect

http://tech1.dccs.upenn.edu/~xconnect/

CrossConnect is a triannual electronic journal examining and presenting contemporary art. It is based at the University of Pennsylvania in Philadelphia. This page is very well-formatted and popular. The current issue is at the forefront, but back issues are available, too.

De Proverbio

http://ftp.utas.edu.au/docs/flonta/

This is an electronic journal of international proverb studies. Several issues are available to be accessed and read, and there are other links available to reach the editors and editorial board of the periodical.

Dimension^2

http://members.aol.com/germanlit/dimension2.html

This is a journal of contemporary German-language literature. It is available in both the original German as well as in English. Also present at this site is original artwork by a contemporary German artist.

The Dr. Susan Block Journal

http://drsusanblock.com/journal.htm

A Journal of Pleasure, Art, Sex, Culture, & Politics. The online version of the Journal is also reader-written.

Early Modern Literary Studies

http://purl.oclc.org/emls/emlshome.html

Dedicated to the English language, literature, and literary culture from the 16th and 17th century, this journal is very interactive, featuring the capability to respond to its published papers in a Reader's Forum.

Exemplaria

http://www.clas.ufl.edu/english/exemplaria/

A journal of theory in medieval and Renaissance studies, Exemplaria is based at the University of Florida. Read articles concerning literature and culture from the formative Middle Ages.

Harvard Gay and Lesbian Review

http://www.hglc.org/hglc/review.htm

Considered the premier journal for gay and lesbian studies, the Harvard Gay and Lesbian Review is now online. There are indexes, articles, and excerpts from big-named scholars in the area of sexuality, such as Camille Paglia and Edmund White.

The Journal of African Travel-Writing

http://www.unc.edu/~ottotwo

The Journal of African Travel-Writing presents and explores past and contemporary accounts of African travel. Scholarly articles, true narratives, fiction, poetry, reviews, and so on.

The Milton Quarterly

http://voyager.cns.ohiou.edu/~somalley/milton.html

A journal related to John Milton and his work. There are abstracts and excerpts from the journal, as well as various other information about John Milton and his work.

Mystery Readers Journal

http://www.slip.net/~whodunit/mystery

Mystery Readers Journal is a quarterly thematic mystery review journal edited by Janet A. Rudolph. Each issue contains articles, reviews, and author essays.

Includes excerpts and table of contents from each issue (13 years). Sample themes include Sports Mysteries, San Francisco, Senior Sleuth, Gay and Lesbian Detectives, and more.

NorthWords

http://www.catalyst-highlands.co.uk/nortword.htm

Produced in the Scottish Highlands, NorthWords is a journal that focuses on the literature of "the North." Their definition of "North" is particularly interesting, though, and doesn't hold any sort of provincial boundary. Not only is creative work featured here, interviews and book reviews also are present.

Plaintext

http://www.plaintext.com/

Plaintext is (amazingly) a self-described "literary daily." Its aim is to present reviews, essays, stories, and articles each day—often in hypertext format. Readers can also submit to this online e-zine by email.

Qui Parle

http://garnet.berkeley.edu:4045/

The home page for the journal of the liberal arts. This periodical covers a wide range of topics, interdisciplinary and otherwise.

Romanticism On the Net

http://users.ox.ac.uk/~scat0385/

A great site about Romanticism in general, this online journal presents many articles, links, and the ability to publish online—that is, if you have something to say about Romanticism.

Sapphic Ink

http://www.lesbian.org/sapphic-ink/

A lesbian literary journal that features fiction, poetry, book reviews, and a hotlist. Also available is the ability to read about and get in contact with the contributors and editors of the magazine.

Science Fiction Weekly

http://www.scifi.com/sfw/

An electronic SF magazine. Covers books, movies, TV, games, artwork, and merchandise, and even some interviews.

Transculture

http://www.ilstu.edu/depts/forlangs/tculture.htm

A journal of interpretations and applications of cultural studies in language. Mostly abstracts from the printed journal, this site invites you to read more about the impact of multicultural studies.

Wespennest

http://www.ping.at/wespennest/wespennest.html

A literary magazine in both English and German. This site has links to literature sites, journals, and specimen articles in the PDF (Acrobat) format. There are also archives, offers, and a form to order this journal in print.

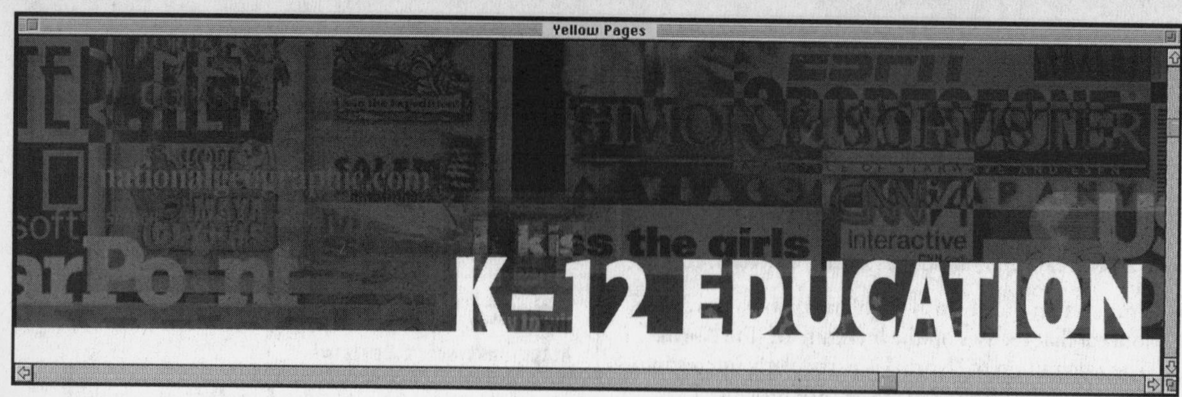

The best teacher is the one who suggests rather than dogmatizes, and inspires his listener with the wish to teach himself.

Edward Bulwer-Lytton

The Cyberspace Middle School
http://www.scri.fsu.edu/~dennisl/CMS.html

Galileo
http://www-hpcc.astro.washington.edu/scied/galileo.html

NASA John C. Stennis Space Center Education Office HomePage
http://wwwedu.ssc.nasa.gov/htmls/eao/eaohome.htm

On-Line Teaching–Examples and Articles
http://www.unl.edu/websat/disted.html

About the NDLC

http://www.occ.uky.edu/NDLC/NDLCexplain.html

Serves as a free resource for K–12, higher education, and adult education, distance learning. Offers a free Telnet database. Explains how to use the database, who to call for help, and NCLD's mission.

Alpine Valley School–Homepage

http://users.aol.com/alpineval/avs.htm

A K–12 independent day school located in Denver at which the students completely design their own education and participate in governing the school. Provides detailed information about the school's philosophy, mission, enrollment process, and generally presents a very bright picture of the school.

ArtsEdge Network

http://artsedge.kennedy-center.org/artsedge.html

Focuses on using technology to increase access to arts resources and increase arts education in the K–12 school environment. Features an online newsletter, an information gallery, curriculum guides, and links to other arts-related online information.

Busy Teachers WebSite K–12

http://www.ceismc.gatech.edu/BusyT/

K–12 Internet resource for teachers. Organized by subject area with annotated links to sites that lead directly to source materials.

Cold Spring Harbor Fish Hatchery and Aquarium

http://www.okc.com/fish

Offers a wide variety of hands-on educational programs for K–12 students. Presents indoor and outdoor displays. Provides trout and other fish to lakes and streams throughout the region.

Columbia Public Schools Homepage

http://www.ims.columbia.k12.mo.us

Serves 15,000 K–12 students. Features student and staff work and technical information for other schools.

Council of the Great City Schools Online

http://www.cgcs.org

Nonprofit organization that represents the nation's largest public school systems. Links to local chapter pages.

The Cyberspace Middle School

http://www.scri.fsu.edu/~dennisl/CMS.html

Contains links to science fairs, *Midlink Magazine* (for kids by kids), and Virtual Bus Stops (links to online middle schools). Also offers many helpful links for students, such as an online Periodic Table, how to read a map, and so on.

FYI, RFC #1578-Schools, and Internet

http://chs.cusd.claremont.edu/www/people/rmuir/rfc1578.html

Provides an Internet FAQ on the Internet and K–12 schools. Offers a clickable table of contents for browsing and contains useful information for anyone considering putting the Internet into a K–12 environment.

Galileo

http://www-hpcc.astro.washington.edu/scied/galileo.html

Offers a downloadable collection of science lesson plans for K–12 science teachers for classroom use.

HotList of K–12 Internet School Sites

http://rrnet.com/~gleason/k12.html

Contains links to all United States K–12 schools with Internet access, divided by state, and lists the level of access each school currently has (Gopher, Web, email only, and so on).

Interactive Educational Simulations

http://www.simulations.com/

This site contains a growing list of educational projects aimed at K–12 schools. Its goal: provide the best in interactive simulations, and stress higher level thinking skills. Plan to do this: use a profit sharing program to reward excellence.

Jerome & Deborah's BIG PAGES of Education Links

http://www.mts.net/~jgreenco/jerdeb.html

A comprehensive listing of K–12 education links for teachers and students. Includes links for Internet use in the classroom, special education, adult education, counseling and reference links.

K–12 Education

http://galaxy.einet.net/galaxy/Social-Sciences/Education/K12-Education.html

Offers many K–12 links, searchable and subdivided into primary and secondary education, and also into document type.

K–12 Technology

http://www.cvu.cssd.k12.vt.us/K12TECH/K12TECH.HTM

Describes what is called "Simple School Internet Protocol"—that is, a way to get schools online.

NASA John C. Stennis Space Center Education Office HomePage

http://wwwedu.ssc.nasa.gov/htmls/eao/eaohome.htm

A broad spectrum collection of K–12 and other educational WWW resources, with special interests toward space and aerospace studies. Includes teacher resources, lesson plans, and links to many other education related topics.

NCSA Education Program

http://www.ncsa.uiuc.edu/Edu/

Seeks to bridge the gap between scientific research and education and make the tools for computation available in the classroom (K–12). Offers jumps for teachers looking for resource materials.

On-Line Teaching—Examples and Articles

http://www.unl.edu/websat/disted.html

The site includes courses using the Internet for communication, research, or for displaying the results of research. Also listed are some online class resources.

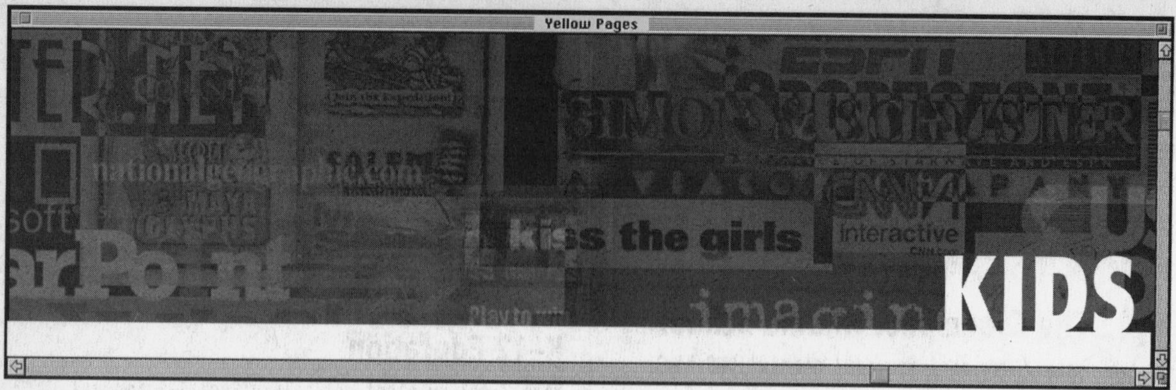

> Children should be taught not the little virtues but the great ones. Not thrift but generosity and an indifference to money; not caution but courage and a contempt for danger; not a desire for success but a desire to be and to know.
>
> *Natalia Ginzburg*

Boston Baked Theatre

http://www.basictheatre.org/

An online version of a theatre in Massachusetts, it's the home of Sprouts Theatre for Children and the Basic Theatre Company. Sprouts Theatre for Children creates humorous and musical productions of fairy tales. Past shows include *The Princess and the Pea, Beauty and the Beast,* and *Snow White and the Seven Dwarfs.* You can even meet the actors.

Building Blocks to Reading

http://www.NeoSoft.com/~jrpotter/karen.html

A reading program for children 3 to 6 years old. Includes activities, crafts, and other fun things for young children who are just learning to read. Links to other places that emphasize learning and links for parents and educators.

Children's Television Workshop
http://www.ctw.org/

Canadian Kids Page

http://www.onramp.ca/~lowens/107kids.htm

This site gives links to Canadian sites for kids—and also, non-Canadian sites. The maple leaf flag indicates the Canadian sites.

Children's Television Workshop

http://www.ctw.org/

Check out all the Sesame Street characters and new games children can play with them. Read interactive stories and discover activities for learning the alphabet, numbers, and shapes. Find out the winners of the Parents' Choice Toy Awards for 1997. Visit the Sesame Street Parents section, with discussions on behavior and discipline, child development, education, and health and safety. Read the reviews of products and check out CTW's favorite books for children.

Color, Cut and Fold Village

http://www.wolfenet.com/~por/foldup.html

Print out houses, stores, a library—a whole village—and children can color and cut them to create a beautiful village. The houses include a rose-covered cottage, a Dutch colonial, and a California Craftsman house. Children can set up the village, deciding where the streets go.

Crafts for Kids

http://craftsforkids.miningco.com/

Explore the many crafts that children can create, including crafts for every holiday and gift ideas. Get creative writing tips and learn how to make a storage box for all your creative writing projects—plus creative writing tips.

CreativeKids

http://www.creativekids.com/

Search for software by topic and child's age. CreativeKids recommended software has been tested, rated, and approved by educational professionals. Read the informative descriptions and check out the testers' personal favorites. You can order software online.

A Girl's World

http://www.agirlsworld.com/

A world created especially for girls. Site includes a clubhouse where girls meet their hosts Amy, Rachel, Geri, and Tessa. Girls can click the picture of each girl and learn more about their new friend. There are also craft, recipe, and other fun areas.

AHA! Kids Network

http://www.aha-kids.com/

Created by Al Hyslop, the producer of Captain Kangaroo, Sesame Street, and 3-2-1 Contact, this site is an interactive playground for kids of all ages. Contains cute graphics, video, and songs. Features an entertaining section for children 2 to 5, mysteries for ages 6 to 12, science for ages 5 to 12, and a section for teenagers.

Art for the Student on the Internet

http://www2.opennet.com/com/schoolhouse/art.html

Part of The Latitude 28 Schoolhouse, winner of a "Top 5% of the Web" award. Has many links to sites where kids can publish their own stories and view art from all over the world, including work by other kids.

Related Sites

http://www.kids-space.org/

http://www.geocities.com/Athens/Parthenon/7726/

Aunt Annie's Crafts

http://www.auntannie.com/

New craft projects every week for kids and adults. Focuses on learning and creativity.

Awesome Site for All Ages

http://www.marlo.com/

Presents witty ClickToons, cartoons for all ages, illustrated children's stories online, and children's jokes. Also allows for the making of customized greeting cards online. Does offer areas for 15- to 95-year-olds.

Berit's Best Sites for Children

http://www.cochran.com/theosite/Ksites_part1.html

Provides links to great Web sites for young kids. The sites are rated out of a possible 5 points. The sites include activity centers with games and opportunities for kids to display art and stories. There are also links to craft and coloring sites.

BigKid Network

http://www.ecst.csuchico.edu/~bigkid/bigkidnetwork.html

Entertaining site containing sections about museums, science, sports, zoos, aquariums, cities and countries, and amusement parks. Also has a fun and games section.

Bookworld

http://www.troll.com/bookworld/index_tzone.html

An online bookstore devoted to children's books, books for parents, and books for teachers. Kids select their age group and topic and Bookworld matches them up with several selections which the kids can then order.

Carlos' Coloring Book

http://www.ravenna.com/coloring/

A coloring site for younger kids. Kids choose a picture to color. Pictures may include an apple, a birthday wish, and other selections.

CHARMAYNE's Kids' Stuff

http://www.bischel.com/%7Echarmayn/kidstuf.html

Provides links for kids which vary from science to homework help. Site also includes poetry geared towards children.

Children Page

http://www.pd.astro.it/local-cgi-bin/kids.cgi/forms/

Web site for children containing many links to other children's Web sites around the world.

The Children's Literature Web Guide

http://www.ucalgary.ca/~dkbrown/index.html

Site provides online children's stories ranging from folklore to classics. There is also an area devoted to stories written by children. Dozens of links to children's books, and links for parents, teachers, storytellers, and writers.

Children's Music Web

http://www.childrensmusic.org/

A nonprofit organization which provides links to anything musical from music reviews to online songbooks. There is a children's concert calendar and a section for music teachers.

Children's Internet Site, Upstate SC

http://www.cris.com/~Tjpsys/community/child/child.htm

For kids, by kids, about kids. Lets kids submit Web art and lets them speak up on the Internet about whatever topics they find important to them. Contains art by kids and other kids' home pages.

Children's Pages at WombatNet

http://www.batnet.com/wombat/children.html

Contains links to Web sites for children about animals, dinosaurs, high schools, libraries, hobbies, magazines, museums, news, space, toys, and travel.

Children's Stories, Poems and Pictures

http://www.comlab.ox.ac.uk/oucl/users/jonathan.bowen/children.html

Contains stories, pictures, sound, and poems. Also features many links to other children's sites.

Club Humongous

http://www.humongous.com/clubhe0.html

Club for kids 3 to 8. Site includes a playroom with games, sounds, and other cool stuff. Also areas for coloring and other activities. There is also a paper, The Club Humongous Gazette, which is published quarterly.

Colgate Kid's World

http://www.colgate.com/Kids-world/index.html

Site contains information about cavity prevention, games, stories, a coloring book, interesting information, and pictures from around the world.

Curious George Rides the Bus

http://www.hmco.com/cgi-bin/trade/george

A mini-adventure game for younger kids featuring the beloved Curious George. Emphasis is on reading and fun. Help Curious George return hats to their rightful owners.

Cyber Stacks for Kids

http://bcn.boulder.co.us/library/bpl/kids/kids.html

A site provided by the Boulder, Colorado Public Library which includes links for learning about other cultures, references, games, a meeting place, and a science center. Also links to other fun places for children.

Cyberhaunts for Kids

http://www.freenet.hamilton.on.ca/~aa937/Profile.html

Site contains links for children of all ages to visit. Features itemized link categories on space, sound, literature, general children's pages, sports, communications, art, computer, science fun, music, misc., animals, and games. Great location to start when browsing the Internet.

Cynthia and Winston's Kids' Page

http://www.webcom.com/~cynspot/kids.html

Features stories by and for children. Also contains many science and reading links appropriate for children to use in learning more about their world.

Eddy the Ecodog's Home Page

http://www.mbnet.mb.ca/eddy

Eddy the Ecodog teaches kids about the environment. Kids can go to four "surfermania" areas by guessing the right password. Once in, there are all sorts of cool places to go. They can send postcards to friends, learn more about Eddy, and sign Eddy's guest book so he can write to them.

Exploring Leonardo

http://www.mos.org/sln/Leonardo/

Learn all about Leonardo da Vinci, the great scientist, artist, and inventor. See sketches of his inventions and see his beautiful masterpieces.

Family.com

http://www.family.com/

This site offers unlimited activities you and your children can share. Make homemade holiday cards and decorate the house. You can also find information on keeping your kids safe on the Internet.

Fiona's Shark Mania

http://www.oceanstar.com/shark/

A site for the shark maniac! Areas include shark art, stories about sharks, and a shark mailing list. Many links are also provided.

Flash Cards for Kids

http://www.wwinfo.com/edu/flash.html

Children can improve their math skills by using these online flash cards. They can try their hand at addition, subtraction multiplication, division, and addition and subtraction, involving more than two numbers. Flash cards are simple (two numbers) to complex (up to 10 numbers).

Fred Penner's Homepage

http://www.fredpenner.com/FredPenner/default.html

Fred Penner is a children's entertainer in Canada. Kids can learn all about Fred, join his fan club, find upcoming concerts, and more! The kids page has coloring pages which kids can print out. Links to other kid sites on the Web are also provided.

FreeZone

http://freezone.com

Web site devoted to children. Contains games, educational areas, comics, e-pal areas, chat areas, and a home page creator for children ages 9 to 15.

The Froggy Page

http://www.cs.yale.edu/HTML/YALE/CS/HyPlans/loosemore-sandra/froggy.html

Everything that kids want to know about frogs! Kids can listen to frog sounds, read frog tales from all over the world, and look at frog pictures. Older kids will appreciate the scientific amphibian section which includes frog anatomy and dissection as well as detailed scientific information on frogs and other amphibians from all over the world.

The Funroom

http://tac.shopnetmall.com/www.funroom.com/

Great games and craft ideas for kids and their parents. The crafts page has eight craft ideas and more to come. Kids can also refer to previous holiday issues for more crafts and games.

FutureScan

http://www.futurescan.com/

Site developed for young adults (ages 11 to 18) to provide helpful information in their career decisions. Featuring actual career stories and FutureScan attempts to help teens in choosing an appealing career to pursue. Although set up for teens, this Web site welcomes anyone that may be curious or interested in a different career.

Girl Talk

http://www.pleiades-net.com/voices/girl/girl.html

Web site where teenage girls can get together and discuss topics relevant to their lives. Features topics on friends, computers, school, pen pals, sexuality, sex, siblings, relationships, and parents. Site is an alternative place where adolescent girls can discuss teen-related issues with others in similar situations.

Global Show-n-Tell Museum Wings

http://www.manymedia.com/show-n-tell/

Site allows for children to submit their accomplishments or projects to "show and tell" about them. Promotes pride and self esteem within children while developing communication skills. Also includes links to other children-related sites.

High School Central

http://www.azc.com/client/enn2/hscentral.htm

An area devoted to high school kids. Includes dozens of net links, a chat area, games, and contests. There are also areas dealing with difficult teen subjects such as violence prevention and drug abuse. New features each month.

Horse Country

http://www.horsecountry.com

Web site for young people interested in horses. Contains information and links to various horse associations, equestrian news and events, the Junior Riders Mailing List, Horse Owners Club For Kids, and the Junior Riders International Pen Pal List. Entertaining site for riders of all ages and skill levels.

Hotlist: Kids Did This!

http://sln.fi.edu/tfi/hotlists/kids.html

A "hotlist" of sites produced by kids for kids. There are seven topics to choose from, such as science, art, and school newspapers. Kids select a topic which will connect them to the "hotlist" of their choice.

Humongous Entertainment

http://www.humongous.com/index.html

This site offers interactive entertainment for children ages 3 to 8. Order games and CD-ROMs online. Meet Freddi Fish, Pajama Sam, Fatty Bear, and Putt-Putt the car. They also offer technical support.

Info Guide—For Kids Only

http://www.theinfoguide.com/kid.htm

Web site containing numerous links around the world devoted solely to children. These sites vary from educational to entertaining.

Interesting Places for Kids

http://www.crc.ricoh.com/people/steve/kids.html

Selected as a "4-Star" site by the McKinley Group, this site contains many entertaining and educational topics for children. Contains sections on getting around the Internet, art and literature, music, museums, science and math, toys and games, movies, and arts and crafts. Also features a collection of art, writing, and other interesting things submitted by children.

Jackson's Page for Five Year Olds

http://www.islandnet.com/~bedford/jackson.html

Site developed for preschool children. Contains activities and games to help with cognitive and recognition skills. Features fun pictures and coloring books along with some adventures of another five year old.

Just 4 Kids

http://www.cottagesoft.com/~jjudkins/4kids.htm

Lists cool links for kids by month and alphabetically. Each month the newest finds are posted.

Kay's Kid's Collection

http://fox.nstn.ca/~tmonk/kayskids/kay.html

Contains a story book, picture page, and a funny page. Has links to sites devoted to crafts, Disney, games, girl guides and Brownies, family and friend pages, pictures, science and history, television, and other fun children's sites.

KID List

http://www.clark.net/pub/journalism/kid.html

More than 100 links to children's sites that are not religious, commercial, or political.

Kidland

http://www.kidland.com/

Kids can leap with Webbie, an animated frog, from site to site. Contains an index of kids' sites, activities, books, cartoons, educational information, games, and other topics related to children.

kidlinks

http://www.carroll.com/ridgewood_elem/kidlinks.htm

Site created by an elementary school in New Jersey. Features numerous links to entertaining and educational sites appropriate for children. Gives good descriptions of individual sites to assist in searching.

KidPub

http://www.kidpub.org/kidpub/

Educational and entertaining site includes over 7,000 stories written by children from all over the world. Also includes a chat area and a message center. The site provides information on how kids can publish their own stories and a story form is provided.

Kids Club

http://www.olworld.com/kidsclub/

Site for children containing online chat, games, stories, and links to other children's sites.

Kids Fun Club

http://www.dcross.com/kidsfun.html

Fun, safe, and educational site for kids of all ages and their parents. Kids can send in drawings, jokes, and stories about themselves. There are computer game reviews, a chat room, and an art gallery. Kids can send in their birth date and it will be posted. Area also provides many links to other Internet places for kids.

Kids Hits

http://www.nchcpl.lib.in.us/Library/LibraryInfo/KidzHitz.html

Contains a large alphabetical listing of sites designed especially for children. Also provides a good description of each site.

Kids on Campus

http://www.tc.cornell.edu/Kids.on.Campus/WWWDemo/

Site developed for children. Contains sections about planets and space, dinosaur and science museum exhibits, disasters (earthquakes, volcanoes, tornadoes) weather, butterfly pictures, and many other exciting areas for children to explore and learn.

Kids on the Web

http://www.zen.org/~brendan/kids.html

Contains valuable information for children and their parents to read before youngsters cruise the Web. Also features links to educational sites, games, and children's books.

Kids Page

http://www.supernet.net/supernet/kids.html

Provides links to sites dedicated to kids' education and interests. Includes links to sports, entertainment, and games and many others.

The Kids' Place

http://www.islandnet.com/~bedford/kids.html

Children's Web site containing a pen pal section, interactive area, children's home pages, online adventures, puzzles and games, fish and marine animal section, and space and astronomy area. Site is a fun and safe place for children of all ages to explore and learn.

Kids' Space Connection

http://www.ks-connection.com/

Guide Bear leads you through the Bulletin Board, where you can post your name on the list and ask questions. Check out the Penpal box and read letters from other children—even post your own letter and become a penpal.

Kid's Web

http://www.npac.syr.edu/textbook/kidsweb/

A World Wide Web Digital Library for school children. Contains information in the categories of art, science, social studies, miscellaneous, and other digital libraries. Within each heading, features several specific subcategories to ease searching.

Kids' Web

http://www.primenet.com/~sburr/index.html

Site developed for children. Contains stories and activities, links organized by topic, software recommendations, children's art gallery, and access to *ComputED Gazette* (a quarterly newsletter devoted to computer education.)

Kid's Window

http://jw.stanford.edu/KIDS/kids_home.html

A Web site in English developed to educate children about Japan and its culture. Contains pictures, a dictionary, and stories.

Kids World 2000

http://www.ecst.csuchico.edu/~bigkid/kidsworldindex.html

Contains hundreds of children's links around the world for children to explore. Primarily educational and entertaining, these are divided into museums, science, sports, fun and games, zoos and aquariums, cities and countries, amusement parks, and government and politics. Also features other interesting sites and a mystery site of the week.

Kid's Zone

http://www.spokane.net/kidzone/

Educational Web site containing areas for children, parents, and teachers. Contains games and stories to help children learn fundamental skills.

KIDS' CLUB

http://mack.rt66.com/kidsclub/home.htm

An exciting site where kids can make friends with other kids from 154 countries and learn about different cultures. Fun and safe for all children. Provides site links for parents and teachers.

KidsHealth.org

http://kidshealth.org/

Site contains interactive articles about children's health care, medicine, surgery, and parenting. There are fun games, kids vote health polls, and Nemours media guide.

KidStuff

http://members.aol.com/vergi/webdetective/kidstuff.html

Contains links to children's sites. Features lengthy descriptions about each site and its offerings.

KidWeb

http://www.teleport.com/~rhubarbs/kidweb/

Contains hundreds of links to sites appropriate for children of all ages. Also features kid's home pages, a survey, and areas divided for different age groups.

Kidworld From Tandem House

http://www.bconnex.net/~kidworld/

Site features stories, articles, and jokes written by kids for kids under 16. There is a pen pal area, a crossword area, and an online magazine.

KidzMagazine

http://www.thetemple.com/KidzMagazine/

A monthly online magazine produced by kids for kids. Includes articles, stories, music reviews, and much more. Kids can have the magazine emailed to them each month for free.

Knowledge Adventure

http://www.adventure.com/

A safe and exciting 3D world for kids. It features educational games, a monthly scavenger hunt with prizes, a complete reference library, and more!

The Learning Company

http://www.learningco.com/

This developer and marketer of educational software offers quality software for children. You'll find ABCs for preschoolers, skill-building math and reading programs, and history and geography software.

LEGO Group

http://www.LEGO.com/

The official LEGO universe: products, services, Legoland, company history, and recent press releases.

Link-4-Kids

http://www.bltg.com/link4kid.html

Site contains many children's links and descriptions to assist the young "surfer." Also features areas for parents that addresses Web safety and offers links to the top Internet security software.

Little Planet Times

http://www.littleplanet.com/

Site modeled after a newspaper for kids from K to 5. Kids can respond to the editor after reading stories. Also includes pages devoted to entertainment and a store where kids can purchase Little Planet products.

Lycos Top 5% Kids Sites

http://point.lycos.com/topics/Kids_Overall.html

Rates top kids' sites based on content, design, and overall rating, and gives the date reviewed. Also lists sites in alphabetical order to help you find a review of your favorite site.

Maddy Mayhem's Kid's Stuff!

http://wchat.on.ca/merlene/kid.htm

A lot of fun kid's links. A safe Web site for children. Links to pen pal connections, fun sites, and more.

Madlibs

http://www.mit.edu:8001/madlib

Kids fill in the blanks using parts of speech such as nouns, adjectives, verbs, and adverbs which are then inserted into a story with hilarious results. A great educational tool and a lot of fun.

Mazes-Hands On Children's Museum

http:www.wln.com/~deltapac/maze/mazepage.html

Fun site for kids who love mazes. Mazes vary from easy to hard. There is also a secret message maze which stresses letters and spelling.

MBG Network

http://MBGnet.mobot.org/MBGnet/

Educational site that has areas for children, schools, and parents. Features pictures and videos of and about the environment. Also offers activities online and projects that can be done at home.

MCA Home Entertainment Playroom

http://www.mca.com/home/playroom/

A safe, fun, and creative place for children of all ages to come and enjoy themselves. Features stories and games that will excite and amuse children.

MidLink Magazine

http://longwood.cs.ucf.edu:80/~MidLink/

This award-winning electronic magazine is written by kids for kids. It's for children in the middle grades—ages 10 to 15. MidLink magazine links children all over the world. Children tell about their role models and can send in stories, poetry, and drama of their own.

Mr. Stix's Electronic Treehouse

http://www.interlog.com/~brucem/

Mr. Stix is an electric drummer and kid's musician. There is a fun center with a lot of activities, a page where kids can find out where Mr. Stix will be performing next, a newsletter, and links to other family-friendly places on the net.

Munchkin Lady

http://www.uncg.edu/~jmarnese/index.html

Contains adventures, cartoons, and coloring books. Also features links to many popular children's sites.

My Little House on the Prairie Home Page of Laura Ingalls Wilder

http://www.vvv.com/~jenslegg/

Kids can learn everything about the *Little House* books, the television show, and special events at the Laura Ingalls Wilder heritage sites. A great introduction to America's frontier history. Provides links to other Little House sites as well.

NFL Kids

http://nflhome.com/kids/kids.html

Site geared for children that contains NFL profiles, statistics, news, and trivia. Also contains a searchable database, index, calendar, and shop.

The NoodleHead Network

http://www.noodlehead.com/

A network devoted to videos made by kids. There is a news page that changes monthly and links to other cool sites. The site is committed to creativity.

Nucleus Kids' Page

http://www.nucleus.com/kids.html

Contains many links to sites for children. Site provides subcategories of education, reading material, places to visit, things to do, movies for kids, TV on the Net, music, toys, kid's work on the Web, pen pals, a variety of links for fun and education, products, and links for parents.

Palos Verdes Kid's Corner

http://wwwsmart.com/~shui/PV/Kids.html

Site developed for kids by kids. Allows for submission of ideas, art, drawings, jokes, and stories. Permits online viewing of submissions from other children.

Pasadena Kid's Pages

http://www.e-znet.com/kids/

Contains a daily calendar of events for children for the Pasadena, California and surrounding suburbs.

Planet Blortland

http://blortland.netserv.com/

Visit the Planet Blortland, an underwater adventure for children. While there, children can take a guided tour, solve a mystery, win prizes, and meet an e-pal!

Platypus Family Playroom

http://www.orst.edu/~dickt/playroom/playroom.html

A Web site for children that offers both English and Spanish versions. Contains self-reading short stories, singing songs in harmony, interactive activities, a maze of the week, map quizzes, and different family activities.

PonyShow's Kids

http:www.PonyShow.com/KidsNet/website.htm

Site developed for children to learn computer skills. This is accomplished through games, activities, and stories. Also features areas on software, art, books, puzzles, travel, and kitchen.

The Preschool Page

http://www.ames.net/preschool_page/

An award-winning site for preschool kids and their parents. Children learn about animals, send in art-work, and view the work by other kids. The site also provides links to other kid-safe pages.

The Prince And I

http://www.nfb.ca/Kids/

Children visit a kingdom with the queen, search for treasure, submit their own drawings and stories, solve puzzles, and play games. The emphasis is on reading, fun, and creativity for kids in grades K through 6.

Rachel's Kids Page

http://exo.com/~jess/

Home page of Rachel, a four year old, site contains children's software and links that will entertain any preschooler.

REACH Summer Science Camp

http://www.ee.mcgill.ca/~reach/

Site contains exciting science projects and experiments for children grades 4 through 9 and teachers. Also features links to other science Web sites designed for children.

Reference links

http://www.lws.com/kidsweb/links.htm

Site designed and ran by children that contains reference links about general history, news, weather, and children's sites. Also features a children's picture gallery.

Rob Jugatic's Home Page: Kid-Friendly Places on the WWW

http://www.icom.ca/%7Erjagatic/kids.htm

Kid-friendly links to the World Wide Web. Includes a link to a Yellow Pages just for kids.

Route 6-16

http://www.microsys.com/616/

An entertaining and educational site developed for kids ages 6 to 16, parents, and teachers. Contains a playground with areas devoted to games and toys, art, music and books, movies and TV, outdoors and sports, oceans and space, animals, vacation and travel, and puzzles and hobbies. Site also features more than 2,000 links.

Safari Touch Tank

http://oberon.educ.sfu.ca/splash/tank.htm

Educational site where kids click different sea creatures and learn what they are and what they do. There are also links to other sea-life sites.

Silly Billy's World

http://www.sillybilly.com/

This site is one of the Top 100 Kids' Sites on the Web. There is a reading series in the site, learning links, stories for kids, and a creative writing area. There is also a section for teachers dedicated to children's reading.

Soap Bubbles

http://www.exploratorium.edu/ronh/bubbles/bubbles.html

Bubbles, bubbles everywhere! Kids love bubbles and this educational site will teach them everything about the chemistry that makes up bubbles. The site also includes links to other bubbly sites.

Stone Soup

http://www.stonesoup.com/

Magazine written and illustrated by writers and artists age 8 to 13. Children can send in their own manuscripts for possible publication. It inspires young writers and contains beautiful stories written by young people.

The Sugar Bush

http://intranet.ca/~dlemire/sb_kids.html

Site where children can enjoy themselves and make friends. Offers stories, crafts, projects, and fun and educational adventures. Also contains a treasure hunt and links to other children's sites.

Terrific Web Sites

http://www.westnet.com/~rickd/Kids.html

Site developed by The Eastchester Middle School provides both educational and entertaining links for middle school students. Featuring two main categories, academic studies and fun sites for kids, several subcategories, and multiple directories within each subcategory, it is easy to locate particular interests quickly.

Tessa's Cool Links for Kids

http://www.islandnet.com/~bedford/tessa.html

Web site created for pre-teens contains links to movies, coloring books, pictures, and software. Features both educational and amusing sites that will entertain your children.

thekids.com

http://www.thekids.com/kids/

Site features extensively illustrated stories, rhymes, fables, folk and fairy tales from around the world, plus discussion groups, games, contests, and information for parents. Also contains to their favorite educational sites.

Theodore Tugboat

http://www.cochran.com/TT.html

Young children can participate in interactive stories and download a page from the coloring book. There is also a section for parents and teacher which includes an email discussion list and many learning tools including synopses of Theodore Tugboat episodes.

Tristan and Tiffany's Daily Cool Stuff for Kids

http://www.polar7.com/tnt/

Created by children for children, this site features links to many entertaining sites.

Ultimate Children's Internet Sites

http://www.vividus.com/ucis.html

Provides links categorized by school ages including preschool and younger, 4 to 9 year olds, middle school, and teenagers. There are also links for kids of all ages and for parents and teachers.

VICNET

http://www.vicnet.net.au/vicnet/kids/youthnet.htm

Thirteen categories of links just for kids. Chat rooms, entertainment, art, trivia, jokes, and more! Created by children in Victoria, Australia. Also provides a link to a site for older cyber surfers and contains pages for music, games, sports, and other neat stuff.

Visa Olympics of the Imagination

http://www.enw.com/visakids/

Art contest challenging children worldwide ages 11 to 13 to draw or paint their own Olympic sport of the future. Includes instructions to teachers and previous winning pictures.

VolcanoWorld

http://volcano.und.nodak.edu/

An educational place for kids to learn all about volcanoes. There are experiments, images, and data, all pertaining to volcanoes and an area where kids can learn where the latest volcanic eruptions have occurred. There is a kids door that opens into a world of art, quizzes, and virtual field trips.

Wangaratta Primary School

http:www.ozemail.com.au/~wprimary/wps.htm

A site created by kids from Australia. Kids can learn about Australia, the kids who created the site, and Australian animals.

Web.Kids

http://www.hoofbeats.com/

Science fiction site for children. Contains stories, graphics, story ideas, and adventures.

Web-a-Sketch

http://www.digitalstuff.com/web-a-sketch/

Kids can sketch on the Internet by selecting a point, clicking, and going from there. Takes some patience so it's probably better for the older child. There are contests and galleries where kids can view sketches done by others.

The White House for Kids

http://www.whitehouse.gov/WH/kids/html/kidshome.html

Kids tour the White House with Socks the cat. Site includes information about the location and history of the White House. Kids can learn about the President and even write to him, the Vice President, and the First Lady using special email addresses!

World Surfari

http://www.supersurf.com/

Monthly virtual tour of a different country. Features information on the people, society, history, and other interesting facts of the particular country.

World Village Kidz

http://www.worldvillage.com/kidz/

Online activities for kids 3 to 13. There are pages for preteens and teenagers and pages for preschool and elementary students. The playground has areas for games, comics, e-pals, puzzles, and provides links to other kid-friendly places on the Internet.

Xplore Kids

http://www.xplore.com/xplore500/medium/kids.html

Web site designed for children to help them learn about animals, find a pen pal, publish art and stories, work on projects for school, or play games and have fun.

Yahooligans

http://www.yahooligans.com/

Web site search engine for children containing sections devoted to history, the arts, politics, computers and games, entertainment, sports and recreation, daily news events weather, and comics. Also features a school section that contains programs and homework answers.

Young Images

http://www.wilmington.net/yi/

A home page written by teens from Cape Fear, North Carolina. Includes articles on issues pertinent to today's teens and provides the readers with the opportunity to publish their owns stories and show their art.

Youth Connection

http://www.ingenius.com/product/cyberhd/youth/youth.htm

A youth-oriented forum which includes sections on art, money, games, and more. Also contains many links designed for children.

The Yuckiest Site on the Internet

http://www.nj.com/yucky/index.html

Young kids who like yucky things will love this site. Wendall the Worm will guide children through the world of worms including different types of worms and what they do for our environment. Rodney the Roach teaches kids about roaches. There are also links to other not-so-yucky kid pages.

Related Sites
http://www.ilos.net/laceplace/
http://ecreations.com/
http://www.sass.ca/
http://www.zdnet.com/familypc/content/9709/farout/index.html
http://imagerystudios.com/onlinecoloring/
http://www.bikesters.com/
http://www.globedirect.com/~pubs/index.htm
http://members.tripod.com/~game_links

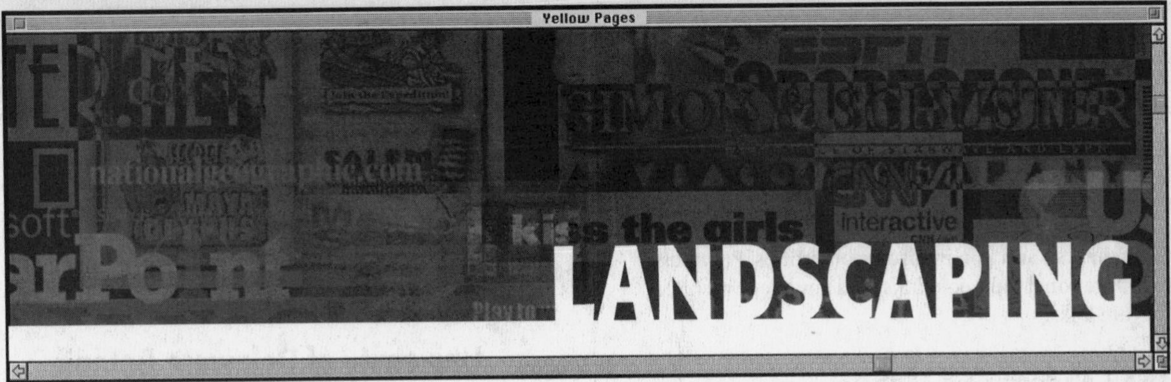

We are stardust. We are golden and we've got to get ourselves back to the garden.

Joni Mitchell

Centre for Landscape Research

http://www.clr.toronto.edu:1080/

Provides a collaborative environment for the exploration of ideas related to the design, planning, and policies of the environment. Focuses primarily on developing and utilizing electronic media to foster more informed decision-making.

Edible Landscaping

http://www.eat-it.com/

An online catalog that describes and enables you to order plants that produce apples, coffee, figs, grapes, herbs, pears, pecans, and so on, as well as some of the lesser-known varieties. Also provides a map of U.S. climate zones, a description of pot sizes, and even a place to read and submit recipes.

Green Landscaping With Native Plants

http://www.epa.gov/greenacres/

Is your goal to restore your land to its pre-settlement appearance? Prevent flooding? Attract wildlife? Sunny? Shady? Wet? This page can help you to answer these questions and others. Also provides a list of suggestions for growing native plants on residential property.

LandNET—American Society of Landscape Architecture Virtual Library
http://www.clr.toronto.edu:1080/VIRTUALLIB/LARCH/comp.html

Green Landscaping With Native Plants
http://www.epa.gov/greenacres/

University of Delaware Botanic Gardens
http://bluehen.ags.udel.edu/udgarden.html

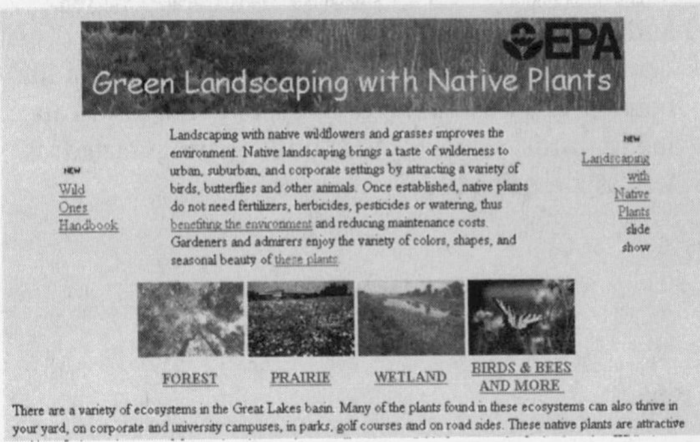

Jeff Chorba Landscape Design

http://home.ptd.net/~jchorba/

Provides design and horticultural documents, links to their related landscaping sites, future site for a BBS Connection, and a photo gallery of various landscape designs.

LandNET—American Society of Landscape Architecture Virtual Library

http://www.clr.toronto.edu:1080/VIRTUALLIB/LARCH/comp.html

Provides valuable links to Internet-based electronic information on a wide range of subjects that pertain to the landscape architecture field.

A B C D E F G H I J K L M N O P Q R S T U V W X Y Z

Landscape Architects

http://www.asla.org/asla/

Learn what ASLA is and how to become a member. Obtain access to the bookstore, marketplace, file library, spotlight (a bi-monthly discussion group that has an online interview with a professional landscape architect), and join in discussion groups. Provides educational links, job links, and landscape architecture links.

The Landscaping Manual

http://204.170.202.2:80/landscape/

Tips on how to increase your money-making capacity in the residential landscaping business. Provides suggestions on acquiring leads, sales techniques, developing your own stockyard, and so on. Includes an order form for this helpful book.

Landscaping to Attract Birds

http://www.bcpl.lib.md.us/~tross/by/attract.html

Tells its visitors how to plant birdbaths and feeders and situate trees and flowers so as to attract the denizens of the air. Also contains descriptions on the benefits of landscaping for birds, basics of landscaping for birds, plants for wild birds, getting started, as well as a reading list.

Pennsylvania Horticultural Society

http://www.libertynet.org:80/~phs/service.html

Provides a library with more than 14,000 types of reference materials. Receive information about garden tours in Pennsylvania, Delaware, New Jersey, New York, and New England. PHS also has their own exhibits and gardens to visit. Learn how to become a member and read various publications.

University of Delaware Botanic Gardens

http://bluehen.ags.udel.edu/udgarden.html

Tour the gardens of the University of Delaware. The tour includes eight different gardens. Descriptions of plants that are contained in the gardens are available.

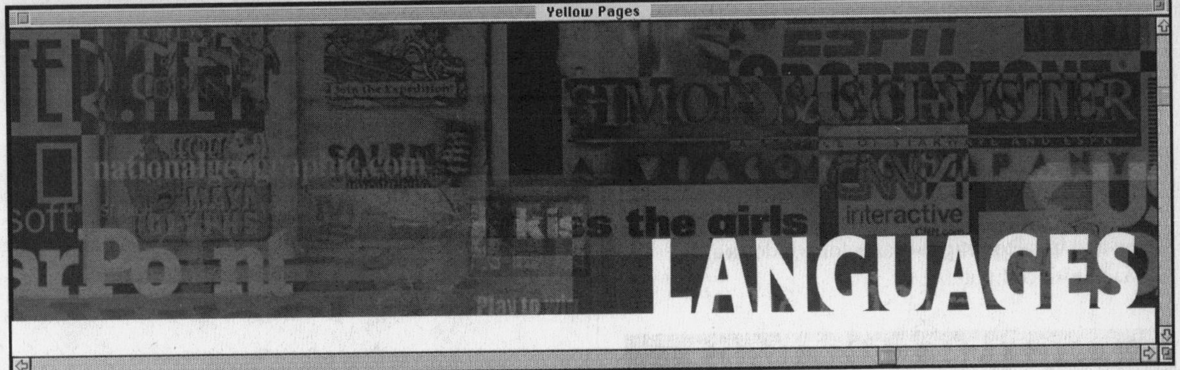

> Life is a foreign language; all men mispronounce it.
>
> *Christopher Morley*

CONSTRUCTED LANGUAGES

Constructed Human Languages

http://www.quetzal.com/conlang.html

A site containing listings and links to further information on constructed human languages. Constructed human languages are planned languages created by humans. The site is a good starting point for any one interested in non-natural languages.

Esperanto Access

http://www.webcom.com/~donh/esperanto.html

Esperanto is the most successful created language and is spoken by some two million people worldwide. Check out this site for a good introduction to Esperanto. The introductions are made available in English, Swedish, Dutch, Spanish, and many other languages.

Esperanto Access
http://www.webcom.com/~donh/esperanto.html

Cool Word of the Day
http://www.edu.yorku.ca/~wotd

The Online Books Page
http://www.cs.cmu.edu/Web/books.html

The Logical World of Etymology
http://www.phoenix.net/~melanie/thelogic.htm

Ergane
http://www.travlang.com/Ergane/

American Sign Language Linguistic Research Project
http://web.bu.edu/ASLLRP/

Home Page on Esperanto Studies and Interlinguistics

http://infoweb.magi.com/~mfettes/

This site is an index to English language sites on "planned" or "international" languages. It focuses on Esperanto because of more than 900 attempts to create international languages, only Esperanto has been successful. Esperanto is thus used as a tool in the branch of linguistics known as interlinguistics, or the study of how languages are used to communicate between two different groups.

The Klingon Language Institute

http://www.kli.org/

This site is for "scholars" wishing to study the Klingon language from the Star Trek TV series. Lots of information is available on the language and you can even learn to speak Klingon using the site.

A B C D E F G H I J K L M N O P Q R S T U V W X Y Z

Tengwar

http://www.dcscomp.com.au/jewell/tolkien/tengwar/

Tengwar is the written language of the elven people described in the books of J.R.R. Tolkien. Here you can find information regarding this interesting constructed language. It includes explanations of Tengwar writing and links to Tengwar fonts for windows and Macintosh computers.

ENGLISH LANGUAGE

American Dialect Society

http://www.et.byu.edu/~lilliek/ads/index.htm

Founded more than a century ago, the American Dialect Society still is the only scholarly association dedicated to the study of the English language in North America, and of other languages, or dialects of other languages, influencing it or influenced by it. The site contains information on ADS activities, including meetings and job offers. An online version of the society newsletter is available.

BritSpeak: English as a Second Language for Americans

http://pages.prodigy.com/NY/NYC/britspk/main.html

Have you ever heard anyone say, "I'll knock you up tomorrow morning"? This statement would be shocking only if you didn't realize that, to the British, the term *knock up* means to awaken someone by knocking on that person's door. This site attempts to clear up many such opportunities for misunderstanding, and provides a dictionary that converts British words and phrases to American and vice versa.

The Collective Nouns

http://www.lrcs.com/collectives/

If a group of fish is called a school, and a group of lions equals a pride, then what is the name of a group of whales? Would you believe a *pod*? This fun site catalogs well over fifty collective nouns, many of them humorous. For example, you might see a colony of penguins, a siege of herons, a bunch of things, or a giggle of girls.

Cool Word of the Day

http://www.edu.yorku.ca/~wotd

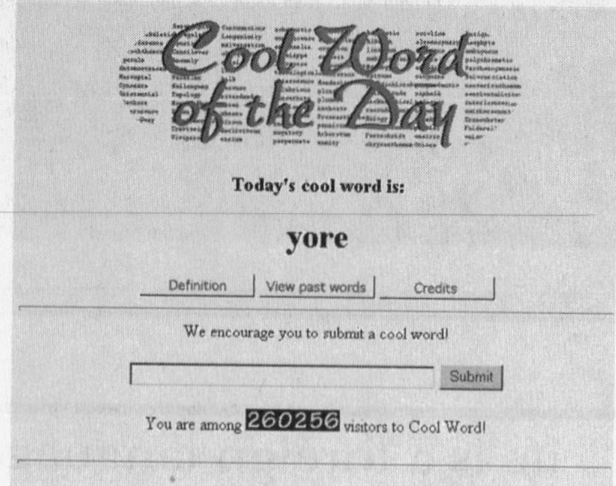

As you might imagine, this site provides an exercise in vocabulary-building. The page's best feature is that, when the page first appears on your screen, all you see is the word itself. If you don't already know the word's meaning, click the Definition link below the word. The interface also allows you to view past words or even submit a cool word of your own.

Cyberbraai

http://mainstreet.t5.com/cyberback.htm

A collection of six lists of words and phrases in South African English, with explanations of their meanings. A very humorous and entertaining site.

The Electronic *Beowulf*

http://www.uky.edu/ArtsSciences/English/Beowulf/

A project of the British Library and the University of Kentucky, the goal of The Electronic *Beowulf* is to make available, on the Web, access to digitized photographs of an early manuscript of *Beowulf*, one of the earliest surviving works of English literature. This project, in addition to making the manuscript much more widely available for study, would also allow the manuscript to be studied through electronic and computerized methods which would otherwise be impossible.

The Electronic Text Center at the University of Virginia

http://www.lib.virginia.edu/etext/ETC.html

This site contains thousands of texts, in Modern, Early Modern, and Middle English, plus French, German, Japanese, and Latin. Here you will find fiction, science fiction, poetry, theology, essays, histories, and many other types of materials. This site is excellent and thorough. Although a huge number of these texts are freely available, some texts are available only to users at the University of Virginia—the licensors of these texts have not permitted the University to make them widely available.

The Etymology of First Names

http://www.engr.uvic.ca/~mcampbel/etym.html

Aaron, Zoe, and all their friends will be interested to learn the origins and meanings of their names at this site, which will also provide plenty of ideas for parents to be.

Grammar and Style Notes

http://www.english.upenn.edu/~jlynch/grammar.html

Quick! What's the difference between affect and effect? Jack Lynch has the answer and he's offered it up on this site, an online guide to the complexities of English grammar. Lynch clearly explains the difference between commonly confused words, defines terms such as dangling participle, and offers his own opinions on a variety of style issues.

History of the English Language

http://ebbs.english.vt.edu/hel/hel.html

Home page for the History of the English Language mailing list (HEL-L). The page includes many resources for English language history studies. Anything from Anglo-Saxon texts to modern American English can be found here.

Larry's Aussie Slang and Phrase Dictionary

http://www.uq.edu.au/~zzlreid/slang.html

A site containing an Australian–English Slang and Phrase dictionary. There are hundreds of colorful Australian phrases to be found here. If you enjoy language, check this site out.

The Logical World of Etymology

http://www.phoenix.net/~melanie/thelogic.htm

Melanie (no last name please), the creator of this site, offers an abundance of information about word origins in this site. In addition to explaining how words are created and providing information about Greek and Latin roots and affixes, she answers etymology-related questions that have been emailed to her. Recent words included jazz, mafia, Cheyenne, and passion.

Old English Pages

http://www.georgetown.edu/cball/oe/old_english.html

Catherine N. Ball, a linguist at Georgetown University, has developed these pages devoted to the study of Old English. The page contains links to electronic texts, manuscript images, and the historical context of the language. Professor Ball has even included downloadable font packages to display Old English characters that no longer exist in our language. The Old English Pages is a vast collection of resources for those interested in the study of Old English and Anglo-Saxon England. This site contains texts, language information, fonts, and sound clips.

The Online Books Page

http://www.cs.cmu.edu/Web/books.html

More than 5000 English-language books are offered on this site, which you can search or browse by author or by title. In addition, you can browse new book listings or browse by subject. Philosophy, religion, science, computer science, literature, law, and medicine are among the subjects you can browse.

The Word Detective

http://www.users.interport.net/~words1/

An online version of The Word Detective, a newspaper column that answers readers' questions about words and language. Back issues of the Word Detective are available. Links to similar, or English language-related World Wide Web sites are included.

The Word Page

http://users.aol.com/jomnet/words.html

Build your vocabulary. (Or, to express it another way, Augment your lexicon!) This page offers ten new words and their definitions a week. This week's offerings included transcendental, soliloquy, aesthete, and multifarious.

Word for Word

http://www.peg.apc.org/~toconnor/welcome.html

Another site detailing the origins of words and phrases, Word for Word reprints installments from Terry O'Connor's column of the same name appearing in the Queensland (Australia) *Courier-Mail.*

WordNet

http://www.cogsci.princeton.edu/~wn/

A lexical reference work, WordNet is designed to map out the relationships and connections between words and their synonyms. Created by the Cognitive Science Laboratory at Princeton University, this site is being developed as an educational tool for improving vocabulary and reading comprehension.

GENERAL LANGUAGE AND LINGUISTICS

Ancient Scripts

http://www-ucsee.eecs.berkeley.edu/~lorentz/scripts/scripts.html

A site devoted to ancient written representations of languages. The scripts are divided in to six geographical categories. Images of these ancient writings are included in each article.

ETHNOLOGUE: Languages of the world

http://www.sil.org/ethnologue/ethnologue.html

One of the most complete sources of information on languages on the WWW, the Ethnologue database contains information on over 360 languages spoken worldwide. Information on languages includes name, number of speakers, and geographical location. The site even contains information on lesser known languages and dialects, such as Gypsy.

European minority languages

http://www.smo.uhi.ac.uk/saoghal/mion-chanain/Failte_en.html

A site dedicated to lesser known European languages. Includes information on languages such as Breton, Basque, and various Celtic languages, that are spoken by small groups of people throughout Europe. Contains links to other sites that specialize in one of the minority languages.

Euskara, the Language of the Basque People

http://www.cd.sc.ehu.es/DOCS/book.SS-G/v2/Euskara.html

Euskara is the language of the Basque people who inhabit northwest Spain and southwest France. This site is an introduction to the euskara language and the Basque people. Euskara is unique in that it is not related to any known language.

Gaelic and Gaelic Culture

http://sunsite.unc.edu/gaelic/

This site contains a good introduction to the Gaelic languages spoken in Ireland, Scotland, and Wales. Information on Gaelic cultures and history can also be found here. Many of the resources listed here are actually in Gaelic, so non-Gaelic speakers/readers beware.

Hindi: The language of songs

http://www.cs.colostate.edu/~malaiya/hindiint.html

Spoken by millions around the world, Hindi is one of the major languages of India. As the site's title implies there is a large archive of Hindi songs available through this site. There are also links to Hindi language and literary resources.

The Human-Languages Page

http://www.willamette.edu/~tjones/Language-Page.html

The Human-Languages Page is an index to sources of language information located throughout the Internet. Examples of resources contained in this guide include online Dictionaries, vocabulary lists, language tutorials, and foreign language software. The page is available in many languages.

Kervarker

http://webbo.enst-bretagne.fr/Kervarker/index.html

Breton is a Celtic language spoken by many of the people in West-Brittany, France. This site provides information about the breton language and culture. A series of lessons in Breton are provided for anyone interested in learning this language. Sound files are included to demonstrate pronunciation.

Kualono: 'Olelo Hawai'i

http://www.olelo.hawaii.edu/OP/help/

A wealth of Hawaiian language information can be found on 'Olelo Hawaii. This site is dedicated to promote and preserve the native Hawaiian language. Available resources include an online dictionary and Hawaiian fonts for IBM PCs and Macintosh computers.

LingNet—The Linguist's Network

http://lingnet.army.mil/

LingNet is a site dedicated to linguistics, the study of language. LingNet is located at the Defense Language Institute Foreign Language Center (DLIFLC) in

Monterey, California. An index of links to other WWW language resources, grouped by language, is available. File libraries and discussion forums are accessible through the LingNet BBS (Bulletin Board System) which has a WWW-based interface.

The LINGUIST Network

http://engserve.tamu.edu/files/linguistics/linguist/

LINGUIST is an electronic network hosted at Texas A&M and Eastern Michigan Universities. LINGUIST is used for research and discussion by linguists worldwide, through the use of its electronic mailing list and World Wide Web site. Archives of past discussions are maintained on the site.

The Logical World of Etymology

http://www.phoenix.net/~melanie/thelogic.htm

If you've ever wondered about the origins of a certain word, this site is for you. There is a featured word of the week whose etymology is discussed. The site also shows one some basic ideas behind etymology and how to apply these ideas logically for the purpose of discovering a word's history.

MERCATOR

http://www.troc.es/mercator/

The MERCATOR Project is an initiative set up by the European community to promote the interests of the minority/regional languages and cultures within the European Union. The site contains information on minority languages found in the EU. There are also links to three MERCATOR departments, and links to a bibliographic database.

The Translator's Home Companion

http://www.rahul.net/lai/companion.html

Sponsored by the Northern California Translators Association, the Translator's Home Companion provides a guide to resources for professional translators. Links to online translation resources, such as dictionaries, are listed on this site. Translation news and product information and reviews can also be found here.

VÍTELIÚ The Languages of Ancient Italy

http://www.netaxs.com/~salvucci/VTLhome.html

Dedicated to the languages of ancient Italy, this site begins with an interesting history of the country's name. Resources include maps showing where these ancient languages were spoken, alphabets of the ancient languages, and fonts for Macintosh personal computers. There is also a section on Etruscan vocabulary.

Yamada Language Center non-English Font Archive

http://babel.uoregon.edu/yamada/fonts.html

If you've ever needed foreign language fonts, this is the site to visit. This archive contains a large number of fonts for foreign languages. Graphic designers and linguists can both benefit from this archive.

LEARNING LANGUAGES

Beginner Level Japanese Course Home Page

http://www.threeweb.ad.jp/threeweb/jpncntrl/bgnr_hp.html

This page teaches the basics of the Japanese language. Lessons are available in two formats, the first is used if your computer is equipped with special software to view Japanese characters, the second uses GIF images to display Japanese characters. Each lesson is made up of three parts, the target material, the explanation, and exercises.

Chinese Language Related Information Page

http://www.webcom.com/bamboo/chinese/

An index of online resources on the Chinese language. There is a featured Chinese site each month. Link categories include literature, software, and Chinese language radio broadcasts.

CLAP—Chinese Learner's Alternative Page

http://www.sinologic.com/clap.html

CLAP offers the Chinese learner great resources that aid in the learning of Chinese. In addition to the standard fare of vocabulary words and dictionaries, CLAP offers information on the latest happenings in Chinese language and culture. For example, there is a section detailing English words in common Chinese usage.

Conjugue

http://www.innoview-data.com/3rdparties/conjugue/

Need a little help conjugating those foreign language verbs? Conjugue is a program that conjugates those tricky verbs for you. It includes support for languages and is for MS Windows computers.

Ergane

http://www.travlang.com/Ergane/

Ergane is a translation program for Microsoft Windows. It includes support for 42 languages. The program uses Esperanto as an intermediate language to translate between the two desired languages. It is available for download on this site and is freeware.

Esperanto Hypercourse

http://wwwtios.cs.utwente.nl/esperanto/hypercourse/index.html

If you've ever had a desire to learn the Esperanto language, this site is for you. The site features a WWW version of a HyperCard stack that will guide you through an introductory course on Esperanto. The lessons are available in English only.

Français à la Carte Formation

http://www.accent.net/falcarte/

Français à la Carte Formation is a company that specializes in French instruction. They provide a writing page to assist those learning French in improving their writing skills. The site also includes many pointers to French language resources available on the Internet.

French Language Course

http://www.kd.qd.se/iii/languages/french/course/index.html

An online course in the French language. The course consists of nine lessons and some additional vocabulary. In addition to the lessons, there is a section describing French expressions and idioms. Also included are pointers to other French language and culture sites.

Focal an Lae: The Word of the Day in Irish

http://www.lincolnu.edu/~focal/

Focal an Lae, literally meaning the word of the day in Gaelic, is a site devoted to the Gaelic Language spoken in Ireland. It includes back issues of Focal an Lae in case you have missed them, or just want to build your vocabulary. The site also features other valuable Gaelic language resources such as a list of useful phrases and links to other Gaelic information sites.

Foreign Languages for Travelers

http://www.travlang.com/languages/

A useful site featuring phrases in several languages that can be used by people who are planning trips abroad. Languages covered include Spanish, Portuguese, German, French, and Dutch. Sound clips demonstrating pronunciation can also be found on the site.

Gaelic Languages Info

http://futon.sfsu.edu/~jtm/Gaelic/

Collection of resources and pointers for learners and speakers of Irish Gaelic. Resources include, Irish Gaelic Web sites, software, and online dictionaries. Although this site mainly lists information relevant to Irish Gaelic, there is some information on other Gaelic languages such as Scottish and Manx.

Greek Through the Internet

http://www.isr.umd.edu/~kanlis/Greek/

Greek Through the Internet provides online lessons in modern Greek. There are five lessons currently available with more to come. Practice exercises are available at the end of each lesson. There are also other sections on grammar, syntax, and vocabulary.

Hebrew: A Living Language

http://www.macom.co.il/hebrew/index.html

Hebrew is one of the world's oldest living languages, and this site is dedicated to the Hebrew language. Basic Hebrew lessons are available on the site, covering topics such as counting in Hebrew. Hebrew stories, and poetry are provided to assist those learning the language. The site even includes Hebrew fonts for those wanting to write in Hebrew on their computers.

Korean Through English

http://ohm.kaist.ac.kr/hangul/

A series of ten lessons written in the English language that teach the basics of the Korean language. The lessons are well organized and include practice exercises at the end of each lesson. A Korean-English dictionary is also available on this site.

LEARN CATALAN

http://www.crocker.com/~lcastro/learncatalan.html

Catalan is a romance language spoken by millions of people along the eastern coast of Spain in the provinces of Catalunya and Valencia. Here you will find an introduction to the language and five lessons teaching the fundamentals of Catalan.

SURVIVAL MALTESE

http://www.fred.net/malta/malti.html

Planning to travel to Malta? If so, Survival Maltese is for you! Survival Maltese focuses on frequently used words and phrases for use by travelers. Phonetic transcriptions of every word and phrase are available so users can see how the language is pronounced. Using Survival Maltese will not only give you a minimum Maltese vocabulary but also helps you get used to pronouncing the language.

Web Italian Lessons

http://www.hardlink.com/~chambers/Italian/

Inspired by the Spanish lessons made available over the Web, Lucio Chiappetti created this site to teach the basics of the Italian language. There are three lessons, available in HTML format for online browsing, and in postscript format suitable for printing.

Web Spanish Lessons

http://www.hardlink.com/~chambers/Spanish/

Online lessons in the basics of the Spanish language. Three lessons are currently available in two formats, HTML for online viewing, and PostScript for printing. A list of helpful resources for people interested in learning Spanish is included.

A Welsh Course

http://www.cs.brown.edu/fun/welsh/Welsh.html

A course in the Welsh language. Welsh is a language related to the Gaelic languages of Ireland and Scotland, primarily spoken in Wales. The course is geared toward beginners. The site also provides links to other Welsh resources on the WWW.

LANGUAGES/LINGUISTICS

The American Dialect Society (ADS)

http://www.msstate.edu/Archives/ADS/

This is the home page of the ADS, the only scholarly association dedicated to the study of the English language in North America—and of other languages, or dialects of other languages, influencing it or influenced by it. Includes membership information, conference schedules, and calls for papers.

American Sign Language Linguistic Research Project

http://web.bu.edu/ASLLRP/

This is a collaborative research project involving researchers at Boston University, Dartmouth College, Rutgers University, and Gallaudet University. Information is provided at this site on the two main parts of this project: investigation of the syntactic structure of American Sign Language (ASL) and development of multimedia tools for sign language research.

The Association for Computational Linguistics

http://www.cs.columbia.edu/~acl/home.html

Includes background information on the Association, conference schedules, abstracts from the Computational Linguistics journal, plus links to related sites.

Australian National Dictionary Centre

http://online.anu.edu.au/ANDC/

This center provides information on research into the usage of Australian English. Includes details on various Australian dictionaries published by Oxford University Press, with plans for an online dictionary.

CELEX Dutch Centre for Lexical Information

http://www.kun.nl/celex/index.html

CELEX has compiled three large electronic databases which can provide online and offline users with detailed English, German, and Dutch lexical data. Aimed at the professional linguist, this database contains representations of the phonological, morphological, syntactic, and frequency properties of lemmata for each of the three languages included.

Center for Machine Translation

http://www.mt.cs.cmu.edu/cmt/CMT-home.html

The Center for Machine Translation (CMT) at the School of Computer Science at Carnegie Mellon University conducts advanced research and development in a suite of technologies for natural language processing. At this site you will find project details, personnel profiles, technical reports, and more.

Center for Spoken Language Understanding

http://www.cse.ogi.edu/CSLU/

This group from the Oregon Graduate Institute of Science and Technology has a mission to perform basic research leading to advances in the state of the art of spoken language systems. Their Web site follows that mission by providing research summaries, publications—including the full text and illustrations of the Human Language Technology Survey—and more.

The Chomskybot

http://www.ling.lsa.umich.edu/cgi-bin/chomsky.pl

The focal point of this site is a Web robot that assembles random phrases from the works of Noam Chomsky into nearly coherent paragraphs. Also provided is a detailed discussion of the programming behind this robot and the linguistic principles it uses.

Colibri Home Page

http://colibri.let.ruu.nl/

Colibri is an electronic newsletter and WWW service for people interested in the fields of language, speech, logic, or information. A searchable index of current and past issues is available, along with subscription directions and many links to related topics.

English as a Second Language Home Page

http://www.lang.uiuc.edu/r-li5/esl/

This home page is a starting point for ESL learners who want to learn English through the World Wide Web. Many people have created ESL learning materials for the Web. This home page links you to those ESL sites and other interesting places. The variety of materials will allow you to choose something appropriate for yourself.

ETHNOLOGUE: Languages of the World

http://www.sil.org/ethnologue/ethnologue.html

If you've ever wanted to know what people are saying all over the world, this is the place to come. This site includes a detailed study of the names, number of speakers, location, dialects, linguistic affiliation, multilingualism of speakers, and much more information on more than 360 languages currently spoken on this planet. A searchable database and clickable maps are provided to help you find just the language you are looking for.

EUROLANG Optimizer

http://www.eurolang.fr/

Provides information on the EUROLANG Optimizer software package. This program is designed to work with the most popular word processors and RDBMS to provide language translation. Download the demo version from this site. Pages available in French or English.

FoLLI, the European Association for Logic, Language and Information

http://www.fwi.uva.nl/research/folli/

This site contains information on FoLLI's background, current and future projects, and publications. Also find out how to join FoLLI and receive their journal.

Haskins Laboratories

http://www.haskins.yale.edu/haskins/inside.html

Haskins Laboratories, New Haven, Connecticut, is a private, non-profit research laboratory. Currently, most of the Laboratories' research projects are focused on problems in human communication and related topics, including speech perception, speech production, reading, linguistics, motor behavior, cognitive science, nonlinear dynamics, medical imaging, functional MRI, and so on.

The Human-Languages Page

http://www.june29.com/HLP/

This page is devoted to bringing together information about the languages of the world. The language resources listed here come from all around the world, and range from dictionaries to language tutorials to spoken samples of languages. Offers the page in several languages. Provides Quick-Jump links for easy navigation, and should soon be searchable.

Journal of Child Language

http://www.cup.cam.ac.uk/Journals/JNLSCAT95/jcl/jcl.html

Journal of Child Language publishes articles on all aspects of the scientific study of language behavior in children, the principles which underlie it, and the theories which may account for it. At this site you will find submission requirements, tables of contents for past issues, and subscription information.

Journal of Pidgin and Creole Languages

http://www.siu.edu/departments/cola/ling/

JPCL presents the results of current research in theory and description of pidgin and creole languages in the wider sense. Includes glossary of linguistic terminology.

The Klingon Language Institute

http://www.kli.org/

Just for fun or for the serious linguist, this site details the development of the "artificial" Klingon language from the Star Trek series and movies. At this site, you can also teach yourself Klingon to speak with your friends.

Kualono: 'Olelo Hawai'i

http://www.olelo.hawaii.edu/OP/help/

This Web site is dedicated to providing information on the native Hawaiian language, both for preservation and teaching. Among its many resources are Hawaiian fonts (Mac and IBM), an online dictionary, and instructional materials for purchase.

Lexeme-Morpheme Base Morphology (LMBM)

http://www.bucknell.edu/~rbeard/

The LMBM lexicon is exclusively the domain of lexemes which are defined specifically as noun, verb, and adjective stems and the lexical categories which define them (Number, Gender, Transitivity, and so on). LMBM distinguishes itself from other lexeme-based theories in that it maintains a pristine distinction between lexemes and grammatical morphemes and consequently predicts this distinction at every level of language and speech.

The Lingua Project

http://www.loria.fr/exterieur/equipe/dialogue/lingua/

This page is devoted to the Lingua Parallel Concordancing Project, which aims at managing a multilingual corpus to ease students' and teachers' work in second language learning. More specifically, some implementation issues of the Text Encoding Initiative guidelines are shown, along with the corresponding tools which have been developed. Currently, this project has translated various texts into English, French, German, Dutch, Greek, or Italian, and cross-referenced each work in a searchable index of the languages.

The LINGUIST Network

http://engserve.tamu.edu/files/linguistics/linguist/

LINGUIST is an electronic network maintained at Texas A & M and Eastern Michigan Universities. LINGUIST serves as a research and discussion facility for the linguistic academic community through an electronic mailing list and its World Wide Web sites. Join a discussion or read archived discussion threads from this site.

Loglan

http://www.halcyon.com/loglan/welcome.html

Loglan is an artificial human language originally designed/invented by James Cooke Brown in the late 1950s. This site details the construction and usage of this language. An HTML primer to learn Loglan is scheduled to be available soon, but some translations are already online.

The Mayan Epigraphic Database Project

http://jefferson.village.virginia.edu/med/home.html

The Mayan Epigraphic Database Project (MED) is an experiment in networked scholarship with the purpose of enhancing Classic Mayan epigraphic research. MED is an Internet-accessible database of primary and secondary sources of epigraphic, iconographic, and linguistic data in a multimedia format.

Model Languages

http://members.aol.com/JAHenning/index.htm

The electronic newsletter contains discussions and articles on made-up languages. Includes subscription information and a software package (Windows) for making your own language.

A B C D E F G H I J K L M N O P Q R S T U V W X Y Z

Multilingual PC Directory

http://www.knowledge.co.uk/xxx/mpcdir/book.htm

The Multilingual PC Directory is designed to help you find products which support non-English languages on PCs and compatibles. A search option by language is available. Includes software reviews, company profiles, and links to Web resources.

Natural Language Computing Home Page

http://www.nyu.edu/pages/linguistics/ling.html

This page is part of a larger Web site that discusses the design and implementation of a computer programming language that works using real English syntax, not the cryptic commands of languages such as C++. This page relates the linguistic theories of Noam Chomsky to the larger project.

Old English Pages

http://www.georgetown.edu/cball/oe/old_english.html

This site contains nearly everything you could want to know about Old English. Includes links to online texts and translations, discussion groups, fonts, audio recordings, course materials, instructional software, and much more.

Russian Manual Alphabet

http://weber.u.washington.edu/~jkautz/russian.sign.html

This small page provides graphics that demonstrate the use of sign language to speak Russian.

Semiotics for Beginners

http://www.aber.ac.uk/~dgc/semiotic.html

As the title suggests, this site provides an online course in the study of signs/communication in society (semiotics). Here you get the history of this discipline, current applications and research, and lists of suggested reading material.

UCREL—University Centre for Computer Corpus Research on Language

http://www.comp.lancs.ac.uk/computing/research/ucrel/

The University Centre for Computer Corpus Research on Language is a Lancaster University research center shared between the Department of Linguistics and Modern English Language and the Department of Computing. Its objective is to carry out computer-based research on the analysis and processing of natural language data. This site provides details on the Centre's research, including data summaries, online papers, and conference schedules.

University of Chicago Press Cognitive Science and Linguistics Catalog

http://www.press.uchicago.edu/Subjects/Linguistics/

This page is the entry-point into U of Chicago's Gopher-based online catalog and ordering system for linguistics texts. Search by author and subject or read the whole catalog, including book summaries.

The Web Journal of Modern Language Linguistics

http://www.ncl.ac.uk/~njw5/

This recently created online journal includes articles, book reviews, and subscription and submission information. (A print version will also be available.) Submissions are encouraged from any branch of Modern Lanquages.

Word Manager

http://www.idsia.ch/wordmanager.html

Word Manager is a system for the acquisition and management of reusable morphological and phrasal dictionaries. Learn about this system developed in Europe; a demo version is downloadable for Macintosh.

WordSmith Tools

http://www1.oup.co.uk/cite/oup/elt/software/wsmith/

Wordsmith Tools is an integrated suite of programs for looking at how words behave in texts. It is intended for linguists, language teachers, and anyone who needs to examine language as part of their work. Download a full demo version from this site at the Oxford University Press.

The Yuen Ren Society

http://weber.u.washington.edu/~yuenren/index.html

Founded for the Promotion of Chinese Dialect Fieldwork, the Yuen Ren Society is a loose group of descriptive linguists working in Hann Chinese. The central focus of this Web site is a guide to Gwoyeu Romatzyh Tonal Spelling of Chinese for the romanization of the Chinese language.

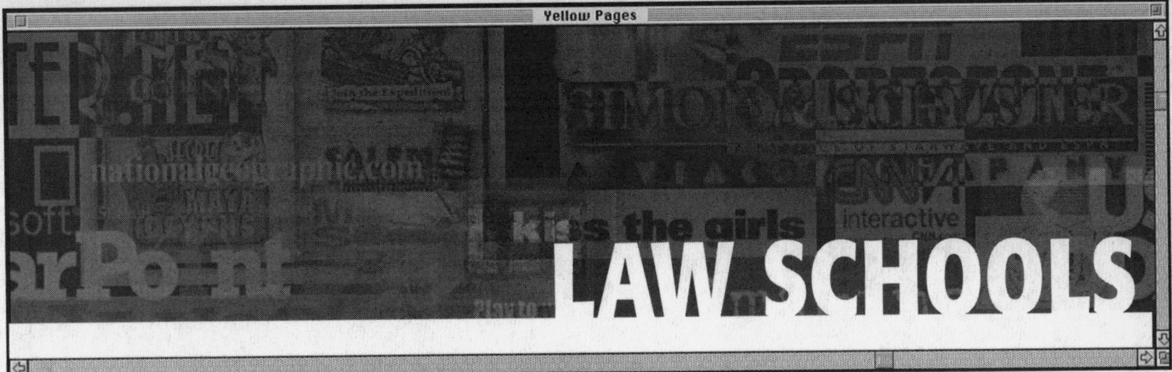

> The Law is the true embodiment of everything that's excellent.
>
> *Sir William Gilbert*

Law School Admission Council Online
http://www.lsac.org/

Law School and the LSAT
http://www.kaplan.com/lsat

Yale Law School Homepage
http://www.yale.edu/lawweb/lawschool/ylshp.htm

FindLaw: Law Schools of Canada

http://www.findlaw.com/02lawschools/canada.html

Part of the FindLaw database. Links to the law schools in Canada. Information given for each school includes a link to the university home page and contact information

FindLaw: US News Top 25 Law Schools

http://www.findlaw.com/02lawschools/USNEWSlist.html

Part of the FindLaw database. Search through the top 25 law schools in the nation based on *US News and World Report*. Each school's listing provides home page links, library links, and snail mail contact information.

Law School Admission Council Online

http://www.lsac.org/

Features "Reggie" the online LSAT registration service. Link to their Web site and get information on law school forums, LSAT preparation materials, and law school financial aid. Page also includes link to WWW sites at LSAC-member law schools.

Law School and the LSAT

http://www.kaplan.com/lsat

From Kaplan, everything you need to know about the LSAT and law school, including scoring, sections, and dates and registration. Page also includes links to help you through law school admission and financial aid. Access to law schools and law student resources also found on the page.

Legal and Political Links

http://www.shore.net/~djn/law.html

A helpful list of law and politics links from all over the Web, including law schools, non-profit institutes, and personal pages.

The Law Student Web

http://darkwing.uoregon.edu/~ddunn/l_schl.htm

The main Web site for law students. A comprehensive index of law student pages, law schools, sites of importance to law students, and strange case law and statutes.

Yale Law School Homepage

http://www.yale.edu/lawweb/lawschool/ylshp.htm

Number one ranked law school in the nation based on *US News and World Report*. Link to admissions information, the 1995-96 Bulletin, faculty biographies, and occasional papers. Also access Dean Kronman's welcoming address to the class of 1998.

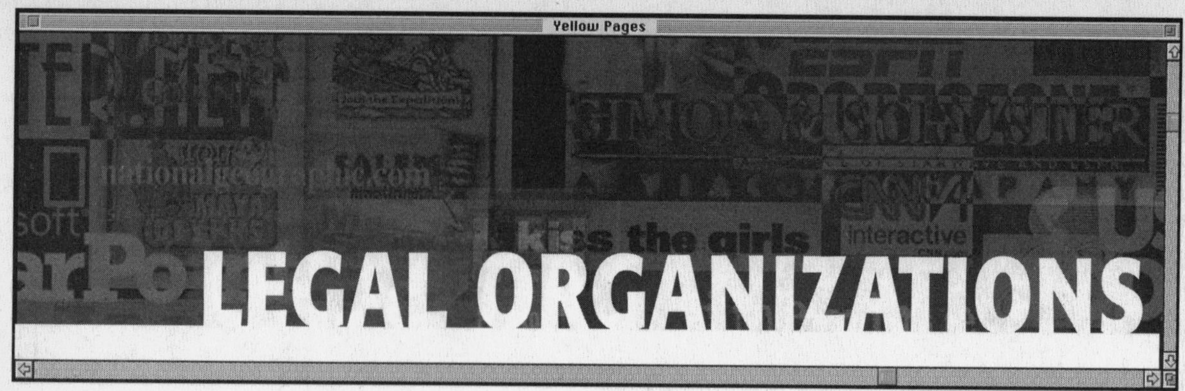

LEGAL ORGANIZATIONS

A B C D E F G H I J K L M N O P Q R S T U V W X Y Z

> Laws are like sausages. It's better not to see them being made.
>
> *Otto von Bismarck*

ACLU Freedom Network
http://www.aclu.org/

American Bar Association
http://www.abanet.org/

NYSDA Public Defense Backup Center Home Page
http://www.nysda.org/

ACLU Freedom Network

http://www.aclu.org/

The home page for the American Civil Liberties Union takes you to the latest happenings from congress, current events, and what's happening in the nation's courts. You can also join the ACLU, browse their cyberstore, and read about current events. Other links take you to highlights of cases that the ACLU has involvement in.

American Bar Association

http://www.abanet.org/

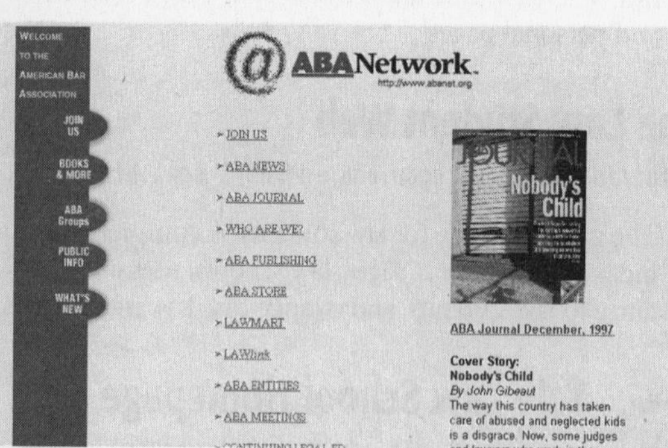

The ABA Network connects you to any information you need pertaining to this world's largest voluntary professional association. Links to information about the various entities of the ABA (each entity has its own link), a calendar of events, and public information are just a few starting points on this top 5 percent Web site.

American Immigration Lawyers Association

http://www.aila.org/

Links to information about the AILA, how to join, and AILA conferences can be found here. Also, writings about immigration as it pertains to America, the role of immigration lawyers, and recent legislative affairs that affect immigration law. Provided, too, is a searchable index of AILA members, and immigration lawyers on the Web.

International Association of Constitutional Law

http://www.eur.nl/iacl/index.html

Provides access to general information about the IACL, an invitation for the adherence to the IACL, a link to more information about the Fourth World Congress, and access to the constitutions of countries of the world, in both the native language and English.

NYSDA Public Defense Backup Center Home Page

http://www.nysda.org/

This is the front page of an extensive collection of links related to the New York State Defenders Association. This not-for-profit organization seeks to improve the quality of defense services in New York State. The site indexes the various departments of NYSDA through various links, including those on membership, the Board of Directors, and the Defender News Archives.

> A verbal contract isn't worth the paper it's written on.
>
> *Goldwyn's Law of Contracts*

ALSO! Main Page

`http://www.lawsource.com/also/`

Provides a comprehensive, uniform, and useful compilation of links to all online sources of American law that are available without charge. Source documents are stored in various file formats in many separately maintained databases located in several countries.

The American Indian Law Review

`http://www.law.uoknor.edu/departments/ailr.html`

This Review is published by the University of Oklahoma College of Law. This site gives background information about the Review, and contact information for getting a copy of the current, or back, issues. The Review is currently not available online.

European Law Journal

`http://www.iue.it/LAW/ELJ/Welcome.html`

Find out about the Journal by clicking the aims and scope link. Get the table of contents, issues covered in the Journal, the editorial board, the advisory board, and information about contributing to the Journal through links from this site.

ALSO! Main Page
`http://www.lawsource.com/also/`

Hieros Gamos
`http://www.hg.org/`

Law Journal Extra!
`http://www.ljx.com/`

LawMarks...The Legal Resource Database
`http://www.cclabs.missouri.edu/~tbrown/lawmarks`

Federal Communications Law Journal

`http://www.law.indiana.edu/fclj/fclj.html`

The official journal of the Federal Communications Bar Association. Site includes links to electronic versions of currently available issues. Access also available to information about the Federal Communications Bar Association and Indiana University School of Law. Journal is maintained by student editorial board at Indiana University School of Law.

Global Legal Studies Journal

`http://www.law.indiana.edu/glsj/glsj.html`

Published by the Indiana University School of Law, this site contains all back issues of the Journal, information on how and why it was started, subscription information, and editorial board information. A search engine is available to help you locate the information you need.

Hieros Gamos

`http://www.hg.org/`

Comprehensive resource for legal professionals, law students, and persons seeking law-related information. Links include bar associations, legal associations, law schools, publishers, law firms, law sites, government sites, vendors, and online services. Site available in English, Spanish, German, French, and Italian. More resources than can be listed.

Journal of Information, Law, and Technology

`http://ltc.law.warwick.ac.uk/elj/jilt/`

This site, home to the e-journal JILT, enables you to access past and present issues, link to what is new, regular features, special features, and information about the people who put JILT together. Also link to information about JILT, how it got started, what its purpose is, and why it is maintained the way it is.

The Journal of Online Law

`http://www.law.cornell.edu/jol/jol.table.html`

E-journal with essays pertaining law and online communications—law and cyberspace. Read the articles, subscribe, get information about the Journal of Online Law, or meet the editorial staff from this Web site.

Law Journal Extra!

`http://www.ljx.com/`

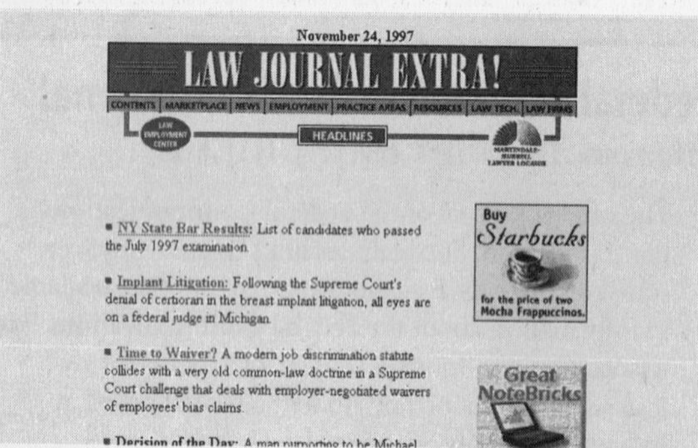

Updated daily, this journal highlights current events that affect the legal and political professions. Articles on high-profile cases and suits, court-room updates, and new rulings are just some of the interesting and resourceful links on this page. Also included is access to national legal journals online, the marketplace, employment center, and law firms online.

Law.Net

`http://law.net/`

A resourceful page that links to a directory of lawyers and law firms separated into specialization. Page also includes how to join information, the newsletter, access to the library, articles of interest.

LawMall

`http://www.lawmall.com/`

A virtual mall for the legal profession with a potpourri of links including classified ads, editorials, articles, expert witness wanted ads, LawMall information, and others. Page also includes links to other law-related resources, and (currently under construction) lawyers and firms by state and city.

LawMarks...The Legal Resource Database

`http://www.cclabs.missouri.edu/~tbrown/lawmarks`

A comprehensive digest of all available legal and law-related resources on the Internet. After reading about LawMarks, choose from the General Directory of Resources menu, or the General Directory of Other Internet Search Engines menu. The General Directory includes links to rules of court, law schools, law journals, legal news, legal directories, federal documents, and law libraries, to name a few.

legal.online

`http://www.legalonline.com/`

Home to the monthly newsletter for legal professional using the Internet. Link to information about legal.online, view a sample issue, check out the index of back issues, fill out the ordering information, read the guide to courts on the Net, and look over the statutes and bill on the Net.

P-LAW Legal Resources Locator

`http://www.dorsai.org/p-law/`

For anyone who is looking for legal resources on the Internet. Link to legislative and other government information sites, multi category reference sites such as universities and the United Nations, specialized topic sites such as advertising law, criminal law, etc., statistical information sites, and miscellaneous sites such as The ACLU Reading Room and The National Criminal Justice Reference Service.

Web Journal of Current Legal Issues

`http://www.ncl.ac.uk/~nlawwww/`

Click and your connected to past and present issues of the Web JCLI. Covers current legal issues. Site also includes other legal links, a welcome message, and information on becoming an author of the Web Journal of Current Legal Issues. A top 5% Web Site by Point.

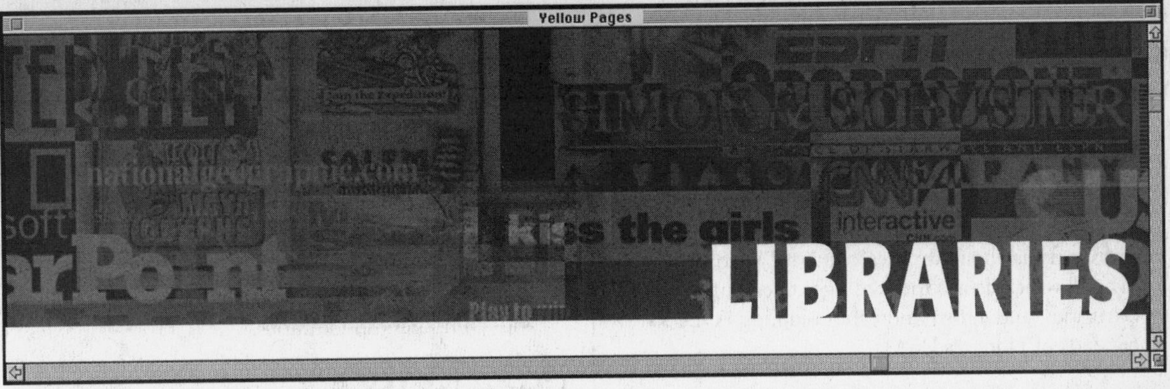

> The more I read, the more questions I have. Everytime I pass a library I get an anxiety attack.
>
> *O'Neill in* SeaQuest DSV *(1993)*

AcqWeb

http://www.library.vanderbilt.edu/law/acqs/acqs.html

This site contains a list of links to information that is especially useful for acquisitions librarians. Some of the links include Telnet links to searchable databases such as OCLC, RLIN, WLN, Dialog, Lexis/Nexis, LOCIS, and HYTELNET; links to Web sites for publishers, vendors, and library associations; links for newsletters and journals; and links to general reference resources.

The American War Library

http://members.aol.com/amerwar/

This library contains data on every military conflict in which the U.S. has been involved since the founding of the country. There is also a veterans' registry, a photo archive section, and many other areas of benefit to veterans and the family. While their catalog listing seems quite comprehensive, no direct way to access the listings seems available, so it may be necessary to email them with your request for information.

Berkeley Digital Library SunSITE

http://sunsite.berkeley.edu/

This site contains "digital collections and services while providing information and support to others doing the same." Essentially an online library.

Portico: The British Library (NRP Top Picks)
http://www.bl.uk

Bibliomania: The Network Library

http://www.mk.net/~dt/Bibliomania/

With more than 40 complete classic novels in HTML and PDF formats, plus reference works such as Gibbon's *Decline and Fall of the Roman Empire* (work in progress) this is a great place to get that classical education you always wanted, but never found the time for.

The Campus Library

http://www.go-campus.com/campus/library.htm

A virtual library for a virtual college campus, called "The Campus," the library is a great source of links to all sorts of information services, such as *DunsLink from Dun & Bradstreet*, lots of news services, and magazine sites—from CNN to *Sports Illustrated* to *Cosmopolitan*. There are book links sorted by topic—poetry, science fiction, mystery, and so forth. In fact, the entire Campus site is a great resource for sites on all sorts of topics.

The C. Christopher Morris Cricket Library and Collection

http://www.haverford.edu/library/cricket/CCMORRIS.HTM

The library, located at Haverford College, has the largest collection of cricket literature and memorabilia in the Americas. With over a thousand volumes, plus related cricket material, the library serves as the leading resource to preserving the history of the sport of cricket in the United States and Canada.

Related Sites

http://www.barthel-memorial.lib.ma.us/

http://www.brooks.af.mil/HSC/AL/SD/DAEDALUS/

A B C D E F G H I J K L M N O P Q R S T U V W X Y Z

Celebrate Libraries

http://www.gale.com/gale/cl.html

This site was established for National Library Week and contains information about Log On Day at Gardiner Public Library in Maine, the library of the year in Charlotte, NC, a quiz about libraries and their history, trivia about libraries, a link to "Who Reads What?", which details the reading interests of various celebrities, and information about joining FOLUSA (Friends of Libraries USA).

Christian Classics Ethereal Library

http://ccel.wheaton.edu/

With hundreds of fiction and non-fiction titles, hymns and choral music, and even a study bible, this site offers an extensive collection of excellent spiritual titles, all in the public domain.

Internet Public Library

http://www.ipl.org/

Includes resources for children, teenagers, and adults. The reference center allows one to ask questions of a live librarian (not a computer). The youth services and teen divisions have links to both books and other resources, such as writing contests, college information, science projects, and author question-and-answer sessions. A section is also devoted to information for libraries and other information professionals. Other features include tutorials, an exhibit hall, reading room with browsable full-text resources, links to Web search engines, and a MOO (Multi-User Object Oriented) environment for browsing the library.

Jonathan Tward's Multimedia Medical Reference Library

http://www.med-library.com/

A comprehensive listing of Web sites on such topics as illness (AIDS, cancer), types of treatments, and medical specialties. It also includes where to get medical shareware, and listings of hospitals and med schools.

Judaica Archival Project

http://www.virtual.co.il/orgs/orgs/archival/

Based out of the Machon Mekorot Institute, located at The Jewish National and University Library in Israel, the JAP has more than a half million pages of rare, out-of-print, and classic material related to Rabbinics. It's possible to view some of the works online or to order reproductions of the classics sent to you. All this from the world's largest Hebrew library.

Librarians' Professional Resources

http://www.cfcsc.dnd.ca/links/lib/index.html

Provides list of links to other library-related sites, arranged into categories of "indexes," "topics in library science," "types of libraries and collections," and "computers and libraries."

Library Job Hunting

http://tigger.cc.uic.edu/~aerobin/libjob.html

Provides information for library professionals who are searching for a job. Contains links to Web sites for library-related associations, Web and Gopher sites for career information, and addresses for library-related mailing lists.

The Library of Congress

http://www.loc.gov/

Provides access to the Library of Congress online catalog through Telnet searches of LOCIS, Gopher searches of LC MARVEL, the Library of Congress FTP site, and the Library of Congress Z39.50 Gateway. Other databases available for searching include Vietnam Era Prisoner of War/Missing in Action database, Task Force Russia database, Global Legal Information Network (GLIN), THOMAS (full-text legislative information), and the National Digital Library. This site is a must for librarians because it includes valuable information about Library of Congress standards for cataloguing, acquisitions, and book preservation; frequently asked reference questions; links to international, federal, state, and local government information; links to Internet search engines and meta-indexes; a link to the U.S. Copyright Office home page; and information about Library of Congress special events and exhibits.

Library Resource List

http://www.state.wi.us/agencies/dpi/www/lib_res.html

This site contains lists of links to other sites, arranged into the categories of Reference Resources, New Sites and Search Engines, Government Resources, Library Sites, Professional Information, and Libraries, the Net, and the NII (National Information Infrastructure). Although the site is geared toward libraries and government information, there is still information here that is valuable for anyone doing research on the Internet or just surfing the net for fun.

Medical/Health Sciences Libraries on the Web

http://www.arcade.uiowa.edu/hardin-www/hslibs.html

A state-by-state listing of all medical and health science libraries on the net. There are also sections for foreign countries, plus an extensive listing of links.

National Archives and Records Administration

http://www.nara.gov/

Includes both searchable and browsable services for locating government information via the Government Information Locator Service (GILS). Has links to the Federal Register, the National Archives and Records Administration Library, and the presidential libraries. The presidential libraries' page also includes the addresses, phone numbers, fax numbers, email addresses, and links to the home pages for the presidential libraries. Also has links for genealogical research.

The National Sporting Library

http://www.nsl.org/index.htm

Containing more than 11,000 volumes on such topics as horse racing, breeding, shooting, foxhunting, angling, polo, sporting art, and more, the NSP serves as a resource for both the interested browser and the serious researcher. With books going back to the 1500s, the library is a storehouse of historical information on these sports. The emphasis is on horse-related sports, plus other sports closely related to the country life, so team sports such as baseball are not included.

North American Sport Library Network

http://www.sirc.ca/naslin.html

NASLIN was developed to facilitate the spread of sports information among sports librarians, archivists, and others through publications, conferences, and educational programs. SPORTDiscus Online, the largest database of its kind, offers coverage of sports, fitness, and recreation-related publications. SPORTDiscus contains more than 400,000 bibliographic citations and "a wide range of information published in magazines and periodicals, books, theses and dissertations, as well as conference proceedings, research papers, and videotapes."

Related Sites

http://lawlib.wuacc.edu/washlaw/reflaw/reflaw.html

http://LCWeb.LOC.Gov/nls/nls.html

OCLC Online Computer Library Center, Inc.

http://www.oclc.org/

Contains information especially useful for librarians and other information professionals. Has links to OCLC documents and forms, a search engine for searching OCLC information, and demonstrations of OCLC services. Actual logon to some OCLC services is available by subscription only.

Perry-Castañeda Library Map Collection

http://www.lib.utexas.edu/Libs/PCL/Map_collection/Map_collection.html

An online map library, with one of the most extensive collections of maps in the world. The online collection is more than just a listing of maps in the library—the maps can be viewed, downloaded, and printed out as the user requires. Be sure to read the FAQ before viewing or printing any of the maps, to be sure that your machine is capable of the task—some of the maps are very large. The site also has links to other map-related sites around the world.

Portico: The British Library

http://www.bl.uk

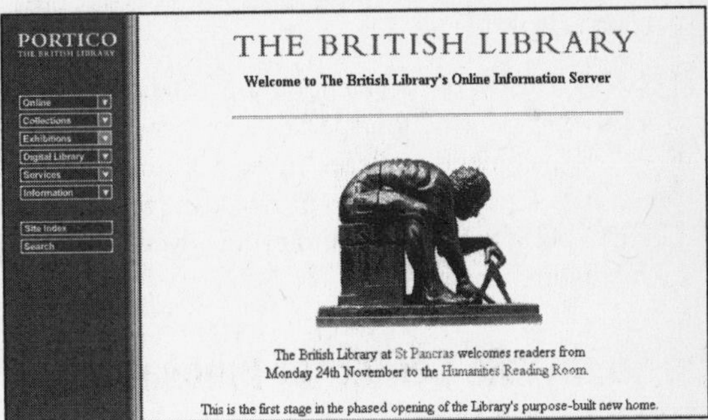

Portico is the online information server for the British Library. From this point, you gain access to the online catalogs, lists of services, collections, and digital library. The site is beautifully rendered, with some documents (including images of actual pages) already available or in progress.

Project Earl: Electronic Access to Resources in Libraries

http://www.earl.org.uk/

With over 40 percent of the libraries in the U.K. joining Project Earl, which intends to put every U.K. library's resources on the net, it's now possible to do research in Britain without ever leaving home. Though the bulk of the site is dedicated to the project itself, there are extensive listings for the individual to do research on such topics as business, arts, government, or history, and to learn of the holdings of libraries throughout the U.K.

School Libraries on the Web: A Directory

`http://www.voicenet.com/~bertland/libs.html`

Contains a browsable list of school library Web pages, arranged alphabetically by state. Also contains links to school libraries in Australia, Canada, Japan, and Sweden.

Smithsonian Institution Libraries

`http://www.sil.si.edu/`

Includes links to the various Smithsonian Museums, a search engine for locating information within the Smithsonian, information about visiting Washington, D.C., information about how to become a member of the Smithsonian, a map showing the locations of most of the Smithsonian Museums, and a browsable shopping area.

Special Library Association

`http://www.sla.org/`

The SLA consists of special librarians who are employed as information specialists by private businesses, governments, colleges, museums, and associations. This site is designed to promote the Special Library specialty and to promote and advertise SLA membership benefits.

The Sunnyvale Center for Innovation, Invention & Ideas

`http://www.sci3.com/`

Established by a unique arrangement between the United States Patent and Trademark Office and the City of Sunnyvale, CA, the Center is able to provide patent and trademark information and research to the entire western United States as well as Pacific Rim countries. This is the only office of its kind in the western U.S. that can provide PTO information outside the Washington, D.C., area.

Related Sites

- `http://metro.org/members/icelib.html`
- `http://nihlibrary.nih.gov/home.html-ssi`
- `http://plaza.interport.net/nypsan/`

Understanding Call Numbers

`http://www.hcc.hawaii.edu/education/hcc/library/callno.html`

This site explains how to read Library of Congress classification call numbers to locate materials on the shelves. The location prefixes information is specific to the Honolulu Community College Library, but the call number descriptions and Library of Congress classification tables are useful for locating materials in any library that uses LC call numbers (as opposed to Dewey Decimal system).

The U.S. House of Representatives Internet Law Library

`http://law.house.gov/`

The library has full-text searchable copies of U.S. Federal Code and U.S. Federal regulations (sorted by agency), federal court decisions, treaties, and links to other sites.

WWW Library Directory

`http://www.llv.com/~msauers/libs/libs.html`

Click a country name to be presented with a list of links to libraries in that country. Most of the countries currently represented are European (both East and West) and North American, although there are a few Asian, Middle Eastern, and South American countries also. Also has links to other library-related resources.

GOPHER SITES

- `gopher://gopher.cni.org/`
- `gopher://gopher.emc.maricopa.edu/7waissrc%3a/library/notablewomen/Notablewomen`
- `gopher://gopher.infor.com/`
- `gopher://musicb.marist.edu/1-gop/fdrg:gopherd.menu`
- `gopher://wiretap.spies.com/11/Library/Classic`

MAILING LIST

- `LIS584-L`

NEWSGROUPS

- `alt.education.research`
- `bit.listserv.libres`
- `misc.education.adult`
- `soc.libraries.talk`

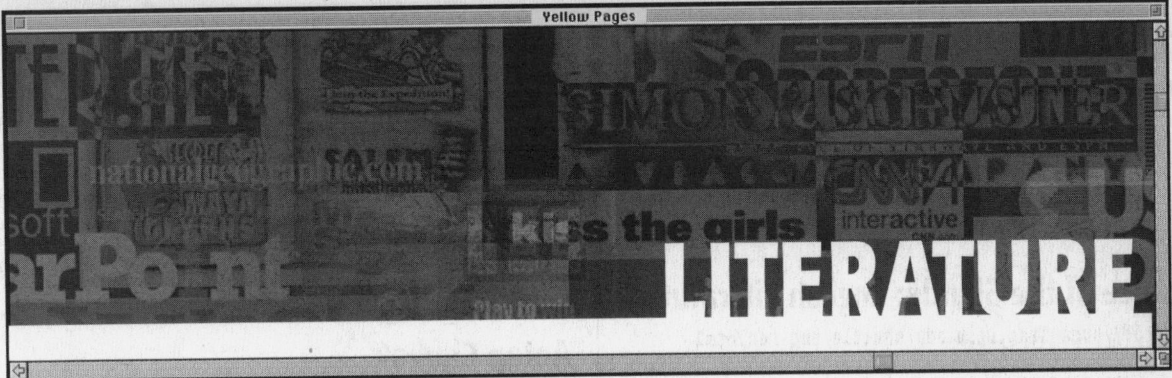

> Great literature is simply language charged with meaning to the utmost possible degree.
>
> *Ezra Pound*

Luminarium
http://www.luminarium.org

Women Writers of the Middle Ages
http://www.millersv.edu/~english/homepage/duncan/medfem/medfem.html

A Dictionary of Sensibility
http://www.engl.virginia.edu/~enec981/dictionary/

Jane Austen: A Collection
http://www.goucher.edu/library/jausten/jane.htm

SEVENTEENTH CENTURY AND BEFORE

Aphra Behn Page

http://ourworld.compuserve.com/homepages/r_nestvold/

This site is dedicated to the first professional woman writer in the English language. A prolific playwright of the seventeenth century (second only to John Dryden in the Restoration), Aphra Behn is known largely for her prose. This site has links to information about Aphra Behn and other women writers.

Luminarium

http://www.luminarium.org

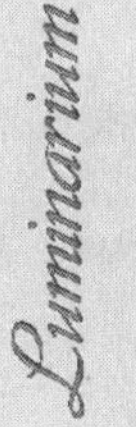

A wonderful site chronicling the lives and work of Medeival, Rennasaince, and 17th century writers, including biography, bibliography, and samples.

Miguel de Cervantes

http://csdl.tamu.edu/cervantes/

A project of the Cervantes International Bibliography Online and Anuario Bibliográfico Cervantino, this site is dedicated to solve the "problem of currency, thoroughness, and accessibility, which now hampers research on Cervantes." Includes a great amount of information on Cervantes, the author of Don Quixote. There is a record of the books, articles, dissertations, reviews, and other points of interest included here to this end.

Shakespeare Web

http://www.shakespeare.com/

This is the site for anyone interested in the plays and writing of William Shakespeare. Includes a listing of festivals and troupes, along with a Web search index for Shakespeare. Provides a feature called "Today in Shakespeare History" and many other related services.

Thomas Middleton

http://www.med.virginia.edu/~ecc4g/middhome.html

Provides information about late 16th century/early 17th century playwright Thomas Middleton. Includes a biography, bibliographical information, and historical perspective of Middleton's work.

Voice of the Shuttle: English Literature

http://humanitas.ucsb.edu/shuttle/eng-ren.html

Provides a wealth of knowledge through links, articles, and essays on literature of the 17th century. Includes an index, database, and many other features. This is a great site for online research.

William Shakespeare: Search the Complete Plays Online

http://www.gh.cs.usyd.edu.au/~matty/Shakespeare/index.html

Provides a search index of the complete plays of William Shakespeare. Includes the capability to search by tragedy, comedy, or history. This is a great site for anyone who is a fan of Shakespeare.

Women Writers of the Middle Ages

http://www.millersv.edu/~english/homepage/duncan/medfem/medfem.html

Provides essays, pictures, and related articles on writers such as Margery Kempt, Hildegard of Bingen, Catherine of Siena, and others. Includes links to many other online related sites. This site is very academically orientated and is recommended to those doing research on writers of the period.

EIGHTEENTH AND NINETEENTH CENTURY

Alfred Jarry

http://www-wane.scri.fsu.edu/~dmorris/jarry.html

Provides a bibliography, biography, and background of French Absurdist playwright Alfred Jarry. Includes links to other literature and Jarry-related sites.

Anna Laetitia Aikin Barbauld

http://www.cs.cmu.edu/afs/cs.cmu.edu/user/mmbt/www/women/barbauld/bal-biography.html

Provides a biography, bibliography, and selections of work by late eighteenth century and early nineteenth century British poet and essayist Anna Laeitia Aikin Barbauld. Site includes a detailed background of Barbauld and links to related pages.

Anton Chekov

http://www.winnipeg.freenet.mb.ca/~vbu053/Anton_Chekhov.html

Provides a profile, bibliography, and essays on late nineteenth century Russian playwright and author Anton Chekov. Includes links to many other sites about Chekov, literature, and theatre.

Charles Dickens

http://lang.nagoya-u.ac.jp/~matsuoka/Dickens.html

This extensive site offers academic resources, chronology, bibliography, and links to many sites about British author Charles Dickens. Dickens, the nineteenth century writer of such classics as *Great Expectations, A Tale of Two Cities, A Christmas Carol,* and many more, is profiled by many pictures, essays, and articles. This site is a definite stop if doing online research of his work.

A Dictionary of Sensibility

http://www.engl.virginia.edu/~enec981/dictionary/

This highly extensive site is dedicated to the understanding of eighteenth century language usage in literature. Includes many essays, a term list, bibliography (both critical and sources), and a detailed introduction to the site. This site is recommended to anyone studying Victorian period literature.

Dostoevsky

http://www.maths.nott.ac.uk/personal/pmyjaw/

This site dedicated to the life and writings of Russian author Fyodor Dostoevesky. Provides full texts of many of Fyodor's novels, a profile, pictures, essays, and much more.

Edgar Allen Poe

http://www.cs.umu.se/~dpcnn/eapoe/ea_poe.html

Author of *The Raven*, Edgar Allen Poe is also famous for his short stories that were meant to "expand the human soul." This Web site is very popular, and deservedly so—it features biography, links to e-text, and a chat room. Includes links to many other Poe and literature-based Web sites.

Edward Bellamy

http://oak.cats.ohiou.edu/~aw148888/bellamy.html

Edward Bellamy is the 19th century writer of *Looking Backward*. This site, evolved from the Center for Utopian Studies, has links to essays and excerpts by Bellamy, as well as links to related sites.

Emily Brontë

http://sunsite.unc.edu/cheryb/women/Emily-Bronte.html

Provides information about nineteenth century author Emily Brontë. Includes information about *Wuthering Heights* and Emily's poetry. Also includes links to other Brontë-related sites.

Emily Dickinson

http://www.planet.net/pkrisxle/emily/dickinson.html

Provides information and background on the nineteenth century American poet Emily Dickinson. Includes a biography, family history, articles, essays, a picture, and links sites that contain Dickinson's poetry.

George Sand

http://www.eden.com/~gebbie/gsand/gs_home.html

George Sand, French writer of the 19th century, finds a very well-constructed Web home here. There are biography, bibliography, and chronology pages present, and perhaps most impressive is the gallery of pictures of Sand.

Herman Melville

http://www.melville.org/

All right, so maybe you didn't like reading *Moby Dick* in high school; that doesn't mean that it wasn't worthwhile, though, right? Melville is actually a pretty approachable author, not to mention his importance to the American tradition. Try him again here—you'll find a comprehensive amount of information about the author of arguably "the great American novel."

Jack London: The Collection

http://sunsite.berkeley.edu/London/

Provides a biography, bibliography, and pictures of *Call of the Wild*, *White Fang*, and *The Sea-Wolf* author Jack London. Includes a collection of London writings, letters, and links to other resources.

Jane Austen: A Collection

http://www.goucher.edu/library/jausten/jane.htm

Provides a wealth of information about the life and works of nineteenth century English writer Jane Austen. This site includes bibliographical information, a profile, and essays about Austen's writing. Includes links to other related Austen sites.

Jules Verne

http://avery.med.virginia.edu/~mtp0f/flips/jules.html

A well-maintained site dedicated to the author of *20,000 Leagues Under the Sea* and *Around the World in 80 Days* (among others), this page is easily navigated and has good links to biography, reviews, pictures, and the like. Includes links to other Verne sites.

Leo Tolstoy—Tolstoy Online

http://www.he.net/~works/tolstoy/index.html

This extensive site is dedicated to Russian writer Leo Tolstoy. Includes quotes, articles about Russia, family background, and more about the author of *War and Peace* and *Anna Karenina*. Includes links to other Tolstoy sites and books.

Lewis Carroll: An Overview

http://www.stg.brown.edu/projects/hypertext/landow/victorian/carroll/carrollov.html

Lewis Carroll (née Charles Dodgson) was not only the writer of the famous *Alice in Wonderland* stories, he also was a mathematician and scientist. This site houses information about Carroll as a whole person—his literary tactics, religion and philosophy, and his work in a political and social context. Also provides links to other Caroll-related sites.

Marcel Proust (Proust Said That)

http://www.well.com/user/vision/proust/

This site calls itself "the highly unofficial organ of the totally unofficial, utterly unacademic Marcel Proust Support Group of San Francisco," but it is probably the best Proust source on the Web yet. There is an interesting hyperlinked biography, as well as some other tidbits, including recipes and articles only slightly relating to Proust.

Mark Twain (Ever the Twain Shall Meet)

http://www.lm.com/~joseph/mtwain.html

Provides a bibliography, articles, essays, and entire novels in HTML of Mark Twain. Includes a great amount of information on Twain, the author of *A Connecticut Yankee In King Arthur's Court, Tom Sawyer*, and many more. This is a great online resource.

The Marx/Engels Internet Archive

http://csf.colorado.EDU/psn/marx/

Provides a comprehensive collection of Marx/Engels writings along with biography and bibliography information. Includes links to other Karl Marx related sites.

Mary Shelley

http://www.netaxs.com/~kwbridge/maryshel.html

This site houses information about Mary Shelley, Percy Shelly Romantics, and, of course, her popular novel *Frankenstein.* Newly updated, there is a gothic air to this site, including a musical background. This site provides a wealth of information about Mary Shelley, the author of *Frankenstein.*

Nathaniel Hawthorne

http://www.tiac.net/users/eldred/nh/hawthorne.html

"Dedicated to enhancing our understanding and appreciation of Hawthorne's writings and life," this site has complete e-texts of his novels and stories. There are readings, pictures, and information about this 19th century American author of works such as *The House of Seven Gables* and *The Scarlett Letter.*

Romanticism On the Net

http://www.stg.brown.edu/projects/hypertext/landow/victorian/litov.html

Provides an online magazine and resource site for Romantic literature. Includes articles, reviews, a chronology, and an index of sites dedicated to Romanticism. This is an extensive site and is well recommended for anyone doing online research on Romantic literature.

Samuel Taylor Coleridge

http://www.lib.virginia.edu/etext/stc/Coleridge/stc.html

This site provides a great amount of S.T. Coleridge writings and poems. Includes a critical essay, time line, and profile of the eighteenth century English poet. Coleridge is famous for *The Rime of the Ancient Mariner, Kubla Khan*, and many others.

Stephen Crane

http://www.en.utexas.edu/~mmaynard/Crane/crane.html

Provides a biography, bibliography, and essays about nineteenth century American writer Stephen Crane. Includes images of Crane and literary analysis of works such as *The Red Badge of Courage* and *The Blue Hotel.*

William Blake

http://www.aa.net/~urizen/blake.html

This site is dedicated to the English Romantic poet and painter William Blake, author of *Songs of Innocence, Songs of Experience*, and *The Marriage of Heaven and Hell.* Includes full color representation of Blake paintings with their accompanying text. Also includes a profile of Blake and links to other related sites.

LISTSERVS

Advanced American Literature List

List Name: advamlit

List Address: advamlit@chaos.taylored.com

Administrative Address: majordomo@chaos.taylored.com

List Type: majordomo

African American Literature

List Name: afam

List Address: afam@henson.cc.wwu.edu

Administrative Address: listproc@henson.cc.wwu.edu

List Type: listproc

American Literature

List Name: AMLIT-L

List Address: AMLIT-L@mizzou1.missouri.edu

Administrative Address: listserv@mizzou1.missouri.edu

List Type: Listserv

American Literature Discussion
List Name: AML-LIT

List Address: AML-LIT@cfrvm.cfr.usf.edu

Administrative Address: listserv@cfrvm.cfr.usf.edu

List Type: Listserv

American Literature from 1600–1870
List Name: AMLIT1B-

List Address: AMLIT1B-@tamvm1.tamu.edu

Administrative Address: listserv@tamvm1.tamu.edu

List Type: Listserv

American Literature from 1640–1900
List Name: AMLIT1-L

List Address: AMLIT1-L@tamvm1.tamu.edu

Administrative Address: listserv@tamvm1.tamu.edu

List Type: Listserv

American Literature from 1880–present
List Name: AMLIT2-L

List Address: AMLIT2-L@tamvm1.tamu.edu

Administrative Address: listserv@tamvm1.tamu.edu

List Type: Listserv

Desire & Literature List
List Name: DESIRELIT-LIST

List Address: DESIRELIT-LIST@listserv.acsu.buffa-lo.edu

Administrative Address: listserv@listserv.acsu.buffalo.edu

List Type: Listserv

German Renaissance and Baroque Literature
List Name: SGRABL-L

List Address: SGRABL-L@listserv.uic.edu

Administrative Address: listserv@listserv.uic.edu

List Type: Listserv

Irish Literature
List Name: irish-studies

List Address: irish-studies@ebbs.english.vt.edu

Administrative Address: listproc@ebbs.english.vt.edu

List Type: Listproc

Modern English Literature
List Name: bie7-l

List Address: bie7-l@uta.fi

Administrative Address: listproc@uta.fi

List Type: Listproc

Romantic Literature
List Name: romantic

List Address: romantic@bgu.edu

Administrative Address: listproc2@bgu.edu

List Type: Listproc

NEWSGROUPS

alt.appalachian.literature

alt.books.arthur-clarke

alt.books.beatgeneration

alt.books.bukowski

alt.books.h-g-wells

alt.books.kurt-vonnegut

alt.books.reviews

alt.books.toffler

asu.books.exchange

aus.books

aus.sf Australian

bit.lang.neder-l

bit.listserv.literary

fj.books.

iijnet.literature

muc.lists.www-literature

pnet.books.review Reviews of books.

pnet.books.talk

rec.arts.books

rec.arts.books.childrens

rec.arts.books.childrens.

rec.arts.books.hist-fiction

rec.arts.books.marketplace

rec.arts.books.reviews.

tnn.books

tnn.literature

uk.media.books

humanities.lit.authors.shakespeare

A B C D E F G H I J K L M N O P Q R S T U V W X Y Z

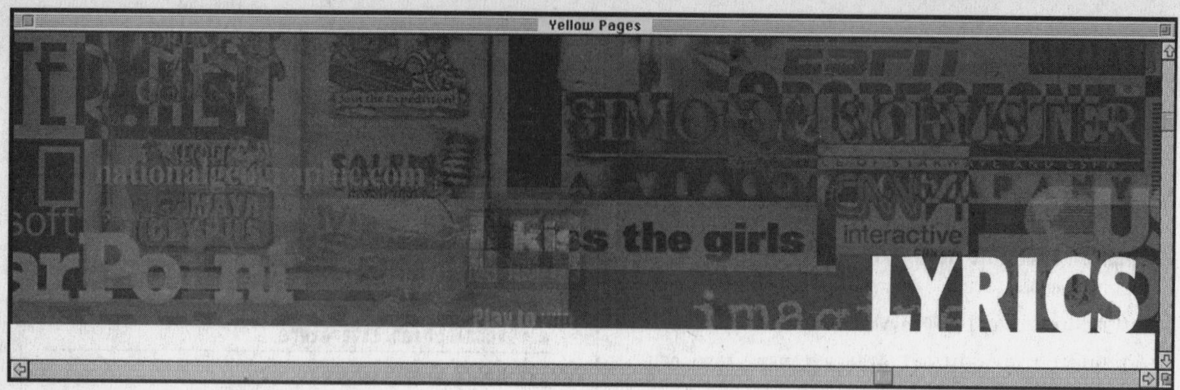

Perhaps all music, even the newest, is not so much something discovered as something that re-emerges from where it lay buried in the memory, inaudible as a melody cut in a disc of flesh. A composer lets me hear a song that has always been shut up silent within me.

Havelock Ellis

Bob Dylan Music

http://http.tamu.edu:8000/~bkf3938/guitar/bob.html

Are you sometimes not sure what the words are when Bob sings? Here are the lyrics to just about every Dylan song ever. There's also a link to the Grateful Dead page, where you'll find even more links.

Candy Apple Pee: Misheard Beach Boys Lyrics

http://www.prairienet.org/~dauber/cap.html

"Good, good, good, good-by raisins," is just an example of the sometimes hilarious mondegreens available on this site. Dozens are listed, and you can contribute one of your own too.

The Lyrics Challenge (NRP Top Pick)
http://www.geocities.com/SunsetStrip/9943/index.html

The Complete Lyrics to 99 Bottles of Beer on the Wall

http://www.virtual-media.com/vm/presents/ouzo/99bottles.html

Well, of course, somebody had to do it. The creator apologizes at the end, but it truly is worth a chuckle. Click the numbers to see the beer bottles disappearing one by one from the wall.

The Cyber Hymnal

http://www.accessone.com/~rwadams/h/

At this site, you'll find the lyrics to hundreds of gospel songs and hymns. With a sound card and speakers, you can hear the music too. There are special areas of Children's, Christmas, and Easter songs along with biographies of song writers and hymn trivia.

EVITA: The Complete Motion Picture Soundtrack

http://turnpike.net/~mosaic/evita/

Here are the lyrics for all the songs from the hit motion picture *Evita*. Just click the song title to see the lyrics.

Jerry's Christmas Jukebox

http://wilstar.net/xmas/xmasjuke.htm

As the site opens, you hear Christmas carols playing. Click the tree ornaments to hear different carols. The lyrics for a couple of Christmas carols are available here, along with a MIDI file of several carols to download.

Jessica Ross and Her Amazing Mondegreen Circus

`http://www.mcs.net/~bingo/lyrics.html`

A site devoted to misunderstood lyrics from all genres. The line, "Sing us a song yellow piano man," is a misunderstood line from Billy Joel's "Piano Man" that goes "Sing us a song, you're the piano man." Contains hundreds of lyrics as well as information on how to submit your own.

Led Zeppelin Lyrics

`http://www.dyadel.net/~lenny/ledzep.htm`

This site contains the lyrics to many Led Zeppelin songs. Just click the song title and read the lyrics. The links will take you to a master index of lyrics for many, many groups.

The Lyrics Challenge

`http://www.geocities.com/SunsetStrip/9943/index.html`

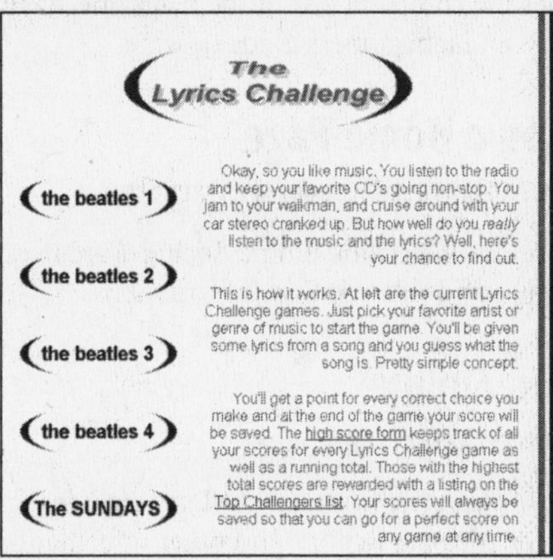

Choose a game. Current choices include the Beatles (four games), grunge, the Sundays, and mazzy star. You'll see a line of lyrics; pick the song those lyrics are from. This is a fun page.

Macarena

`http://www.geocities.com/Paris/2583/macarena.html`

Have you learned to dance the Macarena? And while you're dancing, do you just hum along until the only part you can sing: "Hey, Macarena"? Well, here are the Spanish words and their English translation. There's also a link to another page where you can listen to the song while learning the steps.

Related Site

`http://www.scoutbase.org.uk/camping/campfire/songs.htm`

National Anthems

`http://www.geocities.com/CapitolHill/2975/natanth.html`

The national anthems of 10 countries are available here. You'll find them in their original or in the English translation. Click the speaker to hear the anthem you've chosen. This is a growing site, and you might want to contribute any information you have about other national anthems, their lyrics, music, or history.

Phil's Home Page

`http://www.iinet.net.au/~pgb/`

Phil has chosen quite a few songs to provide lyrics for, and they're all meaningful. He even suggests certain times when each song would be appropriate. Want to tell someone how you feel, but you're at a loss for words? Check these lyrics.

Schoolhouse Rock Lyrics

`http://www.netaxs.com/people/frost/schoolhouse.html`

Here are the lyrics to those cute Schoolhouse Rock songs. Remember "Conjunction Junction"? Just click the title and recall all the words.

Twisted Tunes

`http://www.twistedtunes.com/`

Bob Rivers as Weird Al Yankovic. Features downloadable hits such as "Strawberry Rehabs Forever" and "I Shot the White House."

NEWSGROUPS

`alt.music.lyrics`

`alt.music.prodigy-the.lyrics`

`alt.rap.lyrics`

`fido7.music.lyrics`

`viwa.music.lyrics`

Related Sites

`http://thoth.stetson.edu/users/Bill_Sawyer/Disney/Lyrics.html`

`http://www.acronet.net/~robokopp/shanty.html`

`http://www.usscouts.scouter.com/songs/songbook.html`

`http://www.concentric.net/~Mtspaces/`

`http://www.lyrics.ch/`

`http://bustm.bu.edu:8000/mac/U2/lyrics/index.html`

`http://k2.scl.cwru.edu/~act3/mnintro.html`

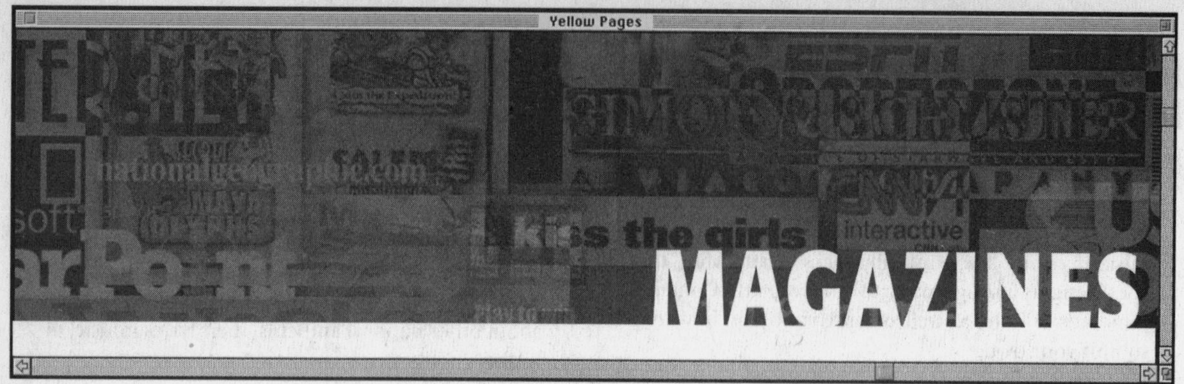

Look Miss Fremont, that feminine intuition stuff sells magazines, but in real life it's still a fairy tale.

Thomas J. Doyle in Rear Window *(1954)*

Acoustic Musician Magazine

http://www.netshop.net/acoustic/

Online edition of the *Acoustic Musician* magazine. Covers all aspects of acoustic music for the folk musician. Features articles, a music festival guide, the table of contents for the forthcoming issue, and a place to submit letters to the editor. Also presents covers of back issues.

Adventure Online Gaming

http://www.gameworld.com

Monthly fantasy fiction Web magazine featuring original art and fiction. Includes exciting interactive graphical hypertext adventures. Describes a human and computer refereed true role-playing game. Features intelligent talking monsters, multiple players, 3D graphics, and advanced chat.

Advertising Age

http://www.adage.com/

Presents images for viewing. Contains archives, ad market information, and a daily top story. Enables you to join the AdAge mailing list.

Discover Magazine
http://www.enews.com:80/magazines/discover/

American Wine

http://www.2way.com:80/food/wine/

American Wine magazine online. Focuses on American vineyards and their products. Features in-depth listings of wine and wine-related links. Also includes the complete text of the magazine, a wine glossary, and a beginners guide to wine.

Architronic Home Page

http://arcrs4.saed.kent.edu/Architronic/

Architectural magazine online. Includes archives of past issues and subscription information.

Asia, Inc. Online

http://www.asia-inc.com/

Business magazine from Asia online. Includes financial news, the Asia Report, and other information for Asian business people.

Astronomer Magazine

http://www.demon.co.uk/astronomer/

A British publication online. Targets the advanced amateur but does contain items for the beginner. Also contains information on comets, asteroids, supernovae, and a variety of other topics that pertain to astronomy.

basilisk

http://swerve.basilisk.com/

Online quarterly journal of film, architecture, philosophy, literature, music, and perception.

Boardwatch Magazine

http://www.boardwatch.com/

Boardwatch magazine online. Focuses on BBSs and the Internet. Provides subscription information (offers the entire publication free online), and enables you to contact the specific departments or editors of the magazine.

BYTE Magazine

http://www.byte.com/

Contains a five year, searchable archive of *BYTE Magazine.* Enter a search term and Presto! Articles that include this word appear in an easy-to-retrieve format. You can download files and shareware mentioned in *BYTE* articles, and download *BYTE*'s benchmark tests. A valuable site worth a bookmark in your browser software.

Car Collector Home Page

http://www.carcollector.com/

Car Collector magazine online. Features back issues, advertising information, subscription information, and automotive news.

Chicago Moving Image Scene

http://www.rtvf.nwu.edu/chicago/

Serves as a resource for media people in Chicago and around the world. Includes links, phone numbers, and information about media production.

Communications Week Interactive

http://techweb.cmp.com/techweb/cw/current/

A colorful site with news for corporate network managers. This publication provides testing, reviews, industry news, and funny tidbits on the world of networking and information management.

Computer Shopper Online

http://www.zdnet.com/cshopper/

Check out the top stories for the latest edition of *Computer Shopper*, considered to be the monthly computer "bible" for computer buyers. Articles on the absolute latest in computer technology can be found in the CyberCentral area.

Cyber Cyclist

http://cyberbike.com:80/E0020/SUI.HpilcNcwU-729cwdFyw9jjMcFjki/index.htm

Web magazine for bicyclists. Includes information about bikes, product reviews, current bicycle events, and other news.

cyberSPOKESMAN

http://tecnet2.jcte.jcs.mil:8000/cybrspke/cybrspke.html

The Air Force online in the form of a magazine. Interesting for military personnel and buffs. Provides information about news and events in the Air Force.

Dirty Linen

http://kiwi.futuris.net/linen/

Abridged edition of top American magazine for folk, electric folk, Celtic, and world music. Features a selection of articles, reviews, interviews, and letters to the editor from the current issue. Also includes a guide to concerts and festivals.

Discover Magazine

http://www.enews.com:80/magazines/discover/

Discover magazine online. Science magazine including text of issues, photos, links related to articles, and a subscription service.

Editor & Publisher

http://www.mediainfo.com/edpub/ep/index.htm

Editor & Publisher magazine online. Offers selected articles from the printed version of the magazine, as well as Web-only content. Offers comprehensive coverage of new media news and trends affecting the newspaper industry.

Electronic Green Journal

http://drseuss.lib.uidaho.edu:70/docs/egj.html

Environmental journal online. Contains information about environmental issues. Also lists the contents of the recent issues of the Journal.

Electronic Newsstand

http://internet.com/

Offers sample articles and subscription information for more than 300 magazines.

Esquireb2b

http://www.esquireb2b.com

An interactive service provided by the publishing operations of *Esquire Magazine.*

Felix Culpa Home Page

http://cq-pan.cqu.edu.au/felix-culpa/felix-culpa.html

Australian student magazine. Provides information geared towards Australian students. Features news, community events, and other school-related issues.

FH: Canada Travel Home Page

http://www.fleethouse.com/fhcanada/fhc_expl.htm

Canada Travel magazine online. Provides information about travel to Canada. Offers information the traveler will want while planing a trip to Canada.

Fix—Funkier Than Blown Vinyl

http://www.easynet.co.uk/fix/fix.htm

Exemplifies twenty-somethings on the Net. Resembles a coffee shop—somewhat pretentious and smoke-filled, frequently raunchy, but interesting nonetheless.

Folk Roots Home Page

http://www.cityscape.co.uk/froots/

Condensed, electronic version of *Folk Roots.* Features their guide to folk and world music events in Britain and Europe, CD reviews, charts and lists of best selling music, a play list from Folk Routes radio program on the BBC World Service, a complete table of contents from the current issue, and much more.

Fortran Journal

http://www.fortran.com/fortran/fug_fj.html

Fortran Journal online. Includes simple form to order the magazine and an in-depth description of the magazine.

FutureNet:.net—Index

http://www.futurenet.co.uk/netmag/net.html

.net magazine online. Covers Internet-related topics. Features their news page. Provides an Internet tutorial, job listings, and back issues. Also provides articles online that don't appear in the published magazine.

Gigaplex

http://www.gigaplex.com/wow

Presents an arts and entertainment Web magazine with departments for film, TV, music, books, theater, photography, food and restaurants, and more. Includes celebrity interviews with actors, musicians, authors, playwrights, directors, and photographers.

Glass Wings: Sensual Celebrations

http://www.aus.xanadu.com/GlassWings/sexual/celebrations.html

Online magazine. Focuses on the sensual side of humanity.

Good Medicine Magazine

http://none.coolware.com/health/good_med/ThisIssue.html

Good Medicine Magazine online. Provides stories and information, such as guided imagery, holistic skin and body care, Reiki (energy healing), and network chiropractic. Proposes that holistic and traditional Western medicine should be combined and considered together as "medicine."

Great Lakes Skier Magazine

http://www.iquest.com/michweb/glskier/

Skiing magazine online. Includes articles and contact information for a subscription. Includes a few skiing links.

HotWired

http://www.hotwired.com/

The slickest mag in the industry has a Web page with articles on the arts, politics, and technology. Before you can access much of anything, however, you have to join (free of charge). If you decide to sign up and are looking for something to do, check out the Arts and Renaissance articles first.

Ice-9 Publications

http://info.pitt.edu/~depst8/

A must-see for the information unconscious. The background completely obscures the text on this page. Fun!

Interactive Age Home Page

http://techweb.cmp.com:80/techweb/ia/current

Interactive Age Magazine online. Focuses on tracking electronic commerce. Enables you to contact the magazine staff, find out the 100 best business Web sites, use their hot link section, or look at their traffic analysis of the most visited Internet sites. Also features daily articles online for registered users.

InterText: The Online Fiction Magazine

http://ftp.etext.org/Zines/InterText/intertext.html

Monthly online fiction magazine. Contains short stories. Features five authors whose work has been published in this magazine and have won awards.

JEST Home Page

http://www.uoregon.edu/~roc/jest/index.html

JEST (Journal of Extraneous Scientific Topics) online. Includes very humorous looks at science.

Knowledge Industry Publications, Inc.

http://www.KIPInet.com/

Offers links to Knowledge Industry's magazines: *AV Video*, *Multimedia Producer*, and *Tape/Disc Business*. Also contains sports links to companies in the audio visual and multimedia fields.

LIFE Photo Home Page

http://www.pathfinder.com/@@egQ6VwAAAAAAAIMR/Life/lifehome.html

The magazine that pioneered photojournalism has re-imaged itself for cyberspace. A visually stunning site that includes many images.

Living Poets, EJournal Home Page

http://dougal.derby.ac.uk/lpoets/

Online magazine. Presents new poetry on the Web.

Logical Alternative—Front Door

http://shell.conknet.com/fusion/

Online magazine that targets multimedia authors. Contains reviews, tips, and other information.

MacNet Journal

http://www.dgr.com/web_mnj/

Contains *MacNet Journal.* Enables you to suggest ideas on improving the Macintosh operating system, peruse a free help wanted page, obtain guidelines for submitting articles, and search past issues. Also enables you to browse the current issue or subscribe (it's free).

MacUser/MacWeek Special on Apple's Future

http://www.zdnet.com/macuser/applefuture/

Interested in the latest on Apple's future? Visit this site for recent information on Apple and all the rumors.

MacWorld Online Web Server

http://www.macworld.com/

MacWorld online. Enables you to search past issues and read articles. Also provides Internet tips.

Mercury Center Home Page

http://www.sjmercury.com/

The *San Jose Mercury* online. Offers in-depth coverage of news events and utilizes hypertext links within stories.

Millennium Whole Earth Catalog

http://www.well.net/mwec/home.html

A limited edition of Howard Rheingold's *Whole Earth Catalog* online. Provides many online excerpts from the catalog book.

MMWIRE WEB

http://www.mmwire.com/

Electronic magazine. Focuses on multimedia and design. Provides much information about current and future multimedia trends.

Mobilia Magazine

http://www.mobilia.com/

Mobilia magazine online. Focuses on the worlds of motoring and collecting. Enables you to read it online and offers subscription information. Includes a classified ad section.

MoJo Wire

`http://www.mojones.com/`

Mother Jones online. Provides insightful information with a Mother Jones slant.

Motorcycle Online

`http://www.motorcycle.com/motorcycle.html`

Online magazine. Covers all aspects of motorcycles. Includes new model reviews, daily news, technical help, pictures, and tours.

Net Traveler

`http://biznetusa.com/nettraveler/`

Contains *Net Traveler* magazine. Provides information about their list of sites and tools. Offers links to brand new things to hit the Internet. Includes a collection of links to sites of importance, as well as a files archive.

Oceanography—The Magazine

`http://www.tos.org/tos/tos_magazine_menu.html`

Does not contain full text versions of the articles, but does list the table of contents and biography information about editors of the magazine.

Online Educator

`http://ole.net/ole/`

Offers lesson plans, sample articles from the *Online Educator* magazine, and many other resources. Offers the magazine itself for subscription in both print and electronic forms.

Outside Online

`http://web2.starwave.com/`

Offers sections on news, going places, activities, and gear for the outdoor enthusiast.

PC-TRANS

`http://kuhub.cc.ukans.edu/~pctrans/`

Provides home site for PC-TRANS, a trade magazine for PC users in the transportation industry. Site provides technical support, discussion forum, and bulletin board. Includes contact information for the group and the magazine.

Penthouse on the Internet

`http://www.penthousemag.com/mg.html`

Penthouse online. Features an Internet edition of the magazine and contains many images. Also includes an erotic toy store.

Perspective

`http://hcs.harvard.edu/~perspy/`

Monthly liberal magazine from Harvard University. Recent issues have focused on the Web.

Playboy Home Page

`http://www.playboy.com/`

Playboy magazine online. Includes interviews, reviews, and a Playboy forum.

PM Zone

`http://popularmechanics.com/`

Popular Mechanics online. Provides movies, pictures, and information about new and useful products and technology.

PurePower a Publication for PowerBuilder People

`http://www.magicnet.net/purepower`

PurePower magazine's Web page provides author contact, Powerbuilder tips, back issues, user group links, and new developments in the Powerbuilder community. You can also download the first issue free.

Redundantly, Online

`http://people.unt.edu/~price/red/`

Presents online version of the printed literary magazine. Concentrates on multimedia and using cyberspace creatively. The print version focuses on the humanities.

Scientific Computing and Automation Magazine

`http://www.scamag.com/`

A colorful Web site for a magazine devoted to computer analysis software for scientists and engineers. Read articles from the latest issue, link to related sites and sites of software developers, such as IBM and National Instruments, or access chemical databases.

Scripps Howard Home Page

http://www.scripps.com/

Presents the media giant on the Web. Scripps Howard owns 18 daily newspapers, 9 TV stations, and a host of other stuff you might want to check out.

Sea Frontiers

http://www.rsmas.miami.edu/sea-frontiers/sea-frontiers.html

Oceanography journal online. Contains full-text versions of articles from recent editions.

Serif: The Magazine of Type & Typography

http://www.quixote.com/serif/

Online magazine that targets the desktop publisher. Features sample articles, subscription information, and desktop publishing links on the Internet.

South Carolina Point

http://www.mindspring.com/~scpoint/point/

Provides online site for *South Carolina Point* news monthly. Includes current and back issues along with contact information.

Tharunka Home

http://www.real.com.au/magazines/tharunka/

Australian university student magazine. Offers a different angle on the news (often quite funny).

The List of Free Computer-related Publications

http://www.soci.niu.edu/~huguelet/TLOFCRP/

If you've ever been buried by catalogs arriving right before Christmas, you'll appreciate this site. Jim Huguelet provides an alphabetical list of addresses and phone numbers for magazines he receives free, yet never asked for. Several publishers that discovered this list requested to be removed; they are listed here, too.

Travel Weekly

http://www.traveler.net/index.html

Travel Weekly online. Serves the travel agency community in the U.S. and internationally. Includes feature travel-related articles and news. Also offers hundreds of links to sites associated with hotels, airlines, cruises, car rentals, railroads, and tour operators.

TravelASSIST Magazine

http://travelassist.com/mag/mag_home.html

Online magazine. Contains articles on travel and travel spots around the United States and the world. Includes back issues for online reading.

Typofile Magazine—Home

http://www.will-harris.com/type.htm

Online magazine. Focuses on type and its uses. Includes articles and links to other type and desktop publishing sites.

UNIX News International

http://apt.usa.globalnews.com/UNI/

Contains the current issue of *UNIX News International*, a monthly publication about UNIX systems.

UT Science Bytes

http://loki.ur.utk.edu/ut2kids/science.html

Online hypertext magazine. Focuses on UT scientists' research projects. Describes the projects at a level appropriate for elementary school students and links any unfamiliar words or concepts to a definition or explanation.

Videomaker's Camcorder & Desktop Video Site

http://www.videomaker.com/

Videomaker magazine online. Includes a product search engine, back issues, and other information about camcorders and video.

Virtual Computer Library Journals

http://www.utexas.edu/computer/vcl/journals.html

Lists a number of Web sites for e-zines and magazines about computers.

Wave~Length Paddling Network

http://interchange.idc.uvic.ca/~wavenet/magazine.html

Kayaking and Paddling magazine online. Includes archives of past articles and current issues with pictures.

Welcome to Computer Shopper

http://www.zdnet.com/~cshopper/

Provides an online edition of the current *Computer Shopper* magazine. Enables you to search through the advertisers for the lost prices on computer components, or browse through current and past articles.

Welcome To HotWired!

http://www.hotwired.com/

Wired! online. Includes information not found in the paper version of the magazine. Offers many links.

Welcome to Infobahn Magazine

http://www.postmodern.com/

Contains *Infobahn* magazine, a publication devoted to covering the Internet from a cultural point of view. Enables you to sign up for a free trial issue, contact the editors, get advertising information and prices, and find out how to submit articles.

Welcome to Pathfinder

http://www.pathfinder.com/@@5NGfxQAAAAAAwIIQ/pathfinder/welcome.html

Time Warner's site. Offers links to *Time* online, *Sports Illustrated* online, *Money Magazine* online, and more.

Welcome to ZD Net

http://www.ziff.com/

Ziff-Davis publishes many computer magazines. Provides articles and information about computers, as well as links to other Ziff-Davis publications, including *PC Magazine, PC Week, MacWeek, MacUser, Computer Life*, and more.

Where the Buffalo Roam

http://internet-plaza.net/wtbr

Presents a cartoon published weekly on the Web. Provides cartoons published in the last five weeks. Tells fans about ordering books and T-shirts.

ZDNet

http://www.zdnet.com/home/filters/maina.html

Home page for Ziff-Davis, the publisher of *PC Magazine, Computer Shopper, MacUser, MacWeek, Computer Gaming World, PC Computing*, and many others. Like other online magazines, access to the really good stuff requires registering. If you decide to join, Ziff-Davis creates a Personal Profile page you can use to customize the types of articles you want to see.

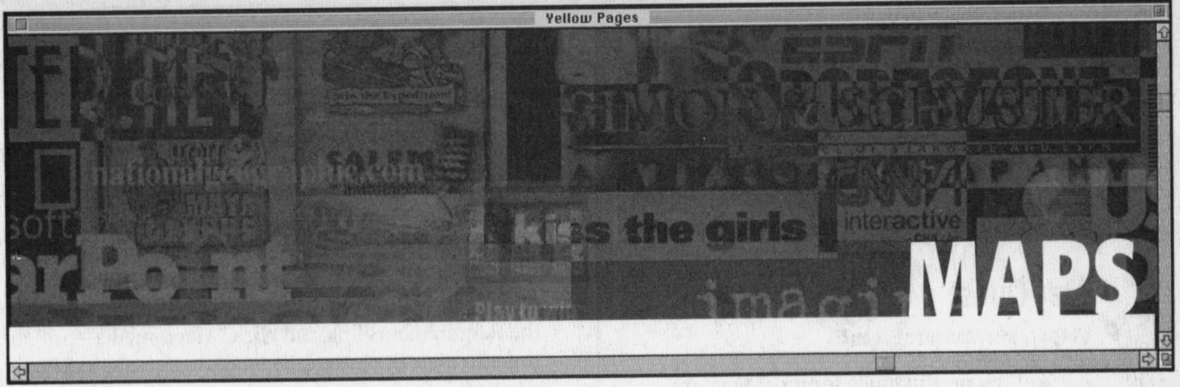

Why doesn't the pursuit of happiness come with a map?

Bernadette McCarver Snyder

Blue Skies for Java
http://cirrus.sprl.umich.edu/javaweather/
MapQuest
http://www.mapquest.com/
OSSHE Historical and Cultural Atlas Resource
http://darkwing.uoregon.edu/~atlas/

Atlas of the World

http://cliffie.nosc.mil/~NATLAS/atlas/

Search by world, continent, city, or image. The maps are not clickable, so you can't zoom in on certain areas, but the maps are large and helpful for students learning about our world's geography.

Blue Skies for Java

http://cirrus.sprl.umich.edu/javaweather/

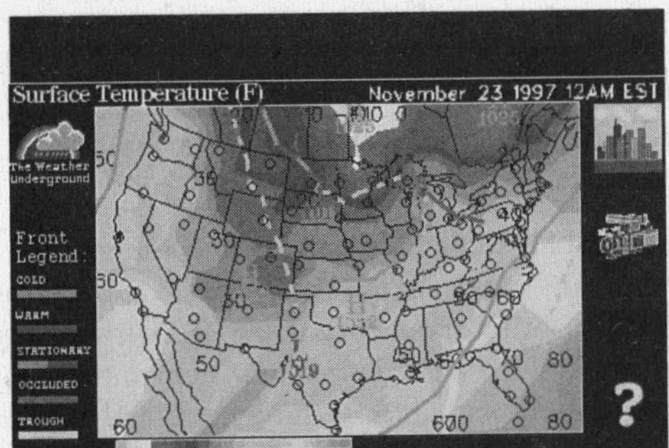

Very interesting site that lets you interact with weather maps. You can view such things as relative humidity, wind, and temperature—and then understand better the meteorological events that come into play with each other. When you select a type of weather map, you can click an area of that map (all U.S. areas) and get the status of what a city's weather is.

Country Maps from W3 Servers in Europe

http://www.tue.nl/europe/

This clearinghouse site offers a clickable imagemap that lists the countries of Europe. Clicking a country's flag takes you to a map of that country. Maps vary in quality (the United Kingdom's map mainly listed universities, not cities or regions, while the link to the European Union didn't even offer a map), but all of Europe is represented. The pages offer English descriptions in addition to commentary in the country's native tongue.

International Map Trade Association

http://www.maptrade.org

Offers links to member stores' Web sites and a geographical directory of map and travel book retailers.

Magellan Maps

http://pathfinder.com/travel/maps/

A great image map of the world is clickable and lets you get more detailed maps for anywhere you want to go. (Be sure to click the country name, not the actual place on the map.) You can also use the search engine to find a particular place. This site also offers maps for sale.

Related Site

http://www.worldtime.com/

MapBlast

http://www.mapblast.com/

Vincinity Corporation's site that helps you create maps of your own. You can also get maps of popular destinations, such as major U.S. cities, national parks, state capitals, attractions, and U.S. regions.

MapQuest

http://www.mapquest.com/

Excellent and resourceful guide for those who are planning to travel in North America. Has travel guides, trip information, clickable maps, directions, and so much more. Share plans and tips with fellow vacationers, get relocation information, or order a road atlas on CD-ROM.

National Atlas of Canada on SchoolNet

http://www-nais.ccm.emr.ca/schoolnet/

This site, offered in both English and French, offers demographic maps based on Canada's languages and aging population, maps of wetlands and natural hazards, an atlas of Canadian communities, and an interactive geography quiz.

> **Lost in Cyberspace: Finding Maps Online**
>
> Online mapping services offer close-up maps, down to the street address. They often include major attractions on the map as well. Excite's City.net (`http://www.city.net/`) is a great example of an online mapping service. The site includes a map and concierge section. You also can check out the top 25 U.S. and international cities. With the map section, you can enter a name and complete address of any business or person you want to visit and then click the Map It button. The site then enters that address into its interactive map system and pulls up a map that shows the address, down to the street and house or business location. While some very small towns do not have street maps available, most U.S. cities will garner results.

One Degree Land Cover Map Derived from AVHRR Data

http://cliffie.nosc.mil/~NATLAS/atlas/

Site that shows phenological data, with 11 types of vegetation areas in the world. You can view the dataset documentation or download binary or ASCII versions of the class maps.

OSSHE Historical and Cultural Atlas Resource

http://darkwing.uoregon.edu/~atlas/

This site was developed for students and aids their learning experience. It offers maps of North America, Europe, the Middle East, and North Africa. Normal maps can be viewed with any JPEG viewer. You need to download Macromedia's ShockWave plug-in—see the Requirements link and click "Macromedia"—in order to view the interactive maps, which are indicated by an icon.

Rare Map Collection at the Hargrett Library

http://scarlett.libs.uga.edu/darchive/hargrett/maps/maps.html

The Hargrett Library, at the University of Georgia Library, offers over 800 rare maps from the16th through the early 20th century. Early maps depict the New World, while others chart Colonial and Revolutionary America, the Civil War, and Georgia's Revolutionary period, cities, and coastal areas. File sizes are large and downloads are slow.

Thomas Bros. Maps

http://www.thomas.com/

Well-known for their street guides, Thomas Bros. now has a site that offers their 1998 CD-ROM. Also, you may browse their online maps of such detailed places as Los Angeles and Orange counties. View their product lines and showcases, too.

World Atlas

http://www.teachersoft.com/Library/ref/atlas/homepage.htm

Great aid for students, this site shows the countries and oceans of the world. Also, view the appendixes to get information about such issues as environmental agreements, the United Nations system, international organizations and groups, and weights and measures.

Related Sites
http://www.webcom.com/~bright/petermap.html
http://wxweb.msu.edu/weather/
http://members.aol.com/oldmapsne/index.html
http://loki.ur.utk.edu/ut2Kids/maps/map.html
http://www-map.lib.umn.edu/news.html
http://www.mapsonus.com/
http://www.census.gov/cgi-bin/gazetteer
http://grads.iges.org/pix/head.html

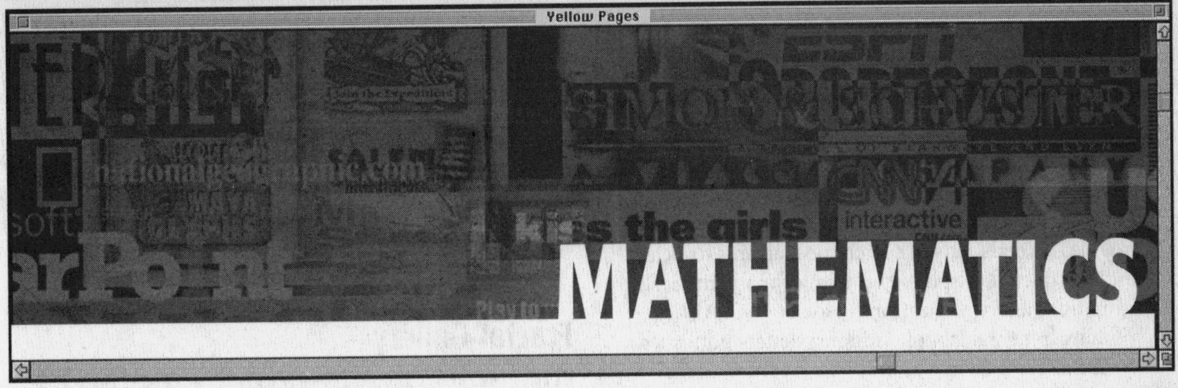

A-Z

As far as the laws of mathematics refer to reality, they are not certain; and as far as they are certain, they do not refer to reality.

Albert Einstein

Chaos at Maryland
http://www-chaos.umd.edu/chaos.html

CSC Mathematical Topics
http://www.csc.fi/math_topics/

e-Math Home Page
http://www.ams.org/

Eisenhower National Clearinghouse DCL
http://www.enc.org/

IMSA Home Page
http://www.imsa.edu/

Mathematics Archives WWW Server
http://archives.math.utk.edu/

Beauty of Chaos

http://i30www.ira.uka.de/~ukrueger/fractals/

Provides interactive journey through fractal images. Takes you through most of the database, which consists of hundreds of images.

Calculus & Mathematica Home Page

http://www-cm.math.uiuc.edu/

Calculus & Mathematica is a calculus-reform project started at the University of Illinois and Ohio State University. Uses Mathematica, a software package from Wolfram Research, to teach calculus to high school and college students.

Chaos at Maryland

http://www-chaos.umd.edu/chaos.html

Provides information on the various applications of chaos theory. Includes dimensions, fractal basin boundaries, chaotic scattering, and controlling chaos. Includes online papers, a searchable database, and general references. Also offers the Chaos Gallery.

Chartwell-Bratt

http://www.studentlitteratur.se/brattint/welcUSE.html

Provides an online catalog for Swedish book publisher, Chartwell-Bratt. Offers English or Swedish databases you can search by title, author, or subject. Includes books on mathematics, computer science, and engineering.

Common Weights and Measures

http://www.cchem.berkeley.edu/ChemResources/Weights-n-Measures/index.html

Contains information on converting to and from metric and United States measurements.

CPLEX Optimization, Inc. Home Page

http://www.cplex.com/

Develops large-scale mathematical programming software and services. Provides lists of products and services and offers linear and mixed-integer programming software.

A B C D E F G H I J K L M N O P Q R S T U V W X Y Z

CSC Mathematical Topics

http://www.csc.fi/math_topics/

Provides information about mathematical software and guidebooks available at the Center for Scientific Computing (CSC, Finland). Also points to application specialists at CSC for help on specific topics. Provides several kinds of search mechanisms to help find documents. Displays examples of mathematical animations and visualizations made at CSC. Also contains some guidebooks and newsletters published by CSC.

Dynamical Systems and Technology Project

http://math.bu.edu/DYSYS/dysys.html

Provides information on contemporary mathematics, such as fractals and chaos. Includes computer demos, as well as movies on some famous fractal sets.

e-Math Home Page

http://www.ams.org/

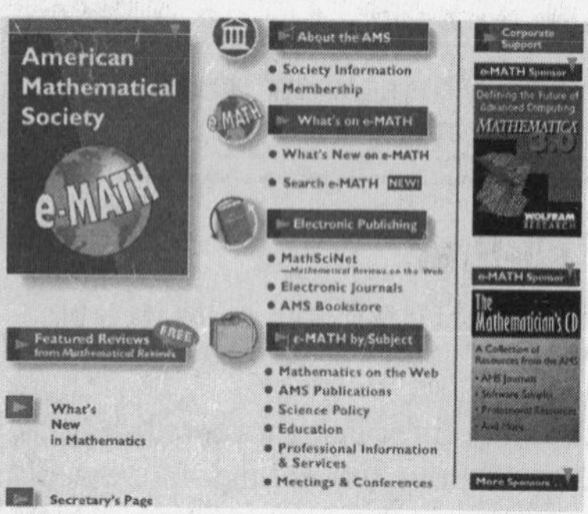

Home of the American Mathematical Society. Offers professional memberships. Publishes electronic journals, books on math, and the fee-based MathSci database, which features comprehensive coverage of research in mathematics, computer science, and statistics.

Eisenhower National Clearinghouse DCL

http://www.enc.org/

Supports improving teaching and learning in math and science in secondary schools. Offers links to other Internet resources. Presents online catalog and databases, as well as a collection of Internet software and information.

Electronic Textbook: Integrated Course in Chemistry, Mathematics, and Physics

http://dept.physics.upenn.edu/courses/gladney/mathphys/Contents.html

Contains information in the areas of trigonomics, velocity, acceleration, Newton's Laws, chaotic systems, and more.

Fractal Gallery

http://eulero.cineca.it/~strumia/FractalGallery.htm

Presents downloadable color fractal images that show different mathematics problems. Includes the Curve of Von Koch, the Mandelbot Set, and trees, ferns, and mountains.

Fractal Microscope

http://www.ncsa.uiuc.edu/Edu/Fractal/Fractal_Home.html

Provides information on basic fractals, why they should be discussed, their purposes in the real world, and why supercomputers are necessary for fractals.

Future Graph, Inc. Home Page

http://forum.swarthmore.edu/~fgi/index.html

Offers many links to math-related sites.

GAMS: Guide to Available Mathematical Software

http://gams.nist.gov/

Gateway to NIST guide to available mathematical software. Allows searching by package name or, more interestingly, by what problem it solves.

Guide to Math Resources

http://www.ama.caltech.edu/resources.html

Offers resource jump list to various math resources, including the Latex, Tex, and Maple packages. Also contains jumps to math-related Gopher sites, newsgroups, math institutes, and a math software index.

History of Mathematics

http://www-groups.dcs.st-and.ac.uk:80/~history/

Contains biographies of mathematicians, searchable by alphabetical or chronological index (and some include pictures).

IMA WWW Server

http://www.ima.umn.edu/

Institute for Mathematics and its Applications. Provides the newsletter and back issues of the newsletters of this professional organization.

IMSA Home Page

http://www.imsa.edu/

Provides information about the Illinois Mathematics and Science Academy, a residential public high school for students talented in the fields of math and science.

Internet Center for Mathematics Problems

http://www.mathpro.com/math/mathCenter.html

Attempts to identify and list all sources of math puzzles on the Internet. Lists problems from back issues of the Missouri Journal of Mathematical Sciences and the Fibonacci Quarterly and contains information about other sources of math puzzlers such as newsgroups and books.

Math Teaching Assistant

http://www.csun.edu/~vcact00g/math.html

Contains a math tutoring program developed for classroom computer labs aimed at secondary school students.

Mathematics Archives WWW Server

http://archives.math.utk.edu/

Provides ftp access to shareware and public domain software for teaching math on the college level. Also provides information and software for people interested in math, as well as links to secondary school software. Includes considerable information on software.

Mathlab

http://www.scar.utoronto.ca/homes/mathlab/mathlab.html

A mathematics computer lab. Features downloadable undergraduate level courseware (designed to run under UNIX and Mathematica) on geometry, graph theory, and complex analysis.

MathSearch—Search a Collection of Mathematical Web Material

http://www.maths.usyd.edu.au:8000/MathSearch.html

Allows you to search a collection of more than 19,000 documents on mathematics and statistics servers.

MathSoft Home Page

http://www.mathsoft.com/

Offers technical support, news, and product catalog.

MathSolutions, Inc. Home Page

http://smc.vnet.net/Christensen.html

Distributes MathTensor, an add-on for Mathematica that performs tensor analysis. Also provides links to resources and offers papers.

MathType Home Page

http://www.mathtype.com/mathtype/

Houses an equation editor for Mac and Windows machines. Offers technical support, registration, and product information.

MathWorks Home Page

http://www.mathworks.com/

Offers MATLAB, a high-end mathematics software package, as well as links to jobs, news, and books. Provides information on the Pentium chip flaw. Also presents products and services and an online copy of the MATLAB newsletter.

More Fractal Pictures

http://www.lerc.nasa.gov/Other_Groups/K-12/fracpage.html

Serves as a resource for fractal images that show the concepts of chaos theory (geared to grades K through 12).

Netlib Repository at UTK/ORNL

http://www.netlib.org/

Contains a large number of downloadable math-related programs (most of the software is share-ware). Contains papers about different research on mathematical topics, many of which involve computers. Also offers links to other math-related databases.

Online Image Archiver

http://www.maths.tcd.ie/pub/images/images.html

Presents math-related images, such as Mobius strips and Kleinband.

Precision Large-Scale Dimensional Metrology/ Measurement

http://worldmall.com/et/ethome.htm

Offers precision large-scale measurement, typically dimensional measurements with .001-inch accuracy.

Principia Consulting Home Page

http://www.csn.net/princon/

Offers training on Mathematica, gives Mathematica support, and does custom programming. Lists fees and availability of training. Provides information on fine-tuning performance with Mathematica.

Quantum Books Home Page

http://www.quantumbooks.com/

Online technical bookstore. Specializes in computer topics such as the Internet, programming, and graphics, as well as in books pertaining to mathematics and physics.

Steven M. Christensen and Associates, Inc.

http://smc.vnet.net/Christensen.html

Offers scientific computing software. Provides information on MathTensor, Schur, and Mathematica. Also offers consulting, which includes porting software to Sun systems. Offers links to Mathgroup, a Mathematica support group.

Transmath—A CBL Mathematics Tutor

http://caliban.leeds.ac.uk/

Offers mathematics courseware using Toolbook (hypertext) documents with Microsoft Windows. Provides instruction on algebra, matrices, vectors, and sequences.

Union Mathematica Argentina

http://www.famaf.uncor.edu/uma/

Organizes workshops, talks, meetings, and conferences, and edits several magazines in mathematics and education.

Video Vita

http://evlweb.eecs.uic.edu/spiff/videovita/index.html

Produces "edutainment" products in mathematics, science, and technology. Offers an online video sample.

Waterloo Fractal Compression Page

http://links.uwaterloo.ca/

Provides information on fractal compression software and papers on fractal compression.

World Wide Web Virtual Library: Mathematics

http://euclid.math.fsu.edu/Science/math.html

Provides links to all things mathematical. Includes jumps to math software, Gophers, newsgroups, electronic journals, preprints, bibliographies, TeX Archives, and high school and university math sites.

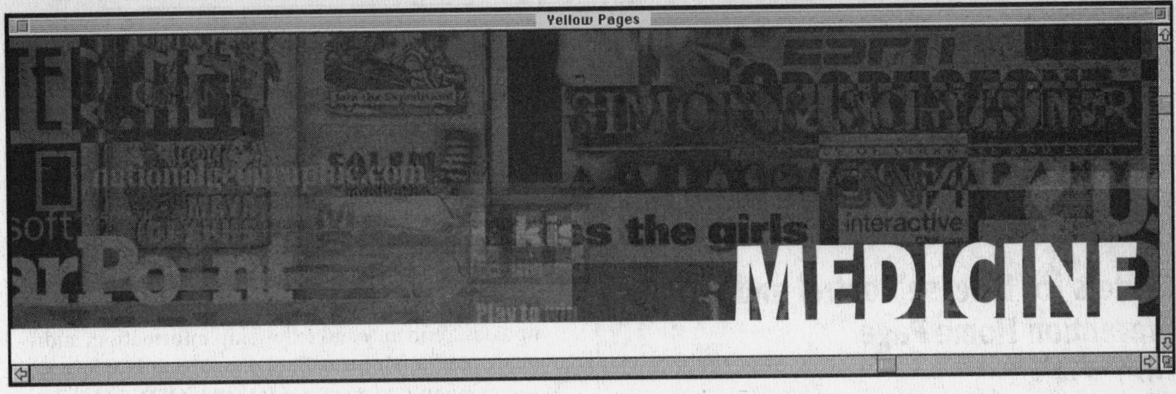

A–Z alphabet tabs: A B C D E F G H I J K L **M** N O P Q R S T U V W X Y Z

> An apple a day keeps the doctor away.
>
> *Unknown*

NRP Top Picks

CDC–Diabetes Home Page
http://www.cdc.gov/nccdphp/ddt/ddthome.htm

Community Breast Health Project
http://www-med.stanford.edu/CBHP/

healthfinder
http://www.healthfinder.gov/

The AAMC's Academic Medicine Web Site

http://www.aamc.org/

Great resource for links to other medicine-related sites. This Association of American Medical Colleges site lists and provides links to accredited U.S. and Canadian medical schools, major teaching hospitals, and academic and professional societies. It provides the latest information on news and events, includes AAMC publications and AAMC information, and presents research and government relations resources. Also includes info and links on education, research, and healthcare and enables you to search the AAMC Web for certain topics.

American Academy of Pediatric Dentistry

http://aapd.org/

Parents can open and read 24 brochures that answer commonly asked questions on topics such as Emergency Care and Diet and Snacking. Includes *E Today*, the electronic newsletter of the AAPD. Also enables you to subscribe to several related magazines. Includes a Directory of Advanced Education Programs in Pediatric Dentistry, with links to each program. Kids can investigate the entertainment section provided just for them.

American Lung Association

http://www.lungusa.org/ndex.html

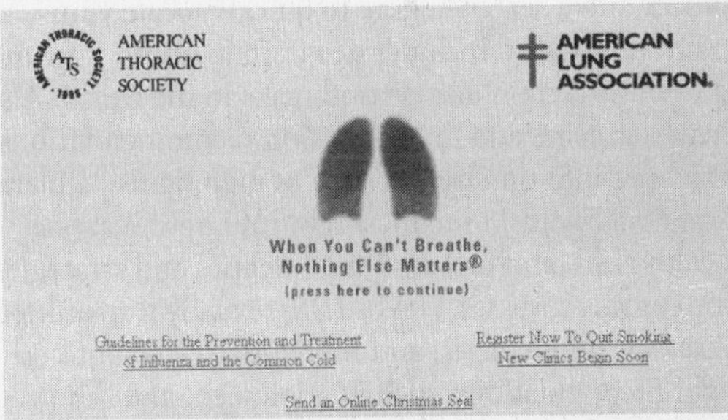

Here, you can find info on the ALA (including research programs, grants, and awards), as well as The American Thoracic Society (the international professional and scientific society for respiratory and critical care medicine). Read the ALA's annual report. Check out info on asthma, emphysema, and other lung diseases; tobacco control; and environmental health. This is a great resource for parents of children with asthma. You'll also find info on volunteer opportunities, special events, and promotions, as well as an extensive list of related links.

CDC–Diabetes Home Page

http://www.cdc.gov/nccdphp/ddt/ddthome.htm

This division of the Centers for Disease Control and Prevention (CDC) is responsible for translating scientific research findings into health promotion, disease prevention, and treatment strategies. Learn about diabetes and what CDC is doing to reduce the burden of this disease. You'll want to investigate the diabetes articles from the CDC and the helpful patients guides on topics such as Keeping Track of Your Blood Glucose and Eye Problems. Also includes an extensive practioners guide, with topics such as Psychosocial Problems and Adverse Outcomes of Pregnancy. Includes links to related sites.

Centers for Disease Control and Prevention Home Page

http://www.cdc.gov/

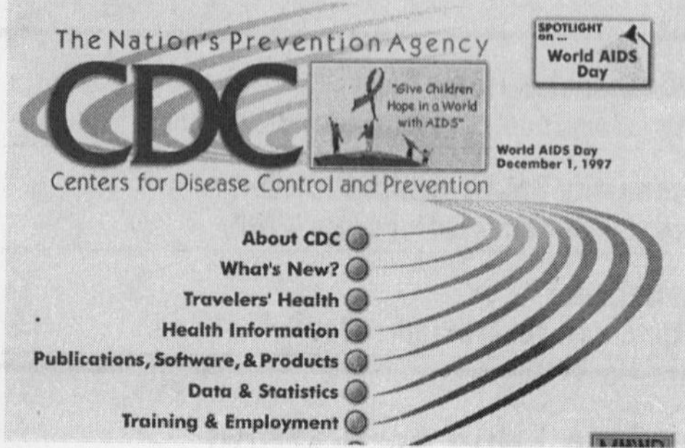

Provides links to the CDC's 11 centers, institutes, and offices and a search engine to quickly locate your point of interest. Includes geographic health info and pinpoints certain disease outbreaks in the world. Also makes vaccine and immunization recommendations. Provides info on diseases such as meningitis, cholera, and malaria, just to name a few. Info on diseases, health risks, and prevention guidelines and strategies for chronic diseases, HIV/AIDS, sexually transmitted diseases, tuberculosis, and more. Also offers info on specific populations, such as adolescent and school health, infants' and children's health, and women's health. Offers helpful links to publications, software, and other products. Also provides scientific data, surveillance, health statistics, and laboratory information.

Community Breast Health Project

http://www-med.stanford.edu/CBHP/

The goal of this project is to improve the lives of people touched by breast cancer by providing information and support, providing volunteer opportunities for breast cancer survivors and friends, and acting as an educational resource and community center for those concerned about breast cancer and breast health. Includes articles from CBHP newsletters and links to cancer-related sites. Also provides a Practical Information section with info about issues such as knowing your family medical leave rights.

Department of Otorhinolaryngology at Baylor College of Medicine

http://www.bcm.tmc.edu/oto/page.html

Provides information from the Department of Otorhinolaryngology (head and neck surgery) and communicative sciences. Potential patients can find information and answers to their questions here. Includes a faculty and resident directory, research updates, residency and fellowship information, audiology program information, grand rounds archives, subscription information for the OTOHNS-Online Otolaryngology discussion group, and links to other otolaryngology resources. Also includes back issues of the *Head and Neck* newsletter.

healthfinder

http://www.healthfinder.gov/

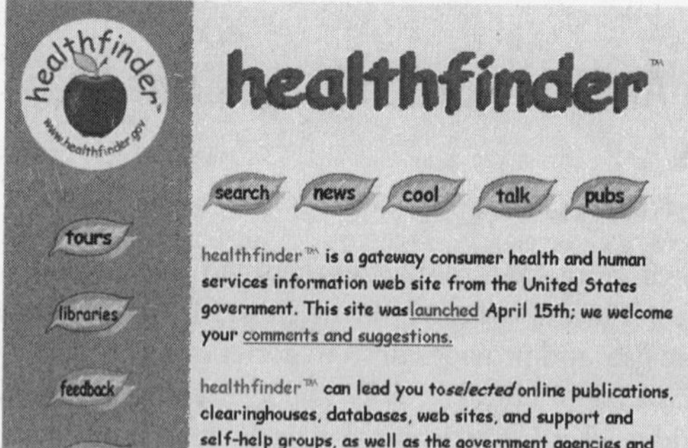

Healthfinder is an information site from the U.S. government. It leads you to selected online publications, clearinghouses, databases, Web sites, and support and self-help groups. It also gives you access to government agencies and not-for-profit organizations that produce reliable information for the public. Includes FAQs on children, older adults, women, and minority health. Also includes FAQs on conditions such as AIDS, allergies, breast cancer, cancer, diabetes, environmental health, food and drug safety, heart disease and strokes, mental health and mental disorders, and substance abuse.

Healthtouch–Online for Better Health

http://www.healthtouch.com/

Lets you look up info on health, wellness, diseases, and illnesses. Topics include prevention and treatment information on AIDS, allergies, asthma, dental health, diet and nutrition, drug and alcohol abuse, eye diseases, eating disorders, family planning, headaches, mental health, poison prevention, sexually transmitted diseases, and other health areas. Includes background about the disease or healthcare issue and product information. You can also look up info about prescription or over-the-counter medications to learn about the proper use of medicines and possible side effects.

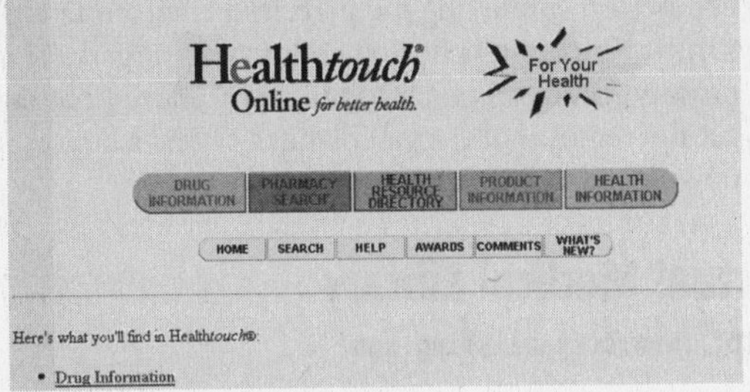

Healthwise@Columbia University

http://www.columbia.edu/cu/healthwise/

Healthwise is the Health Education and Wellness program of the Columbia University Health Service. This site includes highlights from back issues of the *Healthwise* newsletter. Includes the award-winning Go Ask Alice feature—an interactive health Q&A service.

IBMTR's Home Page

http://www.biostat.mcw.edu/IBMTR/

This site is from the International Bone Marrow Transplant Registry (IBMTR) and the Autologous Blood and Marrow Transplant Registry—North America (ABMTR). It includes current IBMTR and ABMTR newsletters, as well as a list of publications produced by both.

Internet Health Resources

http://www.ihr.com

Provides access to Internet-wide health info and local info for the San Francisco Bay Area. Includes resources for dealing with infertility, a wide range of health topics (from allergies to women's health), links to healthcare publications, Internet health newsgroups and Listserv groups, and state and national healthcare organizations. Also includes resources for healthcare providers, including related topics, schools, and publications.

Medical Education Page

http://www.scomm.net/~greg/med-ed

Targets pre-med and medical students. Lists medical schools in the U.S., offers links to medical reference materials and FTP sites, provides lists of specialists, and more.

National Organization for Rare Disorders, Inc. (NORD)

http://www.pcnet.com/~orphan/

NORD consists of more than 140 not-for-profit voluntary health organizations serving people with rare disorders and disabilities. Read the *Orphan Disease Update* newsletter or search the Rare Disease Database, the NORD Organizational Database, or the Orphan Drug Designation Database for info on specific rare disorders. A rare or *orphan* disease affects fewer than 200,000 people in the U.S. There are more than 5,000 rare disorders that affect 20 million Americans. This site includes links to various support groups.

Northwestern University Department of Radiology

http://pubweb.acns.nwu.edu/~dbk675/nwu_radiology.html

Offers links to current radiological information and case presentations, as well as a description of services provided, staff, residency, and fellowship programs.

NYU Medical Center Neurosurgical Department

http://mcns10.med.nyu.edu/

Serves as a resource center on a broad range of neurosurgical issues for patients, families, and healthcare professionals. Includes an introduction to neurosurgery and descriptions and explanations of neurologic disorders. Also describes the surgical specialties and research of the staff of the Department of Neurosurgery at the New York University Medical Center, as well as case presentations.

OsteopathicNet

http://www.osteopathic.net/index.shtml

Targets osteopathic medical students, osteopathic physicians, the allopathic medical community, and people considering medicine as a career. The Osteopathis National Electronic Internship and Residency Database provides free information about every osteopathic post-graduate program in the U.S. This site also includes current and past issues of the *Osteopathic Pulse*—an open-forum newspaper with articles written by medical students, residents, and physicians.

Plink, the Plastic Surgery Link

http://www.nvpc.nl:8080/plink/

Offers a collection of plastic surgery-related links. Targets physicians and interested layreaders. Includes hospital Web pages, journals, books, and general information. Also provides information on societies, departments, physicians, private clinics, conferences, research, and residencies.

Telemedicine Information Exchange–TIE

http://tie.telemed.org/

TIE is a not-for-profit research organization, and its site offers a database of information on telemedicine. *Telemedicine* is the use of electronic signals to transfer medical data (radiological images and patient records, for example) from one site to another in an effort to improve access to medical care for people with substandard access to healthcare. This site also includes Yellow Pages of companies that provide telemedicine products and presents product reviews and technology descriptions. You also can browse through abstracts from current issues of telemedicine journals and newsletters.

Three Dimensional Medical Reconstruction

http://www.crd.ge.com/esl/cgsp/projects/medical/

This site lets you view 3D MPEG format movies of the human brain, skull, colon, lung, heart, torso, and heart arteries. It also provides a simulation of a baby delivery, MR particle flow visualization (in this case, the artery structure of the brain and a visualization of data flow captured by an MR scanner), and a focused ultrasound.

U.S. Department of Health and Human Services

http://www.os.dhhs.gov/

Browse through press releases and fact sheets, speeches, public service campaigns, congressional testimony, and policy forums. Also check out the info on the research, policy, and administration provided by HHS, as well as other federal government research. Use the search feature to find topics from the federal HHS agencies and the Government Information Xchange.

Virtual Environments and Real-Time Deformations for Surgery Simulation

http://www.cc.gatech.edu/gvu/visualization/surgsim/

Focuses on simulating the perceived environment a surgeon encounters during endoscopic surgery. This prototype focuses on abdominal procedures that target the removal of the gall bladder. Offers a large downloadable MPEG movie.

Virtual Medical Library

http://www.ccspublishing.com/

Read current issues of more than 20 medical-related publications and look over the subscription info. Issues include the *Journal of Pediatric Medicine Online, Journal of Psychiatry Online, Emotional and Mental Health Library*, and *Women's Health Library*.

WebMedLit

http://www.webmedlit.com/

Get access to 23 medical journals on the Web. Search through topics such as AIDS/virology, cancer/oncology, diabetes/endocrinology, immunology, neurology, cardiology, dermatology, gastroenterology, medical economics, and women's health.

The WWW Virtual Library: Biosciences: Medicine

http://www.ohsu.edu/cliniweb/wwwvl/

Browse through the extensive listings of and links to institutions and what they offer in their health/medicine fields. Use the search units provided to find answers to questions about topics such as pharmacy, epidemiology, veterinary medicine, and more.

NEWSGROUPS

alt.health.cfids-action

alt.image.medical

alt.med.allergy

alt.med.cfs

alt.support.asthma

alt.support.diabetes.kids

alt.support.eating-disorders

bit.listserv.autism

bit.listserv.deaf-l

bit.listserv.medforum

bit.listserv.medlib-l

bit.listserv.mednews

clari.tw.health.aids

fedreg.health

misc.health.aids

misc.health.alternative

misc.health.arthritis

misc.health.diabetes

misc.kids.health

sci.med

sci.med.aids

sci.med.dentistry

sci.med.diseases.cancer

sci.med.immunology

sci.med.informatics

sci.med.nursing

sci.med.nutrition

sci.med.occupational

sci.med.orthopedics

sci.med.pathology

sci.med.pharmacy

sci.med.physics

sci.med.psychobiology

sci.med.telemedicine

talk.politics.medicine

FTP & GOPHER SITES

ftp://ftp.cdc.gov/pub/

ftp://ftp.uci.edu/med-ed/

ftp://power.ci.uv.es/pub/medicina/

gopher://gopher.niaid.nih.gov/

gopher://gopher.niaid.nih.gov/11/aids

LISTSERV

LISTSERV@listserv.tamu.edu

Related Sites

http://www.ama-assn.org/

http://www.cwhn.ca/

http://www.aafp.org/family/public/publhome.html

http://www.icr.ac.uk/

http://www.medic-online.net/

http://www.mediscene.com/

http://www.uib.no/isf/sats/quality/quality3.htm

http://www.nih.gov/

http://www.nlm.nih.gov/

http://www.who.ch/

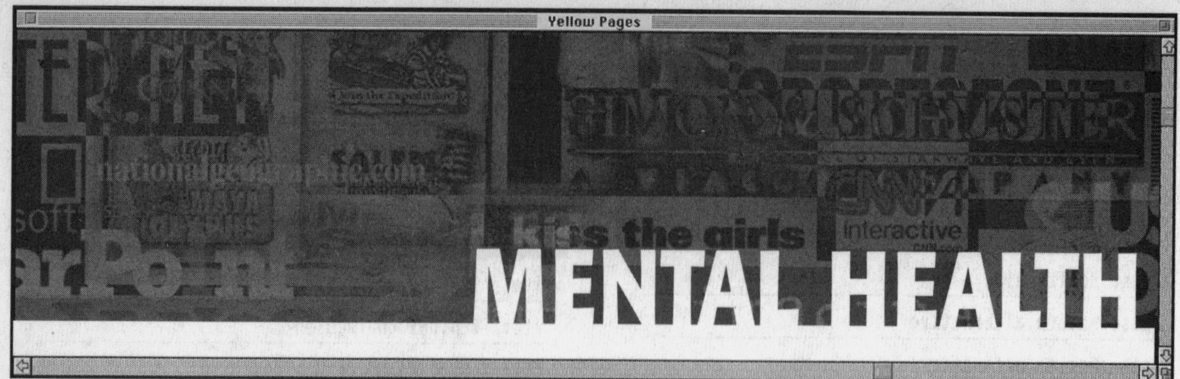

> Don't waste mental energy brooding over past events or worrying about the future. Live a day at a time.
>
> *Dr. Norman Vincent Peale*

American Academy of Child and Adolescent Psychiatry Homepage

`http://www.aacap.org/web/aacap/`

Get info on child and adolescent psychiatry, fact sheets for parents and caregivers on more than 50 psychiatric disorders, and updates on the current research and legislation. You'll find clinical practice guidelines, managed care info, and public health info. You also get links to many related publications.

The American Academy of Experts in Traumatic Stress HomePage

`http://www.aaets.org/`

Read articles from *Trauma Response*—the official publication of the Academy. Articles cover a wide range of trauma—trauma as a result of combat, domestic violence, plane disasters, the Oklahoma City bombing, natural disasters, rape, divorçe, and more. You'll examine case studies and profiles, learn exactly what post-traumatic stress disorder is, look at what causes it, and learn about the various treatments that have been administered.

National Alliance for the Mentally Ill (NAMI) Home Page
`http://www.nami.org/`

Self-Help & Psychology Magazine
`http://www.cybertowers.com/selfhelp/`

The Bipolar Planet

`http://www.tcnj.edu/~ellisles/BipolarPlanet/`

Get info on Bipolar Disorder, which is characterized by mood swings. One variety of this disorder is manic depression. You can search the Mental Health Network database for the topic that concerns you. Includes letters and stories contributed by bipolars. You'll also get a link to a bipolar disorder FAQ and links to other resources.

Center for Anxiety and Stress Treatment

`http://www.stressrelease.com/`

Get resources and services for the treatment of anxiety, stress, panic, phobias, and worry. Includes an online sale of books and audio tapes. Also provides links to treatment centers, workshops, and counseling services.

Cyber-Psych

`http://www.webweaver.net/psych/`

Offers info and advice on topics such as addictions, domestic abuse, eating disorders, anxiety disorders, grief and loss, mood disorders, sexual abuse recovery, transgender info, and trauma recovery. You also get links to various psychology journals and organizations, self-help and support groups, psychology schools, and employee-assistance programs.

Hypochondria and Munchausen Syndrome

http://www.seanet.com/~tzhre/hypochon.htm

Did you know that most people think that hypochondriacs are just pretending to be sick or in pain, but in fact, their symptoms are real? Did you know that people with Munchausen Syndrome or Munchausen Syndrome by Proxy deliberately harm themselves or others to get attention? Learn all about these two disorders at this site. Try the quiz to see whether you're a hypochondriac. And, get up to date on the current research on these conditions.

Institute of Psychiatry

http://www.iop.bpmf.ac.uk/

Post-graduate school at the University of London, recognized by the World Health Organization as a collaborating center for research and training in mental health. Seeks to promote excellence in the research, development, and teaching of psychiatry and its allied subjects, and to apply and disseminate knowledge through the development of treatment for the relief of suffering. Contains info and research on mental health, psychiatry, and neuroscience.

Kindred Spirits—Eating Disorder Info

http://www.geocities.com/Athens/Acropolis/1081/

People with eating disorders are concerned with food, weight, and appearance so much that their health, relationships, and daily activities suffer. They often develop these disorders as a reaction to emotional pain, separation issues, low self-esteem, depression, stress, trauma, or other problems. You'll find info on the causes or factors of eating disorders, treatment, relapse, and recovery. You'll learn about identifying and dealing with anorexia nervosa, bulimia nervosa, and binge eating. The Warning Signs section is helpful for parents, friends, or family who think their loved ones may have an eating disorder; they'll learn what to look for and how to help. Includes poems and essays by those affected, as well as lyrics from well-known artists. You'll also find links to related sites.

Knowledge Exchange Network (KEN)

http://www.mentalhealth.org/

The CMHS National Mental Health Services Knowledge Exchange Network (KEN) provides info about mental health via toll-free telephone services, an electronic bulletin board, and publications. KEN is for users of mental health services and their families, the general public, policy makers, providers, and the media. It gives you info and resources on prevention, treatment, and rehabilitation services for mental illnesses.

Mental Health Net

http://www.cmhc.com/

Get info on disorders such as depression, anxiety, panic attacks, chronic fatigue syndrome, and substance abuse. You'll also get access to professional resources in psychology, psychiatry and social work, journals, and self-help magazines. You can also read articles containing the latest news and developments in mental health.

National Alliance for the Mentally Ill (NAMI) Home Page

http://www.nami.org/

Browse through a host of articles brought to you by NAMI. Learn about the latest treatments and therapy; health-insurance issues; the role of genetics; typical Q&As; and related bills, laws, and regulations. Look into NAMI's campaign to end discrimination against the mentally ill and how you can help. Take advantage of Helpline Online; volunteers talk with you about mental illnesses and the medications that treat them. Examine the scientific aspects of mental illness. Get the facts on depression, schizophrenia, brain disorders, Obsessive-Compulsive Disorder, Bipolar Disorder, Tourette's Syndrome, manic depression, attention deficit, Panic Disorder, and more.

National Coalition of Arts Therapies Associations

http://membrane.com/ncata/

Provides information on six creative arts therapies—art, dance/movement, drama, music, psychodrama, and poetry. These therapies foster good mental health, communication, and expression. They also promote the integration of physical, emotional, cognitive, and social functioning; enhance self-awareness; and facilitate change. Learn all about the therapies at this site.

Obsessive-Compulsive Disorder

http://laran.waisman.wisc.edu/fv/www/lib_ocd.htm

Obsessions are recurring unwanted thoughts or worries, and compulsions are activities or rituals you perform to relieve the anxiety brought on by obsessions. OCD is caused by a chemical imbalance in the brain and has been linked to the neurochemical Serotonin. Learn about the different classifications of OCD and the treatments that have been effective. Find out what the symptoms of the disease are and how to get help. Find out who to contact for more info, and chat with others who are affected by OCD.

Psychiatry and Psychotherapy

http://www-leland.stanford.edu/~corelli/

Offers links to mental health info and resources. Provides info on psychiatric diagnosis, personality disorders, and other areas of psychological interest. Offers links to info on psychotherapy and psychopharmacology. Includes a personal reading list in the areas of psychiatry, psychotherapy, and Jungian psychology.

Self-Help & Psychology Magazine

http://www.cybertowers.com/selfhelp/

The goal of *Self-Help & Psychology Magazine* is to help people improve the quality of their daily lives. You'll find a huge amount of articles and info on topics such as Aging and Aging Parents; Alcohol/Nicotine/Other Drugs; Attention Deficit and Tourette's; Child, Family, and Parenting; Chronic Illness; Depression and Anxiety; Dreams; Eating Disorders; Gay/Lesbian/Bi/Trans; Health and Spirituality; Hypnosis; Internet Psychology; Loss and Bereavement; Mediation and Disputes; Men's Issues; Menopause; Psychotherapy; Relationships; Self-Help; Sex and Lust; Sports/Performance; Stress; Teens; Traumatic Stress; Women's Issues; Work and Finances; and Weight Loss.

Shyness Home Page

http://www.shyness.com/

Helps those with shyness and social phobias so that they can achieve their personal and professional goals by learning new behaviors.

NEWSGROUPS

alt.psychology.help

alt.support.anxiety-panic

alt.support.depression

alt.support.depression.manic

alt.support.depression.seasonal

alt.support.dissociation

alt.support.eating-disord

sci.med.psychobiology

sci.psychology.misc

sci.psychology.psychotherapy

soc.support.depression.crisis

soc.support.depression.family

soc.support.depression.manic

soc.support.depression.misc

soc.support.depression.seasonal

soc.support.depression.treatment

FTP & GOPHER SITES

ftp://ftp.health.org/pub/ken

gopher://gopher.gsa.gov:70/00/staff/pa/cic/health/obsess

gopher://gopher.gsa.gov:70/00/staff/pa/cic/health/schizo.txt

gopher://gopher.nimh.nih.gov/1

gopher://zippy.nimh.nih.gov:70/00/documents/nimh/other/anxiety

gopher://zippy.nimh.nih.gov:70/00/documents/nimh/other/Paranoia

Related Sites

http://www.webhealing.com/

http://www.tezcat.com/~tina/psych.shtml

http://www.teachhealth.com/

http://www.mentalhealth.com/

http://www.med.nyu.edu/Psych/src.psych.html

http://www.cmhc.com/disorders/sx56.htm

http://www.cmhc.com/guide/person.htm

http://www.mediconsult.com/noframes/depression/shareware/amer/amer.html

http://www.nimh.nih.gov/

http://stressrelease.com/qadisorder.html

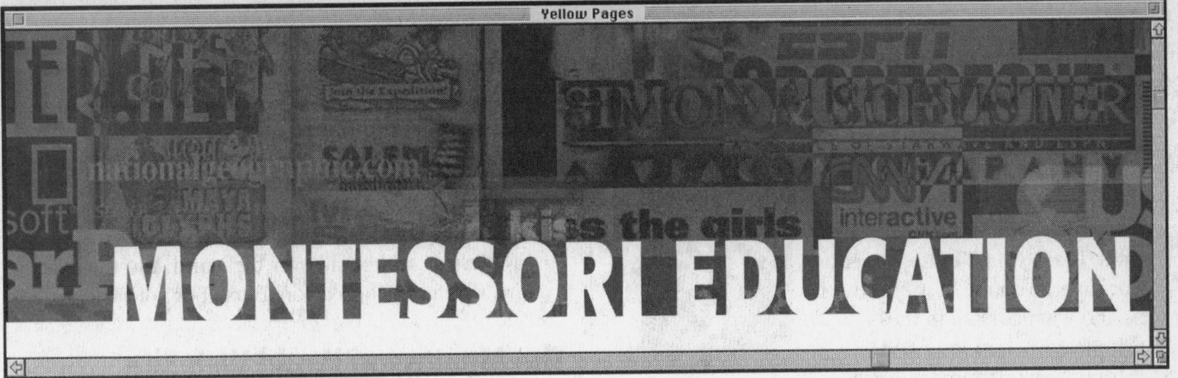

Within the child lies the fate of the future.

Maria Montessori

American Montessori Consulting

http://members.aol.com/amonco/amonco.html

An index of resources for American Montessori Consulting. It has everything from home schooling information to creating your own beginning reading books. You get information about Montessori about preschoolers and elementary-age children. You find links to sites for children, parents, and recommended educational links.

Association Montessori Internationale

http://cyclops.pei.edu:8001/~elem2kc/kcmi/ami.html

Learn about Association Montessori Internationale, the association founded by Maria Montessori in 1929 and guided by her son, Mario, for more than 50 years. Read about the society's objectives and its intensive "training-of-trainer" programs.

The Center for Contemporary Montessori Programs

http://www.stkate.edu/~mdorer/

This site offers information about the Center for Contemporary Montessori Programs' teacher education programs, which are American Montessori Society affiliated. You can get course descriptions and check out links to other Montessori sites.

Related Sites

http://www.slip.net/~scmetro/childco.htm

http://sunrise.byu.edu/~browna/montessori/calder.html

Montessori Education
http://www.amshq.org/

MECA–Montessori Education Centers Associated
http://www.meca-seton.com/

International Montessori Society

http://www.wdn.com/trust/ims/

Learn what Montessori education is all about. Request to receive Montessori publications and get information on the Society's Montessori teacher education program. Find out which schools are recognized by the International Montessori Society. If you'd like to, you can even join the Society by filling out a simple form; when you join, you receive valuable information and materials about Montessori education.

Maria Montessori School and Training Center

http://www.3000.com/montessori_sf/

Read about the school's programs for toddler to high school age children. If you want to be a Montessori teacher, this site tells you how to enroll in the training center and learn Maria Montessori's methods of teaching children. You can also get numerous interactive teaching materials, including materials for instruction in Peace 101, a class that promotes harmony and world unity.

The Materials Company of Boston

http://www.thematerialscompany.com/

This site offers Montessori teaching materials at low prices. It has a Montessori consultant on staff to answer any of your questions. You can buy everything from math beads to furniture.

Montessori Education

http://www.amshq.org/

This site, maintained and updated by the American Montessori Society, has everything you need to know about Montessori education. Learn what Montessori education is all about, how effective it is and what goes on in the Montessori classroom, and Montessori programs in public schools.

MECA–Montessori Education Centers Associated

http://www.meca-seton.com/

MECA is a teacher education program for Montessori teachers and administrators for children 0 to 6 years old. Learn about their Paraprofessional Program for administrators, parents, and assistants, and register for training programs. Discover what fun their summer camp holds for children, with camping for children 0 to 9 years.

Montessori for Moms

http://www.primenet.com/~gojess/mfm/mfmhome.htm

This site offers complete training guides for teaching children by using the Montessori method at home. The lesson plans are appropriate for home schooling and classroom teaching. Montessori for Moms guides are for children ages 2 through 5.

The Montessori Foundation

http://www.montessori.org/

Read about the Montessori Foundation and its purpose, learn about the variety of Montessori schools in America, and subscribe to *Tomorrow's Child*, a magazine for Montessori parents and educators. Check out the Montessori school directory, where you can search for Montessori schools around the world. You can add your school to the directory, too. Visit the Montessori Bookstore, where you can order original works of Maria Montessori translated into English.

Montessori Resources on the Internet

http://www.xe.net/isnet/tms/othrmont.htm

A listing of Montessori schools in Canada and the United States, and a list of American Montessori Society schools around the world.

The Montessori Web Index

http://sunrise.byu.edu/~browna/montessori/montessori.html

At this site, you can check out a huge listing of Montessori schools and add your own school to the list. See what job opportunities are available in Montessori schools all over the world. You can even buy Montessori books for yourself or your friends.

The Montessori World Web Site

http://www.montessori.co.uk/index.htm

This site offers a list of Montessori schools, information about Montessori seminars and workshops, Montessori software, furniture, job listings, and much more. You can also get advice on starting your own Montessori school.

Northboro Elementary Montessori Magnet

http://www.emi.net/~walls/northboro/home.html

This school's site describes the Montessori philosophy and learning environment. Read the principal's message, and soon you can read the parent's comments about the school and Montessori education (the site was under construction as of this writing). Visit a classroom and find out what the students are learning.

Post Oak Printing

http://www.xe.net/isnet/tms/post.htm

Here you find Montessori educational booklets and writing papers to help students with their math skills, geometry, and handwriting. You can also order audio-visual teaching aids.

Related Sites

http://www.learning-tree.com/

http://www.xe.net/isnet/tms/othrmont.htm

http://sunrise.byu.edu/~browna/montessori/data/AI.html#CA

http://sunrise.byu.edu/~browna/montessori/data/NO.html#OR

http://www.comet.net/montessori/

http://sunrise.byu.edu/~browna/montessori/data/PW.html#PA

http://sunrise.byu.edu/~browna/montessori/data/AI.html#AK

http://sunrise.byu.edu/~browna/montessori/data/canada.html#BC

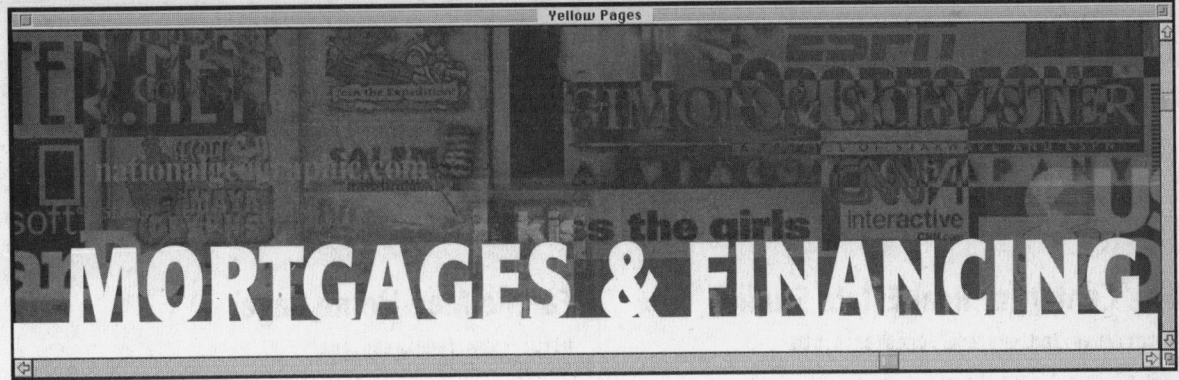

MORTGAGES & FINANCING

> You're not gonna lose the house, everybody has three mortgages nowadays.
>
> *Dr. Peter Venkman in* Ghostbusters *(1984)*

All City Relocation

http://www.idworks.com/allcity/

Provides a wealth of information on cities and towns anywhere in the U.S.. Browsers to the site can review (with pictures and prices) homes, apartments and condominiums for sale or lease in a particular city, as well as an extensive community profile—shopping, recreation, sports, employment, and school and day-care options.

The American Real Estate Society

http://www.uncg.edu/~juddon/

An academically driven organization which produces a number of scholarly journals, including the *Journal of Real Estate Research*, the *Journal of Real Estate Literature*, and the *Journal of Real Estate Management.* The site provides links to the journals, which are archived online.

Related Sites

http://closeprobate.com/_articles/aa_altsolutions.htm

http://ds2.internic.net/cgi-bin/enthtml/business/970516-1125-0003.b

http://www.apollo-usa.com/websites/221288/

http://www.cmacmi.com/

Home Buyer's Vocabulary

http://www.creditinfocenter.com/mortgage/hmvocab.htm

American Relocation Center

http://www.sover.net/~relo/

An extraordinary resource for anyone moving to a new location. Need information on a new community? Select the community information link and get a free relocation/information package for any area in the United States. Looking for the best agent to sell your home? Choose the top producers link to find the leading sales agents in your neighborhood. The site offers links in numerous categories, from private schools to national parks, as well as national access to any Realtor MLS (Multi-Listing Service) system.

The Appraisal Institute

http://www.realworks.com/ai/

This highly regarded group represents real estate appraisers and produces the professionally oriented *Appraisal Journal.* The site provides a number of services to its members and the public, such as the yearly curriculum of courses and seminars, a section on industry news, a bulletin board service, and an online library featuring real-estate papers, articles, and publications.

BCWI Homepage

http://www.island.net/~bcwi/

The first online real estate magazine in British Columbia, B.C. *Waterfront & Island* magazine offers information on the area, new property listings, and the BC Real Estate Navigator, a compendium of links to B.C. realtors, housing, properties, and sales data.

California Real Estate Online

http://www.car.org/calre/

The official publication of the California Association of Realtors offers articles, industry news, and legal information. The site also provides an index to previous issues and links to other publications.

The Center for Real Estate Studies

http://www.indiana.edu/~cres/cres.htm

Housed at Indiana University, the site provides information on Center offerings, including RealSource, a real estate bibliographic database, and the Indiana Housing Affordability Index that tracks the sale of 30,000 homes.

Consumer Mortgage Information Network

http://www.human.com/proactive/index.html

This site is a broad-based primer on home financing. Consumers can download software used for processing mortgages, peruse the extensive file library for articles, government publications and other information, or connect with an extensive collection of related links.

Countrywide Home Loans, Inc.

http://www.countrywide.com/

One of the largest mortgage companies in the United States, Countrywide's Gold Credit page allows consumers to apply for mortgage online. Fill out all the information requested, and receive up to 1.25 percentage points off the loan.

Credit Quality Estimator

http://www.snws.com/loan-bin/credit/

Answer the questions on this page and submit the form to learn how your credit rating is assessed and get an approximate idea of your ranking. Credit is one of the most important factors in obtaining a mortgage. Do your homework here before you apply.

Digital City Real Estate

http://www4.webpoint.com/dci_home/loan_pgm.htm

Check this site for information about obtaining a home loan. If you don't have the traditional 20 percent down payment or are a first time buyer, there are several alternatives mentioned here, including FHA and VA loans.

Eastern Mortgage Services, Inc.

http://www.eastmortg.com/

First mortgage and home equity lender specializing in poor credit loan programs, low-rate mortgages, refinance, debt consolidation, and home improvement loans. 24-hour pre-approval.

Fannie Mae Home Page

http://www.fanniemae.com/

The nation's largest source of home mortgage funds, Fannie Mae works to expand affordable housing opportunities for all. The Fannie Mae site is as diverse as the company. Viewers can search the listing of Fannie Mae properties for sale, read up on the latest news for lenders, or review the latest Housing and Market Outlook.

Federal Home Loan Bank Home Page

http://www.fhlbanks.com/index.htm

Sponsored by the government but privately financed, the Federal Home Loan Bank supports thousands of banks, credit unions, and savings companies as they supply mortgage loans to consumers. They provide lending support for most of the mortgages written in the United States.

Fidelity Union Mortgage

http://www.dirs.com/mortgage/fidelity/

Home loans and mortgages for every purpose: home improvements, purchases, construction, refinancing, equity loans, and more. Strives for fast, professional service.

Freddie Mac Home Page

http://www.freddiemac.com/

Established to support home ownership and rental housing, Freddie Mac has helped to finance one in six American homes. The site explains its role in housing finance, offers investor information on mortgage-backed securities, and offers a comprehensive listing of Freddie Mac homes for sale throughout the country.

Home Buyer's Vocabulary

http://www.creditinfocenter.com/mortgage/hmvocab.htm

Understand the difference between *down payment* and *earnest money*. Learn just exactly what is meant by *points*. When buying or selling a home, you are bombarded with a whole new language. Learn it here.

HomeOwners Finance Center

http://www.homeowners.com/homeowners/index.html

Provides the latest interest rates, rate analysis, market trends, featured loan programs, histories of adjustable rate indices, a mortgage dictionary, a mortgage calculator, and online forms for purchasing and refinancing. Enables you to join a mailing list for updates on the latest news in mortgage rates.

Homes & Land Electronic Magazine & Real Estate Center

http://www.homes.com:8084

Provides real estate information on over 200,000 properties throughout the United States, Canada and Mexico. This "e-zine" also offers an online forum for real estate agents, information on banking services, and a free rental guide.

Homeward Bound Relocation Services

http://www.homeward.com

Homeward Bound provides comprehensive executive relocation services for local, regional, national, and international corporations. In addition to relocation issues, the site itself offers a wealth of information on moving, including employee counseling, moving services, home financing options, and cost of living analysis, among others.

HUD Housing FHA Home Page

http://www.hud.gov/fha/fhahome.html

Information at this site is geared toward both businesses and consumers, with lots of helpful information on buying or renting single and multi-family dwellings. Visitors to the site may also search a directory of HUD housing, participate in online forums or review a number of related Web sites.

Inman News Features

http://www.inman.com/

A wellspring of real estate news and trends, Inman News offers extensive coverage of the industry, with features, a daily mortgage report, and a homebuyer's tip of the day. Another plus—featured articles from past issues are archived for weeks at a time on this site.

Insiders Track Capital Funding Aid

http://www.pennet.net/commercial/itcfa/

Provides an inside view of the capital funding process to start-up or expansion companies. Insiders Track Capital Funding Aid can verify, recommend, or negotiate a capital funding process.

Keystroke Financial Network: How Much Can I Borrow?

http://www.snws.com/mortgage/tools/how_much.shtml

This page is a form where you enter your pertinent financial information and then submit the form to determine the price range of home you can afford. You simply enter your monthly income, all your credit information and monthly debts, banking information, and the amount of your down payment. Then click the Submit button and the calculator determines the price home you can afford.

Kansas City's Guide to New Homes

http://www.kcnewhomes.com/

The online version of this Kansas City magazine is designed with both the real estate professional and consumer in mind. It offers a flexible triple search system (Home Search, Builder Search, Realtor Search) for locating homes in the area.

Mortgage Calculator Input Page

http://www.homefair.com/homefair/mortcalc.html

You can use this page to help determine the amount of your monthly payment. Simply enter the amount of your proposed mortgage, the term of the loan, and your interest rate to check your approximate monthly payment. Then try it at different rates and different terms to see how they will affect your budget.

Mortgage Mag

http://www.mortgagemag.com/mmsubm.htm

Mortgage Mag provides a myriad of information on industry-related issues, such as mortgage and real estate services, commercial and wholesale lending, industry news—even the current interest rates by state!

Mortgage Qualifying Income Calculator

http://www.reslendingsource.com/qual_cl.htm

Use this page to determine the amount of income you need to afford the home of your choice. Just fill in the blanks on the form and click the Calculate Required Income button.

National Mortgage Loan Directory

http://www.mortgageloan.com/search.html

This page has information about current mortgage interest rates across the country. There are 85 loan programs and over 10,000 rates. Check here before you lock in.

National Mortgage Loan Directory: Amortization Schedule

http://www.mortgageloan.com/cgi-bin/amort.cgi

Use this page to find out just how much of each payment actually goes toward your principal balance and how much is earmarked for interest. You might want to use the information to determine how much you'd like to set aside each month to help whittle away at the principal.

Real Estate and Mortgage Library

http://amo-mortgage.com/library/info.htm

Choose your state and search for the information you need. There are links to researching information about credit rating, mortgage insurance, FHA and VA loans, current mortgage rates, title insurance, and much more.

Uncle Sam Offers Financing Breaks to Those Who Serve

http://www.interest.com/editorial/Mortgage_column/mtg_story_970722.htm

If you are a veteran, you'll want to read this article by James R. DeBoth, President of Mortgage Market Information Services, Inc. He details the history of VA loans, why and how they work, and who can benefit.

Union Planters Mortgage, Mortgage Loan Application Checklist

http://www.leaderfederal.com/mortgage.html

Union Planters Mortgage Company has provided this page to help expedite your mortgage application process. Check the information here before making an appointment with your loan officer. You'll save yourself time and headaches by taking the advice you find here.

NEWSGROUP

alt.org.natl-assn-mortgage-brokers

Related Sites

http://www.lendamerica.com/

http://www.mgic.com/

http://www.alaska.net/~premier/

http://www.cmhc-schl.gc.ca/

http://www.cmhc-schl.gc.ca/HealthyHousing/

http://www.first.co.uk/

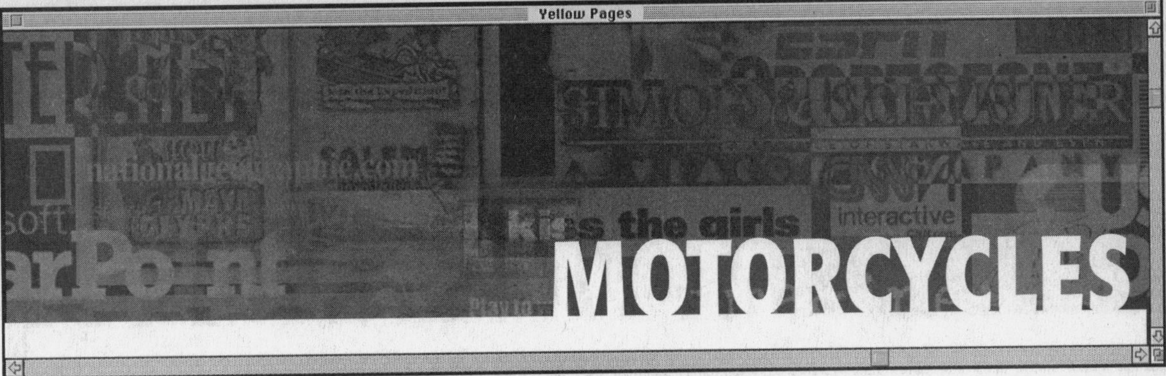

> People are more violently opposed to fur than leather because it's safer to harass rich women than motorcycle gangs.
>
> *Unknown*

AFMWeb

http://www.afmracing.org

Focuses on motorcycle road racing. Offers New Racer School, practices, and schedule of races. Also includes a FAQ, rule book, links, membership information, race results, and a classified section.

Longriders Internet Bikers' Club House

http://www.longriders.com/wwwboard/wwwboard.html

A Web-based chat board of particular interest to bikers. Whether you're looking to buy/sell that rare Harley-Davidson, find a travel partner, or ask fix-it questions, this is the place to go.

Motorcycle Tips and Techniques

http://home.earthlink.net/~jamesdavis/TIPS.html

A collection of tips to keep the potentially dangerous hobby of motorcycling as safe as possible. Read through the collection of tips, peruse a case study on women motorcyclists, and link to a variety of other motorcycle pages.

Motorcycle Tips and Techniques
http://home.earthlink.net/~jamesdavis/TIPS.html

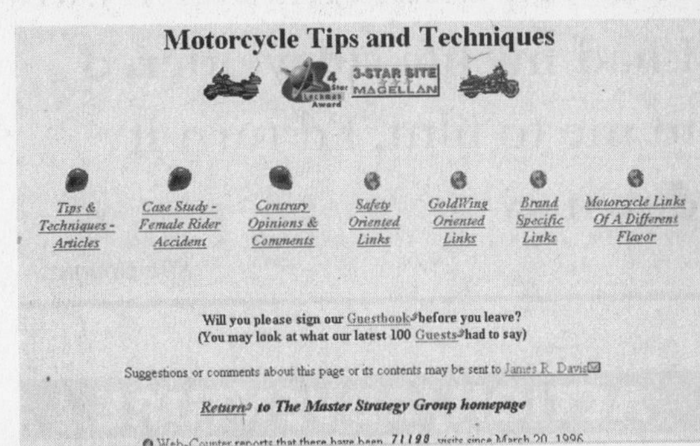

Speedway Home Page

http://www.amg.gda.pl./speedway/speedway.html

Provides links to motorcycle racing forums in Britain, Australia, Canada and the United States. An all event calendar link is provided as well as information involving ice, land, and asphalt track motorcycle racing around the world.

WetLeather Home Page

http://www.micapeak.com/WetLeather/

What is WetLeather? It's what you're wearing if you do much motorcycle riding in America's Pacific Northwest! This motorcycle enthusiast group's Web site features a mailing list, several photos of members at rallies, a registry of members and their bikes, and much more.

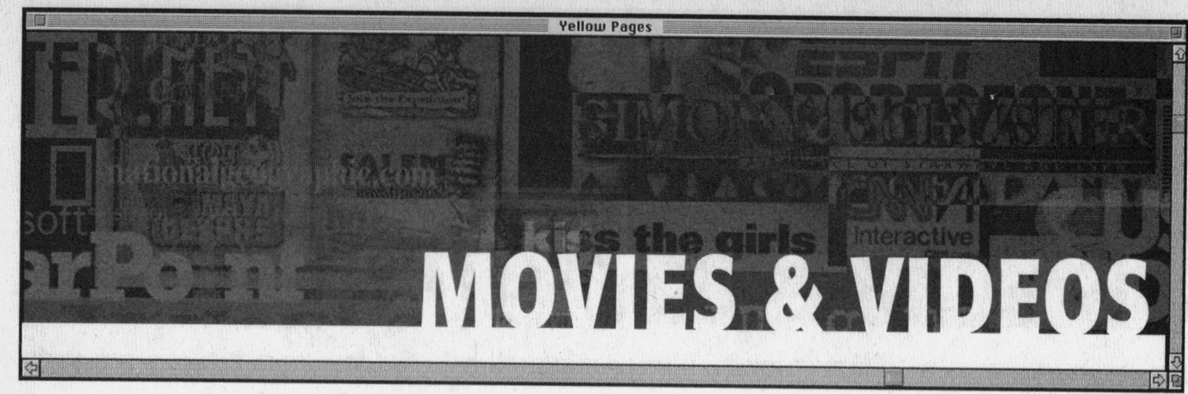

A B C D E F G H I J K L M N O P Q R S T U V W X Y Z

> Life is like a B-picture script. It is that corny. If I had my life story offered to me to film, I'd turn it down.
>
> *Kirk Douglas*

ACTION/ADVENTURE

Braveheart

http://www.aloha.net/~brvhrt/index.html

Maybe you don't share this page creator's opinion that Braveheart is easily the best movie ever made, but it's worth it to let him try to convince you he's right.

Dante's Peak

http://www.dantespeak.com/

She's still as toned as in *Terminator 2*; he's still pumped from his latest role as James Bond. But are they ready to take on a volcano? The site is put together as carefully as the film, with plenty of detail on the reality of volcanic eruption—did you know that director Roger Donaldson once considered a career in geology? For more fascinating facts, clips, sounds, and more, stop by.

Dr. No

http://www.dur.ac.uk/~dcs3pjb/jb/drno.html

This 007 classic, from the period when Sean Connery was still playing Bond, can be found here with raw data, trivia, pictures, and plot summary.

Titanic
http://www.titanicmovie.com/

Tomorrow Never Dies
http://www.tomorrowneverdies.com/

NRP Picks

Escape From L.A.

http://www.escape-la.com/

If you enjoyed the film, be sure to stop by this site. ShockWave games, multimedia adventures, a visit to Los Angeles Island, and, of course, cool graphics from the film.

The Indiana Jones WWW Page

http://www.softaid.net/msjohnso/

From Indy's childhood to what's in store for the fourth installment, this page contains all the theories and artifacts that went into making Indiana Jones an American icon. Links to current Indiana Jones-related sites (novels, CDs, etc.).

James Bond, Agent 007

http://www.mcs.net/~klast/www/bond.html

If you like the Bond genre, you'll enjoy information on the actors, the Bond girls link, previews of the next Bond film, and information on Bond-esque films. Check out the Humor, Trivia, and More section for a little light entertainment.

Jaws

http://www.winternet.com/~tandj04/jaws.html

Bring on the "need a bigger boat" references. Did you remember that Jaws was rated PG? Visit and refresh yourself on one of the most truly frightening movies of our time.

Kansas City

http://www.flf.com/kc/index.html

Did you get a little lost while seeing the film? You can review the synopsis at this site, along with the requisite photos, bios of cast and crew, multimedia experiences, and more.

Killing Zoe

http://w3.nationalnet.com/~berube/kill_zoe.htm

You've never seen a movie like this. Check out images and sounds from what fans consider a masterpiece of filmmaking.

Tombstone

http://www-scf.usc.edu/~garnold/tombston.htm

Not only are there links to the actors from *Tombstone*, links to the characters that they played are available. See how good a job Kurt Russell did as Wyatt Earp when you compare him to the real thing. Tons of great downloadable quotes, too.

ACTORS & ACTRESSES

Looking for information about your favorite movie star? Here's just a sampling of what's available on the Web:

Antonio Banderas	http://www.missouri.edu/~c617756/Antonio.html
Humphrey Bogart	http://www.macconsult.com/mikerose/bogart/bogart.html
Kenneth Branagh	http://www.ultranet.com/~luvvy/kcb/kbfaq.htm
Pierce Brosnan	http://www.goldeneye.com/brosnan.htm
Sandra Bullock	http://www.develop.american.edu/~tlawson/sandyfaq.html
James Dean	http://www.americanlegends.com/jamesdean/
Harrison Ford	http://www.mit.edu:8001/people/lpchao/harrison.ford.html
Jodie Foster	http://weber.u.washington.edu/~jnorton/jodie/jodie.html
Judy Garland	http://www.zianet.com/chrisb/homepage.htm
Tom Hanks	http://www.wsu.edu:8080/~jtwillia/hanks.html
Whitney Houston	http://showbiz.starwave.com/starbios/whitneyhouston/index.html
Raul Julia	http://www.tnef.com/raul_julia.html
Spike Lee	http://www.voyagerco.com/movies/directors/spike/
Demi Moore	http://showbiz.starwave.com/showbiz/memorybank/starbios/demimoore/a.html
Jimmy Stewart	http://www.jimmy.org/
Meryl Streep	http://pathfinder.com/@@TanbUPPMBwAAQBu6/twep/bridges/meryl.streep.html
John Travolta	http://www.execpc.com/~aemog/travolta.html
Elijah Wood	http://www.elijahwood.com/

Clint Eastwood: The World Wide Web Page

http://www.man-with-no-name.com/

Before he was the mayor of a beautiful resort town, Clint Eastwood made a movie or two. In a great Old West style, this page presents everything you could want to know about this king of the screen. When the theme from *The Good, the Bad, and the Ugly* plays, it may jolt you out of your seat.

KeanuNet

http://www.aok.com/keanunet/

Bet you didn't know Keanu Reeves was so well-rounded. Come to this page to see all of his contributions to the arts and catch a glimpse of this dreamy star.

The Marilyn Pages

http://www.ionet.net:80/~jellenc/marilyn.html

Marilyn fans will appreciate the lengthy biography, images, and filmography included on this page. Check out the great images by her photographer and friend, Richard Avedon. Also includes memorabilia information.

StarSite

http://www.webtrax.com/starsite/

Info on some of the industry's biggest stars, indexed by the actor's name or by the title of his or her film or TV show. Want to send your favorite player a birthday card? There's a list sorted by month—and another list of stars' addresses. Go to it!

Welcome to Brandoland

http://www.best.com/~wcleere

Presents Brandoland, an amusement park devoted entirely to Marlon Brando. Enter through to gates to find out more about Brando in every movie he's ever done.

BUSINESSES AND ORGANIZATIONS

The Academy of Motion Picture Arts and Sciences

http://www.ampas.org/ampas/

Check out the latest press releases and new Web features by the Academy. This site also includes the Interactive Guide to the Academy Awards, the winners of the latest Academy Awards, and information on the Academy itself.

The Dove Foundation

http://www.dove.org

Nonprofit foundation that lists "family-friendly" movies and reviews these films. Click the Movies & Videos list to access a searchable index of family-oriented films. Includes links to other family sites on the Web, a Who's Who directory of Dove members and staff, and information on the Dove seal for video retailers.

Elstree Studios

http://www.moose.co.uk/userfiles/elstree/index.html

Don't feel uninformed if you don't remember this studio that's responsible for such classics as *2001*, *The Shining*, and *Star Wars*—they've been on hiatus for a few years. You can still find out about their old productions, though, and what's waiting for them in the near future at this site.

Fine Line Features

http://www.flf.com/

This is the studio that brought you the likes of Robert Altman, *Hoop Dreams*, and the 1996 international sensation *Shine*. Visit and see what they have in store for the coming months, how Cannes went for them, and a list of some of their past films.

Fox Film

http://www.fox.com/film.html

Of course, the primary attraction of this page is its current releases, but there are also links to previews and other "insider" information.

The Lion's Den

http://www.mgmua.com/

Check out new movies and what's been hanging around from Metro Goldwyn Mayer and United Artists. Don't forget to check up on their interactive games for some wild entertainment.

MCA/Universal

http://www.mca.com/

Find out the latest on this mega entertainment company, which includes Universal Pictures, Universal Theme Parks, Spencer Gifts, Winterland productions, and MCA Records. Download stills from current and soon-to-be-released movies, learn about Universal's production studios, Universal Theme Parks' latest rides and events, and upcoming shows and pay-per-view movies on the Universal channel.

Media House Films

http://www.ultranet.com/~msavino/MHFHome.html

Into campy horror films? Good. These guys are, too. Link to some of their recent productions, and enjoy.

Miramar Productions

http://useattle.uspan.com/miramar/

Miramar is a multimedia company, but they're leaders in cutting-edge movies like *The Gate to the Mind's Eye*. They're very happy to have you, and you're encouraged to see what else they have to offer.

Miramax Cafe

http://www.miramax.com/

This studio may be smaller than the other guys, but it more than holds its own when it comes to great movies. Look here for films that are a bit offbeat—that's meant in the best way possible—like the 1996 Golden Globe deluxe, *The English Patient*.

Movies.Com

http://www.movies.com/

Maybe you were looking for information on movies and hit on this site, and to your chagrin found that it was a movie studio. Hollywood Pictures puts out plenty of titles you'll recognize if you decide to stay. It's worth the visit.

New Line Cinema

http://www.newline.com/

As of this printing, New Line is still finalizing their page, but it already includes links to their hot hits, a T-shirt offer, and an interactive memory game. Keep checking back to find out what else they'll have to offer.

October Films

http://www.octoberfilms.com/

For the movies that might not be in your local theater too long (or even make it there), be sure to check out this studio's site.

Paramount Pictures

http://www.paramount.com/homeindex2.html

This nifty site keeps tabs on all the latest releases with links to their individual sites, along with *Star Trek* and Entertainment Tonight Online. If you like trivia games and you're a film industry history buff, be sure to check out the trivia contest.

Sony Pictures Entertainment Page

http://www.spe.sony.com/Pictures/index.html

Find out about Sony's latest movies, theaters, TV shows, and home video. This site also describes their CyberPassage and pay-per-view information. It may take a while to see everything this site has to offer. If you're looking for pictures by Columbia or Tri-Star, look here as well.

Walt Disney

http://www.disney.com/DisneyPictures/index.html

Not only can you read about Disney's current theatrical releases, you can link from here to a host of other pages that deal with their products and productions.

Warner Bros. Online

http://www.movies.warnerbros.com/

Warner Brothers doesn't just do animation (although you can get to their site for that from here); they also make big-name movies. Check here to see what they currently have playing in a theater near you.

Universal Pictures

http://www.mca.com/universal_pictures/

Check out the coming attractions and current in-theaters-now features (including restored classics returning to theaters), see what's new with the company, enter the current contest, add your name to the mailing list—heck, why not email your script ideas direct to headquarters?

Universal Studios

http://www.universalstudios.com/

Yes, there's more to Universal than Universal Pictures. In addition to information and links for their latest films, click the icons to check out the music, interactive, TV, and other divisions.

CHILDREN'S FILMS

101 Dalmatians

http://www.disney.com/101/

Even if you preferred the animated version to the live-action film, you won't be able to resist these adorable puppies on-screen. Behind-the-scenes info on the picture, and a hot shot of Glenn Close that leads to a puppy-search area. Downloadable clips, sweepstakes, and more for kids.

The Adventures of Pinocchio

http://www.pinocchio.com/

Read about Jonathan Taylor Thomas in this movie of the classic children's tale. Pepe (who may remind you of another animated insect) will be your guide on your Internet tour of the film.

Aladdin

http://www.disney.com/Aladdin/

Choose Shocked or non-Shocked versions of the site. Read about the new Aladdin film, third of the trilogy, in which Aladdin and Jasmine finally are getting married. All the usual cast favorites, including a biography of Robin Williams. Download clips and sounds.

A Little Princess

http://http.tamu.edu:8000/~jgh2457/little_princess/littlep.html

Links to online reviews of the movie, plotline, other Princess pages. Interesting link to Japanimation site for animation, version of the main character, Sara Crewe. Links to other Frances Hodgson Burnett sites, including online texts.

All Dogs Go to Heaven 2

http://www.mgmua.com/alldogs2/

If your children enjoyed this movie, show them the Web page so that they can continue the adventure.

Babe

http://www.geocities.com/Hollywood/8713/babe.htm

Something makes this film extraordinarily popular. It's a talking pig—how could it not be? Visit this site to find many other swine-related pages, and maybe get a hint why the movie is such a family favorite.

Beauty and the Beast

http://falcon.jmu.edu/~pollarpe/batb.html

This animated version of the classic fairy tale has a link to the Beast's Page, trivia questions (and answers), as well as pages about the story and music.

Fly Away Home

http://www.spe.sony.com/Pictures/SonyMovies/features/flyaway.html

Details on cast and crew, background information on the history of bird migration. Stills and bios of the film's stars, downloadable Fly Away Home game (ShockWave and non-ShockWave versions), sweepstakes, and links to wildlife sites.

George of the Jungle

http://www.disney.com/DisneyPictures/George_of_the_Jungle/

A great place for kids to play (if they have a fast connection), this site has games and examples of special effects, all under the visual metaphor of an explorer's camcorder. Also contains a special area for downloading sound and video clips.

Homeward Bound II

http://www.disney.com/DisneyVideos/Homeward_Bound_II/

Disney is great at working with animals, and this tale continues the entertaining saga of two lost dogs and a cat with an attitude. Like most Disney sites, this one is equipped with stills, sound bytes, a treasure site for kids, and other goodies.

James and the Giant Peach

http://www.hotwired.com/renfeatures/96/15/index4a.html

It's hard to believe that somebody could do justice to this great Roald Dahl book, but Hotwired has done it. See how the magic was made, and join a discussion about whether the movie lives up to your memories of the book.

The Lion King

http://falcon.jmu.edu/~pollarpe/lionking.html

If you know anyone under the age of ten, you've probably seen this movie at least once. You don't really need the excuse of a niece or nephew to enjoy this movie, though. If nothing else, visit this site to find the hidden Mickey.

The Lion King Web Connector

http://www.geocities.com/Hollywood/6670/

Although this isn't the official site for the film, you can start here to jump to multiple Lion King sites of interest—official, unofficial, and personal.

Mighty Morphin Power Rangers Megadventure

http://www.tcfhe.com/mmpr/

With the White Ranger as your guide, visit this site to see just what being a Power Ranger is all about.

Miracle on 34th Street

http://www.tcfhe.com/miracle/

Visit the site of the remake of this Christmas classic to be reminded of what made it so great, and to remember why it's important to be good the whole year. Santa is always watching.

Muppet Movie Links

http://www.ncsa.uiuc.edu/VR/BS/Muppets/net_movies.html

Start here to find your way to any of the great Muppet movies: *The Muppet Movie, The Great Muppet Caper, The Muppets Take Manhattan, Muppet*vision 3D, The Muppet Christmas Carol, Muppet Treasure Island, The Dark Crystal,* and *Labyrinth.*

The Rescuers

http://members.aol.com/mrbernard/index.html

Your kids may not have recognized the voices of Bob Newhart and Eva Gabor in this movie and its sequels, but they undoubtedly enjoyed the stories of the little mice that saved their friends from kidnappers and other evil types. Although this site isn't particularly graphical, it does provide a lot of details about the films and a number of images.

Snow White and the Seven Dwarfs

http://arti.es/Disneymania/blanci.htm

The arti.es/Disneymania site provides details on a number of the Disney films, including this one, which was Disney's first full-length animated picture. Stills and sound files (in .WAV and Real Audio versions) flesh out the site. Complete text of the film's song lyrics helps out people who want to sing along. For amusement, click the Other Text Files link and look at the list of Walt's rejected dwarf names. (What exactly does Neurtsy mean? I can't even imagine how they'd have drawn Biggo-Ego, or how sad the film would have been with Gaspy.)

Song of the South

http://members.aol.com/mv14/disney/sots/song.htm

Clips from the Disney animated classic, Brer Rabbit stories, and a delightful recording of "Zippidy-doo-dah" that plays when you access the site (requires sound capability, of course).

CLASSICS

Casablanca

http://users.aol.com/VRV1/index.html

Granted, everyone will know you're looking at this site when you can't resist the urge to play "As Time Goes By" while you're looking at it, but this site is well worth any embarrassment you might experience. (If AOL is poking along when you try to access, as is pretty common on weekends and other high-traffic times, you might want to wait and try again later. The home page loading may seem interminable.)

Citizen Kane

http://www.voyagerco.com/movies/directors/welles/p.makingkane.html

This site covers the making of, problems with, and controversy over this American classic. Use this page only as a refresher or an introduction; nothing can substitute for the real thing.

The Jazz Singer (1927)

http://www.cwrl.utexas.edu/~nick/e309k/texts/jazzsinger/jazzsinger.html

Very little information is available on the film, but check out the images that are around, and link to other pages on topics related to one of the first movies to use synchronous sound.

Metropolis

http://members.aol.com/PolisHome/metropolis.html

Even if you aren't already familiar with this Fritz Lang film, once you navigate around the page you're sure to recognize many of the images. Lots of information is out there on the Web about Metropolis, and you can find the links here.

COMEDY

The Addams Family

http://users.deltanet.com/~beaker/movie.html

The one stop for both of the Addams Family movies. You can check out Raul Julia's last film, and then pay homage by linking to all the different Addams Family sites, including the TV show and the cartoon.

A Christmas Story

http://www.fishingworld.com/pdlg/c-story/

Maybe it's the defining difference between generations—now the family gathers around to watch this every Christmas as well as *Miracle on 34th Street.* You can get a taste here with some of the best quotes, but be sure to catch it this year.

A B C D E F G H I J K L M N O P Q R S T U V W X Y Z

A Very Brady Sequel

http://www.thebradybunch.com/

Admit it—you knew the lyrics to the song in the first film, didn't you?! The house, the tic-tac-toe format, and those horrible '70s designs and colors at this site will remind you of the fun and the nonsense of this hit show. It's disgustingly groovy.

Beavis and Butt-Head Do America

http://www.beavis-butthead.com/

This site could also be listed under the heading of "Cult," but most people who can stand this pair think of them as funny. Enter the contest, click various locations on the U.S. map to play interactive games, and of course jump to the MTV Web site, where you can get cool B&B stuff. (Note: Parents might object to some of the language at this site.)

Bogus

http://www.movies.warnerbros.com/bogus/

How do you decide what's real and what isn't? And do your imaginary friends look more like Harvey the rabbit or Gerard Depardieu? In any case, you'll be charmed by the movie and enjoy the site as a place to find out more. Definitely stop by the Cast section and read the bio for Haley Joel Osment. Did you remember him from *Forrest Gump*?

Clerks

http://www.viewaskew.com/clerks/

Haven't heard of Silent Bob? Here's your chance to get acquainted with the crew of this movie that's surely destined for cult classic stature.

Clueless

http://www.paramount.com/Clueless.html

Yes *Clueless* fans, you have a place on the Web, too. Visit Cher Horowitz on her home page and brush up on your Beverly Hills vocabulary and ideas. Jump to the Movie Biz link for background on the filming, the actors, and more.

Fierce Creatures

http://www.fierce-creatures.com/

If the film wasn't in the theaters long enough for you to catch it, stop in here for background details on the film and the cast, assembled again from *A Fish Called Wanda*, before you trot off to the video store. (You might want to turn down your speaker volume a bit before the gunshots start at the site.) Read an interview with John Cleese, laugh again at some of the photos, and definitely check out the drawings in the media section.

The First Wives Club

http://www.paramount.com/motionpicture/fwives/first_wives.html

Lots of images, plenty of background information on the production and the stars, and comments from the actors provide interesting reading at this site. (Note: The links are a bit hard to spot; watch the status bar as you scan over the page with your mouse.)

Four Rooms

http://www.miramax.com/dlpages/fourrodl.html

Catch a lot of pictures and clips from this crazy movie at this site. Tim Roth is the Bell Boy holding together four seemingly unrelated tales.

The Full Monty

http://www.foxsearchlight.com/fullmonty/index.htm

Official site of 1997's biggest sleeper hit. Take a quiz, and find out about the cast of the year's most revealing comedy. Also get a guide to the lingo of the film, in case you're a bloke that's unsure what it means to drop kegs.

Ghostbusters

http://www.okemosweb.com/ghostbusters

Would you qualify to be a Ghostbuster? It's all here at the most comprehensive Ghostbusters site around, including a cool background image of the famous "No Ghosts" symbol.

The Goonies

http://www.mtsu.edu/~m_c_00bc/Goonies.html

This page can take several minutes to load, but it's got some great stills for Goonies fans, along with links to other Goonies pages. Get the scoop on the kids who only wanted to save their homes.

Groundhog Day

http://powered.cs.yale.edu:8000/~miller/hog/groundhog.html

Not just a site about the making of the Bill Murray/ Harold Ramis film, you can also find out a lot about the festivities that surround the town of Punxsutawney, where the story took place during an actual Groundhog Day.

I'm Not Rappaport

http://www.polygram.com/PFE/rappaport/rappaport-home.html

Walter Matthau and Ossie Davis continue to turn in stellar performances as the years pass, and this film of Herb Gardner's play is no exception. This site doesn't provide a lot of detail—just a couple of movie clips and a synopsis—but will at least give you a chance to find out why you need to see this film.

The Jerk

http://www.hirons.com/~lburgess/jerk.html

The page is definitely for fans; otherwise, you'll miss most of the great references to this classic Steve Martin film.

Liar Liar

http://www.mca.com/universal_pictures/liarliar/

Laugh if you will, but this was the third highest grossing movie of 1997. Get up-to-date biographies of the cast, download Quicktime clips from the movie, and even review sounds from the soundtrack album.

Loser

http://www.loop.com/~ecb/loser.html

A low-budget film that's been shown at film festivals around the world. Read its reviews and see whether you think it's worth a trip out to the video store.

Mars Attacks!

http://www.marsattacks.com/

True, this site might be listed under "Science Fiction and Fantasy," but the movie is more silliness than science. The Web site offers just as much humor, with bug-eyed aliens, storyboards, and a Martian-killer game, as well as the usual stills and sounds.

Men in Black

http://www.meninblack.com/main.html

Official site of the top grossing film of 1997. Get background information on the movie that pits Mr. Smith and Mr. Jones against the scum of the universe.

Mother

http://www.mothermovie.com/splash.html

Albert Brooks and Debbie Reynolds provide a lot of the commentary on this official Web site for the movie. View the stills, the teaser, and the trailer, check out the sound clips, and answer an Albert Brooks trivia questionnaire for a little extra fun.

My Fellow Americans

http://www.fellowamericans.com/

Would you choose either of these guys? Hard to imagine. But with James Garner and Jack Lemmon as the stars, the film couldn't help but garner votes. To get a feel for the sequence of action in making a film, read a section of the script, review the story board for that section, and then view the matching clip.

Private Parts

http://private-parts.com/

For adults only. The talk is uncensored and, of course, Howard Stern may drop by at any moment. To access the fun stuff you must click the certification link, indicating that you're at least 18 and have no intention of suing anybody over the site contents. Register your vote about Howard and be sure to play the games.

Rosencrantz and Guildenstern Are Dead

http://www.susqu.edu/ac_depts/arts_sci/english/lharris/class/stoppard/rose.htm

Find out more about the movie that follows Hamlet's friends from college on their misadventures, while things are afoot at the castle.

Smoke

http://www.miramax.com/movies/smoke_.html

This technical page will link you to downloadable stills from the film as well as to the impromptu movie made during the filming of *Smoke—Blue in the Face.*

Space Jam

http://www.spacejam.com/

Whether you're a cartoon fan or a basketball nut, the movie and this site are sure to please. The plentiful graphics are amazing. Souvenirs, Looney Tunes activities for kids, and basketball-related links and stuff will keep you busy.

Tank Girl

http://www.cs.ucl.ac.uk/staff/b.rosenberg/tg/index.html

You know this site has to be good because the studio that made the film has a link to it. Visit the *Tank Girl* gallery, and see what other people have had to say about this futuristic spoof.

CULT

A Clockwork Orange

http://www.lehigh.edu/~pjl2/films/clockwork.html

Every major player is covered in this classic movie's page, from Anthony Burgess to Stanley Kubrick. Full of sound bites and images, as well as links to papers on the film, a chapter from the book that's missing, and other Clockwork Orange pages.

Bloodlust

http://www.ozemail.com.au/~jswjon/

The only Australian film banned in Britain has a site to show you exactly why that's the case. Well-done page, creepy movie.

The Rocky Horror Picture Show

http://www.rockyhorror.com/

This is the official site for the midnight-showing classic, so there aren't any worries about licensing rights that other sites might encounter. You can find background info and memorabilia, as well as ground rules for participation.

This Is Spinal Tap

http://www.spinaltap.com/

As they say, "This page goes to 11." If that means nothing to you, you need to get in touch with Spinal Tap. Devotees will appreciate just how far Spinal Tap can carry out a joke.

DRAMA

Amistad–The Film

http://www.amistad-thefilm.com/

Find out the historical background of the La Amistad mutiny, as well as Debbie Allen's personal quest to turn the story into a movie. Also view a slavery timeline and read extensive production notes about the challenges of assembling the vast African cast.

Boogie Nights

http://www.boogie-nights.com/

Take a trip back into the '70s and '80s in this shag carpet and wood paneled site. Get a feel for what the costume designers were looking for in classic retro fashion. Best seen with at least a 13-inch monitor.

Bound

http://www.polygram.com/PFE/bound/bound-home.html

Like the film, a first-time effort for directors Larry and Andy Wachowski, this site is enticing, dark, and a bit mysterious. They provide a lot of quotes to explain the thoughts behind the film, and plenty of stills and clips. A link on the page leads to OUT.com (an interesting site on its own). Not for kids.

Chasing Amy

http://www.viewaskew.com/chasingamy/

The third installment in Kevin Smith's New Jersey Trilogy (remember *Clerks* and *Mallrats*?), *Chasing Amy* is about friendship, love, and other potentially deadly emotions. Find interesting information on Smith's background, as well as how this film ties into his previous two. Unlike a big studio production, this site has the same honest, rough feel as small, independent-type films.

Evita

http://www.evita-themovie.com/

This film was a long time in coming from Broadway to Hollywood, but well worth the wait. Now that you've seen Madonna's impression of Eva Peron, hop over to this site. Before you click the Enter link at the home page, wait to see all the *Evita* photos displayed in turn above the link. Then check out the other links to cast information, soundtrack, and more.

Ghosts of Mississippi

http://ghosts.msn.com/index.htm

If you're a history buff, or just interested in the past and current state of civil rights, check out the contest at this site. Study guides and a civil rights timeline add to the background info for this moving and dramatic film. Naturally, the site includes info on the history of this infamous murder, the trial, the cast of the film, and more.

The Godfather Trilogy

http://www.exit109.com/~jgeoff/godfathr.html

Focuses on *The Godfather* trilogy. Find out everything imaginable about this famous trio of films. This award-winning site includes pointers to each film, a trivia challenge, soundtrack and dialogue WAVs, stills from the film, and contest information.

Goodfellas

http://www-personal.umich.edu/~geordyg/goodfell.html

This site is still heavily under construction, but you can at least download sound bites and pictures of other great Scorsese films.

Hackers

http://www.mgmua.com/hackers/index.html

Even if you're not a hacker, the site promises that you'll still enjoy this movie (real hackers will enjoy the message it claims). Play the hacking game at the site, read letters from hackers, and link to related sites.

Hoop Dreams

http://www.well.com/user/srhodes/hoopdreams.html

While not very graphical, this unofficial page is full of links to seemingly every article written about this great documentary.

The Ice Storm

http://www.foxsearchlight.com/ice/

Hailed as one of 1997's best films, The Ice Storm stars the versatile Kevin Kline and alien hunter Sigourney Weaver as two people struggling to find meaning in their lives in the strange and not-too-distant early '70s. Find a ton of information about director Ang Lee and the cast, including reviews and historical background.

Il Postino (The Postman)

http://www.cecchigori.com/cinema/postino/home.htm

Visit the site for this Academy Award-nominated picture, and get a glimpse of what's in store for you when you get a chance to see this great film.

In the Company of Men

http://www.spe.sony.com/Pictures/SonyClassics/men/

Opening to rave reviews, this film was a surprise both critically and commercially. The story of two frustrated men in search of revenge and a sense of power, the film explores friendship, love, and anger in a blunt, controversial way. The site contains the standard (but necessary) fare of cast biographies, a brief synopsis, and an interview with director Neil LaBute.

In the Name of the Father

http://www.fsu.umd.edu/students/dhiggins/movies.htm

Look here for sound bites from the film starring Daniel Day Lewis, conveying the tale of the Conlon family.

The Unofficial Jackie Brown Homepage

http://www.geocities.com/Hollywood/Boulevard/9284/jackie.htm

Sometimes the unofficial sites are the most fun. This site has a ton of information about Quentin Tarantino's latest directorial effort. Get trivia, gossip, movie trailers, and join the Tarantino Web Ring.

Jane Eyre

http://www.alliance.ca/theatre/movies/eyre.html

With a stellar cast and Charlotte Bronte's classic work holding it up, this movie holds great promise. Read about the actors and the story itself at this page.

L.A. Confidential

http://www.newregency.com/laconfidential/

This official site is formatted like a tabloid magazine and has a great retro look. Download clips, get the "skinny" on all the stars, and do it all in grand style.

Leaving Las Vegas

http://www.mgmua.com/vegas/index.html

This is the dark film for which Nicolas Cage won Best Actor honors. Be sure to explore Cage, Elisabeth Shue, and others involved in the making of this deeply disturbing movie at their Web site.

Michael Collins

http://www.michaelcollins.com/

QuickTime and Clear Video sound clips from the actors help you get the feeling of what it was like working on this film. Plenty of biographies; click the Casting a Legend link to see how Liam Neeson was chosen for the lead. If you have an interest in the Emerald Isle, be sure to read the sections on shooting on location in Ireland and on some of the locations used in the film.

A B C D E F G H I J K L M N O P Q R S T U V W X Y Z

Othello

http://othello.guide.com/

Read up on interviews with the filmmakers, preview the CD-ROM, and get a chance to learn more about Shakespeare, his other plays, and festivals around the country.

The People vs. Larry Flynt

http://www.spe.sony.com/Pictures/SonyMovies/features/larryflynt.html

Wherever you stood when this case came to trial (and even if you weren't born yet), this film will make you think about free speech, pornography, the Supreme Court, and, of course, Larry Flynt. At the Web site, read the background information, click to see what the First Amendment really says, and review five actual "free speech" cases. Then make your own decision about the film, about the issues, and, of course, about Larry Flynt.

Quiz Show

http://cybermart.com/sundance/movies.html

Because this film is so intricately tied to the Sundance Film Festival, you can view clips from the film and from the Sundance Institute at the site.

Reservoir Dogs

http://www.miramax.com/dlpages/reservdl.html

Here's the place to come to download stills and clips from the film that put Quentin Tarantino on the map.

Scarface

http://www.exit109.com/~jgeoff/scarface/

It would be silly to say anything disparaging about this site, wouldn't it? There's no need to, though. Lots of links for buffs and people who wouldn't know Tony Montana from a hole in the ground—their mistake.

Shine

http://www.flf.com/shine/

Shocked and unShocked versions of this site are available. If you're a music lover and have relatively speedy equipment (and Shockwave), try the Shocked site. You can take the Rachmaninoff challenge and try to click the right keys on the keyboard (in the right order, of course). Plenty of other interesting stuff to enjoy from this award-winning film.

Sleepers

http://www.sleepers.com/

Visit this site for clips, images, filmmaker details, and info on more than just the headliners, in a dark and brooding format that fits the tone of this film.

The Sweet Hereafter

http://www.flf.com/sweet/

This is the official Fine Line Films site for the movie that won three awards at the 1997 Sundance Film Festival. The site's style is fairly sparse and frank, not unlike the film, which chronicles a town's loss and the lawyer who tries to bring compensation to it and himself.

Surviving Picasso

http://www.movies.warnerbros.com/picasso/

Wondering about the history behind the story? Come to this site to get the scoop on Pablo and Francoise, as well as plenty of juicy details about the making of the film, costumes, cast, and, of course, links to other Picasso-related sites.

A Taxi Driver Page

http://pilot.msu.edu/user/svoboda1/taxi_driver/

Even if this movie didn't have Robert DeNiro or Jodie Foster in one of her first roles, it would still be great—hard to imagine, but great. Be sure to check out the counter at the bottom of the first page.

Titanic

http://www.titanicmovie.com/

This is the official Paramount site to James Cameron's huge sea disaster epic. Take a Quicktime tour of the ship, see clips from the movie, and read an interview with James Cameron about the most expensive film ever made.

Tomorrow Never Dies

http://www.tomorrowneverdies.com/

This stylish site commemorates the 18th James Bond feature film. Beyond the traditional cast and production notes areas are sweepstakes and—for all you hardcore action gamers—custom Quake levels with Bond as the lead gunner.

The Usual Suspects

http://www.hollywood.com/movies/usual/bsusual.html

Were you startled by the ending, or did you see it coming? In either case, you'll find the items of interest on this page handy for reviewing why you liked the film. Clips, sounds, trailers, interactive activities, and more.

FESTIVALS

Cinema Festivals

http://www.coproductions.com/cnfestad.htm

This search engine allows you to find specific film festivals by month, home page, topic, name, type of festival (competition or exhibition), city, state, or country, in both French and English.

The Film Festivals Server

http://filmfestivals.com/

What a great site! Whether or not you have the money and time to make it to these festivals, so much information is to be had on these pages that you might feel like you've been there. All the major festivals can be found, plus city guides to go along with them.

Low Res Film and Video Festival

http://www.lowres.com/

This film festival is meant to showcase and encourage young filmmakers by showing just how much can be accomplished on a small budget.

Sundance Film Festival

http://sundancefilm.com/festival/

Take a tour through the independent filmmaker's festival created by Robert Redford. You can look at this year's entries or review past winners.

FILM & PRODUCTION RESOURCES

The Character Shop

http://www.character-shop.com/

This special-effects shop produces some of the most famous animals on the big screen. Read how the Budweiser frogs and anteater were created using puppets and animatronics. Check out the story about the largest animatronic robots ever created for Disney's Operation Dumbo Drop. Includes a resume of every film, TV show, and commercial shot with Character Shop animals, FAQs about their work, a tour of the facility, and semi-regular updates on their work. A fascinating visit!

CinemaSpace

http://cinemaspace.berkeley.edu/

Home page for the film studies program at Berkeley. Choose a department related to science fiction, art direction, Web pages by Berkeley students, and more.

Disney.com Home Page

http://www.disney.com/

Fun things to do for kids and adults. Info on movies, books, and of course the Disney Channel. Order Disney products online, get the latest on the Disney theme parks, cruise for videos of past classics.

DTS Theatrical

http://www.dtstech.com/theatrical/

Visit the Web page of the leaders in movie theater sound if you're going to open a theater, or in the more-likely event that you're just curious. Lists of theaters equipped with DTS sound and past, present, and future films using this technology.

The Independent Film and Video Makers Internet Resource Guide

http://www.echonyc.com/~mvidal/Indi-Film+Video.html

A valuable resource for filmmakers on a professional and political level; there's something here that you need. Special info on Congress and culture, particularly public funding of the arts.

The IMAX Page

http://members.aol.com/neihousej/imax/index.htm

The author of this unofficial page is an IMAX cinematographer and obviously likes the system. If you're interested in what makes IMAX so special, or in how IMAX films are made, this is a good jumping-off point.

A B C D E F G H I J K L M N O P Q R S T U V W X Y Z

Knight Productions, Inc.

`http://www.msen.com/~knight/`

Home page of this film and video production company. Data on their technical capabilities, freelance services. Link to other sites and "tangents," as well as access to informative databases.

LucasArts

`http://www.lucasarts.com/`

Never one to be behind the times in technology, George Lucas' production company has its own site. Come find technical support and sneak glimpses of what they're working on. Multiple formats for viewing, info on LucasArts games and technologies.

Makin' Waves Studio

`http://www.adesign.com/makinwave/welcome.html`

Sample some of their special "Aussie" .WAV files, or order your own custom .WAV. You can even order a broadcast-quality commercial voiceover. Click the .WAV links to hear Aussie pronunciations online (assuming that you have the right audio player available).

Mass F/X

`http://www.ultranet.com/~msavino/fx/fx.html`

A favorite of Media House Films, this group produces special effects props for your film or simply your pleasure.

New York Film and Animation Co. Ltd.

`http://www.okc.com/nyfac`

Home page for NY-based computer animator. Read about NYFAC, check out their gallery of cool graphics, and see what's cooking with current projects.

Production Magic

`http://www.ProductionMagic.com/`

Read about their Shot Logger, a special tool for nonlinear editing. Specifications for the tool, instructions for use, questions and answers, and some examples of it in use are included in the site.

Rhythm and Hues Studios

`http://www.rhythm.com/`

This visual-effects production company has created a number of entertaining rides, exhibits, commercials, and movie effects. Read about their work on the award-winning *Babe* (1995), the Coca-Cola polar bears, and effects for EuroDisneyland. Click Sights&Sounds to see how these special effects are created.

Shades of Light Studios

`http://www.ernestallen.com/shadesoflight/`

A new studio that would like to offer its facilities to those who need a place to film. Read about their specific studios and vision for production and see whether they offer what you need, or just get an inside look at what goes on at a studio.

THX

`http://www.thx.com/thx/`

For home and theater sound, visit this site to see what one of the leaders in effects, LucasFilm, is doing for your listening pleasure.

Virtual Studio Ltd., London

`http://www.vrworlds.com/`

This computer graphics, audio, and custom software studio provides information on virtual reality and links to the biggest VR companies on the Web. Check out the Graphics Studio link to see samples of their work.

WAVE—Wognum Art's Virtual Exchange

`http://www.wognum-art.se/`

Home page for this Stockholm-based art studio. Read about their recent work with clients incorporating interface design, CD-ROM programming, corporate profiling, typography, graphics, 3-D modeling, and animation. Brainwave section offers a variety of interesting "brainscramble" puzzles to solve.

HORROR

The Cabinet of Dr. Casey

`http://www.cat.pdx.edu/~caseyh/horror/index.html`

A great site for horror movie buffs. Check out the extensive Horror Movie Posters Archive, the Horror audio and graphics sections, and Horror in Literature and the Movies.

David Cronenberg Home Page

http://www.netlink.co.uk/users/zappa/cronen.html

Read interviews and reviews, see what's around the corner, and generally be grossed out by this master of horror and creator of many classics of our time.

The Return of the Texas Chainsaw Massacre

http://chainsaw.crimson.com/rtcm/

Because just once isn't enough. Spy on Leatherface, but don't think that he's not looking for you, too. As they say on the page, check out some of their "tasty cuts."

Scream

http://www.dimensionfilms.com/scream/

If you're a fan of horror films, you'll definitely want to check out this site. The "A Stab in the Dark" game is a trip, and you must read the list of serial killers from past gory trips to the theater. Bet you've seen them all.

Scream 2—The Website

http://www.cantnot.org/scream2/

Another unofficial tribute site, this one has a chat area, links to other unofficial *Scream* sites, and loads of information about movie trailers, cast and crew, and soundtrack information. Find out how to get newsletters and join the *Scream* fan club.

The Shining

http://pubweb.acns.nwu.edu/~mdk899/overlook.html

The maker of this page believes that *The Shining* is destined to live on forever in the pages of the movie greats. Visit the Overlook Hotel and let him show you why. He'll take you through all the rooms you remember, and the symbolism that you didn't know was there.

MYSTERY

The Hitchcock Page

http://www.primenet.com/~mwc/

Tribute page to one of the greatest film directors. Read a biography, check out the Filmography and Hitchcock on TV sections, and read about his awards and honors. The Pure Cinema section includes an animation of Hitchcock's famous shower sequence.

PRODUCTS

CyberCinema

http://www.cyber-cinema.com/

Want a movie poster for that bare wall? This online movie-poster store enables you to order posters of the latest hits. Be sure to check out the Classic Movie Catalog and Our Catalog of Favorite Posters. You can order online or send away for their catalog.

HSS Wholesale Home Page

http://www.direct.ca:80/hss

Offers a collection of more than 200 life-sized standup cardboard posters of famous movie stars, singers, *Star Trek* characters, and more. Check their index, or click What's New to see the latest full-size cutouts.

Movie Madness Merchandise

http://WWW.MovieMadness.COM/

If you didn't realize that you liked the movie that much until it was already out on video, here's your chance to still get products that show your devotion.

The Movie Poster Page

http://musicman.com/mp/posters.html

Learn about the movie-poster-collecting frenzy hitting the auction houses. This site includes poster images of leading movies and thumbnails of many other movie posters. You can read about movie poster preservation, poster investing, and the reprint business. This site also includes a movie poster catalog and information on Disney, Elvis, and James Bond movie posters. A busy site!

The Ultimate Resource for Vintage Posters

http://www.chisholm-poster.com/

Visit the only movie-poster search service on the Web. This site also provides examples of extremely rare movie posters and a gallery index for New York.

REVIEWS AND MOVIE LISTINGS

Best Video

http://www.tagsys.com:80/Ads/BestVideo/index.html

This site isn't a must-see movie, it's an online video store that helps you find and buy movies. You have the option of buying previously viewed movies, reading about films in the monthly reviews, or linking to other Web sites. Good when you know what you want but not where to get it.

Bright Lights Film Journal

http://www.slip.net/~gmm/bright.html

This quarterly journal explores the issue of movies as propaganda. They'll take you through all the angles of movie interpretation and impact, and encourage you to give them a piece of your mind.

Cinemania Online

http://Cinemania.msn.com/Default/Home

This site, maintained by Microsoft, will keep you abreast of the newest theatrical releases, allow you to participate in ongoing debates about great actors, or read biographies and regularly updated special features.

Early Motion Pictures 1897-1916

http://lcweb2.loc.gov/papr/mpixhome.html

Download AVI files of early motion pictures of New York, San Francisco before and after the earthquake (1906), and different presidents. This fascinating site also includes essays on film at the turn of the century, the actuality film genre, and early motion-picture information.

Films in the Works

http://www.boxoff.com/cgi/filmwork.pl?filename=filmwork.txt

This kind of site is what the Web is all about, getting information before your friends. You can search for keywords, if you're looking for a sequel, or just browse through the titles and link to information about the movie.

Hollywood Online

http://www.hollywood.com/

News, chat rooms, charts, information on upcoming film festivals, plenty of sound bytes, merchandise, and of course some fun sweepstakes.

The Internet Movie Database

http://www.msstate.edu/Movies/

The Internet movie resource provides information on over 65,000 movies and TV shows. Search for a film of interest to learn about the cast, production company, and staff on the film. This site also includes stills from films, sound clips, and synopses of the films. Check out the Goofs and Location sections for some hilarious info on screw-ups and hellish conditions.

Movie Reviews.com

http://moviereviews.com/

Don't let the name fool you; this site is much more than your ordinary review site. Joining in is more than welcome; you can join experts, or pick a topic such as sex in films or chick flicks to talk about, but, best of all, there's a place to rate the worst movie of all time.

MovieLink 777-FILM Online

http://www.movielink.com

If you live in one of America's larger cities, enter your zip code to see current show times. Local theater locations and up-to-the-minute show times for movies in 25 cities are part of this site. The Cafe includes previews, reviews of films, a parents' guide, and a list of relevant newsgroups.

Movienet

http://www.movienet.com/

Find listings by city or movie of what's showing at Landmark Theaters, read about upcoming films, or just see what's new in the movie business.

Mr. Showbiz

http://web3.starwave.com/showbiz/

A great site for Hollywood gossip queens. Read crazy interviews about the latest films, participate in pure fluff about serious American events, and enjoy it! Not only does this site look good, but it has "substance"!

Popcorn

http://members.tripod.com/~AmyDo/Index.htm

Teen movie reviewer Amy Do looks at popular films from a young person's perspective. She provides a fairly extensive list of titles and reviews, alphabetized for easy access. The color scheme on review pages is a bit much, but kids will enjoy it. Read the celebrity gossip, send email to the reviewer, vote for favorite movies and stars.

Showtimes Home Page

http://www.showtimes.com/

A great place to find links to the pages of movies currently in the theater.

United Film Distributors

http://www.unitedleisure.com/ufd/

A distributing house with some movie names that you may not recognize, but actors you probably will. An interesting look at smaller films.

ROMANCE

Jerry Maguire

http://www.spe.sony.com/Pictures/SonyMovies/movies/jerrymaguire/index.html

This film is full of lovable characters (if you don't end up crazy for Ray, at least, something's wrong with your heart). Lots of interactivity at this site, especially in the Advice Area. Read the archived love lessons, click the character photos to see the advice from each character to Jerry or Dorothy, accept at least some of the advice to see what fun ensues, and more.

The Mirror Has Two Faces

http://www.spe.sony.com/Pictures/SonyMovies/features/mirror.html

Loaded with hearts and a lot of pink, this official Web site for the film provides plenty of multimedia action: video, stills (except, oddly, for having no stills of Barbra Streisand), and sound bytes. An extensive and rather laudatory history of Streisand's work joins short biographies of the other players in the film and other background information.

The Princess Bride

http://faraday.clas.virginia.edu/~dan8s/pbride.html

If you can't recite it line-for-line, you haven't seen it enough times. Link to different parts of the movie by choosing a picture, and then check out how other people have paid homage to Buttercup.

Sabrina (1995)

http://voyager.paramount.com/sabrina/

Okay, maybe we're not talking Bogey and Hepburn, but this remake still has some nice chemistry. The site offers publicity stills, bios of the principal cast members (did you know that Harrison Ford was in the cast of *American Graffiti*?), some nice quotes from the actors in the summation of the film's plot, and of course the requisite background info on the filming.

SCIENCE FICTION/FANTASY

2019: Off-World (Blade Runner Page)

http://kzsu.stanford.edu/uwi/br/

From links to small sites with a few pictures and essays to huge sites with nothing but Blade Runner info, as well as a warehouse of information on the page itself, you won't have any questions left after visiting.

Alien

http://ng.netgate.net/~alvaro/alien/alien.htm

Find behind-the-scenes info, stills, lines, scripts, and lots of other goodies from all three films in the series at this site.

Alien Autopsy

http://www.trudang.com/autopsy.html

It may be a short film, but it had a long impact. More than a year after its premier on the Fox broadcasting network and in video stores, people are still talking about whether the thing is a fake or is based on a real autopsy of a real alien corpse found in Roswell. Check out this site and its links and decide for yourself.

Back to the Future

http://www.pi.net/~eeersel/

The author of this page would like to have an individual page for each installment in this trilogy starring Michael J. Fox, but for now, he has synopses of each on the front page.

A B C D E F G H I J K L M N O P Q R S T U V W X Y Z

Dune

http://www.eerie.fr/~tassin/Dune/dune.html

Frank Herbert's science fiction classic can be found here with links to the main characters, the book, and more information about Herbert's legacy.

Flash Gordon

http://www.geocities.com/Hollywood/4262/

Read other people's comments and contribute your own after you look through the credits, pictures, plot, music, and quotes. You also have the opportunity to buy the movie right off this page.

Independence Day

http://www.id4movie.com/gateway.html

If you loved the movie, you'll be nuts about this interactive Web site in Shocked or unShocked version! Games, an interactive comic book, contests, an extensive "alien" database, and lots of other fun stuff.

The Lost World

http://www.lost-world.com/

In the official site of *Jurassic Park*'s sequel, you can take a Myst-like tour through tons of movie information. Not great with a modem connection; to truly enjoy the site, you need patience or a fast connection.

Mithral Web

http://mithral.iit.edu:8080/highlander/

The unofficial *Highlander* site will link you to many other pages run by people who share a passion for this film, as well as to the pages that fans like to visit.

Phantasm

http://www.phantasm.com/

When a movie's been around this long and still has a unique URL, you know it's here to stay. Take a tour of the Tall Man's Mausoleum, or check out what he has to say to you. It's a site definitely worth checking out, even if it's only for job openings.

The Phantom

http://www.thephantom.com/

If you like the guy in purple, stop by here. Even before the release of the theatrical film based on the comic books, this site was up and running for Phantom fans. Join the Jungle Patrol and explore the Skull Cave, check out the pics and sounds, and be sure to review the production notes for the inside scoop on the "making of."

The Relic

http://www.relic.com/

If the coming attractions didn't scare you, undoubtedly the movie did. The site is creepily reminiscent of the film, and includes extensive background information on the book, the filming, the cast, and the crew.

Star Trek: First Contact

http://firstcontact.msn.com/

Paramount and The Microsoft Network cooked up this joint Web page project. Click the appropriate ENGAGE button to choose a frames or non-frames version, and review the cast and filmmaker information, dossiers on the characters, and plenty of interesting visual images—including a gallery of art created especially for the film.

Star Trek: WWW

http://www.vol.it/luca/startrek/index.html

Not surprisingly, other *Star Trek* pages also abound on the Web. Use this one as a starting point, and then link away to many other pages and see what pieces of Trek lore you can pick up along the way.

The Star Wars Collectors Home Page

http://www.toysrgus.com/

This site has tons of information on *Star Wars* toys, posters, movie props, food, new collectibles, bootlegs, and many more types of *Star Wars* collectibles. This page also has links to Toy Shop, Action Figure Digest, and *The Star Wars Collector Magazine.*

Star Wars Home Page at UPENN

http://stwing.resnet.upenn.edu:8001/~jruspini/starwars.html

A great site that includes *Star Wars* FAQs, art, the Dark Forces Demo, and dozens of articles on different *Star Wars* characters and equipment used in the trilogy.

Until the End of the World

http://www.panix.com/~archii/uteotw/

If you've seen the movie, you'll recognize the wallpaper throughout the site, which is a great effect. Hopefully it'll intrigue you if you haven't seen it. Check out the Themes link, as well as those that take you to the people involved.

MUDS: MULTIPLE USER DUNGEONS

When there are no more dragons to slay, how will you make a living, knight?

Draco in Dragonheart *(1996)*

AmberMush

http://www.amber.godlike.com/

Based on Roger Zelany's Amber series, the site is HUGE with myriad links to all its component parts (how to create a character, how to join, rules, etc.), character pages, artwork, plus links to other Amber sites and games.

Arcadia MUD

http://www.arcadia.net/

Find out if you would like to join this detailed MUD by reading the FAQ and history of Arcadia. See a list of all the characters, contact the game administrators and Web page designers, and check out 3D maps of the Arcadia world.

Avalon: The Legend Lives

http://www.avalon-rpg.com/

Avalon claims to be the biggest game of its kind. A fee-based game, you can review all aspects of Avalon without paying, and then after you join you have five free hours to see whether you like it.

ElendorMUSH
http://www.sitr.on.ca/elendor/

Basic Information about MUDs and MUDding

http://www.lysator.liu.se/mud/faq/faq1.html

Probably the best single FAQ (Frequently Asked Questions) sheet on MUDs and related sites. It covers most of the material you need to know, plus answers to the all-important question: Where do I find MUDs, MOOs, and others?

The Center for Imaginary Enviroments

http://www.imaginary.com/

The CIE is a nonprofit organization that supports multiuser environments and the technology on which such MU*s are based. The CIE membership is most active in developing worlds using LCP and Java languages. They maintain an archive, mailing lists, and a domain for referencing various MUDs.

CWRL MUSH & MOO Page

http://www.cwrl.utexas.edu/moo/

A site based on research projects concerning MUDs, MOOs, MUCKs, and other game environments. While the site is full of suggestions and tutorials on getting started as a player, the page hasn't been updated in a while and some of the links are no longer functioning. But still it looks like a good place to start when you want to learn how to play, or want the theory behind these game worlds.

ElendorMUSH

http://www.sitr.on.ca/elendor/

The oldest (over 2,000 users) and best Tolkien-based MUSH in existence. The site gives information on how to join the game, plus limited information about the world and how to play in it.

FurryMuck

http://www.furry.com/index.shtml

FurryMUCK is a MUD where people assume the roles of Anthropomorphics (the giving of humanlike qualities to non-human animals). Mucks are nothing more than MUDs given another name, though it seems that most MUCKs are light in tone than other MU*s. (MU* refers to *any* multi-user environment: MUD, MUSH, MOO, etc.) FurryMUCK is one of the oldest and largest Furry MU*s around. The site describes what FurryMUCK is about, how to enter, and hints on how to play.

The Imaginative Builders' Guild

http://ibg.bcn.net/

The Imaginative Builders' Guild is designed for people who build MU*s. Its primary function is to serve as the entry point for the mailing list run by the Guild, but it has links to various sites that serve as resources for the world designers to use and study.

LPMud FAQ

http://www.imaginary.com/LPMud/lpmud_faq.html

This FAQ is about LPMuds, a special type of MUD. LP refers to the language in which it was written. The emphasis of LPMuds seems to be on role playing, as opposed to other MUDS, which are often more social in nature. This site also goes into depth on the creation of LPMuds, and where to seek the codes necessary to create one.

MOO-Cows Faq

http://www.moo.mud.org/moo-faq/moo-faq-1.html#ss1.1

MOO stands for MUD, Object Oriented. It's based upon the LambdaMOO server, which is the most commonly used program to run MOOs. Essentially this site is for someone who wants to set up a MU* using the MOO format. It covers all the information necessary for the beginning world builder.

The MUD/MUSH/MOO Catalog of Catalogs

http://www.educ.kent.edu/mu/catofcat.html

This simple site provides links to the largest MUD and other Internet game lists in the country.

The MUDdex

http://www.apocalypse.org/pub/u/lpb/muddex/

A collection of documents and sites pertaining to the history and development of MUDs. It includes logs from various MUDs past and present, plus some tips for play.

MudServices.Com

http://www.mudservices.com/home/why.html

One of several services that permits, for a fee, a MU* to run from their system. Although they don't do code, they do provide a code library for assistance. The descriptions of their services and fee plans seems quite clear and useful.

Outer Space

http://mud.stack.urc.tue.nl/

Check out a new MUD out of the Netherlands. This site provides info on the MUDs setting, FAQs on joining as a Wizard and signing up to play, information on usable domains, and a connection for beginning the game.

PernMUSH Unofficial Homepage

http://www.loach.org/~pern/

An unendorsed site dedicated to the PernMUSH game. The game is based on the *Dragonriders of Pern* novels by Anne McCaffery. This is a very extensive fan site, run by the players themselves instead of the game builders. For a Pern fan, even if you don't play in the MUSH, it's still a fun read.

The Realm

http://www.realmserver.com/

Sierra On-line's graphical MUD promises to be the future in Internet MUD gaming. Create a 3D character and enter him or her into the fantasy world. You can also chat and solve puzzles using this service.

The Unofficial Official Beginners Guide to MUSHing

http://mulberry.com/~tuna/bgm.html

MUSHs are another form of MUDs, but seem strictly aimed at role playing. MUSH itself didn't stand for anything, but later the developers said it stood for Multi-User Shared Hallucination. This site is another FAQ, but without the technical emphasis found on some other sites. It's aimed at the beginner who just wants to play, and doesn't want to develop a world of his/her own.

WebRPG Online

http://www.webrpg.com/?link=gamesystem/index.html

A freeware program that permits players to role play any RPG online together. Essentially a modified chat room, WebRPG serves as the "table" around which the players gather. It includes a dice feature to create random numbers, a toolbox to create maps, customized character sheets, and much more. It's perfect for a few friends who want to game but are scattered around the country—a mini-MU* in real time.

Welcome to the World Wide Web Dungeon

http://www.cling.gu.se/~cl0polau/3wd/3wd.htm

This isn't really a MUD, but is an interesting 3D dungeon you navigate through on the Web. Eventually all MUDs might look like this. The interface provides six arrows; click the direction you want to go, wait a few seconds, and you're closer to your goal.

NEWSGROUPS

alt.mud

de.alt.mud

erml.moo

rec.games.mud

tw.bbs.rec.mud

FTP & GOPHER SITES

ftp.envy.com

ftp.pvv.unit.no

ftp.tcp.com

ftp.warwick.ac.uk

gopher://cyberion.bbn.com/1

gopher://earth.usa.net/11/games

gopher://spinaltap.micro.umn.edu/11/fun/Games/MUDs/Links

MAILING LISTS

benden-l

conjunction-l

CRYSTAL

darkgift

olympia-mush

PERN-RP

urban-legends-l

Related Sites

http://fp.roy.org/

http://scuba.uwsuper.edu/~sfenness/mud.html

http://snowfox.fur.com/tapestries/

http://www.accursed.org/main.htm

http://www.dm.mudservices.com/mainwhole.htm

http://www.geocities.com/TimesSquare/9310/

http://www.mudconnector.com/mud_graphical.html

http://www.shsu.edu/~genlpc/

http://www.webring.org/cgi-bin/webring?ring=muxnmush&id=82&index

http://www.worlds-apart.com/

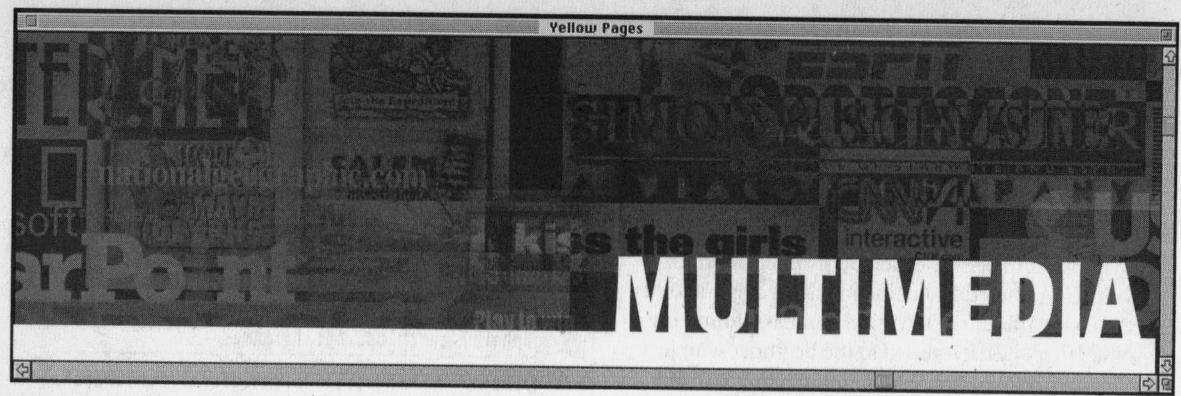

> Microsoft programs are generally bug free.
>
> *Bill Gates*

ASK Multimedia Ltd.

http://www.askm.co.uk/

You can take a guided tour of this Web site, the site of ASK Multimedia, a multimedia producer. Learn about the ASK training management tools, about multimedia, and about the company and how to contact it.

AV Video & Multimedia Producer Magazine

http://165.247.175.190/av_mmp/

This site provides excerpts of articles from *AV Video & Multimedia Producer* magazine, as well as "digital treats," a salute to 100 multimedia pioneers, annual competition and award info, subscriptions, a media kit, and a "meet the editors" page.

Cyberglitz–About

http://www.cyberglitz.com/index.htm

The opening page boasts, "CyberGlitz...because glitz is good!" The company offers custom development of multimedia programs, support for your own projects, and Web page design. The site also offers a color primer, to brief you on the use of color; some animated GIFs to inform you on color theory; and a fun photo essay.

Welcome to Macvideo Interactive
http://www.macvideo.com/

Kennerly Music Productions

http://www.kenmusic.com/index.html

At this site you can order Multimedia Soundtracks, Volume One, a collection of royalty-free production music on CD-ROM. Free samples and demos give you a taste of what's on the CD. You can also learn about the Media Soundtracks browser.

Maris Multimedia Product–Full Catalogue

http://www.maris.com/kdgfolder/ownhtm/catalog.htm

An online catalog of multimedia offerings on CD-ROM. Choose from titles related to astronomy and aviation, plus a few miscellaneous titles. Order online, send in your registration, or get tech support.

MediaBuilder–Multimedia

http://mediabuilder.com/softwaremmedia.html

Use MediaBuilder to build up your software library of multimedia authoring tools, plug-ins, and file managers. From this site you can jump to and download scores of freeware, shareware, and demo programs that will help you work with sound, video, graphics, music, text, and animation.

Mind2Media: Our Team

http://www.mind2media.com/index3.html

The team members of the Mind2Media multimedia company can work with you to make your projects and ideas take shape. Their Web site tells you about who they are and what they do, provides a portfolio of their work, gives you tips and info on the digital industry, and instructs you on how to contact them.

PC-Based Multimedia

http://www.newspage.com/browse/46537/46541/

This page of NewsPage, an interactive news service, offers a line-up of articles on PC-based multimedia. Article categories range from Multimedia Peripherals to Video & Multimedia to Desktop Videoconferencing.

Pixital Imageworks

http://www.pixital.com/

The people at Pixital Imageworks provide graphics, Web page design, art, business presentations, technical support, and video. At their web site, you can look into their rates and read about their clients, plus see what they have to offer in the areas of games, design, art, PC technical aid, tools, and downloads.

Technocrats, Inc. Graphics and MultiMedia Page

http://www.shinycode.com/gmm.html

This company provides Web-site graphics; assistance in producing documents; demonstration and training applications; database design, recovery, and conversion; multimedia creations; and other products and services. Visit the site for details.

The DigiDoc Home Page

http://www.digidocpro.com/

Company info, sales and services, and customer service areas are offered at the site. DigiDoc Productions is a compact disc manufacturing company in California.

Welcome to Macvideo Interactive

http://www.macvideo.com/

Digital video, cross-platform authoring, interactive CD-ROM, and Internet solutions—if you have needs or interests in any of these areas, this is the site to visit. You can contact MacVideo directly via phone, fax, or email.

NEWSGROUPS

comp.multimedia

comp.org.ieee

comp.os.ms-windows.programmer.multimedia

comp.sys.ibm.pc.hardware.video

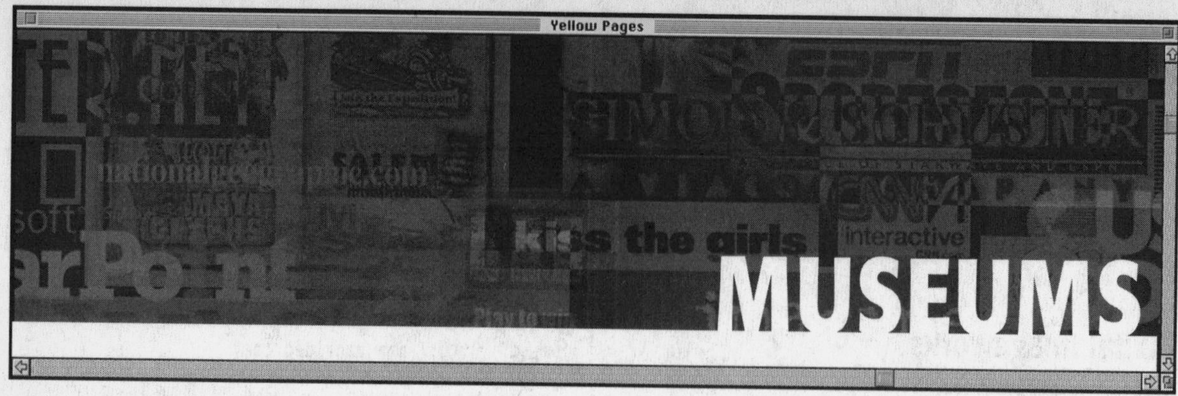

A
B
C
D
E
F
G
H
I
J
K
L
M
N
O
P
Q
R
S
T
U
V
W
X
Y
Z

> I want to make of Impressionism something solid and lasting like the art in the museums.
>
> *Paul Cezanne*

For art lovers, this category will take you through online museums that cover art, architecture, history and culture, photography and film, and sculpture. Here you also will find FTP, Gopher, Listserv, and newsgroups!

ARCHITECTURE

Alvar Aalto Museum

http://192.102.40.8:80/aalto/

The Alvar Aalto Museum preserves, researches, and maintains a permanent display of material related to Aalto's work as an architect and designer. The site contains information about and pictures of Aalto's buildings, which are located around the world.

The Chicago Athenaeum: The Museum of Architecture and Design

http://www.chi-athenaeum.org/

The Chicago Athenaeum features "Landmark Chicago," the first permanent exhibition celebrating Chicago's position as the world capital of historical and contemporary landmarks of modern architecture. This site contains information and photos from this exhibit, as well as other details about the museum and its upcoming schedule.

NRP TOP PICKS

Addison Gallery of American Art
http://www.andover.edu/addison/home.html

The Andy Warhol Museum
http://www.clpgh.org/warhol/

Indianapolis Museum of Art
http://web.ima-art.org/ima/home.html

The National Portrait Gallery
http://www.npg.si.edu/

The Smithsonian Institution
http://www.si.edu/newstart.htm

Museum of Contemporary Ideas
http://toolshed.artschool.utas.edu.au/moci/home.html

The Carnegie Museum of Natural History
http://www.clpgh.org/cmnh/

Berkeley Art Museum/Pacific Film Archive
http://www.uampfa.berkeley.edu/

The Exploratorium
http://www.exploratorium.edu/

Grier Musser Museum

http://www.isi.edu/sims/sheila/gm.html

If you'd like to relive the charm of Victorian Los Angeles, this is the museum for you. The site contains photos of the different rooms of the museum, all of which are decked out in Victorian decor.

National Building Museum

http://www.nbm.org/

The National Building Museum presents permanent exhibitions about the world we live in, from our homes and offices to our parks and cities. This site has online excerpts of exhibits past and present, as well as information about books that complement them. There also are summaries from "The Urban

Forum," a program designed to explore issues related to the design, growth, and governance of American cities.

Netherlands Architecture Institute

http://www.nai.nl/nai_eng.html

Site contains exhibitions, lectures, and other activities from this museum, which houses a vast collection of works from Dutch architects and many others. It contains everything about the epicenter of Dutch architecture, including a link to *Archis*, a Dutch/English monthly magazine about architecture, urban design, and visual arts.

Wharton Eshrick Museum

http://www.levins.com/esherick.html

Site features the life and work of this "Dean of American Craftsmen." Photos include the world-famous spiral oak staircase from his studio in Pennsylvania, and Eshrick's regional influences are discussed.

ART

Addison Gallery of American Art

http://www.andover.edu/addison/home.html

Contains descriptions and photos from current and upcoming exhibits. The museum's permanent collection has over 12,000 works, including significant paintings, prints, works on paper, sculpture, decorative arts, and photography.

The African/Edenic Heritage Museum

http://village.ios.com/~dckog/museum.htm

This traveling exhibit highlights the indigenous African presence in the Holy Land. Among the fascinating subjects explored is scientists' theory that Eve was more likely a dark-haired, black-skinned woman. Site contains pictures and maps from the exhibit.

Agung Rai Museum of Art

http://www.nusantara.com/arma/

This Indonesian museum houses a collection of works by Balinese, Javanese, and foreign artists. Select works are shown on the site, and they're a fascinating display of history and culture.

Alexandria Museum of Art

http://cenla.lacollege.edu/arts/amoa/amoa.html

Recently named "one of the most innovative museums in Louisiana," it contains a collection of contemporary Louisiana art and an array of local, regional, and national exhibits, including the state's largest collection of North Louisiana folk art. The page contains descriptions of the museum's galleries and a calendar of upcoming exhibitions.

The Andy Warhol Museum

http://www.clpgh.org/warhol/

This page contains a guided tour of the Pittsburgh museum that opened in 1994, as well as examples of Andy's artwork. It also describes the work of the Archives Study Center, which collects and preserves anything to do with Warhol's life and work. A calendar details upcoming exhibitions and events.

The Art Institute of Chicago

http://www.artic.edu/aic/firstpage.html

Comprising both a museum and an art school, the institute's 10 curatorial departments have collections numbering more than 300,000 works of art, including one of the finest collections of Impressionist art in the world, with 33 paintings by Claude Monet. The institute also is the home of *A Sunday on La Grange Jatte—1884*, the famous painting by George Seurat that can be seen at this site, and Grant Wood's famous *American Gothic*, among others.

Asian Art Museum of San Francisco

http://sfasian.apple.com/

This is the largest museum in the western world devoted to the arts and cultures of Asia. The museum's collections represent over 40 Asian countries spanning 6,000 years of history. This site provides information about exhibits and programs at the museum, as well as job openings there.

The Brooklyn Museum

http://wwar.com/brooklyn_museum/index.html

The second largest museum in the State of New York, The Brooklyn Museum features a collection of over 1.5 million objects, including works from Ancient Egypt, the arts of Asia, Africa, the Pacific, and the Americas, decorative arts, painting, and sculpture.

Canadian Wildlife and Wilderness Art Museum

http://intranet.ca/cawa/

Contains representative works of Canada's internationally acclaimed wildlife and wilderness painters, sculptors, and carvers. Includes a gallery of artwork, as well as a bio of and artwork by Robert Lougheed, one of North America's best known wildlife and Western artists.

The Chrysler Museum of Art and Historic Houses

http://www.whro.org/cl/cmhh/

The museum's collection of 30,000 objects spans almost 4,000 years of art history. It includes a world-renowned collection of European and American painting and sculpture, an internationally famous glass collection, as well as art from African, Asian, Egyptian, Pre-Columbian, and Islamic cultures.

The Columbia Museum of Art

http://www.scsn.net/users/cma/index.html

The museum's exhibits contain European and American fine and decorative art representing a time period of nearly seven centuries. Its public collections of Renaissance and Baroque art include works by Botticelli, Boucher, Canaletto, Tintoretto, and many others. In 1998, the museum will be moving to a new and larger facility, making it the largest art museum in South Carolina.

The Dallas Museum of Art

http://www.unt.edu/dfw/dma/www/dma.htm

The museum's holdings include ancient American, African, Indonesian, and contemporary art, as well as American decorative arts. The site includes photos from the museum's galleries as well as from several outdoor display areas for large sculptures.

The Finnish National Gallery

http://www.fng.fi/fng/html2/en/

Visit the collections at its three specialist museums—Sinebrychoff, the Museum of Foreign Art; Ateneum, the Museum of Finnish Art; and the Museum of Contemporary Art—which cover a period of eight centuries. Site contains links to the gallery's Central Art Archives as well as the capability to search for information about a particular artist or work.

The Florida Museum of Hispanic and Latin American Art

http://www.latinoweb.com/museo/

This is the first and only museum dedicated 100 percent to Hispanic and Latin American art. (This includes Spain and Latin America, as well as non-Spanish speaking countries such as Brazil and Haiti.) The museum has 11 exhibits per year and is a contemporary art museum, not a historical or pre-Colombian museum. The education department organizes courses in art, literature, music, poetry, and more.

Gallery of Modern Art, Glasgow

http://www.goma.glasgow.gov.uk/

Although this site was still under construction at this book's writing, it has the beginnings of a great Web site. The site has four galleries—Fire Gallery, Earth Gallery, Water Gallery, and Air Gallery. Definitely a site to bookmark and come back to as it progresses.

Guggenheim Museum

http://math240.lehman.cuny.edu/gugg/

Site contains information about the four sections of the museum —the Solomon R. Guggenheim Museum on Fifth Avenue in New York City; the Guggenheim Museum SoHo on Broadway in New York City; the Guggenheim Museum in Bilbao, Spain; and the Peggy Guggenheim Collection in Venice, Italy. Includes some great photos of the museums and their exhibits.

Henie Onstad Art Center

http://www.hok.no/index-e.html

Henie Onstad Art Centre has one of the largest collections of international contemporary art in Norway. Its permanent collection includes works by Picasso, Matisse, Beuys, Vasarely, the COBRA artists and Warhol.

Indianapolis Museum of Art

http://web.ima-art.org/ima/home.html

The nation's seventh-largest general art museum has permanent collections of African, American, Asian, contemporary, decorative, and European art, as well as a textiles and costumes collection, and prints, drawings, and photographs. The IMA complex is surrounded by a 152-acre park, including 50 acres that are accessible to the public and are intensively gardened.

Institute of Contemporary Arts

`http://www.illumin.co.uk/ica/`

Specializes in exhibiting contemporary visual arts, performance art, cultural discourse, and criticism, cinema and video. There is also a substantial archive of video and audio recordings, which can be browsed on the site.

The Institute of Egyptian Art and Archeology

`http://www.memst.edu/egypt/main.html`

Site includes photos and information from its Egyptian artifacts exhibit, and you can take a virtual tour of over a dozen ancient Egyptian sites along the Nile River. Also contains links to other sites that provide information about Egypt.

International Children's Art Museum

`http://www.icamsf.com/`

The International Children's Art Museum in San Francisco features artwork from children around the world. This site has information about the museum and its programs. It also features an online gallery with exhibitions from the museums permanent collection.

The Kemper Museum of Contemporary Art and Design

`http://www.kemperart.org/`

Site includes a calendar of events, the history and architecture of the Museum, images from the collection, and a guest book. The museum also boasts a notable Georgia O'Keefe collection, several watercolors of which can be viewed at this site.

Le Louvre

`http://mistral.culture.fr/louvre/`

Official site of this famous museum, the home of the *Mona Lisa.* Includes information about the museum's seven departments: Oriental Antiquities (with a section dedicated to Islamic Art); Egyptian Antiquities (with a section dedicated to Coptic Art); Greek, Etruscan and Roman Antiquities; Paintings; Sculptures; Objets d'Art; and Prints and Drawings. Site includes many details (a small section of a painting, enlarged so you can see it better) from the museum's collections.

Leonardo da Vinci Museum

`http://www.leonardo.net/museum/main.html`

A virtual museum devoted to the works of da Vinci, and not just his most famous oil paintings, the *Mona Lisa* and *The Last Supper.* Site also includes some of his drawings and sketches, his engineering and futuristic designs, and historical details about his life. Some of the photos of his art are small and hard to see, but there's tons information here.

Metropolitan Museum of Art, New York

`http://www.metmuseum.org/`

One of the largest art museums in the world, its collections include more than two million works of art—several hundred thousand of which are on view at any given time—spanning more than 5,000 years of world culture, from prehistory to the present. Site has an educational section for different age levels and interests, including "Looking at Art," which discusses composition and theme.

Minnesota Museum of American Art

`http://www.mtn.org/mmaa/`

Information about museum hours, tours, classes and exhibits. Read the write up on the exhibit and then visit each Gallery to view the virtual version. Fun and educational.

Museum of American Folk Art

`http://www.folkartmuse.org/`

Site contains samples from traditional and contemporary folk art exhibitions, information about educational programs, and a link to *Folk Art* magazine. Also contains a description of upcoming exhibits and a calendar of traveling exhibits.

Museum of Arts and Crafts

`http://web.cnam.fr/museum/index-a.html`

This French site (viewed in French or English) contains a QuickTime virtual visit to Foucault's pendulum in the Pantheon, a RealAudio tape of a dulcimer player, and a link to online radio. It also has a database of 45,000 objects online. The site can be a little confusing at times, but there are many neat links to follow.

A B C D E F G H I J K L M N O P Q R S T U V W X Y Z

Museum of Bad Art

`http://glyphs.com/moba/`

The Museum of Bad Art is dedicated to the collection, preservation, exhibition, and celebration of bad art. Site contains many examples of bad art, including one rather amusing piece entitled "Sunday On The Pot With George." (Hint: If you don't understand the allusion here, you probably won't understand why this art is so bad and why this museum is so great.)

Museum of Fine Arts, Boston

`http://www.mfa.org/`

Museum prides itself on exhibiting art that is "past and present, old and new, plain and fancy," including masterpieces by Renoir, Monet, Sargent, Turner, Gauguin, and others. The site hosts an online exhibition and contains links to samples from upcoming exhibits.

Museum of Fine Arts, Houston

`http://mfah.org/`

The Museum of Fine Arts, Houston site includes visuals and information about the permanent collection, traveling exhibitions, events, and educational programs. Collections with online links include African sculpture, American painting, ancient art, decorative arts, Impressionist painting, and twentieth-century sculpture.

Museum of Modern Art, New York

`http://www.moma.org/`

Site displays samples from current and future exhibits as well as its permanent collection, which includes painting and sculpture, drawings, prints and illustrated books, architecture and design, photography, and film and video. The collection includes exceptional groups of work by Matisse, Picasso, Miró, Mondrian, Brancusi, and Pollock. The museum owns over 13,000 films, and the site has a calendar of the museum's film and video programs. It also contains links to other Web sites created in conjunction with the Museum of Modern Art and its exhibits.

National Gallery of Canada

`http://national.gallery.ca/`

The National Gallery of Canada is the permanent home of Canada's exceptional national art collection, which includes Canadian art, Inuit art, contemporary art, as well as European, American, and Asian art. It plans to put its entire collection online by the summer of 1998.

Royal Ontario Museum

`http://www.rom.on.ca/`

This large museum has Greek, Roman, and Far Eastern art, archaeology, and natural sciences collections, as well as Native ethnology and natural history collections. Virtual exhibits include educational activities such as games, quizzes, and QuickTime movies, as well as online artifact identification and curatorial research.

Webmuseum

`http://sunsite.unc.edu/louvre/`

Site includes a small tour of Paris, a unique famous paintings collection, and an exhibition of medieval art, "Les tres riches heures du Duc de Ber." The site always features at least one special exhibit—at this book's writing, it was a great collection of works by Paul Cèzanne, one of the greatest of the Postimpressionists.

Whitney Museum of American Art

`http://www.echonyc.com/~whitney/`

Site contains selections from the permanent collection of 20th-century American art as well as links to other art museums. The museum also sponsors artists working on the Web and provides links to some artists' Web projects.

Yokohama Museum of Art

`http://www.art-museum.city.yokohama.jp/index_e.html`

Site provides links and photos from exhibits, past and present. It also gives descriptions and maps of the different areas of the museum.

ART EXHIBITS AND MUSEUMS

Albrecht-Kemper Museum of Art

`http://www.albrecht-kemper.org/`

One of the Midwest's finest American art museums is in St. Joseph, Missouri. The Albrecht-Kemper is home to an extraordinary group of colonial portraits, rich holdings of American landscapes as well as distinguished examples of American Impressionism and post-Impressionist artists of the Boston School. The museum also features work by important 20th century artists and a growing contemporary collection.

The Andy Warhol Museum

http://www.clpgh.org/warhol/

One of the most famous artists of the late 20th century, Andy Warhol's work has influenced an entire generation of fine artists. This site is part of the Carnegie Museums of Pittsburg, and features Warhol images and biographical information.

ArtCity

http://www.artcity.com/

ArtCity is a fine arts multimedia production company that provides Web space to various galleries. Their diverse collection includes glass-blowing, tattooing, sculpture, and more.

The Art Institute of Chicago

http://www.artic.edu/aic/firstpage.html

Everything you always wanted to know about this museum. Includes information about exhibits and collections, the history and layout of the museum site, publications and press releases, gift shop items, and Institute membership information.

Asian Art Museum of San Francisco

http://sfasian.apple.com/

The Asian Art Museum of San Francisco is the largest museum in the western world devoted to the arts and cultures of Asia. The Asian's world-class permanent collections represent over 40 Asian countries spanning 6,000 years of history.

The Electric Art Gallery

http://www.egallery.com/

Features the work of over 200 artists (mostly contemporary) divided into categories such as Haitian, Southwest, Amazon, and Folk. Nicely designed and easy to navigate.

Hot Art Links

http://www.big.com/ae/lnk4.html

Hundreds of diverse links to art-related Web sites.

The Indianapolis Museum of Art

http://web.ima-art.org/ima/

A thorough overview of this Indianapolis museum, its programs, its special events, and its art offerings.

Museum of American Folk Art

http://www.folkartmuse.org/

The Museum of American Folk Art, located in New York City, is dedicated to exploring the diversity of American culture as expressed through folk art. At their site you'll find scanned images of art and artist information, and you can learn about the museum's educational programs and subscribe to *Folk Art Magazine.*

National Gallery of Canada

http://national.gallery.ca/

With text descriptions in both French and English, this well-designed site showcases this large gallery housing the Canadian national art collection.

The National Portrait Gallery

http://www.npg.si.edu/

A fascinating look at history through portraiture. This site features many scanned images of portraits of famous individuals and groups, including portraits of all 41 United States presidents.

The Smithsonian Institution

http://www.si.edu/newstart.htm

Whether you're interested in its museums, tours, events, or shops, you'll find lots of Smithsonian information at this site. Very well organized!

Smithsonian Photographs Online

http://photo2.si.edu/

This site makes the photographic offerings of the Smithsonian available online. Browse the contents, or search a huge library of photographs by keyword.

Viewtopia Online Art Gallery

http://www.viewtopia.com/

This site has lots of scanned images of modern artwork from many different galleries (mostly in Texas) available to view online. You can search by artist, gallery, or category.

HISTORY AND CULTURE

Bosnia & Herzegovina Pavilion at XIX Triennale di Milano

http://www.iht.it/arte/bih/bos-id-e.htm

Contains pictures and a wealth of historical information from the show "Reconstruction of Bosnia & Herzegovina," shown at the Triennale di Milano XIX Esposizione Internazionale. The page is available in Italian, English, and Bosniac, and contains links to other Web sites concerning Bosnia-Herzegovina.

Morikami Museum and Japanese Gardens

http://www.icsi.com/ics/morikami/

The only museum in the United States dedicated exclusively to the living culture of Japan. The museum contains a rare Bonsai collection of miniature trees and has beautiful Japanese-style landscaping. Sample photos from the museum's exhibits of Japanese arts, crafts, and artifacts are included at this site.

Online Museum of Singapore Art and History

http://www.museum.org.sg/

This site contains links to the National Archives of Singapore, the National Museum of Singapore, the Asian Civilizations Museum, the Singapore History Museum, and the Singapore Art Museum. Information about each of these museums is provided, along with calendars, photos, and a plethora of information.

The Smithsonian Institution

http://www.si.edu/newstart.htm

The 150-year-old Smithsonian Institute comprises the National Portrait Gallery, the National Museum of American Art, the National Air and Space Museum, the Sackler Gallery, the Cooper-Hewitt Museum of Design, the National Museum of American History, the National Museum of Natural History and more. This site defies categorization, as it has a lot of everything.

United States Holocaust Memorial Museum

http://www.ushmm.org/

This museum is an international resource for the development of research on the Holocaust and related issues, including those of contemporary significance. Includes a photographic, film, and video archive. Site contains links to museum resources and activities, as well as to related organizations and an internship program.

MISCELLANEOUS

American Museum of Papermaking

http://www.ipst.edu/amp/

This renowned resource on the history of paper and paper technology features a collection of watermarks, papers, tools, machines, and manuscripts. You can go on a virtual tour of the museum and learn about topics such as forerunners to paper, the invention of the paper machine, and recycling in the paper industry.

Art Deco Erte Museum of Fashion and Theater Designs

http://www.webcom.com/ajarts/welcome.html

Cybermuseum in memory of the father of art deco, Romain de Tirtoff (1892-1990), known as "Erté." One of the foremost fashion and stage designers of the early twentieth century, he is remembered for the extravagant costumes and stage sets he designed for the Folies-Bergère in Paris and George White's Scandals in New York, as well as designs for the Broadway musical *Stardust* in 1988. This illustrated museum contains a selection of images drawn from throughout Erté's 80-year career.

Eli Whitney Museum

http://www.eliwhitney.org/

This museum and site are dedicated to exploring people's passion for making things. While this site was being overhauled at the time of this book's writing, it shall once again be a cool site one day. Bookmark it and check back when it's finished.

Graphion's Online Type Museum

`http://www.slip.net/~graphion/museum.html`

This site provides information about the history and practice of typesetting, including biographies of visionary typesetters and elements of typesetting style. There also is a question and answer page where you can request information, make suggestions, or ask any question your heart desires.

Ilias Lalaounis Jewelry Museum

`http://www.addgr.com/jewel/lalaouni/enindex.htm`

A museum devoted to the art of jewelry, its permanent collection houses over 3,000 designs. The gallery is organized into six categories—The Golden Dawn of Art, History of Greek Jewelry, Collections Inspired From 12 Civilizations, Nature, Technology and Biology, and Special Commissions. Photos are available on the site.

The Judah L. Magnes Jewish Museum

`http://www.jfed.org/Magnes/Magnes.htm`

The third largest Jewish museum in North America, it collects and displays treasures of Jewish art, history, and culture. The permanent collection includes paintings, sculptures, prints, drawings, and a film/video and photography collection. The site also provides information about libraries and archives, poetry and video competitions, and books and publications.

Kelsey Museum of Archeology

`http://www.umich.edu/~kelseydb/`

This site contains maps of the ancient world and other online resources for classical art and archeology. It also shows photos of objects on display in the museum's two main galleries, The Greek and Roman Gallery and The Egyptian and Near Eastern Gallery.

Living Museum of Letterpress Printing

`http://www.speakeasy.org/~eoeleven/`

This foundation dedicated to the preservation of the 550 year history of letterpress printing provides links to a reference library, tools of the trade, and much more. (This black-and-white site has some large graphics that take a while to come up. You'll probably need a fast modem and updated browser to view this site most effectively.)

Melbourne Museum of Printing

`http://www.vicnet.net.au/~typo/`

This is a working and teaching museum of type and printing. Its collection includes machines, info about fonts, and other printing items. It also has links to books and records that have to do with printing and businesses of that type (no pun intended).

Museum of Contemporary Ideas

`http://toolshed.artschool.utas.edu.au/moci/home.html`

This unique museum delves into the worlds of the visual arts, the philosophy of science, architecture, technology, performing arts, and off-planet systems. As of this book's writing, for example, the site had a sample chapter of a mystery novel and an Encyclopedia of Superfictions, which forces us to examine what is true and what is false.

Museum of Korean Embroidery

`http://samsung.expo.or.kr/pojagi/poja_m.html`

This museum boasts over 3,000 pieces of embroidery and other handicrafts created by women or used in the women's quarters of traditional Korea. The opening page of the site shows 20 beautiful samples, which you can click to enlarge them and read a description.

Museum of Outdoor Arts

`http://www.fine-art.com/museum/moa.html`

This museum offers people a place to enjoy picnics and concerts in an environment of fine art, architecture, and landscape. Site includes photos of the grounds and sculptures as well as information about the collection, exhibitions, and programs.

National Portrait Gallery

`http://www.npg.si.edu/`

The portraits in the Gallery's permanent collection number more that 7,000, including portraits of all 41 presidents (President Clinton's hasn't been added yet), all of which can be viewed at this site. Portraits of other individuals can be admitted to the collection 10 years after the death of the subject. Other permanent collections include "The Age of Revolution" and "Native Americans" and are supplemented by other special exhibits.

Stephen Birch Aquarium-Museum

http://aqua.ucsd.edu/

Part of the Scripps Institution of Oceanography, this aquarium has volunteer opportunities, educational programs, and summer learning adventures. This home page provides information about all these, plus links to what's new at the aquarium and membership information.

The Victoria and Albert Museum

http://www.vam.ac.uk/

The Victoria and Albert Museum is the largest museum of the decorative arts in the world. Today the beautiful Victorian and Edwardian buildings house 145 galleries containing some of the world's greatest collections of sculpture, furniture, fashion and textiles, paintings, silver, glass, ceramics, jewelry, books, prints, and photographs.

NATURAL HISTORY

American Museum of Natural History

http://www.amnh.org/

The museum's collections include over 30 million items, ranging from "dinosaur fossils, to a sixty-three-foot-long canoe carved by the Haida Indians, to a slice of a giant sequoia tree, to the costume of an African spirit dancer." The site lists a few of its thousands of research projects, along with some photos. The museum displays a wide range of temporary exhibits, which also can be explored at this site.

The Carnegie Museum of Natural History

http://www.clpgh.org/cmnh/

Founded in 1895, the Carnegie Museum of Natural History is one of the nation's leading research museums and is renowned for its Dinosaur Hall. This page was established to provide news the museum's events, as well as developments in the field of natural history in general. It is divided into 13 different and wide-ranging scientific sections, from anthropology and birds to minerals and nature reserves.

The Cleveland Museum of Natural History

http://www.cmnh.org/

This museum has over a million specimens in the fields of anthropology, archaeology, astronomy, botany, geology, paleontology, zoology, and wildlife biology. It also has astronomy programs, live animal shows, and a dinosaur discovery area. Site has links to exhibits and museum news.

Florida Museum of Natural History

http://www.flmnh.ufl.edu/

With over 16 million specimens, this is the largest museum of natural history in the Southern United States. This site features descriptions of its collections in both the Department of Anthropology and the Department of Natural Sciences, which includes mammals, birds, fossils, plants, and more.

The Museum of Natural History of the University of Pisa

http://astrpi.difi.unipi.it/Museo_di_Calci/MusSN.html

Site discusses the museum's natural history collections, consisting of about 200,000 items. The museum's 15 galleries contain exhibits including mineralogy, paleontology, and zoology to name a few, as well as a cetacean gallery that is unique in Europe for its size and number of specimens.

Natural History Museum in the United Kingdom

http://www.nhm.ac.uk/

This site defines and explains each of the museum's five main departments and also discusses its six focus areas for research. For each department (botany, zoology, entomology, paleontology, and mineralogy), the site provides photos and details about several ongoing research projects at the museum. You also can link to the Science Casebook, an interactive exploration of some of the museum's work.

Smithsonian National Museum of Natural History

http://nmnhwww.si.edu/nmnhweb.html

This extensive site has everything you ever wanted to know about this museum, and many things you wouldn't have thought to ask. (Do *you* know what a cephalopod is without looking it up?) The museum's seven scientific departments are: anthropology, botany, entomology, invertebrate zoology, mineral sciences, paleontology, and vertebrate zoology. Online exhibits at the time of this book's publication included "In Search of Giant Squid" and "Hologlobe." This is an amazing site, and even if you're not a science buff, you'll find it fascinating.

Swedish Museum of Natural History

http://www.nrm.se/

The largest museum in Sweden, it has over 18 million objects and is one of the 10 largest natural history museums in the world. The page is divided into research; exhibitions, events and education, and education; Cosmonova, one of the most modern Omnimax theaters in the world; and administration and service.

ORGANIZATIONS

African Americans Museum Association

http://www.artnoir.com/aama.html

AAMA is a nonprofit membership organization serving the interests and needs of black museums and cultural institutions, and black museum professionals. Institutional membership is open to museums, galleries, historical societies, libraries, research centers, and other organizations and agencies that collect, conserve, exhibit, research, and teach the history, science, art, and culture relevant to the African American heritage.

American Association of Museums

http://www.americanmuse.org/AAM/

This organization provides a focal point for professionals in museum and museum-related fields, and currently has over 14,000 members. Every type of museum is represented in its membership, from arboretums to youth museums. Site links to membership information, newsletters, and a bookstore.

Group for Education in Museums

http://www.gem.org.uk/

Group for anyone concerned with education in museums. Site contains links to excerpts from the quarterly newsletter, the annual Journal of Education in Museums, and other publications. Also contains links to lists of museums.

Institute of Museum Services

http://www.ims.fed.us/

This group supports museums' educational roles through grant programs that encourage outstanding museum management and comprehensive collections care practices. This site has links to awards given in 1996 as well as eligibility and deadline requirements for upcoming awards.

James Renwick Alliance

http://www.jra.org/

A national nonprofit organization created to support the Renwick Gallery of the National Museum of American Art, Smithsonian Institution, Washington, DC. Site links to the history of the gallery, membership information, a newsletter, and more.

Mexican Federation of Associations of Friends of Museums

http://www.friendsofmuseums.org.mx/menfem_i.html

This non-profit, non-governmental organization was created to help preserve Mexico's culture. Site links to the information about the organization's activities.

The Museum Security Network

http://www.xs4all.nl/~securma/

This initiative by security managers of leading Dutch Museums aims to present a global platform for all aspects of museum and art security. Site has articles about security matters, law links, and searchable databases. Also links to other similar sites.

PHOTOGRAPHY AND FILM

Berkeley Art Museum/Pacific Film Archive

http://www.uampfa.berkeley.edu/

The visual arts center of the University of California at Berkeley, the UAM/PFA is noted for its thought-provoking exhibitions of both art and film. The museum Web site contains online versions of current and former exhibitions.

California Museum of Photography

http://www.cmp.ucr.edu/

Site contains photos, descriptions, and other information from exhibits at this museum. Also links to a museum store, with copies of featured photos from the exhibit for sale.

International Center of Photography

http://www.icp.org/

Established to collect 20th-century works, this center has a special emphasis on documentary photography. The center, located in New York City, also teaches all levels of photography. Site contains photos from special exhibits.

National Museum of Photography, Film, and Television

http://www.nmsi.ac.uk/nmpft/

This museum contains varied displays, interactive features, large and small screens, and constantly changing special exhibitions, events, theater, and education. Permanent galleries include: The Story of Popular Photography (The Kodak Museum), The IMAX Cinema, Television Galleries, Photography is News, and Pictureville Cinema.

Photo Perspectives

http://www.i3tele.com/photo_perspectives_museum/faces/

An interactive photography museum for the photographic examinations of contemporary society and culture. Site provides links to other sites related to photography or the topics of the current exhibits.

Southeast Museum of Photography

http://www.dbcc.cc.fl.us/dbcc/smp/smphome.htm

Museum has a large collection and hosts exhibitions year round. Site provides descriptions of exhibits and includes sample photos. Museum also focuses on photographic education, with the Southeast Museum School of Photography nearby. Provides links to other museums and galleries.

Virtual Photographic Museum

http://home.pi.net/~patgoos/home.html

Site topics include Photoshop experiments, workshop lighting techniques, and Javascript "TechTalk." Site also links to interesting information such as "Everything about slides and how to present them," "A quest for making even better pictures…," and "A photographic statement for peace in the Middle East."

SCIENCE AND TECHNOLOGY

Carnegie Science Center

http://www.csc.clpgh.org/

Western Pennsylvania's state-of-the-art public facility is committed to educating the public about science and technology through hands-on exhibits and programs. Site contains a calendar of this month's events and featured exhibit, and previews upcoming exhibits.

The Exploratorium

http://www.exploratorium.edu/

The Exploratorium is a collage of 650 interactive exhibits in the areas of science, art, and human perception. It provides access to and information about science, nature, art, and technology. Site has online versions of exhibits and tons of other cool scientific information.

Israel National Museum of Science

http://www.netvision.net.il/n_sci_museum/

A hands-on museum with exhibits that help make science, planning, and technology easy to understand. Provides links to current exhibits and photos, along with general museum information.

The Museum of Science and Industry, Chicago

http://www.msichicago.org/

Site contains online exhibits, such as baby chicks hatching, that provide a sample of the experiences available at the museum. Also provides Omnimax film clips and educational resources for teachers as well as exhibit schedules and general information about the Chicago area.

Museum of Science and Industry, Tampa, Florida

http://www.tampatrib.com/mosi/

This official site of largest science museum in the Southeastern United States is organized by floors. Site also includes updates and previews of exhibits, IMAX films, and events.

National Museum of Science and Technology, Canada

http://www.science-tech.nmstc.ca/

This museum was created to explore "the Transformation of Canada." Different subjects of the museum include: agriculture, communications, energy, forestry, graphic arts, transportation, and many others. Links and descriptions are provided for all subjects as well as for behind the scenes information such as restoration.

Oregon Museum of Science and Industry

http://www.omsi.edu/

Observe vibrations and sound waves in the museum's Electronics Lab, or weave your own piece of the Web in the Computer Lab. This site provides links to all the museum's main areas complete with photos and descriptions of many exhibits. A lot of great information at this site.

Questacon: National Science and Technology Centre

http://sunsite.anu.edu.au/Questacon/

Site includes fun activities, links, and museum information for Australia's national science museum. Take a virtual tour of the galleries and explore the hands-on zone, all without leaving the comforts of home (or paying for a trip to Australia).

Telegraph and Scientific Instrument Museum

http://www.chss.montclair.edu/psychology/perera/telegraph.html

Site contains a list of downloadable illustrations including telegraph instruments, microphones, radios, and wireless-related collections. Also provides links to other collectors' pages.

SCULPTURE

DeCordova Museum and Sculpture Park

http://www.decordova.org/

The only public, year-round sculpture park of changing works in New England. Photos are provided of the grounds' sculptures, as are links to current exhibits and a virtual gallery.

Isamu Noguchi Garden Museum

http://www.inch.com/~snippy/noguchi/entrance.html

This museum was conceived and designed by the artist himself. It contains an extensive collection of more than 250 works of sculpture, drawings, and documentation, and includes an online tour through gardens. Also includes biography info about the artist and links to other sites that display his work.

Laumeier Sculpture Park

http://home.stlnet.com/~jimpotts/fire_ice.htm

This park is a 116-acre venue for contemporary media artists' works. Site contains many images from the park as well as exhibit schedules and other art links.

Sheldon Memorial Art Gallery and Sculpture Garden

http://sheldon.unl.edu/

Together, these two comprise over 12,000 works of art, and the garden contains 33 sculptures exhibited year-round. Site contains photos of several of the sculptures, a schedule of upcoming exhibits, and an artist index.

Storm King Art Center

http://www.skac.org/

This 400-acre sculpture museum in the Hudson Valley area has works from more that 100 different artists. Site gives descriptions and dates of exhibitions.

GOPHER SITES

List of Museums in Greece
gopher://ithaki.servicenet.ariadne-t.gr/11/HELLENIC_CIVILIZATION/MUSEUMS/

Natural History Museum Berne Switzerland (NMBE)
gopher://www-nmbe.unibe.ch:70/

U.C. Berkeley Museum of Paleontology
Information on museum collections and paleontological database information. Also includes nature and science images, images of animals and birds; biology image archive; animal sounds; and an online *On the Origin of Species* complete text.
gopher://ucmp1.berkeley.edu

Yale's The Peabody Museum of Natural History
gopher://gopher.peabody.yale.edu/

LISTSERVS

ACUMGN-L—Assoc. of College & Univ. Museums & Galleries of New England
Brown University, Providence, Rhode Island
You can join this group by sending the message "sub ACUMGN-L your name" to
listserv@brownvm.brown.edu

CHILDMUS—A Forum for Children's Museum Professionals
You can join this group by sending the message "sub CHILDMUS your name" to
listserv@listserv.rice.edu

CIDOC-L—Museum Documentation Discussion List
Swedish Museum of Natural History, Stockholm, Sweden
You can join this group by sending the message sub CIDOC-L your name to
listserv@freeside.nrm.se

COYOTE—Nat'l Museum of American Indian (NMAI) Indian Issues
Smithsonian Institution, Washington, DC
You can join this group by sending the message sub COYOTE your name to
listserv@sivm.si.edu

ICOM-CC—Museum Conservation Discussion List
You can join this group by sending the message sub ICOM-CC your name to
listserv@home.ease.lsoft.com

JAHH—Jane Addams Hull-House Museum
University of Illinois at Chicago, Chicago, IL
You can join this group by sending the message sub JAHH your name to
listserv@listserv.uic.edu

MUSEUM-L— Museum Discussion List
You can join this group by sending the message sub MUSEUM-L your name to
listserv@home.ease.lsoft.com

MUSWEB-L—Museum Web Development Discussion List
Swedish Museum of Natural History, Stockholm, Sweden
You can join this group by sending the message sub MUSWEB-L your name" to
listserv@freeside.nrm.se

NASMNEWS—National Air & Space Museum (NASM) Events at the Smithsonian
Smithsonian Institution, Washington, DC
You can join this group by sending the message sub NASMNEWS your name" to
listserv@sivm.si.edu

NEWMILL—Museums for the New Millennium
Smithsonian Institution, Washington, DC
You can join this group by sending the message sub NEWMILL your name to
listserv@sivm.si.edu

NSOM-L—Nordic School Computer Networks and Museums
Swedish Museum of Natural History, Stockholm, Sweden
You can join this group by sending the message sub NSOM-L your name to
listserv@freeside.nrm.se

USHRI—United States Holocaust Research Institute
U.S. Holocaust Memorial Museum, Washington, DC
You can join this group by sending the message sub USHRI your name to
listserv@listserv.ushmm.org

NEWSGROUPS

alt.culture.usenet

bit.listserv.museum

rec.arts.misc

MUSIC DATABASES

> No, ma'am. We're musicians.
>
> *Elwood Blues in* The Blues Brothers *(1980)*

Alive 93-5's Music Database

http://www.mc.edu/%7Ealive935/music.html

Owned and operated by Mississippi College, in Clinton, MS, Alive 93-5 (WHJT-FM) is a commercial radio station that features adult contemporary Christian music. This Web site offers a searchable index of its Christian music CD collection. Search albums or songs by artist or title.

AMG Online Music

http://allmusic.com/amg/om/omroot.html

Access All-Music Guide's mega music database. Includes articles and reviews of hundreds of titles and artists from more than 200 freelance writers. Includes information on recent and upcoming releases and reissues, the latest in music news, and discographies. Many feature similar and related artist suggestions as well as artists' biographies, their influences, and the time period in which they were popular or active.

Black Music Archive

http://www.blackmusicarchive.co.uk/

Music of black origin (worldwide). Searchable index of 10,000+ albums—search by artist, title, year, or label. Note that results are in alphabetical order, by last name for some artists (for example, you'll find Sergio Mendes under *M*, not *S* as in some databases). Also includes music forums ranging from reggae to hip hop to gospel, a Music Exchange buy/sell/swap area, and music reviews.

Cuban Music Samples
ftp://kiwi.cs.berkeley.edu/pub/music/cuban-music.html

Cuban Music Samples

ftp://kiwi.cs.berkeley.edu/pub/music/cuban-music.html

Cuban Music Samples

Music in the air
I don't get to the Florida Keys as much as I'd like to, but when I do, I always take a recording boom box to tape samples of Cuban radio. The south-facing beaches of the Keys and the 90 miles of salt water separating them from the Havana area create nearly perfect conditions for medium-distance AM reception.

Most of the samples on this page were monitored near Marathon, Florida. All files are in Sun 8-bit .au format, and originated on tapes of the AM radio stations noted below. The recording and reception equipment for most of these samples was a GE Superadio II with built-in cassette; the cassette part no longer works, but the radio continues to work well in my garage.

Musical mélange
Almost no music of contemporary Cuban origination is heard in the USA, as a lasting effect of the trade embargo that's been in place for 30 years. However, Cuba has been listening to the rest of the world. What has evolved is a rich mixture of rock, tropical, Caribbean, and easy-listening love songs. The mix of styles is broadcast all day, every day, to the people of the island of Cuba and those lucky enough to be passing time in the Keys.

About this page

Because of the longstanding trade embargo between the U.S. and Cuba, very little has been imported from Cuba to the States—and that includes Cuban music. The creator of this database records the music with a boom box from the shores of south Florida and then puts some of it online for the rest of us to enjoy. The site even includes lyrics (in Spanish and then English) for some of the songs.

Folk Music Digest Archives

http://www.hidwater.com/fmd/fmd.html

This isn't a database of folk music itself; it's a digest of folk music discussion—the WWW home for Alan Rowoth's *Folk_Music Digest.* Read or search the Folk_Music archives (back issues are available as well). Some of the postings are fascinating, even if folk isn't your favorite genre.

Friedman/Fairfax Publishers

http://www.webcom.com/~friedman/

Freidman Publishing publishes a variety of nonfiction titles and this page provides an overview of their Life, Times, and Music Series. Provides links to jazz, rock, classical, Broadway, weddings, kids, music polls, and so on.

GEMM: Global Electronic Music Marketplace

http://gemm.com

Enables you to search for information about artists, albums, and companies. Lets you register to be notified when a particular item you want is mentioned elsewhere in the marketplace.

German Music Database

http://www.artsci.wustl.edu/~glcory/music/gmd.shtml

For use by teachers in the classroom (or for fun). Songs can be downloaded and printed, or reviewed onscreen. A nice collection of links to other sites as well. The text of the site is in English, but of course the songs themselves are in German. Also includes a collection of MIDI Christmas tunes.

Great Guitar Sites on the Web

http://home.vicnet.net.au/~guitar/

If you're into guitar music—playing, recording, or listening—check out this site. Hundreds of listings for sites: guitar shops, guitar chords, guitar dealers, guitar publications, guitarists…you get the idea. But it's not just guitars—*everything* music seems to be included. (Note: The screen colors may be a little extreme on some browsers.)

Hype! Music

http://www.hype.com/music/home.htm

Provides a searchable database of music reviews for all genres. Enables you to submit your own review of a CD for inclusion in the database. Includes a list of one-hit wonders.

JazzWeb (WNUR-FM)

http://www.nwu.edu/WNUR/jazz/

Based at Northwestern University in Evanston, IL, WNUR-FM plays a variety of interesting music of all genres. The JazzWeb page is devoted to the jazz spectrum. Fairly complete discographies of many popular (and some more obscure) artists. Search for your particular favorites, or roam around in the other sections for something new.

The KFJC Edge of Obscurity Music Database

http://www.spies.com/misc/kfjc/md/db/

KFJC, 89.7 FM, Los Altos Hills, CA, plays a mix of music completely determined by the "on-air host" (note, *not* DJ). You may hear psychedelic, rock, pop, reggae, hip-hop, western, jazz, experimental—all mixed together. No "hits," all new. The database follows the same philosophy, providing a wide array of music, some of it fairly obscure, a lot of it rare. Search by label, artist, reviewer, genre.

Mammoth Music Meta-List @ VIBE

http://www.pathfinder.com/@@DSzPaQAAAAAAANkP/vibe/mmm/

Contains a directory of music-oriented Web sites. Includes folk, bluegrass, blues, jazz, world, classical, rock, and other styles of music.

Mind on Music: On-line Music Database

http://www.cs.uit.no/Music/

Includes lists of the 50 albums voted best, worst, most (?), updated every 10 minutes. Search for favorite artists or albums alphabetically or by individual entry. Lists tracks on each individual album, and includes some reviews.

Music Database (kzsu.stanford.edu)

http://kzsu.stanford.edu/eklein/index.html

Billing itself as "the Web's largest Industrial/Gothic music index," this site offers more than 3,000 listings of titles divided somewhat arbitrarily by the Webmaster into a variety of categories: industrial, techno, Japanoise, atmospheric, gothic, and others. You can also search alphabetically, of course.

Music database (www.cs.nott.ac.uk)

http://www.cs.nott.ac.uk/Department/Staff/ef/database.html

A collection of more than 1,000 traditional British-related folk dance tunes, divided into jigs, reels, hornpipes, and other categories. Most are chords only; some have the score in GIF format. Scores are downloadable in PostScript format in case you want to print them.

The Music Database (musicdatabase.com)

http://www.musicdatabase.com/

Browse over 100,000 CDs and over 1 million songs at this site. Searches the CDDB (otherwise accessible through CDDB-aware CD players—download the information for the CD currently in your CD drive). Search by artist, title—even by song.

The Music Database (music.netsysinc.com)

http://music.netsysinc.com/

Updated daily, this particular database offers more than 35,000 tabs and chords for playing the songs, and more than 5,000 MIDI files. Searchable, of course, by title or artist. Plenty of MIDI files to play or download.

Random Band Name

http://www.terranet.ab.ca/~aaron/band_names.html

Helps you find a name for that band you're starting. Serves entertainment purposes, and generates names that actually come close to some current actual bands. Examples include Bellybutton Fuzz, No Tears of Happiness, and Barking Seagulls.

Rockmine Archives

http://www.rockmine.music.co.uk/

Provides a collection (based on 750,000 text clippings, 7,000 hours of rock video, 25,000 hours of audio material, and various memorabilia) of information about British rock and roll. Includes—among other things—rock film posters and artist information.

Shareware Music Machine

http://www.hitsquad.com/smm

A large collection of downloadable music software for use in recording and playing music with your computer. Instructions and assistance provided by the Webmasters. The Music Machine Bookshop, in collaboration with Amazon.com, offers a nice collection of music-related books you can order from the same site.

Related Sites

http://www.midifarm.com/files/

http://crolinks.cronet.com/cromusic/

http://phys.udallas.edu/rugby/songs/nzsongs.html

Sinhala Music Database

http://www.ifi.uio.no/~kapilae/sindu/

A list of Sri Lankan sheet music and lyrics (in PostScript format) for guitarists and singers. Chords are for rhythm guitar. A link is included to the Ghostview site, in case you prefer to view the files onscreen rather than print them.

Similarities Engine

http://www.ari.net/se/

Enter the names of your favorite artists to receive a list of other bands or artists in which you might also be interested.

Ultimate Band List

http://american.recordings.com/wwwofmusic/ubl/ubl.shtml

Offers links to information about any genre or style of music. Includes information not only on Web pages, but on newsgroups, mailing lists, and more.

Worldwide Internet Music Resources

http://www.music.indiana.edu/music_resources/

Hosted by the William and Gayle Cook Music Library at Indiana University. Contains links to almost every imaginable music-related site—artists/ensembles, composers, genres, publications, the music industry, general and miscellaneous resources, Usenet groups, research, and more.

FTP SITES & GOPHER SITES

file://ftp.cs.ruu.nl/pub/MIDI/index.html

ftp://ftp.cdconnection.com/

ftp://ftp.uu.net/doc/music/

ftp://itre.ncsu.edu/pub/music/

ftp://kiwi.cs.berkeley.edu/pub/music/

gopher://vmsgopher.cua.edu/11gopher_root_music:[_cantus]

gopher://wiretap.spies.com/11/Library/Music/Lists

Related Sites

http://spight.physics.unlv.edu/picgalr2.html

http://www.accsi.com/music/database.html

http://www.austin1.com/JD/

http://www.channel1.com/users/fxxm/

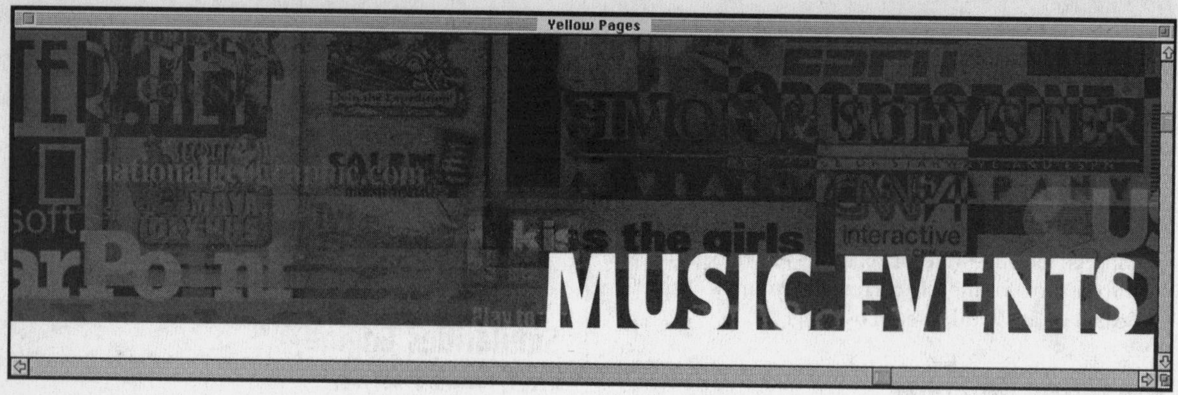

A
B
C
D
E
F
G
H
I
J
K
L
M
N
O
P
Q
R
S
T
U
V
W
X
Y
Z

Lend me your ears, and I'll sing you a song, and I'll try not to sing out of key.

John Lennon and Paul McCartney

Bluesfest Central
http://www.bluesworld.com/fest.html

Jazmin
http://www.batnet.com/jazmin/

ABSOLUTELY WORTHLESS Calendar of New England Folk Concerts

http://theory.lcs.mit.edu/~wald/calendar.html

Offers a calendar of concerts, festivals, and events, organized by month, for folk fans in the New England area. Also contains a guide to other print and electronic folk calendars.

Bluesfest Central

http://www.bluesworld.com/fest.html

A fantastic site full of listings and links to blues festivals nationwide. Bookmark this one—it is a must for any true blues fan.

Creation 97

http://www.creationfest.com/

Provides information on Creation, the nation's largest Christian festival, held annually in Mt. Union, Pennsylvania. Includes what visitors can expect, festival history, schedules, performers, speakers, directions, children's events, and volunteer and merchandise information.

Related Sites

http://www.innotts.co.uk/beat/gigs/

http://www.Roskilde-Festival.dk/

Culturefinder

http://www.culturefinder.com/index.htm

Billed as the "online address for the arts," this site helps you find cultural events in the following major cities: Boston, Chicago, Los Angeles, New York, Philadelphia, San Francisco, St. Louis, and Washington, D.C.

Folk Venue

http://www.hidwater.com/folkvenue/

A comprehensive database of more than 4,000 folk and folk-friendly venues in North America. Also linked to Musi-Cal for event schedules.

Jazmin

http://www.batnet.com/jazmin/

A site promoting women jazz musicians in the San Francisco Bay area. Includes bios of the listed musicians and RealAudio! selections.

Live Online—Music Events Calendar

http://www.live-online.com/cgi-bin/event.pl

A listing of online live concerts, chats, and listening parties complete with date, time, and the name of the featured band. Offers options such as Everyone's a Critic where you can voice your opinion on a Web-only pre-release preview. If they like your critique, they'll post it and you could win some cool stuff.

Mardi Gras Official Web Site

http://www.usacitylink.com//mardigr/

Although it is known primarily as a drunkfest, Mardi Gras includes some fantastic music and draws musicians from all over to join in the festivities. Check this site out for details and schedules of music events.

MBNA College Quartet Contest

http://webpages.marshall.edu/~bennett7/thestation/cqc.html

Includes information on dates, rules, and previous winners of the MBNA Collegiate Quartet Contest. Provides contacts for general information and ways to get involved.

MerleFest

http://www.merlefest.org/

An annual celebration of acoustic music and southern gentility to honor the memory of Eddy Merle Watson, the only son of flat picking legend Arthel "Doc" Watson. Held in April at the natural ampitheather of the foothills of the Blue Ridge mountains.

Music-Cal™

http://concerts.calendar.com/

This site provides access to worldwide live music information about concerts, festivals, and musical events. Search capabilities by performer, venue, city, or event.

New Orleans Jazz and Heritage Festival

http://www.yatcom.com/neworl/jfest/jfesttop.html

Second only to Mardi Gras in the number of visitors it draws to the city, Jazz Fest is much less rowdy and far cooler. Check it out for ticket information and schedule of performers.

Rob Kenney Presents: Kerrville Folk Festival

http://www.fmp.com/~kerrfest/

Provides information about the Kerrville Folk Festival (held in Texas), a major United States folk festival that continues for 25 days starting every May. Contains performance schedules, ticket information, upcoming events, and their limited edition 10-CD set.

Related Site

http://web.tusco.net/jdebevec/amish.htm

The Concert Web

http://www.stl-music.com/events.shtml

An enormous collection of musical event information from around the world. Click the country you are interested in, and up pop the events.

The Foundation Forum

http://www.themusiczone.com/channelf/

This site promotes The Foundation Forum, which is an annual hard rock, heavy metal, hard alternative convention. Includes info on venues, events, bands, and past happenings as well.

The Muddy Awards

http://www.teleport.com/~boydroid/blues/muddies.htm

Cascade Blues Association's annual awards celebration, named for the infamous Muddy Waters, honors local, regional, national, and international blues musicians. Includes a listing of the nominees according to category.

Ron Smith Oldies Calendar

http://www.oldiesmusic.com

A "this week" of events in rock 'n' roll history. Includes charts for the number one songs of the 50s, 60s, and 70s, as well as links to featured artists.

UFOJOE Presents: Information about Canadian Folk Festivals

http://www.interlog.com/~ufojoe/

Provides information and schedules for dozens of Canadian folk music festivals. Also features a festival discussion group and links to other festival information.

Waterfront Blues Festival

http://www.teleport.com/~boydroid/blues/wbfest97.htm

This Portland, Oregon blues festival site lists scheduled performers and date and ticket information. Links to other sites as well.

Related Sites

http://medinfo.labmed.umn.edu/Docs/.www/archives_html/html.9501/msg00040.html

http://www.mosquitonet.com/~gcn/special.htm

http://www.piranha.de/EVE/EVE_01.HTML

http://www.ticketmaster.com/

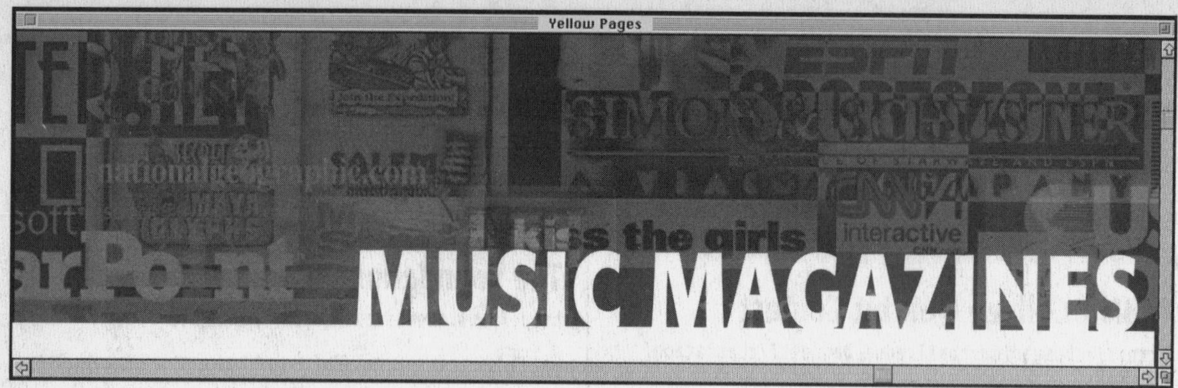

> **To** stop the flow of music would be like the stopping of time itself, incredible, and inconceivable.
>
> *Aaron Copland*

Addicted to Noise

http://www.addict.com/ATN/

Includes interviews with artists like Lou Reed, Iggy Pop, and Neil Young. Provides columns by rock critics, including Dave Marsh and Greil Marcus. Offers daily rock news reports. Serves as a guide to rock spots on the Web. Also offers album reviews with sound bytes, movie reviews, rock book reviews, and music and technology columns. Use RealAudio to listen in on Radio ATN, one of the Internet's only real-time audio radio stations.

Audible Evolution

http://www.seacoast.com/~c/audible-evolution.htm

This site is a boon to all fans of electronic music. Audible Evolution is an online magazine dedicated to all categories of electronic music. Includes reviews, articles, graphics, wave form music files, and much more. Provides links to many other related electronic music sites and much more. A well-organized, great site that is highly recommended.

Related Sites

http://altpress.com/

http://www.audiospank.com/

http://www.fly.co.uk/index.shtml

NRP TOP LINKS

iMUSIC
http://imusic.com/

Latin Music Online
http://www.lamusica.com/welcome.html

Billboard Online

http://www.billboard.com/

This site offers fast and easy access to Billboard Magazine's huge electronic library. Charts and articles from the current issue are available to visitors.

Christian Music Weekly

http://www.jesusfreak.com/cmweekly/

This site features news, reviews, previews, and event listings of Christian musicians and bands. The site is well maintained and contains links to other Christian sites on the Web.

Cosmik Debris E-Zine

http://www.serv.net/cosmikdebris/

Presents articles, features, and interviews with a wide array of musical artists. This electronic magazine focuses on all sorts of music including rock, electronic, jazz, blues, and much more. Provides album reviews, upcoming releases information, and much more. This is a good site with a lot of information and is recommended to all music fans.

Cybergrass—The Internet Bluegrass Magazine

http://www.banjo.com/BG/

Features everything you'd expect in a magazine, including articles, artist profiles, and an events calendar. Includes reader comments and bluegrass want ads. Also includes a guide to magazines and newsletters and offers links to other bluegrass sites.

Electric Magic—The Led Zeppelin Chronicle

http://www.pathcom.com/~rapallof/emagic.html

Online edition of the fan magazine and rated "the best" Zeppelin site on the Net. Features photo and article archives, a video vault, information about the band's appearance on the MuchMusic special and the Montreux concerts, plus much more.

Entertainment Weekly Online

http://cgi.pathfinder.com/ew/

This weekly magazine focuses on movie and television features as well as music info. A good source for general music news.

Feelin' Groovy

http://www.geocities.com/~feelin-groovy/groovy.htm

For anyone who is craving more of the Osmonds, Shaun and David Cassidy, Leif Garrett, or any of the others from the *Tiger Beat Magazine* gang. This is the site to relive your teenage crushes and check out the really cool links.

Flipside

http://www.indieweb.com/flipside/index.html

Provides online site for *Flipside* magazine, which covers punk and independent rock bands. Site includes a record and fan 'zine catalog with ordering information. Also includes magazine advertising rates and contact addresses and numbers.

The Grindstone Magazine

http://members.aol.com/grind55/index.html

A funky '50s retro style guide to roadhouse, roots, and rockabilly. Don't pass up this fun site!

Hyperreal

http://hyperreal.com/

Presents an online collaborative publishing effort that covers rave culture and electronic music. Provides links to a myriad of different rave and electronic music sites. Includes an archive of various sound samples, artwork, articles, and more. This site is very extensive and is highly recommended to fans of the genre and to neophytes.

ICE On-Line

http://www.webcom.com/~ice/

Based on the printed publication and offers a free trial subscription. ICE Provides information and exclusive articles on upcoming album releases. Also includes release dates that are updated weekly.

iMUSIC

http://imusic.com/

News, features, CD reviews, bulletin boards, chat rooms, and even an online music store—this site has it all. Tons of links to individual artists and bands grouped by musical category. If you're into music, definately bookmark this one!

Jelly

http://www.jellyroll.com/

This site has something for almost everyone: jazz, blues, country, soul, and rock & roll. Issues are put online only after the latest issue comes out. If you want the most current issue, you have to subscribe.

Latin Music Online

http://www.lamusica.com/welcome.html

Although Latin music isn't as popular in the U.S. as it is worldwide, this site deserves a look. It is well designed and packed with quality news and features. Who knows, you too might become a fan.

NY ROCK

http://www.nyrock.com/

Daily rock & roll updates, reviews, and articles with that New York flair. Categorized by band, this site also offers gossip, news, and RealAudio sound clips.

OffBeat Magazine

http://www.NeoSoft.com/~offbeat/

Online edition of the monthly print magazine of the same name, "New Orleans' and Louisiana's only music and entertainment magazine." Features interviews, articles, reviews, polls, and more on the New Orleans jazz scene, as well as club, concert, and festival information and classified ads.

A B C D E F G H I J K L M N O P Q R S T U V W X Y Z

POP-i Music Magazine

http://www.popi.com/egotorium.htm

This site features reviews of the latest releases from a variety of bands with downloadable sound bites representing each song on the album, cover art, and photos of band members. Also contains links to audio/video highlights of band interviews.

QUIRK!

http://www.loop.com/~quirkmag/

An online rock & roll magazine full of record and show reviews, articles, and archives of past issues. Also contains links to other music-related sites.

Stirrings Folk Mag

http://www.cityscape.co.uk/users/ah98/

Online edition of the British folk music magazine. Features CD, book, and concert reviews; interviews; concert and festival schedules; news; and more.

VIBE

http://www.vibe.com/

A hip hop online magazine that features daily entertainment updates, preview videos and audio clips, and archives of past issues. A nicely designed and maintained Web site.

Wall of Sound

http://www.wallofsound.com/

A comprehensive site offering artist pages, interviews, news and reviews, new releases, and the ability to track your favorite music star.

Wilson & Alroy's Record Reviews

http://home.dti.net/warr/WAreview.html

Provides reviews of thousands of records, mostly rock and pop. Includes links to hundreds of other related sites. Includes some music book reviews, rock timelines, and other assorted features. This is a good site for any rock music fan.

Related Sites

http://www.gridmagazine.com/

http://www2.cybernex.net/~stegre/headbands/

http://easyweb.easynet.co.uk/~flux/fanzines.htm

http://www2.rocktropolis.com/rt/main.asp?area_id=2&venue_id=16

http://www.musicmagazine.com/showcase/index.htm

http://www.enews.com/

http://tlem.netcentral.net/

http://www.webnoize.com/

http://www.sonances.qc.ca/journals/wnmm.htm

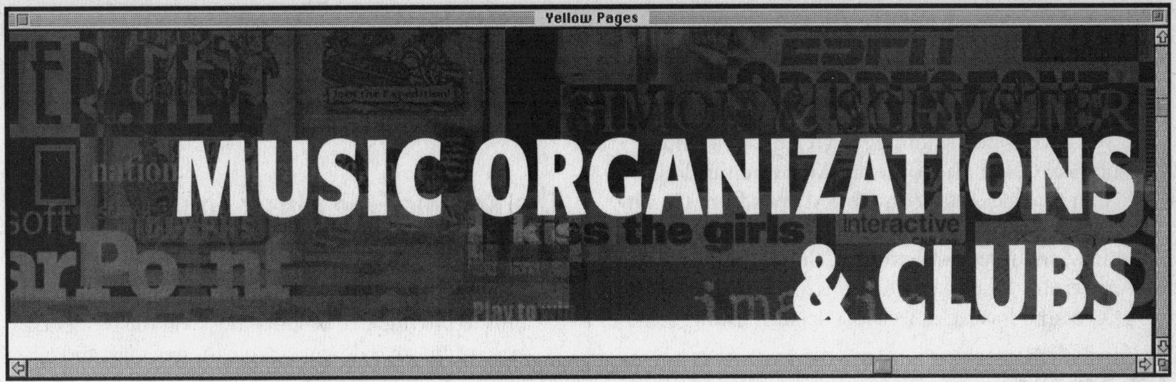

What kind of music do you usually have here?

Elwood Blues in The Blues Brothers *(1980)*

1-800-EVERY-CD

http://www.everycd.com/

Promising that they have every CD you could possibly want (their list includes 7,000 *labels*—not just titles), this site offers a database searchable by the usual artist, label, title, as well as performer, conductor, orchestra, and composer. DVD listings include more than 400 titles. The XPound chat area includes eight different sections for members to enjoy.

Acoustic Performer's Guild

http://www.interlog.com/~robc/apg.html

Here's a new organization (initiated October 7, 1997), dedicated to the performance of music that's strictly acoustic—no amplification, public address systems, or electronic instruments. The founder, Rob Canner, invites musicians to "unite and unplug." Read the initial press release and the introductory fact sheet at this site, or send email to Canner.

Related Sites

http://www.amc-music.com/

http://www.ascap.com/

http://www.cirpa.ca/

http://www.dnai.com/~jinetwk/

http://www.gap.org/

http://www.icomm.ca/macos/

http://www.ifco.org/index.shtml

http://www.ohio.net/~commtech/mindex.html

National Association of Amateur Elvis Impersonators
http://members.aol.com/nudeelvis/index.html

American Federation of Musicians of the United States and Canada

http://www.afm.org/

Professional union of musicians, full- and part-time, as well as students, in all genres. The AFM's goal is to improve musicians' working conditions and wages, and support of the arts and arts education. The Current Events section includes important industry news; the Hiring Musicians section describes how to hire a musician and provides links to booking agents and local musicians. Check the site list for links to related organizations, affiliates, and more.

BMG

http://www.bmg.de/

Lets you explore the universe of music and download sound samples, pictures, and videos of various artists. Provides much of the information in German.

BMI.com

http://bmi.com/

BMI is a nonprofit organization representing hundreds of thousands of songwriters, composers, and music publishers in all genres. This site provides a searchable database of their more than 3 million works. Check the Legislative Update section to keep up-to-date with the latest on copyright laws and other legislation related to intellectual property. The Recommended Reading section tracks all sorts of info on the BMI membership, along with books and articles of interest to the community. The Licensing and Songwriters' Toolboxes provide a wealth of useful material for the professional involved in the music field.

CD Club FAQ

`http://www.blooberry.com/cdfaq/`

If you're considering joining (or rejoining) a "music club" like Columbia House or BMG, read this FAQ first. It provides details on the best deals from the various clubs, strategies on how to get the most for your money, and rules/restrictions of club memberships. Answers to most-asked questions are available in a brief yes/no format, as well as a detailed listing.

CD-Xchange

`http://www.cd-xchange.com/`

A compact disc exchange service that exchanges used CDs between members. A $19.95 membership fee is charged to cover the cost of inventorying the used CDs and listing them online. For each CD you send, you receive one CD of your choice (you pay just postage and handling). Pass along music you're tired of to someone else to enjoy. You also get to try music you might never buy in the shrinkwrap at full price.

Columbia House Music Club

`http://www.columbiahouse.com/repl/mc/tmpls/index.html?8809128272094355147280415 5`

An extensive list of music in a wide variety of categories, but you must be a member to order. Join the club at this location. The current offer is 11 CDs or cassettes free when you sign up—note that you pay for shipping and handling. Catalogs will come to members by mail, but you can also shop online (members get a special site and ordering number).

Creative Musicians Coalition

`http://www.aimcmc.com/`

This international organization represents independent artists and record labels producing music in more than two dozen different styles. Directory of artists, *AfterTouch* magazine/catalog. Search by artist, style, label. The Showcase section offers reviews and samples of new music (some may require plug-ins). Are you ready to experiment?

Hearnet

`http://www.hearnet.com/`

Listening to rock 'n' roll can seriously damage your hearing. If your kids cringe at the idea of turning down the sound, check out this Web site for news that may give them—and you—something to think about. H.E.A.R. (Hearing Education and Awareness for Rockers) is intent on preventing today's Third Eye Blind fans from turning into tomorrow's hearing aid wearers. This nonprofit organization has the support of some seriously heavy medical and musical folks. Definitely worth a look.

The Kosmic Free Music Foundation

`http://www.kosmic.org/`

This international nonprofit (membership about 30) aims to provide free original music on the Net. Each piece of music is downloadable for free play, and takes about 2 minutes at 28.8. WWW, FTP, and BBS sites available for downloading. Check the Kosmic in the Media section for locations where you can hear Kosmic music on the radio, Kosmic mentions in the news, and more. A very interesting organization, and a nicely done site (highly graphical, and you may want the MODplug plug-in to hear the sound).

Muscle Music, Inc.

`http://www.mmusic.com/index.html`

Serves the entertainment industry "through a number of services designed to increase the quality and efficiency of music and audio producers, publishers and record companies." Contains information about music, video, and Web services; previews of artists; and bios of Alabama music achievers.

TuneInn Records Online Record Shop

`http://dspace.dial.pipex.com/tuneinn/tuneinn.html`

Billing themselves as the UK's leading specialists in trance, techno, and acid, this membership-based service provides a lengthy catalog of offerings for ordering online (via email). Descriptions included. Back catalogs and used vinyl are also available. (Note: Graphics-intensive, this site may be very slow to load on some equipment.)

National Association of Amateur Elvis Impersonators

`http://members.aol.com/nudeelvis/index.html`

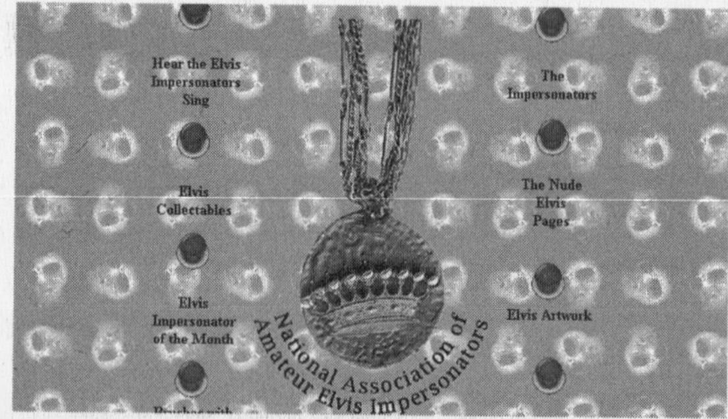

Even if you're not impersonating "The King of Rock 'n' Roll," this site is definitely worth a visit. Be sure to review the Impersonators list (note that Nude Elvis isn't *really* nude), check out the Elvis of the Month, more. Plenty of Elvis links, photos, artwork, and sound bytes from many of the Elvises (Elvi?).

National Music Foundation

http://www.nmc.org/

The nonprofit organization "dedicated to American music and the people who bring it to us." Features a newsletter, press releases, the American Music Calendar, and links to music sites of all types. Also offers a gift shop that includes a cookbook with recipes provided by your favorite country musicians.

Recording Industry Association of America

http://www.riaa.com/

Very cool site. (Note that it carries a parental advisory for possible explicit content.) The RIAA is a trade association representing the U.S. sound recording industry. The thrust of this site is the themes of anti-piracy and artistic freedom. Plenty of interesting reading on these and other topics, as well as a searchable database of gold and platinum record winners, and a short list of related links.

The Unconservatory

http://www.vsuccess.com/unconservatory/index.html

The goal of this nonprofit organization is to support the "creation, performance, recording, and teaching of music." Its site provides access to new publications, and includes a variety of articles of interest to artists in the various music fields. Includes relevant links to other music- and performance-related sites.

Wolverine Antique Music Society

http://www.teleport.com/~rfrederi/

Presents the Wolverine Antique Music Society. Focuses on the preservation of music originally recorded for 78 rpm records. Offers much to the 78 collector and early jazz aficionado. Contains many articles on the music, collecting, and all sorts of technical and resource information pertaining to antique audio. Also contains information on the early record labels, 78 album cover art, and sound clips.

Related Sites

http://www.warchild.org/projects/centre/centre.html

http://www.yca.org/

Women In Music

http://www.womeninmusic.com/

Women In Music (WIM) is a nonprofit organization with the goal of supporting the efforts and careers of women in the music industry. Quite a number of programs are offered at this site, including referrals, newsletters, seminars and workshops, insider's tips, and more. Events and industry news sections provide useful updates on music-related activities.

NEWSGROUPS

alt.guitar.tab

alt.music

alt.rock-n-roll.classic

rec.music

FTP & GOPHER SITES

ftp://ftp.honors.unr.edu/pub/music/

ftp://ftp.visi.com/users/astanley/ambfaq.txt

ftp://ftp.informatik.tu-muenchen.de/pub/rec/music/vocal/lyrics/uwp/

gopher://marvel.loc.gov:70/11/global/arts/music/groups

gopher://runner.utsa.edu:3000/11/Other.Music.Services

gopher://marvel.loc.gov:70/11/research/reading.rooms/perform/music

MAILING LISTS

4AD-L

ALLMUSIC

amslist

CLASSM-L

EMUSIC-L

finlandia

mixmasters

SYNTH-L

themusic

trax-weekly

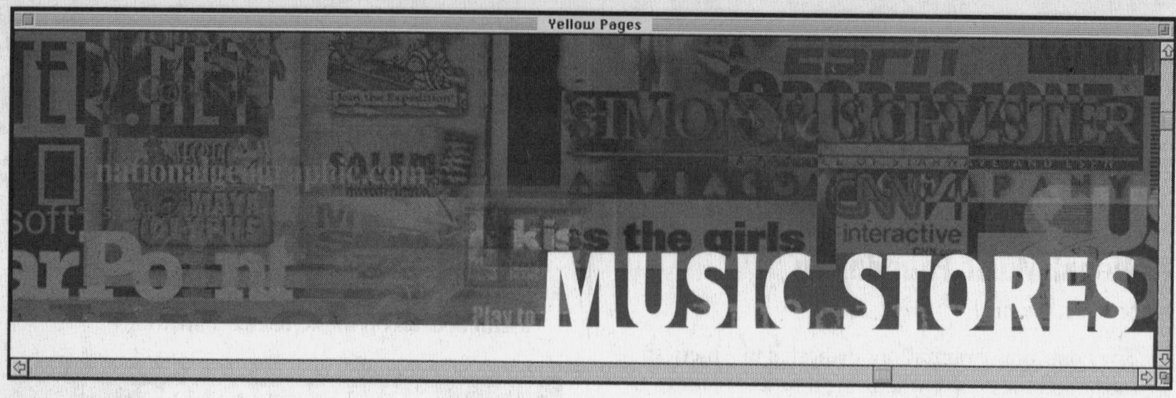

MUSIC STORES

> There's more to music than notes on a page.
>
> *Mr. Glenn Holland in* Mr. Holland's Opus *(1995)*

Abbey Road

http://abbyroad.com/

Specializing in discount CD, video, and DVD, this site also offers stunt kites and kit accessories, believe it or not. These folks are obviously into fun and entertainment—in addition to the serious business of finding and ordering the music and video you want, you can even watch a collection of online movies (Mighty Mouse, Little Lulu, and several more).

Artica—Independent Music CD

http://www.artica.com/

Hear a song clip from the featured artist on the "StarDeck" of this "Music CD StarShip." Recordings are from the labels Heart Consort Music, M-Pire Records, and Russian River Records. Check out the "MissionDeck" to see the goal of this independent-minded group, join the crew, connect to the "top flight" indie links, more.

Blue Vision Music

http://members.aol.com/JamesBVM/homepage.html

Specializing in original contemporary music for kids, this online store offers a small collection of tapes, CDs, and books featuring the work of James Coffey. Sample some of the songs directly from the site (in .au format—requires plug-in or player). The Kid's Club section offers some interesting activities for the younger set (QuickTime or other movie viewer required).

CD Universe
http://www.cduniverse.com/programs/cdubin.exe/tec/?

CD Universe

http://www.cduniverse.com/programs/cdubin.exe/tec/?

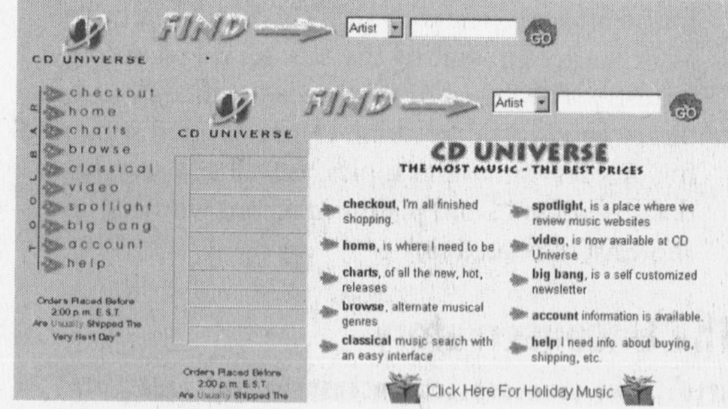

CD Universe promises the most music at the best prices. The interface is particularly easy to use, with graphics augmented by text to explain the purpose of each section (you don't need to spend as much time roaming around to find the section you want). Interested in the top-flight artists in each genre? Check out the Charts section. The "Big Bang" newsletter lets you customize the information that's sent to you (via email) with updates in the musical areas that interest you. A terrific site overall.

CDnow

http://www.cdnow.com/

CDnow claims to be the world's largest music store, and this site seems to back up that statement, with an amazing number of titles available. Search the online database in six different languages for reviews and album info, as well as ordering. Plenty of Real Audio sound clips. Gift certificates for those who have everything; the personalized gift program can also recommend 10 gift ideas based on the names of 4 artists.

There's even a contest in which you can win "music for life"—12 music CDs a year for up to 50 years.

CHILDRENS MUSIC HOUSE

http://www.childrensmusichouse.com/

Releases in the online catalog at this site include CD-ROM, music, video, audiobooks, and books with cassettes from 300 publishers and producers, for the public and the education profession. Specialized services for schools and libraries. Order online or via their toll-free 888 number.

Classical Insites

http://www.classicalinsites.com/live/splash/

Are you a fan of Itzhak Perlman? Yo-Yo Ma? Like to sit back and listen to Maria Callas? Does "anything by Mozart" give you chills? Whatever you like, look for it here, among this site's small gallery of featured artists—composers and performers whose work can be classed as "great." The gallery provides bios, recommendations on which recordings to add to your collection, sound samples, and more.

Music Exoterica

http://www.xme.com/main.html

From a catalog of more than 100,000 CDs in a dozen different categories, this site offers markdowns of 20–30%. Indie bands in several genres are featured. Sound and video clips in RealPlayer format (plug-in required). A custom CD program: Select your favorite cuts from featured artists and have a "collection" CD created the way you like it.

Music World CD

http://www.musicworldcd.com/

Jam-packed with top tracks and a variety of other interesting goodies (175,000 music selections from which to choose), this site guarantees the best prices on the Internet. Currently searchable by artist and title. The planned Reference Library will perform searches based on "artist, group, album, format, label, guest artist, composer, conductor, orchestra, instrument, and over 1 million song titles."

Raag–Indian Music

http://www.webcom.com/raag/

Audio CDs, cassettes, videos (on DVD and laser disk) from India and around the world. According to the site, this store features "Classical, Carnatic, Hindustani, Hindi, Tamil, Telugu, Bengali, Malayalam, Punjabi, Bhangra, Gujarati, Marathi, Ghazals, Bhajans, Meditation, Kundalini, Chakras, etc." Quite a selection! Check out the Buyers' Club page for special discounts.

Siren Disc Online Music Store

http://sirencd.com/

Specializes in imported and alternative music. Two versions of the site; the interactive version uses cookies to track selections in your "electronic cart" until you decide what to order. (A 24-hour phone number is also provided.) Nicely done catalog; search the database alphabetically or browse as you like. Be sure to check the Treasure Chest section for one-of-a-kind or specialty items each time you stop in.

The Sound Connection DJ Music Store

http://www.discjockey.com/store/

Everything the modern DJ needs, including oldies, holiday music, wedding music, dance mixes, novelty tunes, and more. Searchable database—search by title, artist, year (handy for reunion parties). Also offers a variety of equipment, software, and more.

Universal Music Store

http://www.desiboyz.com/

A subsidiary of Desi Boyz Records, Inc., this store has a selection of more than 200,000 music and video titles. Search the database for the desired item; some limited editions are available. Need a unique gift idea? Try a gift certificate to this store—the recipient can do his/her shopping while staying at home! Free shipping on all purchases in the continental U.S.

Related Sites
http://gate.cdworld.com/cdworld.html
http://www.amustardseed.com/homepage.htm
http://www.cdconnection.com/
http://www.cdland.com/
http://www.iglou.com/platterpus/index.html
http://www.lookgreat.com/christianmusic.htm
http://www.microtec.net/~pusher/
http://www.rockfetish.com/
http://www.totalrecall.de/music/_welcome.htm
http://www.turnitup.com.au/
http://www.all-music.com/

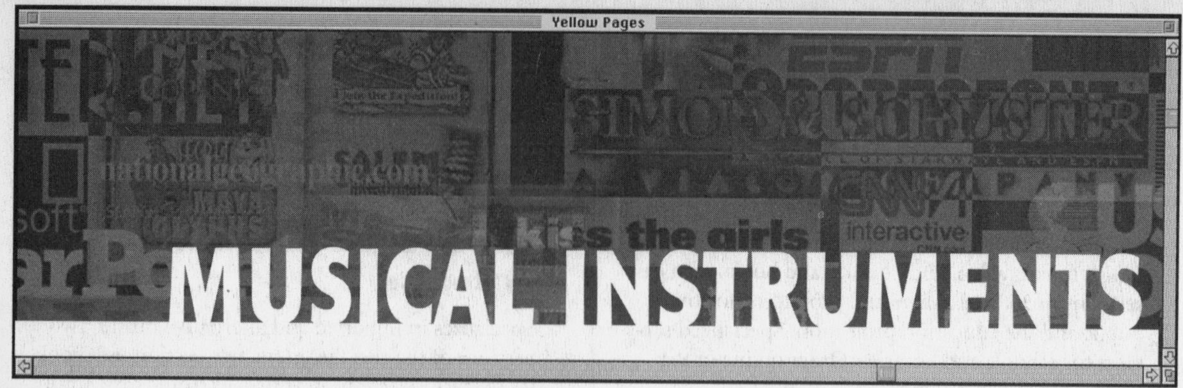

> The noblest thoughts that ever flowed through the hearts of men are contained in its extraordinary, imaginative, and musical mixtures of sounds.
>
> *Henry Higgins in* My Fair Lady *(1964)*

Accordions International

http://www.accordioninfo.com/

Accordion music has come a long way since Lawrence Welk. This manufacturer even offers MIDI kits for electronic accordions! Read about the Concerto, the world's first digital/acoustic accordion. (You can even hear a sample of Bonnie Jo playing the Concerto DA-100 in concert.) Other types of new—as well as used—instruments also available.

The American Nyckelharpa Association

http://www.atmos.washington.edu/~brash/ina.html

This traditional Swedish folk instrument has been around for hundreds of years, but you may not be familiar with it. The author of this page knows of 92 nyckelharpa players in North America. If you're one of them—or you're just curious about this instrument and its players and music—check out this page for details on the association, sound files, and more.

The Barrel Organ Home Page
http://www.geocities.com/Vienna/1444/

American Recorder Society

http://ourworld.compuserve.com/homepages/recorder/

Did you think recorders were just for junior high kids and new age fanatics? Find out more about this instrument and its proponents—more than 3,500 of them in nearly 30 countries. This site is primarily membership-based, but a list of related sites is available as well.

The Barrel Organ Home Page

http://www.geocities.com/Vienna/1444/

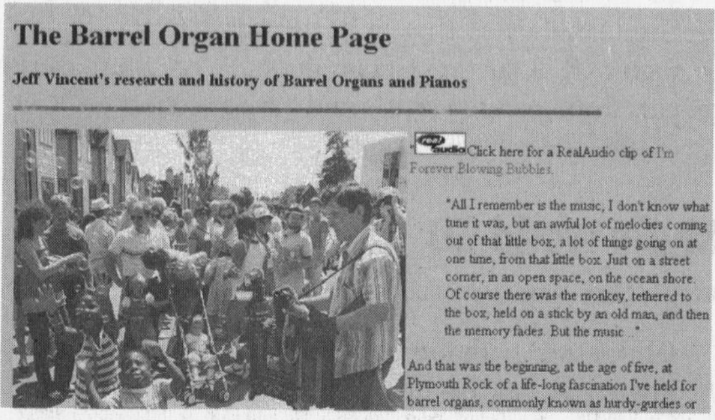

Seeing the photo on the home page at this site may remind you of men with mustaches and garters, and little monkeys with hats. But the barrel organ has a fascinating history that constitutes more than just the prototypical organ grinder. Be sure to read all the pages. If you've never heard a barrel organ (other than in the movies), be sure to try the RealAudio clip of "I'm Forever Blowing Bubbles."

The Bassoon Home Page

http://www.fas.harvard.edu/~tipler/bassoon.html

The author of this site presents a compilation of dozens of links to double-reed pages, music-related sites, and other sites that will be of interest to musicians and bassoon fans alike.

The Ethnic Musical Instruments Co.

http://www.mid-east.com/

This site offers a large selection of "ethnic" musical instruments: sitars, bagpipes, lyres, ocarinas, doumbeks, and many others. Specials, seconds, and repairs—some at great prices—have their own page. Addresses of regional showrooms and related links also included.

Hubbard Harpsichords, Inc.

http://www.hubbard.qds.com/

Hubbard sells completed harpsichords, but also sells kits. Their weekend workshops can help you to put together your own kit, with their help, at a price that's substantially reduced from that of a completely assembled instrument. This site offers details about all the Hubbard products and services, as well as books, CDs, news, events, and general info.

The Internet Cello Society

http://www.cello.org/

With more than 2,500 members in nearly 60 different countries, this organization is an international "cybercommunity of cellists." Learn about the society, connect with other musicians, check out the links, play the many RealAudio sound files. (Note that the file length is not included in the listing—be prepared to wait a while for some files.)

The Music House

http://www.musichouse.com/

Based in Lake Forest, California, this company provides a wide variety of instruments and sheet music to commercial establishments or educational institutions. The service is particularly useful to small music stores that don't have the space or capital to keep a large inventory. Music House School Affiliates can rent or purchase band and orchestral instruments and receive funding assistance.

Northern Sonoran Didjeridoos and DreamTime Pipes

http://members.aol.com/shockleya/dremtime.htm

According to this site, bugs are responsible for some of the most unusual wind instruments in the world—*didjeridoos* are made by aborigines from Australian hardwoods (usually eucalyptus) that are hollowed out by termites. Check out the didjeridoos and DreamTime pipes (a less-expensive version of the didjeridoo, made from agave stalks). Be sure to read the Tip of the Month, and order an instrument of your own, if you're so inclined.

Orange Coast Piano

http://www.forpianos.com/

If your sound system is turned on when you go to this site, be prepared for a pleasant musical interlude that will arrive automatically. This company specializes in rare and antique musical instruments for discriminating buyers and collectors. If you're interested in buying a piano, you may find the Piano Research section to be useful. Want a player piano or new music rolls? Visit a related Orange Coast site at http://www.playerpianos.com/.

¡TchKunG!

http://www.speakeasy.org/~tchkung/

No description for this site could be as good as the one provided there. According to this site, ¡TchKunG! is "a tea cozy, an artist collective, and an experimental percussion and theater troupe. ¡TchKunG! is comprised of musicians, fireworkers, performance artists, martial artists, welders, painters, sculptors, graphic designers, programmers, videographers, activists, and clowns. We are looking to add tattoo artists, acupuncturists, and city planners." Definitely worth checking out.

The Theremin Home Page

http://www.nashville.net/~theremin/

This site is dedicated to a very unusual instrument, named for Leon Theremin. Here's the description from the site: "The theremin is played by waving one's hands near two metal antennas: one for pitch and the other for volume. The antennas vary the frequency of two oscillators." The site offers a rather surprising number of theremin-related links. For a smile, be sure to click the About the Theremin Home Page link and read the history of this site.

Unicorn Strings Music Company

http://unicornstrings.com/

This company specializes in bowed psalteries. You may have seen their unusual instruments in magazines and on TV, such as on the popular science fiction show *Babylon 5*. From this site, you can learn about the company, the instrument and how it's played, the music it produces, and of course how to get one!

UCSC Electronic Music Studios

http://arts.ucsc.edu/ems/music/

This University of California, Santa Cruz site provides a wealth of information on using electronic instruments, some of it in amazing detail. The image map doesn't seem to be working correctly, but the links work just fine. Definitely for "real" musicians and the detail-oriented.

NEWSGROUPS

alt.music.makers

alt.music.saxophone

rec.music.bluenote

rec.music.makers

FTP & GOPHER SITES

ftp://ella.mills.edu/ccm/tuning/papers/bib.html

gopher://wiretap.spies.com/11/Library/Music

MAILING LISTS

BANJO-L

levnet

Recorder-L

TROMBONE-L

TRUMPET-L

Related Sites

http://members.aol.com/jpjonesmi/website/home.html

http://www.cats.se/banjo/

http://www.cnmat.berkeley.edu/~ladzekpo/

http://www.dci.org/

http://www.heartlandharps.com/

http://www.hillside.co.uk/nonsuch/

http://www.hohnerusa.com/

http://www.larkinam.com/

http://www.long-mcquade.com/

http://www.spponline.com.br/drums.htm

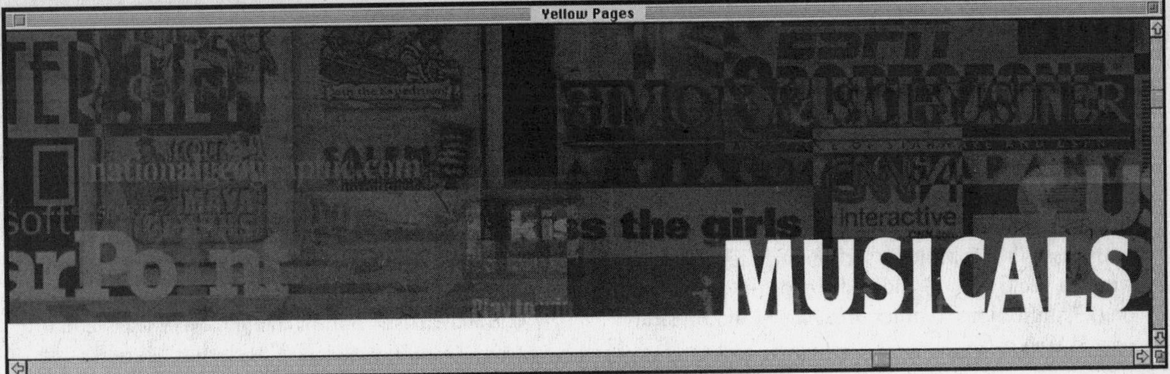

Sure! Make a musical! The new Don Lockwood: he yodels! He jumps about to music!

Cosmo Brown in Singin' in the Rain *(1952)*

The AlftheMerking Page [The Little Mermaid]

http://www.geocities.com/TelevisionCity/8232/

A *Little Mermaid* mania is going on right now, with the Disney film in theaters again. The many graphics on this fun site include Ariel swimming across the opening screen. Play the Java game, where you try to collect the Flounder characters without being eaten by sharks. Includes a collection of links to many, many other Little Mermaid sites, and is itself part of a Little Mermaid Web ring. Lots to do and see.

Beauty and the Beast

http://www.columbia.edu/~zm4/BeautyandBeast/

Zarina Mustapha has put an amazing amount of work into this site, covering in detail both the film and theatrical versions of this timeless tale. It's not surprising that the site has earned quite a number of awards! Read the original fable, heck out the details on the cast of the national tour, view production stills, even the complete libretto. Much, much more.

Musicals.net
http://musicals.net/

Better Living Through Show Tunes

http://www.geocities.com/Broadway/2685/

Okay, the page's title is a little hokey. But the site, devoted to Broadway show-tune fans, is a serious collection of information on Broadway musicals and their composers, with pictures, cast lists, discographies, CD reviews, links to related sites, and more.

Grease Is The Word

http://www.geocities.com/Hollywood/Hills/1173/

The *Grease* phenomenon goes on, with the stage show enjoying a revolving-door cast of stars. This site, part of a Web ring of *Grease* sites, offers lyrics from the songs, including RealAudio clips for some, and a MIDI pack of songs for download. Interviews, biographies, reviews, cast lists, pics, and even *Grease* pen pals.

Livent

http://www.livent.com/livent/home.html

This commercial site represents a company, Livent Inc., based in Ontario, Canada. Livent develops and produces musical theatre productions for their own Canadian theater circuit, including *Phantom of the Opera, Joseph and the Amazing Technicolor Dreamcoat,* and other famous shows, as well as original musical productions. Terrific graphics, audio clips. Browse the concert circuit for the series that interests you (more than two dozen), order tickets online.

Miss Saigon

http://www.clark.net/pub/rsjdfg/

This fan page provides a lot of detail about the show and its history. Cast lists include anyone who has ever played a major role in *Miss Saigon,* as well as pictures and biographies for many of the actors and actresses in the list. The Multimedia section includes video clips (in `.mov` format) and audio clips (in `.au` format). Connections to other *Miss Saigon* and musical-related Web pages.

MovieTunes

http://www.movietunes.com

Part of the Hollywood Online groups of sites, this amazing site receives more than 40,000 hits per week. It's not really surprising—the Soundtracks section alone is worth a visit if you're a music fan. The databases are kept closely up-to-date with new films and productions being premiered. Sound clips require Real Player 4.0 and a fairly fast modem connection. Be sure to check out the connected sites. Multimedia is a favorite for trailers and film clips, MoviePeople for favorite actors and their films. Hours of entertainment about entertainment.

Musical (Dance) Films

http://www.filmsite.org/musicalfilms.html

This site is composed of a lengthy, incredibly detailed document that tells the history of musical film from *The Jazz Singer* (1927) to *The Lion King* (1994). Includes pages on many of the films, with theatrical posters, pictures, and some synopses that tell in great detail the story of each film—including occasional song lyrics and dialogue.

Musicals.net

http://musicals.net/

This page is currently in transition as it changes its name from "The Musicals Home Page" to "Musicals.net." (Don't be surprised if the graphics look different from those shown in the figure.) Listing about 75 popular musicals and plenty of new ones coming up. Click the musical's name to list links, lyrics, media clips, notes, synopsis, and tons of other info. Plenty of details on the news in musical theater.

Performing Arts Online

http://www.performingarts.net/

The Performing Arts Network has put together a great site. Entering from the Navigator 3.0 version of the site plays a lovely electronic tune (you may want to turn the volume up a bit). Links to dozens of performers and companies, sorted by genre—Musical Theatre lists current shows in production. A clickable "featured artists" button changes every few seconds to connect you to performers' Web sites. Hundreds of links to related sites.

RENT - An Unofficial Site

http://www.lifecafe.com/index2.htm

This home page is as unusual as the prize-winning show it describes, with nearly half a million hits in the last year. A discussion board is available for online discussion with other *Rent* fans. A special page is dedicated to Jonathan Larson, who died the day before his dream came true. Plenty of articles are included on the show, its cast, the national tours, and so on.

Sam's Musical Box

http://www.ozemail.com.au/~samoran/index.html

Australian Sam Moran has put together a hefty collection of musical-related links across the world. Included are info on some of the most famous Broadway composers: Andrew Lloyd Webber, the Gershwin brothers, Stephen Sondheim, and others, and links to sites about their shows and others. A section on musical theater performers, as well as "wannabees."

Shadow Song [Phantom of the Opera]

http://www.shadowsong.com/

One of the most fascinating and romantic stage productions ever created, *Phantom of the Opera* now haunts the Internet as well as stages across the world. This site, part of a Phantom Web ring, provides a Virtual Paris Opera. Click the image called The Rotunda to join the mailing list. The Stage takes you to original fiction by *Phantom* fans. Several other images provide more exploring. Be sure to read the section on protecting the Phantom from John Travolta (and the rest of the Hollywood gang).

Tony Awards Online

http://www.tonys.org/mainframe.html

It isn't strictly musicals, of course—plenty of wonderful dramas and comedies take awards in their own categories—but the Tonys are always a guide to what's good in musicals on stage. Stop in at this site for a variety of entertainment: contests, games, a chat page, lists of award winners (and nominees, depending on the season), theater news, and other interesting sections.

Welcome to Halloween!! - The Nightmare Before Christmas

http://www.halloweentown.com/mainindex.shtml

If you missed this fascinating stop-motion animated feature, you may not understand a lot of the stuff at this site. If you're a devotee of this Tim Burton spectacular, on the other hand, you'll find this site a feast. Plenty of pictures and sounds to enjoy—click the pics of Sally, Sandy Claws, Oogie Boogie, and other characters to hear sound bites—and of course tons of detail about Jack Skellington. Did you know he first appeared in *Beetlejuice*? Highly recommended site.

NEWSGROUPS

alt.disney

alt.music.lloyd-webber

rec.arts.theatre.musicals

MAILING LISTS

COLLAB-L

FILMUS-L

Related Sites

http://home1.swipnet.se/~w-18501/Bilder/Star/sib.htm

http://members.aol.com/mgmfanatic/index.html

http://numao-www.cs.titech.ac.jp/~sison/bm.html

http://www.arcana.com/~julie/movie/moviey.html

http://www.foxhome.com/soundofmusic/

http://www.geocities.com/Broadway/4270/

http://www.nykin.com/empress/

http://www.rockyhorror.com/

http://www.tcfhe.com/myfairlady/

http://www1.playbill.com/

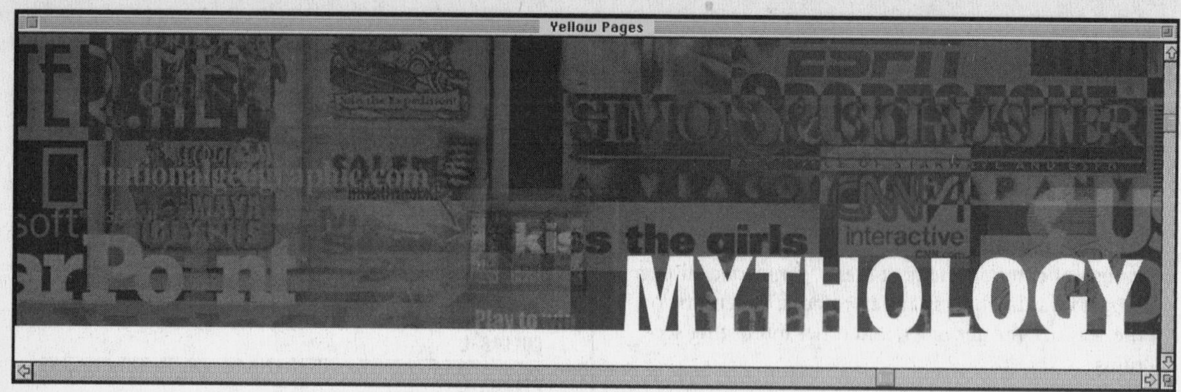

> We live in a fantasy world, a world of illusion. The great task in life is to find reality.
>
> *Iris Murdoch*

Need an escape from reality? Here you'll find sites about mythology, from faeries and folklore to gods and goddess of Greek and Norse mythology. Lose yourself in the mystery of fantasy!

Aeon: The Journal of Science and Myth

http://www.ames.net/aeon/

Journal devoted to investigating and exploring "common patterns of ancient myths from around the world." Takes its viewpoint from scientific studies of archaeology and astronomy. Read articles, subscribe to the mailing list.

The AFU and Urban Legend Archive

http://www.urbanlegends.com/

Here's the site where all the folk tales of city life and urban legends end up (or at least they should). If there's a juicy rumor, or farfetched-but-possible story, there's a good chance it's here, along with the truth of the matter; and if not, you should contact the AFU and urban legend newsgroups.

ARTHURNET Mailing List

http://www.mun.ca/lists/arthurnet/

This is the subscription site for a moderated list on the subject of King Arthur and related subjects. Access to the archives is available at this site.

NRP TOP PICKS

The AFU and Urban Legend Archive
http://www.urbanlegends.com/

Cyberlore Central
http://www.pass.wayne.edu/~twk/cc.html

Encyclopedia Mythica
http://www.pantheon.org/mythica/

Lilith
http://ccat.sas.upenn.edu/~humm/Topics/Lilith/

Parabola Magazine On-Line
http://www.parabola.org/

The Straight Dope
http://www.straightdope.com/

Bullfinch's Mythology

gopher://gopher.vt.edu:10010/11/53

A Gopher site of the famous reference book of mythology.

Creative Minds Presents: Mythology, Legends, & Folklore

http://pages.prodigy.com/myth/mythbb.htm

A monthly forum to discuss various topics on legends, mythology, and folklore.

Cyberlore Central

http://www.pass.wayne.edu/~twk/cc.html

Begin here to explore the folklore that has grown up around computers and the Internet. Full of links to other sites showing the scope of the cyberculture today.

Encyclopaedia of Mythology

http://www.pins.co.uk/upages/probertm/myths.htm

A very brief (usually just a line or two) alphabetical listing of mythical beings (with some concepts and places included). You can search by mythos or by the index, which contains all the listings.

Encyclopedia Mythica

http://www.pantheon.org/mythica/

An extraordinarily well-done encyclopedia containing hundreds of definitions and descriptions of mythic creations: gods and goddesses, supernatural beings, creatures, monsters. It has a search feature for tracking down the entries, and can be viewed in a frames or non-frames format. One of the best sites around.

The Faerie Encyclopedia

http://www.students.uiuc.edu/~rlehmann/fey_denizen.html

A labor-of-love of a true faerie friend, the encyclopedia does a very good job of describing European fairies. Also has a comprehensive links page to other faerie sites.

Folklore and Mythology

http://www.pitt.edu/~dash/folktexts.html

A selection of manuscripts on the WWW concerning mythology and folklore; the emphasis is on Germanic and English tales, but some other cultures are represented.

General Folklore and Mythology

http://pibweb.it.nwu.edu/~pib/mythgene.htm

A fantastic source of links concerning myths, legends, and folklore. If you need a place to start a search, this is it.

Of Gods and Men: The A to Z of Mythology and Legend

http://www.clubi.ie/lestat/godsmen.html

An alphabetical listing of people and places in mythology, legends, and religion. A beautiful site with some excellent images.

Greek Mythology

http://www.intergate.net/uhtml/.jhunt/greek_myth/greek_myth.html

A comprehensive view of the Greek myths with an excellent family tree showing the familial relationships of the gods.

Highlander: The Anthology

http://www.mindspring.com/~vfoster/HL/

Selected links to other Highlander sites, sequels to existing Highlander tales, original stories (some a bit racy for the younger set).

Fan Fiction on the Net

http://members.aol.com/ksnicholas/fanfic/index.html

Extensive list of fiction sites for TV and film—everything from Hawaii Five-O and Miami Vice to Star Trek and Dracula, and everything in between.

Hillhouse Investigations, Inc. Paranormal Detective Agency

http://ic.net/~dunstan/hh.htm

A humorous look at the paranormal; this isn't a real detective agency, but rather a parody of how a "real paranormal agency" would advertise. Read the subheadings on such things as aura imbalance and have a good laugh. Also read the letter columns for other demented humor.

The Holy Grail

http://www.the-spa.com/kirk.burkins/GRAIL.htm

This site is a starting point for researching the myths and legends concerning the Holy Grail; it contains much of the lore surrounding the Grail, as well as book reviews of books about the Grail and related topics. Also has a links page.

The Joseph Campbell Foundation

http://www.jcf.org/

The foundation's purpose is to continue the work of Joseph Campbell in bring the meaning of myth into everyday life. The foundation offers programs and discussion groups to explore Campbell's work and related topics.

Journal of American Folklore

http://ernie.bgsu.edu/~thomasz/JAF/jaf.htm

This site functions as a way of contacting the American Folklore Society online. It gives a brief listing of the contents of previous *Journals* and has links to other folklore Web sites.

Legendary Site of the Week

http://www.web.co.za/arthur/leglist.html

Arthur Goldstuck lists his choice (partially based on nominations by others) of a Web site dealing with mythology, magic, urban legends, the paranormal, and other related topics. Lots of fun.

Legends Unlimited

http://www.Legends-Unlimited.com/

This site is dedicated to the use of myth and legends in fantasy fiction today. It's beautifully done, full of gorgeous graphics and well-written essays and articles. A pleasure to look at and read.

Lilith

http://ccat.sas.upenn.edu/~humm/Topics/Lilith/

A site dedicated to the "first" wife of Adam, Lilith. Said to be the first witch, mother of demons, the first seductress. This site provides a comprehensive view of the origins and myths surrounding this primal character.

LUCKY W Amulet Archive

http://www.sonic.net/~yronwode/LuckyW.html

If you're looking for information on amulets, tokens, talismans, and other symbols of magic and good fortune, this is the site to start your search. The site is very informative and fun to read, and filled with links to other similar sites.

Mythology

http://www.users.csbsju.edu/~djferrar/myth.html

Has a great clickable map of the world; point the cursor to the region you want to know about, and up comes a list of sites concerning the myths of that region. Unfortunately, it covers mainly Europe and the Middle East, with some regions (such as North America) having nothing at the time of this writing. This site welcomes contributions, in case you know of appropriate sites.

Mythology in Western Art

http://lib.haifa.ac.il/www/art/MYTHOLOGY_WESTART.HTML

A collection of .GIF images of the Greek gods, based on scanned images from pottery, architecture, and paintings. The research was done by the University of Haifa Art History, Haifa, Israel.

Mythology on the Web

http://www.unm.edu/~rkoshak/

A collection of sites on the WWW organized by mythos. It seems very complete and far-ranging in scope.

Mythopoeic Society

http://home.earthlink.net/~emfarrell/mythsoc/mythsoc.html

Home page of the Mythopoeic Society, a nonprofit organization interested in studying and discussing literary works, including the myths and legends of Tolkien (the Hobbit tales, and so on), C. S. Lewis, and Charles Williams.

Myths and Legends

http://pubpages.unh.edu/~cbsiren/myth.html

An excellent listing of links on the Net covering many of the world's myths and legends, including medieval and Renaissance periods. It even covers some early fantasy, science fiction, and horror works that are based on mythic and legendary materials.

Napoleon, Russia, and the Olympian Gods

http://www.loop.com/~variagate/olybook.htm

A commercial site selling the book *Napoleon, Russia, and the Olympian Gods: An Illustrated Guide to Greek Mythology*. It explains the nature and significance of the gift that Napoleon sent to Russia, and the artistic and historic importance of the illustrations and the myths depicted.

Norse and Germanic Mythology in *The Wheel of Time*

http://www.dsv.su.se/~k-j-nore/norse.html

Robert Jordan's *The Wheel of Time* series has attracted an enormous following among the reading public, and where the public goes, scholars soon follow, trying to explain where the author got his ideas.

Karl-Johan Norén has written a very detailed scholarly work, comparing key concepts and characters in the series with the Norse and Germanic myths. A must-read for the die-hard Jordan fan, if only to find something else to discuss on the various Wheel of Time forums and lists out there.

Norse Mythology

http://www.ugcs.caltech.edu/~cherryne/mythology.html

A FAQ under construction, it has the basics of Norse mythology, as well as lists of the major gods and goddesses of the mythos. It includes an excellent listing of source materials for those who want to do their own research, and has many links to other sites of related interest.

Parabola Magazine On-Line

http://www.parabola.org/

The online version of *Parabola* magazine, this site contains some articles from the current issue on the newsstand, as well as how to subscribe to the magazine. The purpose of *Parabola* is to show the significance of mythic and spiritual themes in everyday life.

Past, Present, Future: Mythology and Ancient Civilizations in Science Fiction and Fantasy

http://www.missouri.edu/~c570492/capstone.html

A paper on the uses (and misuses) of myths in science fiction and fantasy, with emphasis on recent television shows. While several of the shows are no longer being broadcast (*Earth2*, *Seaquest*) it takes a good look at the new leader of syndicated shows, *Hercules: The Legendary Journeys.*

Pathfinder: Mythologies of the World

http://www.lib.ua.edu/mytholog.htm

This site lists *offline* sources of mythological research that don't include the Greek or Roman mythologies. It also provides online access to AMELIA's catalogue. (AMELIA is The University of Alabama's automated library system.)

The Phantom Bookshop

http://www.phantoms.com/~phantom/index.html

A bookshop in Ventura, California, specializing in books "with an emphasis on the unusual, weird science, older scientific and related material." A fascinating "syte," very visual, but be sure you have plenty of time to look at it all—there's a lot to absorb.

Pleiades Mythology

http://www.astro.wisc.edu:80/~gibson/pleiades/pleiades_myth.html

A small site concerning the mythology of the Pleiades star cluster, also known as the Seven Sisters. The site lists sources that use the Greek legends only. Each of the sisters is briefly discussed, with an explanation of how they became stars in the heavens.

The Practice Hall

http://www.eznet.com/bravo/ph/ph.html

This online companion to the *Tooth & Claw* newsletter explores the use of myths of warriors as a teaching tool to inspire and instruct today's martial practitioners.

The Sacred Landscape

http://www.sonic.net/yronwode/sacredland.html

This site presents a wide variety of astrological discussion, including essays on sacred geometry and the relationship between ancient architecture and astronomy, sundials and other devices, some interesting info on religion and Freemasonry, and other related topics. It also provides a list to join to discuss these topics.

The Straight Dope

http://www.straightdope.com/

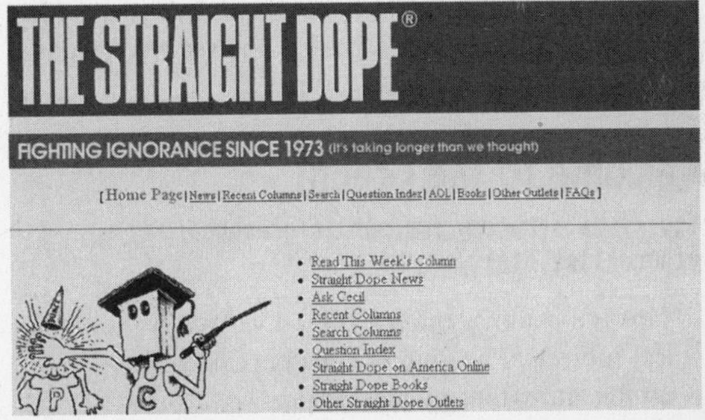

The source for "the truth" on urban legends, old wives' tales, and questions that anyone may have about the strange goings-on in the world. Copies of "The Straight Dope" newspaper columns are available, as well as various FAQs.

Sumerian Mythology FAQ

http://pubpages.unh.edu/%7Ecbsiren/sumer-faq.html

Contains a description of the pantheon and cosmology of the Sumerians, who lived over 4,000 years ago in what is now southern Iraq.

A B C D E F G H I J K L M N O P Q R S T U V W X Y Z

Superstitions

http://www.cam.org/~jennyb/super.html

Listing some of the most popular superstitions, it provides the meaning and possible origins of these well-known beliefs. Done in a frames format; the only problem is that some of the individual frames are hard to read.

UCLA Folklore and Mythology Archives

http://www.humnet.ucla.edu/humnet/folklore/archives/

The Folklore and Mythology Archives are located on the UCLA campus and serve as primary research and instructional resources for the UCLA Folklore and Mythology Program. While the site itself is under construction (most of its listings are empty), it does have a section where questions concerning American folklore can be emailed to the staff there, and a reply will be sent back.

USENET FAQs alt. mythology

http://www.cis.ohio-state.edu/hypertext/faq/usenet-faqs/bygroup/alt/mythology/top.html

Contains the FAQs developed by the alt.mythology newgroup.

The Viking Homepage

http://control.chalmers.se/vikings/viking.html

This is an extremely complete site for legends, myth, lore, and history of the Vikings. It covers everything from myths to language to mead.

Welcome to The Green!

http://www.servtech.com/public/greenman/mythBooklist.html

This is a reading/source list for a variety of mythological subjects. The sources cited have been suggested on the alt.mythology newsgroup.

NEWSGROUPS

alt.arts.storytelling

alt.books.cs-lewis

alt.evil

alt.folklore.computers

alt.folklore.herbs

alt.folklore.internet

alt.folklore.urban

alt.legend.king-arthur

alt.magick.folk

alt.mythology

alt.mythology.mythic-animals

LISTSERVS

ACADEMIC-MYTHS—Academic Myths Discussion Group

You can join this group by sending the message "sub ACADEMIC-MYTHS your name" to

listproc@mailer.fsu.edu

ARTHURNET—King Arthur Mailing List

You can join this group by sending the message "sub ARTHURNET your name" to

listserv@morgan.ucs.mun.ca

KFTLC-L—Kung Fu: The Legend Continues

You can join this group by sending the message "sub KFTLC-L your name" to

listserv@vm.temple.edu

KNIGHTS—Knights of Myth Drannor

You can join this group by sending the message "sub KNIGHTS your name" to

majordomo@efn.org

MYTHUS-L—Mythus Fantasy Roleplaying Game List

You can join this group by sending the message "sub MYTHUS-L your name" to

listserv@brownvm.brown.edu

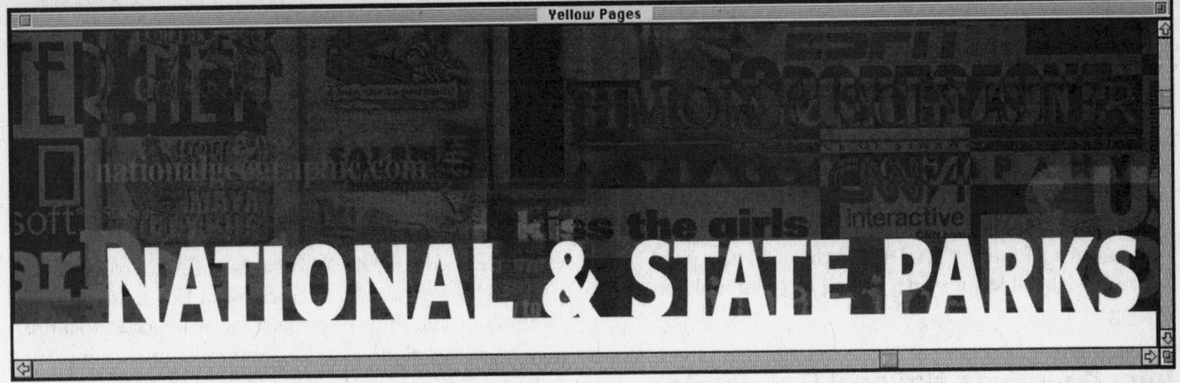

> Come, wander with me,
> for the moonbeams are bright
> On river and forest, o'er mountain and lea.
>
> *Charles Jefferys*

Chaco Communications, Inc.

`http://www.chaco.com/park/`

Find interesting reading about the Chaco Culture National Historical Park, in northwest New Mexico. Archaeological information is provided about this ancient Native American cultural center. Also provided are various photos of the park and links to related sites.

Death Valley National Park

`http://www.desertusa.com/dv/du_dvpmain.html`

The Virtual Visitor Center for Death Valley National Park, in California. You'll find general park information, plus lots of info about what's new at the park, places to go and things to do, and desert life. You can also communicate with others at the Desert Talk message board and mailbag. And be sure to visit the Trading Post to fill up your shopping cart.

NRP TOP PICKS

Grand Canyon Official Tourism Page
`http://www.thecanyon.com/`

L.L. Bean
`http://www.llbean.com/parksearch/`

PARKNET: The National Park Service Place
`http://www.nps.gov/`

Yellowstone Net
`http://www.yellowstone.net/`

Yosemite Park
`http://www.yosemitepark.com/`

Zion National Park
`http://www.infowest.com/zion/`

GORP–Great Smoky Mountains National Park

`http://www.gorp.com/gorp/resource/US_National_Park/tn_great.HTM`

Your first stop for information on the Great Smoky Mountains and the park. You can find out about accommodations, traveling through the Smokies by car, cycling, camping, fishing, hiking and backpacking, horseback riding, the mountain people, and naturalist activities. Also access info on trips and other Internet resources.

Grand Canyon Official Tourism Page

`http://www.thecanyon.com/`

This site provides all the tourism information you'll need when visiting Grand Canyon National Park. You'll get all the standard information on what to do and where to go/stay/eat/shop. Plus, read news bits, get weather info, see photographs, read anecdotes, and learn all about the local area. A great resource.

Harpers Ferry NHP

`http://www.nps.gov/hafe/hf_visit.htm`

If you're interested in history, you'll be interested in this site and its details on Harpers Ferry National Historical Park, located at the confluence of the Potomac and Shenandoah rivers. These pages help you learn about or plan a trip to the area, plus give you insightful lessons on a part of our national heritage.

John Donohue's National Park Photos

`http://www.panix.com/~wizjd/parks/parks.html`

Get a look at a wide array of national parks by viewing photos of their various splendors. Watch a slideshow of the photographer's favorites, or pick a park and see all the related photos. Nice photography.

L.L. Bean

`http://www.llbean.com/parksearch/`

A park-search service covering 766 state parks and 171 national parks, plus wildlife refuges, national forests, and Bureau of Land Management lands. You can search by park name, by the activity you're interested in, or by state. A handy site with volumes of information and many photos. Don't miss this one.

Mesa Verde National Park

`http://www.mesaverde.org/`

This site provides a wealth of information on Mesa Verde National Park, in Colorado. The site also delves into the archaeology of the Ancestral Puebloans and covers the ancient, as well as the modern, culture of the area. Also offers an electronic bookstore selling park-related materials.

National Park Lover

`http://home.sprynet.com/sprynet/schmor/national.htm#Ads`

This is the page for you if you want to explore the national parks and are eager to share your own park-related insights, tips, and stories with others. You can also view pictures and find a park.

National Parks and Conservation Association

`http://www.npca.org/home/npca/`

Site of the NPCA, a citizen action group dedicated to protecting our national parks. Learn about the association and its latest programs, campaigns, and events; search the site to locate topics and information of interest. You can also read the *National Parks* magazine and become a member online.

National Parks Travel Guide

`http://natparks.com/indexf.html`

Locate national park Web pages in several ways: by a listing of regions, via a search, off a U.S. map, or from a rolling slideshow of parks. Gives you access to a full array of travel information. Submit your own info on national parks attractions, add your entry to the Visitor Logs, view a photo gallery, and more.

North Cascades National Park

`http://www.halcyon.com/rdpayne/ncnp.html`

The unofficial guide to North Cascades National Park, in northwestern Washington. The site provides basic park facts and visitor services, informs on the natural history of the area, gives park management info, and leads you to related Web sites. Get everything from the latest conditions to boating information to details on the Alpine plants.

Olympic National Park

`http://www.northolympic.com/onp/`

Provides dozens of links to information on Olympic National Park, in the Pacific Northwest, which has 4 million visitors annually. Also included is a link to a virtual tour of the park. All the information you need in one spot.

PARKNET: The National Park Service Place

`http://www.nps.gov/`

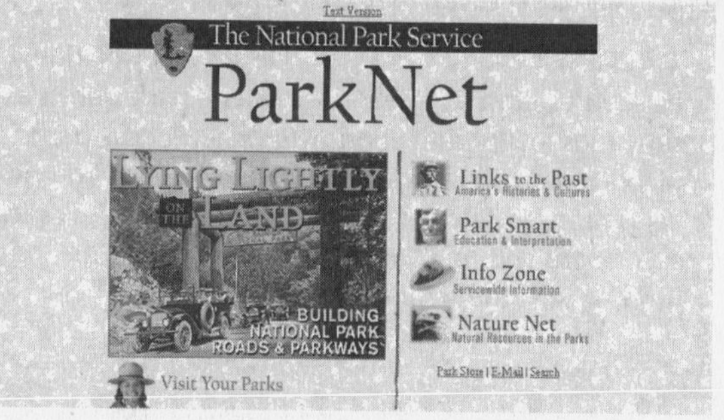

A mandatory stop for anyone interested in our national parks. This is the National Park Service's home page, a searchable site that links to NPS sites for all the parks. Besides finding data on any individual park, you can read special travel features and learn about such topics as natural resources in the parks and America's histories and cultures. Plus, visit the Park Store.

Passport to Your National Parks

http://www.geocities.com/Yosemite/4434/passport.html

Visit this site to learn about obtaining and using the Passport to Your National Parks, a sort of information book and personal travel scrapbook available at national parks. The Passport offers color-coded maps, illustration, visitors' information, and photos, and it can be stamped with an official park "cancellation mark" each time you visit.

Rocky Mountain National Park

http://www.csn.net/~arthurvb/rmnp/rmnp.html

An unofficial site for Rocky Mountain National Park, in Colorado's Rockies. This site offers links labeled What's New, Current Conditions, The Park Service Brochure, Park Information, Park Databases, Current Park Weather, Park Maps, Park Pictures, Park History and Exhibits, and Related Links.

Yellowstone Net

http://www.yellowstone.net/

Site recommended by USA TODAY and others. Visit Yellowstone Net for all kinds of information on the park, news, photos, specialty stores, reservations, related links, and access to the Yellowstone Net community. Check it out.

Yosemite Park

http://www.yosemitepark.com/

Official Web site of Yosemite National Park, in central California. This visually appealing site offers park overview, Yosemite lodging, park activities, dine and shop, special events, gifts and memories, special offers, news releases, and search/index categories for you to explore.

Your Guide to Canyonlands

http://www.canyonlands-utah.com/

Utah's largest national park is profiled at this site. You'll find accommodations, various area destinations, tours, campgrounds, and travel resources via the site.

Zion National Park

http://www.infowest.com/zion/

A sharp-looking home page leads you to a variety of information about Zion National Park, in southwestern Utah. You can choose to jump to general information, maps to and from Zion, walks and hikes, places to stay, things to do, and photo gallery. A nicely done site.

NEWSGROUPS

bit.listserv.travel-1

rec.backcountry

rec.climbing

rec.outdoors.national-parks

rec.outdoors.rv-travel

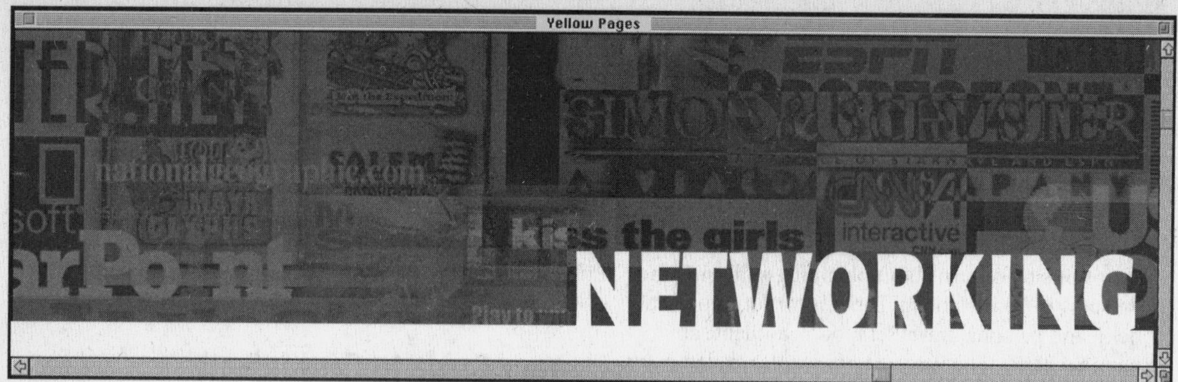

> Networking is an enrichment program, not an entitlement program.
>
> *Susan RoAne*

NRP TOP PICKS
Banyan Systems Inc. http://www.banyan.com/
Florida Atlantic University http://www.fau.edu/academic/cont-ed/compmain.htm
InterWorking Labs http://www.iwl.com/
Network Computing's ISDN Online http://techweb.cmp.com/nc/isdn/
Novell, Inc. http://www.novell.com
PC DOCS, Inc. http://www.pcdocs.com

Alcatel Data Networks

http://www.adn.alcatel.com/

Provides company profile, news releases, product information, and hot topics list for high performance data systems company. Gives full background on Avanza switching architectures and Alcatel platforms. Also provides information, enrolling procedures, and course listings for their Ashburn training facilities.

Banyan Systems Inc.

http://www.banyan.com/

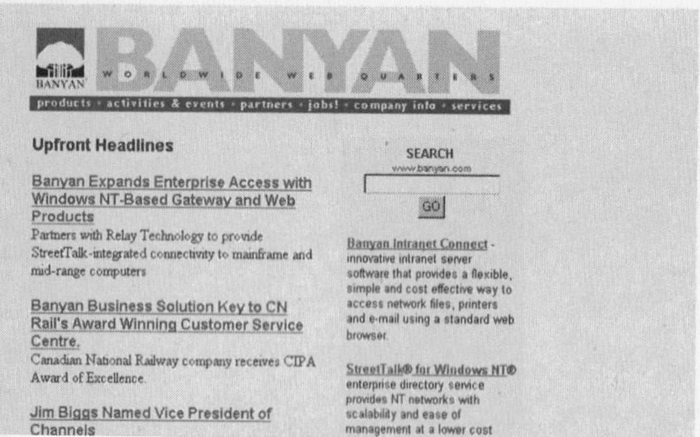

Develops enterprise network software products that allow organizations to integrate diverse computing resources into unified, global networks. Banyan produces TCP/IP products, UNIX/SMTP networking products, the StreetTalk naming service, and the popular VINES network operating system.

Cisco NTI!

http://www.jma.com/

Firewall and network address translation products for your organization. Links to private link information, press releases, contact info, customer support, technical info, and more.

CrossComm Corporation

http://www.crosscomm.com/

Develops and produces network, Internet, and communications products for everything from LANs to workstations. Specializes in ATM technologies and services. Includes information about ClearPath and the XL families of products for use with networks and Internets. Provides technical specifications and applications of CrossComm products. Also includes pricing and ordering information.

CygnaCom Solutions, Inc.

http://www.cygnacom.com/

Produces and provides products and services for service engineering, network creation, server applications, and data security. Includes company philosophies and service listings. Provides company background and profile along with contact information.

Digital Network Product Business

http://www.networks.digital.com/

Researching the purchase of a new server for your business? This site from Digital Equipment Corporation includes extensive technical specifications on Digital's newest server products through the Network Products Guide link. An Application Stories link provides examples of Digital servers currently used in the business environment, and a Seminars, Training, and Events link lets you know when Digital will be demonstrating their products in your town.

Emulex Network Systems

http://www.emulex.com/

Designs and produces hardware and software for network access, communications, and time management. Products specialize in the managing of data between computers and peripheral equipment. Includes detailed product listings, upgrade programs, technical support, and a company profile.

Engage Communication

http://www.engage.com/engage/

Produces routers and other products for networking PCs, Macintoshes, and UNIX networks. Includes product specifications, technical support, and contact information.

Florida Atlantic University

http://www.fau.edu/academic/cont-ed/compmain.htm

Florida Atlantic University offers a one month CNE immersion program through its certified Novell Education Center. This page explains the core courses you will take toward CNE certification taught by veteran CNI Frank Moore, the registration process, lodging, costs, and benefits of the program. Also covers additional courses such as Microsoft certification training.

HDS Network Systems

http://www.hds.com

HDS Network Systems manufactures and sells multimedia X Window stations, and creates software for these systems in a multivendor open-system environment. HDS X terminals offer analog and digital video, IP Multicasting, and live TV/cable displays.

HELIOS Software

http://www.helios.de

Developers of color management and client/server software, including Helios EtherShare, PCShare, EtherShare OPI, and Helios ColorSync 2 Xtension.

Intel Product Info

http://www.intel.com/intel/product/index.htm

A site with links to Intel products and information for your business. Networking, video, conferencing, or Internet are some of the options.

Interphase

http://www.iphase.com/

Products for mass storage and high speed networks. Links to products, support, news, and employment opportunities.

InterWorking Labs

http://www.iwl.com/

Offers Test Suite software products that test SNMP network hardware, such as routers, printers, hubs, servers, and UPSs. Find out about their products, download a free SNMP test suite demo, and contact IWL staff.

ISDN Primer

http://www.interforce.com/technology/isdnprimer.html

ISDN (Integrated Services Digital Network) is another networking technology that provides high-speed phone and data communications. The ISDN Primer site provides an introduction to ISDN, as well as information on where to find additional references on ISDN.

ISDN Tutorial

http://www.ziplink.net/~ralphb/ISDN/

For an introduction to ISDN, including pictures, visit this site. The information is organized in ten pages, including topics on history of ISDN, its advantages, layer protocols, and sources and references. It also includes an ISDN "book store" link to a page that lists some of the third-party reference books available on ISDN.

KarlBridge

http://www.karlnet.com/

Bridges and routers to solve your network security problems. Pictures and links to products and information, applications, and pricing.

Kinesix

http://www.kinesix.com/

Manufacturer of Sammi that enables you to integrate network applications without writing any network or graphical user interface code. Several links to learn more about Sammi, including current users, tech support, employment opportunities, and more.

K-Net Ltd

http://www.k-net.co.uk/

Manufacturer and distributor of Fore Systems ATM switches, adapters, and routers. Our products include a stackable ATM ethernet bridge and stackable ATM video codes. Links to products, support, and employment information.

LAN Solutions

http://www.aimnet.com/~yungi/lansol.html

Based in the San Francisco bay area, the leading Novell network integrator. Check out the long list of services provided by their CNEs.

Lancom Technologies

http://www.inforamp.net/~lancom/

Lancom Technologies provides all the courseware you need to become CNA or CNE certified. Provide this courseware for your students or yourself at reduced costs.

LANology Enterprise Network Solutions

http://www.lanology.com/

Produces a wide array of products for network servers from workstation connectivity to peripheral management and more. Includes product database with technical specifications and support. Provides service listings, contact information, technical partners, and links to related sites.

Maxperts, Inc.

http://www.maxperts.com/

Client/server solutions for SGI platforms and Mac. Create a WAN or get your business up and running on the Internet.

Microsoft BackOffice

http://www.microsoft.com/backoffice

Microsoft BackOffice is a family of products designed to work together, with Windows NT Server its main component. The family includes Microsoft Exchange Server, Merchant Server, Proxy Server, SNA Server, SQL Server, Systems Management Server, Transaction Server, Index Server, and Internet Information Server. This Web site includes information on all these products, as well as how to implement BackOffice in your enterprise.

MONET Home Page

http://fury.nosc.mil

MONET is a Department of Defense network that stands for High Data Rate MObile interNET. This site, which contains no classified information, defines MONET, how it will someday interoperate with the public-carrier networks in the future, and how it will achieve high data rate transfers using mobile RF communication links.

MSI Communications

http://www.msic.com/

Data, voice, and video integration solutions including WAN, LAN, consulting, network engineering and design, management, and maintenance.

Myricom, Inc.

http://www.myri.com/

An inexpensive, high-speed network provider based in sunny California. Myrinet is their LAN based on Mosaic technology and they offer a variety of products, performance info, client info, and more related to Myrinet.

NETiS Technology, Inc.

http://www.netistech.com/

A manufacturer and service provider for all your individual, business, and institutional computer needs. Check out their corporate profile, services and support, product info and press releases, promotionals, and more.

NetMagic, Inc.

http://www.aristosoft.com/ifact/inet.htm?who=unknown

High performance Web servers for Windows 95 and Windows NT, featuring Commerce Builder and Communications Builder. Links to sites that use Commerce Builder, downloading and purchasing information, product information, support and technical info.

Network Communication Computers and Arrays

http://tribeca.ios.com/~ideal/index.html

IDEAL computers, servers for LANs and WANs. Lots of product specs and information provided for your organization.

Network Computing's ISDN Online

http://techweb.cmp.com/nc/isdn/

Network Computing magazine's Web site devoted to ISDN. You can find information about ISDN product and services, the latest news about ISDN, issues and concerns surrounding ISDN, and articles relating to ISDN. The Interaction page includes newsgroups and mailing list information about ISDN.

Networks Incorporated

http://205.138.166.1/networks/

Computer and consulting services for your network installation or troubleshooting. Links to product service and information, the benefits of networks, and more information.

NeuroDimension, Inc.

http://www.nd.com/

A neural network simulation environment that supports any neural models. Check out their product and simulation demos, press releases, screen shots, and more.

Newbridge Networks Corporation

http://www.newbridge.com/

Design, manufacture, sale, and support of multimedia networking solutions for corporations. Links to their products, features, user groups, investors, and more.

Nortel Northern Telecom

http://www.nortel.com/home/home.html

Nortel offers secure networks to ensure privacy. Check out their networking solutions and their training programs to benefit your organization.

Novell, Inc.

http://www.novell.com

The persistent leader in networking software provides information on new products, technical support questions, online manuals, and different networking solutions for business and government. Choose the smart country page for your location to see a neat map of all the countries in your continent. You will end up with information about Novell training courses, conferences, and other events in your city. Neat!

NTG International

http://www.ntg-campus.com/ntg/

The Network Technology group can help you with a small or large project, providing you with network technology solutions and training. Check out their list of products and services, including upcoming conferences.

Onion Peel Software Home

http://www.ops.com/home_net.html

Application developer for HP's OpenView Network Management platform. Download a demo program describing Onion Peel products, including RoboMap for HP OpenView, and ROVE for HP OpenView.

Ornetix Network Computing

http://www.ornetix.com/

Maker of CDVision, a server-based CD-ROM manager that can accommodate up to 392 SCSI CD-ROM drives and multiple users. Download a 30-day full-user version, or practice your German by reading the Deutsch version of this page.

PC DOCS, Inc.

http://www.pcdocs.com

Produces PC-DOCS open document management systems for enterprise networks. Includes product background, press releases, case studies, and sales information. Also includes trade show appearance dates, job openings with PC DOCS, and technical partners listings.

Plaintree Systems

http://www.plaintree.com

Produces the WaveSwitch family of network connectivity products along with other Ethernet switches, converters, and software. Includes product specifications, technical support, and ordering information.

Retix Web

http://www.retix.com/

Creates Internetworking products, applications, and tools. Includes information about the SWITCHStak 500 Ethernet switch, ROUTERXchange 7000 network router, NETXchange400 Ethernet bridges, and the RETIXVision network software. Provides technical specifications, press releases, and contact information.

SNMP and CMIP

http://www.inforamp.net/~kjvallil/t/snmp.html

SNMP is the Simple Network Management Protocol. CMIP is the Common Management Information Protocol. Both of these protocols are very important to the management of networks. If you are new to these protocols or just interested in them, visit this site for "newbie guides" to SNMP and CMIP.

SoftLinx, Inc.

http://www.softlinx.com

Makes Replix Network Fax Software for enterprise-wide networks. This simple site provides traditional services, such as product and price info, technical support, reseller database, and support information.

Strategic Networks Consulting, Inc.

http://www.snci.com/

Provides network design, management, and evaluation consulting services. Includes online essays and articles dealing with computer networking problems and solutions. Also includes job opportunities and contact information.

System Resources Corporation

http://www.srcorp.com/

Provides many different services and network system solutions for corporate, government, and defense clients. Includes company profile, philosophies, and services offered. Also includes client listings and contact information.

TENET Computer Group, Inc.

http://www.tenet.com

A Canadian Novell Netware network reseller and installer. Practice your French on their French version of this page, peruse their links to network-related publications, or find out about their product line.

UniSQL, Inc.

http://www.unisql.com/

The UniSQL server will manage object-relational data better than relational systems, used by leading engineering, telecommunications, health care, manufacturing, and defense groups. Find out about their many products and services.

User's Guide To CMU SNMP for Linux

http://www.cris.ufl.edu/~dadavis/cmu-snmp.html

Carnegie Mellon University (CMU) provides free SNMP software for Linux, a freely distributed Unix version. You can find out about how the CMU SNMP works on Linux, as well as get updated information on SNMP version 2. Some of this information is dated, but this site does provide helpful discussions on using CMU SNMP for Linux.

Word Master, Inc.

http://www.interaccess.com/wmi/wm/

Software developer of relational database managers for client/server environments.

XLNT Designs, Inc.

http://www.xlnt.com/

Includes detailed company profile and product line technical specifications. Also includes technical support, online product registration, and technical partners. Describes their FDDI technology, including a Gigabit Ethernet-capable LAN switch, due in 1997.

Yost Serial Device Wiring Standard

http://www-scf.usc.edu/~khendric/info/yost.html

Describes the Yost serial device wiring standard. Find out why this standard is superior to null modem cables and the many different types of connections that are possible with this standard.

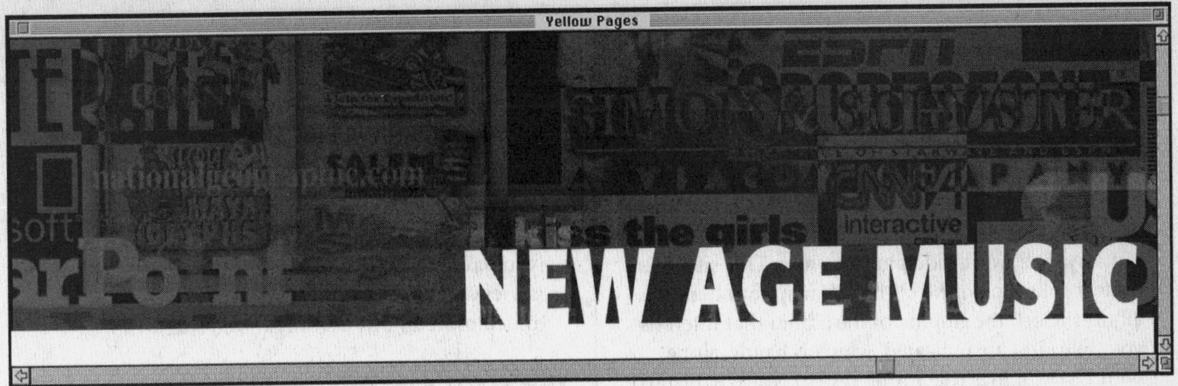

I talked to the woman in musical therapy, and she said that Mozart's the boy for you.

Marjorie 'Midge' Wood in Vertigo (1958)

Amazing Sounds

`http://www.amazings.com/ingles.html`

This e-zine is devoted to alternative music in all forms. Start here to access news and reviews, a gallery of artists who have been reviewed in the past, sources and services (both on and off the net). The Hot Links section is highly recommended—a very thorough list of links to anywhere and everywhere alternative.

Ambient Quantic New Age Music for Relaxation

`http://www.quantikmusic.com/index-a.html`

A series of albums containing music for the body and soul by Micheline Allaire and Alain Lemay, from Quantic Music Productions in Quebec, Canada. (Site may be viewed in French or English.) Click the album cover, read the description, hear the samples.

Arts Online.Com

`http://www.arts-online.com/`

Dedicated to new art forms and the struggling artists who create them—in dance, the visual arts, music, theater, film, and writing. The music section features a different artist each month, as well as an extensive database. Search the list for info on your favorite (or new!) bands, musicians, agents, presenters, record labels, and plenty more. Very cool graphics.

Planet Earth Music
`http://www.planet-earth-music.com/`

Aural Adventures

`http://www.auraladventures.com/`

Supplying "the finest in innovative, unique, and adventurous independent music," this site's catalog includes both music and video. Musicians are invited to submit their work to be sold from the site. Online ordering, of course, as well as bios, artist info, and music clips from the albums. Detailed list of links for musicians trying to get their stuff online.

Backroads Music

`http://www.backroadsmusic.com`

With more than 5,000 titles available from the U.S. and several other countries, this company offers an extensive mail-order service in the following genres: "Ambient, Space, World, New Age, Electronic, Celtic, Native American, Guitar, Piano, and select Vocal Music." The site has a nice, clean look without drowning your modem in graphics. Browse through the new releases, search the online catalog for old faves, check out the "Top 50" list to try something new.

Bjork's—Web Sense

`http://www.centrum.is/bjork/`

Presents the Web site "of the six senses—where sight, hearing, smell, taste, touch, and intuition" serve as the focus.

Crystal Spirit

`http://crystalmusic.com/new_age.html`

Featuring the music of Yatri, a new age musician who plays the glass armonica (invented by Benjamin Franklin, no less), which consists of 35 crystal bowls.

Sample the sound in .wav or .au format. You can order the "Crystal Spirit" album online from this site.

Enya MIDI Archive

http://www2.ucsc.edu/~dego/enyamidi.html

The writers of *South Park* may make fun of her music, but Enya is a worldwide phenomenon. This site offers quite a collection of MIDI files drawn from her albums. Click the graphic of the album that interests you. File sizes are indicated, which is handy, along with EMA ratings (the rating system is also explained at this site). Links to other Enya-related sites as well.

Inner-Media

http://www.inner-media.com/

An unusual use of multiple (sizable) frames, this site offers reviews and interviews of musicians, bands, and their work when you click the Music link. Also includes a book section, updates on activities, publications, and so on that are Earth-related.

Internet Underground Music Archive

http://www.iuma.com:80/

Marketing itself as "the Net's first, free hi-fi music archive," IUMA's site comes in two varieties so folks with slower modems (or who are in a hurry) can choose a version that's slim on graphics. Either version offers tons of info on hot bands, record labels, e-zines, and events. Very up-to-date stuff.

Kaleidospace (Kspace) Independent Internet Artists

http://kspace.com/

These folks are interested in more than music—basically, anything related to the arts and entertainment. Audio clips and descriptions of many artists (whose genres are their own creation—check out the incredibly long list of music genres), in a wide variety of mediums. Zillions of related links and cool sites.

New Age Music Center

http://www.newagemusic.com/

With all the blinking, waving, glittering, color-flashing activities on the home page for this site (frames, too), you may forget why you came. The site belongs to Only New Age Music, Inc. (Onam), which provides services to New Age artists—marketing, packaging, and more. Plenty of sound clips from featured artists, links to related sites. Nice list of online music stores that carry New Age music.

Planet Earth Music

http://www.planet-earth-music.com/

This site offers a large variety of music of all kinds—not just New Age, but jazz, dance, Celtic, and much more. Sign up for a membership to win free CDs; membership is free, and you get free stuff each time you have purchased 10 tapes or CDs. Special offers, reviews of current artists, searchable indexes, and much more in this well-organized site.

The New Age Page

http://www.hal-pc.org/~rich1/midi.html

New Age/synthpop music. On the opening page, click interesting filenames to access sample MIDI files (.mod format to be added later). The My Techno-MIDI page link takes you to the "This is Techno-SOUNDS page," where you can access great music in several formats. New music posted monthly; contributions welcome.

Vangelis—The Man and the Music

http://bau2.uibk.ac.at/perki/Vangelis.html

Provides information about the man and his music and soundtracks (Blade Runner being the most popular so far). Contains an array of pictures, sounds, and digitized film sequences, as well as a page with links to all of the Vangelis fans in the world.

Yanni MIDI Files

http://www.teleport.com/~celinec/music/midi.html

Small but nice collection of Yanni's music in MIDI and MOD formats, along with info/links on where to get players online. Additional files of Yanni material are solicited.

Related Sites

http://infinite.org/newedit/musicoop.html

http://netrover.com/~aviolet/

http://www.artist-shop.com/

http://www.carswellmusic.com/images/buttons/samplemusic.jpg

http://www.cis.ohio-state.edu/hypertext/faq/usenet/music/alt-newsgroup-list/faq.html

http://www.digiserve.com/gaia/

http://www.flexfx.com/newage.html

http://www.jellico.com/doker/age.htm

http://www.mindspring.com/%7Efmacek/

http://www.webcraft.co.uk/webcraft/spiral/spiral.htm

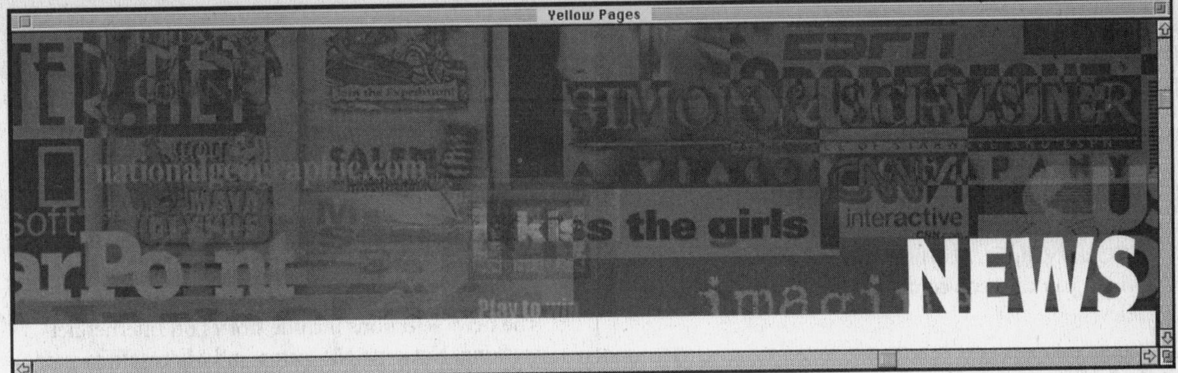

> If all the news is bad, why do I need to hear it?
>
> *Bernadette McCarver Snyder*

American Reporter

http://www.newshare.com:9999/moved.html

A six-day-a-week electronic "newshare" that is free on a trial basis. Set up by the writers whose work it features, it covers most general topics covered by a daily newspaper with wide coverage of foreign news.

Arutz-7 NEWS

http://www.virtual.co.il/news/news/arutz7/sound/

Offers recorded segments of news and commentaries in Hebrew and English, as well as Hebrew broadcasts of news live from Arutz Sheva 24 hours a day (except the Sabbath and holidays). Requires a RealAudio player; you can download RealPlayer from the site if you don't already have it.

Associated Press

http://www1.trib.com/NEWS/APwire.html

The Associated Press online. Requires free login, but then offers full access to the AP news wires.

Bay City News Home Page

http://www.baycitynews.com/

An online regional news service from the San Francisco Bay area that offers these options: Datebook, Entertainment News, General News, Media News, and Legal News. The site also offers info about the news service itself and a fax/email Headline Service.

NRP TOP PICKS

CNN Interactive
http://www.cnn.com/

ESPN SportsZone: Sports, news, scores, statistics
http://espn.sportszone.com/

Infoseek: The News Channel
http://guide.infoseek.com/Topic?tid=1486&sv=A2&lk=noframes

Time Warner's Pathfinder!
http://www.pathfinder.com/welcome/?navbar

Business Wire 1997

http://www.businesswire.com/

Business News distributes news to the media locally, nationally, and worldwide. This wire service offers customized news-release distribution to the news media, online services, the Internet, and the investment community.

CNN Interactive

http://www.cnn.com/

Get all the top news stories at your fingertips, or delve into weather, sports, science and technical news, travel, style, show business, health, and earth topics. Many stories have accompanying QuickTime video segments. This site also lets you in on what CNN has to offer on television.

ESPN SportsZone: Sports, news, scores, statistics

http://espn.sportszone.com/

You can view game scores and statistics, get sports news, participate in fan polls, interact with other sports lovers, get in on fantasy ball games, visit the ZoneStore, get health and fitness info, and much more. And you can get instructions for making ESPN SportsZone your startup page.

FCC Welcome Page

http://www.fcc.gov/

Federal Communications Commission online. Serves as a forum for public discussion concerning FCC issues (including broadcasting). Contains current legislation, full text of relevant speeches, agenda, and the FCC daily digest. Also lists of email addresses to which you can send comments and concerns about television.

infoMCI

http://www.fyionline.com/infoMCI/

Provides news summaries about business, sports, and headlines. Features industry spotlights for the business surfer.

Infoseek: The News Channel

http://guide.infoseek.com/Topic?tid=1486&sv=A2&lk=noframes

You can get top news, weather, stock quotes, even comics at the News Channel, a branch of the Infoseek service. Search all the newswires and national sources for your topic, or jump directly to other news sources, such as *The New York Times.*

International Pages

http://www.omroep.nl/international.html

The Dutch public broadcasting system's Web site. Includes program information and other information about the Netherlands.

Internet Disaster Information Center

http://www.disaster.net/

Offers information about ongoing disasters, historical information about disasters, and links to other disaster sites on the Web.

libraries.americas

ftp://ftp.ping.at/pub/info/internet/libraries/libraries.americas

Provides information on information retrieval from online libraries.

Mercury Center

http://www.sjmercury.com/

This searchable site offers world, national, and local news; business, sports, and entertainment news; feature columns; and other offerings from the *San Jose Mercury News,* a newspaper serving the Silicon Valley and San Francisco Bay area.

NCNS: Network Computer News Service

http://www.ncns.com/andmore2.html

You get three things at this site: computer-related photo links, computer-related news at a glance, and hot links (to such sites as alphaWorks and WebTV). The news selections include stories on Internet networking, Netscape Navigator, and Microsoft, to name a few.

News Front Page

http://www.msnbc.com/news/default.asp

You can personalize the MSNBC news page to get the news you want, the way you want it. Or stick with the standard page for a wide variety of news options. You can also choose news audio headlines to hear the news read to you by newscasters (some video and illustrated audio are also available).

NewsLink Menu

http://www.newslink.org/menu.html

Offers a free service that provides access to many online newspapers, periodicals, and so on, around the world every day.

NewsPage

http://www.newspage.com/

Gives you a daily business briefing, with news from the computing and media worlds, as well as other key industries. Also provides breaking general news and access to CompanyLink, where you can look up news, research, and contacts for more than 65,000 companies. And you can register to create your own individualized NewsPage.

NewsTracker Top Stories

http://nt.excite.com/?uid=

The News option of My Excite Channel brings you this site, filled with news headlines, business, sports, entertainment, sci-tech, nation, world, and lifestyle articles. Sign up for the custom news-clipping service, look through the many pages of news topics, or run a search on the news index.

A B C D E F G H I J K L M N O P Q R S T U V W X Y Z

NJ Online Weather

`http://www.nj.com/weather/`

The Old Farmers Almanac online. Includes weather forecasts for the United States, helpful tips, and other information—just like the hard copy.

NOS TeleTekst

`http://www.nos.nl/cgi-bin/tt/nos/page`

Dutch Broadcasting Service. Provides an interface to news and other information off the Dutch wire services. Includes English menus but provides the articles in Dutch.

Omnivore

`http://way.net/omnivore/`

Provides a free daily news service designed to quickly and concisely deliver coverage of events around the world as they happen (uncensored news, straight from the source and original point of view). Provides many links to other news services.

PR Newswire Home Page

`http://www.prnewswire.com/`

PR Newswire describes itself as "the leading source of immediate news from corporations worldwide for media, business, the financial community, and the individual investor." The site seems to live up to this claim, with a long list of contents that's worth scrolling through.

Reuters: Home Page

`http://www.reuters.com/`

Reuters, a leading news and information company, fulfills the business community's and news media's financial, multimedia, and professional information needs. At this site, you can get online news in these areas or learn more about Reuters.

Time Warner's Pathfinder!

`http://www.pathfinder.com/welcome/?navbar`

The Pathfinder Network can take you to a broad variety of news and information: news, money, business, personalities, entertainment, sports, health, living, and family. It can also jump you directly to the pages of publications such as *People*, *Time*, and *Fortune*. This site also offers a free email service, messageboards, chat, and a search feature.

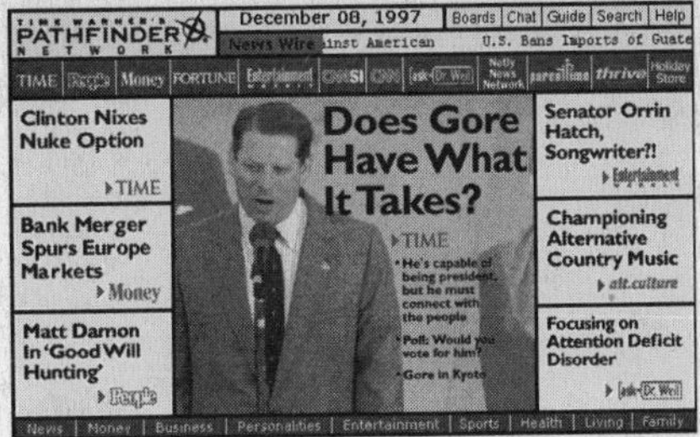

RadioSpace Home Page

`http://www.radiospace.com/index.html`

Serves as a resource for radio-station programming and news staffs. Provides ready-for-broadcast sound bites, news, and programming.

RealAudio: ABC News

`http://www.realaudio.com/contentp/abc.html`

Offers ABC Radio news, available with the RealAudio player. Enables you to download audio files of daily and hourly news broadcasts.

South African Broadcasting Corporation Welcome Page

`http://www.sabc.co.za/`

South African Broadcasting online. Provides many phone numbers and other information. Includes sports scores and news services.

Time Daily News Summary

`http://www.pathfinder.com/time/daily/`

Provides one-paragraph summaries of current stories and provides a search engine you can use for a more in-depth look.

Welcome to PopSci.com | The What's New Website

`http://www.popsci.com/`

This Web site comes to you compliments of the editors of *Popular Science Magazine*. Find out what's news in the automotive, computer, electronics, home technology, and science fields. Plus get other articles from the magazine, various buying guides, and helpful links.

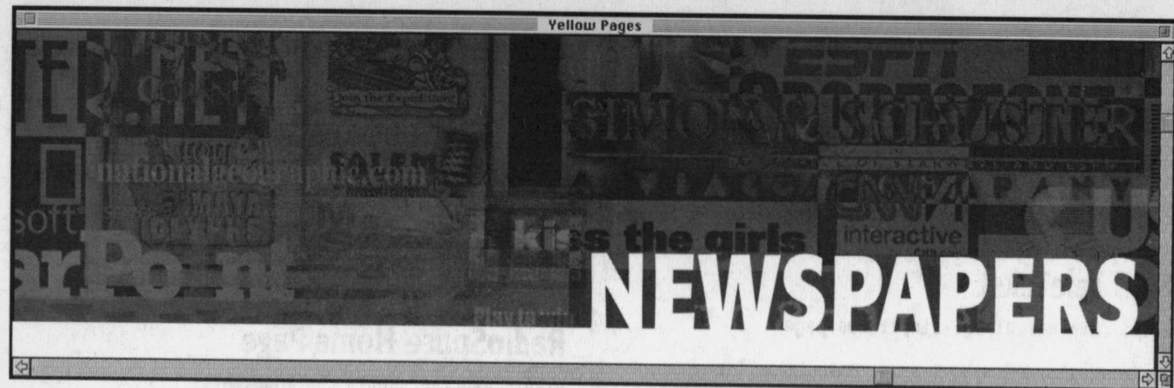

> In these times we fight for ideas, and newspapers are our fortresses.
>
> *Heinrich Heine*

Campus Newspapers on the Internet

http://beacon-www.asa.utk.edu/resources/papers.html

Lists student newspapers available on the Internet. Includes listings for dailies, weeklies, and less frequent publications.

The Capital

http://www.infi.net/capital/

Online site for the daily newspaper for the Anapolis, Maryland area. Provides a supplemental Net version of the paper update five to six times a week. Includes links and area background of the area.

Hastings Tribune Internet Edition

http://www.cnweb.com/tribune/index.html

Nebraska's first online newspaper. Links to news, sports, major stories, subscriber info, comics, want ads, and other info and back issues. Includes color graphics.

Jerusalem Post

http://www.jpost.co.il/

The Internet edition of the *Jerusalem Post.* Access to news, business, features, sports, tourism sections, and more. Includes graphics.

Orange County Register
http://www.ocregister.com

RETRO
http://www.retroactive.com/

Kamloops Daily News–Online

http://www.southam.com/kamloopsdailynews/

A Canadian-based online newspaper with features such as local news, sports, weather, business, opinion page, and more.

Knoxville News Sentinel

http://www.knoxnews.com/

Knoxville, Tennessee newspaper with links to headlines and features stories, sports, news, weather, classifieds, and more. Includes graphics.

Los Angeles Times

http://www.latimes.com/

A practical menu at the top of the home page lets you instantly search in the News, Entertainment, Sports, Business, Classifieds, and So. California sections. An applet ticker runs continuously, updating you with top stories.

Maui News

http://www.maui.net/~mauinews/news.html

The *Maui News* is a local newspaper featuring news, entertainment, classifieds, features, weather, and other sections of the newspaper. The site also features a link to "Maui County at a Glance."

Newspaper/Diario LA NACION–San Jose, Costa Rica

http://www.nacion.co.cr/

Presents news in Spanish. *La Nacion*, the largest newspaper in Costa Rica, provides news and information of Central America and the world.

Orange County Register

http://www.ocregister.com

Great site that includes daily (including Sunday) issues online and boasts Ad Products and Services and Customer Services. The search features in each service category (such as for rentals and classifieds) are very useful. This site also has a SmartFinder engine, in which you can find businesses in Orange County, California.

Private Eye

http://www.intervid.co.uk/eye/

Provides online site for the *Private Eye* newspaper based in London, England. Includes samples of the paper's articles and artwork. Also includes subscription information. This paper is similar to the *National Enquirer*, hence, it is good fun.

Providence Business News

http://www.pbn.com/

Provides online site for the *Providence Business News*. Includes resources, circulation, past issues, and a search index. Also includes subscription information.

RETRO

http://www.retroactive.com/

Newspaper/zine that provides you with up-to-date information about what's around these days that relates to the pop culture of the first three-fourths of this century. Includes retro news, media and music information, shopping guides, classifieds, archives, and so much more. Definitely a hot spot to stop at.

Sydney Morning Herald

http://www.smh.com.au/

Provides home site and online version of the *Syndey Morning Herald*. Includes stories, advertising information, and various features for this Syndey, Australia paper.

Telluride Times-Journal

http://www.adone.com/telluride/

Provides online site for the *Telluride Times-Journal* from Telluride, Colorado. Includes online version of the paper and subscription information.

USA Today

http://www.usatoday.com/

This site is laid out more like a printed newspaper than most, but it also features a search menu. Some of its features are the Inside, Resources, and Top News sections. Check out its Yellow Pages search index at the bottom of the home page.

Vocal Point

http://bvsd.k12.co.us/cent/Newspaper/Newspaper.html

High school newspaper online. Offers monthly news from a teen's perspective. Students from different states collaborate on this site, with future plans to include students all over the world. This site contains current and archive issues.

Wall Street JournalLink

http://journal.link.wsj.com/

Provides an online advertising directory of *The Wall Street Journal*. Contains links to advertiser Web sites and email addresses.

The Washington Post

http://www.washingtonpost.com/

Provides online site for *The Washington Post*. Includes top stories, daily issues, "Style-The Washington Insider's Guide," editorials, and more.

Related Sites

http://weber.u.washington.edu/~vgillis/

http://www.box.nl/~frankhbk/nieuws.htm

http://www.thecrimson.harvard.edu/

http://www.salsgiver.com/icity/newsstand.html

http://www.luc.edu/orgs/phoenix/

http://www.naa.org/hot/

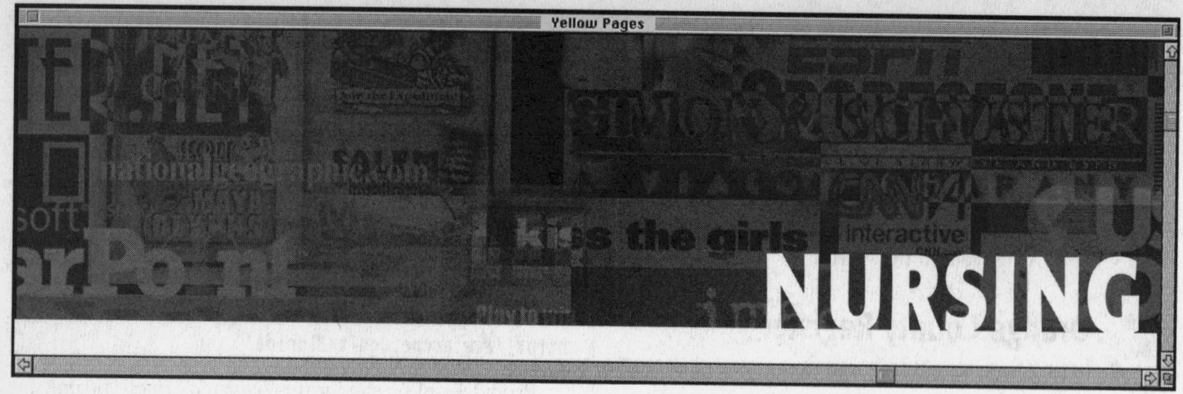

NURSING

> Let me dedicate my life today
> to the care of those who
> come my way.
> Let me touch each one
> with a healing hand
> and the gentle art for which
> I stand.
> And then tonight
> when day is done
> Let me rest in peace
> if I've helped just one.
>
> *Unknown*

ADN/RN Concepts

http://www.azstarnet.com/~jlichty/rn.htm

Forum for current issues, education, health reform, and other nursing topics. Also offers current hot topics and links to other sites.

HomeCareNurse Web Page

http://junior.apk.net/~nurse

Dedicated to providing information to home care nurses. Includes a forms library and "a day in the life of a home care nurse."

International Network for Interfaith Health Practices
http://www.interaccess.com/ihpnet/

WholeNurse
http://www.wholenurse.com/

International Network for Interfaith Health Practices

http://www.interaccess.com/ihpnet/

An electronic forum for resources-sharing among persons of all religious faiths and backgrounds regarding the relationship between spirituality and health.

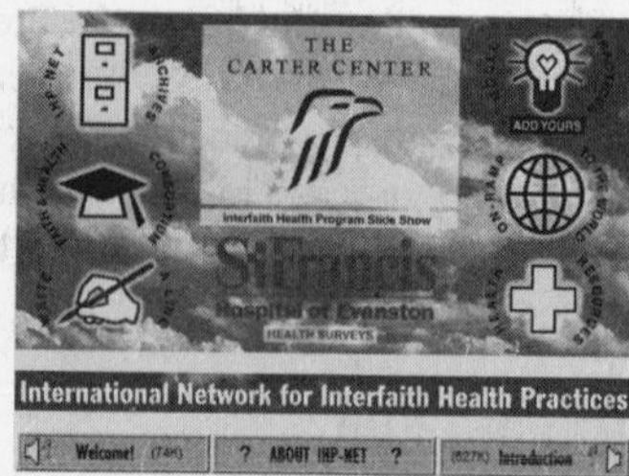

MacNursing

http://www.community.net/~sylvan/MacNursing.html

Offers shareware and freeware, resumes, and hospital unit information systems.

Nursing Lists

http://www.callamer.com/itc/nurse/nrslist.html

Offers links to electronic mailing lists on topics of interest to nurses. Includes lists for opthalmic nurses, intravenous therapy, graduate nursing discussions, and international nursing.

WholeNurse

http://www.wholenurse.com/

Provides information to nurses, patients, and medical personnel of all types in an effort to keep up with the growing amount of information posted online.

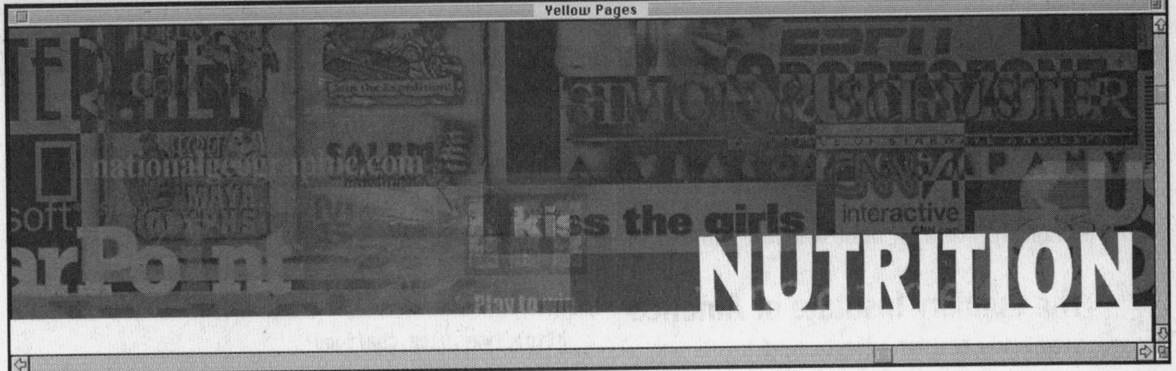

The king of Merigold was in the kitchen cooking breakfast for the queen.

John Lennon and Paul McCartney

American Journal of Clinical Nutrition
http://www.faseb.org/ajcn/ajcn.htm

The Culinary Institute of America
http://www.ciachef.edu/cia.html

The FOOD Museum
http://www.foodmuseum.com/~hughes/first.htm

American Journal of Clinical Nutrition

http://www.faseb.org/ajcn/ajcn.htm

The American Journal of Clinical Nutrition is a peer-reviewed journal that publishes the latest worldwide basic and clinical studies relevant to human nutrition in topics such as obesity, nutrition and disease, energy metabolism, and international nutrition. The AJCN is ranked second in impact factor among 37 nutrition and dietetic journals.

Anne Nicholls' Bonne Bouche School of Cookery

http://www.hi-media.co.uk/bonne-bouche/index.htm

Anne Nicholls' Bonne Bouche School of Cookery provides training for future cooking professionals, cooking holidays, and cultural tours for gourmets.

Austin Reference Guide for Vitamins

http://www.realtime.net/anr/vitamins.html

Contains information on the B vitamins, vitamins C, D, and E, biotin, folic acid, and niacin. Also contains links to reference guides for nutrients, minerals, herbs, and amino acids.

Better Health through Nutrition

http://members.aol.com/healthvis/index.html

Offers alternatives to standard medical practices through balanced and natural nutritional programs. Degenerative diseases can be stopped and reversed with proper nutrition, and nutritional supplements.

Carrie Rehkopf's Homepage

http://www.fullnet.com/u/carrier

Provides links to find nutrition information. Offers a wide spectrum of nutrition topics and provides some nutritional journals to give more information on 'hot' nutrition topics. It also has some links that Carrie enjoys. The page also provides a brief description Carrie and her qualifications.

Center for Food Safety and Applied Nutrition

http://vm.cfsan.fda.gov/list.html

FDA site describing cosmetics, food additives and pesticides, labeling, press releases, and women's health. Also includes a seafood hotline.

Cookery at The Grange - Residential Cookery School

http://www.hi-media.co.uk/grange-cookery

A cookery school in Somerset, UK, established in 1981 to provide intensive training for career cooks, and for holiday breaks for those who love cooking.

The Culinary Institute of America

http://www.ciachef.edu/cia.html

Offering the best culinary education in the world. Associate and bachelor's degrees in culinary arts and baking and pastry arts available for aspiring food service and hospitality professionals. Continuing education programs for current industry professionals offered at the Hudson Valley, NY, and Napa Valley, CA, campuses. Adult education courses for food enthusiasts available in New York. Four student-staffed, on-campus restaurants in New York and one on-campus restaurant in California.

Department of Food Science & Nutrition

http://www.fsci.umn.edu/

Provides information on the programs and courses offered by the University of Minnesota. Offers nutritionists tools that calculate your energy needs and analyze the nutritive value of food items.

Dietetics Online

http://www.dietetics.com/

Home page for the World-Wide Network of Nutrition and Dietetic Professionals. Includes a marketplace and a link to the Dietetics Online archives.

Dole 5 a Day

http://www.dole5aday.com/

A graphics-rich site devoted to the health and nutrition benefits of fruits and vegetables. A fantastic educational tool for teachers.

Foodwine.com

http://www.foodwine.com/

A monthly Internet e-zine devoted to food and cooking. Complete with culinary trivia and articles. Also contains links to any food-related Web site you could possibly want.

Fast Food Finder

http://www.olen.com/food/

Searchable database for information on nutrition and fast-food restaurants.

Food and Nutrition Newsletter

http://www.ext.vt.edu/news/periodicals/foods/

Updated monthly, this newsletter addresses issues in nutrition and food production. Categories include Computer/Internet, Specific Audiences, Dietary Guidelines, Food Products, Nutrition Education, RDA, and Labeling.

Food Fun for Kids

http://www.nppc.org/foodfun.html

Come on in and explore the world of food from a kid's-eye view.

The FOOD Museum

http://www.foodmuseum.com/~hughes/first.htm

The FOOD Museum is a delightful collection of artifacts, ideas, facts, and fun. Community, school, and commercial educational programs related to one of the few things all life on Earth has in common—FOOD—are vitally informative and interesting. They currently have kiosks at The Wild Oats Market chain. Arrange for a program to be presented or museum artifacts to be exhibited anywhere in the world.

French Language and Cooking Chateau

http://3ponts.edu

Enjoy French language and cooking courses in an 18th century French Chateau near Burgundy and Beaujolais. Relaxed, comfortable, family atmosphere. Spacious park and pool. Small establishment.

Getting Well Naturally: CHILDREN'S NUTRITION

http://www.newlifehealth.com/children.html

All natural approaches and answers to your questions right from the doctor's mouth.

The International Kitchen

http://www.intl-kitchen.com

The International Kitchen conducts educational culinary tours of Europe.

Macrobiotics Online

http://www.macrobiotics.org/

Nutrition based on Yin/Yang diet selection and preparation. Includes lifestyle suggestions, classes, recovery stories, recipes, and a FAQ sheet.

MN-NET Home Page

http://www.idrc.ca/mi/mnnet.htm

Provides information on micronutrient malnutrition. Includes discussion of vitamin and mineral deficiencies, current events, and prevalence and control program status.

Mother Nature's General Store

http://www.mothernature.com/

Who better than Mother Nature's General Store to supply healthy, natural, and nutritional foods facts and products including herbs, homeopathic, vitamins, vitamin teas, tea, dental supplies, beauty aids, bodybuilding, housewares, diet products, groceries, and much, much more.

NutriCoach

http://www.nutricoach.com

Reach your nutritional Goals with Vanessa your Internet Nutrition Coach. Nutrition Articles, Free Required Daily Allowance to gain or lose weight, Nutrition Newsletter.

Nutrition Pages

http://deja-vu.oldiron.cornell.edu/~jabbo/index.html

Contains articles discussing current topics such as dairy products, vegetarianism, saturated fat, poisonous plants, and food safety.

Professor Geoff Skurray's Food, Nutrition, and Health Information Page

http://hotel.hawkesbury.uws.edu.au/~geoffs/

An informative site providing such information as: adult recommended daily allowances of nutrients, dietary guidelines, athletic dietary concerns, and links to other nutritional sites. A viable bookmark for health conscious Web surfers.

Sclafani's Cooking School

http://www.gnofn.org/~sclafani

Certified Executive Chef Frank P. Sclafani, Sr. extends you an invitation to join his training as an investment in your culinary career success.

Solar Nutrition

http://www.eatsolar.com

Solar Nutrition is a system of eating designed to maximize the assimilation of light energy from food, and optimize health and vitality. Food charts and recipes included.

Web Nutrition

http://www.c-zone.net/fisher/wn

Your online source for nutritional news with up-to-date articles on health and nutrition. You don't want to miss it!

A B C D E F G H I J K L M N O P Q R S T U V W X Y Z

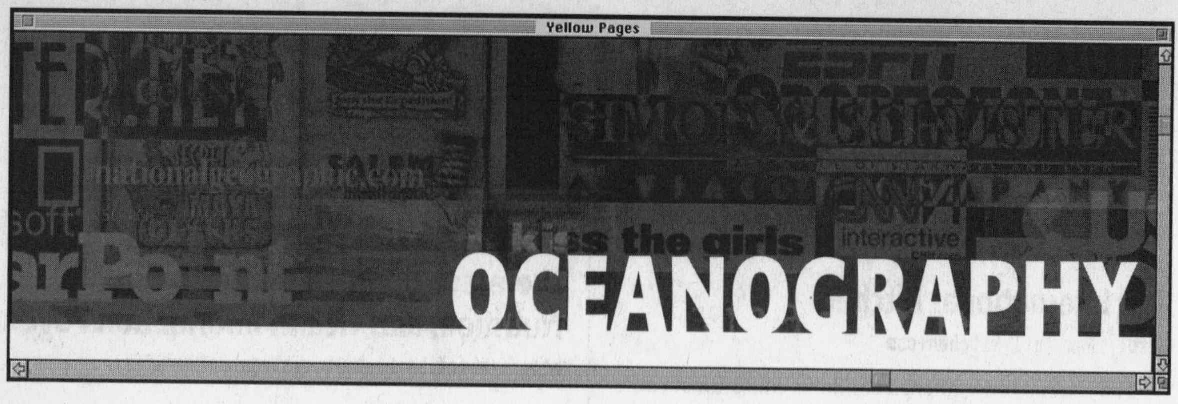

> And murmurs as the ocean murmurs there.
>
> *William Wordsworth*

ASLO Home Page

http://aslo.org/

"The purposes of ASLO are to promote the interests of limnology, oceanography and related sciences, to foster the exchange of information across the range of aquatic science, and to further investigations dealing with these subjects." Contains general information about the organization, as well as information on careers and job listings.

CSIRO Division of Oceanography

http://www-ocean.ml.csiro.au/

Offers two links: The Climate and Ocean Processes link provides information on research in this area, and the Marine Environment and Resources link contains additional information on current research.

El Nino Theme Page

http://www.pmel.noaa.gov/toga-tao/el-nino/home.html

Explains El Nino (frequently referred to on oceanography pages), a disruption of the ocean-atmosphere system in the tropical Pacific that affects weather around the globe.

List of Oceanography Resources

http://www.esdim.noaa.gov/ocean_page.html

Lists oceanography Web sites. Contains a listing of the major NOAA Web sites and links to some of the better Web sites of educational institutions.

NOAA Home Page
http://www.noaa.gov/

Ocean Planet Home Page
http://seawifs.gsfc.nasa.gov/ocean_planet.html

Satellite Oceanography Laboratory
http://satftp.soest.hawaii.edu/

TOPEX/Poseidon—The Ocean Topography Experiment
http://topex-www.jpl.nasa.gov/

National Marine Fisheries Service

http://kingfish.ssp.nmfs.gov/

Provides services and products to support domestic and international fisheries management operations, fisheries development, trade and industry assistance activities, enforcement, protected species and habitat conservation operations, and the scientific and technical aspects of NOAA's marine fisheries program. Offers links to oceanographic information, particularly data concerning fish life.

NEMO—Oceanographic Data Server

http://nemo.ucsd.edu/

Provides a collection of data sets for physical oceanographers. Offers many holdings only to local users. Offers information on shore temperature and winds to all users.

NOAA Coastal & Estuarine Oceanography Branch

http://www-ceob.nos.noaa.gov/

Contains information on the physics of coastal waterways and the movement of the waters and the causes of those movements.

NOAA Home Page

http://www.noaa.gov/

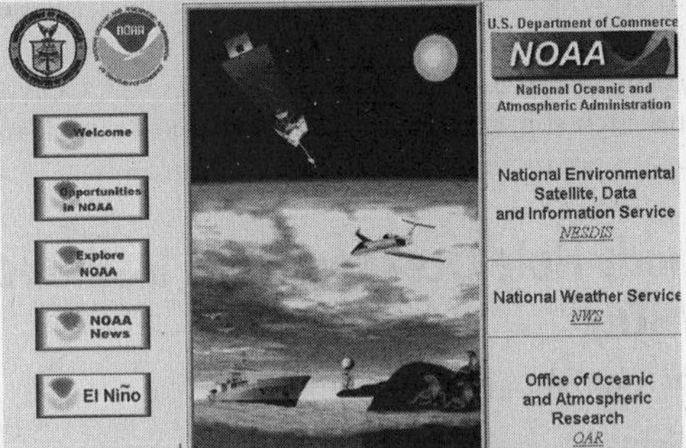

Provides information about National Oceanic and Atmospheric Administration (NOAA) research, current weather information, and links to all other NOAA projects. Also includes latest news involving NOAA and the NOAA mission statement. Includes information about seasonal forecasts, fisheries, protected species, coastal ecosystems, and navigation.

NOAA Paleoclimatology Program

http://www.ngdc.noaa.gov/paleo/paleo.html

Includes searchable databases on climate modeling, ice cores, paleoceanographic, paleovegetation, tree-ring, and other data. Provides alternate search engines for users who cannot use tables.

Ocean Planet Home Page

http://seawifs.gsfc.nasa.gov/ocean_planet.html

Presents an online version of an exhibition at the Smithsonian Institution's National Museum of Natural History. Also contains many resources.

Oceanography Links: Oceanography on the World Wide Web

http://www.eos.ubc.ca/links/

Lists Web sites dealing with the field of oceanography. There are sublistings of educational and government institutions as well as listings of other online resources such as images, project descriptions, and research articles.

Oceanography Society

http://www.tos.org/

Offers general membership information. Maintains a news posting system. Covers a wide variety of topics ranging from highly scientific issues to elementary level oceanography education under the "News System" heading.

Pathfinder Cafe

http://satori.gso.uri.edu/archive/images.html

Contains more than 28,000 images. Serves as resource for finding oceanography images. Provides an interface for acquiring and viewing Pathfinder images.

Safari Splash

http://oberon.educ.sfu.ca/splash.htm

Links people around the world and in classrooms to students and experts diving in an ocean environment. Features the Safari Touch Tank, in which you click on an image of plants and animals to call up a description, large image, 3D animation, and Webster definition of the item you choose.

Satellite Oceanography Laboratory

http://satftp.soest.hawaii.edu/

Contains real-time data for meteorology and oceanography, as well as images and archives of publications. Includes video footage and offers the capability to make comments on the site and its contents.

Scripps Institution of Oceanography Library

http://orpheus.ucsd.edu/sio/inst/index.html

Caters to the information needs of the research and educational activities of Scripps Institution.

Sea Surface Temperature Satellite Images

http://dcz.gso.uri.edu/avhrr-archive/archive.html

Provides access to the University of Rhode Island, Graduate School of Oceanography's archive of sea surface temperature satellite images. Also includes an online lesson plan for teachers who want to incorporate the images into a lesson.

SeaWiFS Project Home Page

http://seawifs.gsfc.nasa.gov/scripts/SEAWIFS.html

Provides access into the background, status, and documentation for NASA's upcoming global ocean color monitoring mission. Offers online documentation on this project, including educational resources.

A B C D E F G H I J K L M N O P Q R S T U V W X Y Z

SelectSite Ocean Technology

http://www.selectsite.com/oceantech/

Provides pointers to businesses that specialize in ocean technology. Also lists conferences and reference sites, some of which might have something to offer someone doing non-business related research.

TAMU Oceanography Welcome Page

http://www-ocean.tamu.edu/welcome.html

Contains a variety of information. Includes a section on questions about careers in oceanography. Also offers links to online journals and research articles and resources related to oceanography.

TOPEX/Poseidon—The Ocean Topography Experiment

http://topex-www.jpl.nasa.gov/

Cooperative project between the United States and France to develop and operate an advanced satellite system dedicated to observing the Earth's oceans. Contains archives and updates for the project.

United States JGOFS Home Page

http://www1.whoi.edu/

Contains information on current professional programs and studies. Includes current images of the world's major oceans as viewed with satellite technology. Also contains recent oceanography references on the Web.

United States WOCE Home Page

http://www-ocean.tamu.edu/WOCE/uswoce.html

Provides information about the present United States WOCE plans and details the status of current work.

Welcome to OCEANIC

http://diu.cms.udel.edu/

Maintains information on World Ocean Circulation Experiment (WOCE), TOGA Coupled Ocean-Atmosphere Response Experiment (TOGA COARE), research ship information and cruise schedules, and other oceanographic information sources.

Woods Hole Oceanographic Institution (WHOI)

http://www.whoi.edu/index.html

Contains general oceanographic information. Includes a listing of oceanography Web sites.

Word about the International Oceanographic Foundation

http://www.rsmas.miami.edu/iof/

Explains the mission of the International Oceanographic Foundation and contains an excellent definition/explanation of the field of oceanography.

World Wide Web Virtual Library: Oceanography

http://www.mth.uea.ac.uk/ocean/oceanography.html

Provides links to a variety of Internet resources on oceanography. Offers links to Web resources by geographic area. Links to the "What's New" link, which contains a listing of sites that have recently announced or renovated their Web sites.

> What is this mess? An empty desk is an efficient desk.
>
> *Mr. Warrenn in* Brazil *(1985)*

Action Office Supplies, Inc.

http://www.actoff.com/

Based in Adelphia, New Jersey, Action offers a wide variety of office equipment and supplies. For details on their offerings, fill in a request for a catalog (several types are offered). Catalogs are sent via snail mail, but you can order online from this site. Includes links to major office equipment/supply manufacturers.

American Business Stationery

http://www.americanbiz.com/

Design and order your business cards online at this site. Raised printing available; multiple ink colors, font styles, paper styles and colors, and more. If your logo, graphics, and so on are available, send the files for ABS to use—in Photoshop, Illustrator, QuarkExpress, or other formats.

Dr. Shredder's

http://www.dr-shredders.com/

Dr. Shredder is the cartoon icon for A&W Business Machines, which supplies equipment to the print community—folders, letter openers, cutters, trimmers, shredders, and all kinds of other goodies, including used equipment. Lines from a number of manufacturers are represented.

OfficeMax OnLine
http://www.officemax.com/

Office Helper

http://www.officehelper.com/catalogs.html

Two catalogs available: Catalog 3, with more than 3,000 items, and Super-Catalog 26, with more than 26,000 items. Order via email (address supplied); online ordering at this site will be available later. Orders delivered by truck next day in the Petaluma, California, area, or via UPS nationwide.

Office Manager.Com

http://www.officemanager.com/

Providing any details about this site would just spoil it (and couldn't come close to how much fun it is). Whether or not you're an office manager, you'll find interesting and useful information here. And definitely play the copier game!

Office Network, Inc.

http://www.accesscomm.net/officenet/

Online shopping, 24 hours a day (especially handy for office slaves who work around the clock). This club of sorts gives its members access to more than 50,000 products and services. When you join the club, a representative installs the Office Network software on your computer and trains you in how to use it to order online. More details at this site.

Related Sites

http://www.acebusinesscards.com/

http://www.businessnw.com/olympic/

http://www.buyersusa.com/nqc/al/crawos.htm

http://www.buyrack.com/

http://www.bxpress.vt.com/

http://www.citysearch11.com/E/V/RDUNC/1003/10/75/

OfficeMax OnLine

http://www.officemax.com/

Ready to shop to the max? Register for free at this business-to-business secure site—registration is required, and you must supply name, address, and billing information to enter the site. Shop through various categories of office equipment, supplies, and services in the OfficeMax, CopyMax, and FurnitureMax sections. If your business has more than 50 office employees, you can sign up to join the OfficeMax Corporate Direct program for perks and savings.

OP Office Plus

http://www.office-plus.com/

The *Online* newsletter promises to keep you up-to-date on the latest in the office products industry—hot topics and products, reviews, and more. Get the details on the OP Office Plus cooperative and its network of dealers.

Paradise Distributing Inc.

http://www2.epix.net/~paradise/

With a limited number of items in its "Para Mall" (and more planned), Paradise provides "unique products" and business supplies. Graphics of most products, along with ordering and shipping information.

Phoenix Direct

http://www.ibp-phoenix.com/

Serving the retail and financial markets, Phoenix Direct carries ink ribbons, rollers, cartridges; all kinds of machine papers, such as fax paper and fanfolds; and more. Send for a catalog from this site—this order and others after it earn you free American Advantage Air Miles.

The Speedy Organiser

http://www.failte.com/cityorg/

Is stationery your bag? How about Montblanc pens? This is the place to come for desk products, including engraving, gift wrapping, and worldwide delivery. A large variety of products. Based in London; prices in pounds (£).

Staples, Inc.

http://www.staples.com/

This office products superstore is pretty familiar to anyone with a small business in a big city—but did you ever think about checking out their Web site? Locate the store nearest you, look over their special deals for contract and commercial customers (government, health care, and educational accounts), and don't forget about the job postings! Fill in your snail mail info for a copy of the Staples catalog.

This Olde Office

http://www.thisoldeoffice.com/

Based in Cathedral City, California, this unique company specializes in equipment that—well, that you can't use to connect to the Internet. Used equipment of all sorts for sale. If you don't see what you're looking for, email and ask; they may have it or be able to find it.

U.S. Office Products

http://www.usop.com/home.htm

This company is into all sorts of things related to business—office furniture and products, school supplies and travel—even coffee! (Click Locations to see the amazing list of divisions, involving more than 19,000 employees.) Click the icon for the area of products or services that interests you to get details on local suppliers as well as overall services available in that area.

word etc.

http://www.wordetc.com/

This group serves "the health care, legal, insurance, financial, education, government, and manufacturing community" nationwide with computer supplies and accessories. Paper supplies, toner/ribbons/cartridges, etc. A links section is supplied to pop you over to a given manufacturer's page.

NEWSGROUP

alt.office.management

Related Sites

http://www.harb.net/ScottOfficeSupplyElectronics/

http://www.misterpaper.com/

http://www.pro-office.com/

http://www.ridgefieldofficesupply.com/

Yellow Pages

ONLINE TEACHING AND LEARNING

> Every moment in life is a learning experience. Or what good is it, right?
>
> *Paul in* Six Degrees of Separation *(1993)*

Canadian Kids' Page

http://www.onramp.ca/~lowens/107kids.htm

Serves as a starting place for parents and children exploring the Web together. This site links to 300 other related sites. Search by topic or title.

Classroom Connect

http://www.classroom.net

Online magazine for K–12 educators using the Internet in the classroom. Both in print and online, Classroom Connect has become a source of pointers and features related to using the Internet in formal education for more than 8,000 monthly readers.

The Community Learning Network

http://cln.etc.bc.ca

Provides information pertinent to United States education as well. Includes distance learning resource information, connections to other educational and Canadian government Gophers and CLN software.

HotList: Virtual Exhibits
http://sln.fi.edu/tfi/jump.html

Cornell Computer Science Graphics Course

http://www.tc.cornell.edu:80/Visualization/Education/cs418/

An online service for the students to review computer graphics lab procedures and results, as well as present lecture material and project animations for all to view.

Distance Education Clearinghouse

http://www.uwex.edu/disted/home.html

Gathers information on teleconferencing technologies, instructional design, programs and courses, and other distance learning resources.

Educational Online Sources

http://netspace.students.brown.edu/eos/main_image.html

Plans to become a central "welcoming" and jump station for educators on the Internet. Contains links to educational conferences, policy and reform archives, and subject guides to online resources.

Exploratorium Homepage

http://www.exploratorium.edu/

Features, among other exhibits, "Diving in to the Gene Pool," "Remembering Nagasaki," "Ask Us A Question," and a digital library. Also offers The Learning Studio, a collection of science resources for parents, teachers, and kids.

Related Sites

http://www.csusm.edu/SUAVE/

http://www.teachnet.com/

HotList: Virtual Exhibits

http://sln.fi.edu/tfi/jump.html

Offers links to many online interactive exhibits, where you control the action on the other end, such as a robot or telescope. Also offers links to online exhibits, such as the Amazon jungle or the Louvre.

Impact! Online Homepage

http://www.ed.uiuc.edu/Impact/impact_homepage.html

Consists of hypertext documents in English, with links giving pronunciation, part of speech, and meaning.

The Interactive Frog Dissection: An On-line Tutorial

http://curry.edschool.Virginia.edu:80/~insttech/frog/

Uses photographs and QuickTime movies to illustrate step-by-step the dissection of a frog. Provides tests along the way to help the student judge mastery of the content.

Intercultural E-Mail Classroom Connections

http://www.stolaf.edu/network/iecc/

Provides listings of teachers and classes needing key-pals for cross-cultural exchanges and partners for online projects at the K–12 and the college level. Also offers links to Listservs and other collections of keypal requests and online projects.

JASON Project

http://www.jasonproject.org/

Collaborative learning experience for students around the world. Each year, a two-week scientific expedition is mounted in a remote part of the world and broadcast in real-time, using state-of-the-art technology, to a network of educational, research, and cultural institutions in the United States, Canada, Bermuda, and the United Kingdom. Lets participating students at the interactive downlink sites "go live" (using telepresence) to the expedition, operate the scientific equipment being used, and talk directly with the scientists at the expedition site.

Related Sites

http://www.twics.com/~comsig/index.html

http://edweb.gsn.org/

http://www.missouri.edu/~rhetnet/interversity/

Landegg Academy Online

http://www.landegg.edu/

Serves as a learning environment in which people from all parts of the world can gather to search for new answers to the needs of contemporary society.

How to Get Freebies Without Dumpster Diving

Keep your money held tight if you are part of an educational institute or government agency. At the Netscape Web site (http://www.netscape.com), you can download and use Netscape for free. It's easy, and Netscape only asks for the name of your school or agency. Another trick of the free trade is to become an active member of Netscape's beta program. In the beta program, you can try out copies of new applications while they are in test phase. Giving a browser the ol' test and retest is a surefire way to figure out whether the browser suits you. Check out Netscape's home page at http://home.netwcape.com to learn more about which applications are currently in beta.

Math Education Resources

http://www.teleport.com/~vincer/math.html

Offers links to many good online math sites. Lists lesson plans, curriculum guides, and interactive links such as the Gallery of Interactive Geometry. Also offers listings of math-related newsgroups.

Online Reference Works

http://www.cs.cmu.edu/Web/references.html

Lists several different online reference sources, such as a hypertext Webster's dictionary, a thesaurus, and an acronym dictionary. Also offers several foreign language dictionaries, and computing dictionaries.

The Open University

http://www.open.ac.uk/

The British institution that pioneered distance education as a way to broaden educational opportunities across the country. Offers a comprehensive program that serves as a model for other programs. Also offers links to other online resources.

Related Sites

http://www.exploratorium.edu/learning_studio/lsxhibit.html

http://www.ncss.org/online/NCSS Online

Netwohttp://www.cc.ukans.edu/~sypherh/bc/onctr.htmlrk

Reed Interactive's Global Classroom

http://www.reedbooks.com.au/index.html

Offers online projects centering around specific themes, and encourages international participation. Also offers an international keypal search and find center and access to education-related newsgroups.

The Study in the USA Online Directory

http://www.studyusa.com/

Serves as a resource for international students seeking to study at a quality American university, college, or English language institute. Lets you browse informative articles and program descriptions, and use the online request information forms to email the school in which you're interested for more information.

Total Recall

http://www.demon.co.uk/sharpsw/total.html

Presents an amazing online training course that teaches you how to dramatically improve your memory powers—improve exam grades, learn foreign vocabulary, and more.

Turner Adventure Learning

http://cee.indiana.edu/turner/tal.html

Contains information about Turner Adventure Learning, electronic field trips for K–12. Contains text documents, graphics, and Web links related to each field trip.

Welcome K–12

http://www.gatech.edu/lcc/idt/Students/Cole/Proj/K-12/K12wel.html

Focuses on teachers learning to use the Internet while online, as well as those who have very limited access time. Arranged alphabetically by subject area with two different tables of content—one with subheadings and pictures for those who want to browse and the other with just plain text links to resources. Addresses the real problem of teachers and time.

Welcome to TEAMSnet

http://teams.lacoe.edu/

Offers information on both distance education and Internet in the classroom. Lists online projects, links to resources, and professional development information. Also offers a page on preservice teacher preparation.

The World-Wide Web Virtual Library

http://www.w3.org/hypertext/DataSources/bySubject/Overview.html

Cross-references everything from aboriginal studies to zoos. Details the links by alphabetical order, by era, and by region. Offers clickable maps of the world and specific information about many countries. Also offers a list of other online resources.

Related Sites

http://www.abacon.com/reynolds/

http://info.ox.ac.uk/jtap/

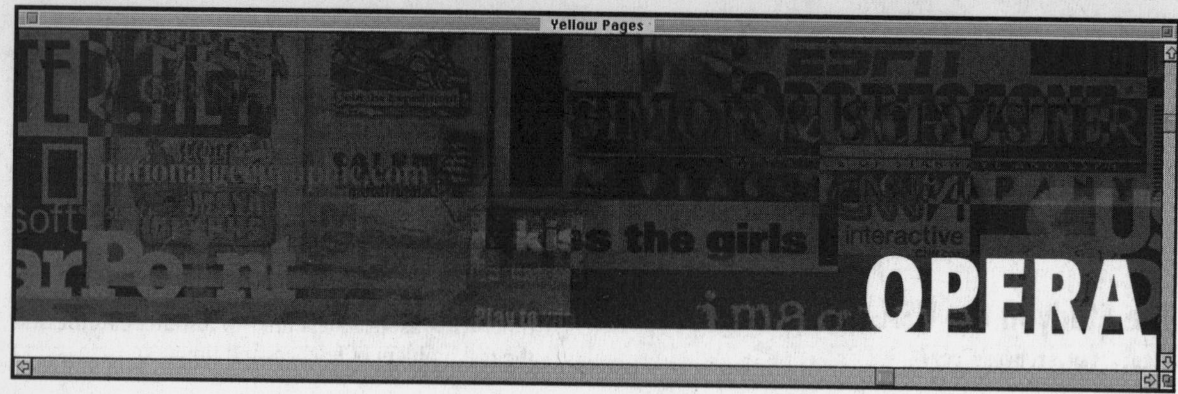

OPERA

Comrade! Why in Beijing opera are woman's roles traditionally played by men?

Song Liling in M. Butterfly *(1993)*

The Aria Database

http://www.aria-database.com/

Would you like to be able to search for info on a particular aria, opera, or composer? This is the place. Search by name, opera, language, or voice type. The database includes MIDI files of some of the music, libretti, translations, and more. Mozart and Verdi are featured, but many other composers are also included. Related links also included.

Báthory Erzsébet - Elizabeth Bathory

http://www.maltedmedia.com/people/bathory/erzsebet/

If you're at all interested in how an opera comes to be, visit this fascinating site. In the Cologne Journal section, Dennis Báthory-Kitsz describes the plans for this semi-historical opera in progress. Check out the history, the bibliography, and of course the castle photos.

BOADICEA.COM

http://www.gen.com/boadicea/

At this location, you can find details on two operas by Clarry Evans and Judy Stevens: *Boadicea - The Celtic Opera* and *Macbeth - The Rock Opera.* Descriptions of the operas, reviews, libretti, a calendar of performances, and tapes of live performances.

The Indiana Opera Theatre and the MacAllister Awards
http://members.iquest.net/~opera/

Bob's Opera Madness

http://www.geocities.com/Vienna/1059/

Bob may be mad, but sure provides an interesting site. The 3-D Opera Gallery is best viewed with 3D glasses. Plenty to see and do here—a collection of opera singers' advertisements for various products, photo essays of singers (some drawn from home movies), even a list of appearances by opera singers in the movies.

Cyberspace Opera Studio

http://home.navisoft.com/cyberopera/

Could you use a customized audiocassette of arias for rehearsal? This commercial site lists prerecorded tapes in various voices for quite a number of arias—and may be able to provide others that don't appear on the menu. Order via mail, email, or fax. Pricing information included at the site.

FanFaire

http://ffaire.com/

A webzine by and for fans of opera and classical music. Updated quarterly. Reviews, slide shows, pics, embedded sound files. For best viewing, you'll need a fairly fast modem and a recent version of Netscape or Internet Explorer. Be prepared for sound at a substantial volume—the Java applets may reset your volume levels.

Field Notes of a Rookie Opera Lover

http://www.alaska.net/~hweaver/opera-index.html

An endearingly personal site at which an opera lover has recorded his impressions about opera performances from 1988 to the present.

The Indiana Opera Theatre and the MacAllister Awards

http://members.iquest.net/~opera/

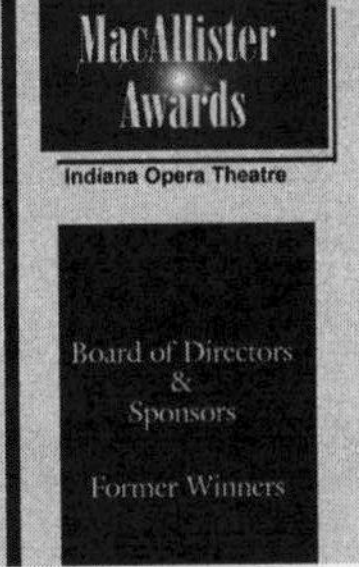

Welcome to the Indiana Opera Theatre and the MacAllister Awards for Opera Singers.
Celebrating its 17th year of nurturing budding opera stars, we at the Indiana Opera Theatre and the MacAllister Awards would like tell you a little about who we are, how we got started, and what we've accomplished.
The Indiana Opera Theatre is a small opera company founded to perform operatic recitals, produce lesser known works of great composers and do contemporary opera. In 1979, as an experiment, we tried a vocal competition. The judges were three or four in number, we had maybe 25 singers and the top prize was $1,500. Thus were the beginnings of the MacAllister Awards.
With some tinkering and expansion, the competition grew slowly and then exploded when we took the action out across the country "to the singers." Scoring was modified to take out politics, judges were invited from out of town, singers escalated in number to over 800 a year and prize money is now over $45,000.
MacAllister Awards
Indiana Opera Theatre
Board of Directors & Sponsors
Former Winners

With prize money of more than $45,000 and competitors numbering more than 800, the MacAllister Awards are a significant competition for opera singers. This site provides all the details on the contest and its sponsor, the Indiana Opera Theatre.

Monsalvat

http://home.sol.no/~deverett/indexns3.htm

This personal site belongs to a real Wagner fan, and are devoted to *Parsifal.* Quite a few articles on various aspects, including a chronology, the libretto (in German), a discography, and so on. Many, many links to related opera sites—both performers and companies.

Musical On Line Companies

http://www.wynn.com/mol/music.on.line.html

Come to Musical On Line when you're in search of professional companies or musicians. Strictly listings and links, except for a musical chat room. The opera company list reaches outside the U.S. into Canada and Europe. Dozens of links.

New York City Opera

http://plaza.interport.net/nycopera/

Information and current schedules for the world-famous New York City Opera. Includes performer biographies.

Opera Companies on the Web

http://musicinfo.gold.ac.uk/index/opera2.htm
http://www.fsz.bme.hu/opera/companies.html

Two different lists of opera companies and opera/voice-related sites.

Opera Glass

http://rick.stanford.edu:/opera/main.html

An opera information server. Here you can get detailed information, including performance histories, synopses, libretti, discographies, pictures, and more on any of a small but rapidly growing number of operas, plus pointers to many other opera servers.

OPERA NEWS Online

http://operanews.com/index.htm

An electronic publication of the Metropolitan Opera Guild, Inc., New York, New York. Historical and musical analyses, performance reviews, profiles and interviews, more. Visitors are welcome to pop in and scope out selected news and articles before subscribing. A subscription gives you access to the full magazine online and via mail.

The Opera Schedule Server

http://www.fsz.bme.hu/opera/main.html

A searchable database providing information about "what's playing" at opera houses all around the world.

Opera Works

http://gray.music.rhodes.edu/operahtmls/works.html

This unusual site, a production of Rhodes College in Memphis, Tennessee, provides a pronouncing dictionary, complete with a brief description and a sound file, for dozens of names associated with opera—names of composers, names of operas. Also connects to the Opera Memphis home page.

Operabase

http://www.operabase.com/

Detailed information on broadcast and performance schedules, festivals, and events; opera houses; reviews and links. Includes opera timelines for viewers seeking a little history. Databases searchable by singer, conductor, producer, composer, and more. A complete and complex site, available in five languages.

OperaFactory

http://www.poptel.org.uk/opera/

Home site for Opera Factory, a London-based company that produces classic and contemporary works, with emphasis on physical as well as musical training. News on current tours and activities.

OperaNet Magazine

http://www.culturekiosque.com/opera/index.htm

An online magazine for opera fans, featuring performer interviews, articles, schedules, and reviews of performances and recordings.

The Ring Disc

http://www.ringdisc.com/

Site for The Ring Disc, a CD-ROM interactive guide to Wagner's *Ring Cycle*, based on the Decca/Solti recording. (Requires Windows 95 or NT on a Pentium system and at least 800×600 resolution.) Includes the score, libretti, translations, and more. This site also includes two thoughtful tributes to Sir Georg Solti, to whose memory The Ring Disc is dedicated.

The Virtual Opera House

http://www.dbn.lia.net/users/dlever/

Information on the great opera composers and their works (including pictures and recommended recordings), singers (by voice type), conductors, and more. Real Audio and WAV files, interesting anecdotes.

NEWSGROUPS

br.opera

humanities.music.composers.wagner

rec.music.opera

GOPHER SITE

gopher://wiretap.spies.com/00/Library/Music/Misc/wagner.rng

MAILING LISTS

C-OPERA

CLASSICAL

OPERA-L

Related Sites

http://www.geocities.com/Vienna/1450/caruso.html

http://www.geocities.com/Vienna/Strasse/1523/callas.htm

http://www.on-luebeck.de/~cdammann/Bernd_Weikl.html

http://www.borlange.se/kultur/jussib/enjussib.htm

http://classicalmus.com/artists/ghiaurov.html

http://www.classicalmus.com/bmgclassics/opera/

http://www.kwf.org/works/m2main.html

http://www.MaxOpus.com/

http://php.indiana.edu/~lneff/libretti/

http://www.china-pages.com/culture/jj_home.htm

http://www.cam.org/~s_lynch/mwoshome.htm

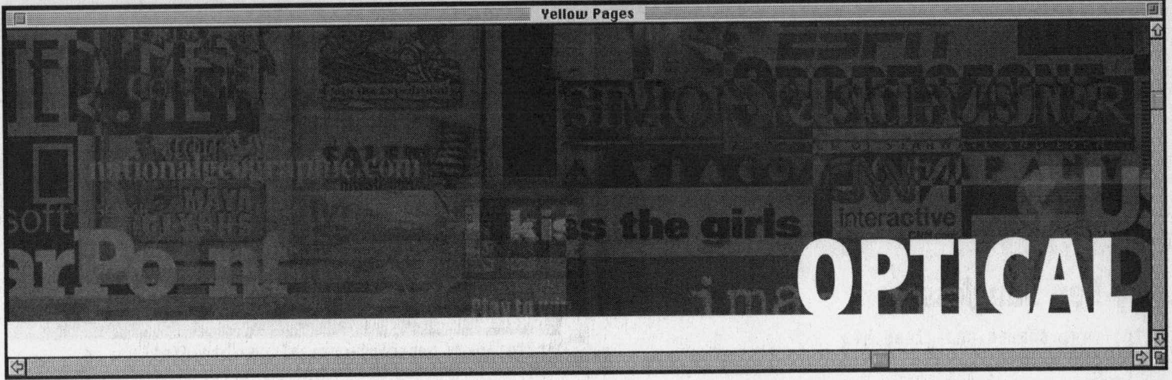

> It's 106 miles to Chicago, we've got a full tank of gas, half a pack of cigarettes, it's dark, and we're wearing sunglasses.
>
> *Elwood Blues in* The Blues Brothers *(1980)*

Aaron Bridges Optical

http://www.aboptical.com/

Order online sunglasses, eyeglasses, frames, safety glasses, sports goggles, and transition lenses. This company also offers a reminder service for a one time fee of only $19.95. Never again forget your mother's birthday or your anniversary!

AB SEE Optical Home Page

http://members.aol.com/absee/index.html

Based in Los Angeles, this company specializes in eyecare for athletes and children. Stop by when you're in L.A.

Absolutely Optical

http://www.aboptical.com/

The site offers glasses, frames, and even eyecare tips, but the real gem here is the actual facility. Anyone in the Tampa, Florida area should look into Absolutely Optical for any eyecare needs. Offers laser correction, orthokeratology, handicapped accessible exam rooms, flexible hours, and an off-site shopping service.

Absolutely Optical
http://www.aboptical.com/

Bard Optical

http://206.158.160.65/bard/

This site offers eye exams, glasses, contacts, and sunglasses. Also fills outside prescriptions, duplicates lenses, and repairs glasses.

Dr. Tavel One Hour Optical

http://www.taveloptical.com/

This nationwide chain store site includes "Ask Dr. Tavel" where you can have your vision care questions answered, order replacement contact lenses online, print coupons good for in-store services, and more. You can even explore employment opportunities with the Doctor.

Harley-Davidson Sunglass Center

http://www.harley-sunglasses.com/

Order online the ultimate sunglasses for riding your hog on a sunny day. Prescription and nonprescription lenses available.

Lens Express

http://www.lensexpress.com/

The world's largest contact lens replacement company. Hey, would Wonder Woman steer you wrong?

Modern Optical

http://www.eye-ware.com/

Offering 50% off frames, sunglasses, and lenses, and 25% off contacts. Get the number or name of the frame, color, and size you want, then send the information along with your prescription and this site will save you big bucks.

Proview Optical Group

http://www.proview.com/

Tons of choices here. If this site doesn't have the glasses you're looking for, forget about it! Safety, welding, sports, night-driving, computer/TV, reading glasses, and more!

Ray-Ban Sunglasses

http://www.shades.com/glass.htm

Stylish sunglasses at 30–50 percent off the retail price. Online shopping with photos and prices.

Shade Brigade™ Sunglasses Online

http://www.shadebrigade.com/

Currently offers Ray-Ban, Serengeti, Bolle, suncloud, Gargoyles, Hobie, Revo, and Vuarnet. According to the site, it will soon offer Swiss Army Brand Sunglasses, Harley-Davidson, Guess, Persol, Killer Loop, Georgio Armani, Maui Jim, and DKNY.

sunglasses.com

http://www.sunglasses.com/def2.htm

Sunglasses by Bolle, Carrera, Gargoyles, Porsche Design, Revo, Ray-Ban, Versace, and more. To speed things up, know your maker and style number before shopping this site, but you can browse through the numerous photos and descriptions online as well.

Related Sites

http://www.benedict-optical.com/benedict/

http://www.compusmart.ab.ca/optical/index.htm

http://www.fastlens.com/index.htm

http://www.colorcontacts.com/

http://netmar.com/mall/shops/guardian/index.html

http://home.earthlink.net/~rixstuff/card.htm

http://www.lyuks.com/johnson.html

http://www.lens4me.com/index.htm

http://www.cyberlens.com/

http://www.giarre.com/store/prodotti.htm

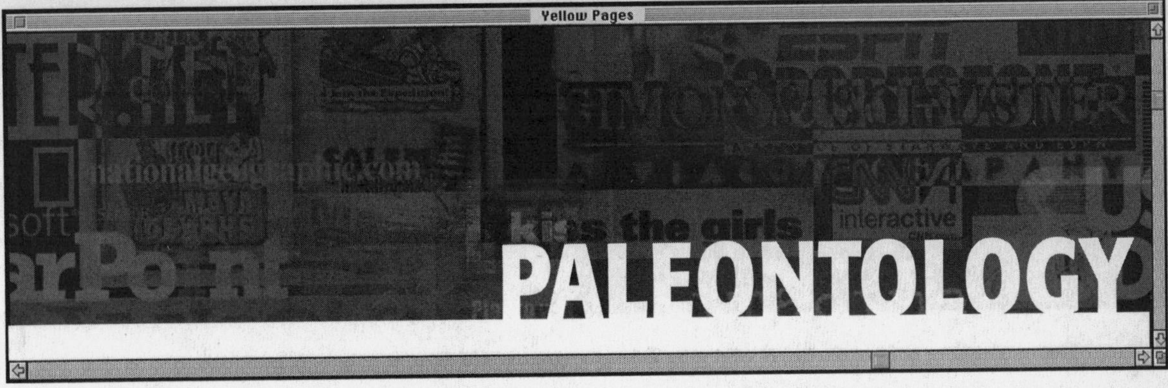

In the tumult of men and events, solitude was my temptation; now it is my friend. What other satisfaction can be sought once you have confronted History?

Charles DeGaulle

Dino Russ's Lair: The EarthNet Info Server

`http://128.174.172.76/isgsroot/dinos/dinos_home.html`

Web site devoted to information about various dinosaurs. Features links to dinosaur and vertebrate paleontology, and earth and geoscience sites. Also contains information concerning contacts for those interested in participating in actual dinosaur digs.

Dinosauria Online

`http://www.dinosauria.com/`

Features dinosaur articles, discussions and essays, reference materials and dinosaur products for sale. Also contains the names and dates of all the geological time periods and links to other dinosaur related Web sites.

Exposure Excursions

`http://dns.magtech.ab.ca/digdino/dinotour.htm`

Vacation planners that arrange paleontological excursions into the "badlands" of Alberta Canada.

Dino Russ's Lair: The EarthNet Info Server
`http://128.174.172.76/isgsroot/dinos/dinos_home.html`

Dinosauria Online
`http://www.dinosauria.com/`

Museum of Paleontology
`http://www.ucmp.berkeley.edu/`

Museum of Paleontology

`http://www.ucmp.berkeley.edu/`

Devoted to the explanation and understanding of paleontology. Also contains sections on phylogeny, geological time, and evolutionary thought.

Palaeolithic Painted Cave at Vallon-Pont-d'Arc

`http://www.culture.fr/culture/gvpda-en.htm`

Presents recently discovered ancient cave paintings from the south of France, created during the last iceage, which makes them between 17,000 and 20,000 years old.

Raymond M. Alf Museum

`http://www.webb.pvt.k12.ca.us/webb/Alf/AlfHome.html`

Features a paleontologic museum tour. Also contains information about various collections that the museum carries.

A B C D E F G H I J K L M N O P Q R S T U V W X Y Z

> We are here and it is now. Further than that all human knowledge is moonshine.
>
> *H. L. Mencken*

ALCHEMY

The Alchemy Virtual Library

http://www.levity.com/alchemy/home.html

This site is one of the first alchemy sites on the Web. It has information ranging from general historic data to alchemical journals and even an image of a reconstructed alchemical laboratory. Chemists and laymen alike will be fascinated by the online translated texts from the journals of alchemists. News of upcoming conferences, recommended books, and mailing lists are included, too, along with many other Web resources.

Black Hole Gallery - The Alchemical Stage of Calcination

http://blackholegallery.com/alchemical.html

Although primarily a gallery of supernatural-themed paintings by VanJohnstone, the page cited here has some interesting basic information on alchemy. I even learned that Grandpa on "The Munsters" was an alchemist, and the character of Dr. Frankenstein, in Mary Shelley's *Frankenstein*, was based on a real-life alchemist. The paintings are sort of cool, especially if you like macabre-sounding names. My favorite title was "Having Tea with Death"—about as anti-Grandma Moses as you can get!

Spagyria
http://www.spagyria.com/

AstroAdvice
http://www.astroadvice.com

Astrology Online
http://www.astrology-online.com/zodiac.htm

Ghosts: The Page That Goes Bump in the Night
http://www.camalott.com/~brianbet/ghosts.html

Ghosts, Spirits, Shades, & Spectres
http://members.aol.com/DWWaldron/home.html

Numerology: 24 Hours a Day
http://www.sun-angel.com/interact/numquest/numquest.html

SpiritLink
http://www.spiritlink.com

Aunt Agatha's Occult Emporium
http://web.idirect.com/~agatha/

Astarte's TarotWeb
http://home1.pacific.net.sg/~mun_hon/tarot/tarot.htm

Learning the Tarot - An Online Course
http://www2.dgsys.com/~bunning/top.html

Michele's Tarot Page
http://www.erols.com/jacksn/

The Extraterrestrial Biological Entity Page
http://www.ee.fit.edu/users/lpinto/index.shtml

Vodun Information Pages
http://www.arcana.com/shannon/voodoo/voodoo.html

Brenna's Page
http://www.argyll.demon.co.uk/

Joan's Witch Directory
http://www.ucmb.ulb.ac.be/~joan/witches/

The Witches' Voice
http://www.witchvox.com/

The Witches' Web Home Page
http://www.witchesweb.com/home.html

The Golden Elixir Home Page

http://www.unive.it/~dsie/pregadio/index.html

Articles, reviews of books, bibliographies—some even in Chinese—and more are available at this site. It's well-organized and gives you handy descriptions of what's available before you go to the trouble of downloading it. "Golden Elixir," by the way, is the translation of *jindan*, one of the Chinese names for alchemy.

The Philosophers of Nature

http://www.mcs.net/~alchemy/

Here's the home page for what claims to be the leading school for "studies in the practical and philosophical aspects of alchemy." The Philosophers of Nature, based in Wheaton, IL (a rather unexotic location for such esoteric studies!), offer videotapes, newsletter articles, links to related sites, a FAQs page, an electronic bookstore, and more, but the courses are the main thrust of the site. The alchemical course consists of two parts: spagyrics (plant alchemy) and mineral alchemy. Check out the fascinating photo of a modern alchemical laboratory.

Robin Murphy's Alchemilla Journal—Alchemy, Astrology, Homeopathy, and Ancient Medicine

http://www.alchemilla.com/

This site, sponsored by The Hahnemann Academy of North Americas, focuses more on the medical aspect of alchemy. Its library offers several sections, however, including one on spiritual alchemy. You can also join a mailing list to get more information on book release and seminar dates.

Spagyria

http://www.spagyria.com/

Spagyria is full of information about spagyrics, the branch of alchemy dealing with plants. Click one of the brightly colored flasks in the navigation bar to go to sections on online publications, products, membership information, and more. The herbal index is particularly interesting; click what ails you and get a list of herbs that just might help. There's even a helpful glossary for all those esoteric terms.

LISTSERVS AND OTHER RESOURCES

Contribute by email to an open discussion forum on alchemy by sending email to `listserv@levity.com` with the words `SUBSCRIBE alchemy-list` and your full name (not your email address) in the message.

Check out `http://www.levity.com/alchemy/new_mail.html` for information on joining email discussion groups on different aspects of alchemy, such as alchemy's influence on art.

You can also try the FTP site at `ftp://ftp.lysator.liu.se/pub/magick/Alchemy/` for more articles.

Try the alt.magick newsgroup, too.

ASTROLOGY

Angelic Astrology

http://www.angels11.com/

For $20.00 (payments are handled through the mail), you can get a personal astrology reading (sorry, folks, but Lisa's too cheap to test it out for you). Click Meet Barbara to see a photo of the blissful-faced woman who does the charts and read about her visits from her guardian angel Abraham. For the reports, you have your choice of your own personality profile, a child's personality profile, seeing what the future holds, finding out how location affects you, what "solar return" can mean for you, and get astrological info on friends and lovers.

Asian Astrology

http://users.deltanet.com/~wcassidy/astro/astroindex.html

Learn all about Asian astrology here. You can find specialized links to Chinese, Tibetan, and Vietnamese astrology. The site also offers current news in Asian astrology, a link to the Asian Astrology bookstore, and a mailing list. If you're so inclined, you can even send a Chinese astrology greeting card to your friends.

AstroAdvice

http://www.astroadvice.com

You have to register to use the services here, but it takes only seconds. Once you do, you can get all kinds of cool information about your astrological profile, including business partnerships, erotic profile (sorry, that information is classified!), your biorhythms, and something called *synastry*, which is your compatibility with a loved one. You'll need to know your birthdate and time and place of birth, of course, with the same data for people whose compatibility factor you're checking. There's also lots of clear, useful info on astrology in general. It's fun and it's free.

Astrology Now

http://www.onesky.com/astrology/

Excellent basic information about each sign. You can also check a compatibility guide to find which out signs you'll love or hate! Nice graphics, and soothing music plays in the background while you peruse the site.

Astrology Online

http://www.astrology-online.com/zodiac.htm

This site claims to be the largest astrology site on the Internet. Could be—it's pretty big! Cool cloud background, attractive graphics, and clean layout, but the content is equally as good. If you're new to astrology, this site is an excellent starting point; even if you're an old hand at astrology, you'll probably learn something new. Very well-written, with clear, in-depth information; you'll find sections on astrology basics, explanations of each sign, weekly and daily horoscopes, compatibility comparisons, and more. You'll also find links to a dream analysis site and many other paranormal/spiritual sites. Michael, the site author, offers an unusual system of handling personalized reports; he sends 'em out first, and you pay later!

The Cosmic Palette

http://nen.sedona.net//haizen/

Features information about current lunar phases and signs, as well as reasons why people believe and disbelieve astrology. Astrologer Haizen Paige, whose interests and qualifications are described, handles personalized astrology reports (and the payments) by mail. You can read an article of his that appeared in *Open Mind* or his musings on why people are attracted to Sedona, Arizona, where he lives.

The Harmony of Heaven

http://ruls41.fsw.leidenuniv.nl/ProZodiac/

This site explains the ProZodiac project, which claims to have musically interpreted the movements of the planets through a "mathematical transformation" (sounds like more fun than an plain ole equation). You can listen to samples of the music (AU or AIFF format), which the site asserts is relaxing when used during meditation.

Horoscopes@SWOON

http://www.swoon.com/horoscopes/

Granted, this site is the online host for *GQ*, *Glamour*, and *Mademoiselle* magazines, so you're not going to find scholarly information here. However, if you're looking for light, amusing horoscopes, and a quick outline to sign and compatibility information, try here. You can also find out your rising sign and moon, if you supply some information. SWOON will even email your dailiy horoscopes to you; occasionally, they're uncannily accurate!

Kramer–Fishing Guide to the Stars

http://www.io.com/~fgs/

One of the wittiest astrology pages on the Web, Kramer gives entertaining horoscopes rather than the usual predigested planetessimal fare. A refreshing look at astrology; for an extra laugh, check out the fine print at the bottom of the welcome page. Kramer will mail you a monthly astrological outlook for all the signs, too; check out the mailto link supplied.

The Metalog Directory of Astrology

http://www.astrologer.com/metalog/

This site maintains links to professional astrologers, student astrologers, national associations, and schools in 48 countries. Get information about how to register with this directory to find local astrologers and astrology-related bookstores in your area. Each entry lists address and phone information, as well as mailto links when email addresses are available.

The Nine Planets

http://seds.lpl.arizona.edu/nineplanets/nineplanets/nineplanets.html

This astounding multimedia tour of the planets offers a wealth of information about the mythological significance and scientific understanding of not only the nine planets, but also their moons and some other small astronomical bodies, such as comets and meteorites. Fascinating facts and images, all neatly organized, make this site an excellent educational tool for the astronomical and astrological novice. There's even a glossary and appendixes for further investigation.

TwoStar Oracle

http://www.twostar.com/astrology

You can get a free reading after supplying some information about yourself. Be forewarned, though: You need to know the latitude and longitude of the place you were born. If you don't have an atlas handy, the site links to a couple of resources where you can figure it out.

The Underground Astrologer

http://www.links.net/astro/

Here's a great introduction to the basics of astrology, written in a light, informal style. Justin, the site author, uses an acting metaphor to describe planets, signs, and houses—an interesting way to look at astrology. I found a few bits of info I hadn't heard before, like the tarot cards associated with each sign. Amusing graphics, plus a bibliography and page of varied online resources with interesting annotations.

USENET NEWSGROUP

alt.astrology

GHOST STORIES AND ANGELS

Angels on the Net

http://www.netangel.com/

All kinds of angel-related features, including a free monthly newsletter, an angel chat room, angel cards you can send by email, stories of angel visitations, and even a "cyber mall" so you can shop for all your angelic needs. Nice graphics and helpful navigation features.

Ghosts: The Page That Goes Bump in the Night

http://www.camalott.com/~brianbet/ghosts.html

Oooooo...scary, kids! Great site, with lots of ghost stories, a sepulchral chat room, a ghostly forum, and lots of supernatural links. Cool graphics (check out the chainlink used as a separator!), and the material is well-written. You can even submit your own tale of terror, if you like.

Ghosts, Spirits, Shades, & Spectres

http://members.aol.com/DWWaldron/home.html

Great-looking site, with organization and content to match. Besides helpful links to other sites, you can learn the difference between banshides and doppelgangers, for instance; find out why some places are prone to hauntings; and read many bone-chilling stories. Great black-and-white photos and illustrations, and the green text on a black background is, well, ghostly!

The Ghost Stories Site

http://www.sitemart.com/ghost/stories.html

More ghost stories than you can rattle a chain at, plus a questionnaire you can submit if you have a ghost story of your own to submit. Lots of links to other ghost sites, too.

Handwriting on the Wall

http://web-star.com/wall.html

Think it's just a photograph of a brick wall? O ye of little faith! The 24-hour-a-day "Web cam" is trained on the brick wall of a building erected on the site of Portland, Oregon's first cemetery, where ghostly handwriting is said to have mysteriously appeared from time to time. The photo is updated periodically throughout the day, and if you see anything, email at once! Comments from visitors who have seen handwriting are included. The eerie music gave me goosebumps, or maybe it was that skull face I saw on one of the bricks...

Obiwan's UFO-Free Paranormal Page - Stories

http://www.ghosts.org/stories/a.html

No, you won't find any UFO stories here! However, you will find all kinds of ghost stories from a variety of sources. Note: When you click a title that interests you, it opens up a new browser window, which I found a little irritating because of my somewhat slow computer. Interesting stories, though.

The Shadowlands Ghost Page

http://users.aol.com/shadoland2/ghost.html

You'll find enough ghost stories here to keep you shivering by your fireplace all winter! Check out the index for a state-by-state listing of haunted places, too. Lots of links to other ghost sites.

The Virtual Library–Angel Encounters

http://www.crown.net/X/AngelStories.html

If you're expecting winged graphics, you won't find them here. However, you'll find many stories about angel visitations written by the page author and other contributors. There are a few links to other related sites.

Welcome to Schloss Reichenstein

http://www.caltim.com/reichenstein/

Beautiful site showing the haunted castle Reichenstein along the Rhine River of Germany. Not only does this site have a story of a man without a head, it gives you an informative tour of the stronghold, along with lots of photos, a map of the area, room rates, and contact information.

The WWW Virtual Library: Archive X, Ghost Stories and Folklore

http://www.crown.net/X/GhostStories.html

This site is a huge collection of ghost stories gathered from many sources. There are also some links to similar sites. No fancy graphics, just text, but some stories are definitely worth reading.

NEWSGROUPS

alt.folklore.ghost-stories

alt.paranet.paranormal

alt.paranet.science

alt.paranet.skeptic

alt.paranormal

NUMEROLOGY

Animals and Karma

http://www.hyperlink.com/weaver/95/25_8/dev/numerol/animals.htm

This article from *The Weaver*, an online spiritual publication, explains the connection between the number seven and the animal kingdom, through the upper and lower astral planes.

Astro-Numerology by Yaakov Kier

http://www.reu.com/kier/

This site acts as an advertisement for numerologist Yaakov Kier, who studied under *National Enquirer* Psychic Frederick Davies. According to Kier, astro-numerology is a powerful combination of astrology and numerology. You can enter personal information and questions and email them to Kier at 150 bucks a pop. But hey, he offers a money-back guarantee if his predictions aren't accurate—what more could you ask for?

Entropic Fine Art Inc - Project Genisys

http://www.entropic-art.com/

This site takes an unusual approach to art based on arcane law, geometry, and numerology. Go on an online quest to decipher and interpret the meaning of five works by Sir Peter Robson.

Numerology

http://www.luna.co.uk/~npharris/number.htm

If you need help discovering your life purpose or determining whether you have "master potential", you might try here. Nigel Harris, founder of the British Numerology Society, gives numerology readings using your name and date of birth. There's also some information about computer programs for numerologists.

Numerology: 24 Hours a Day

http://www.sun-angel.com/interact/numquest/numquest.html

NumberQuest offers a free online numerology service. You'll get a lengthy reading that will surprise you at times and bore you at others. Also, check out the meanings of numbers and how numerology compares to tarot, astrology, the I Ching, and other philosophies, and link to more articles and the Spirit Search Emporium. While you're here, you can have a look at glossaries of the meanings of gemstones and herbs and try "Perfect Planet," an interactive visualization feature. Nice clean graphics in a well-organized site.

SpiritLink

http://www.spiritlink.com

You'll find information on a wealth of different topics at this exceptionally well-organized site, but there's an extensive numerology section. Find out what exactly numerology is, the different types of numerology, how it can help you, and more. The site also offers an "online book" in a zipped format for $4.95 that explains how to do numerology yourself. Check out "The Lighter Side" link in the Numerology section, which explains the best gift and preferred type of music for someone based on the day of the month in which he or she was born.

The Wonderful World of Numerology

http://www.valdosta.peachnet.edu/~abernste/numer.html

This fascinating page gives numerological interpretations into the JFK assassination, Shakespeare's connection to the King James Bible, and presidential deaths.

OCCULT

The Alternative Spiritualites Club Home Page Arts–Esoterica–Hermetica

http://yoyo.cc.monash.edu.au/%7Edarmou/occult/Occult_home.html

This site explores alternative spiritualities and offers links to commercial organizations, pagan sites, rituals, and other spiritual home pages. It also offers a searchable index of pagan and occult groups; the ASC is based in Australia, but groups in other countries are included. You can also get a membership in the ASC.

Anders Magick Page

http://www.student.nada.kth.se/~nv91-asa/magick.html

This site offers resources on a variety of occult, mystical, and "magick" topics. It's still under construction, but it's a good place to check for some of the less-well-known sites and resources, including FTP sites and mailing lists.

Aunt Agatha's Occult Emporium

http://web.idirect.com/~agatha/

This pagan/metaphysical gathering place seeks to promote the occult through links to events, artists, magazines, and, of course, merchandise sales. There's lots of well-organized, easy-to-find information here, including a spell book, an excellent dictionary of occult terms, and links to all kinds of cool places.

Dark Side of the Net

http://www.gothic.net/darkside/

There's an *amazing* amount of information at this site! The author has obviously labored and sweated to search out the Internet for occult-related Web pages, FTP sites, newsgroups, mailing lists, and so on. Everything is neatly alphabetized, and there are descriptions for the newsgroups. The links to Web pages aren't annotated, unfortunately—maybe in the future. Check it out before you start looking elsewhere for pages on supernatural/occult/horror topics.

Shawn's Occult and Religious Resources

http://kosh.dws.acs.cmu.edu/occult/

This is an extremely well-organized site; topics are arranged alphabetically, with links to click for the resource you're interested in. Shawn offers a variety of resources and covers a broad spectrum of subjects.

FTP SITES

ftp.maths.tcd.ie /pub/music/gothic/

ftp.lysator.liu.se/pub/

NEWSGROUPS

alt.horror

alt.magick.chaos

alt.vampyres

REINCARNATION

A.R.E. - Edgar Cayce

http://www.are-cayce.com/reincar.htm

Just for the record, A.R.E. is the Association for Research and Enlightenment. This page discusses Cayce's beliefs on reincarnation and offers links to his thoughts on meditation, ESP, Atlantis, and the millennium, among others.

Human Understood Reincarnation or Resurrecting the Dead

http://www.canuck.com/~akwu/

This site opens to an extremely confusing image map; looks like Jackson Pollock got hold of a typewriter. However, if you scroll down past that, you'll find links to sections that are at least readable. From what I could gather—struggling through the author's misspellings, random use of capital letters, and fondness for exclamation points—the site offers some sort of program you can download that has something to do with resurrecting the dead. Perhaps this site should have been called the Lazarus Home Page...It's oddly entertaining and has some links to other sites that are probably just as bizarre.

Karma and Related Theories

http://users.deltanet.com/~lumiere/karma/mystknow.htm

A very in-depth explanation of the theory of reincarnation and how it works. Joseph Morales examines the philosophical questions raised by the traditional Hindu theory of karma and offers several links to related sites. There's tons of information here, so be prepared to sit down and read.

Regressions and Progressions

http://www.calmness.com/pastlife.htm

You'll find some basic information on what past-life regression and reincarnation are and a short list of related articles. There's no real organization to the list, and the descriptions are brief; however, some are worth a look.

Reincarnation & Karma

http://www.spiritweb.org/Spirit/reincarnation-karma-omni.html

This page in Spirit Web's site discusses reincarnation based on the laws of karma. Author John Payne corrects misconceptions about karma and offers an anecdote, "Charlie, the Soul Story" to clarify the concept. This article is actually an excerpt from the online magazine *Starseeds*, published by Mr. Payne. His email address is included, if you'd like more information.

Reincarnation and Karma

http://www.fst.org/reinc2.htm

This second part of a three-part series of articles by Reverend Simeon Stefanidakis is a fascinating look at reincarnation and karma. The author dispels some of the myths about karma (it's more than just an "eye for an eye," for example) and outlines the degrees of karma, from individual to humankind. Link to Part Three for an absorbing account of the process of rebirth and some of the problems of past-life regression.

Reincarnation Case History

http://www.best.com/~dna/don/CaseHistory.html

Don Showen transcribed this past-life regression session, which he taped in 1976. Written in a question-and-answer format; it makes fascinating—and occasionally eerie—reading.

Reincarnation, karma and past lives

http://inetport.com/~one/bcrkpl.html

Basically, one long essay on reincarnation and its principles by Benjamin Creme, an author, lecturer, and the British chief editor of Share International, a nonprofit organization. He also offers a few links to related sites.

Reincarnation Links

http://www.intercall.com/~joe/reinc.htm

I'm not sure who Joe is, but this page explores Joe's unified spirituality theory and his attempts to understand the meaning of life. He's also a big fan of Edgar Cayce, so he has several links to Cayce's ideas on reincarnation, Atlantis, dream interpretations, and more.

Spiritual Shack

http://www.cs.loyola.edu/~skgupta/

Interesting site—and it wins points for the title! A table of contents leads you to sections on several spiritual topics. Text-heavy, but the information on reincarnation is fairly in-depth, lively, and informative. There are tips on healing, diet, and vegetarianism, as well as a "spiritual tribute" to Edgar Cayce. Links to some related sites, too.

The Weaver Issue No 13 February,1996

http://www.hyperlink.com/E0030/bb8f3dbob82936c50e8440e0721of396be52c392f3f32c8d/weaver/96/25_1/east/buddhism/reincpr.htm

At this online magazine, you can find an article called "The True Reincarnation of the New Panchen Lama," which profiles the Dalai Lama's recognition of a six-year-old boy, Gedhun Choekyi Nyima, as the authentic reincarnation of the 10th Panchen Lama. Contains links to letters to the Chinese government and press releases.

TAROT

Astarte's TarotWeb

http://home1.pacific.net.sg/~mun_hon/tarot/tarot.htm

An excellent site! You can find a brief history of tarot, browse through the FAQs, peruse the list of places all over the country to buy tarot decks, read about the meanings of the cards, find links to many, many tarot sites, and even get a sample reading. This site has great graphics and is extremely well organized. Check out *Divinations: The TarotWeb Newsletter* and The WebWeaver Bulletin Board.

Frank's Cyber-Cafe

http://wwwserv.caiw.nl/~fkuypers/

To give you an idea of what this site is like, when you first reach it, you'll hear a string of WAV files, including one from Homer Simpson! However, for those interested in tarot, check out his CULT-pages section in the navigation bar on the left. You can get an online tarot reading and download a zipped version of WinTarot, as well as check out some good links to other tarot sites. Frank also has a chat corner you can try out, if you like.

InnerSpace Station - Tarot & Spirituality

http://web.idirect.com/%7Einnerspa/

You can get tarot readings and psychic guidance at prices ranging from $20–$75, depending on the scope of the service. Check out the Metaphysical Book store, too, as well as spirital and metaphysical articles, poetry, listings of workshops and seminars, and more. Nice-looking graphics, and the site is well organized. It even offers lots of cool links to more metaphysical/spiritual pages.

Learning the Tarot - An Online Course

http://www2.dgsys.com/~bunning/top.html

Joan Bunning offers an excellent in-depth online tarot tutorial. The entire package can also be downloaded from this site, which is an excellent place to start for those interested in entering the tarot realm. To test out a particular topic in more depth, I looked up the Celtic Cross spread (the most common way to lay out the tarot cards). Wow! Very clear, thorough explanation, including diagrams and a hypothetical example. The information is well written and interesting, too; this is definitely a site to bookmark. She also recommends books and lists links to other interesting sites.

Michele's Tarot Page

http://www.erols.com/jacksn/

A good tarot-for-beginners page, with the information clearly laid out. Michele offers tips, links to other tarot pages (and not-so-tarot pages), places to find tarot books and software, and links to tarot decks.

The Pythagorean Tarot

http://www.cs.utk.edu/~mclennan/BA/PT/PT.html

An interesting take on tarot—its interpretation is based on Pythagorean numerology, although the author also draws on Mediterranean mythology, alchemy, and Jungian psychology, to name a few. The cards are covered in depth, suitably divided into major and minor arcana. Take the time to view the images of the unusual deck created by the author—it's worth it.

Sarena's Tarot

http://www.talisman.net/tarot/

This fascinating site not only covers typical tarot—it also shows you how to do tarot readings with regular playing cards. You'll find tarot FAQs, descriptions of many different, unusual layouts for the cards, tips for tarot experts, tarot spells, recommended books, and links to related sites.

Tarot

http://www.facade.com/attraction/tarot/

This site claims to be the original tarot Web site, and it could well be because it's been offering free tarot readings since 1993. It has several different types of deck readings and covers several schools of tarot thought. One particularly nice feature is that after getting your reading with all the illustrations included, you can choose to get a "print-friendly" format without the graphics, in case you want a paper version to refer to later. You'll also find links to tarot-related topics and other occult interests.

Tarot Inspiration - The Book of Thoth Website

http://www.geocities.com/Paris/2110/index.html

This site gives you information on tarot relating to the Book of Thoth, using the beautifully illustrated Crowley deck. Cool organization—the author has set up the site sections in what looks like tabbed folders at the top of the frame. In the Cards section, there's an interesting interactive feature—you can submit

A B C D E F G H I J K L M N O P Q R S T U V W X Y Z

your interpretation of what a particular tarot card means. Hans (the author) publishes them and responds to many of the comments. A booklist with reviews includes links to Amazon.com, and the links section is short, but illustrated *and* annotated.

Tarot: Tools and Rites of Transformation

http://www.nccn.net/~tarot/

Excellent site, packed full of information. In addition to getting a sample tarot reading with the William Blake deck (beautiful cards inspired by the mystical English writer), you can find newsletters, workshops and seminars, links to other sites, and all kinds of tarot-related resources. It's a great starting point to delve into the world of tarot.

Tarot Weekly

http://tarot.readers.com/

This site from DT King, one of the first to offer a tarot Web site, is now the home of *Tarot Weekly,* an online magazine. Each week features a different article, written in a light, entertaining style.

NEWSGROUPS

alt.divination

alt.tarot

UFOS (UNIDENTIFIED FLYING OBJECTS)

Alien Bob's Command Post

http://www.pnn.com/~boba/alien1.htm

Whew…just goes to show you what happens when you have some spare time on your hands and an active imagination! Find out about the alien invasion that's been taking place since 1923; check out the mischief these aliens have caused (crop circles, to start with), read the "flame" message they've left for us humans, see pictures of the Sinoel Roc's home planet and spacecraft, investigate the government conspiracy (oh, come on! you *knew* there had to be one!) surrounding their invasion, and much more. The featured alien bears an uncanny resemblance to my first boyfriend, by the way.

Area 51

http://www.geocities.com/Area51/Vault/5426/

This site has *got* to be a member of more Web rings than any other I've seen! Start here to get on Web rings for UFOs, conspiracy theories, aliens, and lots more. You'll find a reading list, links to other UFO sites, and more.

Area 51

http://www.ufomind.com/area51/

This page (*not* government sponsored, naturally) is about the secret military instillation that has sparked curiosity and UFO enthusiasts for years. You'll find links to newsletters, testimonials, photos, cartoons, newspaper articles, and more. You can even get a t-shirt with the offical Area 51 warning on it!

BUFORA—British UFO Research Association

http://www.citadel.co.uk/citadel/eclipse/futura/bufora/aboutbuf.htm

This home page for the organization supplies historical UFO information (including the interesting tidbit that Charlemagne supposedly saw a UFO in 810) and outline's BUFORA's research goals. It also discusses BUFORA's publication, *UFO Times,* and annual meetings. BUFORA seems to take a very even-handed approach to UFO sightings, acknowledging that man-made and natural phenomena can account for many.

The Extraterrestrial Biological Entity Page

http://www.ee.fit.edu/users/lpinto/index.shtml

A wealth of information on the cover-up, the conspiracy, sightings, and even a *Newsweek* poll. Even the staunchest skeptic will find enough articles, reports, images, and stories to make him or her think twice. This site also features a helpful search index—great idea—and EBELink, which gives you annotated links to sites on many related topics. For the participation-minded, there are plenty of discussion boards and even a chat room. The author adds a disclaimer, stating he's not responsible for lost time, unexplained scars, brightly colored lights in the sky, or other signs and symptoms.

The EXTRATERRESTRIAL Page

http://www.primenet.com/~kjtar/et.html

Text-heavy site with lots of information; the author's exchange of letters with President Clinton about Area 51, and the responses, are pretty interesting. There's also a NASA links page, where you can see many photos and images, a link to the International UFO Museum and Research Center in Roswell, the author's report of a trip he took to the Little A'Le'Inn and the Area 41 Research Center in Nevada.

PBS' Nova Solves UFO and Alien Abduction Phenomena!

http://lovecraft.cc.utexas.edu/clarity/Nova-Abduction/index.html

Describes the plight of Budd Hopkins' work with PBS, and PBS's handling of the material. Hopkins, who has written two books on alien abductions, accuses the show of a message that "...all people who claim to be abductees are delusional, victims of repeat hallucinations...". The site also has links to letters exchanged between Nova's producers and abductees who were interviewed for the show.

PPG: Faking UFOs

http://www.strw.leidenuniv.nl/~vdmeulen/deeper/Articles/UFOfake.html

For the Web's flip side of the UFO phenomena, try this site. The author explains how to create your own UFOs and crop circles, and apparently, the fakes work quite well! Reports from many contributors relate creating their own pranks or being the victim of one.

UFO Joe, Canadian UFOs & Aliens

http://cron-2.mco.on.ca:80/web/ufojoe/

For our northern neighbors, here's a site devoted to UFO sightings in Canada. You'll also find links to all kinds of Canadian UFO-related organizations, lists of books, and a whole page of links to articles about MIBs (Men in Black—the actual people, not the movie).

UFO Master Index

http://www.ufomind.com/ufo/

This site claims to be the world's largest database of UFO links. I can't verify that, but there *is* a ton o' stuff here. Check out the UFO sightings organized geographically—fascinating. You can also read some detailed reviews of excellent books on UFOs.

The X-Files

http://www.rutgers.edu/x-files.html

You've waited for it, and here it is—the home page for X-Philes. You'll find all sorts of *X-Files* information, from fan club news to episode surveys and guides and frequently asked questions. There are also lots of links to other *X-Files*-related sites.

The X-Files

http://www.thex-files.com/

And here's the more "official" *X-Files* site...You'll find well-organized sections on bios of the principals and staff, an episode guide, show information, videos and collectibles, and a fan forum. This site is one of the *hardest* to see that I've run across; the gray text on a black background is extremely hard to read, and the shadowy photo of Mulder and Scully on the welcome page is barely discernible. (Note for you hardcore X-Philes: They misspelled Mitch Pileggi's name!)

VOODOO

A New Look at Juju

http://www.ulcoa.com/~mcivr/juju.html

This site contains an article from *Djembe Magazine* by N. Adu Kwabena-Essem discussing the Catholic Church's recent recognition of the religions of Africa and its apology for years of scorn. The inner workings of juju and its relation to daily life are covered, along with an interesting explanation of voodoo's move from West Africa to Haiti.

African Religion Syncretism

http://www.ncf.carleton.ca/freenet/rootdir/menus/sigs/religion/pagan/faqs/voodoo

Informative text-only page provides a lengthy discussion about the origins of voodoo and attempts to clear up some misconceptions about the religion. The article also addresses differences in Haitian, Creole, and African voodoo. An interesting tidbit is that the word voodoo, depending on how you spell it, can mean "introspection into the unknown."

Angélique Kidjo - Culture 1

http://www.imaginet.fr/~kidjo/cult1.html

Home page of Angelique Kidjo gives a modern-day look at the role of voodoo practices in daily life of the residents of Benin. There are a few great photos of West African voodoo ceremonies. You can even see a

QuickTime video of a *zangbeto*, an ancestor who comes back to scare off burglars, or listen to Angélique tell you the story of Hwegbaja.

The Electric Gallery—Haitian Voodoo Flags

http://www.egallery.com/flags.html

View—and buy one you like, if you choose—an online gallery of Haitian voodoo flags, called *vevé banners*. An introduction explains what these banners were used for and how they were made. The gallery features several intricate, colorful flags illustrating the hybridization of traditional religions.

Oshun - African Magickal Newsletter, Products, and Info

http://www.tiac.net/users/bpantry/voodoo

This site offers products related to the African-based religious traditions of Voodoo, Santeria, and Ifa to the online shopper. Click, say, vevé offering boxes or voodoo incenses and oils to get price lists and images of the products. Tons of interesting links to African religions and background information on voodoo.

Paranormal New Orleans

http://www.neworleans.com/paranormal/voodoo.html

This site has information about a haunted history tour of New Orleans, which includes a trip to the voodoo cemetery, and a link to voodoo-related products you can buy. Some fun photos and cool, creepy graphics. At one of the links, you can submit an account of your own paranormal experience, if you like.

Vodun Information Pages

http://www.arcana.com/shannon/voodoo/voodoo.html

A thorough table of contents leads you to in-depth information on the history and practices of vodun (voodoo). Click a topic that interests you to go to well-written articles with fascinating photos. I'd suggest checking out the glossary first to familiarize yourself with some of the terms; however, these terms are also hyperlinks within the articles, which makes it easy to look them up as you read. This site even offers a bibliography, index, and list of other Internet resources. The latter is excellent, ranging from a newsgroup (`alt.religion.orisha`) to online voodoo stores.

The Voodoo Queen

http://mardi.gras.com/voodoo.html

Superb graphics make this voodoo page worth visiting. Think of your question, click the "begin" hyperlink, and then take a look at some voodoo tarot cards (with beautiful, compelling illustrations) and an interpretation of their meanings (just for the record, the cards do change with each visit). Links also can be found to Mardi Gras pages.

Voodoo: From Medicine to Zombies

http://www.nando.net/prof/caribe/voodoo.html

This page contains links to articles and reports on African voodoo information, such as the origins of voodoo, gods and goddesses, Afro-Caribbean deities, and other Africa links. Mostly text, but a few excellent black-and white photos are included, some from the Museum of African Art.

Welcome to the New Orleans Historic Voodoo Museum

http://www.neosoft.com/%7Enodust/mus.html

Here's the home page for the New Orleans Historic Voodoo Museum. You can find a brief description of the exhibits and the people who make them happen. Link to a biography of Marie Laveau, the "Popess of Voodoo," or an informative look at voodoo past and present.

WITCHCRAFT

Bewitched

http://www.erols.com/bewitchd/index.html

If you're a fan of Elizabeth Montgomery and *Bewitched*, you've probably already found this page. There's a great record of the '60s TV show *Bewitched* and lots of information about Samantha. Download WAV files of sound clips from the show, read some original scripts, and visit the "Bewitched Bookshelf." The site also features downloadable images of Elizabeth, updates on the original cast members, and a silly slide show.

Brenna's Page

http://www.argyll.demon.co.uk/

You'll find a medley of information here, including a great page of links to sites on pagan and Wicca beliefs. Cool graphics, little animations (I especially liked the one of Felix the Cat), music, photos, and a lively writing style make this an engaging site to visit. And, Brenna is a self-professed pagan and witch who tries to set the record straight on what that means.

Joan's Witch Directory

`http://www.ucmb.ulb.ac.be/~joan/witches/`

This site uses the "Malleus Malificarum," a 15th century witch-hunting manual, as well as other literary and reference resources, to explore witchcraft from a historical viewpoint. The information is well organized with a table of contents, so you can click the subject area that interests you. Check out the Artworks section for a fascinating collection of prints from the 15th through the 17th centuries. There are also assorted witchcraft and neo-pagan (Wicca) links.

Satanism and the History of Wicca

`http://ourworld.compuserve.com/homepages/hpaulis/swc.htm`

Ever wondered what the ties between Satanism and Wicca are? You'll find the answer here. This lengthy text article gives you a historical look at the birth of Wicca from 19th century literary Satanism and the direction of present-day Wiccan philosophy. It also clears up some misconceptions about terminology.

Witches League for Public Awareness

`http://www.celticcrow.com/`

Based in Salem, Massachusetts, this informative witching page offers a resource for witches and pagans to congregate on the Web. You'll find current events links—including articles on portrayals of witches in the media—and many more relevant links. Check out the Craft Community Resource Page to start searching the Web for sites, newsletters, and other resources on witchcraft.

The Witches' Voice

`http://www.witchvox.com/`

Excellent site; this site's founding organization (WVOX) was formed as an educational network to dispel misinformation and myths about witchcraft and pagan religions. Check out the site map at the home page for over 283 pages of up-to date information. The Witches' Voice features an annotated listing of over 800 Web sites devoted to witchcraft/pagan topics and publishes five new essays each month from practicing witches, Wiccans, and pagans.

The Witches' Web Home Page

`http://www.witchesweb.com/home.html`

Great site! It's an excellent place to begin searching for not only historical information about witchcraft, but also modern-day practices and beliefs. Tons of stuff here, including a recipe section, a discussion forum, recommended readings, an online calendar of pagan festivals and important dates, and related links. Cool graphics; very well organized.

The Witching Hours

`http://fox.nstn.ca/~daveman/burning.html`

This site begins with a fitting quote from Edmund Spenser's *The Faerie Queene*, which gives you an idea of the historical/literary focus here. A wealth of reports on many aspects of the witch-hunting craze from 1100–1800 are accompanied by interesting prints, graphics, and paintings. You can also find links to other related sites.

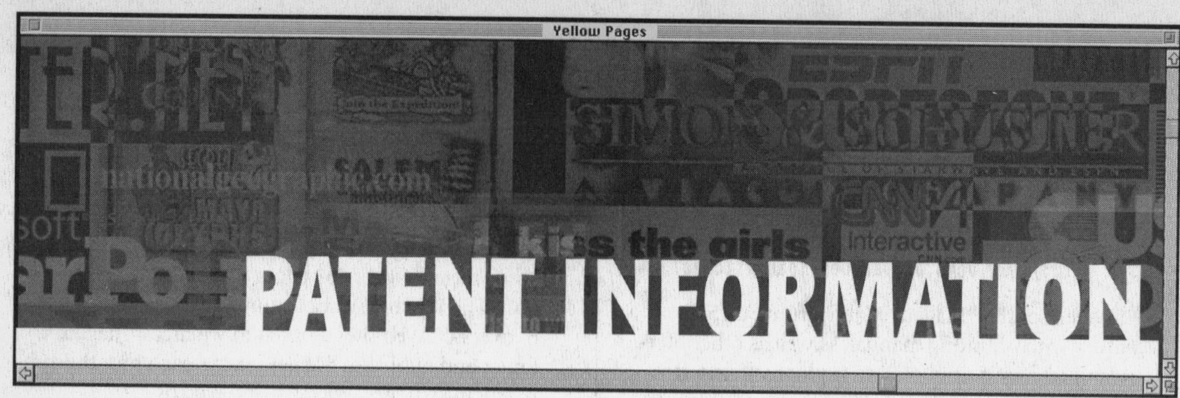

PATENT INFORMATION

When a thing has been said and well, have no scruple. Take it and copy it.

Anatole France

General Information Concerning Patents
http://www.uspto.gov/web/offices/pac/doc/general/

General Information Concerning Patents

http://www.uspto.gov/web/offices/pac/doc/general/

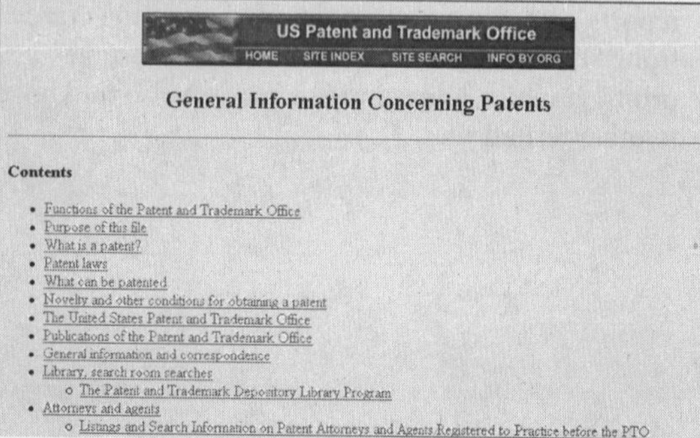
US Patent and Trademark Office

HOME SITE INDEX SITE SEARCH INFO BY ORG

General Information Concerning Patents

Contents

- Functions of the Patent and Trademark Office
- Purpose of this file
- What is a patent?
- Patent laws
- What can be patented
- Novelty and other conditions for obtaining a patent
- The United States Patent and Trademark Office
- Publications of the Patent and Trademark Office
- General information and correspondence
- Library, search room searches
  - The Patent and Trademark Depository Library Program
- Attorneys and agents
  - Listings and Search Information on Patent Attorneys and Agents Registered to Practice before the PTO

Provides general information about application for and granting of patents in non-technical language. Intended for inventors, students, and prospective applicants for patents.

Patent Portal Internet Patent Resources

http://www.law.vill.edu/~rgruner/patport.htm

Serves as an entry point for patent-related information. Identifies resources, organizes and indexes links to resources, and presents new material on patent issues that are currently shaping patent law. Also allows patent searches and searches of patent attorneys and agents.

SBH Patent Marketing Group

http://www.inlink.com/~sbh/index.html

Specializes in licensing and selling existing U.S. patents. Recognizes that many inventors have achieved greater success in creating patents than in selling or licensing them. Acts as an agent for individual inventors, corporations, and institutions in marketing United States patents.

Shadow Patent Office

http://www.spo.eds.com/patent.html

Provides information about United States patents, including a searchable database of the full text of the U.S. Patent and Trademark Office patents issued from January 1, 1972 to the present. Updated weekly.

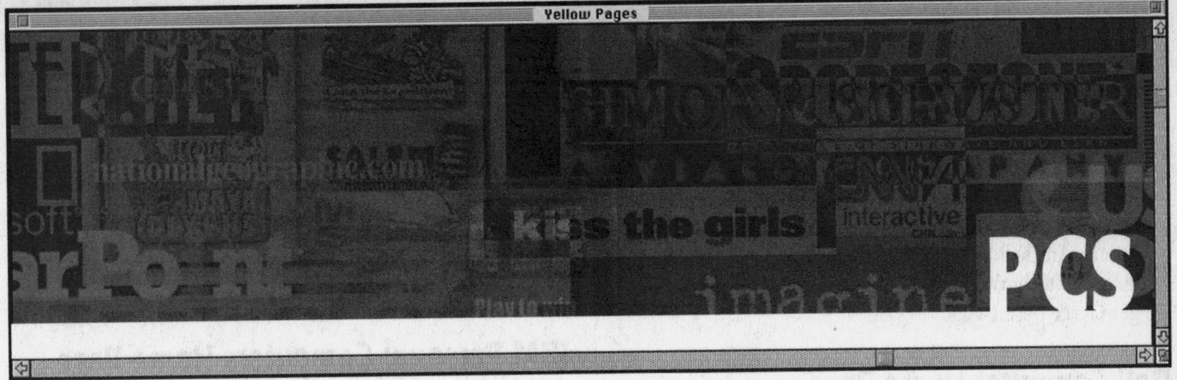

> I try to get people to see what I have… When you run a computer company, you have to get people to buy into your dreams.
>
> *Steve Jobs*

Acer Computer

http://www.acer.com/aac/index.htm

Enter a monthly drawing for a free computer and check out Acer's newest product lines, such as the Aspire. The Windows 95 Information link provides a search feature to help you find information on specific Windows 95 topics—a very helpful feature for Acer owners.

Acorn Computer Group

http://www.acorn.co.uk/

Contains information about Acorn Computer Products. Includes links to Acorn Education, which provides a special program for schools.

amd@work

http://www.amd.com/

Like Intel and Cyrix, AMD is another processor and integrated circuit manufacturer, among other products. Their Web page has specific information for investors and developers, as well as product information for PC processors. The site provides pages for networking, telecommunications, embedded processors, non-volatile memory, and programmable logic.

CyberMax Online
http://www.cybmax.com/

Apple

http://www.apple.com/

Provides news, product updates, customer support, and forms to help you determine your computer needs and financing opportunities. You can order from their online "store" or gather tidbits to build your own Apple.

Build Your Own PC

http://www.verinet.com/pc/

Teaches you how to select components, get them, and put them together. The site discusses operating systems and points to other helpful resources for those who want to be able to bypass big business and do it themselves.

Compaq

http://www.compaq.com/

Compaq Computer's home page offers every advantage that an online store can have: pages for the type of environment the customer is in (business, education, home, and so one), pages for the type of equipment offered (desktop PCs, servers, and so on), and more. Check out their page covering Compaq's coverage of COMDEX 97.

CyberMax Online

http://www.cybmax.com/

Another award-winning company, CyberMax may be most notable for not only great machines at great prices, but the fact that you can order computers with Intel, Cyrix, or AMD chips. Their prices are very competitive and they will custom-build whatever system you want.

Cyrix Online

http://www.cyrix.com/

Cyrix is not a PC maker, but rather the makers of the 6x86 and 6x86MX chips, among others. Cyrix's home page offers quite a bit of information regarding both, as well which motherboards are compatible with it. If you are undecided about what kind of chip you want your PC to have, use this site to learn where you can get Cyrix-based PCs.

Dell Computer Home Page

http://www.dell.com/

The home page for this billion-dollar PC manufacturer requires that you choose from one of 24 countries! The next screen provides choices based on your type of business, such as education, government, home office, or a large or small corporation. After a few more screens, you can examine Dell's latest servers, portables, and desktop computers.

digital

http://www.digital.com/

Beyond the normal sales pages at Digital Equipment Corporation's home page are corporate affirmations regarding community involvement, and environment, health, and safety. You may also learn about present and future Digital products, or see what jobs are available on their Careers page.

Elek-Tek

http://www.elektek.com

Humorous Web site for this computer retailer. Take a survey, check out their online catalog, enter a few contests, and read the latest technology news. Their catalog features more than 8,000 products.

EQUIX

http://www.equix.com/

Based in Cleveland's own Silicon Valley of Beachwood, Ohio, the EQUIX Computer Corporation has its own offerings on the Web. Use their home page to choose systems and components, and learn more about their tech support, company history, and more.

GW2K.COM

http://www.gateway2000.com/

Even if you don't have a Gateway, this site is so well-designed and visually interesting that it is worth a hit. Click on some great graphics to access and join the Gateway club and the kids club. Be sure to visit the Cow Zone, a strange, enjoyable page with contests and cow trivia.

IBM Personal Computers Home Page

http://www.pc.ibm.com/

Home page for IBM U.S. personal computers. Click on Aptiva, Servers, ThinkPad, Desktop, Monitors, or Options to access the type of hardware desired. Click on Options to access the support section and use a searchable database to find patches, software updates, and popular utilities in IBM libraries.

IBM Personal Computers in the U.S. Aptiva

http://www.pc.ibm.com/aptiva/index.html

A colorful page describing the special features of the Aptiva line of PCs. This site also includes links to a searchable database of over 5,000 files and a helpful support library of questions and answers.

Maximus

http://www.maximuspc.com/

This Irwindale, California-based company prides itself on it affordable desktop and laptop systems. You can order online and download any number of drivers and anti-viral scanners, among others.

Micro Express

http://www.microexpress.net/

Micro Express compatibles have been winning awards since their beginning in 11 years ago. Read their Web site to learn more about the company and its products, as well as how to build your own PC. They also provide extensive hardware driver updates.

Micron

http://www.micron.com/

A simple home page for an extremely successful computer company. Find out about Micron's other products, such as SRAM, DRAM, PCBs, radio frequency ID, and field emission display (FED) products used in camcorders. Click on Micron Electronics to access their Web site for Micron computers.

Midwest Micro

http://www.mwmicro.com/

Midwest Micro is another less common brand that's gaining in popularity. Use their home page as the starting point to get information about the company, tech support, and the usual. Be sure to check out the reviews, as well as their BASIC line of machines that get the job done without the high cost.

NEC Home Page

http://www.nec.com/

Besides the common technical support, product info, and news releases, the Research and Development link, Trade Show info, and Career Opportunities may satisfy that insatiable information thirst.

Northstar

http://www.northstar-mn.com/

Computer repair for many manufacturers' laptops, monitors, printers, PCs, and more. Links to pricing and rate information.

Packard Bell

http://www.packardbell.com/index.html

Besides the support, product catalogs, and company news, Packard Bell's unique Home PC User Survey provides important information on trends in home PC use. This link includes charts and articles revealing who is using home PCs (a surprising number of older adults) and how their use is changing with the addition of new technologies.

ProGen Technology, Inc.

http://www.progen.com/

Also known for its multimedia accelerator video graphics adapter cards, this home page offers ProGen multimedia technologies, as well as a simple-to-use page to review their different PC offerings.

Quantex

http://www.quantex.com/

Whereas most PC pages start with desktops, Quantex is so proud of its new line of laptops that it leads their home page. The site also provides a chat area where prospective buyers can interact with other buyers, as well as those who've already chosen a Quantex system.

Swan Technologies

http://www.tisco.com/swan/

PC clone mail order manufacturer. If you're looking for a new system, try out Swan's unique Confi-O-Matic. Choose the features and hardware you want for your PC, and out pops a price on such a system.

Toshiba

http://www.toshiba.com/cgi-bin2/index.cgi

Toshiba is a name synonymous with TV sets and other personal electronics, and in addition to their widely used CD-ROM drives and DVD players, Toshiba has its own line of personal computers, the Infinia. Toshiba touts the usefulness of its InTouch™ Module, which allows users to jump from CD to radio to TV, and so on, with a simple button press.

Vektron

http://www.vektron.com/

Vektron was listed in *Inc.* magazine's fastest-growing private companies list because of its 11,000% increase in annual sales since its start in 1989. Jump to the Trophy Room page to see the many accolades. Vektron is another in a growing list of companies to finally include a 17-inch monitor with each system, rather than forcing you to upgrade.

Xi Computer Corporation

http://www.xicomputer.com/

Xi computer was founded as an engineering firm to design motherboards for Intel processors, but they have expanded and now offer the best machines for CAD workstations—they even earned the coveted Highly Recommended award from *CADalyst Magazine.*

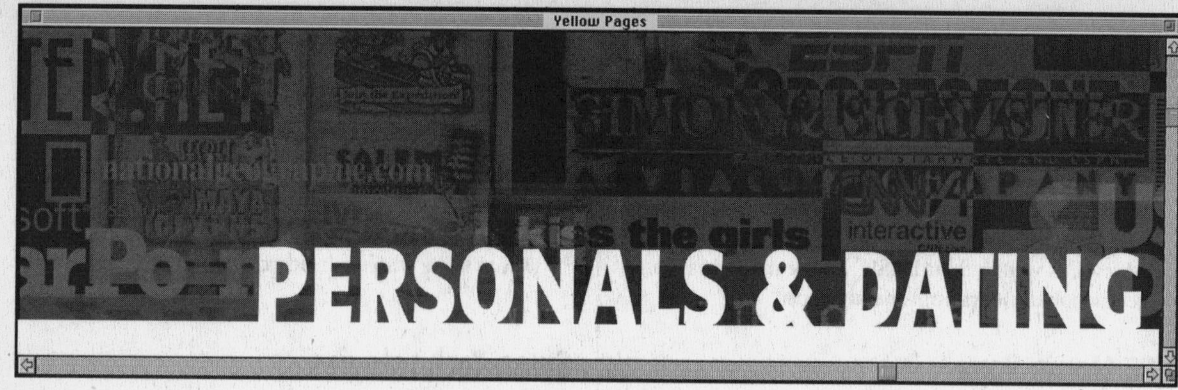

Between you and me, how much do you really know about Roberta? Why didn't you tell me she read the personals? We could have settled this yesterday.

Susan in Desperately Seeking Susan *(1985)*

A Singles Place™

http://asinglesplace.com/

Page after page of links to sites ranging from the unusual (Bosnia Love Page, Cheap and Beautiful Interactive, Pearls from Paradise) to the standard (Christian Registry for Singles, Lifetime Partners, Singles Sanctuary). If you are a man shopping for an overseas bride, this is the site for you!

The Bachelors

http://bachelor.simplent.com/

Hundreds of photos of men for women. Men visiting the site can have their photos added to the list. The guys aren't bad either. They are realistic, normal-looking guys instead of buff models made to look like movie stars. The photos include short bios and stats on the men. Women can email the men they like.

SOLO Lifestyles for Singles
http://www.solosingles.com/

Cupids Network™

http://www.cupidnet.com/

This site offers the standard selection of dating connections. The highlight of this site is the page of links to other cool sites.

Cybertymes

http://www.cybertymes.com/

Full of interesting (and sometimes frightening) selections such as Internet Teen Connections, Inmates in Need, Christian Cybertymes, Campus Singles, and Fetish-Land). Offers free and pay services. Six months are free to anyone buying a membership package ($5 for six months, $8.95 for one year, or $20 for a lifetime).

The Date Doctor

http://www.thedatedoctor.com/

Visiting this site it like a trip to L.A., which is the site's home city. It is filled with choices such as "Power Dating," "Mentor Dating," and "Targeted Intervention." The Mentor Dating option—currently available in L.A. only—walks you through a practice date and gives you feedback, conversation tips, and appearance suggestions for a $300 fee. The Targeted Intervention option—currently available in L.A. only—is designed to help with special dating issues such as shyness, social phobias, lack of assertiveness, and so on for a $100 fee. Other services range from $100 to $1,500. It's a fun site to visit, but anyone with this kind of money to spend shouldn't have any problem finding a date!

Divorce Central

http://www.divorcecentral.com/

Sadly, no relationship category would be complete without a break-up site. This really is a good site for information and support for anyone contemplating, going through, or recovering from a divorce. It addresses legal issues, financial advice, and parenting information. There are also chat rooms and personal ads for when you are ready to rejoin the dating world.

The Internet Computer-Dating Service™

http://computer-dating.com/

This service is free for now, although the site says there will be a low fee in the future. It is a matchmaking service that compares your questionnaire answers to others and notifies you of your matches.

The Most Incredible Dating Service on the Internet!

http://www.lovecity.com/

A fee-based site of personal ads. This site offers three free months with a paid three-month membership ($30) or six free months with a paid six-month membership ($50). Ads are arranged by country and are from the U.S., Canada, Europe, Asia, Austrailia, Africa, the Middle East, and the Caribbean. Visitors can view preview ads, which weren't bad at all. Tons of testimonials from members who have found friendships, relationships, true love, and even marriage through the service.

Single Search

http://nsns.com/single-search/

This site promises it is not a dating service, a 900 number, or a personal ad service; it is a "highly successful method of searching for a soul mate." For a fee of $30 for one month or $60 for three months, the service matches 350 items of compatibility between you and other clients. The service requires 60% or greater compatibility rate according to the questionnaire answers to constitute a match. You can choose how you want to be contacted by your matches—email, snail mail, phone, or indirectly through Single Search.

Singles Alley

http://singlesalley.com/

A cool site with jazzy background music to listen to as you cruise around. Offers a "Meet Market" with singles ads, travel fantasies, book store, psychic advisors (be aware of the $3.96 per minute fee), health store, and music store. The travel packages to well-known destinations such as Club Med, Hedonism II, and Norwegian Cruise Line offer bargains if you're willing to share a room—the rate is as much as 20% more for a single room. Suggestion: Bring a friend you already know, just to be safe.

SOLO Lifestyles for Singles

http://www.solosingles.com/

This site lives up to its claim of being "as current as a newspaper but as thorough as a magazine." It is extremely detailed and offers a wide range of topics of interest to today's singles. Covers everything from tips on looking good, self-improvement, coping with being "suddenly single" as the result of death or divorce. Also offers personal ads and matchmaking services.

USA Singles

http://www.usasingles.com/

A fee-based site offering male and female personal ads grouped by categories such as Christian, U.S., and International. With a paid three-month membership fee of $9.95, you receive another three months free, access to other members' ads, and your own 50 word ad along with free scanning and posting of your photo.

Related Sites
http://www.2ofakind.com/guide.htm
http://nexus.trident.org/cgi/dbf/amour.shtml
http://www.arkline.com/index.html
http://www.connections.email.net/index.html
http://www.ebony.email.net/index.html
http://www.globalsingles.com/home1.html
http://kinky-personals.com/index.htm
http://www.mm.org/
http://www.lyghtforce.com/dateline/index.html
http://www.personal.u-net.com/~america/uk2.htm
http://ourworld.compuserve.com/homepages/ugr/date.html

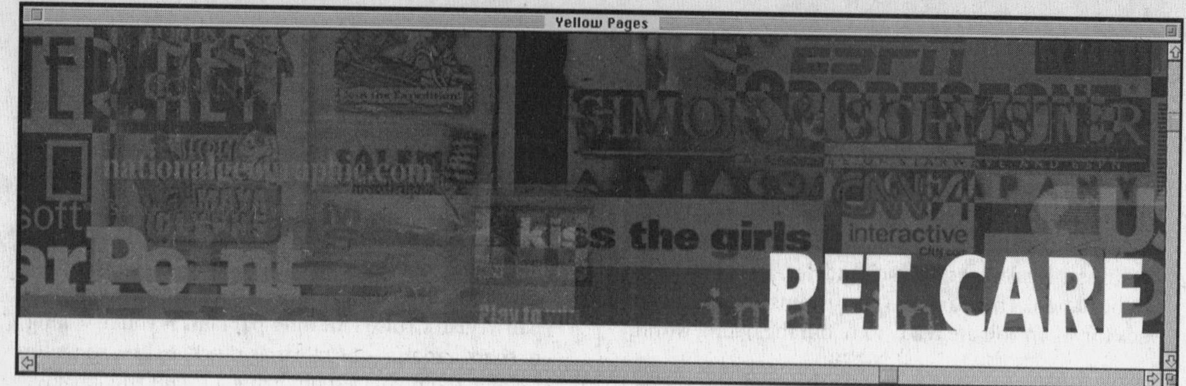

A B C D E F G H I J K L M N O P Q R S T U V W X Y Z

> Animals are such agreeable friends—they ask no questions and they pass no criticisms.
>
> *George Eliot (Mary Ann Evans)*

Animal Health Information

http://www.avma.org/care4pets/avmaanim.htm

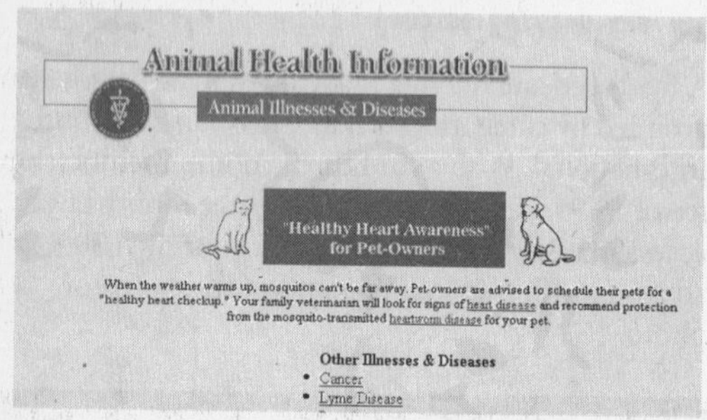

Get info on dental care, pet population control, and vaccinations. Learn how to deal with diseases such as heart disease, heartworm disease, cancer, Lyme disease, parasites, toxoplasmosis, and rabies.

Related Sites

http://www.best.com/~lynxpt/
http://www.cam.org/~biology/pets1.htm
http://www.tattoo-a-pet.com
http://pw1.netcom.com/~eholden/RV122.HTM
http://www.canismajor.com/dog/guide.html
http://www.drjane.com/

Feline Diabetes
http://www.pricemd.com/felinediabetes/

PetView Magazine Online
http://www.petview.com/

Siberian Husky Home Page
http://www.execpc.com/~bbackman/index.html

The AVMA Network American Veterinary Medical Association

http://www.avma.org/

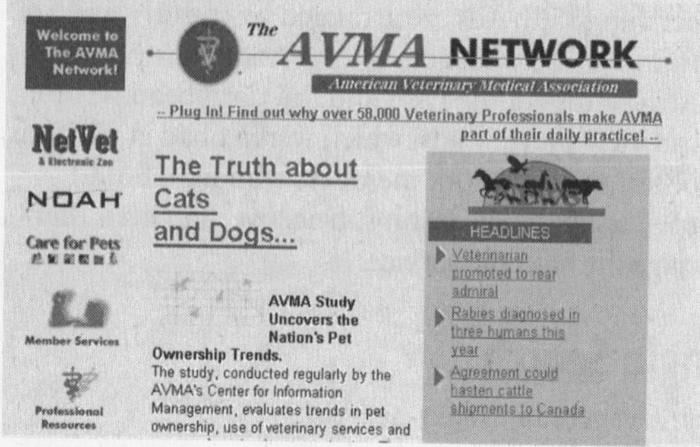

This site is an excellent source for info on caring for your pet. The Health section includes pictures you can print out and let your kids color, and each picture includes an activity or advice on feeding, training, or basic care. Submit a photo or story here about your pet.

Care for Pets

http://www.avma.org/care4pets/

This is the American Veterinary Medical Association's (AVMA) Web page on animal health. It focuses on cats, dogs, and horses. Get tips on dealing with various diseases, selecting the proper pet, and choosing a veterinarian. You'll also find tips on animal safety—dealing with kids, poison control, and first aid.

Exotic Pet and Bird Clinic

http://www.jetcity.com/~exopet/ferrets/nutrion.html

Offers topics such as ferret nutrition and adopting bunnies. Also provides healthcare info on hedgehogs, birds, rats, hamsters, prairie dogs, guinea pigs, mice, geckos, iguanas, turtles, lizards, and snakes.

Feline Diabetes

http://www.pricemd.com/felinediabetes/

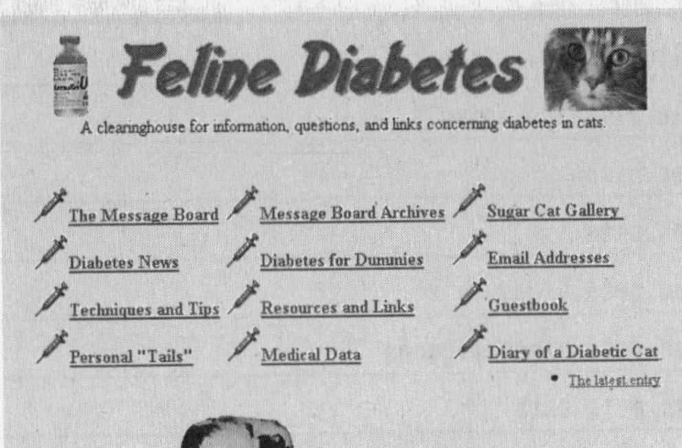

If your pet is faced with this condition, this site should be an invaluable resource for you. You'll find extensive info, Q&As, and links about feline diabetes. You'll get info on urine glucose monitoring, home blood glucose testing, and insulin injections.

NetVet Veterinary Resources and The Electronic Zoo

http://netvet.wustl.edu/

Hosted by Dr. Ken Boschert, a veterinarian at Washington University's Division of Comparative Medicine in St. Louis, Missouri. He lists veterinary mailing lists, and well as FTP, Telnet, and Gopher sites. This site soon will move to AVMA ONLINE.

Oasis Pet Center

http://www.mcs.net/~oasis/saltaqu.html

Tips on setting up and maintaining a saltwater aquarium. Topics include nutrition for saltwater fish, filtration, tank lighting, and choosing the correct salt mix.

Related Sites
http://www.aboutbirds.com/
http://www.petsource.com/ASKDR.HTM
http://planetpets.simplenet.com/choosevet.htm

Pet Care Corner

http://www.pet-vet.com/index.htm

Authored by Lowell Ackermann, a board-certified veterinary dermatologist and author of 34 books on animal health, this site provides answers to owner's questions about their pets' health.

The Pet Channel

http://www.thepetchannel.com/

Get advice from the Ask the Vet and Ask the Pet Therapist sections. Health topics include behavior, internal problems, neurological disorders, reproduction, and skin problems. Covers dogs, cats, horses, and exotic pets.

Pet Lovers Paradise—Pet Care

http://www.rs-kit.com/Pet5.htm

This online pet magazine and encyclopedia includes info on holistic pet care and nutrition. You get access to online magazines such as Dog Fancy On-Line, Cat Fancy On-Line, Aquarium Fish On-Line, Natural Pet, Pet Product News, Bird Talk, and Horse Illustrated On-Line. You'll also get tips on pet care and finding a hospital.

Pet Plan Insurance

http://www.petplan.com/

Pet Plan is Canada's largest pet health insurance company. Hip replacements, ultrasounds, and root canals for pets are becoming more common. Find out how pet insurance can help you avoid making pet health decisions based on your financial situation.

Pet Rats

http://www.icubed.com/users/mfichten/rats/petrats.html

Get advice on pet rat care here. Includes games, news, do-it-yourself projects, and links to other rat Web sites.

PetView Magazine Online

http://www.petview.com/

Advisors answer questions about pet health and care. Read articles on dealing with bugs that affect your pet, allergies, diabetes, genetic testing, ligament surgery, and the needs of a new pet. You'll also get info on senior pets and behavior problems. Back issues available.

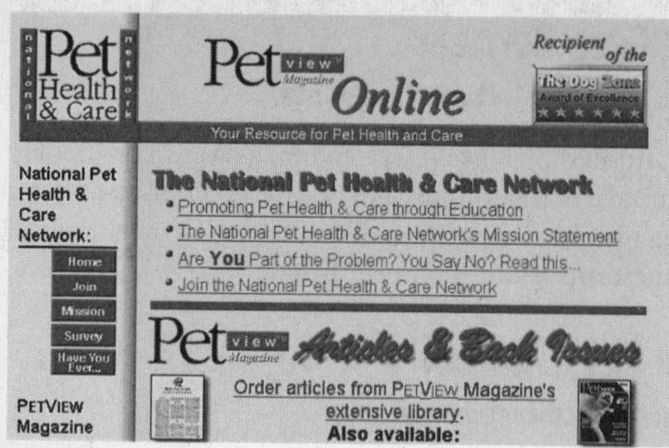

planet pets

http://planetpets.simplenet.com/

Topics include buying a pet, caring for your pet, breeding, characteristics, rescues, and professional services. Get advice on troublesome pet behavior. Check out the book recommendations and the index to products and services. Get info on dogs, cats, birds, fish, ferrets, rabbits, reptiles, snakes, potbelly pigs, llamas, hamsters, horses, and more.

Professor Hunt's Dog Page

http://www.cofc.edu/~huntc/dogpage.html#Message

Get info on rescues, animal health, and socially responsible activities. This site has a special emphasis on herding (working) breeds.

Siberian Husky Home Page

http://www.execpc.com/~bbackman/index.html

Find out how to prepare for your new Husky and what it will need. Browse through the photo gallery and cool sites. Learn about training huskies, keeping them from being bored, and adding them to your family. Includes warnings against pet stores, irresponsible breeders, and puppy mills.

WEBDOCTOR

http://www.primenet.com/~webdoc/

This site focuses on holistic health for animal companions. Includes an animal cancer FAQ and animal arthritis FAQ.

Welcome to Healthy Pets

http://www.healthypet.com/

This site features a pet-care library of info on behavior, common health problems, nutrition, and general care. The American Animal Hospital Association also provides a geographic locator guide for pet hospitals and tips on choosing a vet.

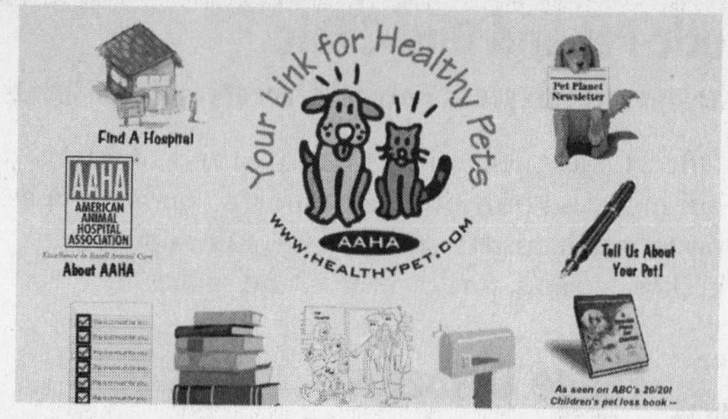

NEWSGROUPS

alt.animals.felines

clari.living.animals

rec.birds

rec.pets

rec.pets.birds

rec.pets.birds.pigeons

rec.pets.cats

rec.pets.cats.anecdotes

rec.pets.cats.announce

rec.pets.cats.community

rec.pets.cats.health+behav

rec.pets.cats.misc

rec.pets.cats.rescue

rec.pets.dogs

rec.pets.dogs.activities

rec.pets.dogs.behavior

rec.pets.dogs.breeds

rec.pets.dogs.health

rec.pets.dogs.info

rec.pets.dogs.misc

rec.pets.dogs.rescue

GOPHER SITES

gopher://adam.greenpeace.org/1

gopher://cas.calacademy.org/11/depts/herp/

gopher://gopher1.cit.cornell.edu:404/00/.files/vetlib

gopher://yfn.ysu.edu:70/11/animal

Related Site

http://www.optics.rochester.edu:8080/users/pgreene/central.html

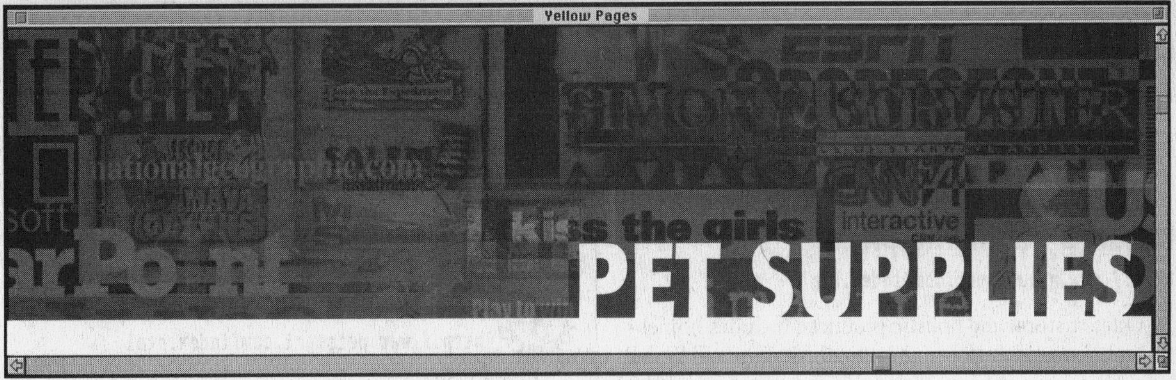

A B C D E F G H I J K L M N O P Q R S T U V W X Y Z

> Animals were once, for all of us, teachers. They instructed us in ways of being and perceiving that extended our imaginations, that were models for additional possibilities.
>
> *Joan McIntyre*

Acme Pet Civic Center

http://www.acmepet.com/civic/

Offers supplies for dogs, cats, birds, fish, horses, reptiles, amphibians, and other exotic animals. Get info on containment, food, health, identification, cleaning, and collars/leads supplies. Also offers books on various pets.

Acme Pet Dogs Marketplace

http://www.acmepet.com/canine/market/k9_col.html

Offers dog collars and leads, clothes, bedding, cleaning products, containment, food, gifts, grooming, identification, and health insurance.

Acme Pet Civic Center
http://www.acmepet.com/civic/
PETsMART
http://www.petsmart.com/index.html

Acme Pet Exotic Marketplace

http://207.226.182.149/exotic/market/ex_sup.html

Offers products for ferrets, including cages, food, nutrition products, toys, and accessories. Includes links to exotic pet supply catalogs.

Healthy Paws

http://healthypaws.com/health.html

Offers health food, vitamins, and books. Includes healing salves, herbs, and ear cleansers. Advertises aids for kidney problems, coughs, breathing problems, feline leukemia, and more. Also offers homeopathic remedies and books on natural animal care.

Kitty Express

http://petstation.com/kitexpo.html

Delivers canned and dry cat food, as well as scoop cat litter concentrate. Not available in stores.

Related Sites

http://www.aardvarkpet.com/

http://www.sonic.net/~melissk/pet_rule.html

Local Pet Store Directory

http://www.actwin.com/fish/stores-usa1.html

Provides a global, alphabetical listing of fish stores, along with a description of what each store offers.

Nature's Pet Marketplace

http://www.naturespet.com/index.html

Offers natural and holistic products. Includes homeopathic remedies, dog and cat food, vitamin and herbal supplements, grooming and skin care products, and flea and tick remedies. Also offers a natural line of bird food and supplements. Includes info such as descriptions and explanations of holistic products.

Pet Botanics by Cardinal Labs, Inc.

http://www.cardinalpet.com/natural/naturepro.html

Offers tea tree spray for flea bite dermatitis, hot spots, and dry skin irritation. Or, check out the oatmeal shampoo for dry, itchy skin and skin irritations. Or maybe your pet just needs the herbal shampoo for cleaning and deodorizing. The cedar shampoo and cedar spray kill infestations of insects (these are natural, non-toxic alternatives to chemical insecticides). Try the herbal collar to repel insects. Includes a glossary of herbs and botanicals.

Pet Lovers Pet Shop

http://www.petloverz.com/

Offers pet stain remover, carpet cleaner, and dog and cat repellent (indoor and outdoor). Also sells dog shampoo, pet Christmas cards, cat postcards, and pet Santa suits. Advertises dog and cat clothes, pet trackers, pet car seat harnesses, gifts, and toys. Includes books on how to groom your dog.

Pet Supplies R Us Cat Products

http://www.petsupplies-r-us.com/cats/

Offers cat beds, books, collars and leashes, carriers, pet doors, feeders and waterers, flea and tick control, furniture, health aids, pans, litter, scoops, medication, repellents, deodorizers, toys, and treats.

Pet Talk, America

http://www.pettalk.com/ptcatalg.htm

Offers informational books, software programs, and videos on pet care. Also sells dog and cat grooming spray and food supplements. Offers a cat catalog of products from all over the country.

Pet Team

http://www.petteam.com/

Click your state on a map to see a listing of all the Pet Team stores in your area. Offers Healthy Harvest Puppy Formula, Adult Dog Formula, Adult Cat Formula, and Lamb Meal & Rice Formula.

PETsMART

http://www.petsmart.com/index.html

PETsMART offers pet food, supplies, and services. Use the search feature to find a PETsMART store near you. Use the Quick Reference Guide to find info on health and nutrition issues that affect your pet. Take a tour of the store, and learn how and where to adopt a pet.

Purina Pet Marketplace

http://www.purina.com/Pet_Marketplace/

Offers cat and dog food: Purina CNM Clinical Nutrition Management brand Veterinary Diets and Pro-Vision Pro Plan brand Pet Food. Also offers Tidy Cat brand products.

Wyld's Wingdom, Inc.

http://www.wingdom.com

Specializes in exotic/pet bird products. Offers bird food, bird toys, and bird-related products. Wyld's doesn't sell directly to the public, but these products may be at your local pet store.

Related Sites

- http://www2.upatsix.com/nacs/articles/finding_petstore.html
- http://www.anjan.com/johnspet
- http://www.johnsonpetdor.com/
- http://noahspets.com/policies.html
- http://www.pet-expo.com/birdbird.htm
- http:/www.vitel.com.au/menus/petshops.htm
- http://pon.com/catalogs.htm
- http://www.wegmans.com/stores/pet/index.html

> Half of the modern drugs could well be thrown out of the window, except that the birds might eat them.
>
> *Dr. Martin Henry Fischer*

PhRMA Home Page
http://www.phrma.org

RxList: The Internet Drug Index
http://www.rxlist.com/

Fischer Pharmaceuticals Laboratories

http://www.dr-fischer.com

Researches, develops, and manufactures dermatology preparations, skin-care lines, sunscreen protection, and eye and cosmetic products.

Hedonistic Imperative

http://www.pavilion.co.uk/david-pearce/hedonist.htm

Believes that within the next 1,000 years, genetic engineering and chemical psychopharmacology will eradicate the biological substrates of suffering.

Pharmaceutical Information Network

http://pharminfo.com/

Discusses publications, conferences, job listings, and software developments related to pharmaceutical care.

pharmacologyPPS OnLine; PPS OnLine

http://www2.pps.ca/pps

Online pharmaceutical product ordering and information service. Targets health care professionals. Presents the PPS Online– Pharma-Response_System, a pharmaceutical information system developed for consumers.

PhRMA Home Page

http://www.phrma.org

Provides an overview of PhRMA, which represents more than 100 U. S. pharmaceutical research companies. Also provides answers to frequently asked questions about pharmaceuticals, the latest news, a health guide series, and an interactive stroke survey.

RxList: The Internet Drug Index

http://www.rxlist.com/

Lets you type in the names of specific drugs, and then returns information regarding generic names, brand names, and categories of classification.

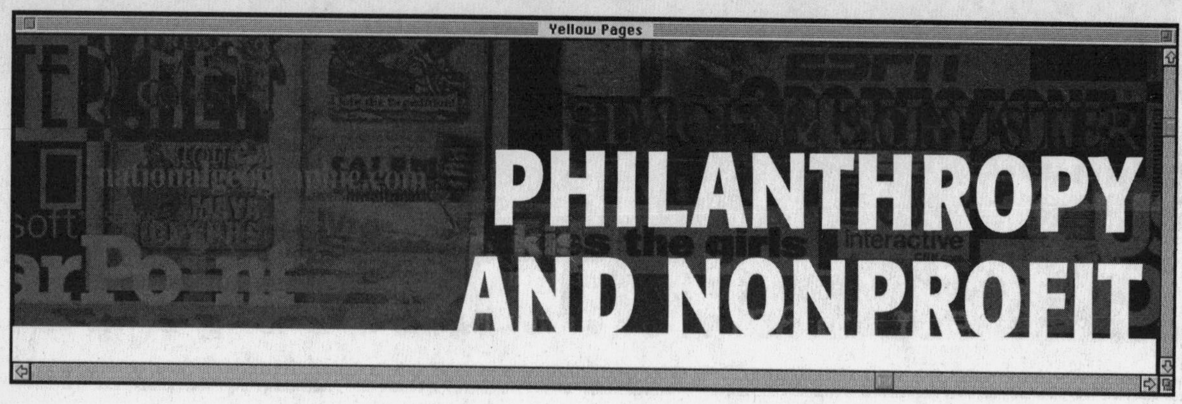

PHILANTHROPY AND NONPROFIT

A B C D E F G H I J K L M N O P Q R S T U V W X Y Z

> Imagine all the people sharing all the world.
>
> *John Lennon*

Adobe Philanthropy Council

http://www.adobe.com/aboutadobe/philanthropy/main.html

This corporate philanthropy arm of Adobe is primarily interested in supporting nonprofit health and human service organizations that in turn provide help to disadvantaged youth, the homeless, victims of abuse, and so on.

Alpha Charitable Foundation

http://www.io.org/~xavier/alpha.html

A charity registered in the U.S. and Canada dedicated to helping the handicapped, the elderly, the poor, and the destitute. They are currently building a large hospital in India.

American Express

http://www.americanexpress.com/corp/philanthropy/

Promotes its own philanthropic goals in areas where they do business or where their employees live. They service three programs: community service, cultural heritage, and economic independence. Makes grants to nonprofit organizations within and outside of the U.S.

NRP TOP PICKS

Ben and Jerry's Foundation
http://www.benjerry.com/foundation/index.html

Electronic Policy Network
http://epn.org/

Foundation Center
http://fdncenter.org/

Philanthropy Archives
http://www-lib.iupui.edu/special/

Project HOPE (Health Opportunities for People Everywhere)
http://www.projhope.org/

United Way of America
http://www.unitedway.org/

AT&T Foundation

http://www.att.com/foundation/

The company's philanthropic arm that helps people to lead self-sufficient, productive lives. They are particularly interested in projects that involve technological innovation. Their four program areas are education, civic programs, arts and culture, and community service.

Ben and Jerry's Foundation

http://www.benjerry.com/foundation/index.html

Seek programs concerned with societal, institutional, and environmental change. The particular areas are children and families, disenfranchised groups, and the environment. Also describes restrictions, types of grants, and how to apply.

Benton Foundation

http://www.benton.org/

Concerned with the information infrastructure. Among their projects: Communications policy and practice, report on public opinion of library leader's visions of future, children's programs, the arts, and public interest organizations.

Carnegie Foundation

http://www.carnegie.org/

Grant-making corporation dedicated to enhancing knowledge. Currently supports education and healthy development of children and youth, preventing deadly conflict, strengthening human resources in developing countries, and other special projects. Also outlines how to submit a proposal.

Commonwealth Fund

http://www.cmwf.org/

Conducts research on health and social policy issues. Programs include improving health care services, improving the health of minority Americans, the well-being of the elderly, developing the capacities of children and young people, and improving public spaces and services.

Corporate Foundations on the Internet

http://fdncenter.org/grantmaker/corp.html

You have two options: from a list of corporate foundations, go directly to the foundation's site, or use a list of annotated links to zero in on a funder.

Council on Foundations

http://www.cof.org/

A membership association composed of over 1,300 nonprofit foundations (independent, corporate, and public). Its programs are in areas such as education, health, human services, science and research, and so on. Also promotes accountability among member foundations.

Deutsches Spendeninstitut Krefeld

http://www.dsk.de/

Note that this page is for speakers of German. Contains 17,000 pages of information on charities and philanthropy in Germany and throughout the world.

Electronic Policy Network

http://epn.org/

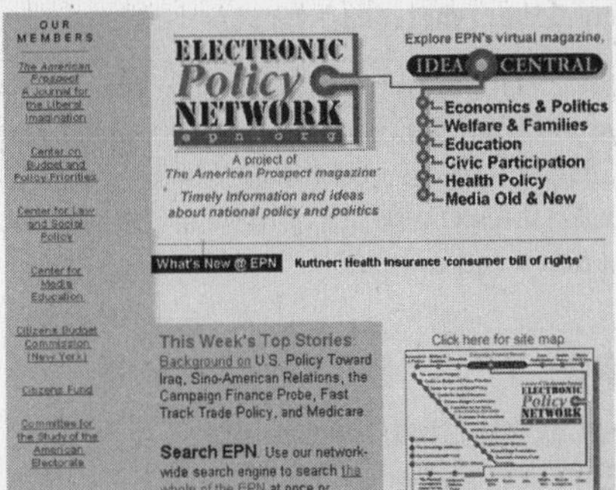

An advocacy association for hundreds of nonprofit organizations. Contains links to current Requests for Proposals (RFPs), information of conferences, legislative actions and other governmental relations, books and publications, education resources, and more.

Environmental Resources

http://www.fiu.edu:80/~time4chg/environmental.html

Links to and lists to environmental resources, including home pages of Greenpeace and the Sierra Club, various resources on the Web and Gopher, a Listserv, and a book recommendation.

FIU Volunteer Action Center

http://www.fiu.edu:80/~time4chg/

Sponsored by Florida International Center, provides opportunities for volunteers, service learning, and advocacy in southern Florida. Includes lists of nonprofit agencies in the area. Enables students to assist faculty in service learning programs. Also links to Volunteer Action Center reading room.

Foundation Center

http://fdncenter.org/

For grantseekers and grantmakers. Contains information on libraries and locations, training and seminars, funding trends and analysis, the fundraising process, and publications and CD-ROMs. Also includes a searchable database and an online reference desk.

A B C D E F G H I J K L M N O P Q R S T U V W X Y Z

Foundation for Individual Responsibility and Social Trust (FIRST)

http://www.libertynet.org/~first/

A nonpartisan, nonprofit foundation for the discussion of national policy relating to our social responsibility. Particularly geared toward those between ages 18–35. Enables you to apply to be an intern. Also discusses news and events.

GE Fund

http://www.ge.com/fund/ibfuna1.htm

A supporter of education grants for people of all ages across the world. Contains lists of programs, grants, staff, committees, and guidelines.

Goodwill Industries International

http://www.goodwill.org/

Provides employment, training services, and removes barriers to people with disabilities. Contains information on the THAP Project, current news, and more. Also enables you to find a donation center, a retail location, and a Goodwill in your area.

IBM

http://www.ibm.com/IBM/IBMGives/index.html

Corporate Philanthropic Arm Concerned with education, the environment, health, human services, arts, and culture.

IdeaList

http://www.contact.org/

Another resource for nonprofit agencies. You can add your own organization. Also a list of nonprofit Web sites, tools for nonprofits, and a searchable directory of public access points to the Web around the world.

Independent Sector

http://www.indepsec.org/frames.html

Through research, promotes understanding of public sector. Dedicated to providing information; advocacy; and service for philanthropy, charities, and voluntarism. Contains updated articles.

Indiana University Center On Philanthropy

http://www.iupui.edu/it/philanth/copwww.html

Arm of Indiana University dedicated to the study of philanthropy and its associated disciplines. Contains links to degree programs, scholarships, fellowships, assistantships, research and books, and publications.

Information for Nonprofits

http://www.eskimo.com/~pbarber/

Information for nonprofit organizations in the United States. Contains a FAQ sheet and information on Washington nonprofits. Information largely drawn from the newsgroup (soc.org.nonprofit).

Institute for Nonprofit Organization Management

http://www.usfca.edu/usf/cps/cs.html

At the University of San Francisco. Teach and training on nonprofits. Offers Master of Nonprofit Administration, Executive Certificate in Nonprofit Management, the Development Director Certificate, Distinguished Public Lecture, and more.

John D. and Catherine T. MacArthur Foundation

http://www.macfdn.org/

A foundation that seeks to improve the human condition through various programs, including peace and cooperation, environment, health, creativity, education, community, culture, and so on. Searchable. Also in Spanish and Portuguese.

Joseph and Matthew Payton Philanthropic Studies Library

http://andretti.iupui.edu/philanthropy/payton.html

A collection of books, dissertations, and audio-visual materials on philanthropy and nonprofit issues. Offers reference service and bibliographic consulting to scholars and practitioners around the world. One of the largest collections of its type in the United States.

Meta-Index for Nonprofit Organizations

http://www.philanthropy-journal.org/plhome/plmeta.htm

Award-winning nonprofit resource. Contains nonprofit organization list, information for nonprofit organizations and activists, human rights, civil liberties and politics, health and human services, environmental issues and animal rights, and more.

National Service-Learning Cooperative Clearinghouse

http://www.nicsl.coled.umn.edu/

ERIC clearinghouse on service-learning programs affecting K–12. Includes links to a National Service-Learning Cooperative Clearinghouse update, the National Society for Experiential Education, the Michigan K–12 Service-Learning Center, Project Bridge the Gap, searchable databases, and other important resources.

Nonprofit Resources Catalogue

http://www.clark.net/pub/pwalker/General_Nonprofit_Resources/

All kinds of resources are available here: from an explorer of Web-based nonprofit resources to a list of nonprofit directories. Contains links to plenty of subcategories.

NPO-NET

http://www.mcs.net/~nponet/nponet/

A resource for Chicago-area nonprofit organizations. Enables you to search for grants and grantmakers, information on fundraising and philanthropy, training for nonprofit management, nonprofit discussions, and more.

Paradigms

http://www.libertynet.org/~rhd/Paradigms/Paradigms2/

A newsletter and posting board for nonprofits. Provides a discussion and announcement forum, idea exchange, snd a searchable directory of project models.

Philanthropic Studies Index

http://andretti.iupui.edu/philanthropy/psl.html

An index of articles on voluntarism, nonprofit organizations, fundraising, giving, and philanthropy in general. Searchable on computer. Also available in paperback. Published three times a year.

Philanthropy Archives

http://www-lib.iupui.edu/special/

Organized and described collection of materials for the intensive study of philanthropy and the history of nonprofit organizations. Includes records of the American Association of Fund-Raising Counsel, Inc., Records, 1935–1992; the Ferry, Carol Bernstein and W.H., Philanthropic Records; the Wheeler Mission; and the Women's Suffrage.

Philanthropy Journal Online

http://www.philanthropy-journal.org/

From North Carolina. A leading Web-based resource for philanthropy and nonprofits. Contains links to several award-winning sites, including the "Meta-Index of Nonprofit Organizations." Also includes information on fundraising, volunteers, foundations, corporate giving, and more.

PRAXIS

http://www.ssw.upenn.edu/~restes/praxis.html

From Richard J. Estes, professor at the University of Pennsylvania. This is a page of resources for social and economic development. Contains a reference room, links to development assistance agencies, organizations, policies, descriptions of levels of social development practice, home pages and news services, and more.

Private Foundations on the Internet

http://fdncenter.org/grantmaker/priv.html

You have two options: from a list of private foundations, go directly to the foundation's site, or use a list of annotated links to zero in on a funder.

Project HOPE (Health Opportunities for People Everywhere)

http://www.projhope.org/

Dedicated to improving health care throughout the world. Provides education, policy research, and humanitarian aid. Also contains links to their research on health policy, their programs, and journal. You can search the HOPE Web site.

Rockefeller Brothers Fund

http://www.rbf.org/rbf/

A private philanthropic foundation. Includes information on the Fund's program guidelines, a list of recent grants, how to apply for a grant, grant restrictions, a list of the Fund's publications, and other programs and foundations.

Seattle's Homeless Newspaper

http://www.speakeasy.org/realchange/

Features past two issues in full, subject index of stories in archives, and directions on organizing a homeless paper in your own city. Contains poetry by those who are homeless.

Service Learning

http://csf.colorado.EDU:80/sl/

A compendium of Web resources on "service learning," a cooperative effort enabling academic programs and communities to interact. Contains articles, bibliographies, dissertations, theses, films and videos, handbooks and manuals, and much more. Also links to archives of two service-learning-related Listservs. Searchable.

UK Charities

http://pitch.phon.ucl.ac.uk/home/dave/TOC_H/Charities/

Information and resources on charities in the United Kingdom. Contains links to UK Charitable Trusts on the Web, useful information on charities, charitable bodies on the Internet, and an alphabetical index of charities.

United Way of America

http://www.unitedway.org/

An organization embracing local community-based United Ways, made up of volunteers, charities, and contributors. Contains information on several of their programs, including Sky Wish, and United Way. Also includes news, a United Way FAQ sheet, and a description of how United Way works.

Urban Institute

http://www.urban.org/

Studies policies surrounding social and economic problems. Contains: annual report, text of current and back issues of publications (for example, *Future of the Public Sector*), and a list of the institute's sites. Site is also searchable.

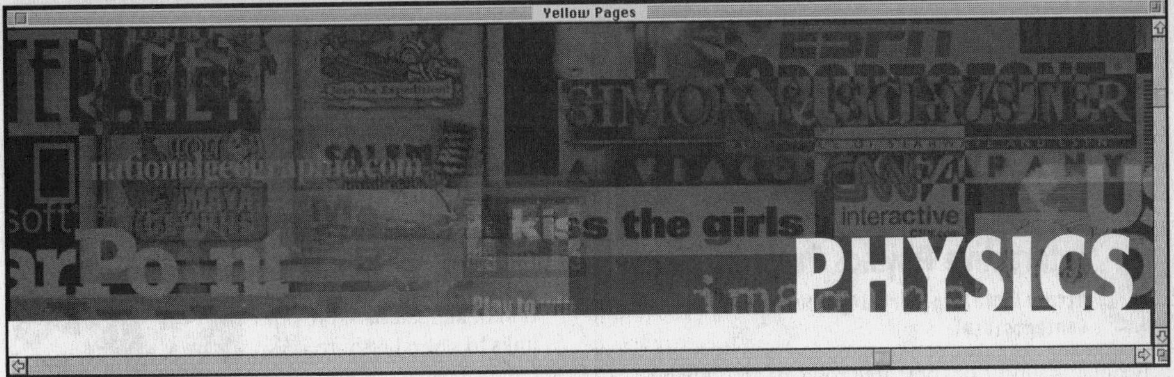

> The world goes round and round.
>
> *Hanson*

American Physical Society

http://aps.org/

American Physical Society is an organization of more than 41,000 physicists. The group publishes research journals, including the *Physical Review, Physical Review Letters,* and *Review of Modern Physics.* Their site contains links to information on the organization's meetings, membership information, and career/employment opportunities, as well as links to their numerous publications.

ASM International Home Page

http://www.asm-intl.org/

Provides information about ASM, the Materials Information Society. Provides a searchable collection of Web sites, a calendar of events, and a collection of materials producers of interest to materials engineers.

CERN European Laboratory for Particle Physics

http://www.cern.ch/

Birthplace of the World Wide Web. Provides general information on the Web and maintains archives of information on particle physics and listings of links to other sites pertaining to the field of physics.

CMB Astrophysics Research Program

http://spectrum.lbl.gov

Surveys ongoing research and lists current personnel in the George Smoot Astrophysics Research Group.

Fermilab—Discovering the Nature of Nature

http://www.fnal.gov/

Site describes the activities of the Department of Energy National Accelerator Laboratory. Features information about the Top Quark discovery, high energy physics, and Fermilab activities.

HyperSpace at UBC

http://axion.physics.ubc.ca/hyperspace/

Contains articles related to gravity and relativity, current news on relativity, job listings, and conference information, among other information.

Institute of Physics

http://www.ioppublishing.com/

An online newsletter. Allows subscribers to receive email that provides up-to-date accounts of news in the field of physics.

Interactive Physics Problem Set

http://info.itp.berkeley.edu/Vol1/Contents.html

Contains almost 100 practice problems accompanied by detailed solutions and interactive computer experiments.

Jean-Marie Vaneskahian's Physics Home Page

http://www.gate.net/~jean/

Offers physics-related links and software, including Net software.

Lawrence Livermore National Laboratory

http://www.llnl.gov/

Provides information about the laboratory and its research projects, as well as links to other sites of general interest. Specializes in the study of nuclear, ecological, and bioscience topics.

Listing of Physics Resources on the World Wide Web

http://aip.org/aip/physres.html

Lists various types of physics resources currently available on the Web.

Livermore Labs Atmospheric Research

http://www-ep.es.llnl.gov/www-ep/atm.html

Provides technical information with research on global and regional climate change, atmospheric physics and chemistry, biogeochemical cycles of anthropogenic gases and aerosols, cloud physics, and real-time modeling of the transport of contaminants in the atmosphere.

Nanotechnology

http://nano.xerox.com/nano

Nanotechnology is an expected future manufacturing technology that should enable us to inexpensively build almost any structure consistent with the laws of chemistry and physics with molecular precision.

Nanoworld Home Page

http://www.uq.oz.au/nanoworld/nanohome.html

Research and service facility dedicated to understanding the structure and composition of all materials. Provides links to several resources. Offers database of microscopic images.

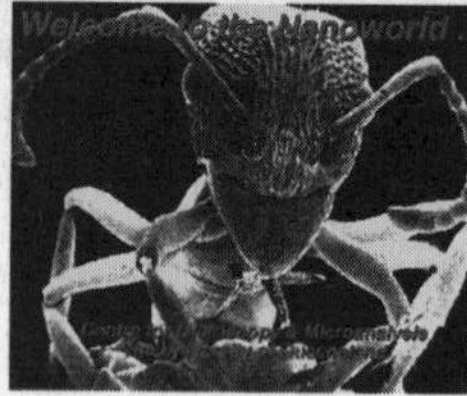

Nuclear Physics

http://www.rarf.riken.go.jp/rarf/np/nplab.html

Contains a catalog of sites pertaining to the field of physics. Contains a variety of links to sites, and an alphabetical listing that consists predominately of links to research centers around the world but that also includes links to a variety of associations.

Physics and Space Technology Directorate

http://www-phys.llnl.gov/

Provides information on physics—particularly physics pertaining to space technology.

Physics around the World

http://www.physics.mcgill.ca/physics-services/

Provides a catalog of physics and related resources on the Web. Includes all major fields in physics, science education, history of science, physical constants, laws, data and tables, journals, software, and more. Also includes bulletin boards for summer schools and workshops and for buying and selling used instruments and equipment.

Physics Demonstrations at UC Berkeley

http://www.mip.berkeley.edu/physics/physics.html

Demonstrations for the subjects of mechanics, waves, heat and matter, electricity, magnetism, and optics.

Physics News

http://www.het.brown.edu/news/index.html

Contains up-to-date information on current events in the world of physics. Offers a listing of various online publications and resource sites.

Physics Problems

http://zebu.uoregon.edu/~probs/probm.html

Contains more than 30 problems in basic concepts, mechanics, and thermal physics.

Quantum Magazine Home Page

http://www.nsta.org:80/quantum/

Provides information about *Quantum* magazine. Contains primarily physics-related contents, but does include a "toy store" of "mathematical amusements." Includes back issues and a sample.

WARP Home

http://www.hia.com/hia/pcr/home.html

Offers a collection of multimedia documents pertaining to various aspects of "alternative" science, including warp technology, fantasy stories of time travel, quantum mechanics, and so on.

Welcome to the Institute of Physics

http://www.ioppublishing.com/iopwelcome.html

Provides information in the field of physics. Restricts use of some items and aspects to registered members only. Users who choose to register can browse text abstracts or download full text versions of any article. To register, you must be a member of a subscribing institution.

Welcome to the Laboratory for Terrestrial Physics

http://ltpwww.gsfc.nasa.gov/

Provides information, documents, and simulations related to terrestrial physics. Features links to images of various terrestrial phenomena, such as magnetic models of the crust.

World Wide Web Virtual Library: Physics

http://www.w3.org/hypertext/DataSources/bySubject/Physics/Overview.html

Offers a general listing of physics sites. Also contains links to listings of more specific sites on geophysics, astrophysics, nuclear physics, and energy science.

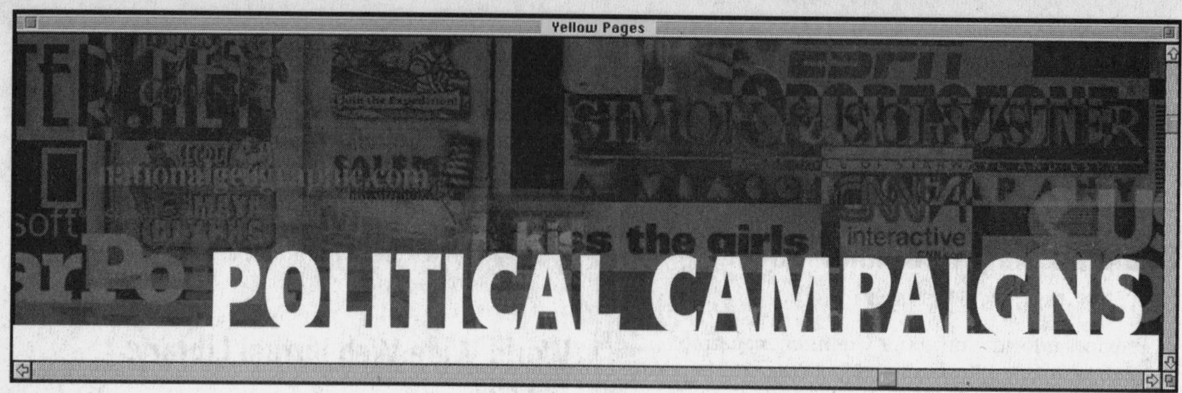

POLITICAL CAMPAIGNS

> Too bad all the people who know how to run the country are busy driving cabs and cutting hair.
>
> *George Burns*

All Things Political

`http://www.federal.com/Political.html`

Brought to you by *Washington Weekly*, this is a look at Washington from the citizen's perspective. Take a look at political speeches from House Speaker Newt Gingrich or President Clinton. Read about political scandals, such as Whitewater. A special section lets you rate some of the news media and submit your input. Includes lists of political newsgroups and links to related sites.

Campaign & Elections

`http://www.camelect.com/`

Campaign and Elections Online! is a magazine for political professionals. Includes a bi-weekly, state-by-state report of upcoming elections (for subscribers to *C&E Magazine* and *Campaign Insider Newsletter* only). You can check out the changing odds on major national, state, and local races across the country. Browse the National Directory of Public Affairs; Lobbying; and Issues Management Consultants, Products, and Services. Or, check out the political analysis section. Get a subscription to *Campaign Insider*—a weekly newsletter for political consultants and committees. Also includes C&E's Buyers Guide; get info on telephone services, media placement, direct mail services, fundraising, and more.

CNN/Time All Politics
`http://allpolitics.com/1997/index.html`

CQ's American Voter
`http://voter.cq.com/`

The MoJo Wire—Interactive Exposes and Politics
`http://www.mojones.com/`

Campaign Finance Reform

`http://www.brookings.org/gs/campaign/home.htm`

This site's goal is to improve the quality of debate on campaign finance reform so that a workable approach can be passed by the 105th Congress and signed into law by the president. Examine new approaches to reform; check out articles analyzing the proposed reforms, related opinion pieces, and proposals to Congress. Go to the Public Forum on Campaign Finance Reform to view others' ideas, analyses, and opinions.

Campaigning On-Line

`http://www.campol.com/`

This site offers Republican campaign consulting for the Web by political consultants to help Republicans create a strong presence on the Web. Campaigning On-Line is a Web-page development service offered at fees starting at about $100 per month. This service puts your campaign on the Web. The Webmaster—whose work has been acknowledged as an Internet standard—is skilled at creating appealing Web sites. The politically savvy campaign team has run (and run in) Republican campaigns. The staff editor knows the art of writing for the Web. And the attorney can help keep your Web site out of trouble. Campaigning On-Line can establish your campaign's Web presence and turn your Web site into an interactive campaign tool. It will also keep your Web site current and up-to-date.

A B C D E F G H I J K L M N O P Q R S T U V W X Y Z

Center for the American Woman and Politics

`http://www.rci.rutgers.edu/~cawp/`

The Center for the American Woman and Politics (CAWP) is a university-based research, education, and public service center. Its mission is to promote greater understanding and knowledge about women's relationships to politics and government and to enhance women's influence and leadership in public life. CAWP is a unit of the Eagleton Institute of Politics at Rutgers, The State University of New Jersey. Learn about CAWP job opportunities and look at general info. Read publications and press releases. Get highlights from reports and order from the list of recommended books. Sample and learn how to order the *CAWP News & Notes* newsletter. Read about female candidates in the latest elections.

CNN/Time All Politics

`http://allpolitics.com/1997/index.html`

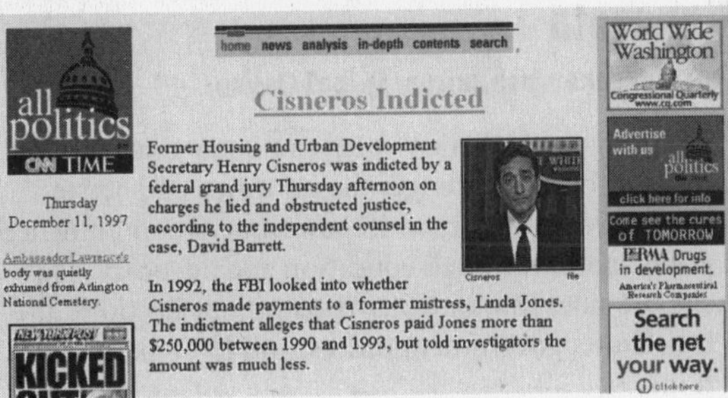

Get breaking news and stories from TIME, CNN, *Congressional Quarterly*, and The Associated Press. Check out the cartoons and opinion pieces from the premier pundits of *Time*, CNN, *CQ*, and the Washington talk show circuit. Or, visit the In-Depth section for interactive features, sights and sounds, and resources such as biographies and transcripts. Check out two of the nation's top political analysts, Stuart Rothenberg and Charlie Cook, who dissect the nation's politics at the Congressional and statewide levels. Offers links to sites about Congress, the White House, think tanks, and political parties. This site is updated continuously, and back issues are available.

Common Cause/Kentucky

`http://nonprofit.venus.net/cmncause/`

Common Cause is a nonpartisan citizen's organization with the goal of ensuring open, honest, accountable, and effective government at the federal, state, and local levels. Check out studies on topics such as the relationship between money, elections, and voting patterns. Includes articles from *Common Cause* magazine, which explores issues such as tobacco's financial ties to Congress, how Congress pays industry—with federal tax dollars—to deplete and destroy the nation's natural resources, and healthcare and Medicare changes. Tells you how to contact elected officials and gives you links to Common Cause sites for other states.

Congress.Org

`http://207.168.215.81/`

Use the U.S. Congressional Directory search engine to look up info on any Congress member, state delegation, House committee, or Senate committee. Also get info on the Congressional leadership. Or, enter your ZIP code to find your Representatives and info about them. Find out who is on the various U.S. House and Senate Committees and view info on each person and committee. The Congress Today section keeps you up to date on the House and Senate schedule, as well as each week's committee hearings.

Congressional Quarterly's VoteWatch

`http://www.pathfinder.com/CQ/`

Get insider access to Congress and your representatives' votes. Get the latest news or search the voting records of the members who interest you. See how the House and Senate voted on the latest issues and get info on those issues. Provides daily coverage of House and Senate actions and debates.

CQ's American Voter

`http://voter.cq.com/`

Congressional Quarterly's American Voter provides comprehensive, impartial news, analyses, and info on government and politics. Get info about members of Congress, bills sponsored, speeches made, and votes recently taken. In the Rate Your Rep section, you can select a member of Congress and fill out a form with 10 Yes/No questions on your outlook on key issues. Your votes are then compared with the actual votes of your Senator or Representative. Get info on the 105th Congress committee rosters; email addresses of Congress, Senate, and House Democratic and Republican leaders; info on Supreme Court justices, and more. Sound Off! provides a forum where you can post and view messages based on certain topics, such as "Next Election Predictions—Who Will Run and Who Will Win." Includes links to the best political sites on the Web.

A B C D E F G H I J K L M N O P Q R S T U V W X Y Z

The Democratic National Committee

http://www.democrats.org/

Read *The Daily News*—news from the DNC—and browse through the archives. Read about where the Democratic party stands on various issues. Check out the transcripts of White House briefings, such as the president's radio addresses. You can also read through the current year of DNC press releases. Includes info on various Senate hearings, as well as a guide to Republican campaign finance abuses. Also includes Democratic National Committee FAQs. The Get Active! section tells you how to join the DNC, volunteer, and register to vote.

DeskTop Candidate–Campaign Management Software

http://www.trilliumsys.com/

DeskTop Candidate is campaign-management software for the campaign professional. Learn how to import any voter data and perform easy voter targeting. Get help on managing voters, volunteers, contributors, and even lawn signs. Maximize your data-entry efficiency with a bar-code reader. Comes with technical support packages.

Elections

http://www.multied.com/elections/

This Presidential Elections Statistics site is presented by MultiEducator. Check out colorful graphs of the electoral votes cast in presidential elections from 1789 to the present. Download photos of scenes from American history. Read selected documents, such as the Articles of Confederation and the Civil Rights Act of 1957. The MultiEducator American History product lets you access events chronologically, alphabetically, or by topic. Access info on major events in U.S. history and get extensive info on each of the presidents. Audio-visuals highlight major periods in U.S. history, and video clips showcase achievements and tragedies. You can order other MultiEducator products and check out pricing at this site.

The Gallup Organization

http://www.gallup.com/

The people who practically invented the political public-opinion poll bring you a site that lets you study all the political trends for the entire election season. Gallup Polls, public releases, and special reports on key social and business-related issues are presented. Get info and poll results on current events. Also includes Gallup Special Reports—in-depth analyses of issues that concern people around the world. Includes comments and suggestions to the editors and archives up to March '96.

gpchome

http://www.governet.com/hdindex.html

The GoverNet Political Channel delivers critical campaign strategy info directly to your desktop. GoverNet offers two primary services for the candidate. The campaign-management software helps organize the campaign, track finances, and create FEC reports. The Political Channel provides current news and info, as well as issues research, to help in the campaign process. You can use the Contacts Database to manage the people involved in a campaign, including voters, volunteers, contributors, consultants, and key contacts—you also can store pictures of these people. GoverNet is designed for every size campaign—local, state, and federal.

The League of Women Voters of Minnesota

http://freenet.msp.mn.us/ip/pol/lwvmn/

The League of Women Voters, a nonpartisan political organization, encourages the informed and active participation of citizens in government and influences public policy through education and advocacy. This site provides info on voter registration, elections, the legislature, government offices, and LWV publications.

The MoJo Wire–Interactive Exposes and Politics

http://www.mojones.com/

Mother Jones is a magazine of investigation and ideas for independent thinkers. Provocative and unexpected articles inform readers and inspire action toward positive social change. Colorful and personal, this magazine challenges conventional wisdom, exposes abuses of power, helps redefine stubborn problems, and offers fresh solutions. The Live Wire Forum lets you participate in several conference discussion areas. The Coin-Op Congress section gives you an in-depth look at what really fuels Washington; you get investigative stories on where the money is going and what it's fueling. A recent article is "The Mother Jones 400: A List of America's Biggest Political Donors and Who They Gave To." You can use the search engine to find certain topics in back issues. This site is updated every Tuesday morning.

National Political Index

http://www.politicalindex.com/

Visit this site for political info for voters, political activists, political consultants, lobbyists, politicians, academicians, and media editors. Offers a wide range of products, services, simulations, games, and polling in an interactive communications environment. Gives political activist organizations tactics and logistics info so that they can compete against the massive TV advertising. Check out the hourly political headlines and the info on federal, state, and local elected officials and candidates. Also includes political humor.

Project Vote Smart

http://www.vote-smart.org/

Project Vote Smart tracks the performance of more than 13,000 political leaders—the president, Congress, governors, and state legislatures. Get info on issue positions, voting records, performance evaluations, campaign finances, and biographies. Enter your ZIP code, and the search engine looks up who represents you and gives you the relevant info and statistics. Or, track the performance of the 105th Congress. Find out how candidates stood on issues before they were elected and see how your Congressperson voted on a bill. Track the status of legislation as it works its way through Congress; read the text of a bill; and find out whether a bill has had committee action, whether it is scheduled for a hearing or a vote, and whether your Congressperson is a cosponsor.

The Right Side of the Web

http://www.rtside.com/

Check out the Popu-List for links to conservative candidates' home pages for the current/upcoming election year. You also get links to sites that reflect the conservative viewpoint on topics such as abortion, legal issues, the family, the second amendment (the right to keep and bear arms), Christianity, media, and more. Read postings from viewers participating in various debates. Take part in several polls and see the results later. Order recommended books reflecting the conservative viewpoint. Read current and back issues of the column *Barely Inside the Beltway*. And, of course, view links to and info about the latest Democratic scandals.

So You Want to Buy a President?

http://www.pbs.org/wgbh/pages/frontline/president/

This site contains a transcript of the program "So You Want to Buy a President," which aired on the show *Frontline* (a weekly public-affairs series on PBS). See what *Frontline* learned about the "rules of the game." See profiles of the interlocking business and political relationships that dominate the presidential fund-raising game. Read excerpts from conversations with a U.S. senator, a former presidential candidate, and political analysts. Get info and resources about politics, campaign financing, and reform.

Support Constitutional Campaign Finance Reform

http://www.aclu.org/congress/campaignfinance.html

This site is brought to you by the American Civil Liberties Union (ACLU) Freedom Network. The ACLU feels that Congress is not addressing real campaign reform; it opposes the proposed constitutional amendment that permits Congress and the states to enact laws regulating federal campaign expenditures and contributions, saying that it gives Congress and the states the authority to restrict speech protected by the First Amendment. Check out this site for a full explanation of the ACLU's views on campaign finance reform and what they've been doing about it, as well as their position on certain court cases. You can also browse the ACLU news archive, learn how to contact members of Congress, learn how to use government research tools, and learn how to lobby Congress.

Welcome to National Journal's Cloakroom

http://www.cloakroom.com/

Cloakroom provides commentary, news, and resource materials on politics and policy. It offers online delivery of most National Journal Group daily publications—*CongressDaily, The Hotline, American Health Line, Greenwire*, and *Daily Energy Briefing*. Includes a database of polling results and trends. Also offers the *1998 Almanac of American Politics*, as well as schedules for Congress. Subscribers to any of National Journal's daily publications receive access to Cloakroom as a benefit of their subscription. Or, you can just purchase a membership to Cloakroom.

Welcome to the C-SPAN Networks

http://www.c-span.org

Check out the C-SPAN schedules (C-SPAN and C-SPAN2) and content. Explore the Public Affairs Video Archives. Or, listen to the show *Washington Journal*. Explore today's headlines from papers such as the *Washington Post, San Francisco Examiner, Chicago Sun-Times*, and more. C-SPAN in the Classroom is a great link for teachers and students. C-SPAN's Majic Bus travels on tours such as one chronicling the history of civil rights in the Deep South. C-SPAN Online Live lets you watch events as they are happening (such as news conferences). Check out the Booknotes program, which presents America's finest authors on reading, writing, and the power of ideas. The C-SPAN Votes Library database contains all votes from the 105th Congress (updated daily) and the 104th Congress, Second Session. Get info on the U.S. House schedule and weekly committee hearings. Check out the C-SPAN School Bus; currently, it is visiting the communities Alexis de Tocqueville visited and the issues he wrote about in "Democracy in America."

WhiteHouse 2000

http://www.niu.edu/newsplace/whitehouse.html

Check out the Democratic possibilities for 2000 for the presidency, House, and Senate. Look at endorsements of certain candidates or reasons why you shouldn't vote for them. Includes info on the Republican players for the Executive office, as well as possible senators and representatives. Check out the links to official pages for Republican and Democratic players. Read statements from and endorsements of third-party candidates, such as Ross Perot. Take a look at the under-35 candidates. Examine current issues, today's news, and party platforms. Includes a history of Campaign 1996.

The Women's Campaign School at Yale University

http://www.yale.edu/wcsyale/index.html

Co-sponsored by Yale Law School and the Women's Studies Program at Yale, the Women's Campaign School teaches a wide range of campaign skills and introduces participants to professionals in the campaign arena. Classes are taught by seasoned campaign strategists and include the latest in campaign techniques. Each student takes part in on-camera training, compiles an individualized campaign manual, and goes on to become part of a close-knit alumnae network. Find out more about the school's programs, alumnae, board members, and upcoming events at this site. You'll also get some to great links to related sites.

Yahoo!–Government: Politics: Elections: 1998 U.S. Elections

http://www.yahoo.com/Government/Politics/Elections/1998_U_S__Elections/

Get links to info on state elections, including Congressional and gubernatorial.

NEWSGROUPS & GOPHERS

alt.dear.whitehouse

alt.politics

misc.headlines

soc.politics

talk.politics.misc

talk.politics.theory

alt.politics.clinton

alt.politics.elections

alt.politics.radical-left

alt.politics.usa.congress

alt.politics.usa.republican

alt.politics.usa.newt-gingrich

alt.current-events.clinton.whitewater

alt.rightside.web

gopher://wiretap.spies.com/11/Gov

Related Sites

http://www.spectator.org/exclusives/97-12-09_update.html

http://www.clark.net/ccentral/

http://www.geocities.com/CapitolHill/1411/index.html

http://www.townhall.com/heritage/library/categories/govern/ib230.html

http://www.rightnow.org/

http://thomas.loc.gov/

http://www.house.gov/

http://www.texas.net/~lookn2it/

http://www.rnc.org/

http://www.whitehouse.gov/WH/Welcome.html

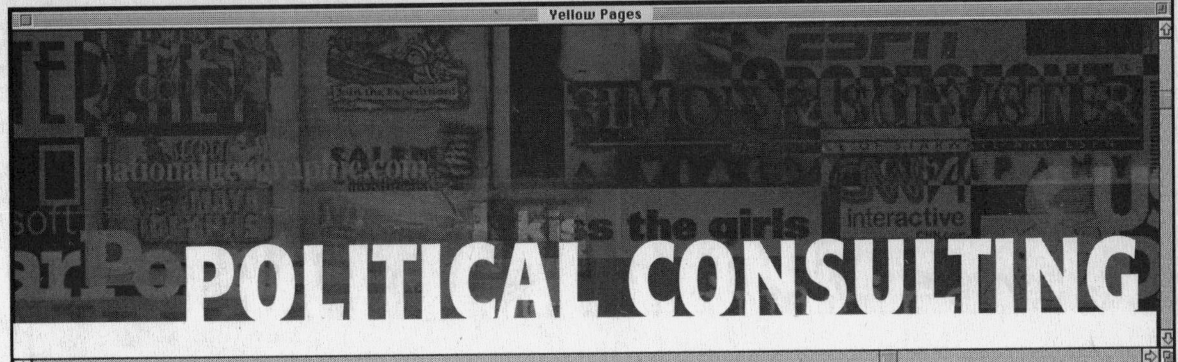

> How can anyone govern a nation that has two hundred and forty-six different kinds of cheese?
>
> *Charles DeGaulle*

Fifty plus One
`http://www.interguru.com/fiftyplusone/`

Redmond & LeCount–Political Management and Research Strategies
`http://www.netcom.com/~redmond/redlec.html`

Devine Advertising Associates

`http://pages.prodigy.com/devine`

A full service advertising, strategy, and management firm that specializes in political campaign consulting, government affairs, and corporate public relations. Let them help you win!

Fifty plus One

`http://www.interguru.com/fiftyplusone/`

Fifty plus One is a grassroots organization training pro-choice women in electoral campaign skills necessary to run for local, state, and national offices.

Greg Stevens & Company

`http://www.mnsinc.com/gscomp`

Greg Stevens & Company is one of the leading Republican media and political consulting companies in America. The goal of the firm is to win with exceptionally creative and well-produced media.

Intermark Communications

`http://www.halcyon.com/jdoman/`

Intermark specializes in enhancing marketing and political campaign tactics with a powerful Internet presence. Intermark also publishes the Executive Technology Letter.

J. Brian O'Day

`http://ourworld.compuserve.com/homepages/jboday/`

O'Day is an independent political consultant, working on Democratic campaigns from his home in Baltimore, Maryland. In the last ten years, he has worked on federal, state, and local campaigns in Maryland, New Jersey, and Pennsylvania.

Kevin LeCount–Political Consultant

`http://www.netcom.com/~redmond/klres.html`

Kevin LeCount is a Louisiana-based political consultant specializing in campaign management and general strategy.

Redmond & LeCount–Political Management and Research Strategies

`http://www.netcom.com/~redmond/redlec.html`

A full-service political consulting firm specializing in campaign management, strategic consulting, and opposition/issue research. Redmond & LeCount services Democratic campaigns at all levels throughout the country.

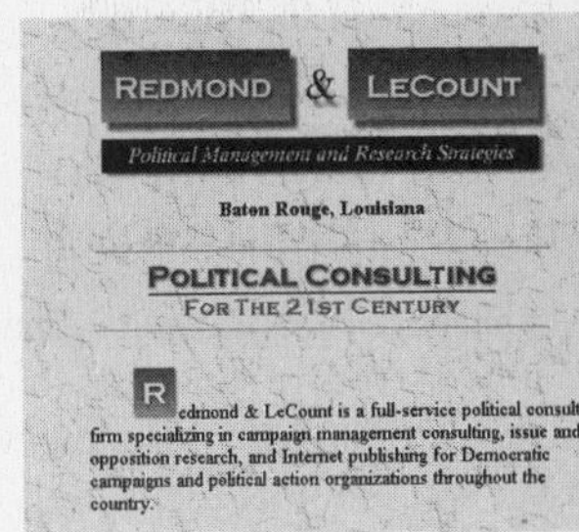

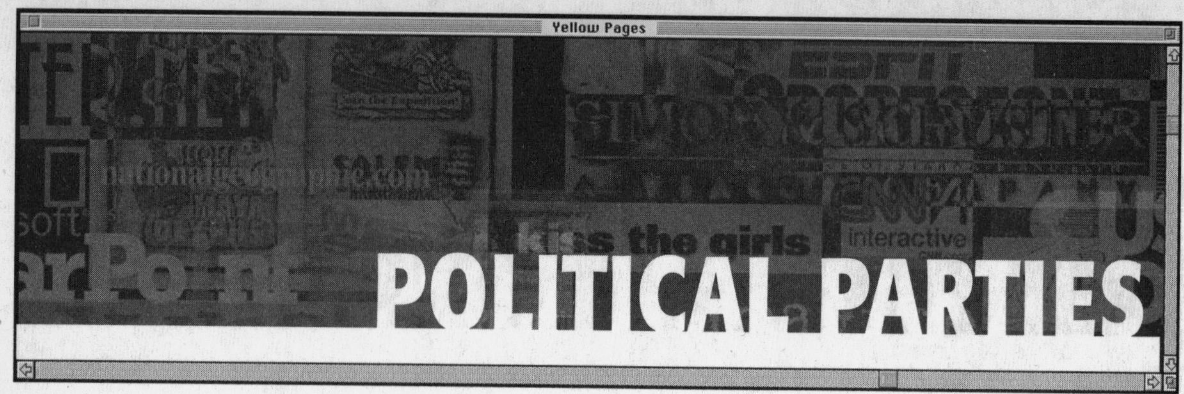

A
B
C
D
E
F
G
H
I
J
K
L
M
N
O
P
Q
R
S
T
U
V
W
X
Y
Z

Politics makes strange bed fellows.

Charles Dudley Warner

The Christian Coalition

http://www.cc.org/

The CC members fight for laws they feel promote the Christian agenda and against those that do not. Their site has reports on every relevant law, as well as how each Congressman voted. The pages include family resources, articles on American Christians, and more.

College Democrats of America

http://www.democrats.org/college_democrats/

The College Democrat site explains the mission, history, and issues of this branch of the party. Membership is also available at this site.

College Republican National Committee Homepage

http://www.crnc.org

Alphabetical listing of College Republican chapters throughout the country.

Common Dreams

http://www.commondreams.org/

This page is considered a "news clipping" service for the progressive American thinker. There's an endless supply of linked articles on every politicial topic under the sun. Another useful, well-designed, quick site.

Pansexual Peace Party
http://www.neosoft.com/~eris/PPPP/

Political Resources on the Net
http://www.agora.stm.it/politic/

Communists Party USA

http://www.hartford-hwp.com/cp-usa/

The American Communists want you if you want to place the tax burden on corporations and the rich; to provide universal health care and college education for all; to maintain strong unions; to ensure the eradication of all discrimination; and much more.

The Constitution Party

http://www.yourworld.com/constitu/constitu.html

The Consitution Party has an interesting balance of liberalism and new-age quirkiness. Their platform includes insituting a 14-percent flat tax, limiting welfare to five years and providing job training, making English the official national language, and protecting the Second Amendment—oh, and releasing all government documentaion regarding unidentified flying objects and any aliens that have been captured.

Democracy*Dynamics

http://www.usa-democracy.org/

Democracy*Dynamics is a political movement to revolutionize the American electoral system and political process through a dynamic process of choice, representation and empowerment.

The Democratic Caucus

http://www.house.gov/demcaucus/welcome.html

This is where the policies of the Democratic Congressional Membership can be accessed. Good research stuff for students.

Democratic National Committee

`http://www.democrats.org/`

Here you can find out everything the Democrats are doing. You can find out about their events, sign up for their electronic newsletter and even join the party.

Democratic Socialists of America

`http://www.dsausa.org/`

The DSA believes that capitalism has failed and that the working peoples of the world are being oppressed and suppressed by a tiny percentage of rich. The DSA works to establish their own humane vision of internationl economic and social order.

Fusion Party

`http://members.tripod.com/~Fusionist/`

The Fusionists believe that there should be no age restrition on the President or other federal positions; that the Electoral College should be abolished, so the elctorate can vote directly (which is what a true democracy allows; we live in a republic, not a democracy); and that welfare should be preserved, in a modified state, because it is ultimately better for the country help the needy.

Green Party USA

`http://utopia.knoware.nl/users/oterhaar/greens/america/usa.htm`

One in a chain of Green Party sites, Green Party USA discusses some slightly recent campaigns, such as the 1996 Presidential campaign when their candidate, Ralph Nader, won .63 percent of the popular vote. Check out the page that explains why eating is a political statement.

Libertarian Party Headquarters

`http://www.lp.org/lp/`

This site isn't very graphics-heavy, but it is dense with Libertarian issues and positions. Those positions are also very Internet-oriented. As with all the political party sites, you can join too.

The John Birch Society

`http://www.jbs.org/`

The JB Society makes the Republican Party look like a bunch of long-haired, New York liberals. Their site dicusses their opinions of "less government, more responsibility," and offers a FAQ, their newsletter, commentary on pending legislation, and more.

Natural Law Party of the United States of America

`http://www.fairfield.com:80/nlp/`

Describes America's fastest growing alternative political party. For those interested in government that is conflict-free, prevention-oriented, and that utilizes proven, field-tested solutions. Features the most comprehensive platform of any U.S. political party.

New Party

`http://www.igc.apc.org/newparty/`

A grassroots, progressive political party running candidates for local elections around the country. They fight for living wage jobs, campaign finance reform, and public education.

Pansexual Peace Party

`http://www.neosoft.com/~eris/PPPP/`

The PPP is a party based on the most humanistic ideals—which makes sense considering that we're all human. The PPP is a grass roots party that believes that "peace is possible," that hierarchic constructs are bad, that crime and punishment in America needs to be retooled, that public-key encryption needs to be expanded for the public good, that the War on Drugs is immoral and hypocritical, and much more.

Patriot Party Internet Home Page

`http://www.epix.net/~dschultz/patriot1.html`

The Patriots are a party dedicated to changing the present de facto two-party system because they believe that this system has deprived the American people of the very rights the government is supposed to celebrate and protect. They want to eliminate contributions from special interests, adopt more stringent term limits, eliminate the electoral college, and more.

A B C D E F G H I J K L M N O P Q R S T U V W X Y Z

Peace and Freedom Party

http://gate.cruzio.com/~pfparty/

The PFP is a self-proclaimed feminist and socialist party that was founded in 1967. They also believe in supporting strong environmentalism, honoring all treaties with Native Americans, respecting all individuals' sexuality choices, providing free health care, and achieving full employment, among others.

The Political Lighthouse

http://www.sjca.edu/~cgillen/lighthouse.html

A comprehensive linked index to most of the major political parties in America today, complete with humorous commentary.

Political Parties and Youth Organizations Around the World

http://www.luna.nl/~benne/pp/index.htm

An extensive list of political parties and youth organizations around the world.

Political Resources on the Net

http://www.agora.stm.it/politic/

An excellent resource, not just for politics, organizations, and political parties in the United States, but all over the world. Definitely worth a visit.

Reform Party Official Website

http://www.reformparty.org/

If there's an aspect to politics and government that can be reformed, this party wants to reform it. Their platform is wide, but highlights include: disallowing all gifts and junkets; requiring the White House and Congress to have the same retirment and health care plans as the rest of us; shortening campaigns to four months; changing Election Day to a Saturday or Sunday so more working people can vote more easily; and more.

Republican National Committee

http://www.rnc.org/

The RNC has a pretty interesting home page. It looks like a small town main street and the icons are the storefront windows. You can link with candidates and get their email addresses and, of course, join the party.

Russell Hirshon for President 2000

http://www.russell.org/

Mr. Hirshon is a bartender from Washington DC who decided to start running for president of the United States. He figured he'd heard enough from the conversations he had had, and it was time to promote his platform, which, for Campaign 96, included having a better comedy act in the Oval Office than has been there, lowering cable rates, outlawing parking tickets, dropping the Cuban embargo so he can have a Cuban cigar, and many more sensible plans.

United States Taxpayers Party

http://www.ustaxpayers.org/

The USTP is a conservative party that believes not only in major tax reforms based on the original text of the Constitution, but also the following: oppose any New World Order, abortion, euthanasia, and Big Government; support a strong military and environmentalism as it suits their needs; and much more.

We the People

http://www.wtp.org/

We the People is an Oakland, California-based party lead by former Governor Jerry Brown that seeks to implement a "sustainability" plan for Oakland, and then, presumably, other cities. Sustainability is a long-term plan that takes into account a city's economy, environment, population, and so forth.

Young Democrats of America

http://www.democrats.org/young_democrats/

This site offers a map of the U.S. that you can click to find the contact information and upcoming YD events for your area.

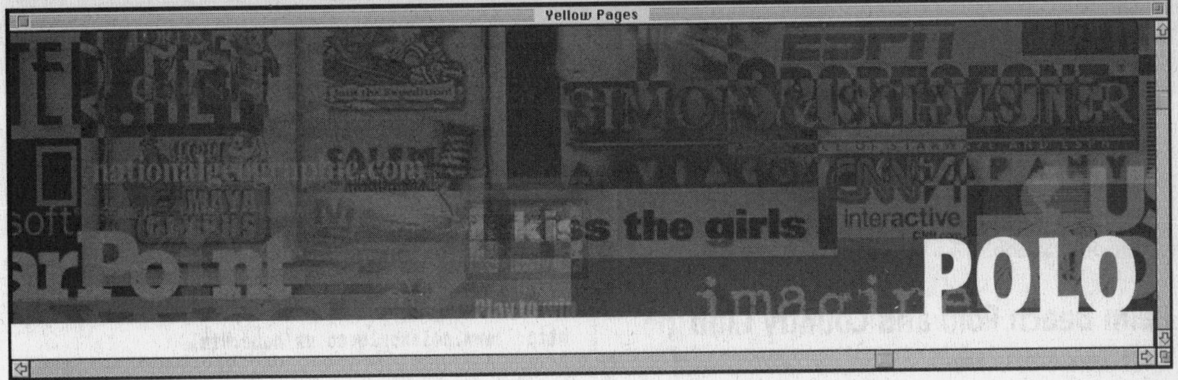

A little neglect may breed mischief: for want of a nail the shoe was lost; for want of a shoe the horse was lost; and for want of a horse the rider was lost.

Benjamin Franklin

American Polocrosse Association

http://www.interlynx-solutions.com/polocrosse/

As the name implies, polocrosse is the hybrid of polo and lacrosse. The sport prides itself as a "one-horse" sport—players may use only one horse per tournament, which levels the field against people who have many horses, that they could replace as they tire. The Web site teaches you more about the sport, the rules, local clubs, and more.

Bicycle Polo

http://www.bikepolo.com/index.html

Based on the equestrian version of the game, bicycle polo is gaining in popularity, presumably because most people can't afford to buy and keep a horse. This site tells you everything you need to get started, including the definition of "chukkar."

Related Sites

http://www.uspolo.org/fip.html

http://www.tackeria.com/

http://www.puntapolo.com/

http://www.corkscrew-balloon.com/polo/96/

http://www.3-cities.com/~bpolo/bikepolo/

Polonet
http://www.polonet.co.uk/

Dallas Polo Club ICQ Communication Panel

http://www.dallaspoloclub.org/Misc/icqpage.html

ICQ continues to grow in popularity. Download it, receive your free identification number, and you will be able to contact other polo players on the network and know exactly who else is online, too.

Elephant Polo

http://www.corkscrew-balloon.com/polo/

This site lists governing rules of elephany polo, whose 1996 tournament was held on an airstrip in Nepal, but the site was created by members of the Screwey Tuskers team. Links are provided for related sites for elephants, Nepal, Thailand, and others.

The Horse Mall

http://www.horsemall.com/

Although not specific to polo, this site offers every kind of riding-related product you could imagine, including clothing and accessories for polo players, such as boots and helmets.

La Martina

http://lamartina.com/

La Martina is both a polo club and a business that sells polo equipment—a natural paring, considering that the players need equipment and know quality. Beyond simply being an online shop, La Martina's site has a clinic, news, photos, and subscription information for *POLO* and *PQ International* polo magazines.

The New Polo Net

http://www.polonews.com/polonet.html

An excellent resource for the polo enthusiast. Polo Net offers everything you could want: polo rules, jobs, events, chat rooms, clubs and associations, supplies and a lot more. Watch out what you say in front of the polo Snoop!

Palm Beach Polo and Country Club

http://www.pbpolo.com/

Perhaps it goes without saying that where the rich go, so do their horse, and that where their horses go, so, too, goes the game of polo. This Palm Beach, Florida, club features 45 holes of golf, 13 polo fields, croquet lawns, and more.

Polonet

http://www.polonet.co.uk/

Polonet is the polo connection for all of Britain. Check out the schedule of tournaments, polo news, equipment, clubs, and more. You can also learn about individual polo players.

Polo Training Foundation

http://www.uspolo.org/ptf.html

The PTF site provides a mission statement and discusses its program and method of funding. An email address is provided so you can get in contact with the staff.

PQ International

http://www.poloworld.co.uk/home.html

This is the online version of the printed magazine. You can subscribe, check out highlights from the current issue, and get your polo calendar.

Rocking Horse Ranch

http://www.rockinghorseranch.com/ponies.htm

If you want an unusual vacation, how about visiting this ranch, which is close to the Black Hill, Yellowstone, and the Bog Horn Mountains. Visitors can laze around, join in the cow-boying chores, or they can join in a game of polo and watch how polo horses are trained.

Sidelines

http://www.sidelinesnews.com/

The online site for the printed polo magazine that covers individual tournaments all over the world, but also contains thoughtful essays and other articles.

United States Polo Association

http://www.uspolo.org/

Begun in 1890, the USPA exists to promote and sustain polo in America. Their site has extensive pages for USPA committees, rules, competition circuits, and more. Their links are a gateway to polo and horses on the Internet.

A B C D E F G H I J K L M N O P Q R S T U V W X Y Z

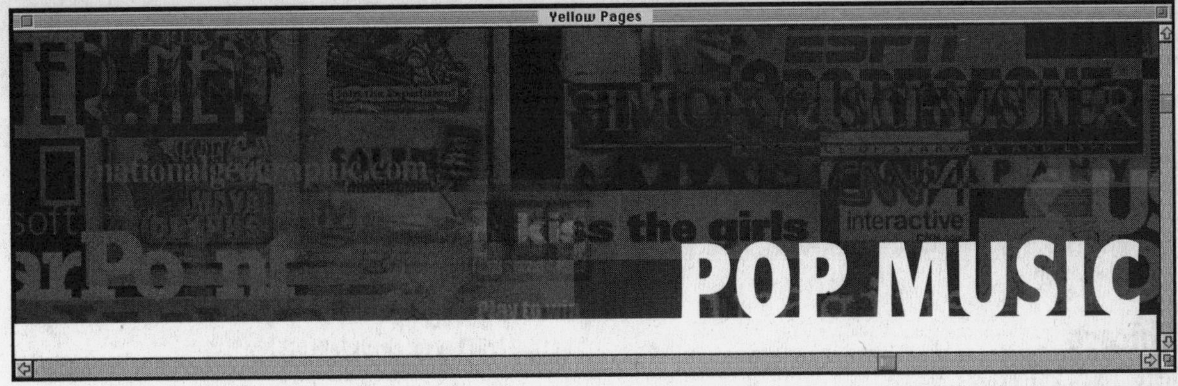

> You really should spend more time on your music, though. The youth of America are counting on you to show the way.
>
> *Frank Zappa in* Head *(1968)*

A House is not a Homepage

http://studentweb.tulane.edu/~mark/bacharach.html

Provides lyrics, biography, news, audio files, lyrics, chord sheets, and news about songwriter Burt Bacharach. Includes articles, pictures, and a list of hit songs. Also provides links to sites where Bacharach's music can be purchased.

ABBAnatic

http://www.sirius.com/~funnyguy/

Serves as a source for all the ABBA lyrics. Also includes pictures and links to other ABBA pages on the Web. Contains information on bootlegs and post-ABBA projects.

Alanis Morissette: Intellectual Intercourse

http://www.sgi.net/alanis/

Provides a home page dedicated to Canadian singer Alanis Morissette. Includes song lyrics, photos, articles, concert reviews, and interviews with Morissette. Also includes a chat room and links to other Alanis-related sites.

Rusted Root
http://www.RustedRoot.com/

and through the wire

http://www.intercenter.net/~jnu/pg/

Offers a collection of goodies about Peter Gabriel. Includes lyrics, pictures, and sound bytes. Also includes excerpts from his authorized biography, recent news, B-side titles, updates on his "Real World" theme park, and Mojo.

Beastie Boys

http://www.grandroyal.com/BeastieBoys/

Contains all conceivable data regarding this raunchy rap band, along with more that you probably haven't conceived of.

Bee Gees Main Page

http://www.beegees.net/main.htm

The ultimate disco group. A great site for true fans to enjoy the Brothers Gibb. Don't forget to order your Bee Gees calendar.

Blues Traveler Home Page

http://www.sgi.net/bluestraveler/

A really thorough site. It offers news, reviews, images, lyrics, tour dates, and more.

Boy George Home Page

http://www.umich.edu/~geena/boygeorge.html

Presents information about Boy George in the form of a fan magazine. Includes a discography with all lyrics, pop chart information, photo gallery, sound bytes, articles, and interviews.

Caribbean Soul: The Jimmy Buffett Parrothead Page

http://www.soasoas.com/

Includes resources for finding Jimmy Buffett on the Net. Offers tour dates, pictures, sound bytes, and the National Parrothead Raffle to benefit the Alzheimer's Association.

Chicago

http://www.chirecords.com/

The official Web site for the legendary music group Chicago. Learn about their music, what's new, talk to the band, look at images, and so on.

Chicago Nation

http://www.mcs.net/~nation/home/cpn.htm

Serves as a resource for Chicago-area fans and collectors about the Artist Formerly Known as Prince and his new wife, Mayte. Also shows the entire Former Prince community what Chicago has to offer.

The Clash

http://www.idiscover.co.uk/paul/rob/clash.html

Features a complete discography of all Clash albums and the lyrics to every track. Also offers a chart history of all the hits that made them big.

Counting Crows

http://countingcrows.com/indexx.html

An index of films, songs, and connections. Also a chance to win an autographed poster of the band.

ELP—Emerson, Lake & Palmer

http://bliss.berkeley.edu/elp/

Provides Emerson, Lake & Palmer (ELP) information. Includes online back issues of the ELP digest and links to other ELP sites.

Elvis Costello Home Page

http://www.east.isx.com/~schnitzi/elvis.html

Focused on Elvis Costello, this site includes mailing lists, concert reviews, lyrics, interviews, photos, guitar tablatures, and a complete discography. Also features a page of closely related artists.

Related Site

http://utopia.knoware.nl/users/ross/ross1.htm

Enigma

http://www.stud.his.no/~joarg/Enigma.html

Provides information on Enigma. Also provides a discography of the band and its founding father, Michael Cretu. Includes mailing list information, a picture gallery, and reviews of Enigma.

Everything But The Girl Web Site

http://raft.vmg.co.uk/ebtg/

This well designed and set up site provides a wide array of information about the English pop group Everything But The Girl. Includes biographies, tour dates, sound bytes, video clips, and more. Also includes tour diaries, a discussion forum, and a museum of guitars and synths.

Frankie Goes to Hollywood Fan Pages

http://www.cs.rulimburg.nl/~antal/fgth/fgth-home.html

Presents Frankie Goes to Hollywood, the band, online. Provides numerous FGTH resources.

Future Love Paradise: The Seal WWW Site

http://pantheon.cis.yale.edu/~ariedels/seal.html

Includes an image oasis, the Seal FAQ file, a lyric library, and more. Also includes transcriptions of online conferences with Seal.

Gaia: Olivia Newton-John Home Page

http://www-leland.stanford.edu/~clem/

Provides information about Olivia. Offers links to SoulKiss, the ONJ Internet Mailing list, movie information, videos, and a photo collection. Also offers information on how to join the fan club.

Gloria Estefan/MSM

http://www.almetco.com/estefan/gloria-1.html

Features Gloria and the Miami Sound Machine. Features background information, photo galleries, album lists, and where to read articles about the artist. Also contains video information, recent news, and fan club and mailing list information.

Related Sites

http://www.geocities.com/SunsetStrip/Palms/4892/indexmc.html

http://www.csoul.com/

Madonna Home Page

`http://www.mit.edu:8001/people/jwb/Madonna.html`

Serves as a means to finding any of a myriad of pages about Madonna on the Web. Includes a link to the Madonna Lyrics Archive, a complete discography, and Madonna's Top 10 List from the infamous Letterman episode. Also includes many pictures.

Men Without Hats: The (Unofficial) Home Page

`http://www.mit.edu:8001/people/tobye/mwh/mwh.html`

Offers all the latest discoveries about this '80s band. Includes a complete discography and a few pictures.

Mike Markowski's Beatles Page

`http://www.eecis.udel.edu/~markowsk/beatles/`

Includes a metaindex of other Beatles resources. Provides all the information you need about the Fab Four, including sounds, pictures, lyrics, merchandise, backwards messages, MIDI files, biographies, bootleg records, and close encounters stories. Even non-fans will enjoy this site.

Natalie Merchant Home Page

`http://www.primenet.com/~infomas/natalie.html`

Provides an unofficial home page for former 10,000 Maniacs lead singer and songwriter Natalie Merchant. Site includes song lyrics, touring information, and a biography. Also includes concert reviews and links to other related sites.

Nicks Fix

`http://web2.iadfw.net/jkinney/`

Features Stevie Nicks, singer of Fleetwood Mac. Contains Stevie news, album and video information, song lyrics, photos, and more. Also includes several links to other Stevie-related pages.

Not Lame Recording Company

`http://www.notlame.com/`

This site has reviews, features, gossip, a listening booth, and Not Lame label releases. Artists include The Rooks and 20 Cent Crush.

Related Sites

`http://www.umo.com/eltonjon.html`

`http://www.rockweb.com/bands/joan-osborne/`

`http://members.tripod.com/~jenilynn/`

Original Unoffical Elvis Home Page

`http://sunsite.unc.edu/elvis/elvishom.html`

Everything you ever wanted to know about Elvis. Reports recent sightings and lets you download some pictures and sounds. Brings Graceland to the Net. Includes lyrics, a collectors' page, a copy of Elvis' will, and links to other Elvis sites. Also lets you make an Elvis connection and find an Elvis pen pal on the Net.

Pete Lambie's Bruce Springsteen Page

`http://www.tiac.net/users/eldeekay/Bruce/`

Provides many pictures, lyrics, and more. Links to people who are willing to help you create your own bootleg collection and suggests a way to bring your bootlegs to life by making your own covers.

Planet Janet

`http://web.mit.edu/afs/athena/user/a/g/agoyo1/www/janet2.html`

Focuses on Janet Jackson. Includes the latest news, tour information, sounds, image gallery, lyrics, and more.

ROSS

`http://www.knoware.nl/music/diana/ross1.htm`

Focuses on singer Diana Ross and includes plenty of reminiscences about the Supremes. Also provides information on how to subscribe to *ROSS*, the official Diana Ross fan club magazine, as well as how to join the fan club.

Roxette: Home Page

`http://babylon.caltech.edu/roxette/roxette.html`

Offers some tour information, an interactive discography, and many pictures. Also includes information on soloists Marie Fredriksson, Per Gessle, and Gyllene Tider.

Rusted Root

`http://www.RustedRoot.com/`

One of most professional-looking sites on the Web. Great use of color and graphics, as well as good quality information for rustheads.

Related Sites

`http://www.uidaho.edu/~wils9231/kennyg/misc.html`

`http://www.celineonline.com/`

`http://www.geocities.com/WestHollywood/9200/`

Sheryl Crow

http://www.cicely.u-net.com/sheryl/news.html

A biography of this recent pop sensation. Concert dates, CD play list, and more.

Sinead O'Connor Home Page

http://www.engr.ukans.edu/~jrussell/music/sinead/sinead.html

Contains an official discography, a biography of Sinead, pictures (including two photos of Sinead with hair), quotations, and additional Sinead information. Serves as a master index to all sorts of goodies.

Sting—The Soul Pages

http://www.ot.com/sting/

Focuses on Sting. Provides the usual information such as lyrics, images, and sounds. Also provides information on Sting's non-musical projects, his work with charity organizations, and his artwork. Includes a personal letter to Sting from the Web page's author.

The Official Hootie and the Blowfish Web Site

http://www.hootie.com/

A good site with a distinctly collegiate feel. Check it out for more info on this longtime college party band.

The Phish.Net Web Site

http://www.netspace.org/phish/

All the Phish you want. FAQs, upcoming Phish events, Phish Tapes and setlists.

Toad the Wet Sprocket

http://www.prairienet.org/toad/

This site includes news, lyrics, scrapbooks, photo gallery, tour dates, and sound clips. Some nice background art too.

Tom Petty Unofficial Home Page

http://www.geocities.com/SunsetStrip/Alley/8813/

A fantastic site featuring tons of information about Tom Petty and the Heartbreakers.

Toni Braxton

http://www.xs4all.nl/~oslu/toni/main.htm

A site full of images, lyrics, and MIDIs of this sultry singer. Also includes her story, her news, and related links.

Tori Amos

http://www.mit.edu:8001/people/nocturne/tori.html

Includes a special link to Really Deep Thoughts, a mailing list digest about the music of Tori Amos. Also includes many pictures and sounds, and a few QuickTime videos.

The Paula Abdul Home Page

http://www.wam.umd.edu/~albert/paula.html

Highlights of her musical and fitness video careers by a very enthusiastic fan.

The Shawn Colvin Website at Plump Records

http://www.plump.com/colvin.htm

Sound clips, lyrics, lots of video and sound clips, and more. Also includes album art.

The Wallflowers Fan Club

http://www.trailerpark.com/phase2/jimd/wf.htm

Join the fan club or just visit the site. Fan club chat room, other Wallflowers links, lyrics, tour dates, and CD cover art.

Weird Al Yankovic

http://www.allamermusic.com/

Provides an unofficial fan home page for pop parody musician/comedian Weird Al Yankovic. Site includes a biography and information about upcoming releases. Also includes links to other Weird Al sites on the Internet.

Welcome to HIStory!

http://www.music.sony.com/Music/ArtistInfo/MichaelJackson.html

Serves as the official Sony page for Michael Jackson. Includes graphics and considerable information and depth of thought.

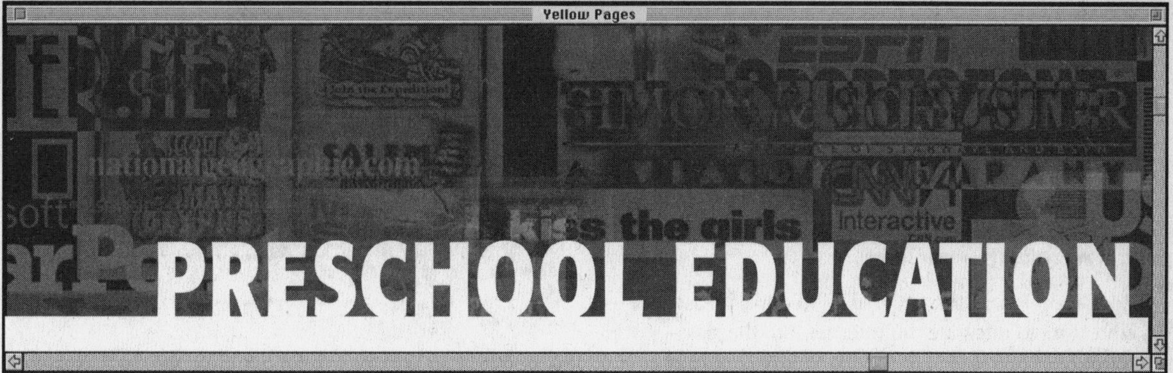

PRESCHOOL EDUCATION

A three year old child is a being who gets almost as much fun out of a fifty-six dollar set of swings as it does out of finding a small green worm.

Bill Vaughan

Child Care Connection for daycare and preschool
http://www.delphi.com/care/

IDEA BOX - Early Childhood Education and Activity Resources
http://www.worldvillage.com/ideabox/index.html

Perpetual Preschool Welcome Page
http://members.aol.com/aactchrday/index.html

Welcome to Knowledge Adventure!
http://www.adventure.com/

Accelerating Your Child

http://www.aycedu.com/

Site details the Accelerating Your Child interactive program of reading and math readiness that parents can follow with their preschool children. You can learn about the AYC staff and the program, see samples of program activities, subscribe to the program online, or enter the Kids Playground, with cool links to kids' sites.

Chateau Meddybemps

http://www.meddybemps.com/index.html

A whimsical site for parents and young children. Among the offerings for preschoolers are: a list of the best books for preschoolers and young readers, fun learning activities designed to develop math, observation, memory, and reasoning skills.

Child Care Connection for Daycare and Preschool

http://www.delphi.com/care/

A colorful, fun, and musical site filled with information, resources, and activities related to daycare and preschool. Geared especially toward child caregivers and the children they care for, with chats, hot links, related forums, and preschool pages. Check out the contents and jump from there.

Early Childhood Educator's and Family Web Corner

http://www.nauticom.net/www/cokids/

Bills itself as "The Place for All Things Early Childhood." Deals with items of interest to early-childhood educators and parents of young children. Offers articles, education debate, family pages, teacher pages, ChildChat sessions, and lots and lots of links. Follow the NEW link for interesting fare.

early childhood.com

http://www.earlychildhood.com/

Offers information for those who are interested in improving the education and experiences of young children. Take advantage of articles and other resources, seek advice from the experts, add to your collection of creative projects, and share your ideas with others in the early-childhood community.

Education World™ Where Educators Go To Learn

`http://www.education-world.com/`

Education World's stated goal is "to make it easy for educators to integrate the Internet into the classroom." Offers articles, lesson plans, school information, employment listings, links, and other resources for educators of preschoolers up through older children. Offers a search engine that searches 50,000 education-specific sites.

Helping Your Child Get Ready for School

`http://ericps.ed.uiuc.edu/readyweb/c4s/doepubs/getready/getready.html`

A Department of Education publication intended to assist you in developing your child's skills so that the child will be equipped to do well in school. Gives detailed instructions on various learning activities for children from birth through age 5. One example: Puppet Magic, instructions on making puppets and getting 1- to 2-year-olds to interact with them.

HOMESCHOOLING PRESCHOOLERS

`http://www.geocities.com/Athens/9094/`

This Web site is designed to help parents easily and inexpensively develop their own Christian preschool program. Covers all aspects of the development of two-year-olds through five-year-olds. You can find everything from resources, supplies, and teaching aids to sample lesson plans to homeschooling software. Plus, this site tackles some of the dilemmas facing homeschoolers and offers suggestions.

IDEA BOX - Early Childhood Education and Activity Resources

`http://www.worldvillage.com/ideabox/index.html`

A bright, informative site that focuses on the education of young children. This site is filled with goodies like projects and games, printable pages, kids' recipes, online stories, links for children, and "Coffee Talk."

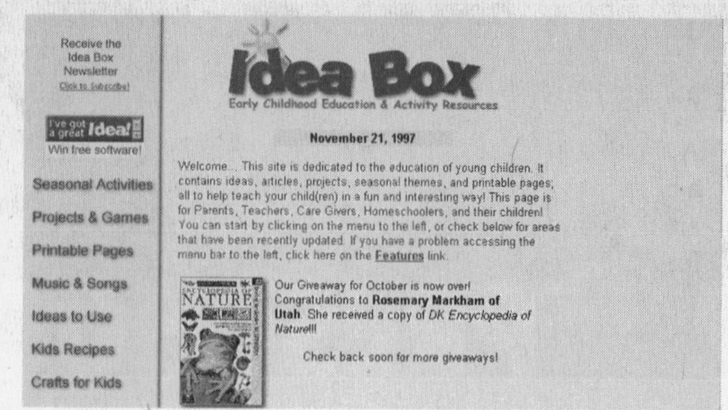

KINDERCARE

`http://www.kindercare.com/`

The home page of KinderCare Learning Centers, Inc., the largest preschool and child-care company in the U.S. You can learn about KinderCare and its programs, find a facility near you, or check out the offered links or the news articles provided.

Learning Fun for Preschoolers and Their Parents

`http://www.yavapai.com/sunny/`

Takes you to Sunny Hollow Press, a fun learning center for preschoolers and their parents and teachers. You'll find an online workshop, games to play, how-to articles, Biblically centered lesson plans, a home teaching kit for preschoolers, a homeschool kindergarten course, and a reading program. Plus, exchange thoughts and questions on the Sharing Page.

NAEYC Online

`http://www.naeyc.org/default.htm`

The site of NAEYC (the National Association for the Education of Young Children). Find out about NAEYC accreditation and membership, check out the searchable online catalog of early-childhood resources, and get information about upcoming conferences. There are pages geared toward parents, early-childhood professionals, and members only.

National Institute on Early Childhood Development and Education

`http://www.ed.gov/offices/OERI/ECI/index.html`

The Institute sponsors various research projects on early childhood. Find out about ECI, its research and development centers, its research and demonstration projects, and the ECI Working Group. Get ECI news or check out the list of related resources.

ONE CHILD, TWO LANGUAGES

http://www.onechild.com/

A site that details *ONE CHILD, TWO LANGUAGES*, a book geared toward teachers of preschoolers who are learning English as a second language. Offers a look at the book's Foreword and Preface, as well as Table of Contents. You can order online or get alternative ordering information.

Perpetual Preschool Welcome Page

http://members.aol.com/aactchrday/index.html

A sort of online preschool for you to explore. Various areas, such as Art Area, Quiet Area, and Science Area, offer ideas and suggestions for specific activities you can enjoy while teaching or playing with preschoolers. Post your own ideas too. A handy source of information.

Preschool Page

http://www.kidsource.com/kidsource/pages/Preschoolers.html

The Preschool area of KidsSource Online. Offers articles that provide information, tips, and suggested activities for children ages 3 to 6. Although part of the site's focus is on education, it also covers safety, recalls, new product information, health, and nutrition.

The Preschool Page

http://www.ames.net/preschool_page/

An award-winning site that children can visit with their parents. Cyberkids will like the features At the Zoo, Other Animals, Frogs and Worms, In the Garden, and At the Circus. And you can submit your child's artwork to be posted on the "Virtual Fridge."

ReadyWeb Home Page

http://ericps.ed.uiuc.edu/readyweb/readyweb.html

Information and resources sponsored by the ERIC Clearinghouse on Elementary and Early Childhood Education. Look into getting your child ready for school by turning to these U.S. Department of Education publications.

SuperKids Software Review

http://www.superkids.com/aweb/pages/reviews/early/3/elmopre/merge.shtml

Provides full reviews of educational software for early learners and older students. The reviews are written by teams of parents, teachers, and kids. Summary ratings of the titles include educational value, kid appeal, and ease of use. Want to know whether Reader Rabbit's Preschool is right for your little one? Want to see whether Elmo's Preschool is worth the money? Find out here.

Welcome to Knowledge Adventure!

http://www.adventure.com/

Sample various Knowledge Adventure educational products (the JumpStart line of software) at this intriguing site. Then get to the Online Store to buy what interests you. A great site that parents, young children, and teachers will love.

NEWSGROUPS

alt.daycare

alt.education

alt.parenting.solutions

misc.education

misc.kids

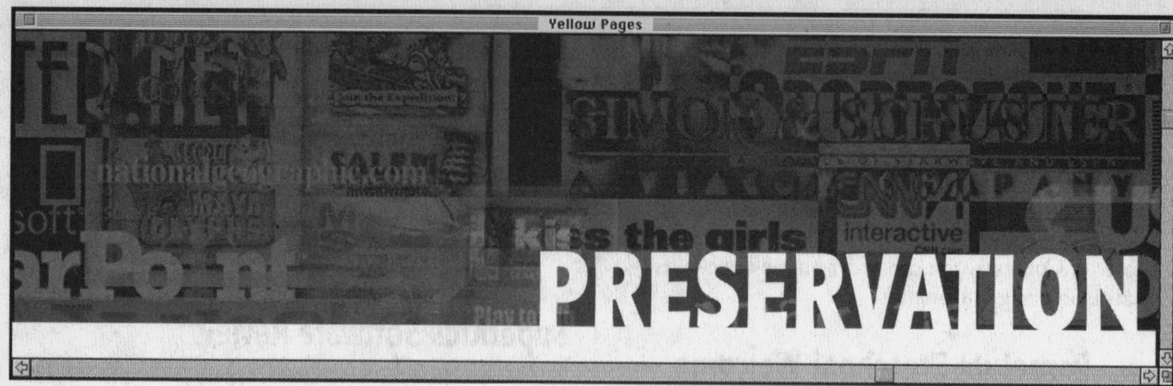

A
B
C
D
E
F
G
H
I
J
K
L
M
N
O
P
Q
R
S
T
U
V
W
X
Y
Z

Let us think of education as the means of developing our greatest abilities, because in each of us there is a private hope and dream which, fulfilled, can be translated into benefit for everyone and greater strength for our nation.

John F. Kennedy

The Air & Waste Management Association

http://www.awma.org/

The AWMA's purpose is "to enhance environmental knowledge and provide quality information on which to base environmental decisions." At their home site, one can find information on becoming a member and a calendar of events that includes annual meetings and workshops. Potential environmental scholars can find a list of schools that offer advanced degrees in environmental science here.

Earthwise Travels

http://www.teleport.com/~earthwyz/

Provides resources for travelers who want to be socially responsible. Explains why socially responsible travel is important, and what can be done to reverse the effects of negative tourism trends.

The Air & Waste Management Association
http://www.awma.org/

Environmental Defense Fund
http://www.edf.org

Greenpeace USA
http://www.greenpeaceusa.org/

Rainforest Preservation Foundation
http://www.flash.net/~rpf/US Environmental

Environmental Protection Agency
http://www.epa.gov/

NRP TOP PICKS

Environmental Defense Fund

http://www.edf.org

The group that formed in 1967 to fight the use of DDT is still going and is more than 300,000 strong. They need your help in addressing what the feel are the nine most critical environmental issues of the '90s. Check out their site to find out what those are and what you can do.

Environmental Protection Agency's Office of Water

http://www.epa.gov/ow

This beautifully produced site explores American water resources with an emphasis on the quality of our nation's water features powerful searching, imagery, animation, kid's pages, valuable publications, and informative hot links.

Fragile Legacy

http://www.npsc.nbs.gov/resource/distr/others/sdrare/sdrare.htm

The endangered, threatened, and rare animals of South Dakota. The site contains pictures, maps, and descriptions of these endangered birds, fish, insects, reptiles and mammals. Information is also provided for what you should do if you happen to see one of the animals on this list.

Greenpeace USA

http://www.greenpeaceusa.org/

As Chief Seattle said in 1854, "The Earth does not belong to us; we belong to the Earth...We did not weave the web of life; we are merely a strand in it. Whatever we do to the web, we do to ourselves." Here you can find out what Greenpeace is all about and get yourself involved in saving our planet.

Headwaters Forest

http://www.igc.apc.org/headwaters/

Headwaters forest is the last unprotected ancient redwood forest on Earth and is about to be cut down by loggers. Get background information on the forest and learn what you can do to help prevent its demise. Includes a list of influential people you can write to for help.

International Greens

http://www.dru.nl/maatschappij/politiek/groenen/intlhome.htm

Read about the developments of green political parties worldwide from 1994–1996, and what the agendas are for the remainder of 1996–1998. Also gives overviews of all green political parties worldwide, sorted by continent.

Rainforest Preservation Foundation

http://www.flash.net/~rpf/

Rainforest Preservation Foundation is a non-profit organization, and a federally registered 501(c)(3) charity that is dedicated to preserving vast areas of rainforest in the Amazon basin.

United States Environmental Protection Agency

http://www.epa.gov/

At the EPA home page, you can access documents such as official EPA press releases, the EPA Journal and more. All EPA programs are documented online, from "Acid Rain" to "Wetlands." Through this page you can send your comments directly to the EPA, as well as apply for employment with them.

Welcome to Sherwood

http://www.sherwoodinitiative.co.uk/

Sherwood Forest, once the great woodland hideout of the famed Robin Hood, is becoming a wasteland. Learn about the Sherwood Initiative and what it's doing to preserve this famous woodland.

The Whale Museum's Orca Adoption Program

http://whale-museum.org

What better way to "save the whales" than by adopting one? By adopting Ralph, Saratoga, Missy, Princess Angeline, Deadhead, Raven, or any of the number of orcas that swim the waters of Puget Sound and southern British Columbia, you'll be supporting Orca research and education.

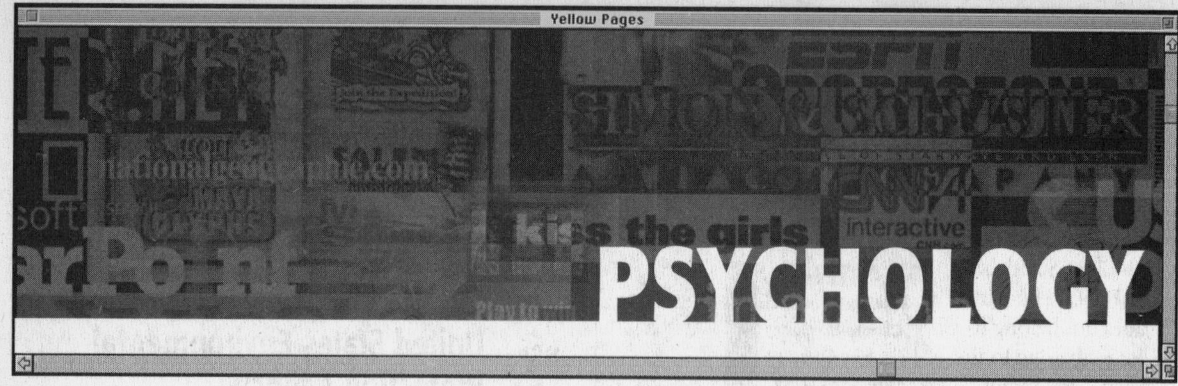

Our minds can work for us or against us at any given moment. We can learn to accept and live with the natural psychological laws that govern us, understanding how to flow with life rather than struggle against it. We can return to our natural state of contentment.

Richard Carlson

Behavior Online

http://www.behavior.net/

Excellent site for behavior analysis. This site offers links to an editorial corner, resources, and organizations. You can also find ongoing discussions about anything from Gestalt theory to organizational development to classical Adlerian psychotherapy. Before you get too serious, though, check out the Diversions section.

Related Sites

http://www.geocities.com/Athens/Parthenon/6469/main.html

http://www.onlinepsych.com/home.html

http://www.psychcrawler.com/

Internet Mental Health
http://www.mentalhealth.com/

JungWeb
http://www.onlinepsych.com/jungweb/

Cognitive and Psychological Sciences on the Internet

http://matia.stanford.edu/cogsci/

An overall resourceful site that links to academic programs, organizations, journals and magazines, newsgroups, publishers, software, and much more—all related to psychology. Learn more about Essex University's Data Archive or join a discussion list.

Cognitive Science Discussion List (COGSCI)

http://coglist.cogsci.kun.nl/index.html

Focuses on cognitive science topics such as connectionism, philosophy, and artificial intelligence. Offers plenty of links to related information on the Web and in listservs. Also check out similar discussion sites and the COGSCI archives.

FreudNet

http://plaza.interport.net/nypsan/

Brill Library's site that focuses on Freud and psychoanalytical studies. The links and information here are many and are very useful for students and professionals alike. Check out the Sigmund Freud and the Freud archives, from which you can read many of Freud's writings, including *The Interpretation of Dreams.*

Related Sites

http://www.geocities.com/RainForest/Vines/6074/psyhohis.htm

http://www.uc.edu/~baimem/

Health Psychology and Rehabilitation

http://www.healthpsych.com/

Focuses on psychomedical disorders and recovery, with information on medicine, therapy, pain and management, and rehabilitation. Offers a page of statistical information ("factoids") from studies done about health/psychology disorders. Also has a forum in which professionals can discuss their points of view about various disorders. This page also offers a few links for further help on the subject.

Internet Mental Health

http://www.mentalhealth.com/

This site is visually and textually appealing. Find what you need to know about mental health, including the most common mental health disorders, diagnoses, and most-prescribed medications. Also check out the several links to related sites and information. This site also has an online magazine that has editorials, articles, letters, and stories of recovery.

JungWeb

http://www.onlinepsych.com/jungweb/

Great site at which you can find anything Jung-related that you need. Get information on listservs and newsgroups, link to related sites, and browse more than 300 books about Jung. You can join a discussion area, take personality tests (including the Meyers Briggs Test - Keirsey Temperament Sorter), and join a mailing list. This site also links to several dream-analysis Web sites.

Psychology.net

http://www.psychology.net/

This site offers help in two areas—psychology and the Internet. Get a unique email account or find newsgroups related to psychology. Download RealAudio or check out some psychology humor. Find out what's new in university psychology departments or download the software for video conferencing. It's all here!

PsycNet

http://www.unipissing.ca/psyc/psycsite.htm

Sponsored by Nipissing University's Department of Psychology, this site serves as a resource for those interested in the science of psychology. Its vast number of links include those to information sources, listservs and newsgroups, downloadable psychology-related software, university and student centers, a message board, research sites, and a chat room.

Psychology Web Archive

http://swix.ch/clan/ks/CPSP1.htm

This site serves as a launch-pad to social psychology links including articles and references, libraries and journals, Gopher sites, and software. Also is a German version of the site.

Quantitative Study of Dreams

http://zzyx.ucsc.edu/~dreams/

This site is from the University of California, Santa Cruz, and offers analytical studies of dreams and why we dream. Offers a scientific approach to researching dreams. See the DreamSAT database, which is downloadable. This site also includes links to tools, a look at Jungian and Freudian studies, and research examples (including case studies and variables such as norms).

School Psychology

http://www.bcpl.lib.md.us/~sandyste/school_psych.html

Good resource for school-related psychology programs. The links are vast and include mental retardation, eating disorders, substance abuse, the gifted and talented, mood disorders, and much more. This site also offers links to journals and articles, as well as many links to related sites.

Self-Help and Psychology Magazine

http://www.cybertowers.com/selfhelp/

E-zine that has more than 75 professionals who contribute to its issues. Offers articles, classifieds, reviews, banner ads, and many links to related information. This site also has psychtoons and postcards. You may subscribe to a free newsletter, too.

ShrinkTank

http://www.shrinktank.com/

This site is great for what it offers, including links to articles and discussions, other related sites, and online personality and psychological tests. This site features tons of downloadable software, most of which is straightforward and of the self-help category.

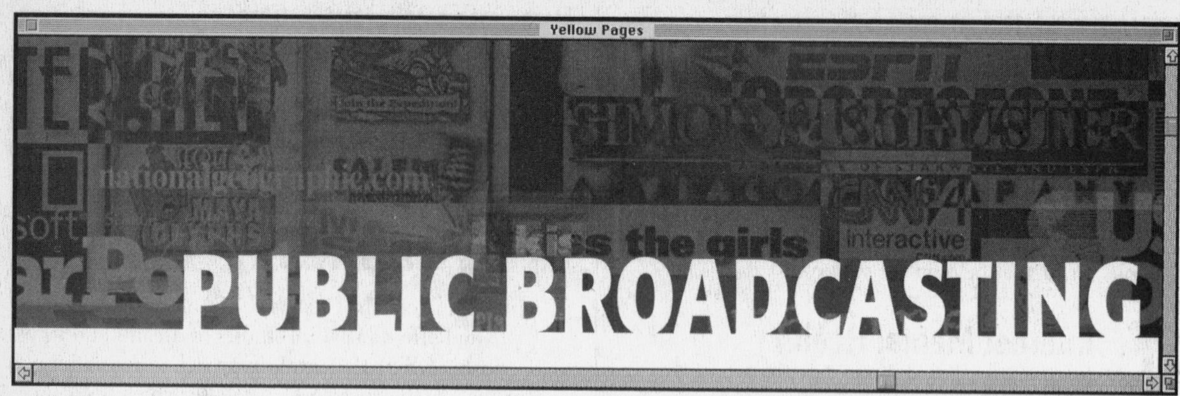

A B C D E F G H I J K L M N O P Q R S T U V W X Y Z

> National Public Radio's vision is to serve the public as the leading provider of high quality news, information, and cultural programming worldwide.
>
> *NPR Vision Statement*
> *(http://www.npr.org/inside/vision.html)*

All Things Considered

http://kcrw.org/c/atc.html

This site provides the current day's summaries of the topics covered on the National Public Radio program *All Things Considered.* You can choose to listen to the entire program or just the topic you're interested in (use a RealAudio Player). You can also see pictures of the ATC hosts, hear the theme music, and find out how to write to the program.

Related Sites

- http://www.geocities.com/Hollywood/Hills/6453/
- http://www.current.org/cm/cm1.html
- http://kera.org/
- http://www.itvs.org/PTV1.html
- http://www.mpbc.org/
- http://www.aspenonline.com/AspenTimes/dir/95/Jan/week4/Opinion.html
- http://www.pcii.net/~udarrell/publicbrcritique.html
- http://the-tech.mit.edu/V114/N66/pbs.66c.html
- http://www.cpb.org/directory/states.html
- http://www-wbgu.bgsu.edu/

ALS: Adult Learning Service Online Homepage
http://www.pbs.org/learn/als/

cartalk.msn.com
http://www.cartalk.com/

PBS Online
http://www.pbs.org/

ALS: Adult Learning Service Online Homepage

http://www.pbs.org/learn/als/

ALS is for both teachers and students. Educators get programming resources and a faculty referral network. Institutions license the right to record programs as they're transmitted via satellite, and they can then use the tapes for educational purposes. Live satellite events give you interactive programs featuring Q&As with nationally known experts. Students can preview and enroll in telecourses and get college credit. In a telecourse, you learn by watching TV programs rather than attending on-campus lectures. You register with a college just as you would for a regular course, study from textbooks, complete assignments, and take exams. Telecourse catalogs are provided online with all the info you'll need. Then, just click a state on the map to find local colleges that offer telecourses. You can also read current articles and back issues of *Agenda,* the PBS ALS online magazine.

The American Experience

http://www.pbs.org/wgbh/pages/amex/

The American Experience is a PBS show about the people and events that shaped America. Some of its programs have included "FDR," "The Kennedys," "Malcolm X: Make It Plain," "Amelia Earhart," "The Great San Francisco Earthquake," "D-Day," "Geronimo," "The Battle Over Citizen Kane," and "The Donner Party." This site gives you a complete listing of its programs for all 10 seasons, along with descriptions and ordering info for videotapes. You can also subscribe to online services, such as *This Week in American History*, the Arthur Channel, and NOVA Online. The Presidents' Teachers' Guide offers activities and resources to help teachers integrate core themes, events, and ideas from the American presidency into the classroom. The Web Site Archives provide pictures and partial transcripts of programs on the show.

cartalk.msn.com

`http://www.cartalk.com/`

You can hear selected replays of the National Public Radio program *Car Talk*, as well as the Weekly Puzzler, at this site. Find out where to tune in to hear Car Talk on NPR stations across the country by searching the directory. You can submit questions in the Ask Tom and Ray section and read answers to others' questions—there's a complete index. Read the latest *Car Talk* column and check out Tom and Ray's mail. There's also a Classifieds section, where you can buy and sell vehicles or just meet other Car Talk fans. Be sure to check out the Car Talk FAQ. This site includes many more features, useful tidbits, and humorous sections.

Current Online: news about public broadcasting

`http://www.current.org/`

This site features selected content from the biweekly newspaper *Current*, which covers public TV and public radio in the U.S. You'll also get links that lead to collected articles on specific topics, such as Children's TV, Religious Programs, Federal and Nonfederal Funding, and more. You'll also get updates on jobs in public broadcasting. Includes an updated guide to the acronyms used for organizations and technologies in the electronic media and public broadcasting.

EduROCK—Reliable Online Curricular Knowledge

`http://www.edurock.com/`

EduROCK is a search engine that maintains a database of educational-related and family-oriented sites. It is an easy way to find Web sites that you're interested in. You use the searchable index of the database to find the name, description, and link of the site you want. EduROCK awards the Public Broadcasting Information Services' (PBIS) seal of approval to Web sites that meet EduROCK's criteria. You'll also learn about the criteria for adding a site to EduROCK.

National Public Broadcasting Archives

`http://www.lib.umd.edu/UMCP/NPBA/npba.html`

The NPBA, from the University of Maryland, brings together the records of major non-commercial broadcasts in the U.S. It offers info and documents on items such as Children's Television Workshop (CTW), America's Public Television Stations (APTS), National Public Radio (NPR), Public Broadcasting Service (PBS), and more. You can also visit this site to read the personal papers of people who have made significant contributions to public broadcasting. Or, you can browse the extensive reference library that contains basic studies of the broadcasting industry, rare pamphlets, and journals on relevant topics, as well as clippings from the PBS press-clipping service. NPBA also offers an audio and video program record of public broadcasting's national production and support centers (NAEB, NPR, CPB/Annenberg) and local stations WETA, WAMU-FM, and Maryland Public Television (MPT).

NOVA Online

`http://www.pbs.org/wgbh/nova/`

Check out the TV schedule for the PBS show NOVA. Read transcripts from the current and past shows. You can make comments and read others' comments on certain programs that aired on the show. Includes tips and ideas for teachers. Visit the shop to buy NOVA books, transcripts, videos, and other products. There's even a Help section in case you're having any technical difficulties while using the site.

NPR—National Public Radio Online

`http://www.npr.org/`

This site lets you listen to NPR news on the hour in RealAudio 14.4 or 28.8. Or, try NetShow 28.8 or higher. View summaries of programs and then listen to them. Or, check out some of the special highlighted stories that you might have missed. Check out the info on the news magazines, talk shows, and cultural and information stories you can listen to—among them, All Things Considered, Morning Edition, Car Talk, and Jazz from Lincoln Center.

OPB On-Line

`http://www.opb.org/`

This is the site of Oregon Public Broadcasting. You'll get TV and radio program previews here. One of the popular TV shows is Oregon Field Guide; you'll see descriptions of upcoming episodes for the year. Northwest News gives you national news at the top of

A B C D E F G H I J K L M N O P Q R S T U V W X Y Z

each hour, 24 hours a day. OPB provides the latest regional news during Morning Edition, Talk of the Nation, The World, and All Things Considered. Or, listen to OPB's daily news magazine Oregon Considered for in-depth coverage of regional stories. Seven Days is OPB's local public affairs program (it's also on OPB Radio). The show brings together a panel of reporters and editors from around Oregon to discuss the major stories of the week. You'll also get Sesame Street, Wishbone, National Geographic, and other popular PBS shows. In the OPB and Me section, you and your kids can get profiles of famous authors and artists, as well as interesting science facts.

PBS Online

http://www.pbs.org/

Check out the PBS picks. Click any program title listed to get info on that show. Or, check your local listings—just click your state and city (the site supplies you with the name of your local station). Click any date on the calendar to get a full listing of programs and times. Find out what's up with the *Sesame Street* gang, *Mister Rogers' Neighborhood, The Magic School Bus, Barney & Friends, Where In Time Is Carmen Sandiego?, Arthur, Wishbone, Bill Nye the Science Guy, The NewsHour With Jim Lehrer, Washington Week in Review, Wall $treet Week, Great Performances, The World of National Geographic, Mystery!, Charlie Rose,* and more. You'll also get *PBS Previews*, a free, weekly, online newsletter.

PBS Scienceline

http://www.pbs.org/learn/scienceline/

Scienceline, a professional development resource for science teachers (grades K-12), is a collaborative effort of PBS and the National Science Teachers Association. Scienceline participants observe teachers in classrooms across the U.S. who are demonstrating effective science teaching. You enroll in the program for one year of professional development. By using modules that incorporate videotape and online learning communities, you'll explore standards-based science teaching with Scienceline colleagues. Scienceline enables you to form professional networks where you can get help, support, ideas, strategies, and reassurance as you facilitate active student learning. See the site for Scienceline fees.

TechnoPolitics Home

http://www.technopolitics.com/

TechnoPolitics is public TV's news-making series on the politics of science, technology, and the environment. It appears for one-half hour each week on public TV stations across the country. Read a complete transcript of the most recent program, or search through the transcripts of all the programs. You can also view a sample clip of the show. In Front Page, newsmakers and the players directly involved in the technopolitical debate are interviewed. In Trade Off, spokespeople for contending interests are pitted against each other in mini-debates. In TP Report, print reporters from leading publications contribute to stories with technopolitical impact.

Welcome to KAOS!

http://www.kaosradio.org/

KAOS is a radio station located at Evergreen State College in Olympia, Washington. It offers traditional and popular music of America and the world, including Jazz, Classical, Swing, Blues, Soul, Rap, R&B, Celtic, new acoustic and electronic music, Native American, Spanish language, rock, and Broadway music. You'll also hear comedy, radio theater, stories from *Pacifica News* and the *Monitor Press*, and news on public affairs. The site includes an on-air schedule, bios of the programmers, and descriptions of the programs. You'll also see KAOS's listing of the current top 30 songs.

World Radio Network Online

http://www.wrn.org/

WRN offers a global perspective on current world events and updates you on news from your homeland. It also covers arts and culture, music, sports, science, and more. WRN via cable, satellite, local AM/FM, and the Internet is used as an educational resource by schools, colleges, and universities. Find out how to hear the broadcasts in your area. You'll also find WRN schedules and learn how to listen to live newscast audio streams in RealAudio and StreamWorks 24 hours a day from 25 of the world's leading public and international broadcasters.

FTP SITE

ftp://ftp.pbs.org/

PUBLISHERS, PUBLISHING HOUSES, AND PRESSES

The man who reads nothing at all is better educated than the man who reads nothing but newspapers.

Thomas Jefferson

Academic Press

http://www.apnet.com/

AP publishes text books on subjects ranging from medicine to economics. AP Professional publishes computer books. The site offers information about their new publications and insight into future releases. Also has a book catalog and textbook shop.

Addison Wesley Longman

http://www2.awl.com/corp/

Addison-Wesley Longman publishes text books and programs for English as a second language. The site is frame-based and provides information about the publishing company and the published titles. The online store lets you purchase books via the Internet.

Alldata

http://www.alldata.tsb.com/

Home site for electronic automotive repair publisher. Provides locations of Alldata repair shops, automotive chat room, recall notices, and technical service bulletin titles for vehicles. Also includes employment opportunities with Alldata, and an extensive link sheet to various automotive sites.

MacMillan Computer Publishing
http://www.mcp.com/

Allen & Unwin Independent Book Publishers

http://www.allen-unwin.com.au

Allen & Unwin is Australia's largest independent book publisher, with links to software, kid's books, academic books, and "great reads."

Association of American University Presses

http://aaup.pupress.princeton.edu/

Features an index of university presses and includes a searchable index of books.

Beach Holme Publishing

http://www.beachholme.bc.ca/

Provides company background, author biographies, bookseller information, and submission guidelines for this Canadian publisher. Beach Holme publishes books in many areas from fiction to children's books. Includes *Swiftsure* online magazine and spiritual titles.

Bioenergetics Press

http://www.msn.fullfeed.com/rschenk/bioecat.html

Publishes books about men's and gender issues. Provides samples of their books, a catalog of tapes and books available, and ordering information. Includes links to sites and newsgroups that deal with men's issues.

A B C D E F G H I J K L M N O P Q R S T U V W X Y Z

Blackwell Science

http://www.blacksci.co.uk/

Publishes medical and scientific journals and books. Provides company news, catalog, upcoming publications information, and service listings of their products. Includes links to all of Blackwell Science's sites world wide.

Blue Heron Publishing

http://www.teleport.com/~bhp/

Provides company profile, catalog, author background, and submissions guidelines for Blue Heron Publishing. Publishes fiction and nonfiction books for adults and children. Catalog also includes information titles for writers, librarians, and teachers.

Bookish

http://www.bic.org.uk/bic/

U.K.-based Book Industry Communications home page that provides links to over 100 publishers and numerous links with booksellers, library suppliers, and service suppliers. A very valuable site for anyone doing business or research on United Kingdom publishers and book industry.

Books @ Random

http://www.randomhouse.com/

Random House Publisher's home page with extensive links to different Random House imprints, such as Kids @ Random, contests, books exerpts, best sellers, and special offers.

BookWire Home Page

http://www.bookwire.com/

This is a fabulous site for authors, publishers, and wholesalers to get the scoop on the book business. Includes indices of book and publishing-related sites, a reading room, the comic of the day, best seller lists, and book reviews.

BradyGAMES Strategy Guides

http://www.superlibrary.com/brady/

Includes a combination of strategies, how-to information, game background, editorial content, valuable "inside" information, interviews with game creators, and more.

Cambridge University Press

http://www.cup.cam.ac.uk/

Features information about the publisher and its different publications. Offers ordering and contact information and other online services.

Carswell Publishing

http://www.carswell.com

Publishes professional books, pamphlets, electronic media, catalogs, and other documents for the legal, medical, banking and corporate fields. Provides company history, services offered, listings of published items, clients served, and additional product information.

CatchWord Ltd

http://www.catchword.co.uk/

Catchword provides electronic publishing for academic journals and scholarly studies. This company is an Internet publishing provider with sites throughout the world.

ChemTech Publishing

http://www.io.org/~chemtec/

Publishes journals, books, and software that deal with the chemical polymers industry. Provides full catalog of products offered and links to related sites. Includes submission guidelines and ordering information.

Cold Spring Harbor Laboratory Press

http://www.cshl.org/about_cshl_press.html

Publishes scholarly journals, books, manuals, and videotapes. Topics covered include biology, genetics, neurobiology, and closely related sciences. Includes information for publishing proposals.

Colorado Independent Publisher's Association

http://www.cipabooks.com/

CIPA is an organization concerned with self-publishing. The site provides information on cooperative marketing and independent publishing. The site provides links to members' sites by book title, subject, or by publishers. Includes contact and membership information. Also includes small publishing links.

Conari Press

http://www.conari.com/index.html

Conari Press publishes the "Random Acts of Kindness" series. The site includes company catalog with cover art and book descriptions. Produces self-spirituality and emotional exploration books. Includes mailing list and ordering information.

David R. Godine, Publisher

http://www.godine.com/

David R. Godine, Publisher, is a literary publisher based in New England. Publishes fiction, essays, non-fiction, art, and books about books. The site provides information about David Godine, an online catelog, and a news link.

Dream Garden Press

http://www.dreamgarden.com/

Provides home site for Dream Garden Press based in Salt Lake City, Utah. Specializes in regional-themed books about Utah and the American West. Includes company catalog, upcoming titles, and ordering information.

East View Publications, Inc. Home Page

http://www.eastview.com/

Offers books, magazines, CDs, maps, microforms and newspapers published in Central Europe, the CIS, and Russia. Offers online delivery of newspapers.

Electronic Journals Ltd.

http://www.electronicjournals.com.uk

Electronic Journals Ltd. is a new, wholly electronic publishing house. Their customized software can publish any document at any price required. Publish academic journals and non-exclusive consultancy reports. Clients with a subscription can download online, fully desktop-published material immediately.

Elsevier Science

http://www.elsevier.nl/

Elsevier Sciencepublishes books about science topics. This beautiful multimedia site provides easy access to information about Elsevier, including customer services, news briefs, book lists, and contact information.

Harper Collins Publishers Home Page

http://www.harpercollins.com

Harper Collins online. Includes information about best sellers, new releases, and an online bookstore.

Harvard Advocate Home Page

http://hcs.harvard.edu/~advocate/

The *Harvard Advocate* is the oldest college literary magazine. This site publishes the online version of the magazine. Offers many links to other online literary resources.

Her Majesty's Stationary Office

http://www.hmso.gov.uk/

Her Majesty's Stationary Office was privatized in 1986 and publishes British royal government information under the name The Stationary Office, Ltd. This publisher specializes in producing the Queen's publications, such as Acts of Parliament. This is the online source of those documents.

International Data Group (IDG.Com)

http://www.idg.com/

This is the corporate Web site for IDG Worldwide. The site provides links to IDG's myriad electronic divisions, as well as its book publishing arm, IDG Books. The site offers news about IDG corporate operations and links to related sites. IDG Books includes the PCWorld and MacWorld imprints as well as the Dummies Press.

Indiana University Press Journals Division

http://www.indiana.edu/~iupress/journals

Non-profit scholarly publisher of the journals *Camera Obscura, differences, History and Memory, Hypatia, Israel Studies, Black Renaissance, Jewish Social Studies, Journal of Women's History, Journal of Modern Literature, NWSA Journal, Religion and American Culture, Research in African Literatures,* and *Victorian Studies.*

John Wiley and Sons, Inc. Publishers

http://www.wiley.com/

Publishing house that develops, publishes and sells both printed and electronic media for educational, professional, scientific, technical, and consumer uses. Features information about the company, press releases, worldwide links, and online products and services.

Karoma Publishers

http://www.infop.com/karoma/

Technical publishers and developers for your business needs. Get your Guide to EDI and International Electronic Trading, links to what's new, learn how to showcase your company.

Koinonia House Interactive

http://www.khouse.org/

Christian book publisher online. Includes information about books and magazines and offers links to other Christian sites on the Internet.

M.E. Sharpe

http://www.mesharpe.com/

A book and journal publisher specializing in the areas of Asian and Russian studies, economics, history and political science. Browse their book listing, which includes the following categories: anthropology, business, education, health journalism, legal studies, literature, philosophy, religion, and much more. Ordering information and manuscript submission guidelines included.

Macmillan Computer Publishing

http://www.mcp.com/

Macmillan Publishing presents this site as a resource to the many computer books it publishes. Provides information on books published by Que, SAMS, New Riders, Brady, The Waite Group, and Hayden, and enables you to review sample chapters of the latest computer books and order online. Enables you to subscribe to *The SuperLibrary Newsletter*, a monthly that offers a wide variety of articles and features. Contains hundreds of Macmillan programs and software packages.

Manic D Press

http://www.sirius.com/~manicd/

Smaller publishing house dealing with books and comics. Features online ordering and a listing of bookstores carrying their works.

McGraw-Hill College Division

http://www.tmhe.com

Publishes printed and multimedia educational products for businesses and schools. Includes online catalog broken down into various imprints and background information. Also provides site search index and complementary copy request forms.

MIT Press

http://www-mitpress.mit.edu/

Offers an online bookstore, search information, journals and textbook information. Also features sale items and links to other sites of interest. Gives previews to new and future releases.

MNE-AESOP(Martin Nobel Editorial)

http://www.martinob.demon.co.uk/mnel.htm

Based in Oxford (UK), Martin Noble Editorial, established for 30 years, offers a wide range of editorial services including editing, proofreading, indexing, novelizations, copy writing, research, and much much more, for any kind of text in paper or electronic publishing. With AESOP (All Editorial Services Online for Publishers) any editorial service can now be ordered online. This site includes a complete directory/guide to editorial services; Index of all editorial services; Graphic chart of how AESOP/MNE can help you at every stage of the publishing process; AESOP/MNE editing style guide; and full details of AESOP's Background, Clients, Publications, Novels and novelizations (including *Who Framed Roger Rabbit, Ruthless People*, and *Tin Men*), Non-fiction publications, and Subject areas.

Monkeywrench Press

http://iww.org/~monkeywrench/index.html

Monkeywrench Press online. Caters to the anarchist in all of us. Features information about authors and current books.

Multimedia Newsstand home

http://mmnewsstand.com/index.html

Offers a collection of subscription information and forms for more than 500 magazines, books, and videos. Also contains a number of different contests sponsored by the various magazines.

Natural History Book Service Home Page

http://www.nhbs.co.uk/

British online bookstore. Focuses on natural history, books on environmental issues, and science books. Provides information in English, Spanish, Italian and German.

O'Reilly Home Page

http://www.oreilly.com/

O'Reilly & Associates publishes highly technical computer books on programming languages and other high-level information. The site provides an online bookstore and information about new pubications, as well as contact information.

Oxford University Press

http://www.oup.co.uk/

Features information about Oxford university Press and its publications. Also includes previews of future titles and links to other Oxford University Press Web sites.

Patrick Cramer Publisher

http://www.cramer.ch/

Patrick Cramer publishes reference books and catalogues raisonnés of works made for publication by major 20th century artists. He also publishes scholarly historical essays. Besides his activity as author and publisher, Patrick Cramer runs an art gallery where he shows contemporary artists. You can choose to browse through the book pile, or view the artist currently showing at the Patrick Cramer Gallery.

Peachpit Press

http://www.peachpit.com/

Provides home page and online ordering for Peachpit Press. Specializes in computer books from personal PC use to online communication service books. Includes indexed catalog, author background, upcoming titles and discussion forums.

Penguin USA

http://www.penguin.com/usa/

Features sections devoted to new titles, a complete reading room, academic books, electronic publishing, and information about Penguin Books.

PennWell Publishing Company

http://www.pennwell.com/

Produces a wide array of magazines, books, newsletters, and trade journals that cover many industries including petroleum, electric utlities, computers, communications, and information technologies. Includes complete company catalog indexed by industry, ordering, and contact information.

pgrmli.txt

http://www.library.nwu.edu:80/media/resources/pgrmli.txt

Burrelle's Transcripts, a leading transcription company for more than 20 years, provides transcripts and, where indicated, videotapes, of more than 75 news, public affairs, health, and talk shows.

Prentice Hall Home Page

http://www.prenhall.com/

Publishes college textbooks and technical books. Offers Prentice Hall's online catalog of books and information, as well as links to their Gopher site and to fun Internet sites, including other Viacom sites. Contains a searchable database by title, author, ISBN number, and subject.

Publishers' Catalogues Home Page

http://northern.lights.com:80/publisher/

Provides a listing of publishers from all over the world and their home pages, indexed by country.

Putnam Berkley Online

http://www.mca.com/putnam/

Provides home site for Putnam Berkley and their related imprints. Includes featured books and a search index of all titles published. Also includes author profiles, book samples, and ordering information

A B C D E F G H I J K L M N O P Q R S T U V W X Y Z

Reed Books Web Site

http://www.reedbooks.co.uk

Reed Books is one of the world's leading publishers of adult and children's fiction and non-fiction books. The site provides links to each of Reed's imprints as well as descriptions of Reed's current catalog.

Reed Education

http://www.reedbooks.com.au/index.html

Provides home site for Reed Educational Publishing and imprints. Beautifully designed site with access to Reed's various imprints and links to kid's places, hot topics, and corporate information.

Resolution Business Press

http://www.respress.com/

Publishes books dealing with the Internet. Includes company catalog, book descriptions, cover art, and ordering information. Also provides links to many family-oriented sites on the WWW.

Saint Mary's Press

http://wwwsmp.smumn.edu/

Publishes Christian religious texts and related books for English and Spanish markets. Includes indexed catalog and links to other religious sites. Provides resources and contact information.

Cyber Publishing Japan

http://www.toppan.co.jp

Cyber Publishing Japan publishes magazines for children, comic magazines, weeklies, dictionaries, encyclopedia, and art books. Features Japanese links, books, and magazines. Provides English and Japanese language versions.

Small Helm Press

http://www.sonic.net/~smllhelm/shp.html

Publisher of nonfiction books. Small Helm Press publishes books on contemporary topics, China, Marx, and faith. The site provides links to author descriptions, a link to thoughts on Petaluma, California, and a description of how to reach Small Helm.

Solo Publications

http://www.solopublications.com

Solo Publications publishes books on the environment, Northern California, poetry, and pottery. The Solo Press also publishes the *Central California Poetry Journal.* The site is not well organized or easy to navigate, but all of the standard publishing information is available.

Springer-Verlag

http://www.springer.de/

Publishing house devoted to scientific, medical, and technical writings. Features press releases, catalogs, and samples of different works. Also contains links to its national Web sites.

Thomas Jefferson University Press

http://tjup.truman.edu/connections/connections.html

A publisher of various scholarly and trade books in such diverse areas as History, Philosophy, Education, Sociology, Literary Criticism, and Poetry. The site provides links to ordering information, the T.S. Elliot Prize, information about their catalog of books, authors, and many related links. The site was under construction and contained links without content.

Time Life Explorer

http://www.timelife.com/

Contains a visual database of all the Time-Life products. Enables you to browse and order products.

Tom Doherty Associates, Inc.

http://www.tor.com/

TOR online. Publishes science fiction and fantasy books. Includes links to other science fiction and fantasy sites on the Web, offers a browseable database of books, and allows online ordering.

W. W. Norton & Company, Inc.

http://www.wwnorton.com/

Provides home site, online catalog, and ordering information for W.W. Norton & Company publishing. Includes a complete catalog indexed and broken down by publishing imprints. Also includes featured books, author profiles, company history, and signing appearance dates.

Web Art Publishing

http://www.webart.com/

Web site publishers devoted to high-quality page production and publishing. Offers information about their services and price structure.

West Publishing

http://www.westpub.com/

West Publishing online, a legal and educational publisher. Includes information on their products. Enables you to use West's Legal Directory to find a lawyer, law firm, or corporate or governmental lawyer located in the United States or Canada.

WWW VL Electronic Journals List: Publishers

http://www.edoc.com/ejournal/publishers.html

Complete listing to publishing companies. Contains listing by: academic, computer, science and technology, electronic, and other commercial publishing companies. Also allows for searching.

Yardbird Books Page of Pages

http://www.yardbird.com

Publisher of challenging, well-made books of fiction, non-fiction and poetry, incorporating the Yardbird Reader, an electronic magazine. Yardbird was founded by writers who write, publish, and print. This is a cool multimedia-based site whose mascot is Charlie Parker and whose frames-based design makes it easy to navigate.

Related Sites

http://mspress.microsoft.com/

http://www.mispress.com/

http://www.waite.com/

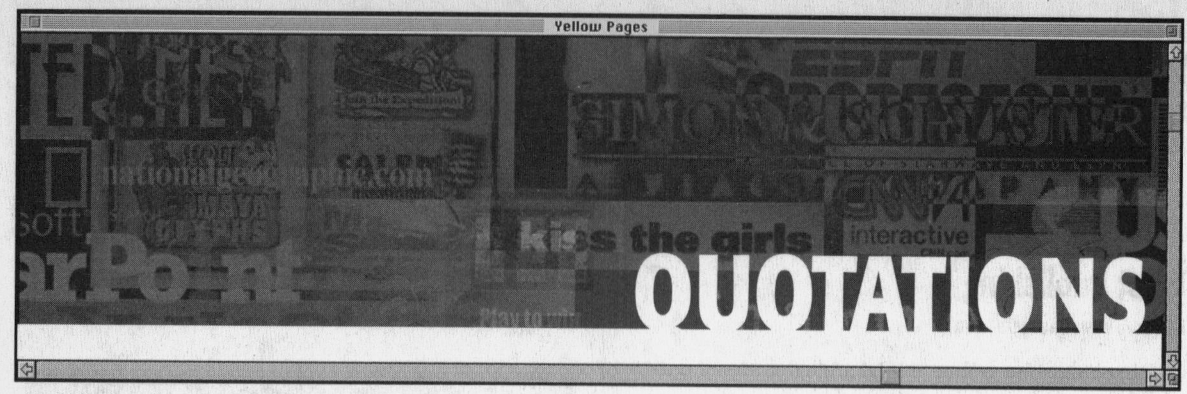

> The wisdom of the wise and the experience of the ages are perpetuated by quotations.
>
> *Benjamin Disraeli*

Advertising Quotes

http://www.utexas.edu/coc/adv/research/quotes/

Jef Richards, an Advertising Professor at the University of Texas at Austin, has collected here a set of quotations about the world of advertising. The Index includes over 60 subcategories, ranging from Advertising Is…to Wear Out. Highlights along the way include Billboards, Critics, Evil, Fantasy & Dreams, Honesty, Manipulation, Morality & Ethics, Puffery, Sex, and Value.

Bartlett's Familiar Quotations

http://www.columbia.edu/acis/bartleby/bartlett/

The Ninth Edition of John Bartlett's famous book, published in 1901, has been converted to HTML format and posted to the Web by Project Bartleby, an extensive Web-based literature library established by Columbia University.

Coles Quotables

http://www2.xtdl.com/~scole/

Offers a search engine that enables you to find quotes on specific subject matter. Also provides links to other quotation sites.

The Internet Movie Database
http://us.imdb.com/

The Kerrie DeGood Quotes Page
http://www.fn.net/~degood/quotes.html

Search Reference – Quotations
http://isleuth.com/quote.html

Dave's Searchable Quote Database

http://www2.vuse.vanderbilt.edu/cgi-bin/cgiuser/~lillyda/bin/search.cgi

This forms-based database contains over 6,500 quotes. Right now, you can only get random quotes, but Dave assures all that he's working on the rest.

Don's Doctor Who Interesting Quote Archive

http://www.mit.edu:8001/people/dasmith/Who/Quotes.html

The quotes originated on the British low-tech science fiction show *Doctor Who*. Topics include art, history, the human race, love, politics, and other pithy topics.

The Internet Movie Database

http://us.imdb.com/

Click the Search button and have a blast. This site enables you to use the search engine to find quotes on all kinds of subject matter. The quotes are referenced by the person who said them, the movie in which the lines were used, as well as the year the movie was produced. Also another great resource for quotes found in this book.

The Kerrie DeGood Quotes Page

http://www.fn.net/~degood/quotes.html

Cool little site that is organized by subject matter. Quotes available for topics that include Abortion, Bores, Cars, Dreams, and more.

The Land of Quotes

http://www.quoteland.com/

Really cool looking site that offers quotes by category. The quotes aren't always the best of the best, but the site is pleasing to look at.

The Official Internet Quayle Quote List

http://www.xmission.com/~mwalker/DQ/quayle/qq/quayle.quotes.html

Okay, maybe we should finally be leaving our former vice-president alone, but when the material he's provided is so funny, how can you refuse to enjoy it? This collection is divided into a number of subcategories, making Quayle's comments on issues such as International Affairs easy to locate. Ironically, though, the Webmaster here has inadvertently included some "Quayle-isms" of his own: In lamenting Quayle's departure from public life, for example, the Webmaster consoles himself with, "We do have his book to look forward to as well as his bid for the presidency in 1994."

Outriders of Reality Reference Manual & Travel Guide

http://www.sols.on.ca/stuff/outriders.html

According to David Harvie, the "Chief Scout" of Outriders of Reality, this oddball listing of quotes "…is a collection of errant pieces of knowledge, quips of non-conventional wisdom found in graffiti, email taglines, bumper stickers, buttons, and snatches of conversions heard while standing in fast-food check-out lines." Subjects are covered with irreverent humor.

Quotation Center

http://cyber-nation.com/victory/quotations/subjects/quotes_subjects_a_to_b.html

Provided by Cyber Nation, this collection of quotes meant to empower and motivate is quite impressive. Alphabetized by category, you can choose from just about any topic available. Very easy to read, although can be a little confusing to navigate through.

Quotation Links

http://www.starlingtech.com/quotes/links.html

Excellent reference for other quotation links. Even provides brief descriptions of what you can expect to find at other links.

Quotations

http://www.jsu.edu/depart/library/graphic/quote.htm

Provides links to other quotation sites.

Quotations About Libraries and Librarians

http://www.nlc-bnc.ca/ifla/I/humour/author.htm

The International Federation of Libraries Associations and Institutions has put together this selection of quotes from authors, statesmen, and celebrities regarding the importance of libraries.

Quotations Home Page

http://www.geocities.com/~spanoudi/quote.html

Another good site that enables you to find quotes by category.

Quotations of William Blake

http://www.mcs.net/~jorn/html/blake.html

This page offers, in somewhat of a hodgepodge, a list of quotations by the radical poet. Note that hodgepodge is the operative word here.

Quotes, Quotes, and More Quotes

www.smackem.com/quotes

Offering quotes from movies and song lyrics, this site also includes quotes about sex, music, love, and God.

Search Reference – Quotations

http://isleuth.com/quote.html

Very cool site in that you can search for quotations from a list of seven different collections. Set up by Michael Moncur, this was used frequently for the quotes in this book. Thanks Michael!

Zappa Quote of the Day

http://www.fwi.uva.nl/~heederik/zappa/quote/

Offers a new random quote each day from one of the geniuses of rock music.

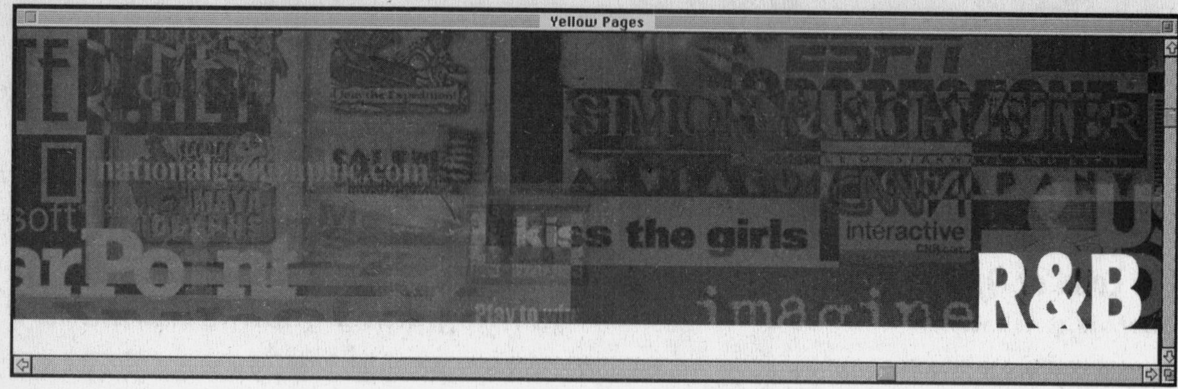

Soul is the music people understand. Sure it's basic and it's simple but it's something else because it's honest, that's it. It sticks its neck out and says it straight from the heart. Sure there's a lot of different music you can get off on but soul is more than that.

Jimmy in The Commitments *(1991)*

Beef Stew's Blues Playground

http://www.neca.com/~bfstew/index.htm

Based on Beef Stew's Blues radio show on 107 FM WCCC out of Hartford, Connecticut. The site includes the current playlist for the show as well as links for blues organizations, record labels, booking agents, tours, bands and musicians, blues festivals, and more.

The Best of Rap and R&B on the Web

http://www.lookup.com/Homepages/82075/favor_sites.html

A fan's page of his favorite groups and artists, has links to other fans' pages for each artist, as well as the artist's home page. A great place to start on a rap and R&B tour of the Web.

The R&B Page
http://www.rbpage.com/

Biscuit Time on Blues Web

http://www.island.net/~blues/

Possibly everything you ever wanted to know about the blues. Offers news, CD reviews, a great selection of audio files, photos, extensive biographies of musicians, articles, links to other blues sites, and more.

Blues Access Online

http://www.bluesaccess.com/ba_home.html

The online version of the magazine *Blues Access.* Provides photos, stories, interviews, articles, tour information, promotions, merchandise, a message board, and of course subscription information. There's also the Essential Blues Album List—the albums the editor believes you *must* have.

Blues Ginza

http://www.wellcomm.co.jp/~blues/

The home site for the blues in Tokyo, Japan. Provides concert information, current news, lists clubs where the blues are played, photos, blues records, and links. English and Japanese versions.

The BluesHarp Page

http://www.axionet.com/bluesharp/

Dedicated to the Blues Harmonica sound, the site contains bios of the "Founding Fathers" of the BluesHarp sound, pictures, lessons, and links.

BluesNet

http://dragon.acadiau.ca/~rob/blues/blues.html

Contains biographies of musicians, an archive of photos (many previously unpublished), a feature on teachers, and many informative articles. Lets you leave your comments in the guest book. Offers links to other major blues sites.

The Blues Site!!

http://www.geocities.com/Nashville/4261/

A *very* basic Web site (originally done for a history project), includes an excellent overview of the history of the blues, with bios of key artists and sound files.

Dallas Blues Society

http://www.metronet.com/~labiche/dbs-main.html

A blues fan's (and friend's) record label dedicated to promoting the blues. The site has a mission statement, current releases, audio clips, and how to order.

Early Blues Legends—The Art of Neal Harpe

http://www.toad.net/~harpe/blues/bhome.html

An online gallery of Neal Harpe's original drawings of blues artists. Prints of each drawing are for sale.

Hip Hop Links

http://www.cs.tut.fi/~p116711/hiphop/hiphop.html

Provides a listing of artists, magazines, businesses, home pages, and other related hip hop/rap links. This site is great for anyone trying to find out information about hip hop/rap music.

House of Blues

http://hob.com/hob.html

Offers QuickTime virtual reality scenes. Includes concert schedules, music and video samples, blues bios, and more.

John Lee Hooker

http://virginrecords.com/jlhooker/

The official site for the blues music of John Lee Hooker. Includes upcoming release information, biography, and a RealAudio slide show. Also includes many pictures, articles, and ordering information.

The Motherpage

http://www.duke.edu/~tmc/pfunk.html

This is an unofficial fan page for George Clinton, Parlament/Funkadelic, and related releases. Includes a lengthy list of answers to frequently asked questions, articles, and P-Funk images. Also provides a full discography and P-Funk samples. This is a great site for fans of funk, rock, and soul music.

The National Blues Pages

http://world.std.com/~bstahl/bluesjams.html

When you're going on the road and need a place to play the blues, check out The National Blues Pages, which lists open blues jams around the country. The list is broken down first by region and then by city. If you need to play, you can find a jam somewhere.

The New Funk Times Home Page

http://ourworld.compuserve.com/homepages/pjebsen/

This is the home page for the official George Clinton Parlament/Funkadelic newsletter. Includes a lot of cool graphics, articles, and details of upcoming releases. Also provides tour dates, related links, and contact and ordering information.

The Official Blues Ring

http://www.geocities.com/BourbonStreet/2690/bluesring.html

A ring is a linked group of Web sites with a common theme; a viewer can go from one site on the ring to another. This ring is dedicated to the blues, so if you have a Web site that's blues-oriented and want to join the ring, here's the place to do it.

The Otis Redding Home Page

http://ernie.bgsu.edu/~adavoli/otis.html

Provides a biography, song list, lyrics, and pictures of soul singer Otis Redding. Includes links to many other R&B sites.

Related Sites

http://acme-atlanta.com/clubs/abs/

http://imp.cssc.olemiss.edu/blues.html

http://nojazzfest.com/97f/97frames.html

http://web.netusa1.net/~kelly/sites.html

The R&B Page

http://www.rbpage.com/

We've been *working endlessly* toward making "*The R&B Page*" the *premier Rhythm and Blues resource* for R&B lovers and *potential R&B lovers* of all ages and types. If you have a wish list, *drop us a line* via email, or share it with us and others through the use of our *Discussion Forum*.

Welcome to The R&B Page. *Instantly access web-exclusive interviews, commentary and music via streaming audio, from R&B legends you know and love...Plus, get the first peek at information available nowhere else.*

The R&B Page **features** *the* **most comprehensive and professionally produced collection of audio-on-demand**

Dedicated strictly to R&B, the site has interviews, audio clips, news, live chat, featured artists and their music on streaming audio, lots of links, and archives to see what you missed. Possibly the premier site for R&B on the Net.

The Rhythm and Blues Music Primer

http://www.zoo.co.uk/~primer/

An excellent site. Includes interviews of favorite blues and soul artists (also audio clips); a voting center to add your favorite artist; the Top Twenty to Try (the 20 artists to hear to begin your R&B and soul education); plus history of the great R&B and soul records labels, info on literature, and plenty of links.

The Rosebud Agency

http://www.rosebudus.com/

An artist management company with strong emphasis on blues musicians. Provides biographies, discography, and tour information. Also booking information.

TSHIRTNOW

http://www.tshirtnow.com/cgi-bin/vsc/tshirtnow/blues.html?E+tshirtnow

Every true fan needs a t-shirt with his favorite artist on it, and this site seems to have every blues and jazz musician known. Photos of each shirt, prices, sizes, and of course ordering information. They do lots of other types of t-shirts as well.

The Unofficial NRBQ Homepage

http://www.ici.net/cust_pages/bad/nrbq.html

Provides home page for the traditional rock and blues band NRBQ (New Rhythm and Blues Quartet). Includes band biography, song lyrics, tour dates, photo album, and fan club information. Also includes quotes from many various famous musicians, such as Paul McCartney and Bonnie Raitt, about NRBQ.

Unofficial Public Enemy Homepage

http://louis.ecs.soton.ac.uk/~rvn95r/public_e/pe.html

Provides profiles, discography, lyrics, and the history of the seminal rap group Public Enemy. Also includes links to many different hip hop sites worldwide.

WavBabe's Blues

http://www.cbminc.com/wavebabe/Blues.htm

A site that has only blues WAV files on it. Something different from the normal text and graphics for those folks interested only in great sounds.

NEWSGROUPS

alt.music.harmonica

rec.music.funky

rec.music.rock-pop-r+b

uk.music.rhythm-n-blues

FTP SITE

yoyo.cc.monash.edu.au

MAILING LISTS

BLUES-L

CTBLUS-L

Harp-L

nw-blues

stlblues-l

Related Sites

http://www.biograph.com/

http://www.bluesfestivals.com/

http://www.galactica.it/101/black/

http://www.island.net/~blues/snake.html

http://www.panix.com/~bsco/

http://www.users.cloud9.net/~leftwich/

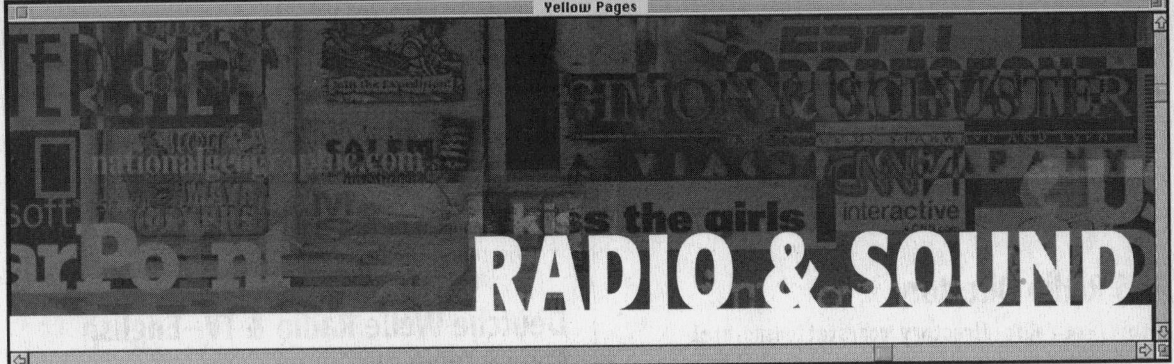

RADIO & SOUND

> Whoever controls the media—the images—controls the culture.
>
> *Allen Ginsberg*

NRP Top Picks

8-Track Heaven
`http://pobox.com/~abbot/8track/`

NPR Online
`http://www.npr.org/`

See Hollywood and Vine
`http://www.hollywoodandvine.com/`

100 Years of Radio Web 1895-1995

`http://www.alpcom.it/hamradio/`

This site contains articles and links regarding Marconi and other points of interest regarding radio history.

440 Satisfaction

`http://www.aloha.net/~hijohn/`

Focuses on the Deejays, news people, and unsung radio people from earlier days in radio. Check out the "Reel Top 40 Radio Depository" to hear sound checks and news from some of the biggest DJs of the sixties and seventies. A real blast!

8-Track Heaven

`http://pobox.com/~abbot/8track/`

Rediscover everything you wanted to forget about the breakthrough 8-track recording technology. Part of the quarterly publication *8-Track Mind* and an extension of alt.collecting.8-track-tapes, this Web page includes a FAQ about the technology, a detailed history, and collector notes. If you grew up on cassettes, feel fortunate and download the sound clip of an 8-track changing programs. Also includes Windows wallpaper and icons, the "8 Noble Truths," and the inquiring 8-Track and UFOs connection. A hilarious site!

The ACE–The Association of Clandestine Enthusiasts

`http://www.frn.net/ace/`

All free radio broadcasters should join ACE, whose offical Web site contains articles, logs, and a link to the Free Radio Network.

Amateur Radio Books and Open Repeater Database

`http://www.artscipub.com/`

Produces amateur radio books, including Radio Modifications, Repeater Mapbook, cartoon license manuals, frequency guides, and reference manuals.

AudioNet–The Broadcast Network on the Internet

`http://www.audionet.com/`

With the RealAudio 2.0 player, you can listen to AudioNet's radio shows, which include sports, talk radio, and specialty programming. Includes live broadcasting from more than 50 college stations, dozens of talk shows from around the country, and news.

A B C D E F G H I J K L M N O P Q R S T U V W X Y Z

The Bob & Tom Show

http://www.bobandtom.com/bobandtom/

Provides home site for the nationally syndicated radio program *The Bob & Tom Show*. Includes show highlights, lowlights, pictures, and much, much more. This site is highly recommended.

BRS Radio Directory

http://www.radio-directory.com/stationsnc.html

A giant directory of links to every public or noncommercial radio station Web page in the net. You can search by call letter, state, format, and others.

CES News

http://www.eia.org/CEMA/cesnews/ontext11.htm

One of the largest trade shows in the U.S., the Consumer Electronics Show, now has an audio/home theater show in Florida every May. Check out the lists of audio exhibitors, learn more about the CES digital fair, and read about other new shows in North America. Download images from recent shows.

Chris Smolinski's Radio Page

http://www.access.digex.net/~cps/radio.html

Provides information (and links to other pages with similar information) about short-wave and amateur radio.

Cinemedia Radio

http://www.afionline.org/CINEMEDIA/CineMedia.radio.html

Provides links to hundreds of radio stations worldwide that have a Web presence. Also includes hundreds of links to radio-related sites for celebrities, shows, directories, controversy, and more. If you're into radio, visit this site first.

Clandestine Radio Intel

http://www.qsl.net/yb0rmi/cland.htm

This Web site acts as a central host among shortwave radio operators and listeners around the globe. These stations often operate under the worst political conditions in order to help a cause, such as democracy in China, peace in the Middle East, or tolerance in Bosnia.

COW: Comedy on the Web

http://www.comedybreak.com/

The COW site helps surfers to find great sources of humor on the Web and used Real Audio so you can listen in. Their three categories are I Can't Believe They Said That, Mental Block (a cartoon), and Wireman (bizarre news).

Deutche Welle Radio & TV—English Home Page

http://www.dwelle.de/english/

Provides online program schedules and news and other reports.

Digital Radio

http://www.magi.com/~moted/dr/

This links page is the perfect stepping stone for information and links about digital radio, which will provide CD-quality sound without interference—after it's fully implemented.

The FCC

http://www.fcc.gov/

Read up on the FCC's Telecom Act of 1996, which will save you from everything evil and sadistic on the Internet and infringe on your First Amendment rights just a little bit more. Here's where it all begins.

Free Radio Network

http://www.frn.net/

More than just a site to get news about pirate radio or complain about the FCC, the FRN Web site also provides True Speech and Real Audio clips of actual show, so that you can learn for yourself what these microstations are about.

HardRadio

http://www.hardradio.com/

Not merely a Web site, HardRadio *is* a radio station of sorts. It uses live Real Audio that streams in hard rock 24/7. The site also provides links to musician pages, concerts, awards, and more.

The Howard Stern Show Sounds Page

http://www2.liglobal.com/stern/

Listen to excerpts from the Howard Stern radio or TV show. Includes sound clips from Stern, his sidekick Robin Quivers, Stuttering John, and others. Also includes sounds about the OJ trial, guests and celebrities on the show, and the usual parade of puppets.

International Broadcasting Bureau

http://www.voa.gov/

The IBB home page acts as the starting point for people interested in their affiliated network: the Voice of America, WORLDNET, Radio and TV Marti, and the Engineering Directorate. The IBB is a bureau of the United States government.

The Internet Karaoke Store

http://www.primenet.com/~karaoke/index.html

One-stop shopping for karaoke laserdiscs and CDs. Includes links to karaoke manufacturers and related Web sites.

Javiation

http://www.demon.co.uk/javiation

Scanner and associated equipment distributor in the United Kingdom. Producer and publisher of the "Airband Guide." Links to products and purchase information and other related sites.

Lucasfilm's THX Home Page

http://www.lum.com:80/thx/

The current leader in audio reproduction for movie and home theaters includes information on the THX sound system, THX-approved equipment, technical specs, and THX laserdiscs at this site.

Media Watchdog

http://theory.lcs.mit.edu/~mernst/media/

This collection of online media watchdog groups includes time-sensitive information, censorship resources, media criticism articles, and dozens of newsletters devoted to the monitoring and analysis of biased media.

The Museum of Television and Radio

http://www.mtr.org/

Take a virtual tour of the museums in New York and Los Angeles. Includes information on their gallery shows, daily screenings of radio and television specials, and an exhibit calendar. Provides visiting hours and directions to museums in Los Angeles and New York.

NPR Online

http://www.npr.org/

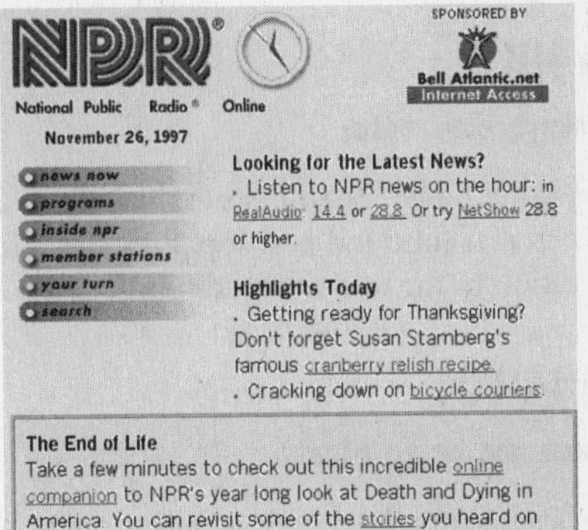

National Public Radio online. Provides information about NPR and other topics. Includes audio version of daily noon news casts, transcripts of other programs, and in-depth looks at current events.

The Official Site for Dr. Laura

http://www.drlaura.com/

Dr. Laura Schlessinger's show is gaining in popularity all over the country. The popular psychotherapist's Web site offers Dr. Larua quotations, fun guest comments and letters, a photo album, and more.

Old Time Radio (OTR) WWW Page

http://www.old-time.com/

Focuses on radio programs from "radio's golden age." Contains pointers to many entertaining and educational areas for fans of nostalgic radio shows.

Pirate Radio

http://www.access.digex.net/~cps/pirate.html

This links page is dedicated to free radio—stations that operate without an FCC license. Free radio broadcasters believe the FCC serves only to protect the interests of the corporate broadcasters.

A B C D E F G H I J K L M N O P Q R S T U V W X Y Z

radioEARTH

http://www.radioearth.com/mainmenu.htm

radioEARTH is the professional broadcaster's organization and Web site. Get all the latest news, download show prep software, the "Radio Ate My Brain" screensaver, and other entertaining and informative tidbits.

Radio History Society

http://www.radiohistory.org/

This Web site features the Society's current exhibit and provides links to realted sites.

Radio HK

http://hkweb.com/radio/

Hong Kong Radio. Broadcasts exclusively into the Internet, real-time and nonstop. Provides information in addition to the real-time radio broadcasts.

Radio JAPAN

http://www.nhk.or.jp/rjnet/

Provides information about Japanese radio. Includes transmission maps and program schedules.

Radio Online—Radio's Starting Point on the Net

http://www.radio-online.com/talent.htm

Click a radio host to see his or her Web page. Includes dozens of deejays. If you're a deejay for a major station, you can submit your URL for review.

RealAudio Audio on Demand for the Internet

http://www.prognet.com/

Download the latest release of the RealAudio player and be part of live Internet audio. This site provides information on the RealAudio player from Progressive Networks, and also its server and encoder products. You can access several Web sites with a significant amount of RealAudio files, including PBS, ABC, NPR, and the Live Events site.

RealTime

http://realtime.cbcstereo.com

Radio show heard across Canada. Includes music and guests. Features a great deal of RealAudio.

Rush Limbaugh Featured Site

http://www2.southwind.net/~vic/rush/rush.html

Dittoheads all over will love this site, which points to the Rush site of the day, as well as featured sites of weeks past.

Secrets of Home Theater and High Fidelity

http://www.sdinfo.com/

Click an object in the home theater room to learn more about that component. This site also includes movie and music reviews for the home theater nut, a "What's New" section that describes the latest gizmos, and a search engine and index to articles. A great place to explore home theater.

See Hollywood and Vine

http://www.hollywoodandvine.com/

This hip site from Capitol Records includes hundreds of sound clips from each of its artists. Choose artists from the list, click Search, and download one of their songs or visit their Web site. Be sure to visit the Hollywood and Vine tourist trap, a collection of attractions with more audio and video than you could ever ask for. Have fun but be patient—takes a while to load!

Sound Site

http://www.soundsite.com/

Provides helpful information on audio and video recording technologies. Help and information includes a troubleshooting guide, history of audio and video, a section on home theater, and setting the time on your VCR. Also includes audio/video industry news, manufacturers lists, and information on new technologies.

Thistle and Shamrock Stations List at the Ceolas Archive

http://celtic.stanford.edu/pmurphy/thistle.html

Provides a list of stations arranged alphabetically by state and city. Broadcasts a popular Celtic music radio program on National Public Radio. Includes broadcast times.

The Voice of America (VOA)

`http://www.voa.gov/text-only.html`

The VOA site has their charter, broadcast schedules, press releases, and texts in different languages of broadcasts to different countries. Texts can be found in Chinese, Albanian, Turkish, and Arabic, among others.

Welcome to BBC Radio

`http://www.bbc.co.uk/`

BBC Radio online. Contains information about program schedules and information about specific programs carried on the BBC radio network.

Welcome to Dolby Laboratories

`http://www.dolby.com/`

If you've ever been confused as to what Dolby actually does, check out the Dolby Technologies hyperlink. Read about Dolby Digital, the latest theater sound; download the Dolby Digital trailer you've seen at theaters; review helpful hints for home theater setup; and see what's on the horizon with theater sound.

World Radio Network

`http://www.wrn.org/`

WRN's is the perfect site to visit if you are an international news hound. You can hear live newscast streams in either RealAudio or StreamWorks, and jump to other live sites to get even more news from around the globe.

Xing Technology's StreamWorks

`http://204.62.160.251/`

Download StreamWorks to play sound files on the Internet. This audio player for Windows, Macintosh, and UNIX lets you listen to live audio. After you download the player, click one of the radio station sites to listen to live radio, or choose other links to download songs and speeches. Neat stuff!

Related Sites

`http://www.comedyorama.com/`

`http://www.hear.com/rw/feature/rrb.html`

`http://www.easylog.com/`

`http://kzsu.stanford.edu/other-radio.html`

`http://www.flash.net/~comedy/`

`http://users.aol.com/cookeh/prep.html`

`http://onairjobtipsheet.com/bumper.html`

`http://www.cab-acr.ca/index.html`

`http://www.norcom.mb.ca/nci/main.html`

`http://www.mrnnet.com/`

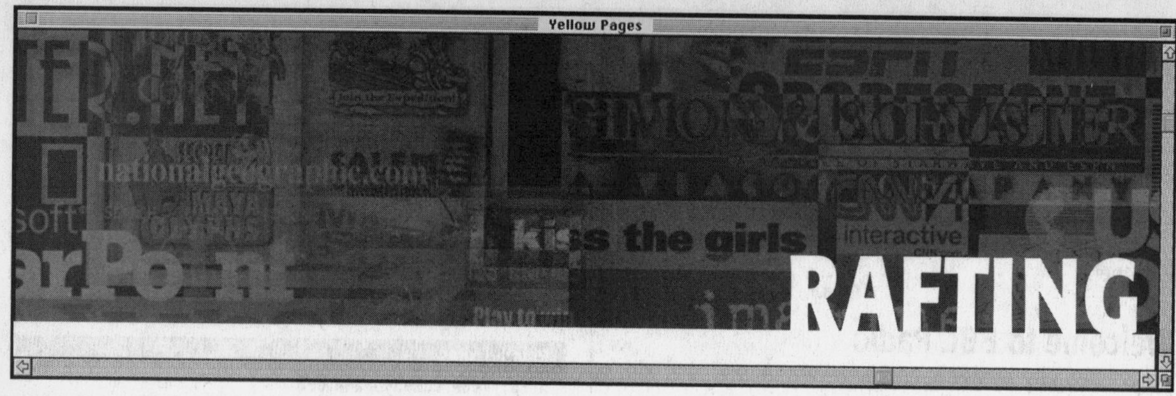

Rivers are highways that move on, and bear us whither we wish to go.

Blaise Pascal

Adrift
http://www.adrift.co.nz/

Grand Canyon River Running
http://www.azstarnet.com/grandcanyonriver/

The River Wild
http://www.nationalgeographic.com/features/96/selway/index.html

ab257's Whitewater Page

http://www.epix.net/~ab257/

A cornucopia of information lies within this site. You can visit the author's favorite rafting sites, view many thrilling photos, get satellite weather maps, and jump to ab257's great collection of links, including hot pages, local sites, online stores and resources, and club sites.

Adrift

http://www.adrift.co.nz/

Explores rivers beyond North America. Visit Uganda, Turkey, Nepal, Zambia, Zimbabwe, Ecuador, and Ethiopa. Adrift does things at the local level, such as buying supplies in the countries they visit. They also leave little impact on the environment. This is a very well-written site that leaves lots to the imagination and will move you to want to go on one of Adrift's tours. However, if you must wait, you can post on their message board and communicate with other rafters that way.

American Whitewater

http://www.awa.org/awa.html

Sponsored by the American Whitewater Affiliation (AWA), this site gives an exhaustive list of information about whitewater rafting. Become a member of AWA and help conserve our country's rivers, browse through the numerous links and resources, or do both. Also, look through this site's white and yellow pages to find rafting products.

GORP Outdoor Recreation Pages: Paddlesports

http://www.gorp.com/gorp/activity/paddle.htm

GORP's paddlesports site is part of a larger network of sites devoted to outdoor recreation. Here, find out what is featured in the rafting news. Jump to river sites all over the country and the world. This site specializes in giving you tips. Learn how to keep from capsizing, get information on clubs, find books and other media about rafting, and join an online forum devoted to whitewater fans who have shared interests.

Grand Canyon River Running

http://www.azstarnet.com/grandcanyonriver/

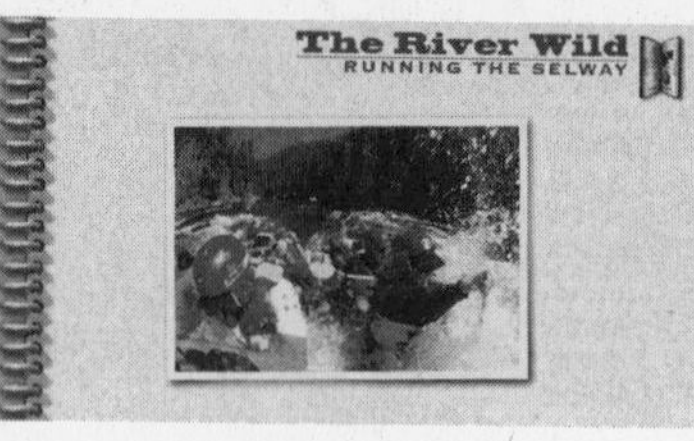

Gives information about private and commercial rafting trips through the Grand Canyon. Also shows beautiful pictures and helpful maps as it guides you through the beginning point, Lee's Canyon, to the ending point, Lake Mead. This site is well-designed, with a Native American motif, in easy-to-follow icons.

National Organization of Whitewater Rodeos (NOWR)

http://www.nowr.org/index.htm

A whitewater rodeo does not involve horses. It is a gathering of river enthusiasts who compete in certain whitewater skills, such as hole-riding. This site explains what the rodeos are all about, everything from rules to judging, and gives calendars of rodeo events—from actual competition to chili cook-offs. The site also links to other rafting URLs.

Outdoor Action Guide to Planning a Safe River Trip

http://www.princeton.edu/~oa/rivplan.html

An article emphasizing river safety, covering accident prevention, river hazards, and how to preplan a trip. This site is written by a director at Princeton and is mostly linear in its sytle. It does provide a few links to other sites, and its graphics illustrate safety and prevention factors. This site also inlcudes a list of other media to turn to when planning a river trip.

Rapid Shooters

http://rapidshooters.com/

A photographer's paradise, essentially, this site has a great photo gallery that features the South Fork American and Kings Rivers. It also offers a message board, a free screensaver for download, and a number of whitewater links. Searching is easy. Just click the "Select your Destination" option, click Go, and you're off.

Southeastern Whitewater Web

http://www.mindspring.com/~whitewater/

Offers some of the usual information you would expect to find on a rafting page, such as what rivers are in the Southeast, expeditions, safety tips, and so forth. But, check out the river tales, quotes, and beer stories! And, on a more serious note, link to the books, movie reviews, H20 reports, or the classifieds. This site has it all.

NRP TOP PICKS

The River Wild

http://www.nationalgeographic.com/features/96/selway/index.html

Offers a cyber tour of the Selway River in Idaho. From the home page, you get full access to a map that shows the course of rafting the Selway. Pictures give you a feel for the lovely mountain scenery. The tour offers hints for camping, navigating the river, speaking in river lingo, and observing the nearby wildlife. Features a QuickTime movie of a rafter running through Lava Falls.

Vince's Idaho WHITEWATER Page

http://www.webpak.net/~rafter/

A charming example of a personal Web site, this offers everything from music for your listening pleasure to a photo gallery. In frames, this site is laid out well and easy to navigate. Plus, it has some extra information not found in most rafting sites, such as political issues surrounding Idaho's rivers. Read "The Bubble Line," a weekly Pacific Northwest newsletter, find out about flow and weather conditions, and read about Vince's personal rafting experiences.

WEBTREKS Whitewater Online

http://www.webtreks.com/whtwater.html

A very simple, easy-to-navigate site with great information and links. From here, you can find out where to order rafting outfits and equipment, link to North American and international paddling organizations, find whitewater associations, get the latest weather and river conditions, and check out whitewater events and other rafting sites.

Wild & Scenic Rivers

http://www.nps.gov/ccso/wildrivers.htm

The Wild and Scenic River Act in 1968 called for preserving rivers and their natural environments. This site tells you the history of the act. An exceptional part of this site's information, however, is in the state listings of rivers, which is fairly exhaustive. Also, find out how you can get involved with agencies whose goal it is to uphold the Wild and Scenic River Act.

Related Sites
http://www.aceraft.com/
http://www.alaska.net/~nova/nova2.htm
http://eagleadventures.com/
http://www.webtreks.com/hudson/
http://www.kingsriver.com/
http://www.whitewater.com/~garland/mww.html
http://www.rroutdoors.com/
http://www.neoutdoors.com/sacobound/
http://206.107.176.4/chp/snkrvadv/
http://www.wildrivers.com.au/

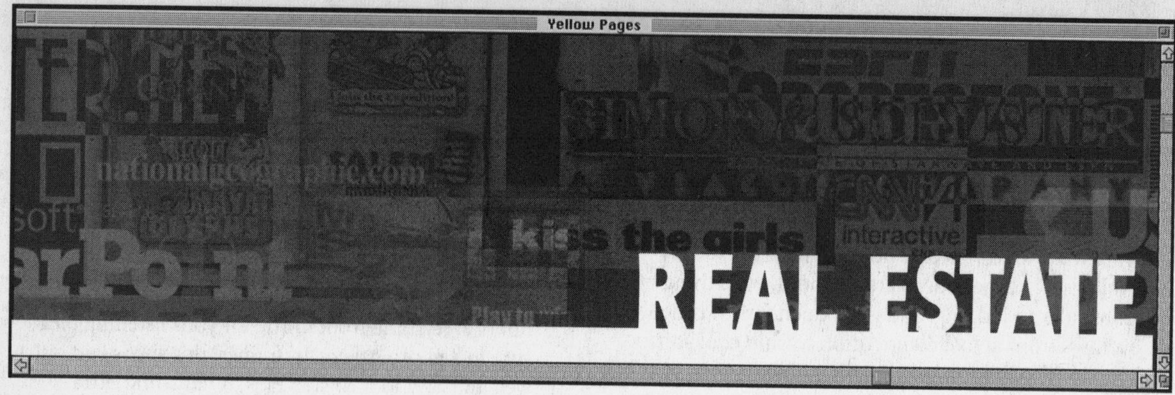

We struck it rich in real estate, making Paris ugly.

Monsieur Arnaud in Nelly & Monsieur Arnaud *(1995)*

A TO Z

The ADLIST Real Estate Database

http://www.adlist.com/re/

Offers opportunities to add your real estate link to the database, search for real estate. Advertise your real estate.

ALWAYS OPEN!—HouseLink US Real Estate Guide

http://www.wirelink.com/houselink/index.html

HouseLink enables you to view and list real estate nationwide. Realtors and brokers can submit their existing sites for a free listing. Can also provide all your Web advertising needs.

bestagents.com

http://www.bestagents.com/

Provides information for home buyers and sellers. Serves as a network of exclusive real estate agents who become your personal advisors, consultants, and negotiators.

Related Sites

http://www.austinre.com/habitat.htm

http://www.houseweb.co.uk/house/index.html

http://www.jaylynn.com/sellhome.htm

Buying and Selling a Home
http://www.mpicture.com/homeguide/buy_sell/buysell.htm

Cabin Country

http://www.frii.com/~buyland/

Since 1974, Cabin Country has offered mountain land and cabins in northern Colorado and southern Wyoming. The site offers a hot list of current properties available, as well as a section explaining what's involved with mountain ownership.

The Commercial Network

http://www.thecomnet.com

A comprehensive resource for securing corporate real estate and facility requirements worldwide, including North America, the Pacific Rim, Latin America, and Europe, among others. In addition to listing properties for sale or lease in more than 150 locations, the site offers an online referral information service and a database that helps members pinpoint market values and property trends worldwide.

Designs Plus—1000s of House Plans

http://www.designsplus.com/

Whether remodeling or starting from scratch, this site can spur numerous ideas with its wide assortment of house plans. The site also provides information on building materials, contractors, and the building process.

The Dream Home Real Estate Network

http://www.islandsd.com/island/dreamhm/

A worldwide online resource for finding or marketing distinctive homes, this creative site allows viewers to browse an "Avenue of Dream Homes" (with listings sorted by location, price, or size) or locate real estate professionals in a particular area through the "Dream Team Real Estate Directory."

ExecuStay. Inc.

http://www.rent.net/ads/execustay/

Find temporary housing accommodations nationwide at this site. ExecuStay offerings range from fully-furnished apartments to private homes, complete with linens, electronics, and cable television!

Exquisite Homes and Properties

http://www.exquisite.com/index.html

Provides a real estate listing service for homes and properties in the U.S., Europe, and the Caribbean. Also includes information on mortgages, title services, lending institutions, realtors, remodeling, and landscaping.

Feng Shui Web Page

http://www.cwo.com/~ashlin/homepage.html

The ancient Chinese philosophy based on harmony and balance in our environment is enjoying a resurgence worldwide. Learn the significance of door, window, and wall placement in housing construction, as well as how to use color and environmental design to optimize the flow of chi, or life energy.

Global Homes

http://www.globalhomes.com/

In addition to property listings, this site provides a variety of resources, such as real estate news and publications, a directory of agents and companies, and databases listing open houses and rental information.

Home Builder's Utopia

http://www.dfw.net/~custmbld/utopia.html

Serves as a guide to links to professional home builders on the Internet. Also lists building associations and products and services.

HomeBuyer's Fair

http://www.homefair.com/homepage.html

Contains classified listings of homes for sale. Provides information on buying, selling, relocating, getting a mortgage, and apartments. Includes a special section for first-time buyers.

HomeScout

http://homescout.com/

This expansive site features more than 350,000 home listings gathered from 130 Web sites in the United States, Canada, and the world. By serving as a one-stop "central listing warehouse," HomeScout minimizes the search effort for consumers. In addition to its phenomenal database, the site offers a FAQ listing, a chat area, and Home Wizard, which provides diverse information on selected geographical areas.

HomeTime

http://www.hometime.com/

Based on the popular broadcasting show, this site is geared toward do-it-yourselfers, tackling home repair or remodeling jobs. The site offers a wealth of information, including highlights from past shows, the How-To Center, a section on tools and materials, and a users forum where readers can share tips.

HomeWeb

http://www.us-digital.com:8080/homeweb/

Provides listings of real estate professionals and corporate relocation managers, as well as a consumer information section on home buying. Check the Home Search page for housing listed at this site.

How I Made 1 Million Dollars In Real Estate With No Money Down

http://www.pwrnet.com/freepage/1million/

Offers strategies for building quick cash and wealth in the '90s. Real estate investor answers questions. Learn how to earn $5,000 to $10,000 in 30 to 60 days.

International Real Estate Council

http://www.boardplace.com/boardplace/intl/intl.shtml

An outgrowth of the Realtor Association of Miami, the Council was created to serve and educate the growing number of real estate marketing specialists. The site provides networking and marketing opportunities, links to international publications, and other information.

International Real Estate Directory

http://www.ired.com

Looking for an independent and all-inclusive source of real estate information? This mega-site is it. The IRED Real Estate Directory offers nearly 10,000 links to real estate Web sites worldwide and can be searched by state, country, or category. The site offers headline news and featured columnists, an events calendar, and a monthly review of the top 10 real estate Web sites.

Internet Real Estate Listings

http://www.map.com/irel

An Internet real estate listing service for anyone wishing to buy or sell real estate.

Internet Real Estate Network

http://www.iren.com/

Free Web pages for real estate properties, professionals, and organizations. Fully searchable database. HTML/CGI authoring and other custom services are also available. Provides answers to frequently asked questions and links to other related sites.

InterOffice Online

http:www.interoffice.com/

Provides accommodations and business services when opening an office. With strong graphics and an attractive presentation, the InterOffice home page enables viewers to visit its 40 nationwide locations, review its office support services, or check out its "Tech Tools": voice, data, and video technology.

land.net

http://www.land.net/

Specializing in vacant land, this multi-faceted site assists customers in buying, selling, and financing land around the world. The site offers local, national, and international listings, an in-depth look at featured properties, and a number of other tools, such as a mortgage calendar, stock quotes, and a page on "Cheap Long Distance!"

MPM Real Estate Tribune

http://www.pmad.com/

This superb service provides information on real estate available within a 50-mile radius of all military installations, bases, and posts. Military personnel can review listings 24 hours a day from anywhere in the world. The Real Estate Guide is initially broken down into the five branches of service (Army, Coast Guard, and so on), then by state and military installation. This inventive site has other good information, too—information on search engines, links to cool sites, and even instructions on navigating the site.

National InterAd Real Estate Page

http://www.nia.com/homes

Offers illustrated listings for real estate, including houses, condominiums, and land. Includes information on real estate agents and services, as well as home buyer's tips.

North American Real Estate Review

http://www.narer.com/fintro.html

Unlike the traditional professional meeting, this online moderated conference allows participants to monitor current issues and expert opinions without the expense of time and travel. Available to registered delegates and invited guests in over 160 countries, the conference debates issues which "influence the development, financing, ownership, management and end-use of real property in America."

RE/MAX Real Estate network

http://www.remax.com/

The corporate site of this nationwide real estate agency offers a lot of material useful to both agents and consumers. Browsers can search a listing of home properties or RE/MAX agents, review commercial or mortgage information, or scan "RE/MAX Times," the in-house publication, online.

The Real Estate Junction

http://www.valleynet.com/~webcity/

Provides real estate listings by category, including residential, farm and ranch, commercial and investment properties, and recreation/resort/retirement properties.

Real Estate Library

http://www.realestatelibrary.com/

A collection of real estate articles of interest to buyers and sellers. Includes links to other "high content" sites.

The Real Estate Pages

http://www.newmarkets.com/real_estate.htm

Real estate listings from all 50 states and around the world.

Related Sites

http://www.dreamhomeloan.com/31.html

http://www.inman.com/news/9608/960821e.htm

Real Estate Shop

http://www.bsoftware.com/reshop.htm

Contains homes, real estate want ads, realtor advertisements, and a unique real estate catalog. Brings together real estate buyers, sellers, and agents. Find the dream house to buy by using Real Estate ON LINE. Sellers can also put their property listings on the ON LINE section. Also helps you locate excellent real estate agents in an area near you.

Real Estate Web

http://www.pilotonline.com/homes

Enables you to browse all listings of property for sale in coastal Virginia, based on price, type of property, and number of bedrooms. Also enables you to view agent profiles or add your own property for sale.

RealtyGuide

http://www.xmission.com:80/~realtor1/

RealtyGuide connects viewers with hundreds of real estate sources on the Internet. The site claims "plenty of links, raw information and a minimum of graphics." A sampling of this site includes a real estate business directory, an electronic newsroom, global finance resources, and a tour of the western mountain states.

Timbergreen Custom Homes

http://www.dfw.net/~custmbld/timbergreen.html

Provides information about Timbergreen Custom Homes, which has been designing and building high-end custom homes in and around Dallas, Texas since 1983. Contains information about the company and present homes available. Also contains photographs, floor plans, and elevations of various projects built by Timbergreen Custom Homes.

Underwater Housing

http://www.cnw.com/~ussubs/searoom.intro.html

For those who can't get enough of the ocean life, U.S. Submarines, Ltd. offers underwater housing units, which provide accommodations above and below water level and can be moored offshore. Developers might want to consider The Searoom Complex, an underwater commercial center that includes luxury hotel suites, a restaurant, and a bar.

Related Sites

http://www.thebuyersbroker.com/html/_buying_right__workshop.html

http://www.tennweb.com/topics/question.html

WebEstate Global Real Estate Web

http:www1.mhv.net/~webestate/misc.htm

Offers online publishing services to the real estate community. The site provides information on publishing and related topics—advertising, sponsorship, and linking pages—along with real estate news, trade tools, newsgroups, and mailing lists.

WRENet–World Real Estate Network

http://www.wren.com

A public real estate search service that includes all types of property (residential, commercial, industrial commercial investment, ranch and land) all over the world. Also includes a list of FAQs.

PUBLICATIONS AND MAGAZINES

Teleres, Daily Commercial Real Estate News

http://www.teleres.com/

A comprehensive resource for commercial real estate information, Teleres offers top news stories, an events calendar, and links to related sites. A frames-capable Web browser is required to view the site.

Wine Country Weekly Real Estate Reader

http://www.rereader.com/

A delightful online magazine with a wealth of information on California wine country real estate. Beyond its extensive listings (recreational, commercial and estate properties, vacation rentals, developments, and homes), the magazine offers real estate articles and sales data.

EXPERT TIPS

Better Homes and Gardens Guide to Buying and Selling Your Home

http://www.bhglive.com/guidpags/resinfo/buyhome/buyhome.html

Better Homes and Gardens offers some sound advice for first-time home buyers, tips about mortgages, relocating, and making your new house a real home. There are links to other BHG pages and lots of good advice.

Buying a House

http://www.burtonc.com/buying.htm

This page contains lots of advice from an experienced realtor. You'll find tips for making the move easier on children; hazards, such as lead paint, to watch out for; a glossary of real estate terms, mortgage rates, a loan calculator, and more.

Buying a House to Remodel

http://www.timelder.com/buyers/remodel.htm

This page, with advice from Tim Elder, a RE/MAX realtor in Greenville, South Carolina, is a must read before you sell your house. You'll learn just what kind of monetary return you can expect for remodeling your kitchen or bath or adding a sunroom. There's lots more good advice too.

Buying and Selling a Home

http://www.mpicture.com/homeguide/buy_sell/buysell.htm

This page contains dozens of articles of interest to those planning to buy or sell a home. You'll find such topics as "How to Afford a Better Location," "Tips for Buying Rural Homes," "Moving Planner," and many more.

Dungeon to a Palace

http://www2.waikato.ac.nz/education/WeNET/nola/TelEd.97/Tui%20Rolleston/contents%20.html

Here's one person's story of the experience of buying, renovating, and decorating a house. This page provides some real world advice about what to expect. It's charming and written from experience.

Experts Tell All About Buying and Selling

http://www.realestate.ca/Toronto/news/REN/doc00100.htm

This site offers two free books, one called *How to Buy Your Home* and another titled *How to Sell Your Home.* The books are described here, and there's an 800 number to call and get them both free.

Related Sites

http://www.amazon.com/exec/obidos/ISBN%3D0517888440/luckystarconsultA/8112-5907399-398805

http://www.amazon.com/exec/obidos/ISBN%3D081292780X/luckystarconsultA/8112-5907399-398805

How Do I Prepare to Make an Offer

http://www.crawfordhomes.com/makeoffer.html

You know the asking price, but what should you offer? Making the offer is tricky. Should you offer the list price? But what if the sellers would have taken less? If you offer too little will they be insulted? Here's a page of advice about how to make this important decision.

How to NOT Screw Up Your Real Estate Deal

http://www.screwup.com/

This well-designed site offers a crash course in real estate. If you're confused about such things as radon, termites, real estate law, for sale by owner, and other intricacies of real estate, check here.

Interactive Home Buying on the Web

http://www.maxsol.com/homes/buytips.htm

This page is just a simple list of things to remember and ways to prepare yourself for buying a house. "Pay off as much debt as possible" and "Get your credit report and correct errors" are just two of the tips you'll find here.

Selling Tips

http://ussweb.com/selltips.htm

This page contains advice for those intrepid people who plan to sell their homes "By Owner." You can save money, but this site offers some good advice about things you may not have thought of.

Selling Your Home Yourself

http://www.fsboconnection.com/yourself.html

This page offers advice about how to prepare your home to sell, whether you plan to do it yourself or hire a realtor. Things you might not ordinarily think of, such as tidying up the garage and adding fresh flowers in strategic spots, can help you market your house.

Ten Things

http://www.goble-assoc.com/kerry/ten.html

Here's a list of ten things you need to know before you enter the heady and frightening world of buying and selling real estate. "Get your mortgage commitment before you go house hunting!" is something you might not have thought of. Check out this site for nine more simple tips.

TIMESHARES

The Cybersharemall

http://www.cybersharemall.com/

A cornucopia of information on real estate—timeshare and resales, resorts and condominiums, vacation, and retirement real estate. The site specializes in tropical locations, especially the Caribbean islands, Florida, and California. An impressive array of photos online allows the viewer to browse for property, resorts, homes, or yachts.

Free Time Share Listing

http://www.apexsc.com/vb/ftp/coop/dough/plant.html

Designed to help owners sell or trade timeshare properties without paying advertising or commission fees. Listings primarily include timeshares in Florida, Mexico, and Hawaii.

Holiday Timeshares: Foreclosed and Discounted Timeshare Properties

http://www.holiday-timeshares.com/

With nearly 8,000 listings, the Holiday Group offers an enormous inventory of foreclosed repossessed or liquidated timeshares. In addition to discounted properties, the site offers a number of timeshare articles.

Interval International

http://www.interval.com/

For those with ownership in a vacation resort, Interval International offers membership services and timeshare exchange opportunities with hundreds of resorts in more than 60 countries. The site includes a FAQ section, a resort directory, resort vacation opportunities at reduced prices, and links to other Web sites.

RCI vacationNET

http://www.rci.com/

Resort Condominiums International (RCI) offers a searchable online directory of 3,000 resorts around the world affiliated with its timeshare exchange program. The site also includes travel tips, a tour of featured resorts, and a section explaining vacation ownership.

Related Site

http://www.nolo.com/ChunkRE/RE.index.html

Resortbase International Timeshare Information Network

http://www.resortbase.com/

This site offers both the consumer and the developer an extensive index of timeshare resorts, as well as a host of information on the timeshare industry, including information on buying, exchanging, or selling a timeshare interval.

TIMELINX

http://timelinx.com/

Timelinx offers an Internet timeshare database for the industry. Members may list units for exchange or sale, regardless of home resort affiliation and without "upfront request fees."

TRI International

http://www.TRI-International.com/

Provides buying, selling, resale, and exchange services of timeshare and resort properties. The site offers a variety of information for buyers, owners, and industry professionals, including a timeshare bluebook of over 2,000 resorts.

Vacation Realty

http://www.webcom.com/

Specializes in timeshare resales without upfront fees. The site offers a worldwide classifieds section as well as an online auction of timesharing properties. Utilizing the online search request form, buyers can search both Vacation Realty's inventory of listings and those of cooperating brokers.

The Worldwide Timeshare Mall

http://timesharemall.com/center.html

Serving as clearinghouse for timeshare information and inventory, the Timeshare Mall has compiled a wealth of information on the subject. Select "The ABCs of Timeshare" a get a better understanding of the concept. Looking for a job? Click "Resort Employment Opportunities." The site also offers a listing of timeshare exchange opportunities.

NEWSGROUPS

alt.invest.real-estate

alt.real-estate-agents

fl.real-estate

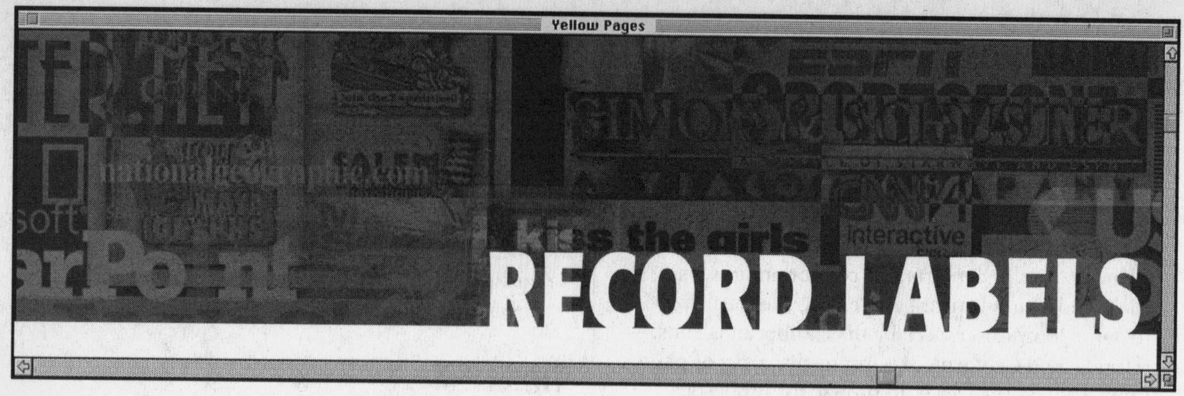

> The best, most beautiful, and most perfect way that we have of expressing a sweet concord of mind to each other is by music.
>
> *Jonathan Edwards*

2.13.61 Records

http://www.21361records.com/

Artist background, pictures, album artwork, and catalog for 2.13.61 Records. The label's artists include Matthew Shipp, Henry Rollins, Mark of Cain, Alan Vega, and many more. Also includes a chat pit and ordering information.

Acorn Music

http://www.sirius.com/~acorn/

Provides a catalog of traditional and nontraditional folk and world music. Includes background of the label and its artists, including tour dates.

Alternet Sonic Realities

http://www.iuma.com/ASR/

Provides label background, artist history, sound clips, and ordering information for this small, independent "cyber-label." Musicians on Alternet Sonic vary from Australian techno to East Coast United States alternative rock.

Related Sites

http://user.aol.com/prodsun/prodsun.html

http://www.execpc.com/~hardrcd/

The Ultimate Band List: Record Labels
http://www.ubl.com/label/

American Gramaphone Records

http://www.amgram.com/

Background and history of the label and their artists. Includes a detailed essay about Chip Davis, the leader of Mannheim Steamroller, Fresh Aire, and American Gramaphone Records. Also includes tour and lecture dates.

American Recordings Home Page

http://american.recordings.com/

The label that publishes acts such as Frank Black, Julian Cope, Pete Droge, Slayer, Lords of Acid, and more. Includes discographies, audio and video clips, tour schedules, online chat with the artists, and more.

Axiom/Laswell Web Site

http://hyperreal.com/music/labels/axiom/

Home site for Bill Laswell and Axiom records. Includes label catalog, upcoming releases, Bill Laswell discography, and links to related musical sites. Also provides an extensive history of Laswell's career in music, which covers all grounds in rock, funk, experimental, and beyond. Fans of eclectic music and those looking for something different would do very well to visit this site.

Badcat Records

http://www.opendoor.com/badcat/BCR_Home.html

The home site for Badcat Records. Includes the label's catalog, artist photos, and downloadable music samples of their records. Provides many choices of information players.

Barking Dog Records

http://www.barkingdogrecords.com/

Provides artist and label information, concert information, sound clips of current albums, current news, and a tour of the Raptor Recording Studios, its recording facility.

Black Rock Coalition

http://users.aol.com./brcny/home.html

To fight the notion that all black artists must play either R&B or hip-hop, the BRC have put out compilation albums containing all rock-n-roll songs recorded entirely by black groups and artists. Check out an overview of the coalition; reviews of their albums; and interviews with progressive black artists, writers, and industry leaders.

Blue Note Records

http://mercury.stumpworld.com/bluenote/

Label history, discography, and ordering information for this classic jazz and blues label. Includes profiles and background on artists such as McCoy Tyner, Ron Carter, Mose Allison, Cecil Taylor, and many others. Includes record reviews and sound bytes.

BMG Classics World

http://classicalmus.com/

Home site for the BMG records classical music division. Includes artist profiles and sound samples for artists such as David Helfgott, Alexander Nevsky, and James Galway. Online catalog and ordering information.

Bogus Records

http://www.w2.com/bogus.html

Founded in 1979 by a guitar shop owner, this label puts out a variety of albums. Check out the records, download some audio clips, and then purchase them online.

Boy's Life Records

http://www.iuma.com/Boy's_Life/

Sound samples, cover art, and catalog for this Los Angeles-based label. Includes ordering information. Boy's Life Records artists' music is described as "psychedelic rock."

C/Z Records Home Page

http://www.musicwest.com/cz/

An online catalog, label biography, artist profiles, and ordering information for C/Z Records. The label's artists include Silkworm, Built to Spill, Engine Kid, and many more.

Capitol Records' Hollywood and Vine

http://www.hollywoodandvine.com/

Online site for Capitol Records, whose artists include The Beatles, George Clinton, The Beastie Boys, Sammy Davis Jr., and many more. This very extensive site includes artist profiles, sound bytes, video files, tour dates, and upcoming release and ordering information. Also includes contests, discussion rooms, and links to many of Capitol's artists' sites.

Castle Communications

http://www.castleus.com/

Provides information on the four labels (Sequel, DOJO, Transatlantic, and Castle Records imprints), plus artist information and current releases. This group includes artists ranging from Ugly Kid Joe to Tangerine Dreams.

Castle von Buhler Records

http://cvb.drawbridge.com/

Home site for this Illinois-based independent, alternative label. Includes band promos and reviews for such acts as Turkish Delight, Splashdown, and sirensong. Sound bytes, album artwork, and ordering information.

Caulfield Records

http://www.acton.com/bernie/

This is the home site for Caulfield Records and their bands. Includes sound bytes, album cover artwork, tour dates, and upcoming releases information. Also includes the Caulfield Web Board for use as a newsgroup.

Curb Records

http://www.curb.com/

Curb Records specializes in—but is not limited to—country and traditional American song forms such as blues and zydeco. Artists on the Curb catalog site include Tim McGraw, Wynonna, Junior Brown, Hank Williams Jr., Lyle Lovett, and Kool and the Gang, to name a few. The site includes artist background, tour dates, record catalog, lyrics, sound bytes, and ample information on Curb artists. Also includes ordering information. This is a nice music site and is highly recommended for fans of these artists.

Death Row Records

http://www.grfn.org/~earthdog/drr/

Home site for Death Row Records, home of rap artists such as Snoop Doggy Dog, 2Pac, and N.W.A. Includes artist profiles and album artwork.

Def-Jam Online

http://www.defjam.com/

Provides label background, artist profiles, tour information, and much more for the Def-Jam label. Artists on Def-Jam include Public Enemy, LL Cool J, Warren G, and many more. Site includes sound bytes and video clips.

Dreamscape Records

http://www.pagelink.com/dreamscape/

The home page for a small independent, this site provides the mission statement for the label, and lists bands currently signed with them. Also some information about the bands.

Geffen Records

http://www.geffen.com/

A very well-put-together page from the giant recording label. Features a variety of information about its various artists, including QuickTime video clips, AU sound files, biographies, rare photos, and more.

Go Kart Records

http://www.w2.com/gokart.html

A record company and link from the World Square home page. Links to recording artists and CD ordering information. Click the CD or song title and download for your viewing and listening pleasure.

Goodlife Recordings

http://www.club.innet.be/~rwcs0127/

Goodlife Recordings is a hardcore music independent (and based on the straight-edge philosophy); the site contains an extensive catalog and includes news and other information.

Hi-Bias Records, Inc.

http://www.interlog.com/~hibias/

A Canadian-based record label, originally developed by DJs and music enthusiasts, producing CDs and music videos. Provides links to their catalog, artists, new releases, features, Club Hi-Bias, and so on.

Hollywood Records

http://www.hollywoodrec.com/

Online site for Hollywood Records. Site includes tour dates, label catalog, artist profiles, and upcoming release information. Also includes information about soundtrack releases and the U.S. distribution of the British Acid Jazz label.

ID&T Records

http://www.dance.nl/id&t/

Originally a rave organizer based in Holland and in Germany, now provides CD releases, album info, DJ info, and fashion and party info to the alternative music enthusiast.

Jazzlogy

http://www.jazzology.com/

Provides information on a series of jazz labels, each with their own catalog, and ordering information. Each label represents a style of jazz: Jazzlogy is Chicago style, GBH Records is New Orleans, Solo Art is piano jazz, and so on.

Magic Island

http://www.magicisland.com/

If you like the music of Bob James, Jazz Stuff, the Island Dwellers, or any other jazz-like sound, check out this site. Links to the home pages of many jazz musicians.

Maranatha! Music

http://www.maranathamusic.com/core.htm

This company, born out of the Jesus Movement of the early '70s, provides Christian music for church worship services. Complete listing of services, artists, releases, worship material, and history of Maranatha! Music.

Related Sites

http://www.geocities.com/Hollywood/Academy/2899/index.html

http://www.humboldt1.com/~etgreen/

Marathon Records

http://www.netads.com/netads/arts/music/marathon/

A group of indie bands who decided to put their pages together on the Internet. Links to alternative bands' pages such as Able Cain, Animator, Fairwell to Juliet, Sunny Day Roses, Soulstice, and others.

Matador Records Central

http://www.matador.recs.com/

Home site for the label and their artists, which include The Jon Spencer Blues Explosion, Liz Phair, Pavement, Silkworm, and many more. Provides links to band pages, articles, reviews, and sound bytes. Includes touring information and a bulletin board.

Maverick Records

http://www.maverickent.com/

This graphics-intensive site seems to take over your screen, providing artist information, new releases, news, employment opportunities, a chat room, and an online store. This is Madonna's label for the artists she's interested in.

Metal Blade Records

http://www.iuma.com/Metal_Blade/home.html

If you like Metallica, check out this Web site of heavy metal, gothic, and doom bands. You can also browse and order from their mail-order catalog.

Moniker Records

http://moniker.org/

Label information, artist info, new release information, tours, reviews, and sound clips. Moniker is a small full-service label (from recording to manufacturing) that's artist-oriented, and handles anything from pop to spoken word, from CDs to 75s.

Monkeyland Records

http://www.monkeylandrecords.com/

Another page for indie music lovers. Includes artwork, CD reviews, sound clips, ordering info, tour dates, and related music links.

Moonshine Music

http://www.moonshine.com/

Musical compilations not often found on top 40 labels. Includes ambient, techno, house, and many more. Links to bands and releases.

Mute Liberation Technologies

http://www.mutelibtech.com/mute/

The Web site of Mute Records, with links to an artist database including Depeche Mode and Erasure, music news, and a full color catalog.

Not Lame Records

http://notlame.com/

Dedicated to "Power Pop"—the music that is "all things melodic, hooky, moderately sugary, and songs that stick like Super Glue to your brain and don't let go!" Provides label infomation, current releases, a mail order music store, samples of what's currently available. Also has vinyl for sale.

Oh Boy Records

http://www.ohboy.com/

Record label formed by John Prine. Contains pages devoted to John and Heather Eatman. Includes discographies, lyrics, pictures, mail-order catalogs, and more. Also covers Red Pajamas Records and Blue Plate Music.

On U Sound

http://server.tt.net/onusound/

Provides a home site for On U Sound, a label headed by music producer Adrian Sherwood. The label carries genre-bending groups such as Dub Syndicate, African Head Charge, Revolutionary Dub Warriors, and much more. Site includes artist profiles, album previews, and cover artwork.

PolyGram Records

http://www.PolyGram.com/polygram/Music.html

From one of the biggest record companies in the world. The site provides artist bios, video clips, sound clips, a complete catalog for PolyGram and its sister labels, tour information, lots of photos, and links to the PolyGram Online site for access to information on Polygram films, videos, and other items.

Propulsion Records

http://www.w2.com/docs2/b/propulsion.html

This home site for Propulsion Records includes an online catalog, sound bytes, album artwork, and artist background. Also includes ordering information.

Putumayo World Music

http://www.putumayo.com/

A leader of independent world music. This site provides Putumayo's catalog of CD releases, news and upcoming information, plus ordering information and other music links.

Rage Records

http://www.w2.com/rage.html

Provides home site and online ordering for Rage Records, a New York City-based hip-hop label. Includes company catalog, artist profiles, and sound bytes.

RCA Victor

http://www.rcavictor.com/

The home site for RCA Victor, home of many great artists from jazz to classical and rock. This site features new releases information, links to artist sites, and sound bytes.

Reservoir Records

http://monsterbit.com/reservoir/reservoir.html

The home site for Reservoir Records provides a catalog, artist profiles, and ordering information.

Restless Records

http://www.restless.com/

Artist profiles, video clips, sound bytes, upcoming release information, and company catalog. Catalog includes artists like the Sex Pistols, Jack Logan, Wire, and many more.

Rhino Records Home Page

http://pathfinder.com/Rhino/

Search for your favorite artist or song in their 2,000-plus title catalog, check out the upcoming releases, chat with an artist, order Rhino merchandise, read the online version of the *Retroactive* newsletter, and enter the monthly contests for free stuff.

Rockadillo Records

http://www.sjoki.uta.fi/~latvis/levy-yhtiot/Rockadillo_Records

Home site for Rockadillo Records, based in Finland. Includes company catalog, artist profiles (not all are Finnish), and contact information. Rockadillo focuses on rock with jazz, ethnic, and country overtones.

Rykodisc/ Hannibal/ Gramavision

http://www.rykodisc.com/3/

Home site for Rykodisc Records and their other subsidiary labels Hannibal and Gramavision. Site includes information about artists such as David Bowie, Frank Zappa, Throwing Muses, and Bob Mould. Also includes artist profiles, album artwork, RealAudio files, and links to many related sites.

Smithsonian Folkways

http://www.si.edu/folkways/

The music recording and music history branch of the Smithsonian Institution. Search the 35,000-track database, visit archives, listen to recent releases, place an order, read the E-zine, and much, much more.

Sony Music Online!

http://www.music.sony.com/Music/MusicIndex.html

The home site for Sony Records and its affiliated labels. Information on artists such as Aerosmith, Miles Davis, Oasis, Shawn Colvin, and many more. Tour dates, artist profiles, pictures, sound samples, and links to their artists' sites. Also includes upcoming releases information.

Sub Pop Records Online

http://www.subpop.com/

Sub Pop Records artists include Sebadoh, The Grifters, Six Finger Satellite, and many others. This site includes artist pages, an online catalog, and ordering information. Also includes links to many different related music sites.

Supernova Records

http://www.intr.net/supernova/

Home site for Supernova Records, based in Arlington, Virginia. Includes background and ordering information for Supernova's artist compilations. Also includes links to many bands, zines, and tour dates.

Surfdog Records

http://www.professionals.com/~surfdog

Artist profiles, label catalog, and contact information. Surfdog artists concentrate on the "surfer music" styles, including reggae and instrumental guitar rock.

Related Sites

http://www.kingsnakecd.com/

http://www.kneelingelephant.com/

The Ultimate Band List: Record Labels

`http://www.ubl.com/label/`

A site designed not only to provide links to hundreds of record labels, but also links for radio stations, artists, clubs and concerts, news, magazines (including E-zines), and even a search engine for your browsing pleasure.

Verb Audio

`http://www.mindspring.com/~brydaguy/verb.html`

The Verb Audio label specializes in electronic dance music. Includes label profile, philosophy, catalog, DJ booking information, and information about the Atlanta dance scene. This site has some unbelievable graphics. Very cool.

Verve Interactive

`http://www.verveinteractive.com/`

The home page for the legendary jazz, blues, and rock label. Includes profiles and sound bytes for artists such as Herbie Hancock, Ornette Coleman, Ella Fitzgerald, and many more. Includes concert dates and links to related sites.

Village Pulse

`http://www.rootsworld.com/rw/villagepulse/outpost.html`

Village Pulse is a record label that specializes in Mandinka drum music and other West African drum artists. Includes label catalog, artist background, photos, and contact information.

Virgin Records America

`http://www.virginrecords.com/homepage.html`

Virgin Records America carries artists such as Smashing Pumpkins, The Rolling Stones, Sex Pistols, and many more. Includes artist profiles, sound files, pictures, tour information, and a chat room.

Walt Disney Records

`http://www.disney.com/DisneyRecords/index.html`

A complete catalog of Disney's children's music, read-a-longs, and movie soundtracks. Also provides a list of stores carrying Disney records, and an online store.

Warner Bros. Records

`http://www.wbr.com/`

Home site for Warner Bros. Records and artists. Includes information about groups such as Van Halen, k.d. lang, Ministry, Lou Reed, The Artist (formerly known as Prince), and many, many more. Also includes discussion groups and links to related sites. There are quite a few famous musicians on Warner Bros.

Windham Hill Records

`http://www.windham.com/`

Includes artist profiles, sound bytes, tour dates, label catalog, and ordering information. Windham Hill artists include George Winston, Michael Hedges, Tuck & Patti, Timbuk 3, and many more.

Your K Homepage

`http://www.olywa.net/kpunk/`

K Records is a punk-and-love rock label based in Olympia, Washington. Includes label discography and a listing of distributed records. Provides profiles of artists such as Beat Happening, Dub Narcotic Sound System, Fitz of Depression, and many more. Includes contact and ordering information.

NEWSGROUPS

`alt.music.4ad`

`alt.music.dream-theater`

`alt.music.producer`

`rec.music.promotional`

FTP & Gopher Sites

`file://ftp.cs.ruu.nl/pub/MIDI/midicomp.html`

`gopher://marvel.loc.gov/11/global/arts/music`

Related Sites

`http://www.mca-nashville.com/`

`http://www.mindspring.com/~david.daniell/samizdat/`

`http://www.obsolete.com/swim/swim.html`

`http://www.wallofsound.com/`

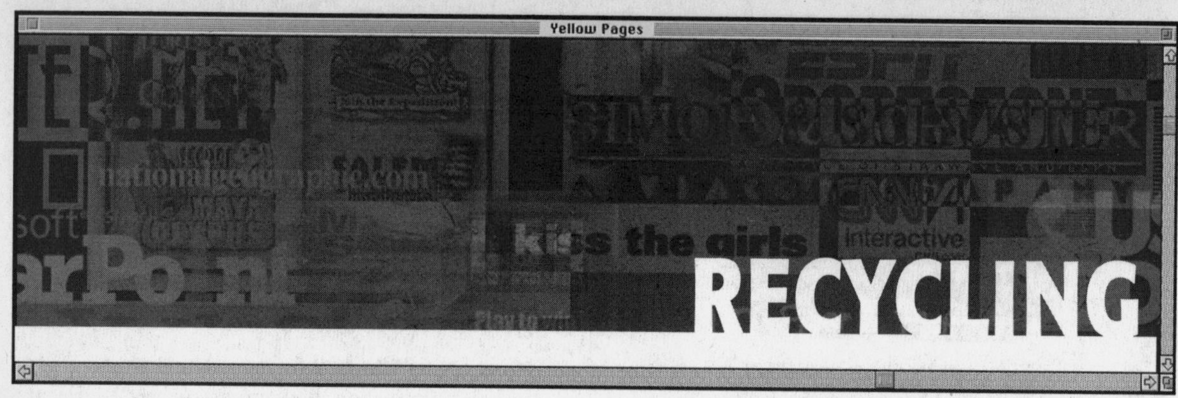

Waste not, want not.

Benjamin Franklin

Commonly Recycled Materials
http://www.best.com/~dillon/recycle/guides/common.html

GREENGUIDE–Reduce/Reuse/Recycle
http://www.pnl.gov/esp/greenguide/appe.html

Recycler's World
http://www.recycle.net/

Cleaning Up C.E. Cole

http://www.enter.net/~tquire/cole.html

The kids of Mr. Yelles and Mr. Kondisko's classes at C.E. Cole intermediate school are concerned about their environment. They started several recycling projects, including this recycling Web page that documents their efforts.

Commonly Recycled Materials

http://www.best.com/~dillon/recycle/guides/common.html

Consider this Web page to be Recycling 101. It explains everything you might not have previously understood about recycling, including those cryptic looking recycling markers. The work here is an effort to make recycling a natural part of everyone's everyday life.

The Consumer Recycling Guide: Index to Local Recycling Centers

http://www.best.com/~dillon/recycle/local/index.html

So you want to become environmentally conscious and start recycling, but you don't know where to do it? Not a problem once you access this index to find a local recycling center near you. The list is always growing and has listings for all 50 states, as well as select international sites.

GREENGUIDE–Reduce/Reuse/Recycle

http://www.pnl.gov/esp/greenguide/appe.html

The table on this page provides valuable information on how to reduce our consumption, reuse frequently discarded items, and recycle materials that can be reprocessed. It also contains special handling instructions for materials from batteries to wood pallets.

The Recycle Link

http://www.recycle.org/

This page, brought to you by Cyber Recycle, Inc., will both help you find a recycling program in your area and teach you what exactly can or cannot be recycled. You can also find information on manufacturers who utilize recyclables and the products they make.

Recycle Locally

http://www.umr.edu/~ems/recycle.html

Did you ever wonder what happens to the materials you recycle once they're out of your hands? The city of Rolla documents its recycling program and tells its citizens exactly where their recycled goods are headed.

Recycler's World

`http://www.recycle.net/`

Recycler's World - Main Menu

Free BUY/SELL/TRADE Listings in

THE RECYCLER'S Exchange

Secondary Commodity Sections

- Automotive Recycling Section
- Battery Recycling Section
- Computer Recycling Section
- Iron & Steel Recycling Section
- Non-Ferrous Scrap Metal Recycling Section
- Precious Metals Recycling Section
- Exotic Metals Recycling Section
- Plastics Recycling Section
- Tire & Rubber Recycling Section

The mother of all recycling sites! You will find pages for every possible recyclable material, from automotive parts to wood and plastics. It even has a section for organic and food waste recycling.

Environmental Issues

`gopher://gopher.well.com/11/Environment`

A variety of stories, essays and book reviews covering various environmental issues and ideas.

EPA Online Library System

`telnet://epaibm.rtpnc.epa.gov`

Search the EPA's online system by author, title, keywords, year of publication and so on.

Great Lakes Information Network

`gopher://gopher.cic.net`

A network to store and disseminate bi-national data and information regarding environmental issues, resource management, transportation, demographic and development data, and other information and resources in the Great Lakes region of the U.S. and Canada.

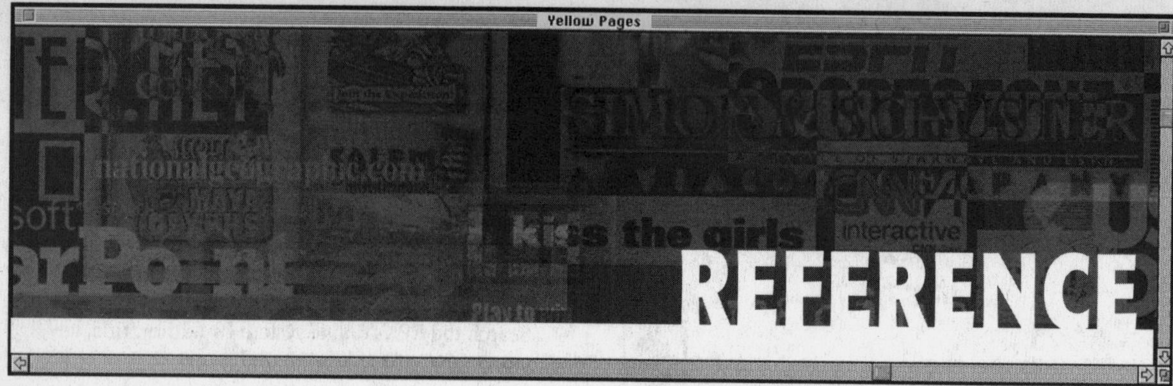

A B C D E F G H I J K L M N O P Q R S T U V W X Y Z

> Knowledge is the small part of ignorance that we arrange and classify.
>
> *Ambrose Bierce*

Betsy Ross Homepage
`http://libertynet.org/iha/betsy/`

The Consumer Information Center
`http://www.pueblo.gsa.gov/`

The Nobel Foundation
`http://www.nobel.se/`

CENSUS

1990 U.S. Census Lookup

`http://cedr.lbl.gov/cdrom/doc/lookup_doc.html`

Contains links to WWW servers for accessing 1990 census data from tapes.

TIGER Mapping Service

`http://tiger.census.gov/`

This site, a service of the United States Census, generates detailed maps of anywhere in the United States. Images are large and, because the service actually *creates* the maps while you wait, download times can be slow.

U.S. Gazetteer

`http://www.census.gov/cgi-bin/gazetteer`

Search engine for retrieving state and local census information from the 1990 census.

FLAGS

Betsy Ross Homepage

`http://libertynet.org/iha/betsy/`

Provides information about Betsy Ross, history of the U.S. flag, pictures of U.S. flags, and links to other flag-related sites. Also has instructions for cutting a five-pointed star in one snip.

The Flag-Burning Page

`http://www.indirect.com/user/warren/flag.html`

Yes, this is the page where you can burn a virtual flag. This site provides information about the proposed Constitutional amendment on flag burning, information on the history of flag-burning, a legal definition of "flag," and information on contacting members of Congress.

The Flag of the United States of America

`http://www.icss.com/usflag/`

Provides flag etiquette, history of the U.S. flag, text of the Declaration of Independence, National Anthem, and Pledge of Allegiance to the flag. The Pledge is in English, German, and Spanish. Information about obtaining a flag that was flown over the U.S. Capitol. Links to other flag-related sites. Poetry, songs, and more about the flag.

Flags of the 19th and 20th Century

http://www.pi.net/~marksens/

Provides pictures of flags, primarily from the Netherlands and surrounding countries, plus a few African countries.

National Flag Foundation

http://www.icss.com/usflag/nff.html

Information about how to become a member of the National Flag Foundation.

Save Old Glory From Flames Home Page

http://www.pic.net/flameout/oldglory/

This site is in response to the Flag-Burning Page. One can add one's name to a list of people that support the Constitutional amendment to outlaw flag burning. Also has links to other politics-related sites.

MEASUREMENTS

Conversion Factor Table

http://www.uwosh.edu/students/wallip27/convert.html

The interface is a bit clumsy, but the information is thorough. Here's how it works: You want to know how many centimeters are in 10 meters. You find meters in the table, see that the conversion factor (or c.f.) is 100 (100 centimeters equal 1 meter), and multiply that number by 10. Ten meters equal 1000 centimeters.

Engineering, Scientific Unit Converter

http://www.webcom.com/~legacysy/convert2/convert2.html

This forms-based tool will convert values in a number of categories: acceleration, angle, area, current, force, inductance, mass, power, time, torque, velocity, volume, and many others.

Measurements Converter

http://www.mplik.ru/~sg/transl/

Select from a list of measurement types that includes weight, volume, length, area, speed, pressure, temperature, circular measure, and time; the script will convert miles to kilometers, ounces to metric tons, and centuries to seconds.

MISCELLANEOUS REFERENCE

Bow Brummell: Where Cyberians Learn the Manly Art of Tying a Bow Tie

http://www.tcf.ua.edu/bowtie/

This humorous page offers diagrams and instructions on how to tie a bow tie. Arguably the most noteworthy thing about the diagrams is that the man in the picture is clearly *not* tying his own tie.

Central Notice

http://www.notice.com/

Billing itself as the place to find information that you aren't aware of not knowing about (as opposed to information that you don't know, but you realize that you don't know it—make sense?). Central Notice posts listings of product recalls, class action lawsuits, and missing children while also assisting with consumer problems and providing lists of holidays, both important and trivial.

The Consumer Information Center

http://www.pueblo.gsa.gov/

With a browsable catalog, consumer news on topics like car- and home-buying and children's health, lists of publications, and links to other consumer sites, the CIC's site is another valuable consumer resource. For other consumer information, see "Consumer Issues," earlier in this book.

The DataStar Information Retrieval Service

http://www.krinfo.ch/

This service of Knight-Ridder Information provides a searchable index to over 400 databases culled widely from sources such as automotive industry data; import/export trade statistics; pharmaceutical, biomedical, and healthcare information; and European news organizations.

Disaster Information Network

http://www.disaster.net/

Offering information about current and historical disasters, this site covers natural disasters, fires (both natural and manmade), and acts of terrorism.

Find-A-Grave

http://www.orci.com/personal/jim/index.html

Listing the final resting places for hundreds of celebrities and VIPs, this macabre site offers notable graves geographically or alphabetically, pictures of famous graves, and links to other tomb-related sites.

Internet Nonprofit Center

http://www.nonprofits.org/

This excellent and extensive grouping of links to non-profit sites offers a search engine that will locate almost any U.S. charity, provides links to home pages for nonprofit groups, and even offers a library of rankings of charities and a "Donor Defense Kit" to help separate the wheat from the chaff when charities contact you for donations.

Morse Code and the Phonetic Alphabets

http://www.soton.ac.uk/~scp93ch/refer/alphabet.html

Contains the phonetic alphabets in British English, American English, international English, international aviation English, Italian, and German and the Morse code equivalent for all letters plus some punctuation marks.

Morse Code Translator

http://www.soton.ac.uk/~scp93ch/refer/morseform.html

Translates typewritten Morse code (dots and dashes) into text and text into Morse code.

MRX—Morse Receive and Transmit Training

http://www.ozemail.com.au/~jwsamin/

Download a copy of MRX from this Web site. MRX is a software program designed to provide training in Morse code. Software system requirements are DOS 4.0, 286 PC, sound card or PC Speaker, VGA monitor, and a joystick port.

My Virtual Reference Desk

http://www.refdesk.com/

This site bills itself as a "one-stop reference for all things Internet." Although it is mainly a collection of links, it maintains a thorough and comprehensive database of references on a vast array of subjects.

The Nobel Foundation

http://www.nobel.se/

In addition to offering a list of present winners, this official site presents a searchable database for past winners. Unfortunately, however, unlike the Nobel Prize Internet Archive, you cannot browse the list of winners or see biographical information about each winner. This site does, however, offer a bio of Alfred Nobel and discusses his motivations for founding the Prizes, in addition to explaining how Nobel Laureates are nominated and selected.

The Nobel Prize Internet Archive

http://mgm.mit.edu:8080/pevzner/Nobel.html

Listing both the 1997 Nobel Prize winners (announced in October) and all previous winners in every category, this site also links to biographical information about many of the winners. The interface is much easier to navigate than the Noble Foundation's official site.

The Obituary Page

http://catless.ncl.ac.uk/Obituary/README.html

This morbidly fascinating page offers death hoaxes, in addition to the life spans of famous figures from literature, movies, music, politics, sciences, sports, radio and TV, and visual arts.

On-Line Reference Works

http://www.cs.cmu.edu/Web/references.html

Carnegie Mellon University provides this list of links to dictionaries, Internet resources, geographical references, bibliographies, and legal and government resources.

The Reporter's Internet Survival Guide

http://www.qns.com/~casey/

Patrick Casey, an Associated Press reporter in Oklahoma, created this online catalog of reference materials for reporters on a deadline. Despite that, this is a valuable reference for anyone needing access to a wide variety of information.

Research-It!

http://www.iTools.com/research-it/research-it.html

This table-based site requires the use of either Netscape Navigator or Microsoft's Internet Explorer. By using forms you can search through dictionaries and thesauri; find acronyms or quotations; translate words between English and French and English and Japanese; find maps, area codes, and 800 numbers; look up currency exchange rates and stock quotes; and even track packages through the United States Postal Service, UPS, and FedEx.

The Scout Report

http://rs.internic.net/scout/report/

Net Scout Services publishes this weekly report (via email and the Web) cataloging new and newly discovered resources and tools available on the Internet. Aimed at researchers and educators, The Scout Report offers its archives on the Web for both browsing and searching.

Standard Industrial Classifications (SIC) Index

http://www.wave.net/upg/immigration/sic_index.html

Browsable list of the 1987 edition of the SIC index (latest available). List is arranged alphabetically by subject.

Ten Codes

http://www.jaxnet.com/~habedd/10codes.html

Lists the official meanings of the 10 codes used by police departments.

THOR+: The Virtual Reference Desk

http://thorplus.lib.purdue.edu/reference/index.html

This information-rich site at the Purdue University Library provides references to many Web resources including the following: government documents, information technology, dictionaries and language reference, phone books and area codes, maps and travel information, science data, time and date information, and ZIP and postal codes.

Tipping

http://www.cis.columbia.edu/homepages/gonzalu/tipping.html

This page offers general guidelines for how much to tip in certain situations: restaurants, hotels, valet parking, train stations and airports, cruise ships, and the like.

UTLink: Resources by Subject

http://library.utoronto.ca/www/subjects.html

The University of Toronto Library maintains this site, which offers lists of resources, at U of T and beyond, in academic fields ranging from African and Black Studies to Women's Studies.

World Population

http://sunsite.unc.edu/lunarbin/worldpop

This site offers an estimate of the current world population at the time you access it.

The WWW Virtual Library

http://www.w3.org/hypertext/DataSources/bySubject/Overview.html

This Web-based library offers hundreds of subjects in science, mathematics, art, literature, music, culture, museums, religion, spirituality, sports, finance, and transportation. Truly eclectic, some of its more unusual categories include beer and brewing, paranormal phenomena, roadkill (!), whale watching Web, and yeasts.

PHONE NUMBERS

555-1212.com Area Code Look-Up

http://www.555-1212.com/aclookup.html

Searchable by city and/or state name for U.S. or Canadian area codes, or browsable by area code or state name. Returns area code and corresponding city/state. Area code links lead to a business look-up directory which is browsable by category or searchable by business name.

Airline Toll-Free Numbers and Websites

http://www.princeton.edu/Main/air800.html

Browsable list of both domestic and international airlines with corresponding 800 numbers and links to Web sites if available.

The AmeriCom Long Distance AREA DECODER

http://www.xmission.com/~americom/aclookup.html

Input city, state, and/or country to receive the area or country code and AmeriCom rates. Input the area code, country code, AmeriCom per minute rate, and/or AmeriCom in state rate to receive the city, state, or country and the AmeriCom rates. Also has information about AmeriCom international business opportunities.

AT&T Internet Toll Free 800 Directory

http://www.tollfree.att.net/dir800/

Browsable by category, or searchable by company name, city, state, and/or category. Also includes information about AT&T.

BigBook

http://www.bigbook.com/

Searchable by business name, category, city, and/or state for a quick search. Search can also be narrowed by using the ZIP code, area code, street name, or map location. Search returns name, address, and telephone number of businesses matching search criteria. Option is available for seeing business locations on a map.

BigYellow

http://s10.bigyellow.com/

Search for businesses by city, state, business name, category, address, and/or ZIP code. Returns full address including ZIP+4 and telephone number for all businesses matching the search criteria. Also includes links to other world-wide telephone directories and Web search engines, business information for setting up Web sites, and advertising information for advertising at this BigYellow site.

The Internet 800 Directory

http://inter800.com/

Searchable by keyword and state. Returns businesses matching the search criteria and their corresponding 1-800 telephone numbers, up to a maximum of 100 businesses.

National Telephone & Communications (NTC) Tele-Locator

http://www.natltele.com/form.html

Searchable by state name, area code, city code, telephone number prefix, telephone number, or country code (for countries outside the United States). Returns city, state, area code, and/or telephone number prefix as applicable.

PC Phone List

http://foundation.mit.edu/cgi-bin/search-phone-list

Provides technical support phone numbers for computer hardware and software. Enter the name of the company or the software, and the program returns all technical support telephone numbers (and bulletin board services if available) that match the search terms.

Period.Com Airlines!

http://www.period.com/airlines/airlines.shtml

Browsable list of domestic, foreign, and shipping airlines with their 800 numbers. Provides links to airline Web sites where available.

PhoNETic

http://www.soc.qc.edu/phonetic/

Enter a phone number to receive all possible letter combinations for that phone number, or enter letters to receive the phone number corresponding to those letters. Also includes information about obtaining phonetic telephone numbers and an explanation for why calculator and telephone keypads are different.

Switchboard

http://www.switchboard.com/

Search for either businesses or people. For people searches, enter last name, first name, city, and/or state to return name, address, and phone number of all people matching the search criteria. For business searches, enter the company name, city, and/or state to return the name, address, and phone number of all businesses matching the search criteria. Registered users may also personalize and update their own listings.

World Telecom Directories

http://infolab.ms.wwa.com/wtx/

Select country name from list, then type in company name. Returns list of companies and corresponding fax numbers. This address is for locating fax numbers for Asian and Pacific region countries.

World Yellow Pages Network (wyp.net)

http://wyp.net/

U.S. and Canadian businesses are searchable by company name and state, phone number, or ZIP code. The white pages are searchable by name, phone number, or keyword. Searches return all entries matching the search criteria, up to a maximum of 100 returns. The white pages also contain search capabilities for locating email addresses of individuals. In addition to providing yellow and white pages searches, this site also allows businesses and individuals to create their own home page for this site and to update it at their convenience.

Yellow Pages Online, Inc.

`http://www.ypo.com/`

Searchable by heading keyword, company name, or brand name. Returns company name and phone number for all entries that match the search criteria.

YellowNet

`http://www.yellownet.com/`

Searchable by geographic area (city, state, county), company name, and/or heading keyword. Returns name, address, and phone number for all entries that match the search criteria.

POSTAL INFORMATION

Geographic Nameserver

`http://www.mit.edu:8001/geo`

Index is searchable by ZIP code or city name. Results returned include city, county, state, country, and ZIP code. Latitude, longitude, population, and elevation are returned if available. If more than one city matches the search criteria, then information on all matching cities is returned.

National Address and ZIP+4 Browser

`http://www.semaphorecorp.com/`

Searchable by company name, street address, city, state, and ZIP code. Returns closest matches along with ZIP+4 code. After information is returned, option is given to browse addresses in the same geographical location. Also includes list of state code abbreviations.

United States Postal Service

`http://www.usps.gov/`

Includes information about stamp releases, pictures of stamps available, searchable index for ZIP+4 codes, state and address abbreviations, preferred addressing methods, size standards for mail, postage rates for both domestic and international mail delivery, history of the USPS, news releases, calendar of events, and other postal-related information. The business section of this Web site includes information both for the mailing needs of businesses and for the business needs of the USPS. Businesses wishing to sell products to the USPS will find a purchasing manual and information about selling products to the USPS at this Web site.

The Zipper

`http://www.stardot.com/zipper/`

Input a five-digit ZIP code to obtain the name, address, and phone number of either the Congressional representative or Senators for that ZIP code. Search returns name, Washington office address, phone number, fax number, and email address (if available) of representative or Senator. A link to the representative's or Senator's home page is provided if available. Also includes a couple of links to other sites for Congressional information.

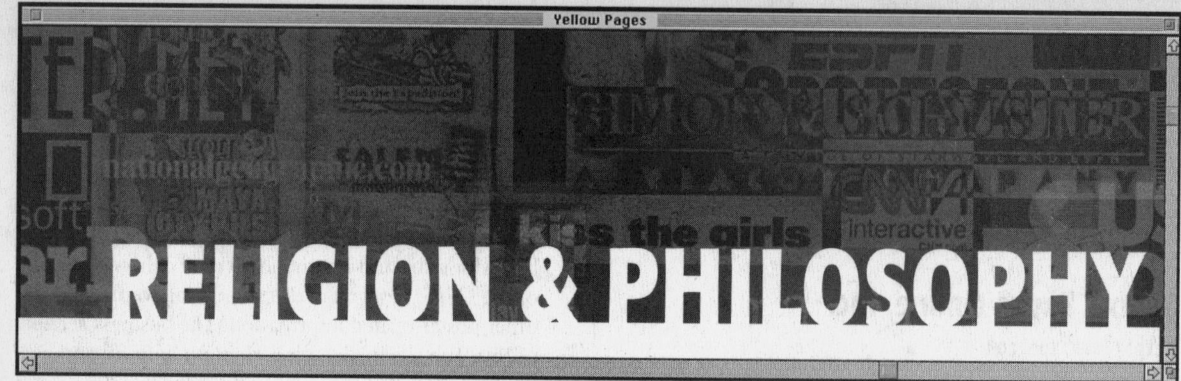

The true meaning of religion is thus not simply morality, but morality touched by emotion.

Matthew Arnold

A–Z of Cults

http://www.guardian.co.uk/observer/cults/a-z-cults/index.html

A list of cults, each with a corresponding entry. Entries include a brief synopsis of the cult, reasons to join, reasons not to join, and the bottom line.

A–Z of Jewish & Israel-Related Resources

http://www.ort.org/anjy/a-z/

Links to a wide variety of Jewish topics, organizations, and resources can be found at this site. The links are organized alphabetically for easy access.

Access to Insight

http://world.std.com/~metta/

Focuses on supporting and deepening Buddhist meditation practice. Emphasizes teachings from the Theravada Buddhist tradition, but represents other Buddhist traditions as well.

NRP Picks

Baha'i Resources on the Internet
http://www.bcca.org/srb/resources.html

Bible Gateway
http://www.calvin.edu/cgi-bin/bible

Catholic Online
http://www.catholic.org/index.html

Ethics Updates
http://www.acusd.edu/ethics/

Finding God in Cyberspace
http://users.ox.ac.uk/~mikef/durham/gresham.html

Judaism and Jewish Resources
http://shamash.org/trb/judaism.html

United Federation of Metropolitan Community Churches
http://www.ufmcc.com/

AFF Cultic Studies

http://www.csj.org/

Studies psychological manipulation and cultic groups, and aims to assist those who have been victims of such. Books and periodicals such as *Cultic Studies Journal*, *Cult Observer*, and *Young People & Cults* are available for order online.

Aish Ha Torah Discovery

http://j51.com:80/~jrsflw

Presents a Jewish adult-education seminar called "Discovery." Provides information ranging from the basics of Judaism to the latest research by mathematicians and computer specialists on the existence of hidden codes in the Bible.

Al Azif: The Manuscript Liber Logaeth

http://www.primenet.com/~ottinge/n.html

Also known as "The Book of the Arab, Abdul Alhazred" and the "Necronomicon," this site provides an electronic version of the manuscript that inspired H.P. Lovecraft to write about the Cthulhu mythos.

Aleister Crowley

http://www.crl.com/~thelema/crowley.html

Learn about the life of the famous mystic. This one-time member of the Golden Dawn is famous for his "Book of the Law," which was dictated to him from behind by the Egyptian god Horus.

Alvin Plantinga Links

http//www.chass.utoronto.ca:8080/~davis/plant.htm

For those of you who've been "Alvinated" or would like to, this is the site. Contains links to several of his articles and even has an interview with the Christian philosopher. Also includes a bibliography of his important works.

American Baptist Churches Mission Center Online

http://www.abc-usa.org/

Contains information about local American Baptist churches, and American Baptist Green Lakes Conferences, as well as national, international, and educational ministries.

American Philosophical Association

http://www.oxy.edu/apa/apa.html

Provides information on how to join APA and offers links to APA's Proceedings and Electronic Bulletin Board. Also offers links to other Web resources for philosophers. Includes information on upcoming events sponsored by APA and/or of interest to philosophers.

ANALYSIS Home Page

http://www.shef.ac.uk/uni/academic/N-Q/phil/analysis/homepage.html

Provides information about the philosophy journal *ANALYSIS* and its monthly email supplement ANALYST. Provides information on how to subscribe to both *ANALYSIS* and ANALYST. Includes recent and current contents of *ANALYSIS*, as well as links to the ANALYST ftp archive.

Answers in Action Home Page

http://answers.org/

Seeks to train Christians to "adopt and promote a Christian world view in every area of their lives." Features book reviews, information on contemporary issues, the Bible, Christian apologetics, and cults.

Arisbe: A Home for Charles S. Peirce Studies

http://204.119.173.21/peirce/

Contains hypertext versions of Charles Peirce's papers and information on various subjects relating to Peirce.

Association of Vineyard Churches

http://www.avc.vineyard.org/

This site supplies information about the Vineyard churches around the world, such as its statement of faith, values, and priorities. There's a directory of Vineyard churches for you to explore, as well as a directory of email addresses of those who attend Vineyard churches.

Augustine

http://ccat.sas.upenn.edu/jod/augustine.html

Contains translations and texts of Augustine. Also includes other research materials and reference aids. Also contains papers from an online seminar and images.

Australasian Philosophy Network: Home Page

http://www.arts.su.edu.au/Arts/departs/philos/APS/APS.home.html

Focuses on philosophy in Australian and New Zealand. Contains information on AP net, Australasian philosophers, departments, conferences, and job postings.

Baha'i Resources on the Internet

http://www.bcca.org/srb/resources.html

A rich collection of links and information for those new to the eclectic and young religion Baha'i. Complete coverage of foundational and institutional texts. Covers IRC fellowship.

Baker Book House

http://www.bakerbooks.com/

Baker Book House publishes approximately 200 Christian books a year in the categories of fiction, non-fiction, children's books, academic textbooks, and references. It also sells BakerBytes reference software. Published authors include Ruth Bell Graham and Robert Schuller, among others.

Baptist Faith and Message

http://www.utm.edu/martinarea/fbc/bfm.html

Contains statement of faith adopted by the Southern Baptist convention.

The Bastard Son of the Lord

http://www.trog.com/jesus/

The home page of Jesus Christ, as maintained by Steve. Jesus visits daily and leaves messages in his "Messiah Log." Site features lists of people that are going to heaven and hell, a 3D stereogram of a nude Jesus, and a downloadable version of Jesus' birthday song, "Spank Me, Jesus." Warning—this page is on the blasphemous side.

BEARS in Moral and Political Philosophy

http://www.netspace.org/bears/

Brown Electronic Article Review Service on Moral and Political Philosophy. Contains short reviews of articles that have appeared in the last six months. Provides information on contributors and a list of reviews.

Bhagavad Gita

http://www.iconsoftec.com/gita/

For students of Hinduism's most revered scripture, this site offers the Bhagavad Gita in the original Sanskrit (requires a PostScript viewer, such as Ghostscript). Also offers Arnold's complete English translation.

Bible Gateway

http://www.calvin.edu/cgi-bin/bible

This award-winning site provides a search form for the Bible and handles many common translations. Lets you conduct searches and output verses in French, German, Swedish, Tagalog, Latin, or English.

Bjorn's Guide to Philosophy

http://www.knuten.liu.se/~bjoch509/

This site is a gold mine for philosophers. Contains information on many philosophers: biography, works, papers, discussion lists, and images. Takes you to various e-journals, other departments around the world, and a library chock full of e-texts.

Campus Observer

http://www.leaderu.com/menus/bldgprss.html

A sort of "virtual newspaper." Covers the latest happenings on college campuses as reported by Leadership University. Contains links to other online journals.

Canada Toronto East Mission

http://www.southwestweb.com/mission/

Sponsored by the Church of Jesus Christ of Latter Day Saints. Provides former missionary email addresses, information about upcoming reunions, mission history and experiences, and access to Toronto resources. A lot of information about Canada too!

Catholic Online

http://www.catholic.org/index.html

Bills itself as the "world's largest and most comprehensive Roman Catholic information service." Provides message centers, forums, and research materials related to Roman Catholicism. There is also information about Catholic organizations, dioceses and archdioceses, publications, software, and doctrines.

Center for Paleo-Orthodoxy

http://capo.org/

This consortium of scholars, think-tanks, and publications is committed to shedding ancient (hence "Paleo") light on modern issues. Links to their award-winning e-journal, Premise. Also links to various institutes (Calvin, Kuyper, Van Til), and PCA mail.

Center for Reformed Theology and Apologetics (CRTA)

http://www.reformed.org/

A nonprofit organization committed to the dispersal of online resources for the edification of believers of a Calvinist leaning. Links to articles on apologetics, the

Bible, Reformed books and commentaries, Calvinism/soteriology, Christianity and science, and so on. Searchable.

Christian Articles Archive

http://www.wilsonweb.com/archive/

Contains articles for Christian newsletters, religious periodicals, brochures, and sermon illustrations. Also provides information about using Internet email conferencing for Christian teaching and discipleship.

Christian Book Connection

http://seercom.com/cbc/

Online bookstore that features nearly 30,000 items. Offers a selection of books, Bibles, software, and research, all of which can be ordered at 20 percent to 50 percent off the retail price.

Christian Classics Ethereal Library

http://ccel.wheaton.edu/

Presents classic Christian literature in electronic format. Contains works from St. Augustine to Wesley. There are also links to a catalog of church music and to the World Wide Study Bible.

Christian Computing Magazine

http://www.website.net/~ccmag/

Online edition of *Christian Computing Magazine.* Contains current as well as back issues of the printed magazine. Provides subscription information and links to Christian resources and literature as well.

Christian Interactive Network

http://www.gocin.com/

A huge Web resource for Christians. Contains links to information on various ministries, missions, publishing, family issues, radio/TV, education, sports, business, shopping, and more. Enables you to enter your business into their directory freely.

Christian Recovery Connection

http://www.fileshop.com/personal/iugm/

Enables you to participate in a 12-step recovery program for abuse, addiction, or grief. Offers links to other recovery programs on the Web that offer support from a Christian point of view.

Christianity Wire

http://www.roehampton.ac.uk/link/wire/

Presents an ecumenical Christian communications periodical, published electronically using the Acrobat PDF format. Includes issues of interest to Christian computer users.

The Church of Scientology vs. The Net

http://www.cybercom.net/~rnewman/scientology/home.html

A Web page put up by a non-Scientologist, who sees the Church as "a religious cult which has unwisely decided to declare war against the Usenet and Internet communities." The page includes information about lawsuits, raids, spams, and more.

Comic Relief: for the Pathologically Philosophical

http://www.webcom.com/~ctt/comic.html

Come here and unload. For the truly zany (or just bored). Philosopher light bulb jokes. Teleology of chicken and road. Weightless philosophy. Causes of death. And more topics that you'd never think of.

Comparison of Calvinism and Arminianism

http://home.earthlink.net/~andrepar/compare.htm

Compares the two theological systems on the points of: the freedom of the will, election (conditional or not), the extent of the atonement, whether or not the call of grace can be resisted, and whether or not one can fall from grace.

Contra Mundum

http://www.wavefront.com/~Contra_M/cm/

"Against the world." This quarterly online journal of reformed thought contains opinion and analysis of issues relevant to reformed thought today. Issues date from 1991 to the present.

Creation Science Home Page

http://emporium.turnpike.net/C/cs/

A site that provides arguments for creationism and against evolutionism. Poses questions to evolutionists. Contains a list of recommended books on the subject of creation and a list of creationist bulletin boards.

Creationism Connection

http://members.aol.com/dwr51055/Creation.html

A wealth of information for creationists. This page provides synopses of creationist books, lists other creationist sites and newsgroups, and maintains a list of creationist organizations sorted by state.

The Critical Thinker

http://rogue.northwest.com/~crt/index.htm

This is the bulletin of the Center for Rational Thought—an atheist hotbed—in Oregon. Contains historical writings, atheism in India, editorials and viewpoints, articles and news, and more. Enables you to subscribe.

Cults

http://www.the700club.org/cbn/teach/cults.html

A teaching sheet for Christians on the subjects of cults and cultism. Provides scriptural references and information on how to recognize a cult.

Cults 'R Us

http://www.mayhem.net/Crime/cults1.html

This "hit list" from the pages of the Internet Crime Archives gives general information about a number of cult figures whose cultish practices included murder, human sacrifice, and suicide.

CyberINDIA: India at your Fingertips

http://www.cyberindia.net/cyberindia/links/i1religi.htm

A component of CyberINDIA focusing on the varied religions of the land of spiritual receptivity. Features links to all the main eastern religions.

CyberMuslim Information Collective

http://www.uoknor.edu:80/cybermuslim/

Provides information and resources regarding Islam worldwide. Offers links to the HyperQur'aan project. Includes information on Islamic culture, schools, computing services, bookstores, and digital activism.

Cybernetics and Systems Theory

http://pespmc1.vub.ac.be/CYBSYSTH.html

Contains information gathered through the Principia Cybernetica Project. Contains general information and background material on cybernetics and systems theory.

D.M. Lloyd-Jones Recording Trust

http://web.ukonline.co.uk/Members/mlj/

Designed to promote, restore, and distribute works by the famous English minister. The Trust has a collection of his sermons on tape. Material by other prominent teachers is available.

DEFA Home Page

http://sunsite.unc.edu/dharma/defa.html

DharmaNet Electronic Files Archive. Contains the online Buddhist libraries maintained by DharmaNet International. Offers links to the Dharma Newsstand, Buddhist Info Web, BBS listings, and more.

Destructive Cults

http://www.algonet.se/~teodor/Cults/welcome.html

Good general information about cults, without going into the various differences between cults. Contains lists of cult characteristics, signs a person might be involved in a cult, recruitment tactics, and the consequences of becoming a cult member.

Dianetics Home Page

http://www.dianetics.org/

Dianetics is a book written by the founder of Scientology, L. Ron Hubbard in 1950. It is used as a basis for the Church of Scientology. More information about the book and its contents can be found at this page.

Dictionary of Philosophy of the Mind

http://artsci.wustl.edu/~celiasmi/MindDict/index.html

A free service. This is a dictionary of words of philosophy of the mind, words such as ontology and behaviorism. Enables you to submit entries and error corrections. Also contains philosophy links.

ECOLE Institute

http://www.evansville.edu/~ecoleweb/

This scholarly site seeks to create a hypertext encyclopedia of the works of early Christian church authors. Covers such "isms" as docetism, mithraism, and stoicism, and their impact on early Christianity, as well as other topics of theological interest. There is also a glossary and links to other sites related to early Church history.

The Egoist Archive

http://pierce.ee.washington.edu/~davisd/egoist/

A collection of resources related to the German philosopher, Max Stirner. Contains information about the philosopher, recent additions, recommended reading, commentaries, and classical musings.

The Egyptian Book of the Dead

http://www.lysator.liu.se/~drokk/BoD/

Learn all about the ancient Egyptian's view on death and the afterlife. The Book of the Dead is here in its full-translated glory, everything from "Hymn to Osiris" to "Making the Transformation to the Crocodile God."

Electronic Book of Common Prayer

http://listserv.american.edu/anglican/bcp

Contains the sacraments, prayers, liturgies, and other rites used in the Anglican and Episcopal Churches. Also contains the Psalms.

Electronic Journal of Analytic Philosophy

http://www.phil.indiana.edu/ejap/ejap.html

Includes three issues in hypertext, simple text, or PostScript; provides analytical philosophy articles. Provides information on how to subscribe to the journal via a Listserv. Includes topics for upcoming issues, and invites submissions. Also contains links to other philosophy sites.

Environmental Ethics

http://www.cep.unt.edu/

Provides information on environmental ethics. Focuses on environmental ethics resources. Provides book reviews and site summaries and links of interest to environmental philosophy.

Ethics Updates

http://www.acusd.edu/ethics/

A resource for both ethics instructors and their students. Provides updates on current ethics related issues. Covers both ethical theory and applied ethics. Takes you to additional resources.

Principal Resources

Ethical Theory			Applied Ethics		
Introduction to Moral Theory	Ethical Relativism	Meta-Ethical Concerns	Abortion	Reproductive Technologies and Bioethics	Euthanasia
Religion and Ethics	Ethical Egoism	Utilitarianism	Punishment and the Death Penalty	Race and Ethnicity	Gender and Sexism
Kant and Deontology	Rights Theories	Contemporary Anti-Theory	Sexual Orientation	Poverty and Welfare	World Hunger
Aristotle and Virtue Ethics	Gender and Moral Theory	Race, Ethnicity, and Moral Theory	Animal Rights	Environmental Ethics	

Additional Resources

Visit the Ethics Forums, An Electronic Agora	The Ethics Calendar A Listing of Forthcoming Ethics Conferences	Broadcast Your Ethics Conference on the Web!

Evolution vs. Creation Science

http://web.canlink.com/ocrt/evolutio.htm

Explains the differences between the various theories of creationism and evolution. Examines what the Bible has to say about creation, how creation scientists believe the Earth was formed, and how evolutionists might interpret the Bible.

.ex-cult Archive

http://www.ex-cult.org/

Contains general information about cults, archives of cult-related Usenet groups, information about specific cults, and a list of addresses for ex-cult support groups. Also includes a list of books that are suggested reading. This is a very informative page.

Famous Unitarian Universalists

http://www.execpc.com/~biblogic/cvuufamo.html

Provides a list of well-known contemporary and historical figures who have been involved with the Unitarian Universalist movement and offers links to sites that provide information about these people.

Finding God in Cyberspace

http://users.ox.ac.uk/~mikef/durham/gresham.html

A guide to religious studies resources on the Internet. Takes you to print, people, digital, gateway resources, starting points for further exploration, e-texts, and so on.

Fire and Ice: Puritan and Reformed Writings

http://ourworld.compuserve.com/homepages/WCarson/

In this case, the name is highly suggestive of the contents. Contains many works of various Puritan writers, from John Owen to Cotton Mather. Also contains history and biography, poetry, new and recommended works, and a quote of the week.

The Five Points of Calvinism

http://www.gty.org/~phil/dabney/5points.htm

R.L. Dabney discusses Calvinism without making use of the well-known acrostic. He discusses original sin, effectual calling, God's election, particular redemption, and perseverance of the saints. Footnotes follow.

Fort: Panth Khalsa

http://www.community.net/~khalsa/

Provides a glimpse into the culture of the Sikh Nation. Posts Hukam-Namah (daily verses from the Sikh Scriptures) in native Gurmukhi format. Contains information about Sikh history and current events relevant to the Sikh people.

Free Daism

http://www.he.tdl.com/~fdac/

Presents Free Daism, the "ancient, eternal, and always new religion of self-transcending God-Realization," based on the teaching of Adi Da (Da Free John). Information on books and other publications.

Friends of Osho

http://earth.path.net/osho/

Introduction to the work of Osho (Bhagwan Shri Rajneesh), popular and controversial teacher of Tantra Yoga.

Gays for God

http://www.gaysforgod.org/

A resource list for the gay and lesbian seeking religious fellowship, this site is home to a great list of links to supportive congregations and organizations from all religious faiths and traditions.

Global Hindu Electronic Network

http://rbhatnagar.csm.uc.edu:8080/hindu_universe.html

Rich site including complete texts of major Hindu scriptures. Contains the `alt.hindu` newsgroup, information on publications, Hindu festivals, and links to Jain, Buddhist, and Sikh dharmas. Also has pictures of famous saints.

The Golden Dawn FAQ

http://www.bartol.udel.edu/~cranmer/cranmer_gdfaq.html

Anything and everything you ever wanted to know about the Hermetic Order of the Golden Dawn, a "society devoted to spiritual, philosophical, and magical development."

GOSHEN Internet Christian Resource Directory

http://www.goshen.net/

GOSHEN stands for Global Online Service Helping to Evangelize Nations. Its goal is to provide free access to Christian resources on the Web. It provides a site for Christian organizations and church-related businesses to add their home pages to the Web with no storage fees. Supplies access to the GoSearch search engine for Christian resources.

Gospel Films, Inc.

http://www.gospelcom.net/gf/

Distributes Christian videos in a range of subjects, from children's tapes to historical/biblical and true life stories. Also features a monthly Bible crossword, Christian games, articles, and news.

Grace To You Ministries

http://gty.org/

The home page for John MacArthur's Bible-teaching media ministry committed to the growth of the Christian church. You can pose a question in the Curiosity Shop. Also contains a Grace To You cybermarket link.

Great Christian Books Online

http://www.greatchristianbooks.com/index.htm

An online Christian resource with a distinctly Reformed flavor (it actually started as "Puritan Reformed Discount Book Service"), although other Protestants will feel at home here. Has links to their author, homeschool, Bible and computer help, commentaries and language help, and new arrivals catalogs.

Greater Grace World Outreach

http://www.ggwo.org/

An international ministry with links to associated ministries including The Grace Hour International Radio Show, missionary outreaches, and the

Maryland Bible College and Seminary. This site also contains daily faith thoughts as well as information about upcoming conferences.

Greek Philosophy Archive

`http://iris.dissvcs.uga.edu/~archive/Greek.html`

Contains the Dialogues of Plato, the works of Aristotle, images of Greek sculptures, works by other Greek philosophers (Epictatus, Plotinus, and so on), and the *Meditations of Marcus Aurelius.*

GROKNet–Comedyatre and Resources

`http://www.ozemail.com.au/~grok/`

Presents an Australian Christian two-man comedy theatrical team. Includes information on GROK's performance history, reviews, and schedules.

Hall of Arguments

`http://www.webcom.com/~ctt/hway.html`

A collection of email exchanges with skeptics, seekers, and the sincere. Also contains articles in response to questions raised by atheists and other skeptics, and questions that other Christians have encountered.

Haqqani Foundation Home Page

`http://www.best.com/~informe/mateen/haqqani.html`

Offers a look into the teachings and precepts of Sufism. Offers many pages of information, pictures, and links intended to spread Sufi teachings of the brotherhood of man. Focuses on Sufi leader Shaykh Muhammad Nazim al-Haqqani.

Hare Krishna Home Page

`http://www.webcom.com/~ara/`

Official ISKCON site, detailing the religion of Krishna Consciousness founded by A.C. Bhakti-vedanta Swami Prabhupada. Identifies spirit as primary and matter as secondary.

Harvest Online

`http://www.harvest.org/`

Provides the history of the Harvest Christian Fellowship. Includes dates for upcoming Harvest Crusades, along with information about the "A New Beginning with Greg Laurie" broadcasts.

Here, Madame

`http://tqd.advanced.org/3075/frames.htm`

Tries to answer man's nagging questions (does God exist, do I have a free will, how do I know I exist?) through the writings of various philosophers. Has information on the various components of philosophy: metaphysics, epistemology, logic, aesthetics, ethics; the history of philosophy, as well as many of the philosophers themselves.

Hinduism

`http://www.geocities.com/RodeoDrive/1415/indexd.html`

An award-winning one-stop overview of the diverse world of Hinduism. Has links to detailed descriptions of the Veda and Vedic literature, Hinduism's secular source. Also discusses Sanskrit, the language of nature, and the main Hindu gods.

Hinduism Today Home Page

`http://www.HinduismToday.kauai.hi.us/ashram/htoday.html`

A Hindu family newspaper online. Provides an index of issues, along with subscription information. Explains vegetarianism, Vedas, and non-violence.

Homeschool Guide

`http://www.ssnet.com/~hsguide/online.html`

You can order this large homeschool guide resource book exploring online services and the Web in general. Can be used right next to the computer. This site also has links to over 100 other recommended sites.

Ibrahim Shafi's Page in Islam

`http://www.wam.umd.edu/~ibrahim/`

Rich in links focusing on the cornerstones of Islamic religious life. Connects to Muslim organizations, texts, FTP, Gopher sites, newsgroups, and other resources. Also offers links to Muslim countries. Great starting point for study of Islam.

ICMC Home Page

`http://www.xc.org/icmc/`

The International Christian Media Commission's vision is to proclaim the Good News through all the types of existing media. This site provides an electronic magazine members can use to browse directories. Maintains a list of links to resources for Christians.

A B C D E F G H I J K L M N O P Q R S T U V W X Y Z

In the Footsteps of the Lord

http://www.xensei.com/users/Angel/Home/CR.html

Created by a Christian from India who is studying at the University of Houston, this site offers testimonials, articles, and many Christian resource links.

Intellectual Sophistication and Basic Belief in God

http://www.leaderu.com/truth/3truth03.html

For those Christians who have struggled with whether or not he or she has a rational foundation for his or her own Christian world view. Among Plantinga's premises are three important propositions: 1) God is speaking to me; 2) God disapproves of what I have done; 3) God forgives me for what I have done.

International Atheistic Secular Humanist Conspiracy [Canada Division]

http://infoweb.magi.com/~godfree/index.html

Provides links to areas of interest to humanists, atheists, agnostics, and freethinkers. Encourages the investigation of a diversity of viewpoints. Features cartoons and On Line Baptism Removal.

The Secular Web

http://www.infidels.org/

A page of interest to atheists, agnostics, humanists, and freethinkers. Links to a variety of Internet resources, including Usenet newsgroups, IRC channels, and other Web pages. The library contains several documents, historical and otherwise.

International Meditation Centres (in the Tradition of Sayagyi U Ba Khin)

http://www.webcom.com/~imcuk/welcome.html

Offers information on 10-day Vipassana meditation courses as well as a newsletter, Theravada Buddhist publications, and images of pagodas.

International Philosophical Preprint Exchange

http://phil-preprints.l.chiba-u.ac.jp/IPPE.html

Part of an international working group coordinating access to philosophy preprints. Provides information in a visual index, as well as a textual one. Includes subject access, submissions, and directory links.

International Research Institute for Zen Buddhism

http://www.iijnet.or.jp/iriz/irizhtml/irizhome.htm

This site contains, among other things, the largest searchable collection of Zen Buddhist primary text materials on the Internet. Also has a searchable database of Zen centers around the world.

Internet Sources for Philosophers

http://www.phil.ruu.nl/philosophy_services.html

This handy resource from the Netherlands gives the cyberphilosopher the basic tools to get started on the Internet. It provides links to information about books and other information, describes various Listservs and Usenet groups, e-journals, electronic texts, and so on.

InterVarsity Christian Fellowship

http://www.gospelcom.net/iv/

The aim of this site is to promote collegiate fellowships and "develop students who employ Biblical values." There are links to affiliated chapters on various campuses. Also offers online ordering for books published by InterVarsity Press.

Islam

http://www-leland.stanford.edu/~yusufali/islam/index.html

Many introductory essays. Includes the Shi'ite encyclopedia and information about the Ahlul Bayt. Features a daily verse from the Qur'an and a daily saying that represents Islamic principles.

Islam's Home Page

http://www.utexas.edu/students/amso/

A valuable Islamic resource containing articles about various Islamic issues including the Renaissance of Islam, women in Islam, and Jesus in Islam. An English translation of the Holy Qur'an and several Islamic prayers can be found at this site, as well as a collection of Islamic images.

Israelite Handbook

http://www.interport.net/~barzel

Serves as the base of operations on the Internet for blacks and Latinos who want to forge a new cultural and religious identity as Hebrew Israelites. Discusses such topics as Islam, Christianity, atheism, Afrocentricity, drugs, and slavery.

Jain Studies

http://www.dmu.ac.uk/~pka/guides/jain.html

Web site of De Montfort University. Provides a starting point for people looking for resources on the Internet for Jainism, a religion of non-violence and avoidance of greed. Offers many links to resources.

Jain World Wide Web Page

http://www.wavefront.com/~raphael/jain/jain.html

Overviews Jain resources on the Web. Describes its Jain mailing list and presents its archives. Offers links to Gopher sites, ftp sites, Web sites, organizations, books, and periodicals.

Jehovah's Christian Witnesses

http://www.eskimo.com/~jcw/index.html

An analytical view of the beliefs of Jehovah's Witnesses. Contains many informative articles, including "A Short History of the Watchtower Organization," "Tips on Dealing with the Witnesses," and "Jehovah's Witnesses a Cult?" The articles are intelligently written and will provide timely information for current, past, or potential members of the group.

Jerusalem One WWW Network

http://www.jer1.co.il/

Calls itself "the most popular Jewish and Israel information source on the Internet." Contains Aliya information, Torah and Judaic studies, a Jewish calendar of events, current news and views from Israel and the world's largest Jewish software, and a clip art library.

Jesus Army

http://www.jesus.org.uk/

What is the Jesus Revolution? Find out on this award-winning British-based site. Contains an electronic magazine and many pictures.

Jesus Fellowship Home Page

http://jf.org/

A family church, a Christian teaching center, a covenant community, a world-wide outreach center, a campus ministry, a neighborhood Bible fellowship, and much more. Links to Miami Christian University, where you can earn theological degrees online.

Jesus Film Project

http://www.mdalink.com/JESUSproject/index.html

Presents the Campus Crusade for Christ Jesus Film project. Includes well-designed graphics pages. Offers links to other Campus Crusade for Christ sites in the United States and abroad.

Jewish Federation/Jewish Exponent

http://www.libertynet.org/~exponent/index.html

The Jewish Federation of Greater Philadelpha has existed since 1901 to serve Philadelphia's Jewish citizens. The Jewish Exponent is the online version of this Philadelphia newspaper that features articles of interest to Jews. This site contains lists of Jewish organizations and referrals in the Philadelphia area.

Jewish on the WELL

http://www.well.com/user/ari/jewish/jewish.html

Contains local religious and cultural information for Jews in the San Francisco area. There are links to the San Francisco Jewish Film Festival home page, and klezmer music pages here.

Jewish Theological Seminary

http://www.jtsa.edu/

Represents this conservative seminary online. Provides a wealth of resources and links to conservative Jewish synagogues and institutions.

Jewishnet

http://jewishnet.net/

Offers a list of Jewish-related sites. Offers links to Gopher sites, home pages, libraries, ftp sites, and provides information on Jewish newsgroups and mailing lists.

Jews for Jesus Home Page

http://www.jews-for-jesus.org/index.html

Serves as a means to finding Jewish Christians. Contains documents on Messianic Judaism, along with a music and concert schedule and a fun quiz.

Journal of Buddhist Ethics

http://www.cac.psu.edu/jbe/jbe.html

The Journal of Buddhist Ethics is a free online publication that promotes academic research in Buddhist ethics. Offers current and back issues. Includes a number of articles in Adobe Acrobat format.

Judaism and Jewish Resources

http://shamash.org/trb/judaism.html

Quite possibly the most complete source of Jewish information and Jewish-related links on the Web. Lists of links include media, singles groups, communities, newsgroups, reading lists, and museums, as well as commerce sites.

Kundalini Research Foundation, Ltd.

http://www.renature.com/krf/

Concerned with the Kundalini Paradigm, an off-shoot of Tantra Yoga and Shaivism. Center for scholarly study of the "serpent energy" and its relationship to higher consciousness. Founded by Gopi Krishna.

L. Ron Hubbard Home Page

http://www.lronhubbard.org/

Read an overview of the life of L. Ron Hubbard, the founder of Scientology. See him portrayed as humanitarian, music maker, poet/lyricist, yachtsman, and philosopher. Also home to an online bookstore, where Mr. Hubbard's work can be purchased.

The Law of Contradiction

http://www.gty.org/~phil/articles/lawofcon.htm

This intriguing piece by the executive director of John MacArthur's Grace To You ministries is a response to the popular notion that there is no absolute truth.

Life and Faith Network

http://www.telos.ca/lf/index.html

Membership in this network enables you to access a group of conferences for people interested in discussing their faith and how it affects their lives.

Logictarian Christian Home Page

http://www.geopages.com/CapitolHill/1205

Focuses on the quest for the meaning of life. Offers a blend of Christianity, Shintoism, martial arts, and science. Also serves as a division of the UFG/ECD, Inc., a Canada-based non-profit research body. Oversized text makes for difficult reading.

Logos Research Systems

http://www.logos.com/

An electronic publishing firm that offers CD-ROMs of biblical translations, ranging from the King James to Revised Standard Version. Also includes many other titles.

Loki Cult Web Page

http://www.memoria.com/loki/

A page for those who profess to worship Loki, the "boogeyman of Norse mythology." Features a variety of articles on Loki worship from "Lokasenna: The Flighting of Loki from the Poetic Edda" to "Loki the Fool."

Lubavitch in Cyberspace

http://www.chabad.org

Offers information pertaining to Chabad philosophy and Chassidic Judaism. Includes Kosher recipe and children's links, multimedia, Listserv, and Gopher resources.

Lutheran Church-Missouri Synod Home Page

http://tcm.nbs.net/~cc/lcms/

The unofficial home page for the Missouri Synod of the Lutheran Church. Provides membership information and other statistics. Contains many useful FAQs, including "What is a Lutheran?" and "What do Lutherans Believe?" Also online is a variety of reference material useful to Christians and links to other Christian sites.

Lutheran Marriage Encounter

http://www.pic.net/~speed/lme.html

Focuses on providing married couples the opportunity to examine their lives together. Contains links to marriage encounters sponsored by other denominations and organizations.

Matthew Henry's Commentary

http://ccel.wheaton.edu/henry/mhc/mhc.html

This is a searchable commentary on the whole Bible. You can search by verse, passage, or book. Also links to Wheaton's "Christian Classics Ethereal Library."

McChurch

http://mcchurch.org/

Over 29,713 saved! The place to go when you need a "Happy Meal" for your eternal soul. Join the Rev. Dr. O.L. Jaggers, D.D. Litt.D. Phd., Miss Velma, and the Holy McDonna (blessed amongst all chicks) as they make McWorship.

Menorah Ministries

http://rainbow.rmii.com/~menorah

Menorah Ministries is a Messianic Jewish resource and referral site. Offers information and articles regarding the Messiah, the Biblical Jewish roots of Christianity, and Israel. There is an "Ask Pastor Reuben" section that answers pertinent questions about Messianic Judaism, such as "Does a Jew stop being Jewish when he/she believes in Jesus?"

Messianic Jewish Alliance of America

http://www.mjaa.org/

Established in 1915 for Jews who believe Yeshua (Jesus) is the Messiah, the MJAA is the largest association of its kind in the world. This site contains information on the MJAA's mission, purpose, and ministries. There are also links to other Messianic Jewish sites.

Methodological Naturalism

http://id-www.ucsb.edu/fscf/library/plantinga/mn/home.html

Plantinga here discusses "methodological naturalism," that is the idea that "science cannot involve religious belief or commitment." He tackles the issue, in part, by addressing whether or not science is religiously neutral.

Minister's Reference Center

http://www.rr-mrc.com/

Serves as a subscription site from which you can download other ministers' sermons for a fee each month. Offers a free trial period as well as a discount for lay members and students.

Misanthropic Philosophy

http://chat.carleton.ca/~rfairchi/order.html

"If I had a lot of oxen, I'd be sexy in some cultures." This site ought to bring a smile to the face of the weary cyberphilosopher. There's a different quote each week. Also contains philosophical anecdotes.

Monastery of Christ in the Desert

http://www.christdesert.org/pax.html

Truly one of the most beautiful Web sites out there! The Benedictine monks of this monastery will help you design and illuminate your home page, and if theirs is any indication, they do an inspired job!

Ms. Guidance on Strange Cults

http://www.t0.or.at/msguide/devilgd1.htm

A plethora of links to all sorts of cult subjects. Several cult categories are addressed, including generic magic, paganism, freemasons, Gnostics, and many more.

National Association of Evangelicals

http://nae.goshen.net/

The NAE is composed of 42,500 congregations across the United States that subscribe to the NAE's statement of faith. The intent of the NAE is to provide cooperation in subsidiary ministries such as the World Relief Corporation. Site contains resolutions, press releases, and the NAE statement of conscience.

National Religious Broadcasters

http://www.mnsinc.com/nrb/

The NRB strives to promote ethical standards in all aspects of broadcasting and exists to safeguard free access to religious broadcasting. You can get information about NRB conventions and publications here, as well as issues of concern to the NRB.

New Kadampa Tradition

http://www.webcom.com/~nkt/

A Mahayana Buddhist organization. Aims to preserve and promote the essence of Buddha's teachings in a form suited to the Western mind and way of life. Offers information on books, meditation programs, and a directory of NKT centers.

New Media Communications

http://www.iac.net/~dlature

Seeks to gather together resources to enable seminaries and theological organizations to bring theological education to all who desire it. Provides links to schools of theology, as well as sociological and hypertext studies.

Nichiren Shoshu Buddhism

http://www.primenet.com/~martman/ns.html

Offers a look into this Japanese school of Buddhism that emphasizes the Lotus Sutra. Includes a list of temples and articles from The Nichiren Shoshu Monthly.

Nietzsche Page at USC

http://www.usc.edu/dept/annenberg/thomas/nietzsche.html

Provides information on all aspects of study. Contains the complete text of Nietzsche's "Thus Spoke Zarathustra"; information on the available email lists for Nietzsche studies; assorted mixed opinions and maxims from Nietzsche; and many other documents and links.

Not Just Bibles

http://www.iclnet.org/pub/resources/christian-resources.html

An incredibly vast collection of Christian resource materials provided for Christians in search of material on "Classical Christianity." Among the myriad of links are mail-based services, Gopher servers, Christian College Web sites, electronic journals, bulletin boards, Usenet newsgroups, and much, much more.

Online Islamic Bookstore

http://www.sharaaz.com

Provides information about the books, tapes, and software. Offers links to Islamic sites and book reviews of important books. "To encourage the Muslim community to read again. To assert the importance of spiritual knowledge especially in this modern age."

Orthodox Christian Page

http://www.ocf.org/OrthodoxPage/

What is Greek Orthodox Christianity all about? This site tells you and provides links to European and American Orthodox sites. There are pages covering scriptures and liturgy, icons, prayers, readings, and links to other resources.

Orthodox Ministry ACCESS

http://goa.goarch.org/access/

Provides information about Orthodox Christianity; the Greek Orthodox Archdiocese; the Orthodox Ministry ACCESS Bulletin Board System (accessible via the Internet); Orthodox Christian resources; Orthodox Christian organizations; and more.

Our Daily Bread

http://www.gospelcom.net/rbc/odb/

Presents a short, daily devotional guide for Christians. Includes an archive page for access to previous months' devotions.

Pagan Pages

http://www.eor.com/pages

Provides free advertising, announcements, and networking for Pagan (witchcraft and nature worship) and Pagan-friendly people and their businesses in hopes of strengthening community ties. The Pagan Pages is arranged as a village setting with subconferences.

Pathways to Metaphysics

http://digital.net/~egodust/

For those involved in the new physics, metaphysics, or the exploration of that which lies beneath the appearance of things. Introduction to Vedanta which explores the manifestation of diversity from underlying unity. Links for novices, veterans, and sadhus.

Perseus Project

http://medusa.perseus.tufts.edu/

This award-winning site is adapted from the Perseus disk. It includes: Greek and translated texts by Aristotle, Plato, Sophocles, art and archaeology, a Greek lexicon, and so on.

Philip E. Johnson

http://www.origins.org/menus/pjohnson.html

Works by the prominent Berkeley law professor are contained here. Articles related to his books, *Reason In the Balance* and *Darwin On Trial* are available. Also contains his speaking schedule.

The Philosophical Gourmet Report

http://www.nyu.edu/gsas/dept/philo/leiter/

Contains the national rankings of graduate schools of analytic philosophy in the U.S. Also includes foreign rankings. Highly detailed.

Philosophy and Religion

gopher://marvel.loc.gov/11/global/phil

Presents the Library of Congress' Gopher guide to philosophy and religion. Contains links and documents relating to philosophy from all over the world.

Philosophy Resources

gopher://gopher.liv.ac.uk/11/phil

Contains a list of all the philosophy departments in the United Kingdom, their addresses, contact information, and their head. Also provides information on conferences, workshops, and calls for papers.

Presbyterian Church USA

http://www.pcusa.org/

Contains news from the Presbyterian News Service, reports and proceedings of the General Assembly, mission news, religious humor, and the PresbyNet conferencing system. There also are links to other Presbyterian-related sites, such as the Web pages of local churches.

Project Wittenberg

http://www.iclnet.org/pub/resources/text/wittenberg/wittenberg-home.html

This award-winning site provides the thought of Martin Luther online. Plans to accumulate all of Luther's work, along with that of other theologians.

PSYCHE: an interdisciplinary journal of research and consciousness

http://psyche.cs.monash.edu.au/

Provides direct access to PSYCHE's archives. Also contains a FAQ associated with the journal that covers the following topics: general introduction; notes for authors; book reviews; subscriptions to the electronic version of PSYCHE; subscriptions to the MIT Press version of PSYCHE; the discussion list Psyche-D; archival information; the executive editor, associate editors, and editorial board.

The Quiet Place: Reformed Baptist WWW Resources

http://www.iserv.net/~mrbill/Quiet.html

This is a veritable cornucopia of resources for the Reformed Baptist Web-head. Here you can find home pages of Baptist churches across the country. You can also fellowship with other Reformed Baptists.

Religion and Philosophy Resources on the Internet

http://web.bu.edu/STH/Library/contents.html

This is an annotated listing of religion and philosophy sites. Covers Asian religions, Christianity, Judaism, and Islam. Also links to library catalogs.

Religious Society of Friends WWW site

http://www.quaker.org/

Offers a list of links about Quakers on the Web. Includes links to sites focusing on Quaker schools, journals, The American Friends Service Committee, genealogy sites, Quaker history, newsgroups, and more.

Renewing Your Mind

http://www.gospelcom.net/ligonier/

The home page of R.C. Sproul's Ligonier ministries. There are plenty of studies from *Tabletalk*, the ministry's ongoing Bible study resource. Also contains information about what you can order from the ministry.

Rivendell Education Archive

http://www.watson.org/rivendell/

This is an educational resource primarily for K–12. Contains information related to many fields, including religion and philosophy, both Eastern and Western.

Saint Mary's Press

http://wwwsmp.smumn.edu/

This award-winning site features St. Mary's Press' online catalog of Catholic-related materials for young people. Their Prophets of Hope series is aimed at Hispanic youths. You can order materials from this site, and access links to other Christian publishers.

Salaam Ailaikum

http://www.wco.com/~altaf/altaf.html

Contains Islamic and social justice poetry, articles, links, and stories. Also contains several articles by the Islamic author, the late Dr. Ali Shariati.

SBC "Maverick" Home Page

http://www.io.com/~tarrytwn/SBC/sbcmain.htm

This unofficial site of the Southern Baptist Convention contains information about this denomination, links to Yahoo and GOSHEN lists of local church home pages, as well as links to an SBC bulletin board and SBC-related sites.

Scientology Home Page

http://www.scientology.org/

The official Web site for Dianetics/the Church of Scientology. Available in English, French, Spanish, Italian, and German, this site is a wealth of information. Features 3D tours of actual Scientology churches, RealAudio lectures from founder L. Ron Hubbard, and complete explanations of the Scientology faith.

Scripture Information Retrieval

http://www.mahidol.ac.th/budsir/budsir-main.html

Promotes the BUDSIR database and search engine for researching the Pali cannon of the sayings of Buddha.

Scrolls from the Dead Sea

http://sunsite.unc.edu/expo/deadsea.scrolls.exhibit/intro.html

This exhibit from the Library of Congress is a great scholastic site. The published text of the Quamran scrolls, commonly known as the Dead Sea Scrolls. These works have been extensively studied by Bible scholars. The site offers a link to the Expo Bookstore where a printed copy of the exhibition catalog can be purchased.

SDANet

http://www.sdanet.org/

This is the site for the Seventh Day Adventist (SDA) WWW server. Links to Gopher sites, SDA institutions, and Bible Study forums can be found here.

Select Plantinga Bibliography

http://www.chass.utoronto.ca:8080/~davis/plant2.htm

This page contains citations on Plantinga's works on a broad spectrum of works related to: epistemology, metaphysics/metaphysical logic, the philosophy, book reviews and correspondence, and autobiographical pieces. Both books and articles are discovered here.

Shamash

http://shamash.org/

This award-winning site run by the Jewish Internet Consortium offers links to various Jewish religious organizations ranging from Hillel to the World Zionist Organization. Includes FAQs pertaining to various facets of Judaism.

Shawn's Rituals Collection

http://www.andrew.cmu.edu/user/shawn/occult/rites/

A collection of rituals from various authors, for a variety of intents and purposes. The rituals included range from "The Lesser Pentagram Banishing Ritual" to "Getting Pop Cans Out of Machines."

Shin Buddhism Network

http://www.aloha.net/~rtbloom/shinran

Award-winning scholarly site. Contains English and Japanese articles on Shin Buddhism, as well as a list of links to Buddhist resources. Includes a self-study course.

Shtetl, Yiddish Language and Culture Home Page

http://sunsite.unc.edu/yiddish/shtetl.html

"Shtetl" means "small town" in Yiddish. This site aims to be a virtual small town on the Web. Provides information on Yiddish culture, as well as resources that point toward a wide range of links—ranging from recommended books to kosher recipes.

Society Hill Synagogue of Philadelphia

http://www-leland.stanford.edu/~nadav/shs.html

An independent, conservative egalitarian synagogue that offers numerous programs in all aspects of Jewish religious and cultural life. Includes detailed descriptions, a brochure, a monthly newsletter, and some nice graphics.

Society of Christian Philosophers

http://www.siu.edu/departments/cola/philos/SCP/info.html

Organized to promote fellowship and intellectual stimulation among Christian philosophers. Goes beyond the usual proceedings of the American Philosophical Association by providing deeper insights on and prolonged discussion of religious issues.

Spirituality, Yoga, and Hinduism

http://www.geocities.com/RodeoDrive/1415/index1.html

A gentle introduction to Hinduism, Yoga, Kundalini, and eastern spirituality. Preaches renunciation and meditation.

The Spurgeon Archive

http://www.spurgeon.org/

This award-winning site is a collection of resources by and about Charles H. Spurgeon, the English preacher and theologian. Contains information on his personal library, the full text of his sermons, his writings, excerpts from *The Sword and the Trowel,* and *The Treasury of David.*

St. Louis Life News

http://www.afn.org/~slli/

Presents pro-life news and information, including opinion pieces and links to pro-life and pro-abortion sites.

Stanford University Zoroastrian Group

http://www-leland.stanford.edu/group/zoroastrians/

Presents a student group interested in exploring the Zoroastrian religion (one of the world's first monotheisms), history, and culture. Presents a short over-view of Zoroastrianism, daily prayers, and links to other Zoroastrian groups.

Talk.Origins Archive

http://earth.ics.uci.edu:8080/origins/faqs.html

A large collection of FAQs generated by the Usenet newsgroup `talk.origins`. The site maintains FAQs on creationism, evolution, flood geology, catastrophism, and more. The collection is basically an argument for evolutionism.

Taoist Resource Center

http://members.aol.com/gr8tao/index.html

A great source of information about Taoism, especially for those just beginning to learn about it. Great explanations of what Tao is, the differences between philosophical and religious Taoism, snippets of wisdom from the "I Ching," and more.

Tarot Reading

http://www.Facade.com/Occult/tarot/

Here you can have your fortune told through the magic of an Internet tarot reading. Choose from five beautifully rendered decks.

Tech Classics Archive

http://the-tech.mit.edu/Classics

Contains full text documents by many philosophers spanning the ages. Includes a full text copy of Candide (English).

Theosophical Society

http://users.aol.com/tstec/hmpage/tsintro.htm

The society was founded in 1875 in an effort to promote the expressed awareness of the Oneness of Life. This site links to descriptions of foundational, esoteric texts by Blavatsky and others. Acts as a guide for personal exploration of truth.

The Thinking Man's Minefield

http://www.ozemail.com.au/~ksolway/index.html

Contains all kinds of worldly insights, including philosophic works, male and female psychology, poetry, quotations, travel in India, atheist archives, and links to articles from *Life and Death Magazine.*

This Week in Bible Prophecy

http://www.niagara.com:80/~twibp/

This Web site supplements a television program on Bible prophecy that is aired over the Trinity Broadcasting network in the United States and over Vision TV in Canada. You can receive transcripts of recently aired programs through this site, as well as read magazine articles and select videos and books.

Tien Dao Christian Media

http://www.webcom.com/~tiendao/tiendao.html

Focuses on Chinese Christianity. Offers software and an online bookstore (includes text in both Chinese and English). Interesting fact—because of the Chinese government's strict laws about Bible distribution/importation, 60 million Christian homes in China do not have Bibles.

Tiger Team Buddhist Information Network

http://www.newciv.org/TigerTeam/

The Tiger Team Buddhist Information Network is a not-for-profit online service dedicated to serving the worldwide Buddhist community. Offers online files, conferencing, and shopping. Includes links to Buddhist resources and to the table of contents for the CyberSangha Journal.

A B C D E F G H I J K L M N O P Q R S T U V W X Y Z

Tough Guys

http://basix.com/~ps91/

Testimonies of drug addicts, convicted criminals, and former gang members who radically turned their lives around after giving themselves to Christ.

Triple Point

http://awsd.com/tripoint/

An online source devoted to the "triple point," the area in which, according to the originator, science, philosophy, and religion meet. Critical examination of and exploration into different world views. Can search the database by keyword(s).

Truth Journal

http://www.leaderu.com/menus/truth.html

A journal for the academic community from a Christian perspective. Covers scientific, philosophical, literary, historical, and theological topics. Contains links to several titillating issues.

United Federation of Metropolitan Community Churches

http://www.ufmcc.com/

Provides resources and information for gay and lesbian Christians. A truly multimedia site, including RealAudio clips, cybercasts, many photos, video, and more.

United Pentecostal Church International

http://www.prairienet.org/community/religion/fire/upc.html

Serves as an unofficial page for this denomination. Contains information about Pentecostalism and the Pentecostal Church on both regional and general levels.

Universal Life Church

http://ulc.org/ulc/about.html

The church that feels that everyone is already a member, they just don't know it yet. This church will ordain anyone that asks, just choose the "Become Ordained" option on their page. There is no fee, and you are taken to a page with a certificate of ordination that you can save and/or print out.

University of Chicago Philosophy Project

http://csmaclab-www.uchicago.edu/philosophyProject/philos.html

Serves as a forum for electronically mediated scholarly discussion of philosophical works. Contains several moderated philosophical discussions between small groups of participants.

University of St. Michael's College, Faculty of Theology

http://www.utoronto.ca/stmikes/index.html

Contains the APS Research Guide to Resources for Theological and Religious Sites—an award-winning guide created by St. Michael's graduate students.

Virtual Vicar

http://ourworld.compuserve.com:80/homepages/Chris_Thackery/index.htm

Provides a practical layout of the essential Christian world view. States and rebuts popular misconceptions. The description of the "Virtual Vicar's sex life" is a hoot! Skeptics are welcome.

Waco Never Again

http://www.mainelink.net/~mswett/

A comprehensive site about David Koresh and the Branch Davidians. Contains many pictures of Koresh, quotes from Koresh, tracts and letters written by Koresh, and a list of strange coincidences between David Koresh and Jesus Christ.

WAMY IslamNet (World Assembly of Muslim Youth)

http://www.cais.com/islamic/index.html

Presents links of interest to students and practitioners of Islam. Includes sounds, magazines, and the Fiqeh database online, among other resources.

Wayfarer's Rest

http://www.compulink.co.uk/~wayfarer/

Articles on mysticism, water healing, and problem solving. Links to various other mystical sites.

Web Chapel—Prayer Request

http://web2.airmail.net/webchap/

Web Chapel is a mission to cyberspace, providing Web access to Christian writings and sermons, an online Bible study and devotional material, information on how to become a Christian, and prayer requests.

Westminster Books and Software

http://www.wts.edu/bookstore/

An online bookstore with discounts ranging from 20 percent to 60 percent off the retail price. Great deals on books, CDs, and commentaries. You can order online. They ship to anywhere in the world.

White Mountain Education—A Source for the Ageless Wisdom

http://www.primenet.com/~wtmtn

Provides articles, lectures, the online publication Meditation Monthly International, esoteric astrology, and psychology.

World ORT Union

http://www.ort.org/

Serves as a host site to ANJY (A Network for Jewish Youth), The Jewish Quarterly, and other Jewish resources. Exhibits on this server are of special interest to young people.

Writing Assessment Services

http://members.aol.com/cmarsch786/index.htm

These writing assessments are offered to homeschoolers to help evaluate children's writing progress. From a woman who was a college English instructor, and is a current instructor for America Online's Online Campus. She's also a homeschooler herself.

Yaohushua, the Genuine Messiah

http://metro.turnpike.net/Y/yaohush/index.html

This site, from Jerusalem, contains information about the original, archaic Hebrew names of the Creator and the Messiah, Yaohushua. Also includes files on various doctrinal beliefs. Topics covered include salvation, health, wealth, love, family, marriage, success, and deliverance.

Zen Mountain Monastery

http://www1.mhv.net/~dharmacom/

Features Questions for Cybermonk, Buddhist resources, a list of worldwide affiliates, Zen art, a Zen environmental studies center, meditation, and a journal.

Zen@SunSITE

http://sunsite.unc.edu/zen

Created as an online home for the Gateless Gate, a collection of koans. New koans presented daily. Features other Zen sites, including links to the Zen Hospice Project and to Zen and Taoist texts.

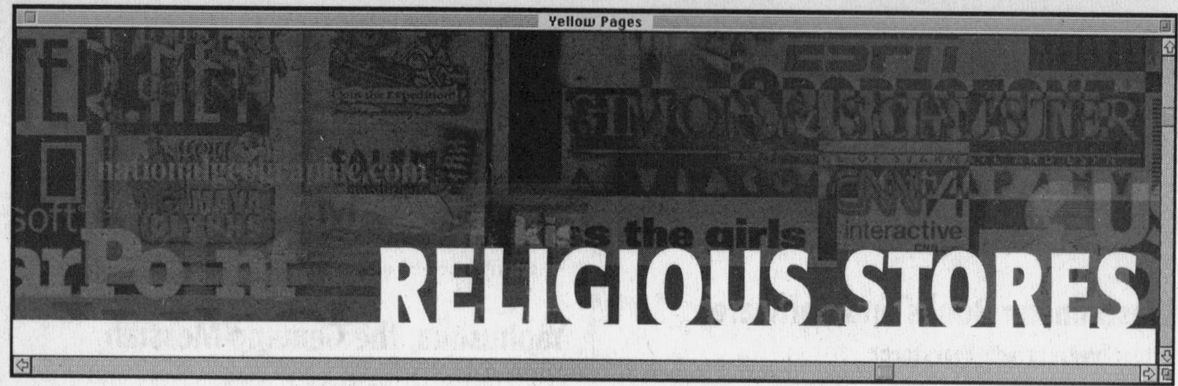

> In order to experience everyday spirituality, we need to remember that we are spiritual beings spending some time in a human body.
>
> *Barbara De Angelis*

Armageddon Books

http://www.armageddonbooks.com/index.html

If you're looking for information on Bible prophesy, this is the site to visit. You'll find books, charts, and videotapes on the subject. You can order online, access prophesy articles and news developments, search the Web, join the chat room, place a classified ad, check out other links, and even win free stuff.

Best Awesome Christian Books!

http://pages.prodigy.com/howtobks/best.htm

Fill your shopping cart with fiction, nonfiction, Bibles, devotional books, children's books, music, and more. Click on R&R to hear customers' rants and raves about their favorite books. Or join in some Christian chat. Site creators are working in association with Amazon.com and CD Universe to provide full customer service and ordering capabilities.

Manna from Heaven, Complete Christian Store
http://www.mannastore.com/

Provident Bookstores Home Page
http://www.mph.lm.com/pbs.html

Zondervan Publishing House
http://www.zondervan.com/

Catholic Market - Books, Magazines, and Newsletters

http://www.maxmarket.com/catholicmarket/books.html

Lists information about and links to various books, magazines, and newsletters. You can also add your business site or place a classified ad from this page.

The Catholic Shopper

http://www.catholicshopper.com/catholicshopper/

An online shopping mall featuring Catholic goods and supplies. Shop for what you want, add items to your order, and then go to the checkout area for purchase. A quick and easy way to get everything from jewelry to statues to gifts and games.

Christ the Way Publications Inc.

http://www.ctwpub.com/index2.html

Jump into the Christ the Way Bookstore to shop for hard-to-get books, Bibles, tracts, comics, videos, and cassettes online. Or check out the special of the week. Order online.

A Christian Apparel Store and More

http://www.teiweb.com/

Choose from a great array of Christian clothing (sweatshirts, ties, and so on) and accessories (WWJD bracelets, mousepads, and more). A searchable site.

Also, from this site you can send a free Devote-a-Note message—an inspirational email with passages and pictures to choose from.

The Christian Link - Stores

`http://www.christianlink.com/store/`

A collection of links to Christian stores, as well as products, catalogs, and reviews. A starting point for surfing the Web when you're looking for religious stores.

The Christian Music Store

`http://www.usgolf.com/music/music.html`

Visit the Christian Music Store for music, as well as books, ministry, and resources. Search music categories by artist, title, or song, and get sound samples for some selections. Get tour info and WWW sites for selected artists. This site also lists some excellent Christian links.

A Christian Store Site For All - Y.O.U.R. Stores

`http://www.yourstores.com/`

Site for the Y.O.U.R. Stores association of more than 200 independent Christian stores. You'll find a secure online catalog and Web site offering Bibles, books, music, art, clothing, gifts, Spanish goods, and more. Get a free subscription to a sales flyer, find stores near you, access customer service, or peruse the online catalog.

Dove Booksellers Biblical Studies Website

`http://www.dovebook.com/index.htm`

Site offers new and used books and software for scholars working in Biblical and ancient studies. Some examples of the offerings: Greek Tutor software, *Calvin's Commentaries* (new book), *Roman Art & Architecture* (used book). Also investigate other useful links this site provides.

Good News Book Store & Religious Gifts

`http://www.goodnewsbooks.com/`

New York store offers church supplies, books, music, and gifts. You can browse and order online—search for the desired product and get availability and pricing info, and a picture of the product. Add to your shopping cart as you go along.

J.M.J. Products: 100% Roman Catholic Merchandise

`http://www.qni.com/~catholic/`

This site showcases three pages of Catholic stuff that you can safely order online. Orders are processed immediately, and most are shipped within 24 hours. You can also sign up for the preferred-customer email list to get coupons and updates on new merchandise.

Logos Bookstore, Springfield, Ohio

`http://www.bookweb.org/bookstore/logos/`

This bookstore stocks Christian reading materials, music, cards, videos, and gifts. They can order any book in print or offer recommendations. Call, fax, or email your order. The site also gives you access to the Christian Search Engine.

Manna from Heaven, Complete Christian Store

`http://www.mannastore.com/`

Browse the online catalog, search for just what you're looking for, or call to order 24 hours a day. Choose from books, gifts, music, audio, and video. Soon you'll be able to listen to audio samples to try before you buy. A nicely done site.

Mustard Seed Christian Music Store

`http://www.amustardseed.com/homepage.htm`

An online Christian music store offering a broad range of tapes, CDs, and videos at a discount. Search the site for artists, producers, song titles, or albums. Order online or by phone. This site is well-organized and easy to navigate.

Provident Bookstores Home Page

`http://www.mph.lm.com/pbs.html`

Focuses on the nine large bookstores of the Mennonite Publishing House, an outreach of the Mennonite Church. See the sale catalog for videos, books, tapes and CDs, and gifts. Look through best-selling book titles and get reviews of new books. Special prices for Internet-BookWeb customers.

St. Gabriel Gift & Book Nook—Your Catholic Virtual Store

`http://www.stgabriel.com/`

Look through the catalog and take note of the free bonus items. While you're at it, mosey down the advent aisle and the sale aisle. You can also enter a free drawing, see what's new at the Gift & Book Nook, or learn more about St. Gabriel Catholic Information Network at this site.

Wear Your Witness! Saved by Grace Club

`http://www.itl1.com/sbgc/`

A source of Christian "witness wear." Choose from exclusive designs, popular scripture jerseys, custom sportswear, and seasonal designs. Place your personal order or learn about selling the items as a fund-raiser for your organization.

William J. Gallery & CO. Home Page

`http://www.wjgallery.com/index.html`

Operating since 1891, the William J. Gallery & Co. sells church goods and other religious items. The store serves the Baltimore/Washington area and now has a Web presence also. You can view and order merchandise securely online. Plus, visit the chat room or follow the offered religious links.

Zondervan Publishing House

`http://www.zondervan.com/`

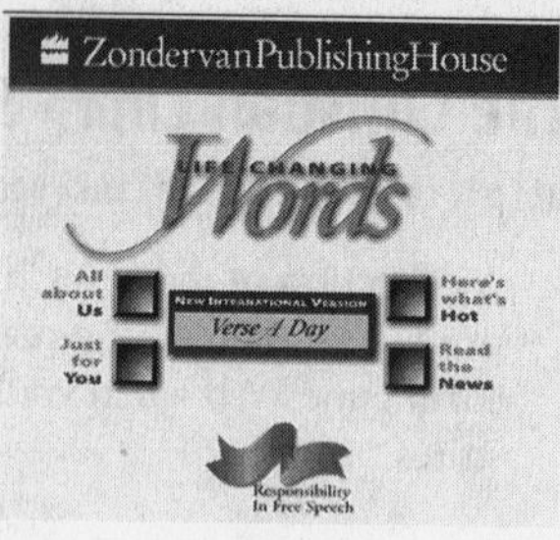

Zondervan's Web site, where you can shop for books, Bibles, gifts, tapes, software, and more. Check out the complete catalog online. You can do other fun things at this site too, like download a free Windows screensaver, participate in Bible surveys, subscribe to the free E-mail Alert Service, and read the news.

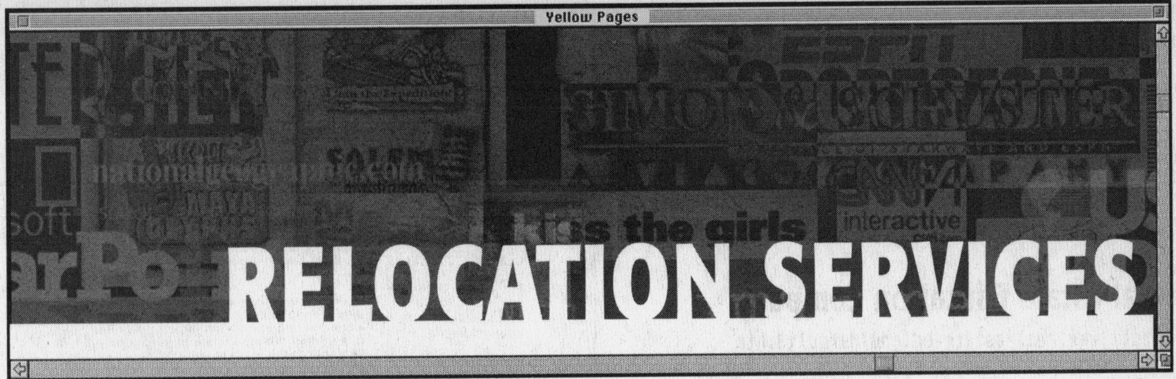

There's no place like home. There's no place like home. There's no place like home.

Dorothy, from the Wizard of Oz

AAA Ameri/Relocators & Super Savers

http://www.amerisavers.com/

Check this site to find help selling your present home and buying one in your new city. The company promises your first month's mortgage payment free if you use one of their agents.

All City Relocation Index

http://www.idworks.com/allcity/

Enter your vital information, the city you're moving to, the date of your move, the price range of the home you're looking for, and a few other informational tidbits, and receive a package made up especially for you. You'll learn about the climate, day care, and many other things you'll need to know before you get there.

American Relocation Center

http://www.kniht.com/

Learn how to save money when you move to a new location. Learn about schools, housing, and property values in the city of your choice. This site promises to save you not only money, but stress, so check it out.

Relocation Services and Information
http://amo-mortgage.com/relocate.htm

Apartments by Rent Net

http://www.rent.net/?ref=homefairapt

Here's a site you'll want to visit if you're looking for short term housing while you relocate. There are links to international rentals, furniture rental, and more. This site provides money-saving links for truck rental and self-storage units too.

Forward Mobility

http://www.forwardmobility.com/

This site provides consulting services for those faced with a move to another city. The service includes international moves. Learn the facts about relocation, including the corporate cost. Check out Forward Mobility's services here, including services at your departure and destination points.

Homebuyer's Fair Address Express

http://homefair.com/homefair/b4u/addexpr.html?NETSCAPE_LIVEWIRE.src=

Fill out the form at this site to receive a change of address kit. They'll help you make sure everyone knows your new address so that you don't miss one *TV Guide* or alumni report.

Military Relocation Network

http://www.milrelo.com/

This site, sponsored by RE/MAX Realty, is specifically aimed at military personnel and their special needs. People in the armed forces move often and sometimes at very short notice, and this site is provided to meet their special needs. Just click the metropolitan area or duty station of your choice to see what's available.

National Online Home Relocation

http://www.wln.com/~exchange/olympia/orelo.htm

Service offers a nationwide network of buyer's agents and marketing specialists. Site includes a substantial real estate needs assessment form for customized services, along with links to a number of related subjects.

Real Estate Education Company

http://www.real-estate-ed.com/default3.htm

Geared toward those interested in a real estate career, the site offers information about training, educators, and REEC products and services.

Real Estate Network International

http://members.aol.com/renintl/homepage.html

Real Estate Network International publishes the Florida Real Estate Journal newspaper and the International Real Estate Investor magazine. The site offers news, features, and commentary from each publication.

Real Estate Recruiting/Careers Education

http://www.realestateeducation.com

Web site with information on real estate careers, recruiting real estate agents, and real estate education on the West Coast.

Relocation Online

http://www.relocationonline.com/

This site provides answers to FAQs, tips for making your move simpler, and a list of the services they offer. Just fill out the Needs Analysis form and submit it to take advantage of their complimentary service.

Relocation Services and Information

http://amo-mortgage.com/relocate.htm

American Mortgage Online's relocation service is quite useful if you're moving to another city. There are links to real estate agents in 2,800 cities, along with advice you'll need if you're moving to a completely new area. Register to receive the free relocation package.

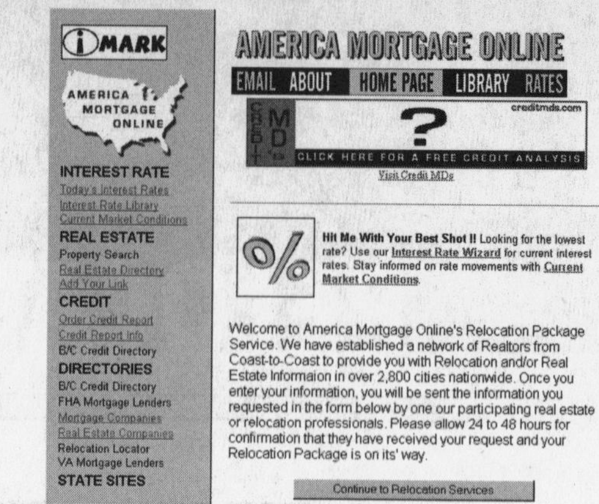

The Relocation Wizard

http://homefair.com/wizard/?NETSCAPE_LIVEWIRE.src=

Answer the questions and submit your information to the Wizard and receive a suggested timeline. Find out here what to do when to make your move go smoothly.

Rent Net: Short Term Furnished Housing

http://www.rent.net/shorterm/homefair.html

This site provides information about short term furnished housing in the area you're moving to. Click the state of destination and see what's available in your new city.

Ryder TRS

http://www.rent.net/trucks.html

You can use this site to contact Ryder Truck Rental and reserve your truck for the day you need it. Just submit the required information, and Ryder will call you with availability and a great rate.

Texas A&M Real Estate Center

http://recenter.tamu.edu/

This is *the* comprehensive source for all things related to Texas real estate. An excellent site design allows viewers to browse efficiently through the myriad of material, including numerous publications, statistical data, an extraordinary collection of real estate articles—even building permit information for all 50 states!

The Relocation Guides

http://www.relocationguide.com/

Search this site for information on cities throughout the United States. The Relocation Guide includes information on health care, education, housing, and other aspects of the community.

The Relocation Universe

http://www.erc.org/

Sponsored by the Employee Relocation Council (ERC), this site covers a myriad of relocation and human resource issues, from transfer costs to family concerns. Sections include a Relocation Career Hotline, information on ERC, and Research and Publications, among others.

Security First Funding

http://www.dirs.com/mortgage/sfft1

They are FHA approved and offer loan programs for home improvement, purchase, or refinancing. FHA Title 1 loans up $25,000 with no equity or appraisal.

NEWSGROUPS

alt.realtor.relocation

alt.relocation

Related Sites

http://www.census.gov/stat_abstract/ranks.html

http://www.erc.org/ecc/eccframe.htm

http://www.projectadvantage.com/

http://www.relomgmt.com/

http://www.relojournal.com/

http://www.ip-solutions.com/tc/index.html

http://www.reloconnect.com/

http://www.io.com/house/tour.html

http://www.home-finders.com/

http://www.relomall.com/relomall/relomall.html

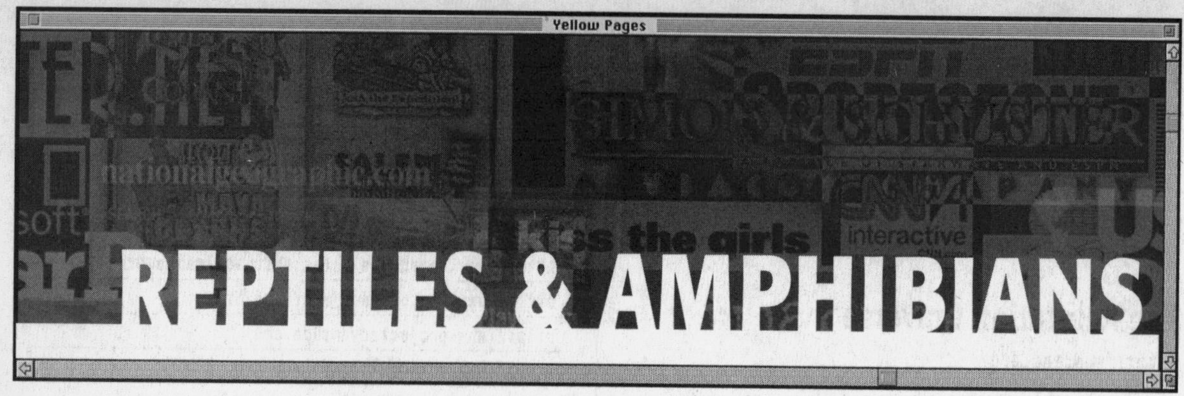

REPTILES & AMPHIBIANS

> I don't like spiders and snakes, but that ain't what it takes to love me.
>
> *Jim Stafford*

Amphibian and Reptile Collection

http://www.mip.berkeley.edu/mvz/mvzherpe.html

Describes the MVZ reptilian/amphibian collection, which includes more than 200,000 specimens from around the world. Includes a few pictures. Also contains a link to information about their animal tissue collection, which can be used for DNA research.

!!!Frogland!!!

http://www.teleport.com/~dstroy/frogland.html

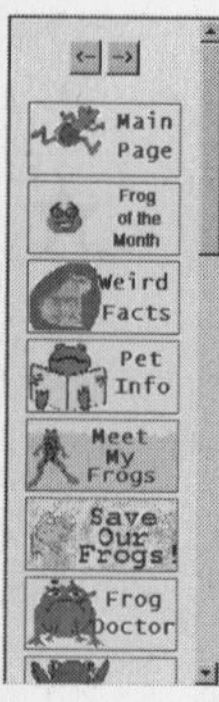

What's the difference between a toad and a frog? This is just one of the FAQs answered on this fun, factual site. You can select sound bytes from a library of frog calls and learn about keeping frogs and toads as pets.

!!!Frogland!!!
http://www.teleport.com/~dstroy/frogland.html

Jason's Snakes & Reptiles
http://www.shadeslanding.com/jas/

Jason's Snakes & Reptiles

http://www.shadeslanding.com/jas/

Jason has assembled an impressive list of Internet sites on the subjects of frogs, snakes, turtle, and even crocodiles. He also provides ordering information for both products and animals and a snake care sheet to keep your pet snake healthy.

Longhorn Lizard Ranch

http://www2.cy-net.net/~maxntim/index.html

The Longhorn Lizard Ranch breeds and sells many varieties of lizards. Their Web site provides an index of care sheets for many these species, including such exotic reptiles as the bearded dragon. View the photo gallery and link to other reptile sites.

Mike's Herpetocultural Home Page

http://gto.ncsa.uiuc.edu/pingleto/herp.html

View the close-up photos and detailed information provided on this Life List which includes newts, salamanders, lizards, terrapins, and much more. Take a photo tour of the Shawnee National Forest, the dwelling place of the cottonmouth water moccasin.

Society for the Study of Amphibians & Reptiles

http://falcon.cc.ukans.edu/~gpisani/SSAR.html

Founded in 1958, the Society for the Study of Amphibians & Reptiles is the world's largest international herpetological society. Find out about meeting dates, membership, publications, and conservation efforts of this group.

Television is now so desparately hungry for material that they're scraping the top of the barrel.

Gore Vidal

The 1st Leave It To Beaver WebSite

http://www.geocities.com/Hollywood/Hills/2993/

More stuff on the Beav and family than we can mention here. If you're a fan, check out this site. Here's just a sampling of what it offers: free newsletter subscription, Beaver FAQs, trivia quizzes, and info on all the actors.

Bewitched And Elizabeth Montgomery Site

http://www.erols.com/bewitchd/index.html

Let this site take you back to Westport, Connecticut, circa 1964. Just wiggle your nose (and click the right spots) and you can learn about the *Bewitched* theme music, hear sound clips, read show scripts, check out the books *Bewitched Forever* and *Bewitched Cookbook*, see a silly slide show, and more.

Bonanza...The Web Site!

http://home.earthlink.net/~deirdre/index.html/

Join the world of the Cartwrights—Ben, Adam, Hoss, and Little Joe. At this site you can read *Bonanza* trivia, FAQs, and the *Bonanza* story; send a *Bonanza* postcard; learn about conventions and available books; join the mailing list; hear the show theme; and check out other *Bonanza* links.

Granada Sherlock Holmes Episode Guide
http://charon.ucsd.edu/kli/HolmesEG/

The Mary Tyler Moore Page
http://www.rust.net/~rkm/mtm/mtm.htm

Nick at Nite & TV Land
http://www.nick-at-nite.com/

Gilligan's Island Archives

http://www.lido.com/tv/gilligan/

At the top of the page, you'll find the opening song ("Just sit right back and you'll hear a tale, a tale of a fateful trip..."). After that, you'll find pictures, FAQ lists, and other Web resources. ("...So join us here each week my friend; you're sure to get a smile, from seven stranded castaways, here on Gilligan's Isle!" Catchy, isn't it?)

Granada Sherlock Holmes Episode Guide

http://charon.ucsd.edu/kli/HolmesEG/

One woman's tribute to the *Sherlock Holmes* series. The site offers lists of episodes with a full range of information, including casts/credits, airdates, lengths, and actual stories. It also offers links relating to cast members, some pictures, an interview with Jeremy Brett, and all the other choice bits fans will be looking for.

Gribble's "Taxi" Pages

http://www.freenet.msp.mn.us/people/gribblea/taxi.html

Choose from the selections History, Cast, Episode List, Trivia, Links, and Home, and go from there. When you click Cast, for example, you'll find a list of regulars and semi-regulars, as well as a list of famous guest stars, such as Tom Selleck, Penny Marshall, and Herve Villechaize (?!).

A B C D E F G H I J K L M N O P Q R S T U V W X Y Z

Gunsmoke

http://comp.uark.edu/~tsnyder/gunsmoke/index.html#basic

The Web page for lovers of *Gunsmoke* starring James Arness. Want to find out the name of the character played by Burt Reynolds for three years? Scroll down a bit. Want to see a picture of Miss Kitty or listen to the *Gunsmoke* theme? Scroll down a bit more. Want to know the name of Festus's mule? Check out the FAQ page.

Happy Days Online

http://www.geocities.com/TelevisionCity/9835/

Sound files, picture galleries, brief and full episode guides, and lots of miscellany—all can be found at this site built around *Happy Days*, the weren't-the-'50s-wonderful show that has been entertaining fans for more than 23 years. One special offering: addresses where you can write all the cast members.

I Love Lucy

http://www.geocities.com/Hollywood/Hills/1684/lucy.html

This site deals with the show-opening sequences of *I Love Lucy*. Did you know that when the show first began in the early '50s, there was no heart on a satin background, but stick cartoon figures of Lucy and Ricky instead? This site has old images of those original openings and tells why they were dropped. Follow the link to The Toon Tracker Animated Lucy Page for more trivia on this subject.

JEANNIELAND

http://member.aol.com/smoke15874/index.htm

The site opens playing the theme from *I Dream of Jeannie*, to get your nostalgic juices flowing. Climb inside the magic lamp to find all the "Jeannie" stuff a fan could dream of, including a chat room, a photo gallery, a newsletter, a special of the week, a treasure chest, message boards, links, animations, music clips, and more.

The Mary Tyler Moore Page

http://www.rust.net/~rkm/mtm/mtm.htm

Source of all things Mary Tyler Moore and *The Mary Tyler Moore Show*. This site consists of a long list of enticing links to such items as episode guides, a list of books about MTM, interesting facts about the MTM kitten, a video clip from the first "MTM" episode, the words from the "MTM" theme song, and Web sites for other "MTM" stars.

The M*A*S*H 4077th Homepage

http://www.netlink.co.uk/users/mash/

Travel to the 4077th to learn all about the *M*A*S*H* series, the characters, the actors, trivia, the *M*A*S*H* movie, and fan interests. One little gem you'll find: a "Where are they now?" page. You'll find other related links here too.

Nick at Nite & TV Land

http://www.nick-at-nite.com/

You can't miss this site—it's your connection to all your favorite classic TV shows. Indulge yourself by exploring the shows, the stars, and the episodes in the TV Shows area. Get show descriptions and schedules for your area, play games and win prizes, and find "TV Treasures." Some pages can be slow to load, but they're worth the wait.

The Prisoner: Joe Brae's Ultimate Village Experience

http://members.aol.com/joebrae/prisoner.htm

If you've seen the show *The Prisoner*, you either love it or hate it. For those in the former category, this Web site serves as a storehouse of opinions and theories about the show and offers a chance to see scores of "Prisoner" images. And while you're there, you must fill out a response form and send it to the site author—after all, you wouldn't want to be *unmutual*, would you?

Star Trek

http://www.startrek.com

One of many sites on the *Star Trek* phenomenon. This one, put out by Paramount Pictures, details not only the original *Star Trek*, which is currently being rerun in more than 200 countries, but also the other shows that evolved from it.

TV Tracker's Classic TV Sounds

http://www.geocities.com/Hollywood/Set/2232/tvtrack.html

Here's an amusing site to visit—as long as you have a 28.8 Kbps or faster modem. Hear theme songs from classic TV shows *The Red Skelton Show, I Love Lucy, Father Knows Best, The Honeymooners, Leave It to Beaver, My Three Sons,* and many more.

The Unofficial Lassie Home Page

http://www.mindspring.com/~jlyoung/lassie.htm

Lassie lovers, unite! This is the place to be for Lassie facts, Lassie photos, and an episode guide. It's also the place for info on Lassie movies, Lassie's other TV series, the new Lassie, and Lassie novels. BTW, did you know that three *Leave It to Beaver* stars—Hugh Beaumont, Tony Dow, and Jerry Mathers—guest-starred in episodes of *Lassie*? Click "Classic Lassie Trivia" for more like this.

Welcome to Total TV Online

http://www.totaltv.com/

Total TV bills itself as "the most comprehensive source for TV information and listings." Although Total TV is not restricted to reruns, its search feature is one great way to find out whether your favorite classic show is currently being given air time, and to see what time you should tune in and what channel to turn to.

"Who's Been Messin' Up the Bulletin Board?"

http://users.aol.com/anewsome/private/home.htm

Whistle along with the "Who's Been Messin' Up the Bulletin Board?" chapter of *The Andy Griffith Show* Rerun Watchers Club (TAGSRWC). Get Mayberry news, FAQs, sounds, and photos; drop in for a chat, leave a message on the message board, check out the Mayberry calendar, find out about joining or starting a TAGSRWC chapter, access a list of other classic TV links, and do lots of other fun stuff.

The Wild Wild West Home Page

http://moose.uvm.edu/~glambert/twww1.html

Currently in syndication on TNT Network, *The Wild Wild West* first came onto the scene in 1965 and was a popular Western/Spy/SciFi fantasy show for four seasons. To relive its glory or glean some new facts for yourself, join 50,000-plus other visitors in browsing through this site.

NEWSGROUPS

news:alt.tv.ilovelucy

news:alt.tv.mash

rec.arts.sf.tv

rec.arts.startrek.misc

rec.arts.tv

GOPHER & FTP SITES

gopher://sunsite.doc.ic.ac.uk/0/public/media/tv/collections/tardis/us/comedy/Taxi/Taxi

gopher://sunsite.doc.ic.ac.uk/0/public/media/tv/collections/tardis/us/sci-fi/TwilightZone/TwilightZoneOld

gopher://sunsite.doc.ic.ac.uk/0/public/media/tv/collections/tardis/us/sci-fi/TwilightZone/TwilightZoneNew.1

gopher://sunsite.doc.ic.ac.uk/0/public/media/tv/collections/tardis/us/sci-fi/TwilightZone/TwilightZoneNew.2

gopher://sunsite.doc.ic.ac.uk/0/public/media/tv/collections/tardis/us/drama/Columbo/Columbo.ed

ftp://src.doc.ic.ac.uk/public/media/tv/collections/tardis/us/comedy/DickVanDyke

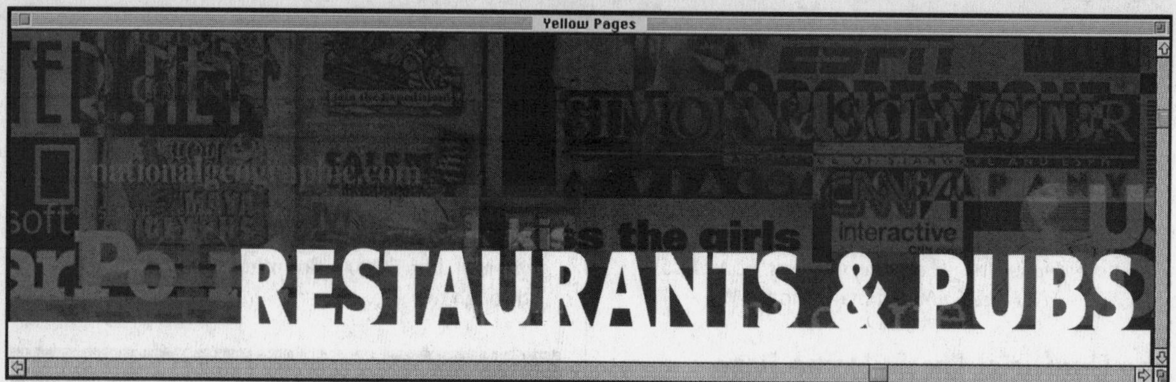

A
B
C
D
E
F
G
H
I
J
K
L
M
N
O
P
Q
R
S
T
U
V
W
X
Y
Z

Part of the secret of success in life is to eat what you like and let the food fight it out inside.

Mark Twain

NRP TOP PICKS

Ben & Jerry's
http://www.benjerry.com/

Chrone's Virtual Diner
http://www.neb.com/noren/diner/Chrones.html

Hot Hot Hot
http://www.hothothot.com/

Ore-Ida Foods, Inc.
http://www.oreida.com/

Ben & Jerry's

http://www.benjerry.com/

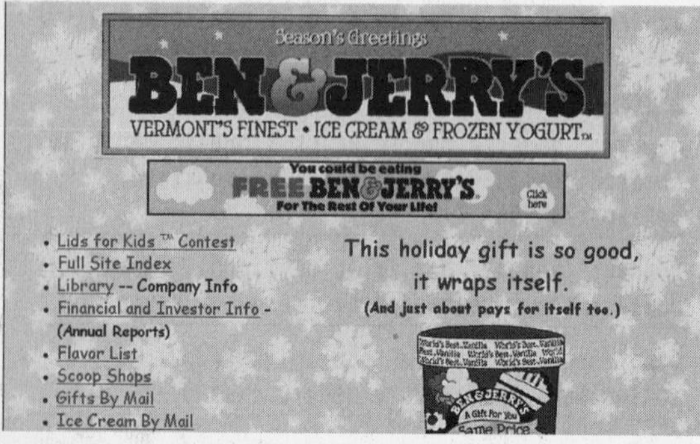

Visit the globally conscious ice cream company that reinvented the way we think about ice cream. Find out what flavors you're missing out on from the complete Flavor List. Find out what flavors you missed in the Flavor Graveyard. Also, learn about the history of the company and the directions it's taking. Stock prices available online soon. Be sure to check out Ben & Jerry's new line of sorbets.

Birds on a Wire

http://www.birdsonawire.com

Restaurant in Columbia, South Carolina! The brain child of a couple of USC students. Try their menu, including the "redneck cuisine."

Borel's Deli and Catering

http://www.americandreams.com/borelsdeli/

This super deli also offers catering with a personal touch.

Boston Restaurant Guide

http://www.hubnet.com/

Provides reviews of recommended restaurants in Boston. Lets you search for your favorite restaurant by name alphabetically, as well as by type of cuisine or location. Includes a list of recently added or closed restaurants. Lets you submit your own reviews.

The Brass Grille

http://www.novia.net/~dwalker/fdc/sponsors/bg.html

The Brass Grille in Omaha, Nebraska's Old Market District is one of the best restaurants in town. Their lunch and dinner menus are online.

Broad Street Deli & Bagel Factory

http://www.busdir.com/broadst/

Tamaqua, PA deli, home of delicious bagels, sandwiches, hoagies, and homemade soups. Stop in to see their daily specials!

Brooklyn Bagel Restaurant and Deli

http://www.magg.net/~brooklyn/index.html

The home page for Brooklyn Bagel Restaurant and Deli, a South Florida bagel chain now offering franchises.

Buckeye Beans & Herbs, Inc.

http://www.buckeyeranch.com/

Black Bean Bart and the Pinto Kid team up to bring you a collection of the finest beans, spices, and pasta around. Dry ingredients are sent straight to your home, where you add ingredients of your own to come up with a flavorful masterpiece.

Cafe Bernardo

http://infovillage.com/cafebernardo/index.html

Cafe Bernardo offers a casual artistic atmosphere to diners in midtown Sacramento. Opened by Randy Paragary. Outdoor seating, creative menu.

CalWine Gourmet Food Shop

http://www.calwine.com/foodshop.html

At CalWine, you can choose from the very best the Napa Valley has to offer. Browse wines by winery or variety, peruse gourmet selections such as chocolate wine sauces and grape seed oil, and then order by fax or toll-free number.

Capt Benjamin's Calabash Seafood Restaurant

http://www.webs4you.com/capt-benjamins/

Capt. Benjamin's Calabash Seafood Restaurant located in Myrtle Beach, SC. They have shrimp, crab legs, and landlubber fare.

Capt. Dave's Dockside Restaurant & Gazebo Bar

http://www.webs4you.com/dockside/

Dockside Restaurant & Gazebo Bar located in Murrells Inlet, SC, south of Myrtle Beach, SC. Serving the finest seafood and steaks for over 20 Years.

Caroline Gold Cheese

http://www.frontiercomm.net/~fkostlev/gold.html

Caroline, Wisconsin is home to Caroline Kountry Gold Cheese, Mehlberg's Maple Syrup, Jim's Blue Ribbon Sausage, and Vern's Cheese Spreads. Order any combination to create a custom gift basket, or choose from a variety of predesigned baskets.

ChefsOnline

http://www.i1.com/chefs/

Provides a selection of gourmet "dinners for four," which are frozen and delivered to your door. You can then prepare them in minutes with a conventional oven, microwave, or just a pot of boiling water and a good pair of scissors.

Chile Today Hot Tamale

http://eMall.com/chile/

Offers Chile, Hot Sauce, and Salsa and Chip of the Month Clubs, as well as dried chiles and exotic sauces from around the world. Also provides a list of spicy recipes to try on your own.

Chrone's Virtual Diner

http://www.neb.com/noren/diner/Chrones.html

Learn all about the American entrepreneurial institution of diners. Get ahold of a menu of a diner in your area, or glance at some reviews listed state-by-state. Learn to distinguish a "real" diner from a hash-slinging restaurant posing as a diner.

Copeland's

http://www.usaol.com/TN/YP/restaurant/Copelands.html

Copeland's of New Orleans in Brentwood, Tennessee offers diners a unique menu of Cajun and Creole dishes in a lively restaurant setting.

CyberExplore Cafe

http://www.cyberexplore.com/

CyberExplore Cafe blends the interactive world of the Internet with the informality of a coffeehouse. Where else can you surf the World Wide Web at blistering speeds, play networked games with friends, and enjoy fresh deli sandwiches, pastries, and Stone Creek Coffee? And all this in the safe, social setting of a neighborhood coffeehouse.

Dean & Deluca

http://www.ishops.com/dd/

Here you can order a variety of kitchen and gourmet products from this New York landmark. Products include copper and stainless steel kitchenware, caviar, jams, coffees & teas, and gifts.

Diner's Grapevine

http://www.dinersgrapevine.com/

The ultimate site for those who like to eat out. Enter specifics of geographic location, price range, ambiance, entertainment, type of cuisine, and special features of the restaurant you're interested in and Grapevine will offer you a variety of selections. A truly invaluable tool for the adventurous diner.

Dining Out on the Web

http://www.ird.net/diningout.html

A comprehensive site that links you to hundreds of restaurant sites and search engines organized by geographical location. Helps you narrow your search to find the restaurant you're looking for. An amazing feat in Web usefulness!

Dragon Spit Flaming Hot Salsa

http://www.shop-utopia.com/dragonspit/

A company specializing in gourmet salsa. Provides a secure online form to order your salsa.

EatHere.com

http://www.eathere.com

An interactive celebration of popular roadside eateries in the U.S. and Canada. Authentic Road Food Recipes, stories. Nominate your favorite eating spots in ten categories, including diners, drive-ins, burgers, barbecue, home cooking, country inns, steak and seafood, and more.

Felipe's Restaurant

http://www.go2mexico.com/pv/food/felipes.html

Felipe's Restaurant has become the preferred destination of visitors wishing to enjoy the best views and best cuisine Puerto Vallarta has to offer.

Frito-Lay Main Menu

http://www.fritolay.com/

The junk food aficionado's guide to Frito-Lay products complete with recipes (Fritos Fixin's). Contains downloadable wallpapers of icon Chester Cheetah.

Garrett's Grille and Grog

http://www.garretts-grille.com

Restaurant and bar in Columbia, South Carolina. Two locations for great food and great sports.

Griffin's Restaurant, Annapolis, Maryland

http://www.griffins-citydock.com

Celebrated by both locals and tourists alike, Griffin's is located in the historic district of Annapolis, Maryland. The restaurant, and the charm of the town, have something for everyone.

Heroes Sports Bar & Deli

http://www.feist.com/oldtown/heroes.html

Wichita's premier sports Bar. Heroes is located in Wichita's historic Old Town District. Stop in for food, fun and excitement.

The Highland Trail Company

http://www.highlandtrail.co.uk/highlandtrail/

Offers online shopping of Scottish products, including smoked salmon, smoked venison, malt whiskey, and gifts.

Hot Hot Hot

http://www.hothothot.com/

If you take a liking to food seasoned with hot sauce named Nuclear Hell or Ring of Fire, Hot Hot Hot is the online hot sauce source for you. Over 100 varieties of sauces from around the globe can be searched by various criteria, including heat level, origin, ingredients, or name. Also contains articles from Chile Pepper Magazine.

Johnnie Fox's Online

http://www.indigo.ie/fox

Johnnie Fox's, one of Ireland's most popular and well-known pubs, goes online.

King David's Glatt Kosher Deli & Restaurant

http://www.angelfire.com/biz/KingDavid

Please visit King David's Glatt Kosher Deli & Restaurant on the Web. The only Kosher Restaurant in Delaware Valley, PA, USA, serving Indian food!

Kisco Kid Deli

http://mtkisco.com/kiscokid.htm

Kisco Kid Deli, located in Mount Kisco, offers quality food at quality prices. They serve everything from

Heros to desserts. Kisco Kid Deli also offers a wide range of catering specials for all of your party and picnic needs. Stop in and check out their party sub specials or just to get a GREAT bite to eat.

Krema Nut Company

http://teraform.com/~schapman/krema/

Established in 1898, the Krema Nut Company offers the old fashioned peanut butter that gave the company its reputation, as well as an overwhelming variety of nuts and nut butter gift packages available through their online catalog. If you like nuts, this is definitely the place for you.

L'Orangerie, The Most Beautiful French Restaurant in Los Angeles

http://www.orangerie.com

The first French restaurant Web site with an interactive menu. L'Orangerie is rated "One of the five best restaurants in the United States" by the press.

The Maine Diner

http://www.biddeford.com/diner/

The Maine Diner in Wells is one of Southern Maine's most popular restaurants. Visit their site, look at the menu, even order a T-shirt!

Mary's Marketplace

http://www.nyackny.com/marys.htm

Mary's is a unique eatery specializing in fresh, great tasting meals at reasonable prices & served with friendly professional service. Visit their indoor/outdoor café.

MenuNet FoodFinder

http://www.foodfinder.com

A restaurant directory structured geographically and by type of food that displays menus and advertising for U.S., Canadian, and European restaurants. The success of this site is largely based upon visitor input. Here's your chance to play restaurant critic!

Michael's On East Restaurant

http://www.bestfood.com

Restaurant, wine store, jazz club, caterer and banquet facility. Located in Sarasota, Florida, adjacent to Longboat Key and Siesta Key. Enjoy fine dining at one of Florida's top 20 restaurants! Award-winning American cuisine, elegant and sophisticated atmosphere, with a new cigar lounge and live jazz club. Features wine list, menus, ballroom, recipes, beers, spirits. Make reservations online!

Misty Moonlight Diner

http://www.berkshire.net/~rshack/misty.html

Classic cuisine in a '50s Theme.

Myer's Gourmet Popcorn

http://www.aus.xanadu.com/GlassWings/arcade/myers/mgp.html

A gift ordering service for the popcorn lover in your life (even if it's yourself). Select from flavors like Cajun, Tutti Frutti, or plain old buttered popcorn. Your gift can be packaged in one of the many decorative tins offered.

National Restaurant Register's Menu Online

http://www.onlinemenus.com/

Welcome to the National Restaurant Register's Menu Online, the interactive restaurant information service providing actual menus and other restaurant information. Select the type of restaurant, location, and price range from thousands of restaurants. Utilize Menu Online and try a new restaurant in your area.

The Old Clam House Restaurant

http://www.iceonline.com/home/echua/oclamh.html

The Old Clam House Restaurant is San Francisco's oldest restaurant, serving the freshest seafood and quality spirits since 1861.

Olympia Bakery and Catering

http://www2.olympiabakery.com/Olympia/

A family-owned bakery and deli since 1924. They offer a full line of cakes including wedding cakes, sculpted cakes, and even x-rated cakes. Located in Tampa, FL, they also do catering for events such as weddings.

Oregon Cupboard

http://amsquare.com/cupboard/index.html

A variety of specialty foods from the artisans of Oregon. Some of the foods featured include jams, pie fillings, honeys, smoked salmon, and coffee syrups. There is also a complimentary recipe exchange maintained at this site.

Ore-Ida Foods, Inc.

http://www.oreida.com/

At Ore-Ida's Web site you can read about their product line, which includes a variety of potato products. Recipes are provided online, as well as some interesting facts, such as how many tater tots you'd have to place end-to-end to circle the Earth.

Pacifico Restaurante Mexicano

http://www.napavalley.com/napavalley/restrnts/pacifico/index.html

Pacifico Restaurante Mexicano claims they feature the finest in Regional Mexican Cuisine that the Napa Valley has to offer. Check it out!

Paolo's

http://www.acoates.com/paolos

Do you know the way to San Jose? If you do, make sure you visit Paolo's for award-winning regional Italian cuisine. Features a seasonal menu and wine list.

Pizza Hut

http://www.pizzahut.com

Order pizza with your favorite toppings with their online order form.

Queen's Kitchen & Pantry

http://www.pantry.com

Internet retail shopping of unusual and exotic foods and related products and services. Contains links to several commercial food sites.

Ragazzi's Italian Restaurant

http://www.webs4you.com/ragazzis/

Ragazzi's Italian Restaurant, located in Raleigh, NC, Cary, NC, and Garner, NC offers Italian cuisine and brick oven pizzas for your dining pleasure.

Restaurant Home Pages

http://www.restaurant-pages.com/pages/

From Gourmet Dining to Fast Food to Juice Bars, a national "billboard" of restaurants and eateries featuring special food, menus, recipes, and wine.

Ristorante Capellini

http://www.capellinis.com

Fine Italian cuisine in the San Francisco area set in a beautiful three level restaurant, designed by the acclaimed restaurateur Pat Kuleto. Come and reserve your special event.

Saguaro Food Products

http://pavilions.com/Saguaro.htm

A chip lover's delight! Products include chips of all sorts: potato, corn, blue corn, and more. Salsas are also on the menu with a full selection available to be shipped anywhere in the continental U.S.

Sally's Place

http://www.bpe.com/

Actually, this site covers a lot more than just restaurants. Food and travel usually come hand in hand and this site blends the two nicely. Sample some ethnically diverse recipes, search for a restaurant on your travels, or find out about your favorite beverages.

Scruffy Murphy's Irish Pub

http://www.magicnet.net/~scruffys

Irish pub located in Downtown Orlando, Florida. Other bars, taverns, pubs, and nightclubs just aren't as fun!

Scubber's

http://www.scubbers.com/

Scubber's provides high-quality Buffalo wings, sandwiches, and finger foods to their in-store customers, but if you're not lucky enough to live close to them, you can still have their products shipped to you via UPS. Shippable products include baskets, bags of wings, and bottles of sauce.

Seasons Restaurant

http://www.go2mexico.com/cabo/food/seasons.html

Excellent Mediterranean cuisine, excellent service, and an excellent atmosphere all add up to the finest dining experience in Cabo San Lucas. Visit their site to learn more about the best new restaurant in Cabo.

Slapstix Pub and Grub

http://www.igateway.net/~bowles/slapstix

Located in Soulard (St. Louis), Slapstix has great food, live music and comedy, and a great atmosphere. Try the Jambalaya!

Steere's Calabash Seafood Restaurant

http://www.webs4you.com/steeres/

Steere's Calabash Seafood restaurant located on Restaurant Row in Myrtle Beach, SC. Their claim to fame is that they offer the best seafood show on earth with the famous all-you-can-eat buffet.

Tabor Hill Winery & Restaurant

http://www.taborhill.com

Join the winery tours to see how fine wines are made. Wine tasting available. Visit the restaurant for a touch of romance or visit their stores to find that perfect gift.

A Taste of Texas

http://www.dallas.net/~atastetx/

A source for authentic Texas sauces and gifts. You can order online from their collection of sauces, which include an award-winning fat-free three-bean salsa. Recipes are provided with every order.

Taste of Texas Market

http://www.cycorp.com/shopping.cgi/tasteoftexas/index.html

A great site for jalapeno lovers and misplaced Texans. A variety of pepper products are available including jalapeno jelly, jalapeno mustard, and Senor Jalapeno's Hot Flash for the more adventurous types.

Tavern On The Green's Info Page

http://www.gate.net/~tavern

Tavern On The Green's Web site provides info about upcoming events to their current customers, and answers questions people might have who haven't been there.

Three Star India Restaurant

http://www.eecs.uic.edu/~jkachapp/3star.html

Conveniently located at Devon and Rockwell in Chicago, Three Star India Restaurant is one of the great Indian restaurants in town.

Tiramesu Restaurant

http://www.winnet.net/tiramesu

Tiramesu Restaurant was established in 1988 in South Beach, Florida. At Tiramesu you will find authentic Italian cuisine. Their dishes are good and healthy, because they use traditional Italian cuisine while maintaining all the nutritional qualities of their fresh ingredients.

Tully Pizzeria and Deli

http://www.angelfire.com/pg1/tullyshop/index.html

Pizza, subs, chicken wings, salads, all in a small town pizza shop in Tully, NY.

Virginia Diner

http://www.vadiner.com/

Provides information about the Diner's history, an online catalog of gifts, some Southern peanut recipes, and other information about peanuts.

A Virtual Pub Crawl of Hull

http://www.arachnid.co.uk/hullpub/index.html

A virtual pub crawl of pubs in Hull City Centre, Old Town and beyond. Includes interactive maps and individual pub pages.

The Whitman House Restaurant

http://www.capecod.net/whitman/

Voted "Best Fine Dining on the Outer Cape" by *Cape Cod Life* magazine for 1995 and 1996, the Whitman House Restaurant offers the best in both cuisine and atmosphere. The Whitman House was also voted "Best Restaurant for a Wedding Reception" in *Cape Cod Life*. If your travels take you to Cape Cod, stop by and experience the Whitman House Restaurant and Quilt Shop. Reservations for dinner are recommended.

J.R. Wood, Inc.

http://www.jrwood.com/

A company that deals in fruits, vegetables, purees, juices, and concentrates, as well as specialty items such as baby food. Information can be requested directly from the company, and corporate contacts are provided online.

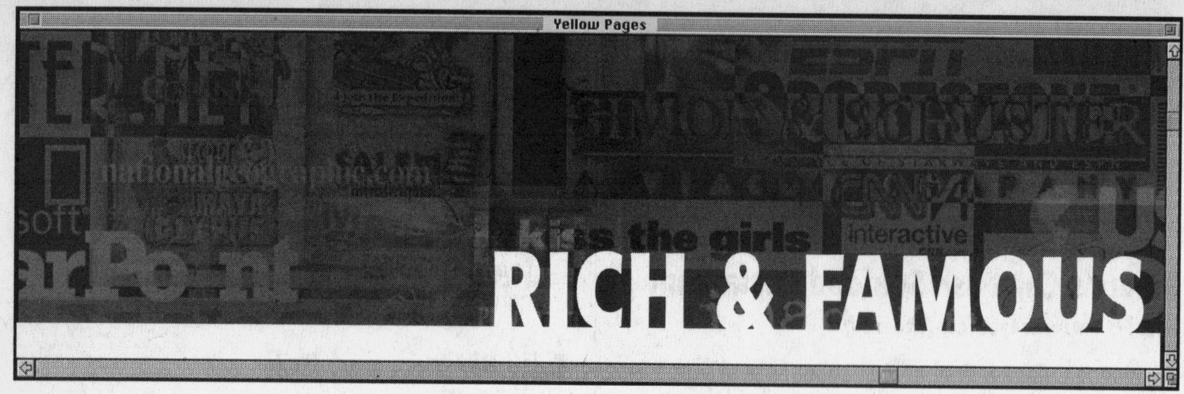

A
B
C
D
E
F
G
H
I
J
K
L
M
N
O
P
Q
R
S
T
U
V
W
X
Y
Z

If you can count your money, you don't have a billion dollars.

J. Paul Getty

GolfWeb–Tiger Woods
http://www.golfweb.com/tiger/news.html

Driveways of the Rich and Famous
http://www.driveways.com

The Official Anne Rice Web Site!
http://www.anne-rice.inter.net/

The Unofficial Twiggy Lawson Homepage
http://www.geocities.com/Hollywood/7308/twiggy.htm

ATHLETES

Cal Ripken, Jr.

http://www.2131.com/

In audio/video, Cal talks about a great '97 season for the Orioles, the American League Championship Series, his back problem, and his consecutive games streak. Take a look at Cal's current stats, career stats, awards, and biography. Get info on the Ripken Museum, or play Cal's Home Run Pinball Game. Includes info on Cal Ripken merchandise.

GolfWeb–Tiger Woods

http://www.golfweb.com/tiger/news.html

Browse through this profile of Eldrick "Tiger" Woods, which includes a list of his major golf victories. You'll also see a FAQ, discussion group, the Tiger Recordbook (starting at age 2), scorecards, tour statistics, features, and news. Be sure to visit the extensive photo gallery and listen to audio clips that include comments from Tiger.

Holyfield/Tyson: TimeLine

http://www.mtyson.com/LONGTIME/HOLIFIEL/RESUME.HTM

Includes bios, resumes, and interviews.

Michael "Air" Jordan–Flight 23

http://zen.res.cmu.edu/~agupta/jordan/

This site includes many pictures, video files, and career statistics of the Bulls star. It also gives you links to other NBA, Bulls, and Jordan sites.

Michael Jordan: A Tribute

http://www.unc.edu/~badgers/jordan.html

Read over the detailed profile with articles about M.J.'s career at North Carolina, as a United States Olympian, and with the Chicago Bulls. Includes video footage, pictures, and much more. Also includes articles and pictures of Jordan's shoes, his try at baseball, and even about his high school basketball career. This is a very detailed and thorough site that no Michael Jordan fan should miss.

The Michael Jordan Virtual Gallery

http://www.wwu.edu/~n9345228/tom1.html

Presents many pictures of Michael Jordan in action. Also includes links to other Jordan and NBA sites.

The Official Dennis Rodman Home Page

http://lonestar.texas.net/~pmagal/

Send mail to Dennis and read mail sent by others. Examine Rodman news, his bio, and his stats. Read quotations about and by Dennis. Be sure to visit the Dennis Rodman Hair Archive. You can also view Rodman merchandise and find out how to join the Dennis Rodman fan club.

PENNY-HARDAWAY

http://penny-hardaway.org/

This site on NBA star Anfernee "Penny" Hardaway includes videos, pictures, statistics, and a profile of the Orlando Magic guard. You'll also see personal information, polls, and even chats with Hardaway.

Shaquille O'Neal

http://www.fiu.edu/~goraczko/bkb/shq/shq.html

Provides pictures, videos, and articles about basketball player/movie actor/rap singer Shaquille O'Neal. You'll see photos of Shaq as a child, in high school, college, and in the pros. You can also read about his history, stats, and much more.

A Tribute To Michael Jordan

http://www.geocities.com/Colosseum/3278/

Provides pictures and a profile of Chicago Bulls basketball star Michael Jordan. This site provides sound bytes, a slide show, and links to related sites.

The Unofficial Penny Hardaway Page

http://remcen.ehhs.cmich.edu/~smurray/pennyh.htm

Provides background, pictures, and statistics on NBA star Anfernee "Penny" Hardaway. Also includes pictures of 'Lil Penny—the costar of commercials with Hardaway.

Wayne Gretzky HomePage

http://www.jetlink.net/%7Espeedy/great1/

This site gives you general info on the famous hockey player, including a history of his awards and records. You'll see a photo album (if you have the patience to wait for it to download), and you can view Wayne in his first Rangers game. You'll also be able to listen to what he said about his trade to the New York Rangers.

NEWSGROUPS

clari.sports.baseball

clari.sports.baseball.games

clari.sports.basketball

clari.sports.basketball.college

clari.sports.golf

clari.sports.hockey

rec.collecting.sport.baseball

rec.collecting.sport.basketball

rec.collecting.sport.football

rec.collecting.sport.hockey

rec.sport.baseball

rec.sport.baseball.analysis

rec.sport.baseball.data

rec.sport.basketball.college

rec.sport.basketball.europe

rec.sport.basketball.misc

rec.sport.basketball.pro

rec.sport.basketball.women

rec.sport.boxing

rec.sport.football.misc

rec.sport.golf

rec.sport.hockey

Related Sites

http://www.sportsline.com/u/palmer/index.html

http://www.emmo.com/

http://www.gabbyreece.com/

http://ww3.sportsline.com/u/football/nfl/elias/1996/FAU460942_bkd.htm

http://www.sampras.com/

http://www.luminet.net/~jurbick/

BUSINESS

Bill & Dave's Excellent Adventure

http://kows.web.net/sarnoff_and_gates/

This site provides a humorous look at the relationship between Microsoft head Bill Gates, NBC founder David Sarnoff, and the cycles of history. Includes a lengthy article, comparisons, and discussion of the similarities between Gates and Sarnoff.

A B C D E F G H I J K L M N O P Q R S T U V W X Y Z

Donald Trump

http://www.cs.uh.edu/~clifton/trump.html

Provides information and background of the Wall Street speculator and famous millionaire. Includes links to articles about "The Don" and pictures of the Trump Castle and Trump Taj Mahal Resort.

The Gates Mandala

http://members.aol.com/mandalagts/index.htm

Styled after Tibetan thangkas, this parody is a wheel-of-life mandala about Bill Gates' accomplishments. The site includes an explanation, commentary, images, and links to related sites.

Perot Periodical

http://www.brainlink.com/~nota/

Provides an online magazine with information and background on Texas billionaire Ross Perot and his Reform political party. You'll find articles, essays, and more about Perot and other independent political parties.

The "Unofficial" Bill Gates

http://www.zpub.com/un/bill/

Take a look at articles, interviews, pictures, and more about Microsoft head Bill Gates. Includes links to Gates, Microsoft, and related sites.

NEWSGROUPS

alt.fan.bill-gates

alt.movies.spielberg

Related Sites

http://www.abbeybooks.com/spielberg.htm

http://www.forbes.com/Richlist/0970.htm

http://detnews.com/menu/stories/13608.htm

http://iisd1.iisd.ca/50comm/panel/pan38.htm

http://www.wmich.edu/com455/murdoch.html

CELEBRITY INFORMATION

Any Day in History

http://www.scopesys.com/anyday/

Look up information about famous people and events by day, month, and year by using the searchable index.

Celebrities On-Line

http://www.mgal.com/links/celeb.html

This site includes a lengthy list of links to official celebrity sites and fan pages on the Internet. It also provides links to related sites that include sound bytes and photos.

Celebrity Addresses

http://mickey.iafrica.com/~cassidy/address.html

Visit this site for a lengthy listing of famous people's addresses. The list covers people from many walks of life. Includes celebrities from Kareem Abdul-Jabbar to ZZ Top.

Celebrity Atheists, Agnostics, and Other Non-Theists

http://www.primenet.com/~lippard/atheistcelebs/

Did you ever wonder about the religious beliefs of some of your favorite celebrities? Well, if they have made statements about being an atheist, agnostic, or otherwise, they might be at this site. Includes celebrity quotations about beliefs and when they first occurred.

Celebrity Bites

http://www.bitesite.com/celeb/bsceleb.html

Visit this site for sound bytes, real audio interviews, and features on many stars and celebrities. Includes downloadable quotations from stars such as Alec Baldwin, Woody Allen, Helen Hunt, and hundreds more. Also includes an archive of sound bytes.

The Celebrity Chronicle

http://www.polaris.net/~merlin/famegov.html

Take a look at civilian brushes with the famous and infamous. These brief celebrity spottings are indexed alphabetically and include icons to describe the encounter. Some of the entries are quite humorous.

The Celebrity Macintosh Page

http://www.owt.com/users/sdechter/celeb.html

Hey, Mac users: Have you ever wondered which famous celebrities use Macintosh computers? Well, you'll find the answer here. Mac users include Dolly Parton, Rush Limbaugh, Steven Sondheim, Ken Kesey, Danny DeVito, Troy Aikman, and many more.

Celebrity Star Bios

http://www.adze.com/bios/celebrty.html

This site provides biographies—from an astrological perspective—of many famous individuals, ranging from Marilyn Monroe to Bob Marley and many more. Includes pictures and links to related sites.

Celebrity Walk of Fame

http://ecinside.interspeed.net/celebrity/cwf.html

Visit this site for news, features, and links to myriad celebrity sites. Browse through lists of stars to find your favorite and read bios, filmographys, and photos. Find info on stars such as Jody Foster, Val Kilmer, Goldie Hawn, and many more.

Ch@T Soup

http://www.chatsoup.com/

This site dishes up celebrity news from chats conducted over the Internet. Includes celebrity postings, gossip columns, and a collection of star quotations. You'll also see a listing of upcoming celebrity chats.

Cyber-Sleaze

http://metaverse.com/vibe/sleaze/index.html

Cyber-Sleaze is a gossip column updated every week day and hosted by Adam Curry (formerly of MTV). You'll get news and info on a variety of stars. This site also provides backlog of daily editions of the site.

Dead Presidents

http://www.csn.net./%7Emhand/Presidents/

So who is buried in Grant's tomb? The question finally might be answered at this Web site. You'll find obituaries and learn about the final destinations of U.S. presidents. You can also view related photos and background info.

Driveways of the Rich and Famous

http://www.driveways.com

This humorous site is the home page for the cable access television show "Driveways of the Rich and Famous." You'll see exciting photos of the driveways of celebrities such as Nicolas Cage, Jim Carrey, and Sharon Stone. Read riveting interviews of a pizza boy straight from the Aaron Spelling mansion, Bill Gates' next-door neighbor, and Barbara Mandrell's carpenter. Other sterling sources include a Beverly Hills fireman, deliverymen, mailmen, gardeners, and others. You'll also be able to read comments from some of the stars about their driveways.

Famous Marriages

http://us.imdb.com/Couples/couples_T.html

Provides information and background on many famous marriages throughout the years. Includes Elizabeth Taylor and Richard Burton, Ted Turner and Jane Fonda, and many more. Also includes links to related sites.

Famous Quotations

http://www.labyrinth.net.au/~pirovich/quotes.html

Visit this site to find quotations from famous people throughout the ages. Use the handy alphabetical index by speaker.

Flashers! The Showbiz Photo Cyberzine

http://www.flashers.com/

Browse through the many stories and photos of stars and their upcoming film releases. Search through the log of past stories and a gallery of other celebrity photos. Also includes links to many other Hollywood sites.

The Forbes 400 Richest People in America

http://www.forbes.com/Richlist/richquer.htm

Do you want to know who is rich in America? This page includes a search index for the *Forbes* magazine 400 Richest People in America list. You can search by state, age, industry, or marital status.

Gems of the Rich And Famous

http://www.gemstone.org/famous.html

Get info about many famous people and their jewelry, including Queen Elizabeth II, Elizabeth Taylor, Ivana, and many more. You'll also find gem tips and links to related pages.

Good Quotations by Famous People

http://www.cs.virginia.edu/~robins/quotes.html

This site has hundreds of quotations from famous people on many subjects—Groucho Marx, Bill Gates, Oscar Wilde, and many more.

Heartland Capitalists

http://www.clark.net/pub/cosmic/96hcr.html

This site gives you info about the Heartland Capitalists—a baseball team in the Cosmic Baseball League that consists of many rich and famous celebrities. This odd site has Donald Trump at first base, Karl Marx as team manager, Lee Iacoca in the outfield, and much more. This site has to be seen to be believed—it's rather strange.

A House of MORPH

http://www.Generation.NET/~max/

Did you ever wonder what Cindy Crawford would look like with a bulldog face? Well, you'll find your long-awaited answer here. You'll also see morphed pictures of famous notables such as Bill Gates, Ingmar Bergman, Steve Jobs, and more. Some of these pictures are very, very strange.

Macarena

http://www.cris.com/~Dcashman/humor/lists/macarena.html

This site is dedicated to that annoying dance, The Macarena. You'll see a list and pictures of many famous people who have been spotted dancing The Macarena. The list includes people as diverse as Neil Armstrong, Dennis Rodman, Barney the Dinosaur, and many more.

Minor Celebrities

http://pw1.netcom.com/~zymrgist/celebrities.html

Are you a minor celebrity? That's the question this Web site wants to answer. You'll see stories and features of everyday people and their brushes with the rich and famous. Read the tales of checking groceries for Michael Jordan, riding elevators with Bill Cosby, and much more.

Mr. Showbiz

http://www.mrshowbiz.com/

This site gives you a plethora of entertainment news and features, including celebrity interviews and profiles. You'll also see star bios, games, and a photo gallery. Make things easier by using the Mr. Showbiz search engine.

Plastic People Page

http://www.geocities.com/Hollywood/7990/plastic.html

View pictures of famous people before and after their plastic surgeries. You'll also see links to related celebrity pages.

The Rich and Famous

http://www.centenary.edu/centenar/alumni/richfam.html

Get email addresses for many famous people, including David Letterman, Tom Clancy, Danny Bonaduce, Rosie O'Donnell, Rodney Dangerfield, and many more.

Stargalaxy

http://www.stargalaxy.com/

This site is dedicated to young actors or celebrities from the past or present. You'll see pictures, profiles, uploads, and trivia quizzes on celebrities such as Isaac, Taylor, and Zachary Hanson; Jonathan Taylor Thomas; and Hayley Mills (remember *The Parent Trap*?).

SUPERSTARS.COM

http://www.superstars.com/

Check out the celebrity news, pictures, and product information here. This site also provides chat forums and links to many related sites of the rich and famous.

The Tombstone Tourist

http://www.teleport.com/~stanton/

Learn the locations of the final resting places of more than 2,000 famous and infamous people. Check out the tombstone of the month, including the history and background of the famous deceased. You'll also find pictures and links to cemeteries around the world. See why Kathy Lee Gifford calls The Tombstone Tourist "the most disgusting page on the Internet." This is a very strange site.

What's in a Name? Trivia

http://www.infocom.com/~franklin/inaname/welcome.htm

Have you ever wondered what a celebrity's *original* name was? Did you know that Cary Grant was born Archibald Alexander Leach? Or that Judy Garland was once called Frances Ethel Gumm? Or that Virginia Patterson Hensley later became Patsy Cline?

NEWSGROUPS

alt.binaries.pictures.celebrities

alt.binaries.pictures.teen-idols

alt.binaries.pictures.teen-starlets

alt.celebrities

alt.fan.actors

alt.fan.elite

alt.fan.teen.idols

alt.fan.teen.starlets

clari.living.celebrities

Related Sites

http://www.net-v.com/csotd/

http://www.eonline.com/Gossip/

http://www.hollywood.com/movietalk/

http://pathfinder.com/people/sp/bw/

MISCELLANEOUS

Elle's Tom Cruise Page

http://www.geocities.com/TheTropics/6761/tom.html

Listen to the background music from Top Gun while reading Tom's bio, or listen to sound bites from his movies. And, of course, no Tom Cruise site would be complete without photos. You can even download the script to *Interview with the Vampire* or *Jerry Maguire*'s mission statement.

Gillian Anderson British Association Home Page

http://terabyte.virtual-pc.com/HawKSanD/gaba/gaba.html

Read through Gillian's personal and professional profiles. You'll get info on her *X-Files* character, Dana Scully, and her history throughout the episodes. Walk through the photo gallery, or check out the "Scullyisms": phrases Scully keeps repeating. Includes messages from fans.

The HOWARD STERN Home Page

http://www.urshan.com/stern/

You'll find news, info, pictures, and articles about radio shockjock Howard Stern here. You'll also get info about books, movies, and links to other related "distasteful" (I say tomAto, you say tomato) sites.

JFK Resources Online

http://users.southeast.net/%7Echeryl/jfk.html

Provides a motherlode of information, speeches, sound bytes, and photos of former President John Fitzgerald Kennedy. Includes many articles about the assassination and links to Kennedy-related sites.

John Grisham

http://www.privat.katedral.se/~nv96gabr/grisham.htm

This site contains info about the novels and related films of popular courtroom author John Grisham. You'll see book artwork, movie stills, and articles about the books and films. You can also read a bio of Grisham and get links to related sites.

Madonna Digest

http://das-www.harvard.edu/users/students/Zheng_Wang/Madonna/

Provides pictures, articles, interviews, lyrics, and many more features about Madonna. Also gives you an extensive index of Madonna news and stories. Includes links to related Madonna and *Evita* sites.

The Official Anne Rice Web Site!

http://www.anne-rice.inter.net/

Get the latest info on Anne, her books, and her latest projects. Periodically, Anne places transcripts of the messages she leaves for her fans on her phone line on this Web site. Anne also answers fans' questions here and occasionally issues letters at the site. You also get a photo gallery and info on Anne Rice-related items and merchandise.

Punch Rush Limbaugh Home Page

http://www.indirect.com/www/beetle87/rush/index.html

Have you ever wanted to punch—electronically, that is—the face of conservative radio personality Rush Limbaugh? Here's your chance.

Robert Pershing Wadlow—Alton's Gentle Giant

http://www.altonweb.com/history/wadlow

Check out the biography and photos of the world's tallest man, Robert Pershing Wadlow. He is cited in the *Guiness Book of World Records* and was 8 feet, 11.1 inches tall. The site includes a chronology of Wadlow's life and much more.

The Rosie O'Donnell Show

`http://www.rosieo.com`

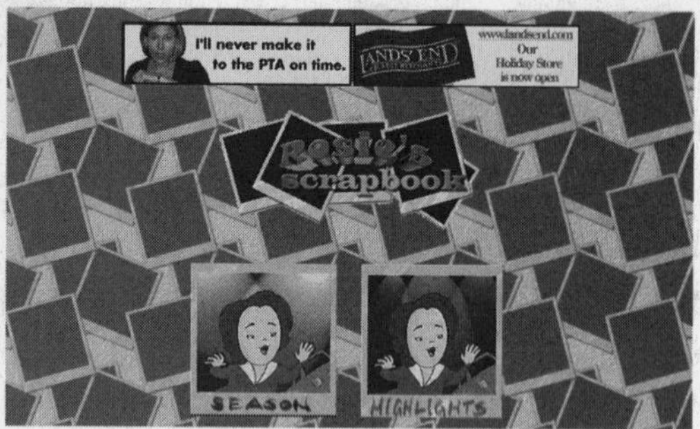

This is the official Rosie site. Rosie's scrapbook includes highlights from all the shows—hear Rosie and John Travolta sing, or see Rosie chat with Mary Tyler Moore. Check out the video and audio clips, as well as pictures from all episodes of her second season. Or, play some of those well-known sound bites, such as "Taped to the desk!" You can also send a message to Rosie, check station listings, and get general info on Rosie's show.

Rush Limbaugh Featured Site

`http://www2.southwind.net/~vic/rush.html`

Enter the Rush chat room, check out the site of the week, or find links to sites dedicated to conservative talk show host Rush Limbaugh. Includes a survey about Limbaugh and some conservative views.

Shrine to Jennifer Aniston

`http://www.lookup.com/Homepages/83766/frame.html`

Visit this site for Jennifer's bio and work history, photos (check out that hair!), a Jennifer test, links to other Jennifer sites and *Friends* sites, and info on *Friends*. You can even download a *Friends* screen saver.

Stephen King

`http://phrtayl0.ucsd.edu/~ed/sk/`

Check out this site for news and info about the books and related films of Stephen King. Includes interviews, articles, reviews, and links to related King sites.

The Stephen King WebSite

`http://www.wco.com/~pace/king.html`

Provides info about the novels of Stephen King. Read through the King FAQ, reviews, articles, survey, and much more. Also includes information on upcoming releases and related films.

A Visit with John Grisham

`http://www.bdd.com/grisham`

Review the profile of author John Grisham and info about his novels. You'll find pictures, articles, and previews of Grisham's work. You'll also find info on Grisham-related films and links to related sites.

NEWSGROUPS

alt-binaries.howard-stern

alt.books.anne-rice

alt.books.crichton

alt.books.john-grisham

alt.books.stephen-king

alt.conspiracy.jfk

alt.conspiracy.jfk.moderated

alt.fan.gillian-anderson

alt.fan.howard-stern

alt.fan.jen-aniston

alt.fan.jim-carrey

alt.fan.pam-anderson

alt.fan.rosieodonnell

alt.fan.rush-limbaugh

alt.fan.schwarzenegger

alt.rush-limbaugh

Related Sites

http://www.geocities.com/Hollywood/7084/index.htm

http://www.virtualvoyage.com/celeb/S_Z/arnoldschwarzenegger.htm

http://miri.simplenet.com/ddeb3/

http://www.forbes.com/Richlist/0886.htm

http://centrifuge.tierranet.com/jcworld/frames.html

http://www.globalnets.com/crichton/crichton.html

http://drh.net/joz/pamela.htm

MODELS

Cindy Crawford Concentration

`http://www.facade.com/Fun/concentration/`

Play a game of concentration using the images of Cindy Crawford. Includes many pictures of Cindy and links to related sites.

Cindymania—For Goddess Cindy Crawford

http://www.geocities.com/Hollywood/Hills/7661/

Browse through the many pictures and articles about supermodel Cindy Crawford. Includes details about Cindy and links to other sites.

Claudia Schiffer Collector Circle—Magic's Corner

http://www.geocities.com/Hollywood/7018/index.html

View hundreds of pictures of model Claudia Schiffer. Find out about the Claudia Schiffer calendar, and check out the links to related sites.

An Ode to Stephanie Seymour

http://www.geocities.com/Athens/1693/steph.html

Visit this site for pictures, a bio, and other facts about model Stephanie Seymour. Includes links to fashion sites and other supermodel pages.

The Official Kathy Ireland Home Page

http://www.kathyireland.com/

Visit this site for pictures, articles, and tips on beauty and fashion. You'll also get Kathy's fitness video info and links to many other fashion sites.

Planet Tyra

http://stallion.jsums.edu/~awil0997/tyra.htm

This is the place to visit for info on Tyra Banks, supermodel and actress. Be sure to visit the photo gallery and check out the biography.

SUPERMODEL.COM

http://www.supermodel.com/home.html

This site has all you'll want to know about your favorite models. Includes news, photographs, links to related sites, and products for sale. You might want to visit the So…You Want to Be a Model? feature, which provides fashion and beauty tips.

The Temple of Kate Moss

http://mastrangelo.polito.it/katemoss/index.htm

Check out this site's bio and many photos of model Kate Moss. You'll find many magazine covers, calendar pictures, and articles about Moss. Includes links to related modeling sites.

The Unofficial Twiggy Lawson Homepage

http://www.geocities.com/Hollywood/7308/twiggy.htm

The Unofficial Twiggy Lawson Homepage

Biography
Albums
SilverScreen
SmallScreen
BlitheSpirit
Books & More

Twiggy's great. I know that. You know that. She's cute, sure. But she's got something else. Her vibrato-laden voice entrances me. The first time I heard it I was awe-struck.

What prompts me to create this page? Well, I've been a fan of Twiggy's since I first saw ***The Boyfriend*** a couple of years ago. I knew that she had been a model, but that didn't really interest me. She was so lovely in that film that I had to find out more about her. And the end result was a better understanding of her life, which she refers to as a "Cinderella tale."

This actress was perhaps the most famous supermodel in the '60s. Check out the detailed biography with pictures. You'll also see descriptions of her albums, movies, and plays, as well as her TV appearances.

The Zone: Celebrities and Supermodels

http://www.thezone.pair.com/celeb/index.htm

Visit this site for a lengthy list of celebrity email and home addresses. Find addresses for many celebrities, including Jenny McCarthy, Pamela Anderson, Brad Pitt, Clint Eastwood, and more. Also provides links other celebrity sites.

NEWSGROUPS

alt.binaries.pictures.supermodels

alt.binaries.pictures.supermodels.kate-moss

alt.fan.kate-moss

alt.supermodels

alt.supermodels.cindy-crawford

Related Sites

http://www.vol.it/mirror/ELLE/elle/elle.html

http://www.algonet.se/~nhaak/iman.htm

http://www.jason.simplenet.com/models/Naomi_Campbell/index.htm

ROYALTY

Flashers! Duke and Duchess of York

http://www.flashers.com/9608/0896yorks.html

Flashers!, The Showbiz Photo Cyberzine, includes articles and pictures related to Fergie and Andrew's relationship after the divorce, including their outings with Princesses Beatrice and Eugenie.

The Palace: Interactive Centre

http://www.royalnetwork.com/palace/index.html

Visit the chat room or the royal message board. Or, check out the create-your-own headline feature covering the English Royal family. This site also enables you to send and read messages in memory of Princess Diana. It also includes pictures, articles, and links to related sites.

Queen Elizabeth II: Queen Of England

http://www2.lucidcafe.com/lucidcafe/library/96apr/elizabeth2.html

Provides a biography, pictures, and articles about Queen Elizabeth II of England. Also includes links to sites about Queen Elizabeth and English royalty.

Romances of the Century Grace Kelly & Prince Rainier III

http://pathfinder.com/@@5keVpQQASiKF*kml/people/romance/kelly.html

Learn how this romantic couple met and then began a correspondence. Read about their famous wedding guests. Learn about their life together and the births of Princess Caroline, Prince Albert, and Princess Stephanie. Also tells about the tragic car accident that took Grace Kelly's life.

The Ultimate Royal Web Page

http://walden.mo.net/~landrum/royal.html

This site begins with a tribute to Princess Diana. It also provides a wide array of information about past and present royalty throughout the world. Read about royal collectibles, news, and pictures. Visit some of the links to the many other royalty sites, and check out the section of related children's stories.

The (Unauthorized) Princess Diana Page

http://members.aol.com/douglasb52/index.html

This site includes letters from people all over the world in memory of Princess Diana.

Welcome to RoyalNetwork

http://www.royalnetwork.com/clubdi/index.html

This site honors the memory of the Princess of Wales. It includes an illustrated history of Diana and a grief support message board. A nice feature is its prayers provided for many religions—Buddhist, Christian, Hindu, Islamic, Jewish, and New Age, just to name a few. Includes thoughts and prayers submitted from around the world. Also provides RealVideo of the funeral and funeral coverage, including the address by the Ninth Earl of Spencer and the lyrics to "Goodbye England's Rose." Also includes a FAQ page.

NEWSGROUPS

alt.gossip.royalty

alt.talk.royalty

clari.living.royalty

uk.current-events.princess-diana

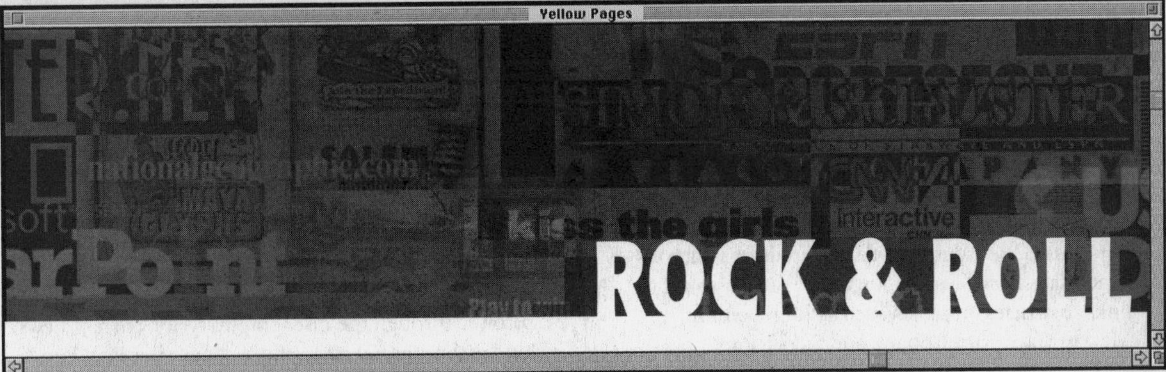

I'm going on down to Yasgur's farm, I'm going to join in a rock 'n roll band.

Joni Mitchell

AC/DC–The Greatest Band

http://www.GeoCities.com/SunsetStrip/Palms/3158/

Take a look at a history of the band, as well as a discography (with album cover pictures and the site author's ratings). Read the lyrics to your favorite AC/DC songs. Be sure to browse through the AC/DC picture gallery, and get links to other AC/DC sites.

Alec Eiffel: A French Pixies Page

http://www.mis.enac.fr/~biel/pixies/

Check out the Pixies' history, discography, pictures, audio, lyrics, articles, reviews, press quotes, and pixies quotes. You'll find a list of bands, people, films, books, and TV shows that referenced or paid homage to the Pixies. Read the FAQ, listen to Pixies tabs and chords, and check out the latest poll results.

Big Star

http://bubblegum.uark.edu/Bigstar/

Get info about the rock group Big Star. Includes guitar tablatures, song lyrics, a band biography, interviews, reviews, and links to related sites. Also includes many pictures of the group.

Related Sites

http://www.pbs.org/wgbh/pages/rocknroll/

http://www7.cddb.com/xm/cd/country/66059409.html

Alec Eiffel: A French Pixies Page
http://www.mis.enac.fr/~biel/pixies/

Pink Floyd -/\= Set The Controls =/|-
http://www.mtnlake.com/~robp/floyd1.html

rockhall.com
http://www.rockhall.com/

Dave Matthews Band

http://redlt.com/dmbandnew/

Provides tour dates, background, sound bytes, photos, and merchandising for the Dave Matthews Band. Includes current band news and links to other Matthews' sites.

Dave's Smithereens Page

http://www.main.com/~persails/

Provides a fan site for the rock group The Smithereens. Includes a band biography, discography, tour dates, pictures, upcoming news, and more. Also includes fan club info and links to related sites.

The David Bowie File

http://liber.stanford.edu/~torrie/Bowie/BowieFile.html

Chronicles the life of David Bowie. Get info and ratings about his albums, movies, and videos. Find out where you can chat with other David Bowie fans. Also, learn about where he'll be touring and making appearances. Includes a search engine so that you can locate the lyrics of specified David Bowie songs.

Related Sites

http://www.datasync.com/~pwkelley/crcmain.htm

http://www.repriserec.com/fleetwoodmac/

http://hem1.passagen.se/kedsfors/index.htm

http://fame2.clever.net/fame/richard.htm

The Death of Rock 'n' Roll

http://weber.u.washington.edu/~jlks/pike/DeathRR.html

Contains samples from Jeff Pike's book of the same name. Features "Untimely Demises, Morbid Preoccupations, and Premature Forecasts of Doom in Pop Music." Sections include heroin deaths, famous death dates, and "Beatles Bugouts." You'll also get links to articles on artists such as John Lennon, Marvin Gaye, Kurt Cobain, and Sid Vicious.

Five Horizons: a Pearl Jam Fanzine

http://www.fivehorizons.com/index2.html

Check out the song of the month, which includes info and sound clips. Listen to a 40-minute phone conversation with Eddie Vedder. Get bios and pictures of all the band members. Check out Pearl Jam's musical influences. Learn about the issues that are important to them (such as PETA and Earth First!). See a concert chronology, a video guide, and tour memorabilia. Includes a discography, reviews, and articles.

FRANK ZAPPA: The Real Frank Zappa Home Page

http://www.zappa.com/

Browse through the complete discography, articles, and answers to FAQs. Get info about Frank's sons Dweezil and Ahmet's musical endeavors. Listen to the "Frank Zappa: American Composer" audio page; it's a two-hour radio documentary that originally aired on U.S. radio in the summer of 1996. Includes a brief biography and interview with Gail Zappa (Frank Zappa's wife, among other things), from *SECONDS Magazine*. Also includes ordering info for Zappa's label, Barfko Swill Records.

The Grateful Highway

http://www.inlink.com/~arbogast/grateful/index.html

You can listen to the Grateful Dead music supplied while you explore this site on the band. Read Grateful Dead song lyrics and original Dead Head poetry. Check out the fractal images created by the site's author. Includes links to other Grateful Dead sites.

Hanspeter Niederstrasser's Def Leppard Page

http://www.princeton.edu/~nieder/defleppard/def.html

Focuses on the band that began in the '80s and defined modern metal. Provides all you might need to complete your collection. Includes complete lyrics, a band history, bios of the group members, images, and sounds. Also presents a guest book and survey to fill out so that you can express your opinion about the band.

Iggy Pop

http://virginrecords.com/iggy_pop/

Browse through the discography, lyrics, current news, and articles about rock singer/songwriter Iggy Pop. Includes a biography, photos, and links to related sites. Also includes video clips, sound bytes, and much more.

Iron Maiden Page

http://www.cs.tufts.edu/~stratton/maiden/maiden.html

Offers a collection of album covers and a running commentary on the meaning and value of each album. Includes many pictures.

Jack's, "The Who" Home Page

http://www.riverdale.k12.or.us/students/jackr/who.html

Get information on the rock-and-roll band The Who. You'll find pictures, info on the band, and info on the Broadway production of its rock opera, *Tommy*. You can also read a history of The Who.

Jane's Addiction

http://www.links.net/vita/muzik/janes/

Contains the latest facts on the band Jane's Addiction. You get detailed discographies, pictures, and sound samples from both Jane's Addiction and Porno for Pyros. Check out interviews, reviews, and opinion pieces. Also contains links to many other Web pages on topics such as Woodstock '94, Led Zeppelin, Grateful Dead, Nine Inch Nails, and more.

Janis Joplin Homepage

http://www.dartmouth.edu/~modred/janis.html

Read Joplin's biography, and browse through her discography. Read song lyrics and reviews. Hear sound bytes, see photos, and get links to other Joplin sites. You can also join a Joplin mailing list.

Related Sites

http://www.worldaccess.nl/~kick/rock_'n'_roll_in_the_american_fifties.htm

http://www.geocities.com/SunsetStrip/8678/

Jerry Lee Lewis

http://www.elektra.com/country_club/jerrylee/jerry.html

This piano-banging rocker of the '50s and '60s had hits such as Whole Lotta Shakin' Goin' On, Great Balls of Fire, and Breathless. Read his interesting bio and the history of his career. Includes a discography, as well as sound and video clips.

Jethro Tull Music Archive

http://remus.rutgers.edu/JethroTull/

Find out how this band that began in 1968 got its name (Jethro Tull is a band, not a person!). You'll get info on album releases and tour dates. Check out the discography, which includes song titles and lyrics. Learn about Jethro Tull with the extensive FAQ. Includes back issues of *St. Cleve Chronicle*—a digest on news, opinions, and anything to do with Tull.

Jiblet's Pretenders Page

http://www.pretenders.org/

Provides song lyrics, pictures, articles, and a discography for the rock band The Pretenders. Get the latest news on the band and a schedule of upcoming tours (or search the archive of tours and live performances from '78 to '96). Includes Chrissie Hynde's writings and links to related sites.

Jim Morrison and The Doors

http://utopia.knoware.nl/users/alienal/ukjimdoors.html

The Doors began in 1965; they took their name from Aldous Huxley's book *The Doors of Perception*, in which the drug Mescaline plays a part. See pictures of Jim (including a mug shot from when he was arrested) and the members of the group. Read Jim's poetry. Includes a history of the band and lyrics from all the albums.

Kinks Web Sites

http://hobbes.it.rit.edu/kinks/kinks.html

Includes info on The Kinks—everything from pictures, sounds, and videos to a complete discography and lyrics database.

Related Sites

http://ubl.com/ubl/cards/012/9/06.html

http://www.idcnet.com/~ecnal/winubj.htm

L.A. Rock & Roll Road Map

http://www.net101.com/rocknroll/page2.html

Check out L.A.-area maps, addresses, and pictures of hangouts where you can run into or reminisce about your favorite musicians and bands. Visit Chateau Marmont, former "home" of the Doors' Jim Morrison; or, visit The Rainbow, the hangout of the likes of Led Zeppelin, Keith Moon, and John Lennon.

Los Lobos

http://www.wbr.com/loslobos/

This is the Web site for the Los Angeles-based group Los Lobos. Los Lobos' 20-year-plus history encompasses punk rock, traditional rhythms, straight-ahead rock 'n roll, and R&B grooves. This site includes articles, interviews, album artwork, and much more. Also includes sound bytes and a comments page.

Marilyn Manson's Misery Machine

http://Www.Utech.Net/Chico/Manson.Htm

Provides info about the gothic horror rock group Marilyn Manson. Includes a Web chat transcript, video clips and sound bytes, lyics, inteviews, album reviews, and articles about the group. You also get a FAQ, band history, newsletters, and a discography. Includes chat rooms, mailing lists, and newsgroups. Also includes many graphics, pictures, and links to other sites.

Meat Puppets Home Page

www.musick.com/puppets/

Offers info on the band Meat Puppets, including photos, sound files, interviews, band art, a discography, and guitar tabs.

Optic Fixations

http://nothing.nin.net/op.html

Includes photo libraries of Nine Inch Nails. View professional photos, live shots, video stills, tour paraphernalia, and promotional items. Also offers video clips of the group.

Past Masters: A Virtual Beatles Tribute

http://members.aol.com/hahahahno/private/frames.htm

Read the lyrics for each song on each of The Beatles albums. Visit the bulletin board or listen to some guitar tabs. Check out pictures from the photo gallery, or

A B C D E F G H I J K L M N O P Q R S T U V W X Y Z

play one of the trivia games. Use The Beatles search engine to find more Beatles pages. Listen to sound clips in Wave format or RealAudio.

Paul K & the Weathermen

http://www.hardmedia.com/paulk/

Provides artwork, lyrics, and a discography for the Lexington, Kentucky-based rock band Paul K and the Weathermen. Includes a bio of Paul K, band news, tour dates, and upcoming release information.

The Phish.Net—Created for Phish Fans by Phish Fans

http://www.phish.net/

Leave thoughts of Wilson behind as you enter this world of FAQs, photos, set lists, and show reviews; and then run like an antelope through links to fan pages, the Helping Phriendly Book, and more. Stay up-to-date on tour info and band rumors. Unite, Lizards, and Free Gamehendge!

Pink Floyd—Set The Controls

http://www.mtnlake.com/~robp/floyd1.html

Visit this site for info on and pictures of the English band that began 30 years ago. Check out the discography: It covers every Pink Floyd release to date. You can view the covers, read the lyrics, and see notes on the production for most of the albums. Includes a special Syd Barrett section, interviews, and info on upcoming tours and releases.

Rave On

http://206.151.68.40:80/kdwilt/

Provides a fan page for great 1950s rock-and-roll hero Buddy Holly. You'll see song lyrics, a discography, a tour background, and a story about "The Day the Music Died." Also provides guitar tabs, interviews, and links to other sites.

Rock and Roll Hall of Shame

http://pathfinder.com/@@VwQROsNXPgIAQJ@8/people/hall/

Features "performers who deserve a very special place on the mantelpiece—right up there with, say, your mood ring collection." Categories includes the Kings Of Shame (Milli Vanilli), Lyrical Letdowns (grand prize goes to MacArthur Park and the cake that was left out in the rain), Haute Rocks (picks for worst clothing and hairstyles), and Rock Flops on Film (remember Sgt. Pepper's Lonely Hearts Club Band in 1978?).

rockhall.com

http://www.rockhall.com/

This is the Web site for the Rock and Roll Hall of Fame and Museum, located in Cleveland, OH. Take a virtual tour of the museum to meet the legends of rock. Read about the songs that made them superstars and the events that made them notorious. Learn how the inductees are chosen, and find out who is being inducted into the Hall this year. You can also view a list of all the past inductees by induction year. Click on any inductee to get a bio, description of impact, song clips, and musical influences. This is a great source of info on all the major influences in rock. Don't forget to visit the Listening Lounge to hear the sounds of your favorite rock legends.

Rolling Stones Web Site

http://www.stones.com/

Contains a vast collection of sounds, pictures, video, and interviews. Check out the discography, chronology, and biography. Also gives you a place to chat with other Stones fans.

St. Alphonzo's Pancake Homepage

http://www.fwi.uva.nl/~heederik/zappa/index.html

This unofficial fan page of Frank Zappa provides articles, photos, and interviews. You'll see a lengthy discography, lyrics, and a FAQ about Zappa and his music. You'll also get many stories and links to Zappa-related sites.

Supersonic

http://members.aol.com/mjwood777/oasis.htm

Provides info about the rock group Oasis. Includes lyrics, band news, articles, sound bytes, and much more. Also includes a fan chat room and a place to vote for your favorite Oasis song.

Tom Petty Homepage

http://www.ugcs.caltech.edu/~hedlund/tom_petty/index.shtml

This unofficial fan page of the rock music of Tom Petty and The Heartbreakers includes album artwork, lyrics, images, and upcoming tour dates. You'll also get guitar tablature, a fan list, and links to related sites.

UBL: Artist Aerosmith

http://ubl.com/ubl/cards/016/0/53.html

"Aerosmith was one of the most popular hard-rock bands of the '70s, setting the style and sound of hard rock and heavy metal for the next two decades with their raunchy, bluesy swagger." This site includes a discography with album releases, reviews, info on who worked on each release, and info about each track. You also get ratings for each album. Includes a bio of the band and links to other Aerosmith sites.

UBL: Artist Aretha Franklin

http://ubl.com/artists/004807.html

Read a bio on The Queen of Soul—singer of "Respect," "Think," and countless other landmark songs. Check out Aretha's roots and influences. Includes a discography with reviews and ratings of her releases. You also get extensive links to related info on Aretha, and you can vote in a poll to rate this artist.

UBL: Artist Jefferson Airplane

http://ubl.com/ubl/cards/002/0/21.html

Jefferson Airplane was the first of the San Francisco psychedelic rock groups of the '60s to get national recognition; later, it became known as Jefferson Starship or just Starship. The group remained quite popular well into the '80s. Read a bio, including info on all the members. Learn who their musical influences were. Browse through the complete discography.

The (unofficial) Elvis Home Page

http://sunsite.unc.edu/elvis/elvishom.html

Listen to songs from early rock-and-roll star Elvis Presley. Includes a tour of Graceland, photos, lyrics, articles, and much more. Also includes links to related sites and an Elvis TV schedule. You'll also find an extensive list of Elvis pen pals you can hook up with. You can read Elvis' last will and testament, and—of course—keep up to date on all the latest Elvis sightings.

Unofficial Soundgarden Homepage

http://www.sgi.net/soundgarden/

This is a site for the Seattle-based rock band Soundgarden (1984-1997). Read a history of the band, and check out the FAQ, discography, tablature, lyrics, articles, and much more. You can also check out the archives of the song-of-the-month sound feature.

Van Morrison: The Man and His Music

http://www.harbour.sfu.ca/~hayward/van/van.html

Provides lyrics, a discography, reviews, and articles about the Irish soul and rock singer Van Morrison. Includes info about Van Morrison's songs, as well as who played what instrument on what song. Also provides interviews and a bibliography.

Warren Zevon

http://www.eecs.tulane.edu:80/www/Morris.Ashley/zevon.html

Includes reviews, tour dates, and a rough guide to the life and music of rock songwriter Warren Zevon. Provides links to related sites and a Top 10 Things Not to Say to Warren Zevon list.

Welcome to Planet Van Halen

http://web.wt.net/~vh5150/

Check out the Sammy versus Dave poll results. Get Van Halen downloads, such as sound bytes and graphics, a bootleg discography, and more VH material. Take a look at *VH Informer*—the unofficial VH newsletter. And, read the interview with Eddie Van Halen from *Guitar World* magazine.

NEWSGROUPS

alt.fan.elvis-presley

alt.fan.frank-zappa

alt.fan.jimi-hendrix

alt.music.billy-joel

alt.music.fleetwood-mac

alt.music.jimi.hendrix

alt.music.pearl-jam

alt.music.pink-floyd

alt.music.texas

alt.music.the-doors

alt.music.van-halen

alt.music.who

alt.music.zevon

alt.rock-n-roll.aerosmith

alt.rock-n-roll.classic

rec.music.beatles

rec.music.beatles.info

rec.music.beatles.moderated

A B C D E F G H I J K L M N O P Q R S T U V W X Y Z

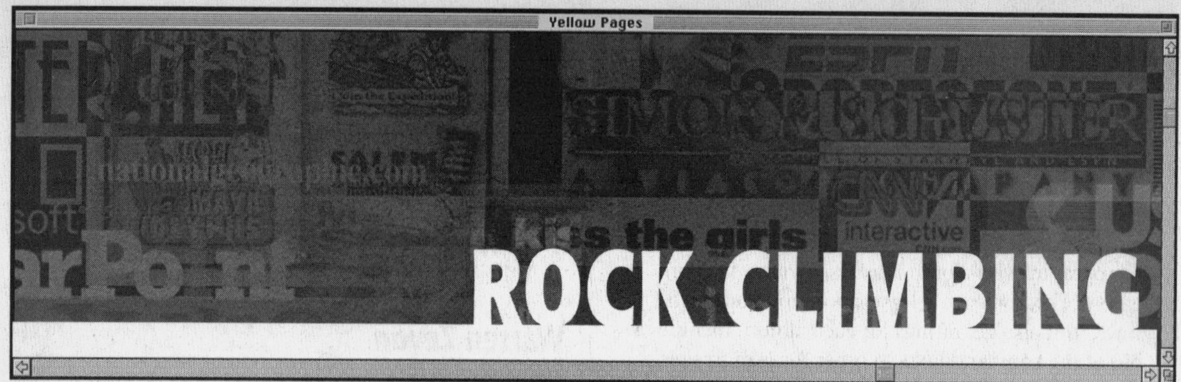

> Don't be afraid to take a big step. You can't cross a chasm in two small jumps.
>
> *David Lloyd George*

American Mountain Guide Association

`http://www.climbnet.com/amga/`

The AMGA's site is aimed mostly at the climbing professional, with pages about certification, but it is helpful to regular climbers with a a page of referrals to certified guides.

Bartley Adventure

`http://www.bcl.net/~dbartley/home.html`

The mountaineering pages of Bartley's site are well-designed and interesting. Learn about the best climbs all over the world, read a journal about a climb up Everest, and much more.

Big Wall Home Page

`http://www.primenet.com/~midds/`

Diehard climbers will appreciate a home page dedicated to intense, multi-day climbs; read about different walls, as well as stories of individual climbs. The big question: What about when you need to go?

CLIMB

`http://www.ozemail.com.au/~climb/`

The e-zine from the South pacific covers rock climbing in Australia and New Zealand. Get the latest news and pictures, but also check out the grade conversion tables and list of new routes.

Himalayas—Where Earth Meets Sky
`http://library.advanced.org/10131/`

ClimbOnline

`http://www.climbonline.com/`

This site has pages about climbers, body and mind, the environment, a searchable database, and many links to related sites.

Expeditions Now!

`http://www.mimer.no/~janhol02/world.htm`

The Expeditions Now! site is geared toward helping climbers find expeditions to join to tackle mountains all over the globe. Articles are provided about medicine, food, safety, and other necessary gear.

Himalayas—Where Earth Meets Sky

`http://library.advanced.org/10131/`

Learn all about the world's tallest mountain range: its geologic past, flora and fauna, environmental concerns, countries that touch these wonders of nature, and more. Other pages have maps, wonderful stories, and quizzes.

Nova Online: Alive On Everest

`http://www.pbs.org/wgbh/nova/everest/`

PBS's *Nova* followed an expedition up the world's highest mountain, and every aspect of the climb can be found on this site, which originally followed them live, in real time.

rock and groove.com

http://www.rockandgroove.com/

An interesting array of articles (such as, is gym climbing the demise of the sport?), interviews, gear advice, and a summary of climbing for visitors new to the sport.

RockByte

http://www.sportiva.com/rockbyte/

RockByte's site specializes in offering every kind of climbing literature you could read: pamphlets, guidebooks, and online guides. They also have videos and calendars, as well as online climbing games and puzzles.

Rock 'n Road

http://www.rocknroad.com/

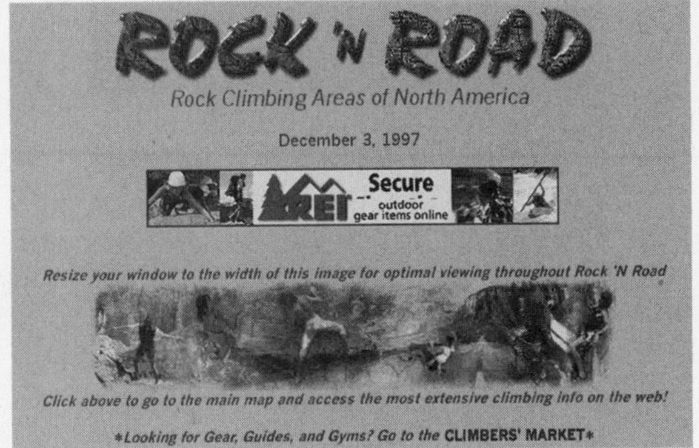

This site carries a lot of helpful information for the beginner and experienced climber. The site's greatest asset is the map to help you find good places to climb in your area. Even the flattest states have some rocks to climb.

Ross Simpson's RockList

http://www.rocklist.com/

Long lists of climbing gyms, alpine clubs, e-zine's and literature, expeditions (including Everest), gear manufacurers, mountain info, and even more.

Shut Up and Climb!

http://www.geocities.com/Yosemite/3664/climbfr.html

This site's greatest pages are its climbing art, graphics, and pics, and its long list of rock gyms—indoor facilities with climbing exercises you can enjoy all year. Check out the WallBangers climbing sim software and the extensive climbing links.

Soleman's Far Out Sports

http://home1.gte.net/soleman/index.htm

An outfitter's site offering new and used rock shoes and other climbing gear. You can see photos of their expeditions, check out today's bargains, and so on.

West Point Mountaineering Club

http://www.toptown.com/CENTRALPARK/armyclmb/INDEX.HTM

Cadets at the Academy enjoy climbing, too, and their site provides the club's history, favorite local climbs, chain of command, and links.

World Climbing Association

http://www.wca-climbing.org/

The WCA's site lists the many benefits of joining their organization, the best of which may be their group climbing insurance, which covers medical, gear, and rescue bills, as well as assistance with travel expenses.

Related Sites

http://Climb-On.com/
http://members.aol.com/osat1996/index.html
http://www.millcomm.com/~kbayne/denali.html
http://volcano.und.nodak.edu/vwdocs/msh/msh.html
http://www.AmericanAlpineClub.org/
http://www.btinternet.com/~mike.franklin/imc/IMC.html
http://www.mtnhighltd.com/
http://www.mtadventure.com/
http://www.DeadVertical.com/
http://AdventuresIntl.com/

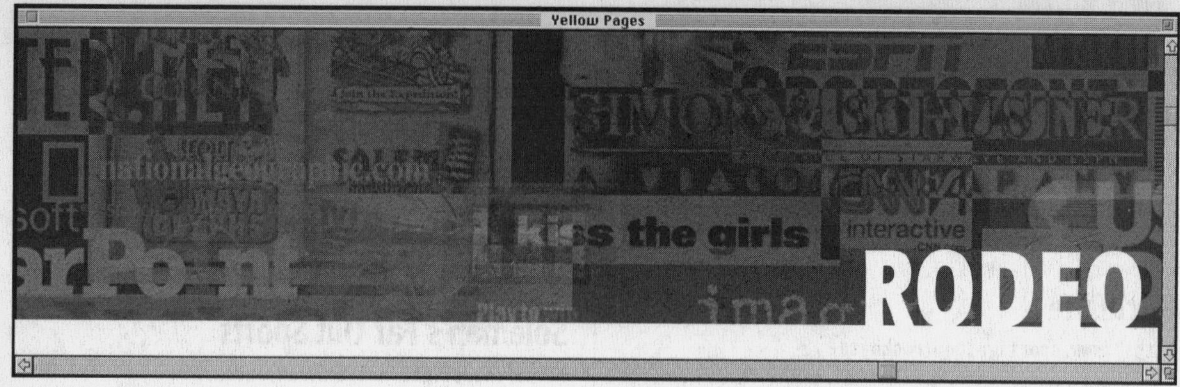

RODEO

> The cowboys have a way of trussing up a steer or a pugnacious bronco which fixes the brute so it can neither move or think.
>
> *Eric Temple Bell*

American Cowboy Association

http://www.amcowboy.com/

With their new presence on the Web, the ACA can keep all cowboy and rodeo fans on top of current events and schedules. You can visit their store, read their news and e-zine, review their stance on animal welfare, and more.

American Junior Rodeo Association

http://camalott.com/~sweetwater/ajra.html

The AJRA was begun when its founder went to rodeos and thought how unfair it was that kids were competing with adults, and so would never win, despite giving it their all. This page has a history of the AJRA, info about the coliseum they use, a schedule, and more.

Billy Joe Jim Bob's Rodeo Links Page

http://www.gunslinger.com/rodeo.html

Perhaps the most complete rodeo index on the Web. Billy Joe Jim Bob takes great care to include links for every rodeo, rodeo association, and rodeo site he could find, which looks to be all of them!

Janet's Let's Rodeo Page
http://www.cowgirls.com/dream/jan/rodeo.htm

Cheyenne Frontier Days

http://www.cowgirls.com/dream/jan/rodeo.htm

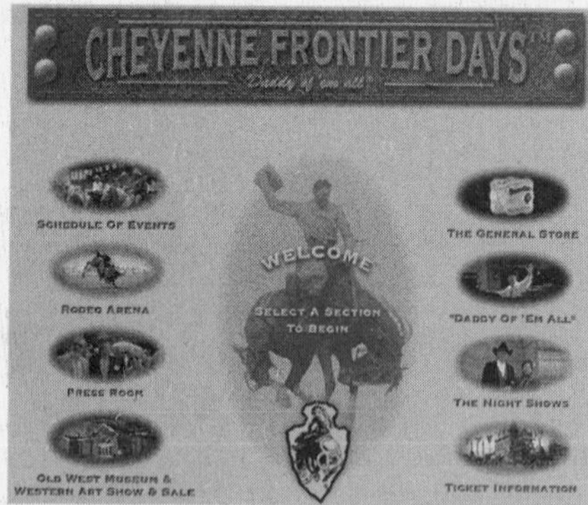

Although not about rodeo specifically, Cheyenne's Frontier Days will be of interest to any latent cowboy or cowgirl. Learn more about their rodeo events, but also about other aspects of Western life.

The Cowboy Page

http://www.imt.net/~mjohnson/carl/frames/hick.htm

Home, home on the page. A well-designed cowboy crossroads. The site offers links to country music sites (especially Garth Brooks), "Western" home pages, and rodeo pages. A great place to start, so pull on your boots, chaps, and spurs, saddle up to your desk, and start hootin' and a-hollerin'.

Cowboys.Com

http://www.cowboys.com/

For the weekend cowboy, as well as the professional rustler, Cowboys.Com offers articles about cowboy art and literature, the Tumbleweeds cartoon, and useful links to everything Western—history, horses, clothes, native Americans, country dancing and night clubs, food, riding clothes, and much more. The site also provides information about a couple dozen dude ranches.

Janet's Let's Rodeo Page

http://www.cowgirls.com/dream/jan/rodeo.htm

Janet's page has some wonderful pictures, links to other rodeo sites, a long list of articles, and countless answers to her question, What do cowgirls dream about?

Jeff's Rodeo World

http://pages.prodigy.com/slyder/rodeo.htm

Jeff appreciates traditional horse, as well as bronco, rodeo riding, and he distinguishes between American and Canadian links on his extensive links page. Related links are provided as well, such as sites for country music performers he likes.

Pro Rodeo Home Pages

http://www.prorodeohome.com/

This site houses personal Web pages for any rodeo personnel who wants one. It's got categories for clowns and bullfighters, announcers, cowboys and cowgirls, ropers, bronco riders, and more.

ProRodeo.Com

http://www.prorodeo.com/index.html

The Professional Rodeo Cowboys Association's official Web site, ProRodeo.Com provides information about rodeo results, individual champions, rodeo publications, and precisely how rodeo animals are treated humanely.

Sarah's Rodeo Page

http://mama.indstate.edu/prentice/sarah/

An excellent rodeo and horse links resource. This site has won awards, and a quick visit is sure to tell you why; it's well-done and simple to use. She also provides a full calendar of events and discussion groups.

Slam Rodeo

http://www.canoe.ca/SlamRodeo/home.html

Interested in what happened at rodeo tournament last night or want to know more about your favorite rodeo stars? Check Slam Rodeo for all your rodeo news needs. Slam also covers other sports.

SpurCrazy's Bareback Page

http://members.wbs.net/homepages/b/a/r/barebackjack1.html

There's rodeo, and then there's bareback. Not just anyone can get on a horse with minimal gearing and hold on for eight seconds, but that's just one reason why this page's author has such a special place for it in her heart.

University of Wyoming Rodeo Club

http://www.uwyo.edu/om/unirel/htm/rodeo/rodeo.htm

It is no surprise that the state university system of Wyoming should represent a sport it helped to make famous. This site discusses the club's schedule, roster, and results from previous tournaments.

Western Wishes Foundation

http://www.westernwishes.com/

Western Wishes is dedicated to granting the wishes of disadvantaged or handicapped children who have Western or ranch backgrounds. They specialize in helping them to meet rodeo personalities and country music singers.

What to Know About Rodeo

http://www.weber.edu:80/library/htmls/spw96/harrison/Title.htm

Angie Harrison's page is a result of research she did because she was curious about rodeo: its history, how it's scored, and so on. People new to rodeo will appreciate the work she's done.

Related Sites

http://www.cowboys.com/nrs/

http://www.cnusa.com/rrt/

http://train.missouri.org/~rclink/depot.htm

http://rodeo.miningco.com/

http://www.pbrnow.com/

http://gowestern.com/link.html

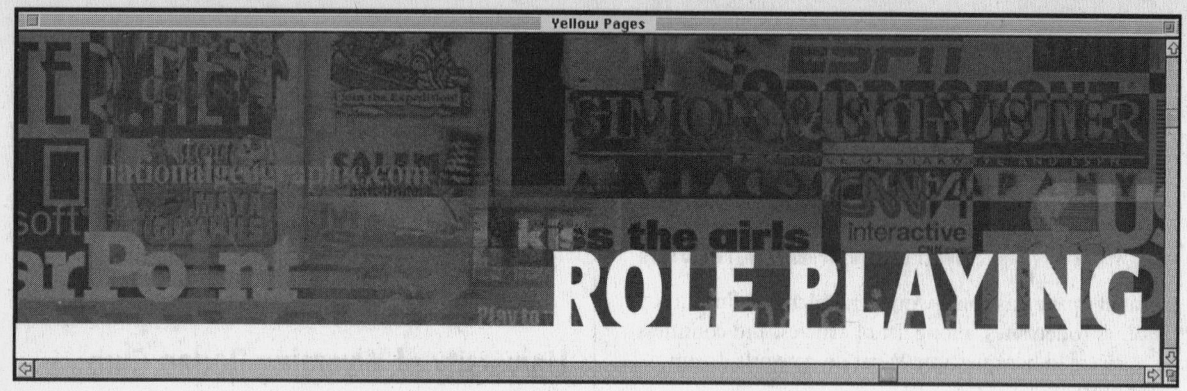

> What you see on these screens up here is a fantasy; a computer-enhanced hallucination!
>
> *Stephen Falken in* WarGames *(1983)*

Biohazard Games

http://www.BiohazardGames.com/

A new company in the field. Its site is very nicely done with neat images, and a great introduction to their main game, "Blue Planet."

B. J. Zanzibar's World of Darkness

http://php.indiana.edu/~adashiel/wod/wod.html

One of the best fan sites for White Wolf's Storyteller series of games (Vampire, Werewolf, Mage Wraith, Changeling). Recently updated in a frames format.

Chameleon Eclectic Entertainment, Inc.

http://www.blackeagle.com/

The producer of the "Babylon Project"—the Babylon 5 role playing game. This site is text only. Covers all their games and also has a download section for some out-of-print information and character information.

Chaosium

http://www.sirius.com/~chaosium/chaosium.html

One of the oldest role playing companies still in existence, its site is very well done, full of graphics, and chockfull of information on its various games, especially Chaosium's primary game, "Call of Cthulhu."

White Wolf Online
http://www.white-wolf.com/

EventHorizons Publications

http://members.aol.com/nowimagine/WBP1.htm

A very well done site, it covers questions about its games and supplements extremely well, and includes examples from the various sourcebooks and supplements.

FASA Corporation

http://www.fasa.com/index1.html

FASA's online catalog covers their Battletech, Earthdawn, and Shadowrun games, along with information on the SF and fantasy novels based on the games.

GameNet

http://www.futurenet.com/gamenet/default.rpg.html

This online magazine from the UK is the Net descendant of *Arcane Magazine,* which folded awhile back. The frames format is very well done. A question remains as to the commitment of the publisher (FutureNet) to the site, as it doesn't appear to have been updated recently.

Game Publishers Association

http://rpg.net/gpa/

A frames-based site, GMA's membership consists of "small and alternative press publishers, focusing on adventure hobby games and related products. With over three dozen members, [its] mission is to improve communication with the industry and the publishing world, and to further the entrepreneurial aims of [its] members." From this site, you can go on to the individual sites of those members.

The Original, Unofficial Castle Falkenstein Home Page

http://daniel.drew.edu/~jmazur/falken.html

If you love the Victorian Age, you must see this site. Centered around the Castle Falkenstein game, it covers or has links to a variety of Victorian-related articles and sites.

Prince Etrigan's Role Playing Gamers Resource Page

http://www.rpg.net/etrigan/rpg.html

One of the best general-purpose game-related sites, it covers industry sites, fan sites, players needing games (and games needing players), among other things, and is fun to look at and read.

RPGnet

http://www.rpg.net/

One of several online magazines, its emphasis is on the industry itself, with plenty of information available for any gamer.

R. Talsorian Games, Inc.

http://www.best.com/~rtg1/toc.html

Full of regularly updated information concerning its games and recent products, Talsorian's site also encourages feedback from gamers, who can submit articles on the various RTG products for appearance on the site itself.

Steve Jackson Games

http://www.sjgames.com/

The producers of the GURPs system of games, SJG is very wired into the Net, even spinning off their own ISP, Illuminati On-line, a couple of years ago. This site is very informative and fun, and SJG isn't afraid to poke fun at itself when cause or need arises.

TSR

http://www.tsrinc.com/

The granddaddy of all gaming companies, TSR had fallen on hard times last year, but with the White Wolf buyout it looks like it's on the road to recovery. The site is well done, with chat and gaming rooms, as well as TSR's catalog.

White Wolf Online

http://www.white-wolf.com/

Probably the best of all the current corporate sites out there (and available in both text and frames versions), it provides not only an online catalog and previews of upcoming products, but also chat rooms and online gaming areas.

Wizards of the Coast

http://www.wizards.com/

The current leader of the RPG industry with its buyout of TSR. This is the home site for information on "Magic: The Gathering," its then-revolutionary collectible card game, which has changed the entire industry. Serves as an online catalog for its games; also has listings of activities and events at the WoTC Game Center in Seattle, WA.

NEWSGROUPS

- alt.games.frp.live-action
- alt.games.frp.nurpg
- bit.listserv.games-1
- rec.games.frp

FTP SITES

- ftp://ftp.cs.pdx.edu/pub/frp/general/
- ftp://ftp.csua.berkeley.edu/pub/btech/
- ftp://ftp.mpgn.com/Gaming/ADND/
- ftp://ftp.netcom.com/pub/ty/typo/rpn.html
- ftp://ftp.sunet.se/pub/pictures/fantasy/
- ftp://rtfm.mit.edu/pub/usenet-by-group/rec.games.roguelike.moria/rec.games.roguelike.moria_Frequently_Asked_Questions

MAILING LISTS

- amber
- dc-heroes
- drago
- earthdawn
- fed2411-digest

fudge-l

gi

HERO

il-north

joang

larp

MYTHUS-L

nero-ashbury

NERPS

PERN-RP

QUILLWRP

rmgame1

ROLEDEV_

rolemaster

roleplay

roleplaying-L

rpgs

sarnath-beta-testers

sfcc-gms

smrpg

spacedock

st-ulysses-rp

SW-RPG

uk-larp

virtual-phantom

webrpg-news

werewolf-narrators

Related Sites

http://ironcrown.com/ICESite/index.html

http://members.aol.com/TerBob/Sworld.html

http://users.aol.com/tritacrep2/index.html

http://www.archongaming.com/

http://www.eternity.com/

http://www.fantasylink.com/paradigma/

http://www.imperiumgames.com/main.html

http://www.pcis.net/ardan/adcom.htm

http://www.starwebs.com/cooperation.html

http://www.student.nada.kth.se/~nv91-asa/mage.html

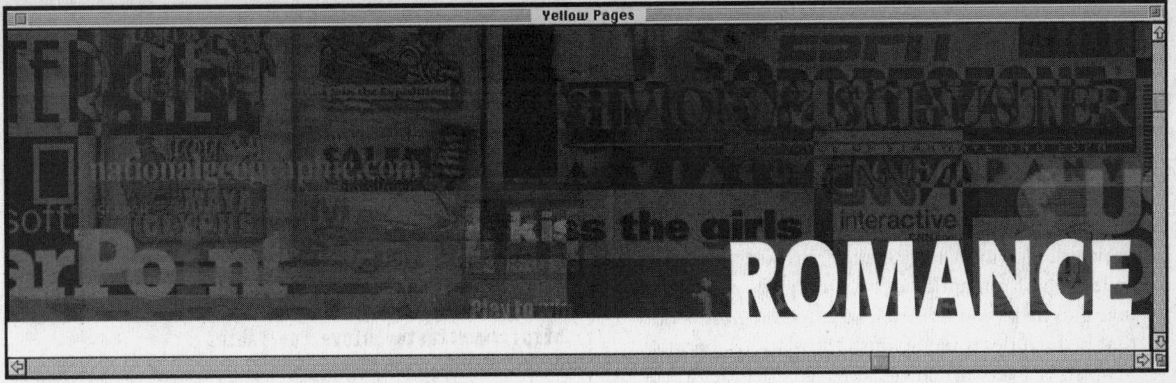

> Romance is great, but I just want to remind you, it don't pay the bills.
>
> *Francis Fitzpatrick in* She's the One *(1996)*

1001 Ways to Be Romantic

http://www.godek.com/1001_1.html

This site contains one-fourth of the book *1001 Ways to Be Romantic*, written by Gregory J.P. Godek and published by Casablanca Press. Get romantic tips and read real-life love stories. Take the romance quiz. View and listen to some segments of the Oprah Winfrey show when Greg appeared as a guest to discuss romance, give advice, and offer tips. Also includes one-fourth of the book *Romance 101, Lessons in Love*, also by Godek. Subscribe to *The Love-Letter*, a newsletter of romantic ideas. Includes links to other romance sites.

amour4u's Home Page

http://www.geocities.com/Paris/9021/

A collection of poetry and writings. Includes published and unpublished works, as well as quotations from well-known people. Learn how to give a sensual massage to your loved one. Learn romance tips and dating info. The Game section includes the Love Calculator, the Are You in Love or Lust quiz, and other interactive games. Learn various amour facts.

Joelogon's Foolproof Guide to Making Any Woman Your Platonic Friend
http://www.wizard.net/~joelogon/platonic/

The Couples Place

http://www.couples-place.com/

A meeting place for people who are thoughtful about committed relationships and want to make theirs a success. Learn what romance is and how to succeed in marriage. Take a relationship quiz for self-reflection. Explore the gap in understanding between partners and the efforts to narrow that gap. Read stories from couples about their successes and failures. David Sanford, the primary contributor to this site, is a psychotherapist and is author of a newspaper column on couple relationships in the *Maine Sunday Telegram*.

Cyber Romance 101

http://web2.airmail.net/walraven/romance.htm

If you've forged a relationship with someone over the Internet and are wondering whether it's love, passion, good communication, or a soulmate phenomenon, this site may give you some perspective. Browse through this compilation of published articles, essays, interviews, and advice columns that provide valuable viewpoints.

Don Juan's Romantic Web Site

http://www.geocities.com/Paris/LeftBank/4528/index.html

Includes a list of movies to watch with a loved one—including *When Harry Met Sally* and *Casablanca*, of course. Each movie serves as a link to the appropriate movie site for more information. Browse through the collection of romantic poetry. Don gives you tips on love and helps you write a love letter. He points out that he includes some Spanish translations, because Spanish is a very romantic language. Includes a section where readers ask Don for advice. Also includes Don Juan's Romantic chat room.

Fabio's Romantic Tips

http://www.tasteyoulove.com/fabio/tips.html

Fabio gives advice on the who, what, when, where, why, and how of romance. Read over letters sent to the Love Guru and the responses they received. Check out the recommendations for romantic getaway spots and read stories of readers' most romantic moments.

Flirting Home Page

http://www.flirts.com/

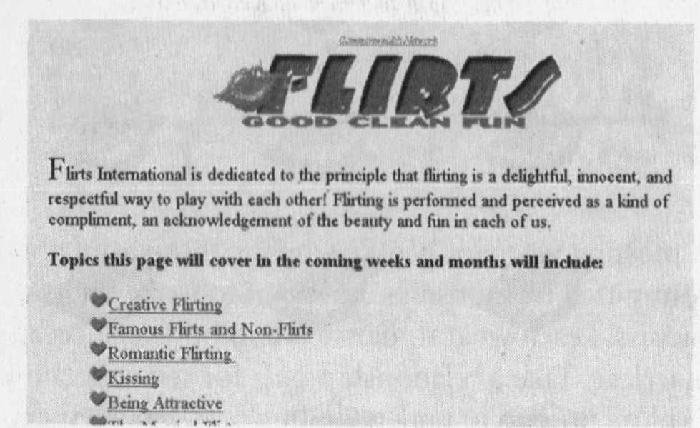

Brush up on your techniques for creative flirting. Includes letters from readers and advice from The Angel of Flirting. Check out the list of famous flirts and non-flirts. Try some of the tips for flirting outrageously with your spouse or lover, or for creative kissing as a romantic flirt. Also includes tips for the married flirt to keep the relationship exciting.

Hopeless Romantics

http://www.primenet.com/~ejones/hrhome.html

This site gives advice and FAQs for the hopeless romantic, and it provides links to sites where you can get advice for more serious problems. Browse through the original poetry and dating advice. Learn about the places to go and what to do. Try out some of the tips on approaching someone for a date. *Do not* try any of the pickup lines provided. (My favorite is "Do you believe in love at first sight, or should I walk by again?") Read stories about readers' most romantic encounters. Be sure to check out the ASCII Art for E-Mails section: learn how to "draw" a carnation on its side, a tulip, a teddy bear, a rose, and more. Or, visit the Hopeless Romantics Java chat room.

I Can't Believe It's Not Butter

http://www.tasteyoulove.com/fabio/

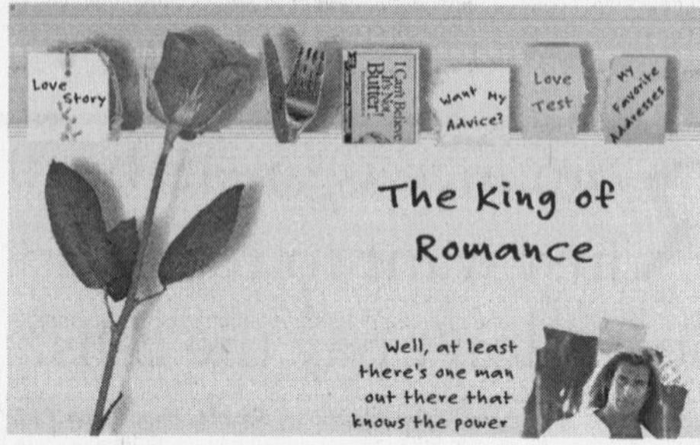

Participate in contests such as your idea of the ultimate dining experience or your recipe for the most romantic dessert (recipes are included on the site). Check out the author's latest romance novel pick. Browse through the Fabio fun facts and the "Fabiography." Learn about the info and tips on all the I Can't Believe It's Not Butter! Products and try out some of the recipes. Check out the advice column—in fact, you can browse through a whole year's worth of Q&As. Or, take the love quiz. Consider the romantic hot spot recommendations, which include links to sites such as Caymans, Great Barrier Reef, and Martha's Vineyard.

Joe's AMAZING Relationship Problem Solver!

http://studsys.mscs.mu.edu./~carpent1/probsolv/rltprob0.html

Don't come here if you need real advice on relationships or romance. This site provides a multiple-choice questionnaire about your problem, and then you are rewarded with an inspired solution somewhat similar to that plastic 8-ball you used to consult for advice.

Joelogon's Foolproof Guide to Making Any Woman Your Platonic Friend

http://www.wizard.net/~joelogon/platonic/

A humorous look at how men are shattered by hearing that all-time dreaded phrase, "I just want to be

A B C D E F G H I J K L M N O P Q R S T U V W X Y Z

friends." Learn some tips for the care of your platonic friend. Joe recommends that you check out the "dos and don'ts of cultivating and maintaining a platonic friendship with a woman you would otherwise want to have a relationship with and quite possibly marry." Read some of the sad stories and killer lines men have heard from the "I just want to be friends" category. Or, use some of those handy rationalizations for why women don't take you seriously. Check out the Excess Bitterness and Other Ramblings section for input from readers. And be sure to read the opening page for a hilarious profile of the site's author.

On Beauty and Love

http://www.cc.gatech.edu/grads/b/Gary.N.Boone/beauty_and_love.html

Browse through this collection of prose and poetry about beauty, love, romance, and life from famous authors. Also includes poetry from the author of this Web site.

Romantic Gestures

http://www.math.swt.edu/~bg01699/

Offers articles related to romance, advice, experiences, and encounters. Includes romantic poetry and prose.

Romantic Getaways

http://site209070.primehost.com/loveandromance/hr-index.htm

Come to this site for descriptions of romantic getaways in the U.S., where you can search for a destination by state. You'll get the name, address, phone number, rates, room types, and other pertinent info for each romantic spot.

SWAK Romantic Tips

http://www.chrsites.com/practicalweb/swak/tips.html

Try some of these romantic tips and ideas from Sealed with a Kiss, which includes low-cost ideas and no-cost ideas. Visit the Sealed with a Kiss Products and Services Showcase, which includes personalized love letters or poems ($10 each).

NEWSGROUPS

alt.love

alt.romance

alt.romance.chat

soc.couples

soc.singles

t-netz.romance

Related Sites

http://www.as.org/as

http://207.87.2.73/tests/lovetest.html

http://www.electpress.com/loveandromance/index.htm

http://www.alienbill.com/romance/

http://www.lovelife.com/love/

http://www.lovestories.com/

http://www.geocities.com/Paris/LeftBank/4120/

http://www.geocities.com/Paris/LeftBank/9340/The-Loveshack.html

http://www.burgoyne.com/pages/jdsquard/index.html

http://www.etoile.demon.co.uk/Love/Love.html

A B C D E F G H I J K L M N O P Q R S T U V W X Y Z

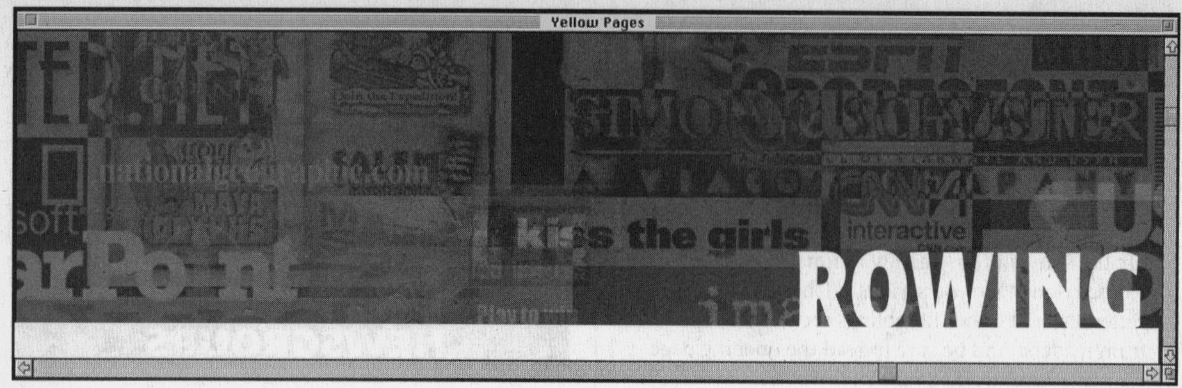

The person rowing the boat seldom has time to rock it.

Unknown

The Coxswain's Locker

http://www.coxing.com/~coxing/

This online store specializes in products for the coxswain—manuals, drill cards, videos, and the like—but the site also contains extensive info, such as the coxswain's role, the landing, and steering.

Godfrey Rowsports

http://www.proweb.co.uk/~godfrey/

View this clothing company's history, peruse their large online gallery of products, and place your order online.

Neczypor Racing

http://www.neczypor.com/

This shell manufacturer's site lets you examine their products' specs and prices, learn about a new product called surfskis, and jump to links.

No Frontiers: A Year in the Life of Fermoy Rowing

http://ireland.iol.ie/~tops/

This video follows eight young rowers going for three Irish titles and an Olympic medal for 1996. See their ups and downs, but be sure to *see* it—the European scenery is beautiful.

Rowing from an Oarsman's Perspective
http://tqd.advanced.org/3265/

The Olympic Tradition

http://www.rowersresource.com/olympics/national.html

Get the rowing results from the 1996 Olympic Games, learn about the rowers and coaches on the team roster, and consider the sport's long history as an Olympic event.

Oxford Rowing

http://www.comlab.ox.ac.uk/archive/other/rowing/oxford.html

Learn about upcoming tournaments, read the results of previous regattas, peruse pictures, and jump to the many rowing links provided.

Regatta Online

http://users.ox.ac.uk/~quarrell/REGATTA/

The sport's premier online e-zine contains a list of records, info on the Henley Royal Regatta, the latest crew news, and much more, including a place where you can vent pet peeves, also known as "row rage."

Regatta Sport

http://www.regattasport.ca/

The official apparel maker for the Canadian National Rowing Team, Regatta Sport also makes jackets, jewelry, and other accessories for the crew enthusiast.

rowersresource

http://www.rowersresource.com/

Get the latest news on regattas around the country and around the globe, learn more about proposed changes to the U.S. Rowing constitution, and check out their store.

Rowing from an Oarsman's Perspective

http://tqd.advanced.org/3265/

This site is great for people new to the sport. You can learn about its history, study the glossary to understand all the terminology, view illustrations of the different kinds of boats, learn about the ergonomics of rowing, understand what the coxswain does, and more.

The Rowing Service

http://users.ox.ac.uk/~quarrell/

This British page offers news, crew notices, race reports, coaching and technical information, and a test to determine whether you are a "rowing geek."

Row Works

http://www.valley.net/~rowworks/

The Row Works Clothing Company makes top-quality suits, shorts, winter gear, insulating Lifa Bodywear, and other fine rowing accessories.

Simply Oarsome

http://www.oarsome.com.au/

This Australian company has been supplying the Australian Rowing Team for nine years. You can download their entire catalog and view their colorful designs.

Vespoli USA

http://www.vespoli.com/

After you've decided that you love racing, you find yourself moving to take a job in North Dakota and leaving your crew behind. Now you need a new shell, which Vespoli has been building since 1980. Their site discusses their shells' speed and value, as well as the company's quality assurance and service.

Yale Crew

http://www.cis.yale.edu/athletic/Showcase/Crew/crew.htm

Yale started the first college rowing club in 1843, and began a long-running rivalry against Harvard in the first intercollegiate sporting event in 1852.

Related Sites
http://www.ecnz.co.nz/sponsorship/rowing/nzra.htm
http://www-atm.atm.ox.ac.uk/rowing/physics.html
http://www.sna.com/rcrc/humor.html
http://www.comlab.ox.ac.uk/archive/other/rowing/quotes.html

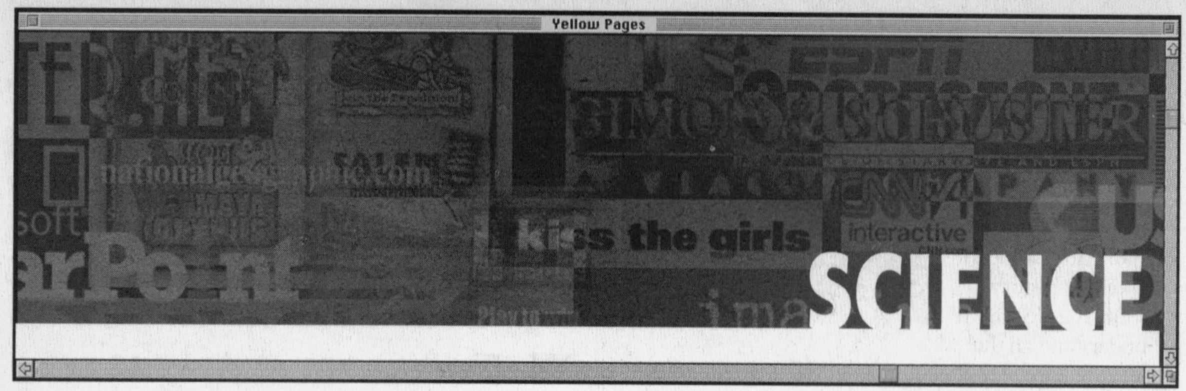

The most beautiful thing we can experience is the mysterious. It is the source of all true art and science.

Albert Einstein

American Institute of Chemical Engineers

http://www.che.ufl.edu/WWW-CHE/aiche/

Provides information on the group's mission, the upcoming world conference, and its programs. Also offers membership information.

Chemical Engineering URLs Directory

http://www.ciw.uni-karlsruhe.de/chem-eng.html

Offers a collection of links to information about chemical engineering resources outside the United States. Also offers a collection of links to chemical engineering sites all over the world. Provides information on upcoming conferences and includes many search links.

D Banks—Microengineering/MEMS

http://www.ee.surrey.ac.uk/Personal/D.Banks/ueng.html

Provides information on microengineering. Offers a small collection of tutorials and documents. Focuses on micromachining and the fabrication of structures the size of microns.

Reliability Analysis Center (RAC) Home Page
http://rome.iitri.com/rac/

Statistical Reports on United States Science and Engineering
http://www.nsf.gov/sbe/srs/stats.htm

World Wide Web Virtual Library: Aerospace
http://macwww.db.erau.edu/www_virtual_lib/Aerospace.html

Fraunhofer Institut for Materials Physics and Surface Engineering

http://www.iws.fhg.de/ext/iwseng.htm

Focuses on basic and applied research for surface processing of materials and components by means of laser and other high-power energy sources.

Institution of Electrical Engineers Home Page

http://www.iee.org.uk/

Provides information about membership in the Institution of Electrical Engineers, upcoming events, information services (including searchable databases), and a collection of links to other Internet resources.

Meetings Information

http://www.tms.org

Provides information about materials-related resources and publications. Also offers a list of national or international conferences and seminars on materials engineering.

Micromath's Home Page

http://www.MicroMath.com/

Develops software for scientists and engineers, primarily for solving equation systems and fitting experimental data. Offers Mac and IBM software. Also offers MMCalc, a downloadable Macintosh desktop utility program (free).

NU Student Chapter ASCE

http://www.civil.nwu.edu/asce/

Provides information regarding the American Society of Civil Engineers. Includes information concerning membership, and offers a calendar and information about other chapters.

Reliability Analysis Center (RAC) Home Page

http://rome.iitri.com/rac/

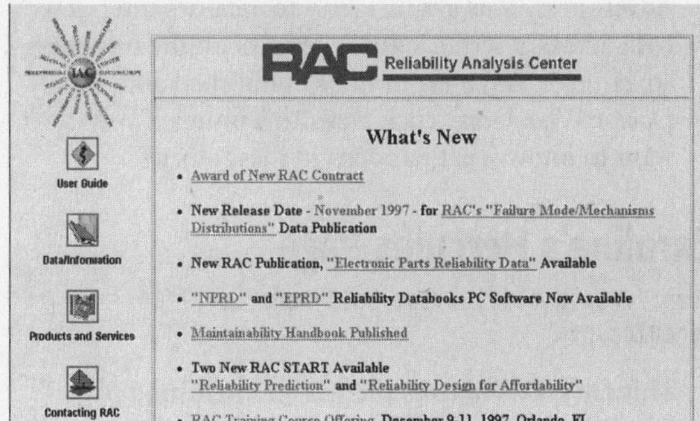

Provides many links to information about reliability engineering. Also provides information on RAC products and offers a large collection of learning resources.

Software Engineering Archives

http://www.qucis.queensu.ca/Software-Engineering/

Provides information regarding software engineering. Offers links to other related information. Includes archives searchable by vendor, category, or name.

Statistical Reports on United States Science and Engineering

http://www.nsf.gov/sbe/srs/stats.htm

Includes the education of scientists and engineers, the science and engineering work force, research and development expenditures and performance, science and technology outputs and impacts, and public attitudes on science.

UCF ASET

http://pegasus.cc.ucf.edu/~aset/

Provides information about the Electric Car project and offers a collection of links to student engineering groups and organizations, along with research-related links.

Virginia Geotechnical Services

http://www.infi.net/~vageo/

Specializes in geotechnical engineering, geoenvironmental services, and construction monitoring. Provides useful information concerning professional consulting, the environment, and business practice.

Welcome to Internet Directory of Biotechnology Resources

http://biotech.chem.indiana.edu/

Provides information on biotechnology engineering on the Internet.

World Wide Web Virtual Library: Aerospace

http://macwww.db.erau.edu/www_virtual_lib/Aerospace.html

Offers collection of links on aerospace engineering; conferences, businesses, publications, and more!

WWW Archive for Electric Power Engineering Education

http://www.uow.edu.au/pwrsysed/homepage.html

Provides resources for electric power educators. Focuses on the Asia-Pacific region. Also provides information about books and software packages.

A B C D E F G H I J K L M N O P Q R S T U V W X Y Z

Yellow Pages

SCIENCE FICTION & FANTASY SHOWS

You wanna hear something really nutty? I heard of a couple guys who wanna build something called an airplane, you know you get people to go in, and fly around like birds, it's ridiculous, right? And what about breaking the sound barrier, or rockets to the moon? Atomic energy, or a mission to Mars? Science fiction, right?

Ellie Arroway in Contact *(1997)*

Ambit

http://www.ambitweb.com/

When you can't find the TV listings for your favorite SF show, check Ambit. It has a 10-day listing for all the regular broadcast and cable shows, but unfortunately lists shows in syndication with no scheduling info (says to check local listings for those). Includes an SF TV newsletter discussing what's going on and upcoming episodes. The site also has access to search engines, non-SF material, and much more.

Mystery Science Theater 3000
http://www.mst3kinfo.com/

Broadsword

http://modjadji.anu.edu.au/steve/broadsword

The Web page for *Doctor Who*, the New and Missing Adventures. This e-zine Web site includes interviews with actors, a writer's guide, articles on the missing adventures, and a list of books published about *Doctor Who*. Don't click New Adventures if you don't want to know what happens in these stories.

Caroline's Hercules Page

http://www.geocities.com/Hollywood/Lot/7194/hercules.htm

This fan's TV *Hercules* site has an interesting page where she compares the TV character to the one in classical mythology. Includes games based on the show, plus upcoming episodes. Has links to other *Hercules* and *Xena* pages.

THE CENTRE

http://www.enteract.com/~perridox/pretender/

Based on the TV show *The Pretender*, this site has episode guides, bios on the staff, and an excellent FAQ that answers most of the questions you might have if you haven't watched every episode. Lots of photos of the program and some audio files.

Dark Shadows

http://members.aol.com/darkkshad/super/natural.htm

Premiering in 1966 on ABC television, this show was a soap opera based on ghouls, goblins, vampires, and the like. There are story lines, photo galleries, fan fictions, and other points of interest for *Dark Shadows* fans at this Web site.

The Dominion Sci-fi Channel

http://www.scifi.com/

Click Table of Contents to see the wealth of info at this site. The Free Zone includes audio clips, images, and video clips. Be sure to check out Sci-fi Live, a CU-SeeMe area that contains live video on the Internet. Nicely designed site.

FanGrok

http://www.roblang.demon.co.uk/fangrok/

A U.K. online zine that satirizes SF television. The site essentially "reprints" an article or two from the paper magazine *FanGrok*. Some of the articles are very funny—be sure to check out the Spice Docs issue. And, naturally, get instructions on how to subscribe to FanGrok so you can get the complete issue.

Forever Knight

http://www.spe.sony.com/Pictures/tv/forever/forever.html

This program chronicles the life of Nick Knight. He is a vampire from the 13th century living in a modern metropolis. He wishes to once again enter the mortal world and end the pain of bloodlust, while keeping his enemies at bay. At this site, you'll find screen savers and other goodies available for download that relate to this show.

Global Episode Opinion Survey

http://www.swd.net.au/geos/

You hate (or love) a particular episode of your favorite sci-fi television show; are you curious whether others agree or disagree? Then join GEOS, where you and others around the world can give your opinions and rate the shows and their episodes.

Hyperlight Enterprises

http://www.iceonline.com/home/roxanneb/www/hyperlight.html

Retailer of *X-Files*, *Star Trek*, and *Star Wars* collectibles and clothing. Click an item of interest in their product line to see what is in stock. Offers many science fiction and fantasy products, including card games and autographs.

In the Buff(y)

http://darklords.simplenet.com/Buffy/Buffy.htm

This shrine to *Buffy the Vampire Slayer* has excellent photos of all the stars, brief character bios, and extensive info on Sarah Michelle Gellar, who plays "Buffy."

Lois & Clark: The Web Server

http://www.webcom.com/~lnc/index.html

If you are a fan of Lifetime's show *Lois and Clark*, then this is the site for you. Includes a great amount of information about the new Superman series with a cast profile, episode guide, picture, and links to many other *Lois and Clark* sites.

Lurker's Guide to Babylon 5

http://www.hyperion.com/lurk/lurker.html

Nice site provides information on the show. Watch out for spoilers if you haven't watched a show yet. Includes info on the making of the show, its cast and characters, images of the amazing special effects, and episode information.

Majel Barrett Roddenberry's RODDENBERRY.COM

http://www.roddenberry.com/

The site has a newsletter from Majel Roddenberry, links to various *Star Trek* sites, and a big section on *Gene Roddenberry's Earth: Final Conflict*. There's also an online merchandise catalog for *Star Trek*. The site is very professionally done—reminiscent of the computer displays on *Star Trek*.

Millennium

http://www.foxworld.com/millnium/main.htm

The official Fox Network site for *Millennium* provides background on the characters, episode synopses, email to the program, collectibles, and more. It's very stylish—very Black.

Mystery Science Theater 3000

http://www.mst3kinfo.com/

SATELLITE NEWS

THE OFFICIAL MYSTERY SCIENCE THEATER 3000 INFO CLUB WEB SITE

THIS DAY IN MSTORY -- 617- THE SWORD AND THE DRAGON
First shown: December 3, 1994

WHAT'S HAPPENING AT BBI THIS WEEK? -- December 1 - December 5
Filming wraps for episode 901- THE PROJECTED MAN and begins for episode 902- THE PHANTOM PLANET

Resumption of studio tours have now been pushed back until AT LEAST December 12.

LATEST NEWS

11/24/97 -- TRACE OFFERS AUTOGRAPHED COMICS
11/20/97 -- MST3K: THE MOVIE DECEMBER AIRDATES
11/18/97 -- EPISODE 902 ANNOUNCED
11/13/97 -- EPISODE 901 ANNOUNCED

Have your friends been talking about the weird TV show where they make fun of old sci-fi and horror movies from a space station? Would you like to know what they're talking about? Then come to the MST3K site and see what all the talk is about. The site has audio and video files, a FAQ, plus info on the stars and writers and lots of other goodies.

The Netpicker's Guide to "The X Files"

http://aea16.k12.ia.us/ricke/netpickhome.html

This a very cool site that points out the "netpicks" in each episode. What are netpicks? "A netpick is a writing/research error, a technical glitch, or a continuity error that made it through post production." A very interesting site, but because it covers only the first three seasons, either this site is inactive, or just running way behind on the postings. But still a lot of fun for the *X Files* fan.

Poltergeist: The Legacy

http://members.aol.com/legacymemb/legacy.htm

This site is presented as the Seattle Legacy House Web site. Not only does it have info in the show itself, but includes fan fiction, character and actor bios, and a Legacy Handbook for aspiring members. Very attractive and well done site.

The Sci-Fi Experience

http://www.geocities.com/Hollywood/Boulevard/4090/

A very well done *Star Trek* site with the emphasis on *Voyager* and *Deep Space Nine* (with *X Files* thrown in for flavor). Episode listings, convention info, crew bios, fan fiction, some great photos, and audio files.

Sliders

http://www.xtc.net/~lucast/sliders/sliders.html

Up-to-date information on the Fox television show, *Sliders*. Description of the latest episodes, a *Sliders* photo gallery, and WAVs of the intro to episodes are included. Includes links to other Sliders sites.

Songs of the Blue Bird

http://www.iquest.net/~jeneric/songs.html

A virtual zine and news source for fans of the former CBS television drama *Beauty and the Beast*. Includes unaired scripts, images and paintings by fans, back issue catalogs, and information about conventions for this cult TV show.

Space Opera

http://fairfax2.laser.net/~epippi/

If you remember *Tom Corbett Space Cadet* or *Video Ranger*, this is the site for you—dedicated to the science fiction shows of the 1950s. You can find listings of articles from various magazines on these shows (sorted by decade) as well as information on the programs; special emphasis is given to *Tom Corbett Space Cadet*.

Star Trek

http://www.netshop.net/Startrek/web/

Provides a good amount of information and links to many sites that cover the television, film, and culture phenomena that is *Star Trek*. This site includes pictures, sounds, quotes, fan information, and much more.

Starship Store

http://www.halcyon.com/uncomyn/startrek.html

Includes collector's items, memorabilia, and clothing of every Star Trek series. Order T-shirts of your favorite characters, key chains, toys, and other items.

Tales from the Crypt

http://www.cryptnet.com/

A huge site from the dungeons that are *Tales from the Crypt*. You can check out the Laboratory, the Vault, the Episode Graveyard, the Screaming Room, and the Cryptique.

Trader 800 Trekker

http://www.scifi.com/trader/

Part of the Sci-fi Channel Web site. The Trader includes collectibles you can purchase of the *X-Files*, *Star Wars*, *Star Trek*, *Doctor Who*, and *Babylon 5*. Click the show you're interested in to see what merchandise is available.

Trek Reviews Archive

http://www.ravenna.com/~forbes/trek-reviews/

This nicely designed Web site for the `rec.arts.startrek.reviews` Usenet group includes an archive of reviews of every *Star Trek* show and episode by season, movie and book reviews, and links to other Star Trek web pages.

TV Century 21: the Gerry Anderson Homepage

http://www.net-gate.com/~simon/tv21.html

A fan's homage to all those great SF puppet shows, especially *Thunderbirds*. It also includes information on other Anderson shows, such as *Space: 1999.* A news section lists upcoming projects; a FAQ is provided for those who need to know.

The TV Sci-Fi and Fantasy Database

http://www.pazsaz.com/scifan.html

If you can't remember the name of a particular episode, or when it ran, just check with the Database. It lists the name and original air date of more than 70 different shows. Please note that no information about the episode is given. Comes in full graphical and less graphical versions.

NEWSGROUPS

alt.tv.highlander

alt.tv.red-dwarf

uk.media.tv.sf

FTP & GOPHER SITES

ftp://198.87.195.20/pub/highlander/

ftp://cathouse.org

ftp://mithral.iit.edu/pub/highlander/FAQ

ftp://sflovers.rutgers.edu

ftp://ziggy.cisco.com/ql-archive/

gopher://sunsite.doc.ic.ac.uk:70/1/media/tv/collections/tardis/us/sci-fi

gopher://wiretap.spies.com/11/Library/Media/

MAILING LISTS

HIGHLA-L

HLFIC-L

SUBSPACE-CHATTER

Related Sites

http://members.aol.com/germainia/ww/home.html

http://www.carol.net/dolphin/ouathome.htm

http://www.dwarflander.com/

http://www.geocities.com/Area51/2653/3rdrock.html

http://www.gis.net/~fm/

http://www.nightman.com/

http://www.public.iastate.edu/~spires/max.html

http://www.scifi.com/kolchak/

http://www.sg-1.com/

http://www.tvplex.com/BuenaVista/Gargoyles/

A B C D E F G H I J K L M N O P Q R S T U V W X Y Z

Yellow Pages

SCOTCHES, BOURBONS, AND OTHER ALCOHOLIC BEVERAGES

Let schoolmasters puzzle their brain,
With grammar, and nonsense, and learning,
Good liquor, I stoutly maintain,
Gives genius a better discerning.

Oliver Goldsmith

The AzureSky Bar Guide

http://www-personal.umich.edu/~azuresky/

Use the search feature by typing in any drink name and then viewing the ingredients and directions for mixing that drink. Learn the basics of stocking a bar—what tools, mixing apparatus, spirits, and mixers you'll need. Check out the guide to glassware, which includes pictures of each type. Also provides info on the techniques of mixology: frappe, blend, heat, shake, stir, and layer. Try out some of the recipes for homemade liqueurs, such as Amaretto, Absinth, sloe gin, Irish Creme, and coffee liqueur. Or, browse through the glossary of liquor terms and view links to liquor-related sites.

Related Sites

http://www.bushmills.com/

http://www.canadianmist.com/

http://www.cutty-sark.co.uk/

http://www.dewars.co.uk/

http://www.schlager.com/home2.cgi

NRP TOP PICKS

The AzureSky Bar Guide
http://www-personal.umich.edu/~azuresky/

Bordeaux
http://www.bordeaux.com/

Samuel Adams
http://www.samadams.com/

Barbancourt English

http://www.cam.org/~interso/srb_eng.html

Check out the general info and brief history about this rum made in Haiti, including the company that produces it. Try out some of the recipes for tasty Barbancourt drinks. Browse through the photo section to see the process of making this drink: harvesting and crushing the sugarcane, extracting the juice, distilling it, and then aging it in oak barrels. Includes extensive listings of Usenet/Netnews groups, mailing list discussion groups, and FTP sites (see the end of this category).

Becherovka

http://www.becherovka.com

Offers information about Becherovka, a liqueur dating back to 1805 that has reigned as Czech's foremost alcoholic beverage for generations. Includes recipes for several exotic drinks and lists distributors in the U.S.

Bordeaux

http://www.bordeaux.com/

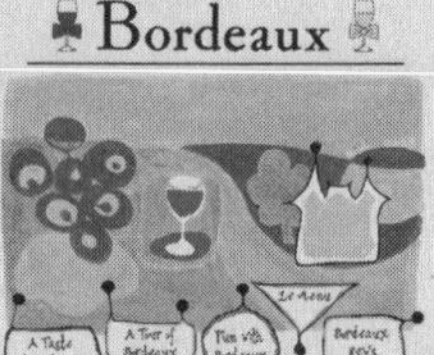

Take a tour of the Bordeaux countryside and learn how this wine is made. You'll even learn where to dine and stay while traveling through Bordeaux. Find tips on enjoying Bordeaux wine and hosting a wine-tasting party. Learn how the wine is made, what restaurants are "Bordeaux-friendly," and how to read a Bordeaux wine label. Learn the basics of grape varieties (Merlot, Cabernet, Semillon, etc.). Investigate the buyer's guide and vintage chart, as well as recipes for French cuisine. Or, check out the glossary of basic wine terms.

Internet Guide to Wine and Frequently Asked Questions

`http://sbwines.silcom.com/usenet_winefaq/`

Read a general intro about what wine is. Learn how wine is made, aged, and stored. Learn the proper way to drink wine, and get tips on buying wine. Check out the varieties of wine, and tour wine countries in France, California, and Canada.

Club Bacardi

`http://www.bacardi.com/`

Try some of the drink and food recipes that use Bacardi Spice and Bacardi Light/Gold Tropical. Enter the Bacardi Select Cigar Lounge for pairing drinks with cigars. Try the Cigar Chat Room and review Cigar Aficionado's more than 1,000 cigar ratings. Learn the Bacardi family history, and take a tour of the Bacardi Museum, the Martini Museum, or the Bacardi Distillery. Use the Bacardi Cocktail Search Engine to learn how to mix a specific drink. Use the Drink Wizard; you tell it what mixes or spirits you have, and it tells you what drinks you can make with them. Learn tips and techniques for professional bartending, and check out the Global Bar Directory for a list of great bars and clubs around the world. Includes a humorous guide on luring the opposite sex.

Cocktail Magazine

`http://www.cocktail.com/`

Another cyberbar beautifully presented. Test your drink knowledge with a quick quiz, brush up on some cocktail alchemy, see what drinks are in season, jump to other mixology sites, and stimulate your brain with Dr. Pseudocryptogram's list of literary interests. Includes back issues of the e-zine.

Courvoisier: A Guide to the Best

`http://www.courvoisier.com/`

Get a quick lesson on pronouncing the name of this cognac by listening to the audio clip. Then move on to the general info and history of Courvoisier and descriptions of the entire line. Check out the dinner and dessert recipes that use Courvoisier. Browse some of the recipes for Courvoisier cocktails. Or, investigate the guide to Arturo Fuente's premium cigars and Courvoisier's choice for the perfect cognac match. Browse the Courvoisier Guide to the Best Restaurants; you click a city on the map provided, and Courvoisier presents its choices for the best restaurants in that city. Includes instructions on judging a good cognac by taste, sight, aroma, and touch. Also features a cognac FAQ.

Cybership 2: Voyage to the Bottom of the Net

`http://www.rum.com/`

This site is brought to you by Captain Morgan's Original Spiced Rum and includes product info on all the Captain Morgan lines. It starts out with a humorous questionnaire to test whether you are 21 or older and therefore allowed to enter the site. Search for a drink, submit a recipe, or look at other users' recipes. Go to the Yo-Ho-Ho Room to download video, audio, and text of Captain Morgan's featured comedian. Submit a joke and read jokes submitted by others. View Captain Morgan's Q&As. Browse the handy glossary of pirate slang and listen to the many sound bites from Captain Morgan so that you'll sound authentic. Learn the Captain's dance moves, browse his semaphore handbook, or follow along with his knot-tying tutorial.

Drunkboy's Virtual Web Bar

`http://www.csh.rit.edu/~tward/vrbar.html`

Visit this virtual bar where people can share and exchange recipes for alcoholic beverages.

Edinburgh Malt Whisky Tour

`http://www.dcs.ed.ac.uk/home/jhb/whisky/`

Learn about the history and manufacturing of malt whisky in Scotland. Check out the image map of Scotland's malt distilleries. You'll also want to take a look at the categories and ratings of various whisky brands and distilleries.

Escapades

`http://www.tanqueray.com/`

This site features some cute graphics and includes info on Tanqueray Escapades Distilled English Gin. Browse through the recipes for drinks and a week's worth of food pairings—including cocktails, appetizers, and entrees. View the tips on throwing a successful party, along with suggestions for party themes. Look through the advertising photo archive and try to match the poster with the decade each ad is from. Also includes a history of the distillation process.

Jim Beam

`http://www.jimbeam.com/`

Play the Find Jim Beam game. Try out some of the drink recipes, including the holiday drinks. Read the history of Jim Beam Bourbon. You can even buy Jim Beam-related merchandise online.

The Miller Genuine Draft Taproom

`http://www.mgdtaproom.com/index.html`

Ask the Brewmaster questions about beer and how it's made. For example, "What is meant by cold-filtered and what is being filtered?" Check out the Brewmaster FAQ. Read the story of Frederic A. Miller, who made a name for himself as a brewer in Germany before moving to New York and then Milwaukee. The Sport-Smash section features schedules for the Indy car, NHRA, and NASCAR races, as well as Miller-sponsored races.

The Pierre Smirnoff Company

`http://www.purethrill.com/`

Try one of the Smirnoff cocktail recipes. Learn about the history of Smirnoff, the distillation process, and the ingredients. Read about the relationship of James Bond with Smirnoff by viewing downloadables (a screen saver, wallpaper, and desktop patterns) and the trailer from Tomorrow Never Dies. Submit stories about the hippest place you've found to sample Smirnoff, your favorite Smirnoff combinations, or where in the world you have enjoyed your Smirnoff and what you were doing at the time. Cast your vote in the Get Real Index. Surveys include deciding which entertainment, media, or sports person is the most pretentious; an example of behavior or a quotation for each celebrity is included.

Related Sites

`http://www.grand-marnier.com/`

`http://www.fujipub.com/scotchmalt/`

REMY-COINTREAU

`http://www.remy-cointreau.com/`

Remy Martin is 100 percent fine champagne cognac from France. Submit questions about Remy Martin and receive a reply via email. Get tips on tasting cognac, hosting a tasting, and "speaking cognac." View descriptions of Remy Martin blends: VSOP (Very Superior Old Pale brand), XO Special, and Louis XIII. Learn what it takes to make a cognac that's second to none, and take an in-depth look at the cognac process—from vine to glass. Includes a history of cognac and Remy Martin. Each month features a portrait of a special guest at the site, such as Jacques Pepin—one of America's best-known chefs, teachers, and authors.

Samuel Adams

`http://www.samadams.com/`

View the extensive guide to the 15 different styles of Samuel Adams beers. Learn about the history, brewing, and flavor characteristics of these hand-crafted beers. Take a virtual tour of the Samuel Adams Brewery, located in Boston, MA. Visit the Samuel Adams store—an online catalog for apparel and beer essentials. Learn the history of the Boston Beer Company and info on beer styles, ingredients, and food matches. Includes beer links.

Scotch.com

`http://scotch.com`

Get tips for preparing food with scotch whisky, and try out the recipes and instructions for two classic malt dinners. Includes general info and a history of scotch whisky. Go to the bulletin board for scotch-related discussions. Check out the extensive info on the fine whiskies of Scotland—blended scotch and single malt scotch. Includes a lesson on and history of the art of blending.

Single Malt Scotch Page

`http://www.kiva.net/~mesh/scotch.html`

This Web site describes and rates approximately 30 single malt scotches. It includes a brief history of the people and their organizations. Also includes several anecdotes about their experiences and words of wisdom to those first-time scotch drinkers or experienced imbibers.

Stoli Central 2.0

http://www.stoli.com/

Stolichnaya, synonymous with vodka, provides a well-designed site for those seeking info about premium liquor of the world via Carillon importers. Visit England for gin, Mexico for tequila, and of course, Russia for vodka. Download Stoli's artistic ads. Online ordering is available.

The Ultimate Internet Beer Guide

http://beer.meccanet.com/beer.shtml

Check out the beer Q&A and the latest beer-related stories in the news. Includes links to a do-it-yourself guide to cask conditioning your beer at home and other home-brewing links. Enter the Beer chat room. Test your knowledge of beer trivia and view the joke of the month.

USENET/NETNEWS GROUPS

alt.alcohol

alt.bacchus

alt.beer

alt.food.wine

fr.rec.boissons.vins

francom.biere-et-vins

rec.crafts.brewing

rec.crafts.winemaking

rec.food.drink

rec.food.drink.beer

uk.food+drink.misc

MAILING LIST DISCUSSION GROUPS

BEER-L

BOP

CANWINE

ENOLOGY

FOODWINE

HOMEBREW

LAMBIC_DIGEST

MALTS-L

MEAD-LOVER-DIGEST

NW-WINE

NZWINE

OZWINE

RBPMail

UK-HOMEBREW

VITICULTURE

WINE

WINE-INFO

FTP & GOPHER SITES

ftp://ftp.netins.net/showcase/fujipub/

ftp://ftp.rtfm.mit.edu

ftp://ftp.stanford.edu/pub/clubs/homebrew/beer/

ftp://ftp.stanford.edu/pub/clubs/homebrew/beer/rfdb/

ftp://ftp.stanford.edu/pub/clubs/homebrew/mead/

gopher.physics.utoronto.ca

Related Sites

http://www.southerncomfort.com/default.asp

http://www.winetitles.com.au/auswine/wineries/tarac/blackjack.html

http://winemag.com/

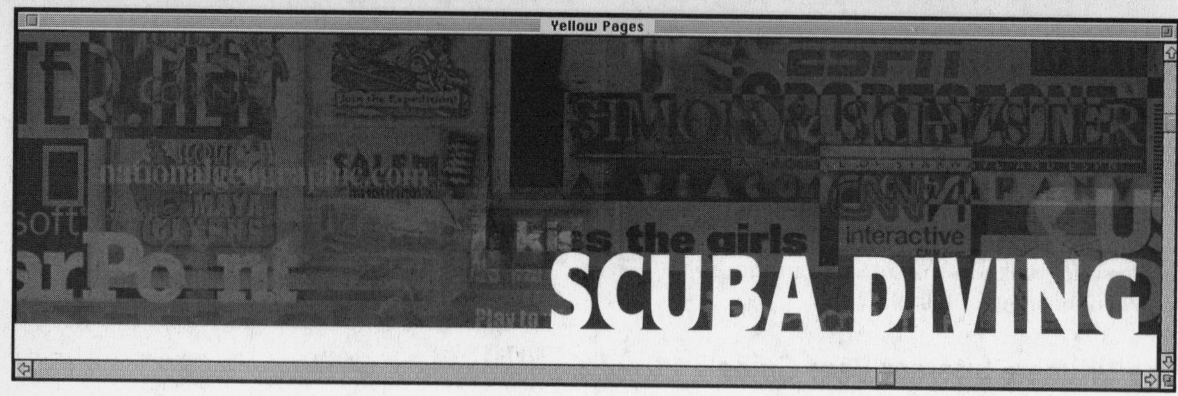

SCUBA DIVING

> I love the sea, so beautiful, so mysterious… so full of fish.
>
> *Luc in* French Kiss *(1995)*

Dive Buddy White Pages
`http://www.divebuddy.com/`

PADI (Professional Association of Diving Instructors)
`http://www.padi.com/`

U.S. Divers Aqua-Lung
`http://www.usdivers.com/`

Dive Buddy White Pages

`http://www.divebuddy.com/`

Promotes the #1 dive rule: Never dive alone. A free registry of more than 455 divers so you can find a buddy to dive with anywhere you want to go. Encourages divers to register and exchange ideas and tips on underwater photography, dive gear, dive locations, and any other dive-related topic of interest.

Divers Dialog

`http://www.datalog.co.uk/`

According the homepage, this was the U.K.'s first Internet directory dedicated to scuba diving. Includes a list of dive shops and clubs, a lost and found registry, and a for sale database. Although the information here is copyrighted, the site encourages visitors to print anything they find helpful for personal or club use.

DiveTravel Net Navigator

`http://www.divetravel.net`

Offers dive packages to the Pacific and Indian Oceans, the Red Sea, the Florida Keys, and every location imaginable in the Caribbean. Contains an online edition of DiveTravel magazine and includes advisor, planner, world directory, travel agents, and information exchange pages.

Diving Equipment & Marketing Association

`http://www.dema.org/`

Dedicated to the dive industry, this site supplies information on how to become a diver, industry news, how to become a DEMA member for those involved in the commercial side of the dive business, and continuing education for certified divers. Also provides information on the annual DEMA trade show in California.

HSA (Handicapped Scuba Association)

`http://ourworld.compuserve.com/homepages/hsahdq/`

The site of this organization dedicated to making scuba more accessible to people with physical challenges appears to be updated frequently. It offers a quarterly journal, travel schedule, guides to wheelchair-accessible dive resorts, an HSA instructor locator page, and training course information for divers interested in becoming an HSA dive instructor.

Moray Wheels

`http://www.moraywheels.org`

Organization founded by a physical therapist to form a group of able-bodied and physically disabled divers. Has more than 100 members and offers certification classes at M.I.T., many local activities in the New England area, and an annual tropical vacation to wheelchair-accessible destinations.

PADI (Professional Association of Diving Instructors)

http://www.padi.com/

A fantastic site with incredibly current information. Updated daily—it even played Christmas music and listed suggested Christmas gifts for divers when I visited the site in November. Offers the usual dive center listings, BBSs, product catalogs, news, and course listings and a wide range of information beyond the usual—a fish quiz to test your knowledge, a map of the ocean floor from NOAA, dive insurance, and more.

Rodale's Scuba Diving

http://www.scubadiving.com

Visitors are offered a free trial subscription to "SCUBA Daily News." Also supplies a guide to dive-related books available on the Web, a humorous top 10 list, and a helpful "Scuba Divers Handbook."

Scottsdale Ski & Sea Club

http://www.9.pair.com/sssc/

A slick, high-energy site with cool background music and sound bites to pump you up. Primarily a ski club, the site also includes scuba diving, water skiing, tubing, roller blading, hiking, biking, camping, vacationing, and partying pages. You get the feeling that these people are quite actively seeking a great time, all the time. With its schedule of trips and monthly meetings complete with open bar, this is the perfect site for anyone who wants to meet people and become active around the Scottsdale, Arizona area.

Scuba Times Online

http://www.scubatimes.gulf.net/

The best feature is a Medical Center page with common questions and answers, tips, quizzes, and information from doctors who will answer divers' medical questions. Also has articles on scuba topics, lots of classified ads, and an offer for a free issue of the actual magazine.

ScubaDuba

http://www.scubaduba.com

Encourages active participation from divers. Requests that visitors submit diving-related articles or stories of interest. It offers classified ads, a buddy directory, chat room, and photos.

Sub-Aqua Association

http://www.saa.org.uk/

This organization was founded more than 20 years ago by various British dive clubs to promote diving issues nationally. The site is extrememly professional and detailed, including an URL minder service to notify you via email any time the site it updated.

TravelBase Scuba Guide

http://www.travelbase.com/activities/scuba

This site offers a link to its featured dive site of the week. Also contains a newsletter, schedule of excursions, underwater photos and video, and directory of dive shops throughout the U.S.

U.S. Divers Aqua-Lung

http://www.usdivers.com/

A visually fun site with an island theme. Click the diver as it swims across your screen to see cool facts of interest to divers. Offers an in-depth look at the Jean-Michel Cousteau Institute, which was founded by the oldest son of the infamous Jacques-Yves Cousteau. Also contains standard business information about the company's catalog, dealer locations, and company contacts.

YMCA Scuba Program

http://www.webcom.com/cscripts/

A good source of general information such as a list of courses offered at the Y. It also contains instructions on how to replace a lost C-card, which is a requirement for any diver. This site offers a quarterly journal too.

Related Sites

http://www.gotropical.com/training.htm

http://www.divemall.com/

http://www.indies-suites.com

http://deckard.mc.duke.edu/scuba/

http://www.nauticalnet.com/

http://pond.net/~bsackett/

http://jwa.com/scubapro/scubapro.html

http://www.ats.com.au/%7Ekingy/

http://www.thescubastore.com/

http://matrix.infomatch.com/scuba/

A B C D E F G H I J K L M N O P Q R S T U V W X Y Z

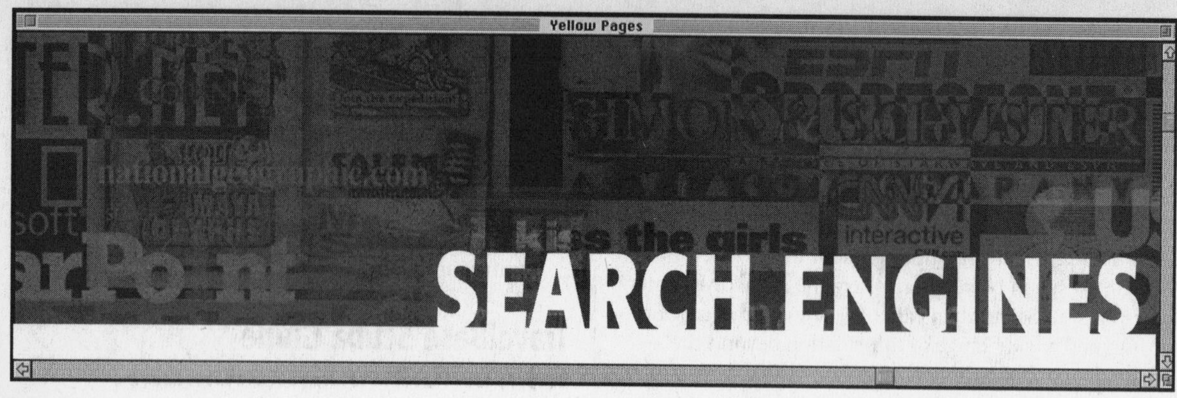

> Often the search proves more profitable than the goal.
>
> *E.L. Konigeburg*

AcqWeb's Guide to Searching the Web

http://www.library.vanderbilt.edu/law/acqs/search.html

Whether you're just learning about the World Wide Web or have been searching successfully for quite some time, this page is highly recommended. In addition to linking to the major (and some "minor" but very useful) search engines, this Vanderbilt University page provides well-written details on exactly how to do your searching—which queries work and why, how not to query, and so on.

All-in-One Search Page

http://www.albany.net/allinone/

The color choices are a bit wild, but this page is one of the most useful places for starting a general search of the World Wide Web and Internet. Includes access to many search engines of all types from a single spot. Add this address to your bookmark list!

AltaVista

http://www.altavista.digital.com/

One of the most thorough search engines, AltaVista (developed by Digital Equipment Corporation) also powers quite a number of other, more specialized engines. On the main page, search for any word in any document published on the Web or in Usenet newsgroups. Multiple language choices. Highly recommended.

Yahoo!
http://www.yahoo.com/

Ask Jeeves

http://www.askjeeves.com/

For people who are familiar with more complicated Boolean queries, this "natural language" search engine may seem like a return to kindergarten. If so, it's kindergarten taught by Albert Einstein. Enter your question in plain language, such as "Where is Afghanistan?" to find answers ranging from where to find a map of Afghanistan to where to find information on the recent conflict in Afghanistan. Extremely useful, especially if you're not sure where to *start* looking for the information you need.

Excite

http://www.excite.com/

With a very readable layout, this site offers both straightforward text querying and several "channel" links that take you to general categories for browsing or more specialized searching. The Exciting Stuff section usually has several special offers for contests, links to new and interesting products, and more. For more specialized services, look to the links at the bottom of the main page. The Penn Jillette column is always interesting (parents, use discretion).

Goto.com [formerly World Wide Web Worm]

http://www.goto.com/

Old address: `http://guano.cs.colorado.edu/wwww/`. Still working, but you'll probably like the new version better anyway. Use a general text search at the top of the page, or scan down through the keyword lists in the overall categories of People, Self, Home, Work, or Play to find what you're looking for. Just browsing on a dull evening? If you live in a major metropolitan area, try out the Dinner and a Movie section. You might find something more fun to do than spending another evening on the Internet (kidding!).

HotBot

`http://www.hotbot.com/`

This is the search engine from the folks at *Wired.* Don't be fooled by the crazy color scheme; it's serious stuff. Conduct searches from general to very specific—including searching Usenet, discussion groups, shareware databases, news and entertainment info, and much, much more. (Parents: This site is for *you,* not your kids.)

Jargon

Bots: Internet robot surfers that travel the Internet, constantly checking out sites and recording information for their masters.

Infoseek

`http://guide.infoseek.com/`

One of the most popular search services, and for good reasons. Very powerful search capabilities. A variety of channel selections make the site friendly to people who are just browsing, in addition to the serious searcher. You can even personalize the service to produce news you can use in a format that fits your information needs. Highly recommended.

More About Infoseek

Infoseek combines a powerful search engine (such as Lycos and AltaVista) with a large Web directory (such as Yahoo!). On its basic search screen, you can enter search keywords or select from dozens of categories.

Lizst, the mailing list directory

`http://www.liszt.com/`

This was already a really useful service, but has recently been improved. Browse through the nearly 85,000 mailing lists in the Lizst database to find something of interest to you—search the general categories of lists, or try specific keywords to find a particular list. Specify the level of "junk filtering" you want for your search; the default setting is Some but you may prefer Lots. Be sure to read the section called "What Do The Color Codes Mean?" before you get started (or in process).

Lycos

`http://www.lycos.com/`

Lycos does a lot of filtering for you—particularly useful when you're in a hurry and looking for sites on very specific topics. When you want the search to be *really* tight, try searching for pages with the topic word in the page's title or in the URL. Of course, you can always do general searches as well, or browse through the channel lists. Note: In support of the National Center for Missing and Exploited Children, Lycos supplies a special section of its site for posting photos of missing children. Please tune in to see whether you recognize any of those faces.

MetaCrawler

`http://www.metacrawler.com/`

Very customizable search engine. You can set up searching to fit your needs, but keep in mind that cookies may be required (some people prefer not to accept cookies). Searching in the "phone book"-style lists is quite handy for anyone who's comfortable using the local Yellow Pages. The Ultimate Directory section provides lots of resources in nine general categories, including some unusual options such as TV listings for your area.

SavvySearch

`http://www.cs.colostate.edu/~dreiling/smartform.html`

Available in multiple languages. Standard keyword querying, but you can specify the exact sections of the Internet you want to search, which narrows down the query and saves search time. You can also indicate how many results you're looking for, and how you want those results displayed—Brief, Normal, or Verbose format.

tile.net

`http://tile.net/`

There's nothing fancy about this engine. It's just straight-up, very powerful searching. Click the check boxes to indicate where you want to search, type your keyword(s), and away you go. The engine searches discussion groups, newsgroups, FTP sites, and a select group of vendors. Very fast!

WebCrawler

`http://www.webcrawler.com/`

Interested in a particular city? Search for it here to get the current weather and a map of the city. General categories as well links to some specialized services;

the upper-right corner lists a few of the top news stories for those who don't have much time for keeping in touch. The Entertainment section is particularly interesting and useful. Provided by the folks at Excite.

Yahoo!

http://www.yahoo.com/

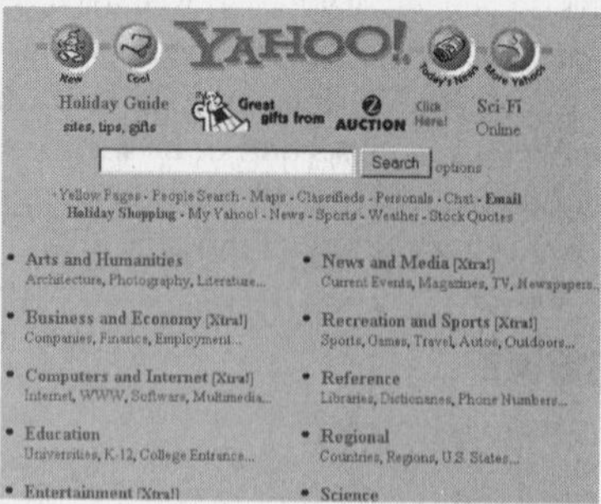

Need some raw power for your search? This is the place. Extremely selective or broad-spectrum searching, plenty of reference sections, people searches, and much, much, much more. One of the very best search engines available. Highly recommended!

Parents and teachers will be especially interested in the Yahooligans! section for kids. Plenty to do, see, and find. Check it out.

> **Engine or Directory?**
>
> Yahoo! Is purely a Web directory. Its main feature is the categories list. You click a category, and then on a subcategory, and so on, until you arrive at the topic you are intersted in. For those of you who don't have time to wade through categories, Yahoo! provides a text box in which you can enter the keywords for which you are searching, but it only searches its own small directory of sites.

NEWSGROUP

alt.fan.dejanews

FTP & GOPHER SITES

ftp://sri.com/netinfo/interest-groups.txt

http://ftpsearch.ntnu.no/

http://www.nexor.com/archie.html/

gopher://gopher.utah.edu/11/

gopher://logic.uc.wlu.edu:3002/7

gopher://veronica.scs.unr.edu/11/veronica

MAILING LISTS

searchlist

searchreport

Related Sites

http://ahoy.cs.washington.edu:6060/

http://catalog.com/vivian/interest-group-search.html

http://gort.ucsd.edu/ejourn/jdir.html

http://n2h2.com/KOVACS/

http://www.bigfoot.com/

http://www.city.net/

http://www.dejanews.com/

http://www.dogpile.com/

http://www.four11.com/

http://www.hotsheet.com/

http://www.ipl.org/reading/news/

http://www.isleuth.com/

http://www.lib.berkeley.edu/TeachingLib/Guides/Internet/FindInfo.html

http://www.mckinley.com/

http://www.nerdworld.com/

http://www.netguide.com/

http://www.nexor.com/archie.html/

http://www.nlsearch.com/

http://www.whowhere.com/

http://www.yahooligans.com/

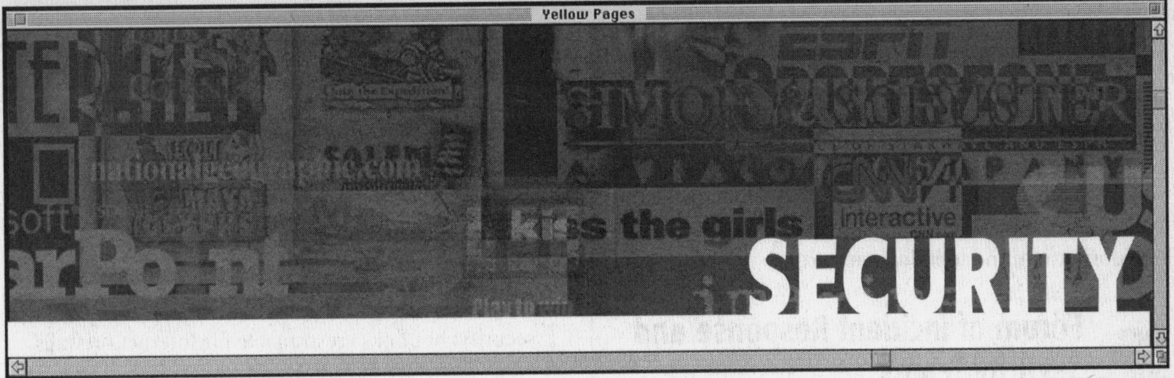

> Security is when everything is settled, when nothing can happen to you; security is a denial of life.
>
> *Germaine Greer*

NRP TOP PICKS

Anonymity and Privacy on the Internet
http://www.stack.nl/~galactus/remailers/

Forum of Incident Response and Security Teams
http://www.first.org/welcome.html

McAfee VirusScan for Windows
http://www.mcafee.com/

National Computer Security Association
http://www.ncsa.com/

VeriSign, Inc.
http://www.verisign.com/

American Power Conversion

http://www.apcc.com/

American Power Conversion is a builder of power surge protection devices. Site provides company background along with a guided tour about power and its capability to damage computers from PCs to networks. Includes a thorough list of customer references, business partners, technical support, and an online "Determine your Risk" quiz.

Anonymity and Privacy on the Internet

http://www.stack.nl/~galactus/remailers/

Informative site discusses how you can protect your privacy and security on the Internet using remailers, encryption software, file wipe utilities, and pass phrases. Download all the software you'll need to keep your computer secure.

Atlantic Systems Group

http://www.ASG.unb.ca/

Designs, consults, and programs security systems including featured TurnStyle Firewall system. Provides ample information and reviews about TurnStyle. Includes trade show attendance listings, product information, dealer and distributor listings.

Byte Box Computer Enclosures

http://www.bytebox.com/bytebox/

Produces and markets Byte Box protective enclosures for computers and other technical equipment. Includes technical specifications and purchasing information.

Computer Security Day

http://www.acm.usl.edu/Home/CSD/

Created by the Association for Computing Machinery, Security Day is intended to remind computer users of the need to see if their computers or data are at risk. This page explains the origins and purpose of Security Day and provides addresses to important figures in public office.

Cryptography and PGP Page

http://rschp2.anu.edu.au:8080/crypt.html

This site includes a detailed discussion of PGP that introduces cryptography to newcomers (the cryptography FAQ goes into more detail). Also included is the actual program for the DOS, MAC, UNIX, and OS/2 environments.

Exide Electronics

http://www.exide.com/exide/

Designs and produces a wide array of power surge protection products. Includes background of products including technical specifications and applications. Provides company profile, ordering information, and technical support.

Forum of Incident Response and Security Teams

http://www.first.org/welcome.html

This site contains information on dozens of security related topics, such as viruses, risks, privacy, conferences, public keys, and trust. The page includes information on security publications, patches, training material, software tools, and alerts.

Index of Privacy Resources

http://www.hotwired.com/Lib/Privacy/

Excellent site for computer users interested in protecting themselves from Net weasels and Big Brother. This Wired magazine archive of government documents, legislation, articles on wiretapping and cryptography, and Internet groups provides useful news about security and the right to privacy.

Information Resource Engineering, Inc.

http://www.ire.com/

IRE specializes in Internet and remote access security. It provides advanced security options, based on standards-compliant encryption technology, that enable you to "confidently" use the Internet and public phone lines instead of expensive private providers.

Internet Firewalls Frequently Asked Questions

http://www.v-one.com/pubs/fw-faq/faq.htm

One of the hottest security topics these days is setting up a shield or "firewall" Web server that separates the Internet from a company's network. This site provides more information than you can probably handle in one sitting, including diagrams of firewall topologies.

McAfee VirusScan for Windows

http://www.mcafee.com/

Makers of the best-selling VirusScan software for Windows 95. Check out McAfee's other products, sign the Guest Book, download evaluation copies of all their software, or read the latest press releases.

National Computer Security Association

http://www.ncsa.com/

The Main Menu for this organization lists conferences, online seminars, and books about computer security; hot links are available for Internet firewalls, virus information, and late-breaking alerts. The Cool Stuff section provides free directories and tutorials created by NCSA; the Hot Links section lists hundreds of important Web sites concerned with security.

Network Systems Corporation

http://www.network.com/

Network security and Firewall systems to protect your valuable information. Check out their disaster recovery plan and information. Links to products and professional services, customer information, and frequently asked questions.

NH&A

http://www.nha.com/

An independent provider of network management, anti-virus, and security software. Check out the many products and companies they represent, including McAfee, TBAV, and others. Downloading information provided.

Raptor Systems, Inc.

http://www.raptor.com/

Develops network security software for use in government and business applications. Includes company profile, product specifications, and articles about their EAGLE Firewall family of products. Includes technical partners listings, network security library, and contact information.

S&S International PLC-Dr. Solomon's Online

http://www.sands.com

Provides online information about computer viruses and security issues. Also provides background of the Dr. Solomon line of computer security and auditing devices including the Anti-Virus Toolkit and Audit. Includes links to other virus-related sites and contact information.

Secure Computing Corporation

`http://www.sctc.com/`

Specializes in security and authentication products for network servers. Includes information about the LOCKout family of identification products. Also includes information about WebTrack security applications and more. Includes technical specifics and product features. Provides investment, technical partner, and contact information.

Security Engineering Services, Inc.

`http://www.blackmagic.com/ses/ses.html`

Provides a wide range of consulting and systems security information and services. Includes information about the COMSEC system, INFOSEC papers, and TEMPEST program management.

UN*X Net for Computer Security in Law Enforcement

`http://fox.nstn.ca/~cooke/`

UNIX security resource with information on PGP, security IDs, anti-virus, and disaster recovery planning. Site also discusses U.N.C.L.E. staff and services.

VeriSign, Inc.

`http://www.verisign.com/`

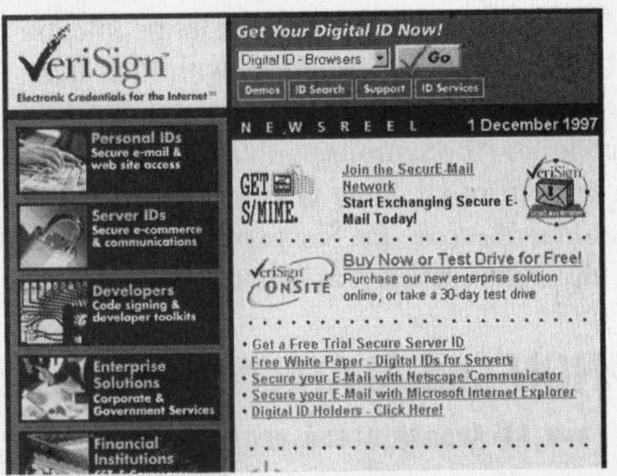

Produces digital authentication products and services. Includes information about the Digital ID Center which provides validity services of identification cards. Also includes facts about the Certificate family of identification products.

ViaCrypt

`http://www.pgp.com/`

Produces encrypting tools and software. Includes product facts, technical support, pricing, and ordering information. Includes press releases and reviews of ViaCrypt products.

The World Wide Web Security FAQ

`http://www.genome.wi.mit.edu/WWW/faqs/www-security-faq.html`

An invaluable resource for Webmasters and employees setting up Web servers. This 120K(!) FAQ includes solutions for protecting documents; creating secure PERL scripts and effective, fair user logs; and security concerns with and reviews of different operating environments. Recently converted to HTML format.

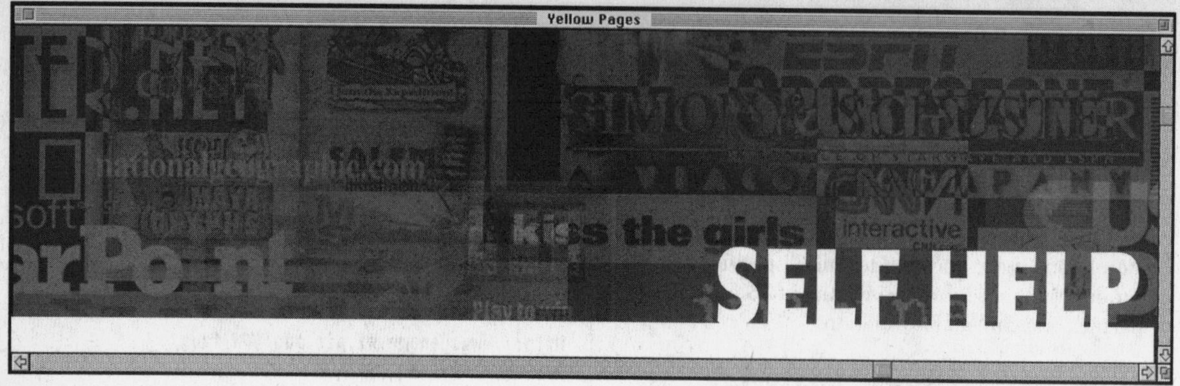

A B C D E F G H I J K L M N O P Q R S T U V W X Y Z

> Miss McFadden, today I begin rehearsals for my first New York play. It will be the most important day of my life. Am I nervous? No, I am not nervous. For I have meditated. I am relaxed. I am calm. I am confident.
>
> *Elliott Garfield in* The Goodbye Girl *(1977)*

Abuse—SafeHaven Organization
`http://www.i-p-d.com/safehaven/`

Nolo Home Page
`http://www.nolo.com/`

Self-Help & Psychology Magazine
`http://www.cybertowers.com/selfhelp/`

Abuse—SafeHaven Organization

`http://www.i-p-d.com/safehaven/`

This site is for people who have been victims of any type of abuse (sexual, emotional, physical, or other) and those whose family members or friends have been abused. This self-help group meets on the Internet to talk, feel safe, and begin or continue to heal. You'll find a helpful library with info on abuse, sexual abuse recovery, helping someone who has been abused, preventing abuse, looking for the warning signs of suicide, and offering family support. Sections are also offered on substance abuse, compulsive behavior, 12-step programs, battering/domestic violence, specific advice for children and young adults, self-mutilation/cutting, and men and abuse. Also includes info on Multiple Personality Disorder (MPD), Dissociative Identity Disorder (DID), trauma, memory, symptoms, illnesses, and recovery.

Adult Children Anonymous

`http://www.ncf.carleton.ca/acainnerpeace/`

Also known as Adult Children of Alcoholics. Read the ACA Personal Bill of Rights; it lists 20 of your personal rights as the child of an alcoholic. Examine the guide to feelings—the process of recovery to your true self. Or, learn about the characteristics people tend to have who grew up in dysfunctional households. Examine the tools and roles people use to cope with alcoholism's interference with their lives. Read about the 12-step recovery program (it's the same as Alcoholics Anonymous, with a few changes). Read excerpts from Dr. Janet Geringer Woititz's book, *Adult Children of Alcoholics.* She explores topics such as Adult Children Guess at What Normal Is.

AL-ANON and ALATEEN

`http://www.Al-Anon-Alateen.org/`

These groups offer self-help recovery programs for families and friends of alcoholics (regardless of whether the alcoholic seeks help or even recognizes the drinking problem). You can view this site in one of 12 languages. You can answer 20 questions to decide whether you need Al-Anon, 20 questions to help teenagers decide whether Alateen is for them, and 20 questions for adults who grew up with an alcoholic. You'll get info on the 12 steps of Al-Anon and the 12 traditions of Al-Anon and Alateen, as well as a guide for personal growth and group unity. You'll be able to find out where a meeting is being held near you. You can also order approved literature and recovery/service material and get links to other online resources.

The Bipolar Planet

http://www.tcnj.edu/~ellisles/BipolarPlanet/

Get info on Bipolar Disorder, which is characterized by mood swings. One variety of this disorder is manic depression. You can search the Mental Health Network database for the topic that concerns you. Includes letters and stories contributed by bipolars. You'll also get a link to a bipolar disorder FAQ and links to other resources.

Bootstraps

http://www.selfhelp.com/bootstraps.html

Bootstraps is a monthly column devoted to self help and self improvement. Read the current column or browse through the archives. Column titles include "Patience," "Making Yourself A Victim," "It's called SELF-help," "Motivation and Anxiety," and more.

COUNSELING CENTER—University at Buffalo

http://ub-counseling.buffalo.edu/

This site offers a wide selection of documents, Internet resources, referrals, and reading lists to help you with day-to-day stresses and difficult periods in your life. Self-help sections include Adjusting to University Life; Stress and Anxiety; Relationships; Alcohol and Drugs; Overcoming Depression and Preventing Suicide; Coping with Death & Grief; Health, Diet, Body Image; and Study Skills.

The Divorce Page

http://www.hughson.com/

This is a support page for those dealing with divorce or the loss of a relationship. It's a great clearinghouse for any divorce-related info you'll need. Includes steps toward recovery, as well as tips on what *not* to do when you are being divorced against your will. Check out the various divorce statistics, and get tips on preventing a divorce and saving your marriage. Get info on helping your children through the divorce, child support, and custody. You'll find the addresses of support groups, as well as links to mental, spiritual, and religious support. Online magazine and book recommendations are provided, as well as links to law and legal resources.

Healself Network

http://www.healself.com/main/

Offers online programs on health education, virtual health consultations, networking opportunities, and comprehensive holistic healthcare info to teach you skills for healthy living. Visit the Reference Desk for links to sites and addresses of organizations that deal with areas such as Acupuncture, Aromatherapy, Ayurvedic medicine (*ayurveda* means "science of life"), Biofeedback, Guided Imagery, Herbal Medicine, Homeopathy, Hypnotherapy, Traditional Chinese Medicine, Yoga, and more. Visit the News Stand for info on recent health-related developments, and learn about the latest research. Online holistic counseling is available, as well as energy-balance evaluations (these consultations are offered for a fee). Join related forums. Visit the Health Store for info on the latest healing aids. Includes a search engine to help you find topics quickly.

Kindred Spirits—Eating Disorder Info

http://www.geocities.com/Athens/Acropolis/1081/

People with eating disorders are concerned with food, weight, and appearance so much that their health, relationships, and daily activities suffer. They often develop these disorders as a reaction to emotional pain, separation issues, low self-esteem, depression, stress, trauma, or other problems. You'll find info on the causes or factors of an eating disorder, treatment, relapse, and recovery. You'll learn about identifying and dealing with anorexia nervosa, bulimia nervosa, and binge eating. The Warning Signs section is helpful for parents, friends, or family who think their loved ones may have an eating disorder; they'll learn what to look for and how to help. Includes poems and essays by those affected, as well as lyrics from well-known artists. You'll also find links to related sites.

Nolo Home Page

http://www.nolo.com/

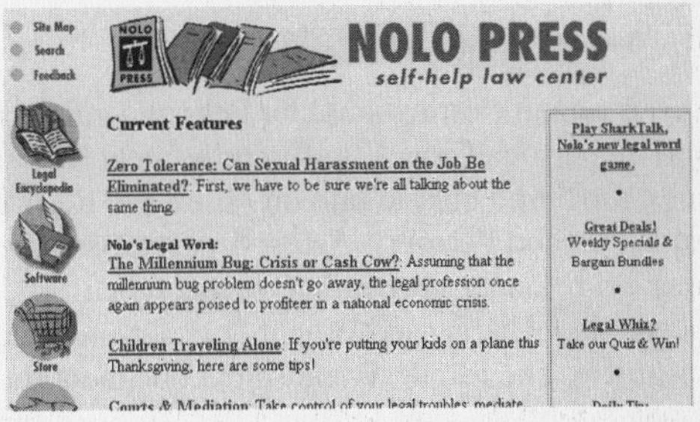

This is the home of Nolo Press, the self-help law center. Get legal info on running your small business; knowing your rights in the workplace; protecting yourself with patents, copyrights, and trademarks; taking control of your legal troubles through courts and mediation; and getting answers to your legal questions. You can also research wills and estate planning; your consumer rights; taking charge of your finances; dealing with tax problems; and learning how to buy, sell, rent, and protect your property. Includes recent articles from Nolo Press on timely issues.

Our-Kids Website

http://rdz.stjohns.edu/library/support/our-kids/

Our-Kids is a support group for parents, caregivers, and others working with children with physical and/or mental disabilities and delays. Members discuss their kids' accomplishments and setbacks in order to help others. Get info and help on feeding, learning, schools, medical resources, techniques, equipment, and coping. Includes inspirational writing, a Listserv (LISTSERV@MAELSTROM.STJOHNS.EDU), book recommendations, links to the home pages of Our-Kids members, and links to other Internet resources.

Self-Help & Psychology Magazine

http://www.cybertowers.com/selfhelp/

The goal of *Self-Help & Psychology Magazine* is to help people improve the quality of their daily lives. You'll find a huge amount of articles and info on topics such as Aging and Aging Parents; Alcohol/Nicotine/Other Drugs; Attention Deficit and Tourette's; Child, Family, and Parenting; Chronic Illness; Depression and Anxiety; Dreams; Eating Disorders; Gay/Lesbian/Bi/Trans; Health and Spirituality; Hypnosis; Internet Psychology; Loss and Bereavement; Mediation and Disputes; Men; Menopause; Psychotherapy; Relationships; Self-Help; Sex and Lust; Sports/Performance; Stress; Teens; Traumatic Stress; Women; Work and Finances; and Weight Loss.

Self Improvement Online

http://www.selfgrowth.com/

This is a great clearinghouse for links and guides to info on personal growth, self-improvement, and self-help. You'll find links to info on Abuse and Recovery; Addiction and Recovery; Aging; Anxiety; Assertiveness; Body Language; Death, Dying & Grief; Depression; Dieting and Weight Loss; Divorce; Eating Disorders; The Family; Friendship; Loneliness and the Single Adult Life; Goal Setting; and Memory Training. Other links offer info on Men's Issues; Pregnancy; Public Speaking; Sexuality, Relaxation, Meditation, & Stress; Speed Reading; and Women's Issues. Further links explore Adult Development; Anger; Building Enthusiasm; Career Development; Child Development and Parenting; Codependency and Recovery; Communication; Exercise; Infant Development and Parenting; Leadership Skills; Longevity; Love, Intimacy, & Marriage; Medical Advice; Positive Thinking; Sales Skills; Stepfamilies; and Teenagers and Parenting.

SELF-Therapy Training Program

http://www.execpc.com/~tonyz/

Get info and tips on dealing with anger, prioritizing your life, and healing from sexual abuse. Take the relationship analysis questionnaire (sexual or nonsexual). Check out the guidelines for emotional health; go through the checklist to see whether you are emotionally healthy. Explore topics on motivation, changing any unhealthy outlooks you have on life, subconscious life scripts, and loving yourself. Includes a humorous discussion of how to have a lousy sex life. New topics are added continuously. You can also get confidential, practical, and free advice from a therapist via email here.

THRIVEnet

http://www.thrivenet.com/

Learn about resilience, thriving, and gaining strength from adversity. Get tips on emotional health and becoming life-competent, resilient, durable, playful, and free. You'll learn the key factors of human resiliency and the barriers to achieving that goal. Read about survivors, such as a woman who was shot in the back of the head by hijackers and a dance instructor who had her leg amputated after a boating accident. Learn about the mindset that helps you survive traumatic events such as these and then go on to thrive in life. You'll also find links to other sites to help you thrive.

NEWSGROUPS

alt.abuse-recovery

alt.abuse.recovery

alt.abuse.offender.recovery

alt.abuse.transcendence

alt.adoption

Alt.child-support

Alt.dads-rights

Alt.mens-rights

alt.psychology.help

alt.sexual.abuse.recovery

alt.sexual.abuse.recovery.d

alt.suicide.holidays

alt.support.abuse-partners

alt.support.anxiety-panic

alt.support.attn-deficit

alt.support.cancer

alt.support.cerebral-palsy

alt.support.crohns-colitis

alt.support.depression

alt.support.depression.manic

alt.support.depression.seasonal

Alt.support.divorce

alt.support.eating-disord

alt.support.ocd

Alt.support.single-parents

alt.support.sleep-disorder

Alt.support.step-parents

bit.listserv.autism

bit.listserv.down-syn

misc.health.alternative

sci.med.psychobiology

sci.psychology.misc

sci.psychology.psychotherapy

Soc.men

soc.support.depression.crisis

soc.support.depression.family

soc.support.depression.manic

soc.support.depression.misc

soc.support.depression.seasonal

soc.support.depression.treatment

Soc.women

FTP & GOPHER SITES

ftp://ftp.damicon.fi/pub/drugs/hyperreal.com/

ftp://ftp.loc.gov/

gopher://cyfer.esusda.gov:70/11/CYFER-net/resources

gopher://gopher.gsa.gov:70/00/staff/pa/cic/children/angry

gopher://gopher.gsa.gov:70/00/staff/pa/cic/children/behavior

gopher://gopher.gsa.gov:70/00/staff/pa/cic/health/schizo.txt

gopher://gopher.uiuc.edu:70/11/UI/CSF/Coun/SHB

gopher://hemp.uwec.edu/

gopher://moose.uvm.edu:70/11/Other%20UVM%20Gophers%20and%20Information%20Resources/University%20Associates%20in%20Psychiatry/Child%20Behavior%20Checklist%20%28Achenbach%20CBCL%29

gopher://tinman.mes.umn.edu:80/11

gopher://tinman.mes.umn.edu:80/11/FatherNet

gopher://zippy.nimh.nih.gov:70/00/documents/nimh/other/alz

gopher://zippy.nimh.nih.gov:70/00/documents/nimh/other/anxiety

gopher://zippy.nimh.nih.gov:70/00/documents/nimh/other/Medicate

gopher://zippy.nimh.nih.gov:70/00/documents/nimh/other/OCD

gopher://zippy.nimh.nih.gov:70/00/documents/nimh/other/Paranoia

LISTSERV

LISTSERV@MAELSTROM.STJOHNS.EDU

Related Sites

http://www.iugm.org/av/

http://www.chriscor.com/linkstoa.htm

http://asa.ugl.lib.umich.edu/chdocs/support/chronic.html#autoim

http://www.teachhealth.com/

http://www.cmhc.com/archives/editor14.htm

http://www.mentalhealth.com/

http://law.net/roundnet.html

http://www.efn.org/~djz/birth/birthindex.html

http://lawlib.wuacc.edu/washlaw/uslaw/statelaw.html

http://www.best.com./~savage/voices/

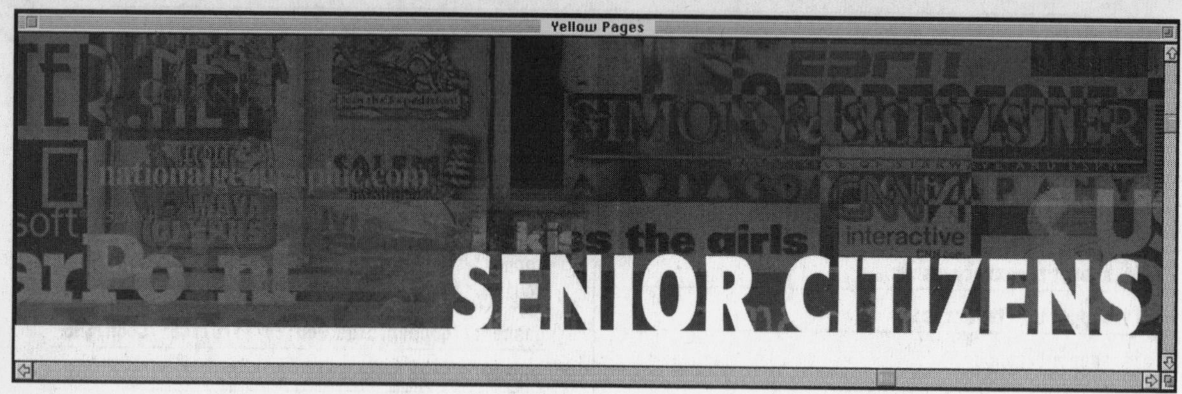

> I'm not interested in age. People who tell me their age are silly. You're as old as you feel.
>
> *Elizabeth Arden*

AARP

http://www.aarp.org/

This very user-friendly site contributes to AARP's goal of allowing senior citizens to lead the rich and fulfilling lives that they are accustomed to. Not only by staying well-informed, but also by staying active.

The Adopt a Grandparent Program

http://hanksville.phast.umass.edu/misc/Grandparents.html

The program's online resource for people interested in volunteering or learning about regional activities.

The Aging Research Centre (ARC)

http://www.hookup.net/mall/aging/agesit59.html

Researchers and laypersons alike can find usable information on aging from the University of Toronto Centre for Studies of Aging. Point and click access to the Real Audio program by or can download as needed. Site includes links to additional university resources.

Related Sites

http://www.americanair.com/aa_home/servinfo/senior.htm

http://www.ageofreason.com/

http://www.alz.org/

http://www.designretire.com/

NRP TOP PICKS

Portals Aging
http://www.portals.pdx.edu/~isidore/aging.html

SENIORCOM Site Map
http://www.senior.com/sitemap.html

Senior Sites
http://www.seniorsites.com/

Burma Shave Signs

http://seniors-site.com/funstuff/burma.html

This is a senior site because if you remember Burma Shave signs, you are a senior citizen. Refresh your memory; share with the grandchildren; if you can remember one that isn't listed here, submit it to the site to share with others.

Caregiver Network Inc.

http://www.caregiver.on.ca/

The Canadian woman who maintains this site became a caregiver herself overnight. She is very aware of what resources you need to take care of someone you care about. Most links are in the United States, and many will refer you to services in your own area.

Continental Airlines–Senior Programs

http://www.flycontinental.com/products/senior/

As a senior citizen, you can take advantage of many discounts available just to you, but first you must know about them. Here's just one of the discount programs available to seniors—one of the best, with 10 percent off offered on most flights. Check this one out.

Related Sites

http://www.aagpgpa.org/

http://www.naela.com/

http://www.on-call.com/

http://www.senioralternatives.com/

Elderhostel

`http://www.elderhostel.org/`

With the fundamental belief that no one should ever stop learning, this site provides access to resources around the world to continue your education. Currently, you must register through postal mail, but all of the registration information is at the site.

Friendly4Seniors Web Sites

`http://www.friendly4seniors.com/`

This site simply offers links to sites that are of interest to seniors. Choose your topic—Government, Financial, Housing, Medical, and many more—click and find what you're looking for.

Grand Times

`http://www.grandtimes.com/`

An e-zine dedicated to the needs of active retirees. Example topics include travel, useful products, beating the casino, high-tech bird feeders, and relief from arthritis, back pain, and migraines.

Illinois State Police–Senior Citizen Scams Alert

`http://www.state.il.us/isp/saf00004.htm`

You've heard it on the news and read about it. You're sure it could never happen to you. But how do those seniors get bilked out of their life savings by fast talking con artists? Check this site to learn just how each scam works. From the Pigeon Drop to Home Repair Fraud, learn how the crook makes his approach and what to be alert for. This is one you should not miss.

InfoSeniors

`http://www.infoseniors.com/`

Aimed at Canadian senior citizens and their families, this site provides one-stop-shopping for all senior services in Canada. Find out what's available to you as a senior citizen of Canada. Some of the information posted here will be of interest to all seniors.

National Center on Elder Abuse

`http://www.interinc.com/NCEA/`

What is elder abuse? Who is in danger? Learn the facts and statistics here. Learn to recognize elder abuse in your community. Learn what you can do to help—hotline phone numbers, who to call, what to do.

National Council of Senior Citizens Home Page

`http://www.ncscinc.org/`

This senior citizen advocacy group, founded in 1961, is a proponent of "senior power." Here you can learn how much you can truly depend on Social Security in your senior years, the truth about the national budget, and more. Take the quiz to find out how much you know about where Social Security dollars go, sign the guest book, learn about the NCSC, and even join from this page.

The National Senior Citizens Law Center

`http://www.nsclc.org`

National Senior Citizens Law Center advocates, litigates, and publishes on low-income elderly and disability issues: including Medicare, Medicaid, SSI, nursing homes, age discrimination pensions.

Over the Hill Gang, International

`http://www.skiersover50.com/`

If you're over 50 and enjoy skiing and other outdoor activities, check out this site. The Over the Hill Gang provides discounts on everything from lift tickets to lodging and ski shop purchases. The group also plans trips to North American, South American, and European ski areas. In the summer, there's whitewater rafting, bicycling, hiking, and golf. If one spouse is over 50, you both qualify for membership.

Portals Aging

`http://www.portals.pdx.edu/~isidore/aging.html`

Provides links to resources for people to find information on the aging process. Covers discussion groups, databases, library catalogs, and aging-related home pages.

SENIORCOM Site Map

`http://www.senior.com/sitemap.html`

There's lots of interest to seniors on this site, including a chat room and message center devoted to the senior citizen community. You'll find articles of interest and links to other pages. Unique features of this page are the chat room and message board. Be sure to read the Solutions column and definitely check the Personals.

Seniors Internet Mall

http://www.ageofreason.com/mall.htm

This is a directory of businesses and services that are geared to the senior or that offer special senior citizen discounts. There are hundreds of links to businesses you'll want to know about.

Senior Sites

http://www.seniorsites.com/

SITES
Welcome to Senior Sites!
Senior Sites is the most comprehensive web source of non-profit housing and services for seniors. With over 5000 listed communities, Senior Sites is a valuable resource for seniors and their families interested in exploring the non-profit housing option. We invite you to search our database for non-profit housing communities in the United States, Guam and Puerto Rico.
Additionally Senior Sites includes links to websites with senior housing resources, information to guide you in selecting a non-profit housing facility, and a directory of national and state senior housing associations. Spend some time looking around Senior Sites exploring the non-profit housing alternative and send us comments so that we may serve you better.

Site that lists nonprofit housing and services for senior citizens. Also includes National and State resources.

Seniors-Site

http://seniors-site.com/

If you're already acquainted with Yahoo!, this site will look very familiar to you. The wide array of links here all keep senior citizens in mind, though, from travel information to fraud, scams, and abuses.

Senior World Tours: Active Travel for Mature Adults

http://www.gorp.com/seniorwo/

This travel company, a subsidiary of Zim Hi-Country Tours, Inc., offers special tours and trips for seniors. A sample listing includes trips to Yellowstone and Alaska featuring snowmobiling and summer adventures.

Social Security Online

http://www.ssa.gov/

Official Web site of the Social Security Administration. Includes announcements and reports on issues related to social security. Contact information and regular updates.

Transitions, Inc. Elder Care Consulting

http://members.aol.com/sudeka/eldercare.html

Transitions locates and arranges services for older adults and their caregivers. Company representatives assess your employees' needs, hold seminars, and provide eldercare counseling.

The Wild, Wacky, Convoluted World of Marty Z, Senior Citizen

http://www.he.net/~martyz/martyz.html

Here's a shining example of what you can do with a personal Web page. Learn about Marty—his adventures in the Navy, as a barbecue chef, and the story of Marty's dental adventures. Marty shares his stock picks and some of his favorite things, including his family.

NEWSGROUPS

ncf.ca.senior

soc.senior.health+fitness

soc.senior.issues

Related Sites

http://www.senioroptions.com/

http://www.seniorlaw.com/index.htm

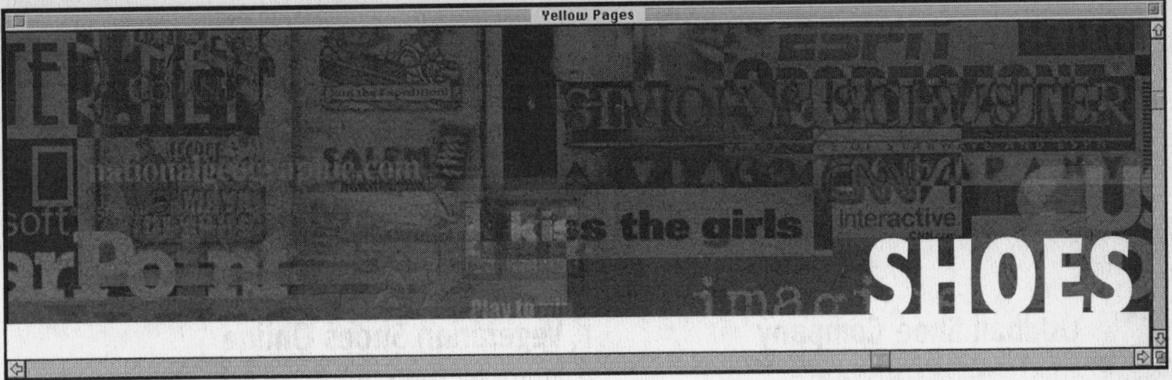

> And I was just thinking: as much as I really admire your shoes, and as much as I'd love to have a pair just like them, I really wouldn't want to be *in* your shoes at this particular time and place.
>
> *C.D. Bales in* Roxanne *(1987)*

Kenneth Cole Shoes
http://www.kencole.com/

Oddball Shoe Company
http://www.oddballshoe.com/

Solemates
http://www.solemates.com/

NRP TOP PICKS

Birkenstock

http://www.birkenstock-shoes.com/

From the company that brought comfort back to footware, this site offers online catalogs and ordering information for adults and a few adorable Birks for kids. Good quality photos, model names, and size and price information.

Dexter Shoe Company Online

http://www.dextershoe.com/

The history of Dexter shoes and online men's and women's catalogs divided by shoe type (casual, walking, saddles, bucks, and so on). If you would rather try the shoes on in person, the company makes it easy to find your nearest Dexter retailer—just enter your ZIP code.

Dexter Shoes Factory Outlet Stores

http://www.dexteroutlets.com/

Visit this site for the same Dexter quality at discount prices. Includes a map of outlet store locations, new store openings, and a brief history of Dexter factory outlets. Unfortunately, there is no online catalog or purchase option at this site.

Etienne Aigner

http://www.etienneaigner.com/

The site of this classic footwear and handbag manufacturer is professional, streamlined, and well organized. Visitors can browse the online catalog and place orders here. Be sure to check the Sale page for good bargains on shoes and handbags that will never go out of style.

J.Amesbury & Co.

http://www.jingo.com/amesbury/

An exceptionally high quality custom shoemaker. The site includes the history of bespoke shoemaking and the company, and customer inquiry forms.

Kenneth Cole Shoes

http://www.kencole.com/

This stylish site reflects the qualities Kenneth Cole shoes are famous for: clean, simple lines with great staying power. Online men's and women's catalogs, company information, retail locations, and a fun stuff page.

Oddball Shoe Company

http://www.oddballshoe.com/

This site belongs to a Portland, Oregon company specializing in large size shoes—available up to sizes 16–20. A nicely done Web site. Take a look here if you are in the large size market.

Rockport Shoes

http://www.walking-shoes.com/

Quality, comfortable walking shoes are available through the online catalog at this site. It also includes a link to The ReSole Center, which is the only authorized Rockport resoling service.

Save Your Soles

http://saveyoursole.com/

This site offers an online catalog of several well-known manufacturers. Currently, the site is advertising a free resole of an old pair when you purchase a new pair of Sebago, Rockport, Sperry, New Balance, or Timberland. Hurry for this deal!

Solemates

http://www.solemates.com/

An ingenious solution to the problem of having two different size feet! This site is a registry of people who have this fairly common foot size problem. It connects you with people who have the opposite sizes as you. For example, if you wear a size 8 on the left, and a size 7 on the right, you need to find someone who wears a size 8 on the right, and a size 7 on the left. Anyone walking around in the wrong size shoes should rush to this site!

The James Clinton Company

http://www.usgator.com/

This site belongs to a company specializing in fine alligator products, including boots, shoes, wallets, and belts. All shoes are 100% handmade, handlasted, and handstitched with leather heels and prime leather soles. Prices aren't low, but neither is the quality.

Vegetarian Shoes Online

http://www.vegetarian-shoes.co.uk/

This site offers shoes made of a synthetic mix of polyurethane and polyester microfibers as an alternative to leather. According to the site, the shoes are highly water restistant, lightweight, scuff-resistant, durable, and comfortable. There is a shoe conversion chart and care and maintainence instructions.

walktall

http://www.walktall.couk.com/

A U.K.-based company that specializes in larger sizes (12–17 U.K. size). Offers name brands such as Teva, Converse, Hush Puppies, Doc Martins, and more. Be sure to confirm your correct size by using the size conversion table on the Ordering Details page!

Related Sites
http://www.netorder.com.au/albundy/
http://www.bikerboots.com/
http://www.bottinoshoes.com/
http://www.globalgateway.com/ni/jackson/index.htm
http://www.thefinishline.com/
http://www.sneakerworld.com/
http://www.sportsitedirect.com/
http://www.onlineshoes.com/
http://www.striderite.com/
http://www.ozemail.com.au/~cyborg6/

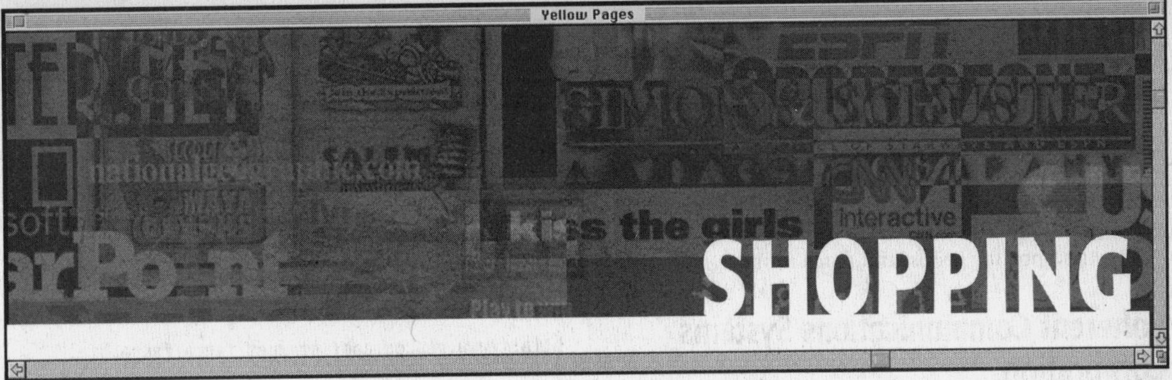

> I love to go shopping. I love to freak out salespeople. They ask me if they can help me, and I say, "Have you got anything I'd like?" Then they ask me what size I need, and I say, "Extra medium."
>
> *Steven Wright*

NRP Top Picks

CouponNet
`http://coupon.com/coupon.html`

Good Stuff Cheap
`http://www.goodstuffcheap.com/index.html`

Magazine Warehouse
`http://cdnow.com/mags`

The Microsoft Plaza
`http://www.eshop.com`

SAM'S Club
`http://www.samsclub.com`

AmericaNet.Com—Free Classified Advertising

`http://www.americanet.com/Classified/`

Provides free national classified advertising, including help wanted, cars, trucks, RVs, commercial real estate, and residential real estate. Lets you submit your ad.

The Americas

`http://www.integctr.com/americas/`

Specializes in folk art and artifacts by Indian and Indigenous peoples of the American Southwest, Mexico, and South America. Includes a catalog and photo gallery of artwork. Email questions are encouraged.

Antiques World

`http://www.antiquesworld.com/`

Features online antique shops, classified ads of antiques and collectibles for sale and wanted, and other resources for collectors and antiquers.

Art of the States

`http://www.pol.com/states/`

Offers limited edition prints and collector series Christmas ornaments. Features a collection of native birds and wildflowers, along with the capital building of its respective state. (All paintings by W.D. Gaither MSB.)

Business and Safety Cartoons by Goff

`http://www.fileshop.com/personal/tgoff/`

Presents samples of cartoons by professional cartoonist Ted Goff. Geared to people who are responsible for an in-house newsletter, training manual, presentation, brochure, or other publication. Available cartoons have safety, teamwork, quality, management, sales, technology, and computer themes. Also provides links to other related sites.

Cartoon Heaven

`http://www.aardvark.ie/cartoon-heaven/`

Presents an animation art gallery in Melbourne, Australia, including artwork from all the major studios. Includes an online catalog and links to related sites.

Catalog Live

http://cataloglive.com

Top shopping site winner! Shop for great upscale items, including Williams Sonoma, Preserves by Viki's, Hoop Backboards, and Golf Gifts. Other shopping categories include wine, flowers, gourmet foods, cookies, sporting goods, and much more.

Coherent Communications Systems Corporation

http://www.coherent.com

Offers voice enhancement technology, including echo cancellation platforms and associated network software. Also provides teleconferencing products for audio, video, and desktop conferencing applications.

CouponNet

http://coupon.com/coupon.html

Do you want to save money? Here is the ultimate online coupon and rebate connection. Includes reference library, recipes, and a coupon trading center. A site for anyone looking to save money while shopping to their heart's content.

Dakota Engraving, Etc.

http://www.uspronet.com/engrave/index.html

Specializes in key tags personalized with your name, URL, email address, and N-Number. Also offers bicycle plates and license plate frames.

Distant Caravans

http://www.greatbasin.com/~caravan/

Serves people interested in the Middle Ages, renaissance, belly dancing, ethnic jewelry, amber, and more. Imports goods from Afghanistan, India, Pakistan, and Poland.

dotSpiegel

http://www.spiegel.com/spiegel/

Spiegel's new online catalog and magazine, including features, merchandise, stories, tips, and contests. Experts also answer questions about interior design, travel, gardening, and more.

Eureka! The Web Junction

http://www.wilder.com/eureka.html

Provides access to an array of unique products. Appellation Spring's Winery T-shirts, Sweet Enhancement candy, solar panel power products, and software can be purchased from this site.

Fanco International Corp.

http://www.webcom.com/~stannet/fanco/fanco.html

Imports PVC laundry, storage, and shopping bags. Also imports slippers and luggage carts from China. Includes an online catalog.

Feathered Friends

http://www.halcyon.com/featherd/welcome.htm

Produces down sleeping bags, outerwear, and accessories. Really, the friends aren't feathered anymore.

Fox Color and Light Home Page

http://www.cyberthings.com/

Creates CyberFashions and CyberToys, including electronic, interactive, programmable clothing, jewelry, gifts, toys, and accessories.

The Front Page

http://www.thefrontpage.com/welcome.html

Offers an extensive mix of shops and services, such as recreational activities, art, computer consulting, and more. American Indian collectibles, telecommunication services, health and weight management products, Havana Cigar Club memberships, and psychic cards included.

Gilltro-Electronics, Inc.

http://www.giltronix.com

Offers remote access systems, local connectivity products, and peripheral sharing devices. Includes product overviews, service and support, and order forms.

Good Stuff Cheap

http://www.goodstuffcheap.com/index.html

Get new, brand-name products below wholesale. Provides an enormous selection of products. Categories include automotive, clothing, baby needs, luggage, tools, and fitness.

The Hahn Company

http://hahncompany.com

The Hahn Company owns and manages more than 40 shopping malls throughout North America. Shop for toys, jewelry, home entertainment, clothing, and more. Also presents retail leasing space information and retail tenant lists. News and games categories offered as well.

Handcrafts Unlimited

http://www.awod.com/gallery/crafts/hu/

Offers a variety of quality hand-crafted items, including clothing, costumes, calligraphy and art, lamp shades, ornaments, miniatures, tole painting, and many other items by request.

Hawaiian Express Unlimited

http://planet-hawaii.com/~hawnexp/

Take a virtual shopping trip to Hawaii. Purchase clothing, coffee, flowers and baskets, hand-crafted jewelry, Hawaiian art, and photos.

Ideal Engraving Co., Inc.

http://www.cybercom.com/~rbeir

Manufactures a complete line of marking products, including steel hand stamps and dies, interchangeable type and holders, numbering heads, and bench presses.

International Craft Directory

http://www.catalog.com/giftshop/icd/icd1.htm

Serves as a guide to crafts and gifts, including clothing, furniture, and jewelry.

Internet Green Marketplace

http://envirolink.org/products/

Features services and products of environmentally and socially responsible companies. Also provides links to related sites.

John Charles Antiques

http://www.londonmall.co.uk/antiques

Deals mainly in furniture originating from the 17th century to the beginning of the 20th century. Buys and sells fine oil and watercolor paintings, old and new prints, clocks, chandeliers, china, glass, mirrors, pewter, copper, brass, bronze, silver, and gold.

Keller's Appaloosas

http://www.babcom.com/keller/

Offers breeding quality Appaloosa horses for sport, halter, and performance. Provides online sales and pedigree information, as well as photos and pricing. Also has links to related sites.

KRAMER Handgun Leather

http://www.kramerleather.com/

Sells horsehide concealment holsters and accessories for the armed professional. Offers specialized designs for government covert operations, military special warfare, undercover police, and dignitary protection details.

Laid Back Designs

http://www.travelsource.com/travelstore/lbd/lbd.html

Offers a catalog of hammocks—high quality, comfortable, versatile, portable hammocks. Great for the office.

Lucia's Little Houses

http://media1.hypernet.com/knight.html

Offers Grand Ideas for Small Houses, a portfolio of 12 designs for small homes by an architectural firm in Maine.

Made in America

http://amsquare.com/america/made.html

Offers American hand-made goods and services. Offers a separate section on career and resume management. Also has links to related sites.

Magazine Warehouse

http://cdnow.com/mags

Offers subscriptions to more than 300 magazines in more than 80 categories, including computing, music, science, sports, fitness, and fashion. What, no million dollar winners?!

Maude Asbury

http://www.deltanet.com/intersphere/ma

Offers distinctive photo albums and desk accessories handcrafted in the United States.

Maverick Communications

http://www.maverickcomm.com

Offers online shopping for radio and communications equipment, as well as repair and customer services for such equipment.

The Microsoft Plaza

http://www.eshop.com

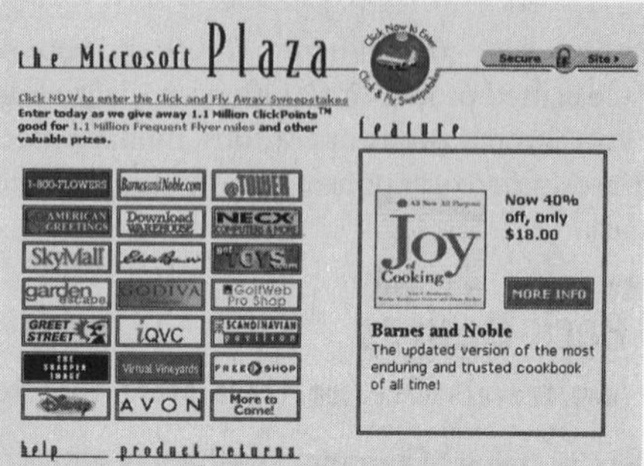

Tower Records, 1-800-Flowers, Spiegel, and more advertise at this site. Job listings also provided. Merchants can create promotions tailored to each shopper.

Musicmaker's Kits, Inc.

http://www.primenet.com/~musikit/index.html

Makers of unusual stringed instruments, kits, plans, supplies, and completed instruments, including dulcimers, mandolins, zithers, banjos, and harps. Provides pictures, prices, and an audio sample of each instrument. Also provides information about the company and links to related sites.

Neuromedical Supplies, Inc.

http://www.neuro.com/

Ordering catalog for neuromedical supplies such as caps, gowns, lab supplies, needs, and more. Check out their catalog for a full list of items available.

Next to Nothing

http://www.winternet.com/~julie/ntn.html

Provides information on getting free stuff both on and off the Internet. Includes free offers from magazines, Internet sites, newsletters, TV, and more.

Paramount Custom Cabinetry

http://www.bizlink.com/paramount

Specializes in custom cabinetry, kitchens, computer furniture, and wall units. Offers the latest computerized designs and layouts.

Perspective Visuals, Inc.

http://www.pvisuals.com/dinosaur_museum/dinosaur_museum.html

Provides information and sales for the Smithsonian Dinosaur Museum CD-ROM. Includes background, sample graphics, and contact information.

The Quiltery

http://mmink.com/mmink/dossiers/quilt/quilt.html

Provides online sales of handmade quilts. Includes photos, pricing, and ordering information.

Roctronics Lighting

http://www.roctronics.com/

Provides lighting, laser graphics, and special effects for nightclubs, theaters, stage performances, exhibits, trade shows, museums, concerts, amusement centers, and special events.

Rubber Stamp Queen

http://www.dol.com/queen/

Provides sales of uniquely designed rubber stamps. Includes catalog information, examples of stamps, links to related pages, and contact addresses.

SAM'S Club

http://www.samsclub.com

SAM'S Club is a membership warehouse club for business and home. SAM'S Club on the Web is your link to SAM'S Club Music Cafe, SAM'S Club Electronics Sampler, SAM'S Club Theater, The VIRTUAL CLUB, SAM'S Club Online Shopping Network, and more! Showcasing the latest in Internet technology, SAM'S Club on the Web has four-color animation and full sound capabilities.

SCHWA Online

http://kzsu.stanford.edu/uwi/schwa/schwa.html

Provides online sales of the SCHWA line of products. What exactly are the SCHWA line of products? Well, let's say they are not of this world—assorted T-shirts, stickers, and other alien defense products. Weird? Yes. Interesting? Yes. Check this site out; it's unlike any other out there.

Scintilla Alternative Lighting, Gifts, and Accessories

http://www.mindspring.com/~bart/scintilla.html

Presents a collection of functional art in forms of lighting fixtures, jewelry, frames, and other choice accessories.

SeaVision USA

http://www.seavisionusa.com

Offers the finest in underwater vision technology, from color-correcting filters to prescription lenses for your diving mask.

Sumeria Product List

http://www.sumeria.com/

Produces and provides sales of CD-ROMs on various subjects. Includes QuickTime movie examples of catalog. Also includes CD-ROM background and ordering information.

Surplus United States Government Sales

http://www.drms.dla.mil/index.html

The Defense Reutilization and Marketing Service sells surplus Department of Defense properties to the general public, including computers, vehicles, aircraft parts, scrap metal, clothing, and furniture.

Tough Traveler Gear

http://www.travelsource.com/travelstore/toughtraveler/toughtraveler.html

Presents Tough Traveler Gear online. Features soft luggage, backpacks, camera bags, duffel bags, and child carriers. Guarantee information available.

Tickets and Travel, Inc.

http://www.inetdirect.net/tnt

Provides online sales for tickets to events including sports, concerts, and more. Also provides travel reservation services and includes company and contact information.

Uncommon Connections

http://www.mps.org/uncommon/

Offers online marketplace. Includes some unique products and unusual gift items such as coffee, off-the-wall checks, sportswear, and art. Provides secure credit card transactions for all online merchants.

The World Shopping & Information Network

http://www.wsin.com

Shopping, travel, real estate, news, entertainment & more. Comprehensive listings, exciting colorful graphics, easy-to-navigate directories and search engines on site to locate anything, anytime!

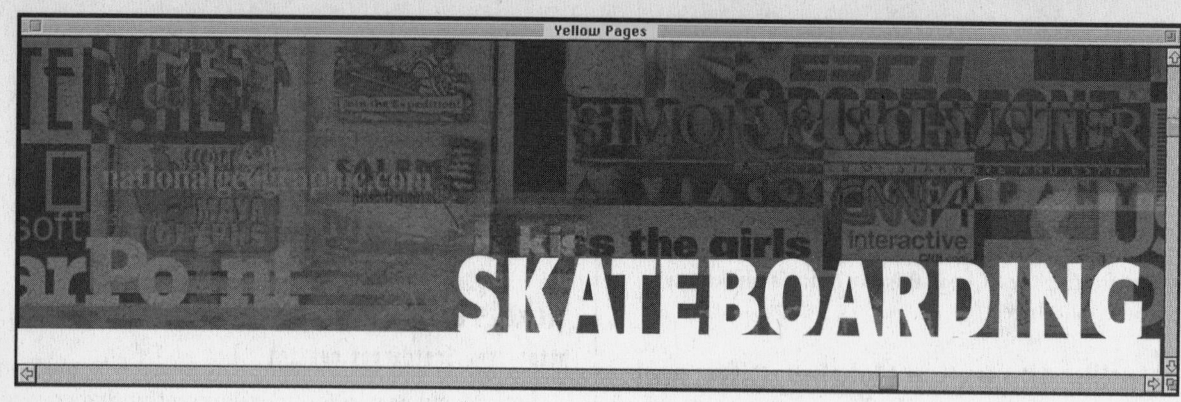

> # Do what you fear most and you control fear.
>
> *Tom Hopkins*

An Interview with Tony Hawk

http://www.burstgum.com/thawk.html

A RealAudio and text interview of skateboard grate, Tony Hawk, after he won Fist Place at Destination Extreme in South Padre Island.

BoardZ Online Magazine

http://www.boardz.com/

This site is for anyone who likes to ride boards, whether on skateboards, surfboards, snowboards, mountainboards, or skis. Check out the numerous articles and back issues for the latest and greatest in the boarding world.

DansWORLD Skateboarding

http://www.cps.msu.edu/~dunhamda/dw/dansworld.html

Dan's is a world of photos, articles, and commentary. Even the non-skater can appreciate the "wisdom" of the *Zen of Skateboarding.*

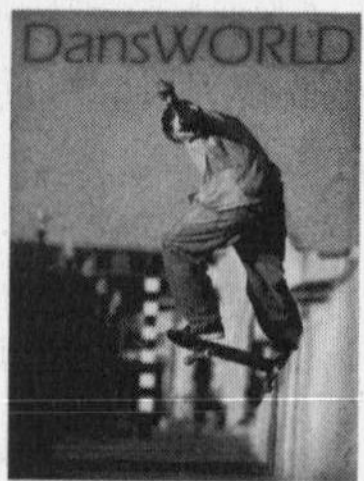

The Skateboarding Legalization Resource
http://www.summersault.com/legalskate/

ESPN X Games Skateboarding

http://espn.sportszone.com/editors/xgames/skate/index.html

ESPN's X Games series includes many "extreme" sports. This page features skating articles, a Q&A with Tony Hawk, and multimedia files of many of the sports other superstars.

THe FLaMMiNG BiSCuiT

http://www.delta.edu/~jdkris/index.html

More photo galleries, links, and skating spots and parks make up the Flamming Biscuit site. There's only one question remaining: What is a "flamming"?

Free Cheese

http://bugsmagazine.com/freecheese/index.html

Although this site is only partially about skateboarding, it's too darned entertaining to pass up. Besides, Andy wants attention, so let's give it to him.

Northern California Downhill Skateboarding Association

http://www.interlnk.net/longboard/default.asp

The NCDSA is dedicated to a different vein of skateboarding, longboarding. The site has articles, chat groups, organization links, equipment, pics, riding techniques, and more. One feature not found anywhere else—a page dedicated to crash stories.

Ryan's Skateboard Page

http://www.geocities.com/Yosemite/Trails/2221/homeset.html

Ryan has a useful page, here. You can learn how to do tricks from the ollie to the varial, read reviews of skate movies, check out skater parks in Colorado, view photos, and jump to other sites with links.

sKATEBOARD.COM

http://www.skateboard.com/tydu/skatebrd/skate.html

This thorough site offers many entertaining articles, skatepark lists, upcoming events, classifieds, ramp plans, and the a huge array of relevant skate links.

Skateboarder's Site

http://www.planet.fi/~hessu9/skate/

This site offers detailed lessons on how to do different tricks, including photos. You can also check out their links and photos.

The Skateboarding Legalization Resource

http://www.summersault.com/legalskate/

Not just another skate page, the SLR actually has a cause! If you are working to ensure the legalization of skateboarding in your town or want to build a skatepark, come here first to get the latest tips, success stories, and other useful links.

Skateworld

http://home.thezone.net/~troy/

This new site offers skate ramp plans, tricks, and links, as well as skater album reviews (and audio clips), a chat page, and more.

Tasmanian Sk8boarding

http://www.tased.edu.au/tasonline/devskate/devskate.htm

Another site of links, tricks, and news, but how often do we see any sites from Tasmania? Looks like there's more to Tasmania than just drooling devils.

Tum Yeto

http://skateboard.com/

Tum Yeto is a commercial skateboarding concern that seems to get mentioned in a lot of other Web sites, so there must be something to that. It offers links to companies that make products that they (an d all serious skaters) seem to approve of. A very colorful site.

Unorganized Skateboard Page

http://www.netpower.no/~troy/skate.html

This site reviews products, skate videos, punk and skate music, and makes sure not to leave out the wives and girlfriends of the pro skaters. Join the chat room, learn the difference between skateboarding and inline skating, and sign the guest book.

Related Sites
http://www.b-house.com/
http://www.magicnet.net/~choux/index.html
http://ireland.iol.ie/~owenh/freeflow/
http://www.geocities.com/Colosseum/Arena/3825/
http://www.krisco.com/home.html
http://www.landsurfer.com/
http://www.teamepic.com/index.html
http://www.souldoubt.com/index.html
http://www.xtremewheelz.com/index2.html
http://www.rollercycle.com/

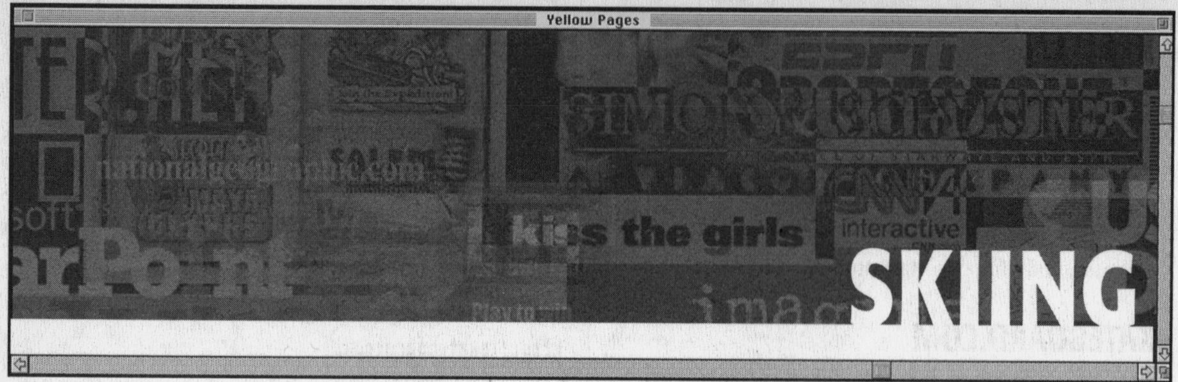

A
B
C
D
E
F
G
H
I
J
K
L
M
N
O
P
Q
R
S
T
U
V
W
X
Y
Z

Cross country skiing is great if you live in a small country.

Steven Wright

Austria Ski Vacation Package

http://www.snowpak.com/snowpak/resorts/austriaresorts.html

Part of the Snow Pak Online site, here you can get quotes for ski vacation packages in Austria, and plan your dream vacation. Be sure to register for full color brochures to be mailed to you and check out the live resort cams.

Bittersweet Ski Resort Online

http://www.mvcc.com/bu/bittersweet/

Here you'll find plenty of information about Bittersweet Ski Resort. Current weather and powder conditions, lessons available, price list, specials, and more. Bittersweet is located close to Chicago, Detroit, and Indianapolis.

Boston Mills-Brandywine Ski Resort

http://www.bmbw.com/

Located in the Cleveland/Akron area of Ohio, these two ski resorts operate jointly. Check out their Home Page for powder and weather reports, services available, rental fees, night skiing info, and lots more.

Related Sites

http://weber.u.washington.edu/~shogun/skiing/school.html

http://vrbo.com/vrbo/532.htm

http://www.acs.ucalgary.ca/~mlroundi/skiing.html

St. Moritz Ski Page (NRP Top Pick)

http://www.skiin.com/switzerland/stmoritz/stmoritze.html

Cool Works' Ski Resorts & Ski & Snowboard Country Jobs

http://www.gorp.com/showme/skirsrts.htm

Ever wondered how those ski instructors get such cool jobs? Check out this site. Pick a state. Pick a resort. Pick a job. Spend the winter playing at your dream job. There are links here to other cool jobs in state parks, on cruise ships, and in camps. Definitely check this out.

CRN—Colorado Resort Net

http://www.toski.com

Serves as a guide to Colorado resort communities, including hotel, restaurant, arts, event, real estate, and shopping information.

GORP Skiing and Snowboarding Tours

http://www.gorp.com/moguls/

GORP, the Great Outdoor Recreation people, have scoured the U.S. looking for great ski deals, and they're all listed here. Click the resort of your choice to learn about package deals available at that resort, or click special trips and tours to see where the very best deals are.

Hyperski—The Magazine for Skiing and Snowboarding

http://www.hyperski.com/

Find out about snow conditions and special packages. Also read the articles about picking the right pair of skis, snowcat skiing, skid chains, and skiing in Austria. This page has a little more than the usual.

Las Lenas Ski Packages

http://www.snowpak.com/snowpak/resorts/laslenas.html

Skiing in Argentina may not be something you've considered before. Check out this page to discover what's available. Get a quote for your vacation plans. Check this one out. It's a little different, but you may like it.

Northern Vermont X-Country, Backcountry, and Telemark Skiing

http://salus.uvm.edu/VTXCSki.html

Provides information about free heel skiing in Northern Vermont. Includes trail maps, trail descriptions, and links to clubs and organizations and resorts related to back-country or telemark skiing.

NRP TOP PICKS

St. Moritz Ski Page

http://www.skiin.com/switzerland/stmoritz/stmoritze.html

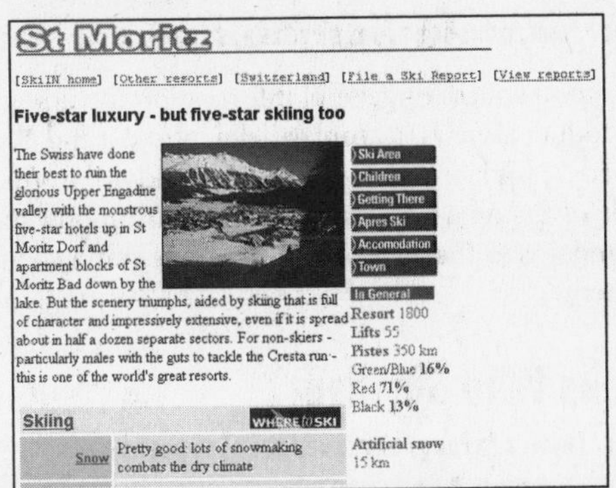

Get an honest appraisal of the world's most luxurious ski accommodations. Find out what to really expect in St. Moritz, what's available to entertain the children, and what to do at night. There's also the usual information about trail conditions and weather and links to other European ski areas.

Skiing in Jackson Hole

http://www.jacksonholenet.com/ski/jacksonh.htm

Extensive information about travel and lodging, the usual weather and powder reports, and information about three different areas. There's also a unique bit of information about ski safety, road safety, and spring skiing safety along with tips on keeping warm.

Stowe Mountain Resort

http://www.stowe.com/smr/index.html

Find out about upcoming package deals at Stowe, Vermont. The latest weather and powder conditions are here, along with FAQs, information about lessons and directions to the resort.

The U.S. Ski Home Team Page

http://www.usskiteam.com/

The official page for the U.S. Olympic Ski Team. Stay informed about all the doings of the ski team all the time, not just during the Olympics. There's also World Cup news, 1998 selection criteria, and more official news.

Winter Sports Foundation's Winter Sports Page

http://www.wintersports.org/

Everything you always wanted to know about all winter sports, including alpine, cross country, and freestyle skiing, bobsledding, figure skating, luge, and more. It's all here on one page. You'll know all about the challenges that face the Olympic competitors in 2002 long before the newscasters start talking about the Winter Games.

World Skiing

http://www.cs.colorado.edu/~mcbryan/bb/ski/ski.html

Provides bulletin boards for reporting world skiing conditions, both Alpine and Backcountry. The lists are extensive, but there is the chance to link a report for your ski area.

NEWSGROUP

rec.skiing.alpine

Related Sites

http://www.northguide.com/terrell/

http://www.itsnet.com/home/getlost/weather.html

http://www.taosnet.com/skiingthenet/

http://www.xcski.org/si.html

http://www.michiweb.com/ski/upcondition.html

http://www.fishweb.com/recreation/ski/index.html

http://www.skicard.com/index3.htm

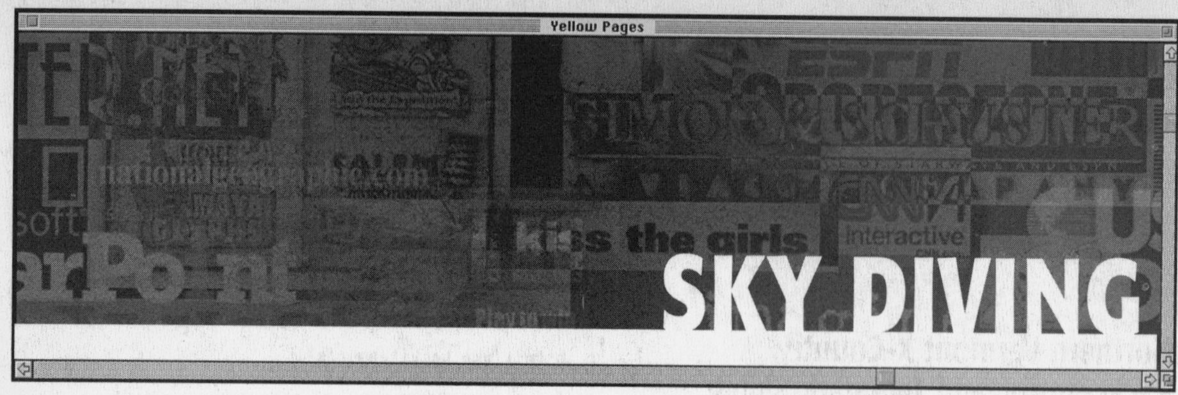

> Yes June, I'm bailing out. I'm bailing out but there's a catch, I've got no parachute.
>
> *Peter D. Carter in* A Matter of Life and Death *(1946)*

Diamond Quest
http://www.voicenet.com/~cheungt/dquest.html

Skydive!
http://www.afn.org/skydive/

Cool & Groovy Fridge Co.

http://www.coolngroovy.com/

This is the site of the makers of the Time-Out!! digital audible altimeter. You can email them for a list of dealers around the world. Offers an "ask the expert" Dive Doctor to diagnose your skydiving troubles.

Diamond Quest

http://www.voicenet.com/~cheungt/dquest.html

This organization is dedicated to CReW (canopy related work)—the intentional maneuvering of two or more canopies in close proximity or contact with another during descent. The organization offers skydiving camps that are open to anyone and the site contains camp journals from actual 1995 and 1996 camp attendees to see what the camp is like. There is a camp schedule and registration information also.

Far West Parachute, Inc.

http://www.pia.com/farwest/index.html

This site belongs to an equipment distributor based in Dallas, Texas. It offers new and used skydiving equipment, clothing, and accessories for sale.

Freefall Photographers Association (FFPA)

http://www.cdnsport.ca/skydive/ffpa/

A good source of general information including product reviews, feature articles, photos, and classifieds. This site has suggestions and advice from other skydivers on a wide range of topics from how to shoot tandems to the latest scoop on photography equipment.

Geeks Who Skydive

http://www.afn.org/skydive/people/geeks/

Who could resist checking out a site with a name like this? It is a handy listing of skydivers' homepages with links to "Geeks in the UK" and "Nordic Geeks" as well. Visiting skydiving geeks are invited to add their names to the list too.

Las Vegas Fly Away

http://www.lvindex.com/vegas/fly.htm

Too cool to pass up, this site belongs to the home of the nation's only indoor skydiving simulators. After a 15 minute training session, participants are able to try out or practice skydiving techniques in a column of air 12 feet across and 21 feet high in vertical wind tunnels with speeds of up to 120 mph. The cost of the ticket includes a flight suit and protective equipment. A video of the experience is available too.

ParaPublishing Skydiving and Parachutes

http://www.parapublishing.com/Catalog-Skydiving@audi/PageIntro.wo

A guide to publications and other information resources. The site has a discussion list for visitors to join if they would like to receive safety bulletins and news. Lots of information on workshops and seminars, presentations, and consulting, as well as an offer for a free information kit.

Skydive!

http://www.afn.org/skydive/

An excellent resource for skydiving enthusiasts. It is full of photos, FAQs, recommended places to skydive, skydiving humor, the sport's history and culture, the latest safety and equipment, training, links to other skydivers, and more. Also includes specific skydiving disciplines such as BASE jumping, paraskiing, relative work and canopy relative work, freestyle, VRW, and sit-flying. It is one of the most extensive Web sites available on skydiving and definitely a "don't miss" for any serious skydiver.

Skydive Kangaroo

http://ourworld.compuserve.com/homepages/skydive_kangaroo/

Although the name of this site seems to imply an Austrailian connection, it offers the visitor a choice of English or German text, which makes it a good page to visit to practice your high school German. Offers a schedule upcoming of trips and a few photos that are worth a look.

SkyPeople

http://www.MakeItHappen.com/spemail/

A directory of skydivers across the country and a huge list of other skydiving links. An exhaustive resource for a variety of skydiving information. Visit this site and cruise the links.

The Parachute Industry Association (PIA)

http://www.pia.com/

This is basically a Parachute Industry Association membership promotion site. It includes technical bulletins and standards, the PIA bylaws and code of professional responsibility, and PIA membership information and an application. Worth a visit if you are interested in joining PIA or curious about what PIA has to offer its members.

UK Skydiving Website

http://www.skydiver.demon.co.uk/

This site contains a list of BPA-affiliated drop zones, classified ads, and a helpful skydiving termonology page that defines common (and not so common) terms and phrases used in the skydiving community. If you're looking for a joke to share with your other skydiving pals, this site offers "Myths, Prayers, and Other Fun Stuff," which is full of skydiving humor.

United States Parachute Association

http://www.uspa.org/

Another great resource for skydivers. This national organization's site promotes parachuting issues in government and legal matters. The site contains safety information, training advisories, details of competitions around the world, and USPA membership information.

Related Sites
http://www.apf.asn.au/~apf/
http://www.cspa.ca/
http://members.aol.com/christskyd/index.html
http://www.skydive.net/compet/
http://www.systemstech.com/paramain.htm
http://www.skydive.net/fsv/
http://www.skydiveu.com/
http://www.skydive.net/
http://www.cityhost.com/skydive/Html/southwest.shtml
http://indigo.ie/~skydive/

A B C D E F G H I J K L M N O P Q R **S** T U V W X Y Z

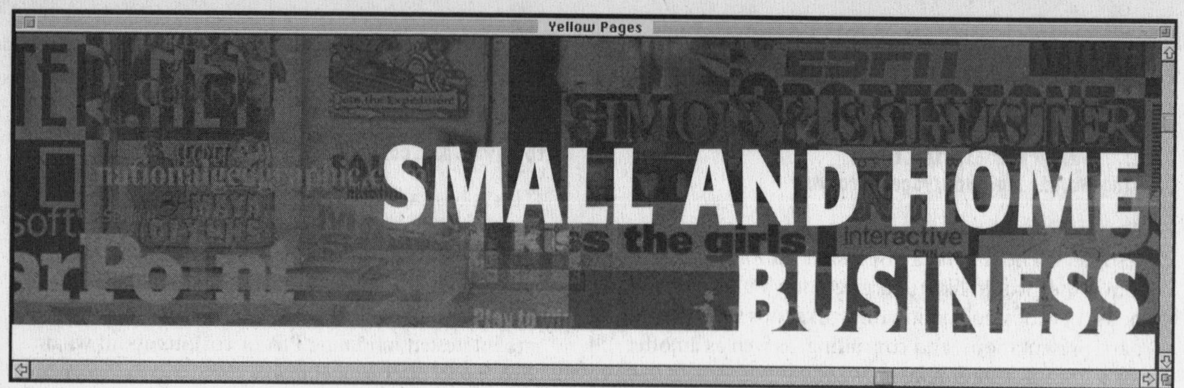

SMALL AND HOME BUSINESS

> I don't want to work, I want to bang on the drum all day.
>
> *Todd Rundgren*

The Apple Small Business Home Page
http://smallbusiness.apple.com/

Home Based Business
http://www.smartbiz.com/sbs/cats/home.htm

The Small Business Advisor
http://www.isquare.com/

Internal Revenue Service
http://www.irs.ustreas.gov/

U.S. Postal Service
http://www.usps.gov/

AT&T Toll Free Directory
http://att.net/dir800/

BUSINESS ADVICE

The American Marketing Association

http://www.ama.org/

The American Marketing Association site offers help for small marketing companies or businesses that use marketing. There is also a classified ad section for job-seekers in the marketing profession.

The Apple Small Business Home Page

http://smallbusiness.apple.com/

Apple Computers answers your small business questions, provides discussion areas, and, of course, recommends genuine Apple hardware that can help you run your business better.

Business Resource Center

http://www.kciLink.com/brc/

Sponsored by Khera Communications, this site contains some great articles about starting, marketing, financing, and managing a small business.

CommerceNet

http://www.commerce.net/

This is a consortium of businesses doing commerce on the Internet. You'll find some excellent resources for entrepreneurs here.

Franchise Handbook Online

http://www.franchise1.com/

A good place to start when considering opening a franchise operation. Includes a directory of franchise opportunities and a message board.

GovCon

http://www.govcon.com/

A wealth of information about how small businesses can bid on and win lucrative government contracts for products and services.

Home Based Business

http://www.smartbiz.com/sbs/cats/home.htm

An assortment of articles, reports, and checklists pertaining to home-based businesses.

Home Office Association of America

http://www.hoaa.com/

The official Web site of the Home Office Association of America (HOAA), the national and local organization for full-time home-based professionals, telecommuters, and others who use a home office.

Info-Net Business Directory

http://www.netime.com/infonet/

Thinking of starting your own home business or a Web site? Here you will find a home-business resource center, information on Web-site management, publishing, database design and management.

Insurance News Network

http://www.insure.com/

A general insurance site, but you'll find answers here to many insurance questions that small business and home office workers often have.

National Federation of Independent Businesses

http://www.nfibonline.com/

An advocacy group for small and independent businesses. Their site provides news items of interest to small business owners, plus forums, contacts, and membership information.

Palo Alto Software

http://www.pasware.com/

This company produces software that helps you plan and start up a small business. Their site not only contains ordering information but also a lot of helpful reference materials that you can use even if you don't want the software.

Small and Home Based Business Links

http://www.ro.com/small_business/homebased.html

A lot of links! Information on franchises, business opportunities, reference material, newsgroups, searching tools, and services for small business.

The Small Business Advisor

http://www.isquare.com/

A diverse, award-winning site that offers articles, reviews, mailing lists, stock quotes, tax advice, and an assortment of other features of interest to the small business owner.

Telecommuting, Teleworking, and Alternative Officing

http://www.gilgordon.com/

This site, sponsored by Gil Gordon Associates (a real estate company), offers some excellent information for people considering telecommuting or currently doing so.

Ten Commandments of Running a Home Business

http://www.tdbank.ca/tdbank/succeed/command.html

A great little article about the important "do's and don'ts" of working at home.

Xerox Small office Home Page

http://www.xerox.com/soho.html

They obviously want you to buy some Xerox equipment here, but this site also contains a Small Business Resources section full of useful small business information.

Yahoo! Small Business Information

http://www.yahoo.com/Business/Small_Business_Information/

Tons of links to small business resources and information.

BUSINESS SERVICES AND PRODUCTS

COPA Connection

http://www.copa.ca/

This Canadian Office Products Association site has a Consumer Connection section with a lot of product information for small and home businesses. Find out about new products, or use the Product Locator to pinpoint the exact product you're looking for. Then check out their Helpful Hints section for business advice.

Credit Card Merchant Accounts for Internet Businesses

http://www.rockmall.com/merchant.htm

This company will, for a fee, set your business up to make secure credit card sales over the Internet.

The Entrepreneur's Wave

http://www.en-wave.com/

An online bookstore specializing in products for the small and home business owner.

Express Digital Images

http://www.expressdigitalimages.com/

A company that offers quick turnaround color printing and scanning. They do small-quantity jobs (typical of small and home business needs) and can make anything from posters to prints to 35mm slides.

The Home Business Bookstore

http://www.homebusiness.com/bookstore/

A handy commercial site where you can browse and order a variety of books and tapes about small businesses and home businesses.

Internet Business Connection

http://www.charm.net/~ibc/

An online shopping mall catering to small businesses.

Little Red Caboose Electronic Publishing Group

http://www.caboose.com/

With this company's software, you can set up an entire mall of stores on the Internet. Try their online demonstration!

GOVERNMENT AGENCIES

Internal Revenue Service

http://www.irs.ustreas.gov/

The IRS has a very helpful site with a lot of information about business tax filing. Includes downloadable tax forms.

Social Security Administration

http://www.ssa.gov/

You'll find a lot of information here about Social Security regulations, benefits, offices, and forms.

U.S. Patent and Trademark Office

http://www.uspto.gov/

Everything you need to know about patenting or trademarking your ideas, logos, and products.

U.S. Postal Service

http://www.usps.gov/

Everything you ever wanted to know about the Postal Service and more, plus a great postage calculator and ZIP code lookup engine.

LEGAL INFORMATION

Legal Information Institute

http://www.law.cornell.edu/topical.html

This server integrates the Gopher and Web offerings of the Legal Information Institute of Cornell University. Read about recent Supreme Court decisions.

The Seamless Website

http://seamless.com/

Legal resources for everyone! A good place for anyone with a legal question to start looking for answers.

PUBLICATIONS

Entrepreneur Magazine

http://www.entrepreneurmag.com/

A lot of helpful articles reprinted from the print version of this publication.

The Home Business Review

http://www.tab.com:80/Home.Business/

The Home Business Review is a monthly online newspaper designed to "educate and promote" the nation's home-based businesses by providing business building articles, information and resources. All of the articles are written at the "how-to" level instead of just theory, providing a News You Can Use approach.

Inc. Online

http://www.inc.com/

A top-notch site based on the print version of *Inc. Magazine.* You can browse hundreds of articles, join discussion groups, check out the list of business resources, and more.

PathFinder

http://www.pathfinder.com

This Time-Warner site has links to articles from a variety of the magazines they own, including Inc., Money, Fortune, Your Company, and Time.

The Small Business Journal

http://www.tsbj.com/

At this site you can review back issues of the publication before deciding to subscribe to the print version.

Your Small Office

http://www.smalloffice.com/

A Web site from the publishers of Small Business Computing and Home Office Computing magazines. Many articles from those magazines are available online, as well as subscription information and columns that cover financial, marketing, managerial, and technical concerns. Recommended!

ZD Net

http://www5.zdnet.com/

Ziff-Davis publishes a wide assortment of computer-related magazines, including *PC Magazine, PC Computing,* and *Computer Shopper.* Browse their articles here, download shareware, and read the latest news about the PC industry.

TELECOMMUNICATION SERVICES

Ameritech

http://www.ameritech.com/

Information about Ameritech services, including small business lines, dedicated Internet lines (ISDN, T1, and so on) and business services. There is also an online Ameritech Yellow Pages.

AT&T Toll Free Directory

http://att.net/dir800/

A search index in which you can look up the toll-free number for any company. Very useful!

Bell Atlantic

http://www.bell-atl.com/html/business/

A lot of information about Bell Atlantic's offerings for businesses of all sizes, including Internet access, ISDN, cellular, and voice and data communications.

BellSouth Telecommunications

http://www.bellsouth.com

An attractive and usable site where you can learn all about BellSouth's home and business services.

BigYellow

http://s11.bigyellow.com/

The NYNEX Yellow Pages online, a searchable database. They claim to have over 16 million businesses in their directory.

Pacific Bell

http://www.pacbell.com/home.html

This site provides solutions to telecommunications problems, ideas for new connections, and occasionally special offers, all for Pacific Bell customers.

U.S. West

http://www.uswest.com/

If you're a U.S. West phone customer, check out their At Work area, with separate sections for home offices, small businesses, and large businesses.

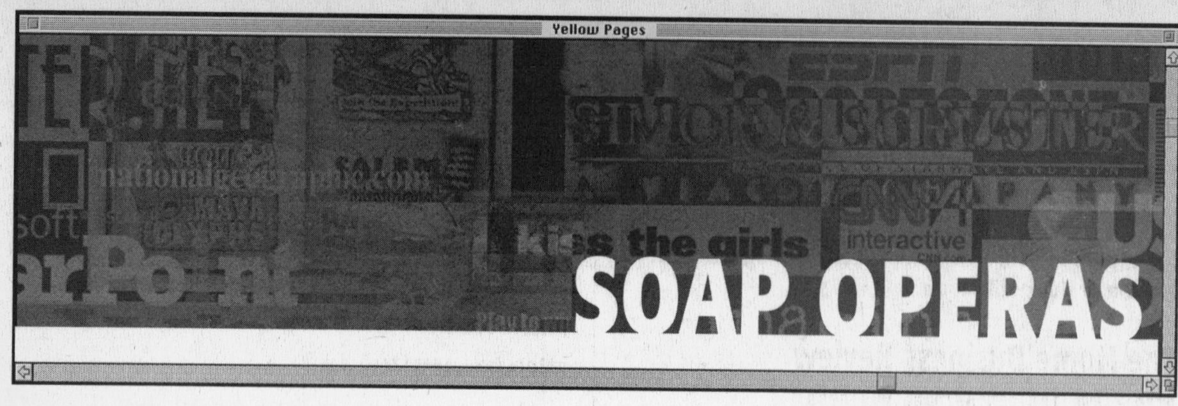

SOAP OPERAS

> Drama is life with the dull bits cut out.
>
> *Alfred Hitchcock*

All My Children

http://www.abc.com/soaps/allmychildren/

See what ol' Erica Kane is up to in Pine Valley these days. This official site includes a daily recap and poll, summaries of years past, and star portraits and bios.

All My Children (unofficial)

http://purplenet.com/soaps/AllMyChildren.html

Read about the show, its characters, and the story line of this successful soap opera. Includes a current cast list and family tree, FAQs about the show, and humor in the press.

All Things Melrose

http://members.aol.com/ALizbth/news.htm

This unofficial site is *full* of gossip, which should suit devotees of this show full of bed-hoppers. It also provides a score sheet (if you don't know what for, you aren't a true fan) and other information related to this love-to-hate-it show.

Another World

http://www.nbc.com/tvcentral/shows/anotherworld/index.html

This official site contains both episode sneak previews and episode archives. View the backstage gallery, peruse transcripts of online chats with AW stars, and read the bio of your favorite cast member.

All My Children
http://www.abc.com/soaps/allmychildren/

Days of our Lives
http://www.nbc.com/tvcentral/shows/daysofourlives/

Port Charles Online
http://www.port-charles.com/

The Another World Fan Club Official Home Page

http://members.aol.com/jensfan/awfc.html

There is loads of information about the popular NBC daytime soap opera here. Cast photos, luncheon schedules, and gossip are plentiful for the perusing.

As the World Turns

http://www.cbs.com/daytime/atwt/

The official site boasts set shots, links, family trees, star bios, and polls. And, if you wish to write to *As the World Turns*, there is a place to write your message.

Bold and the Beautiful

http://www.cbs.com/daytime/bb/

The official home page of *Bold and the Beautiful*. You can take a *Bold and the Beautiful poll*, send email, check out fan club info, and get a sneak preview of what's coming up on the show.

The City and Loving

http://server.Berkeley.EDU/soaps/city/

These shows might be canceled, but they still have devoted fans that love to talk about them! Site includes a Where Are They Now? list, birthday info for the stars, and a link to plot summaries by month. Also links to other sites-in-mourning for these shows.

Coronation Street

http://www.computan.on.ca/~grahame/cs.html

The site for this British soap contains the history of how the show first came to air in December 1960. The show is still going strong today and is the longest running show in the UK. It contains weekly updates, the broadcast schedule for different countries, and info about the official magazine of the show.

Dallas

http://www.wu-wien.ac.at/usr/h92/h9203189/dallas2.html

Contains photos and character descriptions from this hugely popular show that ran for 13 years. There also is a family tree diagram to help with any confusion about who was married to whom, and so on.

Days of our Lives

http://www.nbc.com/tvcentral/shows/daysofourlives/

This show stretches the limits of reality more than any other daytime soap. Contains some classic old photos, although they are a little small. Also offers tributes to some of the show's great supercouples, past and present.

Echo Point

http://yoyo.cc.monash.edu.au/~pilgrim/

This Australian soap opera was not a favorite with critics or the general viewing public. So why the site? According to its creator, why not? Check out this site and see if it's really so bad.

General Hospital

http://www.abc.com/soaps/generalhospital/

If you missed today's show, never fear. This official site can give you all the juicy details. It also has some games and polls, including Daytime Dilemma and What's Going On? Look through a list of characters to find the bios of your favorites.

Guiding Light

http://www.cbs.com/daytime/gl/

Check out what happened last week at this official site of the longest-running drama ever. Read about your favorite stars in their bios, and find out what acting they're doing on the side.

Guiding Light Updates

http://server.berkeley.edu/soaps/gl/update.html

If you missed today's show, you can check out this Guiding Light home page to get the lowdown on what happened. You can also peruse the archives for a past program.

Mediarama's 90210 Weekly Wrapup

http://www.inquisitor.com/~xixax/Mediarama/90210/

This text-only site gets right to the point. Contains both short and in-depth summaries of each episode this season (and the past three seasons). Also provides links to other *90210* sites and a FAQ.

One Life to Live

http://www.abc.com/soaps/onelifetolive/

This official site provides a summary for each year of the show, from 1968 to the present. Read both character bios and actor bios to see who's most like their character.

Port Charles

http://www.abc.com/soaps/portcharles/index.html

Find out what's happening on this new soap, a spin-off of General Hospital. Like other soap sites, this official Web page contains daily and weekly recaps, cast bios, message boards, and photos.

Port Charles Online

http://www.port-charles.com/

Provides daily updates for fans of the daytime dramas Port Charles and General Hospital. Check out the Message Exchange, Cast News, Top Ten lists, and Calendar of Events for the latest on the shows. This site also includes fan clubs, cast birthdays, and filmography info. You can even read about episodes that haven't aired yet. Everything imaginable!

A B C D E F G H I J K L M N O P Q R S T U V W X Y Z

Savannah

http://www.wat136.com/savannah/savannah.html

This show has been canceled, but try telling that to the loyal fans that post to this site. They're writing, emailing, and basically begging for it to return. In the meantime, this site consists of a fact sheet, cast bios, photos, and more.

Suzanne's Pacific Palisades Page

http://people.delphi.com/slanoue/pacific.htm

Even though this show was canceled, it lives on through this site. A cast background is provided as well as links to other pages dedicated to this short-lived show.

Soap Life the 90210 Way

http://home.earthlink.net/~kristinm/9home.html

Come see what it's like to write for the television show *Beverly Hills, 90210*—from an idea becoming a script to the cast stamp of approval. This site is brought to you by the writers of *90210*, who also came up with the Glossary of Nonsense that appears here.

Sunset Beach

http://www.nbc.com/tvcentral/shows/sunsetbeach/

This new soap, the first daytime effort from Aaron Spelling, contains a mix of soap veterans and newcomers (and, of course, a Spelling offspring—this time it's son, Randy). This official site includes episode previews and archives, chat transcripts, and more.

Young & the Restless

http://www.cbs.com/daytime/yr/

Are Nikki and Victor *ever* going to reunite? This official site won't give that info away, of course, but you can find out what's currently happening in Genoa City. Check the cast list to see who plays your favorite characters and find out where to send cheers and jeers.

NEWSGROUPS

alt.tv.90210

alt.tv.another-world

alt.tv.dallas

alt.tv.days-of-our-lives

alt.tv.melrose-place

alt.tv.models-inc

rec.arts.tv.soaps

rec.arts.tv.uk.coronation-st

rec.arts.tv.uk.eastenders

FTP SITES

ftp://ftp.cdrom.com/.12/internet/faqs/tv/soaps

ftp://ftp.cs.columbia.edu/archives/faq/rec/answers/tv/soaps

ftp://ftp.csie.nctu.edu.tw/Documents/FAQ/rec/arts/tv/soaps

ftp://ftp.iem.ac.ru/.1/doc/FAQ/tv/soaps

ftp://ftp.tcp.com/pub/90210/

ftp://ftp.uec.ac.jp/.0/NetNews/news.answers/tv/soaps

ftp://ftp.umr.edu/.pub/faqs/text/tv/soaps

ftp://ftp.uni-rostock.de/FAQs/tv/soaps

ftp://ftp.univie.ac.at/archive/faq/tv/soaps

ftp://ftp.wustl.edu/multimedia/midi/television_theme_songs/melrose.mid

LISTSERVS

GENHOSP-L—ABC Soap Opera General Hospital Discussion List

You can join this group by sending the message "sub GENHOSP-L your name" to

listserv@listserv.aol.com

SOAPRAH-L—Strictly Soaps–The Soaprah Newsletter

You can join this group by sending the message "sub SOAPRAH-L your name" to

listserv@listserv.aol.com

Related Sites

http://members.aol.com/jwhitman1/days.html

http://php.indiana.edu/~kclifton/sunsetbeach.html

http://purplenet.com/soaps/GeneralHospital.html

http://server.berkeley.edu/soaps/gl/update.html

http://web.ukonline.co.uk/tvqueen.t/

http://www.he.net/~dro/soaps/atwtpage.htm

http://www.mediadomain.com/amc/

http://www.serve.com/HeatherC/OLTL/wwwboard.html

http://www.users.globalnet.co.uk/~wayneb/

http://www1.station.sony.com/soapcity/genoa/

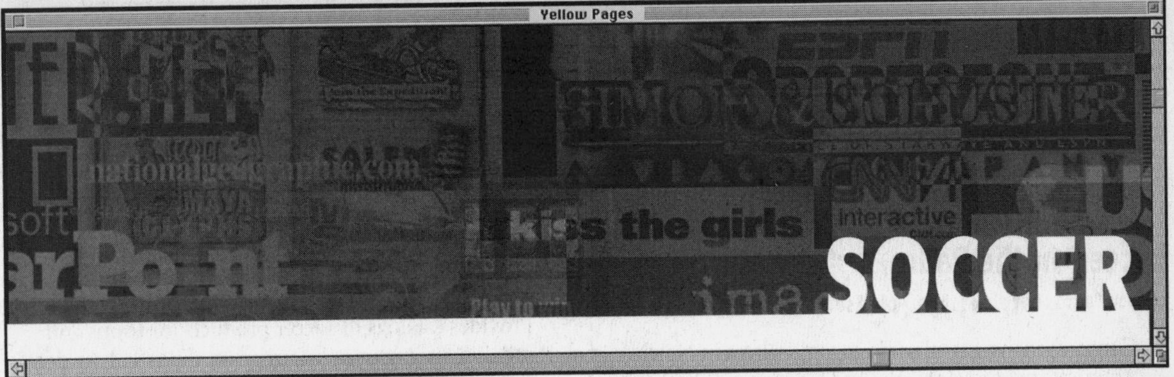

If Britain really wanted to punish Iraq during the Persian Gulf War, it should have sent 4,000 British soccer fans instead of 4,000 British troops.

Angus Jones, Satirist

ESPNet SportZone Soccer

http://espnet.sportszone.com/soccer

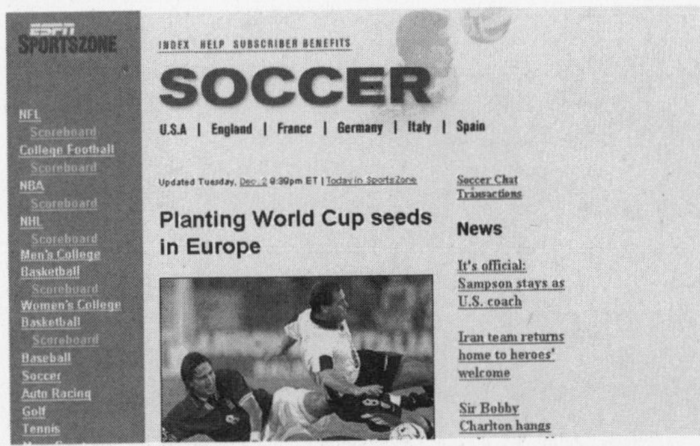

Provides links to soccer's hot zone, Europe, but also to World Cup qualification coverage, worldwide. As Major League Soccer grows in the US, expect ESPN's current coverage to grow with it.

ESPNet SportZone Soccer
http://espnet.sportszone.com/soccer

SoccerNet
http://soccernet.com

International Soccer

http://www2.webbernet.net/~bob/international.html

With links to soccer information the world over, both conferenced teams and clubs, this page is a good place to get soccer facts. Also available is a link to the World Cup history.

The Soccer Homepage

http://www.distrib.com/soccer/homepage.html

Cool page that contains tons of information, from soccer clubs to current standings, events, and game info.

Soccer is Life

http://nextdch.mty.itesm.mx/~rlopez/SOCCER.html

Looking for more information on soccer? This page has a soccer dictionary, links to other cool soccer pages, newsgroups, and mailing lists.

SoccerNews Online

http://www.intermark.com/

Gives you access to soccer information all over the world by linking to the confederation name you want. This site has information about men and women's soccer, their tournaments, players, and national competitions.

SoccerNet

http://soccernet.com

For followers of English and Scottish soccer leagues. You can link to pages for each premiere league team and follow the latest in FA Cup coverage.

Soccer on the Radio

http://sefl.satelnet.org/~philsoc/socrad/

Comprehensive list of audio soccer sources in North America. Includes domestic and international radio stations.

Soccer Yellow Pages

http://www.tdl.com/~chuckn/soc/soc.html

Gobs of listings for soccer sites. Good place to go when searching for more info on soccer.

TSI Soccer

http://www.webpress.net/tsi/

Provides catalogs of soccer products for teams and individuals. Includes information about TSI services. Provides Major League Soccer's schedule, photo gallery, information on "The Instep"— a program to help players get into college. Links to other soccer pages.

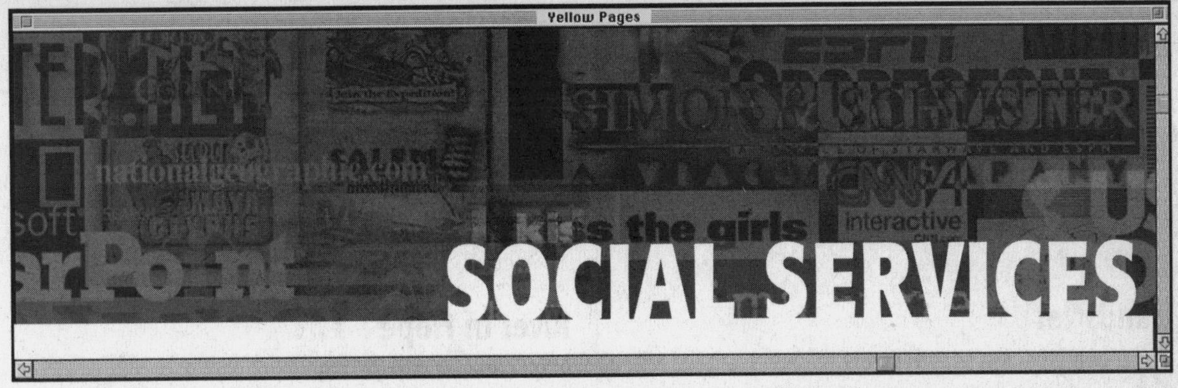

It's a process. No one person can come to a conclusion.

Social Services worker in The Substance of Fire *(1996)*

American Red Cross

http://www.crossnet.org/

Yes, one of the most recognized symbols of help also has a Web page. On their home page, you can find out where the nearest Red Cross is, as well as what projects they are currently working on.

Assist-Net—A World of Difference on the Web

http://www.assist-net.com/

Assist-tech works with nonprofit organizations, health and social services, socially responsible businesses, and arts organizations, to design Web Sites that are inexpensive and effective.

The Carter Center

http://www.emory.edu/CARTER_CENTER/homepage.htm

Atlanta, Georgia is where the former U.S. President and his wife have based their public policy institute. Visit the site to get information about their current and past work, as well as to find out what you can do to help.

American Red Cross
http://www.crossnet.org/

The National Coalition for the Homeless
http://www2.ari.net/home/nch/

Centers for Disease Control and Prevention

http://www.cdc.gov/

Tells about the agency and its services. Links to public health officials and agencies nationwide. Warns travelers of disease outbreaks worldwide. Gives data and statistics. Very informative.

C.R.E.D.E.S.

http://www.mworld.fr/credes/

Using CREDES surveys, as well as data collected elsewhere, statisticians, physicians, and economists bring their combined expertise to the study of all aspects of health economics. Morbidity and health status indicators, health care consumption, social service benefits, hospitals, private practitioners, regional area studies, and international comparisons are some of the main themes.

Contact Center Network

http://www.contact.org/

This group's stated purpose is to provide links to and between nonprofit organizations so that they might better help themselves and each other. You can find groups by country or keyword, or explore how Contact can help your organization.

A B C D E F G H I J K L M N O P Q R S T U V W X Y Z

Evaluation and Training Institute

http://www.otan.dni.us/webfarm/eti/

Established in 1974, ETI is a full-service, nonprofit consulting firm that conducts research, program evaluation, policy analysis, and training with a focus on educational and social services programs and public policy issues.

HandsNet

http://www.igc.apc.org/handsnet/

Intended as a site for sharing information, links can be made to basic information or specific issues, where further links take you to the sites of those who know the topic best. A valuable resource for community service groups.

National Center for Missing & Exploited Children

http://www.missingkids.org/

Offers searchable database records by specific criteria. Short and long indexes of all missing children. Comprehensive site with photographs of some of the children. For more see "Children at Risk" link. Service provided in an attempt to find missing children.

National Children's Coalition (NCC)

http://www.slip.net/~scmetro/ncc.htm

About National Children's Coalition membership, advocacy for kids and teens, KIDS N' NEED radiothons and new WWW Youth and Children Resource Center and its work with street kids and runaways.

National Civic League

http://www.ncl.org/ncl/

When Theodore Roosevelt founded this group with the goal of improving communities, he surely didn't realize how helpful and accessible it would become. This site will link you to mission statements, recent progress in the area, and how you can assist your own community.

The National Coalition for the Homeless

http://www2.ari.net/home/nch/

With the primary goal of abolishing homelessness in mind, this group relates tales of people's struggles with homelessness and provides links to information on recent developments and legislation that pertain to homelessness.

New York State Adoption Home Page

http://www.state.ny.us/dss/adopt/

New York State Adoption Home Page includes information on adoption services and children available for adoption. Adoption Blue Book offers profiles and photographs of some of the children waiting for homes. Support services for those considering adoption.

River of Hope

http://www.riverhope.org/

River of Hope is not itself a service organization; instead it provides links to groups that it believes in. As of this printing, there are links to groups that deal with drug abuse, eating disorders, and emotionally troubled children.

Social Work and Social Services Jobs Online

http://www.gwbssw.wustl.edu/~gwbhome/jobs/swjobs.html

Social work and social services job listings and links to other job resources. Employers can submit job openings online.

Social Work and Social Services Web Sites

http://www.gwbssw.wustl.edu/~gwbhome/websites.html

This 20 page site lists hundreds of links related to social work and social service. Possibly one of the most comprehensive sources to found in any area of interest in this field. Maintained by the George Warren Brown School of Social Work at Washington University in St. Louis.

An Unofficial Guide to Rotary

http://www.tecc.co.uk/public/PaulHarris/

Provides information about the entire history of the Rotary Club, current service projects, and how you can join.

VISTA web

http://libertynet.org/~zelson/vweb.html

Volunteers in Service to America has been around since 1964, and it is now part of the larger AmeriCorps program. Find out about both groups' successes in the past, what they're planning to do in the future, as well as how to find someone that you might have worked with in either group.

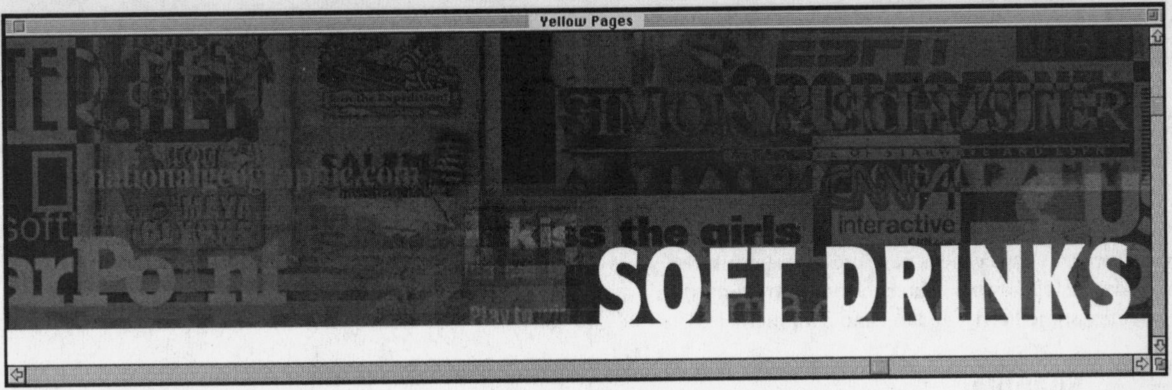

Soft Drinks

It's the real thing!

Makers of Coca-Cola

Jolt Cola
http://www.joltcola.com/

Snapple
http://www.snapple.com/

7Up

http://www.7up.com/index2.html

Official 7Up site that has cool games, opportunities to win 7Up memorabilia, and more.

Almost Official Coca-Cola Page

http://www.geocities.com/capecanaveral/1743/coke.htm

Information on the world's leading soft drink manufacturer. Cool pics and great info.

BYOB: The Soda Page

http://www.634brew.com/Soda.htm

Site that offers recipes and kits for making your own soda. Flavors available include rootbeer, birchbeer (what's that?), and sarsaparilla to name a few.

Coca-Cola

http://www.coca-cola.com

Provides information about the most renowned soft drink company. Buy, sell, and trade Coca-Cola paraphernalia online. Check out Coca-Cola–sponsored sporting events. See how Coca-Cola is doing in the business world before you decide to buy some stock in soft drinks.

DR PEPPER – THIS IS THE TASTE

http://www.drpepper.com/

Official Dr Pepper site. Includes screen savers, recipes, and info on current Dr Pepper contests. Cool graphics!

Gatorade® Thirst Quencher

http://205.217.2.106/gatorade/entry.html

Official Gatorade site that offers the history of Gatorade, products, and timeline quizzes.

Jolt Cola

http://www.joltcola.com/

Arguably one of the best sites on the Web now. With the advantage of having a computer-oriented core audience, Jolt presents a Java-powered site featuring information on the beverage of choice of hackers and college students. Test your vital signs on the Jolt-o-meter. See the impact Jolt has had on the entertainment industry. Get a glimpse of Jolt culture. A good site for pure entertainment value.

Pepsi Russia

http://www.pepsi.ru/

The first Pepsi site in Russia with links to Pepsi New and the history of Pepsi in Russia. You can even see your name appear in Russian atop the Kremlin wall.

Perrier

http://www.perrier.com/

Nature's original beverage refresher in bottled form. Perrier's site provides information about the company and offers a restaurant guide to New York, Los Angeles, Chicago, Washington, D.C., and New Orleans. View Perrier's past, present, and future advertising artwork. Enter the bottle art contest or order some Perrier apparel and paraphernalia.

Snapple

http://www.snapple.com/

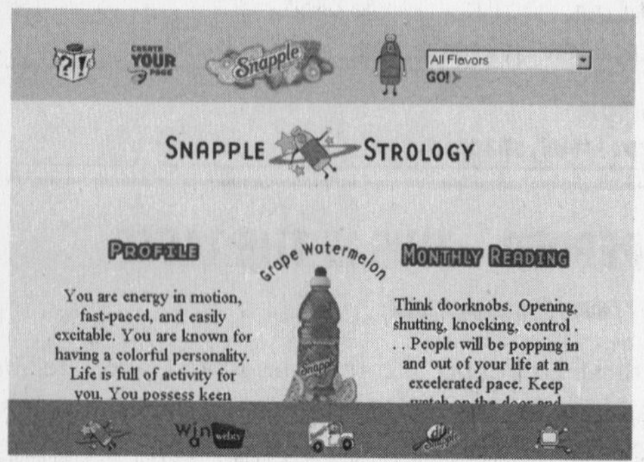

Made from the best stuff on earth, Snapple's site offers information on its current and future flavored beverages. Vote for your favorite! Enter the Snapple-a-day sweepstakes and win free Snapple products.

The Soft Drink Industry

http://www.nsda.org/industry/index.html

Home of the National Soft Drink Association, this site offers market research, information on franchises, as well as fun facts to know and tell.

A B C D E F G H I J K L M N O P Q R S T U V W X Y Z

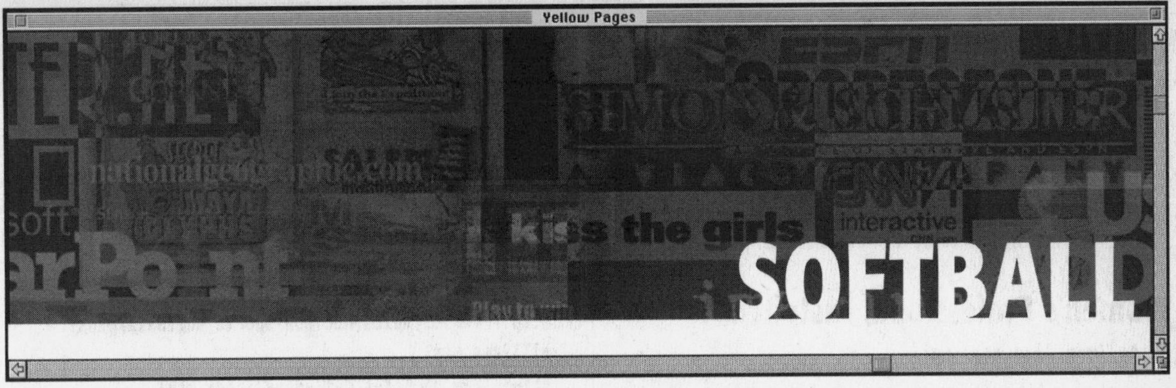

> I like a sporting event in which I know the outcome ahead of time. It's more organized.
>
> *Sgt. Bilko in* Sgt. Bilko *(1996)*

All American Softball School

http://www.kj22.com/default.asp

This site belongs to a school devoted exclusively to developing the skills of athletes interested in playing Olympic-style softball.

America's Finest City Softball League

http://www.geocities.com/WestHollywood/3590/

This site, which is based out of San Diego, includes game schedules for this gay softball league, links to the 1997 Gay Softball World series, team standings, and game results.

Amateur Softball Association

http://www.softball.org/

The ultimate source for information on the latest rule changes for 1998, results, championships, and press releases. Lots of links to other softball sites.

Club Dot

http://members.aol.com/drfc1a/fanclub.html

This site celebrates everyone's favorite Doctor Shortstop from the U.S. gold medal winning Olympic team. Home of the Dot Richardson fan club.

Amateur Softball Association
http://www.softball.org/

Elite Pitching with Michele Smith

http://www.dm-design.com/elite/

Instructional videos for fastpitch softball offered by Michele Smith, a member of the 1996 Olympic gold medal winning team.

National Softball Association

http://members.aol.com/nsamd/index.htm

Features listings of softball tournaments and series happening across the U.S.

National Softball Association of the Deaf

http://home.us.net/~ddstout/nsad/

This site is the home of the nonprofit recreational and competitive organization serving deaf and hard-of-hearing regional softball organizations and players. Includes a directory of affiliates, tournaments schedule, and by-laws and regulations.

Slow Pitch Softball History Page

http://www.angelfire.com/sd/slopitch/index.html

This site features softball national championship and world series history. Also contains links to other softball-related sites.

Townball

http://www.sirius.com/~cmonser/Townball.html

This site describes the rules and history of townball, which is believed to be the game that evolved into today's softball and baseball.

United States Slo-Pitch Softball Association

http://www.usssa.com/

The site of this national organization features the history of slow-pitch softball, major players and rankings, tournaments, state associations, and more.

Women's Professional Fastpitch

http://www.diac.com/~wpf/

This site includes pages for league leaders, team rosters, schedules, press releases, employment opportunities with WPF, and more.

World's Largest Softball Tournament

http://www.richmond-online.com/softball/wlst/

This site contains information about this long-standing (28th year) gigantic softball tournament of more than 400 teams from over 20 states in the U.S. and Canada.

Related Sites

http://www.olympics.nbc.com/sports/softball/bios/williams.html

http://www.magicnet.net/~drss/index.html

http://www.magicnet.net/~dalearob/

http://www.dudleysports.com/

http://wcinet.net/grandslam/

http://www.olympics.nbc.com/sports/softball/bios/berg.html

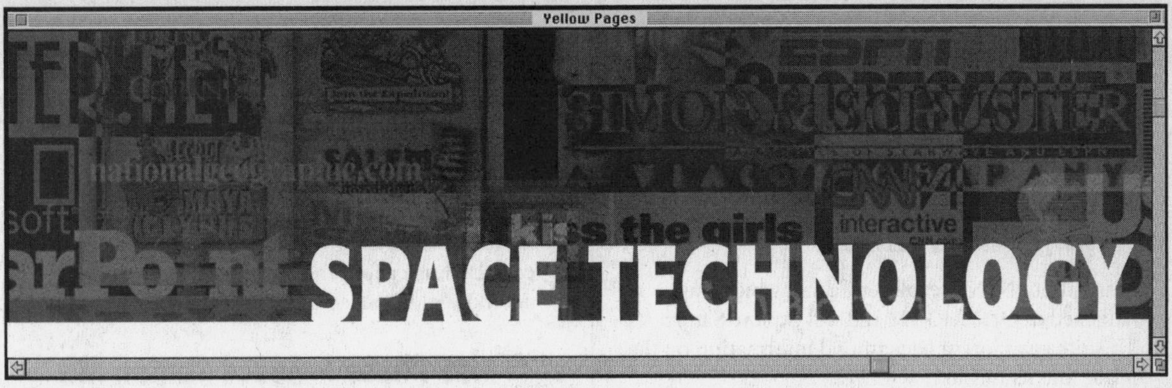

> You know, Hobbes, sometimes even my lucky rocketship underpants don't help.
>
> *Calvin, the comic strip character*

NRP Top Picks
45th Space Wing Home Page `http://www.pafb.af.mil/index.htm`
Bradford Robotic Telescope `http://www.telescope.org/btl/`
ISS Phase I–Space Station Mir `http://www.osf.hq.nasa.gov/mir/`
MIT Center for Space Research `http://space.mit.edu/`
The NASA Homepage `http://www.nasa.gov/`
Stanford SSDL Home Page `http://aa.stanford.edu/~ssdl/`

45th Space Wing Home Page

`http://www.pafb.af.mil/index.htm`

Here you can find the latest schedule of launches from Cape Canaveral as well as learn about the launch vehicles and satellites launched from there. Photos of launches are available.

AIAA Home Page

`http://www.aiaa.org/`

The American Institute of Aeronautics and Astronautics is the main society of the aerospace profession. Look at this site to learn all about it. Find out what's new at the site, read the news bulletin, learn about how to become a member, send email to the staff, and more.

Astronaut Candidates

`http://sauron.msfc.nasa.gov/astronaut-candidates/`

Think you've got the right stuff? Check out this page to find out for sure. It lists minimum requirements for Mission Specialists, the astronaut candidate's ten commandments, and more.

The ATM Page

`http://www.tiac.net/users/atm/`

Are you an Amateur Telescope Maker? This page offers lots of tips and hints on how to build your own telescope.

Basics of Space Flight

`http://www.jpl.nasa.gov/basics/`

As the title suggests, this page presents all the basics of space flight. It comes with a table of contents so you can examine specific topics. It also has a glossary of terms and abbreviations.

Bradford Robotic Telescope

`http://www.telescope.org/btl/`

On this site you can send a request into a robotic telescope in England asking it to take a picture of anything in the northern night sky. This site also has weather reports updated daily. This site also has a comprehensive multimedia guide to stars and galaxies taken from the CD-ROM Earth and Universe from BTL Publishing Limited. It comes with a lot of sound and MPEG format movies.

Cassini: Voyage to Saturn

http://www.jpl.nasa.gov/cassini/

Learn about NASA's explorer Cassini which was launched in October 1997 and will explore Saturn. This site gives lots of background information on the probe and its mission.

Deep Space Network Home Page

http://deepspace1.jpl.nasa.gov/dsn/

Check out this page to learn about the Deep Space Network which is used to support interplanetary spacecraft missions for the exploration of the solar system and universe. The DSN provides a two-way communications link between earth and unmanned planetary explorers such as Galileo.

European Space Agency

http://www.esrin.esa.it/

This is the home page for this European society, which is meant to promote cooperation among its member states in the area of peaceful space research. You can read the latest press releases, learn about the agency's programs and projects, check out their publications, and more.

The First Millennial Foundation

http://www.millennial.org/

This foundation is concerned with the colonization of humans in outer space. This Web site contains information about the foundation's purpose, local chapters, allows you to meet some members, and learn how to join.

Galileo Home Page (JPL)

http://www.jpl.nasa.gov/galileo/

Learn about this planetary probe and its mission. Check up on the latest findings of the mission and look at photos of the planets that have been sent back to earth. The information in the page is so extensive, it comes with its own keyword search.

Institute for Teleoperated Space Development

http://www.teleport.com/~itsd1/

The purpose of this institute is to open space for humankind by early use of teleoperated robots. Learn how and why these robots can benefit mankind. You can also learn about the people in this organization and how you yourself can join.

ISS Phase I—Space Station Mir

http://www.osf.hq.nasa.gov/mir/

Everything you'd want to know about the space station Mir is here. This page comes with a drawing of the space station which you can click to learn more about its specific parts. Details of all the U.S. related missions are given. Lots of pictures and links are available.

Jonathan's Space Report

http://hea-www.harvard.edu/QEDT/jcm/space/jsr/jsr.html

This is a weekly report describing all space launches. It includes piloted missions as well as satellites. Back issues are available.

JSC Home Page

http://www.jsc.nasa.gov/

This is the home page for the Johnson Space Center. Learn all about the center and its purpose within NASA.

Kelly Space Technology Home Page

http://www.kellyspace.com/

This company is concerned with designing low cost, commercial launch vehicles. This page will inform you on their ECLIPSE launch vehicle which is reusable and uses the tow approach to save money. It explains the ECLIPSE, proves that the tow approach can work, provides pictures, and explains their products and services.

Larry's Utility World Home Page

http://www.grove.net/~larry/nasa.html

Want to know the latest up-to-date developments at NASA without watching the news? Here is a listing of the frequencies used by NASA for radio transmission.

Links to other Space Grants

`http://deimos.ucsd.edu/space_grant/sg_homepages.html`

This page offers links to available space grants organized by state and including Puerto Rico.

Long Duration Exposure Facility

`http://setas-www.larc.nasa.gov/setas/ldef.html`

The Long Duration Exposure Facility was a project designed to determine effects of long-term space exposure to space systems and operations. This page gives lots of details of the mission and provides access to the results.

MIT Center for Space Research

`http://space.mit.edu/`

Find out what is going on at MIT involving space technology. This site gives information on all of the ongoing research projects at the school. It also has links to each of the school's observatories. Access to several data resources is given.

The NASA Homepage

`http://www.nasa.gov/`

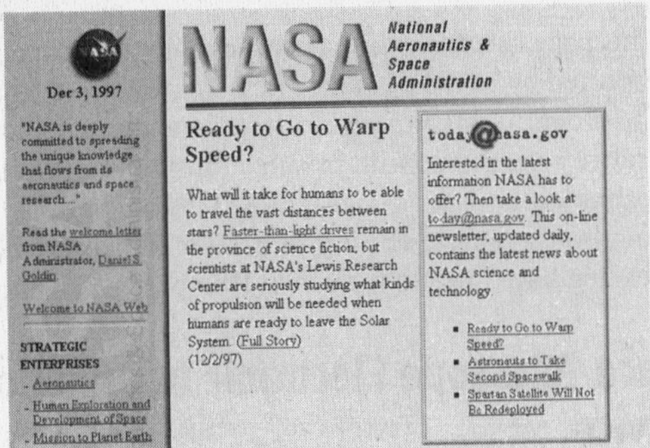

This is the front door to all of NASA's web sites. You can check audio, photo, and video clips, learn about space science, link to NASA's other centers around the world, read the daily NASA news, and a lot more.

NASA/Kennedy Space Center Home Page

`http://www.ksc.nasa.gov/ksc.html`

Come here to find out what's new at the Kennedy Space Center. You can read their online publications and peruse a wealth of educational pages about recent missions. Dozens of links are given.

NATIONAL AIR & SPACE MUSEUM HOMEPAGE

`http://www.nasm.edu/NASMpage.html`

This site describes the museum very well. It includes a very thorough description of the museum's exhibits complete with lots of photos.

National Space Society

`http://www.nss.org/`

The goal of this society is to work toward people living beyond earth. Learn about the society, examine their magazine, pose questions to actual astronauts, contact staff members, become a member, and more on their Web page.

New Space Network

`http://www.newspace.com/`

This site has a Feature Attractions section which offers book reviews, conference reviews, games, and other space-related articles. It also has an industry listing organized by company name or product/service provided. Some publications are linked. Links to other space sites are given.

The Nine Planets

`http://seds.lpl.arizona.edu/nineplanets/nineplanets/nineplanets.html`

The site describes itself as "an overview of the history, mythology, and current scientific knowledge of each of the planets and moons in our solar system." Some pages even have sounds and movies! It also covers asteroids, meteors, comets, and more.

NSSDC Photo Gallery

`http://nssdc.gsfc.nasa.gov/photo_gallery/photogallery.html`

This site offers space photos of planets, nebulae, galaxies, stars, spacecraft, and more. You can even view images taken by specific satellites such as Galileo, Voyager, and the Hubble Space Telescope.

Office of Space Flight

`http://www.osf.hq.nasa.gov/`

This is a great place to learn about ongoing and future space missions at NASA. Read about the shuttle missions and planetary voyagers such as Galileo and Pathfinder. It also holds links to many other space-related pages.

Russian Space Agency

http://liftoff.msfc.nasa.gov/rsa/rsa.html

Learn about the Russian Space Agency. This agency has control of Russia's civilian space program. Learn about its history and about space programs such as the MIR space station and the abandoned shuttle projects.

Satellite Times Home Page

http://www.grove.net/hmpgst.html

Check out what is new in the latest issue of this magazine as well as viewing the table of contents of older issues. This site also contains links to other sites related to satellites. There is an online subscription form.

The Saturn V Launch Vehicle Home Page

http://www.calweb.com/~ccorway/saturn-v/saturn-v.htm

This page offers a lot of information regarding the history and development of the Saturn V launch vehicle. You can even listen to .wav files of its launch and of Neil Armstrong landing on the moon.

SETI Institute

http://www.seti-inst.edu/

Learn about this nonprofit research organization which is dedicated to the Search for Extraterrestrial Intelligence (SETI). Learn about its more than two dozen projects. This site covers the Project PHOENIX very thoroughly.

SETIQuest

http://www.setiquest.com/

Read about *SETIQuest*, the quarterly magazine dealing with the Search for Extraterrestrial Intelligence and Bioastronomy. This site contains some information about SETI. You can even learn how you can get a free copy of the magazine.

SPACE EDUCATOR'S HANDBOOK

http://tommy.jsc.nasa.gov/~woodfill/SPACEED/SEHHTML/seh.html

This is a page created by NASA where you can download an interactive, electronic encyclopedia of information. Windows and Macintosh versions are both supported. The site also contains example math problems applicable to outer space, astronomy information, QuickTime movies from NASA's archives, and more.

The Space Frontier Foundation

http://www.space-frontier.org/

Look here to learn about this foundation. Its principles, philosophy, and programs are all outlined. It also provides many links to other pages including a commercial space links page.

Space News

http://www.spacenews.com/

Check out this newsweekly to read hot news, download images, link to other space-related sites, and more. You have to register online, but it is free.

Space Studies Institute

http://www.astro.nwu.edu/lentz/space/ssi/home-ssi.html

This institute is dedicated to mankind's productive use of the abundant resources in space. You can learn here all about the institute's history and programs. The site also contains assorted information involving the subject of space's colonization.

Space Technology Home Page

http://aesd.larc.nasa.gov/C/CF/STHP.html

This page lists the many space technologies being explored by NASA's Langley Research Center. It gives the program mission, attributes, elements, and cooperative agreements with private industry. Some of the technologies such as laser remote sensing, passive microwave remote sensing, and submillimeter remote sensing have links to their own Web pages.

Space Telescope Electronic Information Service

http://www.stsci.edu/

This site contains a load of information on the Hubble Space Telescope. It provides detailed information about the instruments aboard the HST, information for astronomers proposing HST observations, and lots of pictures and movies of things the HST has photographed.

SpaceBeat

http://www.airspacemag.com/SpaceBeat/Home.html

This is a news magazine covering the aerospace world. It is actually an extension of the Smithsonian Institution's *Air & Space Magazine.*

Stanford SSDL Home Page

http://aa.stanford.edu/~ssdl/

SSDL stands for Space Systems Development Laboratory. Learn about the current research projects at the university. This site also offers admission information and some space-related links.

Trung Tran's Homepage: Technology Links

http://dolphin.upenn.edu/~trant/teklinks.html

You can find some good links here to NASA and other space related pages.

United Nations Office for Outer Space Affairs Portal

http://ecf.hq.eso.org/~ralbrech/un/un-homepage.html

See what programs the United Nations has dealing with outer space. Check out how the organization supports peaceful use of outer space and how it provides member nations with technical information and advice. This site covers a lot of material.

U.S. SPACE CAMP

http://www.spacecamp.com/

Want to learn to be an astronaut? Check out this site. It gives some information about the camp, it's programs, how to register, and more.

WELCOME TO INTELSAT

http://www.intelsat.int/

INTELSAT stands for the international telecommunications satellite organization. Look here to find out what the organization does, what products and services it provides, and who works there.

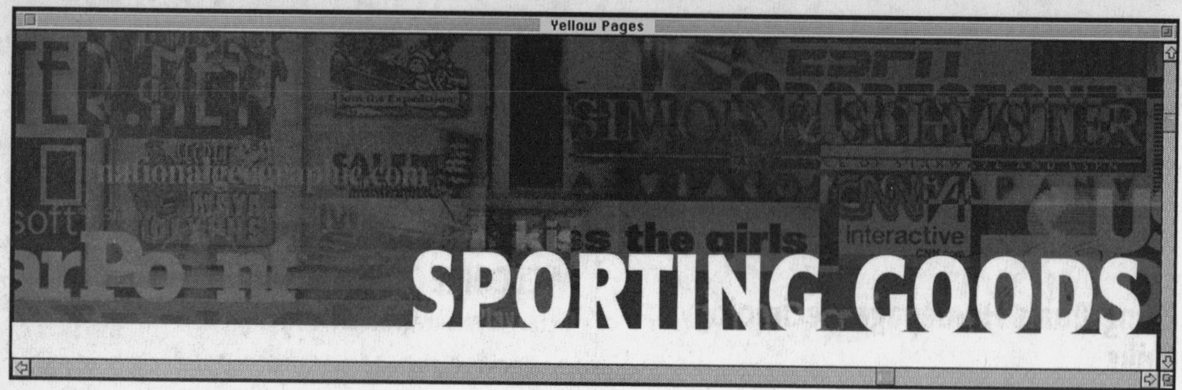

Sports make you grunt and smell. Stay in school, use your brains. Be a thinker, not a stinker.

Apollo in Rocky II *(1979)*

Active Ankle

http://www.activeankle.com/

Athletes everywhere know that the ankle can be a most problematic joint; whether they have first-hand experience or know someone, there's a good chance they'll need a little extra support at one time or another. Active Ankle sells a whole line of ankle supports.

Asian World of Martial Arts, Inc.

http://www.awma.com/

Use the AWMA site to find body padding, clothing, videotapes, weapons, mats, and targets. Check out their custom patches, tae kwon do CDs, silk screening, and books.

Brother Sporting Goods

http://www.brothersportinggoods.com/

If you've gotten sick of going to the gym and want to sweat in the privacy of your home, come to Brother's site to choose from a wide range of exercise equipment, such as bikes, rowers, treadmills, and the like.

Direct Sports

http://www.directsports.com/

This site focuses on brand-name baseball and softball equipment, with links to the home pages of the major manufacturers, such as Louisville Slugger, Rawlings, and Dudley.

Wilson
http://www.wilsonsports.com/

Divots Golf

http://www.capecod.net/divots/chouse.htm

Whether you need new woods, irons, shoes, or bags, Divots has what you need. The site also has pages to help the golfer customize equipment or get his or her hands on a used set.

The Hunter's Mall

http://www.huntersmall.com/

This site is a clearinghouse for e-stores of hunting equipment. You will find everything from camouflage clothing, archery supplies, videos, dogs, guns, ammo, optics, and so on.

Inline Retrofit

http://www.inline-retrofit.com/

This site sells all kinds of inline skates and accessories, including skates for the casual skater, the street hockey player, and the adventurous off-roader who needs skates that look as if they belong on some type of military vehicle.

Nashbar

http://www.nashbar.com/

Nashbar specializes in bicycling and volleyball equipment on their Bike Nashbar and Spike Nashbar pages. Search by manufacturer or choose the item you need (such as cogs, cranks, forks), and the site will provide the appropriate list.

Online Sports

http://www.onlinesports.com/

Online catalog for the secure purchase of any type of sports-related product for every sport known in the universe. You can also sign up for the newsletter, search through a sports career database, and more.

Planet Sports

http://www.planetsports.com/

This online company specializes in equipment for hockey and football, as well as inline skating and other wheeled sports. Check out their "Hot Pick of the Week" and Sports Closeouts.

Play It Again Sports

http://themetro.com/playitagain/

That old bowling ball, gold club set, and polo mallet will no longer have to sit in darkness in the attic. Go to this site to sell, buy, and trade your old equipment for your neighbor's old equipment.

Renee' Paz Swimwear

http://members.aol.com/jawshawaii/index.html

Renee' has been designing swimsuits in Hawaii for almost 20 years. The best thing about her suits is that their custom-designed, so you won't have to worry about being unable to find your favorite patterns in the perfect size.

Score It

http://www.scoreit.com/

Tired of drawing a score card as you watch the Big Game (and all the little games that precede it)? This software provides everything you need to track at bats, player summaries, automatically calculate stats, and a lot more!

Spalding

http://www.spalding.com/

This sport giant's site features goods for basketball, volleyball, baseball and softball, tennis and racquetball, soccer, and women's products.

Sporting Auction

http://www.sportingauction.com/

In categories ranging from snowboarding to hockey, this site enables the Web-surfing athlete to bid on every type of sporting equipment imaginable.

Sportz Outdoor

http://www.sportzoutdoor.com/

This company serves the lifestyles and culture of the hiker, camper, biker, skier, and snowboarder. You can also get great deals on sports adventures, such as ski lift tickets for resorts in New Mexico.

SunFun Collection

http://www.sunfun.com

Offers innovative items for your sun protection, travel comfort, great reading, and sports and outdoor fun.

Sunglasses.Com

http://www.sunglasses.com/def2.htm

Pictorial catalog from which you can order every kind of sunglasses known to sea and sand. Calvin Klein, Bolle, Ray Ban, Vuarnet, and more.

WaterCritters Online

http://www.WaterCritters.com/

With over 11,000 fishing, hunting, and camping products for sale, there's little doubt you'll find what you need. Before you hit the road, you can use provided links to get the weather, fishing reports, and reviews of resorts and lodges.

Wilson

http://www.wilsonsports.com/

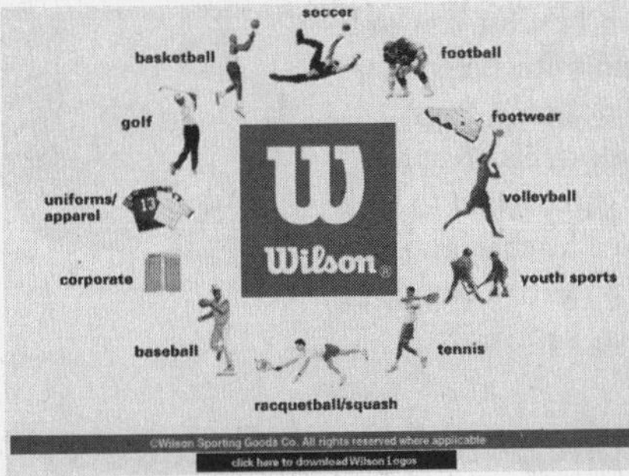

Wilson is perhaps the most popular manufacturer of sporting goods, and their site is a good reflection of this. You can buy Wilson goods for the court, the field, the diamond, the track, and the links, as well as clothing for them all.

Related Sites

http://www.sportswholesale.com/about.html

http://www.planetsports.com/hockeyworld/Edge/

http://www.planetsports.com/hockeyworld/Calcoat/

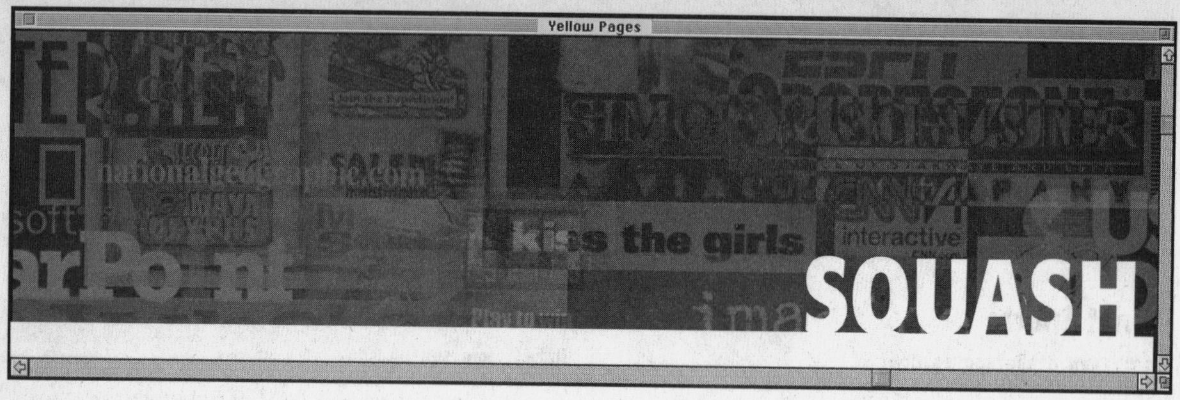

> It's not. I got it at the A&P. It's like... squash.
>
> *Mom in* Breaking Away *(1979)*

Connecticut College Women's Squash

http://camel.conncoll.edu/ccrec/sports/wsqua/index.html

Read about the team's schedule, roster, hall of fame, highlights of past years, and statistics, and view pictures of play.

Dunlap Racquet Sports

http://www.dunlopsports.com/RacquetFront.htm

Use Dunlap's home page to learn which new racquet is best for you and to find out where your local dealer is. Pages include drills great for your game, what to look for in a teacher, and discussion with a couple of Dunlap's pros.

Intercollegiate Squash Racquets

http://www.bates.edu/~hbunker/ISR.html

The ISR home page houses both the National Intercollegiate Squash Racquets Association for men and the United States Women's Intercollegiate Squash Racquets Association for women. Learn about both organizations, read the rules, check the schedule, and consider the rankings.

SquashBusters
http://www.channel1.com/users/clynch/sb/

The Internet Squash Federation

http://www.squash.org/

This very thorough sites covers many issues and topics, including TV coverage, men's and women's regional rankings, rules, clubs, drug policy, ladders and leagues, coaching, and more.

Manta Squash

http://www.nucleus.com/~manta/index.html

Located in Alberta, Canada, Manta specializes in squash equipment and accessories. Peruse their catalog and get details on their racquets or jump to one of the many squash links.

Princeton University Men's and Women's Squash

http://www.princeton.edu/~mwsquash/

Get the team's schedule, see the college team rankings, player rosters and profiles, and learn more about the 1998 squash camp.

Squash: Rules of the World Singles Game

http://www.squash.org/WSF/rules.html

A very thorough page of every aspect of rule of the game. The table format makes finding specific points simple.

SquashBusters

http://www.channel1.com/users/clynch/sb/

This Greater Boston organization uses squash, along with academic and civic participation, to teach young people the importance of hard work, discipline, and concentration to increase their self esteem and social awareness.

SquashPlus

http://www.squashplus.com/

This site is a labor of love for the authors, who see selling squash products as being only one of many services they do or will provide for other enthusiasts. Make and e-appointment with Dr. Lau for advice about fixing squash "ailments."

United States Squash Racquets Association

http://www.us-squash.org/squash/

The USSRA's site provides event information, player and team rankings, and the official game rules. People are asked to volunteer as officials for the 10th World Junior Men's Championship.

Wellesley College Athletics Squash

http://www.wellesley.edu/Athletics/athletics/squash.html

Wellesley's site covers the teams coach, highlights, standouts, roster, and schedule. You can also learn more about the school's other athletic programs.

The World Squash Travel Guide

http://webcom.net/~real/squash/squash.html

The Guide focuses not only on squash itself, but anywhere that squash players can go to have a good time—and still play some squash. Learn about junior squash summer camp, order squash videos, check out the latest health care supplements, and more

Related Sites

http://www.us-squash.org/squash/powerandtheserve_1002.html

http://uts.cc.utexas.edu/~rnr/squash/

http://www.middlebury.edu/~sports/varsityteaminfo/squash.html

http://www.fas.harvard.edu/~athletic/sports/msq/msq_ix.html

http://web.mit.edu/squash/www/

http://ourworld.compuserve.com/homepages/steve_cubbins/tsrc.htm

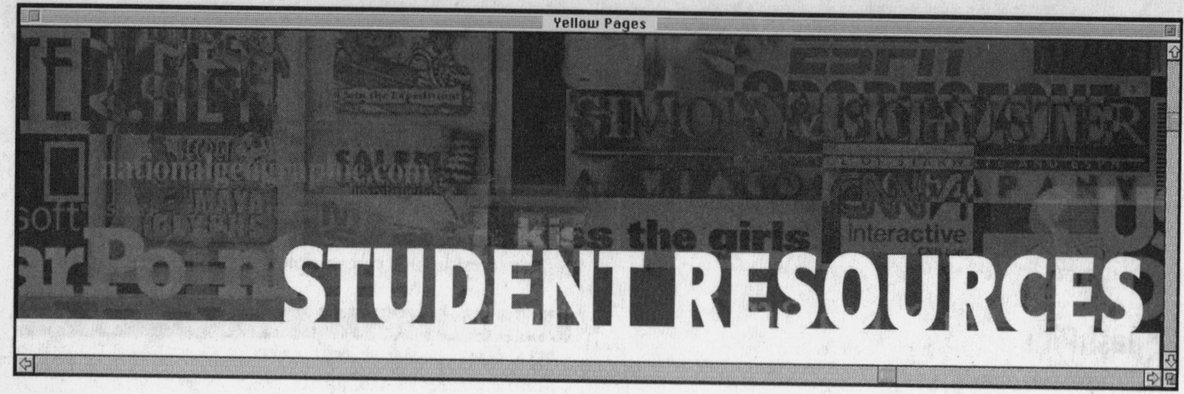

> # My heart is singing for joy this morning! A miracle has happened! The light of understanding has shone upon my little pupil's mind, and behold, all things are changed!
>
> *Anne Sullivan*

CASAA Student Leadership Resource Centre

http://www.sentex.net/~casaa

Focuses on providing fresh student leadership materials, ideas, and support for the student activity advisor.

Children's Literature Web Guide

http://www.ucalgary.ca/~dkbrown/index.html

Catalogs Internet resources related to books for children and young adults. Lists recommended books, recent awards, new authors, resources for parents, teachers, and story tellers, movies based on children's books, and much more. Provides information on how to get your children or class involved in online publication, so the whole world can enjoy their creativity.

Children's Literature Web Guide
http://www.ucalgary.ca/~dkbrown/index.html

CyberKids Home
http://www.woodwind.com:80/cyberkids/

Kids Web at NPAC
http://www.infomall.org/kidsweb/

Writing at MU
http://www.missouri.edu/~writery/

CyberKids Home

http://www.woodwind.com:80/cyberkids/

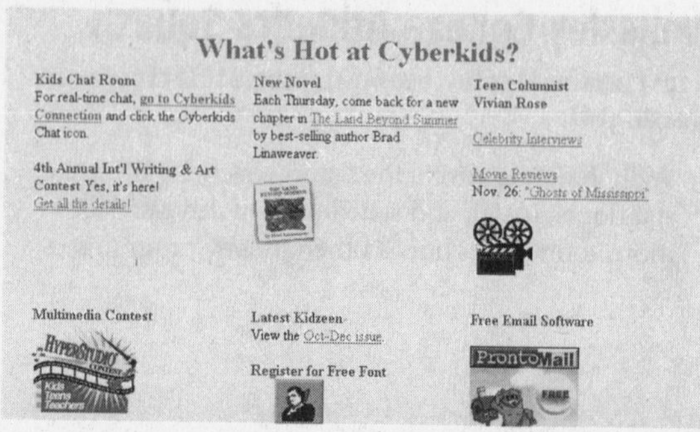

CyberKids was created as a place for kids to learn and have fun. Offers a free online magazine that contains stories and artwork created by kids, as well as online puzzles, games, and more. Also provides keypals from around the globe in CyberKids Interactive.

English as a Second Language

http://www.lang.uiuc.edu/r-li5/esl/

Brings together resources for teaching ES/FL, such as matching audio to text to help comprehension. Also offers links to the Word a Day vocabulary building email service, and idiom of the Week.

Kids' Space

`http://www.interport.net/~sachi`

Kids Space has been planned for children to enhance basic computer skills through their real participation and use of the Internet. Provides tools for creation of student's own Web pages.

Kids Web at NPAC

`http://www.infomall.org/kidsweb/`

Provides a collection of multimedia and other resources useful in education. Caution: The fun and humor link leads to a general Internet humor archive, an area that might not be entirely appropriate for children.

Sylvan Learning Centers

`http://www.educate.com/`

Offers supplemental education to every type of student. Provides information on their services and locations.

Voices of Youth Homepage

`http://www.unicef.org/voy/`

Contains messages from the World Summit for Social Development. Pertains to topics discussed at the Summit, and although the server doesn't currently accept new messages, you can browse and search old messages by topic.

Welcome to RouteICS

`http://ics.soe.umich.edu/`

Provides information to students and attempts to provide them a chance to contribute their own observations, findings, and reflections.

Welcome to Virtual FlyLab

`http://vflylab.calstatela.edu/edesktop/VirtApps/VflyLab/IntroVflyLab.html`

Enables you to play the role of a scientist investigating genetic inheritance: manipulate the matings of different fruit flies and see the genetic results of the matings.

Writing at MU

`http://www.missouri.edu/~writery/`

Online discussion site for writers. Offers four direct links to information exchange with other writers. Includes other links to assorted Internet sites, mostly related to writing, as well. (Note that a few might not be appropriate for children.)

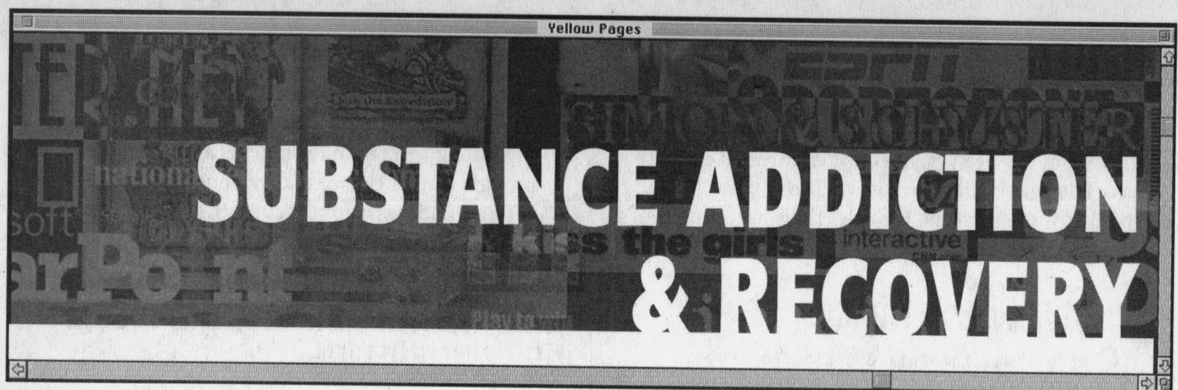

SUBSTANCE ADDICTION & RECOVERY

> There is no moral middle ground. Indifference is not an option…
> For the sake of our children, I implore each of you to be unyielding and inflexible in your opposition to drugs.
>
> *Nancy Reagan*

AL-ANON and ALATEEN

http://www.al-anon-alateen.org/

Answer the 20 questions to help determine whether you'd like to pursue what Al-Anon and Alateen have to offer. Read the 12 Steps and the 12 Traditions of Al-Anon. This site is available in an array of languages, including French, Russian, English, Swedish, and several others. Follow the link to the official Al-Anon/Alateen home page.

The Al-Anon/Alateen Home Page

http://www.al-anon.org/

Explore this site if you feel you are affected by someone else's drinking, or if you grew up with a problem drinker. You'll find 20 questions to answer to determine whether you have a problem. You'll also find 20 questions for the person who grew up with an alcoholic. Answer them to determine whether you're still affected. There's a special section for teens and one for professionals.

Drinking: A Student's Guide
http://www.glness.com/ndhs/

Alcoholics Anonymous

http://www.alcoholics-anonymous.org/

From the home page, choose either the English, Spanish, or French versions of the text, and continue. You'll find 12 questions you can answer to help determine whether A.A. might be helpful. You'll also find local contact information and a special section for professionals.

Betty Ford Center

http://www.bettyfordcenter.org/

Betty Ford Center is the first and most famous of addiction treatment centers, and this is its home page. Here you'll find information about the inpatient and outpatient programs at Betty Ford Center. There's also a codependency treatment plan, along with news of upcoming events and an upcoming alumni event.

Cenikor Foundation, Inc.

http://www.neosoft.com/~cenikor

A nonprofit organization with a focus on assisting people in developing skills they need to live a lifestyle free from substance abuse. Provides free residential, treatment, education, and prevention services to people over the age of 18.

D.A.R.E.

http://www.dare-america.com/index2.htm

This is the home page of the D.A.R.E. to keep kids off drugs people. There's information for kids, parents, and educators. Find out how law enforcement is cooperating in your community and elsewhere to stop drugs. This is a Family Friendly Site.

Definition of Nicotine Dependence

http://www.mayo.ivi.com/mayo/pted/htm/nicdef.htm#retotop

This page, part of the Mayo Clinic's Health O@sis site, provides a clear explanation of nicotine dependence. Do you have a habit, or are you truly dependent on the drug nicotine? Find out here. Also use the Search button to find other pages of interest in the Mayo Clinic site.

Drinking: A Student's Guide

http://www.glness.com/ndhs/

This is a fun site about a serious topic. Aimed at high school and college students, the site presents the facts about binge drinking, alcohol and health, and alcohol and drugs. After reading all the facts, you can do the self-assessment to determine whether you're at risk. If so, there's an extensive list of resources to contact.

Drinkwise

http://www.med.umich.edu/drinkwise/

An educational program that helps people reduce alcohol consumption. Includes a self-evaluation form and phone number to contact Drinkwise for more information.

Habit Smart

http://www.cts.com:80/~habtsmrt/

Provides information about addictive behavior: theories of habit strengths, persistence, and change. Also offers tips for managing problematic behavior.

The Marijuana Anonymous Home Page

http://www.marijuana-anonymous.org/

Learn the facts about marijuana addiction. Take the quiz to find out whether you need help. Learn the 12 steps for recovery. Benefit from the shared experiences of others. Find out how to join Marijuana Anonymous.

The Master Anti-Smoking Page

http://www.autonomy.com/smoke.htm

If you want to quit smoking, check here for cyber-support. Whether you use the patch, taper off, or quit cold turkey, it never hurts to share your experience with others who are exactly where you are. Read about the triumphs and trials of other quitters, and gain support in your own effort.

National Women's Resource Center

http://www.nwrc.org/

This site is devoted to women addicted to alcohol, tobacco, and other drugs or who suffer from mental illness. There are documents on fetal alcohol syndrome and abuse of women as well as a searchable bibliographic database and a library of women's resources.

Partnership for a Drug-Free America

http://www.drugfreeamerica.org/

Check this site for answers to your FAQs about drugs. There's helpful information for parents, and they promise that, unlike some other Internet information, theirs is accurate and up-to-date.

PARTS (Parents and Adolescents Recovering Together)

http://www.parts.land-5.com/

This site contains articles and advice for parents and adolescents who are caught in the maelstrom of drug use. There's advice from parents who have been there and a select list of links where you can find more help.

Prevline: Prevention Online

http://www.health.org/

Provides information for those people battling substance abuse, or who know someone battling substance abuse. Contains press releases, publications, forums, and calendars of upcoming events.

Recovery Home Page

http://www.shore.net/~tcfraser/recovery.htm

Table of contents includes Alcoholics Anonymous information, other 12-step recovery programs, events, treatment centers, commercial recovery sources, and mailing lists.

SOBER VACATIONS INTERNATIONAL

http://www.hpsystems.com/sober/index.htm

Two brothers, one a recovering alcoholic, the other recovering from drug use, sponsor sober group vacations for others. Check it out and join them for fun in the sun that includes speakers and workshops.

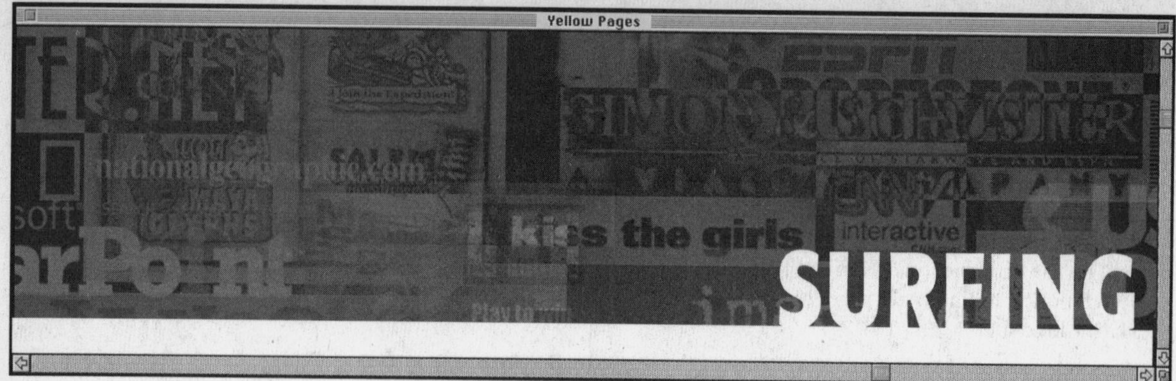

> Remember the tide turns at low water, as well as high.
>
> *Unknown*

Closely Guarded Secrets of the U.K. Surfing World
http://www.britsurf.org/UKSurfIndex/

International Surfing Museum
http://www.surfingmuseum.org/

OceanBlue
http://www.oceanblue.com/

Adventure Surf

http://www.advensurf.com/

This travel and trip planning site is for surfers produced by surfers. Offers info on travel companies, surfboard shapers, surf maps, and more.

Closely Guarded Secrets of the U.K. Surfing World

http://www.britsurf.org/UKSurfIndex/

A thorough and well-designed site for surfing in the U.K. Features include listings of surf clubs and schools, an online surf shop, links to surfing magazines and the British Surfers Association, and much more.

Drop In

http://www.ohana.com/hisurfad/links/links.html

Discover the best places to surf, as well as join Surfrider Foundation USA, an environmental group committed to protecting the beaches and waves.

International Surfing Museum

http://www.surfingmuseum.org/

At this site, visitors can view the collection of surf films, surf music, surfboards, and memorabilia. Visit the current exhibit too. If you like this site, consider becoming a member.

Nancy Emerson's School of Surfing

http://www.maui.net/~ncesurf/ncesurf.html

This school, which is located in Maui, offers classes and clinics taught by international surfing champion Nancy Emerson and other top instructors. The site features a photo of Nancy's dog Apache surfing. If a dog can learn to surf, can't you?

OceanBlue

http://www.oceanblue.com/

This site offers a guide to the best beaches, sea sports, and taking care of the environment. Also contains information on windsurfing, body boarding, boogie boarding, and ocean kayaking. A picturesque site full of useful information.

Real Surfing

http://www.real-surfing.com/

Offers surf weather reports, magazines, health and environmental issues, and more. Also offers a list of the latest surf sites on the Web.

Surf and Sun Beach Vacation Guide

http://www.surf-sun.com/

This site links visitors to beach destinations around the world. Also includes a complete travel planner.

Surfcall

http://www.surfcall.co.uk/indexa.html

Check daily surf conditions for the United Kingdom. Visitors can choose their surf sites according to region.

SurfTrader

http://www.surftrader.com/

This site features surf classifieds that link buyers and sellers of surfing collectibles, art, and memorabilia.

The Surfer's Guide Books and Maps

http://www.vansantcreations.com/surf/

Specializing in East Coast maps and books to help visitors find the best surfing spots. Also offers an online guide to surf colleges.

The Wet Surfing Page

http://members.networx.net.au/~wilcox/

High-graphics site with photos of surfers, their boards and babes, complete with background music. Be aware that this site takes some time to load.

United States Surfing Committee

http://www.ussurfc.org/

This site belongs to a non-profit organization that is dedicated to getting surfing into the Olympics.

Windsurfer.com

http://www.windsurfer.com/

A thorough windsurfing database divided into organized categories. A link to maps and technical info is helpful in using the page and links to member sites and online publications give other areas to explore.

Related Sites

http://infinityweb.com/blueplanet/

http://www.thegrid.net/fleming/

http://www.geocities.com/TheTropics/4271/

http://www.HMBSurfCo.com/

http://www.i-one.com/hisurfad/

http://www.co.la.ca.us/Beaches/scripts/beaches.htm

http://shell2.ba.best.com/~malcolm/surf/legends/

http://www.atlantis-intl.com/tandem_surfing/

http://rodin.cs.uh.edu/~tbone/

http://www.whammer.com/

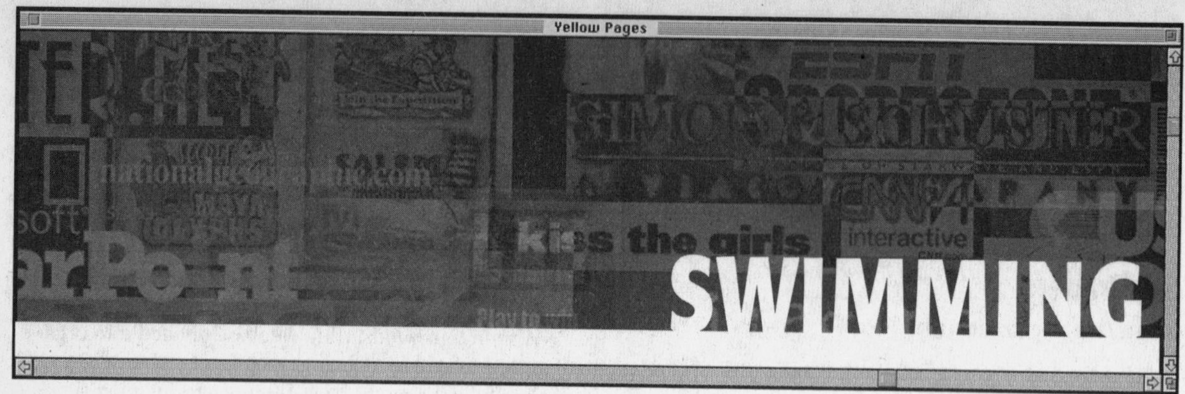

> One time there was this kid, and he went swimming after eating, and he got a stomach cramp and he started to drown, but the sturgeon general grabbed him by his shirt and put him on the shore.
>
> *Eric in* The Cure *(1995)*

8th World Swimming Championships

http://www.iinet.net.au/~wsc1998/

Find out everything you need to know about the 8th World Swimming Championships, held in Perth, Western Australia January 8 through 18, 1998. This aquatic competition features swimming, diving, water polo, synchronized swimming, and synchronized diving. More than 100 countries are expected to compete. Includes recent swimming news on events held in Australia and Australians' swimming accomplishments.

Related Sites

- http://lornet.com/~asca/
- http://www.usswim.org/latest/glossary.htm
- http://hcs.harvard.edu/~swim/links/
- http://www.swiminfo.com/
- http://www.advocatehealth.com/fitness/fitswim.html
- http://www.taper-shave.com/index.htm

Infant Swimming Research, Inc.
http://www.infantswim.com/home.html

STORMFAX Safe Ocean Swimming Guide
http://www.stormfax.com/safeswim.htm

SWIMNEWS ONLINE
http://www.swimnews.com/

Health and Safety Services Aquatics

http://www.redcross.org/hss/aquatics.html

Learn about the courses offered by the American Red Cross for all ages, skill levels, and physical abilities. Children and their families can take courses that teach them how to prevent accidents and enjoy the water safely. They also can learn to swim or improve their swimming with new strokes, stroke refinements, and diving safety tips and techniques. Offers courses for lifeguards, swim coaches, and instructors. A basic sailing course is also available. Use the search engine to find the location of your local Red Cross.

Infant Swimming Research, Inc.

http://www.infantswim.com/home.html

ISR offers a complete program of parent education concerning the many facets of drowning prevention. Examine ISR's lessons and techniques for teaching 6-month to 12-month infants, as well as children who are one year and older. Get drowning-prevention and safety tips. You'll also see info on some of the legitimate concerns about infant swimming programs. This site recommends that you read the *Parent Resource Book*; it is required reading for parents who register their children in ISR lessons. The book covers attitude and emotions; physiology and safety before, during, and after the lesson; factors in learning; behaviorism; family aquatic safety; CCPR; and first aid. Find an ISR instructor near you and learn about the certification requirements each must meet.

SYMPHONY ORCHESTRAS

> Talking pictures, that means I'm out of a job. At last I can start suffering and write that symphony.
>
> *Cosmo in* Singin' in the Rain *(1952)*

Albert Schweitzer Youth Orchestra

http://members.aol.com/JGuntau/asj_eng.htm

For nearly a quarter of a century, the Albert Schweitzer Youth Orchestra, based in Hamburg, has brought teenaged and young adult musicians together for education, rehearsal, and performance. This page provides details on the orchestra—including listing the current performers by name and instrument, upcoming concerts, reviews, and other information. The page is available in English and German versions.

The Children's Orchestra Society

http://www.geocities.com/Vienna/1724/COS.htm

Since 1984, the Children's Orchestra Society (COS) has pursued excellence in musical education for young people, including orchestra and chamber music and private lessons—extending even to master classes with famous guest musicians. This Web site provides details on the history, policies, philosophy, and so on, of COS.

Israel Philharmonic Orchestra

http://www.ipo.co.il/

If for no other reason, go to this site to read the history of the orchestra. It's fascinating. While you're there, though, read about upcoming special concerts, Music Director Maestro Zubin Mehta, the members of the orchestra, and more. Bilingual.

Orchestral News
http://ourworld.compuserve.com/homepages/John_Woollard/

Kammer Sinfonia Berlin

http://www.rewi.hu-berlin.de/~matze/KSB/welcome.html

This relatively young professional orchestra, based in Berlin, performs a wide variety of music. Consisting of an ensemble of 20+ pieces, it can expand to more than 70 as needed. This site provides a brief history of the orchestra and its members, concert information, reviews, and so on. In English and German.

London Symphony Orchestra

http://www.lso.co.uk/

Although the orchestra itself is world-renowned, its Web page is just getting started. All the basic information is provided, though, including a prize drawing (see the guest book), details on booking and concerts, information on sponsorship. The News & Features page is updated monthly with current info. More activities for the Web site are planned in the near future.

National Youth Orchestra of Canada

http://www.nyoc.org/

This interesting site, in English and French versions, is as charming as the young people who make up the orchestra—almost 2,000 of them in the orchestra's nearly 40-year history. Information about the current orchestra and alumni, audition and application details, tour dates, and journal entries from past tours. Related music links.

Related Sites

http://members.aol.com/bayyouthva/byohome.htm

http://www.swilkinson.demon.co.uk/

http://www.geocities.com/Vienna/1724/COS.htm

A B C D E F G H I J K L M N O P Q R S T U V W X Y Z

New World Symphony

http://www.nws.org/

The Web site for this orchestra reflects its Miami Beach location, with refreshingly cool background colors and graphics of palm trees, but that doesn't keep it from being a serious site. Details are provided on the orchestra's 10th anniversary season, 1997–1998. Calendar of upcoming events, biography of founder and artistic director Michael Tilson Thomas, photos, staffing and ticket information.

New Zealand Symphony Orchestra

http://www.nzso.co.nz/

Reading this site's eclectic and entertaining content is almost as enjoyable as attending a good concert. There's plenty to see, hear, and do—be sure to check out the Robo-Critic and the collected links on the Fun page—as well as the expected details on the orchestra, concert dates, news and awards, and much more.

North American Elite Chinese Youth Orchestra

http://uranus.gmu.edu/~rchang/naecyo.html

This orchestra, composed of 88 young Chinese musicians, is only two years old, but already has had an extensive tour through the U.S. and Taiwan. The Web site is even newer. Links to pages for the artistic director, pictures, orchestra members, upcoming tours.

Orchestral News

http://ourworld.compuserve.com/homepages/John_Woollard/

Want to know the schedule for your favorite orchestra? Detailed information on full-sized professional orchestras throughout the world. Information is provided by the orchestras and halls. No graphics; this site is intended for speed. When available, links to the home pages of the orchestras are provided. (Most of the orchestras listed do have Web sites.)

Orchestre Symphonique de Montréal (Montréal Symphony Orchestra)

http://www.osm.ca/

Press releases, details on the orchestra's piano and voice competition, planned concerts for the current and next season, photos, subscription and biography information, and more. This framed site is available in French and English versions.

Radion Sinfoniaorkesterin (Finnish Radio Symphony Orchestra)

http://www.yle.fi/rso/

This bilingual site (in Finnish and English) includes day-by-day details on upcoming concerts and tours (also searchable by artist, type of concert, or composer). Information on musicians and available recordings, photo gallery and listening room. Graphically intense but nicely presented.

Toronto Symphony Orchestra

http://www.tso.on.ca/

Concert schedule, ticket information, press releases, organizational information, subscription and membership details, and the *TSO Gazette*. More contents planned for the future.

Utrechtsch Studenten Concert (Utrecht Student Concert)

http://www.fys.ruu.nl/~usc/Home.english.html

Founded in 1823, the Utrechtsch Studenten Concert is the oldest symphony orchestra of Holland. The orchestra makes an annual trip to perform in foreign countries; this site provides details about the current concert schedule, the orchestra's mascot, and more. Bilingual.

West Australian Symphony Orchestra

http://www.abc.net.au/waso/

This elegant site includes a list of the musicians, a well-organized calendar of events, descriptions of the concert series, and a link to ABC Online (Australian Broadcasting Corporation).

FTP SITE

http://www.iuma.com/IUMA/ftp/indexes/

Related Sites

http://www.csobravo.org/splash.html

http://www.btinternet.com/~nyo/

http://www.nvs.org/

http://www.moccom.com/SJBO/E_HOME.htm

http://www.the-kings-consort.org.uk/

http://www.geocities.com/Vienna/Strasse/3697/

http://www.viola.com/ays/

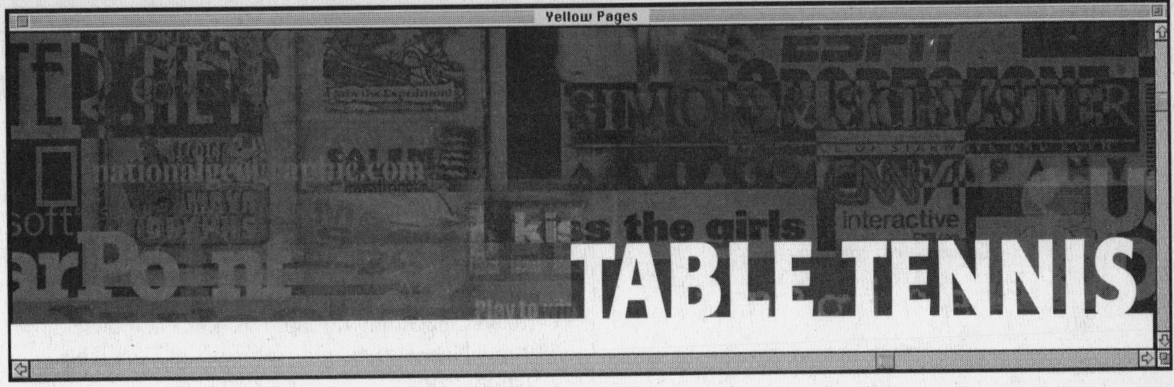

If you can react the same way to winning and losing, that's a big accomplishment.

Chris Evert

BS Table Tennis

http://www.geocities.com/Colosseum/7666/index.html

Check out table tennis rules, rankings, links, the picture gallery, news, and updates.

International Table Tennis Federation

http://www.ittf.com/

Browse through this online magazine for the latest world competition results and profiled players. Also includes links to other table tennis sites.

League of Northeast Intercollegiate Table Tennis

http://www.lnitt.org/

This official LNITT home page promotes college table tennis.

Related Sites

http://www.hal-pc.org/~canupnet/ttworld.html

http://espn.sportszone.com/editors/atlanta96/sports/table/0801men.html

http://www.hamptonsweb.com/sports/tt.htm

http://jtta.ge.niigata-u.ac.jp/index_e.html

http://www.usatoday.com/olympics/ott/ottmrb.htm

Table Tennis FAQ
http://peacock.tnjc.edu.tw/ADD/sport/faq.html

Table Tennis—Home Page from The Mining Company
http://tabletennis.miningco.com/mbody.htm

Sports A to Z: Table Tennis: History

http://www.olympic-usa.org/sports/az_3_36_1.html

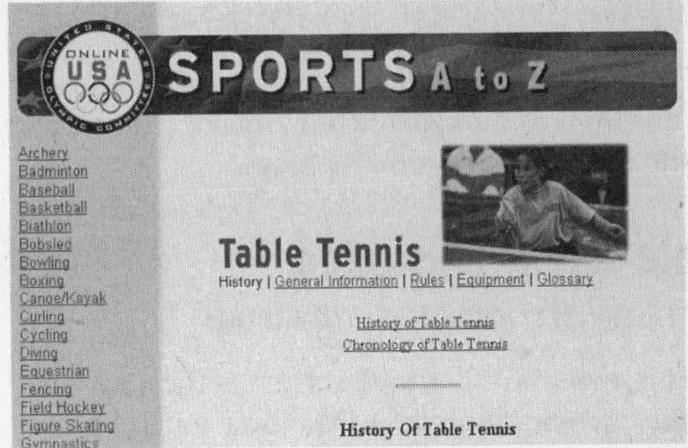

Check out this site for table tennis history, general information, rules, and equipment. If you're unfamiliar with this sport, you might want to read through the glossary of table tennis terms.

Table Tennis Around the World

http://peacock.tnjc.edu.tw/ADD/sport/ww-link.html

Come to this site to consult the schedule of table tennis events around the world. Includes links to the various table tennis clubs hosting the events.

Table Tennis FAQ

http://peacock.tnjc.edu.tw/ADD/sport/faq.html

This site provides great info on rankings, players associations, scoring, and terminology. It's a good place to start if you want to become a table tennis umpire.

A B C D E F G H I J K L M N O P Q R S T U V W X Y Z

Table Tennis—Home Page from The Mining Company

http://tabletennis.miningco.com/mbody.htm

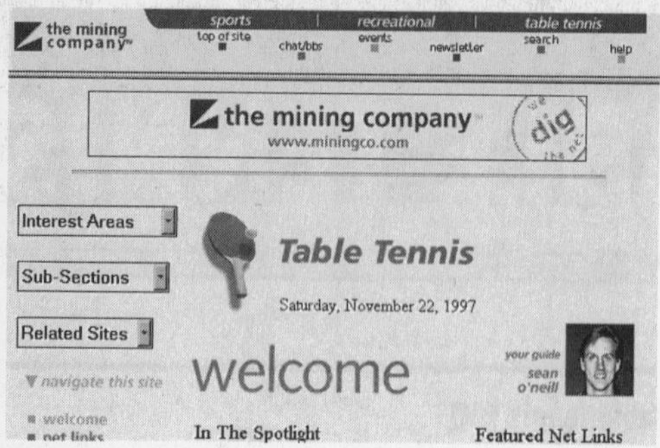

This site provides general table tennis info. Look here for places to play, events, entry blanks, detailed coaching tips, equipment (lists of distributors, dealers, and manufacturers), and book recommendations.

Table Tennis Hub Magazine

http://www.tabletennis1.com/magazine/default.htm

Check here for table tennis competition results. You can also read through the bios of table tennis players and check out the world rankings.

Table Tennis Illustrated

http://www.ittf.com/TTI/GEN/MAG.html

This e-zine is a shortened version of the magazine. *Table Tennis Illustrated* is the official journal of the International Table Tennis Federation. It is distributed worldwide and published nine times a year.

Table Tennis World Championships Videos

http://www.reflexsports.com/wttcfrcopy.html

Offers videos of official table tennis world-class competition. Includes world and European table tennis championships, training, and Olympic competitions.

The Unoffical Ping Pong Home Page

http://www2.cybernex.net/~jfox/jeremy/twopages/pingpong.htm

If you're an amateur player, this Q&A could be quite helpful. Questions include "Is there a best way to serve?" and "What are some of the different shots that you can play?"

USA Table Tennis

http://www.ustta.org/

Check here for news on the USA Nationals, and browse through the Tournament Information Guide. Investigate the info on clubs, hot spots to play, equipment, dealers, USATT rules, upcoming tournaments, and results. Learn how to become a USA Table Tennis member. You can get information on table tennis rules in the Stump the Ump section. Or, browse through the current and past issues of USA Table Tennis e-zine.

WashingtonPost.com: Table Tennis

http://www.washingtonpost.com/wp-srv/sports/olympics/longterm/tableten/front.htm

Come to this site for the latest table tennis news and results.

World Wide Ping-Pong

http://www.asahi-net.or.jp/~SZ4M-KS/wwpp.html

This site gives you a collection of links to table tennis home pages all over the world.

World Wide Web of Sports—Table Tennis (Ping-Pong)

http://peacock.tnjc.edu.tw/sports.html

Gives you info on global tournaments, players, and the current champion.

NEWSGROUP

rec.sport.table-tennis

Related Sites

http://www.nynow.com/nysol/tabten.html

http://point-blockbuster.lycos.com/reviews/OtherIndoorSports_6364.html

http://www.lut.ac.uk/research/paad/ipc/table-tennis/table-tennis.html

http://www.reflexsports.com/linksfr.html

http://www.usatt.org/document/dealers.html

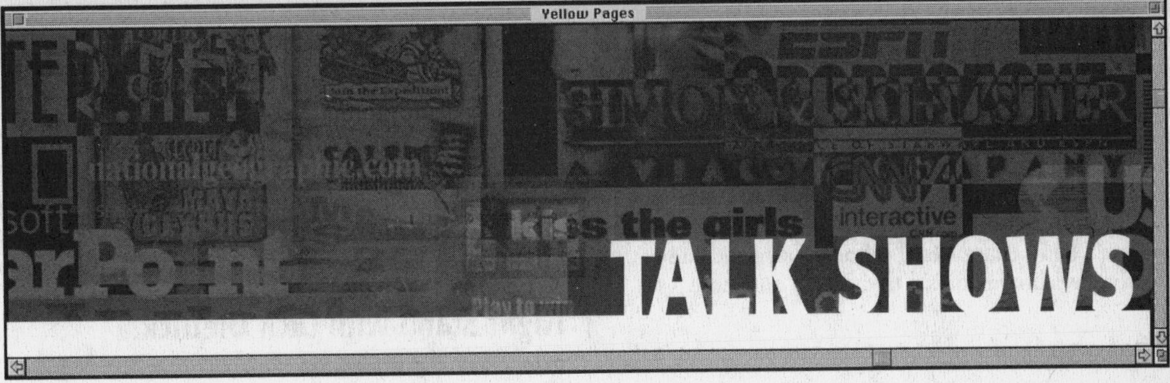

My favorite shows were *Merv Griffin* and *Mike Douglas.* I would literally run home from school everyday and switch them on. I hope we can bring back that kind of show to television.

Rosie O'Donnell

Carol Vitale

`http://www.cvglam.com/`

This centerfold and TV personality is the host of her own cable talk show. Also contains a photo gallery, lace lingerie for the hands, and more. Site has a disclaimer that it is for adults over 21.

Chris Rock

`http://www.hbo.com/chrisrock/`

This hot, in-demmand comedian hosts his own show Fridays at 11:30 p.m. ET on HBO. Site includes weekly show highlights and behind-the-scenes interviews with the show's writers and producers.

Crook & Chase

`http://www.crookandchase.com/`

After a brief stint on national television, can once again be seen every afternoon on cable's The Nashville Network. It features celebrity interviews, comedy sketches, and other informational and entertainment segments.

NRP TOP PICKS

David Letterman
`http://www.cbs.com/latenight/lateshow/`

Home & Family
`http://www.homeandfamily.com/`

Politically Incorrect with Bill Maher
`http://abc.com/pi/`

David Letterman

`http://www.cbs.com/latenight/lateshow/`

Find out who will be on the show each day and check out the latest Top 10 list at this official site for *The Late Show with David Letterman.* Site also contains some of the best quips heard over the past few weeks, ticket information, and Top 10 archives.

The Ed Sullivan Show

`http://www.edsullivan.com/`

Ed Sullivan is the man that they all learned it from: Johnny Carson, David Letterman, Jay Leno, and Conan O'Brien would all have to bow their heads to this man. Now he has a home on the Web. You can order tapes, read bios, and visit the Ed Sullivan store.

Gayle King

`http://members.aol.com/loveugayle/gayle.html`

This is the site for the new talk show hosted by Oprah's best friend, Gayle King. Site contains Gayle's biography and ticket information for the show.

Geraldo

`http://www.geraldo.com/`

Provides a synopsis of today's show and a schedule for the week. Site contains a poll of the week, transcript information, and Geraldo's bio and career highlights. Don't forget to watch Fridays for celebrity gossip!

Home & Family

http://www.homeandfamily.com/

This Family Channel show features hosts Cristina Ferrare and Chuck Woolery. Site offers topics such as In the Kitchen, Parenting, Relationships, Health, and Home Decorating. Also includes a list of classifieds and a Show Diary, which contains video and audio clips, celebrity photos, a trivia game, and more.

Jay Leno

http://www.nbc.com/tonightshow/

Find out who tonight's guests are and who you missed last night. Share a monologue moment and read through some of Jay's famous funny headlines.

Jenny Jones

http://www.jennyjones.com/

This site contains a summary of today's wacky show, a monthly recipe, makeup tips, and show highlights. It also provides contact information for women with breast implant concerns, which is one of Jenny's causes.

Jerry Springer

http://www.universalstudios.com/tv/jerryspringer/

This show can best be explained by its list of show topics for the week. At this writing, they were "I Will Break You Up!", "Surprise! I Have Two Lovers!", "I'm 16 and in a Love Triangle!", "I Know You're Cheating!", and "I Stole My 12-Year-Old's Boyfriend!" (And yes, they all really have exclamation points.) Enough said.

Keenen Ivory Wayans

http://www.tvplex.com/BuenaVista/Keenen/

This show, described here as "talk/variety with an attitude," features celebrity interviews, musical guests, and lots of Keenan's own brand of humor. Best known for the show *In Living Color* (which helped launch Jim Carrey's career), Keenan is a multitalented entertainer who also produces, writes, acts, and directs.

Lauren Hutton and…

http://www.turner.com/laurenhutton/

This interview-format show features Lauren Hutton talking with one guest in depth. According to this site, the show is the first talk show to be shot on film, which lends a unique atmosphere. Site lists this week's guests and offers a quote of the week.

Leeza

http://www.nbc.com/tvcentral/shows/leeza/

This talk show, hosted by former *Entertainment Tonight* personality Leeza Gibbons, attempts to rise above all the filth on other daytime shows. View the show's credits, show schedule, and ticket information here.

Night Stand with Dick Dietrick

http://www.nightstand.com/

This show spoofs other daytime talk shows such as Ricki Lake and Jerry Springer. Actor Tim Stark stars as Dick Dietrick, a fictional talk show host. A great parody of the salacious nature of other shows.

Oprah Winfrey

http://www.oprahshow.com/

This long-running talk show exemplifies the best of daytime TV by far. Site lists this week's topics, which you can rely on to be sensible, not sensational. Read Oprah's bio and find out how to be a guest on the show. For more detailed Oprah information, this site tells you how to get to Oprah Online on AOL.

Politically Incorrect with Bill Maher

http://abc.com/pi/

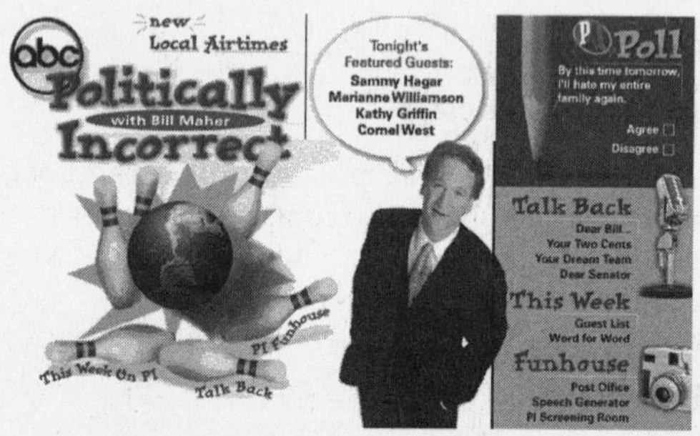

This smart, hip show has found a dedicated following that enjoys its irreverent political discussions. This show provides evidence that some celebs and politicians are smarter than we give them credit for… but most aren't. Site includes a hilarious speech generator that you'll love.

The Politically Incorrect Unofficial Home Page

http://www.netcrusader.net/~olsens/pi/

Bill Maher is the host of this popular ABC panel discussion show. This page is filled with information about him, this show, and other bits of Politically Incorrect trivia.

Regis & Kathie Lee

http://www.tvplex.com/BuenaVista/RegisAndKathieLee/index.html

This site contains interesting facts about both Regis and Kathie Lee, as well as guest and fan club information. You also can enter the daily trivia contest or sign up for the LIVE! newsletter.

Ricki Lake

http://www.spe.sony.com/tv/shows/ricki/index.html

This is the official Ricki Lake home page with audio clips, video and still pictures, and a behind-the-scenes set opportunity.

Rolonda

http://www.kingworld.com/rolonda/index.html

Rolanda Watts' talk show has been on for several seasons. You can visit this Web site to read about its history, Rolanda's biography, or submit show topic ideas.

Rosie O'Donnell

http://www.rosieo.com/

Updated daily, this site has scheduled guests for today and tomorrow, show descriptions, and a list of where you can catch the show.

Sally on the Net

http://www.sallyjr.com/

Send in your favorite show ideas or why you think you should appear yourself. Look to see what happened to past guests after their show aired. Send in your answer to this week's viewer poll.

The Unofficial Talk Soup Web Page

http://home.ptd.net/~mstill/talksoup/index.htm

Mostly filled with sound clips, there are also pictures available at this site dedicated to E! Entertainment Television's *Talk Soup*.

The View

http://www.abc.com/theview/

Take a little time to enjoy The View's Web site. Register your views in today's Hot Topic Poll and answer the Question of the Day. Show archives reveal past guests and topics, and a page is dedicated to viewer responses to the show.

Vibe

http://www.spe.sony.com/Pictures/tv/vibe/

This show has enjoyed a resurgence since Sinbad took over as guest host. See who's on tonight as well as upcoming guests. Listen to audio clips and view video clips from the show. This site is graphics-heavy; people with slower modems beware.

FTP

ftp://ftp.abc.com/Oprah

ftp://ftp.cdrom.com/.12/internet/rtfm/alt/tv/talkshows

ftp://ftp.cs.columbia.edu/archives/faq/alt/tv/talkshows

ftp://ftp.csie.nctu.edu.tw/Documents/FAQ/alt/tv/talkshows

ftp://ftp.eu.net/documents/faq/letterman

ftp://ftp.gwu.edu/pub/rtfm/alt/tv/talkshows

ftp://ftp.sinica.edu.tw/doc/USENET-FAQ/alt/tv/talkshows

ftp://ftp.tol.it/software/FAQ/alt/tv/talkshows

ftp://ftp.uk.psi.net/pub/usenet/control/alt/alt.fan.rosieodonnell.Z

Related Sites

http://dspace.dial.pipex.com/town/estate/gk01/

http://users.cybercity.dk/~dko1225/leno.htm

http://www.candmshow.com/candm/cmhome.htm

http://www.cardnet.net/~alexdiaz/rosie/

http://www.celebsite.com/people/oprahwinfrey/

http://www.channel4.com/entertainment/lunch/

http://www.ils.nwu.edu/~johnson/Letterman/shows.html

http://www.nbc.com/entertainment/shows/conan/index.html

http://www.nbc.com/tvcentral/shows/later/index.html

http://www.pbs.org/charlierose/

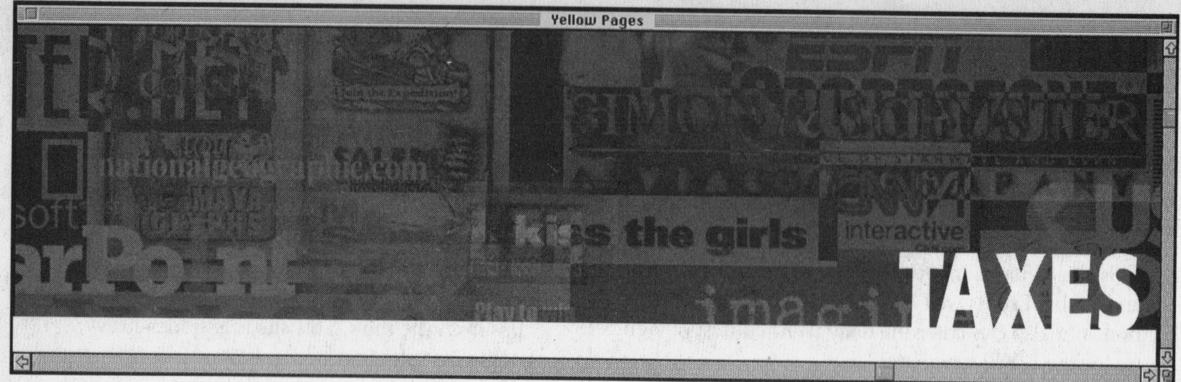

Walk slow, like you do when you come to pay your taxes.

Mayor Hawkins in Meet John Doe *(1941)*

Citizens for an Alternative Tax System

http://www.cats.org/

Houses the national public interest group for an alternative tax system and tax reform. Talks mainly about the group's manifesto and related information.

Citizens for a Sound Economy Foundation

http://www.cse.org/nr-csef-txnbgt092597.htm

This site is devoted to the goal of CSE Foundation counselor Jim Miller's proposal to organize a national tour debate to feature U.S. Representatives Dick Armey and Billy Tauzin. The main question: should the IRS and tax code be scrapped in favor of a national sales tax or flat tax?

Citizens for Tax Justice

http://www.ctj.org/

This is a nonprofit organization that does research to support its advocacy of a fairer tax code for middle- and low-income families, closing corporate tax loopholes, reducing the federal deficit, and requiring the rich to pay their fair share.

Related Sites

http://www.house.gov/democrats/taxplan/taxplan.html

http://www.deathtax.com/

http://www.ctj.org/html/faq.html

Restructuring the IRS
http://www.policy.com/issuewk/97/1103/index.html

The Digital Daily

http://www.irs.ustreas.gov/prod/cover.html

The Daily is the IRS's online newsletter. It provides news, where to go for help, online forms, links, info about record keeping, a commissioner's forum, and a site map.

Electronic Services

http://www.irs.ustreas.gov/prod/elec_svs/index.html

This site serves to help taxpayers deal with the changing landscape of mail delivery. That is, with the advent of online submission of taxes, questions arise regarding what can be sent online and how it is done. The site also provides basic tax info and online forms.

Forms and Publications

http://www.irs.ustreas.gov/prod/forms_pubs/forms.html

This site contains every tax form and publication imaginable. Choose from many formats, including PDF, and you'll never have to drive to the library in the rain to find files they may not have for some reason.

Internal Revenue Service Real and Personal Property Sales

http://www.treas.gov/treasury/services/auctions/irs-auctions/

This IRS site lists all properties up for sale that have been seized for nonpayment, probably from the law-abiding people complaining on the IRS Abuse Reports page!

L.A. Professionals Online

http://www.primenet.com/~laig/proserve

Provides generic information from attorneys, certified public accountants, and medical professionals. Offers a bulletin section that contains information about tax issues, including an analysis of IRS guidelines for independent contractors and employee status.

Online Money: Are You Audit Bait?

http://pathfinder.com/money/features/auditbait_0196/

Money magazine's site provides tips on how to avoid tax audits of your 1996 and 1997 returns by noting items such as what the IRS looks for.

Restructuring the IRS

http://www.policy.com/issuewk/97/1103/index.html

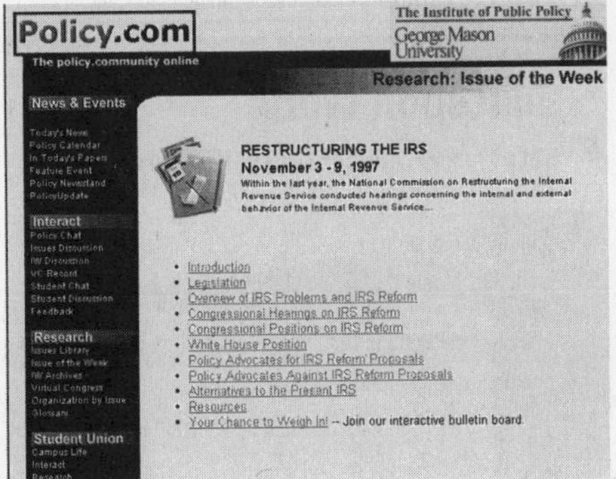

Read news about hearings of the National Commission on Restructuring the Internal Revenue Service, interact with other taxpayers, and do your own research concerning tax code.

A Selection of IRS Abuse Reports for use in Class-Action Lawsuits

http://www.zonpower.com/irs-class-action/1.html#list

This site comes with a warning that the stories become increasingly disturbing and that readers should consider a mild sedative before proceeding. Those with high blood pressure should probably skip it altogether. These stories date back to 1995.

Tax Info for Business

http://www.irs.ustreas.gov/prod/bus_info/index.html

If the individual taxpayer thinks filing is tough, try filing for a business. This site helps to answer all business tax questions, provides more forms, has a tax FAQ, and provides other useful pages.

Tax Info for You

http://www.irs.ustreas.gov/prod/ind_info/index.html

This page will help the individual taxpayer become aware of more exemptions, tax law, and other aspects of filing individually. Like all the IRS-based sites, it provides a search engine for individualized help and more.

Taxpayer Help and Education

http://www.irs.gov/prod/tax_edu/teletax/tc101.html

This site coincides with volunteer-based programs the Service provides to help citizens drudge their way through murky roads.

Tax Regs in Plain English

http://www.irs.ustreas.gov/prod/tax_regs/index.html

According to this site's banners, come here if you want tax questions answered in terms you can follow. Because it is an official IRS site, one must remain dubious.

TaxSites—Income Tax Information in Internet

http://www.best.com/~ftmexpat/html/taxsites.html

Provides income tax-related information. Also contains links to several related sites, including tax forms, FAQs, U.S. and state tax laws, and tax software.

TeleFile

http://www.irs.ustreas.gov/basic/elec_svs/telefile.html

This site explains a relatively new service of the IRS that allows certain citizens to file via the telephone. View an overview, tax statistics, and countless articles that answer just about every question you could have.

United States Tax Code Online

http://www.fourmilab.ch/ustax/ustax.html

Provides interactive access to the complete text of United States Internal Revenue Code.

Yahoo! Full Coverage

http://headlines.yahoo.com/Full_Coverage/US/IRS_Hearings/

With all the hubbub over scandal at the IRS, this page was set up to keep the online taxpayer aware of all breaking news that relates to taxes, the IRS, legislation, Congress, and all things levied.

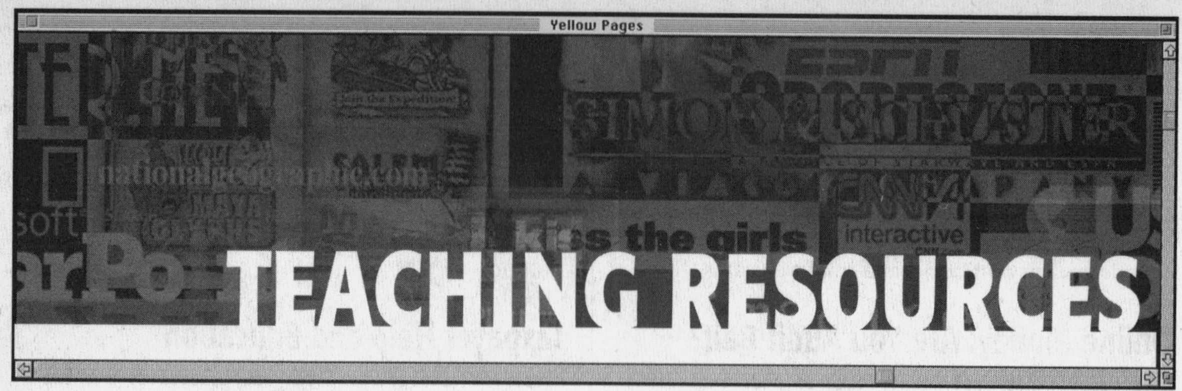

> The best teacher is the one who suggests rather than dogmatizes, and inspires his listener with the wish to teach himself.
>
> *Edward Bulwer-Lytton*

The Book Corner

`http://www.thebookcorner.com`

The Book Corner offers a wide selection of high quality children's books, gifts, and teaching resources, including online secured credit card purchasing.

Early Childhood Educators' and Family Web Corner

`http://www.nauticom.net/www/cokids/index.html`

Early childhood site with teacher resources, original articles, reproducible calendars, and links to other sites with quality content. One of the most complete references for developmentally appropriate practices on the World Wide Web! All things early childhood!

Education World
`http://www.education-world.com`

Selective Learning Network
`http://www.slnedu.com`

A Teachers' Space
`http://www.teleport.com/~atspace`

Education World

`http://www.education-world.com`

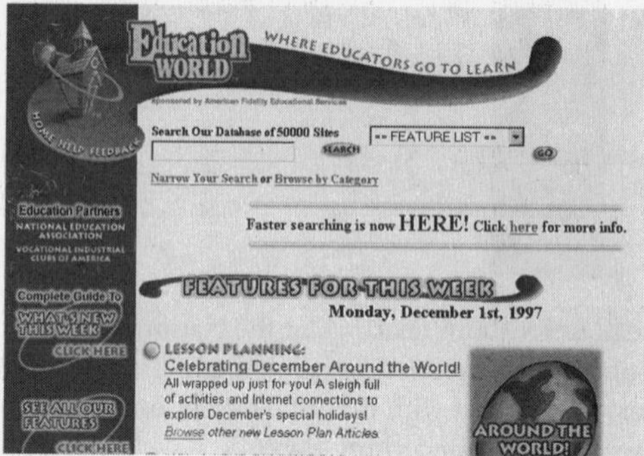

Education World™ is a powerful and free search engine focused on providing information to educators, students, and parents. Use their keyword search, browse by category, or join the Educators' Forum, a message board system to dialogue with educators around the globe. Twenty Education Site Reviews are posted each month.

The Educator's Toolkit

`http://www.eagle.ca/~matink/`

The Educator's Toolkit is a great tool for busy educators. Here you'll find a monthly Internet newsletter, lesson plans, theme sites, teacher resources, and more.

The Puffin House

http://www.puffin.co.uk

The Puffin House contains information about Penguin Childrens' Books. It includes activities for children, teachers' resources, and a searchable database of the full range of book titles.

Selective Learning Network

http://www.slnedu.com

Selective Learning Network is a complete online educational network providing live chat areas in life line mentoring providing support on what students, parents, and teachers face today, educational chat forums with professional in many fields, curriculum lesson plans for teachers, and educational games for students.

Sharon's Page

http://marauder.millersv.edu/~sms60238/

This page has some links to teacher resources as well as some links to entertain such as Winnie the Pooh, Disney, and other cartoon favorites.

A Teachers' Space

http://www.teleport.com/~atspace

A Teachers' Space is an educational resource center in Portland, Oregon. It is a nonprofit organization serving educators and families for the benefit of all children.

TULEP—The Ultimate List of Education Pages

http://userzweb.lightspeed.net/~pmacg/

A growing list of education resources on the Web designed for K–12 educators and technology directors.

Virtual Curriculum Coordinator

http://www.kuvcc.org

The Virtual Curriculum Coordinator is a directory listing of educational resources on the World Wide Web that are useful for K–12 educators and students.

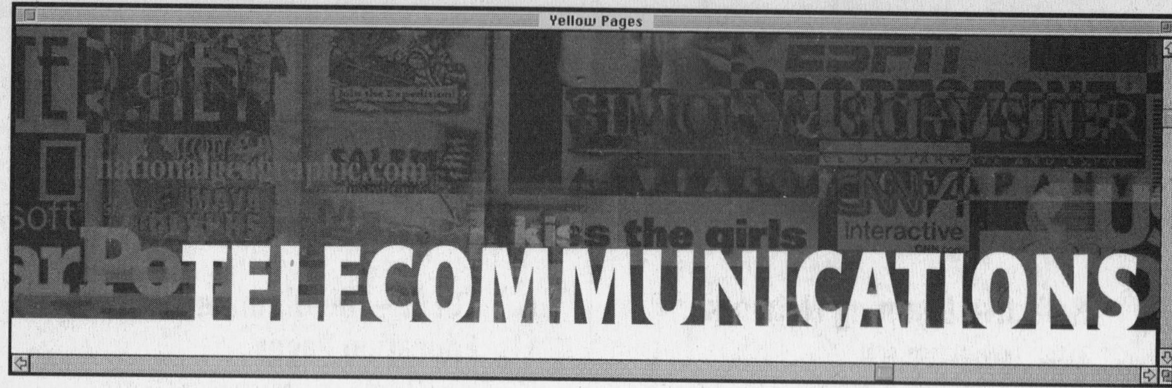

Every improvement in communication makes the bore more terrible.

Frank Moore Colby

EMJ Data Systems
http://www.emj.ca

ISDN Infocentre
http://www.isdn.ocn.com/

Motorola Information Systems Group
http://www.motorola.com/MIMS/ISG/

Applied Signal Technology

http://www.appsig.com/

Home site for design, development, and manufacturer of signal processing equipment for telecommunications signals. Provides company background, product information, and press release file. Includes Applied Signal Techology job opportunities and college recruitment information.

Archtek Telecom Corp.

http://www.archtek.com.tw/

Manufactures SmartLink telecommunications products. Provides company profile, technical partners, support information, and a very comprehensive product line classified by telecommunication needs.

Commercial Speech Recognition

http://www.tiac.net/users/rwilcox/speech.html

This organized site provides hundreds of links to Web pages on Usenet groups, FAQs, ftp sites, mailing lists, research labs, recognition engines, telephony, and text-to-speech vendors. A valuable resource for businesses interested in this technology.

The Computer Telephony Product Group of Artisoft

http://www.stylus.com/stylus

Sells Windows-based tools for building computer telephony and voice processing applications, such as interactive voice response, fax-on-demand, and voice mail. If you're interested in the world of telephony, download one of several interactive tutorials free, or click How to Get Started with Computer Telephony.

Cromack Industries, Inc.

http://www.cromack.com/

Produces Data Communications Equipment and Systems for both network and wireless markets. Includes product specifications, online data sheets, press releases, and contact information. Also includes technical updates and upcoming products release information.

EMJ Data Systems

http://www.emj.ca

Distributes Apple, CAD, UNIX, networking, and telephony products and peripherals in Canada, the U.S., Brazil, and Hungary.

Internet Phone Download a Free Copy

`http://www.vocaltec.com/homep.htm`

Download a working demo of the latest copy of Internet Phone—the "phone" that lets you talk to other Internet users. Besides being one of the top 5 percent most-visited sites on the Web, this software is so hot that hundreds of phone servers have sprouted up on the Internet to handle the "calls."

Internet Telephony Interoperability Consortium

`http://itel.mit.edu/`

Information about the Internet Telephony Consortium (ITC), a group that works on technical, economic, strategic, and policy issues that arise from the convergence of telecommunications and the Internet.

ISDN Infocentre

`http://www.isdn.ocn.com/`

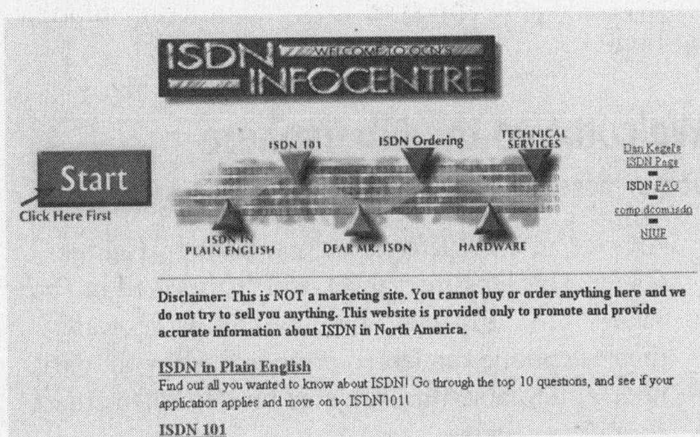

Heard about ISDN but still not sure what it is? Click on the Start Here button to learn about ISDN in plain English. This site's detailed links compare ISDN providers, provide technical help for hooking up ISDN, and review ISDN hardware. An excellent site for the ISDN curious.

M&S Hourdakis SA

`http://www.stepc.gr/~sweetie/hourd.html`

Information technology company located in Greece, serving Europe. Originally a manufacturer of circuit boards, the company has expanded to offer a variety of electronics needs including functionally tested through hole and SMD boards.

MedConnect

`http://netmar.com/medconnect/`

Physician to Patient voice messaging service to provide medical results quickly and securely to your patients by phone.

MediaLogic, ADL Inc.

`http://www.adlinc.com/adlinfo/`

An "Intelligent Data Warehouse" and developer of the first SSA-Capable Tape Library. Check out their long list of products, what's new, press releases and product overviews, ordering information, and more.

MediaSoft Telecom

`http://www.mediasoft.ca/`

Software for interactive communication systems. Check out their consulting services and product line for your organization.

Metricon Welcome

`http://www.metricom.com/`

Home page for a leader in two-way wireless data communication using cellular modems and the Internet. This site discusses Ricochet, their wireless Internet packet radio service, Metricon's cellular modems, UtiliNet, and Metricon's corporate structure. Their coverage maps show where the Ricochet service is available.

Motorola Information Systems Group

`http://www.motorola.com/MIMS/ISG/`

Communications products for the business or the home, including modems, terminal adapters, access devices, routers, and other networking devices.

Multi-Tech Systems, Inc.

`http://www.multitech.com/`

Computer communications and networking products, in particular, modems and multiplexers, to international markets. Links to technical and purchasing info, as well as product and contact information.

Nokia

http://www.nokia.com/

International telecommunications group located in Finland, providing mobile computing products, home and multimedia products, and networking solutions.

Practinet Practical Peripherals

http://www.practinet.com/

Need to upgrade the flash bios in your modem? Are you researching modems before you buy one? Practical Peripherals manufactures some of the fastest and most affordable modems for Macs and PCs. This site is for current modem owners and those who need more information on Practical Peripherals products.

Research Program on Communications Policy

http://far.mit.edu/Pubs/index.html

Home page for MIT's research forum on communications. Lists a number of MIT-related research papers, reports, and articles on future communications-related technology, such as HDTV, high-resolution imaging, Internet broadcasting, electronic media, and many other topics.

Symplex Communications

http://www.symplex.com/

Produces DirectRoute WAN/ISDN routers and other frame relay line applications. Includes product technical specifications, support, company profile, and contact information.

Tascomm Engineering

http://www.tascomm.fi/

Specializes in software telecommunications products. Includes information about the WATER line of router products and DTS family of integration applications. Includes Tascomm profile, product specifications, and contact information.

Terminate Home Page, the Final Terminal

http://www.terminate.com/

Developers of Terminate, advanced DOS communication software for terminal and Internet communication, provides a visually interesting page. Download a working demo of the program, check out some Terminate-related pages in Europe and the U.S., or link to some interesting FidoNet pages.

Universal Group Of Companies

http://www.universalgroup.co.uk/

Provides systems consulting and products for the telecommunications industry. Includes products offered, services provided, and contact information.

Videoconferencing Systems, Inc.

http://www.vsin.com/

Produces the Omega family of video conferencing tools and products. Includes company profile, product capabilities, press releases, and ordering information.

Welcome to the Fibersphere

http://homepage.seas.upenn.edu/~gaj1/fiber.html

An excerpt from *Telecosm*, a new book by George Gilder. This lengthy excerpt, which appeared in *Forbes ASAP* (12/02/92), describes how companies want their telephone carriers to provide them with "dark," fiber-optic, cable-dumb, leased lines for their smart computer systems.

The World Wide Web Virtual Library of Communications and Telecommunications

http://www.analysys.co.uk/vlib/reseller.htm

An excellent resource listing all the U.K. long distance operators. Click a company name to access its Web page.

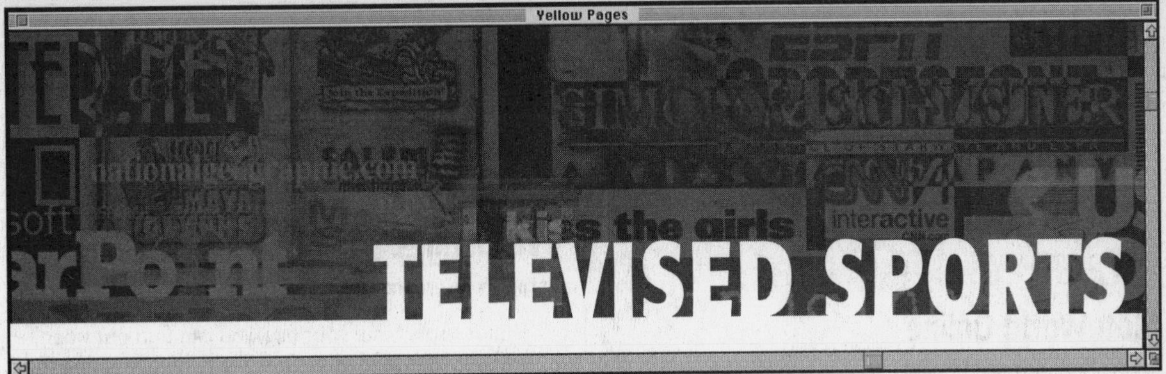

TELEVISED SPORTS

> And this here's the TV. Two hours a day, either educational or football, so you don't ruin your appreciation of the finer things.
>
> *H.I. in* Raising Arizona *(1987)*

ESPN SportZone
`http://espn.sportszone.com/`

FOX Sports Online
`http://www.foxsports.com/`

Monday Night Football
`http://www.abcmnf.com/index.asp`

WeightsNet TV Listing
`http://www.weightsnet.com/Misc/tv.html`

The Best of ESPN

`http://www.duke.edu/~jds13/espn.html`

At this site you can download a complete set of *SportsCenter* commercials in AVI or Quicktime format.

ESPN SportZone

`http://espn.sportszone.com/`

Find out what's going to be on ESPN and ESPN2, and check out the scores for what has already happened. You can also view video clips from recent games and read insightful commentary.

FOX Sports Online

`http://www.foxsports.com/`

This service of the FOX television network tells you what you've recently missed on FOX in the sports department, and provides all the scores and play-by-play to make you wish you had seen it live. It also lets you know what you need to tune in to FOX to watch in the near future.

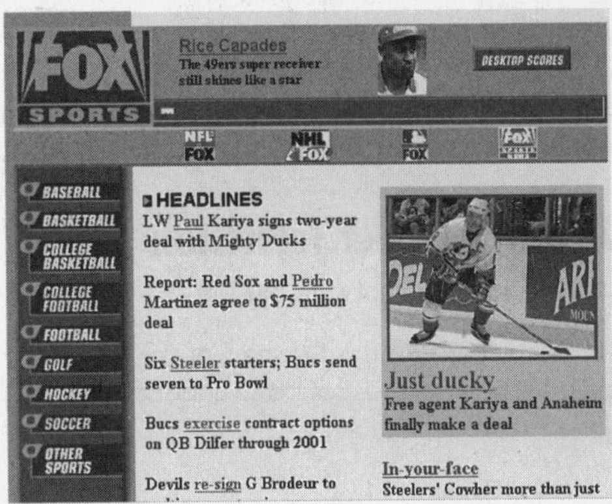

Gladnet II

`http://dspace.dial.pipex.com/town/square/fm71/index.htm`

Everything you wanted to know about gladiators (from the TV show *American Gladiators*) worldwide.

Golf Channel

`http://www.thegolfchannel.com/`

This site lists what you'll be able to watch on the Golf Channel (a cable channel that is available in some areas) and also lists tournament stats and rankings.

Monday Night Football

http://www.abcmnf.com/index.asp

Can't get enough *Monday Night Football* in the precious few hours a week that it's on TV? Visit the official Monday Night Football Web site to relive last week's game and prepare yourself mentally for the upcoming one.

MotoWorld Online

http://www.motoworld.com/

Get the broadcast schedule for this ESPN2 show here.

ORIS Games

http://www.sportsgaming.com/

An innovative online game where players watch televised sporting events and then accumulate points by "trading options" on various players.

Sports Menu

http://www.sportsmenu.com/

If you need to be reminded to watch more sports on TV, this is for you. The Sports Menu is a fax service that delivers a complete listing of all televised sporting events that day. Visit this site to get a free sample copy.

STV: Snowmobiler Television

http://www.snowmobilertv.on.ca/

The home page for the TV show of the same name. Includes how-to, broadcast and channel schedule, classified ads, and more.

Tennis on TV

http://www.mindspring.com/~csmith/docs/tv.html

Use this site to keep up on the tennis events that will be happening on television in the United States.

TVE Listings

http://www.emi.com/tve/tve.html

If motorsports are your bag, you can find out when and on what channel to look for them by visiting this site and perusing the listings.

WeightsNet TV Listing

http://www.weightsnet.com/Misc/tv.html

One-stop listings for all weight-lifting, body-building, fitness competitions, and other muscle-related sports being televised. Very handy!

www.soccerTV.com

http://www.soccertv.com/

The ultimate guide to televised soccer, you'll find out everything you need to know at this site to catch all the soccer action on both broadcast and cable channels.

Related Sites

http://www.adrenazine.com/main.htm

http://www.barklays.com/fnchome.htm

http://www.golftheworld.com/

http://www.hookedongolf.com/

http://www.jimmyhouston.com/

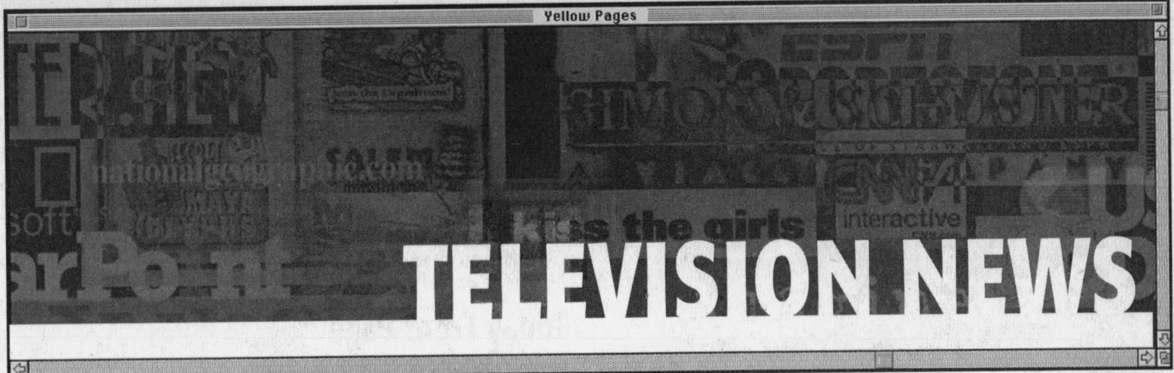

> The one function TV news performs very well is that when there is no news we give it to you with the same emphasis as if there were.
>
> *David Brinkley*

ABCNEWS.com: News Now

`http://www.abcnews.com/newsflash/index.html`

The latest national, international, business, sports, and other news in a well-organized layout. You can also search the site for news dealing with keywords you specify.

CBS News

`http://www.cbs.com/news/`

A very pretty site that ties together all of the news shows offered on the CBS network. You just pick the one you're interested in from a list, and are whisked away to a special home page for that show.

CNET Central

`http://www.cnet.com/Tv/CNETCentral/`

Previews and reviews from CNET's *CNET Central*, a technology/computer news show. Check out the links to CNET's main Web site, one of the best computer-related sites on the Internet.

The Online NewsHour
`http://www.pbs.org/newshour/`

POV Interactive
`http://www.pbs.org/pov/`

Dateline

`http://www.msnbc.com/news/DATELINE_front.asp`

Read about upcoming stories on this popular NBC program, browse or search the archives, and register your opinion in the Talk Back area.

ET Online

`http://et.msn.com/promo/default.asp`

If you consider entertainment news to be a legitimate form of news, you will probably be very interested in this site, which spotlights the current day's *Entertainment Tonight* TV show content and also provides live online events and transcripts.

Eye on Asia

`http://www.eyeonasia.com/`

This companion site to the #1 South Asian American TV program not only spotlights content from the show but also provides many other resources, such as immigration links and news headlines.

Frontline

`http://www.pbs.org/wgbh/pages/frontline/`

For PBS fans, this site has information and pictures from the current *Frontline* show. The nice thing about this site is that they don't take the previous episode's site away when the new one comes out—they continue to make it available and easy to find, so you can check out any of several dozen "back episodes."

MSNBC News

http://www.msnbc.com/news/default.asp

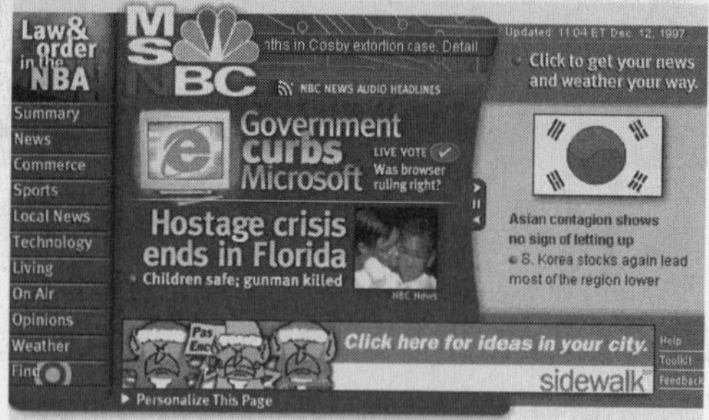

A joint site that combines the strengths of TV news powerhouse NBC News with the online behemoth Microsoft. The result is an interactive site that mirrors and enhances the MSNBC cable network content. Recommended!

The Online NewsHour

http://www.pbs.org/newshour/

Internet version of *The NewsHour with Jim Lehrer.* Includes daily news, chat sessions, essays, and RealAudio recordings of *NewsHour* broadcast segments.

POV Interactive

http://www.pbs.org/pov/

A very content-rich site that is much more than a retelling of the PBS TV show *P.O.V.* Includes film spotlights, archives, a Talk Back section, and lots more.

Sunday Online

http://sunday.ninemsn.com.au/

A public affairs program on Australian commercial television, covering news, politics, current affairs, and investigative journalism.

This Week

http://www.abcnews.com/onair/thisweek/html_files/index.html

ABC News' Sunday morning program co-hosted by Cokie Roberts and Sam Donaldson. The site includes current issues, scheduled guests, and transcripts of past interviews.

Today Front Page

http://www.msnbc.com/news/TODAY_front.asp

The online home of the popular *Today* TV show on NBC. Top stories of the day are highlighted, and you can also check out the archives and request transcripts.

TV Nation

http://www.spe.sony.com/TVN/

Dedicated to the brilliant, short-lived TV news show *TV Nation*, with host Michael Moore. Funny, biting commentary and clips. (There is also a newsgroup devoted to this show at alt.tv.tv-nation.)

Related Sites
http://www.cbs.com/prime/60min/index.htm
http://www.kingworld.com/ajournal/index.html
http://www.desthope.com/
http://www.extratv.com/
http://www.kingworld.com/iedition/index.html
http://www.mclaughlin.com/
http://www.msnbc.com/news/meetpress_front.asp
http://www.rysher.com/strangeuniverse/
http://uttm.com/
http://www.pbs.org/weta/wwir/

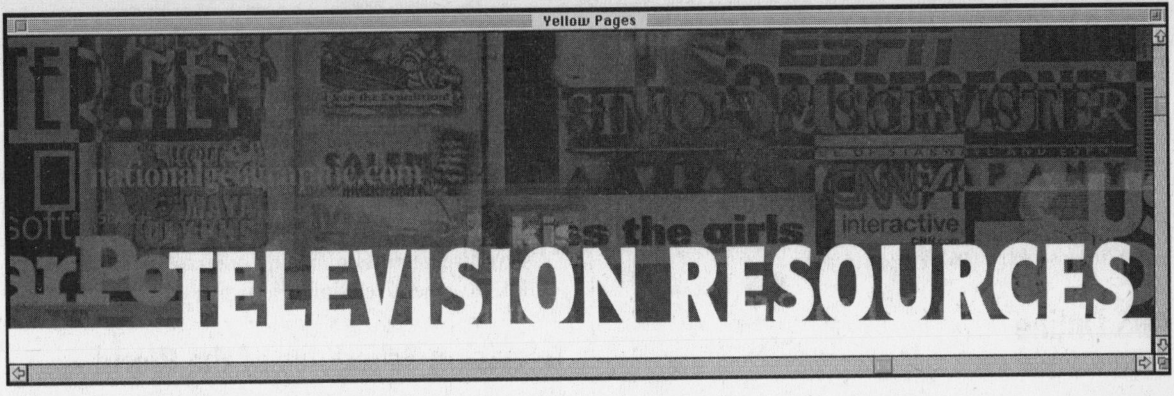

I find television very educating. Every time somebody turns on the set, I go into the other room and read a book.

Groucho Marx

Academy of TV Arts & Sciences

http://www.emmys.org/

This official Web site of the Academy features the TV Hall of Fame and a list of Emmy Award winners from the past few years. Also links to Academy-sponsored education programs and an archive of American television.

CineMedia/Television Sites

http://www.afionline.org/CineMedia/tele.html

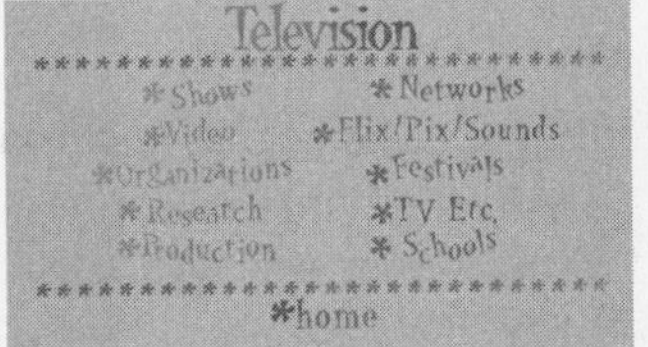

This page is filled with links to TV-related sites including shows, networks, organizations, schools, research, and production. Also links to audio clips, video clips, and photos of different shows and performers.

Related Sites

http://tvchat.ultimatetv.com/

http://vh1.com/

http://www.abctelevision.com/

http://www.cbs.com/

CineMedia/Television Sites
http://www.afionline.org/CineMedia/tele.html

Special TV Resources
http://www.teleport.com/~celinec/tv.shtml

The Ultimate TV List
http://www.ultimatetv.com/

clickTV

http://www.clicktv.com/

A comprehensive guide to TV listings, this site shows listings for your metro area. You also can be become a member of clickTV for more personalized, ZIP code-selected listings. You can try before you buy for complete satisfaction.

Columbia Music Video Resources

http://www.sony.com/Music/VideoStuff/vidfaq.htm

Find out if an alternative to MTV and VH-1 exists in your town. This page includes a list of hundreds of public access and cable shows for music videos.

Comedy Central

http://www.comcentral.com/

The home to many popular comedy shows, there is a download area with QuickTime movies available to fill up that annoying extra space you may have on your hard drive.

EuroTV

http://www.eurotv.com/

Provides a database of the 50 major European television stations. You can access schedules by channels and days. Site also contains popular TV themes and a TV critic.

NBC

http://www.nbc.com/

NBC's home page. Daily updates enable you to access groundbreaking news stories and weather. This site also includes CNBC and sports information. If you like late night TV, be sure to check out Conan O'Brien's Web page.

PBS Online

http://www.pbs.org/

This home page for the Public Broadcasting System includes the latest shows on PBS, classroom resources, an inside look at the corporation, and the PBS store.

Shokus Video/The TV Connection

http://www.shokus.com/

Specializes in classic TV from the 1950s. Watch sample clips online or download QuickTime versions to view later. This site also operates The TV Connection, a service for collectors of TV shows.

Special TV Resources

http://www.teleport.com/~celinec/tv.shtml

This site contains an extensive Usenet newsgroup list and links to Web pages of past and current shows, actors and actresses, magazines, plus other TV-related sites. You also can play Trivia Blitz, a free Java-based game at this site.

Tardis TV Archive

http://src.doc.ic.ac.uk/public/media/tv/collections/tardis/index.html

Archive and database of TV shows, schedules, conventions, awards, and biographies. Also contains photos, mailing lists, scripts, and more. Shows are sorted by country.

Television and Radio News Research

http://www.missouri.edu/~jourvs/index.html

Publishes new mass media research, with an emphasis on long-term trends. Subjects include career entries, women and minorities, salaries and benefits, and more.

Television Pointers

http://www.cs.cmu.edu/afs/cs.cmu.edu/user/clamen/misc/tv/

Links to interesting information about television, but is not meant to be comprehensive. Links are categorized into News and Information, Broadcasters, Advertisements, Humor, and others. Also contains links to other television resources.

Television Schedules of the World

http://www.buttle.com/tel/../tv/schedule.htm

Helps you find out what's on television all around the world. Links to TV guides from many different countries, from Australia to the U.S. Look schedules up before you travel!

Tooncers Web Page Fantasmic

http://www.mind.net/worksj

A crazy site that's the home of the Internet Cola Page, the "UnOfficial" WWIV Web server (a collection of software for Telnetting to BBSs from the Web), and the Toon Town BBS, a collection of animation from cartoons. This site also provides real-time animation and cartoons. Fun!

TradeWave Galaxy's Television Page

http://www.einet.net/galaxy/Leisure-and-Recreation/Television.html

Contains tons of television links including articles, collections, directories, guides, organizations, and much more. Also links to shows by category, such as cartoons, comedy, drama, education, game shows, talk shows, and so on.

TV Guide Entertainment Network

http://www.tvguide.com/

Links to TV Guide Online, FOX Sports, FOX News, and more. Enter your ZIP code to get TV listings specific to your area. Also contains feature articles on your favorite stars.

The Ultimate TV List

http://www.ultimatetv.com/

Describes over 745 TV shows in every genre imaginable. You can find what you're looking for a number of ways: search using the search engine, click on a letter to find an alphabetical list, or choose a genre such as Science Fiction or Comedy. This site also includes pointers to TV-related newsgroups and Web sites.

Vanderbilt Television News Archive

http://tvnews.vanderbilt.edu/

This site may not be pretty, but it includes abstracts of every nightly news broadcast on the big three networks since 1968! See what happened on a particular date over the past 25 years. Be sure to visit the Special Reports and Specialized News Collections areas for news on major events, such as the Persian Gulf War. A service of Vanderbilt University.

The WASHED UP-date

http://us.imdb.com/washed-update/

This weekly column discloses what has happened to former TV stars and other entertainers. The site's archives contain profiles of over 200 celebrities. Also offers a Fun Link of the Week.

Welcome to the BBC

http://www.bbc.co.uk/

The British Broadcasting Corporation on the Web includes pointers to BBC Radio, BBC TV, BBC Internet, BBC Education, and more.

Worldwide TV Standards

http://www.ee.surrey.ac.uk/Contrib/WorldTV/

Explains the different TV standards around the world and why they exist. Also explores solutions to the problem and links to other resources.

X-Files Resources for X-Philes

http://www2.dmci.net/users/jadams/

The ultimate site for *X-Files* fanatics. Includes Web pages, FTP sites, Usenet newsgroups, mailing lists, merchandise, and more. Learn more about the actors and characters, and check out the sound bytes.

GOPHER SITES

Public Broadcasting Service Gopher

gopher://gopher.pbs.org/

Vanderbuilt Television News Archive

gopher://tvnews.vanderbilt.edu/

Voice of America and Worldnet Television

gopher://tvnews.vanderbilt.edu/

LISTSERVS

AHECTA-L—Assoc. of Higher Education Cable Television Administrators

You can join this group by sending the message "sub AHECTA-L your name" to

listserv@uga.cc.uga.edu

ASURTV—ASU Radio and Television Information Distribution List

You can join this group by sending the message "sub ASURTV your name" to

listserv@asuvm.inre.asu.edu

SCREEN-L—Film and TV Studies Discussion List

You can join this group by sending the message "sub SCREEN-L your name"

to listserv@ua1vm.ua.edu

Related Sites

http://www.goforit.com/tsunami/television.html

http://www.qvc.com/

http://www.rcc.ryerson.ca/rta/homerta.html

http://www.tv1.com/

http://www.vortex.com/ProfNeon.html

http://www.weather.com/twc/homepage.twc

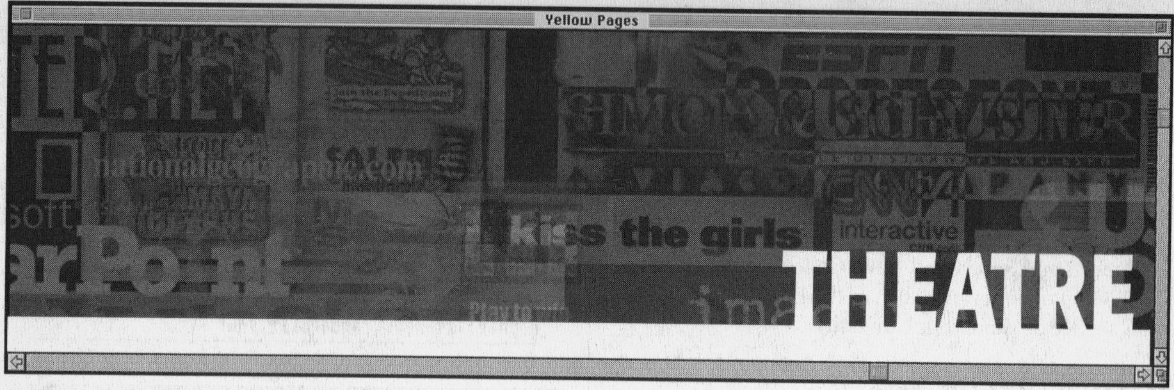

A
B
C
D
E
F
G
H
I
J
K
L
M
N
O
P
Q
R
S
T
U
V
W
X
Y
Z

It takes great passion and great energy to do anything creative, especially in the theater. You have to care so much that you can't sleep, you can't eat, you can't talk to people. It's just got to be right. You can't do it without that passion.

Agnes George DeMille

Actors' Page

http://www.serve.com/dgweb32/

An actor and member of the Screen Actors Guild and the American Federation of Television and Radio Artists has offered a practical *and* entertaining site for those interested in the acting arts as well as finding some contacts in show biz. You can add your URL to the page, check out lists of talent agencies and casting directors in New York City, and join a discussion called "The Actors' Roundtable." And, the theater and actor links at the bottom of the home page are exhaustive.

Aisle Say

http://www.escape.com/~theanet/AisleSay.html

"The Internet Magazine of Stage Reviews and Opinion." Reviews, reviews, and more reviews of stage productions all over the United States and Canada.

Actors' Page
http://www.serve.com/dgweb32/

Vintage Vaudeville and Ragtime Show
http://www.bestwebs.com/vaudeville/

Broadway Play Publishing, Inc.

http://www.BroadwayPlayPubl.com/

A company that adapts American plays has a search engine and several related links. You can order their books, plays, musicals, one-act collections, plays, and play anthologies. See their adaptations of American classics and check out the photo gallery.

Complete Works of William Shakespeare

http://the-tech.mit.edu/Shakespeare/works.html

In addition to providing the complete text of every Shakespeare play and poem, this site includes a discussion area, chronological and alphabetical lists of the plays, Bartlett's familiar Shakespeare quotations, and a funeral elegy by the old man himself. An unbelievable site!

English Actors at the Turn of the Century

http://www.siue.edu/COSTUMES/actors/pics.html

A very straightforward but interesting site, this provides colorful, full photographs of twentieth-century actors in their roles. Just click an actor/movie, and you're there. See many old actors including Maud Jeffries in *Herod*, Sir Henry Irving in *As You Like It*, and George Alexander in *If I Were King*.

Jogle's Favorite Theater Related Resources

http://artsnet.heinz.cmu.edu/OnBroadway/links/

The title says it all. The home page offers a simple-to-navigate listing of anything theater-related that you'd want to know, including where to find books and gifts, tickets and reviews, information about people in theater, and newsgroups and chat rooms.

Larry Stark's Theater Mirror

http://www.theatermirror.com/

Lengthy reviews of new plays in Boston are only part of this rich Web resource. Page includes a calendar of shows, upcoming plays, the casting call board, and notes on recent productions.

London Theatre Guide—On Line

http://www.londontheatre.co.uk/

Use this handy page to find info on West End shows, the Royal National Theatre, and other London theaters. Includes addresses, seating arrangements, reviews of current shows, ballet and opera listings, and a monthly email update service.

New York City Theater

http://www.mediabridge.com/nyc/entertainment/theater/

Provides brief descriptions of plays currently in production on and off Broadway. Addresses and phone numbers are also included.

New York's Capital District Theater Page

http://www.albany.net/~danorton/theatre/

Lists all the plays currently running in Albany, New York. This page also includes audition information, class and workshop information, and active theater company schedules. The "Other Related Web Sites" and "Theater-related Newsgroup" sections provide dozens of links and Usenet addresses.

Playbill Online

http://www1.playbill.com/playbill/

The electronic version of the famous print publication, focusing primarily on Broadway and Off-Broadway theatres. You can purchase tickets online, read reviews, and learn about the stars behind the top productions. A very good site with a strong content offering.

Shakespeare Theatre

http://shakespearedc.org/

Information about the Washington D.C.-based Shakespeare Theatre, including upcoming performances, cast bios, job listings and internships, and acting classes.

SITCOM Home Page

http://www.ccp.uchicago.edu/grad/Dan_Goldstein/sitcom.html

Information on the SITCOM program of improvised half-hour "shows," which mimic rehearsed and planned TV comedy. Provides a blend of structuralist literary criticism and artificial intelligence, a live show that converts audience suggestions into full-length, improvised TV sitcoms that unfold live on stage.

TenEyck Design Studio

http://www.inch.com/~kteneyck/

Web page for a set design company in New York City. Be sure to enter the door to learn more about its designs for plays such as *The Tempest*, and *La Traviata*. The Observatory includes information on all the productions for which TenEyck has designed sets.

Theatre Crafts International Magazine

http://www.etecnyc.net/tci/

Selected articles from the print version of the highly respected magazine for behind-the-scenes theatre professionals, including lighting, sound, production designers, and costume and makeup professionals.

Vintage Vaudeville and Ragtime Show

http://www.bestwebs.com/vaudeville/

Get back to the old ragtime days with this modern site about vaudeville. First, check out the history of vaudeville. Then, view some cool old pictures. Also, get some biographical data on such old stars as Ada Jones and Len Spencer. Best of all, sit back and enjoy some actual music, such as Arthur Collins singing ragtime. There are several RealAudio files to enjoy.

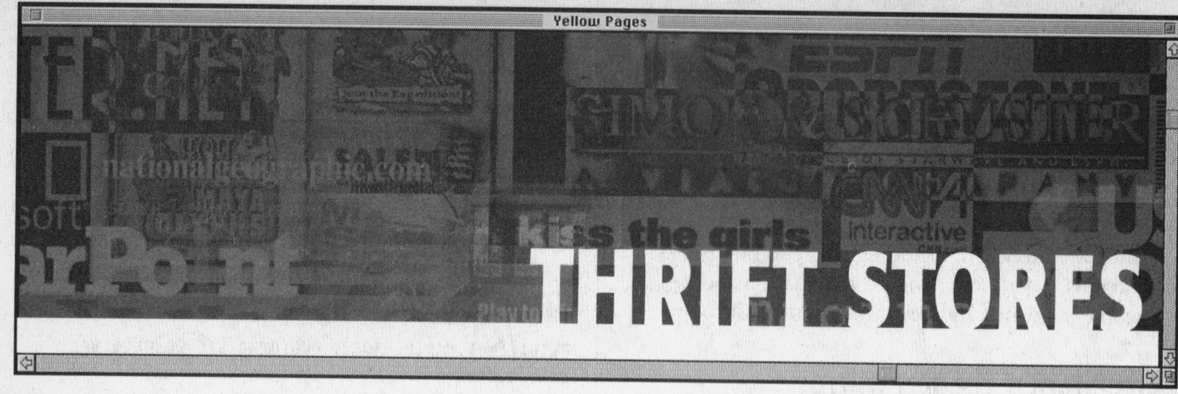

A–Z: T

Mod, funky, rad, grungy—like the fads, I'm fading fast.

Bernadette McCarver Snyder

Rusty Zipper Vintage Clothing
http://www.shopdoor.com/rustyzipper/search/find.cgi?welcome=go

STARticles–Museum of Pop Culture Artifacts
http://www.starticles.com/

Ventura Pacific Limited
http://www.fishnet.net/~sandcat/

American Vintage Classics

http://www.geocities.com/~avintagec/

Check out the pictures and descriptions of men's vintage clothing from the 1930s through the early 1960s. This store specializes in shirts and ties.

Boomerangs

http://www.aac.org/support/boomer/boomer.htm

This AIDS Action Committee resale store offers recycled and new merchandise. The store benefits people with AIDS and supports HIV prevention programs; all profits go to AIDS Action programs. Boomerangs is located in Boston.

Capeway Cards & Music

http://www.capecod.net/capeway/

Offers sports and non-sports collectable game cards, as well as used records, CDs, and tapes. Find imported, out-of-print, and hard-to-find items.

Related Sites

http://www.paperbacks.com/

http://katu.citysearch.com/Portland/Shops_and_Services/Discount_Shopping/

http://www.theclothestree.com/

http://www.rain.org/~carcajou/sbdark/shopping.html

http://www.accessone.com/~philn/findem.htm

http://www.quikpage.com/L/liberia

The Cats Pajamas

http://www.catspajamas.com/

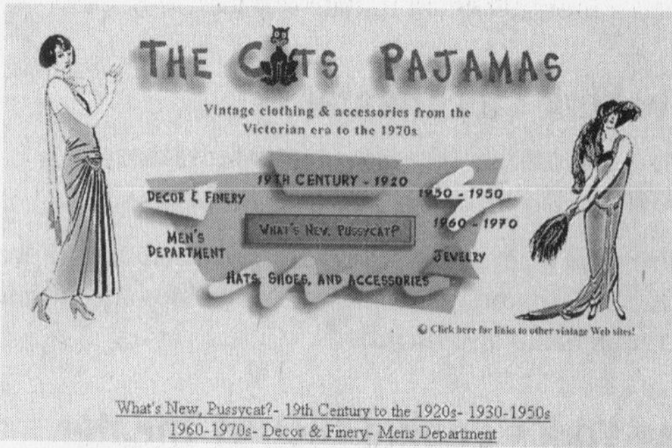

Here, you'll find vintage clothing and accessories from the Victorian era to the 1970s. Includes hats, shoes, jewelry, and accessories.

Glassboro Thrift Village

http://users.comten.com/thrift/default.htm

Find clothing, shoes, vintage jewelry, and toy and sport collectibles. You'll also find items for infants, music (tapes, albums, CDs), stereos, cameras, and more.

Related Sites

http://www.htmp.net/ves/sh-rose/

http://www.southernpride.com/1997/july/economics/salegoddess.htm

http://www.emf.net/~cheetham/kth-es-1.html

The Internet Resale Directory to Secondhand, Surplus, and Salvage

http://www.secondhand.com/

Visit this site for a directory to resale businesses: consignment shops, antique stores, flea markets, thrift stores, secondhand businesses, liquidators, and salvage yards. Covers locations and merchandise in the U.S., Africa, Australia, Canada, and the United Kingdom. These stores offer clothing, furniture, appliances, books, CDs, computers, sports equipment, discounted food, and more.

Mary's Designer Resale Boutique

http://www.marys.com/home/

Shop here for collections from Chanel, DKNY, Escade, Prada, CK, St. John, Armani, Versace, and more.

Play It Again Sports

http://www.playitagainsports.com/

Offers used sporting goods, as well as new merchandise.

Retro: The Tip Tray

http://www.retroactive.com/itinerant.html

Provides hints for living the retro lifestyle. Learn about finding and shopping at thrift stores, and get explanations of thrift store categories: large chains, charity-affiliated, thrift clearinghouses, and consignment stores.

Rusty Zipper Vintage Clothing

http://www.shopdoor.com/rustyzipper/search/find.cgi?welcome=go

Offers vintage clothing, books, patterns, and collectibles. Be sure to check out the Vintage Showcase, where you can browse through all the items, which are presented with pictures, descriptions, and prices. Maybe you're looking for a 1940s necktie. Or maybe you want to try out one of the sewing patterns from the '40s to the '70s. Yep, there are sections for disco items, flares and bellbottoms, and leisure suits.

Savers Value Village

http://www.savers.com/

Provides more than 125 locations of thrift shops. Includes Thrift-via Internet, an online vintage and collectibles thrift store featuring clothing, toys, books, records, glassware, dolls, and figurines.

STARticles—Museum of Pop Culture Artifacts

http://www.starticles.com/

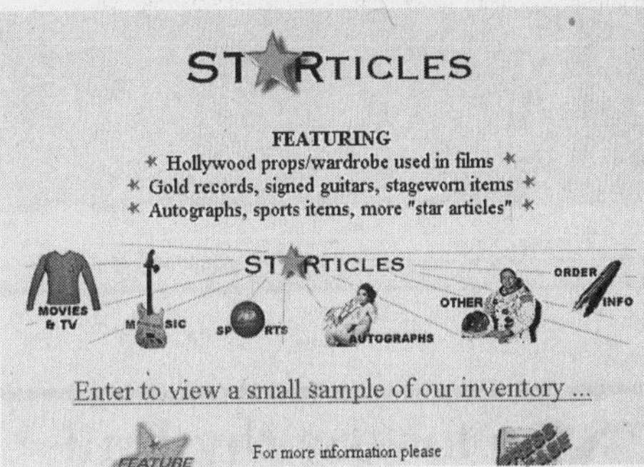

This site offers used Hollywood props, wardrobe used in films, gold records, signed guitars, stageworn items, autographs, sport items, and other celebrity items. Maybe you're interested in Jerry Maguire's prop business cards, Billy Mumy's *Lost in Space* orange velour shirt, or Ralph Kramden's bus driver's uniform jacket from *The Honeymooners.*

The Ultimate Consignment & Thrift Store Guide

http://www.theclothestree.com/branch/ultimateguide/

Get a guide to consignment and thrift stores in the U.S., Canada, England, France, Ireland, and Australia. Investigate info on donating merchandise, check out the pictures, get tips on consignment shopping, and find coupons for certain stores.

The Unicorn Thrift Store

http://www.emq.org/unicorn.htm

Located in San Jose, CA, this store consists of an all-volunteer staff and offers clothing, jewelry, accessories, household items, books, and collectibles. Proceeds benefit Eastfield Ming Quong, a provider of mental health services for emotionally troubled children and their families.

Ventura Pacific Limited

http://www.fishnet.net/~sandcat/

Purchase books, original art, and used photographic equipment. Or, check out the collectible dolls and toys or the handmade teddy bears. Or maybe you'll be interested in the Native American art (ceremonial pipes, buckles, jewelry, and more) or the handmade knives and sheaths. You can also buy antiques, collectibles, and records.

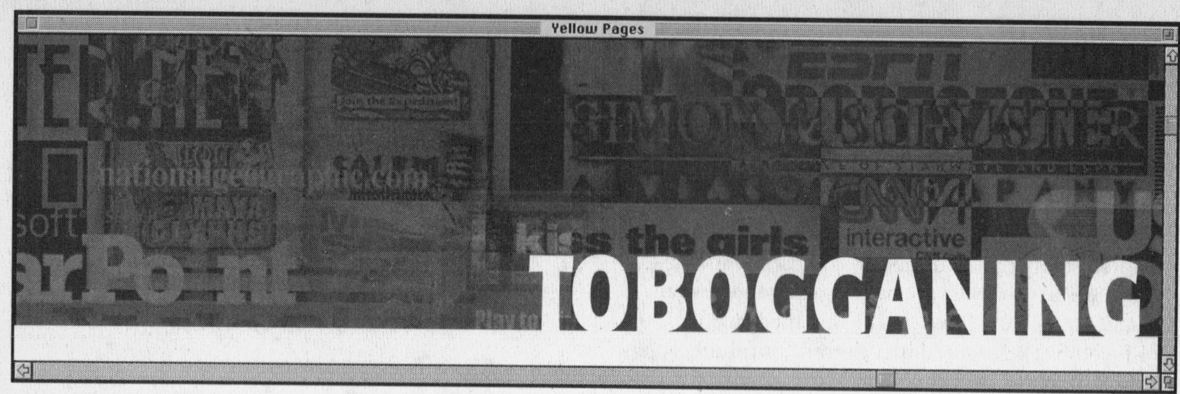

> One for the rhythm! Two for the rhyme! Three for the feeling! It's bobsled time!
>
> *Sanka in* Cool Runnings *(1993)*

Austria National Tourist Office

http://www.anto.com/fandf.html

This site is geared toward Americans who want to visit Austria. Most of the site discusses the great skiing opportunities, but tobogganing is also mentioned. You'll learn about the advantages of the Alps: the vertical drop, altitude, temperature, and atmosphere. Get a description of the nearby resorts and what they offer. Includes a link where you can get the current skiing conditions.

Austria Reports

http://www.wtg-online.com/country/at/res.html

Learn about the recreational opportunities throughout Austria—including Vienna, Burgenland, Carinthia, Lower Austria, the Salzburg Province, Styria, Tyrol, Upper Austria, and Vorarlberg. This site provides a quick reference to these areas. You'll get highlights of the architecture, location, history, and culture. You'll get excursion/sightseeing tips for each area—art, music, churches, museums, historical sites, the stage, museums, shops, and more. You also get a list of resorts for each area and a section specifically devoted to winter sports resorts. If you're interested in a trip to Austria for tobogganing, skiing, sleigh rides, skating, or curling, you'll want to check out this site.

NRP TOP PICKS

Austria Reports
http://www.wtg-online.com/country/at/res.html

Sledding/Tobogganing
http://www.cha.ab.ca/safekids/Sled.htm

B&B Connections of Philadelphia: Pocono Mountains

http://www.bnbphiladelphia.com/pocono/index.html

Check out the places you can stay around the Poconos while enjoying your favorite winter activities: tobogganing, skating, downhill and cross-country skiing, and snowmobiling. Cozy fireplaces await your return from the cold and offer a relaxing escape for the less adventuresome.

Goms Valais Switzerland: General information

http://www.net4u.ch/goms/egoms_in.htm

Goms is the far northern part of the Valais, extending from Grengiols to the Rhone glacier. The countryside by the early reaches of the Rhone is well known for its unspoiled nature and its soothing, peaceful quality; it is accessible by road and rail all year round. This area offers tobogganing runs, as well as other winter sports activities. Learn about the Goms scenery, culture, and events, as well as how to make reservations for your next tobogganing trip.

Great Northern Concrete Toboggan Race 1998, University of Calgary, Alberta

http://www.acs.ucalgary.ca/~jkwong/GNCTR/GNCTR.html

Learn about the 24th Annual Great Northern Concrete Toboggan Race (GNCTR), which was held in Alberta February 4–8, 1998. The University of Calgary Civil Engineers hosts GNCTR, which welcomes students from Canadian, American, and international technical colleges and universities. Teams of students build toboggans with concrete running surfaces and present a paper on the sled's design. Each toboggan carries five students down a snow-packed track. The race is a timed run on a relatively straight course. Prizes are awarded for overall performance, highest speed, shortest stopping distance, best concrete design mix, best team costumes, best team spirit, best newcomer, and more.

Old Sled Works Sled Museum

http://computrends.com/oldsledworks/museum.html

This sled factory is a registered historic landmark in Pennsylvania, and admission to the Sled Museum is free. The Old Sled Works was once the home of Standard Novelty Works, one of the busiest and best-known makers of children's sleds in the country, including Lightning Guider sleds. The museum displays sleds from each decade of operation (some rare), old catalogs and other advertising pieces, patent and trademark papers, tools, early printing and stenciling equipment, and the original sled factory time clock. You can order the book *Flexible Flyer and Other Great Sleds for Collectors* at this site.

OYB#7—The Seasons of the Yurt

http://www.glpbooks.com/oyb/yurt.htm

This is an interesting article from *Out Your Backdoor* magazine. A *yurt*, by the way, is a Mongolian nomad hut. Read about how a group of friends build a yurt in a secluded, hilly area. They discover the joys of tobogganing and build several runs. I especially liked the description of rushing over snowy roads over long hills on old boards at night, although I can't speak to the safety of it all.

Sheffield Ski Village

http://ds.dial.pipex.com/ssv/fram_set.shtml

Sheffield Village is an all-season Alpine resort located in the UK. It's located on a hillside overlooking Sheffield City Centre and provides panoramic views of the Derbyshire countryside. In addition to skateboarding, snowboarding, and skiing, you're encouraged to ride the Thunder Valley Toboggan Run. It's more than 100 meters of twisting and turning track designed to reproduce all the thrills and excitement of the Cresta run.

Sledding/Tobogganing

http://www.cha.ab.ca/safekids/SledKid.htm

Get tips for keeping your kids safe on their toboggan-ing trips. Includes links to safety tips for kids who are biking, having fun on the playground, in-line skating, and playing on the trampoline.

NRP TOP PICKS

Sledding/Tobogganing

http://www.cha.ab.ca/safekids/Sled.htm

Learn about the major causes of sledding injuries and who is at risk (most injuries occur to males between the ages of 5 and 14). Learn how to protect your child from sledding injuries. Learn about SAFE KIDS—an organization that promotes prevention as the key to reduction of deaths and injuries. SAFE KIDS gives you tips on how to check out the tobogganing view, your style, your gear, and the supervision. You also get links to other child-safety sites.

SLEIGH-RIDES & TOBOGGANING in Val Gardena

http://groeden.com/english/sport/sleigh.htm

Val Gardena is in South Tyrol right in the heart of the Dolomites (in the Alps). Learn where the ideal tobogganing runs are located and how long they are. Browse the site for info on other winter activities and learn about the tourist attractions at Val Gardena.

Snowboard Toboggan Pictures

http://www.monmouth.com/~dschutz/pictures.htm

Look at short descriptions and pictures showing the use of snowboards in the operation of ski patrol toboggans in different snow and terrain conditions. You'll also see some of the dos and don'ts of snowboard toboggan operation.

Switzerland Tourism: Ski, Snowboarding, Cross-Country and Tobogganing Snow Report

http://www.switzerlandtourism.ch/snow/snow0_ta.html

This site provides daily snow reports and ski information. Learn about Switzerland's weather and climate, as well as the sports and activities it offers. You'll also get travel tips and info on what you need to know to visit Switzerland.

Sympatico: HealthyWay: Winter Weather Beaters: Tobogganing

http://www.nf.sympatico.ca/healthyway/HEALTHYWAY/feature_dec9c.html

This article in *HealthyWay Magazine* gives you tips on toboggan safety from the Product Safety Inspectors at Health and Welfare Canada. Learn about the SMART-RISK Foundation, which educates Canadians on injury prevention, safety, and smart choices. You'll learn how to make tobogganing a safe activity for you and your children.

TIScover—Austria—tobagganing report

http://www.tiscover.com/1Root/Kontinent/6/Staat/7/AktuelleBerichte/f_rodelbericht...2.html

This site provides a search engine for you to enter the first letter of any town in Austria to get a tobogganing report on the area. You get a summary of tobogganing spots, a rating on the current quality of snow (mountain and valley), info on whether the spot is lit at night, and what establishments are located in the area. You get the latest weather info (including city and mountain weather); satellite images; avalanche info; and snow, ice, and water reports. Includes pictures showing various snow activities around Austria. You also get general info on Austria and things you'll need to know during your stay—such as tips on money, laws, customs, medical care, and more. You can choose to view this site in several languages.

Related Sites

http://www.aaos.org/wordhtml/papers/position/sledding.htm

http://www.iatech.com/tour/loc/loc73.htm

http://www.SledHockey.org/

http://alpha2.bmc.uu.se/~markh/pulka_english.html

http://www.caesars.com/pocono/prwinter.htm

http://www.gala-resort.com/winter.htm

http://www.geocities.com/MotorCity/Downs/3779/

http://www.wellstrails.org/winter.html

http://www.sierra.net/skiconnections/innsbruck.htm

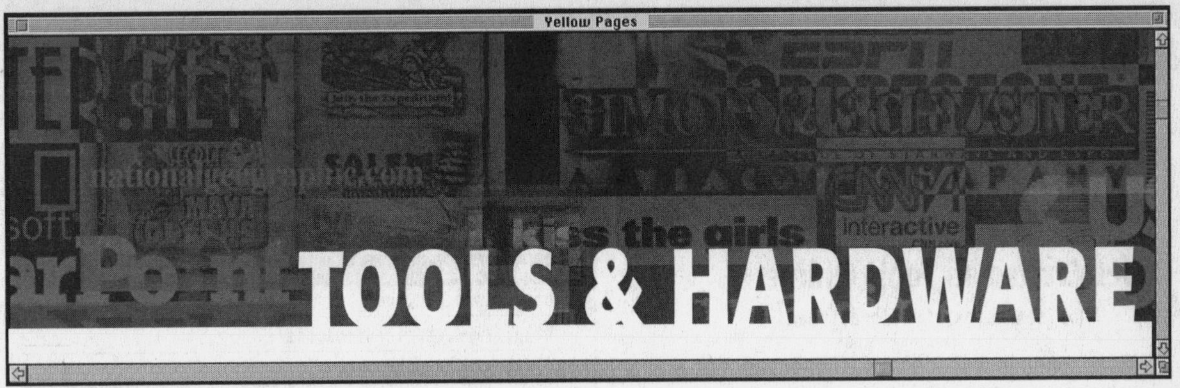

> If the only tool you have is a hammer, you tend to see every problem as a nail.
>
> *Abraham Maslow*

84 Lumber

http://www.84lumber.com/home.htm

Browse home packages or an online catalog, find the store nearest you, or find out how to get a job with 84 Lumber, the largest privately owned retail building materials company in the U.S.

Black and Decker

http://www.blackanddecker.com/

Everything you ever wanted to know about Black and Decker tools. There is even a bridal registry for that handywoman in your life.

Build.com

http://www.build.com/

A large directory and search engine for building and home improvement products and information. Nicely done.

Grainger.com

http://www.grainger.com/

Shop this huge business-to-business hardware house online, or locate a branch near you. Also check out their Resource Center, which includes a chat room.

NRP Top Picks

Build.com
http://www.build.com/

Grainger.com
http://www.grainger.com/

Lowe's Home Improvement Warehouse
http://www.lowes.com/

Hardware World

http://www.hardwareworld.com/

A huge listing of hardware sites on the Net, including products, retailers, distributors, and trade publications.

Home Depot

http://www.homedepot.com/

Shop the Home Depot online, America's largest home improvement retailer. You can also get project advice, read press releases, and investigate the company's finances.

Lowe's Home Improvement Warehouse

http://www.lowes.com/

LOWE'S Home Improvement Warehouse KNOWS Home Improvement

Home Page
What's New
"How-To's"
Home Safety Tips
Product Highlights
Contractor News
Team Lowe's Racing
Company Information
Career Opportunities
Search
Store Locator
Archives
Feedback
Legal Information

The Spirit of the Season

Across many cultures and beliefs, the holiday season is a time of sharing and giving—a time to take a break from the bustle of modern life to be with friends and loved-ones. We appreciate your visit to our site at this special time, and wish you and your family the best of holidays.

Through our Web site, we try to provide how-to and safety information to interested do-it-yourselfers with Internet access. We're proud to announce that for the second year in a row, our site was awarded "Best Educational Value" by Coopers & Lybrand. We hope to continue to add value to your Web experience.

Lowe's is one of the world's largest retailers of home improvement products. We are a Fortune 500 company with over 425 stores located in 25 states.

By the way-if you still haven't caught up with your last minute shopping, visit our gift advisor for great gift ideas for those special people in your life. Convenient Lowe's gift cards are also available. They can be given to allow the gift recipient to choose exactly what they want from our huge inventory of products.

Lots of goodies here, including project tips and tricks, a gift advisor, a store locator, a section for contractors, and of course a display of wares for sale.

A B C D E F G H I J K L M N O P Q R S T U V W X Y Z

NTML

http://www.ntml.com/

A worldwide directory of tooling and machining companies. Organized by categories, the directory can be either browsed or searched.

Order Craftsman Tools Online

http://shop.sears.com/store/craftsman/

As the name implies, this site is a comprehensive online ordering system for Sears Craftsman tools. Even the most hard-to-find model can be safely ordered with their secure ordering system and your credit card. If you're a Craftsman junkie, this site is for you.

The Stanley Works

http://www.stanleyworks.com

A complete online catalog of Stanley products, along with suggested retailers who will sell them to you.

The Toolman Home Page

http://www.thetoolman.com/

Shop for tools online (if this store doesn't have it, it probably doesn't exist), and get tool maintenance and repair tips.

Related Sites

http://www.mmm.com/

http://www.americantool.com/

http://www.fiskars.com/

http://www.jensentools.com/

http://www.masterlock.com/

http://www.pedersenbros.com/

http://www.toolplus.com/

http://www.tooltech.qc.ca/

http://woodworkerstore.com/

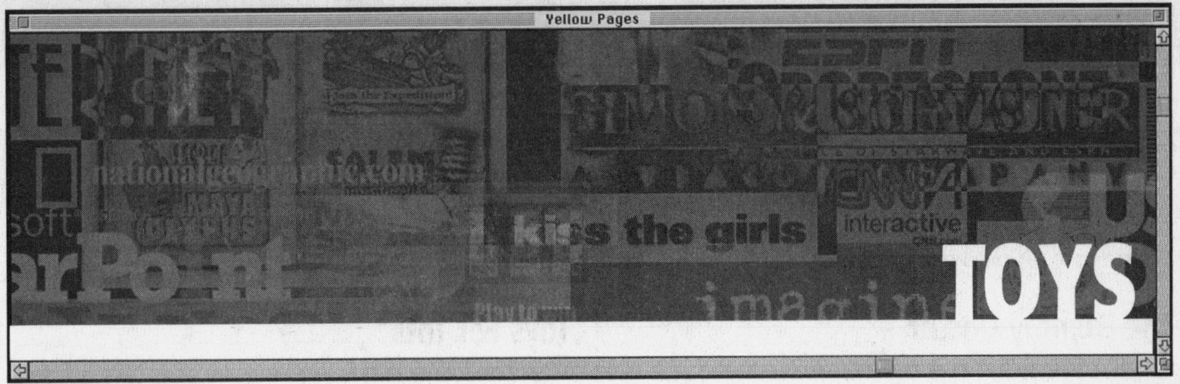

> What chance does a toy like me have against a Buzz Lightyear action figure?
>
> *Woody in* Toy Story *(1995)*

#Cybertron's Web Page

http://www.geocities.com/Hollywood/Boulevard/3156/

If you're a Transformers fan, or you want to talk with other TF fans, you need to see this page. #Cybertron is a channel on the DALNet IRC Network (IRC stands for Internet Relay Chat). The site also provides information on how to join IRCs, where to get the software, and the general rules of conduct.

1-800-BEARGRAM

http://www.beargram.com/

If you need to send a teddy bear anywhere in the country, either personalized or standard, contact these folks. They have bears for every occasion and message.

All Around the World Tams

http://members.tripod.com/~vvillage/tamagotchi.html

A fan's site of Tamagotchi pets, the virtual pets from Japan. While the spelling is a little shaky in spots, the images of "Tamas" from around the world are neat, and the entire site is very sweetly done. A real labor of love.

Trouble in Toyland
http://www.pirg.org/pirg/consumer/products/toy/97/index.htm

The Copernicus Homepage

http://www.1q.com/copernicus/

A store specializing in toys of the imagination for adults—optical illusions, craft kits, puzzles, and the like. You can email for a complete catalog.

CToys® Virtual Beanie Mall

http://www.angelfire.com/nj/beaniebabies/shoplink.html

Tired of standing in line for Beanie Babies? Order them over the Internet! This site lists those stores (including home pages) that will take orders. They also list other Beanie Baby products, links, and services.

Deni's Vintage Barbie Collection

http://www.tir.com/~davidson/

A serious collector of vintage Barbie dolls, Deni lists the things she wants and the items she's selling, and has ID guides available to help identify which doll you have and when it was manufactured. Lots of Barbie and Barbie-related photos.

Doll/Barbie Store Directory

http://www.fix.net/surf/barbie/

This site plans on listing every store in the world that carries dolls or Barbie. If you want to know the stores in your area, or wish to see your store listed, check out this site. If the desired store has a home page, you can jump there from the link at this site.

A B C D E F G H I J K L M N O P Q R S T U V W X Y Z

Dr. Toy

http://www.drtoy.com/drtoy/index.html

Gives advice on what to buy for the children in your family. Rates the 100 best toys, plus sorts them by type (games, books, arts & crafts), and by age. Also includes the best toys to take on vacation—a must during those long hours in the car.

The Dummy Doctor

http://gramercy.ios.com/~asemok/dummies.html

A commercial site offering "handcrafted professional ventriloquial figures," plus puppets and marionettes for both professional and hobbyist. Also does repair and evaluation of vintage dummies and puppets.

The Gallery of Monster Toys

http://members.aol.com/raycastile/page1.htm

The creator of this site says it best: "Vintage monster toys are typically overlooked by collectors, largely because they seem obsolete in today's world. The toys in this gallery are not, for the most part, "slick" or "hyper-detailed." They are humble and imperfect. They depict flawed, tortured creatures. These toys capture a time when horror was fun." A truly fun site for anyone who still loves monster movies.

Moto-Mini Motorcycle Collectibles

http://www.mshopper.eurografix.com/motomini.htm

Presents an online catalog of Moto-Mini's collectible motorcycle models.

The Official LEGO World Wide Web Site

http://www.lego.com/

Aimed primarily at kids, this site lists the LEGO toy groups (LEGO, Duplo, etc.) and provides a parent guide, a Web surfer's club (so kids can list or make their own LEGO sites), and games to play on the Internet. Also has listings of who to contact to get the various toys in every country.

PGT Toys

http://www.tias.com/stores/pgt/

Offers a variety of unusual toys for sale. TV and movie toys, superheroes, and novelty items are included. Prices and purchasing information provided.

Toy Market

http://www.toymarket.com/

An online magazine dedicated to toy collecting and other collectibles. Place an ad yourself, or read the classified ads (updated regularly) to see what items are available. There's also a search engine to speed up your search for that special something.

Toys For Tots

http://www.toysfortots.org/

The U.S. Marine Reserve program Toys For Tots is described in complete detail at this site. It goes into the history, the Foundation that helps to support the program, its corporate sponsors, and most importantly how you can help.

NRP TOP PICKS

Trouble in Toyland

http://www.pirg.org/pirg/consumer/products/toy/97/index.htm

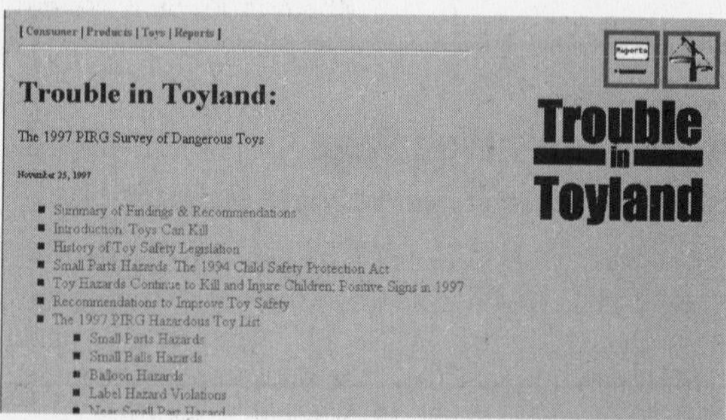

You probably know that some toys are considered unsafe for kids. What you may not know is why—and how that's determined. This Web site discusses the history of toy safety legislation, plus what's currently being done to protect kids from unsafe toys. It also shows how some manufacturers are getting around the legislation.

Truckaholic

http://www.truckaholic.com/

Dedicated to die-cast trucks and other automotive collectibles, the site shows photos of key pieces of the collection, plus items for sale. Also has links to related sites.

The Virtual Toy Store

http://www.halcyon.com/uncomyn/home.html

Targeted toward science fiction and fantasy enthusiasts. Offers a fully interactive toy store, complete with sound and video clips. Specializes in hard-to-find gifts, toys, T-shirts, and jewelry.

The World of Breyer Model Horses

http://www.aa.net/~cascade

A model horse mail-order service that offers all current Breyer model horses and accessories. Also carries a wide variety of discontinued and used models. Includes links to other model horse sites.

NEWSGROUPS

alt.collecting.teddy-bears

alt.fan.plushies

alt.games

alt.toys

rec.games

rec.toys

MAILING LISTS

toy

TOYSTCHR

Related Sites

shttp://ccwf.cc.utexas.edu/~number6/vm/

http://jrscience.wcp.muohio.edu/gene/homepage.html

http://members.aol.com/thedeke/hapmel-f.htm

http://oeonline.com/~slu2/

http://pages.prodigy.com/toys_etc/toys2.htm

http://www.classictintoy.com/

http://www.hotwheels.com/

http://www.mindspring.com/~tmp95/fprice.html

http://www.parentsplace.com/shopping/tnpc/parentalk/toddlers/todd21.html

http://www.stern.nyu.edu/~smalik/matchbox/mbmenu.html

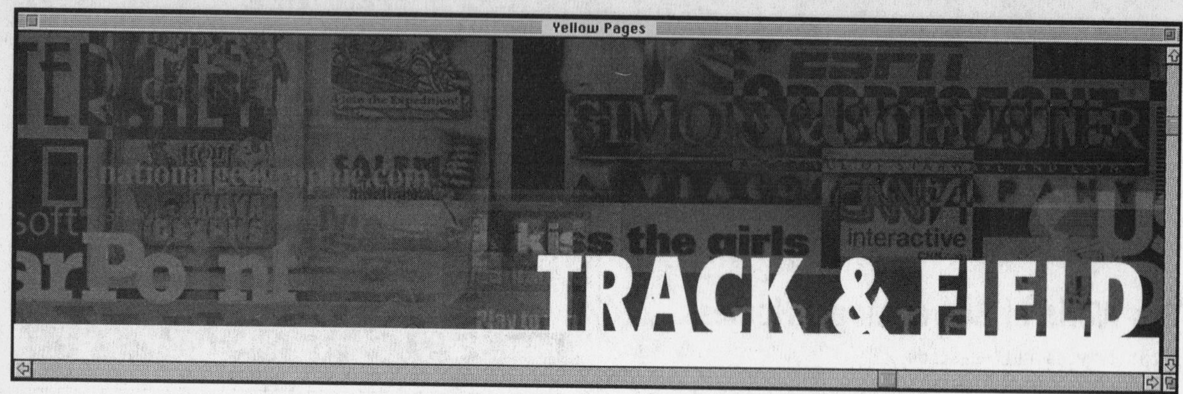

> Now you wouldn't believe me if I told you, but I could run like the wind blows. From that day on, if I was ever going somewhere, I was running!
>
> *Forrest Gump in* Forrest Gump *(1994)*

American Track & Field Online

`http://www.runningnetwork.com/atf/`

Get running tips, news, and links, as well as a track calendar and race results. This e-zine is dedicated to America's 3.6 million T&F participants from the high school to the post-college club level.

Athletics Canada

`http://www.canoe.ca/Athcan/home.html`

As the governing body for Canadian T&F, Athletic Canada's page focuses on Canadian athletes, records, rankings, events, coaching, and news.

Athletics Home Page

`http://www.hkkk.fi/~niininen/athl.html`

A book of records—every record known to the sport is listed here or a link is provided. Want to know track records for Croatia, South Africa, or Bulgaria? Try this page first, and you'll know what to shoot for.

Dan O'Brien
http://www.danobrien.com/

Dan O'Brien

`http://www.danobrien.com/`

Dubbed the World's Greatest Athlete, O'Brien won the gold for the 1996 Olympic decathlon. His home page includes an extensive biography, his schedule, and some words of wisdom regarding the attitude needed to be an athlete or simply to live healthier.

Kangaroo's Triple Jump Online

`http://www.owlnet.rice.edu/~riceroo/`

Not just your casual jumper, this site's author has been studying the biomechanics of jumping since high school. The pages include triple jump and long jump resources, articles, a poll of the best jumpers, and a media archive dedicated to the sport.

Masters Track & Field

`http://members.aol.com/trackceo/index.html`

Young whippersnappers aren't the only people enjoying themselves on the track. This page is dedicated running seniors, some of whom are still breaking records into their nineties.

Pre!

`http://weber.u.washington.edu/~cbeahm/PRE_PAGE/`

A site dedicated to long-distance runner Steve Prefontaine. Read a bio and articles, jump to links, see his stats and photos, and check out the latest about a movie about Steve, who died in a car accident on 1975.

Tommy's Decathlon Page

http://dana.ucc.nau.edu/~tms3/dec1.html

Get the latest on NCAA decathlon competition, learn more about the world championship, view pictures and video clips, and let coaches know that you want to be recruited.

Sydney 2000 Games

http://www.sydney.olympic.org/

The official home pages of the next Summer Olympics, to be held in Sydney, Australia. You can view media releases, environmental guidelines, and other information.

Track & Field News

http://www.trackandfieldnews.com/

Peruse past issues, check up on races, athletes, and records. The countless articles will keep diehard runners busy, until they're rested and are ready to start running again.

Track & Field Online

http://www.trackonline.com/

Although certain pages are reserved for members, this site still offers many T&F resources, such as information about trainers and products, as well as chat forums and athlete interviews.

trackcity.com

http://trackcity.com/

Trackcity caters to runners, coaches, agents, and anyone else with more than a casual appreciation for the sport of running. Catch up on news, read articles from diehard runners and enthusiasts, keep "track" of your favorite track team, run a virtual mile, and create a custom running diary.

Training for 400m/800m: An Alternative Plan

http://www.pnc.com.au/~stevebn/plan.htm

This site shares information gathered by its author regarding better methods to prepare an athlete to run in either the 400 or 800 meter medium sprints. The information includes specific training regimens.

USA Track & Field

http://www.usatf.org/

The official site of track & field's overseeing authority. These pages contain news, national and international records, race walking resources, masters racing, and race numerology.

Vault World (Pole Vault Paradise)

http://www.polevault.com/

Get questions answered in the Coaching Area, see who the top vaulters are this year, jump to link to related sites, view pictures and videos, and read articles about vaulting.

Related Sites
http://www.ocf.berkeley.edu/~justine/hurdle.html
http://www.cs.uml.edu/~phoffman/xc.html
http://www.u-net.com/spiridon/webazine.html
http://www.pentathlon.com/

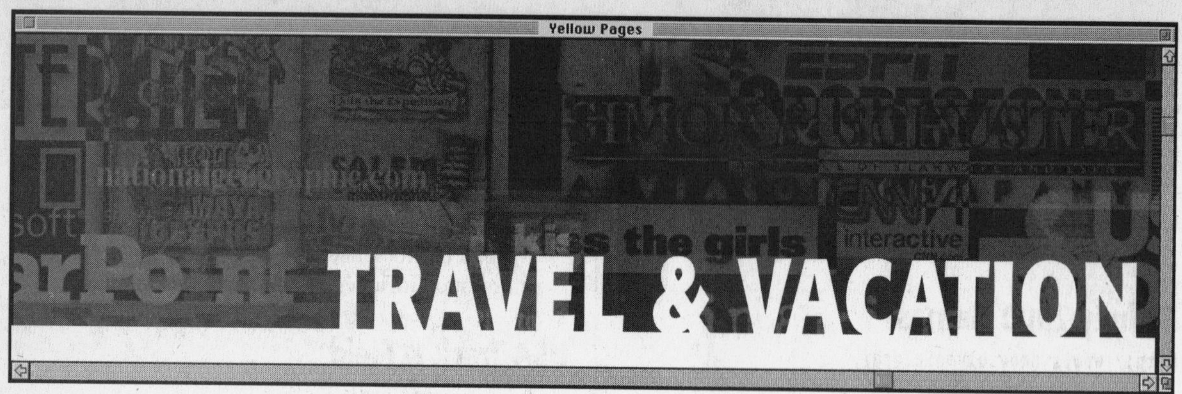

A
B
C
D
E
F
G
H
I
J
K
L
M
N
O
P
Q
R
S
T
U
V
W
X
Y
Z

The world is a book, and those who do not travel, read only a page.

Saint Augustine

AIRLINES

Aer Lingus

http://www.aerlingus.ie/

Ireland's national airline's site, with information for the business traveler, leisure traveler, U.S. traveler, and frequent flyer. Lists flight schedules and gateway cities.

Air Canada

http://www.aircanada.ca/

The official Web site for Air Canada. Includes a news desk, schedules, a program, and a special section called Netguide, which provides information on Internet and HTML basics. Also provides a French version.

Air Charter Guide

http://www.shore.net/acg/

The online edition of *The Air Charter Guide*, a limited version of the book. Serves as a guide for locating charter operators, arranged by state, name. Also includes tips on planning and pricing a charter.

Airlines of the Web

http://w1.itn.net/airlines/

Provides information about airlines, organized by geographic region. Also provides information about cargo airlines, newsgroups, and airports.

Grand Canyon Railway
http://www.thetrain.com/

NRP PICKS

Airlines Online

http://airlines-online.com/airlines/

Airlines-Online is your one-stop Web directory for every airline, airport, and other aviation site that is on the World Wide Web today. This site is the source for aviation links. Airlines-Online is a free service and the site is updated weekly on Monday mornings.

All Airline Sites—the Largest List on the Web

http://www.geocities.com/CapeCanaveral/4285/

The largest list of airline sites on the Web. All airlines on the Web are listed. Cargo and charter airlines too. Updated weekly.

America West Airlines

http://www.americawest.com

The America West Airline's site includes information about both the airline itself and America West Vacations. Travel destinations, flight schedules, hotels and special promotions as well as general information are included.

American Airlines

http://www.americanair.com/

Includes schedules, travel awards program information, special products, and a helpful alphabetical index to access information quickly. Also includes an employment opportunity section.

Ansett Australia

http://www.ansett.com.au/

Provides information, timetables, rates, and special offers on flights. Site has information and links about Australia's currency, history, major cities, and general facts.

Atlantic Southeast Airlines, Inc.

http://www.irinfo.com/asai/

Atlantic Southeast Airlines, Inc. is Atlanta's largest regional air carrier and offers service to 24 cities from a second hub in Dallas, Texas. ASA's stock is traded on The Nasdaq Stock Market's National Market under the symbol ASAI.

British Airways

http://www.british-airways.com/

At this site, you can book and pay for any British Airways flight, check availability, and find out about special ticket offers. Read about packages and tours from British Airways Holidays. There's even a question and answer section where your travel questions can be answered, such as how much baggage you're allowed.

Canadian Airlines Intl

http://www.cdnair.ca/

An airline that obviously cares about its Web presence. Find out flight schedules from a complete searchable index by destination and departure. Find out about business travel fares and accommodation arrangements made in conjunction with Canadian Airlines.

Cathay Pacific

http://www.cathaypacific-air.com/../index2_1.html

The home page of this airline offers information about service to locations in Asia, such as Hong Kong, Bangkok, and Singapore. Includes rates and special deals. Also includes a link to traveling in Hong Kong.

Comair

http://fly-comair.com/

Provides flight schedules, frequent flyer program information, and special weekend fare information for patrons of Comair—a Delta Connection.

Discounts Online

If you want to find discounts online for flights, you have several options. American Airline's Joe Crawley says American offers a special service, called Netsaver Fares, to their patrons that tells them about the weekly specials. While you could look on the home pages of some of your favorite airlines to find this flight information, it might be easier in the long run to check out one of the services offered by major travel sites, such as Travelocity (http://www.travelocity.com), Expedia (http://expedia.msn.com), and Fodor's (http://www.fodors.com).

Each of these travel sites includes a feature for highlighting the lowest fares or super deals on fares. On Microsoft Expedia, you can check out The Real Deal section, which provides tips on bargains all around. You also can find some general advice for the traveler here. Travelocity offers a section called Last Minute Details, which gives discounted information for the last-minute traveler.

Eagle Canyon Airlines

http://cybermart.com/eagle/

Provides air tours of the Grand Canyon, including an extensive air/ground south rim tour. Provides contact information and translations of the site into many other languages.

Frontier Airlines

http://www.cuug.ab.ca:8001/~busew/frontier.html

Provides links regarding the history, development, flight information, and reservation information of Frontier Airlines.

Iberia Airlines

http://www.iberiausa.com/ibusa/home.html

The official North American site of the Spanish international carrier. Find out about special offers, availability, and gateway cities. Book reservations and buy tickets online.

Japan Airlines

http://mmm.wwa.com/travlog/jal.html

Accommodates travelers to Taiwan, Korea, and Japan. Offers frequent flyer information, as well as virtual tours of Asian countries. Also provides a Japanese language version.

A B C D E F G H I J K L M N O P Q R S T U V W X Y Z

Lufthansa Timetable Info

http://www.lufthansa.com/ehome.htm

Focuses on departure information on Lufthansa flights to and from Europe. Furnishes a German version of the page.

Mexicana Airlines

http://www.mexicana.com/

Provides a graphics-intensive airline Web site for Mexico. Includes maps, vacation specials, and online reservations. Also provides links to other travel-related sites.

Mount Cook Airlines

http://www.clearfield.co.nz/mount_cook/

Offers graphics-rich information helpful to those planning to visit New Zealand. Also offers flight schedules, booking arrangements, and exchange rates.

New England Airlines

http://www.ids.net/flybi/nea/

Offers flights to Block Island, Nantucket, Martha's Vineyard, and Cape Cod. Emphasizes Block Island and provides information on the island itself.

Quantas Airlines

http://www.anzac.com/qantas/qantas.htm

Includes a history of the airline, schedules, rates, and links to related sites on Australia and other airlines. Offers pictures of koalas, too.

Virgin Atlantic Airlines

http://www.fly.virgin.com/atlantic/

Provides information about special offers, frequent flyer miles, and more. Lets you plan your flight online from a detailed form. Offers City Guides—travel tips for major North American, Asian, British, Irish, and Greek cities. Also furnishes articles from their magazine, hot air.

Related Sites

http://www.glacierbaytours.com/

http://www.celebrity-cruises.com/

http://www.cunardline.com/

http://www.abercrombiekent.com/

http://www.hideaways.com/

http://www.vacationrentalnet.com/

AUTOMOBILE TRAVEL

ASIRT-Association for International Road Travel

http://www.horizon-web.com/asirt/

Want to know which countries are the most dangerous to drive in? You'll find this fact here, as well as other road information and safety data.

Rental Agencies

http://www.yahoo.com/Business/Corporations/Automotive/Rentals/

Yahoo!'s lengthy list of rental agencies is located here, which includes over fifty rental agency home page links. Also recreational vehicle links are situated here.

Route 66

http://route66.netvision.be/

Get your kicks on the famous roadway route 66. This site is packed with photos, stories, and a wealth of helpful information. Also features a locator map.

Wheels and Deals Online

Rent-a-car services are a must if you need to get around after flying into a location. You can look up each of the companies you are interested in or use a database to locate all of them. You also can use a service, such as Fodor's (http://www.fodors.com), Travelocity (http://www.travelocity.com), or Expedia (http://expedia.msn.com) to help you reserve the car you want.

You should know what kind of car you need before you try reserving anything, though, says Terry Gordon, public relations manager for Avis Ret-A-Car. Think about where you are traveling to—will it be snowing and raining or sunny and beautiful? That should influence your decision regarding what type of vehicle you will want to drive. If you are going to be driving over ice and snow in a state such as Alaska, for example, you might want to think about a 4 by 4. Know what price range you want to stay within and make sure you know how much extra you will have to pay per mile. If you're going to be traveling a long distance and don't want to worry about mileage, you might want to request unlimited mileage for an additional cost.

Related Sites

http://www.all-hotels.com/

http://nthp.org/main/hotels/hotelsmain.htm

http://www.hotelguide.ch/

Scenic Byways and Other Recreational Drives

http://www.gorp.com/gorp/activity/byway/byway.htm

Organized into categories such as Far West, Desert Southwest, Great Plains, and Great Lakes, this site helps you locate the scenic route to your destination. Contains links to a majority of the 50 states.

Traveling in the USA

http://www.travelingusa.com/a1/assistance/youhere.html

These pages will help the U.S. traveler find information on parks, campgrounds, resorts, and recreation. From relief maps to kiddie activities, you'll probably satisfy your travel needs here.

BOOKS AND PUBLICATIONS

Adventurous Traveler Bookstore

http://www.gorp.com/atbook.htm

The claim "The world's most complete source of outdoor adventure books and maps" pretty much says it all. You can search this bookstore's entire database from this site.

Cloudcap Books

http://chatlink.com/~cloudcap/

This site specializes in travel to the Pacific Northwest and Northern California. They offer books on hiking, Mount Shasta, day trips, and dining in southern Oregon.

Lonely Planet

http://www.lonelyplanet.com/

Pick your destination, and away you go! This site offers information on most regions of the world. The information is down to earth and helpful—no fluff. Order your Lonely Planet travel guides online.

Travel Publications

http://www.yahoo.com/business_and_Economy/companies/Travel/publications/Books/

Yahoo!'s list of companies and agencies specializing in travel publications. This list contains sites that deal with a wide spectrum of travel.

Travels with Samantha

http://www-swiss.ai.mit.edu/samantha/travels-with-samantha.html

Philip Greenspun, a graduate student at MIT, provides this summer travel log entirely online. Download chapters or browse the spectacular images; it is worth your time.

World of Maps

http://www.worldofmaps.com/

So you'll never feel lost, a professional cartographer, Brad Green, operates this plentiful online travel site. Mostly Canadian travel information is featured here.

CRUISE SHIPS

Accent's Cruise Connection

http://www.premier.net/~accent/

Provides information about cruises of all kinds, including riverboat, masted sailing ship, European river, and literally worldwide cruising areas ports of call. This site, while still under construction, has ample information about taking cruises in China, Canada's Maritime Provinces, and more familiar destinations in the Caribbean and Mediterranean. Also provided are links to order forms for all said destinations.

America's Cruise Authority: GalaxSea Cruises

http://www.galaxsea.com

GalaxSea Cruises in San Jose, CA is a cruise travel specialist. Their Web site contains the latest GalaxSea featured specials, cruise line specials, recommendations, inside tips, cruise line ratings, cruise ship ratings, plus frequently asked questions about cruising and information on how you can earn a free cruise. Visit often as their pages change frequently!

Cruise Shoppes America, Ltd.

http://www.cruiseshoppes.com/

Provides full-service cruise travel services. Includes destinations, monthly specials, and contact information. Includes an association directory with links to agencies by region.

A B C D E F G H I J K L M N O P Q R S T U V W X Y Z

Cruises Inc.

http://www2.csn.net/cruises/

Provides information and profiles about many different cruises and destinations. Includes company backgrounds, photo albums, cruise reviews, and ordering information. Includes links to cruise lines on the Web.

Cruise with ABOVE ALL TRAVEL

http://www.geocities.com/thetropics/2554

Don't buy your next cruise until you've checked their deals. Honeymoon specials, Bermuda, San Juan, Mexico, and more. Custom phone cards now available.

Disney Cruise Line Profile

http://www.safari.net/~marketc/DisneyProfile.html

Photos of the new Disney Magic Cruise Ship, the lobby and new terminal as well as Cabin Rates and descriptions.

Freighter World Cruises

http://www.gus.com/travel/fwc/fwc.html

Advertises Freighter World Cruises, Inc., a travel agency that focuses on freighter travel. Provides information on various freighter lines and their destinations. Cruise in economy style.

Holland America Line

http://www.hollandamerica.com/

This site has information on Holland America Line's cruises to Alaska, the Caribbean, Hawaii, Asia and the Pacific, South America, Canada and New England, and Europe. You may request literature and order a video on your desired cruise destination.

Norwegian Cruise Line

http://www.ncl.com/

Read about Norwegian Cruise Line destinations and music theme cruises, such as a big band cruise. Sample destinations are Mexico, Hawaii, Alaska, and the Caribbean. Find out about special deals.

Princess Cruises

http://www.awcv.com/princess.html

Cruise on the Love Boat to the Caribbean. Find out about special discounts, 50% or more. You can book your cruise online.

Royal Caribbean Cruise Line

http://mmink.com/mmink/kiosks/costa/rccl.html

A stripped-down overview of cruise destinations, itineraries, and prices offered by Royal Caribbean Cruise Line cruise ships.

Schooner Mary Day

http://www.coastalmaine.com/mainstreet/tours/maryday/index.html

The Schooner Mary Day is a sailing cruise ship (Windjammer) that carries couples, singles, and groups on three to six day cruises among the islands of Midcoast Maine.

Ships Ahoy Cruises

http://www.shipsahoycruises.com

Ships Ahoy is a Florida-based travel agency that sells and specializes in cruises only, therefore, offering the lowest rates available.

Travel Discounts Cruise Index

http://www.traveldiscounts.com/cruises/

Provides discount cruise information, arranged by region and cruise line. Includes up-to-date information and the option to make online reservations.

Travelogic Cruises

http://www.arabian-horses.com/trvlogic/

Travelogic offers discount cruises with all major cruise lines. Come and see their latest hot deals for your next getaway!

INTERNATIONAL TRAVEL

Alchemy of Africa

http://www.icons.co.za/africa/

Provides information all about Africa. Lets you download African music while you stroll through the Art Gallery, browse the Market for shops and business listings, chat online in the chat rooms, armchair travel to African destinations via the Mystical Launch pad, and more.

American International Travel

http://www.aitv.com

A full service travel agency, providing travel planning, online reservations, cruises, tours, car, air, hotel reservations, sports specials, recreational vehicles, honeymoon, vacation, groups, and business travel.

Antigua & Barbuda

http://www.candw.ag/

Provides a guide to Antigua and Barbuda with links to related sites. Home page does not offer detailed information or pictures, but the links to local tourist sites are worthwhile for anyone considering traveling to the area.

Australia Travel Directory

http://www.anzac.com/aust/aust.htm

Offers links to information on tourism, VISA, individual states, and transportation.

Automated Travel Center

http://www.ananda.com/plg/travel/

Provides full online service travel arrangements and reservations. Includes international and domestic United States destination packages for both business and leisure.

Brochure Flow

http://www.broflo.com.au/broflo.html

Provides a home for The Australia Travel Arcade and Brochure Flow Travel agency. Offers full-service travel services, including airline reservations, hotel accommodations, and tourist packages. Includes links by area to any business one might need when planning a trip to Australia. A very handy site for anyone planning to go down under.

Canada Swan International Travel Ltd.

http://www.csit.com/canadaswan

Canada Swan Travel is a full service agency focusing on travels to Asia and Southeast Asia. They have many different clientele ranging from pleasure to last minute to corporate. The agency is a consolidator for many major airlines and therefore is able to give very competitive fares. Their agents are ready to serve you with travels in Canada, the USA, or to anywhere Overseas.

China Circulate International Travel Service (CCITS)

http://china-times.com/ccits/ccits.htm

A travel service that will arrange your tour in China.

The Civilized Explorer

http://www.cieux.com/~philip/

Contains information on the French West Indies and Guadeloupe, including information about beaches, restaurants, activities, and places to stay. Also includes photographs and links to maps, satellite pictures, and other Web resources.

Council Travel

http://www.ciee.org:80/cts/ctshome.htm

Specializes in student and youth budget travelers. Provides information on youth hostels, international student ID cards, and rail passes. Index to study abroad program.

Country Maps of Europe

http://www.tue.nl/europe/

Provides links to sites that detail regional and city maps of Great Britain, European, and Slavic countries.

Cyprus

http://www.wam.umd.edu/~cyprus/tourist.html

Serves as a comprehensive guide to Cyprus—its history, its beauty, and why it's definitely worth planning a trip to. Includes sections on cities and advice on where to stay. Provides information on where to shop, what to buy, the cuisine of Cyprus, music sites, and where to have fun.

Czech Info Center

http://www.muselik.com/

An incredibly well-organized guide to the Czech Republic. Includes general information, bulletin boards (such as finding an ancestor), helpful travel information, and a section on the city of Prague.

Endeavour Travel

http://www.anzac.com/endvr/endvr.htm

Specializes in travel services to Australia, New Zealand, and the South Pacific for both business and leisure. Includes package vacations to exotic locals such as Fiji and the Antarctic. Includes links to Australian and New Zealand sites for travel and information.

European and British Rail Passes

http://www.eurail.com/eurail/passes/passlist.htm

Provides information on the Eurorail pass and rail passes for other countries such as Germany, Austria, Italy, Czech Republic, and Scandinavia. This site is a must for those considering traveling Europe by Eurorail.

Far & Away Travel Services

http://www.faraway.com/default.htm

Provides full travel services to vacation sites worldwide. Includes many package deals and current specials. The site provides ordering and contact information.

FranceEscape

http://www.france.com/francescape/top.html

Informative site on planning and vacationing in France. Includes studies in France, festivals, transportation, and classifieds.

Freesun News

http://www.freesun.be/

This Belgium sight provides links to international travel all over the world. Links to airline information, restaurants, accommodations, bookstores, fairs, and real estate indexed by country.

Going to Belgium

http://www.cais.com/usa/visitors/visitors.html

Provides links to Belgium cities and travel interests, passport and customs information, and information for establishing residency.

Great Australian Travel Co.

http://www.magna.com.au/~hideaway/snow_ind.html

If you like to go skiing, how about skiing in Australia or New Zealand? Check out airfares, ski travel packages, and prices.

Hong Kong Online Guide

http://www.hk.super.net/

A Java-enhanced site providing information about Hong Kong, including shopping, dining, culture, hotel information, and places of interest. Offers links to sites related to Chinese and Hong Kong culture.

Indonesia

http://www.sino.net/asean/indonesa.html

Serves as a guide to Indonesia—its customs, traveling within the country, entertainment, useful phrases, currency, and other traveler tips. Includes a recording of the National Anthem of Indonesia and a soon-to-be-available video clip.

The Internet Guide to Hostels

http://www.hostels.com/hostels/

Includes a Worldwide Hostel Guide for locations throughout the world; "Talk Backpacking," a forum for asking questions; and a guide to Budget guidebooks.

InteleTravel International

http://inteletravel.com/inteletravel/

This is the Web site for one of InteleTravel's Independent Agents. You can book any international travel through this agent. Links to the company, employment travel info, and specials.

International Travel Guide for Mallorca and the Balearic Islands

http://www.mallorcaonline.com

Check out international Travel Guide for Mallorca and the Balearic Islands to plan your next trip to Spain.

Intra Travel

http://qb.island.net/~intra/

Your full-service travel agency based in Vancouver, Canada. Will take care of your travel and accommodation needs, from a cruise to an around-the-world trip.

Jerusalem Mosaic

http://www1.huji.ac.il/jeru/jerusalem.html

Provides a virtual welcome to the city of Jerusalem. Offers many interesting historical and religious facts and pictures pertaining to Jerusalem. Includes a view of Jerusalem from the sky and an option to hear the song of Jerusalem.

Jordan

http://www.mit.edu:8001/activities/jordanians/jordan/

A graphics-rich guide to the Hashemite Kingdom of Jordan, its culture, people, and tourism. Also provides accommodation listings and traveler tips, as well as links to Jordanian sites of interest.

Lanka Internet Services

http://www.lanka.net

The Sri Lanka Web Server page with links to travel and business guides, maps, gems, news, and Internet access info.

Lonely Planet Travel Centre

http://www.lonelyplanet.com.au/

Concentrates on travel in the various regions of India and the attractions of each. These snippets are obviously extracts from the Lonely Planet guides that provide travelers information somewhat off the beaten path (fax an order for your copy today).

Middle World

http://www.centrum.is/english/index.html

Provides home page for Icelandic Internet server service. Interesting site for its links, in English, about Iceland's business, culture, and links to Internet Servers. This site is excellent for anyone interested in Iceland for business or pleasure.

The Monaco Home Page

http://www.monaco.mc/

Presents the Principality of Monaco and its tourism, business, and motor racing. Includes English and French versions.

Salzburg, Austria

http://www.tcs.co.at/fvp.html

Provides seasonal tourist information about Salzburg, Austria and its surrounding regions. Offers alternatives to traditional holiday plans when abroad (in German and English).

Sinbad Travel

http://www.spb.su/ryh/sindbad.html

Provides online travel agency services for Sinbad Travel based in St. Petersberg, Russia. Includes information about student travel packages and hostel information in Russia.

Sydney International Travel Centre

http://www.sydtrav.com.au

Sydney International Travel is an integrated agency, combining corporate, wholesale and retail departments, specializing in individual group arrangements and personalized tour programs.

TGV French High Speed Train

http://mercurio.iet.unipi.it/tgv/tgvindex.html

Features TGV, the French high-speed train. Includes background, graphics, and schedules (in French) and links to other high-speed train sites around the world.

Tour Canada without Leaving Your Desk

http://www.cs.cmu.edu/Web/Unofficial/Canadiana/Travelogue.html

Take a virtual vacation of Canada and each of its provinces via the Web site links provided. This site is a good resource for anything you'd like to find out about Canada and what it has to offer for tourists.

United Kingdom Pages

http://www.neosoft.com/~dlgates/uk/ukindex.html

Provides information about the United Kingdom in many categories: higher education, cities, countryside, culture, government, travel, employment, and other miscellaneous information. Provides more than a thousand links to other sites, primarily within the United Kingdom. Also lists bed-and-breakfast accommodations, picturesque pubs, and so forth. Offers several photo albums of downloadable images, including a page of photographs of the Royals.

Vancouver, British Columbia

http://freenet.vancouver.bc.ca

Provides FreeNet's information and links about Vancouver. Also offers links to the British Columbia home page and other Canadian home pages.

Victoria, British Columbia

http://freenet.victoria.bc.ca/vifa.html

A community-based network available at no cost to residents and visitors of Victoria. Provides easy access to businesses, individuals, government, and more.

Welcome to Future Net—Queensland, Australia

http://peg.apc.org/~futurecom

Future Net's Sunzine presents a collection of graphics concerning life online, from Queensland, Australia. Offers links to many facets of Web life-style, including education, vacationing, and travel. Take a cybertour of Queensland and experience a taste of Australia you might never get to.

ISLAND TRAVEL

America's Caribbean Paradise

http://noc.usvi.net:80/

Provides information about the Virgin Islands, including wedding and vacation information, holidays, carnivals and other events, and weather forecasts. Also offers a section on real estate, vacation rentals, recipes, and Caribbean products.

Bahamas Online

http://TheBahamas.com/

Provides Bahamian facts, available accommodations, restaurants, banks, and bars. A good resource for those looking to visit the islands and sample some Goombay punch.

CaribWeb

http://www.caribweb.com/caribweb/

Serves as a resource for travelers and Caribophiles alike. Provides online travel publications and a conversation area. Also provides information from all the Caribbean tourist-board home pages and other relevant links to the Caribbean. Includes a searchable database, called CaribSearch, which contains information on hundreds of hotels, yacht charter companies, and restaurants.

Charlotte's Caribbean Connection

http://www.coe.uncc.edu/~jcgumbs/ccc.html

Serves as a starting point for the traveler who wants to become familiar with the Caribbean. Jump to island Web pages from a clickable image map of the isles. A good springboard site for those searching for information on the Caribbean.

Galveston Island Official Tourism site

http://www.galvestontourism.com

Your official site for information for Galveston.

Hideaway Holidays—Travel specialists to the Pacific Islands

http://www.magna.com.au/~hideaway/

Specialist tour wholesaler to the exotic islands of the South Pacific. Air/land inclusive or land only packages. Inquiries welcome from anywhere on planet Earth.

Holman Travel

http://www.wwwa.com/holman/

A travel service with links to travel specials and exotic travel, including Hawaii, Tahiti, Fiji, and other islands. Airline, accommodations, and pricing info included.

Isles of Scilly Travel

http://www.islesofscilly-travel.co.uk

Sea and Air Services to the Isles of Scilly from South West UK. Pictures and information about these subtropical islands.

Maldive Islands

http://www.infomaldives.com

Enjoy a perfect holiday for those who seek escape from the ordinary. Hundreds of tropical islands!!

Maui Interactive

http://maui.net/~kelii/MIA/MI.html

A full-blown interactive guide to Maui. Contains information on travel, entertainment, maps, photography, magazines, and art.

NetWeb Bermuda Home Page

http://www.bermuda.com/

Offers links to Bermuda travel and cultural information. Also serves as an advertising site for Bermuda businesses.

The Strawberry Guava

http://www.hawaiian.net/~lauria

The Strawberry Guava is a country bed and breakfast high in Lawai Valley on the quiet and beautiful island of Kauai, the Garden Island.

Turks & Caicos Islands Travel Guide

http://www.ttg.co.uk/t&c/index.htm

Plan a dream holiday in the Turks & Caicos Islands. From details of flight and accommodations to tourist attractions like diving & sightseeing.

Tybee Island Home Page

http://www.tybeeisland.com

The Complete Tybee Island information center.

Washington's Island Sampler

http://www.scenic-cycling.com/northwst/sanjuan5.html

This site gives you a 5-day, 4-night bicycling tour of Washington state's San Juan islands, which boast some of the best bicycling in the country. Check out the itinerary and take in the breathtaking photos.

Western Isles and Outer Hebrides

http://www.tntmag.co.uk/travel/i/west_isle.htm

Read about Scotland's Western Isles and Outer Hebrides and discover their magic. Find out about Skye, Lewis and Harris, and Holy Island, taking in the beautiful photos.

LODGING

1 Stop Shopping Center for Bed & Breakfasts

http://www.zweb.com/lake_hodges_house/bandblis/

This site offers a list of links to North American bed & breakfast guides. You can search by location and fill out a form to specify what things about accommodations are most important to you.

Alaskan Cabin, Cottage & Lodge Catalog

http://www.midnightsun.com

The Alaskan Cabin, Cottage & Lodge Catalog is a comprehensive listing of all the wilderness cabins, cottages and lodges in the State of Alaska. It includes a listing of 200 USFS Recreation Cabins in the Tongass and Chugach National Forests.

Bed & Breakfast Inns Online

http://www.bbonline.com/

Do large hotels have you down? Try this site to find that quaint little hideaway. Pictures and sketches help describe over 600 of these travel gems in the U.S.

Bed and Breakfast Lodgings in the UK

http://www.visitus.co.uk/

Check out over 6,000 accommodations in the U.K., in London, Scotland, Wales, and Northern Ireland. Use the handy map as a reference. Also lists specific cities and regions.

California Travel and Parks Association

http://www.campgrounds.com/ctpa/

This site will help you find camping sites in California, Nevada, and Oregon. Get information on over 400 campgrounds here.

Campground Directory

http://www.holipub.com/camping/director.htm

Look here for a place in the 50 states, Great Britain, or Canada to pitch a tent. Site is still expanding so links are limited.

Choice Hotels

http://www.senior.com/choice/choice.html

Over 3,500 of the Choice Hotels International are available from this site, which includes branches of Econolodge, Clarion, Comfort Inn, and more. Reservations are available from this site.

Colorado Association of Campgrounds, Cabins, & Lodges

http://www.entertain.com/wedgwood/caccl/

The leading source for Colorado campgrounds, cabins, and lodges. Includes Colorado recreation, vacations, adventures, and fun things to do. Come and experience beautiful Colorado!

Colorado Lodging Connection

http://www.colodging.com

Colorado vacation rentals and lodging in Summit County and Vail to include Boulder, Breckenridge, Frisco, Dillon, Vail, Beaver Creek, Silverthorne, and other communities. Offerings include condominiums, private homes, bed and breakfasts, and more.

Holiday Junction

http://www.achilles.net/holiday

Holiday Junction is an online accommodation directory focusing on resorts, lodges and private cottage rentals.

Hostelling International

http://www.taponline.com/tap/travel/hostels/pages/hosthp.htm

Try hostels if you're tired of being overcharged and hate being alone. This page features information about hostels located mainly in France. Site also features a Frequently Asked Questions site.

International Bed And Breakfast Guide

http://www.inntraveler.com/innbook.html

National and international B&Bs dot this site. Countries featured other than the U.S. include Canada, Great Britain, New Zealand, and Argentina.

The National Lodging Directory

http://www.guests.com

The National Lodging Directory, a user-friendly site, contains listings for hotels, motels, bed & breakfasts, and vacation rental property located in the United States.

Nude 2000

http://www.nude2000.com/

You'll satisfy all your needs for a campground here, if you subscribe to the philosophy. Other nudist information available here includes newsletters, updates, and government affairs.

A Place to Hang Your Hat: Hotels Online

You can find hotels from all over the world online. Are you interested in a resort vacation or a simple vacation somewhere in the country? Do you want a small, cozy hotel or do you want something extravagant? What about luxuries? Do you want a pool inside the hotel (or outside during the summer)? What about a whirlpool?

Reserving a hotel room online is an easy way to make sure you are getting the room you want ahead of time. Travelocity (http://www.travelocity.com) offers online registration for some of its over 28,000 hotels in its database. All you have to do is register with Travelocity—and it's free!

Professional Association of Innkeepers International

http://www.paii.org/

You'll find more than just the Innkeeping Weekly at this site, but do look at that, too. The book So You Want to be an Innkeeper is available from this site, as are stimulating topics such as "Cutting Deals with Unlikely Allies" and B&B management tips.

Travel Show Online—Hotels and Lodging

http://www.travelx.com/lodge.html

Travel Show online! Resorts, Hotels, Condos, Lodges, plus more!

Travel Web

http://www.travelweb.com/

This huge travel monster will provide more information than just lodging. This site features a unique section of independent hotels to help you away from the lodging machine of franchised establishments, if that is what you're looking for; however, you can find chain hotels here, too.

Vacation Central

http://www.vacationcentral.com/

Use this site to search for that perfect vacation rental property. Choose from bed and breakfasts, private homes, chalets, condos, or inns.

West Shore Lodging

http://www.tahoecountry.com/wslodging.html

Bed & Breakfasts, guesthouses and lodges along Lake Tahoe's tranquil West Shore, offer visitors peaceful settings and a taste of Old Tahoe.

West Virginia Lodging Guide

http://wvweb.com/www/travel_recreation/lodging.html

West Virginia Lodging, visitors guide to WV accommodations in the West Virginia Web, including bed and breakfasts, camping, hotels, motels, resorts and vacation properties.

World Wide Lodging Guide

http://www.lgww.com/

It's not called the World Wide Lodging guide for nothing. Reservations in most major cities around the world can be made here.

TRAIN TRAVEL

Abercrombie & Kent

http://www.abercrombiekent.com/html/act_ltt.html

Luxury train travel at its best. Visit this site and see how the other half lives. Travel through Scotland on the Royal Scotsman, with tours through England and Wales. Or ride aboard the Venice-Simplon Orient Express. Enjoy gourmet dining and impeccable service. Go ahead—splurge!

European Rail System

http://www.starnetic.com/eurorail/railindx.htm

Get the Eurorail pass information you've been desperately looking for here. You will also find tips about how to travel by train, including the "Plan it, Do it" scheme.

Grand Canyon Railway

http://www.thetrain.com/

Read about the historic Grand Canyon Railway. This site lists timetables and fares, travel packages, and weather information. The opening graphic is wonderful, and when you "climb aboard," listen for the train whistle blowing.

All Aboard!

Liberty's Amtrak Page

http://www.aho.com/amtrak.html

Site provides a more personal look at Amtrak services and train travel in general. Also includes rail-fan information, travelogues, and photos and drawings.

ScotRail

http://www.scotrail.co.uk/

Scotland's official train service. Check out the different itineraries and rail lines—including the West Highland Line, one of the most scenic. Study the timetables to see which routes and times suit your needs. Visit the other useful links.

VI Rail-Canada's Passenger Train Network

http://www.virail.ca/

This is the home page for the railway lining the Great White North. Get travel times, destinations, fares, and more from this iron horse site.

Welcome to Amtrak's Station on the WWW

http://www.amtrak.com/

The country's foremost train authority, Amtrak, is accessed through this page. Find everything from the latest high-speed train info to travel tips and reservations on this useful home page.

TRAVEL DATABASES

America's Best

http://www.americasbest.com/abest/welcome.html

Provides links to the best travel sites of the 50 states. Visit the launch pad to be directed to a random site within the U.S.—a different launch every time. A great resource for travel and historical information about America.

City Net

http://www.city.net/

The first Web site stop any cybertraveler should make. Contains a well organized index of most features of over 2,090 cities and 780 other locations worldwide. Lets you take a virtual tour of Marseille, check the subway schedule for Philadelphia, or find out what types of entertainment are available in Victoria.

GNN Travel Center

http://gnn.com/gnn/meta/travel/

GNN furnishes a Web site for feature stories on special travel sites and links to other travel-related Web sites. A wealth of information for the cybertraveler.

The Inn Traveler–International Bed & Breakfast and Country Inn Guide

http://www.inntraveler.com/

A grant-funded site providing information about bed and breakfast inns. Currently covers the United States (arranged alphabetically) and Canada. Includes room descriptions, reservations (forms), newsletters, and audio clips recorded by the innkeepers. Also offers links to other travel-related sites.

The North American Virtual Tourist

http://www.vtourist.com/webmap/na.htm

An incredible resource for North American travel! One click on the image map of North America will lead you to every WWW resource available for the selected state or region. This site is heaven for those looking for an all-encompassing site on the United States, Canada, and Mexico. Make a bookmark and visit frequently!

rec.travel. library

http://www.solutions.net/rec-travel/

A true library of Internet travel resources. Features a searchable database to find the exact topic you're looking for. Also includes hotel, tour operators, and worldwide rail information.

Round-The-World Travel Guide

http://www.solutions.net/rec-travel/rtw/html/faq.html

Offers links to sites that help you make travel decisions, choose transportation and accommodations, and provide information on money matters, and communications. Covers travel-related newsgroups.

TII–Tourism Info Internet

http://www.tii.de/

Award-winning site providing an index to information on flights, rails, hotels, tourist news, newsgroups, and country information around the world. Includes English and German versions.

Travel & Entertainment Network (TEN-IO) Home Page

http://www.ten-io.com/index.html

Fulfill your personal and business travel needs with a searchable database of travel-related information, including a separate Frequent Flyer information database. Also offers a downloadable demo copy of their Trip Finder for Travelers software.

Travel Information

http://galaxy.einet.net/GJ/travel.html

A searchable index of links to Web sites on domestic and international travel.

The Travel Page

http://www.travelpage.com/

A thorough travel planning site for visitors. Make hotel, airline, and cruise reservations online. Provides vacation recommendations ranging from the more popular to the truly unique.

TravelSearch

http://205.179.48.54/

Provides extensive information from visitors bureaus, offers a searchable database to arrange travel accommodations, and offers a map delivery service to alleviate the hassles of getting your geographical plans together.

TravelSource

http://www.travelsource.com/

Includes information about different vacation packages and locations. Also provides links to travel agents and other travel resources to fine tune your vacation plans. Whether you're looking to scuba dive, white water raft, take a cruise, or simply kick back, this site is your one-stop vacation planner.

Virtual Tourist II

http://www.vtourist.com/vt/

Provides information on various countries, including city information, culture and language, education, maps, news, and so forth. Select the country you're interested in from the globe image map or jump to City.Net for a more precise search. Provides a text-based version for faster access of the information.

The Webfoot's Travel Guides

http://www.webfoot.com/travel/guides/

Serves as a "thinking person's guide" to traveling in Austria, British Virgin Islands, France, Germany, Italy, Spain, Vatican City, and the state of Hawaii. Provides links to good overall information about each location, such as general information, city/site information, public transportation, language, museums, historic sites, literature and culture, and tips for tourists.

The Yankee Traveler

http://www.tiac.net/users/macgyver/ne.html

Provides a compilation of travel-related sources of New England. Includes state Web pages, information on Cape Cod and the Islands, bed and breakfast inns, and map links. Also provides information about real estate, local businesses, and more.

TRAVEL TIPS

Air Traveler's Handbook

http://www.cs.cmu.edu/afs/cs/user/mkant/Public/Travel/airfare.html

Offers links to information on courier travel, consolidators and bucket shops, charters, newsgroups, mailing lists, general travel information, background notes, tourist information, destination information, embassies, car rental agencies, hotels, bed and breakfasts, hosteling, home exchanges health, money and currency, weather, foreign languages, packing, insurance, maps travel publishers, publications, periodicals, travel bookstores, travel software student/budget travel, round-the-world, travelogues, aviation, miscellaneous usage statistics, and entry submissions.

Currency Exchange Rates

http://www.dna.lth.se/cgi-bin/kurt/rates

Presents the exchange rate for 23 currencies. Don't be taken for an ignorant tourist and robbed blind when touring another country. If you need to know what Indian rupees are worth in Dutch Guilders, this site will not let you down. Exchange rates are updated daily.

The Electronic Embassy

http://www.embassy.org/

Serves as a source for information that is useful to the staff of embassies in Washington, D.C., as well as for those interested in embassy affairs. Offers links to embassy Web sites, an index of all D.C. embassies, and jumps to federal executive agencies and a list of Washington events.

Europe Today Travel & Tourist Information

http://europe-today.com

Travel and tourist information covering 16 European countries, regions, resorts, travel tips, excursions, tours, hotels, competitions.

The Executive Woman's Travel Network

http://www.delta-air.com/womenexecs

Delta Air Lines' Executive Woman's Travel Network offers travel tips and discounts, and a Travel Forum where visitors can exchange ideas.

Foreign Language for Travelers

http://www.travlang.com/languages/

Discusses common words and phrases of just about any language you might be interested in, including German, French, Italian, Russian, Czech, Turkish, Finnish, Danish Esperanto, English, Spanish, Portuguese, Dutch, Polish, Romanian, Swedish, Norwegian, and Icelandic. Furnishes sound files for each language. Offers links to other sites that feature translation dictionaries and general information. Won a GNN Best of the Net award.

GNN/Koblas Money Converter

http://bin.gnn.com/cgi-bin/gnn/currency/

Presents a currency converter that is updated weekly for accuracy. Put your calculator to the side and let this site do all the math for you.

Information about Duty Free/Tax Free Shopping

http://www.stelcom.com/duty_free/homepage.html

Provides information on duty-free shopping—allowances, origins, and future developments in this popular method of shopping when traveling.

Interactive Travel Guide

http://www.developnet.com/travel/

Provides information for people traveling on a budget. Includes tips about money, documents, protection against theft, travel organizations, making accommodation arrangements, and lists the essentials for any traveler. Also contains links to other travel-related sites.

International Traveler's Clinic

http://www.intmed.mcw.edu/ITC/Health.html

Provides information about diseases, environmental concerns, and immunizations for travelers. Includes tips on what to pack in your travel medicine kit and concerns for pregnant women who are traveling.

Israel Travel Tips A-Z

http://www.tali.com/israel/tips.htm

A list of valuable travel tips for your visit to Israel. Includes many useful phone numbers and touring ideas.

A B C D E F G H I J K L M N O P Q R S T U V W X Y Z

Journeywoman

http://www.journeywoman.com

From where Queen Elizabeth buys her bras to how to stay healthy in Tibet, to girls-only fly-fishing in the U.S.A., Journeywoman dispenses valuable travel tips gathered from around the world. Written entirely from a female perspective, each 24-page issue contains enough new travel information to keep you smiling.

Mexico: Travel Trips for the Yucatan Peninsula

http://www.geocities.com/TheTropics/5087/

Travel advice for people wanting to go to Mexico or the Yucatan Peninsula. Advice on choosing an airline, resorts, shopping, the best places to see, and many other things.

MU-MU Travel Tips in Japan

http://www.asahi-net.or.jp/~py3y-knd/

Many important tips for travelers to Japan. Culture difference? Don't worry, just visit this home page. Advice on food, money etc.

Railroad Timetables

http://www-cse.ucsd.edu/users/bowdidge/railroad/rail-gopher.html

Offers links to railroad timetables for United (Amtrak) and commuter lines, Canada, Europe, Asia, and Oceania. Also provides links to sightseeing tours by rail.

Travel Discounts

http://www.traveldiscounts.com/

A business travel-oriented site providing information about discounts on car rentals, railroads, tours, cruises, airlines, and specific tour packages arranged by region.

United States State Department Travel Warnings and Consular Info Sheets

http://www.stolaf.edu/network/travel-advisories.html

Provides up-to-date information for international travelers, including warnings, entry requirements, medical requirements, political status, and crime information for travel sites abroad. Also includes the location of the U.S. embassy in each country. Countries are easy to find in an alphabetical index.

U.S. TRAVEL

Access New Hampshire

http://www.nh.com/

A comprehensive guide to the state of New Hampshire, including information about tourism, historical legacy, local happenings, and everything else under the sun.

ACUMUG—Arkansas Index of Internet Resources

http://acumug.ualr.edu/ar-map.html

A clickable image map of the state of Arkansas that allows you to search for information by region whether it's corporate or travel information you're looking for. A valuable reference tool for visitors and residents.

Alabama

http://www.eng.auburn.edu/alabama/map.html

A detailed clickable image map of Alabama by city or region. Provides information of interest to the cyber-traveler in the different regions of Alabama. Offers links to other Alabama-related sites. Awarded an America's Best! site award.

Allons! Acadiana

http://www.allons.com/

A multimedia-enhanced online magazine devoted to the sights, sounds, and smells of Cajun country—southern Louisiana. Provides the What to Do, Where to Go, and How to Get There of traveling through Acadian country. This site is a virtual tour in itself.

America's Land of Enchantment

http://www.nets.com/newmextourism/

A traveler's guide to New Mexico. Provides information about culture, outdoor activities, area ruins, regional events, and skiing. Also includes maps and historical tidbits for travelers.

The Arizona Guide

http://www.arizonaguide.com/

The official site for the Arizona Office of Tourism organized by region in text format and image map format. Provides up-to-date weather information, maps, state information. Features golf resorts and, of course, the Grand Canyon and the many touring packages for exploring it. Well worth visiting even if you're not planning a trip to Arizona any time soon.

Atlanta Web Guide

`http://www.webguide.com/`

Take a virtual tour of Atlanta, Georgia, which was home to the 1996 Summer Olympics. Features businesses, restaurants, historic sites, art galleries, nightlife spots, and other areas worth visiting.

Boston Area Map of WWW Resources

`http://donald.phast.umass.edu/misc/boston.html`

A complete and easily navigable site listing all (or most) sites pertinent to the Boston area. Find what you need from the clickable image map or browse the alphabetized text listing. Everything you want to find out about Boston is right here.

California Do Your Own Thing

`http://gocalif.ca.gov:8000/`

A comprehensive guide to the west coast's tourism mecca. Provides a clickable image map organized by region that delivers the goods on where to stay, eat, shop, visit, and what to do in the various parts of the state. Also offers traveler tips, a calendar of events, and high-resolution downloadable maps of specific areas.

Cambridge, Massachusetts

`http://www.ci.cambridge.ma.us/`

Features Cambridge City resources and more. Offers information on the city's art, entertainment, museums, tourism, and more general information for those looking to relocate.

Chicago Information System

`http://reagan.eecs.uic.edu`

Provides visitor and resident information about Chicago including a calendar of events, tourism, how to get around, government, education, and updated weather forecasts.

CLEVE.NET A Guided Tour of the North Coast

`http://www.en.com/cleve.net/`

Invites you to take a tour of the North Coast. Presents Cleveland, a city once full of urban decay, as a beautiful mecca you can visit and enjoy. Focuses on entertainment, the arts, government, commerce, and other general information for travelers and those considering making Cleveland their permanent residence.

Clickable Connecticut Area Map

`http://www.scsu-cs.ctstateu.edu/lib/map.html`

Just what it says it is. Organized by region, this site offers tourist and general information on the state of Connecticut and its surrounding areas.

Front Desk

`http://www.vegas.com/vegascom/front_desk/front.html`

This link from the Vegas.com page provides other links to restaurants, business services, sports, accommodations, sight seeing, special events, weddings, and more, for the Las Vegas traveler.

Gold Canyon Multimedia

`http://www.goldcanyon.com`

If you're planning a trip to Gold Canyon, Arizona, this site lists business information, history and images of the canyon, desert survival tips, trails and waterways to explore, and other regional sites of interest.

Grand Rapids, Michigan

`http://www.grfn.org/`

A user-intensive searchable index to Grand Rapids, Michigan and what it has to offer for the traveler.

Greensboro Online

`http://www.greensboro.nc.us/gol/`

A comprehensive and visually stimulating site devoted to Greensboro, North Carolina and what it offers to visitors. Contains detailed image maps of the area and its attractions.

Idaho Home Page

`http://www.state.id.us/`

Provides information on regional attractions, state parks, national forests, a calendar of events, and more general information on the state of Idaho.

Index

http://199.201.186.116/info/casinos.htm

If you would like casino information for the Mississippi Gulf coast, look no further. Provides hotels and contact information, including phone numbers, recreational info, maps, and employment opportunities.

Indiana Virtual Tourist

http://www.cica.indiana.edu/news/servers/tourist/index.html

Take a virtual tour of Indiana's diverse offerings via a clickable image map of the state. This site also acts as a directory for all Web servers found in Indiana.

Information Access Websites

http://www.info-access.com/iAW/Contact.htm

Services Web sites featuring most areas of Florida, including Boca Raton, Coral Springs, Ft. Lauderdale, Miami, the Florida Keys, South Florida, and Tampa. Each site features a hotel finder/reservation maker, lists of attractions of the region, corporate information, weather conditions, a map of the area, and links to other Web sites devoted to the region.

Iowa Virtual Tourist

http://www.jeonet.com/tourist/

A detailed clickable image map separated by region linking you to any information resources available on Iowa. Take a cybertour before you go for real or just enjoy the wealth of information.

Kentucky Network Services

http://www.uky.edu/kentucky-network-services.html

A huge clickable image map of recreational and corporate Web sites in the state of Kentucky. Valuable as a reference source as well as a springboard for the cybertraveler.

Las Vegas

http://www.vegas.com

Includes a wide range of vacation-planning information concerning Las Vegas, ranging from hotel information and reservations, to show schedules, sports, conventions, betting tips, employment opportunities, and business services.

Los Angeles Traffic Report

http://www.scubed.com/caltrans/la/la_transnet.html

Features real-time traffic data for Los Angeles, updated once a minute. Contains current areas of congestion, five-minute and real-time maps, and tables of current speeds on freeways.

Maine WWW Resources

http://www.destek.net/Maps/ME.html

An invaluable site containing every Web and Gopher site located in or dedicated to the state of Maine, from the Bangor public library to L.L. Bean.

Minneapolis

http://www.minneapolis.org

The official site of the city of Minneapolis, the city of lakes. Contains a searchable database for narrowing the scope of your search for travel information whether you're in town for a convention or on vacation with the family. From accommodations to dining and entertainment, it's all right here.

Missouri WWW Resources

http://micromedia.com/WWW/StLouis/Missouri.html

A complete alphabetical listing of all corporate Web sites, city home pages, and other recreational sites located in the state of Missouri.

Nashville Scene

http://www.nashscene.com/

An award-winning online newspaper providing the traveler a guide to dining and events in Nashville, Tennessee, in addition to offering some insight into the Tennesseean mindset.

Nebraska Travel and Tourism

http://www.ded.state.ne.us/tourism.html

A well-presented documentation of the attractions, campgrounds, hotels, and tourist sites of Nebraska presented in a colorful interface organized by locale and topic.

Northwest Destinations

http://www.nwdestinations.com

A guidebook of activities and destinations in the Northwest. Visit a place which offers an amazing variety of terrains and cultures.

The Oklahoma Image Map

http://www.mstm.okstate.edu/students/jjohnson2/oklahoma.htm

An attractively laid out site featuring information on Native American culture, regional events and festivals, and an impressive collection of travel and recreation sites highlighting state parks, museums, zoos, and other tourist attractions throughout the state.

Oregon Online

http://www.state.or.us/

Provides information on the government, education, and commerce of Oregon. Of particular interest to the tourist is the section on communities, which provides links to the various regions of the state that may be more pertinent to your travel plans.

Peaks—An Online Magazine About Montana

http://www.cyberport.net/peaks/v01i03/peaks.html

A colorful and clever online magazine focusing on the recreational activities, culture, and art and literature of Montana. Find out about white water rafting and fly-fishing in Montana. Take a virtual tour of Flathead Valley or sample the writing of some local authors.

RING. Online Michigan's Electronic Magazine

http://www.ring.com/michigan.html

Offers comprehensive information on what Michigan has to offer, such as local news and events, sightseeing, travel, entertainment, and more. Make sure to visit this site before you find yourself in Michigan.

Santa Barbara County

http://www.internet-cafe.com/sb/sb.html

Provides information about businesses, community service, events, leisure activities, and visitor information in the sunny county of Santa Barbara.

South Dakota World Wide Web Site

http://www.state.sd.us/

The official state page of South Dakota, replete with travel information including area attractions, available accommodations, events, state parks, outdoor recreation, and travel tips available from an accurate clickable image map. Also provides general information about South Dakota in addition to links to other South Dakota sites.

St. Louis, Missouri

http://www.st-louis.mo.us/

Invites you to visit the "Gateway to the West." Provides information about tourist sites, restaurants, museums, and more.

Tr@vel.Ohio

http://www.travel.state.oh.us

Tr@vel.Ohio is an informative, entertaining site providing details on Ohio's many great travel opportunities. Home to the Rock and Roll Hall of Fame, professional and collegiate sports teams, exciting theme parks, historical sites, world-class art museums and much more, Ohio is quickly becoming a major Midwest travel destination. With Tr@vel.Ohio, visitors can get current information on the many great travel destinations and events awaiting them in the Buckeye state.

USA CityLink

http://banzai.neosoft.com/citylink/

A fantastic guide to touring the 50 U.S. states. This site is organized alphabetically by state and further broken down by city. Offers links to pertinent travel information for each city. A thoroughly indexed site for the virtual or planning tourist.

U/Seattle

http://useattle.uspan.com

Serves as a guide to events, restaurants, accommodations, shopping, sports, and nightlife in the greater Seattle area. Also includes a weather link and news information.

Utah! Travel and Adventure Online

http://www.utah.com/

Visit the Rocky mountains, Sand dunes, and Salt Lake of Utah via a virtual tour. This site also provides general tourist information including maps and travel tips. Find out about a selection of vacation packages ranging from guided adventures to traditional family adventures. A visually breathtaking site not to be missed.

A B C D E F G H I J K L M N O P Q R S T U V W X Y Z

The Vail Valley Home Page

http://vail.net/internetworks/home.html?0

An easily navigable Web site that provides information on what makes Vail famous—skiing. Also offers information about other outdoor activities and what Vail valley has to offer during the summer. Gives a listing of area ski shops in addition to essential travel information such as where to shop, dine, and sleep. Provides a graphic clickable menu in addition to a searchable database.

Vegas.com Online

http://www.vegas.com/

If you're planning a trip to Las Vegas, check out this page for travel and tourist info, shows, casinos, entertainment, real estate, sports, and much more.

Vermont/New Hampshire WWW Resources

http://www.destek.net/Maps/VT-NH.html

A full listing of every Web and Gopher site based in or devoted to the small New England communities located in these adjoining states. Among the links included are ski areas, area universities, museums, and Ben & Jerry's Ice Cream.

Vista Alaska

http://www2.polarnet.com/~vistatrv

A full service Alaskan travel agency specializing in Alaskan tours and cruises. Guaranteed lowest rates for Princess Cruises in the U.S.

VISIT Virginia

http://www2.virginia.org/cgi-shl/VISITVA/Tourism/Welcome

An eye-pleasing site containing general tourism in addition to recreational activities, where to stay, restaurants, local events, theme attractions, and other points of interest in the state for lovers.

The Washington DC City Pages

http://dcpages.ari.net/

Contains information on what the nation's capitol has to offer to visitors and residents alike. Provides content on entertainment, the arts, culture, tourism, travel, dining, and other general information about the city.

Washington State Online Travel Information

http://www.tourism.wa.gov/

Provides things to see and do in the state of Washington, including white water rafting/kayaking, museums, winery tours, whale watches, golf courses, and children-oriented activities. Also provides a regional database of available accommodations in addition to general and historical information about this northwestern state.

Web Texas

http://www.utexas.edu/texas/

A comprehensive searchable index of every Web site connected with the Lone Star state. From commercial to recreational sites, Web Texas' interface makes it easy for the inquisitive visitor to locate what they want.

The West Virginia Web

http://wvweb.com

Serves as West Virginia's main entry ramp to the worldwide information superhighway and the Internet. Pertains to the West Virginia travel industry, economic development, government and virtually any other area of interest within West Virginia.

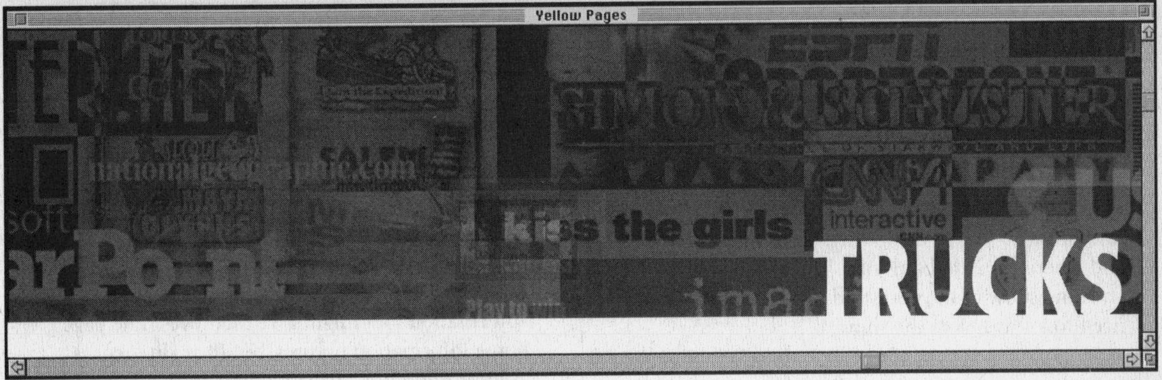

Luxury cars are dead. The future is in trucks.

Jimmy in Les Voleurs *(1996)*

American Truck Historical Society

http://www.aths.org/

You'll like this page if you're interested in the history of trucks, or classic and antique trucks. Subscribe to the magazine *Wheels of Time*, check out the games, go shopping, or just look at the photos of some really neat trucks.

Bigfoot 4×4

http://www.bigfoot4x4.com/

Check this site for news of upcoming 4×4 contests. You'll also find downloadable pictures of some great trucks and a catalog of clothing and collectibles.

The Classic Truck Shop

http://www.classictruckshop.com/

If you're interested in classic trucks, this is the site for you. There are classified ads, a forum for enthusiasts, projects, articles, and history. If you're looking for parts for your classic truck or are just interested in looking at the photos, check here first.

European Trucks

http://www.indigo.ie/poreilly/european-trucks.html

A source of information for those interested in European truck makers. Links to a variety of company home pages, including Scania, Volvo, and Mercedes-Benz. There is also an image gallery with photos of the more popular of the European trucks.

layover.com, Your One Stop Trucking Resource
http://www.layover.com/

Island Rock Crawlers

http://www.off-road.com/~irc/index.html#MainMenu

The Island Rock Crawlers, a group of 4×4 enthusiasts in Vancouver, B.C., has created a very fun site. The pictures of their vehicles are awesome, and there are links to many "way cool" 4WD sites.

layover.com, Your One Stop Trucking Resource

http://www.layover.com/

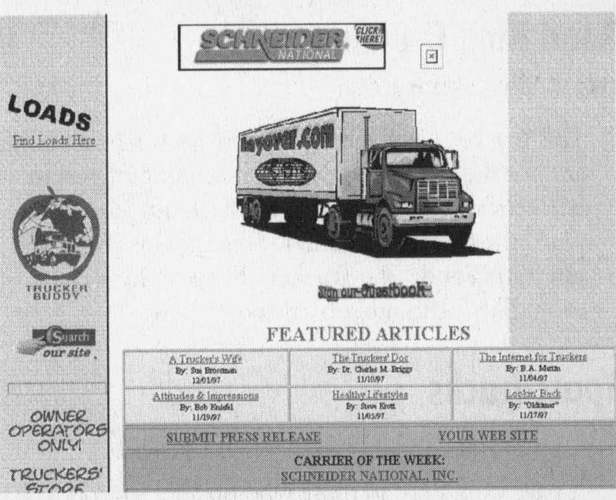

You'll find lots of interest for truckers here: feature articles by truckers' wives, stories from the road, Layover's Lounge, where you can post messages for loved ones, Trucker Talk, a chat room, links to sites of interest, and unique to this site, a load finder. There's more, too much to list here, so check this site.

Related Sites

http://members.aol.com/accestlook/trucks/page1.htm

http://www.fourwheeler.com/adventure/index.html

A B C D E F G H I J K L M N O P Q R S T U V W X Y Z

The Mid-America Trucking Show Home Page

http://www.truckingshow.com/

Yes, this is the home page of the Trucking Expo show in Louisville, Kentucky. Check the schedule of events, find out who will be exhibiting, learn where to stay and where to eat in Louisville. This is the premier trucking show of the year; find out everything you need to know before the show.

Mother-In-Law's Garage

http://milgarage.com/

This site caters to the interests of mudders, monster truck enthusiasts, and tractor pullers. You'll find equipment and parts for sale in the current issue. Browse the table of contents, or use the searchable database if you're looking for something specific.

My Truckin' Bookkeeper and Tax Adviser

http://www.innercite.com/~bjrsales/truckin.html

Here's a site aimed at owner/operators who want to take advantage of the best in tax savings. They provide financial planning, tax service, software, and more—all designed for the trucking owner/operator.

Road King On Ramp

http://www.roadking.com/

This trucker's e-zine has the latest news releases about and for the trucking industry, articles of interest to truckers, and more. Be sure to check out "Break One One," the trucker's forum, for discussions you'll find interesting and "The Trucker's Lounge" for a chat room filled with other truckers.

Sport Trucks

http://home.sprynet.com/sprynet/steinwan/

A page of interest to those who prefer a sportier truck to the traditional rugged look. Information is provided for sport trucks straight from the factory and those that have been custom modified. There is a lengthy image gallery that might take a while to load at slower connection speeds.

TruckDriver.com

http://www.truckdriver.com/

This site provides access to LearnItOnline, where you can learn everything you need to know to become a truck driver (except the actual driving, of course). There's also an online job application. You'll find here links to many sites of interest to truck drivers.

Truck Safety Page

http://www.e-z.net/~ts/ts/ts.html

Professional trucking is a very dangerous occupation, and this page is designed to give truckers some vital information that might save their lives. The page gives some information on fires, but its main focus is rollovers and how to avoid dying in them.

Trucking Times

http://www.ttol.com

The online version of the bimonthly print magazine. Here you will find comprehensive listings of accessories for light trucks and the manufacturers who make them, news stories, and links to other sites of interest to people who own trucks.

Truck.Net Online Trucking Store

http://www.truck.net/store/

Here's convenient shopping while you're on the road. Have gifts delivered from here. You'll find a searchable database with phone cards, T-shirts, trucking software, and lots more.

Yondar, International: The Trucker's Mall

http://www.yondar.com/d.html

Here you'll find an extensive list of products and retailers with products specific to the trucking industry. There's also a collection of writings by truckers, and you'll want to be sure to participate in the reader's survey.

NEWSGROUPS

alt.autos.classic-trucks

alt.autos.dodge.trucks

alt.autos.macho-trucks

misc.transport.trucking

retix.mail.fordtrucks

Related Sites

http://www.fourwheeler.com/adventure/index.html

http://www.truckschool.com/

http://dcweb.designcraft.com/monster/trucks/

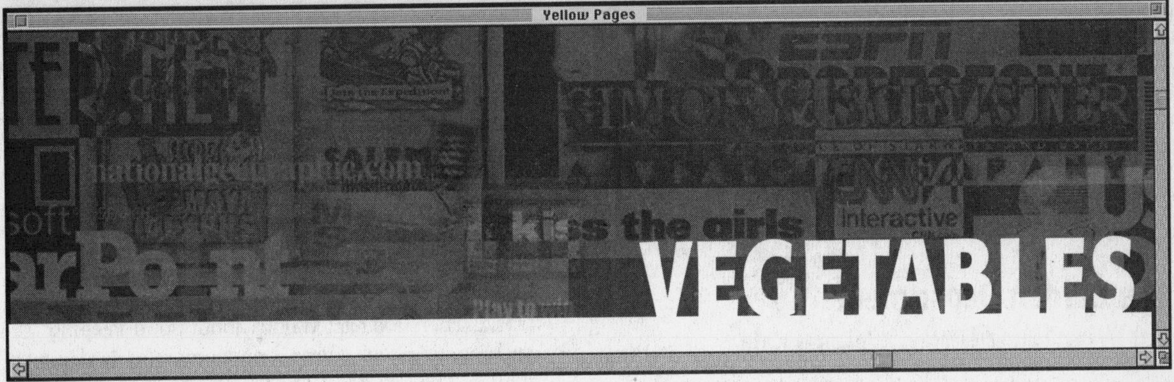

VEGETABLES

A root is a flower that disdains fame.

Kahlil Gibran

Aggie Horticulture

http://aggie-horticulture.tamu.edu/

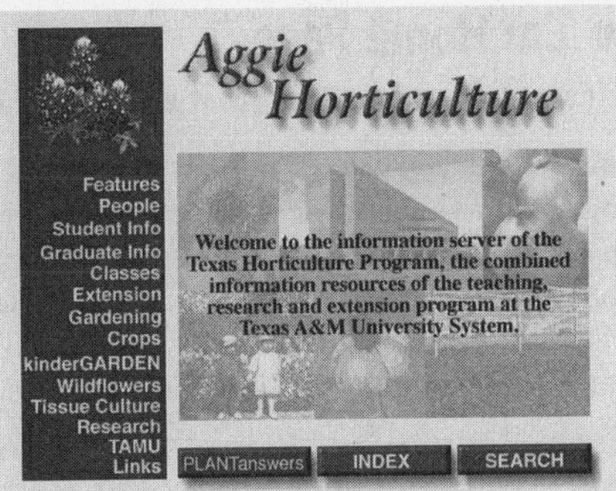

Discusses the horticulture program of the University of Texas, but there is much more here than a collection of mundane course descriptions. Provides intelligent commentary on trends in horticulture, technology and horticulture, and so on. Contains links to sites on topics ranging from extension resources at other sites to commercial sites and other resources. Searchable as well.

The Armchair Gardener

http://armchairgardener.com/

Rated by Lycos as one of the top five percent sites, this contains numerous images, as well as brief but helpful commentary on each subject. Topics range from growing roses to what kind of seeds to plant at a particular time of year. Best of all, the information is kept up to date.

NRP Top Picks

Aggie Horticulture
http://aggie-horticulture.tamu.edu/

The Armchair Gardener
http://armchairgardener.com/

Garden Site Reviews
http://gardening.com/Directory/Default.htm

The Plant Advisor
http://www.plantadviser.com/

The Strawberry Facts Page
http://www.jamm.com/strawberry/facts.html

A Tour of My Garden
http://www.h2net.net/p/cnetter/rose_tour/index.html

Ask Earl, the Yard Care Answer Guy

http://www.yardcare.com/

This site enables you to find answers on common problem areas that gardeners face, including grass, weeds, pests, leaves, and a new lawn. The information is quite extensive, and there is a likelihood that you might find your answer here. Can also search the site via keywords.

Attracting Butterflies and Hummingbirds

http://www.geocities.com/RainForest/1329/butterflies.htm

You probably never knew that butterflies prefer flat, single, daisy-like flowers. Or that hummingbirds prefer red, trumpet-like flowers. A list of the particular plants that attract these creatures is included. Photos abound.

A B C D E F G H I J K L M N O P Q R S T U V W X Y Z

Dig Magazine

http://www.digmagazine.com/

This magazine is directed towards folk living in the eastern states. Has well-laid out and well-photographed articles covering topics such as herb crafting and cooking with basil.

The Garden Department

http://www.lagunabeachca.com/plantman.htm

Courtesy of *Laguna Life International*, formerly *Laguna Life Magazine*. Provides a link to a live chat room with gardeners from all over the world by way of a Java applet. Allows you to look into an indexed version of "A Gardener's Notebook." Furthermore, there is an "Ask the Plant Man Index."

Garden Escape

http://www.garden.com/

This is a professionally run online plant and accessory business. Contains information on products, seasonal collections, and holiday gifts. Click over to the "Garden Escape" magazine which includes tips, resources, and much more. Includes catalogs with plenty of photographs. Ordering items is a snap.

Gardening as an Anarchist Plot

http://www.rain.org/~philfear/garden.html

Here's a guide on how to grow an organic garden—a garden that provides you with food and medicine—in a space the size of a bedroom. Advice on how to grow the various plants. She even provides a diagram of how her garden looks, as well as its component vegetables.

Garden Site Reviews

http://gardening.com/Directory/Default.htm

A database of multiple listings, searchable in three ways: select a keyword; a subject ("Event and Plant-care Calendars"); or region of the U.S. Enables you to further subdivide, or check out the sites. The sites are recommended and reviewed by Garden.com.

Garden Spider's Web

http://www.gardenweb.com/spdrsweb/

A compendium of resources for gardeners. Includes virtual tours (such as the Royal Botanical Garden), horticulture information, guides to "botanical correctness" (for example, what is the difference between an angiosperm and a gymnosperm?), magazines, books, and catalogs, gardening software, newsgroups and mailing lists, and keeping up and finding answers.

Get Set! Yard and Gardening Site

http://www.gardeningbc.com/

A site that provides assistance in gardening and yard keeping alike. Links to online stores from around the world. There are related links about pond-keeping and aquatic plants (there is much more to gardening than one had ever imagined!). Also links to newsgroups for those into gardens and ponds.

Green Thumb Corner

http://www.hht.com/horns

A full service, family owned and operated, home and garden center. Provides information on fall gardening, annuals, perennials, trees/shrubs, landscaping, pest control, and so on. Includes a USDA plant hardiness zone map. You can also ask the Green Thumb a question.

Grow 'Em Home Page

http://personal.nbnet.nb.ca/ppostuma/grow.htm

From this site you can download the updated Grow 'Em, Version 4 shareware, which covers the propagation of plants from seeds, composting, fertilizers, and so on. There are new sections on various topics as well as expanded text. Available in VGA and SVGA formats. Several programming utilities are available as well.

The Grower's Almanac

http://www.jcsolutions.com/jcsgrower/

An online magazine for garden growers in northern climates. Includes a constantly updated almanac of weather conditions, a listing of flowering plants as they actually come into bloom in Northern Michigan, insecticide information, articles, a library, and JCS software. This highly awarded site requires patience for loading but is well worth the wait.

The Hardiest Palm

http://www.libertynet.org/~bgmap/hardiplm.html

You won't believe this! A palm can grow in Philadelphia! The little-known Rhapidophyllum hystrix has been growing in this fellow's backyard for twelve years now. This site contains a description of needle palms, other hardy palms, and other hardy palm links. Pictures are included.

Horticulture Guy

http://www.geocities.com/Athens/4134/

Ask the Horticulture Guy any and all questions and he'll post the answers in a Q & A section. There is also a section on gardening tips for each of the four seasons. Links to a resume about Horticulture Guy. A glossary is added for you convenience.

Living Home Magazine

http://livinghome.com/

A packed online magazine for home and garden design. Contains information on gardening, remodeling, decorating, and design. You can browse their magazine and search the contents of the entire site. Don't miss your chance to order a free copy of the LivingHome CD-ROM, Issue 1—the follow-up to their award-winning Premiere Issue.

Market Information System

http://gnv.ifas.ufl.edu/~MARKETING/MARKET.HTML

A computer information system providing agricultural marketing information from the United States Department of Agriculture (USDA). Allows you to search various reports, including fruit & vegetable reports, from cities across the U.S. and world.

Mike's Back In the Yard

http://www.acs.oakland.edu/~mjthomas/

This site describes the layout and development of a garden in Michigan which was begun in 1989. The page is divided into three parts: an updated "what's new section;" schematics of both old and new layout; and a virtual tour of the garden and pond. Also provides links to other garden-related sites.

The (no) Problem Garden

http://www.netusa1.net/~lindley/

Makes the claim that the problems don't lie with gardens, but with the people who grow them. Whether you agree with this observation or not, you'll find some useful information here. The gardener shares her experiences, and offers advice on appropriate gardener clothing, a description of soil types, and types of growing climates. You can also email her with your questions.

Northern Gardening

http://www.geocities.com/RainForest/1329/

From a newspaper columnist in Minnesota, useful for gardeners everywhere, but geared towards gardeners in the north. Contains downloadable articles. The search engine, "Greensheets," enables you to do keyword searches for horticultural fact sheets.

The Outdoor Power Equipment Institute

http://opei.mow.org/

Contains advice on lawn care tips, including seasonal maintenance, mulching and composting, proper fuel handling, and other tips. Also provides safe mowing tips, mower repair, a guide to outdoor power equipment, and a ride on the cybermower.

Penn State University Horticulture Trial Garden

http://Garden.cas.psu.edu/

One of the premier trial gardens in North America. You can view the results of the trials of New Guinea Impatiens and Spreading Petunias. Also provides discussion of seed and plant sources, garden and plant culture information, events at the garden.

The Plant Advisor

http://www.plantadviser.com/

For the southwestern desert area. A free service deigned to help people make informed decisions about buying plants. Provides an "adviser," a form you can fill out and get feedback on. Also contains a list of plants with their common and botanical names. A glossary of definitions and terms is helpful.

Pond Rushes

http://www.dallas.net/~crush/

Ever consider—er—pondering how to start your own pond? Contains links devoted to research, planning, building, tips, a library, and other links. Even provides a FAQ on questions not related to ponds (such as, "What do I do when my fish get too big?").

Sage Hall

http://www.gardentown.com/chat/sage_display.cgi?1

The dream come true for the virtual gardener. Provides a forum for gardeners to ask all kinds of questions (related to gardens, of course!), make comments, and chit chat in general. Constantly updated gardening questions are asked and answered. There is a form for you to post follow-ups or ask your own. Also enables you to order books, bulbs, fountains, and other gardening supplies.

Southern Garden Gate

http://www.gardengatepress.com/

This site will benefit those gardeners living in Texas, Alabama, North and South Carolina, Florida, Georgia, Louisiana, and Mississippi. Contains information on wildlife, natives, tropical varieties, aquatics, landscaping, herbs, and perennials.

The Strawberry Facts Page

http://www.jamm.com/strawberry/facts.html

A highly awarded and recognized site. Many facts about strawberries are listed here, and the author even lays down a gauntlet for strawberry inquisitors (although she humbly confesses not to be a strawberry-know-it-all). Includes recipes, growing, tending, and history of the strawberry plant, and links to information on other berries. You can also register for email updates.

Sunset

http://pathfinder.com/@@ttlWqAcANl160*rh/vg/Magazine-Rack/Sunset/sunset.html

This journal contains information of interest to Gardeners west of the Rockies. Contains feature articles archived all the way back to 1994. Allows you to do a keyword search of Sunset. Also has a monthly checklist and notebook.

The Telegarden

http://www.usc.edu/dept/garden/

First developed at the University of Southern California, the Telegarden is a tele-robotic installation which permits you to remotely take care of plants in a living garden. Members can plant, water, and monitor seedlings. Plenty of descriptive articles can be found here.

Time Life Gardener Encyclopedia

http://pathfinder.com/@@dmpKhwcAK1160*rh/cgi-bin/VG/vg

A searchable database of almost 3,000 plant species suitable for North American horticultural practice. You can search by name or attribute. For the latter, the breakdown is as follows: lighting, drainage, type, height, color, and blooming season.

A Tour of My Garden

http://www.h2net.net/p/cnetter/rose_tour/index.html

For a collection of some of the best roses on the Internet, take a virtual tour of this person's rose garden in Colorado. Provides links to other gardens in Colorado. Advice on the growth and care of these beautiful plants abounds. Also see and find out here about the blue rose!

Web Server

http://www.mobot.org/welcome.html

A server map with the sites hosted at the Missouri Botanical Garden. It has numerous features, describing the flora of North and South America, Asia, Africa, and other climates. Also has links to a reading room, virtual tours, plants in bloom, a scientific bookstore, and much more.

Weekend Gardener

http://www.chestnut-sw.com/weekend.htm

This weekly electronic magazine promises to be an invaluable tool to the person who loves to garden, but can't seem to find the time. Subscriptions to this resource are free. Provides a daily garden tip, facts on seeds and starting them, links to resources and weather in the U.S., Canada, a resource center, weather lore, and a FAQ sheet.

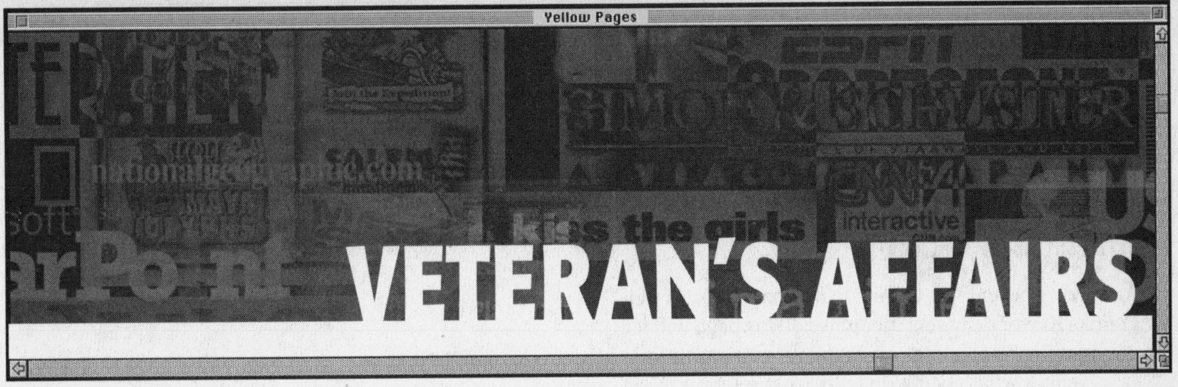

VETERAN'S AFFAIRS

> There is no heroic poem in the world but is at bottom a biography, the life of a man;
>
> *Thomas Carlyle*

The American Legion http://www.legion.org/
Department of Veterans Affairs http://www.va.gov/
Veterans Affairs (VA) Home Loans http://www.va.gov/vas/loan/index.htm

The American Legion

http://www.legion.org/

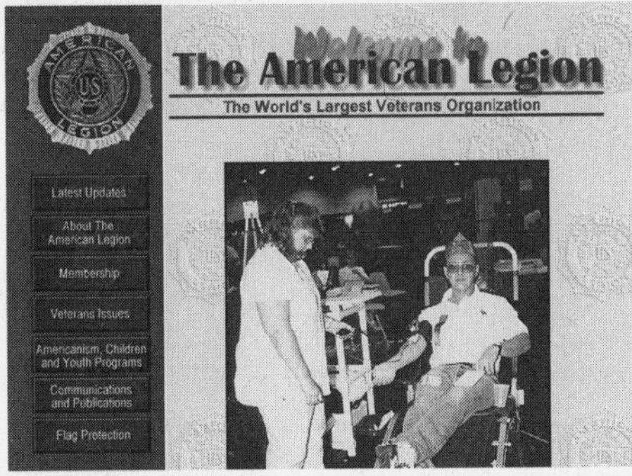

Offers information about the Legion's patriotic programs: education and scholarships, Boy Scouts, flag protection, and more. Also covers veteran health issues and Bosnia topics. See news releases.

Baudo's Vet Links

http://www.teleport.com/~baudo/

A crossroads for veterans and their supporters, this site directs surfers to relevant sites organized as news, chat, support, politics, surveys, and miscellaneous. Interactive site with audio.

Department of Veterans Affairs

http://www.va.gov/

An up-to-the-minute report about where veterans can go to find out about benefits, facilities, and special programs available to them.

Federal Job Search Links

http://www.redrose.net/vidvamc/fedjobs.htm

Site offered by the Department of Veterans Affairs Medical Center of Coatesville, Pennsylvania. Links to Job Web, a federal job database, America's Job Bank, and related Pennsylvania resources.

Military Family Institute

http://mfi.marywood.edu/

This Department of Defense-sponsored research deals with how the entire family is affected by military service. There are also links for "military brats," and be sure to check out the guest book to see if anyone is looking for you.

Veterans Affairs (VA) Home Loans

http://www.va.gov/vas/loan/index.htm

Most of the information needed for veterans wanting to buy a home is here. Refers to a pamphlet to be used as quick reference and one for FAQs, as well as one specifically for veterans needing information on how to use their home-buying benefits. Links to other sites lead to more information.

A B C D E F G H I J K L M N O P Q R S T U V W X Y Z

Veterans Archive

http://www.wavenet.com/~beerborn/index.html

A database of veterans looking for old friends.

Vietnam Veterans Home Page

http://grunt.space.swri.edu/

An index of events pertaining to Vietnam Vets, as well as links to works by vets themselves. This page will let you in on current goings on in the veteran community, as well as what's being done to assist veterans.

U.S. Dept. Of Veterans Affairs

http://www.va.gov/oig/51/51-home.htm

The Office of Inspector General, Office of Investigations Web site. Office makes criminal investigations in veteran-related areas. Includes sample list of investigation areas.

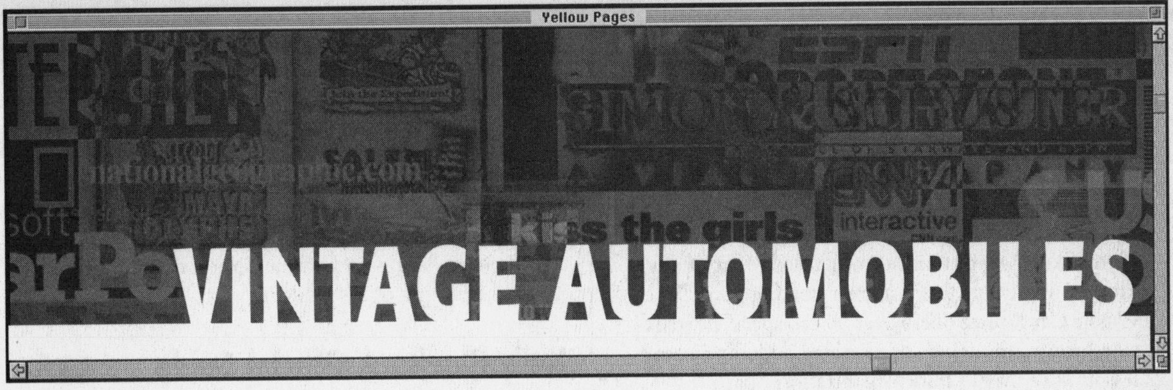

People can have the Model T in any color—so long as it's black.

Henry Ford

AAG: The Auto Appraisal Group, Inc.

http://www.autoappraisal.com/index.html

Wondering what that old Buick on the garage is worth? Need to know for tax returns, divorce, insurance documentation, or another reason? Contact the AAG, and they can help you determine what your collectible is worth, whether you should bother restoring it, and whether it was a good investment.

Ageless Iron

http://www.agriculture.com/contents/sf/ageless/agiindex.html

Ageless Iron is for fans of antique farm machinery, which has been gaining in popularity recently. The library and machine shop offer a ton of information regarding every aspect of collecting and restoring. And you can follow links to related sites. Eli Whitney would be proud.

AMC Rambler Club

http://www.classicar.com/clubs/rambler/rambler.htm

Founded in 1980, the AMCRC is dedicated to the restoration, preservation, and collection of the Rambler during model years 1958 through 1969. Members benefit from a newsletter, free classified ads, a parts source book, and more.

ClassicCarShow.Com
http://www.classiccarshow.com/

The Antique Automobile Club of America

http://www.aaca.org/

The AACA is not just for people who like old cars. Actually, they want to preserve and celebrate all modes of "self-propelled vehicle," by which they mean any vehicle meant to carry people that runs on gasoline, diesel, steam, and electricity. Founded in 1935, the AACA has over 400 chapters all over the world, and their Web site is exhaustive in its coverage of history, legiaslation, film and video, musuems, links, and much more.

Boulder Bob's Roadster Page

http://members.aol.com/boulderbob/roadster.htm

Boulder Bob is a guy from Colorado who took a classic 1929 roadster and turned it into a piece of art. Check out his "rod" and read all the details that went into getting it into the shape it's in today.

Classic Car Gallery

http://www.aclassic-car.com/

View the current inventory in their image gallery. If they don't have what you want, they also provide a locator service to find the car of your dreams. They also maintain a classified listing in which you can advertise your car free for 30 days. They will even appraise your car for a fee.

Classic Car Pictures Archive

http://dutoc74.io.tudelft.nl/voitures/

A collection of over 725 images of classic automobiles, a large number of which are from Bugatti. Take a look at the car of the week, and then browse the subcategories for your favorites. There are over 52 megabytes of pictures available.

Classic Car Source

`http://www.classicar.com/home.htm`

If you like, own, or want to own a classic car of any kind from any era, this is a great starting point. The Classic Car Source offers over 90 car-specific discussion groups, thousands of classified adds, and countless links to events, trade organizations, parts suppliers, musuems, clubs, and much more.

Classic Showcase

`http://www.classicshowcase.com/`

Provides fine vintage cars, automobiles, and motorcycles, as well as a locator service for the machines they don't happen to have in stock. Photos are available for much of their inventory, and an inventory list is available and can be emailed to you on a regular basis.

ClassicCarShow.Com

`http://www.classiccarshow.com/`

Whether you love classic, vintage, historic, or sports cars, ClassicCarShow.Com is the one-stop shop for you. In addition to finding a newsletter, registry, classified ads, and products/parts, this site also houses serious car news and events, a vintage car search engine, and gift shop, and it's even been known to host the occasional Shockwave game contest.

Coys of Kensington

`http://www.coys.co.uk/`

A dealership in England that specializes in historic automobiles. Browse their online showroom for photos of automobiles currently available for sale, or peruse their auction catalogs. They also offer various pieces of automobilia, such as old race posters.

Dave Adnams Art: Scultping with Air

`http://www.hixnet.co.za/adnams/`

Mr. Adnams loves painting vintage cars—loves using them as subjects in paintings, that is! After leaving war-torn England, Adnams came to America, where he started his love affair with the colorful, sparkling autos of the day. He can be commisioned to paint any kind of moving vehicle there is (cars, motorcycles, airplanes, and so on), and his work is so outstanding, you'll swear some of them are photographs.

Horseless Carriage Foundation, Inc.

`http://www.hcfi.org/`

Are you trying to find the specs for a car that hasn't been built for 80 years? The HCFI is dedicated to helping hobbyists, restorers, and scholars find that rare information. Their library includes automotive literature dating back to the earliest days of the car at the beginning of the century.

Kelly Bluebook Official Guide

`http://www.kbb.com/abt_kbb.html?id=excite`

Whether you're looking to buy or sell a used or new car, knowing the Bluebook value helps you to know how much of a bargain you can muster. Enter the make, model, year, equipment, and condition, and the database formulates what you have. A 1991 Toyota Corolla DX four-door sedan in excellent condition with 111,000 miles, power steering, and AM/FM radio-cassette is presently worth $2,970.

Mid-America Old Time Automobile Association

`http://www.classicar.com/CLUBS/MOTAA/MOTAA.HTM`

Noting that all the antique car clubs seemed to be located far away, MOTAA formed in 1958 to provide classic car enthusiasts of the Arkansas, Missouri, Tennessee, Mississippi region a more convenient outlet for their hobby. The club hosts a car show and swap every year in Arkansas, and it has its own newsletter, the *Antique Car Times.*

Model T Ford Club of America

`http://www.mtfca.com/`

The largest Model T club in the world, the MTFCA has chapters all over the globe, offering information, discussion groups, pictures, calender of events, and more to its 20,000 members.

Paul Politis' World Famous Auto Literature Shoppe

`http://www.classicar.com/vendors/litera/litera.htm`

So you have bought, restored, shown, and maybe even driven the vintage car of your dreams. But it's still missing something. Visit the Auto Literature Shoppe, and you can complete the picture with an authentic owner's manual, or perhaps you can cover the garage walls in old sales posters and calendars.

Primarily Petroliana

http://home.stlnet.com/~jimpotts/petroliana/

Because there are no cars without fuel, many collectors steer clear of the super-expensive vintage cars and gas up on vintage filling station memorabilia. Primarily Petroliana provides a list of swap meets and auctions, informational pages and sites, and a host of other links useful to the collector. Junk is in the eye of the beholder.

Steam Automobile Club of America

http://www.classicar.com/CLUBS/STEAM/STEAM.HTM

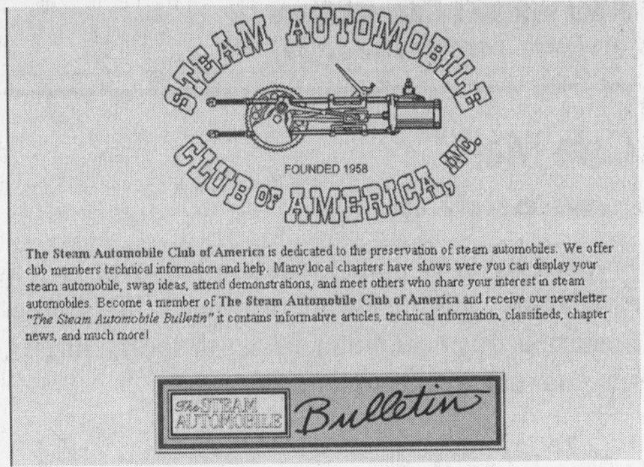

Dedicated to the preservation of steam-powered horseless carriages, the members of SACA have a tough row to hoe, considering the car's rarity. Their Web site presently features a 1906 Vanderbilt Cup racer, whose owner had to be hunted down in Michigan. Members receive the *Steam Automobile Bulletin.*

Strictly Vintage VW's

http://www2.dk-online.dk/users/vwcabrio/index.htm

Focusing on the Volkswagons built from 1938 through 1957, this page offers basic pictures and services, and it goes well beyond the Bug—it offers pages of VW steering wheels, radios, and even the Schimmwagen Page, which features the amphibious VW.

Tangerine Dream Vintage Car Locator Service

http://www.tangerinedream.inter.net/welnt.htm

Having trouble finding that '69 Boss 409? Perhaps Tangerine Dream can help. They specialize in finding vintage Mustangs, Porsches, Volkswagens, big steel, and muscle cars. Browse their FAQ, and then it's as simple as submitting a form telling them what you're looking for.

Thunderbird Cyber Nest

http://www.tbird.org/tcn.htm

If you have an old T-Bird you want to know more about or restore, the Thunderbird Cyber Nest offers resources to find parts, memorabilia, classified ads, and more. If you have ever seen your T-Bird's "date plate," this site offers extensive info to help you decode it. You can sign the registry, subscribe to the mailing list, learn about car shows and other events, and check out the T-Bird of the Month.

The Tucker Automobile Web Site

http://www.tuckerclub.org/

This site contains pages for the Tucker Automobile Club of America, Tucker car fact sheets, pictures, other links, and information about how you might be able to buy one of the 51 original Tuckers, which revolutionized Detroit in the late 1940s, should one come back up for auction. Suggestions are also given about buying Tucker facsimilies, including toys, kits, and Franklin Mint replicas.

The Vintage Triumph Register

http://www.classiccarshow.com/findex.html

All things Triumphant. If you collect or want to collect classic Triumph automobiles, use this site to find information about restoration, competition rules, parts suppliers, mailing lists, other owner Web pages, FAQs, and even a program to help drivers whose cars break down far away from qualified Triumph repair or parts shops.

Wambo!

http://www.kent.net/wambo/

The 10th annual Wallaceburgh Antique Motor and Boat Outing features antique automobiles, motorcycles, fire engines, boats, and tractors. In addition to the antiques, there is entertainment provided for all ages.

XK's Unlimited

http://www.xks.com/

Specializes in Jaguars from 1948 to present, but also deals with other European sports cars of the same era. They have a facility dedicated to restoration, and they maintain a large supply of Jaguar parts. Also, check out some information on the racing of vintage automobiles.

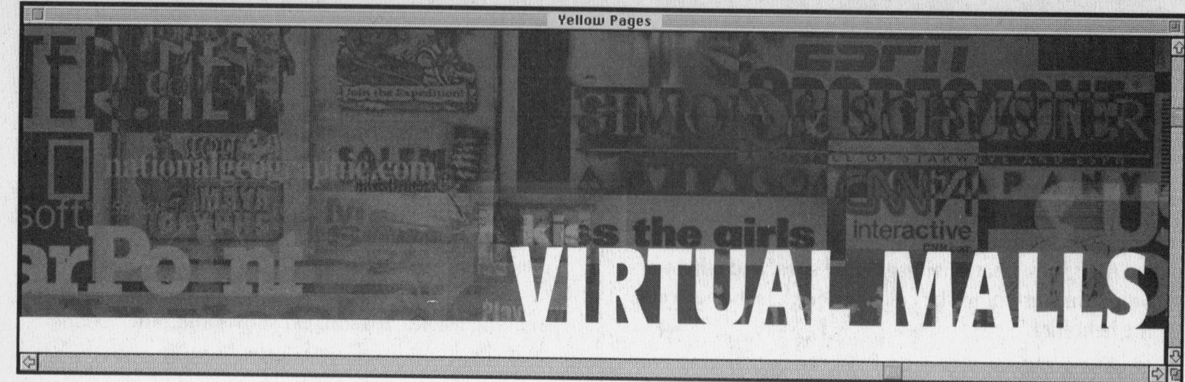

A B C D E F G H I J K L M N O P Q R S T U V W X Y Z

> It's true what they say Oatman, you can never go home again, but I guess you can shop there.
>
> *Martin in* Grosse Pointe Blank *(1997)*

Above & Beyond

`http://www.abmall.com/`

Originally focused on the tall shopper, Above & Beyond now has "wings" of shops for elderly care, gender-issue products, arts & crafts, children, natural health, and more. It also features a search engine to help you find the perfect gift.

Antique Alley

`http://bmark.com/aa/`

Antique Alley's page enables you to search for a specific item or shop; peruse a giant list of shops around the country; or guides you to others antiques pages, in case a search comes up empty.

The Blue Winds Mall

`http://www.bluewinds.com//index.htm`

The Blue Winds site specializes with e-stores that sell hand-crafted products, ranging from jewelry and new age, but it also provides professional services, such as learning workshops. You can also download free flower clipart.

BizCafe Mall

`http://www.bizcafe.com`

Serves as a WWW mall. Includes categories such as travel, books, getting ahead, printing, office, home, consulting, business, financial, legal, sports, fitness, gifts, manufacturing, and autos.

Buy the World

`http://www.buytheworld.com/`

Buy the World's site is separated into its department store, which sells everything under the sun, their Site Design Service, to help you build a site like theirs, and the Outdoor Store, which specializes in products that pay homage to fresh air, water, and sunshine.

The Canyon

`http://www.interart.net/realms/canyon.html`

The Canyon is an award-winning site that sells original artwork, such as paintings and sculpture, original crafts, such as hand-woven clothing, and jewelry, food, wine, and other gifts, such as chilis, sauces, and candy.

The Cyber-Shopping Network

`http://www.cybershopping.net`

Offers a variety of shopping categories, including art and photography, books, pet supplies, real estate, restaurants, formal wear, and sporting goods. Opportunity for free products. Businesses can sign up to advertise on their site.

Flea Market @FUW

`http://info.fuw.edu.pl/market/market.html`

Serves as an online flea market for products. Lets you place ads, as well as search ads in the long and short form, or search for a specific item.

The Front Page

`http://www.thefrontpage.com/`

Specializes in the arts, automotive, building and development, marine supplies, and real estate, all from the Florida perspective.

Great Shops on-line shopping

`http://www.greatshops.com/`

Great Shops specializes in gifts and games, mysteries, and puzzles, including 3D puzzles that stack up as you build them.

iMall Marketplace

`http://www.imall.com/`

The iMall is a fully stocked electronic mall that features a search engine, classified ads, Deals of the Day, and a Flower Club. "Pavilions" allow you to shop by category—from accessories and jewelry to antiques and toys. They also go so far as to sell cars, plane tickets, and other travel arrangements.

IndustryNET Industry's Online Mall

`http://www.industry.net`

Presents up-to-date information about engineering design, automation, and manufacturing news from IndustryNET. Includes application assistance, new products, demo software, online trade shows, tested shareware programs, employment opportunities, and used industrial equipment.

Internet Shopping Network

`http://www.Internet.net:80/`

Enables you to join online shopping club for deals on everything from software to flowers. Provides an alphabetical listing of more than 600 companies.

Mall on the Net

`http://www.mallonthenet.com/directory.htm`

On easy site to use, Mall on the Net has categories for cars, gifts, software, electronics, games, and sports. Their Service area offers Web site design, accounting, and more.

Meetings Industry Mall

`http://www.mim.com`

Serves as a virtual mall specifically for industry professionals. Lets suppliers open shop to meeting planners and buyers throughout the world.

Microplay Video Game Stores

`http://www.canadamalls.com/provider/microp.html`

Have fun in Canada's largest virtual mall. Search the mall by keyword or by store name, browse the new additions, check out the featured store of the month.

Mother Nature's General Store

`http://www.mothernature.com/`

A gigantic e-mall of health foods, supplements, vitamins, teas, books, and so on. If your local store has run out of selenium and St. John's Wort, or the newest book by Dr. Weil, Mother Nature's can help.

Roblyn's Shopping Mall

`http://www.roblyn.com/mallhome.htm`

Offers products and services from Canada's top businesses. 18th century inspired furniture, hydroponics gardening supplies, virtual bookstore, fishing tips, and more.

Rock Mall

`http://www.rockmall.com/`

Not only can you buy recordings of your favorite music and movie, you can also leave reviews, take the trivia challenge, and search by category, such as blues, jazz, and indie rock.

ShoppersUniverse

`http://shoppersuniverse.com/su/welcome.asp`

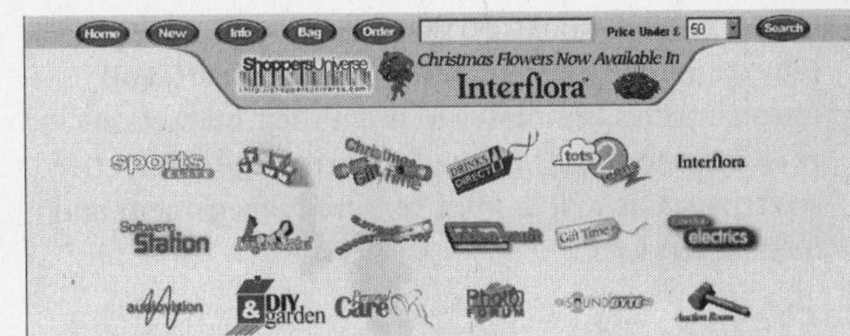

This site is organized by store, such as Video Vault, Interflora, Software Station, Toy Town, Drinks Direct, and so on. You can also conduct searches based on maximum price (in UK pounds).

Shopper's Utopia

`http://shop-utopia.com`

Contains a variety of custom shops, ranging from leather products, fashion jewelry, and salsa, to a full-fledged graphics design shop.

Shop Smart

`http://www.shopsmart.com/ptp.html`

An interesting array of products, from your home and corporate office needs, to "kid stuff," to products for Fido and Fluffy.

Spectra.Net Mall

`http://www.spectra.net/`

Brings the convenience of home shopping to you with electronic classified ads in an array of topics, such as health and beauty and home furnishings. Adds new storefronts, new products, and new services daily.

Star-Byte Shopping Mall

`http://www.starbyte.com/mall.html`

Provides online shopping in numerous virtual stores for many different items. Includes mass media, business, computers, and other products.

Trading Post: The 60s for the 90s

`http://artitude.com/`

Get your counterculture T-shirts, posters, bumper stickers, tie dyes, Web site design, earwear, Grateful Deadorbilia, incense, and the environmental art of Rick Sanders.

The UK Shopping City

`http://www.ukshops.co.uk:8000`

Provides predominantly British products and services. Offers 180,000 books, 56,000 videos, and 14,000 CDs, plus computer software, watches, jewelry, art, and more. Enables businesses to reach their market quickly and economically through Internet and interactive advertising, as well as joint venture management and referral services.

The Village Square

`http://www.villagesquare.com/`

The Village Square is surrounded by the most delectable stores, selling everything from travel arrangements, food, art, and home office needs.

WebMart Virtual Mall and Web Development Services

`http://www.webmart.com/icc/webmart.html`

Provides online shopping and services from the comfort of your own home. Includes links to many different stores based in the eastern United States.

The Web Plaza—Online Marketplace

`http://www.webplaza.com/`

Serves as an online marketplace. Provides categories in employment services, electronics, and real estate. Also provides solutions for effectively marketing products and services on the Web.

Xplore Shopping

`http://www.xplore.com/xplore500/medium/shopping.html`

At Xplore Shopping, you can get almost anything—even your own personal shopper to help you out with those tough shopping decisions. Provides links to FAO Schwartz, L.L. Bean, Land's End, Spencer Gifts, Spiegel, Ticketmaster Online, and more.

Related Sites
`http://www.iboutique.com/`
`http://www.xmission.com/~arts/`
`http://www.csmonline.com/introcsm11.html`
`http://www.deepspace.com/deepspace.html`
`http://www.netoasis.com/`
`http://juniper.mecnet.org/index.html`
`http://www.cityaccess.com/olshopper/default.asp`
`http://www.aaa-mall.com/`
`http://VTGinc.com/uncommon/index.html`
`http://www.virtuallyeverything.com/`

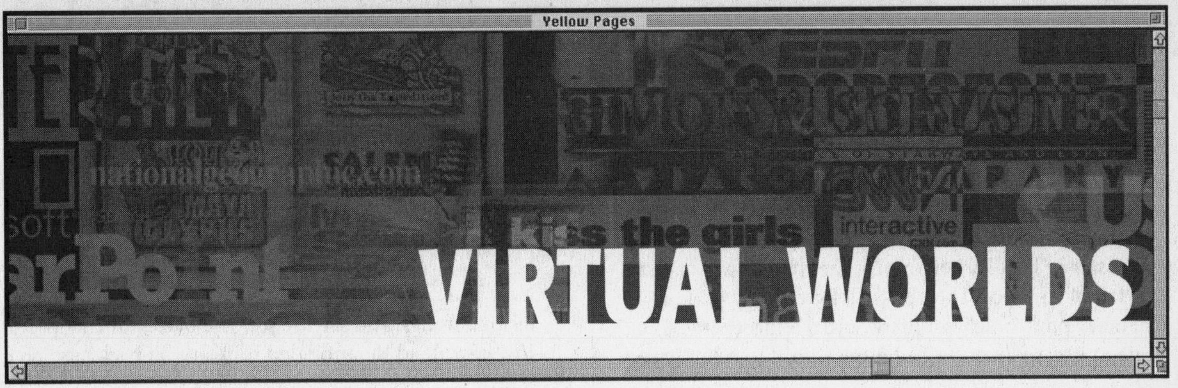

I want to know how virtual reality works.

Sydney Bloom in VR.5 *(1995)*

Aereal

http://www.aereal.com/instant/gziper.cgi?proteinman.wrl.gz

Aereal, an Internet business that develops sites and marketing over the Net, offers free VHML home worlds on its server. Anyone can now create their own world. Check it out.

CYBERspace STUDIOS

http://www.lyrastudios.com/cyberspace/index.html

Better let them describe it. CYBERspace Studios has created "real-time online 3D Virtual Worlds, using a revolutionary new technology that enables fully interactive, fast multiplayer gaming and live chat in an online 3D environment that can accommodate hundreds of visitors simultaneously." The images on the site are very interesting, and you can download demos to see if this is the place for you.

Desiderata—The Reststop

http://www.dfw.net/~custmbld/desid.html

A "rest stop" on the information highway. This site features an annotated version of *Desiderata*, the guide for life.

Related Sites

http://members.aol.com/avfactory/index.html

http://ourworld.compuserve.com/homepages/virtual_design_modeling/

http://www.arch.columbia.edu/DDL/cad/A4535/SUM95/vwcsum95.html

MindWave
http://www.mindwave.com

The Dockingbay

http://www.csd.uu.se/~johnn/

An award-winning interactive tour—one person's view of what a space station might be like in the 2200s. It takes a MYST-like perspective with things to do and discover. An interesting aspect is that the station is recovering from a space battle, and some sections are not available. Looks like a lot of time-consuming fun.

Electric Saloon

http://www.st.rim.or.jp:80/~liliko/e-saloon.html

A fun 3D "saloon" that serves a few drinks and has plenty of characters. Check out the QuickTime movie of the saloon, click on a character to talk to, then see what Web links he or she recommends. Slightly weird, slightly innocent, but still interesting.

The Enterprise City Home Page

http://www.thebook.com/enterprise/city.htm

Take a taxi, ride the monorail, or walk through Enterprise City, a fictitious town with all types of characters and stories. This town comprises a collection of characters, stories, and essays by Dominic R. Villari.

Lost Worlds

http://www.talkcity.com/seismic/

This site offers a virtual tour of the planet: rainforests and ruins, wild and strange places on our planet Earth. The traveler will need the Realspace Viewer plug-in and QuickTime, both of which are available for download. While not all sections of the site are active yet, the ones that are offer interesting tours and conversations with the explorers.

Mariam's Cyberspace Park

http://www.skypoint.com/members/mariam

Nine "parks" await your visit. Take a ride on the roller coaster at EuroDisney, or visit the theme park at the Mall of America. There's also a Psychology park, a Poetry park, a Religion park, and a Sports park. A great way to organize and display links to other pages.

MindWave

http://www.mindwave.com

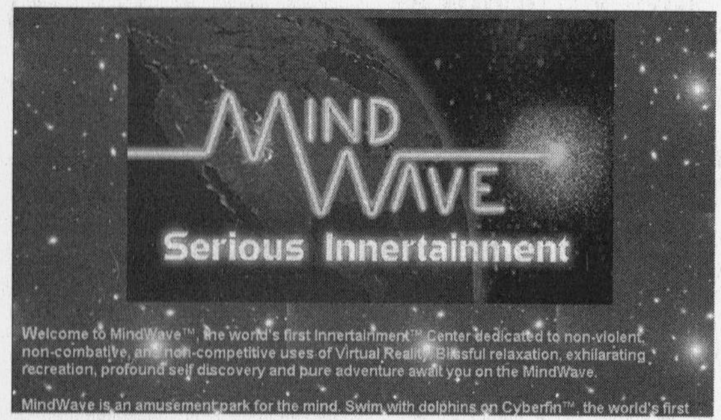

A commercial site, MindWave is both the name of the shop where the VR rides occur, and one of the rides itself. The shop offers a VR swim with dolphins, an exploration of the universe, and much more.

Proteinman's Top Ten VRML2.0 Worlds

http://www.virtpark.com/theme/proteinman/

Links to a rotating list of VRML worlds. You must have have the proper VRML browser to view, but the browers should be accessible for downloading. Very interesting site.

sci.virtual-worlds Introduction FAQ

http://www.lib.ox.ac.uk/internet/news/faq/archive/virtual-worlds.readfirst-faq.html

This is a FAQ for the sci.virtual-worlds newsgroup on Usenet. It describes how to subscribe, what is and isn't accepted for listing, and who moderates the newsgroup. It also includes how to subscribe to Virtua-L, the mirror mailing list, which is unmoderated.

The Social Cafe

http://www.social.com/social/index.html

Become a member (it's free) or just visit and talk with others. This site, by social.com, includes a Sports and Social Clubs area, a message area where you can discuss different topics, the Woman's Page, and the latest news on the social scene. The Fun link includes comics, sports info, and games on the Internet.

Stonehenge

http://connectedpc.com/cpc/ecs/stonehenge/

Now you can visit Stonehenge, learn about these mysterious stones, and see the sun rise over Stonehenge. Just download the provided software, sit back, and go.

The Tin Cup Coffee House

http://www.tincup.com/

Check out Web sites around the Twin Cities (Minneapolis and St. Paul, Minnesota), read the Coffee House Review of all the coffee houses in the area, or listen to great RealAudio files.

Virtex96

http://www.virtex.co.uk/jnindex.htm

A commercial site for a virtual reality trade show exhibition hall for Information Technologies. They provide the browser plug-in for viewing. If you want to exhibit, they'll design your "booth" for you. An interesting site to learn about the latest in I.T.

Virtual Dorm

http://www.vdorm.com/

The Net equivalent of MTV's *The Real World*, in Virtual Dorm you see and chat with real students in their dorm room. The videos are a series of still shots of what's happening in the rooms, and the chat goes back and forth between the student's computer and the viewer's. You can also read online diaries. (One wonders how they got involved in all this.)

Virtual Places

http://home.earthlink.net/~wyvern/vplaces/index.html

Using the VP software and working from the VP server, anyone can both chat and browse while using the net. Groups of people can chat and browse together, visit sites, and discuss them. Choose an avatar to represent you. Play games or just sit in.

Virtual Reality Universe

http://www.vruniverse.com/

An excellent site designed to teach new users of the VRML language. From here, you can go to VMRL 2.0 and the creation of your own worlds. A Lycos Top 5% Site.

The Virtual Society Project

http://www.csl.sony.co.jp/project/VS/index.html

A site for the technically oriented, this home page briefly dicusses the projects and goals for the Sony Corporation in developing virtual worlds and online communities. It also provides links to related sites and virtual world browsers.

Virtual Vegas

http://www.virtualvegas.com

Believe it or not, you can now travel to Las Vegas on your PC. This site provides a virtual trip. Includes casinos (just for fun, of course), the Lizard Lounge, and much more. Also provides links to sites in the "real" Las Vegas. Virtual Vegas is a cool site.

VRML Repository

http://www.sdsc.edu/vrml/

The ultimate site for the individual who wants to become immersed in the technical side of virtual worlds/virtual reality, the VRML Repository has links for authoring and browsing applications, object and sound libraries, documentation, software development, and other information relating to VRML.

Worlds Chat

http://www.worlds.net/wcg/wcg-about.html

A huge real-time chat space where you can create your own avatar (the image that represents you) or use the ones already available. You can visit 8 different worlds from the space station, with more than 800 rooms available. Lots of virtual communites and groups to join. All it takes is to download the free demo software and go voyaging. If you like what you see, purchase the CD-ROM software for complete access.

NEWSGROUPS

alt.cyberpunk.chatsubo

comp.lang.vrml

ed.vr

no.vr

sci.virtual-worlds

uw.virtual-worlds

FTP & GOPHER SITES

ftp://ftp.sdsc.edu/pub/vrml/software/browsers/

ftp://ftp.std.com/bcs/vr/

ftp://sunee.uwaterloo.ca/pub/vr

ftp://sunsite.unc.edu/pub/academic/computer-science/virtual-reality

http://sunsite.doc.ic.ac.uk/usenet/comp.archives/auto/sci.virtual-worlds/

gopher://fdlpc1.scs.unr.edu:2347/7?virtual reality

MAILING LISTS

euro-vrml

evrs

planetx-vre

ukvrsig

VIRTU-L

virtual_reality

vr-net

Related Sites

http://www.best.com/~wooldri/awooldri/vungeon.html

http://www.cs.uidaho.edu/lal/cyberspace/VR/VR.html

http://www.dur.ac.uk/~dla0www/c_tour/tour.html

http://www.ipa.fhg.de/300/vr/homepage.html

http://www.stars.com/WebStars/VR.html

http://www.supersurf.com/

http://www.vwenterprises.com/vwm_hpg.htm

http://www.worldsaway.com/

http://www.worldvirtualcity.com/wvc/

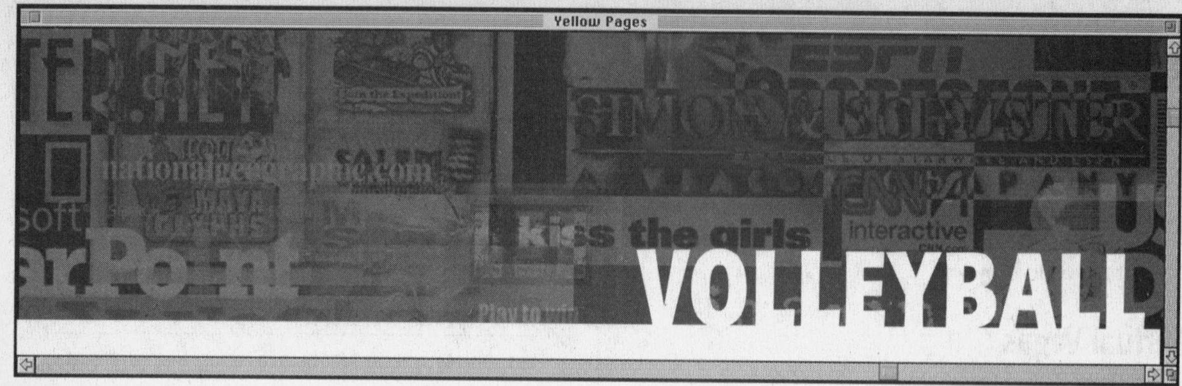

> Today it's Wheaties boxes. Tomorrow it's video games and action figures. The sky's the limit!
>
> *Don Tibbles in* D2: The Mighty Ducks *(1994)*

American Walleyball Association

http://www.wallyball.com/

Walleyball is volleyball played on a racquetball court. Use this site to read the game's rules, order supplies, find out where you can play, and get details about different leagues and tournaments.

Association of Volleyball Professionals (AVP)

http://www.volleyball.org/avp/index.html

Members of the AVP are the best beach vball players in the country. Their site houses their schedule, roster, rankings, awards, history, address, and more.

Backline Sportswear

http://www.backline.com/

Backline is a california-based retailer of the finest in volleyball clothing and equipment. They also sponsor an annual tournament.

Cobra Volleyball

http://www.cobravolleyball.com/

The Cobra net is a popular system easily used on sand or grass that sets up easily for all levels of play, from elementary school gym to professional tournaments.

Gabby Reece Home Page
http://www.gabbyreece.com/

Dylan's I Love Volleyball

http://www.sccs.swarthmore.edu/~dylan/vball/index.html

This Swathmore student wants you—to come play volleyball against his team. His pages have shrines to the great players, pictures, and helpful links.

Evolution Volleyball

http://www.evolutionsport.com/

Evolution is a volleyball apparel company that prides itself on clothes that balance form and function. Check out their clothes, links, and tournament info.

FIVB WWW Home Page

http://www.fivb.ch/

The FIVB is the governing body of international volleyball. Use their site to learn more about upcoming events and tournaments, worldwide beach vball, FIVB meetings, program development, and educational and promotional material.

Gabby Reece Home Page

http://www.gabbyreece.com/

Gabby Reece is volleyball's biggest superstar, which makes sense—she is 6'3"! Her site has a biography, workout tips and words of inspiration, excerpts from her new book, and her vball stats. This site is content-rich and has superior design and interaction.

Related Sites

http://www.seas.ucla.edu/~mcalexan/

http://members.aol.com/Vballxchg/EasterSeals/ESCH.html

http://www.volleyball.org/avca/

Professional Volleyball League

http://www.pvl.com/

This official home page hosts links to the league's five teams, one of which is the longest-running woman's pro sports team, the San Jose Storm. The other teams are from Sacramento, San Bernardino, Utah, and Hawaii.

Schneid's Volleyball Page

http://www.xnet.com/~schneid/vball.shtml

Schneid's excellent content includes the normal links and rules, but also tips on strategy, drills to improve your game, nutritional info for athletes, and advice on training and flexibility.

Todd's Volleyball Page

http://www.io.com/~tdh/vball/

Todd provides comprehensive coverage of the game's rules, according to varying organizations. He also recommends his favorite equipment and discusses volleyball in the opposing towns of Austin, Texas, and Chicago.

UCSB Summer Camps

http://ucsbuxa.ucsb.edu/physical-activities/youthprog/youthprog.html

This site has pages for two programs the university hosts for girls and boys volleyball. Learn more about the program, housing, coaching, highlights, and cost.

Unofficial Volleyball Page

http://www.netwiz.net/~rainmker/

Surf to this page to get the latest news in the world of volleyball, with a focus on how Stanford University's teams are doing.

Related Sites
http://www.borg.com/~uva/
http://www.canuckstuff.com/
http://www.volleyballone.com/

Volleyball Hall of Fame

http://www.volleyhall.org/

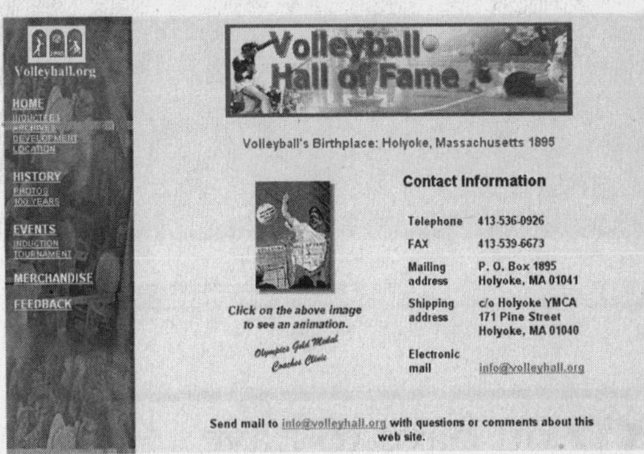

Read the sport's and the Hall's history, view photos, see who's been inducted into the Hall, send feedback, buy a centennial volleyball, and study a map showing where the Hall is located in Holyoke, Massachusetts.

Volleyball Magazine

http://www.volleyballmag.com/

Get the latest schedule of events, scores of recent matches, advice from the sport's biggest names and instructors, and new and articles from the latest edition of the magazine.

Volleyball WorldWide

http://www.volleyball.org/

Fact page and links for both indoor and beach volleyball, men and women's. Provides information for all levels of volleyball: amateur, collegiate and professional. Links to related associations like the US Disabled Volleyball Team home pages also provided.

USA Volleyball Home Page

http://Volleyball.ORG:80/usav/

Links to youth and junior programs as well as rosters for top men and women's teams.

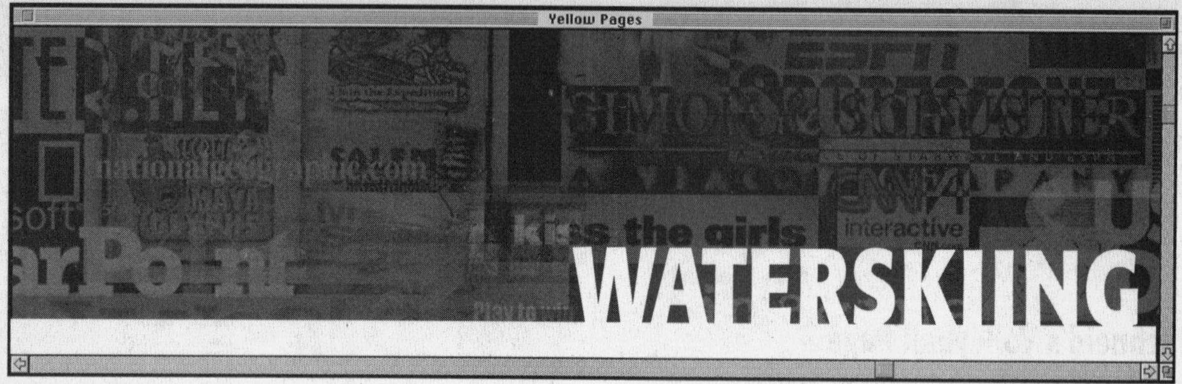

> You have to have courage to stay the course.
>
> *Unknown*

Andy Water Web

http://www.bizlink.co.uk/waterski/index.htm

Andy's site is especially good for beginners. His pages discuss how to get started, what to buy, ski news, and ski schools.

Banana George Blair

http://www.bananageorge.com/

Maybe you've seen him highlighted on a TV show, but now Banana George has his own site. At 80 years of age, Banana didn't even learn to waterski until he was 40. Learn more about him, his favorite food, his favorite color, his movie project, and more.

The Barefoot Media Page

http://waterski.net/foot/media/

See video clips and photos, retrieve tournament info, see what resources other countries have to offer, and use the extensive links to continue your waterskiing journey.

Banana George Blair
http://www.bananageorge.com/

Behind the Boat

http://www.behindtheboat.com/links.htm

A comprehensive waterski links site, with links to boat manufacturers, waterski gear, organizations, schools, teams, and clubs, places to waterski, and pages for specific disciplines (slalom, barefoot, and so on).

British Disabled Water Ski Association

http://www.waterski-uk.com/bdwsa.htm

This page contains contact info for the BDWSA, which promotes and develops the sport for disabled people, and works to invent equipment, so more people can enjoy this exhilarating sport.

The Essential Waterski Links Site

http://194.164.56.2/~chronicle.h2o.ski/links/home.htm

Not only is this site a good starting point for the Web-surfing waterskier, it also contains downloadable waterski scoring software for America, Britain, and France.

Jump: The Water Ski Jumper Web Site

http://pages.prodigy.com/caramedia/jump.htm

Features news and literature about water ski jumping, a directory of jumpers, photos, national standings, and links.

Related Sites

http://www.kneeboard.simplenet.com/

http://waterski.net/foot/media/

National Collegiate Water Ski Association

http://hubcap.clemson.edu/~jhharri/ski_team/ncwsa.html

A compilation of information about college waterskiing and the rise of the NCWSA. The page is part of the Clemson Water Ski Team's site.

National Show Ski Association

http://showski.com/

If water skiing with one foot hooked on the bar or as part of a pyramid sounds like fun to you, consider joining the NSSA. Their site has a schedule of events, results of the Nationals tournament, show ski humor, news, photos, links, and more.

Water Ski News Online

http://www.mooseweb.com/mooseweb/skiEnews/index.shtml

This site provides all the latest news, including video clips of news tricks, feature articles, editorials, classified ads, professional news, and a searchable database.

Water Skier's Web

http://waterski.net/

Every type of water-skimming sport is listed in this links page: barefoot, air chair, wake boarding, and kneeboarding. You can check out the Water Skier's Mall and follow Usenet discussions.

Water Skiers with Disabilities Association

http://www.waterski.net/ski/tourny/wsda.html

Learn about this worthwhile organization—its history, triumphs, and tournament highlights.

Water Skier's Web Mall

http://waterski.net/branch/index.html

This site is a thorough list of vendors for ski schools, equipment, boats, and so on.

The Waterskiing Chronicles

http://194.164.56.2/~chronicle.h2o.ski/

This international site focuses on waterskiing in Europe. Other than articles, links, and news, this site is pushing people to sign their petition to include waterskiing in the Summer Games at Athens in 2004.

USA Water Ski/American Water Ski Association

http://www.usawaterski.org/

The official site of waterskiing's governing body. Learn which man and woman were named Athlete of the Year, see what's in store for 1998, review the bylaws, and much more.

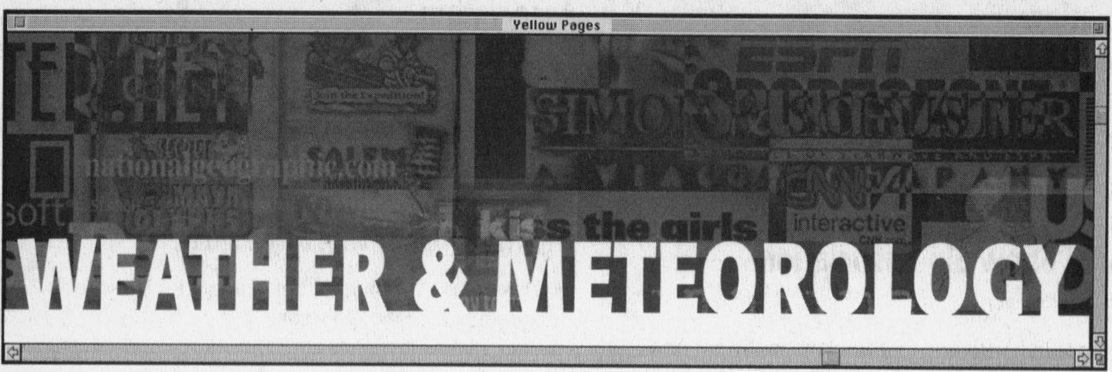

WEATHER & METEOROLOGY

> Rainbows apologize for angry skies.
>
> *Sylvia A. Voirol*

AgriWeather

`http://www.agriweather.com/`

Presents an online catalog of weather instruments and related products. Also offers a customized weather forecast service that provides separate weather forecasts for agricultural, business, and corporate needs.

Alden Electronics

`http://www.alden.com/`

Provides weather data systems, marine electronics, and specialized imaging products and papers. Offers software, hardware, and customized data products.

Atlantic Tropical Weather Center

`http://www.neosoft.com/citylink/blake/tropical.html`

Provides the latest hurricane information and other weather information dealing with tropical cyclones. Also offers images, data, pictures, meteograms, models, and satellite loops.

Automated Weather Source Nationwide School Weather Network

`http://www.aws.com/index.html`

Provides national weather information from images to textual data. Also presents a photo gallery of severe weather by storm chasers throughout the country.

Defense Meteorological Satellite Program
`http://web.ngdc.noaa.gov/dmsp/dmsp.html`

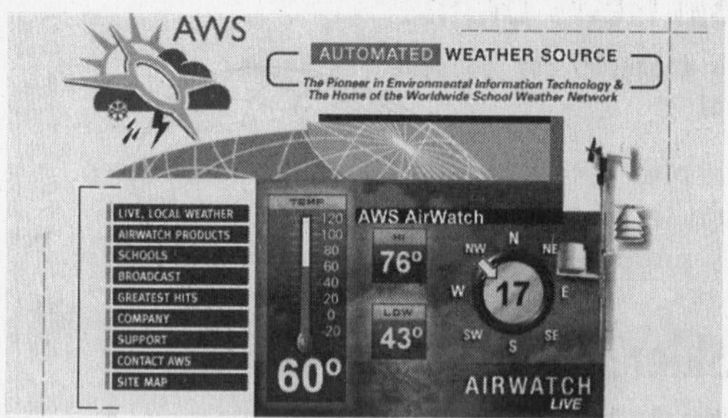

Current World Weather

`http://pw1.netcom.com/~shoote13/home.html`

Offers many links to current U.S. and world weather conditions, other weather-related sites, and Accuweather information. This site gives information provided by major weather organizations, such as CNN weather, The Weather Channel, and Earthwatch Communications, Inc.

Defense Meteorological Satellite Program

`http://web.ngdc.noaa.gov/dmsp/dmsp.html`

Two satellite constellations of near-polar orbiting, sun-synchronous satellites that monitor meteorological, oceanographic, and solar-terrestrial physics environments. Features currently occurring meteorological phenomena.

Earth Watch Communications, Inc.

`http://www.earthwatch.com/`

Contains many images of 3D satellite views from space. Also plugs its 3D software package that integrates 3D weather visualization with a global database to create a virtual world.

El Niño

http://www.enn.com/specialreports/elnino/index.htm

Tells what El Niño is, what past El Niños were like, and how they impact our weather. Also gives news reports on the current status of El Niño and discusses how El Niño systems are measured.

Intellicast

http://www.intellicast.com/

Serves as guide to weather, ski reports, and ocean conditions. Provides information for weather novices and professionals. New to Intellicast are health and travel reports. Also, check out its forecasts for national parks.

Interactive Marine Observations

http://www.nws.fsu.edu

Gives access to meteorological and oceanographic data being reported by buoys and CMAN stations in the Atlantic, United States, and Pacific. Reloads automatically every two minutes if you have Netscape.

International Weather Watchers Official Home Page

http://groundhog.sprl.umich.edu/IWW/

Nonprofit group of weather enthusiasts. Includes information about the group, links to weather-related information, and an offer to receive a free bulletin the group puts out.

NASA Weather Archive

ftp://explorer.arc.nasa.gov/pub/Weather/

Provides archive of weather images taken by the space shuttle and NASA satellite systems.

National Center for Atmospheric Research

http://www.ucar.edu/

Consists of several scientific divisions and programs working together with member universities on research activities to better understand Earth's climate systems. Includes information on resources, facilities, and services; the research data archives; and weather-related information.

National Center for Atmospheric Research

http://www.ucar.edu/

Consists of several scientific divisions and programs working together with member universities on research activities to better understand Earth's climate systems. Includes information on resources, facilities, and services; the research data archives; and weather-related information.

National Hurricane Center Tropical Prediction Center

http://www.nhc.noaa.gov/

Contains resources for the researcher, advanced student, and hobbyist interested in the latest information on tropical weather conditions, as well as archival information on weather data and maps. Provides links to other NOAA information and satellite data.

National Severe Storms Laboratory

http://www.nssl.uoknor.edu/

Provides information about the laboratory, including current research and programs. Does not offer specific information on severe weather but does provide links to sites that do. Also includes an extensive list of links to "Web literacy" sites.

National Weather Service

http://www.nws.noaa.gov/

Provides all information output by the NWS, including national and international weather in graphical and textual formats, and information about regional offices. Also offers links to NOAA and other NWS programs.

Seismological Laboratory

http://www.gps.caltech.edu/seismo/seismo.page.html

Southern California site that provides seismology-related resources, including the record of the day, recent earthquake activity, and publications. A new feature of this site is its Terrascope section, in which you can plot data or get EQ information for recent large earthquakes.

Space Science and Engineering Center (SSEC) Real-Time Data

`http://www.ssec.wisc.edu/data/index.html`

Includes weather information and ocean temperatures. Also offers images, movies, and composites of weather events.

Storm Chaser Home Page

`http://taiga.geog.niu.edu/chaser.html`

Includes information about storm chasers, a photo gallery of storms, and the latest news about the Storm Chasers group. Also provides information about storm chasing at home, including how to contact the NWS.

Warren Faidley's Storm Chasing Home Page

`http://www.indirect.com/www/storm5/`

Presents photos of severe weather taken by Warren Faidley, full-time storm chaser.

Weather and Climate Images

`http://grads.iges.org/pix/head.html`

Offers short- and medium-range forecasts for North America and current weather maps and climate anomaly models for the rest of the world. Provides a key to the weather maps and a table of weather symbols. One of its new features is an El Niño forecast.

Weather and Global Monitoring

`http://www.csu.edu.au/weather.html`

Provides pointers to various weather services worldwide.

Weather Channel

`http://www.weather.com/`

Includes information about the Weather Channel and also provides novice weather enthusiasts with simple weather maps. Provides up-to-date flight information, travel forecasts, and storm watches.

Weather Net

`http://cirrus.sprl.umich.edu/wxnet/`

Tries to list every weather-related link on the Internet. Includes not only WWW sites, but FTP sites, Gophers, and Telnet sites. Includes commercial sites as well as educational and governmental sites.

Weather Page

`http://www.landings.com/aviation.html`

Lists weather links out of Harvard University. Includes brief descriptions of each link. Also provides links to aviation information.

Related Sites

- `http://www.alden.com/`
- `http://www.ems.psu.edu/~fraser/BadMeteorology.html`
- `http://www.atmos.uiuc.edu/`
- `http://www.es.mq.edu.au/ISB/`
- `http://mcc.sws.uiuc.edu/`
- `ftp://explorer.arc.nasa.gov/pub/Weather/`
- `http://pages.prodigy.com/SkyWatch/sw-amain.htm`
- `http://www.indirect.com/www/storm5/`
- `http://www.csu.edu.au/weather.html`
- `http://members.aol.com/Accustiver/wxworld.html`

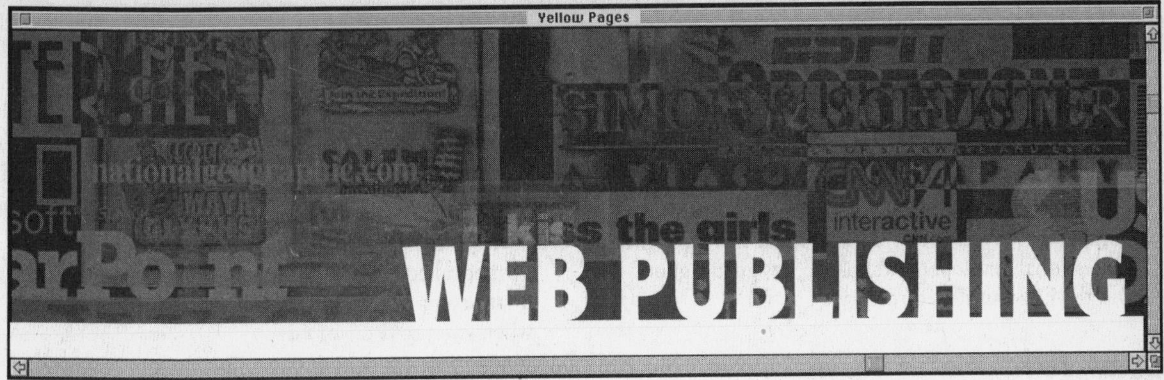

Programming today is a race between software engineers striving to build bigger and better idiot-proof programs, and the universe trying to produce bigger and better idoits. So far, the Universe is winning.

Rich Cook

Artzilla Surf Constructions

`http://www.earthlink.net/~Artzilla`

A group of designers and illustrators who left the corporations and now do what they love—provide the Web with high-quality graphics.

Business of the Internet

`http://www.rtd.com/people/rawn/business.html`

Introduces the Internet for commercial organizations. Offers information about the structure and history of the Internet, how the Internet can help business, and how to connect your business to the Internet.

Copyright Website

`http://www.benedict.com/`

Provides copyright information for the general public and interested parties. Includes categories of fundamentals on copyrights and issues related to copyright over the Net. Also contains a section for relevant sources and links.

NRP TOP PICKS

Dynamic Diagrams Home Page
`http://dynamicDiagrams.com/`

Free Range Media, Inc.
`http://www.freerange.com`

Manhattan MultiMedia, Inc.
`http://www.manhattanmultimedia.com/`

Digital Publishing Ink (DPI)

`http://www.dpinet.com/`

Offers total solutions, including training, programming, graphic design, and server setup. Has very reliable turn-key service options.

Dynamic Diagrams Home Page

`http://dynamicDiagrams.com/`

Focuses on the organization and presentation of information in print and electronic forms, interactive publication and prototype design, SGML applications, Web servers, and computer kiosks for museums.

Four Lakes Colorgraphics, Inc.

`http://www.fourlakes.com/`

This company provides prepress and publishing services to publishers, advertisers, and educational service providers. Four Lakes will design and publish CD-ROMs and home pages. Provides links to its target sights.

Free Range Media, Inc.

`http://www.freerange.com`

A full-scale Web production and Internet services company with expertise in creative design, new technology, and account management. Specializes in keeping track of the newest tools. Produces a wide variety of Web-related products. Also shares many tips and techniques.

FRS Associates Training and Education Division

http://www.frsa.com/

A Web presence provider that specializes in graphics, interactive programming, Java, JavaScript, and animation. Also provides Web training for the novice to the professional developer and links to designed sights and the FRS business directory.

Gates, Jeff

http://www.tmn.com/Community/jgates/home.html

Jeff Gates's personal home page is an example of what he can do for your personal or business use. Provides links to contact Jeff to set up a site of your own.

Headquarters.Com Internet

http://www.headquarters.com/

Internet/intranet Web sites for individuals and businesses. Provides links to current and upcoming projects and their client base. Offers complete multimedia design, including Java, graphics, and CGI scripting, among others.

Hijinx

http://www.hijinx.com.au/

Communications software to give your Web pages memorable pictures and sounds. Provides links to a sample page, product info, and downloading info. Be sure to check out the "latest screen shot."

Home Space Builder

http://www.paragraph.com/whatsnew/homespce.htm

A 3D Web-authoring tool that enables you to create a 3D home space using a standard Windows personal computer. Offers shareware and commercial versions.

HudsoNet

http://www.hudsonet.com/

A New York–based service and Web page designer that will get your business on the Internet. Provides links to client pages and services offered.

Image Alchemy Digital Imaging

http://imalchemy.com

Presents a gallery of digital and traditional art and photography. Offers services such as photo retouching and manipulation. Also designs Web sites.

Image Compression for Publishing Online

http://www.jgc.com

Provides information about Johnson-Grace company, now a part of America Online, a multimedia software development that developed an image compression format called ART. Suggests that using ART enables image compression three times more efficient than when you use JPEG or GIF.

Image House Digital Photography Studio

http://www.concom.com/~whitcomb/ih_home.html

A digital photo studio for your business publishing needs. Provides training and camera installation information, Web site design, and messages from clients.

INTERCAT

http://www.intercat.com/

If you have a catalog or other information you want to get on the Web, Intercat will develop a complete multimedia Web presence for you. Includes links to sample sights, catalogs, and contact information.

Interglobal Mutltimedia

http://www.interglobal.com/

Web solutions for your corporate multimedia Web presence, including Web hosting, design, and security. Provides access to customer profiles, catalog, video, and much more.

Internet Advertising Solutions

http://iaswww.com/

These people will develop your company's Web site and get your information on the Internet. Winner of many awards for innovative site development. Includes links to services, clients, and more.

Internet Business Connection

http://www.intbc.com/

A virtual mall specializing in home page development and marketing services to any business seeking an Internet presence.

Manhattan MultiMedia, Inc.

NRP TOP PICKS

http://www.manhattanmultimedia.com/

Manhattan will help your company plan, develop, and maintain a unique Internet presence by using the most advanced tools possible, including Java, C++, Perl, Oracle, UNIX, Shockwave, and others.

MediaBox Communications

http://www.mediabox.com/

Web publishing, specializing in creative marketing strategies, graphic design and production, multimedia, and advertising for the Web. Click on the MediaBox electronic portfolio to get a sample of its work.

Metrotel Multi-Media Ltd

http://mmm.wwa.com/mmm/why.html

Web design and Internet consulting for your company. Develop a Web presence and find out how to surf the Internet to your advantage.

MGL Systems

http://www.mgl.ca/

A computer technologies firm based in Cambridge, Ontario, offering Web publishing as well as several other cool links to its customer base, shareware sites, search engines, and more.

Moshofsky/Plant Creative Services

http://moshplant.com

Using Shockwave and Director, its creative services can do anything for you or your company, including logos, image manipulation, illustration, presentations, and design. Check out what these folks have already done.

MultiMedia Dimensions New Horizons in Sight and Sound

http://www.mmdimensions.com

MultiMedia Dimensions is a full-service interactive multimedia and Web page design and consulting company helping people find the right business solutions for their needs and budget.

NetCasters, Inc.

http://www.netcasters.com/

Your site for customized Web services, including intranet and database system development, Web publishing, graphic design, site hosting, consulting, and more. Check out NetCaster's electronic portfolio.

NetWorXs of California

http://www.garlic.com/~dennisa/

Offers a full range of Web home page authoring and design services. Also offers full turn-key systems, including training in-house personnel so that you can enhance your Web server as your services or products change.

Program One Online Service

http://www.prgone.com/

Helps businesses and individuals learn and exploit the Internet culture. Provides information about Internet marketing, and explains how companies can survive their ride on the Information Superhighway.

RAMWORKS

http://www.ramworks.com/ramworks/

Provides cutting-edge technology blended with award-winning traditional design to offer interactive multimedia services, Internet presence, Web pages, CD-ROM and CD-I authoring, interactive touch-screen kiosks, and corporate communications.

Stannet WWW Designing and Publishing Company

http://www.webcom.com/~stannet

Focuses on authoring, designing, and publishing Web pages for businesses and individuals. Performs custom graphics work and maintains and upgrades customers' sites as needed. Offers to meet customers in their offices in the greater New York City area.

Vannevar New Media

http://www.vannevar.com

An Internet publishing and applications company that puts businesses on the Web. Located in Houston, it boasts a strong NASA influence.

WebCom Publishing

http://www.webcom.com/html/

A comprehensive guide to Web publishing, this site tells you everything about how to access the Web to how to design your own Web site. It discusses authoring tools, has a FAQ section, and offers an icon index.

Web Developer

http://pubs.iworld.com/wd-online/

An online publication for programmers, Webmasters, network administrators, and other technically oriented personnel, responsible for developing and maintaining software, hardware, and security on the Web.

Web Publishing Australia

http://www.Hughes.com.au/

A professional Web publishing and promotion company based in Queensland, Australia.

WebDesigns

http://www.webdesigns1.com/

A Web page creation service. Focuses on posting and maintenance, logo and graphic design, photography (including improvement of existing photographs), image maps, online newsletters, and getting your page listed in directories like this one, among others.

Related Sites
http://www.3rdeye.net/
http://www.swcp.com/~fugelso/kelley/iworks95/
http://www.ozemail.com.au/~coreweb/
http://www.icox.com/
http://www.xmission.com/~americom/integra-credit.html
http://www.jandaweb.com/
http://www.moonbeach.com/index.html
http://www.bee-eater.demon.co.uk/parity/welcome.html
http://www.protocom.com/protomall/Protocom/bizresrc/WebPAL/
http://www.plonka.com/

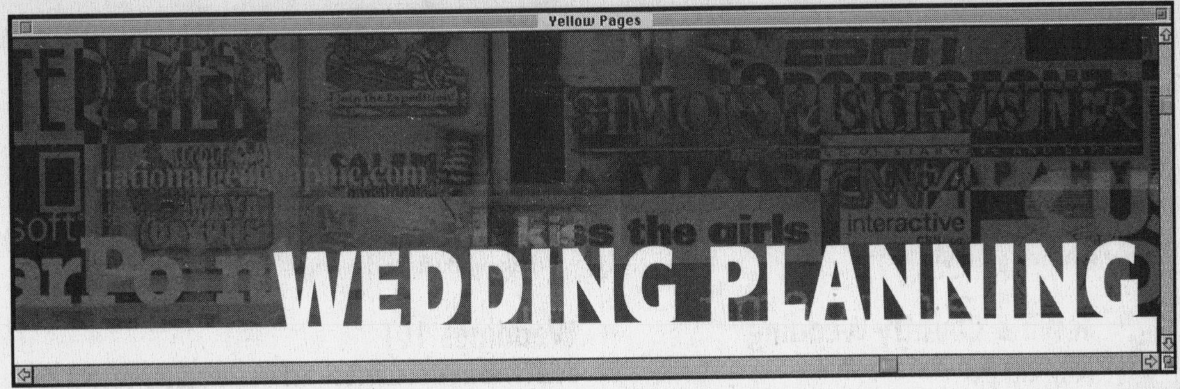

> A wedding invitation is beautiful and formal notification of the desire to share a solemn and joyous occasion, sent by people who have been saying "Do we have to ask them?" to people whose first response is "How much do you think we have to spend on them?"
>
> *Miss Manners*

Bridalink Store

http://www.bridalink.com/store2/

The Bridalink site is an online store known to have low prices on accessories, such as wedding cameras. In addition, visitors can register for monthly give-a-ways.

Great Bridal Expo

http://www.greatbridalexpo.com/

This site features information about the Great Bridal Expo, a bridal show that tours to various cities throughout the United States. From this site you can find out more about the Expo's exhibitors, special events, dates, and locations throughout the U.S. You can even order the tickets for the show online!

The Knot: Weddings For The Real World
http://www.theknot.com/plx.cgi?script=index.html

Modern Bride
http://www.modernbride.com/

Today's Bride Online Magazine
http://www.todaysbride.com/

Town & Country Wedding Registry
http://tncweddings.com/index.html

The Knot: Weddings For The Real World

http://www.theknot.com/plx.cgi?script=index.html

This site is the ultimate wedding resource: 3,000+ wedding-related articles, 6,000 searchable gown pictures, how-to's plus daily hot tips, a 24-hour chat room, and special personalized planning tools. This is definitely one of the most comprehensive, useful bridal planning sites on the Web.

Modern Bride

http://www.modernbride.com/

Features a peak at the current issue of *Modern Bride* magazine. Contains sections covering just about anything wedding-related, plus a chat room and tip of the day.

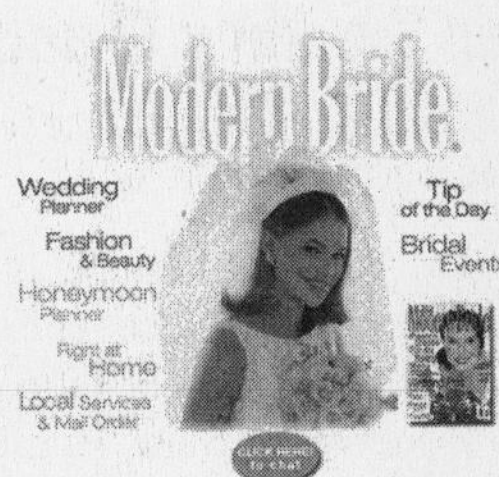

My Wedding Companion

http://www.jaxnet.com/~fivestar/

Offers My Wedding Companion, wedding planning software. From the site, you can download a free trial copy of the software.

Today's Bride Online Magazine

http://www.todaysbride.com/

Picked as a Yahoo! Pick of the Week!, *Today's Bride* magazine's Web site is very user friendly, including a search engine to help you find specific topics. There is even an online bridal consultant to help you with your toughest questions.

Town & Country Wedding Registry

http://tncweddings.com/index.html

From *Town & Country Magazine*, this site contains not only their special wedding issue, but also a wealth of other wedding information. A Registry section allows couples to specify where they are registered, and friends and family can access this information. Overall, this site is a complete source for wedding fashion, planning, and much, much more!

unGROOM'd

http://www.ungroomd.com/home.html

The ultimate wedding site for men, the unGROOM'd home age provides a forum where men can discuss various wedding issues. It also provides helpful wedding information written in a tone especially designed for men.

WayCool Weddings

http://waycoolweddings.com/home.htm

Features an alumni section with links to other couples' personal wedding Web pages. This is a great way to get ideas for your own wedding. In addition, there are links to a variety of wedding resources and a section of humorous wedding stories, called "Giggles."

The Wedding Channel

http://www.weddingchannel.com/go/Gateway/WeddingChannel/Intro

The Wedding Channel is an all-encompassing wedding resource. It contains the following wedding-related sections: Fashion & Beauty, Local Businesses, Honeymoon Suite, Home & Registry, Wedding Planner, and Groom's Corner. The Wedding Planner section has tips from wedding planning expert Beverly Clark, author of the best selling book, *Planning a Wedding to Remember.*

The Wedding Plan-it

http://www.weddingplan-it.com/

Create your personal wedding Web page at no cost through this site. You also will find valuable wedding planning information through "The Wedding Assistant", and by searching a listing of various wedding products and services.

Weddings 101

http://www.geocities.com/Heartland/Plains/6244/

Are you just getting started planning your wedding? This site has great wedding information and advice to help you in planning your perfect day. With information getting organized, all the way to writing thank you notes, this site is a must-see for all wedding planners.

Weddings on Hawaii, Kauai, Maui, and Oahu.

http://www.creativeleisure.com/hawaii/weddings/weddings.html

Are you thinking of marrying in the Hawaiian Islands? This site offers special wedding packages for each of the islands. Your dream wedding could be only a Web site away!

WedNet – The Internet's Premier Wedding Planning Site, Wedding, Bride, Groom, Marriage, Love.

http://www.wednet.com/

Contains numerous wedding-related articles with tips for every aspect of wedding planning. In addition, you can search for other Internet resources and wedding vendors, visit the "WedNet" library, and even register for a free subscription to their monthly newsletter.

Your Formalwear Guide

http://www.tuxedos4u.com/

A complete guide to men's tuxedos. You can view the latest styles in tuxedos, and use the "store finder" to locate the closest place to rent your tuxedo. In addition, the site has a question and answer section to aid you in selecting the appropriate tux for your occasion, and a worksheet to help organize your tuxedo needs.

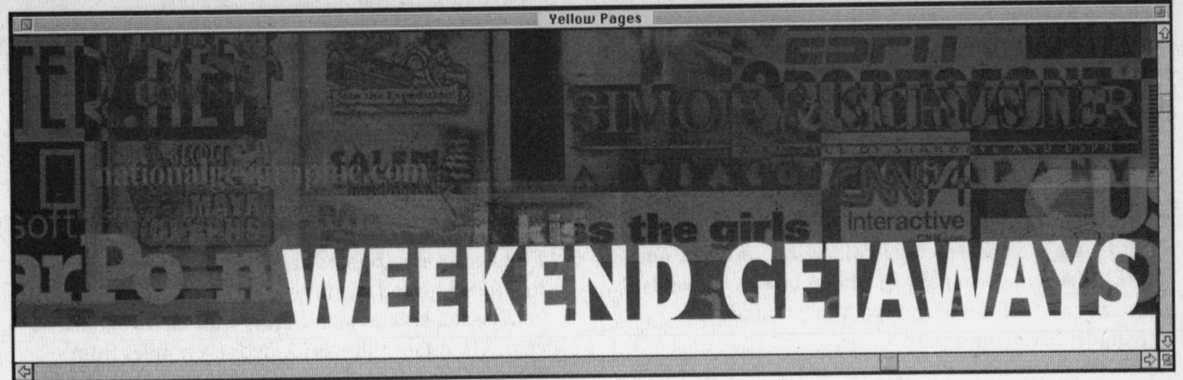

A vacation frequently means that the family goes away for a rest, accompanied by mother, who sees that the others get it.

Marcelene Cox

1st Traveler's Choice: America's Bed and Breakfasts, Country Inns, and Small Hotels

http://www.virtualcities.com/ons/0onsadex.htm

Info on lodging across the U.S., Canada, and Mexico. Search by state, province, type, or languages spoken by innkeepers. Includes *Country Inns* magazine, the *Inn Times*, *Virtual Cities' Trade Show*, and the Gourmet Directory of hundreds of recipes from innkeepers. New inns added weekly.

Amusement Park and Roller Coaster Links

http://users.sgi.net/~rollocst/amuse.html

Here, you'll find links to amusement and theme parks, water parks, fun centers, roller coasters, and Disney parks. Learn about all the Six Flags theme parks; Knott's Berry Farm in Buena Park, CA; Cedar Point in Sandusky, OH; Paramount's Kings Island in Cincinnati, OH; Wet 'N Wild in Orlando, FL; and many more.

1st Traveler's Choice: America's Bed and Breakfasts, Country Inns, and Small Hotels
http://www.virtualcities.com/ons/0onsadex.htm

Amusement Park and Roller Coaster Links
http://users.sgi.net/~rollocst/amuse.html

GORP—Great Outdoor Recreation Pages
http://www.gorp.com/gorp/resource/main.htm

Balsam Shade Resort

http://www.balsamshade.com/

This is country family resort located in the foothills of the Northern Catskill Mountains (Greenville, NY). Activities include springtime whitewater rafting down the Hudson River Gorge, bicycling, and hiking the trails of the Catskill Park. Several golf courses and museums are nearby. Other activities include horseback riding, visiting amusement parks, and taking a trip to Reptiland. Recent events included an acoustic music festival, a biathlon challenge, and the Annual Catskill Mountain Snowmobile Grass Drags.

Cheshire Cat Inn

http://www.cheshirecat.com/cat/

Located in Santa Barbara, CA, this Victorian inn is surrounded by flowers, brick patios, and redwood decks. Features Laura Ashley furnishings, Chinese rugs, and English antiques. Offers 17 guest rooms, suites, and cottages. Some rooms have in-room Jacuzzis, fireplaces, private decks, and outdoor hot tubs. Rates include a full gourmet breakfast and an afternoon wine hour with hors d' oeuvres and crudities. Located four blocks from several shops, restaurants, and theaters. Site includes descriptions (as well as some photos) and rates for each room.

Destinations Magazine

`http://www.travelersguide.com/destinations/destcovr.htm`

Check out the Happenings section for fun things to do around the country, listed by state. Visit Nevada for Rodeo Days, attend the Music Festival in New Jersey, see the horse racing in Maryland, or check out the hydroplane boat races in Arkansas. Recommends eateries and off-the-beaten-path vacation ideas. Includes back issues.

GORP—California National Forests

`http://www.gorp.com/gorp/resource/US_National_Forest/careg.HTM`

GORP (Great Outdoor Recreation Pages) describes all the national forest in California. Click the city you're interested in to view details on activities such as hiking, fishing and hunting, camping, and picnicking, mountain biking, and sightseeing. Also includes descriptions of canyons. You'll also find the locations and phone numbers of the district ranger stations.

GORP—Great Outdoor Recreation Pages

`http://www.gorp.com/gorp/resource/main.htm`

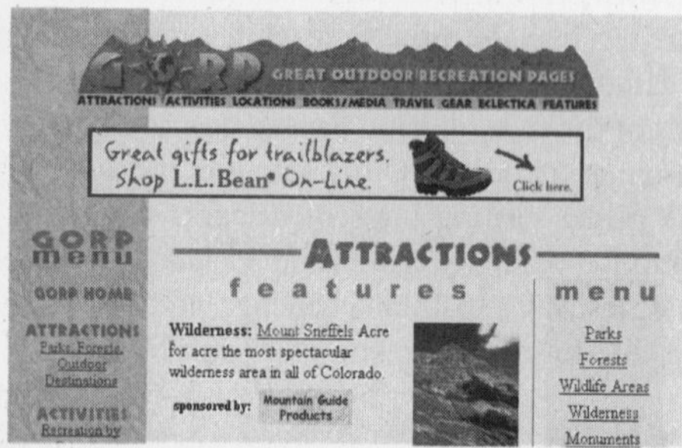

Your guide to U.S. parks, forests, wildlife areas, wildernesses, monuments, rivers, scenic drives, national trails, beaches, recreation areas, historic sites, and archaeology sites. Get advice on equipment, apparel, and accessories; travel and lodging; maps and tours; and features and activities for each destination. Visit the photo gallery of beautiful outdoor scenes, get tips on staying healthy while you travel, and investigate ideas of where to take your kids and pets on your next outdoor adventure. Also includes stories submitted by people who have visited some of these areas. Includes recipes, tips, and cooking gear recommendations. Also lists clubs and associations that promote outdoor recreation, conservation, ecology, and education, and provides a section for outdoor resources for the disabled, including special access and trails.

Mountain Villas

`http://www.digitel.net/smokymtn/mtnvillas/`

Nestled at the foothills of the Great Smoky Mountain Park, The Mountain Villas is a resort community consisting of 50 chalets and villas. The villas feature full kitchens, living rooms, and vary in size from one to four bedrooms (photos provided). The property includes a heated swimming pool, workout room, arcade, and several picnic areas with tables and barbecues. Mountain Villas is located seven miles from Pigeon Forge (home of the Dixie Stampede, Dollywood, and music theaters) and nine miles from Gatlinburg (entrance to the Great Smoky National Park).

The Old Carriage Inn Bed and Breakfast in Shipshewana

`http://www.kuntrynet.com/artoci/`

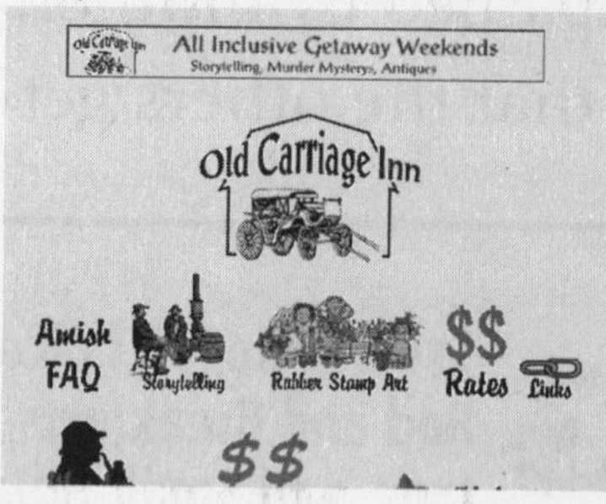

This B&B is located in the midst of Indiana Amish farmlands. You'll have access to crafts boutiques, country stores, specialty shops, and the Shipshewana Flea Market. Features the art of storytelling—each weekend hosts a professional storyteller. Also includes Murder Mystery Weekends; you're an active part in the mystery as it unfolds. Or, attend a Rubber Stamp Art Workshop Weekend to learn new skills and make some great projects. Includes an Amish FAQ and a weather conditions and forecast page.

Romantic Getaways—Bed & Breadfast Inns—Index

`http://site209070.primehost.com/loveandromance/bb-index.htm`

This site enables you to search for romantic B&Bs in the U.S. by state. Each listing provides the name, address, phone number, rates, room types, and other pertinent info for the romantic B&B it describes.

St. Paul Recommends–Destinations (Minnesota)

http://www.wcco.com/bestof/destinations/brainerda.html

One of the 10 best Minnesota sites recommended in *Mpls St. Paul Magazine*, the Brainerd Lakes area is located 125 miles north of the Twin Cites in central Minnesota. It features 450 lakes within a 15-mile radius and access to some of the state's best resorts, golf courses, and fishing holes. This site recommends three places to stay, where to eat, what to see, what to buy, and which local amusements to check out. Don't miss the weekly turtle races during the summer. Also includes Brainerd International Raceway with drag, Classic, and Formula One racing. And, hey—it's the home of Paul Bunyan.

St. Paul Recommends–Destinations (Wisconsin)

http://www.wcco.com/bestof/destinations/wisc/bayfield.html

One of the 10 best Wisconsin sites recommended in *Mpls St. Paul Magazine*, the Bayfield Peninsula is located on the south shore of Lake Superior, east from Duluth-Superior to Ashland. Bayfield is a fishing village, and not much has changed there since the 19th century, except that many of the old homes are now B&Bs. Bayfield offers a quiet countryside and fruitful orchards. Set sail for the 22 Apostle Islands and visit their six lighthouses open to the public. Visit Madeline Island, which features a great golf course, or see rustic Big Bay State Park, which is 20 minutes by ferry from Bayfield. Amusements include Big Top Chautauqua, which features concerts, plays, lectures, and historical re-enactments. Or, visit Isle Vista Casino, Red Cliff Reservation. You'll get recommendations for two places to stay and several places to eat.

Sunrise Farm Bed & Breakfast, Salem, South Carolina

http://www.virtualcities.com/ons/sc/u/scu7701.htm

Sunrise Farm is a restored 1890 Victorian farmhouse inn surrounded by scenic lakes, forests, and waterfalls. It is at the high foothills of the Blue Ridge Mountains and minutes from Clemson University. Offers farmhouse rooms with queen beds and private baths; or, stay in a cottage with a kitchen, fireplace, bedroom, and bath. Each room features unique family antiques and handmade quilts. A country breakfast is served each morning by the fire in the dining room or the parlor. Hike the Blue Ridge mountain trails or ride the white water of the Chattanooga River.

This Is Satya

http://www.montelis.com/satya/backissues/feb97/getaways.html

Satya is a magazine of vegetarianism, environmentalism, and animal advocacy. The February 1997 issue lists vegetarian/vegan B&Bs, hotels, retreats, and yoga centers in upstate New York and New Jersey. Most destinations are two to two-and-a-half hours away by car from New York City.

This Week in the Poconos Magazine Online

http://www.thisweek.net/

This e-zine includes info about B&Bs, country inns, lodging, dining, hiking, and more. Lists airports, upcoming events, church services, libraries, movie theaters, museums and galleries, and points of interest. Also features a guide to searching for antiques, tips on shopping, and information on state parks.

Related Sites
http://www.virtualcities.com/ons/dude.htm
http://www.sunsol.com/ccvd/genlinfo/martinfo.html
http://www.virtualcities.com/ons/fishdex.htm
http://www.gorp.com/gorp/resource/us_nra/main.htm
http://www.gorp.com/gorp/resource/US_National_Park/main.htm
http://www.gorp.com/gorp/resource/US_National_Forest/main.htm
http://www.virtualcities.com/ons/nc/nconydex.htm
http://www.palmsprings.com/
http://site209070.primehost.com/loveandromance/hr-index.htm
http://www.virtualcities.com/ons/skiing.htm

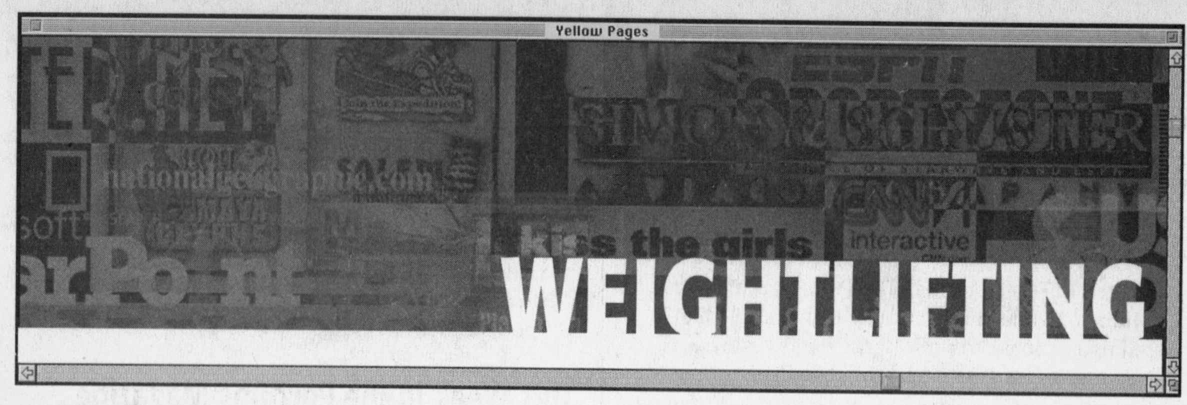

> By constant self-discipline and self-control you can develop greatness of character.
>
> *Greenville Kleiser*

Powerlifting.com `http://www.powerlifting.com/`
Training with Fred Hatfield `http://www.ipf.com/fredhome.htm`
WttP Weightlifting `http://www.waf.com/bin/windex.pl`

Absolute Records

`http://www.geocities.com/Colosseum/3027/lift.htm`

Here you can find out what the world records currently are in almost every imaginable weightlifting and powerlifting event.

American Drug-Free Powerlifting Association

`http://www.adfpa.com/`

Also known as "USA Powerlifting," this site has a lot to offer. It lists match results, contest schedules, drug testing information, and rules, and has links to many other sites, including sports medicine.

International Powerlifting Federation

`http://www.ipf.com/`

Everything a powerlifter needs to know about training, competition, and classification. A great site with tons of links! (Note that this is not the "drug free" type of powerlifting; you'll find info for that sector of the sport at `http://www.adfpa.com` instead.)

Muscle Shack

`http://www.users.zetnet.co.uk/prowland/mshack.htm`

Lots of bodybuilding articles and tips, ranging from leg workout suggestions to dietary supplement advice. A great potpourri for browsers.

Powerlifting.com

`http://www.powerlifting.com/`

A great gateway site that points to almost every imaginable powerlifting site on the Web. Includes federations, match results, how-tos, and lots more.

Training with Fred Hatfield

`http://www.ipf.com/fredhome.htm`

Lots of great articles about powerlifting technique, conditioning, and diet. A must for any serious lifter!

USA Weightlifting

`http://www.usaw.org/`

The home page of the United States Weightlifting Federation, the governing body for Olympic weightlifting in the USA. Includes results of recent matches and organizational info.

Weightlifting: Olympic Lifters on the Web

`http://www.waf.com/weights/lifters.htm`

An alphabetical listing of people on the Internet who have an interest in Olympic-style weightlifting. Browse the list to see if there's anyone you know, or add yourself to the list.

Weights.net

`http://www.weightsnet.com/`

An interactive daily discussion group for people interested in weightlifting. You can browse daily archives or contribute to today's discussion.

WttP Weightlifting

`http://www.waf.com/bin/windex.pl`

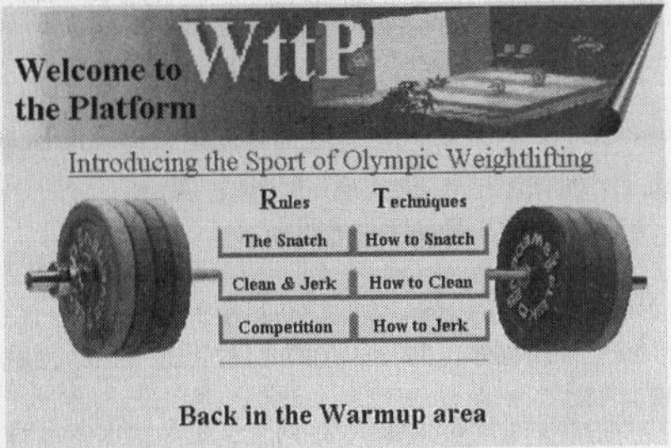

An excellent introduction to Olympic-style weightlifting, including rules, techniques, a calendar, a coaching area, and a message board. A great place for someone with Olympic aspirations to start planning.

NEWSGROUPS

`alt.sport.weightlifting`

`misc.fitness.weights`

Related Sites

`http://www.compusmart.ab.ca/bozena/body.htm`

`http://www.geocities.com/Colosseum/4000/`

`http://www.ironmanmagazine.com/`

`http://ageless-athletes.com/`

`http://www.nasa-sports.com/`

`http://www.powerup.com.au/~miles/`

`http://www.strengthtech.com/`

`http://www.geocities.com/Colosseum/Field/7342/`

`http://student.uq.edu.au/~s315413/uq_power.htm`

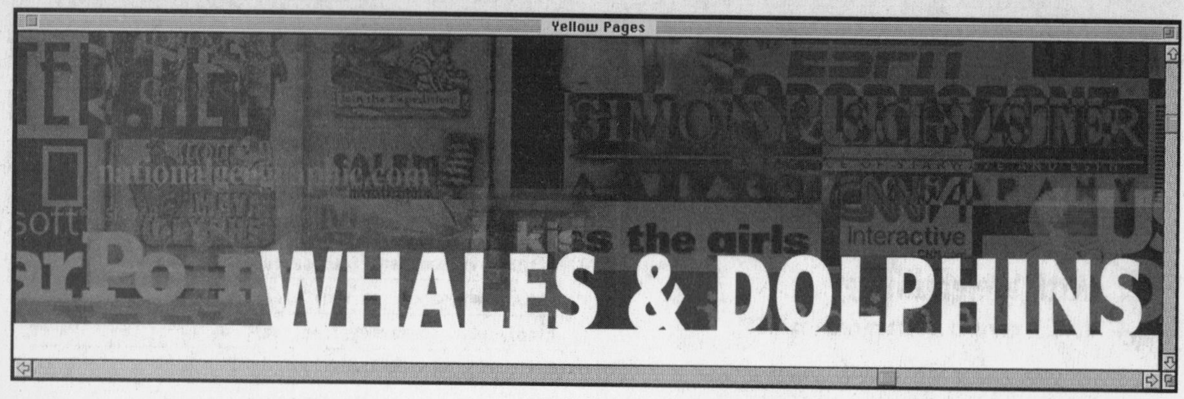

> Though pleased to see the dolphins play, I mind my compass and my way.
>
> *Matthew Green*

Dolphin Information Server—Home Page
`http://elpc54136.lboro.ac.uk/`

Whale Adoption Project Home Page
`http://www.Webcom.com/~iwcwww/whale_adoption/waphome.html`

Whales on the Net
`http://whales.magna.com.au/home.html`

Killer Whales: Birth and Care of Young

`http://crusher.bev.net//education/SeaWorld/killer_whale/birthkw.html`

SeaWorld site that offers images and information about the birth and care of killer whales.

The Dolphin Alliance

`http://envirolink.org/arrs/ahimsa/tda/`

The Dolphin Alliance is a citizen's action group established in 1992 that works to preserve dolphin and whale rights and the protection of their environment. The Alliance has several goals, including working to stop all capture of whales and dolphins within U.S. waters. The group hopes to do this through public education and legislative reform.

Dolphin Information Server—Home Page

`http://elpc54136.lboro.ac.uk/`

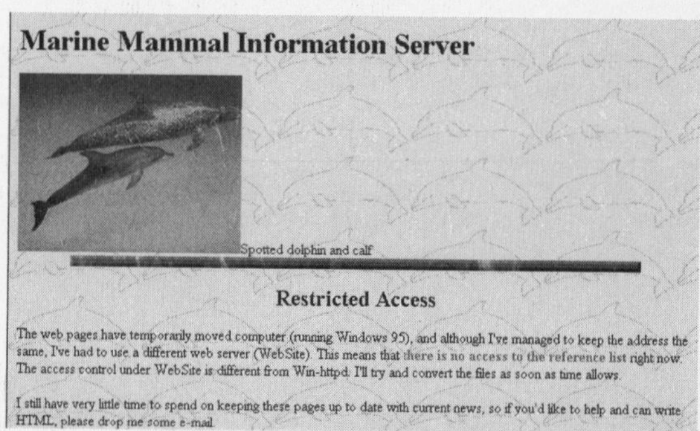

Marine Mammal Information Server
Spotted dolphin and calf
Restricted Access
The web pages have temporarily moved computer (running Windows 95), and although I've managed to keep the address the same, I've had to use a different web server (WebSite). This means that there is no access to the reference list right now. The access control under WebSite is different from Win-httpd. I'll try and convert the files as soon as time allows.
I still have very little time to spend on keeping these pages up to date with current news, so if you'd like to help and can write HTML, please drop me some e-mail

Serves as a simple resource for pictures and information on dolphins, killer whales, and other marine mammals. Includes information about Keiko (the whale in the motion picture "Free Willy").

Marine Mammals

`http://www.earthwatch.org/t/Toceans.html`

The Earth Corps is tracking the migration of marine mammals including whales and dolphins. This site provides links to other centers conducting research, as well as to Wild Dolphin Societies in Florida, Hawaii, and New Zealand. Take the opportunity to sign up for one of several Earth Watch expeditions in 1997 which will focus on exploring dolphin intelligence.

Whale Adoption Project Home Page

http://www.Webcom.com/~iwcwww/whale_adoption/waphome.html

Learn how you can adopt a humpback whale for yourself or as a gift for a friend. View photos of humpback whales and learn how the whaling industry is threatening the survival of this species. Features "Whalewatch," a newsletter of the Whale Adoption Project.

The Whale Rescue Team

http://www.istrada.com/whalerescue/index.html

Site of a group of volunteers that take to the sea to rescue California grey whales from the death grip of commercial gill nets. Check out the latest rescue story.

Whale Songs

http://kingfish.ssp.nmfs.gov/songs.html

Presents the sounds of whales. Includes a small archive of audio files.

The Whale Watching Web

http://www.physics.helsinki.fi/whale/

Serves as the whale-watchers network on the Internet. Offers pictures, information about whales, information about countries around which whales are active.

Whale Watching

http://www.tombarefoot.com/whale.html

Cool site that offers whale watching trips and information on whales and whale watching seasons.

Whales on the Net

http://whales.magna.com.au/home.html

Children will really enjoy viewing the many photographs of whales and then sending a description of their favorite one via email. They'll also find drawings submitted by children, song lyrics, news stories, and even an Exit Exam! The photo galleries and whale watching updates are a big plus.

The Wild Dolphin Project

http://wwwa.com/dolphin/project.htm

The Wild Dolphin Project was started in 1985 to study the history and communication systems of Atlantic spotted dolphins in the Bahamas. The project focuses on understanding dolphin behavior, interactions, and communication. This colorful Web site offers information about the project and includes photos, background info on dolphins, and information on how you can join an expedition.

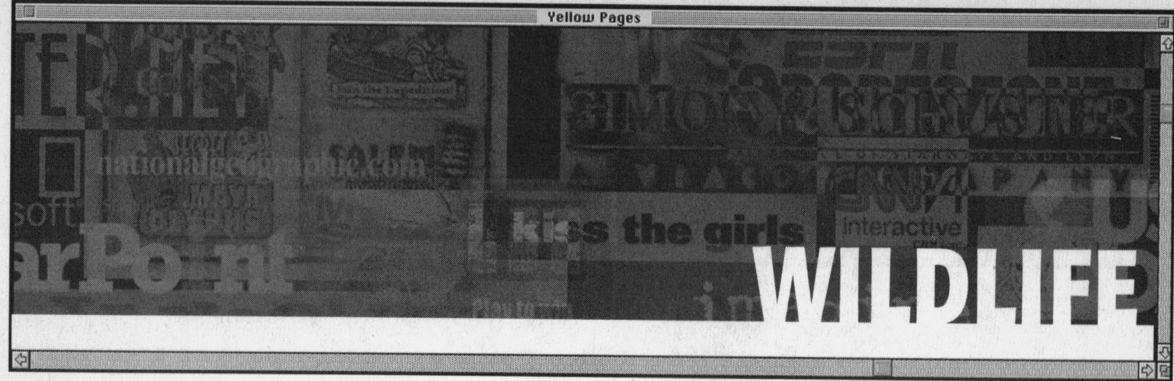

WILDLIFE

> Like the resource it seeks to protect, wildlife conservation must be dynamic, changing as conditions change, seeking always to become more effective.
>
> *Rachel Carson*

NRP Top Picks

Armadillo Online
`http://pilot.msu.edu/user/nixonjos/index.htm/index.htm`

The Bear Den
`http://www.nature-net.com/bears/`

GORP—Nature & Wildlife
`http://www.gorp.com/gorp/activity/wildlife.htm`

LlamaWeb
`http://www.webcom.com/~degraham/`

WWF-Global Network-World Wildlife Fund
`http://www.panda.org/home.htm`

Adam's Fox Box

`http://tavi.acomp.usf.edu/foxbox/`

This colorful, graphics-filled, and award-winning site gives you the scoop on everything you ever needed to know about the fox. Points you to articles, books, stories, songs, and poems, photos, and more. Great site for kids and adults alike.

Animal Lives

`http://gaia.earthwatch.org/ed/olr/animal.html`

How many carnivore species live in the tropical dry forests of southwestern Mexico? Scientists are attempting to answer this and many other questions through the projects they discuss on this Web site. Maintained by Earthwatch, the site also includes photographs of such animals as mountain lions, moose, and wolves.

Armadillo Online

`http://pilot.msu.edu/user/nixonjos/index.htm/index.htm`

Great photos and a lot of fun facts about armadillos. Find out how armadillos are being used in research to cure leprosy and visit the Fast Facts file which dispels some of the common misconceptions about these armored mammals.

Bat Conservation International

`http://www.batcon.org/`

Listen to an audio tape of "Bat Chat", explore the Educator's Activity book, or read the annual report of Bat Conservation International to learn of their accomplishments in preservation, education, and research. Visit the "Masters of the Night Exhibit" to find out the truth about bats.

The Bear Den

`http://www.nature-net.com/bears/`

This site, which contains a wealth of information and photos about bears, provides up-to-date information about initiatives to protect endangered grizzlies. Describes the evolution of bears and details the different species, including the Brown, Polar, and Panda bears. Includes a link to The Cub Den, a new Web site for children that contains bear info geared to young readers. A sound file enables you to hear a bear roar.

Cochrane Ecological Institute

http://www.cuug.ab.ca:8001/~scholefp/swiftfox/

Focuses on reintroducing the swift fox species back into the wild. Stylish, colorful, and contains good reading. Includes links to other sites, such as the International Wildlife Coalition and the African Wild Dog Conservation Fund.

Deer Net

http://www.deer.rr.ualberta.ca/

Focuses on the impact of humans on Canadian wildlife and their habitats. Provides interesting facts on the grizzly and livestock diversification. Provides some species information including the white tail deer, which can be found in every state in the Continental US.

Eastern Slope Grizzly

http://www.rr.ualberta.ca/~lmorgant/grizzly.html

Concerned about human land use and grizzly bear mortality, environmental groups and other agencies formed the Eastern Slopes Grizzly Bear Steering Committee in 1994. This group works to identify and implement research that will predict the effects of development on grizzly bears. This site describes the Committee's activities and also includes photos of grizzlies.

GORP—Nature & Wildlife

http://www.gorp.com/gorp/activity/wildlife.htm

Provides information about almost any conceivable animal-related topic—from bird watching to protection/preservation societies, including the U.S. National Parks, U.S. National Forests, U.S. National Monuments, and U.S. Fish and Wildlife Service.

Hyenas

http://www.csulb.edu/~persepha/hyena.html

Focuses on the much maligned and misunderstood spotted hyena, a carnivore that roams the deserts of Africa. Includes lots of photos. This award-winning site garnered the "Point Survey Top Five Percent of the Web."

Introduced Wild Animals in Australia

http://rubens.anu.edu.au/student.projects/rabbits/wildanim.html

Provides detailed information on Australian wildlife evolution. Takes an intriguing look at the impact of animals, such as the cane toad, English starling, rabbit, and fox, that were introduced into the Australian ecosystem—and subsequently altered the habitat of the wildlife already there.

Kaehler's Mill Farm

http://www.execpc.com/~slc/k-m.html

Contains information about Galloway cattle and Targhee sheep. Describes a farming technique called Management Intensive Grazing. Interesting site for those curious about cattle and sheep farming.

LlamaWeb

http://www.webcom.com/~degraham/

This site focuses on llamas, the South American camelid. Contains pictures of llamas, the lineage of specific llamas, and all about llama shows, products, literature, and llama associations. The site has been voted among the top five percent of Web sites by Point Communications, and also received a four-star rating by Magellan.

Manatees

http://www.bev.net/education/SeaWorld/manatee/manatees.html

Provides information on the habits, habitat, diet, and just about anything else you would want to know about the manatee. Sponsored by Sea World Education Department, this site also contains links to Sea World of Florida, Texas, California, and Ohio.

A B C D E F G H I J K L M N O P Q R S T U V W X Y Z

OSU's Breeds of Livestock

http://www.ansi.okstate.edu/breeds/

Showcases a comprehensive list of the various breeds of livestock, including cattle, goats, horses, sheep, and swine. Sponsored by the Department of Animal Science, Oklahoma State University, this site also provides background information and terminology on animal breeds.

The Polar Regions

http://www.stud.unit.no:80/~sveinw/arctic/wild.html

Offers links to arctic wildlife and resources, including wolves, foxes, polar bears, and Antarctic life.

Turtle Trax—A Marine Turtle Page

http://www.turtles.org

Provides information on marine turtles, which are larger and more interesting than the ones from the store. Also points out that marine turtles are endangered and explains the issue, including how you can help.

The International Wolf Center

http://www.wolf.org/

Provides the history and mission of the International Wolf Center. Features links to related sites and a searchable telemetry database of the movements of wolves through the Superior National Forest. Includes a chance to listen to the howl of the wolf, pictures of wolves, and links to newsgroups that cover wolves.

The Wolf's Den Website

http://www.wolfsden.org/

This site provides information on wolves and wolf recovery, as well as Native American info, amateur radio, and more. Provides updates on brutality incidents against wolves. Includes wolf photos and graphics.

Wolf Resource Page

http://www.greywolf.com/wolf.html

Lists wolf resources and provides special reports on wolf-related news throughout the country.

The Wonderful Skunk and Opossum Page

http://elvis.neep.wisc.edu/~firmiss/mephitis-didelphis.html

Do you know the difference between a possum and an opossum? Find out about that and other interesting facts at this Web site. Contains drawings and newsgroup information, skunk and possum trivia, stories, photos, further reading, and a little historical perspective about these two critters.

The World Wide Raccoon Web

http://www.loomcom.com/raccoons

Features pictures, stories about raccoons, raccoon wildlife management, and links to a raccoon lovers' mailing list.

Wombats, Marsupials, and Other Animals

http://www.batnet.com/wombat/animals.html

Serves as a resource site for marsupials as well as other kinds of existing and extinct species in the animal kingdom.

WWF-Global Network-World Wildlife Fund

http://www.panda.org/home.htm

The World Wildlife Fund is the world's largest independent conservation organization. Read of the history and activities of the WWF and their mission and goals to the year 2000. Also find Weekly Earth Reports, fact sheets, project reports, and a searchable database of publications.

WWF-World Wildlife Fund-Canada

http://www.wwfcanada.org/

This site focuses on conservation efforts in Canada by the World Wildlife Fund. A FOR KIDS ONLY section introduces children to preservation and conservation and how they can help. The site includes detailed maps of Canada, fact sheets about endangered species, and links to other environmental sites.

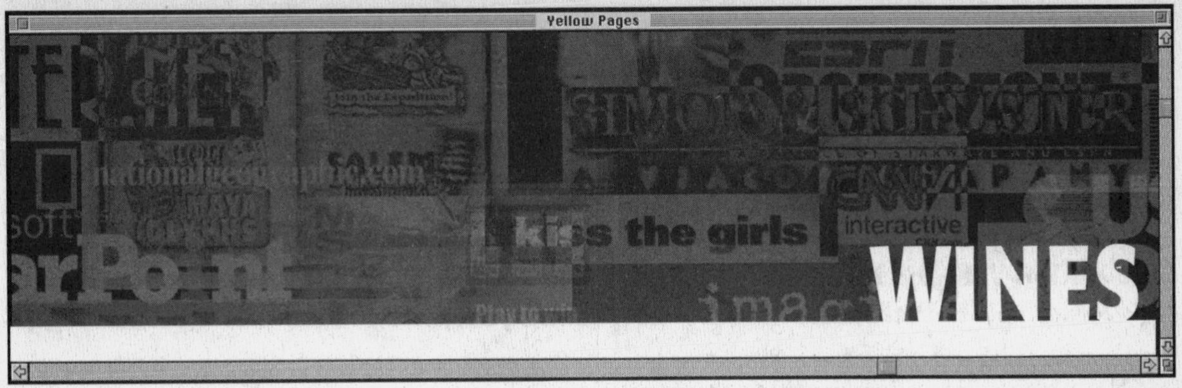

Let schoolmasters puzzle their brain,
With grammar, and nonsense, and learning,
Good liquor, I stoutly maintain,
Gives genius a better discerning.

Oliver Goldsmith

1st Class Wine Accessories

http://www.21stcenturyplaza.com/wine/wine.html

Online catalog offers wine glasses, racks, books, videos, and more. Also contains wine-related gizmos and gadgets, such as bottle tags and a label saver.

Asia Wines

http://www.asiawines.com/

Specializes in wines from the Asia Pacific region. Lists the currently available wine selections, wine clubs, merchants and wholesalers, auctions, and more.

Bordeaux
http://www.bordeaux.com/

Napa Valley Virtual Visit
http://www.freerun.com/cgi-bin/home.o

Virtual Vineyards
http://www.virtualvin.com/vvdata/620506318/main.html

The Wine Broker
http://www.TheWineBroker.com

The Wine Diary
http://www.silcom.com/~wdiary/

WINE: UC Davis Department of Viticulture & Enology
http://wineserver.ucdavis.edu

Bob Levine's Wine Page

http://www.princetonol.com/biz/wine

An independent non-commercial page that recommends current wines, instructs in wine tasting methods, and provides links to other valuable wine pages.

Bordeaux

http://www.bordeaux.com/

Learn all about Bordeaux wines and how they are made. You can download your own vintage chart and learn how to have a wine-tasting party. Even provides recommendations for Bordeaux-friendly restaurants.

Buyers & Cellars

http://www.BandC.com/

This site focuses on wine education. It helps you gain the confidence to enjoy wine and feel comfortable ordering it. You learn how to find bargain wines, the characteristics of different grapes, the correct temperature to serve wine, and more.

California Wine Connection

http://www.wineconnection.com

Specializes in fine and rare wines from California and a few other places. Most of these wines are limited and sold on a first-come-first-serve basis.

Celebration Vineyards

http://www.deltanet.com/intersphere/cv

Offers custom-labeled champagne and sparkling cider table favors for weddings and other special occasions.

Cellar Masters of America

http://www.cellarmasters.com/

Site claims to be "currently the *only* authorized interstate shipper of wine on the Web." Features wines from the United States and imports from Austria, France, and Italy. Site provides a secure online ordering system and a link to pronunciation guides for French food and wine.

The Connoisseur

http://www.theconnoisseur.com/

Showcases a selection of gifts that can be customized with a personal message or a company logo. Gifts include a wooden gift box, a personalized label, and a gift card. Gift categories include wines, novelty, gourmet, wedding, crystal, and more.

Cork n' Beans

http://www.galleria.net/corknbeans//

Cork n' Beans is a specialty retailer in fine wines, gourmet coffee, and custom gift baskets. The home page includes a monthly newsletter, info on free wine tastings, and details on their exclusive wine club. They also are associated with Luau Florist (FTD).

The Cyber Cellars at City Wine

http://www.citywine.com

City Wine, a storefront, sells and ships wines from around the world. Try the monthly features at their double-discounted price.

Fetzer Vineyards

http://www.fetzer.com/

This producer of organically farmed wines is the sixth largest premium winery in the country. In addition to checking out their wine, you can find out more about their environmentally conscious policies.

Grapevine

http://www.terra.net/grapevine

An Internet e-zine that provides reviews and information about international wines and vineyards. Also provides links to wine-related newsgroup archives.

Gruppo Italiano Vini

http://www.giv.it/

This company not only produces and distributes Italian wine, it also manages historic wine cellars. See where the cellars are located on a map of Italy, and read about company news and information.

International Wine Society

http://www.sierra.net/tiws

Become a member of the International Wine Society and order wine and spirits with the Wine of the Month Club. This club offers wine connoisseurs the chance to taste wines from the best vineyards wine country has to offer. Your Wine Club Membership also opens the door to a world of wine accessories and gourmet foods.

Julie's Brewery

http://ourworld.compuserve.com/homepages/d_muir

Wine, wine recipes, and wine tips galore in this straightforward site. No wine snobbery on this winemaking page; just wine, wine, and more wine.

Microsoft Wine Guide Online on MSN, The Microsoft Network

http://www.microsoft.com/wineguide/

The Microsoft Network presents Microsoft Wine Guide, a fun, informative guide for wine lovers offering an extensive wine database, practical information about how to choose the right wine, news about the world of wine, and tips from the world's leading wine experts.

Napa Valley Virtual Visit

http://www.freerun.com/cgi-bin/home.o

Explore various Napa Valley wineries or purchase wines and wine-management software. This site provides sightseeing, dining, and catering ideas, as well as current events. If you're looking to make a "real" visit, check out the information about accommodations. Also contains links to other Valley sites.

Silver Spirits Monthly

http://www.silver-spirits.com/

This site contains a newsletter published monthly by owner Barry Silver that showcases what's best in new and current wine releases. Provides links to domestic wines and wines from other countries. Sign up for the mailing list to be eligible for discounts.

SmartWine Online

http://smartwine.com/

Claiming to be the largest wine-related site on the Web, SmartWine Online provides links to a variety of sites devoted to wine. Peruse some wine tasting notes before you imbibe, select the best wine to complement your meal, glean some health facts about wine, and find out all about the wine industry, all with the click of your mouse.

South African Wines

http://www.capeventures.com/

Describes the history of South African wines as well as the industry today. Also reviews wines, lists distributors, and provides some South African recipes.

Table Wine

http://www.tablewine.com

This page is dedicated to discussing affordable wines. Generally, the selections highlighted range from $10 to $20 a bottle. A different topic is discussed each month, from Sinful Zins to Wines for Winter Stews.

Taste Tour Home Page

http://www.winetaste.com/

Your guide for gaining "instant wine expertise." Have to entertain clients or impress your stuffy boss? The TasteTour WineGuides can get you through. These quick wine references contain all you need to know and can be ordered from this site

Texas Wine Trails

http://www.neosoft.com/~scholars/texas.htm

There's more than just oil in Texas. Site provides information about the Texas winemaking industry. Includes a brief history of Texas wine, a map of the 27 wineries there, and a list of the grapes planted.

Vampire Vineyards

http://www.vampirewine.com/

The Vampire line of wines is imported from Transylvania, Romania, and includes Merlot, Pinot Grigio, Pinot Noir, Sauvignon Blanc, and Cabernet Sauvignon. You also can purchase unique Vampire Vineyards merchandise, including posters, baseball hats, T-shirts, and wine glasses.

Vergina Imports, Inc.

http://www.greekwines.com/

This Canadian company imports Greek wines and spirits. Learn about Greek vineyards, read the company's profile, and view a list of the award-winning wines this company sells.

Vine House Essential—Luxury Wines and Hampers

http://www.vinehouse.co.uk

Vine House provides bulk cases of quality wines, most of which are not available in shops in the UK. Use the search engine for specific wines or browse through the comprehensive wine list. Also sells original bottle stoppers.

The Vineyard Collection

http://www.winecollection.com/

This list-heavy site contains information about French wines. Includes news, specials, label, producer, retailer, price, and awarded wines lists. Also contains links to other wine-related Web sites and to French wine bars.

Vinometer

http://www.vinometer.com/

This thin plastic thermometer can be placed on the outside of wine bottles to monitor their temperature. A demonstration is provided at this site, along with ordering information.

Virtual Vineyards

http://www.virtualvin.com/vvdata/620506318/main.html

Your one-stop wine shop provides online shopping for regional California wines by varietals, wineries, and vineyards. Also provides a section that pairs food with the appropriate wine accompaniment. Be sure to check out What's New at Virtual Vineyards.

A B C D E F G H I J K L M N O P Q R S T U V W X Y Z

What's the Big Occasion?

http://www.topher.net/~occasion/

This company enables you or your business to send personalized greetings or gifts to friends, family, and customers. Send personal or corporate gifts of wine, champagne, coffee, tea—all with your customized label or message.

Wine & Price

http://www.wine-auction-world.com/

The new Wine & Price Yearbook covers all relevant wine auctions worldwide, comprehensively listing all auction results to provide 100,000 prices of more than 15,000 wines from 1,000 wine regions located throughout the world, as achieved in 150 international wine auctions in 1995/96.

Wine Access

http://www.wineaccess.com

A complete guide for all wine lovers. Extensive information highlighted by a wine selection tool. Designed for everyone from the experienced collector to the interested beginner.

The Wine Authority

http://www.wineauthority.com/

This site claims to review wines before most other publications. The editor and publisher of this newsletter personally visits and tastes all wines reviewed. Site also contains hot news from the wine industry as well as member and newsletter subscription information.

The Wine Broker

http://www.TheWineBroker.com

Contains wine and wine-related information for all types of wine lovers, from casual to connoisseur. Site offers holiday gift packages, a monthly wine club, a list of rare wines, and more.

The Wine Diary

http://www.silcom.com/~wdiary/

A wine lover's paradise. This wine guide to France highlights all the best vineyards. Maps identify wine-producing regions and link you to specific descriptions and history.

Wine Enthusiast

http://www.wineenthusiast.com/

This site sells wine-related accessories, from cellars to corkscrews to cigars. Of course, it also sells wine itself, including specials and samplers. Sign up for a free catalog.

Wine Technologies Home Page

http://www.wineprices.com

Site showcases software for serious wine collectors to help manage wine inventory and keep track of aging. Software includes a wine database, a view of your cellar, and The Wine Price File.

Wine Time

http://www.netaccess.on.ca/entrepr/winetime

Established in 1963, Wine Time is a manufacturer and wholesaler of quality wine- and beer-making supplies. Also offers a wide selection of award-winning wine kits.

WINE: UC Davis Department of Viticulture & Enology

http://wineserver.ucdavis.edu

The wine home page of the Department of Viticulture & Enology at UC Davis, the oldest wine and grape research institution in the world, offers information about wine science, home wine making, wine extension classes, wine literature, wine weather, wine aroma, wine URLs, wine and health, wine travel, and more.

Wines on the Internet

http://www.wines.com/

A provocative resource for wine-related topics. Provides links to online wineries and vineyards, features a "virtual" tasting room, online wine shopping, and other notes of interest for the connoisseur and novice wine drinker alike. Also details upcoming events for wine enthusiasts.

World Wide Web Winemaking Home Page

http://www.uidaho.edu/~stevep/wine/winehome.html

Provides recipes and information on making your own wine. Also provides links to suppliers, other recipe pages, downloadable software to make your own wine labels, and other wine-related sites

Your Personal Wine Service

http://www.WineLovers.com/

A personal wine consultant can help you with all your wine questions and needs. Can't find the wine you want? Want something you can afford without sacrificing taste? This is the place to come for guidance. Site also offers help in planning vacation trips to wine country.

FTP & GOPHER SITES

ftp://ftp.catalog.com/aussie/wines

ftp://ftp.demon.net/pub/humour/python/wines

ftp://ftp.doc.ic.ac.uk/park/Events/Cannes/wines.htm

ftp://ftp.hhmi.swmed.edu/pub/private/merlot

ftp://ftp.infohaus.com/infohaus/by-seller/Wine_Tips_Online/Merlot_Magic.free.txt

ftp://ftp.math.ncu.edu.tw/pub/weihan/perl/chap05/sess02/wines

ftp://ftp.ultra.net/pub0/l/landau/public_html/wines

ftp://ftp.wwa.com/pub/wines

gopher://gopher.opal.com/11//grapevine

LISTSERVS

FINEWINE–God Street Wine List

You can join this group by sending the message "sub FINEWINE your name" to

listserv@netspace.org

FINEWINE-INFO–God Street Wine Info List

You can join this group by sending the message "sub FINEWINE-INFO your name" to

listserv@netspace.org

FOODWINE–Discussion List for Food and Wine

You can join this group by sending the message "sub FOODWINE your name" to

listserv@cmuvm.csv.cmich.edu

NEWSGROUPS

alt.food.wine

fj.rec.wine

man.winemaking

niagara.wine

rec.crafts.winemaking

Related Sites

http://WebWinery.com/Hallcrest/

http://www.americanwineries.org/

http://www.awinestore.com/

http://www.kresswine.com/

http://www.kwik-link.com/kwik-link/c/wine.html

http://www.invinoveritas.com/

http://www.primewine.com/

http://www.wchat.on.ca/public/wonderwine/index.htm

http://www.wine.com/

http://www.wineaustralia.com.au/

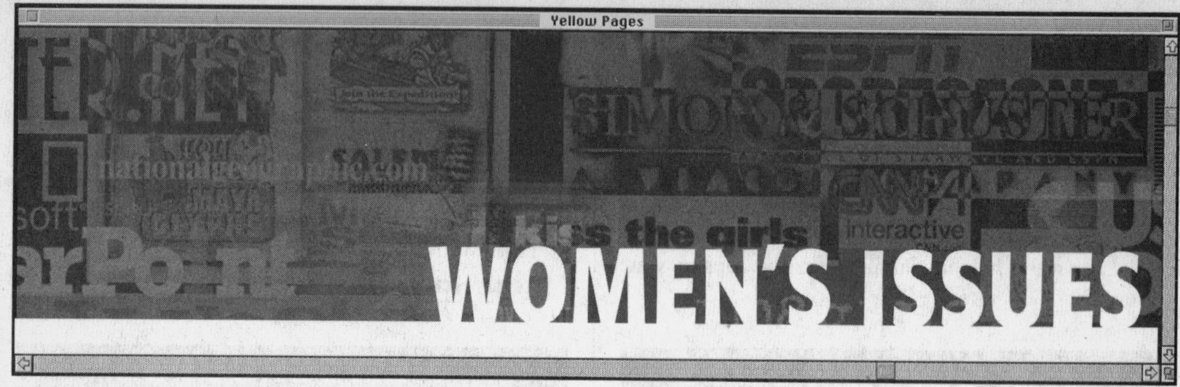

> The only question left to be settled now is: Are women persons?
>
> *Susan B. Anthony*

ACADEMIC/WOMEN'S STUDIES

American Association of University Women (AAUW)

http://www.aauw.org/index.html

The American Association of University Women is a national organization that promotes education and equity for all women and girls. This Web site describes AAUW issues, research programs, grants and fellowships, membership information, and much more.

Artemis Search for Women's Studies Programs

http://www.users.interport.net/~kater/

Search this database for Women's Studies programs in colleges and universities. Great for the high school student preparing to choose a college.

Related Sites

http://eserver.org/feminism/

http://humanitas.ucsb.edu/shuttle/gender.html

http://www.lib.uiowa.edu/gw/wstudies/

http://umbc7.umbc.edu/~korenman/wmst/links.html

Feminist Majority Foundation Online
http://www.feminist.org/

Centre for Women's Studies in Education (CWSE)

http://www.oise.on.ca/webstuff/departments/cwse1.html

This Web server in Toronto, Ontario, Canada is run by the Ontario Institute for Studies in Education. Among its many pages you will find project descriptions, research papers, information on CWSE publications, and links to women's studies sites worldwide.

Feminist Studies in Aotearoa Electronic Journal (FMST)

http://www.massey.ac.nz/~wwwms/FMST/Info.html

FMST is produced by and for those interested in feminist theory, feminist perspectives in philosophy, and contemporary feminist debates, publications and research, and is operated out of Dunebin, New Zealand. Besides an index of issues and online articles, FMST also provides a service called FMST-TALK for service subscribers.

Library Resources for Women's Studies

http://sunsite.unc.edu/cheryb/women/librcws.html

As the site title indicates, this page provides links to university and research center libraries across the U.S. that contain "useful or unique collections" related to women's studies. Includes Telnet, Gopher, FTP, and Web addresses.

Resources for Women's Studies on the Web

http://www.middlebury.edu/~jaj/women.html

An impressive list of links broken down into several major categories, including journals, databases, and history.

Women's Studies Database

http://www.inform.umd.edu:8080/EdRes/Topic/WomensStudies/

The women's studies database serves those people interested in the women's studies profession and in general women's issues. The searchable database contains collections of conference announcements, calls for papers, and employment opportunities, as well as a picture gallery, a significant number of government documents, and much more.

ARTS AND ENTERTAINMENT

Creating A Celebration of Women Writers

http://www.cs.cmu.edu/afs/cs.cmu.edu/user/mmbt/www/women/celebration.html

This site provides links to complete online editions of books by women writers. Currently an index by author is provided, with expansion plans in the works. Volunteers to help with this project are requested; submissions must be either public domain titles (such as the classics) or be authorized by the copyright holder.

Feminist Arts–Music

http://www.feminist.org/arts/linkmusic.html

An annotated list of feminist musicians, with links to the artists' home pages and/or fan club pages where you can get more information.

Feminist Bookstores

http://www.igc.apc.org/women/bookstores/booknets.html

This page provides a comprehensive listing of women's bookstores in the U.S. and Canada arranged by state and province. Includes postal addresses and Internet links (if applicable).

Feminist Science Fiction, Fantasy, & Utopia

http://www.uic.edu/~lauramd/sf/femsf.html

This site provides very detailed information on the page's title topic. An indexed bibliography, book reviews, and author biographies, as well as nonfiction information literary criticism, conferences, and much more. Also included is like information on related literary genres and links to related sites.

Film Reviews

http://www.inform.umd.edu:8080/EdRes/Topic/WomensStudies/FilmReviews/

Part of the inforM site, this page catalogs many feminist reviews of films. There are hundreds of films here, each thoughtfully reviewed.

Flicker

http://www.sirius.com/~sstark/

Flicker is a great source of information about alternative films. You can read about filmmakers, find out what's showing where, and download images from films.

Guerrilla Girls

http://www.voyagerco.com/gg/gg.html

The Guerrilla Girls are a group of women artists and arts professionals who make posters about discrimination. They dub themselves as the "feminist counterparts to the mostly male tradition of anonymous do-gooders like Robin Hood, Batman, and the Lone Ranger." Available online is information on their cause, reactions to their work, and, of course, posters for sale.

Her Own Words®

http://www.netphoria.com/herwords/

This Web site for Her Own Words® Women's History, Literature, & Art Videotapes gives company history, video reviews, an online newsletter, and ordering information. The videos produced by this company all present primary-source, first-person accounts of women's history that are recommended for educational use.

Lifetime Online

`http://www.lifetimetv.com/`

This is the World Wide Web extension of Lifetime Television, the women's network. Provides not only information about Lifetime's television schedule and programs, but articles on health and fitness, parenting, sports, and more. Includes a searchable index of topics covered.

Spinsters Ink

`http://www.lesbian.org:80/spinsters-ink/`

Spinsters Ink publishes novels and non-fiction works that deal with significant issues in women's lives from a feminist perspective. Included on their Web site are book reviews, ordering information, and submission information.

Women in the Arts

`http://www.a1.com/wia/`

WIA is the organization that produces the National Women's Music Festival, the oldest and largest all-indoor festival of women's music and culture, each June. Find out what they have in store for this year's festival, and learn more about this non-profit organization.

Women's Books Online

`http://www.cybergrrl.com/review/`

This site calls itself a cooperative book review, which means that it provides a place for women to post reviews of women's books available at women's bookstores. The only drawback is that submission instructions are not posted.

The World's Women On-Line!

`http://wwol.inre.asu.edu/`

The World's Women On-Line! is an electronic art networking project that was begun in conjunction with the Fourth World Conference on Women in September 1995. The above address takes you to a list of HTML pages; each page represents a particular artist. Unfortunately there does not seem to be a top page linking them all in HTML format.

Related Sites

`http://sunsite.berkeley.edu/Goldman/`

`http://www.nlc-bnc.ca/events/sci-fi/t1-7e.htm`

`http://www.echonyc.com/~women/`

CAREER AND WORK

The Ada Project

`http://www.cs.yale.edu/HTML/YALE/CS/HyPlans/tap/tap.html`

Provides resources and information for women in the computer sciences.

BizWomen

`http://www.bizwomen.com/`

BizWomen provides the online interactive community for successful women in business: to communicate, network, exchange ideas, and provide support for each other via the Internet. BizWomen also provides you with an Internet presence with your online "business card," a colorful online "brochure," or interactive "catalog," to make your products and services available online.

The Business Women's Network

`http://www.tpag.com/BWN/BWN.html`

The Business Women's Network, a division of Public Affairs Group, Inc., was designed to encourage communication and networking between the top businesswomen's organizations in the U.S. BWN is dedicated to the promotion of business and professional women by providing assistance to corporations, businesswomen's organizations and state and federal agencies.

Directory of Women-Owned Businesses

`http://feminist.com/busi.htm`

Categorized list of businesses owned by women. Browse for a business that offers what you need, or list your own business here (for a fee).

Enterprising Women

`http://www.iepublishers.com/EW/Pages/ewmain.stm`

A magazine for women business owners and entrepreneurs. Browse past issues, or subscribe to the print version.

Society of Women Engineers

`http://www.swe.org/`

Information about the Society, plus a resume database and job search help for female engineers. You can also subscribe to their magazine and find out how to submit articles for publication in it.

U.S. Department of Labor–Women's Bureau

http://gatekeeper.dol.gov/dol/wb/

Information about how the Women's Bureau is working to ensure women a level playing field in the work arena, including women's labor statistics and information about current programs the Bureau is sponsoring.

WIDNET (Women In Development Network)

http://www.synapse.net/~focusint/

The WIDNET site presents information pertaining to women's resources throughout the Internet. Also includes the WIDNET magazine, a searchable resource database, business contacts, and much more. Available in English and French.

Women's Business Ownership

http://www.sbaonline.sba.gov/womeninbusiness/

Produced by the U.S. Small Business Association, this page provides information and resource links for women currently running or seeking to run small businesses in the United States.

The Women's Resource Directory

http://www.ghgcorp.com/wordweb/index.html

A Houston-based site focusing on promoting and growing women-owned businesses. Includes a classified ad section, a marketplace, and many articles on business management and ownership.

Related Sites

http://www.aracnet.com/~wmnjourn/

http://www.itis.com/wihe/

http://www.women-networking.com/Welcome.html

FEMINISM AND FEMINIST POLITICS

Colleen's Feminism Home Page

http://pages.prodigy.com/HYEW27A/feminism.htm

This personal home page summarizes many women's issues, including nonsexist language, quotations, women's right to vote, and much more.

Cybergrrl

http://www.cybergrrl.com/cg.html

This site bills itself as the "First Stop on the Web" for women's resources. Includes articles, movie and book reviews, family information, and more. The server for this site also houses many other feminism-related sites.

Feminism and Women's Resources

http://www.ibd.nrc.ca/~mansfield/feminism/

A large collection of feminist and women's resources on the Internet.

FEMINIST.COM

http://feminist.com/

Feminist.com is a site aimed at helping women network more effectively on the Internet. Includes the abridged text of articles and speeches, women's health resources, women-owned businesses, and more.

Feminist Majority Foundation Online

http://www.feminist.org/

This site contains information on government actions for and against women, an online discussion group, publication information, and much more. There is also a shopping area where you can purchase feminist gifts, clothing, and other items.

Gender Equity in Sports

http://www.arcade.uiowa.edu/proj/ge/

Gender Equity in Sports is designed to serve as a resource for any individual investigating the state of affairs in interscholastic or intercollegiate sport. This site provides detailed information on this research project conducted at the University of Iowa.

A B C D E F G H I J K L M N O P Q R S T U V W X Y Z

A B C D E F G H I J K L M N O P Q R S T U V W X Y Z

Global Fund for Women

http://www.igc.apc.org/gfw/

The Global Fund for Women is an international organization that focuses on female human rights. Includes information on supported programs, news articles, a FAQ sheet, and describes what you can do to help.

Internet Resources for Women's Legal and Public Policy Information

http://asa.ugl.lib.umich.edu/chdocs/womenpolicy/womenlawpolicy.html

This guide at the University of Michigan is intended to assist individuals seeking information related to women's and feminist legal, public policy, and political issues. Included are gopher, WWW, and FTP sites; as well as Listservs and Usenet newsgroups. An ACSII version of the index is available for download, if you want a hard copy of the URLs provided.

Linkages FOURTH WORLD CONFERENCE ON WOMEN site

http://www.iisd.ca/linkages/4wcw/

This site provides summary information about the Fourth World Conference on Women that was held in Beijing, China, during September of 1995; the first such conference in 10 years. Includes news articles, photographs, sound files, and more.

The National Organization for Women (NOW)

http://www.now.org/

This home page for NOW offers press releases and articles, issues NOW is currently involved in, information on joining (with email or Web addresses for many local chapters), and the history of NOW. Also provided is a search form if you're looking for a specific topic at NOW's site.

Resources for Feminist Research/ Documentation sur la recherche féministe (RFR/DRF)

http://www.oise.on.ca/rfr/

RFR/DRF is a bilingual (English/French) Canadian scholarly journal at the Ontario Institute for Studies in Education which addresses Canadian and international feminist research issues and debates. At this Web site you will find abstracts of current and back issues, calls for papers, and subscription information.

The United Nations and the Status of Women

http://www.un.org/Conferences/Women/PubInfo/Status/Home.htm

This site from the United Nations provides information about what the UN has done during its 52-year history to further the status of women. Included are conference findings, general articles, and commission reports.

Voices of Women Online

http://www.voiceofwomen.com/VOWworld.html

This online women's group offers articles, an electronic newsletter, snail-mail magazine subscriptions, lists of women's conferences, links to women-owned businesses, and much more. As the site introduction states, "In these pages, real women are telling their stories, discussing issues, sharing hard-won wisdom."

The *Women & Politics* Home Page

http://www.westga.edu/~wandp/w+p.html

Women & Politics is an academic journal published at West Georgia College in Carrollton, GA. The goal of the journal is to foster research and the development of theory on women's political participation, the role of women in society, and the impact of public policy upon women's lives. Included online are article abstracts, calls for papers, and subscription information.

Women Leaders Online (WLO)

http://wlo.org/

WLO is an organization dedicated to stopping the Radical Right/Contract With America agenda. This Web site contains information about Women Leaders Online and a variety of other women-related issues.

WomensNet

gopher://gopher.igc.apc.org:70/11/women

http://www.igc.apc.org/womensnet/

WomensNet is a non-profit computer network for women, activists, and organizations using computer networks for information sharing and increasing women's rights. WomensNet provides email accounts, Internet access, WWW publishing, consulting, and training. Site contains WomensNet's online newsletter and descriptions of projects in which the group is currently involved.

Women's Wire

http://www.women.com/

This online magazine includes sections on news and entertainment, career information, a question and answer area, links to women's businesses, and much more. There is an archive area for perusing back issues, and a "Guide" to find just the subject you're looking for.

Yale Journal of Law and Feminism

http://www.yale.edu/lawnfem/law&fem.html

The *Yale Journal of Law and Feminism* is committed to publishing pieces about women's experiences, especially as they have been structured, affected, controlled, discussed, or ignored by the law. This Web site contains subscription information, Telnet access to past issues, the chance to submit your own article, and even order a T-shirt.

Related Sites

http://www.indiana.edu/~iupress/journals/cam.html

http://www.eskimo.com/~feminist/nownetin.html

http://www.fnsa.org/

GIRLS AND YOUNG WOMEN

Cybergrrl Webstation

http://www.womenspace.com/

Targets young women and girls. Offers promos and free stuff. Sponsored by The Women's Pharmacy, which enables women to shop at home for pharmacy products.

Expect the Best from a Girl

http://www.academic.org/

This site prepared by the Women's College Coalition contains information about what parents and others can do to encourage girls in academic areas, particularly math and the sciences. Includes a listing of programs and institutes that can be contacted.

Feminist Fairytales

http://www.wp.com/Dragontree/fftmenu.html

A collection of non-sexist fantasy stories for children, in which strong heroines succeed.

Girl Power!

http://www.health.org/gpower/index.htm

The national public education campaign sponsored by the Department of the Health and Human Services to help encourage and empower 9- to 14- year old girls.

Girls Incorporated

http://www.girlsinc.org/

An organization dedicated to "Helping girls become strong, smart, and bold." This site includes research and advocacy information, membership info, and more.

Girl Scouts of the U.S.A.

http://www.gsusa.org/

For every girl who enjoys scouting and every adult woman whose life was enhanced by scouting. Girl Scouts can find out about special events and activities, order uniforms and equipment, and read about the history of Girl Scouting; adults can participate in an alumni search, and learn how to volunteer.

Related Sites

http://www.pbs.org/pov/girls/

http://www.teenspeak.com/

http://www.teenworld.com.my/

http://www.kotex.com/girlspace/

HISTORY

Diotima: Women & Gender in the Ancient World

http://www.uky.edu/ArtsSciences/Classics/gender.html

This Web site is intended to serve as a resource for anyone interested in patterns of gender around the ancient Mediterranean and as a forum for collaboration among instructors who teach courses about women and gender in the ancient world. Includes research articles, course materials, a comprehensive bibliography, and more.

Encyclopedia of Women's History

http://www.teleport.com/~megaines/women.html

Part of a "K12-opedia," this site presents essays, stories, poetry, and so on about women in history researched and written by K–12 students worldwide.

Instructions are given for adding your own (or your child's) work to the site. (Sorry, it is requested that submissions be in English.)

Notable Women

gopher://gopher.emc.maricopa.edu/11/library/notablewomen

A database containing information on notable women. Find anything you want on women such as Susan B. Anthony, Annie Jump Cannon, and Blanche Ames.

Upper Midwest Women's History Center

http://www.hamline.edu/../depts/gradprog/whc_html/whc.html

Information about who in Women's History is important, along with a collection of resources, a newsletter, and the center's current program offerings.

Women in Aviation History

http://www.ninety-nines.org/bios.html

Biographies and tributes to the prominent women in the history of aviation, including Louise Sacchi, Fay Gillis Wells, and Bessie Coleman. Interesting!

Women's History Month

http://socialstudies.com/mar/women.html

This Web site, part of the Social Studies School Service, provides teachers with several lessons, student exercises, and reviews of special materials that present exciting ways to bring women's history into their classrooms. Topics include Women in Wartime, American Women at Work, Amelia Earhart, and others.

Related Sites

http://userpages.aug.com/captbarb/

http://scriptorium.lib.duke.edu/wlm/

http://www.niagara.com/~merrwill/

http://pigseye.kennesaw.edu/~ccaldwel/victoria.htm

HOME AND FAMILY

The Child Support Home Page

A direct link to the U.S. Federal Office of Child Support Enforcement, providing policy documents, explanations of current laws, and links to state agencies. There is also a direct email link to the Office.

The CyberMom Dot Com

http://www.TheCyberMom.com/

A cool, kitschy site with a lot of 1950s graphics, where online moms can find information and support. You'll find everything from recipes to video game reviews here, as well as a discussion area where moms can "vent."

The Daycare Page®

http://www.thegrapevine.com/

The Daycare Page® is an information service of the National Daycare Alliance. The highlight of this site is a list of thousands of daycare providers all over the U.S.

Divorce Law Home Page

http://www.agate.net/~corbeau/lyons.html#toc

Essentially an ad for a divorce lawyer offering his services, but with some helpful information and links, including a state-by-state explanation of Family Law, newsgroups and mailing lists, and information about insurance, retirement funds, social security, and other issues involved in a divorce.

The Equal Marriage Rights Home Page

http://www.nether.net/~rod/html/sub/marriage.html

Provides information about laws and statutes currently in force or pending affecting the legality of same-sex marriages in each state of the U.S.

Family.Com

http://www.family.com

An attractive, graphics-laden site that offers fun tips and hints for family life. Offers message boards, chat areas, and articles. The articles are somewhat focused on crafts—a random trip to the site found instructions for making cupcakes, a holiday wreath, and a gingerbread house.

Feminist Mothers at Home

http://www.millcomm.com/~pvallen/fmah.html

Feminist Mothers at Home is a discussion group for thinking women who choose to stay at home with their children. This discussion group offers a positive feminist voice to the issues that surround mothering. It's a LISTSERV you join, but you can get information about the group from the Web page listed above.

Parent Soup

http://www.parentsoup.com/

This aptly-named site is a hodgepodge of helpful information for parents, everything from baby care advice to horoscopes for kids. Also features live chats and online polls.

Rainbow Kids

http://www.rainbowkids.com/

An online publication that supports and encourages international adoption. Many well-written and informative articles, and good-looking graphics.

TASC: The American Surrogacy Center, Inc.

http://www.surrogacy.com/index.html

Comprehensive information on surrogate childbearing, including message boards, classified advertising, a directory of agencies and groups, and articles about surrogacy.

RELATIONSHIPS AND SEXUALITY

alt.romance.chat

In this busy newsgroup, you'll find plenty of people, women and men, eager to talk about romantic relationships, offer advice, and commiserate with your situation. And surprisingly enough, is not a pickup spot, so don't worry about getting hit on!

CRLP: Women of the World

http://www.echonyc.com/~jmkm/wotw/

This site provided by The Center for Reproductive Law & Policy, Inc., provides a review of women's reproductive freedom in six countries around the world—Brazil, China, Germany, India, Nigeria, and the United States. Each country's pertinent laws and policies are discussed on a wide range of topics.

Related Sites

http://www.women.com/work/best/

http://www.millcomm.com/~pvallen/fmah.html

http://www.millcomm.com/~pvallen/fmah/parentin.html

Eve's Garden

http://www.evesgarden.com/index.html

Too embarrassed to shop in your local sex shop? Offended by the sexist images? Then here's a refreshing change! The Eve's Garden catalog of sexual accessories, toys, books and videos is a new and enlightened look at sexuality that celebrates the joy of sex in a sex-positive and non-sexist manner.

Good Vibrations

http://www.goodvibes.com/

Good Vibrations is a worker-owned cooperative with two retail stores, a publishing company called Down There Press and two catalogs, Good Vibrations and The Sexuality Library. They sell quality sex toys for women at a reasonable price, in a straightforward, non-sleazy environment.

Match.Com Online Matchmaking

http://www.match.com

This fun, colorful site is devoted to matching up available and compatible people with one another. Full membership costs around $10 a month, but you can browse for free, and try a 10-day free trial.

Web By Women, For Women

http://www.io.com/~wwwomen/

Lots of solid, unbiased, non-sleazy information about sexuality, pregnancy, contraception, and more.

RELIGION

Bridges

http://weber.u.washington.edu/~iowen/bridges/

This site offers information and support for Jewish feminists. You can find out how to join a Listserv discussion group for Jewish feminist women and how to order a print copy of the Bridges magazine.

Related Sites

http://www.a-womans-touch.com/

http://ng.netgate.net/~allannah/kweb/

http://www.geocities.com/Wellesley/1374/

Christian + Feminist

http://www.users.csbsju.edu/~eknuth/xpxx/index.html

Many articles, reviews, and directories that support the premise that feminism can co-exist peacefully with the historically patriarchal Christian religion.

Christian Women

Christian Women is a women-only discussion forum "for Christian women who use the Internet for personal, domestic, business, and/or ministry activities." To subscribe, send the message SUBSCRIBE CHRISTIAN_WOMEN *YourEmailAddress* to MAJORDOMO@ICLNET.ORG.

CWIA's Women's Spirituality Page

This Canadian-based page provides links and resources to information about a variety of religions as they relate to women and feminism.

Feminist-Theology

FEMINIST-THEOLOGY is an unmoderated forum for the academic discussion of Jewish and Christian feminist theology. Topics discussed include a feminist critique of traditional ways of doing theology and may cover all aspects of theological study. The list will also facilitate the exchange of information about publications and research in this area. To subscribe, send message SUBSCRIBE FEMINIST-THEOLOGY *Your Name* to MAILBASE@MAILBASE.AC.UK.

FEMREL-L

A Listserv devoted to the discussion of women, religion, and feminist theology. You can join this group by sending the message sub FEMREL-L *your name* to listserv@listserv.aol.com.

Machon Chana

http://www.machonchana.org/

A women's institute for the study of Judaism. This nicely done site helps educate Jewish women about their religion and culture.

Related Sites

http://www.cbpwi.com/

http://www.msawomen.org/

http://lark.cc.ukans.edu/cgiwrap/huxtable/home/webofoz

http://www.utoronto.ca/wjudaism/

SisterSpirit: Women Sharing Spirituality

http://www.teleport.com/~sistersp/

A women's spirituality organization honoring the Goddess in all her forms. They publish a print magazine, which you can order from this site.

Women in Islam

http://www.usc.edu/dept/MSA/humanrelations/womeninislam/

Interesting basic information about how women fit into the Islamic religion, mostly oriented toward those unfamiliar with Islam.

WOMEN OF COLOR

AfriNET

http://www.afrinet.net/main/

Although not specifically for women, AfriNET offers a wealth of information for all people of African descent. Especially helpful is their Information Retrieval System (IRS), with which you can search for specific women's issues.

The Amistad Research Center

http://www.arc.tulane.edu/

With more than 10,000,000 documents, the Amistad is acknowledged as the nation's largest independent African-American archives, as well as a leader in automation and advanced techniques. The Center also features extensive collection on Africa, other minorities, and the gay rights movement.

and still WE rise

http://tigger.cc.uic.edu/~vjpitch/

A good list of resources for feminists in general but especially those interested in African-American women's culture.

The Ethnic Woman International

http://www.thefuturesite.com/ethnic/

An online periodical with well-written articles on the political, social, and economic rights and realities of women of color.

Related Sites

http://www.bwip.org/

http://www.corpdiversitysearch.com/

GirlFriend

A Listserv group for black women. You can join this group by sending the message sub GIRLFRIEND *your name* to listserv@home.ease.lsoft.com

WOMEN'S HEALTH

Abortion & Reproductive Rights

`gopher://gopher.well.sf.ca.us/11s/Politics/Abortion`

Whether you are pro-choice or pro-life, this Gopher will be of interest to you. Read Choice Net, a weekly newsletter that has the latest news on reproductive rights around the world. You will also have access to archives of press releases and other informative files on the legal aspects of abortion.

Avon's Breast Cancer Awareness Crusade

`http://www.pmedia.com/Avon/avon.html`

Provides information about breast cancer and breast health. Includes a list of more than 250 breast cancer support groups across the country.

Breast Cancer Information Clearinghouse

`http://nysernet.org/bcic/`

Provides information for breast cancer patients and their families.

Bright Innovations

`http://www.earthlink.net/~bright/`

Provides tutorials and explanations of techniques regarding cervical cancer screening.

Emergency Contraception

`http://opr.princeton.edu/ec/ec.html`

Provides information about prescription emergency contraception such as ECPs, minipills, and the copper-T.

Health and Science

`http://www.polaris.net/~health/`

Offers a specialty health food store and a guide to understanding and controlling PMS, fertility, menopause, and osteoporosis.

Health Articles by Patricia Older

`http://pages.prodigy.com/HYEW27A/womart.htm`

Articles include information on acupuncture, exercise, walking, and "dancing away the menopause blues."

OB/GYN Toolbox

`http://www.cpmc.columbia.edu/homepages/morrowj/tools/tools.html`

An educational resource for the medical community. Contains a body surface area calculator, endometriosis scoring, a gestational age calculator, and an OB ultrasound analyzer.

Planned Parenthood Federation of America

`http://www.igc.org/ppfa/`

Home page for Planned Parenthood, the world's oldest and largest voluntary family planning organization. Includes resources on sexual & reproductive health; contraception/birth control/family planning; pregnancy; STDs, including HIV; sexuality education; abortion; pro-choice advocacy; reproductive rights; and extensive Internet links.

S.P.O.T.: The Tampon Health Web Site

`http://critpath.org/~tracy/spot.html`

Women dedicated to informing other women through "articles and information about the hazards of synthetic tampon use and resources for healthy alternatives."

Web By Women, For Women

`http://www.io.com/~wwwomen/`

Provides feminist information about pregnancy, contraception, abortion, menstruation, censorship, and sexuality.

WomenCare

`http://www.womencare.com/`

For women over 40. Discusses hot flashes, breast exams, PAP tests, and other resources.

Related Sites

`http://www.womenshealth.org/`

`http://www.noah.cuny.edu/pregnancy/pregnancy.html`

`http://www.natlbcc.org/`

`http://www.cancerbacup.org.uk/info/cervix.htm`

If there was a law, they was workin' with maybe we could take it, but it ain't the law. They're workin' away our spirits, tryin' to make us cringe and crawl, takin' away our decency.

Tom Joad in The Grapes of Wrath *(1940)*

American Board of Industrial Hygiene

http://www.abih.org/

This non-profit company administers exams that certify employees in industrial hygiene. You can find out more about the test here, and review past test questions.

American Industrial Hygiene Association

http://www.aiha.org/

"Dedicated to the anticipation, recognition, evaluation, and control of environmental factors arising in or from the workplace that may result in injury, illness, impairment, or affect the well-being of workers and members of the community." Includes links to public relations, continuing education, and government affairs pages.

EMF-Link
http://infoventures.com/

Federal Emergency Management Agency
http://www.fema.gov/

Office of Occupational Safety and Health (OSHA)
http://www.osha.gov/

American Society of Safety Engineers

http://www.asse.org/

This professional organization for safety engineers sponsors an annual conference, which you can read about online, and issues several safety publications.

Bureau of Labor Statistics

http://stats.bls.gov/

If you are interested in the statistical side of workplace safety, you will find plenty of numbers here. Read about current and past surveys and programs, or visit the publication and research paper archive.

Chemical Safety

http://www-portfolio.stanford.edu/100369

Look up a chemical with this searchable index by name, Stanford Number, or Chemical Abstract Number, and find out what the proper handling of the chemical should be. (It doesn't say so on the page, but you can use the * wildcard if you don't know the correct spelling.)

Computer Related Repetitive Strain Injury

http://engr-www.unl.edu/ee/eeshop/rsi.html

Contains an introduction to RSI, symptoms, prevention, and sites to learn more about the problem.

CTD News Online

`http://ctdnews.com/`

Covers repetitive motion injuries. Includes information on massage therapy on the job, tips for safe lifting, carpal tunnel syndrome, and back issues of the *CTDNews* magazine.

Eastern Analytical Services

`http://www.EASInc.com/`

An independent environmental and industrial hygiene laboratory established to provide analytical services for such containments as radon gas, formaldehyde, hydrocarbons, volatile organic compounds, PCBs, pesticides, and metals.

EMF-Link

`http://infoventures.com/`

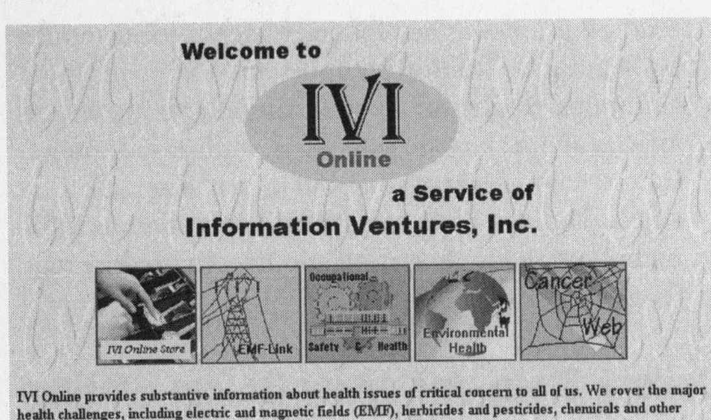

Welcome to
IVI
Online
a Service of
Information Ventures, Inc.
IVI Online Store
EMF-Link
Occupational
Safety & Health
Environmental Health
Cancer Web
IVI Online provides substantive information about health issues of critical concern to all of us. We cover the major health challenges, including electric and magnetic fields (EMF), herbicides and pesticides, chemicals and other hazards in the workplace, pharmaceuticals, and cancer.

Provides information on biological and health effects of electric and magnetic fields from sources such as power lines, electrical wiring, appliances, medical equipment, communications facilities, cellular phones, and computers.

Environmental Health and Safety Information

`http://www-portfolio.stanford.edu/105351`

Many useful articles and procedures, provided by Stanford University primarily for on-campus use, ranging from biohazard information to lab inspection forms.

Federal Emergency Management Agency

`http://www.fema.gov/`

Lots of great stuff here, from an El Niño Loss Reduction Center to an Emergency Preparedness and Training library. You could spend an entire day here browsing.

Human Factors and Ergonomics Society

`http://www.hfes.org/`

This web site contains information about the Society, its member services, and activities. It also allows you to read late-breaking news, shop for HFES products, and submit membership and employment forms.

MSDS's on the Internet

`http://www.msc.cornell.edu/helpful_data/msds.html`

A source of links for Material Safety Data Sheets (MSDS's). There are also instructions for ordering them by fax.

Office of Occupational Safety and Health (OSHA)

`http://www.osha.gov/`

A full-service site containing everything from regulations to statistics. Essential reading for anyone involved in workplace safety!

OSHA-DATA

`http://www.oshadata.com/`

Private corporation offering safety inspection records of companies inspected by the U.S. Department of Labor Occupational Safety and Health Administration. OSHA-DATA will help determine which companies have a better commitment to the workplace environment.

Typing Injury FAQ

`http://www.cs.princeton.edu/~dwallach/tifaq/`

Provides general information about typing injuries, a list of items to replace or update a keyboard, alternative pointing devices, software monitoring tools, and new furniture.

Related Sites
`http://atsdr1.atsdr.cdc.gov:8080/atsdrhome.html`
`http://machine-17.orcbs.msu.edu/absa/`
`http://www.fshi.com/`
`http://www.cdc.gov/niosh/pit/`
`http://www.cdc.gov/niosh/homepage.html`
`http://chppm-www.apgea.army.mil/`
`http://www.nrc.gov/`

A B C D E F G H I J K L M N O P Q R S T U V W X Y Z

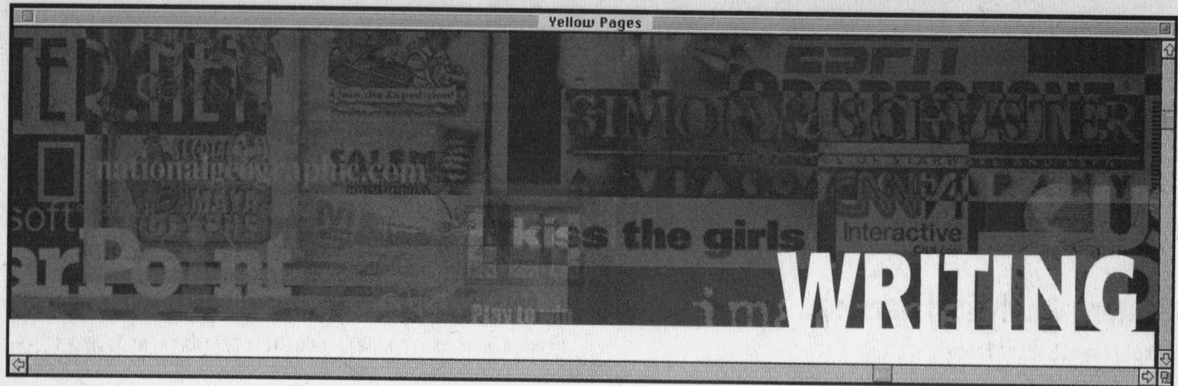

> You must write from the depths of your soul!
>
> *Friedrich Bhaer in* Little Women *(1994)*

Adobe.mag

http://www.adobemag.com/

An online archive of articles from Adobe's desktop publishing magazine. Many "how-to" articles searchable by title, subject, and date. You need Adobe Acrobat to view the articles.

Aspiring Writer

http://www.connet80.com/~aspire/New_aspire/index.html

An online magazine dedicated to new and established writers. Provides a chat room and editors ready to review your manuscripts, plus cartoons to brighten your writing days.

Authorlink!

Http://www.authorlink.com/

A Web site dedicated to authors, literary agents, and publishers. Contains book reviews, business news, competitions, links to publishers and agents, and insights into writing. Very comprehensive and gorgeous to view.

Black Star Press

http://www.blackstarpress.com/

An all-inclusive Web site for writers containing chat rooms, an online bookstore, writer's forums, literary event calendars, and writer's resource links. Also contains a link to Black Star Press itself (a poetry publisher).

Inkspot
http://www.inkspot.com/

Computer Book Cafe

http://www.studiob.com/

StudioB is a new type of literary agency for computer book authors. StudioB sponsors and maintains the Computer Book Cafe to offer computer book writers articles about the computer book industry, its publishers, fellow writers, financial information, tax advice, and a mailing list. StudioB also presents information on the organization and how to become represented.

Dakota State University Online Writing Center

http://www.dsu.edu:80/departments/liberal/cola/OWL/

This site provides writing assistance to students of the University, both on-campus and at remote locations. Among the links on the online writing lab are: how to use the writing lab, other university writing lab resources, and information about the underlying grant.

IAAY Expository Writing Tutorial

http://www.jhu.edu/~gifted/ewt/jindex.html

This cool site provides expository writing instructions for kids in grades 8 through 12. You must be enrolled in the tutorial to access the pages containing the assignements.

Related Sites

http://www.trincoll.edu/~writcent/aksmith.html

http://www.english.uiuc.edu/cws/wworkshop/writer.html

http://www.hooked.net/users/jalsop/bookmarx.html

http://www.lsa.umich.edu/ecb/OWL/owl.html

http://www.aaronshep.com/kidwriter/

Inkspot

http://www.inkspot.com/

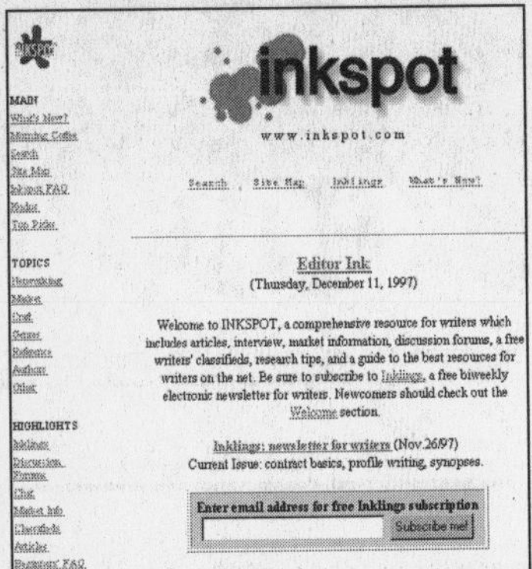

A thorough compendium of writing tools for every genre. The site includes interviews with writers, advice, journals, market information, tax advice, publisher links, and the Inklings newsletter.

Laura Brady's Business Writing Basics

http://www.as.wvu.edu/~lbrady/comm.html

An academic site providing links to course work on business writing, examples, writing help sites, and links to related topics.

Online Magazine Article Writing Workshop

http://members.aol.com/ondeadline/home/bro97.html.htm

A very rich graphical site providing links to the workshop materials, a chat room, and information on how to take the Magazine Article Writing Workshop. You can even order the video online.

Online Writing Centers and Other Resources

http://wilmot.unh.edu/~arm1/wrcenter.html

A comprehensive listing of online writing centers and their links.

Paradigm Online Writing Assistant

http://www.idbsu.edu/english/cguilfor/paradigm/

This excellent site by Chuck Guilford provides extensive instruction on how to write essays for different purposes. Each essay type is presented via a link. A discussion group is provided for sharing writing ideas.

Screenwriters Online

http://screenwriter.com/insider/news.html

This is the only screenwriters tutorial sponsored by professional screenwriters. It consists of a series of chat rooms, forums where screenplays are critiqued, the Screenwriters Insider newsletter, and interview with professionals.

Strunk & White Elements of Style

http://www.cc.columbia.edu/acis/bartleby/strunk/

That most crucial of writing bibles "Strunk and White" is online completely at this site. Chapter by chapter links provide all you want to know about commas, periods, participles, and conjunctions.

Waterside Productions

http://www.waterside.com/

Waterside Productions is a software and print literary agency. The site hosts links to agents, writer's resources, sample contracts, publishers, conferences, and information about how to be represented.

World Wide Web Virtual Library: Electronic Journals

http://www.edoc.com/ejournal/

Everything you ever wanted to know about where to find electronic journals on the Web. Searchable and organized by categories.

Write News

http://writenews.com/

A really neat site presenting everything you ever wanted to know about the publishing business. An industry newsletter online with links for writers, agents, and publishers.

Writer's Resources

http://www.arcana.com/shannon/writing.html

A comprehensive list of agents, publishers, writing tutorials, examples, and essays. Logically arranged in tabular format.

Related Sites
http://www.scbwi.org/
http://www.slip.net/~cluelass/index.html
http://www.internovel.com/novel/
http://www.linkline.com/personal/bbyun/rejection/index.html

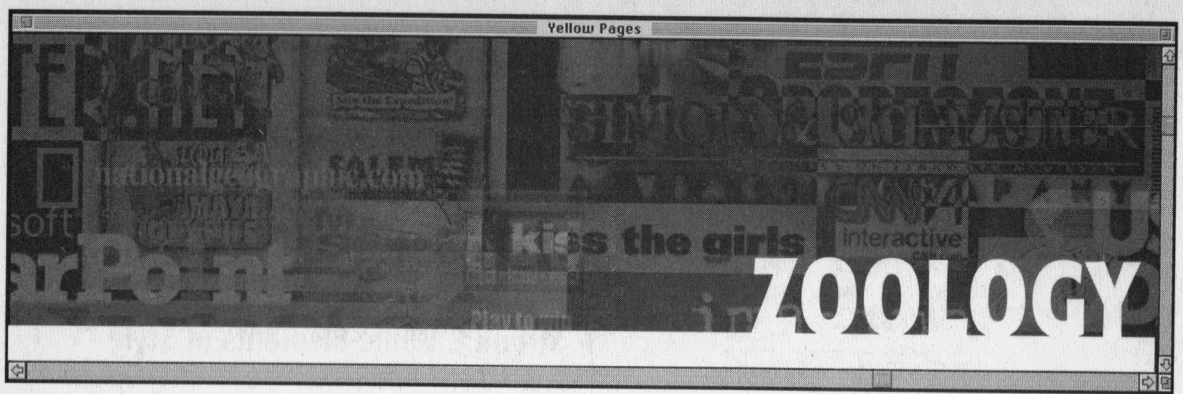

A
B
C
D
E
F
G
H
I
J
K
L
M
N
O
P
Q
R
S
T
U
V
W
X
Y
Z

> Why, it's a push-me-pull-you, of course!
>
> *Dr. Dolittle*

AlpacaNet

http://www.alpacanet.com/

Serves as a resource for Alpaca ranchers, breeders, weavers, spinners, investors, and anyone who wants more information about alpacas.

Australian Herpetological Directory

http://www.jcu.edu.au/dept/Zoology/herp/herp2.html

Anyone interested in studying Australian reptiles needs to check out this index of reptile-related pages.

Biosis Biological Extracts and Zoological Record

http://www.york.biosis.org/index.htm

Contains links to various zoological resources. Provides an online glossary.

Cornell Ornithology Collection

http://muse.bio.cornell.edu/museums/cubird.html

Provides information about the history of the ornithology program at Cornell. Offers a useful link to a Gopher search tool for scientific information on bird species.

Zooary
http://iris.biosci.ohio-state.edu/inscoll.html

Cryptozoology Zone

http://wkweb4.cableinet.co.uk/jdickie/zoology.htm

Cryptozoology is the study of hidden or unknown creatures, such as Bigfoot, Nessie, the Yeti, Mokele Mbembe, and more. A really interesting site, whether you believe or not.

Desert Fishes Council

http://www.utexas.edu/depts/tnhc/.www/fish/dfc/dfc_top.html

The DFC exists to preserve aquatic ecosystems and species found in deserts around the world, including Cichlids, Sticklebacks, freshwater eels, and many more.

Electronic Zoo

http://netvet.wustl.edu/e-zoo.htm

Contains information about animals and animal-related resources. Offers many links to information on nearly any animal.

The Eurosquid Worldwide Web Page

http://www.abdn.ac.uk/~nhi104/

Coming from the University of Aberdeen, Eurosquid is a page dedicated to cephalopods—squid, cuttlefish, octopi, and the like. The site is a collection of links to different publications, Web pages, and other reports.

Fungal Genetics Stock Center

http://www.kumc.edu/research/fgsc/main.html

There's a fungus among us! This University of Kansas site has links to reports and other texts important to researchers in the field of fungus, including the Sordaria, Neurospora, and Aspergillus collections.

Insect Behavior Group

http://www.zoo.utoronto.ca/ibg.html

Site run by zoology professors and students at the University of Toronto. Contains several articles about insect behavior and communication.

Insectcyclopedia

http://www.inscyclo.com/

This site is designed to help the amateur and student identify insects found in Nearctic region. The site is in English and French.

Institute of Ocean Sciences

http://www.ios.bc.ca/

One of Canada's largest marine research facilities, the IOS is located on the west coast of Canada and is responsible to conserve and protect the nation's fish habitat.

National Museum of Natural History

http://160.111.100.64/nmnhweb.html

An excellent site for an excellent museum! Learn about the Museum, the new and existing exhibits, research and collections, and more. Take a virtual tour, view the Museum Directory, and consider their research training programs, among many other things.

NetVet Veterinary Resources

http://netvet.wustl.edu/

Provides information related to veterinary medicine. Offers the Electronic Zoo, a large collection of animal-related computer resources.

The Ohio State University Insect Collection

http://iris.biosci.ohio-state.edu/inscoll.html

This site contains all the information known on Ohio State's collection, including tidbits on loaning items or visiting the collection. View lists of what they have, learn the history of the collection, and more.

The Pelagic Shark Research Foundation

http://www.pelagic.org/

The PSRF is dedicated to help all programs and projects that seek to learn more about sharks. This site provides links, photos, educational items, research information, and video.

Popular Pet Tarantulas

http://inetc.net/Tarantulas/

If the only thing you think when you think of tarantulas is "squish," check out this page, dedicated to the improvement of life through the keeping of pet tarantulas. The site has pictures, a searchable database, chat groups, pet care, a screen saver, and more.

Reef Resource Page

http://www.indiana.edu/~reefpage/

Students of the reef and its environment will appreciate this page, which reports all reef-related news, provides links, and lists reef research institutes.

The Tree of Life

http://phylogeny.arizona.edu/tree/phylogeny.html

The Tree is a collection of WWW pages that together provide a wealth of information about multiple organisms throughout the world. The Tree is presently formed of almost 1,300 pages housed on 20 computers.

Virtual Emu

http://www.vicnet.net.au/~raou/raou.html

A biodiversity and bird conservation group in Australia. Features a library of bird images and listings of threatened birds.

Welcome to the National Zoo

http://www.si.edu/natzoo/

See zoo highlights and animal photos, but also become a Friend of the Zoo, arrange a video conference for your school, or take an audio tour.

Zooary

http://iris.biosci.ohio-state.edu/inscoll.html

This page exists to teach students and teachers about animals so that they may ultimately be conserved because it is a close-held tenet that we will save only the animals that we love, and we love only the animals that we know about. The site offers info about zoological careers, quizzes, pictures, and more.

Zoology Department

http://www.utas.edu.au/docs/zoology/homepage.html

Zoology department at The University of Tasmania Web site. Contains information about the department and its programs. Also has information for contacting the department.

Zoo Book Sales

http://www.zoobook.com/

This company specializes in books about every aspect of zoology imaginable: entomology, ornithology, zoos and their maintenance, animal husbandry, mammology, and more. You can view their catalog, check out their best sellers, or see their favorite links.

Related Sites

http://www.neworleans.net/Audubonsite/html/audubon.html

http://www.bright.net/~vfazio/the-owl.htm

http://www.york.biosis.org/zrdocs/zrprod/zoorec.htm

http://www.spokane.net/cattales/

http://dns.ufsia.ac.be/Arachnology/Arachnology.html

http://www.spacelab.net/~catalj/

http://www.cyborganic.net/people/feathersite/Poultry/BRKPoultryPage.html

http://www.rain.org/~sbzoo/

http://is.dal.ca/~ceph/wood.html

http://is.dal.ca/~ceph/octokeep.html

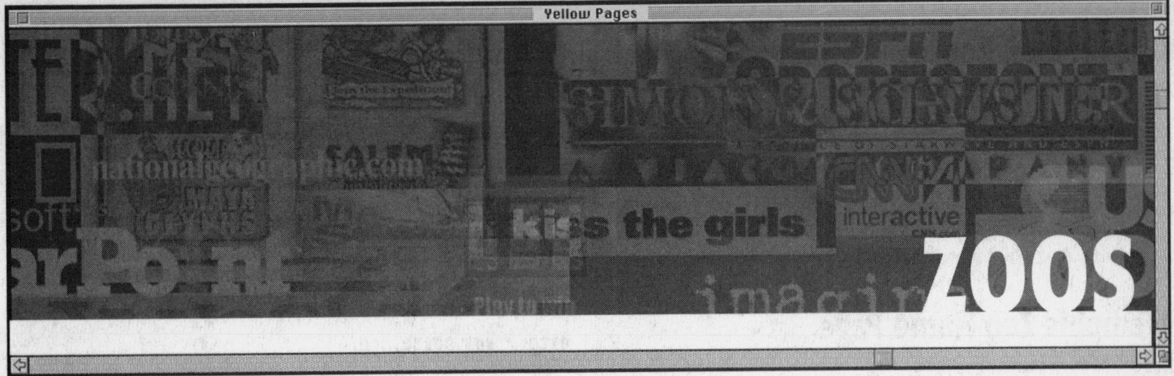

I think I could turn and live with animals, they are so placid and self-contain'd

Walt Whitman

American Association of Zoo Keepers

http://www.aazk.ind.net/

Site of the American Association of Zoo Keepers (AAZK), a nonprofit organization for professionals involved in animal care and preservation. Find out about fund-raisers such as Bowling for Rhinos, join AAZK, view lots of animal images, and find links to other zoological/ecological resources.

Cincinnati Zoo & Botanical Garden

http://www.cincyzoo.org/

Wander through this site to experience the Cincinnati Zoo and the world of nature. Get current events and discover what's new, learn about conservation and how you can help, get info on exotic travel programs, get educated about wildlife, and participate in the weekly animal guessing game.

Cleveland Metroparks Zoo

http://www.clemetzoo.com/

Want to visit the rain forest? Tour the zoo? Learn about conservation? Get educated about the natural world? Read about research being conducted by zoo staff? You can do all this and more at the site of the Cleveland Metroparks Zoo.

Cincinnati Zoo & Botanical Garden
http://www.cincyzoo.org/

The Texas Zoo!
http://www.viptx.net/texaszoo/index.html

Electronic Zoo/NetVet-Animal Image Collection

http://netvet.wustl.edu/pix.htm

This virtual zoo boasts a collection of more than 180 links to photo and image galleries. Among the many offerings are wild and domestic animals, insects, fish, reptiles, and birds. It's hard to imagine there could be an animal *not* pictured at this site.

The Indianapolis Zoo

http://www.indyzoo.com/

Go to the Information Center for who/what/when/where details on the Indianapolis (Indiana) Zoo, or visit the Virtual Zoo for photos and information on the zoo's many inhabitants—both plants and animals. In the Virtual Zoo, you can use the search utility to put the information you want at your fingertips.

Kids World 2000: Animals, Zoos and Aquariums

http://www.now2000.com/bigkidnetwork/zoos.html#zoos

A place where young cyber-travelers can find 60-plus links to animals, zoos, and aquariums. Just click a link to jump to the site of your choice and learn all about the flora.

Lincoln Park Zoo

http://www.lpzoo.com/

This site provides an index of the more than 1,000 animals featured at the zoo. You can also find information on adopting animals, endangered species, and educational programs for schools, families, and adults. A special feature is an online tour of the zoo.

Memphis Zoo Home Page

http://www.memphiszoo.org/

This site provides basic information about the Memphis Zoo, such as hours and prices, educational programs, special events, membership, the gift shop, the animal hospital, and the zoo's history. Good info mainly for those interested in visiting in person.

Metro Washington Park Zoo Official Web Site

http://www.zooregon.org/default.htm

You can search this Portland, Oregon, zoo's site or just jump to one of the offered areas—About our Zoo, About our Animals, Visitor Information, What's Happening, Get Involved, Saving Species, The Group Scoop, Teachers and Educators, No Adults Allowed!, and Site Map. There's something for everyone here.

Montgomery, Alabama - Montgomery Zoo

http://www.city-montgomery.com/discover/zoo.shtml

If you're curious about what a colobus monkey eats, how fast a red kangaroo can run, or what a Canadian lynx looks like, you can find out at this site. You can also find out about the Montgomery Zoo and what's going on there.

National Zoological Park Home Page

http://www.si.edu/natzoo

Web site of the National Zoo. Includes a user questionnaire, news, and information, as well as a photo library. Also includes links to the Smithsonian Institution and educational games that complement the information found on the site. Includes downloadable files that contain press coverage of the zoo. Coffee drinkers, take note: the site contains an interesting legend about Lewak coffee.

Neopolis Zoo

http://www.neosoft.com/neopolis/zoo/default.html

Meet Dupree the iguana at this animal-filled Web site. The page opens with a picture of a panda couple and offers links to other animal photos and sites on the Web.

The North Carolina Zoological Society

http://www.nczoo.org/

This site states that the North Carolina Zoological Park, in Asheboro, is "the country's largest and finest walk-through natural habitat zoo." If you'd like to get a glimpse at this zoo, click "Visit the Zoo" to get a park overview, a park map, visitor's hints, and gift and food info. One tip for real-world visitors: wear good walking shoes, because the zoo spans more than 500 acres.

The OFFICIAL Detroit Zoological Institute Web Site

http://www.detroitzoo.org/

This is where you can find out what's happening at the Detroit Zoo, the Belle Isle Zoo, and the Belle Isle Aquarium. You can join the zoo online, order an interactive CD-ROM, check out current projects and upcoming events, and get the rest of the scoop on all three facilities.

The Philadelphia Zoo Home Page

http://www.phillyzoo.org/

Besides the home page, this site offers an education page, a conservation page, an animals list, the PhillyZoo News page, and an online search engine. You can also enter the Site Index to get all kinds of information—on animals, conservation activities, zoo facts and FAQs, and more.

The Phoenix Zoo Home Page

http://aztec.asu.edu/phxzoo/homepage.html

Offers zoo trails to explore, stuff especially for kids, a calendar of events, animal information, zoo stats, general information, and links to other sites. You can also find out how you can support the zoo—maybe by "adopting" a spectacled bear cub?

The San Antonio Zoo

`http://www.sazoo-aq.org/`

At this site you can get a word from the director, learn what's new at the zoo, get general zoo information, tour the zoo, learn about the "adopt an animal" program, find out about zoo membership, and access links to related sites. The zoo tour was under construction at the time of writing but looked promising.

San Diego Wild Animal Park

`http://www.infopost.com/sandiego/points/sdzoo.html`

Lets you make an online visit to the San Diego Wild Animal Park, a park that features animals in their natural habitats—without fences or cages. Offers a montage of the animals that live in the park.

San Francisco ZOO HomePage/Welcome

`http://www.sfzoo.com/`

Come visit the San Francisco Zoo via a virtual tour. On your explore, be sure to catch the Zoo Talk area, where you can hear animal sounds and try to identify them, and the Insect Zoo (via the Children's Zoo), which gives you a glimpse into the world of these running, leaping, flying, and swimming arthropods. Also be sure to take a look at the Top Ten Animal Exhibits area.

Sea World/Busch Gardens

`http://www.bev.net/education/SeaWorld/homepage.html`

Contains an animal information database maintained by the Sea World Busch/Gardens theme parks. Includes "Ask Shamu," a column that features animal-related questions. Also includes images of numerous zoo species and information on zoological park careers.

Sydd's Internet Zoo

`http://www.clark.net/pub/jrsouza/SyddZoo/home.html`

Sydd's Internet Zoo is an informal, tongue-in-cheek collection of pages that provide links to sites dedicated to particular animals. The more than 385 links are organized into areas much like a zoo is arranged. Or you can jump to an individual animal by using the Animal Index.

The Texas Zoo!

`http://www.viptx.net/texaszoo/index.html`

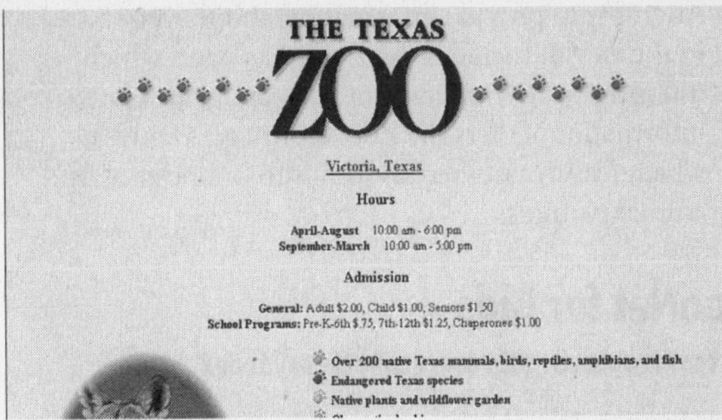

The Texas Zoo, in Victoria, Texas, has set up this site to inform visitors about this zoo, which features only animals indigenous to Texas. You can tour the zoo online to get animal info and some nice photos. You can also check into zoo membership, adopting an animal, and special events.

Zoo Boise

`http://www.sunvalleyski.com/zooboise/`

This site features Zoo Boise, in Idaho, and details the events, animals, education center, upcoming projects, Critter College, and animal adoption aspects of the zoo. It also offers a list of zoo-related links.

The Zoo Bytes Web Site

`http://www.frii.com/~brianw/zoobytes.html`

Zoo Bytes is a handy resource for zoo and animal lovers. Get info on, and some photos of, primates, herbivores, carnivores, and sea life. Interested in visiting a zoo now? Check out the ZooCast to see what the weather will be like at your zoo of choice.

Zoo in the Wild

`http://www.edv.it/naturalia.html`

This "zoo without bars" features animals of the sky and animals of the earth. Each animal is pictured along with pertinent information and a map showing its geographic habitat. Links to the World Conservation Monitoring Centre and an alphabetical index of zoos are also provided.

ZooNet

http://www.mindspring.com/~zoonet/

Attempts to provide information about every zoo in the world. Includes the ZooLinks page, which offers jumps to hundreds of zoos and zoo-related information. Offers the ZooNet Image Archives, which features numerous jumps to online zoos and animal pictures.

ZooNet for Kids

http://members.aol.com/zoonetkids/index.htm

This kid-friendly site will appeal to young animal lovers. They can zip from link to link, exploring such items as Muriel's Traveling Petting Zoo, Whale Times: Kid's Page, Rhinos and Tigers and Bears—Oh My! (Knoxville Zoo), the ZooNet Animal Speller, and Indianapolis Zoo Photos.

Zoos and Aquariums of AZA

http://www.aza.org/

Contains an alphabetical and geographical list of zoos and aquariums worldwide that are affiliated with the American Zoo and Aquarium Association. This site also offers tips on careers in zoology, details conservation programs underway at various zoos, and provides a photo gallery of animals and marine life.

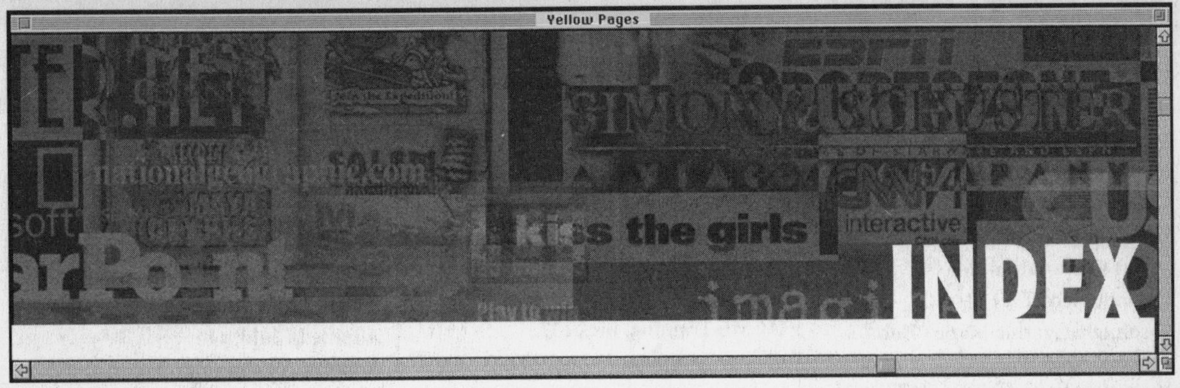

A B C D E F G H I J K L M N O P Q R S T U V W X Y Z

Symbols

A

A B C D E F G H I J K L M N O P Q R S T U V W X Y Z

B

C

A B C D E F G H I J K L M N O P Q R S T U V W X Y Z

D

E

F

A B C D E F G H I J K L M N O P Q R S T U V W X Y Z

G

H

A B C D E F G H I J K L M N O P Q R S T U V W X Y Z

I

J

K

L

M

N

O

P

Q

A B C D E F G H I J K L M N O P Q R S T U V W X Y Z

R

S

T

U

V

W